Anonymous

Williams' Cincinnati directory, city guide and business mirror

Anonymous

Williams' Cincinnati directory, city guide and business mirror

ISBN/EAN: 9783337713621

Printed in Europe, USA, Canada, Australia, Japan

Cover: Foto ©ninafisch / pixelio.de

More available books at **www.hansebooks.com**

No. 141 Main Street.

Railroad and Commercial
PRINTING.

Book and Pamphlet Printing.

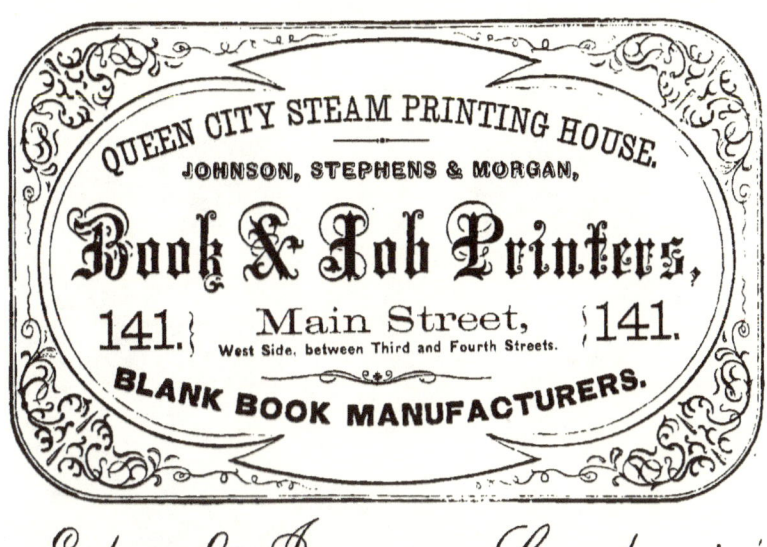

Express & Insurance Companies'
PRINTING.

Blank-Book Manufacturers.

No. 141 Main Street.

WILLIAMS'

CINNATI DIRECTORY

City Guide and Business Mirror,

FOR YEAR COMMENCING

JUNE 1, 1862.

TWELFTH ANNUAL ISSUE.

COMPILED AND PUBLISHED BY
WILLIAMS & COMPANY;
194 Walnut Street.
CINCINNATI.

Wrightson & Co., Printers, 167 Walnut Street, Cincinnati, O.

CONTENTS.

Map of Cincinnati,	In front of City Guide.
Alterations, Omissions, Removals, etc.	8
City Guide,	9
Alphabetical Arrangement of Names,	
Business Mirror,	347
Post Office Directory,	382
Preface,	7
Newspapers,	488
Railroad and Transportation Companies,	435
Indexes,	End of Book.

Entered according to Act of Congress, in the year 1862, by
WILLIAMS & CO.
In the Clerk's Office of the District Court of the United States, for the Southern District of Ohio.

PREFACE.

The present is the TWELFTH annual issue of WILLIAMS' CINCINNATI DIRECTORY, and in presenting the Volume to the public, the Compiler embraces the opportunity to return his thanks to subscribers to the work, for the patronage extended by them, and also to citizens generally for the kind and courteous manner in which they have co-operated with the Publisher, and furnished the information necessary for the preparation of the Directory.

The alteration of the time of the publication of our Volume from the month of January to June, was made by the Publisher under the impresssion that an unusual number of changes in the business locations and residences of our citizens would occur at the commencement of the present Spring. We are now satisfied that we have been enabled by the postponement to make our work much more useful to the public, as the new locations and residences are, in almost every case, noted in the present volume.

Although we can truly state that the City has been thoroughly and faithfully canvassed, square by square, in every part, to obtain the information for the present volume, and that great care and diligence have been exercised to detect errors and prevent omission, yet we can not claim that the work is perfect. Experience has taught us that in the collection, arrangement, and printing of FIFTY or SIXTY thousand names, with numbers attached, errors and omissions will occur in despite of the efforts of the most careful and scrutinizing persons. But the Compiler feels well assured that in the present instance he has as fully overcome these difficulties, and rendered the Directory as reliable as it is practicable to make a work of the kind, and confidently believes that the present volume will be found by our citizens to contain as few mistakes as the Directory of any City of the same population in the United States.

In addition to the usual matter contained in our Directory, we have introduced in this issue a "*Railroad and Transportation Department*," containing information, which will be found of interest to the public. It was prepared for us by S. W. CHAPMAN, Esq., to whom we tender our thanks for the favor conferred.

The "List of United States Post Offices," which we publish in the present volume, although not satisfactory to ourselves, is the best we could prepare under existing circumstances. The names of Post Offices in the Southern States are retained, as postal communication has already been renewed at various points South, and will undoubtedly be soon extended to all the offices where it has been temporarily suspended, and in that case, although somewhat imperfect, the list will be of use to our citizens.

It is important that all persons using the Directory should consult our list of "*Alterations and Removals*," as the latest changes are therein noted, and the *names of all citizens inserted*, that could not be obtained early enough to be arranged in their proper places in the body of the work.

We return our thanks to the Press of the City for notices given during the canvass, and shall aim in each succeeding issue to make the CINCINNATI DIRECTORY more worthy of commendation.

Alterations, Omissions, Removals, &c.

ABEL F. & CO. (F. A. & Henry Hakman), Coal Dealers, w. s. Park b. W. W. Canal and 2d
Abel Hy., grocery, 467 W. 5th cor. Mill
Acklin Maria, bs. Dennison House
Aders Andrew, fruit store, 337 Walnut
Affinger Frank, carp., 151 Everett
Albright, S. & Co. (Strickland A. & Charles A. Johnson) photographists, 20 W. 5th [119 W. 5th
Albright Strickland (S. A. & Co.) bds. co., 74½ W. 3d, h. 219 W. Court
Aldrich H. N., union coal oil and lamp
Allen Hy., bds. Dennison House
AMERICAN WHIP CO., S. E. Beckman, Agent, 17 E. 3d
Andrews & Biggs (Samuel A & Joseph A. B.) wh. boots and shoes, 11 W. Pearl
ANTRAM M. T & CO., Wholesale Fancy Dry Goods, Notions, &c., 47 W. Pearl
ANTRAM Micajah T. (M. T. A & Co.), 570 W. 9th
Ashbrook Benjamin A., photographer, 24 W. 4th, h. Covington
Attersley James, plumber, 321 Vine, res. Indiana
Australian House, John Martin, pro., 273 Walnut
Autenheimer Frederick, lab., City Water Works office
Barrett James, cof. h., 39 W. 3d
BATEMAN WARNER M., Attorney at Law & Notary Public, Office 23 W. 3d, res. Glendale
Beall Geo. E., exchange office, 200 Walnut, h. Newport [George
Beatus Henry, jewelry, 78 Main, b. 325
Beck Andy (Fenton & B.), n. w. c. 6th and Plum
Bell J. B., boots and shoes, 269 Central Av., h. 140 Richmond
Berghaus Barney, mach , h. 164 Clark
Berrett Samuel, butcher, 612 E. Front
Brill Geo. (Jacob & B.) 119 Bremen
Brinkman Christ, (Schell & B.) w. s. Fillmore b. Richmond and Gest
Brown Lewis G., student, 14 E. 2d, h. Mt. Auburn
BRUCK LOUIS, h. 32 Grant
BUCHER JAMES, Superintendent, Memphis and Cin. Packet Co., 16 Pub. Landing
BUSH Wm. S, Editor, Ohio Valley Farmer, n.e.c. 4th and Walnut
Butler Edward S. & Co. (Edward S. B. & Thomas S. Royse) st. bt. agts., and com. mers., 7 E. Front
Butler Edward S. (E. S. B. & Co.), res. Vine St. Hill
Carlton Edward, collector, 419 W. 8th
Carlton Thomas, conductor, h. 419 W. 8th
Carr Hy. L., 52 W. 9th
Carter A. G. W., atty., Odd Fellows' Bldg., n.w c, 3d and Walnut
Cavanaugh Michael, horse trader, w. s. Smith b. 6th and Longworth
Center Hatzel H. (I. S. & H. H. Center) 452 W. 9th
Chamberlin Benj. B., designer and wood engraver, n.w.c. 4th and Race
CLARK John, (C. & Rogers) bds. Walnut St. House

CLARK & ROGERS (John C. & Hiram D. R.) Wholesale Grocers and Produce and Commission Merchants, 28 and 30 E. 2d
Clawson Wm., h. Stone near 3d
COFFIN D. H. B., Wholesale and Retail Groceries, & Produce, 20 E. Pearl
COLEMAN ROBERT S., Cabinet-Makers' Marble Manufacturer, s.w.c. 5th and Broadway, h. 8 Hopkins
Colter Anna, milliner. 154 W. 5th
Cooper Joseph, supt. M. & E. Canal, office 7 W. Canal, h. near Glendale
CURTIS ALVA, Literary and Scientific Institute, and Physio-Medical College. 135 Elm
CUNNINGHAM ANDREW, Edge Tool Manufacturer, s.s. 8th b. Main and Sycamore, h. 37 Hathaway
Daniels Hector L , book bindery, 58 W. 3d, h. n. s. Hathaway b. Jane and Baymiller
Dean Thomas, carp., 32 George
Dornseifer H., watches, &c., 353 Central Av., h. Cumminsville
Duclischer Pierre, furniture, 134 Sycamore, h. s.e.c. Wade and Baymiller
Duerr T. G., clk., 99 Walnut
Ellarman Herman, porter, 11 W. Pearl, h. 22 Woodward
Elias E. H., jewelry and broker, n.w.c. Pub. Landing and Broadway
EVELETH WM. H., Merchant Tailor, 18 W. 4th, bds. 285 Longworth
Eveslage B , cof. h., 7 and 9 12th
FRENCH Lewis, atty., h. 360 W. 6th
Fruhauf Isaac L., barber. 212 Walnut
Fetter Francis, lab., 204 Clark
Focke A. H., clk., 11 W. Pearl, h. 219 Linn
Frey's Exchange 61 W. 5th, Lambert Westerman, pro [Central Av
Garrison D. R., second hand store, 323
Gay James P., agent American Gutta Percha Roofing Co., No. 1 Apollo Building, n.w.c. 5th and Walnut
Gellespie John, carp., 417 W. 8th
Gerkamp Gerhardt, carp., w. s. Coggswell al. b. Franklin and Woodward
Gould R , (Patrick & G.,) New York
Guin Wm., carp , 395 W. 8th
Hackney W. K., salesman, 11 W. Pearl bds. Burnet House
Haddix N., mer. tailor, 229 Walnut
HALL JOSEPH L. & CO., Iron Safe Manufacturers, s.w.c. Pearl and Plum
HALL Joseph L. (Joseph H. & Co.,) 147 Baymiller
HAMMETT HENRY, Hardware and Cutlery, 90 Main, h. Mt. Auburn
HEGNER E. W., Saddle and Harness Manufacturers, 30 W. Court
Henshaw C. H., broker, n.w.c. 6th and Walnut
Heskamp Margaret, grocery, 33 Baum
HOAG David R., (H. & Quick,) 100 W. 4th
HOAG & QUICK, (D. R. H. & Israel Q.) Photograph and Fine Art Gallery, 100 W. 4th
Hornberger F., wood dealer, s.e.c. Race and Elder, h. 682 Vine

Huesman Edward, bk. binder, 262 E. Front
Hughes Edwin, (H. & Reed,) 447 W. 7th
Hughes & Reed, (Edwin H. & Wm. R.,) grain and produce dealers, 37 Water
HUMMEL ANTHONY, Proprietor Frey's Hotel, 421 and 423 Main
JAMES T. M., (Stallo, Tafel & J.) 9 R. R. Bldg., s.w.c. Court and Main
Jonas Frank, carp., 201 Clark
Jonas Michael B., student, bds. 520 W. 7th
Jones Wm. S., printer, 113 George
Jordan Francis, barber, U. S. Hotel
Kemper Hugh F., com. mer., 18 Water, h. Walnut Hills
Kent Thos H., carp., Lawson al. b. 4th and 5th
KETTERLINUS CH. W., Machinist and Locksmith, 408 Walnut, h. 424 Walnut
Kilber Henry, lab., wks 196 W. Pearl
KIMBALL THOS. L., Agent Pennsylvania Railroad 46 W. 6th, res. Linnwood
King Geo. C. & Co., (Geo. C. K., & David C. King.) com. mers. n.w.c. 5th and Walnut, No. 1 Apollo Bld'g
Kinkead Joseph, shoe mkr., wks. 31 12th
Kramer Bernhard, pressman, h. 75 Prince
Kroeger Henry P., dray, 63 Pendleton
Laue Wm., cigar mkr., bds. 65 W. 5th
Lape Jacob S., sash mkr., 379 John
Lauge Chas., gaiter and shoe manufac., 131 12th
Lee Robt., lock mkr., 336 W. 7th
Lubber Julius, b.k. 205 Wade
MATSON & BRO., Dining Saloon, 81 E. Pearl
Milett Richard, lab., e.s. Ramsey n. of Front
Moller John, 44 Findlay
Moore Charles C. M D., 96 Barr
MOORES & CO., (Robt. B. M. & Jas. C. M.) Saddles, Harness, Trunks, &c., 89 Main
Moores Wm. B., lime dealer, 265 Plum
Nulte Fred., shoe mkr., 417 Central Av.
Obere Louisa, n.w.c. Main and Court
Ogborn Edward W., merch., 131 W. 8th
PARKER SEWING MACHINE CO., Thos. L. Kimball, General Western Agent, 46 W. 5th
Reed Wm., (Hughes & R.,) 204 W. Front
Richenbach Michael, teamster. 33 Madison
RODGERS JAMES Y. Attorney at Law, Office Short Bldg. s.e.c. 4th and Hammond
Roelher Henry, meats, 463 Linn
Rougan Margaret, 55 Observatory Road
Schnittker J. Henry, cooper, bds. 20 Buckeye
Shaw Daniel W., 67 Providence
Toban Thos., lab., w.s. Central Av. b. 2d and W. W. Canal Basin
Todd Meritt, sr., pork mer., bds. 319 Longworth
Todd Meritt, jr., pork mer., bds. 319 Longworth
WAYNE Jacob L., jr., (J. L. W. & Co.) 88 Pike

Cincinnati City Guide.

Street Directory.

The STREET DIRECTORY is simply an ALPHABETICAL arrangement of Streets, Alleys, etc., with a sufficient portion of corner numbers attached to such as are of any considerable importance, for the purpose of aiding those who refer to it in becoming familiar with the system of numbering. It will be found by citizens as well as strangers to be a practical guide to the different parts of the City, as far as it has yet been numbered.

EXPLANATIONS.—On streets commencing at and running directly from the River, or others running in the same direction, the ODD numbers are on the West, and the EVEN on the East side of the street, commencing at the River or such other point as the street may commence. On streets crossing Main, the ODD numbers are on the South, and the EVEN on the North side of the street, commencing at and running East and West from Main, thus dividing each into two distinct streets, distinguished by prefixing EAST or WEST to the name. All others running in a similar direction are numbered in the same manner, commencing at the point nearest to Main and running East or West according to the direction of the same. In a very few instances two streets will be found to have the same name, one of them generally in the suburbs, not numbered and of but little consequence—to such A* is prefixed.

In designating the CORNER numbers we have used ODD numbers entirely, except where streets commence at or end upon the side where the EVEN numbers belong.

AARON, al. b. Wood and W. W. Canal, fr. Webb to Avery.
ABBOTT, al. b. Webster and Franklin, fr. Von Seggern al. to College al.
ABIGAIL, e. fr. 488 Main, b. Hunt and Woodward.
 41 Sycamore,
 85 Broadway,
 105 Spring.
ACCOMMODATION, e. and n. fr. 64 con. e. 5th.
ADAMS, w. fr. 519 Elm to Plum.
ADAMS al. b. Findlay and Livingston, fr. Linn to Bell.
ADDISON, n. of Thomas, fr. Central Av. to Valley.
AHLER al. b. Blackford and Clark, fr. Gerrard to Ludlow av.
AILANTHUS, b. Baymiller and Freeman, fr. Bank to Central Av.
ALBION al. b. Wayne and Morgan, fr. Concord to Finch al.
ALEXANDER, n. fr. Baltimore w. of McGrew.
ALFRED, n. of Addison, fr. Central Av. to Valley.
ALLEN al. b. Culvert & New, fr. 6th to North.
ALLISON, w. fr. 573 Main, b. 13th and Liberty, to Vine.
 21 Clay,
 39 Walnut.
AMITY al. e. of Baymiller fr. Bank to Dayton al.
ANDERSON al. b. Park and Mill, fr. Front to 3d.
ANDRESS al b. Patterson and Coleman, fr. Garden to Brighton al.
ANDREWS al. b. 8th and 9th, fr. Vine to Plum.
ANN, w. fr. 447 Plum, n. of 13th to Central Av.
ARCH, e. fr 108 Broadway b. 3d and 4th, to Lawrence.
ASH, n. of Swift, fr. Martin to Collard.
ASHTON al. b. Findlay and Livingston, fr. Baymiller to Werner.
ATKINSON, s. of Renshaw, fr. Elm east.
AUBURN, n. fr. head of Sycamore.

AUGUSTA, w. fr. 47 Central Av. b. w. 2d and W. W. Canal.
AVERY, b. 3d and 5th, fr. e of Park, to a point w. of W. W. Canal.
AVERY al. b. Coleman and Denman, fr. Garden to Brighton al.
BADEAU al. e. of Farmer's al. fr. Front to Fisher al.
BALL. e. of Elm, fr. Atkinson to Renshaw.
BALTIMORE w. fr. 631 Sycamore, n. of Miami.
BANK, w. fr. 883 Central Av n. of Dayton.
 67 Linn,
 191 Piatt.
BANK al. n. fr. 22 W. 3d to W. 4th.
BALDWIN al. e. of Race fr. 7th to 12th.
BARD al. e. of John, fr. Betts to Livingston.
BARNES al. b. Mill and Park fr. Mill to Avery.
BARR, w. fr. 61 Mound b. George and W. 7th.
 59 Cutter,
 123 Linn,
 175 Baymiller.
BARR al. b. 5th and Longworth, fr. Mound to Stone.
BARTON al. b. Ailanthus and Freeman, fr. Bank to Clearwater.
BAUM. n. fr. e 3d, e. of Kilgour to 6th.
BAYMILLER, n fr. 5th, w. of Linn.
☞This street is numbered fr. 418 George, which was formerly its commencement.
 15 Barr,
 27 W. 7th,
 37 Van Horn,
 49 W. 8th,
 71 Kemble,
 91 Richmond,
 113 Catharine,
 141 Cedar.
Piatt street is now attached to this street under the name of Baymiller. ☞See Piatt for the numbers, as they have not yet been changed.
BEDINGER, e. fr. 274 Broadway, b. W. 8th and W. 9th.

BEECH al. b. Liberty and Milton, fr. a point e. of Broadway to Culvert al.
BELL, e. of Linn, fr. Livingston to Findlay.
BEM, n. of Cross, head of Hamburgh.
BENHAM al. w. fr. 141 Race, b. 3d and 4th to Elm.
BENT al. w. of Cutter, fr. David to Melancthon.
BENTON, s. of Elder, fr. Vine to Hamilton Road.
BERK, s. of Windsor, fr. Hathaway lane to Francis lane.
BERKS al. n. of 4th, fr. Vine to Stone al.
BETTS, w. fr. 537 Central Av. b. Laurel and Clinton.
 27 John,
 85 Cutter,
 145 Linn,
 203 Piatt.
BETTS al. b. Dudley & Freeman, fr. Everett to Poplar.
BICKETT al. w. line of Methodist Burying Ground, fr. Court to Clark.
BIGELOW, e. of Walker, fr Channing to Saunders.
BLACKFORD, n. of Espanola, fr. Gerrard to Ludlow av.
BOAL, e. fr. 552 Sycamore, n. of Milton.
BODMAN al. b. St. Clair's al. and Main, fr. 6th to Gano.
BODLEY al. b. Abigail and Woodward fr. Pendleton to Schultz al.
BOGEN al. b. Denman and Freeman, fr. Garden to Brighton al.
BOHN al. b. Ann and 14th, fr. W. Plum to Central av.
BONSALL al. b. 2d and South Pearl, fr. Dart al. to Ormsby's line.
BONTE al. s of Front, fr. Peter al. to French.
BOONE, e. of Lafayette, fr. Marion to McMillan.
BOOTS al. e. of Vine, fr. 13th to Allison.
BORCHER al. b. Fulton av. and Grove, fr. Starr to Vance al.
BORDEN'S al. b. George and 6th, fr. College to Elm.

BOSLEY, s. of Atkinson, fr. Elm east.
BOSTON, e. of Butler, fr. Pearl to 2d.
BRACKETT al. b. Walnut and Clay, fr. 12th to a point n. of 13th.
BRANCH, s. of Stark, w. fr w. line of Sec. 12.
BREMEN, fr. 12th, b. Vine and Race.
 41 13th,
 81 14th,
 119 15th,
 106 W. Liberty,
 211 Green,
 251 Elder.
BRIGHTON, w. of Division, fr. Western av. to Thomas.
BRIGHTON al. s. of Central av. fr. Patterson to Freeman.
BROAD, n. of Reed, fr. the Ohio river to Fulton av.
BROADWAY. n. fr. 55 Front or Pub. Landing, e. of Sycamore.
 25 Yeatman,
 47 E. 2d,
 68 E. Congress,
 81 E. Pearl,
 99 E. 3d,
 110 Arch,
 125 E. 4th,
 159 E. 5th,
 172 Harrison,
 193 E 6th,
 217 New,
 233 E. 7th,
 261 E. 8th,
 276 Bedinger,
 291 E. 9th,
 310 Court,
 353 Hunt,
 387 Abigail,
 407 Woodward,
 427 Franklin,
 445 Webster,
 473 Liberty.
BROMWELL al. b. Rice and Alexander, fr. Mulberry to near Fountain.
BROOKLYN, e. of Waldon, fr. the Ohio river to n. line of Nassau subdivision.
BROOKS al. b. N. Pearl and 3d, fr. Park to sec. line.
BROWNE, parallel to the Miami Canal, fr. Hamilton road to section line.

BUCHANAN, b. 4th and 5th, fr. Lawrence to Pike.
BUCKEYE, w fr. Main, n. of Hamilton Road.
  18 Eden,
  49 Locust,
  107 Poplar.
BUDD, fr. Carr to Horne next n. of Whitewater.
BURNET. w. fr. 137 Walnut, b. 3d and 4th to Race.
BURROWS, w. fr. 69 Race to Elm. b. W. 2d and Pearl.
BUTCHERS' al. b Clearwater and Bank, fr. Clarkson to Starch al.
BUTLER, n. fr. river to E.6th b. Pike and M. Canal.
  11 E. Front,
  41 Congress,
  77 E. 3d.
BYRON, w. of Hamburg, fr. the M. Canal north.
CAIN al. b. Culvert and Hubbard, fr. Culvert to Cork al.
CAMPBELL. w. of Elm, fr. Dick al. to Findlay.
CANAL, EAST, e. fr. 330 Main to Sycamore.
CANAL, WEST, w. fr. 429 Main to Plum.
  24 Clay,
  43 Walnut,
  62 Jackson,
  81 Vine,
  123 Race,
  163 Elm.
CARL al. b. Mill and Stone fr. 3d to Avery.
CARMALT, e. fr. Young, n. of Channing.
CARNEY, e. of Fuller, fr. Pavilion to n. line of sec. 12.
CARR. n. fr. 704 W. Front w. of Freeman.
  79 W. 6th,
  92 Taylor.
  103 Fremont,
  179 W. 8th,
  199 Kemble,
  217 Richmond.
CARTER'S al. b. 9th & Court fr. Walnut to Elm.
CASSATT'S al. e. fr. 500 Main to Broadway, b. Abigail and Woodward.
CATHEDRAL al. b. 7th and 8th, fr. Plum to Central Av.
CEDAR al. b. 9th and Richmond, fr. Freeman to e. of Linn.
CELESTIAL, n. of Oregon, fr. 3d to Observatory road.
CEMETERY, s. of McMillan, fr. Kemper lane to a point e. of Hathaway lane.
CENTER al. b. Druggist al. and Wolf al. fr. 5th to Church al.
CENTRAL AVENUE, n fr. river, b. Plum and John.
  9 Water,
  31 Front,
  49 Augusta,
  67 W. 2d
  85 W. Canal,
  103 W. 3d,
  126 McFarland,
  147 W. 4th,
  170 Perry,
  193 W. 5th,
  215 Longworth,
  239 W. 6th,
  263 George,
  285 W 7th,
  311 W. 8th,
  337 W. 9th,
  346 W. 9th,
  361 Richmond,
  374 Court,
  387 Court,
  413 Elizabeth,
  437 Chestnut,
  459 Clark,
  493 Hopkins,
  504 Ann.

517 Laurel,
539 Betts.
542 14th,
565 Clinton,
583 Everett,
603 David,
629 Wade,
653 Melancthon.
679 W. Liberty,
694 Ash,
609 Oliver,
721 Poplar,
771 Maple,
809 York,
851 Dayton,
883 Bank,
913 op.Mohawk Bridge.
963 Clarkson,
1011 Baymiller,
1075 Freeman.
*CENTRAL av. n. of Miller, fr. Auburn to Hunt.
CHANNING. n. of Ringgold, fr. Price to Bigelow.
CHAPEL, b. 8th and 9th, fr. Walnut to Vine.
CHARLES, w fr, 361 Elm to Central Av.
CHARLOTTE. n. of Findlay, fr. M. Canal to a point w. of John.
CHASE al. b. New and 7th, fr. Scott al, east.
CHEAPSIDE, (East & West) e. and w. side of M. Canal basin. n. fr. e. 8th to Court.
CHERRY al. b. Front and Phœbe, fr. Hughes al. to Plum.
CHESTNUT, w. fr. 433 Central Av. b. Elizabeth and Clark.
  41 John.
CHURCH al. w, fr. 177 Main to Walnut, b. W. 4th and 5th.
CLARK, w, fr. 457 Central av, n. of 12th.
  37 John,
  49 Fulton,
  111 Cutter,
  129 Kossuth,
  149 Rittenhouse.
  161 Hand,
  175 Linn,
  223 Baymiller,
  255 Pine.
CLARK al. b. Commerce and 2d, fr. Vine to Neff al.
CLARKSON, n. fr. 76 B nk to Central Av.
CLAY, n fr. 24 W. Canal.
  41 12th,
  79 13th,
  133 Allison.
CLAYER'S al, b. Clinton and Everett. fr. John to Linn & fr. Baymiller to Freeman.
CLEAR al. b. Frank and Bank fr. Mill Creek to W. Av.
CLEARWATER, w. fr. Clarkson to Freeman,
CLIFTON al. b. Kenton and Kilby, fr. Wayne to Lawyer.
CLINTON, w, fr. 563 Central Av. b. Betts and Everett.
  37 John,
  87 Cutter,
  151 Linn,
  217 Platt.
CLINTON COURT, n. fr. 68 Clinton, b. John and Cutter.
COGGSWELL av. n. of Saunders, fr Auburn east.
COGGSWELL al. w. of Sycamore, fr. Abigail to Liberty.
COLBY al. b. Dunlap and Elm, fr. Forbus al. to Hamilton Road.
COLEMAN, w. of Denman, fr. York al. to Harrison av.
COLEMAN al. b. St.Clair and Main. fr. 9th to Court.
COLLARD, n. fr. river, b. Whittaker and Washington.

COLLEGE. n. fr. 108 W. 6 to 7th. b. Vine and Race,
COLLEGE al.w. of Broadwa fr. Milton to a point e. Abigail.
COMMERCE, w. fr. 39 Wa nut to Plum.
  45 Vine.
CONCORD, e. of Kenton, f Montgomery Pike to McMi lan.
CONES al, e. of Linn, f Clark to Hopkins, and f Laurel to Betts.
CONKLIN, n. of Graham, Race to Ohio av.
CONVENT al. b. 5th and 6t around the Catholic Co vent.
COOK, w. of Central Av. Addison to Alfred.
COOPER al. w, of Elm, fr. 6 to 7th.
COPELEN, e. of Concord, f Montgomery Pike to M Millan,
CORK al. b. 6th and 8th, Culvert to Hubbard.
CORPORATION al. b. Liber and Milton, fr. Wilson Price,
CCURT, EAST, e. fr. 3 Main.
  11 Merchant,
  21 fr. e. front of Cou House,
  37 Sycamore,
  51 Cheapside East,
  61 Broadway.
COURT, WEST, w. fr. 3 Main, b. W. 9th and Can to Central Av.
  25 St. Clair's al.
  49 Walnut,
  103 Vine,
  143 Race,
  183 Elm,
  219 Plum.
☞ W. of Central Av. t street is continued upon wh has heretofore been Cathari street ; but as the old numbe ing has been altered only i few instances, we give t numbers as on that stree starting fr. 285 Central Av.
  45 John,
  81 Fulton,
  137 Cutter,
  154 Kossuth,
  170 Rittenhouse,
  201 Linn,
  249 Baymiller.
CRAMSEY al. b. Mound a Cutter, fr. Court to Penne al.
CRAVEN al. e. of Central fr. 8th to Richmond,
CRIPPEN al. e. of Sycam fr. 7th to 8th.
CROSS, n of Mohawk, Kirby's line to a point e Elm.
CULVERT, n. fr. 206 e. 3d Butler and M. Canal.
  77 W. 5th,
  125 W. 6th,
  157 W. 7th
CUMMINSVILLE SPRING GROVE av. w Cook. fr. Cock's n. line Alfred
CURTIS, s. of McMillan, Montgomery Pike to Ke per line.
CUSHING al. b Goodloe Front. fr. Willow to Ning
CUTS al. b. 5th and 6th, Thomas al to Sycamore.
CUTTER, fr. W. 6th w Mound,
  21 George,
  37 Barr,
  53 W 7th,
  63 Van Horn,
  71 W. 8th,

19 Miller,
37 Walnut,
73 Vine,
109 Race,
145 Elm,
251 Central Av.
281 John,
335 Mound,
383 Cutter,
449 Linn.
495 Baymiller,
539 Freeman,
601 Carr,
643 Harriet.
ELDER, w. fr. 123 Hamilton road,
5 Hamer,
17 Vine,
27 Bremen,
51 Race,
91 Elm,
101 Campbell,
113 Logan,
ELIJAH al. b. Young and Price, fr. Boal to Channing.
ELIZABETH. w. fr. 411 Central Av. to Mound.
39 John.
ELLEN, n. fr. 200 e. of Lock 43 W. 4th.
ELM, n. fr. River, b. Race and Plum.
9 Water,
29 W. Front,
51 Cherry,
71 W. 2d,
103 Pearl,
119 W. 3d,
135 McFarland,
153 W. 4th,
191 W. 5th,
209 Longworth,
243 George,
261 W. 7th,
285 W. 8th,
307 W. 9th,
321 William,
331 W. Court,
351 W. Canal,
385 12th,
405 Grant,
461 14th,
479 Madison,
490 Fifteenth,
521 Adams,
541 Monroe,
550 W. Liberty,
546 Gruen,
619 Elder, .
693 Locust,
693 Cooper,
ELM al. c; of Linn, fr. York to York al.
ELYSIAN, b, Ohio av. and Race, fr. Ohio av. to Graham, and fr. Shawk's n. line to Madeira.
EMERSON al. w. of Elm, fr. Grant.
ESPANOLA, n. of Gest, fr. Freeman to Ludlow av.
EVERETT, n. of Clinton, fr. Central Av. to Freeman.
☞ This street heretofore commenced at Plum, embracing that part of 15th which lies west of the M. Canal—we give the numbers as they stand, commencing at 510 Plum
15 Providence,
29 Central Av,
71 John,
105 Cutter,
144 Jones,
163 Linn,
217 Platt,
244 Dudley.
ENGINE al. b. Franklin and Webster, fr. Long al. to Coggswell al.
ENON al, b. Orchard and Webster, fr. Long al. to Coggswell al.
ERNST al. s. of Harrison av. fr. Barnard to Riddle.

ESSEX al, e. of Baymiller, fr. York to York al.
EVANS al. n of Mulberry, fr, Vine to Race.
EWAN al. b. Brighton and Division, fr. Burnet to Harrison av.
EXETER, s, of Frank, fr. Webster av. to Mill Creek,
FAIRVIEW av. e. of Browne from a point n. of Browne's n. line to the section line.
FALL al, b, Elm and Plum, fr, Wade to Liberty.
FARAN al. b. Kenton and Concord, fr. Wayne to Monroe.
FARMERS al. e. of Lewis, fr. Front to Longworth,
FERGUSON'S al. b. 8th and 9th, fr. Main to Sycamore.
FERN al. b. Frank and Exeter, fr. Mill Creek to Western av.
FIFTEENTH, w. fr. 531 Vine to Central av.
19 Bremen,
39 Race,
57 Pleasant.
FIFTH, EAST, e. fr. 202 Main.
41 Sycamore,
77 Broadway,
95 McAllister,
111 Buchanan,
146 opp. Pike,
181 Butler,
211 M. Canal,
217 Lock.
FIFTH, WEST, w. fr. 193 Main.
41 Walnut,
51 Vine,
167 Race,
181 Elm,
233 Plum,
283 Central Av,
303 John,
361 Smith,
406 Mound,
447 Park,
467 Walnut,
515 Stone,
555 Wood,
601 W. W. Canal,
616 Hannibal,
636 Pierson.
FINCH al. e. of Copelen, fr. Kemper al. to Montgomery Pike.
FINDLAY, w. fr. 153 Hamilton road (junction of Vine and Hamilton road,)
9 Bremen,
35 Race,
73 Elm,
83 Campbell,
97 Logan,
☞ This street is now continued from Plum to Freeman —name changed from Maple —it is partially numbered as Maple.
FLINT, w. fr. 457 Freeman, b. Kenner and W. Liberty
FIRMAN al, b. Freeman and Louisa.fr, Clark to Hopkins.
FIRST al. opp. Green, fr. Hamer to Vine.
FISHERS al, s. of Center, fr. Selas al. to the e. line of Lewiston.
FITCH al. b. Copelen and Concord, fr. Morgan to Montgomery Pike.
FLICK al. n. of Huber fr. Hamer to Goose al.
FOBES al. n. of 14th, running fr. Plum to Providence.
FOLZ al. n. of Pike al. fr. Hamer to Bremen.
FORBUS al. b. Henry and Findlay, fr. Race to Plum.
FORD al. s. of Front, fr. Willow to Leatherberry.

FOSTER, w. of the eastern boundary line of the city, running fr. Front to Wheeler's line
FOUNTAIN, n. of Mound, fr. McGrew to Rice.
FOURTEENTH, w. fr. 489 Vine to Central av.
19 Bremen,
41 Race,
61 Pleasant,
81 Elm.
FOURTH, EAST, e. fr. 150 Main.
37 Sycamore,
77 Broadway,
58 McAllister,
103 Lawrence,
104 Buchanan,
121 Lytle.
FOURTH, EAST, e. fr. 100 Butler to Ellen.
FOURTH, WEST, w. fr. 551 Main,
45 Walnut,
85 Vine,
156 Race,
165 Elm,
205 Plum,
245 Central Avenue,
283 John,
315 Smith,
393 Park,
419 Mill,
461 Stone,
FOURTH al. n. of Benton, fr, Hamar to Vine.
FOWLER, e. of Dover, fr. Lawyer to McMillan.
FOY, w. of Race, fr. Mulberry to Findlay's n. line.
FRANCIS LANE, e. of Hathaway lane, fr. Hathaway lane to Kemper lane.
FRANK, s. of Bank. fr. Western av. to Mill Creek.
FRANK al. s. of Sharp al. fr. Bank to Hamilton road.
FRANKLIN, e. fr. 536 Main, b. Woodward and Webster to Broadway.
21 Hanover,
39 Sycamore,
FREE al. b. Gest and Clark, fr. Israel al. to Luken al.
FREEMAN, n. fr. 664 W Fron', at junction W. 5th,
77 W. 6th,
101 C. H. & D. Railroad,
110 George,
132 Barr.
152 W. 7th,
164 Van Horn,
171 W. 8th.
193 W. 9th,
215 Richmond,
246 Court,
269 Gest,
270 Cedar,
323 Bonita,
351 Hopkins,
372 Laurel,
398 Betts,
418 Clinton,
436 Everett,
457 Flint,
486 Hickory,
529 Liberty,
572 Poplar,
594 Livingston,
608 Maple,
644 York,
678 Dayton,
709 Bank.
FREMONT, w. fr. 103 Carr, (the track of C. H. & D. Railroad.)
FRENCH, e. of Hazen, fr. the Ohio River to the n. line of Carrsville.
FRIENDSHIP, b. Front and Pearl, fr. Lawrence to Butler.
FRONT OR PUBLIC LANDING, e. fr. 2 Main to Broadway.

FRONT, EAST, e. fr. Public Landing, at foot of Broadway.
51 Ludlow,
97 Lawrence,
139 Pike,
183 Butler,
235 Miami Canal,
263 Kilgour,
418 Junction of Pearl,
539 Parsons,
597 Whittaker,
747 Washington.
FRONT, WEST, w. fr. foot of Main,
16 Reynolds,
41 Walnut,
73 Vine,
111 Race,
149 Elm,
185 Plum,
229 Central Avenue,
271 John,
307 Smith,
362 Rose,
479 Mill,
502 Ramsey,
573 Wood,
618 Junction W. 3d,
564 Freeman,
706 Carr,
756 Harriet.
FUGATE al. n. fr. 15th, b. Plum and Central av.
FULLER, e. of Kirby, fr. Pavilion to Court.
FULTON av. n. of Front fr. Washington to Wallace al.
GAGE, n. of Fountain, fr. Rice to Sycamore.
GAMBLE al. w. of Central Av. fr. Betts to Livingston.
GANDOLFO al. w. fr. 367 Vine to Plum.
GANO, w. fr. 273 Main b. 6th and 7th to Vine.
25 St. Clair,
49 Walnut,
67 Lodge.
GARDEN, n. of Dayton, fr. Freeman to Riddle.
GARRARD, n. of Gest, w. of Freeman.
GAS al. n. fr. 382 W. Front to W. 2d, e. s. Gas Works.
GAY al. w. of Baymiller fr. York to York al.
GEORGE, w. fr. 253 Race, b. W. 6th and W. 7th.
41 Elm,
81 Plum,
121 Central Av.
157 John,
195 Smith,
235 Mound,
293 Cutter,
306 Linn,
418 Baymiller.
GERMAN al. w. of Main, fr. 13th north.
GERRARD al. e. of Wallace al. fr. Front n.
GEST, w. fr. 269 Freeman, n. of Richmond (Plank Road.)
GIFFIN, e. fr. Ludlow, b. River and E. Front.
GILMORE al. b. Vine and Race, fr. Water to n. of Pearl.
GLASS al. b. Elder and Green fr. Elm to Race.
GLENN al. s. of Front, fr. Hogarth al. to Hazen.
GOLD al. s. of Charlotte, fr. Proctor al. to Peck al.
GORDON, e. of Wallace al. fr. Front to the n. line of Lewistown.
GORMAN, fr. Everett to Wade b. Linn and Baymiller.
GOOSE al. b. Bremen and Race, fr. 14th to Elder.
GRAHAM. n. of Ohio av. fr. Bremen to Ohio av.
GRAHAM'S al. w. fr. 17 Central Av. to Smith.

GRAND, e. of Old Wal. Hills road, from Morris to Nassau.
GRANT, w. fr. 403 Elm to Plum, b. 12th and 14th.
GREEN, w. fr. 621 Vine, n. of W. Liberty.
  13 Bremen,
  41 Race,
  59 Pleasant.
GREEN al. e. of Badeau al. fr. Front, n. on the e. boundary of Lewistown.
GREANLEAF'S al w. fr. 35 Central Av. b. W. Front and Augusta.
GROVE, n. of Fulton av. fr. Brooklyn to a point w. of Doane.
GUIOU al. e. of Central Av. fr. Court to n. of Canal.
HAFER al. b. Pleasant and Race, fr. Horton al. to Findlay, and fr. Forbus al. to Ham. Road.
HALPIN al. b. Pearl and 3d, fr. Dart al. to w. of Smith.
HAM al. b. Front and Burt, fr. Reed to Waldon.
HAMBURG, n. fr. 334 Hamilton Road, e. of Mohawk Bridge.
HAMER, n. fr. Huber to Elder.
HAMILTON, n. of Fulton av. fr. Wallace to Brooklyn.
HAMILTON ROAD, w. fr. 639 Main.
  63 Walnut,
  78 Locust,
  125 Elder,
  136 Poplar,
  153 Vine,
  221 Race,
  271 Elm,
  291 Dunlap,
  334 Hamburg.
HAMMOND, fr. 18 E. 3d.
HAND, n. fr. West Court to Clark, b. Rittenhouse and Linn.
HANNIBAL, n. fr. 616 W. 5th, w. of W. W. Canal.
HANOVER, n. fr. 18 Woodward to Franklin.
HARMAN al. w. of Jones, fr. Everett to Liberty.
HARRIET, n. fr. 756 W. Front, b, Carr and Horn.
HARRISON, e. fr. 170 Broadway, b. 5th and 6th.
HARRISON, w. fr. s. side of Brighton House.
HATHAWAY, w. fr. Jane to W. W. Canal, b. W. 6th and George.
HATHAWAY LANE, e. of Kemper Lane, fr. McMillan to Kemper Lane.
HATTERS al. b. 5th and Longworth, from Walnut to Central Av.
HAVEN al. w. of Elm, fr. 8th to Richmond.
HAY al. b. 13th and Mercer, fr. Boots al. to Beegar al.
HAZEN, e. of Brooklyn, fr. the Ohio River to the n. line of Carrsville.
HAZEN al. b. Pleasant and Elm, fr. Green to Hamilton Road.
HENDERSON al. w. of Broadway, fr. 7th to 8th.
HENRY, n. of Findlay, fr. Race to Dunlap.
HEUST al. b. Buckeye and Hamilton Road, fr. Vine to Main.
HICKORY, now added to Wade, w. fr. 307 Linn to Freeman, b Everett and W. Liberty.
HIGH, n. of Fulton av. fr. Washington to w. line of Carrsville.

HILL, e. fr. Observatory to Martin.
HIMMELSGARNS al. b. Pendleton and Spring, fr. Hunt to Union al.
HOADLY, w. of Stone, fr. 5th to 6th.
HOGARTH al. b. Brooklyn and Hazen, from Front to Glenn al.
HOLMES al. b. 2d and Pearl, fr. Sycamore to Broadway
HOME, n. fr. 186 W. 4th to 5th, b. Elm and Plum.
HOPKINS, w. fr. 491 Central Av. b. Clark and Laurel.
  30 John,
  103 Cutter,
  163 Linn,
  216 Platt.
HOPPLE'S al. e. fr. 90 Main to Sycamore.
HORNE, w. of McLean av. fr. Front to Mill Creek.
HORNE al. b. 6th and Weller, fr. Harriet to Skaats al.
HORTON al. b. Elder and Findlay, fr. Elm to Race.
HOTEL al. b. Broadway and Ludlow, fr. Front to 2d.
HOUSMAN al. b. Abigail and Hunt, fr. Br'dway to Spring.
HOWARD al. e. of Plum, fr. 5th to 6th.
HUBBARD, on the w. of the M. Canal, 3d to 8th.
HUBER, w. fr Hamer to Vine n. of Liberty.
HUGHES, n. fr. 61 E. Liberty.
  39 Schiller.
HUGHES al. b. Plum and Central Av. fr. 2d to Cherry al.
HULBERT al. b. Riddle and Western av. fr. Dayton to Bank.
HULSE al. e. of Jones, fr. David to Melancthon.
HUNT, e. fr. 442 Main, n. of Canal.
  41 Sycamore,
  81 Broadway,
  90 Spring.
IDA, w. of Parallax, fr. Court to near the north line of section 19.
IRWIN, e. of William, from Morgan to McMillan.
IRWIN al. b. Broadway and Ludlow, fr. Arch to 4th.
ISAAC al. w. of Central Av. fr. Clark to Hopkins.
ISRAEL al. e. of Freeman, fr. Court to Free al.
JACKSON, n. fr. 62 w. Canal b Walnut and Vine, 33 12th.
JAIL al, e. fr. 408 Main to Sycamore, b. Hunt and Abigail.
JAMES, w. of McGrew, fr. Fountain to Mason.
JAMES al. b. Harrison and 6th, fr. Scott al. to a point w. of Werner al.
JANE, n. fr. W. 6th, w. of Cutter.
JOHN, n. fr. River, b. Central Av. and Smith.
  5 Water,
  23 W. Front,
  41 Augusta,
  75 W. W. Canal,
  91 W. 3d,
  111 Webb,
  129 W. 4th,
  167 W. 5th,
  181 Longworth,
  197 W. 6th,
  211 George,
  225 W. 7th,
  245 W. 8th,
  259 9th,
  283 Richmond,
  305 Court,

327 Elizabeth,
349 Chestnut,
377 Clark,
397 Hopkins,
413 Laurel,
437 Betts,
455 Clinton,
479 Everett,
497 David,
513 Wade.
JOHNSON al. w. of Vine, fr. 7th to 12th
JONES, n. fr. 144 Everett to Liberty, b. Cutter and Linn.
JORDAN, w. of Baymiller, fr. Gest to Clark.
JOSEPH al. b. Laurel and Betts, fr. Cones al. to Peru al.
KAUTZ al. b. Broadway and Sycamore, fr. 2d to Holmes al.
KERR al. b. Warner and Baymiller, from Livingston to Ashton al.
KELLY al. b. Poplar and Findlay, fr. Western av. to Kent al.
KEMBLE, now added to W. 9th, w. fr. 335 Central Av.
  45 John,
  101 Fulton,
  223 Linn,
  271 Baymiller,
  349 Freeman,
  397 Carr,
  445 Harriett.
KEMPER al. b. Millan and Wayne, fr. a point w. of Fowler to Finch al.
KENDALL al. b. Cross and Hamilton Road, e. and w. fr. Elm.
KENNER, w. fr. Freeman n. of Hopkins.
KENT al. b. Freeman and Western av. fr. Poplar to Maple.
KENTON, n. fr. Montgomery Pike, e. of Kibby.
KIRBY, e. of Boone, fr. Montgomery Pike to McMillan.
KILGOUR, n. fr. 203 East Front.
KING al. b. Wood and Stone fr. Webb to 4th.
KIBBY, e. of Observatory, fr. Pavillion to Court.
KOSSUTH, n. fr. Court to Clark, b. Cutter and Rittenhouse
LAFAYETTE. e. of Symmes, fr. Short to McMillan.
LAKE al. b. Wade and Liberty, fr. Plum to Fall al.
LANGDON'S al. b. Sycamore and Main, fr. 7th to s. of Cutts al.
LATTA, s. of Cemetery, fr. Kemper lane to Hathaway lane.
LAUREL, al. b. 515 Central Av. b. Hopkins and Betts.
  41 John,
  61 Scott,
  99 Cutter,
  159 Linn.
LAUREL al. b. Freeman and Baymiller, fr. 8th to s. of George.
LAWRENCE, n. fr. River to E. 4th, b. Ludlow and Pike.
  11 E. Front,
  41 Pearl,
  71 E. 3d.
LAWRENCE al. b. Sycamore and Lafayette, fr. Wayne to Short
LAWSON al. n. fr. 10 E. 4th to 5th.
LAWYER, s. of Monroe, fr. Montgomery Pike to Irwin's E. line.
LEATHERBURY, on e. line of sec. 7, running fr. the Ohio River to Front

L'HOMMEDIEU al. b. George and 7th, fr. Mound to College.
LEVI al. b. Green and Liberty fr. Pleasant to Race.
LEWIS, e. of Gordon, fr. the Ohio River to McDowell.
LIBERTY, EAST, (the old Corporation Line,) e. fr. 624 Main.
  16 Hughes,
  37 Sycamore,
  51 Tanner,
  71 Broadway,
  89 Spring,
  98 Wilson,
  105 Pendleton,
  120 Young.
LIBERTY, WEST, (the old Corporation Line,) w. fr. 639 Main.
  21 Clay,
  41 Walnut,
  61 Vine,
  99 Bremen,
  117 Race,
  137 Pleasant,
  155 Elm,
  182 Logan,
  191 Plum,
  207 Providence,
  223 Central Av.
  261 John,
  283 Cutter,
  323 Jones,
  343 Linn,
  409 Baymiller,
  433 Dublin,
  463 Freeman.
LINCK al. s. of Frank al. fr. Bank to Hamilton Road.
LINDEN av. w. of McLean av. fr. Gest to the sec. line.
LINN, n. fr. 306 George, b. Cutter and Baymiller.
  19 Barr,
  33 W. 7th,
  41 Van Horn,
  53 W. 8th,
  69 9th,
  89 Richmond,
  111 Court,
  177 Clark,
  195 Hopkins,
  215 Laurel,
  237 Betts,
  257 Clinton,
  285 Everett,
  309 Hickory,
  349 Liberty,
  369 Oliver,
  387 Poplar,
  407 Livingston,
  427 Maple,
  457 York,
  487 Dayton.
LINNÆUS, n. of York, fr. Central Av. to John.
LITTLE al. b. Plum and Providence, fr. Bohn al. to Forbes al
LIVINGSTON, w. fr. Central Av. n. of Poplar.
  45 John,
  111 Linn,
  141 Werner,
  171 Baymiller.
LOCK, n. fr 249 E. 3d.
  33 E. 4th,
  77 E. 5th,
  113 6th.
LOCKPORT av. on the e. bank of M. Canal, fr. Broadway to Hunt.
LOCUST, n. fr. 78 Hamilton Road.
  27 Buckeye,
  30 Feete.
LODGE, n. fr. 66 W. 5th, b. Walnut and Vine to W. 7th.
  35 W. 6th,
  57 Gano.
LOGAN, n. fr. 182 W. Liberty b. Elm and Plum.
  73 Elder.

CINCINNATI CITY GUIDE. 13

LONG al. e. of Main, fr. Hunt to Liberty.
LONGWORTH, w. from 209 Vine.
  41 Race,
  81 Elm,
  119 Plum,
  161 Central Av.
  195 John,
  227 Smith,
  271 Mound,
  309 Park.
LOUISA, b. Freeman and Garrard, fr. Gest to Hopkins
LUCY, fr. Mary to Liberty.
LUDLOW, n. fr. River, b. Broadway and Lawrence.
  13 E. Front,
  27 E. 2d,
  47 E. Pearl,
  83 E. 3d,
  97 Arch.
LUDLOW av. w. of Garrard, fr. Gest to Flint.
LUKEN al. b. Pine and Freeman, fr. Gest to Flint.
LYTLE, n. fr. 134 E. 3d to E. 4th, b. Lawrence and Pike.
M'ALLISTER, n. fr. 98 E. 4th e. of Broadway to E. 5th.
M'CAMMON al. b. Mill and Smith, fr. Front to the Ohio River.
M'DOWELL, n. of Front, fr. Lewis to Gordon.
M'DOWELL al. n. of Front in McDowell's subdivision.
M'FARLAND, w. fr. 133 Elm. b. 3d and 4th, to Central Av.
M'GREW, n w. of Locust, fr. Mount to Locust.
M'ILVAIN, b. Sycamore and Locust, fr. Mound to Saunders.
M'LEAN av. w of Ludlow av. fr. 8th to Exeter.
M'MILLAN, northern boundary line.
MADEIRA. n. of Conklin, fr. Race to Ohio av.
MADISON, w. fr. 477 Elm to Plum. b 14th and Jefferson.
MAIDEN Lane, b. Front and 2d, fr. Gus al. to Anderson's al.
MAIN, n. fr. Pub. Landing, b. Walnut and Sycamore,
  47 2d,
  81 Pearl,
  90 Hopple's al.
  99 3d,
  153 4th,
  179 Church al.
  201 5th,
  223 Patterson's al.
  249 6th,
  277 Gano,
  303 7th,
  331 8th,
  367 9th,
  401 Court,
  431 Canal,
  444 Hunt,
  469 12th,
  490 Abigail,
  513 13th,
  514 Woodward,
  538 Franklin,
  564 Webster,
  575 Allison,
  590 Orchard,
  629 Liberty,
  641 Ham. Road,
  670 Schiller,
  677 Buckeye.
MALES al. e. of Cutter, fr. Everett to David.
MANSFIELD, n. fr. 58 Webster to Milton, b. Sycamore and Broadway.
  33 Liberty.
MAPLE, attached to Findlay, w. fr. M. Canal, n. of Ash.
  34 Central Av.
  73 John,
  135 Linn,

197 Piatt.
MAPLE, n. of Poplar, fr. Freeman to Western av.
MARGARET, w. of Mound, b 6th and George.
MARION, s. of Lawyer, fr. Montgomery Pike to Symmes.
MARSH al. b. Pole al. and Pearl, fr Park to sec. line.
MARTIN, n. of Front, fr. Pearl to Ash.
MARY, fr. Walnut to Vine, b. Allison to Liberty.
MASON, n. of Gage, fr. Sycamore to Findlay's n. line.
MATHER'S al. w. of Montgomery Pike fr. McMillan to Post al.
MAYNARD, e. of Padget, fr. Miller n.
MELANCTHON, w. fr. 651 Central Av. b. Wade and W. Liberty to Jones.
  43 John,
  65 Cutter.
MERCER, w. fr. 477 Walnut to Vine, b. 13th and Allison.
MIAMI, n. of Mulberry, fr. Sycamore to Locust.
MILK, b. Van Leur and McMillan, fr. Vine to McMillan
MILL. n. fr. 480 W. Front to W. 5th.
  55 W. W. Canal,
  71 W. 3d,
  83 Webb,
  101 W. 4th,
  117 Moses.
MILL al. b Mill and Wood, fr Front to the Ohio River.
MILLER, (new name St. Clair,) n. fr. 28 W. 6th, b. Main and Walnut.
  25 Gano.
  45 W. 7th,
  77 W. 8th,
  108 9th.
MILLER, n of Northern av. fr. Auburn to a point w. of Maynard.
MILTON, e. fr 540 Sycamore n. of E. Liberty.
  25 Mansfield,
  45 Broadway,
  73 Wilson,
  97 Young.
MITCHELL, n. fr. Celestial to Observatory Road,
MOHAWK, n. of Ham. Road, fr. Ravine to w. line of section 13.
MONROE, s. of DeKalb, fr. Montgomery Pike to Irwin's e. line.
MOORE al. e. of Plum, fr. 8th to Richmond.
MORGAN, s. of Wayne, fr. Copelen to Hunt.
MORRIS, s. of Nassau, fr. Eglantine av. to a point w. of Grand.
MORRIS al. b. Elm and Plum fr. 3d to 4th.
MOSES, (new name Avery,) b. W. 4th and W. 5th, commencing with number 55, b. Smith and Park.
  81 Park,
  101 Mill,
  145 Stone.
MOUND, n. fr. 406 W. 5th, b. Smith and Park.
  19 Longworth,
  37 W. 6th,
  47 George,
  63 Barr.
  75 W. 7th,
  83 Van Horn,
  93 W. 8th,
  111 9th,
  131 Richmond,
  151 Court,
  172 Elizabeth,
  196 Chesnut.

MOUNT, w. fr. Sycamore, n. of Reeder.
MULBERRY, EAST, e. fr. head of Main to Sycamore.
MULBERRY, WEST, w. fr. head of Main.
  27 Locust,
  79 Poplar,
NASSAU, s. of Berk, fr. Eglantine av. to a point w. of Grand.
NASSAU al. b. Front and Fulton av. fr. Reed to Waldon.
NEAL al. b. Betts and Clinton, fr. John to Gamble al.
NEFF al. b. Walnut and Vine, fr. Commerce to 2d.
NEST al. w. of Freeman, fr. Front to Sargent.
NEW, e. fr. 212 Sycamore, b. 6th and 7th.
NIAGARA, n. of Weeks, fr. Front to the Ohio River
NILES al. b. Franklin and Woodward, fr. Long al. to Coggswell al.
NINTH, EAST, e. fr. 370 Main.
  41 Sycamore.
NINTH, WEST, w. fr. 365 Main to Central Av.
  17 St. Clair,
  37 Walnut,
  75 Vine,
  109 Race,
  137 Ross,
  145 Elm,
  181 Plum.
☞ Kemble street is now attached to this, but as the numbers are principally the old ones, we refer for numbers to the old name.
NOBLE al. b. Carr al. and Stone, fr. Webb to Avery.
NORRIS al. n. of Mound, fr. McGrew to Norton al.
NORTH, n. fr. 54 E. 6th, b. Sycamore and Broadway.
NORTH al. b. McGrew and James, fr. Fountain to Locust.
NORTHERN av. n. of Coggswell av. fr. Auburn to East.
NORTON al. w. of Locust, fr. Mound to McGrew.
OAK, n. of Locust, fr. Ham. Road to Mulberry.
OBSERVATORY, n. fr. Hill to Hatch.
OBSERVATORY Road, n. & e. fr. Baum to Mitchell.
OHIO al. b. Adams and 15th, fr. Thuber al. to Pitt al.
OHIO av. n. fr. Ham. Road opp. Race.
OLIVER, w. fr. 697 Central Av. n. of Liberty.
  53 John,
  151 Linn.
OLIVER al. b. Reynolds al. and Walnut, fr. 2d to Dunseth al.
ORANGE al. b. Providence and Plum, fr. Ore al. to Fugate al.
ORCHARD, e. fr. 586 Main, b. Webster and Liberty, to Sycamore.
ORE al. s. of 15th, fr. Providence to Plum.
OREGON, n. of Baum, fr. 3d to Observatory Road.
O'RIELLY al. b. Pearl and 2d fr. Lawrence to Dawson al.
ORMSBY al. w. fr. Central Av. b. Augusta and W. 2d.
OWEN al. b. Clearwater and Bank, fr. Freeman to Allanthus.
PADGETT, e. of Auburn. fr. Miller n.
PANCOAST al. b. Main and Watson's al. fr. 7th to Court.

PARALLAX. w of Observatory, fr. Court to the n. line of sec. 12.
PARK, n. fr. 430, W. 2d, b. Smith and Mill, to W. 6th.
  39 W. W. Canal,
  61 W. 3d,
  75 Webb,
  89 W. 4th,
  105 Moses,
  129 W. 5th,
  147 Longworth.
PARK al b. Front and W. W. Canal, fr. Mill to w. of Ramsey.
PARSONS, n. fr. River to E. 3d, at 538 E. Front.
PATTERSON, w. of Coleman fr. Bank to Harrison av.
PATTERSON al. w. fr. 221 Main to Walnut, b. 5th and 6th.
PAVILION. n of Hill, fr. Observatory to Carney.
PEA al. b. Baymiller and Freeman, fr. Clark to Hopkins.
PEARL, EAST, (formerly Lower Market,) e. fr. 80 Main to 45 Sycamore.
☞ From Broadway this street is numbered as Congress. We attach the numbers assigned to that street (Congress.)
  43 Ludlow,
  77 Lawrence,
  123 Pike,
  167 Butler,
  221 Deer Creek Bridge,
  271 Kilgour.
☞ Pearl, north and south, are a continuation of W. Pearl, from Central Av. on the north and south sides of W. W. Canal. It is numbered as W. Canal Basin.
PEARL, WEST, w. fr. 79 Main. b. 2d and 3d.
  41 Walnut,
  77 Vine,
  121 Race,
  171 Elm,
PECK al. b. Proctor al. and John, fr. Gold al. to Charlotte.
PEETE, w. fr. Eden, b. Buckeye and Mulberry.
  31 Locust,
  87 Poplar,
PENDLETON, e. fr. 114 Hunt e. of Spring.
  27 Abigail,
  47 Woodward,
PENN, s. of Morgan, fr. Concord to Irwin's e. line.
PENNOCK al. b. Court and Richmond, fr. Freeman to Baymiller, & Linn to Cramsey al.
PERRY, w. fr. 167 Plum, b. 4th and 5th to Central Av.
PERRY al. w. of Race, fr. 8th to 12th.
PERU al. w. of Cutter, fr. Laurel to Betts.
PETER al. b. French and Hazen, fr. Bonte al. to Front
PHŒBE, w. fr. 53 Plum to Central Av.
PIATT, (now attached to Baymiller, but not yet numbered as part of that street), n. from Clark b. Linn and Freeman.
  97 Clinton,
  121 Everett,
  169 Hickory,
  211 W. Liberty,
  233 Oliver,
  251 Poplar,
  271 Livingston,
  327 York,
  361 Dayton,
  393 Bank,
PIATT al. b. 7th and 8th, fr. Elm to Walnut.

CINCINNATI CITY GUIDE.

PIERCE al. b. Clark and Hopkins, fr. Baymiller to Peaa l.
PIERSON, n. fr. 636 W. 5th, w. of W.W. Canal to W 6th.
PIKE, n. fr. River, b. Lawrence and Butler,
21 Front,
61 Pearl,
95 E. 3d,
123 E. 4th.
Pine, b. Jordan and Freeman, fr. Geat to Clark,
PINE al. b. Elm and Pleasant, fr. 15th to a point s. of 14th.
PINK al. e. of Freeman. fr. s. of Findlay to York al.
PIPE al. s. of Front, from Vance w.
PITT n. of Milk, fr. Vine to McMillan.
PITT al w. of Elm, fr. 15th to Adams.
PLEASANT, n. fr. Washington Park, b. Race and Elm.
10 14th,
57 15th,
115 Liberty,
145 Green.
PLEASANT Court, e. fr. 168 Elm, b. 4th and 5th.
PLOUGH al. b. Orchard & Liberty, from Long al. to Coggswell al.
PLUM, n. fr. River, b. Elm and Central Av.
9 Water,
25 Front,
47 Cherry,
57 Phœbe,
73 W. 2d,
93 Pearl,
111 W. 3d,
133 McFarland,
151 W. 4th,
169 Perry,
191 W. 5th,
211 Longworth,
229 W. 6th,
241 George
261 W. 7th,
291 W. 8th,
311 W. 9th,
323 William,
335 W. Court,
353 Grandin.
401 12th,
449 Ann,
481 Mason,
521 Everett,
571 Wade
601 W. Liberty,
613 Ash,
PLUM, e. side, fr. elbow of M. Canal,
302 W. Canal,
402 12th,
424 Grant,
462 14th,
502 Madison,
524 15th,
548 Adams,
570 Wade,
602 W. Liberty,
662 Elder.
POLE al. n. of 2d, from Park to section line.
POPLAR, w. fr. 719 Central Av. n. of Liberty,
47 John,
123 Linn,
183 Platt,
211 Dudley.
POST al. s. of McMillan, fr. Montgomery Pike to Mothers al.
PRESLEY al. b. Boone and Kilby, fr. Montgomery Pike to Wayne.
PRICE, fr. E. Liberty, e. of Young.
PROCTOR, al. e. of John, fr Findlay to Charlotte.
PRODUCE al. b. Main and Sycamore, fr. Kirby al. to Pearl.

PROSPECT, e. fr. Davis, n. of Boal.
PROVIDENCE, b. Central Av. and Plum, fr. 14th to Liberty, and fr. Oliver to Findlay.
43 15th,
91 Wade.
PUGH al. b. 4th and 5th, fr. Central Av. to Smith.
QUAIL al. s. of 14th. fr. Pine al. to Spruce al.
RACE. n. fr. River, b. Vine and Elm,
7 Water,
21 Front,
43 Commerce,
63 W. 2d.
71 Burrows,
91 Pearl,
99 Union,
107 W. 3d,
151 W. 4th,
191 W. 5th,
211 Longworth,
237 W. 6th,
255 George,
273 W. 7th,
297 W. 8th,
327 W. 9th,
359 W. Court,
381 W. Canal,
415 10th,
453 13th,
491 14th,
427 15th,
479 W. Liberty,
617 Green,
659 Elder,
701 Findlay.
RAMSAY, n fr. 502 W. Front to W. W. Canal w. of Mill.
RANKIN al. b. Clark and Hopkins, fr. Linn to Smith al.
RAVINE, w. of Byron, fr. Browne, north
REED, n. of Lentherbury, fr. Fulton Av. to the Ohio River.
REEDER, w. fr. 659 Sycamore, n. of Dorsey.
RENSHAW, s, of McMillan, fr. Dall east.
REYNOLDS al. n. of fr. 16 W. Front to Pearl.
RICE, w. of Alexander, fr Mulberry to Findlay's n. line.
RICHMOND, w. fr. 319 Elm. This street is from Elm to Central Avenue, a narrow st., (formerly William street,) and numbered as such.
41 Plum.
As Richmond street stands numbered, it commences at
359 Central Avenue,
39 John,
83 Fulton,
143 Cutter,
209 Linn,
555 Baymiller.
RIDDLE, w. of Patterson, fr. York al. to Harrison av.
RIDER, al. b. Dudley and Baymiller, fr. Wade to Poplar.
RIDGWAY al. b. Bremen and Vine, fr. 14th to Liberty.
RINGGOLD, e. fr. Walker, n. of Prospect
RITTENHOUSE, w. of Kossuth, fr. Court to Clark.
ROLL al b. 8th and 9th, fr. Harriet to Horne.
ROOT al. b. College and Race from Borden al. to L'Hommedieu al.
ROSE, n. from 362 W. Front to 3d, b. Smith and Park.
ROSE, al. b. 6th and Gano, fr. Dodson al. to Bodman al.
ROSS al. e. of Elm, fr. 7th to 12th.

ROWLAND al. n. of Fulton av. fr. Leatherbury to Rowland's E. line.
RUSS al. b Green and Fob al. fr. Hamer to Goose al.
RUSSELL, w. of Ida, fron Court, near the n. line o section 12.
ST. CLAIR, n. fr. 20 W 6th b. Main and Walnut to Ca nal.
25 Gano,
45 W. 7th,
77 W. 8th,
109 W. 9th.
SALMON al. b. 6th and New fr. Scott. al. east.
SARAH. b. Clark and Hopkins, fr. Garrard to Firma al.
SARGENT, w. fr. 25 Freema n. of W. Front.
SAUNDERS, n. of Mound, fr Young to Locust.
SAUNDERS al. b. Ludlow and Lawrence, fr. Front t Pearl.
SCHOOL, al. b. 8th and 9th fr. Central Av. w. to Schoo House.
SCOTT, n. fr. 64 Hopkins t Laurel, b. John and Cutter
SCOTT al. e. of Broadway, fr s of Harrison to 7th.
SECOND EAST, e. fr 46 Main to E. Front.
35 Sycamore,
71 Broadway,
113 Ludlow.
SECOND WEST, w. fr. 4 Main,
17 Reynolds,
33 Walnut,
73 Vine,
111 Race,
153 Elm,
193 Plum,
233 Central Av.
271 John,
309 Smith,
357 Rose,
430 Park,
SECOND al n. of 1st al. fr Hamer to Vine,
SECTION n. fr. E. Liberty e of Price.
SEEGAR al w. of Walnut fr 12th to Allison.
SELAS al. of Lewis, fr Front to the Ohio River.
SEVENTH, EAST, e. fr. 30(Main.
SEVENTH, WEST, w. fr. 30 Main.
19 St. Clair,
37 Walnut,
77 Vine,
109 Race,
147 Elm,
183 Plum,
227 Central Av.
263 John,
295 Smith,
333 Mound,
379 Cutter,
439 Linn,
481 Baymiller.
SHARP al. s. of Benton, fr. Beck to Mulberry.
SCHOLL al. b. Everett and Clinton, fr. Bard al. to Gumble al.
SHORT, e. fr. Symmes to Montgomery Pike.
SHORT, al. b. Elm and Plum, fr. Canal to Charles.
SCHULTZ al. b. Broadway and Spring, fr. Woodward to Housman al.
SHUTE al. b. 12th and Grant, b. Plum to Emerson al.
SIDERIAL, n. of Celestial, s. of the Observatory,
SIXTH EAST, e. fr 258 Main.
20 Langdon's al.
33 Sycamore,

CINCINNATI CITY GUIDE. 15

WISS al. b. 2d and Pearl, fr. Ross to section line.
SYCAMORE, fr. 21 Front, or Public Landing, b. Main and Broadway.
  37 E. 2d,
  63 Pearl,
  77 E. 3d,
  123 E. 4th,
  161 E. 5th,
  199 E. 6th,
  214 New,
  231 E. 7th,
  259 E. 8th,
  291 E. 9th,
  327 E. Court,
  351 E. Canal,
  365 Hunt,
  401 Abigail,
  425 Woodward,
  451 Franklin,
  473 Webster,
  495 Orchard,
  511 E. Liberty,
  542 Milton,
  555 Schiller,
  599 Burgoyne,
  615 Miami,
  631 Baltimore,
  647 Dorsey,
  661 Reeder.
SYMMES, e. of Fowler, from McMillan to Montgomery Pike.
TAYLOR, s. of Weller, fr. Carr e.
TAYLOR al. b Front & Pearl fr. Kilgour to M. Canal
THIRD, EAST, e fr 96 Main.
  41 Sycamore,
  77 Broadway,
  107 Ludlow,
  117 Lawrence,
  136 Lytle,
  154 Pike,
  191 Butler,
  208 Culvert,
  231 M Canal,
  242 Lock,
  262 Ellen,
  285 Kilgour.
THIRD WEST, w. fr. 97 Main.
  49 Walnut,
  87 Vine,
  129 Race,
  167 Elm,
  207 Plum,
  249 Central Av,
  277 John,
  313 Smith,
  409 Park,
  441 Mill,
  484 Stone,
  535 Wood.
THIRD al. n. of 2d al. fr. Hamer to Vine.
THIRTEENTH, w. fr. 513 Main.
  21 Clay,
  41 Walnut,
  61 Jackson,
  81 Vine,
  99 Bremen.
THOMAS, n. of Harrison av., fr. Brighton to Valley.
THOMAS al. b Langdon's al. and Main, fr. Cuts al. to 6th.
THORP'S al. b. 6th and Longworth, fr. Lodge to Central av.

THUBER al. e. of Plum, fr. 15th to Liberty.
TORRENCE al. b. Gage and Fountain, fr. Rice to James
TROY al. b. Doan and Starr fr. Grove n.
TRUMAN al. o of John, fr. Clark to Hopkins.
TRUNK al. b. 14th and 15th, fr. Central Av. to Providence.
TUCKER al b. 9th and Richmond, fr. Harriet to Horne.
TUNNEL al. b. Boone and Lafayette, fr. Wayne to Marion.
TURNER al. b. Riddle and Davidson, fr. Hulbert al. to Harrison av.
TWELFTH w. fr. 467 Main to Central Av. n. of Canal.
UNION, w. fr. 97 Race to Elm b. Pearl and 3d.
UNION al. b. Abigail and Hunt, from Pendleton to Spring.
VALLEY, w. of Cumminsville av. fr. Barnard's line to Alfred.
VANCE, e. of French, fr. Hamilton to the Ohio River.
VANCE al. w. of Doane, fr. Fulton av. n.
VAN HORNE, w. fr. 61 Mound b. W. 7th and W. 8th.
  53 Cutter,
  115 Linn,
  161 Baymiller.
VAN LEAR, b. Vine and Ohio av. fr. widow Hammond's n. line to Oh'o av.
VEASY al. b. Dale and Starr, fr. Grove n.
VERNON al. b. Hamburg and Byron. fr. Browne to n. of Mohawk.
VINE, n. fr. river, b. Walnut and Race.
  7 Water,
  21 W. Front,
  41 Commerce,
  57 W. 2d,
  91 Pearl,
  111 W. 3d,
  153 W. 4th,
  193 W. 5th,
  211 Longworth,
  231 W. 6th,
  258 Gano,
  273 W. 6th,
  293 W. 8th,
  727 W. 9th,
  355 Court,
  379 Canal,
  413 12th,
  455 13th,
  491 14th,
  501 Allison,
  533 15th,
  573 W. Liberty,
  594 Huber,
  621 Green,
  646 Benton,
  659 Elder,
  691 Ham. Road,
VON SEGGERN al. e. of Sycamore, fr. Abigail to Boal.
WADE, n. of David, fr. Elm to Jones, and fr. Linn to Freeman.

☞ This street is numbered from Elm to Plum under the old name of Monroe; from 569 Plum to Jones has heretofore been known as Wade and numbered
  21 Providence,
  39 Central Av.
  83 John,
  113 Cutter.
From Linn street this has heretofore been known as Hickory street, for the numbering of which refer to that street.
WALDON, n of Broad. fr. Fulton av. to the Ohio River.
WALKER, e. of Davis fr. Prospect to Auburn.
WALLACE al. e. of Vance fr. the Ohio River to a point n. of Hamilton.
WALNUT, n. fr. River, b. Main and Vine.
  3 Water,
  21 Front,
  41 Commerce,
  57 W. 2d,
  91 Pearl,
  111 W. 3d,
  137 Burnet,
  155 W. 4th,
  193 W. 5th,
  241 W. 6th,
  264 Gano.
  285 W. 7th,
  307 W. 8th,
  333 W. 9th,
  357 W. Court,
  379 W. Canal,
  413 12th,
  451 13th,
  479 Mercer,
  503 Allison,
  563 W. Liberty.
WALNUT HILLS ROAD, e. of Montgomery Pike, from Deer Creek Road to Montgomery Pike.
WARD al. w. of Fowler fr. De Kalb to Penn.
WARNER, s. of Bosley, fr. Wheeler to a point e. of Elm.
WASHINGTON, fr. River. e. Collard.
WATER, w. fr. Pub. Landing, at foot of Main.
  43 Walnut,
  81 Vine,
  121 Race,
  161 Elm,
  201 Plum,
  211 Central Av.
  281 John.
WATSON al. b. Sycamore and Pancoast al. fr. 7th to Canal.
WAYNE, s. of McMillan, fr. Copelen to Irwin's e. line.
WEBB, n. of 3d, from John to Wood, numbered from 103 Smith.
  111 Park,
  141 Mill,
  187 Stone.
WEBSTER, e. fr. 562 Main b. Franklin and Orchard, to Broadway.
  39 Sycamore,
  60 Tanner.

WENDELL al. b. Fox and Rice, fr. Mulberry to Findlay's line.
WERNER, n. fr. Poplar, b. Linn and Platt.
WESTCOTT al. e. of Plum, fr. Charles to 12th.
WEST al. b. Ramsay and Mill, fr. Park al. n.
WESTERN AV. n. fr. W. Liberty, w. of Freeman.
WETSEL al. b. Madison and 15th, fr. Plum to Elm.
WHEELER al. w. of Parsons, fr. Front to the Ohio River.
WHETSTONE al. b. 7th and 8th, fr. Main to Broadway.
WHITE al. w. of Plum, fr. Richmond, north.
WHITEMAN, e. of Linn, fr. Dayton to Bank.
WHITEWATER, fr. Carr, b. Fremont and W. 8th.
WHITAKER, n. fr. River to Morton, e. of Parsons.
WILKINSON, s. of Penn, fr. Montgomery Pike to Irwin's e. line.
WILKYMACKY al. s. of 12th, fr. Main to Walnut.
WILLIAM, e. of Hunt, fr. Morgan to McMillan.
WILLOW, n. of Niagara, fr. Front to the Ohio River.
WILLOW al. b. Madison and 14th, from Plum to Elm.
WILSON, n. fr. e. Liberty to Milton, b Broadway and Young.
WILT al. b. Central Av. and Little al. fr. Bohn to 14th.
WINDSOR, n. fr. 6th, b. Kemper line to Hathaway lane.
WISE al. b. Betts and Clinton, fr e. of Cutter to Freeman.
WOLF al. b. Druggist al. and Walnut, fr. Church al. to 5th
WOOD, n. fr. River, w. of Mill.
  9 Front,
  21 W. 3d,
  48 W. 4th,
  53 Avery.
WOOD al. b. Plum and Central Av. fr. 6th to 7th.
WOODWARD, e. fr. 512 Main b. Abigail and Franklin.
  10 Hanover,
  36 Sycamore,
  81 Broadway,
  90 Spring.
WRIGHT al. b. Mohawk and Cross, e. and w. fr. Hamburg.
XAVIER al. b. Findlay and Charlotte, fr. Snyder al. w.
YEATMAN, e. fr. 16 Sycamore to Broadway.
YORK, w. fr. 807 Central Av.
YORK al. b. York and Dayton, fr. Western av. to Linn.
YOUNG, n. fr. 118 e. Liberty, e. of Wilson.
ZIG ZAG av. s. of the n. boundary of Cincinnati, fr. Fairview av. to the section line.

Church Directory.

BAPTIST.

First Baptist Church, north side Court, between Mound and Cutter; service morning and evening; Rev. E. G. Taylor, Pastor.
High Street Baptist Church, east of City Water Works; service morning and evening; Rev. —— Price, Pastor.
Mt. Auburn Baptist Church, Rev. S. W. Lynd, Pastor.
Ninth Street Baptist Church, south side 9th, between Vine and Race, service morning and evening; Rev. E. T. Robinson, Pastor.
Freeman Street Baptist Church, Freeman, near foot of 5th street; service morning and evening; ——, Pastor.
Welsh Baptist Church, north side Harrison; service morning and evening; Rev. —— Davis, Pastor.
Baker Street Baptist Church (colored), south side Burnet, between Walnut and Vine; service morning and evening; Rev. —— White, Pastor.
Third Street Baptist Church (colored), south side 3d, between Race and Elm; service morning and evening; Rev. Wallace Shelton, Pastor.

CHRISTIAN.

First Christian Church, Longworth, between Central Av. and John; service morning and evening. ——, Pastor.

CONGREGATIONAL.

First Orthodox Congregational Church, north side 7th, bet. Central Av. and John; Rev. Henry M. Storrs, Pastor; service morning and evening.
Second Orthodox Congregational Church, east side Vine, between 8th and 9th; Rev. Charles B. Boynton, Pastor; service morning and evening.
Welsh Congregational Church, west side Lawrence, between 3d and 4th; Rev. Thomas Edwards, Pastor; service morning and evening.

DISCIPLES OF CHRIST.

Christian Church, south-west corner Walnut and 8th; service morning, afternoon and evening.
Christian Church, 6th between Smith and Mound; ——, Pastor; service morning, afternoon and evening.
Christian Church, between T. P 13 and 14. Fulton; ——, Pastor; service morning, afternoon and evening.
Christian Church (colored), north side Harrison; Elder Rufus Conrad, Pastor; service morning, afternoon and evening.
Union Mission Church, north side 9th, between Baymiller and Freeman; Rev. T. J. Melish, Pastor; service morning at 11 o'clock, and afternoon at 4 o'clock.

FRIENDS.

First Friends (Orthodox), 5th between Central Av. & John; services mornings of 1st and 5th days.
First Friends (Hicksite), 6th between Central Av. & John; services mornings of 1st and 5th days.

GERMAN EVANGELICAL UNION.

German United Evangelical Church, corner Bremen and 15th; Rev. Ernst Roos, Pastor; service 10 A. M.
German United Evangelical Church, east side Elm, between 12th and 13th; Rev. Maurice Raschig, Pastor; service 10 A. M.
German United Evangelical Church, north side 6th, between Walnut and Vine; Rev. Augustus Kroell, Pastor; service 10 A. M.
German United Evangelical Church, corner 13th and Walnut ——, Pastor; service 10 A. M.
German United Evangelical Church, corner Race and 15th; Rev. G. W. Eisenlohr, Pastor; service 10 A. M.

GERMAN REFORMED.

First German Reformed Church, north-west corner of Elm and 15th; Hermann Rust, Pastor; service morning and evening.
Second German Reformed Church, south side Findlay, west of Baymiller; Rev. Samuel Mease, Pastor.
Third German Reformed Church, Franklin and Sycamore; Rev. C. Saure, Pastor; services morning and evening.

JEWISH SYNAGOGUES.

Holy Congregation, Children of Israel, south-east corner 6th and Broadway; Rev. Dr. Lilienthal, Rabbi; Julius Freiberg, Parnas.
Holy Congregation, Children of Jeshurun; Lodge, between 5th and 6th; Rev. Dr. Isaac M. Wise, Rabbi; Emil Block, Parnas.
Holy Congregation of Brethren in Love, Race, between 13th and Liberty; M Brown, Parnas.
Polish Congregation of the K. K. Adat. Israel, corner Walnut and 7th; B. Muskewitz, Minister; S. Isaacs, Parnas.
Shearith Israel, Lodge, between 6th and 7th; Nathan Moses, Minister; Nathan Malzer, Parnas.

LUTHERAN.

English Evangelical Lutheran Church, east side Elm, between 9th and Court; Rev. Wm. H. Harrison, Pastor; service morning and evening.
German Evangelical Lutheran Church, east side of Race, between 15th and Liberty; Rev. F. King, Pastor; service morning and afternoon.
German Evangelical Lutheran Church, west side Walnut, between 8th and 9th; Rev. C. Turke, Pastor; service 10 A. E.

METHODIST EPISCOPAL.

East Cincinnati District.—W. Young, Presiding Elder.
Union Ch., north side 7th, between Central Av. and Plum; ——, Pastor; service morning and evening.
Wesley Ch., north side 5th, between Sycamore and Broadway; Rev. J. M. Leavitt, Pastor; service morning and evening.
Trinity Ch., north side 9th, between Race and Elm; Rev. W. X. Ninde, Pastor; service morning and evening
Asbury Ch., south side Webster, between Main and Sycamore; Rev. George Parrot, Pastor, service morning and evening.
McKendree Ch., (Seventeeth Ward). Front street; Rev. C. R. Lovell, Pastor; service morning and evening.
New Street Methodist Ch., (colored), east of Broadway; Rev. ——, Pastor; service morning and evening.
Mt. Auburn Ch., Rev. T. J. Harris, Pastor; service morning and evening.
Collins Ch., T. J. Harris, Pastor.
East Pearl Street Ch., Pearl, between Broadway and Ludlow; Rev. M. J. Cramer, Pastor; service morning and evening.
Walnut Hills Ch., Walnut Hills; Rev. C. R. Lovell, Pastor; service morning and evening
West Cincinnati District—Rev. M. Marlay, Presiding Elder
Morris Ch., west side Central Av. between 4th and 5th; Rev. Wm. H. Fyffe, Pastor; service morning and evening.
Christie Ch., north side Court, between Mound and Cutter; Rev. Wm. I. Fee. Pastor; service morning and evening.
Raper Ch., west side Elm, north of Findlay; Rev. D. J. Starr, Pastor; service morning and evening.
Park Street Ch., south-east corner Park and Longworth; Rev J. T. Mitchell, Pastor; service morning and evening.
York Street Ch., south-west corner Baymiller and York; Rev. John M. Waldon, Pastor; service morning and evening.
Finley Ch., south side Clinton, between Cutter and Linn; Rev. B A. Meharry, Pastor; service morning and evening.
Carr Street Ch., Clark Street Ch., and Mears Ch., Rev. M. Dustin, Pastor.

METHODIST EPISCOPAL—GERMAN.

Cincinnati German District.—Rev. J. L. Klein, Presiding Elder.
First German M. E. Ch., east side Race, between 13th and 14th; Rev. H. D. Schmidt, Pastor; service morning and evening.
Second German M. E. Ch., south side of Everett, near Linn; Rev. C. Gahn, Pastor; service morning and evening.
Third German M. E. Ch., Buckeye, head of Main; Rev. A. Loebenstein, Pastor; service morning and evening.

METHODIST PROTESTANT.

First Methodist Protestant Ch., 6th, between Vine and Race; Rev Joseph White, Pastor; service morning and evening.
Second Methodist Protestant Ch., Elm, between 15th and Liberty; Rev. ——, Pastor; service morning and evening.
George Street Ch., between Cutter and Linn; Rev. —— King, Pastor; service morning and evening.

METHODIST CALVINISTIC.

Welsh Methodist Ch., College, between 6th and 7th; Rev. Howell Powell, Pastor; service morning and evening.

METHODIST—COLORED.

African Ch., Sixth, east of Broadway; Rev. John Warren, Pastor.

NEW JERUSALEM.

Temple, Longworth, between Race and Elm; Rev. Chauncey Giles, Pastor; service morning and evening.

PRESBYTERIAN—OLD SCHOOL.

First Presbyterian Church, 4th, between Main and Walnut; Rev. John E. Annan, Pastor; service morning and evening.
Fifth Presbyterian Church, south-west corner John and Clark; Rev. D. O. Davies, Pastor; service morning and evening.
Seventh Presbyterian Church, west side Broadway, between 4th and 5th; Rev. N. C. Burt, D. D., Pastor; service morning and evening.
Central Presbyterian Church, north-west corner Barr and Mound; Rev. ——, Pastor; service morning and evening.
Ninth Presbyterian Church, David street, west of Cutter; Rev. ——, Pastor; service morning and evening.
First Presbyterian Church (Walnut Hills); Rev. ——, Pastor; service morning and afternoon.

PRESBYTERIAN—NEW SCHOOL.

Second Presbyterian Church, south side 4th, between Vine and Race; Rev. M. L. P. Thompson, Pastor; service morning and evening.

CINCINNATI CITY GUIDE. 17

Third Presbyterian Church, south-west corner 4th and John; ——, Pastor; service morning and evening.
West End Mission Church, Poplar, near Freeman; Joseph Chester, Pastor.
Eighth Presbyterian Church, 7th, between Linn and Bay miller; Rev. George M. Maxwell, Pastor. The hours of service are 11 A. M., and 7½ P. M; Sabbath School in the afternoon, 2 P. M. Weekly lectures on Wednesday evening, and Conference on Friday evening.

PRESBYTERIAN—UNITED.

United Presbyterian Church, 6th, between Race and Elm; ——, Pastor; service morning and afternoon.
United Church, corner Cutter and 7th; Rev. R. H. Pollock, Pastor; service morning and afternoon.
Union Mission Church, Orchard, between Sycamore and Main; Rev. Wm. C. McCune, Pastor.

PRESBYTERIAN REFORMED.

Reformed Presbyterian Church, south side George street, between Race and Elm; Rev. ——, Pastor; service morning and afternoon.
Church of the Covenanters, south side 9th, between John and Mound; Rev. Wm. Wilson, D. D., Pastor; service morning and afternoon.

PROTESTANT EPISCOPAL.

Christ's Church, north side 4th, between Sycamore and Broadway; Rev. ——, Rector, Richard Gray, Missionary; service morning and evening.
St. Paul's Church, south side 4th, between Main and Walnut; Rev. T. Holcomb, D. D., Rector; service morning and evening.
St. John's Church, south east corner Plum and 7th; Rev. Geo. A. Heather, Rector; service morning and evening.
Church of the Advent, Walnut Hills; Rev. Wm. A. Smallwood, Rector.
Church of the Atonement, corner Richmond and Cutter; Rev. Richard Gray, Rector; service morning and evening.
Church of the Redemption, Clinton, between Central Av. and John; B. K. Maltby, Pastor.
Calvary Church, Clifton; Rev. W. F. Lloyd, Rector.

ROMAN CATHOLIC.

St. Peter's Cathedral, south-west corner Plum and 8th; Most Rev. J. B. Purcell, D. D., Very Rev. E. T. Collins, V. G., Very Rev. E. Purcell, V. G., Rev. C. H. Borgess, Rev. W. J. Haily; service morning and afternoon.
St. Francis Xavier, west side Sycamore, between 6th and 7th, Rev. Chas. Driscoll, S. J., Rev. H. Roelof, S. J., Rev. John De Bliek, S. J., Rev. F. Acmal, S. J., Rev. D. Kenny, S. J.; service morning, afternoon and evening.
St. Thomas, west side Sycamore, between 5th and 6th; attended from St. Xavier's, service morning and afternoon.
St. Patrick's, north-east corner 3d and Mill; Rev. F. Cubero, O. S. D.; service morning and afternoon.
Holy Trinity, (German) south side 5th, between Smith and Park; Rev. D. Hengehold, Rev. J. H. Ridder; service morning and afternoon.
St. Mary's (German) south-east corner Clay and 13th, Rev. J. B. Eikmann, Rev. M. Bermann; service morning and afternoon.
St. John's (German) corner Bremen and Green; Rev. Nicholas Wachter, O. S. F., Superior, Rev. Otho Jair, O. S. F., Rev. Dionysius Abarth, O. S. F.; service morning and afternoon.
St. Paul's (German) south-east corner Spring and Abigail; Very Rev. Joseph Ferneding, V. G.; Rev. Herman Ferneding; service morning and afternoon.
St. Joseph's (German), south-east corner Linn and Laurel; Rev. Engelbert Stehle, Rev C. A. Gerst; service morning and afternoon.
St. Philomena (German), north side Pearl, between Pike and Butler. Rev. G. H. Kuhr, D, D., Rev. A. M. Toebbe; service morning and afternoon.
St. Augustine's (German), Bank st; Rev. N. J. Menge, Rev. H. Kehringe; service morning and afternoon.
St. Michael's (German), west side Mill Creek; Rev. M. Deselairs; service morning and afternoon.
St. Francis Seraphicus' (German) corner Liberty and Vine; Very Rev. Eusebius Schmid Custos O. S. F., Rev. Ubald Webersinke, O. S. F., Rev. Anthony Decker, O. S. F.; service morning and afternoon.
St. Anthony's (German), south side Budd, between Carr and Donnersberger; Rev. W. Deiters.
All Saints, corner of High and Court; Rev. David Walker, O. S. F.
Immaculate Conception, Mount Adams; Rev. H. Tappert, O. S. F.
Holy Angels, on Torrence Road (17th Ward); Rev. Thomas Walsh.
St. Francis of Sales; East Walnut Hills; Rev. Aloysius Hattala.
Chapel of Sisters of Charity south side McFarland, between Plum and Central Av.; attended from the Cathedral.
Chapel of the Sisters of Notre Dame, 6th, between Sycamore and Broadway; attended by a Jesuit Father, also from the Cathedral.

Chapel of the Sisters of Mercy, 3d, between Central Av. and John; attended from Cathedral.
Sisters of the Poor of St. Francis (St. Clair's Convent), corner 3d and Lytle; attended from St. Xavier.

UNITARIAN.

First Congregational Unitarian Church, south-west corner 4th and Race; Rev. M. D. Conway, Pastor; service morning and evening.
Church of the Redeemer, Rev. ——, Pastor; services every Sabbath, in the Church, corner of 6th and Mound.

UNITED BRETHREN IN CHRIST.

First Chapel, corner of Mound and Richmond; Rev. ——, Holezinger, Pastor; service morning and evening.
Second German United Brethren Church, west side Rittenhouse, between Court and Clark, Rev. B. Hoffman, Pastor; service morning and evening.

UNIVERSALIST.

First Universalist Church, east side of Plum, between 4th and 5th. Pastorship vacant; Rev. J. D. Williamson, D. D. supplying statedly; service morning and evening.

Public Buildings.

Apollo Building, n.w.c. Walnut and Fifth.
Art Union, n.w.c. Fourth and Sycamore.
Bacon's Building, c Walnut and Sixth.
Bank Buildings, n.w.c. Main and Third.
Brachmann's Building, s.s. Third b. Main and Walnut.
Bromwell's Building, n.w.c. Sycamore and Front.
Boylan's Building, n.s. Fourth, b. Walnut and Vine.
Carlisle Building, s.w.c. Fourth and Walnut
Catholic Institute, n.w.c. Vine and Longworth streets.
Church Buildings, Walnut b. Third and Fourth.
Cincinnati Observatory, Mt. Adams.
Commercial Building, n.e.c. Fourth and Race.
College Hall, Walnut b. Fourth and Fifth.
Court House, Main. opp. Court.
City Hall, Eighth, b. Plum and Central Av.
Court Street Hall, n.s. Court b. Main and Walnut.
Clinton Building, n.w.c. Central Av. and Clinton.
Columbian Hall, n.e.c. Central Av. and Court.
Deholt Building, s.e.c. Court and Main.
Ruqueer Building, c. Vine and Burnet.
Evans' Building, Third, b. Vine and Walnut.
Franklin Rooms, s.w.c. Longworth and Vine.
Gazette Buildings, n.e.c Fourth and Vine.
Greenwood Hall, in Mechanics' Institute, c. Sixth and Vine.
Jefferson Hall, c. Twelfth and Main.
Law Buildings, s s. Third, b. Main and Sycamore.
Lecterum Building, 73 West Third.
Liverpool and London Ins. Co. Building, s.w.c. Main and Third.
Locke's Building. Walnut, b. Third and Fourth, John Locke. Proprietor.
Losantiville Hall, Front, near Deercreek Bridge.
Magnolia Hall (Odd Fellows), n.w.c. Sixth and Walnut.
Marietta Railroad Building, s.w.c. Third and Sycamore.
Masonic Temple, n.e.c. Third and Walnut.
Melodeon, n. w. c. Fourth and Walnut.
Mechanic's Institute, s.w.c. Vine and Sixth.
Medical College of Ohio, Sixth, b. Vine and Race.
Merchant's Block, Walnut, b. Third and Fourth.
Merchants' Exchange, in College Hall.
Meline's Building, 99 West Third.
Metropolitan Building, c. Ninth and Walnut.
National Hall, Vine, b. Fifth and Sixth.
National Hall, Vine, b. Canal and Ninth.
National Theater, Sycamore, b. Third and Fourth.
Neave's Building, n.w.c. Race and Fourth.
Neff's Building, n.e.c. Ninth and Elm.
Odd Fellows' Hall, n.w.c. Walnut and Third
Ohio Valley Bank, Third b Walnut and Vine.
Pike's Opera House, s.s. Fourth, b. Walnut and Vine.
Queen City Hall, c. Eighth and Freeman.
Railroad Buildings, n.w.c. Court and Main.
Reeder's Building, s.s Third, b. Walnut and Vine.
St. John's Hotel des Invalids, n.w.c. Third and Plum.
Selves' Building, s s. Third, b. Main and Walnut.
Short's Building, s. s. Fourth, b. Main and Sycamore.
Skaut's Hall c. Eighth and Freeman.
Smith & Ditson's Hall, 24 West Fourth.
Taylor's Building, s.w.c. Third and Walnut.
Times Building, n.s. Third, b. Walnut and Vine.
Turner Hall, w.s. Walnut. near Allison.
Union Block, n.s. Third, b. Sycamore and Broadway.
U. S. Custom House, c. Fourth and Vine.
Western Museum, e. s. Sycamore, b. Third and Fourth.
William Penn Hall, n.e.c. Eighth and Central Av.
Wood's Theater, s.e.c. Sixth and Vine.

Secret Associations.

Masonic

N. C Harmony Lodge, No. 2. Instituted ——— 1794. Stated meetings, first Wednesday in each month.
Miami Lodge No. 46. Instituted December 21st, 1818. Stated meetings, first Tuesday.
Lafayette Lodge, No. 81. Instituted January 11th, 1826. Stated meetings, first Thursday.
Cincinnati Lodge, No. 133. Instituted Oct. 24th, 1843. Stated meetings, last Thursday.
McMillan Lodge, No. 141. Instituted October 20th, 1847. Stated meetings, last Wednesday.
Cynthia Lodge, No. 155. Instituted October 15th, 1849. Stated meetings, first Friday.
Hanselman Lodge, No. 208. Instituted October 25th, 1851. Stated meetings, fourth Monday.
Yeatman Lodge, No. 162. Instituted September 27th, 1848. Stated meetings, Wednesday, on or before each full moon.
Cincinnati Chapter, No 2. Instituted October 24th, 1816. Stated meetings, first Monday.
McMillan Chapter, No. 19. Instituted October 23d, 1846. Stated meetings, last Tuesday.
Cincinnati Council, No. 1. Stated meetings, third Monday.
Cincinnati Encampment, No. 3. Instituted September 17th, 1841. Stated meetings, second Monday.
Gibulum Lodge of Perfection. Stated meetings, second Thursday.
Dalcho Council of P. of J. Stated meetings, third Thursday.
Grand Chapter of Rose Croix. Meets second Thursday evenings in March, June, September and December.
Grand Consistory of P. of R. Secret, 32. Meets first Thursday evening in January, April, July and October.
The four last named bodies meet in the Hall n.w.c. of Sixth and Main streets. All the others in the hall corner of Third and Walnut streets.

I. O. O. F.

ODD FELLOWS' HALL, COR. THIRD AND WALNUT.
Ohio Lodge, No. 1. Instituted December 23d, 1830. Meets every Monday.
Washington, No. 2. Instituted January 10th, 1832. Meets every Tuesday.
Cincinnati, No. 3. Instituted July 4th, 1832. Meets every Wednesday.
Franklin, No. 4. Instituted May 3d, 1833. Meets every Thursday.
Cincinnati Degree Lodge, No. 1. Meets every Friday.
Wildey Encampment No. 1. Instituted September 10th, 1832. Meets first and Third Fridays.

MAGNOLIA HALL, CORNER SIXTH AND WALNUT.
Magnolia Lodge, No. 83. Instituted March 29th, 1847. Meets every Monday.
Woodward, No. 149. Instituted February 28th, 1850. Meets every Tuesday.
Humboldt, No. 279. Instituted May 18th, 1855. Meets every Wednesday.
Crystal Fount, No. 176. Instituted March 13th, 1851. Meets every Thursday.
Cincinnati Encampment, No. 22. Instituted March 26th, 1847. Meets second and fourth Friday.
Herrman Encampment, No. 16. Instituted September 29th, 1853. Meets first and third Friday.

HALL, ON HIGH STREET.
Vulcan Lodge, No. 178. Instituted March 17th, 1851. Meets every Monday.
Charter Oak Encampment.

EAGLE HALL SOUTH-WEST CORNER OF EIGHTH AND CENTRAL AVENUE.
Eagle Lodge, No. 100. Instituted February 8th, 1848. Meets every Monday.
William Tell Lodge, No. 315. Meets every Wednesday.
Mukatewah Encampment, No. 31. Instituted January 20th, 1849. Meets second and fourth Friday.
Metropolitan Lodge, No. 142. Instituted Janury 23d, 1850. Meets every Tuesday.

HALL, CORNER OF FREEMAN AND EIGHTH.
Queen City Lodge, No. 229. Instituted March 24th, 1854. Meets every Monday.
Pioneer Encampment, No. 72. Meets second and fourth Fridays.

WILLIAM PENN LODGE, CORNER OF EIGHTH AND CENTRAL AVENUE.
Palmetto Lodge, No. 165. Instituted March 14th 1851. Meets every Monday.

William Penn, No. 56. Instituted December 11th, 1845. Meets every Tuesday.
American Lodge, No. 170. Instituted December 19th, 1850. Meets every Wednesday.
Union Degree Lodge, No. 2. Meets second and fourth Thursday.
Washington Encampment, No 9. Instituted March 7th, 1846. Meets first and third Thursday.
Philadelphia Encampment, No. 53. Instituted March 27th, 1853. Meets first and third Friday.

TEMPLE HALL, FULTON.
Fulton Lodge, No. 112. Instituted August 17th, 1848. Meets every Thursday.

GERMANIA HALL, COURT STREET, NEAR MAIN.
Herman Lodge, No. 208. Instituted February 18th, 1853. Meets every Monday.
North Western Lodge, No. 290. Instituted April 1st, 1856. Meets every Tuesday.
Mohawk Lodge, No. 150. Instituted March 2d, 1850. Meets every Wednesday.
Germania Lodge, No. 113. Instituted August 29th, 1848. Meets every Thursday.
Queen City Encampment, No. 43. Instituted January 31st, 1851. Meets first and third Friday.
Schiller Encampment, No. 42. Instituted September, 7th, 1850. Meets second and fourth Friday.

HALL, CORNER WADE AND CENTRAL AVENUE.
Fidelity Lodge, No. 171. Instituted September 23d, 1846. Meets every Monday.
Losantiville Lodge, No. 336. Instituted ———, Meets every Thursday.
Hesperia Encampment, No. 37. Instituted February 19th, 1850. Meets second and fourth Wednesday.

HALL, DEBOLT BUILDING.
Teutonia Lodge, No. 177. Instituted March 15th, 1851. Meets every Monday.

HALL, MECHANICS' INSTITUTE.
Eclipse Lodge, No. 348. Meets every Wednesday.

American Protestant Association.

Augustus Adolphus Lodge, No. 10. Instituted July 8th, 1857. Meets every Tuesday evening, at Hall n.w.c. Eighth and Freeman.
Harmonia Lodge, No. 6. Instituted October 18th, 1854. Meets every Friday, at Hall s.w.c. Court and Walnut.
Liberty Lodge, No. 2. Instituted July 14th, 1853. Meets every Tuesday, at Hall s.w.c. Wade and Central Av.
Martin Luther Lodge, No. 3. Instituted March 2d, 1854. Meets every Monday, at Hall s.w.c. Court and Walnut.
Ohio Lodge, No. 1. Instituted July 12th, 1853. Meets every Monday, at Union Hall, w.s. Plum, b. Seventh and Eighth.
Queen City Lodge. No. 5. Instituted May 27th, 1854. Meets every Friday, at Union Hall, w.s. Plum, b. Seventh and Eighth.
Union Lodge, No. 9. Instituted July, 1855 Meets every Tuesday, at Union Hall, w.s. Plum, b. Seventh and Eighth.
Washington Lodge, No. 4. Instituted April, 1854. Meets every Thursday, at Washington Hall, Mechanics' Institute, s.w.c. Sixth and Vine.
Washington Encampment, No. 1. Instituted December 5th, 1851. Meets every second and fourth Tuesday in each month at Hall, c. Main and Abigail.
William Penn Encampment, No. 1. Instituted August 21st, 1852. Meets second and fourth Monday in each month at Good Fellows' Hall, s.e.c. Main and Court.

Independ't Order of Bene Berith.

District Grand Lodge. No. 2. Instituted 1828. Meets quarterly at Magnolia Hall, Fifth, b. Sycamore and Main J. M. Miller, Grand Massi Ab.
Bethel Lodge, No. 4. Instituted 1848. Meets every Sunday evening at same Hall. Officers elected semi-annually.
Jerusalem Lodge, No. 12. Instituted 1850. Meets every Monday at same Hall.
Mount Carmel Lodge, No. 20. Instituted 1854. Meets every Wednesday at same Hall.
Berith Abraham Lodge. Meets every Sunday evening in Bacon's Building, c Sixth and Walnut.

Druids.

Armenia Grove, No. 3. Instituted 1849. Meets every Monday at Hall, n.s. Ninth. b. Main and Sycamore.
Franconia Grove, No. 8. Instituted 1842. Meets every Wednesday at Armonia Hall on Ninth street.
Germania Grove, No. 5. Instituted 1850. Meets every Wednesday at Druid's Hall, n s. Court b. Main and Walnut.
Jefferson Grove, No. 4. Instituted 1850. Meets every Tuesday at Druid's Hall, n.s. Court, b. Main and Walnut.

Norma Grove, No. 7. Instituted 1851. Meets every Monday at Bacon's Building.
Western Grove, No. 1. Instituted 1849. Meets every Monday at Druid's Hall, n.s. Court, b. Main and Walnut.
Ohio Oak Grove, No. 11. Instituted 1858. Meets every Thursday at Western Grove Hall.

DEGREE GROVE.

Cincinnati Degree Grove, No. 1. Meets second and fourth Friday in each month at Druid's Hall, n.s. Court b. Main and Walnut.

CHAPTER.

Humboldt Chapter, No. 1. Instituted 1853. Meets first and second Friday in each month at Druid's Hall, n.s. Court, b. Main and Walnut.

A. O. of G. F.

Concordia Lodge, No. 11 Instituted November 2d, 1852. Meets every Tuesday at Hall w.s. Walnut b. Thirteenth and Mercer.
Franklin Lodge, No. 2. Instituted May 22d, 1847. Meets every Wednesday at Hall, c. Main and Abigail.
Germania Lodge, No. 5. Instituted February 24th, 1852. Meets every Wednesday at Good Fellows' Hall, s.w.c. Court and Main.
Guttenberg Lodge, No. 10. Instituted October 28th, 1852. Meets every Tuesday at Smith's Hall, n.s. Ninth, b. Main and Sycamore.
Humania Lodge, No. 8. Instituted June 2d, 1852. Meets every Wednesday at Good Fellows' Hall, n.w.c Clinton and Cutter.
Jefferson Lodge, No. 4. Instituted November 2th, 1850. Meets every Monday at Hall c Main and Abigail.
Lafayette Lodge, No. 14. Instituted April 5th, 1853. Meets every Friday at Hall n.s. Fifth, b. Main and Sycamore.
Ohio Lodge, No. 6. Instituted March 6th, 1852. Meets every Saturday at Good Fellows' Hall, s.e.c. Court and Main.
Washington Lodge, No 1. Instituted January 29th, 1840. Meets every Friday at Hall n.s. Ninth, b. Main and Sycamore.

DEGREE LODGE.

Woodbury Degree Lodge, No. 2. Instituted December 16th, 1852 Meets first Saturday in each month at Good Fellows' Hall, s.e.c. Court and Main.

ENCAMPMENTS.

Germania Encampment, No. 2. Instituted December 22d, 1851. Meets every first and third Thursdays in each month at Hall c. Main and Abigail.
Schiller Encampment, No. 5. Instituted November 6th, 1852. Meets every first Monday and fourth Saturday in each month at Good Fellows' Hall, s.e.c. Main and Court.
William Penn Encampment, No. 4. Meets on the first and third Saturday in each month at Good Fellows' Hall, s.e.c. Main and Court.

Improved Order of Red Men.

Matamora Tribe, No. 6. Instituted 1852. Meets every Thursday at Onna Wigwam, Bacon's Building, n.w.c. Sixth and Walnut.
Miami Tribe, No. 1. Instituted April 22d, 1851. Meets every Tuesday at Onna Wigwam, Bacon's Building, n.w.c Sixth and Walnut.
Seneca Tribe, No. 7. Instituted August 4th, 1852. Meets every Wednesday at Onna Wigwam, Bacon's Building, n.w.c. Sixth and Walnut.
Wyandott Tribe. No. 5. Instituted April 17th, 1852. Meets every Thursday at Onna Wigwam, Bacon's Building, n.w.c. Sixth and Walnut.

Sons of Temperance.

Cincinnati Division, No. 2. Meets every Thursday at Hall in Apollo Building, c. Fifth and Walnut.

Templars of Honor.

SUPREME COUNCIL.—The highest legislative body of the Order, meets annually at different points in the United States J. Wadsworth, Most Worthy Recorder. Office and residence 112 Hopkins.
GRAND TEMPLE OF OHIO.— Meets annually in May, at different points in Ohio. J. Wadsworth. Grand Worthy Recorder. Office and residence 112 Hopkins.
Cincinnati Temple, No. 1. Meets every Tuesday in the Hall, s.e.c of Fourth and Vine.
Egeria Social Temple, No. 1, in connection with this Temple. Meets in the same Hall, the second and fourth Friday of each month.
Union Temple, No. 9. Meets every Thursday in the same Hall.
Union Social Temple, No. 2, in connection with this Temple. Meets in the same Hall the first and Third Friday of each month.
Aurora Degree Temple, No. 1, in connection with all the Temples in this city. Meets in the same Hall the last Saturday of each month.
The Council Department meets in the same Hall the first Saturday of each month.
Washington Temple, No. 22. Meets every Tuesday in Odd Fellows' Hall, Seventeenth Ward.

Societies & Associations.

A. B. C. F. MISSIONS' Agency, 28 W. 4th. George L. Weed, Receiving Agent.
ACADEMY OF MEDICINE, organized March, 1857; meets every Monday evening, at the Dental College Building.
ALEMANIA CLUB, Emil Block, President; meets every evening, at Melodeon Hall.
AMERICAN CHRISTIAN MISSION SOCIETY, Rev. Alex. Campbell, President; D S. Burnet, Corresponding Secretary; H. S. Bosworth, Recording Society; office, s.w. c, 8th and Walnut.
AMERICAN REFORM TRACT AND BOOK SOCIETY. Geo. L. Weed. Secretary, 28 W. 4th street.
AMERICAN SUNDAY SCHOOL UNION. Rev. B. W. Chidlaw, Superintendent of Missions for the State, and Secretary; Geo. Crosby, Agent, 44 W. 4th street.
AMERICAN TRACT SOCIETY, Depository and office of Superintendent of Colportage, Melodeon Building, 163 Walnut; Seely Wood, Superintendent.
AMERICAN WINE GROWERS' ASSOCIATION, of Cincinnati, organized 1st, February, 1851, meets on the last Saturday of every month, at the rooms of the Horticultural Society, Bacon's Buildings, n.w.c. 6th and Walnut. Officers elected annually.
BURNS CLUB, of Cincinnati, re-organized January 11th, 1853, meets once a year. Anniversary 25th January.
BUTCHERS' AND DROVERS' STOCK YARD CO., organized May 1st, 1855. Henry Tesch; President; Adam Engle, Vice-President;—Thos. J. F. Weightman, Secretary; Geo. Bogen, Treasurer.
BUTCHERS' MELTING ASSOCIATION, organized September 1st, 1853, Jacob Baumgardner, President; Henry Nicolai, Treasurer,
CATHOLIC INSTITUTE, n.w.c. Vine and Longworth. Wm. Bender, Secretary.
CINCINNATI CHAMBER OF COMMERCE, College Hall Building. President J. W. S bley; Vice-Presidents. Morris Orum, John A. Dugan, Rufus A. Jones. Sam. J. Hale, Thos. Ong and John Dubois; John A. Gano, Secretary; Robert Brown, Treasurer.
CINCINNATI COLLEGE OF PHARMACY, incorporated 1856. Pharmaceutical meetings on third Thursday in every month, in Ohio Medical College Building, s.s 6th b. Vine and Race. Officers elected annally.
CINCINNATI HORTICULTURAL SOCIETY, organized February 17th, 1843. Meets every Saturday in the Lecture Hall of Bacon's Mercantile College, n.w.c. 6th and Walnut. Officers elected annually.
CINCINNATI MEDICAL SOCIETY, organized 1852. Meets first Tuesday in every month.
CINCINNATI STONE CUTTERS' ASSOCIATION, organized May, 1852. Meets every Wednesday evening, at Switzer Hall, e.s. Main, b. Court and Canal. Officers elected annually.
CINCINNATI TURNERS' ASSOCIATION, organized November 21st, 1848. Meets once a month at Turner Hall, w s. Walnut, b. Allison and Liberty, for business. Meets twice a week for exercise. Officers elected semi-annually.
CINCINNATI TYPOGRAPHICAL UNION, No. 3, chartered May 2d, 1852. Meets first Sunday in every month, in the Lecture Hall of Bacon's Mercantile College, n.w.c. 6th and Walnut. Officers elected semi-annually.
CINCINNATI YOUNG MEN'S BIBLE SOCIETY, 28 W. 4th. Wm. Scott, Depository.
GERMAN CARPENTER'S AND CABINET MAKER'S RELIEF SOCIETY, organized November, 1850. Meets first and third Saturday evening in each month, at Working Men's Hall, e s. Walnut, b. 13th and 14th. Officers elected semi-annually.
GERMAN INSTITUTE SOCIETY, organized January, 1852. Meets twice a week at their Hall, n.e.c. Vine and Mercer. Officers elected semi-annually.

GERMAN LADIES RELIEF SOCIETY, founded 1850.
GERMAN RELIEF ASSOCIATION, founded 1855. A. Louis, President.
HISTORICAL AND PHILOSOPHICAL SOCIETY, of Ohio, organized 1824. Meets once a month at the Society Rooms. Officers elected annually.
JEWISH HOSPITAL ASSOCIATION, founded 1850. A. Aub, President; Dr. Bettman, Physician.
JOHN MITCHELL CLUB, organized 1852 Meets every Monday evening, at Hall s.w.c. 8th and Broadway. Officers elected quarterly.
LADIES' BENEVOLENT SOCIETY, founded 1838.
MONTHLY TRACT (VIS.) ASSOCIATION, J. C. Macy, President; H. F. Knowles, General Superintendent. Tract Depository, 163 Walnut.
OHIO MECHANICS' INSTITUTE, s.w.c. 6th and Vine. Chas. F. Wilstach, President; John B. Heich, Clerk.
OLD GERMAN LADIES BENEVOLENT SOCIETY, founded 1841.
OLD WOODWARD CLUB, organized November, 1855. Re-union on last Thursday in September.
PHŒNIX CLUB, founded 1856. Meets every evening at National Hall, 200 Vine.
PIONEERS' ASSOCIATION, of Cincinnati, composed of the early settlers and those born here prior to the 4th of July, 1812. Organized November 29th, 1856. Celebrate the settlement of the State, the 6th of April, and the settlement of the city the 26th of December of each year.
PRESBYTERIAN BOARDS of Foreign and Domestic Missions, Education, Publication, and Church Extension. Agency, 74 W. 4th J. D. Thorpe.
PRESBYTERIAN BOOK DEPOSITORY, for the West and South-west; J. D. Thorpe, Depositary, 74 W. 4th.
PALESTINE RELIEF SOCIETY, founded June, 1853.
TALMID YELSDIM SCHOLASTIC ASSOCIATION, chartered 1849. Henry Mack, President; Isaac M. Wise, Superintendent.
THE SOCIETY FOR THE SUPPORT OF THE INDIGENT, founded 1842.
UNITED IRISH SOCIETY, organized May 22d, 1852. Meets every Thursday evening, at Gordon's Hall, n.e.c. 8th and Central Av. Officers elected semi-annually.
WORKING MEN'S BENEVOLENT UNION ASSOCIATION, organized September, 1857. Meets first Monday in every month, at Gordon's Hall, n.e.c. 8th and Central Av.
YOUNG MEN'S CATHOLIC LITERARY INSTITUTE, organized October 17th, 1852. Meets every Tuesday evening, in basement of St. Thomas Church. w.s. Sycamores b. 5th and 6th. Officers elected semi-annually, first Tuesday in April and October.
YOUNG MEN'S GYMNASTIC ASSOCIATION, organized August 11th, 1855; n.e.c. 4th and Race.

Benevolent Institutions.

Cincinnati Branch of the United States Sanitary Commission, for the immediate relief of our sick and wounded soldiers. Office and Depot, Mechanics' Institute. s.w.c of Sixth and Vine. R W. Burnet, President; George Hoadley, Vice-President; B. P. Baker, Recording Secretary; C. R. Fosdick, Corresponding Secretary; O. M. Mitchell, B. Storer, J. B. Stallo, E. T. Collins, Wm. A. Snively, M. L. P. Thompson, Larz Anderson, G. K. Shoenberger, J. H. Bates, M. E. Reeves, M. Bailey, C. F. Wilstach, A. Aub, Thos. C. Shipley, Robert Hosea, W. W. Scarborough, Eli C. Baldwin, Henry Pearce, Treasurer, W. H. Mussey, M. D., John Davis, M. D., D. Judkins, M. D., Edward Mead, M D., E Y. Robbins, R. S. Brooks, A. G. Burt, G. Mendenhall, M. D., Chas. E. Cist, Thos. J. Odiorne, C. G. Comegys, M. D., J. M. Johnston, Saml. J. Broadwell, S. L'Hommedieu, M. D., Finance Committee; John B. Heich, Storekeeper.
Cincinnati House of Refuge, e.s. Cumminsville Road, about 1 of a mile n. of the Corporation line. Office of Board of Directors. Apollo Building. c. Fifth and Walnut.
House of Employment (Daughters of Temperance), 168 W. Fifth.
City Infirmary, near Carthage. Office w.s. Plum b. Seventh and Eighth.
Home for the Friendless, 464 John.
Lick Run Lunatic Asylum, Harrison Pike.
City Dispensary. c. Longworth and Central Av.
Commercial Hospital, c. Twelfth and Plum.
St. John's Hospital, n.w.c. Third and Plum.

College Information.

Literary.

ST. XAVIER COLLEGE, w. s. Sycamore, b. 6th and 7th.
BOARD OF TRUSTEES.—Most Rev. J. B. Purcell, D.D., Archbishop of Cincinnati; Rev. John Schultz, S. J.; Very Rev. Edward Purcell; Rev.: Charles Driscoll, S. J. Rev. P. J. DeMeester. S. J., Rev. Francis O'Loghlin.
FACULTY.—Rev. John Schultz S. J., President; Rev. T. Kuhlman, S. J., Vice President; Rev. Lewis Heyleu, S. J., Prof. of Mental Philosophy; Rev. Francis O'Loghlin, S. J., Prof. of Natural Philosophy, Chemistry, and Astronomy; Rev. Jos. A. Fastre, S. J., Prof. of Rhetoric and Belle Lettres: Rev. P. J. DeMeester, S. J ; Treasurer; Rev. T. Arnoudt, S. J., Chaplain; C. Coppens, S. J. Prof. of Ancient and Modern Languages and Mathematics; Th. Roose, S. J., Prof. of German Literature; A. Patton, S. J. Assistant Prof. in various branches; J. Mc-Menemy, S. J., Assistant Prof. in various branches; J. Bows. S. J., Assistant Prof. in various branches; H. Gerold and H. Brusselback, Prof's of Music; L. Piket, Prof. of Lineal, and Perspective Drawing.

WESLEYAN FEMALE COLLEGE, Vine bet. 6th and 7th.
OFFICERS OF BOARD OF TRUSTEES.—Rev. Bishop T. A. Morris, D. D., President of the Board; John Reeves, Esq., First Vice-President; D. W. Clark, D. D. Second Vice-President; W. F. Thorne, Treasurer; John M. Phillips, Secretary.
EXECUTIVE COMMITTEE.—The Officers of the Board of Trustees, and John Simpkinson, Wm Wood, E. B. Stevens, M. D, M. B. Hagans, A. N Riddle, John Cochnower, Lewis Fagin, G. Brashears. and J. C. Thorp.
BOARD OF INSTRUCTION.—Rev. Robert Allyn, A. M. President and Prof. of Mental and Moral Science; Mrs. Mary B. Allyn, Governess; Miss A. S. W. S. Bailey, Teacher of Latin and Medical Science; Miss A. H. Gest, Teacher of Natural Science and History; Miss Harriet E. Martin, Teacher 1st Preparatory Department; Miss Mary E. Sackett, Teacher 2d Preparatory Department; Miss Fannie P. Chase, Teacher 3d Preparatory Department; Miss Florence J. Seegar, Teacher 4th Preparatory Department; Charles Barus, Prof. of Music; Miss Julia A. Colburn, Teacher of Music; Henry Worrall Prof. of Drawing; Mrs. Charlotte Cadwell, Teacher of German; Prof. Christine, Teacher of French.

MT. AUBURN YOUNG LADIES INSTITUTE, GOVERNMENT. H. Thane Miller, President; Mrs. L. Burpe, Governess.
INSTRUCTORS. — H. Thane Miller, A. M., Mental and Moral Philosophy, and Evidences of Christianity; Eli T. Tappan, A. M., Mathematics and Natural Sciences; Miss Eliza B. Swan. Composition. Physiology. Latin. Rhetoric and History; Miss C. W. Menzies, Academical Department; Miss E. J. Reynolds, Preparatory Department; F. S. Crawley, Esq., French, Painting and Drawing; Mrs. A. S. Hanks, Theory and practice of Music.

☞In addition to the above Board of Instruction an arrangement has been effected with Prof's. MILTON and NELSON SAYLER, former proprietors of the Cincinnati Female Seminary, and several of their teachers, which will in the main unite the Board of Instruction of that Institution, with this for the coming year. Prof. Milton Sayler will take part in the general superintendence of the school, and in the direction of the studies of the pupils. Prof. Nelson Sayler will occupy the department of Ancient Languages and Natural Science ; Miss Frances C. Bauman will give instruction in Physiology, Botany and Physical Geography; and Miss Jennie E. Newton will teach the entire department of Mental and Written Arithemetic.

Law.

LAW DEPARTMENT OF CINCINNATI COLLEGE. Lecture Room. College Building, over Mercantile Library.
FACULTY.—Belamy Storer, M. H. Tilden, and M. E. Curwen. Dean, M. E. Curwen. The Lectures commence annually on the Wednesday nearest the 15th of October, and continue until the 15th day of the ensuing April, daily.

Medical and Surgical.

CINCINNATI COLLEGE OF MEDICINE & SURGERY. s.w.c. Central Avenue and Longworth.
FACULTY—P M. Crume, M. D., Emeritus Prof of Obstetrics and Diseases of Women and Children; A. H. Baker, M. D. Prof. of the Principles and Practice of Surgery, and Clinical Surgery; B. S. Lawson, M. D., Prof. of Principles and Practice of Medicine and General Pathology; G. R. Chitwood, M D., Prof. of Pathology, Physical Diagnosis, &c.; J. H. Tate, M. D., Prof. of Obstetrics and Diseases

CINCINNATI CITY GUIDE.

of Women and Children; Daniel Vaughn, A. M., M. D.; Prof. of Chemistry and Pharmacy; W F. Thornton, M D.; Prof. of Anatomy and Physiology; M. C. S. Reed, M D. Prof. of Materia Medica and Therapeutics; S. P. Harriman, M. D., Demonstrator of Anatomy. J. H. Baker, President.

ECLECTIC MEDICAL INSTITUTE OF CINCINNATI, n.e.c 6th and Plum.
FACULTY.—H. D. Garrison, M. D., Professor of Chemistry, Pharmacy and Toxicology; L. E. Jones, M. D., Professor of Materia Medica, Therapeutics and Medical Botany; Zoheth Freeman. M. D., Professor of Surgery and Surgical Practice; J. M. Scudder, M. D., Professor of Theory and Practice of Medicine and Pathology; Edwin Freeman, M. D., Professor of General, Special and Pathological Anatomy; A. J. Howe, M. D., Professor of Demonstrative Anatomy and Surgery; R. S. Newton, M. D., Professor of Clinic Medicine and Surgery; W. Sherwood. M. D., Emeritas Professor of Practice of Medicine and Pathology. J. M. Scudder, M. D. Treasurer, office in the College Building.

MEDICAL COLLEGE OF OHIO, s.s 6th b. Vine and Race
FACULTY.—L. M. Lawson, M, D., Theory and Practice of Medicine; Geo. C. Blackman, M D., Surgery, Surgical Anatomy and Clinical Surgery; W. W. Dawson, M. D., Anatomy and Physiology; M. B. Wright, M. D., Obstetrics and Diseases of Women and Children; James Graham, M. D., Materia Medica and Clinical Medicine; Nelson Sayler, A. M., L.L B., Chemistry and Jurisprudence; H. A. Langdon, M. D., Demonstrator of Anatomy,
Geo. C. Blackman, M. D., Dean of Faculty,

PHYSIO MEDICAL COLLEGE, 67 e. 3d st.
FACULTY.—A. Curtis, M. D., Prof. of Theory and Practice of Medicine; J. R. Nichol. M. D., Prof. of Anatomy and Surgery; H. W. Fowler, M. D., Prof. of Botany and Materia Medica; E Hussey, M. D., Prof. of Obstetrics and Diseases of Women and Children; A Curtis, M. D., Lecturer on Chemistry, Toxicology and Medical Jurisprudence, and Dean o the Faculty, office in the College Building.

PHYSIO-MEDICAL INSTITUTE, College Hall, Walnut bet. 4th and 5th.
FACULTY.—S. E. Carey, M. D., Prof. of Theory and Practice of Medicine; D. McCarthy, M. D., Prof. of Medical and Operative Surgery; W. H. Cook, M, D., Prof. of Botany, Therapeutics and Materia Medica; George Hasty, M. D., Professor of Anatomy and Physiology; S, E. Carey. M. D, Prof. of Obstetrics and Medical Jurisprudence; Wm. Lane, M. D.. Prof. of Chemistry and Toxicology.
Wm. H. Cook, M. D., Dean, 113 6th st.

Dental.

OHIO COLLEGE OF DENTAL SURGERY, w.s. College, bet. 6th and 7th.
FACULTY.—James Taylor, M. D., D. D. S., Institutes of Medical and Dental Science; W. H. Atkinson, M. D. D. D.S., Anatomy and Histology; J. Taft, D.D.S., Operative Dentistry; C. B. Chapman, M. D., Chemistry and Physiology. J. Richardson, D.D S., Mechanical Dentistry and Metallurgy. James Taylor, Dean.

Mercantile and Commercial.

BACON'S COMMERCIAL COLLEGE, n.w.c 6th and Walnut. (Bacon's Buildings.)
BARTLETT'S COMMERCIAL COLLEGE, s.w.c. 3d and Walnut.
GUNDRY'S MERCANTILE COLLEGE, n.w.c. Walnut & 5th, (Apollo Building.)
QUEEN CITY COMMERCIAL COLLEGE, s.e.c. 4th and Vine. Richard Nelson.

Cemeteries.

Spring Grove, near Cumminsville, six miles from the city, C. Davenport, Secretary. Office, Melodeon Building, corner Walnut and Fourth.
Wesleyan, at Cumminsville, Samuel W. Williams, Secretary. Office, s.w.c Main and 8th.
Odd Fellows', in Spring Grove.
St. Peter's, at Lick Run, on Harrison Turnpike, three miles north-west of the city.
St. Joseph's, at Warsaw, on Clevestown road, three miles west of the city.
St. Bernard's, Clifton Road, at Howell's Basin, three miles from the city.
St. John's, Vine St. Hill.
German Protestant, Reading Pike, three and a half miles north east from the city.
Carthage Road, three and a half miles from the city.
Walnut Hills.
Presbyterian, Walnut Hills.
Methodist Protestant, Walnut Hills.
Radical, Reading Pike, two miles from the city.

Insurance Companies.

AMERICAN INSURANCE COMAPANY. Capital Stock $100,000 00. Directors—G. Brashears, W H Thompson. Theodore Cook, N. M. Florer. Stephen Morse, S. S. Haines, D. M. Sechler, Benjamin Evans, Lewis Clason. L. Clason, Secretary, Stephen Morse, President. Office, 12 Front street, east of Main.

BUCKEYE STATE FIRE AND MARINE INSURANCE COMPANY. Capital $100,000. Office, 10 Public Landing, b. Main and Sycamore streets, up stairs. Trustees and Directors—Wm. P. Hulburt, David Gibson, A. McAlpin, H. O. Gilbert, A. A. Marsh, Jno. B. Gibson, John Swasey, S. S. Davis, I. W. Parker, Jno. W. Gosling, S. Wilson. E. D. Crookshank, Chas Reakirt, Henry Davis. Isaac C. Fallis, Secretary, W. P. Hulbert, President. W. H. S. Ewell, Surveyor.

CENTRAL INSURANCE COMPANY OF CINCINNATI Office—7 Front street, b. Main and Sycamore sts. Directors—Henry Morton, David Gibson, A. D. E. Tweed, R. M. White, C. W. Magill, M. Swasey, J. H. Baker, S. J. Broadwell. F. Ferry. Francis Ferry, Secretary, Henry Morten, President.

CINCINNATI EQUITABLE INSURANCE COMPANY. 30 West Third street. Directors—Griffin Taylor, R R. Springer, Mark E. Reeves, Geo. Carlisle, B. Matlack, J. W. Canfield, John A. Simpson, S. S. Smith, Charles Andress, John Whetstone, Jos. Jones, A. G. Burt. Griffin Taylor, President; Joseph K. Smith, Secretary.

CINCINNATI INSURANCE COMPANY. Capital, paid up, $150,000. Office in Company's Building, 4 Front street. Directors—John W. Hartwell, Ira Athearn, Jas. Lupton, A. S. Winslow, William Resor, G. S. Williams, R. M. W. Taylor, J. W. Canfield. James A. Frazer, John W. Ellis, Bowman C. Baker, David T. Woodrow, Charles W. Rowland, S. S Boyle. S. N. Pike. G. W. Williams, Secretary; John. W Hartwell, President.

THE CITIZENS' INSURANCE COMPANY, OF CINCINNATI. Capital Stock, $100,000 00. Directors and Trustees—Wm. Wood, Jas. F. Cunningham, Geo. W. Bishop, G. Brashears, Wm. Williamson, John A. Skiff, A. Erkenbrecher, Geo. R. Dixon, John Holden, Geo Keck, S. S. Cooper, Jas. Morrison, Jos. Roakirt, F T. White, Wesley M. Cameron, P. W. Strader, J. N. Kinney. W. W. Wells. Geo. W. Copeland, Secretary; Jas. F. Cunningham, President; A. M. Ross, Surveyor, Office, 18 Main street.

CITY INSURANCE COMPANY, 8 Front Street, east of Main. Capital $150,000. Directors—W. B. Moores, J. W. Donohue, Geo. W. Trowbridge, J. D. Lehmer, Thos. Sherlock, Jos. C. Butler, D. Banning. Thos. Sherlock, President; W. M Richardson, Secretary; W. P. Stratton, Surveyor.

COMMERCIAL INSURANCE COMPANY OF CINCINNATI. Capital Stock $100,000. Directors—Jno. W. Wilson, Wm. H. Dominick, Seymour Straight, R. Macready, J. P. Trumbower, Chas. W. Smith, Adolph Wood, Thomas Sherlock, W. I Whitman, Thos G. Odiorne, Jacob Jones, Martin Dare, Lewis Fagin, Richard Dymond, Henry A. Jones, J. H. French, G. Y. Roots, I. B. Carpenter, Jas. Bugher, Geo. H. Davis, Richard Lloyd. J. A. Townley, Secretary; M. L. Harbeson, President. Office, North west corner Main and Front streets.

EAGLE INSURANCE COMPANY OF CINCINNATI. Edward D. Speer, Secretary; J. W. Garrison, President. Directors—Henry Kessler, Anthony Fay, Wm. Wood, J. W. Garrison, Samuel H. Taft, J. L. Conklin, M. J. Townley. J. B. Lawder, and David Baker, Surveyors.

FIREMAN'S INSURANCE COMPANY OF CINCINNATI. Capital Stock, $100,000. Directors, 1860-61—Edmund Dexter, Robert Andrews. J. P. Tweed, George Wilshire. Jacob Traber, Charles W. West, Samuel J. Hale, John Whetstone, Peter A. White. James Calhoun, John D. Minor, Briggs Swift, J. T. Warren, N. W. Thomas, Pollock Wilson Office in Company's Building, n. e. c. Main and Front Streets. Samuel R. Carter, Secretary; Henry E. Spencer, President.

FRANKLIN INSURANCE COMPANY OF CINCINNATI. Eli C Baldwin, President, James H. Silvers. Secretary. Chas. F. Wilstach, Geo. R. Dixon, Louis Wald, Robert Mitchell, Eli C. Baldwin, Marcus Fechheimer, Darius Eggleston, Hugh Evans, T. H. C. Allen, Directors. Office 31½ West Third street.

GERMAN MUTUAL INSURANCE COMPANY OF CINCINNATI. Office 400 Vine street. Henry Schmidt, President; H. A. Rotterman, Secretary; Joseph Siefert, Treasurer. Directors—George Klotter, Jacob Baumgardner, Frederick Pfiester, Henry Hemelgarn, Michael Eckert, Joseph Siefert, Nicholas Hoeffer, Anthony Bley Christian Moerlin.

MAGNOLIA FIRE AND MARINE INSURANCE COMPANY. Capital Stock $100,000. Directors—W. C. Mann, W C. Vanderbilt, Sol. Levi, Jas. Bugher, George M. Hord, E. D. Gardner, Wm. R. Scott, Jas. T. Fisher, Charles H. Marshall, Secretary; W. C. Mann, President. Office, 15 Public Landing, b Main and Sycamore streets. N. F. Lucky, Surveyor.

MERCHANTS' AND MANUFACTURERS' FIRE AND MARINE INSURANCE COMPANY OF CINCINNATI. Capital $150,000. Office 11 Front street. A. M. Searles, President; B. B. Whitman, Secretary. Directors—A. M. Searles, M. Werk, Robert Hosea, Geo. Dominick, Robert Brown, R. W. Keys, Thomas Emery, W. Henry Davis, A. H. Andrews, S. H. Burton, M. E. Reeves. John A. Dugan, Henry D. Huntington, S. S. Boyle, William Proctor. Branch Office. n.w.c. of Thirteenth and Vine Street, No. 455, W. L. Gaddum, Agent.

NATIONAL INSURANCE COMPANY OF CINCINNATI. Capital $100,000. Office. s w.c. Front and Main 8 reets. Directors—John Burgoyne, William Hepworth, F. X. Wiederner, J. L. Ross, Thomas R. Biggs, Robert Moore, S. W. Smith, Henry Ellis, Marcus Fechhelmer, C. L. Moore. Th. Ong, E. M Smith. Henry C. Urner, Secretary; John Burgoyne, President; P. A. Sprigman, Surveyor.

OHIO LIFE INSURANCE COMPANY, 68 West third street. Capital Stock $100,000. Directors—J. P. Kilbreth, Augustus Isham, Leonard Swartz, Joseph W. Wayne, John W. Donohue. James D Lehmer, J. L. Wayne, B. P. Baker, W. A. Goodman, Augustus Isham, President; John W. Donohue, Vice-President; G. W. Sullivan, Secretary.

PORTSMOUTH INSURANCE COMPANY. Capital $150,000. Jos. S. Ross, President; S. W. Reeder. Secretary; Exekiel Ross, Solicitor. Directors—Jos. S. Ross. Jno. D. Jones. Harvey DeCamp, E. J. Buckingham, I. Shingledecker, Wm. Glenny, S. W. Reeder. Office 110 Walnut street.

QUEEN CITY INSURANCE COMPANY. Office 34 Masonic Temple, Third Street. Capital $100,000. Directors—Wm. McCammon, Wm. A. Stewart. E. M. Shield, Amos Conklin, Dr. J. L. Vattier, Geo. M. Dixon. Daniel McLaren, D. A. Powell, H. Clearwater, William B. Dodds, H. P. Elias, Leonard Swartz, T. M. Farren, R. W. White, Jas. Gordon. James A. Davou, Secretary; William McCammon, President, Hiram Pugh Surveyor.

SUN MUTUAL INSURANCE COMPANY OF CINCINNATI. A. D. Latta, President; E. L Shannon, Secretary. Directors—A. B. Latta, John Mitchell, Geo. Lindeman, Joshua Jones, John Kelly, Wm. T. Phipps, John Curtis, Louis Schnider, J. W. Hughs. Office 75 West Third street, (Evans & Co., Bank Building.)

UNION INSURANCE COMPANY OF CINCINNATI. Capital $100,000. Office, No 5 Front street. b. Main and Sycamore. Directors—E. Henry Carter, S. G. Hubbard, William C. Whitcher, Casper Geist, Wm Wiswell, jr., Geo. F. Davis, A. O. Tyler, Oliver Perin, N. Mitchell. Abm. C. Edwards, Secretary; E. Henry Carter President.

WASHINGTON INSURANCE COMPANY, 41 Main street. Capital $150,000, Directors—S. C. Parkhurst, William Goodman, William Hooper, Gardner Phipps. Joseph C. Butler, Lowell Fletcher, Henry Hanna, John Swasey, Joseph Torrence, C. Taylor Jones, J. W. Sibley, Joseph H. Wilby, Benj. Eggleston, Chas. R. Fosdick, Thompson Dean, A D. Bullock, Wm. H. Woods, B. F. Brannan, John Gould, B. P. Baker, Wm. S. Wright. Wm. Goodman, President; John P. Whiteman, Secretary.

WESTERN INSURANCE COMPANY OF CINCINNATI. Capital $100,000. Office. Second Story of Insurance Building; entrance 2 Front Street, b. Main and Sycamore. Directors—T. F. Eckert, S. W. Pomeroy, A. W. Frank Robt. Mitchell, I. G. E. Stone, Wm. Sellew. Wm. Glenn, Seth Evans, J. H. Tanffe, Geo Stall, H. Clearwater, W. C. Whitcher, D. Gibson, Robert Buchannan, W. H. Comstock, J. W. Wayne, T. Dean, C. G. Shaw, John G. Isham, H. Brachman, J. W. Shipley, Secretary; T. F. Eckert, President; Rudolph Loheyde, Surveyor.

Boundaries of Wards.

1st Ward—Bounded by Main, East Sixth, Liberty and East Third streets.
2d Ward—Bounded by Main. West Seventh, Race, West Third, Walnut and West Pearl streets.
3d Ward—Bounded by Main and East Third streets, the old corporation line and the Ohio river.
4th Ward—Bounded by Main, West Pearl, Walnut, West Third and John streets, and the Ohio river.
5th Ward—Bounded by West Seventh, Main, and West Canal streets and Central Av.
6th Ward—Bounded by John, West Third, Smith and West Fifth streets and the Ohio river.
7th Ward—Bounded by Central Av. and West Canal, Race and West Liberty streets.
8th Ward—Bounded by Central Av. and West Liberty, Baymiller and West Court streets.
9th Ward—Bounded by Main, Hunt and East Liberty streets,
10th Ward—Bounded by Main, West Canal, Race and West Liberty streets.
11th Ward—Bounded by East and West Liberty and Vine streets, the north boundary line, and the old corporation line between the city and Fulton township.
12th Ward—Bounded by West Liberty and Vine streets, the north boundary line and Mill Creek.
13th Ward—Bounded by East Sixth, East Liberty, Hunt and Main streets.
14th Ward—Bounded by Race, West Seventh, John, West Sixth, Smith and West Third streets.
15th Ward—Bounded by Central Av., West Court, Baymiller and West Sixth streets. W. W. Canal and West Fifth, Smith, West Sixth, John and West Seventh streets.
16th Ward—Bounded by West Fifth Street, W. W. Canal, West Sixth, Baymiller and West Liberty streets, M 11 Creek and Ohio river.
17th Ward—Late Fulton Township.

City Water Works.

OFFICE IN CITY BUILDING.

BOARD OF TRUSTEES.

Charles Rule.....................President.
Michael Eckert.
Joseph Torrence.
J. B. Earnshaw...................Superintendent.
George Shields...................Engineer.
J. M. Hanson....................Secretary.
D W. Cunningham.................Clerk.

COLLECTORS.

George B. Williams..............District No. 1.
Valentine Eichenlaub........... "   No. 2.
Alexis Keeler.................. "   No. 3.
F. Blum........................ "   No. 4.

All Water Rent is Payable in Advance.

RULES AND REGULATIONS GOVERNING THE USE OF WATER FROM THE CITY WATER WORKS.

1st. All officers and employees to have free access at all reasonable hours to premises where water is used.
2d. Hydrants. Plugs, Stop Boxes, Hose, and all other attachments must be kept in complete repair by the owner or occupant.
3d. The following ABUSES are absolutely prohibited, to wit: 1. Permitting or allowing the water to be used for any other purpose than those named in the bill. 2. Sprinkling Gardens. Streets, or Sidewalks, or washing Carriages, Omnibuses, Cars, or other vehicles with hose, without a special permit obtained and paid for at the office; and in no case will hose be allowed for the above uses without flows or nozzles, when used for washing carriages and other vehicles greater than one-eighth of an inch, and for any other purpose greater than one-quarter of an inch diameter of circular opening, or their equivalents. 3. Permitting leaks. 4. Allowing water to flow unnecessarily while washing pavements and for similar purposes.
4th. No person, without a written permit from the proper officer, is allowed to turn a public or private stop-cock.
5th. All service pipe must be laid at least three feet below the surface. and all pipe outside the public stop, located on

the upper level of the city must be "STRONG," and all on the lower level must be "EXTRA STRONG."

6th. In all cases where more than one family or other consumer is supplied from a pipe or pipes governed by one stop, some one person must become responsible for the payment of all the bills and the keeping in good repair all pipes, hydrants, etc.

7th. When cisterns are so located as to supply separate premises, and may be filled from a hydrant, water rent must be paid for all families or other consumers having access to said cistern.

8th. Cisterns located on premises where there is no hydrant, must not be filled from the hydrant in any case.

9th. Hydrants must not be located so as to be exposed to use by non-paying consumers, and all hydrants so situated must be removed to some secure location on notice, or the water turned off.

PENALTIES.

Refusal or neglect to conform to the above rules and regulations subjects the parties to have the water turned off—to the forfeiture of the water rent—the payment of penalties varying from fifty cents to five dollars, and to prosecution and fine in the Police Court.

Persons using water from the Works, and any other source, as canals, wells, etc., to be charged full rates for their establishments, except when the amount taken from the Works is determined by meter.

WATER TARIFF.

Houses of 1 and 2 rooms................$3,50 per annum.
" 3 and 4 " .... 4,00 "
" 5 and 6 " .... 5.00 "
" 7 and 8 " .... 6,00 "
" 9 and 10 " .... 7,00 "
" 11 and 12 " .... 8,00 "
" 13 and 14 " .... 9,00 "
" 15 and 16 " .... 10,00 "
" 17 and 18 " .... 11,00 "
" 19 and 20 " .... 12,00 "

Houses containing more than 20 rooms, for each additional room.................... 40 "
Houses occupied by more than one family, extra for each additional family........ 2,00 "
Boarding-houses the following rates in addition to the above
Houses of 7 to 12 rooms, extra.......... 1,50 "
" 13 to 20 " .... 3 00 "
" 21 to 30 " .... 6,00 "
" 31 to 40 " .... 12,00 "
Public baths, warm or cold.............. 8,00 "
Private baths, warm.................... 3,00 "
Private baths, cold.................... 2,00 "
Water Closets, in Public Houses........ 4.00 "
Water Closets, in Private Houses....... 2,00 "
Urinals to be assessed.

Plugs or Hose Hydrants for washing sidewalks, $1.50 for each 25 feet front or less, and six cents for each additional front foot.

Corner Houses and Lots to be charged at the same rate for both fronts.

Plugs for Gardens and other purposes to be assessed.
Barber shops, $1.50 per annum for each chair.
Livery and Private Stables, $1.50 per annum for each stall; for each Carriage, Buggy or Wagon, 75 cents per annum; for each Horse-trough, $5,00 per annum.
Bakers, for each barrel of flour consumed, one-half cent.
Coffee-houses from $5,00 to $20,00 per annum.
Restaurants and Fountains to be assessed.
Stores, Offices, and Sleeping-rooms, $1,00 to $8,00 per annum.
Smith Shops, $1,50 per annum for each forge.
Brick Work, 6 cents per 1,000.
Plastering, 2 cents for each bushel of lime used.
Stone Work 2 cents per perch.
Schools, Asylums, and Churches, $1,50 to $5.00 per annum.
Pork-packers, from $10,00 to $20,00 per annum.
Steam Engines to be assessed by the tables, according to the size of boiler, extent of fire surface, pressure of steam, size and velocity of engines, at the rate of 12 cents per 1,000 gallons, and an additional charge of $4 00 for every fifty hands employed, or the consumption to be determined by meter measurement.
Manufactories, Hotels, Distilleries, Tanneries, Slaughter-houses, Breweries, and all other large consumers, to pay at the rate of 12 cents per 1,000 gallons the amount to be determined by estimation of the Superintendent or Surveyor, or by the meter.

By order of the Board.

Libraries.

CINCINNATI LAW LIBRARY, Court House. Any person who has not been a member for more than three years can have access to the Library, upon paying the annual assessment, from five to ten dollars.

GERMAN LIBRARY ASSOCIATION ROOMS, southwest corner Main and Twelfth.

OHIO PUBLIC SCHOOL LIBRARY OF CINCINNATI, Mechanics' Institute, corner of Vine and Sixth.

The Ohio Mechanics' Institute has deposited their extensive Library with this.

The Managers of the Ladies' Picture Gallery have deposited their superior collection of copies and paintings from the Ancient Masters, and Statuary, with the School Board, which are arranged in the suite of rooms adjacent to the Free Public Library

The residents of Cincinnati are permitted to take books from the Ohio School Library, free, on signing a promise to comply with the rules, and furnish a well-known citizen who agrees to be responsible for any damage or loss.

The Library of the New England Historical Society of Cincinnati is deposited in the Rooms of the Library. To the General Library, known as the Public School Library, there have been added the present year about 7,000 volumes of standard works. This Library contains, at the present time, about 20,000 volumes, and will receive, during the present year, some five or six thousand additional volumes.

ST. JOSEPH CALLASANCTIUS' LIBRARY.
ST. XAVIER'S CIRCULATING LIBRARY.
WESTERN ACADEMY OF NATURAL SCIENCE. College Building, Walnut, between Fourth and Fifth.
YOUNG MEN'S MERCANTILE LIBRARY ASSOCIATION, College Building, Walnut, between Fourth and Fifth.

School Department.

OFFICERS OF THE

Board of Trustees and Visitors

OF COMMON SCHOOLS,

For the School Year, 1862—'63,

RUFUS KING, President.
CHAS. F. WILSTACH, Vice-President.
WM. B DAVIS, Corresponding Secretary.
LYMAN HARDING, Superintendent of Schools.
JOHN McCAMMON, Superintendent of Buildings and Repairs.
W. F. HURLBUT, Clerk.

ROLL OF MEMBERS.

1st Ward—Jas. Watson, Henrie House, Third st..1 year.
T. J. Haldeman.................2 years.
2d Ward—Chas. Bonsall, No. 118 West Sixth St...1 year.
R. S. Newton, n.w.c. Sixth and Vine....2 years.
3d Ward—Rufus King, No. 95 East Third St......1 year.
W. J. Schultz..................2 years.
4th Ward—Robert Hackett, n.w.c. Race and Front.1 year.
George Johnston...............2 years.
5th Ward—John King, No. 85 W. 8th............1 year.
H. M. Bates, 352 Race.........2 years.
6th Ward—John M. Kelly, No. 29 Mill Street.....1 year.
A. Holcomb....................2 years.
7th Ward—John Clark, No. 481 Race Street......1 year.
J. H. Ehlen, No. 373 Elm Street.....2 years.
8th Ward—Thatcher Lewis, jr., No. 5 Gorman st..1 year.
Louis Ballauf, n.w.c. Wade and Linn..2 years.
9th Ward—F. H. Rowecamp, No. 25 Woodward St..1 year.
H. Hemmelgarn, 108 Hunt..........2 years.
10th Ward—F. J. Werner, s.w.c. Walnut & Allison.1 year.
H. Wohmer, 119 Clay..............2 years.
11th Ward—Herman Ekel, 128 Hamilton Road....1 year.
D. G. A. Davenport, Mt. Auburn......2 years.
12th Ward—John Fieber, 636 Central Av.........1 year.
J. M. Doherty..................2 years.
13th Ward—A. W. Armstrong, 29 E. 6th..........1 year.
F. A. Clifford.................2 years.
14th Ward—J. H. Laws, 133 W. 6th..............1 year.
M. E. Reeves, 212 W. 4th........2 years.
15th Ward—Wm. P. Stratton, 261 W. 8th.........1 year
C. B. Evans, 71 Barr...........2 years.
16th Ward—R. K. Cox, sen., 530 W. 9th.........1 year.
J. M. Waters..................2 years.
17th Ward—A. Caldwell, 910 E. Front...........1 year.
Milton Glenn, 1373 E. Front....2 years.

Standing Committees

FOR THE SCHOOL YEAR, 1861—'62.

BUILDINGS & REPAIRS—Messrs. Wilstach, Williams, Cox, Paine and Ballauf.
BOUNDARIES AND STATISTICS—Messrs. Woodward, Watson, Ballauf, Powers, Cox Miller and Davenport.
CLAIMS—Messrs. Reeves, Paine and Kelley.
COLORED SCHOOLS—Messrs. Powers, Newton & Woodward.
COURSE OF STUDY AND TEXT BOOKS—Messrs. Davis, Lilienthal, J. King, Newton and Bonsall.
DISCIPLINE—Messrs. Stratton, Clark, Irwin, Fieber, Laws, Woodward and Rowekamp.
EXAMINATIONS—Messrs. Lilienthal, Bonsall, Glenn, Werner and J. King.
FUEL—Messrs. Paine, Hackett and Lewis.
FUNDS AND TAXES—Messrs. Doherty, Laws, Ehlen, Reeves and Wilstach.
FURNITURE—Messrs Williams, Watson, Lewis, Armstrong and Ehlen.
GERMAN-ENGLISH SCHOOLS—Messrs. Rowekamp, Werner, Eckel, Davenport, Armstrong, Miller, Fieber and Ballauf.
GYMNASTICS—Messrs. Stratton, Rowekamp, Bonsall and Cox, Ballauf.
LIBRARY—Messrs. Bonsall, Reeves, Irwin, Davis and Lilienthal.
LOTS—Messrs. Clark, Davenport, Bates, Fieber and Caldwell.
MUSIC—Messrs. Irwin, Caldwell, Watson, Werner and Davis.
NIGHT SCHOOLS—Messrs. Hooker, Powers, Bates, Kelley and Doherty.
PENMANSHIP—Messrs. Newton, Stratton, Miller, Eckel and Glenn.
PRINTING AND BLANKS—Messrs. Armstrong, Wilstach and Stratton.
SALARIES—Messrs. Cox, Bates, Doherty, Laws, Rowekamp and Clark.
SUPPLIES—Messrs. Kelley, Ehlen, Caldwell, Hackett and Williams.

Local Trustees.

FOR THE SCHOOL YEAR, 1861—'62.

FIRST DISTRICT—Messrs. Miller, Rowekamp and Armstrong.
SECOND DISTRICT—Messrs. Lilienthal, Watson, R. King and Armstrong.
THIRD DISTRICT—Messrs. Williams, Irwin, R. King and Lilienthal.
FOURTH DISTRICT—Messrs. Caldwell, Glenn and Williams.
FIFTH DISTRICT—Messrs. Paine, Hackett, Laws, Newton and Ehlen.
SIXTH DISTRICT—Messrs. Clark, Ehlen, Davis and Fieber.
SEVENTH DISTRICT—Messrs. Woodward, Kelley and Reeves.
EIGHTH DISTRICT—Messrs. Powers, Stratton and Lewis.
NINTH DISTRICT—Messrs. Bates, J. King, Bonsall and Ehlen.
TENTH DISTRICT—Messrs. Werner, Davis and Clark.
ELEVENTH DISTRICT—Messrs. Ballauf, Lewis and Cox.
TWELFTH DISTRICT—Messrs. Wilstach, Cox, Stratton and Werner.
THIRTEENTH DISTRICT—Messrs. Doherty, Eckel and Fieber.
FOURTEENTH DISTRICT—Messrs. Doherty, Fieber and Ballauf.
FIFTEENTH DISTRICT—Messrs. Rowekamp, Davenport and Werner.
SIXTEENTH DISTRICT—Messrs. Davenport, Bonsall and Eckel.
SEVENTEENTH DISTRICT—Messrs. Glenn, Caldwell and Lilienthal.
EIGHTEENTH DISTRICT—Messrs. Watson, J. King and Laws.
ORPHAN ASYLUM—Messrs. Bonsall, Reeves and Irwin.
INDUSTRIAL SCHOOL—Messrs. Powers, Irwin and Reeves.
FIRST INTERMEDIATE—Messrs. Stratton, Wilstach, Reeves, Ballauf and Doherty.
SECOND INTERMEDIATE—Messrs. Irwin, R. King, Lilienthal and Rowekamp.
THIRD INTERMEDIATE—Messrs. Davis, Bates, Laws and Eckel.

Location of School Buildings.

1st District, North side Franklin between Main and Sycamore.
2d District, East side Sycamore, between Fifth and Sixth.
3d " Ellen between Lock and Baum.
4th " Seventeenth Ward (Fulton.)
5th " East side Race between Front and Second.
6th " Corner Elm and Adams.
7th " North side Fourth between Smith and Park.
8th " North side Eighth between John and Mound.
9th " South side Ninth between Vine and Race.
10th " East side Vine between 12th and 13th.
11th " Clinton between Linn and Locust.
12th " Eighth, east of Harriet.
13th " Findlay, west of Vine.
14th " West side Piatt, west of Bank.
Orphan Asylum.
1st Intermediate, Baymiller between Court and Clark.
2d " Ellen between Lock and Baum.
3d " Corner Elm and Adams.
4th " West side Race between Fourth and Fifth.
HUGHES HIGH SCHOOL—South side Fifth, opposite Mound
WOODWARD HIGH SCHOOL—Woodward between Sycamore and Broadway.

Board of Examiners.

E. S. BROOKS, President........Term ending April, 1863.
A. J. RICKOFF.............., " " " "
ELI T. TAPPAN. ...., " " " "
OBED J. WILSON............, " " " 1865.
L. HARDING..............., " " " "
JOHN B. STALLO............. " " " 1864.
ROBERT ALLYN.............. " " " "

REGULATIONS OF THE BOARD OF EXAMINERS OF COMMON SCHOOLS.

The Board consists of seven members, four of whom constitute a quorum at any regular and called meetings.

The regular meetings are held at the office of Public Schools, City Buildings, on the 1st Thursday of each month, except July and August, at 4½ o'clock P. M.* Extra meetings may be called by any three members of the Board, who, in signing the call for such meeting, are understood as pledging themselves to attend it.

The Board grants four grades of Certificates, denominated respectively "Male Principal's Certificate," "Male Assistant's Certificate," "Female Assistant's Certificate, No. 1," and "Female Assistant's Certificate, No. 2."

Candidates for "Male Principal's Certificate" are examined in Natural Philosophy, Constitution of the U. States, Ancient and Modern History. Anatomy and Physiology, Chemistry, Astronomy, Geometry, Plane Trigonometry and Mensuration, and Penmanship.

Candidates for a "Male Assistant's Certificate" are examined in Spelling and Definitions, Reading, English Grammar, Geography, American History, Mental Arithmetic, Written Arithmetic, Algebra, Theory and Practice of Teaching, Natural Philosophy, Constitution of the United States, and Penmanship.

Candidates for a "Female Principal's Certificate" are examined in Spelling and Definitions, Reading, English Grammar, Geography, American History, Mental Arithmetic, Written Arithmetic, Algebra. Theory and Practice of Teaching, Natural Philosophy, Constitution of the United States, Ancient and Modern History, Anatomy and Physiology, Chemistry, Astronomy and Penmanship.

Candidates for a "Female Assistant's Certificate" are examined in Spelling and Definitions, Reading, English Grammar, Geography, American History, Mental Arithmetic, Written Arithmetic, Theory and Practice of Teaching, and Penmanship.

The number opposite to each branch, in the column on the right of the list of studies on the Certificates issued, measures the result of the examination, three being the maximum. Less than two in either English Grammar, Geography, Mental Arithmetic or Written Arithmetic, is a failure. Unless the Spelling is correct, it is marked 0.

The Board has discontinued the Primary Certificate.

A specimen of the handwriting, with a record of the character of the examination of each individual, is preserved in a volume for the use of the Board of Trustees and Visitors.

Candidates must leave with the Clerk of the Board, at least three days before the monthly meeting, a certificate of good moral character, and a written statement of the grade of certificate sought, together with a declaration that they are eighteen years of age (or seventeen, if graduates from the High School, or with similar attainments), and that they design teaching in the Public Schools of Cincinnati, if found

*Candidates are examined in Arithmetic at three o'clock, P. M.

qualified. Candidates are requested to leave their address, and a statement of any experience they may have had in teaching.

Candidates shall be examined in the absence of all spectators, save the Trustees and Visitors of the Public Schools.

Candidates shall not be examined who are not present punctually at the appointed hour. None shall be admitted to a second examination for the same grade of Certificate, or have one already granted improved, till after the expiration of six months.

Communications to the Board to be left with the Clerk, at the Office of Public Schools, in the Mechanics' Institute Building, Sixth street, a few doors west of Vine street, between the hours of 9 A. M. and 12 M., and between the hours of 1 P. M. and 4 P. M.

No Assistant's Certificate shall be issued without an aggregate average of two-thirds of the full number of marks, and no Principal's Certificate shall be issued without an aggregate average of two-thirds of the full number of marks of the additional branches.—*Adopted June 2d*, 1859.

UNION BOARD OF CINCINNATI HIGH SCHOOLS.

WM. GREENE, *President.*
W. F. HURLBUT, *Secretary.*

MEMBERS OF THE BOARD.

DELEGATES FROM THE COMMON SCHOOL BOARD.—James M. Doherty, Louis Ballauf, M. Lilienthal, John S. Powers, Charles Bonsall, Chas. F. Wilstach.
DELEGATES FROM WOODWARD BOARD.—W. G. W. Lewis, Alphonso Taft, Wm. Goodman, S. S. Davis, Mark E. Reeves.
DELEGATES FROM HUGHES BOARD.—Wm. Greene, Wm. Hooper.

STANDING COMMITTEES OF UNION BOARD.

ON TEXT-BOOKS AND SCHOOL-LIBRARIES.—Messrs. Bonsall, Lilienthal and Wilstach
ON COURSE OF STUDY AND CLASSIFICATION.—Messrs. Lewis, Hooper and Lilienthal
ON VOCAL MUSIC.—Messrs Reeves, Doherty and Powers.
ON DISCIPLINE.—Messrs. Taft, Hooper and Goodman.
ON FUEL.—Messrs. Wilstach, Doherty and Ballauf.
ON FURNITURE —Messrs Powers, Davis and Reeves.
ON BUILDINGS AND REPAIRS.—Messrs. Hooper, Goodman and Ballauf.
ON PRINTED QUESTIONS AND ADMISSIONS.—Messrs. Goodman, Taft, Reeves, Wilstach and Doherty.
ON EXAMINATION OF SCHOOLS AND GRADUATES. Messrs. Hooper, Bonsall and Davis.
ON CLAIMS.—Messrs. Goodman, Lewis and Doherty.
SPECIAL COMMITTEES OF EACH SCHOOL.—*Woodward.*—Messrs. Greene, Lewis and Bonsall. *Hughes.*—Messrs. Greene, Hooper and Goodman.

Rules and Regulations

OF THE OHIO SCHOOL LIBRARY OF THE CITY OF CINCINNATI.

ARTICLE 1. The Reading-room shall be open from nine o'clock in the morning to nine o'clock in the evening of all secular days throughout the year, except those days which by custom are regarded as holidays, and to these shall be added any special holidays which may, from time to time, be recognised as such by the Board of Trustees and Visitors of Common Schools of Cincinnati.

ART. 2. All inhabitants of Cincinnati, above the age of sixteen years, of respectable character, and of such orderly conduct and condition as to not interfere with the occupations and comforts of others, shall have free access to the Reading-room during all its regular hours, first signing a promise that they will observe all the existing Rules and Regulations, and all that may be subsequently prescribed by due authority; provided always, that Minors shall bring certificates from their parents and guardians, in a form furnished by the Librarian, setting forth that they are persons who ought to enjoy the privileges of the Public Reading-room, and for whose conduct, while there, such parents or guardians become responsible.

ART. 3. All books belonging to the Library may, at the discretion of the Librarian, be used in the Reading-room—a discretion he is required by the Trustees to exercise, especially in the case of minors.

ART. 4 Every person entitled to use in the Reading-room the books of the Library, shall be furnished by the Librarian with a printed card, on which such person shall designate the particular book asked for, by entering in blanks left for that purpose, the number of the shelf on which it stands, the number of the book on the shelf, and if it be part of a set, the number of the particular volume—all which numbers can be easily ascertained from the printed copies of the catalogue, always on the table of the Reading-room; and this card, which must be presented to the Librarian whenever a book is asked for to be used in the Reading-room, will be retained by him so long as its owner retains the book: but no book, so received, shall, for any reason whatever, be removed from the Reading-room by the person receiving it.

ART. 5. Every person who may visit the Reading-room, shall return each of the pamphlets and periodicals, such person may have used, to its proper place, and any books to the Librarian.

ART. 6. Any person abusing the privileges of the Reading-room by unbecoming conduct there, or by the violation of any of its regulations, shall be at once reported by the Librarian to the Library Committee, and by them excluded from its benefits for a time, or permanently, according to the nature and degree of the delinquency or default: but in case of any gross offense, the Librarian shall act summarily in the matter, and cause the offender to be at once excluded from the room, reporting the case to the Library Committee as soon as possible, in writing, for their future action, if any be required.

ART. 7. An alphabetical list of all the persons enjoying the Reading-room shall be kept by the Librarian, the residence of each person being noted in it.

Colored Schools

BOARD OF DIRECTORS OF THE COLORED COMMON SCHOOLS, FOR 1861—'62.

The Schools are under the control of the following Board, elected by the colored male citizens of Cincinnati:

OFFICERS.

Robert G. Ball..................................President.
Phillip B. Ferguson.......................Vice-President.
Isaac M. Troy...................................Clerk.

ROLL OF MEMBERS AND RESIDENCES.

WESTERN DISTRICT.—Phillip B. Ferguson, Elm st., near Liberty; Coleman Cole, Webb street, between Stone and Wood; Isaac M. Troy, Commerce street, between Elm and Plum.
EASTERN DISTRICT.—Marshall P. H. Jones, Seventh street, No. 12, between Main and Sycamore; Robert G. Hall, Macallister street, between 4th and 5th; Hensley Lewis, Sixth street, east of Broadway.

STANDING COMMITTEES.

ON COURSE OF STUDY AND TEXT BOOKS.—Troy and Jones.
ON DISCIPLINE.—Cole and Ball.
ON FUEL.—Lewis and Troy.
ON PRINTING.—Troy and Jones.
ON SCHOOL-HOUSES, REPAIRS AND FURNITURE.—Ferguson and Lewis.
ON SALARIES.—Ferguson and Ball.
ON BUILDINGS.—Lewis and Cole.
ON LIBRARY.—Jones and Ferguson.
LOCATION OF COLORED SCHOOLS, AND RESIDENCES OF TEACHERS.

WESTERN DISTRICT.—School House on West Court street, between John and Mound.

TEACHERS.

Peter H. Clark, Walnut Hills; Wm. H. Parham, No. 286 Front street, between John and Smith; Miss Lucy A. Blackburn, Smith Court, No. 1.

EASTERN DISTRICT.—School House on Seventh street, east of Broadway.

TEACHERS.

John G. Mitchell, Walnut Hills; Miss Anna E. Ryall; Miss Martha E. Anderson, Park street, between 4th and 5th; Miss Amelia Williams, Water street, between John and Smith.

Foreign Consuls.

Adae C. F., Office southwest corner of Main and 3d; Consulate for the Kingdoms of Prussia, Wurtemberg, Bavaria, Hanover and Saxony; for the Grand Duchies of Oldenburg, Hesse and Baden; for the Electorate of Hesse and the Duchy of Nassau, and for the Free City of Frankfort on the Main.

Eggers Augustus, Office 168 Main; Consul of the Duchy of Saxe Weimer, and of Saxe Coburg-Gotha.

Meline James F, 17 West Third, Consul of Mecklenberg, Schwerin, Holland, Belgium, Hamburg, Lubeck, Sweden, and Norway; Vice-Consul of France, Sardinia, Denmark, Schleswig Holstein, and Lauenburg.

Schmidt Charles, Consul for the Duchy of Braunschweig and Luneburg. Office 632 Main.

3

City Government.

Charter Election first Monday in April.

Regular Meetings of the Board first and third Fridays of each month.

City Officers.

MAYOR.
George Hatch, office City Hall....Term expires April, 1863.

CLERK.
Charles S. Betts.......................Term expires 1863.

CITY COUNCIL.

THEODORE MARSH, *President.*
GEORGE M. CASEY, *Clerk.*

Ward	Member	Term expires
1st Ward	James W. Fitzgerald	April, 1863
"	Jas. H. Walker	" 1864
2d Ward	Peter Gibson	" 1863
"	Finley Latta	" 1864
3d Ward	B. W. Cunningham	" 1863
"	Conrad Schulis	" 1864
4th Ward	J. H. F. Groene	" 1863
"	Wm. H. Glass	" 1864
5th Ward	John H. Carter	" 1863
"	Nathan Bartlett	" 1864
6th Ward	Peter Lavin	" 1863
"	Robert A. Johnson	" 1864
7th Ward	August Rothert	" 1863
"	John Clark	" 1864
8th Ward	James Ashman	" 1863
"	J. Wiseman	" 1864
9th Ward	John B. Warren	" 1863
"	M. A. Cavanaugh	" 1864
10th Ward	M. A. Jacobi	" 1863
"	Wm Seibern	" 1864
11th Ward	Alexander Aupperle	" 1863
"	A. V. Perry	" 1864
12th Ward	Meinrad Kleiner	" 1863
"	Wm. S. Drown	" 1864
13th Ward	Geo. A. Doherty	" 1863
"	Richard Shinnick	" 1864
14th Ward	D. J. Bean	" 1863
"	Thos. H. Wensner	" 1864
15th Ward	Theodore Marsh	" 1863
"	Samuel Stokes, Jr.	" 1864
16th Ward	J. A. Hogue	" 1863
"	S. L. Hayden	" 1864
17th Ward	John W. Scudder	" 1863
"	A. W. Sprague	" 1864

CITY CLERK.
Geo. M. Casey, office City Hall. Term expires April, 1863.
Assistant—J. D. Vanauker.

AUDITOR
George Stackhouse, office City Hall. Term expires April, 1863.
First Assistant—E. B. Townsend.
Second Assistant—John G. Jones.

TREASURER.
J. M. Noble, office City Hall......Term expires April, 1863.

CITY SOLICITOR.
Thos. C. Ware, office City Hall. Term expires April, 1863.
Assistant—William Disney.

CITY CIVIL ENGINEER.
Thos. J. Peter, office City Hall. Term expires April, 1863.
Assistant—George E. Nugent.
Draughtsman—Julius Blackburn.
Recording Draughtsman—John Halpin.
Rodman—Monroe Peter.

CITY COMMISSIONERS.
(Office City Hall.)

Jere. Kiersted.....................Term expires 1863.
Thos. J. Tiernon.................... " " 1864.
Nicholas Hoeffer.................. " " 1865.

WHARF MASTER.
John A. Baker .... Term expires April, 1864.

REGISTER OF PUBLIC LANDINGS.
Herman Ficke.

SUPERINTENDENT OF MARKETS.
R. C. Ashcraft............. .....Term expires April, 1863.
Assistants—John McDonald, Thomas Lippincott, and Thos. J. Brown.

CITY COLLECTORS.
R. P. Spader and S. H. Dunning.

WOOD MEASURERS.
Benj. Jelleffe... ....Miami Canal District.
Joseph Lewis.................................River District.
W. R. Field................................River District.
Bernard Mullen—Market District, including 3d & 17th ward.

CITY SEALER.
William Bellows.

CITY WEIGHER.
E W. Ashley.

HAY WEIGHER.
George Guilford.

INSPECTORS.
Liquors, Oils and Molasses—M. R. Taylor, R. Delavan Mussey, S. Menzies, Hugh Simmons, George Guysi, and Wm. H. Gould.
Flour—J. S. Powers, and Samuel B. Nafew.
Meat—John Schidler.
Tobacco—Joseph Howe.

BOARD OF CITY IMPROVEMENTS.

George Hatch..........................President.
Engineer—Thomas J. Peter.
Commissioners—Jeremiah Kiersted.......Eastern District.
                Thomas G. Tiernon.....Western District.
                Nicholas Hœffer.......Northern District.
Clerk—George Guilford.
Messenger—Frank Kirchner.

POLICE COURT.

Judge—James Saffin..................Term expires 1863.
Clerk—John M. Medary................Term expires 1865
Prosecuting Attorney—F. C. Jones.....Term expires 1863.

CHIEF OF POLICE.

John W. Dudley......................Office City Hall.

LIEUTENANTS.

Thomas Mearn, William Montgomery, Jacob G. Hirst, E. T. Harmon, John G. Kelly, James H. Homer, and J. H. Kramer.

STATION KEEPERS.

J. H. Evans..........................Ninth Street Station.
J. A. Porter.......................... "   "   "
W. H. Phelps........................Hammond Street Station.
Phineas Hudson...................... "   "   "
A Strauss............................Bremen Street Station.
Louis Geier.......................... "   "   "
John McGonagle.....................Pearl Street Station.
James Whalen....................... "   "   "

POLICEMEN.

1st Ward—E. P. Jenkins, Jacob Johnson, Joseph Bolser, Peter Nolan, Daniel Molloy, Emanuel Wolf, Wm. Dwyer, Richard Corcoran.

2d Ward—J. D. Clarkson, F. C. Pearson, John Carney, Thos. Lynch, Thomas Roberts, John McDonald, John G. Gallagher.

3d Ward—M. Ingersoll, S. V. Hammer, Thomas Butler, John Bahmer, John Fortman, Sam. Davis, Jos. Cox.

4th Ward—O. N. Noble, Thos. Moran, Geo. Breaks, Robert Purcell, John B. Molloy, John McCarty, Richd. Carnahan, Wm. Heman.

5th Ward—H. Welsh, H. Butt, F. T. Davis, Wm. Lechman, M. McCaffrey, R. Johnson, I. McFarland, Jno. Truss.

6th Ward—Thos. Mooney, Chas. Bright, Edwd. Mullin, J. J. Williamson, Pat. Day, John Twatchman, Jos. Bunker, James McLean.

7th Ward—Pat Bobbins, E. Wood, Fred. Dressell, Jesse Young, Clements Rewe, H. Korte, John Otte.

8th Ward—Andrew Ross, Richard Bamber, Edw. Tudor, Ed. Weston, H. Kreiger, Thomas S.ewart, Pat Murphy, A. Reide.

9th Ward—Anthony Shafer, John Donohue, J. D. Kornisher, C. Klemper, George Palmer, John Dower, F. Von Seggern, A. F. Secor.

10th Ward—Henry Kusting, M. Liechtendahl, B. Arling, B. Ertle, David Miller, James McKinstry, C. Twatchman, Geo. Smith.

11th Ward—Charles Pepenbring, Charles Crawley, Martin Stahley, John Adams, Jacob Hecht, George Neighber, Wm. Consmiller, James Lyons.

12th Ward—Peter Leiche, Clem Hutman, John Scotchman, James McClellan, John Brown, John Helmich, Jos. Eichelriger.

13th Ward—A. S. Wilson, Thomas Fay, Mich Keating, Dan. Duyler, David Nash, D. Hickey, D. Halcy, William Gettier.

14th Ward—Ben. Smith, M. Haley, Wm. Manneson, Jno. Kline, M. Wheeler, Jerry Twohig, M. Hogan, E. Fitzpatrick.

15th Ward—J. P. Dokes, Jos. Crary, H. H. Wagner, W. L. Morton, Len Bowers, John Weller, Sam. Jenifer.

16th Ward—Edward Hudson, Wm. Walsh, H. Lange, D. T. Hoke, Elias Arnold, John Mahra, Joseph Steele, M. Brogan.

17th Ward—Ludwig Fisher, Thos. J. Weeks, Henry McElhaney, Philip Welsh, Thos. Simpson, James Rowe, A. J. McCall, John Shearer.

RESERVOIR POLICE.

John Martin, Jehu Thomas.

CANAL POLICE.

James McKinley, James Ferry.

RIVER POLICE.

J. H. Riggs, Pat. Flannery, A. Chumley, M. Stevens.

SPECIAL POLICE.

William Garner.

POLICE COURT POLICE.

R. L. Rosebrough, Sam. Simmons, M. Crotty and John A. Watson.

SUBSTITUTES.

J. L Smith, F. Maginniss, Geo. Kelsh, Thomas Fanning, Matthew Ouey, James Cary, Henry Tagge, Thomas Ryan, Maurice Welsh, J. H. Hubing and Fred. Good.

OFFICERS OF THE CITY INFIRMARY AND OUT-DOOR POOR.

James Ayres,
L. L. Armstrong, } Directors.
George Lindeman,
Thomas Winter, Clerk.

CITY INFIRMARY.

Stephen S. Ayers.....................Superintendent.
Elizabeth Ayers......................Matron.
N. S. Armstrong......................Physician.
John C. Hill.........................Property Keeper.
Mollie E. Cox........................School Teacher.

OVERSEERS OF THE POOR.

1st Ward—Mathias Byrne, 69 Baum street.
2d   "   George A. Peters, 127 w. 5th street.
3d   "   A. Kline, 36 Butler street.
4th "   R. P. Cahill, 186 Water street.
5th "   Walter Blackall, 62 Richmond street.
6th "   Anthony Maher, 429 Columbia street.
7th "   Henry Kruse, 424 Elm street.
8th "   John Gerwes, 204 Clark street.
9th "   Richard Zurline, w.s. Main b. 12th and Canal.
10th "   William Leopoldt, c. Main and 12th streets.
11th "   Jacob Hust, 78 Hamilton Road.
12th "   Martin Susner, 1017 Central Av.
13th "   J. V. Hackett, 220 e. 6th street.
14th "   B. Tonies, 335 5t\. street.
15th "   W. Thorburn, 348 George street
16th "   Matthew Hunter 626 Eighth street.
17th "   H. H. Morris, Broad street b. Front and River.

DIRECTORS' REGULATIONS FOR GRANTING OUT-DOOR RELIEF TO THE POOR.

1. Each Ward is one district for providing provisions for the poor, and for this purpose a grocer is to be contracted with in each Ward to deliver, on the order of the Board, such provisions as may be required, the account to be presented and settled on the last day of each quarter, to be sworn to by the grocer, that the articles named therein were all delivered, of good quality, and that the prices charged for the same, are the same as by him charged to his regular cash customers, and no more.

GROCERS.

1st Ward—J. W. Fitzgerald, c. 5th and Broadway.
2d   "   Ira Brickett, c. 6th and Vine.
3d   "   August Rennekamp, c. Butler and Pearl.
4th "   J. H. F. Grœne, c. Race and Cherry Alley.
5th "   Joseph Bushcamp, c. William and Plum.
6th "   John W. Hubing, 452 Columbia street.
7th "   Henry Shornhorst, 543 Race street.
8th "   John G. Kelly, c. Court and John.
9th "   J. B. West, Abigail st., b. Main and Sycamore.
10th "   Conrad Stephen & Co., c. 12th and Main.
11th "   Henry Brethorst, 16 Mulberry street.
12th "   George Helmig, 149 Bank street.
13th "   James O'Conner. Eighth street e. of the Canal.
14th "   Adam Wilson, 224 E. 6th street.
15th "   Martin McCarty, 289 Central Av.
16th "   Clements Haverkamp, Freemen street, b. 7th and 8th.
17th "   John Kramer, Front st. near Jamestown Ferry.

2. For Medical purposes the city is divided into six Medical Districts, as follows, viz:

First District—Eleventh and Twelfth Wards.
Second District—Second, Fifth, and Tenth Wards.
Third District—First, Ninth, and Thirteenth Wards.
Fourth District—Third, Fourth and Seventeenth Wards
Fifth District—Seventh, Eighth and Sixteenth Wards.
Sixth District—Sixth, Fourteenth and Fifteenth Wards.

In each of these Medical Districts there are to be appointed two or more Physicians, one of whom is to be a German; also two or more Apothecaries.

Each Physician so appointed shall attend professionally to the sick poor of his respective District, and shall receive twenty-five cents for each necessary visit: *Provided,* That only such persons shall be paid for as sick paupers who are visited by order of the Directors, on the certificate of the proper Overseer of the Poor; *And Provided further,* That such certificate may be presented to the Board of Directors within two days after the first professional visit. And every Physician appointed by this Board shall present his account for settlement on the last day of each quarter, and shall verify the same by his oath, stating that all the visits charged were necessary for the benefit of the patients therein named. Each Apothecary so appointed shall furnish the medicine ordered by the Physician for the poor in his respective District, and shall file the prescriptions to be delivered to the Board, on presenting his account on the last day of each quarter; and no prescription shall be charged this Board unless the same is signed by the proper Physician of the District, stating the name of the person relieved, and bearing the Physician's mark, "Out-door Poor." And each Apothecary shall verify his account by oath, that the medicines charged therein were actually delivered, and were of good quality, and that the prices are the same as charged to his usual customers, from which prices one-third shall be deducted.

DRUGGISTS.

1st Ward—David Creighton, c. 5th and Broadway.
2d "   John Keeshan, c. 6th and Walnut.
3d "   G. A. Hiller, Broadway, b. 3d and Pearl.
4th "   C. Vilter, s.e.c. Race and 2d.
5th "   H. M. Merrill & Co, c. Court and Plum.
6th "   C. A. Junghanns, n.w.c. 3d and Mill.
7th "   Henry Waffenschmidt, c. 12th and Elm.
8th "   W. H. Runkle, n w.c. Court and Mound.
9th "   A. Langenbeck, c. Abigail and Main.
10th "   Hugo Spamer, 408 Vine street.
11th "   Charles Schmidt, 632 Main street.
19th "   M. G. Helman, c. Findlay and Baymiller.
12th "   Adolph Stierle, c. Race and Elm.
13th "   John T. Toland, s.w.c. 7th and Broadway.
14th "   Joseph Hœveler, n.e.c. 6th and Central Av.
15th "   Albert Ross, s.w.c. 8th and Central Av.
16th "   H. Frisch, c. Gest and Freeman.
17th "   A. Sander, E. Front.

PHYSICIANS.

FIRST DISTRICT—Wards 11th and 12th.

11th Ward—Dr. C. D. Fishburn, 347 Vine street.
12th "   Dr. S. Alexander, c. Baymiller and Central Av.
12th "   Dr. John Greenwald, 998 Central Av.

SECOND DISTRICT—Wards 2d, 5th, and 10th.

2d Ward—Dr. J. A. Thacker, Race above 6th.
5th "   Dr. W. H. Taylor, 140 W 8th.
10th "   Dr. Louis Eyman, 73 Clay.

THIRD DISTRICT—Wards 1st, 9th, and 13th.

1st Ward—Dr. W. Curson, n.e.c. 3d and Broadway.
9th "   Dr. C. C. Richard, Pendleton, b. Hunt and Abigail.
13th "   Dr. George A. Doherty, 228 Broadway.

FOURTH DISTRICT—Wards 3d, 4th, and 17th.

3d Ward—Dr. W. W. Dawson, c. 3d and Broadway.
4th "   Dr. E. H. Johnson, c. Race and Front.
17th "   Dr. J. M. Scudder, 1330 E. Front.

FIFTH DISTRICT—Wards 7th, 8th, and 16th.

7th Ward—Dr. F. Rapp, 483 Elm street.
8th "   Dr. V. Fischer, 137 Laurel street.
16th "   Dr. Joseph Merrill, 8th, b. Carr and Harriet.

SIXTH DISTRICT—Wards 6th, 14th and 15th.

6th Ward—Dr. G. R. Patton, c. 4th and John.
14th "   Dr. J. J. Quinn, 122 W. 7th.
15th "   Dr. F. A. J. Gerwe, c. Longworth and Park.

UNDERTAKERS.

D. Nicholson, 4 New street.
J. Soards & Son, c. 6th and Elm.

Justices of the Peace.

Ferdinand K. Martin.............Term expires Nov. 1862.
F. H. Rowekamp...................   "   Dec. 1862.
C. F. Hanselman..................   "   April, 1863.
David Fisher......................   "   Oct. 1863.
Nathan Marchant..................   "   Nov. 1863.
H. N. Clark........................   "   Oct. 1865.
Benjamin C. True..................   "   Oct. 1863.
William Chidsey...................   "   July, 1864
W L. Aldrich......................   "   Oct. 1863.
Thomas McLean....................   "   April, 1864.

Fire Department.

OFFICE, NORTH SIDE GEORGE BET. PLUM AND CENTRAL AVENUE.

CHIEF ENGINEER—E. G. Megrue, s. s. Longworth, b. Central Av and John.
SECRETARY—Lewis Guelich, No, 208 Longworth.
FIRE DISTRICTS—The city is divided into four Districts, as follows:
FIRST, or South-eastern District, lying south of 6th, and east of Vine.
SECOND, or South-western District, lying south of 6th, and west of Vine.
THIRD, or North-western District, lying north of 6th, and west of Vine.
FOURTH, or North-eastern District, lying north of 6th, and east of Vine.
ASSISTANT ENGINEER FIRST AND FOURTH DISTRICTS—John Doran, east side Mansfield near Liberty.
ASSISTANT ENGINEER SECOND AND THIRD DISTRICTS—Lewis Wisby, s.e.c. 5th and Central Av.

Fire Companies.

No. 1. WASHINGTON, Steam Fire Engine, e.s. Vine. b. Front and 2d. Wm. H Glass, Captain; Otto Raymond, Engineer.
WEST END, Steam Fire Co. No. 2; T. Chambers, Captain; C. Perkins, Engineer.
No. 3. CITIZENS' GIFT, Steam Fire Engine. s.s. 6th w. of Vine. H. R. Leonard, Captain; Finley Latta, Engineer.
No. 4. A. B. LATTA, Steam Fire Engine, e s. Sycamore, b. 7th and 8th. Henry Atkins, Captain; William Piercy, Engineer.
No. 5. JEFFERSON, Steam Fire Co., e.s. Vine, b. Canal and Court. Godfrey Ludwig, Captain, Henry Myers, Engineer.
No. 6. EASTERN. Steam Fire Co., cor. Pearl and Martin. John Shue and H. F. Stewart, Captains.
No. 7. NORTHERN, Steam Fire Co., s.s. Webster b. Main and Sycamore. Jas. Fink, Captain; F. Cammon, Engineer.
No. 8. MARION, Steam Fire Engine, w.s. Cutter, b. Laurel and Betts. Wm. Moore, Captain; Geo. K. Warner, Engineer.
No. 10. DELUGE, Steam Fire Engine, n.w.c. 3d and Lawrence. L. M. Hazen, Captain; Wm. P. O'Rielly, Engineer.
No. 12. MOHAWK, Steam Fire Engine, n.s. Hamilton Road, opp. Vine st. Jacob Hust, Captain; H. Slemmer, Engineer.
No. 13. BRIGHTON, Fire Co., n.s Bank, b. Linn and Baymiller. C. Korzenborn, Captain; Franklin S. Gregg, Engineer.
No. 14. WESTERN, Steam Fire Engine, n.s. 5th b. Smith and Mound. C. O. Andress, Captain; F. G. Miller. Engineer.
No. 15. FULTON, Fire Co., 17th Ward. J. T. Webster and W. C. Morgan, Pipemen.
No. 1. PHŒNIX, Hook and Ladder Co., at 6th and Vine. E. B. Turner, Captain.
No. 2. UNION, Hook and Ladder Co., e.s. Race, b. 13th and 14th.
WATCH TOWER, s w.c. 6th and Vine.
LOCK STREET, Hose Co. No. 2, e.s. Lock b. 4th and 5th. James Pearce, Captain.

Rules and Regulations.

ART. 1. All the Companies of the Department shall be furnished with a copy of the Fire Ordinance and the Rules and Regulations, which shall be framed and placed in their respective houses It shall be the duty of the officers and members of the Department to conform to all the requisitions, and perform all the duties herein required.

ART 2. The Chief Engineer shall have command of the Fire Department, and at all of the fires. and direct the respective Assistant Engineers in any and all matters belonging to the same; he shall lay before the Board of Engineers, and the Board of Supervisors, respectively, all such business as may require their consideration; he shall direct the Assistant Engineers at fires, how to dispose of the respective Companies of their District.

ART. 3. The Assistant Engineers shall examine the condition of the different Companies in their District, and see that the Captain of each Company has the apparatus entrusted to their care kept in good working order, and that the Ordinances and Regulations of the Fire Department are strictly attended to. They shall, in the absence of the Chief Engineer, take the command at all fires in their respective Districts, and receive the report from the Captain of each Company, of any repairs that may be necessary, and report the same forthwith to the Chief Engineer. In the absence of the Ass. Eng. of a District, the Ass. Eng. of the District succeeding shall have th ecommand of the Co's of that District.

ART. 4. The Captain of each Company shall take command at all fires in their Districts, in the absence of the Chief Engineer or his Assistants and when there is more than one Company in a District the Captains of said Companies shall cast lots, who shall have the command, in the absence of the Chief or Assistants. They shall see that the men composing the Companies under their command, comply with the Rules and Regulations of the Fire Department, and shall cause all the orders of the Chief or his Assistants to be strictly obeyed.

ART. 5. The Captain of a Company shall see that all the property in such Company is duly cared for; that the Pipemen, Drivers, Firemen, Watchmen and Engineer attend to their respective duties, and see that they stand their respective watches; he shall direct the members of a Company at fires, call the roll, and report as often as directed, or as he may find necessary, to the Assistant Engineer of his District, or Secretary, respectively.

ART. 6. Alarms are not to be given at any Engine House, unless received from a responsible person or persons, or from another fire bell; the men on duty at the Engine House shall be held answerable for all false alarms given by them.

ART. 7. Racing to or from fires is not allowed under any circumstances, under the penalty of dismissal; and if the apparatus of several Companies proceed on the same street to or from a fire they shall do so in single file.

ART. 8. Any Driver of Steam Engine or Hand Apparatus, Hose Carriages or Hook and Ladder Companies, driving or running over hose, unless it can not be avoided, shall be subject to dismissal from the Department.

ART. 9. The Captain of any Steam or Hand Company shall be at the pipes when at fires, and see that the line of hose are well guarded.

ART. 10. When the Chief Engineer shall find the fire so far reduced that one or all the Companies may cease work, he shall dismiss them, or cause the same to be done.

ART. 11. No officer or member of the Department shall appear on duty, without such badge as may be prescribed by the Board of Engineers, under penalty of twenty-five cents, unless they can furnish a reasonable excuse.

ART. 12. Any officer or stationary member absent from a fire, shall be subject to a fine of *two dollars;* running members, for a like neglect, *one dollar.*

ART. 13. That if a charge of intoxication be preferred and proven against any officer or member of the Fire Department, oftener than once, he shall be discharged; and further, it shall be the duty of every officer or member of the Department to report such member violating this rule to the Chief Engineer or Board of Supervisors.

ART. 14. Members of Fire Companies, or other persons, are not permitted to frequent, meet, or loiter around the Engine Houses, without special permission from their respective officers. Men on duty at the Engine Houses who may allow the same, shall be subject to dismissal.

ART. 15. The Hook and Ladder Companies will take position, when practicable, within the lines and as near the fire, as under all circumstances may be found convenient.

ART. 16. All charges for misconduct against officers or members must be presented to the Board of Supervisors, in writing, and for such charges he or they shall be immediately notified of the same, and stand suspended; and no charge will be recognized unless reported to the Board within thirty days after the misconduct.

ART. 17. Any officer or member of the Fire Department who have charges preferred against them, can or may have a trial within five (5) days from the time the charges have been preferred, and no officer or member shall receive any pay from the Fire Department, during the time he or they stand charged with any misdemeanor or suspension.

ART. 18. Any Company, returning from a fire, finding they have hose which does not belong to them, shall immediately return the same to the Company to which it belongs.

ART. 19. The Captain of each Company shall in no instance allow any person, except the Captain, Pipeman, Engineer or Drivers, to ride on the apparatus, either in going to or from a fire.

List of Cisterns.

Water and Plum streets.
" John
Front and Sportman Hall.
" Toll Gate.
" Lewis.
" Tan Yard.
" Jamestown Ferry.
" Hazen.
" Broad.
" at Wm. Worley's T'rn.
" and Collard.
" Whittaker.
" Junc. of Pearl.
" and Miami Canal.
" Pike.
" Junc. of Second.
" Ludlow.
" Sycamore.
" Main.
" Walnut.
" Vine.
" Race.
" Elm.
" Central Avenue.
" Smith.
" Rose.
Second and Broadway.
" Sycamore.
" Main.
" Walnut.
" Race.
" Plum.
" Central Avenue.
" Smith.
" Park.
Pearl and Kilgour.
" Butler.
" Lawrence.
" Sycamore.
" Main.
" Vine.
" Elm.
Third and Pike.
" Ludlow.
" Walnut.
" Race.
" Plum.
" John.
" Park.
" Stone.
Fourth and Lawrence.
" Broadway.
" Sycamore.
" Main.
" Walnut.
" Vine.
" Race.
" Elm.
" Central Avenue.
" Smith.
" Mill.
Fifth and Lock.
" Pike.
" McAllister.
" Sycamore.
" Main.
" Walnut.
" Race.
" Plum.
" John.
" Mound.
" Stone.
" H. & D. Depot.
Longworth and Park.
Sixth and Baum.
" Broadway.
" Main.
" Walnut.
" Vine.
" Race.
" Elm.
" Central Avenue.
" Smith.
" Cutter.
" Harriet.
Seventh and Sycamore.
" Walnut.
" Race.
" Central Avenue.
" Linn.
" Freeman.
Eighth and Accommodation.

Eighth and Lock.
" Main.
" Vine.
" Elm.
" Mound.
" Carr.
Ninth and Sycamore.
" Walnut.
" Race.
" Plum.
" John.
" Linn.
" Freeman.
Court b. Main and Walnut.
" and Vine.
" Central Avenue.
" John.
" Cutter.
" Linn.
Twelfth and Walnut.
" Race.
" Elm.
Deer Creek Valley.
Broadway and Hunt.
" Franklin.
" Liberty.
" Milton.
Sycamore and Woodward.
" Webster.
" Burgoyne.
" Mount Auburn av.
" opp. Orphan Asylum.
" Corporation Line.
Main and Thirteenth.
" Liberty.
" Buckeye.
" Burgoyne.
Walnut and Allison.
" Liberty.
" Ham. Road.
Vine and Thirteenth.
" Fifteenth.
" Green.
" Ham. Road.
" Mulberry.
Race and Fourteenth.
" Liberty.
" Findlay M'ket space.
" Ham. Road.
Elm and Fifteenth.
" Findlay.
" Ham. Road.
Plum and George.
Central Av. and Elizabeth.
" Laurel.
" Wade.
" Baymiller.
" Brighton.
" York.
John and Augusta.
" Clark.
" Clinton.
" David.
" Poplar.
Mound and Richmond.
" Barr.
" Elizabeth.
Cutter and Laurel.
" Wade.
Baymiller b. George and 6th.
" and Richmond.
" Gest.
" Laurel.
" Liberty.
" Findlay.
" Bank.
Freeman and Gest.
" Hopkins.
" Clinton.
" Findlay.
Linn and Laurel.
" Clinton.
" Poplar.
" Findlay.
Morton and Pierson.
Pendleton and Woodward.
" Liberty.
Spring and Abigail.
Clark and Rittenhouse.
Bank and Whiteman.
Dudley and Everett.
Liberty and Mansfield.

List of Fire Plugs.

Water, b. Main and Walnut.
Water, b. Vine and Race.
Water, b. Elm and Plum.
Water, b. Central Av. and John.
Front, e. of Torrence Road.
Front, w. of Torrence Road.
Front, at Toll Gate.
Front, at Hinkle's Lumber Yard.
Front, at Fulton Engine House.
Front, at Hamilton Ship Yard.
Front, at Marine Railway Office.
Front, at Railroad Crossing.
Front, above old Corporation Line.
Front, at Junction of Morton.
Front, b. Collard and Whittaker.
Front, at the old Engine House.
Front, at the Bagging Factory.
Front, at the east end L. M. Depot.
Front, at the west end L. M. D-pot.
Front, b. Kilgour and Miami Canal.
Front, b. Butler and Miami Canal.
Front and Butler.
Front, opp. Bagging Factory,
Front, b. Pike and Butler.
Front, b. Pike and Lawrence.
Front, b. Main and Walnut.
Front, b. Walnut and Vine.
Front, b. Race and Elm.
Front, b. Central Av. and John.
Front, b. Smith and Rose.
Front, at Hinkle & Guild's Pl'ng Mill.
Front. e. of Mill.
Front, w. of Mill
Front, at Ohio and Mississippi Depot.
Front and 3d.
Front, w. of Wood.
Second, b. Ludlow and Broadway.
Second, at Junction with Front.
Second and Sycamore.
Second, b. Main and Walnut.
Second, b. Vine and Race.
Second, b. Race and Elm.
Second, b. Elm and Plum.
Second and John.
Second, b. John and Smith.
Second and Rose.
Second, b. Park and Mill.
Second, e. of Wood.
Pearl and Martin.
Pearl, b. Kilgour and Miami Canal.
Pearl, b. Miami Canal and Butler.
Pearl, b. Main and Walnut.
Pearl, b. Plum and Central Av. (Sugar Refinery.)
Third, b. Kilgour and Ellen.
Third and Kilgour.
Third and Miami Canal.
Third and Butler.
Third and Lawrence.
Third, b. Broadway and Sycamore.
Third and Hammond.
Third, b. Plum and Central Av.
Third and Central Av.
Third, b. John and Smith.
Third, b. Mill and Stone.
Third and Wood.
Fourth, b. Broadway and Sycamore.
Fourth, b. Main and Walnut.
Fourth, b. Walnut and Vine.
Fourth, b. Smith an ! Park.
Fourth, b. Park and Mill.
Fifth, b. Buchanan and Pike.
Fifth and Broadway.
Fifth, b. Sycamore and Broadway.
Fifth, b. Main and Walnut.
Fifth, b. Walnut and Vine.
Fifth, b. Vine and Race.
Fifth, b. Smith and Mound.
Fifth and White Water Canal.
Fifth and Junction of Front.
Sixth and Culvert.
Sixth and Sycamore.
Sixth, b. Main and Walnut.
Sixth, b. Vine and Race.
Sixth, b. Mound and Park.
Sixth and White Water Canal.
Sixth and Freeman.
Sixth, b. Harriet and Carr.
Sixth near Front.
Seventh, b. Walnut and Vine.
Seventh and Smith.
Eighth and Accommodation.
Eighth and Locke.
Eighth and Broadway.
Eighth, b. Plum and Central Av.
Eighth, b Central Av. and John.
Eighth, b. Cutter and Linn.
Eighth and Baymiller.
Ninth and Broadway.
Ninth, b. John and Mound.
Ninth and Freeman.
Court, at Dominick's Slaughter House.
Broadway, b. Front and Second.
Broadway, b. Second and Pearl.
Broadway and New.
Broadway and Abigail.
Sycamore, b. Sixth and Seventh.
Sycamore, b. Seventh and Eighth.
Sycamore, b. Eighth and Ninth.
Sycamore, b Ninth and Court.
Sycamore, opp. Court.
Sycamore and Orchard.
Sycamore and Boal.
Sycamore and Burgoyne.
Main, b. Second and Pearl.
Main, b. Fourth and Fifth.
Main, b. Sixth and Seventh.
Main, b. Seventh and Eighth.
Walnut, b. Front and Second.
Walnut and Gano.
Walnut, at Greenwood's Foundry.
Wanlut and Mercer.
Walnut and Hamilton Road.
Vine, b. Fron and Second.
Vine, b. Augusta and Commerce.
Vine, b. Court and Canal.
Vine, b. Fifteenth and Liberty.
Vine, b. Liberty and Green.
Vine and Hamilton Road.
Race and Longworth.
Race and George.
Race, b. Thirteenth and Fourteenth.
Race, b. Fifteenth and Liberty.
Elm, b. Sixth and Longworth.
Elm and Fourteenth.
Plum and Fourth.
Plum and Longworth.
Central Av., b. Ninth and Richmond.
Central Av. and Everett.
Central Av. and Laurel.
Central Av. and Liberty.
Central Av., b. Poplar and Findlay.
Central Av., b. York and Dayton.
Central Av., b. Clarkson and Mohawk Bridge.
Central Av. and Baymiller.
Central Av., b. Freeman and Patterson
Central Av., b. Brighton House and Division.
Cutter and Van Horn.
Cutter, b. Court and Clark.
Cutter, b. Laurel and Betts.
Cutter, b. Wade and Liberty.
Baymiller, b. Sixth and George.
Baymiller and Clinton.
Freeman, b. Fifth and Sixth.
Morton and Whittaker
Morton and Pierson.
Morton, n. of Laboratory.
Main and Sycamore.
Front and Second.
Augusta, b. Front and Second
Augusta, b. John and Central Av.
Smith, b. Front and Second.
Locke, b. Fourth and Fifth.
Locke and Fifth.
Locke, b. Fifth and Sixth.
Spring, b. Woodward and Liberty.
Webster, b. Main and Sycamore.
Clay, b. Canal and Twelfth.
Clay and Liberty.
Buckeye and Young.
Buckeye and Poplar.
Burnet, b. Vine and Race.
Hamilton Road, b. Vine and Race.
Hamilton Road, b Hamburg and Canal.
George, b Plum and Central Av.
George and John.
George and Freeman.
Barr, b Cutter and Linn.
Budd and Harriet.
Richmond, b. Cutter and Linn.
Richmond and Harriet.
Longworth, b. John and Mound.
Bank and Brighton Engine House.
Plug, midway in Ham. & Dayton Depot,
Plug. head of Ellen.
Two Plugs in Mudge's Factory, Second b. Vine and Race.
Two Plugs on Eighth, b. Baymiller and Freemen.
Lower end of Clark.

Street Railroads.

CINCINNATI STREET RAILROAD.—Office 162 Vine street. John L. Stettinus, President; O P. Tharp, Superintendent. ROUTE:—Cars start from the corner of Fourth and Vine streets,—thence North on Vine to Seventh street,—thence West on Seventh to Freeman,—thence North on Freeman to Hamilton Road—thence (returning) South on Freeman to York street,—thence East on York to Linn,—thence South on Linn to Ninth street,—thence East on Ninth to Walnut,—thence South on Walnut to Fourth.— thence West on Fourth to Vine street.

PASSENGER RAILROAD.—Office North West corner of Fourth and Main streets. James M. Doherty, President; Seneca W Ely Secretary. ROUTE:—Cars start from the corner of Third and Lawrence streets,—thence North on Lawrence to Fourth.—thence West on Fourth to Smith,—thence North on Smith to Fifth—thence West on Fifth to North West corner of Fifth and Freeman,—thence (returning) East on Fifth (by double track) to Wood street.—thence South on Wood to Third,—thence East on Third to place of beginning.

CITY PASSENGER RAILROAD.—Office, North West corner of Fourth and Main streets. James M. Doherty, President. Seneca W. Ely, Secretary. ROUTE:—Cars start from the intersection of Fourth and Main streets,—thence West on Fourth to John,—thence North on John to Findlay,—thence West on Findlay to Baymiller,—thence North on Baymiller to Bank,—thence West on Bank to Patterson.—thence North on Patterson to Harrison Pike,—thence East on Harrison Pike to Cumminsville Pike,—thence (returning) on Central Avenue to Fifth street.—thence East on Fifth to Main,—thence South on Main to the place of beginning.

PENDLETON AND FIFTH STREET MARKET RAILROAD.—Office, East Front street, East of Washington street. Charles H Kilgour, President; George McLaughlin, Secretary. ROUTE:—Cars start from the corner of Fourth and Walnut streets,—thence North on Walnut to Fifth,—thence East on Fifth to Broadway,—thence South on Broadway to East Pearl street,—thence East on Pearl to Junction with East Front street,—thence East on East Front street to Washington street,—thence (returning,) West on Morton and East Third streets to junction with East Pearl street,—thence West on Pearl to Broadway.—thence North on Broadway to Fourth street,—thence West on Fourth street to the place of beginning.

CINCINNATI AND SPRING GROVE AVENUE STREET RAILROAD.—Office, Cumminsville. Matthew Hopple, President. ROUTE:—Cars start from Brighton House, running to and from Brighton House to Spring Grove, via., Spring Grove Avenue.

County Officers.

PROBATE JUDGE.
Alexander Paddack..............Term expires Feb. 1864.

CLERK OF THE COURTS.
Charles E. Cist....................Term expires Feb. 1864.

SHERIFF.
John B. Armstrong,...............Term expires Jan. 1863.

AUDITOR.
William Ward..................Term expires March, 1863.

TREASURER.
E. D. Crookshank, (present incumbent.) Term expires Sept. 1862.
Oliver H. Geoffroy, Treasurer elect.

RECORDER.
F. H. Oehlmann.....................Term expires Jan. 1865.

PROSECUTING ATTORNEY.
Theophilus Gaines................Term expires Jan. 1863.

SURVEYOR.
Joseph W. Gilbert..................Term expires Oct. 1862.

CORONER.
F. L. Emmerth......................Term expires Jan. 1863.

COMMISSIONERS.
Leonard Swartz...................Term expires Oct. 1863.
John N. Ridgeway .... " Oct. 1862.
Frederick J. Mayer.............. " Oct. 1864.

DIRECTORS COUNTY INFIRMARY.
Samuel Benn.....................Term expires Oct. 1862.
John K. Green................... " Oct. 1863
John H. Tangemann............. " Oct. 1864.

SUPERIOR COURT JUDGES.
Charles D. Coffin.................Term expires May, 1863
George Hoadly, Jr................ " May, 1864.
Belamy Storer.................... " May, 1867.

COMMON PLEAS JUDGES.
M. W. Oliver.....................Term expires Feb. 1867.
Nicholas Hendington............. " Feb. 1867.
Charles C. Murdock.............. " Feb. 1867

HAMILTON
IRON FOUNDRY,

WEST FRONT STREET, NEAR JOHN, CINCINNATI, O.

W. W. HANES.

GRATE BARS,	SOAP KETTLES,	CAST IRON SHAFTS,	FURNACE FRONTS,
TALLOW KETTLES,	HANGERS,	SASH WEIGHTS,	MILL GEARING,
PULLEYS,	CLOCK WEIGHTS,	GUDGEONS,	GUTTER SHOES,
BATTERS PLUGS,	IRON COLUMNS,	&C., &C.	

☞ Steam Engines, Boilers, Circular Saw Mills, Grist Mills, and Wood Working Machinery. Castings and Machinery of all kinds made to order. ☜

DANIEL RAYMOND.   JACOB HILSINGER.   JOHN HILSINGER.

RAYMOND, HILSINGER & CO.,
MANUFACTURERS OF

STEEL MOULD BOARD PLOUGHS,

No. 614 Main Street,
CINCINNATI, O.

☞ STEEL MOULD BOARDS FOR SALE.

CINCINNATI ADVERTISEMENTS.

S. LEVI & BROTHERS,

MANUFACTURERS OF

ALCOHOL,

PURE AND COLOGNE SPIRITS,

PURE CATAWBA BRANDY,

AND DOMESTIC

WINES & LIQUORS

IN GENERAL. DEALERS IN ALL KINDS OF

FOREIGN AND DOMESTIC

WINES, LIQUORS, CIGARS, &C.

A large stock of Pure Catawba Wine, Old Bourbon and Rye Whiskies, always on hand.

Nos. 221 and 223 Walnut St., Cincinnati, O.

J. C. & H. L. TUMY,

BOOK BINDERS,

—AND—

MANUFACTURERS OF

BLANK BOOKS,

(OVER THE BOOKSTORE OF APPLEGATE & CO.)

No. 43 Main Street, below Second Street,

CINCINNATI, OHIO.

WILLIAMS' CINCINNATI DIRECTORY,

FOR 1862.

ABBREVIATIONS.

acct., stands for..accountant.	clk. stands for..clerk.	mkr stands for....maker.
agt ....agent.	cof. h...........coffee house.	M................Miami.
al.............alley *or* allopathic.	com ....commission.	n................north.
atty............attorney.	con ....continuation.	nr...............near.
av..............avenue.	confec...........confectioner.	not..............notary public.
b............between.	dray.............drayman.	opp ....opposite.
bds.............boards.	e................east.	ov...............over.
b. h.............boarding house.	ec ....eclectic.	prov.............provision.
b. k.............book keeper.	ex...............exchange.	r. r..............railroad.
bk..............book *or* brick.	eng ....engineer.	res...............residence.
bar k............bar. keeper.	h................house.	ret...............retail.
bldg.............building.	ham road........Hamilton road.	s................south.
bldr.............builder.	ho ....homœopathic.	tp ....township.
bo..............botanic.	lab..............laborer.	u................upper.
c...............corner.	manufac........{ manufactory *or* manufacturer.	w................west.
cab. mkr.........cabinet maker.	mach............machinist.	wh ....wholesale.
carp.............carpenter.	mer ....merchant.	W. W............White Water.
cig..............cigar		wks ....works.

(ABE)   (ACK)   (ADA)

Aaron Albert, barber, h. 181 Vine
Aarons John, lab., h. 27 Parsons
Abarth Rev. Dyonisus, h. 229 Bremen.
Abba Miss Barbara, tailoress, bds. 501 E. Front
Abbs Mrs. Rose, h. 501 E. Front
Abberly Christopher, moulder, h. 616 W. 8th
Abbett Carver M., b k., 95 Walnut, h. Newport
Abbey Geo. P., bds. Clifton House
Abbiehl Jacob, waiter, Gibson House.
Abbing Bernhard, shoe mkr., bds 677 W. 6th
Abbott Hiram, butcher, h. 409 Baymiller
Abbott James, varnisher, h. 477 W. 3d
Abbott Mrs. Julia, h. 638 W. 6th
Abbott Wm., clk., 259 Cutter
Abby Thos. B., moulder, h 323 Clark
Abel Conrad, mason, e.s. Baymiller b. Wade and Liberty
Abel Daniel, bar tender, 117 E. 8th
Abel F. & Co., (Fred. A. & Henry Hakman) coal dealers, w.s. Park b. 2d and W. W. Canal
Abel Frank, driver, n.w.c. Lawrence and Newport Ferry Landing
Abel Frederick, (F. A. & Co.) 458 W 3d
Abel George, mer. tailor, 959 Central Av.
Abel Henry, grocery, s.w.c. Mill and 5th
Abel John, barber, 719 Race
Abel John, painter, 26 Hamer
Abel Michael, cutter, 114 E. 5th
Abel Theresa, servt., Broadway Hotel
Abeling Frank, shoe mkr., bds. 18 Commerce
Abeling Henry, boots and shoes, 19 River Landing b. Main and Walnut, h. 25 Commerce
Abell Joseph I., clk., 43 Pub Landing
Abell Wm. J, finisher, h. 404 W. 7th
ABER Jacob S., (W. H. Comstock & Co.) res. Lynn, Mass.
Aberle Mrs. Catherine, 5 Lawrence
Aberly Godfried, baker, bds. 1184 E. Front

Abernethy Robert P., mach., 394 Race
Abernethy Wm., (Behrens & A.) h. 34 E. 4th
Abernethy Wm. J., clk., s.w.c. 2d and Broadway, h. 431 W. 4th
Abka Wm., lab., e.s. Anderson al. b. 2d and Pearl
Abke Henry, tanner, n w.c. Elm and Green
Able Jacob, h. 126 Mohawk
Ablet Thomas, paper box mkr., n.s. 6th b. Freeman and Carr
Ablett Isaac, block mkr., wks. 87 E. Ham. Road and Bremen
Abner Pres., bds. Dumas Hotel
Abraham Abraham, b.k., 106 Park
Abraham David, peddler, 452 W. Liberty
Abraham David, peddler, 491 Vine
Abraham Mrs. Johanna, h. s.s. 14th b. Race and Bremen
Abraham John D., 16 Masonic Temple, h. 145 Smith
ABRAHAM JOSEPH, Atty. at Law and Notary, room 16, Masonic Temple, h. 145 Smith
Abraham Mark, 569 Central Av.
Abraham Solomon, (A. & Wagner) bds. 17 Lodge
Abraham & Wagner, (Solomon A. & Bernhard W.) cigar manufs., 191 W 5th
Abramham Louis, b.k. 56 and 58 Main, h. 311 West 6th
Abrams Mrs. Elizabeth, 179 Broadway
Abresa John, 76 Mohawk
Achew Henry, cook, 311 John
Achey Emanuel, 62 Bank
Achsen Anthony, painter, 525 Sycamore
Achteresch Hy., bds. 60 Hunt
Achtermeier August, baker, 51 Kossuth
Achterkelch Wm., lab., bds. 216 W. 7th
Achtermeyer Ernst, s.w.c. Gest and Harriet
Ackenberg Ernst, 53 15th
Acker Andrew, finisher, wks. n.e.c. Walnut and Miami Canal
Acker Emil, mach., bds. 476 Race

Acker Valentine, carpet weaver, h. 24 15th
ACKERLAND ABRAHAM, Manufacturer of Clothing and Importer of Cloths, Vestings, and Gents. Furnishing Goods. 66 W Pearl, h. 242 W. 4th
Ackerland Louis, cigar mkr., 129 Spring
Ackerman Daniel, gardner, w.s. Freeman b. Dayton and Findlay
Ackermann Christian, barber, 3 E. 4th
Ackermann Fred., b.k. 91 Sycamore
Ackermann Geo., moulder, rear 142 Ham. Road
Ackermann Gottlieb F., 10 Webb
Ackermann John, cigar mkr., 127 Clay
Ackermann Thomas, pewter worker, 38 Rittenhouse [Clay
Ackerpohl Frederick, cooper, bds. 171
Ackerstaff John, carp., 11 Orchard
Ackley Abraham, trader, n.e.c. Betts and Cutter
Ackley Abraham, saddler, 204 Clark
Ackley Wm. E., n.w.c 3d and Sycamore, h. Newport
Ackva Wm., pleasure garden, n.w.c. Main and Liberty
Acmal Rev. Francis, w.s. Sycamore b. 6th and 7th
ACTON Clement J., (A. & Woodnutt) h. 342 W. 7th
ACTON & WOODNUTT, (Clement J. A. & Thomas W.) Wholesale Dealers in Dry Goods, 103 W. Pearl
ADAE C. F. & CO., (Carl F. A. & Adolphus Seinecke) German Savings Institution, s.w.c. 3d and Main
Adae Carl F., (C. F. A. Co) Adae's Woods, Cummiusville
Adam Ambrose, tailor, s.w.c. Race and Elder
Adam Mrs. Mary A., 652 Race
Adam Trapert, cab. mkr., 801 W. Front
Adams A., carp., bds. 252 Walnut
Adams A. T., b.k., Queen City Varnish Co. 43 Vine, h. Covington

THOMAS ASBURY.   PRESLEY K. MINSHALL.   WM. REYNOLDS.

THOMAS ASBURY & CO.,

(Successors to MILTON SHUTE.)

 DEALERS IN

NORTHERN ICE!

FOR SALE AT ALL HOURS OF THE DAY,

Corner Plum and Grant Streets,

CINCINNATI, OHIO.

EHRGOTT, FORBRIGER & CO.

PRACTICAL

LITHOGRAPHERS,

Carlisle Block, South-west Corner Fourth and Walnut Streets,

CINCINNATI, OHIO,

Are prepared to execute every kind of work in their line, PLAIN AND IN COLORS, as

Landscapes, Portraits, Show-Cards, Diplomas,

MUSIC TITLES, BOOK ILLUSTRATIONS, MAPS,

BONDS, CHECKS, NOTES, DRAFTS, &C.

We guarantee our work to be equal to any executed in the country, and at the most reasonable cost.

(ADE) CINCINNATI (AHL) DIRECTORY. (ALB) 85

Adams Alex., trader bds. 15 New
Adams Alonzo, chair mkr., 190 Everett
Adams Andrew, carp., 52 Milton
Adams Charles, bk. layer, 427 W. 2d
Adams Chas. F., printer. Cin. Gazette, h. 111 George
ADAMS Christopher T.. (Howell Gano & Co.) h. 254 Longworth
Adams Daniel I., stereotyper, 42 Mansfield
Adams Mrs. Elizabeth, 64 Pike
Adams Miss Emily, bds. w.s. Lawrence b. 4th and 5th
ADAMS EXPRESS COMPANY, Alfred Gaither, Superintendent 67 W. 4th
ADAMS Federal C., (A., Peckover & Co.) res. Covington
Adams Francis, shoe mkr., wks. 53 W. 4th
Adams Hy., cutter, 53 W. 4th, h. Newport
Adams James, baker, Burnet House
Adams James J., finisher, 166 Central Av.
Adams James, walter, 64 Vanhorn
Adams Jesse M., grocer, 815 Vine
Adams John, carp., 82 Abigail
Adams John, carp., 521 W. 3d
Adams John, cook, 13 Race
Adams John, driver, 59 Dudley
Adams John. eng., 37 Pierson
Adams John, carp., s.s. Goodloe b. Willow and Niagara
Adams John, lab., bds. 12 E. Front
Adams John, policeman, 97 Ham. Road
Adams John, river man, bds. 12 E. Front
Adams Mrs. John, 168 Central Av
Adams John E., tailor, s.e.c. Findlay & Race
Adams John W., clk. s.w.c. Main and 5th, h. s.s. 5th b. Vine and Race
Adams Joseph, 250 Longworth
Adams Joseph, eng., 107 Mound
Adams Miss Julia, s s. 3d b. Canal and Kilgour
Adams Miss Louisa, bds. 465 Vine
ADAMS, PECKOVER & CO., (Federal C.A., Joseph P. & John M. Brown), Novelty Iron Works, Stove Founders and Ornamental Pattern Makers, s.w.c. Elm and 5th, foundry s.w.c. Central Av. and Front
Adams Robert F., 14 Stone
Adams Samuel, moulder, s.w c. Front and Central Av
Adams Sylvester, huckster, 40 Race
Adams Solomon, barber shop, e.s. Broadway b. 3d and Pearl
Adams Solomon, cof. h., e.s. Broadway b. 3d and Pearl, h. 109 E. 6th
Adams Solomon (Hughes, A. & Co.), h. 250 Longworth
Adams Valentine, moulder, h. n.s. Corwin b. Walnut and Ham. Road
Adams Wm., 608 Freeman
Adams Wm., 30 Bank
Adams Wm., coal mer. h. 290 Water
Adams Wm , tailor, w.s. Vine b. Milk and Calhoun
Adams Wm., turning shop, n.s. Laurel, nr. John, h. 279 W. Court w. of Central Av
Adams Wm. A., atty., s.e.c. 4th and Hammond, h. 117 Broadway
Adams Wm. H., moulder, 168 Central Av
ADAMS Wm. Q (Buchanan & A.), 290 Water
Adamson Robert, teamster, 108 Water
Addelmen Wm., eng. 214 W. Front
ADDEILEY WILLIAM H., Druggist and Apothecary, n.e.c. 6th and Mound, h. 44 Mound
Adders Hy. tanner, bds. 701 Elm
Addis Thomas L , varnisher, bds s.e.c. Richmond and Carr
Addis Wm., Odd Fellows' regalia manuf. 260 Walnut, h. nr. Cheviot
Addison Cyrus, trader, bds. Black Bear Hotel
ADDY Matthew, (Robert Moore & Co.), 95 W. 8th
Ade Geo., cooper, 445 Main
Ade Michael G., tailor, 244 Pleasant

Ade Mrs. Caroline, 1015 Central Av
Adel John, lab. 510 Plum
Adelman Wm., wks. John Mitchell's
Adelsdorfer Sigmund, b.k., 74 Main, h. 342 Walnut
Adelsdorfer Theodore, b k., 82 W. Pearl, h. 117 W. 8th
Ader Anthony, fruit dealer, 337 Walnut
Ader Anthony, lab., 126 Clay
Ader Frank, grocery, 120 Clay
Ader Jacob, peddler, 102 Clay
Ader Wm., lab. 169 Webb
Adger Richard, b.k., bds. 272 W. 7th
ADKINS DUDLEY M., Wholesale and retail Hats, Caps & Furs, 144 Walnut, h. Columbia, O.
Adkins Silas, carp. 1722 E. Front
Adler Benjamin, 39 Race
Adler Bernhard, (Karlsruhar & A.), s.w.c. Walnut and 7th
Adler Bernhard, paper dealer, 281 W.7th
Adler Bridget, servt. National Hotel
Adler David, loan office, 195 Elm
Adler Mrs. Fanny, 207 Main
Adler Frederica, servt. National Hotel
Adler Leonard, turner, 589 Walnut
Adler Michael, cigar mkr. bds. 17 Lodge
Adler Mrs. Sarah, 20 Betts
Adleta Marlin, cof. h. 580 Central Av
Adlinger Charles, composer, bds. 502 Walnut
Adolphus Louis, phys., 124 Betts
Adolph August, walter, Walnut Street House [Pearl
Aeck Francis, cab. mkr. wks. 196 W.
Aeck John A., cook, 185 Laurel
Aelars John, varnisher, 270 Longworth
Aelixman Hermann, mason, 594 Race
Aelken Ignatz, 34 Abigail
AETNA INSURANCE CO., of Hartford, Conn. J. B. Bennett, General Agent. Branch Office, 171 Vine
Aetzel Michael, 42 Mohawk
Aftermask Hy. lab. 684 Main
Agadair Mrs. Anna, 400 W. 7th
Agan Barney, lab. h. s.s. 8th b. Accommodation and State
Agan Constantine, lab. s.w.c. W. Court and Linn
Agan Martin. lab. 142 George
Agars John, lab., wks. c. 3d and W. W. Canal
Agen John, waiter, Spencer House
Agin John, lab. 913 Water
Agin Miss Kate, tailoress. bds. 206 W. Front
Agne August, turner, 445 W. 2d
Agnes Sister St. Clare Convent, n.w.c. 3d and Lytle
Agnes Sister. St. John's Hospital, n.w.c. 3d and Plum
Agnew James, carp., n.s. Front e. of Ferry
Agnew Wm., hatter, 149 Main, h. 440 W. 9th
Ahans Joseph, grocery, s.e.c. Dudley and Liberty
Aharn Owen, contractor, 279 W. 9th
Ahe John Geo., b. k., 281 Ham. Road
AHL Daniel, jr. (R. M. Pomeroy & Co.) bds. Gibson House
Ahlborn Wm., sen., boots and shoes, 499 John
Ahlborn Wm., jr., wks. 499 John
Ahlborn Mrs. Mary, 164 Dayton
Ahlenfeld Leopold, express man, 135 W. Front
Ahlensdorf Hermann, shoemkr. n.e. Long al. b. Woodward and Franklin
Ahlfeld Frederick W., cigar mkr., 480 Walnut
AHLERING Herman H. (J. B. Brummer & Co.) bds. 130 E. 4th
AHLERING JOHN F, Merchant Tailor and Clothier, 39 Broadway, h. 135 E. 3d
Ahlers Charles, cof. h., 69 W. Court
AHLENS CONRAD, Family Grocery. 628 Main
Ahlers Rembert, porter, 70 Vine
Ahlers Frederick H., grocer, 771 Vine
Ahlers John, grocery, 185 Ham, Road
Ahlers John B., milk dairy, junction Bernard and Division

Ahlers John H., shoemkr. 404 Sycamore
Ahlers Wm. H., grocery, 24 Buckeye
Ahn Frederick, cook, 130 W. Liberty
Ahn Lewis, cigar manuf., bds. s.w.c. Race and 3d
Ahn Louis, cigar mkr., 114 13th
Ahouse Hy., lab. e.s. Anderson b. 2d and Pearl
Ahr Charles, tailor, 51 13th
Ahr Conrad, paper store, 616 Central Av
AHRENFELDT Charles, (F. Schultze & Co.) res. Paris, France
Ahrens Miss Caroline, saleswoman, s.e.c. Woodward and Sycamore
Ahrens Christopher, mach. 125 W. 2d
Ahrens Fred (Melcher & A.), 55 W. Liberty
Ahrens Herman, grocer, s.e.c. Mound and Richmond, h. 130 Mound
Ahrens John G. stone yard, 341 Broadway, h. 422 Sycamore
Ahrens J Peter, grocer, s.e.c. Sycamore and 7th
Ahrens William, chair mkr., 24 W. Mulberry
Ahrens Wm. porter, 50 Mulberry
Aichele Frederick, lab., bds. n.s. Flint b. Freeman and Mill Creek
Aiken Charles A. clk. 50 W. 2d, h. 152 E. Liberty
Aiken Chas., music teacher, 152 E. Liberty
Aiken Mrs. Johanna, 24 Hughes
Aiken Patrick, 297 John
Aiken Thos., brass finisher, s.s. 5th b. Vine and Race
Aiken William, stone mason, 153 Cutter
Aiken Wm. H. clk. 152 E. Liberty
Airns Hy., lab. bds, n.e.c. Sycamore and Abigail
Aitchison Robert, porter, American Ex. Co
Akemyer Martha A., 61 E. 8th e of Lock
Akins Samuel, grocery, 842 E. Front
Akof Hy. lab. 52 Laurel
Alback Paul, house furnisher, 196 W. 3d
Albeest Wm., porter, 56 W. Liberty
Alber Casper, barber, 92 E. 2d
Alberger Mrs. Ellen, b.h. 104 Plum
Albers Clemens, chair mkr. 70 12th
Albers Mrs. Emma, 99 W. Court
Albers Fred., foreman, 9 and 11 E. Canal, h. 113 Clay
Albers Hy. clk. 223 Central Av
Albers Hy. lab. w.s. Goose al. b. 14th and 15th
Albers Jackson, clk. n.w.c. 4th & Race
Albers John. 33 Buckeye
Albers John C., lab., 32 Jackson
Albers Joseph, tailor, bds. n.s, 5th, opp. Wood
Albers Lanan, servt., 195 W. 4th
Albers Mathias J., boots and shoes, 31 Green
Albershardt Henry F., shoe mkr., bds. 51 W. 5th
Albert Adam, pilot, 724 E. Front
Albert Mrs. Elizabeth. 63 Lodge
Albert Henry. bds. 514 Main
Albert Henry, stone mason, 52 Webster.
Albert Jacob, (Jacob Gaminger & Co.,) 149 E. 3d, s. of Collard
Albert Jacob C., yawl builder, 149 E. 3d, e. of Collard.
Albert John, cooper, s.w.c. Elder and Logan
Albert Lewis, cof. h., 115 Ham. Road
Albert Paul R , clk. 329 Central Av., bds. 196 W. 3d
Albert Rudolph, piano dealer, bds. s.w.c. 3d and Broadway
Albert Wm. H., messenger Homans & Co., h. 44 Pleasant
Alberts Amelia, servt. wks. 448 Broadway.
Alberts John, (Wm. & John A.) h. 88 Bremen
Alberts Michael, huckster, h. 535 Race.
Alberts Wm., (Wm. & John Alberts,) h. 84 Bremen.
Alberts Wm. & John, (Wm. & John,) marble yard, 88 13th
Albertshardt Christina, servt , 64 Cutter
Albertzat Dietrich, brick layer, 15 E. Liberty.
Albes C. H., clk., 190 Central Av.

FRANKLIN
Type and Stereotype Foundry,
168 VINE STREET,

BET. FOURTH AND FIFTH, - - - CINCINNATI, OHIO.

R. ALLISON, Superintendent,

MANUFACTURERS OF, AND DEALERS IN

NEWS, BOOK AND JOB TYPE,

Printing Presses, Cases, Galleys, Etc., Etc.

INKS AND PRINTING MATERIAL OF EVERY DESCRIPTION.

STEREOTYPING

OF ALL KINDS—BOOKS, MUSIC, PATENT MEDICINE DIRECTIONS, JOBS, WOOD ENGRAVINGS, ETC., ETC.

BRAND AND PATTERN LETTERS,

OF VARIOUS STYLES,

ELECTROTYPING IN ALL ITS BRANCHES.

NCINNATI (ALL) DIRECTORY. (ALT) 87

.e.c. Alf Frank, cab. mkr., 187 Hopkins
Alf Herman, lab., n.e.c. Sycamore and Webster
Alf Henry, carriage trimmer, 159 Laurel
Wal- Alf John D., boots and shoes, 822 E. Front
Alf Mrs. Mary, grocery. 9 Woodward
Alf Wm. wagon mkr., 229 W. Liberty
A.) Alfers B. H. & J. Nilling (Bernard H. A. & Joseph N.) feed store, 434 Vine
loose Alfers Bernard H., (B, H. A. & J. Nilling.) 454 Vine
re Alfisi Andrew C., professor of music, 334 George
. 54 Alfken Henry D. shoe mkr., s.w.c. Milton and Price
s. 54 Algiers Harris, mach., 12 Commerce
i.e.c. Algoe Mrs. Mary T., millinery, 222 W. 5th, h. 162 Plum
. M. Alich Adam, cook, Galt House.
Alig John, cigar store, 119 Bremen
, res. Alig Peter, cigar mkr., 119 Bremen
Alik Lena, servt, 367 Central Av.
Saw Alimann John, finisher, 163 Buckeye
tory, Allan Geo, (A & Kettell.) 430 George
. Allan Mrs J., fancy store. 136 W. 4th
b. 3d Allan James, mach., n.s Front, e. of Kelly
it, Allan & Kettell, (Geo. A. and Terence K.,) painters, 201 Plum.
h, w. ALLAN & KLISTER (Peter A. & Herman K.,) Fashionable Boots and Shoes, 147 Main
w. of ALLAN Peter (A. & Klister,) h. n.w.c. 4th and Elm
e. of Allan Theodore F., b. k. Commercial office, bds. Walnut St. House
anu- Allard Lewis D., carver, 99 Bremen
, 126 Allbrink Fred., grocer, 133 Bank
Alleghany House, John Long, n.e.c. Walnut and River Landing
ALLEMONG A. W., (Mitchell A. & Co.) bds. 36 Longworth
Alli- Allen ———, bds. 174 Plum
Syca. Allen Mrs , s.e.c 3d and Walnut
Allen A., 142 W. 4th
rt. Allen Albert H., 235 Walnut
.,) h. Allen Albert J., salesman, 104 W. 5th
ALLEN Alfred F., (A. & Co.,) res. Covington
h Allen Miss Ann. h. 61 Vine
l and Allen Mrs. Ann H., physician, 365 Central Av.
m & Allen Bridget. servt. 119 Broadway
h Allen C. & W. H., (Caleb & William H.) watches, jewelry, &c , 117 Main
f the Allen Caleb. (C. & W. H..) 255 Walnut
West Allen Mrs. Carrie, bds. 96 E. 4th
Cen- Allen Chas. H., (A. & Co.,) res. Glendale
Long- Allen Cornelia, teacher, 204 Sycamore
Main ALLEN & CO., (Samuel B. A., Chas. H. Allen, & Alfred F. Allen) Wholesale Druggists, s.w.c. Main and 5th
ymil-
more ,
CO.,
Daniel Allen David, 343 W. 6th
loods, Allen David P., brick layer, 310 George
Allen Mrs. Elizabeth, 112 Laurel
plar Allen Henry, clk. 154 Main
Main, Allen Henry, h. s.s. Friendship al., b. Pike and Butler
Front Allen J. T., teller, s.w.c. 3d and Walnut, h. Covington [John
Allen Jacob H., paper hanger, h. 114
i door Allen James, s s. Webb b. Wood and Stone
Court Allen James, blk. smith, 454 E. Front
[Race Allen James, cof. h. 371 W. 2d
. 307 Allen James, pipe fitter, wks. n. e.c. Walnut and Canal
s. 125 Allen John. fish monger, 255 W. 3d
. wks. Allen John R., butcher, 459 W. 5th
il Allen John R. Jr., actor, 459 W. 5th
k Co.) Allen Joseph M., assistant teacher, 13th District School, h. Covington.
R. R. Allen Joshua, carp., 454 E. Front
Allen Kate, servt., 133 Broadway
5 Cen- Allen Lewis E., mach., 351 John
Allen Luman S.. clk., 66 W. 5th
Clin- Allen Mrs Margaret, 224 Longworth
Allen Matthew W., chair mkr., bds. 343 W. 6th
ont Allen Miss Mary, bleacher and presser, bds. 175 W. 4th
Plum
m and Allen Mrs. Mary, 33 Webb b. Wood and Stone

Allen Nicholas C., wh. liquor mer., h. s. e.c. 6th and Lodge
Allen M., phys. 95 W. 7th
Allen Peter L., driver, 29 Grant
Allen Richard, agency office, 25 E. 4th
Allen Robert, dray. 13 David
Allen Mrs. Salina, 182 W. Front
ALLEN Samuel B. (A. & Co.) res. Glendale
Allen T. J., bds. Walnut Street House
ALLEN Thomas H C., (J. N. Harris & Co.) res. Mt. Auburn
Allen Wm., baggage master C. H. & D. R.R., h. 637 W. 6th
Allen Wm., second hand clothing, 1026 Central Av.
Allen Wm. H., (C. & W. H. A.) 174 W. 4th
Allen Wm. M. sawyer, h. 44 Richmond
Allen W. N., printer, bds. 539 W. 5th
Allendorf Hy., cooper, wks. J. Kauffman & Co.
Allendorf Joseph, tinner, bds. 231 Walnut
Allert Wm., cap mkr., 25 Monre
Allen Mrs. Anna, h. 367 W. 8th
Alley Benjamin R., hats, caps, furs, &c., 41 Broadway
Alley Chas. C , candy manuf. and hoop skirts. 220 W. 5th
Aligaier Sebastian A., (Scott & A.) bds. n.s 7th b. Plum and Central Av.
Allgeir Patrick, teamster, 286 Water
Alligham Richard, dray, 136 Water
Allison Alex., clk., 242 Longworth
Allison Amos, printer, s.w.c. 5th and Plum
Allison Alexander, lab., wks. C. H. & D. R.R Depot
Allison James, plumber, wks. 200 Vine
ALLISON ROBERT, Superintendent Franklin Type Foundry, 168 Vine h. 59 W. 7th
Altmann Abe. mason, 639 Vine
Altmann Peter. lab., 410 W. Liberty
Allyn Mrs. Mary D., governuess, Wesleyan Female College
ALLYN REV. ROBERT, A. M., President and Professor of Moral Science Wesleyan Female College, w.s. Vine b. 6th and 7th.
Almond Timothy, lab., 56 Melancthon
Alms Gerhard H., furniture store, 115 Liberty
Alms H. August, dry goods, 571 Vine
ALMS HENRY, Proprietor Verandah Restaurant, 27 and 29 W. 3d
Alms Wm., millinery store. 642 Race
Alms Wm. H., clk. 115 W Liberty
ALMY STEPHEN O., Physician and Surgeon, 161 W. 4th
Alpha Martin, butcher, s.s. Montgomery Turnpike nr. Lebanon Road
Alpleens John, lab., wks. 222 E. Front
Alrink Henry H., tailor, 130 E. 4th
Alsheimer Geo., blk. smith, 617 Vine
Alsheimer John G., blk. smith. 617 Vine
Altenao William, lab., n.s Sloo E. of Harriet
Altendick Ferdinand, cigar mkr., 114 Hunt
Altenhoff Herman, 48 Elm
ALTER Frank, (R. W. Booth & Co.) bds. Burnet House
Altermeier Hermann, miller, 24 Brighton
Altevers John tailor, 181 Hopkins
Althammer Godfried, shoe mkr., 16 Bremen
Althammer Wm. F, salesman, 85 Bremen
Althauser Andrew, lab., w.s. Western Av. b. Bank and Harrison Road
Althauser Mrs. Anna, w.s. Western Av. b. Bank and Harrison Road
Althauser Fredrick, w.s. Western Av. b. Bank and Harrison Road
Althauser Jacob, carp., w.s. Western Av. b. Bank and Harrison Road
Althof Leopold, peddler, 5 Mary
Althoff Casper, cooper, 519 Sycamore
Altmann Jacob, lab., e.s. Plum b. Adams and Liberty
Altmann John, cigar mkr., 90 Findlay

J. BECKLEY & CO.

MANUFACTURERS OF

IMPROVED FIRE AND WATER PROOF

ASPHALTUM

Cement Roofs,

OFFICE:

No. 112 Pearl St., one door east of Race,

CINCINNATI, OHIO.

MATERIALS FOR SALE, WHOLESALE AND RETAIL.

☞ We are extracting the acids from our Cement, that have been so destructive to Roofs heretofore. By calling at our office, 112 Pearl Street, or at our Chemical Works, all can be convinced of the fact.

J. & R. HUTTON,

WAGON MANUFACTURERS,

Front Street, between Elm and Plum,

CINCINNATI, OHIO.

B. D. WHEELER,

Dentist,

Office and Residence, No. 95 Seventh St., bet. Vine and Race,

CINCINNATI, OHIO.

W. W. WINDER,

HOUSE, SIGN AND BANNER PAINTING,

No. 120 WEST THIRD STREET,

Between Vine and Race,

CINCINNATI, OHIO.

AMERICAN WHIP CO., S. E. Beckman, Agent, 17 E. 3d
AMERICAN YEAST PLANT CO., A. J. Wright, Secretary, Office, 128 W. 5th
Ames Mrs. Anna, h. 512 Sycamore
Ames Fisher W., phys., 18 Hathaway
Amick Mrs. Margaret, n.s. Vanhorn b. Cutter and Linn
Amier Hy., tailor, 137 Baymiller
Amill John, clk., h. s.e.c. Smith and 3d
Amis Christian, hatter, 23 15th
Amiss Robert B., pattern mkr., wks. n, e.c. Miami Canal and Walnut
Amlung Jacob, peddler, h. 115 Clay
Amman Anthony, clk., 77 E. Pearl, h. Newport
Ammann Benedict, grocer, 47 Dunlap
Ammann Joseph, cof. and b.h. 346 Main
Ammann Phillip, h. 338 Ham. Road
Ammet Geo., cigar mkr., n e c. 9th and Central Av.
Amons John J., mach., h 13 W. 4th
Amos August, 275 W. Liberty
Amrehn Bartholomeus, bakery, 547 Race
Amshler John, cooper, 181 York
Amsted Charles, whitewasher, 91 Freeman
Amtaur Henry, cof. h., 124 Linn
Anchutz Chas. lab., wks. 728 Central Av.
Ancker Hart P., 32½ Hathaway
Ande Jacob, shoe mkr., 154 Linn
Ande Mary, servt., 532 Main
Andee Phillip, tailor, 9 Pendleton
Andemark Mrs. Ann, 104 W Front
Anderle Prokop, cab. mkr., 557 Race
Anders Mrs. Mary, 92 W. Front
Anderson —, carp., 382 W. 7th
Anderson Alonzo W. jr., carp., h. 207 Water
Anderson Alonzo W. sen., wood carver, 152 W. 3d, h. 207 Water
Anderson Benjamin, h. n.s. Phoebe al. b. Plum and Central Av.
Anderson Mrs. Bethia P., tailoress, 445 W. 4th
Anderson Mrs. Catharine, laundress, rear 490 Walnut
Anderson Chamberlain, h. 73 E. 7th
Anderson Chas., instrument mkr., bds. 223 W. 6th
Anderson Charles R., salesman, 83 and 85 Walnut, h. 413 W. 4th
Anderson Miss Cornelia A., bds. e.s. Sycamore b. 7th and 8th
Anderson Daniel, barber, 4 W. 4th
Anderson Daniel, coach painter, wks. 64 E. Front, h. Covington
Anderson Edward, shoe mkr., 322 W. 6th
ANDERSON Edwin, (A. & Hannaford) h. 168 Mound
Anderson Mrs. Eliza, 104 John
Anderson Geo., hinge fitter, wks. n.e.c. Walnut and Canal
Anderson Geo. M., clk., 27 W. 3d, bds. 29 W. 7th
ANDERSON & HANNAFORD, (Edwin A. & Samuel H.) Architects, n.e.c. 3d and Race
Anderson Hy., tent mkr., s.s. Mount or Sycamore
Anderson Hy. A., bds. 413 W. 4th
Anderson Hy. H., clk., bds 368 W. 8th
Anderson Jacob, plasterer, 179 Mound
Anderson James, brush mkr., bds. 247 W. 6th
Anderson James, carp., h. 196 W. Court w of Central Av.
Anderson James, chandler, 201 W. Liberty
Anderson James, shoe mkr., h. w.s. Mound b. Longworth and 6th
Anderson John, h. 413 W. 4th
Anderson John, carp., s.e c. Front and Brooklyn
Anderson John, carp. and box mkr., e.s. Bank al. b. 3d and 4th, h. Vine street Hill
Anderson John, printer, bds. s.e.c. Sycamore and 5th
Anderson John, shoe mkr., h. w.s. Baymiller b. Clinton and Betts

ANDERSON John A., (Shaw & A.) 103 E. Pearl
Anderson John A., shoe mkr., h. 48 Cross
Anderson John S., carp., bds. 207 Water
Anderson John W., b.k., 187 Mound
Anderson John Wm., printer, wks. s.w. c. Canal and Bedinger, res. Mt. Healthy
Anderson Mrs. Julia, washer woman, e.s al. b. 4th and 5th and Park and Mill
Anderson Kate, servt., 98 Broadway
Anderson Larz, n e.c 3d and Pike
Anderson Lefferson D., clk., 439 W. 5th
Anderson Louis, turner, 177 Clinton
Anderson Marmaduke S., b.k., n.w.c. 3d and Central Av., bds. 104 John
Anderson Miss Martha E. teacher Park b. 4th and 5th
Anderson Mrs. Mary A., bds. 644 E. Front
Anderson Mrs. Mary A., 101 Poplar
Anderson Mrs. Nancy, 110 W. 5th
Anderson Nathaniel T. car man, 160 Linn
Anderson Pembroke S. clk. s.e.c. 12th and Central Av, h. 15 Hopkins
Anderson Samuel, blksmith, 61 Barr
Anderson Thomas, dray, 395 Race
Anderson W., whitewasher. h. 4 North
Anderson Wm. salesman, 87 Main. h. 438 W, 4th
Anderson Wm. trunk mkr. 69 W. 3d, h. Newport
Anderson Wm. C., conductor. bds. 191 Poplar
Anderson Wm. H., cigar mkr. 223 W. 6th
Anderson Wm. W., car man, 160 Linn
Anderson Yeatman, clk. 77 and 79 Walnut, h. 377 6th
Andrew Moses L. mach. 212 W, Front
Andres Ernst, butcher, bds. 701 Elm
Andres Hy. G music teacher, 333 Vine
Andres Jacob, 120 Mohawk
Andres John, 36 Pleasant
Andres Joseph, trader, 21 Webb
Andress Andrew, shoemkr. 1113 Central Av
Andress August, finisher, 361 Cutter
Andress Augustus H clk, 144 W. 7th
Andress Charles, (F. & C. A,) 378 W. 6th
Andress Chas. O. agt. wall paper, 163 Main. h. 110 George
Andress F. & C. (Frederick & Charles A.) paper hangings, 60 W. 4th
Andress Frederick (F. & C. A.) 134 W. 7th
Andress H. W. clk. 60 W. 4th, h. Peru, Ind.
Andress John, cigar mkr. 455 Sycamore
Andress Powell, cooper, 309 Findlay
Andressen Peter, tailor, h. 317 W. 6th
Andrew Janet, h. 100 Baum
Andrew Mary, bds. 110 Baum
ANDREW P. & CO. (Peter A., Richard Lloyd & George M. High), Forwarding and Commission Merchants, n.w.c. Front and Kilgour
ANDREW Peter, (P. A. & Co.), h. 84 Baum
ANDREWS Alex. II. (Minor & A.) h. 419 W. 6th
ANDREWS Daniel (Tweed & A.) 65 W. 8th
Andrews Jacob, pipe fitter, wks. n.e.c Walnut and Canal
Andrews James, bds. 98 Broadway
ANDREWS James (Tweed & A.), Clifton
Andrews Mrs. Jane, 65 W. 8th
Andrews Joseph, 254 Vine
Andrews Joseph, clk. bds. 65 W. 8th
Andrews Miss Louisa, 105 W. 3d
Andrews Mrs. Margaret, 98 Broadway
Andrews Mrs. Maria, bds. 149 Elm
Andrews Mary, servt. s.c.c. Pike and 3d
Andrews Moses, mach. bds. 212 W.Front
Andrews Miss Nancy, bds. 65 W. 8th
Andrews Robert, com. and liquor mer., 58 W. Front, h 333 W. 7th
Andrews Rupert R. tinner, 247 Cutter
Andrews Samuel, (A. & Biggs), 65 W. 8th
Andrews Thomas. 98 Broadway

CINCINNATI ADVERTISEMENTS.

O. E. NEWTON, M. D.
OFFICE, No. 90 West Seventh Street, bet. Vine and Race. Residence, No. 102 Seventh St., bet. Vine and Race. Office Hours, from 7½ to 8½ A. M., 1½ to 2½ P. M., and 7 to 8 P. M.

R. BRINKMAN,
Manufacturer of STOCKS AND DIES. **No. 246 West Court Street.** Stocks and Dies constantly on hand for sale. Repairing and Blacksmithing promptly done.

WESTERN CHAIR AND FURNITURE MANUFACTORY.
JOHN GEYER, Manufacturer of Chairs and Furniture, **No. 6 East Fourth Street, Cincinnati.**

T. S. HUNTINGTON,
Civil Engineer and Surveyor,
Ninth St., opp. City Buildings,   CINCINNATI, O.

ADAM GEIS,
WHOLESALE AND RETAIL MATTRESS AND BEDDING MANUFACTURER,
No. 67 Fifth St., bet. Walnut and Vine, Cincinnati, O.

MARSH & HARWOOD,
Manufacturers of Sulphuric, Nitric & Muriatic Acids,
HAMILTON ROAD, NEAR MOHAWK BRIDGE,
CINCINNATI, O.

WILLIAM NABER,
WHOLESALE
STEAM CHAIR FACTORY,
567 RACE STREET,
Bet. Fifteenth and Liberty Sts.,   CINCINNATI, O.

ROBERT GORDON & CO.
COAL YARD,
OFFICES AND YARDS:
171 SIXTH STREET, N. W. CORNER MIAMI CANAL,
—AND—
235 East Front St., Cor. Miami Canal, CINCINNATI, O.
The best Youghiogheny and Pomeroy Coal always on hand. All orders promptly attended to.

J. E. HULL,
MANUFACTURER OF
Tin and Sheet Iron Workers' Tools,
Of all descriptions,
No. 93 East Eighth Street, Cincinnati, O.

WESTERN ROW MILLS.
L. CAMERON,
Manufacturer of that Celebrated Fancy Brand
"CAMERON'S SNOW FLAKE,"
AND OTHER CHOICE
BRANDS OF FAMILY FLOUR,
ALSO,
GRAHAM FLOUR, CRACKED WHEAT, CORN MEAL, &C.
Corner Central Avenue and Clark Sts.,
CINCINNATI, O.

HIBBERT BROTHERS,
FASHIONABLE
HATTERS,
WHOLESALE AND RETAIL.
STORES, 210 FIFTH ST., bet. Elm & Plum,
51 Lower Market St., bet. Sycamore and Broadway,
CINCINNATI, OHIO.
Corner Madison and Pike Streets, Covington, Ky.

BISHOP'S
DAGUERREAN AND PHOTOGRAPHIC
GALLERY,
No. 58 Fourth Street, bet. Vine & Walnut,
CINCINNATI, OHIO.
He is prepared to take every variety of Picture in the best style and on very reasonable terms. Call and see.

S. WARDLE,
Dentist,
No. 97 West Seventh Street,
CINCINNATI, OHIO.

L. FAY,
Manufacturer of Patent Galvanized Sheet Metal Air-Tight

BURIAL CASES AND CASKETS,
Also, PATENT ROOFING MACHINES, METAL & SLATE ROOFER
No. 349 PLUM STREET, - - - CINCINNATI, O.

R. M. WHITE,
—DEALER IN—
LUMBER, SHINGLES,
LATH, DRESSED FLOORING, SHELVING,
AND ALL KINDS OF SAWED TIMBER,
No. 422 CENTRAL AVENUE,
East side, above Court Street,   CINCINNATI, O

W. K. LANPHEAR & CO.'S
STENCIL ROOMS,
No. 102 West Fourth St., second story,
CINCINNATI, OHIO.
Marking Plates cut for 5 cents per letter. Old Coins bough and sold.

Anus Ann, servt. n.e.c. 3d and Pike
Anwyl Thomas, stone cutter. 8 Lock
Apel Justus, blksmith. n.s. 6th b. Harriet and Horne
Apfel Jacob, cof h. 464 Walnut
Apfel Lewis J. cigar mkr. 91 Bremen
Apfel Louis. cigar mkr. 89 Bremen
Apollo Billiard Rooms. E. P. Johnson, pro., n.w.c. 5th and Walnut
Apollo Building, n.w c. Walnut and 5th
Appel Adam, h. 147 Bremen
Appel Justus, blksmith. s.s. 6th b. Harriet and Horne, h. n.s. 6th b. Harriet and Horne
Appel Kunigunde, servt. e.s. Johnson al. b. Canal and 12th
Appel Martin. shoemkr, 140 Bremen
Appelmann Geo. tailor, 586 Race
Appelhaus Hy. cab. ware, 14 Dudley, h. 236 Everett
APPENZELLER JOHN C., Manufacturer Indigo Blue, Mustard and Coffee Essence, n.w.c. Oliver and Plum
Apple Jacob, shoemkr, 126 Mohawk
Apple Peter, h. 28 Brighton
Apple Wm. blksmith, wks. Niles Works. h. Newport, Ky
Appleby Andrew E. 23 Hannibal
Applegate Basil W., carp. shop, 191 Mound, h. 32 Clark
APPLEGATE & CO., (Arthur H Pounsford & Jesse H. Lacey,) Booksellers, Stationers and Publishers, 43 Main
APPLEGATE James R. (A., Tyler & Co.) bds. Clermont Hotel
APPLEGATE JOHN W. Attorney at Law, room 6 Carlisle Building, h. Colerain Pike
APPLEGATE, TYLER & CO , (James R. A. & Edward M. T.), Photographers. 26 W. 5th
APPLEGATE Wm. A. (Chas. L. Moore & Co.) h. 456 W. 9th w. of Central Av
Appler Hy. cab. mkr. 557 Race
Appleton Miss E. H., young ladies' school, 232 W. 4th
Appleton Hy. J. clk. 413 W. Front, bds. 230 W 4th
Aqua Herman, lab. 196 Clark
Araldo Vincent, cof. h 84 W. Front
Arand August, printer. 341 Main
Arand Frank F., b.k. n w.c. Race and 6th
Arata Lewis, h. 116 W. Front
Arata Louis, clk. bds. 206 W. 5th
Arata Stephen, 116 W. Front
Arath Mrs. Rosa, confec. 57 Broadway
Arbeiter Halle, e.s. Walnut b. 13th and Allison
Arceno Lawrence, watch mkr bds. 60 W. 5th
Archer Wm. A., dray. 508 W. 3d
Archibald Alex. carp. 127 Baymiller
Archibald James. baker, 113 W. Front
Archy Zeigle lab. 49 Providence
Arcorn Wm , lab. n.s. al. b. 12th and Canal and Vine and Race
Arend J. W., chair mkr., wks. John Mitchell's.
Arendt Daniel, grocery, n.e.c. 6th and Lock.
Arendt John, clk., bds. n.w.c. Clinton and Central Av.
Arendt John, grocer, s.w.c. Whiteman and Bank.
Arens August A., (Bickenhorst & A.) 65 Mansfield.
Arens Bernard H., lab. 53 Woodward.
Arens Francis. moulder, 65 Peete.
Arens John F., cab. mkr. 55 W. Liberty.
Arens John G., tailor, 9 Moore.
Arens Wm , porter, 60 Mulberry.
Ares Mrs. Laura. e.s. John b. Elizabeth and Chestnut.
Argus Charles. barber shop, 724 e. Front.
Arhmann Francis, box mkr. 142 Buckeye.
Arins Bernhard. tailor, 61 Ham. Road.
Arins Gerhard, tailor, 61 Ham. Road.
Arins Herman, tailor, 61 Ham. Road.
Arkenbeck Frank, chair mkr. h. 418 Longworth.

Arkenberg Frank, carp. 418 Longworth.
Arling Miss Lizzie, 273 Richmond.
Arlinghaus Frank, clk 59 E. 3d.
Armand James, salesman, 297 Baymiller.
Armbruster Mrs. Ganyvia, 62 Peete.
Arnbruster Louis, butcher, 43 Moore.
Armender Henry, bar k. n.e.c. Court and Elm.
ARMEL DANIEL, (Cobb A. & Fletcher,) and (Cobb & Armel,) res. Aurora Ind.
Armel Wm. b. k. (Cobb & Armel,) bds. 310 Elm.
Armeling Henry, shoe mkr. 610 Central Av.
Armes Frank, lock mkr. wks. n.e.c. Walnut and Canal.
Armstead Miss Louisa, select school, n. w.c. Hopkins and Cutter, bds. 80 John.
Armitstead James, dray. Richmond b. Harriet and Millcreek.
Armitstead, Wm. C., driver 119 Baymiller.
Armleder Fiedel, shoe mkr. bds 671 Race.
Armstead Herman, b'k. mkr. h 194 Hopkins.
Armstead John mach. 34 Mitchell, Mt. Adams.
Armstroff Gustave, saddler, 43 1'th.
Armstrong A. W., deputy sheriff, h. 36 Dayton.
Armstrong Aaron D., carp. 157 W. Court W. of Central Av.
Armstrong Arthur E., (J. M. & A. E. Armstrong,) 30 Richmond.
Armstrong B. D. Black Bear Hotel, s.w.c. 8th and Sycamore.
Armstrong C. W. bds. Clifton House.
Armstrong Edward C., bds. 226 Sycamore.
Armstrong Eugene, civil eng. 57 W. 3d. bds. 165 Elm.
Armstrong Frank, N. dep. sheriff, 226 Sycamore.
Armstrong Frank A., receiver, W. U Telegraph Co., h. 226 Sycamore.
Armstrong Geo. W. carp. 518 W. 7th.
Armstrong Gustavus, harness mkr. s.w.c. Race and 14th.
Armstrong Mrs. Harriet, 1182 E. Front.
Armstrong Mrs. Harriet T., 592 W. 5th.
Armstrong Henry, pyrotechnist, Observatory street, Mt. Adams.
Armstrong J.. painter. bds. cor. Richmond and Baymiller.
Armstrong J. M., & A. E. (James M, & Arthur E.,) flour dealers s.e.c. Walnut and Canal.
Armstrong Jackson. painter, bds. n.w.c. Richmond and Baymiller.
Armstrong James, 322 Baymiller.
Armstrong James, lab. w.s. Pole al. b. 2d and Pearl.
Armstrong James, tailor, 31 W. Court w. of Central Av.
Armstrong James A., tinner, h. 193 Mound.
Armstrong James M., (J. M., & A. E. A.) n.e.c. Clark and John.
Armstrong James T., (McNutt & A.,) 423 W. 4th.
Armstrong John A., clk. L. M. R. R. Depot, h. 32 Harrison.
Armstrong John A., foreman press room Meth. Book Concern. h. 23 Barr
ARMSTRONG JOHN B., Sheriff Hamilton County, Office Court House, h. 325 Elm.
Armstrong John Y., 100 E. Liberty.
Armstrong Leonard L., director City Infirmary. 231 Broadway.
Armstrong Mrs. Mary, 12 Hannibal.
Armstrong Robt. G., conductor, bds. 226 Sycamore.
Armstrong Samuel, clk. bds. Madison House.
Armstrong Mrs. Sarah S., 22 E. 6th.
Armstrong Wm. janitor Union Block, 60 E. 3d.
Armstrong Wm. H., telegraph clk. I. & C. R. R., h 226 Sycamore.
Armstrong Wm. J., clk. 24 E. 2d. h. 30 Richmond.

McCORMICK, GIBSON & CO.

MANUFACTURERS OF

LEAD PIPE, SHEET AND BAR LEAD,

AND DEALERS IN

PIG LEAD BLOCK TIN AND PATENT SHOT,

NINTH STREET,

BETWEEN MAIN AND SYCAMORE. — — — CINCINNATI, OHIO.

Being exclusively in the Lead Trade, we can furnish the above to better advantage to DEALERS, and on BETTER terms than can be had elsewhere. No insurance effected unless by special orders.

JOHN H. DETERS,

Manufacturer and Wholesale Dealer in Gentlemen's, Ladies and Children's

BOOTS AND SHOES,

And Importer of French and English Lastings, Galloons, French Blacking, etc.

☞ ALWAYS ON HAND A GOOD ASSORTMENT OF UPPERS, OF ALL DESCRIPTIONS

No. 53 West Fourth Street, Cincinnati, O.

G. W. SHOLL,

MANUFACTURER OF

TRUNKS, VALISES, AND CARPET BAGS,

57 Walnut, Cor. West Second, and 507 Plum Street,

CINCINNATI, OHIO.

A NEWLY INVENTED PATENT TERRA COTTA BURIAL CASE

INVENTED BY  **DAVID SHOLL.**

This Case is made of material which is everlasting—neither water nor dampness has any effect upon it. We warrant them to neither rust nor decay. They are truly the everlasting Burial Case. Persons wishing to obtain the right of any State, will call upon

G. W. SHOLL,

North-west corner Second and Walnut Streets, Cincinnati, Ohio

---

JOSEPH MERNA,

WHOLESALE AND RETAIL DEALER IN

TRUNK MAKERS' MATERIALS, HOOP AND SHEET IRON

PUMP CHAINS & UTENSILS.

HARDWARE IN GENERAL,

Iron and Brass Wire, House-Carpenters, Machinists, and Coopers' Tools. Truss Hoops, etc.

HOUSE FURNISHING GOODS,

No. 192 Main Street, between Fourth and Fifth, Cincinnati, Ohio.

(ARU) CINCINNATI (ATE) DIRECTORY. (AUF) 43

nd Francis, carp. wks. n.w.c. 15th and Goose al.
nd Leopold, tanner, 66 Dunlap.
ndt Bernhard, cigar store, 351 Vine.
net Christopher, bk mkr. 651 W. 8th.
net David, 101 Baymiller
net John T. bds. 103 Baymiller
netz Peter, cof h. 92 W. Court.
nhold Augustus, bakery, 551 Central Av.
nhold Henry, turner, bds. 495 Main.
nhold Henry, turner, 594 Main.
ning Henry C., porter, 113 Clay.
nink Geo., l. h. 286 Water.
nn Mrs Sarah, 380 W. 8th.
nold Chas., cab. mkr. 11 Madison.
  RNOLD & CRAWFORD. (Mont-
L   gomery A., & Wm. D. C.,) Com-
    mission Mer. 22 E. Canal.
nold Eliah, policeman, 13 Carr.
nold Franklin E., salesman, 11 W. 6th. h. 10 George.
nold Geo., cooper, 130 Bremen.
nold Henry, varnisher, 130 Bremen.
nold Henry F., cof h. 470 Vine.
nold Jacob, varnisher, bds. n.w.c. Smith and Augusta.
nold John, bds. 293 W. 5th.
nold John G. gardener, 96 Bremen.
nold John P, eng. wks. 50 e. 8th. h. Newport. Ky.
nold Joseph, lab 152 Baymiller.
nold Joseph, lab. n.s. 6th b. Harriet and Horne.
nold Leopold, lab. 66 Dunlap.
nold Lesier, notion store, 11 W. 6th n 10 George.
nold Mrs. Margaret, grocery, 64 Elder.
nold Matheuin, 356, W. 5th.
nold Minn, servt. 438 Main.
NOLD Montgomery, (A. & Crawford,) h. Hamilton.
nold Peter, stone mason, 177 Clinton.
nold Phillip, lab. w.s. Harriet b. 6th and Sloo.
nold Simon, cab. mkr. 69 W. Liberty.
nold Wm, glazier,625 Vine.
nold Wm. trunk mkr. 139 Bremen.
not J. W., carp. bds. n.e.c. Walnut and River Landing.
noudt Rev. Peter, w.s. Sycamore b. 6th and 7th.
nschler Frank, match mkr. 181 York.
nsperger G., watch mkr. 173 Elm.
nsperger, Henry, clk. s.s. Schiller, b. Hughes and Main.
sperger Mrs. Magdelene, s w.c. Schiller and Hughes.
nt John, w. s. Lebanon Road near Channing.
nzen Bernard, clk. 55 Jackson.
nzen John H., salesman, h. 24 Dudley.
ons Wm. C. 233 George.
  RECO ANTONIO, Barber Shop and
    Hair Dye Manuf., 108 W. 4th, h.
L   379 George.
rico Louis, barber, 444 W. 7th.
srun Barney, lab. wks. 63 and 70 Water.
stingstall James S., Hammond St. Stable 20, 22. and 24 Hammond.
szmanz John C., teamster, 196 Pleasant
szmann Joseph, n.s. Dayton, b. Western Av. and Coleman.
t Mrs Catharine, cof. h. 510 Plum.
t John Henry, porter. 32 Main. h. e.s. Plum b. 13th and 14th.
thur Edward, hinge fitter, wks. n.e.c Walnut and Canal.
thurs Joseph G. rope manuf. e.s. Baymiller b. Clark and Court.
tman Frank, (Monnig & A.) h. 4. Smith Court.
tman Wm., stove mounter, 97 Pendleton.
tmann Bernhard, prop. Mechanics Hall s.e.c. Smith and Front.
tos Rudolph, engraver, bds.21 Franklin
tsman Frederick, s.s. Calhoun b Mc-Millan and Clifton Av.
uschler John, cooper, 181 York.

Arzeno Joseph, confec. 69 W. 5th,
Asbury Frank, clk. 40 Grant.
Asbury Stephen, driver, 54 W. Front.
ASBURY Thos., (Thos. A. & Co.,) 40 Grant.
A SBURY THOS. & CO , (Thos. A.,
    Presley, K. Minshall, and Wm.
    Reynolds.) Northern Ice House
    s.e.c. Grant and Plum.
Asbury Wm., 40 Grant.
Aschenbach Joseph, peddler, 473 Walnut.
Aschendorf Wm., porter, 11 12th.
Aschermann Fred. porter, 103 W. 5th.
Aselarge Henry, grocery, 548 Walnut.
Arzenhaimer Adam, coppersmith, 50 Abigail.
Ash George, s.w.c Culvert and 7th.
Ash James, 77 E. 7th.
Ashar Joseph W., carp. 436 W. 5th.
Ashbaw Joseph, pattern mkr. wks. n.s. Front b. Lawrence and Pike.
Ashbaw Joseph jr., pattern mkr. wks. n.s. Front, b. Lawrence and Pike.
Ashbrook Benj. A. photographer, 106 W. 4th, h. Covington Ky.
Ashby Mrs Elvira, 938 E. Front,
Ashby Reuben, carp. n.s. Burt b. Broad and Reed.
Ashcraft Jessie. coal yard, 131 E. Front h. Avondale.
Ashcraft Robert C., market master, 54 Ludlow.
A SHCRAFT SAMUEL S., Iron Foundry, n w.c. Wade and Plum, h 353 W. 4th.
Asher Wm., lab. n.s. Front e. of Foster.
Ashford Charles S ,352 W. 4th.
Ashford Emily, music teacher, 352 W, 4th.
Ashley E. W., city weigher, 1 Water, h. 222 Clinton.
Ashman Charles, shoe mkr. 298 Linn.
Ashman James, boot and shoe store, 519 Central Av. h. 31 Jones.
Ashman Miss Lydia, teacher, 208 Linn.
Ashmore Chas., carp. 57 Wade.
Ashron C. lab. wks. John Mitchell's.
Ashton John, lab. wks. Cincinnati Stone Works.
Ashton John T., lab. 631 W. 7th.
Ashton Mary, teacher, 631 W. 7th.
Ashton Wm A., 334 Cutter.
Ashworth John, mach 296 W. Front.
Askew Thos. E., clk. 40 Main, bds. s.w.c. Pearl & Ludlow.
Askren Wm. H. Turner, h. 316 W. 8th.
Asman Louis, shoe mkr. bds. 48 E. Pearl.
Asniet Theodore, 105 E. 2d.
Aspak August, basket mkr. w.s. Western Av. b. Bank and Harrison Road.
Aspak Henry, basket mkr. w.s. Western Av. b. Bank and Harrison Road.
Aspen Henry, lab., h. n.s. Channing, b. Price and Young
Aspenleider Nicholas, cooper, bds. 403 Vine
Aspenleiter Sebastian, mason, n.s. Mercer, b. Walnut and Vine
Aspinwall Chauncey B., agt. and collector, n.e.c. Betts and John
Aspinwall Horace Z., mach., bds. n.e.c. Betts and John
Assum Andrew, shoe mkr., 59 Martin
Assum Henry P., boots and shoes, 508 Vine
Assur Adolph, dry goods, 120 W. 5th, bds. 281 W. 4th
Assur Alex., h. 281 W. 4th
Ast John A. attorney at law, s.e.c. Main and Court, h. 30 Jackson
Astermau Theodore, cooper, 41 E. 7th
Aston John, blk. smith, wks. J. A. Fay & Co's., res. Covington
Aston Thos. P., clk., 100 W. 5th, h. 145 Longworth
Astroth Frank, lab., 63 Woodward
Asylum for Colored Orphans, s.s. 9th, b. Elm and Plum
Aszharn Bernhard. lab., 122 Abigail
Aszmann Henry F., dry goods, 363 Central Av.
Atchison James, chandler, 50 Betts
Aten A. M., student, bds. 110 W. 5th

A THEARN & SEDAM, (Ira A. & J.
    P. S.,) Steamboat Agents and
    Commission Merchants,5 E. Front
ATHEARN Ira, (A. & Sedam,) bds. Madison House
Athern ———, rooms 60 E. 3d
Atherton Charles H., bds 98 Broadway.
Atherton George, coach-trimmer, bds. 21 George
ATKIN M. H. A., (Charles J. Buckingham & Co.,) res. Mt. Auburn
Atkins Benjamin R., salesman, s. e. c. Pearl and Walnut, h. 219 Richmond
Atkins Emery, carp., h. n s. Burt, e. of Broad
Atkins George. fancy goods and trimmings, 102 W. 5th, h Clifton
Atkins Henry, foreman, 148 Spring
Atkins James. printer, bds. 307 W. 6th
Atkins John, 594½ Freeman
Atkins Richard L., piano tuner, 72 W. 4th. h. 594½ Freeman
Atkins Thomas piano tuner, 307 W. 6th
Atkinson Mrs., 792 E. Front
Atkinson Edward, distiller, wks, Foote, Nash & Co., h. Newport
Atkinson Edward, (R. B. McCrackin & Co.,) h Newport
Atkinson Edward J., 121 Baymiller
Atkinson Mrs. Elizabeth, grocery, 62 Butler
ATKINSON George V., (McDonnell & A.,) h. 34 Richmond
Atkinson Mrs. Harriet, milliner, 121 Baymiller
Atkinson John V., china, glass, &c., 23 E. 4th. h. 34 Richmond
Atkinson Mrs. Mary, 28 Accommodation
Atkinson Mrs. Mary, 253 Freeman
Atlantic Fire Insurance Company, Taylor & Anthony, agts. 76 W. 3d
Attee Mrs. Elizabeth. 209 W. 4th
Attee John G., clk , 209 W. 4th
Attee Mary E., teacher, 209 W. 4th
Attee Wm. R., clk., 397 Longworth.
Attermeir Andreas, mason, 677 Race
Attermeyer Henry, h. n.w.c. Race and Green
Attleman Louis, lab., 146 Clinton
Attick Peter, teamster, wks. 1365 E. Front
Attig Lewis, clk., 1273 E. Front
Attig Peter, lab., n s. Front e. of Lewis
Attig Philip, 1273 E. Front
Attlesey James, plumber, 321 Vine, res. Ind.
Attwell Mrs Amanda, 199 Everitt
AUB Abraham. (A. Frenkel & Co.,) h. 26 Longworth
AUB, FRENKEL & CO.. (Abraham
A , Benedict F., & Nathaniel Newburgh,) Wholesale Clothiers, 30 W. Pearl
Aub Samuel, salesman, bds. 28 Longworth
Auberger Valentine, porter, 62 W. Pearl h. n.w.c. Linn and Findlay
Aubery John, artist, 14 E. 4th, h. 317 Vine
AUBERY William, (Traber & A.,) East Walnut Hills
Aubke Francis, tailor, h. 603 Main
Aubke G. Henry, clk., 18 Buckeye
Auhke Henry, tailor, h. 285 W. 9th
Aubke Henry G., tailor, 18 Buckeye
Aubrey Madam, bds. Henrie House
Auburn Mission Sunday School, n.s. Webster, b. Main and Sycamore
Auel Conrad, saloon, 277 Freeman
Auell Henry, blk. smith, 6 Miami
Auer Frederick, tailor, bds. 90 E. 2d
Auer John, tobacconist, 17 Main. h. e.s Baymiller b. Clark and Court
Auflerherr Rudolph, lab., rear 517 Main
Auflerheide Bernhard H., grocery, 469 W. 8th
Auflerheide Henry, driver, 136 Vanhorne
Auflerheide Henry, lab., 64 Hughes
Auflerheide Rudolph, wagon mkr., 31 Webster
Auferheck Alfred, painter, 432 Sycamore
Aufenberg Wm., lab., 24 W. Mulberry
Aufertianut Henry, tailor, w.s. Fountain b. Rice and Alexander
Aufterheide Rudolph, lab., 301 Linn

CINCINNATI ADVERTISEMENTS.

JACOB TRABER, JR.   WM. AUBERY.

TRABER & AUBERY,

WHOLESALE

GROCERS, COMMISSION MERCHANTS,

—AND—

DEALERS IN PIG IRON,

No. 7 PUBLIC LANDING, CINCINNATI, OHIO.

Agents for the sale of Fairbank's Scales, and Coal Grove Fire Brick and Clay.

R. BARTLETT & CO.
(Successors to B. BARTLETT & CO.)

COMMISSION MERCHANTS,
—AND DEALERS IN—

Oil, Turpentine, Alcohol, Camphene, Burning Fluid, Lamps, (Coal Oil and Fluid,) Varnishes, White Lead, Potash, Glue, &c. Also, Agents for the sale of Coal Oil.

S. W. COR. WALNUT AND FRONT STS., CINCINNATI, OHIO.

JAMES A. FRAZER.   S. G. CHAPMAN.

JAMES A. FRAZER & CO.,

WHOLESALE GROCERS AND COMMISSION MERCHANTS

Nos. 66 and 68 Walnut St., Cincinnati, O.

Always on hand Shot, Lead, Lead Pipe and Sheet Lead, Tar, Pitch, Rosin Oakum, Manilla and Hemp Cordage, Cotton Yarns, &c. Fish of all kinds and in all sized packages. Foreign Fruits Nuts, Sardines, Pickles, &c. Pure Old Bourbon and Rye Whisky.
Particular attention paid to Consignments of and orders for Produce, Oils, Whisky, Cincinnati Manufactured Goods, &c

---

H. W. BROWN.   **H. W. BROWN & CO.,**   R. K. BROWN.

FREIGHT AGENTS

PENNSYLVANIA CENTRAL & PITTSBURGH, FORT WAYNE & CHICAGO RAILROADS

STEAMBOAT AGENTS,
—AND—

GENERAL COMMISSION & FORWARDING MERCHANTS,

No. 25 East Front Street, bet. Broadway and Ludlow, Cincinnati, O.

J. W. GILBERT.   J. JONES.   I. A. OGBORN.

GILBERT, JONES & OGBORN,

GENERAL COMMISSION AND FORWARDING MERCHANTS,

Nos. 595, 597 and 599 Fifth Street, opp. C. H. & D. R. R. Depot,

CINCINNATI, OHIO.

afterheide Wm., turner, 301 Linn
ufheupper John, 115 Carr
ug August, lab., 73 Green
ug Jacob, painter, 649 Vine
uger Charles, watchman, al. b. Charlotte and Findlay, and Plum and Central Av.
ughinbaugh Barnett, carriage mkr., 161 George
ughinbaugh Barnett A., carriage mkr., 161 George
ughinbaugh W. L., printer, Press Office, bds. 161 George
ngar Daniel, tanner, h. 1224 E. Front
UGUR James S., (Dubois & A.,) h. 82 Hopkins
ugur Wm., eng., n.s. Railroad, e. of Hazen
uguat Lewis. horse dealer, 163 W. 5th
ukenu Hy., lab., h. 41 Race
ull Conrad A., cutter, 122 Walnut, h. 284 W 8th
ull Jacob, salesman, 32 W. Pearl, h. 2.2 Laurel [2d.
ull T., tinner. wks. n.w.c. Race and ulman Barney, finisher, wks. n.e.c. Walnut and Canal
ultemier Hy., tailor, 186 Everett
ultheizer Frederick, w.s. Western av., b. Bank and Harrison Road
uman John, clk., s.w.c. Cutter and H ɔpkins, h. 166 Cutter
uperker Ferdinand, n.w.c. Linn and Findlay
UPPERLE ALEXANDER, Hardware Store and Lock Manufactory, 24 Hamilton Road, h. 14 Wilson
upperle Mrs. Christiana D., 26 Ham. R >ad
ur Mrs. Charlotte Elizabeth, 386 Broadway
urbecker Peter, lab., 87 Wade
usd-nmoore Mrs. Anna M., n. w. c. Pleasant and Green
usdenmoore Bertha Hy., shoe mkr. bds. 467 W. 9th. w. of Central Av
usdenmoore Hy., boots and shoes, 59 Central Av., h. 27 W. 3d.
usdenmoore Herman, jewelry, 663 Central Av.
usdenmoore John B., shoe mkr., bds. 467 W. 8th. w. of Central Av.
usdenmoore Mrs Mary, 663 Central Av.
USTIN Alvin. (A. & Smith) bds. s.w.c. Broadway and 3d
ustin Carrie, servt., 43 Ellen
ustin Charles. barb.r, e.s. Pancoast al. b. 7th and 8th
ustin George, blk. smith, bds. Bevis House
ustin Major Gen. T., paymaster U. S. A., bds. 29 W. 3d
ustin Henry. tinner, h. 141 W. 3d
USTIN JAMES S., Staple and Fancy Groceries. n.e.c. 5th and Elm, h. s.w.c. 4th and Elm
ustin James W., clk., n.e.c. 5th and Elm, bds. s.w.c. 4th and Elm
ustin Mathias, 17 Kossuth
ustin Prince A., 119 W. Court, w. of Central Av.
USTIN & SMITH, (Alvin A. & Louis N. S.,) Wholesale Confectioners and Powder Dealers, 8 E. 2d
ustin Theodore. shoe mkr., 329 Cutter
usting Barney, lab., 92 Woodward
USTING Frank, (Litner & A.,) h. 455 Broadway
usting John D., grocery, 60 and 62 Abigail
USTRALIA House, 273 Walnut, John Martin, Proprietor
utenrieb Hy., stone mason. 57 14th
utenrieb John M., lab., 103 Ham. Road
utenrieth Frederick F., paper hanger, 69 15th
AUTENRIETH LEWIS, Engraver, and Die Sinker, and Engine Turner s.w.c. 4th and Walnut, h. 549 Vine
utenrieth Mrs. Mary, w.s. Goose al. b. 14th and 15th
uth Nicholas. 226 Linn
avani Thomas L., tailor and renovator, 47½ Sycamore, h. Covington

Avelbeck Herman, blk. smith. n.s. Cassatt al. b. Sycamore and Main
Avelive William C., watchman, Gibson House
Averbeck Barney, lab., 25 Mill
Averbeck Ferdinand, variety store, 362 Broadway
Averbeck Frederick, driver, 444 Sycamore
Averbeck Hy., lab., n.w.c. Ramsey and Park al
Averdick Martin, dray., bds. 114 Hunt
Averdick Matthew, dray., bds. 49 Pendleton
Avermatt Geo., bds. 165 Bremen
Avermatt Hy., 315 Findlay
Avermatt John, grocery, 165 Bremen
Averwater Barney. box mkr., wks. Livingston near Linn
AVERY CHARLES, Furniture Manufacturer, 277 Main. h. 355 John.
AVERY CHARLES L., Physician and Surgeon, 99 West Seventh.
Avery Mrs. Lydia, 274 Race
AVERY Seymour B., (Ringwalt & A.,) 435 W. 6th
Avery Wm. L., atty., 21 W. 3d, bds. 274 Race
Avey Mrs. Prudence, h. e.s. Park, b. Longworth and 6th
Avis Mrs. Matilda, s.w.c. Central Av. and Everett
Avritt Thomas, restaurant, 43 E. 4th
Awwerwater Casper, fam grocery, n.e.c. York and Linn
Axtmann Alois, porter, 91 W. Pearl, bds. 55 Sycamore
Aydelott Benjamin P., physician, 37 Linn
Aydelott John H., (Roots & Co.,) 270 W. 4th
Aver Thomas, lab., 109 Clark
AYERS James W, (Barr & A.) 469 W. 9th
Aylward Mrs. Ann, 381 W. 8th
Aylward Nicholas, plumber, wks. 230 Main, b. Covington
Ayrea Benjamin, chair mkr., 176 Longworth
Ayres Isaac W.. cof. h. 401 Central Av.
Ayres James, director city infirmary, 176 Longworth
Ayres James A., bk. layer, 176 Longworth
Ayres Miss Josephine, music teacher, 119 E. 3d
Ayres Richard, teacher, 12 Ann
Ayres Stephen, clk., 12 Ann
Ayres Stephen, ice dealer, 12 Ann
Ayres Wm. clk., 12 Ann

B

BABB CLEMENT E., Editor Christian Herald, 26 W. 4th, res. College Hill
Babb Robert E., carp., 50 Kossuth
BABBITT Calvin, (B., Good & Co.) h. 2n George.
BABBITT, GOOD & CO.. (Calvin B. John G. & Edmund B. Gardner) Wholesale Grocers and Commission Merchants, 18 and 19 Public Landing
Babcock C. II., steward, Dennison House
Babcock George W, clk., 49 Main, h. 102 W. 5th
Dabe Mrs. Catharine, seamstress, 18 Hughes
Baber John, cook, s.s. Goodloe b. Willow and Niagara
Baber Mrs. Mary A., tailoress. s.s. Goodloe b. Willow and Niagara
Babka Mathias, gilder, bds. 347 Walnut
Babke Matthew, gilder, 347 Walnut
Babst Wm., clk., n.e.c. 4th and Main, bds. 76½ Broadway
Bacciocco John, confec., 124 W. 5th
Bacciecon Joseph, confec., n.e.c. 4th and Elm
Baccineco Santino, confec., 176 W. 5th
Baccus Mrs. Levinia, 45 Lodge
Bach Adam, lab., 60 Allison

Bach Casper, blk. smith, 419 Longworth
Bach Geo., (Niehaus & D.)
Bach Lewis, lab., 570 Elm
Bacharach Solomon, clk., bds. 61 E. Pearl
Bachegalope Charles, musician, 100 W. Front
Bachelor Charles R., (B, DeCamp & Co.) Lockland
Bachelor. DeCamp & Co, (Charles R. B., Harvey DeC., & Samuel H, Bachelor) paper manuf., 61 Walnut
Bachelor Samuel H., (Bachelor, DeCamp & Co.) h. Lockland
Bacher John, barber, 1186 E. Front
Bacher Valentine, cooper, s.e.c. Bank and Baymiller
Bachle Peter, carp., 257 Clark
Bachmann Abraham, clk., 191 Main, bds. 319 Vine
Bachmann B., lab., w.s. Chamberlain & Co.
Bachmann Chas. G., tailor, 8 Moore
Bachmann Miss Eva, bds. w.s. Ridgway al. b. Liberty and 15th
Bachmann James, bar k., n.e.c. Walnut and River Landing
Bachmann Gertrude. 203 Pleasant
Bachmann John, (Knus & B.) s.e.c Harrison Pike and Division
Bachmann Mrs. Kunigunde, bds. 13 15th
Bachmann Leopold, tailor, 72 Bremen
Bachrens Chas. R., carp., 131 Clark
Bachring U. C., clk., C. H. & D. R. R. Depot
Back Anthony, lab , 20 Woodward
Back Anthony, lab., e.s. Hanover b. Woodward and Franklin
Back Mrs. Catharine, bds. e.s. Hanover b. Frankl n and Woodward
Back Geo., tanner, 661 Vine
Back Hy., clk., 680 Central Av.
Back Hy., lab., 416 Sycamore
Back Henry, lab., e.s. Sycamore b. Abigail and Woodward
Backes Peter, cab. mkr., 142 Wade
Backhaus Frank. tailor, 549 Main
Backhaus Frederick, lab., 9 Peete
Backhaus Hy., wagon mkr., n.e.c. Hunt and Broadway
Backhaus John, lab., Findlay b. Central Av. and John
Backhaus John, lab., 83 Findlay
Backherm Bernard, lab, 57 Riddle
Backman Frederick, cab. mkr., 184 Everett
Backman Reinhart, cigar mkr., 63 Walnut, h 17 Clinton
Backman W. W., b.k. Cobb, Armel & Fletcher's, bds. 310 Elm
Backmann Geo, 613 Elm
Backmann Hy., shoe mkr., 436 Linn
Backmann Peter, shoe mk., 436 Linn
Backmeier Frederick, cab. mkr. 49 Pleasant
Backmoyer Mary, servt., 373 George
Backus Eliza, servt , 311 Longworth
Backus George M., clk., 53 W. Pearl, h. 219 Cutter
Backus J. M., salesman, bds. 78 Mound
Backus Julius N., clk., 78 Mound
Bacon Mrs. Adelaide, 349 W. 8th
Bacon's Building, n.w.c. Walnut and 6th
BACON'S MERCANTILE COLLEGE, n.w.c 6th and Walnut, J. H. Doty Principal.
Bade Hy., lab , 24 W. Mulberry
Badenhop Frederick H., tailor, 72 Bremen
Bader John, butcher, 113 Gest
Bader John, collar mkr., 69 Main, bds. 61 W. 5th
Badgeley Miss Harriet, bds. 13 W. 6th
Badger Miss Harriet, seamstress, 423 Sycamore
Badger Hy P., carp., bds. s.s. Dayton b. Coleman and Western Av.
Badger Samuel, clk., s.w.c. Main and 5th. res. Covington
Badger Wm., sexton, n.s. Pearl b. Lawrence and Pike
Badrack John, peddler, 176 Broadway
Badrack Samuel, cof. h., 172 Broadway
Barhmer Hy., cooper, bds. 61 Bremen
Baehr Mrs. Barbara, 50 Findlay

CINCINNATI ADVERTISEMENTS.

WOODWORTH'S
Planing Machines,
STOVER'S PATENT
Planing Machines,
Tenoning Machines,
MOULDING & SASH-STICKING MACHINES,
Chair-Seat Machines,
POWER-MORTISING MACHINES,
BLANCHARD'S SPOKE LATHES
Felloe-Bending Machines,
SCROLL SAWS,
RAILWAY SAWS,
LATH MACHINES,
Shingle Machines,
SAW MANDRELS,
Grind-Stone Saw Gummers,
TURNING LATHES,
Hub-Boring Machines,
Hub-Hewing Machines,
Especial attention given to all kinds of
Wheelrights' Machinery,
—ALSO—
Full equipments of Furniture and Chair Makers' Machi-

LANE & BODLEY,

Founders and Engine Builders,

MANUFACTURERS OF

CIRCULAR SAW MILLS,
—AND—
WOOD-WORKING MACHINERY,

Corner John and Water Streets,

CINCINNATI, OHIO.

LANE & BODLEY'S CIRCULAR SAW MILL,

(PATENTED JULY 7, 1858, AND JULY 26, 1859.)

Combines many improvements of detail and convenience found in no other mill, among which may be enumerated the Simultaneous and independent Head Blocks, and the new and unequalled "Friction Feed," which gives the sawyer the most perfect control over his mill. These improvements, together with the unusual strength of its parts, beauty of design, and excellence of workmanship, are its recomendations.

$8 00 PER HUNDRED POUNDS.

SHAFTING ACCURATELY TURNED AND POLISHED. PULLIES TURNED AND BALANCED.

With Sellers' Patent Self-adjusting Hanger, Bearings, mounted on Ball and Socket Joint runs with much less than ordinary friction. $10,00 per hundred pounds.

LANE & BODLEY,
Corner John and Water Streets.

Backermeyer Geo., lab., 223 Betts
Bacler Joseph, tailor, s.e.c. 4th and Walnut
Baenford Hy., clk., 101 W. 4th, h. 7th b. Sycamore and Broadway
Baen John W., genl. index. clk., Recorder's Office, h. Symmes Tp.
Baenkampan Mrs. Charlotte, w.s. Western Av. b. Dayton and Bank
Baenninger Solomon, h. 542 Race
BAENZIGER CONRAD, Importer and Dealer in Liquors, Groceries, Swiss, Limberg and Sapsago Cheese, 404 Vine
Baer Chas., lab., 624 Race
Baer Conrad, grocer, 705 Vine
Baer Hy., upholsterer, 67 Pleasant
Baer Jacob, cof. and b.h , 37 Ham. Road
Baer Joseph, grocer, 170 Ham. Road
Baer Michael, tailor, bds. 48 Rittenhouse
Baer Mrs Rosella, 145 Hopkins
Baeracker John, chair mkr., 57 Wood
Baertlein Albert, lab., 39 Moore
Baetz Wm., carver, 620 Vine
Baeumer Bernhard, porter. 51 Peete
Baghy Geo., molder, wks. 222 E. Front
BAGGE Frank, (Vallo & B.) h. 89 Spring
Bagge Hy., carp., 69 Spring
Baggs James, lab., n.e.c. Vine and Water
Bagley Mrs. Jane, b.h., 61 E. 4th
Bagley Wm. A., clk., U. S. Express Co.
Bagnell Richard L., shoe mkr., bds. 91 W. 8th
Bagnell Robt., shoe mkr., 91 W. 8th
Bagott James, tinner, 59 W. Court w. of Central Av.
Bagott Thomas, butcher, n.e.c. Mound and 9th
Bagott Wm., butcher, 61 Hopkins
Bahlandorf William, tailor, 53 David
Bahler John, lab., 67 Butler
Bahlman Caspar, cof. h., 612 Race
Bahlman Frank, chair mkr., 610 Central Av.
BAHLMANN Albert, (Kruse & B.) 389 Main
Bahlmann Conrad, cab. mkr., 660 Elm
Bahlmann Geo. J., lab., s.w.c. Abigail and Broadway
BAUMANN Frederick, (Diebold, B. & Co.) 646 Vine
Bahmer Hy., cab. mkr., 147 Clark
Bahn Fred., 11 Ann
Bahn Herman, harness mkr., 112 Main, h. s.s. 9th w. of Freeman
Bahn Mrs. Jennie, dress mkr., 174 Broadway
Bahn Wm., printer, bds. 91 Longworth
Bahn Wm. H., Bahn Saloon, s.w.c. 6th and Elm, h. 18 George
Bahue Andrew, grocery, 24 W. Court w. of Central Av.
Bahnus Christian, cooper, s.e.c. Milton and Broadway
Bahr Francis, tailor, 543 Race
Bahr Isaac, trader, 549 Central Av.
Baier Geo., 8 15th
Bailer Casper, cab. mkr., 197 Elm
Bailer Joseph, tailor, bds. s.w.c. 3d and Race
Bailer Martin, lock smith, 17 Mary
Bailey Miss A. S. W. S., teacher, Wesleyan Female College
Bailey Alfred F., carp., 762 Central Av.
Bailey Chas., lab., Commercial Hospital
Bailey Daniel, asst depot master, n.w.c 4th and Baum
Bailey Daniel, freight master, 43 Ellen
Bailey & Decamp, (John B. & John D.) furniture store. 133 E. Front
Bailey Edward N., trunk mkr., 89 Main, h. Newport
Bailey Mrs Eliza, s.s. New b. Culvert and Broadway
Bailey Emanuel, mach. n.s. Water b. Smith and Cass
Bailey Frederick, lab., n.s. Railroad e. of Wallace al.
Bailey Henry, lab, 170 Cutter
Bailey James, driver, 67 E. 8th e. of Lock
Bailey John, (B. & Decamp) h. Walnut Hills
Bailey John, dray, 59 Pendleton

Bailey John, box mkr., 36 E. 8th e. of Lock
Bailey John A., b.k., 29 E. 3d, h. 28 Pike
Bailey John A., grocery, 425 Sycamore, h. Walnut Hills
Bailey Joseph B., tinner, 317 W. 6th
BAILEY Kennedy, 43 Ellen
Bailey M. & Co., (M. B. & Charles Berrall) provision broker, s.w.c. Walnut and 2d
Bailey Emanuel, mach., 314 Water
Bailey Martin, bakery, 347 W. 5th
Bailey Micajah, (M. B. & Co.) 134 W. 8th
Bailey Patrick H., boatman, 92 Longworth
BAILEY Samuel, stone cutter, 43 Ellen
Bailey Samuel, jr., clk., Adams Express Co., h. 43 Ellen
Bailey Sarah, servt., 556 W. 9th w. of Central Av.
Bailey Wm. W., printer, 62 W. 3d, h.
Newport
BAILIE Benjamin, (John Bailie & Co.) s.e.c 2d and Ludlow
BAILIE John, (John B. & Co.) s.e.c. 2d and Ludlow
BAILIE JOHN & CO., (John B. & John W. Hastie & Benjamin Bailie) Steam Bakery, s.e.c. 2d and Ludlow
Bailie Thomas, s.e.c. 2d and Ludlow
Bailing Frederick, driver, h. 100 Cherry al. h. Plum and Central Av.
Baily Wm W., dray, 279 W. Front
Baily Elizabeth, servt, 430 W. 8th
Baily Ezra, lumber yard, 518 W. Front, h. 138 Smith
Baily Hy., lab., wks. n.e.c. Elm and Miami Canal
Baily Hezekiah B., with Ezra Baily, 518 W. Front, h. Covington
Bailie Isaac S., carman, 154 Longworth
Baily John, 24 Abigail
Baily Mrs. Mary, 59 Pendleton
Bain Mrs. Adelia, dress mkr, bds. 171 W. 3d
Bain Miss Elizabeth, dress mkr., bds. 171 W. 3d
Bain James, finisher, bds. 171 W. 3d
Bain Miss Mary, dress mkr., bds. 171 W. 3d
Bain Mrs Mary. dress mkr., 171 W. 3d
Bain Patrick, huckster, 32 Race
Bain Miss Sarah, dress mkr., bds. 171 W. 3d
Bain Thomas, clk., n.w.c 4th and Central av
Bainbridge Jerome, lab., 101 Mound
Bainbridge Wm., paver, 400 W. 7th
Baine John, bksmith. wks. 23 Freeman
Baine Mark, blksmith., bds. 35 Ludlow
Bains Mrs. Mary, fruit dealer, 152½ Walnut, h s w.c. 3d and Elm
Baird John T., 16 Plum
Baird Mrs. Sarah, 137 W. 6th
Baird Wm., 16 Plum
Baird Wm., clk., s.w.c. Walnut and Pearl, h 16 Plum
Baird Wm., cooper shop, 39 Bremen, h. 143 Clinton
Baird Wm. jun., clk., bds. 16 Plum
Baird Wm. M., cooper, 143 Clinton
Baiter Jacob G., cab. mkr., 153 Everett
Benting George, painter, wks. Crane, Breed & Co's
Bake W. M. A., cof. h., n s. Ham. Road, nr. Mohawk Bridge
Bakeman John, pork packer, 38 McFarland
Baker, b.k., bds. 168 W. 4th
BAKER ABRAHAM H., Physician and Surgeon, 316 W. 6th
Baker Adam, lab., 458 E. Front
Baker Albert, (Fox & B.,) 17 Madison
Baker Alex. n.w.c Bank and Central av
Baker Mrs. Amelia, 474 W. 8th
Baker Andrew, 71 Mohawk
Baker Andrew, brklayer, n.s. Corporation al., b Price and Young
Baker Arthur W., bds 168 W. 5th
Baker Mrs. Augusta, bds. 99 Mound
Baker Augustus, lab., bds. 60 Broadway

BAKER B. P. & CO., (Benj. P. B., Orville R. B , and Sam'l C. Emley,) wh. Grocers and Com. Merchants, 54 and 56 Walnut
Baker Mrs. Barbara, 257 Clark
BAKER Benjamin P., (B. P. B. & Co.,) h. 124 W. 8th
Baker Benj. R , printer, bds. 316 W. 6th
BAKER Bowman C., (B. & Co.,) h. 306 W. 6th
Baker Charles. 52 Mohawk
BAKER Charles E., (Fallis, Young & Co.,) E. Walnut Hills
Baker Christ., cigar mkr., h. 74 Clark
BAKER & CO., (Bowman C. B., Nimrod H. Sinclair. Joel Baker, and James P. Garvey,) wh. Grocers, 29 Main
Baker Darley, b.k., 371 W. 6th
Baker David, ins. surveyor, 73 W. 3d, h. n s. Grant, b. Elm and Canal
Baker David F., salesman, 144 Walnut, h. 309 Longworth
Baker Mrs. Dianna, 140 W. Pearl
Baker Ernst, cig. mkr., 670 Main
Baker Frank, moulder, 237 Clark
Baker George, 337 Longworth
Baker Geo., tailor and clothier, 63 Broadway, h. 99 E. 2d
Baker Hamilton, brklayer, n.w.c. Bank and Central av
Baker Miss Hannah, bds. 333 Cutter
Baker Hy., chairmkr., 187 Linn
Baker Hy., lab., 141 Abigail
Baker Hy , printer, wks. 170 Sycamore, bds. Planters Hotel
Baker Hy, tinner, 14 Jackson
Baker Hy., willow-ware, &c., 349 Vine
Baker Horatio O ,'saddler, 363 W. 4th
Baker Increase, coal measurer, s.e.c. Front and Butler, h. s.e.c. Baum and Observatory Road
Baker J. H , shoe mkr., s.s. 6th, b. Vine and Race
Baker J. Samuel, b k , Hieatt & Woods, h. Newport, Ky.
Baker, James J., brush mkr., wks, 190 Walnut, res. Covington
Baker James M., tailor. 74 W. 6th
Baker Mrs. Jane, 422 Broadway
Baker Mrs. Jane, 337 Longworth
BAKER Joel, (B. & Co.,) h. Newport
Baker John, 767 Vine
Baker John, c'k., bds 445 Main
Baker John, lab.- s.s. Friendship al., b. Pike and Butler
Baker Jno. A., wharf-master. 270 Richmond
Baker John H., chair mkr., 187 Linn
Baker John R., penny-post, 178 W. Court, west of Central av.
Baker Jno. S., atty., 148 Walnut, h. E. Walnut Hills
BAKER John W., (B. & Von Phul,) h. Covington, Ky
Baker John H , driver, e s. Poplar, b. Linn and John
Baker Leopold, cof. h., 807 Vine
Baker Lewis, packer, 53 W. Pearl, h. 31 Plum
Baker Lewis, salesman, 144 Walnut, h. 309 Longworth
Baker Lewis H., clk., 31 Plum
Baker Lewis H., salesman, 144 Walnut, h. 363 W. 4th
Baker Mrs. Mary, n.e.c. 7th & Sycamore
Baker Miss Matilda, teacher, 20 Longworth
Baker Nath., (Langley & Kinkend's,) h. 118 Plum
Baker Nathan F., admr. Jno. Baker, 39 W. 4th, h. E. Walnut Hills
Baker Nathaniel, b k., 277 George
BAKER Orville R., (B. P. Baker & Co.,) bds Gibson House
Baker Peter, 86 Mohawk
Baker Peter, carp., 142 Wade
Baker Mrs. Rose, 104 Butler
Baker Ruffin, steward, 140 W. Pearl
Baker. Solomon T., ticket agent, L. M. R. R. Depot
Baker Thomas, lab., 18 Park
BAKER THOS. F. Ornamental Iron Works, Iron Railing Manuf. and Jail Works, cor. Harriet & Front, and 273 W. 5th, h. 345 W. 7th

GEO. F. DAVIS.   A. JUDSON DAVIS.

GEO. F. DAVIS & CO.

WHOLESALE DEALERS IN

PROVISIONS,

AND CURERS OF THE

STAR BRAND HAMS,

NO. 11 SYCAMORE STREET,

CINCINNATI, OHIO.

(Star logo: GEO. F. DAVIS & CO. EXTRA SUGAR CURED HAMS & BEEF.)

G. & P. BOGEN,

PORK PACKERS,

CURERS OF

EXTRA SUGAR-CURED FANCY CANVASSED HAMS,

AND

FRENCH BOLOGNA SAUSAGES.

Manufacturers of Still and Sparkling Catawba Wines.   *Also Manufacturers of Sausage Skins.*

NEAR THE BRIGHTON HOUSE, CINCINNATI, OHIO.

S. DAVIS, Jr., & Co.,
PORK & BEEF PACKERS.
AND
CURERS OF EXTRA FAMILY HAMS,
DIAMOND BRAND.

A Diploma and Silver Medal were awarded them by the State Board of Agriculture, at the Fair held in Cincinnati, Oct., 1850, "For the best cure of Hams."

WAREHOUSES,
303 to 313 Broadway,
S.W. COR. COURT,
CINCINNATI,
O.

CHARLES JACOB, JR.   GEORGE WUST.

CHARLES JACOB, Jr. & CO.

PORK & BEEF PACKERS,

PRODUCE & COMMISSION MERCHANTS,

And Wholesale Dealers in Bacon, Lard, Dried Beef, Hams, Beef Tongues, Shoulders, and Bologna Sausages,

No. 50 WALNUT STREET, between Front and Columbia, CINCINNATI, O.

Banziger Chas., cof. h. 404 Vine,
Banziger Hy., lab., n.w.c. Plum and Wade.
Bappart Peter, porter, 41 Walnut, h. s.e.c. Front and Walnut.
Baptista Sister, St. Clare Convent, n.w.c. 3d and Lvile. [worth.
Baragin Elizabeth, serv't., 315 Long-
Barameir Herman, 223 Betts
Barameir Hy., driver, 17 Betts.
Barbaro Dominick S., cigars &c., 10 Dd'way, h. Newport.
Barbe Mrs. Eliza, h. 529 W. 5th.
Barbenchon Felix G., (B. & Jones,) 17 Abigail.
Barbenchon & Jones, (Felix G. B., & James V. J.,) painters, n.e.c. Walnut and 6th.
Barbenisch Jacob, brewer, bds. 493 Vine.
Barber Catharine, serv't, 173 W. 4th.
Barber Edward H., (Choate, B. & Evans) 20 Clinton.
Barber Mrs. Emma, bds. 89 E. 3d.
Barber John, oysters fish and game, 77 W. 5th, h. 451 W. 9th.
Barber John, mach., wks. n.s. Front b. Lawrence and Pike.
Barber Wm., mach., 672 E. Front.
BARBJUR ADIN R.. Boots and Shoes,140 W. 5th, bds. 355 W. 8th.
BARBOUR Goodrich H., (Shaw, Barbour & Co..) bds. Burnet House.
BARBOUR Lucius, (Shaw B., & Co.,) Hartford Ct.
Barbur Joseph N., Supt., Industrial School, n.e.c. Race and Commerce.
Barch Simon, tailor, 45 Wade.
Barchard John H., mach., 168 Linn.
Barclay James, foreman, Cin. Gazette, h. 151 Central Av.
Bard Archibald, cab. mkr., wks. n.w.c. Smith and Front.
Bard David, moulder, 24 W. Court w. of Central Av.
Bard Silvester W., Livery Stable, s.w.c. John and Everet, h. 56 Betts.
Barden Michael, 95 Mulberry.
Bardes Christian, butcher, 655 Vine.
Bardes Hy., meat store, 667 Vine.
Bardes Jacob, meat store. 536 Vine.
Bardes Louis C., book binder, e. s. Walnut b. 4th and 5th, h. 605 Elm.
Bardo John, cof. h. 290 Ham Road.
Bardsley Thos., paper hanger, 60 W. 4th, h. Newport, Ky.
Bare Hy. lab., wks. 25 Water.
Bare Martin, (Hammar & B.,) h. Covington.
Bare Sam'l, peddler, h. 585 Central Av.
Bareiter Mrs. Catharine, 130 Pleasant.
Bares Martin, painter, 82 Mound.
Barey Mrs. Ann, seamstress, w.s. Walker b. Ringgold and Boal.
Barey James, moulder, w.s. Walker b. Ringgold and Boal.
Barfoot Edward, 366 W. Liberty.
Barg Frederick, cooper, 18 Madison.
Barg John, dray, 53 Rittenhouse.
Bargan Morton, dray, 546 Sycamore.
Bargelt George, optician, 164 Mound.
Barger L., conductor, 91 Sycamore.
Barger Peter, lab., wks. 21 Webster.
Bargling Geo., cigar mkr., 195 Clinton.
Bargmann Hy., tailor, 417 Longworth.
Barhr Conrad, brewer, wks. s.w.c. Plum and Canal.
Barkaling Hy., tailor, h. 149 Abigail.
Barkan, Hy., cof. h. n.w.c. Browne and Vernon Av.
Barker Albert, tailor, 246 Clark.
BARKER EDWARD, Carriage Manufacturer, 11 E. 6th, h. 32 E. 6th.
Barker George, bk. binder, 43 Main h. Covington Ky.
BARKER, HART & COOK, (Jonathan H. B., Matthew H., & Theodore C.,) Grocers, Ship Chandlers and Boat stores, 44 Pub. Landing.
Barker Israel, peddler, h. 205 Elm
Barker James, bk. layer, 135 Baymiller
Barker John, lab, 403 W. 3d.
BARKER Jonathan H., (B. Hart & Cook,) 143 Elm.

Barker Louis, carpet weaver, 13 E. 3d e. of Parsons.
Barker Mrs. Margaret, rear 221 Water.
Barker Robert, 148 Baymiller.
Barker Mrs. Susan, bds. 148 Baymiller.
Barker Wm., h. 7 Harrison.
Barker Wm., 52 E. 5th.
Barker Wm., mach., n.s. Channing b. Price and Young.
Barkhaus Geo , porter, 26 Main.
Barkhouse Julius, jeweler, 35½ ⅔ George.
Barkof Harmon, shoe mkr., w.s. Sycamore b. Abagail and Woodward.
Barkon Margaret, serv't. 84 E. 3d.
Barksoll Philip, basket mkr., w.s. Western Av. b. Bank and Harrison Road
Barkshire Mrs. Virginia, dress mkr., 12 Webb.
Barlage Clemens, cigar mkr., bds. Baymiller nr. Liberty.
Barlage Geo. H. varnisher, 462 John
Barlage Frank, lab. 379 Broadway
Barlage Frank, lab. 382 Broadway
Barlage Hy. finisher. 75 Spring
Barlage Hy. shoemkr. 223 Baymiller
Barlage Wm. tailor, 71 Baymiller
Barlar Frank, moulder, wks. n.e.c. Canal and Walnut
Barler Edwin A. b.k. s.e.c. 2d and Main, h. 36 Richmond
Barliga,H. shoemkr, 181 Baymiller
Barllmann Richd, hostler, bds s.w.c. 6th and Smith
Barlosius Ludwig, glove cutter, 314 Main, bds. Napoleon Tavern
Barlow Danforth, agt Middleton, Strobridge & Co., h. 179 W. 9th
Barlow Hy. cooper, h. 442 Sycamore
Barlow Hy. fir isher, wks. n.e.c. Walnut and Canal
Barlow Joel J., clk. n.e.c. 5th and Race, h. 166 Central Av
Barlow John, cooper, 442 Sycamore
Barlow Warren S., agt. 108 Linn
Barlow Wm. finisher, wks. n.e.c. Walnut and M. Canal
Barlow Wm. moulder, 444 Sycamore
Barmann Barney, cof. h. 185 W. Canal
Barnard Alanson, office n.s. 8th b. Br'd way and Sycamore. h 120 Spring
Barnard Christian, 29 Providence
Barnard David, teacher, 492 W. 5th
Barnard Geo. clk. 295 Clark
Barnard Geo. wks. Cin. type foundry
Barnard Wm., stencil cutter, bds. s.e.c. 9th and Walnut
Barnes Anne, seamstress, 233 Betts
Barnes George D., butter and eggs, 322 W. 6th, h. 151 Cabot, Newport
Barnes Hy., printer, 21 Grant
Barnes John, 462 W. 5th
Barnes John, cigar mkr., wks. 223 Vine. h. 519 W. 8th
Barnes John H., carp., 988 E. Front
Barnes Lyman L , salesman, 93 W. Pearl, h. 375 W. 6th
BARNES RICHARD G. Merchant Tailor, 155 Main
BARNES Wm. H. (D. B. George & Co.) h. 174 Pearl b. Broadway
Barnett James. barber shop and chiropodist, 137 Sycamore
Barnett James, confec. 60 Mound
Barnett James E., b.k. Gilmore, Dunlap & Co.'s, bds. 107 Pike
Barnett John, dray, 491 W. 4th
Barnett John, mach. bds. 79 George
Barnett John, mach bds. s.e.c. George and Plum
Barnett Ralph, eng. 26 Observatory Road
Barnett Mrs. Ruth E. e.s. Whittaker b. Front an d 3d
Barnett Wm. barber, 278 W. 6th
Barney Hy. lab. 983 Linn
Barney Howard, salesman, 55 W. 4th, bds. 258 Longworth
BARNEY Roderick D., (Robert Clarke & Co.) 258 Longworth
Barney Theodore, cab. mkr. 114 Betts
Barneygrevers Barney, box mkr., wks 54 Elm
Barnhorn Clemens, cof. h., 50 and 52 W. Court

Barnhorn Hy. carp. 99 W. 2d
Barnhorn John H., box mkr., wks. 54 Elm
DARNING Bernard. (Grothe & B.) Gest b. Freeman and Carr
Darnitz M. C. (Mumford & Co) 328 W. 3d
Barnitz Mack R., sec'y. for Mumford & Co). h. 328 W. 3d
Barns Mrs. Eliza, h. 33 Rittenhouse
Barns George R. clk. 337 Main, bds. 195 Broadway
Barns Wm. carp. n.s. Goodloe b. Willow and Niagara
Baroshaw Joseph, surveyor and civil eng. n.w.c. 4th and Race, bds. 167 Plum
Barntz Herman, porter, 23 Commerce
Barolesius Lewis, cutler, bds. 442 Main
Barnwell George, shoemkr, 401 W. 6th
Barr Amos, 22 H.thaway
BARR & AYERS. (Baldwin B. & James W. A.) Carpenters & Builders, 120 Central Av
DARR Baldwin (B. & Ayers) h. 555 Freeman
Rarr Benjamin, b.k. 22 Hathaway
Barr Charles H. molder, wks. Wm. Resor & Co.'s
Barr Geo. printer, 181 Race
Barr George R. molder, s.s. Front b. Plum and Central Av
Barr Geo. W. molder, 503 Water
Barr & Gudgeon (Hy. H. B. & Wm. A. G.) feed mill, n.s. Front b. Torrence and Keily
DARR Hy, (Frazer & Co.' n.s. Hathaway b. Jane and Dunlop
Barr Hy. H. carp.n.s. Front, b. Torrence and Kelly, h. Barr at. b. Front and R ver
Barr Miss Jane, bds. 159 Clinton
Barr John, grocer, 34 George
Barry John, lime dealer, 16 Oliver
DARR Lewellyn (A. G. Wright & Co.), 87 Baum
Barr Martin, painter, 82 Mound
Barr Mrs. Mary, 61 Mound
Barr Rachael, h. 159 Clinton
Barr Samuel, lumber mer., s s. Torrence nr. Railroad
Barr Stephen, teamster, n.s. Front e. of Lumber
Barrett Edward, carp. 123 Lock
Barrett Edward, eng. 219 George
Barrett Elizabeth E. dress mkr. 485 W. 8th
Barrett Mrs. Emma, 310 Elm
Barrett Geo W., cof. h. 205 W. 6th
Barrett James, bar k. n.e.c. Front and Broadway
Barrett James, lab. 70 Kossuth
Barrett John, lab. 25 8th above Lock
Barrett Lawrence, lab. n.e.c. Vine and Water
Barrett Leonard, clk., 52 W. Pearl, bds 91 E. 3d
Barrett Mrs Mary, 91 E. 3d
Barrett Michael, s.e.c. Front and Ludlow
Barrett Michael, dray, 13 Carr
Barrett Michael, driver, 487 W. 8th
Barrett Michael, huckster, 60 W. Front
Barrett Oliver R. carp. 105 Clinton
Barrett Patrick. lab. h. 58 Water
Barrett Mrs. S. E., music teacher, bds. Spencer House
Barrett Samuel, furnishing goods, 115 Walnut, bds. 77 Laurel
Barrett Samuel lab. 137 E. 6th
BARRETT Silas M. (Tylor & B.) h. 309 Richmond and Avondale
Barrett Theodore, caulker, n.s. Railroad e of Hazen
Barrett Wm. lab. 57 Pendleton
Barrett Wm wks. J. Whittaker's, Deer Creek Valley
Barrick Eliza t acher, 147 E. 3d
Darrick Louisa, teacher, 147 E. 3d
Barrick Mary, teacher, 147 E. 3d
Darrick Rebecca, 147 E. 3d e. of Collard
Barrick Wm. carp. 117 Martin
BARRINGER GEORGE L., General Freight Agent, Indianapolis and Cin. R R. Co., 66 W. 3d, h. 144 Smith

CINCINNATI ADVERTISEMENTS.

BERTRAM & CO.

Successors to CANFIELD & BERTRAM,

DEALERS IN COAL & COKE, FIRE BRICK & CLAY,

OFFICE & YARD, 197 East Front St., south side, bet. Butler St. & Miami Canal,

CINCINNATI, OHIO.

Constantly on hand a supply of Youghiogheny, Peach Orchard, Cannel and Hartford City Coal, City Manufactured and McKeesport Coke, Fire Brick and Clay.

E. HUTCHISON,

WHOLESALE AND RETAIL DEALER IN

Youghiogheny, Peach Orchard, Syracuse, Hartford City, and Cannel

COALS, COKE, FIRE BRICK AND CLAY;

OFFICE AND YARD AT THE OLD STAND OF PEACH ORCHARD COAL CO.,

South-East corner of Front and Butler Streets, Cincinnati, Ohio.

M. TEMPEST.   **TEMPEST & CO.**   F. DALLAS.

MANUFACTURERS OF AND DEALERS IN

YELLOW & ROCKINGHAM WARE,

HAMILTON ROAD POTTERY.

Nos. 283, 285 and 287 Hamilton Road, head of Elm St., CINCINNATI, O.

To reach our Pottery by the Street Railroad, take the Cars on Fourth and Main Streets, get out at Bank Street, and turn eastwardly to the Mohawk Bridge, which cross, and go on to the Pottery; or take the Omnibus which starts from the corner of Fifth and Main streets, and passes the Pottery.

HENRY FAEHR.   CHAS. BOTTLER.   E. CULMANN.

FAEHR, BOTTLER & CO.

IMPORTERS OF

RHINE AND MOSELLE WINES,

Manufacturers of SPARKLING NATIVE, HOCK and MOSELLE WINES. Wholesale Dealers in all kinds of STILL NATIVE WINES.

NO. 438 MAIN STREET, CINCINNATI, OHIO.

GEORGE STACEY,

MANUFACTURER OF

GASOMETERS, WROUGHT-IRON ROOFS,

And all kinds of Wrought-Iron Work, used in the erection of Gas and Coal Oil Works; Wrought-Iron Bridges, for Railroads and other purposes. Wrought-Iron Joists and Girders, for buildings; Wrought-Iron Jails and Bells.

Manufactory, Ramsey Street, opposite Ohio & Miss. R. R. Depot, Cincinnati, O.

REFER TO: Cincinnati Gas Light and Coke Company; Cleveland Gas Company; Lexington, Ky., Gas Company; Springfield, Ills., Gas Company; Baton Rouge, La., Gas Company; Davenport, Iowa, Gas Company, and John Jeffrey, Esq., Gas Engineer, Cincinnati, O. N. B. Roofs covered with either Corrugated Sheet Iron or Slate.

JACOB FRIDGER,

BRASS FOUNDER & MACHINIST,

Manufacturer of PATENT FIRE PLUGS, HOSE COUPLINGS, of all sizes, Gas, Steam, and Water Cocks, Gauge and Cylinder Cocks, Globe, Angle and Check Valves, Wrought-Iron Pipe and Fittings, Steam and Water Gauges, Signal Bells and Improved Metallic Packing, Steamboat Whistles of all sizes. Iron and Brass Pumps, of all descriptions. All kinds of Distillery and Steamboat Work done at short notice. Shafting, Hangers, Pulleys, and Engines made to order. SECOND-HAND ENGINES FOR SALE. Steamboats fitted out with PIPES AND FIRE PUMPS. All sizes of GUM AND LEATHER HOSE.

No. 48 PUBLIC LANDING, CINCINNATI.

(BAR) CINCINNATI (BAT) DIRECTORY. (BAU) 53

Barrington James, reporter, Merchants' Exchange, h. 41 Gest
Barrington Mary A. servt. 142 Broadway
Barrington Wm., b k. Merchants' Exchange, h. 49 Gest
Barron Bridget, seamstress, wks. 53 W. 4th

BARRON JOHN, Currier, 28 Water h. 323 John
Barrond John B. lab. s.s. Harrison Pike b. Riddle and Division
Barrows Ira F, coach mkr., 21 W. 7th h. Walnut Hills
Barry Mrs. ——, w.s. Langdon al. b. 6th and 7th
Barry Dennis, painter. 22 Ann
Barry Ellen, 149 George
Barry James, tobacco presser, 137 W. Canal
Barry John, shoemkr, w.s. Langdon al, b. 6th and 7th
Barry Mary, 429 W 2d
Barry Richd. blksmith. 28 Broadway
Barry Patrick, lab. 447 W. 2d
Barry Purce I C. bds. 240 W. 3d
Barry Richd. blksmith, 58 Broadway
Barry Sarah A. 31 Race
Barry Thos. P. (Wm. B. B. & Co.) 240 W. 3d
Barry Thomas P clk. s.e c. Front and Broadway, bds 240 W. 3d
Barry Wm. B, & Co.. (Wm. B. & Thos. P. B.) foreign exchange office, 76 W. 3d
Barry Wm. B. (Wm. B. B. & Co.), 240 W. 3d
BART Edwin R. (B. & Hickox), 248 Race

BART & HICKOX, (Edwin R. B. & Wm, C H) Goodyear's India Rubber Goods. Importer of Fancy Goods and Toys. 49 W. 4th
Bart Nicholas, 731 Elm
Barta T. blksmith, 16 Green
Bartal Frederick turner, 70 Rittenhouse
Bartalenk Joseph, bender, 41 Gest
Bartel Charles, cab. mkr. Oehler al. b. Freeman and Garrard
Bartel Wm, H, molder, 172 Everett
Bartele Michael, lab. wks, n.o.c. M. Canal and Walnut
Bartels Charles, ailor, 767 Vine
Bartolt Martin. lab. e.s. Sprig b. Abigall and Woodward
Barter Barney, lab. wks. 335 Broadway
Barter John, cof. h. 672 Central Av
Barth Frederick, jeweller, 367 Vine
Barth Frederick, meat store, 104 and 106 W. Liberty
Barth H,. Cin. type foundry, h. Newport, Ky
Barth Herman II., butter store, 295 W. 6th
Barth John. lab 54 Mohawk
Barth John, tailor, 62 Bremen
Barth William clk,, 295 W. 6th, b. 315 Mound
Barthel Frederick. phys. 389 Vine
Barthold Bernard H. R. blksmith, n.w,c. Wilson and Milton
Barthold Hy. 71 Milton
Bartils Augustus, cof. h. 14 Sycamore
Bartlett Brewer. b k. 88 and 90 W. Pearl, h. Glendale
Bartlett D. bds. Dennison House
Bartlett John, lab. wks n.e.c. Park and Marsh
Bartlett Nathaniel, 119 W. 9th
Bartlett Nathaniel P. salesman, 55 W. Pearl, h. 119 W. 9th
Bartlett Nelly, s.s. 6th b. Broadway and Culvert

BARTLETT R. & Co., Commission Merchants,Oil Dealers.Naval Stores, &c. s.w.c. Walnut and Front

BARTLETT R. MONTGOMERY, Bartlett's Commercial College, s.w. c. 3d and Walnut, h. Sedamsville
Bartlett Reed (R. B. & Co.) res. Glendale
Bartley Mary, bds. 240 E. 6th
Bartley John, driver, bds. s.e.c. Pearl and Pike
Bartley John, lab. 240 E. 6th
Bartley Patrick, blksmith, 30 Abigail
Bartley Pat. nail mkr. 65 Abigail

Bartley Peter, waiter, 200 Plum
Kartling Phillip, barber, bds. 22 W. 9th
Birtmann Peter, 178 Richmond
Barton Ann,, seamstress, 224 W. 6th
Barton Benjamin, clk, 32 W. 3d
Barton Elizabeth, teacher, Everett b. Central Av. and John
Barton George, contractor, 421 W. 8th
Barton Mrs. J. N. ladies' caps, head dresses, &c. 22 E. 4th
Barton Lafayette, marble cutter, 976 E. Front

BARTON ORLANDO F., Wine Merchant, bds. 37 Longworth
Barton Wm., carp., 162 E. 6th
Barton Wm. C., b.k., 59 Everett
Barton Wm. C., deputy sheriff, h. Delhi
Barton Wm. H. bds, 59 Everett
Barton Wm. H. H., type founder, 59 Everett
Bartshe Edward, miller, 385 Broadway
Bartscher Arnold, bk. bindery, 25 14th
Burtze Harmon, cab. mkr., s.e.c. Mound and Clark
Barumar Arnold, shoe mkr., s.e.c. Abigall and Broadway
Barus Charles. prof. music, 59 Webster
Burwise Geo., fireman, s s. Vanhorn b. Baumiller and Freeman

BARWISE & KING, (Luther T. B. & Joseph K.) Merchant Tailors and Clothiers. 171 Main
BARWISE Luther T., (B. & King) 415 W. 7th
Baschang George, carpet weaver, 273 W. 5th
Bascher Philip, grocery, 436 Linn
Bascoe Mildred, 119 W. 2d

BASCOM SILAS, Exchange Broker 15 W. 3d. bds. 52 W. 9th
Base Charles, cigar mkr., s w c. 15th and Pleasant

BASFORD DR CHAS. F., Manufacturing Physician, 103 Darr
Basford Frances C., bds. 97 Laurel
Baskerville R bt., lab., 58 Carr
Baslar John, gun mkr., 50 Dunlap
Basler Frank, 45 14th
Bas er John, cof. h., 661 Vine
Bass Thomas, willow ware, 208 W. 5th
Bassaka Francis. finisher, wks. n.e.c. Walnut and Broadway
Basse Gerhard L., saddler, 98 13th
Dassenkamp Fred.. cigar mkr., 73 David
Bassett Geo. P., clk., 564 W. 9th
Bassett Geo. W.. teamster, 1316 E. Front
Basset James L., moulder, bds. 305 W. Front
Bass-tt Joel, 110 E. Liberty
Bassett Joseph, teamster, s.s. Front b. Foster and Kelly
Bassett L, b.k., bds. 242 Plum
Bassett Luke. A., (Spear & Co.) bds. 242 Plum
Bassett Theodore, conductor, bds. Brighton House
Basso Mary, 510 Race
B sswell John, tanner, 33 Pleasant
Bast John, architect, 125 Hopkins
Bast John jr., 125 Hopkins
Bastele Michael, lab., wks. n.e.c. Canal and Walnut
Bastian Jacob, shoe mkr., 587 Race
Butchelder Geo. H., (Cutaiar & B.) 275 W. 8th
Batchelor Frank Y., steamboat capt., 275 W 7th
Batchelor John K., bds. 7 Pine
Butchelor Stanton. clk., 23 Pine
BATE Samuel, (Jas. D. Smith & Co.) h. Newport
Bateman Mrs., 57 7th
Hateman Aaron E., mach., 49 Webster
Bateman F. A., b.k., 84 E. Pearl, h. 48 Webster
Bateman Hy., eng.. 13 Providence
Bateman John T., b.k., 38 McFarland
Bateman Miss M. O., clk., 575 Central Av., h. 190 Everett
Bateman Thos., clk., 211 Laurel
Bateman Thos., painter, 211 Laurel
Bateman Thomas, shoe mkr., 254 W. 9th

BATEMAN WARNER M., Attorney at Law and Notary, Office, 30 W. 4th, res. Glendale
Bates Caleb, lab. Burnet House
Bates Caroline, bds. 270 W. 3d
Bates Caroline, 15 Stone
Bates Edward, barber, 15 Stone
BATES Edward (Johnson & B.) s.s. Webb b. Mill and Stone
Bates Eliza G.. b k. binder, wks. 137 Walnut, bds. Covington
Bates Geo., bds. 270 W. 3d
Bates Henry M., painter, 11 W. 9th, h. 352 Race

BATES JOHN, Wholesale Dealer in Liquors,Cigars and Fine Groceries, and Proprietor National Theater, e s Sycamore b. 3d and 4th
Bates John S, 79 Providence
BATES Joshua H, (B. & Scarborough) h. e. Walnut Hills
Bates Lizzie, 429 Broadway
Bates Sarah, bk. binder, bds. 296 W. 5th
BATES & SCARBOROUGH, (Joshua H. B. & Wm. S S) Attorneys at Law, Room 58 W. 3d
Bath Francis, cooper, 38 Findlay
Bathelor Mary, 184 W. Court

BATHGATE CHARLES, Grocery and Spice Mills, 242 W. 6th

BATHGATE JAMES, Family Grocery and Provisions, 67 W. Court, h. 264 W. 6th
Bathgate Richard. grocer. 201 W. 6th

BATHIANY RUDOLPH, Coffee House and Billiard Saloon, 475 and 477 Walnut
Batline Albert dray, n.s. Front b. Lawrence and Pike
Batsche Frank, saloon, n.e.c. Smith and Water
Dattel Joseph, 308 Main
Battel Rachinel, e.s. Carl b. 3d 4th and Mill and Stone
Batter Dietrich, shoe mkr., 9 Buckeye
Batter John T., grocery, 204 Linn
Battersby Mary. 538 W. 8th
Bottey Ellen, 69 E. 8th e. of Lock
Battles James, 310 W. 7th
Battles William, lab., 312 W. 7th
Battle Daniel, huckster, 210 W. 6th
Battles Jennie. bds. s e c. 6th and Smith
Butty Wm., molder, 636 W. 6th
Batzsch Chas. Win., cap mkr., 540 Race
Bauer Adam, lab. 76 Buckeye

BAUER ADOLPHUS A., Physician,
Office and res. 744 Race
Bauer Adolph, tailor, 121 Ham Road
Bauer August, printer, 16 Jackson
Bauer Catharine. peddler, 165 Carr
Bauer Casper, paper carrier, 309 Cutter
Bauer Charles, baker, wks 63 Bremen
Bauer Christian. shoe mkr., 71 Green
Bauer Conrad, cof. h , 133 Ham. Road
Bauer Conrad, shoe mkr., 15 Abigail
Bauer F., lab., wks. 335 Broadway
Bauer Francis. mason, 19 Green
Bauer Frank, bk. mkr., 910 Central Av.
Bauer Frank, trimmer, 127 Clay
Bauer Frederick, cooper, s.e.c. Elm and Findlay
Bauer Geo., blk. smith, 540 Race
Bauer Geo., cooper. wks. G. Bricka's
Bauer George, lab., 986 Central Av.
Bauer Geo., tailor, 537 Walnut
Bauer Gottfried, grocery, 73 Peeto
Bauer Gustavus A., clk. P. O., h. 344 Race
Bauer Hans, carriage trimmer, 127 Clay
Bauer Jacob, cof. h , s.e.c. Pearl and Pike
Bauer Jacob, stone mason, 165 W. Liberty
Bauer John, w.s. Vine b. Milk and Mulberry
Bauer John, bk. mkr., 116 Carr
Bauer John, clk., 550 Walnut
Bauer John, cof. h., 29 W. Front
Bauer John, cof. h., 187 Ham. Road
Bauer John, express driver. 622 Vine
Bauer John, lab., 14 W. Mulberry
Bauer John, lab., 584 Plum
Bauer John, tailor, 172 Ham Road
Bauer John, tailor, 168 Hopkins

JOHN JOHNSTON. JAMES M. JOHNSTON.

J. & J. M. JOHNSTON,
LUMBER DEALERS,
Corner of Third and White Water Canal.

We have constantly on hand a large and general assortment of

PINE, POPLAR, WALNUT AND CHERRY LUMBER,

Also, FLOORING, WEATHERBOARDING, SHINGLES, LATH, SCANTLING, JOIST, &C.

Orders left at our ICE CHEST & PACKING BOX FACTORY, 219 and 221 West Third Street, promptly attended to.

JOHN JOHNSTON. JAMES M. JOHNSTON.

J. & J. M. JOHNSTON,

Nos. 219 and 221 WEST THIRD STREET, CINCINNATI, OHIO,

MANUFACTURE BY STEAM POWER

MAISH'S PATENT REFRIGERATOR,

ICE CHESTS, BATH TUBS, PACKING BOXES, &C.

A liberal discount to Dealers in Refrigerators. Also, a general assortment of LUMBER,— Pine, Poplar, Walnut and Cherry, Weatherboarding, Flooring, Shingles, Lath, &c.

JETHRO MITCHELL. T. C. ROWLAND.

MITCHELL & ROWLAND,
DEALERS IN
LUMBER, LATH, SHINGLES AND SAWED TIMBER,

No. 522 VINE STREET, CINCINNATI, O.

OHIO RIVER SALT COMPANY,
MANUFACTURERS OF
COMMON FINE, AND SUPERIOR DAIRY AND TABLE SALT.

W. A. HEALY, Sole Agent.

Stores, Nos. 27 West Front Street, and 61 West Canal St., Cincinnati, O.

All kinds of Country Produce and Provisions received in exchange for salt.

THEODORE DREIDEL,
MANUFACTURER OF
ESSENCE AND GROUND COFFEE,

Indigo, Prussian and Wash Blue, Stove Polish and British Lustre,

No. 10 North Providence Street,   CINCINNATI, O.

(BAU) CINCINNATI (BEA) DIRECTORY. (BEC) 55

Bauer John B., stone mason, 607 Race
Bauer John M., cooper, 715 Race
Bauer Joseph, boiler mkr., 20 Ham. Road
Bauer Joseph, lab., e.s. Young b. Ringgold and Channing
BAUER Leonard, (Beck & B.) 57 Harrison Pike
Bauer Louis, baker, 160 Ham Road
Bauer Michael, cab. mkr., 119 Providence
Bauer Michael, lab., 57 Hamer
Bauer Ulrich, cof. h., 347 Walnut
Bauer Robert, clk., 71 Green
Bauer Valentine, lab., 57 Bremen
Bauer Valentine, stone cutter, 709 Central Av.
Bauer Wm., carriage painter, n.e.c. Hughs and Schiller
Bauerem Geo., 207 Clinton
Bauerfeld Charles, cof. h., n.e.c. Harrison Pike and Spring Grove Av.
Bauersfelt Chas., cab. mkr., 214 Laurel
Baughman Isaac, b.k., 4 Pub. Landing, h. Newport
Baughman Jacob, painter, 51 Webster
Bauhtman Hy., cab. mkr., 194 Clark
Bauknecht Frank. cof h., 68 13th
Bauland Hy., lab, 29 Hannibal
Bauling Christopher, box mkr., 23 Pierson
Bauling Geo., cab. mkr., 192 Clinton
Baum Catharine, 503 Vine
Baum Esther, 30 E 5th
Baum Geo., carriage smith, 558 Vine
Baum Geo., cooper, 1001 Central Av.
Baum Geo. W., molder, 173 E. Front
Baum Hy., mach., bds. 158 W. Front
Baum Hermann, lab., 141 Abigail
Baum John, bk. smith, 7 Bank
BAUM JOHN C., Postmaster; office, s w.c. 4th and Vine, and Manufacturer of Prussiate of Potash, e.s. Canal b. Findlay and Ham. Road, h. 53 Dunlap
Baum Joseph, clk., bds. 349 W 6th
Baum Louis, peddler, 569 Central Av.
Baum Mrs. Louisa, bds. 173 E. Front
Bauman Alfred W., h. 91 W. 5th
Bauman Andrew, carp., 7 E. 3d e. of Parsons
Bauman Edward, lab., 144 E. Front
Bauman Frederick C., paper carrier, 531 Walnut
Bauman Geo., teacher, 206 Linn
Bauman John, cof. and b. h., 74 E. Pearl
Bauman Louis, clk., w.s. Lawrence b. 2d and Pearl
Bauman Michael, stone mason, n.s. Nassau b Broad and Waldon
Baumann Anthony, carp., 7 High
Baumann Catharine, 1 Mary
Baumann Charles, foreman. 161 W. 3d
Baumann John A., driver, 140 Bremen
Baumann John G., bds. 680 Vine
Baumann Louis, (M. H. Lewis & Co.) 3 Lawrence
Baumbush Charles. carp., 24 Charlotte
Baumeister Bernard, varnisher, 649 Central Av.
Baumeister Wm., clk., 114 13th
Baumer Barney, tailor, 51 Peete
Baumer Christ, cigar mkr., 1 Mary
Baumer Engelger, shoe mkr., 378 Broadway
Baumer Hy., cutter, 67 Green
Baumer Hermann, shoe mkr., 300 W. 8th
Baumer Joseph, lab., 67 Spring
Baumer Theo. W., feed store, s w.c. Findlay and Central Av
Baumgard Damian, lab., 366 Race
Baumgardner Jacob, butcher, 700 Elm
Baumgardner John, lab., e.s. Young b. Ringgold and Channing
Baumgardner Joseph, cooper, 416 Longworth
Baumgardner Louisa, 6 Providence
Baumgarten Martin, cooper, wks. 543 W. 3d
Baumgarten Simon, peddler, 47 Clinton
Baumgarten Wm., clk., 359 Race
Baumgartner J. & Co., (Joseph B. & Francis Jacob) millinery, 592 Vine
Baumgartner Jacob, meat store, 626 Race

Baumgartner Joseph, (J. B. & Co.) 592 Vine
Baumgartner Leonard, mate, w.s. Lawrence b. 2d and Pearl
Baumgratz John, tailor, 109 Buckeye
Baumkamp Hy., lab, e.s. Front e. of Kelly
Baur Adolphus, printer, 16 Jackson
Baur Casper, lab., 801 W. Front
Baur Theodore, clk., C. F. Adae & Co., h. 79 Milton
Baurean Thomas, grainer, 37 Barr
Baurittel Wm. Henry, phys., 42 12th
Baursfeld Frederick, bedstead factory, 23 Harrison
Baus Joseph, white washer, 22 E. Liberty
Baute Ann, servt., 102 Abigail
Baute Eliza, seamstress, 102 Abigail
Baute Frank, lab., 102 Abigail
Baute Hy., lab., 13 Peete
Baute John H., cooper, 55 Buckeye
Baute Wm., jr., tailor, 102 Abigail
Bavenger John, carp., wks. n.e.c. Canal and Walnut
Baxter David, carp., 142 E. 3d e. of Colllard
Baxter Dennis, eng., bds. 10 Sycamore
Baxter Hiram J., driver, e s. Ludlow b. Pearl and 3d
Baxter John, carp., 590 W. 6th
Baxter John, lab., n.w.c. 7th and Plum
Baxter John, saddler, 4 North
Baxter Mary, 29 E. Liberty
Baxter Mary Ann, s s. L'Hommedieu al. b. Central Av. and John
Baxter Sarah, 281 Longworth
Baxter W. D., 962 Race
Bay Christian, 3 Mulberry
Bay Geo., blk. smith, n.e.c. Front and Foster
Bay Michael, cooper, 597 Sycamore
Bayens Joseph, painter, 17 15th b. Elm and Plum
Bayer Jacob, phy., 58 14th
Bayer Martin, shoe mkr., e.s. Vine nr. Liberty
Bayer Mary, teacher, 383 Vine
Beyersdoerfer John, cof. h., 640 Vine
Bayland Hy., cooper. 67 Dayton
Bayles Stephen A., driver, 780 E. Front
Baylis Samuel, (J. L. Ruffin & Co.) 404 W. 4th
Baynes John H., agt. bone-dust manuf., 244 Clark
Baynes Joseph, carver, bds. 206 Linn
Baynum Edward, eng., n.s. Front e. of Washington
Bazing Thomas, distiller, 24 Rittenhouse
Bazlie John J., tailor, 225 W. Front
Bazuden Hy., 100 Everett
Beach Albert D, student, bds. 318 Clark
Beach Andrew S., jeweler, bds. 54 Broadway
Beach Joseph, carriage mkr., bds. 203 Elm
Beach Julia, 8 Home
Beach Richard, jeweler, wks. 6 W. 4th
Beach Sarah M., 54 Lock
Beach Wm., b.k., 44 Elizabeth
Beadford Ann, servt., 170 Broadway
Beadle Geo. W., painter, bds. 53 E. 3d
Beadle John, cab. mkr., 181 Laurel
Beagle Jacob, lab., wks. w.s. Lock b. 4th and 5th
Beahn Andrew, driver, 98 Pike
Beahr Jacob J., salesman, 53 W. 4th, bds. 92 Perry
Beahring Wm., clk., 494 W. 5th
Beal John, carp., 603 Elm
Beal R. & Co., (Richard B. & Nicholas D. Redhead) druggists, n.e.c. Freeman and Everett
Beal Richard, (R. B. & Co.) bds. 442 Freeman
Bealage Herman, cooper. 71 Abigail
Beale Chas., driver, wks. s.e.c. Grant and Plum
Bealer Cornelius, liquor dealer, 18 Broadway
Bealink John, sawyer, 454 W. Liberty
Beall Charles, bds. 333 Cutter
Beall George H., clk., 359 George
Beall John, s.e.c. Broadway and Milton
Beall Joseph, carp, 321 George
BEALL Peter, (Graveson & Co.) res. Newport

Beall Theodore, plasterer, bds. 487 W. 7th
Beall Wm. B., hatter, 487 W. 7th
Beals James W., millwright, 794 E. Front
Beals Wm., foreman, n.e.c. Park and Marsh, h. 65 Avery
Beam Alexander, 988 E. Front
Beam Lycurgus, carp., n.s. Goodloe b. Willow and Niagara
Beam Margaret, 988 E. Front
Be m Wm., carp., 988 E. Front
Beaman Fred., dray, w.s. Harriet b. 6th and Sloo
Beaman Wm. H., trunk mkr., 31 Broadway, h. Covington
Bean Anna, 40 Race
Bean Dabney J., printer, 136 Vine, h. s. e.c. 6th and John
Bear Charles, butcher, 50 Findlay
Bear Wm., s.e.c. 2d and Whittaker
Beard Gabriel H. blk.smith, 213 W. 2d
Beard Jacob, clk., bds. 22 Perry
Beard James C., prin. Cin. Art Academy, s w.c. 4th and Walnut, h. Covington
Beard James H., artist, 6 Carlisle Bldg., res. Covington
Beard John H., clk. 49 W. 4th, h. 303 W. 4th
Beard T. Frank, student, s.w.c. 4th and Walnut, h. Covington
Beard Wm. A., clk., 42 Jackson
Beard Wm. Allen. b.k., 51 Jackson
Beardsley Flint, printer, n.e.c. 3d and Sycamore
Beardwell Walter, printer, 140 W. 3d, h. 196 W. 7th
Bears John R. G., cutter, 95 W. Court w. of Central Av.
Bearly George carp., s.s. Clinton b. Linn and Baymiller, h. 192 Everett
Beasley Wm. A., printer, 345 Longworth
Beaton Robert, millinery, 144 W. 5th
Beats Jane, trimmer, 186 W. 9th
Beattie James M., clk. w.s. Central Av. b Court and Elizabeth
BEATTIE JOHN, Commission Merchant, 51 and 53 W. Front, h. 170 Longworth
BEATTIE JOHN & CO., (John B. & Peter Andrew) Maltsters, s.s. Front e of Water Works
BEATTIE John H., (Carter & B.) and Not. Pub., 63 Clinton
Beattie Ruth, al. b. Central Av. and John and Augusta and Front
Beattie Wm., carp, 1205 E. Front
Beatton Louisa, n.w.c. Broadway and 6th
Beatty Chas. H., printer, bds. s.e.c. Plum and 5th
Beatty J. F., printer, bds. s.e.c. Plum and 5th
BEATTY James, (James B. & Co.) res. Jones' Station, C. H. & D R. R.
BEATTY JAMES & CO..(James B. & Geo. W. Trowbridge) Pork Packers and Commission Merchants, s.w.c. Race and Miami Canal
Beatty Mary, 71 E. 8th
Beatus Hy., dealer in watches, clocks and jewelry, 78 Main, h. 325 George
Beaty C. H., printer, bds. 192 Plum
Beaty J. H., printer. bds. 162 Plum
Beauchamp Jane, 161 Longworth
Beaugrand Louis, saloon, 58 E. 5th
Beaugureau Philibert, artist, 358 Freeman
Beaumont Wm., clk., 131 Central Av.
Benver Hy., 193 Everett
Beazell Jasher, b.k, 7 College Building, res. Pendleton
Bebb David O., b k. 29 W. Pearl, h. 91 Darr
Bechdel Louis, lab., 142 Clay
Becheer Frederick, carp., 47 Observatory
Becher Hy., tailor, n.w.c. 15th and Elm
Bechert Philip, lab., 69 Buckeye
Bechler Jacob, 22 Allison
Bechler Jacob, mason, 26 Peete
Bechler Lena. servt., 422 Monroe
Bechmann Chas V., clk., Co. Recorder's Office, h. 544 Elm
Bechmann Frederick W., moldings, 261 Ham. Road

CINCINNATI ADVERTISEMENTS.

BRODFUEHRER & BROTHER,
FASHIONABLE BOOT AND SHOE MAKERS,
No. 52 WEST SIXTH STREET,
North Side, bet. Walnut and Vine.   CINCINNATI, OHIO.

Constantly on hand, a large assortment of French Calf Skin Boots and Shoes, also Patent Leather Congress Boots and Oxford Ties, and will make the same to order at the shortest notice.

JOHN W. GOSLING,
CARRIAGE MANUFACTURER,
Corner Sixth and Sycamore Sts., Cincinnati, O.

HOLSTEIN & HAMMER,
MANUFACTURERS OF
Serpentine, Gothic and other
MOULDINGS IN ALL KINDS OF WOOD,
ALSO OF
OVAL LOOKING GLASS FRAMES,
No. 31 Smith, corner Augusta Street, Cincinnati, O.

H. CUMMINGS & BERNE,
PLAIN AND ORNAMENTAL
HOUSE AND SIGN
PAINTERS,
North East Corner Race and Third Streets,   CINCINNATI, O.

Fresco and Kalsomine Painting, in all their various branches; Imitations of Woods and Marbles, Plain, Ornamental and Stained Glass Damask, Tapestry, and Morocco. Specimens of each may be seen by calling at the store. Wall Painting in Oil, Turpentine, and other Composition Colors. Paints, Oils and Glass constantly on hand and for sale. Block Letters Cut to Order.

CINCINNATI (BEC) DIRECTORY. (BEE) 57

Becker Clemens, tailor, 5 Wade. b. Elm and Plum
Becker Edward. butcher, e.s. Gamble al. between Melancthon and Liberty
Becker Edward, horse shoer, 91 E. Front, h. Newport
Becker Elizabeth candy store. 66 14th
Becker Ernst, cab. mkr., bds. 65 W. 5th
Becker Ferdinand, clothing, 3 Sycamore, bds 4 Sycamore
Brcker Francis, carp., 519 Race
Becker Francis, shoemkr., 161 Pleasant
Becker Frank, lab., 478 Walnut
Becker Fred., cooper. 113 Ham. Road
Becker Fred., ment store, 87 Bremen
Becker George, carp, 256 Walnut
Becker Geo., clothing, 97 E. 2d
Becker Geo, molder, 87 Bremen
Becker Gertrude 320 Longworth
Becker Hans, gilder, 5 2 Main
Becker Harmon, painter, 519 Elm
Becker Heinrich, finisher, wks. s.w.c. Elm and Front
Becker Hy., cab. mkr., 411 Sycamore
Becker Hy., cigar mkr., 53 Woodward
Becker Hy., painter, 118 Clay
Becker Hy. G., lab., 35 Buckeye
Becker Jacob, barber 4 Sycamore
Becker Jacob, cof. h., 634 Race
Becker Jacob B., lab., wks. 438 Main
Becker John, 47 Allison
Becker John, cof. h., 596 Vine
Becker John, gilder, bds. 532 Main.
Becker John C., painter. 111 Ham. Road
Becker John F., tailor, 26 Mulberry
Becker Joseph. caudle mkr., 124 W. Liberty
Becker Joseph, carriage smith, 15 Mary
Becker Joseph, cof. h., 7 Buckeye
Becker Joseph, shoe mkr., 179 Barr
Becker Leonhard, lab., 123 W. Liberty
Becker Lewis, butcher, s.e.c. Clark and Baymiller
Becker Lewis, mason, 63 Ham. Road
Becker Mary C., 66 W. Liberty
Becker Matthew, tailor, 27 E. Liberty
Becker Nicholas, millinery, 122 W. 5th
Becker Peter A., n.s. Thuber al. b. Wade and Adams
Becker Philip, candy mkr., 168 W. 5th
Becker Rosy, 1 Mary
Becker Sebastian, lab., 18 Hamer
Becker Simon, boots and shoes, 42 Pike
Becker Sybilla, 81 Bremen
Becker & Tebelman. (Christian F. B. & John T.) cigars and tobacco, 148 Walnut
Becker Theodore, fresco painter, bds. 532
Becker Theodore, currier, 12 Jackson
Becker Valentine, carriage painter, 81 Bremen
Becker Valentine, teacher, 540 Race
Becker Victor, lab., 71 Hughes
Becker Wm., cab. mkr., n.s. L'Hommedieu al. h. Central av. cnd John, h. 71 David
Becker Wm., mason, 7 Wade, b. Elm and Plum
Beckers Hy., clk., 60 E. Pearl, h. 74 E Pearl
Becket Arthur, h. 236 W. 9th
Becket Frank J., gardener, Denman, b. Kenner and Flint
Becket Geo., carp., s.s. 6th, b. Main and Sycamore. h 256 Walnut
Beckett Arthur, plumber. 321 Vine
Beckett Ellen, actress, National Theatre
Beckett Susan, actress, National Theater
Beckhaus John, wagon mkr., wks. 109 Hunt
Beckhaus Wm., tailor, 149 Bank
Beckhouse Barney, 50 Pleasant
Beckler Benjamin, lab., 245 Linn
Beckler George L., lab., 584 Plum
Beckler Ioseph. tinner 14 E. 6th
Beckler Michael, 15 E. 6th
Beckler S., stone mason, 15 E. 6th
BECKLEY Jesse, (Jesse D. & Co.,) 265 W. 3d
BECKLEY, JESSE & CO., Fire and Water Proof, Asphaltum Cement Roofing, 110 W. Pearl
Beckley Michael, 286 Main
Beckley Wm., huckster, 134 W. 3d
Beckman A. H., sawyer, wks. 304 Broadway

Beckman Barbara. servt., 365 W. 8th
Beckman Chas, tin shop, 535 W. 6th
Beckman Frederick, tinner, 103 Everett
Beckman Harmen, lab., 43 Elm
Beckman Hy., clk., 292 Main
Beckman Hy., cof. h. s.w.c. Broadway and Hunt
Beckman Hy., lab., 170 Everett
Beckman Hy., stoves and tin ware, 109 Everett
Beckman Hy., wagon makr., 43 Elm
Beckman Herman, tailor, 607 W. Front
Beckman John, shoe mkr., wks. 83 E. Pearl
Beckman John H., boots and shoes, n.w. c. Wade and Baymiller
Beckman Joseph, driver, 43 Elm
Beckman Joseph, lab., al. b 13th and Mercer. and Vine and Walnut
BECKMAN S. E., Agent American Whip Co. Also, Manufacturer and Dealer in Foreign and Domestic Cigars, 17 E. 2d
Beckman Adam, lab., s.e.c. Brighton and Harrison Pike
Beckmann Anthony, tailor, n.w.c. Abigail and Pendleton
Beckmann August, stoves and tin-ware, 571 Race
Beckmann Bernhard, finisher, 80 Pendleton
Beckmann Caroline, servt,, 273 Richmond
BECKMANN GEORGE H., Family Grocery, 458 W. 3d
Beckmann Gerhard, stone cutter, 22 Mansfield
Beckmann Theodore, boots and shoes, 615 Race
Beckmann Henry, blk smith, 50 Pleasant
Beckmann Hy., driver, wks 450 Walnut
Beckmann Hy., grocery, 106 Clay
Beckmann Hy., lab., 15 Abigail
Beckmann Hy., lab, 103 Clay
Beckmann Hy., shoe mkr., 17 Green
Beckmann Herman, lab, 608 Elm
Beckmann Herman, lab., 393 Broadway
Beckmann John, shoemkr., 374 Broadway
Beckmann John H., cof. h., 109 E. 2d
Beckmann John H., salesman, n.e.c. Milton and Sycamore
Beckmann Joseph, tailor, 106 Abigail
Beckmann Reinhard, cigar mkr., 17 Clinton
Beckmann Wm. C., upholster, 49 Betts
Beckroege Henry, lab., 53 Hughes
Becksmith Frank. cof. h., 169 W. 5th
Becksmith Hy., cof. h. and White Hall, s.w.c. 9th and Broadway
Becktel Geo., corp., h. 114 Clay
Beckvermart George, lab., 158 E. 5th
Beckwerment Herman, dray., 114 Butler
Bectee John B., turner, bds. s.w.c. Pearl and Ludlow
Bedar John, huckster, 96 Clay
Bedding Gustave. brewer. 64 Dunlap
Bedel Jacob, carp., 123 Ham. Road
Bedel John. cab. mkr., 181 Laurel
Bedel Thomas, bakery. 342 Ham. Road
Bedenharn Hy., polisher, 100 Carr
Bedenzarn Harmer, polisher, n. e. c. Broadway and Hunt
Beders Eberhard, chair mkr., bds. 76 Spring
Bedford Erastus T., 335 Cutter
Bedgood Carroll. lab., n. e. Webb, b. Stone and Wood
Bedgood Martha, 19 Gest
Bedker Ann, n.e.c. Central Av. and Court
Bedmann Wm., tailor, wks. s.w.c. Plum and Longworth
Beebe Edward M., teamster, s.w.c. Laurel and John
Beebe Lorenzo, teamster, s.w.c. Laurel and John
Beebe Samuel, dray., 207 Hopkins
Beeber Max, 276 W. 4th
Beeche Fidel, 43 E. Front
Beecher James E., drawer, s.w c. 4th and Walnut, h. 90 Wade
Beeching John, clk., 171 W. Court w. of Central Av.

H. P. HOPKINS,

HOUSE, SIGN, AND ORNAMENTAL

PAINTER!

FLAGS, BANNERS,

PICTORIAL SIGNS

—AND—

GLASS GILDING.

183 VINE STREET,

CINCINNATI, O.

(BEH) CINCINNATI (BEL) DIRECTORY. (BEN) 59

Deegan John W., grocery, s.e.c. Plum and Longworth
Beehler Gottlieb, tanner, 50 Dunlap
Beehler John, 70 Peete
Bechler John, bar k, s. w. c. 7th and Main
Beehler John A., tanner, h. 642 Elm
Beel Francis, lab., h. 150 Pleasant
Beel John, carp., 75 Pendleton
Beeler John, blk. smith, 48 E. 3d
Beeler John A., tanner, 642 Elm
Beermann Frederick, cooper, wks., 39 Bremen
Beers Charles H., cof. h., 68 E. Pearl, b. 136 E. Liberty
Beesley Harry, b. k., Henry Nye's, b. 151 John
BEKSLEY JOHN W., Merchant Tailor, 105 Main, h. 151 John
Beeson R. S., salesman, 19 E. 2nd, b. 411 W. 8th
Beetson Wm., butcher, 62 Accommodation
Beevy Daniel, teamster, 174 W. Front
Degel Jacob, stone mason, 249 E. 5th
Begemann Caroline, 25 14th
Begemann Charles F. W., carriage painter, 25 14th
Begemann William, carriage painter, 25 14th
Begge August, lab., 99 Spring
Beggs Caroline, h. 14 Lock
Beggs J. P., n s. Coggswell nr. Auburn
Begham David, clk., s. w. c. 9th and and Race
Degley Patrick, lab., 301 John
Degrore Ily., lab., wks. s.e.c. 5th and Culvert
Beh Frederick, cab. mkr., 170 W. Liberty
Behel Catharine, 18 Mansfield
Behlan Charles, (Charles B. & Co.,) 17 Mary
Behlen Charles & Co., (Charles B. & Francis J. Erd,) carriage manuf., 578 Vine
Behle F. edrick, confec., 310 Linn
Behle Frederick, varnisher. 310 Linn
Behlen Geo., clk., bds. 74 W. Court
Behler Adam, cooper, 27 Brighton
Behler Frank L., shoemkr. 172 W. Front bds. e s. Front b. Elm and Plum
Behler Herman, cooper, 27 Brighton
Behler Joseph, e s. Campbell al. b. Elder and Liberty
Behm Fredericke, tailor, bds. 701 Elm
Behm Jacob, express, e.s. Ohio av. b. Corporation line and N. Elm
Behm Phillip, lab., e.s Ohio av. b Corporation line and N. Elm
Behmann Ily., tailor, 615 Race
Behmer August, boots and shoes, 40 E. 5th
Dehmer Ily., carp., 147 Clark
Behner Ily., cooper, 602 Main
Dehner John, cooper, 60 Elder
Dehner John, jr., cooper, 602 Main
Behning August, tailor, 25 Abigail
Behning Charles, tailor, rear 64 W. Mulberry
Behr Augustus, clk. in Clerk's Office U. S. Court, h. Vine St. Hill
Behr Nicholas, cab. mkr., 749 Race
Behren Henry W., stoves and tin ware, 537 Race
Behrens Bernhard, carp. 25 Franklin
Behrens Frederick, grocery, 33 E. 9th, e. of Lock
Behrens Hammond, clk., s.w.c. Broadway and New
Dehrens & Abernethy (Henry D. & Wm. A..) carps., s.s. Baker b. Walnut and Vine
Dehrens Henry, (B. & Abernethy,) 75 Melnenhton
Behrens Ily., lab., h. 19 Mulberry
Behrens John J., grocery, 102 Elder
Behrens Wm., cigar mkr., h. 692 Main
Dehrens Wm., tailor, h. e.s. Anderson, b. 2d and Pearl
Behring Frederick, mach., h. 90 Pleasant
Dehringer Ily., cigar mkr., 551 Vine
Behringer Ignatius, tailor. 506 Vine
Dehringer John, carp., 535 Walnut

Behrle Elizabeth, 620 Main
Behrle John, gilder, 6.0 Main
Behrle Lucas, painter, wks. Crane, Breed & Co's
Behrling Geo., cigar mkr., 195 Bremen
Dehrman Ily., tailor, 195 Everett
Behrmann Ily., tailor, 61 Bank
Behrmann John, barber, 107 W. Liberty
Behrmann John tailor, 107 W. Liberty
Behrman Margaret, 2 5 Bremen
B hrmann Michael, 78 Mohawk
Behrwinkle Henry, tailor, 301 Linn
Behse Charles, lab., 130 Ham. Road
Beidel Anna, 70 Rittenhouse
Beiderkellen Lewis, lab., 90 Pleasant
Reiderwelle Jo n H., lab., 36 Pleasant
Heier August, tanner, 34 Mulberry
Beier Bernhard, lab., 122 Abigail
Beierbaum Ily., mach., 172 Baymiller
Baierle Charles, butcher, w.s. Bremen b. Elder and Findlay
Beierlein Francis, grocery, 96 Bremen
Beierlein John, lab., 154 Ham. Road
Beierlein Michael, carpet weaver, 142 Buckeye
Beierlein Michael, jr., tailor, 142 Buckeye
Deigel Leonhard, lab., 8 Henry
Beigler Jacob, lab., s s. al. b. Clay and Main b. 12th and M. Canal
Beikers Ily., 72 E. Pearl
Beil George, lab., 11 Pendleton
Beil Joseph, cigars and tobacco, 108 Hunt
Beile Joseph, finisher, 11 Pendleton
Beiler John, 164 E. Front
Beimeier Joseph shoemkr. 112 Buckeye
Beinert Geo., painter, 96 Ham. Road
Beinhardt Magdelena, 167 W. Liberty
Beinhardt Martin, cigar mkr., 167 W. Liberty
Beinhardt Michael, cigar manuf., 167 W. Liberty
Beinker Wm., lab., 170 Everett
Beinstroh Henry, c oper, 24 Orchard
Beir Margaret, 55 Plum
Beis Frederick, shoemkr, 57 14th
Deiser Andrew, lab., 65 Oliver
Beiser Frederick, lab., 7 E. 3d, e of Parsons
Deiser John, cutter 471 Vine
Deising Frank, 502 Join
Beistmann Barney, lab., wks 97 E. 2d
Beiswinger Chas., shoemkr., 567 Sycamore
Beiswinger Chas., shoemkr., 571 Sycamore
Beiter Jacob, cab mkr, wks. 153 Everett
Beitmann Charles. leather and findings, 238 Main, h. 31 Milton
Beizer Louis, cab. mkr., n e.c. Liberty and Vine
Bekel Godfrey, cooper, s.w.c. Dayton and Linn
Beken Mrs. 130 Pleasant
Belcher George, teamster, 10 Carr
Belcher Thomas, fireman, wks. Gas Works
Belden H. S., bds. Dennison House
Beler James, driver, bds. Pennsylvania Hotel
Delfor Henry, bds. 086 Central Av.
Beling Hermann, cooper 167 Woodward
Belker Conrad, cooper, 768 Central Av.
BELKNAP BOYD P., Dentist, Office and residence 137 W. 4th.
Belknap Ily., teacher, 569 W. 9th
Belknap Henry P., carp, 569 W. 9th
Belknap Laura E., teacher, 569 W. 9th
Bell Mrs., huckster, w.s. Langdon al. b. 6th and 7th
Bell A., sawyer, wks. John Mitchell's
Bell Albert, carp., 328 W. 6th
Bell Charles, 146 Richmond
Bell Charles, painter, bds. Ludlow House
Bell Conrad, foreman Eggers & Co's., 3 8th Vine
Bell David B., carp, n s. 6th, e. of Lock
Bell Emma, bds. 476 W. 5th
Bell Ferdinand B., bk. layer, n.s. Taylor, b. Carr and Freeman
Bell Frank, dentist, 95 W. 7th
Bell George W., painter, 134 Clark
Bell George W., steam pipe fitter, n.s. 6th, e. of Lock

Bell George W., teamster, 619 Central Av.
Bell Henrietta, e.s. Mound b. Longworth and 5th
Bell J. B., bds. Burnet House
Bell James, harness mkr., 201 Broadway
Bell James, stone cutter, 32 Water
Bell James B., shoe dealer, 140 Richmond
Bell Jane, 232 W. 5th
Bell John, bk. layer, 158 Spring
Bell John, mach, 184 E Pearl
Bell John, mer., bds Madison House
Bell John E., deputy co. auditor, 446 W. 7th
Bell John W., s e.c. 3d and Walnut
Bell Joseph, finisher, 22 12th
Bell Joseph G., collar mkr., 89 Main, bds. F0 e. 5th
Bell Juliet, teacher, h 146 Richmond
Bell Mary, millinery. 232 W. 5th
Bell Mary A. E. teacher, 123 Elm
Bell Max tailor 161 Main, h. 67 W. 6th
BELL PETER, Attorney at Law, 10 Court House Building. res. Sharpsburg
Bell Robert M., blksmith, 32 Mound
Bell Samuel W. 164 Poplar
Bell Silver, cab. mkr. 135 Bremen
Bell Thomas, horse shoer, 152 W. Court
Bell Wm. dray, 74 Rittenhouse
Bell Wm. L. saw mkr. 28 Rittenhouse
Bellamy Mary, 247 Cutter
Belle James B. boots and shoes, s.w.c. Barr and Linn, h. 140 Richmond
Belle Lewis B. teamster, 211 Wade
Belleden Francis J. grocery, 95 E. 5th
Bellenger John P. conductor, bds. 575 W 5th
Beller Geo. cab. mkr. 24 Mansfield
Beller Jacob, porter, 14 E. 2d, h. 57 Everett
Bellfore Arthur, cooper, s.s, 8th b. Br'dway and Sycamore
Belliew John. blksmith. wks. s.s. 8th b. Main and Sycamore
Belliew Patrick, blksmith, s.s. 9th b. Sycamore and Main, h. w.s. Langdon al. b. 6th and 7th
Bellman E. coppersmith, 77 Spring
Bellmann Ily. lab. 176 Bremen
Bellows Wm. eng. w.s. Kilgour b. 3d and 4th
Bellows Wm. inspector and sealer of weights. 7 Pub. Landing, h. n.e.c. 6th and Plum
BELLOWS Wm H (Wilder, Robinson & Co.) 204 W 4th
Belman Ily. porter, 64 Walnut, h. 106 Bremen
BELMAN J. C., Local Editor, Daily Enquirer h. 164 Plum
Belmer Anna, 17 Madison
Beiser Chas C. clk. 102 W. 5th
Belsford R. L. baggage master, L. M. depot. bds. 22 Baum
Belsher Thomas, fireman, 441 W. 2d
Belt Sarah, 44 E 3d
Beltermann E. tailor, s.s. 12th b. Vine and Race
Belt r Edward, express, 98 Baymiller
Belvile Mrs. Amanda D. 124 Laurel
Belville James S. pipe man, 124 Laurel
Belzer Charles C. tailor, 5 Pleasant
Bemer Wm . watchman on firetower, s.s. 5th nr. Pike
Bemforde Bernhard, porter, 390 Broadway
Bemforde Ily. porter, 31 E. 7th
Bemis Warren B. clk. 32 W. 5th, bds. Dennison House
Bemsel John lab 43 Jones
Benard Jane, 36 W. 9th w. of Freeman
Benbridge Susan, 117 Broadway
Denckenstile Charles, clk. n.w.c. Harrison Pike and Spring Grove Av
Denckenstein Christian, gander, n.w.c. Harrison Pike and Spring Grove Av
Denckenstein's Garden, e. Harrison Av. and Spring Grove Av
Bender Anthony, lab. 145 W Liberty
Bender Francis X. saddler, 651 Vine
Bender George, cooper, Oehler al. b. Freeman and Garrard
Bender John, bakery, 461 Elm
Bender John, plow mkr. wks. 10 W. 7th

WELLS'
CINCINNATI TYPE FOUNDRY,

Where we Manufacture not only the

TYPES,

BUT THE

PRESSES, CASES, GALLEYS,

STANDS, CHASES,

Composing Sticks, Rules, Cuts, &c.

STEREOTYPING, ELECTROTYPING,

WOOD TYPE, PRINTERS' INKS, &C.

And as we make a manufacturer's profit on all, we can, and will, sell a better outfit for less Cash, than any establishment which makes only half of what it sells; and ours is the only one in the Union, manufacturing all these articles.

ESTIMATES

Of Cost of Material to print any Book, Newspaper or Job,

FURNISHED ON APPLICATION.

(BEN) CINCINNATI (BEN) DIRECTORY. (BER) 61

Bender Joseph, baker, bds. 176 W. Front
Bender Mary A, 133 York
Bender Peter, cof. h., 17 E. 8th
Bender Peter W., clk., 474 John
Bender Wm. cab. mkr. 114 W. Canal
Bender Wm., liquor mer., 474 John
Bender Wm., liquor and vinegar manuf. 582 Central Av
Bender Wm. tinner. al. b. Linn and Baymiller and Liberty and Wade
Dendorf August, plater, al. b. Vine and Walnut and 13th and Mercer
Bene Gerhard II., cutter, 64 14th
Bene Hy. G., tailor, 64 14th
Benedick Less, porter, 102 Butler
Benedict Abraham, peddler, 205 W. 6th
Benedict Alexander, carp., 427 W. 9th
Benedict Benjamin, cof. h. 222 Vine, h. n.e.c Court and Plum
Benedict Emanuel, 205 W 6th
Benedict Isaac, 218 W. Court
Benehaus George, lab. 52 McFarland
Beneke John. prop. Front St. House, 55 W. Front
Benge Frederick, cigar store, n w.c, Liberty and John
Bengel Geo., bakery, 69 Wade
Bengel Philip, bakery, 625 Vine
Benger Chas., lab. wks 315 Broadway
Beniam Alfred, b.k. Frey's hotel
Benhart Sarah, e.s. Western Av. b. Poplar and Findlay 'eve
Benhogen Joseph, cooper. bds. 27 Buckenighaus John, lab. 173 Clay
Benike Christian, blksmith, 448 Main
Beninger Jacob, 83 Cross
Beninger Jacob, n.w.c. Browne and Vernon al
Beninger Jacob, butcher, n.s. Corp. Line nr. Auburn
Benites Manuel, tailor, 301 W. 2d
Benjamin Bernhard, cof. h., 25 Providence
BENJAMIN & CO. (James B., Hugh McDonnald & James W. Riley.) Commission Merchants, 190 Walnut
Benjamin Elizabeth, 91 St. Clair
BENJAMIN James (B. & Co.) bds. Dennison House
BENJAMIN James (McDonnald & B.), h. Putnam, O
Benjamin Joseph, hat and cap store, 327 Central Av
Benke Diederick, lab. 293 Water
Benker Hy. lab. 323 Plum
Benkeser Leonhard, lab. 69 Buckeye
Benkner Pankraz, eng. n.e.c. Smith and Water
Benna Frank, lab , 135 Abigail
Bennaeyer Hy., Pavillion b. Observatory and 3d
Benne Frank, 135 Abigail
Benne Hy , 91 Clay
Bennedich Edward, cook, Frey's Hotel
Bennemyer Margaret, 24 13th
Benner Chas., bds. Cincinnati House
Benner Chas., jeweller, 26½ Broadway
Benner Jacob, meat store, 198 Linn
Benner Peter, 98 W. Liberty
Benniger Louis, butcher, 1902 Freeman
Benning Barney, lab , bds. 14 13th
Benning Chas., h.k., 441 Sycamore
Benninger Geo., butcher, Junction Walnut Hills and Reading Road
Benninger H., 16 E. Front
Benninger Wm., mach., wks. 222 E. Front
Benninghouse George, driver, h. 52 McFarland
BENNET Alonzo (Cunningham & B.) Newport, Ky
Bennet Jane, fruit store, 423 Sycamore
BENNETT August A., (B , Kittredge & Co.) bds. 335 Longworth
Bennett Benjamin T., clk., 142 W. 3d, h. 420 Freeman
Bennett Charles Edward, b.k., n.e.c. 2d and Walnut, bds. 167 Plum
Bennett Chas. H., bakery, 89 W. Court, h. 175 Laurel
Bennett Chauncey, pattern mkr. 466 W. 4th
BENNETT DEROBIGNE M., Drug Store, s.w.c. Chestnut and Central Av. h 21 Chestnut

Bennett F. C., adjuster, Ætna Ins. Co., 171 Vine, h. 299 Baymiller
Bennett Geo., eng., 93 Clay
BENNETT GEO S., Local Editor, Cin. Enquirer, h. 263 Everett
Bennett H. S., bds. Dennison House
BENNETT H. THORNTON, At Cincinnati Directory Office, 194 Walnut, h. n.w.c. Cabot and Bellevue. Newport
Bennett James, tinner, 30 Mound
Bennett James, tinner, 202 Livingston
Bennett James, tinner, n e.c. Betts and Cutter
Bennett John, lab., wks. Central Saw Mill, 17th ward
Bennett John, sawyer, n.w.c. Reed and Nassau
Bennett John H., carp., 479 Plum
Bennett June, 72 Laurel
BENNETT JOSEPH B., General Agent. Ætna Insurance Co.; Office 171 Vine, res Clifton
Bennett Lewis, huckster, 67 Wade
Bennett Maxwell, brk. mkr., Richmond h. Harriet and Mill Creek
Bennett Michael, brush mkr., n e c, Betts and Cutter
Bennett Michael, foreman, 107 Walnut
Bennett Morris, painter, 292 Elm
Bennett Robert, clk., 171 Vine, h. 67 Clinton
Bennett S. S., salesman. rooms Selves' bldg
Bennett Simon, mailer. bds. 37 Broadway
Bennett Smith. 167 Plum
Bennett Washington, molder, 90 Barr
Benoit Octave, traveling agt., 326 Main
Bens John, butcher, bds. 9 45th
Bens John, roller, 86 W. Front, h Covington
Bens John, tailor, 130 Pleasant
Bense James, printer, 165 Barr
Bensen John, dray. 37 York
Bensing Jacob, carp., w.s. Linn b. Dayton and York
Benson Benjamin W., eng., 500 W. 4th
Benson Mrs. E. J., 333 Vine
Bin o i Fr in 1 . c k., bd., 110 W, 6th
Benson John, molder, 455 W. 2d
Benson John P., clk., s.w.c. Broadway & 7th
Benson Mary, 455 W. 2d
Benson Wood, actor, bds. Clifton House
Bente Hy., grocer, s w.c. Wood and 5th
Bentel Lewis, fin sher. 102 Bremen
Bentel Wm., cof. h., 67 Elder
Benten Hermann, saddler, 652 Race
Benter Benj., britania worker, 38 Rittenhouse
Benter Wm., pewter wkr., 391 W. Liberty
Bentley Albert, lab. 359 Broadway
Bentley Edward, brush mkr., bds. 324 W. 6th
Bentley Edward, molder, 321 W. 6th
BENTLEY LEWIS P., Printer, Daily Press Office, res. Ludlow, Ky.
Bentley Milton, wh ite washer, 202 Betts
Bently Sarah, h. 51 W. 7th
Bently David, printer, n.w.c. 3d and Main
Benton Count. mach., 206 W. Court
Benton Daniel, lab , gas works
Benton Duritt L., toll gate keeper, gate no, 1. Carthage Road
Benton Hy., molder. s s. Hathaway b. Jane and Baymiller
Benton James, molder, wks, n.w.c. Plum and Wade
Benton John. finisher. wks. n.e.c. Walnut and Miami Canal
Benton Mary, 341 Central Av.
Bents Benjamin, driver, bds. n.e.c. Elm and Pearl
Bentz Simon, tailor, 1232 E. Front
Benus Christian, cooper. s.s. Schiller b. Hughes and Main, h. s.w.c. Milton and Sycamore
Benz Anton, carp., 89 Dank
Benz Charles, cooper, bds. s.w.c. Freeman and Liberty
Benz Francis, carp., 15 Bank
Benz Gottlieb K., shoe mkr., 135 Pleasant

Benz Philip, tailor, 253 E. Pearl e. of Broadway
Benzer Charles, boots and shoes, 437 Walnut
BENZIGER BROTHERS, Publishers, Book Sellers and Stationers, Catholic Institute, n.w.c. Vine and Longworth
BENZIGER J. N. Adelrich, (B. Brothers) 137 Race
Benziger Meinrath, lab., 640 Race
Benzing Al., n s. Dayton b. Western Av. and Coleman
Benzing Christopher, bds, n s. Dayton b. Western Av. and Coleman
Benzing Geo., painter, 24 15th
Deodker Theodore, cigar mkr , 319 John
Beorde Fred., watch mkr., 444 Sycamore
BEPLER Augustus, (Bepler & Co.) s. w.c. Denman and Ham. Road
Bepler Chas.. clk., 354 Main
BEPLER & CO., (Edward B. & Augustus Bepler) Bankers, and Publishers German Bank Note List, 314 Main
BEPLER Edward, (B. & Co.) 354 Main
Bepler Jacob, tanner, 474 Race
Ber John, tailor, s.w.c. Hughes and Schiller
Berberich Chas., umbrella mkr., 32 Hamer
Berberich Franz, huckster, 245 W. 6th
Berberich John, cof. h , n.w.c. Pearl and Kilgour
Berberich Peter, waiter, Galt House
Bercaw Amos H., clk. C. H. & D. R.R Depot, bds. 22 Hathaway
Berch John, tailor. al. b. Charlotte and Findlay and Plum and Central Av.
Bercke Chas., lab., 62 Hunt
Berckhemer Charles, mach., 610 Main
Berckley Christian, cab. mkr., 313 Cutter
Berckmeier Hy., saddler, bds. 519 Main
Berde Hy., blk smith, 170 Charlotte
Berde Joseph, lab., 52 Riddle
Berdeker Elizabeth, 113 Woodward
Berderkamp Hermann H., lab., 53 Pendleton
Berensen Hendricus, shoe mkr., w.s. Goose al. b. Green and Elder
Beresford Francis, slaughter house, junction Walnut Hills and Reading Road. h. n.s. Deer Creek Road
Beresford Francis. jr., 423 Sycamore
Beresford James D , lab., 318 Broadway
Beresford Richard, butcher, n.s. Deer Creek Road e. of Liberty
Beresford Samuel, butcher, 97 Dudley
Beresford Samuel, butcher, h. n.s. Deer Creek Road e. of Liberty
Berends Christian, printer 141 Main; bds. 401 Elm
Beremdsen John, shoe mkr., 457 Walnut
Berens Theodore J., grocery, s.w.c. Water and Plum
Berens Wm., cigar mkr., 622 Main
Berg Anton, lab., wks. Cincinnati Chemical Laboratory
Berg August. coppersmith. 134 W. Court
Berg Bernhard, s.w.c. Race and 3d
Berg John, huckster, 66 Pleasant
Berg Margaret, n.s. Browne w. of Ravine al.
Berg Phillip, dray, n.e.c. Abigail and Spring
Berga Joseph, 116 W. Front
Bergan John, lab., 11 Bedinger
Borgberrer Lawrence, finisher, 49 Observatory
Bergen Wm., lab., w.s. Miller, nr. 7th
Bergenoder Emanuel, butcher, n.s. Deer Creek Road e. of Liberty
BERGER ALEXANDER M., Medicinal Mineral Water, 128 W. 4th, h. 204 Elm
Berger August, lab., 33 Baum
Berger Franz Joseph, tailor, 512 Walnut
Berger Fritz, cartman, n.s. Taylor al. w. of Kilgour
Berger Geo., blk smith, 14 W. 13th
Berger Hy., driver 65 Hunt
Berger Hy., lab., 439 Plum
Berger Hermann H., boots and shoes, 61 E. 5th

D. HILLS & CO.   C. F. O'DRISCOLL.

STEREOTYPE
AND
ELECTROTYPE FOUNDRY

No. 141 MAIN STREET, - - CINCINNATI, O.

HILLS, O'DRISCOLL & CO.

STEREOTYPERS, ELECTROTYPERS

AND DEALERS IN

Type, and Printing Materials generally,

Leads, Cases, Galleys, Brass and Metal Rules, Quoins, Furniture, &c., &c., always on hand.

STEREOTYPING,

OF ALL KINDS.

Books, Music, Pamphlets & Jobs of every description,

Done at short notice and in the best manner.

ELECTROTYPING OF CUTS, JOBS, &C., &C.,

Done at short notice.

(BER) CINCINNATI (BER) DIRECTORY. (BES) 63

Berger Hy., lab., 31 Baum
BERGER JOHN,
  Cigars and Tobacco 223 Vine
  h. s.w.c. Buckeye and Poplar
Berger John, lab., wks. Henry Nye's
Berger John T., boots and shoes, 438 W. 5th
Berger Joseph, lab., 412 E. Front
Berger Leander, cigar mkr., s.w.c. Buckeye and Poplar
Berger Mathias, gardener, n.s. Poplar b. Western Av. and Mill Creek
Berger Meinrod, cigar manuf., 100 Buckeye
Berger Peter, pattern mkr., 109 W 2d
Borger Peter, teamster, 557 Walnut
Berger Stephen, carp., n.s. Charlotte b. Linn and Baymiller
Berger Victor, 30 Perry
Berger Wm., mach., 112 Abigail
Berger Wm., sawyer, 664 Sycamore
Bergfeld Hy., grocery, 93 Spring
Bengfeld Hy., (Munnig & B.) 93 Spring
Berghaus Barney, lab., 164 Clark
Berghauss Geo., blk.smith, bds. s.w.c. Bank and Whiteman
Herghnuss Gerhard, lab., 169 Oliver
Berghegger Geo., lab., 30 Jones
Berghold Francis, wire mkr., 34 Ham. Road
Bergi Frederick, lab., 12 Eden
Bergin James, lab., rear 14 Richmond
Berglohann Hy. J., blk.smith, 147 Pleasant
Bergman Benjamin, n.e.c. Smith and August
Bergman Hy., cab. mkr., wks. s.w.c. M. Canal and Elm
Bergmann Anna M. C., tailoress, 549 Main
Bergmann Francis, lab., 8 Buckeye
Bergmann Geo. A., lab., 67 W. Liberty
Bergmann Geo. A., lab., 594 Vine
Bergmann Hy., cigar mkr., 310 Cutter
Bergmann Hy., gardener, n.s. Corporation Line nr. Auburn
Bergmann Otto, lab., e.s. Hamburg b. Mohawk and Cross
Bergmann Peter, cooper, bds. 615 Main
Bergmann Wolfgang, lab., n.s. al. b. Poplar and Vine and Ham Road and Buckeye
Bergmeier Frederick, lab., 43 Race
Bergmeier John, bk layer, 55 Hughes
Bergmeyer Jacob, gardener, n.s. Corporation Line nr. Auburn
Berhans David, carp., 53 Clinton
Berheide Diana, 592 Race
Berhman John, cab. mkr., 149 Poplar
Berhrman Mrs., s e c. Clinton and Cutter
Bering Mary, servt., 30 W. 7th
Bering Rosanna, n.e.c. 2d and Broadway
Beringer Theresa, 180 Buckeye
Berkemeier Alexander, baker, 596 Main
Berkemer John, varnisher, h. 509 Elm
Berkenkemp Hy., teamster, 503 W. 8th
Berker Clemens, lab., 149 Abigail
Berker Fred., carp., 106 Hunt
Berkhofer Geo., carp., 72 Bremen
Berkin Antone, lab, 517 E. Front
Berkli Edward, molder, wks. n.e.c. M. Canal and Walnut
Berkmann John F., 5 Melanthon
Berkmeier George, finisher, s.e. c. Hoadly and Longworth
Berkmeier Hy., tailor, e s. Stone al. b. 5th and Longworth
Berlekamp Fred., 19 Bedinger
Berlekamp Hy., bk. molder, 57 Buckeye
Berle Reimond, printer, 533 Sycamore
Berleman Wm., tailor, 604 Race
Berlew W., tobacconist, bds. Madison House
Berler Jacob, 57 Everett
Berliner Sol., second hand store, s.e.c. Main and 6th, h 264 Main
Berliner Abram, clothing, 189 Broadway
Berliner Meyer, clk. 65 W. Pearl, h. 239 W. 7th
Berling Hy., boots and shoes, 682 Central Av.
Berling Hy., shoe mkr., 11 12th
Berling Hermann, cooper, 107 Woodward
Berling Hermann G., lab., 596 Race

Berling Hermann H., boots and shoes, 917 Central Av.
Berling Peter, cork mkr., 172 W. Court w. of Central Av.
Bermann David, clothing, 5 Bd'way, and 54 Pub. Landing, h. 98 W. Front.
Berman Wilhelm, blksmith, 193 Clark.
Bermker Bernhard, shoe mkr., 606 Race.
Bornacker Chas., harness mkr., bds. 36 E. 5th.
Bernard Arneen clk., 55 Jackson.
Bernard Christian, boots and shoes, 612 Vine.
Bernard Daniel, salesman, 194 Main, h. 492 W. 5th.
Bernard Ellen. 240 Hopkins.
Bernard Frederick. lab., 111 Browne.
Bernard Geo. H., baggage master, O. & M. R. R., h 13 Hathaway.
Bernard Nicholas L., prod. and com. mer., 59 W. Miami Canal, h. 197 W. 7th.
Bernbeck Frederick, finisher, 118 Bremen.
Bernbeck Frederick, mach., 15 Bremen.
Bernderf Andrew, lab., wks. n.e.c. Walnut and Canal.
Berndt Augusta, 78 W. Liberty.
Berndt Chas.] walter, Walnut St. House.
Berndt Ernst. blksmith, 159 Gamble.
Berndt J. bds. s.w.c. Race and 3d.
Berne Christian, porter, 15th District School.
Berne Elizabeth, 66 Barr.
Berne Elizabeth J., teacher, 66 Barr.
Berne Jacob, blksmith, 127 York.
Berne Jonathan J., ins. agt., 33 W. 3d, h. 66 Burr.
Berne Joseph J., painter, 66 Barr
BERNE Wm. J., (H. Cummings & B.,) 199 Poplar.
Berneng Bernard, lab., n.s. Rail Road e. of Vance.
Bernes Joseph, grocery, 369 W. 5th.
Berner Barney, cab. mkr., 304 Longworth.
Berner Frederick, finisher, 111 Brown.
Berner Jacob, finisher, s.w.c. Elm and 2d.
Bernet Frank, carriage mkr., 403 Broadway.
Berney Barney, wks, 1563 E. Front.
Bernhard Mrs. Bluemelein, bds. 505 Vine.
Bernhard Paul, lab., 101 Bremen.
Bernhardt Andrew, lab., e.s. Vine b. Milk and Mulberry.
Bernhardt Bernard, chandler, w.s. John b. Liberty and Oliver.
Bernhardt Jacob, molder, 16 Moore.
Bernhardt John, 101 Bremen
Beruhardt John, lab., wks. 728 Central Av.
Bernhardt John P., gardener, s s. Liberty b. Freemen and Ludlow.
Bernhardt Peter, shoe mkr., 587 Walnut.
Bernhardt John, shoe mkr., 553 Walnut.
Bernheim S., clk., h. 246 Walnut.
Bernheimer Zacharias, clk., 7 Race.
Berning Anthony Wm., boots and shoes, 7 Pleasant.
Berning Barney, (Grothe & B.,) 770 W. 6th.
Berning Benj., shoe mkr., bds. 361 W. 5th.
Berning Casper, boots and shoes, 364 W. 5th, h. 370 W. 5th.
Derning Hy., cigar mkr., s.e.c. Buckeye and Poplar.
Berning Hy, tailor, n.w.c. Hopkins and Baymiller.
Berning John, tailor. 924 Hopkins.
BERNINGHAUS RICHARD,
  Wholesale Manufac. Ink, Vinegar, Book Binding Varnish and Perfumery 13 Carr.
Dernreuther Ernst tanner. 61 Findlay.
Berns Bernhard, tailor, 111 Woodward.
Bernshorn John. lab., s.w.c. Freeman and Richmond.
Bernstein Ferdinand, clk., 174 Linn.
Bernstein Mrs. J. D., 174 Linn.
Bernstein Samuel, clk., 174 Linn.
Bernt Catharine, 16 E Mulberry.

Bernum, Chas., bk. dealer, bds. 206 W. 5th.
Berold Frederick, musician, 518 Main.
Derold Mary, 518 Main.
Berrell, Chas., (M. Bailey & Co.,) 112 Mill.
Berre Hy., huckster, 208 Laurel.
Berrelsheimer M., peddler, 91 Sycamore.
Berrigan James, hostler, s.e.c. Elm and Longworth.
Berrigan Patrick, lab., 236 E. 6th.
Berrigan Patrick jr., lab., 236 E. 6th
Berringer Frank X., boiler mkr., w.s Butler b. Pearl and Front.
Berringer Fred, boiler mkr., wks. Jones Evans & James.
Berringer Wm., teamster, w.s. Butler b. Pearl and Front.
Berry Augustus, watchman, 560 E. Front.
Berry Blufford, bar k., 64 B'dway.
Berry Eugene, Steward, 56 E. 7th.
Berry James, 48 Longworth.
Derry John, lime dealer, 600 Central Av.
Berry John C., baker, 121 W. Court w. of Central Av.
Berry Robt., s.e.c. 7th and Broadway.
Berry Thos., plasterer, 121 W. Court w. of Central Av.
Berry Thos. C., Clk. Co. clks. office 73 Betts.
Berry Wm. H., b. k., 77 Hopkins
Berry Willis H., lumber mer., 77 Hopkins.
Berschmann Chas., cab. mkr., 90 Pleasant.
Berseng John, driver, wks. 450 Walnut.
Bersicker Frederick, varnisher, s.s. Niles al. b. Main and Sycamore.
Derska John. lab . 149 Carr,
Bertel Hy., P. tailor. 57 Fountain.
Bertelsmann Wm., lab., 24 Buckye.
Bertelt Frank, shoe mkr., 179 Linn.
Bertenshaw James. tailor, 32 North.
Berter Bernhard, dray, e.s. Race b. 12th and 13th.
Berter Theodore. blksmith, 26 Green.
Berthmann John, lab., n.s. al. b. Canal and 13th, and Vine and Race.
Bertholf Sarah, 422 Broadway.
Bertken Richard, cof. h. 71 Sycamore.
Bertlen John, cooper, 264 Ham Road.
Bertling Adolphus, tanner, 23 Dunlap.
Bertling Ernst, jewelry 426 Walnut.
Bertling Hy., clk., 426 Walnut.
Ber ling John, dyer, bds 19 Abigail.
Bertling, John, lab., s s Montgomery Turnpike nr. Reading Road.
Bertling Matthew, grocery, 706 Central Av.
BERTRAM Alex F., (B. & Co.,) 88 E. 4th.
Bertram Benjamin, bakery, 522 Race.
BERTRAM & CO.
  (Alex. F. B. & Co.) Coal Yard, 197 E. Front.
Bertram Hy., tool mkr., wks. 8 Main.
Bertram Peter, dray, s.w. E. 3d b Butler and Canal.
Bertsch Frederick, lithographer, h. 542 Race
Bertschinger Chas., gardener, h. s.e.c. Pearl and Pike.
Berty Joseph, dray, 58 W. 6th.
Berz Chas., wine dealer, 101 Clinton.
Bescheker Margaret, 63 W. Front.
Beacher Antony, (Reinstelter & D.) s.w.c. Race and 2d.
Bescher Philip, carp., 436 Linn.
Berclier Philip, salesman, 140 Main, h. 436 Linn.
Beschman Theodore, molder, 522 Race.
Beseck Jacob, gilder, bds. 79 Peets.
Besegar Louisa, servt. 757 W. 7th.
Besing Christian, bk. binder, 501 Main.
Besing Thos., lithographer, wks. 64 W. 4th.
Bessardt Mrs. M., 64 Kossuth.
Besson Franklin B., shoe mkr. 387 W. 2d.
Best Adam, cooper, 277 Ham. Road.
Best John, cooper 723 Race.
Best Joseph. 717 Elm.

CINCINNATI ADVERTISEMENTS

W. F. & V. WHITNEY,
(SUCCESSORS TO TAFT, WISE & CO.,)

Dealers in Lumber, Shingles & Lath.

Constantly on hand, Flooring,

SASH, BLINDS & DOORS.

YARD AND OFFICE,

Cor. Central Avenue & Laurel Sts. Cincinnati.

ANDREW A. EYSTER,
Importer, Wholesale & Retail Dealer in

CLOCKS, WATCHES,

Jewelry, &c.

Nos. 271 & 341 Central Avenue,

CINCINNATI, OHIO.

D. B. PIERSON.   R. M'CULLOUGH.

DANIEL B. PIERSON & CO.,

LUMBER DEALERS,

Keep constantly on hand all kinds of Pine Lumber, for Building, purposes. Flooring, Joist, Shingles, &c.

381 Plum St., at Elbow Miami Canal,

CINCINNATI, O.

ADAM EPPLY,
WHOLESALE DEALER IN

EMBROIDERIES,

Dress and Coat Trimmings,

Millinery Goods, Notions, &c.,

No. 20 PEARL STREET,

Between Main and Walnut Streets,

CINCINNATI.

WM. PEARE & H. WINTER,
SUCCESSORS TO CONWELL & GAITHER,

PLUMBERS,

PUMP & HYDRANT MAKERS,

No. 296 West Sixth Street,

CINCINNATI, O.

Baths, Water Closets, &c.

☞ Orders from the Country promptly attended to.

A. C.
WHOLESALE A

READY-MA

No. 194 MAIN ST.

Opposite A

CINC

T. H. WEASNER.

T. H. WE

DEALERS

BUILDIN

371 PLU

CINCIN

C. CURRY

PAPER

NO. 85 M

ONE DOOR

CINCIN

FRENCH BURR M
Genuine Dutch Ant
numbers, Mill Castings,
Damsel Irons, Tempering
chines. Portable Mills, al
BRADFORD & CO., Offi
2d Street, bet. Race and

C. W. C.

DEALER

Office & Wood Yard 115

UNION HOTEL
Sts., (261 W. 5th St
Travellers and Boarder
modations.
☞ Boarders by the m

HENRY MARTIN.

H. & C.

TANNERS & L

No. 694 Elm Street,

M. D.

Manufacturer of Hard
of every description. P
Rags, &c. No. 2 College
Fourth and Fifth, opp. Gi

Best Richard, carp., 279 Cutter.
Best Wm., 223 Betts.
Beste Christian, upholsterer, n.s. Kilgour b. 3d and 5th.
Beste Hy. A., china, 538 Main.
Bestermann Barney, conductor, 448 E. Front.
Bestermann Hy., watchman, 450 E. Front.
Besuden Frederick, b. k. 93 Walnut, b. 109 Everett.
BESUDEN HENRY, Dealer in all kinds of Leaf Tobacco, 93 Walnut. h. E. Walnut Hills.
BESUDEN HERMAN, Eating Saloon 59 E. Pearl, h. 471 Elm.
Betchen Frederick, turner, 11 15th b. Elm and Plum.
Betel Joseph, matress mkr., 16 Hamer.
Betenhon Wm., blksmith, wks. n e.c. Walnut and Canal.
Bethel Chapel, 30 Pub. Landing.
Betker Theodore, cigar mkr , 349 John.
Betling Peter, brewer, s.s. Montgomery Turnpike near Reading Road.
Betlinger, Mathias, pattern mkr. 14 Milton.
Betner Catharine, h. 674 Central Av.
Bets Maria, 742 W. 6th.
Betscher Caspar, phys., 65ª Vine.
Bettigheimer Frank, ice mer., 11 Jackson.
Bettinger Jacob. cab. mkr., wks. s.w.c. Canal and Elm.
Bettinger Peter, book store. 3 Budd.
Buttman Meier, (M. Hess & Co.,) 100 W. 0th.
Bettmann Abraham, phys . 245 Elm.
BETTMANN Bernhard, (Simon Shohl & Co.,) 1260 W. 7th.
Bettmann Mauritz, hosiery, 80 W. 5th, h. 270 W. 9th.
BETTS Aaron S., (R. M. Pomeroy & Co.,) bds. Burnet house.
Betts Addison. 16 Clark.
BETTS CHAS. S., Clerk Mayors Office, h. 283 Richmond.
Betts Hy., inventor, bds. s.w.c. Franklin and Broadway.
Betts Isaac, 16 Clark.
Betts Joseph W. clk , 13 Gorman.
Betts Oliver C. 66 Clark.
Betts Smith, n.e.c. Hopkins and John.
BETTY EDWARD, Reporter Commercial Office, h. 346 George.
Betty William, jr., dry goods, 160 W. 5th. h. 119 Mill.
Betty William, Sr., b. k., 119 Mill.
Betz Frederick, shoe mkr., 522 Walnut.
Betz Jacob, lab., 6 Walnut.
Betz Martha. 63 W 6th.
Betz Wm., stone mason, bds. 680 Vine.
Betzer Frank, butcher, bds. 17 Wade.
Betzer Frank, driver, bds. 57 E. Pearl.
Betzer Geo., shoe mkr., w.s. Ludlow b. Front and 2d.
Betzer Mary, 63ª Elm
Betzing Conrad drays. 679 Sycamore.
Betzing Conrad, mason, 18 Hughes.
Beumer Bernhard, lab., 593 R ice.
Beumler John, molder, 136 Pleasant.
Beuse Gebhard barber, 921 Central Av.
Beuse Louis, 607 Vine.
Beuter Alois, foreman 89 16th.
Beurkley Gabriel, mohler, 17 Mary.
Bevan John, n.s Summit w. of Auburn av
Bevan John, jr., atty., room 13, Masonic Temple. res. Mt. Auburn
Bevens Martha, 550 Race
Bevermann Conrad, tailor, 231 Hopkins
BEVIS Alfred, (Leavitt & B ,) 97 Pike
BEVIS HOUSE, s.e.c. Court and Walnut

Bevis J. W., 79 W. 5th
Bevis Jesse, (John B. & Co.,) h. Bevis, Butler co
Bevis John, (John B. & Co.,) h. Bevis, Butler co
Bevis John & Co., (John B. & Jesse B.,) prs., Cin., Colerain, Venice & New London Omnibus Line, 160 Walnut

BEVIS MARTIN, Proprietor Bevis House, s.e.c. Court and Walnut
Bevis Uriel, bk , Bevis House
Bexell & Hill. (John B. & E. H. H.,) watches and jewelry, 103 Main
Bexell John, (B. & Hill) 322 John
Beyland Emma, 488 Main
Beyland Francisca, seamstress, 488 Main
Beyland Gottlieb, E. D., copper smith, 488 Main
Beyland Mathilda, seamstress, 488 Main
Beyer Fred, cigar mkr., 400 Vine
Beyer John, 593 Elm
Beyer John, cooper, 468 Linn
Beyer John N., lab , s.s. Findlay, b. Freeman and Western av
Beyer Josephine, servt., 546 W. 5th
Beyer Michael, brewer. s.s. Montgomery pike. nr. Reading Road
Beyerle Catharine, grocery, n.w c. Park and Longworth
Beyerle Wm , clk., n.w.c. Park and Longworth
Beyerlein Frederick, finisher, 1¹ Moore
Beyers Nich. stoneware, 1068 Central av
Beyland Christian F., baker, s.s. 14th, b. Rice and Bremen
Beyrer John N., dentist, 96 Ham. Road
Buffer Wm., saddler, bds. 125 W. 5th
Bhar John, confec., 568 Central av
Bhile Frederick, butcher, wks. 72 13th
Bian Ferdinand, cigar mkr., wks. 107 W. Liberty
Bice Edward, fireman, 479 W. 7th
Bice Eliza, milliner, s.e c. 7th and Baymiller
Bice Geo , lab., n.s. Augusta, b. John and Smith
BICHARD PETER, Furniture Store, 547 Vine
Bichart Peter, c rp., e.s. Ridgway al. b. Liberty and 15th, h. 547 Vine
Bichsel George. jeweler, 19 Main
Bick Bernhard. driver, 61 Pendleton
Bickel Edward A.. stoves, 236 W. 5th
Bickel Rev. Wm. P., 81 Pendleton
Bickenhauser Philip, barber, 993 Central av.
Bickers Hy., varnisher, 590 Race
Bickerstaff Samuel. eng., 109 Baymiller
Bickett Isabella, 183 Cutler
Bickett John, collector, 184 Cutter
BICKHAM WM. D., Journalist, Commercial Office, h. 269 Richmond
Bickhouse Barny, blk. smith, Hill, opposite Catholic church, Mt. Adams
Bickley Geo , locksmith, wks. 182 Central av
Bickley Humphrey T., preserved fruit, &c., 111 E. Pearl, h. Newport
Bickman Margaret, washwoman, 52 Everett
Bicknell Edward M., (Stinford & B.,) 73 Longworth
Bicknell Ira, express, s.s. Front, opp. Torrence
Biddle Frank J., atty., 22 W. Court, h. Walnut Hills
Diddle Hester, w.s. Cogswell al. b. Franklin and Woodward
Biddle Mary. 119 Broadway
Biddle Wm. P , atty., 34 Bank Bldg., h. 41 Everett
Bidenharn Anthony, (Vierschilling & B ,) 25 Green
Biderwelle Christica, seamstress, 74 Dudley
Biderwelle Minie, match mkr., 74 Dudley
Bidlingmeyer John, tailor 564 Elm
Bidwell Emma, h. h , 408 W. 7th
Bieber Andrew, (B. & Bro.,) 595 Walnut
Bieber & Bro., (Andrew & Nicholas,) tailors, 230 Main
Bieber Elizabeth, 33 Locust
Bieber Frederick, jeweler, 516 Main¹
Bieber Nicholas, (B. & Bro.,) 90 Peete
Biebinger Geo., tailor, 490 Walnut
Biecker Francis L , carp., 196 Pleasant
Biedemeier Ferdinand, lab., 660 Main
Biedenbach Geo., finisher, 116 Clay
Biedenbender Adam, lab., 118 Clay
Biedenbender Frederick, salesman, 118 Clay

Biedenbender Jacob, hats and caps, 212 and 226 Main
Biedenbender Kate, 118 Clay
Biedenharn Bernhard, lab., 4 Lucy
Biedenhoke Barney, lab., 46 Dunlap
BIEDINGER PETER, Paper and Rag Dealer, 548 Elm
Biedinger Peter, jr., student, bds. 548 Elm
Biegelman Frank A., lab., 118 Abigail
Biegler Francis, bk. layer. 699 Race
Biehle Geo., cooper, 284 W. Liberty
Biehrmann Frederick, cooper, 78 Bremen
Bieker Godfried, shoe mkr , bds. 65 W. 5th
Bieknuver Barney, lab., 145 Baymiller
Bielefeld Dietrich, lab., 537 Main
Bi-ler, Geo , salesman, 370 Elm
BIELER Hy., (Nickel & B.) Delhi Tp
Bieler Peter. lab., 56 Buckeye
Bieler Mrs. Rachael, 56 Buckeye
Bieman Hy., stone cutter, bds. 12 Mulberry
Biemann John, lab., 12 E. Mulberry
Biemann Reinhart, marble dresser, 12 Mulberry
Bien Anthony, grocery, 772 W. 6th
Bien Moses, 65 Providence
Biengelman Hy., carp., 387 W. Liberty
Bier Ceif., 569 Central av
BIER Emanuel, (Steiner & B.,) 271 W. 9th
Bier John, carp., n.e.c. Plum and 6th
Bierbaum Hy., lab., 172 Baymiller
Bierbaum Peter, painter. 11 Whiteman
Bierding Peter, 172 W. Court, w. of Central av
Biere Frederick W., piano tuner, w.s. Vine, b. Milk and Calhoun
Biermann August, w.s Bremen, b. Elder and Findlay.
Biermann Conrad, tailor, 229 Betts
Biermann Francis, cooper, 756 Pleasant
Biermann John, w.s. McGrew, b. Alexander and Fountain
Biermann Mrs. Mary, w.s. Jordan, b. Clark and Gest
Bierre Bernard. tinner, wks. 5 W. 5th
Biers Ann, 17 Mucalister
Bieser Charles, barber, 28 E. Front
Bigeon Mrs. Mary, millinery, 231 W. 5th
Bigelow Horace G., coach mkr., 443 W. 3d
Bigelow Silas II., eng., 366 W. Liberty
Biggen Felix, s.e.c. New and Broadway
Bigger Elizabeth S., bds. s.w.c. Franklin and Broadway
Bigger ly., c.of. h., 21 E. 5th, h. 25 Harrison
Bigger James W., saddler, 213 Laurel
Biggers Hermann, lab., 3 8 Baymiller
Biggins Patrick, lab., e.s. Oregon, b. 3d and 6th
Biggs George. presser, 86 W. Front
Biggs James L , s.b. runner, bds. s.s 3d, b. Canal and Kilgour
Biggs John S., auction stable 24 E. 5th, res. Delhi
Biggs Joseph A., (Andrews & D.,) 55 Gest
BIGGS T. R. & CO., (Thomas R. B. & David A. White.) Wholesale Grocers, s.w.c. Main and 2d
Biggs Thomas, bds. 104 Broadway
Biggs. Rev. Thomas J , 382 Vine
BIGGS Thomas R., (T R. B. & Co.,) res. Milford
Bigham David L., clk., s.e.c. Main and 6th, h s.w.c. 9th and Race
Bigham W. D , clk., s. s. 6th b. Vine and Race
Bighan Wm. D., coach mkr., 155 W. 4th
Bigle George, 307 Findlay
Bigler & Co.. (Daniel M. B., & Jacob A. J. B.,) grocers 155 W. 5th
Bigler Daniel M., (B. & Co.,) 155 W. 5th
Bigler Elbert F., printer, 115 Douglass
BIGLER GEO. W., Physician, Office and Residence, 59 W. 7th
Bigler Jacob A. J., (B. & Co., 155 W. 5th
Bieles Margaret, 26 Abigail
Bihl Adam, cab. mkr., 603 Elm

CINCINNATI ADVERTISEMENTS.

 # CINCINNATI BLIND FACTORY.

A. VIETH,
VENETIAN BLIND MANUFACTURER,

No. 140 SYCAMORE STREET,
Bet. Fourth and Fifth, East side, CINCINNATI, O.

Venetian Blinds made to order in the most fashionable and durable manner. Blinds of all styles and finish on hand, and will be disposed of at the lowest prices. OLD BLINDS REPAIRED AND PAINTED. *First Premium awarded at the Ohio State Fair, 1857, and at the U. S. Fair, 1860.*

SAMUEL BLAIR. ## SAMUEL BLAIR & CO. R. S. ZILAR.
DEALERS IN

PURE NORTHERN ICE!
Office, N. E. Cor. Twelfth and Plum Streets,
CINCINNATI, O.

This engraving represents SAMUEL BLAIR & CO. cutting Ice on their Basin at Rasinburg, 114 miles north of Cincinnati, Shelby county, O., on a surface of water 20 acres: depth 15 feet. Fed by Miami and Loramie rivers.

D. K. CADY,
DEALER IN
FANCY GOODS & TOYS,

FRENCH, ENGLISH, GERMAN AND BOHEMIAN MANUFACTURES.

Tortoise Shell, Ivory and other Combs, Brushes, Fine Cutlery, Beads, Needles, Rubber Goods, Portmonnaies, Sporting Flasks, Work Boxes, China Ornaments, Vases, &c.

NORTH-EAST CORNER FIFTH AND WALNUT, CINCINNATI, O.

A large stock of Fishing Tackle and Children's Carriages, (from $2,50 to $25,00) always on hand.

JOHN G. DOUGLASS,
ATTORNEY AT LAW,
North-East Corner Fourth and Walnut Streets,
CINCINNATI, OHIO.

NOTARY PUBLIC AND COMMISSIONER,

For Kentucky, Illinois, Michigan, Pennsylvania, Missouri, Virginia, Wisconsin, Indiana, Tennessee, Kansas, Mississippi, New Jersey, Arkansas, Iowa, Alabama and New York.

(BIR) CINCINNATI (BIS) DIRECTORY. (BLA) 67

Bihl John, cab. mkr., 592 Elm, h. 603 Elm
Bihlman John. bar k., bds. 437 Vine
BIIN ANDREW, Pottery, 237 and 239 Hamilton Road
Bile John, lab , 492 E Front
Biles Geo. butcher 51 Pendleton
Biles Martha, nl. b. Linn and Baymiller, Dayton and Bank
Bilks Charles. (James White & Co.,) h. Newport
Bilks Edmund. bksmith, wks. James White & Co.'s
Bill Hy., lab., 102 Abigail
Bill John, rope mkr., 4-1 W. 3d
Bill Peter, molder. wks. n.e.c. Canal and Walnut
Billamann Theodore, lab., bds. n.e.c. Poplar and Linn
BILLAU ADAM, Merchant Tailor, 97 E. Pearl
Billenstein John, lab., 664 Elm
Billenstein Joseph, lab., 651 Elm
Billerbeck Clements A., Ale and Porter manufac., 189 E. Pearl, h. Newport
Billerbeck Mary, bds. 32 Harrison
Billermann, Geo., barber, 68 Freeman
Billet Joseph, cutlery, 26 13th
Billian Michael, tailor, 13 Mary
Billigheimer Joseph, 17 14th, b. Central av and Plum
Billigheimer Louis, meat store, 180 W. 6th, h. 49 George
Billing John M., teamster, 49 Rittenhouse
Billings Chas., b.k. layer, 66 Richmond, E. of Central av
BILLIODS FREDERICK. Lafayette Brewery, n.s Ham. road, b. Vine and Race, h. 719 Vine.
Bilou Geo., bar. k., 454 Walnut
Bitming Gerhard, cooper, 692 Main
BILTZ AUGUST Dealer in Cigars, Tobacco, &c., 521 Main
Biltz Charles, blk. smith bds. 109 E. 2d
Bimbel Frank, lib. bds. 140 Carr
Bimgleman Benjamin, carp., 22 Dudley
Bimgleman John B., carp. 22 Dudley
Bind Samuel, salesman, 130 W. 5th
Binder Anthony. 497 Elm
Binder Jacob, cof. h . s e c 6th and Freeman
Binder Joseph, varnisher, 128 Pleasant
Binder Oswald, c. h., 24 E Front
Binder Sigmund, coach mkr., bds. 24 E. Front
Binder Theodore, painter, 510 Race
Bindhammer, Powell, b. h., 3 0 Vine
Bindley James, carp., w.s Lawrence b. 2d and Pearl h. 3 5 W, 3d
Bindsack John, painter, 71 Hughes
Bing M. & Brother, (Moses & David,) clothing, 391 Main
Bing David, (M. B. & Bro.,) h. Washington, O.
Bing Isaac, clk., bds 243 Broadway
Bing Moses, (M. B. & Bro.,) 243 Broadway
Bing Moses jr., clothier, 243 Broadway
Bing Nathan, 243 Broadway
Bing Samuel, student, bds. 391 Main
Bingham Ann, variety store, h. 1310 E. Front
Bingham Harriet A., s.s. 3d, b. Canal and Kilgour
Bingham Thomas, shoe mkr., 1310 E. Front
Bingham Wm., clk., bds. 153 W. 4th
Binhelm Harman, grocery, 67 Hughes
Binker Chas , lab., 115 Woodward
Binney Geo., lab., wks. n.e.c. Walnut and Canal
Binsack Peter, shoemkr., 34 Green
Binsack Wm., painter., 25 14th
Birce John, baker 10 W. 5th
Birch John, b.s., 236 Race
Birch Peter. clk , 314 Main
Birch Peter. salesman, bds. s.e.c 9th and Walnut
Birch Sarah A., bds. s.w.c. 4th and Race
Birchler Anson, turner, wks 825 Central Av.
Bird Abraham, clk., 66 Richmond

Bird, Burrows & Co., (Henry N. B., George B. & Wm. W. Cooper,) chair manuf., 20 E. 3d., factory, w.s. John b. Front and Augusta
Bird Charles, clk., s.w c 3d and Walnut
Bird Henry N., (B., Burrows & Co) 269 W. Court, w. of Central Av
Bird Herbert, b., 33 W. 3d
Bird Ira H., 239 Longworth
Bird J. N., b.k. Dennison House
Bird Joseph, river man, bds. 14 E. Front
Bird Joseph, sexton, e.s. Freeman, b. 5th and 6th
Bird Mary. 132 W 3.1
BIRD MICHAEL H , Books, Stationery and Pictures, 297 Central Av., bds. s.w.c George and Elm
BIRD NICHOLAS, Attorney at Law, s w. c. 3d and Sycamore, h. 102 George
Bireline Frederick, mach., wks., n. s. Front b. Lawrence and Pike
Birger Elizn, servt., 238 W. Court, w. of Central Av.
Birgler Catharine, washerwoman, 419 W. Liberty
Birgler John, brass finisher, 419 W. Liberty
Birgler Wm., waiter, 29 W. 5th
Birk Jacob, tailor, 150 Bremen
Birk Martin, soap mkr., s.e.c. Findlay and Rice
Birken Hermann. saddler. 427 Sycamore
Birkin Frederick, bds 427 Sycamore
Birkmeyer Wm., cab. mkr , Oehler al. b. Freeman and Gurrard
Birmingham Anna, se vt., 50 Pendleton
Birmingham D ra, servt., 33 Harrison
Birmingham Kate, chambermaid, Burnet House
Birmingham John, wks. J. Whitaker's, Deer Creek Valley
Birmingham Martin, lab , 334 W 8th
Birmlen Mary, 66 Stark
Birnb um t atharine, 62 Broadway
Birnbryer Adolph, clk., Broadway Hotel, h. 620 Elm
Birney Barney, bk. mkr., 351 W. 7th
Birney James, clk., 78 W. 5th
Birney John, lab., wks., C. H. & D. RR. Depot
Birtsch John, bakery, 637 Central Av.
Birtwhistle Richard printer, 21 Webb
Birty Harry, tailor, bds. 97 W Court
BISBY WM. B. & CO., (Wm. B. B., B F N chols & S. Stevens,) Lumber Dealers, 133 Freeman
BISBY Wm. B., (Wm. B B. & Co.,) 2 Jane b. 6th and George
Bische Helena, 438 Main
Bischer Henry, cooper. 684 Main
Bischer Wm., molder, 684 Main
BISCHOF Bernhard, (B. & March,) h. 24 E. 7th
BISCHOP & MARCH. (Bernhard B. Sisel M.,) Wholesale Clothiers, 35 W. Pearl
Bischof Mary, s.s. E. Pearl, b. Pike and Butler
Bischof Sebastian, boiler mkr., wks. McIlvain Spiegel & Co's
Bischoff Anthony, express, 38 Elder
Bischoff Anthony. tailor. 13 Mercer
Bischoff Samuel, grocery, 19 Mercer
Bischop Christopher, lab., 63 Clay
Bischter Christian, peddler, e.s. Clarkson b. Bank and Central Av.
Bishop A. W., b k., 34 W. Pearl, bds. Henrie House
Bishop Alex. D. 36 Main, h. 13 Chestnut
Bishop C. H., clk., 77 Spring
Bishop Chaplin J., b. k., 32 Walnut, bds. 442 W. 7th
Bishop Charles, lab., wks. n.e.c. Canal and Walnut
BISHOP George W. (B. M. B. & Co) 101 W 7th
Bishop Herman, blk. smith, 52 Everett
Bishop J. G. & J. W., (Jacob G. B. & James W. B.,) grocers, 16 Main
Bishop Jason G., (J. G. & J. W. B.,) 115 W. 9th
Bishop James W., (J. G. & J. W. B.,) 14 E. 6th
Bishop Jennie servt., 126 E. 4th

Bishop John, clk., bds., 206 W. 5th
BISHOP John W , (Dickinson, Price & B .) 101 W. 7th
BISHOP JUSTIN R., Photographic Artist, 5 W, 4th, h. Newport
Bishop Mrs. L. L., b. h., 137 W. 7th
BISHOP R. M & CO.,(Richd. M. B., Geo. W. Bishop, & Wm. T. Bishop) Wholesale Grocers and Commission Merchants. 36 Main
BISHOP Richd. M., (R. M. B. & Co.,) n.e.c. 6th and Mound
Bishop S., cigar mkr., 22 Hamer
Bishop Samuel P., clk. 17 W. 3d, h. 137 E. 5th
Bishop Stephen, cab. mkr., 95 Richmond
Bishop Wm. II , painter, 267 W. 3d
BISHOP Wm. T., (R. M. B. & Co.,) 104 Richmond
BISHOPRICK H & CO., Manufac. of Baking Powders, 111 W. 5th
BISHOPRICK Henry, (H. B. & Co.,) 134 W. 9th
Bising Celestine, musician, 51 14th
Bising Thos., lithographer, 173 W. Court w of Central Av
Bisker Frederick, lab., 17 E. 3d, e. of Parsons
Bisman Frederick, blk. smith, bds. 320 E Pearl
Bismeier Matthews Chris., carp., 175 W. Liberty
Bissell Mrs. E. F., b. h. 111 W. 5th
Bissell Henry B., assistant cashier Bank of Ohio Valley, 120 E. 5th
Bisset Robert, mach., 453 W. 7th
Bithemorn George, lab., 57 Butler
Bitte Charles I., cab mkr., w.s. Ridgway al, b. 14t and 15th
Bittel Eva, tailoress, r. 156 Ham. Road
Bittel Jacob, basket mkr., r. 78 W. Mulberry
Bittel Michael, dray., 136 Ham. Road
Bitter Frederick. tailor, 120 Ham. Road
Bitter George, tailor, 717 Elm
Bitter Peter, tailor, 210 W. 6th
Bittinger Jacob, cab. mkr., 87 Ham. Road
Bittle John, finisher, 153 Clinton [Av.
Bittlinger Charles, lab., wks. 798 Central
Bittner Caroline, seamstress, wks, w.s. Goose al., b. Green and Elder
Bittner Catharine, seamstress, wks. w.s. Goose al., b. Green and Elder
Bitner John, 72 Hunt
Bitzer John, lab., 107 W. Liberty
Bitzer Philip, brewer, n.e.c. Front and Parsons
Bixler Frederick, lab., 55 Martin
Braak Peter, miller, wks. 143 Race
Black A. H., clk., 101 W. 4th
Black Ambrose, eng., 211 Freeman
Black Anna B., 103 W. 5th
Black Bear Hotel, B. B Armstrong, proprietor, s w.c. 9th and Sycamore
Black Catharine, bds. 1248 E. Front
Black Charles, cook. 43 E. 4th
Black David, b. k., 41 Walnut
Black David, druggist, 392 Findlay
Binck George. dray., 505 W. 4th
Black James, h 101 Betts
Black Honora, 303 W 6th
Black Hugh, hinge fitter, wks. n. e. c. Walnut and Canal
Black Isabella, 165 W. 6th
Black James. carver, 150 Barr
Black Jacob, clk., bds. 175 W. 5th
Black James shoemkr , bds. 2 9 Broadway
Black Jane, 497 Sycamore
Black John, 157 W. 5th
Black John, printer. 75 Spring
Black L. H , clk. Adams Express Co., h. Newport
Black Letty, 270 W. 7th
Black Peter, stable. s.s. Patterson al. b. Main and Walnut, bds. Dennison House
Black Samuel, 486 W. 4th
Black Samuel, boiler mkr., n.s. Cherry al. b. Plum and Central Av.
Black Samuel F., atty., 33 E. 3d, h. 417 Broadway

| WM. GLENN. | JAS. M. GLENN. | R. DYMOND, JR. | O. T. GLENN. |

WM. GLENN & SONS,
WHOLESALE GROCERS,
70 and 72 Vine Street, between Second and Pearl Streets,
CINCINNATI, O.

| JAMES BEATTY. | | GEO. W. TROWBRIDGE. |

JAMES BEATTY & CO.
(Successors to TROWBRIDGE & BEATTY.)

PORK PACKERS, COMMISSION MERCHANTS,
AND CURERS OF EXTRA SUGAR-CURED HAMS.

"Non Est Melior" Brand.

South-West Corner of Race Street and Miami Canal,   CINCINNATI, OHIO.

| ROBERT MOORE. | | MATTHEW ADDY. |

ROBERT MOORE & CO.,
PRODUCE & GENERAL COMMISSION MERCHANTS,
No. 49 Walnut Street, Cincinnati, Ohio.

Bacon, Flour, Grain, Cheese, Butter, Seeds, Oils, Soap, Candles, White Fish, Cordage, Cotton, Pig and Bloom Iron, and articles of Domestic Manufacture, and Produce generally.

JAS. MAGILL,
PORK & BEEF PACKER,
—AND—
COMMISSION MERCHANT,
No. 52 West Court Street, Cincinnati, Ohio.

| N. W. THOMAS. | | E. L. THOMAS. |

N. W. THOMAS & CO.
CURERS OF EXTRA HAMS, PORK PACKERS,
—AND—
COMMISSION MERCHANTS,
Corner of Walnut and Canal Streets,   CINCINNATI, O.

| ROBT. CLARKE. | R. D. BARNEY. | J. W. DALE. |

ROBERT CLARKE & CO.
(Successors to H. W. DERBY & CO.)
LAW PUBLISHERS & BOOKSELLERS,
STATIONERS, IMPORTERS, AND DEALERS IN THEOLOGICAL, SCIENTIFIC, SCHOOL AND MISCELLANEOUS BOOKS

No. 55 WEST FOURTH STREET, CINCINNATI, O.

Foreign Books, old or new, imported to order. Particular attention paid to the collection of rare works. Catalogues furnished gratis, on application. Harpers' Books, Magazine and Weekly.

ck Stephen, mate, 25 Pierson
ck Wm., carp., bds. 70 Sycamore
ck Wm., lab., 11 14th, b. Central Av. and Plum
ckall Walter A., painter, 62 Richmond b. Plum and Central Av.
ckburn Christopher C., photographer, 268 W. Front
ckburn Edward, butcher, al. b. Linn and Baymiller, and Bank and Central Av.
ckburn Frances, seamstress, 421 W. 3d
ckburn Francis A., b. k., 93 W. Pearl, h. Covington
ckburn Geo. S., 59 W. 7th, h. 71 Laurel
ckburn Hy., cof. h., 440 W. Front
ckburn Jacob C., clk. P. O., h. 119 W. 6th
ckburn John. butcher, al. b. Linn and B ymiller, and Bank and Central Av.
ckburn John. butcher, 89 Bank
ckburn Jonathan, 14 Harrison
ckburn Julius F, 424 W. 8th
ckburn Lucy A., teacher, 1 Smith Court
ckburn Richard, whitewasher, 2 Smith Court
ckburn Robert, coachman, 113 Pike
ckburn Robert, coachman, 2 Fmish Court
ckburn Thos. R., piano manuf., 223 Main, h. 71 Laurel
cke Catharine, 37 Green
cke John H., shoemkr, 401 Broadway
cker Mary, 414 Longworth
cker Thos. J., sexton, n.s. 7th b. Central Av. and John
cket Francis, molder, 31 Observatory
ckett Edwd, molder, Observatory, Mt. Adams
ckett Francis, molder, wks. 250 E. Front
ckford Jos. bds., Dennison House
LACKFORD PRICE, Proprietor Monongahela House, 12 E. Front
ckford Joseph, clk., bds 50 Elizabeth
LACKMAN GEO. C., Physician and Surgeon, h. 113 W. 8th
LACKMAN JOHN L., Wood and Coal Yard, 68 Smith
ckman Miuny, servt. 288 George
ckmann Herman H., 92 Dudley
ckmore Dawson. clk., 87 W. 2d
ckston Susan, 63 E. 7th
ckwell Mary, 326 Main
ckwood Robert, shoemkr, bds. 281 Central Av
ckwood Thomas, clk. L.M.R.R. Depot
demeier Frederick, blksmith, bds. 452 W. 2d
des James, omnibus driver, bds. 97 Freeman
etterbauer Wenzel, lab. 37 Green
gard Chas., barber, 69 15th
gg B. W., st. bt. captain, bds, 149 Elm
in Joseph, clk., bds. Madison House
indells John, foreman, bds. 170 W. 4th
ir Charles T., b.k. at Charles Rule's, bds. 394 W. 9th
ir Francis, cutler, 105 Main
ir Geo. W., bds. 329 Central Av
ir John, eng., n.e.c. Pearl and Pike
ir John, mach., bds. n.e.c. Pearl and Pike
ir John M., bklayer, 394 W. 9th w. of Central Av
ir John R., ice dealer, 78 Providence
ir Joseph D., bklayer, 240 W. Front
ir McLean J., clk., 48 Pub, Landing
ir Robert, plasterer, 29 Pine
ir Russell, clk., 99 12th
AIR Samuel, (Saml. B. & Co.), 90 15th
LAIR SAMUEL & CO., (Saml. B. & Reuben S. Zilar) Northern Ice House, n.e.c. 12th and Plum

Blaisdell Octavius, mach,, bds. 170 W. 4th
Blake James, tailor, 209 W. 3d
Blake Peter, foreman, n s, 5th b. Hannibal and Freeman
Blakely J. Lauriz. not. pub, and phonographer, 53 W. 3d, h. 221 Broadway
Blakemore Frank, pipe fitter, wks, n.e.c. Walnut and Canal
Blakemore John K., japanner, 14 David
Blaker Barney, lab., 219 Betts
Blakeslee Edward, clocks, 229 Main, h. 66 Franklin
Blakeslee George B. clk., 55 Webster
Blakeslee Lyman W , clk., 25 North
Blakey John, carp., n.e.c. Elm and Court
Blanc and Frank, shoemkr., bds. s.w.c. Betts and Linn
Blanchard Geo. S., bookseller, 39 W. 4th, h. 140 Richmond
Blanchard John, tanner, bds. 70 Sycamore
Blanchard Wm. A., pork mer., 138 Smith [Elm
Blanck John, s.g. Dover al. b. Plum and Blanckemeier Catharine, 130 Ham. Road
Blancker Wm., clk., bds, 71 W. 9th
Blandull Burnhard, tailor, 67 Bremen
Blaney Ambrose, carp., 507 W. 5th
Blaney Geo. S., tinner, 35 Elizabeth
Blaney Wm. M., carp. 112 Park, h. 49 York
Blangey George W., teamster, 96 Water
Blaugey Rob rt M., teamster, 91 Water
Blangy Wm. F., wood yard, r. 109 Water, h. 130 Water
Blank Anna, 566 Elm
Blank Francis, saddler, bds. s.w.c. 12th and Main
Blank Jacob, baker, bds. 176 W. Front
Blank Robert, conchman, 560 Elm
Blanke Frederick, porter, 56 W. 2d, h. Covington
Blankemeier Hy., cooper, 130 Abigail
Blankenbuhler John, lab , 29 Hughes
Blankenfeld Charles, butcher, 91 Bank
Blunkenheim John, cigar mkr, 118 Bremen
Blanker John, bds. Pennsylvania Hotel
Blankey Hy., lab., wks. n.w.c. Plum and Wade
Blannerhassett Arthur T., turner, n.e.c. Avery and Stone, h. 371 Longworth
Blargman Joseph, lab.. wks. n.s. Frout b. Lawrence and Pike
Blase Anthony, teamster, 105 Buckeye
Blase Gottfried, cooper, n.e.c. Clark and Cutter
Blase Jacob, shoemkr., n.w.c. Cutter and Clark
Blasse Adam, 101 Hunt
Blasy Hy., tanner, s.s. Liberty b. Linn and Baymiller
BLATCHFORD & CO., Refrigerators and Ice Chests, 166 Vine, Factory 205 Freeman
BLATCHFORD Hy. S. (B. & Co.), h. 26 W. 8th
Blattau Peter, grocery, 618 Vine
Blatter John, cof. h., 454 Walnut
Blattner Jacob, lab. 664 Race
Blau Frederick M., cof. h., 277 W. 5th
Blau Meyer, peddler, 47 Clinton
Blau Peter, shoemkr, bds. 1034 Central Av
Blautt Martin, hostler, h. e.s Sycamore b. 3d and 4th
Blazer Christopher, finisher, wks. 141 W. 2d
Bleak's David M., police. 260 Hopkins
Bleaks Dorcas, 217 Water
Bleaks George, policeman, 184 Water
Bleaks Wm., mate, 217 Water
Blease Samuel, w.s. Western Av. b. Findlay and Dayton
Blebaum Charles, plasterer, 25 Hammond
Blecker Hy. W., tailor, bds. 105 Barr
Blecker John, 105 Barr
Blecker Joseph M., carp., bds. 105 Barr
Bleckman Hy. C., blksmith, w.s. Ruth b. Laurel and Betts, h. w.s. Linn b. Hopkins and Laurel
Dlee Wm. 11 , conductor, bds. Spencer House

Bleier Maurice, hide dealer, 63 12th
Blesi Mathias, shoemkr, 1 Mary
Bieska Hy., finisher. 89 Pleasant
BLENDINGER JOHN, Coffee House, 510 Central Av
Blenke Hy., lab. n.s. Charlotte b. Linn and Baymiller
Blenkemeier Theresa, 69 Abigail
Blese Christian, finisher, 7 W ide b. Elm and Plum
Blettner Hy., bar k., 24 Allison
Blettner John, blksmith, 3 Hamer
BLETTNER Joseph B , Fritsch, Burkhardt & Co.), 470 Race
Bleuler Felix A., paper hanger, 520 Walnut
BLEY A. & BRO., (Anthony & Wm.) Carpenters and Builders, n.e.c. Liberty and Baymiller
Bley Andrew, carp., 135 Bank
BLEY Anthony (B. & Brother), 135 Bank
Bley Hy., carp., s.s. Liberty b. Linn and Baymiller
Bley Theodore, carp., 42 Elm
BLEY William, (B. & Brother), 137 Bank
Bleyle Roman, shoemkr, bds. 556 Vine
Blezer May, 65 12th
Blick Robert F., (S. Mauning & Co.) h. Covington, Ky
Blickerbuum Charles, tailor, 623 Elm
Blickle Christian, salesman, 107 W. Pearl, h. 15 W. 8th
Blicklin Mathilde, 526 Main [Av
Blight Wm , shoemkr, bds. 281 Central
Blil Louis, baker, 71 E. Front
Blimmer Bernard, s.s. Charlotte b. Linn and Baymiller
Blimmer Clemens, lab., s.s. Charlotte b. Linn and Baymiller
Bling John, liquor dealer, 419 Central Av
Blinker Joseph, cab. mkr., 362 Broadway
Blinn O. & Co., (Orange B. & William A. B.) furniture, 201 W. 5th
Blinn Ozias, clk., 201 W. 5th
Blinn Orange (O. B. & Co.) 201 W. 5th
Blinn Wm. A. (O. Blinn & Co.) 201 W. 5th
Bliss Asa, n.s. Taylor b. Carr and Freeman
Bliss Hy., jeweler, 103 Broadway
Bliss Hy., lab., bds. 404 W. 5th
Bliss John C., driver. 631 W. Front
Bliss Morris. tailor, 269 Main
Blittersdorf Chas., baker, 189 Bremen
Blitz Issac. clk., 348 Main
Bloch Abraham, shoe store, 268 W. 6th
BLOCH & CO. (Edward B. & I. M. Wise), Publishers of the Israelite and Deborah, Books, &c., 32 W 6th
Bloch Charles, cof. h., 541 Elm
Bloch David, clk., 197 Central Av
BLOCH Edward (B. & Co.) 13 George
Bloch Jacob, peddler, 28 Allison
Bloch Joseph, 99 Betts
Bloch Lazarus, h. 18 W. 8th
Bloch Leonhard, rag dealer, 136 W. Liberty
Bloch Martin, 113 Laurel
Bloch Constantine, clk., bds. 353 Central Av
Block E. & L. (Elias & Lazarus), rectifiers, 28 Sycamore
Block Edward, salesman, 71 15th
Block Elias (E. & L. B.) 53 W. 9th
Block Emil, liquor mer., 28 W. 8th
Block Herman, peddler, n.s. Everett b. John and Cutter
Block Lazarus (E. & L. B) 113 Laurel
Block Leonard, n.s.c Broadway and 8th
Block Leopold, (E. Block & Bros.,) 152 George
Block Louis, clk., 53 W. 9th.
Block Louis, second hand store 193 B'dway.
BLOCK Leopold, (Marienthal, Lehman & Co.,) 200 George.
Block Maurice, (J. Dube & Maurice,) 194 & Co.
Block Wm. L., carp., bds. 70 Sycamore.
Blocker John, cook, bds. Ludlow House.

CINCINNATI ADVERTISEMENTS

A. KRAMER

Manufacturer and Wholesale Dealer in all kinds of

FURNITURE AND C[HAIRS]

WAREROOMS, No. 530 Main Street, east side, bet. Woodward and

STEAM FACTORY, No. 11 FRANKLIN STRE[ET]

Keeps constantly on hand a large stock of well made Furniture, of all kinds, at the lowe[st]
All orders received through the Post Office will be promptly attended to.

H. McALPIN.   B. P. HINMAN.

McALPIN, HINMAN

DEALERS IN CABINET HA[RDWARE]

Upholsterers and Undertakers' Mat[erials]

No. 103 WALNUT STREET, - - - - - - CINCI[NNATI]

J. F. COATE[S]

MANUFACTURER OF

SOFAS, SOCIABLES, PARLOR

—AND—

GENERAL UPHOLSTE[RY]

No. 150 Eighth Street, near Elm, -CIN[CINNATI]

CABINET MAKERS' UNI[ON]

Factory, Augusta Street, below Smith

JACOB DIEHL, Agent.

Manufacturer of Bedsteads, Sofas, Chairs, Bureaus and all oth[er]

CHAS. WOLF[F]

Manufacturer of and Dealer in all kinds of

FASHIONABLE CABINET FU[RNITURE]

Warerooms, No. 85 Sycamore Street, between Third a[nd]
and No. 52 Eighth Street, East, CINCINNATI

N. B. Work done to order; Furniture Repaired; Upholstery done with neatness and di[spatch]

J. C. RINGWALT.

RINGWALT & AVERY,

IMPORTERS OF & DEALERS IN C[ARPETS]

PIKE'S OPERA HOUSE BUILDING, No. 69 WEST [FOURTH ST.]

CINCINNATI, OHIO.

Blump George, lab , 604 Main.
Blundell Anna, bds. 116 Smith.
Blundell Joseph M., 364 Freeman.
Blunt Edmund B , kitchen range manufac. 224 Main, res. Mt. Auburn.
Blnst Robert, carp, 71 Hages,
Blute Michael, lab , s.w. Yeatman b. Broadway and Sycamore.
Bly Douglass, manufac, of artificial limbs s.w c. Vine and 6th.
Bly Frederick, chair mkr., 34 Smith.
Bly Hy , carp., al b. Linn and Baymiller and Liberty a'd Wade.
Blymeyer Frederick, express driver, 90 W. 2d.
Blythe John, carp., 235 E, 5th.
Blythe W N., carp , 235 E. 5th
Boake John, wagon manufac. 64 W. Canal h. 70 W. Canal
Boake John L., clk., 70 W. Canal.
Boake Wm , painter, 70 W. Canal.
Boate Geo. F., salesman 30 W. 4th.

BOARD OF CITY IMPROVEMENTS, Office City Hall.

BOARD OF TRUSTEES, AND VISITORS COMMON SCHOOLS. Office City Hall.

Bobert Francis, huckster, 2 Mary.
Bobo Charles pilot, n.s. Goodloe b. Willow and Niagra.
Bocakel R., servt , 71 Barr,
Bochtmann. Hy., h. w. end of Mohawk.
Bock George, tanner, 661 Vine,
Bock John, lab. 228 Everett.
Buckhast Barney, lab. 364 Broadway.
Buckholt Frederick, cof. h, 51 W. 5th,
Buckholt Hy. B., cof. h 216 Walnut.
Buckhop Frederick H., lab., 131 Pleasant.
Bockhop Hy., turner, 11 Adam.
Buckhurst Geo., lab.. 162 E. 5th.
Bocking Adolph H., atty., Carlisle Building. h. 69 Webster.
Bocklage Hy., lab. wks. Hy., Nye's.
Bocklage Herman, 390 W 5th.

BOCKLAGE JOHN H., Family Grocery, s.w.c. 2d and Smith.

Bocklage Mrs. Mary, 53 Woodward.
Bockl k Herman, dray. 172 Webb,
Bockman Anthony, tailor, n.w.c. Abigail and Pendleton.
Bockmann Joseph, shoe mkr., 75 Pendleton.
Bockm nn Joseph, tailor, 106 Spring.
Bockshorn Hy., varnisher, 13 moore.
Bockshorn John, varnisher, 20 E. Liberty.
Bockstegel Hy., cooper, 147 Pleasant.
Buckweg Adelaide, bds. w.s. Goose al. b. Green and Enter.
Bockweg Bernhard, tailor. 628 Race,
Bockweg Hy., lab , 599 Race.
Bode August, lab., 436 E. Front.
Bode August, horse shoer, wks. 702 Vine.
Bode Chas., (G. Muench & Co.,) 644 Vine.
Bode Chas. H , apothecary, n.w.c. Linn and Hopkins.
Bode Christian H., cof. h. 592 Main.
Bode Ferdinand; watch mkr., 414 Sycamore.
Bode Frederick, lock mkr., n.e.c. Sycamore and Milton.
Bode Frederick, wagon mkr., 592 Main.
Bode Frederick, wagon mkr., bds. 592 Main.
Bode Hy., bksmith. wks. 10 W. 7th.
Bode Hy., grocery. 59 Findlay,
Bode He., lab., bds. 592 Main.
Bode Margaret, cof. h. 537 Elm.
Bode Mary, 441 Sycamore.
Bode Wm., bksmith, wks 10 W. 7th.
Bodecamp H., wks. Wood & McCoy's.
Bodecker Frank, bds 90 E, 2d.
Bodeker, John H., packer. 271 W. 3d.
Bodeker John H., porter, 77 Walnut. h. 299 W. 2d.
Bodeker Wm., tailor, 139 Plum.
Bodemer Elizabeth, 11 Moore.
Boden August, baker, 511 Sycamore.
Boden Michael, bksmith, wks. s.e.c. Race and Water.

Boden John, stone mason, 64 Richmond.
Bodenberg Richard, carpenter, shoe mkr., 409 W. 8th,
Bodhast Wm., tailor, 20 Madison.
Bodkin Samuel, cof. h. 11 Vine.
Bodley A. M., foreman, D. S. Carrick's h. Newport.
Bodley Anthony P., pattern mkr., 397 W. 8th.
Bodley Clara, Observatory, b. Hatch and Court.
BODLEY Joseph T., (Lane & D ,) 390 Longworth.
Bodley Rachel L., teacher, 397 W. 8th,
Bodley Richard P , carp., 434 W. 9th.
Bodmann Charles, state tobacco ware house. 59 and 61 W. Front, h. Mt. Auburn.
Bodmann F., tanner, s.s. 6th b. Harriet and Horne. h. Mt. Auburn.
Bodmann Fe dinand, cigars &c., 973 Main. h Mt. Auburn.
Boelin Frank. baker, 65 Abigail.

BOEBINGER A. & J., (Adam & John) Merchant Tailors, 490 Walnut.

BOEBINGER Adam, (A. &. J. B.,) 490 Walnut.

Boebinger Adam, shoe mkr., 18 Ham. Road.
Boebinger Geo., tailor, 487 Walnut.
Boebinger J coh, shoe mkr . 67 14th.
Boebinger John, clk., 490 Walnut.
Boebinger John, (A. & J. B.,) 12 Mary.
Boebinger Lewis. cof. h. 531 Vine.
Boebinger Michael 460 Walnut,
Boechtle Lewis, bksmith, wks. n.e.c. Walnut and Canal.
Boecker Geo. B , barber, 679 Race.
Doechle Christian, cab. mkr., 367 Cutter.

BOECKLEY CATHARINE, Hardware 557 Vine.

Boecklin Werner, bds. s.w.c. 3d and Broadway.
Boeckman Geo., lab., 320 Broadway.
Boeckmann John H. Sen., 251 W. 5th.
Boeckmann John H. Jr., clk., 258 W. 5th.
Boeckmann Joseph, shoe mkr., 75 Pendleton.
Boeckmann Theodore. lab., u.s. Cassatt al. b. Main and Sycamore.
Boedker Harman, grocery, s e c. Court and Cutter
Boeter Fred., lab., 304 Vine
Boeger Geo , wks. Cin. Type Foundry
Boeger Geo., finisher, 12 Madison
Boeger Hy., bk. mkr., n.e.c. Price and Liberty
Boeger John, cof. h., 34 Butler
Buehl Hy., cigar mkr , 37 13th
Boehle Anthony, (John & Anthony P.) bds 511 Sycam re
Boehle Wm., cooper. 420 W Liberty
Boehle John, (John & Anthony B.) bds. 511 Sycamore
Boehle John & Anthony, coopers, n.s. Liberty b. Main and Sycamore
Boebler Charles, printer, n.w.c. Race and Green
Boehm Adam, tailor, bds. 704 Elm
Boehm Anthony, tanner, 26 Elder
Boehm Barbara. servt . Galt House
Boehm Conrad, hostler, 103 Ham. Road
Boehm David, clk. 120 Main, h. 19 Home
Buehm Frederick, box mkr., 148 Buckeye
Boehm Frederick, carp., 140 Buckeye
Buehm George, basket mkr, w.s. Milk b. Vine and Cath u t
Soehm Gottlieb, artist. 417 Vine
Buehm Wilhelm, confec.. 417 Vine
Buehme Edward, tailor. 541 Elm
Boehmer Albert, painter, w.s. Goose al. b. Green and Elder
Boehmer Bernhard, bds. w.s. Goose al. b. Green and Elder
Boehmerle John, cof. h., 468 Main
Boehme Henry, 161 Clay
Boehning Herman, 64 Findlay
Boehning Wm H., clk., bds. 35 Jackson
Doehringer Wolfg ng. lab, 35 Buckeye
Baehrs Hy., stone mason. 235 Bremen
Boehrs Elizabeth. 69 Abigail

APPLEGATE & CO.,
BOOKSELLERS, STATIONERS,
PRINTERS AND PUBLISHERS
—OF—

Clark's Commentary, Dick's Complete Works, Rollin's Ancient History, Plutarch's Lives, Spectator, Tattler and Guardian, Mosheim's Church History, Josephus, Gathered Treasures from the Mines of Literature, Dick's Theology, Chain of Sacred Wonders; Complete Works of Lorenzo Dow, Farmer's Hand Book; Shakspeare, Soden's German Grammar, Peterson's Familiar Science, Speeches of Hon. Thos. F. Marshall, Life of Dr. Daniel Drake, Guizot's History of the Decline and Fall of the Roman Empire, Nightingale, Universal Musician; Etc., Etc.; Etc.

ALSO, JUST PUBLISHED

WEBB'S FREEMASON'S MONITOR,

The best Masonic Book extant. Also,

THE BROTHERHOOD, OR ODD FELLOWSHIP, PUBLISHED IN ENGLISH AND GERMAN.

We invite the attention of Booksellers, Druggists, and General Dealers to our stock of Books, Paper and Stationery, Blank Books, etc., suitable to the wants of City Jobbers and Country Dealers. In addition to our own large list of Publications, we supply the trade with all books at Publisher's Prices. We manufacture every variety of

BLANK BOOKS,

And offer them to the trade, at the lowest Wholesale Rates of Eastern Markets. Our extensive assortment of

LETTER, CAP AND NOTE PAPERS, ENVELOPES,

Wrapping Paper, Bonnet Boards, Etc.

Enable us to compete successfully with Eastern Houses in supplying the Jobbing Trade with these articles and Stationery of every description. Our large and well furnished

Printing Office and Bindery,

Enable us to do JOB PRINTING of every description, and publish Books for Authors in as good style and on as favorable terms as can be done anywhere.

JOBBERS and DEALERS are invited to call and examine our stock.

All orders received by mail filled promptly, and with strict attention to the wishes of the customer.

APPLEGATE & CO.,
43 Main Street, Cincinnati, O.

(BOH) CINCINNATI (BOL) DIRECTORY. (BON) 73

Boeker Frederick, cigar mkr., bds. 115 Ham. Road
Boekested Elizabeth, 6 Pleasant
Boellner John H., dry goods, 517 Race
Boelsker John, quarryman, 67 Pendleton
Boemmel Michael, stone mason, 132 W. Liberty
Boeniker Christian, blk.smith, wks. 602 Main
Boer Jacob, produce, n.s. Corp. al. b. Price and Young
Boeracker John, cab. mkr., 57 Wood
Boerdering Ily., w.s. Vine b. Milk and Mulberry
Boeres John, boots and shoes, 660 Elm
Boerger Francis, cooper, 637 Race
Boertger Geo, blk smith. bds. 13 14th
Boerger Ily., porter, 8 13th
Boericke Oscar, b k. S P. Thomas', h. 5 Jackson
BOERNER Chas. G., (Smith & B.) 70 Barr
Doesch Frank, tinner, 9ª Barr
Boese Frederick, wagon mkr., 634 Main
Boeshirz John, barber, 433 Vine
Boeshausen Andrew, lab., 186 Everett
Boesher Jacob, tanner, 443 Main
Boeter Ily., lab. bds. 24 Woodward
BOETIG TRAUGOTT, G , Looking Glass and Frame Maker, Ornamenter and Decorator, s.e c. John and 2d, h. 181 Richmond
Boetker Wm., 59 Riddle
Boettcher Wm, druggist, s.w.c. Vine and Findlay
Boetter Ily., lab. 67 Pendleton
Boettger Ily., porter, 60 13th
Boetticher Michael, eng., 244 Pleasant
Boewing Herman. lab., 2 Lucy
Bofinger Augustus G., clk., bds. 167 W. 9th
Bofinger Benjamin, atty., 241 W. 9th, h. 167 W. 9th
Bofinger Carrie, 167 W. 9th
Bofinger Wm. H , clk., 167 W. 9th
Bogart Isaac, sen., (D. & Son) res. Carthage
Bogart John H., banner painter, 25 W. 4th, bds. 485 W. 9th
Bogart Samuel, meat store, 325 Central Av., h. n.w.c. 4th and Smith
Bogart & Son, (Isaac D., sen. & Isaac B., jr.) painters, s.s Vanhorn b. Baymiller and Freemen
Bogart Thos. O , mach., 107 Mound
BOGEN G. & P., (George B. & Peter B.) Pork Packers and Ham Curers, also, Manufacturers of Catawba Wine and Sausage Skins,' Ham. Road nr. Brighton House
BOGEN George, (G. & P. D.)- Ham. Road nr. Brighton House
Bogen George, jr., with G. & P. Bogen, h 127 Dayton
Bogen Jacob, with G. & P. Bogen, h. 158 Dayton
Bogen Joseph lab., 391 W. Front
BOGEN Peter, (G. & P. B.) Ham. Road nr. Brighton House
Bogenleck Ily., 88 Stark
Boger Ily., lab., 20 Madison
Boger Michael, mach., wks. n.s. Front b. Lawrence and Pike
Bogershausen Julius, bakery, 347 Central Av.
Bugert Hannah, confec., 46 E. 6th
Boggert David, silver plater, s.e.c. New and Broadway
Boggs George W., blk smith, 336 W. 7th
Boggs James, b k. 747 Central Av
Boggs Robert, candle manuf., 747 Central Av., h. 96 David
Boggs Samuel, blk.smith, 124 E. 2d, h. 356 W. 7th
Bogner John, carp., 682 Main
Bogus --, molder, 29 E. 3d e. of Parsons
Boham Daniel, carriage mkr., 130 Clinton
Bohan Patrick, lab., s.s. 6th e. of Lock
Bohart Cornelius, porter, 19 Woodward
Bohatek Joseph, saddler, 41 Elder
Bohein Catharine, 134 Bremen
Bohen Cornelius, huckster 29 Cutter

Bohen Dennis, porter, Burnet House
Bohen Michael, huckster, s.s. Hunt e. of Liberty
Bohen Thos., servt., Burnet House
Bohen Wm., porter, Burnet House
Boher George, lab., 164 Everett
Bohl Cecilia, servt., 286 Longworth
Bohl Jacob, shoe mkr., bds. 10 Sycamore
Bohl John, boots and shoes, 10 Sycamore
Bohl John, driver, American Express Co
Bohl Peter, butcher, h. n.w.c. Pub. Landing and Sycamore
BOHL PETER, New Orleans House, 19 Sycamore
Bohl Valentine, millinery, 73 E. Pearl
Bohland Dena. 18 Commerce
Bohland Francis. stone cutter 631 Vine
Bohlander Emma, 52 Everett
Bublander George, wood yard, n.s. Ham. Road nr. Mohawk Bridge, h. 377 Baymiller
Bahlander Ily., clk., bds. 377 Baymiller
Bohlander John, meat store, 59 W. Court w. of Central Av., h. Findlay b. Central Av. and Canal
Bohlender John, cigar mkr., wks. 438 Main
Bohler Jacob, baker, bds. 199 W. 6th
Bohling Ily., 128 Poplar
Buhlinger Anthony, trunk mkr., 27 Buckeye
Bohlinger Michael, cigar mkr., 196 Clinton
Bohlke George H., grocer, 305 Freeman
Bohlman Ily., chair mkr., 104 Clark
Boldmrn Joseph, molder, 132 Clinton
Buhlmann Bernard, cab. mkr., 20 Mansfield
Bohlmann Conrad, cab. mkr., wks. 128 W 2d
Bollmann Elizabeth, 132 Clinton
Bohlmann Ily., carman. 41 E. 7th
Buhlmann Ily., lab . 132 Clinton
BOHM Abram, (B., Mack & Co.) 80 Barr
BOHM Joseph, (Bohm, Mack & Co.) 349 W. 6th
BOHM, MACK & CO , (Abram B , David M. & Joseph Bohm) Wholesale Dealers in Notions, Fancy Goods, &c. 80 W. Pearl
Bohm Moses, paper hanger, 12 Home
Bohmer Frances, bds. 164 E. 5th
Bohmer Wm., watchman, 481 W. 8th
Bohn John, meat store, s.w.c. Liberty and Baymiller
Bohn John, wagon mkr., bds. 343 Walnut
Bohn Joseph lab., 108 Ham. Road
Bohn Lewis, peddler, 67 Buckeye
Bohne Fred., tailor 65 12th
Bohnert B. & J., (Bernhard & Joseph) curled hair, &c., 704 Race
Bohnert Bernhard, (B. & J. B.) 463 Vine
Bohnert Joseph, (B. & J. D.) 187 Ham. Road
Bohnkamp Ludwig, 20 Milton
Bohnsack John, lab , 293 Water
Bohon Elijah. printer, 77 Pendleton
Bohr John, lab., wks. s.e.c. Canal and Vine
Bohrer Eberhard. tailor, 13 Hunt
BOHRER GEORGE A , Livery Stable and Undertaker, 551 Elm, h. 540¾ Elm
Boia Ily., cof. h., 86 W. 2d
Boice Ed., bk. binder, 447 W 2d
Boll Thomas, blk. smith. bds. 19 Abigail
Boll William, 398 Broadway
Bolla Rachael, 187 W. Court w. of Central Av.
Bollney Newton, carp., s.s. Taylor b. Freeman and Carr
Bojer George. lab., 148 Laurel
Bokap Fredericka, servt., 31 Clark
Bokmann Geo., car mkr., wks C. T. Dumonts
Bolan Edward. lab., 67 Cherry al.
Bolan Eliza, servt., 116 E. 4th
Bolan John, lab., 51 E. 8th e. of Lock
Boian Sarah, 614 W. 6th
Boland Conrad. butcher, e.s. Milk b. Vine and Calhoun
Boland Dennis, lab., 116 Barr 6

Boland Fred., wks Cin Type Foundry
Boland John, lab., 155 Water
Boland John, lab , 19 Central Av.
Boland Lizzie, servt., 293 Richmond
Boland Richard, currier, 83 Spring
Boland Wm., teamster, n s. Liberty b. John and Linn
Bolander Nathaniel, meat store, w.s. Pike b. Pearl and 3d
Bolaur John, lab., wks. s.w.c. Broadway and 5th
Bole Robert, blk.smith, wks. n.s. Front b. Lawrence and Pike
Boleter George, lab., 91 12th
Boles Bernhard, cab. mkr , bds. 16 Abigail
Bolford John, carp., 671 W. 6th
Bolger John, lab., e.s. Reading Road nr. Montgomery Pike
Bolla Chas., lab., 235 Bremen
Bolinger Jacob, cab. mkr. 35 W. Court w. of Central Av.
Bollard Fred., mach., n.e.c Hunt and Broadway
Bolle Martin, harness mkr., 49 Bremen
Boller John, 78 Mohawk
Boller Louis, carp., 68 Rittenhouse
Bollers Bernard, carp., bds. 16 Abigail
Bolles David, marble works, 243 Vine, h. Mill Creek Tp.
Bolles Lemuel. b k., 6 E. 4th, h. Covington
Bolles Thomas, lab., 185 W. Canal
Balles Wm. T., clk., 215 Baymiller
Bolley Alexander, confec., n.s. 6th, b. Baymiller and Jane
Bollin Basilius, bk. binder, 29 Elder
Bolling Chas. Ily , carp., 654 Main
Bolling Francis. varnisher, 91 W. Court
Bolling Ily , chair mkr , c. Elm & Green
Bollinger Mary, wks. Ilieatt & Woods candle factory
Bollinger Peter, saloon, 120 Clinton
Bollmann Dietrich, stone mason, 63 Observatory
Bollmann Frank, hostler, 66 Richmond
Bollmann Frederick G., conf h. 38 Green
BOLLMANN J. B. & CO., (John B., B. & Ed. Hoenig,) props., Teutonia Hotel. 15 and 17 E. 9th
Bollmann John, lab. wks. 11 Franklin
BOLLMANN John B., (J. B. B & Co.) 15 9th
Bollmann Theodore, boots and shoes, 35 Baum
Bollmann Wm., watch mkr., bds. 369 Main
Bollmann Wm., bar k., 218 Vine
Bolls Geo., shoe mkr., 1 Smith Court
Bo'mer Barney, lab., 25 Mill
Bolser Chas W , 53 Clay
Bolser Geo., painter, 53 Clay
Bolser Joseph, policeman, 53 Clay
Bolser Wm. H., 53 Clay
B dt Francis, seamstress, 154 Ham. Road
Bolt Mrs. Mary, dress mkr., 416 Walnut
Bolte Anna M , seams'ress, 102 Abigail
Boltes Wm., clk., bds. 162 Elm
Bolthaupt John F , molder, 7 15th, b. Elm and Plum
Bolton Margaret, servt., 422 W 6th
Boltz John, cooper, bds. 277 Ham. Road
Bolz Adam, turner, n.w c. Laurel and Central av. h. 529 Plum
Bolz Daniel, barber, bds. 139 E. Front
Bolz Jacob, barber, 555 W. 5th, h. 490 W. 3d
Boman Hy., 28 Mohawk
BOMAN LEWIS, Propr. Brighton House, Harrison Pike, Head of Central Avenue
Bomberger Aaron, mer., h. 240 Broadway
Bonan Theodore. cab. ware, w.s. Cutter, b. Clinton and Betts, h. 114 Betts
BONAPARTE Edmund, (B. & Reynolds,) 182 Sycamore
BONAPARTE & REYNOLDS, (Edmund B. & Edward B. R.,) Physicians, 182 Sycamore
Bond Chloe, 135 Everett
Bond Elizabeth, dress mkr., bds. 199 Webb
Bond Enos. bds 199 Webb
Bond Francis, lab., 199 Webb
Bond Sarah, 199 Webb
Bond Sophia, 55 George

JAMES SKARDON,

AGENT FOR

SINGER'S SEWING MACHINES,

For Manufacturing and Family use,

NEW COMMERCIAL BUILDING,

Corner of Fourth and Race Streets,   CINCINNATI, O.

Machine Needles, Silk, Thread, Cotton, Oil, and every article connected with the Machine business, can be procured at the above Office.

To ascertain the immense superiority of Singer's Machines, it is only necessary to inquire of any mechanic or manufacturer who uses one.

NATIONAL INSURANCE COMPANY,

OF CINCINNATI, OHIO.

CAPITAL, - - - - - - - - - - $100,000.

Office, South-West Corner of Front and Main Streets.

Marine, Inland Transportation, and Fire Risks taken at current rates.

DIRECTORS:

JOHN BURGOYNE,	THOS. R. BIGGS,	MARCUS FECHHEIMER,	WILLIAM HEPWORTH,
ROBERT MOORE,	C. L. MOORE,	F. X. WIEDEMER,	S. W. SMITH,
TH. ONG,	J. L. ROSS,	HENRY ELLIS,	E. M. SMITH.

HENRY C. URNER, Secretary.   **JOHN BURGOYNE, President.**

G. A. MENZEL & CO.'S

(Formerly Klauprech & Menzel's.)

Lithographic Establishment,

Nos. 257 and 259 WALNUT STREET,

Opposite Walnut Street House, - - CINCINNATI, O.

Portraits, Landscapes, Show Cards,

MAPS.

CARDS, NOTES, BILL-HEADS, CHECKS, DRAFTS,

Labels of every kind, &c., &c., done in the best style and on the most reasonable terms.

(BOO) CINCINNATI (BOR) DIRECTORY. (BOS) 75

Bond Wm., printer, bds. 91 Longworth
BOND Wm Key, Receiver Cincinnati, Wilmington and Zanesville Railroad Company. h. 114 Broadway
Bonditz Ch rles, painter, 138 W Liberty
Bone Hv., cigar mkr., 393 Broadway
BONER JOHN, Importer and Dealer in Military and Fancy Goods, 35 W. 5th, h. 47 George
Boney Joseph, lab., bds. 239 Barr
Boney Louis, bds. 163 Sycamore
Bonfanti Anselmo, tailor, 29 W. 8th
Bonfanti Samuel, fruit stand, n.w.c. 4th and M din, h. 29 W. 8th
Bonham Nehemiah A., carp., 672 W. 6th
Boningle Sophia, 559 Sycamore
Bonjarts E J., clk., bds. 360 Elm
Bonker Joseph, watchman, n.w.c. Plum and 9d
Bonlaar Ann, servt., 72 Pike
Bonn H., cigar mkr., 15 Madison
Bonn John, shoe mkr., h. 12 15th
Bonn John shoe mkr, 66 Rittenhouse
Bonn Wm., tailor 35 Moore
Bonner John, confec., 461 W. 5th
Bonner J hn, omnibus driver, 112 Baum
Bonner R., white washing, 45½ E. 3d
BONNER STEPHEN, Physician and Surgeon, Office and Residence, 189 W. 7th
BONNER STEPHEN, Physician, 189 W 7th
Bonnet John, lab., E. 3d, b. Baum and Parsons
BONNEVILLE James E., (J. C. Towers & Co.) 149 Main
BONNY Andrew, (Shaw & B.,) n w.c. Court and Cutter
Bonny John lab. 463 George
BONSALL CHAS., General Insurance Agent, 4 Public Landing, h. 118 W. 6th
Bonsall Chas. P. J, ins. agt., 118 W. 6th
Bonsall Eliza, 297 Longworth
Bonsall Franklin millwright, 480 W. 4th
Bonsall Geo. W., printer, 430 W. 4th
BONSALL ISAAC H., Photograph and Ambrotype Gallery, 14 W. 5th
Bonsall John, mach., 480 W. 4th
Bonsall Robt T., salesman, 39 W. 4th, h 118 W. 6th
BONTE ALBERT P. C., Oval and Squire Frame Manufac., 118 W. 4th, h. 141 Linn
Bonte Charles E., frame mkr., bds. 22 Perry
Bonte Edward, bds. 22 Perry
Bonte Frank, varnisher, 61 Abigail
Bonte Hy., hatter, 14 W. 9th
BONTE John, (John B. & Co.,) res. Springdale
BONTE JOHN & CO., (Jno. B. & Wm. Hasson.) Ropes and Cordage, 8 Commercial Row
Bonte John H, wagon mkr., s.e.c. 9th and John. h. 252 John
BONTE PETER C., Pork Packer, 619 Central av , h. 16 David
Bonte Wm., wagon mkr , h 252 John
Bontel Louis, mach , 102 Bremen
Boobe Hy , lab., 144 Baymiller
Boogaart Cornelius, lab , n.s. Cassatt al. b. Main and Sycamore
Boohan Dennis, grocery, 29 Accommodation
Book John, carp., bds. 15 Commerce
Brooke Jacob, carp., 285 Linn
Dooker Fanny, 24 E. 7th
Bookwood Chas., cof. h., 238 Vine
Boone Joseph C., express driver, 435 Sycamore
Boone Joseph T., express driver, 435 Sycamore [Vine
Boone Mary, n.s Mulberry, b. Rice and
Doorman Thomas, plasterer, 213 Everett
Boos August, mach., 41 Moore
BOOTH R. W. & C ., (Ralph W. B., Frank Alter. John Young & Adolphus D. Rodgers.) Importers and Jobbers of Hardware, Cutlery and Guns, s.w.c. Pearl and Walnut
BOOTH Ralph W., (R. W. B. & Co.,) h. New York city

Booth Waldo C., salesman, s.w.c. Walnut and Pearl h. 146 Smith
Booth Wm. J., box mkr., hds. 158 W. 3d
Boothm Mary. 517 E. Front
Boots Deborah, 369 W, 8th
Buran Michael, lab., n.s. Cherry al., b. Plum and Central av
Borch Alexander, copper smith, bds. 426 Vine
Borchard Christopher, cab. mkr., wks. 11 Franklin
Borcherding Conrad, stone mason, 189 Oliver
Borcherding Conrad, tailor, 72 Rittenhouse
BORCHERDING Henry, (R. & H. B.,) bds. 503 Freeman
Borcherding H rman, lab., 173 Oliver
BORCHERDING R. & H., (Rudolph & Henry,) Hardware Store, 503 Freeman
BORCHERDING Rudolph, (R. & H. B.,) 503 Freeman
Borchers George J. F , printer, bds. 4 Mary
Borchers Hv., carp., 588 Race
Borchers Hv., lab., wks. 196 W. Pearl
Borches Sophia 4 Mary
Borckenhagen Wm., wagon mkr., 537 Walnut
Borckmeier Chas. L., molder, 43 Pleasant
Bordeck Christian, meat store, 168 Linn
Borden Geo. W., saddler, bds. United States Hotel
BORDEN HENRY C., United States Pension Agent, 75 W. 3d, h 411 John
Dord n Samuel, clk., h. 411 John
Borgan Joseph. lab., 68 Peete
Borgard Herman H., stone cutter, 68 Green
Borgeding B rney, shoe mkr., bds 22 E. Front
Borgeding Frank shoe mkr..66 W. Front
Borgeding Hermann H., 176 Pleasant
Borgumecke Christopher, cab. mkr., 246 Clark
Borgemenke Elizabeth. 246 Clark
Borgender Herman, lab., wks. N. W Thomas & Co.
Borgender Rodolph, wks. N. W. Thomas & Co.'s
Burger Fred., boots and shoes. 459 Main
Borger George, teacher, 625 Vine
Burger John, 70 Race
Borger Peter. finisher, 8 Moore
Borger Wendel. blk. smith, s.w.c. Vine and Findlay
Borgerding Francis. tailor, 612 Elm
Borgerding Hy., lab., 613 Race
Borgerding J. Hv., confec., 8 E. Front
Borgershausen Herman, jeweler, bds. 347 Broadway
Borgert John, tailor, n.s. Goose al. b. Green and Elder
Borges Mary, 278 George
Borges Rev. Casper, s.e.c. 8th and Central av
Borget Hy , watchman. n.s. Front, e. of Kelly
Borginaun Darney, box mkr., wks. Livington, nr. Linn
Borgmann Hy., dray, 55 Hughes
Borgmann. Hy., box mkr., wks. Livingston. nr. Linn
Borgmann John. lab , e.s Sycamore, b. Abigail and Woodward
Borginann Joseph, lab, 24 Abigail
Bargo Vincent, huckster. 59 Vine
Dorhen, varnisher, 205 W. Front
Borherding Wm., dry goods, 143 Everett
Bork Hermann, b.k., 64 W. Pearl, h. 117 Laurel
Bork Wm. carp., 18 Hughes
Borkkenbolt Fred., shoe mkr., bds. 37 Ludlow
Borlace Hamilton, clk., bds. 44 W. 7th
Borland Hy , lab., 62 W. Mulberry
Borland Hy., molder, wks. n.e.c. Canal and Walnut
Borland John. molder, wks. n.e.c. Canal and Walnut
Borland Mrs. P., 34 Longworth
Born Eva. e.s Vine, b. Calhoun and Auburn av

Born & Greiwe, (Jacob B. & Christoph, G.,) mineral water manuf, 530 Walnut
BORN Hy., (B. & Steidel) 564 Vine
Born Hy., cigar mkr., 15 Madison
B rn Jacob. (B. & Greewe) 530 Walnut
Born Nicholas. bds 3 3 Walnut
Born Philip, liquor store. 665 Race
BORN & STEIDEL, (Henry B. & Jacob S.) Millinery Store, and Hats, Caps, &c., 564 Vine
Bornickhouse Hy. G., clk., bds. 52 McFarland
Bornman Charles, butcher, 331 Baymiller
Borns Christian, cof. h., 517 E. Front
Bornschein Edward, watch mkr., 594 Central Av.
Bornstein Henrietta, 16 Richmond
Bornstein Leopold, com. mer., 35 W. Front, h. 16 Richmond
Borntrager Valentine, tailor, 130 W. Liberty
Boro & Bro., (James & Vincent) confec., 89 Broadway
Boro Dominick, (Boro & Bro.) n.e.c. 3d and Elm
Boro James, (B & Bro.) n.e.c. 3d and Elm
Boro V. & Bro., (Vincent & Dominick) confec., n.e.c. 3d and Elm
Boro Vincent, (B. & Bro) n.e.c. Elm and 3d
Borrington James, tailor, bds. 70 Sycamore
Borst Charles, painter, w s. Thuler al. b. Wade and Adams
Borwinckel Hy., lab., 65 Abigail
Bosch John, confec., 302 W. 8th
BOSCH NICHOLAS, Agent German Emigration and Relief Society, s. w c. Court and Walnut, h. 24 Mercer
Borcha F., tinner, wks. n.w.c. Race and 2d
Bosche Caroline, seamstress, 95 Woodward
Boschen Robert, printer, 510 W. 3d
Boschert Bernhard, cof. h., 620 Main
Bose Chas. L . cigar mkr , 57 15th
Bose John, cooper, 9 Accommodation
Boser Frederick, clk., 81 Clay
Bosfeld Christian, plasterer, w.s. Thuber al b Wade and Liberty
Bosh Benjamin, shoe mkr., 160 Freeman
Boskan John, salesman, 110 Carr
Boskermul er William, lab., n.w.c. Ramsey and Park al.
Bosley James E., conductor, bds. 142 W. 7th
Bosley Thos. A., paper hanger, n.s. 7th b. Race and Elm
Boss Christien, (B & Co) 54 Franklin
Boss & Co , (Christian B , Geo. B. & Julius Gebhard) brewers, s.e c. Sycamore and Abigail
Boss Frantz, carriage mkr., bds. 343 Walnut
Boss Geo., (B. & Co.) s.e.c. Sycamore and Abigail
Boss Harriet. bds. 87 E. Front
Boss Jacob, tailor, bds. 31 Buckeye
Boss Louis, clk., c. 5th and Pike
Boss Robert, pilot, n.w.c. Front and Elm
Bosse Frank, mason, 391 Broadway
Bosse Hy., furniture 50 W. 5th, h. 132 Clark
Bosse Mary, servt., 252 Longworth
Bosse Wm., upholsterer, 187 Clark
Bossenmeier Robert, brewer, 669 Vine
Bossey Wm., cof. h., n.e.c. Linn and Bank
Bossinger John, tailor, wks. 547 Vine
Busaman Conrad, watchman, n.s. Cherry al. h. Plum and Central Av.
Bosso Antony, brush mkr., 84 W. Front
Bost John, carp., 129 York
Bost John, trunk mkr., w.s. Jordan b. Clark and Gest
Bostler John, grocery, n.w.c. Lewi and Front
Bostler Margaret, 714 Vine
Bostwick Hy., printer wks. 2 Baker
Bostwick Sarah, 337 W. 8th
Boswell Geo., lab., 33 Pleasant

H. HOMAN,
MANUFACTURER OF
BRITANNIA WARE & CANDLE MOULDS,

AGENTS AND MANUFACTURERS OF

Stainthorp & Co's Patent Candle Mould Machine,

And Dealers in Block Tin, Antimony, and Tinners' Soder,

No. 11 East Seventh Street, between Main and Sycamore Streets, north side,

CINCINNATI, OHIO.

PAPER WAREHOUSE.

LOUIS SNIDER,
Franklin Paper Mills,   HAMILTON, O.

MANUFACTURER OF

FOURDRINIER, SIZED, CALENDERED, FINE & COMMON

BOOK PAPERS.

Also, SUPERIOR NEWS PRINTING PAPER,

AND DEALERS IN

Manilla and Colored Papers, Bonnet and Book Boards, Also, Wrapping, Ham, Roofing Papers, &c., &c.

WAREHOUSE, 232 WALNUT STREET,

JOHN McCALL, Agent.   CINCINNATI, O.

CURLED HAIR, BRISTLE, AND GLUE MANUFACTORY.

A. D. BULLOCK & CO.

Nos. 12 and 14 West Second Street, CINCINNATI, O.

Manufacture and keep constantly on hand a full stock of all kinds of

CURLED HAIR,

PURE LONG, SHORT AND MIXED,—Suitable for the use of Cabinet Makers, Upholsterers, Carriage Makers, Car Builders and Saddlers. Also, Dealers in GLUE, and the different descriptions of AMERICAN BRISTLES. We respectfully solicit your orders for goods in our line.

(BOW) CINCINNATI (BOY) DIRECTORY. (BRA) 77

Boswell Joseph, s.w.c. 6th and Broadway
Bosworth H. S , publisher, 28 W. 4th, res. Walnut Hills
Bosworth H S.. (M. J. Dennis & Co.) res. Walnut Hills
Bosz Paul lab., 640 Race
Bote August, baker, wks. 347 Vine
Bothe Bernard, tailor 2 2 Clark
Bothe Hy., blk smith, 34 Smith
Bothner Louis, cof. h., 430 Main
Butter Geo.. lab., 50 Rittenhouse
Botlers Miller. tailoress, 164 Everett
Bottenus Daniel. tailor, 63 Bremen
Butter Gerhard H., cof. h. 18 13th
Butter Mary. tailoress, 62 Hunt
Bottger John H. D., shoe mkr , s.s. Calhoun b. Clifton Av. and McMillan and Clark
Botthoff John, e.s. Hand al. b. Court and Clark
BOTTLER Chas , (Fachr & B) 64 Webster
Bottler F. Wm., 542 Main
Bottler Philip, cigar mkr.. bds. 622 Vine
Bottler Wm., lab., wks. 478 Main
Bottner Charles, tailor, w.s. Dayton b. Western Av and Coleman
Bottonhern John A., trimmer, s.w.c. Brown and Byron
Botts —, jewelry, bds. 34 Longworth
Botts Arthur F., teamster. 216 W. Front
Botts Hannah, s.s. 6th b. Broadway and Culvert
Botts John. b. h., 212 W. Front
Botts John S.. lab., 101 W. Front
Botts Wm.. lab , 219 Water
Bouchard Edwin H., shoe mkr., 281 W. 6th
Boucker Fred. Hy., carpet layer, 375 W. 5th
Boudry David, photographer, wks. 30 W. 4th [24
Boapher Thomas, mach.. wks. 116 W.
Boul John. tailor, 32 Sycamore
Bou ; Mary, servt , 100 E. 4th
Bour Philip A., clk. n.w.c. 7th and Broadway
Bourbring Barney, teamster, 225 Cutter
Bourbring Hy.. teamster 2.25 Cutter
Bourke Pat.. lab., 50th John
Bourman Ferdinand, 253 Clark
Bourman Hy., carp., 53 Pine
Bourmann John, cab mkr., 433 Clark
Bourne Oswin, clk., 337 W. 4th
Bourne Richard, shoe mkr., wks. 231 Race
Boushauen August, gilder, 186 Everett
Boustanger Israel, peddler. e.s. Baymiller b. Liberty and Wade
Bouts Frederick, watch mkr , 34 Longworth
Bowan David, harness mkr., bds. 109 W. 5th
Bowder Louisa, n.e.c. Sycamore and Abigail
Bowdle Daniel, 299 Walnut
Bowdle Daniel D , atty., bds. 299 Walnut
Bowden Julia, servt , 109 Pike
Bowdre David, artist, 423 W. 3d
Bowe John, teacher. St. Xavier College
Bowen Aaron S , com. mer., 5 E. Front, res. Clifton
Bowen David, harness mkr , bds. 109 W. 6th
Bowens Sarah, 147 Clark
Bower George, carp., s.e.c. Bank and Baymiler
Bower Joseph, driver, wks. n.w.c. Court and Race
Bower Moritz. sprinkler, 23 Bremen
Bower Timothy, carp., 952 E. Front
Bower Wm., mason, 32 Jones
Bowering Geo , teamster, bds. 112 Laurel
Bowers A. L., bls. s.w.c. Race and 3d
Bowers Anna, 346 W. 5th
Bowers E. E., clk, 56 W. 3d
Bowers Geo. W., clk, 56 W. 3d
Bowers Harrison, teamster. 75 Pleasant
Bowers Hy., pattern mkr., 199 Richmond
Bowers Isaac W., general supt. Greenwood's Foundry
Bowers J F, bk. binder bds. 296 W. 5th
Bowers John, cooper, 105 W. M. Canal
Bowers Lindolf, bk. layer, 424 W. 8th
Bowers Matthew, lab., 69 Observatory Road

Bowers Robert. shoe mkr., 61 W. 4th
Bowers Robert. shoe mkr., 242 Broadway
Bowers Val.. lab., wks. Henry Nye's
Bowers Wm. T., bk. layer, 140 Daymiller
Bowersfield Chas. W., rope mkr., 240 Laurel
Bowersfield Herman, bk. layer, 184 Everett
Bowes Emeline, 483 Race
Bowie Archibald, mach , s.w.c. Ludlow and 3d
Bowie Donald clk., 210 Sycamore
Bowie Lock, driver, e s Ludlow b. Pearl and 3d
Bowker Chas. H., clk, 101 W. 4th
Dowlby William, painter, bds. Indiana House
BOWLER G. W., Veterinary Surgeon, n.w.c. 6th and Walnut
BOWLER ROBERT B , Proprietor Kentucky Central Railroad, Office, 90 Broadway, res. Clifton
Bowles Fred. A., clk., 174 Elm
Bowley George J. engraver, s.w.c 4th and Walnut, bds. Newport
Bowling Jean, wks. Cin. Type Foundry
Bowman A., bds. Dennison House
Bowman Amos, white washer, s.s. 6th b. Broadway and Culvert
Bowman & Co., (Henry P. B.. H. A. B. Wm. Heatt & Wm. H. Woods) slaughter house, s.s. Deer Creek Road n. of Court
Bowman H. A.. (B. & Co.) 392 W. 9th w of Central Av,
BOWMAN Hy. P.. (Heatt & Woods) h. Pleasant Ridge, O.
Bowman John L., salesman, e.s Broadway nr. 4th
Bowman Joseph, cigars and tobacco, 279 Walnut
Bowman Mary, 462 W. 5th
Bowman Mary, 82 Peete
Bowman Mrs. P., b ds. 231 Walnut
Bowman Robert T., salesman 11 E. 4th
Bowman Thomas, roller, Race b. Court and Canal
BOWN Benj . (B. & Deming) 40 Main
BOWN & DEMING, (Benj. D. & John D) Wholesale Candy Manufacturers, Foreign Fruits and Nuts, 40 Main
BOWN THOMAS, Ornamental Composition Works and Gilding, and Manufacturer of Mirrors, 30 E. 4th. h. country
Bowyer Lewis W., dray, 281 W. Front
Box —, grocery, bds. 192 Sycamore
Box Joseph, shoe mkr.. bds. 31 Hopkins
Box Wm., feed store. 203 Broadway
Box'aiter Frederick, varnisher, 115 Carr
Boxleider Margaret, 13 E. Liberty
Boyce Wm., hinge fitter, works n.e.c Walnut and Canal
Boyces Anna. 28 Lock
Boyd Aaron, molder, wks. s.w.c. Front and Central Av
Boyd Adaline, teacher, 186 Mound
BOYD ALEXANDER, Merchant Tailor, 33 E. 3d, Railroad Building
Boyd Clara E , bds 194 E. 6th
Boyd David, lab., h. s.w.c. Vine and Water
Boyd Eliza, laundress, 66 George
Boyd Hy., bk, binder, wks. s.w.c. 8th and Walnut
Boyd Hy. mer.. 15 New
Boyd John, 765 Vine
Boyd John C., car builder, 14 Dayton
Boyd John W., bk., 10 W. Court w. of Central Av
Boyd Jos. B.. printer, 25 W. 4th, bds. Dennison House
Boyd Maria F., h. 10 W. Court w. of Central Av
Boyd Matthew, lab., bds. 35 Ludlow
Boyd Peter, tailor, 33 E. 3d
BOYD R. R., (R. G. Dun & Co.) h. New York City
Boyd Rachel, 139 Plum
Boyd Robert, b.k., 52 W. 2d, h. 74 Barr
Boyd Samuel, tailor, 27 E. 4th, h. 88 12th
Boyd Thomas L., agt., 65 W. 4th, h. 449 Linn

Boyd Thos. M. printer. 114 E. 3d
Boyd Wm.. driver, n.s. Pearl b. Lawrence and Pike
Boye Fred W., b.k., 319 Main, h. 20 W. 8th
Boyer Frank, baker, 444 W. 5th
Boyer Frank, baker, wks. s.e.c 2d and Ludlow
Boyer Hy., waiter, 60 E. 7th
Boyer John L., b.k., 42 W. 2d, bds, 229 W. 4th
Boyer Wm, D., clk., 42 W. 2d bds. 269 W. 7th
Boylan E , bds. Burnet House
Boylan James, cutter, h. 94 Bremen
Boylan Junius A., mer., bds. Spencer House
Boylan Thomas, mer., bds. Spencer House
Boyle Ann, waiter, Commercial Hospital
Boyle Charles, b k., bds. 109 E. 3d
Boyle Charles, carp., e.s. Smith b. 2d and Augusta
BOYLE & CO., Wholesale Liquor Dealers, 49, 51, 53 and 55 E. 2d
Boyle Dennis, bksmith. wks. 60 Hunt
Boyle Edward, paving, 90 Richmond
Boyle Hannah, 67 Cherry al
Boyle James bds. Railroad House
Boyle James, atty.. n.w.c. Main and Court, h. Mill Creek tp
Boyle James, dray, 58 Pierson
Boyle James. lab., 546 E. Front
Boyle John, (B. & Roach) 144 Linn
Boyle John, blksmith, 67 Commerce
Boyle John, coach smith, 67 Cherry al
Boyle John, contractor, 144 Linn
Boyle Mary, servt., 419 W. 6th
Boyle Mary, 126 Water
Boyle Mary, 176 Water
Boyle Michael, blksmith, bds. s.w.c. 5th and Broadway
Boyle Patrick 249 W Front
Boyle Patrick, driver, wks. 165 Central Av
Boyle Patrick, lab., e.s. Garrard n. of Gest
Boyle & Roach (John B. & Patrick E. R.) liquors, 269 Main
Boyle Rachael, 187 W. Court w. of Central Av
BOYLE Stephen S. (B. & Co.), res. near St. Mary's College. Warsaw Pike
Boyle Wm. H , harness mkr., bds. 241 W. Court
Boyles C. C., b.k., 74 W. 4th, h. 169 E. 3d
Boylson Bridget, 231 W. Court
Boynton Chas. A.. teller. A. L. Mowry & Co., h. n.s. Ringgold b. Price and Young
Boynton Rev. Chas. B., n.s. Ringgold b. Price and Young
Boynton Hy. V. N., n.s. Ringgold b. Price and Young
Boynton Samuel W., phys., 424 W 5th
Boynton Wm. McLean, clk., n.s. Ringgold b. Price and Young
Boys Thomas, wks. n.w.c. Freeman and 9th
Boyus James, 23 Madison
Braam Cornelius M., Cin. type foundry, h. 19 Mulberry
Braam John, carp.. 29 Schiller
Braam Nicholas, painter. 6 Mulberry
Braam Peter. painter, 5 Mulberry
Brabender Hubert, cof. h., 18 Mercer
BRACE Julius, national claim agency, 66 W 3d, h. Newport
Brace Thomas D , conductor, bds. Spencer House
Bracel George, cab. mkr , 53 Jones
Brach Susanah, laundress. 207 Clinton
BRACHMANN HENRY, Importer & Dealer in Wines and Liquors, 81 W. 3d, and C. N. Morris & Co., h. 399 W 5th
Brachmann Wm, b.k, 81 W. 3d, bds. 399 W. 5th
Brachmann Wm., cooper, bds. 172 Clay
Bracken Elisabeth, ironer. Spencer H use
Bracken James, driver, wks. n.w.c. Court and Race
Bracken Rebecca, 253 Laurel

CINCINNATI ADVERTISEMENTS.

E. & J. McARDLE,
Fashionable Merchant Tailors,

176 Vine St., bet. Fourth & Fifth,

CINCINNATI, O.

☞ A choice selection of Gent's Furnishing Articles always on hand.

G. W. SHEPPARD & CO.,
Manufacturers of

GOLD PENS,

No. 6 W. Fourth St., up Stairs,

BET. MAIN AND WALNUT, CINCINNATI, OHIO.

A large stock of superior Gold Pens, Gold and Silver Pen and Pencil Cases, always on hand, at liberal prices, wholesale and retail.

Pens neatly repaired and repointed to order. Orders by mail promptly attended to.

CHARLES GRAHAM.   ROBERT GRAHAM.

CHAS. GRAHAM & BRO.,
MACHINE BLACKSMITHS

277 West Front Street,

CINCINNATI, OHIO.

Manufacturers of Bridge Bolts and all kinds of Blacksmithing.

I. O. GESNER,
(Agent for Graniss & Co.,)

MONUMENTAL OYSTER CO.,

BALTIMORE, MD.

Wholesale and Retail Depot, 222 Walnut St.,

BET. FIFTH AND SIXTH STREETS,

CINCINNATI, O.

☞ Fresh Oysters received daily by Adams Express Co.

MEIER & RIEMEIER,
LUMBER DEALERS,

Hamilton Road, opp. Race St.,

CINCINNATI, O.

Keep constantly on hand an assortment of Pine Framing Timber, Pine and Poplar Joists, Scantling, White and Yellow Pine Flooring, Shelving, Weather Boards, Shingles and Lath.

Orders promptly filled.

THOMAS W. FARRIN.   JOHN K. GREEN.

T. W. FARRIN & CO.,
Dealers in all kinds of

PINE, POPLAR & OAK BUILDING LUMBER,

CEDAR, LOCUST & OAK FENCING POSTS.

Yard on Freeman St., opp. George.

FRAZER & CO.,
DEALERS IN LUMBER,

No. 404 NORTH SIDE SIXTH STREET,

Ten doors east of Cincinnati, Hamilton and Dayton R. R. Depot. Offer for sale a large assortment of Dry White and Yellow Pine, and other Lumber, Shingles, Shelving, Weather Boards, Partition Boards, Lath, Flooring, Sash and

SAW MILL TIMBER,

At the Lowest Cash Prices.

LANG & WANNER,
TANNERS & CURRIERS,

No. 39 DUNLAP STREET,

Between Henry Street and Hamilton Road,

CINCINNATI, O.

T. WICKERSHAM,
ARTIST.

Portrait and Photograph Painter.

Photographs taken and Portraits of all sizes painted on canvas.

Rooms No. 19 Pike's Opera House, 3d Floor,

CINCINNATI, O.

R. WALKER.
Dyer and Gents' Clothing Renovator, Repairing, &c.

65 EAST THIRD ST., CINCINNATI, O.

Clothing taken in every disfigured condition, and made to look equal to new. Orders by express promptly attended to.

MIDDLETON, STROBRIDGE & CO.,
LITHOGRAPHERS,

Engravers and Plate Printers,

No. 64 W. Fourth St. Cincinnati O.

J. W. BEESLEY,
MERCHANT TAILOR,

No. 105 Main Street,

Four doors above Third,   CINCINNATI, O.

Bracken Wm., cof. h., 8 Landing, h. s.e. c Ludlow and Front
Bracken Wm., teamster, 192 Clark
Brackenmann Herman, eng., 64 Elder
Brackland Hy., cigar manuf., 579 Main, bds. 577 Main
Brackman Hy., cooper, wks. Deer Creek Mills
Brackmann Herman, 46 Elder
Brackmeyer Bernhard, wagon mkr., w.s. Ridgway al. b. 14th and 15th
Bradbury Anni R., 43 E. Liberty
Bradbury C. N., b k., 256 Broadway, h. Walnut Hills
Bradbury Roxana, 121 Betts
Bradbury Vincent, saw mkr., 235 E. 6th
Bradbury Vincent C., salesman, 134 Main, h. 140 E. Liberty
BRADBURY WM. E., Flour Mill, 260 Broadway h. 276 Longworth
Bradenbach Fred., lab., 110 Clinton
Bradenbich Margaret, 112 Clinton
Bradenberger Martin, mason, w.s. Vine b. Mulberry and Milk
Bradford Miss ——, actress, National Theater
Bradford Frank, hostler, bds. Indiana House
BRADFORD James (James B. & Co.), 349 George
Bradford James, power, 401 George
Badford James, well and cistern bldr., 685 Sycamore
BRADFORD JAMES & CO., Manufacturers of Portable Flour Mills and Mill Stones, 65 Walnut, Factory 70 Elm
Bradford John, carp., wks. n e c. Canal and Walnut
BRADFORD John (T. Bradford & Co.), 338 George
Bradford Joseph, painter, 71 W. Court w. of Central Av
Bradford Louisa P., teacher, 38 Harrison
Bowford Maria, bds 71 Baker
Bradford Mary A., 375 W. 7th
BRADFORD T & CO. (John Bradford & David McGraw), French Bure Mill Stone and Portable Mill Manufacturers, 59 Walnut and 135 W. 2d
Bradford Thos. J., turner, 401 George
Bradler John, baker, e.s. Anderson al.b. 2d and Pearl
Bradley ——, 249 W. Front
Bradley C., conductor, bds. Burnet House
Bradley Charles, 193 Lock
BRADLEY Charles F. (B. & Webb), h. 4104 W. 9th
Bradley Dannis, blksmith, 199 E. Front
Bradley Edward M., clk, Chamberlain & Co.'s, h. w.s. Wilson b. Liberty and Milton
Bradley Ellen, 61 Barr
Bradley Geo. B., b k., Gaylord, Son & Co., bds. Henrie House
Bradley Giles, porter, w.s. Lock b. 8th and 6th
Bradley Hy., blksmith, bds. s.w.c. Plum and 6th
Bradley Hy., coachman, 355 W. 4th
Bradley Hy., painter, 115 Mound
Bradley Hy. M., varnisher, 115 Mound
Bradley H'ram., c irp., 46 Milton
Bradley Hiram A., moller.bds. 46 Milton
Bradley James, blksmith, 12 E. 8th
Bradley James, coach trimmer, bds. 21 George
Bradley James, lab., 418 W. 2d
Bradley James, lab., 420 W. 2d
Bradley John, carp., 494 W. 5th
Bradley John, lab., 60 Baum
Bradley John, molder, wks 267 W. 5th
Bradley John F., molder, bds. 41 Milton
Bradley John W., blksmith, 136 W. Pearl
Bradley Patrick, lab., n.s. Front e. of Lumber
Bradley Maria, 53 Everett
Bradley Mary, e.s. Crippen al. b. 7th and 8th
Bradley Richael, s.s. 6th b Broadway & Culvert
Bradley Thomas, 458 Elm

Bradley Thomas, dray, 73 14th
Bradley Thos., lab., n.s. Oregon b. 3d and 5th
Bradley W. P., clk., O, & M. R R. office, bds. 242 Plum
BRADLEY & WEBB. (Charles F. B. & Wm. A. W.) Stationers, Steam Printers Binders and Blank Book Manufacturers, 135 Main
Bradshaw Wm. Milton, (Byron & Co.), s.w.c. 5th and Central Av
Bradstucker Joseph, lab., 164 Everett
BRADSTREET EDWARD P., Attorney and Notary, 25 W. 3d h. Newport
BRADSTREET Hy (John M. B. & Sons), h. N. Y. City
BRADSTREET John M. (John M. B. & Sons), res. N. Y. City
BRADSTREET JOHN M & SONS, (John M. B. & Henry B.) Improved Mercantile Agency, 21 W. 3d. C. F. Brooke, Agent
Brudt uller Hy., cooper, 64 David
Brady Alice, e.s. M. Canal b. 6th and Court
Brady Anna, servt., 10 Elizabeth
Brady Bernhardt, chair mkr., wks. John Mitchell's
Brdy Francis, lab. 154 George
Brady James cof. h., 207 John
Braly John, currier, 15 W. Court w. of Central Av
Brady John, fireman, bds. 12 Landing b. Main and Walnut
Brady John, lab., 96 W. Mulberry
Brady John, lab., 602 Race
Brady John, porter, s.w.c. Elm and Pearl
Brady Jos. C., carp., 124 Cutter
Brady Martin, express man, 104 Clinton
Brady Mary, 31 E. 9th
Brady Michael, coachman, 361 W. 4th
Brady Patrick, lab., 32 Mulberry
Braly Solomon, baggage car, 61 Findlay
Brady Terrence, lab., 109 Mul erry
Brady Thomas, lab., n s. E Front e. of Leatherbury
Brady Thomas, teacher, w.s. Sycamore, b. 7th and 8th
Brnetzer Jacob, tailor, 26 Mohawk
Bruennig Joseph, painter, 491 Main
Braeutigam Anthony, shoe mkr., 650 Vine
Braeutigam Ernst, stone cutter, 43 Pleasant
Braeutigam John, chair caner, 78 W. Liberty
Braeutigam Sabina, mid wife, 78 W. Liberty
Brager Mary, 48 Lock
Brahm Barney, lab., w.s. Spring, b. Abigail and Hunt [way
Brahm John H., cof. h., 3 Landing, b. Broadway and Ludlow, h. 53 Broadway
Brahm Mary L., servt , 521 Vine
Brahu John B. h. 149 Abigail
Braidy Mary, cook, Dennison House
Brairton Martin, lab , 181 E. 3d
Braker David D., fish-dealer, s.s. Court, e. of Broadway
Brakman Henry W., cooper. 19 Adams
Bramble Alfred F., (Gerard & Co.) bds. s.e.c. Poplar and Freeman
Brames Frank, porter, rear 14 13th
Brammer Hy., porter, 130 Sycamore
Bramshoe George F., carp., 207 W. Court w. of Central Av.
Branagan Patrick, coachman, 441 Longworth
Brman Patrick, grocery, n.s. Cherry al. b. Plum and Central Av.
Branch M etha. 273 George
Branch Peter P., tailor, 24 Elder
Brand Charles. blk smith, n s. Poplar b. Freeman and Western av
Brand Francis W., druggist, s w.c. Race and 15th
Brand George, cigar mkr., 648 Vine
Brand George, ck., h. 83 E. Pearl
Brand Gottlieb, cooper, wks 33 Bremen
Brand Hy., carp., 553 John
Brand Hy., cooper, 61 David
Brand Hermann, cab. mkr., 53 Woodward

Brand John, lab., w.s. Campbell al., b. Elder and Findlay
Brand Margaret, 130 W. Liberty
Brand Peter, cooper, 94 Betts
Brand Peter, cooper, s.e.c. Harrison Pike and Brighton
Brand Peter, cooper. 147 Livingston
Brand Richard 475 Broadway
BRANDECKER Frank X., editor Wahrheitsfreund, s w.c. Vine and Longworth, h. Newport
Brandenstein Judah, lab., 487 Central Av.
Brandes George, bds. 86 e. 3d
Brandewiede Bernhard, lab., 671 W Front
Brandhorst Henry J., porter, n.e c. Race and 15th
Brandhorst Wm., lab., 684 Main
BRANDIS Charles (Weisker Brothers,) 121 Main
Brandis Henry, lab , 31 Pleasant
Brandis L., atty., 91 Sycamore
Brandle John, 110 Mohawk
Brandner, Anton, cab. mkr., wks. 468 W. 6th
Brandmeier Jacob, shoemkr., 280 Linn
Brando n Minerva, 416 W. 9th
Brandsta' r Frank, cooper, h. 377 Bay-miller
Brandstetter Joseph, lab., 103 Hamilton R ad
BRANDT ALBERT R., Malt House, 113 John, corner of Webb, h. 385 George
Brandt Andrew, cigars, &c.. 648 Vine
Brandt August, shoemkr., bds 65 W 5th
Brandt Charles. musician 12 E. Liberty
Brandt Charles, saddler. bds. 463 Vine
Brandt Conrad, tailor, 443 Main
Brandt Ernst. w.s. Campbell al ,b. Elder and Findlay
Brandt Frederick. clk.. 365 Cutter
Brandt Frederick, grainer, 90 Pleasant
Brandt Frederick C.. clk., 389 Main. h. w s. John nr. Wade
Brandt Gottlieb C. cooper, 26 Pleasant
Brandt Hy., painter, wks. Chas. Behlen & Co's. [3d
Brandt Hy., porter, bds. s.w c. Race and
Brandt Hy , shoemkr., 2 Lucy
Brandt Herman, bar k., bds. 216 Walnut
Brandt Herman. cab. mkr., 53 Woodward
Brandt John, musician, bs 22 Ham. Road
Brandt John. porter, 27 Cherry al
Brandt John C., lab., 29 Commerce
Brandt John H . lab . 2 Lucy
Brandt John H., shoemkr., 108 Walnut
Brandt Lewis (Angelbecks & B.,) n.e.c. Walnut and 9th
Brandt Lewis cab. mkr., 70 Buckeye
Brankamp Joseph, clk., s.e c. Linn and 8th
Brannan Anna, servt., n.e.c. 4th and Broadway
BRANNAN D. F., (Tweed & Andrews,) 133 W 7th
Brannan Martin servt., Burnet House
Brannan Patrick, lab., 68 Butler
Brannan Peter. lab.. 33 Race
Brannin James, stone cutter, 253 W. Court
Branning Carl. blk. smith, s.s. Reading Pike nr. Tunnel
Brannock Hy., carp., n e c. Reed and Nassau
Brannon, John. hostler, 70 Gano
Brannon Timothy, lab. 132 Central Av
Brannon Timothy, lab., w.s. Langdon al. b. 6th and 7th
Bransell John, lab., 26 E. 8th e. of Lock
BRANSON MISS SUSAN. Agent f r Aikens Family Knitting Machines. 104 W. 4th
Brant Barney, weaver, 303 W. 8th
Brant Michael L. musician, 422 Walnut
Brantis Sophia, seamstress, 52 Webster
Branton M.. molder, wks. Chamberlain & Co's.
Brann Mary, 206 E. 6th
Branmich Hy., lab., n.s. Sloo, e. of Harriett
Braraton Edward, h. 53 E. 8th, e. of Lock

Wrightson's Steam Printing House.

WRIGHTSON & CO.

BOOK & JOB PRINTERS

NO. 167 WALNUT STREET,

CINCINNATI, OHIO.

The attention of Publishers and Authors is respectfully directed to our superior facilities for doing

Printing, Stereotyping, & Binding,

In every style that may be required, promptly, and on reasonable terms.

CARDS,

ORNAMENTAL, COLORED, AND PLAIN,

GOLD, BRONZE, CRYSTAL AND FLOCK.

PICTORIAL AND ILLUSTRATED PRINTING.

PARTICULAR ATTENTION GIVEN TO THE PRINTING OF
Tinted Checks, Notes, Drafts, Stock Certificates, Lawyers' Blanks
BILL HEADS, BILLS LADING: CIRCULARS & MERCANTILE WORK.
RAILROAD BLANKS, TICKETS, &C.

Brartton Michael, molder, h. 53 E. 8th, e. of Lock
Braring Lizzie, 674 Central Av.
Braser Penn., clk., bds. 292 Race
Brashear Herman F., student, cor. 66 W. 3d, h. w.s Ohio av. nr. Elm
BRASHEARS G. & LAWS., (Gassaway B. & James H. L.) Auction and Commission Merchants, 57 and 59 Main
BRASHEARS Gassaway, (G. B & Laws) h. 84 Mound
Brashears Gassaway, jr., b. k., 57 Main, bds. 84 Mound
Brashears Joseph, clk., 65 Walnut
Brasher Albert, 190 W. 9th
Brasher B. Penn., salesman, 262 Race
Brasher Robert. 90 W. 9th
Brass C J., clk. R. G. Dunn & Co's.
Brassar Theodore, 78 Abigail
Brassartz Frank, cof. h., 97 W. M. Canal
Brassel Thomas, teamster, 50 E. 7th
Bratfisch August C , tailor, 665 Vine
Bratfisch Theresa, bds. 665 Vine
Brats Laurenz, currier, 209 Smith
Bratzler Charles, cof. h., 238 E. Front
Brauer Anna, 22 Hughes
Braurr Anthony, stone cutter, 207 W. Front
Brauer Edward, salesman, bds. 30 Broadway
Brauer John, porter, n.e.c. Bank and Linn
Brauer Joseph, carp., 213 Hopkins
Brauer Michael, barber, 672 Vine
Braumas Frank H., porter, 14 13th
Braun Anton, lab., 100 W. Liberty
Braun Bernard 309 W. Liberty
Braun Bernhard, bk. layer, 127 Ham. Road
Braun Engelbert, molder, w.s. Goose al. b. Green and Elder
Braun Ferdinand, grocery, 99 Hamilton Road
Braun Frederick, clk, 454 Walnut
Braun Geo., brush mkr., 36 Ham. Road
Braun Geo carp , 566 Elm
Braun Gottlieb, grocery, 454 Walnut
Braun Hy., tailor, 585 Walnut
Braun Jacob, tanner, 10 Dunlap
Braun John, baker 681 Race
Braun John, brush mkr , 507 Sycamore
Braun John, carp., 546 Sycamore
Braun John, policeman, 52 Elder
Braun Josephine, servt., 172 Sycamore
Braun Lewis, butcher, h. 576 Elm
Braun Peter, lab., 170 Clay
Braun Sophia, 70 Pleasant
Braun Wm., druggist, 696 Race
Braunstein Frank X., 71 Pike
Braunts George, mobler, 30 Jackson
Braunts Hy., lab., 389 Vine
Braunwerth Michael J., baker, n. s. Charlotte, h. Linn and Baymiller
Brausch Mathias, lab., 666 Race
Brausch Peter, coach mkr., 666 Race
Brauss Ferdinand, steward, St. Charles Exchange
Brawdy Rufus, barber, e.s. Pancoast al. b 7th and 8th
Bray C. W., painter, 221 Elm
Bray George R., b. k., 364 W. 5th
Bray Job F., pipeman, 364 W. 5th
Bray John, marble cutter, wks. n.e.c. Elm and Canal
Bray Patrick, stone cutter, w.s. Mulberry al., b. Pearl and 3d
Bray William J., printer Press Office, h. Pendleton
Brayer Nicholas, molder, 64 Elder
Brazel George, (B & Tasnacht.)
Brazel & Tasnacht, (Geo. B. & Fred. T) cab. makers n.w.c Laurel and Central Av.
Brazell John, salesman, 196 Main, h. Mt. Adams
Brazil Martin, painter, e.s. Whittaker, b. 3d and Front
Breakheart Catharine, n.s. Sloo, w. of Freeman
Brechtmann Bernard, 57 Riddle
Brechtner Casper, dry goods, 1064 Central Av
Breckat John, peddler, 102 W. Front
Brecount Geo. S., agt D. & M. R.R., office 5 College Bldg., h. 187 George

Bredell Wm., shoemkr., 170 W. 5th
Bredemeier Carolina, seamstress, 22 Hughes
Bredemeier Henry W., lab., 115 W. Liberty
Bredemeier Wm., 22 Hughes
Bredull Reinhold, phys., 21 Franklin.
Bree George, box mkr., s.s. Front b. Vine and Walnut.
Bree John, hatter, 137 Clark.
Breeding Conrad, teamster, n.s. Front e. of Kelly.
Breem Cornelius, salesman, 19 Mulberry
Breem Mathias, dray, 26 Peete.
BREED Abel D.. (Crane B. & Co., A. L. Scovill & Co) bds. 102 W. 7th.
BREED RICHARD E., Tobacco and Cigar manufac. 120 W. 2nd, h Covington.
BREED Wm. J., (Crane, Breed & Co.) bds. 102 W. 7th.
Breen Edward, shoe mkr , 22 Richmond.
Breen James, cooper, Crippen al, b. Broadway and Sycamore.
Breen James shoe mkr., 22 Richmond.
Breen John, lab., 221 E. 6th
Breen John shoe mkr., 22 Richmond.
Breen Margaret, seamstress, Burnet House.
Breen Michael, waiter, Spencer House.
Breen Pat, shoe mkr., 22 Richmond.
Breene Mary, bds s.s. Phoebe al. b. Plum and Central Av.
Breene Wm., lab., s.s. Phoebe al. b. Plum and Central Av.
Brees Thomas, express wagon, 41 Jackson.
Brehe J. Rudolph. carp., 104 Abigail.
Bretm Andrew, 775 Vine
Breidheil John, carriage mkr., 13 Mercer.
Breidenbach George, mach., 86 Betts
Breidenbaugh Wally, varnisher, 90 Gest
Breidenbuecher Geo., stamp cutter, 492 Vine.
Breidenstein Lucas, stone cutter, 142 Pleasant.
Breiding Hannah, 57 George.
Breier Frederick, wagon mkr., 214 Clark, h. 177 Hopkins.
Breier Nicholas, molder, 64 Elder.
B eightly Hy., miller, 227 E. 5th.
Breiling Arnold, bakery, 167 Pleasant.
Breinar John, cooper, n.e.c. Linn and Bank.
Dreininger, Michael, baker, 55 Allison.
Breunker Theodore, blksmith, wks. 136 W. Pearl.
BREISCH J. F., Book Bindery, 1 Court House Building, h. n.w.c. Broadway and Court.
Breitbeil John, carriage mkr., wks. Ch. Behlen & Co's.
Breitenbach Valentine, painter, 90 Gest
Breitenbuecher, silver plater, bds. 490 Vine.
Breitenstein John, stone cutter, n.s. Jail al. b. Sycamore and Main.
Breitenstein Lucas, stone cutter, 142 Pleasant.
Breitfeld Wm., bar k., 589 Walnut.
BREITHAUPT Bernhard, Editor Volksblatt, 511 Race
Breitling Simon G., cab. mkr., 713 Race.
Breitmeyer Frederick, lab., 661 Race
Breits Jacob cooper, al. b Charlotte and Findlay and Plum and Central Av
Brekel Christopher, baker, n.s. 6th b. Horne and Harriet.
Brelenx Charles, clk., w.s. Lawrence b 2d and Pearl
Brell Andrew, tailor, 11 Budd
Brelman David, fish dealer, n s Calhoun b. McMillen and Clifton Av
Brelsford R. S., baggage master, L. M. R. R. Depot.
Bremann Fred, lab., 372 Broadway.
Bremen S reet Station House, w.s. Brem n h. Liberty and 15th.
Bremenkamp Hy., tinner, 462 Walnut.
Bremer Anna, 141 Everett.
Bremer George, porter, 24 Hughes.
Bremer Hy., cooper, 18 Mulberry.

Bremer Joseph, cab. mkr., wks. s.w.c Canal and Elm.
Bremke Ferdinand, dray, 105 Woodward.
Bremmer Barney, lab., wks. 120 W. 2d.
Brenan James. lab., 405 Sycamore.
Brennan James H., bar k. n.w.c. 4th and Walnut.
Brenan Thomas, lab., 405 Sycamore.
Brendamour Francis, carver, 407 Central Av.
Brendamour Susanah, millinery, 407 Central Av.
Brendel Amelia, seamstress, 18 Hughes.
Brendel Frederick, 671 W. Front.
Brendel Geo., bakery, 535 Walnut.
Brendel Jacob, grocery, 20 Hamer.
Brendel Margaret, 594 Race.
Brendel Peter, edge tool mkr., n.s. Wade b. Plum and Elm.
Brendt Hy., shoe mkr., 154 Sycamore.
Brenen George, drays, 191 Water.
Breneng Christopher, dray, 20 Mansfield.
BRENEMAN Hy. H., paper hangings, and window shades, 57 W. 4th, h. 26 Hathaway.
Brenfus Margaret, servt., 256 W 4th
Brenker George, shoe mkr., bds. 65 E. Pearl.
Brenkman Hy., lab. e.s. Kilgour b. 3d and 5th.
BRENKMAN R., blksmith, and stock and die sinker, 246 W. Court. h. 70 Kossuth
Brenkmann Barney, cooper, 245 Clark.
Brennan Edward, mach., wks 110 W. 3d.
Brennan Edward, finisher, bds. 70 Sycamore.
Brennan Ella b he, servt 105 Broadway
Brennan George J., porter, 5 Melancthon.
Brennan James. 163 E. 3d.
BRENNAN James P., (Alexander B. & Co.) h. 436 W. 4th.
Brennan John, shoe mkr. 5 Melancthon. (Av
Brennan Michael carp, bds 221 Central
Brennan Michael, lab., 163 E. 3d
Brennan Thomas, bk layer, w.s. Central Av. b. W. W. Canal and 3d
Brennan Thomas, lab., 234 Carr
Brennegan Wm , cooper, 65 Pleasant
Brennan George, dr. y, 191 Water
Brenner Conrad, shoe mkr., 281 W. 6th
Brenner Geo., brewer, 59 Abigail.
Brenner Gottlieb, tailor, 548 Walnut
Brenner Gottlieb, tailor, 580 Walnut
Brenner John, cof. h. 80 W. Court
Brenner John, cooper, 65 Bank
Brenner John C., boots and shoes, 139 York
Brenner Joseph, lab , 538 Plum
Brenner Philip A., baker, 351 Vine
Brennin Barney, driver, 305 Freeman
Brenning John A., brush mkr , 211 Hopkins
Brenon Ellen, 21 E, 8th
Brensel Jacob, millwright. 522 Race
Brent Armistead, janitor, 179 Smith
Brent Elizabeth dress mkr , 179 Smith
Brentano Emile, cigar mkr., 196 W. Court
Brenzbach Geo., tailor, 488 Race
Brerink Mary. 249 Clark
Bresslmann Martin, lab., 14 E. 8th e. of Lock
Breslan Timothy, stone cutter, 210 Sycamore
Bresler George. 40 Dunlap
Breslin Michael, grocery, 109 Woodward
Breslin Patrick, lab., 210 Sycamore
Breslin P. H., lab., Water Street House
Bresnan Daniel C., grocery, 61 E. 8th
Bresnan Eugene, policeman 221 Freeman.
Bresnan Michael, porter, 69 Woodward
Bresslin Pat, shoe mkr., n.s. Whetstone al. b. Broad av and Sycamore
Bresser Hy., blksmith, c. Pendleton and Woodward
Bresser Hy., lab., 113 Woodward.
Brestel Valentine, show case mkr., 1039 Central Av

CINCINNATI ADVERTISEMENTS.

THEODORE ROYER. JOSEPH SIMONTON. JOHN YOUNG.

GREAT WESTERN
SPOKE, HUB AND FELLOE
MANUFACTORY.

ROYER, SIMONTON & CO.,

Manufacture and keep constantly on hand, a large supply of

SPOKES, HUBS, FELLOES, SHAFTS, BOWS, &C., &C.

Factory, Nos. 340 & 375 Third Street, below Smith,

CINCINNATI, OHIO.

Mr. Simonton being a practical Carriage Maker, our customers may depend upon having their Orders filled correctly.

C. DIEBOLD. F. BAHMANN. J. KIENZLE.

IMPROVED FIRE AND BURGLAR PROOF
SAFES,

Manufactured by
DIEBOLD, BAHMANN & CO.,
S. W. Cor. Elm and Front Sts., CINCINNATI, O.

☞ THESE SAFES ARE WARRANTED DRY AS WELL AS FIRE PROOF. ☜

CINCINNATI COACH AND CARRIAGE WAREHOUSE AND MANUFACTORY.

Nos. 55 and 57 Fifth Street,

Between Sycamore and Broadway, South side, Cincinnati, O.

B. R. STEVENS,
COACH AND CARRIAGE MAKER,

Keeps constantly on hand a large assortment of Carriages of his own manufacture, which he will warrant and sell low for Cash. ☞ Orders received for all kinds of Carriages, and promptly executed. Also, repairing done on the shortest notice, and at the most reasonable rates.

THOMAS DODSWORTH. M. DODSWORTH.

T. & M. DODSWORTH,
DEALERS IN

YOUGHIOGHENY, BIG SANDY, PEACH ORCHARD, POMEROY, HARTFORD CITY,
SYRACUSE, AND CANNEL COALS,

ALSO, COKE, FIRE BRICK AND CLAY.

Offices: Corner Lawrence and Front and Corner of Court and Walnut Streets.

AMERICAN BANK NOTE CO.,

S. E. Corner of Fourth and Main Streets,

CINCINNATI, OHIO.

GEO. T. JONES, Superintendent.

Brestel Wilhimena, servt., 365½ W. 7th
Bresting John, cook, 197 Webb
Brestle Conrad, mach., 68 Luck
Brestler Geo., blksmith, w.s. Bank al. b. 3d and 4th.
BRETANO Emil, (Eggert & B.) 196 Court
Brethorst Hy., grocery, 16 W. Mulberry
Brethauer Hy., lab., 4 Hamer
Breuel Lowry E., cla., 76 Main, h. 50 W. 5th
BREUER FREDERICK, Cigars and Tobacco 53 13th
Breuer Jacob, printer, 98 h. Ham. Road
Breuleux Charles, clk., e.s. Ludlow b. 2d and Pearl
Breumer Geo., scale mkr., wks. 392 Vine.
Breur John B., meats, 521 Main.
Brew James, dray, 24 Commerce
Brew Thaddeus, truss mkr., 24 Commerce
Brewe Regina, 169 Clay
Brewer August, tanner, 679 W. 6th
Brewer Mrs. B., 215 W. 9th w. of Central Av
Brewer Ferdinand, pattern mkr., n.s rail road e. of Kelly
Brewer Sarah, 180 W. Court, w. of Central Av
Brewer T., tinner, wks. n.w.c. Race and 2d
Brewer Tunis, surveyor, 11 Pierson
Brewster Perscilla E., 24 Hopkins
Brewster Horatio S., clk. Co. clks office 84 Hopkins
Breyer Frederick, wagon mkr., 177 Hopkins.
Breyer G., blksmith, 903 Central Av
Briant Isaac, molder, 146 Carr
Brick Gottfried, cooper, 258 pleasant
Bricalara Helena, seamstress. 5 Pleasant
Bricalara Vincent. 5 Pleasant
Brichler Barbara, 54c Race
Brichler Geo., cof. h. n.e.c. Elm and Green
Brichler John, carp., n.w.c. Front and Wood
Brichler Thomas, cigars. 96 Ham. Road
Brickell George, clk., 265 W 7th
Brickel Sebastian, carp., 61 Ham. Road
Brickell Wm., carriage mkr., 7 Sargent
BRICKETT & CO., Groc'rs, n.e.c. 6th and Vine
BRICKETT Irad, 765 Elm
Brickler Joseph, lab., 69ⁿ W. Front
Drickler Joseph teamster, n.s. Front opp. 5th St Ferry
Brickley Hy., teacher, 187 Livingston
Brickley Margaret, b. h 158 W. 3d
Brickley R. H. & Co., book binders, 160 Vine
Brickley Robert H., (R. H. & Co.) bds. 158 W. 3d
Brickman Mary seamstress, n.w c 15th and Elm
Brickmann John H., mach., 57 12th
Brickner Matthew, carp., s e.c. Locust and Baltimore
Brickwedde Hy., porter, 22 13th
Brickwedde Joseph, clk., 15 Franklin
Briddle John finisher, wks. n.e.c. Walnut and Canal
Bridenbick Benjamin, carp., 55 Betts
Bridenbaugh George, carp., n.e.c. Betts and Clifton
Bridenbick John, pipeman, 112 Clinton
Bridge Amanda, bds. n.s. Nassau b. Reed and Broad
Bridge Geo. W., clk., s.w.c. 6th and Mound
Bridge Josiah, teacher, s.w.c. 6th and Mound
Bridgeman Agard H., clk. 133 Freeman, bds. 2 Jane
Bridges George, lab., 25 Commerce
Briedle Theodore, lab. 602 Race
Briehl John, lab., 63 Laurel
Brienkman Chris., painter, w s. Fillmore b. Gest and Richmond
Brier Lottie, laundress. 34 Mulberry
Brietling Franz, sen., baker, bds. 313 Walnut

Brietling Franz, jr., blk.smith, bds. 343 Walnut
Briggenman Margaret, 50 Race
Briggmann Hy. J., cooper, junction W. 5th and Front
Briggemeier John H., lab., 66 Dudley
Briggs John T., cof. h., 2 Commercial Row, h. 209 Water
Briggs Nelson, painter, 167 E. 6th
Brigham Chas. F., news dealer. 79½ Walnut
Brigham John C., conductor, 197 Freeman
Brigham Susan. bds. 248 Longworth
Brigham Thomas R.. messenger, room 203 Burnet House
Bright Charles, bds. 158 W. 3d
Brightman Frank, cigar mkr., bds. 117 Providence
Brightman Joseph, cigar mkr., 117 Providence
Brightmore Geo. T., carp, bds. 49 Everett
BRIGHTON HOUSE, L Boman Proprietor, Harrison Road head of Central Av.
Brighton Stock Yards, head of Central Av.
Brigman Hy., eng., wks. Crane, Breed & Co's.
Brigman John, lab., 578 Richmond
Brigman John A., dray, Richmond b. Freeman and Carr
Brill Adam, shoe mkr., 648 Vine
Brill Andreas lab., 159 Bremen
Brill Chas., painter. 134 Bremen
Brill Ellus tailor. 708 Vine
Brill Geo., 24 15th
Brill Samuel, peddler, 572 Elm
Brilling Franklin, 167 Oliver
Brimmer Hy., steward. Galt House
Brimstone John, janitor, 154 Mound
Brincker Joseph, cab. mkr., 364 Broadway
Brinckhof Emily, millinery, 378 Broadway
Brinckman Harmon, 362 Freeman
BRINCKMAN HENRY, Proprietor Buckeye Mills, 11 Hunt, h 63 Bremen
Brinckman H., lab., 71 Abigail
Brinckman Hy., porter 32 W. Pearl
Brinckman Hy., lab., 72 Hunt
Brinckmann Christian, dray. 12 Abigail
Brinckmann Christian lab., 20 Abigail
Brinckmann Eberhard, cab. mkr., 593 Walnut
Brinckmann Frederick, lab., 196 Clinton
Brinckmann Hy., express driver, 11 Buckeye
Brinckmann Hy., lab., 18 Abigail
Brinckmann John, sawyer, n.s. Cassatt al. b. Main and Sycamore
Brinckmann Lewis, blk.smith, 25 Moore
Brinckmann Wm., tailor, 20 Buckeye
Brinckmeier Frederick, tailor, 464 Elm
Brincus Hy., chair mkr , 29 Commerce
Bringmann Wm., cutter, 88 Buckeye
Bringemann Wm , molder, wks. n.e c. Canal and Walnut
Bringmann Theodore, 23 Gano
Brink Anna, servt. 504 W. 5th
Brink Benedict O., painter, bds. 146 Clark
Brink George, bk. mkr., s.e.c. Dudley and Liberty
Brink Hy., rear 107 Clay
Drink Joseph, carp., 124 Clay
Brink Wm., lab., 171 Oliver
Brinkelsetz Chas., wagon mkr., 46 Findlay
Brinker H rney, tailor, 151 Abigail
Brinker Bernhard, soap factory, w.s. Goose al. b. Liberty and Green
Brinker Gerhard. dray, 31 Madison
Brinker Hy., tailor, 299 W. Front
Brinker Hy., tailor, 151 Abigail
Brinker Joseph, dray, 172 Spring
Brinker Theodore, blk.smith, 102 Abigail
Brinkers Hy., chair mkr. 27 Commerce
Brinkers John B., porter, 62 Abigail
Brinkley John, plasterer, 67 W. Court
Brinkman Albert, horse shoer, wks. 132 W. Court
Brinkman Barney, cooper, 245 Clark

Brinkman Casper, lab., 104 Everett
Brinkman Clements, chair mkr., 24 Abigail
Brinkman Edward, coffin mkr., wks. 450 Walnut
Brinkman Edward, dray, 67 Martin
Brinkman Fred., dray, wks. 21 W Front
Brinkman Geo., dray, 21 W. Front
Brinkman Hy., carp., 84 Abigail
Brinkman John H., dray, u s. Pearl b. Smith and Pearl
Brinkman John H., lab., wks. Mitchell & Rammelsberg's
Brinkman John H., teamster. 413 W. Front
Brinkman Kate, servt . 43 W. 9th
Brinkman Rudolph O., blk.smith, 67 Koesuth
Brinkman Wm., dray, 69 Martin
Brinkman Wm., finisher, wks. C. T. Dumont's
Brinkmann Christian, tailor. 3 Lucy
Brinkmann Ernst, teamster, 7 Wade b. Elm and Plum
Brinkmann Ferdinand M., lab., 91 Woodward
Brinkmann Frank, lab., 589 Race
Brinkmann Fredrick, s.s. Milton b. Pri e and Young
Brinkmann Frederick, carp , 7 Wade b. Elm and Plum
Brinkmann Fredrick Wm., carp., 4 Mansfield
Brinkmann Geo., dray, bds. 468 Main
Brinkmann Gerhard. tailor. 62 Findlay
Brinkmann Hy., 49 Fountain
Brinkmann Hy., 3 Lucy
Brinkmann Hy., miller, 63 Bremen
Brinkmann Hermann H., meats, 90 Woodward
Brinkmann Martin, porter, wks. 215 Main [Main
Brinkmann Theodore J., baker, 522
Brinkmann Wm., cof. h., 344 Main
Brinkmeier Gerhard, lab., 109 Clay
Brinkmeier Hy., lab., 602 Race
Brinkmeier Hy., lab., 60 Abigail
Brinkmeier Hy., molder, wks. n.e.c. Canal and Walnut
Brinkmeier Joseph, carp., 97 Pendleton
Brinkmeier Mary. 1 c Bets
Brinkmeier Wm., tailor, 30 Adams
Brinkmeyer Fred , cutter, 464 Elm
BRINKMEYER FREDERICK W., Family Grocery, 410 W. 3d
Brinkrui c J., carp., n.ks. Chamberlain & Co's
Brinsel Hy., dray, 302 W. Liberty
Brislan John, dray, bds. 249 E. Pearl e. of Broadway
Brisbo Francis, bakery, 22 Findlay
Brischo Charles, barber 20 E. 5th, h. w. s. Stone b. 5th and Longworth
Brischo & Gordon, (James B & Andrew J. G.) barbers, 95 W. 5th
Brischo James, (B. & Gordon) h. Mt. Pleasant
Bristol Emanuel, bk. layer, 24 Hughes
BRISTOL WHEELER H., (McCallum Bridge Company) h. Oswego, N. Y.
Bristol Wm. H . omnibus stable, n.e.c. Park and Marsh, h. 404 W 3d
Bristow Isaac, clk John Bates', h. 116 Smith
Britenback Elizabeth. servt 372 W. 6th
Britenback Benjamin, mach.,, bds. 55 Betts
Britner Wm., shoe mkr., wks 230 W. 5th
Britt Catharine, servt., 279 George
Britt Charles, clk., 132 Linn
Britt Elizabeth, e.s. Smith b. 2d and Augusta
Britt Harvey, policeman, 244 W. Court w of Central Av.
Brit Ida, teacher, 132 Linn
Britt Lawrence, foreman, 209 Smith
BRITT Nelson A., (Kelly & B.) 132 Linn
Britt Nelson A. jr., carp., bds. 132 Linn
Britt Oliver S., b.k. s c.c. John and Water
Britt Patrick, salesman, 13 E. 7th
Britt Peter, tin ware, &c., 42 Pub. Landing. h. Newport

CINCINNATI ADVERTISEMENTS.

JOHN ROWE,
MANUFACTURER OF
SAWS,
No. 238 SEVENTH ST., CINCINNATI.

EXTRA CAST STEEL CIRCULARS,
(All Sizes,—Fully Warranted.)

MULAY MILL, CROSS-CUT, VENEER AND WEBB SAWS,
Plastering Trowels, Machine Knives, Springs, &c.
PARTICULAR ATTENTION PAID TO REPAIRING ALL KINDS OF SAWS.

Cincinnati Chemical Laboratory,
JUNCTION OF CONGRESS and FRONT STREETS.
EUGENE GRASSELLI, Proprietor,
MANUFACTURING, ANALYTICAL AND CONSULTING CHEMIST.

MANUFACTURES

OIL VITRIOL,	PURE HYDRIODATE OF POTASH,	COPPERAS,
PURE VITRIOL,	SULPHURIC ETHER,	AQUA FORTIS,
MURIATIC ACID,	AQUA AMMONIA, ACETIC ETHER,	NITROUS ETHER.

ALLEN & CO., Agents,
South-West Corner of Main and Fifth Streets,   CINCINNATI, OHIO.

ALL ORDERS PROMPTLY ATTENDED TO.

J. J. BUTLER'S
EXCELSIOR FLUID INKS,
**MERCANTILE, for general Purposes,
RECORD, for Ledgers and Records,
COPYING, for Letter Press,
CARMINE, of Brilliant Hue.**

Celebrated for :—1st. Intense Black Color (at first of a greenish hue.) 2d. Easy flow from the pen. 3d. Permanency, (will never fade by exposure.) 4th. Economy. (EXPLANATION.—These Inks can be satisfactorily used to the last drop. Other domestic Inks in a brief time grow too thick for use, and are only fit to be thrown away before half consumed.) The Carmine may be exposed to the action of the air without injury.

FACTS CONFIRMING THE ABOVE QUALITIES.

1st. These Writing Fluids are now in general use throughout the United States, with an increased demand. 2d. They have been analyzed by Dr. Chilton, the celebrated Chemist of New York City, and pronounced "equal in quality and durability to the best imported English Fluids."

Manufactured by J. J. BUTLER, Agent,
No. 39 VINE STREET, CINCINNATI, O.

Britt Peter H., carp., bds. 132 Linn
Britt Thomas, dray, e.s. State b. 8th and Accommodation
Brittain John, cof h., 204 W. 6th
BRITTING & BRO., (George M. B. & Julius D) Piano and Melodeon Manufacturers and Dealers. 227 W. 5th
BRITTING Geo. M., (B. & Bro) 74 W. Canal
Britting John, pianos, &c., 236 Vine, b. 74 Canal
BRITTING Julius, (B. & Bro.) 74 W. Canal
Britting Louis, 72 W. M. Canal
BRITTING M. & P., (Margaret & Pauline) Millinery Goods, 227 W. 5th
BRITTING Margaret, (M. & P. B.) 74 W. Canal
BRITTING Pauline, (M. & P. B.) 74 W. Canal
BRITTINGHAM JOHN W., Commercial Editor Daily Times, bds Madison House
Britton Benj. W., paper hanger, 60 W. 4th
Britton James, lab., 355 Broadway
Britton John D., cof. h., 4 W. 3d
Britton Joseph, dray, 150 E. Liberty
Britton Matt., clk., bds. 177 Sycamore
Brizolara Charles, confec., n e c Front and Elm, and n.e.c. Front and Race
Brizolara John, confec., 28 E. 4th, h. 24 E. 4th
Broadbey Robert, currier, n.e.c. Betts and Cutter
BROADWAY EXCHANGE, n.e.c. 2d and Broadway, Frank Piepenbring, Proprietor
Broadway Hall, n.e.c. Hunt and Broadway
BROADWAY HOTEL, s.e.c. 2d and Broadway, Joseph H. Cromwell, Proprietor
Broadwell Charles O., weigher, 446 Elm
Broadwell & Edwards, (Mahlon L B & Joseph E) grocery, 1454 E. Front
Broadwell Linius, 331 George
Broadwell Mahlon L, (B. & Edwards) 1451 E. Front
Broadwell Mary, 90 Broadway
BROADWELL Samuel J., (Hagans & D.) 93 Broadway
Broadwell Wm. H., weigher 13 Water, bds. 446 Elm
Broarmann Hy., dyer, n.e.c. Pendleton and Abigail
Brobeck Lewis, 115 Browne
Brobinder Martin, lab., 65 Riddle
Brobst Peter, tailor, 303 W. 5th
Brocump Barney, lab., wks. n.e.c. Walnut and Canal
Brock Joseph, cooper, s.w.c. Abigail and Spring
Brock Louis, cof. h., 184 Walnut
Brock Samuel, carp, 313 Water
Brock W. W., conductor, bds. Burnet House
Brockamp Agnes, bds. 588 Race
Bruckamp Eliza, bds. 588 Race
Bruckamp Hy., tailor, 116 Betts, h. 54 Butler
Brockamp Lina, 588 Race
Brockame Tony, lab., 169 Linn
Brockhaus Hy., carp., 466 Main
Brockhaus Margaret, grocery, 270 Longworth
Brockhaus Samuel, potter. 164 Bank
Brockhoff Gustav, lab., 193 Baymiller
Brockhoff John A., dry goods, 121 Hopkins
Brockhoff Joseph, tailor, 30 Observatory
Brockington John C., millinery, 150 W. 5th
Brockman Barny, cab mkr., 212 Laurel
Brockman Barney, molder, wks. n.e.c. Canal and Walnut
Brockman Barney H., cab. mkr., 214 Laurel
Brockman Eliza, 151 Clark
Brockman Elisabeth, n.e.c. Hunt and Broadway
Brockman George, porter, wks. n.w.c. Race and 2d [way
Brockman Hy., n.e.c. Hunt and Broad

Brockman Hy., grocery, s.e.c. Elm and Water
Brockman Hy., lab., 188 Betts
Brockman Wm, molder, 75 Pendleton
Brockman Wm., shoe mkr., 153 Everett
Brockmann Barney, lab., 118 Abigail
Brockmann Bernard, harness, &c , 112 Pearl. E. of Broadway
BROCKMANN CHRISTIAN E., China. Glass and Queensware, 234 Main
Brockmann Harmon, 319 Findlay
Brockmann Hy., cooper, 147 Pleasant
Brockmann Hy., shoe mkr., 84 Hunt
Brockmann Herman, cooper, 25 Moore
Brockmann Herman H., grocery, 373 Broadway
Brockmann John B., lab., 120 Abigail
Brockmann John H., cooper, 120 Abigail
Brockmann Joseph, finisher, 460 W. 8th
Brockmann Joseph, harness mkr., 112 Pearl. E. of Broadway
Brockmann Kate, 151 Webb
Brockmann Mary, 120 Abigail
Brockmann Theodore, cof h., 73 W. 6th
Brockmann Theodore, jr., bar. k , 73 W. 6th
Brockmeier Amelia, servt., 118 E. 5th
Brockmeier Hy., bk. layer. 72 Hughes
Brockmeier Hy., porter, 99 W. Front
Brockmeyer Frederick, shoe mkr., 8 J. ckson
Brocks Francis, cab. mkr., 13 Woodward
Brocks Louisa. 700 Race
Brockschmidt Hy., blk. smith, 543 Race
Brockschmidt Hy. W., cigar mkr., 490 Race
Brocksmith Hermann, 477 Broadway
Brocksmith John, cig. mkr., s.s. 14th, b. Bremen and Race
Brocksmith Mary, 110 Avery
Broadbeck Andrew, box mkr., wks. Livingston, nr. Linn
Brodbeck John, tailor, 467 Walnut
Drodbeck Joseph, 22 Mercer
Broderick D. vis tailor, 191 W. 5th
Broderick Jno., waiter, Burnet House
Broderick Margaret, dress mkr., 130 Central av
Broderick Martin, shoe mkr., bds. 222 Broadway
Broderick Michael, fireman, 445 W. 2d
Broderick Patrick, dray., 38 Kossuth
Brodersen Gottfried, salesman, 91 W. Pearl
Brodersen Hy. C. N., b. k., 537 Walnut
BRODFUEHRER & BROTHER, (Chas. H. & G M. B.) Boots and Shoes, 52 W. 6th
Brodfuehrer Catharine, 231 Richmond
BRODFUEHRER Charles H., (B. & Brother,) 231 Richmond
BRODFUEHRER G. M., (B. & Brother,) 231 Richmond
Brodhag Wm., meats, 40 Lock
Brodhag Wm., porter, 400 Vine
Brodrick Dennis, turner, 178 Cutter
Brodrick Patrick, dray., 38 Kossuth
Brodtman Edward, carp., bds. s.w.c. 3d and Wood
Brodwolf John, cab. mkr., 107 Carr
Brody James, lab , 208 E. 6th
Broeckerhoff Anthony, cof. h , 519 Main
Broehe Adam, carp., s.e.c. Allison and Clay
Broemann Adolph, lab., 12 Madison
Broemann August, cigars, &c , 573 Main
Broemann Christian cooper, 3 Mulherry
Broemann Frederick, lab., 49 Pendleton
Broermann John, packer, wks. 131 Race
Broesamle Frederick, painter, 600 Elm, h. 64 Findlay
Broeth Lizzie, servt., 445 Sycamore
Brogan Ann, servt., 419 W. 6th
Brogan John, mach , 64 Barr
Brogan Michael, policeman, n e.c. Budd and Donnersberger
Brogan Nancy, n.e.c. Budd & Donnersberger
Brogan Wm., penny post, 231 E. 5th
Brogeman M., lab., wks. Wood & McCoy's
Brokamp A., tailor, 110 E. 2d
BROKAMP Bernard, (B. & Lake,) 62 Abigail

Brokamp Bernard, eng., 166 Spring
Brokamp Francis, stone setter, e.s. Kilgour, b. 3d and 5th
Brokamp Hy., cof. h , n.w.c. Hunt and Pendleton
Brokamp Hy., lab., 388 Broadway
Brokamp Hy , porter. 195 Laurel
Brokamp John D., bds. 193 Laurel
Brokamp John H., clk., 54 Butler
Brokamp John H., lab., 102 Abigail
BROKAMP & LAKE, (Bernhard B. & Bernhard L.,) Merchant Tailors, 464 Main
Brokemann Geo., molder, wks. n.e.c. Canal and Walnut
Broker Geo , shoe mkr., 389 W. Liberty
Broker Hy., lab , 70 W. 6th
Broker Johanna. 22 Mill
Broker Wm., lab., 145 Baymiller
Broking Diana, e.s. Hand al. b. Court and Clark
Brokopp Frank, 549 Main
Broksmidt Fred., lab., 40 Rittenhouse
Brombe Ludwig, tanner. 205 Ham. Road
Brombair Louis, s.e.c. Ham. Road and Elm
Bronkamp Chas., cigar mkr., bds. 61 Hughes [tral av
Bromley Thomas, potter, bds. 170 Central av
Bromley Wm., pottery, 1077 Central av
Bromm Caspar, painter, 144 Pleasant
Brommelkamp Hy., carp., 9 Franklin
Bromstrobe Hy., carp , 16 Hughes
Bromstrup Philipp F., molder, 27 Woodward
Bromwell Andrew J., 272 Longworth
Bromwell Elizabeth, 272 Longworth
Bromwell Hy., hose mkr., 410 W. 6th
Bromwell Margaret, 446 W. 9th
Bromwell Oliver, 272 Longworth
Bromwell Robert R., fireman, 421 W. 7th
BROMWELL Wm., (Wm. B. & Co.,) 359 W. 7th
BROMWELL WM. & CO., (Wm. B. Thos. J. Melish and Stants G. Burnet.) Brushes and Wire Goods, 151 Walnut
Bronche Richard, lab., 226 Water
Brond Chs. Wm., blk. smith, Poplar, nr. Freeman
Bronles Nancy, s.s. Goodloe, b. Willow and Niagra
Bronnen Christopher, lab., n.s. Sloo E. of Harriett
Brons Gasper, lab., 257 Carr
Bruns Hy. R., carp., 7 Goorman
Bronsman Hy., lab , 13 Bremen
Bronston Thos J., printer, 58 W. 6th
Bronkbank Anderson K., sawyer, 1228 Front
Brookbank James B., sawyer, n.s. Nassau. b. Reed and Broad
BROOKE J. H., Merchant Tailor, and Boys and Youth's Clothing, 66 and 68 W. 5th, h. Newport.
BROOKE Charles F., agent for John M. Bradstreet & Sons 27 W. 3d, h. 44 Clinton
Brooke Hy., n.e.c. Linn and Everett
BROOKE J. H., h. Newport, Ky
Brooke Leighton, 272 W. 7th
Brooker Geo., shoemaker, 656 Vine
Brookfield Edward V., marble worker. 583 Freeman
BROOKFIELD Wm., Marble Works, s. e c. Plum and 8th, h. 111 Laurel
Brookmeirer Hy., shoemaker, bds. 52 Dudley
Brookmeyer Hy., lab., 99 W. Front
Brooks, clk., bds. 272 W. 7th
Brooks Mrs. D., bds. s.s. 6th, E. of Lock
Brooks E. S , teacher, 459 W. 6th
Brooks Eliza J., bds. 22 Harrison
BROOKS F. F., Queen City Varnish Co., 43 Vine, h 331 W. 4th
Brooks John. harness mkr., lds. s.w.c. 5th and Broadway
Brooks John F., grocer, 8 Jane
Brooks Kate J , teacher, 111 Clinton
Brooks Michael, molder, wks. n.w.c. Plum and Wade
Brooks Nathaniel, barber. 106 Vanhorn
BROOKS Oliver A., (Huntington & B) h. Cleveland, O.

CINCINNATI ADVERTISEMENTS.

JAMES TODD,
STEAM ENGINE BUILDER AND MACHINIST,
Corner of Seventh and Smith Streets, Cincinnati, Ohio.

Manufacturer of Noye's New Improved Planing Machine—on iron or wood frames—for Tongueing, Grooving, Flooring, and any other kind of Lumber. Also, Sash, Mulay and Circular Saw Mills, and Mill work generally. Portable Corn and Flouring Mills, Horse Powers, Cotton, Hay, Lard, Tobacco, and Wine Screws. Also, Castings of every description, furnished to order. Planing Machines, on Iron and Wood Frames.

J. H. BROOKE,
MANUFACTURER OF
MENS, YOUTHS, BOYS, AND CHILDREN'S CLOTHING,
AND DEALERS IN
FURNISHING GOODS,
Nos. 66 and 63 WEST FIFTH STREET, CINCINNATI, OHIO.

E. MENDENHALL,
MAP AND BOOK PUBLISHER,
PRINTSELLER AND STATIONER,
No. 157 Main St., adjoining N. W. C. Fourth and Main Sts., CINCINNATI, O.

Maps of all other Publishers on sale.

D. M. SECHLER. ## SECHLER & PORTER, **W. H. PORTER.**
SOLE AGENTS FOR
LAWRENCE ROLLING MILL
OF IRONTON, OHIO,

Dealers in Pig Iron, Bar, Boiler, and Sheet Iron, Plow Slabs and Wings, Axles, Springs, Nails, Steel, Window Glass, Sugar Cane Mills and Evaporators, and Castings generally.

Warerooms, No. 54 Second Street, bet. Walnut and Vine, Cincinnati, Ohio.

WM. KIRKUP & SON,
BRASS FOUNDERS, STEAM PIPE FITTERS,
AND MANUFACTURERS OF
STEAM AND WATER GAUGES, LOCOMOTIVE SPRING BALANCES AND SIGNAL BELLS.

Dealers in Wrought Iron Pipe and Fittings, Globe, Angle, and Check Valves, Gas, Steam, and Water Cocks, &c., &c.

No. 250 East Front Street, opp. Little Miami R. R. Depot, Cincinnati, Ohio.

WESTERN UNION TELEGRAPH,
CINCINNATI OFFICE,
Derby's Building, South-West Corner of Third and Walnut Streets.

ANSON STAGER, Gen'l Sup't.   *CHAS. DAVENPORT, Sup't Southern Division.*

Brooks S. A., bds. Walnut st. House
Brooks Saml., baggage-master Ohio and Miss. R R., bds. 502 W. Front
Brooks Saml. H., baggage-must r O. & M. R.R, bds. Western Hotel
Brooks Sarah A., 111 Clinton
Brooks Theodosia, music teacher, bds. n w.c. Longworth and Central av
Brooks Wm., porter, 12 E. 7th
Brooks Wm A., carp, 194 Barr
Brookville House, n.w.c. Front and Central av
Broom Geo, D, plasterer, bds. s.w.c. Franklin and Broadway
Broome Geo, carp., 328 Linn
Broomer Barney, lab, 40 Gest
Broomer John B., tailor, 130 E. 4th
Brophill Thomas, dray.. 12= Webb
Brophy Ann servt, 254 W. 3d
Brophy James, blacksmith, works Niles Works
BROPHY JOHN L., Tin, Copper & Sheet Iron Works. 114 W. 9th, h. 210 E. 6th, E. of Baum
Brophy Joseph, bx. layer 350 Cutter
Brophy Maria, servt, 254 W. 3d
Brophy Mary, 210 E. 6th
Broring Arnold, grocer. 312 Baymiller
Broring Hy., clk. bds. 674 Central Av.
Bros John, carp, 53 Woodward
Broschermann Ernst, shoemkr., 51 15th
Brosey Frederick. clk., 37 E. Front
Broshart Chas., bill poster, bds. Tremont Hotel
Brosmear Joseph, cigar mkr., bds. 50 Dudley
Brosser Jacob. lab., wks 21 E. Canal
Brosshart Peter, molder, s.w.c. Vine and 12th
Brossmer Francis S., cof h., Hill b. Celestial and Observatory
Brosz Paul, cooper, rear 463 Sycamore
Brothers Hy., bar. k., bds. Pearl Street House
BROTHERTON & CO., Bankers, 23 W. 3d
BROTHERTON James H., (B. & Co.,) res. Chicago
Brotherton John G., teller Gilmore, Dunlap & Co's., h. 59 Milton
Brough Chas. M. Elk., bds. 172 Vine
Brous Berny, porter, 411 Baymiller
Broutts Louis, molder, 300 Vine
BROWER ABRAM, Jr, Attorney at Law, room 4, Masonic Temple, res. Delhi township
Brower Wm W., gilder, 69 Barr
Brown Mrs. dress mkr., bds. 297 W. 6th.
Brown Alfred, molder, wks n.e.c Canal and Walnut
Brown Allen, s.e.c. John and Court
Brown Alonzo C., carp., 371 W. 9th
Brown Amelia. cook, n.s. Grandin al. b. Elm and Plum
Brown Ann. e.s. Pendleton, b. Woodward and Liberty
Brown Anna, Richmond, b. Harriet and Mill Creek
Brown Anna. 25 Abigail
Brown Annie, servt., 305 W. 7th
Brown Anton, lab., 113 Browne
Brown Augustus C., woolen mach. manufacturer, 27 Walnut, h. 290 W. 3d
BROWN & BROTHER, (George and Richard.) Livery and Sale Stable, 9 E. 6th
Brown Charles, lab., 136 W. 3d
Brown Charles, lab., wks. s.e.c. Canal and Vine
BROWN Charles, (Spining & Brown,) 115 W. 7th
Brown Charles, varnisher. 13ª Findlay
BROWN CHARLES BRADY, Attorney at Law, 19 W. 3d, h. n. e. c. Plum and Pth
Brown Charles D., bell hanger, 2 B Mulberry
Brown Charles E., b. k. 62 Walnut, h. Mt. Auburn
Brown Charlotte, servt., 140 E. 3d
Brown Conrad, cooper, s.w.c. Linn and Clinton [and Smith
Brown David lab., n.s. Augusta, b. John
Brown David M., clothing inspector, 32 Elizabeth

Brown Dennis, blk. smith, n.w.c. 3d and Ellen
Brown Dennis, jr., blk. smith, e. 3d and Lock
Brown Duncan D., 343 Central Av.
Brown E S. salesman. bds 409 W. 5th
Brown Edward. clk., bls. 409 W. 5th
Brown Eliza. 35 e. 3d, e of Parsons
Brown Eliza L, 327 Longworth
Brown Elizabeth, bds. 21 Hathaway
Brown Emery, mer., w.s. Auburn av. nr. Central Av.
Brown Ephraim T., (O. & E. T. Brown,) h. Mt. Airy
Brown Eustus lab., s.w.c. Riddle and Harrison Pike
Brown Ferdinand, drover, 183 Bremen
Brown Francis, cab. mkr., 217 E. 3d
Brown Frank, cab mkr., 277 Betts
Brown Frederick, tinner. 27 Abigail
Brown G. B., agt. C. O. & P. C. & C. RR., 77 W., d. h. 212 Poplar
Brown George, barber. 27 Gano
BROWN George, (B. & Bro.,) 228 Sycamore
Brown George, shoe mkr, s.s. George b Race and Elm
Brown George, shoe mkr., bds. 65 W.5th
Brown George O., b. k., 23 W. 4th, h. Mt. Auburn
Brown George S. b k, 398 W 9th
Brown H. b. bds. Dennison House
BROWN H W. & CO., (Hugh W. B., Robert K. Brown,) Freight Agents Pennsylvania Railroad, Steamboat Agents, Forwarding and Commission Merchants. 25 E. Front
Brown Hannah, w.s. Pancoast al., b. 7th and Pth
Brown Hy., butter and eggs, s.s. Sloo. e. of Harriett [Elm
Brown Hy., cigar mkr. n.e.c. Court and
Brown Hy., lab., 29 Spring
Brown Hy., molder, 71 Clay
Brown Hy., tobacconist, bds. 170 West Court
Brown Hy. L. clk., c.s. Freeman, b. York and Findlay
Brown Hiram D. eng., bds. 284 W. 9th, w. of Central Av.
BROWN Hugh Wilson, (H. W. B. & Co.,) 372 W. 8th
BROWN IRA. Dealer in Guns and Pistols, 238 Main, h. n.e.c. Elm and 7th
Brown Isaac, bds 3 al. b. 4th and 5th, Park and Mill
Brown Isaac C. harness mkr., 103 Vine, h. Walnut Hills
Brown Isaac I., plasterer, 203 Sycamore
Brown Isabella, 327 Longworth
Brown Isam. lab. 173 W. Pearl
Brown Israel J., atty., s.w.c. Court and Main, h. Mt. Airy
Brown James, baker. 74 E. Pearl
Brown James, blk. smith, 46 Barr
Brown James, carp, 180 Central Av.
Brown J mies. driver, bds. 575 W. 5th
Brown James, paper carrier, 49 Chestnut
Brown James tailor, 119 W. 5th
Brown James D. printer, Cincinnati Gazette, h. 110 Butler
Brown James J., grocery. 64 Cutter
Brown James S., carp., bds n.s. Front, e. of Foster
Brown Jane S. 327 Longworth
Brown Jefferson, pipeman. 100 E. 5th
Brown Jeremiah, mach., 129 E. 3d
Brown John, 56 E. 7th
Brown John, 466 Linn
Brown John, 40 Mohawk
Brown John, carp, 4 Jordon
Brown John. lab., s.s. 6th b. Broadway and Culvert
Brown John, lab., 32 Mulberry
Brown John, lab., 429 W 8th
Brown John, steward, bds. 74 E. Pearl
Brown John, grinder, 64 W. 4th
Brown John D., lamps, &c., 4 e. 4th, h. Covington
Brown John H., carp., 301 Clark
Brown John M., dental depot. n.w.c. 4th and Walnut, h. s w.c 4th and Smith
Brown John S., b. k., 217 Main, h. 136 W. 7th

Brown John W., 133 Wade
Brown Joseph, express waggon, 49 Water
Brown Joseph, lab., 32 Mulberry
Brown Joseph, shoemkr., bds. 92 Central Av.
BROWN Joseph R., (J. R. B. & Co.,) s.w.c. Richmond and Harriet
BROWN JOSEPH R. & CO., Commission and Produce Merchants, Manufacturers of Brooms, and Dealers in Flour, Grain, &c., 2 Walnut
Brown Julia, n.s. Augusta, b. John and Smith
Brown Julia A. h. 39 Pike
BROWN LEONARD W., Coal Yard, Offices, n.w.c Vine and 7th. and s.w c. Plum and Court, h. 662 W. Front
Brown Levin, coachman, 40 Webb
Brown Lewis. clk., 21 Harrison
Brown Lewis G., atty., 14 E. 2d, h. Mt. Auburn
Brown Louisa, servt., 178 Sycamore
BROWN M. J., Who esale Grocer and Liquors, Produce and Commission Merchant, s.e.c. Main and 7th, h. 64 Cutter
Brown Marceilus L., clk., 308 W. 9th, w. of Central Av
Brown Marcus, clk., h. 26 W. 8th
Brown Margaret, tailoress, 507 W. 9th, w. of Central Av.
Brown Martha, n.e.c. Walnut and 6th
Brown Martin, lab, 761 W. Front
Brown Martin, lab., 310 Longworth
Brown Mary, 157 Plum
Brown Mary. cof. h., s.s. 6th b. Broadway and Culvert
Brown Mary, grocery, s w.c. 4th and Stone
Brown Mary, servt., 415 W. 6th
Brown Mary Jane, nurse, Commercial Hospital
Brown Matilda. servt, Dumas House
Brown Michael. shoemkr., bds. 7th. b. Broadway and Sycamore
Brown Michael, lab., 142 Longworth
Brown Michael, lab.. 431 George
Brown Nancy, w.s. Henderson al. b. 7th and 8th
Brown Nesbitt L., trimmer, bds. s.e.c. 5th and Vine
Brown Nichols., lab., 144 Van Horne
Brown Noah. lab., s s. 6th, b. Broadway and Culvert
Brown O. & E. T., (Oliver & Ephraim T. B.,) attys. s.w.c. Court and Main
Brown Oliver, (O. & E. T. Brown.) h. Mt Airy
Brown Patrick, lab., n.w.c. 3d and Ellen
Brown Patrick, pipe fitter, wks. n.e.c. Walnut and Canal
Brown Patrick H., cof. h., 20 River Landing
Brown Peter, candle mkr.. 797 Celestial av.
Brown Peter, mate, s.w.c. Railroad and French
Brown Peter L., (B., Stout & Butler,) res. Clifton
Brown Philip, lab., s s. Harrison Pike, b. Riddle and Brighton
Brown Phillip Y., clk., 572 W. 9th
Brown R & Co., (Robert B., Wm. White & Wm. B. Craig,) hosiery, s.e.c. Pearl and Walnut
BROWN Richard, (B. & Bro.,) h. country
Brown Robert, brass finisher. 299 John
Brown Robert, dray., 55 Commerce
Brown Robert, (R. B. & Co.) 315 Freeman
BROWN ROBERT, Pork Packer and Commission Merchant e.e.c. Court and Sycamore, h. e.s. Ohio avenue. south end
Brown Robert, jr, with Robert Brown, h. e.s. Ohio av. south end
Brown Robert H., clk., 110 W. 7th
BROWN Robert K, (W. Brown & Co.,) bds. s.e.c. 3d and Broadway
Brown Robert W., clk, 44 Walnut, h. Clifton
Brown Rosa, s.e.c Elm and Union

CINCINNATI ADVERTISEMENTS.

A. ROSS.   A. PETTIBONE.   G. W. ROSS.

ROSS, PETTIBONE & CO.,
COAL DEALERS,

YARDS:

358 Central Avenue,

Corner of Richmond,

Corner Third & White Water Canal,

Bet. Baymiller and Freeman,

—AND—

406 West Fifth St.,

Corner of Mound,

CINCINNATI,

OHIO.

Orders also received at Railroad Freight Office, 115 Vine Street, under Burnet House.

Constantly on hand a supply of Superior

YOUGHIOGHENY, HARTFORD CITY, CANNEL, AND OTHER COALS.

Customers may depend upon a pure article. All Orders left at either Yard promptly attended to.

C. G. SIEWERS,
SAW & CABINET TOOL FACTORY,
No. 93 East Eighth Street, Cincinnati, O.

TRY SQUARES,	BRACES,	SURGEON SAWS,
BEVELS,	SAW FRAMES,	PRUNING SAWS,
GAUGES,	BUTCHER SAWS,	MACHINE WEBS,
PLUMB AND LEVELS,	BUCK SAWS,	NACK AND FRET SAWS,
SPOKE SHAVES,	COMPASS SAWS,	COACH ROUTERS,
SAWPADS,	WEB SAWS,	TRUSS SPRINGS,

On hand and made to order, at lowest rates.

C. H. WATERS.   EBEN DOLE.

CHARLES H. WATERS & CO.
Manufacturers and Wholesale Dealers in

WOODEN AND WILLOW WARE, CORDAGE AND TWINES,
BROOMS, BRUSHES, MATS, MATCHES, BUCKETS, TUBS,

Churns, Measures, Zinc Washboards, French and German Fancy Baskets, &c.

Nos. 4 MAIN ST., and 3 PUBLIC LANDING, CINCINNATI, O.

GEO. B. DIXON.   I. W. PARKER.

GEO. R. DIXON & CO.,
OHIO MUSTARD MILLS,

Wholesale Dealers in FRESH ROASTED AND GROUND COFFEE, Spices, Mustard, Pepper Sauce, Tomato Catsup, Baking Powder, Peanuts, Indigo, Nutmegs, &c.
Highest Cash Prices paid for MUSTARD SEED.

Nos. 243, 245, and 247 Sycamore Street, Cincinnati, Ohio.

Bruce Wm., finisher, wks. n.e.c. Walnut and Canal
Bruch John, tailor, 569 Vine
Bruckle John, mach., 50 Dudley
Bruck Bernard, tailor, 106 Browne
BRUCK LOUIS, 32 Grant
Bruck Nicholas, 74 Stark
Bruck Valentine, cof. h., 458 E. Front
Brucker Chas., basket mkr., 559 Vine
Brucker John, carp., 337 Clark
Brucker Regina, bds. 559 Vine
Bruckert Eve, 773 Vine
Bruckmann Joseph, lab., 128 Clay
Bruckner Matthew, carp., s.s. Baltimore b. Locust and Sycamore
Brudder Varsiliam, cooper, 137 Livingston
Bruder Geo., grocery, 560 Vine
Bruder John G., tailor, 11 Moore
Bruechler Anthony, tin smith, wks. 533 Vine
Brueck Chas., confec., 522 Main
Brueckel Geo., stone cutter, e s. Ridgway al. b. W. Liberty and 15th
Brueckner August, copper smith, 90 Buckeye
Brueckner William, bakery, 623 Main
Bruegge Bernhard, shoemkr,n.w.c. Race and Green
Brueggemann Adolph, grocery, n.w.c. Liberty and Walnut
Brueggemann Anna, bds. 14 Mary
Brueggemann Bernhard, cof. h., 602 Elm
Brueggemann Chas., chair caner, 26 Abigail
Brueggemann David, safe mkr., 26 Abigail
Brueggemann Francisca, 19 Pendleton
Brueggemann Mary, 26 Abigail
Bruegier Chas., lab., 273 Bremen
Bruehl Edward W., marble cutter, 600 Elm
Bruel Lawrence, clk., bds. 50 W. 8th
Bruel Samuel, letterer, 50 W. 8th
Brummerkamp Lambert, carp., bds. 9 Franklin
Bruen Isaac N., feed dealer, 54 Laurel
Bruen Kate, 113 E. Front
Bruen Mary, servt., 110 E. 4th
Bruening John F., lab., bds. 468 Main
Bruenn Adolphus, phys., 180 Sycamore
Bruer Hy., carp., s.w.c. Gest and Carr
Bruer John, mach., 604 Elm
Bruerman Hy., dray, wks. 450 Walnut
Brueesselbach H. J., teacher,n.w.c. Vine and Longworth
Bruetsche Frederika, 13 15th
Bruggemann August, bakery, 456 Vine
Bruggemann Chas., cab. mkr., 50 Race
Bruggemann Fred., porter, 504 W. 3d
Bruggemann Hermon, bk. mkr., 192 Hopkins
Bruggemann John, lab., 97 Pendleton
Bruggemann Wm., molder, 19 Pendleton
Bruhl Gustavus, phys., 146 Laurel
Bruin Bernard H., lab., 59 14th
Bruinstrob Rudolph, dray, 6 Mulberry
Bruissebach Hy.,music teacher,591 Main
Bruker Mary, servt., Galt House
Brukemann Gerhard H., varnisher, 73 Abigail
Brukmann Frederick, lab., 207 Webb
Brulport Maria, 155 Sycamore
Brum Adam, cooper, 253 Clark
Brum Hermann, tanner, s.s. Liberty b. Linn and Baymiller
Brum Moritz, tanner, 195 Everett
Bruman Adam, cooper, 253 Clark
Bruman Barney, driver. 305 Freeman
Bruman Hy., lab., 151 Everett
Brumen Louisa, servt., 105 W. 4th
Brumerthal Michael, drover, 32 Providence
Brumme Frederick W., baker. n.s. al. b. Canal and 12th, and Vine and Race
Brummer Ferdinand, brewer, 674 Race
Brummer J. B. & Co. (John B. B. & Herman H. Ahlering), tailors, 244 Main
Brummer John B. (J. B. B. & Co.) 130 E. 4th
Brun Barney, blksmith, s.e.c. Front and John
Brun Hy., teamster, s.e.c. Front and John

Brunabel Mary, servt., 427 W 6th
Brunar W. H., clk., 101 W. 4th
Brunce John. lab., e.s. Anderson al. b. 2d and Pearl
Brund Fred., lab., wks. Wnod & M'Coy's
Brune Catharine, 113 W. Front
Brune Frederick, bakery, 134 W. Front
Brane I., packer, wks. 728 Central Av
Brune Ludwig, 20 Mansfield
Bruner Benjamin, blksmith, 262 W. Front
Bruner John F., boiler mkr., 20 Ham. Road
BRUNER MARTIN. Attorney, 20 W. Court, h. 540 Elm
Bruner Wm. H., clk., bds. 409 W. 5th
Brunes Frank, finisher, wks. n.e.c, Walnut and Canal
Brunes Joseph, lab., 239 Hopkins
Bruning Fred., grocery, 52 Baum
Bruning Hy., lab., 211 Hopkins
BRUNING Hy. (Miller, B. & Dieckmann) 118 E. 5th
Brunke August, carp., bds. 37 Ham. Road
Brunklaus G. L., tailor, Moore al. b. W. 8th and 9th and Plum and Elm
Brunland Phillip, tailor. rear 176 Clay
Brunn Jacob, clk., 253 Main
Brunnan Ellen, 61 Mill
Brunne Joseph, molder. 114 Clay
Brunner Alphonse, teacher, n.w,c. 4th and Central Av
Brunner Francis, 104 Bremen
Brunner H., lab., wks. Hieatt & Wood's
Brunner John, shoemkr, w.s. Fountain b. Rice and Alexander
Brunner Peter, tanner, 601 Vine
Brunner Philip, finisher, 104 Bremen
Brunner Samuel, peddler, 25 15th
Brunner Sophia, servt., e.s. Race b. W. Liberty and 15th
Brunner Theodore, teacher, 47 Milton
Brunning J., molder, wks. n.s. Front b. Lawrence and Pike
Bruns Anthony, (B. & Wisher) Pennsylvania Hotel
Bruns Anthony, grocery, 183 Hopkins
Bruns Anthony, tinner, 180 Hopkins
Bruns Catharine, 141 Clay
Bruns Chas., cigar mkr., 38 Findlay
Bruns Doris, midwife, 38 Findlay
Bruns Frank, cigar mkr., 788 Central Av
Bruns Frederick, lock mkr., 91 Clay
Bruns Hy., lab., 91 Woodward
Bruns Hy., w. end of Mohawk
Bruns Hy., lab., wks. n,e.c. Walnut and Canal
Bruns John, lab., bds. s.w.c. Vine and 15th
Bruns John B., furniture. 50 Lock
Bruns John B., shoemkr, 201 Clark
BRUNS JOHN B., Coffee House, 480 W. Front
Bruns Joseph, grocery, 98 Clay
Bruns Joseph, porter, 239 Hopkins
Bruns Maria, seamstress, 91 Clay
Bruns & Wisher (Anthony B. & Barney W.) Pennsylvania Hotel, s.w.c. Pike and Front
Brunsen Hy., shoemkr, 98 W. Front
Brunsen Sarah, 58 Providence
Brunsmann Bernhard H., shoemkr, 233 Bremen
Brunsmann Geo., mach., bds. 233 Bremen
Brunsmann Hy., dray, 23 Grant
Brunsmann Hy. R., porter, 136 Hopkins
Brunsmann John H., b.k., 27 Observatory Road
Brunsmann Joseph, express, e.s. Bremen b. Elder and Findlay
Brunson Daniel, builder, 117 Hopkins
Brunssen Helena, servt., n.s. al. b. Canal and 12th and Vine and Race
BRUNSWICK John M., (J. M. B. & Brother) 437 Walnut
BRUNSWICK J. M. & BROTHER, (J. M. & Joseph B.) Manufacturers of Billiard Tables, 8 W 6th
BRUNSWICK Joseph, (J. M. B. & Brother,) n.w.c. 8th and Walnut
Brunt Catharine, 52 Webster
Brunt Peter, lab., wks. 80 Poplar

UNDERTAKER,

SOLE AGENT FOR

Cincinnati and Hamilton County, O. Also, Kenton County, Ky.

—FOR—

I. C. SHULER & CO'S

WROUGHT

GALVANIZED IRON

AIR-TIGHT

METALLIC

Burial Case.

I refer especially to my stock of Mahogany, Rosewood, Walnut and White Wood Coffins, Walnut covered with Black Cloth, and Merino or Satin. Furnishing Goods, as follows, always on hand, viz: Black Cloth, Merino, Velvet, Satin, Flannel, Luster Shrouds, Robes, Gloves, Hosiery, Ribbons, and Laces, &c. Brilliant and Cambric, Coffin Handles, Name Plates, Silver Plating, Finishing Tacks and Ornaments of all kinds for Undertakers' use, on hand and for sale. Also constantly on hand a large supply of Ready-made Coffins, at low rates to the Trade in and out of the city.—with competent assistants to attend funerals. First Class Hearses and Carriages furnished. First Class Pleasure Carriages, for Families and Parties. I have extensive accommodations for Private Horses and Buggies, on board, by the Day, Week, or Month.

MANUFACTORY AND STABLES, Nos. 182, 184, and 186 NINTH STREET,

Opposite the City Park, running through to Richmond Street,

Office corner of Ninth and Plum Streets, CINCINNATI, OHIO.

Residence, 326 Plum Street.

CINCINNATI (BUC) (BUC) DIRECTORY. (BUE) 91

Bruntz Sophenia, e.s. Vine b. Milk and Mulberry.
Bruntz Wm, lab., wks. 630 Central Av
Brunzt Peter, barber, 554 Vine
Brusecker John. mach., 336 Hopkins
Brusel Jacob, millwright, h. 522 Race
Brusker Herman, lab., s.s. Taylor b. Carr and Harriet
Bruss Peter, tanner, wks. H. & G. R. Martin's
Bruss Wm., tanner, 165 E. 5th
Brussert John, tailor, 63 Clay
Brust Margaret, 216 Bremen
Brutter Hy., lab., 1019 Central Av
Brutton Ambrose, carp., 284 W. Liberty
Brutton Capt. Charles H., 320 Findlay
Bryan Alfred, b. k. 76 Main, h. 381 George.
Bryan Clarence, clk., 65 W. 4th, h. Covington
Bryan Ely W., salesman, 138 Walnut, h. 250 Longworth
Bryan James, egg packer, 62 Gano
Bryan James, eng., h. 491 W. 4th
Bryan Luke, millinery, 240 W. 5th
Bryan Malcolm, clk., Suire Eckstein & Co., h. Covington Ky
Bryan Patrick, cooper, 91 W. Front
Bryan Rebecca, servt., Henrie House
Bryan William. 332 W. 6th
Bryant Alfred, b. k., 381 George
Bryant Charles W., brk mkr., bds, 173 Linn
Bryant George A., painter, 247 Everett
Bryant Harriet J., 381 George
Bryant Harvey, express wag., 19 Accommodation
Bryant Jane, servt., s.w.c. Franklin and Broadway
Bryant Jerome B., teacher, 71 Betts
Bryant Kate, teacher, 207 Mound
Bryant Mary, 71 Betts
Bryant Samuel L., pipe fitter, wks. n.e.c. Walnut and Canal
Bryant Samuel M., finisher, 94 Ludlow
Bryant Wm., shoe mkr., 120 E. 8th
Bryarley Thos. J., b. k. bds. 204 W. 4th
Bryce Dunhan, shoe mkr., h. 24 E. 4th
Bryce Peter F., bakery, 506 Sycamore
Bryce T., 449 Linn
Bryce Samuel G., collar mkr, wks. 208 Central Av
Bryer Frank, bar k., 222 Vine
Bryson Chas., grocery, 634 W. 5th
Bryson Isaac, pilot, 79 Mill
Bryson Mick, lab., wks. C. H. & D. R.R. Depot
Bube Nicholas, cab. mkr., 31 Madison
Buchanan A. M., (B. & Adams.) h. Brooke Co., Va
Buchanan & Adams, (A. M. B. & Wm. Q. A) coni yard 333 W Front.
BUCHANAN ALFRED, Coal Yard, 333 W. Front h. 300 George.
BUCHANAN Chas. M., (B. & Co., & R. Buchanan & Son,) h. Clifton Ohio
BUCHANAN & CO , (Chas. M. B. & Wm. R. Scott,) Wholesale Liquor Merchants 12 Pub. Landing
BUCHANAN R. & SON, (Robert B., & Chas. M. B.,) Commission & Forwarding Merchants 26 E. 2d.
BUCHANAN Robert, (R. B. & Son,) res. Clifton
Duchanan Mrs. Sarah, h. 14 Oliver
Buchanan Thomas, 192 W. Court
BUCHANAN W. R., Proprietor Dennison House, s.s. 5th b. Main and Sycamore
Bucher Frederick, cof. h. 16 E. Front
Bucher Fred. shoe mkr., 273 Walnut
Buchione Barney, cab. mkr. wks. s.w.c. Canal and Elm.
Buchheit Mary, huckster, s.s. Ohio al. b. Elm and Plum.
Buchheit Peter, toys, &c., 62 Martin
Buchhoff Hy., turner, 11 Adams
Buchholts,Frederick, hostler, bds. 216 W. 7th
BUCHHOLZ GEO., Livery and Sale Stable, 216 and 218 W. 7th
Buckholz Hy , hostler, bds. 216 W. 7th
Buckholz Mathias, cof. h. 41 14th

Buchmann B , printer, bds. s.w.c. Race and 3d.
Buchman Nicholaus, tailor, 53 Hamer.
Buchman Bernard, stationery &c., 26 W. 3d h. 28 Longworth
BUCHMAN Raphael, (Rindskopf Bros. & Co.) 175 George
Buchner John, lab , 59 Martin
Bucholt Mary E., 67 Pendleton.
Bucholtz Fred, driver, 407 Elm
Buchner Geo., cooper, 553 Vine
Buchta Hy., stone mason, 29 Dunlap
Buchtmann Hy., shoe mkr. bds. s.s. Harrison Pike b. Division and Brighton.
Buck Chas., chair mkr., bds. 9 Franklin
Buck Frederick 120 Linn
Buck Frederick, cab. mkr. 56 Elder
Buck Frederick, cooper, 91 W. Front
Buck Frederick A., seamstress, rear 31 Hughes
Buck Fred Wm., cigar box mkr., 73 Hughes
Buck Gerhard, cigar mkr., bds. 59 W. Liberty
Buck Hy., dray, n.s. Corporation al. b. Price and Young
Buck Hy. J., tailor. 115 Ham. Road
Buck Hermann, h. 25 Abigail
Buck James, porter, 25 Abigail
Buck John, bk. layer, 15 Hughes
Buck John W., clk. n.w.c. George and Central Av. b. 24 Bremen
Buck Michael, wagoner, 66 W. Liberty
Buck Wm., meats, s.s. Harrison Pike b. Brighton and Division
Buckel Barbara, servt., 466 Main.
Buckel Jacob, saddler, bds. 47 12th
Buckels Francis, carp, 1158 and 1160 E. Front.
Bucker Clements, lab., rear 92 Dudley
Bucker Eleseta, 92 Dudley
Bucker John, lab., 177 Hopkins
Bucker John F., lab., w.s. Broadway b. Hunt and Abigail
BUCKEYE DINING SALOON, McDonnell & Atkinson, proprietors 170 and 172 Vine,
BUCKEYE STATE FIRE AND MARINE INSURANCE CO., Isaac C. Fallis Secretary, W. P. Hulbert President, 16 Pub. Landing
Buckhard Basslie, lab., rear 206 Cutter
Buckhardt George, 66 Martin
Buckhardt Mary, tailoress, 66 Martin
Buckhorst Geo., polisher, n.s 5th b. Pike and Butler
Buckhurst Eliza, servt., 409 W. 6th
BUCKINGHAM Charles J., (Charles J. B. & Co.,) res. Miamisville
BUCKINGHAM CHARLES J. & CO. (Charles J. B., & M. H. A. Atkin) Flour, Grain, Produce & Commission Merchants, 117 E. Pearl
BUCKINGHAM E. J., (B. & Mathers) 334 Race
BUCKINGHAM Edson G., (Spencer & Co.) 135 George.
BUCKINGHAM & MATHERS (E. J. B. & Richard M.) Pork and Beef Packers, 114 W. Court
Buckler Mary, s.s. 6th b. Broadway and Culvert
Buckler Hy., grocery, 63 Woodward
Buckles J. C., (J. C. B & Co.) Louisville
Buckles J. C. & Co., com. mer. 20 Broadway
Bucklet John, 118 Mohawk
Buckley Benjamin, express, 478 W. 3d
Buckley Dennis, lab., h. 263 John
Buckley Elizabeth, s.w.c. Court and Walnut
Buckley Elizabeth,, 58 Gano
Buckley Francis, matt. mkr., bds. s.w.c. Court and Walnut
Buckley Frank, molder, wks. n.e.c. Canal and Walnut
Buckley Hy., packer, 87 Main
Buckley James, lab., e.s. Ramsey b. Front and W. W. Canal
Buckley Johanna, w.s. Langdon al. b. 6th and 7th
Buckley Margaret, w.s. Langdon al. b. 6th and 7th
Buckley Mary, servt., 292 Longworth

Buckley Mary, bds. 203 Richmond
Buckley Patrick, express driver 99 Clark
Buckley Stephen, peddler, 56 Kossuth
Buckley Thos., iron worker, e.s. Ramsey n. of Front
Buckley Timothy, wks. 247 W. 5th .
Buckman Jacob, peddler, 12 Charles,
Buckman Joseph, saloon, c. Newpor Ferry Landing and Lawrence
Buckmann Frank, hostler, 95 E. 2d
Buckmann Fredericka, grocery, 57 12th
Buckmann Hy., chair mkr., 110 Betts
Buckmann John, finisher, 37 12th
Bucknell Thomas, 140 Dayton
Buckner Commodore F., phys., 10 Pancoast al. h. 10 E. 7th
BUCKNER James H., (Taliaferro & B.) 52 W. 7th
Buckner Kingan, phys., w.s. Henderson al. b. 7th and 8th
Buckner Mary, 50 E. 2d
Buckner Wm., porter, 10 Pancoast al
Backshorn Hy., wks. 196 W, Pearl
Buckton Abram, cooper. 33 Vine
Buckton Wm., eng., n.w.c. 3d and Park
Budde Barney, shoe mkr., 170 Linn
Budde Hermann, cooper, 307 Findlay
Budde Peter, porter, 92 Broadway
Buddeke Joseph G., salesman, 287 George
Buddeker Frank, lab., 482 W. 5th
Buddelmeier Wm. II., lab., 568 Race
Buddemeyer Louis H., (B. & Ummethen,) h. 351 W. 7th
Buddemeyer & Ummethen, (Louis H B., & Gerrard W U.,) dry goods, 307 Central Av
Budden Edward R., engraver. n.w.c 3d and Main, res. Walnut Hills
Buddendick Hy., molder, 49 Pendle'on
Buddendick John, molder, w.s. n.e.c. Miami Canal and Walnut
Buddick Frank, lab., wks. s.w.c. Park and W. W. Canal
Budger Glade, painter, 257 Clark
Budke Arnold, tailor, 50 W. Mulberry
Budke Conrad, cigar box mkr., 126 Spring
Budke Hy., clk., h. 214 Water
Budke Hy., lock smith, wks. J. H. Schroders
Budke Wm., baker, bds. 94 W. 6th
Budke William, lab., wks. s.w.c. Elm and 5th
Budkem Wm., lab. 19 Mulberry
Budmeier Francis, 50 Melancthon
Busch Christian, carp., e.s. Kilgour b. 3d and 5th
Buecker August, boots and shoes, 382 Race, h. 120 W. Canal
Buecker Frederick H., cigar mkr., Pleasant b. Findlay and Henry
Buecker Garrett, shoe mkr., n.w.c. Elm and Liberty
Buecker Hy., saddler, 155 Pleasant
Bueckr Wm., blk.smith, 19 E. Liberty
Bueckmann Frederick, lab., n.s. Ridgway al. b. 14th and 15th
Buehl John A., tailor, 604 Elm
Buehler A., cook, Burnet House
Buehler Andrew, cof. h , 187 Vine
Buehler Conrad, lab., bds. 125 Ham. Road [lin
Buehler Frederick, shoe mkr., 24 Franklin
Buehler Mary, 116 Liberty
Bueker Agathia, 143 Abigail
Bueker Joseph, hatter, 139 Walnut
Buckhols Frederick, stable, 348 W. 6th, h. 350 W. 6th
Buel R. H., clk., 90 Pike
Buell Hy., clk., s.e.c. Pike and 3d
Buellow Hy., phys., 551 Sycamore
Buelte Barney, molder, 124 Clark
Buening Anthony, groceries, 590 Elm
Buening Geo. II., molder, 501 Race
Buening Jacob, finisher, 38 Green
Buening Johanna, 590 Elm
Buenter Louis, stone cutter, 75 Milton
Buenter Louis, 75 Milton
Buerkle John C., furs, gloves, &c., 137 Main
Buerckie Gabriel, lab., 17 Mary
Buerge John, lab., 23 Green
Buerger Chas., stone dresser, 620 W. Front

CINCINNATI ADVERTISEMENTS.

JULIUS J. BANTLIN.   W. A. COMPTON.

BANTLIN & COMPTON,

DEALERS IN

SADDLERY HARDWARE,

Leather and Findings,

S. E. Cor. Main and Court House Building, CINCINNATI, O.

WM. C. KELLAR, Salesman, late with Wilson & Hayden.

P. CODY,

Commission Merchant,

AND WHOLESALE DEALER IN

GROCERIES,

FOREIGN & DOMESTIC LIQUORS,

17 & 19 WATER STREET,

BETWEEN MAIN & WALNUT,   CINCINNATI, O.

KOLKER & McCAMMON,

STAIR BUILDERS,

SASH, BLIND AND DOOR MANUFACTURERS,

Cor. of John and Laurel Streets,   CINCINNATI, O.

Large assortment of Newell's and Banisters constantly on hand. Window Frames, Mantels, Mouldings, and every thing pertaining to BUILDING furnished at the shortest notice

---

SAMUEL A. SARGENT,

REAL ESTATE AND LOAN BROKER,

No. 2 Apollo Buildings,

Cor. of Fifth and Walnut Sts., Cincinnati, O.

Dr. J. H. PULTE,

HOMEOPATHIC PHYSICIAN, Office, 293 Walnut Street, between Seventh and Eighth.
OFFICE HOURS.—Seven to eight in the morning, two to three in the afternoon, and six to seven in the evening.

JOS. A. SAVAGE,

MACHINIST, Manufacturer of Converse and Burdge's Simultaneous Bed Screw Cutter. Particular attention given to Cutting Gearing for Patterns and Sewing Machines, 93 East Eigth Street,   CINCINNATI, O.

JOHN STANTON,

STAMP, BRAND AND STENCIL CUTTER AND Manufacturer of Baggage Checks, 139 Fifth Street, South side, 2 doors West of Race,   CINCINNATI, O.

DR. JAMES G. HUNT,

HOMEOPATHIC PHYSICIAN & SURGEON,

NO. 278 Walnut Street,

Special attention paid to diseases of the EYE and EAR CANCERS, FISTULA IN ANO (cured without the knife,) and all Chronic Diseases.
References given to patients cured.

S. T. CRAWFORD,

Attorney at Law & Notary Public,

Office No. 30 West Fourth Street Cin., O.

JAMES FOSTER Jr. & CO.,

OPTICIANS,

Mathematical and Philosophical

INSTRUMENT MAKERS,

S. W. Cor. 5th and Race Sts. Cincinnati, O.

And 60 Dearborn Street,   CHICAGO, ILL.

M. H. BIRD,

Print Publisher, Bookseller, Stationer,

And Dealer in RELIGIOUS and FANCY PICTURES.
Also, Fine Line Engravings.

297 Central Avenue, Cincinnati, Ohio.

JOSEPH BUSSE,

STOVES & TIN WARE MANUFACTURER, No. 495 Main Street, West Side, between Twelfth and Thirteenth Streets,   CINCINNATI, O.

P. C. BROWNE,

PLAIN AND FANCY

BOOK, CARD, AND JOB PRINTER,

South=East Corner of Third and Sycamore Streets,

(Entrance on Third, Browne's Row.)

CINCINNATI, OHIO.

Buerger Geo. M., tailor, 244 Pleasant
Buerger Jacob, shoe mkr., e.s. Bremen b. Elder and Findlay
Buerger John L., barber, 160 Ham. Road
Buerglin Frank, shoe mkr., s.s. Oliver b. John and Linn
Buerkle Harer, cab. mkr , 41 Jones
Buerkley Franklin, cab. mkr., 41 Jones
Bueschelmann Elizabeth, 278 W. Front
Buesching Mrs. Catharine, 46 Buckeye
Buetker Mathias, carp., 17 Green
Buettner Bernhard, lab., 33 Buckeye
Buettner E , teacher, 24 E. 4th
Buettner Geo. A., shoe mkr , 36 Green
Buettner Hy., tailor, 133 Bremen
Buff & Blossfeld, (John B. & Frederick B.) tailors, 313 W. 6th
BUFF JOHN, Merchant Tailor and Renovator, 126 Vine, h. 70 W. 6th
Buffington M., clk., h. 629 Front
Buffington Jessy, carp., 57 Pierson
Buffington Robert, carp., 629 W. Front
Bugbie Mrs. M. A , bds. 120 John
Bugel John A., shoe mkr., n.s. Vine b. Mulberry and Milk
Bugganner Peter, vof. h., 1502 W. 3d
Bugher Jas., st.bt. capt , 126 W. 6th
Bughnar Chas., carp., 306 Elm
Buggy John W., 410 Longworth
Buggy Mary, 209 W. 4th
Buggy Patrick, coachman, n.s. 3d b. Elm and Plum
Bugsbager Louis, mach., wks. n.w.c. Pearl and M. Canal
Buhene Derack, currier, 392 Broadway
Buhland Herman, cooper, 12 Buckeye
Bubler Michael, lab., w.s. Kilgour b. 3d and 4th
Buhlmann John, mason, s.w.c. Bank and Whiteman
Buhr Joseph, finisher, wks. 141 W. 2d
Buhrlage Frederick, cooper, 18 Buckeye
Buhrlage Frederick, boots and shoes, n. e.c. 15th and Plum
Buhrlage Herman, cooper, 12 Buckeye
Buhrmann Geo. L., boots and shoes, 579 Central Av.
Buhrmann Hy., upholsterer, 41 Pleasant
Buicker Catharine, laundress, 167 W. Liberty
Buicker Leo, 167 W. Liberty
Buker August, bar k. s.e.c. 5th and Elm
Buker Harmon, carp., n.w.c. Elm and Liberty
Bulach Conrad, 114 W. Canal
Bulde Bonny, molder, 124 Clark
Buidmann Lewis, box mkr., 93 13th
Buidmann Louisa. 464 Main
Buldock Milton, dray, 87 E. Front
Buldman W., painter, 464 Main
Bulger James, cof. h., n.e.c. E. Front and Washington
Bulger John, eng., wks. J. Whitaker's, Deer Creek Valley
Bulger Patrick, finisher, n.s. Augusta b. John and Smith
Bull Frank, lab., bds. 115 Carr
Bull Wm., bds. 98 Broadway
Bulle Martin, saddler, 49 Bremen
Bullerdick Frederick, chair mkr., 22 Madison
Bullet Louisa, music teacher, 499 Walnut
Bullet Ami. stone cutter, 29 Race
Bullmann Joseph, lab., wks. 68 Water
BULLOCK A. D. & CO., (Anthony D. B., Henry Lewis & Wm. B. Bullock) Wool Dealers and Commission Merchants, 12 and 14 W. 2d
BULLOCK Anthony D., (A. D. B. & Co.) h. Mt. Auburn
BULLOCK Wm. B., (A. D. Bullock & Co.) bds. Burnet House
Bulmer John, wks. J. Whittaker's, Deer Creek Valley
Bulscher Jacob, shoe mkr., bds. 64 E. 5th
Bulter Herman, tailor, 186 Clark
Bultermann Hy., lab., 23 Mill
BULTMAN CHRISTIAN F., Hardware and Cutlery, s.e.c. Main and 9th, h. 9 W. 9th
Bultman Hy. T., cab. mkr,, 144 Baymiller

Bultman Julius, clk. s.e.c. Main and 9th, h. 9 W. 9th
Bultmann D. Lewis, box factory, 141 Water, h. 98 13th
Bultmann Diedrich, cab. mkr., 141 W 5th, h. e.s. Baymiller nr Clark
Bumillor Theodore H., bk , bds. 83 W. 9th
Bumpville Lewis. 20 Harrison
Bunce Hy., s.s. Dorsey nr. Sycamore
Bunce James W., b.k. 120 E. 2d, h. 262 W. 8th
Bunckenburg August tinner, 199 Pleasant
Bund Hy., driver, 29 Commerce
Bund Hy , mach., 410 Broadway
Bunder Albertine, seamstress, 21 Hughes
Bungener Barney, cab. mkr., wks. 468 W. 6th
Bunger Louis carp., wks. 13 Ham. Road
Bunghost Hy., watchman, 108 Hunt
Buning Frank, grocery, s.w.c. Freeman and Dayton
Buning Hy., bds. 83 Baymiller
Buning Jacob, lab., wks. n.w.c. Plum and Wade
BUNING JOHN H., Family Grocery and Feed Store, 81 and 83 Baymiller
Buning Joseph, porter, 38 Pub. Landing
Buning Wm., bds. 83 Baymiller
Bunkenburg August, tinner, wks. 149 W. 5th
BUNKER CHARLES W., Reporter Daily Times, h. 168 Smith
Bunker John, jailor, 375 Sycamore
Bunker Richard, cof. h , n.e.c. Plum and River
Bunnell Susan, b.h., 209 Central Av.
Bunnemeyer Barney, porter, w.s. Observatory b. Hill and Pavillion
Bunnemeyer John B., porter, 79 W. Pearl
Bunnemeier Herman, tailor, 538 Plum
Bunning Hy., lab., wks. 108 E. 2d
Bunny Joseph, lab., 297 Barr
Bunselmieur Wm., 300 Linn
Bunsmeyer Hy., stone cutter, 213 Findlay
Bunst James, lab., n.s. Front e. of Kelly
Bunte Frank, clk., 61 Abigail
Bunter Clinton, carp., s.e.c. York and Freeman
Bunton Clinton, carp , e.s. Freeman b. York and Findlay
Bunton Phoebe, n.s. Oregon b. 3d and 5th
Bunyan Maurice, shoe mkr., 207 Broadway, h. 202 Broadway
Burbacker Geo., coachman, 17 Macalister
Burbage Robert, s.s. 8th b. Broadway and Sycamore
BURBECK Andrew C., (B. & Haight) res. Locklaud
BURBECK & HAIGHT, (Andrew C. B. & Jered. H.) Flour and Grain, Commission and Forwarding Merchants, 107 and 109 E. Pearl, and Bakery 58 and 60 Commerce
Burch John W., agt. H. & St. Jo. R. R., 35 W. 3d
Burchfield James, printer, n.w.c. 5th and Vine
Burchhart Philip, lab., 79 Hughes
Burck Mary, 196 Ham. Road
Burck Patrick, lab., 309 W. 8th
Burckard Geo., cof. h., 100 W. Liberty
Burckhalter George, cutter, bds. s.w.c. Race and 3d
BURCKHARDT & CO., (Leopold & Fred B.) Commission Merchants, Lard Oil and Stearine Manufacturers 107 Sycamore
Burckhardt Edward, huckster, 626 Vine
BURCKHARDT Fred., (B. & Co.) 61 W. 9th
Burckhardt Fred., molder, wks. 222 E. Front
BURCKHARDT Leopold, (B. & Co.) 142 Smith
Burckhardt Louis, butcher, 54 Dunlap
Burckhardt Michael, huckster, 54 Buckeye
Burckhart Peter, 64 Elder
Burd Jasper N., clk. n.e.c. 4th and Main, bds. Dennison House

Burd Thomas M., clk. Co. Recorder's Office, res. Spencer Tp.
Burdeck Hy., peddler, n.e.c. 3d and Wood
Burdge Elizabeth, 125 Longworth
Burdge Jonathan E. sewing machine manuf., 327 W. 3d
Burdge Sarah, 403 W. 3d
Burdick Anna, 91 Clay
Burdick Bernard, shoe mkr., w.s. Linn b. Clark and Hopkins
Burdick Frederick, blk.smith, n.s. 12th b Vine and Bremen
Burdorff Hy., blk.smith 103 Hunt, h. e.s. Spring b. Hunt and Abigail
Burdsal Alfred, b.k. Wood & McCoy's, h. 416 Broadway
BURDSAL & BRO., (Henry W. & James S.) Wholesale Druggists, n, w.c. Main and Front
Burdsal Elijah, b k. n.w.c. Main and Front
BURDSAL Henry W., (B. & Bro.) h. College Hill
BURDSAL James S., (B. & Bro.) h. 118 E. 5th
Burdsal Joseph W., clk., 206 Longworth
Burdsal Samuel, drugs, &c , 409 Main, h. 448 Broadway
Burdsal Thomas C., druggist, 416 Broadway
Bureau L B., bds. Madison House
Burford Robt., clk., n.s. Corporation Line nr. Auburn
Burford Robert G., tailor, 227 Central Av.
Burg Ludwig, cof. h., 53 Ham. Road
Burg Nicholas, lab., 36 Mohawk
Burganey Josephine. 613 Elm
Burgard Prosper, finisher, bds. 199 W. 6th
Burger Albert, tailor, 76 W. 3d, h. 248 Clark
Burger Barbara, 106 Buckeye
Burger Catharine, seamstress, 108 Buckeye
Burger Frank J., boots and shoes, 328 W. 8th
Burger George, lab., 671 W. 6th
Burger Hy. G., teacher, 625 Vine
Burger John, salesman, 324 Main
Burger Philip H., boots and shoes, 324 Main
Burger Simon, clk., 120 W. 5th, bds. 30 Perry
Burger Valentine, cab. mkr., 305 Freeman
Burzerdink Hy., bedstead mkr., 185 W. 2d
Burgers Edward. porter, 100 Spring
Burgert Paul, 58 Dudley
Burgert Peter, daguerrean art., s.w.c. Dudley and Liberty
Burgert Peter (B., Sand & Co.), bds. 58 Dudley
Burgert, Sand & Co. (Peter B., Adolphus S. & David Kruger) match factory, 60 Dudley
Burgess Jemina, 106 Barr
Burgess Perry, n.e.c. Smith and Augusta
Burgess Thomas Hy., bds. 75 Park
Burgess Wm., driver, American Ex. Co. bds. Evans' Hotel
Burgess Wm., lab., n.e.c. Abigail and Spring
Burgess Wm., wire weaver, 75 Park
Burgett Daniel, 185 W. 6th
Burggraf Ernst, carp., bds. w.s. Ridgway al. b. 14th and 15th
Burghardt Cecilia, milliner. 571 Vine
Burghardt Jacob, mach., wks. 264 Central Av
Burgmann Engel, 46 Buckeye
Burgon Michael, waiter, n.w.c. Vine and Longworth
Burgoyne Alex., 92 Sycamore
BURGOYNE JOHN, President, National Insurance Co., s.w.c. Main and Front, h. Glendale
Burgoyne John, jr., atty. s.e.c. Main and Court, h. 40 Mansfield
Burgoyne Mary F., 517 Freeman
Burgoyne Wm., salesman, 99 W. Pearl, h 470 John
Burgoyne Wm. M., b.k., 85 Main

CINCINNATI ADVERTISEMENTS.

OCULIST!
E. WILLIAMS, M. D.

Gives his exclusive attention to the Treatment of Diseases of the

EYE AND EAR,

OFFICE, 163 RACE STREET, between Fourth and Fifth, CINCINNATI, OHIO.

ARTIFICIAL EYES INSERTED.

R. M. BISHOP.   G. W. BISHOP.   WM. T. BISHOP.

R. M. BISHOP & CO.

(Formerly BISHOP, WELLS & CO.)

WHOLESALE GROCERS, FORWARDING & COMMISSION

MERCHANTS,

Dealers in Hemp, Grass Seeds and Produce generally,

No. 36 MAIN STREET, BET. FRONT and SECOND,

CINCINNATI, OHIO.

DAVID KIRK,

Plumber, Pump & Hydrant Maker,

No. 215 Walnut St., west side, bet. Fifth and Sixth,

CINCINNATI, OHIO.

Keeps constantly on hand, and makes to order, Water Closets, Hot and Cold Baths, Shower Baths, Hydrants, Cistern, Well, Force and Beer Pumps, Sheet Lead, and Lead Pipe. Repairing neatly done. All orders promptly attended to.

ADOLPHUS LOTZE,

MANUFACTURER OF LOTZE'S PATENT

WARM-AIR FURNACES,

Registers and Ventilators, Stoves, Grates, Tin, Copper and Sheet-Iron Ware, Ventilating and Chimney Caps, Metallic Roofing. All Jobbing done with neatness and dispatch.

No. 219 WALNUT STREET; ABOVE FIFTH; CINCINNATI, O.

WALNUT STREET DYE HOUSE.

JOHN HARMEIER,

FANCY DYER AND SCOURER,

OFFICE, 218 Walnut Street, bet. Fifth and Sixth, east side, CINCINNATI, O.

☞ Dyes and Prints all kinds of Silk and Woolen Goods, to any color. Also, cleans Ladies and Gentlemen's Wearing Apparel, Shawls of every description, Curtains, Carpets, &c., at the shortest notice.

(BUR) CINCINNATI (BUR) DIRECTORY. (BUR) 95

BURGUND HENRY,
  Glass Stainer, 47 E. 3d,
  h. 139 Linn
Burgunder Saml., trader. h. 239 W. 7th
Burhans David J., carp., Lawson's al. b.
  4th and 5th, h. 102 Clinton
Burhen Reinhardt, varnisher, 295 W.
  Front
BURHOFF BARNEY,
  Coffee and Boarding House,
  s.w.c. 5th and Smith
Buring Frank H., varnisher, bds. s.s.
  Clark b. Baymiller and Freeman
Burk Catharine, tailoress, 223 Cutter
Burk Charles, hinge fitter, wks. n e c.
  Walnut and Canal
Burk Edward, lab., 245 Clark
Burk Harman, 117 Laurel
Burk James, painter, n.e.c. 6th and
  Baum
Burk Johanna, servt., 126 Barr
Burk Martin, cooper, 500 W. 6th
Burk Mary, servt , 124 E. 4th
Burk Mary, 28 Accommodation
Burk Michael, lab., 493 W. 3d
Burk Patrick, lab , 7 Jackson
Burk Patrick, tailor, 23 E. 7th
Burk Pierce, fireman, e.s. Park b. 2d and
  W. W. Canal
Burk Richard, shoemkr, n.s. Front e. of
  Kelly
Burk Richd. S. clk., n.e.c. 4th and Main
Burk Thomas E., 410 Longworth
Burk Thomas I., shoemkr, 147 Main
Burk Wm , teamster, 49 Hopkins
BURKAM Chas. B. (E. G. Burkam &
  Co.) bds. s.e.c. 6th and Race
BURKAM E. G. & CO.,
  (Elzy G. & Joseph H. B., Chas.
  B. B., Wm. D. B), Bankers, 19 W.
  3d
BURKAM Elzy G., (E. G. B. & Co.),
  res. Chicago
BURKAM Joseph H. (E. G. Burkam &
  Co) res. Lawrenceburg, Ind
BURKAM Wm. D. (E. G. Burkam & Co.)
  res. Chicago
Burkard Anna, 233 W. 6th
Burkard Joseph, gardener, 229 Carr
Burkard Anna C., 37 Ham. Road
Burke Antony, lab., 21 Commerce
Burke Barney, tailor, e.s. Stone al. b. 5th
  and Longworth
Burke Bridget, servt., 248 Longworth
Burke Catharine, 165 W. 5th
Burke Chas., waiter, 171 Walnut
Burke Cornelius, lab., 103 Central Av
Burke Dennis, shoemkr, bds. 12 Commerce
Burke Edward, lab., n.s. Augusta b. John
  and Smith
Burke Ed., waiter, Burnet House
Burke Hy., cab mkr., wks. 126 W. 2d
Burke Hy., safe mkr., 95 Pleasant
Burke James, lab , 191 E. Front
Burke James, lab , w.s. Central Av. b.
  Front and Water
Burke James, painter. 71 E. 8th
Burke James J., bk. binder. 131 W. Front
Burke John, grocer, 150 E. 6th
Burke John, wks. n.w.c. Plum and Wade
Burke John, lab., 54 George
Burke John, lab., 133 W. Front
Burke John, wks. J. Whittaker's, Deer
  Creek Valley
Burke Joseph, mach., bds. 512 W. Front
Burke Kate, n.w.c. 6th and Harriet
Burke Kate, servt., 883 E. Front
Burke Mrs. M., h. 291 Vine
Burke Maggie, servt., 101 Pike
Burke Martin, bar k., Thomas Sand's
Burke Martin, peddler, 7 Lock n. of 8th
Burke Mary, w.s. Pole b 2d and Pearl
Burke Mary, n.w.c. 6th and Harriet
Burke Mary, grocery, 121 Lock
Burke M9ry, servt., 422 W. 6th
Burke Mary A., 238 Broadway
Burke Milo. dray,"e.s. John b. Elizabeth
  and Chestnut
Burke Michael, lab., w.s. Collard b.
  Front and 3d
Burke Patrick. fireman, Spencer House
Burke Patrick, lab., 126 Carr
Burke Pat., lab., s.s. Friendship al. b.
  Pike and Butler
Burke Patrick, lab., s.e.c. 6th and Baum

Burke Pat., waiter, Burnet House
Burke Perry, lab , n.s. al. b. Pole and
  Park and 2d and W. W. Canal
Burke Peter, finisher, wks. n.e.c. Walnut and Canal
Burke Thomas. bds. 61 E. 4th
Burke Thomas, chair mkr., 118 Everett
Burke Thomas, cof h., 401 W. 2d
Burke Thomas, lab., 62 Butler
Burke Thomas, lab., s.s. 2d b. Park and
  Rose
Burke Thomas, Union Exchange, 512 W.
  Front
Burkeberle Charles, butcher, 363 Cutter
Burkemeler Hy., harness mkr., 519
  Main
Burkenkamp Hy., b.k., 91 Sycamore
Burkhard Frederick B., mach., 279 Bremen
Burkhard John, blksmith. w.s. Lebanon
  Road b. Liberty and Corp. Line
Burkhard Peter, molder, 643 Vine
Burkhardt Andy, 29 Grant
Burkhardt Chas., harness mkr., 11 12th
Burkhardt Christian, bar k., 225 W. 6th
Burkhardt Hy., upholsterer. 72 Bremen
Burkhardt John, tailor, 469 Elm
Burkhardt John, tailor, 74 Dudley
Burkhardt Matthias, molder, 61 Observatory
Burkhardt Mathias G., foreman, h. 75
  Observatory
Burkhardt Peter J., (Fritsch, B. & Co.),
  645 Vine
Burkhardt Wm., driver, 29 Grant
Burkhardt Andreas, lab., 675 Race
Burkhart Francis X., stoves, &c., 393
  Vine
Burkhart Frank. bakery, 584 Central Av
Burkhart Michael, 45 E. Front
Burkhart Wm., butcher, bds. 640 W. 6th
Burkhart Dyonisius, sawyer. 23 Abigail
Burkhuus John H., lab., 149 Carr
Burkhemmer George, h. 377 Longworth
Burkholz John, brewery, e.s Walnut b.
  Ham Road and Liberty, b. 49 Ham.
  Road
Burkle Martin, cof. h., 78 Mohawk
Burkley John, mach., bds. 355 Central
  Av
Burkmann Hermann, box mkr., 158
  Oliver
Burkshire Garrard, boatman, s.e.c. 8th
  and Lock
Burman Thomas, bk. layer, 156 Linn
Burman Valentine, driver, 21 Lodge
Burmeyer John, tailor, 16 Dudley
Burl Clara, 234 Longworth
Burlage Geo., 115 Avery
Burland Herman, lab., 17 Mulberry
Burlew Hy., tobacconist, b ls. Madison
  House
Burley C. J. F., messenger. 65 W. 3d
Burley Eliza J., teacher, 50½ Milton
Burley Thomas, clk., 23 W. 3d. bds. 127
  W. 5th
Burley Wm. finisher, 59½ Milton
Burling Adolph, varnisher, bds. 91 W.
  Court
Burlinggame Margaret, n w.c. 4th and
  Sycamore
Burnd Daniel, blksmith, 919 Central Av
Burnd John, blksmith, 127 York
Burnes Wm., butcher, n.s. Deer Creek
  Road e. of Liberty
BURNET HOUSE,
  T. P. Saunders & Co., Proprietors,
  n.w.c. 3d and Vine
BURNET Jacob, (Jones & B.) res. nr.
  Cumminsville
Burnet Jacob, jr., boots and shoes, 93 W.
  Pearl, h. 109 Mill
Burnet Jacob T., atty., 168 W. 7th
Burnet James C., s.w.c. 5th and Plum
Burnet John. lab.. wks. n.w.c. Pearl and
  M. Canal
Burnet John G., 168 W. 7th
Burnet Mrs Rebecca, 150 W. 7th
Burnet Richard, weaver, s.w.c. Cutter
  and Betts
Burnet Richard, lab., 427 W. 3d
Burnet Robt. W., 158 W. 7th
BURNET STAATS G.
  (Wm. Bromwell & Co.)
  h. 217 Mound
Burnett Alfred, h. 59 David

Burnett P. C., china, glass, &c., 392
  Central Av
Burnett Thos. N., bakery, 217 Freeman
Burney Hy. A , bk. binder, w.s. Main b.
  Buckeye and Ham. Road
Burney Jos., peddler, 126 Walnut
Burnhagen Clemens, shoemkr, 100 W.
  Court
Burnham Daniel, huckster, 257 Richmond
Burnham John, trader, 40 Linn
Burnham John T., wks. 310 Main
Burnhan John, shoemkr, 46 Stone
Burnhan Mary, 16 Stone
Buruhan Victor, bds. 16 Stone
Burns Alice, s.s. al. b. Pike and Lawrence and 3d and Pearl
Burns Ann, h. 3 New
Burns Ann, s s. al. b. Pike & Lawrence
  and 3d and Pearl
Burns Anna, servt., wks. 519 W. 7th
Burns Barney, waiter, Burnet House
Burns Bridget, 156 George
Burns Bryan, lab., 550 Race
Burns Cath rine. 28 Accommodation
Burns Chas. S., salesman, s.s. 3d e. of
  Kilgour
Burns Cornelius A., carp., 240 Vine
Burns Cornelius, peddler, 327 W. 2d
Burns Delia, 113 George
Burns Dominick. lab., 381 W. 2d
Burns Edward, shoemkr, 160 Cutter
Burns Eliza, laundress, 220 Central Av
Burns Elizabeth, n.e.c. Abigail & Spring
Burns Fred., lab., s.s. 6th, nr. Harriett
Burns Geo. W., cigars, &c , 31 E. 3d,
  res. Newport
Burns Hy., (Robinson & B.) Charlotte,
  b. Central av. and John
Burns Herman, lab. 25 Commerce
Burns Hugh, lab., 52 E. 8th, E. of Lock
Burns James. foreman. 296 W. Front
Burns James, lab., 419 George
Burns James, lab., 4 Charlotte
Burns James, lab., 203 W. 2d
Burns James, lab., 546 Race
Burns James, lab., w.s. Whittaker, b. 3d
  and Front
Burns James, lab., b. 4th and 5th and
  Central av and John
Burns James, mach., 419 George
Burns James A., coppersmith, wks. 21
  E. Front
Burns James M., printer. bds. 298 W. 5th
Burns John, 976 E. Front
Burns John, foreman, n.w.c. Smith and
  Front
Burns John, lab., n.s. Front. e. of Kelly
Burns John, lab., 203 W. Front
Burns John, lab., w.s Central Av., b. 2d
  and W.W. Canal
Burns John, painter, Burnet House
Burns John, painter, 47 E. 4th
Burns John, shoe mkr., bds 138 Longworth
Burns John B., tailor, 33 Jackson
Burns John H , Mill street House, n.w.
  c. Mill and Front
Burns Julia, 64 Melanthon
Burns Lawrence, shoe mkr., 477 W. 3d
Burns Lewis, tailor, 104 Gest
Burns Margaret, 46 Lock, n. of 8th
Burns Mrs. Margaret, s.s. al. b. Pike
  and Lawrence, and 3d and Pearl
Burns Mary, dress mkr., 156 George
Burns Mary, n.s. Front, e. of Foster
Burns Mary, n.s. Taylor, b. Curr and
  Freeman
Burns Martin, molder, s.s. 6th, b. Broadway and Culvert
Burns Matthew, lab., 29 E. 3d, e. of Parsons
Burns Michael, lab., 412 W. 3d
Burns Michael, lab., 71 Richmond
Burns Miles, hostler, 78 W. 6th
Burns Pat., lab., n.s. Front, e. of Kelly
Burns Pat., lab., 213 E. 3d
Burns Pat., lab., bds. n.e c. 3d & Butler
Burns Stephen, dray., s.s. Avery al. w.
  of Wood
Burns Theodore, lab., 214 Water
Burns Thomas, bds. 41 Pub. Landing
Burns Thos., lab., n s. Front, e. of Kelly
Burns Thos., lab., s.w.c. Freeman and
  Richmond
Burns Timothy, porter, 69 W. Front

Burns Wm., rooms 14 E. 5th
Burns Wm., blk smith, 404 George
Burns Wm., lab., 448 George
Burnsey Wm., lab., e.s. Little al. b. 14th and 15th, and Central Av and Plum
Burpe Mrs L., governess, Mt. Auburn Institute
Burridge Edward, eng., e.s. Freeman, b. Wade and Liberty
Burris Maria, teacher, 575 8th
Burris Sarah, 201 Broadway
Burridge John, wks. Cin. type foundry
Burris Sylvester H., lab., 808 W. Front
Burrop Hy., bIksmith, 76 Spring
Burroughs Amos, cooper, 181 Linn
BURROWES Grant H., (C. B. Evans & Co.,) 375 W. 8th
Burrowes Hy., clk., 76 W. 5th
BURROWES WM. S.,
Attorney at Law,
6 W. 4th, bds. Gibson House
Burrows Geo., (Bird B. & Co.,) 312 Plum
BURROWS J. H. & CO., (Joseph H. B. & Abel Kimball,) Foundry and Machine Shop, 180 W. 2d
Burrows James B., salesman, bds. 177 W. 3d
Burrows John T., with Davidson & Bro., n.e.c. Main and 5th
Burrows Joseph H., mach., 177 W. 3d
Burrows Joseph H., (J. H. B. & Co.,) 177 W. 3d
Burrows Robert, plasterer, 212 W. Court w. of Central av
Burrows Sylvester H., molder, 808 W. Front
Burse Bernard, lab., 663 Central Av
Burstinger Joseph, fringe manuf., 352 Main
BURT A. G. & CO., (Andrew G. B. & John T. Hooper,) Bankers and Exchange Dealers, 101 Main
BURT Andrew G., (A. G. B. & Co.,) h. 338 W. 4th
Burt George, carp., bds. 420 W. 8th
Burt John S. G., 172 Race
Burt Margaret, servt., 317 W. 6th
Burt Nancy, w.s. Whittaker, b. 3d and Front
Burt Rev. Nathaniel C., 71 E. 3d
Burt Pitts H., teller, 101 Main, bds. 338 W. 4th
Burt Samuel T., millwright, s.s. Front w. of Hill
Burt Wm., clk., w.s. Whittaker, b. 3d and Front
Burt Wm., shoe mkr., 182 W. Court
Burtmenger Aaron, dry goods, 48 Elder
Burte John, porter, n.s. 6th, b. Walnut and Vine
Burteling Joseph, mec., wks. n.w.c. Freeman and 9th
Burterner Frank, boots and shoes, 5 Landing, b. Broadway and Ludlow
Burtner Peter, carp., 272 Hopkins
Burton Alice, bds. 200 Webb
Burton Ann, 61 E. 7th
Burton Gideon, wh. boots and shoes, 32 W. Pearl, h. 118 Broadway
Burton James H., bds. 208 W. 5th
Burton O., 77 E. 7th
Burton Robt. B., b.k., 32 W. Pearl, h. 118 Broadway
BURTON S. H. & CO., (Stephen H. B., Miles Greenwood, and James G. Clarke,) Manuf. of Stoves, Hollow Ware, &c., 11, 13 & 15, W. 2d
BURTON Stephen H., (S. H. B. & Co.) h. Avondale
BURTON Stephen R., (Redway & B.,) res. Avondale
Burton Wm. T., clk., 32 W. Pearl, h. 118 Broadway
Burwinkel Anthony, grocery, 24 Woodward
Burwinkel John, lab., 103 Clay
Bury Andrew, lab., n.w.c. Liberty and Dudley
Bury Andy, lab., 76 Dudley
Bury John, lab., 76 Dudley
Busa Hy., porter, 92 Broadway
Busam Engelbert, baker, w.s. Goose al., b. Liberty and 15th
Busam Michael, cof. h., 652 Central Av
Busch Andrew, chair mkr., wks. John Mitchell's

Busch Andrew, cab. mkr., 5 Melancthon
Busch Andrew, cooper, 50 Dudley
Busch August, dray., bds. 546 Central Avenue
Busch Anna, seamstress, 71 Hughes
Busch Catharine, 658 Elm
Busch Charles barber, 232 W. 6th
Busch Charles, carp., wks. n.s. Front, b. Lawrence and Pike
Busch Christian, brewer, 566 Elm
Busch Christopher. clk., bds. 513 W. 5th
Busch Edward, barber. 334 Central Av
Busch Elizabeth, 104 Avery
Busch Frederick, lab., 72 Hughes
Busch Francis X., cof. h., 654 Race
Busch John, cof. h, 68 E. Front
Busch John, tinner, n.s. Montgomery Pike, nr. Madison Road
Busch Michael, dry goods, 400 Broadway
Busch Wm., (Thueringer & B.,) 526 Race
Busche Wm., 18 Mansfield
Buscher Anthony, cutler, 61 Richmond
Buscher Fred., lab., s.s. Beal, b. Broadway and Sycamore
Buscher Frederick, shoemkr., n.w.c. Pendleton and Abigail
Busching Hy., varnisher, 31 Ham. Road
Busching Richard, varnisher, 31 Hughes
Buschir Antony, tailor, 61 Richmond
Buschklaus Richard, carp., n.e.c. Pleasant and Green
Buschle Frederick, (Schaefer & B.,) 49 Canal
Buschmann F. & Co., (Fred. R. & Anthony Schiffmacher,) painters, 500 Sycamore
Buschmann Fred., (F. B. & Co.,) 17 Mansfield
Buse Lewis, lab., n.s. Goose al. b. Green and Elder
Busean Herman H., carp., 76 Spring
Bush Adolph, cooper, 52 Dudley
Bush Amanda, chair caning, 30 Rittenhouse
Bush B. F., tel. op., 162 Broadway
Bush Christopher, teamster, 25 Dudley
Bush Frank, tel. op., bds. 162 Broadway
Bush Ferdinand, meats, 223 Freeman
Bush George, 121 York
Bush H. G F., b.k., H. Homan's, h. 66 Milton
Bush Hy., clk., 69 E. Pearl
Bush Hy., gasfitter, 50 Webster
BUSH Obadiah N., (Chamberlain & Co.) b. Mt. Auburn
Bush Sandford S., clk, 124 Main, bds. 52 W. 9th
Bush Wm., butcher, 194 Clinton
BUSH Wm. S., (Sanford & B.,) res. Loveland
Bushler Theodore, 769 Central Av
Bushman Hy., blksmith, wks. 11 W. 9th
Bushmuller Richard, roller, bds. Mechanics Hall
Bushnell Hy., finisher, wks. n.w.c. Plum and Wade
BUSHNELL JOSEPH,
Coal Agent, e.s. Central Avenue, b. 2d and Pearl, h. Mt. Auburn
Bushnell Thomas C., c.k., Wm. G. Warden's, bds. Spencer House
Busing Bernard H., lab., n.s. Browne, b. Ham. Road and Mohawk
Buskamp Joseph, grocery, 323 Plum
Buske Hy., cig. mkr., bds. 14, 13th
Buske Hermann, dray., 41 Mansfield
Busken Geo. H., (J. H. Busken & Bro.) 234 W. 6th
Busken J. H. & Bro., (John H. & Geo. H.,) dry goods, 234 W. 6th
Busken John H., (J. H. B. & Bro.,) 234 W. 6th
Busker Elizabeth, 464 Main
Busker Wm. K., blk. molder. 337 Clark
Buskerding Rodolph, lab., 503 Bremen
Buskirk Wm. H., clk., 14 Jackson
Busmann Catharine, 1 Budd
Busmann Joseph, cab mkr., 1 Budd
Busmann Mary, 1 Budd
Busmend John, helper, wks. n.e.c. Walnut and Miami Canal
Buss Charles, printer, 51 Allison
BUSS Jacob, (P. Eckert & Co.,) 51 Allison
Bussall Andrew T., stable, s.s. Patterson al. b. Main & Walnut, h. 227 Laurel

Busse Frank., lab., 349 Broadway
Busse Frederick, shoe mkr., 60 Plum
Busse Hy., wks. 218 Sycamore
Busse Hy., lab., w.s. Western Av. b. Bank and Harrison Road
Busse James, stone cutter, 23 Harrison
BUSSE JOSEPH,
Stoves, Hollow-ware, Tin and Copper-ware, 45.5 Main
Busse Louisa, 511 Sycamore
Busse Wm., lab., 187 Clark
Bussell Anderson T., horse trader, 227 Laurel
Bussert Thomas. (Van, Winkle & B.) bds. Burnet House
Bussi Fred, blk.smith, 218 Clark
Bussi Theo., cooper, 200 Linn
BUSSING G. H., (G. H. B. & Co.) 250 Race
BUSSING G. H. & CO., (G. H. B. & George C. Glass) Bankers and Exchange Dealers, n.w.c. Walnut and 3d
Bussing Nicholas, varnisher, 21 Hughes
Busink George H., banker, 244 Race
Bussmann Bernard, cof. h, 155 Front
Bussmann Christopher, baker 64 David
Bussmann Hy., molder, 414 Longworth
Butcher Frederick, shoe mkr., 326 Main
Butcher's Melting Association, n.w.c. Central Av. and Findlay
Butchert Margaret, seamstress, 191 W. Canal
Buten Barney, carp., s.s. Calhoun b. Vine and Walnut
Buten Hy., harness mkr., wks. 30 W. Court
Buter Elizabeth, 144 E. Front
Buter Theodore, clk., bds. 97 W. Court
Butke Wm., lab., 97 Woodward
Butker Hy., stone mason, 64 Wade
Butkle Elizabeth, 214 Water
Butler Albert, plasterer, bds. 124 York
Butler Amelia, n.s. 8th b. Broadway and Sycamore
Butler Arthur T., clk, 104 W. 6th
Butler —, traveling agt., bds. s.w.c. 3d and Broadway
Butler Barney, 7 Jackson
Butler Ben., pattern mkr., wks. n.e.c. Miami Canal and Walnut
Butler Bridget, 994 E. Front
Butler Catharine, laundress, Spencer House
Butler Chas., artist, 532 Elm
Butler Conrad. carp., e.s. Bremen b. Elder and Findlay
Butler D. C., salesman, n.s. McFarland nr. Elm
Butler David M., dray, 26 Lock n. of 8th
Butler Edward, 66 Avery
Butler Edward, lab., 928 E. Front
Butler Edward S, 30 Sycamore, res. Vine St. Hill
Butler Engelbert, lab., 150 Pleasant
Butler George, carp., 518 W. 9th
Butler George, lab., n.s. E. Front e. of Lentherbury
Butler George H., shoe mkr., bds. w.s. Smith b. Augusta and 2d
Butler Grauger T., whitewasher, 123 W. Court w. of Central Av.
Butler Harrison H., steward, 20 Macalister
Butler Isaiah Z., cooper, 1162 E. Front
Butler James, lab., 544 W. Front
BUTLER JAMES J. Agent, Butler's Mercantile, Record and Copying Fluid Ink, 30 Vine, h. 160 W. 8th
Butler John, lab., bds. 73 E. Front
Butler John, mach., n.s. Pearl b. Lawrence and Pike
Butler John B., carp., s.w.c. Longworth and Elm
Butler Joseph C., Lafayette Banking Co., 396 W. 6th
Butler Julia, 398 Broadway
Butler Margaret, n.s. al. b. Pearl and 3d and Lawrence and Pike
Butler Mary, w.s Central Av. b. 2d and W. W. Canal
Butler Mary C., trimmer, n.s. Oliver b. Linn and Baymiller
Butler Michael, dray, 107 Baum
Butler Michael M., driver, bds. 26 Lock n. of 8th

(BYL) CINCINNATI (CAH) DIRECTORY. (CAL) 97

Butler Richard, lab., 374 Broadway
Butler Richard, lab., wks. 335 Broadway
Butler Richard, lab., wks. Henry Nye's
Butler Richard, tailor, n.s. 6th e. of Lock
Butler Richard A., (Brown, Stout & B.) 411 Broadway
Butler Thomas, clk. 94 W. Pearl, bds. 192 W. 7th
Butler Thomas, cooper, 44 E. 2d
Butler Thomas, policeman, n.s. Pearl b. Butler and Pike
Butler Thomas C., 104 W. 6th
Butler Thomas S., agt. Butler's IXL oil blacking, 39 Vine, h. 453 W. 7th
Butler Virginia, 367 W. 7th
Butler Wm., 64 E. 8th
Butler Wm., carp., s.s. Front b. Broad and Waldon
Butler Wm., eng., 15 Arch
Butler Wm., lab., 54 Baum
Butler Wm., printer, bds. e.s. Ludlow b. Pearl and 3d
Butler Wm., salesman, bds. 186 Race
Butler Wm., stable, 183 W. 6th
BUTLER Wm. H., (J. C. Parr & Co.) bds. 554 W. 5th
Butler Wm. J., clk. 101 W. 4th
Butley John, tailor, 57 E. 7th
Butsha Frederick R., cof. h., 463 Vine
Butscher Jacob, cab. mkr., 74 W. Liberty
Butscher John, carp., 74 W. Liberty
Butscher Valentine, cab. mkr., 74 W. Liberty
Butscher Wm., boiler mkr., wks. McIlvain, Spiegel & Co.
Butt Frederick, artist, e.s. Coleman b. Dayton and Findlay
Butt James B., cooper, 48 Clark
BUTTEMILLER'S HOTEL, John Buttemiller Proprietor, 40 W. Court
BUTTEMILLER JOHN, Proprietor Buttemiller's Hotel 40 W. Court
Buttenbaum Deidrich cooper, s.e.c. Jones and David
Buttenweiser Bunet, compositor, bds. 477 W. 8th
Buttenweiser Isaac, peddler, 477 W. 8th
buttenwieser L, (Heller, Bros. & Co.) 246 Plum
Buttenwieser Samuel, h. e.s. Plum b. George and 7th
Butter Barney, lab., 72 Hunt
Butter John, lab., e.s. Goose al. b. Liberty and Green
Butterfass Philip, (Mayleben & B.) 41 Commerce
BUTTERFIELD A S., Saddle, Harness and Trunk Manufacturer, 242 Main. h. 150 York
Butterfield Cummings, 95 Race
BUTTERFIELD Jones, (Jennings & B.) 31 George
Buttermann Hy, lab., 70 Buckeye
Butternut Herman, cigar mkr., 21 Gano
Butters Edmund, carriage manuf., 599 Central Av., h. 7 David
Butterworth Joseph, bk. layer, 464 W. Front
Button Chas., city weigher, 239 Clinton
Butts James, cooper, 248 W. Liberty
Butts Samuel A. jr., teacher, bds. 253 W. Court w. of Central Av.
Butz Christian, brewer, 13 Hughes
Buiz John, s.s. Henry b. Elm and Dunlap [more
Butz Mrs. Margaret. cof. h., 365 Sycamore
Buxe John G., lab., e.s. Kilgour b. 3d and 5th
Buyon Lewis. 403 Linn
Byurl Margaret, servt., 435 W. 6th
Byatt Wm., butcher, s.e.c. 5th and Wood
Bydermuhle Hy., lab., bds. 450 Sycamore
Byers Charles, finisher, n.s. Raiload e. of Hazen
Byers Chas. A., harness mkr., 85 14th
Byers E. M., bds. Walnut St. House
Byers Wm. J., (James Dunlap & Co.) 214 Richmond
Byington John O., 557 Freeman
Byington Theresa, teacher. 22 Milton
Byington Wm. H., clk., 786 E. Front
Byl Leendert, sink and vault cleaner, 30 Stone

Bylon James, lab., 1 York
Byran Wm. H., tinner, 38 E. Pearl
Byres E. M., salesman 69 W. 4th, bds. Walnut St. House
Byrian Nora, servt., 407 W. 6th
Byrn John, carp. n.w.c 5th and Stone al., h. s.w.c. Harriet and Canal
Byrn Mary, servt., 457 W. 6th
Byrn Thomas, lab., 172 Cutter
Byrna Margaret, grocer, s.e.c. 9th and Elm
Byrna Thomas, furnace man, 592 E Front
Byrne Charles J., clk., 107 Clinton
Byrne & Co., (Peter B. & Co.) com. mer., 63 W. Miami Canal
Byrne Eugene, shoe mkr., 5 E. 7th
Byrne J. & Co., (James B, & Ephraim Morgan) book binders, 111 Main
Byrne James, (J. B. & Co.) 63 Pike
Byrne James F., b.k 107 Clinton
Byrne John. clk. 134 Main
Byrne Mathias, clk., h. 62 Baum
Byrne Maurice W., com. mer., 107 Clinton
Byrne Morris W., clk., 107 Clinton
Byrne Patrick, lab., 40 Mitchell, h. Mt. Adams
Byrne Peter, (B. & Co.) 107 Clinton
Byrne Peter P., clk., 107 Clinton
Byrnes F. T., commissary, bds. s.w.c. Race and 3d
Byrnes Thomas, mer., 106 Gest
Byron & Co., (John B. & Wm. Milton Bradshaw) liquors, &c., s.w.c. 5th and Central Av.
Byron Ellen, servt., 288 Longworth
Byron John, (B. & Co.) s.w.c. 5th and Central Av.
Bywaters Edward, carp., 186 Cutter

C

CABINET MAKER'S UNION, Jacob Diehl Agent, n.s. Augusta b. Smith and Rose
Cable Emily, 87 Race
Cachard Francis O., clk. 109 E. Pearl
Cade Perlina, dress mkr., 244 Longworth
Caden John, cof. h., n.w.c. Ludlow and River
Cadenbaugh Mary, 158 W. Front
Cadmes Chas., carp., 148 Clark
Cadwell Charlotte, teacher, Wesleyan Female College
Cadwell H. W., trunk mkr., 317 Vine
Cadwell Humphrey, saddler, 317 Vine
Cadwell John, foreman, 109 Martin
Cady Anna, seamstress, wks. 53 W. 4th
CADY DAVID K., Dealer in Fancy Goods, Toys, &c., n.e.c. 5th and Walnut, h. 76 W. 8th
Cady D. K., jr., atty. 57 W. 3d, bds. 76 W. 8th
Cady Hutch. C., b.k. D. K. Cady's, h, 76 W. 8th
Cady James, shoe mkr., 28 Broadway
Cady Nicholas, shoe mkr , wks. 53 W. 4th
Cady Rebecca, dress mkr., 28 Broadway
Caen V, bds. Dennison House
Caffrey & Hunt, (Wm. A. C. & Wm. J. H.) barbers, 330 W. 5th
Caffrey James, sewing mach. manuf., s.w.c. John and Augusta, res. Covington
Caffrey Owen, lab., 15 W. Court
Caffrey Wm. A., (C. & Hunt) 367½ W. 7th
Caffrey Edward, finisher, wks. 62 W. 4th
Cahill Bridget, laundress, 142 Longworth
Cahill Dennis, lab., 1182 E. Front
Cahill Hugh P , fireman, 186 Water
Cahill James. lab., 24 W. Court w. of Central Av.
Cahill John, boots and shoes, 52 W. Pearl, h. s e.c. Freeman and York
Cahill John. dray, 72 Holcombe
Cahill John F., O. & M. R. R., 443 W. 6th
Cahill Margaret, 138 Longworth
Cahill Mary, 35 Accommodation
Cahill Michael H., b. k., bds. s.e.c. Freeman and York

Cahill Patrick, cof. h., 53 Commerce
Cahill Patrick, lab., 12 W. Court, w. of Central Av.
Cahill Richard, waiter Spencer House
Cahill Thos., cooper, bds. Central House and Harriet
Cahill Wm., lab., h. s.s. Weller, b. Carr and Harriet
Cahn Ferdinand, periodicals, &c., Burnet House, h. 146 John
Cahn Jacob, 146 John
CAHN Julius, (L. Cahn & Bro.,) 146 John
CAHN L. & BRO., (Lee & Julius,) Dealers in Cigars, Tobacco, &c., Spencer House, Cincinnati, and Galt House. Louisville
CAHN Lee, (L. C. & Bro.,) res. Louisville
Cain Alexander, tailor, 201 Broadway
Cain Bridget, chambermaid, Burnet House
Cain E. D., clk., 123 W. 7th
Cain Hy., lab , s.w.c. 8th and Broadway
Cain James, lab., n.s. Pearl, b. Smith and Park
Cain Jane, 60 E. 7th
Cain John, carp., 62 Hunt
Cain John, lab., s.s. Arch, b. Ludlow and Lawrence
Cain John, mach., 36 Elizabeth
Cain Mary, chambermaid, Burnet House
Cain Maurice, blk. smith, bds. 177 East Front
Cain Michael, finisher, 52 Baum
Cain Richard, lab., n.s. Whetstone al. b. Broadway and Sycamore
Cain Wm., bk. mkr., W. 9th, b. Harriet and Mill Creek
Cain Wm., lab, 654 W 8th
Caine John H., b. k., 123 Laurel
Caiter John, finisher, wks. n.e.c. Walnut and Canal
Calaban Pat., waiter Burnet House
Calaway Walker, lab., n s. Whetstone al. b. Broadway and Sycamore
Caldenbuch Hy., turner. 56 Ham. Road.
Culdow James, lab., 203 Richmond
Caldow Robert, clk., 203 Richmond
Caldow Robert P., clk., L. M. R. R. Depot, 259 Richmond
CALDWELL ANTHONY, Carpenter and Joiner, 910 E. Front. h. High, b. Kemper lane and Weeks
CALDWELL & CALDWELL, (John W. & Samuel,) Attorneys at Law, 379 Main
Caldwell Hattie, dress mkr., 57 Plum
CALDWELL J. C. & CO., (James C. C. & Co.) Outcalt's Metallic Roofing, 132 W. 2d
CALDWELL James C., (J. C. C. & Co.) res. Walnut Hills
CALDWELL JAMES H., President Gas Company, 260.Vine, res. New Orleans
Caldwell John D., reporter, h. 25 Ellen
CALDWELL JOHN D., Tin Shop, 509 Central Av., h. 57 Clinton
CALDWELL John W., (C. & C.) h. College Hill
Caldwell Joseph, roller, bds., c. 2d and Smith
Caldwell Joseph J., salesman, 56 W. 5th
Caldwell Robert W., clk., City Treasurer's Office, h. Covington
CALDWELL Samuel, (C. & C.,) h. College Hill
CALDWELL SYLVESTER G., Carpenter and Builder, 130 Race, h. 11 Linn
Caldwell Terrence, hostler, whs. 177 W. 6th
CALDWELL William B., (Wm. B. C., & M. H & W. Tilden) h. Avondale
CALDWELL WM. B. & M. H. & W. TILDEN, (Wm. H. C., Myron H. T. & Wm. T.) Attorneys at Law, 9 Masonic Temple
Calender Thomas, carp., 157 Baymiller
Cales Andrew. finisher, wks. n.e.c. Walnut and Canal
Calfield Patrick, carp., 37 W. 9th, w. of Central Av.
Calhoun Agnes, bds. 498 W. 3d

98 (CAM) CINCINNATI (CAM) DIRECTORY.

Calhoun Chas., tinner, bds. 250 Walnut
Calhoun Crawford, 370 W. Liberty
Calhoun Jas., 79 Dayton
Calhoun John, teamster, w.s. Butler, b. Pearl and Front
CALKINS J. P. & CO., (John P. C. & Jacob Debnor,) Produce and Commission Merchants, 23 Walnut
CALKINS John P., (J. P. C. & Co.,) bds. e.s. Kilgour, b. Pearl and 3d
Call Elizabeth, 34 Carr
Callaidan Bridget, servt., 94 E. 4th
Callaghan Eugene, 237 Broadway
Callaghan Honora, 123 Betts
Callaghan John, 237 Broadway
Callaghan Margaret A., dress mkr., 13 E. 7th
Callaghan Mary, 13 E. 7th
Callaghan Michael, second hand store, 237 Broadway
Callaghan Patrick, tailor, 391 W. 2d
Callaghan Peter, lab., 17 Jones
Callahan Geo., cab. mkr., h. 38 Grant
Callahan James, bar k., Spencer House
Callahan James, lab., 185 Cutter
Callahan James, lab., s.s. Phœbe al., b. Plum and Central Av.
Callahan John, carp., 11 Elizabeth
Callahan John, lab., e.s. Oregon, b. 3d and 6th
Callahan John, tailor, s.s. 6th, b. Broadway and Culvert
Callahan Margaret, 52 McFarland
Callahan Mary, n.s. Channing, b. Price and Young
Callahan Michael, lab., 643 W. Front
Callahan Michael, lab., s.s. Avery al., w. of Wood
Callahan Michael, lab., 44 Accomodation
Callahan Patrick, porter, 58 Water
Callahan Patrick, tailor, 26 Broadway
Callahan Thomas, lab., 185 Cutter
Callan James, grocery, n.w.c. 7th and Cutter
Callaway Joseph, bolt works, 71 12th, h. 73 12th
Callaway Philip, carp., 63 W. 7th
Callihan David, clk., 26 Broadway
Callihan George, cab. mkr., 38 Grant
Callihan Jeremiah C., lab., 6 Crippen al.
Callihan Patrick, molder, bds. 221 Central Av.
Callihan Patrick, tailor, bds. n.e.c. River and Ludlow
Callinan Patrick W., grocer, 57 w. 7th
Callinge Bridget, 619 Central Av.
Calloway Caleb, carp., 63 W. 7th
Calmeaze Benjamin, sexton, s.s. 3d, b. Race and Elm
Calvert Albert L., salesman, 124 Walnut
Calvert H. A., salesman, 23 W. Pearl, bds. Spencer House
Calvert Hannah J., dress mkr., 22 McFarland
Calvert Wm., molder, 22 McFarland
CALVERT Wm. H., (W. H. C. & Co.,) h. w s. N. Elm, b. Corp. line and H'm. Road
CALVERT WM. H. & CO., (W. H. C. & D. A. Calvert.) Wholesale Fancy Goods, 67 W. Pearl
Calvin Benjamin, shoe mkr., bds. 22 Home
CAMARGO MANUFACTURING CO. Paper Hangings & Window Shades, 57 W. 4th
Camass John, 593 Elm
Camben Ann, 92 Baum
Camerer Valentine, lab., s.e.c. 6th and Curr
Cameron A. J., carp., 391 John
Cameron Alonzo, freeman, 391 John
Cameron Dell, carp., 391 John
Cameron Ebenezer D., carp., 85 Barr
Cameron Hester M., 262 Clark
Cameron John, dray., 287 W. Front
Cameron Joseph, dray., 224 Water
Cameron Joseph, dray., bds. 150 West Front
CAMERON JOSEPH G., Dentist, 140 W. 6th
CAMERON LYCURGUS, Flour & Grist Mill, s.w.c. Clark and Central Av., h. 83 Laurel

Cameron Melinda, 105 Poplar
Cameron Norval, clk., 32 W. 2d, h. 226 Clark
CAMERON, STORY & MALONE, (Wm. C., J. H. S. & W. H. M.,) Mill Creek Saw Mill, Storrs Tp.
CAMERON W. M. & CO., (Wesley M. C. & Otis B. Little,) Franklin Planing Mills, s. e. c. Sixth and Hoadly
CAMERON Wesley M., (W. M. C. & Co.,) b. 391 John
CAMERON William, (C., Story & Malone,) 9 Clark
Camman Frank H., eng., 24 Orchard
Camman Joseph, cigar mkr., wks., 218 W. Front
Cammerer David, 11 Dunlap
Cammon Frank, turner, 52 Laurel
CAMP C. B. & CO., (Calvin B. C. Frank T Lockwood, Geo. Williams & Wm. N. Nichols.) Ladies Furs, Hats, Caps, and Straw Goods, 95 West Third.
CAMP Calvin B., (C. B. C. & Co.,) h. New York City
Camp Lizzie, servt., 408 W. 7th
Camp Martha, 151 Cutter
Campbell Abraham, brass molder, wks. 247 W. 5th
Campbell Alexander, electrotyper, 241 Longworth
Campbell Allen, peddler, bds. 177 East Front
CAMPBELL Angus, (McIlvain, Spiegel & Co.,) res Madison. Ind.
Campbell Anselm, pork packer, 457 Sycamore
Campbell Archibald, mer., bds. 57 Broadway
Campbell Asbury, lab., 101 E. 6th
Campbell B., surveyor, 77 W. 3d, h. 312 W. 9th
Campbell Benjamin, 310 Cutter
Campbell Calvin H., bds. 974 E. Front
Campbell Calvin W., 346 W. 6th
Campbell Charles, lab., 11 8th above Lock
Campbell Charles C., mach., h. 97 E. 3d
Campbell Conrad, agt., 16 Hamer
Campbell Cornelius, bar k., foot 5th, nr. Freeman
Campbell Edward, oil mkr., 151 E. 3d e. of Collard
Campbell Elijah, 177 Oliver
Campbell Eliza, 11 8th above Lock
CAMPBELL, ELLISON & CO.(Hiram C., William E., Robert Scott, & D. T. Woodrow,) Manufacturers of Stoves and Castings, Hot and Cold Blast Pig Iron, and Dealers in Sheet Iron, 21 E 2d
Campbell Frank, salesman, 148 W. 4th
Campbell George, painter, bds. Bevis House
Campbell George W., pilot, 211 George
CAMPBELL H. & CO., (Hiram C., John C., John Peters, Isaac Peters, D. T. Woodrow. Addison McCullough, George P. Rogers, Samuel McConnell, Wm. Ellison, & Robt. Scott,) Manufacturers of Bar, Boiler and Sheet Iron, 19 E. 2d
Campbell Hy., pork mer., 12 Grant
CAMPBELL Hiram, (H. C. & Co.,) h. Ironton, O.
Campbell Hiram, driver, 463 W. 3d
Campbell Hugh, 226 E. 6th
Campbell James, wks. Meth. Book Concern
Campbell James, (Cunningham & Co.,) res New York City
Campbell James, dray., 63 E. 8th, e. of Lock
Campbell James, lab., 1458 E. Front
Campbell James, shoemkr., s.s. 5th, b. Main and Sycamore
Campbell James C., phys., 180 George
Campbell John, 173 Oliver
Campbell John, carp., rear 33 Hughes
Campbell John, clk., 103 Smith
Campbell John, grocer, n.w.c. John and Betts
CAMPBELL John, (H. Campbell & Co.) h. Ironton, O.
Campbell John D., phys., 195 Longworth

Campbell
Campbell
Campbell
Campbell
Campbell and J
Campbell
Campbell W. of
Campbell
Campbell New
Campbell erett
Campbell way
Campbell
Campbell worth
Campbell
Campbell
Camper
Campett Plum
Campsmi Sprin
CANA 1st 7
Candler
Candler
Candon 4th
Candy and
Cane Is ter
Cane Th sau
Cane W Woo
Canfield
CANFII n.w.
CANF W!
7
Canfoald
Canida J
Canisius Vine
Canna I
Cannell
Cannon Mill
Cannon
Cannon
Cannon
Cannon
Cannon
Cannon Joh
Cannon
Cantwel way
Capp H
Capp Jo
Capp W wor
Cappel
Cappelle kins
Cappeln
Capus Mill
Carber J and
CARI Fo
Carbin
Carbin Wa
Carbot J
Carby J
Carciott
Card El
Card Sa
Card Tl pot
Cardem
Ceret F
Carey rel

Carey Ann M., e.s. Macalister b. 4th and 5th
Carey Areen, e.s. Macalister b. 4th and 5th
Carey Bridget, servt., Burnet House
Carey Dennis, grocer, 142 E. 6th
Carey Edward H., harness mkr., 47 Oest
Carey Eliza, 195 Vine
Carey Geo. A., 217 Plum
Carey Geo. W., student, 23 W. 3d
Carey James, lab., e.s. Kilgour b. 3d and 5th
Carey Milton C., phys., 207 Everett
Carey Patrick, molder, wks. Chamberlain & Co's
Carey Samuel D , b.k. 299 W. 8th
Carey Thomas M., flour inspector, 388 W. 7th
Carey Wilson, b. k., bds. 264 Elm
Cargen Stephen, 68 Richmond b. Plum and Central Av
Caring Francis C., laundry, 77 W. Front
Carithers Moses, stocking manufac., s. w.c. Cutter and Betts
Carius John P., cutter, 31 Jackson
Carl Daniel, shoe mkr., bds. Pennsylvania Hotel
Carl Hy., carp., bds. Indiana House
Carl Patrick, lab., n.s. E. Front, e. of Leatherbury
Carl Wm., clk., s e.c. Elm and Ham. Road
Carland Anthony, teacher, 205 Linn
Carland Barney, hostler, bds. 20 Baymiller
Carle Margaret, 649 W. Front
Carleton Benjamin F., agt. powder Co., n e.c. Walnut and 2d., bds. Gibson House
Carley Ellen, servt., 377 W. 6th
Carley Samuel T., jewelry, s.w.c. 4th and Main, h. Clifton
Carlin James, clk, County Treasurer's office, h. Cleves
Carlin John, trunk mkr., wks. 509 Plum
Carlin Joseph, wood yard s.e.c. W. W. Canal and Smith
Carlin Owen, butcher, n.s. Montgomery Pike nr. Reading Road
Carlin Rose, 102 Baymiller
Carlisle Building, s.w.c. 4th and Walnut
CARLISLE GEO., Lafayette Banking Company, (Stedman C., & Shaw) h. 119 W. 4th
Carlisle George W., salesman, 17 W. Pearl, bds. 119 W. 4th
Carlisle James, eng., bds. 12 E. Front
CARLISLE JOHN, Office s.w.c. 4th and Walnut Carlisle Block, h. 384 W. 6th
Carlisle Mary Ann, b. b. 37 Longworth
Carlisle W. carp., bds. 37 Longworth
Carlos Hester, h. 154 E. 6th
Carlow Thomas, waiter, Clifton House
Carls Hermann, tanner, 170 Ham. Road
Carlsbath Marcus, peddler, 10 Home
Carlton Edward, 153 George
Carlton James, butcher, 61 Oliver
Carley Mary, 168 Linn
Carman Caleb, expressman, 265 Cutter
Carman Julia, dress mkr., 31 W. 8th
Carman Nelly. bds. 71 Baker
CARMICHAEL Robert, (Stewart C. & Co.,) 235 Longworth
Carns Andrew, bds. 687 Central Av
Carnahan Frank, printer, bds. 149 Elm
Carnahan Gustavus A., teacher, bds. s. w.c. Broadway and Franklin
Carnahan Isaac V., pork mer., s.e.c. Pike and 3d
Carnahan J. R., prof. book keeping, n. w.c. Vine and Longworth
Carnahan Richard, policeman, 457 W. 5th
Carneal Louis, 110 E. 4th
CARNELL Wm., (Peat & C.) Lockland O.
Carnes Adolphus, grocery, 238 W. 6th
Carnes Augustus A., clk., 233 W. 6th
Carnes Guilford. 227 Everett
Carnes James K., clk. P. O., 238 W. 6th
Carnes Joseph, lab., s.w.c. Kelly and rail road
Carnes Kate, servt., 258 W. 7th

Carnes Wm., lab., rear 52 Plum
Carney Andrew, w.s. Central Av. b. Liberty and Oliver
Carney Ann, grocer, h. 126 E. 6th
Carney Bridget, servt., 12 Arch
Carney Bridget, 462 George
Carney Daniel, stable, 19 E. 5th, h. 28 E. 7th
Carney Ellen, h. 249 W. Front
Carney Elnora, huckster, w.s. Langdon al. b. 6th and 7th
Carney James, eng., Burnet House
Carney John, fireman, Burnet House
Carney John, lab., e.s. Ludlow b. Pearl and 3d
Carney John, police, bds, 186 Race
Carney John, waiter, Clifton House
Carney Mary, servt., Burnet House
Carney Michael, grocer, n.s. 6th b. Culvert and Broadway
Carney Patrick, clk., 19 E. 5th, h. 414 Sycamore
Carney Patrick, lab , s.s. Phoebe al. b. Plum and Central Av
Carney Sarah, servt., 312 Longworth
Carney Thos , clk., 239 Broadway
Carney Timothy, huckster, 326 Main
Carney Tobias, fireman, 563 W. 5th
Carnighan Wm. F., b k. 171 Vine h. Mill Creek Township
Carnighan Robert H., upholsterer, rear Morris Chapel Central Av. b. 4th and 5th
Carnighan Wm. W., clk., h. s.s. Coggswell Av., nr. Auburn [Pearl.
Carothers John S., dining saloon ,21 E
Carpenter Abel B.. 77 Wade
Carpenter Daniel H , com. mer. s. W. W. Canal b. Central Av. and John, h. 217 W. 4th
Carpenter & Ford, (Isaac D. C., & Smith F.) tobacco 14 W. Front
Carpenter Horace, E , bds. 46 W. 9th
Carpenter Isaac B., (C. & Ford,) 46 W 9th [ter
Carpenter Jacob, shoe mkr., 220 Cutter
Carpenter Jennie, bds. s.e.c. 6th and Smith
CARPENTER M. K., Millwright, at Miles Greenwood's h. 6 12th
Carpenter Marion, photographist, 22 W. 5th, res. Avondale
Carpenter, Mary, 117 Mound
CARPENTER SAMUEL S., Attorney at Law, Notary Public, Commissioner of Deeds &c., 23 W. 3d h. Springfield
CARPENTER Wm. W., (Wm. W. C. & Co.,) h. 128 E. Liberty
CARPENTER WM. W. & CO., (Wm. W. C. &,Henry Schlotman,) Venitian Blinds, 82 W. 6th
Carr Alfred S., type foundry, 261 Hopkins
Carr Andrew, lab , 458 W. 8th
Carr Andrew, peddler, 321 W. 2d
Carr Anrill, butter dealer, 226 Longworth
Carr Catharine, 20 Commerce
Carr Elizabeth tailoress, 188 Everett
CARR Frederick M., (Clark & C.,) h. 34 Jefferson St., Newport
Carr Chas., lab., wks. 509 Plum
Carr Geo. W., constable, 116 W. 5th
Carr Henry H., bk. laye 54 W. 8th
Carr Hy., L , salesman. 49 W. 2d, bds. 310 Elm
Carr James, mach., E. 3d b. Baum and Parsons
Carr James, porter, 87 Race
Carr John, 130 Baum
Carr John, dray, 16 Charles
Carr John, supt., 284 Broadway
Carr Margaret, ironer, Commercial Hospital
Carr Mary, 269 W. 3d
Carr Michael biksmith, wks. Niles Works
Carr Michael. lab., 30 Lock
Carr Moses, white washer, 127 Avery
Carr Perry, carp., 444 W. Front
Carr Samuel, 476 John
Carr Wm.. barber, w.s. Elm b. Front and Cherry al., h. s.w.c. Plum and Water

Carragen Bridget, servt., Burnet House
Carragen Catharine, servt., Burnet House
Carrel Edw. T., printer, h. n.e.c. Pike and Pearl
Carrell Maggie, waiter, Dennison House
Carrett I. F., teacher, h. 333 Vine
CARRICK ANTHONY L., Physician and Surgeon, office and residence 226 Broadway
CARRICK DAVID S., Saddles, Harness and Trunk Maker, 112 Main, h 295 Richmond
Carrigan John, tailor, 858 E. Front
Carrigan John W., clk., bds. 200 Richmond
Carrigan Mary, n s. Cherry al. b. Plum and Central Av.
Carrigan Michael, lab., 405 Sycamore
Carrigan Philip, grocery, n.e.c. 3d and Butler
Carrigan Wm., driver, 65 Abigail
Carrigan Wm., carp., n.s. Railroad e. of Hazen
Carrlin Mary A., 102 Baymiller
Carroll Barney, lab., 654 W. 8th
Carroll Amasa P., trader, w.s. Wheeler's Av. n. of Front
Carroll Anna, servt., 193 W. 7th
Carroll Bernard, watchman, s.s. Budd b. Fremont and 8th
Carroll Charles, 53 W. Front, bds. 400 W. 3d
Carroll Charles, printer, 136 Vine, bds. n.w.c. 9th and Central Av.
Carroll David, 478 W. 4th
Carroll Dennis, dray, s.e.c. E. Pearl and Pike
Carroll Dennis, shoe mkr., bds. s.w.c. Front and Pike
Carroll Edward T., printer, bds. n.e.c. Pearl and Pike
Carroll Elizabeth, cof. h., 42 Lock n. of 8th
Carroll Ellen, 333 Central Av.
Carroll Ellen, 16 E. 8th e. of Lock
Carroll Hamilton, dray, 77 Walnut
Carroll Hy., fireman, No. 4 Engine House
Carroll James, 32 Lock n. of 8th
Carroll James, porter 21 E. 2d
Carroll Johanna, confec., 97 Central Av.
Carroll John, butcher, 162 Poplar
Carroll John, cof. h., n.w.c. Carr and W. W. Canal
Carroll John, currier, 32 Lock n. of 8th
Carroll John, lab., 44 Lock n. of 8th
Carroll John. shoe mkr., 398 Broadway
Carroll M., lab., Burnet House
Carroll Margaret, n.s. Taylor al. w. of Kilgour
Carroll Margaret, 32 Lock n. of 8th
Carroll Mary, 35 Accommodation
Carroll Michael, lab., bds. n.s. Augusta b. John and Smith
Carroll Michael, lab., 15 W. Court w. of Central Av.
Carroll Michael, lab., bds 399 Sycamore
Carroll Owen, porter 21 E. 2d
Carroll Patrick, cof h., 238 Water
Carroll Patrick F., waiter, Spencer House
CARROLL Robert W., (Rickey & C.) 358 W. 6th
Carroll Rosa, e.s. Vine b. Milk and Mulberry
Carroll Samuel, s.s. 6th b. Broadway and Culvert
Carroll Thomas, biksmith. n.s. New b. Broadway and Culvert
Carroll Thomas, horse dealer, 21 Lock n. of 8th
Carroll Thomas, phys., 358 W. 6th
CARROLL Wm., (Hall, C. & Co.) 400 W. 3d
Carroll Wm., lab., 46 E. 8th e. of Lock
Carroll Wm., saloon, 245 W. 3d
Carrolton Antony, hackman, s.e.c. Elm and Water
Carrolton Thomas, hackman, 146 Water
Carron Robert, dray, bds. 399 Sycamore
Carruthers Wm., clk. 42 W. 2d, bds. 134 Broadway
Carson & Dexter, (James C. & Harrison D.) lumber yard, 449 Freeman

100 (CAS) CINCINNATI (CAS) DIRECTORY. (CEN)

Carson Ellen, 28 W. Court w of Central Av.
CARSON ENOCH T., (McHenry & C.) Collector of Customs, office Custom House, h 298 Richmond
Carson Hy. T., clk., 189 Barr
Carson Isaac S., bk. layer, bds. 176 Barr
Carson James, (C. & Dexter) h. Glenn Grove
Carson Margaret, 414 W. 9th
Carson Oliver P., yard master, 189 Barr
Carson R. & W., (Robert & William) carps., 414 W. 9th
Carson Richael, teacher, 414 W. 9th
Carson Robert, (R. & W. C.) 414 W. 9th
Carson Robert, lab., 197 Barr [Tp.
Carson W. L., (Wilson & C.) h. Green
Carson Wm., (R. & W. C.) 414 W. 9th
Carson Wm., carp., 184 Cutter
Carson Wm., paper carrier, 355 Elm
Carson Wm., phys., n.e.c. 3d and Broadway, h. 138 E. 3d
Carlee Frank, chair mkr., 15 Madison
Carter A. G. W., atty., 8 Masonic Temple, bds. Madison House
Carter Ann, matron Cin. Orphan Asylum, Mt. Auburn
Carter Anna, laundress, Gibson House
CARTER & BEATTIE, (James H. C. & John H. B.) Agents Ætna Insurance Company, 171 Vine
Carter Benj., lab., s.w.c. Abigail and Spring
Carter Chas. C., 28 W. 7th
Carter Chas., roller, bds. 94 Everett
Carter Deborah, bds. 105 Longworth
CARTER E. Hy., Prest Union Ins. Co., h. Storrs Tp.
Carter Edward, 144 E. 6th
Carter Eliza, 208 George
Carter Isaac, clk. 230 W. 5th
Carter James, ladies shoes, 230 W. 5th
CARTER James H., (C. & Beattie) 80 W. 8th
Carter John C., bds. 28 W. 7th
Carter John H., bds., 28 W. 7th
Carter John S., lab , 5 Pine
Carter John W., cab. ware, 132 Sycamore, h. 602 W. 9th
Carter Joseph, 284 Baymiller
Carter Joseph H., s.e.c. Baymiller and Findlay
Carter Margaret, n.s. Patterson al. b. Main and Walnut
Carter Mary, 236 Vine
Carter Mary, 408 W. 4th
Carter Mathilda H., 28 W. 7th
Carter Niles, steward, s.s. New b. Culvert and Broadway
Carter Restore O., phys , 112 George
Carter Samuel B., atty. at law s.w.c. Main and Court, h. 64 W. Court .
Carter Samuel R., Secy. Fireman's Ins. C , h. 268 Longworth
Carter Tabitha A., 26 Elizabeth
Carter Thos. P., clk. 24 Main, h. Covington
Carter W. Byron, clk., 290 Longworth
Carter Wm., furniture 34 E. 5th, h. 110 Everett
Carton Chas., bds. 109 Freeman
Cartwright J. M., bk. layer, bds. Bevis House
Carty E. B., b. h., 29 W. 7th
Carver Hy., cab. mkr , 412 W. 4th
Carver Leander R., clk., n.w.c. Hunt Broadway
Carver Thomas M., hat block mkr., wks. 63 E. 3d
Carver Wm. H., hat block manuf., 63 E. 3d, h. Covington
Carvin Frank, eng., bds. 10 Sycamore
Carvin Mary, servt., 3 Harrison
Carwin John, conf. h., 587 W. 5th
Cary Alonzo, blksmith, 222 Laurel
Cary Martin W., hatter, 95 W. 3d
Cary Olive, trimmer, 226 Barr
Cary Pat., molder, bds. 114 Hunt
Casanler Jacob, cab. mkr., 96 Clay
Case Darine H., student, bds. 47 W. 7th
Case Dominick, porter, 35 Main
Case Geo., 161 Longworth
Case John, cigar mkr., bds. Cincinnati House
Case Julia A., 187 W. Court w. of Central Av.

Case Lewis L., mach., 4 Crippen al.
Case Loyd, pilot. h. 10 Race
Case Wm., captain, 72 Water
Casey Eliza, 136 Sycamore
CASEY GEO M., City Clerk. Office, City Buildings, h. 349 W. 7th
Casey John, lab.. e.s. M. Canal b. 8th and Court
Casey John, lab., n.w.c. Pike and 3d
Casey John, lab., 163 E. 3d
Casey John, lab., 214 Sycamore
Casey John F., cooper, s.s. 3d b. Canal and Kilgour
Casey Maria, 101 Park
Casey Martin, waiter, 111 Pike
Casey Mary, servt , 272 Longworth
Casey Mary, 134 W. 6th
Casey Matthew, lab., 708 E Front
Casey Michael, lab., wks. Niles Works
Casey Michael, watchmun, w.s. Lock b. 8th and Court
Casey Pat., hackman, 20 W. Court w. of Central Av.
Casey Robert, lab., 219 W. Front
Casey Wm., fireman, 45 Race
Casey Wm., lab., 50 McFarland
Cash Geo., blksmith, wks. n.e.c. M. Canal and Walnut
Cash Spencer, n s. 6th b. Culvert and Broadway
Cashen Wm., grocery, 208 W. 7th
Cashen Wm. H., sawyer, n.s. Cassatt al. b. Sycamore and Main
Cashion Margaret, 44 Accommodation
Cashion Thos., blksmith, 44 Accommodation
Cashman Geo. W., blksmith, 311 Elm
Cashman Mary, 24 W. Court w. of Central Av.
Casiday Wm., b.k , 19 Webb
Caskey Matilda, 144 Baymiller
Caslor R. N., express messenger, bds. Broadway Hotel
Casley Patrick, dray, 348 Race
Casting Frank, plasterer, 374 W. Liberty
Casner Susan, 128 Mound
Casner Wm., 44 Freemen
Casper Ernst, tailor, 49 Fountain
Casper Harris, tailor, 155 W. 5th
Casper Jacob, carp., 200 Hopkins
Cass Abbey, 199 E. 6th
Cass Adam, mattress mkr,, wks. 51 E 3d
Cass Andrew, mattress mkr,, wks. 51 E. 3d
Cass Geo., molder, wks. n.w.c. Plum and Wade
Cassady Frank, bds. n.e.c. Plum and River
Cassady & Glass (Jas. C. & Wm. H. G.) confec., 26 Vine
Cassady Jas., (C. & Glass) 92 Water
Cassady James, drug, 54 Baum
Cassady Joseph, lab., 12 Hannibal
CASSADY Michael, (C. & Stewart), h. Miamisburg
Cassady Patrick, lab., 740 W. 6th
CASSADY & STEWART, (Michael C. & Chas. S.), Linseed Oil Manufacturers, Office s.e.c. 9th and Sycamore
Cassatt Gilbert H., pork packer, 61 Hunt, h. 371 W. 9th
Cassat Davik C., 504½ Main
Cassedy Charles L., b.k., bds. 158 Barr
Cassedy Hiram D., mailer, 158 Spring
Cassedy Jas. A., bk. binder. 143 Mound
Cassedy Lee C., wood yard, n.w.c. W. W. Canal and Smith, h. 158 Barr
Cassedy Wm. H., b.k., 19 Webb
Cassellmann Anthony.molder, 114 Hunt
Cassellmann Mary E., 60 Spring
Cassiday Bridget, servt., Burnet House
Cassidhy Mary, servt., Burnet House
Cassidy Frank, lab., 395 Walnut
Cassidy Fred., lab., wks. n.e.c. Walnut and Canal
Cassidy James, cof. h., h. 102 Water
Cassidy James J , printer, s.e.c. 8th and Sycamore
Cassidy Mary, 163 Oliver
Cassidy Rose, s.e.c. 8th and Sycamore
Cassidy Wm., eng., wks. w.s. Western Av. h. Bank and Harrison Road
Cassidy Wm. H., bk. layer, 27 Dudley

Cassilly Catharine, servt., 386 W. 6th
CASSILLY CHARLES P., Banker, 63 E. 4th
Cassilly Sophia B., 119 Broadway
Cassilly Thomas A., clk., 44 Pub. Landing
Cassilly Wm. B., 119 Broadway
Cassler Conrad, candy mkr., 180 Barr
Cassuelle Nich., clk., 31 W. 5th
Castel Mary, 180 Barr
Castello Angelo. musician, 100 W. Front
Castello Peter. molder, wks n.e.c. Walnut and Canal
Caster Anna, servt., Henrie House
Castigan Dan., lab., Burnet House
Castillo Anthony, dray, 547 W. 7th
Castillo Joseph, lab., 464 E. Front
Casting Fred. L.,tobacconist,s.s. Young b. Ringgold and Channing
Castle Edmund I., druggist, n.e.c. Clinton and Linn
Castle Nicholas, bk. layer, bds. Black Bear Hotel
Castle Patrick, b.k., s.e.c. Main and 7th
Castle Peter, 180 Barr
Castner Peter, lab., 27 Moore
Caston Saml. B., clk., 20 W. 6th, h. 190 W. 7th
Cathell J., bds. Dennison House
Cathell John, wks Cin. type foundry
Cathmann Joseph. grocery, 459 W. 5th
Catholic Institute,n.w.c. Vine and Longworth
CATHOLIC TELEGRAPH, Jos. A. Hemann, Editor and Pro., s.w.c. Vine and Longworth
Catlone Robert. mach., 114 E. Liberty
Caton John, cigar mkr., wks. 213 Walnut
Caty Thos., fireman. Burnet House
Caufield John. lab., 27 E. 8th
Caufield Margaret, h. 285 Vine
Caulfield James, lab , n.s. Augusta b. John and Smith
Caulfield Jenny, bds. 375 W. 8th
Caughlin John, lab., wks. C., H. & D. R R. depot
Caughling Patrick, lab., 13 Lock n. of 8th
Caulkin Margaret, 453 W. 5th
Caulkin Patrick, 453 W. 5th
Cauther John, 343 Main
CAVAGNA BARTHOLOMEW, Family Grocery and Bakery, 31 W, 5th
CAVAGNA PETER, At 31 W. 5th, , h. 144 W. 4th
Cavally Lewis. saloon, 97 St. Clair
Cavanagh Daniel, lab., 41 Race
Cavanagh Ellen, 239 Broadway
Cavanagh Martin, blksmith, 80 Butler
Cavanaugh Bridget, seamstress, wks. 53 W. 4th [Front
Cavanaugh Edward, blksmith, 202 W.
Cavanaugh John, blksmith. 219 W Front
Cavanaugh John, tailor, 102 Baymiller
Cavanaugh Patrick, cutter, 63 W. 5th
Cavanaugh Patrick, lab., w.s Oregon b. 3d and 6th
Cavanaugh Thos., hostler, wks. n.w.c. Race and Longworth
Cavanaugh Wm., 253 Broadway
Cavell Hy., painter, 112 George
Caven Wm., pattern mkr., n.w.c. Elm and 9th
Caveney Thomas, lab., 16 Dublin
Cavermann Barney. sawyer, 74 Dudley
Caylor Wm., dray, 22 Dudley
Cecil & Clark, 'James B. C. & John G. C.), com mers., 19 E. M. Canal
Cecil James B., (C. & Clark), res. Middletown
Ceck Conrad, finisher, 186 Clark
Cehagen Ludwig, cigar mkr., 15 Lock
Cells Anthony, clk., 60 Broadway
Cement John, gilder, bds. Teutonia Hotel
Cemon Michael. barber, 4 E. 6th
Center Hartson H.. (I. S., H. H. & T. B. Center) 184 Barr
Center I. S., H. H. & T. B., carps., 56 George
Center Ira S. (I. S., H. H. & T. B. Center,)53 Barr

(CHA)   CINCINNATI   (CHE)   DIRECTORY.   (CHR)   101

Center T. B. (I. S., H. H. & T. B. Center) 18 Everett
Centner Christoph, cab. mkr., 189 Bremen
Centner Elizabeth, 129 W. Liberty
Centner Francis H., shoemkr, Goose al. b. Liberty and Green and Vine and Race
Centner Martin J., shoemkr, 164 Pleasant
Centner Philip, cigar mkr., h. 109 Ham. Road
CENTRAL Christian Herald, office 28 W. 4th
CENTRAL INS. CO. OF CINCINNATI. Francis Ferry, Secretary, Henry Morton, President, office, 7 Pub. Landing
Central Saw Mill, Nathan R. Morton, 1379 E. Front
Cerf Isaac, barber, 278 Cutter
Chadwick Darwin A., dray, 306 Water
Chadwick James B., 304 W. 4th
Chafer F. A., tinner, wks. n.w.c. Race and 2d
CHALFANT F. P. (Morris & Co.), h. Newport
CHALLEN James R. (Cranch & C.), res, Spring Garden
CHAMBER OF COMMERCE, w.s. Walnut b. 4th and 5th, Wm. Smith, Superintendent
CHAMBERLAIN Addis E. (C. & Co.), h. 253 W. 7th
CHAMBERLAIN & CO. (Addis E. C., Franklin V. Chamberlain & Obadiah N. Rush) Anchor Iron Works. Stoves and Hollow Ware, s.s. Hunt, e. of Broadway, Store 51 and 53 Vine
Chamberlain Frank N., bleacher, bds. 175 W 4th
CHAMBERLAIN Franklin V. (Chamberlain & Co.), 166 Linn
Chamberlain J. L., salesman, 22 Main, h. 102 Longworth
Chamberlain O. Stafford, clk, 51 Vine, h. 253 W. 7th
CHAMBERLAIN WM. G., Pressman, 167 Walnut, h. Clifton
Chamberlin Benj. B., engraver, s.e.c. Main and 4th, bds.s.w.c. George and Race
Chamberlin Theodore, clk., Adams' Ex. Co., h. Newport, Ky
Chambers C. C. & W. (Charles C. & Wm.) dry goods, 53 E. Pearl
Chambers Charles C. (C. C. & W. C.), 53 E. Pearl
Chambers Elizabeth, 150 W. 5th
Chambers George, lab, 126 W. Front
Chambers Hy., wagon mkr., 682 Freeman
Chambers Isaac, cooper, bds. s.e.c. Brighton and Harrison Pike
Chambers James, cooper, bds. s.e.c. Linn and Liberty
Chambers Jane, 22 Perry
CHAMBERS Josiah (C Stevens & Co.) h. Aurora Ind
Chambers Lewis B., 754 E. Front
Chambers Nicholas, cof. h., 132 W. Front
Chambers Pius, finisher, h. 193 Laurel
Chambers Samuel F, harness mkr., bds. Bevis House
CHAMBERS, STEVENS & CO (T. Shotwell. Josiah C., Levi E. S., W. F. S. & Francis Wymond) Wholesale Dry Goods, 23 W. Pearl
Chambers Theodore, mach., 88 Barr
Chambers Wm. (C. C. & W. C.) 17th ward
Champlin Chas. C., b.k, 143 E. 3d
Champlin John M., b. k. Geo R. Dixon & Co., h. 338 Richmond
CHAMPLIN Louis D. (Stone & C.) 330 W. 7th
Champlin M, F., mer., 167 Elm
Chance Hiram, salesman, 61 Hopkins
Chandler Edward A., b.k., h. 240 Longworth
Chandler Joseph, 173 Poplar
Chandler Lewis L., agency, 203 Plum, h. 291 W. 5th
Chandos Leonna, bds. Black Bear Hotel

Chanpeuter Michael K., pattern mkr., wks. n.e.c. Canal and Walnut
Chapin Hy. L., cutter, 118 Richmond
CHAPIN, JONES & CO. (N. J. C, & M. L. J.) General Produce, Forwarding and Commission Merchants, 33 Water and 17 Gilmore's Wharf
Chapin Lorenzo, boots and shoes, n.s. 6th nr. Main, h. 118 Richmond
CHAPIN N. J. (C., Jones & C.), h. Mt. Hope
Chaplin Hy., meat store, n.w.c. Park and 4th
Chapman Frederick, teamster, wks. G. & H. Muhlhauser's
Chapman Hy J., clk., s.w.c. 6th and Vine, h. 73 Laurel
Chapman John C., supt. Franklin Cotton Factory, h. 303 W. 3d
Chapman John Q. A.. bill poster, Enquirer office, h. 55 Clay
Chapman Mrs. Lisetta, seamstress, 128 Spring
Chapman Margaret, seamstress. 128 Spring
CHAPMAN Noah H (J. E. Wynne & Co.) bds. Gibson House
CHAPMAN SIDNEY W., General Freight Agent, Cin. and Chicago Air Line R.R., res. Chicago
CHAPMAN Stephen G. (J. A. Frazer & Co.) h. Newport, Ky
Chapman Wm., lab., 14 Sargent
Chapman Dr. Wm. B , 73 Laurel
CHAPMAN Wm. C. (Shuesler & C.), 73 Laurel
Chapman Wm. S., carriage shaft fastener, s.e.c. 3d and Vine, h. Spencer tp
Chappe Andrew confec., 45 Pub. Landing
Chapple John, tailor. wks. 257 Walnut
Chapple John T., miller, 301 Clark
Chard James, painter, 180 Oliver
Chard Sophia, 141 Hopkins
Chard Thomas J., mach., 141 Hopkins
Charles C., fruits, Vine opp. P. O., h. n.e.c. Vine and Baker
Charles Ellen, 345 Clark
Charles John, teamster, 345 Clark
Charles Mary, 135 Poplar
Charles Wm., bds. 135 Poplar
Charles Wm., teamster, 345 Clark
Charlton Geo., bar k., 150 Main
Charmbury Hy., mach., 37 Parsons
Charter Oak Life Ins. Co. Agency, 65 W. 3d   [5th
Chase Amelia, e.s. Macalister, b 4th and
Chase Andrew J., 93 Longworth
Chase Chas., 98 W. 6th
Chase Isaac. carp , bds. 445 Main
Chase Jennie P., teacher, Wesleyan Female College
Chase R., lumber mer., bds. 22 Home
Chase's Building, n.s. 3d, 3d door e. of Main
Chatfield Thomas, clk., bds. 283 W. Court. w. of Central Av
CHATFIELD Wm. H.. (Nixon, C. & Woods,) h. 283 W. Court, w. of Central av
Chatten Mary, e.s. Pendleton b. Woodward and Liberty
Chatwith Wm., tailor, 424 Freeman
Chavanu Frank P., saddler, 171 Central Avenue
Cheany John, bds. 365 W. 7th
Cheeseman Sarah A., teacher, 14 Elizabeth
Cheeve Hy., foreman, 14 Elizabeth
Cheeve Hy., chair mkr., 220 George
Cheever A. G., (A. G. C. & Co.,) 134 E. 5th
Cheever A. G. & Co., (A. G. C. & Chas Harkness,) candle manuf., 11 W. 5th
Cheever Chas. S., 17 Hathaway
Cheever George E., clk., 53 W. Pearl, bds. 134 E. 5th
CHEEVER John H., (Kirk & Co.) res. Mt. Auburn
Cheever Maria, teacher, 17 Hathaway
Cheney Caroline, 49 David
CHENOWETH Wm. B., (Swain & C.,) 322 Clark

Chernbeck Hy., lab., wks. 375 W. 3d
Cheron Narcisse, clk., 6 W. Front
Cherrer Marion. 961 Central Av
Cherry John A., student, bds. 238 Race
Cheshire Thomas, pattern. mkr , 212 W. Front
CHESELDINE Samuel P., (Hammett & Co.,) bds. Broadway Hotel
Chessley Charles, conductor, bds. Brighton House
Chessley Wm., mach., bds. 29 W. 7th
Chester Rev. Joseph, 32 York
Chevallo John, carp., bds. 355 Central Avenue
Chevallo John, marble cutter, wks. n.e.c. Canal and Elm
Chew James F., furniture auction, 21 E. 4th, res. Lawrenceburgh
Chiappe Andrew, confec., 5 E. Front
Chick James, carp., 1019 Central Av., h. 106 Central Av
Chick Wm., farmer, 334 Clark
Chickering J. B., Academy, n.s George, b. John and Smith, h. 152 W. 4th
Chicsa John, confec., n.w.c. Race & 9th
CHIDLAW BENJAMIN W., Missionary Supt. American Sunday S. Union, 41 W. 4th, res. Cleves
Chidsey Joseph, pipe fitter, wks. n.e.c. Walnut and Canal
CHIDSEY WILLIAM, Justice of the Peace and Notary Public, office 20 W. 6th, h. 232 Richmond
Child Isaac S., wood dealer, 440 George
Child James W., plasterer, 347 W. 7th
Child John R., 27 W. 6th
Child S. D., dress maker, 347 W. 7th
Child Sarah J., 347 W. 7th
Child W., bds. 27 W. 8th
Childen John, pipe fitter, wks. n.e.c. Walnut and Canal
Childen Michael, pipe fitter, wks. n.e.c. Walnut and Canal
Childs Charles, shoe mkr., 222 Central Avenue
Childs Elizabeth, 221 Laurel
Childs M., carp., 40 E. 2d
Childs Nathan, bds. Harts Hotel
Childs Solomon A., 43 W. 9th
Childs Thomas, lab.. 39 Plum
Childs Wm. E, 98 W. 9th
Chilling Ernst, carp., 287 W. Liberty
Chipman Horace D , com. mer., 161 Linn
CHIPMAN W. DOUGLAS, Agent, Flour Produce and Com. Mer., s.s. W. W. Canal. b. Central Av. and John, h. 454 W. 3d
Chisholm Benjamin, s s. Accommodation, E. of 8th
Chisholm Geo., carp., 424 W. 8th
CHOATE Alonzo B., (C. Barber & Evans,) h. 297 Findlay
CHOATE, BARBER & EVANS, (Alonzo B. C., Edward H. B. & John T. E.) Box Manuf. & Proprs. Race st. Planing Mill, 567 Race
Choate Evan P., cof. h., 271 Main
Cholar Caroline, 105 Van Horn
Cholerd Patrick, lab., 69 Woodward
Chons Michael, saddle-tree mkr., 153 Carr
Chree Margaret, n.s. al. b. Pearl and 3d, and Lawrence and Pike   [lay
Chrisling Bernard, box mkr., 314 Findlay
Chrisman Mary, 610 Central Av
Chrisman Peter, cooper, 623 Central Av
Christ Bertha, seamstress, wks. 537 Vine
Christ Edward, tinner, wks. John K. Coolidges
Christ Joseph, cooper, 64 Hughes
Christ Philip, tailor, 144 Spring
Christel Sebastian, cab. mkr., 632 Race
CHRISTIAN APOLOGIST, Dr. Wm. Nast, Editor, s.w.c. Main and 8th
Christian Ernst, carp., 76 Buckeye
CHRISTIAN George H., (J. E. Wynne & Co.) bds. 52 W. 9th
Christian John, grocery, 654 E. Front
Christian John, wagon mkr., e.s. Kilgour, b. 3d and 5th
Christian Margaret, 80 Gest
Christian Martin, wagon mkr., e.s. Kilgour, b. 3d and 5th
Christian Peter, lab., bds. 80 Gest
Christian Press, monthly, Dr. Geo. L. Weed, editor, 28 W. 4th

102   (CIN)   CINCINNATI   (CIN)   DIRECTORY.

Christie David, blksmith. 144 W. 6th
Christie Ebenezer, bakery, 146 W. 6:h
Christin J. C., teacher, 124 Betts
Christin John C., clk., 136 Hopkins
Christine ——, Prof, teacher of French, Wesleyan Female College
Christmann John, lab., 520 Main
Christmann Michael, tailor, 39 Milton
Christmann Peter, tailor, 31 Buckeye
Christofel John, butcher, 263 Pleasant
Christopher Adam, cigar mkr., 95 Elder
Christopher Alex. C., 243 Laurel
Christopher Alfred H., carp., 27 Clinton
Christopher Alfred H.. com. mer., 20 W. Front, bds. Madison House
Christopher Gustavus, blksmith,10 Buckeye
Christopher Hy., lab., 195 Laurel
Christopher Kate, wks. Hieatt & Woods candle factory
Christopher Mary, 105 Pleasant
Christopher Oliver P., conductor, 189 Poplar
Christy David, 278 W. 4th
Christy Hy., hackman, 53 Elizabeth
CHRISTY James W, (Cobb, Williams & Co.,) 401 W. 8th
Christy Jane, 420 W. 2d
Christy John, blksmith, 54 Lock
Christy John, boiler mkr, 13 E. 3d, e. of Parsons
Christy John T., boiler mkr, 15 High
Chron Sarah, 22 Union
Chruler Christ, cigar store, 210 W. Liberty
Chumard John, carriage mkr., 192 E. 5th
Chumley Armstrong, policeman,81 Clinton
Chumley Franklin, 130 Livingston
Chumuey Frank, driver, wks. n.w.c. Court and Race
CHURCH CHARLES, Coal Dealer, n w.c. 3d & John, bds. 120 John
Church H. A, printer, Cin. Gazette, bds. Tremont House
Church Hy. E., news-stand, s.e.c. 4th & Vine. h e.s. Elm, b. 8th and 9th
CHURCH JOHN, Jr., Publisher of Music and Dealer in Music Books, Pianos and Musical Instruments, 66 W. 4th
Church John, porter, 27 Arch
Church Wm. F., adjuster Ætna Ins. Co., 171 Vine. h. 334 W. 8th
Churchill Alonzo W., inspector, 361 Walnut. h. 175 Mound
Churchill George W., baggage master C. H. & D. R.R., h. 333 Clark
Churchill Franklin. clk., h. 333 Clark
Chuck Anna, n.s. Pleasant Court, e of Elm [and John
Ciario Joseph, grocery, s.w.c. Chestnut
Cider August, helper, wks. n.e.c. Canal and Walnut
Cincinnati Aid Association, Dr. Chas. H. Cleaveland, manager, 263 W. 4th
Cincinnati Art Academy. Jas. C. Beard, prin., s.w.c. 4th and Walnut
CINCINNATI CHEMICAL LABORATORY, Eugene Grasselli Prop. junction of E. Front and Pearl
Cincinnati Chess Club, s.e.c. Vine and 4th
CINCINNATI & CHICAGO AIR LINE R.R. Freight Office. W. O. White Ft. Agt., 115 Vine
Cincinnati & Chicago Dispatch, 5 College bldg
Cincinnati, Colerain. Venice and New London Omnibus Line, John Bevis & Co, proprietors 69 Walnut
Cincinnati College of Medicine and Surgery, s.w.c. Longworth and Central Avenue
CINCINNATI COMMERCIAL, M. D. Potter & Co., Proprs. n.e.c. 4th and Race
Cin. Detective Police Agency, n.w.c. 3d and Main
CINCINNATI DIRECTORY OFFICE, 104 Walnut, cor. 5th
CINCINNATI ENQUIRER, Faran & McLean, Proprietors, n.e.c. Vine and Burnet

CINCINNATI EQUITABLE Insurance Company, 30 W. 3d
Cincinnati Female Seminary, Wellington H Tyler, principal, s.w.c. 7th and Mound
CINCINNATI FIRE DEPARTMENT, Chief Engineers Office, n. s. George, b. Central Av. & Plum
CINCINNATI FUEL CO., Coal Dealers, s.w.c. 3d and Ludlow
CINCINNATI GAS LIGHT & COKE CO., 269 Vine H. J Miller, Pres. pro tem
CINCINNATI GAZETTE CO.,, (Joseph Glenn, Richard Smith, E. T. Kidd & J. T. Perry,) n.e.c. Vine and 4th
CINCINNATI, H. & D., L. M. and all connecting Railroads, Office 115 Vine
CINCINNATI, HAMILTON & DAYTON Railroad Depot and Offices, s.s. 6th, b. Hoadly & W. W. Canal
Cincinnati, Hamilton and Dayton Railroad round house, blksmith, paint and car shops, n.s. 6th, nr. W.W. Canal
Cincinnati, Harrison and Brookville omnibus line, 169 Walnut
Cincinnati House, John Friedlein, 55 Sycamore
CINCINNATI HOUSE OF REFUGE, Office City Hall, W. Leuthstrom, Secy.
CINCINNATI INSURANCE CO., Fire & Marine, Geo. W. Williams, Secy., John W. Hartwell, Prest., Office 4 Pub. Landing
Cincinnati Lancet and Observer, 130 Richmond
Cincinnati Law Library, Court House
CINCINNATI LAW SCHOOL, M. E. Curwen, Dean, 66 W. 3d
CINCINNATI LEAD WORKS, McCormick, Gibson & Co., Props. s.s 9th, b. Main and Sycamore
Cincinnati and Lebanon omnibus line, 169 Walnut
Cincinnati Machine Works, n.e.c. Front and Lawrence
Cincinnati and New Orleans Pilots Association, 4 Public Landing
CINCINNATI OIL WORKS, Burckhardt & Co., 12 Hammond, salesroom 107 Sycamore
Cincinnati Orphan Asylum. s.w.c. Summit and Auburn Av., Mt Auburn
CINCINNATI POST OFFICE, s.w.c. 4th and Vine, J. C. Baum. Postmaster
CINCINNATI PRESS, Daily and Tri-weekly, Vine, opposite Post Office
CINCINNATI PRICE CURRENT, Office Merchants Exchange, Wm. Smith, Proprietor
Cincinnati and St. Louis omnibus line, c. Park and Mursh
Cincinnati and St. Louis Pilot Benevolent Association, 7 Pub. Landing
Cincinnati Saw Mill. H. Whateley & Co. junction 6th and Front
CINCINNATI STONE WORKS, Graveson & Co, s.e.c. 3d and Lock
Cincinnati Street Railroad Co., 162 Vine
CINCINNATI TIMES, Daily and Weekly, C. W. Starbuck, Pro., 62 W. 3d
Cincinnati Truss. Brace and Bandage Institute, 318 Main
CINCINNATI TYPE FOUNDRY, s.w.c. Longworth and Vine
CINCINNATI UNION, Chas. A. Hertzsch, Editor 9 W. Court
CINCINNATI VOLKSBLATT, Court House Building
CINCINNATI VOLKSFREUND, s.w.c. Longworth and Vine

(CLA) CINCINNATI (CLA) DIRECTORY. (CLA) 103

Clapp Orville S., carriage mkr., bds 303 Water
CLAPP WILLIAM B., Wholesale Jeweler, 81 W. 4th bds. Spencer House
Clara Sister, St. Clare Convent n.w.c. 3d and Lytle
Claray Michael, shoe mkr., n.w.c, Rittenhouse and Court
Clare John, tailor, h. 86 Mill
Claridge Mrs. Isabella, 329 Central Av
Clare Theresa, servt., 419 W. 6th
Clark Mrs, 104 Clinton
CLARK Alex, (Gaston Dickson & Co.,) bds. Walnut St. House
Clark Alex P., boots and shoes, 338½ W. 5th
CLARK Alexander R., (C. & Carr,) h. 68 Jefferson Newport
CLARK Amos B., (C. & Carr,) h. 90 Jefferson, Newport
Clark Andrew, lab , 281 John
Clark Ann, 454 W. 3d
Clark Asa A., b. k., Cin. Daily Times, h. E. Walnut Hills
Clark Augustus, tobacconist, 174 W. Front
CLARK Augustus J., (Wilson & C.,) 84 W. Court w. of Central Av
Clark Benjamin, turner. 150 W. 6th
Clark Bridget, servt., 107 Broadway
CLARK & CARR, (Amos B. C. Frederick M Carr & Alex. R C.,) Wholesale Grocers and Commission Merchants, 29 Walnut
Clark Carvil, cooper, s.s. Court e. of Broadway
Clark Catharine, h. 196 Broadway
Clark Catharine, n.s. W. W. Canal b. Smith and Park
Clark Cecilia, 112 Avery
Clark Charles, sawyer, n.s. Goodloe b. Willow and Niagra
Clark Charles, shoe mkr., h. s.s. Accommodation e. of 8th
Clark Chas. E., barber, 4 Burnet House, h. 26 Harrison
Clark Charles H. riverman, bds. 12 E. Front
Clark Charles T., mach., wks. 137 W. 2d
Clark Charles W.. shoe mkr., 338 Accommodation
Clark Chester M., painter, 72 W. 3d, h. 78 Clark
Clark Clem M., painter, 261 W. 5th. h. 14 W. 5th
Clark D. Lawler, bds. 67 E. 3d
Clark Danl. W , mach., 103 W. Court w. of Central Av
Clark David C., paper hanger, 122 Clinton
CLARK Rev. Davis W., editor Ladies Repository, s.w.c. 8th and Main, h. 139 W. 9th
Clark Dennis, lab., 32 Lock
Clark Edward, mach., bds. s.w.c. 5th and Broadway
Clark Elliott, barber, 9 Broadway, h. 28 Harrison
Clark Elizabeth, n.e c. 6th and North
Clark Enos B., carp., 328 Cutter
CLARK ERASTUS, Freight Agent Little Miami R R., Office at Depot, h. 191 George
Clark Fanny J., teacher, 7th district School. res. Walnut Hills
CLARK FRANK, Agent American Express Company 92 W. 4th, h. Newport
Clark Frazee, grocery, 1524 E. Front, h 1522 E. Front
Clark G. W., riverman, bds. Henrie House
CLARK GEORGE, Merchant Tailor, 146 Walnut h. 113 Mound
Clark George F., 102 W. 4th
Clark Geo. G., clk., American Express Co., bds. Spencer House
Clark Geo. J., b. k. 496 W. 7th
Clark Geo. W., b. k., 180 Main, res. Covington
Clark George W., broker, 75 Barr
Clark Gibbs, actor. bds. 206 W. 5th
Clark Gus, clk., 174 W. Front

Clark H. N., justice of the peace, 10 Court House Building, bds. Buttemiller's Hotel
Clark Harrison, dry goods, bds. 27 Longworth
Clark Henen, 67 E. 3d
Clark Hy., apothecary, 165 Elm
Clark Hy., carp., 132 Butler
Clark Hy. S., phys., saddle bags, e.s. Walnut b. 5th and 6th
Clark Hugh. lab., 186 Central Av
Clark J. F. & J. W., (John F. and Joseph W.,) fish, game &c., 163 W. 5th
CLARK JAMES L., Oysters, Fish, and Game, 55 W. 5th, h. 585 Freeman
Clark James. blksmith, bds. s.w.c. 5th and Broadway
Clark James, carp., 208 George
Clark James, carp., 440½ W. 5th
Clark James, lab., 33 Observatory Road
Clark James, lab., 32 Race
Clark James G., stove manufac, 134 Longworth
Clark James M., salesman, s.e.c. Elm and 7th
Clark Jeremiah M., clk., Co. Recorders office, h. 122 Clinton
Clark Jerome M., b. k., 122 Clinton
Clark John, bds. Walnut St. House
Clark John, broker, 52 W. 3d, h. Covington
Clark John lab., n.w.c. 3d and Park
Clark John, silver plater, 10 E. 6th, h. 481 Race
CLARK John A., (Jno. A. C. & Co.,) h. 84 W. Court w. of Central Av
CLARK JOHN A. & CO., (Jno. A. C. H.. St. Clair & B, Fogel,) Grocers and Commission Merchants 32 Vine
Clark John C., mach., bds. s.w.c. 5th and Broadway
Clark John F. (J. F. & J. W. C.,) bds. Fremont Hotel
Clark John G., (Cecil & C.) res. Middleton
Clark John O., b. k., St. Nicholas, h. 342 W. 4th
Clark John S., foreman, 52 Lock
Clark John T., steward, 32 Race
Clark Joseph, chair mkr., 372 W. 4th
Clark Joseph W , (J. F. & J. W. C.,) bds. United States Hotel
Clark Julia, bds. 335 Walnut
Clark Luke, 127 W. Front
Clark Luke, brush mkr. 96 W. Front
Clark Margaret L., 215 Richmond
Clark Martha, seamstress 55 12th
Clark Mary, n.s Patterson al. b. Main and Walnut
Clark Mary, servt., 290 Longworth
Clark Mary, servt., 441 W. 7th
Clark Michael, bar k., 119 W. 5th
Clark Mollie J., seamstress, 257 W. 9th
Clark Nelson, shoe mkr., 169 Cutter
Clark Patrick, bds. 124 E. 8th
Clark Patrick, cof. h. 253 W. 6th
Clark Peter H., b. k., 25 Macalister
Clark Priscilla, dress mkr., 50 Longworth
Clark Reuben, carp., n.s. Front e. of Lewis
CLARK S. & S. S., (Samuel and Sidney S.,) Saddlery, Hardware and Carriage Trimmings, 180 Main
Clark Sallie, nurse, Commercial Hospital
CLARK Samuel, (S. & S. S. C.) res. Covington
CLARK Sidney S., (S. & S. S. C.) res. Aurora Ind
Clark Stephen, atty., 22 W. Court
Clark Sue, 59 W. Court
Clark Susan, servt., 107 Broadway
Clark Thomas, hostler, 339 Central Av
Clark Thomas H., waiter, bds. Indiana House
Clark Walter, St.Bt. Agent, 36 Central Av
Clark Webster, lab., 32 Race
Clark Wm., grocery, 85 E. 3d, e. of Whittaker
Clark Wm., lab., h. 29 Webb
Clark Wm., porter, 29 Webb

Clark Wm., stone cutter, 439 Sycamore
Clark Wm. B., pipeman, n.s. 5th nr. Smith
CLARK Wm. H., Cast Steel, Iron, Amalgam Bells, Cane Mills &c., 122 Main, h. 509 Freeman
Clark Wm. P., surveyor, n.e.c. Walnut and 9th, h. 461 Race
CLARKE C. R., Importer of Brandies, Wines, Liquors, Cigars, &c., 11 Walnut, h. Covington
Clarke David, carp., 420 Broadway
Clarke Eliza, 149 George
Clarke Frederick, tailor, n.w.c. 5th and Sycamore
Clarke George, clk., bds. 406 W. 7th
Clarke James, clk., 55 W. 4th, bds. 420 Broadway
CLARKE James G., (S. H. Burton & Co .) h 134 Longworth
Clarke John N., blk. smith, 36 E. 6th, h. 34 E. 6th
Clarke Luke, brush mkr., 96 W. Front
Clarke Margaret, h. 333 Central Av
Clarke Nelson, F. shoemkr., 169 Cutter.
CLARKE PETER, General Engraver, 1 W. 4th, c. Main. h. 440 Broadway
CLARKE Robert, (Robert C. & Co.,) h. 420 Broadway
CLARKE ROBERT & CO., (Robert C., R. D. Barney & J. W. Dale,) Law Publishers and Booksellers, 55 W. 4th
Clarke Thomas, carp. 333 Central Av.
CLARKE WM. L., Secretary Gas Company, 269 Vine, h. 495 W. 7th
Clarke Wm. M. T., clk., 498 W. 7th
Clarkson John D., 294 Linn
Clarkson M. M. L., n.e.c. Perry and Central Av.
Clary Catharine, servt., wks. 503 W. 7th
Clary Daniel, lab., 395 W. 2d
Clary Frederick, cooper, 24 Hughes
Claser Chas., butcher, 636 Elm
Clason Lewis, Sec'y. Amer. Ins. Co., h., 207 W. 7th
Clason Marshall B., atty., 21 W. 3d, bds. 36 Longworth
Class Charles, cof. h. 168 Vine, h. s.s. 5th, b. Vine and Race
Class Hy., clk., n.e.c. 4th and Main
Classick Michael, tailor, 134 Main
CLATWORTHY A. C., Reporter Cincinnati Gazette, bds. 170 W. 4th
CLATWORTHY F., Reporter Cincinnati Gazette, h. 148 Walnut
Clatworthy Wm., b. k., 81 W. 2d, bds. 170 W. 4th
Clauder Moritz, waiter, Walnut Street House
Claus Elizabeth, servt., 286 George
Clausheide Henry, cooper, 75 Buckeye
Clausing Clements, tailor, 353 Main
Clauson Frank, mach., bds. 575 W. 5th
Claverkamp Joseph, lab., 65 Woodward
Clavin James, sawyer, 38 E. 8th e. of Lock
Clawson Andrew J., tailor, 136 Betts
Clawson Charles H., conductor, bds. 81 Mill
Clawson Isaac, cab. mkr., 110 Avery
Clawson John. shoemkr., 73 Hathaway
Clawson Samuel, mer., 107 Barr
Clawson Wm., bedstead factory, 81 Mill
Clawson Wm., H., bds. 81 Mill
Clay Marilla, w.s. Henderson al. b. 7th and 8th
Clay Lucy A., h. 266 Everett
Clay Thomas, carp., 40 W. Court
Clayer Barney, file cutter, 9 Franklin
Caymeyer Hy., cooper, 73 Wade
Claypoole Nancy, teacher, 435 Broadway
Claylon C., bds. Freys Hotel
Clayton Geo. N., clk., bds. N. 296 Race
Clayton Margaret, confec., 323 W. 9th, w. of Central Av.
Clayton Richard, jeweler, bds. Broadway Hotel
Clayton Rosa, 59 Gano [nut
Clayton William M., salesman, 34 Wal-

104   (CLI)   CINCINNATI   (COA)   DIRECTORY.   (COE)

Clearwater, Hiram, butcher, 391 Baymiller
Cleary John, boots and shoes, 128 Lock
Cleary Mary, servt., 99 Broadway
Cleary Michael, 91 Sycamore
Cleary Michael, clk., rooms International Hotel
CLEARY Pat, (A. D. Schram & Co.,) 129 Richmond
Cleary Pat., cooper, 5 Crippen al.
Cleaveland Chas. H., phys., 203 W. 4th, bds. 204 W. 4th
Clebrew Robt. S., pipe fitter, wks. n.e.c. Walnut and Canal
Clegg Thomas, basket mkr., 'n.s. Mulberry, b. Rice and Vine
Cleland Alicia, teacher, 82 W. 9th
Cleland Anna teacher, 82 W. 9th
Cleland Fanny, 17 McAlister
Clelend Ann, teacher, h. 330 W. 9th w. of Central Av.
Clemann Anthony, tailor, 150 Hopkins.
Clemens B., porter, wks 21 and 23 W. Front
Clemmens Jeremiah, cook, n.w.c. Bank and Central Av.
Clemens Thomas, trunk mkr., wks. 509 Plum
Clement John, gilder, bds. Teutonia Hotel
Clement Robt. M., b. k. 14 W. Pearl, h. 219 Poplar
Clement Wm. B., b. k., 222 Betts
CLEMENT WM. H., President Little Miami Railroad, Office s e c. Pearl and Kilgour, h. Morrow
Clements ——, clk., rooms, 56 E. 3d
Clements Geo., broker. bds. 65 Broadway
Clements Martin, currier, n.s. Railroad e. of Wallace al.
Clements Mary, 597 W. 8th
Clements Michael, foreman. 597 W. 8th
Clements T. D., surveyor Cin. Ins. Co., n.s. 3d, b. Broadway and Sycamore
Clements Thomas, trunk mkr., h. 597 W. 8th
Clements W. M., clk, O. & M. R. R., freight office, h. 433 W. 2d
CLEMMER J. H., Attorney at Law, n.e.c. Main and Seventh, h. 370 W. Eighth
Clemmer John, cigar mkr., 89 Richmond
Clemons Chas. C., clk., bds. 238 Race
Clemons Wm., eng., 1300 E. Front
Clency Bridget. servt., 414 W. 6th
Clendenin Annie, tailoress, 327 Central Av.
CLENDENIN WM., Physician and Surgeon. s.e.c 7th and Vine
Cleneay Chas. P., clk., 143 W. 4th
Cleneay Francis G., (Wm Cleneay & Son,) h. 3d6 W. 4th
Cleneay Geo., W. B., (Joseph S. C. & Co ,) 437 W. 8th
Cleneay Joseph S., (Joseph S. C. & Co.,) 443 W. 8th
Cleneay Joseph S. & Co., (J. S. C. & G. B. Cleneay,) com. mer., 42 Vine
Cleneay Thomas. 143 W. 4th
Cleneay Wm., (Wm. C. & Son,) 143 W. 4th
Cleneay Wm. & Son, (Wm. C. & Francis O. C.,) com. mer., 51 Walnut
Clenen Mrs. Mary A , 50 Barr
Clericus Lewis, bk. binder, 569 Sycamore
CLERK OF POLICE COURT, Office, City Building
Clerks Office U. S. Circuit and District Court. John McLean, Clerk, Custom House Building, s w.c. 4th and Vine
Clermont Hotel, Marshall & Robbins, Proprietors, e.s. Broadway b. 3d and Pearl
Clery Bridget. servt., 90 E. 3d
Cless G. F., cigar mkr., bds. 130 West Court
Cleveland, Columbus & Cincinnati Railroad, office 4. Colledge Bldg.
Clifford Alice, folder, bds. 179 Lock
Clifford Kate, bds. 448 Elm
Clifford Patrick, lab., 43 Plum
Clifford Patrick A., b. k., 43 Lock, n. of 8th

Clifford Samuel, bk. layer, 26 Abigail
Clifford Thomas, cooper, 43 Lock, n. of 8th
Clifford Wm., plumber, 309 W. 8th
Clifton S , steamboat mate, 196 George
CLIFTON HOUSE, Samuel Johnson, Proprietor, s.e.c. 6th and Elm
Climer Hy., carp., s.s. Charlotte b. Central Av. and Linn, h. Charlotte, b. John and Linn
Climperman Bernhard, lab., n.s. 6th, b. Horne and Harriet
Clinch Patrick, eng., 583 W. 5th
Cline Alexander, grocery, 26 Butler
Cline Casper, 68 Mohawk
Cline Hy., cof. h., n.s. Front, e. of Kelly
Cline John, planing mill, 139 E. Front, h. Mt. Vernon, Ky.
Cline Martin, stone cutter. 162 E. 5th
Cline Michael, polisher, 136 Water
Cline Wm., sheet iron wkr., bds. Pennsylvania Hotel
Clineburg Hy., lab., n.e.c. 3d and Wood
Clinger Geo., auctioneer, 154 Main, h. 264 W. 8th
Clinger John, finisher, 148 W Pearl
Clingman Geo. E., clk., 68 Walnut, bds. 59 E. 4th
Clingman John, finisher, s.w.c. 3d and Smith
Clingman Sarah, 39 Jones
Clink Joseph, porter, 25 Franklin
Clinker Barney, lab., 416 Longworth
Clinker H , lab., wks. Chamberlain & Co's.
Clinst Adam, lab., wks. 335 Broadway
Clinton John, lab, 135 W. Front
Cliphane Margaret. n.s. Patterson al., b, Main and Walnut
Clishy Thomas, agt., 610 W. 9th
Clisby Thomas W., ale and porter depot, 31 Vine, h. n.s. 9th, w. of Freeman
Clive Geo., school, 204 W. 7th
Clo Mathias, finisher, e.s. Hand al., b. Court and Clark
Clobby John. lab 990 E. Front
Clock Hy., lab., bds. 56 W. Court
CLOON P. B , 21 Public Landing, h. Avondale
CLOON Samuel, (Samuel C. & Co.,) h. Avondale
CLOON SAMUEL & CO., (Samuel Cloon, James E. Tylor. Erastus D. Tylor & Samuel T. Tylor,) Bakery and Flour Store, 21 Public Landing
Closs Frederick. jewelry, 57 Ham. Road.
Closs Hy., 10 Hughes
Closs John, lab, 535 Freeman
Closs John, organ builder, 407 Central Av. h. 13 Elizabeth
Closterman George. lab., 130 Betts
CLOSTERMAN HENRY, Chair Manufacturer, s.e.c. Augusta and Smith h. 368 W. 3d
Closterman J., Brookville House, n.w.c. Front and Central Av.
Closterman Joseph, cab. mkr., wks. 126 Sycamore
Closterman Wm., moulder, bds. 412 Vine
Clotilday Sister, St. John's Hospital, n.w.c. Plum and 3d
Cloud Francis, 225 W. Front
Clouds George, carp., 1192 E. Front
Clough William, patent atty., 122 Main, bds. Gibson House
Clous Theodore, carp., 511 Race
Clowser Andrew J., shoemkr., 202 Richmond
Cloyer Andrew J., teamster, 149 Van Horn
Cloyer Elizabeth, 187 W. Court, w. of Central Av.
Cloyer Elizabeth. bds. 148 Van Horn
Cloyd Julian, cof. h., 193 w. 6th
Clucas John, finisher, 65 Vine
Cluff Julia, 243 Longworth
Clyde Adam, mach., 247 Everett
Clyde Andrew, builder, 142 Clinton
Clyman Joseph, penny post, 373 Sycamore
Clymer John D., salesman, 143 Walnut, bds Walnut Street House
Coakly Thomas, cof. h., 127 Water

Coalhouse Geo., lab. wks. Niles' works
Coniscolt Thomas H., dray., 116 Laurel.
COAN B. F., Ticket Agent Marietta and Cincinnati Railroad, Office No. 3. Burnet House, boards Burnet House
Coan John porter, 122 Cutler
Coates Francis J.. clk., 20 Grant
COATES JOHN F., Furniture Warerooms, 150 W. 8th, h. 20 Grant
Coates Joseph M., (C. & Lecount,) 55 Laurel
Coates & Lecount, (J. C. & F. L.) painters, 119 Laurel
Coats M. H., b.k. 104 W. 4th
Coats Paxson, alcohol manuf.; s.w.c. John and W.W. Canal, h. 287 Water
COBB & ARMEL, (John C. & Danl. A.) Stock Dealers, 335 Broadway
COBB, ARMEL & FLETCHER, (John C., Danl. A. & Wm. F. F.) Pork Packers, 335 Broadway
COBB John, (C & Armel, & Cobb, Armel & Fletcher) 335 Broadway, res Aurora, Ind.
Cobb John, lab., wks. 335 Broadway
Cobb Nancy, dry goods, 515 W. 5th
COBB O. F., (C., Williams & Co.) res, Aurora, Ind.
Cobb P. W., s.s. 6th b. Vine and Race
Cobb Rachael, laundress, 456 W. 4th
Cobb Samuel, undertaker 143 Sycamore, h. 221 Baymiller
Cobb Sylvanus G., printer 62 W. 3d
COBB, WILLIAMS & CO., (O. P. C., P. W. W. & J. W. Christy) Com mission Merchants, 35 Water and 19 Pub. Landing
Cobb Zachariah B., clock repairer, 515 W. 5th
Cobbin Alexander, clk., e.s. Lock b. 8th and Court
Cobbs Margaret, bds. 35 Parsons
Cobe John A., locksmith, bds. 53 Broadway
Cobler Froney, laundress, 144 Van Horn
COBURN Augustus S., (Nichols & C.) bds. Clifton House
Cochland Thomas, n.e.c. North and New
Cochnower John, coal, 28 W. 3d. h. 329 W. 4th
Cochnever, John L., b.k., h. 329 W. 4th
Cochran Alex., painter, 287 Vine
Cochran Daniel, fireman, 177 Webb
Cochran David C., hinge fitter, wks. n.e. c. Walnut and Canal
Cochran Geo. S., 335 W. 4th
Cochran Geo. W., n.e.c. 3d and Race, h. 333 W. 4th
Cochran John A., clk., 593 W. 5th, bds. 108 Smith
Cochran Joseph, plumber. 227 Vine
Cochran Mary, servt., 99 Broadway
Cochran Paul, cooper, 36 North
Cochran Philip, fireman, n.e.c. 5th and Park
Cochran Robert. mill stone mkr., 44 W. Front, h. 59 George
Cochrane Joseph, plumber. 269 Vine
Cocilot John, lab., s.e.c. McDowell and Hill
Cock Griffin, 518 Elm
Coddington Mary E , 601 Freeman
Coddington Sarah, 439 John
Coddington Wm. S., bds. 28 Hathaway
Code Patrick, lab., 238 Water
Cody David, printer, bds. 49 Race
Cody J. E., clk. P. Cody's, h. 65 McFarland
Cody Mary, servt., 506 W 5th
Cody Mary, servt., 373 George
CODY PATRICK, Commission Merchant and Wholesale Grocer. 17 and 19 Water, h. 65 McFarland
Cody Wm E., clk. P. Cody's, 17 and 19 Water
Coe A. J., clk. n.w.c. Main and Front, bds. 89 E. 4th
Coe Erastus P., (Roots & Coe) 502 W. 7th
Coe J. C., bds. Dennison House
Coe Lydia L., 480 W. 8th
Coe Thomas, carriage painter, bds. Dennison House

Coesmeler Barney, grocer, 18 Donnersberger
Coffey Mary, 651 W. Front
Coffey Mary, 72 Rittenhouse
Coffey Patrick, wire wkr., wks. 181 Walnut
Coffield David, lab., 212 W. 2d
Coffield James, lab., 42 E. 8th e of Lock
Coffield John, lab., 8 Linneus
Coffield Pat., blksmith, wks. w.s. Butler b. E. Pearl and Front
Coffin Chas. D., judge Superior Court of Cincinnati, bds. Burnet House
Coffin D H. B., grocer, 20 E. Pearl, res. Newport
Coffin G. W. & Co., (Geo. W. C., Ezra W. Vanduzen & Cornelius T. Tift) bell and brass founders, 102 and 104 E. 2d
Coffin Geo. W., (G. W. C. & Co.) 136 Broadway
Coffin H. W., salesman, h. 417 Broadway
Coffin Levi, grocery, n.w.c. Hunt and Broadway, h. s.w.c. Franklin and Broadway
COFFIN CHAS. D., Judge Superior Court of Cincinnati, bds. Burnet House
Coffin Moses, 390 W. 5th
COFFIN & SON, (Wm. C. & W. R. C.) Oil Dealers and Engineer's Supplies 3 Water
COFFIN W. R., (C. & Son) h. Newport
COFFIN Wm., (C. & Son) h. Newport
Coffin Wm. G., clk., 93 Smith
COFFIN Wm. G., (F. H. Lawson & Co.) h. 326 W. 7th
COFFIN Z. B., Wholesale and Retail Grocer and Tea Dealer, 32 W. 5th res. Newport
Coffin Edwin, b.k., 128 W. 5th
Coffman John M., leather dresser, 31 Observatory
Cogen Patrick, lab., 97 Hopkins
Coggie Annie, servt., 392 Longworth
Coghill Mary A., milliner, e.s. Central Av. b. Laurel and Betts
Cogin John, lab., 133 E. 6th
Cogswell John, pipe fitter, wks. n.e.c. Walnut and M. Canal
Cohen A. & Co., (Abram & Isaac) clothing 41 E. 4th
Cohen Abram, (A. C. & Co.) 353 W. 5th
COHEN ABRAHAM, Wholesale and Retail Clothing, 194 Main, h. 317 Walnut
Cohen Benj., salesman 194 Main
Cohen Bridget, 32 Pierson
COHEN GUITERMAN & CO., (Hy. C., Joseph G., & Frederick & Wm. Guiterman) Manufacturers of Clothing and Wholesale Dealers in Merchant Tailoring Goods, 82 W. Pearl
COHEN Hy., (C. Guiterman & Co.) at 82 W. Pearl
Cohen Isaac, (A. Cohen & Co.) 41 E. 4th
Cohen Isaac, lead pencil mkr., h. 222 Walnut
Cohen Isaac, pawn office, 96 W. Front
Cohen Isidore M, b.k. 130 Main
Cohen Lewis A., mer., 163 W. 5th
Cohen Louis, clk. 79 W. Pearl
Cohen Martin S., 210 W. Front
Cohen Mendle A., liquors, 185 John
Cohen Sim., lead pencil mkr., 222 Walnut
COHEN SIMON M., Yankee Notions, Ladies and Gents Furnishing and Fancy Dry Goods, 130 Main, h. 161 Race
Cohen Solomon, cutter, n.e.c. 4th and John
COHEN WOLF, Wholesale Clothing, and Dealer in Gent's Furnishing Goods, 191 Main, h. 319 Vine
Cohl Wm., 519 W. 7th
Cohn Barney, lab., wks. C. H. & D. R. R. Depot
Cohn Conrad, cartman, 88 Hunt
Cohn Gottlieb, peddler, 72 Bremen
Cohn Hy., peddler, 142 Bremen
Cohn Jacob, tailor, 43 Wade
COHN Jacob, (May & C.) bds. 210 George

Cohn Levi, furniture, 367 Central Av.
Cohn Louis, peddler, 20 Harrison
Cohn Marcus, 210 George
Cohn Matthew A., cof. h., 68 W. 6th
Cohn Michael, produce dealer, 163 W. Liberty
Cohn Solomon, mer., 30 Perry
Cohorst Hermann H., salesman 51 W. Pearl, h. 485 Main
Cohrs Hy. C., groceries, 71 Elder
Cohrs Hermann F., dry goods, 501 Vine
Coin Frank, lab., 61 Mill
Coine Mrs. bds. Dennison House
Coinan Frank, roaster, wks. 131 Race
Cokely Thomas, lab., 60 Pierson
Cokeley Wm., lab., n.s. Butler b. Pearl and Front
Cokman Geo., hinge fitter, wks. n.e.c. Walnut and Canal
Colahan Mary, 128 Mound
Colahan Patrick, carp., 44 Kossuth
Colbert Ellen, bds. 139 Clinton
Colburn Charles L., salesman 55 W. Pearl, h. Mt. Auburn
Colburn Ezekiel. 337 W. 8th
Colburn Frederick, 337 W. 8th
Colburn Geo. M., clk. Burnet House
Colburn Julia A., music teacher Wesleyan Female College
Colburn Wm. F., pianos, &c., 94 W. 4th, h. 396 W. 9th w. of Central Av.
Colbus Wm., carver, 308 George
Colby Anahstatia, teacher, 212 W. Court
Colby Geo. W., printer, 117 York
Colby Isaac, 214 W. Court
Colby James, lab., s.s. Montgomery Pike nr. Madison Road
Colby Samuel, dept. marshal, 216 W. Court
Colcher Gus., (J. L. Ruffin & Co.)
Colder John, roofer, bds. 158 W. Front
Coldkemp Frederick, teacher, 18 Donnersberger
Cole —, cab. mkr., bds. n.s. Augusta b. John and Smith
Cole Alexander A., clk., 308 Richmond
Cole Coleman, cook, 202 Webb
Cole Crawford, cook, Madison House
Cole David, bar k., 107 W. 3d
Cole Jacob F., bds. Burnet House
Cole James, baker, 194 W. 6th
COLE JAMES C., Umbrella, Parasols and Cane Manufacturer, 98 W. 4th, h. 30 Harrison
Cole John K., com. mer., 42 Sycamore
Cole Joseph, painter, wks. n.e.c. 3d and Race
Cole Julia, 72 E. 7th
Cole Lewis, lab., 40 Central Av.
Cole Lewis Cass, clk. U. S. Express Co.
Cole Lydia A., 129 Water
Cole Maria, 303 Richmond
Cole Nancy, s.s. Goodloe b. Willow and Niagara
Cole Robert, h. n.s. Burt b. Broad and Reed
Cole Sarah Ann, servt., 313 Longworth
Cole Thomas G., salesman 83 and 85 Walnut, h. 308 Richmond
Cole Walter A., cooper, 15 E. 2d, h. s.w. c. 8th and Sycamore
Cole Wm., bklayer, 194 W. 6th
Cole Wm. bk. molder, 758 W. Front
Cole Wm , finisher, 10 Observatory
Cole Wm., shoe mkr., n.s. Railroad e. of Stone al.
Cole Wm, Archibald, salesman, 83 Mill
Coleman Adbeel, plasterer, 142 John
Coleman Andrew, lab., 700 W. Front
COLEMAN Arnold H., (Nordloh & C.) w.s. Park b. 2d and W. W. Canal
Coleman Augustus, carp., 63 Laurel
Coleman Augustus, varnisher, 311 Findlay
Coleman B. S., blksmith, n.e.c. Freeman and Poplar
Coleman Bluffard S., clk., n.w.c. Freeman and Poplar
Coleman Clement, butcher, 235 Everett
Coleman Daniel, molder 63 Laurel
Coleman Daniel B., molder, 63 Laurel
Coleman David, lab., 86 Water
Coleman Mrs. E., teacher, 154 W. 4th
Coleman Elizabeth, 432 Sycamore
Coleman Elizabeth T., bds. s.w.c Franklin and Broad

Coleman Evaline, 14 Hannibal
Coleman Geo., butcher, 75 Poplar
Coleman Geo. D., steward, Burnet House
Coleman Geo. W., wood dealer, s.w.c. 5th and Front. h. 4 Sargent
Coleman Georgianna, cook, 47 W. 7th
COLEMAN James (J. C. & Co.), 102 John
COLEMAN JAMES & CO. (James C. & Wm. F. Mitchell), Plow Handle and Washboard Manufacturers, s.s. E. 8th e. of Broadway
Coleman Rev. John, 4 Sargent
Coleman John, tailor, 130 W. 5th, h. 39 Plum
Coleman John, teamster, Richmond b. Harriet and Millcreek
Coleman John W., molder, 349 Central Av
Coleman John W., pork dealer, 13 W. Court
Coleman John W., shoemkr, wks. 34 W. 5th
Coleman Joseph, lab., 100 Carr
Coleman Kate, b. h., s.w.c. Broadway and 5th
Coleman Louis, turner, wks. 468 W. 6th
Coleman Margaret, 177 W 9th
Coleman Marion, driver, 672 E. Front
Coleman Mary, h. rear 58 Hunt
Coleman Mary, h. n.s. Patterson al, b. Main and Walnut
Coleman Michael, dray, 502 Sycamore
Coleman Michael, lab., 68 Butler
Coleman Nancy, 6 North
Coleman Patrick, grocery, 40 Kossuth
Coleman Peter, clk., 628 W. 6th
COLEMAN Robert B. (Foster & C.), 8 Hopkins
Coleman Samuel, teamster, 13 Sargent
Coleman Saml. T. J., banker, 57 W. 3d, h. 462 W. 7th
Coleman Sylvanus B., conductor, 146 E. 3d e. of Collard
Coleman Thomas, printer, bds. 63 Laurel
Coleman Thomas, steward. 174 Webb
Coleman Thos. teamster, 414 John
Coleman Wm., lab., 153 Water
Coleman Wm., porter, 17 Commerce
Coles Mrs. A. B., 132 Smith
Coles Abraham, finisher, 152 Spring
Coles Albert B., pork packer, 139 Smith
Coles Stephen, atty., 120 Main, h. 229 Baymiller
Colfish Herman, lab., wks. 33 Lock
Colina Patrick, lab., 42 Kossuth
Colina Thomas, drover. 189 Laurel
Colkmeier John, lab., 50 Webster
Collahan James, carp., 303 W. 5th
Collamer Stephen P., boots and shoes, 224 Central Av., bds. 281 Central Av
Collan John J., porter, 79 W. Pearl
Collepy John, butcher, bds. 48 E. 6th
Collet John, cigars, &c., 1111 Central Av
Collet Peter, tailor, 16 Hamer
Collett Annette. bds. 279 W. Front
Collett Francis, blksmith, n.e.c. 3d and Wood
COLLIER Allen, (Jno. Swasey & Co.), 300 Richmond
COLLIER Chas. B., (Johnston & C.), res. Walnut Hills
Collier John, teamster, w.s. Jordon b. Clark and Gest
COLLING J. TH., Secretary Western Insurance Co., h. 310 Walnut
Collingwood Thomas, porter, 414 W. 6th
Collins ——, bds. Dennison House
Collins Cadwallader J., clk., 41 Harrison
Collins Catharine, 32 North
Collins Chas., lab., 91 Sycamore
Collins Charles, sawyer, w.s. Mulberry al. b. Pearl and 3d
Collins Charles H., bds. 342 W. 4th
Collins Charles W., vet. surgeon, 24 Dayton
Collins Dennis, fireman, Spencer House
Collins Edward, bds. 333 Central Av
Collins Edward, pressman, E. Morgan's printing office
Collins Rev. Edward T., s.e.e. 8th and Central Av
Collins Elizabeth, 50 Mound
Collins Geo., cab. mkr., e.s. al. b. 4th and 5th and Park and Mill

106 (COL) CINCINNATI (CON) DIRECTORY. (CON)

Collins Geo. T., treasurer, Wood's theater, bds. Clifton House
Collins Hy., atty., 41 Ludlow
Collins Hy., boots and shoes, 251 Central Av., h. 141 George
Collins Hy., cutter, 63 W. Pearl
Collins Hy., lab, s.s. 6th b. Broadway and Culvert
Collins Hy., lab., bds. s.w.c. Race and 2d
COLLINS & HERRON, (Isaac C. C & John W. H.) Attorneys at Law, 148 Walnut
COLLINS Isaac C. (C. & Herron) h. E. Walnut Hills
Collins James, furniture, &c., 350½ W. 5th
Collins James H., driver, U S. Express Co, bds. 182 Race
Collins Jeremiah, lab., w s. Culvert b. 5th and 6th
Collins Jesse, river man, 15 Webb
Collins John, dray, 236 Walnut
Collins John, dray, n.s. 6th e. of Lock
Collins John, dray, 802 Central Av
Collins John, finisher, 30 Lock
Collins John, lab., s.s. 6th b. Broadway and Culvert
Collins John, printer, 74 W. 3d, bds. 104 Commerce
Collins John C., chair mkr., 9 Gest
COLLINS JOHN F, National Claim Agency, 66 W. 3d, h. New York
Collins Josephine, photographic artist, s.w.c. Main and 9th, h. s.s. Green nr. Race
Collins Joshua, whitewasher, 131 W. M. Canal
Collins Julius B., teacher, 123 Linn
Collins Letty, select school, 299 Clark, bds. 141 George
Collins Margaret, w.s. Crippen al. b. 7th and 8th
Collins Martha, 289 Water
Collins Martin, lab., 104 Cherry al
Collins Mary, bds. s.s. 6th b. Broadway and Culvert
Collins Mary, 31 W. Court w of Central Av
Collins Mary V., h.h., 206 W. 5th
Collins Maurice, lab., 90 Hunt
Collins Michael, foreman, wks. 830 Central Av
Collins Michael, lab., 4 Charlotte
Collins Patrick, huckster, 29 E. 8th
Collins Richard, lab., wks. n.w.c. Freeman and 9th
Collins Richard H., publisher, 25 W. 4th, h. Covington
Collins Samuel D., foreman, S. Roberts' bds. Dennison House
Collins Thomas, dray, n.s 6th e. of Lock
Collins Thomas, harness mkr, bds. Farmers' Hotel
Collins Timothy, lab., 30 Lock n of 8th
Collins W. M. (Harrison & C.)
Collins Washington M., b.k., s.o.c. Vine and Front
Collins Wm, cof. h., n.s. 6th e. of Lock
Collins Wm., lab., wks. s.e.c. 9th and Sycamore
Collins Wm., steward, 206 W. 5th
Collins Wm. E., shoemkr, e. end of Harrison
Collis Robert O, sporting apparatus, bds. s.w.c. 5th and Broadway
Collison Catharine, 67 E. 8th e. of Lock
Collopy John J., molder, 146 W. Court w. of Central Av
Collard Rev. Isaac, 41 York
Collard Newton B., b.k., 34 Walnut, h. 41 York
COLLORD W. A. & CO, Bankers and Exchange Dealers, 3 W. 2d
COLLORD Wm. A., (W. A. C. & Co.), 118 Hopkins
Collum Geo., pilot, bds 305 W. w. of Central Av
Colonna John, confec, 154 Sycamore
Colquhoun John, porter, 408 W. 3d
Colshear Lucinda, laundress, 146 Vanhorn
Colston Thomas, huckster, 450 W. 5th
Colter Aaron A., grocer, 319 Main, h. Mt Washington

Colter Alexander, mer., 450 W. 9th w. of Central Av
Colter Elizabeth, teacher, 450 W. 9th
Colter Ellen, servt., 275 George
Colter Martha, 169 Mound
Colter Nathaniel, fruits, bds. 294 W. 5th
Colton Frederick, atty., 17 E. 3d, bds Broadway Hotel
Colton John B., stone mason, 112 Richmond
Colville Andrew B., dep. sheriff, 263 Cutter
Colville Hugh, teller, Com. Bank, res. Covington
Colville James, b.k.. 57 Main
Colville Thomas, salesman, s.w.c. Walnut and Pearl
Colvin Sylvia, teacher, bds. 15 George
Colvin Miss S., teacher, 15 George
Colvin Sylvia M., teacher, 249 W. Court
Colwin Benj., pilot, bds. 141 Sycamore
Combrinck Bernhard, grocery, 140 Hopkins
Comegys C. P., asst. librarian, public library, bds. 137 W. 7th
Comegys Cornelius G., phys., n.e.c. W. 7th and Elm
Comegys W. D., 23 W. 3d, h. n.e.c. 7th & Elm
Comens Michael, clk., bds. 210 Sycamore
Comer John, sawyer, wks. n.w.c. Freeman and 9th
Comfort James, lab., 74 E. 3d e. of Whittaker
Comfort Margaret, 93 Hopkins
COMMERCIAL (Daily and Weekly,) n.e.c. 4th and Race, M. D. Potter & Co., Proprietors
Commercial Bank of Cincinnati, 132 Main. James Hall, Pres
Commercial Hospital, 12th b. Plum and Central Av
Commercial House, n.e.c. Central Av. and 7th
COMMERCIAL INS. CO., n.w.c. Main and Front, W. L. Harbeson, Pres't
Commercial Office Building, n.e.c. 4th and Race
Commercial Row, Main b. Water and Front
Commons Bridget, 25 8th above Lock
Commonwealth Ins. Co. agency, 62 W. 3d
Compass George, lab., 422 Sycamore
COMPTON Wm. A. (Dantlin & C.), 88 E. 5th
Comschmidt Arnold, tailor, s.w.c. Linn and Hopkins
COMSTOCK Wm. H. (Wm. H. C. & Co.) 261 W. 4th
COMSTOCK WM. H. & CO, (Wm, H. C. & Jacob S. Aber) Wh. Boots & Shoes, 14 and 16 W, Pearl
CONAHAN Charles (Jones & C.) 442 W. 6th
Conahan James, 26 Laurel
Conaley Harney, porter, n.s. Commerce b Walnut and Vine
Concannon John, carp., 269 W. 3d
Conclin Fannie, lab., 92 Barr
Conclin Phoebe, bds. 92 Barr
Conclin Wm., grocery, 95 W. 5th, res. Campbell county, Ky
Condan Michael, lab., n.s. Patterson al. h. Main and Walnut
Condlan Bridget, bds. 198 E. 6th
Condon John, lab., s.s. 6th b. Broadway and Culvert
Condon Patrick, lab., 34 Kossuth
Condron John, dray., 31 Gest
Condroy Michael, lab., 69 W, Mulberry
Condroy Thomas, lab., bds. 466 George
Cone Chas. S, Treas. O. & M. R. R., n.s. Front b. Mill and Wood, bds. Burnet House
Cone Isaac, 2nd hand store, w.s. Elm b. Front and Commerce
Cone J. H., bds. Gibson House
Cone L. C., harness mkr., bds. 143 Sycamore
Conrey Mrs, Susan, 177 Barr
Cones Mrs. Mary, 273 George
Conet Henry, bds. 63 Baymiller [Av
Coney Dennis, mach., bds. 35 Central

Coney George C., clk. P. O., 58 Hopkins
Coney James, lab., 249 Broadway
CONEY Martin R., (Hubbel & C,) 47 Mansfeld
Coney Robert, eng., 222 E. Front
Conger Daniel, s.s. Charlotte b. Linn and John
Conger John. cooper, s.s. Charlotte b. Linn and John
Congress Exchange, s.w.c. Pearl and Ludlow
Conie Joseph, confec., 19 Broadway
Conigton Patrick, lab., bds. n.w.c. Mill and Front
Coningham J. H., shoe mkr., bds. 65 W. 5th
Conk George H., miller, 101 Abigail
Conklin Amos, com. mer., 94 Richmond
Conklin David, clk., bds. 124 Mill
Conklin Ellen, 591 W. 6th
Conklin Ellen, 60 Pierson
Conklin George, gilder, bds. 459 W. 8th
Conklin Jerome B., lawyer, 18 David
Conklin John, atty., bds. 198 W. 3d
Conklin Jno., painter, 113 W. Court w. of Central Av
Conklin Oliver P., teacher, 94 Richmond
Conklin Patrick, lab, 591 W. 6th
Conklin Patrick, lab., wks. C. H. & D. R R. repair shops
Conklin Truman, atty. and notary, 245 W. 9th
Conkling David, clk. P. O., h. 124 Mill
Conkling Edgar. 64 W 4th, res. country
Conkling J. L., lard oil manuf., 109 E. 5th, res. Avondale
Conkling Mary, 44 Harrison
CONKLING R. & CO., (Richard C. & Robert Hogue,) White Lead Manuf., 272 Broadway
CONKLING Richard, (R. Conkling & Co.) res. Indian Hill
Conkling W. H. & Co , (Wm. H. C. & Wm. W. Andrews,) com. mer., 56 W. Front
Conkling Wm., (C. Young & Co.,) 286 Broadway
Conkling Wm., cooper, 286 Broadway
Conkling Wm. H., (W. H. C. & Co.,) Ohio Av. Vine St. Hill
Conkling Wm. H., deputy Post Master, h. Vine St. Hill
Conkling, Young & Co., (Wm. C., John Y., B. W. Oliver & Mark Mocar.) keg manufs., 20 Spring
Conlan Abbie, 31 W. Court w. of Central Av
Conlan Hugh, cooper, 39 E. 8th e. of Lock
Conlan Michael, cooper, n.s 7th b. B'dway and Sycamore
Conlan Michael, jr., n.s 7th b. Broadway and Sycamore
Conley Ann, 1 New
Conley Edward, bds. 244 Broadway
Conley John, lab., wks. Chamberlain & Co's
Conley Lawrence, porter, 28 Commerce
Conley Margaret, 35 E. 3d e. of Parsons
Conley Mary, s.e.c. 7th and North
Conley Mollie, 102 W. 4th
Conley Sarah I., 297 W. 3d
Conley Wm., 114 Barr
Conlin Agnes. 21 E. 8th
Conlin Patrick H., dray., bds. 249 E. Pearl e. of Broadway
Conlon James, lab., 404 E. Front
Conlon Michael, cooper, wks 44 E. 2d
Conlon Michael, saddler, 63 Vine
Conlon Pat., blk.smith, bds. V Hughes
Conlondy Wm., blk.smith, 157 Linn
Connahan Gustavus, teacher, bds. s.w.c. Franklin and Broadway
Connahan Patrick, bk. binder, 192 Betts
Connahan Patrick, gardener, s.s. Montgomery Pike nr. Madison Road
Connecticut Fire Ins. Co., agency, 80 W. 3d
Connel Patrick, lab., 84 Water
Connell Ann. nurse, 57 Kossuth
Connell Catharine, 63 W. Front
Connell Charles, lab., wks. 100 Sycamore

Connell Charles, shoe mkr., s.e.c. 14th and Race
Connell Daniel, 82 John
Connell Ellen, 104 W 8th
Connelly Jas., blk.smith, 144 W. Court w. of Central Av
Connell James, lab., s.e.c. 2d and Ludlow
Connell Jeremiah, lab., wks. s.w.c. 5th and Broadway
Connell John, lab., 448 George
Connell John, shoe mkr., bds. 407 W. 3d
Connell Kate, e.s. Henderson al. b. 7th and 8th
Connell,Michael, cab. mkr., wks. 133 E. Front
Connell Michael, lab., bds. n.w.c. Front and Central Av
Connell Patrick, lab., e.s. M. Canal b. 8th and Court
Connell Peter, huckster, 446 W. Front
Connelly Ann, s.s. Phoebe al. b. Plum and Central Av
Connelly Bridget, servant, Galt House
Connelly Bridget, 50 Race
Connelly Catharine, bds. e.s. Pancoast al b. 7th and 8th
Connelly Coleman, lab., 36 Butler
Connel'y Frank, dray., 31 Webb
Connelly Fisty. cof. h., 70 E. Front
Connelly Gregory, lab., 84 Water
Connelly James, cooper. rear 194 E. 6th
Connelly James, lab., 70 E. Front
Connelly James. printer, bds. 16 Harrison
Connelly James W.,s.s. al: b. Pike and Lawrence and 3d and Pearl
Connelly Jefferson,lab.rear 14 Richmond
Connelly Jennie. s.s. al. b. Pike and Lawrence and 3d and Pearl
Connelly John, carp, 20 Richmond
Connelly John, eng., 56 Butler
Connelly John, lab., 326 Main
Connelly John, lab., 15 Vine
Connelly John H., clk., 42 Main, h. 20 Richmond
Connelly Joseph. carp., 66 W. Court w. of Central Av
Connelly Mary, 87 Longworth
Connelly Michael, cooper, 34 E. 8th e. of Lock
Connelly Michael, dray, 172 W. Front
Connelly Michael, porter. 21 E. 2d
Connelly Patrick, 976 E. Front
Connelly Patrick, cof. h. 51 Commerce
Connelly Patrick, copper smith, 1455 E. Front
Connelly Patrick, dray, 31 Webb
Connelly Patrick, lab., 132 W Front
Connelly Peter, baker, c Harriet and Weller
Connelly Richard, lab., wks. at J. A. Fay & Co's
Connelly Richard, blk. smith, bds. n.s. Augusta b. John and Smith
Connelly Thomas, cof. h., 46 Pike
Connelly Thomas, b. and cof. h., n.e.c. Vine and Water
Connelly Thomas, lab., 176 E. 3d e. of Collard
Connelly Thomas, painter, 87 Longworth
Connelton'Andrew, mach., 49 Pendleton
Conner Ben., finisher, wks. n.e.c. Walnut and Canal
Conner Charlotte, 221 Everett
Conner Edmond A., moulder, 154 Webb
Conner Hannah, 243 Laurel
Conner James, blk. smith, 185 Baymiller
Conner James, lab., wks. 222 E. Front
Conner Jeremiah, lab., w.s. Spring b. Liberty and Woodward
Conner John, 57 W. 5th
CONNER John, (P. Lukens & C.,) bds. Walnut St. House
Conner John, mason, 394 Broadway
Conner John. steward, Madison House
Conner John Q. A., dining saloon, 197 Vine, h. 405 Longworth
Conner Kate, servant, s.w.c. 3d and Broadway
Conner Mary, servant, 383 W. 6th
Conner Mary, 100 Baymiller
Conner Richard, clk., 18 Perry

Conner Richard J., salesman, 94 W. Pearl, h. 18 Perry
Conner Wm., cof. h., n.e.c. Front and Ludlow
Conner Wm. H., clk., O. & M. R. R., bds. 238 Longworth
Conner Wm. J., phys., bds. 326 W. 6th
Conner Wesley, 164 Livingston
Conners Dennis, lab., n.s. Augusta b. John and Smith
Conners Johanna, s.w c. 5th and Central Av
Conners John, lab., 130 Central Av
Connerton Andrew, mach., 49 Pendleton
Connerty James, lab., 67 Cherry al
Connerty Patrick, lab., 67 Cherry al
Connet Abel C., carp., 335 Clark
Conney Joseph, finisher,bds. 247 W. 6th
Connolly Bernard, joiner, 210 Cutter
Connolly Dennis, lab., w.s. Kossuth nr. Clark
Connor Benjamin, finisher. 206 Darr
Connor Dennis, cooper, 170 Central Av
Connor Eliza, servant, 422 W. 7th
Connor Frank, lab., 43 Observatory Road
Connor James, blk. smith, 185 Baymiller
Connor John, carp., 100 Race
Connor John, salesman, 30 W. 4th, bds. 151 Broadway
Connor Margaret, servant, 284 Longworth
Connor Martin, lab., bds. 10 Landing b. Main and Walnut
Connor Michael G., foreman, at George Dominick & Bros.
Connor Norn, servant, 562 W. 9th
Connor Phillip, lab., bds. 333 W. 2d
Connor Sauvier D., 238 Longworth
Connor Thomas, com. mer., bds 95 W. 8th
Connor Thomas, lab., 65 E. 8th
Connor Wm..speculator, 470 Elm
Connors James, lab.,n w.c. Fremont and Harriet
Connors Michael, dray., 96 Cherry al
Connors Michael, lab., 19 Mill
Conolly Ann, servant, 124 E. 4th
Conoway Mat., lab., 63 Pierson
Conrad Absolom, whitewasher. e.s. John b. Betts and Clinton
Conrad Casper, lab., at G. & P. Bogen's
Conrad Charles, bar k., 30 Broadway
Conrad Christian.cof. h.,797 Central Av
Conrad George, trunk mkr., 144 Bremen
Conrad George, (Willingter & C.) 598 Walnut
Conrad Jacob, Cin. Chemical Laboratory
Conrad James. h. 56 E. 7th
Conrad John, 77 Mohawk
Conrad John, tailor, 60 13th
Conrad Margaret. 144 Bremen
Conrad Michael, Findlay, b. Central Av. and John
Conrad Monroe. carp., 88 Freeman
Conrad Peter, blksmith, 150 Pleasant
Conrad Peter, boots and shoes, 553 Walnut
Conrad Peter, fruits, 687 Vine
Conrad Peter, lab., 770 W, Front
Conrad Rufus, clk., 24 Harrison
Conrad Valentine, shoe mkr., 21 Clinton
Conradi Chas., finisher, 28 Ham. Road
Conradi Christian, n.s. 12th b. Bremen and Race
Conradi Frederick, carriage manuf., n. w.c. Bremen and 12th, h. n.s. 12th b. Bremen and Race
Conradi Hy., lab , 12 Hughes
Conradi Nicholas, tailor, 106 Bremen
Conradi Peter, blksmith, 150 Pleasant
Conradi Wm., blksmith, 157 Linn
Conradt Frank P., clk., 53 W. Pearl
Conrat Barbara, servt., 333 W. 8th
Conrath Joseph, bds. Cincinnati House
Conrath Peter S., clk. Cincinnati House
Conrey Mary, servt., 457 W. 6th
Conrey Peter, lab., 110 E. 2d
Conrod Nancy, s.s. 6th b. Broadway and Culvert

C ONROY CHARLES,
Family Grocery,
n.e.c. 3d and Central Av

Conroy Dennis, lab., 63 Kossuth
Conroy Michael, tailor, 673 W. 6th
Conroy Patrick C., stewart, 157 Cutter
Conroy Sarah, s.e c. 5th and Butler
Conroy Winnie, clk., n.e.c. 3d and Central Av
Consmiller Fred, lab., 1031 Central Av
Constable A. G. A., atty., room 11 Short's Building

C ONSTANT HENRY,
Wines, Liquors. Cigars, &c., 58 E. 2d, h. 300 Walnut

Constantine W. L., paper hanger, 100 W. 6th, bds. United States Hotel
Constans Charles, cof. h. 460 Vine
Constine Catharine, 624 W 6th
Con.s ate for Duchy of Braunschweig and Luneburg, 632 Main
Continental Ins. Co., agency 65 W. 3d
Conton David, lab., bds. s.w.c. 6th and Plum
Conton Wm., stone mason, bds. s.w.c 6th and Plum
Contun'M'dlle. recluse, Convent of the Good Shepherd
Convent of the Good Shepherd, n.w.c Baymiller and Bank
Conway Catharine, servt., 68 Cutter
Conway Catharine, servt., n.e.c. 3d and Pike
Conway Catharine, 70 Laurel
Conway & Co., printers, 8 W. 3d
Conway Cornelius, (C. & Co) 202 Longworth
Conway James, produce, 434 Sycamore
Conway John, hutcher. 25 State
Conway John, dray, 136 W. Front
Conway John, porter, s.e.c. Race and 3d
Conway John M., carp., 304 Plum
Conway Lawrence, blksmith,3d b. Baum and Parsons
Conway Louis. pipe fitter, wks. n.e.c. Walnut and Canal
Conway M., lab., wks. Chamberlain & Co's
Conway Mason A., painter, e.s. Central Av., b. 7th and 8th, h. n.w.c. Richmond and Baymiller
Conway Mathias, lab , n.s. Taylor b. Carr and Freeman   [worth
Conway Maurice, printer. bds. 202 Longworth
Conway Michael, carp., 58 Elm
Conway Michael, cof. h. s.e.c. 8th and Sycamore
Conway Michael, lab., 57 Pendleton
Conway Michael, pattern mkr., 193 Mound
Conway Michael, teamster, 50 E. 7th
Conway Rev. Moncure D., bds. 435 W. 4th
Conway Patrick, shoe mkr., 101 Smith
Conway Patrick, shoe mkr., bds. 138 Longworth
Conway Rosa, 57 Pendleton
Conway Stephen, lab., s s. Weller b. Carr and Freeman
Conway Thomas, dray. 386 Broadway
Conway Thomas, lab., 91 Hopkins
Conway Thomas, painter, bds. 138 Longworth
Conway Thomas A., n.w.c. Richmond and Baymiller
Conwell Miss, actress, National Theatre
Coogan Michael, grainer, 88 Carr
Coogan Timothy. 88 Carr

C OOK ALBERT L.,
Physician s.w.c. 4th and Broadway
h. n.w.c 6th and Broadway

Cook Alfred M., (M. H. Cook & Co.) res. Delhi Tp.
Cook Ambrose W., 94 Gest
Cook Andrew J., coal measurer, s.e.c. Front and Butler, h. 274 Richmond
Cook Anthony. furniture, 531 Central Av., h. 209 Hopkins
Cook Areanus, h. 163 W. Pearl
Cook August. 139 Wade
Cook Augustus, dray, 156 Wade
Cook Ban. cab. mkr., 233 Hopkins
Cook Barney, carp., 219 Betts
Cook Barney, cof. h. 600 Central.Av
Cook Barncy, lab., wks. Wood and McCoy's

108 (COO) CINCINNATI (COO) DIRECTORY. (COR)

Cook Benj., store fitter, 469 W. 4th
Cook Catharine, phys., 40 Gest
COOK CARTER,
   Stoves and Tinware,
   n.w.c. Richmond and Central Av
Cook Charles, jewelry, 370 W. 5th
Cook Chas., carriage trimmer, wks. 11 Freeman
Cook Cornelius G., wks., 340 W. 3d
Cook Edward, (Edward C. & Co.,)
Cook Edward, driver, 197¼ Plum
Cook Edward & Co., (Edw. C. & Benjamin Hill,) candle manuf., 79 Poplar
Cook Elizabeth, 41 Observatory
Cook Elizabeth, laundress, b. 500 E. Front
Cook Ernst, lab., wks. n.e.c. 7th and Walnut
Cook Fred., bk. mkr., s.s. Ringgold b. Price and Young
Cook Frederick, sexton, s.s. 6th b. Race and Elm
Cook Fritz, lab., wks. Wood and McCoy's
Cook George, clk., 208 Hopkins
Cook George, lab., 12 Dunlap
Cook Hy., bk. mkr., s.s. Ringgold b. Price and Young
Cook Hy., brick yard, s.w.c. Ringgold and Price, h. s.s. Ringgold b. Young and Price   [Av
Cook Hy., cab. mkr., wks. 531 Central
Cook Hy., saddle tree mkr., 654 W. 8th
Cook James, lab., 119 Broadway
Cook James, lab., s.s. Sloo W. of Freeman
Cook James W., bk. layer, 76 Gest
Cook John, 346 Ham. Road
Cook John, cab. mkr., Schiller b. Main and Hughes
Cook John, (Leonard & C.,) n.e.c Findlay and Elder
Cook John G., saddler, 189 Mound
Cook John H., chair mkr., 234 Everett
Cook John L., 267 Walnut
Cook Joseph, cab. mkr., 208 Hopkins
Cook Joseph, cab. mkr., 180 W. Court w. of Central Av
Cook Joseph, clk., 208 Hopkins
Cook Joseph, tailor, 9 David
Cook Joseph S., plants and trees 197 Walnut, h. Walnut Hills
Cook Lizzie, 208 Hopkins
Cook M. H. & Co., (Milton H. C. & Alfred M. Cook,) planing mill, w. s. W. W. Canal b. 5th and 6th
Cook Mahala, s.w.c. Mound and Longworth
Cook Martin, lab., 206 Cutter
Cook Mary, 362 Cutter
Cook Mary Ann, 400 W. Front
Cook Mary E., 365 W. 4th
Cook Michael, blksmith, 666 Race
Cook Michael, shoe mkr., 80 Mill
Cook Milton H., (M. H. C. & C.,) 361 W. 4th
Cook Nicholas, trunk mkr., 49 Bremen
Cook Richard, bds. Dumas Hotel
Cook Seth H., printer, Cin. Gazette, h. 109 George
Cook Theodore, (Barker, Hart & Co.,) 428 W. 6th
Cook Thomas, bds. 166 Vine
Cook Thomas, eng., s.s. Front b. Niagara and Willow
Cook Valentine, cigar mkr., 247 W. 6th
Cook Webster H., b. k., M. H. Cook & Co.,
Cook William, tailor, 30 Pub. Landing, h. 238 Broadway
Cook Wm. D., tinner, wks. n.w.c Richmond and Central Av
Cook Wm. H., plasterer, 137 Clinton
Cook Wm. H., phys, 113 W. 6th h. 151 George
Cooke George, driver, bds. Pennsylvania Hotel
Cooke Geo. T., (Geo. T. & Wm. E. C.,) e.s. Coleman b. Dayton and Findlay
Cooke Geo. T. & Wm. E., pattern mkrs. s.w.c. John and Augusta
Cooke Grant F., clk., 77 W. 3d, bds. s.e.c. 6th and Race

Cooke Jane, 232 E. 6th
Cooke John T., clk., 72 W. 4th, b. 512 W. 9th
Cooke Michael, boiler mkr., 35 Lock n. of 8th
Cooke Richard, carp. and bldr., 45 E. 3d, h. 90 Barr
Cooke Wm. E., (Geo. T. & Wm. E. C.,) n.s. 9th, e. of Baymiller
Cooke Wm. E., clk., auditor's office, L. M. R. R., h. 512 W. 9th w. of Central Av
Cooke Wm., teamster, n.e c. 3d and Wood
Cooley Bridget, servt., 391 W. 6th
Cooley Geo. W., bds. Burnet House
Cooley Matthew, lab., w.s. Pole b. 2d and Pearl
Coolidge Mrs. E. T., 3 George
Coolidge Edwin C., b. k., 185 W. 5th, bds. Spring Grove
Coolidge Elizabeth, bds. 116 John
Coolidge John K., furniture, 185 W. 5th, res. Spring Grove
Coolidge Wm. H., drugs &c., n. e. c. Pearl and Sycamore
Cooling John, pipeman. 1 Crippen al.
Coombe Elijah, cutter, 73 Barr
Coombs David., rope mkr., 207 Everett
COOMBS SAMUEL B.
   Manufacturer of Venetian Blinds,
   230 Vine
Cooms James, carp., 101 Dudley
Coon Barbara, bds. s.e.c. 9th and Walnut
Coon Catharine, bds. s.e.c. Walnut and 9th
Coon Geo., 958 Central Av
COON George, (G. S. C. & Co.,) h. 147 Dayton
COON GEORGE & CO., (George C. John Taylor, & Joseph Taylor,)
   White Mills Distillery, n.e.c. Riddle and Bank
Coon John, carp., 291 Livingston
Coon Levi, 49 Clinton
Coone John J., eng., 932 E Front
Cooney John, lab., s.w.c. Pearl and Butler
Cooney Mary, 18 Commerce
Cooney Patrick, conf. h., 972 E. Front
Cooney Patrick, lab., n.s. Augusta b. John and Smith
Coons Hannah B., teacher, 101 Broadway
Coons Harrison, belt mkr., bds. 97 E. 3d
Coons Hy., eng., n.s. E. Front e. of Washington
Coons Rev. John F., bds. 101 Broadway
Cooty John, eng., 35 Central Av
Coony Judy, laundress, Spencer House
Cooper Abner M., real estate, 35 W. 3d, h. 97 E. 4th
Cooper Abram N., h. 484 John
Cooper Allen, porter, 93 Pleasant
Cooper Andrew J., real estate, 75 W. 3d, h. 18 Richmond
Cooper Andrew S., finisher, 67 Richmond
Cooper Barney, tinner, 304 Longworth
Cooper Barney, watchman, n.e.c. Front and Foster
Cooper Caroline, 72 E. 7th
Cooper Casper, carp., 878 E. Front
Cooper Chas., cab. mkr., s.w.c. 9th and Central Av.
Cooper & Co., (Wm. C. & Rudolph Meyer) cigars. &c., 10 E. Front
Cooper Eliza J., 272 W. 4th
Cooper Enos, teamster, 124 Laurel
Cooper George, mach., wks. 116 W. 2d
Cooper George W., blksmith, n.e c. 3d and Central Av
Cooper Hy., tinner, 304 Longworth
Cooper I. R., salesman, 142 Laurel
Cooper James, (C. & Stokes) b. 365 John
Cooper James C., bakery, n.e.c. Walnut and Water
Cooper John, blksmith, 103 E. 3d e. of Whittaker
Cooper Joseph, 142 Laurel
Cooper Joseph, eng., bds. 31 Hathaway
COOPER Joseph M., drugs, &c., s.w.c. Cutter and Court

COOPER DRS. L. & J. M.
   (Lot & Joseph M.) Physicians,
   s.w.c. Cutter and Court
COOPER Lot, (J L. & J. M. C.) s.w.c. Court and Cutter
Cooper Maria, chamber maid, 196 Plum
Cooper Mary, 136 Linn
Cooper Mary E., 309 W. 4th
Cooper Robert A., grocer, 28 and 30 E. Pearl, h. 129 Dayton
Cooper Samuel S., com. mer. 59 Walnut, h. 333 W. 4th
Cooper & Stokes, (James C. & Samuel S.) auctioneers and com. mer., 14 E. 4th
COOPER THOMAS,
   Coffee House,
   76 W. 3d, h. 38 Race
Cooper Wm., (C. & Co.) res. Newport
Cooper Wm. G., varnisher, 112 Gest
Cooper Wm. W., (Bird, Burrows & Co.) 300 Baymiller
Coopie Wm., lab., 132 Ham. Road
Coors Frederick, Farmers Hotel, 1312 E. Front
Coos Fred., lab., wks. n.w.c. Plum and Wade
Cootz Joseph, porter, 553 Main
Cope Herman, shoe mkr., 79 Spring
Cope John, lab., Pennock al. b. Cutter and Linn
Cope John, lab., al. b. Court and Richmond and Cutter and Linn
Cope John C , bklayer, 193 W. Court w. of Central Av.
Cope Mary, 74 Bank
Cope Wm., bklayer, 654 W. 8th
Copeland Archibald, cook. 54 Richmond
Copeland E., b.k., bds. 160 W. 6th
Copeland Geo. J., b.k., 302 George
Copeland Ira, porter, 31 W. Front
COPELEN G. W., Sec'y Citizens' Ins. Co., n. W. Washington, O.
COPEN ALFRED P.,
   Cooperage and Cooper's Stuff,
   99 Water, bds. 111 W. 5th
Copen Robert, salesman, bds. 31 W. Front
Coppens Charles, teacher St. Xavier College
Coppin Daniel C., pattern mkr., 427 W. 5th
Coppin Joseph, carp., 427 W. 5th
Coppin Wm. G., carp., 140 Spring
Coppock Wm. J. atty., 9 Masonic Temple, bds. 236 Race
Coppresa Joseph, 17th Broadway
Cops Louis, mach., 172 W. 6th
Coquain Wm., huckster, 21 Elizabeth
Cora Nicholas, lab., wks. 25 and 27 Water
Corbets Michael, confec., 210 Sycamore
Corbin Elizabeth, bds. 419 W. 7th
Corbin Geo., bds. 22 Cutter
Corbin John H., auctioneer, 35 Plum
Corbin John S., roofer, 291 W. 5th
Corbin Joseph C., clk. 65 W. 3d, bds. 141 Smith
Corbin Mary J., teacher, 62 Cutter
Corbin Richard, tobacconist, e.s. John b. Betts and Clinton
Corbin Wm., 141 Smith
Corbit Michael, stone mason, 64 Avery
Corbley Francis M., farmer, 595 Central Av.
Corbley Nellie, servt., 103 W. 7th
Corbley Owen, pipe fitter, 465 Plum
Corbus James, cartman, 99 Baum
Corby F. P., 4 Pub. Landing, bds. Winnie House
Corcoran Bridget, chambermaid Black Bear Hotel
Corcoran Dennis, 39 E. 7th
Corcoran Edward, cof. h , 232 Elm
Corcoran Edward, grocery, n.w.c. Smith and Longworth
Corcoran Edward, hostler, n.e.c. 6th and Elm
Corcoran Elizabeth, 223 Hopkins
Corcoran Ellen, tailoress, 158 Baymiller
Corcoran James, cooper, bds. n.e.c. Smith and 6th
Corcoran James, salesman, e.s. Kilgour b. 3d and 5th
Corcoran John, clk., 446 W. 5th
Corcoran John, lab., 458 W. 5th

Corcoran John, molder, 80 Butler
Corcoran John, sawyer, 11 8th above Lock
Corcoran Mary, 232 Elm
Corcoran Mary, servt., 273 W. 4th
Corcoran Michael. cof. h., 18 Landing b. Ludlow and Broadway
Corcoran Nancy, 444 W. 5th
Corcoran Patrick, cooper, n.e.c. Smith and 6th
Corcoran Patrick, dray, 29 Lock n. of 8th
Corcoran Philip, fireman, 444 W. 5th
Corcoran Thomas, cof. h. s.w.c. Vine and Water
Corcoran Thos., porter. 60 Hunt
Corday Wm., porter, bds. 23 Water
Corde Hy., blksmith, 67 Pendleton
Cordege Mary, servt. Broadway Hotel
Corderman Geo., bklayer, bds. 11 Chestnut [nut
Corderman John W., bklayer, 11 Chestnut
Corders Christopher, butcher, 61 Ham. Road
Cordes Cort., 40 Mohawk
Cordes Diedrich, grocery, n.w.c. York and Baymiller
Cordes Sophia, 18 Allison
Cordesman H. J. & D. Dierker, (Hy. J. C. & Deidrich D.) foundry, 137 W. 2d
Cordesman Hy. J., (H. J. C. & D. Dierker) 339 Clark
Cordesman Wm. A., b.k., 339 Clark
Cordon Gerhard, cooper, bds. 61 Bremen
Cordray David, bds. 172 W. 6th
Cordry John J., carp., h. n.s. Nassau b. Reed and Brond
Cordukes John, b.k. 69 Vine, b. 74 W. 4th
CORDUKES Jonathan, (Gilmore & Co.) h. Belfast, Ireland
CORDUKES Thomas. (Morrison, C. & Co.) bds. Burnet House
Corehouser John, lab., wks. s.e.c. Canal and Vine
Corel John, coach mkr., Vine Street Hill
Corell Chas., compositor, w.s. Vine b. 14th and 15th
Coren Daniel, painter, bds. 109 Longworth
Cores Frederick, lab., 684 Main
Corey Leander H., supt Niles Works, h. Spencer Tp.
Corhaus John, lab., 52 Abigail
Coriell Levi T., b.k. A. L. Mowry's h. 589 W. 8th
Corigan Philip, lab., bds. 247 W. 6th
Cork Michael, lab., 93 Water
Corken Patrick, cooper, 328 W. 6th
Corken Peter, bklayer, bds. 74 Longworth
Corkhill Philip, n.e.c. Liberty and Pendleton
Corkin Hugh, lab., s.s. McFarland e. of Hill
Corkmeier Fred., hostler, bds. 24 Gano
CORLISS Daniel G., (S. N. Marsh, C. & Co.) h. 178 Elm
Cormack Robert, finisher, wks. n.e.c. Walnut and Canal
Cornamus Jacob, dray, 93 Martin
Cerneau Charles H., clk. 16 W. 2d, bds. 73 Clinton
Corneau D. Ellis, clk. 12 W. 2d, h. 73 Clinton
Corneau Rebecca, 73 Clinton
Cornelius Conrad, barber. 610 Vine
Cornelius Elizabeth, 546 Race
Cornelius Geo., scale mkr., bds 426 Vine
Cornelius John G., lab., 114 W. Liberty
Cornelius Lorenz, porter, s.s. Allison b. Walnut and Vine
Cornelius Maxwell, foreman C. H. & D. R R. blacksmith shop
Cornelius Michael, blksmith, bds. 674 W. W. 6th
Cornelius Mrs. R. A., confec., 234 Elm
Cornelius Valentine, cab. mkr., 299 Clark
Cornelius Valentine, shoe mkr., h. rear 176 Clay
Cornelius Wilbur F., painter, 142 Clinton
Cornell Wm., baker, wks. 118 W. 5th
Corner David L., salesman 90 W. 5th, bds. 131 Longworth

Corners John, lab., 69 Richmond
Corney Jane, servt., 109 Pike
Corney Wm., s.s. 6th b. Vine and Race
Cornish Ann. 21 Hannibal
Cornman L. E., lab., wks. John Mitchell's
Cornman S., lab., wks. John Mitchell's
Cornwell Smith, molder, 222 E. Front
Corr Michael, lab., 30 Lock
Corragan Martin, lab., 391 W. 8th
Corre Albert, bar k. National Theater Bldg.
Correvont Francis, cof. h. 1112 Central Av.
Correvont Joseph, barber, 447 W. 2d
Correvont Leonard, barber, s.s. Pearl b. Pike and Butler
Correvont Rudolph, barber, s.e.c. Everett and Cutter
Corrigan Hugh, plasterer, 487 W. 5th
Corry James C, 96 Longworth
Corry Thomas F., 96 Longworth
Corry Wm., mach., s.s. 7th b. Freeman and Curr
CORRY WILLIAM M., Attorney at Law, Metropolitan Building. n.e.c. 9th and Walnut, h. Vine Street Hill
Corry Wm. P., 96 Longworth
Corte Frederick, lab., 173 Oliver
CORWIN DANIEL W.. Wholesale Dealer in Foreign and Domestic Dry Goods, 88 and 90 W. Pearl, b. 151 W. 4th
Corwin Frank W., clk., 88 W. Pearl, h. 151 W. 4th
Corwin Henry R., lumber, 244 E. Pearl e. of Broadway, h. 121 E. 3d
Corwine James B., n.e.c. Dayton and Whiteman
CORWINE RICHARD M., Attorney at Law, room 7, Short's Building, bds. Burnet House
Corwine Samuel L., 339 George
Cory Johanna, bds. 57 Broadway
Cose Margaret, 180 E. Pearl
Cosgriff Edward, lab., 67 E. 8th, e. of Lock
Cosgriff James, lab., 42 Accommodation
Cosgrove Burnett, lab., 651 W. Front
Cosgrove John, lab., 16 E. 8th, e. of Lock
Cosgrove Peter, expressman, n s. 7th, b. Broadway and Sycamore
Cosgrove Otway, 8 E. 7th
Cosgrove Thomas, cof. h., n.s. 8th, b. Broadway and Sycamore
Cosgrove Thomas, carp., 74 Gest
Coshutter Mary, servt., 124 E 4th
Coslowe Michael, lab., 740 W. 6th
Coss Christopher, lab., h. n.s. Avery al. w. of Wood
Coss Daniel, lab., n.s. Augusta, b. John and Smith
Cossen James, cook n s. Grandin al. b. Elm and Plum
Cossen Mrs. Mary, cook, n.s. Grandin al. b. Elm and Plum
Cost Hy., 84 Laurel
Costello Mrs. Catharine, 153 W. Front
Costello Edward, lab., n.s. Friendship al. b. Lawrence and Pike
Costello Ellen, 58 W. Court
Costello John, blk. smith, 48 Pierson
Costello John, clk., n.s. Corp. line, Mt. Auburn
Costello John, huckster, 92 W. Front
Costello John, lab., 556 W. Front
Costello John, lab., 151 W. Miami Canal
Costello Michael, dray, 76 Pierson
Costello Thomas, clk., 138 W. 5th
Costello Thomas, lab., 136 Water
Costello Thomas, millinery, 138 W. 5th
Costello Timothy, tailor, 106 E. 6th
Costello William, clk., 138 W. 5th
Costello William, lab., s.s. Friendship al. b. Pike and Butler
Costello William, marble cutter, 156 Cutter
Coster James, lab., w.s. Langdon al., b. 6th and 7th
Costigan Mary, servt., Burnet House
Costigan Mary, servt., 520 W. 7th
Costigan Nora, servt., 520 W. 7th
Costigan Wm., porter, 539 W. 8th

Cotney Barbara, seamstress, 510 Plum
Cottenbrink Rudolph lab., 54 Kossuth
Cotter Henry, (C. & Wessing)
Cotter Patrick, tailor, 105 Main
Cotter & Wessing, (Henry C. & Frank H. W.,) cof. h., 9 Landing, b. Broadway and Ludlow
COTTERAL & GOLDSWORTHY, (J. W. C. & T. G.,) Carpenters and Builders, 328 Elm
COTTERAL Joseph W., (C. & Goldsworthy,) 324 W. 9th
Cotterell Nellie. bds. 51 Broadway
Cottle Rodman H., bk. mason, 158 Cutter
Cottle Wm. F., house mover, 220 Cutter
Cottman N., mach., wks. n.s. Front, b. Lawrence and Pike
COTTMAN Thomas, (Garrett & C.,) 332 Race
Cottom Even J., clk., 59 W. Pearl, h. 280 George
Cottom John W., 59 W. Pearl, h. 280 George
Cotton Lyman S., civil eng. L. M. R. R. bds. 36 Longworth
Cottonbrook Hy., clothier, 88 E. Pearl, e. of Broadway
Cottrell Geo. W., liquors, 164 Spring
Cottrell Ida, bds. 43 Lodge
Cotts Mary, h. 417 Broadway
Cotty Wm., carp., 19 Hathaway
Couch John R., eng., w.s. Ramsey n. of Front
Couch Wash., eng., w.s. Ramsey, b. Front and W. W. Canal
COUDEN MISS E. B., Millinery Store, 7 E. 4th.
Coughlan James, bds., 64 Gest
Coughlan John, 64 Gest
Coughlan John, jr., eng., bds 64 Gest
Coughlan John, lab., bds. 64 Gest
Coughlan Michael, lab., bds. 64 Gest
Coughlan Daniel, cooper, 41 Lock, n. of 8th
Coughlin Jerry, 39 Lock, n. of 8th
Coughlin John, cooper, 41 Lock n. of 8th
Coughlin Joseph B., clk., 310 Main
Coughlin Margaret, bds. 379 W. 8th
Coughlin Thomas, cooper, 41 Lock n. of 8th
Coughlin Thomas, lab., w.s. Langdon al. b. 6th and 7th
Coughlin Thomas, printer, n.s. Hathaway, b. Jane and Baymiller
Coughlin Wm., 80 Baum
Cousins Mrs. Sarah A., 20 E. 7th
Coulter Bernhard V., clk., bds. 463 W. 7th
Coulter David, 46 E. Front
Coulter Wm., glass cutter, 102 E. 2d
Coultry John, lab. bds. 48 W. Front
Coultry Martin, cof. h., 48 W. Front
Coultry Patrick, lab., bds. 46 W. Front
Counte Joseph O., porter, w.s. Henderson al. b. 7th and 8th
Counterman Daniel, h 39 Jones
COUNTY AUDITOR'S OFFICE, Court House,
  William Ward. Auditor.
COUNTY CLERK'S OFFICE Court House,
  Charles E. Cist. Clerk.
COUNTY COMMISSIONER'S OFFICE in Auditor's Office, Court House.
COUNTY SHERIFF'S OFFICE, Court House,
  John B. Armstrong, Sheriff.
COUNTY TREASURER'S OFFICE, Court House,
  O. H. Geoffroy, Treasurer.
Court House, e.s. Main, opp. Court
Courtes John, shoemkr., 402 Elm
Courtman Theodore. carp., 240 Clark
Courtney John, harness mkr., 59 Observatory
Courtney Mary, dress mkr., h. 214 W. Court, w of Central Av.
Courtney Michael L., student, bds. 214 W. Court, w. of Central Av.
Courtney T. F., river man, bds. 10 Sycamore

110 (COY) CINCINNATI (CRA) DIRECTORY. (CRA)

Courtly Thos., lab., 84 Water
Courtwright Geo. S., phys. Commercial Hospital
Courtwright Jennie, bds. s.e.c. 6th and Smith
Cousins Samuel, dray., wks. n.e.c. Elm and M. Canal
Cousins Wylie, barber, 234 Longworth
Couson John, lab., bds. n.w.c. Mill and Front
Coussin John, tobacconist, 140 Longworth
Coutou Peter, tailor, bds. 125 Main
Coutts James, lab., 128 Mound
Coverdale Robert T., gas fitter, 262 W. Court w. of Central Av.
Covert Preston, harness mkr., bds. 185 Barr
Covington Eli, white-washer, 435 George
Cowan Fred., 164 Dayton
Cowan George, janitor, 335 Walnut
Cowan Hy., photographs, 92 W. 5th, b. 119 Elm
Cowan James, lab., 401 Sycamore
Cowan John H., shoemkr., 556 Central Av.
Cowan Thos., lab., 30 Lock
Cowe Hy., 53 W. 3d
Cowen James, shoemkr., 13 Hannibal
Cowey Charles, shoemkr., wks. Pavillion b. Observatory and 3d
Cowey Thomas, lab., 30 Lock
Cowgill Eliza, 469 Elm
Cowgill Wm., b. k., 51 W. Front, bds. 107 Pike
Cowing E. H., b. k., 11 W. Front
Cown John, tailor, 213 W. 3d
Cowpland John C., mer., 309 Clark
Cox Abel, mach., 261 W. 5th, h. 28 Betts
Cox Alexander H., mach., bds. 214 W. Front
Cox Ann, n.s. 6th, e. of Lock
Cox David, chair mkr., 72 Clark
Cox Edwin, notary public, 23 W. 3d, h. 530 W. 9th
Cox Eliza, 507 Sycamore
Cox Geo B., carp., 240 Cutter
Cox John, clk., 435 W. 5th
Cox John, eng., 48 Baum
Cox John, lace manuf. 16 E. 4th
Cox John H., laces, &c., 16 E. 4th
Cox John S., carp. 300 W. Front
Cox John S., druggist, 493 Central Av.
Cox Joseph, atty., n.w.c. Walnut and 5th. h. Storrs Tp.
Cox Joseph, coachman, 505 Race
Cox Joseph B., watchman, 377 W. 9th, w. of Freeman
Cox Lucy, 16 Union
Cox Margaret O., teacher, 498 Central Av.
Cox Myron S., atty., 3 Apollo Bldg., h. 167 Baymiller
Cox Patrick, blk. smith, 26 15th
Cox Richard K. sen., foreman 221 W. 5th h. 530 W. 9th
Cox Richard K. jr., chief clk. co. treas. office, h. 267 Richmond
Cox Robert, w.s. Lawrence b. 4th and 5th
Cox Robert, blk. smith, bds. 319 Baymiller
Cox Robert S., 224 Clinton
Cox Susan, 469 W. 3d
Cox Thomas, carriage mkr., bds. 319 Baymiller
Cox William R., painter, 455 W. 3d, h. 367 W. 4th
Coxson James, fireman, 136 W. 3d
Coyle & Co., (Phillip C., Patrick Lavalle & John Coyle,) fruits, &c., 25 Broadway
Coyle Mrs. Elizabeth, 319 John
Coyle Fletcher, speculator, 118 John
Coyle Hugh, clk., h. 249 Sycamore
Coyle John, (C & Co.,) 249 Sycamore
Coyle Michael, bds. 249 Sycamore
Coyle Peter W., clk., 249 Sycamore
Coyle Phillip, fruits, n.e.c. 5th and Walnut, h. 249 Sycamore
Coyle Robert K., salesman, 89 E. 4th
Coyle Rosa, 53 Spring
Coyle Thomas D., carp., 473 W. 7th
Coyn James, lab., n.e.c. 4th and Wood
Coyn John, bds. 1234 E. Front
Coyne Ann, 61 E. 4th
Coyne Owen, cooper, 122 E. 6th

Coyne Patrick, 50 McFarland
Coyne Patrick, lab., Maiden Lane, b. Gas al. and Anderson al
Coyne Patrick, walter, Madison House
Coyne Vincent, gold pen mkr., bds. Dennison House
Cozine Jacob, rope mkr., 133 Wade
Cozine Jane D, 655 Elm
Cozine James C., belt mkr., 417 W. Liberty
Cozzens Alfred A., cooper, bds. 57 E. 3d
Cozzens John, roller, 140 Longworth
Crade John, fireman, n.e.c. Smith and Water
Craddick Martin, hostler, bds. 229 W. 6th
Cradduck Susan, 201 Betts
Cr ft Isaac, eng., 212 Elm
Craft Jacob, foreman, 465 2d
Craft Jacob, salesman, bds. n.w.c. Mill and Front
Craft James, teamster, 207 W. Front
Craft Jenny, w.s. St. Clair, nr. 7th
Craft Lizzie, s.e.c. North and New
Crager Louis, wagon mkr., Mansfield, b. Sycamore and Broadway
Cragg Frank T., b.k., w s. Freeman, ft. George, bds. 218 Barr
Cragg Hy., clk., bds. 27 Longworth
Crago Wm., cof. h., 202 W. 6th
Craig ——, bds. 185 W. 3d
Craig Alexander, baker, 59 E. 7th
Craig Andrew W., mach., 42 Plum
Craig Hy., mer., bds. 27 Longworth
Craig Isabella, 38 New
Craig J. C., bds. Dennison House
Craig James, carp., 216 Cutter
Craig James. 477 W. 4th
Craig James C., 485 Broadway
Craig James G , atty., Masonic Temple, h. 5 Harrison
Craig James H., finisher, 42 Plum
Craig James S., carp., 216 Cutter
Craig John, 129 W. Front
Craig John R., com. mer., 5 Harrison
Craig Lucinda, h. 5 Harrison
CRAIG ROBT. S., Brush Manufacturer, 240 Central Av., h. 324 W. 6th
Craig Thomas, bk. binder, n.s. New e. of Broadway
Craig Wm. B., (R. Brown & Co.,) 5 Harrison
Craighton Peter, carp., 58 Clark
Crail Milton, salesman, 53 W. Pearl, h. s.w.c. 5th and Park
Crain Hy., driver, 102 Bank
Crain Martin, grocery, 47 Plum
Crain Michael, blksmith, 130 E. 6th
Crambert Lawrence, box mkr., 199 W. Front
Crameng Bernard, cooper, 140 Abigail
Cramer Agnes, servt., 385 W. 5th
Cramer Anthony, furniture, 68 Clinton
Cramer Chas. F., cigars, 67 Wade
Cramer Edward, cigar mkr., bds. 127 Ham. Road
Cramer George R., 65 Clinton
Cramer Jennie, bleacher, bds. 69 Bank
Cramer John B., grocer, 322 W. 9th, w. of Central Av
Cramer Joseph, meats, 253 Broadway
Cramer Rev. M. J., bds. 80 Lawrence
Cramp Michael, cof. h., 460 Elm
Crampelman John C., dray, 772 W. Front
Cramsay Wm., upholsterer, s.w c. Mound and Longworth, h. 141 Mound
Crance August, lab., 158 E. 5th
CRANCH & CHALLEN, (Edward P. C., & James R. C.,) Attorneys at Law and Solicitors for Soldiers Claims, Notaries and Commissioners, s.c.c. 4th and Vine
CRANCH Edward, (C. & Challen,) res. E. Walnut Hills
Crandall Solomon S., shoe mkr., 273 Cutter
Crane Abbie C., teacher, 328 W. 8th
Crane Aurelia F., teacher, 139 Barr
CRANE, BREED & CO., (Martin H C., Abel D. B & Wm. J. Breed,) Metalic Burial Cases and Hearses, Office and Manufactory s.s. 8th, West of Freeman
Crane Celia, e.s Mound, b. Longworth and 5th

Crane Hy. L., salesman, 426 W. 4th
Crane James, carp., 70 Laurel
Crane James C., com. mer., 346 Walnut, h. Mt. Auburn
Crane John C., pipe fitter, wks. n.e.c. Walnut and Canal
Crane L. M., furniture, 81 Sycamore
CRANE Martin H., (Crane, Breed & Co.,) h. 193 W. 7th
Crane Mary, e.s. Kilgour, b. 3d and 5th
Crane Patrick, lab., n.s. Augusta, b. John and Smith
Crane Sarah F., 139 Barr
Crane Wm. L., bds. 426 W. 4th
Cranley John, fireman, 2 Race
Cranley John, shoe mkr., w.s. Race, b. Front and Water
Cranmer Joseph, fireman, Madison House
Cranston Wm. B., watchman, n.w.c. Hazen and Railroad
Crapo Wm., meats, 169 Richmond
Crapsey Mrs. Edward, bds. w.s. Ohio Av., b. Calhoun and North Elm
CRAPSEY JACOB T., Atty. at Law, n.w.c. 6th and Walnut, h. Ohio Av. b. Calhoun and North Elm
Crapsey Thomas G., student, bds. Ohio Av. b. Calhoun and North Elm
Crary Charles L., clk., h. 55 Clinton
Crazy Samuel, 926 Central Av
Craschy Hy., Allauthus, b. York and Dayton
Cratec Elizabeth, 557 W. 8th
Craven Ezekiel, 170 Smith
Craven Francis A., bds. 451 W. 8th
Craven G. T., salesman, 25 W. 4th
Craven Moses, paper dealer. 12 E. Pearl, h. s.s. 9th, b. Main and Walnut
Craven Nancy, 118 Everett
Craven Sarah, 170 Smith
Craven Thomas, b. k., 267 Richmond
Craven Wm., foreman, 170 Smith
Crawford Andrew, 105 Betts
Crawford Andrew, 376 Clark
Crawford Benjamin, mach , 374 Clark
Crawford Benjamin J. express driver, 376 Clark
Crawford Charles, actor, 44 E. 3d
Crawford David, 143 Race
Crawford Elizabeth, bds. 61 Everett
Crawford Frank, painter, 591 Main
Crawford Frank, painter, bds. 462 Sycamore
CRAWFORD Geo., (George C. & Co.) 11 George
CRAWFORD GEORGE & CO., (Geo. C., Geo. W. C., & John S. C.,) Com. Mer. and Importers of Soda Ash, Sal Soda, and Caustic Soda, 209 Walnut
CRAWFORD Geo. W., (George C. & Co.,) h. 11 George
Crawford James, molder, wks. C. T. Dumont's
Crawford James A., salesman, 352 W. 6th, b. Mound and Smith.
CRAWFORD JOHN, Dry Goods, 76 W. 5th, h. s s. Dayton, b. Linn and Baymiller
Crawford John, plasterer, rooms 300 John
CRAWFORD John S., (George C. & Co.,) h. Glendale
Crawford Louis V., wheel-wright, 163 Linn
Crawford Mary, 55 Hopkins
CRAWFORD S. T., Atty. at Law, 30 W. 4th, h. e.s Freeman, 2d door above Findlay
Crawford Thomas, bds. Clermont Hotel
Crawford Thomas, paper carrier, 102 Baum [more
Crawford Wm., s.s. Mount, nr. Sycamore
Crawford Wm., dray, 63 Observatory
Crawford Wm., wks. J. Whitaker's, Deer Creek Valley
Crawford Wm , lab., Franklin Brewery, s.s. Reading Pike
Crawford Wm., turner, 570 Central Av
CRAWFORD WM. A., (Henry Marks & Co.,) h. Covington
CRAWFORD Wm. D., (Arnold & C.,) h. Hamilton

Crawford Wm M. painter, 54 York
Crawley Edwin, bk. binder, 43 Main
Crawley F. S., teacher, Mt. Auburn Institute
Crawly Johanna, waiter, Dennison House
Crawly Wm., sawyer, n.s. Nassau, e. of Broad
Crayberker Joseph, mach., 420 Sycamore
Creager Albert, blksmith, wks. 55 and 57 E. 5th
Crenin George, horse trader, 357 W. 7th
Crealmon James, baker, wks. 118 W. 5th
Creary Charles, 53 Clinton
Credon Mary, servt., 181 W. 4th
Creed Dennis, grocery, n.e.c. Jackson and 12th
Creedon Peter, tailor, s.e.c. 7th and Broadway
Creelman Solomon, baker, 409 W. 4th
Creer Charles, lab., wks. n.s. Front, b. Lawrence and Pike
Cref Mary, seamstress, n.e.c. Linn and Betts
Cregar Bernard, mach., 490 W. 3d
Cregar Jonathan, mach., 424½ George
Cregar Samuel P., cof. h., n.e.c. Elm and 15th
Crehore James, 134 Richmond
Creiger August, cof. h., 718 Central Av
Creiger Casper, peddlar, 363 Central Av
Creighton Peter, carp., Burnet House
Crellen Hy., shoe mkr., 379 W. 2d
Cremering Barney, cooper, 149 Abigail
Cremm John, molder, 147 Bremen
Creppel Frederick, cof. h., s.s. Front w. of Hill
Creppel Hy., saloon, 325 W. 5th
Cresap Daniel J., tailor, 144 Clark
Cresap Margaret, 62 Barr
Cress M. M. V., driver, 688 W. Front
Cress Theodore M., driver, 3d and 4th St. R. R
Cress Wm. L., checkman, I. C. R. R., 91 Carr
Cressler John, bds. Dennison House
Crete John, lab., n.e.c. Smith and Water
Creutz J., atty., s.e.c. Main and Court, h. 484 York
Crever J. A., teacher. 192 Oliver
Crewel Samuel, driver, wks. s.e.c. Grant and Plum
Crews James II., bds. 206 W. 5th
Crews S P., phys., bds. 318 W. 5th
Crewsan Wm., lab., 131 W. Front
Cribb Bernhard, baker, wks. 118 W. 5th
Crichton David, druggist, s.e.c. 5th and Broadway
Crichton Wm., salesman, at Gaylord, Son & Co., bds. Burnet House
Cridland C. E., portrait painter, 60 E. 3d, h. Newport
Crigley Michael, lab., 136 Water
Crimon Charles, musician, 538 Main
CRIPPEN ABRAHAM T., Eating Saloon, 212¼ W. 6th
Crippen Arthur, watchman, 122 W. 9th w. of Central Av
Crippen Ellen, 3 Gorman
Crippen Lydia, 122 W. 9th w. of Central Av
CRIPPEN WM. G., Editor Cin. Daily Times, 62 W. 3d h. 448 W. 6th
Cripple Jerry, bds. 3 Gorman
Criscall John, stone cutter. 32 12th
Criss Joseph, mate. bds. 12 E. Front
Crist Peter, lab., 87 Martin
Cristman Jacob, 228 Clinton
Critchell Robert S., clk., 171 Vine
Critchell Mrs. S. A., 171 Vine
CRITTENDEN L. B. & CO., Coal Dealers, 46 Mill
CRITTENDEN Lyman B., (L. B. C. & Co.) 507 W. 8th
Crittenden Solomon A., clk., bds, 507 W. 8th
Croaker Wm., express, 49 Mill
Croake Wm., lab., e.s. Anderson al. b. 2d and Pearl
Crocamp Henry, moulder, wks. n.w.c. Plum and Wade
Croche Christopher, finisher, 101 Woodward

Crocker Louis H., moulder, wks. n.w.c. Plum and Wade
Crotcker Valentine B., painter, 46 Observatory
Croell Sylvanus, blk. smith, 612 E. Front
Croffort Mary, 41 Elm
Crofton Edward C., carp.. 943 Elm
Crofton Mary, servant, 288 Longworth
Croghen Mary, s.s. 6th b. Broadway and Culvert
Crokeman Henry, lab., wks. 91 M. Canal
Croley James, hinge fitter, wks. n.e c. Walnut and Canal
Croley John, molder, wks. Chamberlain & Co's
Crolie Cornelius, e.s. Pancoast al. b. 7th and 8th
Croll Theodore, trunk mkr., wks. 509 Plum
Crolley Sarah, 173 Longworth
Crome August, eng., 11 Madison
Crompton Ebeneezer, tin ware, n.e.c. Central Av. and George, h. 214 W. 5th
Crompton Margaret, fancy goods, 214 W. 5th
Cromwell Chas. L., supt., Broadway Hotel
Cromwell Eliza, s.e.c. Front and Brooklyn
CROMWELL JOSEPH H., Prop'r., Broadway Hotel, s.e c. 2d and Broadway
Cromwell Peter, stone cutter, Pennock al b. Mound and Cutter
Cronamus George, dray, 103 Martin
Cronan Catharine, servant, 426 W. 6th
Cronan Cornelius, 48 Lock b. of 8th
Cronan Cornelius, drays, s.s. Webb b. Wood and Stone
Cronan Daniel, shoe mkr., 28 Jackson
Cronan Dennis, lab., s.s. 6th b. Culvert and Broadway
Cronan Jeremiah, dray, 516 W. 3d
Cronan Jeremiah, dray, bds. 261 W. 9th
Cronan John, lab , 225 E. 6th
Crone B., tinner, wks. n.w.c. Race and 2nd
Crone Barney, rope mkr., h. 25 Mill
CRONE BENJAMIN, Carpenter shop w.s. Cutter b. Betts and Clinton, h. 121 Clinton
Crone George P., grocer, 147 Clinton
Crone Joseph, clk., 24 W. Pearl, h. 524 W. 7th
Crone John, 524 W. 7th
Cronemus George, 83 Martin
Crones Henry, pipe fitter, wks. n.e.c. Walnut and Canal
Cronin Andrew, wks. 222 E. Front
Cronin Cornelius, plain mkr., 48 Lock
Cronin Dennis, dray, 202 E. 6th
Cronin Dennis, lab., wks. 200 Vine
Cronin Dennis J., mer., 468 Broadway
Cronin Ellen, chambermaid, Burnet House
Cronin Jeremiah, 468 Broadway
Cronin Julia, 468 Broadway
Cronin Martin, shoe mkr., 26 12th
Cronin Mary, chambermaid, Burnet House
Cronin Michael, tailor. 32 North
Cronin Patrick, lab., 24 Lock n. of 8th
Cronin Stephen, huckster 131 Spring
Cronin T. & C , lard oil manuf., 28 Water
Cronin Timothy, (T. C. & Co.,) 141 W. Front
Cronin Timothy, lab., 38 Lock n. of 8th
Cronin Wm'. shoe mkr., n.s. 7th b. Sycamore and Broadway
Croning Morris, lab., n.s. Elder b. Campbell al. and Elm
Cronon Margaret, 386 Broadway
Crooker Eliza, 359 George
Crooks Charles T. clk., s.e.c. Main and 6th, h. 268 Main
Crooks John, boots and shoes, 268 Main
CROOKSHANK E. D., Treasurer Hamilton County, Office Court House, h. Cheviot
Crookston J. H., salesman, 200 Smith
Crookston James, clk., bds. 209 Longworth

Cropper A. H , phys. 133 Laurel
Cropper Cyrus, bk. binder, 111 Main, h. Cumminsville
Crosby Frederick L., clk., bds. 121 E. 3d
CROSBY GEORGE, Bookseller and Stationer, 41 W. 4th, res. Spring Garden
Crosby James, mach., w.s. Ruse b. Front and 2d
Crosby W. E., principal 6th dist. school, res. Avondale
Crosdale —, driver, bds. 65 Broadway
Croset Sarah, 16 Abigail
CROSLEY Josiah, (Matson & C.) Mt. Washington
Crosley Ross. painter, 219 Broadway
Cross David T., mach., 10J Baymiller
Cross C., blk. smith, 169 Water
Cross Christopher, lab., 492 E. Front
Cross Hannah B., 441 W. 8th
Cross John B , b.k., 107 Baymiller
Cross John C., clk. Co. Recorder's office, h. s.s. Mercer nr. Walnut
Cross Julius, goldsmith, 16 Mercer
Cross Truman, 63 E. 7th
Cross Wilson. mach., 231 Richmond
Crosset Joseph, lab., 343 Broadway
Crosset Margaret, s.s. Court b. Main and Sycamore
Crosset Wm., dray, 10 Clinton
Crossley Reuben, driver, h. 76 Richmond
Crossman John, janitor, 354 W. 4th
CROSSMAN WM., Agent for Clark Williams, room No. 1, Art Union Bldg., h. 309 W. 6th
Crostone Marg., n.e.c. 7th and Sycamore
Crother John H., grocery, 582 Central Av
Crothers Wm., lab., 50 Abigail
Crotty Edward, lab., 102 Butler
Crotty Edmund, lab., 518 John
Crotty Francis M., clk., 101 W. 4th, bds. E. 5th
Crotty John, lab., 152 John
Crotty Mary, 156 Mound
Crotty Michael, shoe mkr., bds. 136 Mound
Crotty Thos., clk., 161 W. 4th, h. 343 E. 5th
Crotty Thos., porter, 351 W. 5th
Crotty Wm., lab, 102 Butler
Crotty Thomas, stone cutter, bds. 156 Mound
Crouch Geo. W., plasterer, 190 Betts
Crouch James M., plasterer, 190 Betts
Crouch D , cooper, 190 Betts
Crouch Wesley, photographer, 92 W. 5th, bds. 190 Betts
Croughan John tinner, w.s. Pike b. Pearl and 3d
Crouse Geo. W., cigars, s.w.c. Court and Central Av
Crouse Jacob S., auctioneer, 17 E. 5th h. 225 Baymiller
Crout Henry, flour mill, junc. Leatherburry and E. Front, res. Covington
Crouts George W., foreman, 457 Sycamore
Crow Emily P. dress mkr., 83½ George
Crow James, gold pen mkr., 3 Park'
Crow Matthew, printer, 19 Butler
Crow Patrick, lab., 138 Mound
Crow Thomas,'98 Cherry al
Crowder Jacob, cook, 11 Pancoast al
Crowder James, wagon mkr., s w.c. Vance and E. Front, h. 1258 E. Front
Crowe Matthew, printer, bds. 86 Butler
Crowel John, 466 John
Crowell Samuel, ice dealer, 47 Elizabeth
CROWLEY Albert G., (C. & Co.) 328 W. 5th
Crowley Alvin, 147 W. Pearl
Crowley C. J., compositor, Cin. Gazette h. 297 W. Front
CROWLEY & CO., (Albert G. & John Seeman,) Grocery, 328 W. 5th
Crowley Cornelius J , printer, 70 Gano
Crowley Frank, chair mkr., 225 Cutter
Crowley Henry, molder, 166 Spring
Crowley J. F , printer, bds. s.e.c. 9th and Walnut
Crowley John, lab., w.s. Langdon al. b. 6th and 7th

112 (CUL) CINCINNATI (CUN) DIRECTORY. (CUR)

Crowley John B. moulder, bds. 114 Hunt
Crowley Lizzie, dress mkr., bds. 328 W. 5th
Crowley Mary, servant, Burnet House
Crown Anthony, lab. 446 W. 3d
CROWTHER EDWARD W., Drugs, Medicines, Chemicals, &c., n.e.c. 7th & Mound and s.w c. 6th and Central Av
CROWTHER F. A. & BRO., (Fred. A. C. & Edward W. C.) Drugs, Medicines, Chemicals, &c., n.w.c. Richmond and Baymiller
CROWTHER Fred A., (F. A. C. & Bro.) h. n.w.c. Richmond and Baymiller
CROWTHER George H., (Morrison & C.) 26 W. Court w. of Central Av
Crowther Henry, clk., n.e.c. 7th and Mound
Crowther John, finisher, wks. 141 W. 2d
Crowther Phillis, h. 101 Mound
Crozier Sophia, servant, 94 E. 4th
Cruger Peter, eng., 581 W. 5th
Cruise Hunt D., clk., 410 W. 4th
Cruise Jane, bds. 77 Baymiller
Cruise John J., b.k., 14 E. 2d, h. 56 Mound
Cruise John J., clk., bds. 125 W. 5th
Cruise Mrs. M. T., bds. 125 W. 5th
Cruise Wm., bds. 125 W. 5th
Cruise Wm. G., bds. 125 W. 5th
Cruitt Listen, fireman, e.s. Stone b. 4th and 5th
Cruter John, tailor, bds. 64 Barr
Crum Chas., lab., 202 Cutter
Crumir Wm., mach., 542 E. Front
Crumley Hugh, collector, 36 Butler
Crumley Thos., mach., 354 W. 6th
Crumpton Samuel E., japanner, 209 W. 5th. h. Covington
Crundell John, bklayer, 247 Hopkins
Crusaw Wm., lab., wks. 196 W. Pearl
Cruse Frank, teamster, s.s. Friendship al. b. Pike and Butler
Cruser Christopher, teamster, 91 and 93 Martin
Crusoe Geo., fireman, 1 Crippen al.
Crusoe Mary, grocery, 250 Broadway
Crutchfield Mrs. Nancy, 161 Longworth
Cubero Rev. Francis, 433 W. 3d
Culbertson Hy. C., clk. Culbertson, Kilgour & Co., h. 386 W. 6th
Culbertson John, pipe fitter, wks. n.e.c. Walnut an l Canal
CULBERTSON John C., (C., Kilgour & Co.) h. 386 W. 6th
Culbertson John M., 386 W. 6th
Culbertson Joseph A., 386 W. 6th
CULBERTSON, KILGOUR & CO., (John C. C., Chas. H. K. & John Kilgour) Bankers, n.s. 3d b. Main and Walnut
Culbertson Robert, tanner, Elm nr. Findlay, h. 343 W. 8th
Cullan Michael, second hand store, 175 W. Front
Cullan Robert, mach., bds. 221 Central Av.
Cullan Wm., shoe mkr., 129 Smith
CULLEN JAMES, Dealer in Ice, Vegetables, Preserves, Fruits, &c., 46 Public Landing, Ice House 365 Plum, bds. 137 Broadway
Cullen James, gardener, 55 Observatory Road
Cullen James, lab., 576 E. Front
Culley John W., printer, 141 Main, h. Newport
Cullen Wm., mach., 230 Barr
Cullen Winnie W., 412 Sycamore
Cullfink Fred. W., dray. 364 Broadway
Cullien Agnes, bds. 98 Broadway
Cullien Kate, bds. 98 Broadway
Cullien Thos., bds 98 Broadway
Cullin Robert, stereotyper, 255 Main
Cullinan Thos., carp., 200 E. 6th
Cullinan Thos., clk., bds. 98 Broadway
Cullinghum Kien, melter, 500 W. 8th
Cullmann Geo., confec , 537 Race
Cullom Mrs., seamstress, 424 Freeman
Cullom A. G., agent, bds. Henrie House
Cullom Wm. F., watchman, 124 Hopkins
Cultum David P., eng. Times office
Cullum James, clk., 624 Race

Cullum Robert, stereotyper, 255 Main
CULMANN Ernst., (Faehr, Bottler & Co.) 438 Main
Culver Hy., carp , 1290 E. Front
Culver L., carp., s.w.c. Railroad and French
CULVER J. D., Physician, Office, 216 Walnut
CULVER J D., Exchange Broker, Office, 216 Walnut
Cumberger Gustavus, bds. 362 Ham. Road
Cummerer Joseph, blksmith, bds. n.e.c. Buckeye and Vine
Cumming James, express driver, 90 W. 2d
Cummings Andrew, shoe mkr., 17 Betts
CUMMINGS & BERNE, (Hamilton C. & Wm. J D.) House and Sign Painters, n.e c. 3d and Race
Cummings Eliza, 106 E. 3d
CUMMINGS Hamilton, (C. & Berne) h. Covington
Cummings James, blksmith, 163 W. Front
CUMMINGS James P., (Samuel C. & Son) h. 48 York, Newport, Ky.
Cummings John, tinner, 49 Race
Cummings John, shoe mkr., 17 Betts
Cummings Joseph D., b.k. 43 Walnut, res. Covington
Cummings Martin, huckster, s.w.c. 3d and Central Av.
Cummings Michael, cigar mkr., h. 163 W. Front
Cummings Rebecca, h. 409 Broadway
CUMMINGS Samuel, (Samuel C. & Son) h. Mt. Vernon, Ky.
CUMMINGS SAML. & SON, (Saml. & Jas. P.) Brass Founders and Machinists, 162 E. Front
Cummings Wm., tinner. 105 Laurel
Cummins Catharine. 47 Pleasant
Cummins James, driver U. S. Express Co.
Cummins James, jr., (Jas. Cummins & Son) 12 David
Cummins James, sen., (James Cummins & Son) 56 Everett
Cummins James & Son, (James sen. & James jr.) boots and shoes, 56 Everett
Cummins John, shoe mkr., wks. 56 Everett
Cummins Martin, lab., s.e.c. Lawrence and Pearl [5th
Cummins Patrick, shoe mkr.; wks. 34 W.
Cummins Wm., shoe mkr., 15 Race
Cummins Wm. L., saddler, 333 Race
Cunniskey Samuel, currier, 311 W. 2d
Cunning James, turner, w.s. Lawson al. b. 4th and 5th, h. 493 W. 5th
Cunning James, jr., clk., 403 W. 5th
Cunning Sophia, n.w c. Main and Court
Cunningham Ellen, seamstress, 162½ W. 3d
CUNNINGHAM Albert J. (French & C.) h. nr. Camp Dennison, O.
CUNNINGHAM ANDREW, Edge Tool Manufacturer, s s. 8th b. Main and Sycamore, h. 496 W. 9th w. of Central Av
CUNNINGHAM & BENNET, (Jos. C. & Alonzo B.) Steamboat Agents and Commission Merchants, 20 Pub. Landing
Cunningham Bernard W., clk. City Water Works office
CUNNINGHAM Briggs S., (C. & Son) 32 W. 8th
Cunningham & Campbell, (Daniel C. & James C.) Irish linens, 350 W. 5th
Cunningham Daniel, (C. & Campbell) 350 W. 5th
Cunningham David, bklayer, 200 Richmond
Cunningham David. clk. R. G. Dunn & Co., h. 200 Richmond
Cunningham Elizabeth, foot of Harrison
Cunningham Elizabeth, 130 York
CUNNINGHAM Elmore W., (C. & Son) 32 W. 8th
Cunningham Feliz, boots and shoes, 37 Central Av.

Cunningham Hy., lab., wks. s.w.c. W. W. Canal and Smith
Cunningham James, lab., al. b. Cutter and Linn and Richmond and Court
CUNNINGHAM JAMES F., (J. F. C. & Co.,) and President Citizens Insurance Company. 337 W. 4th
CUNNINGHAM JAMES F. & Co., (Jas. F. C. & Co.,) Commission Merchants, 20 Public Landing
Cunningham John, 39 Plum
Cunningham John, baker, 46 E. 7th
Cunningham John, driver, 204 Betts
Cunningham John, stair builder, 327 Clark
CUNNINGHAM JOHN P., Carpenter and Builder, 410 George, h. 405 George
CUNNINGHAM Joseph, (C. & Bennet) 130 Barr
Cunningham Margaret, 146 Spring
Cunningham Margaret, 208 W. 7th
Cunningham Margaret, servt., 16 Hathaway
Cunningham Maria, servt., 375 W. 6th
Cunningham Martin, stone cutter, 200 Cutter
Cunningham Michael, cartman, 64 Richmond
Cunningham Patrick, lab., wks. 375 W. 3d
Cunningham Patrick, lab., s.s. Pearl b. Smith and Park
Cunningham Patrick, printer, 146 Spring
Cunningham R , cupola-tender, wks. Crane, Breed & Co's
Cunningham R C., printer, bds. 141 Sycamore
CUNNINGHAM & SON, (Elmore W. & Briggs S.) Pork Packers and Commission Merchants, 284 Sycamore
Cunningham Thos., clk. s.e.c. Front and Ludlow, h. 146 Spring
Cunningham Thomas, lab., n.s. Pearl b. Smith and Park
Cunningham Thomas, lab., w.s. W. W. Canal b. Park and Rose
Cunningham Terrence, lab., 45 E. 8th e. of Lock
Cunningham Wm., carp., 49 E. 8th e. of Lock
Cunningham Wm., dray, 327 W. 8th
Cunningham Wm., printer, 140 Betts
Cunningham Wm. C., harness mkr., bds. 74 Longworth
Curd Thomas H., collector, 334 Richmond
Curin Patrick, cab. mkr., n.s. Augusta b. John and Smith
Curlan James, dray, e.s. Ludlow b. Pearl and 3d
Curlen Wm., lab, 379 W. 2d
Curley John, lab., wks. gas wks.
Curley John, lab., 170 Cutter
Curley John, lab., 182 Cutter
Curley Luke, boots and shoes, s.s. Pearl b. Pike and Butler, h. 48 Butler b. Pearl and 3d
Curley Thomas, lab., s.e.c. Celestial and Mitchell
Curn Hannah, servt., 389 Sycamore
Curr Kate, bds. 51 Stone al.
Curran Bridget, servt. Burnet House
Curran Catharine, 63 E. 8th
Curran Eliza, 61 E. 6th
Curran Elizabeth, tailoress, bds. 29 Parsons
Curran John, huckster, s.e.c. 6th and Plum
Curran Mary, 792 E. Front
Curran Patrick, lab., wks. 205 Freeman
Curren Wm. F., blksmith, 29 Parsons
Curren Mary, servt , 55 Barr
Curren Patrick, lab , n.e.c. Baymiller and Richmond
Curry Hugh, painter, 82 Mound
Curry Mrs. clk. bath room Burnet House
Curry Alexander E., printer, 87 Pike
Curry Catharine, e.s. Crippen al. b. 7th and 8th
Curry Edward P., box wood, 120 Main, h. Walnut Hills
Curry Ellen, n.w.c. Hopkins and Baymiller
Curry Henrietta, 61 Vine

(DAE) CINCINNATI (DAL) DIRECTORY. (DAM) 113

Curry Jacob J., agt. C. O. & P. C. R. R., s. e. c. Front and Broadway, h. 100 E. 5th
Curry James, bds. 475 W. 7th
Curry John, lab., bds. 18 Landing b. Broadway and Ludlow
Curry Martin, finisher, wks. 247 W. 5th
Curry Mary, h. 236 Hopkins
Curry Richard L., engraver, h. Walnut Hills
Curry Samuel, teamster, s. s. Taylor b. Freeman and Carr
Curry Thos. II., 21 Betts
Curry Thomas II., eng., 61 Betts
Curry Wm. B., printer, 22 W. 4th, res. Walnut Hills
Curtain Mary, servt., 27 Harrison
Curth H., cutter, bds. Teutonia Hotel
Curtin Francis, lab., h. 140 Freeman
CURTIS ALVA, Physician, 87 E. 3d
Curtis John, lab., s. e. c. 7th and Broadway
Curtis Jonas, tobacconist, wks. 12 Main
Curtis Jno., s. b. capt., 336 Richmond
Curtis John A., clk , 70 E. Pearl, bds. Dennison House
Curtis Jonathan, bds. 191 Smith
Curtis Julia, 30 Baum
Curtis Lewis, mach., bds. Evans House
Curtis Richard D., 244 Elm
Curtis Thomas, dye-house, 244 Elm, h. 351 W. 6th
Curtner Hy , b. k., n. w. c. Main and 2d, bds. 89 E. 4th
CURWEN MASKELL E., Atty. at Law, and Dean of Law School, 65 W. 3d, h. 144 Elm
CUSCADEN ALEXANDER, Family Grocery, s. w. c. Elm and 3d
Cushin Jno., lab., 90 W. Court, w. of Central Av
Cushing Anna, bds. 64 Richmond
Cushing Louis, hostler, 2 New
Cushing Thomas, lab., 273 John
Cushing Timothy, lab., 64 Richmond
Cushion Johanna, s. s. Phœbe al. b. Plum and Central Av
Cushion Mary, s. s. Phœbe al. b. Plum and Central Av
Cushman John, coachman, 408 W. 6th
Cushman Wm., bds. 125 W. 5th
Cusick Patrick, lab., 614 W. 8th
Custard John, embroidery, 260 W. 5th
Custard Lane R., mach., 260 W. 5th
Custard Leonard, finisher, wks. C. T. Dumont's
Custer Fred., tailor 225 Everett
Custer George, molder, s. w. c. 3d and Smith
Custermann Hy., lab., w. s. Cutter, b. Liberty and Melancthon
CUSTOM HOUSE, Wm. Holthenrichs, 13 E. Pearl
Cutaiar & Batchelder, (Joseph C. & Geo. H. B.,) cigars, &c., 237 Main
Cutaiar Joseph, (C. & Batchelder,) 126 Dayton
Cutler Eliza, 447 Linn
Cutler Hy., molder, 30 Parsons
Cutler Phœbe, 454 E. 3d
Cutler Spaulding, mach., 108 E. Liberty
Cutler Volney, sewing machine manuf., 447 Linn
Cutter Alpheus, stable, 78 W. 6th, h. 138 W. 7th
Cutter Mrs. Amelia M., 210 Water
Cutter Barney, carp., wks. 1565 E. Front
Cutter Ezekiel, flour dealer, 249 Walnut, h. 447 Linn
Cutter Harmon, teamster, 195 Freeman
Cutter Hy., eng., 70 Lock
Cutter Martha, 428 W. 5th

D

Daase Catharine, 190 Linn
Dabert John, lab., 695 Race
Dabney Harry, tobacconist, 95 W. Front
Dacey Ellen, 131 E. 6th
Dacey Michael, lab., 133 E. 6th
Dadrick Mary, 341 Central Av
Daegge Hy., policeman, 50 Bremen

Daekee Gerhard, shoe mkr., 76 Bremen
Daeling John, porter, 18, 13th
Daen John S., s. s. Poplar, b. Linn and John
Daernkamp Conrad, tailor, 76 Dudley
Daernti Charles, bkksmith, n. s. 13th, b. Main and Walnut
Daeschler John, tailor, 682 Vine
Daeshey John, candy mkr., 36, 12th
Daganer Hy., blksmith, 907 Central Av., h. 319 Baymiller
Daganer Louis, grocer, 309 Findlay
Dugen John, cooper, s. s Poplar, b. Freeman and Western Av
Dagen Phillip, 337 Ham Road
Dogenhart August saddler, 734 W. 6th
Daggett Alfred, 102 Milton
Daggett Hy. J., w. s. Ohio Av. b. Calhoun and North Elm
Daghan Patrick, dray., 168 Cutter
Daglan Bernhard, lab., bds, 19 Landing, b. Broadway and Ludlow
Dahlinghaus Hy., shoe mkr., s. e. c. 6th and Central Av
Dagnan Mrs. Anna, 493 W. 3d
Dagner Hy., blksmith, 319 Baymiller
Daguet Alfred, molder, wks. n. e. c. Canal and Walnut
Daguet Anna, 489 Sycamore
Dahlke Gottlieb J., cab. mkr., 503 Walnut
Dahlstrom Frederick, cooper. 165 Clay
Dailey Alfred H., b. k., 175 Main, res. Newport
Dailey Andrew, lab., s. s. Front, e. of Torrence
Dailey David T., painter, 95 W. Court, w. of Central Av
Dailey John, lab., 130 Central Av
Dailey Martha, 519 W. 8th
Dailey Patrick, bar k., 25 Webb
Dailey Patrick, lub., 123 W. 9th, w. of Central Av
Dailey Timothy, lab., 55 Mill
Dailey William, lab, 55 Mill
Daily Bridget, s. s. Front, e. of Torrence
Daily Carl, carp , 199 Cutter
Daily Christopher, lab., 84 E. 5th
Daily Ellen, bds. Frey's Hotel
Daily James, lab., n. w. c. Union & Race
Daily James, porter, Dennison House
Daily John, lab., s. e. c. Elm and Water
Daily Julia, 249 Broadway
Daily Margaret, dress mkr., 222 W. 5th
Daily Nugent, lab , bds. 239 Barr
Daily Thomas, lab., s. s. Front, e. of Torrence
Daily Thomas, lab., wks. n. w. c. Plum and Wade
Dain James, lab., n. s. Marsh, b. Smith and Park
Dair Miss, dress mkr., bds. 297 W. 6th
DAIR John F., (John F. D. & Co.,) h. 64 W. 7th
DAIR JOHN F. & CO., (John F. D. & Wm. Stoms.) Seed Store and Agricultural Implements, 40 & 42 E. Pearl
Dair Wm., conductor, bds. 442 W. 7th
Dais John, carriage mkr., 51 W. 5th
Daisey Cornelius, mach., 92 Broadway
Daisey John, lab., 184 E. Pearl
Daisey Michael, boiler mkr., wks. s. s. 3d, b Butler and Miami Canal
Daisey Timothy, blksmith, 36 E. 6th
Daitmering Harmon, lab., 240 Hopkins
Dale Ann, s. w. c. E. 3d and Collard
Dale Geo. C., carp., 54 Laurel
Dale Hy., col. h., 59 Allison
Dale James, plasterer, 38 Mansfield
DALE John W., (Robert Clarke & Co.) h. 96 E. Liberty
Dale Mary, 11 Bedinger
Dale Nathaniel, shoe mkr., 11 Skaats
Dale Samuel, sexton church, s. s. Webster, b. Main and Sycamore
DALE THOS N. & CO , Importers and Manufacturers of Clothiers and Tailors Trimmings, 90 W. 3d
Dalem Charles, lab., 115 Carr
Daley Andrew, lab., 187 W. Canal
Daley Dennis, lab., 236 E. 6th
Daley James, lab , 57 E. 8th, e. of Lock
Dalhelm Geo., billiards, n. w. c. Vine and Longworth, h. 228 Walnut
Dall Theodore, bds. Cincinnati House
Dallahant Catharine, 57 8th, e. of Lock

Dallahant John, lab., 57 8th, e. of Lock
DALLAS Frederick, (Tempest & Co.,) h. 697 Elm
Daller John, jeweler, 391 Vine
Daller Joseph, watch mkr., 301 Vine
Dallert John, chair mkr., 130 W. Miami Canal
Dallinghaus Catharine, seamstress, s. s. Cassatt al. b. Sycamore and Main
Dallinghaus Catharine M., s. s. Cassatt al. b. Sycamore and Main
Dallinghaus Elizabeth, seamstress, s. s. Cassatt al. b. Sycamore and Main
Dallinghaus Hy., shoe mkr., s s. Cassatt al. b. Sycamore and Main
Dallinghaus Joseph, chair mkr., s. s. Cassatt al. b. Sycamore and Main
Dalliman F. H., foreman, 134 Sycamore, h. 512 Race
Dallman Herman, stone mason, 24 W. Mulberry
Dallmann Francis, lab. w. s. Hanover, b. Franklin and Woodward
Dallmann Hy., 18, 13th
Dallmann Hy., cab. mkr., 528 Main
Dallmann Hy. E., cab. mkr, 528 Main
Dallmann Herman H., brush manuf, 438 Main
Dallmann Rudolph, stone mason, 24 W. Mulberry
Dallmann Wm., varnisher, 26 Orchard
Dalm Charles, varnisher, 115 Carr
Dalton Evans E., cooper, 429 Sycamore
DALTON JAMES, Staple and Fancy Dry Goods, 146 W. 5th
Dalton James, lab., 130 Mound
Dalton James T., conductor, 429 Sycamore
Dalton Jane, 149 Livingston
Dalton John, lab., 14 Plum
Dalton Margaret, 103 W. Front
Dalton Mary Ann, tailoress, s s. Phœbe al. b. Plum and Central Av
Dalton Milton A., salesman, 28 Main, h 359 W. 7th
Dalton Thomas, huckster, w. s. Langdon al, h. 8th and 7th
Dalton Thos. J., clk., 282 Main
Dalton Wm. D., clk. L. M. R R , h. 282 Longworth
Dalwig Catharine, 65 Buckeye
Daly Abby, servt., 115 Pike
Daly Andrew H., lab , 185 Canal
Daly Bridget, 140 John
Daly Dennis, hostler, bds. 51 W. 5th
Daly James, lab., n. s. 6th, b. Broadway and Sycamore
Daly James P., marble cutter, wks. s. w. c. Broadway and 5th
Daly John, huckster, 247 W. 3d
Daly John, lab., wks. Cincinnati Gas Light Co.
Daly John, lab., s. s. al. h. Pike and Lawrence, and 3d and Pearl
Daly Kate, seamstress, Broadway Hotel
DALY M. V., (King & D.,) h. Newport
Daly Mary, chambermaid, B'dway Hotel
Daly Mary, servt., 147 Broadway
Daly Mary, servt., 115 Pike
Daly Patrick, barber, 13 Arch
Daly Patrick, bar k., Madison House
Daly Patrick, lab., n. s. Front, e. of Kelly
Daly Thomas, lab., 36 North
Daly Wm., lab., 18 Landing, b. Broadway and Ludlow
Dalzell Jane, nurse, Cin. Orphan Asylum
Dam Charles, barber, 250 W. Front, h. 572 Race
Damarell Wm., roofer, 172 W. Front
Damen Wm., furniture, 517 Main
Damm Chas. J., barber, w. s. Goose al. b. Liberty and 15th
Damm Conrad, barber, 100 Buckeye
Damm John, lab , 57 Peete
Damm Peter, lab., w. s. Vine b. Milk and Mulberry
Damm Peter, shoemkr. wks. 612 Vine
Damme Cornelius, tanner, bds. 111 Clay
Damme Hy., lab., rear 16 Madison
Dammeier Augustus, chair mkr, 190 Clinton
Dammeier Louisa, seamstress, h. 62 Bremen
Dammeyer Hy., mason, 13 Mulberry

114   (DAR)   CINCINNATI   (DAV)   DIRECTORY.   (DAV)

Damon Fred., lab., wks. Crane Breed & Co.'s
DANBY Chas. (Vall & D.) 556 W. 9th w. of Central Av
DANDRIDGE A. S., Physician and Surgeon, n.e.c. 3d and Broadway, h. 93 E. 3d
Dane Patrick, stone mason, 57 W. 9th w. of Central Av
Dancker Geo. J., clk., 53 York
Danenhower John W., clk. 146 W. 3d, b. 262 Hopkins
Danforth Elizabeth, s.e.c. 5th and Elm
Dangel Francis, teamster, wks. J. Kauffman & Co.'s
Danger Ferdinand, cab. mkr, 209 Baymiller
Daniel Fanny, 160 Longworth
Daniel Hy., lab., 177 Hopkins
Daniel Hiram, com. mer., 41 Vine, h. 96 Barr
Daniel James, lab., 55 Gano
Daricl James S., 29 Vine
Daniel Margaret, s.e.c. 7th and Broadway
Daniel Solomon, 524 Race
Daniels D. N., truss manuf., 2 W. 4th
Daniels Geo., messenger, 3 W. 3d
Daniels Hector L., book bindery, 38 W. 3d, h. n.s. Hathaway b. Jane and Baymiller
Daniels Hy., clk., n.w.c. John and Clinton
Daniels J. A., 47 George
Daniels Jacob, saddles, &c., 205 W. 6th, h. 152 W. 6th
Daniels James A., clothing, 47 George
Daniels Mrs. L. D., b.h , 77 E. 3d
Daniels Lettia, 494 W. 9th
Daniels Stacy, plasterer, 494 W. 9th
Dankel Frederick, grocery, 9 Franklin
Danker Hy., eng., 71 Spring
Danky Dora, 24 Parsons
Danky Phillip, pyrotechnist, 24 Parsons
Dann Joseph, carp., 543 W 3d, h. Ludlow, Ky
Dannbaum Wm., teamster, 18 Mansfield
Dannecker Geo. J., rope mkr, 118 Findlay
Dinnecker Jacob P. J., rope walk, 118 Findlay
Dannemann John, shoemkr, 510 Sycamore
DANNENHOLD B. (D. & Nock), w.s. Dudley b. Poplar and Liberty
DANNENHOLD & NOCK, (B. D & Wm. S. N.) Steam & Gas Fitters, 99 W. 5th
Dannenhold Walter, gas fitter, h. 117 Dudley
Danner Anna M., b.h., 216 Plum
Danner Hy., driver, wks. 25 and 27 Water
Dannerberg Hy., porter, 11 Wade b. Elm and Blum
Danner Mary A., h. 143 Everett
Danneteuther Abraham, piano manuf., 407 Central Av
Dannevan Daniel, lab , 608 W. Front
Dant Richard, lab, h. s.s. Pearl b. Pike and Butler
Dapp John, porter, 61 W. Pearl, h. 91 Ham. Road
Daupen Edward, turner, 587 Race
Darbller Frederick, lab., s.s. Charlotte b. Linn and Baymiller
Darby James A., silver plater, wks. 10 E. 6th
Darc Clement, civil eng., 286 Longworth
Dargent August, foreman, s.s. 6th b. Broadway and Culvert
Daring James, steward, h. 13 Plum
Daring Martin, cigar mkr. n.w.c. Cutter and Clark
Daring Thomas, lab., 160 Webb
Darion Hugh, tailor, 70 Gano
Dark Ebenezer, b.k., 341 Clark
Dark Eliza, 341 Clark
Dark Rose E., bds. 341 Clark
Darling Jeremiah, wood dealer, F9 W. Court, w. of Central Av. b. 5 Clinton Court
Darling Mary, b h., s.w.c. 7th and Race
Darlis Andrew, cof. h., e.s. Reading Road nr. Montgomery Pike
Darnbush Fred., carp., 211 Clinton

Darnell Albert, barber, 130 W. 3d
Darnell James, barber, 130 W. 3d
Darock John, mach , wks. 222 E. Front
Darp Hy., cooper, 67 Green
Darr Charles, clk., 272 Race
Darr Frank. 272 Race
Darr Joseph, 272 Race
Darr Joseph Jr., 272 Race
Darrow George P., 445 John
Darsey John, lab, wks. Queen City Distillery
Dart Charles, b.k., 38 W. 4th, h. 496 W. 3d
Dart Elvira, 496 W. 3d
Dart Thomas M., bds. 496 W. 3d
Dartnell W. B., b.k. Gilmore, Dunlap & Co., res. Newport
Daruck Andrew, butcher, 113 Pleasant
Darnsmont Alexis, 721 Vine
Darvett Anthony, lab., 186 W Front
Dasch Chas., cof. h., 617 Vine
Dashney Findley, tailor, 109 Longworth
Dasinger Wm., lab., n.s. Ham Road, head of Elm
Dass Martin, grocery, 834 E. Front
Dassell Anton, watch mkr, 109 Linn
Dasy John, lab., 184 E. Pearl
Dater Adam, dray. 145 Poplar
Dater Peter, com. mer., 66 W. Court
Daterman Hy., lab., 43 Race
Daters Frank H., foreman, w.s. Bremen b. 12th and 13th
Daters Hy., 323 Plum
Dates Christopher, stocking mkr, wks. 413 Main
Dates John, stocking mkr., wks. 413 Main
Dau Charles, cab. mkr., 422 Vine
Daubenbis Frederick, bds. 28 14th
Daubenbis Frederick, foreman, 473 Race
Daudistel Adam, coffee roaster, 40 Jones
Dauenhuwer Geo., bk. binder, 627 Vine
Dauenhauer Hy., varnisher, n.s. Adams b. Plum and Elm
Dauer Francis, blksmith, 4 Moore
Dauer Frank, blksmith, 585 Walnut
Daugherty Alice, 63 Observatory Road
Daugherty John, lab , 10 Mill
Daugherty John, lab., 105 W. 2d
Daugherty Michael, lab., 435 W. 3d
Daugherty Michael, lab., rear 211 Water
Daugherty Patrick, dray. 194 Water
Daugherty Wm., lab , c. 8th and Accommodation
Daum Barbara, milliner, 109 Mulberry
DAUM MICHAEL, Globe Saloon and Billiards. 30 Broadway
Dauman Hy., porter, 74 W. Pearl, h. 125 Ham. Road
DAUMANN HENRY, Coffee and Boarding House, 125 Ham. Road
Daumann Hy., shoemkr, bds. 125 Ham. Road
Daumiller Geo., painter, 570 Race
Daummeier Hy., carp., bds. 139 Baymiller
Dauner John, tailor, 637 Race
Daunhauher Hy., varnisher, 15 Plum
Daus Andress, cigar mkr., 602 Elm
Daut Elnora, 21 Mercer
Dauth Jacob, bds. 118 Bremen
Davenport ——, bds. 207 W. 6th
DAVENPORT CHARLES, Division Superintendent W. Union Telegraph Co., office s.w.c. 3d and Walnut, h. 216 Richmond
DAVENPORT CYRUS, Sec'y Spring Grove Cemetery, office Melodeon Bldg., n w.c. 4th and Walnut, h. 283 W. 7th
DAVENPORT D G. A., Auditor. L. M. R. R. Co., office s.e.c. Pearl & Kilgour, res. Mt. Auburn
Davenport Isaiah, com. mer., 168 Barr
Davenport John D., clk . 125 Carr
Davenport Susanna, teacher, 125 Carr
Daverset Peter, peddler w.s. Denman b. Central Av and Bank
DAVEY John R. (A. H. Hinkle & Co.), n s. Hopkins b. John and Central Av
David Daniel, clk., 271 Central Av., h. 23 Clinton

David Hy., soaps, &c., 278 Main, h. 22 W. 7th
David Jacob, clk. co. treasurer's office, h. 2d W. 7th
David Joseph, bar k., Clifton House
David Mary, servt., 421 Freeman
David Thos., lab., s.s. Friendship al. b. Pike and Butler
David Wm. H., clk., Adams' Express Co., bds 22 W. 7th
Davidson Alex. G., 169 E. 3d
Davidson George, lab., n.w.c. Central Av. and Pearl
Davidson Henry C., printer, bds. 361 George
Davidson John, blksmith. 17 15th
Davidson John, eng., 29 Providence
Davidson John B., printer, Commercial office, h. 361 George
Davidson John M., 361 George
Davidson L. W., clk., 101 W. 4th
Davidson M W., bds. 77 E. 3d
Davidson Rodger J., baggage master, O. & M. R. Rv, bds. 420 W. 4th
DAVIDSON Tyler (Tyler D. & Co.) bds. Burnet House
DAVIDSON TYLER & CO. (Tyler D., Henry Probasco & Caleb P. Marsh) Wholesale Hardware, 140 and 142 Main
Davidson Rev. Wm., 320 Plum
Davidson Wm. A., watch mkr, bds. 348 George
DAVIDSON Wm F., Wholesale and Retail Drugs, Medicines, Paints, &c., n.e.c. Main and 5th, h. 10 E. 5th
Davie Melancthon O., b.k., 294 W. 8th
Davies Rev. D. Owen, bds. Clifton House
DAVIES GEORGE C., Insurance Agent, 67 W. 4th, h. 191 W. Court w. of Central Av
Davin Patrick, blksmith, n.s. Front e. of Kelly
Davis Abraham, peddler, 324 Main
Davis Adolph, tailor, 76 E. 5th., h. 60 E. 5th
Davis Chas. A., grainer, 342 Richmond
DAVIS A. Judson (Geo. F. D. & Co.) h, 585 W. 8th
Davis Ann I. 127 W. Court w. of Central Av
Davis Annie, servt, 415 W. 6th
Davis Barbara, seamstress, 8 W. Mulberry
Davis Benjamin, drover, 61 E. 8th e. of Lock
Davis Benj. B., local mail agent P. O., h. Delhi Tp.
Davis Caroline, 64 Bremen
Davis Chas., cigar mkr., 792 E. Front
DAVIS Chas., (Chas Davis & Co.,) h. 57 W. 9th
DAVIS CHAS. & CO., (Chas. D., John H. Porter and Nathaniel Goldsmith,) Pork and Beef Packers, n.w.c. 6th and Sycamore
Davis Chas. W. bds 127 W. Court w. of Central Av
Davis Charlotte, school, s.s. 5th b. Central Av. and John
Davis & Co., (Samuel D. jr., G. M. High & P. Andrew,) slaughter House s.s. Deer Creek Road n. of Court
Davis C. White, upholsterer, 508 Sycamore
Davis Cynthia, 6 E. 8th, e. of Lock
Davis Daniel J., bds. 158 W. 3d
Davis Daniel S., eng., h. 158 W. 3d
Davis David, porter, 10 W. 2d, b. 260 E. Front
Davis David B., boiler, bds. c. 2d and Smith
Davis David E , dray, 325 Clark
Davis Deborah, 300 Water
Davis Edward, 36 Ellen
Davis Edward, dentist, bds.. 81 Everett
Davis Edward, saddler, bds. 110 W. 6th
Davis Eli, bridge framer, 221 Freeman
Davis Eli M., watchman, w.s. Cutter nr. Clark
Davis Eliza, hoop skirt mkr., 433 W. 5th
Davis Elizabeth, confec., s.e.c. Findlay and Baymiller

Davis Elizabeth, 472 W. 3d
Davis Elizabeth K., servt. 16 McFarland
Davis Elizabeth, tailoress, bds. 472 W. 3d
DAVIS F. P. & CO., (Franklin P. D., & Wm. O. Davis,) Iron Founders, Stoves, &c., n.w.c. Main and 2d
Davis Frank, lab., s s. Pleasant Court e. of Elm
Davis Franklin, painter, 49 Jones
DAVIS Franklin P., (F. P. D. & Co.,) 413 W. 3d
DAVIS Franklin S., (S. S. Davis & Co.,) h. 278 W. 7th
Davis Franklin T., police, 129 George
DAVIS Geo. F., (Geo. F. D. & Co.,) Southern Av., Mt. Auburn
DAVIS GEORGE F. & CO., (Geo. F. D., & A. Judson Davis,) Wholesale Dealers in Provisions and Curers of Extra Family Hams, 11 Sycamore
DAVIS George H., (N. H. & G. H. D.,) 53 W. 8th
Davis George W., conductor, 380 Baymiller
DAVIS H. H., Proprietor Walnut Street House, e.s. Walnut b. 6th and 7th
Davis Harvey, barber, 71 W. 9th w. of Central Av
Davis Henry D., driver, wks. 131 Race
Davis Henry L , clk., County clks. office, h. 251 W. 4th
Davis Hugh D. lab., bds. 974 E. Front
Davis I. B., coal agt., 25 W. Front, h. 279½ Longworth
Davis J. M., bds. Clermont Hotel
Davis Jackson, 22 Logan
Davis Jacob, tailor, 58 E. 5th
Davis J. B., builder, 80 Hopkins
Davis Rev. James, foot of Harrison
Davis James, lab., s.s. 6th b. Broadway and Culvert
Davis James, porter, 24 W. Pearl
Davis, James, printer, bds. s.e.c. Walnut and 9th
Davis James E., (Feigley & D.,) Perry County O.
Davis James H., (James H D. & Co.,) 286 John
Davis James H. & Co., (James H. D., John G. Davis & Saml. O. Davis,) carps., 38 W. 9th, w. of Central Av
Davis James J., foreman, 36 Ellen
Davis James W., driver. 101 George
Davis Jane, 323 W. 9th, w. of Central Av.
Davis Johanna, n.e.c. Richmond and Cutter
Davis Jennie, bds. 272 Main
Davis John, 427 W. 3d
Davis John, 260 E. Front
Davis John, 82 W. 8th
Davis John, blksmith, 19 15th, b. Central Av. and Plum
Davis John, dray., 4d Lock
Davis John, lab., 289 Water
DAVIS JOHN, Physician, Office and Residence 323 Elm
Davis John, pressman, s.e.c. 3d and Vine
Davis John C., clk., bds. 82 W. 8th
Davis John D., miller, 49 New
Davis John G., (James H , Davis & Co.,) 286 John
Davis John G., finisher, foot of Harrison
Davis John, 427 W. 5th
Davis John O , watchman, 591 W. 5th
Davis, John P., vault builder, 12 Chestnut
Davis John R., 498 W. 9th
Davis John V. S., harness mkr., 34 Stone
Davis John W., carp., 24 Hill
Davis Jno., W., clk., 12 George
Davis Joshua, at Charles Davis & Co's, res. W. Walnut Hills
Davis Joseph, lab., 606 W. 8th
Davis Joseph, lab., n.s. Carr nr. Harriett
Davis Joseph M., painter, 276 W. 9th
Davis Mac, fireman. 188 Cutter

Davis Manuel, barber, bds. 72 E. 7th
Davis Margaret, servt., n.e.c. 3d and Lawrence
Davis Margaret, wks. 278 W. Court w. of Central Av
Davis Maria, 328 Baymiller
Davis Mary, bds. 163 E. 3d
Davis Mary J., tailoress, bds. 472 W. 3d
Davis Michael. G., carp., w.s. Whittaker b. 3d and Front
DAVIS N. H., & G. H., (Nathaniel H., & George H. D.,) Dealers in Bourbon Whiskey, and Importers of Wines and Liquors 69 Walnut
DAVIS Nathaniel H., (N. H. & G. H. D.,) 21 W. 9th
Davis Newton C., printer, bds., s.e.c. 9th and Walnut
Davis O. H., b. k., bds. s.e.c. 9th and Walnut
Davis Oliver, mach., 134 Pleasant
Davis Reese, 437 W. 2d
DAVIS S. Jr. & Co., (Samuel D. Jr. & Wm., H. Davis,) Pork Packers. and Ham Curers, 303 to 313 Broadway
DAVIS S. S. & CO., (Simon S. & Franklin S. Davis,) Bankers, 61 W. 3d
DAVIS Samuel Jr., (S. D. Jr. & Co.,) 46 W. 8th
Davis Samuel, carp., n.w.c. John and 5th, h. 173 John
Davis Samuel, lab., bds. 150 W. Front
Davis Samuel, police, 27 Parsons
Davis Samuel O , (Jas. H. Davis & Co.) 286 John
Davis Sarah, 116 Butler
Davis Sarah, n.s. R. Road e. of Hazen
Davis Sarah C., 413 W. 3d
DAVIS Simon S., (S. S. D. & Co,,) 430 W. 8th
Davis Stephen A., foreman, 50 Pearl, h. 197 W. Front
Davis Susan, res. at Geo. F. Davis' Mt-Auburn
Davis Thomas, bds. 83 Baymiller
Davis Thomas, cook, Clifton House
Davis Thomas, dray, wks. 109 E. Pearl
Davis Thomas, printer. bds. 170 W. 5th
Davis Thomas B., marble cutter, bds. 82 W. 8th
Davis Theodore D., barber shop, 382 Central Av.
Davis Thomas D., distillery, w.s. Western Av. b. Bank and Harrison Road, h. Covington
Davis Thomas F., grainer, bds. 342 Richmond
Davis Thomas H., printer, Cin. Gazette, h. 170 W. 5th
Davis Thomas J., clk., 242 W. 6th
Davis Thomas M., mate, 87 Mill
Davis Wm., 9 Harrison
Davis Wm., bk. gilder, bds. 119 W. 6th
Davis Wm., driver, 513 W. 8th
Davis Wm., tailor, 33 E. 3d
Davis Wm., tailor, 145 Clinton
Davis Wm. B., b.k., 27 W. 3d, h. 75 Clinton
Davis Wm. B., eng., n.s. McDowell e. of Mill
Davis Wm. B., phys., 315 Elm
DAVIS Wm. C.. (F. P. Davis & Co.,) res. Dayton
Davis Wm. E., mail agt., 142½ Laurel
Davis Wm. H., dining saloon, 14 E. 5th
DAVIS Wm. H., (S. Davis Jr., & Co.,) 124 E. 4th
Davis Wm. M., bds. 52 W. 8th
Davis Wm. M., astronomer, Cin. Observatory
Davis Wm. M., baggage man bds. Spencer House
Davis Wm. M , clk., 82 W. 8th
Davis Wm. M., sewing machine manuf., 247 W. 5th. h. Cin. Observatory
DAVIS WILLIAM W., Wholesale Dealer in Provisions and Curer of Hams, Dried Beef and Beef Tongues, 40 W. Front, h. 56 W.9th
Davis Wilson S., clk., P. O., h. 430 George
Davison Geo., eng., 535 W. 5th
Davison H. B., clk., 101 W. 4th bds. 98 Broadway

Davison James, silver plater, 178 Longworth
Davison James M., clk., 178 Longworth
Davison John L., clk., 101 W. 4th
Davison P. R , bds. s.e.c. 9th and Walnut
Davison Wm. C., silver plating, 72 W. 8th, h. 29 George
Davitt Martin, lab., 30 Water
Davock John, finisher, 49 E. 8th e. of Lock
Davey Edwin, harness mkr., bds. 116 W. 6th
Davlin Catharine, servt., 395 Richmond
Davy Mrs Ann, 100 Baymiller
Davy Catharine, 135 W. Front
Davy James, bds. w.s. Lawrence b. 4th and 5th
Davy John R., (W. B. Smith and Co.,) 14 Hopkins
Davy Michael, lab., 143 E. 2d
Dawson, phys., bds. Madison House
DAWSON BENJAMIN, Stoves, Tinware &c., 254 W. 6th h. 167 Richmond
Dawson Edward A., b. k., 29 W. 3d, h. 319 Elm
Dawson Eliza. h. 319 Elm
DAWSON JAMES, Boarding House, 298 W. 5th
Dawson James J., paper carrier, 297 W. 5th
Dawson John, cab. mkr., s.e.c. Channing and Young
Dawson Sarah, h. 108 Baum
Dawson Theodore, teamster, 94 W. Court
Dawson Wm., cab. mkr., s.e.c. Channing and Young
Dawson Wm., lab., s.s. 2d b. Rose and Mill
Dawson Wm., printer, s.w c. 3d and Sycamore
Day Berry, (D. & Woodruff,) 424 John
Day & Brother, (Alexander M. D . & Timothy C. D.,) confec., 259 Walnut
Day Hy. M., atty., 58 W. 3d, h. 229 W. 4th
Day Israel, driver, 68 Avery
Day James, printer, bds. 74 Longworth
Day James R., (W. T., & S. D. Day & Co.,) 328 W. 9th
Day Jeremiah, J., cooper, wks. 39 Bremen
Day John, plasterer, 220 Cutter
Day Mary, 167 E. 3d
Day Michael, lab., n.s Patterson al. b. Main and Walnut
Day Nathan, conductor, e.s. Freeman b. Barr and George
Day Patrick, policeman, n.s. Patterson al. b. Main and Walnut
Day Ruth, bds. 42 Stone
Day Samuel D., (W. T. &, S. D. D. & Co) res. Canton Ohio
Day Sarah, 167 E. 3d [3d
Day Timothy C., (D. & Brother) 167 E.
Day W. T. & S. D. & Co., (Wm. T., Samuel D. D. & James R. Day) manuf. printing presses, 173 W. 2d
Day Wm., jeweler, wks. s.w.c. 4th and Main
Day Wm T., (W. T. & S. D. D. & Co.) res. Columbus, O.
Day & Woodruff, (Berry D. & Job W.) stables 26 E. 5th
DAYTON & CINCINNATI (Short Line) Railroad, 13 W. 4th, Samuel H. Goodin, President
DAYTON & MICHIGAN RAILROAD, Office, 5 College Building, e.s. Walnut b. 4th and 5th
Daywald Jacob, lab., 90 York
Dazenbrack Fred., chair mkr., wks. John Mitchell's
Deakmann Herrod, 135 Abigail
Deakmann Martin, 133 Abigail
Deal David S., painter, 185 W. Court w. of Central Av.
Deal Mary, 180 Elm
Deal Nicholas, 759 Vine
Deal Philip N., painter, 185 W. Court w. of Central Av.

Dealin Robert, carp., 1265 E. Front
Deamon John, cof. h., 67 W Liberty
Deams Conrad, b k., 461 W. 7th
DEAN & HALE, (Thompson D. & Sam'l J. H.) Commission Merchants and Wholesale Dealers in Flour and Whisky, 19 and 21 Sycamore
Dean J. D., clk. Adams Express Co., h. Newport
Dean James H., shoe mkr., 231 Central Av
Dean James T., mach., 451 W. 7th
Dean James T., painter, 451 W. 7th
Dean John, stone mason, 127 W. 9th w. of Central Av.
Dean John H., salesman 17 W. Pearl
Dean Kate, nurse, John Bates'
Dean Michael, carp., 168 E. 3d
Dean Michael, fireman, s.s. 2d b. Rose and Park
Dean Patrick, lab., w.s. Central Av. b. 2d and W. Canal Basin
Dean Philip N., barber, s.s. 6th b. Broadway and Culver
Dean R. L., bds. National Hotel
DEAN Thompson, (D. & Hale) 200 W. 4th
Dearing J., bds. Burnet House
Dearing Thos., eng. Burnet House
Dearl Lizzie, servt., 169 E. 3d
Dears Frederick, chair mkr., e.s. Fountain b Rice and Alexander
Dears Wm., e.s. Fountain b Rice and Alexander
Deartstock Benjamin, finisher, wks. n.e. c Walnut and Canal
Dearwaters James R., fireman, 107 Betts
Deasy Cornelius, mach., 92 Broadway
Denters Ferdinand, cigar mkr., 401 Broadway
Debbler Barney, bar k., 90 E. 2d
DeBeck B. O. M., teacher, 230 Betts
DeBeck Joseph, lab., n.s. Front e. of Kelly
DeBeck Wm., n.s. Poplar b. Freeman and Western Av.
Deberetz Michael G., molder, 47 Findlay
Debler Charles, bar k., wks 480 Vine
Debohr Charles, h. 58 Stark
Debold Anthony, pattern mkr., 503 W. 4th
Deboll A. L., bksmith, 194 Bremen
Debolt Building, s.e.c. Main and Court
Debolt Chas, box mkr., 11 Moore
DEBOLT EXCHANGE, John C. Flach, Proprietor, s.e.c. Main and Court
Debolt Joseph H., druggist, 1216 E. Front
DEBOOR Jacob, (J. P. Calkins & Co.) 41 Milton
DEBORAH, Bloch & Co. Publishers, I. M. Wise Editor, 32 W. 6th
Debre Nicholas, trunk mkr., 235 Bremen
Drebretz Peter, finisher, 9 Mary
Debus Louis, still tub and cistern mkr., 167 W. 2d
DeButts Archibald S., tailor, 107 Dudley
DeButts Benjamin F., b k., 204 Poplar
Deby Frederick, carp., bds. 67 1 W. 6th
DeCamp Asbury, (Miller & D) 303 5th
DeCamp Caleb D., b.k., h. 288 W. 7th
DeCamp Christopher C., carp., 148 Cutter
DeCamp Daniel, (J. & D. DeC.) res. Glendale
DeCamp David, carp., 306 George
DeCamp E. L., atty., bds. 21 Barr
DeCamp Edwin F., clk. Hand, Whitehouse & Co's
DuCamp Harvey, (Bachelor, DeC. & Co.) 339 W. 4th
DeCamp Hiram, bk. layer, 288 W. 7th
DeCamp J. & D , (Joseph & David) carps., 130 W. Court w. of Central Av.
DeCamp Mrs. James, 306 George
DeCamp James F., b.k., 19 Barr
DeCamp Job, bk. layer, 78½ Laurel
DeCamp John, (Bailey & D.) Branch Hill
DeCamp Joseph, (J. & D. DeC.) 282 George
DeCamp Lambert, bk. layer, 78 Laurel

DeCAMP & NIEHAUS, (Thos. L. DeC. & Joseph N.) Dealers in Hardware and Manufacturers of Locks, 270 Central Av.
DeCAMP Thomas L., (DeC. & Niehaus) res. Glendale
DeCharms Mary, teacher, 453 W. 6th
DeCharms Richard, printer, bds. 453 W. 6th
Dechs Julius, 379 Elm
Deck Abraham, cof. h., s.w.c. Clarkson and Central Av.
Deck David K., real estate, 567 Freeman
Deck Frederick, cooper, h. 12 Orchard
Deck Jacob, butcher, bds. 125 Ham. Road
Decke Frederick, cooper, h. 12 Orchard
DECKEBACH F. C. & CO., (Fred. C. D. & John Groenewold) Coppersmiths, Brew and Still Kettle Manufacturers, 171 W. Court
DECKEBACH Fred. C., (F. C. D. & Co.) 171 W. Court
Deckebach Geo., carpet manuf., 173 W. Court
Deckebach Hy., 151 W. Court
Deckebach Philip, grocery, 286 W. Liberty
Deckelmann Hy., shoe mkr., 1205 E. Front
Deckelmeier Francis, tailor, 70 Pleasant
Decker Charles, lab., bds. 140 Carr
Decker Daniel, 140 E. 6th
Decker George, grocery, s.s. Harrison Pike b. Brighton and Western Av.
Decker Gerhard, druggist, bds. 493 Vine
Decker Hy., cooper, 24 Abigail
Decker Hy., lab., 103 Wade
Decker Hy., watch mkr., 24 Abigail
Decker J. C., printer, wks. s.e.c. 3d and Sycamore
Decker Jacob, grocer, s.s. Harrison Pike b. Division and Brighton
Decker John H., watch mkr., 24 Abigail
Decker Joseph, lab., 674 Race
Decker Michael, bk. layer, n.e.c. Rice and Mulberry
Decker Wm , tanner, 701 Elm
Duckert Elizabeth, 654 Race
Deckman Frank, box mk., e.s. Kilgour b. 3d and 5th
Deckman Rosina, h. 168 W. Liberty
Deckman Wm , lab., n.s. Broad e. of Lewis
Deckwetz August, gror. &, 26 Madison
Decrrer J. C., bds. Dennison House
DeCurdin Anthony, carp , 543 Sycamore
Decy John, lab., 228 E. 6th
Dedenbeck Joseph, finisher, wks. C. T. Dumont's
Dederlin Mary, 185 W, 4th
Dedling Geo., cab. mkr., 17 Ham. Road
Dedrick David, carp., 119 Clinton
Dee James, printer, bds. 74 Longworth
Dee Michael, cof. h., 33 Race
Deeds Wm., tinner, wks. 393 Vine
Deeming George, stocking weaver, rear 567 Sycamore
Deeming John, sen., stocking weaver, rear 567 Sycamore
Deepe Hy., chair mkr., 407 Elm
Deer Creek Mills, w. s. Lock b. 3d and 5th
Deering Lewis, shoe mkr., n.e.c. Water and Central Av.
Deerman Hy., lab., 709 Freeman
Deery Sarah. 60 Stone al. b. 5th and 6th
Dees Andrew, watch mkr., 309 Main
Deery Wm., sawyer, 60 Stone al. b. 5th and 6th
Deffenbach Frederick, 80 Mohawk
Deford A. J., printer Commercial office, h. Newport
DeForest Deluzun, bk. binder, 62 W. 3d, h. 29 Freeman
DeForest Wm. S., type mkr., n.e.c. George and Linn
Defoy Mary, 61 Richmond
Degenhard Chas., cab. mkr., bds. s.s. 6th b. Harriet and Horne
Degenhard Georg , shoe mkr., bds. s.s. 6th b. Harriet and Horne
Degenhard Philip, boots and shoes, s.s. 6th b. Harriet and Horne
Deger Chas., bk. layer, 192 W. 5th
Deger George, lab., 613 Main

Deger Hy., lab., rear 3 Wade b. Elm and Plum
Degischer Ernst, porter, 13 E. Pearl
Degner Ernest L., willow ware, 164 Ham. Road
Degner John, 57 Rittenhouse
Degner John, waiter Burnet House
Degraw Abram, grocery. 246 W. 6th
DeGraw Daniel, carp., bds. n.s. Nassau b. Reed and Broad
DeGraw Wesley L., builder, 400 W. 9th
Degray Lewis, steward. 74 Pleasant
Degroot Anna M., 119 Spring
Dehler Clemens, stone setter, 52 Abigail
Dehls Martin. varnisher, 104 Butler
Dehls Mary, dress mkr., h. 104 Butler
Dehmer Ernst M., lab., 299 W. Front
Dehmer Lewis, shoe mkr., 107 Pleasant
Dehmer Daniel, grocer, s.s. 6th b. Harriet and Horne
Dehner John, brush mkr., wks. 190 Walnut
Dehner John, carp., 115 Laurel
Deho Catharine, 113 Martin
Deho Wm., hat store, 119 Laurel
Deic John, tailor. 110 W. Liberty
Deiche Louis. cigar mkr. 564 Elm
Deichmann Albert, shoe mkr., res. Vine St. Hill
Deicke Hy. F., cab. mkr., 564 Elm
Deicke Theresa, seamstress, 564 W. Liberty
Deickman Hy., bds. Railroad House
Deickmann Geo., leather dealer, 446 Walnut
Deidling Heinrich, finisher, 207 Clinton
Deie Anthony, lab., 538 Plum
Deie Dina, seamstress, 536 Plum
Deier A., tailor, wks. 269 Main
Deierlein Frederick, painter, 27 Bremen
Deierling Jacob, cof. h., 546 Race
Deierling Jacob, grinder, 20 Green
Delhi Hy., lab., wks. 120 W. 2d
Deihl Jacob, clk., 444 Walnut
Deihl Wm., miller, wks. Queen City Distillery
Delling Mary. 362 Broadway
Deimann Chas. baker, wks. 549 Vine
Deiner Anton, butcher, 560 Central Av.
Deinhart John, stocking weaver, w.s. Goose al. b. 14th and 15th
Deininger Henry, cof. h., 34½ E. Front
Deinlein Dorothea, 9 Allison
Deinlein Pankras, shoe mkr., 66 Ham. Road
Deis Herman, baker, w.s. Campbell al. b. Elder and Findlay
Deis John, car mkr., bds. 51 W. 5th
Deiss John, cigar mkr., wks. 191 W. 5th
Deitemeier Adam H., packer, 25 Franklin
Deitemeier Adam H., packer, h. 138 Pleasant
Deiterle John, foreman, n.s. Augusta b. John and Smith
Deiters Rev. Wm., s s. Budd b. Carr and Donnersberger
Deitsch Jonas, exchange office, n.w.c. 4th and Sycamore, h. 143 Longworth
Deitsch Julius, h. 143 Longworth
Deitz Louis, pipe fitter, wks. n e c. Walnut and Canal
Deiweig John Phillip, cof. h., 550 Walnut
Dekert Wm., lab., 417 Freeman
Dekins Sarah, teacher, E. Front b. Hill and Stone
Delader John, porter, 126 Clay
Deladron Leonardt, 32 Dunlap
Delainey John, tailor, 66 Butler
Delainey Martin, lab., 28 Lock n. of 8th
DeLAND Chas. W., (DeL. & Gossage.) bds. Burnet House
DELAND & GOSSAGE, (Chas. W. DeL. & Chas. G.) Staple and Fancy Dry Goods, 74 and 76 W. 4th
Deland Henry, clk., 79 Wade
Delaney Anna, s.e.c. North and New
Delaney Catharine, 341 Central Av
Delaney Catharine, servant, 275 George
Delaney Cornelius, grocery, s.e.c. North and New
Delaney Daniel, 69 Avery

Delaney Daniel, lab., 414 George
Delaney Eliza, 130 Water
Delaney Henry, hostler, bds. 138 Longworth
Delaney James, grocery, 184 W. Front
Delaney John, clk., 184 W. Front
Delaney John, lab., 442 W 7th
Delaney John, lab., n.e.c. Front and Plum
Delaney John, lab., n.s. Van Horn w. of Carr
Delaney John, tailor, 66 Butler
Delaney Martin, box mkr. bds. 612 W. 6th
Delaney P. F., bds. Dennison House
Delaney Philip, blk. smith, n.s. 7th b. Plum and Central Av
Delaney Richard, dray, n.w.c. 3d and Ludlow
Delaney Thomas, carp., 475 W. 3d
Delaplain Frances, bds. 303 George
DeLaroy John D., eng., rear 188 Cutter
DeLarue Maria, saleswoman, 518 Water
DeLarue O., locksmith, 518 Walnut
Delb Jacob, lab., 273 Freeman
Delbrugge Ernst, tailor, bds. 45 Elder
Delcksen Henry, grocery, 23 Green
Deleany Daniel, lab., 414 George
Delehenty Pat., servant, Burnet House
Delg Jacob, 310 W. Liberty
Delin Herman, cab. mkr., 109 Findlay
Deling John, lab., 164 Carr
Delker Mary, 61 Lock
Dell Adams, lab., 14 Hamer
Dell Frederick, agent, 56 13th
Dell N. C., auction, 219 Main, h. 39 W. 6th
Dell Nicholas, tailor, 36 Peete
Dellbrugge Wm., lab., s.s Findlay b. Freeman and Western Av
Dellehunt James, lab., 28 E. Front
Dellen John, lab., wks. 222 E. Front
Deller Henry, shoe mkr., al. b. 13th and Mercer and Vine and Walnut
Deller John, bk. binder, 140 Buckeye
Deller John, brewer, n.s. al. b. Poplar and Vine and Ham. Road and Buckeye
Deller John, cof. h. 140 Buckeye
Deller Peter, 101 Ham. Road
Deller Peter, express driver, 77 Ham. Road
Deller Peter, ice dealer, 140 Buckeye
Dellhoff Frank, cooper, 133 Baymiller
Dellinger Henry A., tailor, 60 W. Mulberry
Delkamp Catharine, 12 Abigail
Dellman Henry, dray, n.s. 6th b. Freeman and W. W. Canal
Dellmann Anton, cigar mkr. s.w.c. Woodward and Pendleton
Dells David, currier, bds Bevis House
Delmel Miss, actress, National Theatre
Delorac James R., clk., 284 Main, bds. U. S. Hotel
Delorac Michael, agent. 180 Linn
Delphin Theodore, molder, 458 E. Front
Demai Sarah, bds. 30 W. Court w. of Central Av
DEMAND MATHIAS, Wholesale Candy Manufacturer and Dealer in Fire Works, Toys, Fruits and Nuts, 207 Main, h. 216 Sycamore
Demann Clemens, cab. mkr., 122 Richmond
Demaree Amanda, 362 Freeman
Demarest Emma L., teacher, s.s. 3d b. Park and Smith
DEMAREST G. L, (Nye & D.) 381 W. 3d
Demcker Robert, teacher, 22 Arch
Deme John, 765 Vine
DeMeester Rev. Peter J., w s. Sycamore b. 6th and 7th
DeMeyer Peter, porter, St. Xavier College
Deming Charles, printer, 52 Clark
Deming Geo., carp., Spencer House
DEMING John, (Down & D.) Melyme, Ohio
DEMING Wm. S., (Straight, D. & Co.) Ashtabula Co
Demler John, cigar mkr., 69 Mohawk
Demmer Charles, tinner, 103 York
Demmer Francis, brewer, wks. J. Kauffman & Co's

Demmet Wm. 374 Elm
Demmitt John, hatter, bds. s.s. Pearl nr. Broadway
Demmett Mrs. Julia A., millinery, 162 W. 5th, h. s.s. Pearl nr. Broadway
Demmon Chas. H., 52 Clark
DeMott Thomas G., clk., bds. 113 Smith
Dempker Adolph, teacher, 22 Arch
Dempsay Henry, tailor, 143 W. Front
Dempsay Lewis, lab., 587 Central Av
Dempsay Michael, grocer, n.w.c. North and New
Dempsey John S.,grocery, s.e.c. 6th and Plum
Dempsey Michael, tinner, wks. 149 W. 5th
Dempsey Thos., salesman, 140 Main, h. 68 Barr
Dempster Mary A., 5 Jane
Dencken Henry, eng., 71 Spring
DeNeal Thomas, cutter, 66 Pike
Denecke Ferdinand, tailor, 60 Ham. Road
Denecke Henry A. T., student, h. 60 Ham. Road
Denghausen Frederick, (Koehnken & Co.) 16 Milton
Dengler Francis X., atty., 22 W. Court, h 120 Betts
Dengler Frederick, wagon mkr., bds, 606 Vine
Denham Alfred C., coal mer. 453 W. 4th
Denham Kate, seamstress. 53 W. 4th
Denham Margaret, seamstress, 53 W. 4th
Denhover George, lab., bds. 19 Abigail
Denigan John, 204 Cutter
Denio Joseph, lab., 1162 E. Front
Denisch John, 128 Mohawk
Denk Joseph, janitor, 99 Woodward
Denker Barney, painter, 589½ W. 6th
Denker Frederick, tailor, n.w.c. Mansfield and Liberty
Denker Henry, 493 Walnut
Denkerlcker John, butcher, e.s. Logan b. Elder and Liberty
Denzinger Frank, shoe mkr., rear 13 E. Liberty
Dennavan John, lab , 678 W. Front
Dennedy Margaret, 48 Plum
Dennedy Patrick, lab., n.w.c. Plum and 3d
Denner Gilge, stone cutter, 124 Clay
Dennett John, wood worker, bds. Farmers Hotel
Denney Maria, bds. 31 Chestnut
Denning Henry. lab., n.s. Corporation Line nr Auburn
Denning Henry, tailor. bds. 14 13th
Dennis Ann M., 114 W. Liberty
Dennis Christopher, hostler, s.s. Patterson al. b. Main and Walnut
Dennis Louis, bk. store, 375 W. 5th
Dennis M. J., (M. J. D. & Co.) res. Walnut Hills
Dennis M. J. & Co., (M. J. D. & H S. Bosworth,) photographers, 28 W. 4th
Dennis Martin, finisher, 239 Bremen
DENNIS O. F., Plasterer, 183 Oliver
Dennis Robt., gas fitter, 35 Hamer
Dennis W. B. & Co., (Warden B. D. & Andrew J. Mullane,) real estate agts. 146 Plum
Dennis Warden B., (W. B. D. & Co.) 99 Dudley
Dennison Mrs , bds. 119 W. 6th
Dennison Edward, peddler, 66 Richmond
DENNISON HOUSE, Wm. R. Buchanan, Proprietor, s.s. 5th b. Main & Sycamore
Dennison Joseph, cooper, 28 Lock n. of 8th
Dennison Luther, stencil cutter, 135 Central Av.
Dennison Mary, teacher, 56 Richmond
Densch Barney, tailor, wks. n.w.c. Main and Court
Densch Michael, cof. h., 704 Central Av
Denser Elizabeth, servant, 261 Richmond
Denser Fidele, brick mkr., 195 Carr
Denver James, cooper, 429 W. 3d

Denz Joseph,tailor,s.w.c. Peete and Poplar
Deopke John H., dry goods, 615 Central Av
Deps Bernhard, shoe mkr., 112 Clay
Depenbrock Barney, rear 72 Hunt
Depenbrock Frederick, horse shoer, wks. 702 Vine
Depenbrock Henry, shoe mkr ,70 Pleasant
Depenbrock Rudolph, tanner, 72 Hunt
Deperets Daniel, cof. h., 156 Ham. Road
Depinel Christopher. salesman, s.s Weller b. Carr and Harriet
DePinal John, clk., 8 E. 4th, h. s.s. W. W. Canal nr. Harriet
DePinal Wm., bleacher, n.w.c. Court and Broadway
Depker Benjamin H., driver,n.e.c. Wood and 3d
Depker Hy., lab., h. 444 W. 3d
Depkins Barney, shoemkr., s.e.c. Main and 6th
Depner Joseph, tailor, 140 Hopkins
Deppe Hy., cigar mkr, 128 Clark
Deppe John, molder, wks. 137 W. 2d
Deppe John H., blksmith, wks. Niles Works
Deppel Andrew, painter, 53 Gest
Deppermann Edmund, jeweler, 289 W. Liberty
Deppray Peter, lab., 9 Mary
Deppri Theodore, bk. layer, 140 Buckeye
Doppleman Edmond, jeweler, 290 W. Liberty
Deppler John. lab., 32 E. Front
Deppy John A., blksmith, 23 Observatory Road
DeRasy Peter, saloon, n.w.c. 7th and Plum
Derbra Nicholas, trunk mkr., wks. 509 Vine
Derby James, 2 E. 7th
Derby Nicholas. salesman, s.e.c. 4th and Vine, bds. Burnet House
Derecamp George, lab., wks. 375 W. 3 d
Deremo John, boots and shoes, 1029 Central Av.
Derencamp Bernhard, lab., 286 Water
Derer Casper, e.s. Hamburg b. Mohawk and Cross
Dererline Lewis, 97 Findlay
DeReuter Cornelius, wks. Cin. type foundry
Derfus Geo., bk. layer, 229 Everett
Derfus Robt., cigar mkr., 87 Ham. Road
Derham Dominick, lab., 65 Vine
De Ricqi s J., music teacher, 118 John
Dering Joseph, peddler, 612 Race
Dering Wm., 52 Dudley
Derman Hy., 28 Pierson
Dermann Hy., driver, 700 Freeman
Dermody Andrew, lab., e.s. State b. 8th and Accommodation
Dermody Joseph, cof. h., 35 Accommodation
Derneady Wm., porter, Burnet House
Dero Leonhard, broom mkr , 597 Race
Derow Jas., broom mkr., e.s. Coggswell al. b. Woodward and Abigail
Derow Peter, broom mkr., e.s Coggswell al. b. Woodward and Abigail
Deroy Amel, druggist, 80 Abigail
Derrenkamp George, bender, 416 Longworth
Derry Joseph, lumber mer., bds. 141 Carr
Dersom Peter, lab., City Water Works office
Derstock Bernhard, tailor, 124 Clay
Derstock Elizabeth, laundress, 124 Clay
Derstok Herman, lab., h. s.s. College al. b. Hunt and Abigail
DeSales Sister, St. John's Hospital, n.w. c. 3d and Plum
DE SAX PLACIDE S., Tell City Dining Saloon, 80 and 82 Walnut, h. 57 W. Front
Desch Phillip, driver, s.s. Pearl b. Pike and Butler
Descher Dietrich, basket mkr., n.e.c. Sycamore and Milton
Deshauer Aaron 24 W. Court
Desilver Anson E., bds. 225 Laurel
Desilver Francis, salesman, 225 Laurel

118 (DEV) CINCINNATI (DHL) DIRECTORY. (DIC)

Desmond John C., mach., bds. 214 W. Front
Desmond John J., china, glass, &c., 330 Central Av
Desmond Michael, eng., 31 York
Desmond Patrick, blksmith, n.s. Patterson al b. M in and Walnut
Dessar Julius H., prof. of languages, 172 Longworth
Dessar Lewis, b.k., 74 W. Pearl, bds. 172 Longworth
Dessauer Levi, barber, n.w.c. Main and Court
Dssum Peter, lab., 94 Betts
Dessmann Hy., lab., s.s. Hubbard b. 5th and 6th
Detch Geo., wood and willow ware, 211 W. 5th, h. Ludlow, Ky
Detchan Hy., 101 W. 6th
Detchen Hy., carp., 295 Elm
Detenbeck Joseph, mach., 25 Observatory Road
Determann Al., shoemkr, 96 W. Front
Determann Franz H., fireman, 16 Milton
Determann J., 497 Race
Determann Hy., express driver, 99 Buckeye
Deters Frank, grocery, 50 Race
Deters Francis H., lab., 13 Bremen
Deters Gerhard H., carp., 587 Race
DETERS JOHN H., Wh. Manufac. Boots, Shoes and Uppers, 53 W. 4th, h. 580 W. 8th
Deters Joseph, cooper, bds. 693 Main
Deters Mary C., h. 21 Abigail
Deters Theodore, box mkr., bds. 70 Sycamore
Detling Geo., carp., 17 Ham. Road
Detling John, stone cutter, 172 Baymiller
Detmer George, cooper, 58 David
Detmer Herman, teamster, 101 Pleasant
Detmer Richd., stone mason, 28 Mansfield
Detmering Apollonia, midwife, 149 Bremen
Detmering Frederick, lab., w.s. Ridgway al. b. W. Liberty and 15th
Detmering Hy., mach., 15 W. Liberty
Detmering Hy. L., 149 Bremen
Dettermann Hy., 19 Milton
Dattert Gerhard H., 301 W. Front
Dattert Hy., tailor, 11 Court House Bldg.
Dattmann John, carp., 599 Elm
Dattmer Bernhard, tailor, 183 Walnut
Dettmer Catharine 83 Spring
Dettmer Hy., plasterer, 378 Broadway
Detzel Michael, American House, 30 E. Front
Deubel F., cab. mkr., 458 W. 5th
Deubel Joseph, cooper, s.s. Findlay b. John and Central Av [5th
Deubel Theobald H., cab. mkr., 458 W.
Deucker Wm., lab., 18 Donnersberger
Deumann Jacob, lab., 609 Main
Deunt Robert D., lab., E. 3d b. Baum & Parsons
Deupener Anton, plasterer, w.s. Hamburg b. Mohawk and Cross
Deuschle Michael, cooper, 264 Sycamore
Deuser Chas. W., baker, 40 Findlay
Deuser Joseph A., lab., 273 Frauz nr. Elder
Deuszer Wm., tailor, bds. 93 Ham. Road
Deutch Phillip, 72 12th
Deutemeier Frederick, blksmith, 416 Sycamore
Deutsch Mary, laundress, 70 12th
Deutsche Leopold, cigar mkr, 110 Bremen
Deutschle Helena, 110 Bremen
Devanna James, bds. 687 Central Av
DeVault Martin, box mkr., wks. 509 Plum
Deveney James, grocery, n.w.c. Cutter and Barr
Deveney James, tailor, 29 Cutter
Devenney Michael, lab., 126 W. Front
Devenney Patrick, 56 Water
Devenny James, dray, s.s. 5th b. Wood and Stone
DEVENNY LAFAYETTE, General Agent Central Ohio, & Pittsburgh, Columbus and Cincinnati, Pennsylvania and Baltimore and Ohio Railroads, 77 W. 3d, h. 359 W. 7th

Deveren John, ink manuf., 149 George
Devereux Lorenz, blksmith, wks. n.e.c. Front and Lawrence
Devery John, lab., n.s. E. Front e. of Leatherbury
Devine Edward, lab., 305 Water
Devine Frederick, lab., 359 Ham. Road
Devine John, dray, bds. 174 E. Pearl
Devine Margaret, servt., 23 8th above Lock
Devine Michael, huckster. 70 Spring
Devine Wm H., cooper, 210 E. 6th
Devinney Wm., lab., 83 Barr
Devit Catharine, 186 Race
Devlin Patrick, shoemkr, 70 W. Court w. of Central Av
Devling Mary, servt., 99 Longworth
Devoe John, 779 Vine
Devol H., lab., wks. Chamberlain & Co's
Devoto A. & Co. (Angelo D. & John Devoto), confec., 6 W. 5th
Devoto Angelo (A. D. & Co.) 70 W. 8th
Devoto Chas., clk., 70 W. 8th
Devoto John (A. Devoto & Co.), h. 172 Bremen
DEWALD MICHAEL, Family Grocery, s.w.c. Linnaeus and Central Av.
De Wald Phillip, hatter, 532 Sycamore
Dewaed Susan, seamstress, wks. 19 Abigail
Dewein Christian, pressman, h. 490 Race
Dewein F., tanner, 267 Ham. Road
Dewein Nicholas, lab., 26 Madison
Dewein Wm., cof. h., 385 W. 4th
Dewerk Martin, lab., n.s. Front e. of Kelly
Dewey Julius E., photographer, 112 W. 5th
Dewgar Alexander, carp., h. E. 6th
Dewin John, grocery, 537 Front, h. 533 E. Front
DeWire Lizzie, servt., 116 Broadway
Dewire Timothy, lab., c.s. Mill b. 2d and W. W. Canal
Dewire Wm., blksmith, wks. n.s. Front b. Lawrence and Pike
DeWitt Garrett V. H., h. 116 E. 4th
Dewitt Ross, 50 E. 2d
DeWolf Theodore, mach., bds. 136 John
Dewyer Bridget, 150 E. Pearl
Dewyer Bridget, n.s 6th e. of Lock
Dewyer James, blksmith, 198 Culvert
Dewyer John, lab., bds. 121 Lock
Dewyer Michael, bds. rear 203 E. 6th
Dewyer Michael, lab., n.e.c. 3d and Butler
Dewyer Patrick, 80 Butler
Dewyer Patrick, blksmith, s.s. 6th e. of Lock
Dewyer Patrick, lab, 16 E. 8th e. of Lock.
Dexheimer Chas. blksmith, 600 Main.
Dexheimer John, blksmith, 559 Walnut n. 601 Walnut.
Dexter Chas. (Edmund D. & Sons) 91 E. 4th.
Dexter Edmund (Edmund D. & Sons.)
Dexter Edmund Jr. (Edmund D. & Sons) n.e c. 4th and Broadway.
Dexter Edmund & Sons. (Edmund, Chas & Edmund Jr.) liquors 51 Sycamore.
Dexter Harrison, (Carson & D) 507 Freeman
Dey John, lab, 444 W. 3d.
Dey Timothy, lab. s.s. 6th b. Broadway and Culvert.
Deyer John, cof. h., 27 Mercer
DeYound Mrs. E., 260 Walnut.
Dezas Chas., tinner, 465 Vine.
Dhaniel Hiram, produce. 96 Barr.
Dhaniel James, clk., bds. 96 Barr.
Dhler Hy., leather mer., 373 Elm.

Dhonau Jacob, harness mkr., e.s Vine b. Auburn Av. and Calhoun.
Dial Frank A., bk. h. 104 Broadway.
Diamon Mary, 54 Kossuth.
Diamond Edward, varnisher, 477 W. 3d.
Diamond John, lab.. 55 E. 8th e. of Lock.
Diamond John, marble cutter, wks., n. e.c. Miami Canal & Elm
Diarstock John. moulder, wks., n.e c. Canal and Walnut.
Dibone Rebecca, 13 Abigail.
Dick Catharine, h. 639 Vine.
Dick Elizabeth, dress mkr., bds. 227 Cutter.
Dick Harvey, clk., bds., Frey's Hotel.
Dick Hy., 137 Livingston.
Dick Hy., hinge fitter, wks., n.e.c. Walnut and Canal.
Dick Hy., 60 Abigail.
Dick Hy., lab., 702 Freeman.
Dick John, lab., 702 Freeman.
Dick Lizzie, seamstress, 630 Vine
Dick Martin, dairy e.s. Western Av. nr. Harrison Pike.
Dick Wm., cab. mkr., bds 97 Jackson.
Dick Wm. A., watchman, 87 Milton.
Dick Wm. U., carp., 42 Barr.
Dicker Ursula, servant, bds., n.w.c. 12th and Vine
Dickerson John H., Ass. Q. M. U. S. A. 56 W. 3d, bds. Clifton House.
Dickerson Wm., barber s.s. Cherry Al., b. Elm & Plum.
Dickescheid George, shoe mkr., 313 Main
Dickescheid Peter, dining hall 171 Walnut, h. 183 Walnut.
Dickescheid V., saloon, 183 Walnut.
Dickescheid Wendel, bar k., 183 Walnut.
Dickey Elizabeth, 459 Sycamore.
Dickey James B., porter, 450 Sycamore.
Dickey Nancy J., 60 Water.
Dickhaus Frederick, cutter, 116 Abigail
Dickhaus Frederick, lab, 37 Hughes.
Dickhoff August, finisher, 14 Mary.
Dickhoene August, lab., 114 Carr.
Dickhouse Hy., porter, 143 W. 3d.
DICKINSON D. L., Produce & Commission Merchant, 11 and 13 W. Front, h. Lockland.
DICKINSON, PRICE & BISHOP. (Wm. S. D., John Z. P. & John W. B.,) wh., dealers in Hats, Caps & Straw Goods, 102 and 104 W. Pearl.
DICKINSON Wm. S. (D. Price & Bishop.) 347 W. 7th.
Dickman Garret, clk., n.w.c. Plum and 2d.
Dickman John, saw filer, wks., 1565 E. Front.
Dickman Henry J., foreman, 22 Lodge.
DICKMAN MARTIN, Family Grocery, n.w.c. Plum and 2d.
Dickmann Geo. H., potter. 135 Abigail.
Dickmann Hy., chair mkr., 418 Longworth.
Dickmann Hy., porter 13 Madison.
Dickmann John H. tailor, 597 Race.
Dickoff Hy., lab wks., n.e.c. Walnut and Canal.
Dicksmann Wm., cab. mkr., 110 Pleasant.
Dickson Alice, h. 132 Central Av.
Dickson C., eng., 304 Broadway.
Dickson James, Gas Al. b. 2d and Front.
Dickson John. 21 George.
Dickson John. w.s. Ohio Av., b. Calhoun and N. Elm.
DICKSON John, (Gasten D. & Co.) 165 Race.
Dickson Loyd, cooper, 40 Peete
Dickson Martha, 48 Milton.
Dickson Mary, n.w. 4th and Sycamore.
Dickson Rob. B., clk., n.w.c. 5th and Sycamore.
Dickson Samuel, painter, 191 W. 4th.
Dickson Thomas, bds., e.s. Macalister b. 4th and 5th.
Dickson Wm. B., painter, 48 Mound.
Dickson Wm. J., salesman, 104 Walnut.
DICKSON WM. M. Atty. at Law 6 E. 3d Chase's Bldg. h 321 Longworth.

CINCINNATI (DIF) DIRECTORY. (DIN) 119

Dieker Hy., cooper 37 Buckeye.
Diekhart Martin, lab., rear 524 E. Front.
Diekhaus Catharine, 112 Buckeye.
Diekler Chas., e.s. Vine near Auburn Av.
Diekman Frank, box mkr., wks., s.w c M.. Canal and 5th
DIEKMANN GERHARD, Leather & Findings, 349 Main, h. 448 Walnut.
Diekmann Hy., tailor. 60 13th.
Diekmann & Stiens (Herman H. D., & Francis S.) stables 627 Race.
Diekmeier Henry P., lab , 7 15th b. Elm and Plum.
Diekmeier John H., clk., 7 15th b. Elm and Plum.
Diel Christian, dray, rear 507 Elm.
Diel John, tailor, 277 Freeman.
Diemann Christian, tailor, 7 Wade b. Elm and Plum.
Diemann Elizabeth, seamstress. Hay Al. b. 13th and Mercer and Vine and Walnut.
Dienst Ernst, cab. mkr., 491 Race.
Dieringer Celestin. cooper, Pleasant b. Findlay and Henry.
Dierken Bernhard, lab., 22 Woodward.
Dierker Deitrich (H. J. Cordesman & D. D.) 290 W. Front.
Dierker Richard, molder, W. Front.
Dierkers Elizabeth, 97 Milton.
Dierkers Hy., tailor, n.e.c. Pendleton and Abigail.
Dierkers Hermann, lab., n.e.c. Pendleton and Abigail.
Dierkes Barney, painter, 97 Pendleton.
Dierkes Bernard, collar mkr., 15 Commerce.
Dierkes Catharine, 19 Mulberry.
Dierkes Gertrude, 97 Pendleton.
Dierkes Hermann, tailor, 76 Dudley.
Dierkes Miss Mary, seamstress, 19 Mulberry.
Dierks Barney, marbleizer, wks. 267 W. 5th
Diers Frederick, tailor, 13 Wade, W. of Jnn
Diers Herman S., Fountain st. Jackson hil
Diers Hy. W., sawyer, wks. Meader & C 's
Diers Vm., mach., wks. n.w.c. Smith & Front
Dies Louis, cab. mkr., e.s. Main b. Schiller and Liberty
Diesle Michael, cooper, 366 Sycamore
Dieterich Samuel, carp., s.w.c 2d and Ludlow
Dietermann Anton., lab., 59 Abigail
Dieterle Andrew, cof. h., 019 Central Av
Dieterle John, shoe mkr., 125 E. Pearl
Dieterly Jacob, carp., 44 Hamer
Dietmann Jacob, dray, 64 Ham. Road
Dietmier Adam, packer, wks. 131 Race
DIETRICH CLEMENT, Pres. Dayton & Michigan R.R. Office 5 College Building, h. Glendale, Ohio
Diettrich Francis, carriage mkr., 101 Ham. Road
Dietrich Francis, peddler, 91 Ham. Road
Dietrich Jacob, tailor, 185 Bremen
Dietrich Herman, carriage mkr., 589 Walnut
Dietrich Peter, trader, 91 Martin
Dietrichs Carl, silver-smith, 364 Broadway
Dietrick John, bar k., bds. Teutonia Hotel
Dietsch Dora, servt. 489 Vine
Dietterich Michael, b.k. 380 Main, h. 555 Sycamore
Dietz Catharine, 716 Vine
Dietz Frederick H., porter, n.s. Schiller, b. Main and Hughes
Dietz Fred. W., book store, h. 611 W 8th
Dietz John, boots and shoes, 928 Central Av
Dietz Louis, machinist, 718 Vine, h. 716 Vine
Dievenbach Frederick, bds. 920 Central Av
Diewald Jacob, stone cutter, 157 York
Diewald Phillip, hatter, 532 Sycamore
Diffley James, lab., 54 Rittenhouse
Diffley James, jr., plasterer, 54 Rittenhouse

Digan James, lab., 184 E. Pearl
Digman M., lab., wks. Chamberlain & Co.'s
Dignan Bridget, servt., 273 George
Dignan Jeremiah, 20 Pierson
Dignan John, lab., s.w.c. 5th and Central Av
Dignan Mary, 163 E. 3d
Dignen John, carp.. 445 W. 3d
Dih Hy., lab.. bds. s.s. Liberty, b. Freeman and Mill Creek
Dihm Michael, cab. mkr., e.s. Goose al. b. Liberty and 13th
Dile Phillip, express, rear 91 Findlay
Dildine George, painter, 466 W. 5th
Dilg Adam, hall keeper, 38 W. Court
Dilg Peter, tanner, bds. n.w.c. Linn and Poplar
Dilg Wm., clk., U. S. Express Co.
Dill Anna, bds. 146 E. 5th
Dill James, jr., salesman, 94 W. Pearl, bds. Walnut-st. House
Dill Julia E., 148 W. 8th
Dillan Mary, 301 W. 6th
Dille Salathiel, jr., carp., s.w.c. John & Richmond
Dillean Anthony, lab., w.s. Langdon al. b. 6th and 7th
Dillhoff Anna, 133 Baymiller
Dillhoff Hy. J., cooper. 9 Woodward
Dillhoff Theodore, butcher, 133 Baymiller
Dillhough George, cooper wks. s.s. Gest, b. Freeman and Carr
Dillinger John, tailor, 58 Ham. Road
Dillman Hy , dray, 584 W. 6th
Dillman Hy.. mill wright, wks. n.w.c. Pearl and M. Canal
Dillman Willis, carriage smith, 222 Broadway
Dillon Amelin, 128 Walnut
Dillon Catharine, 92 Baymiller
Dillon Catharine, 311 John
Dillon Garrett, bds. e.s. Main, b. 8th and 9th
Dillon Hannora, servt., 431 Broadway
Dillon James, shoe mkr., 15 E. 8th
Dillon Maria, 245 W. 7th
Dillon Mary, chambermaid, Burnet House
Dillon Phillip, bds. s.s. 8th, b. Sycamore and Broadway
Dillon Phillip, lab., n.s. Whetstone al. b. Broadway and Sycamore
Dillon Thomas, bk. layer, 138 Dayton
Dillon Thomas, lab., Maiden Lane, b. 2d and Front
DILLS W. R., Commission Merchant, and Dealer in Grain and Feed, 91 & 93 W. Miami Canal, h. 645 Elm
Dilly Salathiel, mach., s.e.c. Richmond and John
Dilsor Joseph, 44 Sycamore
Dimick Miss Ada, phys., 171 W. 4th
Dimick Otis W., horse trainer, 41 Cutter
Dimons Barnhard, molder, 1518 E Front
Dinan Daniel, collar mkr., 89 Main
Dinan James, lab., 293 E. 6th
Dinckhuf Joseph, plumber, wks. 397 Vine
Dingelstedt Charles, shoe mkr , 569 Main
Dingelstedt Otto, shoe mkr., 569 Main
Dinger Jane, 138 Dayton
Dingess John A., agt., 134 George
Dinginhausen Fred, 16 Milton
Dinidy Ellen, servt., 430 W. 6th
Dink Hy., lab., 21 Lodge
Dinkel George, boatman. 42 W. Front
Dinkel Margaret. 42 W. Front
Dinkel Mary, 42 W. Front
Dinkel Stephen, driver. 15 Poplar
Dinkelacker C. & F., (Charles & Frederick D.,) meats, 139 W. 5th
Dinkelacker Chas., (C. & F. D.,) 742 W. Front
Dinkelacker Frederick, (C. & F. D,) 742 W. Front
Dinkelbihler John, tailor, 708 Vine
Dinkelman August, shoe mkr., bds. 32 Rittenhouse
Dinkelman Geo. H., boots and shoes, 32 Rittenhouse
Dinkelmann Wm., cooper, 147 Pleasant
Dinnebache. carp., bds. 225 W. 6th
Dinneen Marg., servt.. Burnet House
Dinner George, stone cutter, 124 Clay

120 (DOB) CINCINNATI (DOE) DIRECTORY. (DOL)

Dinner Hy., varnisher, bds. n.w.c. Pike and Pearl
Dinsdale Owen, lab., s s. Dorsey, near Sycamore
Dinsdale Thomas, carp., s.s. Dorsey, nr. Sycamore
Dinsmore Samuel J., mach., 193 W. Court, w. of Central Av
Dipold Lorenz. blksmith, 194 Bremen
Dipper Frederick, plasterer, 647 W. Front
Dir Edward, blksmith, 608 Elm
Dircks Barney, mach., 71 Spring
Diring Wm., lab., wks. 728 Central Av
Dirk Lewis, lab., 808 W. Front
Dirker Wm , porter, 53 Hughes
Dirkers Barney, harness mkr., bds. 15 Commerce, b. Walnut and Vine
Dirks August, grocery, n.w.c. Grant and Elm
Dirmuller Joseph, cab. mkr., 202 Clark
Dirrick Lewis, butcher, 560 Elm
Dirsch Casper, lab., wks. Queen City Distillery
Dischmeier Frederick, cooper, w.s. Pendleton, b. Abigail and Woodward
Discher Dietrich, (Eppens & D.,) n.e.c. Sycamore and Milton
Dischinger Raymond, cab. mkr., 629 Vine
Dischler Wm., lab., bds s.w.c. Clifton Av and Corporation line
Discon Michael, lab., s.s. Friendship al , b. Pike and Butler
Diserens Frank L., bar k., 29 W. 5th
DISERENS FREDERICK, Proprietor Wm. Tell Exchange, 29 W. 5th
Diserens Frederick, jr , clk., 24 W 5th, bds. Wm. Tell Exchange
Diserens Hy., 71 Clinton
Disman Hy., lab., wks. 222 E Front
Disney Mrs. David T., 29s W. 7th
Disney T. Bishop, clk., 141 Main, b. 357 W. 9th
Disney Wm., asst. city solicitor, 298 W. 7th
Diss Louis, cab mkr , wks. 41 W. 2d
Distel Conrad, cof. h., 52 Elder
Distel John, tanner, 58 Stark
Distler Conrad, 705 Elm
Distler Geo., shoe mkr., w.s. Lebanon Road, near Montgomery Pike
Distler John, 705 Elm
Distler John G., paper carrier, 53 Peete
Ditchen Phillip J., bk binder, 51 Laurel
Ditcher Charity, e.s. Pancoast al. b. 7th and 8th
Ditcher Moses, cock, 27 Race
Ditenhaver Margaret, washwoman, 175 W. Canal
Ditmars Isaac V., cutter, 106 W. Pearl, h. 413 W. 8th
DITSON Oliver, (Smith & D.,) h. Boston, Mass.
Ditten James P., 185 W. M. Canal
Dittman Isadore, boots and shoes, 140 Walnut, h. s.e.c. 9th and Vine
Dittmann Jacob, lab., 11 Buckeye
Ditton Paul, 187 W. Canal
Dittus Frederick, baker, 431 Sycamore
Divine Wm., carp., wks. C. H. & D. R. R paint shop
Dixon Charles, eng., e.s. M. Canal, b. 8th and Court
Dixon Chas. P., fruits, bds. 473 W. 5th
Dixon George, lab., h. n.s. Railroad, e. of Hazen
Dixon George H., fruits, 103 W. 5th, h. 473 W 5th
DIXON Geo. R., (Geo. R. D. & Co.,) h. 156 W. 9th
DIXON GEO. R. & CO., (Geo. R. D. & Isaac W. Parker,) Ohio Spice & Mustard Mills, 243, 245 and 247 Sycamore
Dixon Helen, 235 W. 7th
Dixon Humphrey, porter, 22 Union
Dixon Peter J., lab., 170 E. Pearl
Dixon Saml. B., driver, bds. 473 W. 5th
Dixon Joseph, bk binder, c.s. Park, b. Longworth and 5th
Dioupf John, peddler, 63 Kossuth
DOANE Wm. H., (J. A. Fay & Co.,) 137 W. 7th
Dobhelling Fred., clk, 434 Plum, h. 562 Freeman

DOBBELING JOHN F., Stone Yard, 434 Plum h. 562 Freeman
Dobbins Thomas, tin shop, h. 68 W. Court, w. of Central Av
Dobell Edwin B., furniture warehouse, 22 E Pearl, e. of Broadway, h. 257 W. 3d
Dobell Mary A., bds. 257 W. 3d
Dobell Wm. T., grocery, 288 W. 6th, h. 337 W 5th
Doberle John, baker, 585 Walnut
DOBMEYER JOSEPH G., Attorney at Law, n.w.c. Court & Main, h. 80 W.9th
Dobmeyer M. A., teacher, h. 109 Betts
Dobmeyer Michael, teacher, bds. 137 Race
Dobney Benjamin, tobacconist, 15 Stone
Dobson Mary Ann, dress mkr., n.e.c Longworth and Plum
Docker Frank, lab., 137 Laurel
Docker John A., grocery, 91 Hopkins
Dodd Edward, tailor, 290 E. 6th
Dodd Edward, banker, 33 E. 3d
DODD EDWIN D., (D. & Huston,) h. 430 W. 9th w. of Central Av.
Dodd Edward S., (Wm. Dodd & Co.,) bds. 366 W. 4th
DODD Geo. S., (Wm. Dodd & Co.,) 114 W. 7th
Dodd Hy., hatter, 366 W. 4th
DODD & HUSTON, (Edwin D. D. & Alex. B H.,) Attorneys at Law, 14 E. 9d
DODD Wm., (Wm. D. & Co.,) h. 366 W. 4th
DODD WILLIAM & CO., (Wm., Geo. S. & Edward S. Dodd,) Wholesale and Retail Dealers in Hats Caps and Furs, 144 Main
Dodds James, card writer, Burnet House
Dodds John, molder, bds. 214 W. Front
DODDS Wm N., (W. B. D. & Co.,) h. s.e.c Plum and McFarland
DODDS WILLIAM B. & CO., (Wm B. D. & N. Mackeel,) Fire and Burglar Proof Safe Manufacturers, s.s. Pearl b. Elm and Plum
Dodey John, blksmith, wks. 11 W. 7th
DODGE ISRAEL F., Physician and Surgeon, Office and Residence 313 Race
Dodge Wm., shoe m kr, 174 W. 9th
Dodson Chas. A., clk., n.w.c. 3d and Walnut, res. Walnut Hills
Dodson Wm. B., mate, 414 W. 3d
Dodsworth Edward locksmith, s.w.c. 8th and Central Av.
Dodsworth Edward, mach., wks. Geo. L. Musters & Co's
DODSWORTH Marmaduke, jr., (T. & M. D.,) h. 52 Lawrence
Dodsworth Martin, salesman, 85 Main, h. 61 Everett
DODSWORTH T. & M. (Thomas D. & Marmaduke D., Jr.,) Coal Yards s.e.c. Front and Lawrence and n.e.c. Walnut and Court
DODSWORTH Thomas, (T. & M. D.,) h. 56 Lawrence
Dodt Bernard H., wagon mkr., 68 Spring
Dodt Clemens, wagon mkr., 347 Broadway [Hughes
Doebbeling Frederick, blksmith, 49
Doebben John, shoe mkr., 192 Pleasant
Doeding Hermann, lab., bds. 468 Main
Doeflinger Frederick, lab., 40 Ham Road
Doegen Wm., b. k., 51 Hopkins
Doehn Peter, butcher, 177 W. Liberty
Doel Hy., watch mkr , 386 Vine
Doelk Christian, 50 Dunlap
Doell Adam, lab., 14 Hamer
Doell Geo., bark., s.w.c. 19th and Main
Doeller August, calico printer, 15 14th b. Central Av. and Plum
Doeller Leopold, n.s. Rice near Fountain
Doenselmann Hermann, dry goods, 31 Ham. Road
Doepke Philip, grocery, 16 Mulberry
Doepker Catharine, servt., 91 Woodward
Doepker Elizabeth, seamstress, 91 Woodward

Doepker Gertrude, 91 Woodward
Doepp John., porter, 91 Ham. Road
Doer Patrick, wagon mkr., 251 W. 3d
Doerer Michael clk., bds. 445 Main
Doerfler John, lab., 246 Pleasant
Doering John H., cab. mkr., 170 Ham. Road
Doerler Jacob, lab., 640 Vine
Doerler John, tinware, 292 Broadway
Doerner Andreas. shoe mkr., 25 15th
Doerr Andrew, tailor, 57 W. Liberty
Doerr Chas., cutter, 387 Vine
Doerr Chas., tailor, e.s. Johnson al. b. Canal and 12th
Doerr George, tailor, n.w.c. Pleasant and Green
Does Conrad, dray, 495 Walnut
Doescher Albert, candy manuf., 36 12th
Doescher John, molder, 402 Vine
Doetcker Hermann, cooper, 71 Buckeye
Doetmann Margaret, 27 Franklin
Dohannay Bridget, s.s. 6th b. Broadway and Culvert
Doheen John, gold pen mkr., 198 E. 6th
Doherty Anna, tailoress, 266 W. Water
Doherty Bernard, 68 Cutter
Doherty Bridget, servt., 416 W. 4th
Doherty Charles, clk., s.s. 12th b. Vine and Race
DOHERTY Chas. C., (Chas. C. D. & Co.,) 31 W. Pearl
DOHERTY CHARLES C. & CO., (Chas. C. D. & Co.,) Wholesale Millinery and Silks. 34 W. Pearl
Doherty Edward, driver, 25 Accomodation
DOHERTY GEORGE A., Physician and Surgeon, Office and Residence 223 Broadway
Doherty James, clk., 41 Elm
Doherty James M., pres. City Pass. street R. R., 160 York
Doherty John, 196 E. 6th
Doherty John, lab , 28 Broadway
Doherty John, lab., wks. 18 Sycamore
Doherty John, mate, 89 E. 5th
Doherty Joseph M., clk., s.w.c. 9th and Central Av
Doherty Nicholas, dray, 361 Broadway
Doherty Michael, fireman, 334 W. 3d
Doherty Mary, laundress Spencer House
Doherty Paul, bk. binder, 12th b. Vine and Race
Doherty Patrick, hatter, al. b. 4th and 5th and Central Av. and John
Doherty Timothy A., mach., 225 Race
Doherty Wm. F., cutter, 155 Hopkins
Dohr Jacob, painter. 144 Bremen
Dohrman Dietrich, hostler, 177 W. 6th
Doisy Adelbert E., salesman, 113 W. Pearl.
Dokenwadeh Johanna, w.s. Goose al. b Green and Elder
Dokes Jacob P., watchman, 148 Barr
Dolan Bridget, laundress, n.e.c. 3d and Butler
Dolan Caren, lab., rear 970 E. Front
Dolan Catharine, 405 Race
Dolan John, carp., Celestial St. Mt. Adams
Dolan John, driver, s.s. Hubbard b. 5th and 6th
Dolan M., clk., bds. 186 Race
Dolan Patrick, lab., 108 Culvert
Dolan Patrick, lab., 253 Freeman
Dolan Patrick, lab., 35 E. 8th e. of Lock
Dolby Noah, steward, s.e.c. 3d and Mill
Dold Chas., blksmith, bds. 13 Freeman
DOLE Eben, (Chas. H. Waters & Co.,) 245 Hopkins
Dole Marion R., teacher, 61 W. 8th
Dole Mary A., teacher, bds. 61 W. 8th
Duley Patrick, lab., 35 E. 8th e. of Lock
Dolf Hy., tailor, 553 Walnut
Doll Francis. watch case mkr., s w.c. 4th and Walnut, h. 386 Vine
Doll Geo. J., cof. h. 58 W. Liberty
Doll Jacob, cof. h. 76 Ham. Road
Doll Joseph, tailor, 222 Clark
Doll Robert, cof. h. 554 Walnut
Doll Robert, coffee roaster 544 Walnut
Doll Rose, 62 Butler
Dell Samuel, coffee roaster, 466 Walnut
Dollanty Wm., hostler, 78 W. 6th

Dolle Geo., bottler, s.s. Atigail b. Sycamore and Main
Dolley Ellen, 204 Plum
Doller Adam, cof. h. 321 Broadway
Doller Hy., 431 Plum
Doller Jacob, carp., 105 W. Liberty
Dollmann Anthony, cigar mkr. 115 Woodward
Dollmann Frank H., 79 Pendleton
Dollmann Wm., varnisher, 26 Orchard
Dolloer Michael, 300 Vine
Dollmann Isaac, peddler, 726 Central Av
Dolph A. M., salesman, s.e.c. 4th and Walnut, h. Walnut Hills
Dolph Mary, waiter, Dennison House
Dolph Moses, show case manuf., s.e.c. 4th and Walnut, h. Walnut Hills
Dolwig Valentine, tailor, bds. 628 W. 6th
Dombaugh Val., printer, bds. 243 W. 5th
Domeier Henrietta, 424 W. Liberty
Domhof Hy., tailor, 556 W. Walnut
Dominica Sister. St. Clare Convent, n.w.c 3d and Lytle
DOMINICK Geo., (Geo. D. & Bro.,) 93 E. 4th
DOMINICK GEORGE & BRO., (Geo. D. & Wm. H. D.,) Beef and Pork Packers, Ham Curers and Dealers in Provisions. 25 and 27 Water
DOMINICK Wm. H., (Geo. D. & Bro.,) h. Avondale
Donahue Ann, 539 W. 8th
Donahue Dennis, lab., 351 W. 5th
Donahue James, waiter, Walnut Street House
Donahue John, lab, 168 Freeman
Donaldson Alex, mach., s.w.c. John and Augusta, h. 70 Avery
Donaldson Andrew, clk., 39 W. 4th h. e. s. Park b. 4th and 5th
Donaldson Thomas, baggage master, O. & M. R. R., h. 190 Mill
Donaldson W. M., lithographer, 64 W. 4th
Donavan Wm., lab., w.s. Lock b. 8th and Court
Donbusch Frederick, shoe mkr., 185 W. 2d
Donderos D., confec., 93 W. 5th
Donela James, porter, 369 W. 7th
Donela Peter, clk., 369 W. 7th
Donelan Peter, salesman. 43 Main
Donelly Margaret, laundress, Gibson House
Donevan Dennis, finisher, 14 E. 8th e. of Lock
Doney Chas. bk. layer. 100 Hopkins
Doney Nancy A , 162 Clark
Donge August, shoe mkr., 579 Main
Donigan James, lab., n.s. Avery al. w. of Wood
Donkman Christopher, cab. mkr., 242 Hopkins
Donlan Martin, lab., 50 Pike
Donien Bridget, servt., 50 Mound
Donling Patrick, lab , 203 W. Front
Donlon James, porter, 309 W. 7th
Donn David, lab., 936 W. Front
Donnagan Bridget, 647 W. Front
Donnavan Corydon, printer, 411 Longworth
Donnavan Wm., blksmith, 19 E. 8th
Donnegan Joseph, lock mkr., wks n.e.c. Walnut and Canal
Donnegan Wm., lock mkr., wks. n.e.c. Walnut and Canal
Donnahue, porter, n.e.c. 3d and Vine
Donnahue Bernard, lab., n.w.c. 3d and Collard
Donnahue John, lab., 19 Mill
Donnellon Thomas, bds. 158 W. 3d
Donnelly Anna, h. e.s. Crippen al. b. 7th and 8th
Donnelly August, printer, 99 Mound
Donnelly Cornelius, lab , 175 E. 6th
Donnelly Francis M., 207 W. 3d
Donnelly John, b.k., 40 York
Donnelly Kate, dress mkr., 235 Cutter
Donnelly Michael, cof. h , 189 W 6th
Donnelly Patrick, clk., bds. 227 Broadway
Donnelly Patrick, driver, 52 Elizabeth
Donnelly Patrick, lab., Weller nr. Mill Creek
Donnelly Patrick, tinner, 78 Race 10

Donnelly T., bds. 158 W. 3d
Donnelly Thomas, 50 E. 2d
Donnelly Thomas, s.e.c. 7th and Broadway
Donnelly Thos., lab., wks. n.e.c. Walnut and Canal
Donnelly Thomas, varnisher, s.s. Phoebe al. b. Plum and Central Av.
Donnelly Wm., bk. layer, 297 W. 3d
Donner Frederick, cooper, 149 Poplar
Donnerberg Christ., cooper, 16 Hughes
Donnersberger Anthony, s.e.c. 8th and Donnersberger
DONNERSBERGER Joseph, (Fredewest & D.) h. 613 W 8th
Donnewald Christopher, meats, 94 Dudley
Donnivan Cornelius, lab., 238 Water
Donnohoe Edward, lithographer, s.s. O'Reilly al. b. Pike and Lawrence
Donnohoe Patrick, lab., w.s. Central Av. b. 2d W. W. Canal
Donohue Frank, lab., 97 Clark
Donohue Ann, servt., 390 George
Donoghue Florence, dray, 718 W. 6th
Donoghue Michael, dray, 718 W. 6th
Donoghue Michael, lab., 238 Water
Donohue John, grocery, 62 W. Court w. of Central Av.
Donohue John, jr., bds. 62 W. Court w. of Central Av.
Donohue Cornelius, 444 W. 4th
Donohue Edward, s.s al. b. Pike and Lawrence and 3d and Pearl
DONOHUE J. W. & CO., (John W. D. & Wm. Galway) Dealers in Coal Oil and Gun Powder, s.e.c. Walnut and 2d
Donohue James, lab., 126 Carr
Donohue James, roller, bds. s.e.c. 2d and Smith
Donohue Jeremiah, porter, 26 Commerce
Donohue John, blksmith, n.s. 6th b. Carr and Harriet
Donohue John, cof. h. s.e.c. 3d and Walnut, h. 111 Mill
Donohue John, lab., n.e.c. Richmond and Freeman
Donohue John, police, Von Seggern al. b. Abigail and Woodward
DONOHUE John W., (J. W. D. & Co.) h. 105 Broadway
Donohue Margaret, s.s. al. b. Pike and Lawrence and 3d and Pearl
Donohue Mary Ann, servt., 324 Longworth
Donohue Oliver, bds. 106 Broadway
Donohue Patrick, lab., Von Seggern al. b. Abigail and Woodward
Donohue Patrick, sergeant-at-arms Co. Auditor's office
Donohue Rosa, 578 W. 9th
Donohue Thomas J., eng. 26 Brighton
Donohue Wm., lab., bds. 126 Carr
Donovan Bartholomew, lab., 71 E. 8th
Donovan Mrs. Catharine. 109 Mulberry
Donovan Catharine, s.e.c. 6th and Sycamore
Donovan Cornelius, dray, 110 Betts
Donovan Daniel, clk., 23 E. 7th
Donovan Ellen, s.e.c. 8th and Sycamore
Donovan Jeremiah, gardener, 110 Betts
Donovan John, blksmith, s.e c. 8th and Sycamore
Donovan Mary A., 107 Mulberry
Donovan Patrick, lab., 201 Broadway
Doolan Charles, lab., n.s. 6th e of Lock
Doolan Mary, servt., 321 Longworth
Doolan Sarah, laundress, e. 6th and Accommodation
Dooley Patrick, teamster, 441 Sycamore
Dooley James, porter, 62 Hunt
Dooley John, cof. h., 23 Accommodation
Dooley Julia, State b. Deer Creek Road and Accommodation
Dooley Mary, servt., 111 Pike
Dooley Patrick, teamster, s.s. Coggswell al. b. Franklin and Woodward
Dooley Richard, horse trader, bds. 96 Gest
Doolittle Amos H , b.k. 93 Main, bds. s. e.c. 3d and Broadway
Doorley James, lab., 111 E. 3d
Doorley John. shoe mkr., 68 Butler
Dopp John, shoe mkr., bds. 249 W. 6th
Dopp Solomon, carp., rear 986 E. Front

Dopke Frederick, millinery, 91 and 93 Martin
Doppelmann Frank, shoe mkr., bds. 261 W. 3d
Doppes John D., clk. w.s. Freeman opp. George, h. 3 Pine
Doppler Andrew, cof. h., 764 Central Av.
Dor John, lab , wks. Lane & Bodley's
Dora Wm. N., real estate, 37 W. 3d, h. Covington
Doram Catharine, 43 Barr
Doram Jane, matron of Asylum for colored orphans, s.s. W. 9th b. Elm and Plum
Doramday Margaret, servt., 296 W. 6th
Doran Anna, h n.w.c. 3d and Ellen
Doran Edward, tinner. bds. s.s. Fremont b. Carr and Harriet
Doran Ellen, 12 E. 6th
Doron John, asst. eng. fire dept., 45 Mansfield
Doran John, sawyer, 170 Cutter
Doran Paul, lab., w.s. Central Av. b. 2d and W. W. Canal Basin
Doras Charles, harness mkr., bds. 173 W. 3d
Dorches John, express driver, 172 Spring
Dore Patrick, turner, 251 W. 3d
Doren John, wks. junction 6th and Front
Dorenkamp Mary. servt., 116 E. 5th
Dorfeuille Jennette. 351 W. 8th
D'Orfeuille M. J., teacher, 351 W. 8th
Dorgan Stephen, grocery. 381 W. 2d
Doris Hy , cigar mkr., 452 Elm
Doriss James, lab., 30 Lock n. of 8th
Dorland Alex. M., salesman n.w.c. Main and Pearl, h. 233 W. 4th
DORLAND GARRET T., Watches and Jewelry, n.w.c. Main and Pearl, h 61 McFarland
Dorland Luke, lab., wks. C. T. Dumont's
Dorle Mathias, lab., n.w.c. Ramsey and Park al.
Dorley Eliza. servt., 96 E. 4th
Dorman Christ.. s.s. Calhoun b. Clifton Av. and McMillan
Dorman E. E., b.k., 227 Broadway
Dorman Harriet, 98 E. 5th
Dorman John, carp., wks. W. M. Cameron's & Co's
Dorman John C., periodicals, 462 Broadway
Dorman Sidney A., 462 Broadway
Dorman Wm., driver, bds. 62 Richmond
Dormann Hy., express man, e.s. Oregon b. 3d and 6th
Dormandy Wm.. lab.. 224 E. 6th
Dormer Arnold. b.k. 111 W. Pearl, bds. 172 Longworth
Dormity Philip, lab., 611 W. 8th
Dormor Samuel P., mach., wks., 659 Vine
Dorn Bernard, lab., 22 Commerce
Dorn Catharine. 550 W. 3d
Dorn Conrad, blksmith, 600 Walnut
Dorn Frederick. baker, 271 Freeman
Dorn Kate. 116 W. Liberty
Dorn Philip, meats, 93 Ham. Road
Dorn Thomas, boiler mkr., 43 Mill
Dorna Christian, cof. h., 529 E. Front
Dorna Nicholas, lab., wks. Cincinnati Chemical Laboratory
Dorna Peter, lab., n.e.c Front and Parsons
Dornberg Leander, printer, 383 Vine
Dornberger Frank, cooper, wks. 30 Webster
Dornbusch Adolph, lab , 1 Mulberry
Dorna Nicholas. lab. 54 Martin
Dorney Mrs Adeline M., 377 W. 4th
Dornhager Philip, hostler, 95 E. 2d
Dornhoefer Moritz. cof. h., 94 Buckeye
Dornkamp Kate. servt., 201 Richmond
Dorr A. K., 14 Main, h. 31 George
Dorr Eliza, e.s. Cutter b. Betts and Clinton
Dormind John, peddler, 207 W. 2d
Dorries Hy., cigar mkr., 452 Elm
Dorrmann Frederick, blksmith, 509 Elm, h. 507 Elm
Dorrna Peter, lab., 544 E. Front
Dorsch John, (D. Torner & Co.) s.e.c. Freeman and Findlay

122 (DOU) CINCINNATI (DRA) DIRECTORY. (DRE)

Dorsch, Torner & Co., (John D., Hy. T. & Joseph Kleber) coopers, s.s. Dayton b. Freeman and Western Av.
Dorse Jacob, tailor, n.s. al. b. Race and Ham. Road n. of Findlay
Dorsey John E. P., printer, 12 Jane
Dorsey Garrett, lab., 96 Brighton
Dorsey Patrick J., lab., 976 E. Front
Dorst Barbara, w s. Ridgway al. b. 14th and 15th
Dorst Catharine, 129 Bank
Dorst Dietrich, cab. mkr., 86 Vine
Dorst Isaac, n.w.c. Browne and Ravine al.
Dorst Isaac, tannery, rear 23 Dunlap, h. 19 Dunlap
Dorst John, harness mkr., 129 Bank
Durst Valentine, finisher, 2 Lucy
Dory James, driver, 53 Pendleton
Dory Peter, publisher, 85 Darr
Dosch Frederick, lab., 583 Walnut
Dosh Daniel, bk. layer, 164 York
Doss Robert, carpet mkr., 203 W. Front
Dossatt James, bds. 444 W. Front
Dossmann Anthony F., 20 Webster
Dothage Wm., lab., 20 Commerce
Dotkarte Chas., 281 W. Liberty
Dotkarte Frank, cab. mkr., 281 W. Liberly
Dotmann Bernhard, teamster, 293 Water
Dott Nicholas, box mkr., 18 Allison
Doty Hannah, 600 Freeman
DOTY J. H., Principal of Bacon's Mercantile College, n.w.c. 6th and Walnut
Doty John M., clk. 101 W. Pearl, h. 193 Longworth
Doty Linna, 193 Longworth
Doty Robt., steward, s.w.c. Freeman and Richmond
Doty Wm. A., carp., h s.s. Liberty b. Elm and Plum
Dotzauer Frederick, cof h., 353 W. 6th
Dotzauer John, mason, 38 Peete
Double Harriet, bds. 267 ½ George
Doubleday Hy. J., show cards, 120 Main
Dougherty Chas., porter, w.s. Johnson al. b. Canal and 12th [Av
Dougherty David, cof. h., 618 Central
Dougherty Daniel, lab., 132 Central Av
Dougherty Edward, e.s. Central Av, b. Clinton and Everett
Dougherty Edward, grocery, 544 E. Front
Dougherty Eliza, servt., 280 Longworth
Dougherty Hy., molder, bds. n.w.c. Front and Central Av
Dougherty James, foreman, 41 Elm
Dougherty John B., porter, 103 W. 2d
Dougherty Joseph M., clk., s.w.c. Central Av. and 9th
Dougherty Mary, 143 Clark [eity
Dougherty Mary, laundress, 29 E. Liberty
Dougherty Louise, bds. 143 Clark
Dougherty Patrick B., porter, n.s. Water b. Elm and Plum
Dougherty Pierce, lab., w.s. Johnson al. b. Canal and 12th
Dougherty Terrence, lab., w.s. Wood b. 3d and Front
Doughty Geo. E., b.k., 142 Walnut, h. 71 Longworth
Doughty Hy., molder. bds n.w.c. Front and Central Av
Douglas Alonzo, b.k. Lafayette Banking Co., h. 67 W. 7th
Douglas Peter, 62 E. 4th
Douglass Abby, 230 Barr
Douglass Amelia, 36 E. 3d
Douglass Benj. blksmith, 90 Carr
Douglass Chas. C., bds. 209 George
Douglass Eliza, 209 George
Douglass F. M., salesman. 434 W. 4th
Douglass John E., clk., 101 W. 4th, h. 209 George
DOUGLASS JOHN G., Attorney at Law, Notary and Commissioner of Deeds, n.e.c. 4th and Walnut, h. 160 W. 4th
Douglass John M., messenger, U. S. Express Co
Douglass Sarah Ann, 67 W. 7th
Douglass Stephen M., bds. 209 George
Dounheen John, gold pen mkr., 199 E. 6th
Dourson Fred., cab. mkr., n.e.c. Young and Channing

Dourson Jno. cab. mkr., 560¼ Sycamore, h. n.e.c. Young and Channing
Douse Anthony, 532 Walnut
Dovey Edward G., 84 Bank
Dow Louis, pipe fitter, wks. n.e.c. Walnut and Canal
Dow Mary A, 131 Sycamore
Dowd'James, produce, &c., 434 Sycamore
Dowd John, policeman, 33 E. 8th e. of Lock
Dowd Mary, servt., 343 George
Dowd Pat., waiter, Burnet House
Dowd Thomas, lab., 35 E. 8th e. of Lock
Dowdell Francis, lab., n.s. Augusta b. John and Smith
Dowdell James, n.s. Augusta b. John and Smith
Dowdell Michael, lab., n.s. Augusta b. John and Smith
Dowdy James, lab., al. b. 4th and 5th and Central Av. and John
Dowe Patrick, lab., 72 Richmond
Dowell J., bds 41 Pub. Landing
Dowery Agnes, 61 Richmond
Dowling Catharine, 66 Woodward
Dowling James, lab., 45 Wood
Dowling John, lab, 69 Kossuth
Dowling Patrick, tailor, 3 New
Dowling Thos. M., clk , 24 W. Pearl, h. 3 E. 7th
Downard Mary A., dry goods, 154 W. 7th
Downes Peter, trunk mkr., 123 Baymiller
Downey Ann, dress mkr., bds. 17 Stone
Downey James, hostler, 165 Central Av
Downey James, printer, 17 Stone
Downey Julia, 116 Lock
Downey Kate, dress mkr, bds. 17 Stone
Downey Margaret, 17 Stone
Downey Michael, dray, 128 Webb
Downey Patrick, tinner, bds. 158 W. 3d
Downey Wm., wks. junction 6th and Front
Downhor Geo, bk. binder, 627 Vine
Downing Robt., periodicals, 283 W. 6th
Downing Wm., waiter, Burnet House
Downton Thomas, roller, bds. 444 W. Front
Doyle Ann, 37 New
Doyle Bridget, 331 W. 8th
Doyle Catharine, 152 Linn
Doyle Christopher, eng., 453 W. 2d
Doyle Edward, blksmith, 465 W. 9th
Doyle Edward, dray, 768 E. Front
Doyle Hy., lab., w.s. Denman b. Kenner and Flint
Doyle James, carp., s.e.c. Elm and 3d
Doyle Joseph, carp., bds. 119 Longworth
Doyle Maggie, waiter, Dennison House
Doyle Michael, driver, 63 Butler
Doyle Owen, e.s. M. Canal b. 8th and Court
Doyle Patrick, cof h., 100 Freeman
Doyle Patrick, lab., 493 W. 3d
Doyle Patrick, lab., 17 Accommodation
Doyle Thos., whitewasher, 17 8th above Lock
Doyle Wm., printer, 74 W. 3d, b. Covington [ward
Drace Gerrard, bk. layer, rear 33 Woodward
Drace Herman, cab. mkr., 216 Laurel
Drach Chas., bar k., n.w.c. Vine and Longworth
Drach Chas., lock smith, 652 Race
Drach Louisa, printer, 63 Providence
Drack Conrad, cab. mkr., h. 146 Hopkius
Draddy John J., stone cutter, 37 Baum
D.ach Chas. A., stereotyper, 618 Sycamore
Dracus Wm, lab., bds. 686 W Front
Drager Drege, lab., 18 Mansfield
Drager Edward, porter, s.s. 2d. b. Broadway and Ludlow
Drager Richard, cigar mkr., wks. n.e.c. 2d and Ludlow
Drahaus Hermann, cab. mkr., 46 Pleasant
Drahmann Anthony, sawyer, 662 Race
Drahmann J. H. & Co. (John H. D., John H. Enneking & John D. Drahmann), tailors, 56 Sycamore
Drahmann John B. (J. H. Drahmann & Co.), 19 Commerce
Drahmann John H. (J. H. D. & Co.), 56 Sycamore

Drake Alice, 161 E. 3d e. of Collard
Drake Chas., stereotyper, 616 Sycamore
Drake David H., tinner, 9th E. 5th
Drake Edw. G., roofer, 219 Mound
Drake & Fillmore (Thomas M. D. & Wm. A. F.) groceries, &c., 249 W. 4th
Drake Francis K., blksmith, n.s. R. Road e. of Kelly
Drake J. T., clk., 140 Main, h. 422 Longworth
Drake James H., clk., 101 W. Pearl, bds. 61 Longworth
Drake Joseph N., clk., 249 W. 4th, bds. n.e.c. John and Hopkins
Drake Josiah, 392 Longworth
Drake Julius A., salesman, s.e.c. 3d and Vine, h. Covington
DRAKE LOUIS P., Shirt, Collar and Bosom Manufacturer. 58 W. 4th, 2d floor, h. 176 Baymiller
Drake Mary, bds. 23 E. 7th
Drake Matthias K , 392 Longworth
DRAKE SAMUEL C., Dry Goods, 449 W. 5th, h. 24 Hathaway
Drake Thomas M. (D. & Fillmore), bds. 386 W. 7th
DRAKE Wilson T. (Evans & Co.), 331 W. 7th
Drake Wm. H., carp., 1524 E. Front
Drake Wm. H., carp , 399 John
Dransfield Hy. F., stoves, 624 Central Av.
Dransman Hermann, mach., 227 Betts
Draper Joseph, jewelry, &c., 16 W. 4th, h. 233 W. Court w of Central Av.
Dras Herman, tailor, 408 Longworth
Draude August, cof. h., 961 Central Av
Draude Hy. W., cof. h., 691 Elm
Drautmann Chas., 53 Gest
Drawes Wm., lab, h. 33 Rittenhouse
Drayman Barney, clothing, 19 Commerce
Drech Louis, cof. h., 647 Sycamore
Dreckhoff Barney, 229 Betts
Drees Herman, cab. mkr., 216 Laurel
Drees Margaret, servt., 504 Vine
Dreese Wm., tanner, s.s. Liberty b. Linn and Baymiller
Dreft Gotleib, tanner, 770 W. 6th
Drege Frederick, rear 524 Sycamore
Dreher Frederick, cab. mkr., 465 Walnut
Dreher Frederick, tinner, rear 176 Clay
Dreher Maria, seamstress, 465 Walnut
Dreher Martin, cigar store, 33 Green
Drehm Frank, turner, 498 Walnut
DREIDEL THEODORE, Essence of Coffee Manufacturer, 10 North Providence, h. 74 Betts
Dreidon George, lab., n.s. 6th b. Culvert and Broadway
Dreier Frederick, cartman, rear 12 15th
Dreifus Abraham, 64 W. 5th
Dreifus Athen, 337 W. 6th
Dreifus Mrs C., millinery, 64 W. 5th
Dreifus David, peddler, 568 Elm
Dreisback Hy., Findlay b. Central Av. and John
Dreiser Daniel, b.k., 5 Whiteman
Dreister Mrs. C., 76 Peete
Dreisz Philip, 700 Race
Dreling Balser, tailor, 61 York
Dremmel George, tailor, 25 Commerce
Drendle Fred., tailor, 660 Sycamore
Drening Chas, gardener, 278 W. Liberty
Drenham Eliza, bds. 206 W. 5th
Drennan Martin, lab., 710 Vine
Drennen James, lab., h. 30 Lock
Dresbach James E , grocer, 146 Longworth
Dresbach Joseph, grocer, s.e.c. Linn and 9th, h. 146 Longworth
DRESCHER CHARLES, Proprietor Rosing House, 251 W. 6th
Dresing Fred. H., (D. & Otting), res. Newport
Dresing & Otting (Fred. W. D. & Geo. H. O.) cigars, &c., 7 Sycamore
Dresler Fred., butcher, bds. 408 Main
Dress Christian, lab., 73 Hughes
Dress Geo., tailor, bds. 257 Main
Dress Hy., lab., n.s. 6th b. Harriet and Horne
Dresse Hy. tanner, s. s. Liberty, b. Linn and Baymiller

(DRU) CINCINNATI (DUF) DIRECTORY. (DUL) 128

Dressel Fred., watchman, 72 Providence
Dressell Hy, 32 Bank
Dressell Wm., molder, 594 Freeman
Dressmyer Isaac, tailor, e.s Vine, b. Liberty and Green
Dreve Fred., cabmkr., 22 Grant
Drew C. P., painter, 21 W. 7th
Drew James S., printer, 386 W. 7th
Drew John, lab., n.s W. W. Canal, b. Smith and Park
Drewes Wm., cab. mkr., 33 Rittenhouse
Drewes Wm., finisher, wks. 340 W. 3d
Dreyer Hy., grocer, 913 Central Av
Dreyer Hy., carp., rear 5 Wade, b. Elm and Plum
Dreyer Hermann P., carp., s s Charlotte, b. Linn and Baymiller, res. Fairmount
Dreyer John, n.w.c. Liberty and Mansfield
DREYFOOS Samuel, (Pappenheimer & D.,) 266 Vine
Dreyfoos Wallace, salesman, 36 W. Pearl, h. 264 Vine
Dreyling Wm., tailor, 495 Walnut
Driden Peter, bk. binder, 603 Elm
Driehaus Hermann, cab. mkr., 46 Pleasant
Driehouse Wm., 46 Pleasant
Driefer Barney, blksmith, bds. 229 W. Liberty
Driemeier Hy., shoe mkr. rear 32 Hughes
Drier Frank. clk, 60 E. Pearl
Driesden Emmaline, washwoman, n.s. Grandin al. b. Elm and Plum
Drieser John, 709 Central Av
Driessmann John F., grocery, 135 Laurel
Driffill Mrs. Mary A., 114 Betts
Driscoll Rev. Chas., St. Xavier College, w.s. Sycamore, b. 6th and 7th
Driscoll Eliza, chambermaid, Burnet House
Driscoll Ellen, chambermaid, Burnet House
Driscoll Hy., carp., 65 Barr
Driscoll James W., b.k, 123 Linn
Driscoll John, foreman, 32 12th
Driver Mary Ann, 431 W. 9th
Drobderman Richard, 451 Plum
Droege Hy., tobacconist, 18 Mansfield
Droege Lewis, tobacconist, 25 Ham.road
Droeger Frederick, lab., 15 Hughes
Droll Athnas, lab., 41 Peete
Droll Lewis. cook, 407 Vine
Droppelman John H., boots and shoes, 345 Central Av
Droppelmann Joseph, tobacconist, 17 Main
Dropper Herman, lab., 667 W. Front
Droste Gerhard, printer, 55 Pendleton
Droste Henry H., (Droste & Kuhn,) h. Newport
Droste Hy. R., driver, 74 Laurel
Droste & Kuhn, (Henry H. D. & Wm. K.,) vinegar manuf., n.s Yeatman, b. Broadway and Sycamore
Drought Ellen, Cramsey alley, b. Mound and Cutter
Drought Richard, lab., wks. Hieatt and Wood's
Drout Edward, wks. J. Whitaker's
Drowery Wm., barber. 90 Park
Druan John, lab., 52 Water
Drubbel Barney, lab., n.w.c. Pierson and 5th
Druck Frank, cof. h., 33 E. 3d, e. of Parsons
Druck Fred., finisher, wks. C. T. Dumont's
Drucker Chas., tailor, 69 Wade
Drucker Isaac, 473 Plum
Drucker Nathan, clk., 108 W. 5th, bds. 471 Plum
Druensmar Hermann, cab. mkr., 227 Betts
Druffel John H., saloon, 90 E. 2d
Druid Hall, 36 W. Court
Druke Frank, lab., bds. 90 E. 2d
Drum Catharine, grocer, s.c.c. 7th and North
Drum Jacob, n.w.c. Elm and Liberty
Drum Thomas, brewery, n.w.c. 2d and Smith, h. 301 W. 3d
Drumbar Enos, curp., w.s. Sycamore, b. Hunt and E. Canal. b. Walnut Hills
Drummond Lucy, 189 Oliver
Druppelmann Mary, servt., 274 George

Drury Thomas, clothing, 146 W. Front
Dryden Geo., porter, wks. 30 Vine
Dryer A. H., peddler, 163 W. 5th
Dryer Gerhard, lab., s.e.c. Hopkins and Baymiller
Dryer James, confec., 172 W. 6th
Dryer John H., porter, n.w.c. Liberty and Mansfield
Dryer Salome. b.h. s e c. Plum and 5th
Drynan Margaret. 412 Sycamore
Duane Margaret, 145 W. Pearl
Duhe John, 200 W. 5th
Dubeck Christ, cof. h., n.n.c. Central Av. and Court
Duble John A., st.bt. capt., h. 204 Sycamore
Dubois & Augur, (John D. & James S. A.,) com. mer., 67 W. 2d
Dubois John, (D. & Augur.) 33 York
Dubois W. S., bds. 109 W. 5th
Ducane Ada 476 W. 5th
Duchemini Peter, painter, 61 Avery
Duchemini Wm., painter, 223 George
Duchemini Wm., paper carrier, 61 Avery
Duchscher Peter, furniture, 209 W. 5th, h. 160 Baymiller
Duckweitz J. Charles D., baking powder manuf., 506 John
Duddy John, (Hafer & D.,) 26 E. 7th
Dudley Hy., shoemkr., bds. 149 George
Dudley James, shoemkr., 149 George
Dudley John, pattern mkr., wks. Fritsch, Burkhardt & Co.'s

DUDLEY JOHN W., Chief of Police, Office City Hall, h. 293 Richmond

Dudley John D., pattern mkr., 179 Court, w. of Central Av
Dudley Mary, 208 W. 7th
Dudley Samuel, 179 W. Court, w. of Central Av
Dudlinger John, millwright, 600 Main
Dody John blksmith, 21 W. 7th
Duebel John, finisher. 769 Central Av
Dueber John C., watch case mkr., s.w.c. 4th and Walnut
Dueber Michael B., clerk, 65 East Pearl, bds. 403 W. 8th
Duebuis Ernst, lab, s.s. Dover al, b. Elm and Plum
Duecher Nicholas, cab. mkr., bds. 160 Baymiller
Duecher Peter. lab., 160 Baymiller
Duensing Lewis A., b.k., Wahrheitsfreund Office, h. 414 Longworth
Dueper Pauline, seamstress, s.e.c. 4th and Vine
Duerig Sebastian, barber, 432 Sycamore
Duerlein John, tailor, 180 Walnut
Duerr Andrew, lab., 670 Vine
Duerr George, clk. 45 Vine, h. 518 Main
Duerr Geo., baker, 669 Vine
Duerr Joseph, clk., 518 Main
Dues Hy., coffin mkr., 686 W. 6th
Duesher Nicholas, eng., 160 Baymiller
Duesher Peter. furniture, 231 Clinton, b. 160 Baymiller
Duesher Theodore, cab. mkr., 240 Betts
Duesher Thomas, cab. mkr., 160 Baymiller
Duesing Franz, cooper, 524 Walnut
Duesing Louisa, servt., 542 W. 9th
Duffel Casper, boots and shoes, 37 Ludlow
Duffey Ann, washwoman, Commercial Hospital
Duffey Anna, servt., 185 E. 3d
Duffey Barney, lab, 229 E. Front
Duffey Bridget, e.s. Pleasant Court, e. of Elm
Duffey Francis, carp., 200 E. 6th
Duffey Hugh, lab., 60 Water
Duffey James, grocer, 78 E. 7th
Duffey James, lab., 55 E. 8th, e of Lock
Duffey John, lab., 505 E. Front
Duffey John, lab., 55 E. 8th, e. of Lock
Duffey Joseph, lab., 53 E. 8th, e. of Lock
Duffey Lawrence, lab., 19 Lock, n. of 8th
Duffer Margaret, s.w.c. 3d and Central Avenue
Duffey Martin, lab, 61 Mill
Duffey Patrick. rubber, wks. n.e.c. Canal and Elm
Duffey Rose, e. end of New
Duffey Terrence, 137 W. 6th
Duffield Benj. C., carp., 169 George

Duffield David, cooper, 169 George
Duffner Wenderlin, grocer, s.w c. Poplar and Linn
Duffy Andrew, blksmith, 37 Central Av.
Duffy Andrew, blksmith, 4 Greenleaf al.
Duffy Barney, lab., 114 E. 3d, e. of Whittaker
Duffy Bridget, servt., Burnet House
Duffy Daniel, carp., bds. 260 E. 6th
Duffy Edward, blksmith, 416 W. 2d, h. n.w.c. Longworth and Stone
Duffy Ellen, 62 Lock
Duffy Francis, 171 Water
Duffy Francis, carp., 200 E. 6th
Duffy Frank, currier, rear of 72 Hunt
Duffy George, cooper, 62 Lock
Duffy James, butcher, s.s. Oliver, b. John and Linn
Duffy Johanna, n.s. Front. e. of Kelly
Duffy John, n.s. Water, b. Walnut and Vine
Duffy John, lab., 134 Clark
Duffy John, lab., 500 E Front
Duffy Martin, lab., al. b. 4th and 5th and Central Av. and John
Duffy Michael, lab., 112 W. Pearl
Duffy Michael T., teamster, n.s. Front, e. of Kelly
Duffy Pat., waiter, Burnet House
Duffy Patrick, carp., n.s. Burt, b. Reed and Brond
Duffy Patrick, carp., bds. 200 E. 6th
Duffy Patrick, lab., 76 E. 3d, e. of Whittaker
Duffy Patrick, lab., rear 182 Cutter
Duffy Terrence, porter, 76 W. 7th
Duffy Thomas, lab., n.w.c. Front and Vance
Duffy Thomas D., 494 W. 5th
Duffy Wm, salesman, 144 Linn
Dugan Hugh, com. mer., 37 Walnut, b. Covington
Dugan John, molder, wks. at Goodhue and Co's
Dugan John, lab., n.w.c. Fremont and Harriet
DUGAN John A., (John A. D. & Co.) h. 361 W. 5th
DUGAN JOHN A. & CO., (John A. D. & Richard W. Keys,) Wholesale Grocers, 21 and 23 W. 2d
Dugan Maggie, servant, 625 Freeman
Dugan Margaret, servant, n.e.c. 3d and Lawrence
Dugan Mary, laundress, Spencer House
Dugan Mary, n.s. Front. e. of Kelly
Dugan Matthew, lab., 175 Hopkins
Dugan Patrick, hackman, 198 Water
Dugan Rosa, chambermaid, Broadway Hotel

DUHME & CO., Watches, Jewelry and Silverware, s.w.c. 4th and Walnut

DUHME H. H., Staple and Fancy Dry Goods, 74 W. 5th

Duhme Herman, clk., at Duhme & Co's h. 27 W. 3d
Duhme John H.. brewery, 432 Main
Duhme Margaret, 432 Main
Duidmann Mrs. Mary, 579 Main
Duir Nicholas, carp., 18 Allison
Duirrstock John, molder, n.w.c. Hughes and Schiller
Duke John blk. smith, 24 E. 8th, e. of Lock
Duke Margaret, bds. 184 Barr
Duke Mary, s.e.c. Court and Mound
Dulanty Patrick, waiter, 13 W. Court w. of Central Av
Dulen Patrick, lab., 203 W. Front
Duley Chas., lab., n.s Montgomery Pike nr. Reading Road
Duley Margaret, n.e.c. 8th and Central Av
Dullanty Rudolf, stone cutter 50 Hunt
Dull Catharine, 15 Green
Dulle Bernard, shoe mkr., bds. 281 Central Av
Dull George, lab., bds. 13 Abigail
Dulle Joseph, expressman, s.w.c. Laurel and Baymiller
Duller Gerhard, lab., 56 W. Liberty
Dullheinty Bridget, 385 Vine
Dullheinty Miss Mary, 385 Vine

Dulweber Theodore, 119 Hunt
Dumas Hotel, e.s. Macalister b. 4th and 5th
Dumhoff Henry, lab., 114 Betts
Dumhoff Henry, tailor, rear 555 Walnut
Dumkorst John, porter, 17 Madison
Dumler George, (D. & Bro.) bds. 47 12th
Dumler & Bro., (John & George D.) collar manufa., 35 Bremen
Dumler John, (D. & Bro.) bds. 47 12th
Dumier Joseph, saddler, bds. s.s. 12th b. Bremen and Vine
Dumler Martin, meats, n.e.c. Linn and Betts
Dumler Philip, saddler, bds. 47 12th
Dunmeier Henry, dray, 55 Hughes
Dummiller Elizabeth, seamstress, 53 W. 4th
Dumont Chas. T., machinist, 65, 67 and 69 E. Front, res. Walnut Hills
Dumont Richard, bds. 325 W. 3d
Dumont Richard S, (Holabird & D.) h. 449 W. 4th
DUN R. G., (R. G. D. & Co.) h. New York City
DUN R. G. & CO, (R G. D. & R R. Boyd,) Mercantile Agency, s. w.c. 3d and Walnut
Dunagan Birney, lab., h. w.s. Macalister b. 4th and 5th
Dunahoe James, blk. smith, bds. 674 W. 6th
Dunavan Wm., dray, 48 Look n. of 8th
Dunaway Margaret, h. n.w.c. Budd and Harriet
Dunbacher Frank, cooper, 417 Longworth
Dunbar Robert, cooper, bds 445 Main
Duncall & Co., (R. L. D. & J. E. Meredith.) dentists, 92 W. 7th
Duncall E. L., (D. & Co.) 92 W. 7th
Duncan Andrew, builder, 133 York
Duncan Anthony, grocer 323 Clark
Duncan George, 223 Broadway
Duncan Hannah, 424 George
Duncan James, 103 Betts
Duncan John, blk. smith, h. Everett b. Wood and Laurel
Duncan John, carp., n.s. Goodloe b. Willow and Niagara
Duncan John, finisher, s.w.c. 3d and Wood
Duncan John G, brush mkr., 310 W. 3d
Duncan Mary, 112 Avery
Duncan Mary, 308 W. Liberty
Duncan Morris L, 312 W. 6th
Duncan Nancy, 316 W. 3d
Duncan Samuel W., b.h., 312 W. 3d
Duncan Thos., lab., bds. n.s. Augusta b. John and Smith
Duncan Thos. H., artist, 103 Betts
Duncan Thomas M. N., porter, 204 W. 6th
Duncan Townsend, carp., bds. 215 Mound
DUNCAN WM. C., Dentist h. 156 W. 6th
Duncanson Robert S., artist, 54 Pierson
Dunckmann Rudolph, cab. mkr., h. 188 Clark
Dunes Michael, carp, 82 Mohawk
Dundon Ann, al. b. 4th and 5th and Central Av and John
Dundon Edward, lab, n.s. Pew al. b. Central Av. and John
Dunelius Herman K., dry goods, 395 Elm
Dunnemann Louisa, servant, 65 Broadway
Dunfield Henry, gardener, w.s Culvert h. 5th and 6th
Dunham Esther, seamstress, wks. 53 W. 4th
Dunham Frank W., salesman, 70 Vine, h. 148 Richmond
Dunham & Higdon, (Levi D. & Benj. H.) stable, 177 W. 6th
Dunham Joseph C., bk. binder, 609 W. 6th
Dunham Levi, (D. & Higdon,) 98 Carr
Dunham Mrs. R., 93 W. 7th
Dunham Rhoda, 178 Barr

Dunham Wm., salesman, bds. 107 Pike
DUNHOLTER HENRY, Bakery, 244 W. 6th
Dunkhorst Fred., porter, 40 Walnut
Dumkhorst John, porter, 40 Walnut
Dunker John, cigar mkr., 179 Bremen
Dunker Toney, lab., 179 Hopkins
Dunkerlay Joshua, stone cutter, bds. 631 W. 7th
Dunkmann Bernard, 13 Adams
Dunkmann Rudolph, cab. mkr., 188 Clark
Dunkinann Wm., cooper, 179 Baymiller
Dunlap Chas. C., b.k., 12 Pine
Dunlap J. D. & Co., (James D. & Wm. J. Byers,) lumber yard, 435 Freeman and 534 Vine
Dunlap James, (J. D. & Co.) res. Cedarville, O
Dunlap James. steward, 450 W. 4th
Dunlap John, clk , Burnet House Restaurant
Dunlap John, clk., s.w.c. Walnut and 2d, bds 12 Pine
Dunlap John, walter, n.e.c. Ludlow and Pearl
Dunlap Robert. eng., Pike's Opera House
Dunlap Robert A., b.k., bds. 449 W. 4th
Dunlap Robert E., teller, Gillmore & Dunlaps, h. 449 W. 4th
Dunlap Thomas, foreman, 160 Main. bds. 21 George
DUNLAP Wm. J., (Gilmore, D. & Co.) h. 377 W. 4th
Dunlavy Annie, servant, 422 W. 5th
Dunlavy Bridget, servant, 375 W. 6th
Dunlavy Matilda, 43 Everett
Dunlay Dennis, lab., wks. 207 W. 5th
Dunlea Hannah, tailoress, 177 W. 9th
Dunlea Johanna, tailoress, 177 W. 9th
Dunlevy Ann, tailoress, h. 423 W. 3d
Dunlevy Bridget, m.s. al. b. Park and Pole and 3d an1 W. W. Canal
DUNLEVY D. B., (Ferris, D. & Fowler,) e.s. Lawrence b. 3d and 4th
Dunley James, agent, h. 40 E. 7th
Dunlop Wm., 449 E. Front
Dunlop Wm., clk., h. s.s. 3d b. Canal and K Igour
Dunlope Robert, lab., s.e.c. North and New
Dunmeyer Mary, 67 W. Court
Dunn Alexander M., patent roofing, 451 W. 4th
Dunn Ann, 710 Vine
Dunn Bridget, n.s. Water b. Walnut and Vine
Dunn Bridget, servant, 40 Cutter
Dunn Cornelius, cof. h. 120 E. 8th
Dunn Dorsey W., carp., 47 W. 7th
Dunn Edward, boatman, n.s. Water b. Walnut and Vine
Dunn Edward, lab., n.w.c. Plum and 2d
Dunn Elizabeth, 303 W. 2d
Dunn Harriet, s.e.c. Elm and 3d
Dunn Hy. carp., 23 Mill.
DUNN Hy., C., (Woodrough & McParlin,) res. Hamilton, O.
Dunn Ignatz, salesman, n.e.c. Vine and 5th h. Vine St. Hill.
Dunn James, 54 Laurel.
Dunn James, cutter 82 W. Pearl, h. 63 George.
Dunn James, saloon, w.s Central Av. b. 2d and W. W. Canal
Dunn John, boatman n.s. Water b. Walnut and Vine.
Dunn John, lab., bds. 187 Cutter.
Dunn John, lab., 113 W. Front.
Dunn Joseph, dray, 578 E. Front.
Dunn Margaret, seamstress, wks. 53 W. 4th
Dunn Margaret, servt. 375 W. 6th.
Dunn Mary, servt Burnet House.
Dunn Mary s.s. 6th b. Broadway and Culvert.
Dunn Mary, 47 W. 7th.
Dunn Peter, porter, 139 Walnut. h. 69 Avery.
Dunn Philip, clk., 323 W. 2nd.
Dunn Philip, lab., rear of 632 W. 6th.
Dunn Philip, tailor 323 W. 2d.
Dunn Richard, lab n.w.c Main and Court.

Dunn Sarah, s.s. 6th b. Broadway and Culvert.
Dunn Thomas, lab., 311 W. 2d.
Dunn Thomas, wks. n.e.c Smith and 2d
DUNN Wm., (D. & Witt.) 230 W. 3d.
Dunn Wm., lab., 10 Race.
DUNN & WITT, (Wm. D. & Richard W.) Tin, Iron and Slate Roofing, 144 and 146 W. 3d.
Dunnavan Bartholomew, edge tool mkr. 23 6th above Lock.
DUNNAVANT Josiah H. clk. 461 Plum
Dunneducker Joseph, grocer 205 Laurel
Dunnegan Michael, driver, wks. n.w.c. Court and Race.
Dunnegan Patrick, driver, wks. n.w.c Court and Race.
Dunnican Kate, servt. Burnet House.
Dunnigan Catharine, n.s. Pearl b. Smith and Park.
Dunnigan Michael tailor, s.e.c. 5th and Wool.
Dunnigan John, gardener, n.w.c. 3d and Ellen.
Dunning Robert S., st. bt. clk., 521 W. 7th.
Dunphy Michael, grocery s.e.c. 5th & Butler.
Dunseng Louis, printer, 414 Longworth
Dunseth J., mach. wks. n.e.c Front b. Lawrence and Pike.
Dunsmore Mary A., bds . 660 Race.
DUNSTORF WM., Bakery, 176 W. Front.
Dunwoodie Thomas, hatter, n.w.c. Main and Court.
Dunzelmann John H., tailor, bds. 498 W. Front.
Dupell Wm., scale mkr. bds. n.e.c. Elm and Pearl.
Dupes Christian, 611 Elm.
Dupey John C., pipe fitter, wks n.e.c. Walnut and Canal.
Dupler Mary A., bds . 660 Race.
Duprey Wm., br k., Madison House.
Dupuys Paul, saloon mkr. 492 Race.
Durain Anna, bds. s.e.c. 6th and Smith.
DURAIN CHARLES, Coffee House, 336 Central Av.
DURAND John, Supt. Marietta & Cincinnati R. R., Office no 3 Burnet House, h. 413 W. 6th.
Durant Martha, 240 Longworth.
Duravan Ann, 962 E. Front.
Duravan James, lab., bds. 962 E, Front.
Duravan John, lab. 964 E. Front.
Duravan Mary, 962 E. Front.
Duravan Patrick, lab bds. 912 E. Front.
Durbeck John C., coal oil manuf., bds. 138 Carr.
Durham Elizabeth, dress mkr., 274 Walnut
Durham James, porter, 70 Vine, h. 63 Walnut
Durkee Wm. H., clk. n.e.c. Pearl and Sycamore, bds 23 E. Pearl
Durkin Ellen, huckster, 282 W. 6th
Durkin Pat., lab, 151 E. Pearl.
Durkin Patrick, lab 333 W. 5th
Durman Mathew, lab., 106 Hunt.
Durning Bernard, tailor, n.w.c. 5th and Sycamore
Durning James, bds. National Hotel.
Durper Hy., lab., 255 Hopkins
Durr E., lab , wks. n.s Front, b. Lawrence and Pike
Durr Christopher, driver 410 Longworth
Durrauh Mary Ann, w.s. Pleasant Court e of Elm
Durrell Friend, cooper, 30 Pleasant
Durrell James E., watchman 513 W. 3d
Durrell John, teamster 167 Clinton
Durrell Joseph, deputy sheriff, 69 Providence.
Durrett Warren, barber 491 W. Front.
Dury —, National Theater
Dury Chas. W., stencil cutter, 70 W. 4th
Dusch Geo., shoe mkr., s.e.c. 12th and Vine
Duschengall John, shoe mkr., 1469 E.
Dusenberry Saml. N. H., trader, bds. s. e.c. 9th and Walnut
Dusing Frank, rear 31 Hughes
Dusing Frank jr., cooper rear 31 Hughes

Dusing Frederick, lab., 95 Pendleton
Dusing Wilhemina, servt., 330 George
Dussour Joseph t ilor, 36 Ellen
Dussour Martin jr., tailor, 36 Ellen
Dussour Martin sen , tailor, 36 Ellen
Dust Bernard Hy., porter 512 Walnut
Dust Gerhard Hy., lab , 512 Walnut
Dust Hy., lab., e.s. Walnut b. Liberty and Allison
Dust Kate, milliner, 512 Walnut
Dusterberg Adam, clk.. 450 Walnut
Dusterberg Christ, driver, wks., 450 Walnut
DUSTERBERG John H., (Hackmann & D.) 450 Walnut
Dustin Rev. Miles, 480 W. 7th
Duitlinger John G., mach., 600 Main
Duttman Casper, (Dellenbeck & D.) 378 Broadway
DUTTON AARON R., Attorney at Law, 6 E 3d, Chase's Bldg. bds 270 W. 3d.
DuTowr Mrs M. bds. s.w.c. Race and 3d
Dutzer Frederick, cooper, 689 Main
Dutzhour John, lab., wks. N, W. Thomas & Co's.
Duval Joseph, peddler, 84 W. Front
Duval Maria, bds.113 Barr
Duvall Hy., painter, 22 Abigail
Duvall Otho, eng. 361 W. 3d
Duvall Mary, 102 W. 4th
Duvelius Bernard, huckster, 484 W. 6th
Duvencok Frank, shoe mkr., bds 478 W. 5th [Elm
Duverney Antoinette, dress mkr. 203
Duverney Joseph, bk layer, 203 Elm
Duwolios Hy., lab., 57 Buckeye
Duwolius Christian, cigars, 530 Main
Duwellius Hy. H., dry goods, 375 Elm
DUZAN WM. W., Clk., 194 Walnut, rooms s.s. 5th opp. Old Fellows Hall Covington
Dwibel Geo., lab., n s. R. Road e. of Lewis
Dwier Lawrence, lab.. n.s. Fremont b. Harriet and Millcreek
Dwyer —, blksmith, bds 65 Broadway
Dwyer Anthony, painter 20 New
Dwyer Bridget, laundress, 220 Central Av
Dwyer John, lab., 21 Main
Dwyer John, lab., 673 W. 6th
Dwyer Martin T., box mkr., 213 E. 3d.
Dwyer Patrick, (Meyor & D.) 6th Street Hill
Dwyer Thos., waiter, Burnet House
Dwyer Wm., packer, wks. 141 Race
Dwyer Wm., policeman 62 E. 5th
Dwyre Ann., 64 Freeman
Dyal Edward, lab., rear 210 Cutter
Dye Daniel, lab. 343 Broadway
Dye Julia, b. h. 495 W. 6th
Dye Moses lab., s.s. 6th b Broadway and Culvert
DYER CHAS. S. Notion Dealer. 37 Everett
Dyer Elisha, chair mkr., 9 Race.
Dyer Geo. E., deputy U. S. marshal, s.s. E. 3d b. Canal and Kilgour
Dyer James, copper smith, w.s. Lock b. 8th and Court
Dyer Thomas, saddletree mkr , 151 Carr
Dyer Wm. H., clk., 135 Main
Dyett Joshua A., b. k. 482 John.
Dykins Anna, bds., 166 Central Av,
Dykins Robert A., b. k. 21 W. Front b. 166 Central Av.
DYMOND Richard, (Wm. Glenn & Sons) 400 W. 6th
Dymond Wm., clk. 70 Vine, bds. 409 W. 6th
Dzierzanowsky Christ, dray, 51 Kossuth
Dzierznowsky Louisa, 42 Rittenhouse

E

Eads John, eng., c. Burt and Waldon
Eagan John, lab., 50 E. 7th
Eagan John, ped ller. 183 W. 2d
Eagan John, ticket clk., O. & M. R. R., h. Ludlow, Ky.
Eagan Elizabeth, 209 Cutter
Eagan Margaret, n.s Patterson al., b. Main and Walnut

Eagel Cynthia, servt., 93 E. 3d
EAGLE BREWERY, Joseph Schaller, Prop'r s.e c. Plom and Canal
Engle Emrea, seamstress, 202 W. Court
EAGLE INSURANCE CO., 73 W. 3d, Ed. D. Spears, Secretary
Eagle Joseph L, carriage mkr., 133 York
EAGLE MATCH COMPANY, Office and Factory, corner Freeman and Flint
Eagle Quintin, mach., 25 David
Eagleman John, salesman, 20 E. 2d, h. 146 Buckeye
Eagon Virginia, e.s. Cutter b. Betts and Clinton
Eahmann Hy., finisher, wks. n.e.c. Walnut and Canal
Eakle Jacob G., bk. layer, 148 W. 8th
Earhart Elizabeth, 3J W. Court w. of Central Av.
Earhart Phillip, driver, 34 Butler
Earls John H., cigar mkr., 64 Linn
Earl Benjamin W., b.h.. 162 Broadway
Earley B., lab., wks. 18 Sycamore
Earley John, drays, 740 Vine
Earley Peter, tailor, 284 W. 8th
Earley Peter J., s.e.c. Sycamore and New
Earley Rachael, 740 Vine
Earley Robert, drays, 740 Vine
Earley Robert, sawyer, 153 Buckeye
Earley Thomas, grocer, 128 Linn
Earls Catharine, bds. 47 W. 7th
Early Andrew, blksmith. 153 Buckeye
Early Catharine, 230 Water
Early James, lab., 104 Spring
Early Margaret, 153 Buckeye
Early Mary, 108 E 6th
Early Mary A., 153 Buckeye
Early Michael, s.e.c. Forbus al. b. Elm and Canal
Early Patrick, dray, 240 Barr
Early Robert, lab., 153 Buckeye
Early Thomas, (Gibson, E. & Co.) 123 Linn
Early Wm.. teamster, 517 W. 8th
EARNSHAW JOHN B., Superintendent City Water Works. Office, City Hall, h. E. Walnut Hills
Earnshaw Hy., surveyor, 207 Clark
Earnst Albert, clk. 123 W. 3d
Easly John, butcher, s.w.c. Liberty and Baymiller
Eastermann Bernard, shoe mkr , h. 135 Hopkins
Eastman Harry, dairy, n s. Friendship al. b. Pike and Butler, h. Mainesville, O
Easton Benj. P., b.k. 232 Main, res. Covington
Easton Blanche, bds. 51 Stone al. b. 5th and 6th
Easton Mrs. F. C., 232 Main
Easton James S., clk. 232 Main, h. Covington
Easton Lydia E., teacher, 232 Main
EASTON SHADFORD, Tanner and Currier, and Dealer in Leather, Hides and Oil, 234 Main, res. Covington
Eaton Alonzo, clk.. bds. 161 Livingston
Eaton Andrew B., b.k.., 43 George
Eaton Brewer D. M., printer Press office, bds. 269 W. 7th
Eaton Eben, printer, 161 Livingston
Eaton Chas. B., distiller, 223 Baymiller
Eaton Chas. P., student, bds. 269 W. 7th
Eaton Frederick O., student, bds. 269 W. 7th
Eaton Hy. G., b.k. 18 Pub. Landing, h. 315 George
Eaton J. O., portrait painter, room 27 Pike's Opera House, bds. 330 W. 4th
Eaton Jane, dry goods, 136 Dayton
Eaton John B., atty., n.w.c. 6th and Walnut, res. Avondale
Eaton Martin P., carp., 409 George
Eaton Wm., engraver, n.w.c. 3d and Main, res. Walnut Hills
Eaton Wm., printer, bds. 161 Livingston
Eaton Rev. William W., 269 W. 7th
Eavis Mary, 405 Race

Eberle Julius, bar k., 123 W. Liberty
Ehbers Hy., tailor, 414 Walnut
Ebbert Peter, wks. junction 6th and Front
Ebbett James, lab., 477 W. 3d
Ebbing Joseph, shoe mkr., 11 12th
Ebling Christian, cof. h., 4 Moore
Ebeler Barney, grocery, 474 Linn
Ebeler Louis. bir k., wks Arbeiter Halle
Ebelhner Fred., pipe fitter, wks. n.e.c. Walnut and Canal
Eben John, painter, 20 Hamer
Ebensing Henriett., polisher, bds. s.w. c. 14th and Bremen
Eberhardt F., wagon mkr., rear 363 Ham. Road
Eberhardt Geo. J., (Geo. J. & John J. E.) 373 Main
Eberhardt Geo J. & John J., dining saloon, 25 W. 3d
Eberhardt Gertrude, 108 Buckeye
Eberhardt John, 355 Ham. Road
Eberhardt John J. (Geo. J. & John J. E.) 343 Main
Eberhardt Martin, tailor, 506 Vine
Eberhardt Max. student, 343 Main
Eberhardt Valentine, C. (E. & Wust) 352 Ham. Road
Eberhardt & Wust, (Valentine C. E. & Frederick C W) wagon mkrs., n.s. Ham. Road nr. Mohawk Bridge
Eberhart Christian, cab. mkr , 630 Main
Eberhart Joseph, lab., 548 Walnut
Eberhart Phillipine, seamstress, 548 Walnut
Eberhart Rosa, seamstress, 548 Walnut
Eberle Andreas, gunsmith, 545 Vine, h. 475 Vine
Eberle August, b.k. Denziger Brothers bds. 137 Race
EBERLE CHARLES, Druggist. s.e.c. 5th and Central Av.
EBERLE CLEMENTS C., Barber Shop and Dentist, 91 Spring
EBERLE CLEMENTS C., Family Grocery and Coffee House, s.e.c. Abigail and Broadway, h 91 Spring
Eberle Hy., cab., mkr., 579 Main
Eberle Jacob, carp., 164 Richmond
Eberle John, tailor, 108 Buckeye
Eberle Mary, 57 Chestnut
Eberle Philip, 674 E. Front
Eberlein John potter, 73 Peeto
Eberlein Pankrus, shoe mkr., 599 Sycamore
Eberling John, trunk mkr., 175 Clay
Ebers Hy.. tailor, 363 W 8th
Ebert Conrad, hotel, River b. Ludlow and Lawrence
Ebert Frederick, cof. h. 353 Main
Ebert Philip L., carver, 170 Spring
Ebers Lisette, seamstress, 13 Madison
Ebesmeier Frederick, cigar mk., 149 Everett
Ebinger Mina, seamstress, 449 Linn
Ebke John F., cigars, 443 Central Av.
Ebker John H , grocer, 195 Gest
Eble Anthony, wagon mk., 126 Ham.
Eble Frank, 576 E. Front
Ebmeier Hy , driver, 112 Gest
Eccles Ann, 39 Pike
Eccles Hy.. mach., 120 Plum
Ecc es James, lab., 290 Main
Echemeier Mrs. Bernhardine, 401 Sycamore
ECHERT P. & CO , (Peter E. & Jacob Buss) Wholesale Candy Manufacturers, 81 Walnut
ECHERT Peter, (P. E. & Co.) 13 Mary
Echtermeier Mary, 31 Green
Eck Jacob G., salesman 23 Woodward
Eck Peter, boots and shoes, 623 Central Av.
Eck Peter, miller, 612 Sycamore
Eckardt Chas., cof. h., 84 W. 3d
Eckel Chas., gunsmith, 380 Walnut, h. 128 Ham. Road
Eckel Ch rlotte L.. 129 Ham. Road
Eckel Herman, druggist, 128 Ham. Road
Eckel John, 37 Ludlow
Eckie Philip, carpet mkr., 75 W. Liberty
Eckelman Mary, 610 Central Av.

126 (EDM) CINCINNATI (EGA) DIRECTORY.

Eckelman Theodore, britannia wkr., 38 Rittenhouse
Eckelmann Benjamin, shoe mkr., bds. 283 W. 6th
Eckelmann Hy. B., boots and shoes, 6 E. 5th, h. 24 Milton
Eckelmann Rudolph D., shoe mkr., 24 Milton
Eckelkamp Geo., 436 Broadway
Ecker Michael, mason, 27 Moore
Eckerle Hy., wagon mkr., wks. 600 Walnut
Eckerle Michael, meats, 72 13th
Eckerle Paul, meats, 47 12th
Eckerman John, cigar mkr., wks. n.w. c. 2d and Sycamore
Eckermann John, finisher, 158 W. 2d
Eckert Conrad, lab., 162 Baymiller
Eckert Fred., lab., 30 York
Eckert Gottfried, white washer, e.s. Walnut b. Allison and Liberty
Eckert Hy., cof. h., 630 Central Av.
Eckert John, butcher, 700 Freeman
Eckert John S., plasterer, 154 Carr
Eckert Lewis, carp., 34 Ham. Road
ECKERT LORENZ, Books and Stationery, n.w.c. Walnut and 13th, h. 47 Jackson
Eckert Mariana, Wade b. Elm and Plum
ECKERT MICHAEL, Dealer in Leather, Shoe Findings, Hides, Oils, &c., 179 Main, Tannery 964 Central Av., h. 86 Bank
Eckert Philip, barber, 628 Central Av.
Eckert R., painter, 227 Clark
Eckert Susan, seamstress, 168 Hopkins
ECKERT Thos. F, Pres't Western Ins. Co., h. Mill Creek Tp.
Eckert Wm. H., tel. op., C. H. & D. R. R. Depot, bds. Burnet House
Eckford James, mach., 453 W. 8th
Eckhardt Adam, tailor, wks. 13 Hunt
Eckhardt Conrad, varnisher, 162 Baymiller
Eckhardt Hy., clk., 492 Race
Eckles Maria, 175 Elm
Eckloff Geo., lab., n.s. Adams b. Plum and Elm
Eckman Bernard, dray. 28 13th
Eckman Margaret, 60 McFarland
Eckstein Miss E. C., n e.c. 8th and Central Av., h. Glenda's
ECKSTEIN Fred'k, (Suire, E. & Co.) h. River Road
Eckstein Paul, lab., 244 Bremen
Eckstein Peter J., bds. 508 Race
ECLECTIC MEDICAL INSTITUTE, John M. Scudder, Dean, n.w.c. Court and Plum
Eddingfield John, lab., s.s. E. 3d b. Parsons and Baum
Eddison James, watchman, 294 W. Front
Eddy Spencer, mach., 180 E. Pearl
Eddy Solomon, lab., 180 E Pearl
Ede Wm, upholsterer, 392 Central Av.
Edelmann Michael, cof. h., 17 Ham. Road
Edelmann Hy., gilder, 4 Lucy
Edenger John, varnisher, 65 Abigail
Eder John, grocer, n.e.c. Jones and Melancthon
Edgar Richard J. C., b.k. Stewart, Carmichael & Cu's. h. 7th nr. John
Edgar Samuel M., box mkr., bds. s.e.c. John and 9th
Edge B. O., bds. Burnet House
Edgley Edwin G., mach., 42 Central Av.
Edgley Thos. M., eng., n.w.c. Mill and 4th
Edimeyer Chas., foreman 18 Hammond
EDMESTON Mrs. Louisa B., (Hunter, E. & Co.) h. n.w.c. Longworth and Mound
Edmonds John A., brush mkr., bds. 331 W. 3d
Edmonds Theodore, bk. layer, 48 Baum
Edmonds Thos., cooper, 67 W. Court
Edmondson Dr., bds. 297 W. 6th
Edmondson Andrew, white washer, 234 Longworth
Edmondson James, shoe mkr., s.s. Baum b. 3d and 5th
Edmondson Robert, boots and shoes, w. s. Broadway b. 3d and Pearl, h. 99 Baum

Edmonson James, barber, 201 Central Av., bds. 207 George
Edwards A. G., bds. Clifton House
Edwards Abraham C., Sec'y Union Ins. Co., h. 317 Longworth
Edwards Arthur D., carriage mk., bds. s.s. 5th b Main and Sycamore
Edwards Catharine. 176 Barr
Edward Charles, bds. n.w.c. Longworth and Central Av.
Edwards Curtis O., clk. Methodist Book Concern, h. 84 Wade
Edwards David, egg packer, bds. 25 Richmond
Edwards Daniel I., clk., 82 Laurel
Edwards E. D., comb mkr., bds. 22 W. 7th
Edwards E. Alphonso, salesman 146 W. 5th, h 6 Pine
Edwards Edwin, atty., 148 Walnut, h. s. w.c. Richmond and Central Av.
Edwards Evan, spoke mkr., 25 Richmond b. Elm and Plum
Edwards Hy., eng., 50 Pierson
Edwards Humphrey, driver, 110 Longworth
Edwards Isaac, bds 83 Baymiller
Edwards Isaac, butter dealer, 25 Richmond b, Elm and Plum.
Edwards Isaac N., 1456 E. Front
Edwards Jemima, s.s. 5th b. Central Av. and John
Edwards John, mailer Times office, s.s. Richmond nr. Harriet
Edwards John M., teacher, bds. 160 Longworth
Edwards John N., molder, 517 W. 3d
Edwards Joseph. (Broadwell & E.) n.s. Front e. of Hill
Edwards Jos. F., clk. 112 W. 5th
Edwards Julia, 20 Harrison
Edwards Maggie, servt., 21 Hathaway
Edwards Mary, 186 Central Av
Edwards Mary, servt., 146 E. 5th
Edwards Mathias, M., bds. 177 W. Court w. of Central Av.
Edwards Roderick, bds. 464 W. Front
Edwards Rowland L., stove mounter, h. w.s. Oregon b. 3d and 6th
Edwards Samuel, malt mkr., bds. 399 Sycamore
Edwards Sarah, 300 W. 8th
Edwards Thomas, 437 W. 2d
Edwards Thomas, (Holtzinger & E.,) Richmond nr. Freeman
Edwards Wm., bds. n.w.c. Longworth and Central Av
Edwinkel Wm., plasterer, 58 W. 6th
Eferlin Frederick, butcher, 268 E. Pearl e. of Broadway
Effing Arnold, painter, w.s. Goose al. b. Green and Elder
Effing El'za, e.s. Goose al. b. Liberty and Green
Effing Hermann, carp, bds. w.s. Goose al. b. Green and Elder
Effinger Barney, cab. mkr., 428 Sycamore
Effinger John, cof. h. 6 Sycamore
Effinger Martin, lab., 8 Henry
Effkermann John, 496 W. Front
Effland Frederick, cof. h. 194 Broadway
Effland John, teamster, rear 16 Milton
Edray Alexander, gents' furnishing goods, 174 Vine
Efter Hy., grocer, e. s Logan, b. Elder and Findlay
Efkermann Barney, lab., e.s. Anderson al. b. 2d and Pearl
Egalbrink John, lab., 17 E. Mulberry
Egan Catharine, 214 Cutter
Egan Constantine, drny. wks. Cincinnati Stone Works
Egan James, plumber. 310 W. 3d
Egan Jno., cutter, 113 W. Court w. of Central Av.
Egan Mary A., e.s. Johnston, al. b. Canal and 12th
EGAN Sanford K, (E. & Slocomb,) h, Covington
EGAN & SLOCOMB, (Sanford K. E. & Rufus T. S.,) Jobbers, Commission Merchants, Wholesale Dealers in Boots and Shoes, 73 W. Pearl

Egan S
Egbers
Egbus G
Ege Fre
Egelbren and
Egelhoff
Egelmar way
Egelstor and
Egelton b. P
Egemele
Egen Je
Egert H
Eggeme
Eggers
EGGER Elm
Eggers
EGGE H. tu Fr
Egg bli &c
Eggers
Eggers ler
Eggers
EGGER Mai
Eggers and
EGGE gu St M
EGGE & In m
Eggert
Eggert and
Eggert
EGGER Cen
EGGLE " 78
Egglest nal,
Egglest
Eggleso
Eglema
Eggleston
EGLES " Co
Egly J and
GLY
E R. nt
Egner J
Egner J
Egolf C
Eha Gc Rac
Ehay N
Ehearht
Ehemar igai
Ehinger
Ehkels
Ehlen C
Ehlen C b. C
Ehlen 216
Ehlel U Cou
EHLEL
Ehler Fro 3d
Ehler E
Ehler E
Ehler T
Ehlerd lay

(EIC) CINCINNATI (EIS) DIRECTORY. (ELL) 127

Ehlerding Wm., (Schaeffer & Co.,) 717 Freeman
Ehlermann Fritz, lab., 5 Whiteman
Ehlers Christian. driver 16 Mulberry
Ehlers Hy., shoe mkr., 91 W. 12th
Ehlers John, clk., wks. 507 Sycamore
Ehlers Rebecca, 525 Sycamore
Ebling John, lab., h. n s. Abigail b. Broadway and Spring
Ehlinger Jacob, mach., 52 Baum
Ehll Casper, grocer, c. Harriet and Front
Ehlmann Herman B., (H. B. E., & Seelen,) 660 Main
Ehlmann H. B., & Seelen, (Herman B. E. & August S.,) stable and undertakers. 593 Main
Ehlmann Wm., steam pipe fitter, 29 Ham. Road
Ehman Frank, lab., 142 Buckeye
Ehman John, bksmith, 593 Walnut
Ehmann Andrew, tailor. 688 Vine
Ehmann Chas., cook, 518 Main
Ehmann Christopher, box mkr., 15 Abigail
Ehmen Wm., tinner, bs. 199 W. 6th
Ehmer Joseph, cof. h. 166 Bremen
Ehreck John, shoe mkr., bds. 22 E. Front
Ehrendraut Ernst F., tanner, 31 Buckeye
Ehrenmann John, tailor, 124 Spring
EHRGOTT FORBRIGER & CO., (Peter E., Adolph F., & J L. Westheimer,) Lithographers and Engravers. and Printers, s.w.c. 4th and Walnut
Ehrghott Martin lithograph printer, 22 Charles
EHRGOTT Peter, (E. Forbriger & Co.) 55 Allison
Ehrhard Francis, shoe mkr., 719 Race
Ehrhard Geo., tailor, wks. 107 W. Liberty
Ehrhardt Christian, lab., rear, 526 E. Front
Ehrhardt Daniel, 613 Elm
Ehrhardt Frederick J., 568 Vine
Ehrhardt George, lab., rear 526 E. Front
Ehrhardt Wm., lab., e.s. Hand al, b. Court and Clark
Ehrhard Ann, h. 512 Race
Ehrhardt Frederick, cigar mkr., 613 Race
Ehrhardt Jacob, harness mkr., wks. 59 Ham. Road
Ehrich Frederick, soap mkr., 206 Pleasant
Ehring Louis, s.e.c. Baymiller and Central Av
Ehrlberling Frank, shoe mkr., s.e c Water and Walnut
Ehrlich Joseph. clk. 86 W. 9th
Ehrman Mrs. Barbara, 174 W. 6th
EHRMANN BERNARD, Physician Office and Residence 46 W. 4th
Ehrmann Fannie, 21 15th b. Central Av and Plum
Ehrmann Fred. phys., 84 W. 7th
Ehrmann Michael, eng., 400 Sycamore
Ehrmann Winzens, clk., 66 Main h. 142 Buckeye
Ehrmantraut Theresa, h. 136 Pleasant
Ehrmatral M., molder, wks. Chamberlain & Co's.
Ehrt Francis, lab., 67 Buckeye
Eibeck Peter, peddler. 30 Hughes
Eich Frederick. (Leetsch & E.,) n. e. c. Pearl and Race
Eich Peter, cof. h., 282 W. Liberty
Eichacker Geo., carp., 475 Vine
Eichberg Frederick, furnishing store 199 Longworth
Eichberg Lewis. mer., 31 Longworth
Eiche G., pro. Phoenix Hall, 200 Vine
Eicbe Oscar, barber, 181 Vine
Eichelberger Andrew, butcher, bds. 434 W. 7th
Eichelberger Hy., lab., bds. 197 Baymiller
Eichelberger Jacob, grocery, 108 W. Liberty
Eichelberger Joseph, watchman, 197 Baymiller
Eichelman Josephine, 110 Mohawk

Eichengruen Chas., peddler, 62 Find lay
Eichenlaub Frederick, grocery, 280 W. Liberty
Eichenlaub Geo., eng., rear 21 Mercer
Eichenlaub Geo. F., b. k., 240 Bremen
Eichenlaub Geo. F., cof. h. 543 Central Av.
EICHENLAUB Geo. F., (J. Kauffman & Co.,) 605 Vine
Eichenlaub John A., molder, 187 Ham. Road
Eichenlaub Mrs. Regina, 226 Bremen
Eichenlaub Valentine, collector, 240 Bremen
Eichels Peter, steward, 277 George
Eichensberger Christian, 310 W. Liberty
Eichera Michael, 33 York
Eichert Barbara, s.s. Hubbard b. 5th and 6th
Eichert Peter. candy mkr., 13 Mary
EICHHOLZ M. & BRO, (Mayer & Solomon,) Cigars and Tobacco, 318½ Main
EICHHOLZ Mayer, (M. E. & Bro.,) res. Philadelphia
EICHHOLZ Solomon, (M. E. & Bro.,) 318½ Main
Eichhorn George, cof. h., 601 Main
Eichenger Elizabeth, e.s. Ridgway al, b. W. Liberty and 15th
Eichluum Fred., millwright, wks. 825 Central Av
Eichler Charles F.. cigar mkr., 559 Vine
Eichler Peter, tailor, 101 Pleasant
Eichman Chas., box mkr., wks. Livingston nr. Linn
Eichner Conrad, tailor, 112 Ham. Road
Eichner Michael E., s.s. Hardson Road b. Riddle and Brighton [Av
Eichorn Frank, lab., wks. 830 Central
Eick Francis, cab. mkr., wks. n.w.c. Elm and Pearl
Eick Fred., cab. mkr., 124 W. 3d
Eickbush Henry, lab., 80 Melancthon
EICKENHORST & ARENS, (Henry E., & August A. A.,) Flour Dealers, s.w.c. Canal and Main
Eickenhorst Fred. H., dray, 12 Milton
EICKENHORST Henry, (E. & Arens,) 28 Milton
Eickhof Henry, cartman, 13 Mulberry
Eiden Martin, lab., 642 Elm
Eigholt Julius, cab. mkr., 277 B'dway
Eikmar James, dray. n.e.c. 3d and Lock
Ellermann Flefrau, 95 Clay
Ellermann Henry, bk. layer. 95 Clay
Ellermann Herman, porter, 22 Woodward
Eilers Bernard, turner, 79 Augusta
Eilers Gerhard. lab., w.s. Goose al. b. Liberty and 15th
Eilers Henry, lab., w.s. Broadway b. Hunt and Abigail
Eilers Henry, shoe mkr., 92 Hunt
Eilers Hermann, shoe mkr., 572 Race
Eilers John, furniture, 47 W. 5th, h. 596 Race
Eilhardt Fred, lab., al. b. Vine and Walnut and 13th and Mercer
Einhaus Oswald, clk., 64 W. 2d, bds. s.e. c Front and Race
Einstein Samuel, 56 W. 7th
Eirhaus Frank H., grocery, 414 Linn
Eirich James, molder, wks. n.e.c. Walnut and M. Canal
Eisle John, baker, 38 Elder
Eisele Francis X., printer, 571 Race
Eisele John B., brush mkr., 69 W. Liberly
Eiseman Abraham, (Fleischbauer & E.) bds. Sylvester House
Eisemann Abo, peddler, e.s. Ridgway al. b. Liberty and 15th
Eisemann Anthon, carp., 613 Race
Eisenacher John, grocer, 310 Cutter
Eisenhardt Benjamin A., salesman, 67 W. Pearl, h. 127 Betts
Eisenhardt Chas., tailor, 636 Race
Eisen Anton, saloon, s.w.c. Freeman and Dayton
EISENLOHR Rev. Gustavus W., editor Prot. Zeitblaetter, s.w.c. 15th and Race
Eisenmann Anton, cigar mkr., s.w.c. Green and Race

Eisenmann Bernhard, tailor, 19 Hamer
Eisenmann Jacob, cooper, n s. Charlotte b. Linn and Baymiller
Eisenmann Samuel, peddler, 124 W. Liberty
Eisenschmidt Julius, baker, 120 Ham. Road
Eisfelder Louis, cof. h., 22 Bank
Eisie Joseph, cof. h., 37 Dunlap
Eisley Francis, boots and shoes, n.w.c. 6th and Freeman, h. 195 Freeman
Eistacher Margaret, bds. e.s. Ridgway al b. W. Liberty and 15th
EITH BERNHARD, Union Garden, n.s. Ham. Road b. Race and Elm
Ekelmann Bernhard, cab. mkr., Cramsey al. b. Mound and Cutter
Eker Raymond, glass molder, 303 Clark
Ekert Daniel, bakery, n.w.c. 6th and Culvert
Elbat Catharine, servant, 437 W. 6th
Elberg Geo. J., marble cutter, bds. 412 Vine
Elbert John, baker, wks. 176 W. Front
Elble Chris., cof. h., 106 Walnut, h. 432 Walnut
Elble Joseph, brewer. wks. s.w.c. Plum and Canal
Elbrecht Wm., lab., 56 W. Liberty
Elbreg Frederick W., atty., bds. 395 B'dway
Elbreg Henry, shoe mkr., 17 Gorman
Elbreg Henry, vinegar mkr., 305 Broadway
Elbring Mary, 501 Race
Elbring Wm., molder, 501 Race
Elder Rudolph, butcher, 133 Ham. Road
Elder Sylvester, bar k., 113 W. M. Canal
Eldis H. H.., clk., American Ex. Co.,bds. Spencer House
Eldrege Judson, clk., bds. s.e.c. Race and 6th
Elenbaas Peter, porter, 496 Linn
Elf Jacob, lab., 804 W. Front
Elfela Joseph, grocery, 509 W. 7th
Elfers Antony, printer, 335 W. 5th
Elfers Barney, varnisher, 403 Longworth
Elfers Francis A., printer, 335 W. 5th
Elfers Helena, 72 Abigail
Elfers Henry, cigar box mkr., 20 W. Mulberry
Elfers John, lab., 104 Spring
Elfhaus Barney, 117 Findlay
Elfring Henry, teamster, 28 Mansfield
Elgerts John, 995 Central Av
Elias E., 53 George
Elias Ellis, mer., 96 W. Front
Elias Ellis H., jeweler, 44 E. 4th
Elias Wm. M., clk., 16 W. 4th, bds. Dennison House
Elias R. H., clk., Dennison House
Elig Mathias, lab., 105 Ham. Road
Elker Christian. carp., 26 Logan
Elking Ferdinand, clk., 20 E. Liberty
Elkins John, porter, h 72 Gano
Eliott Wm. W., clk., 103 W. Pearl, h. Glendale
Elitzer John, shoe mkr., wks. s.w.c. Bremen and Findlay
Ell Philip, sawyer, wks. at John Mitchell's
Ellard George D., n.w.c. 4th and Race
Ellard John, moves bs. n.w.c. 4th and Race
Ellerbrock Geo., cab. mkr., 493 Race
Ellerhorst Casper, tanner, 28 Canal
Ellerhorst Gerhard, copper smith, s.w.c. Front and Pike
Ellerhorst Lewis, shoe mkr. 67 Peets
Ellermann Bernhard, baker, 128 W. Liberty
Ellermann Christian, bds. 61 Hughes
Ellermann Frederick, porter, 70 Vine, h. 5 Whiteman
Ellermann Gerhard H., cab. mkr., 50 Rittenhouse
Ellermann Henry, gardener, w.s. Western Av. b. Findlay and Dayton
Ellers John T., shoe mkr., 293 Hopkins
Ellery Eben H. R., printer, 289 W. 8th
Ellinwood Samuel, American Ex. Co., bds. Broadway Hotel
Ellgas Anthony, mason, 62 Buckeye

Ellick John, carp., 531 Sycamore
Ellick John, jr., 83 Cross
Ellinger Jacob, finisher, 52 Baum
Elliot Mary, 28 W. 6th
Elliot Samuel B., b.k., 21 W. 5th
Elliot Sarah, 583 W. 5th
Elliot Wm., lab., 583 W. 5th
Elliott Alexander, (Harwood & E.) res. Glenn Grove
Elliott Daniel J., barber, 109 E. 6th
Elliott Elizabeth, 14 Park
Elliott Elizabeth, 66 Milton
Elliott Harvey, bds Burnet House
Elliott James, clk., 520 W. 3d
Elliott James, clk. Custom House, h. Millcreek Tp
Elliott James, marble cutter, 42 Mansfield
Elliott Margaret, 301 W. 6th
Elliott Margaret, 301 W. 6th
Elliott Peter, lab., wks. s.s. Court e. of Broadway
ELLIOTT Thos. R., (G. W. Ball & Co.) 540 Freeman
Elliott Wm., machinist, bds. 140 Carr
Elliots John, boatman, 92 Longworth
Ellis Alex, hack-man, bds. 5 New
Ellis Chas., stair builder, n.s. Corporation al. b. Young and Price
Ellis Charles B., clk., bds. 462 W. 7th
Ellis Chas. W., 2-6 W. 8th
Ellis David, s.s. 7th b. Linn and Baymiler [worth
Ellis E. C., clk., 110 Main, h. 211 Longworth
Ellis Flora, 3 e.c. 8th and Lock
Ellis Franklin. 292 Linn
Ellis George, (E. & Richardson,) 216 Vine
Ellis Granville S., ments. s.e.c. Mound and Longworth, h. 30 Mound
Ellis H. & J., (Henry & John,) produce, 21 Water
Ellis Henry, (H. & J E.) 371 Vine
Ellis Henry, tinner, bds 161 Baymiller
Ellis Henry, shoe mkr., 91 12th
Ellis Herbert, e.s. Linn b Everett and Wade
Ellis James, blk. smith, bds. 5 New
Ellis John, (H. & J. E.) 467 W. 7th
Ellis John, foreman Queen City Distillery
Ellis John, produce, bds. 126 Mill
ELLIS John W., (E., McAlpin & Co.) 260 W. 6th
Ellis Jonathan, boots and shoes, 193 Smith, h. 117 Park
Ellis Louis, waiter. bds. 5 New
ELLIS, McALPIN & CO., (John W. E., Geo W. McA. and James E. Polk & Jed. Heberd.) Importers and Wholesale Dealers in Dry Goods, 118 W. Pearl
ELLIS R. Jr. & CO.,
(Rowland E. jr. & Jas. W. Vinton,) Bankers, 15 W. 3d
Ellis R. Gordon, salesman, 53 Main, h. 54 E. 6th
Ellis Rebecca. 63 E. 7th
Ellis Richard G., salesman, 54 E. 6th
Ellis Richard, watchman, 349 John
Ellis & Richardson, (Geo. E. & John W. R.) cof. h., 199 Vine
ELLIS Rowland jr., (R. E. jr. & Co.) 238 W. 4 b
Ellis Rowland, sen., 15 W. 3d, h. 211 Longworth
ELLIS ROBERT, Mattress Manufacturer Upholsterer and Dealer in Window Shades, 136 Sycamore
Ellis Samuel, stair builder, 444 W. 5th
Ellis Thos. A., clk., 112 Hopkins
Ellis Wm., porter, bds. 5 New
Ellis Wm., riverman, bds. 206 W. 5th
Ellis Wm. R., sutler, bds. 326 Central Av
Ellison A., bds Gibson House
Ellison Abner, blk. smith, 22 Plum
Ellison Archey, clk. L. M. R. R., rooms 30 W. 4th
Ellison Geo., porter, 20 E. Pearl
ELLISON Wm., (H. Campbell & Co.) h. Manchester, O
Elithorp Mary, servant, 412 Race
Ellman Joseph, cof. h., 5 Landing b. Broadway and Ludlow, h. 37 Broadway

Ellseinheimer John, wagon mkr., 149 Bank
Ellston Wm. H., bonnet presser, 200 W Front
Ellstrip Thomas, butcher, n.w.c. Cutter and Richmond
Elmanhaus Henry T., carp., bds. 412 Vine
ELMER & FORKNER, (Willard E. & Jas. F.) Manufacturer of Stoves and Hollow Ware, 600 and 602 W. 5th
Elmer Geo., molder, wks. n.e.c. M. Canal and Walnut
Elmer Julia. h. 56 Rittenhouse
ELMER Willard E., (E. & Forkner,) bds. 345 George
Elmes Henry, lithographic printer, 64 W. 4th
Elmiger Aloys, tailor, 530 Plum
Elmore Michael, lab., e.s. Auburn nr. Bigelow
Elsas Isaac, porter. 20 Pearl, h. 143 W. Pearl
Elsas Jacob, manuf., of clothing, 109 W. Pearl, h. 126 E. 4th
Elsas Jacob, jr., clk., h. s.w.c. 7th and Walnut
Elsaszer John, cooper, Pleasant b. Findlay and Henry
Elsbernd Hy., cigar mkr., 51 Mulberry
Elsche Geo. H., express driver, 497 Sycamore
Elsenheimer Geo., carp., 562 E. Front
Elsenheimer J. Geo., cof. h., 412 Vine
Elsenheimer John J., confec., 409 Vine
Elster Hy., bklayer, al. b. Linn and Baymiller and Liberty and Wade
Elstner & Fisher, (Wm. C. & Wm. M. F.) flour mill, w.s. Lock b. 4th and 5th
Elstner Chas. E., 177 Broadway
Elstner Geo. R., drill master, 177 Broadway
Elstner Joseph, agent flour mill 294 Broadway, h. 124 E. Liberty
Elstner Mary, 177 Broadway
Elstner Wm. C., (E. & Fisher) 177 Broadway
Elstner Wm. C., b.k., h. 177 Broadway
Elstro Christian, bklayer, 477 Broadway
Elwood Frank, cutter, 313 Findlay
Elworth Margaret, servt., 532 W. 5th
Ely John H., clk. 140 Main, h. 197 Longworth
Ely Seneca W, sec'y and treas. City Pass. and Pass. St. R.Roads, h. 197 Longworth
Elzer Joseph, bds. 281 W. 7th
Elzner Chas., 422. Vine
Elzner Fredericka, midwife, 422 Vine
Elzner Hermann A., music teacher, 422 Vine
Elzner Hugo, clk. 49 W. 4th, h. 422 Vine
Emanuel John, bar k., 183 W. 3d
Embers Margaret, rear 432 Sycamore
Embus Barney, lab., n.s. Liberty b. Main and Sycamore [8th
Emclutz Helena dress mkr., bds. 616 W.
Emery Barney, 674 Central Av.
Emerson Daniel G., mach., 307 Richmond
Emerson Edwin A., auctioneer, bds. 103 Broadway
EMERSON EDWIN S., Drugs, Chemicals, Paints, &c., s.e c. Pearl and Broadway, h. 161 York
Emerson Hy., (N. W. Emerson & Co.) 64 E. 4th
Emerson Hy. B., horse dealer, 84 12th
Emerson Jas., brush mkr., 249 W. 4th
Emerson Jas, horse dealer, 84 12th
Emerson Jas. P. clk., 84 12th
Emerson John, driver. 64 12:h
Emerson N. W., (N. W. E. & Co.) 114 Broadway
Emerson N. W. & Co., (N. W. E., Hy. E. & T. L. Macdonald) grocers, 147 Walnut
Emerson Samuel W., painter 44 E. 3d, h. Newport
Emerson Wm., 84 12th
Emery J. Howard, b.k. s.e.c. Vine and Water, h. 301 W. 4th
Emery Rev. Joseph, city missionary, 212 Richmond

EMERY Josiah J., (Thomas E. & Sons) 301 W. 4th
Emery Kezia, 301 W. 4th
Emery Mary, 117 Betts
Emery Mrs. Thomas, 301 W. 4th
EMERY Thomas J., (Thomas E. & Sons) 301 W. 4th
EMERY THOMAS & SONS, (Thos. J. E. & Josiah J. E.) Lard Oil and Candle Makers, s.e.c. Vine and Water
Emig Elizabeth, 9 Moore
Emig Jacob, cigar mkr., 9 Moore
Emig Philip, lab., 9 Moore
Emigholtz Frederick, shoe mkr., 334 Main
Eminger Joseph, turner. 162 Clark
EMLEY Samuel C., (B. P. Baker & Co.) 136 E. 3d
Emling Hy., shoe mkr., 610 Central Av.
Emmeluth John J., cab. mkr., 616 W. 8th
Emmelth Justice, cab. mkr., 616 W. 8th
Emmert Frederick L., coroner, 16 Court House Building, h. s.w.c. 13th and Jackson
Emmerson Mrs. B., 31 Gano
Emmett Samuel, carp., 490 John
Eminick Hy., carman, 9 Webb
Emmig Bernard, tailor, 601 Sycamore
Emmigholz Hy., cab. mkr., 16 Dudley
Emmling Wm., 44 Cross [ter
Emmons Emma, actress National Thea-
Emrich Michael J., bar k., 13 Bremen
EMRICH Philip, (Sprenger & E.) h. 349 Main
Emrick David L., druggist, n.w.c. John and Clinton
Emrickmeier Eliza, 52 Dudley
Emshoff Geo., dray, 24 Mansfield
Emsike Joseph, 43 Jones
Emskamp Hy., shoe mkr., 434 Sycamore
Emwille Geo., blksmith. n.e.c. Abigail and Sycamore
Endaredan Frederick, dray, 16 Commerce
Endebrock Frederick, 65 Oliver
Endebrock Hermann H., porter, 65 Oliver
Endebrock Lewis, trunk mkr., bds. 65 Oliver
Endebrock John H., mason, 50 Pleasant
Endebrock Wm., porter, rear 9 Liberty
Endereden Anthony, blksmith, rear 50 Webster
Enderlen Joseph, clk., 17 E. 3d e. of Parsons
Enderlen Peter, lab., 17 E. 3d e. of Parsons
Endres John, 189 Bremen
Endres Nicholas. tailor, 618 Vine
Endres Philip, teacher, 47 Findlay
Endress John A., cigar mkr., 455 Sycamore
Endress John A., salesman 81 W. Pearl, h. 22 W. 9th
Eng Fred., cooper, 89 12:h
Eng Joseph, lab., 63 Clay
Engar Daniel, lab., wks. 141 W. 2d
Engbert John, barber, 184 Linn
Engberson Wm., grocery, n.s. Front e. of Foster
Engbessen Bernhard, blksmith, 38 Abigail
Enge Emma M., 604 Race
Engel Adam, butcher, 74 Dunlap
Engel Adam, butcher, 88 Findlay
Engel Caroline, bds. 388 Baymiller
Engel Francois, shoe mkr., w.s. Poplar b. Duckeye and Ham. Road
Engel Frank, cooper, 132 Hopkins
Engel Frederick, cof. h., 675 Vine
Engel Frederick, lab., 534 Plum
Engel Geo., bar k., 675 Vine
Engel Geo., butcher, 723 Vine
Engel Geo., porter 11 Main, h. 29 Ham. Road
Engel Hy., teamster, 32 Dudley
Engel John, butcher, 723 Vine
Engel Margaret, 29 Ham. Road
Engel Mary, bds. 536 Race
ENGEL Wm., asst. editor of the Christian Apologist, s.w.c. Main and 8th, h. Covington

Engel Wm., lab. 32 Adams
Engelbrest August, comb mkr., 104 Butler
Engelcamp John, trimmer, 67 Spring
Engelhard Joseph, confec., 265 Main
Engelhard Mary, h 205 W. Front
Engelhard Hy., cab. mkr., 305 Clark
Engelhardt John, cof. h., 575 W. 5th
Engelhart Elizabeth, 51 Allison
Engelhart Frederick, tailor, 535 E. Front
Engelhart J. Conrad, finisher, wks. Crane, Breed & Co's
Engelhart Jacob. cof. h., 247 W. 6th
Engelhart John, finisher, 143 Buckeye
Engelthorn Philip J., stone cutter, 59 Findlay
Engelke Fred., bakery, 635 Central Av.
Engelke Frederick, lab., 218 W. Front
Engelke Frederick, sawyer, 70 Pleasant
Engelke Wm., meats, 59 Abigail
Engelmeier Wm., lab., 143 Abigail
Engelo Chris., porter, 20 Abigail
Engels Joseph, tailor, 646 Vine
Enger Andreas, trader, 58 Elder
Enger Bullig, shoe mkr., e.s. Western Av. b. Dank and Harrison Pike
Enger Joseph, trader, 729 Race
Engert Michael, 26 Schiller
Engert Peter, cooper. 132 W. Liberty
Enghusch Barney, blksmith, wks. n.e.c. Walnut and Canal
Enginger Andreas, tailor, 29 Elder
England John, lab., wks. n.e.c. Walnut and Canal
England John, painter, 240 Vine
Engle John, lab., wks. Queen City Distillery
Englebrecht August, varnisher, 104 Butler
Englehardt Frederick, tailor, 778 E. Front
Englehuff Hy., cab. mkr., 305 Clark
Engleman Andrew, 23 Providence
Englert Frederick, boots and shoes, 116 Ham. Road
Englert Joseph, huckster, w.s. Bremen b. Elder and Findlay
Engles Joseph W., carriage trimmer, 319 W. 3d
Engles Nathan, cab. mkr., wks. 196 W. Pearl
Englet John J., lab., 31 Buckeye
English Chas., paver, 98 Gest
English Charles, pewter smith, 114 Clinton
English Charles, tinner, n.e.c. Clinton and Baymiller
ENGLISH CLEMENT L., Portable Forge, Bellows and Brush Manufacturer, 41 E. 2d
English Horace B., driver, bds. s.w.c. Longworth and Stone
English Isaac, hose mkr., 125 Clinton
English Isaac H., collector, 125 Clinton
English Jacob, molder, s.e.c. 3d and Whittaker
English James, bellows manuf., wks. 41 E. 2d, res. Newport
English John, cof. h., 290 Broadway
English Mary A., Western Museum 78 Sycamore
English Owen, painter, 250 E. 6th
English Theodore, mach , bds. 9 Race
English Wm. P., b.k. 221 W. 5th, h. 125 Clinton
Enkel Herman, cigar mkr., 678 Vine
Enneking Mrs., 128 Pleasant
Enneking Frederick, clothing, 355 Main
Enneking & Huwe, (John B. E. & Hy. H.) tailors, 7 Broadway
ENNEKING J. B., (Kleine, Hegger & Co.) 216 Vine
Enneking John D., (E. & Huwe) h. E. Walnut Hills
Enneking John B., stencil cutter, 128 Pleasant
Enneking John H., (J. H. Drahman & Co.) 56 Sycamore
Enneking Lewis, b.k. 127 Walnut, bds. E. Walnut Hills
Ennis Catharine, servt., 420 W. 5th
Ennis Mrs. Eliza, 48 Kossuth
Ennis Margaret, millinery, 194 W. 5th
Ennis Martin, upholsterer, 321 John
Ennis Patrick, cooper, 114 Gest
Ennis Patr'ck, hinge fitter, wks. n.e.c. Walnut and Canal

Ennis Patrick G., cooper, bds. 118 Gest
Ennis Thomas, lab., 4 Linnaeus
Enright Daniel, plasterer, 43 David
Enright Geo., tailor, s.w.c. Mound and Longworth
Enright Johanna, 208 W. 7th
Ense Wm. P., tinner, wks. 17 W. 5th
Ensign Hy. foreman, wks. n.e.c. Walnut and Canal
Ensign Horton, molder. 449 John
ENSLIN ADOLPHUS, Apothecary and Druggist, n.e.c. Main and Orchard
Enslin Chas. F., lithographer, bds. 533 Walnut
Enslin Frederick C., clk., 533 Walnut
Ensner Stephen, shoe mkr., 530 Plum
Enters Louis, turner, 177 Clinton
Enthoff Catharine, 29 Abigail
Entwisel James, painter, 41 New
Entres Philip, teacher, 47 Findlay
Entrysel Andrew, lab., n.s. Pearl, b. Smith and Park
Enyart Carlon, tinner, 233 Barr
ENYART Chas.. G., (Gardner, Phipps & Co.,) bds. Burnet House
Enyart Charles L., clk., 1000 Central Av
Enyart Elizabeth, n.e.c. Baymiller and 9th
Enyart Jacob L., grocery, 1000 Central Avenue
Enyart John C., clk., n.e.c. Baymiller and 9th
Enyart Salem, 39 Hathaway
Enyart Wm. W., mach., bds. 233 Barr
Enz Edward, finisher, 96 Ham. Raad
Enzinger Mary, 162 Bremen
Epinger Wm., clk., bds. 333 Race
Epke Anna C., 54 Rittenhouse
Epke Francis, teamster, 27 Dudley
Epker Hy., 593 Elm
Epker Martin, cooper, s.w.c. 5th and Hannibal
Eppens & Bro., (Bernhard & Christian E.,) grocery, 9 E. Liberty
Eppens & Discher, (Frederick E. & Dietrich D.,) basket manufacturers, 560 Main
Eppens Frederick, (E. & Discher,) 17 Mulberry
Eppens Hy., shoe mkr., bds. 17 Mulberry
Epperle Jacob, mach., 164 Richmond
Epperle Louisa. 545 Main
Eppich Phillip J., cab. mkr., 671 Race
Epping Anthony peddler, 26 Green
Epping John, lab., 124 Clark
Epping Joseph H., lab., 590 Elm
Epping Wm., shoe mkr., 386 Baymiller
Eppinger Abraham, e.s. Pleasant, nr. Findlay
Eppinger Gotfried, cooper, 449 Linn
Eppinger Julius, butcher, 132 W. 6th
Eppinger Lewis, butcher, 35 Gano
Eppinger Solomon, b.k., 13 Sycamore, h. 47 14th
Epple Christian, cook, Burnet House
Epple Jacob, dray, 127 York
Epplete Margaret D., teacher, 10th district school
EPPLY ADAM, Wholesale Millinery and Notions, 20 W. Pearl. h. 133 W. 9th
Epply F. G., clk., 20 W. Pearl, h. 133 W. 9th
Epply Jacob. salesman, 57 W. 4th, h. 83 Hopkins
EPPLY JOHN P., Undertaker and Livery Stable, 182, 184 and 186 W. 9th, opp. City Park. h. 326 Plum
Epply Lizzie, teacher, 133 W. 9th
Epps Jesse, peddler, 524 Elm
Epps Martha, 31 David
Epstein Hermann, peddler, 572 Elm
Erasmus Gerhard, cab. mkr., 25 Ham. Road
Erb John, cooper, 139 Wade
Erbecker John, wagon mkr., n.s. Front, e. of Lewis
Erchinger Christian, lab., bds. 680 Vine
Erd Francis J., jr., (Chas. Behlen & Co.,) Lexington, Ky.
Erd Herman F., b.k., 74 W. Court
Erdmann Elizabeth, 462 Elm
Erdmann Ferdinand, bk.layer, s.w.c. Vine and Findlay

Eramann Zacharias, cutter, 74 Broadway
Erforth Charles, wagon mkr., 528 E. Front
Erhardt George, lab., wks. Cincinnati Chemical Laboratory
Erk Martin, stone mason, 540 Plum
Erke Peter, cooper, bds. e.s Western Av. b. Dank and Harrison Pike
Erkel Hy., painter, 449 Linn
ERKENBRECKER ANDREW, Manufacturer Pearl and Wheaten Starch, 87 Lock, h. 46 Harrison
Erkenbrecker Fred., tailor, 415 Main
Erkenbrecker Frank, chair mkr., 418 Longworth
Erlemoein Peter, carp., 59 Findlay
Erler John S.. carp., h. 51 Jones
Ermandtraut Michael, molder, 125 Pleasant
Ernhoff Jacob, wks. n.w.c. Smith & 2d
Ernst Anton, tanner, 28 Canal
Ernst August, cab. mkr., 9 Wade, b. Elm and Plum
Ernst August, porter, rear 66 Hughes
Ernst Christopher H., tailor, 81 Spring
Ernst Franklin, quarter mast., 359 W. 9th, w. of Central Av
Ernst George, grocery, h. 578 Elm
Ernst Hy., carriage mkr., rear 886 Central Av
Ernst Hy., hinge fitter, wks. n.e.c. Walnut and Canal
Ernst Hy. M., (Jacob Ernst & Co.,) h. 23 Ellen
Ernst Hiram, lab., 82 Abigail
Ernst Jacob, (Jacob E. & Co.,) 23 Ellen
Ernst Jacob, b.k., 538½ Elm
Ernst Jacob & Co., (Jacob E. & Henry M. Ernst,) booksellers, &c., 107 Main
Ernst John, 24 Brighton
Ernst John, 551 Sycamore
Ernst John, buckskin dresser, 267 Ham. Road
Ernst John, tanner, wks. 183 Ham. Road
Ernst Louis, butcher, 28 Brighton
Ernst Ludwig, shoe mkr., 13 15th, b. Elm and Plum
Ernst Mary, 26 Pleasant
Ernst Parker, painter, 420 John
Ernst Phillip. 26 Mohawk
Ernst Rudolph, pyrotechnist, 533 W. 8th
Ernst Rudolph. tailor, 533 W. 8th
Ernst Thos. J., stencil cutter, 187 Walnut
Ernst Wm., cab. mkr.. 7 15th, b. Elm & Plum
Ernst Wm. H., carriage manuf., 886 Central Av
Ernst Wm., tailor, 140 Hopkins
Erpienstein Joseph, grocery, h. s.s. Budd b. Donnersberger and Harriet
Erbick Casper, lub., wks. n.w.c. Plum and Wade
Erschell Frederick, salesman, 20 W. 2d
Erskine Peter, 39 Jones
Ertel Bernhard, policeman. 78 Bremen
Ertmann Ferdinand A., cab. mkr., 112 Pleasant
Ertmann Ludwig, carp., 60 Findlay
ERVING Luther, (Macy, Rankin & Co.) h. 286 George
Ervin Mary, 203 W. Court
Erwin G., riverman, bds. 12 E. Front
Erwin J. C., clk., 101 W. 4th
Erwin James, hatter, 225 Broadway
Escales Moritz, jewelry, 140 Walnut, bds Silvester House
Eschbach John, tailor, 546 Walnut
Eschen Catharine E., 407 Central Av
Eschenbach Charles, baker, f 41 Race
Eschenbach John, cof. h , 157 Pleasant
Eschenbrenner Chas., grocery, 793 Race
Eschmann Andreas, butcher, wks. 466 Main
Eschmann Magdalena, s.w.c. Vine and Main
Escmus Jacob, carp., wks. 74 Pendleton
Esdus Mille, 87 Race
Eshelby James, mer., 361 W. 9th, w. of Central Av
Eske Hy., tailor, 251 Hopkins
Eskens Leroy, 116 E. 6th
Esler John, baker, wks. 104 W. 6th
Eslinger Michael J., lab., 359 Race
Esmann Joseph, cof. h., n.w.c. Walnut and Court

130 (EVA) CINCINNATI (EVA) DIRECTORY. (EWI)

Espel Hy., grocery, 52 Elm, h. n.e.c. Sycamore and 6th
Espenleiter, John, lab , 636 Vine
Espenscheid John, paver, 220 Bremen
Esper Catharine. 6 Buckeye
Esper John. 40 Dunlap
Espich Chas., bird store, s.s. 6th, b. Main and Walnut
ESPY James, (Kinney, E. & Co.,) h. Clifton
ESSELBORN Julius, (Weisker Brothers) 121 Main
Essen Clement, lab., 222 Clark [6th
Essenback Charles, baker. wks. 244 W.
Essens Frank, finisher, wks. n.e.c. Walnut and Canal
Essert Christian, tailor, bds. s.w.c. Pearl and Ludlow
Esses Anton, shoe mkr., 459 Main
Esses Jicob, shoe mkr., 459 Main
Essex Eliza washwoman, h. 68 George
Essip Patrick, blksmith. 57 Sycamore
Esslair Ferdinand. cigar mkr.. 565 Vine
Esslinger John, cof. h., 446 Main
Esslink Hy., lab., wks. 106 W. Pearl
Este Mrs , bds. 89 E. 4th
Este David K., jr, 379 W. 4th
Este David K.. sen., 379 W. 4th
Este Wm. M., 379 W. 4th
Estell D. & Son, (Daniel & Levi,) woodyard, n.e.c. Elm and river
Estell Daniel, (D. E. & Son,) 168 W. Front
Estell John, vet. surgeon, 168 W. Front
Estell Levi, (D. Estell & Son,) 168 W. Front
Estell Samuel C., b.k.. n.e.c. Elm and River. h. 168 W. Front
Estep Benj. D., cab mkr., w.s. Baymiller, b. Clark and Hopkins
Estep Richard P., foreman, 479 W. 4th
Estep Thomas B., b.k., 206 W. Court
Estep Thomas C., undertaker, 52 Richmond
Estep Wm., fireman, 80 Bank
Estep Wm. H., fireman, w.s. Jackson, b. Canal and 12th
Esterly Catharine, servt., 367 W. 8th
Esterman John B., shoe mkr., 135 Hopkins
Estermann Bernhard, chair mkr., 197 Pleasant
Estlinger Wm., lab..n.s. Kemper's Lane, b. Hill and E. Front
Estus Holmes J., painter, 23 Richmond, b. Elm and Plum
Etgerson Robt., porter, bds. s.w.c. Pearl and Ludlow
Fther Hy.. lab., 601 Walnut
Etly Jacob H., bar k., 179 W. 3d
Etna Fire Insurance Co. agency, 76 W 3d
Etter Louis, cab. mkr., wks. 45½ E. 3d
Etter Wm., lab., 122 Clay
Ettinger Geo., porter, bds. 74 E. Pearl
Ettley J. H., bar k., Burnet House
Eucler Jacob, varnisher, 20 Hannibal
Euler Mary, milliner, wks. 492 Vine
Euling Samuel, carp., 14 Hannibal
Euphrat Charles, cigars, &c., 77 Walnut, h. s.s. Mercer b. Walnut and Vine
Euphrat Louis, cigars,&c.,160½ Walnut, h. e.s. Walnut b. 4th and 5th
Euphrat Siegmund, cigar mkr., n e.c. 13th and Jackson
Eusterkemper Bernhard H., lab., 8 Buckeye
Eusterkemper John H, 8 Buckeye
Eustis Marvin, lab.. 108 West
Eustis George, teller, 65 W. 3d, b. 438 Freeman
Evans Ann, servt., 420 W. 6th
Evans Ann J., servt , 418 W. 5th
Evans Arthur, foreman, 214 George
EVANS Benj. (Swift, E. & Co.,) 14 W. 9th
Evans Benj. A., baker, 245 W. 6th
EVANS C. B. & CO. (Caleb B. E.. E. Loring & Grant H. Burrowes) Enameled Grates and Mantels, 142 W. 3d
EVANS & CO. (Jason E., Briggs Swift, Hugh W. Hughes & William T. Drake), Bankers, 75 and 77 W. 3d

EVANS Caleb B. (C B. E. & Co.), 71 Barr
Evans Catharine L., 260 W. 9th
Evans Daniel D., b k., 215 Main, bds. s. e.c. 3d and Broadway
EVANS Daniel O. (Jones, E. & James), s s. 3d b Butler and M. Canal
Evans David, b.k., 65 W. 3d, h. 249 Laurel
Evans David. eng., 35 New
Evans David E., stair bldr , 237 Laurel
Evans David G., saddler, 37 Hathaway
Evans Ebenezer, grocery, 178 Broadway
Evans Edward, blksmith, 37 Jackson
Evans Edward D., cab. mkr., 380 George
Evans Edward E. (E. & Williams) 235 Laurel
Evans Elizabeth, 37 Jackson
Evans Evan, hinge fitter, wks. n.e.c. Walnut and Canal
Evans Evan, lab., 23 College
Evans Evan, boiler mkr., wks., s.s. 3d b. Butler and M. Canal
Evans Evan, stair bldr.. 237 Laurel
Evans Evan E. (E. & Williams), 237 Laurel
Evans Evan R., grainer, 508 Walnut
Evans, Gaines & Co. (Hugh E., G. J. G. & Owen Gaines), pork packers, n.e. c. Broadway and Court
Evans Georgianna, bds. 431 Central Av.
Evans Geo. T., 237 W. Court
Evans Harriet, 306 George
Evans Hy., harness mkr., bds. 250 Walnut [Park
Evans Hy., wks. rolling m■■, rear 24
Evans Hy. C , foreman, 102 Liberty
Evans Hester, 89 E. 3d
Evans Hester, clk., 202 Betts
Evans Hester, tailoress, 25 Martin
Evans Hotel, 65 Broadway
Evans Hugh (Evans, Gaines & Co.) 102 Liberty
Evans James, clk.. 16 Barr
Evans James, painter, 37 Jackson
Evans Jane, servt , 140 John
EVANS Jason (E. & Swift & E. & Co.), h. 59 W. 5th
Evans Job., carp., Observatory st., Mt. Adams
Evans John, rear 144 Culvert
Evans John, bk. layer, 127 W. 9th
Evans John H.. station house keeper, 237 W. Court
Evans John P., lock smith, 21 Melancthon
EVANS John T. (Choate, Barber & E.), 290 Findlay
Evans Lewis. lab., 517 W. 3d
EVANS & LINDSEY, (Wm. L. E. & Henry K. L.) General Insurance Agts. 65 W. 3d
Evans Maria, 80 E. 3d
Evans Maria, servt., s.s. 3d b. Butler & M. Canal
Evans Maria. tailoress, 25 Martin
Evans Martha, Observatory st., Mt. Adams
Evans Mary, 214 George
Evans Mary, 134 W. 9th
Evans Mary. 135 W. 3d
Evans Mary, milliner, bds 141 Carr
Evans Moses, chemist. 141 Carr
Evans Nellie, 157 Central Av.
Evans R. N., clk., bds. n.e.c. 6th and Race
Evans Richard b.k., 20 E. 2d, res. Covington
Evans Richard, clk., bds. 238 Race
Evans Richard, mach., 37 Jackson
Evans Robert. finisher, wks. n.e.c. Walnut and Canal
Evans Sarah J , dress mkr., 206 John
EVANS Seth (Alex. Swift & Co. & McKeehan & K.) h. Avondale
Evans Stephen. carp., 288 W. Front
EVANS & SWIFT. (Jason E. & Briggs S) Pork Packers and Ham Curers 21 E. 9th
Evans Theodore A., engraver, 93 Mill
Evans Thos., blksmith, 37 Jackson
Evans Thomas. clk., n.w.c. 6th & Freeman, h. 9 Pine
Evans Thos. C., salesman, 146 W. 5th, bds. n.w.c. Longworth and Central Av.

Evans Thomas L., lab., 9 Pine
Evans Mrs. W. F., b.h., 239 Race
Evans Wm , n.s. New b. Culvert and Broadway
EVANS Wm. L. (E. & Lindsay) h. Walnut Hills
Evans Wm. M., watch mkr., 206 John
Evals & Williams (Evan E. E., Ed, E. E. & Thos. S. W) stair bldrs., 519 Central Av.
EVELAND Harmon (French, Wilson & Co.) h. Loveland, Ohio
Eveleth Mary, 129 Barr
Eveleth Wm. H., mer. tailor, 18 W. 4th, h. 127 Barr
Evens Edward, carp., n.s. Railroad e. of Hazen
Evens John G., finisher, n.s. Railroad e. of Vance
Evens Joseph, carp., s.s. Railroad e. of Stone al
Evens Lewis, wks. junction 6th and Front
EVENS PLATT, jr., Seal Engraver and Variety Machine Works, 64 W. 4th, up stairs, h. Covington, Ky.
Evens Thomas A., engraver, s.w.c. 4th and Walnut
Everett Geo , porter, h. 15 Commerce
Everett George H., tel. op., 162 Broadway
Everhard Mary, clk., 83 E. Pearl, bds. 152 W. 5th
Everhardy Mathias,butcher, 5 Whiteman
Everley David, lab , 234 W. Front
Everly June, h. 135 W. Pearl
Evers Bernard, cigar mk.., 12 Madison
Evers Chas., hats and caps. 35 E. Pearl, h. 379 Walnut
Evers Diedrick, lab., 12 15th
Evers Frederick, 570 Walnut
Evers Frederick, cooper, wks. 9 Orchard
Evers John Hy., grocer, 87 Wade
Evers Herman, shoemkr, 98 Clay
Evers Joseph, lab., 9 Woodward
Eversfield John, cof. h.,14 E. 7th
Eversfield Michael, 175 Longworth
Eversman Fred., huckster, 104 Betts
Eversmann Charles D., clk., n.w.c. Cutter and Richmond
Eversmann Herman H , grocery, n.w.c. Richmond and Cutter
Eversmann Peter, grocery, 644 W. 5th
Eversol Sarah, 300 W 8th
Everson Albert, eng., Burt e. of Broad
Everson Benjamin, carp. 1166 E. Front
Everson James, mach., 9 Pierson
Everson John, bk. binder, 9 Pierson
Everson John, carp., 121½ E. Front
Everson Kate, 266 Cutter
Everson Thomas. blksmith, 9 Pierson
Everson Wm., blksmith, 9 Pierson
Eveslage Benjamin, cof. h., 9 12th
Eveslage Bernard, cof. h., 47 Pendleton
EVESLAGE JOSEPH, Staple and Fancy Dry Goods, 472 Main
Eveslage Otto H., boots and shoes, 171 W. 5th
Evet Francis, lab., wks. s.e.c. Canal and Vine
Evis Joseph, lab., wks. 222 E. Front
Ewald Catharine, 80 Milton
Ewald Elizabeth, 523 W. 7th
Ewald Frank, tailor, 157 Central Av.
Ewald John H. turner, w.s. Ridgway al. b. Liberty and 15th
Ewald Joseph J., boots and shoes, 383 Main
Ewald Wm., tailor, 95 Buckeye
Ewan Evan, prop. Ewan House, 326 Central Av.
Ewan Isaac, dray, rear 586 E. Front
Ewell Benjamin F., clk., C., H. & D. R. R. depot
Ewell W. H. S., surveyor Buckeye State Ins. Co., h. Fairmount
Ewers Geo. H., tailor, 10 Woodward
Ewighaus Chas.. lab., 66 Ham. Road
Ewin Hy., 270 Main [9th
Ewin John, banker. 54 W. 3d, h. 39 W.
Ewing Etna, bds. 353 Central Av.
Ewing Elizabeth, 466 W. 7th
Ewing George lab., 216 Water
Ewing George W., teamster, 216 Water

| CINCINNATI | (FAN) | DIRECTORY. | (FAR) | 131 |

Co's, h.

nd Carr
all al. b.

Avery b.

&c., 403

Main

Central

mkr., 74

Hamilton

more
d, h. 68

8 Vine
printer,

m

ade
more
more
(Henry
ulman).
le Deal-
Catawba
le Deal-
Wines,

Co.), 436

8 Main

W. Lib-
, bds. 15

W. 7th
6th

r
Pearl
h. 319

ler, 299

c. Court

Mills,
erchant,
anal and

an Mills,
L. Canal

h. New-

rt, w. of

rt & F.,)

147 Ham.

rear 94

st
er
wks. 11

n

Faby Matthew, lab., 36 Butler
Failey James F., wheelwright, bds. 316 W. 3d
Failey John W., carriage mkr., bds. 316 W. 3d
Fairbanks John, stone mason 82 Water
Faircamp Lucas, porter, 265 Main
Fairchild D M., salesman, 29 W. Pearl, h. Covington
Fairchild Elijah B., porter, n.w.c. Pearl and Walnut, h. Covington
Fairchild J. B., solicitor, 68 W. 3d, h. Covington, Ky.
Fairclough Thomas, plasterer, 193 Richmond
Fairley Alexander, dray., 15 Grant
Fairley Wm., carp., 74 E. 3d, e. of Whittaker
Fairris Mary, w.s. Langdon al., b. 6th and 7th
Fairweather Geo. M., carp., bds. 132 Linn
Fais Leo, tin smith, e.s. Bremen b. Elder and Findlay
Fais Peter, shovel manuf., rear 180 Buckeye
Faisz Pius. tinner, 628 Vine
Faler Joseph, lab., s.s. Bank b. Freeman and Coleman
Falk Adolph, cab. mkr., 96 Ham. Road
Falk Charles W., boots and shoes 526 Sycamore
Falk Fiedel, 67 Peete
Falk Michael, bk. layer, 22 E. Liberty
Falk Placidus, lab., 700 Race
Falk Simeon, shoe mkr., 286 Ham. Road
Falkansten Frank, dray., 36 Parsons
Falke Frank H., horse shoer, wks. 702 Vine
Falkenhan Adam, porter, 99 Pendleton
Falkner Charles, eng., 1202 E. Front
Fallada Anna, 42 Race
Fallada Francis, cap mkr., 42 Elder
Fallan Patrick, lab., 192 Water
Fallbush Chas., b. k., 5 Jackson
Faller Charles, cigar store, 215 W. 6th h. 93 Richmond
Faller John, carp., 544 Race
FALLIS David J., (F. Young & Co..) h. Covington
FALLIS Isaac C., Sec'y. Buckeye State Ins. Co., h. 265 Hopkins
FALLIS YOUNG & CO., (David J. F., John Y., & Charles, E. Baker,) Bankers. s.w.c. 3d and Walnut
Fallon Bernard, lab., 422 W. 3d
Fallon Betty, servt., 27 Harrison
Fallon Catharine, servt., 113 Pike
Fallon Edward, lab., s.w.c. 5th and Central Av.
Fallon Hy., 251 W. Front
Fallon James, finisher, 92 Avery
Fallon Patrick, carp., s.s. Front e. of Hazen
Falls Elizabeth, 73 W. 7th
Falls John, ice mer., 17 Grant
Fals M., tinner, wks. n.w.c Race and 2d
Falter Frank, harness mkr., bds. e s. Vine b. Calhoun and Auburn Av
Fanaholt Wm., peddler, 464 W. 5th
Fancees Louis, tailor, n.e.c. 9th and Walnut
Fandel Pierre, carver, 128 Ham. Road
Fandell Peter, carriage mkr., wks. 55 E 5th
Fandriel Cornelius, lab., 110 Clay
Fanger John,shoe mkr., 83 E. Pearl
Fangman Barney, porter, 66 W. Front
Fangman Hy., locksmith, 121 Pleasant
Fangman Joseph, boots and shoes, 66 b. 3d and 5th
Fangman Joseph, cooper, 102 Abigail
Fanker Wm., carriage painter, 85 12th
Fankhouse Wm., baggage master, 83 E 3d e. of Whittaker
Fankmann Joseph, cooper, n.s. Abigail b. Broadway and Spring
Fannan Mary, s s. 6th b. Broadway and Culvert
Fannegin James, blksmith, 89 12th
Fannen Pat. W. S., blksmith, 28 Accommodation

Fannesy Patrick, grocery, s.e.c. 3d and Mill
Fannin Mary, 189 Cutter
Fanning Bartley, driver, n.e.c. Ludlow and 3d
Fanning Geo., coach mkrs., wks. 21 W. 7th
Fanning Patrick F., silver smith, 91 Longworth
Fanning Roxanna, 234 W. Front
Fanning Thomas, 506 W. 6th
Fannon Julia, servt, s.w.c. 3d and Broadway
Faraly Nicholas, lab., 223 E. 6th
FARAN James J., (Faran & McLean,) h. 122 E. 3d
FARAN & McLEAN, (James J. F., & S. B. W. McL.,) Editors and Proprietors Cincinnati Enquirer, n.e.c. Vine and Burnet
Farbach Gottfried P., driver, 147 Ham. Road
Farbeck Benjamin, lab., 59 Woodward
Farber Charles, tanner, rear 11 E. Liberty
Farber Hy., driver, 110 Avery
Farbourn Hy., b. k., 293 W. 5th
Farden Maria, servt., 109 Pike
Fareline Albert. clk., bds. 158 Cutter
Fareline Philip. clk., bds. 158 Cutter
FARES & MILLER, (Sebastian F., & Wm. M.) Dealers in Stoves, 5 W. 5th
FARES Sebastian, (F. & Miller,) 449 Broadway
Farington Peter, dray, 237 Everett
Faris Davis, bar k., 79 Barr
Faris John, box mkr., wks. 219 W. 3d
Faris Samuel M., watch mkr., wks. 6 W. 4th
Farl Thomas, lab., 32 Lock
Farley Hugh, lab., 71 Richmond
Farley James, bas. 518 John
Farley James, 85 E. 3d e. of Whittaker
Farley James, blksmith, bds. n.w.c. Front and Central Av.
Farley James, huckster, 146 W. Court. w. of Central Av.
Farley John, 67 Oliver
Farley John, lab., 30 David
Farley Julia, s w c. 6th and Broadway
Farley Patrick, lab., 18 Kossuth
Farlin Dudley II , clk., O & M. R. R. Freight Office, h. 329 Clark
Farlindi Antony, lab., wks. 830 Central Av
Farmer Ellen, 21 Mill
Farmer Ellen, 67 Woodward
Farmer Mary, servt., 437 Broadway
Farmer Thomas, lab., wks. s.w.c. Broadway and 5th
Farmers' Hotel. 1512 E. Front
FARMERS' HOTEL,
Geo. I., Fey & Co., Proprietors n.e c. Court and Race
Farney John, driver, 234 E. 6th
Farning John, boots and shoes, 174 Broadway
Farnsworth. Paul M., 52 Pierson
Farnsworth Wm., messenger, 19 W. 3d h. 52 Pierson
Farry Chas., 219 Ham. Road
Farny Heury P., b. k., 83 W. Pearl, bds. Spencer House
Farran Bernard, lab., 83 Race
Furran Hy., printer, 44 Lock
Farran Hermann 46 Lock n. of 8th
Farrar Betsy, 189 W. 3d
Farrell Andrew, huckster. 227 W. 6th
FARRELL BERNARD,
Printer, bds. Clifton House, rooms 41 George
Farrell Bernard, saw setter, e.s. Kilgour b. 3d and 5th [rail
Farrell Bernard H., carp., rear 69 Abigail
Farrell Bridget, servt., 358 George
Farrell Christina, 155 Cutter
Farrel Daniel, lab., 29 Commerce
Farrell Mrs. E., 78 E. 7th
Farrell Edward, lab., 143 Clark
Farrell Franklin, lab., w.s. Cutter, b. Melancthon and Wade
Farrell James, clk., bds. 137 W. 9th
Farrell James, lab., cor. Front and Central Av

132   (FAU)   CINCINNATI   (FEE)   DIRECTORY.   (FEL)

Farrell James, painter, wks. 144 W. 3d
Farrell James, printer, s.s. 6th b. Broadway and Culvert
Farrell James, teamster, 94 Baymiller
Farrell John, eng., 70 Richmond b. Plum and Central Av.
Farrell John, lab, n.w c. 3d and Collard
Farrell John, tinner, wks. s.w.c. Sycamore and 7th
Farrell Joseph M., b. k., 23 Walnut h. 155 Cutter
Farrell Kate, bds. 163 E. 3d
Farrell Maria, servt., 315 George
Farrell Martin, lab., 774 W. Front
Farrell Martin, pipeman, 370 W. 5th
Farrell Mary, s.s. 6th b. Broadway and Culvert
Farrell Mary, 255 W. Court
Farrell Michael, lab., 49 Mill
Farrell Michael, lab., 85 W. 9th w. of Central Av.
Farrell Michael, 92 Baymiller
Farrell Michael T., (Higdon & F.) 94 Baymiller
Farrell Philip, wks. 57 W. Miami Canal
Farrell Richard, lab., 163 Central Av.
Farrell T. J, molder, wks. 200 Vine
Farrell Thomas, bk. layer, 402 W. 5th
Farrell Thomas, lab., 41 Rittenhouse
Farrelly Nicholas, lab., wks. s.e.c. 9th and Sycamore
Farrelly Owen D. (Rocap & F.) res. Millcreek tp.
Farren Hy., lab., 89 12th
Farunkopf Michael, baker, 36 Findlay
FARRIN THOS. W., (Thos. W. F. & Co.) h. 218 Barr
FARRIN THOS. W. & CO., (Thos. W. F., & Jno. K. Green,) Lumber Dealers, w.s Freeman ft. of George nr. C. H. & D. R. R.
Farris James, stone cutter, s.s. 6th e. of Lock
Farris Margaret, rear 144 Culvert
Farro John, carp., 1518 E. Front
Farro John, lab., wks, 1565 E. Front
Farrow John, cof. h., 134 Culvert
Farry John, 33 E. 3d
Farry Mary, seamstress, 33 E. 3d
Farthing Richard C., 28 E. 2d, h. 127 W. 7th
Faruchler Joseph, lab., 69 Buckeye
Farwick John. teamster, 21 Carr
Farwick Richard, wood dealer, 16 Carr
Fasig Mary C., music teacher, 254 George
Faske Herman, grocery, 185 Hopkins
Faske Joseph, tailor, rear 60 Abigail
Fasnacht Gotfried, cab. mkr., 590 Elm
Fasold Hy., cooper, 31 Dunlap
Fass Amelia, 276 Central Av.
Fass Chas., clk., 276 Central Av.
Fass Joseph, clk., s.e.c. Pearl and Vine, bds. U. S. Hotel
Fassenden Stephen G., bk. layer, 551 Race
Fassmann Wm., lab., bds. 24 Abigail
Fastre Rev. Joseph, St. Xavier College, w.s. Sycamore b. 6th and 7th
Fastrick Hy., lab., w.s. Harriet b. 6th and Sloo
Fastrow Hermann, molder, n.s. 6th b. Harriet and Horne
Fasy John, huckster, 641 Elm
Fat Adam, mattress mkr., 934 Central Av.
Fath Adam, tailor, 642 Race
Fath Daniel, molder, 618 W. 5th
Fath John, cooper, s.s. Hubbard b. 5th and 6th
Fatte Hy., carriage smith, 93 Spring
Faubel Hy., 691 Elm
Faught Jacob, lab., wks. n.w.c. Plum and Wade
Faulkner Abigail, 115 W. Court w. of Central Av.
Faulkner Bridget, servt., 186 Race
Faulkner Jeremiah, printer, 55 Everett
Faulkner John, cof. h., 49 W. 5th
Faulkner Jno. A., carp., Junction of 6th and Front
Faulkner Stephen, (Taylor & F.) bds. 568 Freeman
Faulwetter Chas H., printer, 8 15th
Faulwetter Theodore, jeweler, 8 15th

Faurekell Carl F., blksmith, 628 Race
Faus Andrew, cigar mkr., 802 Elm
Faus Michael, 235 Findlay
Faust Henry, distiller, 363 W. 6th
Fawcett Mrs. Price, 81 Longworth
Fawcett Snelling P., pilot, 81 Longworth
Fawn John, clk., 518 W. 5th
Fay Adolphus, conductor, O. & M. R.R. bd 339 Longworth
Fay Anthony (F. & Stickney), h. 58 Franklin
Fay Calvin C., furniture car, 186 W. 4th
Fay Edward, bds. 444 W Front
Fay Ellen, servt., 309 Longworth
FAY J. A. & CO., (Wm. H. Doane, Caleb B. Rogers, Edward Joslin & Wm. E. London,) Wood working and Stave Machinery and Engine Builders, &c., s.w.c. John and Front
Fay Jas., carp., 29 Commerce
Fay Jas., lab., w.s. Central Av. b. 2d and W W. Canal
FAY LUCIAN, Metallic Burial Cases & Caskets, Patent and Roofing Machines, 349 Plum, h. 433 W. 7th
Fay Mary, c. 3d and Hill
Fay Peter, rubber, wks. n.e.c. Canal and Elm
FAY & STICKNEY, (Anthony F. & Daniel S.) Planing and Flooring Mill, 304 Broadway
Fay Thomas, policeman, E. 3d b. Parsons and Baum
Fay Walter, carp., 224 E. 5th
Fays James, clk., Cin. Gazette Co., h. 164 Vine
Fazzi James. plaster paris worker, 47 E. 4th, h. Newport
Fchring Anna A., vest mkr., h. 109 Woodward
Feakins Margaret, millinery, 24 E. 4th
Fealey Jas., wheelwright, bds. 316 W. 3d
Fealey John, wheelwright, bds. 316 W. 3d
Fealey Mary, servt., n.e.c. 3d and Pike
Fearle Michael, lab., Findlay b. Central Av. and John
Fearn Geo., jr., b.k., 36 Walnut, bds. 88 E. 4th
Featherly Truman, bds. 51 Gest
Featherman Nancy, 187 W. Court w. of Central Av.
Featherstone Wm., finisher, n.s. Charlotte b. Linn and Broadway
Fechenbach Samuel, peddler, 402 Race
Fechhelmer Hy. S., salesman, 84 W. Pearl, h. 86 W. 8th
Fechheimer Kate, 818 Walnut
Fechheimer Leopold S., salesman, 84 W. Pearl, h. 86 W. 8th
FECHHEIMER MARCUS, Wholesale Clothier and Dealer in Cloths, Cassimeres, &c., 84 W. Pearl, h. 86 W. 8th
Fechheimer Max, clk., bds. 318 Walnut
Fechheimer Max. M., salesman, 84 W. Pearl, h. 343 Vine
Fechheimer Wolf, clothing, 627 Vine
Feckers Hy., lab., n.e.c. Budd and Donnersberger.
Fedders B. F., agt., v.s. Abigail e. of Pendleton
Fedders Hy., tailor, 333 W. 5th
Fedders John H., lumber dealer, 151 Abigail
Feder Chns., clk., s.w.c. 3d and Park
Federle Gottlind, cooper, 378 W. Liberty
Federle Joseph, gardener, s.s. Liberty b. Freeman and Mill Creek
Federle Peter, stone mason, 124 W. Liberty
Federley Gottleib, 391 W. Liberty
Federspell August, lab., 207 Broadway
Fedick Jacob, lab., 87 Martin
Fee Mary, s.s. Phœbe al., b. Plum and Central Av.
Fee Rev. I., 132 Richmond
Feefler John. pattern mkr., bds. s.e.c. 2d and Plum
Feek Peter, carriage trimmer, 504 Sycamore
Feelner Fred., carp., 223 Central Av.
Feeney Michael, lab., 180 Water
Feeney John, dray, 123 W. 9th w. of Central Av.

Feeney John, tailor, 46 E. 7th
Feeney Michael, 31 W. Court w. of Central Av.
Feeney Patrick, driver, rear 32 Mulberry
Feeney Patrick, lab., 550 Race
Feery Frank, lab., s.s. Hunt, e. of Liberty
Feeser Louis, phonographic law reporter, 9 W. 4th
Feeway John. stocking weaver, 544 Sycamore
Fegel Lizzie, n.e.c. Allison and Clay
Fegel Wm., baker, wks. 532 Main
Feger Frances, 150 Pleasant
Fehr Chas., barber, 1112 Central Av.
Fehrenbach, John, cab mkr., 136 Pleasant
Fehring John G., lab., 109 Woodward
Fehrmann —, lab., 66 Hughes
Fehrmann Christian, cooper, 59 W. Liberty
Fei Mingus, lab., 191 Hopkins
Fei Wilhemina. millener, 407 Central Av.
Feibe Geo., lab., 200 Linn
Feibelman Aaron L., clk., 82 W. Pearl, h. 81 W. 4th
Feiber Simon, dentist. 65 Clay
Feichspan Geo , saddler, 404 Vine
Feick Valentin, dray, 642 Race
Feierstein Barbara, servt., 468 Main
Feiertag Geo., cigar stor., 59 15th
Feiertag Martin, lab., bds. 622 Vine
Feigel Margaret, servt., 436 Main
Feigery Kate, servt., 570 W. 9th
Feigle Theodore, lab., 143 Pleasant
Feigley & Davis, (Sam'l F. & James E. D) com. mer., 247 Walnut
Feigley Samuel, (F. & Davis,) h. 379 Elm
Feiler Christopher, tailor, 25 Mulberry
Feilhamer Magdalena, music teacher, 453 Vine
Feindel Jacob, wines, &c., 13 Hunt
FEINTHEL Jacob, (Fischer & F.) h. Iowa
Feiny Peter, lab., 20 Logan
Feistel Leopold, liquors, &c., 112 W. Canal
Feit Louis, tailor, 484 Elm
Feitz John, lab., 202 Linn
Feken Aaron H., grocery, s.e.c. 4th and Lock
Felbier Franz, locksmith, 3 Wade, b. Elm and Plum
Felch Mary, tailoress, 164 Everett
Feld Christian H., lab., 536 Race
Feld Hy., cab. mkr., 554 W. Front
Feld Hy., lab., 110 Clay
Feld John H., lab., 293 W. Front
Feldauer Chas., painter, e.s. Ridgway al. b. Liberty and 15th
Feldcamp Hy., porter, 407 Central Av.
Feldcamp Martha, bds. 116 Betts
Felden Frederick. shoemkr., 341 Freeman
Felders Chas., mach., 18 15th b. Central Av. and Plum
Feldhaus John, tailor, 207 Linn
Feldhause John H., mason. rear 5 Wade b. Elm and Plum
Feldkamp Bernard, grocer, 391 W. Liberty
Feldkamp Bernhard J., carp. shop, w.s. Cogswell al., b. Woodward and Franklin, h. 25 Franklin
Feldkamp Geo., paper carrier, 4 Oehler al. b. Freeman and Garrard
Feldkamp H. D., porter, 25 Franklin
Feldkamp Hy., carp., 664 Race
Feldkamp Hy., trimmer, 407 Central Av
Feldkamp Hermann, lab n.s. Niles Al. b. Main and Sycamore
Feldkamp Hermann, paper carrier Oehler al. b. Freeman and Garrard
Feldkamp John H., carp., 25 Franklin
Feldkamp Joseph, h. Oehler al b. Garrard and Freeman
Feldkamp Mary, rear 93 Woodward
Feldkamp Rudolph, cigar mkr., 226 W. 5th
Feldkamp Wm., cooper, bds. 19 Adams
Feldman Hy. J., grocer 295 Linn
Feldman Hermann, card writer, 594 Race
Feldman John B., paper carrier, 295 Linn

(FEL) CINCINNATI (FER) DIRECTORY. (FET) 133

Feldmann Barney, blksmith, 75 Abigail
Feldmann Christian, cab. mkr , 566 Race
Feldmann Francis, carp., 639 Vine
Feldmann Hy., ex. driver, 53 15th
Feldmann Hermann cooper, 109 Woodward
Feldmann Hermann, lab., 26 13th
Feldmann Hermann, dry goods, 29 Green
Feldmann Hermann, shoe mkr. 55 Pendleton
Feldmann Hermann G., boots and shoes 630 Race
Feldmann J. Hy., cooper 109 Woodward
Feldmann John, cooper, 110 Pleasant
Feldmann John W., dry goods, 644 Race
Feldmann Joseph, lab., 73 Abigail
Feldmann Valentine, carpet weaver 666 Main
Feldmann Wm., dry goods, 585 Race
Feldwisch J. Hy., grocery, 36 Hughes
Feleng Wm, bakery, 20 W. 4th
Felheimer Solomon, mer 163 W. 9th
Felicitas Sister, superior, St Clare Convent, n.w c. 3d and Lytle
Felinger G., blksmith, wks. C. T. Dumont's
Felix Adam J., cooper, 244 Pleasant
Felix Francis, tailor, e.s. Johnson al. b. Canal and 12th
Felix Frederick, cab. mkr., 13 E. Liberty
Felix Geo. M., blksmith 997 Central Av.
Felix John. lab., 37 Baum
Felix John A. 244 Pleasant
Felix John J., lab. 37 Baum
Felix Mathew, cof. h. w.s. Browne, nr. Ham. Road
Felix Michael tailor, s.s. Henry b. Elm and Dunlap
Felix Peter, 284 W Liberty
Felix Sabastian, tailor, 244 Pleasant
Felkamp Franklin, tailor. 63 David
Fell Jacob F., tannery. s.e,c. 5th and Culvert, b. 43 Mansfield
Fell Mathews, tailor. h. 410 W. Liberty
Feller Chas, cigar mkr. 98 Richmond
Feller John, 500 W. Front
Feller Nicholas. 240 E. Front
Follermeier Frederick varnisher w.s Long Al, b. Woodward and Franklin
Fellermann John A., lab., 22 Orchard
Fellis Edward, bk, layer, 393 Race
Fellis Peter, butcher, w.s. Reading Road nr. Montgomery turnpike.
Felock Hy. C., bds. 61 E. Pearl
Felpmann Casper. molder, 41 W. 3d
Fels Mathias, peddler 87 Ham. Road
Fels M., propr. Mt Auburn omnibus line, res. Mt. Auburn
Felsenden Jacob, peddler, 199 W. Liberty
Felt Clements, lab., e.s. Ramsey b. W. W. Canal and Front
Felt Hy., meats, 14 15th b. Central Av. and Plum
Felter Barney lab. wks. s.w.c. W. W. Canal and Smith.
Felter Sarah G., seamstress, 193 Mound
Felthaus Frederick, watchmkr, s.e.c. 2d and Sycamore
Felthvester Hy. F., turner 94 15th
Felthouse Hy., grocer, n.e.c. Liberty and Broadway.
Feltkamp Bernhard, waiter Gibson House
Feltkamp Mary, servt, 359 W. 7th
Feltlow H., chair mkr. wks. John Mitchell's
Feltman B., lab., wks. n.s. Front b. Lawrence and Pike
Feltman Barney, blksmith, wks. n.e.c, Walnut and Canal
Feltman Hy., tailor, 236 Hopkins
Feltman John, 418 Longworth
Feltmann Casper H., lab., 451 W. 3d
Feltmann Francis, tailor, n.e.c. Abigail and Pendleton
Feltmann Geo. H., boots and shoes, 283 W. 6th
Feltmann Hy. 141 Abigail
Feltmann Hy. jr., cooper, 109 Woodward
Feltmann Hy. sen., cooper, bds. 109 Woodward
Feltmann Hy., shoe mkr., wks s.e.c. Main and 6th

Feltmann Hy., tailor, 48 Woodward
Feltmann Hermann, blksmith 388 Broadway
Felton Willis, huckster, 214 E. 6th
Feltrop Dena, 50 Plum
Feltrup Herman, cooper, bds 695 Main
Feltrup Joseph, wks., 137 W. 2d
Feltus Lambert M., b k. 117 John
Felty Augustus W., 647 Elm
Female City Prison, n.w.c. Parsons and E. Front
Fench Pardon, carp., 30 Parsons
Fenelon Thomas, porter 113 W. Pearl
Fenemann Geo., porter 62 Pierson
Fengel Louis, painter, 65 David
FENGER ANTHONY,
Coffee House
500 W. Front
Fenger John, cof. h., 5 Lawrence
Fenity Dennis, lab., n.w, c. 6th and Harriet
Fenker Bernard H., lab. 61 Abigail
Fenker Hy., huckster, e.s. Race, b. W. Liberty and 15th
Fenker John, grocer, e.s. Ramsey nr. Park Al,
Fenker John F., molder, 6 Ramsey
Fenley Patrick, feed store. 170 Water
Fenmann Hy., cab. mkr. 16 Hughes.
Fenn Orlonzo, cooper 344 George.
Fennefron Herman, cooper, s.e.c. Longworth and Hoadly
Fennel Adolphus, druggist, 444 Sycamore
Fennemann Elizabeth, 362 Broadway
Fennemann George, porter, 86 W. 2d
Fennemann Geo , salesman, 62 Pierson
Fennemann H. H., dray, 537 W. 6th
Fennemann Herman, shoe mkr , 77 W. Front
FENNESSY EDWARD,
Family Grocery
s.e.c. Race and Commerce
Fensley John, capt,, bds Walnut st, House
Fenstermacher Chas., finisher, 80 W. Liberty
FENTON AARON B., Atty. and Agt. for the firm of S. Fenton & Co., 38 Walnut. h. 152 W. 4th
FENTON & BECK, (Roswell H. F. & Andy B.) Daily Market, n.w.c. Plum and 6th
Fenton John W., carp., al. b. Cutter and Linn and Court and Richmond, h. 193 W. Court
Fenton Julia, 176 W. Court w. of Central Av
FENTON Roswell H., (F. & Beck.) h. Cheviot
FENTON S. & Co., (Solomon F. & Aaron B. F.) Produce and Com. Merchants, 38 Walnut
FENTON Solomon, (S. F. & Co.) res. Erie Co. N. Y,
Fenton Susan. b. 464 W. 4th
Fenton W. W., pilot, bds. Madison House
Fenton William, cab. mkr. 123 Richmond
Fenton Wm., lab., 19 E. 8th
Fenton Wm. W., clk. L. M. R. R. depot h. 123 Richmond
Fenup Hy., s.s. Alexander b. McGrew and Fountain
FENWICK & CO.,
India Rubber Goods,
56 W. 4th
FENWICK Wm. (F. & Co.) bds. Gibson House
Fenzer Casper. cooper, 706 Race
Ferdelmann Hy., lab., n.w.c. Pleasant and Green
Ferdinand Chas., saloon, 78 Sycamore
Ferdinand Hy., photographist 414 George
Ferera Andrew, cof. h. 102 W. Front
Ferguson Mrs., n.w.c. Smith and Longworth
Ferguson Benham P., carp., 537 Elm
Ferguson Chas. K., clk., bds. 345 Race
Ferguson Daniel, dray, 145 W. Front
Ferguson David, upholsterer, 191 Laurel
Ferguson David J., driver, 39 Plum
Ferguson David S., stencil cutter, 162 Plum

FERGUSON Edward Alex., (F. & McGinnis,) h. 423 W. 8th
Ferguson Eliza. b.h., 102 Plum
Ferguson Miss Ella, teacher, 191 Laurel
Ferguson Miss Emily, teacher, 191 Laurel
Ferguson James, dray, 501 Sycamore
Ferguson James, lab., 12 Commerce
Ferguson James W., tanner, s.s. Front e. of Ferry
FERGUSON JOHN,
Family Grocery, s.e.c. 9th & Vine,
h 345 Race
Ferguson John J., clk., bds. 345 Race
Ferguson Margaret, mid wife, s.s. 5th b. Wood and Stone
FERGUSON & McGINNIS, (Edward A. F. & James McG.) Attorneys at Law, 65 W. 3d
Ferguson Phillip B., carp., 547 Elm
Ferguson Robert G., dray 458 W. 7th
Ferguson Wm., n.w.c. Washington and 3d
FERGUSON WM., Messenger Commercial Bank, h. 242 Court w. of Central Av
Ferkheimer Samuel, peddler, 555 Race
Ferl Wm., lab., n.s. Marsh b. Smith and Park
Ferlminn Henry, bk. mkr., e.s. Western Av. b. Dayton and Bank
Ferman Bernhard H., grocery, 18 Abigail
Fermburg Louis, furniture, 632 Central Av
Fern Frederick, painter, bds. 65 Broadway
Fern Geo., clk., bds, 88 E. 4th
Fern John, lab., h. 36 Butler
Fernaux Geo., bk. binder, 43 Main
Ferneding Rev. Herman, s.e.c. Spring and Abigail
Ferneding Rev., Joseph, s.e.c. Spring and Abigail
Fernich Jacob, (Kaufman & F.) 26 W. 6th
Fernin Miles, cof. h., n.s. Montgomery Pike nr. Reading Road
Fernkaes George, paper carrier, 48 Ham. Road
Ferrari & Co., (Geo. F. & F. Pedretti,) cof. h., 177 Vine
Ferrari Geo., (F. & Co.) 101 Race
Ferrari Giovani, cof. h., h. 101 Race
Ferree Wm. M., carp., 256 Hopkins
Ferrell Anna M., cof. h., 176 Central Av
Ferrell Michael, plumber, n.e.c. Baymiller and Richmond
Ferrell Thomas. molder, 36½ Barr
FERRIS, DUNLEVY & FOWLER, (Wm. T. F., D. B. D. & S. N. F.) Produce and Commission Merchants, 51 W. 2d
Ferris Fred. J , salesman, s.w.c. Walnut and Pearl, h. 136 Broadway
Ferris John, painter, bds. s.w.c. Race and 2d
FERRIS Wm. T., (Ferris, Dunlevy & Fowler,) e.s. Lawrence b. 3d and 4th
Ferris Willis, conductor, bds. 572 W. 9th
FERRY & CO., (Lewis V. F. & P. B Hayward,) Tattersall's Saloon, 20 E. 5th
FERRY FRANCIS,
Sec'y Central Ins. Co. of Cincin'ti, h. 573 W. 8th
Ferry Hannah, cof. h., n.e.c. North and New
Ferry James, saloon, 212 W. 7th
FERRY Lewis V., (F. & Co.) 20 E. 5th
Ferst Ludwig, lab., 641 Elm
Fesenbeck Rosina, 110 Pleasant
Fessa August, hostler. 175 W. 6th
Fessel Casper, brewer, s.e.c. Grant and Elm
Fessel Lorenz, cooper, wks. s.e.c. Plum and Canal
Fessel Matthias, brewer, wks. s.e.c, Plum and Canal
Fessey C. carp., wks. 304 Broadway
Fester Bernhard, lab., 3 Mulberry
Fester Geo., carp., 241 Clark
Fester Leonard, pyrotechnist, 83 Kilgour
Fetch John A., candy, 631 Vine

134 (FIE) CINCINNATI (FIN) DIRECTORY. (FIR)

Fetherlen Eliza, h. 209 Barr
Fetsch Nicholaus, tailor, 49 Elder
Fette Fred., waiter, Galt House
Fette Henry. blk. smith, 89 Spring
Fette Ludwig. tailor, e.s. Milk b. Vine and Calhoun
Fetterspille Anton. finisher, wks. n.e.c. Walnut and Canal
Fetterstone Wm., mach., wks. n.s. Front b. Lawrence and Pike
Fetting Wm., sawyer, 76 Dudley
Fettleman Henry, finisher, wks. n.w.c. Plum and Wade
Fettleman Herman, lab., wks. n.w.c. Plum and Wade
Fettweis Chas. L., marble yard w.s. Ham. Road b. Findlay and Race, h. n.s. Findlay b. Race and Ham. Road
Fettzer Ulrich, lab., 96 Ham Road
Feucht Simon, liquors, bds. s.w.c. Race and 3d
Feulner Henry J., mechanic, 95 Bremen
Feurbach Dora, 63 Green
Feuerstein Frank, stone cutter, 178 Clay
Feuerstein Henry, cof. h. s.s. Harrison Pike b. Riddle and Brighton
Feuerstein Valentine, shoe mkr., 660 Vine
Feuriger Chas. A. F., helper, n.s. Goose al. b Green and Elder
Feuss Wm., bakery, 207 Cutter
Feust H. F., prof. of music, bds. Teutonia Hotel
Ferwry Peter, blk. smith, h. 172 Water
Fey Adelaide, 421 Vine
Fey Conrad lab., 28 Elder
Fey Francis, tailor. 28 Elder
FEY GEO. P. & CO., Farmers Hotel, n.e.c. Court and Race
FEY Geo. P., (Geo P. F. & Co.) n.e.c. Court and Race
Fey Henry, cof. h., 235 Bremen
Fey John, lab , 36 Elder
FEY SEBASTIAN, Coffee House, 621 Vine
Fey Valentine, shoe mkr., 68 Rittenhouse
Fey Wm., cooper, n.s. Bank b. Central Av. and Clarkson, h. 991 Central Av
Fey Wm., student, bds. 621 Vine
Feye Geo., grocery, n.e.c. Sycamore and Woodward
Fibbe Geo., lab., wks. 179 W. Canal
Fibbe Herman, grocery, s.w.c. 12th and Race
Fibich Mary, trimmer, s.w.c. Elm and 13th
Fichmann August, carp. 67 Wade
Fichter Jacob, clothing, 100 W. 9th
Fichter Nicholas, lab., 10 Abigail
Fick Frederick, painter, 133 Clinton
Fick Mary, seamstress, 12 W. Mulberry
Ficke Bernard, tailor, 603 Walnut
Ficke Henry, clk., 219 Linn
Ficke Herman, china, &c., 60 E. Pearl, h. 427 Walnut
Ficke James, n.s. Corporation Line nr. Auburn
Ficke John, driver, 323 Plum
FICKEN JOHN, Wholesale Grocer & Liquor Dealer, 16 E. Pearl
Ficker Bernhard. lab., 50 Buckeye
Ficklest Conrad, cab. mkr., wks. 115 Buckeye
Fiddler John, lab., 49 E. 3d e. of Whittaker [Vine
Fidel Andreas, cigar mkr., bds. 680
Fideler Geo., bk. layer, w.s. Ridgway al. b. 14th and 15th
Fidler Frederick, lab. 159 Pleasant
Fidler John W., pattern mkr., 127 Bremen
Fidley Effort. cof. h., 195 Vine
Fiebelmann Leopold, cigars, 81 W. 4th
Fiber Frank, currier, bds. 967 Central Av
Fieber John, 392 Baymiller
Fieber John, butcher, 355 Central Av
Fieber Samuel, 104 Brown
Fieber Wm , clk., 107 Sycamore, h. 256 Central Av

Fiedler John, carp., 38 Mohawk
Fiedel Wette, carp., 56 Elder
Fiedeldey Henry. butcher, e.s. Logan b. Elder and Liberty
Fiedeldey Hermann, lab., 118 Abigail
FIEDELDEY JOHN C., Pork and Beef Packer, 54, 56 and 58 E. Pearl
FIEDELDEY JOHN H., Leather and Findings, 5 12th, h. 96 Hunt
Fiedler Daniel, carp., 130 Pleasant
Fiedler Edward, cof h., 206 Vine, h. n. w.c. 5th and Vine
Fiedler Fred., grocery, n.w.c. Court and Elm
Fiedler Louis, tailor, 286 W. Liberty
Fiedler Ludwig, tailor, 258 W. Liberty
Fiefhaus Henry, lab., 17 Mulberry
Fiehe Catharine, b.h. 113 Clay
Field Catharine, 32 12th
Field J. D., bds. Gibson House
Field Owen, lab., 54 Richmond b. Plum and Central Av
Field Michael, lab., rear 188 Cutter
Field Richard B., baker, 118 W. 5th, h. Clifton Heights
Field Wm. R., wood measurer, 200 Freeman
Fielding Michael, 122 Cutter
Fields Ann, 52 McFarland
Fields George, whitewasher, n.s. Phoebe al. b. Plum and Central Av
Fierlein Albert G. W., clk , 158 Cutter
Fierlein Phillip, clk., e.s. Cutter b. Court and Clark
Fiersattle John S., meats, 560 Main
Fieth Joseph, expressman, 131 Clark
Fifer John T., molder, s.s. Weller b. Freeman and Curr
Fifield M. B., sexton, W. Court b. Mound and Cutter
Fifth Mission Sunday School, e.s. Freeman b. 5th and 6th
Figalist Conrad, cab. mkr., 66 W. Liberty
Fige Wm., tailor, 17 Mary
Figer Margaret, seamstress, 44 Peete
Fihe John H., dry goods, 610 Central Av
Fihe Sophia, 610 Central Av
Fike Bernard. blk. smith, 705 Vine
Fillan Francis, barber. 89 Ham. Road
Filler John, lab., 154 Ham. Road
Filling F , eng., bds. 91 Sycamore
Filling Hy., teamster, 91 Sycamore
Filling Mary, servt., 91 Sycamore
Fillmore Comfort L., ship carp., s.e.c. Reed and E. Front
Fillmore Ebenezer H., carp. s.w.c. Front and Lawrence, h. 26 Parsons
Fillmore H. B., bds. Dennison House
Fillmore H. E., asst receiver Pendleton and 5th St. R.R., 26 Parsons
Fillmore Wm , stone mason, 153 Everett
Fillmore Wm. A., (Drake & F.) 26 Parsons
Filtuan Mathilda, dress mkr. 78 W. 4th, h. 169 Baymiller
Finagin Geo. C., paper carrier, 29 Buckeye
Finan Bridget, 65 Rittenhouse
Finan Kate, servt , 100 E. 4th
Finch Benoni P., carp., s.s. George b. Baymiller and Freeman, h. 91 Laurel
Finch Daniel W., carp., 91 Laurel
Finch Edward, b.k., bds. n.e.c. 5th and Broadway
Finch George M., b.k. 63 W. Pearl, h. 188 Richmond
Finch Hy. H., huckster, 330 Clark
Finch Mary H , teacher, 21 Grant
Finch Parkin M., carp., 30 Parsons
Finch Thomas J., salesman 139 Walnut, h. 3¾ W. 4th
Finder Maurice, tailor, e.s. Johnson al. b. Canal and 12th
Findlay Ellen P., teacher, 159 Baymiller
Findley Wm., baker, h. 194 W. 6th
Findly Fenton, tailor, 47 E. 3d
Finger Chas.. hinge molder, wks. n.e.c. Walnut and Canal
Finigan Ellen, 12 Skaats

Finister James. porter, 148 Water
Fink Adam, driver, 69 E. Pearl
Fink Anthony. cigar mkr , 66 Abigail
Fink Francis M., salesman 170 W. 6th
Fink Fred., molder, wks. n.e.c. Canal and Walnut
Fink Frederick, porter, wks. 359 Walnut
Fink Jacob, lab., 132 Bremen
Fink James, organ builder, 18 Milton
Fink John, cigar mkr., 132 Bremen
Fink John P., boots and shoes, 94 W. Court
Fink Valentine, lab., wks. n.e.c. Park and Marsh
Finke August, chair mkr., 301 Linn
Finke Barney, boots and shoes, 50 E. Pearl
Finke Frederick, grocery, 312 Linn
Finke Frederick, porter, 27 Ham. Road
Finke Frederick, molder. 61 Pendleton
Finke Frederick J , porter. 517 Race
Finke Hy., horse shoer 702 Vine, h. n.e. c. Vine and Peete
Finke Hy., tanner, s.s. Liberty b. Linn and Baymiller
Finke Hy. A., boots and shoes, 717 Race
Finkelstein Adam, painter, 201 George
Finkenstedt Frederick. lab., 723 Race
Finkler John, bksmith, 674 Race
Finkman Frederick, agt, bds. 579 W. 5th
Finkmeier Christopher, wagon mkr., 225 Betts
Finian Peter, lab., 243 W. 3d
Finlay Albert A., printer, wks. 168 Vine
Finley Alice, h. 13 Arch
Finley Andrew, baker, bds 320 W. 6th
Finley F. F., tinner, 26 George
Finley James H., paper carrier, bds. 233 John
Finley John, tailor, 231 E. 5th
Finley Mary, 233 John
Finley Mary J., teacher, 233 John
Finley Rose. 26 George
Finley Samuel B , 159 Baymiller
Finley Thomas P., clk., 59 Cutter
Finley Wm., confec., 89 Sycamore
Finn Adam, n.s. Browne b. Ham. Road and Mohawk
Finn Bridget, 460 W. 5th
Finn Edward, lab., 197 E. 6th
Finn Ellen, 67 Kossuth
Finn James, driver, 118 Butler
Finn Jas., lab., 101 Hunt
Finn John, lab., s. Macalister b. 4th and 5th
Finn Margaret, 29 Webb
Finn Martin, collar mkr., e.s. Lock b. 6th and 8th
Finn Mary, 67 Kossuth
Finn Thomas, actor, 154 Sycamore
Finnan Bernard M., 172 Poplar
Finnarn Michael, grocer, n.w.c. Wade and Cutter
Finnegan Louis, hinge filter, wks. n.e.c. Walnut and Canal
Finnegan Mary, 165 Mound
Finnegan Owen, driver, 165 Mound
Finnegan Patrick, lab., 107 Baum
Finnegan Richard. saloon, n.s. Augusta b. John and Smith [Av.
Finnell James, lab., wks. 830 Central
Finnell Wm., carp., 62 Butler
Finnerty Thomas. lab. 228 E. 6th
Finney John, tailor, 120 W. 6th, h. 46 E. 7th
Finney R., pilot, 12 Home
Finnigan Ellen, h. w.s. Culvert b. 5th and 6th
Finnigan John, lab, bds. n.w.c. Mill and Front
FINNIGAN MICHAEL, Steam Free Stone Works, n.e.c. Hoadly and Longworth, h 407 W. 3d
Finnity T., lab., wks. Chamberlain & Co's
Finsterle Gottlieb, tailor, 602 Elm
Finton John, shoe mkr , 52 Barr
Finton Wm., janitor, s.s. Front e. of Lewis
Fippen James, driver, 3d and 4th st. railroad
FIREMAN'S HALL. George Morscher, proprietor, 65 W. 5th

Fireman's Hall, 17th Ward, n.e.c. Vance and E Front
FIREMEN'S INSURANCE COMPANY. Fire and Marine; Samuel R. Carter, Sec'y; Henry E Spencer, Pres't; Office, n.e.c. Main and Front, up stairs
Firth John F., tinner, wks. 21 E. Front
Firth Joseph, brass finisher, wks. 120 E. 2d
Firth Thomas, supt., 120 E. 2d, h. 14 W. Court w. of Central Av
Fisbigh Wm , (Strietmeier & F.) 92 Bank
Fischel Solomon. cigar mkr., 323 W. 6th
Fischens Anna, 451 W. 3d
Fischer A. W., salesman. bds. 648 Main
Fischer Adolph. mer., 644 Main
FISCHER Albert, (F. & Feinthel) 34 W. Court
Fischer Alois, tanner, 656 Elm
Fischer Barney. box mkr., bds. n.s. 2d b. Park and Mill
Fischer Bernhard, grocery, 34 Abigail
Fischer Casper, cigar mkr., 22 Hamer
Fischer Chas., tailor, 68 Hughes
Fischer Chas. Wm. Ferdinand, phys., 648 Main
Fischer Christian, bakery, 272 Main
Fischer David, carp , 6 Moore
FISCHER & FEINTHEL, (Albert F. & Jacob F.) Cork Cutters and German Produce, 34 W. Court
Fischer Francis B., clk., 231 Main
Fischer Frederick, cigar manuf., 495 Elm
Fischer Frederick, cof. h., 214 Vine
Fischer Frederick, tailor, 68 Hughes
Fischer Frederick, tailor, 570 Elm
Fischer Frederick H., tanner, 55 Milton
Fischer Gerhard, hardware, 156 Baymiller
Fischer Gerhard L., cooper, 150 Pleasant
Fischer Hy., basket mkr., 547 Main
Fischer Hy., cigar mkr., 495 Elm
Fischer Hy., clk., bds. 648 Main
Fischer Hy., lab., rear 72 Hunt
Fischer Jacob, cof. h., 617 Main
Fischer Jacob, shoe mkr., 136 Liberty
Fischer John, barber, 935 Central Av
Fischer John, bk binder, 273 Bremen
Fischer John F., blksmith, n.e.c. Liberty and Freeman, h. 434 W. Liberty
Fischer Julius, millinery, &c., 77 E. Pearl, h. 630 Main
Fischer Lawrence, brush mkr., 6 Mulberry
Fischer Louisa, rear 66 Hughes
Fischer Louis, tanner, 20 Dunlap
Fischer Maria, midwife, 21 15th b. Central Av. and Plum
Fischer Martin, carp., s.s. Charlotte b. Linn and Baymiller
Fischer Martin, lab., 1 Mary
Fischer Martin, molder, 118 Ham. Road
Fischer Martin, shoe mkr., 233 Bremen
Fischer Mathias, eng., 20 Dunlap
Fischer Mary, servt., 23 Harrison
Fischer Michael, lab., 72 Hughes
Fischer Michael, turner, 233 Bremen
Fischer Nicholas, foreman, 141 Clay
Fischer Peter, finisher, 114 W. Canal
Fischer Peter J.. tailor, w.s. Bremen b. Elder and Findlay
Fischer Valentine, cigar store, 405 Central Av.
Fischer, Valentine, phys., 137 Laurel
Fischer Wm., confec., s.e.c. 6th and Walnut
Fischer Wm., mer., 648 Main
Fischer Wm., musician, bds. 47 12th
Fischer Wm., varnisher, 20 Mansfield
Fischfot Rudolph, wood dealer, bds. 468 Main
Fish Hanford H., eng., n.w.c. Goodloe and Willow
Fish Wm. B., 288 Longworth
Fishburn Cyrus D., phys., s.e.c. Vine and Ham. Road
Fishbyrn Rosana. 471 George
FISHEL & BRO., (Morris & Edward F.) Wholesale Clothiers, 60 Main
FISHEL Edward, (F. & Bro.) 367 W. 9th
Fishel Edward, clk., 367 W. 9th w. of Central Av.
FISHEL Morris, (F. & Bro.) 367 W. 9th

Fisher Adolph, clk., h. 644 Main
Fisher Albert, sawyer, 177 Clinton
Fisher Annie B., servt., 343 W. 7th
Fisher Anthony, w.s. Jordan, b. Clark and Gest
Fisher August, shoemkr, 137 Linn
Fisher Bernard, watchmkr, 62 Main, h. w.s. Main, b, 5th and 6th
Fisher Brownlow, printer, bds. 36 Longworth
Fisher Charles, paper box mkr., s.e.c. 5th and Main
Fisher Charles A., eng., bds. 131 Carr
Fisher Charles W., eng., s.s. Front, E. of Vance
Fisher David, (John W. Fisher & Co.,) 14 Ann
FISHER DAVID, Justice of the Peace, n.s. 9th. b. Plum and Central Av. h. 20 Perry
Fisher Daniel M., plasterer, 241 Findlay
Fisher David W., clk., 20 Perry
Fisher Frederick, n.e.c. Linn & Everett
Fisher Frederick, blksmith, wks. n.w.c. Race and Burrows
Fisher Frederick, cab. mkr., 211 Clinton
Fisher Fred. O., dry goods, 131 Carr
Fisher Frederick W., pattern mkr., 413 W. Front
Fisher Geo. box mkr., 54 Elm
Fisher Geo., carp., 106 Browne
Fisher Geo., mer. tailor, 257 Walnut, h. 270 George
Fisher Geo., trimmer, 666 Central Av
Fisher Hy. W., eng., s.s. Front, e. of Foster
Fisher James A., clk., 20 Perry
Fisher James L., (Isham, F. & Co.,) 372 W. 6th
Fisher John, bk. mkr., 33 Gest
Fisher John, cig. mkr., 170 Clinton
Fisher John, f reman, 177 Clinton
Fisher John, lab., 30 York
Fisher John, lab., 173 Charlotte
Fisher John S , druggist, bds. 149 Elm
Fisher John W., carriage trimmer, 51 Clinton
Fisher John W., (J. W. Fisher & Co.,) 426 John
Fisher John W. & Co., (John W. F. & David Fisher,) feed store, 539 Central Av
Fisher Joseph, 194 Oliver
Fisher Joseph, lab., e.s. Anderson al., b. 2d and Pearl
Fisher Joseph, lab., wks, 114 W. Court
Fisher Joseph, lab. wks, 375 W. 3d
Fisher Julia A., h. 150 John
Fisher Kate, 55 George
Fisher Lawrence, lab., w.s. Garrard, b. Hopkins and Kenner
Fisher Lewis. blksmith, 796 Central Av
Fisher Ludwick, policeman, n.s. Railroad, e. of Hazen
Fisher Maria, dress mkr., 175 Spring
Fisher Martin, lab., 195 W. Front
Fisher Martin, molder, wks Chamberlain & Co.'s
Fisher Martin, porter, 1 Mary
Fisher Martin R., clk., 1092 E. Front
Fisher N. H., phys., Commercial Hospital
Fisher Peter, baker, wks. 224 W. 6th
Fisher Peter, finisher, wks. n.e.c. Walnut and Canal
FISHER Samuel S., (Lee & F.,) 545 W. 8th
Fisher Solomon, cigar mkr., 323 W. 6th
Fisher Thomas, dray, bds. 195 W. Front
Fisher Wm., 202 Ham. Road
Fisher Wm., 196 W. 7th
Fisher Wm. C., dray, bds. 159 W. Front
Fisher Wm. J., grocery, 446 W. 3d
Fisher Wm. M., (Elstner & F.,) h. Linwood
Fishman August, cab. mkr., 162 Clark
Fishman George, lab., 159 Everett
Fishwick Elizabeth, clk. 415 Central Av
Fishwick James, mach., 415 Central Av
Fishwick Mrs. James, variety store, 415 Central Av
Fisk Amos, carp., n.s. 4th, b. Park and Mill
Fisk Mrs. J. C., s.w.c. 5th and Plum
Fisk W., agent, 174 Vine, h. Covington, Ky.

Fiske G Hermann, cooper, n.s. Abigail b. Broadway and Spring
Fisler Louis, hats and caps, 502 Vine
Fisse J , tinner. wks n.w.c Race & 2d
Fister Leonard, fire-works, e.s. Kilgour, b. 3d and 5th
Fitch Morgan L., printer, 350½ W. 5th
Fitch Wm., caulker, 460 W. 4th
Fither Stephen, 273 Clinton
Fithian Daniel, b.k., 407½ John
Fitten John, tailor, s.s. 9th, b. Cutter & Linn
Fitterrer Joseph, lab., 668 Vine
Fitting James, lab., 180 Carr
Fitts L. E., b.k , 16 W. Front
Fitzgibbon Jane, 118 Everett
Fitty Frederick, waiter. 52 Abigail
Fitz Patrick, lab., rear 515 E. Front
Fitzdam Hy., tailor. 771 Vine
Fitzgerald David, lab., 1 Budd
Fitzgerald Ellen, servt . 360 W. 7th
Fitzgerald Frederick, carver, 418 W. 5th
Fitzgerald Gerald, waiter. Burnet House
Fitzgerald & Jackson. (Peter F. & John A. J.) liquors, 112 E. Pearl
Fitzgerald James. lab. 132 Central Av
Fitzgerald James E , clk., h. w.s. Mansfield. b. Liberty and Milton
FITZGERALD JAMES W., Dealer in Family Groceries, s.w c. 5th and Broadway, h. 175 Broadway
Fitzgerald John, tailor, 95 Park
Fitzgerald Lorenz, cooper, n.s 6th, e. of Lock
Fitzgerald Michael, 483 Race
Fitzgerald Michael, lab , 50 McFarland
Fitzgerald Michael, lab., s.s. 2d, b. Rose & Park
Fitzgerald Michael, jr., bds. s.s. 2d, b. Park and Rose
Fitzgerald Oliver, cof. h., s.w.c. Race and Pearl
Fitzgerald Patrick, foreman, 323 Plum
Fitzgerald Patrick, lab , n.s. Fremont, b. Carr and Harriot
Fitzgerald Peter, (F. & Jackson,) 57 Mansfield
Fitzgerald Wm., conc' man, 167 E. 3d
Fitzgibbon Thomas. servt tender, s.e.c. Freeman and W.W. Canal
Fitzgibbons John, cooper, 7 Lock, n. of 8th
Fitzgibbons Maurice, carp., 205 Baymiller
Fitzharris Andrew, dray, 462 George
Fitzmoran M. . - iter, Burnet House
Fitzmorris Bridget, 61 Mill
Fitzmorris Catharine, 60 E. 5th
Fitzpatrick Dennis, carp., 153 W. 9th
Fitzpatrick Edward, watchman, 409 W 7th
Fitzpatrick James, lab , 593 W. 8th
Fitzpatrick James, lab., s.w.c. 8th and Carr
Fitzpatrick James, lab., 48 Butler
Fitzpatrick John, cook, s.e.c. Mansfield and Liberty
Fitzpatrick John, lab , 539 W. 8th
Fitzpatrick John, lab., s.e.c. Liberty & Mansfield
Fitzpatrick John, lab., n.e.c. Vine and Water
Fitzpatrick Kate, servt , n.w.c. Longworth and Central Av
Fitzpatrick Kyren, carp., 52 Kossuth
Fitzpatrick Margaret, servt., 136 Broadway
Fitzpatrick Mary, 265 John
Fitzpatrick Mary, servt , 436 W. 4th
Fitzpatrick Mary A., 128 Elm
Fitzpatrick Martin, lab., s.s. Friendship al., b. Pike and Fulton
Fitzpatrick Mathew, lab. 464 George
Fitzpatrick Michael, dray,. 405 Race
Fitzpatrick Michael, grocery, 136 W. Front
Fitzpatrick Michael G., 90 W. 5th, bds. 265 John
Fitzpatrick Moses, carp., 523 Freeman
Fitzpatrick Patrick, molder, 135 E. 6th
Fitzpatrick Thomas. lab. 158 W 3d
Fitzsimmons Anna E., bds. 57 E. 3d
Fitzsimmons Bernard, 45 Peete
Fitzsimmons Hy., lab., wks. 46 Public Landing
Fitzsimmons John, b.k., 70 Walnut

136 (FLA) CINCINNATI (FLE) DIRECTORY. (FLO)

Fitzsimmons John, clk., 65 Hopkins
Fitzsimmons Margaret, rear 71 Abigail
Fitzsimmons Matthew, clothing, 155 W. 3d
Fitzsimmons Patrick, bds. 158 W. 3d
Fitzsimmons Patrick, drayer, rear s.e.c. Lawrence and Pearl
Fix John, 16 Hamer
Fix John A., 537 Race
Fix August, paper hanger, 557 Race
Fiva H., stocking mkr., wks. 413 Main
Flach Charles, slaughter house, n.s. Montgomery Pike, nr. Reading road
Flach Frances, cof. h., n.s. Webster Av., b. Bank and Harrison road

FLACH JOHN C., Proprietor Deholt Exchange, s.e.c. Main and Court
Flack Frederick, porter, 10 W. Front
Flack Mrs. Lucinda, h. 13 Arch
Flack Martha, bds. 104 Plum
Flacke august, porter, 517 Race
Flade Hy., lab., wks. n.e.c. Canal and Walnut
Flade Herman, cab. mkr., 257 Clark
Flagg Asa F., britannia manuf., 196 E. 6th
Flagg George, molder, Hill, nr. 3d
Flagg Mary B., bds 27 Chestnut
Flagg Saml. M., 135 George
Flagg Wm. J., bds. Nicholas Longworth's
Flagge Francis H., carp , 145 Baymiller
Flaherty Andrew, lab., 36 Butler
Flaherty Catharine, 207 W. Front
Flaherty James, lab., 177 E. Front
Flaherty John, lab., 177 E. Front
Flaherty Patrick, bksmith, wks. C. H. & D. R.R. bksmith shop
Flaherty Pat., cof. h., 177 E. Front
Flaherty Winnifred, c. 8th and Accommodation
Flaig Andrew, boots and shoes,613 Race
Flaig Jacob M., saloon, 82 E. Pearl
Flaig John, shoe mkr., 633 Sycamore
Flaig John, tailor, bds. 488 Race
Flamm Bernard, mer. tailor, 43 W. 5th
Flamm Christian, clk., 596 Freeman
Flanagan Bridget, e.s. Court, b. 6th and Observatory Road
Flanagan Daniel, printer, 186 Race
Flanagan James E., harness mkr., 32 Rittenhouse

FLANAGAN JOHN, Coffee House, n e.c. Ludlow and Pearl
Flanagan Mary, 127 Wade
Flanagan Nicholas, lab., 109 Mulberry
Flanagan Patrick, carp., bds 158 Cutter
Flanagan Patrick, carp., n s Patterson al. b. Main and Walnut, h. 221 Longworth
Flanagan Robert, lab., 32 Rittenhouse
Flanedy Pat , shoemkr., e.s. John b. Elizabeth and Chestnut
Flannagan Mrs. ———, 155 Water
Flannagan Edward, cof. h., n.s. Front e. of Leatherbury
Flannagan James, hostler, 32 David
Flannagan Michael, lab., s.s. Sico w. of Freeman
Flannagan Patrick, hostler, 203 Race
Flannagan Robert, bksmith, 124 Central Av.
Flannegan Mary, 132 Central Av
Flannegan Michael, lab., 207 Smith
Flannegan Michael, lab., 123 E. 6th
Flannegan Nicholas, lab., 107 Mulberry
Flannelly Brian, lab., wks s.w.c. Broadway and 5th
Flannery Barney, stone cutter, bds. 70 Sycamore
Flannery Catharine, c.s. Hand al. b. Court and Clark
Flannery James, agt., 371 W. 7th
Flannery John, lab., 48 E. 7th
Flannery Martin, cof. h., 12 Landing b. Main and Walnut
Flannery Martin, lab., 60 W. Front
Flannery Patrick, policeman, 46 E. 3d
Flannery Patrick, lab., 69 Richmond
Flannery Patrick, lab., 122 Accommodation
Flannery Thos., lab. 69 Richmond
Flannery Thomas, lab., rear 58 Mulberry
Flannery Thomas, lab., 58 Abigail
Flannery Timothy, dray, 71 Pendleton

Flannigan Bridget, 68 Butler
Flannigan Daniel, printer, bds. 186 Race
Flannigan Hy., bksmith, n.s. Augusta b. John and Smith
Flannigan John, lab., 143 E, 2d
Flannigan Michael, 68 Butler
Flannigan Patrick, wks. n.w.c. Freeman and 9th
Flannigan Patrick, molder, s.w,c. Central Av. and McFarland
Flannigan Patrick, servt., 425 W. 6th
Flannigan Robt., bksmith, 124 Central Av.
Flarney John, lab., n.w.c. 6th and Harriet
Flashtel Moses, 161 W. 9th
Flaspoehler Angel, 113 Woodward
Flaspoehler Hy., shoemkr., 448 Main
Flatau Joseph, peddler, 397 Main
Flatterman Hermon, cooper, 217 Betts
Flattery Martin, lab., s.s. Taylor, in rear 632 W. 6th
Flattich Jacob F., cof. h., 469 Vine
Flatley Ann, servt., s.w.c. 3d and Brdway
Fleak Elizabeth, 64 Pike
Fleake Martin, fireman, 1562 E. Front
Fiechtell Moses, clk., 61 W. 9th
Flechter Joseph, carver, 14 Home
Flechter Rebecca, variety store, 188 W. 5th
Flechter Simon, dry goods, 196 W. 5th
Fleckenstein Elizabeth, 139 W. Liberty
Fleckstener Alex., bksmith, 35 Bremen
Fledderman George, teamster, 203 Water
Freeman D. R , steward, Burnet House
Fleet Margaret, servt., 357 W, 8th
Fleetwood Anthony, lithographer, 132 Betts
Fleetwood Chas. W., lithographer, 33 E. 3d, b. 132 Betts
Flege Hy., porter, 21 Hughes
Fleharty Delia, servt., 372 W. 7th
Flelloger Frederick, 55 Riddle
Fleischer Emil, paper hanger, 321 Central Av.
Fleischhauer Adolph (F. & Eiseman), 13 Richmond
Fleischhauer Caroline, servt., s.s. Oogeswell al. b. Abigail and Woodward
Fleischhauer & Eiseman (Adolph F. & Abraham E.) wool, hides, &c., 25 W. Miami Canal
Fleischmann Chas., cab. mkr., 176 Charlotte
Fleischmann Israel. clk., bds. 161 Broadway
Fleischman Joseph, tailor, 128 W. 5th
Fleisharver Benjamin, peddler, 142 Everett
Fleisman Samuel, b,k., 78 W. Pearl, h. 349 W. 6th
Fleishmann George, cooper, e.s. Elm b. Findlay and Green
Fleissner Geo. W., clk., 651 Vine
Fleming Eliza, 297 John
Fleming Hy. W., bk. layer, n.e.c. North and New
Ficuing James H., grocer, 333 Cutter
Fleming John, lab., n.e.c. Elder and Logan
Fleming John (John & Jas. H. F.), bds. 333 Cutter
Fleming John & James H., grocery, 339 Central Av.
Fleming Matthew, eng., 105 E. 3d e. of Whittaker
Fleming Thomas,lab., 200 E. 6th
Flemming Andrew,bds. junction Ludlow and Lawrence
Flemming Hy., driver, e.s. Ludlow b. Pearl and 3d
Flemming Jacob J., cab. mkr., s.s. 6th b. Harriet and Horne
Flemming John, shoemkr. 565 W. 9th
Flemming Patrick, bksmith. wks. C.H. & D. R. R. bksmith shop
Flemming Wm., bksmith, wks. C., H. & D. R R. bksmith shop
Flemons Mrs. ———, 22 E. 7th
Flenner John, cutter, 66 W. Pearl, bds. Madison House
Fletcher Emma, 184 Central Av
Fletcher James, lab., b. 585 E.Front
Fletcher John F., brush mkr, 444 George

FLETCHER L., HOBART & CO.(Lowell F., Wm. N. H. & Wm D. Harrison), Alcohol Manufacturers, s.e. c. Vine and Front
FLETCHER Lowell (L. F., Hobart & Co ,) 232 W. 4th
Fletcher Maria, seamstress, 114 Betts
Fletcher Mollie, 55 George
Fletcher Richard, stone cutter, 35 E. 3d e. of Parsons
Fletcher Robt., surgeon, U. S. A., bds. Burnet House
Fletcher Robert, currier, 440 W. 8th
FLETCHER Wm. (Cobb, Armel & F.), bds. Walnut St. House
Fletcher Wm., collar mkr, bds. 171 Sycamore
Fletcher William, tinner, bds. 428 Sycamore
Fletcher Wm. D., 252 W. 4th
Flewellen John N., clk., 75 E. 7th
Flichman Fred., 475 Plum
Flick Albert, shoemkr, 59 14th
Flick Barbara, 388 Baymiller
Flick Daniel, lab., 609 Vine
Flick Frank, glazier, 567 Main
Flick Frederick, cab. mkr. 485 Walnut
Flick Jacob, stone cutter, 502 Walnut
Flick John, rear 767 Vine
Flick Joseph. cof. h., w.s. Lebanon Road nr. Channing
Flick Joseph, lab., 632 Vine
Flick Peter, tanner, s.s. Cross, 1st h. w. of Hamburg
Flick Rudolph, shoemkr, 107 Pleasant
Flick Sophia, nurse, 439 W. 6th
Flickinger Samuel, clk., 43 Main, h. 302 Richmond
Flickner Jacob O., leather, 235 Main, b. 150 Barr
Flinker Christina, rear 420 Sycamore
Flinker Hy. J., lab., 9 Mary
Flinn Christopher, driver, n.e.c. Court and Baymiller
Flinn Dennis, lab., bds. 164 W. 8th
Flinn Ellen, b. e.s. Pancoast al. b. 7th and 8th [Wade
Flinn Hy., lab., wks n.w.c. Plum and Flinn Hy., painter, 95 Oliver
Flinn Jacob, atty., 1 Richmond)
Flinn John, drover, 349 John
Flinn John, finisher,93 Martin
Flinn Kate, servt. Spencer House
Flinn Margaret, servt., 59 Pendleton
Flinn Mary, servt., n.e.c. 4th and Brdway
Flinn Mary, s.s. 6th b. Broadway and Culvert
Flinn Mary, servt., 398 W. 6th
Flinn Mary, servt., s.w.c. 3d and Broadway
Flinn Michael, lab., 175 Water
Flinn Michael, lab., 673 W. 6th
Flinn Thos., carp., 24 W. Court w. of Central Av.
Flinn Timothy, grocery, 53 E. 8th
Flint Andrew, mach., 275 John
Flint E. J., teacher, room 26, Union Block
Flint J. D , cashier O. & M. R.R. freight office
Flint Tobias E., tailor, 173 E. Front
Flischman Simon, bk., 349 W. 6th
Fliszner August, carp., wks. 365 W. Front
Flock Solomon, horse trader, 187 Bremen
Floger Abraham, tailor, 60 Ham. Road
Flohr. Chas. F., finisher, 60 Ham. Road
Flohr Frederick, painter, 281 Bremen
Flohr John, cook, St. Charles Exchange
Flood Ann, 925 E. 6th
Flood Bernard, lab., 116 Barr
Flood Edward, s.s. 3d b. Canal and Kilgour
Flood Frank, clk., 628 W. 8th
Flood Jennie, servt., 216 Richmond
Flood Joel D., boatman, 138 W. Front
Floor Sarah, 130 W. 5th
Florer James, lab., Broad b. Front and Bur

FLORER N. M., Wholesale Pork, Bacon and Lard Dealer, 9 Sycamore, h. 117 W. 7th
Florian Rieger, tailor, n.s. Garden b. Freeman and Western Av.

(FOE) CINCINNATI (FOL) DIRECTORY. (FOR) 137

Florn Dena. servt., 432 W 4th
Flospole Barney, lab., 391 Broadway
Flotem-sch Geo., bk layer, 97 Bremen
Floth Margaretha, 38 Elder
Flotker Geo., lab., n.w.c. Liberty and Baymiller
Floto Carl, b.k. 7 Pub. Landing, h. 648 Vine
Flottamesh Joseph, blksmith. 22 Abigail
Flottmann Hy., cooper, 171 Clay
Flottmann Hy. porter. 207 W. Front
Flowers Mrs. Dorcus, 117 W. Court w. of Central Av.
Floyd Geo., watchman steam engine fire company No. 3
Floyd John. trader, bds. 403 Sycamore
Floyd Thomas. cooper, 112 Smith
Fluerken Anton. brewer, s.w.c. Riddle and Harrison Pike
Flugel Louis. tinner, 566 Race
Flugen Lewis, lab., w.s. Goose al. b. Liberty and 15th
Flugil Frederick, hostler. 83 Baymiller
Fluhr Oswabl, bk. binder. 19 Abigail
Fluker Andrew, printer, s.e c. 13th and Elm
Flur Oswald, millinery. 492 Vine
Flutcher George, lab., wks. N. W. Thomas & Co's.
Flutt Wm., huckster, 626 W. 8th
Flynn Andrew, bar k., 21 E. 5th bds. 25 Harrison
Flynn Elizabeth, s.s. E. Front, e. of Reed
Flynn Ellen, servt., 109 Mill
Flynn Hy., varnisher, n.w.c. Plum and 2d
Flynn James, lab., s.s. al. b. Pike and Lawrence and Pearl and 3d
Flynn John, finisher, 93 Martin
Flynn John, lab., n.s. Rail Road e. of French
Flynn John, tailor. 35 Lock n. of 8th
Flynn John C, exchange office, 191 Broadway. h. 135 Lock
Flynn Margaret, servt., Burnet House
Flynn Michael, dray, bds. 140 Water
Flynn Michael, dray, n.s. Rail Road e. of Vance
Flynn Michael, hostler, s.w.c. Freeman and Front
Flynn Michael, lab., s.s. al. b. 9th and Richmond and Baymiller and Linn
Flynn Patrick, carp., 506 W. 9th
Flynn Patrick, lab., 213 W. 3d
Flynn Patrick, lab., 213 W. 3d
Flynn Thomas, lab., 24 Bank
Flynn Thos. printer. bds. 35 Lock
FLYNT MRS M. D., Book and Periodical Store, n.w.c. Court and Central Av.
FLYNT MARTIN D., Trunk Manufacturer, 2 College Building, e. s. Walnut n. 4th and 5th, h. 387 Central Av.
Flynt Patrick, lab., 157 Hopkins
Fobes John, lab., wks. 267 W. 8th
Fobing Frank, tailor, s.s. Charlotte b. Linn and Baymiller
Fock Maria, 720 Vine
Focke Hy., porter, Andrews & Biggs'
Focke Joseph, feed store s.s. Harrison Road b. Western Av. and Mill Creek
Focks John, dry goods, 571 Main
Foda Hy., driver, 525 Freeman
Foddy John. clk., 313 W 6th
Foehel Gottfried, shoe mkr., 96 Ham. Road
Foegel Hy., cooper, 156 Clay
Foegler Anton, brewer, 264 Ham. Road
Foehr Edward, butcher, 680 Main
Foeniges Ferdinand, lab., 12 Eden
Foerst John B., gilder, 71 Woodward
Foerster Andrew, col. h, 257 Ham. Road
Foerster Daniel, salesman, at G. & P. Bogen's
FOERTMEYER Adolphus W., (Johnson & F.,) n e c. 6th and Elm
Foertmeyer Charles, clk., bds. Teutonia Hotel
Foertmeyer Wm., clk., s.e.c. Main and 9th, h. 9 W. 9th
Foese August, tailor, 6 Buckeye 12

Foet Charles, lab., w.s. Carr nr. Gest
Fogarty J. U., 13 Central Av.
Fogarty James, grocery, 613 Central Av.
Fogarty James, jr., clk., 613 Central Av.
Foga t/ John, lab., 65 E. 8th
Fogarty Patrick, lab, 65 Green
Fogel Adolph, lab., 7 Wade b. Elm and Plum
Fogel John, lab., 166 E. Front
Fogelman John, clk., 171 Laurel
Fogelman Wm., clk, 160 W. 5th
Fogelpohl Hy, blksmith, 52 Commerce
Fogelsang Geo, lab., 360 Broadway
Fogelsang John, lab., rear 71 Abigail
Fogerpol Hy., blk-mith, 52 Elm
Fogerson Geo., lab., wks. 335 Broadway
Fogerty John, lab., s.s. Hunt e. of Liberty
Fogerty Margaret, e.s. State b. 8th and Accommodation
Foget Charles, cigar mkr., w.s. Cutter b. Wade and David
Foginson Hy., lab., s.s. Front b. Smith and John
Fogle Albert, carp., s.s. Taylor b. Carr and Harriet
FOGLE Benj., (Jno. A. Clark & Co.,) 49 Cutter
Fogle John, 480 Linn
Fogleman John, salesman, 67 W. Pearl, h. 128 Laurel
Foglepool John, lab., 79 Gest
Foglesein Barney, bds. 6-7 Central Av.
Fozleson Hy., lab., 164 Clark
Fohimer John, porter, 406 Walnut
Fohr John, lab., 143 Everett
Fohrmann Ferdinand, lab, 46 Buckeye
Foil James, 54 E 7th
Fokerbercer Mrs. Catharine s.e.c. 9th and Harriet
Foley A'fred. teamster, 174 W. Front
Foley Anna, n.e.c. 5th and Race
Foley Bridget, s.s. Yeatman b. Broadway and Sycamore
Foley Happy, h 23 Webster
Foley Happy #2 12th
Foley Hy., 277 W. 5th
Foley James, lab., 56 Water
Foley John, carp., 138 Race, b. 30 Elizabeth
Foley Keziah, 23 Webster
Foley Margaret, servt., e.s. Auburn nr. Bigelow
Foley Mary, servt., Spencer House
Foley Mary A., servt., Henrie House
Foley Patrick, roofer. 126 Lock
Foley Peter, lab., 126 Freeman
Foley Timothy, lab., n.s. Taylor b. Freeman and Carr
Foley Susan, 186 W. Court w. of Central Av.
Folgele George, shoe mkr., 660 Ham. Road
FOLGER Chas. R., (M Greenwood & Co.,) 106 Richmond
Folger George M.. mach., 162 Spring
Folger James, molder, 355 Clark
Folger Louis R., clk., 106 Richmond
Folger Mary A.. dress mkr., 238 Cutter
Folger Peter, carp., 40 Stone
Folger Seth W, bk. mason, 485 W. 9th
Folger Wm. B., clk., bds. 103 Richmond
Folk Chas., painter, 559 Race
Folk Phillip. blksmith, 701 W. 6th
Folk Thomas, tailor, 105 Mulberry
Folk Wm., carp., n.s. 6th b. Harriet and Horne
Folke Frank, w.s. Vine b. Mill and Mulberry
Folker Hy., finisher, 772 W. Front
Folkner, Amelia. s.s. Goodloe, b. Willow and Niagara
Foll Casper, 351 Vine
Follen Patrick, lab., n.s. Railroad e. of French
Follencamp Hy., tailor, 19 Commerce
Follmer Christian, lab., 35 Rittenhouse
Follmer Julia, servt., 395 W. 8th
Folmur Wm., tinner, 85 Rittenhouse
Folsom Richard, atty., s.w.c. 4th and Walnut h. Madison Pike
Foltmann John, tailor, 407 Walnut

Foltz Andrew, tailor, e.s. Logan b. Greene and Elder
Foltz Frederick, 30 Peete
Foltz Max, cigar mkr., 68 Buckeye
Foly Michael, wks. A. G. Cheever & Co's.
Foly Michael, hostler, 15 W. 6th
Folz Hy., tailor, w.s. Fountain b. Rice and Alexander
Folz Martin, butcher, 143 Buckeye
Folz Theresa, servt., n s. Liberty b. Freeman and Mill Creek
Fonbolo Ardof, chair mkr., 21 Commerce
Fonda Christopher Y., music and musical instruments, 72 W. 4th
Foning Hy., cooper, 552 John
Fontayne Albert, mach., 162 Richmond
Fookes Irwin. bds Rail Road House
Foot Frank B. jr., bar k., bds 7, Baymiller
Foot Frank H., cof. h., 71 Baymiller
Foote Andrew R., mer., 100 Burr (merce
Foote Charles B., cashier, Com. Bank, h. E. Walnut Hills
Foote Chas. G., locksmith, wks. 182 Central Av.
Foote Charles S., contractor, 16 Dayton
FOOTE GEORGE F., Dentist, 55 W. 7th
Foote Hy., varnisher, 157 Linn
Foote Hy. K., phys., 263 W. 4th
Foote John P., 204 W. 3d
FOOTE John T., (F. Nash & Co.,) 117 E. 3d
FOOTE JOSEPH W., Cincinnati Butter Store, 199 Central Av, h. 457 W. 7th
FOOTE, NASH & CO., (John T. F, Job, M. N. & Samuel M. Murphy,) Wholesale Liquor Merchants and Distillers, 17 and 19 W. 2d, Distillery s.w.c. Pearl and Kilgour
Foote Oliver P., lab., n.s. 8th b. Broadway and Sycamore
Foppe John, (F. & Longland,) h. 402 W. 4th
Foppe & Longland, (John F. & Joseph L.,) Boots and Shoes 403 W. 5th
Foppiani Frank, ice dealer, s.s 12th b. Race and Elm
Foran James, 46 Lock n. of 9th
Forawalt Henry, tanner, 223 Betts
Forberg Charles, 303 Cutter
Forbes Alex, eng., Geo. R. Dixon & Co.'s h. Covington
Forbes B. M.. trader, 25 W. 3d, bds. Burnet House
Forbes George W., tanner, 322 Findlay
Forbes George W., clk., 65 W. 3d, bds. 291 Plum
Forbes Miles, painter, Observatory st. Mt. Adams
Forbes Valina, nurse, 94 Betts
FORBRIGER Adolph (Ehrgott F. & Co) 60 13th
Forbriger Arthur, painter, 492 Sycamore
Forbus John F., (F. and Stevenson) n. w c. Elm and Findlay
Forbus John F. morrocco dresser e.s. Plum n. of Findlay, h. 601 Elm
Forbus Shaffer, 1 Providence
Forbus & Stevenson, (John F. F. & Peter G. S.) hides and leather, 254 Main
Forbus Wm. H., b. k. 254 Main, h. n.w. c. Elm and Findlay
Forbush Ann, 188 W. Court
FORCE Manning F. (Kebl r. Whitman & F) 9 Masonic Temple
FORCHHEIMER MEYER S., Manufacturer and Wh. Dealer in Hats and Caps and Straw Goods, 64 W. Pearl, h 99 E. 3d
Ford Alonzo J., phys., 131 Race
Ford Mrs Ann., 89 Water
Ford Bridget, servt., 221 W. 4th
Ford Elijah, 58 New
Ford Eliza 44 Hughes
Ford Geo., clk., 27 W. 5th
Ford Geo., trader 138 Bremen
Ford Geo. W. 180 W. 4th
Ford Green, lab., s.s. 6th b. Broadway and Culvert
Ford Hy., lab., s.s. 6th b. Broadway and Culvert

Ford James stone mason, 180 E. Pearl
Ford John, baker. 64 Avery
Ford John, lab., s.s. Poplar b. Linn and John
Ford John, lab., s.s. 6th b. Broadway and Culvert
Ford Jesse. lab. s.s. 6th b. Broadway and Culvert
Ford John F., mach., n.s. Fremont b. Carr and Harriet
Ford John H.. finisher, wks. n.e.c. Walnut and Canal
Ford Joseph, capt., 263 Clark
Ford Lida, bds, 61 E. 4th
FORD LUCIAN C., Publisher Christian Herald, 28 W. 4th, res. Walnut Hills
Ford Michael, lab., 172 Cutter
Ford Pat., driver, 165 E. Pearl
Ford Pat., lab., w.s Butler, b. E. Pearl and Front
Ford Samuel, lab., s.s. 6th b. Broadway and Culvert
Ford Peter, lab., s.s. 6th b. Broadway and Culvert
Ford Sarah, h. 105 E. 6th
Ford Smith, (Carpenter & F.) 124 W 9th
Ford Toby lab , s.s. 6th b. Broadway and Culvert
Ford Thomassen., lab., s.s. 6th b. Broadway and Culvert
Ford Thomas jr., lab., h. s.s. Cth b. Broadway and Culvert
Ford Wm , lard oil factory, s.s. Front b. Reed and Broad, h. n.s. Duit b. Reed and Broad
Ford Wm. H., lab., s.s. 6th b. Broadway and Culvert
Fordingham Thos., carp., n.s. Avery nr. Wood
Fore P. G , phys., n.e.c. Vine and 7th
Forewach John, lab. 218 W. Liberty
Forewald Barney, driver, s.s. Ringgold b. Young and Price
Forewald Hy., lab., 223 Betts
Forgatas Clements, finisher, 129 Linn
Forgerding Barney, blind mkr., 622 Race
Forgey Jacob, P., b. k. 20 W. 2d h. 334 Linn
Forhmann Christopher. carver, 105 Curr
Forkner G H , salesman 136 Walnut bds 199 W. 3d
FORKNER James, (Elmer & F) res Centerville Ind.
FORMAN Wm. H.. (VanDokkum & F.) 17 George
Formberger H. porter, 22 Mansfield
Formore Antony lab., s.s 6th b. Harriet and Horn
Fornholz John, umbrella mkr. 371 W. 5th
FORREST Wm. T. (Warden F. & Sheppard.) 130 W. Court
Forrester Barnhard, bds 74 E. 5th
Forrester Daniel, S., carp., 165 W. 5th
Forrester Elizabeth, h 403 W. 8th
Forri-tall Chas. T. sign painter, 122 Vine, bds. 37 Burr
Forristall Hy. B., painter, bds 37 Burr
Furristall Jas., japanner, wks. n.w.c. Race an 1 2d
Forristal Jane, 37 Burr
FORSBERG A. O , Manufacturer of Trusses, Shoulder Braces and Supporters, 5 E 4th
Forschein John, driver. 407 Elm
FORSE & CO (Wm. & Wm. H.) Exchange Office, 14 E. 3d
FORSE Wm. (F. & Co.) h. Covington
FORSE Wm. H. (F. & Co.) h. Covington
Forsha Samuel W., fam. medicines 413 W. 5th
Forst Frederick, boots and shoes, 164 Richmond
Forster Hy., lab., 230 Water
Foston Richard, barber, bds 272 W. 3d
Furten C J., tinner, wks. n.w.c. Race and 2d
Fortman Anthony, mach. 71 Abigail
Fortman Anthony, potter, 73 Spring
Fortman C., lab. wks. n.s. Front, b. Lawrence and Pike
Fortman Francis brewery, s.w.c. Clay and 12th, h. 46 Jackson

Fortman Hy., carp., 203 Hopkins
Fortman Hy. N., salesman, b. 3. Spring
Fortman John, police,. 50 Lock
Fortman John, cooper, bds, 118 Gest
Fortmeier Chas. Wm., clk., 9 W. 9th
Fortney Hiram. caulker, 970 E. Front
Fortney Meredith, lab., 970 E. Front
Fortune Christop'er, molder, wks. n.w, c. Plum and Wade
Forwald Fritz, lab. w.s. n.w.c. Wood an 1 3d
Forward James. bds. Brighton House
Forwold Hy., baker, 21 David
Fory Daniel, lab. 412 Sycamore
Fos Barney, shoe mkr 65 Abigail
Fos Hy. lab. 185 Hopkins
Fosdick Chas. R , com. mer. 46 Walnut, h. s.w.c 9th and Race
Fosdick Margaret. 20 W. 4th
Fosdick Margaret, 153 York
Fosdick Samuel, (Harkness, Stader & F.) office 46 Walnut, h. Glendale
Foshold Hy., cooper 31 Dunlap
Fuskuhln Hy , tanner, n.s. Rail Road e. of Lewis
Fosler Geo., tailor, bds. s.s. Front e. of Lewis
Fosmer Kate 127 Everett
Fosmeyer John H., wood yard, 500 W. 5th
Fosmeyer Mary Ann, 568 W. 5th
Foss Barnard. cooper. 42 Evans
Foss Henrich, lab , 131 Abigail
Foss Stephen. phys. 53 W. 6th
Foss Wm. tailor, h. n w.c. Melancthon and Cutter
Fossett Jesse 12 Webb
Fossler John, porter, 42 W. Front
Foster Miss Catharine. 4 Webster
Foster David, carp., 273 George
Foster David M. G , s e.c. Pike and 3d
Foster Edward, bds. 624 E. Front
Foster Elizabeth, 200 W. 4th
Foster Enoch, carp. bds 204 W. 6th
Foster Francis, bk binder, 233 Richmond
Foster G W. & Co., (Geo. W. F & Lemuel T. Wells,) copper face type manufacturers. 139 W. 5th
Foster Geo.. porter, 23 E 5th
Foster Geo. W. (G. W. F. & Co,) 128 W. Court, w. of Central Av
Foster Hartman c b mkr. , 161 Clay
Foster Hattie A., 204 W. 4th
Foster James, s.s. Front b. Foster and Kelly
Foster James, lab., s.e.c. Elm and Water
FOSTER James jr., (J. F. jr. & Co.) h. 136 W. 8th
FOSTER JAMES, JR. & CO (James F. jr. & Hy. Twitchell,) Opticians, Mathematical and Philosophical instrument mkrs. s.w.c. 5th and Race
FOSTER Joab. G., (Hughes & F.) 292 Water
Foster John, lab., Spencer House
Foster John H., printer, bds 186 Race
FOSTER JOSEPH. Steam Marble and Free Stone Works, n.e c. Elm and Miami Canal, h. 414 Elm
Foster Mary 101 Butler
Foster Nathaniel, phys , n.e c. 3d and Broadway, h. 96 Broadway
FOSTER Seth C., (Stearns & F.) res. Clifton
Foster Stephen H., b. k 210 Everett
Foster Theodore, varnisher, 17 15th
Foster Thomas, grocer, 110 Pearl e, of Broadway, h. n.w.c. Pearl and Broadway
Foster Washington, conductor, bds. 81 E. Pearl
Foster Wm. L , cooper 112 W. Pearl
Foster Wm. S , receiver Cin. St. R. R. Co., 160 Vine, h 200 W. 8th
Fosthoff Theodore, varnisher, 17 15th b. Elm and Plum
Foswinkel John, lime burner, w.s. Goose al b. 14th and 15th
Fotheringham Thos.. carp.. 10 Avery
Foulds Martin, cof. h., 15 Water
FOULDS Thomas H , (F. & Wright,) 280 Longworth

FOULDS & WRIGHT (Thomas H. F. & Nat. W. jr) Commission and Forwarding Merchants. 596 and 598 W. 5th
Poulk Hy., 20 Dunlap
Foulke Philip, lab., Harriet, b. 6th and Front
Foults Samuel. bds Harts Hotel
Fountain Mrs Ann, cof. h. 317 Elm
Foutty Geo W., depot master 131 George
Foutty Isaac N., mate. 80 Mill
Foutty Joseph P.. clk. C. H. & D R. R. h. 434 George
Powee John. shoe mkr., 171 W. 5th
Fowler Absalom W , clk., 204 Richmond
Fowler Chas., finisher. 28 Lock
Fowler Henry C., carp., n.s. Front w. of Hill
Fowler Henry W , phys., 87 E. 3d, bds. n.s 5th b. Main and Walnut
Fowler Jane, bds. 135 W 3d
Fowler Joseph, huckster, 124 E. 6th
Fowler Josiah, mach., e.s. Lock b. 3d and 5th
Fowler Mary, seamstress, e.s. Carr b. 6th and Taylor
FOWLER S. N., (Ferris, Dunlevy & F.) 83 Everett
Fox A., egg packer, 84 E. Pearl
Fox Abraham, Hebrew writer, 482 Central Av
FOX Adam C., (Luthy & F.) 129 Clinton
Fox Alexander, lab., 80 Gest
Fox & Baker, (Geo. F. & Albert D.) coopers, 414 Elm
Fox Barney, bds. Walnut St. House
Fox Bernhard, horse trader, bds. 61 W. 6th
Fox Catharine, h.h., 214 W. Front
FOX Charles, (T. Harris & Fox,) h. 123 W. 9th
Fox Charles, cooper, 100 Browne
Fox Chas., waiter. St. Nicholas
FOX Chas. H., (Fox, Harris & F.) 123 W. 9th
Fox Chas. J., turner, 133 Smith
Fox Chas. N., (F , Thomas & Wardlow,) 601 Freeman
Fox Conrad, lab., 24 Brighton
Fox E., lab.. wks. Chamberlain & Co's
Fox Edward, horse shoe nail mkr., h. 137 Cutter
Fox Edward, lab., 81 Spring
Fox Eliza J., b.h , 159 W. Front
Fox Elizabeth, 34 Findlay
Fox Elizabeth, servant, 356 W. 7th
Fox Elizabeth, servant, 409 W. 5th
Fox Frank, shoe mkr.- 634 Race
Fox Frederick, b.k., Gibson House, h. 247 Cutter
Fox Geo. (F. & Baker.) 27 Pleasant
FOX Geo., (Larkin, Fox & Bro.) res. Glendale
Fox George, (T. & G. F.) res. Glendale
Fox Geo. D., bar k, 27 Pleasant
FOX, HARRIS & FOX. (Charles F., Samuel T. H. & Charles H. F.) Attorneys at Law, 116 Main
Fox Henry, tinner, 29 Moore
Fox Hester, 601 Freeman
Fox Jacob, umbrellas, &c., 253 Central Av
Fox John, 34 Campbell al
Fox John, lab.. Burnet House
Fox John, plasterer, 320 W. 6th
Fox John, porter, wks. 12 and 14 E. Canal
Fox John, lab. e.s. Kilgour b. 3d and 5th
Fox John A., lab., 91 Woodward
Fox John E., cooper, 316 Water
Fox Louis, butcher, w.s. Division b. Bernard and Bank
Fox Martin, lab., 35 Ludlow
Fox Martin, moulder, rear 310 Cutter
Fox Noah, bds. 139 W. Front
Fox Patrick, trailer. 22 E. 5th
FOX Thomas, (Larkin, Fox & Bro.) res. Lockland
Fox Thos., lab., 65 Barr
Fox Thomas, marble cutter, 54 Richmond b. Plum and Central Av
Fox Thomas B., polisher, wks. n.e.c. M. Canal and Elm

(FRA) CINCINNATI (FRA) DIRECTORY. (FRE) 139

Fox Thos. & Geo., starch manuf., 71 Walnut
FOX, THOMAS & WARDLOW, (Chas. N. F., Alfred C. T., Jas. K. T. & Chas. H. W.) Forwarding and Commission Merchants, 21 E. M. Canal
Fox Wm. lab., bds. 9 Landing b. Main and Walnut
Foy Anthony, painter, n.w.c. Broadway and 6th
Foy Bridget, grocery. 40 Pierson
Foy John, lab, 500 W. 8th
Foy Mary, n.w.c Broadway and 6th
Foy M'chael, cof. h., 9 Landing b. Main and Walnut
Foy Thomas, J., b.k., 40 Pierson
Frans James, upholsterer, 25 E 3d. b. Newport
Frach Frederic. dray, 57 Everett
Frackmann Margaret. S., servt., 77 Barr
Frade Wm., lab, 141 York
Frade'a'ce Barney, lab., n.s. 2d b. Park and Mill
Fraenk Isaac, peddler, n.s. Bremen b. Elder and Findlay
Fraenkel Lewis, cap mkr., 46 Hamer
Fraenzel Fredericks, s.w.c. Bremen and Findlay
Frailey Joseph, shoe mkr., w.s. Miller nr. 7th
Fraley George, drav, 24 Kilgour
Fraley Mary, 24 Kilgour
France James D , clk., Spencer House
Frances Wm., lab., wks. s.w.c. Broadway and 5th
Francis Abraham, W., blksmith, rear 93 E 8th. h. 114 E. Liberty
Francis Frederick, lab., wks. James White & Co.'s
Francis Henry, carp., 41 Hathaway
Francis Peter, grocery. 591 W. 6th
Francis Richard, foot of Harrison
Francis Robert moulder, wks. n.e.c. Canal and Walnut
Francis Wm., stone cutter, bds. 35 Harrison
Francisco. A. W., business manager Cin. Daily Times, 62 W. 3d, h. E. Walnut Hills
Francisco Geo. W., butcher 107 Dudley
Franc' e Albert, finisher 114 W. Liberty
Franey Joseph, lab., 536 W. 7th
Frank Abram. 2 Harrison.
Frank Alexander, paper dealer, 33 Gano
Frank Ann , 184 W. Court
Frank Anton, saloon, 08 Geat
Frank Ant'ny, plaster paris moulder, w.s. Langdon al. b. 6th and 7th
FRANK AUGUST W., Wholesale & Retail Groceries, n.w.c. 6th and Race. h. 241 Race
Frank Burney, (F. & Jones) 138 E. 5th
Frank Benedict. 473 Race
Frank Casper, blk. smith, 47 Pleasant
Frink Chas., (Chas. F. & Co.) 173 George
Frank Chas. & Co., (Chas, F. & Leo Frank,) liquors. 38 W. Court
Fronk Chas. J , clk., n.w.c. Elizabeth and Central Av
Frank David, express driver, 718 Vine
Frank David, peddler, 189 Longworth
Frank Emanuel, A., peddler, 22 Ham. Road
Frank, Ewl. I., cof. h.. 74 W. Court
Frank Francis, wks. Hleatt & Wood's candle factory
Frank Francis, peddler, 32 Pleasant
Frank Fred., mer., h. w.s. Auburn nr. Central Av.
Frank George, dray, 170 Poplar
Frank George, dray, n.e.c. Vine and Buckeye
Frank Godfrey, cab. mkr., 28 Bremen
Frank Godfrey, A., grocery, n w.c. Elizabeth and Central Av.
Frank Gottfried. carp. w.s. Bremen b. Elder and Findlay
Frank Henry, cooper. 66 Dudley
Frank Henry, lab., 712 Central Av.
Frank Hermann, 36 Dunlap
Frank Isaac, mer., 99 W. 9th W. of Central Av
Frank Isaac, b.k., 106 W. Pearl bds. 2 Harrison
Frank Isidor, phys., 216 Elm

Frank Jacob B , grocer, 51 Elizabeth
Frank John. currier, wks. s.w.c. Front and Butler
Frank John, lab , 549 Plum
Frank Joseph, b. k , 106 Plum.
Frank Joseph, printer, s.s. Friendship Al. b. Pike and Butler
Frank Leo. N., (Chas. Frank & Co.), 173 George
Frank Marx, driver. 674 Race
Frank Mary. s.s Friendship Al. b. Pike and Butler
Frank Mary, tailoress. rear 421 Vine
Frank, Peter. driver 27 Providence
Frank, Philip A., peddler, 22 Ham. Road
Frank. R chel. 269 John
FRANK SAMUEL H., Family Groceries, Provisions, &c , 379 Vine
Frank Simon, painter. 40½ 12th
Frank, Wm., c'k., 14 Hamer
Franke August (F & Fleischman) s.e. c. 5th and Race
Franke Catharina, tailoress, h. 19 Webster
Franke Clamor A. T., b.k., 109 W. Pearl b. Newport
Franke Clements, barber, 649 Central Av
Franke Frank. cab. mkr. , s.w.c. Laurel and Baymiller
Franke Fred.. lab. 407 Central Av
Franke Fredericka, 18 Webster
Franke & Jones. (Barney F. & John F. J) saw mill, 128 W. 2d.
Franke Josephine, tailoress. 18 Webster
Franke Wm.. cigar mkr., 6 Hamer
Frankel B. & W. (Benj. & Wm.) clothing. 68 Findlay
Frankel Benj. (B. & W. F.) 68 Findlay
Frankel Wm. (B. & W. F.) 68 Findlay
Frankenherr Isaac, drover, 446 John
FRANKENSTEIN GEO., Local Editor Commercial, h. 117 Mill
Frankenstein Jacob, barber, 705 Elm
Frankenstein John, sculptor. 14 E. 4th
Frankland Thomas, (F. & Tidball) res. Cumminsville
Frankland & Tidball (Thos. F. & V. C. T.), printers, 28 W. 4th
Franklin. Rev. B., pastor Bethel Chapel, 30 Pub. Landing
Franklin Benj., editor. 396 W. 3d
Franklin Bldg., s.w.c. Vine and Longworth
FRANKLIN COTTON FACTORY, (Siml. Fosdick, E-tate of Anthony Harkness & Jac b Struder deceased) n.e.c. 3d and Smith
Franklin Frank. tinner. 576 E. Front
Franklin Harriett 159 R'chmond
Franklin Henry, 78 Main. h. 328 George
FRANKLIN INSURANCE CO OF CINCINNATI, 31½ W. 3d, James H Silvers, Secy.
Franklin L. M., fancy goods, 94 Main, h. 201 W. 4th
Franklin Max. fancy store. 201 W. 4th
Franklin Melinda. 18 Union
Franklin Milton, steward. 14 Woodward
Franklin Michael, tailor, 248 Broadway
Franklin Peter. cooper. w.s. Western Av. b. Bank and Harrison Road
FRANKLIN TYPE & STEREOTYPE FOUNDRY, R. Allison Sup't, 168 Vine
Franklin Wm., express driver, s.w.c. Laurel and John
Franklin Wm. H., carp., s.w.c. Laurel and John
Frankman Caroline. 623 Elm
Franks Frederick, wks. Auburn Av. nr. Central Av.
Franks Robert, carp., 633 W Front
Frantz Alexander, baker, wks. 176 W. Front
Frantz John H., mach., 10 Observatory Road
Frantz M. Mechanics Hall, s.e.c. 2d and Plum
FRANZ CONRAD, Gas Fitter. 58 and 60 W. Court
Franz Geo , lab., 222 Linn
Franz Frederick, 609 Race

Franz Geo., shoe mkr., 85 George
Franz Gottlieb, lab., bds. 32 E. Front
Franz Hy., cooper. bds. 66 Dudley
Franz Herman, cooper. 66 Dudley
Franz John, driver, 609 Freeman
Franz John finisher, wks. n.e.c. Walnut and Canal
Franz Killian, lab., n.s. Mulberry b. Main and Sycamore
Franzen Bernhard, lab., 591 Elm
Franzman Ludwig, cigar mkr., 623 Elm
Franzmeier Fred., baker, 623 Elm
Franzreb Hy., grocery, 135 W. Liberty
Franzreb Jacob, cof h., 412 Freeman
Frary David, carp., 51 E. 3d
Fraser Thomas, bds. n.e.c. 2d and Broadway
Frats John G . 481 W. 8th
Fritz John Geo., clk., 1015 Central Av.
Fraund Jacob, 405 W. 6th
Frawley John, lab. h. 98 Lock
Frayne F J., actor, 38 E 4th
Frazee Clark. grocery, 1524 E. Front, h. 1522 E. Front
Frazer Abner L., clk., 66 and 68 Walnut. bds. 461 W. 8th
Frazer Alexander, (F. & Meyers,) 25 Longworth
Frazer Augustus B., distiller, bds. 287 Water
FRAZER & CO., (John F. & Henry Barr,) Lumber Yard, n.s. 6th, e. of R. R. Depot
Frazer Hy., lab., 26 Mansfield
Frazer Hiram T., Solicitor Central Ins. Co., 298 W 4th
FRAZER. James A., (J. A. F. & Co.,) 103 Pike
FRAZER JAMES A. & CO., (James A F., & Stephen G. Chapman). Wholesale Grocers and Commission Merch'ants, 66 and 68 Walnut
FRAZER John, (F. & Co.) c. Hunt and corp. line
Frazer & Meyers (Alexander F. & Henry M.) paper hangings. 161 Walnut
Frazer Robert A., shoe mkr.. 212 E. 8th
Frazier Andy S. pilot. 174½ Baymiller
Frazier Geo., 479 W. 5th
Frazier James K., butcher, 9 Wade w. of Linn
Frazier James A., pilot, 365 W, 9th, w. of Central Av.
Frazier John, lab., wks. Henry Nye's
Frazier Melvin. caulker, 958 E. Front
FRAZIER SAMUEL, City Meat Inspector, 134 Vine, h. 219 Baymiller
Frea Fred , lab., 139 Everett
Frebhon Michael. lab., 275 Bremen
Frech Fredericka variety store, 636 Main
Frech Geo., J., lab., 634 Elm
Frech Jacob. cooper. 634 E'm
Frecke Frank, baker, 231 Clark
Frecking Benj., foreman, 442 W. 2d
Fredelocke Hy., lab., 203 Water
Frederich Chas , butcher, bds 701 Elm
Frederick Conrad, vinegar manuf., 660 Central Av.
Frederick Hy., 643 Central Av.
Frederick Hy., brewer, bds. 652 Main
Frederick Hy., tailor, n.s Browne, b. Ham. Road and Mohawk
Frederick Joseph, cab. mkr., 276 W. Front
Frederick Peter, molder, c. Cutter and David
FREDEWEST & DONNERSBERGER (Joseph F. & Joseph D.), Book and Job Printers, 422 Main
FREDEWEST Joseph, (F. & Donnersberger,) 617 W. 8th
Free Fred.. sawyer. 139 Everett
Free Jacob, box mkr , wks. 219 W. 3d
Free Joseph W., lab., n.s. Nassau b. Reed and Broad
"FREE Nation," Ames Moore, pub., 247 W. 5th
Free Samuel, caulker, s.s. Goodloe, b. Willow and Niagara
Free Watkin, 54 W., h. b. 464 W. 8th
Freely Eliza. servt . Burnet House
Freeman D. H , clk., 376 Van Horn
Freeman Edwin, phys., 276 W., 6th
Freeman Ellen. teacher, 1526 E. Front

Freeman Frances, 553 Race
Freeman Hy., porter, 19 Carr
Freeman James, 422 W. 5th
Freeman John, barber, bds. 204 Broadway
Freeman Lafayette, salesman, 422 W. 5th
Freeman Lafayette, salesman, 66 W. Pearl, h. Covington
Freeman Lewis, teacher, bds. 408 Sycamore
Freeman Lewis, teacher, 6th District School
Freeman Mary, 3 al. b. 4th and 5th Park Mill
Freeman Mathias, carp., 19 Providence
Freeman Philip, lab., 558 E. Front
Freeman Wm., lab., 43 Rittenhouse
Freeman Wm. B., painter, 106 Barr
FREEMAN ZONETH, Physician and Surgeon, Office and Residence 270 W. 6th
Freers Herman, blksmith, 93 Pleasant
Freese Hy., lab., wks. 17 Webster
Freeze Jefferson, cutter, 103 Smith
Freehoff Louisa, n.e.c. Elm and Court
Frehse Joachim, tailor, 532 Main
Freiberg Herman, clk., h. 104 E. 3d
FREIBERG Julius, (F & Workum,) h. 104 E. 3d
Freiberg Lewis, clk., 9 W 5th
Freiberg Morris. 9 W. 5th
FREIBERG & WORKUM, (Julius F. & Levi J. W.) Wholesale Dealers in Wines and Liquors. 13 Sycamore
Freidel Barbara, h. 118 Mohawk
Freidel Charles, 138 Mohawk
Freidenburg Hy., clk., s.e.c. 5th and Main, h. 90 W. 7th
Freidlander Moses, 314 Elm
Freier John, stone mason. 521 Sycamore
Freiheit Andrew, brewer, 61 Buckeye
Freil John, 112 Mohawk
Freimuth Louis, bar k., Frey's Hotel
Freis Jenny, 13 Woodward
Freis John H., porter, 446 Walnut
Freis Otto, tailor, 61 York
Freise John L., pipe fitter, wks. n.e.c. Walnut and Canal
Freisens John, painter, 6 Hamer
Freisenss Christopher, painter, 648 Vine
Freitag Fred., musician, 589 Race
Freitag Hy., musician, 16 Moore
Frekes John, molder, 11 Pendleton
Freking Bernard, dry goods, 459 W. 2d
Freligh Mrs. Eliza, bds. 315 Ham. Road
Frelinger Gregory W., blksmith, 174 Cutter
Frembach Jos., eng., w.s. Bank al. b. 3d and 4th
Fremont August., harness mkr., bds. Phœnix Hotel
French Chas. A., clk. P. O., 134 Race
FRENCH & CUNNINGHAM, (Lewis F. & Albert J C.) Attorneys at Law, 57 W. 3d
French Eliza, 267 W. 3d
FRENCH J. H. (Tweed & Sibley), h. Covington
French J. W., baggage man, Spencer House
French Jacob, (F. Wilson & Co.) 109 Mulberry
French John, b. k, Gilmore, Dunlap & Co., res. Carthage
FRENCH Lewis, (F. & Cunningham,) 21 W. 7th
French Lizzie, 794 E. Front
French Maynard, e.s. Auburn b. Coggswell Av. and Central Av.
French Maynard, jr., clk., 171 Vine, h. Mt. Auburn
French Michael, clothing, 367 W. 3d
French Sarah, 120 Hopkins
French Theophilus, b. k., 131 Race, h. Carthage
French Wm. K., photographer, 204 Mound
French. Wilson & Co. (Jacob F., Wm. S. W., & Harmon Eveland,) commer., 27 E. Front
Frendenberger Barbara, bds. 150 Bremen
Frenlenberger Hy., saddler 150 Bremen
Frendhoff Theresa, 112 Buckeye
Frenge Philip, lab., s.e.c. 3d and Whittaker

Freniger Florence, carp., 703 E. Front
FRENKEL Benedict, (Aub, F. & Co.) h. 108 E. 4th.
Frenker Hermann, shoe mkr., 20 Madison
Frenselmeier Harmon, carp., 234 Everett
Freou Jozef, atty., n w.c. 3d and Main, h. 191 Barr
Frerich Clemons, box mkr., h. 191 Baymiller
Fresch Francis, 316 Main
Frese Hy., clk., 360 Central Av.
Frese Johnnna. bds. w.s. Main b. Liberty and Ham. Road
Frese Joseph, peddler, 622 Main
Frese Rudolph, lab., rear 31 Hughes
Frese Wm., coffin mkr., 9 Franklin
Fresenberg Hy., tailor, 202 Broadway
Fresenberg Mary, tailoress, 116 Abigail
Fresenborg August, (Wm. Wenning & Co.) 118 Laurel
Freudenreich Gotthard mach., 527 Race
Freulke Hy., carman. 158 Clay
Freund August, w.s. Vine b. Milk and Mulberry
Freund Ernst, meats. 1106 Central Av.
Freund Jacob, lab., s.s. 6th b. Linn and Baymiller
Freund Michael, lab., 100 Buckeye
Freund Valentine, mason, 1 Mary
Frey Adolph, teacher, 433 Vine
Frey August, cof. h., 18 W. Court
Frey Chas.. carp., 23 Mulberry
Frey Charles, cof. h., 583 Main
Frey Christian, distiller, 161 W. 3d
Frey Elizabeth, laundress, 19 Mercer
Frey George, lab., 225 George
Frey Geo. F., cigar mkr., bds. 503 Vine
Frey Hy., 299 W. Front
Frey Hy., clk., bls. Pennsylvania Hotel
Frey Hy., lab, 99 Bremen
Frey Hy., mach., 38 Harrison
Frey Hy., mach., 28 Harrison
Frey Jacob, paper carrier, 433 Vine
Frey John, s e.c. Baymiller and York
FREY JOHN, Proprietor Pearl Street House, s.w.c 3d and Race
Frey John Henry, printer, bds. 18 E. Liberty
Frey Joseph, molder. 104 E. 5th
Frey Lavina, dress mkr., 80 Pleasant
Frey Lewis. meats. 16 Mary
Frey Nallerton, cab. mkr., 190 Linn
Frey Valentine, cab mkr., 190 Linn
Freyberg Anthony, tailor, 36 Elder
Freye Hy., printer, 18 E Liberty
Freye Herman, foreman, 18 E. Liberty
Freyer Philip, wagon mkr., 529 E. Front
Freyermuth Peter, cof. h., 607 Elm
FREY'S HOTEL, A. Hummel Proprietor, 421 and 423 Main
Freytag John, cigar mkr., 13 Madison
Frich George, gardener, e.s. Western Av., b. Poplar and Findlay
Friche Lewis, cooper, rear 143 W. Court, w. of Central Av
Frick, cig. mkr., bds. 577 Main
Frick August, cig. mkr., 62 Allison
Frick Christian, cab. mkr., s.e.c. Front and John
Frick Constantine, s.w.c. Melancthon and Central Av
Frick Ferdinand, cig mkr., 5º0 Main
Frick Francis, brewer, 10 Hamer
Frick John, lab., 612 Vine
Frick ——, cab. mkr., s.e.c. Front and John
Fricke Barney, carpet weaver, 422 Race, h. n.e.c Buckeye and Poplar
Fricke Christian, shoemkr., bds. 16 E. Liberty
Fricke Clements, lab, 223 W. Front
Fricke Francis, lab., 563 Race
Fricke Frederick. carp., 483 Walnut
Fricke Frederick, carpenter, 57 13th
Fricke Frederick L., confec., 235 Sycamore
Fricke Hy., cab. mkr, 643 Central Av
Fricke Jeanette, 13 Bremen
Fricke Lewis, cooper. 148, W. Court
Fricke Wm., driver, 34 Butler
Fricke Wm. F., tailor, 494 Elm
Friday John, butcher. 417 Baymiller
Fridethe Mrs. Catharine, 13 Dudley

FRIDGER JACOB, Brass Founder and Machinist, 48 Public Landing, h. 91 E. 3 l, e. of Whittaker
Fridger Jacob, lab., 310 E. Pearl
Fridger John, lab., 310 E. Pearl
Fridger Peter, lab., wks. n.e.c. Front & Lawrence
Frie Barney, lab., 104 Clay
Fried Jacob, butcher, 102 Baymiller
Fried Jacob, cooper, wks. J. & A. Propheter's
Fricde Jacob, butcher, bds. 201 Baymiller
Friedeborn Jacob, 107 Bremen
Friedeborn Wm, baker, 543 Race
Friedenberger Hy., trunk mkr., wks. 33 W. 5th
Friedenburg Herman, clk., 91 W. 7th
Friederick Bernard, wagon mkr., bds. 347 Walnut
Friederick Christopher, cof. h., 502 Walnut
Friederick Francis, tinner, 61 Hamer
Friedhoff Wm.. carp., 163 Clay
Friedland B., peddler, n.w.c. Broadway and 6th
Friedlander Abram, clothing, 194 W. Court
FRIEDLANDER Abram J., (Heidelbach, Wertheimer & Co.,) h. 398 W. 7th
Friedlander Isaac J., salesman, 86 W. Pearl, h 53 Longworth
Friedlein Geo., cof. h., 62 Buckeye
FRIEDLEIN JOHN, Proprietor Cincinnati House, 55 Sycamore
Friedman Morris, (Zeiller & F.,) 175 W. 3d
Friedman Levy, (F. & Stern.) 59 W. 7th
Friedman Samuel, clk., 111 Main
Friedman Solomon, mer., 6 George
Friedman & Stern, (Levy F. and Saml. S.,) clothiers. 52 W. Pearl
Friedmann Ambrose, teamster, 13 Thuber al
Friedmann Geo., lab., s.s. Findlay, b. Bremen and Franz
Friedmann Jacob, tailor, n.s. Franz, b. Elder and Findlay
Friedmann Joseph, coffee roaster, 171 Clay
Friedrich Catharine, 142 Buckeye
Frieker Jacob foreman, 14 Martin
Frieker John, lab., wks. Cincinnati Chemical Laboratory
Frieker Mathias, driver, 23 E. 3d, e. of Parsons
Friel Daniel, bds. 1026 Central Av
Friel & McGuire. (Patrick F. and Thos. McG.,) tailors, 256 Walnut
Friel Patrick. (F. & McGuire.) h. Lexington, Ky
Frieling Bernhard, dry goods, 248 W. 6th
Friend Jacob H., liquors, 123 W. 3d, h. 376 Race
Friend Louis, clk., 121 Main
Frier Frederick. lab. 186 Pleasant
Fries Adam, 72 Dunlap
FRIES ALEXANDER, French Chemical Works, Office, 104 Main
Fries Balthasar, tailor, 25 Mulberry
Fries Barney, finisher, wks. n.e.c. Walnut and Canal
Fries Ferdinand butcher, 72 Dunlap
Fries Frederick, lab, 1 8 Pleasant
Fries Geo., gardener, 108 13th
FRIES GEORGE, Physician and Surgeon, Office and Residence, 74 W. 8th
Fries Hy., clk. county Treasurers office, bds 74 W. 8th
Fries John, clk., 58, 12th
Fries John, driver, n.s. 12th, b. Vine & Race
Fries Jchn, grocery, 218 Findlay
Fries Louis. 72 Stark
Fries Michael, cooper, e.s. Brighton, b. Bernard and Harrison Pike
Fries Michael, meats, 671 Vine
Fries Philip, meats. 642 Vine
Fries Wm., grocer, s.e.c. Cutter and Peete
Frieser Geo., shoemkr., 46 Peete
Frietman David, furnishing goods, 30 Longworth

(FRO) CINCINNATI (FUC) DIRECTORY. (FUL) 141

Frietsch Sigmund, pork packer, n.w.c. Ohio Av. and North Elm
Frigge Frederick, tailor 115 Mohawk
Frill Chas., tailor, 118 Mohawk
Frilling Chas., blksmith. wks. C. H. & D. R R blksmith shop
Frilling Frederick, shoe mkr., 630 Race
Frim Peter, carp., Hill, nr. 3d
Frincker Jacob, bklayer, 28 Brighton
Fringint Peter. tobacco mer., 173 Elm
Frink Geo. stone cutter, e.s. Vine, junction of Buckeye
Frintz Anna, 113 Buckeye
Friutz Juliana, 111 Buckeye
FRINTZ MICHAEL, Merchant Tailor, s.w.c. 4th, h 367 W. 3d
Frisbie John L., foreman, 97 Laurel
Frische Hy. J., 19 Green
Fristch Mary, bds 9 David
Fritch Anthony. cooper, 541 Sycamore
Fritch Mrs. Barbara, n.e.c. Elder and Logan
Fritsch. Burkhardt & Co., (Francis E., Peter J. B., and Joseph B. Blettner.) foundry, 546 Vine
Fritsch Dorothea. teacher, Everett, b. Central Av. and John
Fritsch Elizabeth, 9 David
Fritsch Francis, (F. Burkhardt & Co.,) 102 Liberty
FRITSCH HENRY, Druggist, n w.c. Freeman and Gest
Fritsch Joseph, 103 Gest
Fritsch Matthew, saddler, 304 Findlay
Fritsch Peter, mech., wks. Fritsch. Burkhardt & Co.'s
Fritsch Wm. J., druggist, n.e.c. 6th and Main [Elder
Fritsche E., w.s. Goose al., b. Green and
Fritsche Martin, lab., 163 Pleasant
Fritz Blaseus, carp., 92 Hunt
Fritz Frederick, grocery, 43 Moore
Fritz Hy., 641 Central Av
Fritz Hy., blksmith, 139 Ham. Road, h. 156 Ham Road
Fritz Jacob, 94 Betts
Fritz John, bakery, 609 Vine
Fritz John, butcher, 62 Dudley
Fritz Matilda, 156 Ham. Road
Fritz Nicholas, molder, wks. C. T. Dumout's
Fritz Phillip, lab., w s. Division, b. Bank and Hamilton Pike
Fritz Wm., tanner, Oehler al., b. Freeman and Gerrard
Fri'zzell John. peddler, 128 Lock
Frizzell Michael, peddler. bds. 128 Lock
Frizzell Wm., peddler, h 116 Lock
Froehlich Adam, baker, 134 Linn
Froehlich Chas., cof. h., 527 Central Av. h. 2 & Clark
Froehlich Chas. D., billiards, n.w.c Main and 7th, h. 526 Elm
Froehlich Christian, musician, 1 Mary
Froehlich Jacob, finisher, 150 Clay
Froehlich John, bakery, 134 Linn
FROELKING August, (F. & Marmet,) 9 Bank
FROELKING & MARMET, (August F. & Otto M.,) Hardware and Cutlery. 1013 Central Avenue
Froescher Anton, clk., 8 W. 6th
Froescher John, grocery, 30 Peete
Froese Catharine. servt., 412 W. 5th
Froese Hy., tailor, w.s. Goose al., b. Green and Elder
Froese Hermann, bds. w.s. Goose al., b. Green and Elder
FROESE RUDOLPH, Watch Maker, 240 Vine
Frohle Joseph, boots and shoes, 33 W. 7th
Frohlich Bernard, cigar mkr., w.s. Vine, b. 12th and 13th
Frohlich Catharine, 150 Clay
Frohlich Frederick, dray, e.s. Kilgour, b. 3d and 5th
Frohman Andreas, cab. mkr., 103 Carr
FROHMAN Edward, (Menderson & Frohman) 301 W. 9th w. of Central Av.
FROHMAN Lewis, (Menderson & F.) 301 W. 9th w. of Central Av.

Frohmann Chris., carver. 105 Carr
Frohmeyer Joseph, tanner. 368 Broadway
Frohmuller The., lab., 211 Hopkins
Frohoff Anthony, finisher. 7 John
Froleich Joen, mattress mkr., wks. 51 E. 3d
Fromeyer Francis. clk., 629 W. 7th
Fromeyer Hy., japanner, wks. 142 W. 3d
Fromeyer Joseph, lab., wks. s e c. 5th and Culvert
Fromherz Joseph, dyer, 98 Ham Road
Fromholz Ferdinand, harness mkr., 25 13th
Fromiller Philip, stone cutter, 534 Plum
Fromm Anthony, cab. mkr., 598 Elm
Fromm Balthaser, picture store, 703 Vine
Fromm Conrad. tailor, n.e.c. Race and 15th
Fromma Joseph, driver, 172 Webb
Fromme Gerhard, carp., 595 Race
Frommeier Fred., lab, 114 Abigail
Frommeier Hy., lab., n.e.c. Pendleton and Abigail
Frommeier Joseph, dray, n.e.c. Pendleton and Abigail
Frommel Frederick, (F., Kramig & Co.) 578 Walnut
Frommerer Francis G., salesman, h. 629 W. 7th
Frommeyer J. F. & Son, (John F. & Wm H.) flour dealers. 432 Main
Frommeyer John F., (J. F. & Son) 451 W. 5th
Frommeyer Mrs Mary, 29 Hannibal
Frommeyer Wm H., (J. F. Frommeyer & Son) 451 W. 5th
Frondhoff Francis, painter, 10 Woodward
Frondhoff Mrs. Gertrude, 10 Woodward
Front Street House, John Beneke, 55 W. Front
Froome Samuel.office.s w.c. 3d and Vine, h 525 W. 5th
Froomer Jacob. meats. 57 15th
Frost Geo T., printer, Cin. Gazette, 110 Smith
Frost James H., printer, 56 W. 4th
Frost Mary, 56 W. 4th
Frost Sarah, wks. 137 Walnut
Frost Thomas. carp., s.s. 3d b. Sycamore and Broadway
Froulier Hy., carp., s.s. 8th b. Harriet and Mill Creek
Frovaga Mary, h 118 W. Front
Frowley Ellen. servt., 20 Barr
Frowley Mary A, bds. 65 Linn
Frown Frank. carp., 671 W. 6th
Frucauf George, 579 Race
Fruhwald Mathias. cof. h., 64 Lock
Fruth Valentine. fireman. 706 E. Front
Fry Rev. Benjamin J., 34 Findlay
Fry Frederick, cab. mkr., 64 Barr
Fry Hy., clk. 17 E. 3J, h. s.w.c. Pike and Front
FRY HENRY L., Wood Carver and Pattern Maker, 324 Central Av., h. Pleasant Ridge
Fry Isaac D., clk. Custom House, h. Walnut Hills
Fry John, carp., 222 Sycamore
Fry John, clk., 376 Elm
Fry John, mach., wks. n.s. Front b. Lawrence and Pike
Fry Joseph. carriage trimmer, n.s. Front b. Louis and Vance
Fry Joseph, molder, wks. n.s. Front b. Lawrence and Pike
Fry Kate, 730 W. Front
Fry Ursus. clk 30 Pub. Landing
Fry Wm. R.., cigars. 133 Vine, bds. e.s. Race b. 6th and 7th
FRYE HENRY, Chair Factory, 367 Broadway, h. 362 Broadway
Fryer Jacob, 60 Stark
Fryer Lewis, (Rentz & F) h. Newport
Fuchs Adam, huckster, 42 Findlay
Fuchs Adam. lab., h. 612 Elm
Fuchs Conrad. waiter St. Charles Exchange
Fuchs Fred., 663 Central Av.
Fuc's Geo., dray, 30 Allison
Fuchs Gottlieb, wagon mkr., 11 Adams
Fuchs Hy., trunk mkr., wks. 509 Plum

Fuchs Hy. A., tinner, 29 Moore
Fuchs Hy. B., harness mkr., bds. e.s. Vine b. 9th and Court
Fuchs Jacob, trunk mkr., wks 509 Plum
Fuchs John, meats. 17 Allison
Fuchs Julius, cof. h., s w.c. Melancthon and Central Av.
Fuchs Lorenz, cof. h., 75 Elder
Fuchs Michael butcher. 17 Allison
Fuchs Peter, cof. h., 424 Vine
Fuchs Simon, printer, wks. Volksblatt office
Fuchshuber Rev. Joseph, 101 E. Pearl
Fuechs Philip. policeman. 20 Jaeger
Fueger Hy., lab., h. 44 Peete
Fuehr Adelaide. servt., 660 Race
Fueller Mrs. Elizabeth. 594 Vine
Fueller Oswin, lab., wks 438 Main
Fuersattel John S. ments, 580 Main
Fuerst Helena, 5 Buckeye
Fugal Frederick, lab., 83 Baymiller
Fugate Thomas. plane mkr., 407 Plum
Fuglin Michael, porter, 249 Clark
Fugman Joseph, cheese depot, 56 Buckeye
Fugsberger Robert, peddler. 607 Race
Fuhlger Hy., lab., s w.c Gest and Carr
Fuhr John, wood' worker., s.s. Everett b. Cutter and Linn
Fuhrke John, cigar mkr., wks. 213 Walnut
Fuhrmann Frederick, 151 Clay
Fuhrmann Joseph, brewer 696 Race
Fuhrmann Louis, tannery, Deer Creek b, rth and Court, h. 43 Franklin
Fuhrmann Peter, molder 151 Clay
FUHRMANN VALENTINE, Manufacturer and Dealer in Cigars Tobacco. &c., 7 Main, h. 151 Clay
Fuiglein Andrew sawyer, h. 1 Wade b. Elm and Plum
Fnirste Frederick, lab., 143 Clay
Fuirste Hy., shoe mkr., 14 Hughes
Fuldner John, cof h., 192 Clinton
Fuldner Philip, cigars, 196 Clinton
Fulgerve Chas., cigar mkr., n.e.c. Liberty and Main
Fulin Michael, molder, 249 Clark
Fullam Timothy S., foreman, 367 W. 4th
Fullbright Alfred. lab., s.s. 6th b. Broadway and Culvert
Fuller Albert, (Albert F. & Co.) 315 Longworth
Fuller Albert & Co., (Albert F & Niles works foundry) water faucet manufa., 118 E. 2d
Fuller Anton, clk, bds. Pennsylvania Hotel
Fuller Chas. H., brass worker, bds. 315 Longworth
FULLER E. F., general ticket agt. O. & M. R.R., bds. Burnet House
Fuller Evaline, servt., n.e.c. Wade and Dudley
Fuller Fred., lab., wks. n.e.c. Canal and Walnut
Fuller Frank, lab., 473 Broadway
Fuller James M, clk. 337 John
Fuller James M., phys., 185 Richmond
Fuller Julia, seamstress, Cin. Orphan Asylum, Mt. Auburn
Fuller Lewis. lithographic printer, s.w.c. 4th and Walnut
Fuller Louis, plasterer, 255 Hopkins
Fuller S. L., clk., bls. 337 John
Fuller Samuel. driver, 357 John
Fuller Samuel B, foreman. wks. n e c. Canal and Walnut
Fuller Sarah, 149 Carr
Fuller Sydney B., blksmith, 159 Richmond
Fuller Wm F., st bt. capt., 286 W. 7th
Fullermer Margaret, 412 Sycamore
Fullerton Wm. R., salesman 55 W. Pearl, h. 172 Plum
Fulliston Elisa. s s. Phoebe al. b. Plum and Central Av.
Fullriede Louis, stone mason, rear 521 Sycamore
Fultner J c h, 212 Laurel
Fulton Abraham, miller, 112 Baum
FULTON Chas. E., (F. & Karr) 148 Walnut
FULTON & KARR, (Chas. E. F. & John K.) Attorneys at Law, 148 Walnut

142 (GAE) CINCINNATI (GAL) DIRECTORY. (GAN)

Fulton James T., clk. Burnet House
Fulton Wm R., salesman, bds. 172 Plum
Fultz Mrs., 83 E. Pearl
Fulweiler Abra am, tanner, 72 Clinton
Fulweiler Jacob, finisher, 37 Moore
Fulweiler John, clk., bds 274 W. 7th
Fulweiler John H., tailor, 160 Vine, h. 274 W 7th
Fummner Hy., polisher, h 86 Freeman
Funck Charles R., clgars, 178 W. 6th
Funcke Wm, porter "O" Race
Funcke David, cab mkr, wks, 198 W. 2d
Funikow John, lab., rear 26 Lock n. of 8th
Funk Frederick, porter 165 Pleasant
Funk Hy., foreman, 64 Bremen
Funk Hy B., 1st Hopkins
Funk Isaac B., carp., 1180 E. Front
Funk John O., clk., h 1s. 473 Walnut

FUNK JOHN R.,
China, Glass and Queensware, n. w. c. Vine and Court

Funk Lewis A., carp., bds. 189 E. Front
Funke Charles, cab. mkr., 133 Baymiller
Funke Frederick H., boots and shoes, 582 M. In
Funke H. W., p cker, 307 Race
Funke Hy. L., lab., 62 Bremen
Funke Mary, milliner, 5-7 Races
Furber Chas. E., cook, 207 George
Furgeson Edward, porter, 91 George
Furgia Kivin U. S. A., 626 W. 6th
Furkov B., blksmith wks. n.s. Front b. Lawrence and Pike
Furling Frederic, lab., 81 Martin
Furlong James, driver, 40 Freeman
Furman John, molder, wks. n.e.c. Canal and Walnut
Furnam Geo., finisher, 80 E. 3d
Furn'er Andrew, e.s Division b. Bernard and H m s in Pike
Furselli Frank, upholsterer, 181 Laurel
Furst Abraham tra ler 54 Rittenhouse
Furst Charles, cof h., 44 E. Pearl
Furst Jacob, 311 Vine
Furst John, gilder 71 Woodward
Furst= August. tailor b. 315 Vine

FURSTE FRIEDERICK,
Boot & Shoe Manufacturer, 40 W. 5th

Furst= Frederick J. carp., 11 Hughes
Furste Wm., silver smith, 4 O W. 5th
Furster Fred Julius, cooper, rear 34 Mulberry
Fury Bernard, cof. h., 94 Freeman
Fury John, fireman, n w c 2d and Rose
Fury Peter, ta lor 162 W. Front
Fusgreen Henry, lab., wks. John Mitchell's
Fusler Conrad, carp, 13 Ann
Fusnecker John, farrier, 19 Green
Fusner John, cof. h., 561 Walnut
Fust Michael, cooper, 7-8 Central Av.
Fusz John, carp., 113 Buckeye
Fusz Joseph, carp., h 143 Buckeye
Futing Wm., lab., 680 Main
Fyfe John salesman, 21 W. Pearl, h. Newport
Fyffer Rev Wm. H., 488 W. 4th

G

Gaab Jacob, lab., 216 Walnut
Gabenmesch Christopher, cof. h. n. s. Harrison Pike, b. Brighton & Riddle
Gabers Joseph, lab. rear 55 Woodward
Gable Leonard, 291 W. Liberty
Gabler Charles silver smith, Duhme & Co.'s, 136 Hopkins
Gabriel James, lab., 128 Mound
Gabriel John cooper, n.s. Charlotte b. Linn and Baymiller
Gabriel Michael, brach mkr., 195 Linn
Gabriel Peter, finisher, Observatory st. Mt. Adams
Gabriel Rayena, second hand store, 31 E. 5th
Gabriel Richard, lab., s.s. Weller b. Carr and Harriet
Gabriel Thomas, lab., 5 Weller, b. Carr and Harriet
Gaculu Samuel, 135 W. 5th
Gaddam Wm. J., ins. agt., 455 Vine, h. 174 York
Gaeber Geo., shoe mkr, 184 W. Court

Gae le Frank, cooper, 63 Bremen
Gaeney Daniel, molder, wks. n. e. c. Canal and Walnut
Gaentner Joseph, cundy mkr., 21 13th
Gaeringer Juliana, servt., wks. 523 Main
Gaeth Ernst. cab. mkr., 107 W. Liberty
Gaetlein John, lab., Pleasant, b. Findlay and Henry
Gaertner Sebastian, tin ware etc., 566 Vine
Gneeling Catharine, millinery, 518 Main
GAFF James W., (Perin, Gould & Co.,) h. Aurora, Ind.
Gaff John, (Horner & G.) 422 W 7th
GAFF Thomas, (Perin, Gould & Co.,) h. Aurora, Ind.
Gifeney C. O'Brien. cupping and leeching, 276 Walnut
Gaffner Peter, drmy. 41 Gest
G ffney Edward, distiller, 303 W, 3d
Gaffney John. lab , 431 W. 3 d
Gaffney John, polisher, 431 W. 3d
Gaffney Peter, porter, h. 276 Broadway
Gifney Mary, servt, 435 W. 6th
Guge Thomas, lab., e s. Vine b. Milk & Mulberry
Gage Will M., clk., 101 W. 4th, bds, 52 W. 9th
Gager John H , lab., 1162 E. Front
Gugher Andrew, cab. mkr., bds. n. w. c. Smith and Augusta
Gahazan John, c b. mkr., wks. s. w. c. Canal and Elm
Gahn Rev. Conrad, 127 Everett
Gahr George, brewer, 337 Ham. Road
Gainer John, boots and shoes, s.w.c. Vine and Court
Gaines Austin, cooper, 61 Woodward
Gaines G. J., (Evans G. & Co.) res. Boone co, Ky.
Gaines Lou sa, h. 39 New
Gaines Owen, (Evans G. & Co) res. Boone co., Ky

GAINES THEOP?TILUS, Prosecuting Attorney Hamilton County Office Court House, h. 3 3 Richmond

Gainor Wm., molder, wks. n.s. Canal w. of Elm
Gair Rev. Otto 229 Bremen
Gaisendorf Andrew, sawyer, 565 Race
Gaither James E., printer, bds. 102 R ce
Gaisser Benjamin, cap mkr. 145 Main, h. s.w.c. 13th and Clay

GAITHER ALFRED,
Superintendent Adams Express Co. h 87 E 5th

Gaither Thomas, mess. I. & C. R. R., rooms 100 Burnet House
Gaites Joseph, boots and shoes, 446 W. 8th
Gakens Catharine, 72 Abigail
Galagher John, watchman, 402 W. 3d
Galbraith W. H. b. s., 30 M in
Galbreth Geo., butcher, 201 Poplar
Galbreath M. B., saddler, bds. Dennison House
Galbreath Nancy, 96 W. 7th
Galbreath Robert H., salesman, Dahme & Co 's, bds. 26 W. 7th
Gale John, lab., 1 York
Gale John A., com. mcr., 80 W. Front, h. 214 Findlay
Gale Wm. M., finisher, 191 Poplar
Galison Wm., draftsman, bds. 252 Walnut
Galisque Joseph, bds. 51 W 5th
Gall Frederick baker, 632 Race
Gall J. A. & W. B. (John A. & Wm. B.) butchers, n. w. c. Clarkson, b. Bank & Central Av.
Gall John A., (J. A. & W. B. G.) 505 Linn
Gall Louis, 80 Mohawk
Gall W. B. (J. A. & W, B. G.) h. s.w.c. Clarkson and Bank
Gallager Wm. D., salesman, 101 W. Pearl, h. 24 Hopkins
Gallagher Anna, servt., 7 Harrison
Gallagher Catharine, tailoress, h. 27 Arch
Gallagher David carp, wks. s.s. Baker b. Walnut and Vine
Gallagher Edward, lab., 92 Avery
Gallagher Edward, lab., wks. 196 W. Pearl

Gallagher Eliza G., h. 267 W 3d
Gallagher Geo W., salesman, 383 W 3d
Gallagher Jacob, blksmith, 990 Central Avenue
Gallagher James R., foreman, 227 Central Av.
Gallagher John, 427 W. 3d
Gallagher John, carp, 93 Hopkins
Gallagher John, drw. Pennock Alley b. Mound and Cutter
Gallagher John, driver, e. s. Walnut b. 5th and 6th
Gallagher John J., clk., 427 W. 3d
Gallagher Louisa, milliner bds. 27 Arch
Gallagher Kate, servt , 112 Mill
Gallagher Kate milliner, bds. 27 Arch
Gallagher M. J., tobacconist. R ce
Gallagher Maggie tailoress, 27 Arch
Gallagher Mary, 164 E Pearl
Gallagher Mathew, jeweler, h. 278 Clark
Gallagher Michael, hackman. 213 W 7th
Gallagher Michael, lab., 114 W. Front
Gallagher Michael. lab. 183 W. 2nd
Gallagher Patrick, lab. 3 3 W. 5th
Gallagher Richard, 108 W. 6th
Gallagher Sarah, servt., 423 W 6th
Gallagher Sarah A., 102 W. 4th
Gallagher, Simon, lab., wks. C. T. Dumont's

GALLAGHER THOMAS J,
Attorney at Law, 148 Walnut, h. 30 W. 8th

Gallan Mary, 13 Arch
Galle Augu t, lab , 3d Dudley
Gallear Wm., bds. 444 Front
Gillenbeck Wm., tailor bds. 110 B. 2nd
Gailer Casper, cooper, 432 Linn
G llese Barney. lab., 29 Acc ommodation
Galleson Wm. H., p it ern mkr., wks. n. e. c. Walnut and Canal
Galliece Michael, lab., 329 W 2d
Gallighan Daniel, lab , 23 Landing, b. Ludlow and Broadway
Gulligher Chas., cooper, bds. 61 W. 6th
Galligher Mary, e.s. Pancoast st. b. 7th and 8th
Galligher Patrick, drsy, 333 W. 5th
Gallinger Jacob, millwright, wks. 825 Central Av
Gallmann Louis, cof. h., 14 E. 8th
Galloway John M., carp. n.s. Railroad e. of Stone al
Gillivan Hannah, 48 E. 7th
Galt Elizabeth, h. 302 Longworth

GALT HOUSE,
Wm. E. Marsh, Proprietor, s.w.c. 6th and Main

GALVAGNI JOHN,
Books, Fancy Goods, &c., 513 Vine

Galvin M. & T. (Maurice & Thomas), blksmiths, n.w.c. Sycamore and Canal
Galvin Maurice (M. & T. G.) 78 Mulberry
Galvin Thomas (M. & T. G) 119 Lock
GALWAY Wm. (J. W. Donohue & Co.) 303 W. 9th w. of Central Av
Galwin John, bk. binder, wks. 162 W. 3d
Gamble Andrew, butcher, s w.c. Freeman and Dayton
Gamble Anna, bds. 101 W. 5th
Gambly George, student, 20 Clark
Gamble Henry E., shoemkr, bds 208 W. 5th
GAMBLE James, (Proctor & G.) 27 Clark
Gamble James M., clk. 26 Clark
Gamble John, clk., bds. 304 Vine
Gamble Thomas, chandler, 37 York
Gamble Wm. cor. driver,bds. e.s. Kilgour b. 3d and 5th
Gambs Martin, tailor, 93 Ham. Road
Gambun Morris, lab., s.s. Budd b. Harriet and Mill Creek
Gamel John, shoemkr. 615 Race
G imel John P., boots and shoes, 567 Race
Gamel Wm., express driver, rear 52 Plum
Gamer Hy., b iler mkr., wks. s.s. 3d b. Butler and M Canal
Gammer Hy., lab., w.s. Kilgour b. 3d & 5th
Gans Casper, cof. h., 519 Walnut
Gander Jacob, fringe mkr., 132 W. Liberty

Gandolfo August. n w c Elm and 12th
Gandolfo Peter, confec., n.w.c. 5th and Broadway
Gandolfo Peter, ice house, n.w.c. Elm & 12th, h. 375 Elm
Gandolph Frank, cof, h., 59 Vine
Ganey Ellen, e.s. Court b. 6th and Observatory Road
Ganehen Bartholomew, lab., 792 W. 3d
Gangin James, blksmith, 11 Providence
Gangon James, wks. s. Vanhorn b. Linn and Cutter
Ganhimer Mary, 23 E 3d e of Parsons
Gaulan Edward, lab 47 E. 3d
Ganner Chrl.s. lab., 52 Mohawk
Gannon Bridget, servt., 398 W. 6th
Gannon Peter, s.w.c. 7th and Plum
Gannon Stephen, lab., n e c Barr and Freeman
Gansenmuller Fred., brewer,Clearwater b. Baymiller and Freeman
Gano —, mach., b ls. 60 Broadway
Gano Eliza, h. 16 E 5th c. of Lock
GANO Gazzam (Howell Gano & Co.) h. Clifton
Gano George, b.k., 138 Walnut, bds. 23 Longworth
GANO Howell (Howell G. & Co.), h. Clifton
G ANO HOWELL & CO. (Howell G., Gazzam Gano & Christopher T. Adams), Wholesale Dealers in Hardware. 138 Walnut
G ANO JOHN A.
"Financial Editor" Commercial, h. 41 W. 7th
Gano John S, asst. clk., Police Court h 87 W. 9th
Gano Peter, finisher, 138 Walnut
Gano Sarah, 26 E. 8th e. of Lock
GANO Stephen, manager at B. G. Dun & Co's, h. Avondale
GANO W. G. W., cashier, Lafayette Banking Co., h. Clifton
Gano Wm., tailor 40 W. Court w. of Central Av
Gans Benjamin, clk., bds. n.e.c. 6th and Elm
Gans Danl. S., phys., h. 348 Race
Gans Gustavus, peddler 530 Elm
Gans Isaac, lab., s s. Ohio al. b. Elm and Plum and 15th and Adams
Gans Joseph, auction 1005 Central Av
Gans Michael, meats, 53 13th
Gant John, hackman, 5 North
Gantenberg Bernhardt, sewing machine manuf , 264 Central Av
Ganthamer Adam, lab., wks. W. W. Thomas & Co's
Gantz Isaac clk., rear 579 Main
Gany Bridget, 251 Broadway
Garaty Thomas, box mkr., n.w.c. 5th and Smith
Garbaum Elizabeth, 232 W. Court
Garbott James, cab. mkr, 744 W 6th
Garbrock Casper, locksmith, 426 Sycamore, h. 424 Sycamore
Gardiner Mrs. —. bds 117 John
Gardiner Eleazer M , auctioneer, 390 W. 9th w. of Central Av
Gardiner George M., supt. h. 365½ W. 7th
Gardiner L., blksmith, wks. n s. Front b. Lawrence and Pike
Gardiner Robert, b.h., s.e.c. Walnut and 9th
Gardner Adam. cof. h., 673 Race
Gardner Amos, pilot, 64 Vanhorn
Gardner Andrew, b.k , 49 W. Pearl
Gardner Anna, servt., 225 W. 6th
Gardner Arthur, shoemkr, 272 W. Liberty
Gardner Benjamin. cab. mkr, bds. Olean Hotel
Gardner Carlisle D., plumber, 287 W. 6th, h. 177 Poplar
GARDNER Edmund B. (Babbitt, Good & Co.) h. Mt. Auburn
Gardner Hannah, seamstress, 177 John
Gardner Jacob, coal yard, 523 E. Front, h. 70 High
Gardner Jacob, cof. h., 70 E. 3d e. of Whittaker
Gardner James, bds. 162 Plum
Gardner John, 6d Dudley
Gardner John, finisher, 428 Walnut

Gardner John, sexton, s.w.c. Torrence and Front
Gardner Jos. clk., 140 and 142 Main
Gardner Judson, (G. & Magee) h. Quaker Bottom
Gardner Lawrence, blksmith, 27 Observatory Road
Gardner Lizzie seamstress, 177 John
Gardner & Magee (Judson G. & Augustus M) com. mers., 20 Water
Gardner Peter, bk. mkr., 60 Dudley
Gardner Phillip, trunk mkr, 97 Wondward
Gardner Robert, bds. s e.c. 9th and Walnut
Gardner Robert, bk. layer w.s. Coggswell al b. Woodword and Abigail
Gardner Samuel, boatman, n.s. Accommodation e. of 8th
Gardner Stephen A., jr., b.k., 173 W. 2d, h. 502 W. 7th
Garehan Thos., wood dealer. 57 Mill
Gareis John, peddler, e.s. Vine nr. Auburn Av
Garethy James, lab , 20 Rittenhouse
Garhind Herman, cigars, &c , 451 W. 3d
GARLICHS Geo. H. (Eggers & Co.) 39 Harrison
Garlick Hy. S., b.h., 72 W. 4th, h. 41 Baum
Garman M. B., 128 Walnut
Garner Hy., dray, 101 Gest
Garner Hy., lab , wks, C., H. & D. R R. depot
Garner Jacob, dray, bds. 92 Gest
Garner John, molder, 166 Carr
Garner Wm S., policeman, 166 Carr
Garney John, lab., n.w.c. Union and Race
Garnor Ernst, carp., 487 Walnut
Garoute Archibald M., 133 George
Garran Peter, lab., w.s. Langdon al. b. 6th and 7th
Garrard Jephtha, atty., s.e.c. 4th and Vine
Garraty Jas., lab., 85 W. 9th w. of Central Av
Garraty Julia, 145 W. Pearl
Garre Bernhard, paper hanger, 591 Main
Garre Hy., chair mkr., wks. F. Kanemann & Bro's
Garre M. & E. (Misses Mary & Elizabeth G) millinery, 591 Main
Garre Elizabeth (M. & E G.) 591 Main
Garre Mary (M. & E. G.) 591 Main
Garretson Geo. W., jr. carp., 71½ Laurel
Garretson Geo. W., carp., 71½ Laurel
Garretson Hy., molder, bds. 69 Elm
Garrelson James, clk., 187 George
G ARRETSON JESSE, Physician,
Office & Residence. 274 W. 4th
Garretson Sarah, 479 W. 9th w. of Central Av
Garretson Wm. A., carp., 71½ Laurel
Garrett & Cottman (C. G. & Thos. C.), plow manufs, 9 W. 7th
Garrett Cyrus (G. & Cottman), 19 W. 8th
Garrett Eliza A., bds. 106 Longworth
Garrett J., bds. 81 E. Pearl
Garrett Louisa, 340 Main
Garrott Patrick, lab. 103 W. Front
Garrett Samuel F., packer, 113 Abigail
Garretty James, sawyer, wks. 196 W. Pearl
Garvey John, tailor, 403 Central Av
Garretty Thomas, hostler, bds. Bevis House
Garretty Catharine, 143 Clark
Garretty Thomas, sawyer, s.e.c. 5th and Smith
Garribaldi Antonio, lab., wks. 137 W. 2d
Garrigan James, lab., 654 W. 8th
Garrigan Michael, salesman, 26 Commerce
Garrigan Patrick, lab. 56 Elm
Garrigan Thomas, lab., n s. 6th e. of Lock
Garrigan Thomas, salesman, 20 E. 2d, h. Covington
Garringer Phillip, trunk manuf., 637 Elm
Garris Wm., cooper, wks. s.s. Gest b. Freeman and Carr
Garrison D. N., 369 W. 5th
Garrison Elizabeth, 109 Pike

Garrison Frances, teacher, 75 Hopkins
G ARRISON H. D.
Physician and Surgeon, 235 Central Av , bds. 271 W. 6th
Garrison H.. cab mkr., wks. 168 W. 2d, res. Covington
Garrison James, clk , Madison House
Garrison Jerre. pattern mkr., bds. s.w.c. Pearl and Ludlow
G ARRISON JOHN W., President Eagle Insurance Co., and Prop'r Madison H use, 19, 21 & 23 Main
Garrison Mary J., 75 Hopkins
Garrison Saml T., agt., 128 W. 5th,bds. 27 Longworth
Garrison Stephen R., prop. Sportsman's Hall. s s Front e. of Corp. line
Gurits Gershom G., exchange once, 14 E 3d, b ls. Broadway Hotel
Gars Barney, eng. 74 Abigail
Garsombrukar Henrietta, servt., 603 Freeman
Gartrell C. H., dry goods, bds. 232 Walnut
Garty Terry, hostler, bds. n.e.c. Linn and Everett
Garven Rosey. bds. 333 W. 2d
Girver Nicholas. dray, 57 Martin
Garver Theobald, lab. 57 Martin
Garver Wm., 19 R chmond b. Elm and Plum
Garvey Dan'l. lab. 63 E. 8th
GARVEY James P., (Baker & Co.,) h. Newport Ky
Garvey John, cutter, 23 Webb
Garwe John, cooper, w.s. Wood, b. 3d and Front
Garwood Harriett, 446 W 5th
Gasenhaus Hermann, lab., bds. n.w.c. Linn and Clark
Guskill Isaac, shoe mkr., 38 E. 5th
Gaskill Wm , tailor, 38 E 5th
Gasner John, bakery, 74 H m. Road
Gass Adam, mattress mkr., 106 Pleasant
Gass Henry, cof. h., 177 Clay
Gass Henry W., turner, 58 Everett
Gassanala John B., 177 Clay
Gassaway H C., b. k., 14 Pub. Landing h. Newport
Gasselbracht Wm , janitor, s.s. 8th b. Linn and Mound [Elm
Gassenschmidt Mathias, blksmith, 462
Gasser Anthony, basket mkr., 271 Linn
Gasser Benjamin. grocer. 603 W. Front
Gasser John J , attorney, n.w.c. Main and Court. h. Newport
Gastdorf Christpher, whitewasher 131 K. Pearl
G ASTEN, DICKSON & CO., (Robert G . John D. & Alex Clark) Importers and Jobbers of Hardware, 53 W. Pearl
GASTEN Robert, (G. Dickson& Co.), 191 W. 7th
Gastinger Robert, porter, Al. b. 13th and Merce and Walnut and Vine
Gastner Nicholas, wagon mkr. 31 J Ham. Road, h 237 Ham. Road
Gastol Morris G , carp., 37 Parsons
Gasz John, cof.h., 650 Vine
Gatchell Nathan, clk., R. G. Dun & Co.'s, h. Newport
Gate John, grainer, bds. 155 Clark
Gate John, lab., wks, 335 Broadway
Gates D. W. C., b. k., 51 W. 3d, h. Walnut H.l s
Gates Geo., bakery, s.w.c. Pike and Butler
Gates James, books, 268 W. 7th
G ATES JAMES,
Union Envelope Manuf. s e.c. 4th and Hammond
GATES John, (John G. & Co.) 414 W. 6th
G ATES JOHN & CO., (John G. & Joseph Gates). Wholesale Dealers in Boots and Shoes. 54 W. Pearl
Gates John, lab. wks. Henry Nye's
GATES Joseph, (John G. & Co) 446 W. 8th
GATES Nelson, (Miles Greenwood & Co .) 393 Walnut
Gates Wm., molder, 793 Elm
Githaus Henry, grocery, 70 Hunt
Gutlay Bernard, dray, n.s. Court E. of Broadway

144 (GAZ) CINCINNATI (GEI) DIRECTORY.

Gats A., bds. Bevis House
Gats N., bds. Bevis House
Gattemeier Bernhard, lab., 73 Buckeye
Gattertem Christina, 49 E. 3d
GATTI G. & ZANONE (Guiseppe G. & John D. Z.,) Com. Merchs. and Dealers in Foreign and Domestic Fruits, Wines, Liquors, &c., 60 Broadway
GATTI Guiseppe, (G. G. & Zanone,) h. 60 Broadway
Gattmann Barney, lab., s.e.c. Hopkins and Baymiller
Gattman Isaac M., chemist, 282 Broadway
Gatto Antonio, peddler, 122 W. 3d
Gatto John B., (John B. G. & Bro.,) 122 W. 3d
Gatto John B. & Bro., (John B G. & Thos. G.,) confect. 122 W. 3d
Gatto Mary, h. 122 W. 3d
Gatto Thos., (John B. Gatto & Bro.,) 122 W. 3d
Gau Joseph, painter, 14 15th
Gawbley Christopher, lab., 164 Everett
Gauckler Henry, pipeman, n.w.c. Ludlow and 3d
Gault Edmond, mach., 17 Observatory Road
Gault Edward, finisher, wks n.e.c. Walnut and Canal
Gault Granville C., (G. & Sackett,) 81 High
Gault John H., b,k , 679 Freeman
Gault & Sackett, (Granville C. G. & Geo. H. S.,) painters, s.s. Front, E. of Leatherbury
Gault Samuel C., clk., 99 Walnut, bds. 416 Broadway
Gause Henry, tailor, bds. s.w.c. 5th and Broadway
Gausepohl Anna, 91 Woodward
Gausepohl Fred., cab. mkr., 25 Clinton
Gausepohl Gerhard, clk , 27 Madison
Gausepohl Henry, stoves &c., 598 Main
Gausepohl John B., grocery, s.e.c. Front and Plum
Gausepohl John B., porter, 91 Woodward
Gaussen Thos. B., inspector Cincinnati Gas Co., bds. National Hotel
Gausen Wm. E., cof h. 71 W. 3d
Gausz Chas. J., cigar mkr., 118 Clinton
Gausz Justus, cigars. &c., 118 Clinton
Gauwatz Henry, tinner, 430 Walnut
Gauf Philip, carp., Ham. Road b. Elm and Plum
Gavegan Edward, bar k. 25 E. 5th
Gavel. John, coachman, 129 W. 3d
Gavin David, carp., s.s. 6th b. Harriett and Horn
Gavin John, lab., 130 W. 3d
Gavin Michael, cof. h., 16 Landing b. Broadway and Ludlow
GAY JAMES P., Agent for American Gutta Percha Roofing Co., Office 273 Sycamore, h. 146 Broadway
Gay Joseph W., b. k , s.w.c. Walnut and 2d, bds. s e c. 3d and Broadway
Gay Lewis W., gutta percha roofing, 273 Sycamore
Gay Walter. author, bds, 176 John
Gayle Wm. H , salesman Duhme & Co., h. Newport
Gayles Moses, lab , 99 E. 6th
Gaylor Harry, hatter, 576 E. Front
GAYLORD Benjamin B., (Gaylord Son & Co.,) res. Portsmouth
GAYLORD SON & CO., (Thomas G. G. & Benjamin B. Gaylord,) Bloom Forge Iron Works, 90 and 92 Broadway
GAYLORD T. G. & CO . (Thos. G. G. & Wm. F. Gaylord,) Iron Pipe & Rolling Manufs., Foundry Newport. Warehouse 92 Broadway
GAYLORD Thomas G., (G. Son & Co.,) 100 E. 4th
Gaylord Wm. F., Iron mer., bds. Spencer House
Gaxlay Allen W. 418 W. 6th
Gaxlay James W., 418 W 6th
Gazollo Anthony, confec., 56½ Broadway, h. 49 Public Landing
Gazolo Catharine, 172 Broadway
Gazolo James, confec., 45 Public Landing

Gazolo Peter, confec 26 Public Landing
Geagan Ann, servt., 360 W. 6th
Geary Peter fireman, Burnet House
Gebauer Peter, butcher, bds. 19 Wade
GEBBE Hy., (Rattermann, G. & Co.) 125 W. Liberty
Gebbe Hy., varnish manuf., 107 W. Liberty
Gebel Hy., tailor 464 Walnut
Gebert Frederick, meats, 107 Clark
Gebhard Anthony, butcher. 609 Race
Gebhard Julius, (Boss & Co) 400 Sycamore
Gebhart Samuel, finisher, wks. n.e.c. Walnut and Canal
Gebhardt Edward. b k., 60 Allison
Gebhardt Magdalen, 38 Peete
Gebhardt Wm., (Hopf & G) 48 Ham. Road
Gebhart John, mason 64 W. Liberty
Gebhart John, varnisher, 38 Peete
Gebhart Joseph, tanner, n.s. Rail Road e of Stone al
Gebhart Martha, 81 Cross
Gebler Hy., mach. 23 Mercer
Geckel Andrew, c. Smith and Augusta
Gecks Anthony, meats. 50 E. Front
Gecks Peter musician, 556 Vine
Gedney Ann E., 274 Longworth
Gee Gordon, plasterer, 63 E. 7th
Gee James, carp., wks. 20 Lodge
Geering Hy., dray, e.s. Ludlow b. Pearl and 3d
Geers Mary, 197 Bremen
Geeske Caroline, servt., 149 Elm
GEFFROY O H. & CO. (Oliver H. G. & Peter Gibson,) Proprietors Gibson House, w.s. Walnut b. 4th and 5th
GEFFROY OLIVER H., County Treasurer. Office Court House, res. Gibson House
Geggus Phillip, stone mason, n.s. R. Road e. of Lewis
Geglein Andrew, tail r 33 Peete
Gegner Geo., miller, 62 Lock
Gegner John, bakery, 211 W. 6th
Gegner John, butcher, 727 Race
Gegner Lorenz, saddler, wks. 59 Ham. Road
Gehbauer Mary, 68 Ham. Road
Gehefer Cornelius, barber, 575 Main
Gehegan Michael, 163 Central Av
Gehm Wm., lab., 101 Ham. Road
Gehnke Chas., tailor, 584 Walnut
Gehoeffer Hy., 61 Findlay
Gehring August, lab., 99 Clay
Gehrung Benedict, tinner, 402 Race
Gehring Hy., dray, wks. 109 E. Pearl
Gehring Joseph, shoe mkr., w.s. Plum nr. 15th
Gehring Nicholas, tailor, 207 Broadway
Gehrung Amelia, teacher, 225 Vine
Gehrke August, tailor, 16 15th
Gahrlein Frank, meats, 268 E. Pearl, e. of Broadway
Gehrlich Thomas M., basket mkr. 239 Bremen
Gehrmann Michael, tinner, bds. 435 Walnut
Gehrum John, butcher, 202 Ham. Road
Geiber Chas., dray, 21 York
Geider George, finisher, 141 Pleasant
Geier Anthony, tailor, 5 Buckeye
Geier Francis, driver, 91 Bremen
Geier Frederick, turner, 231 Hopkins
Geier Jacob, turner, 231 Hopkins
Geier Jacob, turner. 385 W. Liberty
Geier John lab., 40 Peete
Geier Phillip, turner, 231 Hopkins
Geiger Albert, pattern mkr., 52 Allison
Geiger Andrew, lab., 99 Barr
Geiger Anthony, cigar mkr., 512 Vine
Geiger Chas F., clk. 512 Vine
Geiger Christina, servt., 537 Vine
Geiger Geo., biksmith, 343 Ham. Road, h. 345 Ham. Road
Geiger George, porter, 25 Vine
Geiger Hy., 66 Sturk
Geiger John, biksmith, 52 Mohawk
Geiger John, grocer, 70 Pleasant
Geiger John, molder, n.w.c. McDowell and Lewis
Geiger Robert. bk. binder, 193 Pleasant
Geiger Romann biksmith, 14 Madison
Geiger Wm., printer, 512 Vine

(GER) CINCINNATI (GER) DIRECTORY. (GET) 145

Geller Amelia, servt., Galt House
Gelvin Jehu, sand dealer, e.s. John, b. Oliver and Liberty
Gemahlen John, harness mkr., 709 Central Avenue
Genaly Antony, lab., n.s Pearl, b Smith and Park
Genau Adam, stone cutter, 249 Everett
Gener Frederick, s.s. Ohio al., b. 15th and Adams, and Elm and Plum
Gener Herman W., sawyer, 101 Pleasant
Genley Patrick, fireman, n.s. W. W. Canal, b. Park and Smith
Gennon Thomas, tailor, 38 E. 5th
Gensheimer Adam, lab., 46 Buckeye
Gensling Michael, painter, h. 248 Clark
Genter Michael, lab., wks. s.e.c. Canal and Vine
Gentrub Wm., cab. mkr., 16 Hughes
Gentrup Hy., eng., 520 Main
Gentrup John H., eng., 622 Main
Gentsch Lewis, stone mason, 557 Vine
Gentsch Wm., cof. h., 393 Vine
Genty James, rubber, wks. n.e.c. Canal and Elm
Geobel Chas., 49 Clay
Geoble Wm., carp., 207 Mound
George Adolphe. lab., 572 Race
George C. F., clk., 102 Walnut, h. 131 W. 9th
George Charles L., painter, 374 Clark
George Chas. S., foreman Times pressroom, h. 372 Clark
GEORGE D. B. & CO., (Daniel B. G., Wm. H. Barnes, & John W. Kain, Wholesale and Retail Grocers. n.e.c. Pearl and Broadway
GEORGE Daniel B., (D B. G. & Co.,) h. 196 W. 4th
George Frank, lab., w.s. Western Av., b. Bank and Harrison Road
George Geo., lab., wks. 222 E. Front
GEORGE GEO. W., Wholesale Boots and Shoes, 102 Walnut, h. 131 W. 9th
George Rev. H. H., bds 242 Plum
George Hy. B., b.k., 102 Walnut, h. 131 W. 9th
George Henry W., salesman, 16 Main, h. s.s. 9th, b. Freeman and Carr
George Hugh McKane, pilot, e.s. Park, b. Longworth and 6th
George James, pattern mkr., 29 Milton
George Sarah, 325 W. 9th, w. of Central Avenue
George Wm., n.e.c. Ludlow and Pearl
Georgi Adolph C., cab. mkr., w.s. Goose al , b. Liberty and 15th
Geotkamp Mrs. Mary, seamstress, 442 Linn
Geottle Albert, 37 Dayton
Geotlie Joseph, architect, 37 Dayton
Geotlie Joseph, clk., 37 Dayton
Gepfet John, plasterer, 657 Vine
Gepferi John, butcher, 240 Hopkins
Gephart Peter, lab., wks. 76 E. Front
Geppert John, baker, 240 Hopkins
Geppert Michael, 731 Elm
Gerard & Co., (Dewitt W. C. G. & Alfred F. Bramble,) grocers, n.w.c. Pearl and Sycamore
Gerard Dewitt W. C., (6. & Co.,) 76 Pike
GERARD John H., (John H. G. & Co.,) h. Mt. Washington
Gerard John H., jr., deputy clk. Probate Court, res. Newtown
GERARD JOHN H. & CO , (John H. G., David A. Huston & Stephen C. Gerard,) Pork Packers and Commission Merchants, 295 and 297 Broadway
GERARD Stephen C., (John H. Gerard & Co.,) s.s. Richmond, b. Baymiller and Freeman
Gerbe Richard, 593 Elm
Gerber Charles, lab., w.s. Western Av., b. Bank and Harrison Road
Gerber Hy., wks. w.s. Brighton, near Benckenstein's Garden
Gerbhard Andreas, s.e.c. Elm and Findlay [Co.'s
Gerbig Hy., molder, wks. Wm. Resor &
Gerd Krzst, lab., 22 Madison
Gerde Hy., blksmith, 156 Pleasant
Gerdes Bronk, box mkr., e.s. Main. b. Woodward and Franklin 13

Gerdes Hy., cig. mkr., 575 W. 5th
Gerdes John R., 310 Water
Gerdess Herman, clk., 220 Walnut
GERDSEN HERMAN H., Family Grocery and Provisions, 519 Vine
Gerdt Ernst, sawyer, 22 Madison
Gerdewien Caspar, bds. 2 Abigail
Gere Albert H., b.k., 68 Water, h. 495 W. 7th
Gerhard Christian., lab., 198 Pleasant
Gerhard Conrad, 926 Central Av
Gerhard John, lab., 114 Bank
Gerhard John C., drugs, &c., n.w.c. Cutter and Clinton
Gerhard Jno. K., printer, 25 W. 4th
Gerhard Joseph, varnisher, 371 W. 5th
Gerhard Louis, peddler, 496 Linn
Gerhard Wm., butcher, 50 Findlay
Gerhardt Krasmus, carp., 25 Ham. Road
Gerhardt Lewis, carp., 107 Ham. Road
Gerhardt Lewis, pattern mkr., 507 Walnut
Gerhardt Valentine, finisher, 78 12th
Gerhart Hy. teamster, 225 Cutter
Gerhart Joseph, lab., 371 W. 5th
Gerheiser John, baker, w.s. Pancoast al., b. 7th and 8th
Gerhold Louis., cof. h., 240 E. Front
Geringer John. shoe mkr., 540 Plum
Gerke Hy., 424 Freeman
Gerke John F., dray, 53 Pendleton
Gerke Joseph, tailor, 62 Broadway
Gerke Richard, boots and shoes, 426 Freeman
Gerkepott Ernst, cab. mkr., 210 Mound
Gerlach Herman, lithographer, 27 Betts
Gerlach John, carp., 139 W. Court
Gerlach John, cooper, wks. 94 Water
Gerlach Louis, lithographer, 65 Pleasant
Gerlach Philip, cigar mkr., 50 15th
Gerlach Philip, tailor, 10 Walnut
Gerlag John. cooper, bds. 32 E. Front
Gerland Frederick, lab., 38 Hughes
Gerland Hy., hinge fitter, wks. n.e.c. Walnut and Canal
Gerland Hy., lab., 38 Hughes
Gerland Wm., cigars, &c., 146 E. Front
Gerlemann Bernhard H., cooper, n.w.c. 9th and John
Gerling Basil, terra-cotta molder, rear 14 15th
Gerling George, finisher, 458 E. Front
Gerling Hy., lab., 71 Woodward
Gerling Herman, hinge fitter, wks. n.e.c. Walnut and Canal
Gerling Jacob, tailor, 159 Bremen
Gerling Wm., tailor, 459 W. 5th
GERMAN EMIGRANT and Relief Society, s.w.c. Court and Walnut, Nicholas Bosch, Agent
GERMAN GYMNASTIC SOCIETY, Walnut, near Allison
GERMAN MUTUAL INSURANCE Company, 400 Vine, H. A. Rattermann, Secretary
GERMAN SAVINGS INSTITUTE, C. F. Adae & Co., s.w.c. 3d and Main
Germania Fire Insurance Co , agency, 76 W. 3d
Germania Hall, 22 W. Court
Germann Mary, grocery, n.w.c. 12th and Main
Germann Michael, tinner, 435 Walnut
Gernes Robert, dray, 654 Sycamore
Gerold Herman, music teacher, 300 Elm
Gerrahan Pat., lab., 67 Mill
Gerrard Mrs., 239 Barr
Gerretsen John, miller, rear 656 Walnut
Gerrish James, upholsterer, 290 W. Front
Gerrity Thomas, lab., e. s. Fountain b. Rice and Alexander
Gerrott Joseph, cooper, n.w.c. Linn and Findlay
GERRY Arad, (Wooley & G.,) 219 Longworth
Gerry Daniel, molder, bds. Bevis House
Gerry Wm., grocery, 368 Central Av.
Gers Hy., clk., bds. 464 W. 9th
Gers Napoleon, peddler, 137 E. 3d
Gerson Bernard, bds. 334 Vine
Gerst Mrs., n.s. Augusta b. John and Smith

Gerst, Rev. Casper A., 206 Linn
Gerst Frank, shoe mkr., n.w.c. George and Cutter
Gerst Frank A., salesman, s.w.c. Clark and Mound
Gerstle Gustav, clk., 179 Longworth
Gerstle Samuel, teacher, 179 Longworth
Gerstle Wm., musician. 494 Walnut
Gerstner Simon, lab., 124 Pleasant
Gertel Jacob, lithographer, n.w. c. 3d and Main
Gerten Theresa, teacher, 241 Clark
Gerterman Alexander, clothier, 343 Race
Gerth Valentin, cof. h., 110 W Liberty
Gertner Elizabeth, rear 95 Woodward
Gerton Frank, shoe mkr., 241 Clark
Gerty Catharine, rear 206 Cutter
Gerum Jacob, butcher, 11 Mulberry
Gerum John, carp., 143 Buckeye
Gerung Elizabeth, h. 525 Vine
Gerve John B., tailor, 287 George
Gervers Hy., finisher, 133 Linn
Gervers N., mach., wks. n.s. Front b. Lawrence and Pike
Gerves John, Ins. agt., 204 Clark
Gervey Geo., driver, 160 Bank
Gervy John, tailor, e.s. Stone al. b. 5th and Longworth
Gerwe Frederick A. J., phys., 306 Longworth
Gerwe Geo., driver, Bank b. Ailanthus and Freeman
Gerwe Hy., lab., 57 Riddle
Gerwe Joseph. tailor, 636 Vine
Gerwe Mary, dress mkr., 512 Walnut
Gerwe Peter, tailor, bds. 636 Vine
Gerwes John, cigar mkr., 467 Walnut
Gerwin Joseph, lab., s. s. Niles al. b. Main and Sycamore
Gescher Casper, meat store, 799 Central Av.
Gesler Valentine, cab. mkr., 715 Race
Gesling Frank A., boots and shoes, 388 Baymiller
Geschwind Balthazar, tinner, n.s. 13th b. Walnut and Vine
Geschwind Constantine, tailor. 518 Main
Gesendoerfer Sebastian, lab., 246 Pleasant
GESNER ISAAC O., Agent for Grannies, Taylor & Co., Wholesale and Retail Dealers in Oysters, 222 Walnut, bds. Gibson House
Gessart Hy., 29 York
Gessen John, tailor, e.s. Kilgour, b. 3d and 5th
Gessert Jacob, b. k., Cab. Mkrs. Union, h. Cumminsville
Gessner John, cab. mkr., 86 Pleasant
Gest Miss A. H., teacher, Wesleyan Female College
Gest E., office, 101 Main, h. 637 W. 8th
Gest Joseph J., b. k., n.e.c. 4th and Walnut. h. 637 W. 8th
Geszer Christian, carp., h. 714 Vine
Getche Wm., driver, s.e.c. Freeman and Liberty
Getle Joseph, blksmith, h. n.w.c. Ham. Road and Findlay
Getler John. lab., 673 W. 6th
Getler Christian, wks. w.s. Brighton, nr. Benckenstein's Garden
Gettier Thomas J., agt. C. C. & C. R.R. College Bldg., h. 398 W. 7th
Gettier Wm., policeman, 351 Elm
Gettis Frank, meats, n.s. Ham. Road, head of Elm
Gettman Frank, grocery, 213 Cutter
Getz Frank, clk., 47 Pub. Landing
Getty Jas., compositor, wks. Methodist Book Concern
Getz Chas. A., clk., 108 Smith
Getz Christopher, lab., 164 E. Front
Getz Conrad, stove mkr., e.s. Ohio av. b. Corp. Line and North Elm
Getz Ed. J., salesman, 23 W. 4th, h. 108 Smith
Getz Geo. W., b. k., 107 Sycamore, bds. 574 W. 9th
Getz Herman, brewer, n.s. Montgomery Pike, nr. Madison Road
Getz John, b. k., h 108 Smith
Getz Lewis B., clk., 108 Smith
Getz Matthew, pleasure garden, 781 Vine

146 (GIB) CINCINNATI (GIE) DIRECTORY. (GIL)

Getz Samuel, 316 Main
Getzendanner Hy., marble cutter, 162 W. 9th
GETZENDANNER JACOB H., Attorney at Law, 15 W. 3d, h. 135 Smith
Geuer Caroline, servt., 490 Main
Geuff Mary, seamstress, 424 Freeman
Geuter Michael, watch mkr., 141 Buckeye
Gevrin Mary, servt., 124 E. 4th
Geyer's Assembly Rooms, 30 W. Court
Geyer Frederick, 717 Elm
Geyer Geo., butcher, 218 Findlay
Geyer Geo., lab., wks. 180 Poplar
GEYER JOHN, Cabinet Furniture Manufacturer, 8 E. 4th, h. Delhi Tp.
Geyer John, dancing teacher, 30 W. Court
Geyer Joseph, watchman, wks 728 Central Av.
Geyer Lewis. Station House keeper, h. 442 Linn
Geyer Martin, 442 Linn
Geyer Samuel, bds. 34 Longworth
Gfroerer Peter, printer, 422 Bremen
Gfroerer Raphael, express driver, s.e.c. 3d and Whittaker
Ghal Fred., lab., 692 Race
Ghio A. J., confec., 136 Vine, h. s.e.c. Race and Burnet
Ghiradelli Jerome, confec., s.w.c. Pike and 3d
Gialliece Michael, lab , 329 W. 2d
Gialliece Patrick, fireman, 327 W. 2d
Gibbert Mary. servt., 171 E. 3d
Gibbner Geo., eng., 445 Linn
Gibbons Ellen, dress mkr., at 9 Walnut
Gibbons Harriett, 218 George
Gibbons James, b.k., 11 W. 5th, bds. 162 Broadway
Gibbons Jas. T., painter, 218 George
Gibbons John, baker, 129 W. Front
Gibbons John, cof h., 15 Landing b. Broadway and Ludlow
Gibbons John, lab., 131 Front
Gibbons John, lab., 187 Water
Gibbons John E., clk., 460 Broadway
GIBBONS JOSEPH G., Attorney at Law, 35 W. 3d, h. 217 W. 4th
Gibbons Mary, servt., 388 W. 4th
Gibbons Mary A., dress mkr., s.e.c. 6th and Linn
Gibbons Mary A., saloon, River b. Ludlow and Lawrence
Gibbons Thomas, s.s. Yeatman b. Broadway and Sycamore
Gibbs David O., cook, 175 Webb
Gibbs Edward B., carp., 212 Plum
Gibbs H. & Co., (Mrs. H. G. & R. G. Russell,) dye house, 212 Plum
Gibbs Mrs. H., (H. G. & Co.) 212 Plum
Gibbs Ira, 135 Barr
Gibbs John, carp., 218 Livingston
Gibbs Joshua, 246 Broadway
Gibbs Mary, nurse, 56 Richmond b. Plum and Central Av.
Gibbs Sally, seamstress, 208 Livingston
Gibbs Shelby, bds. 144 W. Pearl
Gibbs Thos., s.e.c New and Broadway
Gibbs Wm. H., clk., s.w. c. Main and 2d, bds 315 George
Giblan Mrs. Catharine, 147 Clark
Gibney Chas., carp., 548 Race
Gibner & Hall, (James G. & George H.) flat boat dealers, n.e.c. Race and Landing
Gibner James, (G. & Hall,) 44 Plum
Gibner John, molder, 44 Plum
Gibner Joseph, lab., 200 W. Front
Gibner Samuel, 44 Plum
Gibner Theodore, driver, 44 Plum
Gibner Wm., n. e. c. Richmond and Mound
Gibner Wm. H., pl'ot, 44 Plum
GIBSON & CO. (Stephen G. & Robert H. Gibson), Lithographers and Paper Dealers, n.w c. 3d and Main 466 W. 4th
Gibson Daniel, clk., Adams Express Co. 466 W. 4th
Gibson Daniel. wire weaver. 390 W. 7th
Gibson Daniel W., porter, 266 W. 9th
GIBSON David, (D. G. & Co.) 261 Vine

GIBSON DAVID & CO. (David G., Henry Grotenkemper & W. C. Vanderbilt,) Commission Merch'ts, 48 W. 2d
Gibson, Early & Co. (Henry G., Thomas E. & Wm. Stewart), grocers, 50 W. 2d
Gibson G. B., pass agt., N. Y. Cen. R R. s e.c. Front and Broadway, h. 238 W. 3d
Gibson G. & J., (George & John.) dry goods, 8 W. 5th
Gibson Geo., lithographer, 573 Sycamore
Gibson Geo. (G. & J. G.), 10 Hopkins
Gibson Henry, (G., Early & Co.,) h. Avondale
GIBSON HOUSE, O. H. Geffroy & Co., Proprietors, w. s. Walnut, b. 4th and 5th
Gibson Hugh, wire worker, 370 W. 7th
Gibson Isaac, driver. 107 E. 6th
Gibson Isabella, teacher, 415 W. 3d
GIBSON J. B. & T., (John D. & Thomas.) Plumbers, Brass Founders and Gas Fitters, 200 and 202 Vine
Gibson J. T., bds. Dennison House
Gibson James, molder, wks. Chamberlain & Co's
Gibson James E., molder, 490 Sycamore
Gibson John, 318 W. 3d
GIBSON John, (John G. & Co.,) h. 290 Main
Gibson John, lithographer, 318 W. 3d
GIBSON John B., (J. B. & T. G) bds. Gibson House
GIBSON JOHN & CO., (John G. & Michael Heberger) Practical Plumbers, 290 Main
Gibson John H., agt., n.e.c. Wade and Freeman
Gibson John J., carriage trimmer, bds. 44 Mansfield
Gibson John N., (G. & J. G.) 10 Hopkins
Gibson Mary, 1 York
Gibson Mary, seamstress, 157 Baymiller
GIBSON Peter, (O. H. Geffroy & Co.) Gibson House
GIBSON Robert H., (Gibson & Co.) h. 362 W. 7th
Gibson Stephen, b.k. 13 W. 4th, h. 44 Mansfield
Gibson Stephen, sen., collector, h. 44 Mansfield
Gibson Stephen, jr. artist, bds. 44 Mansfield
GIBSON Stephen, (G. & Co.) 362 W. 7th
GIDSON Thos., (J. B. & T. Gibson) h. 17 Elizabeth
Gibson Wm., 39 Jones
GIBSON Wm., (McCormick, G. & Co.) h. 63 W. 8th
Gibson Wm A., bds. 44 Mansfield
Giddings James, boot stores, 38 Pub. Landing
Giddis James, carp., bds. 199 E. Front
Giehel Hy., carp., 373 Cutter
Giehel Hy., clk., 34 Walnut
Giebel Hy., clk. n.w.c. 4th and Elm
Giebelmeier Fred , hinge fitter, wks. n. c. Walnut and Canal
Giebemeier Rudolph, lab., 36 Hughes
Gienand Geo., 448 Race
Gier John, weaver, bds. 19 Abigail
Giering Hy., distiller, bds. 42 Elm
Gieringer Stanishaus, barber. 41 Race
Giese Barney, shoe mkr , 681 Sycamore
Giese Charles L., agt., grocery, 56 Rittenhouse
Giese Ferdinand, boots and shoes, 63 E. Pearl
Giese Hy., cab. mk., 362 Broadway
Geise John W., lock smith, bds. 7 Mary
Giese Joseph, boots and shoes, 55 E. Pearl
Giese Wm., lab., h. 623 Race
Giese Wm , tailor, 50 12th
Giesecke Chas., tailor, s.w.c. 9th and Central Av.
Gieseking Hy., clk. 70 Main
Giesen Jacob, carriage mkr., 98 Hamilton Road
Gieske Herman, carp., 5 Mary
Gieaker Herman, carp., 5 Mary
GIESTING George, (J. D. & G. G.) 408 Longworth

GIESTING J. D. & G., (John D. & George) Boots and Shoes, 52 W. 5th
GIESTING John D, (J. D. & G. G) 400 George
Giffin Andrew, 20 Rittenhouse
Giffin Ann, seamstress. 424 Freeman
Giffin Chas. M., clk., 20 Rittenhouse
Giffin James A., clk., 20 Rittenhouse
Giffin P. C., grainer, 221 Elm
Giffin Wm., bk layer, rear 133 York
Gifmeier Joseph, lab., rear 512 Walnut
Gilb Joseph, mach., 320 Main
Gilb Mathias, lab , 6'6 Vine
Gilb Mathias, lab., Franz nr. Elder
Gilb Simon, lab., 165 Ham. Road
Gilb Theodore, letter carrier, 491 Walnut
Gilbert Alfred, molder. 77 Abigail
Gilbert Alfred, w.s. Ohio Av. b. Calhoun and North Elm
Gilbert George, boots and shoes, 279 W. 6th
Gilbert Geo. H., stage manager, 24 E. 6th
GILBERT Hy. O., (Smith & G.) 218 W. 4th
Gilbert Jacob P., foreman, 79 Gano
Gilbert James. dairy , 109 E. 6th
Gilbert James. painter, bds 231 Laurel
Gilbert John E., painter, 13 Betts
GILBERT, JONES & OGBORN. (Joseph W. G., Jacob J. & Isaac A. O.) Commission Merchants, 595, 597 and 599 W. 5th
Gilbert Joseph W., Co. Surveyor, office, Court House, h. 77 Bank
GILBERT Joseph W., (G., Jones & Ogborn) 44 W, 9th
Gilbert Josiah, painter, bds. 231 Laurel
Gilbert Richard, painter, 231 Laurel
Gilbert Sere., watch case mkr., h. n.s Front b. Canal and Kilgour
Gilbert Thos., farmer, 111 W. Court w. of Central Av.
Gilbert Warren, auction, n.e.c. Darr and Freeman
Gilday Catharine, servt , 373 W 6th
Gilday Catharine, h. 183 W. 2d
Gilday James, lab., 59 Race
Gilday Mary, servt., 100 E 4th
Gilday Michael, lab., 155 Water
Gildhaus Elizabeth, lab. w.s. Mulberry al. b. Pearl and 3d
Gildhaus Hy., watchman, w.s. Mulberry al. b. Pearl and 3d
Gildhause L. M., bds. Cincinnati House
Gildhos Hy., millstone mkr., n s. Cherry al. b. Race and Elm
Giles Rev. Chauncey, 261 Longworth
Gillolle James, cooper, s.e.c. New and Broadway
Gilford George, n.w.c. 6th and Carr
Gilfoy Dr. Raymond. teacher, St. Francis school
Gilfoy Daniel, porter, Burnet House
Gilfroy Mary, chambermaid, Burnet House
Gilham Alfred, teamster, 110 Water
Gilham Oliver P., salesman 10 Main, bds. Dennison House
Gilhous Geo., driver, 146 Clark
Gilivan James, tinner, wks. 600 and 602 W. 5th
Gilker Wm., harness mkr., wks. 112 Pearl e. of Broadway
Gilkerson H. N., printer, bds. 110 W. 6th
Gilkison H. N., compositor, Cin. Gazette, bds. 110 W 6th
Gill Alice, bds. 59 Gano
Gill Ann, e.s. John b. Betts and Clinton
Gill Bridget, servt., 396 W. 6th
Gill Bridget, 67 Cherry al.
Gill Charles, cof. h., 49 Water
Gill D. L , conductor C., H. & D. R.R., bds. 283 W. 7th
Gill Geo. F., blksmith, 152 Linn
Gill James. clk , 218 W. Court w. of Central Av.
Gill James, tailor, 48 Butler
Gill John, clk., n.s. Augusta b. John and Smith
Gill John, lab., bds. 48 Butler
Gill John, lab., wks 830 Central Av.
Gill John, lab., n.s. Augusta b. John and Smith

(GIL) CINCINNATI (GLA) DIRECTORY. (GLE) 147

Gill Joseph, finisher, w.s. Pancoast al. b. 7th and 8th
Gill M. G., commissary, bds. s.w.c. Race and 3d
Gill Margaret, h. 320 John
Gill N., mach., wks. n s. Canal w. of Elm
Gill Nicholas, planer, 488 Elm
Gill Patrick, lab., bds. 48 Butler
Gill W Capt., U. S. A., bds. Madison House
Gill Winnifred, bds. 48 Butler
Gill Wm. P., clk., 201 W. 4th
Gillan Maria, servt., 564 W. 9th
Gillan O. P., bds. Dennison House
Gillan Patrick, lab., 9¤2 E. Front
Gillard George H., painter, ¤3 Mill
Gillard Wm., bk. store. 182 W. Court
Gillard Wm., carp., 68 Longworth
Gillaspey Mrs Sarah, 190 John
Gillenny Patrick, lab., n.w.c. 3d and Collard
Gillegan Mary, 49 Plum   [man
Gillegan Michael, tinner, wks. 205 Free-
Gillen Archibald, lab., w.s. Ramsey n. of Front
Gillen Mary, dress mkr., 64 Hughes
Gillespie Christopher, peddler, 444 W 3d
Gillespie John W., carp., 138 Clark
Gillespie Wm. F., b k. Franklin Type Foundry, 168 Vine, h. Covington
Gillett Joel, clk. 32 W. 3d
Gillham John, clk , 413 W. 9th
Gillhoff Theodore H . lab., 133 Baymiller
Gilliard N., carp., wks. 304 Broadway
Gillias John, 231 W. 4th
Gillich Louisa, h. 131 Bremen
Gilliece James J., molder, bds. 327 W. 2d
Gilligan Bartholemew, brush mkr., 63 George
Gilligan Bartley brush mkr., 63 George
Gilligan Edward, constable, 84 Butler
Gilligan Eliza, bds. 84 Butler
Gilligan Ellen, 84 Butler
Gilligan James, lab , 183 W 2d
Gilligan Maggie, milliner, 183 E. 2d
Gilligan Michae¹, copper smith, 48 Plum
Gilligan Michael, lab., 13 Commerce
Gilligan Pat., servt., Burnet House
Gilligan Thomas, lab., s.s. 8th b. Harriet and Mill Creek
Gillivan James, tinner, 222 Central Av.
Gillmour Michael, lab., n.w.c. Parsons and E. Front
GILLON JAMES F., Proprietor Stan⁴ix Hall, 7 E. Pearl
Gilman Wm., eng., 153 Baymiller
Gilmartin Anton, 126 E. 6th
Gilmartin Mary, servt , 110 E. 4th
Gilmor Rev Robert. (Pollock & G.) Neave's Bldg., n.w.c. 4th and Race
Gilmore Alfred, lab., e.s. Lock b. 8th and Court
Gilmore & Cordukes, (Edward G. & Jonathan C.) pork packers, e.s. Sycamore b Court and Canal
GILMORE DUNLAP & CO., (James G., Wm. J. D , Thomas G. Robinson, and Edward W. Mullikin,) Bankers, 26 and 28 W. 3d
Gilmore Edward, (G & Cordukes,) h, Belfast Ireland
Gilmore Geo. W., saddler, Henrie House
GILMORE James, (G , Dunlap & Co,) bds. Burnet House
Gilmore Patrick, lab., 12 Hannibal
Gilmore Phoebe, 92 W. Front
Gilmore Thos , stucco worker, 137 Elm
GILMOUR REV. RICHARD, Pastor St. Patrick's Church, n.e.c. 3d & Mill, h. 453 W. 3d
Gilner Frederick, n.e.c. Clifton Av. and Calhoun
Gilp Ferdinand, bar. k., 72 Broadway
Gilp John, cooper, 127 York
Gilp Samuel, barber, 198 Sycamore
Gilpin Charles, b. k. Evans, Gaines & Co., n e.c. Broadway and Court
Gilpin Charles C., teacher, 54 Betts
Gilpin Thomas, planing mill n.s. Miami Canal w. of Elm, h. 130 W. 8th
GILPIN WM H., Commission Merchant, 17 E. Miami Canal, h. 433 Broadway

Gilroy Mrs. Helen, 198 W. 3d
Gilroy James, lab., w. s. Culvert, b. 5th and 6th
Gilroy Robert, carp., 209 W. 4th
Gilsey Henry, cigar mkr., bds. Teutonia Hotel
Gilster Wilhomina, servt., wks. 95 E. Liberty
Gilt Barbara, 767 Vine
Giltenan Daniel, hostler, bds. 163 Central Av.
Gilthaus Christ, cigars, etc., bds. 53 Sycamore
Giltrap Lucy, servt., Burnet House
Gimperling J. E., conductor, bds. Broadway Hotel
Ginan Bartholemew, wks. 340 W. 3d
GINANDT GEO., Saloon 349 Walnut, h. e. s. Race opp. City Park
Ginandt John, fruits. 107 Ham. Road
Ginandt & Rehse, (Wm. G. & Fred R.) cab. mkrs., 148 W. 6th
Ginandt Wm., (G. & Rehse,) h. 464 W. 5th
Gindelin Max, brewer, 740 Vine
Ginder Annie, e.s. Carr, b. 6th and Taylor
Ginder Hattie, bds. 101 Gest
Ginn Wm., clk. L. M. R. R. Depot, h. Newport
Ginochio Angustin, confec., 210 Vine
Ginochio Domonick, confec., 6 E. 3d and 28 E. 5th
Ginochio Louis, confec., n.w.c. Broadway and 6th
Gintert Edward, tailor, 416 Vine
Ginther John, grocery, 182 Clark
Gintman Wm., 210 Hopkins
Giovani Thomas, tailor, bds. 81 Front
Girard Laura, n.w.c. 4th and Sycamore
Girardez Henri, porter, 30 W. 4th, h. 120 Spring
Girden Christ, shoemkr., 559 Race
Girding Henry, shoemkr., 455 Sycamore
Gire John, lab., 68 Water
Gireghty Margaret, 183 Cutter
Girpenpot Hans, cab. mkr., 210 Mound
Girt Ernst, carp., rear 422 Walnut, h. 107 Liberty
Girten Christian, shoemkr., w. s. Race b. 15th and Liberty   [Vine
Girten John, tailor, n.e.c. Liberty, and
Girty John S., R. R. Pass. agt. s. e. c. Broadway and Front, h. Newport|
Girty Wm H. R. R. Pass. agt. s. e. c. Front and Broadway, res. Newport
Girtz Charles, baker, wks 224 W. 6th
Girvin Robert sr , lab., bds. 389 Sycamore
Gislar John, blksmith, wks. 64 E. Front
Gissman Martin, carp., 51 Jones
Git Wm , 157 Linn
Gittermann Anton, tailor. 361 Cutter
Given James, mill wright, 173 Baymiller
Given James, molder, 406 W. 5th
Given John, molder, bds. 297 W. 6th
Given Robert H., b. k 305 W. Front, h. 233 Laurel
Given Michael. lab., s.s. Phoebe al b. Plum and Central Av.
Givens James, pattern mkr., wks. n.e.c. Walnut and Canal
Giveny Michael, express driver, 10 Kossuth
Glaab Adam, meats, 112 Buckeye
Glaab John C., huckster, 35 Elder
Glab Adam, cooper, n.e.c Vine and Allison
Glab Adam P., cooper, 506 Vine
Glab Wm., cooper, 327 Race
Gladden George W., carp., 112 Water
Gladen Henry, tinner, h. n.s. Pearl, b. Pike and Butler
Gladen John B., coppersmith, 33 Observatory
Gladon Bernard, coppersmith, 24 Observatory
Gladwell Geo. W , eng , 850 E. Front
Glaerl Frederick, carp., 24 Hughes
GLAESCHER GOTTLIEB W., Hardware, Cutlery, etc , 534 and 536 Main, h- 144 Spring
Glaeser Frederick, meats. 510 Vine
Glaesner Maria, 540 Sycamore
Glancey Lavinu, milliner, 159 Spring
Glandolf Herman, chair mkr., h. 203 Hopkins

Glandorf Herman, chair mkr., wks. F. Kabeman & Bro.'s
Glannan Pat blksmith, 139 E. Pearl
Glauville Saml , agt., 128 W. 5th, bds. Farmers' Hotel
Glardor John, driver, 3d & 4th Sts. R. R.
Glardor Joseph, driver, Vanhorn b. Freeman and Carr
Glascoe James S., druggist at Wm. G. Davidson's, h. 34 York
Glase Henry J., lab., 606 Race
GLASER & BROTHERS, (Samuel, Lewis. Julius & Max G.) wh. Clothiers, 98 and 100 W. l'earl
Glaser Jacob, cof. h , 417 Main
GLASER Julius, (G. & Brothers,) h. Indianapolis, Ind.
GLASER Lewis, (G. & Bro.'s) 379 W. 6th
GLASER Max, (G. & Bro.'s) 379 W. 6th
GLASER Samuel, (G. & Bro.'s) 357 W. 5th
Glasgow Geo. C., carp., 222 W. 9th
Glasgow Hugh, carp., 134 Race, h. 222 W. 9th
Glasgow John, chair mkr., s w.c, 3d and Wood
Glason James, blksmith, 33 Front b Kelly and Foster
Glass Elizabeth, 27 Longworth
GLASS George C., (G. H. Bussing & Co.) 252 Longworth
Glass Lorenz, grocery, s e c. 3d & Smith
Glass Roberta, b. h. 204 W. 4th
Glass Wm. H., deputy sheriff, 265 W. Front
Glassford Henry A., 408½ W. 9th w. of Central Av.
Glatz Mrs. Pauline, 530 Elm
Glaub Valentine, gunsmith, wks. 134 Main
Glazier Andrew J., cof.h., 178 Central Av.
Glazier Charles A., clk., 405 W. 3d
Glazier John S , dep. agt. Union R. R. Ticket Office, bds. 405 W. 3d
Glazier Wm. B., atty., s.e.c. 9th & Central Av.
Gleason Bridget, servt., 404 W. 6th
Gleason Catharine, 504 W. 3d
Gleason Edward, lab., 64 Pierson
Gleason Ellen, servt., Burnet House
Gleason James, lab., W. 9th b. Harriet & Millcreek
Gleason James, lab., s.s. 6th b. Broadway and Culvert
Gleason John, 26 George
Gleason John, blksmith, 61 Observatory Road
Gleason John, lab., 109 E. 2nd
Gleason John, lab., 64 Pierson
Gleason John, lab., 97 E. 2nd
Gleason Martin, waiter, 110 E. 4th
Gleason Mary, 53 E 8th e. of Lock
Gleason Michael, baggage master, 260 E. Front
Gleason Michael, lab., 64 Pierson
Gleason Michael, lab., 64 Pierson
Gleason Michael, servt., 380 W. 6th
Gleason Patrick, lab., 231 W. Front
Gleasou Thomas, grocery, 587 W. 6th
Gleason Timothy, lab., 16 E. 8th e. of Lock
Gleason Wm., lab., s.e.c. 5th and Butler
Gleeson Michael, stone mason, 559 Sycamore
Gleich Adam P., butcher, n. s. Henry near Elm
Gleich Dolser, drum manuf., 61 Clay
Gleich John F., musical instrument mkr., n.e.c. Walnut and 9th
Gleick Leopold, tailor, 268 Central Av.
Glein George, carp., 64 Stark
Gleiser Timothy, carp, 376 Broadway
Glemser Frederick, carp., rear 480 Walnut, h. 525 Vine
Glenn Alfred, machinist, 13 Betts
Glenn James, lab., 131 W. 7th
Glenn James, lab., rear 830 Central Av.
Glenn James K., room 8 s.w.c. 4th and Walnut, h. 365 W. 7th
GLENN James M., (Wm. Glenn & Sons,) 188 George
GLENN JOSEPH, (Cin. Gazette Co.) h. 382 W. 4th
GLENN Lewis, (M. & L. G.) h. 1206. E. Front

148 (GOD) CINCINNATI (GOH) DIRECTORY. (GOL)

GLENN M. & L., (Milton & Lewis,) Saw Mill and Lumber Yard, 1565 E. Front
Glenn Martin, lab., 27 Commerce
Glenn Mary, 1296 E. Front
Glenn Mary A., e.s. Freeman b.5th & 6th
GLENN Milton, (M. & L. G.) 1569 E. Front
Glenn Nicholas, lab., a. s. Friendship Al. b. Pike and Butler
Glenn Susan, servt., 361 W. 7th
GLENN Omer T. (Wm. Glenn & Sons,) 132 W. Ninth
GLENN Wm. (Wm. G. & Sons,) 328 W. 4th
GLENN WM. & SONS, Wm. G. & James M. Glenn, Richard, Dymond & Omer T. Glenn,) Wholesale Grocers, 70 and 72 Vine
Glennon Mary A., St. Aloysius school, 40 E. 5th
Glenney Auther E., clk., 56 Clark
Glenny Ann, 383 Central Av.
Glenny Wm., paints, &c., 383 Central Av., h. 221 Poplar
Glensman John H.. salesman, 25 Main, h. Prospect Hill
Glescher Gottlieb W., hardware, 144 Spring
Glessner ——— artist, a.s. 6th b. Vine and Race
Gleves Elizabeth, washerwoman, 115 E. 6th
Glicker Michael, finisher, wks.n.e.c.Walnut and Canal
Glindmeyer Frederick, foreman, n. w. c. Baymiller and Wade
Glindmoor Frederick, butcher, n. w. c. Wade and Baymiller
Gling Louis, 34 Mohawk
Glinnen James, lab, 98 Race
Glipfer Gottlieb, glazier, al. b. 13th and Mercer and Vine and Walnut
Glipfer Hy., al. b. 13th and Mercer and Vine and Walnut
Glissman Hy., dray, 26 Jones
GLOBE IRON WORKS, (Worthington & Co.,) 413 W. Front
Gloss Edward, cigar mkr., 405 Vine
Glossner & Bro. (Charles & Daniel A.), brewery, 436 Vine
Glover Joseph, huckster, 131 W. Pearl
Glovercomp Joseph, distiller, bds. 19 Elm
Gluchowsky Jacob S., cab. mkr., 66 Rittenhouse
Gluck Gottlieb, porter, s.e.c. 14th and Bremen
Glueck Geo J., lab. e.s. Goose al. b. Green and Elder
Gluck Gottlieb, lab., 78 Bremen
Glueckert Adam, lab., rear 122 Clay
Glynn Wm., mess., 70 W. 9th w. of Central Av
Gnau Catharine, w.s. Bremen b. Elder and Findlay
Gnewikow Frederick, rope mkr., s.s. Budd b. Harriet and Mill Creek
Goas Edward, pattern mkr., wks. n.e.c. Canal and Walnut
Gons John H., 11 Dunlap
Gobel Jacob, cab. mkr., n.e.c. Freeman and 8th
Gobel Philip, cab. mkr., 153 Carr
Gobel Philip, cab. mkr., 272 Carr
Goble Elizabeth, teacher, h. Dayton nr. Freeman
Goble Wm., carp., 191 Mound, h. 207 Mound
Gobrecht Augustus, musician, 433 Walnut
Gobrecht Christian (Snyder & Co.) s.s. Harrison Pike b. Division & Brighton
Gobrecht Wm., lab., 173 Clay
Gock Hy., driver, 275 Bremen
Gocke August, tobacconist, 78 Abigail
Gocke Peter, cab. mkr., wks. n.w.c. Elm and Pearl
Gockel William, brass founder, 17 Richmond
Gockel Wm., cab. mkr., 17 Richmond
Gockenbach John, painter, 13 Mercer
Goda Hy., cooper, bds. 695 Main
Godar John, steward, 125 Ham. Road
Goddard Catharine, servt., 345 W. 8th

Goddard Joseph A., clk, 61 Longworth
Goddard Richard, cof h., 192 W. 6th
Goddard Mrs. S., 55 Clinton
Godden Sarah W., bds. 458 W. 7th
Goderwis John, porter, 125 W. 2d
Goderwis John H., porter, s.w.c. Main and 2d
Godfrey Mary, s.s. al. b Pike and Lawrence and 3d and Pearl
Goebel Chas., cab. mkr., 557 W. 8th
Goebel Christian, carp., w.s. Goose al. b Green and Elder
Goebel Hy., cab. mkr., 557 W. 8th
GOEBEL HENRY, Coffee House. 584 W. 6th
Goebel Jacob, cab. mkr., 558 W. 8th
Goebel John, painter, 162 Bremen
Goebel John, teacher, 32 Jones
Goebel Leonhard, driver, s.w.c. Pearl & Pike
Goedard Richard, lab, wks. n.w.c. Plum and Wade
Goeddell Hy., molder, 127 Bremen
Goehbinghorst Hy., lab., 461 Sycamore
Goeking George, teacher, E. Front b. Hill and Torrence
Goelkel Adam, furniture, 45½ E. 3d, b. 67 E. Pearl
Goetz Lewis C., baker, e.s. Johnson al. b. Canal and 12th
Goemann Hy. J., cab. mkr., 516, Vine
Goens Robert, lab., e.s. Sycamore b. 7th and 8th
Goepf Valentine, mason, 102 Ham. Road
Goepper Catharine, dress mkr., 510 Walnut
Goepper Chas., dray, 160 Spring
Goepper Herman, student, bds 424 B'dway
GOEPPER MICHAEL, Commission Merchant and Dealer in Hops, 3 Court House, h. 424 Broadway
Goering Hermann, porter, 116 Abigail
Goerkemeier August, porter, 517 Main
Goernand Gottfried, peddler, 8 Buckeye
Goes Frederick carp., 35 Mercer
Goesser Christian, cab. mkr., 747 Vine
Goetce August, salesman, 217 Cutter
Goetle Martha, wks. Hieatt & Wood's candle factory
Goetle Mary A., wks. Hieatt & Wood's candle factory
GOETHEIM Francis (Wernert & G.) 600 Race
Goetke Wm., bk., w.s. Goose al. b. Green and Elder
Goetle Joseph, jr., teller, 25 W. 3d, rooms 17 W. 3d, Selves' bldg
Goetz Andreas, lab., 102 W. Liberty
Goetz Jacob, driller, wks. s.w.c. Elm and Front
Goetz Jacob, lab., 100 Buckeye
Goetz Jacob, lab. 133 Bremen
Goetz John, hostler, bds. 577 Main
Goetz John, lab., 150 Bremen
Goetz John, whitewasher, 417 Sycamore
Goetz John G., cof. h., 507 Elm
Goetz Phillip, cof. h., 357 Ham. Road
Goetze August, brewer, 795 Race
Goetzel Chas., grocery, 572 Race
Goff Mary M., grocery, n.s. Front e. of Kelly
Goff W. D., barber, 120 W. 6th
Goforth Elizabeth H., seamstress, h. 302 W. 3d
Goforth Jemima D., teacher, 10th district school
Gogens Wm., stone cutter, bds 138 Longwort
Goggan Thos., clk., 94 W. 4th
Goggan Wm., clk., 94 W. 4th
Goggans Patrick, blksmith, 78 Race, bds. 58 W. Court
Goggin Wm. H., stone cutter, 138 Longworth
Gogh Frank, cooper, 13 Wade b. Linn & Baymiller
Gogreke Willibald P., 137 Bremen
GOUREVE Christian H. (Mueller & G.) h. 82 E. Pearl
Gohen Richard, 29 Mohawk
Gohen Thomas, 317 Ham. Road
Gohlinghorst Hy., lab., wks. 17 Webster
Gohlke John, shoemkr., bds. 426 Vine
Gohman Dietrich, lab., 105 Woodward

Gohmenn John H., sawyer, 122 Pleasant
Gohn Harris, glazier, e... Gamble al. b. Melanchon and Liberty
GOHS E. & CO. (Elizabeth G. & Herman Stratigher) Staple and Fancy Dry Goods, 478 & 480 Main
GOHS Elizabeth (E. G & Co.) 480 Main
Gohs Hermann, clk., 478 Main
Gohs Joseph H., clk., 478 Main
Gohs Joseph H, sen., bds. 478 Main
Going Hy., teamster, 44 Findlay
Going John H., teamster, 44 Findlay
Goings Nancy, laundress, 116 Avery
Goke Hy., 484 W. 6th
Goke John, blksmith, bds. 218 Clark
Gokel Mary, 174 Charlotte
Gokermann Hy., lab., wks 108 E. 2d
Golau James, painter, 345 Broadway
Golatzke Anna, 71 E. Front
Golcamp Wm., carp., wks 48 E. 8th
Gold Eugene, bds. 339 W. 5th
Gold George, grocery, 70 Martin
Gold Hy. S., salesman, 137 Walnut
Gold John G., s.w.c. 2d and Ludlow
Gold Louisa, 21 Mulberry
GOLD PETER, Family Grocery and Rope Store, s.w.c. 2d and Ludlow
Gold Wm, 273 Cutter
Goldberg Annette, teacher, 323 Vine
Goldberg Jacob, clk, 167 Sycamore
GOLDBERG JOSEPH, Agent for Myer Goldberg, Pawn Broker, 323 Vine
Goldberg Leopold, 16 W. 8th
Goldberg Mary, seamstress, 22 Woodward
GOLDBERG MYER, Pawnbroker, Office, 173 Vine Joseph Goldberg, Agent
Golde John, tinner, 541 Main
Golden Ann. 345 Central Av
Golden David, tailor, 63 E. 8th
Golden Elizabeth, 686 W. 6th
Golden Geo., clk., 172 Elm
Golden Hy., tanner, 111 W. M. Canal
Golden Isaac (Estate), grocery, 172 Elm
Golden Mary, teacher, 713 Elm
Golden Mary, w.s. Butler b. E. Pearl and Front
Golden John, lab., 60 W. Front
Goldenberg Richard, cigar mkr., bds. 252 Walnut
Goldenberger John, millinery, 429 Vine
Goldgreve Herman, stone cutter. 517 Sycamore
Goldman Flora, w.s. Pancoast al. b. 7th and 8th
Goldmeier Wm., cooper, n.e.c. York and Baymiller
Goldmeyer Hy., dray, 19 Dudley
Goldmeyer Wm, cooper, n.e.c. York and Baymiller
Goldreiner Xenophon, cab. mkr., s.s. W. W. Canal b. John and Smith
Gohlschmidt Abraham, 103 Longworth
Goldschmidt Hy., rags, 39 Adams
Goldschmidt John B., lab, 68 Hunt
Goldschmidt Jos., store keeper, Burnet House
Goldschmidt Levy, peddler, 116 W. Canal
Goldschmidt Phillip, dray, 60 Hunt
Goldschmit Marcus, 52 Elder
Goldsmith Benj., second-hand store, 639 Central Av
Goldsmith George, harness mkr., 103 W. 3d
Goldsmith Israel, jeweler, 384 W. 7th
Goldsmith Joseph, carp. wks. 34 E. 5th
Goldsmith Joseph, clk., 98 13th
Goldsmith Leopold, jeweler, 446 Main
Goldsmith Michael, peddler, 146 Everett
Goldsmith Nathan, 546 Race
GOLDSMITH Nathaniel, (Chas. Davis & Co.) 55 W. 9th
Goldsmith Nicholas, meats, 206 W. Liberty
Goldsmith Samuel, clk., 78 12th
Goldsmith Sarah, 16 Race
Goldsmith Solomon, salesman, 78 W. Pearl, h. 30 Grant
Goldson Thos., carp., 14 Hannibal
Goldstein David, glazier, 485 Walnut
Goldstein Wm., clk, n.e.c. Public Landing and Sycamore

Goldsticker Herman, daguerreotypist 53 Bremen
GOLDSWORTHY Thomas, (Cotteral & G.) s.s. Dayton b. Freeman and Coleman
Goldthwaite Frank, lab. bds. 12 E. Front
Goldvogel Samuel, butcher, 97 St. Clair
Golegly James, n.s. 6th b. Culvert and Broadway
Gollar Andrew, driver, 589 Plum
Gollenstein Joseph, barber, 45 E. Front
Gollinger Frederick. bakery, s.e.c. Baymiller and Central Av
Gollmer Hugo, lithographer, 516 Walnut
Golsch Chas., cigar mkr., 552 Elm
Goman Hyppolite, mach., 501 Plum
Gominger J. & Co., (Jacob G. & Jacob Albert,) yawl builders, 704 E. Front
Gominger Jacob J., (G. & Co.) 752½ E. Front
Gonder Margaret, laundress, n.w.c. 2d and Broadway
Gonzalez Francis, cigar, mkr, bds. 80 E. 5th
GOOCH CHAS., Hardware and House Furnishing Goods, 353 Central Av h. College Hill
Good Burcell, grocer, 364 W. 8th
Good Frederick, policeman, 529 Elm
Good James, clk. Quarter Master's Office U.S.A.
Good James lab, al. h. 4th and 5th and Central Av. and John
GOOD John. (Babbitt, G. & Co.) w.s. Ellen b. 3d and 5th
Good John, huckster, 96 W. Court
Good John, mach., wks., n.s. Front b. Lawrance and Pike
Good Louisa, wks. Hieatt and Woods candle factory
Good Matthew, cof. h. 462 Race
Good Michael, 399 W. 3d
Goodale Samuel D., n.s. Oregon, b. 3d and 5th
Goodall Ann, 119 Everett
Goodall Catharine, 13 Clinton
Goodall Geo., foreman, 268 Main
Goodall James, stone cutter, 121 Everett
Goodall Joseph, bk. layer, e.s. Hanover b. Woodward and Franklin
GOODALL WM. Marble Works, 244 W. Court
Goodberlt F., tanner, 664 Elm
Goodbrad John L, eng., 17 Betts.
Goode Burwell P., phys., 304 Baymiller
Goode Burwell S.. (Wm. H. Thompson & Co.) 364 W. 6th
Goode Harmon, tanner, 293 Linn
Goode Thomas J., painter, 6 North
Goodell Hy., molder, 127 Bremen
Goodell Rich., eng bds. Sportsman's Hall
GOODHART J. H. & CO. (Julius H. G. & Chas. Hyman.) Produce and Commission Merchants. 7 W Front
GOODHART Julius H., (J. H. G. & Co) 335 W. 6th
Goodheart Arnold, (Leopold & G.) 45 W. 8th
Goodheart Caroline, dress mkr., bds. 335 W. 6th
Goodheart Wm. (Leopold & G.) 125 W. 8th
Goodhue Daniel F., (G. & Co.) h. Storrs Tp.
Goodhue & Co., (Daniel F. G. & Saml. Williamson.) foundry n.w.c. Plum and Commerce
Goodhue Cornelia, 631 W. Front
Goodhue Fire Insurance Co., agency 76 W. 3d
Goodhue Geo. W. 165 Plum
Goodin James, Office 13 W. 4th, h. 330 Vine
GOODIN Saml. H., 'Prest. Dayton & Cin. (short line.) R. R. Co.. office 13 W. 4th, b. Delhi Station
Goodin Wm. I., b. k. 226 Main, h. 330 Vine
Gooding James, lab. bds. 60 Baum
Goodman Adolph, (G. & Vornholz,) 4 E. 7th
GOODMAN Chas. (T. S. G. & Co.) res. E. Walnut Hills
Goodman Conrad, foreman 145 Clark

Goodman Frank. clk. 65 W. 3d, bds. s' e.c. 6th and Race
Goodman Hannah, 672 Central Av
Goodman Israel, tailor, 8 E Front
Goodman Jacob E., bds. 362 John
Goodman Rose, servt., Burnet House
Goodman Roanna, 46 Sycamore
Goodman Samuel, tailor, 156 W. Frout
Goodman Simon, peddler, 542 Main
GOODMAN T. S. Notary Public, Office 17½ W. 3d, Selves Bldg res. E. Walnut Hills
GOODMAN T. S. & CO. (Chas. G & Wm. A. G.) Office 17½ W. 3d, Selves Bldg
Goodman & Vornholz, (Adolph G. & J. Hy. V.) clothing 307 Main
GOODMAN Wm., Prest. Washington Ins. Co., 41 Main, h. 330 W. 4th
GOODMAN Wm. A., (T. S. Goodman & Co.) cashier Bank of the Ohio Valley, h. E. Walnut Bills
Goodman Abraham, 18 Gano
Goodmann David, peddler 542 Main
Goodnough Erastus P., b. k. s.w.c. Main and 5th, h. 256 Richmond
Goodoff A., mach,, wks. n.s. Front b. Lawrence and Pike
Goodrich Chas. T., salesman, 95 W. 3d
Goodrich Hy., bds. 123 W. Court w. of Central Av
Goodrich John, bridgebuilder, 142 Linn
Goodson Edward W., phys. n.w.c. 3d and Plum.
Goodwin Alex, bakery 43 Public Landing
Goodwin James S., dray, 170 Linn
Goodwin Samuel W., clk. 43 Public Landing
Goose Hy., tailor, bds. Galt House
GOOSMANN Fred., (G. & Nietert.) 87 W. Court
GOOSMANN & NIETERT, (Fred. G. & Hy., N.) Wines and Liquors, 133 W. Court
Goosterholt Geo., boots and shoes, 11 12th
Goprever John, lab., 70 Abigail
Gordon A. Eliza, teacher, Eastern Av above Selas
Gordon Andrew J. (Brischo & G.) 95 W. 5th
Gordon Catharine, servt, 12 Arch
Gordon Eliza, laundress 187 W. 3d
Gordon Geo., awnings &c., 150 Sycamore
Gordon Harriet, 63 E. 7th
Gordon Hy., clk., bds. 369 W. 9th w. of Central Av
Gordon James, lab., 448 George
Gordon James, oil manuf., n.w.c. 4th and Lock, bds. Broadway Hotel
Gordon John, compositor, Cin. Gazette, h. 18 Hannibal
Gordon John M. H., paper carrier 565 W 9th
Gordon Jonathan B., s.s. Front e. of Selas
Gordon Nathan, whitewasher, 234 Longworth
Gordon Nettie, 266 Baymiller
GORDON Oliver F., (W. J. M. Gordon & Bro.) 292 Richmond
GORDON ROBT., Coal Yard, s.w.c. Front and Miami Canal and n.w.c. Miami Canal and 6th, h. 10 8th Street Hill
Gordon Robert, lab., 614 E. Front
Gordon Thos., printer, bds. 18 Hannibal
Gordon Wm, 35 Webb
Gordon Wm. painter, n.e.c. 5th and Lock
GORDON Wm. J. M. (Wm. J. M. G. & Bro.) 292 Richmond
GORDON WM. J. M. & BRO. (Wm. J. M. G, & Oliver F. G.) Druggists and Pharmaceutists, n.e.c. 8th and Central Av. Laboratory 107 E 8th
Gorges Christian, lab., e.s. Fountain, b, Rice and Alexander
Gorges Hy., lab., 12 Hughes
Gorien Patrick, cof. h. n.w.c. Race and Water
Goringflo Peter, tanner, 95 Ham. Road
Gorman Barney, lab., 614 W. 8th

Gorman Catharine, rear 24 W. Court w. of Central Av
Gorman Catharine, s.s. 6th b. Broadway and Culvert
Gorman Edward J., carp., s s. David, b. John and Cutter
Gorman Ephriam J., carp. 12 David
Gorman Hanora, servt., 182 Broadway
Gorman Hugh, shoe mkr., 187 Cutter
Gorman James, shoe mkr., bds. 65 W. 5th
Gorman James J., painter 45½ E. 3d h. 26 New
Gorman John, cof. h. 179 W. Court
Gorman John, lab., 592 E. Front
Gorman John, lab., bds. n.w.c. Front and Central Av
Gorman Lawrance, tailor, 8 W. 3d, h. W Covington
Gorman Margaret, lab., w.s. Pike b. Pearl and 3d
Gorman Michael, lab., wks. n.w.c. Plum and Wade
Gorman Patrick, lab. 13 Providence
Gorman Patrick, lab. wks. n.w.c. Plum and Wade
Gorman Pierce, clk. w.s. Ailanthus, b. Bank and Clearwater
Gorman Rose, 5½2 E. Front
Gorman Thos., cof. h. s.w.c. Court and John
Gorman Thos., lab., 183 W. 2d
Gorman Wm., auctioneer 192 W. 6th
Gornall Ellen, 445 W. 4th
Gornall Hy., molder, bds 445 W. 4th
Gornger Theresa, servt. 79½ Pike
Gornham Joseph, awning mkr. 114 Sycamore
Goronfio Peter, lab. 95 Ham. Road
Gorrer John, cof. h. 17 Poplar
Gorrien Hy., cof. h. 78 Water
Gorsley John, tailor 564 and 586 Race
Gorsuch Howard. 149 Spring
Gorsuch Lowry F, hatter 129 Spring
Gorton Anson, exp. agt., bds. 354 W. 8th
Gorton E. B., clk. Adams Express Co., bds. 107 Pike
Gosenmeier Ann, w.s. Goose al. b. Green and Elder
Goshen John G., blksmith, 372 W. Liberty
Goshen Frank B., molder, bds. 138 Longworth
Goshorn Alban O., clk. 383 Central Av, b. n.e.c. 8th and Cutter
GOSHORN Alfred T., (Mills & G.) 380 W. 8th
Goshorn Nicholas, 380 W. 8th
Goshorn Oliver, mer., 380 W. 8th
Gosiger Frederick J., grocery, s.e.c. George and Cutter
Gosker Joseph, (Hathrew & G.) 103 Carr
Gosling Alice, bds. 90 Barr
Gosling Frederick, grainer, 402 Longworth
GOSLING JOHN W., Carriage Manufacturer, s.w.c. 6th and Sycamore, h. 417 Freeman
Gosling Margaret, servt., 496 Main
Gosling Thomas, blksmith, 69 Hunt
Gosman A., bds. Dennison House
Gosinger Joseph, molder, 83 Spring
Gospol Frederick, cab. mk., 25 Clinton
Goss Frederick, carp., rear 480 Walnut
Goss L. W., teacher, 207 Mound
GOSSAGE Chas., (DeLand & G.) bds. Burnet House
Gossin ——, blksmith, bds. n.e.c. 7th and Central Av.
Gossin Benj. F., at J. B. Green & Bro's, res. Storrs Tp.
Gossin Hy. H., blksmith, h. 484 W. 8th
Gossman John F., mess. Ky. C. R.R., 27 Elizabeth
Gost Ilyncinthe, seamstress, 72 Abigail
Gosterder Margaret, 93 12th
Goszler John, lab. 29 Peete
Goszmann Hy., lab., 600 Elm
Gotfried Ruppert, cooper, 174 Charlotte
Gothart Daniel, servt., 419 W. 6th
Gotlieb Hy., bk. mkr., 12 14th b. Central Av. and Plum
Gotlieb Jacob, 63 Longworth
Gotsweiler John, lab, 267 Cutter
Gott Frederick, lock smith, 92 Clinton

150   (GOW)   CINCINNATI   (GRA)   DIRECTORY.   (GRA)

Gott Hy. A., clk P. O., 29 E. 7th
GOTT Herman J., (H. Schrader & Co.) h. Covington
Gott Hubert, lock smith, 92 Clinton
Gott Sarah, n.s. Sloo w. of Freeman
Gottlehoede Bernhard H., grocery, 113 Woodward
Gottemiller Hy., shoe mkr., bds. 484 W. 5th
Gotthewit Daniel, coachman, rear 204 Richmond
Gotlheim Francis, grocer. 610 Race
Gotti John, cof. h., 35 W. 3d, h. s.e.c. 8th and Walnut
Gottkamp Hy., bds. s.e.c. Elm and Findlay
Gottlieb & Bro., (Joseph & Solomon) clothiers, 1107 Central Av.
Gottlieb Caroline, 58 Providence
Gottlieb Catharine, 58 Providence
Gottlieb F. A., clk. 73 W. 4th
Gottlieb Hannah, 311 Main
Gottlieb Joseph, (G. & Bro.) 1107 Central Av.
Gottlieb Simon, peddler, 103 W. Liberty
Gottlieb Solomon, (G. & Bro.) res. Sacramento, Cal.
Gottman Augustus, 403 Central Av.
Gottman Philip, clk, 455 Main
Gottman Wm., tailor, 9 Wade b. Elm and Plum
Gottmoller Julia. servt., 20 Hathaway
Gotto John, 44 Pub. Landing
Gottschalk Conrad, carp., 543 W. 3d, b. s.w.c. 3d and Wood
Gottschalk Frederick, cof. h., 982 Central Av.
Gottschalk Gustaf, carp., bds. s.w.c. 3d and Wood
Gottschink Robert. ments, 523 W. 8th
Gotzell Wm., porter, 50 15th
Gotzinger Andrew. turner, 406 Clark
Gouben Mrs. Catharine, midwife, 53 W. Liberty
Gould Michael, 331 W. 6th
Gould Alice, servt, 103 Pike
GOULD Charles H., (G. & Wells & G. Pearce & Co) 304 John
GOULD GEO. W., Produce and Commission Merchant, 11 and 13 E. 9th, h. 263 W. Court w. of Central Av.
Gould J. N., salesman 69 W. 4th, b. Newport
GOULD John, (Peris, G. & Co.) 278 W. Court w. of Central Av.
Gould John, bklayer. 332 George
Gould John B., clk 11 E. 9th, h. 263 W. Court w. of Central Av.
Gould John P., office 25 W. 3d, h. Mt. Auburn
Gould John Q., supt. at I. & B Bruce's w.s. Baymiller b. Poplar and Liberty
GOULD, PEARCE & CO. (C. H. G., James P. & Henry P.) Manufacturers and Dealers in Cotton Goods, n.w.c. 5th and Lock, warehouse 43 Walnut
Gould R., (Patrick & G.) res. New York City
GOULD & WELLS, (Charles H. G. & W. W. W.) Manufacturers and Dealers in Cotton Goods, 46 Walnut
Goull Wm., agt., 44 Stone
Gould Wm., carp., n.s. Kemper's Lane b. Hugh and E. Front
Gould Wm. H., gauger, 12 W. Front, h. 483 W. 7th
Gould Wm. S., salesman, 15 E. 9th
Goulding S. P , law student, bds. 179 Broadway
Goule Frederick, clk., 178 York
Gouryeon Edward, steward, 26 Abigail
Gouvion John. blksmith., 21 W. 7th
Gove Charles G., clk., bds. 566 W. 8th
Gove Louisa, 456 W. 8th
Gove Mary, 460 W. 8th
Gove Wm. H., salesman 194 Main, h. 466 W. 8th
Gow John. polisher, s.e.c. New and Broadway
GOW & SHARP, (Walter G. & Jos. S.) Belting and Hose Makers, 63 Walnut
Gow Thomas, cab. mkr., 137 Webb
GOW Walter, (G. & Sharp) 266 Clark

Gowan Edward, 231 Central Av.
Gowzing Hy., blksmith, wks. n.e.c. Canal and Walnut
Goydet John H., cof. h., 687 Central Av.
Gozzolo Simuel, fruit stand n.e.c. 4th and Walnut, h. 155 W. 5th
Graab Geo., tailor, 168 Sycamore
Grabbage Nicholas, cof. h., 63 Vine
Grabee Hy., finisher, wks. n.e.c Walnut and Canal
Grabee Peter, finisher, wks. n.e.c. Walnut and Canal
Grabeng Philip, lab., s.e.c. Bank and Baymiller
Grabenstein Charles, mattress manuf., 224 Central Av., h. s.s. 15th b. Elm and Pleasant
Grabfield Philip, 68 W. Pearl, h. 86 E. 3d
Grabham James, plumber, 232 W. Court
Grabuth George, lab., h. s.s.s. Taylor b. Carr and Harriet
Grace Catharine, 83 Barr
Grace Mary, servt., 168 Broadway
Grace Robt. A., clk., 376 W. 7th
Gracey Robert Capt., bds. s.e.c. Sycamore and 5th
Gradel Andrew, shoe mkr., 13 Moore
Gradel John, boots and shoes, 587 Walnut
Grady John, dray, 585 W, 5th
Grady John, lab., 81 Baymiller
Grady John, lab., Mt. Adams
Grady John, paper hanger, 45 Betts
Grady John, stone cutter. 58 Hunt
Grady Martin, lab., 366 Broadway
Grady Mary, s s Phoebe at. b. Plum and Central Av.
Grady Mary, servt., Burnet House
Grady Michael, lab., 928 E. Front
Grinly Patrick, lab., 21 E. 8th
Grady Patrick, dray, 585 W. 5th
Grady Thomas, hostler, bds. 81 Baymiller
Grady Thomas, lab., h. w.s. Central Av. b 2d and W. W. Canal
Grady Timothy, lab., 368 Broadway
Graebe Frank, butcher, s.s. Sloo w. of Freeman
Graef Frank, baker. 72 Allison
Graemer Francis, tailor, s.s. Liberty b. Vine and Race
Graenland Herman M., map mounter, 1 Court House Bldg., b. 250 Walnut
Graeser Lewis, teacher, n.w.c. Vine and Longworth
Graeser Wm., varnisher, s.w.c. Allison and Main
Graeslin Chas., cof. h., 435 Vine
Graf Adam, blksmith, 34 Harner
Graf Albert, 67 Webster
Graf Andreas, instrument mkr., bds. 47 12th
Graf Anthony, cigar mkr., 290 Hunt
Graf Catharine, 105 Ham. Road
Graf Chas., cab. mkr., wks. 71 W. 5th
Graf Chas., cigar mkr., wks. 405 Vine
Graf Chas., varnisher, 406 Vine
Graf David, sergeant-at-arms Co, Clks. Office
Graf Elizabeth, 76 E. Front
Graf Guerinus, tailor, 601 Sycamore
Graf Joseph, cof. h., 209 W. 6th
Graf Joseph, shoe mkr., 26 Schiller
Graf Leonard, shoe mkr., 712 Vine
Graf Nicholas, butcher, 67 Elder
Graf Nicholas, agt., 97 Buckeye
Graf Norbert, nail mkr., 1104 Central Av.
Graf Peter, porter, wks. 341 Walnut
Graf Theresa, servt., 595 Vine
Grafe F., salesman, bds. w.s. Race and 3d
Grafe Ferdinand, clk. 69 E. Pearl, bds. 70 Sycamore
Greif Bernhard, teamster, 301 W. Front
Grafeukamp Hy., blksmith, 67 Spring
Graff Alexander C., coal yard s.e.c. Central Av. and 2d, bds. Broadway Hotel
Graff Andrew, tinner, 99 Barr
Graff Benjamin, salesman, bds. 569 W. 5th
Graff Charles F., 49 E. 4th
Graff Daniel, lab., wks. n.e.c. Park and Marsh

Graff Herman A. W., bk. mkr., 47 Rittenhouse
GRAFF Jacob, (Jacob G. & Kohl) 282 Longworth
GRAFF JACOB & KOHL, (Jacob G. & Chas. C. K.) Auctioneers and Commission Merchants, 20 E. 4th
Graff Joseph H., waiter, 91 E. 3d
Graff Paul C., mess. Am. Exp. Co., bds. Broadway Hotel
Graff Philip, 357 Ham. Road
Graff Valentine, lab., wks. Hieatt & Wood's
Graff Wilhemina, 47 Rittenhouse
Graffansteeler Barbara, 995 Central Av.
Graft Andrew, weaver, 15 Ham. Road
Graft Jacob, driver, s.s Front b. Smith and John
Gragan Patrick, lab., 21 Kilgour
Graham Anna M., h. 328 W. 6th
Graham Barney, fireman Clifton House
Graham Bartholomew, 35 New
GRAHAM Charles, (C. G. & Bro.) Harriet nr. 8th
Graham Chas., shoe mkr., 327 Cutter
GRAHAM CHARLES & BRO., (Charles & Robert) Blacksmiths, 277 W. Front
Graham Chas. F., janitor, n.w.c. 6th and Walnut
Graham Daniel A., (W. M. Graham & Co.) h. Covington
Graham Elizabeth, 135 E. 6th
Graham Geo. W., b.k. Spencer House
Graham James, plys., 119 W. 7th, bds. Gibson House
Graham James, grocery, 131 Hopkins
Graham Lida, bds 9s George
Graham Michael bar k. 71 W. 3d
GRAHAM Robert, (Chas. Graham & Bro.) 405 W. 3d
Graham Wm., foreman, 328 W. 6th
Graham Wm. lab., 178 Water
Graham Wm. M., (Wm. M. G. & Co.) 64 Laurel
Graham Wm. M. & Co., (Wm. M. G. & Daniel A. Graham) grocers, 4 and 5 Commercial Row
Grahn Chas., gilder, 533 Walnut
Grahn Lewis, painter. 533 Walnut
Graim John, lab., 14 Surgent
Grainger George, shoe mkr., n.s. Railroad e. of Vance
Grainger Wm., driver, bds. 188 E. Pearl
Graman John, painter, n.e.c. Carr and W. W. Canal
Gramann Caroline. 94 Bremen
Gramann Elizabeth, bds. 94 Bremen
Gramer Hy., porter, 81 Spring
Gramer Joseph, stone cutter, n.s. Goose al. b. Liberty and 15th
Gramke Hy., lab. bds. 34 Abigail
Gramkow Mrs. Mary, h. 229 E. 5th
Grammlich Henry, lab., 625 15th
Grammer Barney, cooper. s.s. Hopkins b. Linn and Baymiller
Grampp Michael, janitor, 44 Jackson
Gran Chas., carp., 674 Race
Granberger Frederick, peddler, bds. 442 Main
Grandin Wm. S., 57 E. 4th
Grane Jacob O., peddler 103 Clinton
Graney Peter, lab., 170 E. 3d e. of Collard
Graney Thos., baggage master I. & C. R. R., bds. 511 W. Front
Granger Major R. R., 101 E. 3d, bds. Clifton House
Granger Wm. W., b.k., 12 W. 8th, h. Newport
Graninger P. Joseph, patterns, &c., 233 Central Av
Graninger Peter J., soda water, 53 Pub. Landing, h. Newport
Grannam Joseph, bds. 243 W. 5th
Grannemann Caroline, bds. 134 Ham. Road
Granner Elizabeth, servt., 393 Vine
Granner Margaret, 108 Ham. Road
Grannin James, cof. h., n.e.c. 9th and Central Av
Grant Alex, carp., 68 E. Pearl
Grant Amanda, servt., 37 McFarland
Grant Hiram. dray, 9th b. Harriet and Millcreek
Grant Jacob L., plasterer, 222 Freeman

(GRA) CINCINNATI (GRE) DIRECTORY. (GRE) 151

Grant James B., broker, 39 Walnut, h. n.w.c. Harriet and 7th
Grant John, (Grant & Pittman) 230 Main
Grant Mary 182 E 6th
Grant & Pittman (John G. & Isaac A. P.), printers. 8 W. 3d
Grant Samuel S., trader, 113 Dudley
Grant Thos., bds. 113 Dudley
Grant Wm., b.k., 508 W. 9th
Grant Wm. W., dray, 596 W. 3d
Grapevine Absalom, furnace man, 572 E. Front
Grapevine Geo., furnace man, 29 E. 3d e. of Parsons
Grapevine Hudson, 29 E. 3d e. of Parsons
Grapevine John, eng., 590 W. 6th
Grapevine John, eng., n.s. 3d b. Wood and Canal
Grapperhaus Henry, carriage mkr., n.s. 13th nr. Walnut
Grapperhaus John, CO 13th
Grarsh Ann. 154 Richmond
Grascain, William, cooper, bds. 504 W. 3d
Grasin Mary, 19 15th b. Central Av. and Plum
Grason Wm. M., shoe mkr., 282 Baymiller
GRASSELLI EUGENE, Proprietor Cincinnati Chemical Laboratory, Junction of Pearl and E. Front
Grassenger Margaret, 33 E. 8th e. of Lock
Grassmuck A., tailor, 168 Pleasant
Grasson Deborah, 54 W. Front
Gratbitch Hamlet, 502 Linn
Grater Christian, bakery, 71 E. Front
Gratwohl Aaron, peddler, 378 Elm
Grau George, tailor, 97 E. Pearl
Grau Julius, wire cage mkr., 692 Main
Grautmann Frederick, hair mat manuf., rear 15 E. Liberty
Grautner Geo. F., mach., 58 Hunt
Grave Edward, clothier, 139 Abigail
Grave Mary, servt , 130 E. 4th
Grave Wm., cab. mkr., 17 Providence
Grave Wilhelm C., wooden shoe mkr., 37 Observatory
Gravenger Joseph, blksmith 502 John
Graver John, eng , wks. n.s. Front b. Lawrence and Pike
Graves George, varnisher, 402 Longworth
Graves Henry, shoe mkr., 207 W. Court w. of Central Av
Graves Hiram D., clk., bds. 31 George
Graves Mary, s.e.c. Freeman and W. W. Canal
GRAVESON & CO., (Isaac G., Wm. Graveson & Peter Beall) Cincinnati Stone Works, s.e.c. 3d and Lock
GRAVESON Isaac, (G. & Co) 286 Richmond
Graveson Wm. sen., lock smith, 20 Linn
GRAVESON Wm. jr., (G. & Co.), 20 Linn
Gravis Henry, box mkr., 71 Abigail
Graw Hermann, lab , 180 Pleasant
Grawe Anna, servt , 395 Broadway
Grawe Bernhard, (G. & Hullman,) 131 Bank
Grawe & Hullman. (Bernhard G. & Theodore H.), com. mers., 424 Race
Grawe Wm., cab. mkr., wks. s.w.c. Canal and Elm
Grawey Dorney, 131 Bank
Grawey Joseph, grocery, 136 Bank
Gray Anna D., 217 Longworth
Gray Anna M., teacher, 207 Barr
Gray Darlington, shoe mkr. 276 Hopkins
Gray David. expressman, 144 W. Pearl
Gray Frederick, saddler, 150 Everett
Gray George A., b.k., 66 Gest
Gray Geo. A., Jr., mach., bds. 66 Gest
GRAY, HEMINGRAY & BRO. (Ralph G., Robt. H & Sam. J. H.), Flint Glass Manufacturers, 20 E. 2d
Gray Henry, lab., wks. n.w.c. 4th & Lock
Gray James, porter, 136 W, Front
Gray James H., tinner, 439 W. 6th
Gray Jane, 35 Milton
Gray John, formn. 439 W. 6th
Gray John, pilot, 277 W. 7th

Gray John, tinner, 207 Barr
Gray John D., tinner, 439 W. 6th
Gray John E., clk. L. M. R. R. Depot, res. Loveland
Gray John M., real estate, 189 w. 4th
Gray Jno. N., tinner, 207 Barr
Gray John R., 211 Everett
Gray Louisa. 38 Elder
Gray Melchior W., clk., 120 W. 2d
Gray O. P., clk.. 69 W. Front
Gray Phebe, 61 Mound
GRAY Ralph, (Gray, Hemingray & Bro.), res. Covington
Gray Rev. Richard, h. 221 Richmond
Gray Richard, tailor, 127 Barr
Gray Thomas, drover, w.s. Western Av. b. Bank and Harrison Road
Gray Thomas, lab., s.s. Weller b. Carr and Freeman
Gray Wm. C., clk., 17 W. Front, h. Covington
GRAY WM. I., Commission Merchant, 17 W. Front h. Covington
Gray Wm. T., b. k.. bds. 66 Gest
Graybill Emanuel K., clk., s.w.c. Pearl and Walnut
Graydon Alexander, cashier I. & C. R. R. freight depot. h. 302 Longworth
Graydon Alexander, clk. I. & C. R. R., 392 Longworth
Grayman Elizabeth, servt., 235 W. 4th
Grayson Edward S., shoe mkr., 104 Longworth
Graywink Margaret, 74 Abigail
Gready Martin, brass molder, bds 174 E. Pearl
Greany Thomas, mess. O. & M. R. R., bds. Dennison House
Greany Timothy, painter, 228 Elm
Grear Robert D., butter dealer, 94 Longworth
Grear Mary, talloress, 462 W. 8th
Groasa George, cof. h.. 227 E. 5th
Greatrick Elizabeth. 81 Betts
GREAT WESTERN COAL & OIL CO. of Newark. Ohio, H. Worthington. Pres., F. A. Savage, Secy., Office 13 W. 4th
Great Western Despatch, John McCune, agt., 122 W. 4th.
Grebenstein Chas.. mattrasses, 234 Central Av. h. 67 15th
Greble Joseph R., cooper, 49 Commerce
Grebner J no., co oper, 267 Cutter
Greble/Wm., jew ly, 517 Vine
Grebs John F., tailor, 15 E. 3d e. of Parsons
Grebuhl John, butcher, n.s. Harrison Pike b. Brighton and Western Av
Greeble Mrs. & Bro. (Mrs. Mirium G. & Nathan Malzer), dry goods, 331 Central Av
Greeble Miriam, (Mrs. Greeble & Bro.), bds. 331 Central Av
Greeg John, conductor, bds. Brighton House
Greely Hiram F., pattern mkr., bds. 174 E. Pearl
Green A. H., porter, 57 W 4th
Green Alanson, clk., bds. 31 W. Front
Green Albert G., blksmith, 1272 E Front
Green Alex, saddler, wks. 242 Main
Green Alfred, lab., s.s. Front w. of Hill
Green Ann M., 200 W. 3d
Green Mrs. B., seamstress, 91 Sycamore
Green Bartholomew, 99 W. Court w. of Central Av
Green Belle, servt., n.w.c. Longworth and Central Av
Green Benjamin, bds. Clermont Hotel
GREEN Chas S.. (J. B. Green & Bro.), h. Storrs Township
Green Columbus W., lab. 313 W. Liberty
Green Elizabeth, 305 Race
Green Elizabeth, talloress, bds. 214 W. Front
Green Frank. lab., w.s. Anderson b. 3d and Pearl
Green Frank, porter, Broadway Hotel
Green Frederick, carp., 50 Melancthon
Green Geo., (Geo. & John) 203 Plum
Green, (George & John), boots and shoes, 201 Plum
GREEN Jared B., (J. B. G. & Bro.), Storrs Township

GREEN J. B & BRO.. (Jared B. & Chas. S), Railroad Chair & Spike Manufacturers, 4 Pub Landing
Green Jacob, cap mkr., 375 Central Av
Green James, cof. h., 151 Culvert
Green James E., mill w ight, 10 Clinton
Green Joel, bds. 305 Race
Green John, e.s. Campbell al. b, Elder and Findlay
Green John, (George & John G.), 107 George
Green John, boots and shoes, 142 Vine, bds. Pearl St. House
Green John, driver, wks s.e.c. Grant and Plum
Green John, lab , 67 Cherry al.
GREEN John K., (Thos. W. Farrin & Co.), res. Carthage
Green John W., 65 Abigail
Green Julia, s.s. 6th c. of Lock
Green Leroy A , teller A. L Mowry & Co. s, h. 214 W 4th
Green Lizzy, servt., 237 Walnut
Green Miletus, teacher, 187 Longworth
Green Moses, cooper, s.s. 8th b. Broadway and Sycamore
Green N., lab., wks. n.s. Front b. Lawrence and Pike
Green Nath, bell hanger, bds. 170 W.4th
Green Ory, s.s. Front w. of Hill
Green Richard H., sheet iron worker, 79 E. Front
Green Robert, molder, wks. n.e.c. Canal and Walnut
Green Robert B. (Quinlan & G.), 176 Race
Green Robert C., broker, 183 E. 3d
Green Russell, 1523 E. Front
Green Silvester A., b. k., 251 W. 4th
Green Solomon L., phys., 1521 E. Front
Green Thomas J , chair mkr., 235 W. 3d
Green Wm., coal yard, 1313 E. Front, h. 1523 E. Front
Greenbach Mrs., 92 W. Front
Greenbaum Moses, huckster, 20 Providence
Greenbrier Fanny, servt., 51 Stone al.
Greenburg August, eng., 10 Commerce
Greenbury Wm., harness mkr., wks. 208 Main
Greene Anne. teacher, 66 Milton
Greene Caleb B , druggist, 24 E. Pearl, h. 9 George
Greene Chas. A.. lamps, &c., 184 W. 5th, res. Walnut Hills
Greene Ellhue, 264 Baymiller
GREENE John H., assistant editor Catholic Telegraph, s.w.c. Vine and Longworth, h. 137 Race
Greene Lewis H., clk., 49 E. 2d, bds. 9 George
Greene Math., dray, 171 Baymiller
Greene Miss Sarah, teacher, 66 Milton
Greene Wm., 66 Milton
Greene Wm., 165 W 7th
Greene Wm. S., clk., 49 E. 2d, res. 9 George
Greener John C., mach., s.s. Ham. Road nr. Pleasant
Greenfield Fred., tinner, rear 569 Sycamore
Greenfield Mary, rear 569 Sycamore
Greenfield B., chair mkr., wks. John Mitchell's
Greenfield Hy., tailor, 424 Sycamore
Greeninger Christian tinner, 44 Linn
Greenland Paulina, b h., 236 Walnut
Greenleaf Emma, bds. 204 Plum
Greenleaf Mrs. Henry L , music teacher, s.w c. 3d and Broadway
Greelee John, riverman, bds. 10 Sycamore
Greenlees Archibald, sexton, 86 12th
Greenlees Colin, clk., 41 W. 4th, h. 86 12th
Greenlees John, carp., n.s. Dayton b. Western Av. and Coleman
Greenlees Wm., 89 E. Front
Greenless J., carp , wks. 701 Broadway
Greenless Wm., clk., 101 W. 4th, h. 80 12th
Greenlow Elizabeth, servt, h. 12 Cutter
Greenough John, bds. 98 Broadway
Greens Mrs. M., h. 27 Gano
GREENWALD Ezra, (I. & E. G.) 239 E. 5th, c. of Lock

152 (GRE) CINCINNATI (GRI) DIRECTORY. (GRI)

GREENWALD I. & E., (Isaac & Ezra,) Iron Foundry and Machine shop, n.w.c. Pearl and M. Canal
GREENWALD Isaac, (I. & E. G.) 483 W. 4th
Greenwald John, phys., 998 Central Av.
Greenwalt Wm., lab., 101 Martin
Greenwood Jas. F., 74 Abigail
GREENWOOD MILES, Eagle Foundry and Machine shop, n.e.c. M. Canal and Walnut, res. Avondale
GREENWOOD MILES & CO. (Miles G., Chas. R. Folger & Nelson Gates,) Manufacturers of Hardware, 396 Walnut
Greer Fred., lab., 89 12th
Greese Chas., finisher, n.e.c. Walnut and Canal
Gref Elizabeth, 71 E. Front
Greger Hy., turner, n.w.c. 2d and Smith Newport
Gregg Daniel, blksmith, w. s. Sycamore b. Hunt and Abigail
Gregg Elias, blksmith, 123 Betts
Gregg Harriett, 54 14th
GREGG & HARVEY, (Jno. M. G. & Joshua H.,) Real Estate Agents and Brokers, 19 W. 3d
Gregg Harriet J., teacher, 55 Betts
GREGG Jno. M., (G. & Harvey,) 188 W. 4th
Gregg Theodore E., salesman, 91 W. Pearl, h. 188 W. 4th
Gregg Wm. L., n.s. Corp. line, near Auburn
Gregor John, driver, n.s. al. b. Poplar and Vine, and Ham. Road and Buckeye
Gregory Amanda C., 112 Broadway
Gregory Anna, tailoress, bds. 355 Central Av.
Gregory Dudley, 112 Broadway
Gregory Hannah, 18 New
Gregory Saunders, junction High and Kemper's Lane
Gregson John, cof. h., 182 W. 6th
Gregson John, lithographer, 182 W. 6th
Gregston Samuel, trader, 47 Cutter
Greefenkemp Bernard, (Kessing & G.) 92 Clay
Greiffer Louis, 29 Providence
Greig Frank, eng., 10 Whiteman
Greiz John, lab, 138 Oliver
Greiker Wm., 64 Stark
Greilich Martin, baker, 501 Sycamore
Greemann Michael, carp., 299 Clark
Greeman Nicholas, carp., 299 Clark
Greiner ——, cab. mkr., bds. 225 W. 6th
Greiner Fred., (G. & Mueller,) 128 Walnut
Greiner John, cab mkr., 493 Vine
Greiner & Mueller, (Fred. G. & Ludwig M.) glass blowers, 24 E. 4th, (up stairs)
Greiner Peter, glass blower, w.s. Bank al. b. 3d and 4th
Greinner George F., 503 John
Greis John, painter, 578 Elm
Greiselbach Edward, teacher, 69 Clay
Greiser Michael, s.s. Henry b. Elm and Dunlap
Greivenkamp Hy., tailor, 53 Pine
GREIVING G. H., Family Grocery, s.w.c. Elm and Longworth
Greivy Hy., cab. mkr., 145 Baymiller
Greiwe Christopher, (Born & G.,) 530 Walnut
Greiwe E., clothing, 353 Main, h. 139 Abigail
Greiwe Hy., b. k., 70 Abigail
Greiwe John H., lumber, Hunt e. of Broadway, h. 70 Abigail
Greiwekamp Bernhard, lab., rear 94 Clay
Grells Bridget, 50 Race
Grem Mat. dray, 171 Baymiller
Grema David, lab., 127 Betts
Gremaessan Jacob, varnisher, bds. 170 Clinton
Grene John H., grocer, 61 Mill
Greps Mary, servt., 54 Franklin
Gresch Hy., lab, 5 Linnaeus
Grese Margaret, servt., 322 George
Greser Wm., varnisher, 577 Main
Greshof Gerhard H., wagon mkr., bds. 229 W. Liberty

Greskamp Hermann, tailor, 123 W. Liberty
Greslin Carl, wines. &c., 348 Main
Gress Lewis, mason, 57 Hamer
Gresse Joseph, marble works, n.s. Betts b. Linn and Baymiller
Gresser Geo., bar k., 25 Moore
Greswold Thomas E., druggist, 329 Cutter
Gretsch John, cooper, 54 Buckeye
Greule Lawrence, porter, Pearl b. Pike and Butler
Greulitz Adam, porter, St. Nicholas Restaurant
Greuzer Christian, cab. mkr., 568 Race
Greve Adam H., 378 Broadway
Greve Gerhard, 372 Broadway
Greve Hy., baker, 130 Pleasant
Greve J. C. D., cutter, 64 W. Pearl, h. Newport
Greve John G., eng., 47 Pendleton
GREVE THEODORE L. A., Drugs, Medicines, &c. s.e.c. John and 6th
GREVER Frank, (Kleine, Hegger & Co.) 11 Jackson
Grevers John, harness mkr., bds. Phœnix Hotel, 17th ward
Greves Geo., painter, 402 Longworth
Grew John, dray, 559 Sycamore
Grewald Hy., tailor, 404 Vine
Grewe Edward J., varnisher, 477 W. 3d
Grewe Geo., grocery, 665 Vine
Grewe Hy., shoe mkr, 25 Commerce
Grewe Henry C., clk., 65 E. Pearl bds. Cincinnati House
Grewe Theresa, 128 Clay
Grewe Wm., 70 Hunt
Gribus Hy., clk.) 12 Wilson
Grielig Agnes, 129 Linn
Grielig Clemmons, finisher, bds. 129 Linn
Grienberger John, saddler, bds. 249 W. 6th
Grienewald Valentine, lab., 111 Buckeye
Grienneger Chas., 242 Ham. Road
Grierson Robert C., actor, 245 W. 6th
Griese Benj. H., com. mer., 3 Com. Row, h. s.s. Everett b. Linn and Baymiller
Griese Christian, meats, 84 Buckeye
Griese Emily, 169 Pleasant
Griese Joseph, porter, 108 Clinton
Griese Samuel, porter, 138 Walnut, h. 16 Madison
Griesenberger Hy., clk., bds. 205 W. Front
Grieshaber John, instrument mkr., n.e.c. Walnut and Allison
Grieshaber Lewis, lab., 120 Pleasant
Griesheimer Jacob, cof. h., 359 Ham. Road
Griest E. H., (Lukens & Co) bds. Walnut St. House
Grietz Daniel, wagon mkr., n.s. Ham. Road b. Dunlap and Hamburg, h. 361 Ham. Rond
Grieumard Chas., prof., 97 Mound
Grieumard Julius, b.k., bds. 97 Mound
Grieve Adam H., s. e. c. Abigail and Broadway
Grieve Christoph., mineral water manuf. 70 Abigail
Grieve John, lab., 137 Bremen
Grife Wm., blksmith, wks. 108 E. 2d
Griffey Mrs. David, 108 Broadway
Griffin Patrick, lab., w.s. Lebanon Road b. Liberty and Corp. Line
Griffin Patrick, lab, h. n.s. Montgomery Pike nr. Reading Road
Griffig Ernst J., bakery. 106 Buckeye
Griffin A. D., tel. op, 131 Longworth
Griffin Anna, bds. 71 Baker
Griffin Chas., asst. baggage master, C.H. & D. R.R. depot, 561 W. 5th
Griffin Conrad, lab, 513 W. Front
Griffin Harvey, lab., 207 Plum
Griffin James lab., 451 W. 2d
Griffin John, bds. 102 E. 3d
Griffin John, binder, bds. 203 W. Front
Griffin John, expressman, 153 W. Pearl
Griffin Mary A., seamstress, 137 Linn
Griffin P. J., grainer, 120 Cutter
Griffin Patrick, huckster, 92 W. Front
Griffin Thos., blksmith, n.e.c. Plum and Water

Griffin Thos., lab., 196 Water
Griffin Thos., lab., Torrence, nr. Front
Griffis Mary, 60 Everett
Griffith Alex., teamster, 1564 E. Front
Griffith David, Sr., carp., 51 Barr
Grifuth David, Jr., carp., 51 Barr
Griffith G. P., clk., 171 Vine, h. n.e.c. 8th and Plum
Griffith Geo. T., printer, 14 Jane
Griffith Hannah, book-folder, 108 W 6th
Griffith James T., carp., h. 136 E. 5th
Griffith John A., (John A. G. & Co.,) bds. Burnet House
GRIFFITH JOHN A. & CO., (John A. G. & James O'Neil,) Importers and Dealers in Tailors Trimmings, s.w.c. 4th and Walnut
Griffith John S., builder, 19 Elm
Griffith Michael, 108 E. 6th
Griffith Robert, barber, 6 E. 2d, h. 25 McAllister
Griffith Saml., cab. mkr., 23 Elizabeth
Griffith Saml , cof. h., 31 W. Front
Griffith Smith A., druggist, 51 Broadway
Griffith Thomas, dray, n.s. Sloo, E. of Harriet
Griffith Thomas, molder, foot of Harrison
Griffith Thomas H., butcher, 5 Harrison Pike
Griffith W., clk, bds 31 W. Front
Griffiths Catharine, 31 Harrison
GRIFFITHS GRIFFITH, Tea Dealer, n.w.c. 5th and Central Av., h. 201 Longworth
GRIFFITHS JOHN, Gun and Pistol Manufacturer, 165 Main, Residence Walnut Hills
Griffiths Richard, clk., n.w.c. 5th and Central Av., bds 201 Longworth
Grigg Jacob, driver, 181 Clinton
Griggs Lewis, pork packer, 80 Plum, h. 477 W. 5th
Griggs Otis, waiter, bds. 59 E. Pearl
Grigois Christopher, cof. h., 180 Buckeye
Grillo Joseph J., confec., 232 W. 5th
Grim Anton, tailor, rear 64 Hunt
Grim John, horse-shoer, wks. 152 W. Court
Griman Hy., bds. Pennsylvania Hotel
Grimer Wm., painter, 247 Clark
Grimes Hiram B., clk., bds. 31 George
Grimes Kate, bds. 138 W. 8th
Grimes Wm., 212 Walnut
Grimm Catharine, tailoress, 570 Walnut
Grimm Dina, servt., 19 Abigail
Grimm Dominick, lab., 530 John
Grimm Dorothy, 56 Kossuth
Grimm Gallus, (Koehnken & Co.,) 27 Schiller
Grimm John, molder, 147 Bremen
Grimm Joseph, 10 13th
Grimm Michael, prop. Ludlow House, n.w.c. 2d and Ludlow
Grimm Nicholas, tailor, 570 Walnut
Grimme Barney, 189 Hopkins
Grimme Bernhard, cigar mkr., bds. 514 Main
Grimme Harmon, cof. h , 7 Landing, b. Main and Walnut
Grimme Herman H., tailor. 46 Buckeye
Grimme Lena, servt., 508 Main
Grimmeisen Nicholas, cab. mkr., 299 Clark
Grimmelsmanh Frank, fam. grocery, n.w.c. 5th and Hannibal
Grimmelsmann John H., painter, 19 Franklin
Grimmer Conrad, eng., 295 W. Front
Grimmer Peter, lab., bds. 73 E. Front
Grimmer Thos., waiter, 28 W. 6th
Grimmmlger Lewis, soup mkr., 102 W. Liberty
Grimshaw James, mach., 202 W. Court
Grindley Wm. T., carriage mkr., bds. 120 E. 5th
Grinkemeyer Herman, hinge molder, wks. n.e.c. Walnut and Canal
Grinston Robert, lab, s.w.c. 6th and Broadway
Grinthal Christopher H., 16 Buckeye
Grintkemeier Hy., finisher, 14 Allison
Gripner John, (Peter, Jacob & Co.,) w. s. Cutter, b. Betts and Laurel

(GRO) CINCINNATI (GRO) DIRECTORY. (GUD) 153

Grischy Hy., cigar mkr., 1015 Central Avenue
Grisenbrocker Mrs. F., 593 Elm
Grisenbrocker Philip, cigar mkr., 593 Elm
Griser John, stone cutter, bds. 24 Woodward
Grisman Mathias, carpet weaver, 121 York
Griswold Geo. H., com. mer., 313 George
Griswold Thomas H., clk., 52 W. 2d, h. 329 Cutter
Grive Hy. J., cab. mkr., 145 Baymiller
Groaf Andrew, instrument mkr., s.s. 12th, b. Vine and Race
Groat D. B., conductor, bds. Burnet House
Groat Francis, salesman, 152 E. 3d, e. of Collard
Grob George, lab., w s. Freeman, b. Findlay and Dayton
Grob John, bds. 624 Vine
Grob Michael, tailor, 681 Race
Grockowitsch Bartemas, tailor, 209 Wade
Grocott John, potter, 376 W Liberty
Grodder Hy., bar k., bds. 445 Main
Grode George, cab. mkr., s e.c. Jones and Melancthon
Grode John H., cab. mkr., 90 Melancthon
Grodhaus Hy., cab. mkr., 497 Elm
Grodhaus Mary, 41 Race
Groe Hy., dray., 63 Pendleton
Groene Frederick H., (Rothert & G.), s.w.c. Race and Cherry al
Groene John H. F., grocery, 43 Race
Groenefeld Benjamin, chair mkr., 593 Race
Groener John, eng., 243 Ham. Road
GROENEWOLD John, (F. C. Deckebach & Co.), 171 W. Court
Groesbach Jennie, servt., 126 E. 4th
Groesbeck John, office 68 W. 3d, h. 178 W. 7th
GROESBECK WM. S., Attorney at Law, 21 W. 3d, h. 163 W. 7th
Groeser Louis, teacher of gymnastics, 150 Clay
Groetze August, porter, 217 Cutter
Groetsicki Anthony, 19 14th
Groetzinger John, brewer, 31 Bremen
Groezinger John, brewer, wks. e.s. Walnut, b. Ham. Road and Liberty
Grof Daniel, driver, 468 W. 3d
Groffs Hy., dray, 26 Mansfield
Groff Wm. T., physician, 400 W. 4th
Grogan Bridget, n.s. E. Front, e. of Leatherbury
Grogan John, cartman, 172 Cutter
Grogan Lawrence, lab., n.e c. River and Ludlow
Grogan Richard, dray, 161 Gest
Grogur Theodore W., grocer, 411 W. 8th
Grogg Aldrich, lab., 150 Clay
Groh Jacob, tailor, 18 Hamer
Groh Peter, express driver, 19 Ludlow
Groha Geo., tailor, 239 Hopkins
Grohss Hy., carp., n.e.c. Court and Elm
Groll Geo., stone cutter, bds. 556 Walnut
Grondemann Fred., shoemaker, rear 50 Webster
Groneweg Frederick, grocery, 501 Walnut
Groneweg Hermann, constable, 49 Allison
GRONEWEG LEWIS, Druggist and Chemist, s.w.c. Court and Walnut, h. 61 Webster
Gronninger Anna, 148 Laurel
Gronotte Barney, grocery, s.w.c. Union and Race
Groof Benjamin, clk, bds. 569 W. 5th
Groom A. D., painter, wks. 27 W. 7th
Groom J. A., coach mkr., 21 W. 7th
Groom Thomas, lab., 162 John
Grooms Richard, carp., 186 Cutter
Groot Geo. R., supt., 52 E. 6th
Groover John, cab. mkr., n.s. Railroad, e. of Kelly
Gros Hy., baker, wks. 43 Pub. Landing
Gros Joseph, finisher, 55 Elder
Grosardt Geo., shoe dealer, 410 Freeman
Grossardt Marie, grocery, 168 Clay
Grosenbrink Wm., chair manuf., rear 15 Mercer

Groskopf Theresa, servt., 339 W. 8th
Groskordt Hermann, 48 Dunlap
Grosman Adam, harness mkr., bds. Dennison House
Grosman Peter, harness mkr., bds. Dennison House
Grosmink Michael, cooper, 95 York
Gross A., bds. 701 Elm
Gross A., Vice Pres. D. & M. R.R., 5 College building, h. Glendale
Gross Albert, cooper, wks. 830 Central Avenue
Gross Charlotte, 55 Webster
Gross Chas., painter. 117 Bremen
Gross Chas. C., baker, wks. 118 W. 5th
Gross Chas. W., clk., 136 Walnut, bds. 248 Race
Gross Conrad, cooper, wks. 330 Central Avenue
Gross Conrad, lab., 91 Findlay
Gross Frederick, cab mkr., w.s. John, b. Pleasant and Oliver
Gross Frederick, meat inspector, 10 Pleasant
Gross George, lab., 4 Hughes
Gross Hy., lab., 515 E. Front
Gross Jacob, boots and shoes, 77 W. 5th, h. 79 W. 5th
Gross Jacob, driller, wks. s.w.c. Elm and Front
Gross Jacob, lab., 173 E. Front
Gross Jacob, lab., 146 Clay
Gross Jacob, varnisher, rear 432 Sycamore
Gross Lizzie, servt., 329 George
Gross Joseph, finisher, wks. s.w.c. Elm and Front
Gross Peter, huckster, 17 Clinton
Gross Peter, shoemkr. bds. 524 Sycamore
Gross Philip, lab., 34 Peete
Gross Rev. T., 123 Longworth
GROSSIUS JOHN, Tin and Coppersmith, 33 W. Court
Grosskopf Barbara, shoe store, w.s. Baymiller b. George and Barr
Grossman Adam, molder, n.s Augusta b. John and Smith
Grossman Joseph, tanner, n.s. Front w. of Hill
Grossman Wm., 50 Wade
Grossmann Bertha, teacher, 50 Wade
Grossmann Geo., lab., bds. 19 Abigail
Grosvenor Mason, atty., n.w.c. 6th and Walnut
Grosz Frederick, shoemkr, 605 Elm
Grosz Jacob, lab., 85 Pleasant
Grosz Philip, cab. mkr., 129 Ham. Road
Grosz Philip, dentist, 143 Ham. Road
Grossheim Joseph, sawyer, 137 Pleasant
Grossmann Geo., lab., 106 Buckeye
Groszmann Herman C., actor, 519 Walnut
Groszmann Julius, actor, 403 Vine
Groszmann Louisa, servt., 81 Bremen
Grote Bernhard, lab., 13 Mill
Grete Catharine, h. 13 Hunt
Grote Charles, lab., 13 Hunt
Grote Clemens, grocery, s.w.c. Linn and Hopkins
Grote Ernst, lab., 53 Pleasant
Grote Gerhard, 55 Biddle
Grote Hy., finisher, w.s. Main b. Canal and 12th
Grote Hy., street sprinkler, 379 Broadway
Grote John F., upholsterer, 106 Pleasant
Grote Joseph, varnisher, 52 McFarland
Grote Tony, 361 Broadway
GROTENKEMPER Hy. (David Gibson & Co.) h. Spring Garden
Groters Hy., cab. mkr., 56 Rittenhouse
Groth Bernhard, cab. mkr., bds. 514 Main
Groth John, finisher, wks. Crane, Breed & Co's
Grothaus Hy., bds. 179 Baymiller
Grothaus Herman, lab., h. 209 Wade
Grothaus Mary, servt., 385 Sycamore
Grothe & Barning (George G. & Barney B.) feed store, 770 W. 6th and 267 Freeman
Grothe Bernhard tailor, rear 103 Woodward
Grothe George (G. & Barning), 770 W. 6th

Grothen John, blksmith, rear 680 Main
Grothoff John, grocery. 399 Sycamore
GROTHUES JOSEPH H., Coffee House, 494 Main
Grothues Ludwig A., groceries, (42 Elder
Grotiann Mrs. Margaret, dairy, 6 Miami
Grotjohn Frank. finisher, n.s. Court b. Vine and Walnut
Grotkass August, cooper, 54 Dudley
Grotlische Hy., bar k., 571 Vine
Grotluech Hy., s.w.c. Vine and Liberty
Grottendieck Hermann, teamster, 12 Orchard
Grouse Andrew, lab., n.s. Rice, head of Fountain
Groutman Hy., mer. tailor, 76 W. Front
Grove August, shoemkr, 209 Elm
Grove Hy., shoemkr, 25 Commerce
Grove Margaret Ann, 62 Webster
Grover B., lab., wks. Hughes & Foster's
GROVER & BAKER'S Sewing Machine Co. G. D. V. Rollo, Agent, 58 W. 4th
Grover John H, phys., 443 Sycamore
Grover Wm., baker, bds. 143 Linn
Groves Noah, 573 Central Av
Groves Stephen, carp., rear 956 E. Front
Groves Wm. J., scale mkr, s.e.c. Broadway and Milton
Grow John, 151 W. Pearl
Growe Mrs. ———, midwife, 122 Abigail
Growe Bernhard, 122 Abigail
Growe Joseph, wagon mkr, 173 Hopkins
Growar Clara, rear 70 Hunt
Groweg Fred., driver, 400 Sycamore
Gruala Lorenz, clk., n.s. Pearl b. Pike and Butler
Grubb John, clk., 56 W. 3d
Gruber Fridolin, tailor, 642 Elm
Gruber Wm., rope mkr, w.s. Carr b. 7th and 8th
Gruenstein Abraham, peddler, 530 Elm
Gruenthal Hy., cooper, 703 Main
Gruese Herman, porter, 16 Madison
Gruesser Benedict, cof. h., 633 Vine
Gruesser David, mason, 635 Vine
Grueter Wm., jeweler, bds. 371 W. 5th
Gruimme Bernard, cigar mkr., bds. 514 Main
Gruiter Gerhard, paper carrier, 371 W. 5th
Gruka Frank, lab. 90 E. 2d
Grumbine Jeremiah, trunks, &c., 204 Vine, h. 308 Linn
Grumman Chas. H., b,k.. 20 Pub. Landing, h. 149 Longworth
Grummon Ichabod, clk., h. 435 W. 5th
Grundhoefer Chas., confec., 630 Vine
Grundhofer Lewis, finisher, n.e.c. Race and 15th
Grundhoefer Peter W., clk., 105 Pleasant
Grundner Andrew, grinder, 39 Ham. Road
Grundy James, lab., 420 W. 2d
Grundy John, bds. 441 W. 2d
Grunkemeier John, shoemkr., n.w.c. Pearl and Central Av
Grunkemeyer H. & J. (Hy. & Joseph), saloon, n.w.c. W. W. Canal & Central Av
Grunkemeyer Hy. (H. & J. J. G.) n.w.c. Central Av. and W. W. Canal
Grunkemeyer Joseph, (H. & J.J.G.) n.w. c. Central Av. and W. W. Canal
Gruner Jacob, lab., 105 E. 2d
Gruner Robt., tobacconist, w.s. Bank al. b. 3d and 4th
Grunthal Hy., cooper, 694 Main
Grantzes John, cab. mkr., 512 Plum
Grupia Frederick, lab., 160 Carr
Grussel Hy., tailor, 218 John
Grusz Wm., cutter, 397 Elm
Grutges John, carp., 512 Plum
Gryden Hans P., carriage mkr., 20 Dayton
Gschwend Franz, lab., 154 Baymiller
Gubel Gabriel, cof. h., n.e.c. 6th and Walnut
Gud Peter, express driver, 82 Pleasant
Guddle Patrick, lab., E6 Front
Gude August, cigar mkr., 61 Dudley
Gude John, lab., 70 Water
Gudgeon Hiram, carp., s.s. Front b. Foster and Kelly

Gudgeon Wm. (Barr & G.) junction of Torrence and R.R.
Gudhart Herman, tailor, 126 Gest
Gudmann August, finisher, 22 Orchard
Guelich Jacob, 33 Arch
Guelich John W., saloon, 153 Central Av
GUELICH Lewis, sec'y, fire dept., office 192 George, h. 194 Longworth
Guenter Geo., tailor, 163 Buckeye
Guenter Hy., porter, h. s.s. Court b. Walnut and Vine
Guenther Conrad, lab., 122 Mohawk
Guenther Elizabeth, seamstress, wks. 154 Bremen
Guenther John S., lab., 138 Mohawk
Guenther John, jr., 138 Mohawk
Guenther Lewis, lab, 620 Vine
Guenther Nicholas, lab., w s. Goose al. b. 14th and 15th
Guerin Hy, W., b.k., Western Union Telegraph Co.
Guerin Laurence, b.k., 217 Richmond
Guerin Mathias, tailor, 97 E. 7th
Guerin Matthew, tailor, e.s. Crippen al. b. 7th and 8th
Guertler Peter, cab. mkr., 64 W. Liberty
Guesler August, butcher, 666 Race
Guess Catharine, 105 W. Front
Guest M. K., cooper, wks, 33 Lock
Guethermann Barbara, bds. 636 Vine
Guethlein John, tailor, 29 Elder
Guetle Joseph, blksmith, 165 Ham.Road
Gugenberger Charles, grocery, 717 Elm
Guggenheimer Sarah, 348 Main
Guhan Jeremiah, lab., 135 E. 6th
GUHE HENRY, Merchant Tailor and Clothier, n.e.c. Central Av. and Front
GUHL EDWARD, Queen City Exchange, n s 8th b. Freeman and Carr
Guhmann Jacob, cof. h., 491 Vine
Guhmann John, trader, 112 W. Liberty
Guhrauer Oscar, clk., bds. 142 Sycamore
Guibert Benjamin J., b k., 124 Main, h. 323 W. 3d
Guilan Edward, lab., 47 E. 3d
Guild Ann M., h. 354 W. 8th
GUILD Charles(L. B, Crittenden & Co.) 156 Livingston
Guild Geo., cooper, n.s. Miami Canal b. Main and Walnut, h. 443 Main
Guild H. M., clk., 101 W. 4th, h. 248 Race
GUILD Joseph (Hinkle, G. & Co.), h., Walnut Hills [mnn
Guilfil John F, contractor, h. 239 Free-
Guilford Chas. C, teacher, 54 Betts
GUILFORD GEO. J., Clerk, Office Board City Improvements, h. 509 W. 8th
Guilford Harriet E., teacher h. 54 Betts
Guilford June, dry goods, 363 W. 5th
Guilford M., clk., L. M. R. R, rooms 39 W. 4th
Guilford Nathan, clk., bds. Spencer House
Guilfoy Francis, lab., 301 John
Guilfoyle Daniel, lab., 75 E. 8th, e. of Lock
Guilfoyle James, cof. h., 62 E. 8th e. of Lock
Guiling Phillip, lab., 155 Everett
Guillerme Chas., tailor, 374 Broadway
Guillon Antoine, macaroni mkr., 374 Walnut
Gulman Fabian, bk.binder, bds. 426 Vine
Gulmner Thos jr., waiter, Burnet House
Guin John, clk , U. S. Express Co
Guin Wm., carp., 400 W. 7th
Guinan Wm., blksmith, 181 Plum
Guinan Wm., paver, 13 W. Court w. of Central Av
Guinean Wm., blksmith, 65 Butler
Guinen Mrs. Sarah, 522 John
Guion Chas. H , b.k., Adams, Peckover & Co., bds. 90 Perry
Guion David D., 164 W. 9th
Guion Eliza J , t acher, 104 W, 9th
Guion Peter C., bed fastener manuf.,257 W. 7th, h. 255 W. 7th
Guion Wm. A., b.k., 19 W. 4th, h. 20 Perry
Guiterman Alex. (Loewenstein & G.) 348 Race

Guiterman Emil, b.k., 82 W. Pearl, bds. 117 W. Court
GUITERMAN Frederick, (Cohen, G. & Co.) bds. 117 W. Court
Guiterman Henrietta, 271 W. 8th
GUITERMAN Joseph, (Cohen G. & Co) 54 W. 7th
Guiterman Marks, (G. & Sulzbacher,) h. 84 W. 8th
Guiterman & Sulzbacher, (Marks G. & Hy. S) clothiers 60 W. Pearl
GUITERMAN Wm., (Cohen, G. & Co.) 117 W. Court
Gukelberger Geo. cof. h. 462 Walnut
Gulde Joseph, carp., 490 Race
Gulden Chas., carp, 600 Race
Gulden Francis, saddler, 561 Vine
Guler Joseph, cab. mkr. 490 Race
Gulfoyl John, driver, 34 Lock n. of 8th
Gulick Geo. H. saloon, 346 W. 6th, h. 944 Hopkins
Gulker Hy., shoe mkr. wks. n.s. Pearl b Pike and Butler
Gulow John, W. C., tailor, n.s. al. b. Canal and 12th, and Vine and Race
Gulow Wm., tailor, 55 12th
Gundersdorf Casper, wire wkr. 65 Wade
Gundrum Peter, mason, 490 Walnut
GUNDRY JOHN, Mercantile College, Apollo Bldg. n.w.c. 5th and Walnut, bds. 47 W. 7th
Gunginch Adam, varnisher 150 Clay
Gunkel Ernst, nail mkr. 62 W. Liberty
Gunkel Jacob wks. w.s. Brighton near Benckensteins Garden
Gunn Margaret. 48 Butler
Gunnel —, shirt mkr. 180 Elm
Gunning Daniel, (Morgan & G.) Newport Ky
Gunniss David C., tailor, 45 Elizabeth
Gunter Augusta, 102 W. 5th
Gunter Geo., lab. s.e.c. 3d and Whittaker
Gunther Anton, cab. mkr. 142 Wade
Gunther Miss Antoinette, milliner bds. 91 W. Court
Gunther Casper, N., watchmkr., wks. n. w.c. Main and Pearl
Gunther Conrad, cab. mkr., 148 Pleasant
Gunther Francis, cab. mkr. 148 Pleasant
Gunther Hy., clk. bds. 91 W. Court
Gunther Ludwig, cab. mkr. 150 Pleasant
Gunther Nicholas, cigars &c., 98 W. Court
Gunther Sophia, 91 W. Court
Guntsch Wm. M., tailor, 154 Pleasant
Guntter Wm., tailor, n.s. Findlay, b. Elm and Logan
Gunzelles Sarah J , n.e.c. Richmond and Cutter
Gurckemeier Herman, lab., bds. 216 W. 7th
Gurdon John, fruits, n.w.c. Main and Court
Gurney J. H. (G. & Tucker,) 92 E. 5th
Gurney & Tucker. (John H. G. & James H. T.) meats, 92 E. 5th
Gurth John, lab., 160 Peete
Gurvis Joseph, eng., 184 Hopkins
Gury John F. J., mach. 90 W. Court
Gury Victor, brewer, wks. s.w.c. Plum and Canal
Gusdorf Jacob, bds. s.w.c. 3d and Race
Gusdorf Morris, cigars &c., 140 Vine bds. s.w.c. 3d and Race
Gusdorf T., cigars &c., bds. s.w.c. 3d and Race
Gusemeyer J., molder, wks. Chamberlain & Co's
Guspohl Barney, porter, 43 Race
Gustand Bernhard, varner 648 Elm
Gustavus Catharine, w.s. Bank al. b. 3d and 4th
Gustetter Hy., clk. 234 Main
Gusweiler Daniel, tinner. 91 Freeman
Gut Anthony, molder, 192 Clinton
Gutbelet John, tanner, 664 Elm
Gutenberger John, tailor, 7 Buckeye
Guth Jacob, cof. h. s.w.c. 2d and Vine
Guthardt Conrad, cof. h. s.e.c. Melancthon and John
Guthardt Elias, tailor, 565 Vine
Guthrie Emma, 140 Laurel
Guthrie Geo., bk. molder, 135 Poplar
Guthrie Geo., saddler, 366 Sycamore

Guthrie Grey's Armory, n.w.c. 5th and Walnut
Guthrie James V., U. S. steamboat inspector, h. 3 Harrison
Guthrie Jane, 53 Woodward
Guthrie John, roller bds. 464 W. Front
Guthrie Martha, teacher, 15th District
Gutke Mary, 403 Longworth
Gutkin Catharine. nurse, 385 George
Gutlieb Mrs. Caroline, 58 Providence
Gutling Elizabeth, h. 582 Elm
Gutling Michael, molder, 582 Elm
Gutling Wm., molder, 582 Elm
Gutman Mary, seamstress, 447 Main
Gutmann Martin, shoe mkr 14 Mary
Gutswiller Geo., dray, 91 Ham. Road
Gutswiller Joseph, trunk mkr. 579 Race
Guttenburg Fred , cof h. 394 Vine
Gutzwiller H. A., porter, 267 Cutter
Guy Douglas, dray, 10 Pleasant
Guy Edward, upholsterer, bds. 28 Rittenhouse
Guy Hy., driver, 3d and 4th St. R. R.
Guy Jane, 61 Barr
Guy John. tailor, 16 E. 4th
Guy Saml., dray, 25 Pleasant
Guyo Eliza J., 2,594 W. 5th
Guyser J ihn, cooper, wks, s.s. Gest b. Freeman and Carr
Guysi Geo. W., gauger office Minor and Andrews, h. 376 W 9th
Guysi John R. billiards, w.s. Celestial b 3d and Observatory road
Guystuff Geo., cab. mkr. wks. s.w.c. Canal and Elm
Gwire Pat., lab. 16 6th
Gwene John H , driver wks. b Allanthus and Freeman
Gyer Saml., bds 34 Longworth
Gyler Barney, blksmith., wks. 825 Central Av.

H

Haab Adam, s.s Henry b. Elm and Dunlap
Haab Fred., carriage painter, bds s.w.c. Elm and Henry
Haab John, blksmith. 58 Bank
Haack Geo bellows mkr, bds. 346 Main
Haacke Hy., teacher, 591 W. 8th
Haaf Martin, mason, rear 60 Mohawk
Haafkens Peter, bds 158 W. 3d
Haag Fred. G , carp., bds. 346 Main
Haag Michael, grocery, s.s. Central Av. nr. Brighton House
Haage Hy., tailor, 90 Pleasant
Haagen John, grocery, 60 Ham. Road
Haah John shoe mkr 542 E. Front
Haahs Jacob, lab. wks. Hieatt & Wood's
Haake Anthony, saloon, 107 E. 2d
Haameier August, clk., 226 Linn
Haan Benjamin, salesman, 35 E. Pearl
Haar Herman, lab., bds. n. s. Pearl opp. Depot
Haarmann Barney, meats. 94 Abigail
Haarmeier Hy. C., carp. e.s. Hanover b. Franklin and Woodward
Haarmeyer, H. August, clk., 92 W. 5th
Haas Chas., baker. 552 W. 5th
Haas Chas. J. cof. h. 493 Vine
Haas Francis, tailor 33 Peete
Haas Geo., 367 Linn
Haas Gottleib, brewer. s.w.c. Clifton Av. and corp. line
Haas Jacob, chandler, bds. 114 Hunt
Haas Jacob, grocery. 61 Peete
Haas Joseph, lithographer, 113 Ham. Road
Haas Joseph, 564 Elm
Haas Nicholas, grocer, 521 Sycamore
Habedank Wm. V., salesman, 417 Pleasant
Habekotte Gerhard, F., varnisher, 517 Race
Habekotte J. G. Fred., watchman, 69 Milton
Haben Joseph, lab., bds. 90 E. 2d
Habening Philip, trunk mkr. w.s. Goose al. b. Green and Keller
Haberich Christian, rear 509 Sycamore
Habermann Philip, porter, 110 Pleasant
Habighorst Wm., cab. mkr. n.s. Cherry al. b. Plum and Central Av.
Habing Joseph H., clk., 470 Main

(HAD) CINCINNATI (HAG) DIRECTORY. (HAH) 155

Habler Hermann, driver, n.s. Water b. John and Smith
Hablitz Fred , bakery, 720 Vine
Hablitz Mary, 720 Vine
Hablitzel Christian, clk. P. O, h 600 Elm
Hablizer Fredericka, servt., 10 Abigail
Habiy Mary, servt., 199 W. 4th
Habrank Mathias, blksmith, wks. 469 Walnut
Hachstuhl Martin, porter, 601 Vine
Hacht Abraham, trader, 51 George
Hack Andrew. butcher, 38 Elm
Hack Josephine, servt. 105 Broadway
Hacker Theresa, 456 W. 5th
Hackett Geo. chair mkr., n.e.c. Smith and Augusta
Hackett James, 220 E. 6th
Hackett James B., shoe mkr., bds. 281 Central Av
Hackett James E., carp., 517 W. 3d
Hackett John, lab.. 65 Abigail
Hackett John, molder, wks.. n e c. Lawrence and Front
Hackett Mrs Mary, 43 E. 8th. e. of Lock
Hackett Robert, cof. h. 134 Water
Hacking Ann. 47½ W. 8th
Hacking Ann, teacher, 472 W. 8th
Hacking Elizabeth, teacher, 472 W. 8th
Hacking Martha H., teacher 472 W. 8th
Hackinger Jennie, bds. 150 Sycamore,
Hackinger Joseph, clk., 629 W. 7th
Hackinger Thomas, produce &c., 144 Dayton
Hackle Casper, cab. mkr. s.s. Liberty, b. Linn and Baymiller
Hackle Hy., lab. 81 Melancthon
Hackman Geo , cooper. wks. 577 W. 6th
Hackman Gerhard E. furniture &c., 79 W Court
H ACKMAN H JOSEPH, Family Groceries, Provisions, &c., s.e.c. Longworth and Hoadly
Hackman Harmon, lab., 152 Baymiller
Hackman Hy., s.e.c. Mound and Longworth
H ACKMAN JOHN G., China, Glass, Queensware, &c.. and House Furnishing Goods, 164½ W. 5th
Hackmann Barney, foreman, bds. 450 Sycamore
Hackmann Caspar, turner, w.s. Coggswell al. b. Franklin and Woodward
H ACKMANN & DUSTERBERG, (Henry H. & John H. D.) Undertakers and Livery Stable, 450 Walnut, and n.s. 13th b. Walnut and Clay
Hackmann Frederick, lab., 44 Pleasant
Hackmann Frederick, teamster, 170 Spring
Hackmann Geo , lab., 550 W. 3d
Hackmann Hy., blksmith. 158 E. 6th
HACKMANN Hy., (H. & Dusterberg) 450 Walnut
Hackmann Hy., (H. & Springmeier) w. s. Coggswell al. b. Woodward and Franklin
Hackmann Herman, tanner, 154 Baymiller
Hackmann John, turner, 26 Woodward
Hackmann Mary A. w.s. Coggswell b. Franklin and Woodward
Hackmann & Springmeier, (Hy. H. & Ferdinand S.) painters, 26 Woodward
Hackney W. K., salesman Andrews & Briggs, bds. Burnet House
Hackstad Frederick, sawyer, 181 W. 2d
Hackstate H., sawyer, wks. 304 Broadway
Hackstedle Hy., lab., 472 Freeman
Hacktmann Maggie, cap mkr., wks. 327 Central Av.
Hackwelder Geo. W., canvasser, 51 Laurel
Hackwelder Wm. H., 116 Laurel
Haddix N., tailor, 260 Walnut, h. Vine St. Hill
Haddix Wm. C., paper hanger, s.s. Rail road e. of Stone al.
Haddley Mary, bds. s.e.c. Plum and 5th
Haders John, cof. h., 763 Vine
Hadiet Thomas, lab., bds. n.w.c. Hill and Front
Hadler Mary, 453 Sycamore
Hadler Mary J., teacher, 453 Sycamore

Hadley Geo. D., mach., 460 W. 3d
Hadley Louis, cook, Burnet House
Haecker John G., b.k, 169 Main, h. 243 Everett
Haecker John G., b.k., 208 Vine
Hnedacker Wm., box mkr., 67 14th
Haedecker Hy., lab., s.w.c. Gest and Harriet
Haefner Charles. shoe mkr., s.s. Harrison Pike b. Division and Brighton
Haehl Jacob, carp., Freeman b. Bank and Central Av.
Haehl Jacob, wagon mkr., s.s. Bank b. Freeman and Coleman
Haehn Peter, (Stock & Co) 674 Race
Haelker Deitrich. lab , 66 Spring
Haelker Francis. lab., 301 W. Front
H ielscher Catharine, 17 E. Liberty
Haem Hy.. mach., wks. 90 W. Court
Haemann Wm., blksmith, 52 Dudley
Harmon Fritz. lab., wks. 222 E. Front
Haendle Gottlieb. lab., 612 Elm
Haenlein Adam, lab., 570 Elm
Haens Wm., lab., 606 E. Front
Harring Chas. P., molder, 139 Bremen
Haering John, express driver, 512 Vine
Haeringer Joseph, tailor, 179 W. Liberty
Haerrwig John G., shoe mkr., wks. 382 Race
Haese Ernst, wagon mkr., 26 W. Mulberry
Haeseler A., lock smith, 530 Main
Haeseler Ernst, cab. mkr., 466 Elm
Haeusler Jacob, (Wartman & H.) 675 Elm
Haeusler Mary, laundress 686 Main
Haeuseler John, veterinary surgeon, 669 W. Front
Hafutaber Hy., carp., 236 Hopkins
Hafenbroedel Joseph, musician, 4 Louisa
Hafer Catharine, 73 E. Front
Hafer & Duddy (Geo. H. & John D.) com. mer., 65 Walnut
Hafer Frederick H., dray, 103 Wade
Hafer George. (H. & Duddy) 80 Clinton
Haferkamp Hy., lab., bds. 19 Abigail
Hafermann Theodore, lab., 194 Clark
Haffein Bridget, servt., Henrie House
Hafferty John. lab., 450 W. 2d
Haffner Ferdinand, gold smith, 31 Bremen
Hafner John, cooper, w.s. Western Av. b. Bank and Harrison Road
Hafner Adam, dry goods. 10 Abigail
Bafner Anton, baker, 42 Pike
Hafner Doris, actress, 47 Jackson
Hafner John A., (Schwartz & H.) 10 Abigail
Hafner Stephen, cof. h , 707 Elm
Hafter R mount, carp., n.w.c. Front and Whittaker
Hagan James, bds. 90 Freeman
Hagan James, cof. h. 258 Walnut, h. 197 Court
Hagan John, blksmith, bds. 140 John
Hagan John S., clk., bds United States Hotel
Hagan Louis lab. 24 Mansfield
Hagan Mary, servt., 197 W. 4th
H AGANS & BROADWELL, (M. B. II. & Samuel J. B) Attorneys at Law, 146 Walnut
HAGANS Marcellus B., (H. & Broadwell) 434 Broadway
Hagarty Catharine, 333 W. 5th
Hagarty & Co., (John H. & S. E. Hagarty) ship chandlers, 48 Pub. Landing
Hagarty John, (H. & Co.) bds. Spencer House
Hagarty S E., (H. & Co) 48 Pub. Landing
Hagebneck Bernhard, tailor. 12 Green
Hagedorn Bennett. finisher, wks. s.w.c. Plum and Pearl
Hagedorn Frederick, foreman, 365½ W. Front
Hagedorn Frederick, lab., 559 Race
Hagedorn Hy., chair mkr., wks. John Mitch-H's
Hagedorn Hy., lab., 71 Spring
Hagedorn Hermann, b.k. Volksfreund office, L. s.w.c. Melancthon and Cutter
Hagedorn John, feed store, 500 Walnut

Hagedorn Wm., cigar mkr., bds. 26 Mulberry
Hagedorn Wm., plasterer, rear 26 Mulberry
Hagel Barnard, lab , 52 McFarland
H igelstein Wendelin, lab., 660 Vine
Hageman Hy., tailor, 156 Baymiller
Hagemann Anthony, finisher, wks. n.w. c. Race and Burrows.
Hagemann Diedrich, carp., 22 Hughes
Hagemann Hy., tailor, n e.c. Hunt and Broadway
Hagemann Mary, 73 Abigail
H igemeyer Wm., cigar mkr. 80 Milton
Hagen Frederick, 961 Central Av.
Hagen Geo., clk. Galt House
Hagen Geo. J., huckster, 285 Pleasant
Hagen John, tailor, 334 Ham. Road
Hagen Joseph. wagon mkr., 21 Bank
Hagen Josephine, servt., Galt House
Hagen Kate, servt., Galt House
Hagen Wm., cooper. w.s. Western Av. b. Bank and Harrison Road
Hagenbuch Hy., grocery, 28 Mercer
Hageney Anton W., books, 191 Linn
Hagency Wm. A., teacher, 206 Linn
Hagenhoff John, varnisher, n e.c. Findlay and Ham. Road
Hager Bernard, teamster, 145 Abigail
Hager Caroline, 52 Webster
Hager Dominicus, blksmith, wks. I. & B. Bruce's
Hager John, blksmith, e.s. Anderson b. 2d and Pearl
Hager Simon, s.s. Oliver b. John and Linn
Hager Wm., lab., e.s. Price b. Milton and Black
Hagerdorn Conrad, grocer, s.s. Calhoun b. Vine and Madison
Hagerlee John, finisher, wks. n.e c Walnut and Canal
Hagerman Joseph, barber. Dennison House. h. 38 McFarland
Hagerman Wm., blksmith, wks. n.e.c. Walnut and Canal
Hagermann Adam. grocer, 114 Bank
Hagermann Anthony, blksmith, 342 Baymiller
Hagermann Herman, lab., 639 W. Front
Hagerty Mrs., bds. Spencer House
Hagerty Antony, lab., n.s. al. b Pole and Park and 2d and W. W. Canal
Hagerty James H., shoe mkr., 210 Cutter
Hagerty Mary. servt., 21 Barr
Hagerty Patrick. lab., n.s. Montgomery Pike nr. Reading Road
Hagerty Samuel, harness mkr., 209 Central Av.
Hagerty Wm , hackman. 183 Water
Haggarty Robert, blksmith, w.s. Cutter b. Wade and David
Haggerty Alexander, hackman, 188 Water
Haggerty Alex , lab., bds. rear 70 Hunt
Haggerty Anthony. lab., wks gas works
Haggerty Barney, lab., bds. rear 70 Hunt
Haggerty James. 242 Broadway
Haggerty Wm., hostler. 13 Rittenhouse
Hagie Jacob, molder, 40 Pike
Hagmaier Geo , tailor, 685 Race
Hagner Martin, shoe mkr., s.e.c. 7th and Freeman
Hahmann Elisabeth, 36 Hamer
Hahmann Valentine. 36 Humer
Hahn Barbara, 59 Baymiller
Hahn Emanuel, paper dealer, 543 Elm
Hahn Frederick A., bds 914 E. Front
Hahn H., music teacher, 157 Smith
Hahn Hy., bklayer, 25 Observatory Road
Hahn Hy., cab. mkr., 340 Vine
Hahn Hy., drover, 30 Perry
Hahn Hy.. tailor. 680 Main
Hahn Hy. T , confec., 530 Elm
Hahn Jacob, teamster, bds. n.e.c. Elm and 15th
Hahn Joseph, butcher, 49 Findlay
Hahn Joseph, finisher, bds. 44ᵈ Elm
Hahn Louis, finisher, bds. 44ᵈ Elm
Hahn Ludwig, porter, 170 Clay
Hahn Philip, finisher, 448 Elm
Hahn Wm., tailor, 107 Clay
Hahneberg Clemens, cigar mkr., bds. 494 Main
Hahnemann Chas., bakery, 549 Vine

156 (HAL) CINCINNATI (HAL) DIRECTORY. (HAL)

Hahner John, varnisher, 527 Race
Hahr Christian, blksmith, 164 Ham. Road
Hahsenmeier Chas., lab., n.s. Browne w. of Ravine al.
Haider Joseph, shoe mkr., 422 Walnut
Haig Alex, musician, w.s. Broadway b. Hunt and Abigail
Haig Margaret, w.s. Broadway b. Hunt and Abigail
Haig Mrs. Mary, s.e.c. 3d and Whittaker
Haight James, huckster, 13 W. Court w. of Central Av
HAIGHT Jered (Burbeck & H.), 109 E. Pearl
Haight Jered, 1525 E. Front
Haight M. G., riverman, bds. 12 E. Front
Haile James R., b.k. 59 Walnut, bds. 333 W. 4th
Haile Robert, lock smith, 648 Vine
Hailemann Henry, box mkr., wks. Livingston nr. Linn
Hailemann Sander, box mkr., wks. Livingston nr. Linn
Hailes Mrs., 18 Union
Hailey B. & Bros., (Bernard, Henry & Frank), com. mers., 5 Water
Hailey Bernard, (B. H. & Bros.), 599 Race
Hailey Chas., 6 E. 7th
Hailey Frank, (B. H. & Bros.), Race b. Liberty and 15th
Hailey Frank, (H. & Bros.), 683 Central Av
Hailey Henry, (H. & Bros.), 685 Central Av
Hailey Henry, (B. H. & Bros.), 71 Woodward
Hailey Humphrey, lab., 23 E. 8th
Hailey John B., (H. & Bros.), 509 Race
Hailey Mary, w.s. Langdon al. b. 6th and 7th
Hailey Patrick, lab., n.s. Front b. Foster and Kelly
Hailing Henry, lab., 75 Abigail
Hailly Thomas, 218 Cutter
Hailstock Robert, lab, s.s. 6th b. Culvert and Broadway
Haims Charles, sawyer, 323 Clark
Hainbuck John C., carp., 6 Peete
Haine James R., mer. 333 W. 4th
Hainebach Herman, cutlery, 248 W. 5th h. 415 Elm
Hainer Catharine, tailoress, 299 Linn
HAINES Ezekiel S., (H. Todd & Lytle) s.e.c. 4th and Lawrence
HAINES Seth S, (Wynne & Co.), h. Waynesville. O.
HAINES, TODD & LYTLE, (Ezekiel S. H., Alex T. & Wm. H. L), Attorneys at Law, 15 W. 3d
Haines Wm., cupalo tender. 608 Front
Halo Nicholas, cof. h., 564 E. Front
Haisch Gottlieb, tailor, 28 Allison
Haizelmann Gregor, bk. layer, 273 Franz nr. Elder
Hake Charles, packer, wks Mitchell & Rammelsberg
Hakemoeller Bernhard, cooper, wks. 586 Walnut
Hakenhoff John, varnisher, 160 Ham. Road
Haking Hermann. lab., 91 Pendleton
Hakle John, e s Branch b. Ham. Road and Findlay
HAKMAN HENRY, (F. Abel & Co.), Rope and Cordage Manufacturer, 442 W. 2d. h. 406 W 3d
Hakstat Henry, mach., s.s. Findlay b. Freeman and Western Av
Halburns Anton, lab., 255 Hopkins
Halcomb Mrs. Louisa, 17 Union
Halde Lewis, cook, 63 W. Court
Haldeman L. S., salesman, 239 Race
Haldeman Robert A., mach., h. 57 E. 4th
Haldeman Thos. J., U. S. steamboat inspector, 57 E. 4th
Haldmeyer Frank, 132 Clinton
Haldgrawe Henry. lab., 27 Dudley
HALDY FRANK P., French Boot and Shoe Manufacturer, 61 W. 4th h. 411 Elm
HALE Alden J., (H. & Co.), 128 Walnut
Hale Allen O., stable, 22 Lodge, h. 263 Vine

Hale Beale, printer, 301 Longworth
HALE & CO, (Alden J. Hale & E. Knight), Real Estate and General Agency, 128 Walnut
Hale Geo. S. com. mer., 25 West Front, h. Covington
Hale H. W., salesman, 23 W. Pearl, bds. Gibson House
Hale Howard, clk. M. & C. R. R. 301 Longworth
Hale Jno. R., (Richardson. Wilson & H.), h. 177 Sycamore
Hale Joseph, attorney, 17 W. 3d, bds. 244 Broadway
Hale Louis, tailor, 64 Dunlap
Hale Margaret, 49 E. 3d
HALE Samuel J., (Dean & H.), 128 W. 8th
Hale Thomas M., varnisher, bds. 36 E. 5th
Halenbeck Mary, 265 Everett
Halenkamp George H., grocery, 20 Cutter
Halenkamp Wm., organ mkr., 144 Baymiller
Haley Henry, carp., wks. 413 W. Front
Haley James, lab., 77 W. Front
Haley John, finisher, wks. 247 W. 5th
Haley John, buckster, 195 Vine
Haley Mary, 60 Gano
Haley Michael, finisher, 50 Race
Haley Patrick, b. k., 35 Ludlow
Haley Patrick jr., dray, 8 Jackson
Haley Patrick sen., dray. 8 Jackson
Haley Thos., cof. h., 10 Landing b. Main and Walnut
Halihan Lizzie, Dennison House
Halinan Daniel, lab., 14 Race
Haling Jacob, bk. binder.610 Central Av
Haliron John, cof. h., 229 W. 6th
Halker Frank, syrup mkr., 157 Front
HALL B. E., (Hatch & H.), h. Covington
Hall Bishop, cof. h., 201 Vine
HALL, CARROLL & CO., (Joseph L H. & Wm. C.) Manufacturers of Fire and Burglar Proof Safes, s.w.c. Pearl and Plum
Hall Charles, brush mkr., 126 Smith
Hall Chas., cigar mkr., bds. 69 W. 6th
Hall Mrs. Chas. F., seal engraver, 14 W. 4th
Hall Edward H., s.e.c. Plum and 2d
Hall Edward H., meats, &c., 571 Central Av
Hall Edwin R. b k., 458 W. 9th
Hall Elizabeth, 282 Longworth
Hall Elizabeth, 308 W. 6th
Hall Ezra, agt., 297 W. 3d
Hall Geo., cook, Dennison House
Hall George, (Gibner & Hall), 206 W. Front
Hall George, printer, 399 W. 8th
Hall George cook, 48 Lodge
Hall Harry D., bds. Burnet House
Hall I P., harness mkr., 89 Main
Hall Isaac, hinge fitter, wks. n.e.c. Walnut and Canal
Hall Isaiah, turner, 13 Betts
Hall James, bk. layer, 9 Wilson
Hall James, clk., n e.c. 4th and Smith
Hall James, lab., 25 W Court w. of Central Av
Hall James, pres. Com. Bank, h. 123 E. 3d
Hall James, plasterer, n.s. Corporation al. b. Young and Price
Hall James F., b.k., 103 W. 4th, h. Covington
Hall John, b.k., at Cyrus Welch's, res. country
Hall John, bk. layer, 625 Sycamore
Hall John D., salesman, 36 Main, h. 137 W. 7th
Hall John C., upholsterer, 299 Longworth
Hall John W., architect, 141 W. 6th
Hall Joseph B., shoe mkr., bds. 126 W. 5th
HALL Joseph L., (H., Carroll & Co.), 147 Baymiller
Hall Leander, agt., bds. 149 Elm
Hall Maria, servt., 189 Sycamore
Hall Martha, 29 Buckeye
Hall Mary E., 187 W. Court w. of Central Av

Hall Mary, 14 Charlotte
Hall Ozni, carp., 32 North
Hall Perley, molder, 13 Betts
Hall Perry, harness mkr., 188 W 5th
Hall Mrs. S. P., phys., 56 W. 4th
Hall Samuel, variety store, 242 W. 5th
Hall Samuel H., n.s. Burt b. Broad and Reed
Hall Sam'l P., 87 Laurel
Hall Sarah, e.s. John b. Betts and Clinton
Hall T. J., basket mkr., rear 78 W. Mulberry
Hall Thomas, blksmith, 422 John
Hall Wm., b. k. 19 W. Pearl
Hall Wm., carp., 206 W Front
Hall Wm., cof. h., 1234 E. Front
Hall Wm., grocer, n.s. Harriet and Millcreek
Hall Wm., pilot, bds. 131 Longworth
Hall Wm., plasterer, 14 Rittenhouse
Hall Wm., showman, 326 Main
Hall Wm. H., clk., 13 Betts
Hall Wm. H., 175 W. Court w. of Central Av
Hall Wm. H., cab mkr., bds. 175 W. Court w. of Central Av
Hallam Ambrose, wagon mkr., 34 Race
Hallam Chas. A., clk, daily Times, bds. Mt. Adams
Hallam John, tinner, 110 Vanhorn
Hallam John H., lab., 36 Mitchell
Hallenbeck Adam, tailor, 202 Linn
Hallenbeck William, hostler, 149 John
Hallenkamp George H., grocer, s.w. c. George and Smith
Hallenbeck W. H, boots and shoes, bds. 27 Longworth
Haller Frederick, n.w.c 3d and Main
Haller Frederick, grocer, 290 Linn
Haller Frederick, hardware, bds.137 Race
Haller Gabriel, brewer, Clearwater b. Baymiller and Freeman
Haller George, wagon mkr., 691 Central Av.
Haller Herman, blksmith, bds., Anderson al. b. 2d and W. W. Canal
Haller Jacob, clk., 31 Bremen
Haller Jacob, lab, 271 Franz nr. Elder
Haller Jacob, tailor, 25 14th
Haller John, cigar mkr., 25 14th
Haller Justus, blksmith, 41 W 9th w. of Central Av
Haller Kate, 64 W. Court w. of Central Av
Haller Mary, 473 Vine
Haller Wm., blksmith, bds. 41 W. 9th w. of Central Av
Haller Wm. F., molder, 52 W. Court w. of Central Av.
Hallero Morris, tailor, E. end of New
Hallesson Daniel, molder, n.s. Front e. of Kelly
Halley Albert M., b.k., 73 W. Pearl, bds. 274 Clark
Halley Daniel, lab., 17 Lock n. of 8th
Halley Emanuel G., 274 Clark
Halley John, lab., 28 Accomodation
Halley Lydia C., bds. 407 W. 4th
Halley Patrick, lab., 28 Accomodation
Halley Rachel P., 274 Clark
Halley Wm., 158 Livingston
Halley Mrs. W., 28 Accommodation
Hallgate Thos., driver, 173 E. 3d
Halligath Joseph, st. boat agent, h. 19 Clinton
Halliday Franklin, U. S. Com., s.w.c. 4th and Vine, h. Oxford, Ohio
Halliday Susan, 195 Mound
Halligan Patrick, tailor and renovator, 50½ E. 5th
Halligan Richard, dray, e.s. Hand al. b. Court and Clark
Hallinger Matthew, 225 Findlay
Hallmann Fred., lab., 28 Madison
Halloran James, stone cutter, bds. 25 W. Court w. of Central Av.
Hally Rev. Wm., s.e.c. 8th and Central Av.
Halm Conrad, shoe mkr., bds. 365 W. 5th
Halm Victoria, laundress, 489 Walnut
Halmer Charles, boots and shoes, 414 Vine
Halmer Philipp, shoe mkr., 131 Bremen
Halorn Mary, n.w.c. Elm and Water

(HAM) CINCINNATI (HAM) DIRECTORY. (HAN) 157

Halpin John, baggage master, L. M. R. R. Depot
Halpin John, draughtsman, at city eng. office, h. 255 W. Court
Halpin John, dray, 481 W. 9th
Halpin Michael, lab., n s. E. 3d, nr. Martin
Halpin Michael, peddler, 65 Vine
Halping Antony, carp., 740 W. 6th
Halping Michael, lab., E. 3d b. Parsons and Baum
Halseman Joseph, lab., wks. 68 Water
Halsey Enos, clk., 76 E. 5th
Halsey John, clk., 76 E. Pearl
Halsher Hy., lab., s. s. Court e. of Broadway
Halsschneider Theodore, lab., 51 Rittenhouse
Halsted E. O. H., driver, Walnut b. 6th and 7th
Halstead Edward O., fireman, 88 Longworth
Halstead Elihu O., 88 Longworth
HALSTEAD MURAT, (M. D. Potter & Co.,) h. 266 W. 7th
Halstermann Clemmers, 9 Barnard
Halstine John, lab., bds. 17 Wade
Haltenhof Chas., stone cutter, 533 Walnut
Haltel John, wks. 222 E. Front
Haltes Wm., carp., 187 Linn
Halthaus Hy., carp., 115 Martin
Halvorsen John, mach., 102 W. 5th
Halvorsen Mary, dress mkr., 102 W. 5th
Halwig Joseph, clk., wks. 23 W. 5th
Ham Gustavus C., boatman, 304 W. 6th
Ham John, (H. & Savill.) 20 Betts
Ham & Savill, (John H. & Leonard S.) paper hangings, 211 Central Av.
Haman Andrew, blksmith. s.s. Budd b. Donersberger and Harriet
Hamann Benj., cooper, College al. b. Woodward and Abigail
Hamann Lewis, meats, e.s. Race, b. W. Liberty and 15th
Hamant Lambert, blksmith, bds. 936 Central Av.
Hamar Reuben, lab., 46 Baum
Hamasot Wilhemina, 593 W. 3d
Hambacher Jacob, boots and shoes, 537 Vine
Hamberg Armean, 415 Elm
Hamberg Ferdinand, saddler, 9 Woodward
Hamberg Hy., tailor, 183 Linn
Hamberg Herman, boots and shoes, 200 Linn
Hamberg John H., grocery, n.e.c. Pearl and Pike
Hamberg Moses, peddler, s.s. al. b. Clay and Main and 12th and Canal
Hamberg Otto, 72 Peete
Hambleton Edward R., clk., 1200 E. Front
Hambleton James H., carp., 1263 E. Front, h. 1235 E. Front
Hambleton S. T. & Co. (Samuel T. H. & Wm. L. Hambleton), st. bt. builders, s.s. Front e. of Hazen
Hambleton Samuel T. (S. T. H. & Co.) 1262 E. Front
Hambleton Wm. L. (S. T. Hambleton & Co.) res. Mound City, Ills.
HAMBO MRS. MARY, Trimmings and Fringe Manufacturer, 142 W. 5th
Hambrock Harmon, lab, wks. 267 W. 5th
Hambruck Hy., clk., 455 Sycamore
Hamburg Hy., lab., wks. 179 W. Canal
Hamburger Jacob, bar k., 214 Vine
HAMBURGER JACOB, Staple and Fancy Dry Goods, n.w.c. Race and Elder
Hamburger S., cof h., 22 W. 6th
Hamer Henry, boiler mkr., 70 Lock
Hamer Henry, molder, 189 W. Front
Hamer John H., blksmith, 222 Linn
Hamer Thos. molder, wks. n.e.c. Canal and Walnut
Hamer Wm. W., flour mills, 120 W. 3d
Hamilton Alex , baker, 530 Main
Hamilton Alex., clk., Union R.R. ticket office, b. 144 W. Front
Hamilton Alex., lab., 614 E. Front

Hamilton Andrew, teamster, bds. w.s. Jordon b. Clark and Gest
HAMILTON BREWERY, Geo. Kinter & Co., 331 Hamilton Road.
Hamilton Chas., stocking mkr., 427 W. 3d
Hamilton County Jail, w. s. Sycamore, b. Canal and Abigail
Hamilton Edward R , carp., 45½ E. 3d
Hamilton Elizabeth, teacher, 403 W. 8th
Hamilton H. D , bds. Dennison House
Hamilton Hy , clk , 316 W. 8th
Hamilton James, lab., s. Avery b. Mill and Stone
Hamilton James, clk., s. e. c. Sycamore and Liberty
Hamilton James, driver, 513 W. 3d
Hamilton James, teamster, w.s. Jordan, b. Clark and Gest
Hamilton James W., lab., wks. n.e.c. Park and Marsh
Hamilton Jenny, bds. n.s. Edward b. Mill and Stone
Hamilton John, gilder, bds. n.s. Avery b Mill and Stone
Hamilton John, lab., 80 Race
Hamilton Lucy, 314 W. 7th
Hamilton Margaretha, wks. Times office
Hamilton Mary A., s.e.c. Sycamore and Liberty
Hamilton Nicholas, conductor, rear 109 Park
Hamilton Robert S., atty, 180 Walnut, res. Newport
Hamilton Thomas, bds. n. s. Avery b. Mill and Stone
Hamilton Thomas, pilot, 220 Water
Hamilton Wm. teamster, 302 Water
HAMLEN Shephard L. (H. & Smith,) h. 163 Elm
HAMLEN & SMITH, (Shephard L. H. & Harris R. S.,) Dentists, 3 W. 4th
Hamlin Chas., blksmith, 116 E. 3d e. of Whittaker
Hamlin Edward S., atty., 142 Elm
HAMLIN Europe W., (E. G. Leonard & Co.) 91 Pike
HAMLIN HANNIBAL G., Jr., Wh. & Retail Dealer in Military Goods, &c., 63 W. 4th, h. 91 Pike
Hamlin Hannibal G., Sen., 91 Pike
Hamman Bernhard, cooper, wks. 586 Walnut
Hamman Hy., eng., 111 Clark
Hamman Hy., shoe mkr., 543 Sycamore
Hamman J. C., printer, 543 Sycamore
Hamman John, molder, 695 Race
Hamman Mary, 695 Race
Hamman Mary, servt , wks 27 Mercer
Hammann Abel, cof. h., 1 Mary
Hammann Anton, boots and shoes, 75 12th
Hammann Christopher, clk., 353 Main
Hammar & Bare, (Francis H & Martin B.) com. mers., 52 Walnut
Hammar Benj. E., bds. 7 Longworth w. of Stone
Hammer Francis, (H. & Barc,) h. Covington
Hammeier John G., saddler, bds. 9 Woodward
Hammel Chas., sawyer, 671 Race
Hammel Conrad, butcher, s.s. Findlay b. Bremen and Franz
Hammel Jacob, varnisher, 130 W. Liberty
Hammell Abraham, painter, 67 W. 3d, h. 64 Clinton
Hammelle Chas. harness mkr., 548 Walnut
Hammelmann Fred., printer, 35 Hamer
Hammelmeyer B., lab. s.w.c. Broadway and Hunt
HAMMER Gustavus, (Holstein & H.) 541 Race
Hammer Hy., blksmith, wks. Ch. Behlen & Co.'s
Hammer John, mate, 68 E. 3d, e. of Whittaker
Hammer John M. whitewasher, 695 Race
Hammer Lawrence, bds. 74 E. Pearl
Hammer Leopold, mason, 697 Race
Hammer Minnie, 526 E. Front
Hammer Theresa, midwife, 540 Walnut

Hammer Valentine, tailor, wks. 604 Elm
Hammerschmidt Martin, butcher, 624 Vine
Hammerstein Jacob, baker, bds. 546 W. 5th
HAMMETT & CHESELDINE, (Jas. H. & Samuel P. C.) Staple and Fancy Dry Goods, Carpets, &c., s.e.c. Main and Pearl
Hammett Hy., hardware, e.s. Auburn nr. Central Av.
HAMMETT James, (H. & Cheseldine,) bds. Dennison House
Hammler Henry, lab., 70 Lock
Hammon Elizabeth, 415 Central Av.
Hammon Jacob, s.w.c. Corp. Line and Clifton Av.
Hammon Joseph, driver, wks. s. e. c. Grant and Plum
Hammon Wm., carp, n.s. Goodloe b. Willow and Niagara
Hammond Andrew C., carp., 776 E. Front
Hammond Chas. F., baker, 776 E. Front
Hammond Fred , lab., 62 Lock
Hammond Geo. C., carriage painter, n.w.c. Clinton and John
Hammond Jas., paper carrier, 128 Barr
Hammond John, mach., 18 Rittenhouse
Hammond John S., tinner, 18 Rittenhouse
Hammond Joseph W., molder, 516 Plum
Hammond Marian, seamstress, 516 Plum
Hammond Martin, 267 Ham. Road
Hamon Fred., painter, 117 Betts
Humpa Chas., dray, 17 Mansfield
Hamp Hy., cab mkr., 245 Clark
Humpe August, cab. mkr., 15 Adams, b. Plum and Elm
Hampe Joseph, tailor, n.s. Abigail b. Broad ay and Spring
Hampson John, hatter, 95 W. 3d
Hampson Richard, photographer, 100 W. 4th
Hampson Thomas, photographer, 100 W. 4th
Hampton Clap, clk., bds. 321 Walnut
Hampton Daniel, lab., 1232 E. Front
Hampton James, carp , 636 E. Front
Hampton Wm. F., butcher, b. n.s. 6th e. of Lock
Hamsley Ralph, 73 Bank
Hamsontt Frank, 375 Broadway
Han James, lab., bds. n. s. Augusta, b. John and Smith
Hanaway Ephraim, tinner, 262 W. 6th
Hanbold Jacob, tailor, 553 Vine
Hancarling Henry J ; tailor, 196 Clinton
Hancock Isabella, 233 Laurel
Hancock John, teacher, 25 Betts
Hancock L. B., (Decamp & H.) 34 Laurel
Hancost Joseph, gas fitter, s. s. Charlotte, b. Central Av. and Linn
Hand Benj., engineer, 136 George
Hand Caleb C., variety store, 147 Linn
Hand Chas. C., finisher, wks. n. e. cor. Walnut and Canal
Hand Firman, carp., 133 George
Hand James, fireman, bds. n. s. Augusta b. Smith and John
Hand John J., printer, s. e. c. 9th and Walnut
Hand Joseph, blacksmith, 440 W. 6th
Hand Kate, servt., 341 Walnut
Hand Owen, tailor, 52 E. 2d
HAND Sylvester, (H. Whitehouse & Co.) res. Spring Grove
Hand Thomas, lab., s. s. 6th, b. Broadway and Culvert
HAND, WHITEHOUSE & CO., (Sylvester H , Joseph W. & Daniel Decamp) Queen City Marbleized Iron Mantel and Grate Works, 265 and 267 W. 5th
Hand Wm. G., blksmith, 205 Barr
Handerhin Edward, tailor, s. s. 6th, e. of Lock
Handle Christopher, baker, 43 Public Landing
Handle John, baker, 43 Pub. Landing
Handlan Alexander H., pilot, 209 Everett
Handlan Eugene, wire weaver, 209 Everett
Handley J. bez B., painter, 113 E. 3d, e. of Whittaker

Handley James W., engineer, n. s. Railroad, e. of Hazen
Handman Frederick, safe maker, 5*0 Elm
Handman Lewis, carp., bds. 526 E. Front
Handman Charles, eng., 116 High
Handorf John Henry, shoemkr., 373 Broadway
Handrehan Catharine, bds. 210 E. 6th
Handsmith Arnold, lab., 633 W. Front
Handwerk, Catharine, 585 Race
Handwerk Elizabeth, 585 Race
Handy & Bro., (Henry F. & Truman B.) carp. and builders, e. s. Pendleton, bet Woodward and Liberty
Handy Henry F., (H. & Bro.) e. s. Auburn near Bigelow
Handy Martin E., 493 Elm
Handy Robert L., 51 Mansfield
Handy Truman B., (H. & Bro.), e. s. Auburn. near Bigelow
Hane Augustus, lithographer, bds 65 Broadway
Haneberg, Francis C., cigar mkr, bds. 494 Main
Hanen Charles, cab. mkr., 303 Freeman
Hanengild Michael, painter, 21 Bremen
Hanes Peter, carp., Burt, b. Reed and Broad

HANES, WM. W.,
Hamilton Foundry and Machine Shop. 259, 261 and 263 W. Front, res. Covington

Hanney Arthur, s. s Front bet. Niagara and Willow
Haney Daniel, porter, W. Douglas Chapman's
Haney Ellen, 135 E. 6th
Haney, James, finisher, 10 Observatory
Haney Mrs Margaret, 303 W. 2d
Haney Martin, shoemkr., s.w.c. 6th and Harriet
Haney Mrs. Mary. 639 W. 6th
Haney R. H., bds. Dennison House
Haney Thomas, lab., n.s. W. W. Canal, bet. Smith and Park
Haney Thomas, moulder, s s. 6th, bet. Carr and Freeman
Hanfbauer Conrad, cooper, 258 Pleasant
Hanfbauer John, pattern mkr., 55 Hughes
Hanfbauer Leonard, 95 Ham. Road
Hanhanser Anthony, cigar mkr., 20 Ham. Road
Hanhauser Anthony, cigar mkr., 94 Woodward
Hanhausen Jacob, baker, 215 Linn
Hani Augustus, lithographer, 14 E. 4th
Hanibal John, dray, n.w c. Lodge and Gano
Hanigan Pat., tailor, 39 E 7th
Hanitton Henry, clk., 316 W. 8th
Haninger Henry, carver, 60 Mohawk
Hanivan J. C., bds Dennison House
Hanks Mrs. A. S., teacher, Mt. Auburn Institute
Hanks Charles, locksmith, wks. 270 Central Av.
Hanks Mrs Geo. L. 262 W. 8th
Hanky Louis, 240 Betts
Hanks Richard, grocer, 32 Vine, res. Covington
Hanky Louis, plasterer, 525 Freeman
Hanlein John A., blksmith, 135 Wade, h. 137 Wade
Hanlein Joseph, blksmith. bds. 137 Wade
Hanley Bartholomew, driver, 48 Butler
Hanley Edmond, driver, e s. Central Av. b. 2d and Pearl
Hanley John, express man, h. 222 Central Av.
Hanley Mary. bds. junction High and Kemper's Lane
Hanley Nelson. cook. 293, W. 5th
Hanley Roger, lab., junction High and Kemper's Lane
Hanley Wm. lab., wks, n.e.c. Park and Marsh
Hanlin John, lab, h. 517 W. 3d
Hanlin John J., wire worker, bds. 229 Baymiller
Hanlin Wm., druggist, n.w c. Front and Elm. bds. 21 Barr
Hanlon Betsy, h. n w.c 3d and Ellen
Hanlon David, pressman, bds. 246 Clinton
Hanlon Michael, stone mason. rear 66 Woodward

Hanly Edward K., shoemkr, bds. 281 Central Av.
Hanly John, clk., 47 W 9th
Hanly Joseph C., (Wentworth & H.) 47 W. 9th
Hanly Margaret. 50 E. 7th
Hanly Patrick, lab., h. 61 Barr
Hanly Thos., shoemkr., h. n.s. 7th, b. Broadway and Sycamore

HANLY, WM. W.,
Wholesale Grocer and Com. Mer., 25 Main. res. Covington

Hanmon Anthony, carp., h. 118 E. 3d e. of Whittaker
Hann Adam, h. n.e.c. Milton and Sycamore
Hann John, h 69 Mulberry
Hann Kate, bds. Dennison House
Hann Philip. finisher, h 448 Elm
Hann Geo W., painter, h. 56 Avery
Hanna James, (James H. & Co.,) 161 Clinton
Hanna James & Co , lumber dealers, n. w.c Linn and Clinton
Hanna John H , painter, 29 W. Court, w. of Central Av.
Hanna Mary, h. 54 Kossuth
Hanna Sarah, 54 Kossuth
Hannaford John W., receiver, 3d and 4th Street Railroad, h. 8 Pine
HANNAFORD SA 4'L, (Anderson & H.,) res. Cheviot
Hannah F.. bds. 310 W 5th
Hannan Bridget. h. 400 W. 5th
Hannan Daniel, (H. & Lyons,) 48 E. 6th
Hannan Dennis, lab.. res. n. s. 8th, b. Broadway and Sycamore
Hannan Eliza, h. 90 Richmond
Hannan James F., teacher, h. 521 W. 5th
Hannan Jeremiah, lab., h. 311 E. 6th
Hannan Johanna, h. s. w.c. John and 5th
Hannan & Lyons, (Daniel H. & Frank L.,) meats, s.e.c. 6th and Sycamore
Hannan Mary. h. 210 E. 6th
Hannassy John, stone cutter, h. 88 Wade 15th
Hannay Hugh H., photographer, 26 W.
Hanney Martin, shoe mkr., n.w.c. 6th and Harriet
Hannibal & St. Joseph R.R., 35 W. 3d, John W. Burch gen'l. agt.
Hannibell Fred., turner, wks. 625 Central Av.
Hannigan Mich. walter, Burnet House
Hanning Barney, foreman, 214 Water
Hanning Henry, shoe mkr., rear 658 Main
Hanno Gustavus, painter, 215 W. Front
Hannon Mich , lab., s.s. Pleasant Court e of Elm
Hannon Sarah, 54 Barr
Hannosie John, mustard mkr., n.s. 13th b. Main and Walnut
Hannsi John, mach. bds. 523 Main
Hannum Elizabeth, 948 E. Front
Hannum John. 944 E. Front
Hanny Pat., lab., 83 Barr
Hanover Harriet A., millinery, 190 W. 5th, bds Dennison House

HANOVER JOHN C., Auctioneer and Conveyancer of Real Estate and Notary Public, 57 W. 3d bds. Dennison House.

HANOVER M. D.,
Attorney at Law, Office 57 W. 3d bds 135 W. 9th

Hanover Sarah, huckster. 180 W. 6th
Hanrahan Cornelius, finisher, bds. 302 E. 6th.
Hanrihan Jeremiah, shoe mkr., 130 Mound
Hans Catharine. laundress, 437 Walnut
Hans Frederick. lab., w.s. Browne near Ham. Road
Hans Henry, butcher, w s. Lebanon Road near Montgomery pike
Hans Jacob, barber, 504 Main
Hans Jacob. lab., c.s. Western Av. b. Poplar and Findlay

HANS JOHN,
Proprietor Fremont Hotel, s e.c. Vine and 5th

Hansberg Michael, boiler mkr., bds Pennsylvania H tel

Harding Lyman, jr., teacher 15th district school
Harding Mrs. Mary C., 104 York
Harding Susan, servt., 295 Longworth
Harding Wm., dining saloon. 263 W. 6th
Harding Wm C., teacher, 153 W. 4th
Hardinghaus Hy., 61 W. Miami Canal, b. 58 Clay
Hardinghaus Martin, clk., bds. 58 Clay
Hardie Hy., cof. h., 762 Central Av
Hardleib John, cigar mkr., 647 Central Avenue
Hardling John, cof. h., s.w.c. John and Wade, h. 503 John
Hardon Augustus, clk., 185 Poplar
Hardor Bewls, clk., 185 Poplar
Hardt Herman, porter. 15 Pub, Landing
Hardt Philip, grocery, 623 Vine
Hardway F., music teacher, s.e.c Everett and John
Hardwick Wm., lab., wks. Queen City distillery
Hardy Benjamin, brush mkr., 387 Main
Hardy Catharine, 614 E Front
Hardy Charlotte, 254 W. 9th
Hardy Dexter D., mach., 265 Freeman
Hardy Ephraim, teacher fourth district school
Hardy Jenny, 214 Plum
Hardy John, clk., 241 W. Court
HARDY JOHN Q., Dentist. 87 W. 7th
Hardy Maria 152 E. 5th
Hardy Mrs. R. B., dress mkr., 350 W. 8th
Hardy Wm., brush mkr., bds. 249 W. 6th
Hare James O., printer, bds. U. S. Hotel
Hare Patrick O., grocery, n.e.c. Smith and 4th, h. 268 W. 4th
Hare Samuel, plumber, bds 290 Main
Harey John, carp., 358 Clark
Harford Christopher, sawyer, e.s. Linn, b. Everett and Wade
Harge Andrew, lab., rear 55 Woodward
Hargedon Hermann, s.w.c. Melancthon and Cutter
Hargot Barney, lab., wks. 15C5 E. Front
Hargot Wm., lab., wks. 1565 E Front
Hargrave Geo., eng., 177 W 9th
Hargrave Joseph, b.k., 145 Walnut, h. 170 Plum
Hargrave Wm., lab., 22 Richmond, b. Elm and Plum
Hargy John, cab. mkr., 187 Richmond
Hargy John W., foreman, 241 W. Court
Harig John, carp., n.w.c. Clark and Garrard
Harigan Wm., carp., 548 Race
Hariger Lewis, saddler, bds. s.w.c. 6th and Plum
Harima Hy., finisher, wks. n.w.c. Plum and Wade
Harkemeyer Charles, 120 Gest
Harkins Ellen, servt., 375 W. 8th
Harkins John, lab., s.s 2d, b. Rose and Mill
Harkins Peter, dray, n s. Augusta. b. John and Smith
Harkness Charles, (A G. Cheever & Co.) h. near Lockland
Harkness R. F., salesman, 18 and 19 Public Landing, bds. 107 Pike
Harkness, Struder & Fusdick, cotton factory, n.e.c 3d and Smith
Harlam Emanuel, tailor, 210½ Central Avenue
Harlam Michael, tailor, 210½ Central Av
Harlan Geo W., b.k., J. W. Gosling's, bds. 61 Longworth
Harlan Jessie J., plasterer, 460 W. 3d
Harlan W. W., printer, bds. Dennison House
Harle Geo., molder, 228 Clinton
Harle Jane T., teacher, 16 Rittenhouse
Harle Mary Ann, 16 Rittenhouse
Harlers Herman, shoe mkr., rear 176 Clay
Harley Bridget, 63 E. 7th
Harley Daniel, lab., s.s. 6th, b. Broadway and Culvert
Harlingen August, sausage manuf., 27 Campbell al
Harlin N. W., bds. Dennison House
Harlos Jacob, teamster, 268 E. Pearl, e. of Broadway
Harlow John, stock dealer, 271 W. 3d

Harman Angeline, 59 Rittenhouse
Harman Edwin T., 36 Parsons
Harman Eliza, servt., 26 Harrison
Harman H., molder, wks. Chamberlain & Co.'s
Harman Jane, washwoman, w.s. Lawrence, b 4th and 5th
Harman Joseph, cooper. 367 Linn
Harmann Barney, meats, s.s. Abigail, b Broadway and Spring, h 94 Abigail
Harmann Fred, tobacconist, bds. 76 W. Court
Harmann Gerkard H., porter, 659 Walnut
Harmann Hy., carp., 21 Kossuth
Harmann Wm., bksmith, wks. s.w.c. Freeman and Front
Harmeier Anna E., 26 Franklin
Harmeier Augustus, clk., bds. 61 E, 4th
Harmeier Ernst F., clk., 128 W. 5th, bds. 10 Woodward
Harmeier Frederick, tailor. 61 Hughes
Harmeier Hy., lab., bds. 113 Clay
HARMEIER JOHN, Walnut Street Dye House, 218 Walnut
Harmeier John F, Sr, bds. 10 Woodward
Harmeier John F., printing calico, 10 Woodward
Harmening Mrs. Louisa, shoe binder, 524 W. 7th
Harmes Hy., clk., 189 Laurel
Harmes Richard, finisher, 98 13th
Harmeyer Hy., grocery, s.e.c. Liberty and Logan
Harmeyer Ily., porter, 76 Melancthon
Harmi Harmon. lab., wks. 229 E. Front
Harmon G., lab., wks. n.s. Front, b. Lawrence and Pike
Harmon Hy., shoe mkr., 323 Plum
Harmon John, 34 Dunlap
Harmon Louis, baker, 616 Central Av
Harmon Matthew, butcher, n s. Corporation Line, nr. Auburn
Harmon Peter. tailor, 106 Plum
Harmond Mrs P., 45 W, 7th
Harms Charles, lab. sawyer, 321 Clark
Harms Hy., lab., 43 Pleasant
Harmyer Lewis. cigar mkr., 44 Lodge
Harmer Geo. W., clk., 197 W. 3d
Harnish John, sawyer, 77 Laurel
Harnold Jacob, cof. h., 638 Vine
Harnold Louis, shoemkr., 42 Findlay
Haroch John, lab, wks. n.s. Front, b. Lawrence and Pike
Haron John, tailor, 336 W. 5th
Harpel Jeremiah, printer and phys., e.c. 3d and Vine, h. 452 W. 9th
Harpel Luther M., printer, bds. 452 W. 9th
Harpel Oscar H., printer, 213 Laurel
Harpenao Frank, porter, 194 Clark
Harper B. A., 21 Barr
Harper Daniel, (H. & Winall,) res. W. Walnut Hills
HARPER David, (David H. & Son,) 88 E. 4th.
Harper David, Jr., salesman, 36 Walnut, bds. 68 E. 4th
HARPER DAVID & SON, (David H. & Hy., E. H) Produce and Commission Merchants, 36 Walnut
Harper George W., teacher, Woodward High School
HARPER Hy. E. (David Harper & Son) bds. 88 e. 4th
Harper James W., salesman, s.e.c. Vine and Pearl
Harper Joseph, wheelwright, wks. P. J. Marqua & Co's
Harper Micajah A., tailor, e.s. Walnut b. 5th and 6th. bds. 154 Broadway
Harper Lilly, bds. 71 Baker
Harper P. M., bds., U. S. Hotel, h. 21 Barr
HARPER THOMAS L., Physician and Surgeon, h. 215 Plum
Harper Wilhelmina, bds. 398 Race
Harper Willa, teacher, 6th dist, school
Harper Wm., carriage mkr., 403 Baymiller
Harper & Winall (Daniel H. & Saml. J. W.) com. mers , 12 E. 2d
Harperink Otto, tanner, 590 Elm

Harpst Christ, cigar mkr., 75 Commerce
Harran Mrs. Mary, 86 W. Liberty
Harrell Elmore, 312 Elm
Harrell Guo., 312 Elm
Harrell Nathan, 312 Elm
HARRIS DAVID, Brewery, 100 Sycamore, bds Burnet House
Harriett Margaret, 323 W, 6th
Harrigan Andrew J., agt., bds. w.s. Observatory b. Hill and Pavillion
Harrigan Charles, dray 65 Observatory
Harrigan Fanny, 65 Observatory
Harrigen Patrick. foreman, s.e.c. Mitchell and Celestial
Harrigan Peter jr., lab., n.w.c. Observatory and Hill
Harrigan Peter. sen., w.s. Observatory b. Hill and Pavillion
Harrigan Thomas H., saloon, 62 E. 5th
Harring John, brewer, 624 Vine
Harrington Alfred, phys 490 John
Harrington Mrs B., cof h., 11 Landing b. Main and Walnut
Harrington Dennis, cutter, 146 Walnut
Harrington Denny, lab., 240 Barr
Harrington Jeremiah, lab., 359 Broadway
Harrington John, lab., Oregon nr. Observatory Road
Harrington John, meats, bds. 33 W. Front
Harrington Nath., lab., 109 E. 8th
Harrington Patrick, lab , s s. 6th e. of Lock
Harrington Sarah, bds. 230 W. Court w. of Central Av
Harrington Thu., bds. Railroad House
Harris Abraham, clothing, s.e.c. 5th and Main. h. 189 Broadway
Harris B. W., salesman, 55 W. Pearl, b. 181 Longworth
Harris Burrell, servt., n.e.c. 3d and Pike
Harris Charles O., clk., 159 E. Front, h. Newport
Harris Chas. P., b.k., 175 W. 2d, h. 232 Baymiller
Harris Charles M , b.k., n.w.c. 4th and Lock, h. 254 Hopkins
HARRIS Conrad, (H. & Zoiner), Mt. Hope
Harris Daniel, roller, 95 W. Front
Harris David H., bksmith, s.e.c. Front and Plum
Harris E. J., clk., 140 Main
Harris Elijah, painter. bds. 266 Clark
Harris Eliza. 290 W. 4th
Harris Esther, dye house, 374 W. 5th
Harris Fanny, 91 W 8th
Harris Harris A., 89 W. 8th
Harris Frederick, clk ,bds. 27 Longworth
Harris George, fireman, s.e.c. Elm and Pearl
Harris Geo., waiter, bds. w.s. Lawrence b. 4th and 5th
HARRIS GIBSON & CO., Mattress Ma. uf. & Upholsterer, 130 Sycamore
Harris Harry, bds. 83 Baymiller
Harris Hester. 238 Main
Harris Hester, laundress. 12 Webb
Harris Isaac, salesman, 4 Harrison
HARRIS J. N. &CO. (Jonathan N. H., Perry Davis & Son and Thomas H. C Allen), Southern and Western Proprietors Davis' Pain Killer, Richardson's Sherry Wine Bitters, Weaver's Syrup and Cerate, 7 College bldg., Walnut b. 4th and 5th
Harris James, 647 Sycamore
Harris James, finisher, 51 E. 3d e. of Whittaker
Harris James, fireman, 24 Commerce
Harris James, fish, &c., 611 Vine
Harris James, lab., wks. 179 W. Canal
Harris James, lab., 611 Vine
Harris John, hostler, 60 Gano
Harris John, pattern mkr., bds. s.w.c. Pearl and Ludlow
Harris John, tobacconist, 72 W. 3d
Harris Jno. H., carriage mkr., 74 Richmond
HARRIS Jonathan N. (J. N. H. & Co) res, New London, Conn
Harris Mrs. L. L., bds 304 W. 5th
Harris Col. Len. A., 490 W 4th

Harris Levi C., salesman, n.e.c. 3d and Vine. h. 282 Longworth
Harris Lewis cap mkr., 20 Home
Harris Nathan C., pass. agt., C., C. & C. R.R., s.e.c. Front and Broadway
Harris O. C, tobacconist, 95 W. Front
Harris Philip, molder, wks, s.w.c. Front and Central Av
Harris Robert J., collector, 39 Jones
HARRIS Samuel T., (Fox, H. & Fox) h. Glendale
Harris Susan B., 111 Broadway
Harris Rev. Thomas, e. s. Auburn b. Northern and Central Av's.
Harris Wm., molder, 162 Linn
Harris Wm. B., clk., bds. 281 Longworth
Harris Wm. H., stone cutter, 423 Sycamore
HARRIS & ZOINER (Conrad H. & Paul W. Z.) Stove and Ornamental Pattern Makers. foot of 8th
Harrison ——, carp., National Theater
Harrison Alfred, steward, 115 E. 6th
Harrison Amos A., coffee packer, 141 Sycamore
Harrison Barney, carp, 257 Clark
Harrison C. S., painter, 449 George
Harrison Chvs. A., asst. librarian, Y.M, M. Library Association
Harrison & Collins (Wm. H. & W. M. C.), billiards, n.w.c. 5th and Central Av
Harrison Daniel, lab., 257 Clark
HARRISON Daniel Y., (H. & Wilson), Fairmount
Harrison Dennis, carp., 257 Clark
Harrison E., bds. 182 W. 4th
Harrison Edwin, 246 Hopkins
Harrison Edwin W., conductor, bds. 246 Hopkins
Harrison Eliza, 215 Mound
Harrison George, twister, 86 W. Front
Harrison Hy., carp., 143 Hopkins
HARRISON & HOOPER (L. B. H. & Wm. H.) Grocers and Commission Merchants, 50 W. 2d
Harrison James, bds. 1258 E. Front
Harrison James, supt., s.w.c. Baymiller and Freeman, bds. 83 Baymiller
Harrison James, trader, 272 W. 6th
Harrison John, lab., 222 Central Av
Harrison John jr., currier, 29 Kossuth
Harrison Joseph, river man, 604 W. 9th Landing
HARRISON L. B. (H. & Hooper) 234 W. 4th
Harrison Louisa, bds. 183 Race
Harrison Mary, 164 E Front
Harrison Mary, 47 W. 8th
Harrison Mary, 300 W. 8th
Harrison Mattie, bds. 483 W. 5th
Harrison Michael, lab, bds. n.w.c. Mill and Front
Harrison Reuben P., eng , 260 Clark
Harrison Robert A., clk , 215 Mound
Harrison Susan. w.s. Plum b. Water and River
Harrison Thomas, engraver, Am. Bank Note Co.. h. Clifton
Harrison W. H. conductor, h. 641 W. 5th
HARRISON W. H. & CO., Wholesale Dealers in Paints, Oils, Varnishes, French and American Window Glass, &c., 23 W. 4th
Harrison Wm., 103 W. Pearl
Harrison Wm. (H. & Collins) n.w.c. 5th and Central Av
Harrison Wm., car. driver, bds e.s. Kilgour b 3d and 5th
HARRISON Wm. D., (L. Fletcher, Hobart & Co.), bds. 252 W. 4th
Harrison Wm. E., mach., 227 Harr
HARRISON Wm. H. (Wm. H. H. & Co.) h. 49 W. 4th
Harrison Rev. Wm. H., 64 Clark
HARRISON & WILSON (Daniel Y. H & Edward Y. W.) Coffee and Spice Mills, 131 and 133 Race
Harrlinger George, lab., 149 Poplar
Harrman Hy., cab. mkr., 21 Kossuth
Harrold Charles, finisher, n.e.c. Central Av. and Pearl
Harrold Johanna, 718 W. 6th
Harrold John, carp., 2 New

Harroway Samuel lab., 107 E. 6th
Harry Molton R . clk., 47 Pub. Landing, bds. Broadway Hotel
Harry Wm., salesman, 34 E. 4th
Harry Wm. C. (Isham. Fisher & Co.), bds. Broadway Hotel
Harsch Christian, stone cutter, 57 14th
Harsch Dorothea 540 Walnut
Harsch Elizabeth, 57 14th
Harsch John. cof. h , 52 Water
Harsch Margaret, 6ª W. Mulberry
Harspring Michael, cigar mkr., bds. 53 W. 5th
Harstman August, eng., 4 Mary
Hart Anthony, lab., s.s. Friendship al. b. Pike and Butler
Hart Benjamin, mach., gas works
Hart Bridget, servt., 349 W. 8th
Hart Catharine, 320 W. 7th
Hart Chas.. lab., 241 Clark
Hart Cornelius, lab., bds. n.w.c. Front and Central Av
Hart David, Hart's Hotel, 21 W. 6th
Hart Henrietta, e.s. Cuggswell al. b. Abigail and Woodward
Hart Hy., b. k., 33 Plum
Hart Hy., weigher, n. w. c. Vine and Front
Hart Isaac. clothing. 613 Vine
HART Isaac (Hart & Watt) 3ª Pierson
Hart Jacob, lab., rear 529 E Front
Hart James D., clk., 126 Dayton
Hartman Jno. A., waiter, Burnet House
Hart Joseph W., engraver, n.e.c. Burnet and Vine, h. Newport
Hart Judah H., paper cutter, bds. 33 Plum
Hart Mary, w.s. Kilgour b. 3d and 5th
HART Mrs. Mary C. (Wm. Hart & Co.) 320 W. 7th
HART Matthew, (Barker, H. & Cook,) res. E. Walnut Hills
Hart Philip, butcher bds. 505 Linn
Hart Thomas, dray, 67 Cherry al.
Hart Thomas, lab. s.s. Friendship al. b. Pike and Butler
Hart Thomas, lab., s.s. Friendship al. b. Pike and Butler
Hart Thos. watchman, bds. Tremont House
Hart W. D , salesman, 74 W. 4th, bds, Clifton House
HART & WATT, (Isaac H. & Andrew W.) Book and Job Printers, 25 Broadway
HART Wm. (Wm. H. & Co.) h. 320 W. 7th
Hart Wm , clk., h. 36 Harrison
HART WM. Exchange Office 8 E. 3d, h. 36 Harrison
Hart Wm., trader, 13 E. Liberty
HART WM. & CO., (Wm. H. & Mary C. Hart.) Wh. Boots and Shoes, 95 Walnut, and 18 W. 5th
Hart Wm. M. dentist, 97 W. 7th, h. 318 W. 7th
Hartburn Anne, 96 E. Liberty
Harte August, bakery, s w.c. 8th and Linn
Harte Barney, carriage mkr., 139 Daymiller
Harte Hy., tinner, 195 Everett
Harten Fred., bds. 248 Race
Harten Philip, baker, w.s. Long al. b. Woodward and Franklin
Harter Benedict, brewer, 19 Abigail
Harter Hy., cof. h. 421 Vine
Harter Joseph, stone cutter, Ailanthus b Bank and Clearwater
Harter Mathias, carp., e.s. Goose al. b. Liberty and Green
Harteste Mary A., seamstress, 25 E, 4th
Hartfield Matthew, lab. 48 Pleasant
Hartford Fire Insurance Co, agency 80 W. 3d [worth
Hartford Seth, civil eng., bds. 34 Longworth
Harth Charles, cab. mkr. 663 Vine
Harth Chas., J. carp., 663 Vine
Hartig Lucian. lab., 60 Ham. Road
Hartig Peter, lab. 56 Ham. Road
Hartig M., lab. 23 Abigail
Hartigan Michael, lab., s.e.c. Freeman and W. Canal
Hartigan Mrs. S. B., music teacher, h. 165 Poplar

Hartigan Strange B., 185 Poplar
Harting Susan, 126 Spring
Hartke Gerhard, lab. 105 Buckeye
Hartke Hy., lab. 105 Buckeye
Hartken Hy., shoe mkr. n.w.c E. Front and Washington
Hartkey Fred. lab., wks. n.w.c. Plum and Wade
Hartkle Bahron, carriage painter, wks. 55 E. 5th
Hartkle Joseph, blksmith, wks. 55 E. 5th
Hartlaub Frank, finisher, wks. 14 W. 2d
Hartlaub Peter, grocer, 60 Observatory
Hartleb Carl, Olive Branch House, s.w.c Ludlow and Front
Hartleb Joseph, huckster, 34 Hamer
Hartleb Philip, cab. mkr. 17 Mary
Hartleib Elizabeth, bds. 19 Hathaway
Hartley Geo. F., dray, 169 W. Court w. of Central Av
Hartler James H., tinner, 19 Kossuth
Hartley John. frame mkr. 94 Hunt
Hartley John, shoe mkr. 166 E. Front
Hartler Rob., lab. n s. Pearl b. Smith and Park
Hartley Robert F., dray, 476 W. 9th
Hartley Thomas, teamster, bds. 445 W. 4th
Hartlieb Jacob, cab. mkr. 49 14th
Hartling Geo. grocer, 262 Baymiller
Hartling Michael, brewer, wks. s.w,c Plum and Canal
Hartman G. G., clk. 13 Water
Hartman Conrad. shoe mkr. 52 W. 5th
Hartman Francisca. 49 Ham. Road
Hartman Frank., basket manuf., 76 W. Mulberry
Hartman Fred., blksmith, bds. 570 Race
Hartman Fred. W., lumber yard, 184 Everett [terman's
Hartman Geo., fireman, wks. H. Closterman's
Hartman Geo., lab., 662 Main
Hartman Geo , waiter, Gibson House
Hartman Gerhard. eng., 301 W. Front
Hartman Hy., blksmith, 158 W. 6th
Hartman John, 150 Everett
Hartman John, carp., bds. 412 Vine
Hartman John, clk., 170 E. 5th
Hartman John, lab., n.w.c. Everett and Linn
Hartman Joseph, cutter, 110 E. 2d
Hartman Joseph, porter, n.e.c. 6th and Sycamore
Hartman Louis, cab. mkr. wks. Augusta b. Smith and Rose
Hartman Mic ael, lab., wks., n.e c. Walnut and Canal
Hartman Robt., liquors., 236 John
Hartmann Anton, w.s. Vine b. Milk and Mulberry
Hartmann Conrad, mason 45 W Liberty
Hartmann Dietrich, lab.. 113 Clay
Hartmann Elizabeth, 49 Ham. Road
Hartmann Frank., willow ware, 76 W. Mulberry
Hartmann Frederick W., carp., 184 Everett
Hartmann Mary, 72 W. Liberty
Hartmann Michael, blksmith, 550 Walnut
Hartmann Michael, stone cutter, 179 W. Liberty
Hartmann Valentine. carp., e.s. Goose al. b. Green and Elder
Hartmann Valentine, 239 Bremen
Hartmann Wm., b. k. 30 W Pearl, h. 242 Baymiller
Hartnagel Joseph, tailor, 168 Pleasant
Hartner Geo., painter, bds. 112 Ham. Road
Hartnett Jeremiah, stone cutter, 19 W. Court w. of Central Av
Harton Chas., b. k., bds. 149 Elm
Harton Geo., W., salesman, 136 W. 2d, bds. n.e.c. Pearl and Elm
Harton James, lab., s.s. 6th b. Broadway and Culvert
Harton Mary E., 278 Richmond
Hartry Michael blksmith, n.w.c. John and David
Hart's Hotel, David Hart prop., 21 W 6th
Harts John W. clk., bds. 47 W. 7th
Hartshorn Asher. (Loring & H.) 266 George
Hartshorn Chas., claim agt., 101 E. 3d h n.w.c. 5th and Lock

(HAS) CINCINNATI (HAT) DIRECTORY. (HAU) 161

Hartshorn John D., paper carier, 89 Barr
Hartsock Emanuel, carp., 50 Dudley
Hartun Fred., lab., e.s. Oregon b. 3d and 6th
Hartung Fred., lab., 33 Lock
Hartung Valentine, barber, 9 13th b. Elm and Plum
Hartwell Geo W., clk, 723 E. Front
Hartwell John W., Prest. Cin. Ins. Co. b. Walnut Hills
Hartwell Seth W., surveyor, 174 Vine bds. 34 Longworth
Hartwell Winthrop D., books &c. 193 W. 5th
Hartwig Augustus, china painter, 421 George
HARTWIG John B., (C. Pürrmann & Co) 353 Elm
Harty Mary, s.w.c. 9th and Central Av
Hartye Hy., lab., wks 728 Central Av
Hartye John H., tailor 51 Plum
Hartz August, cab. mkr., h. s.s. 6th b. Harriet and Horne
Hartzel Thos., grocery 168 W. 3d
Hartzhorn Thos., 175 W 5th
Harvedear Jacob, lab, 93 Central Av
Harvermeler Hy., lab., 101 Hunt
Harvermeier John, blksmith, s.s. Harrison Pike b. Brighton and Western Av
Harvey Chas. A., student, bds 322 Elm
HARVEY, COLLINS & BRACE National Claim Agency, 66 W. 3d
Harvey Edward, blksmith, 189 Barr
Harvey Edward, driver, 322 Elm
Harvey Edward T., grate setter, bds. 451 W 7th
HARVEY FRED. L. National Claim Agency, 66 W. 3d h Washington D. C.
Harvey Geo., grate setter, 451 W. 7th
Harvey Geo. E., salesman 180 Main, bds 322 Elm
Harvey Hy., finisher, wks. C. T. Dumont's
Harvey Hugh K., n.w.c. Ludlow and Front
Harvey James, pipe fitter, wks. n.e.c. Walnut and Canal
Harvey Jane, bds. 98 Broadway
HARVEY Joshua, (Gregg & H.) 306 W. 9th, w. of Central Av
Harvey & Kemper, Wm. H. & Hugh F. K) com. met. 14 Water
Harvey Lock, clk., h. 519 W. 8th
Harvey Saml. G., teacher, bds. 451 W. 7th
Harvey Thos. clk. 322 Elm
Harvey Wm. (H. & Kemper,) h. Avondale
Harvey Washington lab., wks., n.e.c Park and Marsh
Harvey Wm. H., huckster, 241 Clark
Harvie A. H., finisher, 131 Spring
Harvie Chas. S., stencil cutter, 50 Mansfield
Harvle Maria, 131 Spring
Harwell Geo., saddler, bds. 47 W. 7th
Harwell Wm., saddler, bds. 47 W. 7th
Harwey Harris C., clk., 304 W. 9th
Harwig Eliza, servt., 94 E. 5th
Harwich Joseph, teamster, bds. 17 Wade
HARWOOD Edward, (Marsh & H.) 131 Dayton
Harwood H. Elliott, (James C. H. & Alexander E.) carps. s.s. Avery b. Park and Mill
Harwood Geo., collar mkr., 47 W. 7th
Harwood Geo. C., clk. C. H. & D. R. R. n.e.c. 4th and Mill
Harwood Geo. H. clk. n.e.c, 4th and Mill
Harwood James C., (H. & Elliott,) res. Glenn Grove
Harwood Jenny, bds. 262 George
Harwood Mary, bds 264 George
Harwood Mary F., teacher, 381 George
Harwood Robt., W., salesman, 64 E Pearl
Harwood Thos. H., salesman, 185 Richmond
Harwood Wm., collar mkr., bds 47 W. 7th
Harzog Hy., carriage painter, wks, J. W. Gosling's
Hasbe Mary, servt, 429 Broadway 15

Huse August, gardener, 175 W Liberty
Hiselbeck Peter, lab., 111 Bank
Husemeyer Ferdinand, tanner, 26 Canal
Husenauer Mrs Mary A., 56 Dudley
Husenkamp John whitewasher, 448 John
Hasenmeier Hy. A., cigars, 50 W. Liberty
Hisenohr Albert, shoe mkr., bds. 22 E. Front
Hasenohr Gustave, shoemkr., 50 E. Pearl
Haenstup John, lab., e.s. Vine, b. Mulberry and Milk
Hashworth John, mach., 292 W. Front
Haskamp Joseph, lab., bds. s e.c. Clinton and Linn
Haskamp Kasper, cigars, 105 W. 2d
Haskell Joseph. b h., 110 W. 6th
Haskell Joseph T., clk., bds. 110 W. 6th
Haskell Phineas B., clk., bds. 110 W. 6th
Haskell W. P., b k, bds. 110 W. 6th
Haskin Wm., miller, wks. G. & H. Muhlhauser's
Haskins Jennie, 282 John
Haskins John, huckster, 66 E. 7th
Huslebacher Andrew, printer, bds. n.s. Court, b. Walnut and Vine
Hasler John F., butcher, 257 Carr
Hasler R. N., mess Am. Ex. Co., bds. Broadway Hotel
Haslit Mary, 636 W. 6th
Hislocher Joseph, painter, 33 Buckeye
Huss Hov. H., molder, 612 Sycamore
Hisse Chas., cab. mkr., 210 Barr
Hissel Mary A., 55 Woodward
Hasselbeck John, tanner, 263 Pleasant
Hasselbeck Peter, cab. mkr., 201 Pleasant
Hasselbeck Valentine, 709 Central Av
Hisselbrook Hy., cutter, 628 Race
Hasselbush Jacob, tailor, 31 Hughes
Hassenbush Bennett, 2d handstore, 148 Sycamore
Hassenbush Lazarus, 2d bandstore, 103 W. 5th
Hassenpflug Daniel, cab. mkr., 66 Wade
Hissett Dr., 233 W. 7th
Hasslet Maria, washwoman. 23 E. 3d
Hassmann Hy., tailor, 67 Green
HASSON Wm., (Jno. Bonte & Co.,) h. bs. 164 W. 9th
HASTIE John W., (John Bailie & Co.) 183 E. 3d
Hasting John, tailor. wks. 8 W. 3d
Hastings Mrs. A., 251 Walnut
Hatfings Elizabeth A., bds. 445 W. 7th
Hastings Hezekiah, shoemkr. 124 W. 3d
Hastings James, lab., wks. Foote, Nash & Co.'s
Hastings Jno. L., printer, 276 Clark
HATCH GEO. Mayor, Office City Buildings, h. 96 W. 9th
HATCH & HALL, (Benj. E. Hall & J. L. Egleston,) Wholesale Grocers, Commission and Forwarding Merchants, 36 Vine
Hatch Horatio N., salesman, bds. 121 E. 3d
Hatch John, 70 W. 7th
Hatch John, tailor, n.s. Front, e. of Kelly
Hatch John B., 70 W. 7th
Hatebeck Joseph, lab., wks. 335 Broadway
Hatfield C. F., druggist, bds. Madison House
Hatfield Clark S., (Williamson & H.,) 41 Walnut
Hatfield David T., 87 Everett
Hatfield George, mer., 63 Everett
Hathaway John A., fruits, 6 College Hall Bldg., h. 169 Walnut
Hathaway James T., printer, n.w.c. Washington and Front
Hatherly George D., clk. R.G. Dun & Co.'s. h. 108 Broadway
Hathrew & Gosker, (Samuel H. & Joseph G.,) saddle tree mkr., 151 Carr
Hathrew Samuel, (H. & Gosker,) 151 Carr
Hatke Bernhard, (H. & Larbes,) 610 Race
Hatke Bernhard, cof. h., 13 Landing, b. Broadway and Ludlow, h. cor. Lawrence and Landing
Hatke Catharine M., 610 Race

Hatke Geo., blksmith, 93 Pendleton
Hatke Geo., milliuery, 104 13th
Hatke Hy., chair mkr. 610 Race
Hatke Hy., lab., bds. 141 Pleasant
Hatke & Lurbes, (Bernhard H. & Joseph L.,) furniture. 610 Race
Hatkin Lindley, s. s. 64 Accommodation
Hitley Hy H., shoemkr, 42 Elm
Hatmaker Benjamin, butcher, bds. 17 Wade
Hatsuf Eliza, servt., 316 Longworth
Hatt Mary J., bds. 216 Longworth
Hatten Patrick lab., e.s. Vine, b. Milk and Mulberry
Hatten Michael, clk., bds. Dennison House
HATTERSLEY JONATHAN, Agent, Parkins Bros. & Hodgson, 24d W. 7th, h. Walnut Hills
Hattersley Saml, cof h, 514 W Front
Hattmann David, 294 Findlay
Hattmann Michael, stone cutter, 179 W. Liberty
Hattmann Wm., molder, 622 Main
Hatton M.. bds. Dennison House
Hatzenbihler Abraham, locksmith, 66 Hughes
Hatzig John, stocking mkr., 33 Moore
Haubold Elizabeth, 34 Ham. Road
Hauold Fred rick, grocery, 141 Everett
Hauck Achade, 30 Jackson
Hanck Caroline, seamstress, 30 Jackson
Hauck Catharine. 148 Findlay
Hauck Catharine, servt., 609 Vine
Hauck Charles, cigar mkr., 499 Vine
Hauck Christopher, shoemkr., 39 Hamer
Hauck Geo., carver, 395 Sycamore
Hauck Jacob, cig r mkr., 110 W. Liberty
Hauck Jacob, cigar mkr., 196 Clinton
Hauck Jacob, cof, h., s.e.c. Findlay and Race
Hauck John, bds. 74 E. Pearl
Hauck John, (John H. & Co.,) 395 Sycamore
Hauck John, maltster, n.w.c. Abigail and Sycamore
Hauck John & Co., (John H. & Bernhard Pengeman,) flour dealers, 372 Walnut
Hauck Joseph, molder, 30 Jackson
Hauck Joseph, cab. mkr., 212 Laurel
Hauck Julian. 30 Jackson
Hauck Maria. 30 Jackson
Hauck Nicholas, carriage trimmer, 395 Sycamore
Hauox Wm., cof. h., s.e.c. Wade and John
Hauck Hy., tinsmith, n.w.c. Main and Court
Haucker Rudolph, clk., bds. n.w.c. Court and Main
Hauenhorst Albert, mach., 418 Longworth
Hauenschild Hy. C., cof. h, 577 Main
Hauenstein Caspar, 170 Charlotte
Huenstein Geo. H., shoemkr, 72 Bremen
Haud John, finisher, 303 Clark
Hauffmeyer Herman, driver, 83 Findlay
Haufley Paul, tanner, 5 Melanethon
Haug Jacob, furniture. 541 Race
Haugh Jacob, carriage painter, wks. 57 E. 5th
Haugh Thos., cutler, 241 Cutter
Haughton John E., b.k., 243 E. Pearl, h. E. Front, opp. Jamestown Ferry
Haughton Josephine, 65 Pike
Haughton & Reid, (Samuel M. H. & James R.,) pork packers, s.w.c. Canal and Sycamore
Haughton Samuel M., (H. & Reid,) 88 Clark
Hauk Andrew J., butcher, 28 Pub. Landing, h 38 Elm
Hauk Chares, cab. mkr., 533 E. Front
Haukenspink Morris, lab., 25 Dudley
Haukker Hy . 374 W. Liberty
Haun Charles, cab. mkr., 305 Freeman
Hauns Jacob, lab., bds. s.s. Liberty b. Freeman and Mill Creek
Haunsz Anselm, lab., 673 Race
Haupe Geo, hinge fitter, wks. n.e.c. Walnut and Canal
Haupt Conrad, varnisher, 349 W. 5th
Haupt George. cab. mkr., 551 Sycamore
Haupt George, finisher, 53 13th

162 (HAW) CINCINNATI (HAY) DIRECTORY. (HEA)

Haupt Matthew, tailor, 664 Main
Haupt Moritz, furniture, 348 W 5th
Hauptmann Jacob, teamster, 57 Harrison Pike
Haus John, 66 Stark
Haus John, lab., w.s. Fountain, b. Rice and Alexander
Hause Charles, meats, 288 Linn
Hausen Jacob, lab., 708 Freeman
Hauser Angeline, n.s. Front. e. of Ferry
Hausen Anna, 278 W. Front
Hauser Frederick, b.k., 376 Main
HAUSER JACOB, Napoleon Tavern, Restaurant and Boarding House, 442 Main
Hauser John, carp., 682 Vine
Hauser John. lab., 187 W. Court, w. of Central Av
Hauser John, tailor, 55 Elder
Hauser Matthew, liquors, &c., 70 13th
Hauser Stephen, cooper, 675 Vine
Hauser Stephen, cooper, 305 Vine
Hausfeld Angel, n.w.c. Abigail and Pendleton
Hausfeld Barney. lab., 36 Abigail
Hausfeld Benjamin, clk., n.e.c. Pearl and Pike
Hausfeld Hy., lab., 53 Pendleton
Hausfeld Hy., painter, bds. 473 Broadway
Hausman Hy., cab. mkr., 213 W. Court, w. of Central Av
Hausmann Caroline, seamstress, 159 Bremen
Hauss John, lab., s.e.c. Riddle and Harrison Pike
Haustein Emil, store keeper, Burnet House
Haut Lorenz, 172 W. Liberty
Hauth Elisabeth, teacher, 11th district school
Hauttenhaus Hy., mer., 56 Clay
Hauttenhaus Hy., jr., clk., 56 Clay
Hauttenhaus Martin clk., 56 Clay
Hauzenvinkel Hy., clk., bds. 98 Pearl e. of Broadway
Havalin Samuel, molder, 1230 E. Front
Havelin Gilbert, painter, s.s. Front e. of French
Havely Joseph, porter, Sylvester House
Haven Augustus, cashier, 177 W. 2d
HAVEN James L., (James L. H. & Co.) h. Avondale
HAVEN JAMES L & CO., (James L. H. & Benjamin F. Paddack) Iron and Brass Founders and Manufacturers of Hardware, 173, 175 and 177 W. 2d
Haven Mary, servt., 486 W. 7th
Havens James, driver, bds. Brighton House
Haverdill John, 292 Broadway
Havercamp Hy., lab, wks. n.w.c. Plum and Wade
Havercamp John, wks. 310 W. 3d
Havercamp Jos., salesman 38 W. Pearl, h. 531 W. 7th [man
Haverkamp Clemens, grocery, 160 Freeman
Haverkamp Hy. J., tailor, 25 Buckeye
Haverkamp John, lab., 76 Melancthon
Haverkamp Wm., porter, 236 Everett
Haverkotte Louis, blksmith, 76 Melancthon
Haverly Mary, 1290 E. Front
Havies John J., finisher, wks. n.e.c. Walnut and Canal
Havink Gerhard J., shoe mkr., 30 Green
Havlin Hy., teamster, 296 Water
Havlin James M., lab., 974 E. Front
Havling Mary M., n.w.c. Hopkins and Baymiller
Havries John W., pattern mkr., wks. n.e.c. Canal and Walnut
Havy Elnora, s.s. 6th b. Broadway and Culvert
Haweker Barney. lab., 686 W. 6th
Hawekotte Angeline, 34 Pleasant
Hawekotte F., mach., 38 Pleasant
Hawekotte W. H., clk. 175 Main, h. 38 Pleasant
Hawickhorst Hy., tailor, 560 W. 5th
Hawken Wm., lab., 83 W. Front
Hawkey Hy., molder, wks. n e.c. Plum and Wade
Hawkins Alfred, janitor, s.w.c. 7th and Mound

Hawkins Alice, bds. Dumas Hotel
Hawkins Augusta, 139 Plum
Hawkins Edward, shoe mkr., 532 W. 6th
Hawkins Edward H., harness mkr., 215 W. 7th
Hawkins Eliza, 1232 E Front
Hawkins Hy., lab., 92 W. Front
Hawkins Jane, 164 Smith
Hawkins John, 124 Mill
Hawkins John, porter. 15 Stone
Hawkins Joseph lab., 563 Elm
Hawkins Julius, (Smith & H.) 4 Home
Hawkins Mary, 136 Mound
Hawkins Sarah, 59 Gest
Hawkins Wm., trunk mkr., 17 Observatory Road
HAWLEY David, (Smith & H.) 106 John
HAWLEY J. R., Stationer and Publisher, 164 Vine, h. Covington
Hawley Susan, 514 W. 9th w. of Central Av.
Hawn Andrew J., chair mkr., bds. 19 Union
Hawn George W., bk. mason, bds. 19 Union
Hawn Nancy, 19 Union
HAWORTH OWEN W., Horse Dealer, 13 E. 5th. h. 124 E. 5th
Hay James, bds. Dennison House
Hay James, lab., 590 E. Front
Hay John E., huckster, 514 W. 3d
Hay Wm. B., plane mkr., wks. 196 Mound
Haybrok John. lab., wks. Henry Nye's
Haycock Isabelle, 518 Sycamore
Hayden Deborah, 159 George
Hayden Esther, bds. 144 John
Hayden Frisbee W., barber, bds. 226 W. 7th
Hayden Harry, porter, 61 W. 3d
Hayden Patrick, watchman, bds. 883 E. Front
Hayden Richard B., clk., n.e.c. Freeman and 6th
Hayden Samuel L., druggist, n.e.c. Freeman and 6th
HAYDEN Peter, (Wilson & H.) h Columbus, O.
Hayes C. & Bro., (Calvin & Job M.) com mer., 15 Walnut
Hayes Galvin, (H. H. & Bro.) 365 W. 3d
Hayes Frank, carp., s.s. Accommodation e. of 8th
Hayes James Q., b.k. s w.c. John and Front, bds. 462 W. 7th
Hayes Job M., (C. Hayes & Bro.) 365 W. 3d
Hayes John, lab., 71 E. 8th e. of Lock
Hayes John C., gas fitter. 274 W. 9th
Hayes Lawrence, tailor, 8 W. 3d
Hayes M., clk. 101 W. 4th, h. 14 E. 7th
Hayes Mary, 1 E. 7th
Hayes Mary, 1516 E. Front
Hayes Oliver C., 216 Longworth
Hayes Rutherford B ., atty., 383 W. 6th
Hayes Wm., grocery, 133 E. 6th
Hayes Wm., lab., s.s. 6th b. Broadway and Culvert
Hayes Wm., porter, 49 Race
Haygh Mary, 161 W. 5th
Hayman Benj. F., eng., 47 E. 7th
Hayman Harmon H., lab , 139 Plum
Hayman John, clk., s.w.c. 3d and Smith
Haynes & Bro., (Edward T. & Geo. S.) painters, 132 Race
Haynes Edward T., (H. & Bro) 313 Clark
Haynes Geo. S., (H. & Bro.) 311 Clark
HAYNES Ira, (H., Lewis & Spencer) h. 432 W. 7th
Haynes James E., carp., 5 Observatory Road
HAYNES, LEWIS & SPENCER, (Ira H., Chas. R L. & Wm. F. S.) Wholesale Dealers in White Goods, Notions and Staple Dry Goods, 136 Walnut
Hayes David D., carp., 330 Clark
Hays Eliza. n.s. E. Front e. of Leatherbury

Hays Euphemia, bds. 296 W. 5th
Hays Isaac M., saw mkr., 418 John
Hays James, clk., bds. 462 W. 7th
Hays James, finisher, wks. C. T. Dumont's
Hays James, fireman, n.s. 2d b. Park and Rose
Hays James, lab., junction High and Kemper's Lane
Hays James, lab., w.s. Pole b. 2d and Pearl
Hays James, molder, bds. Bevis House
Hays John, atty., 88 12th
Hays John, eng., wks. central saw mill
Hays Rev. John S., 290 Richmond
Hays Miss Mary, n.e.c. 6th and John
Hays Mary, 13 E. 7th
Hays Mary, rear 53 E. 3d e. of Whittaker
Hays Michael, salesman, 13 E. 7th
Hays Patrick, stone yard s.e.c. Plum and Adams, h. 12 Oliver
Hays Mrs. Robert M., 502 W. 5th
Hays Simeon, bk. mkr., n.s. 6th b. Harriet and Horne
Hays Thomas, lab., 35 W. Court w. of Central Av.
Hays Thos. B , 85 George
Hays Wm., lab., bds. 49 Race
Hays Wm., tanner, 62 Dunlap
Hays Winston, eating house, 43 E. 4th
Hayse John, lab., 274 W. 9th
Hayt Augusta, teacher, 93 14th
Hayton John, mach., wks. J. A. Fay & Co's
HAYWARD P. B., (Ferry & Co.) 19 Harrison
Hazard Wm. S., com. mer., 65 W. Miami Canal, h. 500 W. 7th
Hazen Burton, real estate agt., s.w.c. 6th and Vine, h. Brooklyn, Ky.
Hazen Edward, carp., 1294 E. Front
Hazen Hanora, 187 E. 3d
Hazen John T., clk. 93 W. Pearl, bds. 103 Broadway
Hazen Larry M., policeman, 187 E. 3d
Hazen Nathan, clk , bds. 103 Broadway
Hazlett John, boat stores 13 E. Front, h. 100 E. 5th
Hazlett Joseph, lab., e.s. Macalister b. 4th and 5th
Hazelton Thos., finisher, 95 E. 3d e. of Whittaker
Head Jas. E., b.k., 71½ Betts
Head Samuel H., bill poster Commercial office, h. 124 Mound
Headington Nicholas, Judge Court of Common Pleas, res. Mill Creek Tp.
Hendley Hy., watchman, 86 W. 2d
Headley Herman, cab. mkr., 86 W. 2d
Headrick Ann, w.s. Bank al. b. 3d and 4th
Heads James F., painter, n.s. Channing b. Price and Young
Heal Wm., 552 Central Av.
Healey Bridget, servt., 332 W. 7th
Healey James, stone cutter, 63 E. 8th
Healey Martin, grocery, s.e.c. Court and Mound
Henley Wm., stone cutter, 63 E. 8th
Healing Geo., printer, 106 W. 7th
Healy Albert M., 258 Longworth
Healy Bartley, lab., 59 Race
Healy Catharine, 65 E 8th
Healy Cornelius, tailor, 346 12th
Healy Hannah, servt , 310 W. 7th
Healy James, lab., 260 Water
Healy James, lab., wks. s.w.c. Broadway and 5th
Healy Jas. N., carp., 120 Baymiller
Healy John C., student, 6 E. 3d
Healy John P., grocery, 278 Central Av.
Healy P., finisher, wks. n.e.c. Walnut and Canal
Healy Thos., saloon, 163 Central Av.
Healy Wm., lab., wks. s.w.c. Broadway and 5th
HEALY WM. A., Agent Ohio River Salt Company, 27 W. Front, h. 279 Longworth
Hebbler Hy., teamster, 50 Wade
Hebenstreet Peter, driver, 528 Main
Heaney James, painter, 288 E. 6th
Heanue Patrick, blksmith, w.s. Freeman b. 5th and 6th

(HEC)　　CINCINNATI　　(HEG)　　DIRECTORY.　　(HEI)　　163

Heard John, lab., 260 Water
Hearn Ellen, 46 E 5th
Hearn Michael, lab., 86 E. 5th
Hearn Patrick, cof. h., 86 E. 5th
Hearn Stephen J., sawyer, 144 Carr
Heart Bridget, servt.. Henrie House
Heart Elijah, dray, 193 W Front
Heart Samuel, bds 193 W. Front
Hearty Ellen, servt., 2°0 Longworth
Heath Alfred, tailor, 68 E Pearl
Heath Augustus, bk. layer, 395 Central Av
Heath Thos. H., bk. layer, s.e.c. Betts and John
Heath Thos. H. jr., bk. layer, bds. s.e.c. Betts and John
Heathrington John S., lab., s.s. Front b. Waldon and Broad
HEATON Daniel, (Hubbard & H.), 321 Walnut
Heaton John, painter, 28 Mohawk
Heaton Kate, bds. 57 E. 3d
Heaton Thomas, n.s. Coggswell al. nr. Auburn
Heaverin Wm. II , 9 Sycamore
Hebbler Herman, teamster. 7 John
Hebel Wm. F., cigars, 64 W. Liberty
Hebeler Wilhelmina, 146 Buckeye
Hebenk Henry. chair mkr., 435 W. 2d
Heber Lewis, cigar mkr., 635 Vine
HEBERD Jed., (Ellis McA. & Co.), 176 Elm
Heberger Francis, plumber. 197 Bremen
HEBERGER Michael, (John Gibson & Co.). 309 Main
Heberling John, saddler, bds. 493 Vine
Hebern Catharine, confect., 22 Central Av
Hebron Patrick, lab., 156 Mound
Hechler Peter, stone mason, 69 Green
Hecht Elias, broker, w.s. Walnut b. 13th and Mercer
Hecht Ernst F., tailor, 649 Vine
Hecht Henry, peddler, 19 15th b. Elm and Plum
Hecht Jacob. police man, 54 Hamer
Hecht Marcus, exchange office, 231 Walnut. h 360 Walnut
Heck Adam, butcher nt G. & P. Bogen's
Heck Adam, quarryman, 708 Vine
Heck Bernhard tailor, 639 Vine
Heck Florian, harness mkr., bds. 347 Walnut
Heck Geo., shoe mkr., bds. 80 W. Liberty
Heck H.. bds. Dennison House
Heck Jacob, brewer, s.w.c. Divison and Harrison Pike
Heck Jacob, lab., w.s. Coleman b. Bank and Central Av
Heck John, lab., wks. N. W. Thomas & Co.'s
Heck John, n.w.c. Browne and Vernon al
Heck Louis, lab., w.s. Riddle b. Bank and Harrison Pike
Heck Peter H.. hinge mkr., 589 Race
Heck Simon, peddler, 709 Central Av
Heckadore John, plasterer, 32 Mulberry
Heckel Edward, mach., 7-8 Central Av
Heckel Henry, foreman, wks. 728 Central Av
Heckel Jacob, molder, 40 Pike
Heckelrath John, clk., 105 Sycamore, bds. 91 Sycamore
Hecker Frederick J., bar k., 481 Vine
Hecker Jacob, cof. h., 481 Vine
Hecker Jennie, 161 Longworth
Hecker John. cab. mkr., 50 Lock
HECKERT HENRY F.. relght Agent Baltimore and Ohio Railroad, 3 E. Front, h. 78 Pike
Heckert Mrs. Mary, 57 E. Woodward
Heckewelder George W., mer., 319 W. 8th
Heckewelder John Y., mer., 319 W. 8th
Hecklaw Frederick. butcher, s.e.c. Findlay and Race
Heckle Joseph, trimmer, bds. w s. Walnut b. 4th and 5th
Heckle Wm., pocket book mkr., 145 Ham. Road
Heckleman George. dray, 165 Carr
Heckmann David. blksmith, 262 Pleasant
Heckmann John D., blksmith, 262 Pleasant

Heckrotte Henry J., carp., 317 W. 6th
Hector Ellen. servt., 31 McFarland
Hector Patrick, lab., 415 W. 2d
Hector Thomas, lab., n.s. E. Front e. of Leatherbury
Hedderton Thos., lab., w.s. Ramsey n. of Poplar
Heddinger Lorentz, 607 Elm
Heddirington Ann, 211 Poplar
Heddirington Leonora, teacher, bds. 211 Poplar
Heddirington Martha, teacher, bds. 211 Poplar
Heddirington Mary Ann, laundress, Gibson House
Heddirington Nora. teacher, h 101 Dudley
Heder John, blksmith, 263 Vine
Hedgelan Jacob. watchman, 511 W. 3d
Hedger Robert, 28 Hathaway
Hedges D. O., baggage master C. H. & D. R. R., n e.c. Carr and Taylor
Hedges Isaac A , miller, 442 W. 7th
Hedges James blind manufac. 236 Vine
Hedges John K , clk., 83 E. 3d
Hedges Sherman, cashier C. H. & D. R. R., 92 Carr
Hedley Broughton, salesman, 58 W. 5th
HEDRICK HENRY, Insurance Agent, 60 W. 3d, h. Glendale
Heedkamp Frank, cooper, 149 Bank
Heeg Adam. cigar mkr., n.s. Corwine b. Walnut and Ham. Road
Heeg Henry, bar k., 24 W. Court
Heeke Clemmens, (H. & Scheve). n.s. Ham. Road nr. Mohawk Bridge
Heeke & Schleve, (Clemmens H. & John S.) chair mkrs., n.s Ham. Road nr. Mohawk Bridge
Heekin Ellen. e.s. Carl b. 3d and 4th and Mill and Stone
Heekin Mary, e.s. Carl b. 3d and 4th, and Mill and Stone
Heely Bridget, servt., 376 W. 7th
Heemann Henry, cooper, rear 176 Clay
Heemann Lambert, iron railing, 467 Walnut, res E. Walnut Hills
Heenan Mary. bds. 355 Central Av
Heerbaum Henry, lab., 56 Poplar
Heerdt Adam. clothing, 558 Central Av
Heerdt Conrad, tailor, n.w. c. Linn and Findlay
Heerdt Leonhardt, rear 122 Mohawk
Heermance Henry, druggist. 933 E. Front, h. n.e.c. Broad and E. Front
Heermann Frederick W., grocer, 927 Central Av
Heermann John, cooper, 50 York
Heery Chas.. brush mkr., 26 Ham. Road
HEET BARNEY G., Family Grocery, 654 Sycamore
Heet Harwey, bk. layer, 101 Richmond
Heffer John, lab., 588 Race
Hefferman T., sawyer, wks. 304 Broadway
Hefferman Thomas, carp., 328 Race
Hefferman Thomas W., pattern mkr., 165 Cutter
Hefferman Wm. C., carp., 394 W. 5th
Heffling Henry, bar k. s.e.c. 5th and Vine
Heffner Daniel, driver, n.s. al. b. Poplar and Vine and Ham. Road and Buckeye
Heffner James, plasterer, s.s Charlotte b. Central Av. and Linn
Heffner Mary, laundress, 396 Broadway
Hefley Anna J., teacher, 267 W. 7th
Hefley Isaac, (Marshall & H.) 267 W. 7th
Hefling Adam, huckster, 338 Clark
Hefner Geo., shoe dealer, 184 W. Court
Hefren John, lab., 188 Water
Heft Casper A., carp., w s. Goose al. b. W. Liberty and 15th
Heftlein Martin, baker, 362 Broadway
Hegedom Jane, n.e.c. Pendleton and Liberty
Hegel Charlotte, seamstress, 639 Vine
Hegel Nicholas, 639 Vine
Hegens Henry C., harness mkr., 68 W. Court
Heger Leiers. 394 Broadway
Heger Simon, cof h., 95 W. Miami Canal
Hegerle Joseph, lab., n.e.c. Madison and Plum

Hegermeier Charles, cooper, wks. 216 Clark
Hegge Herman B., barber, 102 Hunt
Hegger Barney, lab , bds. 90 E. 2d
Hegger Barney, 102 Butler
Hegger Bernard H., lab., rear 512 Walnut
HEGGER J. Fred. (Kleine, H. & Co.), 108 Butler
Hegger John, blksmith, 449 W, 2d, h. Anderson al. b. 2d and W. W. Canal
Heggerman Wm., blksmith, 19 Observatory Road
Hegian William, carp., 509 W. 3d
Hegmier John, lab., 1365 E. Front
Hegner Christopher, (L. & C. H.), 68 W. Court
Hegner L. & C., (Lawrence & Christopher), harness mkrs., 30 W. Court
Hegner Lawrence. (L. & C. H.), bds. Buttemiller's Hotel
Hehe Christian, lab., w s. Coggswell al. b. Franklin and Woodward
Heheman Herman H., porter, 139 Plum
Hehemann Frank, clk., n.w.c. Vine and 2d, bds. 145 Race
Hehemann Henry, clk., n.e c. 6th and Central Av
Hehmann Frederick F., carp., 93 Pendle
Hehmann Henry, mason, 161 Pleasant
Hehmann Henry, teamster, wks. G. &. H Muhlhauser's
Hehmann Wm., bar k., 9 12th
Hehn Michael, plumber, w.s. Harriet b. Sloo and Front
Heibel Valentine, gardener, Garden of Eden
Heiberger John, harness mkr., 624 Central Av
Heiberger John, saddler, 504 Elm
Heich John B , clk. O. M. Institute. h. 111 Everett
Heid John, finisher, 16 14th
Heidacker Joseph, cof. h., s.e.c. Ham. Road and Elm
Heidacker Fred., grocery, 678 Main
Heidacker Louis, clk., 413 Elm
Heidebrink Henry, cigar mkr., wks. n.e. c. 2d and Ludlow
Heidebrink John H., salesman, 61 Hughes
Heidecker L., salesman, 413 Elm
Heidel Helena, seamstress, s.s. W. Liberty b. Bremen and Race
Heidel Joseph, shoe mkr., 107 W. Liberty
Heidel Michael, Heidel's Cornet Band, 197 Vine, h. 501 Vine
Heidelbach Louis, 51 W. 3d, h. 224 W. 4th
HEIDELBACH Marum, (Heidelbach, Seasongood & Co.), h. New York City
Heidelbach Michael, clk., s.w.c. 3d and Vine. bds. 26 E. 3d
HEIDELBACH Moses, (H. Wertheimer & Co.), 49, E. 5th
Heidelbach Nathan, salesman, s.w.c. 3d and Vine, bds. 224 W. 4th
HEIDELBACH Phillip, (H. Seasongood & Co.) 224 W. 4th
HEIDELBACH, SEASONGOOD & CO., (Phillip H., Jacob S. & Marum Heidelbach, Lewis Seasongood & Samuel Thorner), Importers and Wholesale Dealers in Dry Good, Furnishing Goods and Clothing, s. w.c. 3d and Vine
HEIDELBACH, WERTHEIMER & CO., (Moses H., Arnold W. & Abram J. Friedlander). Manufacturers and Wholesale Dealers in Clothing, and Importers of Cloths, Cassimeres, &c., 86 W. Pearl
Heidelman Bernhard, porter, 14 Providence
Heidelmeyer Josephine, 24 Hamer
Heidenreich Chas., tailor, 57 W. Liberty
Heidenreich Lorenz, cab. mkr., 81 Bremen
Heider Christian, chair mkr., 43 R ce
Heidkamp Barney, clk., bds. 411 Main
Heidkamp Bernhard, tailor, rear 95 Woodward
Heidkamp Ferdinand, tailor, w.s. Observatory b. Hill and Observatory Road

164 (HEI) CINCINNATI (HEL) DIRECTORY. (HEL)

Heidkamp Frederick, lab., rear 93 Woodward
Heidkamp Joseph, clothing, 411 Main
Heidlebach Anthony, harness mkr., 205 W Liberty
Heidleman Barney, 464 Linn
Heidleman Joseph, cigars. 464 L'nn
Heidmann Henry, carp., bds. 577 Main
Heidman Hy., lab., wks. s.e.c. Vine and Front
Heidman John, cigar mkr., 526 W. 8th
Heidmeyer Anard, lab., 42 Elm
Hekischuh Geo., coffee dealer, h. 126 Pleasant
Heidsick John P., express man, 20 Mercer
Heidt Geo., stone mason, 15 Wade w. of Linn
Heidt Henry, printer, bds. 51 W. 5th
Heiffmann Hy., lab., 97 Buckeye
Heiger Richard, bds. 151 Abigail
Heighway Eliza, 496 Vine
Heighway Wm. H , 25 Jackson
Heil Hy., corp., 639 Vine
Heil Phillip. tailor. 657 Vine
Heiland John, cooper, s.s. 6th b. Broadway und Culvert
Heilbran Levi, tailor, 20 Providence Av.
Heileman Jacob, lab , wks. 830 Central Av.
Heileman John, tailor, 204 Linn
Heileman Bernard H., shoe mkr., 497 Race
Heilemann John, cigar mkr., 106 Elder
Heilemann John B., boots and shoes, 497 Race
Heilemann John B., bar k., n.w.c. Walnut and Court
Heilman Hermann H., lab., 171 Oliver
Heilmann Jacob., n s. Charlotte. b. Linn and Baymiller
Heilermann Mrs. Mary, 106 Elder
Heilers Theodore. finisher, wks. Mitchell & Rammelsberg
Heilos Lawrence. lab , bds. s.s. Harrison Road b. Riddle and Brighton
Heim Casper. cab. mkr., 205 Providence
Heim Hy , finisher, s s. Ohio Al. b, Elm and Plum
Heim Phil'p, lab., 77 Peete
Heim Wm., printer 157 Pleasant
Heimann C., tailor. 155 Water
Heimann Fred., teamster. 524 John
Heimbach Peter, lab. 758 W Front
Heimerling Wolf, h, 102 Brown
Heimgrider Frank. lab , s.s. Charlotte b. Linn and Baymiller
Heimler Geo., tailor. e. end of Mohawk
Heimoos Jacob. tailor. 137 Wade
Heimoos Nicholas, 127 York
Heimrod Adolph, printer. 504 W. 4th
Heims Nathan, actor, 195 Vine
Heims ith Casper H., grocer, 20 Milton
Heinn Barney, bds. s. w. c. Race and Henry
Heinan Gustav A., coppersmith, c. 14th and Race
Heinbach Phillpp, carp., 118 Bremen
Heinberger Christiana, cap mkr., 97 Brown
Heinbuch John C. H., lab., 5 Mulberry
Heinck Hy , dray, s. e. c. Front and John
Heine Chas., tailor. 9 Mary
Heine Chas. F. W., shoe mkr., 41 12th
Heine Elizabeth. 430 Pleasant
Heine Henry, walter, Gibson House
Heine Joseph, teamster, wks. 830 Central Av.
Heinebach Christian, varnisher, 118 Bremen
Heinebach Louis. 415 Elm
Heinemann Abraham, 80 George
Heinemann Chas., harness mkr., 524 Sycamore
Heinemann Gertrude, seamstress, 24 13th
Heinemann Magnus, cab. mkr., 102 Ham. Road

H EINEMANN OTTO. Drugs, Medicines, Chemicals, &c., n.e c. Linn and Laurel

Heinen Jacob, tailor, 50 Bremen
Heinen Joseph, tailor, 63 Ham. Road
Heiner Geo., waiter, 31 W. 2d
Heing Herman H., lab., 103 W. Front
Heinich Wm., cab. mkr., 87 Ham. Road
Heinicke Edward H., tailor, 510 Race

Heinking Chas., b k., 50 W. 2d, h. 152 Clark
Heinrich Joseph, porter, 55 12th
Heinrichsdorff Otto, bakery, 19 W. 5th
Heinrick Hy , tailor, 26 Mill
Heins Hy., blksmith, n.s. Front. h. M. Canal and Kilgour
Heinsheimer D., jr., not. public, 10 W. Court
Heinsheimer David, (J. H. Heinsheimer & Co.) 169 John
Heinsheimer J. A., (J. H. Heinsheimer & Co) 3'1 George
Heinsheimer J. H. & Co., (J. H. H , David H. Louis H. & J. A. H.,) clothing, 195 Walnut
Heinsheimer Joseph H., (J. H. H. & Co) 301 George
Heinsheimer Louis, (J. H. Heinsheimer & Co) 62 Mound
Heinsheimer N. E., c'k., bds. 301 George
Heinsmann Elizabeth, restaurant, 12 W. Court
Heinsmann Henry, miller. 294 Broadway, h Vine Street Hill
Heintz Bartholomew, tailor, 615 Central Av.
Heintz Chas., brewery, s s. Montgomery Pike nr. Reading Road
Heintz Philip, cab. mkr., 505 Race
Heintz Philip, carp , 6 16 Elm
Heinz Chas., tanner, 259 Ham. Road
Heinz Joseph, teamster 52 Findlay
Heinzenberger Louisa. teacher. 53½ Elm
Heinzheimer Lewis, mer., 62 Mound
Heinzelman Geo., cab. mkr., 140 Barr
Heir Theodore, porter, 3 Lucy
Heireman Hy., instrument mkr., 57 Clay
He'schman Henry, lab., wks. Wood & McCoy's
Heisel Fred , painter. 266 Hopkins
Heisel Geo., cab mkr., 266 Hopkins
Heiser Anna. 72 12th
Heiser Joseph, lab , 165 W. Liberty
Heiser Peter, cigar mkr., 165 W. Liberty
Heising Theodore, lab , 22 Commerce
Heising Wm., sawyer, wks. 128 W. 2d
Heisman Mark, cigar mkr., 50 Friendship al.
Heisner Frank, varnisher, bds. s.s. Front b 3d and 5th
Heister Adam, bar k., Walnut Street House
Heister, Hy., janitor. College Building, e.s Walnut b. 4th and 5th
Heister Michael Dining saloon, 123 Main, h. 130 Main
Heisterman Barbara, n.s. Friendship al h. Lawrence and Pike
Heit Balser, lab., 25 Providence
Heit Fred , driver, 63 Providence
Heit John mach., wks. 408 Walnut
Heitacker Hy., cab. mkr., 67 14th
Heitacker Herman, lab., 67 14th
Heitacker Wm., box mkr., 67 14th
Heithrinck Adam. mason, 411 Sycamore
Heitkamp Francis, cab, mkr , n.w.c. 3d and Stone
Heiter Adam, pocket book mkr., n.e.c. Buckeye and Main [Hunt
Heithaus Benj., boots and shoes, 104
Heithaus Bernard, shoe mkr , 66 Spring
Heitkemper John G., cigar mkr , 19 Mulberry
Heitmann Clemens, police, 61 Findlay
Heitmann Frank, watchman, 611 Race
Heitmann Hy., tailor, bds. 1 Budd
Heitmann James, finisher, wks. n.e.c. Walnut and Canal
Heitmann Wm., laundry, bds. 577 Main
Heitmeier John F., porter, 474 Race
Heitmeyer Arnold porter. 42 Elm
Heitz Chas.. tanner, 259 Ham. Road
Heitz Gertrude, seamstress, 24 13th
Heitzer Frank, 125 York

H EKER JACOB, Coffee and Boarding House, 481 Vine

Hekhof Hy., cartman 61 Kossuth
Helber John, peddler, e.s. Vine b. Mulberry and Milk
Helbers Geo , 486 Broadway
Hell ush Clemens, clk., 62 Main
Helcher Hy., lab., bds. n.e.c. Linn and Poplar

Held Chas , upholsterer, 603 Main
Held Christ F., mach., 195 Clinton
Held Fred., cab mkr., 195 Clinton
Helde Jacob, conf. h , 164 Freeman
Heldwein Margaretha, 673 W 6th

H ELFFERICH FRANCIS, Coffee House, 387 Main

Helfferich Francis, jr., bds. 387 Main
Helfferich J , clk., Adams Express Co. h. 387 Main
Helfrich Frank, frame mkr., rear 26 Franklin
Helgenhold Hy., grocery, 1256 E. Front
Helle Barney, feed store. 599 Race
Helle Richard, grocery, 599 Race
Helkee Herman. lab., s.e.c. Clark and Rittenhouse
Helle Elizabeth. 162 E. 5th
Helleberg Charles G , daguerreotypist, 164 Ham. Road
Hellencamp Catharine, servant, 284 George
Hellenger John, coppersmith, bds. n.w. c 2d and Lawrence
Heller Asher, (H. Bros. & Co.,) 246 Plum
Heller Barney, lab., wks. Hieatt & Woods
Heller Bernhard. lab., 600 Race
Heller Bros. & Co., (Asher H., Solomon H., & L Buttenwieser,) furnishing goods, 228 W. 5th
Heller Chas., bk. binder 143 Pleasant
Heller David, b. k., 246 Plum
Heller Francis. druggist. e.s Auburn b. Central Av. and Corp. Line
Heller Francis P., (H. & Young.) res. Jamestown. Ky.
Heller John, lab., w.s. Goose al. b. 14th and 15th
Heller Kalman L., teacher, 246 Plum
Heller L. , mer., 246 Plum
Heller Mathias, clk., 2 6 Plum
Heller Solomon W., (H Bros. & Co.,) 246 Plum
Heller Wm., tinner. 500 W Front

H ELLER & YOUNG, (Francis P. H. & Elias Y.) Manufacturers of Kitchen Ranges and Warm Air Furnaces. 292 Main

Helling John H , grocery, n. w. c. 3d and Stone
Hellinger Mathias, cab mkr., 225 Findlay
Hellman Henry, varnisher, wks. Mitchell & Rammelsberg's

H ELLMAN Max., (Meyberg & H), 140 E. 3d

Hellmann Christian A., porter, 17 Abigail
Hellmann Frederick G., agt. boots and shoes, 486 Main
Hellmann Geo , tailor, 9 Woodward
Hellmann Herman, file mkr., bds. 19 Abigail
Hellmann Joseph, inspector, 43 Race
Hellmich Henry, lithographer. 154 Bremen
Hellmig Henry, 708 Freeman
Hellmig John, wagon mkr., 103 Bank
Hellmond Wm., tailor, 727 Elm
Hellmuth Joseph, lab., 110 W Liberty
Hellstern Joachim, cof h., 552 Vine
Hellworth Raymond, bar. k., 26 E. Canal
Helm A L., engraver, Am. Bank Note Company
Helman Albert M., tailor, 101 Betts
Helman Chas. F., clk., n.w.c. Findlay

H ELMAN CHAS M., Druggist and Apothecary, n.w.c Findlay and Baymiller

Helman Max., mer., 140 E. 3d
Helman Orlando A., clk., 132 W. 6th
Helmann George. molder. 14 Abigail
Helmas Barney, lab , wks. n.w.c. Plum and Wade
Helmcamp Frank, b.k. Julius Balke's 568 Race
Helmech Charles, porter. 524 Sycamore
Helmerich Chas., gilder, 69 W. Liberty
Helmers Barney, lab., s.w.c. Logan and Green

H ELMERS CLAUS. Leather and Findings 356 Main

(HEM) CINCINNATI (HEN) DIRECTORY. (HEN) 165

Holmers Herman, foreman, s.s. Green b. Elm and Pleasant
Helmers Toney, lab, 62 Pierson
Helmes Barney, lab., wks. s.w.c. Park and W W. Canal
Helmes Herman, tailor, 636 Main
Helmholz Wm., cooper 296 Findlay
Helmich Eliza, 166 E Front
Helmich Fred., ci zar mkr., 71 Elder
Helmich Frederick, painter, bds. 399 Sycamore
Helmich Henry, boots and shoes, 154 Bremen
Helmich Wm. cigar mkr., 57 Mulberry
Helmick Isaac, cook, s.w.c. Lewis and Front
Helmig Barnard, 151 Abigail
Helmig Bernhard, cab mkr., 371 Broadway
Helmig Geo., (Rattermann, Gebbe & Co.) res. Mill Creek Tp.
Helmig Geo., grocery, 149 Bank
Helmig Henry, confec. 1269 E. Front
Helmig Henry driver, n s. Dayton b. Western Av. and Colem n
Helmig Henry, turner, s.e. c. Bank and Freeman
Helmig Joseph, grocery, 708 Freeman
Helming Henry, lab. bds 19 Abigail
Helming Henry, tailor. 207 Linn
Helming John, boot and shoe mkr., n.w. c Elm and 6th
Helmink Stephen, 71 Abigail
Helmkamp Ann M 59 Race
Helmkamp John H. lab. 171 Buckeye
Helmke B., cigar mkr , 532 Elm
Helmke Gerhard, cigar mkr , 532 Elm
Helms Antony, lab., e.s. Anderson b. 2d and Pearl
Helms Barney, box mkr., 11 Budd
Helms Caroline, watch mkr., 420 W. Liberty
Helms Geo., lab., 420 W. Liberty
Helms Henry, lab., 12 Mary
Helms John, lab., n.s. Sun b. Mill and Park
Helms Toney, cooper. 91 Dudley
Helms Wm , clv., 926 Main
Helmsdorfer Frederick, cof h 1121 Central Av.
Helmsing John, tanner, 83 Woodward
Helmuth Barney, 2 Logan
Help Max., mer., 24 Longworth
Helscher Bernhard, carp., s. s. Green b. Race and Pleasant
Helskamp Mrs. Elizabeth. 72 Abigail
Helsmann Henry, la'., 42 Elm
Helt John, lock smith, 10 Hughes
Helters, John B., lab., 378 Broadway
Heltman John, cigar mkr., wks. 579 Main
Heltmon John, driver, 702 Freeman
Helweg Herman 381 Broadway
Helwick John, cth mkr.. 495 W. 6th
Helwig Wm., bk. layer. 6 S Main
Heman A., pattern dresser, wks. Crane, Breed & Co.'s
Heman Henry, carp., s.e.c. Liberty and Lucy
Heman Rudolf, teamster, 524 John
Hemann Francis, blk. smith, 13 Woodward
Hemann Henry T. carp , 61 W. Liberty
HEMANN JOSEPH A, Editor and Proprietor of Daily and Weekly Volksfreund ; also Proprietor of Wahrheitsfreund and Catholic Telegraph s w.c. Vine and Longworth h, 130 Longworth
Hemann Louis. clk., 170 Longworth
Hemann Wm. blk. smith, 53 Dudley
Hemann Wm., (Strubbe & Co), 40 Pleasant
Hemberger Joseph, lab., 500 Linn
Hembhoff Henry, shoe mkr., 75 Milton
Hembrock Christian, tailor, 111 Woodward
Hembrock Geo., 123 Clay
Hembrock Hermann. lab., w.s. Goose al b. Green and Elder
Hembrock Joseph, tailor, 123 Clay
Hemenway Artemus P., mach., 212 W. Front
Hemesath Henry, dray, 23 Buckeye
Hemmer Jacob, w s. Vine b. Milk and Mulberry

Hemefling John, cof. h., 48 Ham. Road
HEMINGRAY Robert, (Gray, H. & Bro), res Covington
HEMINGRAY Saml. J., (Gray, H. & Bro) res. Covington
Hemler Michael foreman, 16 15th
Hemmelkatk Henry, cooper. 380 Sycamore h. n s Hunt b. Spring and Pendleton
Hemmer Henry, clk., bds. n.e.c. Clay and Liberty
Hemmer Jacob, cof. h., 2 3 Ham. Road
Hemmerle Adolph, saddler, 348 Walnut
Hemmerle Joseph, finisher, 56 Elder
Hemmert Andrew, lab., 61 Buckeye
Hemmet Lorenz, lab., 31 Buckeye
Hemmes John mate, 124 Clay
Hemmet Lawrence, clk., s.e.c. Walnut and 6th
Hemminghaus Henry J., molder, 563 Vine
Hemmler Michael, 14 Mary
Hempe Dora, seamstress, 15 Mansfield
Hempel Frederick, furniture, 36 W. Court
Hempel Godfreid, cab mkr., 473 Walnut
Hempel Nicholas, shoe mkr., 12 Buckeye
Hempelman Bernard, grocer, n. w. c. Linn and Findlay
Hempelmann Fred , harness mkr., n.e.c. 7th and Broadway
Hemphill Alexander, tailor, 213 Wade
Hemphill, Elizabeth, s.s. Front. e. of Hazen
Hemphill Griffin, carp., n.s.E. Front e.of Vine
Hemp ill James, teamster, 46 W. Mulberry
Hempsared Henry, carp., wks. J. Whittaker's Deer Creek Valley
Hencher Henry, grocery, 409 W. 7th
Heuchli Geo., molder, 37 Chestnut
Henchman R. B., clk., 101 W. 4th
Hencke Charles, cab mkr., 517 Elm
Hencke Vincent, shoe mkr , 18 Hamer
Hordehaw James, pipe fitter, wks. n.e.c. Walnut and Canal
Hendel mez Henry, cooper. 608 Freeman
Henderson Annie, servt., 428 W. 6th
Henderson Archibald, molder, 159 George
Hend rson Charlotte, servt., 127 E. 3d
HENDERSON Dewitt C., gen'l agt. D & M. R. R. 5 College Building h. 132 Longworth
HENDERSON EDWIN, Reporter Cincinnati Gazette, bds 65 Laurel
Henderson Geo., 18 W. 5th
HENDERSON JULIA A., Millinery Cloaks and Fancy Goods 18 W. 5th
Henderson James, writing academy Ohio Medical College h. 130 W. Miami Canal
Henderson Jardine J., finisher, s.s. 3d b. Canal and Kilgour [way
Henderson John, mech., bds. 177 Broadway
HENDERSON JOHN J., City Editor, Cincinnati Gazette, n. e.c. Vine and 4th h. 50 Laurel
Henderson Thomas J., atty., 15 E. 3d h. 130 W. 9th
Henderson Wm. C., coal oil, 48 Public Landing, rooms Short's bldg
Hendley Edward K., shoe mkr., wks. 261 W. 6th
Hendley George W., hats and caps, 262 W. 5th, h. Stoor's Tp
Hendley Louisa, servt., 78 Pike
Hendrick H. H., finisher. 461 Broadway
Hendric's Julia, servt., 61 Mound
Hendrick Leonard A. jr., dentist, 56 W. 4th h. Milford O
Hendrick Miles. lab , n.s. Fremont b.Carr and Harriet
Hendrick Sarah, bds. 105 Broadway
Hendricks August., printer, 441 Sycamore
Hendricks Geo W., atty., 241 W. 9th
Hendric'ts Gerhard. sawyer, 10 Webb
Hendricks John G., coal yard, n. e. c. Hunt and Main, h 136 W. 5th
Hendricks Elijah, carp., 378 W. Liberty

Hendrix Sidney G., carp., 467 W. 4th
Hendy Frank T., jewelry, 6 W 4th, res.
Hendy Samuel, porter, n e.c. John and George
Hone Henry H., painter, 34 Pleasant
Henefeld Frederick, cooper, 48 Milton
Hener Ferdinand L. brewer, 719 Race
Henertzet Henry, tailor. 484 Linn
Henessy Thomas, moulder, wks. 137 W. 2d
Henfeld Henry, driver. 29 Ham. Road
Henge Paul, wagon mkr., 702 Central Av.
Hengehold Rev. Bernard. Trinity Church s.s. 5th, b. Smith and Park
Hengehold Wm , baker, h. 73 Spring
Heneker Christian. 584 Plum
Henghan Mary, 174 Water
Hengler Peter, tinner, 79 Jones
Hengolds Wm., baker. 73 Spring
Hengsler Martin, brewer, 1 Hamer
Henhart John, b.h., 3 4 Ham Road
Henimen Hermann. lab., b 4 Everett
Henis Chas F, mach., wks. 64 W. 4th
Henisee Ellen, 153 E 6th
Henke Bernhard, gardener, 154 Ham. Road
Henke Hy., lab., wks. s.w.c. W. W. Canal and Smith
Henke Hy. lab., 69 Race
Henke John H., boots and shoes, 209 Elm
Henke Vincent, shoe mkr., 18 Hamer
Henke Wm L. tailor. 493 Race
Henkler John, cab mkr., n.s. Betts b. Linn and Baymiller
Henklin Valentine, lab., 464 E. Front
Henlein Nicholas, cooper 201 Pleasant
Henley Claus, butcher. 93 Findlay
HENLY Harry. (I. & H. II.) 204 W. 6th
HENLY I. & H. (Isaac & Harry) Wholesale Dealers in Millinery Goods, 21 W. 4th, un stairs
HENLY Isaac (I. & H. II.) 132 W. 8th
Henly Peter, tailor, s.e.c. Anderson and Pearl
Henne Antonia, music teacher, 476 Race
Henne Henrietta, music teacher, 476 Race
Henneberg Wilhemina, 566 Race
Hennecke Frank, watch mkr., 16 Sycamore
Henneckes H., jeweler, 658 Clark
Hennefeld Francis. lab., 380 Broadway
Hennegin Wm. tanner 28 Canal
Henneke Francis, blksmith, 467 Walnut
Henneke Louis, blksmith, w.s. Main b. Allison and Liberty
Henneke Lucas, 91 Clay
Henneker H., cof b , 537 Main
Henneker Mary, cof. h. 53 Main
Hennekes Geo. teamster, rear 558 Walnut
Hennekes Geo H., turner, s.e.c. Walnut and Liberty
Hennemeyer Fred., lab., c. Linn and Everett
Henner Geo., lab., 8 13th
Henness Brothers (W. T. H. & O. A. II) com. mer., s.w.c. Canal and Vine
Henness O A , (H. Brothers) 757 John
Henness W. T. H. (Brothers) 357 John
Hennessey Ann, 41 W 9th w. of Central Av.
Hennessey Martin, bolt mkr., 52 Accommodation
Hennessey Owen, baker, wks. 118 W. 5th
Hennessey Thomas. shoe mkr., Pavilion h. Observatory and 3d
Hennessey Thomas B , molder, bds. 49 Race
Hennessy Alice L., bds. 170 W. 5th
Hennessy John. porter n.e.c 4th and Main, bds. 50 Bedinger
Hennessy Joseph, mason, 320 John
Hennessy Thomas, cof. h., 40 Accommodation
Henney Michael J., shoe mkr., 463 W. 3d
Henniball Wm , 60 Wade
Henniger Diedrich drav, 4 Pleasant
Henniger Margaret, 4 Pleasant
Henniges Fred. tanner 11 Mulberry

166   (HEN)   CINCINNATI   (HER)   DIRECTORY.   (HER)

Hennika Frederick H., coach mkr., 195 Everett
Henning Frank, cof. h., 513 Main
Henning Hy. D., artist, 5 Mulberry
Henning John, carp., 7 Home, h. 43 Cutter
Henning Louisa, 513 Main
Henning Mary, 513 Main
Henning Wm., blksmith, 725 Race
Henninger Hy., tanner, 60 Mohawk
Henninger Laney, servt., 165 E. 3d
Hennings Hermann, cab. mkr., 13 Woodward
Hennington Surry, huckster, rear 61 Woodward
Hennix Hy., dray, wks. 109 E. Pearl
Henochsberg Joseph, frame mkr., 283 Main
Henochsberg Moses, frame mkr., 283 Main
Henoson James, tinner, 254 W. 6th
Henri Alexauder, millinery, 138 W. 5th
Henrich Joseph, porter, 55 12th
Henrich Joseph, carver, wks. n.w.c Elm and Pearl
Henrich Wm., shoe mkr., 34 Pleasant
Henrichs Hy., sawyer, 10 Webb
Henrichson John W., instrument mkr., e.s. Johnson al. b. Canal and 13th
Henricks Christopher, lab., 293 W. Liberty

HENRIE HOUSE, James Watson, Proprietor, 16 E 3d

Henrie John W., b.k. Gibson House
Henrie Mary, 13 Providence
Henry Mrs., 118 Laurel
Henry A. D., carp., 91 Sycamore
Henry Barlley lab., 50 Race
Henry Catharine, servt., 503 W. 7th
Henry Chas., 105 E. 6th
Henry Elisa E., 54 George
Henry Elisabeth, servt., n.w.c. Pike and Pearl
Henry Ellen, 550 Race
Henry Ellen, 325 W. 9th w. of Central Av.
Henry Frederick, wagon mkr., 195 Everett
Henry George, 105 E. 6th
Henry Geo., confec., 12 13th
Henry George D., salesman 78 W. Pearl
Henry Hugh, carp., s.s. Front e. of Brooklyn (9th
Henry Jacob, wks. n.w c. Freeman and Henry Jacob Central Av.
Henry Jacob, 948 Central Av.
Henry Jacob, confec., 479 Main
Henry Jacob, pork packer, 249 Cutter
Henry James, chair mkr., 12 Race
Henry Jennie, 30 Patterson al.
Henry John, cooper. bds. n.s. Melancthon b. Cutter and Jones
Henry John, lab., 50 Race
HENRY John. (Poland & H.) bds. Broadway Hotel
Henry John W., bds. 54 George
Henry Joseph, carp., n.s. E. Front e. of Vance
Henry Lawrence, lab., 585 W. 5th
Henry Lucia, 71 W. 9th w. of Central Av.
Henry Margaret, dress mkr., 475 W. 8th
Henry Mary, 227 Race
Henry Patrick, hackman, 142 Water
Henry Peter, finisher, 144 Hopkins
Henry Richard, plow mkr., n.e.c. York and Baymiller
Henry Robert, 350 Ham Road
Henry Robert A., carp., 13th b. Collard and Washington
Hense Chas. F., plasterer, rear 184 Cutter
Hensel Hy., driver Am. Exp. Co.
Henshall J. G., phys., 106 W 6th
Henshall James A., phys., 106 W. 6th
HENSHAW Edward, (G. H. & Sons) 157 Dayton b. Baymiller and Freeman

HENSHAW G. & SONS, (George, Edward & George. Jr.) Furniture Manufacturers, 26 Sycamore, Factory c. Elm and Canal

HENSHAW Geo., sen., (G. H. & Sons) 166 W. Court w. of Central Av.
HENSHAW Geo., jr., (G. H. & Sons) 312 Clark

Henshaw Hy., 166 W. Court w. of Central Av.
Hensing Barney, lab., 91 Dudley
Hensius F., wks. s.w.c. Vine and Longworth
Hensler Mrs., bds. s.w.c. Race and 3d
Hensler Joseph, finisher, wks. n.e.c. Walnut and Canal
Hensler Lewis, n.s. 6th b. Culvert and Broadway
Henson Elizabeth, 63 E. 7th
Henson Frances, seamstress, s s. 6th b. Broadway and Culvert
Henssler Jacob, blksmith. 44 John
Henssler Jacob, finisher, 163 Buckeye
Henter C., lab., wks. John Mitchell's
Hentsman Hy., molder, wks. n.e.c. Canal and Walnut
Hentz Frederick, carp., 490 John
Hentz John C..cab. mkr., n.s. Augusta b. Central Av. and John
Hentz Louis, blksmith, n.s. 6th b. Carr and Harriet
Henwright George, tailor. 15 Mound
Henz Roselle, h. e.s. Fountain b. Alexander and Rice
Henzerling Conrad, 474 Freeman
Henzi Helena, 76 Ham. Road
Henzie Michael, cof. h., 544 W. Front
Hensler John N., (H. & Molk) h. 799 Central Av.
Hensler & Molk, (John H. & Christian M.) terra cotta works, w.s. Plum b. Everett and Wade
Hepler Hy., driver, n.s. Wade b. Central Av. and John
Hepner Chas., lab., 40 15th
Hepp Charles, lab., wks. s.e.c. Canal and Vine
Hepp George, cooper, n.s. Charlotte b. Linn and John
Hepworth Wm., tanner, Deer Creek Valley, bds. Galt House
Herancourt Barbara, seamstress, 708 Vine

HERANCOURT GEO. M., Brewery, Malt House and res. Harrison Pike w. of Mill Creek Bridge, and Brewery s.w.c Freeman and Denman

Herancourt Lizzie, seamstress, 27 Everett
Herancourt Peter, cof. h., 1060 Central Av.
Heratage John, wks. Cin. type foundry
Herberding Frank, confec., s.w.c. Walnut and 9th
Herbers Herman, shoe mkr., bds. 10 Sycamore [tral Av.
Herbert, Andy, 187 W. Court w. of Central
Herbert Andrew J. painter,167 W. Court w. of Central Av.
Herbert Bridget. 126 Smith
Herbert Fred., 440 Linn
Herbert Hy., steam fitter, w.s Goose al. b. Green and Elder
Herbert Mary, servt., 116 E. 5th
Herbert Patrick, stone mason, 187 W. Court w. of Central Av.
Herbert Robt., (Jackson, H. & Co.) 167 Sycamore
Herbert Wm., lab., 442 Linn
Herbes Hy., grocery, 108 Baum
Herbes Hy., varnisher, 369 W. 5th
Herbig John F., harness mkr., 61 Allison
Herbison Peter, 220 Broadway
Herbist J. Joseph, lab., w.s. Goose al. b. Green and Elder
Herbolsheimer Clementine, music teacher, 19 14th
Herborn Conrad. shoemkr., 101 Pleasant
Herbrich Felix, fringe manuf., 29 15th b Elm and Plum
Herbslich August, tailor, bds. 51 W. 5th
Herbstrith Frank, repe mkr., 821 Vine
Herbst Christian, tanner, n s. Cassatt al. b. Main and Sycamore
Herbst John, 130 Mohawk

HERBSTREIT MATHIAS, Wines. Liquors, &c. 461 Vine

Herckelrath C. & H., (Chas. & Henry), liquors, 115 Sycamore
Herckelrath Chas. (C. & H. H.), bds. 91 Sycamore

Herckelrath Hy (C. & H. H.) res. Germany
Herckelrath John, 91 Sycamore
Hercules Mary, 096 Central Av
Herd John. driver, 260 Water
Herder Gustav., hardware, 338 Main, h. 7 W. 9th
Herder Mary, notions, &c., 85 E. Pearl, h. 152 W. 5th
Hereman John B., lab., 67 Clay
Herhammer Mary, 602 Elm
Herich Christopher, tailor. 803 Vine
Hering Augustus, cigar mkr., 63 Walnut
Hering Ernst, s.s. Calhoun b. McMillan and Clifton Av.
Heritage Mrs. Jane, w.s. Coggswell al. b. Woodward and Abigail
Heritage Diana, 416 John
Herkenhoff Frank. cooper, bds. 118 Gest

HERKER JACOB, Coffee and Boarding House, 481 Vine

Herking Wm. (Tewes & H.) n.s. Front e. of Kelly
Herlihy Bart. clk., s.w.c. 8th and Sycamore
Herlinger George, soap mkr.. wks. 728 Central Av
Herman Frederick, lock smith, 519 Sycamore
Herman Gabriel, peddler, 30 E. 5th
Herman Helmeng J., shoemkr, bds. 191 W. 6th
Herman Hy., lab, 458 W. 5th
Herman Jacob, porter, 38 Plum
Herman John, brush mkr., 34 Dunlap
Herman Mary, s.e.c. 5th and Race
Hefmann Adam, lab., wks. s.e.c. Canal and Vine
Hermann Adam, lab., 96 Clay
Hermann Christian, porter, 17 Abigail
Hermann Christine, seamstress, 458 W. 5th
Hermann Christopher, cab. mkr., 48 Ham. Road
Hermann Conrad, carp.. 570 Race
Hermann Geo., cab mkr., 62 Buckeye
Hermann Hy., cooper. s.w.c. Linn and Poplar
Hermann Hy., lab., 46 Findlay
Hermann J. Paulus, whitewasher, 585 Race
Hermann Jacob, salesman,106 W. Pearl, h. 220 Race
Hermann Jacob, tailor, 41 Milton
Hermann John, cab. mkr., 62 Buckeye
Hermann Maggie. 105 W. 3d
Hermann Theodore, lab., 74 Dudley
Hermann Theresa, laundress, 156 Ham. Road
Hermann Victor, compositor,wks. Meth. Book Concern
Hermann Wm., 302 W 8th
Hermes Francis J., exchange office. 97½ E. Pearl, h. 107 E. 2d
Hermesch Hy., porter, wks. Cobb, Williams & Co's
Hermeyer Herman, lab., 35 Baum
Hermien Elizabeth, tailoress, 297 Linn
Herming John, cab. mkr., 37½ Broadway
Hermleis Bernard, tanner, s.s. Liberty b. Linn and Baymiller
Hermon Jacob, 529 Plum
Herms Hy., box mkr., 1 Budd
Hermsenn Joseph, lab., 10½ Buckeye
Hern Bridget, servt., 145 Elm
Hern John J., molder, e.s. Oregon b. 3d and 5th
Herns John, lab., n.s. Montgomery Pike nr. Reading Road
Herod Edw. A., salesman, 81 W. Pearl
Herold Herman A., barber, 10 13th
Herold John, meats, 94 W. Front
Herold Michael, mercantile academy, n. w.c. 4th and Race, h. 185 Longworth
Herold Susanna, 53 Hamer
Heron Cornelius, bk. layer, 150 Carr
Herpat Herman, tinner, 223 Linn
Heraberger Adam, clk., 203 Richmond
Herran Frank, hostler, wks. n.w.c. Race and Longworth
Herchert Philip, stone cutter, 705 Race
Herrell Charles, 138 Everett
Herrell John, 16 15th b. Central Av. & Plum
Herren Stephen, wks. 340 W. 2d

Herrfurth Wm., mach., w.s. Vine b.15th and Liberty
Herrich Caspar, lab., 150 Pleasant
Herrick Miss D., bds. 84 Butler
Herridan Mary, s.s 6th b. Broadway and Culvert
Herriott Edgar, bds. 80 E. 5th
Herring Margaret, w.d. Ramsay n. of Front
Herrington James, dray, 58 Pierson
Herritage John, bds. 213 George
Herrlinger Andrew, cigar mkr., 463 Linn
Herrman Gottlieb, lab., s.s. Front e. of Kelly
Herrman Joseph, shoemkr., 33 Providence
Herrman Stephen, lab., n.s. Front e. of Kelly
Herrmann Am and, cab mkr., 11 Bremen
Herrmann Charles, express man, 568 Elm
Herrmann Elizabeth, n.s. 12th b. Race and Bremen
Herrmann Ernst, cof. h., n.w.c. Lawrence and 24
Herrmann Frederick, safe mkr, 519 Sycamore [15th
Herrmann Frederick, shoemkr, rear 16
Herrmann George, cab. mkr., wks. 11 Franklin
Herrmann John, carver. 65 Findlay
Herrmann Lawrence, tailor, 73 E. Front
Herrminck Stephen, rear 71 Abigail
Herrold John. butcher, 92 W. Front
Herron Andrew C., land agt , 65 W. 4th, h. 166 Smith
Herron Andrew Clark, jr., clk., bds. 166 Smith
Herron David, Capt., 381 John
Herron Hy., lab., Burnet House
Herron Jane, seamst. ess, n.e.c. Central Av. and Court
Herron John, lab., n.s. Goodloe b. Willow and Niagara
Herron John K., eating saloon, 115 Baymiller
HERRON Jno. W. (Collins & H.) h. 135 E. 5th
HERRON JOSEPH, Principal Herron's Seminary, 64 W. 7th
Herron Sarah, 593 Central Av
Herron Thomas G., student, bds. 64 W. 7th
Herron William C., b.k.. n.w.c. 2d and Broadway, h. 64 W 7th
Herrzog Bernard, painter, 17 15th b. Elm and Plum
Hersberger Adam. 203 Richmond
Herach Nathan, butcher, 47 Longworth
Hersch Samuel, b.k., 54 Main, h. s.s. 8th b. Elm and Race
Herschauer Nicholas, boiler mkr., 37 E. Pearl
Herschede John, finisher, 114 Abigail
Herschel Barney, 22 Logan
Herschel Frank, b.k, w.s. Spring Grove Av., rear of Benckenstein's Garden
Hershhauer Fredrick, brewer, wks. s.w. c. Pearl and Pike
Hertel John, baker, s.w.c. 9th and Elm
Hertell John, cook, Madison House
Hertenstein Frederick, shoemkr., 6 Louisa
Herter Ernst, cigar mk.., rear 12 Mulberry
Herterich George, cooper, 380 Baymiller
Hertig Hannah, 29 Elder
Hertkorn Ulrich, brewer, wks. s.w.c. Pearl and Pike
Hertlein John, baker. bds. 91 Bremen
Hertlein John, baker, bds. 650 Vine
Hertry Michael, bds. 43 David
Herty Daniel, cof. h., 205 E. 6th
Hertwig Baptist, carp , 244 Bremen
Hertzig Andrew, shoemkr, 654 Walnut
Hertzek Joseph, dray, wks. 450 Walnut
HERTZSCH Chas. A., editor Daily Cincinnati Union, 9 W. Court, h. 54 Allison
Hertzsch Gottlieb, mach., 520 Walnut
Hervey James B., salesman. 58 E. 2d, res. Walnut Hills
Herwerg Herman, cab. mkr, s s, Niles al. b. Main and Sycamore

Herwegen Hy., furniture. 241 W. 5th
Herweh Adam. 261 Ham. Road
Herwig Frederick, lab., 92 Woodward
Herwig H., 197 Vine
Herwig Hy., cab. mkr. 24 Woodward
Herwig Hy., cigar mkr, 510 Main
Herwig John F., saddler, 61 Allison
Herze Julius, lab., wks. 728 Central Av
Herzen Isaac, lab., 71 Providence
Herzog Aloisius, tailor, 636 Vine
Herzog Bernard, driver, n s. Frienship al. b. Law ence and Pike
Herzog Catharine. 682 Vine
Herzog F., blksmith, wks. 103 Hunt
Herzog Hy., carp., 566 Race
Herzok Anthony, lab., 67 Butler
Heschong Michael, vermicelli manuf., 571 Walnut
Hesing Caspar (H. & Co.) 51 12th
Hesing & Co. (Henry H. & Casper Hesing,) carriage manufs., 58 12th
Hesing Hy. (H. & Co.) 51 12th
Hesing Peter F., blksmith, bds. 47 12th
Heskamp Barney, porter, 98 Hunt
Heskamp Herman, porter, 98 Spring
Heskamp Herman, shoemkr, wks. 457 Walnut
Heskamp John, cooper, 19 Pendleton
Heskamp John G., grocer, 65 Hunt
Heskamp Lisetta, servt., 9 Woodward
Hesler Joseph, molder, 103 Woodward
Hesnink Herman, miller, 31 Pierson
Hespe John, cooper, 33 Vine, bds. s.e.c. Wade and Central Av
Hesping Herman, grocery, n.w.c. Liberty and Baymiller
Hess Abraham, 19 W. 9th
Hess Adam, mach., 406 Longworth
Hess Casper, cigar mkr., wks. 213 Walnut
Hess Chas., music teacher, s.s. Coggswell al. nr. Auburn
Hess Chas., tailor, w.s. Vine b. Milk and Mulberry
Hess Chas. V., cook, 602 Race
Hess Conrad, brewer, 866 Race
Hess Edward. mer., 107 W. Court
Hess Elias, watch mkr , 22 G no
Hess Elizabeth, n.e.c. Front and Parsons
Hess Emanuel trader, 450 W. Liberty
Hess Fred., boiler mkr , 175 E. Front
HESS Hy.. (A. & J. Trounstine & Co.) 17 W. 9th
Hess John, butcher, 106 Clinton
Hess Jonas, b.k.. bds. 70 W. 9th
Hess Ludwig, 142 Wade
Hess M. & Co., (Moses H., Jacob Victor & Meier Bettman) clothing, 347 Main
Hess Michael, mer., 19 W. 9th
Hess Moses, (Hess, M. & Co.) 17 W. 9th
Hess Samuel, butcher, 9 Melancthon
Hess Samuel, clk. 164 Main, bds. 22 Gano
Hess Susan, 796 E. Front
Hess Wm. J., b.k., 441 Sycamore
Hesse Ernst H., cof. h., n.e.c. Pearl and Race
Hesse Frederick, boiler mkr., 175 E. Front
Hesse John C. W., barber, 5 E. 4th, h. n.w.c. Dayton and Central Av.
Hesse Wm., barber, n.w.c. Central Av. and Dayton
Hesse Wm , lab., 472 Freeman
Hessel Hy., sawyer, wks. Mitchell & Rammelsberg's
Hessel John H., cooper, 100 Abigail
Hesselberger Samuel, second hand store, 334 W. 5th
Hesselberger Theodore II., grocer, s.e.c. W. 9th and Mound
Hesselbrock Barney, dray, 665 Central Av.
Hesselbrock Hy , soap factory, s.s. Deer Creek Road n. of Court, h. n s. Accommodation
HESSELER WM. II., Union Venetian Blind Factory, 147 Sycamore, h. 88 Hunt
Hessell Nathan, tailor, 187. W. 6th
Hessen Jane, 209 Broadway
Hesses Philip, 64 13th
Hessing Bernardina, servt., 47 12th
Hessing Eliza, 62 Bremen
Hessing Peter, blksmith, bds. 47 12th

Hessler Frederick, finisher, 530 Main
Hessler Fred., grocer, 174 W. 6th, h. 159 Pleasant
Hessler Hy , clk., 159 Pleasant
Hessler Joseph, eng., rear 103 Woodward
Hessler Philip, carp. 172 Baymiller
Hessling John, wks. junction 6th and Front
Hesslink Bernard, lab., 772 W. Front
Hesslink Herman, miller, 31 Pierson
Hessman Frank, lab., 107 Sycamore, h. 67 Abigail
Hester Barkley, waiter, Burnet House
Hester Catharine, servt., Burnet House
Hester Jas., lab., Burnet House
Hester John, lab., 197 Cutter
Hester Michael, lab , 50 Race
Hester Mich., waiter, Burnet House
Hester Michael, watchman. 55 Plum
Hester Pat , lab., Burnet House
Hester Patrick, lab., 200 Cutter
Hester Thomas, saloon, s.w.c. 6th and John
Hester Thomas, shoe mkr., bds. 91 Longworth
Hester Thomas, waiter, Clifton House
Hesterberg Hy., (Mosig & H.) 139 Bremen
Hesterer John. tailor, 1 Harrison Pike
Hesterkamp Hy., 207 Clinton
Hesz Casper, mason, 5e5 Walnut
Heszler Robert, c rp., 55 Ham. Road
Hetchner John. butcher, e.s. Clarkson b. Bank and Central Av.
Hetenmeier Hy., stone mason, bds. 428 Sycamore
Hetmann Francis, jr., b.k., 59 W. Front, h 611 Race
Hetsel Anna, servt., 400 Longworth
Hetsler Blasey, grocery, 636 W. 6th
Hett Magdelane, millinery, 926 Central Av.
Hetterich Bernard, finisher, 621 Sycamore
Hetteseimer Franz, tailor, 508 Walnut
Hettler Chas. F., bar k , 294 Main
Hettner John, teamster, 466 E. Front
Hettrick Chas., 50 Milton
Hetze Philip, photographer, n.w.c. Elm and Court
Hetzel Dominick, bk. binder, 41 Race
Hetzel Louis, weaver, wks. s.w.c. Cutter and Betts
Hetzner Geo., ham curer, n.s. Central Av. nr. Freeman
Heuck Herbert, clk. G. M. Herancourt's, e.s. Harrison Road nr. Mill Creek
Heuckmann Barney, bakery, 257 Pine
Heuel Frank, shoe mkr., wks. s.e.c. Main and 6th
Heuer Bernard, bklayer, 293 W. Liberty
Heuer Mary, 31 Pleasant
Heuermann Bernard, tanner, 290 Linn
Heuermann John, stable, 15 W. 6th
Heule H. A., porter, 21 Franklin
Heun Bernard. salesman 83 W. Pearl, h. Vine St Hill
HEUN EDWARD, Druggist and Apothecary, s.w.c. 5th and Vine
Heupel Peter. bar k., 1 E 6th
Heur John, bklayer, 680 Sycamore
Heuser Mrs. Anna, 70 12th
Heuser Gerhard, molder, 11 Bremen
Heuszmann Hy., lab., 479 Walnut
Heutenrick Lawrence, carp., wks. 205 Freeman
Heutle John, teamster, 170 Clay
Heuver Mrs. Gertrude, seamstress, 106 Woodward
Heuver Maria, vest mkr., 106 Woodward
Heuver Mary G , seamstress, 106 Woodward
Hevern Miles. lab., 116 Barr
Hevern Mrs. Mary, blksmith, 131 W. Front
Hevren Patrick, lab., s.w.c. Central Av. and W. Canal
HEWES John II., (H. & McCann) h. 162 George
HEWES & McCANN, (John H. H. & Wm. McC.) Boots and Shoes, 34 W. 5th and 264 W. 5th
HEWES Orrin, (Morrison & H.) 163 George
Hewett Geo., lab., rear 50 Plum

Hewitt Joseph R., salesman s.e.c. 2d and Broad
Hewitt Lucinda, w.s. Henderson al. b. 7th n 18th
Hewitt Wheeler B, clk. 26 W. 5th, h. 201 W. 4th
Hewlett J. L., rooms 60 E. 3d
HEWLETT Jeremiah S., (M. Werk & Co,) h. College Hill
Hewson J. H., receiver, 75 W. 3d, h. Clifton
Hewson John. city order, 110 Longworth
HEWSON WM. M. F.,
  Stock and Bill Broker,
  21 W. 3 t, h. 97 E. 3d
Hewston James, box mkr., s.s. Charlotte b. John and Linn
Hexter Caroline, dress mkr., bds. 35 Longworth
Hexter S., cutter, 33 Longworth
Hey Albion M., mach., 216 W. 2d, h. 146 George
Hey Chas . 7 Pierson
Hey Geo., blksmith, 7 Pierson
Hey Geo., gas fitter. 7 Pierson
Hey Jacob, cnf. h . 585 Walnut
Hey Jas. H., b k. Queen City Distillery, 199 Freeman
Hey Margaret. caf. h., w.s Lebanon Road near Montgomery Turnpike
Hey Wm., plasterer 235 Hopkins
Hey Wm . saloon, 326 Main
Heyds Wm., hds. 4 Hughes
Heyer Chas. F., lab. 4 Moore
Heyer John J., porter, 56 W. Liberty
Heyer Mary, 18 Woodward
Heyer Theodore, porter, 2 Lucy
HEYKER F. & M . (G. Frederick & Ma thew) Manufacturers of Heyker's Stomach Bitters, 308 Cutter nr Clinton
HEYKER G. Fred., (F. & M. H.) 92 Clinton
HEYKER Matthew, (F. & M. H.), h. 305 Cutter
Heyker Theodore M., manuf. stomach bi ters 305 Cutter
Heyl Hy., cab. mkr. 639 Vine
Heylen Rev. Lewis, St. Xavier College w.s. Sycamore b 6th and 7th
Heymann Alex., saloon, n.e.c. Hopkins and Linn
Heymann Chas., American Hotel, n.s. Front e. of Lewis
Heyn John, tailor, 277 Bremen
Heyn Philip, lab., 57 Peete
Heyne Herman W., cigars &c., 409 Walnut
Heyner Barney, finisher, wks. 825 Central Av
Heynes James E., carp., s.s Baker b. Walnut and Vine, h. 5 Observatory Road
Heys Casper, e.s. Branch, b. Ham. Road and Findlay
Heysler Jacob, tobacconist, bds, 72 W. Court
Heywood James, lab. n.s. Augusta, b. Smith and John
Hiatt Marvin, carp., 105 Cutter
Hibben J. H., with Ellis McAlpin & Co. 108 Pearl, h.is. Gibson House
HIBBERT Alfred, (H. Bros.) 210 W. 5th
HIBBERT BROS.,
  (John & Alfred,) Hats and Caps,
  51 E Pearl and 210 W. 5th
HIBBERT JOHN, (H. Bros.), 51 E. Pearl
Hicks Patrick, clk., 62 Clark
Hickenlooper, Andrew, civil eng., 108 Betts
Hickens Hy., cook, 140 W. Pearl
Hickey Alice, chambermaid, Burnet House
Hickey Ann. cof h., 33 Lock, n of 8th
Hickey, Daniel lab., 13 Accommodation
Hickey David R., Clifton House, s.w.c. 6th and Elm
Hickey James, hds. Rail Road House
Hickey James T., mach., bds. 28 Laurel
Hickey John S., gen., cof. h., s.w.c. 6th and Pierson
Hickey, John S. lab., n.s. Taylor b. Carr and Freeman
Hickey Kate, bds. 103 E. 2d

Hickey Mary, w s. Stone al. b. 6th and Longworth
Hickey Mary, 132 Central Av.
Hickey Michael. lab , 228 E. 6th
Hickey Patrick F., roofer. 247 George
Hickey Rich., butcher, 222 Findlay
HICKMAN Hy. J , (Trumbower & H.), 386 George
Hickman J. L & Co., real estate agts. and note brokers 60 W. 3d
Hickman Jesse B , shoe mkr , s.e.c. Melancthon and John
Hickman Josiah L., (J. L. H. & Co.) 92 Hopkins
Hickman Catharine, 416 John
Hicks A. W., clk., bds. 170 W. 4th
Hicks C. D., student, 297 Main
Hicks Chas., H. mess. superior court 297 Main
Hicks Geo. W., mach., 39 Pierson
Hicks Hy. C., carp., 39 Pierson
Hicks James, 231 Vine
Hicks John A., 297 Main
Hicks John M., carp., 39 Pierson
Hicks Joseph, 672 W. Front
Hicks Levi T., (Wilson, H. & Kinsey), b. Lexington Pike. Kenton Co., Ky
Hicks Matilda, 138 W. 9th
Hicks Rob., carp , 207 Main
Hicks Wm , driver, Freeman nr. Central Av
Hickok Mary A., bds. 120 John
Hickox Hiram S., carp., h. 238 Hopkins
HICKOX Wm. C., (Bart & H.) 262 Longworth [3d
Hidden Otis, b.k. 12 W. Pearl, h. 453 W.
Hieatt Dudley E., inspector, 50 W, Front h. 181 W. Court w. of Central Av
HIEATT Wm., (H. & Woods,) h. Montgomery O.
HIEATT & WOODS. (Wm. H., Wm. H. W. & Hy. P. Bowman,) Lard-Oil and Candle Manufactory. s.s. Deer Creek Road n. of Court
Hieber Danl. Fred., dairyman, 26 Mulberry
Hieber Jacob Fred., wagon mkr., 26 W. Mulberry
Hieber John, cab. mkr., 636 Race
Hieber Nannie servt. 370 W. 7th
Hieber Rickey. servt 366 W. 7th
Hiede Hy., lab., r6 Hunt
Hiedgerken John, col., h. 404 W. 5th
Hiedt Michael, col. h. 464 E. Front
Hief Jacob, lab., bds., s.w.c. Race and 2d
Hiefer Jacob. cab. mkr w.s. Long al. b. Woodward and Franklin
Hiem John, carp., 260 W . Liberty
Hieneman Geo., bakery , n.s. 6th b. Harriet and H orne
Hients Geo., blksmith. e.s. Bremen, b. Liberty and 15th
Hier Thos. B., carp., 539 Freeman
Hiersing Herman carp., 145 Livingston
Hiftline, Louisa, servt. n.e.c. 3d and Ellen
Higbee Israel, paver, bds. 421 W. 6th
Higbee James G., (W. W. Higbee & Co) 439 W. 4th
Higbee Wm., wharf master, 95 Water
Higbee Wm. W., (W. W H. & Co.) h. 95 Water
Higbee Wm. W. & Co (Wm. W. H. & James B, Higbee), lumber yard, n.e c. Elm and Water
Higby Ira B., expressman, 22 Betts
Higdon Benj., (Dunham & H.) 307 George
Higdon & Farrell, (Peter H. & Michael T. F.), carps., 117 Linn
Higdon Peter, (H. & Farrell,) 83 Gest
Higdon Thos., 131 W. Court w. of Central Av
Higgerson Bridget, servt., 365 W. 7th
Higginbotham R. W., salesman, 137 W. 7th
Higgins Anna, servt., 206 W. 5th
Higgins Chas., lab., 651 W. 8th
Higgins E. P., policeman, s.e.c. 8th and Walnut
Higgins Elizabeth, cigars &c., 28½ Broadway
Higgins James, shoe mkr., s e c. Front and Ludlow
Higgins Jno., painter. w.s. Bank al. b. 3d and 4th

Higgins Julia, servt . 490 W 7th
Higgins Lawrance, lab., bds. w s. Western Av b. Blank and Harrison Road
Higgins M., 183 W. 2d
Higgins Margaret. 186 Cutter
Higgins Mary. cook, Black Bear Hotel
Higgins Michael, lab. 299 W. 2d
Higginson Michael, lab., 7 Crippen al.
Higginson Thos. D, gas fitter 176 Broadway
HIGH Geo. M , (Davis & Co. and P. Andrew & Co,) ard W. 8th
Highland Pat., lab., s.s 8th b. Broadway and Sycamore
Highland Wm., agt. O. & M. R. R. 96 Race
Highlands John S. teacher, 1289 E Front
Higledick Wm., dray, 491 Race
Higman Wm, butcher, 5 Wade b. Elm and Plum
Higney Martin, shoe mkr., 140 Freeman
Hinkemann Frank, shoe mkr. bds. 023 Central Av
Hiib Max, liquors &c., 376 Main, h. 24 Longworth
Hilbers Herman, shoe mkr., bds. 404 Sycamore
Hilbert Benj., mach., 205 13th
Hilbert Benj., finisher, 108 Linn
Hildebeidel John, tailor, 179 W. Liberty
Hildebrand Hy , bk. layer, 47 Allison
Hildebrand Hy., porter, n.w.c. Allison and Walnut
Hildebrand Leopold bk. binder 61 Findlay
Hildebrand Wm. wks. 361 Vine
Hildebrand Wm. cigar mkr., 9 Wade b. Elm and Plum
Hildebrand Wm., b.k. 124 Walnut, h. 39 George
Hildebrandt Barney, 414 Longworth
Hildegard Sister, St Clare Convent, n.w. c 3d and Lytle
HILDRETH DAVID,
  Family Groce ry.
  s.w.c. Cutter and 7th
Hildreth Geo. C. clk., bds., s.w.c. Cutter and 7th
Hildreth Lewis A., b. h. s.w.c. 3d and Broadway
Hildreth Wm. J., carp., n s. Rail Road e. of Hazen
Hilebrand Hy., varnisher, Oehler al. b Freeman and Garrard
Hileman John M., currier, bds. Fireman's Hall
Hilles A aron, s.s. Front b. Reed and Broad
Hillge Ernst, lab. 20 Madison
Hillge Hy., lab., 22 Madison
Hillgefor Hy., porter, 109 Hunt
Hillgemaier Herman, tailor. 173 Clay
Hillgemann Ernst, lab., 26 Madison
Hillgemann Fred., cigars &c , 5nd Elm
Hillgemann Fred., cigars &c., 55 12th bds. s.w.c. Vine and 12th
Hillgemann Fred., cooper, 529 Sycamore
Hilgemann Wm. K., foundryman 234 Everett
Hilgerfnott Hy., porter, 109 Hunt
Hilker Barney, cab. mkr., 218 John
Hilker Herman, H., dray, 427 Walnut
Hilkie B chair mkr., wks. John Mitchell's
Hill Dr., bds. 164 Elm
Hill Alexander, foreman wks. 304 Broadway
Hill Alexander, 140 E. Liberty
Hill Alex., salesman, 41 W. 4th, h. 204 W. Court
HILL ALFRED C
  Druggist and Apothecary, s.w.c.
  3d and Smith, h 553 W. 6th
Hill Alfred F., atty , 54 Bank Bldg., h. n s. York b. Freeman and Baymiller
Hill Arthur, 201 W. Court
Hill Asa, railroad agt., bds. 171 Broadway
Hill August, finisher, s.s. Front e. of Kelly
Hill August, 51 Martin
Hill Benj., (Edward Cook & Co.)
Hill C. W., forwarding agt.. bds. 80 E 5th
Hill Chas., paper mkr., 525 Vine
Hill Chas , carp., n.w.c. George and Central Av

Hill Chas., printer, bds. 61 Longworth
Hill Daniel, rear 11 E. Liberty
Hill David, constable, 274 E Front
Hill Detty M., 29 Cutter
Hill Edmund, locksmith, 13 Betts
Hill Edward D., cigars, &c., 5 Main, h. 175 Poplar
Hill Edward H., (Daxell & H.,) 69 Laurel
Hill Elizabeth, 07 George
Hill Elizabeth J., 454 Broadway
HILL Mrs. F. D., (H. H. H. & Co.,) 392 W. 3d
Hill Frank, salesman. 280 W. 7th
HILL George H., (George H. H. & Co. and Hunnewell H. & Co.,) 280 W. 7th
HILL GEORGE H. & CO., (Geo. H. H., Daniel H. Hunnewell and Joseph S. Hill,) Soap and Candle Manufacs., 31 Main, Factory 612 Plum
HILL H. H. & CO., (H. H. H. and Mrs F. D. Hill,) Wholesale and Retail Druggists, s.e.c. 5th and Race.
Hill Henry, baker, wks. 118 W. 5th
Hill Henry, cof. h., 114 Baum
Hill Henry, steward, 236 W. 8th
HILL Hiram H., (H. H. H. & Co.) 264 W. 8th
Hill Jacob, rear 11 E. Liberty
Hill James, saloon, 41 Pub. Landing
Hill John, carp., s.e.c. Ludlow and Arch
Hill John, driver, 178 E. Pearl
Hill John. lab., 5 John
Hill John B., clk., 189 Mound
Hill Jonathan M., carp., n.s. Railroad, e. of Vance
Hill Joseph, s.e.c. 9th and Mound
Hill Joseph, baker, wks. 118 W. 5th.
Hill Joseph M., 454 Broadway
HILL, Joseph S., (Hunnewell, Hill & Co.) h. 123 W. 5th
Hill Kate, 10 New
Hill Margaret, bds. 25 Lock, n. of 8th
Hill Margaret E., 453 George
Hill Martha. 97 W. Court, w. of Central Av.
Hill Mary, 63 e. 7th
Hill Mary, 107 W. Court, w. of Central Av.
Hill Mary A., 454 Broadway
Hill Mary A., servt, 107 Broadway
Hill Mary A. T., grocery, n.e.c. Baum and Observatory
Hill Mary E., teacher, E. Front, b. Hill and Stone
Hill Nathaniel, phys., s s. 6th, b. Broadway and Culvert, h. 170 Webb
Hill Peter, saddler, bds. 80 E. 5th
Hill Philip, n.e. Friendship al., b. Lawrence and Pike
Hill Reuben, printers' furniture, 168 W. 2d, res. Covington
Hill Richard, b. k., n.w.c. 3d and Sycamore, h. 49 Ellen
Hill Robert, carp., 613 Central Av.
Hill Robert, cutter, 194 Main, bds. 170 W. 5th
Hill Robert, saddler, bds. s.w.c. 6th and Plum
Hill Sarah, grocery, 19 E. 8th
Hill Thomas, wagon mkr., 524 Central Av.
Hill Wm., barber, 32 Central Av.
Hill Wm., dray, 390 Broadway
Hill Wm, F. M, clk., 29 Cutter
Hillard Elizabeth, bds. 385 W. 3d
Hillbeck John, finisher, wks. n.e.c. Walnut and Canal
Hille Wm., bk. layer, 21 Madison
Hillebrand Barney, mach., 414 Longworth
Hillebrand Frank, cooper, 107 Clay
Hillebrand Frederick, grocery, 30 Dudley
Hillebrand Henry, clk., bds. 30 Dudley
Hillebrand Joseph, eng., s.w.c. Front and Central Av.
Hillebrand Wm., b. k., 390 George
Hilleman Barney, tailor, 26 Race
Hiller J. F. E., painter, s.w.c. 4th and Walnut
Hillenkamp Henry, clk., 17 Mulberry
Hiller Chas., b. k., Volksblatt office, h. Vine St. Hill
Hiller Francis 703 Vine   16

HILLER GUSTAVUS A., Druggist and Apothecary, 76 Broadway, res. Mt. Auburn
Hillerman Geo. J., harness mkr., 115 Park
Hillert Lewis, (H. & Fahlbusch,) 447 Sycamore
Hillert Lewis. salesman, 69 W. 4th, h. 447 Sycamore
Hillert & Fahlbusch, (Lewis H & Frederick A. F.,) grocery, 449 Sycamore
Hillgardner George, n.s. Front, e. of Foster
Hillman Ernst, tailor, 181 Baymiller
Hillman Lena, e.s. Anderson, b. 2d and Pearl
Hillman, Frederick, locksmith, 26 Schiller
Hillman Wm., tailor, 598 Elm
Hillmeyer Wolfgang, tanner, s.s. 6th, b. Harriet and Horne
HILLS David, (H. O'Driscoll & Co.,) 78 Betts
Hills John, cof. h., n.w.c. Front and Butler
Hills John E., salesman, 227 Richmond
HILLS, O'DRISCOLL & CO., (David H., C. F. O'D. & Co.) Stereotype and Electrotype Foundry, 141 Main
Hills Sarah, teacher, 24 Richmond
Hills Wm. F., foreman, 24 Richmond, b. Elm and Plum
Hilshoff Henry, tanner, 604 Elm
Hillyer Anna 20 Mohawk
Hillyer Catharine C., 46 Everett
Hillyer E. G., b. k., 140 Main, h. 20 Mohawk
Hillyer Frederick, rear 623 Elm
Hillyer John, foreman, 49 Everett
Hilman, John, cigar mkr., 520 W. 8th
Hilman Peter, lab., 367 Linn
Hilmer Joseph, carpet weaver, 173 W. 5th, h. s e c. Linn and George
Hilms Barney, shoe mkr., 89 Clay
Hilp Jacob, grocer, s.w.c. John and W. 9th, h. 265 John
Hilrich Matthias, clk., bds. 72 W. 5th
Hils Conrad, teamster, 45 Pleasant
Hils Henry, tailor, s.w.c. Bremen and Findlay
Hils Henry, Jr., clk., s.e.c. 6th and Walnut
Hilschoff Henry, tanner, 604 Elm
HILSINGER Jacob, (Raymond H. & Co.,) 587 Main
HILSINGER John, (Raymond H. & Co.,) 587 Main
Hilsinger Michael, wagon mkr., s w.c. Vine and Findlay
Hilskamp Catharine, tailoress. 72 Abigail
Hilsman Wm., butcher, 59 Martin
Hilterman Henry, tailor, 610 Race
Hilterman Mary G., 610 Race
Hilton Emma, teacher, 265 Richmond
HILTON GEO. H., Attorney at Law, 13 W, 3d, b. 293 W. Court, w. of Central Av.
Hilton Samuel G.,) barber, 6 E. 2d, h, 12 E. 8th
Hilton Lucy B., 145 Hopkins
Hilton Theron S., agt, 538 W. 8th
HILTS CHAS. Attorney at Law, 22 W. Court, h. 158 Richmond
Hiltz Eliza, servt., s.w.c. 3d and Broadway
Hiltz Kate, servt., s.w.c. 3d and Broadway
Hilzinger Henry, brush mkr., 105 W Court
Himan Henry, 128 W. 9th
Hime Sarah A , 225 Elm
Himmelfart Joseph, tanner, n.w.c. McDowell and Lewis
Himmelgrand Henry, cooper, 110 Hunt
Himmeller John H., soap mkr., 63 David
Himmelreich Sarah, clothing, 511 Vine
Himmlein Geo., brewer, 12 Hamer
Himmler John G., carp., 685 Race
Hinchay Wm., lab, 403 Sycamore
Hinchman Allen, b. k., 95 W. Pearl, h. 350 W 8th
Hinchy Thomas, cof. h., 546 W, Front
Hind Isabella, teacher, 330 Cutter
Hinde Eliza Jane, bds. 124 Everett
HINDE John D., (H. & Porter,) h. Newport
Hinde Malinda, 124 Everett

HINDE & PORTER, (J. D. H. & Thos. P., Jr.,) Commission Merchants, 47 W. 2d
Hinderberger Andrew, printer, 610 Vine
Hindersman Henry, lab., 17 15th, b. Elm and Plum
Hindersman Hy., boots and shoes, 116 W. Liberty
Hindley Hy. P., cutter, s.w.c. 3d and Vine, h. Mt. Adams [5th
Hindman Eliza, e.s. Kilgour, b. 3d and
Hindman Ida, bds. e.s. Kilgour, b. 3d and 5th
Hindy Saml., clk., 154 George
Hine C. C., trav. agt. Ætna Ins. Co., res. Covington
Hine Joseph, 144 Laurel
Hiner David, capt., 411 W. 7th
Hines Abner, co., 110 Barr
Hines Adam, s.w.c. Longworth and Elm
Hines Bridget, 1564 E. Front
Hines John, clk., bds. 120 and 128 Central Avenue
Hines Valentine, teamster, 502 E. Front
Hiney Joseph, finisher, 872 E. Front
Hingen Thomas, lab., 109 Laurel
Hinger Jacob, lab., 504 E Front
Hinghaus Wm., grocery, 46 Rittenhouse
Hinke Barney, lab., n.s. Front, e. of Kelly
Hinkelmann Louis, cof. h., 300 Findlay
Hinken George, (J. & G.,) 118 Water
Hinken Hermann, 95 Clay
Hinken J. & G., (John & George,) grocery, n.e.c. Race and Water
Hinken John, (J. & G. H.,) 118 Water
Hinkle A. H. & Co., (A. H. H. & John R. Davey,) book binders, 137 Walnut
Hinkle Anthony H., (A. H. H. & Co.,) 592 W. 8th
HINKLE, GUILD & CO., (Phillip H., Joseph G. & Edward R. Loughead,) Planing Mill and Lumber Yards. 365 W. Front
HINKLE Philip, (H. Guild & Co.,) 311 W. 4th
Hinkler John, cab. mkr., 240 Betts
HINMAN Benj. P., (McAlpin & Co.,) bds. Burnet House
HINMAN E. D., (Rawson, Wilby & Co.,) bds. Burnet House
Hinnau Frederick, cigars, &c., 441 Vine, bds. s.e.c. 12th and Vine
Hinnau Gustav, coppersmith, 45 13th
Hinnechett Chas , lab., wks. n. e. c. Walnut and Canal
Hinnen Emanuel, boots and shoes, 1113 Central Av
Hinnenkamp Geo., hostler, 592 Main
Hinrachs Chris., porter, 231 W. Liberty
Hins Hy., lab., 303 Front
Hinsdale Loring, clk., 88 W. Pearl, h. 14 McFarland
Hinsdale Susan M., 14 McFarland
Hinshey Robt , pork cutter, 13 New
Hinsler John, carp., 609 Vine
Hinsley Wm., coachman, 142 Broadway
Hintermesch Frederick, cooper, e.s. Freeman, b. Findlay and Poplar
Hintermeyer Franklin, porter, 45 Findlay
Hinternish Barney, blksmith, 186 Clark
Hintley Artlet, 770 W. 6th
Hintreck Bernhard, huckster, 638 Elm
Hintze Ehrbardt, sewing machine factory, h. 259 W. 3d
Hipp Herman, cig. mkr., bds. 577 Main
Hipp Herman, b.k , 105 Sycamore, bds. 91 Sycamore
Hipp Jacob, cab. mkr., 203 Freeman
Hipp Sebastian, finisher, 60 Findlay
Hipp Wm., 403 Race
Hipp Wm. C., b.k., 31 Main, h. 403 Race
Hippler Sebastian, lab., Denman, b. Kenner and Flint
Hird Isaac, turner, s.s. E. Front, e. of Reed
Hirsch A., liquors, 109 W. 6th, h 15 and 17 Lodge
Hirsch Anthony, foreman, 53 W. 4th, h. 146 Barr
Hirsch F., salesman, 28 W. 7th
Hirsch Frederick, sawyer, n.s. Ridgway al., b Liberty and 15th
Hirsch Herman, exchange office, 601 Main

170 (HOB) CINCINNATI (HOE) DIRECTORY. (HOF)

Hirsch John, lab., 27 Buckeye
Hirsch Joseph, peddler, 491 Vine
Hirsch Meyer, b k., 126 Main, h. 14 W. 8th
Hirsch Morris, b.k., 26 W. Pearl, h. 25 W. 9th
Hirsch Wm., peddler, 520 Main
Hirschauer Nicholas; boiler mkr., 123 E Pearl
Hirschauer Paul, wagon mkr., 607 Race
Hirschauer Phillip, boiler yard, 147 E. Front, h. 110 E. 3d
Hirschberg Jacob, clothing. 287 Main
Hirschhiel Jacob, 30 Mercer
Hirschbrunner Gottlieb, bk. binder, e.s. Ridgway al., b. Liberty and 15th
Hirschfeld Isaac, turner, 722 Central Av
Hirschland H., bds. 92 W. 8th
Hirschmann ——, shoemkr, 566 Elm
Hirschmann Geo., blksmith, 29 Abigail
Hirsh Aaron, liquors, bds. 17 Lodge
Hirsh Alexander, mer., bds. 33 Longworth
Hirsh Bernhard, dry goods, bds. 17 Lodge
Hirsh Joseph C., clk., s s. 3J, b. Elm and Plum
Hirsh Nathan, tailor, 212 Vine
Hirshberg Meyer, agt., groc'y, 573 Central Av
Hirshburg Hannah, 573 Central Av
Hirshburg Simon, clk., 513 Central Av
Hirspieler Lorenz, blksmith, 33 Moore
Hirst Ella, s.e.c. Parsons and 3d
Hirst Geo., eng., 636 E. Front
Hirst Jacob G., policeman, s.s. 3d, b. Whittaker and Washington
Hirst James, 359 W. 3d
Hirst P. M., b.k. Com. Bank, res. Clifton
Hirst Theresa, 247 W. 3d
Hirtzel Martin, carp , 70 W. Mulberry
Hischauer Frederick, brewer, bds. n.w.c. Pike and Pearl
Hiseman John H., pipe fitter, wks. n.e. c. alnut and Canal
Hisen Frederick, painter, 266 Hopkins
Hisen Jacob, trunk mkr., 266 Hopkins
Hisen John Geo., cab. mkr., 266 Hopkins
Hisner Louisa. servt., 231 W. 4th
Hitchcock B I., clk., Methodist Book Concern, bds. 313 Longworth
Hitchcock Bennett, b.k., 78 Richmond
Hitchcock Coleman, shoe manuf., 26 Dayton
HITCHCOCK Luke, (Poe & H.,) 313 Longworth
Hitchell John, tinware, 433 Central Av
Hitchens Hamilton, tinner, 202 Poplar
Hitchens John, blksmith, n.s. Railroad, e. of Vance
Hitchens William. lab., 29 Carr
Hitchins Thos., blksmith, 149 George
Hite Rebecca, 169 Sycamore
Hitkamp Frank, cab. mkr., n.w.c. Stone and 3d
Hitton Hy., shoe mkr., wks. 98 Race
Hitzemann Frederick, 20 Hughes
Hitzman Augustus, cigar mkr., 15 Webb
Hively John, carp., 34 Rittenhouse
Hoadly Geo., Judge Superior Court of Cincinnati, h. E. Walnut Hills
Hoag David R., (H. & Quick,) 100 W. 4th
Hoag Mary L., n.e.c. Pendleton and Liberty
Hoag & Quick, (David R. H. & Israel Q.,) photographers, 100 W. 4th
Hoak Hy., sawyer, rear 71 Abigail
Hoard ——, clk., bds. 152 W. 4th
Hoban James, mach., s.e.c. Mill and Race
Hoban John, collector, 67 W. Court, w. of Central Av
Hoban Joseph, grocery, 392 W. 3d
Hoban Mary Ann, bds. s e c. 3d & Mill
Hoban Patrick, hoop poles, 51 Water, h. 56 Water
Hoban Thomas, lab., s.e.c. 3d and Mill
HOBART Wm. N., (L. Fletcher. H & Co.,) bds. s.e.c. 6th and Race
Hobbs C & Quick, salesman, 10 Main, h. 200 W. 8th
HOBBS Hy. K., (H. & Parker,) 260 W. 4th
Hobbs James, molder, 50 Betts
Hobbs John W., clk., bds. 47 W. 7th

Hobbs Mary C., teacher, 85 Pendleton
HOBBS & PARKER, (Henry K. H. & Joseph W. P.,) Wholesale Grocers and Commission Merchants, 10 Main
Hobbs Richard, lithographer, 85 Pendleton
HOBBS WM. H., Coffee House, 166 W. 6th
Hobby Mary L., bds. 371 Central Av
Hoben James, painter, s w c. Mound and Longworth
Hoben Martin, blksmith, 47 Plum
Hoben Patrick, trunk mkr., wks. 509 Plum
Hoberg Hy, cooper, w.s. Cutter, b. Wade and David
Hoberg Harman C., salesman, 79 Martin
Hobern Thomas, lab., 38 Rittenhouse
Hobin Peter, lab., n.s. Friendship al., b. Pike and Butler
Hobson Geo., bds. 571 E. Front
Hobson James, finisher, 39 Pike
Hobt Fridolin, express wagon, 14 15th
Hoch Geo. J., 562 E. Front
Hoch Jacob, brewer, n s. Franz, b. Elder and Findlay
Hoch Jacob. lab., 594 Elm
Hoch Roman, saw mkr., wks. 93 E. 8th
HOCHENLEITNER JOSEPH, Brighton Brewery, s.w.c. Division & Harrison Pike
Hochstetter Wm., 106 W. Pearl, h. 73 Hopkins
Hochstrasser Mary, dress mkr., 422 Vine
Hochstuhl Martin. porter, e.s. Goose al., b. Liberty and Green
Hock Chas., butcher. 1055 Central Av
Hock .ly.. tailor, 25 Dudley
Hock John, blksmith, bds. Justus Appel's
Hock John, plumber, 48 E. 2d
Hock Joseph, tailor, bds. 678 W. Front
Hock Matthew, lab., w.s. Lebanon Road, b. Liberty and Corporation Line
Hock Michael, wks. n.w.c. Smith & 2d
Hocker Christ, porter, n s.c. 6th & Ma'n
Hocker Frank, boots and shoes, 467 W. 9th, w. of Central Av.
HOCKER GEO., Boot and Shoe Manufacturer, s.w.c. Richmond and Central Av.
Hocker Hy., teamster, n.w.c. Plum and 2d
Hocker Herman B., boots and shoes, 39 Elm
Hocker Martin, shoe mkr., 92 Central Avenue
Hocker Theodore. lab , 230 Hopkins
Hocker Wm , tailor, s. s. Melancthon, b. Cutter and Jones
Hockins Ann, laundress, s. s. 6th, b Broadway and Culvert
Hockloe Geo., carp., n.s. Front e. of Kelly
Hockman Caroline, servt., 197 W. 7th
Hockmann Catharine, 40 Rittenhouse
Hockmann Geo., lab., 33 Rittenhouse
Hockmann Hy., lab., 40 Rittenhouse
Hocks Hy., lab., 310 W 2d
Hock? John, lab., s.s. Weller, b. Carr and Harriet
Hochstetter Wm., b. k., 106 W. Pearl, h. 73 Hopkins
Hoctor Patrick, lab., 445 W. 2d
Hodge Alexander, dray, 124 Lock
Hodges Geo., n.e.c. Plum and 6th
Hodgson Geo. B., brush mkr., 46 Mansfield
Hodgson George B. II., salesman, 11 Main, h 384 W. 4th
Hodgson Thos., mach., wks. 162 E. Front
Hodgson Wm., mach., 45 Mansfield
Hodgson Wm. H., salesman, 30 Walnut, h. 361 W. 9th
Hodson James, 23 Dank
Hodson Kate. milliner, 18 W. 5th
Hoeb Thomas, express, 271 Bremen
Hoechst Jacob, cutter, 659 Vine
Hoecker Hermann P., lab., 536 Race
Hoeckzema Lizetta, seamstress. 99 Clay
Hoefelgunner Bernard, lab., 512 Walnut
Hoefer Geo., painter, 151 Bremen
Hocter Hy., cab. mkr., 581 Race

Hoefer Hy., cab. mkr., w.s. Goose al. b. 14th and 15th
Hoefer Joseph, wks. Oehler al. b. Freeman and Garrard
Hoeffer Francis. gardener. 320 Freeman
Hoeffer Geo., bk. layer, 281 Bremen
HOEFFER GEO. F., Jr., (Long & H.) 320 Freeman
Hoeffer Joseph, butcher, 311 Freeman
Hoeffer Nicholas, city commissioner N. Dist., office, City Hall, h. e.s. Race n. of Elder
Hoeffer Nicholas, jr., feed store, n.w.c. Baymiller and 8th. h. 311 Freeman
Hoeffling John F., tailor, bds. 11 Mulberry
Hoeffler John, brush mkr., 93 Bremen
Hoeft Hy., cof. h., 600 Main
Hoeger Benedict, lab , 59 Buckeye
Hoehn Christian, lab., 602 Main
Hoehn Jacob, carp., 26 Peete
Huehn Michael, plumber, wks. 221 W. 5th
Hoel Edmund, 361 W. 7th
Hoeland Fred., painter, 473 Race
Hoeler Samuel. salesman, 92 Main
Hoeller Fred., cik., 137 Race
Hoeller H. S., clk., bds. Teutonia Hotel
Hoelscher August, blksmith, 17 E. Liberty
Hoelscher Fred , clk., 17 E. Liberty
Hoelsher Francis H , cutter, 54 Sycamore
Hoeltge Augustus, surgeon, U. S. A., 240 Richmond
Hoeltge Louisa E., 500 Richmond
Hoeltze Wm., tinman, w.s. Cutter b. David and Wade
Hoendorf Chas , saddler, 468 Walnut
Hoendorf Gottfried, sa.idler, 385 Vine
Hoendorf Robert, saddler, 3s5 Vine
Hoendorf Robert, saddler, al. b. Charlotte and Findlay and Plum and Central Av.
HOENIG Edward, (J. B. Bollmann & Co.) h. 15 and 17 E. 9th
Hoepink Bernhard, cab. mkr., 514 Elm
Hoer Catharine, cof. h.. w.s. Fountain b Rice and Alexander
Hoere James, painter, 17 Ann
Hoereth John N., mas'n, e.s. Goose al. b. Green and Elder
Hoerner Michael, foreman, 485 E. Front
Hoernermann Hy., tailor, 61 W. Liberty
Hoernschemeir Frank H., tailor, n.w.c. Cutter and Clark
Hoers Phillip H., dry goods, 486 Walnut
Hoersting Hy., marble works. 201 Linn
Hoerstmann Fredericka, 108 Abigail
Hoerstmann John, molder, Spring, b. Woodward and Abigail
Hoerz Hy., blksmith, 56 Ham. Road
Hoesse Jacob, carriage mkr., 25 Mulberry
Hoess Anthony, cof. h., 56 Ham. Road
Hoeveler Elizabeth, n.e.c. 6th and Central Av.
Hoeveler Geo., clk., n.e.c. 6th and Central Av.
HOEVELER JOSEPH, Drugs, Medicines, Chemicals, &c., n.e.c. 6th and Central Av.
Hof Fred., cooper. rear 533 Sycamore
Hof Geo., cooper, 150 Spring
Hof Gustave. clk., 577 Sycamore
HOF GUSTAVUS, Wholesale Paper Dealer, 2nd Main, h. 577 Sycamore
Hof Margaret, rear 533 Sycamore
Hof Martin cooper, rear 533 Sycamore
HOFACKER CHRIST, Coffee House, 35 E. 3d
Hofehulti Wm., e.s. Park b. Longworth and 6th
HOFER CHARLES, Wines and Liquors, 208 Vine, h. 111 Smith
Hofer Jacob. tailor, 145 Clay
Hoferkamp Hy., clk., 63 Baymiller
Hoff Geo., cooper. 170 Spring
Hoff Jacob, lab., 38 Findlay
Hoff John, cap mkr., bds 602 Walnut
Hoff Joseph, bar k., Galt House
Hoffer Geo., cooper, 797 Central Av.

(HOF) CINCINNATI (HOF) DIRECTORY. (HOH) 171

Hoffer Nicholas, 660 Race
Hoffsuemmer Mrs Gertrude, n.s. 13th b. Walnut and Vine
Hoffhelmer Abram, (H. & Brothers,) 132 W. 8th
Hoffheimer, Brothers, (Solomon, Max, Abram & Isaac H.) liquors, &c., 32 E. 2d
Hoffheimer Isaac, (H. & Brothers,) res. St. Louis
Hoffheimer Max, (H. & Brothers,) h. 129 W. 6th
Hoffheimer Solomon, (H. & Brothers,) 132 W. 8th
Hoffman Abram S, (Kraft, H. & Co.) 72 Longworth
Hoffman Mrs. Anna, tailoress, 720 Vine
Hoffman Rev. B., 11 Rittenhouse
Hoffman Chas., stone mason, 123 Richmond
Hoffman Christian, tinner, bds. 115 Clinton
Hoffman Daniel, molder, 16 Jackson
Hoffman Daniel, lab., 66 Martin
Hoffman Edward, cap mkr., bds. 115 Clinton [man
Hoffman Elizabeth, servt., 1517 Freeman
Hoffman Elizabeth, 115 Clinton
Hoffman Francis, packer, wks. 728 Central Av.
Hoffman Fred., chair mkr., bds. 115 Clinton
Hoffman Fred., grinder, Linn b. Clinton and Everett
Hoffman Fred., lab., e.s. Kilgour b. 3d and 5th
Hoffman Fred., w.s. Browne near Ham. Road
Hoffman Geo., baker, 21 David
Hoffman Geo., molder, 21 David
Hoffman Geo. L., rear 133 York
Hoffman Geo. L., paints, 488 Race
Hoffman Hy., clk., 33 Milton
Hoffman Hy., driver, 191 Hopkins
Hoffman Hy., dray, e.s. Kilgour, b. 3d and 5th
Hoffman Hy., salesman, 63 Webster
Hoffman Hy. L., carp., 225 W. 3d
Hoffman Isaac, American Express Co.
Hoffman J., japanner, wks. n.w.c. Race and 2d
Hoffman Jacob, cutter, 258 Carr
Hoffman Jacob, lab., wks. 13 E. Front
Hoffman Jacob, porter, Gibson House
Hoffman Jacob, porter, 54 Martin
Hoffman Jacob H., paper ruler, 66 Martin
Hoffman John, 88 Stark
Hoffman John, butcher, 58 Dunlap
Hoffman John, cab. mkr., 468 W. Front
Hoffman John, cof. h., 10 Landing, b. Broadway and Ludlow, h. 35 E. Front
Hoffman John, confec., 35 E. Front
Hoffman John, instrument mkr., s.e.c. Abigail and Sycamore
Hoffman John A., 494 W. 9th
Hoffman John S., carp., 140 Mound
Hoffman Joseph L., carver, 468 W. Front
Hoffman Louis, (Kiersted & H.) 148 George
Hoffman Mary, bds. 110 13th
Hoffman Mathias, cof. h., 1462 E. Front
Hoffman Meyer, boots and shoes, 105 E. 6th
Hoffman Michael, butcher, w.s. Browne nr. Ham Road
Hoffman Peter, driver, s.s. Grant b. Elm and Plum
Hoffman Renhold B., n.s. 6th b. Harriet and Horne
Hoffman Sophla, 116 Betts
Hoffman Viola, bds. 187 W. Court. w. of Central Av.
Hoffman Wm., dray, 52 Baum
Hoffmann Adam, baker, 73 Green
Hoffmann Adam, (H. & Kroder,) rear 30 Webster
Hoffmann August, brewer, bds. 652 Main
Hoffmann Barbara, 305 Sycamore
Hoffmann Bernhard, comb mkr., w.s. Goose al. b. Green and Elder
Hoffmann Chas., tailor. 536 Main
Hoffmann Chas. G., confec., 441 Sycamore

Hoffmann Christian, cab. mkr., 217 Ham. Road
Hoffmann Christian, grocery, 46 Hamer
Hoffmann Christopher, lab., 7 Miami
Hoffmann Eliza, seamstress. 133 York
Hoffmann Emil, clk. Co. clerk's office, h. n.e.c Main and Orchard
Hoffmann Emilie, 526 Main
Hoffmann Fred., cab. mkr., 115 Clinton
Hoffmann Frederick, cof. h., 132 Bremen
Hoffmann Frederick, lab., 521 Sycamore
Hoffmann Frederick, tailor, 14 Mary
HOFFMANN George, (H. & Moser), res. Covington
Hoffmann Geo., shoe mkr., 88 Buckeye
Hoffmann Henry, boots and shoes, 38½ E. Front
Hoffmann Henry, lab., 418 Walnut
Hoffmann Henry, lab., 174 Webb
Hoffmann J. Philip, barber, 82 Ham. Road, h. 96 Ham. Road
Hoffmann Jacob, boots and shoes, 494 Walnut
Hoffmann Jacob, carp., e.s. Bremen b. Elder and Findlay, h. 677 Vine
Hoffmann Jacob, lab., 119 Bremen
Hoffmann Jacob, porter, 125 Bremen
Hoffmann John, 700 Vine
Hoffmann John, cab. mkr., 408 W. Front
Hoffmann John, cigar mkr., 677 Vine
Hoffmann John, instrument mkr., 395 Sycamore
Hoffmann John, lab., 538 Plum
Hoffmann John J, furniture. 677 Vine
Hoffmann Julius, cof. h., n.s. 13th b. Walnut and Vine, h. 436 Vine
Hoffmann & Kroder, (Adam H. & Frederick K.), coopers, 30 Webster
Hoffmann Margaretha, seamstress, h 1 Wade b. Elm and Plum
Hoffmann Margaretha, 612 Sycamore
Hoffmann Mary, 110 13th
Hoffmann Michael, butcher, n.s. Henry nr. Elm
Hoffmann Michael, slaughter house, 421 Baymiller
HOFFMANN & MOSER, (George H. & Charles Moser), Paints, Oils, Brushes, Varnish, Artist's Materials, &c., 222 Main, and White Lead Manuf., s.w.c 6th and Miami Canal
Hoffmann Peter, cab. mkr., 56 Elder
Hoffmann Peter, cab. mkr., 562 Vine
Hoffmann Phillipp, cigars, 1013 Central Av
Hoffmann Sebastian, weaver, 96 Bremen
Hoffmann Valentine, blksmith, wks. 600 Walnut
Hoffmann Wm., dry goods, 213 W, Front
Hoffmeier Wm., saddler, 72 Rittenhouse
Hoffmeister Charles, finisher, wks. C. T. Dumont's
Hoffmeister Ferdinand, trimmings, 114 W. 5th, h. 217 W. 7th
Hoffmeister Henry, wood dealer, 21 Hughes
Hoffmeyer Herman, dray, 10 Hughes
Hoffmeyer Geo., lab., 266 Water
HOFFNER JACOB. Stoves, Tin and Sheet Iron Ware 34 E. Pearl
Hoffner Jacob, trunk mkr., 34 Adams
Hoffner James, lab., 563 W. 5th
Hoffner Stephen, gardener, n.s. Corporation Line nr. Auburn
Hoffstetter Wm. H., lab., n.s. Front e. of Kelly
Hofgesang Caspar. lab., 37 Green
Hofgesang Margaret, midwife, 37 Green
Hofhus G. Theodore, lab., 101 Woodward
Hoflin Michael, butcher, 109 Clinton
Hofinghoff Chas., grocer, 110 W. Court
Hofman Casper, shoe mkr., 440 W. 5th
Hofman Chas, saddler, rear 16 E. Mulberry
Hofman Frederick, cigar mkr., 232 Main
Hofman John, butcher, Junction Walnut Hills and Reading Road
Hofmann Catharine 660 Vine
Hofmann Jacob, upholsterer, 204 Elm
Hofmann Laura, 48 Ham. Road
Hofmann Peter, express man 460 Main
Hofmeier Wm., saddler, 72 Rittenhouse

Hofnau Annanias, tailor, bds. s.e.c. 7th and Central Av
Hofoge Henry. shoe mkr., 166 Spring
Hofsechutte. carriage trimmer, 124 Clark
Hofstetter Stephen, tailor. 442 W. 5th
Hogan Ann, servt., 141 Barr
Hogan Anthony, huckster. 58 E. 5th
Hogan Arthur, carp., n.e.c. Richmond and Freeman
Hogan Bridget, grocery, 321 John
Hogan Daniel, lab., n.s. Front e. of Lumber
Hogan Dennis, shoe mkr., wks. 53 W. 4th
Hogan Eliza, 110 Broadway
Hogan Ellen, servt., n.s 3d b. Elm and Plum
Hogan Ellen, servt., 267 George
Hogan Fannie. actress, National Theater
Hogan Geo., collar mkr , 255 W. 3d
Hogan James, lab., s.s. Friendship al. b. Pike and Butler
Hogan James, lab., h. n.s. Fremont b. Carr and Harriet
Hogan Johanna, cof. h., s.s. 6th b. Broadway and Culvert
Hogan John, bds. 41 Pub. Landing
Hogan John, saloon, 189 Central Av
Hogan Julia, servt., n.s. 3d b. Elm and Plum
Hogan M., carp., National Theater
Hogan Margaret, laundress, Gibson House
Hogan Martin, lab., 130 Central Av
Hogan Mary, seamstress, wks. 53 W. 4th
Hogan Mary, n. s. Fremont b. Harriet and Mill Creek
Hogan Mary, servt., Henrie House
Hogan Michael, police, n.s. 7th b. Central Av and John
Hogan Patrick, cof. h. 241 W. 6th
Hogan Patrick, dray, s.s. Court e. of Broadway
Hogan Patrick, driver, 137 W. 3d
Hogan Patrick. lab., 63 Barr
Hogan Peter, lab., s.s. Sloo w. of Freeman
Hogan Peter, blksmith, wks., C. H. and D. R. R. blksmith shop
Hogan Stephan, shoe mkr., wks. 53 W. 4th
Hozan Terrence, porter, 405 Race
Hogan Thomas, clk., bds. 346 Race
Hogan Thomas, grocery, 45 E. 3d e. of Whittaker
Hogan Thomas, lab., e.s. Oregon b. 3d and 6th
Hogan Walter, boiler, bds. s.e.c. 2d and Smith
Hogan Wm., carp., 171 Sycamore
Hogbin Thomas, confec., 210 Central Av
Hogoback John H., lab., 20 Woodward
Hogeluch Henry, teamster, n.s. Railroad e. of Kelly
Hogeluch Herman. chair mkr., n.s. Railroad e. of Kelly
Hogen Patrick, trunk mkr., 23 Providence
Hoger Theodore, bk. binder, bds. 550 Main
Hoggart Edw., barber, 150 Baymiller
Hoggart Miss Missouri, bds. 130 Baymiller
Hograver Frank, cigar mkr., 92 Baum
Hogreve Detrich, cab. mkr., wks. 123 W. 2d
Hogrife, Wm., tailor, s.w.c. Cutter and Melancthon
Hogue Jacob A., cab. mkr., 300 Richmond
HOGUE Robert, (R. Conkling & Co.), bds. s.w.c of 4th and Broadway
Hohan Ann. 436 W. 6th
Hohenzullern John, baker, 492 W. Front
Hohit Nicholas, shoe mkr., 3 Harrison Pike
Hohhas Martha, seamstress. 418 Race
Hohinsollern Geo., 21 David
Hohman Isaac, salesman, 158 Sycamore
Hohman Jacob, dray, 114 W. Liberty
Hohman John, cab. mkr., 607 Race
Hohmann Henry, cooper, 9 Buckeye
Hohmeier Albert, lab., 10 Buckeye
Hohmeier Bernard, tanner, e s. Logan b. Elder and Findlay
Hohn Andrew, lab. 189 Linn

172 (HOL) CINCINNATI (HOL) DIRECTORY. (HOL)

Hohneck Catharine, e.s. Johnson al. b. Canal and 12th
Hohneck Valentine, cof. h., 614 Vine
Hohnhorst Geo. H., clk., 213 Longworth
Hohnhorst John, T., shoe mkr., 77 E. Pearl
Hohnhorst Wm. H., clk., h. 213 Longworth
Hohnstedt Henry, grocery, 490 Race
Hohrmann Henry, cooper, 60 Wade
Hoke David T., watchmann, 142 Carr
Hokengos Magdalene, dress mkr., 422 Vine
Holabird A. B. & Co., machinists, 355 W. Front
Holabird & Dumont, boilers, 355 W. Front
Holbrook Anna, servt., 29 W. 3d
Holch Mathias, tailor, 476 Vine
Holcher Herman, dray, 444 W. 3d
Holcomb Ann, 57 Gano
Holcomb Alonzo, deputy sheriff, 443 W. [2d
Holcomb Asa, peddler, s.w.c. Richmond and Linn
Holcomb John D., lab., s w.c. Richmond and Linn
Holcomb Richard, fireman, 213 W. Court w. of Central Av
Holcomb Rev. Theodore I., bds. s.w.c. 3d and Broadway
Holden David, painter, 93 Freeman
Holden Kate. milliner, bds. 97 W. Co[urt
Holden Oliver, mach., 202 Richmond
HOLDEN R. A. & CO., (Reuben H. & Chas. Houghton), Commission Merchants and Feather De[alers], 67 Vine
HOLDEN Reuben A., (R. A. H. & [Co.]), s.w.c. Auburn and Mason Mt. Auburn
Holden Robert, manufac. of sewing machines, 202 Richmond
Holden Wm., carp., 70 Laurel
Holderbrink John, molder, 73 David
Holders Henry, finisher, 419 Longworth
Holdheid Herman, lab. 126 Clay
Holdmann Louis, lab., wks. C. H. & D. R. R. depot
Holdmeier Christian, cooper, n.e.c Pleasant and Green
Holdmin, Louis, lab., 62 Pierson
Holdridge Ami, boots and shoes, n.s. 6th nr. e. Main. h. 204 Freeman
HOLENSHADE Jacob W., (H. Morris & Co.), 174 Elm
HOLENSHADE, MORRIS & CO., (Jacob W. H. Edward C. M.), Hardware, Iron and Stoves, 553, 555, 537 Central Av., Bolt Works 535 and 537 Central Av.
Holford Ann, 510 W. 8th
Holford Geo., clk., bds. n.w.c. Clinton and Central Av.
Holford Peyton, lab., 638 E. Front
Holford Phoebe, asst. matron Cin. Orphan Asylum, Mt. Auburn
Hollabird Leah, 47 W 7th
Holland Bridget, 246 Sycamore
Holland Eliza, tailoress, 485 Walnut
Holland George, whitewasher, 92 W. Front
Holland Jas , box mkr., 612 W. 8th
Holland James, messenger, 15 W. 3d
Holland James, sawyer, 612 W. 8th
HOLLAND John, (G W. Sheppard & Co. 246 Sycamore
Holland John, mach., w.s. Kilgour b. 3d and 5th
Holland John W., finisher, wks. n. e c. Walnut and Canal
Holland Kate, bds. n.s. R. Road, e. of Lewis
Holland Lawrence, fireman, n.s. R. Road e. of Lewis
Holland Patrick. trimmer, 238 Broadway
Holland Richard. bk. layer, n. e. c. Barr and Baymiller
Holland Thomas, tailor, s e. c. 7th and Broadway
Holland Wm. H., trav. agt. Aetna Ins. Co., 171 Vine, h. 101 Richmond
HOLLANDER Adam, (G. P. & A. H.) 397 Walnut
HOLLANDER G. P & A., (Geo. P. H. & Akam H.) Venetian Blind Manufacturers, 397 Walnut

HOLLANDER Geo. P., (G. P. & A. H.) 397 Walnut
Hollander Joseph, clk., Co. Auditor's Office. h. 57 Ham. Road
Hollander Samuel, phys., 159 W. Court
Holle Chas.. ale and porter manufac., 126 Cutler, h. 147 W. Court, w. of Central Av.
Holle Theodore, musician, 35 Jackson
Holle Wm., carp., 66 David
Hollebach George, painter, 929 Central Av.
Hollebeck Valentine, carpet weaver, 78 Buckeye
Hollen Stephen W., 34 Grant
Hollenbeck Martin, shoe mkr., 188 Everett
Hollenbitter Peter, carriage smith, 69 Young
Hollenkampe Henry, clk., 238 Main, bds. s.w.c. Milton and Spencer
Holler Joseph. eng., 10 Webb
Hollerbach John, prop. Missouri House, 43 E. Front
Hollerbach Valentine, carpet mkr., 78 Buckeye
Holleran Martin, lab., n.s. R. Road, e. of Vance
Hollering Wm., 223 Betts
Hollester Wm., sawyer, junction of Torrence and Front
Holley John, lab.. 5¢ Gano
Holley Robert, dray, 419 Sycamore
Hollywood Job., plumber, s. e. 6th b. Broadway and Culvert
HOLLIDAY & SMITH, (Thomas H. & John W H. S.) Hardware, Tools and Cutlery, n. e. c. 5th and Central Av.
HOLLIDAY Thomas, (H. & Smith,) 130 John
Hollican Julia, bds. 206 W. 5th
Hollin James, lab., 133 W. Front
Hollinger Henry, lab., 49 Observatory
Hollinger John, gilder, wks. Eggers & Co., Mt. Adams
Hollingber John M., coppersmith, bds. n.w.c Lawrence and 2d
HOLLINGSHEAD MARK, Insurance Agent, & Agent for Payson's Sash Balance, 77 W. 3d, h. 375 George
Hollingsworth E. T., clk., Cin. Enquirer, h. 46 Hathaway
Hollingsworth Rosanna, 169 Sycamore
Hollins Henry, lab., 80 Baum
Hollins John W., 709 E. Front
HOLLISTER GEO. D., Attorney at Law, 230 Walnut, up stairs, h. s.s. Coggswell, Mt. Auburn
Hollister Wm., sawyer, wks. 1565 E. Front
Hollman Barney, chair mkr., 369 W. 5th
Holiman Henry, (Tobe & H.) bds. Fremont House
Hollmann Theodore, painter, 371½ Broadway
Holloway Green, lab., 52 Lodge
Hollway Saml., currier, bds. 114 Hunt
Holloway Samuel, whitewasher. 66 Peete
Hollstein Louis, 343 Vine
Hollwede Conrad, clk., bds. 207 W. Front
Holly John, lab., 187 Water
Holly Mary, servt., 343 W, 8th
Holman Charles, conductor, bds. Spencer House
Holman John D., mer., 137 W. 9th
Holmann Bernard, watch mkr., 369 W. 5th
Holmes Catharine, 68 Rittenhouse
HOLMES Charles S., (Rawson, Wilby & Co.) 35 McFarland
Holmes & Co., (Isaac I. H.) dealers in liquors, 19 E. Front
Holmes Henry, barber, s. e. c. 6th and Lock. h. 24 E. 6th g. of Lock
Holmes Henry S, clk, Quarter Master's Office, h. Clifton
Holmes Isaac I., (H & Co.) res. E. Walnut Hills
Holmes J. & Co., (Jane H & L. R. Holmes) grocers, s.w.c. 5th & Plum
Holmes Jane, (J. H. & Co.) 438 George
Holmes John, shoe mkr., s.w.c. Pearl and Butler
Holmes Lovick R., (J. Holmes & Co.) 438 George

Holmes Martin, lab., n. s. W. W. Canal b. Smith and Park
Holmes Mary, s.w.c. Pearl and Butler
Holmes P., lab., wks. Chamberlain & Co.'s
Holmes Patrick, lab., n.s. Pearl b. Smith and Park
Holmes Perry B., eng.. h. 114 Baum
HOLMES S & Son., (Southworth H. & Wm. N. Holmes,) Manufacturers and Importers of Paper Hangings, 65 W. 4th
HOLMES Southworth, (S. H & Son) h. Clifton
Holmes Thomas, lab., 10 Race
Holmes W. Porter, clk., 19 E. Front, res. E. Walnut Hills
Holmes Walter G.. clk., 19 E. Front, res. E. Walnut Hills
Holmes Wm. cab. mkr., 355 Clark
Holmes Wm. N., (S. Holmes & Son,) h. Walnut Hills
Holoren Bridget, 254 W. 7th
Holroyd E., clk., 101 W. 4th
Holscher August., horse shoer, 17 Liberty
Holscher Bernard, cab mkr., 351 W. 6th
Holscher Fred. H., clk., 17 E. Liberty
Holscher Herman, dray, 444 W. 3d
Holse Eliza., n.w.c. Cutter and Everett
Holsen Elizabeth, Moore al. b. 8th & 9th and Plum and Elm
Holsher Henry W., bk. maker, s. e. c. Western Av and Findlay
Holsmann Henry, blk. smith, 172 Spring
Holst Henry, painter, 54 Dudley
HOLSTEIN Augustus, (H. & Hammer,) 334 W. 6th
HOLSTEIN & HAMMER. (Augustus H. & Gustavus H..) Steam Moulding and Oval Frame Factory, s.w.c. Augusta and Smith
Holster Wm., finisher, 501 Race
HOLT AMOS, Butter and Egg Depot, Basement 32 W. 5th, h. 50 Elizabeth
Holt John, constable, 46 Freeman
Holt John A., 584 E. Front
Holt Josiah, lab. Richmond b. Harriet and Mill Creek
Holt Mary, 55 Observatory Road
HOLT WM., Wholesale and Retail Groceries and Produce, 84 and 86 E. Pearl and 29 W.5th, h. Newport
HoRcamp Barney, lab., 43 Race
Holtel Henry, carp , 715 Race
Holteman Frank, chair mkr., wks. 517 Main
Holtenkamp Joseph, 179 Hopkins
Holterhoff Godfred, clk., 200¼ Barr
Holterman Henry, clk., 14 W. Pearl, bds. Madison House
Holtermann Francis, chair mkr., 21 Abignil
HOLTERS B., Alhambra Saloon, n.w.c. Main and River Landing, h. 104 Longworth
Holters Benj.. (B. H. Trame & Co.,) 104 Longworth
Holters Bernhard J., confec., 104 Longworth
Holters Henry, finisher, wks. 142 W. 3d
Holtge Frederick, tinner, 131 Linn
Holtge Wm., tinner, 307 Linn
Holtgrave Herman, mach., 525 Freeman
Holthage Gerhard, lab., bds. 113 Clay
Holthaus Bernhard H., boots and shoes, 62 E. Front, h. 22 E. Front
HOLTINRICHS WM., Custom House Saloon, 13 E. Pearl
Holthoefer Bernhard, baker, 10 Hughes
Holthof Frederick, lab , wks. S. Robert's
Holthouse Abraham carp., al. b. Linn & Baymiller and Wade and Liberty
Holthouse Barnard, cof h., n.s. R. Road e of Stone al.
Holthouse Henry, lab., 18 Commerce
Holthouse Josephine, servt., 285 George
Holthouse, Wm., lab., w.s. Kilgour b. 3d and 4th
Holtman Rev. Anthony. n.w.c. Vine and Liberty
Holtmann Frank, lab., 100 Abigail
Holtmeier Francis, cabmkr., 35 Buckeye

(HON) CINCINNATI (HOP) DIRECTORY. (HOP) 173

Holtmeier Henry, finisher., bds. w. s. Race b. Liberty and Green
Holtmeyer Annie, servt. 340 W. 7th
Holton Mary, teacher, 264 W. 9th
Holton Thomas, mess. American Ex. Co. bds. Broadway Exchange
Holtz Albert, harness mkr., bds. 620 W. Front
Holtzinger, D. Wesley, 22 Perry
Holtzinger & Edwards, (Henry E. H. & Thomas E.,) carps., 167 George
Holtzinger Henry, carp., bds., 22 Perry
Holtzinger Henry E., (H. & Edwards,) 167 George
Holtzinger John S., frame mkr., bds. 22 Perry
Holtzman John, porter, 94 Hunt
Holvas Sophia, 190 Walnut
Holwedel John, s.e c. Main and Orchard
Holz Frederick, builder, 14 Allison
Holzbach Wm., painter, 766 Central Av.
Holzhauer Jacob, lab., 146 Clay
Holztel Andrew, bar. k., 51 W. 5th
Holzer Ferdinand, carp., 130 Ham. Road
Holzgrarfe Wm., tailor 29 Ham. Road
Holzhalb John C., 236 Broadway
Holzman Joseph, (Samuels & H./ 174 W. 3d
Holzman Saml., b.k., 18 W. Pearl, bds. 116 E. 5th
Holzmann John, porter. 94 Hunt
Holzmeister Jacob, blksmith, 23 Mulberry [eye
Holzmeister Michael, blksmith. 31 Buck-
Holzmeister Michael, blksmith, 31 Locust
Homan Albert, tanner, n.s. Railroad e. of Lewis
Homan Chas., mach 65 12th
Homan Chas., plumber, wks. 200 Vine
Homan Fred.. 65 12th
HOMAN HENRY, Britannia Ware Manufacturer, 11 E. 7th, h. n.w.c. Walnut and 12th
Homan Hy. O., foreman, 25 W 4th, h. 155 Richmond
Homan Henry, lab., n.s. Railroad e. of Lewis
Homan Herman, tanner, n.w.c. McDowell & Lewis
Homan Isaac, clk., 158 Sycamore
Homan James, eng. 470 Elm
Homan John, lab., 60 Bank
Homan Joseph, mason. 107 Woodward
Homan Louis, mach., 65 12th
Homan Louis, pipe fitter, wks. n.e.c. Walnut and Canal
Homan Martha, servt., 16 Barr
Homan Wm., shoemkr, n.s. Railroad e. of Vance
Homann John, soap mkr, wks. 830 Central Av
Homann John H., 60 Abigail
HOMANS Benj., jr., (H. & Co.) h. Covington
HOMANS & CO. (Benj. H., jr. & J. Smith Homans, jr.) Bankers. 13 W. 3d
HOMANS J. Smith, jr. (Homans & Co.) h. New York City
Homberg Fred. Wm., phys., 415 Walnut
Homberg Peter, miller, 163 Clay
Home Insurance Co., of New Haven, Agency, 76 W. 3d
Home Insurance Co., of N. Y., Agency, 65 W. 3d
Home of the Friendless, Mrs. N. B. Smith, matron, 37 W. Court w. of Central Av
Homer Jacob. s.s. Reading Pike nr. Franklin Brewery
Homer James. policeman, 405 W. 4th
Homer Thomas, confec., bds. 49 Elizabeth
Homeyer Bernard, tanner, s s. Liberty b. Linn and Baymiller
Homeyer John, e.s. Logan b. Elder and Liberty
Homler Frank. tailor, w.s. Vine b. Mulberry and Milk
Hommann Martha, 571 Race
Hone Frank. teacher, bds s.w.c. Smith and 2d
Honecke John, lab., wks. n.w.c. Plum and Wade

Horek Anthony, carp., 41 Elder
Honsmeier Hy., dray, 459 W. 2d
Honemeyer Hy., rope mkr., 442 W. 2d
Honer Catharine, seamstress, 273 Franz nr. Elder
Honer Chas., cab. mkr., wks. 71 W. 5th
Honer John D., watch mkr, 203 Walnut, h, 134 Hopkins
Honerkamp John H.. carp.., 114 Abigail
Honerlage Hy.. soap factory, s.e.c. Dudley and Liberty
Honert Hy., cigar mkr., 14 15th b. Elm and Plum
Honey Hy.., cab. mkr., n.e c. Clark and Baymiller
Honhauser Bernard, bakery, 63 E. 8th
Honhauser T., cigar mkr., 20 Ham. Road
Honhauser John, bakery, 90 Hunt
Honhorst Joseph (F. B. James & Co.), 35 Baum
Honing Frank, cof. h., 470 Main
Honka Hy., lab., wks. 222 E. Front
Honkamp Hy. H., eng., 47 Pendleton
Honkamp Frederick, cof. h.. 145 W. 5th
Honkomp Hy., bar k., 145 W. 5th
Honley Thomas, lab., 47 Mill
Honneck Michael, bar k., 403 Vine
Honnen John. lab., 5 Providence
Honnerborn, Benjamin, lab., wks. 196 W. Pearl
Honnig John, cab. mkr., 115 Woodward
Honnigfort Hermon B., b.k., 139 Pleasant
Honnestein Casper, lab., wks. Hieatt & Wood's
Honroth Wm., bk. yard, w.s. Western Av. b. Bank and Harrison Road
Hood Archibald, eng,, w.s. Kilgour b 3d and 4th
Hood Barbara, e.s Anderson b. 2d and Pearl
Hood James, omnibus driver, n.s. Front e. of Kelly
Hood John, carp., s.e.c. Parsons and E. 3d
Hood John, hostler, bds. 19 W. 7th
Hood John, lab., 19 E. 7th
Hood John, lab., 259 W. Front
Hood Newman, bk. mkr.. c. Horne and Harriet
Hoods Sarah, 155 W. Pearl
Hook Benjamin, lab., w.s. Carr nr. Gest
Hook Tony, lab., wks. Hy. Nye's
Hooke Andrew, miller, 61 Lock
Hooker Frances, 125 Avery
Hooker John J., atty., n.s. Front w. of Kill
Hooker Wm. J., ins. agt, 1312 E. Front
Hoole Edmund A., clk., 29 E. 2d, h. 252 Hopkins
HOOLE JOHN R., Book Furnishing Store, 29 E. 3d, res. New York
HOOLE SAML. R., Agent for John R. Hoole, Book Binders' Stock, 29 E. 3d, h. 259 Hopkins
Hoon Wm., blksmith, 82 Butler
Hoop Dorothes, 13 E. 3d e. of Parsons
Hopp Hy., lab., 13 E. 3d e. of Parsons
Hooper Ellen, e.s. Macalister b. 4th and 5th
Hooper Hy., teller, 101 Main, bds. 334 W. 4th
HOOPER John T. (A. G. Burt & Co), bds. 338 W. 4th
HOOPER Wm. (Harrison & H) h. Walnut Hills
Hooping F., lab., wks. Chamberlain & Co's
Hoopmann John D., lab.. 506 Race
Hoops Hy., lab., wks. 222 E. Front
Hoot David, pattern mkr., 13 E. 3d e. of Parsons
Hoover Adam, lab., wks. w.s. Lock b. 4th and 5th
Hoover August, baker, 480 Vine
Hoover Benjamin, lab., 59 Observatory
Hoover Catharine, servt., 54 Franklin
Hoover Elizabeth, 174 Webb
Hoover Jacob, rope mkr., 174 Webb
Hoover John, 47 Jones
Hoover Wm., tanner, 20 Dunlap
HOOVER Wm. H., (Murray, Shipley & Co.), h. 204 W. 4th
Hope Insurance Co. Agency, 76 W. 3d

Hopf Bernhard (H. & Gebhardt) 48 Ham. Road
Hopf & Gebhardt (Bernhard H. & Wm. G.) file cutters, 28 Ham. Road
Hopf Peter, cigars, 62 Ham. Road
Hopf Valentine, finisher, wks. s.w.c. Elm and Front
Hopkins Andrew, cooper, n.s. 6th b. Harriet and Horne
Hopkins Ann. servt., 498 W. 7th
Hopkins Bartley, lab., 259 W 2d
Hopkins Benjamin E., teller, Gilmore, Dunlap & Co's, h. 313 W. 8th
Hopkins Edmund S., 125 Cutter
Hopkins Edw., clk., 397 Central Av., h. 420 Freeman
HOPKINS HENRY P., House and Sign Painter, s.s. Baker b. Vine and Walnut. h. 215 Poplar
Hopkins Hy., dray, 424 Freeman
Hopkins Hy. F., printer, 42 Mansfield
Hopkins John. lab., 116 Barr
HOPKINS JOHN B., Tinware, &c., s.w.c. Sycamore and 7th, h. Mt. Adams
Hopkins John G., harness mkr., 47 E. 8th e. of M. Canal
Hopkins John H.. clk., 21 Elizabeth
Hopkins John T., b.k., Elstner & Fisher's, h Newport
Hopkins John W., salesman, Methodist Book Concern, h. 125 Cutter
Hopkins Joseph, finisher, 58 Providence
HOPKINS L. C. (L. C. H. & Co.) b. 1st dwelling n. of Cin. Orphan Asylum, Mt. Auburn
HOPKINS L. C. & CO., Staple and Fancy Dry Goods, n.e.c. 5th and Vine
Hopkins Martin, lab., 15 Water
Hopkins Mrs. Mary, 45 E. Front
Hopkins Mary J., bds. 519 Freeman
Hopkins Michael, lab., 54 Rittenhouse
Hopkins Patrick, dray, 423 George
Hopkins Thomas, 458 Elm
Hopkins Thos., fireman, n.s. Van Horn nr. Carr
Hopkins Thomas, molder, wks. 222 E. Front
Hopkins Wm., morocco dresser, 47 E. 8th e. of Lock
Hopkins Wm., tailor, bds. 158 W. 3d
Hopkins Wm. A., eng., bds. 21 Elizabeth
Hopkins Wm. H., finisher, wks. n.e.c. Walnut and Canal
Hopkinson Norman A., painter, 536 W. 8th
Hopp Hy., mach., 147 Clark
Hopp John, 691 Elm
Hoppe D. & Co. (Dominick H. & Geo. H. Vanderahe) com. mers., 25 Walnut
Hopps Dominick (D. H. & Co.) 546 Central Av
Hoppe Frederick. tailor, n.e.c. Linn and Betts
Hoppe Gustavus, tailor, 482 Walnut
Hoppe Joseph, bds. Cincinnati House
Hoppen Moses, hinge fitter, wks. n.e.c Walnut and Canal
Hoppengans Wm., lab., 158 E. 5th
Hopper Alfred, inspector, Cin. Gas Co.,. bds. National Hotel
Hopper Eliza A., 221 Cutter
Hopper Hermon, mach.. s.w.c. 9th and Walnut
Hopper Livingston, bklayer, bds. 158 Cutter
Hopper Maggie, teacher, bds. 23 George
Hopper Miss Mary G., teacher, 143 George
Hopper Morris S., boots and shoes, 25 E. Pearl
Hopper Samuel, collector, 164 Longworth
Hopper Wm., bklayer, 50 Clark
Hopperton John, butcher. 55 Wade
Hopple Jacob, coppersmith, 247 Plum
Hopple John J., 11 E. 3d, h. 247 Plum
Hopple Joseph, 11 E. 3d, h. Camp Washington
Hopple Matthew, attorney, 11 E. 3d, h. Camp Washington
Hopple Richard B., 11 E. 3d, h. Camp Washington
Hopwood. Cordelia J., bds. 121 E. 3d

174 (HOR) CINCINNATI (HOT) DIRECTORY. (HOW)

Horak John, blksmith, 70 Abigail
Horber Jerry, finisher, 409 W. 7th
Horch Louis, cooper, 31 Dunlap
Hord Elias R., b.k., 92 W. Pearl, bds. 132 W. 4th
Hord George M., (G. M. H. & Co.,) 325 W. 7th
Hord George M. & Co., (G. M H & Albert W. Mullen,) com. mer., 60 W. Front
Hordelbrink Geo. H., chair mkr., 610 Race
Hore Patrick, lab., 365 Sycamore
Horel Jno. B., shoemkr, 351 Central Av
Horen Mary, servt, 114 Broadway
Horgan Abbe, servt, Henrie House
Horlacher Conrad, safe mkr, 661 Race
Horman Christian, boots and shoes, 76 W. Court
Hormann Hy., clk., 628 Main
Hormann Hy., tob cconist, 76 W. Court
Hormann Wm., cooper, 179 Baymiller
Hormberg Hermann H., rear 26 Franklin
Hormsbey Thos., porter, 63 Lodge
Horn Charles, clk., bds. 44 E. 4th
Horn Christian, 181 Linn
Horn Eckhard, shoemkr., 46 Hughes
Horn Geo., cof. h., 272 Main, h. 59 St. Clair
Horn Hy., stone mas n, 143 Wade
Horn John, bklayer, n.w.c. Cutter and Hopkins
Horn Patience, 450 W. Liberty
Horn Reinhold, soap mkr., 538 Main
Horn Wm., bar k., 272 Main, h. 59 St. Clair
Hornbach Louis, lab., n s. Mulberry, b. Main and Sycamore
Hornberger Andrew, teamster, 606 Vine
Hornberger Frederick, wood yard, s.e c. Elder and Race, h 632 Vine
Hornberger Jacob, wood yard, s.e.c. Plum and Liberty, h. 177 W Liberty
Hornblow Wm., frame mkr, * E. 6th
Horubrook Richard, carp., 186 Cutter
Horne Mrs. Caroline, 273 Freeman
Horne Charles. 23 W. 3d, h. 178 Sycamore
Horne Chas. W., law student, 178 Sycamore
Horne Daniel H., 178 Sycamore
Horne Daniel H., jr, com. mer., 212 George
Horner & Gaff. (Geo. S. H. & John G.,) com. mer., 38 Main
Horner Geo. S., (H. & Gaff,) 291 Richmond
Horner Jacob, cof h., s.s. Reading Pike, nr. Franklin Brewery
Horner Thomas D, painter, 536 W. 8th
Horner Wm., druggist, bds 31 Longworth
Horner Wm. D., clk., 110 W. 3d
Horney Thornton F., roller, s.s. Front, e. of French
Horning John, baggage master, Broadway Hotel
Hornle Frederick. tailor, 935 Central Av
Hornschemeyer Hy., bklayer, 225 Cutter
Horning Adam S., deputy sheriff, 454 Elm
Hornung Christian, wagon mkr., 169 Pleasant
Hornung Eberhard, dray, 14 Mercer
Hornung John, 9 Hughes
Hornung Peter, grocery, 19 Hughes
Horr Elizabeth, 351 W. 5th
Horrack John, blksmith, 70 Abigail
Horragan John, lab., Cassatt st, b. Sycamore and Broadway
Horran Edward, blksmith, 316 W. 5th
Horrin August, cooper, e.s. Oregon, b. 3d and 6th
Horrocks Hy. R., (J. R. H. & Son,) 17 Race
Horrocks J. R. & Son, (Jas. R. H & Henry R. H.,) tinware, 6 Commercial Row
Horrocks Jas. R., (J. R. H. & Son,) 15 Race
Horrocks John, tinner, 187 Barr
Horrock Joseph, baker, 376 Broadway
Horsford Hy., tailor, 55 Woodward
Horsley Charles W., carp., 20 McFarland

Horsley Burton, sexton, 15 George
Horsley & Ehler, (Wm. H. & Elias E.,) planing mill, 248 W. Front
Horsley Wm., (H. & Ehler,) 20 McFarland
Horsley Wm, jr., carp, 20 McFarland
Horsley Wm. Geo., musician, bds. 15 George
Horst Andrew, musician, 129 W. 6th
Horst August, clk., 19 Green
Horst Hy., clk., 19 Green
Horst Hermann, mach., 495 Vine
Horst Jefferson, carp., w.s. Ohio Av., b. Calhoun and North Elm
Horst Mary, 19 Green
Horstman Francis H., collar mkr., 181 Spring
Horstman Frederick, porter, 459 Broadway
Horstman George, lab , 29 Abigail
Horstman Joseph, hinge molder, wks n.e.c. Walnut and Canal
Horstman John, lab., 58 Abigail
Horstmann August, eng., 4 Mary
Horstmann August, lab., 1 Lucy
Horstmann Dieterich, tailor, 11 Mulberry
Horstmann Frederick, tailor, 9 Peete
Horstmann Gerhard, sawyer, 8 E. Canal
Horstmann Hy., carp., bds. 519 Sycamore
Horstmann Hy., dray, 47 Pleasant
Horstmann Hy., molder, w.s. Broadway. b. Hunt and Abigail
Horstmann Hy., porter. 32 Walnut
Horstmann Hy., rope mkr., 442 W. 2d
Horstmann Herman, shoemkr, 9 Peete
Horstmann Nicholas, carpet weaver, 14 Abigail
Horstschneider Joseph, boots and shoes, 165 W. 5th
Hortelbrink Geo , chair mkr., 610 Race
Hortens Arnold H., tailor, rear 69 Abigail
Hortinger Mrs. Maria, 90 Mohawk
Hortmuth Philip, 903 Central Av
Horton Caroline W., select school, 119 E. 3d
Horton David C., b.k., 63 E. Front, h. E. Walnut Hills
Horton Eliza, w s. Ohio Av., b. Calhoun and North Elm
Horton Gilbert, eng., bds. 303 W. 6th
HORTON HENRY V., Real Estate Agent, n.w.c. 5th and Walnut, h College Hill
Horton John, 713 Elm
Horton Josephine D., teacher. 71 Barr
Horton L. V., b.k., 7 Carlisle Bldg., bds. Clifton House
Horton Mary A., teacher, 73 Elm
Horton Smith W., eng., s.s. Charlotte, b. Linn and Baymiller
Horton Timothy, salesman, 17 W. Pearl, bds. Madison House
Hortsinger Michael, brewer, s.s. Harrison Pike, b. Division and Brig ton
Hortsman August, blacksmith, bds. 13 Freiman
Horwerth Frank L., cab. mkr., 43 Miami
Horwerth Wm., jr, cab. mkr., 11 Mulberry
Horwitz David, peddler, 467 Vine
Hosmus Adolf., turner, 233 Betts
Hosea Lucy, 273 W. 4th
HOSEA Robert, (Robert H. & Co.) 273 W. 4th
Hosea Robert, jr., clk., 273 W. 4th
HOSEA ROBERT & CO., Wholesale Grocers and Commission Merchants, s.w.c. Front and Main
Hoskamp Margaret, grocery, 33 Baum
Hosken Wm., miller, 93 Findlay
Hoskins W. O., b.k. 73 W. 4th, h. Covington
Hospe Anthony, frame manuf., 16 E. 4th, h. 88 Woodward
Hoss John, lab., 25 Abigail
Hoss John J. F., stone cutter, 25 Abigail
Hossemans Cornelius, peddler, 550 Race
Hossler Chas., mach., 209 Barr
Hostmann Hy., rope mkr., 17 Park
Hustreckt Fred , cab. mkr., 4 W. Canal b. John and Smith
Hotchkiss O. E. & Co , (Osamus E. H. & Geo. Simmons) liquors, 86 Broadway

Hotchkiss Osamus E., (O. E. H. & Co.) 86 Broadway
Hotchkiss Vail, bds. 144 W. 7th
Hotel Geo., cof. h., s.s. Budd b. Harriet and Mill Creek
Hotke Barney, cof. h., n.w.c. Lawrence and Ferry Landing
Hottendorf Louis, clk., 1015 Central Av.
Hottke Joseph, driver, n.s. Livingston b. John and Linn
Hotz John, carp., 119 Bremen
Hotzman Joseph, clothing, 174 W. 3d
Houber Jacob, lab., 114 Gest
Houck Adam, cooper, 15 Bank
Honck Chas. A., carp , 101 Hopkins
Houck Geo. cooper shop, 29 Bernard
Houck Geo. W., boots and shoes, 354 W. 6th, Christian Church n.s. 6th b. Mound and Smith
Houck Joseph, plasterer, 71 Mohawk
Houck Peter. w.s. Riddle b. Bank and Harrison Pike
Houe Wm., carp., wks. 48 E. 8th
Hough Daniel, teacher, 519 Freeman
Hough H. A., bds. Dennison House
Hough Mary, teacher, bds. 221 Longworth
Hough Rev. Sabin, pub, New Church Herald, College B'dg , h. 105 Smith & Co.) h. Mt. Auburn
HOUGHTON Chas. E., (R. A. Holden & Co.) h. Mt. Auburn
Houghton Louis M., teacher 3d district school
Houk Chas A., carp., 101 Hopkins
Houk Hy., lab., 550 E. Front
Houland Chas., ambrotype gallery, n.w. c. 5th and Main
Hour John, tobacconist, 144 Baymiller
Houre John, lab. 130 Mound
House Alfred. miller, bds. 47 New
HOUSE Erwin, assistant editor Western Christian Advocate, s.w.c. 8th and Main, h. Mt. Auburn
House Hy., bar k., bds. 10 Sycamore
House John, tar k., bds. 10 Sycamore
HOUSE OF REFUGE, Office, City Buildings, Wm. Leuthstrom, Secretary
Housefield Hy., lab., wks. n.w.c. Plum and Wade
Houseman F., lab, n.s. Front b. Lawrence and Pike
Houseman Hy., blksmith, wks. n.s. Front b. Lawrence and Pike
Rouseman J., tinner, wks. n.w.c. Race and 2d
Houser John, cab. mkr., 684 Vine
Houser Martin, n.e.c. Linn and Everett
Housling Hy., lab , h. n.s. Front e. of Kelly
Housman B., Woodward b. Sycamore and Broadway
Housman Benj., constable, 23 Franklin
Housman Frederick, blksmith, s.s. Sycamore b. Abigail and Woodward, h. 27 Spring
Housman Mary, 67 Spring
Houston Alice, bds. 107 Broadway
Houston Allen E., molder. 310 Clark
Houston Miss Mary, bds. 107 Broadway
Houston Wm. C., clk., bds. 413 W. 3d
Houts Joseph, cooper, s.s. Harrison Pike b. Division and Riddle
Hove Anton, chair mkr., bds. 192 Hopkins [Bank
Hover John, wagon mkr., bds. rear 7
Hovestadt John H , salesman, 246 Main
Hovey Benjamin P., barber, 938 E. Front
Hovey Delos W., phys ,53 E. 3d
How Elbridge, grocer, 193 George
HOW Fulton M., (Phister & H.) res. Walnut Hills
Howard Ann, n.e.c. Clark and Garrard
Howard Ann, rear 14 Richmond
Howard Ann, 150 E. 3d e. of Collard
Howard Anna, millinery. 216 W. 5th
Howard Catharine, 3 North
Howard Geo. P., salesman 139 Walnut, h. 60 Clinton
Howard John, 216 W. 5th
Howard John, lab., n.e.c. Clark and Garrard
Howard John, printer, bds. s.e.c. 9th and Walnut
Howard John W., rope mkr., wks. 498 John

Howard Johnson, cook, 278 W. 6th
Howard Kate, n e.c 7th and Sycamore
Howard Margaret, 81 W. Front
Howard Martha, 150 E. 3d, e. of Collard
Howard Minerva, 150 E. 3d, e. of Collard
Howard Olivia, 278 W. 8th
Howard Peter, lab., 17 Jordan
Howard Samuel, carp., 176 W. 5th
Howard Samuel, finisher, wks. n.e.c. Walnut and Canal
Howard Samuel F., (Ordelmundt & H.) h. 176 W. 5th
Howard Stella, bds. 272 Main
Howard Stephen, finisher, 16 14th b. Central Av. and Plum
Howard Thos., 50 E. 7th
Howard Walter, shoe mkr., s.e.c. W. Court and Cutler
Howard Wm., printer, bds. s.e.c. Walnut and 9th
Howarth Dennis H., printer, bds. Buttemiller's Hotel
Howarth John, printer, wks. Times office
Howatt Wm., sailor, s.s. Front e. of Vance
Howcroft Jonathan H., clk., 46 Barr
Howdon & Co., (Robert H. & Bart. Kane) foundry, 714 W. 6th
Howdon Robert, (H. & Co.) n.e.c. Everett and Freeman
Howe A. Jackson, surgeon, 2 W. 4th, h. 258 Longworth
Howe Chas., clk , bds. Fremont House
Howe Charles, distiller, 483 W. 7th
Howe Chas. F., file mkr., wks. 93 E. 8th
Howe Ernst, teamster, 68 Findlay
Howe E. H., salesman, 193 George
HOWE HENRY, 111 Main, h. 140 E. 5th
Howe J., shoe mkr., bds. 231 Walnut
Howe John, wks. junction 6th and Front
Howe Thos. R., harness mkr., bds. s.w. c. 5th and Broadway
Howe Wm., harness mkr., bds. s.w.c. 5th and Broadway
Howe Wm., mach , wks. n.s. Front b. Lawrence and Pike
Howell Dav'd, eng., bds. 120 E. 5th
Howell Elizabeth, saloon, 154 Baymiller
Howell George, roofer, 463 W. 9th w. of Central Av.
Howell James, lab., 25 W. Court w. of Central Av.
Howell John, miller, 104 Spring
Howell Joshua, cutter, 73 George
Howell Richard S., car and omnibus manuf., 56 Bank, h. 28 Dayton
Howell Stephen, n.s. McDowell e. of Hill
Howell Thos. W., salesman f6 W. 2d, res. Fairmount
Howells Mary, select school, 162 Oliver, h. 462 W. 9th
Howells R. S., carriage manuf., 28 Dayton
Howells Richard, carp , 78 Clark
Howells Samuel, carp., wks. n.e.c. Canal and Walnut
Howells Sylvanus, pattern mkr., 34 Mitchell
Howelt Wm., carp,, 1312 E. Front
Howind Hermann, finisher, 100 Bremen
Howitt Elizabeth, 98 E. 3d
Howitt John, bksmith, wks. C. T. Dumont's
Howley Jas., lab., s.s. Weller b. Carr and Freeman
Howley Thos., lab., 51 Mill
Howlso —, cattle dealer, 973 W. 3d
Howly Jas., bksmith, wks. C., H. & D. R R.bksmith shop
Hoy —, tobacco mer., bds. 61 E. 4th
Hoyt Angelo, clk., cigars Burnet House
Hoyt Ellen, bds. 178 Elm
Hoyt Fannie G., teacher, 98 14th
Hoyt Sarah M., teacher, 98 14th
Hozfeld Mary, servt., 38 W. Court w. of Central Av.
Hronne Joseph, lab., 102 Abigail
Hronne Louisa, seamstress, 102 Abigail
Hubb Joseph, lab., w.s. Goose al. b. 14th and 15th
Hubbard Chas., broom mkr., h. 68 Lodge

Hubbard Daniel M., salesman 103 W. Pearl, h. 98 Longworth
HUBBARD & HEATON, (Sherman G. H. & Daniel H.) Auction and Commission Merchants, 21 W. 5th
Hubbard John, porter, 155 W. Pearl
Hubbard Joseph B., (H. & Worrel) Mt. Harrison
HUBBARD SHERMAN G., Book Trade Sales Rooms, 21 W. 5th, up stairs, h. s.w.c. 7th and Race
Hubbard Sidney, 794 E. Front
Hubbard Mrs. T. A., 72 Betts
Hubbard Timothy, bk. 21 W. 5th
Hubbard Wm., clk. 108 W. Pearl, bds. 93 Longworth
Hubbard & Worrell, (Joseph B. H. & C. R. W.) com. mer., 33 Walnut
Hubbell Ann, 166 Central Av
Hubbell Chas. H., (Ogden & Co.) 101 Park
Hubbell and Coney, (Ephraim T. H. & Martin R. C.) grocery, 626 Main
Hubbell E. C., 3cH W. 4th
Hubbell Ephraim T., (H. & Coney), 498 Sycamore
Hubbell Hy., compositor, 188 Everett
Hubbell Jacob A , salesman, 53 W. Pearl, bds. 357 W. 8th [port
Hubbell John, clk. 104 Walnut, h. Newbell Nathaniel S., agt. Cin. fuel co., h. 113 E. 3d
Hubbell Jampson H., 59 W. Pearl, h. 357 W. 8th
HUBBELL Wake, (Jno. Swasey & Co.) h. 270 Richmond
Hubbell Wm. M., sec. Cin. fuel co , s.w. c. 3d and Ludlow, h. 388 W. 4th
Hubbell Wm. R., salesman, 81 W. Pearl, bds. 484 W. 4th
Hubber Hy., watchman, wks 500 Plum
Hubbers Lambert, watchman, 468 W. 3d
Huber —, conf. h., h. 450 Vine
Huber Adam, candle mkr., 530 Plum
Huber Amsel, candle mkr., 20 Hamer
Huber Andreas, safe mkr., 661 R ce
Huber Andrew, w.s. Vine b. Milk and Mulberry
Huber Anna, 564 Race
Huber August, baker. e.s. Johnson al. b. Canal and 12th
Huber Chas., printer, e.s. Race b. 4th and 5th
Huber Eli, foreman, Thos. Emery & Son's, s.e.c. Vine and Water
Huber Francis. X., bksmith. 179 Bremen
Huber Fred., brewer, 544 W. 5th
Huber Fred., cigar mkr., wks. 438 Main
Huber Fred., rope mkr., 442 W. 2d
Huber Fred., lab., n.s. 5th b. Stone al. and Hoadly
Huber Geo., 2:9 Bremen
Huber Geo. W., b.k. 6 W. Front
HUBER J, EDWARD, Saloon, 56 W. 3d
Huber Joseph, finisher, 551 Central Av
Huber Jacob, mach., 549 Central Av
Huber John, lab , n.s Rice b. McGrew and Fountain
Huber John, printer, 97 Smith
Huber John, tanner, s.e.c. Henry and Dunlap
Huber Joseph, bksmith, 29 W. 6th
Huber Joseph, box mkr., s.s. Taylor b. Carr and Harriet
Huber Joseph, expressman, 68 Pleasant
Huber Peter A., finisher, n.w.c. Pearl and Pike
Huber Philip, 72 Peete
Huber Philip, clk., 216 Sycamore
Huber Mrs. Rebecca, 601 Sycamore
HUBER, SCHEU & LEIST, (Wm H. Geo. S. & John L.) Tanners and Curriers, 6(9 Elm
Huber Theresa, 26 Hamer,
Huber Thos., plasterer. 612 Vine
Huber Wm., butcher, 143 Pleasant
HUBER Wm., (H., Scheu & Leist) h. s.e.c. Henry and Dunlap
Huber Xavier, bksmith, wks., n.w.c. Race and Burrows,
Hubert Eliza 607 Vine
Hubert Elizabeth 29 Buckeye
Hubert John C., clk. 38 W. 3d, h. s.w.c. Vine and 12th

Hubert Wm., liquor mer., bds. 236 Race
Hubing John, police, 22 Mill
HUBING JOHN W. Family Grocery, 452 W. 2d h. 450 W. 2d
Hubner Wm., dyer. 351 Race
Huck Frank, (H. & Landre,) n.e.c. 2d and Ludlow
Huck Geo., upholsterer, 69 Allison
Huck & Landre, (Frank. H. & Hy., L.) cigars &c. n.e.c. 2d and Ludlow
Huckins Catharine, 55 Cutter
Huddart Wm., (Wm. H. & Co.) 373 George
Huddart Wm., & Co , (Wm. H., & Isaac Rigdon) scale manuf. 8 W. 2d
HUDEPOHL LOUIS, Wines, Liquors &c., 372 Main
Hudepohl Louis jr., truss mkr., bds. 372 Main
Hudnell Narcissa, 02 12th
Hudson —, lab., 55 Gano
Hudson Barney, lab., s.s. 15th b. Elm and Plum
Hudson Ceylon, 23 W. 4th, res. Storrs Tp.
Hudson Edward, molder, 97 Richmond
Hudson Elizabeth, 58 Elm
Hudson Fred., b.k. bds., 271 W. 7th
Hudson Fred. V., clk. 54 W. Pearl
Hudson Geo. M., huckster, 26 Richmond
Hudson Harriet, 130 Clark
Hudson Isaac Porter. 17 Woodward
Hudson J. Q. A , trav. agt. Ohio River Salt Co., bds. Madison House
Hudson Jas. T., druggist, 125 W. Court, w. of Central Av
Hudson Jno., servt., Burnet House
Hudson Joseph, sawyer, bds. 1234 E. Front
Hudson Julia L., teacher, 20 Richmond
Hudson Maria, s.w.c. Rail Road and French
Hudson Peter, lab., 58 Hunt
Hudson Philip, hatter, bds. 174 Plum
Hudson Phineas, turnkey, 46 Richmond
Hudson Polly, 8 Commerce
Hudson Wm., painter, n.s. Rail Road e. of Lewis
Hudson Wm. Hy., clk., bds. 361 W. 9th w. of Central Av
Hudson Mrs Wm. L.,335 Longworth
Hudson Wm. S.. saloon, 2:0 Central Av
Hudson Wilson, fireman, 84 W. 2d
Hudspith Wm., stone cutter, 322 Plum
Hueber Francis A., 233 Bremen
Hueber John, carp., bds. 674 W. 6th
Huebner August, apothecary, 497 Elm
Hueging Gerhard, cigar mkr., 7 15th b. Elm and Plum
Huel Jacob, lab , 121 Gest
Huelbeck Joseph, lab., 103 Woodward
Huele Adrian, porter, 21 Franklin
Huelgemann Fred., cooper, 525 Sycamore
Huelmann Henry, cigars, 131 Clay
Huelsman Anton, porter. 28 13th
Huelsman Ferdinand, lab., 166 Spring
Huelsman Henry, shoe mkr., 29 Green
Huelsmeier Henry, lab., n.s. Niles al. b. Main and Sycamore
Huemmer Joseph, tailor, 76 Buckeye
Huenefeld Frederick, cooper, wks. s.s. Orchard b. Main and Sycamore
Huenefeld Henry, driver, wks. 400 Sycamore
Huenemeier Frederick, lab. 13 Jones
Huenmann W. A., paper hanger, 424 Walnut [Clark
Huepel John H., lab. n.w c, Cutter and
Huermann Franz bk. layer, 416 Vine
Huermann Henry, cigar manufac., 416 Vine
Huesgen John H., salesman, 208 Vine
Huesman & Co., (John H. H.), cigars &c., 15 Broadway
Huesmann Edward, bar k., 202 E. Front
Huesmann Herman, clk., 15 Broadway, res. Broadway Hill
Huesman John B., cigars 15 Broadway, h. 251 W. 5th
Huesman John B., 15 Broadway, res. Broadway Hill
Huesmeir Wm., bksmith. w.s. Hughes b. Schiller and Mulberry

176 (HUG) CINCINNATI (HUL) DIRECTORY. (HUM)

Hueston W. C., clk., 101 W. 4th, h. 413 W. 3d
Huette Adam, cooper, 6 Buckeye
Huette John H., shoe mkr., 112 Ham. Road
Huette John H., shoe mkr., 22 Orchard
Huettenbauer Simon. butcher, 5 Mary
Huewe John H., leather, 359 Vine
Huf Frederick, lab., 140 Carr
Huff Henry, lab. 215 Betts
Huff James R., saddler, bds. 309 Main
HUFF JOHN, Money Loaner, Office n.e.c. Main and 7th, h. 491 Sycamore
Huff Thomas, lock mkr., wks. n.e.c. Walnut and Canal
Huff Valentine, teamster, n.s. Front e. of Kelly
Huffmann Mary, 227 Betts
Huffsky Frederick, 362 Freeman
Hufker Herman, cooper, 36 Pleasant
Hufnagel Lorenz, tailor, 75 Peete
Hufty Julia, seamstress, 424 Freeman
Hug Max, candle mkr., 529 Race
Hug Rosina, 36 Green
Hug Rudolph, surgical inst. manuf., 540 Central Av., h. 49 14th
Hagal James, dray, 468 W. 8th
Hugart John, salesman, 182 W. 4th
Huge Ernst Wm., carp., rear 526 Sycamore
Hugel John, clk., bds. 10 Abigail
Hugel John, cof. h., 6 Buckeye
Hugelar Hubert, painter, 207 Clinton
Hugenberg Frederick, clk., 52 Clay
Hugenschmidt John, tailor, 79 Gest
Hugger August, meats, n.e.c. Sycamore and Milton
Hugger Theresa, 161 Pleasant
Huggins Thomas, w.s. Auburn Av. head of Southern Av
Huggins Wm., carriage mkr., 79 Clinton
Hughes Adams & Co., (Joshua W. H., Solomon A. Thomas Kinsey & Jno. D. Hinde) office 138 Walnut
Hughes Alexander C., student, 238 Race
Hughes Alexander E., foreman Commercial office h. 490 W. 4th
Hughes Alice, servt., s.w.c. 3d and Broadway
Hughes Ann, 91 Barr
Hughes Ann, servt. 120 E. 3d
Hughes Augustus, b.k., 301 Longworth
Hu.hes Bridget, 209 W. 4th
Hughes Charles, 130 Water
Hughes Edward, (H. & Reed), 407 W. 7th
Hughes Edward, finisher, 123 Avery
Hughes Eliza M., confec., 225 Central Av
Hughes Enoch, 437 W. 2d
Hughes Frederick B., expressman, 490 W. 4th
HUGHES & FOSTER, (Hudson E. H. & Joab G. F.) Planing and Flooring Mill, Sash, Door, and Blind Manufacturers, s.w.c. John and Augusta
Hughes Geo., expressman, 131 E. Pearl
Hughes Geo., molder, bds. 265 W. Front
Hughes High School, s.s. 5th oppos. Mound, Joseph L. Thornton, principal
Hughes Hugh, lab., 50 Mound
HUGHES Hugh W., (Evans & Co.), bds. s.w.c. 3d and Broadway
HUGHES Hudson E., (H. & Foster), 304 Longworth
Hughes Israel. (H. & Sharp), res. Green Township [8th
Hughes James, blksmith, 29 Lock n. of
Hughes James, lab., 59 Pendleton
Hughes James, carp., 214 cutter
Hughes James G., 284 W. 7th
Hughes James A., b. k., s.w.c. Augusta and John, bds. 304 Longworth
Hughes James, finisher, wks. n.e c. Walnut and Canal
Hughes James, lab., bds n.w.c. Mill and Front
Hughes James E. clk., s.e c. 2d and Central Av
Hughes Jane, 437 W. 2d
Hughes John, 174 E. Pearl
Hughes John, hostler, wks. e.s. St. Clair b. 8th and 9.h

Hughes John, lab., 407 W. 7th
Hughes John, waiter, Clifton House
Hughes John, carp., bds. 204 W. 6th
Hughes Joshua W., (H. Adams & Co.), 156 Richmond
Hughes Joshua W., 156 Richmond
Hughes Leopold F., 323 Longworth
Hughes Maria, servt., n.s. Nassau. b. Reed and Broad
Hughes Martin. shoe mkr., 39 Race
Hughes Mary, dress mkr., bds. 70 Laurel
Hughes Mary F., e.s. McAlister, b. 4th and 5th
Hughes Michael, lab., 262 Water
Hughes Patrick, dray, 60 E. 2d
Hughes Pat., lab., s.s. al. b. Hunt and Abigail and Broadway and Sycamore
Hughes Patrick, tailor, 85 Race
Hughes Peter, painter, 938 E. Front
Hughes Peter, lab, bds. n.w.c. Mill and Front
Hughes & Reed (Edward H. & Wm. R.,) com. mers., 123 W. 2d
Hughes Rose, 29 Lock, n. of 8th
Hughes Samuel, lab., n.s. Goodloe, b. Willow and Leatherbury
Hughes & Sharp, (Israel H. & Isaac S.,) carps., 5 Augusta. b. John and Smith
Hughes Thomas, lab., 12 Commerce
Hughes Thomas, lab., 71 Richmond
Hughes Thomas, lab., wks. 375 W. 3d
Hughes Thomas, hostler, Commerce, b. Race and Elm
Hughes Thomas, sawyer, 359 W. 3d
Hughes William, lab., 16 Commerce
Hughes Wm. H., driver, c. Plum and George
Hughes Wm. P., h. 243 Plum
Hughey Isaac N., 431 Central Av.
Hughey Samuel, type mkr., 238 Clinton
Hughey Turzah, teacher, 238 Clin,on
Huging Gerhard, cigar mkr., 7 15th
Hugle Gideon, dray, 91 W. 9th, w. of Central Av.
Hugle James H., dray, 456 W. 8th
Hugle John, dray, 166 Richmond
Hugle Wm., dray, 58 Rittenhouse
Hugo Joseph, teamster, bds. 17 Wade
Hugo Louis. carman, 73 Hughes
Hublfeld Gerhard, sawyer, 121 Pleasant
Huhn Conrad, umbrella mkr., 61 15th
Huhn Henry, paper hanger, 28 Ham. Road
Huie John, wh. notions, 104 Walnut, b. 36 Munsfield
Hullefeld Elizabeth, seamstress, 5 Wade b. Elm and Plum
Huilsmann Franz, presser, 40 Webb
Huiser Geo., finisher, wks. n.e.c. Walnut and Canal
Huiwe Frederick, tailor. 141 Clay
Huk Felix, huckster, 97 Park
Hukill Frederick, salesman, 67 Main. b. 185 Barr
Hukill Frederick E., salesman, b. 185 Barr
Hukill Hanson, exchange office, 47 Sycamore, b. 40 Plum
Hukill Johnson, carp., 113 Betts
Hukill Michael, molder, wks. n e.c. Canal and Walnut
Hukill Montravile, molder, 118 E. Liberty
Hukill Richard, cof. h., 156 Main, h. 123 Water
Hulbers Gerhard, molder bds. 468 W. 3d
Hulbert Lambur, grocer, n.w.c. Linn and Court, h. 119 Linn
Hulbert Margaret, 17 Carr
Hulbert Nathan, 501 Freeman
HULBERT Wm, P., president of Buckeye Ins. Co., h. 625 Freeman
Hulburt Samuel cooper, 185 W. Court, w. of Central Av.
Hulcher Ann M., s.s. Court, e. of Broadway
Hulker Francis J., tailor, 154 Hopkins
Hull Clarence M., harness mkr, 153 Barr
Hull David, cashier C. W. Z. R. R., 203 Barr
Hull George, bk. layer, bds. 153 Barr
Hull George, clk., bds. 16 Perry
Hull George H., clk., bds. n.e.c. 4th and Plum
Hull Geo. M., Jr., bk. layer, 247 Hopkins
Hull James, clk., 285 Plum, b. 153 Barr

HULL John S., (Spear & Co.,) 143 Court, h. Cutter and Linn
HULL JOSEPH E., Manufacturer of Tinners' Tools, 95 E. 8th, bds. 136 John
Hull Julius, com. mer., 7 W. Canal, h. Covington, Ky.
Hull Kate, 176 Central Av.
Hull L. R., b. k., 17 W. Pearl. bds. 204 W. 4th
Hull Mary M., e.s. Sycamore, b. 7th and 8th
Hullman Theodore, (Grawe & H.,) 11 Bremen
Huls Wm., fish dealer, 13 Home
Hulseiman Samuel, helper, wks. n.e.c Canal and Walnut
Hulseman Anton, porter, 28 13th
Hulsman Barney, dray, 41 E. 7th
Hulsman F., lab., wks. n.s. Front, b, Lawrence and Pike
Hulsmanñ Bernhard, lab., 120 Pleasant
Hulsmann Henry, painter, 17 Jones
Hulsmeir Barney, carp., 245 Laurel
Hulsmeir John, shoe mkr., 83 Findlay
Hultouse Herman, cab. mkr., 16 Commerce
Hultsman Henry, blksmith, wks. 10 W. 7th
Hulvershorn C. A., clk., 99 Walnut, bds. 345 Vine
Hulz Jacob, brewer, 553 Elm
Humfel Peter, stone cutter, 36 New
Humbert Geo. I., lab., 67 Pleasant
Humbert Henry, tanner, 297 Linn
Humbert Jacob, baker, bds. 172 Sycamore
HUMBLE J. & P., (James H. & P. H.,) Stone Cutters and Builders, 288 Broadway
HUMBLE James, (J. & P.,) 122 E. Liberty
Humble James M., b. k 148 E. Liberty
Humble John, 148 E. Liberty
HUMBLE Peter, (J. & P. H.,) 36 New
Humbolt Henry. carp., 565 Elm
Hume Ann, 183 Cutter
Hume Chas., huckster, 5 Crippen al.
HUME JAMES, Brass Foundry, 65 Lodge, h. 393 Elm
Hume James, shoe mkr., 220 Betts
Hume Mary J., bds. 456 W. 8th
Hume Robert, mach., 161 Cutter
Hume Wm., paper hanger. 183 Cutter
Humes Gerhard, lab., 478 Main
Humes Samuel C., mer., 140 Broadway
Humler Charles, tailor, 652 Race
Humler Francis X., tailor, 652 Race
Humler Gustav, tailor, 652 Race
Humme Mary, servt., 490 Main
HUMMEL ANTON, Proprietor Frey's Hotel, 421 and 423 Main
Hummel Christian, brewer, 171 W. Liberty
Hummel Christian, porter, wks. 221 Walnut
Hummel David, s.s. Calhoun, b. Madison and Vine
Hummel David, stone yard, 586 Plum, h. 674 Freeman b. York and Dayton
Hummel Gottlieb, blksmith, 600 Race
Hummel Jacob, carp., 509 Elm
Hummel Jacob, nail mkr., 670 Central Avenue
Hummel John, shoe mkr., 70 W. Liberty
Hummel John, vinegar manuf., n.e c. Hopkins and Linn
Hummel John H., student, Freeman b. York and Dayton
Hummel Joseph, clk., n.e.c Hopkins and Linn
Hummel Leo. G., clk., n w.c. Linn and Hopkins, b. 160 Hopkins
Hummelmeier Ferdinand, drays, n.e.c. Pendleton and Abigail
Hummel Henry, lab., 9 John
Hummel Joseph, watch mkr., 526 Main
Humphrey Hugh, pattern mkr., bds. 196 W. Front
Humphreys Edward, bk. layer, bds. 56 Avery
Humphreys Eliza, 99 E. 3d, e. of Whittaker
Humphreys John, 407 John

HUNTER, EDMESTON & CO., (Nathaniel D. H., L. B. E. & Henry L. Kemper,) Importers and Manufacturers of Saddlery Hardware and Carriage Trimmings, 168 Main

Hunter Edward, tailor, bds. s.w.c. 5th and Broadway
Hunter Frank M., molder, 507 Vine
Hunter Garrett V., meats. s.e.c. Linn and Richmond, h. 184 Richmond
Hunter Gavin R., stair builder, 438 W. 9th w. of Central Av.
Hunter Geo., tailor, 53 Broadway
Hunter Geo. W., stair builder, n.e.c. 6th and Hoadly, h. n.s. 9th b. Cutter and Linn
Hunter Henry S., carp., 118 E. 3d e. of Whittaker
Hunter James, huckster, 43 Mill
Hunter James. sheet iron wkr., 51 Mill
Hunter John K., atty., 75 W. 3d, h. 183 Richmond
Hunter John Y., carp., n.w.c. Washington and 3d
Hunter Matthew S., paper carrier, 626 W. 8th
HUNTER Nathaniel D., (H. Edmeston & Co.) res. Covington
Hunter Thos., saddler, 1304 E. Front
Hunter Wm., stone cutter, 176 W. 3d
HUNTER WM. M., Dentist, Office and Residence 296 Vine
Hunting Richard C., (S. W. Smith & Co.) h. 14 Perry
HUNTINGTON Albert W., (H. Bros. & Co.) h. 179 Elm
HUNTINGTON & BROOKS, (H. D. H., O. A. B. & H. Huntington,) Importers and Dealers in China, Glass and Queensware, Dealer's Warehouse n.s. Freemont b. Carr and Harriet, Office s.w.c. 4th and Walnut
HUNTINGTON BROS. & CO., (Albert W. H., John C. H. & Wm C. Huntington,) Importers and Dealers in China, Glass, Queensware and House Furnishing Goods, &c. 119 Main
Huntington Chas., silver plater, bds. 243 W. 5th
HUNTINGTON Fred. G., (Jones, Bros. & Co.) res. 155 John
HUNTINGTON Henry D., (H. & Brooks.) 133 Broadway
HUNTINGTON Horace (H. & Brooks), bds. Burnet House
HUNTINGTON John C. (H. Bros. & Co.) 121 W. 9th
HUNTINGTON THOS. S. Civil Engineer and Surveyor, 222 W. 9th, h. 117 Clinton
HUNTINGTON Wm. C., (Huntington Bros. & Co.) 179 Elm
Huntshe Fred. C., lab., 524 John
Huntsman Elizabeth B., teacher, 290 W. Court [Court
Huntsman Lucretia W., teacher, 290 W.
Huntsman Samuel, clk., bds. 116 E. 5th
HUNZICKER JACOB, Coffee House and Family Grocery, 118 Bremen
Hup Peter, grinder, 5 Buckeye
Huping Fred., locksmith, 696 Race
Hupp John, lab., 116 Ham. Road
Hurberger John, lab., s.s. Sloo w. of Freeman
HURD EDWARD, Carpets, Oil Cloths, Curtains, &c., 11 E. 4th, b. Main and Sycamore, h. 31 Clark
Hurd Ethan O., 11 E. 4th, h. E. Walnut Hills
Hurd Julia, 154 Richmond
Hurd Mrs. M., 154 W. 5th
Hurd Patrick, lab., 91 Sycamore
Hurd Rukard, 11 E. 4th, h. E. Walnut Hills
Hurd Sarah, teacher, 71 E. 3d
Hurdlebring Jacob, molder, wks. n.e.c. Canal and Walnut
Hurdman Chas. P., shoe mkr., 219 Clinton
HURIN JAMES K., Commission Merchant, 577 and 579 W. 6th, h. 293 Longworth

Hurlbut Samuel, cooper, 185 W. Court w. of Central Av.
HURLBUT WM. F., Clerk of Public Schools, Office, City Building, h. 68 Hopkins
Hurley Daniel, cof. h., 36 Lock n. of 8th
Hurley Daniel, driver, 113 W. M. Canal
Hurley Ellen, 171 W. 9th
Hurley Francis, lab., 47 E. 4th
Hurley James, 286 Main
Hurley James, cooper, bds. 41 Lock n. of 8th
Hurley Mary, 52 Rittenhouse
Hurley Michael, lab., s.w.c. 3d and Central Av.
Hurley Patrick, lab., 240 Barr
Hurley Richard, n.s. 6th b. Culvert and Broadway
Hurley Thos., lab., Mt. Adams
Hurley Timothy, pipe fitter, wks. n.e.c. Walnut and Canal
Hurley Timothy, lab., 230 Barr
Hurlhey Daniel, shoe mkr., 251 Sycamore
Hurly Peter, 40 Elizabeth
Hurm Wendel, mason, 114 Bremen
HURRELL WM. F., Ladies' Shoe Store, 104 W. 4th, h. 509 Freeman
Hurst Phoebe, 318 Plum
Hurst Wm., clk., wks. 152 Ham. Road
Hurster David, baker, 430 W. 3d
Hurstmann John, porter, 106 Abigail
Hurt John, baker, 205 Vine
Hurtig, Daniel, 289 W. 5th
Hurtig Louis, painter, 163 W. 5th
Hurtkopf Charles, bar k., 123 Main
Hurion —, pork packer, 18 Clark
Husemann Theodore, b.k. C. F. Adae & Co.'s bds. n.e.c. 7th and Central Av
Huser Edward, atty, bds. s.w.c. Race and 3d
Huser Gustave A., brewery, e.s. Colerain Pike and north of corp. line
Huser John, lab., s.w.c. Main and Liberty
Hushfield Lewis, 420 W. 7th
Husing Hermann, carp., s.s. Wade bet. Linn and Baymiller
Husing Wm., sawyer, 213 W. Front
HUSMAN ANDREW, Coffee House, s.e.c. Ann and Central Av.
Husman Darney, coachman, bds. 576 Elm
Husman Henry, molder, wks. n. e. c. Canal and Walnut
Husman Henry, 370 Broadway
Husman John H., sawyer, 459 Broadway
Husman Joseph, cigar mkr., wks. 503 Main
Husmann Anthony, cutter, 150 Laurel
Husmann Barney, grocery, 49 Woodward
Husmann Fred., blk. smith, 72 Spring
Husmann Frederick J., lab., 593 Walnut
Husmann Henry, blk. smith, 410 Broadway
Husmann Mary, 13 Hunt
Husmann John, saddler, bds. 508 Main
Husmann Joseph, 49 Woodward
Husmann Joseph, blk smith, w.s. Broadway b. Abigail and Hunt
Huss Charles, grocery, 1116 Central Av.
Huss David, cab mkr., 213 W. Front
Huss John, cigar mkr., 422 Walnut
Hussey Edward H., salesman 95 W. 3d, bds 155 W. 4th
Hussey John, lab., wks. 222 E. Front
Hussey John, lab., 210 E. 6th
Hussey Wm. C., phys., 56 W. 4th
Hussey Z., phys. at., 135 Elm
Hust Adam, e.s. Riddle b. Bank and Harrison Pike
Hust Andrew, lab., 388 Baymiller
Hust Henry, stable, n.w.c. Ham. Road and Locust
Hust Jacob, (Stahl & H.,) h. 80 Ham. Road
Husta John, potter, 124 Findlay
Hustede Frank, lab., 132 W. Liberty
Hustedder Gerhard, cooper, 61 Abigail
Hustedt Charles, shoe mkr., 462 Race
Huster Frederick, saloon, 137 Everett
Huster Henry, 153 York

Huster Henry, cooper, al. b. 13th and Mercer and Vine and Walnut
HUSTON Alexander B., (Dodd & H.,) n e.c. Plum and 6th
Huston Benjamin, clk., 73 W. 4th
HUSTON David A., (John H. Gerard & Co.,) h. Mt Washington
Huston James box mkr., s.s. Charlotte b. Central Av. and Linn
Huston Jas A., salesman 36 Main, h. 391 W. 4th
HUSTON JOSEPH M., House and Sign Painter, 67 W. 3d, h. 126 Longworth
Huston Priscila, 356 E. Front
Huston Samuel M., clk., 113 W. Pearl bds. 121 W. 4th
Huston Wm., cook, n.s. Grandin al. b. Elm and Plum
Husucker Henry F., dray. 24 Gano
Husxfeld Andreas, lab., f6 Findlay
Hut Andreas, lab., s.s. Goose al., b. Liberty and Green
Hutchens Anna, 4'6 W. 9th
Hutchenson John, wagon mkr., bds. 112 Laurel
HUTCHESON ERSKINE E., Attorney at Law, 65 W 3d, h. 395 John
Hutchings Newton, 78 Sycamore
Hutchings Wm. S., museum, 16 Pine
Hutchins E. W., salesman, 92 W. Pearl, bds Walnut Street House
Hutchinson Edward J., clk., 161 High
Hutchinson Edwin A., clk., bds. s. w. c. 3d and Broadway
Hutchinson Henry R., painter, 161 E. 3d e of Collard
Hutchinson Mary, 161 E. 3d e. of Collard
Hutchinson Samuel E., mach., bds. 351 W. Front
Hutchinson Wm., bds. 77 E. 3d
Hutchinson Wm. T., turner, 107 E. 3d, e. of Whittaker
Hutchinson Wm. H., salesman, 94 W. Pearl bds. s.e.c. 3d and Broadway
HUTCHISON EDWARD, Coal Yard, s. s. Pearl bet. Pike and Butler, and s.e.c. Front and Butler, h. Hamilton
Hutfilter Frederick, painter, 43 Pleasant
Huth Anthony, turner, 112 Avery
Huth Jacob, brush mkr., 34 Dunlap
Huth John, lab., 599 Sycamore
Huthsteiner Edward, cigars, 405 Vine
Huthsteiner Gustav., cigar mkr., 405 Vine
Hutman Geo., frame mkr., s.w.c. Laurel and John
Hutman Joseph, shoe mkr., 1017 Central Av
Hutte Bernhard, lab., 4 Mary
HUTTON B. & R., (John & Robert,) Wagon Manufacturers, 164 W. Front
HUTTON John, (J. & R. H.,) 19 Betts
HUTTON Robert, (J. & R. H.,) 217 W. Front
Hutzler Frederick, piano teacher, 159 Pleasant
Huvrt Hermon, boots and shoes, 556 Central Av
Huwe Benjamin, clk., bds. 96 Butler
Huwe Bernard, clk., 51 Public Landing
Huwe Henry, (Enneking & H.,) 96 Butler
Hux Mrs. Barbara 90 Peete
Huxer Hermann, lab., bds., 15 Abigail
Huxoll Ernst, dray, 24 Mansfield
Huyc John. variety store, 36 Mansfield
Huxmann Wm, hk layer, 19 Oliver
Hyams Abraham, (H. & Marks.,) h. 100 Water
Hyams Isaac, clk., 12 Race
Hyams & Marks, (Abraham H. & Alex. M.,) renovators, 10 E. 6th
Hyams Nathan, pawnbroker, 2001 Walnut h. 172 W. 3d
Hyatt Charles B , student, 139 Hopkins
HYATT JOHN T., Collector, 29 W. 3d, h. 139 Hopkins
Hyatt Joseph B. P., student, bds. 139 Hopkins
Hyatt Sarah, bds. 15 Stone

Hyatt Wm., mach., s.w.c. Mill and 5th
Hyde Charles, clk., Auditor's Office, h. 95 Laurel
Hyde Henry, pressman, 167 Walnut
Hyde Michael, lab., n.w.c. Wade and Baymiller
Hyer Frank, bar k., Tremont Hotel
Hyller John, brass finisher, wks. 250 E. Front
Hykley Geo., driver. 200 Linn
Hyland Margaret, tailoress, bds. 214 W. Front
Hyland William, janitor. 96 Race
Hyle John A., cooper, bds. e.s. Cutter b. Laurel and Betts
HYMAN Charles, (J. H. Goodhart & & Co.,) 335 W. 8th
Hymann Morris, clk., 205 W. 5th
Hyndman Geo., hinge fitter, wks. n.e c. Walnut and Canal
Hyndman Mary, brush mkr., n. w. c. Sycamore and Orchard
HYNDMAN WM G., Bellows and Patent Portable Forge Manufacturer, 54 E. 2d, h. 101 Mulberry
Hyne Edward, carp., 919 Central Av
Hynes John, shoe mkr., s s. al. b. Pike and Lawrence and 3d and Pearl
Hynes Mary, s s. al. b. Pike and Lawrence, and 3d and Pearl
Hynes Thomas, tailor, 17 North
Hynson George W., b k., 3×3 W. 8th
Hynson Peter. lab., 172 Water
Hyre Mary, 461 Walnut
Hyre Wm., carp., 525 W. 8th
Hywarden Louis J., barber, 186 Walnut

I

Iang John, vinegar mkr., 104 Abigail
Iauch John, maltster, 59 Abigail
Ibeck Casper, driver, 471 Vine
Icefelder Louis. cof. h. 22 Bank
Ichleholf Charles, 278 Main
Ida Miss, millinery, 137 W. 4th
Iddings James C., b.k. 9 Pearl, h. Walnut Hills
Iddings Nathan, student, bds. s ec. 6th and Race
Ieixy Phillip, lab., 346 Ham. Road
Iferd Belle, actress, National Theater
Iferd Elizabeth, 162 W. 3d
Igebrink John, lab., 17 Mulberry
Ivenhorst Theodore, shoe mkr., 40 Gest
Iglaur Arnold, clk., bds 391 W. 7th
Iglauer Leopold, clk., 164 Main bds. 156 W. Court w. ot Central
Igmier Martin, driver, n. w.◆◆◆h and Hannibal
Igo Bridget. servt., 119 Broadway
Ihle Charles, gardener, 520 Freeman
Ihle Michael, china, &c., 479 Vine, h. 64 Milton
Ihlle Christian, gardener, 26 Abigail
Iland John, lab., 7 John
Ihrock Dietrich, sawyer, 131 Pleasant
Ihrock Wm., lithographer, 131 Pleasant
Iler Hy., paper carrier, 367 John
Ilg Anthony, cof. h , 106 Ham. Road
Ilg Geo., cof. h., 478 Vine
Iliff Archibald M., currier, 83 Clinton
Iliff James, clk., 380 W. 4th
Iliff Marilan. school, s.s Clinton, b. Cutter and Linn, h. 251 Everett
Iliff Wm. H., contractor, 38 York
Ill Barney. vinegar manuf., 8 Ann, h. 419 Plum
Ill Mary, 138 Buckeye
Imbus Harney, lab., rear 101 Woodward
Imbusch Fred., tailor, s.w.c. Abigail and Spring
Imbusch Hy., wks. w.s. Brighton, nr. Benckenstens Garden
Imhof John, cof. h., 345 Broadway
Imhof John, tanner. s.s. Liberty, b. Linn and Baymiller
Imhof John J., tailor, 230 Bremen
Imhof Michael, cooper, s.s. Hubbard, b. 5th and 6th
Imhoff Jacob, lab., 305 W. 2d
Imholdt Annie Maria, 55 Jackson
Imholz Dietrick, porter, 92 Mulberry
Imm Charles, grocer, n.w.c. Linn and Poplar
Immeng John, lab., 158 E. 5th

Immenhart Hy. W., grocery, 511 Race
Imsande Dietdrich, lab., rear 19 Mulberry
Imsech Joseph, painter, 43 Jones
Imthun Hy. B., clk , 39 Broadway
Imwalle Barnard, boots and shoes, 67 Butler
Imwalle Hy., boots and shoes. 60 E. 5th
Imwalle Hy. C., wagon mkr., 636 Race
Imwalle Herman, shoemkr, 11 Pendleton
Imwalle Rudolph, shoemkr, 60 E. 5th
Imwalle Wm., sawyer, 404 Longworth
Inbusch Hy., 89 Bank
Incroft Barnard, lab., 285 Linn
Incrot Barney, baker, wks. 217 Everett
Indemnity Fire Insurance Co. Agency, 76 W. 3d
Inderrieden Joseph, baker, 515 Main
INDIANA HOUSE, Gideon E. Ryman, Proprietor, 139 W. 5th
INDIANAPOLIS AND CINCINNATI Railroad Company, Office 66 W. 3d
INDIANAPOLIS AND CINCINNATI Railroad Depot, e.s. Front, nr. foot of 3d and Wood
Industrial School, n.e.c. Race and Commerce, Joseph N. Barbur, supt.
Ingalls Jane, seamstress, 162 W. 7th
Ingalls Mrs. Nellie, 135 W. Pearl
Ingalls Theodore F., b.k , bds 174 Plum
Ingelkan Frederick, lab., 212 W, Front
Ingelard Ignatz, lab., 61 Walnut
Ingels Boone. clk., n.w.c. Main and 2d, bds. 413 W. 3d
Ingersoll ——, policeman, bds. 65 Broadway
Ingersoll Samuel D., 714 E Front
Ingham Thos., foreman 174 W. Front
Ingle Randolph, cab. mkr., 15 Hannibal
Ingleback Joseph, coachman, 17 Macalister
Inglemeyer Wm., lab., 143 Abigail
Inglert Joseph, cooper, h. 28 Brighton
Ingles George, carriage trimmer, 319 W. 3d
Ingles John, lab., n.s. Garden, b. Freeman and Western Av
Ingles John E., printer, wks. Times office, h. Newport, Ky
Ingram John R., b.k., bds. Bevis House
Ingram Thos., sexton, n.s. Clinton, b. Central Av. and John
Inloes Edward, cooper, 4 Crippen al.
Innes Robert D., bkbinder, 200 Barr
Inneccentia Sister, St. Clare Convent, n. w c. 3d and Lytle
Inott Wm., grocery, 589 Central Av
INTERNATIONAL SALOON AND Billiard Rooms, Phil. Tieman, Proprietor. 91 Sycamore
Irtlekofer Edward, lab., 79 Pleasant
Inwalle Benjamin J., bar k., bds. United States Hotel
Inwalle John H, expressman, 451 W. 6th
Inwalle John H., jr., cof. h., 451 W. 6th
Inwaller George, blksmith, n.e.c. Sycamore and Abigail
Iredale John, shoemkr, 709 W. Front
Iredle John, shoemkr. 209 W. Front
Irelan Eliza, tailoress, 3 Garrow
Ireland Aaron, lab., 285 Linn
Ireland Alexander, bk. layer, 183 Oliver
Ireland F. Geo., b.k., Walnut St. House
Ireland Geo. N., foreman, 28 Jackson
Ireland John, bklayer, 19, 15th
Ireland Richard, bklayer, 139 Everett
IRELAND Thomas S., (Rindskopf, Bros. & Co.,) Harrison Pike
Ireland Wm., bklayer, w.s. Providence, b. Wade and Liberty
Ireland Wm., carp., 382 W. Liberty
Ireland Wm., provisions, 597 Central Av
Irelen Elizabeth, 187 W. Court, w. of Central Av
Ireton Edward, clk., 33 W. 3d, h. 25 Pine
Irey Otho, bkmkr., n.w.c. Harriet and Roll al
Irion Jacob, brewer, bds. William Tell
Irion Thomas, 568 Vine
Irish James, shoemkr, 104 Hunt
Irvin Ellen. 169 Avery
Irvin Jacob, brewer, wks. s.w.c. Plum and Canal

Irvin James, bds. Railroad House
Irvin John, selvemkr, 53 Plum
Irvin Margaret, 13 8th, above Lock
Irvine Celia, dress mkr,, bds. 201 W. Liberty
Irvine Robert W., b.k., 105 W. Pearl, h. Covington
Irving Mrs. J. S., millinery, 164 W. 6th
Irving John S., tailor, 164 W. 6th
Irwin Geo. A., 32 Broadway, bds. Spencer House
Irwin Geo. W., bklayer, 3 York
Irwin James, mach., 108 Longworth
Irwin James F., 142 E. 5th
IRWIN James T., (Taylor & I.,) 169 Race
Irwin Jared J., salesman, 53 W. 4th, bds. 253 Walnut
Irwin Patrick. lab., 17 8th, above Lock
Irwin Robert, lab., 139 Plum
Irwin Samuel, surveyor, 221 Vine, h. Walnut Hills
Irwin Narah A., 64 Pike
Irwin Stephen, lab., 16 Union
Irwin Wm. C., n.w.c. Linn and 9th
Isaac Isaac, 150 George
Isaac Morris, olk. 287 Main
Isaacs Geo., bds. Walnut St. House
Isaacs Geo.. salesman, 109 W. Pearl, h. 382 W. 4th
Isaacs Max., saiesman, 299 Main
Isaacs Samuel, agt., military caps, 104 Main, h. 6 Harrison
Isaacs Simeon, variety store, 289 Main
Isaacs Susanna. 392 W. 4th
Isbell Everett E., watch mkr., 174 Plum
Isdell Lloyd P., wks. n.w.c. Freeman and 9th
Isenhort Benjamin A., comb mkr., 127 Betts
Iserman Mary, rear 60 Abigail
ISHAM Augustus, President Ohio Life Insurance Co., h 137 Broadway
Isham Fisher & Co., (John G. I., James T. F. & Wm. C. Harry,) ship chandlery, 47 Public Landing
Isham John G., (I. Fisher & Co.,) 137 Broadway
Ishen Edward, painter, bds. 192 Sycamore
ISHERWOOD GEO. W., at Cincinnati Directory, 194 Walnut, h. e.s. Moss, one door n. of Bellevue, Newport
Islaus J., lub., wks. 18 Sycamore
Ismael George A., n.s. Cherry al., b. Pluic and Central Av
Ismael Matilda, bds. n.s. Cherry al., b. Plum and Central Av
Isolo Joseph, musician, 84 W Front
Isop Patrick, boiler mkr., 59 Rittenhouse
Ispacht Mrs. Mary, n.s. Ham. Road, head of Elm
ISPHORDING Anthony, (Meier & I.,) 499 Race
Issick Wm., baker, 619 Central Av
Istell Lloyd, carp., bds. 575 W. 8th
Itchenbach Rosier, cigar mkr., 116 W. Liberty
Ittig Wm., marble cutter, wks. s.w.c. Broadway and 5th
Iuppenlatz Mrs. Anna C., 119 Central Avenue
Ivens & Co., cloaks, &c., 28 W. 4th
Ivers Edmond J., drover, bds. Brighton House
Ivers Patrick, drover, bds. Brighton House

J

Jabbert Hy., turner, 74 Rittenhouse
Jack George W., carp, 35 Parsons
Jack Perry, cab. mkr., bds. w.s. Sycamore, b. 5th and 6th
Jack Samuel T., carp., 119 Martin
Jack Thomas P., carp., 119 Martin
Jackers John, butcher, h. n s. Montgomery Pike, nr. Reading Road
Jackers Louis, h. n.s. Montgomery Pike, nr. Lebanon Road
Jackert Charles, reporter, bds. 137 Race
Jackson Albert G., cof. h., 205 Elm
Jackson Alice, s.w.c. 6th and Broadway
Jackson Andrew, egg packer, bds. 57 E. Pearl
Jackson Chas., carp., 232 Betts
Jackson Chas. H., 403 Vine
Jackson Chas. H, 204 W. Court
Jackson David H., 437 John
Jackson Edwin, stereotyper, bds. 361 W. 6th
Jackson Egbert. (J. Herbert & Co.,) res. Philadelphia
Jackson Elizabeth, teacher, 259 Clark
Jackson Elizabeth J., teacher. 32d Linn
Jackson Elmore W., clk. M. & C. R. R., bds. 403 Vine
Jackson Gamaliel, dentist, 131 W. 4th
Jackson George, steward, 547 Elm
Jackson Geo. E, clk. Culbertson, Kilgour & Cd.'s, h. Storrs tp.
Jackson, Herbert & Co., (Egbert J., Robert H. & Eugene Velphue,) National Dispensary, 167 Sycamore
Jackson Jane, 361 W. 6th
Jackson John, bds. Dumas Hotel
Jackson John, blksmith, bds. 112 Laurel
Jackson John, blksmith, bds. 25 W. Court, w. of Central Av
Jackson John, driver, 13 Accomodation
Jackson John, hatter, 21 George
Jackson John, lab., 673 W. 6th
Jackson John, liquors, 60 Clark
Jackson John, steward, 42 W. Court, w. of Central Av
Jackson John, teamster, wks. John Mitchell's
Jackson John A, 140 E. 6th
Jackson John A., (Fitzgerald & J.), n.s. Clark b. Mound and Cutter
Jackson John P. (Jackson and Johnson), res. Newport
Jackson John W. sen., 403 Vine
JACKSON JOHN W., JR., Wholesale and Retail Dealer in Cigars, Tobacco, Snuff, &c., 429 Central Av. h. 403 Vine
Jackson John W., whitewasher, s.s. 6th b. Broadway and Culvert
Jackson & Johnson, (John P. J. & Edgar M. J.), attorneys, 15 Masonic Temple
Jackson Joseph, carp., 259 Clark
Jackson Kate, s.s. New b. Culvert and Broadway
Jackson Lizzie, 361 W. 6th
Jackson Maggie, teacher, 323 Race
Jackson Margaretha, 13 Sargent
Jackson Margaret, teacher, 259 Clark
Jackson Matthew, lab., 53 Ellen
Jackson Milton, finisher, n.s. Railroad e. of Kelly
Jackson Moses, lab., 107 E. 6th
Jackson Murray M., grocery, s.s. Front e. of Brooklyn
Jackson Rachel, bds. 177 W. Court w. of Central Av
Jackson Ralph, paper carrier, 361 W. 6th
Jackson Richard, caulker, 956 E. Front
Jackson Robert, lab., n.s. Pearl b. Smith and Park
Jackson Thomas M., cashier Culbertson, Kilgour & Co., h. Storrs tp
Jackson W. G , salesman, bds. Dennison House
Jackson Wm., lab., 90 Carr
Jackson Wm., P., distiller, 403 Vine
Jacob & Brill, (Christ J. & Geo. B.), pork packers, 214 Walnut
Jacob Christ, (Jacob & Brill), 214 Walnut
JACOB Charles, (Charles & Louis J.) n. e.c. 2d and Sycamore
JACOB Charles jr., (C. J. jr. & Co.), 478 Elm
JACOB CHARLES, JR. & CO. (Charles J. jr. & George Wust), Pork and Beef Packers, 50 Walnut
JACOB CHARLES & LOUIS, Pork and Beef Packers, n.e.c. 2d and Sycamore
Jacob David, lab., 740 Vine
Jacob Francis, (J. Baumgaertner & Co.) 592 Vine
Jacob Henry, lab. 60 Buckeye
Jacob Henry, turner, 6 Mulberry
Jacob Henry H., (Samuels & J.), 57 Longworth
Jacob Hermann, cooper, wks. 9 Orchard
JACOB ISAAC, Sole Appointing Agt., for the U. S. for L. Lyon's Pure Ohio Catawba Brandy, 45 E. 2d, h. 57 Longworth
Jacob John, lock mkr., 661 Race
Jacob John, tailor, 458 Walnut
Jacob John Peter, shoe mkr., 599 Sycamore
Jacob Louis, beef packer, 858 Central Av
Jacob Louis sr., pork packer, 16 E. 2d, h. 24 Charles
Jocob Louis jr., salesmann, 16 E. 2d, h. 24 Charles
JACOB Louis. (Charles & Louis J.), n.e. c. 2d and Sycamore
Jacob Moses, peddler, 71 15th
Jacob Peter, (Peter J. & Co.), Kossuth b. Court and Clark
Jacob Peter & Co.. (Peter J., John Gripner & Frank Post), coopers, s.w.c. Cutter and Clinton
Jacob Samuel, pipe fitter, wks. n.e.c. Walnut and Canal
Jacob Simon, tailor. 102 Hunt
Jacob Wm., carp., 6 Mulberry
Jacoba Sister, St. Clare Convent, n.w.c. and Lytle
Jacobi Ernst A.. clk., 533½ Elm
Jacobs Alfred, driver, 444 George
Jacobs Balthazar, barber, 594 Elm,
Jacobs Benjamin, photographer, n.w.c. 5th and Main
Jacobs Bernard. shipping clk., 27 Main, h. 483 W. 3d
JACOBS CHARLES C., Rope and Cordage Manufacturer, s.s. Budd below Harriet, Office 34 W. Front
Jacobs Christopher, grocer, 118 Gest
Jacobs Christopher, lab., e.s. M. Canal b. 8th and Court
Jacobs Eliza, 444 George
Jacobs Elizabeth, 483 W. 3d
Jacobs Ellis, lab., wks. s.w.c. Park and W. W. Canal
JACOBS Enoch, (Valleau & J), Walnut Hills
Jacobs F. & Son, (Feist & Henry), clothiers, 483 Vine
Jacobs Feist, (F. J. & Son), h. 483 Vine
JACOBS GEO., Carriage and Spring Wagon Manufacturer, 86 and 88 Ham. Road
Jacobs Henry, clk., 18 Main, h. 483 W. 3d
Jacobs Henry, (F. Jacobs & Son), 483 Vine
Jacobs Jacob, 16 Oliver
Jacobs Jane, cof. h., foot 5th nr. Freeman
Jacobs John, porter, 483 W. 3d
Jacobs John, watchmann, s.s. 9th b. Harriet and Mill Creek
Jacobs Joseph, cof. h., n s. Vine b. Milk and Mulberry
Jacobs Margaret, 142 Longworth
Jacobs Mary, 36 W. 4th
Jacobs Peter, cooper, s.e.c. Clark and Kossuth, h. 55 Kossuth
Jacoby Peter, tailor, w.s. Milk b. Calhoun and Vine
Jacocks Ann M., seamstress, 150 Clark
Jacopi Henry, stone-mason, 90 Gest
Jacquet Joseph, cof. h. 68 12th
Jacquis Mary, e.s. Auburn nr Bigelow
Jaeger Francis, lab., 491 Vine
Jaeger Francis A., cooper, 18 Hamer
Jaeger Gottlieb, boots and shoes. 666 Elm
Jaeger Henry, mason. 70 W. Liberty
Jaeger Jacob, baker, 293 Freeman
Jaeger Jacob. cigar mkr., 126 Bremen
Jaeger Jacob, lab., 505 Race
Jaeger John, mill stone cutter, s.w.c 5th and Smith
Jaeger Lena, seamstress, 180 W. Liberty
Jagemann Andrew, stone cutter, 589 Race
Jagen Michael, lab., 61 Mill
Jager John N , butcher, 124 Clark
Jahn Chas. A., clk., w.s. Franz b. Elder and Findlay
Jahn Ignatius, cab. mkr., 56 Elder
Jahn Jacob, baker, 56 Elder
Jahn John, lab., 635 Vine
Jahnsen Catharina, 22 Abigail
Jahnsen Geo., 145 W. 3d

180 (JAS) CINCINNATI (JEN) DIRECTORY. (JOH)

Jahr Bernhard, bakery, 532 Main
Jakli Valentine, billiard table mkr., 76 Abigail
James, bds. 167 Elm
James Mrs. A. C , 173 Broadway
James Alex., tobacconist, 12 Main
James C. J., bds. 453 W. 6th
James, C. H , dentist, 97 W. 7th, h. Glendale
James Charles, 105 E. 2d
James Charles E., trimmings, 206 W. 5th h 334 George
JAMES CHARLES P.,
   Attorney at Law, Room 15 Masonic Temple. h. 87 W. 7th
James David A., glue factory, Cumminsville. h. 33 McFarland
JAMES David H., (Jones, Evans & J.), 443 W. 3d
James Dora, teacher 10th district school, 171 Broadway
James Edward J., molder, wks. W. W. Hano's
James F. B. & Co., (Francis B. J. & Joseph VonHost), sheet iron workers, 35 E. Front
James Francis B., (F B. J. & Co.), 443 W. 3d
James Frank B., clk., 70 Walnut, h. 33 McFarland
James George C., clk., 488 W. 8th
James H. P., clk., bds. s.w.c. Race and 3d
James Johanna, rear 567 Sycamore
James John, molder, wks. s.w.c. 7th and Smith
James Joseph A., book's, 428 W. 8th
James Letetia, 130 Water
James Mary A., 173 Broadway
JAMES ROBERT,
   Manufacturer of Ladies Shoes, 172 W 5th, h. 75 Longworth
James Thomas, clk., 171 Vine, h. 79 George
James Thomas, lab., 171 Water
James Thomas M., attorney, 3 Masonic Temple. h. Walnut Hills
JAMES URIAH P.,
   Publisher and Bookseller
   167 Walnut, h. 12 Arch
James W. P., real estate agt., 9 Water, h. Covington
James Wm., painter, 17 David
James Wm. H., molder, wks. 267 W. 5th
Jameson Alex I., clerk U. S. Clerk's Office, h. Covington
Jamison Harriet, teacher, 122 Everett
Jamison Harry, lab., 611 W. 8th
Jamison Jane, servt., 625 Freeman
Jamison Mary, millenery, 121 W. 5th
Jander Gustavus, saddler, 59 Ham. Road
Janes Edward, carp., s.e.c. Hazen and Railroad
Janes Harvy, carp., 167 E. Front, h. n.e. c Reed and Water
Janninck Wm. J., cooper, 11 Peete
Jannings Mary, dry goods, 139 Laurel
Jansan Chas., cigar mkr., 17 Mulberry
Jansen Anthony, cigar mkr., bds., 17 Mulberry
Jansen Chas., cigar mkr., 17 Mulberry
Jansen John, barber, 31 15th b. Plum and Elm
Jansen Peter, brushmkr., 22 Peete
Jansen Wm., agt., Pavillion b. Observatory and 3d
Jansen Wm., tailor, 17 Mulberry
Janser Michael, carriage smith, 156 Bremen
Janssens Elizabeth, h. 10 Webb
Janson Martin, grocery, 15 Mulberry
Jantz Anthony, carp., 197 Pleasant
Jantzen Julius F., b.k., 330 Ham Road
Jaques Catharine, 174 Broadway
Jaquillard Christian, grocery, 030 Central Av
Jaquish Nancy, 69 George
Jarbury John, piano mkr., wks. 236 Vine
Jarvis C., haggageman, Spencer House
Jarvis John, grinder, 27 Broadway
Jasaph Charles, varnisher, 174 Richmond
Jasper, E. W., cigar mkr., 126 Findlay
Jasper Wm., cooper, wks. Foote, Nash & Co.'s

Jasper Wm., porter, 123 Clay
Jaup Charles, bds. 206 Everett
Jaup Louisa, teacher, 202 Everett
Javor Mathias, shoe mkr., 59 Abigail
Jay John, driver, s.s. Canal b. Race and Vine
Jeckel George, cof. h , 60 Mulberry
Jeckel Henry, (Lammers & J.), 268 Central Av
Jeckel Joseph, shoe mkr., 414 Longworth
Jedelhauser Catharine, 68 Hughes
Jefferies Robert, dray, 445 W. 4th
Jeffers James, cof. h., 58 Water
Jeffers John, conductor, 44th W. 5th
Jeffers John W., lab., 309 W. 8th
Jeffers Nathan, merch., bds. 36 Longworth
Jeffers Wm. H , clk., bds. 22 Stone
Jefferson Charles, barber, 149 W. 4th
Jefferson Hall, s.w.c. Main and 12th
Jefferson Thomas, lab., 208 W. 7th
Jefferson Wm., driver, s.e.c. North and New
Jefferson Wm., driver, 3d and 4th st. R. R.
Jeffras Nathaniel A., clk., 95 W. Pearl, bds. 36 Longworth
Jeffrey John, supt. & eng. of gas works, h. 241 W. 4th
Jeffries Geo. H., lumber inspector, 27 Pine
Jeffries Hy., porter, 20 Stone
Jeffries Rebecca, 160 Freeman
Jehle Geo. J. shoemkr., w.s. Ridgway al. b. 14th and 15th
JELKE Ferdinand, (David Harper & Son), 295 Vine
Jelleff Benjamin, wood measurer, h. 410 Race
Jelleff Charles E., clk., bds. s.s. Findlay b. Freeman and Western Av
Jelleff Chas. S., tailor, 323 Central Av
Jemison Geo., bk layer, 251 Hopkins
Jenewein Peter, 753 Vine
Jenifer Benjamin, stable, s.w.c. 12th and Walnut, h. 10 Jackson
Jenifer Mary, 5 North, h. 76 E. 7th
Jenifer Samuel, policeman, 619 W. 9th
Jenkins Albert, tobucconist, 9 Pancoast al.
Jenkins Azubah, n.e c. 4th and Wood
Jenkins Berry, porter, 10 E. 7th
Jenkins Chars. H., undertaker, 79 Martin
Jenkins Charles W., (J. & C. W. J.) 79 Martin
Jenkins Charlotte, 343 Central Av
Jenkins E. A., bds. Dennison House
Jenkins Edward, foreman, J. Beckley & Co's
Jenkins Edward, sawyer, wks. Hughes & Foster's
Jenkins Edwin P., police, 14 Harrison
Jenkins Fannie, s.w.c. 3d and Broadway
Jenkins Hy., clk., Duhme & Co., h. 324 Longworth
Jenkins Hy., lab., s s. 6th b. Broadway end Culvert
Jenkins J. & C. W. (John & Chas. W.) undertakers, 138 Sycamore
JENKINS J. & T. & CO. (John & Thomas J. & Godfrey Ludwig) Carpenters and Builders, 390 W. 8th
Jenkins James, n.s. Augusta b. John & Smith
Jenkins John (J. & C. W. J.), 138 Sycamore
JENKINS John (J. & T J & Co.) Storrs tp.
Jenkins John, pattern mkr. 24 Hill
Jenkins Martha, bds. s.w.c. 3d and B'd way
JENKINS Thomas (J. & T. J. & Co.), 231 Barr
Jenkins Wm., janitor, s.w.c. 6th and Vine
Jenkins Wm. H., clk., 224 Walnut
Jenkinson Robert, painter, 126 Daymiller
Jenks Lucilla, n.e.c. Frout and Washington
Jenks Wm., eng., n.s. Goodloe b. Willow and Niagara
Jennebeck John, n.s. al. b. Pearl and 3d and Lawrence and Pike
Jenner Peter G., lumber, 650 Elm

Jennewein Peter, cigar mkr., wks. 549 Main
Jenncy Herbert, notary, Masonic Temple, h. 229 W. 4th
Jennings Annie, servt., 492 W. 4th
JENNINGS & BUTTERFIELD,
   (Edward J. & Jonas B.), Grocers and Commission Merchants, n.w.c. Main and 6th
Jennings Catharine, bds. s.w.c. 5th and Broadway
JENNINGS Edward (J. & Butterfield,) h. Albany, O.
Jenni Hy., cof. h., 550 Main
Jennings Jno , dray, 24 Commerce
Jennings John, lab., 13 Lock n. of 8th
Jennings John, lab., w.s. Central Av. b. 2d and W. Canal
Jennings Jno., waiter, Burnet House
Jennison John S., carp., 129 Betts
Jennings Kate, bds. s.w.c. 5th and Br'dway
JENNINGS M. C.,
   Merchant Tailor, 11 W. 4th,
   h. 132 Smith
Jennings Silas T., carriage mkr., 425 Freeman
Jennison James S., printer, "Commercial office," h. Newport
Jenny Carolina, h. 492 Race
Jenny Frederick, molder, 485 Sycamore
Jenny Jacob, cigar mkr, 550 Main
Jennys Wm. C , cof. h., 286 Main
Jenuine Joseph, trunk mkr., wks. 509 Plum
Jeng Geo., cof. h., s.w.c. 15th and Plum
Jepp Frederick, tailor, bds. 90 E. 2d
Jeque James, farmer, bds. 61 W. 6th
Jerker August, barber, 3 E. 4th
Jerow Jacob, cutter, bds. 320 W. 3d
JESSOP WM. & SONS,
   (Augustus Wessel, Agent,)
   Steel Manufacturers, 7 W. 2d
JESSUP Firman (Miller & J.) bds. s.e. c. Main and Court
Jessup Thos. C., dentist, 318 W. 7th
Jesterman George, lab., bds. 64 Abigail
Jesterman Hy., lab., 64 Abigail
JEUP John B., editor, Volksfreund, 139 Plum
Jevens Wm., mach., 292 W. 5th
Jevett Thomas, traveling agt., 353 Race
Juvons Wm.. mach , 292 W, 5th
Jew John, lab., 55 Martin
Jewell Clark, carp., 59 Dudley
Jewell George W., bds. 170 Barr
Jewell Robert C., milkman, 179 Barr
Jewett Decatur S., eng., bds. 471 W. 5th
Jewett E. C., salesman, 73 W. 4th, bds. 169 E. 3d
Jewett H. P. B., clk., 73 W. 4th, bds. 169 E. 3d
Jewett Hy., clk., bds. 209 Longworth
Jewett Joseph F., bag manufac., 465 W. 9th w. of Central Av
Jewish Hospital, n.w.c. Cutter and Betts
Jewish School House, e.s. Lodge b. 5th and 6th
Jillelhauser Catharine, seamstress, 581 Sycamore
Jinger Sebastian, porter, 105 E. 2d
Jirauth Emil, cigars, 597 Vine
Jirgens Frederick L., hatter, 24 Mercer
Joachim Jacob, painter, 679 Race
Joachim Michael, cigar mkr., 685 Race
JOACHIM WENDELL,
   Attorney at Law and Notary Public
   22 W. Court, h. 32 Grant
Joas George, tailor, 59 Martin
Jobe Daniel, penny post, 07 Barr
Jobe Hannah, dye house, 134 W. 6th
Jobert Emil, carver, wks. n.w c. Smith and Front
Jobert Joseph, mach., wks. n.w.c. Smith and Front
Jobson Mattie S., 403 John
Joehring Ferdinand, saddler, 526 Sycamore
Joering Frederick. boots and shoes, 5½ Landing b. Broadway and Ludlow
Joh John, lab., e.s. Bremen b. 14th and 15th
Johan Fred, 65 Clay
Johanger Peter, mach., 76 E. Front
Johannes John P., barber, 633 Vine

Johannigmann Mathias, coal dealer, 611 Elm., h. 610 Race
Johanning Carolina, servt., 520 Main
Johanning Hy., 60 Observatory
Johantgen Peter, mach'., 71 E. Front
John Catharine, b.h.. 27 Jackson
John Chas., cab. mkr., 27 Jackson
John James C., com. mer., 199 W. 5th
John John S., cab mkr., 513 W. 3d, h. s.e.c. Mound and Court
John Moses, lab. s.s. 6th b. Broadway and Culvert
John Wm. S , Clifton House, h. n.e.c. Hathaway and Baymiller
Johns Asa S., carp., bds. 174 E. Pearl
Johns August, plater, 26 Ham. Road
Johns David V., molder, w.s. Kilgour b. Pearl and 3d
Johns James, bksmith, E. 3d b. Parsons and Baum
Johns James H., carp.. 666 E. Front
Johns Joseph, painter, 15 Stone
Johns S. W., b.k., wks. 41 Vine
Johns Samuel, b k., n.s. Hathaway b. Jane and Baymiller
Johnsing Bernard H., 151 Abigail
Johnson A. W., vinegar manuf., 47 E. 2d. h. Walnut Hills
Johnson Alexander, express man, 92 W. Front
Johnson Andrew, paper dealer, 45 W. 2d, h, 151 W 8th
Johnson Ann, 616 Sycamore
Johnson & Bates (Moses J. & Edward B.) barbers, e.s. Central Av. nr. 6th
Johnson Benjamin, scale mkr., 92 Avery
Johnson Benj., teamster, 619 Central Av.
Johnson Benj. F., cooper, 61 Buckeye
Johnson Beverly, steward, s.s. Pancoast al. b. 7th and 8th
JOHNSON Brooks (Brooks J. & Co.), 206 W. 4th
JOHNSON BROOKS & CO. (Brooks J & Eli J.) Provision Brokers, Enquirer Building, 134 Vine
JOHNSON BROS. & CO., Proprietors of Lord's Detector, and Bankers, n.w.c. 3d and Main
Johnson C., oof. h., 186 Central Av
JOHNSON C. E. & CO. (Charles E. J. & Co.) Manufacturers, and Wholesale Commission Dealers in Boots, Shoes and Brogans, 51 W. Front
Johnson Catharine, 402 W. 7th
Johnson Charles, barber, s.s. 6th b. B'dway and Culvert
Johnson Chas., lab., 359 Broadway
Johnson Chas., whitewasher, n.s. Margaret b. Jane and Baymiller
JOHNSON CHAS. A., Photograph Gallery, s.w.c 9th and Main
Johnson Charles B., clk., bds. Gibson House
JOHNSON Chas. E. (C. E. J. & Co.), rooms Selves' Bldg., 17 W. 3d
Johnson Chauncey M , bds. 14 Stone
Johnson Christian, carriage mkr., 4 Peete
Johnson D. T., foreman, bds. 95 St. Clair
Johnson David, bds. 1060 Central Av
Johnson David, clk., n.w.c. Court and Mound, bds. 80 Clark
Johnson David, liquors bds 525 W. 7th
Johnson Diederich, grocery, n.e.e. Barr and Baymiller
Johnson E. B., clk., Lafayette Banking Co., h. Covington
Johnson Edgar M. (Jackson & J.), 56 Richmond
Johnson Edward H., phys., 139 W. 6th, h. 119 W. 6th
Johnson Edward P., billiards, n.w.c. 5th and Walnut [5th
Johnson Edward T., student, bds. 80 E.
JOHNSON Eli (Brooks Johnson & Co.) 381 W. 6th
Johnson Elijah C. (J., Stephens & Morgan) s.e.c. Mound and Elizabeth
Johnson Elizabeth, 477 W 4th
Johnson Emma, ladies' furnishing goods, e.s. Walnut b. 5th and 6th
Johnson Frances, w.s. Plum b. Water & River

Johnson Francis, porter, 161 Bremen
Johnson Frank, watchman, bds. 206 W. 5th
JOHNSON Frederick A. (J. Bros. & Co.) bds. 59 Richmond
JOHNSON, FRY & CO.
  Publishers, 65 W. 4th
  Richard C. Pelling, Agent
Johnson Geo. (Stanley & J.) 96 Dudley
Johnson Geo., barber, 235 Broadway
Johnson George H., pyrotechnist, bds. Celestial st., Mt. Adams
Johnson Harriet, 331 W. 5th
Johnson Hy , butcher, e.s. Linn b. Poplar and Findlay
Johnson Hy., carp , h. 377 Broadway
Johnson Hy., molder, wks. n.e.c. Canal and Walnut
Johnson Hy., police, 170 Mound
Johnson Hy., sexton, 170 Mound
Johnson Hy., whitewasher, 329 W. 6th
Johnson Hy. C., plumber, 440½ W. 5th
Johnson Hy. H , box mkr., 501 Vine
Johnson Isaac D., livery stable, w.s St. Clair b. 8th and 9th
Johnson J., bds. Dennison House
Johnson James, caulker, s.s. Goodloe b. Willow and Niagara
Johnson James, cooper, 183 George
Johnson James, dray, 264 Richmond
Johnson Jas., lab., 53 E. 3d
Johnson James, pilot, s.w c. Broadway and New
Johnson James F., lab., Cramsey al., b. Mound and Cutter
JOHNSON JAMES W.,
  Attorney at Law,
  17 Bank Building. h. 56 Richmond
Johnson Jerome B., marble works, e. s. Central Av. b. 12th and Ann, h. 82 W. 8th
JOHNSON John, (J. Morton & Co.,) bds. Broadway Hotel
Johnson John, cab mkr., 26 Commerce
Johnson John, carp., s.s. 2d b. Smith & Rose, h. s.e.c. Smith and 2d
Johnson John, porter, U. S. Hotel
Johnson John, shoe mkr., bds., 1113 Central Av
Johnson John A., clk., 140 Main, h. s. w.c. Broadway and Franklin
Johnson John H. (Parvin & J.,) 54 W. Court w. of Central Av
Johnson John H., porter, 550 Walnut
JOHNSON John T., (Roberts & J.) 160 Barr
Johnson Joseph, cutter, E. 5th. h. Mt. Adams
Johnson Julia A., 133 Longworth
Johnson Julia E , 67 Hopkins
Johnson Justus, car mkr., 247 W. 6th
Johnson Lafayette M., 250 Longworth
Johnson Lloyd, 27 E. 8th e. of Lock
Johnson Louisa, bds. 69 George
Johnson Martha, servt., 454 W. 5th
Johnson Mary, bds s. w. c. Court and Mound
Johnson Mary, bds. 103 E. 3d e. of Whittaker
Johnson Mary, e.s. Pancoast al. bet. 7th and 8th
Johnson Mary, eating saloon, 84 W. Front
Johnson Mary, tailoress, bds. 355 Central Av
Johnson Mollie, bds. 204 Plum
JOHNSON, MORTON & CO.,(John J. Daniel H. M. & Samuel Startsman) Queen City Saw Mill, s.s. Front b. Kelly and Foster, office 102 E. Pearl e. of Broadway
Johnson Moses, (J. & Bates,) 6 Home
Johnson Overton J., prop. Dumas Hotel, e.s. Macalister, b. 4th and 5th
Johnson Perre, bds. 477 W. 4th
Johnson Rosa, servt., 297 Richmond
Johnson Rufus H. bds. Broadway Hotel
Johnson S. J. & Co., exchange office, 30 W. 3d
Johnson Samuel, bds. 77 E. 3d
JOHNSON SAM'L..
  Proprietor Clifton House,
  s.e.c. 6th and Elm
Johnson Samuel A., salesman 124 Main, bds. s.e.c. 3d and Broadway

Johnson Samuel J., (S. J. J. & Co., 433 W. 5th
Johnson Sarah, h. 45 E. 8th
Johnson, Stephen & Morgan, book and job printers, 141 Main
Johnson Susan, cook, s.s. 6th b. Broadway and Culvert
Johnson Thomas, bk. layer, 117 Carr
Johnson Thos. A., blk. smith, 28 W. 6th
Johnson Timothy F., sexton, s. w. c. 4th and Race
Johnson Thomas H., 349 W. 8th
Johnson Thos. J., pyrotechnist, bds. Celestial st., Mt. Adams
Johnson Wm., (T. Whitmore & Co.,) h. w.s. Central Av. b. 3d and 4th
Johnson Wm., bk. layer, 12 14th
Johnson Wm., blk. smith, 212 Laurel
Johnson Wm., brakesman, bds. 302 W. 5th
Johnson Wm., dray, bds. 92 Gest
Johnson Wm., lab. 316 Water
Johnson Wm , painter, 302 Plum
Johnson Wm., tailor, 27 Broadway
Johnson Wm. A., clk., s. w. c. 3d and Walnut
Johnson Wm. W., b.k., Burnet House
Johnston Mrs., 333 W. 5th
JOINSTON Alex. M., (J. & Foertmeyer,) 20 Clark
Johnston Anna M., 275 Walnut
Johnston Augustus, wagon mkr., bds. 247 W. 6th   [W. 6th
Johnston Benjamin F., painter, bds. 69
JOHNSTON & COLLIER, (Wm. J. & Chas. B. C.) Attorneys at Law, Room 13, Masonic Temple
Johnston Daniel, lab., 452 W Liberty
Johnston Edward P., billiards, 15 David
JOHNSTON & FOERTMEYER, (Alex. M. J. & Adolphus W. F.,) Chemists and Druggists, n.e.c. 6th and Elm
Johnston Francis, grocery, 46 E. Front
Johnston George, lab., n.w.c. Plum and Water
Johnston George, lab., n. w. c. Central Av. and Pearl
Johnston Geo. W., barber, w s. Broadway b. 7th and 8th
JOHNSTON GEO. W. C.,
  Wood Yard, 145 Water
  h. 15 Plum
Johnston Hannah D., 334 George
JOHNSTON Henry M., (Hugh, McBirney & Co.,) 18 Hopkins
Johnston Hugh, mach., wks, 116 W. 2d
Johnston Hugh A., carp., 52 Race
Johnston Isaac, clk., n.s. corp. line Mt. Auburn
JOHNSTON J. & J. M., (John & Jas. M.,) Bath Tubs, Refrigerators and Box Manufacturers, 219 and 221 W. 3d
Johnston J. Wilson, clk., Custom House h. 250 W. 7th
Johnston James D., carp., 52 Race
Johnston John E., clk., s.e.c. Main and Pearl, bds. Dennison House
JOHNSTON James M., (J. & J. M. J.,) 246 Longworth
JOHNSTON John, (J. & J. M. J.,) n.s. Hathaway b. Jane and Baymiller
Johnston John, (McNair & Co.,) res. country
Johnston John K., h. 423 W. 9th, w. of Central Av
Johnston John S., (W. & J. S. J.,) 429 Central Av
Johnston John W., gun smith, bds. 24½ E. 4th
Johnston Julia, 645 Sycamore
Johnston Joseph M., conductor, 222 Water
Johnston Louisa, teacher first district school
Johnston Miss M. C., bds. 50 Gano
Johnston Margaret, 52 Race
Johnston Matilda, 15 Plum
Johnston Mrs. Matilda, 323 W. 9th w. of Central Av
Johnston Moses, barber, 6 Home
Johnston Robert, plumber, 186 E. 6th
JOHNSTON ROBERT A., Attorney at Law and Notary, Room 4 Masonic Temple, h. 433 W. 4th

182 **(JON)** CINCINNATI **(JON)** DIRECTORY. **(JON)**

Johnston Robert M., b.k., 117 Central Av
Johnston Samuel B, foreman. 332 Clark
Johnston Thomas, auction, 93 Main, h. Mt. Auburn
Johnston Thomas, steward, e.s. Haven al. b. 8th and 9th
Johnston W. & J. S., (Wm. & John S.) die sinkers, 429 Central Av
JOHNSTON Wm., (J. & Collier,) res. Clifton
Johnston Wm., (W. & J. S. J.) 429 Central Av
Johnston Wm,, carp., 63 E. 3d, res. Mt. Auburn
Johnston Wm., cutter. n.e.c. Pub. Landing and Sycamore
Johnston Wm. A., n. w. c. Main and Court
JOHNSTON Wm. B., (Winston & J.,) 398 W. 6th
Johnston Wm. H., 421 Freeman
Johnston Wm. S., 189 W. 4th
Johnston William W., salesman, 378 George
Joice Chas. T., lab., 301 W. 8th
Joice Michael G, reporter, 2ᵈ Race
Joice Timothy, fireman, 301 W. 8th
Jokers Michael, grocery, 355 Ham. Road
Jokers Magdaline, 74 W. Liberty
Jolliffee John, atty., 60 W. 4th h. 248 Race
Jolly Alsabide, pilot, 402 W. 3d
Jolly John, pilot. 402 W. 3d
Jolly Oscar B , pilot. 402 W. 3d
Jolly Wm , 314 W 6th
Jonas Henry, carp., 190 Clark
Jonas Jacob, 190 Clark
Jonas John, cigar mkr., wks. 213 Walnut
Jonas Joseph, 520 W. 7th
Jonas Martin. clk., Stewart, Carmichael & Co.'s, bds. s.s. 6th b. Baymiller & Freeman
Jonas Wm., bds. 362 Ham. Road
Jones —, conductor, bds. 422 W. 7th
Jones A. B., student, bds. 140 W. 6th
Jones A. E., phys., 806 E. Front, h. Walnut Hills
Jones Abraham, hats and caps, 49 E. Pearl
Jones Abraham, lab., 45 Race
Jones Amanda M., dress mkr., 548 Sycamore
Jones Anna, 314 W. 7th
Jones Ann E., w.s. Sycamore, b. 7th & 8th
Jones Benj., bds. 206 W. 5th
Jones Benjamin V., 316 Plum
JONES BROTHERS & CO., (Jones Caleb, Geo. W., John J., John D. & F. G. Huntington,) Wholesale Dry Goods. 19 W. Pearl
JONES & BURNET, (Talbot J. & Jacob B.) Attorneys at Law, Room 5, Masonic Temple
JONES C. Taylor, (J. & Conahan,) 132 W. 7th
JONES Caleb, (J. Brothers & Co.,) res. Philadelphia
Jones Chas., painter, 123 Hopkins
Jones Charles P., (Syfers & J.,) bds. 289 W. 6th
JONES & CONAHAN, (C. Taylor J. & Chas. C.) Oil, Soap and Candle Manufactory, 724 Central Avenue, Office, 39 Walnut
Jones Cornelius, driver, 65 Avery
Jones Daniel, carp., s.s. Goodloe, b. Willow and Niagara
Jones David, 242 E. 6th
Jones David, finisher, wks. Fritsch, Burkhardt & Co.
Jones David, lab., 444 W. Front
Jones David, paver. 73 Pike
Jones David, stone cutter, 242 E. 6th
Jones David, sawyer, wks. 128 W. 2d
Jones David H., cheese dealer, 215 Laurel
Jones David S., bds. 158 W. 3d
Jones David W., salesman, 186 Main, h. 64 Rittenhouse
Jones Douglass. mer., bds. Frey's Hotel
Jones E. P. & Sons, (Enoch P. J., John J. & Isaiah J.) coal yards, s.w.c. Front and M. Canal

Jones Edward, clk., s.w.c. W. W. Canal and Smith
Jones Edward, eng., wks. 128 W. 2d
Jones Edward, lab., 11 Wade w of Linn
Jones Edward G., (Pogue & J.,) h. Fairmount
Jones Eliza, servt., 406 W. 6th
Jones Eliza J., bds. 455 W. 7th
Jones Elizabeth, 387 W. 3d
Jones Elizabeth, servt , 381 W. 6th
Jones Ellen, servt., 120 E. 5th
Jones Enoch P., (E. P. J. & Sons,) res. Walnut Hills
Jones Evan, boiler mkr., bds. s. e. c. Smith and Front
JONES EVAN W., Family Grocery, 513 W. 5th
Jones Evan W., pattern mkr., wks. 222 E. Front
JONES, EVANS & JAMES. (Robert J., Daniel O. E. & David H. J.,) Boiler Makers, s.s. Pearl 1 door e. of Ludlow
Jones F. E., engraver, s.w.c. 8th and Main, h. 481 W. 7th
Jones Francis, 550 Sycamore
Jones Francis, waiter, 10 Jackson
Jones Frank, cigar mkr., 192 Mound
Jones Frank, deputy sheriff, bds. Buttemiller's Hotel
Jones Frank, tinner, 32 Main
Jones Frank G., porter, res. Sycamore Hill
Jones Geo., caulker, n.s. R. Road e. of Hazen
Jones Geo., roller, bds. s.e.c. 2d and Smith
Jones George E., phys., 481 W. 7th
JONES GEO. T. Superintendent American Bank Note Co., s.e.c. 4th and Main, h 569 W. 5th
JONES George W., (J. Brothers & Co.) res. Jones' Station
Jones Geo W., salesman, 134 Walnut, h. 126 E. 5th
Jones Griffith, shoe mkr., bds. 174 E. Pearl
Jones H., b. k., bds 162 Elm
Jones Hayward, b. k., 42 Vine, h. 162 Elm
Jones Hy., lab., 59 E. 3d e. of Whittaker
Jones Henry A., Pres. of Niles' Works, h. 97 Pike
Jones Henry C., clk., 96 W. 4th, h. 414 W. 4th
Jones Hy. W., confec., 59 E. 4th
Jones Hugh, carp., w.s. Plum b. Canal and Court
Jones Isaac, boot black, 6 E. 3d, h. 58 E. 7th
Jones Isaac N., paper hanger, bds. 513 W. 5th
Jones Isaiah, (E. P. J. & Sons,) res. Walnut Hills
Jones Israel, bk. layer, 204 George
Jones J. Colegate, printer, 17 Hannibal
JONES J. Dan, (Baldwin & Co.) h. Columbia tp.
JONES Jacob, (Gilbert, J. & Ogborn,) bds. Burnet House
Jones Jacob, tailor, bds. 628 Race
Jones James, dry goods, 53 Hopkins
Jones James B., painter, 133 Smith
Jones James J., clk., 53 Hopkins
Jones James V., (Barbenchon & J.,) 131 Walnut
Jones James W., salesman, 101 W. Pearl bds. Burnet House
Jones Jane, wks. 278 W. Court w. of Central Av.
Jones Jeremiah H, atty., 148 Walnut
Jones Jesse, cooper, 175 W. Court w. of Central Av.
Jones John, 33 New
Jones John, 47 New
Jones John, 244 Broadway
Jones John, bds. 73 Pike
Jones John, (E. P Jones & Sons,) h. E. Walnut Hills
Jones John, carp , 213 Wade
Jones John, carp., 102 Baum
Jones John, cigar mkr., 21 Hopkins
Jones John, dray, 214 Cutter
Jones John, paver, e.s. Davis b. Doal and Ringgold

Jones John, plasterer, bds. n.e.c. Elm and 15th
Jones John, whitewasher, e.s. Sycamore b. 8th and 9th
JONES John D., (J. Brothers & Co.) res. 393 W. 6th
Jones John D, baker, n.e.c. Barr and Freeman
Jones John C., printer, 17 Hannibal
Jones John E. com. mer., 105 W. 5th
Jones John F., (Franke & J.,) 3d, 2d door e. of Butler
Jones John G., 2d asst. city auditor, 296 W. 6th
Jones John G., b. k., 91 W. Pearl, h. 437 W. 7th
JONES John J. (J. Brothers & Co.) s.w.c. Walnut and 4th
Jones John X., boiler, foot of Harrison
Jones John L., clk., 79 E. Pearl, bds. 81 E. Pearl
Jones John M., fireman, 58 Elm
Jones John R., miller 53 Ellen
Jones John S., driver, Am. Ex. Co., 95 E. Pearl
Jones Jonathan H., finisher, 294 W. Front
Jones Joseph, bar k., rooms 58 Broadway
Jones Joseph, blksmith, 66 E. Front
Jones Joseph, cutter, 408 W. 5th
Jones Joseph, lab., s. w. c. Vine and Front
Jones Joseph, surveyor, Cin. Equitable Ins. Co., 129 Pike
Jones Joseph A., clk., 102 Baum
Jones Joshua, mer., 303 W. 9th w. of Central Av.
Jones Leroy, molder, wks. 600 W. 5th
Jones Littleton, barber. 42 E. 3d
Jones Lizzie, bk. folder, bds. 225 Richmond
Jones Lizzie, servt., 86 E. 3d
Jones Lorenzo E., phys., 302 Race
Jones Loton, dyer, 271 Clinton
Jones Lucy, 18 Richmond b. Elm and Plum
JONES M. L., (Chapin J. & Co.) 444 W. 8th
Jones Margaret, 62 Clark
Jones Margaret, e.s. Linn b. Poplar and Findlay
Jones Margaret, rear 70 Hunt
Jones Margaret, servt., 545 W. 8th
Jones Marshall, hackman. 12 E. 7th
Jones Martha A., teacher, 105 W. 5th
Jones Martin L., com. mer., 444 W. 9th w. of Central Av.
Jones Mary, bds. 17 Hannibal
Jones Mary, 245 Broadway
Jones Mary, servt., 155 John
Jones Mary, servt., 275 Longworth
Jones Mary, servt., bds. 353 Central Av.
Jones Mary A., 71 E. Front
Jones Mary A., 29 Webb
Jones Mary A., teacher, h. 47 New
Jones Nancy, 493 W. 3d
Jones Nathaniel S., clk., 132 W. 7th
Jones Oliver, cook, 5 New
Jones P. J., salesman, bds. 360 W. 4th
Jones Paul. bk. layer, 134 Betts
Jones Peter, lab., 281 W. 7th
Jones Prucilla, cof. h. 138 Culvert
Jones Pryce J., clk., 53 Hopkins
Jones Rudolph, cof. h. 4 Home
Jones Rebecca, 3 al. b. 4th and 5th and Park and Mill
Jones Rebecca, w.s. Henderson al. b. 7th and 8th
JONES Robert, (J. Evans & James) w.s. Baum b 3d and 5th
Jones Robert, boiler mkr., 29 Baum
Jones Robert, carp., w.s. Plum b. Canal and Court
Jones Robert, plasterer, 17 Grant
Jones Robert N., b.k. 99 W. 4th, h. 481 W. 7th
Jones Rowland J., eng., 129 Butler
Jones S. L., blksmith, 21 W. 7th
Jones Samuel, butcher, 131 Everett
Jones Samuel G., wagon mkr., bds. 316 W. 3d
Jones Samuel W., salesman, 89 E. 5th
Jones Sarah, 54 W. Front
Jones Susan, 225 Richmond

JONES & SHARP, (Wm. E. J. & Thomas T. S.), Attorneys at Law and Notaries, room 8, Masonic Temple
Jones T. A., b k. Geo. Dominick & Bro's, h. n.w.c. 6th and Race
Jones T. H. D., exp. mes., bds. Broadway Hotel
JONES Talbot, (J. & Burnet) bds. Burnet House
Jones Theodore, wood engraver, s.e.c. 4th and Walnut, bds. Wm. Tell
Jones Thomas, barber, n.s. 7th b Broadway and Culvert
Jones Thomas, fireman, bds. 35 Hathaway
Jones Thos , lab , bds. 444 W. Front
Jones Thos., salesman 99 W. 4th, h. 481 W. 7th
Jones Thos. C., cab. mkr., 25 E. 3d e. of Parsons
Jones Thos D., sculptor, 47 E. 4th, bds. Henrie House
Jones Thos E., fireman, 35 Hatteras
Jones Trum in B., enz., 422 George
Jones Wilkinson, 548 Sycamore
Jones Wilson, blksmith, bds. 66 W. Court
Jones Wm., bds. 81 E. Pearl
Jones Wm , 209 W. Front
Jones Wm., boatman, 124 Lock
Jones Wm., 1 b., 239 Barr
Jones Wm., lab., wks. C., H. & D. R.R. Depot
Jones Wm., painter, 400 Race
Jones Wm., presser, wks. 830 Central Av
Jones Wm. B., cigars, 14 Pub. Landing, h. 556 Freeman
JONES Wm. E., (J. & Sharp) res. Newtown
Jones Wm. H., blksmith, wks. n.e.c. Walnut and Canal
Jones Wm. H., carp., w.s. Lewis b. River and Front
Jones Wm. H., clk., 92 Ludlow
Jones Wm. H., lab., 101 E. 6th
Jones Wm. J., bds. 236 E. 6th
Jones Wm. J., clk., bds. 1216 E. Front
Jones Wm. O., boiler mkr., 76 E. 3d e. of Whittaker
Jones Wrightson, clk., 227 Broadway
Jonkin Bernhard, tailor, e.s. Ridgway al. b. Liberty and 15th
Jonte Alfred, (J. & Bro.) 154 Poplar
Jonte & Bro., (Alfred & Robert) coopers, 158 Poplar
Jonte Mary E., teacher, 486 Race
Jonte Mollie A., saleswoman 53 E. Pearl
Jonte Peter, 765 Vine
JONTE PETER N., Cooper Shop, 484 Race, h. 486 Race
Jonte Robert, (J. & Bro.) 156 Poplar
Jordan Aaron M., pilot, 264 Clark
Jordan Annie M., bds. 53 E. 5th
Jordan C. D., molder, wks. 267 W. 5th
Jordan Caleb D., foreman, b. 166 Longworth
Jordan Charles, actor, National Theater
JORDAN CHAS. W., Paper Box Manufacturer, n.e.c. Walnut and 5th, up stairs, res. Celestial street, Mt. Adams
Jordan D , engraver, rooms 56 E. 3d
JORDAN DANIEL B., Fancy Paper Box Manufacturer. 187 Main, h. Celestial st., Mt. Adams
Jordan Delia, 468 Broadway
Jordan Edward T., teamster, 44 Kossuth
Jordan Francis, barber, 212 Walnut
Jordan Harry, actor, 171 Sycamore
Jordan Hy. J., white washer, 108 W. Liberty
JORDAN Isaac, (Ball & J.) bds. Broadway Hotel
Jordan John, contractor, 202 George
Jordan Mary, bds. 18 Hamer
Jordan Mary, 108 W. 5th, bds. 202 George
Jordan Michael, 905 Central Av.
Jordan Morton, lab., 138 Freeman
Jordan Nicholas, weaver, n.w.c. Baymiller and Gest
Jordan Richard M., cutter, 474 W. 3d
Jordan Sullivan, lab., bds. 67 Oliver

Jordan Thos., shoe mkr., s.w.c. 5th and Central Av.
Jordan Wm., molder, wks. 267 W. 5th
Jordan Wm., porter, res. Walnut Hills
Jordan Ann, 342 Clark
Jordan Jas., lab , 425 W. 2d
Joring Barney, tailor. 403 Broadway
Joring Hy., boots and shoes, 249 Hopkins
Jorling Barney, carp., 213 Hopkins
Joseph Adolph, clk. s.e.c. Vine and Pearl, h. 303 Race
Joseph & Brother, (David J. & Solomon J.) clothing, 253 Main
Joseph Chas. painter, 174 Richmond
Joseph David, (J. & Brother) 276 George
Joseph Joseph, jeweler, 402 W. 4th
Joseph Levi, clk., 78 Hopkins
Joseph Sister, St. Clare Convent, n.w.c. 3d and Lytle
Joseph Solomon, (J. & Brother) 311 Main
Joslin Allen T., carp., 24 Betts
JOSLIN Edward, (J. A. Fay & Co.) res. Keene, New Hampshire
Joslin Elizabeth, servt., 49 Webster
Joslin Louisa, 150 Everett
Joslin Lydia, servt., 49 Webster
Joslyn John J., 60 W. Court w. of Central Av.
Joslyn Wm. H., lab., wks. Hiatt and Wood's
Journal of Rational Medicine, Chas. H. Cleaveland, M. D., Editor, 203 W. 4th
Joss Frederick, lab., 310 Linn
Jost Anthony, cab. mkr., 72 Abigail
Jost Catharine, servt., s.e.c. 2d and Plum
Jost John, wks. junction 6th and Front
Jostwerts Wm., carp , 11 Pendleton
Jouvet John H., sewing silks, 72 W. 4th, h. 420½ W. 7th
Jow John, grinder, s.e.c. New and Broadway
Joy John, lab., 48 Lock
Joy Morris, lab., h. 15 Carr
Joy Morris, lab., h. 15 Park
Joy Mary Ann, 136 Linn
Joy Thomas, cof. h., 48 Lock
Joyce Edwin, boots and shoes, 122 Lock
Joyce Garrett clk., n w c. Court and Mound, bds. 301 W. 8th
Joyce James, pattern mkr., wks. n.e.c. Canal and Walnut
Joyce Michael, grocery, 982 E. Front
Joyce Nancy, s.e.c. Front and Hazen
Judah J., barber, 4 E. 6th
Judd O. E., watchman. 2 Horne
Judge Ann, servant. Burnet House
Judge John, dray, 27 Arch
Judge John F., phys., 116 Dudley
Judge Martin. huckster, 308 W. 7th
Judkins David. phys., 301 Race
JUDKINS JESSE P., Physician, 137 W. 6th h. 38 Longworth
Judkins Mary, 38 Longworth
JUNGLING Hy., (J. & Woodburn,) 6 York
JUEGLING & WOODBURN (Henry J. & Robert W.,) Plumbers, 602 Central Av
Juergens F. L , hatter, 481 Vine
Juhars Louis, bakery, n.s. Pearl b. Butler and Pike
Juilg Michael, tailor, 120 Pleasant
Jukter Michael, 267 Ham. Road
Julius M., clk., s.w.c. 6th and Plum
Jull George, turner, 530 Plum
Junas Jacob, carp., 190 Clark
Junas Peter, cab. mkr., 190 Clark
Junck Chas. H., shoe mkr., 108 W. Liberty
Junck Creighton, cof. h. s.s. Court b. Main and Sycamore
Juncker Philip, lab., 12 Abigail
Jung Adam, cooper, 23 Abigail
Jung Christian, carp., 18 Hamer
Jung Christopher, steward, St. Nicholas Exchange
JUNG Daniel, (Weyand & J.,) 1033 Central Av.
Jung Ignatz, lab., 601 Vine

Jung Jacob, butcher, 226 Linn
Jung Jacob, cooper, 93 Abigail
Jung Jacob, saddler, 64 Findlay
Jung John, peddler, 51 12th
Jung John tailor, 88 Bremen
Jung John, tailor, rear 12 E. Mulberry
Jung John, tailor, 3 9 Vine
Jung Peter, cigar mkr., 600 Race
Jung Philip, shoe mkr., 139 Bremen
Jung Mrs. Susanna, 63 Buckeye
Jungclut Chas., lab., 11 Peete
Jungclut Wm., lab., 30 Buckeye
Jungclus John, 30 Miami
Jungling Wm , cooper. s. s. Brighton b. Bernard and Harrison Pike, h. 14 Brighton
Jungmann Adam, painter, wks. s.w.c Elm and Front
Jungmann Mary, 243 Ham. Road
Jungmann Susanna, seamstress, s.w.c. Pleasant and Ham. Road
Junion John H., tanner, 29 Kossuth
Junium Chas., carp., 151 Bremen
Junk Hermann, tailor, bds. 298 Central Av.
Junker Frank, tailor, 148 Hopkins
Junker John, butcher, b. u.s. Corp. Line nr Auburn
Junkins Samuel, whitewasher, s. s. L'Hommedieu al. b. Central Av. and John
Jurenk Ferdinand, saddler, 526 Sycamore
Jurgens John F., butcher, 146 Buckeye
Justice Wm., carp., s.s. 9th b. Harriet and Mill Creek
Justice Wm. H. H., b. k., 95 Main, h. Newport
Justis C. H., salesman, 140 Main, h. 285 George
Justis Frederick, porter, 57 Main, h. 51 W. 5th
Justis Harriet, 285 George
Justis John, bds. 400 Longworth
Justis John, b. k., 49 Barr
Justis John J., b.k., Suire Eckstein & Co.,
Justis Thomas T., 285 George
Justus Frederick, clk., bds. 51 W. 5th
Jutzler Heinrich, cof. h., 443 Vine

K

Kabbas Conrad, packer, 62 Lock
Kabbas George, fireman, 17 Commerce
Kahel Balser, butcher, 400 Baymiller
Kabcs Hy., tanner, 91 Bremen
Kabs Wilhelmina, chair caner, rear 535 Main
Kadeker Annie S., saleswoman, 78 W. 4th, bds. 149 Linn
Kadel Adam, cab. mkr., 50 Allison
Kaefer Jacob, lock smith, 143 Clay
Kaefer John, tanner, 40 Dunlap
Kaelin Marus, lithographic printer, s.w.c. 5th and Bremen
Kaehr Mary, servt., Gilt House
Kaell Robert, cooper, s.w.c. Freeman and Dayton
Kaelch Catharine, laundress, n.s. Long al. b. Woodward and Franklin
Kaelin Alois, painter, s.w.c. 9th and Elm
Kaelin Maurice, lithographer, 119 Bremen
Kaemerling Gustavus n.e.c. Liberty and Vine
Kaemper William, lab., 176 Clay
Kaen Frederick, lab., 517 E. Front
Kaen James, harness mkr., 3 North
Kaes Joseph, lab., 42 Peete
Kaes Joseph, stone cutter, s.w.c. Laurel and Baymiller
Kaesler Frederick, lab., e.s. Anderson b. 2d and Pearl
Kafer John, 40 Dunlap
Kafer John, shoe mkr., 911 Central Av.
Kager Hy., lab., 300 Vine
Kahl Nicholas, carp., 100 Linn
Kuhle Wm., lab., w.s. Goose al. b. Liberty and 15th
Kahles Charles, tailor, 538 Plum
Kahn Abraham, sutler. 62 Richmond
Kahn Andrew, lab., 71 Poplar

184 (KAL) CINCINNATI (KAM) DIRECTORY. (KAS)

Kahn Andrew W., clk., n.e.c. 5th and Sycamore
Kahn Caroline, 64 Findlay
Kahn Charles, 73 Everett
Kahn Charles, peddler, 57 14th
Kuhn Charles slaughter house, n.e.c. John and Poplar
Kahn Charles Jr., butcher, 19 14th b. Central Av and Plum
Kahn Delphin E., peddler, 544 Race
Kahn Francis, varnisher, 38 E. 5th
Kahn Hy., meats 31 W. 6th
Kahn Isaac, 206 Elm
Kahn Jacob M., saddler, 133 Sycamore
Kahn Julius, auction, 9 W. 5th
Kohn Louis, 359 Ham. Road
Kahn Michael, 84 E. 3d
Kahn Moses, meats, s.w.c. 7th and Walnut, h. 468 John
Kahn Philip, peddler, 21 David
Kahn Samson, 600 Bremen

KAHN SAMUEL, Proprietor American Hotel, n.e.c. 5th and Sycamore

Kahn Solomon, butcher, 19 14th b. Central Av and Plum
Kahtenbrink Hy., lab., 12 Orchard
Kaiber Chas., butcher, wks. 47 12th
Kaighn Phillip, T., salesman, 30 W. 4th, res. Covington
Kaile Chas., blksmith, wks. 9 W. 7th
Kailer Augustus, tailor, 397 Broadway
Kailer Peter. t ilor, 397 Broadway
Kain Anna, 15 Abigail
Kain Antony, lab., 193 Water
Kain George, lab, 13 Accommodation
Kain James, harness mkr., 2 North
Kain John. cof. h., 34 E. 6th e. of Lock
Kain John, mach., wks. n.s. Front b. Lawrence and Pike
Kain John, tea dealer, 2 North
KAIN John W., (D. B. George & Co.,) res. Batavia
Kain M., mach., wks. n.s. Front b. Lawrence and Pike
Kain Mary, 200 Cutter
Kain Mary, 49 Rittenhouse
Kain Mary, 173 Water
Kain Michael, blksmith, 58 Baum
Kain Michael, lab., wks. 165 Central Av.
Kain Patrick, lab., 95 Clark
Kain Patrick, lab., 173 Water
Kaine Rosanna, waiter, Dennison House
Kaise Anna D., 38 Elder
Kaiser Anton, cigar mkr., bds. 463 Sycamore
Kaiser Caroline, h. 137 Pleasant
Kaiser Charles, cigars. 202 W. Front
Kaiser Charles, cooper, wks. 161 W. 3d
Kaiser Conrad, finisher, 611 Main
Kaiser Conrad, lab., wks. w.s. Ham. Road b. Findlay and Liberty
Kaiser Frank, (K. & Kohler,) 475 Walnut
Kaiser Genevieve, rear 13 E. Liberty
Kaiser Hy., cigar mkr., n.s. Green b. Race and Pleasant
Kaiser Hy., clk., 52 E. Pearl, bds. 59 Allison
Kaiser Hy., lab., rear 512 Walnut
Kaiser Hy., varnisher, 611 Main
Kaiser John, mach., wks. n.s. Front b. Lawrence and Pike
Kaiser & Kohler (Frank K. & Wm. K.) musical instruments, 473 Walnut
Kaiser Louis, bar k., 390 Vine
Kaiser Louis, cooper, 2 Mulberry
Kaiser Mathias, carp., 116 W. Liberty
Kaiser Mathias, watchman, 167 Clay
Kaiser Matthew, cab. mkr., n.e.c. Liberty and Race
Kaiser Peter, stone mason, 194 Bremen
Kaiser Phillp, cof. h., n.s. Harrison Pike b. Brighton and Riddle
Kaiser Wm., 611 Main
Kaiser Wm., butcher, 209 Race
Kaiser Wm., cof h., 15 W. Canal
Kaiser W m., plasterer, 137 Pleasant
Kaiser Wm. H., cigar mkr., 137 Pleasant
Kaiser Xavier, cof. h., 390 Vine
Kaisser Albert, lab., wks. n.w.c. Plum and Wade
Kaisser Chas., millwright, 142 Clay
Kalaham Daniel, lab., 63 Vine
Kalb Philip, cab. mkr., 141 Daymiller

Kalbfell Wm., (Wm. K. & Co.), 21 E. 3d
Kalbfell Wm., & Co. (Wm. K., Stephen Gibson and Robt. H. Gibson,) printers, 21 E. 3d
Kalemburger Lewis C., clk., 464 Elm
Kalenback Annie, servt., 140 E. 3d
Kaley Catharine, s.s. 12th b. Walnut and Clay
Kaley Wm., lab., 990 E. Front
Kalflasch Herman, miller, 63 Lock
Kalicinski Vincent, tailor, 5 Mary
Kalihan John, lab, 35 Accomodation
Kalla Joseph, carp., 186 Clark
Kallenberger Jacob, whitewasher, rear 458 Walnut
Kallendorf Dederich, carp., 26 Logan
Kallendorf Chas., carp., 26 Logan
Kallendorf Fred., carp., 26 Logan
Kaller Adam, blksmith, 126 Bremen
Kaller Anton, carp, 108 Avery
Kallery Luke, dray, 141 Pleasant

KALLMEYER FRED., Harness, Saddles, Trunks Whips, Carpet Bags &c., 508 Main

Kallmeyer Geo. H. boots and shoes 357- Main
Kallmeyer Hermann, boots and shoes 255 Richmond
Kallmeyer Louis, cigar mkr. 14 Orchard
Kally Wm., lab., 207 W. 9th w. of Central Av
Kalmear Mary, servt., 457 Broadway
Kalnsberg Hy., dray, e.s Fountain, b. Rice and Alexander
Kaltebrunn Anthony, lab., 65 Buckeye
Kaltenbach Heronomus, wagon mkr., 56 13th
Kaltenbach Martin, 54 Ham. Road
Kaltenbach Mathias, 54 Ham. Road
Kaltenbach Moses, blksmith, wks. Chas. Behlen & Co's
Kaltenbach Rosalie, 56 Ham. Road
Kalthoff Hy. W., teamster, 723 Race
Kalthoff Harmon, 140 Green
Kalthoff Herman H., blksmith, n.e.c. Pleasant and Green
Kambhaus Wm., carp., 572 Race
Kamfer Barney, lab., 674 Central Av
Kamm Chas., wks. 8 W. 6th
Kamm Dani., cab. mkr. 126 Clay
Kamman Frank H. B., lab. 103 Clark
Kammann Francis, mason, 102 Bremen
Kammann Frank, eng., 24 Orchard
Kammann Frank, turner, 52 Laurel
Kammunn Fred.. cooper. 181 York
Kammann Hy., mason, 484 Elm
Kammann Hy. W., dry goods, 499 Vine
Kammerer David, 11 Dunlap
Kammerer Joseph butcher, 486 Walnut
Kammerling Fred., baker, 542 Main
Kamp Bernard C., shoe mkr., wks. s.e.c Main and 6th
Kamp Chas., molder, 179 W. 2d
Kamp Frank. lab. 81 Martin
Kamp Frederick, lab., bds. 14 13th
Kamp Gerhard H., boots & shoes, 124 W. 3d
Kamp Joseph, lab., 118 Abigail
Kamp Joseph, salesman, 427 Freeman
Kamp Peter, blksmith, 150 W. Court, w. of Central Av., h. 14 Rittenhouse
Kampe Chas. A., clk., n.e.c. 4th and Main, bds. 109 W. 3d
Kampe Fred, tailor, 109 W. 3d
Kampe Hy., tailor, 549 Race
Kampel Wm. L., tailor, s.w.c. Race and Elder
Kamper Eliza, n.s. Sloo e. of Harriet
Kamper Hermon D., cooper, 563 Walnut
Kamper John, cooper, n.e.c. Logan and Green
Kamphouse Joseph, lab., 103 Woodward
Kamphus Geo., lab., 422 Sycamore
Kamping Bernard, molder, 66 Spring
Kamping Caroline, servt., 341 George
Kamping John A., teacher, 397 Elm
Kampman Geo , box mkr., wks. Livingston near Linn
Kampman Hy., 40 Rittenhouse
Kampman Jacob, hinge fitter, wks n.e.c Walnut and Canal
Kampmann Geo., 84 Melancthon
Kampmayer, & Bro., (John & Henry,) chair factory, 175 Clinton ton
Kampmayer Hy., (K. & Bro.) 175 Clin-

Kampmayer John, (K. & Bro.) 175 Clinton
Kamp Louis, barber, bds. 379 W. 3d
Kanalty Thos., lab., 435 W. 3d
Kandel Hy, varnisher, 97 Buckeye
Kane Bart, (Howdon & Co.) 233 Hopkins
Kane Ellen, servt., Dennison House
Kane Jane, 250 Walnut
Kane John, lab, 198 Culvert
Kane John D., printer, 332 W. 9th
Kane Kate. servt, 100 E. 4th
Kane Louis lab, 109 Mulberry
Kane Margaret. candy &c., 108 E. 5th h 28 Lock
Kane Michael, hostler, 138 George
Kane Nancy 493 W. 3d
Kane Patrick, lab., e.s. Anderson b. 2d and Pearl
Kane Thos., 223 John
Kane Thos.. caulker. rear 970 E. Front
Kaneridge Patrick, lab. s.s. 6th b. Broadway and Culvert
Kanett Michael, 197 Goose al. b. Liberty and Green
Kaney Thos., lab., 462 W. 5th
Kanicke Hy., tinner, 531 Sycamore
Kanickmaer Ernst, coachman, 384 W. 6th
Kannay Stephens, lab., bds. e.s. Central Av. b. 12 and 14th
Kant Thos., 357 cooper Broadway
Kants Philip, stone cutter, 76 W. Liberty
Kaper Jacob, upholsterer, h. 68 Wade
Kaper Peter, scroll mkr., 251 Laurel
Kapp Hy., cooper, 548 Race
Kapp John carp., 522 Main
Kappel Adam, 596 Central Av
Kappel John A., cof. h., 259 Everett
Kappes Peter, cab. mkr., 512 Vine
Karb Conrad, lab., 464 E. Front
Karch John, lab, 661 Race
Karcher Sophia, 165 Ham. Road
Karcuk Herman, hinge moulder, wks. n e.c Walnut and Canal
Karger, Zacariah, printer. 687 Sycamore
Karhof Gerhard, lab. 599 Race
Karhof Barney, lab., wks. 600 W. 5th
Karhoff Geo., finisher, wks. 55 E. 5th
Karhoff Hy., lab., 114 Abigail
Karl Mary, servt, 389 Vine
Karl Wm., clk., 265 Ham. Road
Karle Catharine, seamstress. 688 Main
Karle Xavier, rag dealer, 605 Race
Karls Herman, 170 Ham. Road
Karlsruher & Adler, (Hirsh K. & Bernhard A.), paper dealers. 344 Walnut
Karlsruher Hirsh, (K. & Adler,) 86 W. 9th
Karman Andrew, cof. h., s.e.c. Cutter and Liberty
Karman Anthony, cof. h., s.w.c. Wade and Central Av
Karman John lab., 196 Clark
Karman Louisa. servt, 340 George
Karnelka Hy., porter, 531 Sycamore
Karnen Rudolph, wks., s.w.c. Vine and Longworth
Karnes Archy, hostler, 524 W. 5th
Karney Ellen, s.s. Poplar b. Linn and John
Karr James, steward Gibson House
KARR Jno., (Fulton & K.) 148 Walnut
Karr Patrick, porter, 389 W. 8th
Karrin Michael, lab., n.s. Cherry al. b. Plum and Central Av
Karrmann —, tailor, 22 Mercer
Karrmann Ferdinand, bk. binder, 95 Dayton
Karrmann Wm. druggist, n.w.c 5th and Smith
Karsh John, Walnut Hills
Kershner Wm. phys., 219 W. 9th, w. of Central Av
Karsker Gerhard H., molder, 136 Pleasant
Karskcr John G., grocery, 144 Pleasant
Karsteng Antony, cab. mkr., n.s. Abigail, b. Sycamore and Broadway
Karthman Barney, carp., 158 E. 5th
Kartmann Deitrich, lab., 43 Race
Kartschoke Henrietta, candy shop, 599 Sycamore
Kasander Jacobus, carp., 26 Clay
Kaschner Peter, lab., 97 Moore,

Kauber Hermann, lab., 138 W. Liberty
Kauber Wm., tailor, 138 W. Liberty
Kauch Lewis, cooper, 21 Bank
Kauder Bernard, lab. 42 Jones
Kauderer Marcus, waiter, Galt House
Kauffman Edward, lab., n s. al. b. Canal and 12th and Vine and Race
Kauffman Geo., lab., wks. 222 E. Front
KAUFFMAN J. & CO., (John K., Geo. F. Eichenlaub & Rudolph Rheinhold), Brewers. 604 Vine
KAUFFMAN John, (J. K. & Co.), 10 Hamer
Kauffman Michael, 69 Wade
Kauffmann Mrs. Caroline, w. s. Pancoast al. b. 7th and 8th
Kauffmann Lewis, millwright, bds. 493 Vine
Kauffmann Mary E., 151 George
Kauffmann Sam'l, (S. Kauffmann & Bro), h. 7 George
Kauffmann S. & Bro., (Sol. K. & Sam'l K.), liquors, 31 Sycamore
Kauffmann Solomon, (S. Kauffmann & Bro.), 195 W. Court
Kaufhold John, painter. al. b. Vine and Walnut and 12th and Mercer
Kaufholdt Barney, lab., wks. n.e.c. Walnut and Canal
Kaufman Barbara, seamstress, 612 Sycamore
Kaufman C. Stoner, phys. 190 Richmond
Kaufman & Fernich, (Marcus K. & Jacob F.), confec., 26 W. 6th
Kaufman Frank, molder, 612 Sycamore
Kaufman H., peddler, 22 Gano
Kaufman Henry, (Rosenfeld & K.), 277 W. 8th
Kaufman Jacob, tinner, 88 Woodward
Kaufman Julius, com. mer., 22 W. Front, h. 51 Longworth
Kaufman Marcus, (K. & Fernich), 26 W. 6th
Kaufman Samuel, mer., 10 George
Kaufmann John, 42 Cross
Kaufmann John, lab., wks. 728 Central Av
Kaufmann Julius, com. mer., 51 Longworth
Kaufmann Mary, 612 Elm
Kaufmann Michael, 10 Hamer
Kaufmann Mina, seamstress, 112 Elm
Kaufmann Valentine, molder, 160 Pleasant
Kaufmann Victor J., finisher, e.s. Vine b. Liberty and Green
Kauper Henry, grocer, n.w.c. Linn and Oliver
Kauper John, shoe mkr., wks. s.w.c. Bremen and Findlay
Kaurs Hermann, cooper, wks. Philip Dagen's
Kaus Adam, (K. & Bachmann), s.e.c. Division and Harrison Pike
Kaus & Bachmann, (Adam K. & John B.), bksmiths, s.e.c. Harrison Pike and Division
Kausmann Henry, cooper, s.e.c. Central Av. and Liberty
Kausmann Herman, cooper, 15 15th
Kauther Bernhard, tailor, 146 Clay
Kauther John. stocking mkr., 345 Main
Kauther Philip J., tailor, 107 Martin
Kauntrup Henry, porter, 139 Baymiller
Kautz Mary, notion store, 650 Central Av
Kautzmann Geo., lab., 62 Ham. Road
Kavanaugh Daniel, lab., 41 Race
Kavanaugh Daniel J., pilot, 23 Richmond
Kavanaugh Edward, bksmith, 202 W. Front
Kavanaugh Ellen, servt., s.w.c. 3d and Broadway
Kavanaugh James, lab., 479 W. 9th w. of Central Av
Kavanaugh John, bksmith, 219 W. Front
Kavanaugh Michael, w.s. Smith b. Longworth and 6th
Kavanaugh Michael, eng., 676 W. Front
KAVANAUGH MICHAEL A., Family Grocery, n.e.c. Hunt and Broadway

Kavanaugh Patrick, n.e.c. Poplar and Western Av
Kavanaugh Patrick, lab., al. b 4th and 5th and Central Av. and John
Kavanaugh Patrick, shoe mkr., bds. 74 Longworth
Kavanaugh Rose, 559 Sycamore
Kavanaugh Thos., hostler, wks. n.w.c. Race, and Longworth
Kavanaugh Thos., lab., 16 Dublin
Kavaney Bartholomew, lab., 16 Lock n. of 8th
Kavaney Thos., lab., 16 Lock n. of 8th
Kavelman Henry, lab., e.s. Ramsey n. of Front
Kaveman Charles, (F. K. & Bro.), 116 Hopkins
Kaveman F. & Bro., (Frederick & Charles). chair manufac., 116 Hopkins
Kavemann Frederick, (F. K. & Bro.), 116 Hopkins
Kaven Gavert, boots and shoes, 222 W. Front
Kaven John, shoe mkr., 223 E 6th
Kaver George, brick mkr., e.s. Garrard n. of Gest
Kay James W., cab. mkr., bds. n.s. 3d 2d door w. of Smith
Kay Mary, bds. w.s. Freeman b. Liberty and Poplar
Kay Richard M., butcher, w.s. Freeman b. Liberty and Poplar
Kay Wm. L., bds. w.s. Freeman b. Liberty and Poplar
Kayler Casper, tailor, s.s. Calhoun b. Clifton Av. and McMillan
Kaylor Daniel, carriage mkr., 144 Baymiller
Kaylor John, 747 Vine
Kaylor John, lab., s.e.c. Liberty and Logan
Kaylor John, shoe mkr., 31 Dunlap
Kealey James, lab., n.s. Friendship al. b. Pike and Butler
Kealin Nicholas, teamster, 256 Carr
Kearns Alexander, porter, Madison House
Kean Andrew, lab., 63 Clay
Kean John, painter, 276 W. 8th
Kean Michael, boot and shoe mkr., 222 Broadway
Keanan James, walter, bds. 59 E. Pearl
Kearney Bridget, servt., Burnet House
Kearney Edward (Turner & K.), 135 W. 4th
Kearney James, lab., 56 Elm
Kearney Michael, huckster. w.s. Central Av. b. 2d and W. W. Canal Basin
Kearney Michael, lab., n.w.c. Dudley and Wade
Kearney Michael, lab., n.s. Wade b. Freeman and Dudley
Kearney Patrick, tailor, s.w.c. 6th and Broadway
Kearney Prudence, 149 George
Kearns John, tailor, 8 W. 3d, h. Covington
Kearns Thomas, lab., 63 Avery
Kearny Bridget, servt., 99 E. 4th
Kearny Patrick, lab., bds., 26 E. 5th
Keas Richard, lab., 115 Martin
Keating Catharine, n.w.c Lock and 6th
Keating Frank J., clk. 325 Central Av., bds. s.e.c. Perry and Plum
Keating James, 47 E. 3d
Keating Julia, servt., w.s. Ludlow b. 3d and 4th
Keating Lawrence, 47 E. 3d
Keating Mary 148 Everett
Kenting Mary, bds. 428 W. 4th
Keating Stephen, tinner, s.w.c. 8th and Sycamore
Keaton Thomas, 106 E. 6th
Keats Thomas, lab., 336 W. 5th
Keavet John, bk. mkr., rear 23 Bank
Kebler John, 4 Miami
KEBLER John, (K., Whitman, & Force) 340 W. 4th
KEBLER, WHITMAN & FORCE, (John K., Henry C. W., Manning F. F.). Attorneys at Law, 11 Masonic Temple
Kebner Xavier, lab., 112 Pleasant
Kech Geo.. blksmith, 96 Ham. Road
Kech John, cab. mkr., rear 14 15th
Kechwebe Nicholas, carp., s.w.c. Linn and Charlotte

186 (KEE) CINCINNATI (KEI) DIRECTORY. (KEL)

Keck Adam, deputy sheriff, res. Spencer tp.
KECK Geo., (K. & Shaffer), 61 W. 8th
Keck Geo., clk., bds. 61 W. 8th
Keck Gustav, copper smith, 57 Allison
Keck Hermann, jewelry, 2 W. 4, h. 530 Walnut
KECK Josiah L., (Keck & Shaffer), 420 W. 9th w. of Central Av
KECK & SHAFFER, (Geo. K., Wm. S., & Josiah L. Keck & Barker B. Palmer), Pork Packers and Com. Merchants, 9 and 11 E. M. Canal
Kecke George, wagon mkr., wks. 109 Hunt
Keckeler Adolphus T., b.k, 200 Vine, h. 324 W. 4th
Keckeler Theo. T., asst. sec'y Cin. Equitable Ins. Co., h. 107 Park
Keddis Samuel, b.k. 103 W. 4th
Kedel Adam, cab. mkr., 59 Allison
Keean Michael, lab., 50 Elm
Keef Maggie, bds. s.w.c. 3d and Mill
Keef Patrick, waiter, Walnut St. House
Keefe Bartholemew O., cutter 106 Pearl, h. 17 Chestnut
Keefe Bridget, 444 W. 3d
Keefe Daniel, lab., e.s. John b. Elizabeth and Chestnut
Keefe Daniel, shoe mkr., 63 E. 8th
Keefe Dennis, eng., 53 E 3d
Keefe Joseph, contractor, 18 Dayton
Keefe Kate, laundress, Spencer House
Keefe Mary, 45 Race
Keefe Pat., waiter, Burnet House
Keefe Wm., bds. Cincinnati House
Keefe Wm., tailor, 52 Main
Keefe Wm., tailor, s.w.c. 3d and Mill
Keefer D., 345 Main
Keefer Geo., blksmith, 24 Hannibal
Keefer Geo., blksmith, 24 Pierson
Keefer Jacob, carpet weaver, w.s. Kilgour nr. 3d
Keefer John, saddler, 89 Main, bds. Cincinnati House
Keefer Samuel, driver, American Exp. Co.
Keefer Wm. M., blksmith, bds. 94 Pierson
Keegan Catharine, 48 Butler
Keegan Jas., grocery, 48 Freeman
Keegan John, carp., 161 Longworth
Keegan John, lab., rear 95 Clark
Keegan John, lab., 171 Water
Keegan John. salesman 200 Main, h. n. w.c. Pearl and Rose
Keegan Matthew, cof. h., 61 Water
Keegan Stephen, shoe mkr., bds. 917 Central Av.
Keehan Michael, lab., w.s. 7th b. Broadway and Sycamore
Keehan Michael, porter, n.w.c. 7th and Broadway
Keehan Thos., 254 W. 7th
Keehner Christopher, butcher. 262 Daymiller
Keel Chas., blksmith, wks. 9 W. 7th
Keelan Mary, servt., 142 E. 5th
Keeland John, lab., bds. n.s. Augusta b. John and Smith
Keeler Alex., collector City Water Works, h. 465 W. 7th
Keeler Andrew, pipe fitter, wks. n.e.c. Walnut and Canal
KEELER ISAAC M., Dealer in Stoves and Hollow Ware, 13 and 15 W. 5th, h. 253 W. 7th
Keeler Nelson. blksmith, wks. n.e.c. Canal and Walnut
Keeler Susan S., 299 W. 5th
KEELER WM. HENRY, Newspaper Depot, 504 W. Front, h. 164 Broadway
Keeller Sarah, 212 Findlay
Keelor John, blksmith, wks. n.e.c. Walnut and Canal
Keelty Thos., huckster, w s. Langdon al. b. 6th and 7th
Keely Ann, 64 Richmond
Keely Catharine, servt., 380 W. 6th
Keely Julia, 299 W. 5th
Keely Margaret, servt., 423 W. 6th
Keen Dudley M. 1., salesman 113 W. Pearl, bds. 187 George
Keen J. M, clk., bds. Henrie House
Keenan Bridget, servt., 110 E. 4th

Keenan Chas., bk. binder, 1 New
Keenan Jerry C., finisher, 385 Vine
Keenan John, w.s. Stone al. b. 5th and Longworth
Keenan John, lab., at 625 Freeman
Keenan Lawrence, 243 W. Front
Keenan Mary, 1 New
Keenan Newton E., photographer, 100 W. 4th
Keenan Nicholas, cof. h., n.e.c. Richmond and John
Keenan Pat. J., saddler, bds. 186 Race
Keenan Rosa Ann, bds. 207 Everett
Keene John M., clk. 105 W. Pearl, bds. Henrie House
Keene Lewis, finisher, 564 E. Front
Keeni John, lab., wks. 222 E. Front
Keeper Chas., cab. mkr., wks. 71 W. 5th
Keeper Jacob, cab. mkr., wks. 71 W. 5th
Keese Michael, shoe mkr., Mt. Adams
Keeshan Ann, s.s. 6th b. Broadway and Culvert
KEESHAN EDWARD, Family Grocery, n.e.c. 9th and Elm, h. 153 W. 9th
Keeshan John, druggist, n.w.c. Walnut and 6th, h. 140 W. 8th
Keeshan John, huckster, 119 Hopkins
Keeshan Michael F., clk., 119 Hopkins
Keever L. C., b.k. 70 Vine, h. 154 Broadway
Kefakurdas Theodore, harness mkr., 186 Hopkins
Keffe Dennis, lab., 398 Broadway
Kuffman Hamer, lab., wks. 114 W. Court
Kegan James, lab., n.s. Pearl b. Smith and Park
Kegan Patrick, Commerce b. Race and and Elm
Kegan Patrick, cooper, rear 194 E. 6th
Kegan Thomas, lab., wks. s.w.c. Broadway and 5th
Kegan Wm., fb, 22 Commerce
Kegbert Anna, w.s. Harriet b. 6th and Sloo
Kegel Elizabeth. landress, 486 Walnut
Kegel Helena, laundress, 486 Walnut
KEHLENBACH WM., Produce Exchange and Dealer in Liquors, Cheese, &c., 418 Main c. Court
Kehn Augusta, 49 Bremen
Kehna Hy., 524 John
Kehoan Hy., clk., 193 Baymiller
Kehnan Stephen, dray, 193 Baymiller
Kehoe Dennis, distiller, wks. Foots, Nash & Co.'s
Kehoe John, boatman, 46 E. 8th e. of Lock
Kehoe Michael, dray, 62 Melancthon
Kehoe Patrick, lab., wks. 45 E. 4th
Kehoe Patrick, plumber, 59 E. 7th
Kehoe Thos., dray, s.w.c. Wade and Central Av.
Kehr Elizabeth, 109 Ham. Road
Kehr Mary, 247 Ham. Road
Kehrstein Mary, e.s. Goose al. b. Green and Elder
Kehsen Hy., feed store, 1114 Central Av.
Keibler Gottlieb, baker, 302 Broadway
Keidel Wm. H., grocery, 606 Race
Keif Arthur, lab., n.s. Patterson al. b. Main and Walnut
Keifel Frederick, pattern mkr., 406 Sycnmore
Keifer Jacob, carpet weaver, e.s. Kilgour b. 3d and 5th
Keifer Michael, cook, 59 E. Pearl
Keifer Samuel, driver, 174 E. Pearl e. of Broadway
Keifer.Wm., clk. s e.c. Vine and Pearl, bds. 315 W. 6th
Keil Geo., huckster, 460 Main
Keil John, tailor, 90 Peets
Keily Ann, servt., 107 Clinton
Keimel Michael, mill stone mkr., 286 Water
Kein Geo., chair mkr., n.s. Front e. of Kelly
Kein John, tailor, 37 Moore
Keiner Geo., locksmith, bds. 622 Vine
Keiselkamp Frederick, lab., 491 Race
Kaiser Anthony, cof. h., 65 Wade
Keiser C., lab., wks. 13 E. Front
Keiser Coleman, baker, bds. 470 Main
Keiser Conrad, stone mason, 559 Vine

Keiser David, teamster, 9 Pendleton
Keiser Diedrich, cigar mkr., s.w.c. Cutter and Melancthon
Keiser Frederick P., tailor, 54 Ham. Road
Keiser Hy., cigar mkr., bds. s.w.c. Cutter and Melancthon
Keiser Hy., lab., 138 W. Liberty
Keiser Herman. cab. mkr., 367 Cutter
Keiser Jane 65 Abigail
Keiser John F., lab., 277 Broadway
Keiser Mary, 91 Dudley
Keisler Mark, baker, wks. 118 W. 5th
Keisweitter Godfreid, tailor, 222 W. 6th
Keiter Hy., lab., s.w.c. Abigail and Spring
Keith Albert, express driver, 85 Pleasant
Keith Charlotte, 467 W. 9th w. of Central Av.
Keith Daniel, driver, 88 Freeman
Keith Francis, 104 George
Keith Ishmael, 87 Pleasant
Keith J. M., canvasser, bds. Henrie House
Keith Robert, fish and game, 81 W. 5th, h. 45 Everett
Keith Wm. B., clk., bds. 45 Everett
Kelber Michael, 66 Dunlap
Kelbert Herman, saloon, s.w.c. Gest and Harriet
Kelee Harry, painter, 244 Elm
Keleher Matthew, lab., 26 Brighton
Kelevorn Hy., mason, 392 Broadway
Keliher Patrick, lab., 130 Central Av.
Kelker Catharine, 56 Martin
Kelkerstein Edward, lab., 33 Lock n. of 6th
Kellar Hy., miller, rear 61 Abigail
Kellar Wm. C., salesman Bantlin and Compton's, res. West Fairmount
Keller Adam, grinder, 118 Pleasant
Keller Adam A., cab. mkr., 104 Avery
Keller Anthony, grinder, 129 Bremen
Keller August, tailor, 123 Mohawk
Keller Bernard, lab., w.s. Campbell al. b. Elder and Findlay
Keller Catharine, seamstress, rear e.s. Plum b. Adams and Liberty
Keller Chas., soap mkr., wks. 729 Central Av.
Keller Chas. J., dyer, 407 Elm
Keller Ellen, servt., 182 Broadway
Keller Francis P., cab. mkr., n.e.c. Water and Smith
Keller Frank, butcher. h. 168 Clay
Keller Frederick, cooper, 225 Cutter
Keller Hy., lab., w.s. Goose al. b. Green and Elder
Keller Hy., tailor, 61 15th
Keller Jacob, dyer, rear 543 Main
Keller Johanna, nurse, 432 W. 4th
Keller John, lab , 41 Ham. Road
Keller John, lab., 337 Ham. Road
Keller John, lab., 87 Martin
Keller John, saddler, bds. 674 W. 6th
Keller John, stone cutter, 27 Mercer
Keller John C., steward, n.e.c. 3d and Lock
Keller Joseph, 33 Dunlap
Keller Lewis, cook, 11 Mary
Keller Nicholas, shoe mk., 186 W. Court w. of Central Av.
Keller Patrick, lab., wks. n.s. Front b. Lawrence and Pike
Keller Rebecca, 49 Plum
Keller Rebecca, 16 Race
Keller Samuel. cap mkr., n.s. Browne b. Ham. Road and Mohawk, h. 102 Ham. Road
Keller Stephen, watch mkr., 43 W. Court
Keller Valentine, cof. h., e.s. Vine, b. Auburn Av. and Calhoun
Kellerman Joseph, teamster, 558 W. 8th
Kellermann Henry, lab., 625 Main
Kelley Amos, turner, s.w.c. Harriet and W. W. Canal
Kelley Ann, servt., Burnet House
Kelley Ann, 3 E. 7th
Kelley Mrs. Ann, 299 Plum
Kelley Antony, dray, 148 Water
Kelley Burney, porter, 58 W. 5th
Kelley Bernard, n.s. 6th, b. Culvert and Broadway
Kelley Catharine, s.e.s. 7th and Broadway

Kelley Charles, optician, 198 W. Front
Kelley Daniel, lab., 14 Plum
Kelley Daniel F, b.k., bds. 157 Elm
Kelley Edward, lab., 544 Race
Kelley Edward, lab., e. s. Ludlow b. 3d and Pearl
Kelley Edward A., teamster, bds. 270 Everett
Kelley Erastus, fireman, 88 Longworth
Kelley Frank, lab., n. w. c. Front and Vance
Kelley Geo. A, clk., Geo. R. Dickson & Co.'s, bds. Dennison House
Kelley Hugh, stone yard, n. e. c. 2d and Central Av
Kelley J., bds. Dennison House
Kelley James, b.k., bds. 210 Sycamore
Kelley James, dray, 24 Commerce
Kelley Jas., lab., 658 W. Front
Kelley Jas., lab., 62 Gano
Kelley Jas. T., dray, bds. 29 Mill
Kelley Jane, 69 Richmond
Kelley John, 149 John
Kelley John, 97½ Central Av
Kelley John, cab mkr., 149 John
Kelley John, lab., wks. 267 W. 5th
Kelley John, lab. 124 E 8th
Kelley John, stone cutter, 9 Park
Kelley John G., grocery, n.w.c. John and Court
Kelley John M., bds. 29 Mill
Kelley John, bar k., U. S. Hotel
Kelley Joseph, lumber, bds. 22 Home
Kelley Margaret, servt., 163 E. 3d
Kelley Martin, grocery, n.e.c. Linn and Poplar [12th]
Kelley Martin, lab., s. e. c. Walnut and Plum
Kelley Martin, lab., n. e. c. Walnut and Plum
Kelley Martin, mach., 177 W. Front
Kelley Michael, boots and shoes, 152 E. 6th
Kelley Michael, carp., 40 Linn
Kelley Michael, tailor, 33 E. 3d
Kelley Morris, conductor, 132 Baymiller
Kelley Nathaniel, shoe mkr., 103 Clark
Kelley Owen, eng., 77 Plum
Kelley Patrick, box mkr., 49 Plum
Kelley Patrick, dray, 47 Betts
Kelley Patrick, hostler, bds. w. s. Lawrence b. 4th and 5th
Kelley Phillip, n.s. Cherry al. b. Plum and Central Av
Kelley Rossanna, n.s. Goodloe b. Willow and Leatherbury
Kelley Rose, 77 Plum
Kelley Sarah, servt., 115 Pike
Kelley Thomas, b.k., 151 Sycamore
Kelley Thomas, lab., 29 Mill
Kelley Thomas, lab., wks. 375 W. 3d
Kelley Wm., cof. h., 30 Water
Kelley Wm., dray, wks. n.w.c. Freeman and 9th
Kelley Wm., lab., 58 Pike
Kelley Wm. F., b k., P. Andrew & Co's, h. 123 Cutter
Kelley Wm G., bds. 397 W. 4th
Kelliner Fred., butcher, n. s. Rice. near Fountain
Kellogg Chas. H. jr., clk., 19 W, 2d, h. 190 E. 4th
Kellogg C. W., liquor mer., bds. Spencer House
Kellogg Chas. F., w.s. Ohio Av., b. Calhoun and North Elm
Kellogg Eleanor, teacher 435 Broadway
Kellogg Elizabeth, 435 Broadway
Kellum Mrs. Catharine, 8 Wilson
Kelly —, clk., bds. 61 E. Pearl
Kelly Mrs., 366 Sycamore
Kelly Mrs., 576 E. Front
Kelly Ann, seamstress, wks. 53 W. 4th
Kelly Ann, 36 W. Court w. of Central Av
Kelly Ann, h. 65 Vine
Kelly B rtholomew, foreman, n. w. c. Front and Kelly
Kelly Bridget, Torrence nr. Front
Kelly Bridget, servt., 333 Longworth
KELLY & BRITT, (Nathan D. K. & Nelson A. B.,) Architects and Builders, Office 75 and 77 W. 3d, shop n e.c. Richmond and Linn
Kelly Catharine, 89 E. Front
Kelly Chas., expressman, bds. 201 W. 9th

Kelly Charles spectacle mkr., 198 W. Front
KELLY CHAS. J., Marble Works, s.e.c. Linn and Hopkins, bds. 123 Linn
Kelly Denis, harness mkr., wks., 208 Main
Kelly Edward, carp., 198 Linn
Kelly Edward, lab., 80 Gest
Kelly Edward G., clk., 47 Ellen
Kelly Ellas, 158 W. 6th
Kelly Elias, steersman, 104 George
Kelly Elizabeth, nurse, n. w. c. 3d and Ludlow
Kelly Ellen, 48 E. 7th
Kelly Erastus, pipeman, cor. Longworth and Elm
Kelly Ewing, stone cutter, 9 Park
Kelly Frances, 373 W. 7th
Kelly Francis, shoe mkr., 130 W. Front
Kelly Harriet, laundress, 212 Central Av
Kelly Henry, eng., n.s. Friendship al. b. Pike and Butler
KELLY HUGH, Stone Cutter and Steam Saw Mill, n.s. 2d bet. Plum and Central Av., h. 9 Park
Kelly James, carp , 197 Cutter
Kelly James, clk., 152 W. Front
Kelly James, dray, n. s. al. b. Pike and Lawrence and 3d and 4th
Kelly James, finisher, 137 Linn
Kelly Jas , lab., 254 Water
Kelly Jas. C., clk., wks. s.w.c. Elm and Water
Kelly James W. B., china, &c., 123 W. 5th, bds. 125 W. 5th
Ke'ly Jane, 65 Vine
Kelly John, dray, n. e. c. Baymiller and Richmond
Kelly John, lab., wks. Chamberlain & Co.'
Kelly John, lab., s.s. Arch, b. Ludlow & Lawrence
Kelly John, lab , w.s. Central Av. b. W. W. Canal and 3d
Kelly John, lab., w.s. Langdon al. bet. 6th and 7th
Kelly John, lab., n.s. 6th b. Horn and Mill Creek
Kelly John, saddler, bds. 309 Main
Kelly John R., carp., 343 W. 7th
Kelly Joseph, baker, w.s Langdon al.b. 6th and 7th
Kelly Joseph M., b.k., 24 E. 3d, h. Covington
Kelly M., mach., wks. John Michell's
Kelly Margaret, 65 Barr
Kelly Maria, chambermaid, Dennison House
Kelly Martin. bds. 365 W. 5th
Kelly Mary, 209 Cutter
Kelly Mary, n. s. R. R. e. of Kelly
Kelly Mary, servt., 396 W. 6th
Kelly Mary, servt , 254 W. 3d
Kelly Mary, waiter, Dennison House
Kelly Mathew, grocery, 307 W. 3d
Kelly Michael, gardener, 130 Clark
Kelly Michael, lab., 80 Baymiller
Kelly Michael, lab , 295 E. 6th
Kelly Michael, mach., s.s. al. b. Pike & Lawrence and 3d and Pearl
Kelly Michael, tailor, bds. n.e.c. Elm & Pearl
Kelly Nancy J., h. 274 W. 8th
KELLY Nathan B., (K. & Britt,) 397 W. 4th
Kelly Patrick, 54 E. 3d
Kelly Patrick, blk. smith, 130 Central Av.
Kelly Patrick, dray, 137 W. Front
Kelly Patrick, lab., 249 W. Front
Kelly Patrick, lab., 48 E. Pearl
Kelly Patrick, walter, Burnet House
Kelly Peter, lab., Burnet House
Kelly Sarah, servt., Broadway Hotel
Kelly Solomon, barber, Clifton House, h. 120 E. 6th
Kelly Thomas, clk., 151 Sycamore
Kelly Thomas, lab., h. n.w.c. Vine and 2d
Kelly Thomas, lab., 35 E. 8th e. of Lock
Kelly Winnifred, servt., 110 E. 4th
Kelly Wm., teamster, 576 E. Front
Kelly Wm F., b.k., 123 Cutter
Kelly Wm. G., student, bds. 397 W. 4th

Kelly Wm. J., b.k., 37 Main, h. Covington
Kelner Christina, 604 Elm
Kelpan James, driver, 188 Betts
Kelpen John D., carp.; 314 Plum
Kelpen Thos., carp , 314 Plum
Kelsall Thos., school furniture manufac. s.s. George b. Baymiller and Freeman, h. n.w.c. 7th and Baymiller
Kelsch Joseph, lab., 112 Ham. Road
Kelsch Michael, lab., 538 Plum
Kelsey B. W., commissary, bds. s. w. c. Race and 3d
Kelsh George, policeman, 121 Linn
Kelsh John, fireman, n.s. Buckeye bet. Poplar and Locust
Kelshaw John, boiler mkr., 465 W. 6th
Kelso Stephen, yard master O. & M. R. R., 92 Carr
Koltenburg Caroline, 361 W. 8th
Keltharter Henry, turner, 49 W. 15th
Keltz Frederick, lab., 293 Linn
Keltz Henry, shoe mkr., s.s. Montgomery Pike, nr. Madison Road
Kemann John. n.e c. Elm and Court
Kember Henry C., carp., e.s. Hand al. b. Court and Clark
Kemenic Henry, lab., 99 Pendleton
Kemerlin Frederick, baker, 542 Main
Kemerling Frederick, tailor, 507 Walnut
Kemker Henry, foreman, 143 Abigall
Kemme Henry, soap factory. e.s. Western Av., b. Dayton and Bank
Kemmer Ferdinand, porter, 115 Woodward
Kemmer Joseph, pipe fitter, h. s. w. c. Pendleton and Woodward
Kemmerer Benedict, lab., 48 Ham. Road
Kemna Hy., boots and shoes, 412 W. 3d
Kemp Philip, lab., 11 Mary
Kemp Philip, shoemkr., 538 Plum
Kemper Arnold, lab., 9 Pendleton
Kemper Barney, lab., 385 Broadway
Kemper Bernard, tailor, 11 Budd
Kemper Catharine, 120 W. 5th
Kemper Harmon, cab. mkr., 230 Betts
Kemper Hy., baker, wks. 119 W. 5th
Kemper Hy., peddler, 26 Green
Kemper Hy. J., grainer, 41 Pleasant
KEMPER Hy. L., (Hunter. Edmeston & Co.,) res. E. Walnut Hills
Kemper Hy. W., landscape painter, 25 W. 4th
Kemper Hugh F., (Harvey & K.,) h. Walnut Hills
Kemper James L., salesman, 70 Vine, h. Walnut Hills
Kemper John, finisher, wks. n e. c. Walnut and Canal
Kemper Joseph, lab., 120 Abigall
Kemper Phillip, tailor, 8 Pleasant
Kemper Samuel, deputy sheriff, 108 E. Liberty
Kemper Theophilus, notary public, 8 E. 2d
KEMPER WASHINGTON, Plumber and Lead Pipe Manufacturer, 230 Main, h. cor. Hathaway and Windsor, Walnut Hills
Kemper Wm., lab., 152 Baymiller
Kempf Charles. 566 Elm
Kempf Joseph, shoemkr, 538 Plum
Kempf Laurence, porter, 314 Longworth
Kempfer Antony, manuf. stomach bitters. 403 W. 8th
Kemphaus Joseph, lab., 103 Woodward
Kempheil H., lab., wks. Chamberlain & Co.'s
Kemphouse Joseph, wood yard, h. 560 W. 5th
Kempig B., molder, wks. Chamberlain & Co.'s
Kempner John, cab. mkr. 136 Bremen
Kems John H., lab., 15 Green
Kempus Adam, lab., 63 Clay
Kempus Frank, grocery, 250 Clark
Kendall Charles, baker, bds. 172 Sycamore
Kendall Chas. F., carp., 1089 E. Front
Kendall David H., steward, 211 Water
Kendall Ellen F., teacher, 120 John
Kendall Fanny, 59 Gano
Kendall Franklin, eng., bds. 35 Hathaway
Kendall Geo., blksmith, 468 W. 3d

Kendall Henry, varnisher, 97 Buckeye
KENDALL Hy. H., (Rowe & K.,) 22 Rittenhouse
K ndall Hy. jr., clk., 140 W. 5th, bds. 256 Clark
Kendall John McD., b.k., n w.c. 3d and Main, h. 137 Main
Kendall Luke, 22 Rittenhouse
Kendall Omar H., burning fluid, 98 Betts
Kendall Uzziah, sr., 91 Pleasant
Kendall Uzziah, horse shoe mkr., 693 Central Av., h. 602 Freeman
Kendle Lydia, 71 Baker
Kendy James, lab., e.s. Macalister, b. 4th and 5th
Kenemond Chas., cab. mkr., 636 Main
Kenifech Mrs. Susan, dress mkr., n.e.c. 9th nd John
Kenkel Caspar H., jewelry, 516 Main
Kenkel Clemens, lab., 25 Abigail
Kenkel Clemens, shoemkr. 595 Race
Kenkel Daniel, saloon, 105 E. 2d
Kenkel Theodore, lab., 79 Pendleton
Kenkle John G., jewelry, 550 Central Avenue
Kenler Michael, cof. h., 482 Linn
Kennady John, lab., E. 3d, nr. c. of Hill
Kennard Franklin, 188 W. Court
Kenne Frank, lab., bds. 60 Hunt
Kenneally Mrs. M. E., dress mkr., 112 W. 4th
Kenneally Patrick, confec., 122 Central Avenue
Kenneally Wm H., 137 W. 9th
Kennedy Albert, auctioneer, 138 Clay
Kennedy Andrew, porter, s.e.c. 4th and Vine, h. 30 E. 4th
Kennely Bridget, 15 Water
Kennedy Catharine, servt., 350 W. 7th
Kennedy Catharine, washwoman, 431 George
Kennedy Chas., 237 Findlay
Kennedy Daniel, lab., 20 E. 8th, e. of Lock
Kennedy Daniel, tailor, 163 Central Av
Kennedy Dennis, lab., 330 W. 6th
Kennedy Ellen, servt., 346 W. 7th
Kennedy Geo. W., carp., 231 John, bds. 55 Sycamore
Kennedy Hy. P., produce, 31 Vine, h. 249 Laurel
Kennedy James, w.s. Miami Canal, b. 6th and 8th
Kennedy James, butcher, bds. w.s. Lock, b. 8th and Court
Kennedy James, driver, 48 Freeman
Kennedy James, grocery, 54 E. 8th, e. of Lock [Central Av
Kennedy James, lab., bds. c. Pearl and
Kennedy James, lab., 199 Cutter
Kennedy James, lab., 12 Kossuth
Kennedy James, porter, 54 E. 8th
Kennedy James, sawyer, 199 Cutter
Kennedy Johanna, 227 Cutter
Kennedy Julia n l., servt, 86 E. 4th
Kennedy John, dray, 30 E. 7th
Kennedy John, teamster, w.s. Central Av., b. 2d and W.W. Canal Basin
Kennedy John, walter, Clifton House
Kennedy John, walter, Burnet House
Kennedy Joseph, eng., 413 W. Front
Kennedy Joseph, lab., 37 Mill
Kennedy Joseph, shoemkr, bds. Indiana House
Kennedy Joseph F., shoemkr, bds. 159 W 5th
KENNEDY Lewis, (J. M. McCullough & Son,) bds. s.e.c. 3d and Broadway
Kennedy Margaret, 27 E. 8th
Kennedy Margaret, cof. h., 117 Sycamore
Kennedy Margaret, servt., 560 W. 9th
Kennedy Martha, bds. 135 Central Av
Kennedy Mary, 99 E. 2d
Kennedy Mary, 108 Vanhorne
Kennedy Mary. 61 Mill
Kennedy Mary, servt., 103 Broadway
Kennedy Mary, servt , 386 George
Kennedy Michael, 50 New
Kennedy Michael, cof. h., 111 W. 3d
Kennedy Michael, lab., wks. 333 W. Front
Kennedy Michael, lab , 40 Elisabeth
Kennedy Michael, marble cutter, wks. n.e.c. Elm and Canal
Kennedy Michael, tailor, e.s. Haven al., b. 8th and 9th

Kennedy Nicholas, butcher, 23 State
Kennedy Owen, e.s. M. Canal, b. 8th and Court
Kennedy Owen, lab., 100 Race
Kennedy Owen, walter, Burnet House
Kennedy Patrick, clk., 433 W. 2d
Kennedy Patrick, clk., 150 E. 5th
Kennedy Patrick, grocery, 217 E. 6th
Kennedy Patrick, lab., 40 Elizabeth
Kennedy Patrick, lab., 435 W. 3d
Kennedy Patrick, lab., 18 Ludlow
Kennedy Patrick, lab., 34 Butler
Kennedy Patrick, lab., w.s. Central Av. b. W.W. Canal Basin and 2d
Kennedy Patrick, lab., s.e.c. 5th and Smith
Kennedy Patrick, lab., w.s. Whittaker, nr. Front
Kennedy Peter, bds. 1026 Central Av
Kennedy Robert, sexton, n.s. 4th, b. Main and Walnut
Kennedy Sallie, e.s. Crippen al., b. 7th and 8th.
Kennedy Stephen, lab., 30 Lock
Kennedy Thomas, butcher, bds w s. Lock, b. 8th and Court
Kennedy Thomas, lab., 61 Butler
Kennedy Thos., lab., bds. n.w.c. Mill and Front
Kennedy Thos., lab., s.s. 6th, b. Broadway and Culvert
Kennedy Thomas, lab., 99 E. 2d
Kennedy Thomas, lab., s.w.c. Central Av. and W.W. Canal
Kennedy Thomas, wks. J. Whitaker's, Deer Creek Valley
Kennedy Timothy, lab., 99 E. 2d
KENNEDY WARREN, Bookseller and Stationer, 160 Vine, bds. 172 Vine
Kennedy Wm., butcher, 32 Lock, n. of 8th
Kennedy Wm., dray, bds. Pennsylvania Hotel
KENNEDY Wm. B., (Baldwin & Co.,) 73½ Betts
Kennedy Wm. J , clk., bds. 330 W. 6th
Kennel Obadiah G., tinner, bds 196 Race
Kennell George. hose al. 1 belt manuf., 19 W. Front, h. Covington
Kennely Patrick, blksmith. n.s. W.W. Canal, b. Central Av and John, h. 122 Central Avenue
Kennely Patrick, cooper, 37 W. 9th, w. of Central Avenue
Kennett Charles, cof. h., 619 Elm
Kennett Hy. G., 28 Macfarland
KENNETT JOHN, Wholesale Tobacco and Cigars, 14 Public Landing, h. Newport, Ky
Kenneweg Christ., cigar mkr., 80 Milton
Kenney Cornelius, lab., 153 Cutter
Kenney David, white washer, 200 Webb
Kenney Elizabeth, bds. n.e.c. 3d and Central Av
Kenney Frank. lab., bds. n.w.c. Mill and Front
Kenney John, plumber, 138 George
Kenney John, printer, 421 W. 4th
Kenney Martin, blksmith, 438 W. 2d
Kenney Mary A., tailoress, bds. 123 Vanhorn
Kenney Moses, 65 W, 7th.
Kenney Robert A., lab., n.s. Pearl, b. Butler and Pike
Kenney Wm., s.w.c. Pearl and Butler
Kenney Wm., watchman, 38 E. 8th, e. of Lock
Kenning Anthony, tailor, 96 W. Court
Kenning Joseph, cigar mkr., 96 W. Court
Kenning Mary, saleswoman, 96 W. Court
Kenny Mrs., 305 Water
Kenny Rev. Dennis, 'St. Xavier College, w.s. Sycamore, b. 6th and 7th
Kenny Edward, cof. h., 740 W. 9th
Kenny John, silver plater, 65 W. 4th, h. 47 Betts
Kenny Margaret, 221 Central Av
Kenny Patrick, lab., 3 Oliver
Kenny Patrick, tailor, bds. s.w.c. 5th and Broadway
Kenny Thomas, lab , w.s. Anderson al. b. 3d and Pearl
Kensch John, tailor, 38 Buckeye
Kent Andrew, molder, 650 Central Av

Kent Edward, huckster, 17 Jordan
Kent John, fireman, 606 E. Front
Kent Ellen, 1 New
Kent John, porter, e.s. Kilgour b. 3d & 5th
KENT LUKE, Dealer in Watches, Jewelry, &c., s w.c. 6th and Main, h. 133 Richmond
Kent Thomas R., carp., 20 Lodge, h. 91 E. 5th
Kent Thomas, cooper, 357 Broadway
Kent Thomas, foreman, 214 W. Court w. of Central Av
Kent Thomas, huckster, 17 Jordan
KENT Wm. (Wm. K. & Co.) 126 W. 5th
Kent Wm., molder, 650 Central Av
KENT WM. & CO. Dealers in Boots and Shoes, 126 W. 5th
Kentner Burgia, 481 W. 5th
Kentner Frederick, clock mkr., 478 W. 5th
Kentner Michael, weaver, 478 W. 5th
Kentrup Hy., polisher, 97 Buckeye
Kentrop Hy., porter, 139 Baymiller
Kenyon Martha. bds. 115 Broadway
Kenzel Ferdinand, driver, 198 Linn
Keoff Hy., lab., wks. 222 E. Front
Keolmell V., porter, 97 Buckeye
Keon John, lab., 436 Linn
Keon Margaret, 414 Smith
Keon Michael, 114 Smith
Keonig Charles, butcher, 708 Vine
Keopher Augustus, scissors mkr., bds. 347 Walnut
Keough Bridget, bds. s.w.c. 5th and B'd-way
Keough Mary, bds. s.w.c. 5th and Br'd-way
Keough Timothy, walter, Spencer House
Keown Daniel, lab., s.s. Phoebe al. b. Plum and Central Av
Keown James, horse farrier, 136 W. Front
Keown & Manly, (Michael K. & Wm. M.) saloon, n.e.c. Front and Broadway
Keown Michael (K & Manly) 114 Smith
Kepp August. cigar mkr., b 330 Walnut
Kephart Maria, nurse, bds. 462 George
Keppel Caroline, servt., 379 Vine
Keppenbrock Bernard, painter, n.w.c. Broadway and Wood
Keppler Geo., confec., 253 W. 4th
Keppler Jacob, salesman, 11 E. 9th, b. 263 W. Court w. of Central Av
Keppler Ludwig, shoemkr., 20 Webster
Kepple Michael, butcher. e s. Lebanon Road nr. Montgomery Turnpike
Keppler Wm., confec., bds 253 W 4th
KEPPNER L. A., Shirt Manufacturer and Gents' Furnishing Goods, 107 W. 6th, h Ludlow, O.
Keramig Franz. cof. h., 578 Walnut
Kerbert Hermon, feed store, s.w.c. Gest and Harriet
Kercher Chas., brewer, 95 Buckeye
Kerchner George, teamster. 192 Clinton
Kerdolff John A., meats, 360 George, h. 153 George
Kerger Andreas, baker, n.s. Cassatt al. b. Sycamore and Main
Kerhof Barney, lab., 275 Betts
Kerk Louis, tailor, 282 W. Liberty
Kerke August, lab., 165 Oliver
Kerkling Hy., cab. mkr., 100 Buckeye
Kerler Matthew, shoemkr, bds. 275 Freeman
Kern Ann K., midwife, 217 Linn
Kern Geo., brewer, n.s. Augusta b. John and Smith
Kern Frank, grocery, 694 Central Av
Kern John, carp., 65 David
Kern John, saloon, bds. 273 Walnut
Kern Leonard, tailor, 26 Pleasant
Kern Michael, lab., n.s. Cassatt al. b. Sycamore and Main
Kern Paul, e s. Baymiller b. Wade and Liberty
Kernan Chas., finisher, wks. n.e.c. Walnut and Canal
Kerner Christian, finisher, 118 Bremen
Kernebeck Wm., cooper e.s. Western Av. b. Bank and Harrison Pike
Kernen Gottlieb, attendant, bds. 14 E. 6th

(KES) CINCINNATI (KIB) DIRECTORY. (KIL) 189

Kernen John, blksmith, bds. s e.c. Harrison Pike and Brigton
Kerner Frederick, cooper, 11 Mohawk
Kerner John, baker, 8 Walnut
Kerner Wm., lab., 76 Mohawk
Kerney Francis, shoemkr, 221 George
Kerney John H., grocery, n.e.c. 3d and Stone
Kerney Mary, 456 W. 5th
Kernig Joseph, lab., 191 Hopkins
Kerns Rosina, 961 Central Av
Kerr Ellen, teacher, 313 Clark
Kerr George, hats and caps, 92 W. 5th, bds. 110 W. 6th
Kerr James, clk., bds. 389 W. 8th
Kerr Margaret, s.w.c. Vine and Findlay
Kerr Patrick, clk., bds. 389 W. 8th
Kerr Robert H., dept. sheriff, 325 Elm
KERR Wm. H., asst. prosecuting atty., Ham. co., h. 273 Richmond
Kerren Thomas, lab., wks. 375 W. 3d
Kerrick Edward, 402 Baymiller
Kerring Caspar, lab., s.w.c. Abigail and Spring
Kerrison Dena, servt., 167 E. 3d
Kerry John, lab., s.s. Pleasant Court e. of Elm
Kersey Ely C., cooper, 49 12th
Kershermau Michael, lab., 293 Freeman
Kerwker Hy., porter, s.e.c. Green and Pleasant
Kerstiens Herman, blksmith, 546 Sycamore
Kerstiens John H., blksmith, 546 Sycamore
Kerstig Bernhard, tanner, e.s. Goose al. b. Green and Elder
Kersting Bernard, tanner, s.s. Findlay b. Elm and Plum
Kersting Hy. J., policeman, 5 12th
Kerstner Ulrich, lab., bds n.s. 6th b. Canal and Freeman
Kerth Miss ——, actress, National Theater
Kerth George, e s. Clarkson b. Central Av. and Bank
Kerwa John M., lab., 225 W. Front
Kerwalt Charles, finisher, wks. C. T. Dumont's
Kerwick Patrick, box mkr., 330 W. 6th
Kerwin Ann, servt., 111 Pike
Kerwin Mich., waiter, Burnet House
Kerwin Wm., lab., 25 Webb
Keshan John, lab., w.s. Reading Road, nr. Montgomery Turnpike
Keskar Fred., tailor, s.e.c. Young and Ringgold
Kesker Hy., lab., 369 Broadway
Kesker John G., grocery, s.e.c. Pleasant & Green
Kesley Ellen, servt., 114 E. 3d
Kessel Christian, tanner, 246 Bremen
Kesselring Martin, tannery, 64 Bank
Kessen Geo., tailor, 148 Hopkins
Kessen Hermann, jr., chair mkr., 304 Water
Kessen J., Herman, chair mkr., 304 Water
Kessen Maria, rear 512 Walnut
Kessens Theresa, servt., 496 Main
Kesserman Martin, varnisher, 293 Freeman
Kessing B F., clk., bds. 56 Sycamore
Kessing Bernard (K. & Greifenkemp), bds. 56 Sycamore
KESSING FRANK, Family Grocery, 49 Plum
Kessing & Greifenkemp (Bernard K. & B. G.) clothing, 4 Landing b. Main and Walnut
Kessinger C., molder, wks. Chamberlain & Co's
Kessler Charles, butcher. 923 Richmond
KESSLER Chas. H. (H. Kessler & Son), 24 D vid
Kessler Francis, lab., 9 John
Kessler Frank, tailor, 188 Clark
Kessler Frederick, upholsterer, s.w.c. Elm and 6th
KESSLER H. & SON (Henry & Chas. H.) Dealers in Leather, Hides, Findings, Furs, &c., 215 Main
KESSLER Hy. (H. K. & Son) 212 Barr
Kessler John, huckster, bds. 466 W. 7th
Kessler Valentine, tailor, 466 W. 7th

Kessleg Mary, 435 Linn
KESSLING HENRY J., Bakery and Confectionery, s.e.c. Clinton and Linn
Kessnen Herman sen., 304 Water
Kest Rienhart, lib., e.s. Western Av. b. Poplar and Findlay
Keste Nicholas, dyer, e.s. Ridgway al. b. Liberty and 15th
Kesten Gertrude, laundress, 109 Clay
Kesten Herman, lab., 119 Clay
Kesten Louis, lab., 24 Brighton
Kester John, lab., n.e.c. Abigail and Spring
KESTNER AUGUST H., Family Grocery, 432 Main
Kestner Felix, shoemkr, bds. 140 Carr
KESTNER GEO. F. Grocery and Provisions, s.e.c. Main and Canal
Kestner John R., pork house, 8 E. Canal, h. n.e.c. Main and Canal
Kestner Wm., saloon, 140 Carr
Kesy Patrick, 72 Water
Ketcher John, coach mkr., bds. Ludlow House
Ketcham James, lab., 626 W. Front
Ketchum F. H., express mess., 278 Race
Ketchum J. B., salesman, 310 Elm
Ketchum Kate, seamstress, n.s. Mulberry b. Main and Sycamore
Keter Wm. A., porter, 58 15th
Ketis Valentine, meats. 731 Elm
Ketscher John, coach mkr., bds. n.w.c. 2d and Ludlow
Ketteler Charles, baker, 29 Jackson
KETTELER WM., Union Saloon and Billiard Saloon, 442 Sycamore
Kettell Terrence (Allan & K) n.s. Budd w of Harriet
Kettels Wm., watchman, 164 Dayton
Kettemann George, S., tailor, 74 Ham. Road
Ketterer Andrew, cof. h., 712 Vine
Ketterer Charles B., tobacconist, bds. 347 Walnut
Ketterhenrich Frederick, tanner, 226 Findlay
Ketteritzsch August, stone yard, 597 Elm, h. e.s. Baymiller b. Wade and Liberty
Ketterlinus Chas. W., mach., 408 Walnut, h. 424 Walnut
Ketters Bernhard. lab., 149 Pleasant
Kettich Margaret, boots and shoes, 278 W. Liberty
Kettle Peter. painter, 357 Elm
Kettler Charles, baker, 29 Jackson
Kettler Edward, gunsmith, 641 Central Av
Kettler Geo., eng., 297 W. Front
Kettler Hy., chair mkr., 45 Jones
Kettler Louis, baker, bds. 222 W. 6th
Kettler Wm., b. k., 64 W. 2d, bds. Teutonia Hotel
Kettles Geo., eng., wks. Hughes and Foster's
Kettman Hy., tanner, 127 Pleasant
Kettner Christian, carp., bds, 123 Ham. Road
Kettner Henry L., shoe mkr., 67 Pendleton
Kettner Solomon, cutter, 51 George
Kettridge August, stone cutter, e.s. Baymiller b. Liberty and Wade
Keuney Geo., blksmith, 247 W. 6th
Keuper Theodore, blksmith, 52 McFarland
Keuthen Henry, cutter, 79 W. Pearl, h. Newport
KEUTZ BARNARD H., Proprietor, Liberty Tree House, 70 Sycamore
Keyer Ludwig, pipe mkr.. 64 Abigail
Keyler Fredericka, 245 Linn
Keys James, eng., 56 Providence
KEYS Richard W., (John A. Dugan & Co.) b. Glendale
Keys Robert T., provision broker, n.s.c. 2d and Walnut, bds Spencer House
KEYS Samuel B., (Moore, Wilstach, K. & Co.) h. E. Walnut Hills
Kialy Thos., cof. h., 152 Freeman
Kibby Milton, painter, 3 Wilson

Kichner Frank, mess., e.s. Vine b. 9th and Court
Kick George W., student, bds. 61 W. 8th
KIDD EDWIN T., (Cincinnati Gazette Co.) 324 W. 7th
Kidd Geo., 324 George
Kidd Geo. W., jr, clk., 18 Sycamore, h. 324 George
Kidd Hy., teamster, 79 Abigail
Kidd John S., clk., 324 George
Kidd Robert, boatman, 30 Mansfield
Kidelmann John H., sawyer, 164 Clay
Kidner Daniel, grocery, 140 Water
Kidney Robert, checkman, 478 W. 9th w. of Central Av
Kieb Michael, cigar mkr., 499 Vine
Kieber Adam, carp., w.s Denman, b. Bank and Central Av.
Kieborth Barbara, 312 Findlay
Kiechler Christopher, tin ware, 110 Baymiller
Kief Daniel, teamster, 54 Rittenhouse
Kiefenmeier Hermann, lab., bds. 19 Abigail
Kiefer Catharine, 608 Vine
Kiefer Caroline, 47 Allison
Kiefer Charles, (A. & J. Trounstine & Co.) 345 W. 6th
Kiefer Fred., 73 Green
Kiefer Geo., sen., egg dealer, 47 Findlay
Kiefer Geo., jr. egg dealer, 49 Findlay
Kiefer Ignatius, carp., 25 Carr
Kiefer Jacob, cooper, 76 Melancthon
Kiefer John, cof. h., 1828 Central Av.
Kiefer John, lab., n.s. Front b. Foster and Kelly
Kiefh John, malt mkr., 9th b Harriet and Mill Creek [erett
Kiegler Christin, shoe mkr., 164 Everett
Kiehborth Conrad, 312 Findlay
Kiehfuss Christian, bk. binder, bds. 468 Vine
Kiel John, pattern mkr., wks. n e.c. Walnut and Canal
Kielkenstein Kate, 696 Race
Kiely John, hostler, 15 W. 6th
Kiely John M, salesman, s.w.c. 4th and Walnut, h. 122 Lock
Kiem Joseph, turner, 276 W. Front
Kien Joseph. chair mkr., 276 W. Front
KIENZLE Jacob, (Diehold, Bahmann & Co.) c. Henry and Race
Kiepfuss Christian, bk. binder, 568 Vine
Kieran Thos., boiler mkr, 297 W. 3d
Kiernon Anthony, contractor, 131 Sycamore
Kiersted Hezekiah, (K. & Hoffman,) 197 E. 3d
Kiersted & Hoffman, (Hezekiah K. & Louis H.) coppersmiths, 87 E. Front
Kiersted Jeremiah, city coms, western dist., office, City Hall, h. 827 E. 3d
Kies Barney, lab., 111 Woodward
Kieser Christian, porter, 39 Ludlow
Kiesewetter Gotfried, tailor, 219 Elm, h. 222 W. 6th
Kieske Augusta, s.w.c. Race and Elder
Kiesling Jacob, locksmith, wks. 30 W. 6th
Kiess John H., contractor, 51 Allison
Kievet Wm., lab, bds. 16 Abigail
Kifdochf John, butcher, 151 George
Kifel Chas., confec., 52 Sycamore
Kiggen Thos., lab., 16 E. 5th e. of Lock
Kigney Michael, lab., e.s Oregon b. 3d and 6th
Kihl Jacob. pattern mkr., 55 W. Liberty
Kihn Valentine, cof. h., 55 Elder
Kilb Michael, cigar mkr., 499 Vine
Kilb Sebastian, eng., wks. 728 Central Avenue
Kilborn Marcus P., b. k., 30 Butler, h. 317 George
Kilbreth James P., trustee Ohio Life Ins. Co. and Trust Co., 17 W. 3d, h. 422 W. 6th
Kilbreth John W. 64 Walnut, h. 423 W. 6th
Kilburn C. L., Major U. S. A., 107 Pike
Kilday John, lab., wks. 33 Broadway
Kilday John, polisher, 33 Observatory Road
Kilday Thomas, lab., 66 Mulberry
Kilduff John, clk., bds. s. w. c. John and Elizabeth

Kilduff Margaret, grocery, s.w.c. John and Elizabeth
Kilduff Thomas, lab., 54 Baum
Kiles Geo. H., mason, 82 Gest
Kiley James, molder, bds. 96 Gest
Kiley John, shoe mkr., bds. 65 W. 5th
Kiley Thomas, molder, 96 Gest
Kilfilin Wm., blksmith, n.w. c. Longworth and Stone
Kilfoil J., waiter, Burnet House
Kilgarf Margaret, servt., 394 Longworth
KILGOUR CHARLES H., (Culbertson, K. & Co) Sec'y L. M. R. R., h. n.e.c. Pearl and Kilgour
Kilgour Mrs. E. C., n e.c. Pearl and Kilgour
KILGOUR John, (Culbertson, Kilgour & Co.) n.e.c. Pearl and Kilgour
Kilian John, bk. binder, b. 35 Elder
Kilian W., watch mkr , 440 Walnut
Kiling Hy., teamster, n.s. Augusta b. John and Smith
Kilkenstine Edward, lab., 32 Lock, n. of 8th
Kilkoin John, lab., 137 W. Front
Killday Eliza, laundress, 66 Mulberry
Killday Margaret, tailoress, 66 Mulberry
Killfilan Chas., printer, bds. 510 W. 3d
Killgallan Daniel, lab., 132 Front
Killian Herman, lab., bds. 48 E. Pearl
Killin Jacob, driver, 35 Elder
Killion Mary, servt., Henrie House
Killkelly Patrick, painter, wks n.e.c. Carr and W. W. Canal
Killroy Bridget, n.s. Friendship al. b. Pike and Butler
Killner Robert, cigar mkr., 140 Green
Kilroy Andrew, lab., 654 W. 6th
Kilroy Anna, servt., 421 W. 8th
Kilwer Hy., lab., 521 Sycamore
KIMBALL Abel, (J. H. Burrows & Co.) 191 W. 3d
Kimball Augustus, mach., bds. 191 W. 3d
Kimball Cyrus, 30 Hathaway
Kimball Hy., molder, bds. 191 W. 3d
Kimball Isaac, (K. & Wiltsee,) h. Walnut Hills
Kimball Thos. L., agt. P. Cen. R R., 46 W. 5th, h. Linnwood
Kimball Wm. J., artist, 58 Broadway, h. Walnut Hills
Kimball & Wiltsee, (Isaac K. & J. W. W.) saw mkrs., 41 W. Court
Kimber Hy., variety store, 327 Findlay
Kimber Jerome, shoe mkr., 62 W. Liberty
Kimerle Christian, driver, 30 York
Kimih John, stone cutter, 138 Clinton
Kimerle Christ., millwright, wks 825 Central Av.
Kimmig Jacob, stone cutter, bds. n.e.c. Linn and Clinton
Kimsted Wm, lab., rear 14 Allison
Kimstman Sebastian, shoe mkr., 54 Mohawk
Kimtzelmiller Wm., watchman, 74 Milton
Kinam Frank, turner, wks. 340 W. 3d
Kinan Barney, lab., n.s. Pearl b. Smith and Park
Kincannon Michael, lab., s.e.c. Pearl and Butler
Kincannon Thos., lab., s.e.c. Pearl and Butler
Kind Anne, midwife, 652 Central Av.
Kind Hy., cab. mkr., 168 Baymiller
Kindel Gabriel, cooper, n.s. Charlotte b. Linn and Baymiller
Kindel Joseph, blksmith, wks. C. H. & D. R R. blksmith shop
Kindel Joseph, molder, n.s. Charlotte b. Linn and Baymiller
Kinder Geo., blksmith, wks C. T. Dumont's
Kindervater Theodore, cof. h., 202 Vine
Kindle Geo., blksmith, 468 W. 3d
Kindle Joseph, harness mkr., bds. 1076 Central Av
Kindley Leonard, 95 St. Clair
Kindt Henry F., cab mkr., 160 Baymiller
Kine Peter, lab., 189 E. Pearl
Kineen Martha L., teacher, 115 Broadway

King ——, servt., 443 Broadway
King Abraham, cab. mkr., 34 Barr
King Andrew, (J. McMullen & Co.,) h. New York
King Andrew L., 30 McFarland
King Ann, e.s. M. Canal, b. 8th and Court
King Antony, lab., 80 Race
King Catharine, al. b. Augusta and Front and Central Av. and John
King Carrie E., teacher, 34 Barr
King Chas. C., rope walk, 493 John, h. 53 Wade
KING & DALY. (Michael J. K. & M. V. D.) Importers and Dealers in Brandies, Wines, Teas, Tobaccos, Cigars and Domestic Liquors, s w.c. 2d and Sycamore
King Daniel, grocery, s.s. 8th b. Broadway and Sycamore
King David C. (Geo. C. King & Co.), 86 E. 4th
King David P., harness mkr., wks 9 W. 6th
King Edward, cook, 120 E. 6th
King Eliza. bds. 131 W. 5th
King Rev. Enoch, bds. 349 W. 5th
King Frederick B., clk., 69 E. Pearl, bds. 62 W. 5th
King George, sutler, 672 E. Front
King George, eng., 475 W. 4th
King George, harness mkr., bds. Phoenix Hotel
King George, stone mason, 131 Everett
King G orge, lab., 564 E. Front
King George, lab., 74 Dudley
King George C., (Geo. C. K. & Co.,) 86 E. 4th
King Geo. C. & Co., (Geo. C. K., & David C. King,) com. mers., 273 Sycamore
King George E., eng., h. 475 W. 4th
King George J., b. k., n.w.c. Pearl and Walnut, h. 34 Barr
King George W , painter, n.s. Taylor b. Carr and Freeman
King Gilbert H., salesman, 103 W. Pearl h. 30 McFarland
King Harmon, clk., bds. 85 W. 8th
King Hy., s. s. Milton b. Price and Young
King Hy., carp., 7 Gorman
King Hy. R., carp , 501 Race
King Hy. L., mess. Adams Express Co., bds. 149 Longworth
King Hy , L., blacking manufac., bds. 273 Walnut
King Hy. W., mer., 378 W. 4th
King Hy. W., real estate agt., s.w.c. Poplar and Dudley, h. 111 Dudley
King Horace C., bds. 193 W. 7th
King James boots and shoes, 91 W. Court w. of Central Av.
King James B., clk., 25 E. Front, bds. s.e.c. 3d and Broadway
King James J., rectifier, s.w.c. 6th and Freeman
King Jeremiah F., clk. 69 E. Pearl, bds. Dennison House
King John, boatman, 72 Water
King John, clk. 18 E. 4th, h. 36 E. 4th
King John, cooper, wks. 33 Lock
King John, dray, 232 W. Court
King John, Drover's Inn, 883 E. Front
King John, phys., 25 W. 8th
King John, Jr., bds. 85 W. 8th
King John W., tinner, 224 George, h. 222 George
King Jonathan, butcher, n.s. Deer Creek Road e. of Liberty
KING Joseph (Barwise & K.,) 191 Longworth
King Julia, cof.h., 8 Commerce
King Kate, b. h., n.w.c. Longworth and Central Av.
King Mrs. Lewis. b. h., 38 E. 4th
King Lewis, confec., n.e.c. 4th and Sycamore
King Martha J., teacher, 302 George
King Mary, 97 W. Court, w. of Central Av.
King Mary, servt., 322 Longworth
King Michael, n.w.c. 3d and Ellen
King Michael, cutter, n.e.c. 9th and John

King Michael, lab., 77 Plum
King Michael, lab., 58 Plum
KING Michael J., (K. & Daly,) h. Newport, Ky.
King Patrick, boatman, n.e.c. Vine and Water
King Patrick, lab., 50 Race
King Peter, blksmith, 1032 Central Av
King Robt., w.s. Langdon al. b. 6th and 7th
KING Rufus, (K. & Thompson,) 95 E. 3d
King Rufus, printer, 141 John
King Thomas, carp., 153 Longworth, h. s.w.c. 5th and Central Av.
King Thomas, grocery, 71 W. Court w. of Central Av.
King Thomas E., conductor, 90 Wade
KING & THOMPSON, (Rufus K., & Samuel J. T.,) Attorneys at Law, 23 W. 3d
King Victoria, 240 E. Front
King Walter, carp., n s. Rail Road opp. French
King Willard C., b. k., 30 McFarland
King Wm., clk., s.e.c. 4th and Sycamore
KING WM. H., Boots and Shoes, 27 E. Pearl h. 472 W. 7th
Kingan & Co., (Samuel K., Wm. Kingan, & Thos. D. Kingan,) pork packers, n.e.c. Court and Sycamore
Kingan Samuel, (K. & Co.,) h. Belfast Ireland
Kingan Thos. D., (K. & Co.,) bds. s.e.c. Court and Main
Kingan Wm., (K. & Co.,) h. Belfast Ireland
Kinghorn John, brewer, 13 Abigail
Kinghorn John, foreman, 391 Sycamore
Kingsbury ——, tel. op., bds. 174 E. Pearl
Kingsbury Horace, watch mkr., 443 W. 3d
KINGSLEY Rev. Calvin, Editor of Western Christian Advocate, s.w.c. 8th and Main, h. 147 John
Kingston Thomas, lightning rod fitter, 37 Jones
Kininho Barney, finisher, wks. C. T. Dumont's
Kinkaid Alexander, cooper, 477 W. 9th w. of Central Av.
Kinkaid Alexander Jr., clk., 225 W. 9th
Kinkaid Wm., wood wkr., 16 W. Court w. of Central Av.
Kinkead Elisabeth, dress mkr., 30 12th
Kinkead Jos. D., (Langley & K.,) h. Covington
Kinkead Oscar. S., b. k., 30 12th
Kinkead Samuel, sawyer, bds. 14 Rittenhouse
Kinker Frank, (K. & Sasse,) 412 Broadway
Kinker, Mary E., seamstress, 100 Abigail
Kinker & Sasse, (Frank K., & Frank S.) carriage manufac., 16 & 18 E. 8th
Kinley James, lab., 112 W. 9th w. of Central Av.
Kinley John H., baker, 66 Pike
Kinimick Geo., lab., 126 Clinton
Kinnan Mrs. Wm., dress mkr., 171 Sycamore
Kinnen Hy., porter, 193 Baymiller
Kinner Ernestine, seamstress, 662 Main
Kinner Gottlieb, lab., 662 Main
Kinner William, cigar mkr., 662 Main
Kinney Ann, 45 Rittenhouse
Kinney Ann, e s Macalister. b. 4th and 5th
Kinney Catharine. 544 W. 5th
Kinney Dennis, dray, 182 Cutter
KINNEY Eli, (K. Espy & Co.,) s.e.c. 5th and Pike
KINNEY, ESPY & CO. (Eli K., James E., & M. W. Lodwick,) Bankers, 51 W. 3d
Kinney Geo., gardener, 436 W. 4th
Kinney James, lab., 132 W. Front
Kinney James, teamster, 544 W. 5th

Kinney John printer, 164 Elm
Kinney John, silver plater, 47 Betts
KINNEY JOSEPH N.,
　General Freight Agent, Office at L.
　M. R.R. Depot, res. Walnut Hills
Kinney Mrs M., e.s. Vine b. Calhoun
　and Auburn Av.
Kinney Mary, s.s. 6th b. Broadway and
　Culvert
Kinney P. S., coach painter, n.w.c.
　Plum and Perry
Kinney Patrick, bds. 502 W. 4th
Kinney Patrick, lab., 176 Cutter
Kinney R. D., clk. L. M. R. R., h. w. s.
　Kemper nr. Madison Pike
Kinney Thomas, chair mkr., 29 Webb
Kinney William, lab., 176 Cutter
Kinnicutt H. W., mess. Adams Express
　Co., room 199 Burnet House
Kinnig Wm., grinder, 63 David
Kinnig Louisa, servt., 18 Barr
Kinsbach Catharine, 534 Main
Kinsbach Ferdinand, drugs &c., 515
　Vine
Kinsclee James, striker, wks., C. H. &
　D. R. R. blksmith shop
Kinsel Eugene, glass stainer, bds. s.w.c.
　Walnut and Mercer
Kinsella James, clk., 46 Pub. Landing,
　bds. Madison House
Kinsella Patrick, blksmith, wks. C. H &
　D. B. R. blksmith shop
Kinssler James, clk., bds. Madison
　House
Kinsey C., bds. Dennison House
KINSEY DAVID,
　Manufacturer of Silver Ware and
　Jewelry, 24 W. 5th
Kinsey Edward, jeweler, e.s. Broadway
　third door below 4th
Kinsey Frank, bds. 83 Daymiller
KINSEY Joseph. (Worthington & Co.,)
　res. Mt. Auburn
Kinsey Nathaniel, 2166 Richmond
Kinsey Pierson, plasterer, 165 W. Pearl,
　h. 208 Richmond
Kinsey Samuel foreman, n.s. Front b.
　Lumber and Kelly
KINSEY Thomas W., (Wilson Hicks &
　K,) 205 Longworth
Kinsey Wm., leather, 696 Central Av.
Kinshler John, lab, n.s. Fremont b. Har-
　riet and Mill Creek
Kinshler Patrick, blksmith, n.s. Fremont
　b. Harriet and Mill Creek
Kinshler Wm., carp., n.s. Fremont b.
　Harriet and Mill Creek
Kiesler Jacob, safe mkr., 717 Race
Kinsley Hannah, 55 E. 8th e. of Lock
Kinsley James, blksmith e.s. Oregon b.
　3d and 6th
Kinsley John R., silver plater, 193 Long-
　worth
Kinsley Mat, bds. 100 Freeman
Kinssella Ellen, s.w.c. Smith and Long-
　worth
Kionle Hy., cigar mkr., 459 W. 5th
Kipperle Xavier, cooper, bds. 172 Clay
Kipgen Michael, finisher, wks. n.e.c.
　Walnut and Canal
Kipler Catharine, bds. 468 W. 3d
Kipler Margaret, bds. 468 W. 3d
Kipp Bernard, box mkr., 391 W. Lib-
　erty
Kipp Frederick, blksmith, 617 Elm
Kipp Gottlieb, painter, bds. c. 9th and
　Walnut
Kipp Wm. H., clk., bds. 378 Baymil-
　ler
Kipp Herman, cigar mkr., 577 Main
Kipp Joseph, 315 Findlay
Kipp Louis, teamster, 162 Freeman
Kipp Sarah S., 378 Daymiller
Kippel John, stone cutter, 4 Miami
Kipper Elizabeth, seamstress, 666 Race
Kippinbrouck John, painter, 96 Hunt
Kiran Thomas, boiler mkr., wks. s.s. 3d
　b. Butler and M. Canal
KIRDY CLINTON,
　Attorney at Law and Notary, n.w c.
　6th and Walnut, h. Glendale
Kirby Daniel, (J. J. & D. K,) e.s. Lud-
　low second door s. of 3d
Kirby Ellen, bds. 123 Vanhorne
Kirby J., butter mer., bds. 318 W. 5th
Kirby James F., plasterer, 201 Wade

Kirby J. J. & D., (John J. & Daniel,)
　lumber yard, 93 E. Front, near Law-
　rence
Kirby James, butcher, 166 Mound
Kirby James H., hostler, bds. 201 Wade
Kirby John, 561 Central Av
KIRBY John, (M. Werk & Co.,) s. w c.
　Central Av. and Clinton
Kirby John, shoe mkr.) 123 Vanhorne
Kirby John J., (J.J. & D. K,) 9 Harri-
　son
Kirby John S., bds. 561 Central Av
Kirby Josiah, bung factory, cor. Watson
　al and Whetstone al., h. 114 Rich-
　mond
Kirby Margaret, tailoress, bds. 123 Van-
　horne
Kirby Mary, grocery, 67 Observatory
　Road
Kirby Mary, 477 Vine
Kirby Patrick, hatter, 117 Main
Kirby Roht., butcher, 162 Mound
KIRBY Thomas, (M. Werk & Co.,) 477
　Vine
Kirby Timothy, n.w c. 6th and Walnut,
　h. Cumminsville
Kirby Wm., butcher, 12 Clinton
KIRCHENBOTE & VOLKSBOTE,
　Published by Fredewest & Don-
　nersberger, 428 Main
Kircher Francis, porter, 165 W. Front
Kircher Geo., box mkr., 27 Commerce
Kirchhoefer G. W., chemist, bds. Teuto-
　nia Hotel
Kirchhof Ludwig, baker, 642 Main
Kirchhoff Christopher F., clk, 336 W.
　7th
Kirchhoff Harman, painter, 574 Free-
　man
Kirchner Christian, black smith, 14
　Moore
Kirchner James M., tannery, 936 Cen-
　tral Av
Kirchner John, cigars, &c., 88 W. Court
Kirchner Nicholas, lock smith, 487 Wal-
　nut
Kirk Bridget, servt., 136 Broadway
KIRK & CHEEVER, (John W. K. &
　John H. C.) Pension and Govern-
　ment Claim Agency, 37 W. 3d
Kirk Daniel L., dray, Pennock al. bet.
　Cutter and Linn
KIRK DAVID,
　Plumber and Hydrant Maker
　215 Walnut
Kirk Edward H., salesman, 221 Mound
Kirk Fred., 10 Jackson
Kirk Geo W., porter, 10 Jackson
Kirk John, coach trimmer, bds. 298 W.
　5th
Kirk John W., (K. & Cheever,) res. E.
　Walnut Hills
Kirk Pryor, 221, Mound
Kirk Robert, coach trim m r, bds. 298 W.
　5th
KIRK Wilson J., (Sawyer & K.,) 221
　Mound
Kirker D., bds. Dennison House
Kirker David, lithographer, 64 W. 4th
Kirker John, (J. K. & Co.) 12 Elizabeth
Kirker John & Co., (John K , Thomas
　Kirker and David Kirker,) grocery,
　32 E. 5th
Kirker Margaret, bds 320 W. 5th
Kirker Sarah J., bds. 320 W. 5th
Kirker Thos., lithographer, 12 Elizabeth
Kirkhoff Henry J., clk., P. O, bds. s.e.c.
　5th and Vine
Kirkland James, salesman. 30 W. 4th
Kirkland John A., dry goods, 58 W. 5th,
　h. Covington
Kirkland Joseph M., saloon, 54 Broad-
　way
Kirkpatrick Mrs. Agnes, 587 Central Av
Kirkpatrick Eliza, 249 Hopkins
Kirkpatrick Wm., cof. h., s.e.c. 6th and
　Culvert
KIRKUP Joseph, (Wm. Kirkup & Son)
　15 Harrison
KIRKUP Wm., (Wm. K. & Son,) 15
　Harrison
KIRKUP WM. & SON, (Wm. K. &
　Joseph K.,) Brass Founders, 250
　E. Front
Kirland Jas., dray, 65 Walnut
Kirman Edward, 26 Lock

Kirsch John, gardener, Garden of Eden
Kirschbaum Andrew, lab., 646 Vine
Kirschberg Mrs Therese, s w.c.Peete and
　Poplar
Kirschner Gottfried, mach., 683 Race
Kirschner, John, finisher, 683 Race
Kirshner Adolphus, furniture, 59 Broad-
　way, h. 608 W. 8th
Kirspert Geo., saddler, 405 Vine
Kirthner Christian, carriage smith 16
　Moore
Kirtley Milton, b.k., 32 Vine, h. Coving-
　ton
Kirton Wm., foreman, J. Whittaker's,
　Deer Creek Valley
Kirwan Michael, lab., 253 W. 3d
Kiser Henry, cab mkr., 59 Allison
Kisker Henry, lab., 692 Main
Kisker Wm., lab., 28 Mansfield
Kisling Mrs. Catharine, 550 Race
Kispert Geo., saddler, bds 405 Vine
Kissick Jas., auction, 217 Main, h. 64
　Baum
Kissick Jas. B., clk., 217 Main, res. New-
　port
Kissinger Charles, molder, 676 Main
Kissinger Geo. W., bk. layer, n.s. Schil-
　ler, b. Hughes and Main
Kissinger Wm., bk. layer, 676 Main
Kistener Frederick, clk., 110 Clay
Kistener Johanna W., 110 Clay
Kistener Wm., cab mkr., rear 116 Clay
Kisting Barney, lab., s.s. Woodward bet.
　Sycamore and Broadway
Kistner Adolph, clk., bds. 492 Main
KISTNER EDWARD,
　China, Glass, Queensware, &c.,
　341 Main, h. 56 Franklin
Kistner Felix, shoe mkr., bds. e.s. Carr,
　b. Weller and 8th
Kistner Fred , clk., 110 Clay
Kistner Henry. mer , 03 St. Clair
Kistner John, millwright, wks. 825 Cen-
　tral Av.
KISTNER JOHN,
　Scale Manufacturer,
　392 Vine
Kistner John D., cab mkr., 153 Pleasant
Kiszling Frederick, tailor, 585 Walnut
Kiszling Jacob, lock smith. 33 Moore
Kitchell Joseph S., clk., 41 Main b. Col-
　lege Hill
Kite Elisha, lab., 435 George
Kite Henry, cab mkr., wks. 45½ E. 3d
Kite Joseph, 116 E. 6th
Kite Nicholas, photographer, n. s. 6th b.
　Broadway and Culvert
Kite Thos. b.k., 93 W. 2d, h. 489 W. 4th
Kitt Frank, trunk mkr., 25 Providence
Kitt Nicholas, trunk mkr., 25 Provi-
　dence
Kitte Bernhard, lab., 14 Buckeye
Kitte Henry, driver, 600 Race
Kitte John, lab., n.s. Cassatt al. b. Main
　and Sycamore
Kitte Mary, servt., 644 Race
Kitten Henry, foreman, 107 Woodward
Kittin Elizabeth, 314 Clark
Kitlemann Henry, dray. 11 Hannibal
Kittner David, b.k., bds. Silvester House
Kittner David, b.k. 25 Vine, h. 28 Long-
　worth
KITTREDGE B. & CO., (Ben. K. &
　Augustus A. Bennett.) Guns and
　Sporting Apparatus. 134 Main
KITTREDGE Ben., (B. K. & Co ,) res.
　Red Bank
Kittredge Chas., salesman, 134 Main, h.
　322 Linn
Kittredge E. W , atty., s. w. c. 4th and
　Walnut, h. Madison Pike
Kizer Andrew, pork cutter, 317 Broad-
　way
Kizer John, 14 Barr
Kizer John, jr., 14 Barr
Klassen Henry. box mkr., 606 Race
Klabeln Francis, porter, 524 Sycamore
Klaehaker Anton, driver, 35 Smith
Klaer George. chair mkr., 164 Everett
Klafor Benj., clk., 5 12th
Klaier Ernst. carp , n. w. c. Wade and
　Daymiller
Klair Geo., chair mkr., wks. John Mitch-
　ell's
Klam Mrs. Johanna, e. s. Davison, bet.
　Harrison Pike and Bernard

Klamire Chas., lab., 52 Webster
Klanke Fred., lab., 685 Race
Klank Henry, tanner, 619 Elm
Klansing Alex., tinner, w.s. Main b. 8th and 9th
Klapake George, lab., 402 Longworth
Klaproot August, 138 Everett
Klapper Lewis, carp., 9 Buckeye
Klaproth Aug., lab., 685 Central Av
Klar Ignatius, cooper, 579 Main
Klar Mrs Maria F., 579 Main
Klare Fred., car driver, 54 Kossuth
Klare Rudolph, lab., 74 Rittenhouse
Klarenaar John Francis, b.k. 54 McFarland
Klarmann George, cab mkr., 79 Augusta
Klarmann John G., cab mkr. 79 Augusta
Klasmeier John, tailor. 145 Bremen
Klass John, tailor, bds, 84 W Court
Klatte John, lab., 65 Pleasant
Klaw Matilda. 93 W. 8th
Klauer Balthasar, lab., 38 Ham. Road
Klauer Fred.. cooper., 244 Bremen
Klaus Christian. 159 Pleasant
Klaus Henry, bds. s. w. c. Race and Henry
Klaus Joseph, lab., Oehler, al. b. Freeman and Garrard
Klausing Bernard, 278 W. Front
Klausing Clemens, watch mkr., 485 Main
Klausing Joseph, blk. smith, 278 W. Front
Klausmann Francis, tailor, 29 Moore
Klausmeier Deitrich, tailor. 63 Dudley
Klausmeyer August H., baker, 100 Bremen
Klausmeyer Wm., music teacher, 413 Elm
Klaustermann Bernard, tailor, 65 David
Klaustermann John, tailor. 65 David
Klaustermeyer Wm., bar k., n. w. c. Front and Central Av
Klaver Eliza, servt., Mill, junction of 2d and Front
Klaverskamp John, molder. wks. n. e. c. Canal and Walnut
Klayer Henry. carp., 137 Everett
Klayor Wm H., clk., bds. 137 Everett
Klear Caspar, sash mkr., 64 David
Kleb Christian, blk. smith. 506 Elm
Kleber Joseph, (Dorsch. Torner & Co.,) s.w.c. Dayton and Freeman
Kleck Mathias, tailor, 705 Vine
Kleckamp Henry, express, 382 Baymiller
Kleemann Peter, furniture, 991 Central Av
Klefot Fred., fam. grocery, 96 Hunt
Kiel Barney, lab., 222 Linn
Kleiber, Jno., watch mkr., bds. 134 Hopkins
Kleier Ernst A , carp., bds. n. w. c. Wade and Baymiller
Kleier Frank, tailor, 63 Dudley
Kleier George T., sawyer, 99 Bremen
Kleiman Wm , agt., 63 Walnut, h. 361 John
Kleiman Wm., grocer, e.s. Fountain b. Rice and Alexander
Kloimeier Theodore. tailor, 534 Main
Klein Anthony, grocery, n.w.c. Court and Baymiller
Klein Caroline, seamstress, 534 Plum
Klein Catharine, n.w.c. Main and Court
Klein Charles jr., clk., 534 Plum
Klein Charlotte, 141 Clay
Klein Christian, clk., 83 W. Pearl, bds., Debolt Exchange
Klein Christian, miller, 163 Clay
Klein David, driver, 156 Bremen
Klein Francis, carp , 55 Findlay
Klein Frank, lab., wks. 114 W . Court
Klein Frederick, tailor, 141 Clay
Klein Frederick, tailor, 192 Clinton
Klein Frederick, tailor, 207 Clinton
Klein Geo.. (H. Vondergotten & Son), 99 E. 2d
Klein Geo. P., grocery, 660 Vine
Klein Henry, lab., bds. 469 Main
Klein Henry, saddler, bds. 125 W. 5th
Klein Jacob, grocery, 63 Ham. Road
Klein John, molder, 604 Vine
Klein John, musician, 147 Carr
Klein John, tailor, 707 Race

Klein Rev. John A., 87 Milton
Klein Joseph, fireman, 682 Vine
Klein Mary, servt., s.w.c. Pearl and Ludlow
Klein Michael, gas fitter, 562 Elm
Klein Nicholaus, tanner. 648 Elm
Klein Peter, cigar mkr., 67 Elder
Klein Peter, cof. b., 147 Carr
Klein Peter, umbrella mkr., 67 Elder
Klein Phillip, cigar mkr., 707 Race
Klein Phillip, tailor, 207 Clinton
Klein Regina, al. b. 13th and Mercer and Vine and Walnut
Klein Samuel, molder, 116 Clinton
Klein Sebastian, cigar mkr., 67 Elm
Klein Solomon, 534 Plum
Klein Valentine, butcher, n.s. Corwine b. Walnut and Ham. Road
Kleinbeck Joseph, tailor, 675 Race
Kleinberg Dietrich, driver, rear 107 Clark
Kleinberg Herman, driver, 107 C ark
Kleinbohnhorst Frank, boots and shoes, 8½ Landing b. Broadway and Ludlow, h. 53 Broadway
Kleine Charles, cab. mkr., 249 Clark
Kleine Dorothea, 54 15th
KLEINE Frederick, (K., Hegger & Co.), h. E. Walnut Hills
KLEINE, HEGGER & CO., (Frederick K., J Fred. H., Frank Grever & J. B. Enneking), Cloths and Gents Furnishing Goods,, 127 Walnut
Kleine Henry, 71 Clay
Kleine Henry, lab., wks. s.w.c. W. W. Canal and Smith
Kleine William, cutter, 20 Hughes
Kleinehellmann Bernhard, lab., 15 Franklin
KLEINER & BRO., (Fridelin K. & Meinrad K.), Jackson Brewery, 284 Ham. Road
KLEINER Fridelin, (K. & Bro.), h. 284 Ham. Road
KLEINER Meinrad (K. & Bro.), 284 Ham. Road
Kleinmann Dina, 502 Race
Kleinmann Magdalene, 107 Pleasant
Kleinochle Wm., b.k. 50 Walnut, h. 467 Walnut
Kleintank Anthony, shoe mkr., 677 W. 6th
Kleintank Hermann, shoe mkr., bds. 686 W. Front
Kleintank John, boots and shoes, 686 W. Front
Klem John, cooper, e.s. Western Av. b. Bank and Harrison Pike
Klemeier Clements, shoe mkr., bds. 357 Main
Klemeier Frederick, ham packer, 12 15th
Klemeier John, dray, 4 Pleasant
Klemeier Wm.. shoe mkr., bds. 357 Main
Klemm Chas., shoe mkr.. 94 Mansfield
Klemm Charlotte, 525 Vine
Klemm Ernst, trimmer, Leon Marks & Co.
Klemper Henry, grocer, 492 W. Front
Klensch Frederick, cof. h., 78 W. Liberty
Klengenberg Geo., tailor, 360 Broadway
Klenk Christian, varnisher, 163 Clinton
Klenke Henry, watchman, 115 Woodward
Klenke John, hinge molder, wks. n.e.c. Walnut and Canal
Klenke Joseph, lab., rear 115 Woodward
Klennanberg Henry, shoe mkr., bds, 412 W. 3d
Klensmith Herman, porter, GibsonHouse
Klepper Wm., cab mkr , 640 E. Front
Klett John, sawyer, s.s. Oliver b. John and Linn
Klevnow John, shoe mkr., 62 Lock
Klewerkamp Henry, lab., wks. 68 Water
Kleyer Bernard, carp., 146 Clinton
Kleyer Fred., lab., 146 Clinton
Klinch Frank, lab., Junction High and Kemper's Lane
Klie Conrad, lab., 164 Carr
Klier Caspar, cab. mkr., wks. s.w.c. Canal and Elm
Klier Wm., cab. mkr., wks s.w.c. Canal and Elm
Klile Casper J., carp., 22 Dudley
Klimper Fred., salesman, s.w.c. 3d and Vine, h. 19 Baum

Klimper Henry J., salesman, n.e.c, 3d and Lock
Klindtworth Doris, seamstress, 84 Bremen
Kline Adaline, second hand store, 567 Central Av
Kline Anthony H., stone cutter, 210 Mound
Kline Benneville, (Mills & K.), h. Covington
Kline Mrs. Catharine, 249 Everett
Kline Chas., finisher, 249 Clark
Kline Charlotte, grocery, n.s. Goodloe b. Willow and Niagara
Kline Daniel, cigars, &c.. 38 E. 3d
Kline Daniel E., (L. E. Steinman & Co) 55 Barr
Kline David, dray, wks. 117 E. Pearl
Kline Eugene F., clk., bds. s.e.c. Barr and Cutter
Kline Henry, bds. s.w.c. Poplar and Baymiller
Kline Henry, huckster, n.e.c. Front and Kelly
Kline Jacob, carp., n.s. Goodloe b. Willow and Niagara
Kline John, molder, wks. Chamberlain & Co.'s
Kline John jr., cooper, bds. n.s. Front e. of Kelly
Kline John H., dray, 27 Kossuth
Kline Joseph, pipeman, 683 Vine
Kline L., servt., s.w.c. Franklin and Broadway
Kline Martin, student, bds. 137 Race
Kline Mrs. Mary, bds. 29 Kossuth
Kline Patrick, molder, wks. Chamberlain & Co.'s
Kline Samuel, molder, s.s. Betts b. Linn and Cutter
Kline Thomas, lab , 164 Freeman
Kline Valentine, butcher, 142 W. Liberty
Kline Wm. blksmith, n.e.c. Front and Kelly
Klinebag Mary, 124 Clark
Klinebornhorst Frank, shoe mkr., 53 Broadway
Klineman John, clk., Findlay b. Central Av. and Canal
Kliner Benj., teamster, 299 W. 2d
Kliner Frederick, clk., bds. 771 Vine
Klineschmidt Adam, baker, 369 Central Av
Kling Catharina, hats and caps, 495 Vine
Kling John, eng., 242 Main
Kling Joseph, harness mkr., wks. 23 E. 5th
Kling Ludwig, cap mkr., 109 Pleasant
Kling Phillip. lithographer, 477 Elm
Kling W., bds. Dennison House
Kling Wm., harness mkr., wks. 23 E. 3d
Klingberg Geo., tailor, 360 Broadway
Klinge Frederick, cigars, &c., 107 W. Liberty, h. 109 W. Liberty
Klingelberg Jacob, finisher, 9 Moore
Klingelhofer F., painter, 57 W. 3d, bds. Cincinnati House
Klinger Anna, 41 Race
Klinger Anthony, cab. mkr., 163 Pleasant
Klinghefer Fred., bds. Cincinnati House
Klingler Joseph, driver, 138 Bremen
Klingler Joseph C.. cof. h.., 144 Bremen
Klingmer John Fred., 25 Hughes
Klink Chas., porter, 25 Findlay
Klink Leander, broom mkr., 528 Main
Klink Martha, 528 Main
Klinkenberg Jacob, currier, 9 Moore
Klinker Barney, porter, 416 Longworth
Klinker Mary, bds. 207 Webb
Klinler Geo., lab., n. w. c. Lawrence and Newport Ferry Landing
Klinney George, liquors, 437 W. 8th
Klipper Henry, s.w.c. Melancthon and Cutter
KLISTER Herman, (Allan & K.), 93 Woodward
Klits Henry, tailor, 41 E.7th
Klits Theresa, 87 Spring
Klos John, bk. layer, rear 71 Abigail
Klock Henry, lab., bds. 56 W. Court
Klocke Ernestine, 916 Race
Klocke Henry J., cutter, 59 19th
Klocke J. H., cutter, 78 W. Pearl, h. s.e. c. 12th and Race

(KLU) CINCINNATI (KNI) DIRECTORY. (KNO) 193

Klockenbrink Henrietta, s.s. Abigail b. Main and Sycamore
Klocker Albert, cigar mkr., 590 W. 6th
Klocker Louis, cigar mkr., 590 W. 6th
Kloeffler Frederick, cab. mkr., bds. 444 Sycamore
Kloeker Wm, stone mason, 11 Adams
Kloke Peter, cigar mkr., 122 Linn
Kloing Henry, molder, 166 Spring
Kloman F., tanner, 262 Ham. Road
Klomann John, rear 264 Ham. Road
Klonck Lewis, baker, 397 Broadway
Klonna Bernard H., lab., 17 Webb
Klonne A. Henry, tailor, 218 Linn, h. 228 Linn
Klonne John H., tailor, 152 Laurel
Klopf Joseph, porter, 81 Pleasant
Klopfer John, lab, 3½ E. Front
Klopfer Morris, bds. 362 John
Klopp Francis, lab., 79 Pleasant
Klopp Jacob, basket mkr., 86 Pleasant
Klopp John wagon mkr., w.s. Race b. 14th and 15th
Klopp John J., 86 Pleasant
Klopp Joseph, porter. 81 Pleasant
Klopp Michael, lab., 505 Race
Klopp Peter. lab., 86 Pleasant
Klopp Philipp, (Schroeder & K.) 499 Vine
Klosterman Catharine, bds. 89 Spring
Klostermann Charles A., express man, 391 Baymiller
Klostermann Eliza, servt., 12 Green
Klostermann John, tailor, 12 Green
Klostermann Joseph, shoe mkr., wks. n.e.c. Barr and Linn
Klostermann Mary, servt., 70 Sycamore
Klostmeyer Joseph, carp., 70 Hunt
Klostermeyer Wm., bds. 42 Elm
Klotter Frank, prop. National Hall, 402 Vine
KLOTTER Geo., (Geo. K. & Co.) 322 Ham. Road
Klotter Geo., b. k , 183 Laurel
Klotter Geo, jr., clk. P. O., 183 Laurel
Klotter Geo , grocery, 119 Browne
KLOTTER GEO & CO., (George K. & John G Sotu) Hamilton Brewery, 330 Ham. Road
Klotter Hy., (Wiebold & K) 477 Main
Klotter Louis, brewer, bds. 322 Ham. Road
Klotter Michael, 337 Ham. Road
Klotter Phillip, 66 Mohawk
Klotz Matthew, mach., 280 W. Liberty
Kluba Paul, lab., 97 Buckeye
Kluber John, grocery, 102 Baymiller
Klueher August, cigar mkr., bds. 624 Vine
Klueher Valentine J., cigars, &c., 646 Race
Kluge Wm., mer., bds. 51 W. 5th
Kluzman John N., cigars, &c , 452 Main h. s.s. al. b. Walnut and Vine and W. Court and 9th
Klumann Hy., n.e.c. York and Linn
Klumb Henry, meats, 26 Central Av., h. n.e.c. Water and Central Av.
Klumb Peter, butcher, 61 Dudley
Klump Andrew cab mkr., 24 Grant
Klump Peter, butcher, 137 Wade
Klump Peter, lab., 116 Ham. Road
Klumper Fred., policeman, 73 Pendleton
Klumper Joseph, grocery, n.w.c. George and Cutter
Klupf Mrs. Mary, 186 W. Court w. of Central Av.
Klundt Peter, s.w.c. 15th and Plum
Klunz John, 56 Findlay
Klusmann Fred., lab., bds. 9 E. Liberty
Klusmann Fred, lab., 23 Peete
Klusmann H. Gottlieb, boots and shoes, 544 Main, h. 542 Main
Klusmann Hy , carp., 600 Race
Klusmann Hy., miller, 63 Woodward
Klusmann Louis, lab., 698 Main
Kluss Bernhard, tanner, 119 Dunlap
Kluss Joseph, tanner, wks. s.s. 6th b. Harriet and Horne
Klussmann Hy., lab., 538 Plum
Klute John, lab., s.s. Montgomery Pike nr. Lebanon Road
Klute John H., boots and shoes, 634 Main
Kluver Fred., lab., 108 Baum
Kluz John, 19 Ann

Klyman Julius, liquors, 39½ Hathaway
Knabbe Mary, 183 Hopkins
KNABE ALBERT, Staple and Fancy Dry Goods, 116 W. Liberty, h. Richmond, Ind.
Knabe Christopher, cooper, 183 Hopkins
Knabe Frank A., salesman, 116 W. Liberty
Knabe Gottlieb, carp., s.w.c. Freeman and Dayton [erty
Knabe Joseph A., salesman, 116 W. Liberty
Knable Geo., sheet iron worker, wks. C. T. Dumont's
Knacht John, carp., 53 Plum
Knaebel Geo. L., cigars. 634 Central Av.
Knagge John T., 663 Vine
Knagge Miss L. F., saleswoman, 30 W. 4th, h. 663 Vine [Park
Knaggs Thos., painter, n.e.c. 3d and res. College Hill
Knup Charles B., carp , 790 E. Front
Knap Leonard, lab., wks. n.w.c. Plum and Wade
Knapke John B., clk., 260 Main
Knapke Mary, s.s. Hunt b. Sycamore and Main
Knapky Francis J., blksmith, 434 Sycamore
KNAPMANN J. H., Merchant Tailor, 11 Court House Building, h. n.e.c. Laurel and Linn
Knapmeyer John S., sawyer, wks. 128 W. 2d
Knapp Bridget, 974 E. Front
Knapp Chas. T., barber, 602 Central Av
Knapp Frank H., cab. mkr., 66 David
Knapp Frederick W., music teacher, 60 Elder
Knapp Henry, 66 David
Knapp Hy., lab., 104 Clinton
Knapp Hy., painter, wks. 15 Mercer
Knapp Hy., lab., 674 Central Av
Knapp Jacob, tobacconist, w s. Bank al. b 3d and 4th
Knapp Mary, 110 Clinton
Knapp W. H., porter, 109 E. 3d
Knapp Wm., shoe mkr , 143 Clark
Knapperts Henry, carriage trimmer, 125 Clay
Knappmeyer Theodore, 141 Abigail
Knauber Geo , cof. h., 19 Providence
Knauft Christian, cigar mkr., 56 Elder
Knauft Edward, varnisher, 56 Elder
Knaul & Co., (Peter K. & Michael Knaul,) bakery, 137 York
Knaul Michael, (K. & Co.) 137 York
Knaul Michael, molder, wks. n.e.c. Walnut and Canal
Knaul Peter, (K. & Co.) 137 York
Knauper Francis, mason, 34 Peete
Knear Jacob, roller, 520 E. Front
Kneass C., bds. Burnet House
Kneass Mrs. Nelson, actress, 171 Sycamore
Knebel Geo., lab., 42 Peete
Koechler Eva, e.s. Race b. Liberty and 15th
Knecht Geo., barber, bds. Front Street House
Knecht Geo., lab. 26 Abigail
Knecht Jacob, molder, 26 Abigail
Knecht John, varnisher, 110 W. Liberty
Knecht Louis, molder, 616 Central Av.
Knecht Wm., grocery, 509 John
Kneiper Henry, 45 Jones
Knelbnck Joseph F., tailor, 164 Everett
Knell Andrew, teacher. 32 Jones
Knemoller Wm., lab., 138 Pleasant
Knepp Casper, lab., 46 Gest
Knepp Wm. H., porter, 109 E. 3d
Kneppe Hermann, lab., 102 Clay
Knepper Wm. J , molder, 425 W. 7th
Kner Valentine, mason, 58 Elder
Knese Bernard, phys., 371 W. 5th
Knese Hy., blksmith, 683 Central Av.
Kniar Hy., lab., 658 E. Front
Knickel Jacob, shoe mkr., s.e.c. Main and 6th
Knickmeier Christopher, cab. mkr., 67 15th
Knicht Geo., lab., 26 Abigail
Knight Alpha, 182 Race
KNIGHT BROTHERS, (Geo. H. K. & Octavius K.) Solicitors of Patents and Counsellors in Patent Cases, Gazette Building, n.e. c. 4th and Vine

Knight Catharine, 115 Avery
Knight D., policeman, bds. 37 Longworth
KNIGHT E., (Hale & Co.) h Carthage, Ohio
Knight Edward S., saddler, bds. 273 Walnut
Knight Emma, teacher, 104 York
Knight Geo. C., real estate agt., Apollo bldgs., n.w c. 5th and Walnut, res. College Hill
KNIGHT Geo. H. (Knight Brothers,) h. Mt. Auburn
Knight Jacob, meats, s.e.c. 6th and Harriet
Knight M. Lizzle, teacher, 507 Freeman
Knight Michael, lab., 251 W. Front
KNIGHT NORRIS S., Real Estate Agent. n. w. c. 5th and Walnut, res. College Hill
KNIGHT Octavius, (Knight Brothers,) h Washington. D. C.
Knight Richard, b.k., 23 Sycamore, h. 81 Everett
KNIGHT Robert, (K. & Warren,) 361 W. 8th
KNIGHT & WARREN, (Robert K. & Wm. W.) Agents Liverpool and London Insurance Company, s.w. c. 3d and Main
Knipker Wm , driver, 79 Augusta
Knippen John H., lab., n.w.c. Broadway and Woodward
Knippenberg Eberhard, rear 32 E. Mulberry
Knippenberg Hy., bklayer, rear 16 E. Mulberry [Vine
Knipper August, brush mkr., wks. 309
Knipper Jacob, cooper, bds. s.w.c. Dudley and Liberty
Knirham Joseph, clk., bds. 51 W. 5th
Knittel Alexander, painter, 64 Elder
Knoasal John, 37 Baum
Knobbe Lucena, bds 435 W. 2d
Knobel Joseph, tailor, w.s. Vine b. Milk and Mulberry
Knobelsdorf Nellie, cook, 60 Broadway
Knoblaugh Frederick H., at 126 Sycamore, h. 239 W. 3d
Knoblaugh Leroy E., furniture, 137 John
Knoblaugh Wm., cab. mkr., 194 W. Court w. of Central Av
Knohloch Frank, barber, 62 W. Court
Knode Leander, lab., n.w.c. Linn and Findlay
Knodel Mrs. Ebhardine, 664 Elm
Knodel F., tailor, 81 W. 5th
Knodel Frederick, butcher, n.s. Browne nr. Ham. Road
Knodel Jacob. tailor, 548 Vine
Knoepfler Michael, carp , 299 W. Front
Knole James, lab., n.s. Front e. of Kelly
Knolenberg Geo., chair mkr., bds. 212 W. Front
Knollenburg Gen., chair mkr., wks. John Mitchell's
Knoll Wm , tailor, n e.c. George and Central Av., h. 40 W. Court w. of Central Av.
Knollman Andrew, lab., 641 Elm
Knollman Frank, lab., s.s. Weller b. Carr and Harriet
Knollman Hy., 148 Findlay
Knollman Herman, grocer, n.e.c. Betts and Cutter
Knollmann Gerhard. lab , 136 Pleasant
Knollmann John, lab., 136 Pleasant
Knolmann Frederick. lab., Oehler al. b. Freeman and Gerrard
Kneltbush Hy., 34 Campbell al.
Knooh Jacob, painter, 75 Clay
Knopf Constantine. saddler, 75 14th
Knopf Julius, cigar mkr., 310 Vine
Knopfer Michael, box mkr., 299 W. Front
Knoploth Nicholas, wks. 108 E. 2d
Knopp Gustavus, teacher penmanship Polytechnic College, h. 206 W. 6th
Knorbert Jacob, butcher, 25 Dunlap
Knorr A. & H , (Adam & Hy.) Ice, s.e. c. Plum and Findlay
Knorr Adam, (A. & H. K.) s.e.c. Plum and Findlay
Knorr Hy , (A. & H. K.) s.w.c. Elm and Henry

19

Knost Frederick, cab. mkr., 95 Pleasant
Knost Frederick, cooper, s.s. al. b. Race and Ham. Road n. of Findlay, h. 694 Race
Knost Hy., cab mkr., 95 Pleasant
Knost Hy., lab., 16 W. Mulberry
Knost Herman, clk. 70 Main, bds. 66 W. Court
Knost Julius, clk. 70 Main, bds. 66 W. Court
Knostman Chas., boots and shoes, 27 Pub. Landing
Knott Amanda, 431 George
Knott Elisha, shoe mkr., 19 Abigail
Knowlden Miss M. A., 43 Chestnut
Knowles Hanibal F., b.k. 163 Walnut, h. Covington
Knowlmann Hy., painter, bds. 641 Elm
Knowlton Mark, 43 Chestnut

KNOWLTON DR. P.,
Dentist,
136 W. 4th

Knox Edward C., millinery, 120 W. 4th, h. 169 Elm
Knox Fanny, bds. 138 Longworth
Knox John, paper hanger, 58 Observatory
Knox Reuben E., finisher, 224 W. 6th
Knox Thos., huckster, 6 North
Knox Thos., huckster, bds. 204 Broadway
Knoxall B., lab., wks. Wood & McCoy's
Knue Anthony, lab., 46 Woodward
Knuepfer Hy. J., cof. h., 657 Vine
Knuszmann Philip, lab., 43 Moore
Knuven Barney, porter, 9 Woodward
Knuwer August, lab., e.s. Kilgour b. 3d and 5th
Knuwer Clemens, porter, 11 Hannibal
Kob Lewis, tinner, 22 Commerce
Kobbe John A., bar k., 3 Cassilly's Row
Kobbes Geo., lab , 17 Commerce
Kobel Geo , finisher, 566 Vine
Kobelmann Reuben, dray, 65 Oliver
Kober Leonard, lab., 11 Logan
Koberg Hermann H., tailor, rear 115 Woodward
Koberg John H., tailor, 115 Woodward
Kobie Hy., lab., wks. n.w.c. 4th and Lock
Koble Michael, cof. h., Findlay b. Central Av and John
Kobmann Frederick C., cof. h., 81 Bremen
Koch A., lab., s s. Findlay b. Elm and Plum
Koch Adam, brewer, 71 Buckeye
Koch Adam, lab., 685 Race
Koch Balser, teamster, 59 Harrison Pike
Koch Baptist, (Bristel & K.) 82 Buckeye
Koch Bernhard, bklayer, 112 Ham. Road
Koch Chas. L., grocer, 267 Ham. Road
Koch Christian, brewer, 406 Longworth
Koch Emil, b k. 123 Main
Koch Ernst, lab., 577 Walnut
Koch Frank, shoe mkr., 97 York
Koch Frederick bklayer, 120 Ham. Road
Koch Frederick, cooper, 2 Peete, h. 1 Mulberry
Koch Frederick, lab., 536 Race

KOCH H. & J., (Henry & John D.)
Merchant Tailors,
178 Walnut

KOCH Henry, (H. & J. K.) h. 192 W. Court
Koch Hy., 131 Everett
Koch Hy., cigar mkr., 76 Buckeye
Koch Hy., feed store, 610 Main
Koch Hy., lab., 130 Ham. Road
Koch Jacob, mason, 117 Buckeye
Koch Jacob C., molder, 543 Race
Koch John, bklsmith, 577 Walnut
Koch John, cof. h., s.s. Harrison Road b. Coleman and Patterson
Koch John, feed store, 728 Elm, h. 265 Ham. Road
Koch John, lab., w.s. Franz b. Elder and Findlay
Koch John, shoe mkr., n.w.c Hughes and Schliter
Koch John teamster, 126 Ham. Road
Koch John, trunk mkr., n.e.c. Elm and Elder
Koch John D., (H. & J. K.) 50 W. 9th
Koch John Geo., tailor, 617 Vine
Koch Joseph, cooper, 155 Clark

KOCH LOUIS,
Coffee House,
59 W. 3d

KOCH MARCUS,
Jeweler and Watchmaker,
585 Central Av.

Koch Mary C., bds. n.s. Jail al. b. Sycamore and Main
Koch Melchior, tailor, 1 Lucy
Koch Michael, grocery, 660 Race
Koch Nicholas, lab., 49 Bremen
Koch Paul, shoe mkr., bds. 40 E. Front
Koch Peter, lab., bds. 577 Walnut
Koch Peter, tailor, w.s. Franz b. Elder and Findlay
Koch Regina, 69 Buckeye
Koch Solomon, peddler, 55 15th
Koch Wm., grocery, 211 Clinton
Koch Wm., lab. 55 Peete
Koch Wm., teamster, 668 Vine
Kochmann Joseph L., confec., 79 Sycamore
Kochmann Miss Mina, seamstress, wks. 36 Elder
Kock Barney, eng., 410 Broadway
Kock Frederick, shoe mkr., 109 Clay
Kock Hy., blksmith, 107 Woodward
Kuck Joseph, cooper, 155 Clark
Kockenge Mary, servt., 172 Sycamore
Kockler Herman, cigar mkr., 106 Clinton
Kockman Hy., 43 Race
Kocks Hy. H., confec., 322 Central Av.
Koda Mary, servt., 94 E. 3d
Kuebbe John A., tailor, 93 Woodward
Koebbing Hy., lime burner, n.s. Goose al. b. 14th and 15th
Koebel Geo., lab., 665 Vine
Koebel Joseph, cof. h., 43 Riddle
Koebel Magdalena, bds. 665 Vine
Koeble Paukraz, cof. h., n.w.c. 12th and Vine
Koeblein G., mach., wks. n.s. Front b. Lawrence and Pike
Koeck Amadeus, 229 Bremen
Koeffler Ignatz, lab., 670 E. Front
Koehl Jacob, teamster, 38 Dunlap
Koehl John, grocery, e.s. Reading Road nr. Montgomery Pike
Koehler Albert F., cof. h., 349 Walnut
Koehler August, eng., 161 W. 3d

KOEHLER CHRISTIAN, Fashionable Boot and Shoe Manufacturer, 169 Main, h. 199 Hopkins

Kuehler Frederick, barber, 95 E. Pearl, h n.e.c. Pearl and Broadway
Koehler Frederick, cof. h., 11 E. Liberty

KOEHLER Gottfried, (J. K. & Co.) 93 Buckeye

KOEHLER GOTTFRIED & CO., (G. K. & John Koehler) Maltsters and Brewers, 93 Buckeye and 124 Ham. Road

Koehler Hy., huckster, 636 Vine
KOEHLER Henry, (G. Koehler & Co.) 93 Buckeye
Koehler John, bar k., wks. n.e.c. Vine and Mercer
Koehler Josephine, 15 Poplar
Koehler Mary, bds. 136 W. Liberty
Koehler Nicholas S., clk., 99 Hopkins
Koehne Theodore, lithographer, 108 W. Court
Koehnig Chas., butcher, 708 Vine
Koehnig Mary E., 1 Wade b. Elm and Plum
Koehnig Wm., lab., 525 Sycamore

KOHINKEN JOHN H. & CO., (John H. K , Frederick Denghausen & Gallus Grimm) Organ Manufacturers, 555 Sycamore

KOEHNKEN John H., (John H. K. & Co.) 18 Milton
Koekle Casper. 73 Mohawk
Koelbin Gottlieb, liquors &c., 22 E. 2d
Koelbin Gottlieb, finisher, 103 Bremen
Koelker Bernhard, lab. 301 W. Front
Koelker J. Hy., tailor, 12 Buckeye
Koelling Fred., cof. h. 559 Race
Koellmer John, baker, 630 Race
Koelmel Vincent, lab., 97 Buckeye
Koelner Barney, lab., bds. 519 Main
Koen Carmick, broker, 65 Vine
Koene Antony, carp. 297 W. Front
Koenenkamp Ernst H., tailor, 525 Vine

Koenig Rev. Fred., trinity church, e.s. Race b. Liberty and 15th
Koenig Fred., lab., 538 Plum
Koenig Herman H., grocery, 27 Buckeye
Koenig Johana, 44 Pleasent
Koenig John, cigar mkr., bds. 249 W. 6th
Koenig Louise, 44 Pleasant
Koenig Raymond, grocery, 98 Ham. Road
Koenig Valentine, 32 Hamer
Koeniger Philip, tailor, s.e.c. Race and 12th
Koeninger Bernhard, lab., e.s. Goose al. b. Green and Elder
Koepf Geo., F, brush manuf. 41 Ham. Road
Koepfer Jacob, porter, 179 Main
Kuerditz Emil, drugs &c., s.w.c. Vine and Green
Kuerner Chas., cab. mkr., n.w.c. Pleasant and Green
Koernlein Chas., engraver, s.w.c. 4th and Main, h. 606 W. 8th
Koester John, cooper, 171 Clay
Koester Louis, wks., w.s. Brighton nr. Benckenstein's Garden
Koestermann Lena, 19 Mulberry
Koesters John G., lab., 9 Woodward
Koeth Valentine, lab., 12 Bremen
Koetter John, lab, H 15th b. Elm and Plum
Koetters Barney, sawyer, 147 Pleasant
Koewold Hy., tinner, 430 Walnut
Kuffman Powers, bds. 81 E. Pearl
Koglar Herman, cigar mkr., 13 Jones
Kohane Mary, 55 Plum
Kohl Chas., tanner n.w.c. Elm and Green
Kohl Chas. C., b. k 459 W. 8th
Kohl Frank, bklayer, 449 Linn
Kohl Frank, shoe mkr., 165 Carr
Kohl Fred, cab. mkr., 115 Carr
Kohl Geo., n.s. Browne b. Ham. Road and Mohawk
Kohl Geo., lab., wks., 196 W. Pearl
Kohl Geo. J., shoe mkr. 76 Abigail
Kohl Hy., 90 Rice
Kohl J. T., cupper and leecher, 98 W 7th
Kohl John, tailor 633 Race
Kohl Joseph, driver, 60 York
Kohl Mahlon M., salesman, 118 W. 4th h. 81 Barr

KOHL WM M., Picture and Looking Glass Frame Manufacturer, 3 College Bldg. e.s. Walnut b. 4th and 5th, h. 519 W. 7th

Kohlberg Joseph, peddler, 223 Cutter
Kohlbrand August, hats and caps, 452 Walnut, h. n.s. 13th b. Walnut and Clay
Kohlbrand Chas , hatter, 24 Grant
Kohlbrand Kate, milliner, 502 Main
Kohler Anton, 68 Peete
Kohler Bernhard, plasterer, 712 Vine
Kohler Christian, blksmith, 36 Elm
Kohler Hy., hinge fitter, wks. n.e.c. Walnut and Canal
Kohler Louis, lab., 76 Abigail
Kohler Wm., 465 Walnut
Kohlenberg Wm., cab. mkr., al. b. 13th and Mercer and Vine and Walnut
Kohlfaken Richard, lab., e.s. Anderson al b. 2d and Pearl
Kohlhater John, tailor, s.w.c. 3d and Vine
Kohlka Julius, cof. h., 27 13th
Kohlman Chas., b.k. bds. 296 W. 6th
Kuhluien, Chas., boots and shoes, 97 W. 3d, h. 296 W. 6th
Kohlman Chas., shoe mkr., 409 Elm
Kohlman David, lab., 188 Hopkins
Kohlman David, shoe mkr., 556 Central Av
Kohlman Hy., 45 Clay
Kohlman Hy , lab., wks. Fritsch, Burkhardt & Co's
Kohlman John, lab, 55 Ham. Road
Kohlman Joseph, porter, 50 Plum
Kohlmann C., baker, e.s. Vine, b. Calhoun and Auburn Av
Kohlmann Hermann, shoe mkr., n.e.c. Sycamore and Abigail
Kohlmann John, butcher, s.s. Oliver b. John and Linn

(KON) CINCINNATI (KOR) DIRECTORY. (KRA) 195

Kohlmeier Hy., harness mkr., 447 Main
Kohlmeyer Catharine, 253 Laurel
Kohls Barney, lab., s.s. 3d, b. Park and Mill
Kohlsdorf John, tailor, 723 Race
Kohmescher John M., police, 62 Hunt
Kohn Isaac, 362 John
Kohn Isaac, furnishing goods, 111 Main (Morris Ohlmann agt.)
Kohn Simeon, painter, 16½ W. 5th
Kohnan Hy., lab., s.s.Budd b. Harriet and Mill Creek
Kohne W., tailor, n.s., a! h. Canal and 12th and Vine and Race
Kohnen Hy., tailor, 129 Pleasant
Kohnle Anton, 674 W. 6th
Kohnradt Christian, 42 Mohawk
Kohrmann Barney, lab. 30 Pierson
Kohrmann Hy., (Veluve & K.) 680 W. 6th
Kohrmann Jacob, lab., 19 Mercer
Kohus Harmon, shoe mkr., £60 E. Front
Kohus John, (K. & Moormann,) 84 Broadway
Kohus & Moormann, (John K. & Louis M.) tailors, 84 Broadway, and 260 E Front
Koke Hy., bk. layer, 27 Dudley
Koke Hy., bksm th, 207 Webb
Koke Joseph, clothing 10 Pub. Landing b Broadway and Ludlow, res. Newport
Kokenbrink Barney, lab., rear 72 Hunt
Kolb Chas. M., drugs &c, 214 Elm
Kolb Gertrude, 524 Race
Kolb John, brewer, 172 Ham. Road
Kolb Philip, bk. binder, 6 Hamer
Kolb Philip, cab. mkr., 141 Baymiller
Kolbe Hy., pattern mkr. wks. C. T Dumont's
Kolbe John, b k. Hoffmann & Moser's b 63 Bremen
Kolbe Werner, china glass &c., 522 Main h. 63 Bremen
Kolbe Wm., weaver, bds. 273 W. 6th
Kolbus Christian, mach., bds 264 Central Av
Kolbus Hy., H., chair mkr , 105 Pleasant
Kolby John, clk., 63 Bremen
Kolckmeier Mrs. Mary, 46 Pleasant
Kolen John. baker, 42 W. Front
Kolhenberg Hy., tailor, 455 Main
Kolhoff Joseph, tailor, 165 W. 5th
Kolker Hermon, box mkr.. wks. Livingston near Linn
KOLKER John H., (K. & McCammon) 131 Clinton
KOLKER & McCAMMON. (J. H. K. & J. McC.) Stair Builders, n.w.c. John and Laurel
Kolkmeier Francis, cooper, 695 Main
Kolkmeier John lab., 50 Webster
Kolkmeier Miss Mary, seamstress, 46 Pleasant
Kolkmeier Wm., stone cutter, 18 Madison
Koll John, cab. mkr., w.s. Walnut b. 13th and 14th
Kollefrath Jacob, 1114 Central Av
Kolker Herman, 42 Jones
Ko'lmann Mary, tailoress, 99 Clay
Kolp Chas., b ls. 85 Gest
K lp Geo., butcher, 159 Clay
Kolp Jacob, edge tool mkr., 85 Gest
Kolp Louis, saddlery &c., 621 Central Av
Kolsthorf Frank, tailor. 103 York
Kolve John, b k. 222 Main, h. 63 Bremen
Komer Rich., wks. 222 E. Front
Komming Christian, whitewasher 4 Hughes
Komming Hy., eng., 4 Hughes
Komming Wm., lab , 4 Hughes
Konan Barney, baggage master C. H. & D. R. R., 62 Pierson
Konemann Adolph, teamster, s s. Liberty b. Linn and Baymiller
Konermann Henry, grocery 207 W. Front
Konermann Anthony H., carp., w.s Goose sl. b. Green and Elder
Konig Fred., bksmith, wks 103 Hunt
Konig Fred , bksmith, 116 Betis
Konig Hy., wood dealer, 513 Plum

Konigkramer Ernst shoe mkr., bds. 52 Dudley
Konigkramer Kate, 52 Dudley
Konkel Constans, huckster, 35 Buckeye
Konsheim August, stoves &c., 103 Ham. Road
Konsler Peter, 149 Poplar
Konzheim Wm., brewer, n.s. Henry nr. Elm
Kno Wm., cof. h., 90 Freeman
Koob, Mathias. tailor. 240 Bremen
Koogle Ellen 331 Cutter.
Kooj John, cab. mkr., 467 Walnut
Kooman Anthony. n.s Hanover b. Franklin and Woodward
Koons John, wagon mkr., 520 Main
Koons John, wagon mkr., n.e.c. Clinton and Baymiller
Koop August W., cab. mkr., 520 Main
Koop Bernard, cigar mkr., 403 Longworth
Koop Hy., cigar mkr., wks. s.w.c. Canal and Elm
Koop Hy., cigar mkr., 252 John
Koop Jacob, tailor, 26 12th
Koop Wm., cigar mkr., 46 Rittenhouse
Koor S, clk., bds., Teutonia Hotel
Koors Barney, cooper, 504 W. 3d
Koors Barnard H , coopers, 504 W. 3d, b 504 W. 3d
Koors John. salesman, s.w.c. W. W. Canal and Smith
Kop Annie M., 403 Longworth
Kop Benjamin, cigar mkr., 403 Longworth [Linn
Koper Hermann, wagon mkr., bds. 150
Kophman John, tinner, bds. 347 Walnut
Kopmann Caroline, seamstress, wks. 93 Woodward
Kopmann Chas., tailor, rear 176 Clay
Kopp Felix, cof. h., 468 Walnut
Kopp Geo , tailor, 13 Poplar
Kopp John, lab., 495 Walnut
Kopp John. musical instr. mkr., 17 Mary
Kopp John, tailor, 13 Poplar
Koppe Ferdinand, cab mkr., 156 Ham Road
Koppmann Christopher, carp., w. s. Goose al., b. Green and Elder
Koppmann Wm., tailor, 573 Main
Kopps Warner. rope mkr., s.s. Budd, b. Harriet and Milcreek
Korden John, finisher, bds. s.e.c 2d and Plum
Kordes Hy., varnisher, 143 Pleasant
Kordes John F., bksmith. 669 Vine
Kordes John F.. blksmith. 674 Vine
Korf Hy., jewelry, &c , 369 Main
Korff Harmon, bds. s.w.c. Walnut and 9th
Korff Jacob, s.e.c. Riddle and Harrison Pike
Korher Nicholas, lab., 96 Bremen
Korhoff ——, mach., 599 Race
Koring Louisa, 61 Buckeye
Korman Jacob. lab., wks. City Water Works office
Kormann Cornelius, basket mkr., 38 Findlay
Korn David, basket mkr., 70 W. Mulberry
Korn Jacob, cap mkr., 516 Vine
Korn John L., cashier Marietta and Cincinnati R.R. freight office, bds. Henrie House
Korn Joseph, turner, wks 128 W. 2d
KORNLITH J. & CO., (Jacob K. & Moses Newburger,) Wholesale Clothiers and Dealers in Cloths, Cassimeres and Tailors' Trimmings. 70 W. Pearl
KORNBLITH Jacob, (J. K & Co.,) 113 Elm
Kornblith Jane, 49 Longworth
Korndring Theodore, tailor, 204 Linn
Korner John. shoemkr, 779 Vine
Kornmann Hy., harness mkr., 52 Mercer
Kornmann Jacob, 16 Madison
Kornmann Mrs. Sophia, 69 W. Liberty
Korrell Chas., printer, bds 413 Vine
Kors Barney, varnisher, wks. 408 W. 6th
Kort Peter, broom mkr., bds. 111 Clay
Kort Peter, lab., 160 W. Front
Korte Albe t, grocery, n.w.c. Sycamore and 7th

Korte Frank, chair mkr., 17 Madison
Korte Franz Henry, boots and shoes, 17 Mulberry
Korte Hy., blksmith, 67 Pendleton
Korte Hy., lab., 149 Carr
Korie Hy., lab , wks. 120 E. 2d
Korte John F., cof. h., 42 E. 5th, h. 128 Hathaway
Korie M.. sawyer, wks. 304 Broadway
Korte Matthias, mach., 74 Abigail
Kortgardner Frederick, clk., bds. 70 Broadway
Kortkamp John H., tanner, 195 Everett
Kortman Hy., driver, w.s. Reading Road, nr. Montgomery Pike
Kortmann Clemens, bds. 191 Baymiller
Koske John, tailor, 110 E. 2d
KOST August, assistant editor Volksfreund, h. 367 Vine
Kost Frederick. 549 Vine
Kostars Frank, shoe mkr., 363 George
Kosten Alexander, confec., 64 Butler
Koster Hy., packer, 140 Main
Koster Hy., porter, 373 Broadway
Koster John, packer, 140 Main
Kosters Frank, shoemkr., n.e.c. Barr and Linu
Kosters Gerhard, baker, 257 Pine
Kotcampe Hy., tanner, 195 Everett
Kotenkamp Josephine, 164 Spring
Kotenkamp Margaret, 164 Spring
Kotenkamp Wm. F., printer, 164 Spring
Kothe Charlotte, 396 W. 7th
Kothe Eugene, bds. 396 W. 7th
Kothman Richard, porter, wks. 131 Race
Kothmann Hermann, 142 Pleasant
Kotkemeyer Hy., cab. mkr., wks. 128 W. 2d
Kotte Anthony, porter, s.e.c. Front and John
Kotte John, lab., 297 W. Front
Kottenbrock Hy., clothing, 2 Landing, b Broadway and Ludlow, h. 88 E. Pearl
Kottkamp Hy., lab., s.e.c. Elm and Findlay
Kottman Bernhard, stone mason, 9 John
Kottman Herman, grocery, 9 John
Kottman John, shoemkr., bds. 62 Hunt
Kottman Anthony, bar k., s.e.c. Smith and Front
Kottmann Bernard. tailor, 486 Broadway
Kctz Hy. lab., 764 W. Front
Kovermann Edward, grocery, 30 Buckeye
Kovermann Frederick, shoemkr, bds. 1684 Central Av
Krabs John, waiter. Gibson House
Kracht Theodore. cof. h., 679 W. Front
Krucke Herman. tailor, 100 Buckeye
Krackenberger Louis, express, 206 Clark
Kraemer Catharine, 547 Main
Kramer Charles, boots and shoes, 681 Vine
Kraemer Charles, carp., bds. 90 Woodward
Kraemer Felix, butcher, e.s. 15th, b. Plum and Elm
Kraemer Hy., lab., 551 Sycamore
Kraemer Hy. W., express man, wks. 530 Main
Kraemer Jacob, flour dealer, 568 Vine
Kraemer Nicholas, lab., 541 Main
Kruenz Henrietta, seamstress, wks. 674 Race
Kraeper Wm. F., tailor, 507 Race
Kraft Andrew, weaver, wks. 22d Walnut
KRAFT FRANCIS, Coffee House, 467 Vine
Kraft Hy., bds 109 E. 2d
Kraft, Hoffman & Co , (Isaac K., Abram H. & M. Kraft,) Clothiers, 88 Main
Kraft Isaac, (K. & Hoffman & Co.,) 72 Longworth
Kraft Mary, 230 Bremen
Kraft Max, (Kraft, Hoffman & Co.,) h. Columbus
Kraft Michael, cooper, 29 Hughes
Kraft Michael, cooper, wks. 30 Webster
Kraseck Paul, mason, 98 Buckeye
Krager Charles, dray, w.s. Kilgour, b. 3d and 4th
Krager George, lab, 29 Commerce
Krager John, carp., 137 Linn

196   (KRA)   CINCINNATI   (KRE)   DIRECTORY.   (KRI)

Krager John B., 172 Sycamore
Krager Louis, blksmith, 13 Mansfield
Krahenbrink Hy., molder, wks. n.e c. Walnut and Canal
Krahn Charles, currier, 500 Linn
Krais Wm., leather and findings, 557 Main
Kraiser Jacob, lab. wks. Cincinnati Chemical Laboratory
Krakeler Lewis, porter, 137 Water
Kralik Wenzeslaus, tailor, 41 Elder
Kralik Wenzeslaus, tailor, 40 Hamer
Kmlin Jacob, bkbinder, 910 Central Av
Kraman Hy., saddler, 81 Spring
Kraman Hy., lab., 679 W. 6th
Kramer Mrs., 191 Hopkins
Kramer Adam, liquors, &c., 135 Central Avenue
KRAMER Adolph, (K. & Kroger,) 64 Franklin
K RAMER ANTHONY, Cabinet Furniture Factory, 11 Franklin, Wareroom 530 Main, h. 68 Clinton
Kramer Anton, carp., 65 Oliver
Kramer August, turner, 114 Carr
Kramer Barney, printer, 75 Spring
Kramer Barney, shoemkr, bds. 492 W. Front
Kramer Bernard, porter, 31 E. 7th
Kramer Bernard, sr., tailor, 54 Peete
Kramer Bernard, jr., tailor, 54 Peete
Kramer Bernhard, porter, 597 Race
Kramer Catharine, 547 Main
Kramer Catharine, furniture, 535 Main
Kramer Charles, 582 Walnut
Kramer Chas., leather, &c., 150 Bremen
Kramer Clement, grocery, 159 Laurel
Kramer Edward, cigar mkr., bds. 127 Ham. Road
Kramer Fidel, cab. mkr., 72 Ham. Road
Kramer Frank, lab., 175 Hopkins
Kramer Frederick, grocery, 83 W. Front
Kramer Fred., lab., wks. n.w.c. Plum and Wade
Kramer Frederick R., lab., 70 Pleasant
Kramer George, chair mkr., 478 W. 5th
Kramer George, cof. h., 57 E. Front
Kramer Hy., blind mkr., wks. 147 Sycamore
Kramer Hy., lab., 77 Abigail
Kramer Hy., lab., 104 Clay
Kramer Hy., lab., e.s. Anderson, b. 2d and Pearl
Kramer Hy. B., tailor, 81 Pleasant
Kramer Mrs. I., 9 College
Kramer John, 117 Providence
Kramer John, s.s. Mohawk, b. North Elm and Hamburg
Kramer John, cab. mkr., 69 W. Liberty
Kramer John, grocery, s s. Front, e. of Ferry
Kramer John G., porter, 21 Anderson al.
Kramer John G., boots and shoes, 132 Butler
Kramer John H., clk., n.e.c. Hunt and Sycamore
Kramer John S., policeman, 69 Bank
Kramer Joseph, cutler, 252 Main
Kramer Joseph, sawyer, e.s. Race, b. 15th and Liberty
Kramer Julia, servt., 141 Spring
K RAMER & KROGER, (Adolph K. & Bernhard K.,) Tailors and Clothiers, 62 Broadway, and 252 Main
Kramer Magdalena, 136 Pleasant
Kramer Moses S., b.k., 236 Walnut, h. 9 College
Kramer Theresa, servt., 32 McFarland
Kramer Theresa, servt., 387 Vine
Kramers Elizabeth, 55 15th
Kramig F. & Co. (Francis K. & Frederick Frommel) flour dealers, 603 Walnut
Kramig Francis (F. K. & Co.) 578 Walnut
Kramig Frans, cof. h., 578 Walnut
Krammel Wm., copper smith, 477 Main
Krammer C., eng., wks. Hughes & Foster's
Krammer Daniel, tailor, 419 Sycamore
Krammer Fred., cooper, 181 York
Krammer Joseph, tailor, 127 Ham. Road
Krampe Wm. J., cab. mkr., 19 Buckeye
Kramschuster Michael, cooper, 267 Cutter

Krane Anton, cooper, n.e.c. Green and Race
Krantz John F., lab., 170 Everett
Kranz Christian. cab. mkr., bds. n.w.c. Smith and Augusta
Kranz Mathias, lwb., 456 E. Front
Krapes Michael, 310 Cutter
Krapf Eliza, bds. 465 Vine
Krapf Valentine, lab., 52 Baum
Krapp Frederick, lab., wks. n.s. Front b. Lawrence and Pike
Krapp Geo., shoemkr. e.s. Goose al. b. W, Liberty and 15th
Krapps Anthony, shoemkr., 53 Plum
Kras Herman. cab. mkr., s.w.c. Laurel and John
Krass Michael, miller, w.s. M. Canal b. 5th and 6th
Krass Anthony, cooper, n.w.c Race and Green
Kratz John, 129 Mohawk
Kratz Paul, cigar mkr., s.s. Ohio al. b. Elm and Plum and 15th and Adams
Krauger Albert, blksmith, n.e.c. Logan and Green
Krauger Hy., wagon mkr., n.e.c. Green and Logan
Kraul Fred., molder, wks. n.e.c. Canal and Walnut
Kraulaus Fred., wagon mkr., 691 Central Av
Kraus Chas., cof. h., 87 Ham. Road
Kraus Chas., cigar mkr., 30 Peete
Kraus Chas., tailor, 20 Hamer
Kraus Christian, baker. 21 Kossuth
Kraus Christopher, lab., 82 Mound
Kraus Conrad, sawyer, 160 Freeman
Kraus Elizabeth, 666 Elm
Kraus Francis, clk., 438 Main
Kraus Frederick, boot and shoemker, 66 Wade
Kraus John, cooper, 55 Elder
Kraus John, sewing machine manuf., 492 Walnut
Kraus Julia A., 518 Freeman
Kraus Max, mer., 217 George
KRAUS Wm, (Stadler, Bro. & Co.) 22 Longworth
Krausart John, e.s. Plum b. Adams and Liberty
Krause Charles, tanner, 703 Elm
Krause Eliza, servt., 65 Broadway
Krause Ferdinand, sawyer, 143 Everett
Krause Max, mer., 132 W. 6th
Krause Rachael, h. 132 W. 6th
Krause Wm, gas fixtures, 14 W. Court, h. 494 Walnut
Krause Wm., mer., 132 W. 6th
Krauser Ferdinand, lab., 143 Everett
Krauss Christian, baker. 21 Kossuth
Krauss Frederick, 557 Main
Krauter Chas., lab., 23 Mill
Krauth Jacob, molder, wks. C. T. Dumont's
Krauth John, molder, s.s. 3d b. Butler and M. Canal
Krautwasser John, barber, 45 E. Front, h. 94 E. 2d
Krautzberg Anton, hostler, wks. w. s. Lodge b. 5th and 6th
Krayenbrook Charlotte, servt., 356 George
Krebs Antone, shoemkr, 53 Plum
Krebs August, barber, 91 Spring
Krebs Casper, tailor, 47 E. 4th
Krebs Conrad, mach., 330 Plum
Krebs Hy., liquor mer., 91 Spring
Krebs John J., tanner, 145 Livingston
Kreba Peter, flour store, 157 Everett
Kreckel Chas., tailor, bds. n.w.c. Walnut and 9th
Kreeken Hy., tailor, rear 376 Broadway
Kreel Frederick, finisher, bds s.e.c. 2d and Plum
Kreft Barney, driver, bds. 388 Sycamore
Kregar John, carp., wks. 296 Carr
Kregor John, tanner, h. 691 Elm
Krehenbrink Hy., clk., 75 Abigail
Krehenbrink Henry, lab., wks. 222 E. Front
Kreider George, cab. mkr., 144 Pleasant
Kreidler Mathias, baker, 506 Walnut
Kreienhagen Wm, painter, 6 Miami
Kreiger Barney, lab., 57 Martin
Kreiger Hy., policeman, 222 Cutter
Kreihenbach Juergen, tanner, wks. 183 Ham. Road

Kreimborg John, blksmith, 19 Ham. Road
Krein Nicholaus, lab., 155 Pleasant
Kreinbaum Hy., lab., 91 Woodward
Kreinbruch Frederick, lab., al. b. 13th and Mercer and Vine and Mercer
Kreinhagen Wm., stone cutter, 461 Sycamore
Kreis Hy., clk., bds. n.w.c. Race and 6th
Kreise Jos., porter, 108 Clinton
Kreiser Elizabeth, 180 Buckeye
Kreiss Casper, lab., 261 Pleasant
Kreitel Joseph. cab. mkr., 126 Ham. Road
Kreizer Joseph, lab., 107 Ham. Road
Kreke Arnold, cab. mkr , 18 Hughes
K RELL ALBERT. Musical Instrument Manufacturer and Dealer, 180 Vine, n. 36 Jackson
Kremer Frederick. tanner, 72 Dunlap
Kremer Gerhard H., cooper, 55 Buckeye
Kremer John, baker, bds. 516 W. 5th
Kremer Nicholas, vinegar mkr., 541 Main
Krenig Martin, lab., 84 Melancthon
Krenuling Wm., carp., 15 Jones, h. rear 290 Linn
Krentz Frederick, tanner, 28 Canal
Krenz Fred., tinner, 170 Everett
Kreps John, tanner, 145 Livingston
Kreskamp Wm., cooper, bds. 207 Webb
Kress Conrad, actor, 9w 13th
Kresz Hy., cof. h., 1000 Central Av
Kreuger August, painter, 426 Walnut
Kreulich Constantine, butcher, 1 9 W. Liberty
Kreusmeyer C., lab., wks. 18 Sycamore
Kreusmeyer Wm., lab, wks. 18 Sycamore
Kreuter Eberhard, varnisher. 69 Green
Kreutz John M., butcher, 12 Betts
Kreutz Ludwig, cigar mkr , 502 Elm
Kreutzer Frank, cutter, 476 Race
Kreutzer Regina washing fluid, 476 Race
Kreutzmann Joseph, bar k., 66 W. Court
Kreuzberger Adam, lab., bds. 624 Vine
Kreuzer Christian, cab. mkr., 558 Race
Kreuzer Geo. lab., 30 Mercer
Kreusberg Ignatz, rear 461 Walnut
Krevet Ferdinand, A. tanner, bds. n.w.c. Linn and Poplar
Kreyenbrink Hy., lab., 75 Abigail
Kreyenbrock John C., grocery, n w.c. George and Central Av
Kreyenhagen Christ., drover, s.w.c. Freeman and Liberty
Kreyling Geo., carp., rear 24 W. Court w. of Central Av
Kreyser John, cab. mkr., 62 Findlay
Krick John, tailor, 25 Hughes
Krick Wm., blksmith, 183 Hopkins
Krider Charles, lab, wks. Queen City Distillery
Krider Joseph, 138 Culvert
Krieg Barbara, servt., 438 Main
Krieg Charles, locksmith, 14 Allison
Kriege Rudolph, baker, bds. 174 Sycamore
Krieger Chas., tinner, bds. 65 W. 5th
Krieger Christ., clk., wks. 825 Central Av.
Krieger Christian, clk., 59 Findlay
Krieger Frank, finisher, 91 Hopkins
Krieger Geo. mach., 819 Central Av
K RIEGER JOHN F, Machinist and Finishing Shop, 825 Central Av
Kries Frank, driver, n.s. Augusta b. John and Smith
Kriese John, rear 70 Hunt
Kriese Margaret, rear 376 Broadway
Krieslauber Ethedore, lab., rear 529 E. Front
Krietz Daniel, 361 Ham. Road
Krigbaum Adam W., eng., 172 Linn
Krile Joseph, finisher 123 E. Pearl
Krill Anna, 64 W. Liberty
Krimm Anna M., 95 Ham. Road
Krimm John G., b. k. 93 Ham. Road
Krimpleman Elizabeth, tanners, n.e.c., 2d and Broadway
Kringel Gustav, cof. h., 218 Vine
Krintzer George, lab., wks. s.e.c. Canal and Vine

(KRO) CINCINNATI (KRU) DIRECTORY. (KUE) 197

Krinz Christopher, cab. mkr., bds. 33 Augusta
Krippner Adam, saloon, n.e.c. Clark and Baymiller
Kris Bartholomew, tailor, 10 Commerce
Krische Charles, lab., 104 W. Front
Kr s t Geo., bar k., 25 Moore
Kritzer Jacob, lab., 310 E. Pearl
Krobfeld Kunigunde. 87 W. Liberty
Krockel Chas., tailor. bds. 422 Walnut
Krode Barney, feed store, 192 Hopkins
Kroder Frederick (Hoffman & K.), rear 30 Webster
Kroe Barbara, servt. s.w.c. Race and 3d
Kroeger August F., painter, 426 Walnut
Kroeger Cecilia tailoress, 532 Main
Kroeger Euphemia, servt. 10 4 13th
Kroeger Hy., tailor. 516 Race
Kroeger John H, tailor. 99 W. 2d
Koeke Anna M., servt., 34 Elder
Kroell Rev Augustus 54 W 6th
Kroell Francis, lab., 145 W. Pearl
Kroell Hy., white washer. 22 Mercer
Kroeniger Frederick Ch., tanner, s.w.c. Ham Road and Elm
Krog Julius cof. h. w.s. Ham. Road near Brighton House
Krogar Hy., cab mkr., 406 Longworth
Kroger Anton, grocery, 1 Pine
Kroger Barney, cof. h., 1 Budd
KROGER Bernhard, (Kramer & K.,) 83 Pike
Kroger Chas., tinner, bds. Fireman's Hall
Kroger Fred. molder, wks. n.e.c. Canal and Walnut
Kroger Hy., bksmith, bds. 454 W. Liberty
Kroger Hy., chair mkr., 406 Longworth
Kroger H., lab., 18 Baum
Kroger Hy., lab., 59 Martin
Kroger John H, dry goods, 548 Central Av.
Krogman Hy., bksmith, 3d near Lock
Krogman Joseph H., finisher, s.s. 3d b. Canal and Kilgour
Krogman Josephine. cap. mkr., s.s. 3d b. Canal and Kilgour
Kroh S., auctioneer, 309 Walnut
Krohmer John, carp., 25 W. Liberty
Krohner Nicholas, e.s. Vine b. Calhoun and Auburn Av.
Krolage Frank, chair mkr., 225 Cutter
Kroll Conrad, w.s. Walnut b. Allison and Mercer
Kroll Conrad, clk., 35 E. 3d, h. s.w.c. Allison and Walnut
Kroll Frederick, tailor, n.w.c. Wade and Baymiller
Kroll John, bar k., 29 W. 3d
Krollmann Geo., bk layer, e s. Goose al. b. Liberty and 15th
Krombring John, box mkr., wks. Livingston near Linn
Kromm Catharina, servt., 28 14th
Kronacher Jacob, b. k., 38 W. Pearl, h. 263 Longworth
Kronauer John, musician, 18 Woodward
Krone Andy, lab., 76 Dudley
Krone Bernhard, varnisher. 25 Mill
Krone Geo., shoe mkr., 63 E. Pearl
Krone Harmon, s.w.c. Price and Millron
Kronenurger Hy., lock mkr., wks. n.e.c. Walnut and Canal
Kronenberg Edward, blksmith, 512 Race
Kronenwald Bonifacius, candle mkr., bds. 442 Main
Kroner Chas., lab., 60 Pleasant
Krones John. express, 740 Vine
Kronlacke Frederick, tailor, 50 Melancthon
Kronlage Berhard, cof. h., 636 Walnut
Kronlage Hy., family grocery, 384 Sycamore
Kronlage Julia, servt., 411 Broadway
Krons John P., tailor, 656 Vine
Kropp Frederick, blksmith, 63 Bremen
Kroth Frank, lab. 39 Observatory
Kroth Isaac, molder, 37 Observatory

Krothup Joseph, lab., w.s. Clay b. 13th and Allison
Krotman Antony, chair mkr., 563 W. 5th
KROUSE Jacob, (Stix K. & Co.) 327 Walnut
Krouse John, 55 Fountain
Krouse Peter, wagon mkr., 163 Bank
Krouse Simon, 302 George
Krouss John, n.e.c. York and Baymiller
Krow Catharine, chambermaid, Black Bear Hotel
Krow S'mon. salesman, 184 Main, bds. Tentonia Hotel
Kroyer Andrew, 18 Baum
Kruher El'jah, 163 W. 5th
KRUCH LOUIS, Coffee House and Boarding House, 252 Walnut
Kruckemeyer Hy., turner, 12 Mary
Kruckemeyer Justice, silversmith, Duhme & Co., hds. 74 W. 6th
Krucker Francis, salesman, 32 W. Pearl, h. 206 George
Krucker John, clk., 49 Walnut, h. 206 George
Krucker Louisa. 206 George
Krueck Jacob, huckster, 552 Elm
Krueger Catharine servt., 10 Green
Krueger Fred, boots and shoes, 633 Central Av.
Kruehiemer Moses, peddler, 159 W. Court
Kruemmel Frank, tailor. al. b. 13th and Mercer and Vine and Walnut
Kruere Victor, brewer, 396 Central Av.
Kruetzelmann Geo., stoves &c., 526 Main
Krug Adolphus, carp., bds. 9 E. Liberty
Krug Frederick, brick yard, bds. 140 Carr
Krug Gebhard, mach., 127 W. Liberty
Krug Kephart, mach., 123 Race
Krug Martin, shoe mkr., 138 Everett
Krug Peter. mach., wks. 365 W. Front
Kruger David. (Burgert, Sand & Co.,) h. Sedamsville
Kruger Fred, mach., cor. 13th and Clay
Kruger Hy., trunk manufac. 479 Central Av
Kruger Margaret, servt., 397 Broadway
Kruimpelbeck Francis, tailor, 685 Race
Krull Fred, tailor, 267 Main
Krum Christ. cab. mkr., wks. s.w.c. Canal and Elm
Krum David K., molder, 46 Pierson
Krum Joseph, clk., bds. 5 W. 7th
Krum Wm., printer. 5 E. 7th
Krumberg Theodore, dry goods, 399 Main
Krumbhols John, butcher. 52 Martin
Krumdieck Fred., (J. C. Nolker & Fred. K.,) 64 Richmond
Krumie John, porter, 579 Sycamore
Krumka Joseph, 22 Logan
Krumler August, tailor, s.e.c. Young and Ringgold
Krumm Hy. fireman, 556 E. Front
Krumm John H, barber, w.s. Sycamore b. 8th and 9th
Krumm Wm., printer, 5 E. 7th
Krumme Barney, cab. mkr., 205 Hopkins
Krumme Frank, chair factory, 230 Hopkins
Krumpe Frederick, 66 Stark
Krumpe Harmon, 66 Stark
Krumpe Margaret, 149 Pleasant
Krunler George, shoe mkr., bds. n.w.c. Elm and 6th
Krup Frank, lab., 87 Elm
Krupp Hy., lab., 430 Walnut
Krurra Agnes. 11 Pendleton
Kruse Agnes, 18 13th
Kruse Agnes, h. 167 Linn
KRUSE & BAHLMANN, (Lewis K., & Albert Bahlmann,) Hardware, Cutlery &c., 389 Main
Kruse Bernhard, bk. layer, 4 Mary
Kruse Bernhard, chair mkr., 167 Linn

Kruse Christian, 61 David
Kruse Christian, clk., 10 Orchard
Kruse Christ H., grocery, 58 15th
Kruse Elizabeth, 10 Orchard,
Kruse Ernst, carp., 95 Pleasant
Kruse Frederick, dray, 12 Hughes
KRUSE Hy., (J. F. & H. K.,) s.w.c. Race and Elder
KRUSE Hy, (Kasting & K.,) 10 Orchard
Kruse Hy., cab. mkr , 537 Race
Kruse Hy., grocery, 97 Woodward
Kruse Hy., grocery. 602 Race
Kruse Hy., F. W., grocery. 464 Elm
Kruse Hy., upholsterer, 223 Betts
Kruse Herman, bk. layer, 68 Buckeye
KRUSE J F. & H., (John F. K., & Henry K.,) Dry Goods Store, s.w.c. Race and Elder
KRUSE John F., (J. F. & H. K.) s.w.c. Race and Elder
Kruse John H., cab. mkr., 537 Race
KRUSE Louis, (K. & Bahlmann,) 496 Sycamore
Kruse Wm. C., tailor, 95 Pleasant
Kruser Frederick, driver, 536 Main
Kruseling Barney, box mkr., wks. Livingston near Linn
Krusemeier Conrad, porter, 96 Clay
Krusemeier Herman, (K. & Rosing,) 92 Clay
Krusemeier Joseph, teamster, 547 Walnut
Krusemeier & Rosing, (Herman K., & Anton R.,) Feed Store, 362 Ham. Road
Krusszmann Frederick, lab., wks. 17 Webster
KRUTHAUPT JOHN J. F., Family Grocery, n.e.c. Butler and Pearl
Krutzelmann Frederick, harness mkr., 130 Sycamore
Kruz Jacob, 40 Providence
Kruzius John G., cof. h., 766 E. Front
Krysher T. A., bds. Dennison House
Kubach Frederick, painter, bds. 9 15th
Kuball Adolph, book binder 26 Pleasant
Kubbeng Hy., box mkr., bds. 143 Carr
Kubler Victor, cab. mkr.. s.e.c. Jones and Melancthon
Kuchenbuch Chas., baker, wks. 35 Elder
Kuchenbucher Theresa, 145 Bremen
Kuchler Adolph, cab mkr.. 39 Ludlow
Kuchler August, saloon, 39 Ludlow
Kuchler Casper, cof. h. s.e.c. Brighton and Harrison Pike
Kuck Bernhard, porter, n.s. Green b. Race and Pleasant
Kuckmeier Hy., paper mkr., 595 Race
Kuckmeyer Wm. J., shoe mkr., 18 Woodward
Kuder Joseph, cigar mkr., bds. 117 Lodge
Kueck Bernard, porter. 146 Pleasant
Kueckmeier Christ, mach., 67 15th
Kuegler Chas., cof. h. w.s Central Av. b. Findlay and Poplar
Kuehl Adolph, 28 Mercer
Kuehl Hy., tailor, 99 Woodward
Kuehn Adolph, 28 Mercer
Kuehn Emil, brush mkr., rear 36 12th
Kuehn F., 197 Vine
Kuehn Henriette, brush mkr., rear 36 12th
Kuehn John, baker, 15 nr, Vine
Kuehn Louisa, 712 Vine
Kuehn Theodore, brush mkr., rear 36 12th
Kuehne Francis, musician, 135 Bremen
Kuehne Louis, musician, rear 13 E. Liberty
Kuehner Chas. F., brass worker, 9 Allison
Kuehnle Elisabeth, 66 Ham. Road
Kuehnle Philipp, finisher, 16 14th
Kuel'porth Mrs. Anna, 9 Mary
Kuell George, turner, 530 Plum
Kuelling Martin, sawyer, w. s. Goose al. b. 14th and 15th
Kuemmerling Frederick, tailor, 570 Walnut
Kuemecke Frederick, teamster, bds. 105 Buckeye
Kuenemund Chas., billiard table builder, 636 Main

Kuenneman Chas., cab mk., 14 Moore
Kuennen Catharine, 15 Franklin
Kuenzbach Henry, watch mkr., 34 Green
Kuerkel Geo., brewer, bds. 493 Vine
Kuertz Wm., butcher, 128 Clay
Kuerz Richard, steward, Galt House
Kuesz Geo., dray, w.s. Bremen b. Elder and Findlay
Kuettich Magdalene, 144 Bremen
Kuffer Edward, paper carrier, 550 Walnut
Kuglin Samuel, tinner, wks. 11 E. Front
Kuhl Bernhard J., lab., 606 Race
Kuhl Chas., painter, 38 Green
Kuhl Conrad, tailor, 599 Elm
Kuhl Gerhard J., lab., w.s. Goose al. b. Liberty and Green
Kuhl Herman J., bk layer, 4 Mary
Kuhling John, porter, 21 Commerce
Kuhlenbook John, dray, 84 Melancthon
Kuhling Clement, feed store, 220 Clark, h. n.e.c. Baymiller and Clark
Kuhling Frank, clk., 147 W. 5th, h 25 Commerce
Kuhlkamp Henry, shoe mkr., bds. 438 W. 5th
Kuhlman Casper H., clk., 49 Pub. Landing, h. e.s. Kilgour b. 3d and 5th
Kuhlman Geo. D., dye-house, 44 E 6th
Kuhlman Henry, shoe mkr., wks. 101 E. Pearl
Kuhlman Louisa, 498 Vine
Kuhlman Martin, carp., n.s. Charlotte b. Linn and Baymiller
Kuhlmann B. H., b.k., 8 Main, h. 141 E. 3d
Kuhlmann Casper, salesman, e. s. Kilgour b. 3d and 5th
Kuhlmann Chas , shoe mkr., 409 Elm
Kuhlmann Egidius, clk., 66 Findlay
Kuhlmann Frederick, shoe mkr., bds. 399 Sycamore
Kuhlmann Fred. J., lab., 141 E. 3d
Kuhlmann Geo., dye-house, 142 W. 4th, h. 44 E. 6th
Kuhlmann Geo., veterinary surgeon, 44 E. 6th
Kuhlmann Henry, blk. smith, 533 Walnut
Kuhlmann Henry, carp., 143 Baymiller
Kuhlmann Henry D , boots and shoes, n.e.c. Vine and 6th, h, 432 Sycamore
Kuhlmann Hermann, shoe mkr , n. e.c. Abigail and Sycamore
Kuhlmann John H., shoe mkr., w.s. Smith b Augusta and 2d
Kuhlmann Joseph, grocery, 704 W. 6th
Kuhlmann Joseph, porter, 50 Plum
Kuhlmann Lewis, carp., 139 Baymiller
Kuhlmann Rev. Theodore, St. Xavier College, w.s. Sycamore bet. 6th and 7th
KUHN Abraham (K., Netter & Co.,) h. New York
Kuhn Adam, e. s. Baymiller north of Central Av
Kuhn Bernard, chair mkr., bds. 606 Race
Kuhn Christian, cooper, 177 Providence
Kuhn David, barber, e. s. Johnson al. b. Canal and 12th
Kuhn David J., barber, 225 Vine, h. 387 Vine
Kuhn Ferdinand, bar. k., 38 E. 5th
Kuhn Rev. G. H., n.s. Pearl b. Pike and Butler
Kuhn Geo. M., shoe mkr., 677 Elm
Kuhn Joseph, box mkr , 21 Clinton
Kuhn M., butcher, 333 Ham. Road
Kuhn Michael, lab., wks. n. w. c. Plum and Wade
Kuhn Michael E., clk., 512 Vine
Kunn Moses, 197 Elm
KUHN, NETTER & CO. (Abraham K., Jacob N. Samuel Kuhn and Solomon Loeb,) Importers and Dealers in Dry Goods, Clothing and Furnishing Goods, n.e.c. 3d and Vine
Kuhn Phillp, porter, 400 Walnut
Kuhn Richard, tanner, 10 Dunlap
KUHN Samuel, (K., Netter & Co.,) 332 W. 4th
Kuhn Wm., (Droste & K.,) 57 Allison

Kuhne Chas., box mkr., 17 Elm
Kuhne Henry, shoe mkr., 583 Main
Kuhuer Chas., cigar mkr., 197 W. Liberty
Kuhner Theodore, carp., 57 14th
Kuhnke Chas., barber, 370 W. 2d
Kuhnle Anthon, 699 Race
Kuhr Chas., salesman. bds. 137 Race
Kuhn John H., lab , 2d 13th
Kuhr Mary, bds. 9 Woodward
Kuhner Henry, shoe mkr., 585 Main
Kuister Chas., 10 E. Liberty
Kulenburg Henry, tanner, 28 Canal
Kuling Joseph, chair mkr., wks. H. Clostermann's
Kulke Barney, lab., 301 W. Front
Kulke Joseph, lab., 188 Barr
Kull Christopher, grinder, 69 W. Liberty
Kullenkamp Chas., 30 Broadway
Kuller Charlotte, servt., 343 Richmond
Kullmann Henry, lab., 50 Buckeye
Kullmann Henry B., carp., 50 Buckeye
Kullmann Henry, lab., rear 50 Mulberry
Kummer Andrew, porter, 154 Bremen
Kummer Catharine, 144 Bremen
Kumpe Carolina, bds. 10 Abigail
Kmnper Bernard, s.w.c. Abigail and Broadway
Kunckel Deborah, grocery, 1476 E. Front
Kunckel Edmund, clk., s e.c. Pearl and Broadway, bds. Dennison House
Kundrenk Herman, bk. layer, 157 Everett
Kunen Cornelius, lab , n. s Mercer bet. Vine and Walnut
Kung Peter, cof. b,, s. e. c. Riddle and Harrison Pike
Kungel Theodore, huckster, 203 Pleasant
Kunk Gerhard H., lab., 106 Abigail
Kunkel Balthasar, candle mkr., 86 W. Court
Kunkel Chas , pianoist., 151 Richmond
Kunkel Geo., stone cutter, 149 Bank
Kunkel Jacob, music teacher, 10 Richmond
Kunkel John, 708 Freeman
Kunkler Edmund P., (K. & Peters,) 235 W. 9th w. of Central Av
Kunkler & Peters, (Edmund P. K. & Chas H. P.,) tin ware, 241 Vine
Kunning Henry, cof h. and b h., s.w. W. Canal b. John and Smith
Kurns Lewis wks. junction 6th and Front
Kunsmann Lorenz, sawyer, 56 Dudley
Kunst Benj., dry goods, 283 Linn
Kuntz Anthony, shoe mkr., bds. 149 Carr
Kuntz Christian, lab., 50 Dunlap
Kuntz Frank, cigar mkr , 41 Mulberry
Kuntz Geo., barber 453 Main
Kunts Geo. F. 14 Hamer
Kuntz Henry. wks. 6 W 6th
Kuntz Jacob, lab., 660 Vine
Kuntz John, 647 Sycamore
Kunts John, boiler mkr., e s. Kilgour b. 3d and 5th
Kuntz John, cook, 53 13th
Kuntz John, cook, n w. c. Vine and Longworth
Kunts John, dray, 75 Pleasant
Kunts Joseph, tinner, 109 Clay
Kuntz Louis, waiter, 29 W. 3d
Kuntz Mrs. Mary, 62 Bank
Kunts Michael, barber shop, 453 Main
Kuntz Peter, col. h., 634 Vine
Kunts Valentine, nail mkr., 628 W. 6th
Kuntzelmiller Wm., watchman, 74 Milton
Kuntzler John, mach., e.s. Bremen bet. Liberty and Green
Kuntzmann John, meats, s.w.c. Liberty and Broadway
Kunz Casper, lab., 216 Bremen
Kunz Conrad, lab., 9 Lucy
Kunz George, clk., bds. 62 Bank
Kunz Geo., clk., n. e. c. York and Baymiller
Kunz John, bottler, 609 Main
Kunz John, butcher, 51 Dudley
Kunz Kate, bds. 216 Bremen
Kunz Philippina, 395 Vine
Kunz Rosine, 418 Vine

Kunz W., tailor, bds. 90 E. 2d
Kunze Frederick W., dray, n.e.c. Liberty and Broadway
Kinze Henry, dray, 60 13th
Kunze John, lab., wks. James White & Co.'s
Kunzen F. Y., n.e.c. Liberty and Broadway
Kunzler Nicholas, turner, 462 W. 5th
Kunzler Nicholas, wagon mkr., 462 W. 5th
Kuper Frank, lab., 304 Longworth
Kuper Joseph, blk. smith, bds. w. s. al. b. Vine and Walnut and 13th and 14th
Kupfer Henry, b.k., 164 Main, h. 88 Hopkins
Kupierle Geo., (Max. Mosler, & K.,) 269 Walnut
Kuny Wm., butcher, 126 Ham. Road
Kure Wm., basket mk., e. end of Mohawk
KURDLEMEYER Geo., (Rogers & K.) 13 Mansfield
Kurfeso Frederick, baker, s.s. Taylor al. w. of Kilgour
Kurns Lewis, sawyer, n.s. 6th b. Harriet and Horne
Kurre Elizabeth, seamstress, 410 Broadway
Kurry August, varnisher, 224 Baymiller
Kurte Frederick J., 20 Hathaway
Kurte John, tin smith. bds. 628 Race
Kurts Christian, painter, 43 14th
Kurtz Frederick, tailor, 31 Webster
Kurtz John, boots and shoes, 100 W. Court
Kurinkel Anthony, cab. mkr., 278 W. Front
Kurz Leonhard, shoe mkr., 161 Bremen
Kurz Margaret, servt., 269 George
Kurzlieb Wm., mach., bds. 9 15th
Kuse John, lab., 28 Hunt
KUSGOERD Anthony, (H. & A. K.) s. w.c. 3d and Park
KUSGOERD H. & A., (Henry & Anthony) Family Groceries. Provisions, &c., s.w.c. 3d and Park
KUSGOERD Henry, (H. & A. K.) s.w. c. 3d and Park
Kushman Louis, hostler, 2 New
Kushmann Frederick, steward, 16 Baum
Kusman Fred., lab , 22 Grant
Kussmaul John, shoe mkr., 1017 Central Av
Kustaman H., molder, wks. Chamberlain & Co's
Kuster Christian, cooper, bds. 12 Buckeye
Kuster Hy. W , tanner, 308 Race
Kuster Lewis. lab., 154 Pleasant
Kusterer Amelia, seamstress, 26 Mercer
Kustermann Hy., molder, 72 W. Liberty
Kustermer John, salesman, 59 Ham. Road
Kusz Chas. foreman. 40 12th
Kutcher Frank, 165 W. Front
Kutter Barney, carp., n s. Railroad e. of Vance
Kutter Frederick, soap mkr., 470 Main
Kutz Joseph, porter, 553 Main
Kutzep Wm C., mach., wks. 543 Vine
Kwasneski Stanislaus, bklayer, 165 Linn
Kygin Jane, 13 8th above Lock
Kyler Stephen. lab., s.s. 6th b. Broadway and Culvert
Kylius Ferdinand, finisher, 29 Hughes
Kyser Mary, dress mkr., 51 W. 7th
Kyte Joseph T., grocery, n.w.c. Lock and 8th

L

Laacke Henrietta, 10 Moore
Laacke Henrietta, seamstress, 566 Race
Laacke Mrs. Mary, 10 Moore
Laacke Mary, 10 Moore
Laacke Mary, 516 Race
Laake Barney H., Lab., 100 Carr
Labbe Francis, shoe mkr., 563 Vine
La Belle Florence, bds. s.e.c. 6th and Smith
Laboau Jacob, molder, 21 Clinton
Labold Herman, grocer, n.w.c. John and Everett

(LAH) CINCINNATI (LAM) DIRECTORY. (LAN) 199

Labold Isaac H., b.k. 121 Main, h. 481 John
LABBOT AUGUSTUS A., Commission Merchant and Importer of Wines, Brandies and Havana Cigars, 6 W. Front, h. South Covington
Lace Wm., tailor, 6 Clinton Court
Lacey Cowper, saddle tree mkr., 73 Baymiller
Lacey Edward, mach., wks. n.w.c. Freeman and 9th
LACEY Jesse H., (Applegate & Co.)
Lacey Lute, dress mkr., 139 W. 4th
LACEY Nicholas, (Murdock & L.) 46 E. 3d
Lacey Thos., currier, bds. s.e.c. 9th and Walnut
Lacey Thos., clk., 139 W. 4th
Lacey W. B., b.k. 23 W. Pearl, bds. 108 Broadway
Lacheby Jas., eng., 160 W. Front
Lachlan Robt., 205 W. 3d
Lachtrop Hy., cof. h., 18 Webster
LACK CHAS., Importer and Dealer in Rhine and Catawba Wine, 342 Walnut
Lackener Frank, 128 Clay
LACKMAN Herman, (Sandman & L.) n s Longworth 2d door from Stone
Lackner Andrew, gas fitter, wks. 62 W. 4th
Lackner John, cigar mkr., 120 Clay
La Count Frederick C., painter, 82 Betts
Lacy Edward, finisher, 31 Kossuth
Lacy L., rooms 60 E. 3d
LADD Thos. W., (Mitchell & L.) 61 Longworth
Ladd, Webster & Co's sewing machines, 94 W. 4th
Ladeberger John, lab., 62 W. Liberty
Ladenburger Christopher, s.w.c. 3d and Walnut
Ladenkotter Jos., grocery, 106 Abigail
Laderbier Susan, s.s Harrison Pike b. Riddle and Division
Ladewig Chas., shoe mkr., 489 Walnut
LADIES' REPOSITORY, Rev. D. vis W. Clark, editor. s.w.c. 8th and Main
Ladkin James D., tailor, s.e.c. 4th and Vine, h. Newport
Ladley John J., painter, wks. 43 E. 2d
Ladley Salathiel W., s.s. Findlay b. Freeman and Western Av.
Ladogar Jacob, lab., s.s. 6th nr. Harriet
Laekamp John A., lab., 31 Buckeye
Laeher John, cooper, 102 Clay
Laeubly John, cab. mkr., 79 Pleasant
Laeukering Hy. J., cof. h., 520 Main
LAFAYETTE BANKING CO., Geo. Carlisle, President, n.s. 3d b. Main and Walnut
LAFAYETTE BREWERY, Fred. Billiods, Proprietor, n.s. Ham Road b. Vine and Race
Lafayette Hall, 6:4 Race
Lafeld Wm., cab. mkr., s.w.c. 6th and Smith
Lafferty Archibald B., clk. C., H. & D. R.R., 324 Clark
Lafferty Isaac, carp., 812 E Front
Laffey Andrew, lab., 256 Water
Laffey Wm., 118 W. Front
Laffler Francis, seamstress, 172 Baymiller
Lafon Felix, b.h., 87 E. 5th
Laga Joseph, teamster, 242 Hopkins
Lagemann Joseph, shoe mkr., al h. 13th and Mercer and Vine and Walnut
Lagorio Joseph, 461 W. 5th
Laha Mary, 28 Accommodation
Lahae John, wks, 340 W. 3d [8th
Lahan Matthew, driver, 39 Lock n of
Laheney Thos., lab., 385 Vine
Laher David, cor., 204 Clark
Lahey Mary, servt., 61 E. 4th
Lahey Tim., lab., 61 Pierson
Lahmann Hy. A., grocery, 170 W. Court w. of Central Av.
Lahring H. & J. (Hy. & John) cof. h., 496 W. Front
Lahring Hy., (H. & J. L.) 496 W. Front
Lahring John, (H. & J. L.) 496 W. Front
Lahrman Geo. A., turner, bds. 27 Commerce

Lahrman John H., box mkr., n.s. Commerce b. Race and Elm, h. 27 Commerce
Lahy Annie, servt., 404 W. 6th
Lahy Timothy, lab., 648 W. Front
Laig Ernst, lab, 11 15th b. Elm and Plum
Laile Louis, lab., 142 Buckeye
Laing Barney, salesman 12 Pearl, bds. n.e.c. Pearl and Butler
Lainos John, carp., 360 Clark
Laird Clarence, teacher, E. Front b. Vance and Stone
Laird Elisa, millinery, 250 W. 5th
Laird Hannah, 162 Spring
Laird Jas. A., driver, U. S. Exp. Co.
Laird John M., printer Cin. Gazette, 111 W. 6th
Laird T. A., tel. op., 195 W. 3d
Laire James A., collector, 129 E. 3d
Laiser Geo. cab. mkr., 20 Dunlap
Laitsch Godfrey, bellows mkr., wks. 41 E. 2d
Lakamp Hy., wagon mkr, bds. 615 Elm
Lakamp John, s.e.c. Liberty and Sycamore
Lake Amanda, seamstress, 108 13th
Lake August eng., 447 W. 3d
LAKE Bernhard, (Brokamp & L.) 404 Main
Lake Jacob, tailor, 141 Abigail
Lake Wm., circus manager, bds. U. S. Hotel
Laker Barney, dray, n.e.c. Carr and W. W. Canal
Laley John, lab., 414 Sycamore
Lallance James B., carp., 353 George
Lalley Martin, lab , 16 Landing b. Broadway and Ludlow
Lalley Michael, tinner, 29 Race
Lally Elisa, 45 Rittenhouse
Lally John, lab., Cassatt al, b. Sycamore and Broadway
Lally Patrick, lab., bds. s.e.c. Front and John
Lally Wm., lab., rear 180 E. 6th
Lamade Lewis, foreman, 131 Pleasant
La Mair Chas., salesman 12 E. 4th, bds. s.e.c. 3d and Broadway
Laman Edward, butcher, 43 Mill
Lamar Fire Ins. Co., agency, 76 W. 3d
LAMB ANDREW, Agent for N. Longworth, h 20 Harrison
Lamb Geo. W., boots and shoes, 269 Central Av., h. 166 Barr
Lamb James, civil eng., bds 198 W. 3d
Lamb John W., boots and shoes, 281 Central Av.
Lamb Mary bds. 119 W. 6th
Lambdin Thomas, clk., 131 Longworth
Lambe Jas., lab., 304 Elm
Lambe Jeremiah, rear 427 W. 5th
Lambe Wm., clk., 21 W. 5th, h. 427 W. 5th
Lambeke Wm., lab. 496 W. Front
Lamberd Amann. lab., bds. n.s. Flint b. Freeman and Mill Creek
Lambers George, blksmith, wks. n.e.c. Walnut and Canal
Lambers Herman, shoemkr., 64 Hunt
Lambers John H., grocer, n.e.c. Budd and Donnersberger
Lambersick Wm., 51 Kossuth
Lambert Barbara, n.s. al. b Poplar and Vine and Ham. Road and Buckeve
Lambert C., pattern dresser, 99 Pendleton
Lambert Henry, bk. layer, 11 15th b. Elm and Plum
Lambert Ignatius, bk. layer, 165 Pleasant
Lambert James, lab., n.w.c. 6th and Harriet
Lambert John H., shoe mkr., 165 W. Court w. of Central Av
Lambert Mary A., bds. 165 W. Court w. of Central Av.
Lambert Sarah, 136 Linn
Lambes John G., blksmith, 20 Abigail
Lambing Francis, blksmith, bds. 16 Abigail
Lambre Barney, blksmith, 22 Woodward
Lambur Anthony, grocery, s.e.c. 2d and Smith
Lamcol Henry, porter, 15 E. 8th

Lamer Henry, turner, wks. 825 Central Av
Lamers Bernhard, blksmith, 22 Woodward
Lamerie Lewis, roofer, 131 Pleasant
Lamertine Mary, 623 Central Av
Lamie Bridget, 154 Freeman
Laming John, 88 W. Court w. of Central Av
Lamker Henry, chair mkr., bds. 662 Race
Lamker Henry, tailor, s.w.c. Linn and Hopkins
Lamlean Francis, saddler, bds. 674 W. 6th
Lamm Paul, cigar mkr., 17 Allison
Lammars Fred., cab. mkr., 234 Betts
Lammart Frank, 15 Commerce b. Walnut and Vine
Lammas Wm., cab. mkr., 234 Betts
Lammeier Henry, lab., w.s. Goose al. b. Green and Elder
Lammering Benjamin, bds. 83 Baymiller
Lammers Andrew, foreman, 99 W. 4th, h. 51 15th
Lammers Geo., carp , 96 Clay
Lammers Henry, cab. manufac. al. b. Vine and Walnut and 13th and Mercer
Lammers Henry, lab., 65 Pendleton
Lammers & Jeckel. (Joseph L. & Henry J.), tailors, 208 Central Av
Lammers John W., carp., 143 Baymiller
Lammers Joseph, (L. & Jeckel), 5 Jane
Lammers Joseph, tailor, 524 W. 7th
Lammers Joseph. 5 Jane
Lammers Mary, 55 15th
Lammert Geo., clk., 305 Main
Lammert Joseph, trimmings, 505 Main
Lammus Wm., cartman, n.s. Taylor al. w of Kilgour
Lamout Henry, lab., wks. Campbell al. b. Elder and Findlay
Lamour Philip, fireman. River b. Ludlow and Lawrence
Lampe Albert, cab mkr., 704 W. 6th
Lampe Anthony, lab., 20 Abigail
Lampe Barney, porter, 100 W. Pearl
Lampe Bernard, porter, 106 W. Pearl
Lampe Bernard, shoe mkr., 667 Sycamore
Lampe Francis, stone mason, 44 Gest
Lampe Frederick, clk., 238 Main
Lampe Geo , lab., n.e.c. Pendleton and Abigail
Lampe Gerhard, wagon mkr., rear 19 Ham Road
Lampe Henry, tailor, 64 W. Mulberry
Lampe Henry, wagon mkr., rear 19 Ham. Road
Lampe Henry, watch mkr., bds. 369 Main
Lampe John, lab., 59 E. 8th e. of Lock
Lampe John, porter, 13 Woodward
Lampe John, shoe mkr., bds. 65 W. 5th
Lampe John B, boots and shoes, 6 E. Canal, h. 667 Sycamore
Lampe John F., varnisher, 90 Peete
Lampe John H., porter, 9 Woodward
Lampe Sarah, seamstress, 15 15th
Lampe Sophia, dress mkr., 549 Central Av.
Lamper Christian, cab. mkr., n.s. 6th b. Harriet and Horne
Lampers A., lab, wks. n.s. Front b. Lawrence and Pike
Lampert Christopher, butcher, 55 Hamer
Lampert Joseph, driver, wks. 450 Walnut
Lamping Bernhard H., grocery, 491 Race
Lamping Franz, wagon mkr., bds. 16 Abigail
LAMPING Frederick, (Myers & L.), 397 Vine
Lamping Henry A., grocery, 19 Franklin
Lamping John B., cof h., 193 W. 6th
Lamping John H., boots and shoes, 191 W. 6th
Lamping Joseph, 17 E. Liberty
Lams Philipp H., shoe mkr., 703 Main
Lamv Edmund, lab., n.w.c. Fremont and Harriet
Lanagan Margaret, servt., 390 Longworth
Lanahan Edward, carp., 67 W. Court w. of Central Av

CINCINNATI ADVERTISEMENTS.

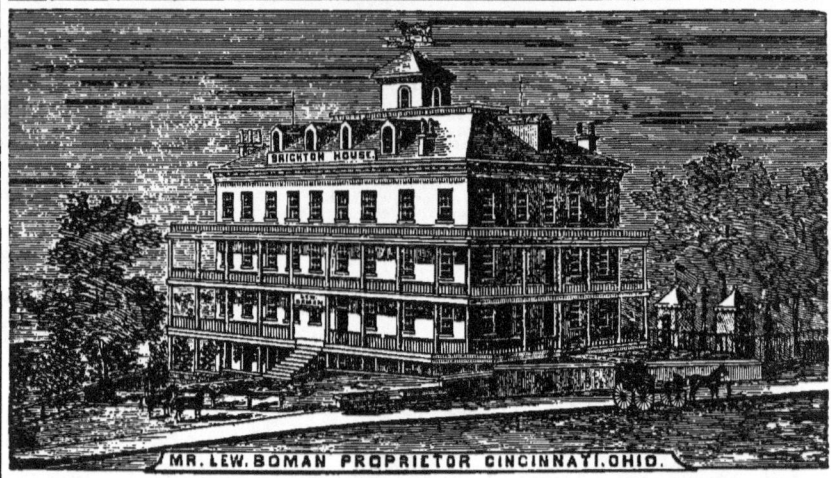

BRIGHTON HOUSE,
LEWIS BOMAN, Proprietor,
Harrison Pike, Head of Central Avenue, - - - CINCINNATI, OHIO

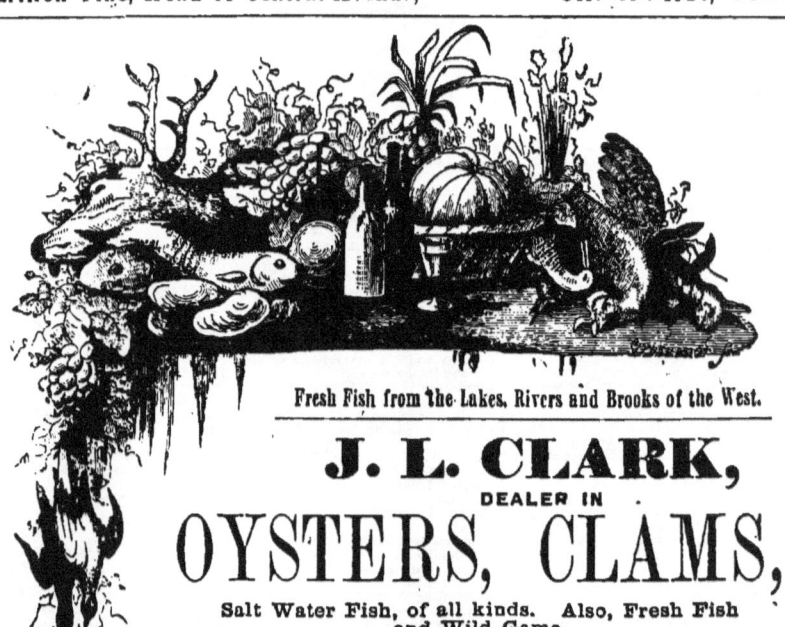

Fresh Fish from the Lakes, Rivers and Brooks of the West.

J. L. CLARK,
DEALER IN
OYSTERS, CLAMS,
Salt Water Fish, of all kinds. Also, Fresh Fish and Wild Game.

DEPOT, 55 WEST FIFTH STREET, CINCINNATI, O.
WILD GAME, OF ALL KINDS, IN SEASON.

Lancaster Isaac, wood dealer, s s. 8th b. Broadway and Lock, h. n.s. 6th b. Broadway and Culvert
Lance Sarah E., 105 W. 3d
Lancer John, molder, 20 Commerce
Lancing Anthony, lab., 602 Elm
Land Jno., box mkr., bds 6 Cheapside al.
Land Wm., box mkr., 6 Cheapside al.
Landaman Henry, molder, wks. n e.c. Canal and Walnut
Landauer Aaron, clothing, 473 Vine
Landauer Jacob, bds. 239 Main
Landauer Nathan, clk, bds. 31 Longworth
Landegan Julia, laundress, Spencer House
Landeg John, lab., e.s. Anderson b. 2d and Pearl
Lander Max, cof. h. 567 W. 5th
Landerdan Bridget, servt., 426 W. 6th
Landers Wm., porter, 142 Spring
Landfried Mathilda, 650 Vine
Landherr Theodore, carp., 573 Main
Landman John, cigar mkr., wks. 6 W. Pearl
Landman John, porter, 200 E. Front
Landmeier Henry, lab., 48 Pleasant
Landmeier Wm., teamster 234 Everett
Landre Henry, (Huck & L), 22 Orchard
Landsberg Abraham, b.k., 52 George
Landsberg Gerson, teacher. 52 George
Landsiegel Wiegand, tailor, 512 Vine
Landstrom Reinhold. bds. 296 W. 5th
Landt Bell, confec., 207 Walnut
Landwehn Diedrich W., cab. mkr., 28 Madison
Landwehr Anthony, grocer, s.e.c. Liberty and Hunt
Landwehr Bernhard, varnisher, 55 Pendleton
Landwehr Christian, stone mason, 67 Green [son
Landwehr Dietrich W., porter, 28 Madison
Landwehr Henry H., carp. 15 Rittenhouse, h.172 W. Court w. of Central Av
Landwehr Wm., lab., 36 Mansfield
Lane Ann, 12 Kossuth
Lane Bertha, 376 Broadway
LANE & BODLEY, (Philander P. L. & Joseph T. B), Iron Founders, Engine Builders. Circular Saw Mills, Woodworking Machinery, Steam Pipe, &c., s.e.c. John and Water
Lane Celia, servt., 325 Longworth
Lane Chas. M., foreman, wks. n.e.c. Walnut and Canal
Lane Edward, driver, e s. Aburn nr. Bigelow
Lane Fredericka. servt , 171 E. 3d
LANE GEO., Pork Packer and Ham Curer, 23 and 25 E. M. Canal, h. 434 Broadway
Lane Geo. M , saddler, bds. 177 Sycamore
Lane Henry, b.k. 23 E. Canal, h. 434 Broadway
Lane Henry M., mate, 1188 E. Front
Lane James, printer, 6 Wilson
Lane John, tailor, 8 W. 3d, h. Covington
Lane John I., 85 Laurel
Lane Mary. 934 E Front
Lane Nancy. bds. 46 Linn
Lane Patrick, lab., 207 E. 6th
Lane Patrick, tailor, bds. 49 W. 5th
LANE Philander P., (L. & Bodley), s.e. c. John and Water
Lane Wm., cigar mkr., bds. 65 W. 5th
Lanendaw Thomas, n.s. Front e. of Foster
Lanfred Adam. e.s. Vine b. Calhoun and Auburn Av.
Langanke Edward A., music teacher, 24 E. 4th
Lanferman Henry. sawyer, 207 Hopkins
Lanfersieck Adam J., stone mason, 53 Kossuth
Lang Anthony, cigar mkr., 19 Franklin
Lang Anthony, huckster. s.s. Ohio al. b. Plum and Elm
Lang August, mason, n.s. al. b. Poplar and Vine and Ham. Road and Buckeye

Lang Chas., cof. h., 544 Race
Lang Christian, tailor. 662 Race
Lang Elizabeth, dress mkr., bds. 75 Mill
Lang Frank, shoe mkr., 524 W. 7th
Lang Frederick, carriage trimmer, 137 Bremen
LANG Frederick, (F. Lang & Co.), 9 W. Court
LANG FREDERICK & CO., (Fred. L. & Edward Becht), Publishers and Proprietors Daily Cincinnati Union, 9 W. Court
Lang Geo. artist, n.w.c. Poplar and Ham. Road
Lang George, brewer 34 Abigail
Lang Geo , maltster, n.s. Abigail b. Sycamore and Main
Lang John, cof. h., 649 Vine
Lang John, mason, 69 Buckeye
LANG Julius, (L. & Wanner), h. 693 Elm
Lang Lewis, cab. mkr., 10 Abigail
Lang Louis, jeweler, 12 Ge t
Lang Michael, saddler, 548 Walnut
Lang Robert, sen.,grocer, n.e.c. 7th and Linn
Lang Robert, jr., mach., h. n e c. 7th and Linn
Lang Thos., cof. h., 18 Ham. Road
LANG & WANNER, (Julius L. & Herman W.,) Tanners and Curriers, 39 Dunlap
Lang Wm., tailor, 116 Ham. Road
Langdon E Bassett, atty., n.e.c. 9th and Walnut
Langdon Elam P., 14 E. 6th
Langdon Elam W., 12 E. 6th
Langdon John C., cof. h. 119 W. 5th, h. 61 W. 7th
Langdon Oliver C., s.e.c. Longworth and Plum
Langdon Solomon, salesman, 109 E. Pearl, h. 60 W. 7th
Langdon Thomas, blksmith, n.s. Barr al., near Stone al
Lange Anton J., boots and shoes, 460 W. 8th
Lange Bernhard, driver, s.s. Hunt, b. Sycamore and Main
Lange Mrs Bernhardine, 2 Louisa
Lange Chas., baker. bds. 28 W. 5th
Lange Charles, finisher, wks. Crane, Breed & Co.'s
Lange Francis, cooper, 66 Spring
Lange Frederick H., eng., 503 Race
Lange Hy., lab., 8 E. Canal
Lange Hy., teamster, 304 Water
Lange Hy. Wm , tailor. 517 Sycamore
Lange J. & Brother, (Julius & Louis,) jewelry, 32 W. 4th
Lange John G., grocery, 363 George
Lange John H , mover, 16 13th
Lange John H., policeman, 357 George
Lange Joseph, lab. bds. 8 E. Canal
Lange Julius, (J. L. & Brother,) bds. Gibson House
Lange Louis, (J. L. & Brother,) 12 Gest
Lange Miss Mary E., bds 2 Lucy
Lange Paul. wheelwright. 50 Plum
Lange Wm., cooper, e.s. Dudley, b. Everett and Liberty
Langeinge Joseph, lab., 660 Race
Langeller Charles. shoemkr, 181 Cutter
Langemeier Frederick, molder, 290 W. Front
Langemeier Bernard, lab., 122 Abigail
Langemier Hy., lab., 143 Abigail
Langemeier Herman, molder, 303 W. Front
Langenbach Catharine, 34 Ham. Road
LANGENBECK ADOLPH, Drugs, Medicines, Chemicals, &c., 490 Main
Langenbeck Frederick, druggist, 490 Main
Langenbein Charles, restaurant, 36 E. 5th
Langenberg William, shoemkr, n.e.c. Hughes and Liberty
Langenstoer Bernard, shoemkr, 373 W. 5th
Langenstro Casper, lab., 213 Hopkins
Lager Daniel, lab. 679 Vine
Langerman August, cigar mkr., 293 Elm
Langerman Chas., cigars, &c., 623 Central Av

Langeman Chris., cigar store, 293 Elm
Langerman Ferdinand, cigar mkr., bds. 293 Elm
Langerman Michael, lab., 16 Commerce
Langermeyer Joseph, lab., 660 W. Front
Langforder Frederick, lab , 114 Carr
Langfritz Frederick, plasterer, 49 Findlay
Langheinrich Christian, paper box mkr. 90 Clay
Langhorn Wm., cooper, bds. 74 Bremen
Langhorst August, clk, 29 Buckeye
Langhorst Charles, carriage mkr., 29 Buckeye
Langhorst Daniel, 29 Buckeye
Langhorst Fred., carp., 115 Laurel
Langhorst Hy., bds. 309 Central Av
LANGHORST HENRY A., Hardware, Cutlery, &c., 510 Main, h 29 Buckeye
Langhost Anthony, painter, rear 558 Walnut
Langinbrummer Bruno, collar mkr., 198 Sycamore
Langius Joseph F., bk. layer, 104 Bremen
Langley & Kinkead, (Lewis W. L. & Jos. D. K., com mer., 31 Water
Langley Lewis W., (L. & Kinkead,) 45 George
Langluett Jacob, cooper, 519 Sycamore
Languened John, boots and shoes, 295 Central Av
Langmead Wm., shoemkr., bds. 295 Central Av
Langstaff James, (L. & Wanzer,) h. 138 Smith
Langstaff & Wanzer, (James L. & John W.,) pork packers, e.s. Miami Canal, near Mohawk Bridge
Langtry Miss C. E., bds. 170 Longworth
Langtry Charlotte E., teacher, 95 Pike
Langtry James, 102 Milton
Langtry James W., 201 W. 5th
Langtry Wm T., compositor, wks. Methodist Book Concern
Lanham R. J., liquors, 9 Water, res. Vevay, Ind.
Laning Benjamin, porter, 446 W. 4th
Lankhorn Wm., cooper, bds. 74 Bremen
Lann Jackson, blksmith, h. 63 W. Court, w. of Central Av
Lannagan Ellen, 39 Plum
Lannen Pat., jeweler, 88 W. Court, w. of Central Av
Lanon Matthew, stone cutter, 182 Cutter
Lanphear Edward P., real estate agt., 82 W. 3d. h. 330 Linn
Lanphear Joseph, land agt., 324 Linn
LANPHEAR Wm. K., (Wm. K. L. & Co.,) 135 Central Av
LANPHEAR Wm. K. & Co., stencil cutters, 102 W. 4th
Lansaur Hy., tailor, 704 Freeman
Lanser Peter. carp., 219 Betts
Lansing David F., ornamenter, 133 Smith
Lansing Harmon, skin finisher, 986 Central Av
Lanug Vincent. carp.. 222 Baymiller
Lantry John, lab., wks. 46 E. 2d
Luntry Patrick, cartman, 56 Kossuth
Lantseter Hy., tailor, 101 Pleasant
Lanze Fred., turner, wks. 825 Central Avenue
Lanzer Hy., carp., 804 W. Front
Laomen Hy., cooper, 76 Abigail
Loxtermann David. box mkr., 11 Pine
Lape Benjamin b.k., 379 John
LAPE JACOB S., Queen City Flooring Mill, 512, 514, 516 and 518 Central Av, h. 379 John
Lape Wm. H., (Wm. H. L. & Co.,) res. Newport
Lape Wm H. & Co., tin ware, 21 E. Front
Laperman Ferdinand, River, b. Ludlow and Lawrence
Lapham Charles. 139 Plum
Laphan P. F., printer, 13 W. 4th
Laporte Celestine, bds. 215 Longworth
Laporte Victoria. 215 Longworth
Lapp Charles. butcher, 58 Hughes
Lapp John. paper hanger, 224 Betts
Lapp Michael, 224 Betts
Lapp Solomon, 224 Betts

J. M. BRUNSWICK & BROTHER,

BILLIARD TABLE

MANUFACTURERS,

No. 8 West Sixth Street, - - - CINCINNATI, O.

BRUNSWICK'S PATENT COMBINATION CUSHIONS,

Approved by PHIL. TIEMAN, Cincinnati, O., JOHN SEEREITER, Detroit, Mich., and many other scientific and amateur players in the United States.

AIKEN'S KNITTING MACHINES,

FOR FAMILY AND MANUFACTURER'S USE.

These Machines knit Hosiery of all sizes and textures, Fancy Articles, such as Shawls, Nubias, Sontags, Hoods, Capes, Rigolets, Undersleeves, Head Dresses, Millitary Sashes, Comforts, etc.

They knit a Pair of Socks in Fifteen Minutes.

And require less skill to work them than Sewing Machines. The Foot Power is represented in the cut. The Portable and the Power Ribbed Machine operate by Hand or by Power.

ALL MACHINES WARRANTED.

ORDERS FOR CUSTOM WORK PROMPTLY FILLED.

Office 104 West Fourth Street, Second Floor,

Miss. S. BRANSON, Ag't.

S. L. HAMLEN.   H. R. SMITH.

DRS. HAMLEN & SMITH.

DENTISTS,

No. 3 West Fourth Street,

CINCINNATI, OHIO.

G. G. WRIGHT, Agent,

(Successor to A. C. PORTER,)

MANUFACTURER AND DEALER IN EVERY DESCRIPTION OF MODERN & IMPROVED

LIGHTNING RODS,

No. 23 WEST SIXTH STREET, CINCINNATI, O.

N. B. Lightning Rods put up at the shortest notice.

Laque Nicholas, barber, 97 E. Pearl, h. 100 E. Pearl
Laral Martin, carp., wks. w.s. Western Av., b. Bank and Harrison Road
Laralde Edward, broker, 47 Walnut, h. 67 E. 3d
Larbes Joseph, (Hatke & L.,) 600 Race
Large John, hostler, s.w.c. Freeman and Front
Large Samuel, b.k., s.w.c. Court and Walnut
Larison Mary, 115 Betts
Larison Samuel, brush mkr., 115 Betts
Larkby James, lab., 160 W. Front
Larkey Bridget, n.s. Goodloe, b. Willow and Leatherbury
LARKIN, FOX & BRO., (Joseph F. L., Thomas F. & George Fox,) Bankers, 25 W. 3d
Larkin James, driver, 114 Webb
LARKIN Joseph F., (L. Fox & Bro.,) 27 Ellen
Larkin Mary, n.s. Front, e. of Washington
Larkin Patrick, messenger, bds. 74 E. 5th
Larkins Thomas, teamster, 50 E. 7th
Larkin Wm. F., clk., 25 W. 3d, bds. n.e.c. Ellen and 3d
Larnes Wm., lab., w.s. Lebanon Road, b. Liberty and Corp. Line
Larose Peter, tailor, 99 E. 2d
Larrance Isaac, map publisher, 235 E. 6th
Larrison Enoch, wagon mkr., n.e.c. Front and Washington
Larrison Joseph, farmer, 115 Betts
Larrison Mary, seamstress, 115 Betts
Larrison Samuel, brush mkr., 115 Betts
Larue Charles, b. h., 180 Broadway
Lary Jeremiah, lab., 48 Lock, n. of 8th
Lasance Augustus, tailor, 120 W. Front
Lasance Hermann, painter, 570 Elm
Lasch Chas., cof. h., 52 W. Liberty
Lascia Miss Louisa, servt., 417 Freeman
Laseke Hy., salesman, 17 W. 5th, h. 190 Clark
Lasha Mrs. Margaret, s.e.c. Riddle and Harrison Pike
Lasker Barbett, furniture, 101 Sycamore
Lasker Gustav, second hand store, 149 Sycamore
Lasker Myer, clothier, 154 Sycamore
Lass Frank, tailor, 703 Vine
Lassig Theodore, clk., 56 13th
Lastrode Laurence, upholster, 11 E. 4th
Lusz Frank, 740 Vine
Lusz Joseph, shoe mkr., 740 Vine
Latcha Sebastian, finisher, w.s. Goose al., b 14th and 15th
Later John D., porter, 126 Clay
Latham Allen, 105 Broadway
Latham Edward T., (John A. Shaw & Co., h. New York
Latham J. W., bds. Dennison House
Lathrop Mrs. G., b. h., 174 Plum
LATHROP W. H., atty., 9 Masonic Temple
Latemore Maggie, bds. 243 W. 5th
Latsch John, last manuf., 670 Central Avenue
Latscha Chas., finisher, 10 Abigail
Latt John, varnisher, wks. Mitchell & Rammelsberg's, res. Covington
Latta A. B. & E., (Alexander B. L. & Edmiston L.,) steam fire engine builders, 179 Race
Latta Alex. B., (A. B. & E. L.,) 179 Race
Latta Edmiston, (A. B. & E. L.,) 179 Race
Latta Finley, eng., 119 W. 6th
Latta Leonard, clk., n.e.c 5th and Elm
Latta Rebecca, h. 179 Race
Latter John P, clk., 406 George
Lattner G. A., confec., 282 Walnut, h. 497 Vine
Lattura Anna, 59 Vine
Latz Mary, servt., 34 Harrison
Lau Herman, teamster, bds. s.e.c Smith and Front
Laub Chas., stone cutter, 482 Walnut
Laubach Christian, shoe mkr., 773 Vine
Laube John R., stone cutter 29 Madison
Laube Rudolph, stone cutter, 29 Madison
Lauber Lisetta, bds. 463 Vine

Laubernd Henry, lab., 18 Buckeye
Laubernd John cooper, 18 Buckeye
Laubly Henry, 159 Pleasant
Laubly Henry, blk. smith, wks. s. w. c. Elm and Front
Lauchermer Christian, bk. binder, 92 Clay
Lauck Maria, s.e.c. Clinton and John
Lauck Michael, cof. h., n. s. Ham. Road b. Poplar and Vine
Laudeman David, saddler, 222 Barr
Laudenschlager David, butcher, rear 26 Mulberry
Laudenschlager George, tinner, 57 14th
Lauderback Geo., wagon mkr., wks. 169 Hunt
Lauderback Hermann, wagon mkr., 109 Hunt
Laudon Danl., lab., 10 Hughes
Laudon Jacob, cook, St. Charles Exchange
Lauenstein Ernst A., miller, 129 Butler
Lauer Jacob. cigar mkr., 402 Vine
Lauer Wm., tailor, 669 Race
Lauer Wm., tailor. 662 Race
Laufer Abraham, salesman, 124 Walnut, h. 66 W. 7th
Laufer Adam, shoe mkr., 523 Sycamore
Laufer Michael, cof. h., 24 W. 6th
Lauferman Bernard, cooper, s. w. c. 8th and Broadway
Laufersick Wm. H., bonnet presser, 54 Rittenhouse
Laugel Anton, mason, 12 Green
Laughlin Hugh, lab., 20 Pierson
Laughlin James, lab., n. w. c. Main and Court
Laughlin John, lab., 187 Water
Laughlin Patrick, lab., 187 Water
Laughlin Peter O., currier, bds. 158 W. 3d
Laughlin Rose, servt., 116 E. 4th
Lauk Frank, harness mkr., 89 Main
Laumann John, cooper, 20 Peete, h. 37 Buckeye
Laundau Morris, peddler, 335 Walnut
Launer Barbara, 97 Park
Laurence Francis, cook Burnet House
Laurens John, feed store, s s. Harrison Pike, b. Riddle and Division, h. 763 Vine
Laurens Charles, lab., e.s. M. Canal, b. 6th and Court
Laurozia Frank, lab., 162 E. 5th
Lauser Geo., tailor, 20 Dunlap
Laut Henry, 10 Orchard
Lautenschlerger John, bu.cher, Central Av. nr. Mohawk bridge
Lauterbach Diedrich, cigar mkr., bds. s. e.c. Mercer and Vine
Lauterbach Maida, 511 Vine
Lauth Jacob., driver, 390 Sycamore
Lauther Adam, bakery, 62 13th
Lauther John, grocery, 930 E. Front
Laux Joseph, cof. h., 608 Vine
Lauxtermann David. planer, 11 Pine
Lavalle Patrick, (Coyle & Co.,) n. w. c. 5th and Race
Laven Bridget, chambermaid Dennison House
Lavender Michael, porter, s.e.c. John & Front
Lavender Thos. F., salesman, 57 and 59 Main, h. 412 Longworth
Lavenson Isidore, liquors, h 55 Gano
Lavercomb Wm. H., upholsterer, 58 Hopkins
Lavercombe Jenny, dress mkr., 164 Plum
Lavery Patrick, porter, 1 Central Av.
Lavey Peter, lab , Pennock al. b. Cutter and Linn
Lavin Edward, lab., 82 Water
Lavin John, lab., 471 George
Laviu Peter, grocery, 425 W. 2d
Lavon Martin, mach., 56 Water
Lavoy Alonzo carriage trimmer, n. s. Milton e. of Young
Lavry Patrick, porter, al. b. 4th and 5th and Central Av. and John
Law Building, s.s. 3d b. Main and Sycamore. M. Hopple proprietor
LAW BULLETIN, W. W. Warden, Proprietor 19 W. 4th

Law John, trader, 151 Longworth
Law John H., ins. agt., 62 W. 3d, h. Hamilton co., opposite Loveland
LAW DR. JOHN S., Agent Royal Fire and Life Insurance Company, 62 W. 3d, h. Hamilton co., opposite Loveland
Law Robt., trader, 151 Longworth
LAW SCHOOL OF CINCINNATI COLLEGE, M. E. Curwen, Dean, 66 W. 3d
Lawerre Nicholas, lock smith. 235 Elm
Lawder J. B., surveyor, 73 W. 3d, bds. 162 Plum
LAWDER John F., (Spooner & L.,) h. 130 York
Lawler Ann, s.s. Charlotte b. Central Av and Linn
Lawler Daniel lab., n. s. Wade b. Freeman and Dudley
Lawler Davis B., 113 Broadway
Lawler Elizabeth, cof. h., 371 Sycamore
Lawler Jas., 65 Vine
Lawler James M., clk., 14 W. Pearl, h. s.w.c. 9th and Central Av
Lawler John, lab., s. s. Phoebe al. bet. Plum and Central Av
Lawler John, lab, 83 Barr
Lawler Mary, bds. 206 W. 5th
Lawler Michael J., porter, s.w.c. 9th & Central Av.
Lawler Thomas, s.s. 3d b. Canal and Kilgour
Lawler Thomas, lab., 700 Central Av
Lawler Wm. J., clk., bds. 226 Sycamore
Lawless Edward, lab., 180 E. 6th
Lawless Michael, 98 Race
Lawless Patrick, plumber. 186 E. 6th
Lawless Pat., lab., cor. 6th and Lock
Lawn Oliver, boatman, 19 Melunction
Lawrence Arthur, lab., 48 Plum
Lawrence Augustus, b.k., 29 Main, h. 110 E. 4th
Lawrence B. S., clk., bds. 41 George
LAWRENCE CHAS., Gunpowder, Sporting Ammunition, &c, 50 Main, h. 110 E. 4th
Lawrence E. M., clk. 567 W. 9th
Lawrence E. W., clk , 14 W. Pearl, bds. s e.c. 3d and Broadway
Lawrence Edward, foreman, h. 567 W. 9th
Lawrence Elnora, dress mkr., 220 Findlay
Lawrence Geo., butcher, 64 Accommodation
Lawrence Gee., cab mkr., 533 E. Front
Lawrence Gibson, lab., 179 W. Front
Lawrence Harriet, bds. 150 Sycamore
Lawrence Hiram B., plasterer, 9th, bet. Harriet and Mill Creek
Lawrence Jas , lab., 311 W. Liberty
Lawrence James M., bk., layer, 1 Hopkins
Lawrence John, butcher, n.s. Deer Creek Road b. Liberty and Tunnel
Lawrence John, carp., 170 Poplar
Lawrence John, tanner, bds. 92 14th
Lawrence Mary, 105 W. 3d
Lawrence Michael, tinner. h. 535 E. Front
Lawrence Nicholas, cab mkr., 182 Linn
Lawrence Peter, mason, s. s. Cross 1st h. w. of Hamburg
Lawrence Sister, St. John's Hospital, n. w c. Plum and 3d
Lawrence T. H., tobacconist. 12 Main
Lawrence Thos. A., type caster, s. s. Mount nr. Sycamore
Lawrence Thos. M., produce, 239 Clinton, bds. 132 Baum
Lawrence Uriah, shoe mkr., s.w.c. Hopkins and Central Av.
Lawrence Wm. G., salesman, 145 Main, h. 189 Clinton
Laws Alex. R., b.k., 70 Vine, h. 52 Mansfield
Laws Dniel, bds. 52 Mansfield
Laws Daniel, clk., bds. Gibson House
LAWS James H., (G. Brasheurs & L.,) 133 W. 6th
Laws S , salesman, bds. Devis House
Laws Wm H , salesman, 57 Main, bds. 133 W. 6th
Lawson D. W., clk., 65 W. 3d., bds. 359 W. 6th

MILES GREENWOOD,

MANUFACTURER OF

STEAM ENGINES,

AND ALL KINDS OF MACHINERY,

WROUGHT AND CAST IRON WORK,

FOR

Stores, Dwellings, Jails, Etc.

GAS & STEAM FITTINGS & BRASS WORK;

HEATING APPARATUS

FOR DWELLINGS AND PUBLIC BUILDINGS.

CAST BUTT-HINGES, AXLE PULLIES, ETC.
WROUGHT STRAP & "T" HINGES
AND WASHERS.

HEAVY AND LIGHT CASTINGS, OF ALL DESCRIPTIONS,

North East Corner of Canal and Walnut.

I. H. BONSALL'S

Photographic Rooms,

No. 14 WEST FIFTH ST.

Bet. Main and Walnut,

CINCINNATI, O.

Small Pictures copied and enlarged and colored in Oil or Water Colors. Special care taken with Card Photographs and Ivorytypes.

All Styles of Pictures made satisfactory and warranted.

CINCINNATI (LEE) DIRECTORY. (LEH) 205

Leary Cornelius, molder. rear 58 Hunt
Leary Michael, cooper, bds 118 Gest
Leary Robt. L., cigars, &c., 166 Vine, h. 237½ Longworth
Leasburgh Christopher, wks. 340 W. 3d
Leatherbery Alexander, 401 W. 3d
Leathercoop John, lab , 235 Carr
Leaver Barney, tailor, 250 Clark
LEAVITT & BEVIS (Joseph P. L. & Alfred B.) Ladies and Gents' Hosiery and Furnishing Goods, n.w.c. 5th and Vine
Leavitt Frank J., b.k., 24 W. 2d, h. 85 E. 5th
Leavitt Humphrey H., District Judge, U. S. Court, southern dist. of Ohio, h. 85 E. 5th
Leavitt John B., 328 Clark
Leavitt Rev. John W., 66 E. 5th
LEAVITT Joseph P. (L. & Bevis) 272 Richmond
Leavitt L T., printer 200 W. 3d
LEAVITT Wm. D. (Lee & L.) 69 Clinton
Leavittson ———, 32 George
Leavy Eliza. servt., 384 W, 6th
Leavy Mary, servt., 384 W. 6th
Lebbe Barney, peddler, 550 Central Av
Lebeau John J., molder, 21 Clinton
Lebenstein August, butcher, 504 John
Lebish Anthony, collector. 426 Sycamore
Lebke Joseph, lab., s.s. Taylor b. Carr and Harriet
LE BLOND J. FREDERICK, Printer, 167 Walnut, bds. 320 Findlay
LE BLOND ROBERT E., Printer, 167 Walnut, bds. 320 Findlay
Le Blond Robert. agt., stationery, 321 W. 6th. h. 312 Clark
LE BOUTILLIER Chas. (J. Le Boutillier & Bros.) res. Philadelphia
Le Boutillier Geo., mer., 2 Hopkins
LE BOUTILLIER J. & BROS. (Jas. Charles & Thomas) Staple & Fancy Goods. 30 W 4th
LE BOUTILLIER James (J. Le B. & Bros.) h. 173 Plum
LE BOUTILLIER Thomas (J. Le Boutillier & Bros) res. New York
Lebrecht Geo., huckster, 55 Findlay
Lebrecht Salome, w.s. Ridgway al. b. Liberty and 15th
Lech Valentine, lab., 205 W. Liberty
Lechdine Ferdinand, lab., 6 Pleasant
Lechemier Edward lab., n.s Montgomery Pike nr. Madison Road
Lecher Christ . finisher, wks. n.e.c. Walnut and Canal
Lechner Frances, 651 Vine
Lechner Fred., wks Cin. type foundry
Lechner Frederick, finisher, w.s. Sycamore b. Hunt and Abigail
Lechner Josephine. h. 651 Vine
Lechrick John, 709 Central Av
Lecht ———, lab , 418 Walnut
Lecht John H., turner, 386 Vine
Lecht la Christian, lab., 164 Carr
Lechtler Christ , cof. h., s.w.c. Liberty and Plum
Leckemeyer Hy. C. F., match mkr, bds. Western Av, nr. Bank
Luckenmeier Hy . e.s. Western Av. b. Bank and Harrison Pike
Leckermeier Hy., carp., 654 Race
Leckermeier Hy., cab. mkr, n.e.c. Elm and Elder
Leckerfield Barney, driver, s.e.c. Hoadley and Longworth
Lecount F. (Cont's & L)
Lecount Wm. H., fireman, 238 Cutter
Lecquire Fred. H., salesman, 87 Main, h Newport
Leddy Daniel. cof. h., 137 E. 6th
Lederer Geo., brewer, n.w.c. Hamburg and Mohawk
Lederer Jacob, clk., 16 Home
Ledger Hanna, cof. h., 175 W. Court
Ledlie Geo., b. k. 103 W 4th, h 562 W. 9th
Ledman John L., bds. 24 W. 9th
Ledwidge Peter, dray 36 Elizabeth
Lee Alfred, brakesman. 134 Barr
Lee Burney, bds 204 Broadway
Lee Eliza, tailoress, 154 Baymiller

Lee Elizabeth, 97 W. Court w. of Central Av.
LEE & FISHER, (Geo. M. L. & Saml. S. F.,) Attorneys at Law. 53 W. 3d
Lee Geo., cof. h., 414 W. Front
LEE Geo., M., (L. & Fisher,) h. Fairmount
Lee Isaiah, blksmith, wks. 64 E. Front
Lee John, baker. 188 W. Court
Lee John, lab., 50 Baum
Lee John, lab., bds., Mechanics Hall
Lee John, lab., bds. s.e c Smith and Front
Lee Joseph, 154 Webb
Lee Joseph, dray, 13 Lock n of 8th
LEE & LEAVITT, (Rufus S. L. & Wm. D. L.) Manufacturers of Circular Saw-Mill Machines, 130 W. 2d
Lee Margaret, 95 Mulberry
Lee Michael, lab., n.s. Rail Road e. of Kelly
LEE R. Wilson, (Adolph Wood & Co) 69 W. 9th
LEE RENSAELAER W , Resides one mile south of Covington nr. Turnpike Gate on the Bank Lick Road Leading to Latonia Springs. Post Office address Cincinnati
Lee Rich., 131 Poplar
Lee Robert, locksmith, n.w.c. Mound and 7th
Lee Rob., E., ticket agt., Union R. R. ticket office, s.e.c. Front and Broadway, res. E. Walnut Hills
Lee Rob. R., awning mkr., s.w.c. Central Av. and 6th
LEE Rufus S., (L. & Leavitt) 202 Mound
Lee S. W., door kpr., National Theatre
Lee Saml., watchman, 152 W. 6th
Lee Sylvester, baggage master, 269 W. 3d
Lee Thomas, lab., 184 Central Av
Lee Thos., shoe mkr., 53 Broadway
Lee Wm., 332 W. 5th
Lee Wm., boots and shoes, 138 Vine, h. 34 E 3d
Lee Wm., H., awnings and tents, 222 Central Av
Leech Maria, 411 Broadway
Leech Mary, 83 Mulberry
Leech Roswell upholsterer, 237 Clinton
Leech Wm. C , phys., 55 W. 7th
Leedom Thos., L., 101 W. 4th, h. 416 W 4th
Leeds Mary, 62 Gano
Leeds Wm., cooper, 653 W. Front
Leeke Catharine, teacher, bds. 144 Longworth
Leeke H., tinner, wks. n.w c. Race and 2d
Leekel Herman H., lab., 536 Race
Leeker John, porter, 10 W. Front
Leen B., lab., n.s. Front, E. of Foster
Leen John, lab., s.s. Front E. of Torrence
Leese Geo., tinner, bds. 186 Race
Leese Manuel J., foreman, 30 Butler
Leetsch & Eich, (John L. & Fred. E.), carps., s.s 12th b. Vine and Race
Leetsch John, (L. & Eich.) s.w.c. Race and Commerce al
Lefering Henricks, weaver, 15 Green
Leffingwell M. W., actor, 142 W. 4th
Lefl Jacob, saddler, bds. 609 Walnut
Lefkin Joseph, bar k. s.e.c. Ann and Central Av
Leforce Saml., policemann, 79 Bank
Lefson C., carp., 345 Main
Legg Elizabeth, b. h. 208 W. 5th
Legg Geo. W., cooper, wks., n.w.c. Freeman and 9th
Legg Joseph F., cooper 707 Clark
Legge Elizabeth, bds. 515 W. 8th
Leggatt Chas., butcher 151 Baymiller
Leginger Elizabeth, 494 Walnut
Legler Joseph, stewart, e.s. Park b. Longworth and 6th
Legner Geo., tailor 29 Elder
Legner John, cab. mkr., 540 Plum
Legras E., clk., D. & M. R. R. 5 College bldg., h. Newport
Lehan John, lab., s.e.c. Pearl and Butler
Lehany Alice, 20 Lock n. of 8th

ECLECTIC MEDICAL INSTITUTE,

College Building, Cor. Court and Plum, CINCINNATI.

WINTER SESSION.

The Winter Session *commences on Monday the 13th of October*. Preliminary Lectures and Clinical Instruction, from Monday, September the 29th.

EXPENSES.

Fees for Lectures and Matriculation, $60. Demonstrators and Hospital tickets, each, Five Dollars.

Good boarding can be obtained at from $2 50 to $3 50 per week.

For *One Hundred Dollars*, paid in advance, the Institute issues a CERTIFICATE of SCHOLARSHIP, entitling the holder to three, four or more Courses.

Matriculation, Demonstrators, and Hospital Tickets, each, $5 00, to be paid at the Commencement of each Session.

Requisites for Graduation.

The candidate must be twenty-one years of age, must possess a good moral character, must have read medicine two years, and to have attended two courses of Lectures, one of which, must have been in this Institutue; or he must have attended three courses with intermediate reading; or he must have practiced four years, and have attended one course of Lectures.

INFORMATION.

Students visiting the City, will call at the College Building, where they can matriculate with the Treasurer, Prof. J. M. SCUDDER, who will likewise assist them in procuring suitable boarding houses.

For further information, address

JOHN M. SCUDDER,
Box 2209 Cincinnati, O.

Lehany Mary, laundress, 27 Lock, n. of 8th
Leheay John, wheelwright, 63 Avery
LEAMAN Gerson, (Marienthal, L. & Co.) 149 W 6th
Lehman Hy., clk., 326 Main
Lehman Herman, carp., 26 13th
Lehman Jacob, cab. mkr, 186 W, 9th
Lehman John, harness mkr*, 466 Main
Lehman Leopold, student, 201 Elm
Lehman Lewis, lock mkr, 531 Vine
Lehman Moses, lock mkr., 532 Vine, h. 531 Vine
Lehman Nason, shoe mkr., 60 David
Lehmann Amelia, seamstress, 148 Ham. Road
Lenmann Christian, 805 Vine
Lehmann Fred., shoe mkr., 22 W. Mulberry
Lehmann Hart, grocery, 201 Elm
Lehmann Hy, carp, 578 Elm
Lehmann Jacob, lab., 34 Hamer
Lehmann John, blksmith, 154 Pleasant
Lehmann John, saddler, 466 Main
Lehmann Lewis, lock smith, 531 Vine
Lehmanowsky, Louis L., watchman, 3 Clinton Court
Lehmeier Joseph, lab., 65 Green
Lehmer Hy., lib., wks. 222 E. Front
LEHMER JAMES D., Commission Merchant, 81 and 83 W. 3d, n.w c. Ludlow and Arch
Lehmhous Wm., lab., n.s. Yeatman b. Broadway and Sycamore
Lehmkueler Wm., blksmith, 39 Moore
Lehmkuhl Barney, porter, 613 Race
Lehmkuhle Dietrick, cooper, n.s. Rail Road e. of French
Lehmkuhler, Bernhard, lab., 612 Race
Lehmkuhler Ernst H., grocery, 173 Clay
Lehmuth Fred., cooper, 47 W. Liberty
Lehnes John, shoe mkr. 125 E. Pearl
Lehuer John W., oven builder, e.s. Goose al. b. Green and Elder
Lehnkring Hy. D., clk., 65 E. Pearl, bds Cincinnati House
L'Hommedieu Dr. S., bds. Burnet House
L'HOMMEDIEU STEPHEN S., Prest C. H. & D. R. R.; Office s.s. 6th b. Hoadly and W. W. Canal, res. Storrs tp
Lehr Jacob, cigar mkr., wks. 381 Vine
Lehr John, cooper, wks. 586 Walnut
Lehy Peter J., shoe mkr., 320 John
Leibenberg Bernhard, clk., 282 Main h. 164 W. 6th
Leibold John, cab. mkr., 71 Green
Leibold John, lab 34 Mohawk
Leibold John, lab., 492 Vine
Leibrandt Christian, cap mkr., 530 Walnut
Leicht Peter J., carp., 211 Clinton
Leicht Michael, teamster, 15 Adams
Leichtenburg Michael, lab., wks. n.w.c. Plum and Wade
Leichtle Francis J., barber 127 Ham. Road
Leichtle John, carp, 127 Ham. Road
Leick John, tailor, 490 Walnut
Leidel Peter, barber, 221 W. 6th
Leiendecker Peter, tailor, 5 37 Vine
Leiermau Peter, shoe mkr., 495 Walnut
Leighton Chas, H., clk., 138 E Liberty
LEIGHTON E. & CO., (Elliott L. & G. Tompkins.) Pork and Beef Packers. 270 Sycamore
LEIGHTON Elliott, (E. L. & Co.,) 138 E. Liberty
Leighton Geo., clk., 380 R c.s
Leihkauf Leonard, lab., 76 Buckeye
Leiker Martin, lab., bds. 70 Sycamore
Leiland John, 686 Vine
Leimann Anna, rear 26 Franklin
Leimann Peter, shoe mkr., 485 Walnut
Leimann Rudolph, carp., 600 Main
Leimer Charles, shoe mkr., 538 Plum
Leinen Peter, shovel mkr., wks. rear 180 Buckeye
Leininger George, furnaceman, 99 E. Pearl
Leininger Hy., carp., al. b Walnut and Vine and 13th and Mercer
Leininger Jacob, finisher, 58 Ham. Road

LEININGER JOHN G., Merchant Tailor, and Boots and Shoes. 315 and 317 Vine
Leinweber Hy., bds. 94 Central Av.
Leinweber Mary, 94 Central Av.
Leins Wm., cab. mkr., 519 Elm
Leis Geo., scale mkr., wks. 392 Vine
Leis Louis, clk., 614 Sycamore
Leiser David, clk., bds. 29 Longworth
Leiser Marx, clothing, 359 Main, h. 29 Longworth
Leiser Theodore H., tailor, e.s. Race b. Liberty and 15th
Leisker Frank, baker, College al. b. Woodward and Abigail
Leisler William, shoe mkr., 665 W. Front
Leisman Hy, dray, wks. 51 W. 2d
Leist Jacob, stoves and tinware, 128 W. Liberty
LEIST John. (J. L. & Co. Huber, Scheu & L.) 84 Woodward
LEIST JOHN & CO., (John L., & John Riley,) Leather and Findings, 313 Main
Leist Peter. tanner, 1460 E. Front
Leist Philip, tanner. n.s Front w. of Hill
Leist Valentine tanner, 1460 E. Front
Leisitkon Charles, cab. mkr., 165 Carr
Leisure Samuel, caulker, n.s. Goodloeb. Willow and Niagra
Leithold Hy., cab. mkr., res. Vine St. Hill
Leitlein Conrad, 705 Elm
Leive Hy. H., cab. mkr., 12 Mary
Lekamp Geo. O , lab., 148 Clinton
Lekamp John F., lab, 517 Sycamore
Lekamp Wm., cooper, 16 Mulberry
Leland John, batter, 431 W. 5th
Leland John, printer, 431 W. 5th
Leland Patrick. stone cutter 28 Lock
Leland Thomas A., mess. O. & M. R. R. h. 484 W. 4th
Leman Mathias, tailor, 409 Elm
Lemcole Hy., porter, 15 E 8th
Leming Nathaniel, mach. 637 W. Front
Lemker Hy., tailor, 185 Linn
Lemman John, foreman, John Mitchell's h. 229 Longworth.
Lemming George, plow mkr., wks. 9 W. 7th
Lemming Hy., plow mkr., wks. 9 W. 7th
Lemming John, plow mkr., wks. 9 W. 7th
Lemming Martha, 637 W. Front
Lemmon Abraham, candy mkr., s.e c. Poplar and Dudley
Lemmon Hy., blksmith, e.s. Kilgour b. 3d and 5th
Lemmon J. P., printer, bds. 217 Plum
Lemon Alexander H., clk., 171 Clinton
Lemon Eliza, 325 W. 9th w. of Central Av.
Lemon Wm., painter, 165 Mound
Lemuth Frederick, cooper. 29 Hughes
Lencke Frederick. cab. mkr., 148 W. Court w. of Central Av.
Lendamann Frank, blksmith, 48 Pleasant
Lender August, shoe mkr., bds. 925 Central Av.
Lender Frederick, hardware, 1065 Central Av.
Lender Mary, teacher, 18 W. 9th
Lender Joseph, 361 Ham. Road
Lendert Wm tinner, wks. 378 Main
Leneke Frederick, cab. mkr., 148 W. Court w. of Central Av.
Lenkersdoerfer George, tailor, bds. 576 Elm
Lennamore Wm, cof. h. 277 Walnut
Lenneman Geo.. molder, wks. n.e.c. Walnut and Canal
Lennert Wm., lab., 200 Pleasant
Lennon Mrs. A. millinery, 218 W. 5th
Lennon Andrew, 217 W. 5th
Lennon Washington H., lab., wks. Evans Gaines & Co's.
Lense Chas., cof. h. 35 Moore
Lents Jacob, brewer, s.w.c. Division and Harrison Pike
Lentz John, paper box manufac., 76 W. 3d

Lentz Julius, paper carrier, 98 W. Court
Lenwer George, lab., 509 Main
Lenz Catharine M., lab. 152 Bremen
Lenz Geo., lab., 152 Bremen
Lenz Geo., molder, 99 Clay
Lenz Mathias, shoe mkr., 121 Providence
Lenzius Christian, tailor, 116 Ham. Road
Leo ———. cab. mkr., 208 Clark
Leo Margaret, servt., 93 E. 3d
Leo Mary, 83 Barr
Leohr Hy., b. k. at 39 Walnut
Leon Joseph, 226 Walnut
Leon, Marks & Co. (Marks L , Hy. M., Emanuel M. & Moses C. Marks) Clothing, 5 W. Pearl
Leon Marks. (L., Marks & Co.) 299 W. 9th
Leonard A. W., bar k., Burnet House
Leonard Bridget, 33 Kossuth
Leonard Aaron. blksmith, 104 Broadway
Leonard Bernard, lab., 357 Cutter
Leonard Catharine, servt., 349 W. 7th
Leonard & Cook, (Louis L. & John C.) trunk manuf., n.e c. Main and 2d
LEONARD E. G. & CO., (Ezra G. L. & Europe W. Hamlin) Importers and Wholesale Dealers in Hardware, 55 W. Pearl
Leonard Edward, teamster, wks. 830 Central Av.
LEONARD Ezra G., (E. G. L. & Co.) h. Avondale
Leonard F., finisher, wks. C. T. Dumont's
Leonard G. W., pipeman, 107 W. 5th
Leonard Geo., dray, 393 Race
Leonard Geo. W., clk., bds. 104 Broadway
Leonard Hy., (H. L & Co.) 468 Elm
Leonard Hy. & Co., (Hy. L., & Hy. R. Leonard) pork packers, 487 Elm
Leonard Hy. R., cistern builder, 63 Hopkins
Leonard Jas., lab., e.s. Henderson al. b. 7th and 8th
Leonard Jas., mach., rear 24 W. Court w. of Central Av.
Leonard John, h. 514 Sycamore
Leonard John, bklayer, 304 Linn
Leonard John, dray, s.s. 3d b Canal and Kilgour
Leonard John, lab., n.s. Cherry al. b. Plum and Central Av.
Leonard John, lab., s.s. 9th b. Harriet and Mill Creek
Leonard John, pipeman, 544 Sycamore
Leonard John, stone mason, 116 Butler
Leonard John, tailor, 102 W. 5th
Leonard John, jr., clk., 468 Elm
Leonard John B., bklayer, 304 Linn
Leonard John D., clk., 110 W. 3d
Leonard John W., printer, bds. 104 Broadway
Leonard Miss L., millinery, 150 W. 5th, bds. 67 W. 6th
Leonard Louis, (L. & Cook) 40 Bremen
Leonard Margaret, servt., 349 W. 7th
Leonard Mary, servt., 396 Longworth
Leonard Michael, lab., 297 John
Leonard Michael, lab., n.s. Montgomery Pike nr. Reading Road
Leonard Patrick, dray, bds. n.w.c. Pike and Pearl
Leonard Patrick, grocery, 31 Race
Leonard Patrick, watchman O. & M. R. R., 744 W. 5th
Leonard Robert, box mkr, 217 W. 3d
Leonard Mrs. S. J., 70 Longworth
Leonard Samuel, 157 Livingston
Leonard Thos., 20 Mohawk
Leonard Thos., s.s. Langdon al. b. 6th and 7th
Leonard Thos., lab, s.s. 6th b. Broadway and Culvert
Leonard Thos., lab., n.w.c. Ludlow and River
Leonard W. B., (Miller & Co.) n.s. 5th b. Sycamore and Main
Leonard Wm, porter, 200 Pleasant
Leonards Robert, lab., wks. c. 3d and W. W. Canal
Leonhard Christian, wagon mkr. 412 Vine

CINCINNATI ADVERTISEMENTS.

M. D. FLYNT,
MANUFACTURER OF HARD LEATHER & TRAVELLING

TRUNKS,

OF EVERY DESCRIPTION.

PACKING TRUNKS, VALISES, CARPET BAGS, &C.

NO. 2 COLLEGE BUILDING,

Walnut Street, between 4th and 5th, opp. Gibson House, - - - - CINCINNATI, OHIO.

L. F. POTTER & WILSON,
MANUFACTURERS OF STEAM ENGINES,
AND DEALERS IN
MACHINERY,

98 and 100 East Columbia Street, bet. Broadway and Ludlow, Cincinnati, O.

Offer for sale Marine, Stationary, Portable, Pumping and Hoisting Engines, Boilers, Fire Fronts and Grate Bars, Portable and Stationary Saw and Grist Mills, Wood-Working Machinery and Machinist's Tools of all descriptions, Slide Lathes, Drill Presses, Planers, Screw Cutters, Ratchets, Stock and Dies, Shafting, Pulleys and Hangers; Leather, Gum and Gutta Percha Belting, Blacksmith's Tools, Anvils, Vizes, Bellows, etc. Wrought Iron Pipe and Fittings. Steam Guages, Chain Cables, Wire Cordage, etc. etc. Second Hand Machinery bought and sold on Commission. Also, Machinery built and repaired at short notice. Cash Advances made on Machinery left with us for sale.

A. E. CHAMBERLAIN.   O. N. BUSH.   F. V. CHAMBERLAIN.

CHAMBERLAIN & CO.
PROPRIETORS OF THE
ANCHOR IRON WORKS,
MANUFACTURERS OF EVERY DESCRIPTION OF
COOKING AND HEATING STOVES,

Hollow-Ware, Dog Irons, Sad Irons, Tea Kettles, Cauldron, Potash and Sugar Kettles, and Castings in general.

OFFICE, SAMPLE AND SALE ROOMS, Nos. 51 and 53 VINE STREET,

FOUNDRY, on Hunt Street, east of Broadway.

Leonhard John, tailor, 109 York
Leonhard Philip, music teacher, 3 Pleasant
Leopold & Goodheart, (Morris L. L. & Wm. G. & Arnold Goodheart,) clothiers, 74 W. Pearl
Leopold Lorenz, shoe mkr., bds. 671 Race
Leopold Morris L., (L. & Goodheart) 101 W. 8th
Leopold Moses, peddler, 402 Vine
Leopold Otto G., civil eng., 126 Betts
Leopold Samuel, clk. 74 W. Pearl, h. 101 W. 8th
Leovy D. J., chiropodist. 275 W. 6th
Leowen Jacob. cigar mkr., 402 Vine
Leowenstein Ily , 402 Vine
Lepage Elizabeth. 448 George
Lepelane John. artist, bds. 293 W. 5th
Lepere Valentine, ale and porter manuf., 144 Buckeye
Lepere Wm , 144 Buckeye
Lepker Geo., box mkr., 60 Findlay
Leppelmann Hy. H., wood yard, 424 Central Av.
Lepper Adam, mess. Lafayette Banking Co., bds. n w.c. 9th and Walnut
Loppert Chas.. molder, 59 Martin
Leppert Christian. lab., 1 Lucy
Leppert Lawrence, screw cutter, 99 E. Pearl e. of Broadway
Leppert Leonard, mason, 698 Vine
Leppert Lorenz, 99 E. Pearl
Leppert Wolfgang, lab.. 141 Pleasant
Lerch Theodore, butcher, 25 Dunlap
Lerep John, cigar mkr., wks. 503 Main
Leribus B.. chair mkr., wks. John Mitchell's
Leribus Joseph, chair mkr., wks. John Mitchell's
Lesaint Frank, tailor 700 Vine
Lesaint Peter, tailor, 700 Vine
Leseberg Christian, spoke mkr , 508 W. 9ch
Leseke Hy., lab., 190 Clark
Leser Christian, lab , 682 Vine
Lesher Wm., pipe fitter, wks. n.e.c. Walnut and Canal
Leslie A. M., jr., clk. n.w.c. 4th and Race bds. 278 W. 7th
LESLIE JAMES, Dental Depot and Gold Foil Manufacturer. n.w.c. 4th and Race. (up stairs) h. 278 W 7th
Leslie John. artist, National Theater
Leslie Robert, clk. 100 W , 5th, h. 243 W. Court near Baymiller
Lees Benedict. porter, 102 Butler
Lessel Peter. potter, 99 Hunt. b. 04 Hunt
Lessly Julius, bar k., n.e.c. 6th and Walnut
Lester John, fireman, 35 Hathaway
Leszmann Anthony, lab., 286 Water
Letle Frank, tailor, 346 Ilam Road
Letle Thos., w end of Mohawk
Lettenbaur Francis, tailor, 180 Walnut
Letzenberger David, 767 Vine
Letter John. lab., bds. n.s. 6th b. Canal and Freeman
Letter John P.. clk., bds. 406 George
Letlerler Mrs. Louisa, 76 Peete
Letsche Matthew, grocery, 613 Elm
Letzer Jacob, lab., 481 W. 8th
Leuba Hy., b k. 62 W. 4th, h. Covington
Leuchtenburg John F., cigars, 626 Central Av

LEUCHTWEIS AUGUST, Brass Founder and Finisher, 46 12th
Leuck Anton. lab., bds. 341 W. 6th
Leuderalbert Herman H., cooper, 19 Pendleton
Leudhart Louis, lab., 375 W. 5th
Leuenberger James, eng., 469 George
Leuenberger Rudolph. eng., 469 George
Leusenbach Michael, lab., e.s. Bremeu b. Elder and Findlay
Leussink Reinhold, tailor, w.s. Goose al. b. Green and Elder

LEUTHSTROM WM.,
Secretary House of Refuge, Office, City Buildings, res. Glendale
Leuting Christiana, seamstress, wks. 12 Green
Leuve Leonard. 503 Elm
Leuxenburger Peter, cartman, 70 E. 3d e. of Whittaker

Levebre Lewis, shoe mkr., e.s. Coggswell al. b. Woodward and Franklin
Levendorf Soloman, second hand store, 180 W. Front, h. 182 W. Front
Levenstein Hy., lab., rear 194 W. 5th
Lever Hepsa, dress mkr , bds. 123 Mill
Leverony D., cof. h., 68 W. Front
Levi Abraham J., missionary, 392 W. 7th
Levi Albert, liquors, 347 Race
Levi Amelia. grocery, s.s. Front b. Broad and Waldon
Levi Barney, driver, 105 Providence
Levi Chas , peddler, 69 W. 7th
Levi David, 4 Metropolitan Bldg., h. 471 Race
LEVI Herman, (S. Levi & Brother) 201 Race
Levi Isaac, books, &c., 191 John
Levi Isaac, cutter, 72 Longworth
Levi Isaac. peddler, 163 W. 9th
Levi Jacob, cigar mkr., 205 Elm
Levi Jacob horse trader, bds. 17 Lodge
Levi James, clk., 347 Race
Levi Joseph, cigar mkr., 128 Walnut
Levi Joseph, fancy goods, 1 8 W. 5th
LEVI Leopold, (S. Levi & Brothers) 311 Walnut
Levi Lewis, peddler, 201 George
Levi Lipman, peddler, 201 George
Levi Louis, peddler. 73 Providence
Levi Louis, tailor, 197 W. Liberty
Levi Mary, n s. Pearl b. Smith and Park
Levi Mrs. Mary A., 249 W. Front
Levi Mrs. Isabella, dress mkr., 204 Everett
Levi Moses, peddler, 356 W 5th
Levi Nathan, peddler, 33 Chestnut
Levi Rachael, 92 W. Front
Levi S., bds. 35 Longworth
LEVI S. & BROTHERS, (Solomon L., Leopold L. & Herman L.) Distillers and Dealers in Wines and Liquors, 221 and 223 Walnut
Levi Samuel, s.s. E. Front b. Broad and Waldon
Levi Samuel, 178 Central Av.
Levi, Senior & Co., (Sigmund L., Abraham S. & Abraham Mayfield) liquors, 103 Sycamore
Levi Sigmund, (L. Senior & Co.) 322 Walnut
LEVI Solomon, (S. L. & Brothers) 18 E. 6th
Levi Wm., cap mkr., rear 16 15th
Levi Jacob, b.k., 204 Everett
Levie Barbara, 59 W. Court
Levin David F., janitor, s.w.c. 3d and Walnut
Leving Geo., wks. Junction 6th and Front
Leving Hy., wks. Junction 6th and Front
Levings Jeremiah W., b.k. 27 W. Pearl. bds. Madison House
Levinson David S., sexton, c. Walnut and 7th, h. 114 E. 5th
Levinson J. & M., (Jacob & Meyer L.), clothiers, 170 Broadway
Levinson Jacob. (J. & M. L.), 248 Br'd. way
Levinson Leah, trimmings, 268 W 5th
Levinson Meyer, (J. & M. L.), 160 Br'dway
Levits Mary, rear 524 E. Front
Levoy Michael, harness mkr., 188 Mound
Levoy Wm , 112 Milton
Levy, hatter, bds. 65 Broadway
Levy Albert, (Jas. Levy & Bro.), 347 Race
Levy Babette, 467 Vine
Levy Ellis, carp., 439 W. 2d
Levy James, (Jas. L. & Bro), 346 Race
Levy James & Bro., (James & Albert L), liquors, 7 W. Front
Levy Joseph, bds. Silvester House
Levy Joseph, (Nathan & L.), 135 Central Av
Levy Joseph, peddler, 195 W. Liberty
Levy Joseph J., cigar mkr., 128 Walnut
Levy Lipman, b k., 37 W. Pearl, h. 473 W. 5th
Levy Peter, hat., al. b. Court and Richmond and Cutler and Linn
Levy Sam'l, second hand store, 115 W. 5th
Lewe Henry, shoe mkr., 373 W. 5th

Lewis, actor, National Theater
Lewis A. H., ass. supt. O. and M. R. R., office n.s. Front b. Mill and Wood, h. 404 W. 8th
Lewis Abigail, 4 Webster
Lewis Agnes, 76 Pleasant
Lewis Albert, conductor, bds. Brighton House
Lewis Anna. servt , 545 W. 8th
Lewis Arathusa, 4 Webster
Lewis Arthur, bds , 109 E. 2d
Lewis B. F., salesman, n.e.c. 5th and Vine, h. Reading
Lewis Bolly, bds 290 W. 6th
Lewis Charles, brush mkr., bds. 41 E. 2d
Lewis Charles, grocery, 64 and 66 E. Pearl
LEWIS Charles, (W. & C. L.), 108 Broadway
Lewis Chas. A., clk., 101 W. 4th, rooms n.w.c. 4th and Race
LEWIS Chas. R., (Haynes L. & Spencer), 136 Walnut
Lewis Christopher. lab., 830 W. Front
Lewis Clara. 454 W. 5th
Lewis Edward. tinner, 148 W. Court w. of Central Av
Lewis Elizabeth, s.w.c. Court and Walnut
Lewis Ellen, 4 Webster
Lewis Fanny, 91 St. Clair
Lewis Fountain, (L. & Tosspot), 266 Longworth
Lewis Frances, 264 George
Lewis Frank, miller, 31 Pierson
Lewis Frank B.. clk, bds. 191 Smith
Lewis George, clonks, &c., 92 W. 4th, bds Gibson House
LEWIS GEO. N., Books and Stationery, 28 W. 6th. b 327 Baymiller
LEWIS Henry, (A. D. Bullock & Co.), h Walnut Hills
Lewis Henry, mail agent, bds. 125 Longworth
Lewis Hensler, n.s. 6th b. Culvert and Broadway
Lewis J., actor, bds. 38 E. 4th
Lewis Jane, bds. 183 Race
Lewis Mrs. Jane. washwoman, w.s. Mulberry al. b. Pearl and 3d
Lewis Mrs. Jane M., bds. 244 Hopkins
Lewis John, boiler mkr., h. 98 E. 5th
Lewis John confec. and notion store, 24 Broadway
Lewis John. lab., h. 37 Daum
Lewis John C., bill poster, h. 221 Hopkins
Lewis John H., clk., h. 202 W. 4th
Lewis John H., attorney at law, n.w.c. Main and Court, h. 135 Baymiller
Lewis John V , clk., 202 W. 4th
Lewis Joseph, h. 98 E. 3d
Lewis Joseph M., boiler mkr., bds. 297 Water
Lewis Joseph P., wood measurer, wks. rear 109 Water, h. 143 W. 3d
Lewis Laura, 339 W. 6th
Lewis Lloyd S., colorer, 429 W. 5th
Lewis M. H. & Co., (Matthew H. L & Louis Baumann), liquors, 16 Broadway
Lewis Martha, teacher. 5 Gorman
Lewis Matthew H., (M. H. L. & Co.), h. Newport
Lewis Nanette, notion store, 136 W 9th
Lewis Reuben, eng., 18 E. 8th E. of Lock
Lewis Nicholaus. 104 W. 8th
Lewis Robert, boiler mkr., 56 Lock
Lewis Robert, horse dealer, 212 Betts
Lewis Robt., freshwater. e s. North b. New and 7th
Lewis Robert C., 130 Butler
Lewis Samuel, lab., bds. n.s 6th e. of Lock
Lewis Samuel, tailor, 46 Rittenhouse
Lewis Samuel, whitewasher, 108 Central Av
Lewis Sandford A., barber, 379 Central Av., h 538 Central Av.
Lewis Sarah. 58 E. 4th
Lewis Sarah, 341 Central Av
Lewis Thatcher, bk. layer, 5 Gorman
Lewis Thomas, potter, 73 Bank
Lewis Thomas, tinner, 213 Plum

CINCINNATI ADVERTISEMENTS.

EVENS' VARIETY WORKS,

64 West Fourth Street,

CINCINNATI, O.

ALL KINDS OF **Sewing Machines,** REPAIRED.

SEAL PRESSES FOR THE USE OF COURTS, LODGES, SOCIETIES, AND BUSINESS SEALS.

SEND FOR SAMPLES. A LIBERAL DISCOUNT TO STATIONERS AND AGENTS.

EVERY DESCRIPTION OF **Light Machinery,** MANUFACTURED.

SEAL ENGRAVING, —AND— ## DIE SINKING.

I have the most complete, Jobbing and Light Machine Works in the Country, driven by ERICSSON's CALORIC ENGINE, where every requisite is provided. Fine Tools and Material for Making and Repairing every variety of Light Machinery in a perfect and workmanlike manner.

P. EVENS, JR.

(LIG) CINCINNATI (LIN) DIRECTORY. (LIN) 211

Lewis Thomas M., clk., bds. 338 Richmond
Lewis & Tosspot, (Fountain L. & George T), barbers, 4 W 4th
Lewis Vena. 200 Plum
LEWIS W. & C. (Wm. & Chas..), Ladies and Children's Shoes, 82 W. 4th
Lewis Wm., clk., 34 W. Court w. of Central Av
LEWIS William, (W. & C. L.), bds. 108 Broadway
Lewis Wm. H., porter, 34 W. Court w. of Central Av
Lewosk Betsy, h. M Mill
Leydon Michael, grocery, s.w.c. Central Av. and W. W Canal
Leyendecker Michael lab., 549 Race
Leyman John, cof. h . 562 W. 5th
Liala Louis, finisher, wks. n.e.c. Walnut and Canal
Libeau Mary. 366 Clark
Libeck Mary, wks. Hieatt & Wood's candle factory
Libeck Rosey. n.s. Flint b. Freeman and Mill Creek
Libel Michael, tailor, 179 W. Liberty
LIBERTY TREE HOUSE, 70 Sycamore

Libker Gerhard H., chair mkr., 295 W. Front
Libler Nicholaus, carp., 681 Vine
Lichtenberg Herman, lab., 22 Mill
Lichtenfels Jacob, lab., 548 Vine
Lichtenstein Alex., peddler, bds. n.e.c. 5th and Sycamore
Lichtenthal Bernhard, carriage mkr., 572 Race
Lichtenthal Mathias J., policeman, 572 Race
Lichtfers Peter, compositor, e.s. Jackson b 12th and 13th
Lickner Joseph, cooper, 56 Peete
Liddell Andrew, 23 Park
Liddell Andrew, bolsterer, 270 Clark
Liddy Hugh, s.s. Poplar b. Linn and John
Liddy Michael, s.s. Poplar b. Linn and John
Liddy Peter, clk., 90 Butler
Liddy Thos., paper dealer. 90 Butler
Liddin John, saloon, 108 Sycamore
Lidmann Frank, lab. 110 Clay
Liebenstein Isaac, clothier, 9 E. Pearl, h. 267 W Court
Lieber Wm., lab., lab., 149 Carr
Lieberherr Christian G., teacher, 64 Milton
Liebermann Francis. tinner, 602 Elm
Liebler Thomas, cab. mkr , 39 Moore
Liebmann Anthony, dry goods, s.e.c. Elm and Elder, h. s.e.c. Elm and Ham. Road
Liebshutz Marx, cutter, 459 Vine
Liech Peter, watchman. 21 York
Lieckeng Joseph, clk , 461 Main
Lied Conrad. lab., 21 Wade w. of Linn
Liedjger August, tailor, wks. 6 W. 9th
Liefert Henry, tailor, 225 Everett
Liele Henry, wks. Cincinnati Type Foundry
Lieman Henry, salesman, 130 W. 5th
Liemfelt Anthony, weaver, 26 Green
Lien Bryant, lab., wks. 1565 E. Front
Lienhard Catharine, s.w.c. Court and Linn
Lienhard Charles, barber, s.w.c. Court and Linn
Liening Juhn B., cigar mkr., 360 Broadway
Liening John H., porter, 50 Plum n.e.c. 2d and Walnut
Lennebrink Henry, mason, 592 Main
Lier Joseph, shoe mkr , 515 Vine
Lierup George, shoe mkr., n s. Woodward b. Main and Sycamore
Lieser John F., tailor, n.s. 6th b. Culvert and Broadway
Lieveding John, porter, 22 Abigail
Lievre Lewis, bk. layer, 26 Green
Lizenmeyer John, lab , 140 Pleasant
Liggins John, whitewasher, 133 Avery
Light Amos, tanner. 75 Bank
Ligt Henry, cook, 103 K. 2d
Light Jacob, steward, 37 Baum

Light John L., clk., 75 Bank
Light Peter, steward, s.w.c. 4th and Park
Lighten John, lab., s.w.c. Vine and Water
Lightfoot Wm. shoemkr., wks. s.e.c. 6th and Central Av
Lightner James, upholsterer, wks. 11 Franklin
Lightweight Adam, carp., 252 Carr
Ligner Joseph, lab., 644 Race
Lihman Henry, tailor, 53 Pendleton
Lilge Wm., tin smith, 641 W. 6th
Lilgebeck Mrs. Anna F., dressmkr., 25 Clinton
Lilgebeck Matilda, dressmkr.. 25 Clinton
Lilgenkamp Fred., dray, 19 Mansfield
Lille Frederick, grocery, n e.c. Wade and Dudley
Lilienthal Rev Max E., 209 Broadway
LILLER J hn, (M. & J. L.). 533 Vine
LILLER M & J., (Michael & John), Tin. Copper and Sheet Iron Ware, 533 Vine
LILLER Michael, (M & J. L.), 533 Vine
Lillis Patrick, lab., 52 Barr
Lilley Matilda, 567 Vine,
Lilley Wm., trunk mkr., wks. 509 Plum
Lilling Bernard, carp s.s. Boal b. Broadway and Sycamore
Lillis Martin lab., bds. n.w.c. Front and Central Av.
Lillis Patrick, lab., n.s. Cherry al. b. Plum and Central Av.
Lillis Patrick, porter, Madison House
Limb Jeremiah, lab., 2 New
Limberg Fanny, teacher. 344 Race
Limberg Francis, clk., s.w.c. Vine and Longworth, h 125 Linn
Limberger Wm., lab , 510 Race
Limebaugh Samuel, blksmith, 123 W. Front
Limer Charles, fireman, 126 Avery
Limke Francis A., groceries, 68 Green
Limppel Joseph, lab., 50 Brighton
Linamer George, lab , 72 Abigail
Linbart Ann, e.s. Price b. Milton and Slack
Linbert Harmon, lab., e.s. Price b. Milton and Slack
Linbert John, lab., e.s. Price b. Milton and Slack [6th
Linch James, lab., e.s. Oregon b. 3d and
Linch Mary. 500 E. Front
Linch Richard, molder, bds. n.s. al. b. Canal and 12th and Vine and Race
Linck John, lab., w.s. Campbell al. b. Elder and Findlay
Linck Joseph A., 77 Ham. Road
Linck Mrs. W , e.s. Branch b. Findlay and Ham. Road
LINCOLN F D., Attorney at Law, 50 Main, bds. Burnet House
Lincoln Hart, shoe mkr., 16 Elizabeth
Lincoln John R., news stand, 26 W. 5th
LINCOLN Preston, agent McCallum Bridge Co.. 75 W. 3d, h. 25 Gest
LINCOLN SMITH & WARNOCK, (Timothy D. L., Fayette S. & James W .) Attorneys at Law, 8 E. 2d, up Stairs
LINCOLN Timothy D., (L. Smith and Warnock,) 296 W. th
Lincoln Wm.. blksmith. 126 Lock
Lind John, tailor, 107 Martin
Lindaman Dora, servt., 276 W. 4th
Lindaman Hy., molder, wks. n.e.c. Canal and Walnut
Lindaman John, coach mkr., 147 Abigail
Lindaman Wm , molder, wks. n.e.c. Canal and Walnut
Lindauer Chas., printer, 57 Providence
Lindauer David, liquor mer., 16 W 9th
LINDAUER David H. (Amberg and L.,) 201 Race
Lindauer Jacob, 315 Walnut
Lindauer M., 246 Walnut
Lindeman Hy., driver, 111 E. 3d
Lindeman John, varnisher, 89 Bremen

Lindemann Anton, cab. mkr., bds 365 W. 5th
Lindemann Charles, rear 13 E. Liberty
Lindemann Dorothea, 16 Buckeye
Lindemann Fred., (L. & Wehrmann,) 70 12th
Lindemann Frederick W., carp., 688 Bremen
Lindemann Geo., director City Infirmary, 557 Walnut
Lindemann Hy., dry goods, 531 Main
Lindemann Hy., molder, 484 Elm
Lindemann Hy., porter, 15 Hughes
Lindemann Hy. E., lab., 68 Bremen
Lind-mann Hermann, carp., bds. 9 E. Liberty
Lindemann Hermann, clk., n.e.c. Webster and Mansfield
Lindemann Joseph, porter, 65 W. 12th
Lindemann Theodore, lab., wks. n.e.c. Walnut and Canal
Lindemann & Wehrmann, (Frederick L., and Joseph W.,) boots and shoes, 70 12th
Lindemann Wilhelmina, seamstress, 153 Bremen
Lindemann Wm., carp., 153 Bremen
Linden Thomas, shoe mkr., 78 Bremen
Linder Catharine, seamstress, 448 Race
Lindermann Hy., carp., 88 Freeman
Lindermuller Leonard, saddler, bds. 65 W. 5th
Lindheimer Rosine. rear 49 Hughes
Lindkamp John, 64 Peete
Lindineyer Hy., sawyer, h. 48 Pleasant
Lindner Charles. 367 Linn
Lindner Frederick, tailor, 628 Main
Lindner George, painter, 403 Longworth
Lindner John, turner. 403 Longworth
Lindner Joseph, e s. Denman b. Bank and Central Av.
Lindner Michael, lab , 403 Longworth
Lindsay Alex Y., cigars &c., 375 Central Av. h. 220 Barr
Lindsay Elizabeth, 2:0 Barr
Lindsay James P., b. k., bds 220 Barr
Lindsay John F., carp., 1 Hopkins
Lindsay Thomas C., artist, 2d W. 4th bds. 220 Barr
LINDSEY Henry K., (Evans & L.,) h. Walnut Hills
Lindsey Margaret, 151 Mohawk
Lindsey Margaret, 53 E. 3d
Lindsey Sarah, 20 Gest
Lindsley Hy., cutter, 70 Broadway
Lineback James, cooper, bds. 170 Clay
Linenaugh Samuel, blksmith, 143 Water, h. 123 W. Front
Lineman Louis, butcher, Bank b. Baymiller and Freeman
Linemann Hy., cab. mkr., 255 Hopkins
Linemann John, carriage mkr., 147 Abigail
Linesch Hermann, carp., 69 Pendleton
Linfert Joseph, tailor, bds. 144 Pleasant
Linfoot Christopher W., cab. mkr., 274 John
Lingelbach Ferdinand, clk., bds. 444 Sycamore
Lingemann Joseph, lab., 160 Freeman
Linger Barney, plasterer, 126 Pleasant
Lingers Hy.. stable. 341 W. 6th
Lingner Michael, lab., rear 91 Findlay
Linhard Andrew, baker, rear 3 Wade, b. Elm and Plum
Linhart Andrew, baker, 133 Ham. Road
Linhs Jacob, tailor. 46 Observatory
Linicos Joseph, lab., 21 Commerce
Link Frank, lab. e.s. Plum b. Adams and Liberty
Link Frank, tailor, 27 Ham. Road
Link Jacob, lab., 680 Vine
Link Martin, bakery, w.s. Elm b. 3d and McFarland
Link Valentine, finisher, n.e.c. 3d and John
Linke Louis. eof. h. n.w.c. 9th and Walnut

CINCINNATI ADVERTISEMENTS.

DR. JAS. G. HUNT,
HOMŒOPATHIC PHYSICIAN & SURGEON,
No. 278 WALNUT STREET.

Special attention paid to diseases of the EYE and EAR. CANCERS, FISTULA IN ANO, (cured without the knife,) and all chronic diseases. *References given to patients cured.*

McKEE & ROTH,

Merchant Tailors,

No. 48 West 4th Street,
AND
No. 159 Walnut Street.

CINCINNATI, OHIO.

E. E. C. SWIFT,   H. C. SWIFT.
E. E. C. SWIFT & CO.

Commission Merchants,

AND DEALERS IN

Grain, Gunny, Flour and Ham

BAGS,

Cor. Walnut & Water Sts. Cincinnati, O.

Highest Cash Price paid for GINSENG, FEATHERS and BEESWAX. Orders for above articles solicited and promptly filled.

F. C. DECKEBACH & CO.
COPPERSMITHS,
AND MANUFACTURERS OF

Brew and Still Kettles,

Generators and Soda Fountains,

No. 171 COURT ST.

South Side, bet. Race and Elm Sts. - - CINCINNATI, O.

Jobbing of all kinds in Copper or Brass done to order.

J. D. MACKENZIE,
STENCIL ESTABLISHMENT, No. 180 Walnut Street, between Fourth and Fifth, (opposite Gibson House,)
Cincinnati, O.
☞ Brushes, Marking Ink, Alphabets, Figures, &c., always on hand.

H. BURGUND,
GLASS STAINER,
No. 45 East Third Street.

J. TAFT.
DENTIST
No. 58 West 4th St., bet. Walnut and Vine, CINCINNATI, O.
☞ Editor Dental Register.

J. BIEDENBENDER, **236 MAIN STREET.**

PAPER BOX FACTORY.

D. B. JORDAN,

Wholesale and Retail Dealer in

PAPER BOXES,

No. 187 Main Street,

CINCINNATI, O.

PERSONAL.

FURNITURE--If you want to buy Furniture, Carpets, Oil Cloths, Matting, Books, Pictures, in fact almost any thing very cheap, go to   H. E. SHAW,
No. 18 East 4th Street.

J. C. WILMS, DEALER IN WATCHES, JEWELRY, CLOCKS, &c. COLLEGE BUILDING CINCINNATI, O.

(LIS) CINCINNATI (LIV) DIRECTORY. (LOC) 213

Linkenbach Philip, lab., s.w.c. Bank and Baymiller
Linkenfels Theodore, finisher, 160 Freeman
Linkenstein Jacob, mason, 661 Vine
Linman Jacob, carp., n.s. 9th b. Plum and Central Av.
Linn Christopher, cooper, 97 York
Linn Hy., carp., bds. 143 Carr
Linn Johanna W., teacher, 5th District School
Linn Martha I., teacher, 7th District School
Linne Ernst, painter. 29 Buckeye
Linneman J. ., shoe mkr., 171 W. 5th
Linnemann Frederick, blksmith, 48 Pleasant
Linnenbaum Theodore, lab., w.s. Clay b. 13th and Allison
Linnenbry Hy., molder, 51 15th
Linnenkugel George, lab., 50 McFarland
Linnenhugel Richard. lab., 50 McFarland
Linner Margaret 554 Vine
Linsenmeyer Christine, seamstress, 546 Walnut
Linson Elizabeth, 251 Clark
Linsted Joseph tailor, 468 W. 5th
Lint Lumburtus V., bk.binder, 459 Main
Lintner John, turner, bds. 403 Longworth
Linville Mary, Observatory St. Mt. Adams
Linville Wm , painter, w.s. Oregon b. 3d and 6th
Linz Edward, student, bds. 178 W. 5th
Linz Lorenz tailor, 520 Freeman
Linz Madison waiter, 29 W. 5th
Linz Michael, 178 W. 5th
Linz Pius, gardener, n.s. Liberty b. Freeman and Mill Creek
Linzen John II., clk., n.w.c. George and Central Av., h. 251 Clark
Lions Michael, driver, s.s. 3d b. Ludlow and Lawrence
Lipman Jacob M., pawn broker, s.e.c 4th and Sycamore
Lipman Lewis, clk, 107 W. Pearl, b. 436 Main
LIPMAN MIKE H., Exchange and Loan Office, 131 Sycamore, bds. Gibson House
Lippard Amelia, s.w.c. 3d and Smith
Lippard Gustavus, lab., bds. s.w.c. 3d and Smith
Lippen Catharine 71 Buckeye
Lippert Karl tailor, 150 Clay
Lippert Ludwig. clk., 74 Broadway
Lippert Mary, 149 Everett
LIPPERT OTTO. Drugs. Medicines, Chemicals &c., 913 Central Av.
Lippert Paul, jeweler Duhme & Co's., bds 74 W. Court w. of Central Av.
Lippes Philip, waiter, Gibson House
Lippncott Edwin, supply agt. and paymaster O. & M. R. R., h. 144 smith
Lippencrate Mary. 192 Smith
Lipple Matthew, stone mason, rear 49 Hughes
Lipplemann Hy., teamster, n.w.c. Freeman and Richmond
Lippman Barnard. tailor, 460 W. 8th
Lippman Hirsch, trader, 597 Vine
Lippman Lewis, clk , bds. Silvester House
Lippman Louis, pedd'er. 12 Charles
Lippold Hy., teamster, 550 Main
Lipps John, turner, wks. 825 Central Av.
Lipps Philip J., gilder, s.e.c. Findlay and Race
Lipscomb Daniel, servt., 111 Broadway
Lipscomb Mary, h. 13 E. 8th e. of Lock
Liser Sebastian, butcher, 681 Elm
Lishawa Catharine. 81 Wate
Lishawa Philip. conductor. bds. 81 Wade
Lisker Chas.. weaver, 40 Pleasant
Lister George, eng., s.e.c. North and New
Lister George. lab., w.s. Phuber al. b. Elm and Plum

Lister Sarah, w.s. Phuber al. b. Elm and Plum
Listermann William, driver, bds. n.w.c. Mill and Front
Liston James, lab., 160 Carr
Litch Xavier, gardener, n. s. Flint bet. Freeman and Mill Creek
Litenbarger John, lab., 6½ Liberty
Litherbary Chas., carp., s.w.c. Goodloe and Willow
Litherbury John, st. bt. builder, s. e. c. Litherbury and Front, h. 131 E. 3d
Litherbury John W., clk., 8 E. 2d, h, 131 E. 3d
Litler Leonard, driver, n.s. 9th b. Plum and Central Av
Litner & Austing, (Casper L. & Frank A.,) distillery, s s. Pearl bet. Canal and Kilgour
Litmer Casper. lard oil factory, 63 Hunt b. 74 Spring
Litmer Henry, bar. k., 70 Sycamore
Litmer Henry, grocery, 528 Main
Litmer Hermann, clk., 528 Main
Litmer Joseph, lard oil mkr., 76 Spring
Litsch Bernhard, harness mkr., 620 W. Front
Littecken Catharine. 22 Peete
Littell Samuel S., salesman, 18 and 19 Pub. Landing, h. 321 W. 9th
Littell Wm M , dray, 321 W. 9th w. of Central Av.
Littelmann F. Herman, cof. h., w.s. Vine b. Mulberry and Milk
Litten John, carp., 100 Water
Little Catharine, talloress, 257 W. 9th
Little Catharine, 35 Cutter
Little Chas. plumber, 337 George
Little David W., clk., bds. s.w c. 7th and Race [Road
Little Ebenezer, lab., 59 Observatory
Little George, 337 George
Little John, carp., 156 Spring
Little Julia, 36 E. 3d
Little Mary A., bds. 292 Water
Little Matthew, fitter, e.s. Kilgour b. 3d and 5th
LITTLE MIAMI RAILROAD CO., Offices s.e.c. Pearl and Kilgour. General Ticket Office s. e. c. Front and Broadway
LITTLE MIAMI RAILROAD, Freight Office and Depot n. e. c. Front and Kilgour, Erastus Clark General Freight Agent
LITTLE MIAMI RAILROAD, Passenger Depot s.s. Front e. of Miami Canal
LITTLE Otis B., (W. M. Cameron & Co.,) h. 33 Clark
Little Robt dray, h. 6 Lock
Little St George, clk. 64 George
Little Sarah. seamstress, 156 Spring
Little Thomas, eng., 150 Spring
Little Win.. express. 132 Everett
Littleberry George, stone cutter, 59 Clinton
Littlefield Albert H., music teacher, 289 Longworth
Littlefield Henry, confec., 399½ W. 5th
Littleford John § S., baker. 14 E. Pearl
Littleton Vanburen, lab., 838 E. Front
Littsler G. R., salesman. bds, 239 Race
Litz Frederick, blk. smith, 105 Ham. Road
Litz Herman, lab., w.s. Wood b. 3d and Front
Lively John, lab., s.s. Sloo w. of Freeman
Livellari John B , confec., 70 W. 3d
Livermore Marshall bds. w.s. Ohio Av. b. North Elm and Calhoun
Liverpool Francis, 46 Race
Liverpool John, barber, 5 Walnut, h. 48 Race
Liverpool John H., barber, 129 Race
LIVERPOOL AND LONDON INSURANCE CO., Knight and Warren, Agen's. s w c. 3d and Main
Liverpool Thos. N. C., barber, Gibson House. h. 4 Race
Living Annie, servt., 136 Broadway
Living Henry, lab., s. s. 6th b. Harriet and Horne
Livingston A. B., printer, Cin. Gazette, h. 32 George

Livingston Chas. E., manuf. of military goods, w.s. Kilgour b. 3d and 5th
Livingston Herman, butcher, 142 Everett
Livingston J. J., clk., County Treasurer's Office, 199 Poplar
Livingston John M., cook, 71 W. 9th w. of Central Av
Livingston Julia, 53 George
Livingston Nathan, drover, 21 David
Livingston Phoebe S., 92 W. Front
Livingston S , bds. 91 Sycamore
Livingston Thos. H., clk., 101 W. 4th, bds. Walnut Street House
Livingstine Bernard, peddler, 23 Clinton
Lloyd ———, actor, National Theater
Lloyd Rev.. e.s Auburn b. Coggswell Av. and Central Av
Lloyd Alfred, clk., 8 W. 3d
Lloyd Hannah, e.s. Ludlow b. Pearl and 3d
Lloyd J. C., mess. I. & C. R. R., bds. Broadway Hotel
Lloyd J. H., bds. Dennison House
Lloyd Jas.. lab., e s. Macalister bet. 4th and 5th
Lloyd John, blk. smith, 65 Observatory Road
Lloyd John, mach., wks. n.s. Miami Canal w. of Elm
Lloyd John, pattern mkr., w.s. Pike bet. 3d and Pearl
LLOYD Richard, (P. Andrew & Co.,) 25 Pike
Lloyd Samuel, carp., 218 W. 9th w. of Central Av
Lloyd Wm., caulker, 960 E. Front
Lloyd Wm. P., tinner. 130 Baymiller
Loar Apollas, phys., 933 Clark
Loar Jas. A , clk., 933 Clark
Lobb John, 24 E. 5th
Lobbe Henry carp., 161 Clay
Lobeck Henry, tailor, 293 W. Front
Lobenstein Anthony, clothing, 37 Broadway
Lobker Geo., box maker, wks. Livingston's, near Linn
Lobker Henry, chair mkr., s.s. Front b Smith and John
Lobker Henry, grocery, 39 Pike
Lobker Hermann G., grocery, 201 Clark
Lobker Mary, 39 Pike
Lobmiller Theodore, teacher, Allanthus b. Bank and Clearwater
Lobner John B., teacher, St. Francis school
Locher John, clk., O. & M. R. R., e. s. Ramsey n. of Front
Lochner Fred., cof. h., 753 Vine
Lock Gebhard, shoe mkr., 179 Barr
LOCKARD Chas. O., (L. & Ireland,) 23¼ Findlay
Lockard & Ireland (Chas. O L. & Thos. S. I.,) wh d'y goods, 88 & 90 Pearl
Locke Elisha, music teacher, 144 George
Locke Jas., 341 George
Locke John, 341 George
LOCKE JOSEPH M., Chemist and Mineralogist, 31½ W. 3d, h. 341 George
Locke Mary, 311 George
Loc e O. M., clk., bds. Walnut Street House
Locke Peter, mason, 486 Walnut
Locke Wm. R., student, 341 George
Lockhorn George, boots and shoes, 62 & 64 Hunt
Lockland Derby, porter. John Bates'
Lockman Herman, brewer, n. s. Longworth n. stone all'y
Lockman Jefferson T., molder, h. 204 Barr
Lockman Wm., policeman, 14 Richmond b. Elm and Plum
Lockwood Augustus, hatter, 190 Oliver
Lockwood Chas. L.. gents furnishing goods, &c., 14½ W. 4th, res New York
LOCKWOOD Danl. H., (Henry Marks & Co ,) res. Loveland
LOCKWOOD Edward A.. hatter, 190 Oliver
LOCKWOOD Frank T., (C. B. Camp & Co.,) 157 John
Lockwood Horace H., salesman, 95 W. 3d, h. Mt. Auburn

CRANE, BREED & CO.

MANUFACTURERS OF
PATENT METALLIC
BURIAL CASES AND CASKETS, AND HEARSES,

OFFICE AND MANUFACTORY,
EIGHTH STREET, WEST OF FREEMAN STREET, CINCINNATI, O.

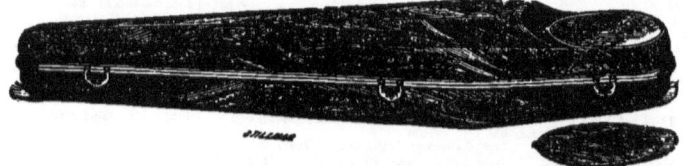

Under their present *improvements* these Burial Cases are entirely free from those revolting suggestions which have heretofore been connected with their name.

THE METALLIC BURIAL CASKET

Is entirely devoid of those unpleasant associations which usually accompany the form of a coffin. Heavy Polished Plate Glass extends nearly its whole length. With the elaborate Silver-Plated Mountings, as represented in the above engraving, it surpasses in elegance anything of the kind which has ever before been offered to the public.

These Burial Cases and Caskets are beautifully finished in imitation of the finest rosewood. Their *invaluable qualities* for *ordinary interment*, for *transportation*, and for *preservation*, are now universally acknowledged. They *protect* the remains of the departed from *water*, *vermin*, or other *intrusion*. *Future removal*, should it ever be desired, may be accomplished without inconvenience. A *delay of days* or *weeks*, awaiting the arrival of absent friends, is entirely practicable. When due attention is given to sealing, which may, with care, be accomplished by any one, (printed instructions accompanying each Case and Casket,) bodies may be carried to *any part of the globe at any season of the year*, with perfect safety. They are, moreover, a sure *safeguard* against *contagious diseases*. These advantages render them unequalled by anything which either in ancient or modern times has been invented for the reception of the human body after death.

Our facilities for the manufacture of HEARSES, of every style, and of the best qualities, are unequalled by any establishment in the country.

(LOE) CINCINNATI (LOH) DIRECTORY. (LON) 215

Lockwood James D., carp., 6 W. 2d, h. Covington
Lockwood John, sawyer, wks. 1565 E. Front
Lockwood John, tailor, bds. 23 Elizabeth
Lockwood Maguire, (Wm. H. L. & Jas. M.,) gold beaters, 181 Walnut
Lockwood Nathan S., salesman, 13 Main b. 406 W. 3d
Lockwood Thomas, mach., 107 Baum
LOCKWOOD Walter, (Henry Marks & Co.,) rooms 229 W. 4th
Lockwood Wm., carp., 102 E. 6th
Lockwood Wm. H., (L. & Maguire,) bds. 190 Oliver
Lodder Louis, bds. Cincinnati House
Lodders John F., grocery, 549 Race
Loder Benj., (W. & B L.,) 53 W. 7th
Loder W. & B., (Wm. & Benj.,) foreign and domestic liquors, 270 Main
Loder Wm., (W. & B. L.,) 53 W. 7th
Loderbine Adolf, lab., 295 Linn
Lodge Joseph B., mach., 38 Central Av
LODGE Wm. H., (J. A. Loudon & Co.,) bds. 189 Richmond
LODWICK M. W., (Kinney, Espy & Co.,) n.w.c. 3d and Pike
Loeb —, 213 Elm
[Ills
Loeb Adolph, (L. & Bros.,) h. Cairo,
Loeb & Brothers, (Isaac L., Adolphus L. & Simon L.,) tailors, 2 Burnet House
Loeb Isaac, (L. & Bros.,) h. Nashville, Tenn
Loeb Jacob, printer, 116 W. 5th
Loeb Leopold, 133 Central Av
Loeb Leopold, clk. 2 Burnet House, h. 269 W. 9th
Loeb Louis, peddler, 21 David
Loeb Marcus, liquors, 273 W. 9th
Loeb Simon, (L. & Bros., h. Caudleville, Ind.
LOEB Solomon, (Kuhn, Netter & Co.,) 333 W. 6th
Loebenstein Alois, 93 Milton
Loebker Barney, sawyer, 543 Sycamore
Lobnit Chas. F., turner, n.w.c. Freeman and Gest
Loebnitz Fred. J., turner, n.w.c. Freeman and Gest
Loehschuetz Loeb, 479 Vine
Loebstein Caroline, h. 365 Cutter
Loeffler Theodore, lab., 120 Ham. Road
Loehider Rudolph, 24 Milton
Loehmann Hy., tailor, 19 14th
Loehmann John, cigar mkr., bds. 29 Abigail
Loehmann Miss Maggie, seamstress, 29 Abigail
Loehmann Wm., (Wm. L. & Co.,) 106 E. Pearl
Loehmann Wm. & Co., liquors, 37 E. Front
Loehmann Wm. J., cooper, 29 Abigail
Loehr Christopher H., b.k., 615 Central Av
Loehr John H., 615 Central Av.
Loehr John A., 615 Central Av
Loehrlein John, tanner, 682 Vine
Loepker Anthony, lab., 11 Mary
Loerberheimer Mary, s. s. Charlotte bet. Linn and Baymiller
Loerger Jacob, tailor, 456 Elm
Loerhrlein Hy. A., clk., 164 Main, h. 193 Ham. Road
Loesch Frederick, tinner, 1046 Central Avenue
Loesch Mathias, shoemkr. 57 Buckeye
Loesche Mrs. Mary, washwoman, 571 Race
Loescher Caspar H., lab, 165 Ham. Road
Loeva Christopher, 773 Vine
Loewe Hartman. cab. mkr., s.s. Weller, b Carr and Harriet
LOEWE JOSEPH O., Proprietor Loewen Garden, 437 Vine
Loewen Peter, cigars, &c., 331 Vine
Loewenberg Amelia. 84 Bremen
Loewenger Charles, lab, 15, 15th, b. Elm and Plum
Loewenstein clothing, bds. Silverster House
Loewenstein Adolphus, clk., 110 Park

Loewenstein & Guiterman, (Julius H. L. & Alex. G.,) clothing, n.e.c. Sycamore and Public Landing
Loewenstein Hy., foreman, 110 Park
Loewenstein Herman, meats, n. w. c. John and 9th, h. 142 Everett
Loewenstein Julius H., (L. & Guiterman,) n e.c. Public Landing and Sycamore
Loewenstein Morris, carver, 110 Park
Loewenstein Simon, shoemkr. e. s. Coggswell al. b. Abigail and Woodward
Loewenstine & Brothers, (Jacob H., Morris R., David C., & Henry M.,) clothiers, 50 W. Pearl
Loewenstine David C., (J. H. L. & Bros.,) h. Peoria, Ill
Loewenstine Hy. M., (J H. L. & Bros.) h. Peoria, Ill
Loewenstine Jacob H., (J. H. L. & Bros.,) 197 Broadway
Loewenstine Morris R., (J. H. L. & Bros.,) h. Pekin, Ill
Loewenstine Moses, h. 197 Broadway
Loft Chas. walter, 171 Walnut
Lofthouse Thomas, lab., 162 John
Loftis James, expressman, 58 Hunt
Loftis Pat., lab., e.s Crippen al., b. 7th and 8th
Loftis Sarah, 131 W Front
Loftus John, lab. bds. 512 W. Front
Loftus Michael, lab., s.w.c. 3d and Central Avenue
Loftus Patrick, lab., wks. 49 E. 2d
Logan Alex. A., tailor, 31 Chestnut
Logan Christ., wks. Wood & McCoy's
Logan Edward, 63 E. 7th
Logan Elizabeth, 136 Linn
Logan James, molder, s.w.c. Cutter and Betts
Logan Jane, 148 W. Pearl
Logan John, molder, wks. n.e.c. Canal and Walnut
Logan Phoebe B., teacher, 31 Chestnut
Logan Robert S., n.s. Avery, b. Mill and Stone
Logan Robert S., 308 Main
LOGAN THOMAS A., Attorney at Law, 73 W. 3d, h. 264 Longworth
Loge John P., 270 W. 8th
Logermann Bernard, soap factory, n.s. Bank. b Riddle & Division
Logue John, dray, 25 Lock, n. of 9th
Lohde Adolph, jeweler, 75 Clay
Loheking Hy., bds Cincinnati House
Lohayde R., surveyor, n.s. Milton, opp. Mansfield
Lohius Andrew, box mkr., wks. Livingston, near Linn
Lohle Rebecca, 59 14th
Lohler Patrick, lab., 540 W Front
Lohman Benjamin, cigar mkr., 554 W. Front
Lohman Richard, porter, 3 Mary
Lohman Wm. H., omnibus driver, 209 Barr
Lohmann Anthony, tailor, 524 Main
Lohmann Bernhard H., lab., 107 Clay
Lohmann Dietrich, porter, 3 Lucy
Lohmann Edward, bakery, 33 Mulberry
Lohmann George, bds. n.w.c. Race and 14th
Lohmann Hy., plumber, wks. 397 Vine
Lohmann Hy., lab., 491 Race
Lohmann Johanna, servt., 486 W. 4th
Lohmayer John H., tinner, wks. 21 E. Front
Lohmeyer Christian, tailor, 622 Main
Lohmueller Hy., lab., 170 Spring
Lohn Frederick, grocery, n.w.c. Freeman and Poplar
Lohn John. tinner, 533 W. 5th
Lohns Adolph. lab., 94 Dudley
Lohnsbeck Gustave, agt., 117 W. 5th
Lohnsbeck Harriet, paper boxes, 117 W. 5th
LOHR JOHN H., Hardware Tools, Cutlery, &c., n.e.c. Main and 9th
Lohren Mary, tailoress. 164 Everett
Lohrer Bernhard, stone mason, bds. 680 Vine
Lohrer Jacob, cof. h., 576 Elm
Lohrer Martin, shoemkr., 138 Clinton

Lohrey Geo., finisher. 533 Walnut
Lohrey Peter, basket mkr., e.s. Milk, b. Vine and Calhoun
Lohrlein Hy., clk., 123 Ham. Road
Loman Charles, blksmith, wks. 347 Broadway
Lomas Wm., cof. h., 33 W. Front
Lomix Gabriel, rear 245 Broadway
Lomping John, cooper, 59 E. 8th
Lon John, finisher, wks. n.e.c. Walnut and Canal
Londargan Edward, shoemkr, 50 Longworth
London Catharine, 269 Longworth
LONDON Wm. E., (J. A. Fay & Co.,) h. 441 W. 8th
Londwaer Frederick, tailor, 418 Longworth
Lonergan John, lab., 58 Accomodation
Longacre Isaac L., wheelwright, wks. Royer. Simonton & Co.'s
Longacre Wm L., foreman, 183 Barr
Long Abby, 931 Central Av
LONG Alex., (L. & Hoeffer,) 387 John
Long Alexander N., printer, bds. 16 Harrison
Long Andrew, expressman, 175 E. Front
Long Bartholomew, lab., rear 95 Woodward
Long Charles, harness mkr., bds. 173 W. 3d
Long Daniel W., janitor U. S. Courts, 32 Barr
Long David, lab, 118 Everett
Long Edwin, painter. 46 York
Long Eli, lab., n.s. Liberty, b. Freeman and Mill Creek
Long Frederick, janitor, 179 W. 2d
Long G. B., bds. Clifton House
Long Gibson. drays 552 Sycamore
Long Henry K., n.s. Everett, b. Jones and Linn
Long Hy., harness mkr., bds. 173 W. 3d
Long Hy., sr., auctioneer, 19 E. 5th, h. 54 E. 5th
Long Hy. H., auctioneer, h. 131 Barr
LONG & HOEFFER, (Alex. L. & Geo. F. H., Jr.,) Attorneys at Law, Office 25 W. 3d
Long J. M., conductor, bds. Spencer House
Long John, Alleghany House, n. e. c. Walnut and River Landing
Long John, blksmith, bds. Brighton, b. Division and Western Av
Long John, 221 W, 5th
Long John, carp., 616 Sycamore
Long John, hostler, bds. 51 W. 5th
Long John, hostler. 203 Race
Long John, lab., 160 Peete
Long John, shoemkr, 311 John
Long John, tailor, s s. Friendship al., b. Pike and Butler
Long John C., phys., 278 W. 6th, h. 222 Longworth
Long Joseph, butcher, bds 137 W. 7th
Long Julius, 693 Elm
Long Kate, servt., 216 Richmond
Long Mary, 160 Peete
Long Mary, 16 Harrison
Long Patrick, lab., 67 Cherry al
Long Paul, chair mkr., 50 Plum
Long Rebecca, bds. n.s. al. b. Canal and 12th, and Vine and Race
Long Robt., drays, 20 Milton
Long Robert, pattern mkr., wks. n.e.c. Canal and Walnut
Long Reuben H., carp., 390 Race
Longe Jar d, grocery, 52 Abigail
Longenecker Alfred P., clk., s.w.c. 3d and Walnut, h. Fai mount
Longfellow Margaret, bds. s.w.c. E. 3d and Collard
Longinotti J. B., (J. B. L. & Bro.,) 216 W. 6th
Longinotti J. B. & Bro, (J. B. L. & James L.,) confec., 216 W. 6th
Longinotti James, (J. D. Longinotti & Bro.,) 216 W. 6th
Longland Joseph, (Foppe & L.,) 402 W. 5th [4th
Longley Albert S., student, bds. 293 W.
Longley Alcander, clk. P. O., 417 Central Avenue
Longley & Bro., (S. & S. H. L.,) flag manuf. 164 Vine

CHOICE FAMILY FLOUR.

LEWIS FAGIN, - - No. 33 Lock Street.

(LOR) CINCINNATI (LOV) DIRECTORY. (LOY) 217

Longley Elias, phoenetic publisher, Neave's bldg., n.w.c. 4th and Race, b. Loveland, O
Longley Septimius H., (L. & Bros.,) res. Foster's Crossings
Longley Servetus, (L. & Bro.,) 295 W. 4th
Longmeier Frederick, molder, 290 W. Front
Longmeyer George, stamper, wks n.w.c. Race and 2d
Longshaw John, tinner. 73 W. 12th
Longshore Abner, route agt. M. & C. R.R., 79 Baymiller
Longshore James, deputy sheriff, 159 W. Front
Longshore John, confec., 73 12th
Longshore Theresa, bds. 261 Richmond
Longstreet Stephen H., b.k., 20 Clinton
Longwaer Frederick, tailor, 418 Longworth
Longweiler Mena, bds. 476 John
Longwish Hy., meats, s.e.c. Baymiller and Court
Longworth Joseph, at N. Longworth's, e.s. Pike, b. 3d and 5th
LONGWORTH NICHOLAS, e.s. Pike, b. 3d and 5th

Lonkenheimer Fred., pipe fitter, wks. n.e.c Walnut and Canal
Lont Philip, mechanic. 4 Horne
Looker Hy., wks. 340 W. 3d
Looker Hy. carriage mkr., 213 Water
Looker Lewis V., painter. 404 W. 7th
Looker Mary E., teacher, 161 Baymiller
LOOKER, PURCELL & CO. (Saml. C. L. John C. & Patrick Sullivan) Carriage Manufacturers, w.s. Central Av., b. 4th and 5th
Looker Richael, 101 Baymiller
LOOKER Saml. C., (L., Purcell & Co.,) 165 Central Av
Looker Wm. R., printer, 243 Hopkins
Lookhouse Frank, lard oil manf., b. 309 W. Liberty
Lookinbaer B., lab. wks. n.s. Front b. Lawrence and Pike
Loolhoffer Wm., nurse Commercial Hospital
Loomis. M. D. W., 409 W. 5th
Loop Jacob, printer, 116 W. 5th
Loos Geo., tailor, e.s. Bremen b. Green and Liberty
Loos Ily., foreman. 140 Charlotte
Loos Joseph, clk., bds. e.s. Bremen b. Liberty and Green
Loose Lewis. clk., 601 Vine
Loraine Lewis H , trader, 255 Race
Lorch Alexander, confec., 111 W. 6th
Lord Ammi W., 74 W. 4th, b. 435 W 4th
Lord Alfred, shoe mkr., 201 Broadway
Lord Frank B., conductor, I. & C. R.R. bds 201 W. 4th
Lord Geo H., conductor, bds. Burnet House
LORD HENRY C . President Ind. & Cin R. R. Company, 66 W. 3d h. Sedamsville
Lord Rev N. L., district secy. A. B. C, F. M., 28 W. 4th res. Walnut Hills
Lordin John clk., bds. 556 W. 9th
Loree Samuel, cof. h , s.e.c. 6th and Lodge
Lorence Basilius, cof h., 40 Pike
Loreng Joseph, lab. 147 Abigail
Lorensen L , bds. 438 Sycamore
Lorentz Joseph, carp., 115 W. Liberty
Lorenz Barnard, tailor, w.s. Vine b. Mulberry, and Milk
Lorenz Ily., teamster, 14 Dunlap
Lorenz John, lab. s. s. Harrison Road b. Riddle and Brighton
Lorenz Joseph, s.s. Charlotte b. Linn and Baymiller
Lorenz Philip, bds. 763 Vine
Lorillard Fire Insurance Co., agency 76 W 3d
Loring David. (L. & Hartshorn) n.w.c. Plum and McFarland
LORING E., (C. B Evans & Co.) s w.e 4th and Walnut
Loring & Hartshorn, (David L. & Asher H.) billiards, 761 W. 4th
Loring J F., billiards. 19 College
Lortz Lewis, varnisher, 621 Race

Lortz Philip, 621 Race
Lory Adam, coop., e.s. Western Av., b. Bank and Harrison Pike
Lory John, cooper, e.s. Western Av. b. Bank and Harrison Pike
Losekamp Geo., s w.c. Peete and Poplar
Losekamp Hy., J., chair mkr., 205 Hopkins
Losekamp Joseph, cab. mkr. 230 Betts
Losi r David finisher, 181 W. 2d
Lososs Martin, tailor, 41 Elder
Loster Hy., lab. bds., 130 W. Court
Loth Chas.. tailor, e.s Bremen b. Elder and Findlay
Loth Hy., tailor, n.s. Mulberry, b. Main and Sycamore
Loth John, mach., 142 Clay
Loth Joseph, tanner, 47 Findlay
Loth Moritz, embroideries, 121 Main, h. 287 Longworth
Loth Philip, brewer, 142 Clay
Lothas, Edward, lab., 275 Ham. Road
Lotler John, lab., 47 Rittenhouse
Lott Fred., carp., 28 Dudley
Lott Saml., carp., bds , 420½ George
Lotte Celestine. 132 W. Liberty
Lotter Casper, 625 Main
Lotter John, weaver, wks. s.w.c. Cutter and Betts
Lotterhoss Catharine, 116 Ham. Road
Lotters Lawrence, cooper, rear 29 Hughes h. 25 Hughes
Lottler Saml., manager, 14 W. Front, bds. Madison House
Lottman Barney brick yard 230 Hopkins
Lotz Antony, saddler, bds. 734 W. 6th
Lotz Catharine, servt., 327 Walnut
Lotz Ernst, bk. mkr., 464 Freeman
Lotz Hy., cab. mkr., 10 Webb
Lotz Hy., shoe mkr , 708 Freeman
Lotz Hy , white washer, 20 Mercer
Lotz John, harness manuf., 612 Central Av
Lotz John, shoe dealer, 616 Central Av
Lotz Joseph J., tailor, 543 Race
Lotz Peter, cof. h. 40 Findlay
Lotz Wm., express. 767 Vine
LOTZE ADOLPHUS. Warm Air Furnace and Cooking Ranges, 219 Walnut, h. 115 W. Court
Lotze Frank, wheel wright, Clark, b. Linn and Baymiller
Lotze Laurence, lab., 266 Clark
Loizer Frank, finisher, wks. 340 W. 3d
Lotzers Harris. peddler, 473 Plum
Loucheim Saml., cigars &c., 115 Main h 161 Race
Louchen James, foreman, 117 W. 5th
Louck W m , pipe fitter, wks. n.e.c. Walnut & Canal
Louderback Jacob P., 489 W. 8th
Louderback Mary, confec., 489 W. 8th
Louderbuck Michael, baker, 489 W 8th
LOUDON J . A. & CO., (Jas. A. L. & Wm. H Lodge), Commission Merchants, 301 Vine
LOUDON Jas. A., (J. A. L. & Co.), 189 Richmond
Loudon John, n.e.c. Hill and Observatory
Luer Peter. feed store, 171 E. Front, h. 109 E. Front
LOUGHEAD Edward R., (Hinkle, Guild & Co.) h. 301 Richmond
Loughlin Daniel, lab. 51 Mill
Loughlin Daniel, lab , h. s.s. Taylor b. Freeman and Carr
Loughman Michael, cof. h, 460 W Front
Louis A. & Co.. (Adolph L. & Hy. Roesham) liquors &c., 56 and 58 Main
Louis Adolph, (A. L. & Co,) 273 W. 4th
Louis Hannah, 34 Hughes
Louis N.. tailor, bds. s.e.c, 9th and Walnut
Louis Susan. servt., 100 E. 4th
Lounsbery O. H., salesman, 23 E. 2nd h Loveland Ohio
Lounspech John, cooper, 129 Livingston
Louttenbach Herman, 135 Abigail
Loutenshier Geo., blksmith, 57 14th
Loutenslicker John, lab., 961 Central Av
LOVE ALEX. H., Family Grocery, n.w.c. 5th and Sycamore. h. 134 E. Liberty
Love Charlotte, house kpr., Spencer House

Love J. E , bds. Dennison House
Love Sevara, n.e.c Goodloe and Niagara
Love Mary, 154 E Liberty
Lovejoy Cynthia, 60 Hopkins
Lovelace Benj. F., shoe mkr., 118 Baymiller
Lovell A.fred. confec.. 93 W. Front
Lovell Rev Chas R., s.e.c. Front and Ferry
Lovell Edward D., 89 W. 9th
Lovell J. D & Co.. (John D. L. and Oliver L.) painters, 43 E. 2d
Lovell John D., (J. D. L. & Co.) 89 W. 9th
Lovell Oliver, (J D. L. & Co.,) res. Clifton
Lovell Sturgis O , 89 W. 9th
LOVELL THOS., Watchmaker and Jeweler, n.w.c. 5th and Race
LOVETT THOS. D., Civil Engineer at Ohio and Miss. Railroad Office, h. 396 Longworth
Loventhal Benj. S., grocery, s.e.c. Race and 3d
Lovering E T., salesman, n.e.c. 5th and Race
Lovie Hy., artist, 265 Everett
Loving Lucia, 11 Home
Low James, bds. 1934 E. Front
Low Minerva, 166 W. 8th
Lowden Ann teacher, 3d district school h. Mt Adams
Lowden Wm., blksmith, 98 E. 3d
Lowdon Martha, 137 E. 3d
Lowe Chas. W., turner, 870 E. Front
Lowe Cornelia T., teacher, bds 411 Longworth
LOWE Ed. S., gen. t'cket agt., C. W. & Z. R. R , s.w.c. 3d and Sycamore h 237 Longworth
Lowe Geo., lab., 80 Baymiller
Lowe Geo., shoe mkr., n.s. Montgomery pike h near Madison Road
Lowe Geo. W., saddler 230 Main
Lowe James F., blksmith, Observatory St. Mt. Adams
Loweman Wm. H. driver, 209 Barr
Lowenstein Simon 142 W. 6th
Lowenthal Saml., (L. & Windler,) 18 E. 6th
Lowenthal & Windler, (S L. & Benj. W.) cigars &c. 6 W. Pearl
Lowery Conrad, foreman. 16 Jackson
Lowery Mary, servt., 51 Mound
Lowes Cyrenius. packer, 99 W. 4th bds. Bevis House
Lowler Thos., carp., wks. 830 Central Av
Lowman Deterich, cigar mkr., n.s. Pearl b. Smith and Park
LOWMAN Isaac, (J. Lowman & Bro.) 292 Walnut
LOWMAN J. & BRO., (Jas. & Isaac Shirt manuf. and dealers in Gents Furnishing Goods, 38 W Pearl)
LOWMAN James, (J. L. & Bro.) 389 W 7th
Lowman Rebecca, 59 Martin
Lownds Wm.. n.s. Corporation al. b. Price and Young
Lownie John, steam pipe fitter, 403 Plum
Lowery Jacob S., paver, 203 Race h. Walnut Hills
Lowry Eli j h exchange office, 8 Sycamore. h. Covington
Lowry Ellen 326 Broadway
Lowry Geo . molder, wks. n.e.c. Walnut and C nal
Lowry John, molder, wks. n.w.c. Plum and Wade
Lowry John, lab., 83 Providence
Lowry Monroe, c irp, 453 W. 4th
Lowry Patrick, lab., n.e.c. Sycamore and Abigail
Lowry Rebecca, bds. 295 Longworth
LOWRY Samuel (Procter & Gamble) 19 George
Lowry Thos., bds. s.s. Cassatt al. b. Sycamore and Main
Lowry Wm., mer. 19 George
Lowvenstein Hy., cutter, s.w.c. 3d and Vine, b. 101 Park
Loyd Rev. Samuel, h. e.s. Auburn b. Northern and Central Av's

218 (LUD) CINCINNATI (LUI) DIRECTORY. (LUT)

Lubbe Geo. (R. & G. L.) 480 W. 5th
Lubbe R. & G. (Rudolph & George) grocery, 480 W. 5th
Lubbe Rudolph (R. & G. L.) 480 W. 5th
Lubbelman Geo., grocery, 430 Walnut
Lubbermann Bernhard, tailor, 142 Pleasant
Lubbermann Hy., lab., 71 Woodward
Lubbers Albert, blksmith. 181 Hopkins
Lubbink Hy., lab., 772 W. Front
Lubeka Frederick, shoemkr., 170 Charlotte
Lubeka Gerhard, 170 Charlotte
Lubeka Rudolph, 170 Charlotte
Lubermann John T., 95 Clay
Lucas Alfred, lab., 92 W. Front
Lucas John. fireman, e.s. al. b. 4th and 5th and Park and Mill
Lucas London, huckster, 212 Central Av.
Lucas Robert E., mess. Adams' Express Co. bds Burnet House
Lucas Win, lab., s.s. 6th b. Harriet and Horne
Lucht Martin C., salesman, 28 Main, h. 308 Race
Lucht P. H., b k., s.w.c. Main and 2d
Luchte Anton, shoemkr, 131 Clark
Luchte John, lab., e.s. Hand al. b Court and Clark
Lucius Charles A., jeweler, 428 Main
Luck Anthony B., brass molder, 109 Laurel
Luck Barney, watchman, n.e.c. Front and Foster
Luck Jacob. butcher, bds. 151 Baymiller
Luck Thomas, tanner, w.s. Western Av. b. Dayton and Bank
Luck Wm. finisher, bds. w.s. Western Av. b Dayton and Bank
Luckan George, tailor, 177 Hopkins
Lucke Henry, huckster, 76 E. 2d e. of Whittaker
Luckener Barney, lab., w.s. Kilgour b. 3d and 4th
Lucker George, lab., n.s. Railroad e. of Vance
Luckerd Christian, blksmith, 157 Bremen
Luckey George H., clk., 79 Vine, b. Fairmount
Luckey Mary, servt., 386 W. 6th
Luckhardt Caroline, bds. 444 Sycamore
Luckman Adolph, lab., wks 196 W. Pearl
Luckman George, cab. mkr., wks, 196 W. Pearl
Luckmann John, teamster, 124 Clark
Luckmann Phillipp, tailor, 474 Freeman
Lucky Hy. B., bk. layer, 2 3 Findlay
Lucky Mary, bds. 511 W. 5th
Lucky N. N., surveyor, h. 121 Laurel
Lucky Nathaniel F., bk. layer, 121 Laurel
Lucy Ellen, bleacher, bds. 175 W, 4th
Lucy Patrick, lab., 56 Abigail
Ludders Dederich E., cof. h., s.e.c. Bank and Whiteman
Ludeke Christian, bakery, 565 Main
Ludeke Christian, picture gallery, 565 Main
Ludemann Chas. H., lab., 97 Woodward
Ludwig Chas., carp., 388 Race
Ludington A. (Meader M.) h. 66 E. Pearl
LUDLOW AUGUSTUS S., Attorney at Law, s.e.c. 4th and Vine, h. 225 Baymiller, near Liberty
Ludlow Elizabeth, 431 Sycamore
Ludlow House, n.w.c 2d and Ludlow, Michael Grim, prop'r
Ludlow John, 139 Race
Ludlow Philo, 243 Laurel
Ludlow W. S., salesman, 140 Main, h. 199 Race
Ludlum Mary 21 Clinton
Ludinm Priscilla, 261 W. 9th
Ludneer Hy., lab., 20 Mansfield
Ludwick John. gardener. s.s. Liberty b. Freeman and Mill Creek
Ludwig Caroline, cutter bds n.w.c. 12th and Vine
Ludwig Chas., jr., clk., bds. 177 Hopkins
Ludwig Chas F., carp., 137 Hopkins
Ludwig Christian, printer, e.s. Main b. Schiller and Liberty

Ludwig Christian, tailor. 200 Pleasant
Ludwig Francis K., porter, 6 W. Front
Ludwig George, carp., wks. 304 Broadway
LUDWIG Godfrey (J. & T. Jenkins & Co.) 136 Laurel
Ludwig Hy. carp., 2 Hamer
Ludwig Hy., cigar mkr, 50 Pleasant
Ludwig Hermon, clk., 794 Central Av.
Ludwig Martin, tailor, 6 R Vine
Ludwig Philip, tailor, 41 Hamer
Ludy Judy, servt, Spencer House
Lue Thomas, lab., n e.c. 4th and Wood
Luebbe Louis, cigar mkr.. 26 Orchard
Luebmann Jno., carriage trimmer, n.w c. 13th and Clay
Lueck Oswald, varnisher, 447 W. 3d
Luecken Elizabeth, 46 Findlay
Luecken Hy., shoemkr, wks. 596 Main
Lueckens Wm., varnisher, 558 Race
Luecking Benj., bk. binder, 549 Sycamore
Luecking Gertrude, 549 Sycamore
Luecking John, lab., 19 Pendleton
Luedecke Ann, cap mkr, bds. 10 Orchard
Luedecke August, tailor, bds. 592 Main
Luedecke Charles, carp., 31 Werster
Luedemann Claus H., lab., 26 Abigail
Lueger Amelia, seamstress, bds. n.w.c. 12th and Vine
Luehn Mrs. Mary, 66 Dudley
Luehrmann Anna M., bds. 536 Race
Luehrmann Christian H., carp., 536 Race
Luehrmann Hy. W., boots and shoes, n. e.c. Race and 14th
Luehrmann John, planer. 247 Clark
Lueff Wm., cab. mkr., 69 Kossuth
Luenebrinck Jno. F., cooper, 577 Walnut
Luenemann Heinrich G., blksmith, 236 Water
Luenemann Stephen, cutlery, al. b. Vine and Walnut and 13th and Mercer
Luepke Hy., tanner, wks. 183 Ham. Road
Luepker Lizzie, seamstress, 53 Hughes
Luercke Louis, glass stainer, 96 Hunt
Luers Frank, miller. 58 Pierson
LUERS MRS. JOHN B., Bakery, 174 Sycamore
Luetkehaus Frank, (Rehe & L.) 309 W. Liberty
Luetmers Mary, bds. e.s. Hanover b. Woodward and Franklin
Luft Christopher, cutter, 92 Dudley
Luftenberg Peter, 58 Stark
Lugars Helena, 482 W. 5th
Luger Joseph, 52 Dunlap
Lugton Joseph J., painter, 122 Linn
Lugton George R., painter, foot of Harrison
Luhan Mathias, lab, 96 Bremen
Luhman ——, s.s. Calhoun b. Vine and Madison
Luhmann G. H., cab. mkr., 12 Mercer, res. Vine St. Hill
Luhn Agnes. match mkr., 66 Dudley
Luhn Hy., box mkr., 11 Budd
Luhn Herman, tailor, 407 Central Av
Luhn John B., tailor, 36 Ellen
LUHN JOHN H.,
Merchant Tailor, 8 E. 5th,
h. w.s. Kilgour b. 3d and 4th
Luhn John H., box factory, s s. Willow b., Curr and Harriet near W. W. Canal
Luhn J. Wm. salesman 93 Kilgour
Luhn Wm., tailor. w.s. Kilgour b. 3d and 4th
Luhr John, baker, 370 Elm
Luhring Caroline, 48 Rittenhouse
Luhring Fred. brush mkr, 48 Rittenhouse
Luhring & Michael (Wm. L. & John H. M.) leather and findings, 334 Main
Luhring Wm. (L. & Michael) 334 Main
Luhrman Caroline, seamstress, wks. 53 W. 4th
Luibker Hy., shoemkr., 159 Clay
Luick Emanuel, butcher, 583 Race
Luinebrink Frederick, cooper, 577 Walnut
Luinnemann Hy., molder. 51 13th [13th
Luinnemann Stephen, knife mkr., 53

Luisker Mary, 2 W. Mulberry
Luithart Louis, mach., h. 375 W. 5th
Luke Mary, servt., Burnet House
Luke Richard, 144 Longworth
Luke Winn. servt., Burnet House
Luken Barney, carp., 215 Baymiller
Luken Barney, porter, bds. 300 W. 5th
Luken Benjamin, tailor, s.w.c. Linn and Hopkins
Luken Edmund J., clk., 49 E. 4th
Luken John B., chair mkr., bds. 177 Hopkins
Luken John B. mer tailor, 285 Main
LUKEN JOHN GERHARD,
Merchant Tailor, 285 Main, h. E. Walnut Hills
Luken Joseph, grocery, 36 Elm
Luken Wm., tailor. bds. 285 Main
Lukens Abraham R., 49 E. 4th
Lukens Edwin J., salesman, bds. 49 E. 4th
Lukens P., (P. L. & Co.,) b. Springborough, Ohio
Lukens P. & Co. (P. L., Jos. Worwick, E. H. Griest & Jno. Conner,) Provision brokers, s.w.c. Walnut and 2d
Luking John, finisher, wks. n.e.c. Walnut and Canal
Lukins Wm., varnisher, 559 Race
Lulf Wm., cab. mkr., 69 Kossuth
Lullmann Rebecca M., dry goods, 22 13th
Lumbly Robert. 287½ Longworth
Lumley Jane. 2 Wilson
Lumley Samuel A., carp., 293 W. 8th
Lumney Harry, shoe mkr., wks. e.s. Baymiller b George and Barr
Lump Catharine. 607 Elm
Lumpp Hermann, cap mkr., 507 Walnut
Lunan Kate. servt., Burnet House
Lund Chas. A., b. k., 149 W. 5th
Lundaman Henry, molder, wks. n.e.c. Canal and Walnut
Lunin Dennis, cartman. 50 Wade
Luning Frank. cof. h., 467 Walnut
Luning Fred., cof. h. 497 Main
Luning Henry. J. & H. L.) 499 Main
Luning J. & H., (Joseph & Henry.) tailors, 110 E. 2d
Luning Joseph, (J. & H. L.) 150 Hopkins
Lunkenheimer Frederick, finisher, 458 Broadway
Lunt James M., train master, L.M. R.R. 14 Freeman
Lunum John, finisher, wks. n.w.c. Plum and Wade
Lupton David B.. Sec'y Cin. & Chicago R.R., 178 W. 4th
Lupton James, 53 W. 2d, bds. 178 W. 4th
Lupton Thompson N., clk., 108. W. Pearl, h. 178 W, 4th
Lushy John R., photographs, 58 Broadway, res. Walnut Hills
Luscum John, bk layer, 19 15th b. Central Av and Plum
Lusher Joseph, w.s. Lebanon Road b. Liberty and Corp. Line
Lusk James, bk layer, 306 W. 9th
Luster Chas., peddler 622 Main
Luster John, fireman, bds. 25 Hathaway
Lustig Chas. J., b. k., 507 Walnut
Lusty Thomas, carp., 36 Stone
Lute ——, photographist, bds n.w.c. Central Av. and Longworth
Lutebeck Bernard, lab., e. s. Lebanon Road, nr Montgomery Pike
Luther C. T. Edward printing office, 432 Walnut, h. 39 Mansfield
Luther Martha, 444 W. 5th
Lutherback Barney lab., 426 Sycamore
LUTHY & FOX, (Richard L & Adam C. F.,) Wholesale Grocers, n.e.c. Main and 7th
LUTHY Richard, (L. & Fox,) n.e.c. Main and 7th
Luthy Samuel, confec., 598 Walnut
Lutierbein Rodolph, teamster, h. 152 Baymiller
Lutman O. G., foreman. 17 Freeman
Lutmeding Ferdinand, tailor. 301 W. 2d
Lutmehr Barney, lab., 209 Linn
Lutmer Barney. porter, 999 Linn
Lutterbel Hy., lab. 68 Findlay
Lutterbei Sophia, 68 Findlay

Luttman George, 17 Freeman
Lutwig Chas., 958 Central Av.
Lutz Anna Maria, midwife, 175 W. Liberty
Lutz Anthony, lab., 71 Buckeye
Lutz Augustus, tinner, wks. n.w.c. Race and 2d
Lutz Caroline, variety store, 458 Vine
Lutz Casper, tailor, 152 Hopkins
Lutz Geo., drove ard., 6*6 Main
Lutz Hy., b. k., Broadway Hotel, h. 39 Broadway
Lutz Henry, stone cutter, 507 Elm
Lutz John, 175 W. Liberty
Lutz John, bksmith, wks. 414 W. M. Canal
Lutz Julianna, 243 Ham. Road
Lutz Julianna, seamstress, s.w.c. Pleasant and Ham. Road
Lutz Lawrence curp., 50 Wade
Lutz Lewis, lab., 188 Everett
Lutz Lorenz, cof. h., 154 Ham. Road
Lutz Lorenz, cooper, 154 Ham. Road
Lutz Michael, hostler, 418 W. 6th
Lutzberger Jacob, cap mkr., e. s. Vine b. Calhoun and Au'urn Av.
Luvy John, lab., rear 291 Elm
Luxius Philipp, barber, 63 W Court
Lyde Michael, lab, bds. 317 W. 2d
Lyden Ellen, Maiden Lane, b. Gas al. and Anderson al.
Lyden Patrick, trunk mkr., wks. n.w.c. Main and Patterson al.
Lyden Wm., carp., 149 George
Lydon Bridget, servt, Galt House
Lydon Bridget, 62 Water
Lyer Nicholas, brewer, 286 Ham Road
Lyford John, cab. mkr., bds. 170 Burr
Lyford Lewis, painter, 154 W. 3d, b. 484 John
Lykins Marcus D., (L. & Son,) h. Se damsville
Lykins & Son, (Marcus D. & Wm.) com. mers., s.w.c. Main and Water
Lykins Wm., (L. & Son,) h. Sedamsville
Lyle Chas., coal measurer, 160 Clinton
Lyle John M., bk. layer, bds. 169 Clinton
Lyle Margaret, w. s. Auburn Av. ar. Central Av.
Lyle Mary, teacher, 169 Clinton
Lyle Rebecca, teacher, 169 Clinton
Lymus Eliza J., e.s. Pancoast al. b. 7th and 8th
Lynagh Peter, cooper, 505 W 5th
Lynah John F., clk, County Treas. office
Lynch Absalom, teamster, 130 Smith
Lynch Ann, laundress, 142 Spring
Lynch Chas., finisher, 456 W. 5th
Lynch David, teamster, 131 Smith
Lynch Elizabeth, cof. h., 18 Lock n. of 8th
Lynch Eunice, 483 W. 9th w. of Central Avenue
Lynch Geo., molder, wks. W. W. Hanes'
Lynch Harriet, 5 North
Lynch James, finisher, wks. n.e.c. Walnut and Canal
Lynch James, lab., 19 Mill
Lynch James, lab., 55 E. 8th e of Lock
Lynch Jeremiah, mill builder, 370 Clark
Lynch John, hostler, 7** W. 6th
Lynch John, lab., 15 E. 7th
LYNCH JOHN A., Attorney at Law, Notary Public and Commissioner of Deeds. Room 7, Short's Building, h. 219 Laurel
Lynch Michael, n.s. New b. Culvert and Broadway
Lynch Michael, lab., 52 Rittenhouse
Lynch Michael D., grocery, 1216 Central Av.
Lynch Nora, 208 W. 7th
Lynch Patrick, cof. h., 22 Lock, n. of 8th
Lynch Pat, porter, s.w.c. 2d and Sycamore
Lynch Pat, shoe mkr., n.s. 7th b. Broadway and Sycamore
Lynch Peter, lab., s.s. Hunt, b. Sycamore and Main
Lynch Robert, peddler, 158 E. 5th
Lynch Thomas, lab., n.w.c Elm and Water

Lynch Thomas, cof. h., 227 W. 6th
LYND ROBERT R., Physician and Surgeon, Office and Residence 281 W. 8th
Lynd Rev. Samuel W., w.s. Auburn Av. nr. Central Av.
Lynd Staughton, atty., 7 Masonic Temple, res. Mt. Auburn
Lynde Leander F, clk., 166 Main, h. 219 Longworth
Lynde Wm W., salesman, 35 Main, h. 220 Laurel
Lynn Caroline, bds. rear 515 E. Front
Lynn Conrad, lab., rear 515 E. Front
Lynn James E., (L. & Morse,) h. Covington, Ky.
Lynn & Morse, (James E. L. & Edward M.,) real estate brokers, 227 Vine
Lyon Benj. C., atty., 123 Mound
Lyon Elizabeth G., dress mkr., 148 Longworth
Lyon Frank, e. s. Milk b. Vine and Calhoun
Lyon Gilson, driver, 179 W. Front
Lyon Hamilton, pattern mkr., bds. 68 E. 4th
Lyon Hamilton S., student, 341 W. 8th
Lyon James J., bk. layer, 317 Findlay
LYON JOHN, Wholesale Ladies Shoe Manufacturer, 281 W. 6th, h. 564 W. 9th w. of Central Av.
Lyon Jonathan W., carp., 172 Plum
Lyon Michael, lab., 556 W. Front
Lyon Sarah J., dress mkr., 395 W. 4th
Lyons Abraham, exchange broker, 422 W. 3d
Lyons Alfred, (J. H. Smith & Co.) 325 Longworth
Lyons Daniel, lab., 312 Sycamore
Lyons Dennis, lab., n s. 8th bet. Broadway and Sycamore
Lyons Edward, lab., 176 E. 3d, e of Collard
Lyons Ella, 64 Plum
Lyons Frank, (Hannan & L.,) 48 E. 6th
Lyons Helen, n. e. c. Central Av. and Court
Lyons Hy., carp., 134 George
Lyons Hy., lab., wks. 222 E. Front
Lyons John, bds. 168 W. 3d
Lyons John D., clk., 27 W. 3d, h. 325 W. 4th
Lyons John G., carp., 302 Clark
Lyons Joseph C., shoe mkr., 289 Central Av.
Lyons Martin, huckster, s.e.c. Sycamore and 7th
Lyons Michael R., grocery, h. s.s. 6th b. Macalister and Lawrence
Lyons Pat, dray, 312 E. Pearl
Lyons Perry, bds 553 W. 5th
Lyons Simon, 40 W. Court, w. of Central Av
Lyons Simon, jr., bds. 40 W. Court w. of Central Av
Lyons Wm., finisher, 101 E. Front
Lytle David, salesman, 59 W. Pearl, bds. s.w.c. Race and 7th
Lytle Geo. W., porter, 16 W. Front
Lytle Kate, servt., Galt House
Lytle James L., b k., 59 W. Pearl, bds. s.w.c. Race and George
Lytle Thos., mate, 17 Kossuth
LYTLE Wm. H., (Haines, Todd & L.,) 15 W. 3d
Lyttle Catharine, wash woman, bds. s.s. 6th b. Broadway and Culvert

Mc

McAfee Joseph, lab., 8th above Lock
McAleer Michael, lab., 71 Observatory Road
McAlister Alexander, steward, 121 Avery
McAlister James, fireman, 121 Avery
McAlister Michael, grocery, n.w.c. Race and Front
McAlister, Pat., 311 W. 2d
McAlister Daniel, lab., n.s. Friendship al. b. Lawrence and Pike
McAllister John, n.s. 6th b. Culvert and Broadway

McAllister Richard V., bar k., n. s. Leatherburry b. Willow and Reed
McALPIN Andrew, (McA., Hinman & Co.,) 66 W. 8th
McAlpin Andrew, clk., bds. 66 W. 8th
McALPIN G. W., (Kilis, McA. & Co.,) h. Clifton
McALPIN Henry, (McAlpin, Hinman & Co.,) 66 W. 8th
McAlpin Henry, clk., bds. 66 W. 8th
McALPIN, HINMAN & CO., (Andrew McA., B. P H & Henry McAlpin,) Wholesale Cabinet Hardware, 99, 101 and 103 Walnut
McALPIN Wm., (Smith & McA.,) res. Ernst Station. C. H. & D. R. R.
McAlpin Wm, clk., 99 Walnut, h. 66 W. 8th
McALPINE W. J., Vice President and Superintendent O. & M. R. R., office n.s. Front b. Mill and Wood, bds. Burnet House
McAlroy, Bernard, huckster, 382 Race
McAnally John, lab., 187 Water
McAndrew John P., miller, s s Dayton b. Coleman and Western Av
McAndrew Pat., lab., s.s. 8th b. Accomodation and State
McAndrews Ann, 37 New
McAndrews Thomas, porter, 43 Race
McAnnally Francis, nail mkr., 614 W. 6th
McAnrow John, horse trader, 405 Sycamore
McARDLE E. & J., (Edward & Jas.,) Merchant Tailors, 176 Vine
McARDLE Edward, (E. & J. McA.,) 326 W. 8th
McARDLE James, (E. & J. McA.,) 326 W. 8th
McArdle Pat., blk. smith, 200 6th Street Hill
McAroy Wm., huckster, 164 W. 8th
McArthur John, finisher, wks. n. e. c. Walnut and Canal
McArthur Andrew J., (McA. & Son,) bds. 162 W. 5th
McArthur Daniel, mach., 20 Linn
McArthur John, lab., n.s. Augusta bet. John and Sulith
McArthur & Son, Andrew McA. & Andrew J. McA.,) booksellers, 162 Vine
McAteer John, dray, 56 Mansfield
McAten Aaron M., student, bds. 110 W. 6th
McAuliff John, hatter, 91 Longworth
McAvoy Alex. B., clk., 6 E. 4th, h. Mt. Vernon
McAvoy Daniel, gardener, Garden of Eden
McAvoy Elizabeth, 544 W. 5th
McAvoy Emma, teacher third district school, h. t. Adams
McAvoy Frank, lab., 33 Kossuth
McAvoy Mary, cof. h., n e c. Ludlow and 3d
McAvoy Peter, bk. binder, 25 W. 4th, h. 347 W. 9th
McAvoy Peter, molder, wks. s. w. c. 7th and Smith
McAvoy Wm., fireman, on railroad, n.s. Taylor b. Freeman and Curr
McBIRNEY Hugh, (H. McB & Co.,) 20 Hopkins
McBIRNEY HUGH & CO., (Hugh McB. & Hy. M. Johnston,) Commission Merchants, 69 Vine
McBride Arthur, lab, 4" Mill
McBride Jas., bds. Clifton House
McBride Jas., lab., 414 Sycamore
McBride Jas. S., pilot, bds 138 Barr
McBride John, finisher, wks. n. e. c. Walnut and Canal
McBride John, w.s. Park b 4th and 5th
McBride John S., paper hanger, bds. 138 Barr
McBride Joseph, finisher, 34 Mulberry
McBride Louisa, 130 Burr
McBride Lyman, carp., rear 173 Elm, h. 205 Water
McBride Saml., pilot, 48 Plum
McBurnie Mrs. Theophila, 135 W. 9th
McBurns Barney, lab., 220 E. 6th
McCabe Alexander, tanner, Deck Creek, foot of 8th, h 352 Main

220 (McC) CINCINNATI (McC) DIRECTORY. (McC)

McCabe Chas., shoe mkr., bds. Pavillion b. Observatory and 3d
McCabe Edward, lab., 25 Martin
McCabe Francis, fireman, Burnet House
McCabe Francis, lab., n. w. c. Vine and 2d
McCabe Isaac, w s. Miami Canal bet 6th and 8th
McCabe J. C., clk., 101 Sycamore, h. Sedamsville
McCabe Jas., bds 150 E. 6th
McCabe Jas., dray, 99 Bremen
McCabe Jas., waiter, Burnet House
McCABE John W., (Pfaff, Webb & McCabe,) hds. s.w.c. 7th and Race
McCabe Michael, 860 Central Av.
McCabe Michael, lab., 138 George
McCabe Owen, lab., s.e.c. Chestnut and John
McCabe Owen, lab., s.s. Phoebe al bet. Plum and Central Av.
McCabe Patrick, lab., wks. 830 Central Av
McCabe Peter, driver, al. b. 4th and 5th and Central Av and John
McCabe Ross, foreman, 83 Pendleton
McCabe Thomas, eng., 107 Baum
McCafferty Jas., blk. smith, 14 Race
McCaffray Nicholas, grocery, 71 Richmond
McCaffrey Barney, lab., n. s. R. R. e. of French
McCaffrey Jas., wagon mkr., 14 Race
McCaffrey Michael, policeman, 208 W. 7th
McCaha Thomas, hackman, 137 W. 3d
McCaig Robert, bk. layer, 35 Jones
McCain Richard. lab., wks. s.w.c. Broadway and 5th   [Lock
McCalion Jas., carp., 61 E. 8th e. of
McCall David. carp., 1224 E. Front
McCall Jas. E., clk., P. O., 232 Sycamore
McCALL John, agt. Louis Snider, 232 Walnut, h. 437 Plum
McCall John W., 222 Sycamore
McCall John W, type founder, bds. 222 Sycamore
McCall Wm. A., 307 W. 4th
McCall Wm A., bds. 202 Sycamore
McCalligan Joseph, huckster, s.s. Carl b. 3d and 4th and Mill and Stone
McCallister John, lab., 150 W. Pearl
McCallister Wm., tailor, n.s. Goodloe b. Willow and Leatherbury
McCALLUM BRIDGE CO., (Daniel C. McC., Wheeler H. Bristol & Simeon S. Post,) Bridge Builders, 75 W. 3d
McCALLUM Daniel C., (McC. Bride & Co.) h. Owego, N Y.
McCallum John, driver, 62 Butler
McCallum John, foreman, 100 Baum
McCalwey Jas., lab. s.s. Avery al. w. of Wood
McCam Jas. P., bds. 37 Longworth
McCammant Joseph, pilot, 244 Richmond
McCammon Charles E., clk., 89 Hopkins
McCammon Geo., b k., bds. s. e. c. Pike and 3d
McCammon Jas, belt mkr., 55 Observatory Road
McCammon John, builder, 69 Hopkins
McCAMMON John, (Kolker & McC.,) res. Mt. Hope
McCAMMON WM., President Queen City Insurance Company, h. Storrs Township
McCann Michael, horse trader, 91 E. 5th
McCandless Sarah, h. 121 E. 5th
McCandless Mary A., 69 W. Court w. of Central Av
McCandless Truxton, clk. L. M. R. R., 121 E. 5th
McCandra Michael, 138 George
McCandra Peter, lab., s. s. al. bet. Pike and Lawrence and 3d and Pearl
McCandre Bartley, lab., 221 W. Front
McCandre Pat., lab., 221 W. Front
McCandry Bridget, n.s. Augusta b. John and Smith
McCandry James, n. s. Augusta b. John and Smith

McCane Melvina, 662 E. Front
McCane Thomas, caulker, 668 E. Front
McCann ——, actor National Theater
McCann Annie, servt., 390 W. 6th
McCann Catharine, 516 W. 3d
McCann Jas., dray, 516 W. 3d
McCann Jas., gas fitter, 48 Barr
McCann Jas. P., carriage trimmer, wks. 11 E. 6th
McCann Joseph, printer, 54 Barr
McCann Margaret. 13 W. 3d
McCann Margaret, servt., 150 Broadway
McCann Pat., dray, e.s. Macalister b. 4th and 5th
McCann Pat., printer, 54 Barr
McCann Pat., tailor, 23 Webb
McCann Thos., type finisher, 97 W. Court w. of Central Av
McCANN Wm., (Hewes & McC.,) 194 George
McCann Mary, rear 40 Sycamore
McCanne Edward. lab., 451 Plum
McCrachen Louisana, trimmer, s. s. Richmond b. Plum and Central Av
McCarder John, s. w. c. 3d and Central Av.
McCardle Rose, 541 W. 5th
McCardy ——, dray, rear 367 Sycamore
McCarrell Jane, n.s. 7th bet. Harriet and Mill Creek
McCarrell Mary, n.s. 7th b, Harriet and Mill Creek
McCarren Ellen, servt., 409 W. 7th
McCarred Peter, 21 Accommodation
McCarthy Adelia. tailoress, 171 Main
McCARTHY D. W., Physician and Surgeon, 110 W. 6th
McCarthy Daniel. grainer, 100 W. 6th
McCarthy Dennis, coach' trimmer, bds. 57 Broadway
McCarthy Josiah, carp., 204 Clark
McCarthy James, clk., s.s. Sloo e. of Harriet
McCarthy Jas. J., tailor, 38 New
McCarthy Jeremiah, 109 W. Front
McCarthy Johanna, servt., Henrie House
McCarthy John, box mkr, 141 E. 3d
McCarthy John, hats and caps, 172 E. 5th
McCarthy John, lab., 31 Ann
McCarthy John, tailor, n.w.c. Union and Race
McCarthy Kate, 653 W. Front
McCarthy Margaret, s.e.c. 7th and Broadway
McCarthy Margaret, servt., 371 W. 6th
McCarthy Margaret, servt., n.s. Wade b. Freeman and Dudley
McCarthy Mary. servt., 317 Longworth
McCarthy Michael, carp., 251 Clark
McCarthy Peter, lab, 265 John
McCarthy Susan, 653 W. Front
McCarthy Timothy T., undertaker, 221 Sycamore
McCarthy Wm., grocery, 97 Sycamore
McCarthy Wm., lab., 91 Sycamore
McCarthy Wm., tailor, 211 W. Front
McCartney Jane bds. 30 Chestnut
McCartney John, bakery, 444 W. 5th, h. e.s. Park b Longworth and 5th
McCartney Kate, bds. 32 Chestnut
McCartney Peter, harness mkr., 151 George
McCartney Sarah, bds. 36 Chestnut.
McCarty Annie, 1203 E. Font
McCarty Anna M, servt, 2 5 W. 8th
McCarty Bernard, lab., 307 W. 2d
McCarty Bridget. servt 133 Broadway
McCarty Cecelin, servt., 282 Longworth
McCarty Chas., blacksmith, wks. s.e.c. Miller and 7th
McCarty Chas., cook, bds. n.e.c. Front and Ludlow
McCarty Charles, tailor, 321 W. 6th
McCarty Chas., tailor, 238 Broadway
McCarty Daniel. finisher. 40 Linn
McCarty Dan!., lab., wks. Hy Nye's
McCarty Dennis, lab., 48 Lock n. of 8th
McCarty Dennis, lab., 60 Woodward
McCarty Dennis, lab., 202 W. Front
McCarty Dennis, n.s. 5th b. Broadway and Sycamore
McCarty Elizabeth, bds. 48 Lock n. of 8th

McCarty Eliza, 51 E. 3d e. of Whittaker
McCarty Ellen. s.s. 6th b. Broadway and Culvert
McCarty Florence, 125 Lock
McCarty Florence, lab., 48 Lock n. of 8th
McCarty Jas., carp., 29 Parsons
McCarty Jas., driver, 51 E. 3d e. of Whittaker
McCarty Jas., rear 37 New
McCarty Jas., driver, 189 E Pearl
McCarty Jas sr., bds. n.e.c. 3d and Stone
McCarty Jas., jr., lab., n.e.c. 3d and Stone
McCarty Jas. J., tailor, h. 38 New
McCarty Jeremiah, lab., w s. Central Av. b. W. W. Canal and 3d
McCarty John, carriage mkr., 394 Broadway
McCarty John, cof. h., n.s. Front w. of Hill
McCarty John, lab., wks. s.w.c. Broadway and 5th
McCarty John, lab., e s. Crippen al. b. 7th and 8th
McCarty John, lab., e.s. Macalister b. 4th and 5th
McCarty John, lab., wks. Hy. Nye's
McCarty John, lab., wks. Foote, Nash & Co.'s
McCarty Julia, servt., 99 Broadway
McCarty Margaret 141 E. 3d
McCarty Margaret, Gas al. b. Front and 2d
McCarty Margaret, servt , 90 E. 3d
McCarty Martin, grocery, 239 Central Av.
McCarty Martin, lab., e.s. Garrard n. of Gest
McCarty Mary, e.s. Pancoast al. b. 7th and 8th
McCarty Mary, servt , 404 W. 6th
McCarty Michael, driver, bds. 26 Lock n. of 8th
McCarty Peter, wks J. Whittaker's, Deer Creek Valley
McCarty Patrick, dray, 109 Cutter
McCarty Patrick, lab., s.s. 6th b. Broadway and Culvert
McCarty Patrick, waiter. Madison House
McCarty Randall, cot. h , 16 Lock n. of 8th
McCarty Randall, lab., 16 Dublin
M Carty Thos., lab., 180 E. Pearl
McCarty Timothy, dray, 188 Cutter
McCarty Timothy, lab., 142 Spring
McCarty Wm., blacksmith, 89 Richmond and Culvert
McCarty Wm , lab., s.s. 6th b. Broadway and Culvert
McCasker Jane, bds. 202 Broadway
McCauley James, driver, n.e.c. 6th and North
McCauley Margaret, 209 E. 6th
McCauley Patrick, lab, w s. Culvert b. 5th and 6th
McCaven Patrick, molder, wks. n.e.c. Canal and Walnut   [3d
McCendrick Patrick, shoe mkr., 113 W.
McChesney Margaret, 199 W. 3d
McChester Samuel, printer, Cin. Gazette, h 125 W. 5th
McClain Mary, n.s. Cherry al. b. Plum and Central Av.
McClane Wm , hostler, 303 Sycamore
McCleary Samuel, variety store, 170 Central Av.
McCleley Anderson, lab., s.s. Taylor rear of 632 6th
McClellan Jas., cof. h., 1072 Central Av.
McClellan Robt., lab Indiana House
McClenn in Lizzie, 21 Carr
McCleod Jane. rear 204 Richmond
McClintock Geo., lab., s.s. Front e. of French
McClintock Jas. D., printer, h. 230 W. Court w. of Central Av.
McClintock Samuel E., saddler, bds. 120 E. 5th
McClintock Sarah J., bds 179 Broadway
McCloskey Geo., gas fitter, wks. n.e. c. Walnut and Canal
McCloskey Hy., lab., wks 166 W. Pearl
McCloskey Mary, servt., 301 Longworth
McCloskey Wm., hinge fitter, wks. n.e. c. Walnut and Canal

McCloskey Wm., mach., n.s. Augusta b. John and Smith
McClosky Chas., conductor, Augusta b. John and Smith
McClosky Elizabeth, 402 Baymiller
McClosky Margaret, servt., 499 W. 5th
McClosky Mary, n.s. Augusta b. John and Smith
McCloud Margaret, bds. 159 W. Front
McCloud Wm., cutler, 395 Vine
McCloushy ——, 65 Butler
McCloy Hy., grocer, 10 Freeman
McClum David, wagon mkr., bds. 112 Laurel
McClung Jas., clk. L. M. R.R. Depot, bds. Spencer House
McClure Alex., clk. water works, h. 408 W. 7th
McClure David, grocery, 35 Cutter
McCLURE EMILY, Fashionable Millinery, 111 W. 4th
McClure John, mach., 161 Cutter
McClure Sarah, 187 W. Court w. of Central Av.
McClure Wm., carp., 54 Lock
McClury Bishop, eng., bds. 10 Sycamore
McCluskey Mary, servt., 264 Longworth
McClymon John B., atty., n.w.c. 3d and Main. h. Walnut Hills [Pearl
McCollif Daniel, lab., w.s. Pole b. 2d and
McCOLLUM HUGH, Plumber, Pumps, Hydrants, &c., 101 W. 6th, h. 413 Broadway
McCollum Hugh, plumber, 413 Broadway
McCollum Joseph, b.k. 101. W. 6th, bds 413 Broadway
McCollum Robt., plumber, bds. 413 Broadway
McColmack Ann, servt., w.s. Broadway b. 4th and 5th
McColmack Bridget, servt., w.s. Broadway b. 4th and 5th
McComas Evalyn, teacher, 178 Race
McComas Maria, teacher, 178 Race
McComas Richard P., dry goods, 575 Central Av., h. 199 Betts
McComas Richard T., b.k., 178 Race
McComba Mart. clk., 138 W 9th
McComman Samuel, salesman 134 Walnut
McConba Samuel S., clk., bds. 363 W. 4th
McCONNELL Samuel, (H. Campbell & Co.) h Portsmouth
McCONNELL THOS S., Carpenter and Builder, 467 W. 8th, bds. 138 Smith
McConville John, grocery. 754 E Front
McCOOK Robert L., (Stallo & McC) h 19 W Court
McCord B., lab., wks. Wood & McCoy's, 20 Spring
McCord Barney, lab., 98 Hunt
McCord Chas., plasterer, 127 Elm
McCord Daniel, clk. s w.c. 8th and Central Av., h. 106 George
McCord David A., (J. S. & D. A. McC.) 261 W. Court w. of Central Av.
McCord J. H., painter, 178 W Court
McCord J. S. & D. A., (Joseph S. & David A.) carps., n.e.c. Pine and Gest
McCord Jackson, carp., 166 George
McCord Jas. W., b.k. 11 W. Pearl, h. 130 Linn
McCord John R., bds. 178 W. Court w. of Central Av.
McCord Joseph S., (J. S. & D. A. McC.) 255 W. Court w. of Central Av.
McCORD Wm., Merchant Tailor, 292 W. 6th
McCormack Chas., molder, 460 W. 8th
McCormack Eliza, servt., Burnet House
McCormack Jas, bksmith, 22 E. 5th
McCormack Jas., painter, w.s. Collard b. Front and 3d
McCormack John, groceries, s.e.c. 5th and John
McCormack John, shoe mkr., wks. 34 W. 5th
McCormack John, wire weaver, 61 Water
McCormack Joseph W., seive mkr., 63 Everett

McCormack Mat., dray, 94 Cherry al. b. Plum and Central Av.
McCormack Michael, blksmith, bds. 51 W. 5th
McCormack Rody, upholsterer, 19 North
McCormack Thos., cof h., 25 E. 5th, h. w.s. Kilgour b. 3d and 5th
McCO MICK Andrew, (McC., Gibson & Co.) h. Mt. Auburn
McCormack Christopher, molder, 252 Water
McCORMICK, GIBSON & CO., (Andrew McC., Wm. G. & John Mc Cormick) Lead Pipe and Sheet Lead Manufacturers, s.s. 9th b. Main and Sycamore
McCormack H. G, clk. 171 Vine, res. Clifton
McCormick Hy., carp., w.s. Oregon b. 3d and 6th
McCormick J., bds. Dennison House
McCormick James W., auctioneer 154 Main, bds. Dennison House
McCORMICK John, (McCormick Gibson & Co.) h. Mt. Auburn
McCormick John B., molder, bds 49 Race
McCormick John B., molder, n.s. Water b. Central Av. and John
McCormick Margaret teacher, bds. n.s. Poplar b. Freeman and Western Av.
McCormick Mary, n.w.c. 3d and Ellen
McCormick Mary A., rear 149 Cutter
McCormick Matthew, grocery, 319 E. 6th
McCormick Michael, b. 143 E. 2d
McCormick N. W., auctioneer, bds. Henrie House
McCormick Norah, chamber maid, Dennison House
McCormick Patrick, blksmith, n.s. Patterson al. b. Main and Walnut, h. 21 North
McCormick Pat, silver smith, h. 99 W. Court w. of Central Av.
McCormick Patrick, tailor, s.e c. 4th and Vine
McCormick Phillip, cof. h., 56 Accommodation
McCormick Phillip, lab., wks. 179 W. Canal
McCormick Rosette, h. 203 W. 2d
McCormick Thomas, porter, 24 E. 2d
McCormick Wm., 312 Longworth
McCormick Wm. C.. clk., 318 Clark
McCourt Mary, servt., 150 John
McCowen Lawrence, 29 Gest
McCowlif Jerry, n.s. Patterson al. b. Main and Walnut
McCoy Dennis, 175 Water
McCoy James, painter, 61 George, h. 74 Hopkins
McCoy Samuel, painter, 164 W. Court w. of Central Av.
McCoy Thomas H., b. k., 99 Walnut, h. 337 Vine [Vine
McCoy Thos J., (Wood & McC.,) 337
McCoy Wm. G., agt., 460 W. 6th
McCracken James. clk , s.s. Richmond b Plum and Central Av.
McCracken Louisa, u. s. 9th b. Plum and Central Av.
McCracken R. B. & Co., (Robert B. McC., & Edward Atkinson,) fire brick, and furnace builders, 76 E. Front
McCRACKEN RALPH C , Shirt Manufacturer and Gents' Furnisher 19 W. 4th, h 66 Longworth
McCracken Robert, lab., s.s. Cassatt al. b Sycamore and Main
McCracken Robert B., (R. B. McC. & Co.) h. Newport
McCracken Simon, clk. 98 Water
McCracken Thomas, carp., bds. 158 W. 3d
McCray John, plumber, bds. s w.c. 5th and Broadway
McCrea Charles T., salesman, 103 W. Pearl, h. 16 Clark
McCrea John, lab., 43 Wade
McCready James W., carp., 18 David
McCreata Wm., butcher, 48 E. 6th
McCrett Wm., butcher, 48 E. 6th
McCrevy Mary, s.s. Cassatt al. b. Sycamore and Main

McCristle Ellen, n.s. Taylor al. w. of Kilgour
McCrodden James, 297 W. 2d
McCrory Annie, servt., 359 George
McCrory Hugh, porter, bds. 23 Longworth
McCrory Philip, carp , 404 W. 5th
McCue Edward, s.s. Pearl b. Pike and Butler
McCue Francis, lab , 127 Webb
McCue James, lab., bds. n.e.c. Vine and Water
McCue Michael, s.s. Charlotte b. Linn and Baymiller
McCue Michael, lab., s.w.c. Front and Smith
McCue Michael, lab., s.s. S100 w. of Freeman
McCue Thomas, s.s. Charlotte b. Linn and Baymiller
McCullan James, grocer, 159 E. 6th
McCullen Alexander, carp., 161 Cutter
McCULLACH JOSEPH B., Reporter Cincinnati Commercial bds. Walnut Street House
McCullough A., 37 New
McCULLOUGH Addison, (H. Campbell & Co.,) h. Ironton Ohio
McCullough Alexander, molder, 491 W. 5th
McCullough Anna A. R , 44 Lock
McCullough Chas., cof. h., 320 Broadway
McCullough Edward, clk., 317 Broadway
McCullough Edward, 379 Main, h. n.w.c. Broadway and Court
McCullough Eliza, bds. 390 W. 7th
McCullough Hezekiah, mach., n.s. Front E. of Foster
McCullough Hugh, boots and shoes, 29 Broadway
McCullough J. B., bds. Walnut Street House
McCULLOUGH J. M. & SON, (James M. McC., and Lewis Kennedy.) Agricultural Implement and Seed Store, 200 Main and 3 E. 5th
McCullough James A., molder, 491 W. 5th
McCULLOUGH James M., (J. M. McC. & Son) h. Pleasant Ridge
McCULLOUGH Robert, (D. B. Pierson & Co.,) 39 W. Court, w. of Central Av.
McCullough Wm. R., clk., bds. 1170 E. Front
McCully Rachael, 35 Elizabeth
McCune Barney, lab., n e.c. Front and Ludlow
McCune Ellen, 118 Everett
McCune Ellen, s.s. Pearl b. Pike and Butler
McCune James, lab., 15 W. Court w. of Central Av.
McCune John, agt. Great Western Dispatch. bds. Burnet House
McCune John, molder, 12 Race
McCune Joseph S., broker, 208 Barr
McCune Pat, lab., wks., C. T. Dumont's
McCune Samuel A., clk., C. H. & D. R. R., h. 208 Burr
McCune Rev. W. C., 40 W. Mulberry
McCurdy Samuel, b. h., 69 E. 4th
McCurdy Wm., cab. mkr., s.w.c. 9th and Central Av.
McCusker John, lab., 49 Water
McDaniel Patrick, lab , n.s. Montgomery Pike near Reading Road
McDevitt John. dray, 23 8th above Lock
McDelmott Jonn J., blksmith, 178 Linn
McDermott Charles, lab., w.s. Anderson b 3d and Pearl
McDermott Cornelius, tailor, bds. 186 Race
McDermott John, lab., 134 Water
McDermott John Co., lab., n.w.c. 6th and Harriet
McDermott Larey, tinner, 17 Elm
McDermott Thomas, hackman, 134 Water
McDermot Martin, waiter, Burnet House
McDermot Mary, 208 W. 7th
McDermot Michael, grocery 493 W. 4th
McDermott, lab., 31 Mill

McDermott Alice, 50 E. 8th e. of Lock
McDermott Anna, bds. Dennison House
McDermott Mrs. B., cof. h., 8 Landing b. Main and Walnut
McDermott Bridget, servt., 31 McFarland
McDermott Cornelius, tailor, bds. 166 Race
McDermott Ella, bds Dennison House
McDermott Mrs. J. R., dress mkr., 167 Race
McDermott James, shoe mkr., 283 W. 6th
McDermott John, lab., 54 Melancthon
McDermott John, shoe mkr., 58 Abigail
McDermott John, teamster, bds. 207 Wade
McDermott L., tinner, 9 Wade
McDermott Mary, milliner, 207 Wade
McDermott Mary A., bds. 254 E. 6th
McDermott Michael, lab., 49 E. 8th e. of Lock
McDermott Roseanna, bds Dennison House
McDevitth Mary, seamstress, wks 53 W. 4th
McDevitt Charles, dray, 479 Broadway
McDevitt Wm, dray, 546 Sycamore
McDiarmid Annie, teacher 4th District School
McDiarmid William, printer, 62 W. 3d
McDoll Wm, mate, n.e.c. Richmond and John
McDonald Alfred, bk. layer, 462 W. 8th
McDonald Alexander, bk. seller, bds. 467 W. 8th
McDonald Alexander, 179 Mound
McDonald Alex., lab., Burnet House
McDonald Alex, lab., w.s. Pancoast al. b. 7th and 8th s.
McDonald Alonzo, hostler, n.s. Court b. Central Av. and Plum
McDonald Andrew, printer, 45 Pub. Landing
McDonald Anthony, lab., s.w.c. Central Av. and W. W. Canal
McDonald Anthony, tinner. 120 E. 8th
McDONALD & BENJAMIN (Hugh McD. & James B.), Wholesale Stone Ware Depot), 14 and 16 Water
McDonald Charles H., house furnishing goods, n e.c John and 5th
McDonald Dan'l, pattern mkr., 128 Walnut
McDonald Edward, 180 E. 6th
McDonald Ellen, 52 Rittenhouse
McDonald Geo., n e.c. John and 5th
McDonald Hugh, (McD. & Ross), res. Covington
McDONALD Hugh (Benjamin & Co.), bds Dennison House
McDONALD Hugh, (McD. & Benjamin) h. Putnam, O.
McDonald James, boiler mkr., 516 E. Front
McDonna'd James A., porter, Adams Express Co.
McDonald Jane, laundress. Gibson House
McDonald Johanna, 28 W. 6th
McDonald John, asst. market master, n. s. Augusta b. John and Smith
McDonald John, gas fitter, 107 Baum
McDonald John, lab., 560 E. Front
McDonald Joseph, peddler, 41 Ludlow
McDonald Kate, n.s. Front e. of Washington
McDonald Margaret, 54 Barr
McDonald Margaret, servt., 438 W. 4th
McDonald Mary, clk., bds. 41 George
McDonald Mary, cof. h., 113 W. 3d;
McDonald Mary, s s. 6th b. Broadway and Culvert
McDonald Michael, lab., s.s. Yeatman b. Broadway and Sycamore
McDonald Michael, carp., Observatory at , Mt. Adams
McDonald Patrick, carp., 129 Butler
McDonald Patrick, lab., 188 W. Front
McDonald Patrick, polisher, wks. n.e.c. Canal and Elm
McDonald & Ross, (Hugh McD. & Chas. W. R.), liquors, &c., 22 Water
McDonald Thomas, dray, 22 Hughes
McDonald Thomas, lab., 449 W. 2d
McDonald Thomas, stone cutter, 52 Rittenhouse

McDonald Thomas, lab., 700 Race
McDonald Thomas, tailor, 67 W. Court w. of Central Av
McDonald Wm., wks. 340 W. 3d
McDonald Wm., carp, 958 E. Front
McDonald Wm., chair mkr., 363 W. 3d
McDonald Wm., dry goods, 230 W. 6th
McDonald Wm., saloon, 64 Broadway, h. 31 Parsons
McDonald Wm., 197 Vine
McDonald Wm., wheel wright, 263 W. 3d
McDonnell Alexander, lab., 132 Central Av.
McDONNELL & ATKINSON, (J. N. McD. & G. V. A.), Buckeye Dining Saloon, 170 and 172 Vine
McDonnell Harriet, 197 George
McDonnell John, police, 68 W. Court w. of Central Av
McDONNELL John N., (McD. & Atkinson), h. 75 Richmond
McDonnell Matthew, driver, bds., 518 W 3d
McDonnell Mathew, lab., wks. c. 3d and W. W. Canal
McDonnell Michael. carp., n.s. Patteral. b. Main and Walnut, res. Mt. Adams
McDonnell Michael, saloon, 323 W. 8th
McDonnell Patrick, stone cutter, 57 Kossuth
McDonnell Wm., bar. k., 31 Parsons
McDonnoll Susan, 254 W. 6th
McDonnough Bernard, lab., n.w.c. 3d and Collard
McDonough Bridget, servt , 27 Chestnut
McDonough D., lab., 214 Sycamore
McDonough Hugh, hackman, 14 Race
McDonough James V., marble cutter, n. s. Augusta b. John and Smith
McDonough John, clk., 50 Race
McDonough John, hackman, 125 W. Front
McDonough John, lab, 131 W. Front
McDonough John, lab., rear 52 Plum
McDonough John. stable, s.s. 5th b. Broadway and Pike, h.w.s. Lawrence b. 4th and 5th
McDonough Mary, servt., Henrie House
McDonough Miles, roofer, 17 E. 6th
McDonough Patrick, lab., 243 W. Front
McDonough Patrick, lab., 50 Elm
McDonough Peter, droyer, 93 Hopkins
McDonough Phillip, clothing, 218 Plum
McDonough Thomas, lab., s.s. 2d b. Mil and Smith
McDormand John R., bds. 273 Walnut
McDormott John, 33 New
McDougal Addison B., clk. Co. Auditor's office, h. 300 John
McDougal Chas., bds. Dennison House
McDougal Joseph, atty. 57 W, 3d
McDougall Allen. boatman, 60 W Fron
McDougan Joseph, bds. Olean Hotel
McDOWELL ALEX., Wholesale and Retail Dealer in Carpets, Oil Cloths and Curtain Goods, 100 W. 4th, bds. Clifton House
McDowell Ellen, bds 228 Barr
McDowell James, tinner, 42 Pub. Landing
McDowell Jane, al. b. Mound and Cutter, from W. Court to Pennock al
McDowell John J., teller, Com. Bank, bds. Burnet House
McDowell John S , tinner, 42 Pub. Landing
McDowell Joseph, s.s Front e. of Ferry
McDowell Joseph E., lab., s.s. Front e. of Ferry
McDowell Malcolm, n.w.c. Front and Hill
McDowell Matthew, driver, bds. 130 W. Court
McDowell Rebecca, bds. e.s. Macalister b. 4th and 5th
McDowell Robert V., mate, 52 W. Court w. of Central Av
McDuffy Ann, 257 Plum
McEauliff Jerry, hostler, n.s. Patterson al. b. Main and Walnut
McElevey Louisa, 168 W. 4th
McElhaney Hy., police, n.s. Railroad e. of Hazen
McElhaney William H., shoemkr., 42 Pierson

McElroy Michael, lab., s.s. 6th e. of Lock
McElroy Patrick H., bk. layer, 168 Linn
McElroy Patrick J , mach., 112 John
McElroy Sabrina, teacher. 429 W. 4th
McElvain Alonzo. eng , 253 Laurel
McElwee Wm., foreman, Niles' Works, 40 Harrison
McElwee Wm. J., mach., wks. Niles' Works
McFadden G. & H. (George & H. McF.) notions, &c., 98 W. 5th
McFadden George (G. & H. McF.) res. country
McFadden H. (G. & H, McF.) h. New York
McFadden John, clk., 96 W. 5th
McFadden John, stone cutter, 295 W. 8th
McFadden Michael, lab., s.s. Front e. of Reed
McFall Edward, pilot, 260 Clark
McFall Francis M., clk., bds. 110 W. 6th
McFARLAN James (Straight, Deming & Co.) 464 W. 9th
McFARLAN Thomas (Steptoe & McF.) res. Covington
McFarland Andrew, paver, 193 Cutter
McFarland Augustus, clk., bds. 73 W. 7th
McFarland Caroline A., teacher, 519 Freeman
McFarland Charlotte, 245 Broadway
McFarland Francis. dray, bds. 171 Baymiller
McFarland Isaac, 22 David
McFarland Jas , cooper, bds. 143 Baymiller
McFarland James, plasterer, 21 Melancthon
McFarland John, stable kpr., 131 E. 5th
McFarland John F., wood., 576 W 9th
McFarland John R., molder, 3 Gorman
McFarland Margaret, 143 Baymiller
McFarland Robert G., reporter Merchants' Exchange, bds. s.e.c. 7th and Vine
McFarland Wm. A., mer., n.w.c. 4th and John
McFarland W. Y., with Geo. W. Phillips, Jr., rooms Selves' Bldg
McFarrall Daniel, lab., 458 W. 5th
McFeely James J., phys., 105 W. Front, h. Covington
McGamitt Patrick, lab , 31 Mill
McGann Michael, al. b. 5th and Longworth and Elm and Plum
McGannes Anna, 197 Richmond
McGarhan Mary. servt., n.e.c. 3d and Ellen
McGarry Bridget, n.s. Augusta b. John and Smith
McGarvin Mary, servt., 237 W. 4th
McGary Anna, laundress, Gibson House
McGary Annie. servt , 372 W. 7th
McGary Hy., steward, 11 8th above Lock
McGEGHIN THOMAS, Wholesale Grocer. s.e.c. Main and 6th, h Reading Road
McGee Clement, cooper 906 Central Av
McGee Elizabeth, bds. 404 W 4th
McGee James, clk., 33 W. 3d, h. Covington
McGee Julia, seamstress, 118 Laurel
McGee Mary, 133 E. 6th
McGee Patrick, tanner, wks. 183 Ham. Road
McGee Wm., bds. 112 E. 3d
McGechan Patrick, tanner, 155 Pleasant
McGeorge Geo , blksmith, 12 Grant
McGeorge John, stocking manuf , 130 Betts
McGeorge Jotham H., mach , 19 Kossuth
McGeorge Wm. G. M., 12 Grant
McGhee Archie, lab., s.e.c. 4th and Wood
McGhee Wm., porter, bds. 108 Central Av
McGibbon Mary, 382½ W. 7th
McGibbons David L., blksmith, 97 Longworth
McGill Elizabeth, teacher, 147 W. 5th
McGill Margaret, 147 W. 5th
McGill Margaretha, 61 W. 6th
McGill Wm., 69 W. Court w. of Central Av
McGill Wm., stone mason, 309 E. Front

CINCINNATI (McG) DIRECTORY. (McI) 223

McGraw Ellen, servt, n.w.c. Longworth and Central Av
McGraw James, lab., bds. n.s. Augusta, b. John and Smith
McGraw Patrick, driver, 242 E. 6th
McGraw Patrick, lab., s.s. Front. e. of French
McGray John, plumber, bds. s.w.c. 5th and Broadway
McGray John, porter, 303 W. 2d
McGreen Thomas, dray, 676 W. Front
McGregor Alexander, finisher, wks. 216 W. 2d
McGregor Benj., locksmith, 173 Mound
McGregor Elizabeth, dry goods, 116 Lock
McGREGOR GEO., Locksmith and Bell Hanger, 133 W. 5th, h. 187 Mound
McGregor James, bds. w.s. Auburn Av., near Central Av
McGregor James, shoemkr, 112 Bremen
McGregor John, plumber, wks. 46 E. 3d
McGregor Robert, n.e.c. Central Av. and Lebanon Road
McGregor Wm., clk., 77 Walnut, bds. Mt. Auburn
McGrevey Daniel, boatman, 49 Water
McGrew Ann, seamstress, 206 Hopkins
McGrew Ann P., 253 W 7th
McGrew Hy., carp., 12 E 5th
McGrew Hy., shoemkr, 512 Race
McGREW HENRY C., Printer, 30 Milton
McGrew James, coal agent, s.e.c. Front and Lawrence. bds. Broadway Hotel
McGrew John S., phys., bds 408 W. 7th
McGrew Joseph A., salesman, 23 W. 2d, h. 258 W. 7th.
McGrew Robert, harness mkr., 378 Vanhorn
McGREW ROBERT, SR., City and County Inspector of Lumber and Shingles, 53 Laurel
McGrew Robert B., 240 W. Court, w. of Central Av
McGREW Samuel P., b.k., 97 Dayton
McGrew T. O., bds. 80 E. 4th
McGrew Wm., bk. layer, 134 Baymiller
McGrew Wm. A., bk. layer, 309 Baymiller
McGREW WM. WILSON, Watches, Jewelry. &c., s.w.c. Main and 4th, h. 194 Richmond
McGroarty Catharine, 132 Barr
McGroarty John J., druggist, bds. 132 Barr
McGROARTY Patrick, (McG. & Rogers,) 132 Barr
McGROARTY & ROGERS, (Patrick McG & Robert C. R.,) Attorneys at Law, room 2 Short's Building, s.e.c. 4th and Hammond
McGroarty Stephen J, 132 Barr
McGroarty Capt. Wm. H., bds. 132 Barr
McGuckan Michael, tailor, 73 Mulberry
McGuffin John, lab., 55 Observatory Road
McGuffin Thos., lab., 55 Observatory Road
McGUFFEY ALEX. H., Attorney at Law, 120 Main, h. 148 W. 4th
McGuin Patrick, lab., 30 Observatory
McGuinness Archibald, plumber, 27 Hannibal
McGuire Ann, 131 E. 6th
McGuire Austin, cof. h., 9 E. 4th, h. 215 Longworth
McGuire Burney, porter, w.s. Pierson b. 5th and 6th
McGuire Bernard, lab., n.s. Court e. of Broadway
McGuire Catharine, n.s. Oregon b. 3d and 5th
McGuire Cornelius, blksmith, 86 Butler
McGuire Edward, lab., 13 Commerce
McGuire Jas., wks. 127 W. 2d
McGuire Jame, tailor, 238 Broadway
McGuire John, carp., bds. 138 Longworth
McGuire Joseph, plumber, wks. 46 E. 3d
McGuire Margaret, n.s. Front e. of Washington
McGuire Martin, lab., 65 Vine

McGuire Mary, bds. 17 Lock n. of 8th
McGuire Matthew, collector, s.w.c. 5th and Broadway
McGuire Michael, bds. n.w.c. Pike and Pearl
McGuire Michael, trunk mkr., bds. 483 Broadway
McGuire Patrick, clk. 19 E. Canal, h. 483 Broadway
McGuire Peter, lab., 518 John
McGuire Philip, driver, 131 E. 6th
McGuire Philip, lab., bds. 60 Baum
McGuire Rose, n s. 6th e. of Lock
McGuire Rosey, bds. 17 Lock n. of 8th
McGuire Terry, lab., bds. 60 Baum
McGuire Thos., (Friel & McG.) bds. Walnut St. House
McGuire Thomas, grocery, s.e.c. 6th and Baum
McGuire Wm., blksmith, 3 North
McGuire Wm., blksmith, bds. s.w.c. 5th and Broadway
McGurvin Edward, wire wkr., 51 W. Court w. of Central Av.
McGurk Bernard, mach., n.w.c. 3d and Collard
McGurren Edward J., wire wkr., 53 W. Court
McGwin Mark, lab., n.w.c. 3d and Collard
McHale Martin, confec., e.s. Walnut b. 5th and 6th
McHENRY & CARSON, (John McH. & Enoch T. C) Gas Fixtures, Lamps, Gas and Steam Pipe Fittings, 162 Main
McHenry James, lab., s.s. Montgomery Pike near Reading Road
McHENRY John, (McH. & Carson) res. country
McHenry Patrick, driver, 187 W. 6th
McHugh Bartley, lab., Burnet House
McHugh Bridget, servt., Burnet House
McHugh Du-sen, tobacconist, 26 Observatory Road
McHugh Edwd., lab., s.s. Pearl b. Pike and Butler
McHugh Elijah, 824 W. 6th
McHugh Jas., lab, 1-6 Cutter
McHugh John, bar k., 110 W. 4th
McHugh John, carp., 611 W. 8th
McHugh John, carp., n.s. Vanhorne w. of Carr
McHugh John, lab., s.s Marsh b. Park and Smith
McHugh John, lab., wks. 100 Sycamore
McHugh John, stone mason, 26 Observatory Road
McHugh Judy, s.s. Friendship al. b. Pike and Butler
McHugh L., molder, 186 E. 6th
McHugh Mary, chambermaid, Burnet House
McHugh Michael, tailor, 7 Water
McHugh Mich , waiter, Burnet House
McHugh Patrick, cof. h. 320 Plum
McHugh Patrick, lab., c Park and Marsh
McHugh Thos., baker, Burnet House
McHugh Wm., cof. h., 17 Landing b. Broadway and Ludlow
McHughes John, lab., n.s. Patterson al. b. Main and Walnut
McIlvain Hugh L., liquors, &c., 5 E. Front, h 432 W. 4th
McILVAIN. SPIEGEL & Co., (Thos. McI., Wm. S & Angus Campbell) Boiler Makers, w.s. Lawrence b. 2d and Pearl
McILVAIN Thos., (McI., Spiegel & Co.) h Newport
McIntire Geo. G., gas fitter, 296 W. 5th, h. 503 W. 5th
McIntosh John, blksmith, 281 Central Av.
McIntosh Wm. L., clk., 166 Carr
McIntyre Ellen, 278 W. Liberty
McIntyre Jas., carp., 934 E. Front
McIntyre Martin, hostler, 222 Broadway
McIntyre Michael, gas fitter, 90 Clark
McIntyre P. W., shoe mkr., bds. 65 W. 5th
McIntyre Samuel, lab., s.s. Friendship al. b. Pike and Butler
McIntyre Sterling, conductor, bds, 91 W. 8th
McIntyre Wm. F., conductor, bds. 91 W.

224   (MoK)   CINCINNATI   (McL)   DIRECTORY.

McJunk Alexander, bds. 158 W. 3d
McJunkin Alexander, wheel mkr., bds. n e c. 3d and Elm
McKahan Eliza, servt., Burnet House
McKanna Geo., clk. n.w.c Main and Court
McKay Arthur, painter, 54 Baum
McKay Geo., wks. Cin. type foundry
McKay Geo., brass rule mkr., 155 Carr
McKay Leroy, printer, bds. s.e.c. Plum and 5th
McKay Neil, carp., foot of W. 9th
McKayle Cecelia, 383 W. 2d
McKeag Hannah, 182 Everett
McKeag Robert, bklayer, 456 John
McKean W. D., salesman 142 Walnut, h. n.s. 14th b. Elm and Plum
McKee Chas , paper box mkr., 102 Gest
McKee Eliza, b.h., 170 W. 5th
McKee Johu, box mkr., bds. 158 W. 3d
McKee John. box mkr., 210 W. 3d
McKee Patrick, lab., 260 E. Front
McKee Robt , b.k., bds. 170 W. 5th
McKee Robert R., salesman 90 W. 5th, h. 131 Longworth
McKEE & ROTH. (Samuel McK. & Joseph R.) Merchant Tailors, 48 W. 4th and 159 Walnut
McKEE Samuel, (McK. & Roth) 89 E. 4th
McKee Wm. clk. n.e.c. 5th and Elm, bds. 170 W 5th
McKERHAN & EVANS, (James McK. & Seth E.) Pork Packers and Commission Merchants, n.e.c. and s.e.c. 9th and Sycamore
McKERHAN James. (McK. & E & Swift, Evans & Co.,) h. 357 W. 4th
McKeens James, finisher, s.s. Front b. Foster and Kelly
McKeever Daniel, lab., 563 W. 5th
McKeg Ann, servt., 319 Longworth
McKelvey Wm., horse dealer, 215 W. Court
McKenna Arthur, bklayer, w.s. Central Av. b. 2d and W. W. Canal Basin
McKenna Geo., lab., 98 Cherry al. b. Plum and Central Av.
McKenney Mary, 92 E. 5th
McKenzie Mrs s.s 6th b Vine and Race
McKenzie Chas., scale mkr., n.e.c. Bay-miller and Richmond
McKenzie Duncan, boots and shoes, 10 W. 6th
McKenzie Jas. M., express man, 14 Rittenhouse
McKenzie John. mach , 581 W. 5th
McKenzie Margaret. 49 Water
McKenzie R. H., mer., 358 W 8th
McKenzie Robert, lab., 27 E. 3d e. of Parsons
McKenzie Robert D., lab., 27 E. 3d e. of Parsons
McKenzie Stephen M., clk., 209 W. Court w. of Central Av.
McKenzie T. K., carp , 503 Mound
McKeon Char es. express man. 88 Gest
McKeon Daniel, fireman, Phoebe al. b. Plum and Central Av.
McKeon Jas., shoe mkr., 26 Kossuth
McKeon John, lab., 202 W. Front
McKeon Patrick, dray, 495 W. 9th w. of Central Av.
McKeon Patrick, lab., 202 W. Front
McKeon Patrick. lab., 96 Gest
McKernan John, Jefferson House, n.e.c. Ludlow and River
McKernan Thos , lab., 33 Race
McKibben G. H., bds. Dennison House
McKim Marietta, 13 W. 4th
McKim Chas. S A.. box mkr., 102 Gest
McKimmie Annette, teacher, 214 Betts
McKimmie Wm., shoe mkr., 214 Betts
McKindley Margaret, h. 504 W. 4th
McKinley Benj.. ca p , n.s. Goodloe bet. Willow and Niagara
McKinley Jas., policeman, 28 12th
McKinley Wm., clk , bds., 434 W. 7th
McKinney Robt., foreman, wks. n. e. c. Walnut and Canal
McKinney Wm. H , b.k., 15 Hathaway
McKinsey Mary Ann, dress mkr., 180 Smith
McKinsey Thomas, huckster, 21 Elizabeth

McKinstry Jas., policeman. 110 13th
McKitrick John. paint, 469 W. 5th, h. 415 Longworth
McKitrick Julia, 341 Central Av.
McKitrick Noah, carp., n. s. Burt e. of Broad
McKitrick Saml., carp., 1294 E. Front
McKinzie Agnes. 483 Race
McKinzie John, eng., 581 W 5th
McKinsie Joseph, driver. 483 Race
McKnight Benj.. bk. mason, 12 15th
McKnight John, blk. smith, wks. 211 W. 2d
McKnight Sarah, e.s. Henderson al. bet. 7th and 8th
McKnight Wm. D., printer, 47 Plum
McKone Luke, blk. smith, w. s. Butler b. Pearl and Front, h. n.s. Pearl bet. Butler and Canal
McKune Luke. blk. smith, 170 E. Pearl
McLACHLAN JOHN Ropes. Cordage, &c.. n.w.c. Main and Water, h. 25 Madison
McLachlan R. B., b.k., n.w.c. Main and Water. h. 25 Madison
McLane David, foreman, bds. s. e. c. Plum and 5th
McLane Wm , cof. h., 42 E. Front
McLane Wm., lab.. n. s. Hopkins bet. Freeman and Garrard
McLane Thomas, shoe mkr., bds. n.e.c. 5th and Mound
McLAREN DANIEL, Superintendent C H. & D. R. R., Office in Depot, h. 412 W 7th
McLaughlin Mrs. Ann. 34 North
McLaughlin Bridget. 230 Broadway
McLaughlin Chas. A., (Tomlinson, McL. & Co.,) h. Covington
McLaughlin Chas., d ay. 60 Hunt
McLaughlin Christopher, lab., n. e. c. George and Cutter
McLaughlan Eliza, servt , 93 E. 3d
McLaughlin Geo., boatman, n.e.c. Vine, and Water
McLaughlin Geo.. treas. Pendleton and 5th St. R. R., h. 123 Central Av.
McLaughlin Hy., bk. layer, 53 Observatory Road
McLaughlin James, lab., 91 Sycamore
McLaughlin James, lab., 207 E. 6th
McLaughlin James, lab., 580 E. Front
McLaughlin James, lab., 62 Daum
McLaughlin James, lab., 170 E. Front
McLaughlin James, stone cutter, 35 E. 3d, e. of Parsons
McLAUGHLIN JAMES W., Architect, 123 Central Avenue
McLaughlin John. dray, bds. s. s. Pearl b. Pike and Cutler
McLaughlin John. lab., n.s.W.W. Canal b. Smith and Park
McLaughlin John, lab., w.s. Central Av. , b. 2d and W.W. Canal Basin
McLaughlin John, saloon, 74 E. 5th
McLaughlin John B., clk., 46 Walnut, h. Covington
McLaughlin J., n. s. 6th b. Culvert and Broadway
McLaughlin Julia, 35 E. 3d w. of Parsons
McLaughlin Margaretta, teacher, 443 W. 7th
McLaughlin Mary, 134 Longworth
McLaughlin Mary, 74 W. 6th
McLaughlin Mary, grocery. 117 Lock
McLaughlin Patrick, lab , 91 Mill
McLaughlin Peter, bds. 158 W. 3d
McLaughlin Phillip, cooper, 46 Lock n. of 8th
McLaughlin Samuel, lab., Iver arr
McLaughlin Sarah, servt., et House
McLaughlin Thos., fireman, bds. n.w.c. Front and Central Av.
McLaughlin Thomas, lab., 212 E. 6th
McLaughlin Thomas, lab., 60 Gano
McLaughlin, Tomlinson & Co. (Chas. A. McL. & James T.) Tobacconists, 46 Walnut
McLaughlin Walter, blksmith, bds. s.w.c. 5th and Broadway
McLaughlin Wm., b. k., 83 Walnut, h. 123 Central Av.
McLaughlin Wm.. cof. h., 157 W. 5th, bds. Indiana House

McNamara Thomas, lab., 660 E Front
McNamara Thomas, paver, 122 Lock
McNamara Thomas L., civil eng., 262 Water
McNamara Wm., mach., n.s. 6th e. of Lock
McNee Mary, 211 Smith
McNeff Ann, s.e.c. 6th and Culvert
McNeff Peter, lab., 66 Butler
McNeal Robert J., wire weaver, 220 W. 9th
McNeil Gordon, b.k. n.e.c. 7th and Walnut, bds 252 Walnut
McNEIL JOHN, Plumber, Pump and Hydrant Maker, n.e.c. 7th and Walnut, bds 252 Walnut
McNeil John, clk., 79 W. 4th
McNeil Wm., carp., wks. C. H. and D. R. R. repair shops
McNeill John, b.k., s.w.b. 3d and Vine
McNeill John, mach., 273 John
McNeill John S., cab. mkr., n.s. Front e. of Lumber
McNeill Richard J., clk., 58 Richmond
McNespy James, blksmith, wks. C. H. and D R.R. blksmith shop
McNespy James, lab., 423 George
McNespy Patrick, lab. 469 George
McNichol Ellen, 59 Woodward
McNichol Jas., cutter, bds. Clifton House
McNichols James, huckster, 10 Richmond
McNicols James K., gaiter, s.e.c. 4th and Vine, bds. Clifton House
McNicolson Elizabeth, 239 W. 6th
McNight John, printer, s.e.c. 3d and Lock
McNoite Thomas, chair mkr., 304 Plum
McNullen Michael, lab., 629 W. Front
McNultey Wm., hostler, 467 W. 9th w. of Central Av
McNulty Ann, 110 W. Front
McNulty Chas., hostler, bds. 256 W. 9th w. of Central Av
McNulty Charles, lab., 506 W. 9th
McNulty John, 170 W Front
McNulty John, dray, 137 W. Front
McNulty Peter, lab., 143 E. 2d
McNulty Patrick, lab., s.s 6th b. Broadway and Culvert
McNulty Rhody, lab., s.s. Friendship al. b. Pike and Butler
McNulty Sarah, 162 Clark
McNulty Sarah, servt., 297 Longworth
McNulty Thomas, hostler, 256 W. 9th w. of Central Av
McNulty Thomas, lab., 506 W. 9th
McNulty Wm, watchman, s.s. 9th b. Linn and Cutter
McNurty Bridget, servt., 338 W. 7th
McNutt & Armstrong, (Samuel McN. & James T. A.), trunk manuf., 69 W. 3d
McNutt Samuel, (McN. & Armstrong), 460 W 5th
McOmber J. R., b k, Clifton House
McPaddon Dominick, lab., 269 W. 4th
McPARLIN Michael (Woodrough & McP.) 1 3 W. 6th
McPeak Henry, lock mkr., wks. n.e.c. Walnut and Canal
McPeak James, upholsterer, 204 Hopkins
McPharen John, mach., 269 W. 8th
McPhetrin John, finisher, bds. 269 W. 8th
McPherson George, porter, 15 Home
McPhermon J. Aaon, periodicals, bds. 27 Mound
McPherson Lewis, 236 Race
McPherson R. B., clk. American Express Co., bds. Burnet House
McPhillips Bernard, bds. 71 Sycamore
McPlek Samuel, lab., 206 Hopkins
McQuau Patrick, lab., s.e.c. Park and Marsh
McQuaid John F, salesman, 187½ Barr
McQuaid Wm. S., grocery, 258 W. 6th
McQuade Ann, 369½ W. 7th
McQuade James, 369½ W. 7th
McQuade Jane, 369½ W. 7th
McQueety John, b.k., 148 Smith
McQueety E C., b k., 148 Smith
McQuillen Milton F., Journalist Cin. Gazette Co., h. Walnut Hills
McQuillen Wm., lab., 53 Mill

McQuithey Louis B., student, bds. 139 Hopkins
McRoberts Wm., clk., 49 E. 2d, h. 11 David
McShane Daniel, cook, bds. 59 E. Pearl
McShane James, eng., 33 Webb
McSharry Josephine, bds. 306 Clark
McSherry Elias, lab., 65 Abigail
McSimon Walter, agt., bds 19 Longworth
McSorley Daniel, cooper, 239 Broadway
McSorley Terrence, clk., bds. 239 Broadway
McSweeny John, cooper, 105 E. 2d
McSweeny Hannah, rear 61 Barr
McSymon Walter, river reporter Merchant's Exchange, h. s. s. Longworth b. Baymiller and Stone
McTagg Mary, chambermaid, Burnet House
McTaig Farrell, 59 E. 7th
McTaig Patrick, lab., 57 E. 7th
McTey Wm., lab., 249 W. Front
McVean Peter, fruit dealer, 222 Walnut, res Country
McVey Martin, lab., 170 E. Front
McVicker Jane, 191 Linn
McVitie Robert, carp., 520 Elm
McWiel James, mach., al. b. 4th and 5th and Central Av. and John
McWilliams Mary, actress, 16 E. 4th

M

Maag Barney, shoemkr., bds. 72 Abigail
MAAG FRED. & SON. (Fred & Frank) Proprietors Western Hotel, 443 Main
MAAG Frank, (Fred. M. & Son), 443 Main
MAAG Fred., (Fred M. & Son) 443 Main
Maag Henry, chair mkr., 15 15th b. Elm and Plum
Maag Henry, cof. h., s.e.c. 6th and Vine, bds. 443 Main
Maag Frank, h. 77 Abigail
Maas Benjamin, tailor, 420 W. 12th
Maas Garrett W., cab. mkr., 240 Everett
Maas Leonard, shoemkr., n.s. Front e. of Foster
Maasse Lewis, lab., bds. s.e.c. 2d and Plum
Mabry Mary, e. s. Sycamore b. 7th and 8th
Mabus John, cutter, 210 Mound
Mabus Michael, lab., 110 Ham. Road
Mackauley Richard E. bakery, 278 W. 5th
Macavoy Eliza, bds. 35 Kossuth
MacBrair Archibald, lithographer, 14 E. 4th, h 158 W 5th
MacBrair Robert, lithographer, 14 E. 4th, h. 158 W. 8th
Macci Dionysius, 44 Hughes
MACDONALD ALEX.
  Book Seller and Stationer,
  9 W. 4th, h. 467 W. 8th
MacDonald Jno. C., gas fitter, w.s. Baum nr. 5th
Macdonald Thomas L., (N. W. Emerson & Co.), h. 517 Freeman
Mace Benjamin, tailor, 418 Walnut
Mace Eliza M., 328 W. 6th
Mace Elizabeth, tailoress, 158 Baymiller
Mace John, lab., e s. Anderson b. 2d and Pearl
Macelmore Rachael, w.s. Henderson al. n 7th and 8th
Machle Adam, billard table builder, 5 Pleasant
Machmeier Herman, porter, 445 Main
Mack Alexander, salesman, 68 W. Pearl, h. 168 Plum
Mack Bernard, tailor, a.s Woodward b. Sycamore and Broadway
MACK & BROTHERS. (Harmon, Henry & Simon), Wholesale Clothiers, Importer of Cloths, Cassimeres, &c., 78 W. Pearl
Mack Charles G., conductor, bds. Spencer House
Mack Charles W., 86 Pike
Mack Christian, lithograph'er, 64 W. 4th
Mack David, salesman, 80 W. Pearl, h. 382 Elm.

MACK David, (Bohm, M. & Co.), 382 Elm
Mack Edward, lab., n.s. 6th b. Freeman and Pierson
Mack Fred., cigar mkr., w.s. Vine b. 4th and 5th
Mack George, roller, 26 W. Front
MACK Harmon, (M & Bros.), 336 Vine
MACK Henry, (M. & Bros.), 26 Longworth
Mack Isaac, salesman, 78 Pearl, h. 336 Vine
Mack Jacob L., clothing, 17 Arch
Mick James, lab., 1202 E. Front
Mick James, lab., 466 George
Mack James, lab., 44 Pierson
Mack James, lab., 16 Lock n. of 8th
Mack John, bk. layer, w.s. Pierson b. 5th and 6th
Mack John, lab.,w.s. Weller b. Carr and Freeman
Mack John, lab., n.s. Fremont b. Harriet and Mill Creek
Mack John, lab, 52 W, 9th
Mack John, lab., 462 W. 5th
Mack Julius, salesman, 78 W. Pearl, h. 336 Vine
Mack Leonard W., 111 Elm
Mack Lewis, baker, 109 Bremen
Mock Margaret, 385 Vine
Mack Margaret, 15 Commerce
Mack Martin, (M. & Worms), 153 W Court
Mack Martin, lab., 44 E. 8th e. of Lock
Mack Martin, mach., 473 Walnut
Mack Martin W., clk., 78 W. Pearl, h. 111 Elm
Mack Max, mer., 141 W. 8th
Mack Mix J., b.k., 70 W. Pearl, bds. 45 W 7th
Mack Melissa, servt., 163 W. 4th
Mack Owen, shoemkr., 435 W. 3d
MACK Simon, (M. & Bros.), 266 W. 8th
Mack Thomas, lab. 591 W. 6th
Mack Wm., fireman, n.s. Taylor b. Freeman and Carr
Mack & Worms, (Martin M. & Herman W.) clothiers, 190 Main
Mac Known Joseph, box mkr., 17 Elm
Mickavoy Ellen, 962 E. Front
Macke Bernard, tailor, 42 W. Front
Macke Dietrich, cigars, 86 Hunt
Macke Francis, groceries, 278 W. Front
Macke Frank, cof. h., n.e.c. Sycamore and Abigail
Macke Frank, finisher, 16 13th
Macke Fred., porter, n.e.c. Richmond and Freeman
Macke Geo., cirman, 72 Hunt
Macke H. H. & Co., (Henry H. M. & Henry Snippel) Phoenix Hotel, n.s. Front e. of Lewis
Macke Hy., finisher, bds. 300 Sycamore
Macke Hy., lab., 368 Broadway
Macke Hy., lab e.s. Kilgour, b. 3d and 5th
Macke Hy., H., (H. H. M. & Co.) n.s. Front e. of Lewis
Macke Herman blksmith, 16 13th
Macke Herman F., grocer, 213 Freeman
Macke John shoe mkr., 509 Main
Macke Mary, bds. s s. Abigail b. Main and Sycamore
Micke Moses, s.e.c. 5th and Race
Macke Wm., boots and shoes, 509 Main
Mackelfresh Chis. W., tinware and stoves, 291 W. 5th, bds. 238 Longworth
MACKENTEPE BERNARD, F..mily Grocery, and Coffee House n w.c. Vine and 2d, h. 145 Race
Mackenzie —, clk. 140 Main
MACKENZIE JOSEPH D., Stencil Cutter, 180 Walnut. h. 124 W. Court w. of Central Av
Mackenzie Robert H., liquors &c. 306 Main, h. 358 W 8th
Mackenzie Wm. D , salesman, 13 W. 2d h 251 or 501 W. 9th
Macker David, lab., wks. n.w.c. Pearl and M. Canal
Mackey —, cof h. 107 W. 3d
Mackey Andrew, barber, w.s. Mulberry al. b Pearl and 3d
Mackey Christopher, cof. h., s.s 6th e. of Lock
Mackey Fred., W., driver, 178 E. Pearl

Mackey James, lab., 60 Mill
Mackey John, clk., 467 W. 4th
Mackey John, sr., cof h., n.w.c. 4th and Walnut, h. 470 W. 5th
Mackey Peter, lab , 56 Poplar
Mackneme Mary, laundress, 100 Butler
Mucknight Wm., printer c. Plum and Commerce
Mackwoy Thos., driver, 11 Abigail
Macky Julia, servt., 396 W. 5th
Maclane David. supt. Israelite, 32 W 6th bds. 162 Plum
Maclish Chas, C., prop. U. S. Hotel, s.w c Walnut and 6th
MACNEALE Neil, (W. B. Dodds & Co) 168 Broadway
Macrae Major N. C., supt. of recruiting service for the State of Ohio, 101 E. 3d h. 106 E. 6th
MACREADY ROBERT, Wholesale Druggist. 58 and 60 Walnut, h. 247 W. 7th
Macy John M., clk., bds. 52 W. 9th
MACY John C., (M. Rankin & Co.) res Mt. Auburn
MACY, RANKIN & CO. (John C. M., Chas. S. R., Joshua P. W iton, & Luther Erving) Grates. Mantels. Ornimental and Architectural Iron Works, s.w.c. Elm and Pearl, Salesroom 8 Burnet House
Madaka Hy., butcher, 302 Baymiller
Maddegan Ellen. 333 W. 5th
Madden Ann, 173 Hopkins
Madden Edward, lab., 70 Rittenhouse
Madden John, cutter, 23 North
Madden Kate, servt., 118 Linn
Madden Michael, lab., 21 Mill
Madden Timothy lab., wks. gas works
Madden O , expressman, 78 Pleasant
Madden Mrs. bds. 27 Longworth
Maddix James, 33 Goodloe b. Willow and Niagara
Madilock Joseph, printer, wks. 140 W. 3d
Muddock Philip, drainer, 9th b. Harriet and Mill Creek
Maddock Stephen J., mach., 190 Walnut h 530 W. 4th
Maddock Thos., janitor, 167 Mound
Maddon John, turner, wks. 375 W. 3d
Maddon Martin, lab., s.s. Friendship al. b. Pike and Butler
MADDUX BROTHERS, (Lewis, Thos. & Wm. B.) Wholesale Dealers in Tobacco and Teas, 27 W. Pearl
MADDUX Lewis, (M. & Bros.) 236 Longworth
MADDUX Thos. (M. & Bros.) bds. s.w c. Race and 7th
MADDUX Wm. B., (M. Bros.) 75 Laurel
Maden Timothy lab. 61 Mill
Mader Agnes, bds. 87 W. Front
Mader Chas. L., rooms 56 W. 3d
Mader Edward, painter. 70 Martin
Mader Mathias. tailor, 21 Mulberry
MADISON HOUSE, 19 21 and 23 Main. John W. Garrison Prop'r.
Madison Jacob, driver, 107 E. 6th
Madison Mary, laundress, n.s. Grandin al. b. Elm and Plum
Madlinger Ottilla, seamstress. 102 Clay
Madower Wm., carp., 172 Charlotte
Madule Patrick, lab., wks Queen City Distillery
Maegly Jacob F , mason, 279 Bremen
Maegly John, stone mason. e.s. Logan b. Green and Elder
Maegly Michael, shoe mkr. 442 W. 5th
Muchrlein Daniel, boots and shoes, 658 Vine
Maenle Amelia, 24 Green
Maenle Elizabeth, 136 W. Liberty
Maenz Adolph, wagon mkr., bds. 1032 Central Av
Maerckle Theodore, butcher. 63 Hamer
Maeringer Nicholas, tailor, w.s Bremen b. Elder and Findlay
Maerlein Andreas, barber. 35 Green
Maerlein John, 720 Elm
Maerts Bernhard, cof. h., 201 W. 6th
Maertz Leo , cutter. s.e.c Vine and Pearl, h. Vine St. Hill
Maers Clemens, lab., 62 Bremen
Maers Michael, porter, 536 Race

(MAH)   CINCINNATI   (MAL)   DIRECTORY.   (MAL)   227

Maguire Mary, servt. 435 Broadway
Maguire Sarah, 203 Water
Maguire Thos, cof. h., s.e.c. Central Av and Pearl
Maguire Thos., tailor, h. 403 Central Av
Magonnager Catharine, servt., wks., 391 W. 8th
Magurk Michael J., salesman. 144 Main
Magure Owen, lab , s.s. 2d b. Rose and Mill
Magurne Pat., lab., 30 Observatory
Magveny Anna, servt., 502 W. 7th
Maha John, lab., 93 E. 8th
Mahan Hannah, serv., 91 Sycamore
Mahan John, dray, 31 Parsons
Mahan John, grocer, n.s. 6th b, Broadway and Culvert
Mahan John, tailor, n.e.c. 3d and Central Av
Mahan Margaret. 217 E. 6th
Mahan Mary, 173 Water
Mahan Michael. lab, s.s. Friendship al. b Pike and Butler
Mahanna Sylvester, dray, 180 Water
Mahaney Mrs. Ann. 78 E. 7th
Mahanna Matthew. lab., 19 Mill
Mahany Dennis, lab., e.s. Court b. 6th and Observatory Road
Mahany Wm. G., eng., s.s. Front e. of Brooklyn
Mahar Frank, lab., 58 Accommodation
Mahar James, boatman, bds. 9 Walnut
Mahar Patrick, lab., 546 W. Front
Maher Ann 297 John
Maher Ann, 34 Lock n. of 8th
Maher Ann, 453 W. 2d
Maher Anthony, grocery, 429 W. 2d
Maher Dennis, driver, 34 Lock n. of 8th
Maher James, lab., s.s. Webb. b. Mill and Park
Maher James, lab., 127 Webb
Maher Johanna, 333 Central Av
Maher Johanna, servt., 407 W. 8th
Maher John, cof. h., n.e.c. 8th. and Sycamore
Maher John, driver, h. 34 Lock n. of 8th
Maher John, lab , 412 Sycamore
Maher Kate, servt., 329 Central Av
Maher Margaret, bds. s.w.c. 5th and Broadway
Maher Mary, e.s. Macalister b. 4th and 5th
Maher Michael, lab., 440 W. Front
Maher Timothy. lab., 453 W. 2d
Maher Wm., driver, 34 Lock n. of 8th
Mahl Geo., pipeman, 20 Jackson
Mahl John, bksmith, 151 Hopkins
Mahl Michael, butcher, 112 13th
Mahly Thomas. peddler, 138 Baum
Mahl John, bksmith, wks. 55 E. 5th
Mahlenkamp Barney, lab , 435 W. 2d
Mahler Anthony, engraver, Carlisle bldg h. 340 Main
Mahler Anthony, painter, bds. 550 Main
Mahmault Hannah, servt , 84 Pike
Mahon Ellen. bds. 220 Central Av
Mahon Robert, molder, bds. 87 Longworth

MAHON THOMAS,
    Marble Works, 339 Broadway
    h. 466 Broadway

Mahon W. O., foreman, wks. n.w.c. Race and 2d
Mahon Walter, japanner, wks. n.w.c. Race and 2d
Mahone A. C. (Lum. M. & Co.) 76 Clark
Mahone Lum. & Co. (A. C. M. & Jacob S. Lape) turning shop, 518 Central Av.
Mahoney Daniel, 53 E. 8th e. of Lock
Mahoney Dennis, lab., E. Court above 6th
Mahoney Eugene, 53 E. 8th e. of Lock
Mahoney Eliza, cof. h., 209 E. 6th
Mahoney Jas. B., mach., 100 Broadway
Mahoney John F., dray, 53 E. 8th e. of Lock
Mahoney Julia, 189 E. 6th
Mahoney Mary E., grocery, s.e.c. 4th and Wood
Mahoning Mary, servt., Broadway Hotel
Mahony Catharine, bds. 385 Vine
Mahony Daniel, wire mkr., n.s. Augusta b. John and South
Mahony David, lab., 65 Barr [8th
Mahony Eugene, stereotyper, bds. 53 E.

Mahony Jeremiah, shoemkr., 385 Vine
Mahony John, lab., n.w.c. Pierson and 5th
Mahony John B., painter, 161 Cutter
Maibach Hy., shoemkr., e.s. Bremen b. Elder and Findlay
Maid Mike, 13 W. Court w. of Central Av.
M iids Chas , agt., 402 W. 8th
Maier August, stone cutter, bds. 502 Walnut
Maier Christian, blksmith, h. 125 E. Pearl
Maier Geo., express man, junction Vine and Ham. Road
Maier John, bakery, 118 Pleasant
Maier John, tailor. 42 Elder
Maier Matthew, plasterer, 91 Pendleton
Maier Nicholaus, shoemkr, 31 Pleasant
Maier Simon, cof. h., n.e.c. Vine and Ham. Road
Maier Wm., shoemkr, 21 Elm
Maiten John, lab. bds. 70 Sycamore
Ma ley June, servt., 206 W 5th
Main Joseph, plasterer, 38 Pierson
Mainers Geo , lab., 236 Pleasant
Mainger John. butcher, bds. 17 Wade
Mains Hy., teamster, wks. n.w.c. Vine and River
Mains James W., driver, bds. 200 W. Front

MAINS JOHN, SEN.,
    Wood Yard, n.w.c. Vine and River,
    h. 200 W Front

Mains John, jr., teamster, 200 W. Front
Mains Joseph, clk., wks. n.w.c. Vine & River
Mains Stephen, teamster, wks. n.w.c. Vine and River
Mains Mrs W. dress mkr., 9 W. Court w. of Central Av
Maisch Wm. cigar mkr., 129 W. Liberty
Maish Andrew C., tinner, 213 W. 6th, h. 277 W. 6th
Maisinger Anna Maria, servt., 53 Bremen
Maithre Peter, tailor, 175 E. Front
Maitland Samuel, lab., wks, 16 E. Canal
Maixner Josephine, 109 Ham. Read
Maixner Paul, lab.. 107 Ham. Road
Majer Mathias. tailor, 610 Vine
Makin James. printer, e.s. Haven al. b. 8th and 9th
Makin Patrick, lab., e.s. Haven al. b. 8th and 9th
Making W.. blksmith, 468 Main
Malacky Mary, servt., 280 George
Malaley Joanna, 182 E. Pearl
Malany Margaret, 446 W 3d
Malakey Mary, 14 Lock n. of 8th
Malay Patrick, over. 221 Clinton
Malay R., bds. Dennison House
Maldamer Barbara, servt., 549 Vine
Malden Wm. B , tent mkr., 464 E. Front
M ellen James, s.s. Court e. of Broadway
Males Wm., 51 Providence
Maley Audrew, cab. mkr., 274 Cutter
Maley Bessie, dress mkr., 478 W. 3d
Maley Rev. Geo. W., 307 Baymiller
Maley Margaret, dress mkr., 478 W. 3d
Maley Martin, watchman, h. w.s. Smith b. 4th and 5th
Maley Patrick, lab., 61 Mill
Maley P. F., phys., 146 W. Front, h. 153 W. Front
Malinee Enoch T , 169 E. Front
Maling John, finisher, wks. n e.c. Walnut and Canal
Malinn Wm., dray, s.s. Marsh b. Park and Smith
Malique Fred., blksmith, wks, n.e.c. Canal and Walnut
Malkmus Joseph, carp., 757 Bank
Malley Michael, lab , 6½ Freeman
Malling Martin, lab., n s. al. b. Canal and 12th and Vine and Race
Mallon Bridget, servt., 273 Longworth
Mallon Catharine, servt., 273 Longworth
Mallon John, dray, wks. 100 Sycamore
Mallon M. Rosina, h. 91 W. 9th w. of Central Av

MALLON & VON SEGGERN (Patrick M. & Christopher Von S.) Attorneys at Law, Debolt Building, s.e.c. Main and Court

MALLON PATRICK,
    (M. & Von Seggern)
    res. Mt. Auburn

Malor James, express man, h. s.s. Pearl b. Pike and Butler
Mallory Jerry, lab , s.s. 6th b Broadway and Culvert
Mallory Lawrence, clk., 95 Main, h. Mt. Auburn
Mallory Mrs. Lucy. bds. 218 E. 6th
Mallory Michael, lab., h. 110 Culvert
Malloy Catharine, servt , Burnet House
Malloy Daniel, policeman, 80 Butler
Malloy James, blksmith. 26 Baum
Malloy John, stone cutter, 59 Rittenhouse
Malloy Mike, lab., wks. 222 E. Front
Malloy Parker, trader, 165 Mound
Malloy Thomas, lab., 163 E. 3d
Malonay Thomas, lab., 36 Ellen
Malone Ann, rear 61 Barr
Malone Edward, tailor, 162 W. 5th
Malone Frank, wagon shop, s s. Front b. Lawrence and Pike, h. 139 E Pearl
Malone Hezekiah B., saw mill, bds. 25 Gest
Malone Hugh, porter, 85 Race
Malone James. 144 Carr
Malone John, lab., bds. 144 Carr
Malone John, s.e.c. Corporation line and North Elm
Malone Joseph M., molder. 37 Chestnut
Malone Mary, servt , 35¼ Central Av
Malone Matthew. lab., 191 Cutter
Malone Michael, 27 W. Court w. of Central Av
Malone Michael, shoemaker. 45½ E. 3d
Malone Patrick, bds 191 Cutter
Malone Patrick, wks. n.w.c. Smith and 2d
Malone Patrick. tailor, 526 Plum
Malone Peter W., phys., 87 Broadway, bds. Spencer House
Malone Thos., eng., 27 W. Court w. of Central Av

MALONE Wm. H., (Cameron, Story & M.) 25 Gest

Maloney Bridget, h. 44 E. 8th e. of Lock
Maloney Martin, blksmith, e. s. Front e. of Weeks, h 766 E. Front
Maloney Mary, h. 63 W. Front
Maloney Michael, blksmith, n.e.c. Barr and Freeman
Maloney Michael, blksmith, 766 E. Front
Maloney Michael, clk, cigar stand Burnet House
Maloney Michael, lab., e.s. Court b. 6th and Observatory Road
Maloney James, lab , wks 222 E. Front
Maloney John, fireman, Burnet House
Maloney John, shoemkr. 19 Abigail
Maloney Jno., waiter, Burnet House
Maloney Patrick, driver, wks. n.w.c. Court and Race
Maloney Patrick, lab., n.e.c. River and Ludlow
Maloney Wm., bk. mkr., 199 Clinton
Malony David, dray, 203 W. 9th
Malony Frank, wagon mkr., 133 E. Pearl
Malony James, lab., s.w.c. Pearl and Canal
Malony James, lab., wks. 690 W. Front
Malony Michael. lab., 15 Water
Malony Thomas, lab., 36 Ellen
Malott Isaac L , carp., Front. opp. Ferry
Malott Samuel, conductor, bds. Front opp. Ferry
Maloy Daniel, lab., 259 W. Front
Maloy Hy., carp., 16 Charles
Maloy James, blksmith, 26 Baum
Maloy James, cof. h., 125 Water
Maloy James, lab., 47 Observatory Road
Maloy John, butcher, s.s. Montgomery Pike near Reading Road
Maloy John, lab., 15 Water
Maloy Mary, b h., 162 W. 5th
Maloy Michael, lab., n s. Montgomery Pike, nr. Reading Road
Maloy Patrick, lab., n.e.c. Ludlow and 3d
Maloy Patrick, lab., 54 B um
Maloy Peter, lab., Anderson al. b. Front and 2d
Maloy Thomas, blksmith, 32 Lock
Maloy Thos., tailor, 162 W. 5th

228 (MAN) CINCINNATI (MAN) DIRECTORY. (MAR)

Maloy V. C., saloon, O. & M. R.R. depot, h. 498 W. Front
Malsacher Sebastian, cof. h., s.s. Front, b. Lawrence and Pike
Maltby Rev. Benj. K., 93 Laurel
MALTBY C. S., Dealer in Oysters, 11 W. 5th, Robert Orr, Agent
Maltis John, peddler, 63 W. Front
Maltoner Joseph, shoemkr, s.s. Ohio al. b. Adams and 15th and Elm and Plum
Maly Andrew, cab. mkr., 274 Cutter
Maly Mrs. W., 15 Water
Malzer Nathan, (Mrs. Greeble & Bro.,) 331 Central Av
Mammel Frederick, carver, 118 Laurel
Man Abraham, peddler, e.s. Race, b Liberty and 15th
Manague Thomas, second hand store, n.s. Pearl, b. Ludlow and Lawrence
Mandary Mary A., servt., 27 Clark
Mandel Edward, cooper. 66 Bank
Manderlick Joseph, bds. Clifton House
Manderman Honora, 206 E. 6th
Mandeville Ed., lab., wks. 413 W. Front
Mandeville Mary, dress mkr., bds. 206 E. 6th
Mandler Chas., barber, 291 Central Av
Mandler Hy., barber. 291 Central Av
Mandler Herman, barber, 248 E. Front, h. n w.c. Pearl and Kilgour
Mandler Paul, cof. h., s.e.c. Walnut and 19th
Mandley Edward, lab., e.s. Ramsey, n. of Front
Maneely Robert, painter, bds. 429 W. 8th
Manery Wm., lab., 193 Carr
Mang Gustav, tanner, 14 Logan
Mangan Andrew, porter. 86 W. Front
Mangan James, teacher. 228 Broadway
Manger Augusta, seamstress, 630 Vine
Manger John, painter, h. 233 Bremen
Mangmon James. 78 E. 7th
MANGOLD ADAM, Family Groceries and Provisions, 107 W 5th. h. 30 Jackson
Mangold Casper, lab., 57 Everett
Mangold Charlotte, n.s. Budd, b. Harriet and Millcreek
Mangold Ferdinand, 41 Jones
Mangold John, 79 W. 5th
Mangold John F., cigar mkr., 652 Race
MANGOLD Matthew (Stetter & M.,) 233 W. 6th
MANGOLD SIMON, Confectionery, 577 Central Avenue
Manhart Hy., bksmith, 987 Central Av
Manhattan Life Ins. Co. Agency, 76 W 3d
Maniel James, lab., e.s. Pike, b. E. Pearl and Front
Maniel James, lab., s.s. Pearl, b. Pike and Butler
Maniel John, lab., s.e.c. Pearl and Butler
Maning R., bds. Dennison House
Manion John, lab., s.e c. Butler and 3d
Manis Daniel, bksmith, 15 W. Court, w. of Central Av
Manison Wm. S., policeman, 210 W. 6th
Manker Benjamin, lab., e.s. Anderson al. b. 2d and Pearl
Mankhaus David, pattern mkr., 71 Abigail
Manley Patrick, lab., 112 13th
Manly D. I., trav. agt., 5 W. 4th, h. 345 W. 4th
Manly Lizzie. 178 Central Av
Manly Richard, carp., n s. Goodloe, b. Willow and Niagara
Manly Wm., (Keown & M.,) 114 Smith
Mann Abraham, student. bds. 200 Laurel
Mann Albert P., clk., 123 Main, h. 184 Vine
Mann Allen A., b k., 119 Spring
Mann Andrew J., clk., 32 W. 3d
Mann Anson, com. roofer, office 146 Plum, h. 174 W. 4th
Mann Anthony, whitewasher, 179 E. Front
Mann Elizabeth, Maiden Lane, b. Gas al. and Anderson al
Mann Hiram F., clk. in P. O., 142 Betts
Mann Isaac, 200 W. 5th

Mann Jno., tailor, 499 Walnut
Mann John H., dry goods, 200 W. 5th
Mann John R., ticket agt., 78 Sycamore
Mann M. P., b.k. bds. 184 Vine
Mann Martin, dray, 237 Everett
Mann Mary, 464 W. 4th
Mann Philip, cooper, bds. 346 Main
Mann Mrs. Sarah. 309 W. 5th
MANN WM. C., President Magnolia Ins. Co., h. 249 W. 7 h
Mann Wm. H., shoemkr. rear 220 Broadway
Mann Zadock H , designer railroad machinery 142½ Betts
Manne Charles, grocery, s 13th
Manney Ellen, servt., Henrie House
Mannion Thomas, dray, 52 Kossuth
Mannion Margaret, 35 Observatory Road
Manning Augustus, shoemkr, bds. 92 Central Av
Manning Mrs. Betsy, e.s. Crippen al. b. 7th and 8th
Manning Chas G., regalia, &c., 126 Walnut, h. 13 Chestnut
Manning James, lab., n.e.c 4th and Lock
Manning James T., (S. Manning & Co.) 25 W. 7th
Manning John, grocery, 126 W. Front
Manning Joseph, lab., rear 908 E. Front
Manning Lewis D , atty., 230 E. 6th
Manning Michael, w.s. Central Av., b. 2d and W.W. Canal
Manning Patrick, lab., w. s. Vine, b. Milk and Mulberry
Manning Robert, marble cutter, wks. s.w.c. Broadway and 5th
Manning S. & Co , (Samuel M., Robert F. Blick & James T. Manning,) grocers, 64 Walnut
Manning Samuel, (S. M. & Co.,) bds. Walnut St. House
Manning Thos., molder, 540 W. Front
Mannix Samuel, bksmith, 15 W. Court, w. of Central Av
Mannix Daniel S., clk. Spencer House
Manns Francis, tailor, n.s. Avery al. w. of Wood
Manns John A., clk., 174 W. 5th, bds. 12 Avery
Manns Wm., jeweler, Duhme's & Co., 546 Main
Manorgan Geo., molder, 660 E. Front
Manseng Charles. tailor, 35 Milton
Manser Andrew, tailor, 66 Dudley
Manser Rebecca, n e c Pearl and Pike
Manser Wm., sr., 68 E. 4th
Manser Wm., jr., salesman, 34 W. Pearl, bds. 68 E. 4th
Mansey Herman, foreman, n.w.c. Elm and Pearl
Mansfield Bridget, servt. 140 Broadway
Munsfield Chas. D., notary, 6 E. 5th, res. country
Manson Wm. L., 54 Clinton
MANSS Henry, (L. M. & Sons,) 79 E. Pearl
MANSS John, (L. M. & Sons) bds. 79 E. Pearl
MANSS L. & SONS, (Louis, Henry, Louis, jr. & John,) Wholesale and Retail Dealers in Boots, Shoes, Hats and Caps, 39, 41 and 79 E. Pearl
MANSS Louis, (L. M. & Sons,) 79 E. Pearl
MANSS Louis, jr., (L. M. & Sons,) 37 E. Pearl
Mantel Hy., dry goods, 701 W. 6th
Mantel Wilhelmina, 398 Race
Mantelbaum Moses, cigar mkr., 47 Clinton
Manthey Charles, b.k., 46 W. 2d, h. 45 Findlay
Manuel John, cof. h., 182 Walnut, h. 183 W. 3d
Manwood Charles. stone cutter, Pennock al. b. Mound and Cutter
Many Mary, s s. 6th, b. Broadway and Calvert
Manz Frank, lab , n.s. Liberty, b. Freeman and Mill Creek
Manz Lorenz, lab., n.s Liberty, b. Freeman and Mill Creek
Manzer Joseph, cooper, bds. s.w.c. Freeman and Dayton

Mapes Abner, gunsmith, bds. 326 W. 9th, W. of Central Av
Mapes Elizabeth, b. 326 W. 9th. w. of Central Av
Mappes Hy., pottery, s.e.c. Vine and Mulberry
Mappes Michael, box mkr., Vine St. H.l.
Mara John, lab., s.s. Pearl, b. Lawrence and Pike
Mara Michael, lab., c. 8th and Accomodation
Mara Patrick, lab , 108 Culvert
Mara Patrick, currier, 11 rth, above Lock
Mara Thomas' lab., s.e c. Lawrence and Pearl
Marnesch Wenzel, brush mkr., wks. 93 Bremen
Marah Patrick, lab., 435 W. 3d
March David, mer., 34 Perry
March Hy., cook, 392 Broadway
MARCII Sisel, (Bischof & M.,) 21 Longworth
Marchant Isaac. sen., keeper female city prison. n.w.c Parsons and Front
Marchant Nathan justice of the peace, 42 E. 2d. h. 34 Elizabeth
Marck David, cof. h., 14 Landing, b. Broadway and Ludlow
MARCKWORTH Herman, local editor, 571 Sycamore
Marcus August, dentist, 151 W. 6th
Marcy James, cab. mkr , 13 Plum
Mardin Sarah, nurse, n.e.c. Central Av. and Court
Mardock Thos., office n.e.c. 3d and Race, up stairs
Mardon Chas., tobacconist, n.s Bank al. b. 3d and 4th
Mareschen John H., planer, 293 W. Front
Marcus Barney. molder, wks. n.e.c Walnut and Canal
Margraf John, stone cutter, h. 133 Everett
Marhand Hy., molder, W. 9th, b. Harriett and Mill Creek
MARHOFFER PHILLIP, Coffee House, 590 W. 6th
MARIENTHAL Israel, (M. Lebman & Co.) 211 W. 7th
MARIENTHAL LEHMAN & CO., (Israel M., Gerson L. & Leopold Block,) Importers of and Dealers in Foreign and Domestic Liquors, Cigars, and Rectifiers, 236 Walnut, and 36 W. 6th
Marietta Ambrose, peddler, 172 Broadway
MARIETTA & CINCINNATI, & Baltimore & Ohio R.R. Through Freight and Ticket Office No. 3 Burnet House; A. B. Waters, Freight Agent. M. & C. R.R.
MARIETTA & CINCINNATI Railroad Depot, s.s. E. Front, e. of Water Works
MARINE Railway and Dry Dock Company, s.s. Front, b. Waldon and Brooklyn
Marini Isadore, clk., h. 31 W. 5th
Maringer Hy., cooper. 314 Findlay
Maringer Peter, tailor, 123 E. Pearl
Marischen Hy., sawyer, wks. Hughes & Foster
Marischer Bernhard, shoemaker, 107 Woodward
Marishen Bernhard, shoemkr, 107 Woodward
Mark Andrew, shoemkr, bds. n.w.c. Elm and 6th
Mark Philip, baker, 194 W. 6th
Marken August, varnisher, 90 E. Liberty
Markson Alexander, tailor, 59 St Clair
Market Fire Insurance Co. Agency, 76 W. 3d
Markland Anna, millinery, 166 W. 5th
Markland Mary, 89 E. Front
Marklein Michael, 57 Mulberry
Marks Alex., (Hyams & M.,) 59 St. Clair
Marks Anna, millinery, 70 W. 5th
Marks Conrad. 148 Abigail
Marks David, boots and shoes, 436 Main

CINCINNATI (MAR) DIRECTORY. (MAR) 229

Marquis John, 14 Hannibal
Marr Lizzie, servt., 110 E. 4th
Marr Peter, bk. layer, 235 Hopkins
Marr Thomas, cigar mkr., 65 Oliver
Marran Bridget, walter, Dennison House
Marrat John, 44 E. 3d
Marriet Ann, 430 Linn
Marriner Daniel N., painter, 132 Baum
Marron Jas., lab., w.s. 267 W. 5th
Marsch Wenzel. lab, 96 Bremen
Marsden Geo., carp . s s. Bank b. Free man and Coleman
Marsfelter Daniel, carp., wks. Moore & Richardson's
Marsh Aaron. bk. layer, 20 George
Marsh Aaron B , bk. layer, 20 George
Marsh Aaron P., bk. layer, 302 Linn
Marsh Alfred A , (M. & Co.,) h. 133 Pike
MARSH Augustus W., (Geo. D. Winchell. M. & Co.,) 226 Richmond
MARSH Caleb P , (Tyler, Davidson & Co .) bds Burnet House
Marsh Chas. E , clk., s. w. c. Walnut & Pearl. h 111 W. Court
Marsh Christian. 23 Woodward
Marsh & Co., (Edward L. M., Geo. A. Marsh & Alfred A. Marsh.) plaster and cement, s.w.c. 4th and Sycamore
MARSH David M., (M. & Harwood,) h. 102 Dayton
Marsh Edward L., (M. & Co.,) 277 Longworth
Marsh Elbert, 111 W. Court
Marsh Emma A.. seamstress 17 Gest
Marsh Geo., grinder, 79 Abigail
Marsh Geo. A , (Marsh & Co.,) 137 Plum
MARSH & HARWOOD, (David M. M. & Edward H.) Oil Vitrol Works. 313 Ham. Road
Marsh Hy., bds. 47 W. 7th
Marsh Hy C., bds. 47 W. 7th
Marsh Isaac, jr., bk. la er, 388 George
Marsh Isaac W.. lock smith, 153 Burr
Marsh Jas , checkman O. & M. R. R., 105 Park
Marsh James, brass finisher, bds. 174 E. Pearl
Marsh John, n s. York b. Linn and Baymiller
Marsh John, blk. smith, 388 W. 6th
Marsh John W., 91 Mill
Marsh John W., clk., 25 W. 4th
Marsh L. H., bk. layer, bds. 110 W. 6th
Marsh Mary A., 261 W. 9th
Marsh Nathan B., phys , 107 Laurel
Marsh Phoebe A., seamstress, 17 Gest
Marsh Richard. com. mer., 20 W. Front, h. 724 E. Front
Marsh Robt., 77 Dayton
Marsh Robt, S., paper carrier, 17 Gest
MARSH S. N., CORLISS & CO, (Seymour N. M , Daniel G. C. & Joshua Read.) Truss, Brace, Bundage and Artificial Limb Manufacturers, 5 W. 4th
MARSH Seymour N., (S. N. M., Corliss & Co ,) h. New York
Marsh Theo., 302 George
Marsh Thomas, coffin mkr., wks. 175 W. 6th
MARSH WM E. Sr., Proprietor Galt House, s w.c. 6th and Main
Marsh Wm. E., jr., clk., 23 W. 2d, h. 438 W. 7th
Marsh Wm. N . note and bill broker, 59 W, 3d. h. Covington
Marshall Alvira, 1 0 Sycamore
Marshall Andrew, blk. smith, s.e.c. Sycamore and Webster
Marshall Ann, 119 Broadway
Marshall & Brothers, (George, James & Thos. H.,) dry goods, 56 W. 5th
Marshall Chas. C., eng., 25 Cutter
Marshall Chas. D , 217 Poplar
Marshall Chas E., b.k., 369 Longworth
Marshall Chas. E., clk., Adams Ex. Co., h. 244 Clark
Marshall Chas. H., Sec. Magnolia Ins. Co., h. 437 W. 6th
Marshall Edgar, clk., 267 Central Av. h. s.s. 12th b. Race and Elm
Marshall Elijah, mate, 314 Water

Marshall Geo , bds. 107 Broadway
Marshall Geo.. (M. & Brothers) h. Harrison Pike
Mars all & Hefley. (Robt. N. M. & Isaac H.,) printers. 6 W. 2d
Marshall Hugh. 53 Clinton
Marshall J.. bds. Dennison House
Marshall Jas., lab., 554 E. Front
Marshall James, (M. & Brothers,) 83 Wade
Marshall John, porter, rear 648 E. Front
Mars all Julius, bds. Du nas Hotel
MARSHALL Levi G., (M & Robbins,) Clermont Hotel
Marshall Margaret. 82 Wade
Marshall Montgomery, cook, 171 Water
Marshall Oliver, 415 W. 4th
Marshall Robt., painter, 40 Sycamore
Marshall Robert N., (M. & Hefley,) Mt. Hope
MARSHALL & ROBBINS. (Levi G. M. & Wm. M R.,) Proprietors Clermont Hotel, e.s Broadway b. 3d and Pearl
Marsh ll Thos., shoe mkr., 105 Vine
Marshall Thos H., bds. Dennison House
Marshall Thos. H., (M. & Brothers,) 97 Betts
Marshall Thos W., carp., 25 Cutter
Marshall Wm. S., b k , 2nd George
Marshuetz Adolph G., b k. 78 W. Pearl, h. 191 W. Court w. of Central Av
Marshuetz Leo., wks. Cin. type foundry
Marston Augustus, 313 Findlay
Mart Michael, lab., 140 Carr
Martes Anton, barber, n. s. Front e. of Lewis
Martelsmann John C., lab., 55 W. Front
Marten Andreas, cage mkr., 602 Race
Martens Anton, cooper, bds. e s. Western Av. b. Bank and Harrison Pike
Martens Chas., tailor, 9 Hughes
Martens Henry, b. h. 137 Race
Marthens Albert H . 3.4 W. 7th
Marthens Albert W., cigars, 63 Walnut, h. 3;4 W. 7th
Marthens Chas E., b k. 63 Walnut, bds. 354 W. 7th
Marthis Andrew H.. millstone cutter, u. s. Goodloe b. Willow and Leatherbury
Martin Absalom. lab., bds. 434 George
Martin Albert, brewer, 1031 Central Av
Martin Amand, peddler, 94 Clay
Martin Aurelia, 52 15th
Martin Andrew. tinner, 602 Race
Martin Ann, 217 E 6th
Martin Anna, n4 Melancthon
Martin Ann A., 176 E 3d e. of Collard
Martin Barbara M., 50 Bremen
Martin Bernh., baker, 203 Main
Martin C., clerk, 140 Main, h. 536 W. 5th
Martin Caroline, dress mkr., 15 Elizabeth
Martin Catharine, 57 Buckeye
Martin Chas.. engraver, 988 John
Martin Chas. C., bds. 385 W. 3t
Martin Chas. C., engraver, 988 John
Martin Christian, instrument mkr., 337 Walnut
Martin Claud, clk., bds. s w c. 5th and Broadway
Martin Daniel D. D., salesman 26 Main, bds. Henrie House
Martin Dell clk. 11 E. 3d, h. 394 W. 3d
MARTIN EDWARD, Wholesale Clothier, 134 Walnut, h 27 E. 7th
Martin Edward, lab., n.w.c. Wood and Avery al.
Martin Ellen, s.w.c. Longworth and Elm
Martin Emil, steward, 65 W. Court
Martin F. K. justice of the peace, 11 E. 3d, h. 394 W. 3d
Martin Ferdinand, lab , 583 W. 5th
Martin Frederick, barber, 60 Ham. Road
Martin Francis, carp., 82 Clifton
Martin Francis. dray. e.s. Pendleton b. Woodward and Liberty
Martin Geo., bds. 98 Broadway
Martin Geo., mate, bds 12 E. Front
Martin Geo . lab., bds. 575 W. 5th
Martin Geo. D.. b.k. Commercial office, bds. 107 Pike

230 (MAR) CINCINNATI (MAS) DIRECTORY. (MAT)

Martin Geo., scale mkr., 30 Rittenhouse
Martin Geo. H., b.k., 167 Race
MARTIN Geo. R., (H. & G. R. M.) h. 480 Elm
Martin Gustav., instrument mkr., 337 Walnut
MARTIN H. & G. R., (Henry & G. R.) Tanners and Leather Dealers, 649 Elm
Martin Hamilton, 138½ Betts
Martin Harriet E., teacher, Wesleyan Female College
Martin Harrison H , molder, wks. Lane & Bodley's, res. Covington
Martin Hy., bds. 85 Milton
Martin Hy., carp., n.s. al b. Poplar and Vine and Ham. Road and Buckeye
MARTIN Henry, (H. & G. R. M.) Philadelphia
Martin Isaac S., printer, bds. 290 Race
Martin Jas., carp. at gas works
Martin Jas., roofer, bds 298 W 5th
Martin Jas. A., cik., canal collector's office, bds. 19 Milton [5th
Martin Jas. H., real estate agt., 536 W.
Martin Jas. W., sgt. Dr Bly's artificial legs. s w.c. 6th and Vine, bds. Dennison House
Martin J ne, 519 W. 8th
Martin John, bds. Pennsylvania Hotel
Martin John bklayer, at gas works
Martin John, cof. h., n.e.c Vine and Milk
Martin John, dray, 16 Baum
Martin John, dray, e.s. Pendleton b. Woodward and Liberty
Martin John, foreman, s.w.c Court and St. Clair
Martin John, policeman, 590 E. Front
Martin John, Australian House, 273 Walnut
Martin John, pro. Washington House, 231 Walnut
Martin John, stone cutter, 57 Buckeye
Martin John, sawyer, w.s. Goose. al. b. Green and Elder
Martin John, whitewasher, 62 Ham. Road
Martin Joseph, mason, 92 Buckeye
Martin Mrs. L . 59 St. Clair
Martin Laura, bds. 301 W. 5th
Martin Lloyd L , tel. op , 138½ Betts
Martin Martha J., laundress, 20 L'Hommedieu al.
Martin Michael, lab., 91 Johnson
Martin Morris, peddler, 41 W. 6th
Martin Owen. eng., 110 W. 3d
Martin Pat., miller, 110 W. 3d
Martin Patrick, bds. 158 W. 3d
Martin Peter, lab , 80 Gest
Martin Peter, tailor, 408 Longworth
Martin Peter, tanner bds. 106 York
Martin Peter, tinsmith, 149 W. 5t
Martin Philip, frame mkr., 23 Barr
Martin Robert, s.w.c. Mill and Park al
Martin Sallie, servt. 10 Broadway
Martin Samuel, 3-5 W. 3d
Martin Thos., bds. Dumas Hotel
Martin Thos., dray, bds. 309 Sycamore
Martin Thos. P carp., 326 W. 6th
Martin Thos. W., clk. C., H. & D. R.R., bds. 434 George
Martin Valentine, eng , Gibson House
Martin Valentine, mach., 97 Baum
Martin Valtin sawyer, wks. n.w.c Freeman and 9th
Martin Wm., foreman, 176 W. 3d
Martin Wm., hatter, 322½ W. 6th
Martin Wm., lab , 70 Lock
Martin Wm., lab . 30 Lock
Martin Wm , salesman, 322½ W. 6th
Martin Wm. H., civil eng., 120 York
Martin Wm. J., saloon, n.w c Front and Ludlow, h. w.s. Plum b. Wade and Liberty
MARTIN WILSON, Eldorado Coffee House, 210 W. 6th
Martin Wilson, scale mkr., 30 Rittenhouse
Martin Xavier, harness shop, w.s. Ludlow b. Front and 2d
Martines Ferdinand, clk., 32 Main, bds. s.w.c 4th and Central av.
Martines Madam J. A., teacher of French, 247 W. 4th

Martinger Nicholas, mason, 716 Vine
Martins Herman, cab. mkr , 108 Avery
Martins Peter, tailor, 40s Longworth
Martinschang Joseph, clk., 243 Ham. Road
Martischang Joseph, b.k., 243 Ham. Road
Marty Francis J., grocer, s.w.c. 8th and John
Marty Louis, 258 W. 8th
Martz August, tailor, w.s. Vine, b. Milk and Mulberry
Martz Michael, s.e.c. Baymiller and Central Av.
Marvin John J., teacher, bds. 64 Webster
Marvin John J., teacher, 80 W. 7th
Marrol Bridget, 164 Cutter
Marwietz Florence, lab., n.s. Front e. of Ferry
Marx Gottfried, lab., 62½ Race
Marx John, blksmith, 704 W. 6th
Marx John, cig'r mkr., 55 Sycamore
Marx Nicholaus, tailor, 246 Vine
Mary Sister, St. John's Hospital, n.w.c. 3d and Plum
Marz Philip, lab., 558 E. Front
Mas Felix, barber, 51 W. 5th
Maschinot Mathias, sailor, 46 Peete
Muschmeier Hy., lock smith. 22 Hughes
Maschmeier Herman cooper, 686 Main
Mascomeier Hermann, porter, 94 Clay
Mase Chas., second hand store, 351 Central Av.
Mashly Nicholaus, trunk mkr., 87 Pleasant
Masker John Hy., lab., 140 Hopkins
Masker Joseph, warehouseman, 45 Walnut
Maslow Frederick, driver. 675 Vine
Musmnin Bernard cab. mkr., 54 Jones
Masminster Laura, notions, &c., 83 E. Pearl
Mason Alexander C., bklayer, 28 Bank
Mason Caroline, 61 E. 7th
Mason Cuthbert H., clk., 213 Everett
Mason David, box mkr., 77 Plum
Mason Edwin, hats and caps, 42 W. 5th, h. 32 Gest
Mason Eliza, e.s. John b. Betts and Clinton
MASON GEO., Wholesale Dealer in Hats, Caps and Straw Goods, 73 W. Pearl, h. Covington
Mason Georgianna, bds. 208 Broadway
Mason Jas., stone cutter, 77 Pendleton
Muson Jas. P., clk , s.s. Findlay b. Freeman and Western Av.
Mason John, peddler, n.w.c. York and Baymiller
Mason Luther W., music teacher, 36 Barr
Mason Richard, student, bds. 50 E. 5th
Mason Robert, lab.. 77 Plum
Mason Thomas J., carriage mkr., 169 Barr
MASONIC REVIEW, C. Moore Editor and Proprietor, 117 Walnut
MASONIC TEMPLE, n.e.c. 3d and Walnut
Masque M. J., carver, 510 Race
Mass Jacob, porter, 4 Pub. Landing, bds, Cincinnati House
Mass Wm., cab. mkr., wks. s.w.c. Canal and Elm
Massa Joseph, 246 W. 5th
Massa Nicholas, confec., 246 W. 5th
Massard Wm., cooper, 164 Dayton
Massbaum Wm., stone mason, 24 W. Mulberry
Masse Francisco, peddler, 59 Vine
Masse Frank, fruits, 59 Vine
Masseron Theodore, lab., 142 Ham. Road
Massey ——, w.s. Langdon al. b. 6th 7th
Massey Daniel, sen., coach painter, 36 Providence
Massey Daniel, jr., painter. 36 Providence
Massey Edward, blksmith, 36 Providence
Massey Francis, 178 Broadway
Massey John, 72 Dudley
Massey John B., fruits 174 Broadway
Massman Lewis, jr., b k Thomas Emery & Sons, h. 90 Woodward

Massmann Thos., cooper, bds. 25 Buckeye
Masson Mansfield B., carp., s.s. Liberty b. Broadway and Mansfield, h. 98 E. Liberty
Masson Wm., b.k., bds. Deholt Exchange
Master Caspar, grocery, 29 13th
Master Chas., watch mkr., s.w.c. 4th and Main, h. w.s. Vine b. 8th and 9th
MASTERS Geo. L., (Geo. L M. & Co.) bds. 170 W. 4th
MASTERS GEORGE L. & CO., Manufacturers and Dealers in the "Braman" Sewing Machines, s.w. c. John and Front
Masters John, 123 Main
Masters Stephen, dray, 301 W 2d
Masterson Mrs., 5 3 Sycamore
Masterson Edward, clk., bds 23 Longworth
Masterson Edward W., clk., 23 Longworth
Masting Francis, tailor, 528 Main
Masting Frederick, tailor, 528 Main
Maston Anthony, carp., 142 E. 3d e. of Collard
Mastrup Frank, lab., 89 Bank
Maszmann Louis. enameler. e.s. Spring b Woodward and Abigail
Masteer Margaret, 58 Richmond b. Plum and Central Av.
Mater Joseph, w.s. Vine b. Milk and Mulberry
Mathaeus Chas , confec., 515 Main
Mathiesz Paul mason, 41 Findlay
Mather Benj. C., mach., 508 Sycamore
Mather Fred., lab., 150 Pleasant
MATHERS Richard, (Buckingham & M.,) res Walnut Hills
Mathers Wm., s e.c. 9th and John
Matheus Peter, cof h., 177 W. Liberty
Mathews D. G., m ss., M. & C. R. R., bds. Dennison House
Mathews Mary, 14 Race
Mathews Wm. R., grocery, 174 Barr
Mathewson Brown. drays, Richmond b. Harriet and Mill Creek
Mathias Daniel, lab., bds 101 E. 6th
Muthias Eliza H , 317 Broadway
Matluck Bowen, dry goods. 256 W. 4th
Matle Anna, s.s. Charlotte b. Linn and Baymiller
MATSON & CROSLEY, (Isaac M. & Josiah C.) Proprietors Union Dining Saloon, 61 E. Pearl
MATSON Isaac, (M. & Crosley,) 61 E. Pearl
MATSON Isaac B., (M. & Paxton,) rooms n.w.c. 4th and Sycamore
MATSON & PAXTON, (Isaac B. M. & Thomas B. P.) Attorneys at Law, 21 W. 3d
Matt Francis, b.k., C. T. Adae & Co.'s, h. 413 Elm
Matt Geo , boiler mkr., 176 E. Pearl
Matt M., w. s. Poplar b. Buckeye and Ham. Road
Mattakey Kate, junction High and Kemper's Lane
Mattakey Matilda, junction High and Kemper's Lane
Mattens Herm nn, lab., bds. 19 Abigail
Matthes Fred., tailor, 547 Vine
Matthews Benjamin, pipe fitter, wks. n.e.c. Walnut and Canal
Matthews Bentley, clk., C.H. & D. R.R., 319 Longworth
Matthews Elizabeth, w.s. Bank al. b. 3d and 4th
Matthews Frank H., clk., C. H. & D. R.R., 319 Longworth
Matthews Hannah, 208 John
Matthews Henry, (Sliker & M.,) h. Covington
Matthews Henry C., b. k., bds. Broadway Hotel
Matthews Herman, chair mkr., 108 Mill
Matthews Hugh C., 59 E 6th
Matthews James, 126 Mill
Matthews James, teamster, n.s. Front e. of Lumber
Matthews John, n. s. Corporation Line nr. Auburn
Matthews John, tailor, 306 E. 6th
Matthews Miss L., bds. 43 Lodge

Matthews Mary, 60 Everett
Matthews Robert. clk., 217 Clinton
Matthews Robt. L., b.k., s.w.c. Clinton and Baymiller
Matthews Samuel R., atty., 23 W. 3d, h. 319 Longworth
Matthews Stapley, atty., 23 W. 3d, h. Glendale
Matthews Thomas. lab, 306 E 6th
Matthews Mrs. Thos. J., 319 Longworth
Matthews Wm. E., 192 W. Court e. of Linn
Mattick Jacob, varnisher, 31 Ham. Road
Mattler John, bds. 73 E. Pearl
Mattoon J. C. tcl. op., 195 W. 3d
Matts Conrad, lab., wks. n.w.c. Plum and Wade
Mattscheek Philip, lab., 206 Clark
Mattson Hezekiah A., paver, 477 Plum
Matuska Joseph, safe mkr., bds. s.w.c. Elm and 2d
Matz Conrad, boiler mkr., 17 15th b. Elm and Plum
Matz Geo , tailor, 96 Ham. Road
Matz John. tailor. 71 Green
Matz Peter, lab., 52 Mohawk
Matzdorff Adolph, clk., 76 Broadway
Matzloff Ernst, cook, 187 Vine
Matzner Gottfried, upholsterer, 136 Carr
Maudery Jacob, baker, wks 217 Everett
Maue Frederick, clothing, 70 Broadway
Maue Louisa, 178 Clay
Maul Geo., blksmith, 55 Elder
Maul Robert, cof. h., 511 Plum
Maule Daniel, sign writer, bds. e. s. Broadway b. 5th and 6th
Maunder John, lab., 13 Bremen
Mauntel Fred., lab., 67 Pleasant
Maure John, s.w.c. Cutter and Melasthon
Maurer Christian, wagon mkr., 919 Central Av.
Maurer Henry, boots and shoes, s. s. Harrison Pike b. Riddle and Division
Maurer John. carp., 598 Vine
Maurer Nicholaus. carp., 321 Hamer
Maurer Rachael, bds. 212 W. Liberty
Maurice Francis, tailor, 399 Broadway
Maus Hy., cigar mkr., 36 W. 12th
Maus Mathias, trunk mkr., 28 14th
Maus Nicholas, blksmith, 337 Broadway h. 49 Hunt
Maus Wendel, musician, 36 12th
Mause Joseph, currier, 24 W. 8th
Mauser Joseph, tanner, 24 W. 9th
Maushard Francis X., mason, 493 Vine
Mauthe Christian. clock mkr., 34 Adams
Mauthe Magdalena, 576 Elm
Mautrer Theresa, 566 Elm
Maux Mary, seamstress, 447 Main
Maux Wm., plasterer, 185 Laurel
Mauzy Ann, 79 Barr
Maxwell Chas., bds. 41 Pub. Landing
Maxwell Geo., bds. Burnet House
Maxwell Geo., jr., bds. Burnet House
MAXWELL REV. GEO. M., Pastor 8th Presbyterian Church, h. 196 Richmond
Maxwe'l Jackson, shoe mkr., s.s. Front w. of Hill
Maxwell James R., pattern mkr. 90 E. 5th
Maxwell John, molder, wks. n. w. c. Plum and Wade
Maxwell John, shoe mkr., n.s. Front e. of Stone al.
Maxwell Lawrence, plumber, n.e.c. 3d and Lock
Maxwell Marcellus J., b. k., 95 W. 3d, bds. 310 Elm
Maxwell Margaret, 28 Kossuth
Maxwell Mary, 23d Hopkins
Maxwell Mary, 51st John
Maxwell Patrick, lab. 3.1 W. 2d
May Benno, clk., bds. 320 Walnut
May Benno M., clk., 121 Longworth
May Bridget, servt., Galt House
May & Cohn. (Henry W. M. & Jacob C) clothing, n w c. 5th and Main
May Emil, b k. 8 W 6th
May Henrietta, 329 George
May Henry W., (M. & Cohn.) 36 E. 7th
May Isaac, peddler. 60 Richmond
May Isaac, b. k., Muller & May's, bds. s.w.c. Main and 7th
May Jacob, clk., bds. 322 George

May Levi. sexton 104 E. 5th
May Madison, bar k., Gibson House
May Nathan, (Muller & M ,) res. Kentucky
May Pat. lab., s.s. Friendship al. b. Pike and Butler
May Peter carp., 183 Barr
Maybach Fred.. clk., 33 12th
Maybach John F.. lock manuf., 33 12th
Mayberry Willie. 66 Avery
Mayer Abraham, jewelry, &c., 72 Main. h. 47 E. 5th
Mayer Andy, bk. mkr., n.s. Prospect b. Young and Sycamore
Mayer Anthony C., carp., 191 Baymiller
Mayer Chas., clk., 72 Main
Mayer Chas., shoe mkr., 21 Franklin
Mayer Chas., tinner, 478 Walnut
Mayer Chas. H., brush manufac., 399 Vine
Mayer Charles W., b. k., 107 W. Pearl, h. 26 Grant
Mayer Chas Wm., tailor, 542 Race
Mayer David, 184 Vine
MAYER ELIAS, Exchange and Loan Office, 164 Vine, h. 311 W. 6th
Mayer Francis. painter, 494 Race
Mayer Fred., dray. 416 Walnut
Mayer Fred. J., County commissioner's office, Court House, h. 388 Race
Mayer Geo., cof. h., 527 Main
Mayer Hy., 165 Clinton
Mayer Jacob, 47 E. 5th
Myer Jacob. wig mkr., 152 Walnut
Mayer John, barber. 560 Central Av.
Mayer John, grocer. 13 Jones
Mayer John lab., 430 Plum
Mayer John H. dr er, wks. 450 Walnut
Mayer Joseph cab. mkr. 524 W. 3d
Mayer Joseph clk., 447 Main
Mayer Joseph. clk., bds. 174 Plum
Mayer Joseph, lab . .... Prospect b. Young and Sycamore
Mayer Joseph P . foreman, pipe laying at City Water Works, h. Walnut Hills
Mayer Louis, clk., bds. Gibson House
Mayer Richard B., plate printer, s.w.c. 5th and Main
Mayer Theodore. clk., bds. 99 W. 8th
Mayer W., driver, wks. 450 Walnut
Mayer Wm., tailor, n.s. Buckeye b. Main and Walnut
Mayers tailor, 27 E. 4th, h. 12 Jackson
Mayers R., 110 Webb
Mayfield A vi, Senior & Co.) 15 Cou
Mayhew per hanger, e. s. Mound b. Wortz
Mayhew Sam , Corp. Line nr. Auburn
Mayhew Thos. W., carriage smith, 317 Baymiller
Mayhew Wm., lab., n. s. Slack al. b. Ringgold and Boal and Price and Young
Mayhugh Wm., produce dealer, 328 W. 5th
May'orr Le Roy, teamster, 460 W. 8th
Mayle Ebenezer, books &c., s.e.c. Walnut and 5th, store 384 Central Av.
Mayle Geo, D., clk., bds. 30 W. Court
Mayle Sarah, 30 W. Court w. of Central Av.
Mayleben & Butterfass, (John M. & Philip B.,) cof. h. 2 Walnut
Mayleben John, (M. & Butterfass,) 14 Walnut
Mayleben Philip, cof. h. 16 Walnut
Maylon James, cooper, bds. n.w.c Pike and Pearl
Maynard Anson W., 236 Richmond
Maynard Geo. C., bds. Burnet House
Mayner Jane. 136 W. 5th
MAYO ENOCH M . Stocks, Dies, Screw Cutting Machinery and Lightning Rod Manufacturer, 245 Sycamore, h. 10 Hopkins
MAYOR'S OFFICE, City Buildings, George Hatch, Mayor
Mays S. P., produce, 76 W. 6th
Maytum James, bk. layer, 61d W. 6th

Mazze Francisco, teacher, h. 50 Vine
Mead Edward, phys., w.s. Ohio Av. b. North Elm and Calhoun
Mead George N., teacher, 17th District School
Mead Oscar, miller, n.s. Goodloe b. Willow and Niagara
Mead Rebecca. n.s. Poplar b. Freeman and Western Av.
Mead Richard, lab., 59 Mill
Meadel Anton, w.s. Vine b. Mulberry and Milk
Meaden John, salesman, n.e.c. 7th and Plum
Meader Amanda, 612 W. 8th
MEADER & CO., (Daniel F. M., O. D. M., J. F. M. and Thomas B. Smith,) Chair and Furniture Manufacturers, 41 and 43 W 2d
MEADER Christopher D., (M. & Co.) 159 W. Court w. of Central Av.
MEADER Daniel F., (M. & Co ,) 136 Smith
Meader Hy., dray, n. s. al. b. 14th and 15th and Central Av. and Plum
Meader Hy. C., w.s. Walker b. Ringgold and Boal
MEADER J. F., (M. & Co.) res. Covington
Meader Joseph A., w.s. Walker b. Ringgold and Boal
Meader & Ludington, (N. R. M. & A. L.) grocers, 32 E. Pearl
Meader Nathaniel R.. (M. & Ludington,) w s. Walker near Ringgold
Meader Webster, clk., Daily Times, 136 Smith
Meader Wm., lab., 120 Carr
Meagher Bridget, servt., 140 Broadway
Meagher John, grocery, 52 Plum
Mengher Thomas J., cook, 3 . Moore
Meal J. W. & Co., (John W M. & Otto Von Bargen,) com. mers., 12 and 14 Walnut
Meal J. Wesley. flour mill, 260 Broadway, h Covington
Meal John W., (J. W. M. & Co.,) h. Covington
Mealea Patrick, lab., s.w.c. Mill and 3d
Mealy Margaret, servt., 164 Broadway
Mealy Thomas, s.s. 6th e. of Lock
Means Thomas W., (Sinton & M.,) Union Furnace Landing, Lawrence Co. O.
Meara James, lithographer. n.s. 8th b. Lock and Accommodation
Meara Thomas, policeman, s.s. Hathaway b. Jane and Baymiller
Meara Wm., lab., 52 E. 2d
Meara Wm. H., salesman, 163 Main, h. 276 John
Mears Daniel H., 21 E. 2d, h. Mill Creek Tp.
Mears Hiram A., mach., s.s. Front e. of Vance
Mears John B., clk. 21 E. 3d, h. Mill Creek Tp.
Mears Richard, brass finisher, s.s. M. Canal b. Elm and Plum
Mease Rev. Samuel, 231 Findlay
Measher John, bds Cincinnati House
Measson Isaac C., clk., 153 W. 4th
Meason Narcissa, 153 W. 4th
Mebus John, tailor, 2 O Mound
Mechanics' Hall, s.e.c. Front and Smith Bernhard Artmann, prop.
MECHANICS INSTITUTE s.w.c. Vine and 6th
Mecheler Bernard, tailor, 18 Hamer
Mechenburg Ann, 11 14th b. Central Av. and Plum
Mechley Adam, wks. 8 W. 6th
Mechnit Matthias, tailor, s.s. Charlotte b. Linn and Baymiller
Mechnot Nicholas. tailor, s s. Charlotte b. Linn and Baymiller
Meck Martin, mach., h. 473 Walnut
Mecke Wm., cab mkr., 472 Freeman
Mecklenborg Wm., printer, 11 W. 14th
Meckler John, finisher, 119 Mohawk
Meckler Joseph, 114 Mohawk
Meckler Salma, 14 Hamer
Mecky James, lab., 61 Mill

(MEI) CINCINNATI (MEI) DIRECTORY. (MEI)

Medairs Shadrick, carp., 233 Hopkins
Medary Fanny, s.w.c. Front and Broad
Medary Jacob, lab., wks. Queen City Distillery
MEDARY JOHN M., Clerk Police C't Office City Hall, h. 169 Baymiller near Clark
Medary Mary B. bds. 134 Burr
Meddend Iph Chris', cab. mkr., wks. n.w.c. Smith and Front
Meddendorf An rew, locksmith, n.w.c. Broadway and Woodward
Meddendorf Augustus, blin l mkr., n.w.c. Broadway and Woodward
Meddenlorf Barney, n.w.c. Broadway and Woodward
Meddendo f Frank, watch mkr., n.w.c. Broadway and Woodward
Meddendorf Frederick, lab., 226 Water
Meddend rp Hermann, carriage trimmer 148 Abigail
Meddick Peter. stone cutter, wks. Cincinnati Stone Works
Medeke Hy., 40 Mohawk
Medical College of Ohio, s.s. 6th b. Race and Vine
Medkerk Anna, 451 Freeman
Medkerk Josephine, teacher, 451 Freeman
Medkerk Rachael J., teacher, 451 Freeman
Meehan Charles J., shoe mkr., 8 Clinton
Meehan John, carp., n.s. al. b. Pike and Lawrence and 3 l and 4th
Meek John P. (Harcourt & M.) h. Newport
Meeker Frank, clk., Court House, res. Coventry
Meeker Jonas B., photographer, 424 W. 5th
Meeker Wm., lab wks. n.e.c. Walnut and Canal
Meeker Wm., carp., 472 Freeman
Meerfold Mattias, cooper, n.s. Charlotte b. Freeman and Baymiller
Meerhof Hy. H., pipe fitter, 65 Kossuth
Meersman Hy., mer., 10 Perry
Meersman Hy., lab. wks. 222 E. Front
Mecaler Joseph, molder, wks. n.e.c. Canal and Walnut
Medford Anna, bds. 204 Richmond
Megan Ann, 1 New
Mogerle Anna, 539 Race
Meginn John, pedler, 2 Crippen al.
Megrue C horace C., h. 229 Richmond
MEGRUE ENOCH G., Chief Engineer Fire Department, Office 92 George, h. 160 Longworth
Megrue Francis, bk layer, s.s. Dayton b. Column and Western Av
Megrue Joseph R., student, bds. 169 Longworth
Megrue Lewis C., plasterer, 230 Richmond
Mehan James, lab., 203 E. 6th
Mehan James, shoe mkr., 173 Water
Mehan John, miller, 16 Abigail
Mehan Wm., carp., 34 Kossuth
Mehaney Mrs. Ann, s.e c. 7th and Broadway
Meharry Rev. Alexander, 119½ Clinton
Mehl Fredericka, h. 259 Ham. Road
Mehle Hy F., clk., bds. n.e.c. Water and Central Av.
Mehler Simon J., shoe mkr., 626 Race
Mehltop J hn, cutter, 62 W. Pearl h. 22 Mulberry
Mehlmann Ernst, cab. mkr., wks. John K Coolidge's
MEHMER CHARLES, Proprietor of Deutsches Theater, Billiard and Lager Beer Saloon, n.g.c. Vine and Mercer
Mehner Louis, grocer, 31 E. Pearl, h. 530 W. 8th
Mehring Hy., pipeman, 20 Webster
Mehring John H., pipeman 20 Webster
Mehung Leonard V., tailor, 28 Hughes
Mu rincer Joseph, shoe mkr. 612 Race
Maichel Geo., shoe mkr., 67 Homer
Mews Hy., wagon mkr., 599 Walnut, h. 21 Ham Road

Meidel Anton, grocer, w.s. Vine b. Milk and Mulberry
Meier ——, peddler, 387 Main
Meier Mrs., seamstress, al b. Vine and Walnut and 13th and Mercer
Meier Adolph F. turner, 23 Mill
Meier Andreas. stone cutter, 509 Vine
Meier Anthony, carp., 191 Baymiller
Meier Anthony, lab. 55 14th
Meier Anthony, plasterer, 89 Pendleton
Meier Anthony, tanner, 60 Elder
Meier Anton, brewer, bds. 480 Vine
Meier August, cof h. s.e.c. 5th and Elm
Meier Barbara, 13 Pendleton
Meier Bavard, cooper, 73 Dudley
Meier Bernhard, lab., 211 Hopkins
Meier Casper, lab., s.s. Division b. Bank and Harrison Pike
Meier Catharine, 135 Pleasant
Meier Chas. E., tailor, 508 Walnut
Meier Christian, bk. layer, 678 Main
Meier Christian, carp., 29 Commerce
Meier Christian, cigar mkr., 525 Sycamore
Meier Christian, expressman, 678 Main
Meier Christian, lab., 525 Sycamore
Meier Clemens, cigars &c, 382 Race
Meier Conrad, meats 662 Main
Meier Conrad F., cooper, 78 Bremen
Meier Dietrich, dray, 49 Pendleton
Meier Dietrich, musician, 535 Main
Meier Doris, bds. 519 Vine
Meier Ferdinand, lab., 628 Main
Meier Francis, 261 Pleasant
Meier Frank, bksmith., 173 Hopkins
Meier Frank, eng., Cin. Gazette Office, h. E Walnut Hills
Meier Frank, lab., 67 Cutler
Meier Frank tailor, W. Woodward
Meier Fred. baker, 74 E. Front
Meier Frederick, expressman, 105 Pemm
Meier Fred, lab., 69 Hughes
Meier Frederick, molder, 46 Pendleton
Meier Geo., cigar mkr., 112 Clay
Meier George, plasterer, 371 Broadway
Meier Gerhard, tailor, 75 Bremen
Meier Gertrude, 97 Woodward
Meier Gertrude, tailoress, W. Woodward
Meier Harmon, tailor, bds 104 Clinton
Meier Helena, 364 Walnut
Meier Heinrich, 20 Milton
Meier Henry. bds Raffel al
Meier Henry sr., 187 Clay
Meier Henry, h.f.e.W., ... of Central Av
Meier Henry, bk...
Meier Henry, cigar...
Meier Henry, cooper...
Meier Henry, grocery...c. Mansfield and Webster
Meier Henry, hostler, 106 Ham. Road
Meier Henry, lab., 167 Clay
Meier Henry, lab., 54 Dudley
Meier Henry, lab., 147 W. Court w. of Central Av
Meier Henry, lab., Wm. H. & G. R. Martin's
Meier Henry, lab., 608 Vine
Meier Henry, lab., s.w.c. Abigail and Spring
Meier Henry, lab., 104 Clay
Meier Henry sr., mason, 56 Allison
Meier Henry, stone mason, 179 Baymiller
Meier Henry, tailor, 70 Dudley
Meier Henry, tailor, 160 Peete
Meier Henry E., driver, w.s. Goose al. b. Green and Elder
MEIER Henry W. (M. & Remeier), 725 Race
Meier Hermann H., stone mason, 11 Madison
Meier Herman T., lab., 667 Race
MEIER & ISPHORDING (John H. M. & Anton I.), Dealers in Leather, Hides, Furs, Findings and Shoemaker's Tools, 8 Main
Meier Jacob, baker, bds. 90 Hunt
Meier Jacob, expressman, 67 Bremen
Meier Jacob, shoe mkr., bds. 65 E. 3th
Meier Jacob, tailor, 700 Freeman
Meier John carp., E. end of Mohawk
Meier John, dray, 105 Bremen

Meier John, eng., 53 Pendleton
Meier John, photograph gallery, 519 Vine
Meier John, shoemkr., 267 Cutter
Meier John G., expressman, 108 Ham. Road
Meier John H, cab mkr., 509 Race
MEIER John H, (M & Isphording), 205 Clinton
Meier John H., lab. Drum al. b. 13th and Allison and Main and Clay
Meier Joseph, cab. mkr., 64 Elder
Meier Joseph, lab., 175 Water
Meier Joseph, lab., rear 375 Broadway
Meier Julius, lab k., 186 Vine, bds. s.s. 5th b. Vine and Race
Meier Julius, cigar mkr., 538 Walnut
Meier Katz, 634 Race
Meier Lewis, expressman, 105 Bremen
Meier Louis, brush mkr., 20 Orchard
Meier Louis, w.s. Denman b. Bank and Central Av
Meier Louis, shoemkr., 104 Hunt
Meier Margaretha, bds 382 R. ce
Meier Mary, servt., wks 61 Pendleton
Meier Mary, 50 Allison
Meier Phillip, box mkr., 13 Mulberry
Meier Philip, lab., 601 Walnut
MEIER & REMEIER, (Henry W. M. & John D R.) Lumber Dealers, n.s. Ham. Road Head of Race
Meier Samuel, porter, 106 Clay
Meier Sarah, 166 Clay
Meier Sophia, 504 Race
Meier Theodore, c'air mkr., 642 Elm
Meier Wm., carp., bds 42 Sycamore
Meier Wm., shoemkr., 571 Race
Meier Wm., tailor, bds. 577 Main
Meier Wm., 678 Main
Meier C. V., expressman, 74 Bremen
Meier Xivier, E. end of Mohawk
Meier decks Gerhard. lab . h. 49 Plum
Meier Jacob, lab., 24 Peete
Meier Henry, cab. mkr., 210 Linn
Meier Francis J., paper carrier, 213 North
Meier Frederick, cigar mkr., 539 Main
Meier John, carp., 83 Cross
Meier bds. 479 Race
Meier John, cab. mkr., 324 W. 3d
Meier molder, 106 Hunt
Meier liquors, 207 Cutter
Meier ine, porter, 352 Main
Meifeld John G., tailor, 147 W. 5th, b. 205 W. Front
Meifeld Joseph, cigar mkr., wks. 554 W. Front
Meighlen Joseph, lab., wks. Queen City Distillery
Meigle Jacob, lab., 226 Water
Meikel Michael, peddler, 401 Vine
Meil Anna M., 11 Wade b. Elm and Plum
Meil Hermann, lab., w.s. Goose al. b. Green and Elder
Meiler Bastian, lab., 120 Gest
Meimeyer Theodore, teamster, 263 Clinton
Meinard George, carp., 26 Mohawk
Meinberg Conrad H., tailor, 83 Pleasant
Meinders Henry, lab, 256 Water
Meinecke Gottlieb, mach., 184 Vine
Meineke Wm., machine shop, 105 Ham. Road
Meinecke Henry, cooper 694 Race
Meiner Richard, brush mkr., 20½ Hopkins
Meiners Anna, seamstress, wks. w.s. Goose al. b. Green and Elder
Meinert Herman, stone mason, 26 Madison
Meines Geo., sawyer, wks. n.e.c. Elm and Canal
Meinhard Christian, baker 625 Vine
Meinhardt Henry, molder, wks. Crane, Breed & Co's.
Meinhardt Henry, tailor, 16 W. Mulberry
Meiniger ——, shoe mkr., 5½3 Main
Meiniken John, tailor, bds. 511 Sycamore
Meininger Carl, cof. h., 184 Walnut
Meininger Chas., 479 Elm
Meininger Sophia, 100 13th
Meincke Henry, carp., 64 Ham. Road
Meinking Frederick H., shoe mkr., 583 Main

MENDENHALL EDWARD,
Map and Book Publisher,
157 Main, h 150 Livingston

MENDENHALL GEO.,
Physician and Surgeon,
Office and Residence 197 W. 4th

MENDERSON & FROHMAN, (Nathan M. & Lewis & Edward F.),
Wholesale Dealers in Cloths and Clothing, 111 W. Pearl

MENDERSON Nathan, (M. & Frohman) 316 W 9th w. of Central Av
Meng Sebastian, carp., 105 Ham. Road
Mengdehl Theodore, collector, n.s. Liberty b. Main and Walnut
Menge Robert C., cof. h., 134 Bremen
Menges Geo., cigar mkr., 634 Race
Menges Henry, porter, 16 Hammond
Menges John, cigar mkr , s.s. Pleasant b. Green and Elder
Menges John G., 103 Pleasant
Menhoff Hermon, saddler, 136 W. M. Canal
Menick Frederick, blksmith, 145 Livingston
Menk Eberhard, lab., 159 Clay
Menke Charles, finisher, wks n.w.c. Race and Burrows
Menke Arnold, boots and shoes, 72 Sycamore, h. 62 E Pearl
Menke August, tinner, 20 Woodward
Menke Barney, pattern dresser, 99 Pendleton
Menke Bernhard H., finisher, 99 Pendleton
Menke Dietrich H., blk. smith, 20 Woodward
Menke Gerhard H., shoe mkr., 10 Buckeye
Menke Gerhard M., grocer, n.e.c Cutter and Clinton
Menke Hy., blk. smith, 20 Woodward
Menke Herman, 63 David
Menke Hermon H., shoe mkr., bds. cor. Pike and Front
Menke John B., blk. smith, 65 12th
Menke John G., dry goods, 205 W. Front
Menke Joseph J., lock smith 151 Hopkins
Menke Mary, w. s Sycamore b. Mount and Saunders
Menke & Schulte, (John G. M. & Herman S.,) dry goods, 91 W. Court
Menke Wm., lab., 17 Mulberry
Menkedieck An .. i , rear 97 Woodward
Menkedieck Hy., drayman, rear 97 Woodward
Menken J. A., (S. M. & Sons,) 62 W. 5th
Menken J. S., (S. M. & Sons,) 62 W. 5th
Menken Jacob, millinery, e. s. Lodge nr. 5th   [5th
Menken N. D., (S. M. & Sons) 62 W.
Menken S. & Sons, (J A. M., J. S. M. & N. D. M.,) millinery, 62 W. 5th
Menker Hy., shoe mkr., bds. Pennsylvania Hotel
Menkhaus Casper, cab. mkr., 27 Buckeye
Menkhaus Fred., lab., 104 Abigail
Menkhaus John F. carp., 202 Pleasant
Menkhouse David, pattern mkr., 71 Abigail
Menning Geo., varnisher, 13 Adams
Menning Francis, rear 34 Mulberry
Menning John, carp., al. bet. 13th and Mercer and Vine and Walnut
Menninger John E., lab., 34 Elder
Menninger John O., druggist, n. w. c. Cutter and Clinton
Menninger Paul, bar k., 218 Vine
Menninger Wm , lab., bds. 34 Elder
Menogue Nicholas, second hand store, 142 Race
Menogue Peter, hackman, 219 E. 6th
Mensing Hy , tailor, 32 Milton
Mental Henrich, dry goods, 313 Freeman
Menticis Martin, shoe mkr., 54 W. 5th
Mente Louis, druggist, Commercial Hospital
Menter Almon, cof. h. 81 W. 4th, h. 111 Park

Menter Valentine, 72 Gest
Menton Martha, 159 Clark
Menton Mary, 159 Clark
Mentz Edward, carriage mkr., 528 Race
Menz Jacob F. J., barber, 504½ Main
Menze Anton, lab , 188 Clifton
Menzel August A., lithographer, 380 Elm
Menzel Conrad, cigar mkr , 494 Walnut

MENZEL G. A., (G. A. M. & Co.,) 380 Elm

MENZEL G. A. & CO.,
(G. A. M. & Herman G. M.,)
Lithographers, 257 Walnut

MENZEL Herman G., (G. A. Menzel & Co.,) h. 257 Walnut
Menzel Jacob, cof. h., 10 Walnut
Menzell Hy., cooper, bds. n.e c. Clarkson and Central Av
Menzer Engelbert, basket mkr, 121 Pleasant
Menzies Miss C. W., teacher, Mt. Auburn Institute
Menzies Samuel G., phys., 186 Richmond
Meorn Thos. J., tinner, 281 W. 7th
Mercantile Fire Insurance Agency, 62 W. 3d
Mercer Chas., lab., s. e c. Central Av. and Pearl
Mercer Dennis, 50 E. 2d
Mercer Dennis D., river man, 109 Sycamore
Mercer Hy., lab., wks. s.w.c. Canal and Vine
Mercer Mary, 169 Sycamore
Mercer Thos., 116 E 6th
Merchant Anderson, tobacco presser, 135 W. Miami Canal
Merchant Eliza. 291 W. 9th
Merchant Wm., tobacconist, 11 W. Court w. of Central Av.

MERCHANTS EXCHANGE,
e.s Walnut, b. 4th and 5th,
Wm Smith Superintendent

Merchants Insurance Company, agency 65 W. 3d

MERCHANTS & MANUFACTURERS INS. CO., A. M. Searles President, B. B. Whiteman Secretary, Office, 11 Public Landing

Merchutz Chas., tailor, 149 Bank
Merck Modest, carriage mkr., wks. Ch. Behlan & Co.'s
Merckel August, tanner, 58 Stark
Merckle Chas. blk. smith, 15 Hughes
Merckle Chas., lab., 71 Buckeye
Merdian Barbara, 700 Race
Meredith David, lab., 62 Rittenhouse
Meredith Ephraim, molder, 57 Observatory
Meredith Mary, 241 W. Court
Meredith J. E. (Duncall & Co.,) 92 W. 7th
Meredith Joseph, watchman, 76 Laurel
Meredith Philip, dentist, 132 W. 6th, h. 179 W. 4th
Meredith Robt. P., carp., 239 Broadway
Mergenthaler Charles A., bk. layer, 45 Mulberry
Mergenthaler Dorseth, 52 Peete
Mergenthaler Jacob F, carp., 52 Peete
Mergenthaler Johanna, 636 Main
Mergenthan Casper, 124 Mowhawk
Mergle Joseph, meats, n. w. c. 3d and Park
Merhart Andrew, salesman, 256 Main
Merkel John, bakery, 72 E. Pearl
Merker August. varnisher, 20 E. Liberty
Merker Chas., blk. sm th 15 Hughes
Merker Fanny, teacher, 415 Elm
Merker Paul, salesman, 150 Walnut, h. 415 Elm
Merkle Barbara, 600 Elm
Merkle Jacob, tailor, 38 Elder
Merkle Xavier, baker, 41 4th
Merkler John, lab. 961 Central Av
Merlein Francis, shoe mkr., 1 Lucy
Merlet Geo., lab., wks. 1– Sycamore

MERNA JOSEPH,
Hardware, Cutlery, &c.,
192 Main, h. 42 Lock

MERRELL Ashbel S., (Wm. S. Merrill & Co) 220 Longworth
Merrell Dwight, druggist, 625 W. 7th
Merrell Elizabeth, bds. 73 W. 7th

234 (MES) CINCINNATI (MET) DIRECTORY. (MEY)

MERRELL Harlow M., (Harlow M. M. & Co.,) 58 Richmond
MERRELL HARLOW M. & CO., (Harlow M. M. & I. Blackford Stevens) Chemicals, Drugs and Medicines, n.w.c Court and Plum
Merrell Laura, bds. 295 John
Merrell Wm. H., barber, 135 W. Miami Canal
MERRELL Wm. S., (Wm. S. M. & Co.) h. 166 Elm
MERRELL WM. S. & CO.. (Wm. S. M. & Ashbel S. M.,) Wholesale Druggists, 110 and 112 W. 3d
Merrett Wm. H., clk., 166 Elm
MERRIAM Andrew B., (Suire, Eckstein & Co.,) h. Clifton, Ohio
Merrick Hart J., shoe mkr., bds. 314 W. 9th w. of Central Av.
Merrie Hugh. fin'sher, 46 Baum
Merrihew Kelley E., 501 W. 7th
Merrill August F., salesman, 21 Public Landing, h. 274 W. 3d
Merrill Elou, lab 67 Richmond
Merrill Henry, printer, 13 Arch
Merrill Hugh, mach., 46 Baum
Merrill John F., stoves, &c., 219 W, 5th h. 17 York
Merrill Joseph, phys., 610 W. 8th
Merrill Wm., huckster, 295 John
Merriman John P., carp , 119 Cutter
Merriman Wm., carp , Burt e of Broad
Merring Elijah, plasterer, 124 York
Merritt John T., ambrotype gallery, 188 W 5th, res. Covington
Merritt Mary. servt., 324 Longworth
MERRITT Wm., 77 Laurel
Merry Jackson, hack, 14 New
Mersch Hy , lab., 75 Abigail
Mersel Geo., tailor, 463 Linn
Mersmann Hy., tobacconist, 17 Main, h. 10 Perry
Mersmann Samuel, b.k., 17 Main, h. 62 Laurel
Mertens Rudolph, butcher, 427 Sycamore
Mertine John. japanner, wks. n.w.c. Race and 2d
Mertz Martin, cigar mkr., 105 Pleasant
Merworth Geo., lab., wks. n.e.c. Walnut and Canal
Merz Benedict. cof. h., e.s. Vine b. Milk and Mulberry
Merz Geo., 557 Elm
Merz John, rag dealer, 557 Elm
Merz John M., cutter, 524 Sycamore
Merz Leo, tailor, e.s. Vine b. Milk and Mulberry
Merz Mary. seamstress, 557 Elm
Mesoh John II., shoe mkr,, 111 W. Court, h. 130 W. Court
Mesch Joseph, lab., 240 Barr
Mescher Frederick. grocery, s.w.c. Longworth and Smith
Mescher J. Bernhard, varnisher, 52 McFarland [way
Mese John G., shoe mkr , 388 Broadway
Meser Bertha, seamstress, 604 Elm
Meser Louisa, seamstress, 604 Elm
MESEROLE Wm. H., Canal Collector. 7 W. Canal, h. 19 Milton
Nesker Joseph, porter. 50 Plum
Meslow Frederick, teamster, 675 Vine
Mesmann Hy., 64 Laurel
Mesmann Hy . lab., wks. 114 W. Court
Mesmann Hy., sawyer, wks. w s. Sycamore b. Woodward and Franklin
Mesmann Joseph. driver, 406 W. Front
Mesmer Martin, teamster. 717 Race
Mess Simon, lab., wks. Deer Creek Mills
Messang Frank J., lab., 111 Carl
Messang Frank J., stereotyper, 111 Mill
Messenger Chas., finisher, wks. n.e.c. Walnut and Canal
Messenger Jno., lab., Burnet House
Messer George. lock smith, 449 Walnut
Messer Peter, molder, 449 Walnut
Messer Wm , lock smith, 449 Walnut
Messer Wm., plate printer, s.w.c. Walnut and 13th
Messersmith George, bk. binder, 46 Jones
Messick George, lab., 95 Freeman
Messick Sallie A., dress mkr., bds. 167 Cutter

Messik Ely, dray, h. 163 Mound
Messing Frederick. lab., n.e c. Elm and Elder
Messinger Chas., lab., 103 Ham. Road
Messinger Geo. J., grinder, 16 Hamer
Messinger Joseph. molder, 799 Race
Messier Wm., finisher, 43 Moore
Messman Hy., lock smith, 132 Hopkins
Messman Hy., porter, 277 George
Messman John H., lock smith, 132 Hopkins
Messman Joseph, lab., wks. s.w.c. Park and W. W. Canal
Messman Wm., carp., 55 Pendleton
Messmer Wm.. e.s Linn near Poplar
Messner Gottfried, tailor. 554 Vine
Messner Nicholaus, tailor, 554 Vine
Mest Simeon, lab., wks. Deer Creek Mills
Mestemaker Franz, chair mkr., bds. 13 Bremen
Mestemaker Joseph, furniture, 15 Bremen. h. 13 Bremen
Mester Charles, tailor, e.s. Oregon b. 3d and 6th
Mester George, baker 215 W. Front
Messman Fred, 157 Everett
Meszner Chas., finisher, 103 Bremen
Metakotte Hy., lab., 32 Dudley
Metcalf Alfred, stone cutter, 46 E. 7th
METCALF Chas. W.. (M. & Ross), 193 Barr
Metcalf Geo. T., bds. 89 E. 4th
Metcalf Hiram, printer, bds 50 Mound
Metcalf James L., carp., 195 Barr
Metcalf Martha A., b.h., s.e.c. 6th and Smith
Metcalf Mary, 193 Barr
METCALF & ROSS (Chas. W. M. & Frederick R) Columbian Saloon, n.e.c. Main and 8th
Metcalf Sarah, 50 Mound
Metcalf Thomas, harness mkr,, bds. 141 Sycamore
Metcalf Thomas, tobacconist, 17 Main
Metcalf Wm , carp , bds. 193 Barr
Metcket Peter, stone cutter, 196 Linn
Metendor Margaret, 149 Carr
Methe John cab. mkr., 257 Clark
METHODIST BOOK CONCERN, Poe & Hitchcock, Agents, s.w.c. Main and 8th
Methven Alexander, boots and shoes,538 Central Av
Methven James, baker. 509 Sycamore
Methven John E., grainer,158 Clark
Metker Antony, lab., 305 W. 3d
Metropolitan Building, n.e.c. 9th and Walnut
Metsker Philip, butcher, 423 W. 7th
Metsker Philip F., butcher, 43 W 7th
Mette Wm., mer. tailor, 76 E. Front and 137 E. 2d
Mettey Geo , cooper. 502 Vine
Metz Adam. harness mkr., 25 13th
Metz B. & E. (Barney & Edward) cigars, &c., n.w.c. Sycamore and 2d
Metz Barney (B. & E. M.) n.e.c. David and Jones
Metz Edward, (B. & E. M.) 12 Harrison
Metz Geo., cigar mkr., 645 Central Av
Metz Jacob, blksmith, wks. n.w.c. Pearl and M. Canal
Metz Lewis (M. & L. M.) 103 Longworth
Metz M. & L. (Morris M. & Lewis M.), dry goods, 50 W. 5th
Metz Martin, cooper, 265 Pleasant
Metz Morris (M. & L. M.) 50 W. 5th
Metz Pauline 12 Harrison
Metz Peter, lab., wks. 335 Broadway
Metzel Geo., provisions, &c., 63 Elder
Metzeier Paul (M. & Von Bund) 8 Miami
Metzeler Paul, brush mkr., 8 Miami
Metzeler & Von Bund (Paul M. & J. Von B.) brush manuf., 93 Hughes
Metzer Michael, 2 W. Mulberry
Metzger Barney. bk. molder, 53 Pine
Metzger Hernhard, lab., 193 Pleasant
Metzger Dorritt, midwife, 73 Buckeye
Metzger Elizabeth, 193 Pleasant
Metzger Geo., bakery, 91 Bremen
Metzger George, janitor. 13 Adams
METZGER Gottlieb (Pfister & M.), 99 Pleasant
Metzger Gottlieb. paper hangings, 455 Main, h. 99 Pleasant

Metzger Jacob, baker, bds. 480 Vine
Metzger Jacob, lab., wks. 488 Main
Metzger John, watch mkr., h. 59 E. 3d
Metzger John A., gardener, Garden of Eden
Metzker Gottlieb, paper store, 455 Main
Metzker Isaac. bds. Hart's Hotel
Metzler Eusepius. tailor, e.s. Bremen b. Elder and Findlay
Metzler Geo., mason, 160 Buckeye
Metsler Hermann, painter. 657 Vine
Metzler Jacob, grocery. 147 Bremen
Metzlof Lena, 50 Dunlap
Meuer Martin. cigar mkr., 571 Race
Meuhof Diebrich, tailor, 517 Sycamore
Meulengraf Geradus, cab. mkr.,510 Plum
Meuler Hy., 45 Clay
Meumeier Joseph, h 247 W. 4th
Meurer Hy.. clk., 72 Bremen
Meuret Frederick, comb mkr., rear 557 Elm
Meury Franz Martin, tailor, n.e.c. 15th and Plum
Meuttmann Anna, milliner, 518 Race
Meuttmann Jacob, painter 433 Walnut
Mevrie Wm., hinge fitter, wks. n.e.c. Walnut and Canal
Mewhinney David, n.e.c. Poplar & Freeman
Mewhinney James, cutter, 367 Longworth
Mewhinney Sylvanus, grocery, s. e. c. Poplar and Freeman
Mey Lewis G., carp., 503 Race
Meyberg Benedict, (M. & Hellman,) 88 W. 7th
Mayberg Hellman, (Benedict M., & Max H.) hats and caps, 124 Walnut
Meyenschein John, cof. h. 194 Pleasant
Meyer Adam, carriage trimmer, 60 Allison
Meyer Adam F., cooper, 368 W. 9th w. of Freeman
Meyer Adolph, (Weil & M.,) bds. 257 W. 8th
Meyer Agnes, 588 Race
Meyer Albert, porter, 54 Rittenhouse
Meyer Albert, teamster, 717 Race
Meyer Albert N., clk., C. F. Adae & Co's, h. 73 Milton
Meyer Andrew, bds. 687 Central Av.
Meyer Andrew. wks. 690 W. Front
Meyer Andrew, tailor, 14 Jackson
Meyer Andrew tailor, 492 Elm
Meyer Anna 613 Race
Meyer Anton. brewer, 91 Ham. Road
Meyer Anton. teamster, s.e.c. Hunt and Pendleton
Meyer Antony ice dealer, Weller near Horne
Meyer Augutt, 42 Cross
Meyer August, (C. F. Meyer & Bro.) 477 Race
Meyer August, dray, 599 R ce
Meyer August, hinge fitter, wks. n.e.c. Walnut and Canal
Meyer August, marble cutter, wks. e. s. Central Av. b. 12th and Ann
Meyer August, porter, 517 Race
Meyer Barney, lab., s. s. Railroad e. of Brooklyn
Meyer Barney, shoe mkr., bds. 42 Elm
Meyer Barney, tailor, 65 12th
Meyer Barney, varnisher, h. 165 Carr
Meyer Barney H.. cof h. 42 Elm
Meyer Bernard. cooper.73 Dudley
Meyer Bernard A., (C. F. Meyer & Bro.) 70 W. Court
Meyer Bernhard, match box mkr., 106 Buckeye
Meyer C., clk.. 562 Vine
Meyer C. F. & Bro.,) Charles F. & Bernard A.) cigars &c.. 70 W. Court
Meyer Casper. coal yard, s.w.c. Cutter and Hopkins, h. 402 Cutter
Meyer Catharine, n.e.c. Front and Parsons
Meyer Charles, e.s. Mill b. Vine and Calhoun
Meyer Charles, n.s. Corporation Line near Auburn
Meyer Charles, cab mkr., wks. 71 W. 5th
Meyer Charles, lab., 99 York
Meyer Charles, meats, 536 Central Av.
Meyer Charles, tailor, 60 15th

(MEY) CINCINNATI (MEY) DIRECTORY. (MEY) 235

Meyer Charles F., (C. F. M. & Bro.) 70 W. Court
Meyer Charles H., cof. h. 52 15th
Meyer Charles W., clk., 24 Grant
Meyer Christian, 163 Clay
Meyer Christian, carp., wks. s.w.c. Elm and Front
Meyer Christian, cof. h. n.w.c. Front and Wood
Meyer Christian, cof. h., 165 Clay
Meyer Christian, cooper, e. s. Western Av. b. Bank and Harrison Pike
Meyer Christian, cooper, 365 Cutter
Meyer Claus, Fred, shoe mkr., 148 Clay
Meyer Conrad, h. w. s. Sycamore b. Mount and Saunders
Meyer D. salesman, 121 Main
Meyer Daniel, lab., s.w.c. Auburn Av. and Corporation Line
Meyer David, salesman, 211 Main
Meyer Dedrich, shoe mkr., 681 Sycamore
Meyer Dietrich, cigar mkr., n.e.c. Main and Franklin
Meyer Dietrich, shoe mkr., 90 Buckeye
Meyer Dietrich B., clk., s.e.c. Wilson and Milton
Meyer & Dwyer, (Luke M., & Patrick D.) blksmiths, 27 Lodge
Meyer Elizabeth, tailoress, 135 Hopkins
Meyer Francis, painter, bds. 9 15th
Meyer Francis, wood cutter, e.s. Lebanon Road, nr. Montgomery pike
Meyer Francis J., box factory 117 Race, h. 150 Water
Meyer Frank, clk., 36 E. Pearl, h. 34 Harrison
Meyer Frank A., cof. h. 14 13th
Meyer Franz, lab., 2 W. Mulberry
Meyer Fred bk. mkr., s.s. Ringgold b. Price and Young
Meyer Fred., boots and shoes, 50 Sycamore, h. 153 Bremen
Meyer Fred., cab. mkr., 16 15th
Meyer Fred., carp., 91 12th
Meyer Fred., cigar mkr., 151 Clay
Meyer Fred., cigar mkr., n.e.c. Betts and Cutter
Meyer Fred., driver, 89 12th
Meyer Fred., grocery, 34 Harrison
Meyer Fred., lab., 195 W. Canal
Meyer Fred., lab., 55 12th
Meyer Fred., lab., n.s. Front e. of Fo
Meyer Fred., shoe mkr., 153 Bremen
Meyer Fred., shoe mkr., 1017 Centr Av.
MEYER Fred., (Sommer & M.) 84 Harrison
Meyer Fred., tailor, 19 12th
Meyer Fred., tailor, 674 Central Av
Meyer Fred., teamster, 299 W. Front
Meyer Fred., wagon mkr., wks. Miami Canal
Meyer Fred., watchman, 70 Lock
Meyer Frederick A., saloon, n.w.c. man and Richmond
Meyer Fred. H., porter, 146 Buckeye
MEYER FREDERICK W., Family Grocery s.w.c 4th and Park
Meyer Fred. W., lab., 25 Ham. Road
Meyer Geo, 438 Linn
Meyer Geo, baker, 35 Elder
Meyer Geo., butcher, 713 Central Av
Meyer Geo., cof. h., w.s Western Av. b. Dayton and Bank
MEYER GEO., Coffee House, 117 Bremen, h. 23 15th
Meyer Geo., driver, s.s. al. b. 15th and 14th and Central Av. and Plum
Meyer Geo., lab., 134 Linn
Meyer Geo., peddler, 126 Bremen
Meyer Geo., watchman, 91 W. Court
Meyer Geo., F, bk. layer, 83 Ham. Road
Meyer Gerhard, cab. mkr., 139 Plum
Meyer, Gottlieb, lab., 10 Buckeye
Meyer, Hy., blksmith, 74 Gano
Meyer Hy., box mkr., bds., 14 13th
Meyer Hy., cab. mkr., 642 Elm
Meyer Hy., carver, 55 Court
Meyer, Hy ; cigars &c., 347 Vine
Meyer Hy., clk., n.w.c. York and Baymiller
Meyer Hy., clk., bds. 583 Race

Meyer Hy., cooper, 86 Bremen
Meyer Hy., omnibus driver, 17 Park
Meyer Hy., gardener, s.s. Montgomery pike near Madison Road
Meyer Hy., lab., 409 Elm
Meyer Hy., hinge fitter, wks. n.e.c. Walnut and Canal
Meyer Hy., huckster, e.s. Vine, b. Calhoun and Auburn Av
Meyer Hy., lab., 20 Commerce
Meyer Hy., lab., 608 Elm
Meyer Hy., lab., bds., 347 Walnut
Meyer Hy., lab., 25 Commerce
Meyer Hy., mach.. wks. s.w.c. 7th and Smith, 63 E. 12th
Meyer Hy., jr., mason, 66 Allison
Meyer Hy., shoe mkr. w.s. Coggswell al. b. Franklin and Woodward
Meyer Hy., tailor, w.s. Lebanon Road near Channing
Meyer Hy., tanner, n.s. Wade b. Dudley and Baymiller
Meyer Hy., teamster, wks., 304 Broadway
Meyer Hy., varnisher, 165 Carr
Meyer Hy., varnisher, 165 Clay
Meyer Hy., whitewasher, 20 E. Liberty
Meyer Hy. A., carp., 21 Franklin
Meyer Hy. A., (Stall & M.) 115 Richmond
Meyer Hy. C., clk n.w.c. York and Baymiller
Meyer Hy. G., cigar mkr., 51 15th
Meyer Herman, chair mkr., 15 15th b. Elm and Plum
Meyer Herman H., grocer, s.w.c. Cutter and Melancthon
Meyer Isaac. com. men, 447 Main
Meyer Ignatz, tanner e.s. Branch b. Findley nd Ham. Road
Meyer Jacob, cof h., 16 W. Court
Meyer Jacob, cook, Spencer House
Meyer Jacob, cook, 473 Vine
Meyer Jacob, cook, n.e.c. Broadway and 3d
MEYER Jacob, (Faehr & M.) 438 Main
Meyer Jacob, lab., s.w.c. Auburn Av. and Corporation line
Meyer Jacob, lab., s.s Montgomery pike near Reading Road
Meyer Jacob F., carp., 18 15th
Meyer Jane, lab., 142 Broadway
Meyer Jane, rear 623 Elm
Meyer John, n.s. Ham. Road, head of Elm
Meyer John, bk. mkr., w.s. Price b. Channing and Ringgold
Meyer John, cooper. 73 Wade
Meyer John, eng., 53 Pendleton
Meyer John, driver. 705 Freeman
Meyer John, lab., e.s. Vine b. milk and Mulberry
Meyer John, lab., n.n.c. Milton and Sycamore
Meyer John, lab., n.s. Front w. of Hill
Meyer John, lab.. 712 Central Av
Meyer John, lab., 171 Oliver
Meyer John B., grocery, 189 W. Front
Meyer John B., tailor 23 Broadway, b. Newport
Meyer John D., clk.. s.w.c. Pike and Pearl, bds.. 55 W. Front
Meyer John, D., (L. E. Steinman and Co.) 399 Longworth
Meyer John F, 588 Race
Meyer John F., cigar mkr., 448 Race
Meyer John F., painter, 690 Race
Meyer John G., cigars &c., 549 Main, h. 112 Clay
Meyer John H., grocery, 218 John
Meyer John K., veterinary surgeon, s.e c. Pearl and Pike
Meyer John L., cab. mkr., 63 David
Meyer Joseph, blksmith, bds. 86 W. Court
Meyer Joseph, bk. mkr., w.s. Price b. Channing, and Ringgold
Meyer Joseph, cab. mkr., wks. 71 W. 5th
Meyer Joseph, cigar mkr., 624 Race
Meyer Joseph, cooper, 463 Linn
Meyer Joseph, lab., bds. s.s. Harrison pike b. Coleman and Denman
Meyer Joseph, lab. n.s. Browne b. Mohawk and Ham. Road
Meyer Joseph, lab., 512 Walnut
Meyer Joseph, shoe mkr., bks. 486 Main

Meyer Joseph, tailor, 35 Elder
Meyer Kate, bds., 91 W. Court
Meyer Lizzie, seamstress 623 Elm
Meyer L., bds. Gibson House
Meyer Lawrence, lab., wks., 690 W. Front
Meyer Leopold, jewelry &c., 189 Walnut, h. 405 W, 8th
Meyer Mevi. furniture &c., 336 W. 5th
Meyer Lewis, lab., 585 Race
Meyer Lewis, undertaker, 69 12th
Meyer Louis, bds. 67 W. 9th
Meyer Louis, brush mkr., 26 Orchard
Meyer Louis, carp, 678 Sycamore
Meyer Louis, cof h. w.s. Ham. Road nr Brighton House
Meyer Luke, (M. & Dwyer,) n.s. Gano nr. Vine
Meyer Margaret, 154 Pleasant
Meyer Martin, bar. k. 116 Main, h 76 W Liberty
Meyer Martin, cof. h. 76 W. Liberty
Meyer Martin, currier, wks. 166 Main
Meyer Mary, 259 Everett
Meyer Mary, 181 York
Meyer Mary, h. 511 Vine
Meyer Mathias, cigar mkr., 69 W. Liberty
Meyer Michael, soap mkr., s.s Browne, cor. of Byron, h. n.e.c. Browne and Byron
Meyer Motts, plasterer, 215 Betts
Meyer Nicholas, bk. binder, 485 Sycamore
Meyer Nicholas, shoemkr, 669 Vine
Meyer Phillip, bds. 90 Freeman
Meyer Phillip, cof. h., 1034 Central Av
Meyer Philip, lab., 17 Mulberry
Meyer Rachael, 193 Everett
Meyer Richard, lab., wks. n.s. 9th, b. Plum and Central Av
Meyer Rudolph, (Cooper & Co.,) 134 Wade
Meyer Selma, 69 W. Liberty
Meyer Samuel. 2 Providence
Meyer Samuel, liquors. &c., 141 W. Pearl
Meyer Sigmund, 4 Clinton Court
Meyer Sophia, 22 Orchard
Meyer Theodore, clk., bds. 99 W. 8th
Meyer Theresa, 652 E. Front
Meyer Werner, tailor, 24 13th
Meyer Wm, bds. 90 Freeman
Meyer Wm., boots and shoes, 184 E. 6th
Meyer Wm., cof h., n.e.c Elm and Pearl
Meyer Wm., shoemkr, 62 Bremen
Meyer Wm., tailor, 740 Vine
Meyer Wm., watchman, 440 Linn
Meyer Wm. B., clk. C. F. Adae & Co.'s h. 73 Milton
Meyerhoper Jacob, brewer, s.e.c. Hoadley and Longworth
Meyerman J. B. H., storekeeper, Commercial Hospital
Meyerrose Mrs. Wilhelmine, 511 Sycamore
Meyers Adam A., cooper, 368 W. 9th, w. of Central Av
Meyers Antony, driver, 46 14th
Meyers August, molder, bds. 35 15th
Meyers Frank, butcher, 63 Providence
Meyers Frank, lab., 371 W. 3d
Meyers Frederick, molder, wks. Chamberlain & Co.'s
Meyers Frederick W., porter, 25 Ham. Road
Meyers George, finisher, 278 W, Front
Meyers George, paper hanger, wks 161 Walnut
Meyers Geo., roaster, w.s. Main, b. 8th and 9th
Meyers Hy., cigar mkr., 149 Poplar
Meyers Hy, eng. 98 W. Court
Meyers Hy., (Frazer & M.,) h. Walnut Hills
Meyers Hy., grocer, n.w.c. Cutter and Everett
Meyers Hy., lab., 121 Harrison Pike
Meyers Jacob, cigar mkr., 210 Hopkins
Meyers Jacob, tobacconist, bds. 88 W. Court
Meyers Jacob B., shoemkr., 284 Main
Meyers James, molder, wks. 137 W. 2d
Meyers Jere. steward, Broadway Hotel
Meyers John, boots and shoes, 65 Dayton
Meyers John D, jr., grocery, n.e.c. Water and Central Av

236 (MID) CINCINNATI (MIL) DIRECTORY. (MIL)

Meyers John, tailor, 608 Central Av
Meyers John D., cof. h., 20 Central Av., h n.e.c. Water and Central Av
Meyers Joseph, cigar mkr., bds. 608 Vine
Meyers Joseph, molder, wks. Chamberlain & Co.'s
Meyers Joseph, shoemkr, 65 Dayton
Meyers Kate, wks. Hleatt & Wood's candle factory
Meyers Lewis, 26 Pleasant
Meyers Manuel, clk., 5 Broadway, bds. 98 W. Front
Meyers Mary, 14 Providence
Meyers Matilda, 308 Findlay
Meyers Peter, tailor, 434 Linn
Meyers Richard, turner, wks. 340 W. 3d
Meyers Wm., clk., n. w. c. Cutter and Everett
Meyers Wm., cooper, 134 Wade
Meyers Wm., eng., bds. n.s. Augusta, b. John and Smith
Meyers Wm., grocery, 676 Central Av
Meyersick Frederick. cigar mkr., 7 Main
Meyhew Rufus D. 317 Baymiller
Meyn Johanna, 439 Walnut
Meyrose Fred., tailor, 333 Walnut
Meysner John, butcher, 52 Dunlap
Miami Oil Works, (Walter, Smith & Co.) 9 W. 2d [Elm
Miami Planing Mill, n.s. M. Canal, w. of
Michael Andreas, cab mkr., 56 Findlay
Michael Andreas, 132 Mohawk
Michael August, huckster, 10 Pleasant
Michael Conrad, lab., 108 Culvert
Michael Francis, carp., 216 Bremen
Michael Hy., blksmith, 172 Spring
Michael John, lab., wks. n.w.c. Plum and Wade
Michael John, lab., 16 Mulberry
Michael John C., tailor, 172 Spring
Michael John H., blksmith, 172 Spring
Michael John H., (Luhring & M.,) 59 Abigail
Michael Harz, tanner, 246 Pleasant
Michael Nicholas, lab., bds. s.s. Liberty, b. Freeman and Ludlow
Michael Richard, lab., 63 Pleasant
Michael Wm., stone mason, 74 Rittenhouse
Michaela Sister, St. Clare Convent, n.w. c 3d and Lytle
Michaels Alex., b.k., 317 Broadway
Michaels Conrad, lab., 108 Culvert
Michaels Dieterich, lab., 63 Pleasant
Michaels Jacob, dray., 187 Poplar
Michaels Morris, shoemkr, 55 E. 8th
Michel Daniel, stoves, &c ; 145 E. 2d
Michel Geo., glazier, 23 W. Court
Michelson John, barber, 78 Bremen
Michelson John P. C., barber, 76 Bremen
Michener Israel, pork packer, 126 W. Miami Canal, res. Philadelphia
Michie James C., watch mkr., 45 Franklin
Michie Wm., watch mkr., 45 Franklin
Michie Wm., jr., wat h mkr., 45 Franklin
Michler Francis, weaver, 9 John
Mick Miss Anna, seamstress, wks. 547 Vine
Mick Joseph, cigar mkr., 180 Buckeye
Mick Mary, rear 180 Buckeye
Micke Herman, lab., wks. n.w.c. Plum and Wade
Micke John, lab., wks. n.w.c. Plum and Wade
Middeke Hy., clk., 218 Main, h. 419 Sycamore
Middcke Phillip, wagoner, 419 Sycamore
Middelhoff Gerhard, lab., 107 Clay
Middendorf Clements, cutter, 62 Broadway
Middendorf Hy., barber, 316 Main
Middendorf Hy., lab., 113 Clay
Middendorf John, lab., 30 Pierson
Middlebuck Fred., tailor, 91 Spring
Middlehoff Geo., sawyer, wks. John Mitchell's
Middleton E. C., portrait publisher, 118 W. 4th. h. Columbia Township
Middleton Edwin, carp., s.s. Front, e. of Ferry
Middleton George, 229 W. 4th
Middleton Geo. A., salesman, bds. n.e.c. 4th and Plum
Middleton Maria A., electrician, s.s. Front, e. of Ferry

Middleton Robt., 130 Smith
MIDDLETON, STROBRIDGE & CO. (Hines Strobridge.) Lithographers, Engravers and Publishers, 64 W. 4th
Middleton Wm., b.k., 436 W. 8th
Middleton W. C., b.k., 435 W. 8th
Middleworth Wm., driver, 39 Plum
Midel Roman, e.s Milk, b. Vine and Calhoun
Midgley Ann, propr. Evans Hotel, 63 and 65 Broadway
Midgley Mrs. Ernstein, variety store, 419 Central Av
Midgley Harwood, steward, 65 Broadway
Midgley John. 65 Broadway
Midwenwarp Hermann, carriage mkr., 148 Abigail
Miedden Geo. H., 60 Hunt
Miedeking Hy., grocery, n e.c. 9th and John
Miefield John G., tailor, 205 W. Front
Mieh Hy.. blksmith, wks. 825 Central Avenue
Mier Frederick, peddler, 390 Central Av
Mierenfeld John, carp., 676 E. Front
Mierenfeld John A., carver, 272 Linn
Miers Andrew, 60 Elder
Miers Hy., e.s. Elm, b. Elder and Findlay
Miers Leopold, jeweler, 407 W. 8th
Mies John. butcher, 435 W. 2d
Mieth Gottlieb, instrument mkr., 29 Jackson
Migel Bernard, bds. Hart's Hotel
Mikale Mary, bds. 162 Elm
Mike Andrew, 112 Clinton
Mike Andrew, cook, St. Charles Exchange
Mikel Nathan, clk., 193 Broadway
Mikolajowsky Francis, shoe mkr., 463 Vine
Milam Geo. W., baggage master O. & M. R.R., h. 419 George
Milan Catharine, 64 Abigail
Milan Eliza, bds. s.s. 6th, b. Broadway and Culvert
MILES H. S., (Wells & M.,) 268 Longworth
Miles John M, tailor, 33 E. 3d, h. Covington
Miles Martha, 202 W. Front
Miles Mrs. N., 218 George
Miles Rawley, lab., 202 Broadway
Miles Theodore, clk., bds. n.w.c. Central Av and Longworth
Miles Thomas, lab., s.s. Front, b. Smith and Mill
Miles Winnefried, 150 Water
Milos Wm., servt., 197 W. 4th
Milius Ferdinand, 147 Longworth
Milius Labon, 120 W. 7th
Milkebuck Daniel, lab., 9 Pendleton
Mill Street House, J. H. Burns, propr., n.w.c. Mill and Front
MILLAR Constantine D., (M. D Potter & Co) 252 W 3d
Millard Chas., carp., wks. 40 E. 2d
Millberger Catharine, s.e.c. Elm and Findlay
Miller ——, lab., 20 Jackson
Miller A., cigar mkr., 47 Milton
Miller Adam, n.s. Mulberry b. Race and Vine
Miller Adam, blksmith, 704 W. 6th
Miller Adam, lab., wks. 120 W. 2d
Miller Adam, paver, 155 Clark
Miller Adam, printer, n.w.c. Court and Main
Miller Adam, printer, bds. 442 Main
Miller Adam, teamster, 422 John
Miller Agatha, servt., 493 Vine
Miller Albert W. W., b.k. 14½ W. 4th, res. Covington
Miller Alfred, 447 W. 2d
MILLER Alfred, (M. & Jessup) 188 E. 6th
Miller Altha, teacher, 132 Spring
Miller Andrew, dray, 353 Elm
Miller Andrew, grocery, 78 Buckeye
Miller Ann, 184 Richmond
Miller Ann T., 184 Richmond
Miller Anna, servt., 124 Betts
Miller Anna, 132 Spring
Miller Annie, n.e.c. Longworth and Plum

Miller Anthony, box mkr., 169 Webb
Miller Anton, blksmith, 701 W. 6th
Miller Antone, baker, 63 W. Court
Miller August, baker, 46 Rittenhouse
Miller Augustus bar k., 222 Vine
Miller B , lab., 416 Longworth
Miller Benjamin. lab., 140 Carr
MILLER, BRUNING & DIECKMAN., (Fred. M , Henry B. & Wm. D.) Wholesale Grocers and Commission Merchants and Dealers in Liquors, 33 Sycamore
Miller C. R , teacher, Bacon's Mer. College, n.w.c. 6th and Walnut
Miller Caroline E., dress mkr., bds. 11 Linn
Miller Carrie, seamstress. 516 Walnut
Miller Caspar, lab., 113 Buckeye
Miller Catharine, 293 Elm
Miller Chas , brewer, rear 62 Mohawk
Miller Chas., clk., 91 Sycamore
Miller Chas., shoe mkr.. 14 Milton
Miller Chas., tailor, 13 Pendleton
Miller Chas. H., plow manuf., bds. 23 W. 7th
Miller Chas. L.. clk., 47 Ellen
Miller Christopher, trunk mkr., wks. 479 Central Av.
Miller Christopher, rope mkr., 169 Webb
Miller Clark R., teacher, Bacon's Mer. College
Miller Conrad, fireman, n.e.c. Front and Parsons
Miller Conrad, 11 Jordan
Miller D. S., gardener, n.s. Liberty b. Freeman and Mill Creek
Miller Daniel, lab., e.s. Mill Creek b. Fremont and 6th
Miller Daniel, trimmer. 65 Ham. Road
Miller David S., reaper maker, 132 Spring
Miller David S., policeman, 30 12th
Miller David W., carp , (M. & DeCamp) 193 Barr
Miller & DeCamp, (David W. M. & Asbury DeC.) carps , 458 George
Miller Drake, bklayer, 226 Clinton
Miller Edward A., clk., bds. 463 W. 78th
Miller Edward M., engraver, n.e.c. Burnet and Vine, h. 141 Longworth
Miller Edward R., carp., 463 W. 8th
Miller Eliza, 45 Wade
Miller Elisabeth, bds. 65 W. Court
Miller Elisabeth, h. e.s. Plum b. Adams and Liberty
Miller Elizabeth C., 340 Richmond
Miller Emil, cab. mkr., Oehler al. b. Freeman and Garrard
Miller Emil, chair caner, 19 15th b. Elm and Plum
Miller Emma, binder, 155 Hopkins
Miller Esther, s.s. Wade w. of Baymiller
Miller Eve, servt., 178 Sycamore
Miller Eve, 39 Jones
Miller Ferdinand, lab., 16 Walnut
M r Francis, drover, 417 Sycamore
Miller Francis G., blksmith, 488 W. 8th
MILLER FRANCIS W.. Attorney at Law and Notary Public, 65 W. 3d, h. 72 Barr
Miler Frank, 481 W. 5th
Miller Frank, finisher, wks. Lane & Bodley's
Miller Frank, huckster, 434 Linn
Miller Frank, lab., 242 Hopkins
Miller Florence, clk., 46 Woodward
Miller Frederica, rear 420 Sycamore
Miller Frederick, driver, 531 W. 8th
Miller Frederick, grocery, 118 E. 5th
Miller Frederick, lab., wks. 413 W. Front
MILLER Fred., (M., Bruning & Dieckman) 116 E. 5th
Miller Frederick, tailor, 475 W. 8th
Miller Geo , baker, bds. 65 W. Court
Miller Geo., bird dealer. 28 W. Court
Miller Geo., chair mkr., 572 Broadway
Miller Geo., dray, 304 W. Liberty
Miller Geo., lab., wks. n.e.c. Park and Marsh
Miller Geo., plumber, s.w.c. Freeman and Liberty
Miller Geo., printer, 516 Walnut
Miller Geo. A., cooper, Charlotte b. Linn and Baymiller
Miller Geo. A., tobacconist, 132 W. Miami Canal

Miller Geo. C., (Geo C. M. & Sons) h 23 W. 7th
MILLER GEO C. & CO.,
Plow Manufacturers,
11 and 13 W. 7th
MILLER GEO. C. & SONS, (John G. M. & Jeptha G. M.) Carriage Manufacturers, 19 and 21 W. 7th
Miller Geo. W., printer, 516 Walnut
Miller Geo. W., real estate dealer. n.w.c. 3d and Walnut, h. 145 Sycamore
Miller Geo. W. J., confec.. 166 W. 5th
Miller Gustav, grocery, s.e.c. 6th and Central Av.
Miller H., clk., bds. 61 Longworth
Miller H., lab., wks. n.s. Front b. Lawrence and Pike
MILLER H. J.,
President, pro tem., Cincinnati Gas Co. 209 Vine, h. 108 E. 4th
MILLER H. Thane, Pres't Young Ladies' Mt. Auburn Institute, h. w.s. Auburn Av., Mt. Auburn
Miller Hamilton, clk. 14 W. 4th, res. Covington
Miller Hamilton J., b.k. 49 E. 2d, h. 159 Living-ton
Miller Harmon, lab., w.s. Sycamore b. Mount and Saunders
MILLER HARVEY,
Gold and Silver Plater
217 Elm, h. 39 Barr
Miller Henrietta. 615 Vine
Miller Henrietta, rear 420 Sycamore
Miller Hy., n.w.c. Linn and Poplar
Miller Hy., s.s. Coggswell av. near Auburn
Miller Hy., b.k. Commercial office, 151 Barr
Miller Hy., blksmith, bds. 412 Vine
Miller Hy., buck skin dresser, wks. Deer Creek foot of 8th
Miller Hy., gas fitter, 541 Elm
Miller Hy., miller, 156 Spring
Miller Hy., porter, s.w.c. Main and Court
Miller Hy., stereotyper, wks. 169 Vine
Miller Hy. F., molder, c. Hunt and Pendleton
Miller Hy. G., b.k., 151 Barr
Miller Hester, milliner, bds. 238 Race
Miller Horace T., (C. A. Stuart & Co.) 154 Broadway
Miller Ignatz. clk., bds. 249 W. 6th
MILLER ISAAC J. Attorney at Law and Notary Public, 34 Bank Bldg., h. 541 John
Miller Isabella. 615 Vine
MILLER J. & CO., (Joseph M. & W. B. Leonard) Sale Stable, 234 Walnut
Miller Jacob, brewer, s.s Montgomery Pike near Reading Road
Miller Jacob, grocer, n.w.c. Mound and 8th. h. 338 W. 8th
Miller Jacob, lab., e.s. Ohio Av. b. North Elm and Corporation Line
Miller Jacob, mach., c Race and Liberty
Miller Jacob, phys., bds. 633 W. Front
Miller Jacob, trunk mkr., 66 W. Court
Miller Jacob L., clothier, 234 W. 3d
Miller Jas., eng., 101 Gest
Miller Jas., hatter. 302 W. 8th
Miller Jas. H., clk. 101 W. 4th, bds. 61 Longworth
Miller Jane, 147 W. Front
MILLER Jeptha G., (Geo. C. Miller & Sons) h. Walnut Hills
MILLER & JESSUP, (Alfred M. & Firman J.) Bucket Manufacturers, s.s. Court e. of Broadway
Miller Job Wm., pattern mkr., 384 W. Liberty
Miller John, 75 Mohawk
Miller John, 150 Broadway
Miller John, 58 Providence
Miller John, barber, bds. 447 W. 2d
Miller John, bar k., 91 Sycamore
Miller John, bar k., 263 Clinton
Miller John, box mkr., 544 Vine
Miller John, brewer, 601 Vine
Miller John, brush mkr., wks. 41 E. 2d
Miller John, cab. mkr., 21 Bank
Miller John, carp, 21 Bank
Miller John, carp., 534 Vine
Miller John, carver, 108 Everett
Miller John. cof. h., 263 Clinton
Miller John. cooper, s.w.c. Findlay and Bremen
Miller John, cooper, bds 305 Linn
Miller John, finisher, 401 Longworth
Miller John, finisher, 502 Vine
Miller John, carman, 475 Race
Miller John, huckster, 486 Walnut
Miller John, lab., 676 Main
Miller John, lab., 434 Linn
Miller John, porter, Spencer House
Miller John, saddler. 150 Water
Miller John, tailor, 518 E. Front
Miller John, tailor, E. 3d b. Baum and Parsons
Miller John, tobacconist, 161 Longworth
Miller John A., lab., c. 6th and Front
Miller John D, tanner, 557 Race
MILLER John G., (Geo. C. Miller & Sons.) h. Walnut Hills
Miller John H., mach, 635 W. 7th
Miller John J., butcher, s.s. Findlay b. Bremen and Franz
Miller John P., lab., 124 Carr
Miller John W., carp., wks. n.e.c. Canal and Walnut
Miller Jonas, wks. Mitchell & Rammelsberg's
Miller Joseph, wks. junction 6th and Front
Miller Joseph, blksmith, 137 Pleasant
Miller Joseph, boots and shoes, w.s. Smith b. 2d and Augusta, bds. 34 Smith
Miller Joseph, finisher, wks. Crane, Breed & Co.'s
Miller Joseph, lab., 151 Clark
Miller Joseph, lab., rear 52 Abigail
MILLER Joseph, (M. & Co.) h. 206 Sycamore
Miller Joseph, meats, 40 Race
Miller Joseph, nurse, Commercial Hospital
Miller Joseph, tinner, 225 Hopkins
Miller Joseph J., 369 W. 9th w. of Central Av.
Miller Joseph R., foreman, 205 Freeman
Miller Judy, 54 W. Front
Miller Kate, seamstress, 10 Pleasant
Miller Lewis, turner, 299 Linn
Miller Lewis, shoe mkr., 28 Commerce
Miller Louis, 602 Elm
Miller Louis, clk., w. s. Spring b. Hunt and Abigail
Miller Louis, lab., 176 E. 5th
Miller Louis, servt, 114 Broadway
Miller Louisa, n.w.c. Elm and Court
Miller M. R., printer, 25 W. 4th, bds. Bevis House
Miller Magdalena, laundress, 29 Hughes
Miller Margaret, Walnut
Miller Margaret, saut
Miller
Miller Margaret, W. Court
Miller Martin, p...., s.w.c. Vine and Findlay
Miller Martin, stone mason, 19 Hughes
Miller Mary, s.w.c. Race and 3d
Miller Mary, teacher, 113 Barr
Miller Mary, seamstress, 10 Pleasant
Miller Matilda, teacher, 420 Sycamore
Miller Michael, 171 W. 6th
Miller Michael, finisher, wks. s.w.c. Front and Smith
Miller Michael, lab., 463 W. 3d
Miller Michael, leather, &c., 158 Sycamore
Miller Milton H., b. k., 30 Findlay
Miller Milton H., b. k., s.w.c. Elm and Water
Miller Morgan, barber, 61 E. 7th
Miller Morris, tailor, 397 Main
Miller Nicholas, 68 Mohawk
Miller Nicholas, cof. h., n.s. R. Road e. of Wallace al.
Miller Patrick, steward, n. s. 6th e. of Lock
Miller Pauline, bds. 65 W. Court
Miller Peter, bar k., 442 Main
Miller Peter. cigars, &c., e. s. Vine nr. Auburn Av.
Miller Peter, mach., h. 491 Elm
Miller Peter, jr., driver, 491 Elm
MILLER PETER,
Lumber Dealer,
567 Elm, h. 491 Elm
Miller Peter, tailor, w.s. Goose al. b. Green and Elder
Miller Peter, tailor, 157 W. 6th
Miller Phillip, bakery, 65 W. Court
Miller Phillip, cof. h., s.s. Calhoun b. Madison and McMillan
Miller Richard, sen., b. k., 150 Broadway
Miller Richard, jr., 150 Broadway
Miller Richard, meats, 47 Court
Miller Robt., lab., bds. 10 Sycamore
Miller Rudolph, grocer, n.w.c. Liberty and Mansfield
Miller Ruth 72 Barr
Miller Samuel, mach., wks. 137 W. 2d
Miller Samuel B., grocery, s.e.c. Sycamore and Webster, h. 489 Sycamore
Miller Sarah, 30 12th
Miller Sarah, 132 Spring
Miller Simon, coachman, 396 W. 6th
Miller Simon L., clothing, 147 Race
Miller Sophia, servt., 119 E. 5th
Miller Theodore, carp., n.s. Wade b. Dudley and Baymiller
Miller Thomas, lab., 176 Water
Miller Thomas, meats, 096 Central Av.
Miller Thomas B., currier. 247 Clark
Miller Thos. H., clk., 303 Central Av. bds. 353 Elm
Miller Thos. S., clk., 82 Richmond
Miller Wm., blksmith, 39 Moore
Miller Wm., cab. mkr, 113 Barr
Miller Wm., cigars, &c., 325 Main
Miller Wm., clk. bds. Bevis House
Miller Wm, cof. h., 100 Elm
Miller Wm., cook, 21 15th b. Central Av. and Plum
Miller Wm., cupola-tender, wks. Chamberlain & Co.'s
Miller Wm, eng., 229 W. 3d
MILLER Wm, (Fares & M..) 451 Broadway
Miller Wm., foreman, 353 W. Front
Miller Wm., lab., 185 W. 2d
Miller Wm., lab., 492 E. Front
Miller W m., porter, 185 W. 3d
Miller Wm., tailor, 176 Webb
Miller Wm. B. b. k., 100 Sycamore, res. Covington
Miller Wm. B. R., deputy sheriff, h. College Hill
Miller Wm. H., bds. 98 Broadway
Miller Wm. J., cigar mkr., bds. 325 Main
Miller Wm. T., clk., bds. Bevis House
Millery Frank, foreman, 417 Sycamore
Millet Patrick, cof. h., 82 Water
Millin John, sexton, w. s. Broadway b. 4th and 5th
Millinger Wm., cab. mkr., n.e.c. Smith and Water
Milliner Wm., carp.. n.e.c. Smith and Water
Milloy John, driver, 3d and 4th St. R.R.
Mills Chas S., salesman, 18 and 20 Main h. 296 Richmond
MILLS D. H., (M. & Woodruff,) res. New York
Mills David, jr., 499 W. 7th
MILLS Edward, (M. & Goshorn,) 99 Pike
MILLS & GOSHORN, (Edward M., Lewis E. M. & Alfred T. G.) Attorneys at Law, 17 W. 3d
Mills Hy., lab., bds. 130 W. Court
Mills Isaac. bds. 24 W. Court w. of Central Av.
Mills Isaac L., carriage smith, 441 W. 9th w. of Central Av.
Mills James, carp., 16 Perry
Mills James R., salesman, 137 Walnut
Mills Johanna, bds. 24 W. Court w. of Central Av.
MILLS John, (John M. & Co.) 47 Chestnut
MILLS JNO. & CO.,
Staple and Fancy Dry Goods,
303 Central Avenue
Mills Joseph F., (M. & Kline,) 296 Richmond
Mills & Kline, (Joseph F. M. & Benneville K.,) Grocers, 15 Perry
MILLS Lewis E., (M. & Goshorn,) 99 Pike
Mills Margaretha, 441 W. 9th w. of Central Av.

238   (MIT)   CINCINNATI   (MIT)   DIRECTORY.

Mills Philemon E., bk. layer, bds. 441 W. 9th w. of Central Av.
MILLS Samuel, (M. & Spellmire,) 49 Everett
MILLS & SPELLMIRE, (Samuel M. & Joseph H. S.,) Carpenters and Builders, 49 Everett
Mills Wm., shoe mkr., 241 Central Av.
Mills Wm. A., boots and shoes, s. e. c. Poplar and Dudley
MILLS & WOODRUFF, (D. H. M. & C. S. W.,) Wholesale Dry Goods, 1 and 3 W. Pearl
Millson James, bleacher and presser, 139 W. 6th
Millson Joseph, bar k. 175 W. Court
Millus Chas., carp., h. n.s. Montgomery Pike nr Reading Road
Millwood Chas., carp , 92 W. Front
Milner A. S., mate. bds. 12 E. Front
Milott Johanna, 482 W. 5th
Milson John express. 54 Jones
Milton Thomas. clk., 23 E. 3d
Mimes Elizabeth, 99 E. 6th
Mimms Shedrick, bds. 25 McAllister
Mims James, janitor. 4 Baker
Mims James J., steward, bds. 26 Elizabeth
Minaud C., lab , wks. n.s. Front b. Lawrence and Pike
Minderman Albert, cab. mkr., 58 David
Mindermann Hermann, cigar mkr., 467 Walnut
Mineare Samuel, captain, 33 Parsons
Minehardt John, e.s. Clarkson b. Bank and Central Av.
Miner Chas. W , 319 W. 4th
Miner Herman, bds. 270 Everett
MINER JOHN L., Attorney at Law, 57 W 3d, h. 319 W. 4th
Minerd Joseph. brewer s.s. Montgomery Pike nr. Lebanon Road
Minerd Richard, brush mkr., 201 Hopkins
Minger Wm., blksmith. 29 Carr
Minier E. P., phys., 444 W. 5th
Minister Geo E., trunk mkr., 7 Harrison Avenue
Mink Frank, tailor, 7 Wade b. Elm and Plum
Minker Herman H., lab., 176 Clay
Minkhaus Frank, lab , n.w.c. Broadway and Woodward
Minkhouse Fred., lab., 204 Abigail
Minkhouse Martin, steward, n.w.c. Front and Elm
Minnadier Fred., turner, w.s. Bank b.t. 3d and 4th
Minnermann Albert, cab. mkr , 58 David
Minneropp Fritz, miller, n.w.c. Hannibal and 5th
Minnes Edward, porter, 157 W. Pearl
Minning Geo., varnisher, 13 Adams
Minning Hy., varnisher, 125 Bremen
Minning Wm., sawyer, 125 Bremen
Minning Wm., shoe mkr., 125 Bremen
Minuis Edward, porter, Broadway Hotel
Minogrm Thos., 44 E. 8th e. of Lock
Minor Alice bds 37 Hathaway
MINOR & ANDREWS, (John D. M. & Alex. H. A.,) Wholesale Grocers and Commission Merchants, s.e.c. 2d and Main
Minor Ann, 47 Plum
MINOR John D., (M. & Andrews,) 390 W 6th
Minshall Mrs. Presley K., 122 Everett
Minstus J., blk. smith, 70 Abigail
Minton Luke, lab., Mt. Adams
Mirkel John, bakery. 72 E. Pearl
Mirrielees Archibald, com. mer., 22 Water. bds. 112 E Liberty
Mirrielees Benj., 112 E. Liberty
Mirrielees Jas , 112 E. Liberty
Mischler Louis, s.w.c. Corporation line and Clifton Av.
Misener John B., plasterer, 253 Everett
Missemer Andreas, huckster, 32 Elder
Missouri House, 43 E. Front
Mistler M ydalene servt., 91 E. Liberty
Mitch Wm , clk., bds. 496 W. 7th
Mitchell Mrs., s s. 6th b. Vine and Race
Mitchell Albert H., clk., 99 W. 4th, b. Avondale

MITCHELL, ALLEMONG & CO., (D. A. M., A. W, A. & G. W. Smith,) General Produce and Commission Merchants, 13 Water
Mitchell Andrew, lab., 44 Hughes
Mitchell Caroline, binder, bds 57 Broadway
MITCHELL D. A, (M. Allemong & Co.,) bds. 152 W. 4th
Mitchell Dan., molder, 46 Mulberry
Mitchell David S., b.k., 110 W. Pearl, h. 78 Laurel
Mitchell Dom., lab., 171 Water
Mitchell E. B., pressman, wks. Times office, bds Covington, Ky
Mitchell Franklin, police, 205 Webb
Mitchell Geo., pork mer., 48 Clinton
Mitchell Geo., clk., wks. 350 Plum
Mitchell Isaiah, barber, 36 Broadway
Mitchell James H., harness mkr, 163 W. 5th
Mitchell Jas. W. molder, 462 W. 9th w. of Central Av.
MITCHELL Jethro. (M. & Rowland,) res. Mt. Auburn
Mitchell Jethro, G , b.k., s.w.c. Pearl and Elm, res. Mt. Auburn
Mitchell Johathan, blk. smith, s.s. 5th b. Vine and Race
MITCHELL JOHN. Chair Manufacturer, s.s. 2d b. John and Smith, h. n.e.c. Longworth and John
MITCHELL. JOHN, Commission Merchant, 39 Water. h. 496 W 7th
Mitchell Jno , lab , W. 9th, b. Harriet and Mill Creek
Mitchell John, lab., s.s. Friendship al. b. Pike and Butler
Mitchell John, waiter, bds. 30 Public Landing
Mitchell John F., 38 York
Mitchell John G., teacher Walnut Hills
Mitchell John L., janitor, s.e.c. Front and Broadway
Mitchell John T , brush mkr., s.s. Charloite b. John and Linn
MITCHELL Rev John T., pastor Park Street Chapel, 316 Longworth
Mitchell John W , shoe mkr., bds. n.s. North side Goodloe, b. Willow and Niagara
MITCHELL & LADD, (Newton M. & Thomas W. L.,) Pork Packers and Commission Merchants, 357 and 359 Plum
Mitchell Lizzie. bds. 184 Race
Mitchell Margaret, servt., 25 State
Mitchell Mary, 98 Butler
Mitchell Michael, lab., 6th near Mill ree'k bridge
Mitchell Michael, lab., W. 6th
Mitchel, Mrs. N. J., N., orge
Mitchel Nelson, shoe mkr., bds. n.s. Goodloe b. Willow and Niagara
MITCHELL Newton, (M. & Ladd,) 377 W. 6th
Mitchell Oscar, bds. 16 Stone Front
Mitchell Owen, conductor, bds. 786 E. Front
M'tchell Owen, dray, bds. 171 Baymiller
Mitchell P., bds. 107 Broadway
Mitchell Pat. s.s. College al. b. Hunt & Abigail [& Co.'s
Mitchell Patrick, lab., wks. Chamberlain
Mitchell Pat., shoe mkr., 130 Spring
Mitchell Pat. F., bk. binder, 25 W. 4th, h. 333 W. 5th
Mitchell Pierson R., b.k., 12 and 14 W. 2d, bds. 107 Broadway
MITCHELL & RAMMELSBERG, (Robt M. & Fred. R.,) Wholesale and Retail Furniture, Pianos and Looking Glasses, 99 W. 4th, and 23 and 25 E. 2d. Factory and Warerooms cor. John and 2d
MITCHELL Robt., (M. & Rammelsberg.) h. Avondale
Mitchell Robt , porter, 499 Sycamore
Mitchell Robt., porter, 8th and Accommodation
MITCHELL & ROWLAND, (Jethro M. & Thomas C. R.,) Lumber Dealers, 522 Vine
Mitchell Samuel, hinge fitter, wks. n.e.c. Walnut and Canal

(MOL) CINCINNATI (MON) DIRECTORY. (MOO) 239

Mogean F. H., clk., bds. 426 Vine
Mogly Andreas, shoe mkr., 149 Bremen
Mohan Catharine, servt., 265 W. 3d
Mohl Frank, lab., 759 Freeman
Mohlenhoff Fred., clk., bds. 81 Milton
MOHLENHOFF JOHN A.,
China, Glass and Queensware
44 W. 5th, h. 81 Milton
Mohlenkamp Mary, 20 Mansfield
Mohlmin John, shoe mkr., s.s. Front b. Vine and Race
Molmin John, lab., 439 W. 2d
Mohn John, 406 Vine
Mohn Marie, 51 13th
Mohnlein Casper, sawyer, e.s. Main b. Schiller and Liberty
Mohr Amelia, bds. 163 Oliver
MOHR August, (M., Solomon & Mohr), 163 W. 3d
Mohr Chas, baker, 635 Vine
Mohr Chas., bk. binder, 677 Vine
Mohr Geo., butcher, 62 Ham. Road
Mohr John, carp., 169 Pleasant
Mohr John D., auctioneer, 28 Race
MOHR Paul, (Mohr, Solomon & M.) 185 W. 4th
MOHR. SOLOMON & MOHR, (August M., William S. & Paul M.), Wines, Liquors, &c., 159 and 161 W. 3d
Mohring Henry, cooper, 179 Baymiller
Mohrhaus Bernard, grocery, 540 Plum
Mohrmeier Margaret w.s. Goose al. b. Liberty and 15th [Walnut
Mohrstadt Adolph, copper smith, 486
Moinning Frank, tailor, 116 Betts
Moise Chas., b.k., 159 Dayton
Mokler Charles, waiter, Gibson House
Mokler Michael, lab., 110 Avery
Molan Jonathan, lab., s.s. 6th b. Broadway and Culvert
Molars Elizabeth, servt., 163 E. 3d
Molengraff George, lab., wks. 196 W Pearl
Molenhoff Frederick, clk., bds. s.w.c. Race and 3d
Molenkamp Barney, lab., 435 W. 2d
Molier Dr. D., bds. Indiana House
Molique Frank Joseph, blksmith, 45 Wood
Molique John, cof. h., 13 Freeman
Moliquer Bernard, tailor, 26 Hamer
Molitohn Christopher, lab, 2d 13th
Molitor Casper, salesman, 228 Main
Molitor Martin, paper carrier, 64 W. Mulberry
MOLITOR STEPHEN,
Proprietor Volksblatt, Office Court House Building, h. Vine Street Hill
Molk Christian, (Hengler & M.), 58 15th
Mollally Mary, w.ss Langdon al. b. 6th and 7th
Moller Anthony T., lab., 137 Pleasant
Moller Franklin, carp., 11 Adams
Moller Joseph, dry goods, 101 Woodward
Mollers Theodore, finisher, wks. n.w.c. Race and Burrows
Mollott Andrew, lab., n.s. Kemper'sLane b. High and E. Front
Mollott Marshall A., dr'y, 1254 E. Front
Molloy Betsey, b h 318 W. 5th
Molloy Dennis. lab, 136 W. Front
Molloy Frank, shoe mkr., 179 Cutter
Molloy Hugh. lab., 71 E. Front
Molloy John, blksmith., M. & C. R. R., n.e.c. 3d and Butler
Molloy John carp., w.s. Cutter b. Wade and David
Molloy John, lab., 90 W. 2d
Molloy John B , policeman, 56 Avery
Molloy Michael, carp., 168 Cutter
Molloy Patrick. blksmith, wks. Looker, Purcell & Co's.
Molloy Thos. blksmith, 32 Lock
Molloy Timothy, shoemkr., 179 Cutter
Moloney James, mach., 44 Central Av
Moloney Patrick, mach., 44 Central Av
Moloney Patrick. molder, 197 E. 6th
Molony John, lab., w.s. Stone al. b. 6th and Longworth
Molony Patrick, lab., w.s. Stone al. b. Longworth and 6th
Moly John H., carp , 71 E. Front
Molster Cornelius, n.e.c. Front and Whittaker

Molter Charles, saddler, bds. 333 Walnut
Moltz John, blksmith, wks. n.e.c. Walnut and Canal
Molwes Frederick J., molder, 16 Madison
Moly Bridget, 554 Sycamore
Momberg Henry, w.s. Vine b. Milk and Mulberry
Mom erg Justus, shoemkr., 562 Race
Momberg Lewis. wks. 8 W. 6th
Momburg Minnie, bds. 2 Louisa
Momke Clements, tailor, s.w.c. 9th and Walnut
Monague Ellen, 48 Elm [miller
Moncke Francis, n.w.c. Liberty and Baymoncke Fred. H., n.w.c. Liberty and Baymiller.
Mondare Peter, turner, w.s. Freeman b. Clark and Hopkins
Mondary John, tailor, 141 Wade
Monday Joseph, cof. h., s.w.c. Dudley and Liberty
Mondeke Joseph, teamster, s.e.c. Hunt and Pendleton
Monderer Jacob, w.s. Riddle b. Bank and Harrison Pike
Mondowney Jeremiah, grocer, 314 W. 7th, h. 198 Webb
Mondt Ludwig, tailor, 56 13th
Mone Nicholas, grocery, 624 W. 6th
Monehen Wm., grocery, n.s. Pearl b. Smith and Park
Money Mary, 176 Webb
Money Patrick, lab., 61 Butler
Money Thomas, lab., 58 Gano
Money Thomas, poll s, 176 Webb
Monfort Alden, st. bt. capt , 322 W. 9th w. of Central Av
MONFORT Jos. G., (M. & Wampler), h. Glendale, O.
MONFORT & WAMPLER, (Joseph G. M. & Jno. M. W.), Editors and Proprietors of "The Presbyter," 25 W. 4th
Monfort Wm. P., 13 Gest
Monfort Wm. P. jr., printer, 13 Gest
Monger Terre...ce, lab , 193 Water
Mongey Peter, clk., 319 Main, bds. 13 Orchard
Monheimer Isaac, liquors, 67 Walnut, h. 324 Walnut
Monheimer Theresa, servt , 84 E. 3d
Monigan John, lab., 36 Elizabeth
Moning Lary, dray, 304 Plum
Moning George, s.w.c. Brighton and Harrison Pike
Monjar Peter, shoemkr., bds. 142 Linn
Monkadick August, chair mkr., wks s. e c. Hunt and Pendleton
Monkadick Theodore, chair m'r., s.e.c. Hunt and Pendleton
Monkedesk Mrs. Ellen, seamstress, 102 Abigail
Monkerheu Her, lab., w.s. Campbell al. b. Elder a 'ulley
Monkhof Elisa, 30 Jone.
Monnig & Artman, (Ferdinand M. & Frank A.), iron rolling maauf., n.w. c. Race and Burrows
Monnig & Bergfeld, (Fred. M. & Henry B.), flour store. 83 Spring
Monnig Ferdinand, (M. & Artman), s.s. Livingston b. Linn and Baymiller
Monnig Fred., (M. & Bergfeld), 81 Spring
Monnig George, cooper, bds. s.w.c. Harrison Pike and Brighton
Monnig Henry, blksmith, bds. 617 Elm
Monnig Kate, servt., 120 Broadway
Monohan Lawrence. dray, 86 Gest
Monongahela House, 12 E Front
Monroe Albert, carp., s.s. Goodloe b. Willow and Niagara
Monroe Alex, asst. b.k. Sellew & Co.'s
Monroe James, lab., 65 W. 7th
Monroe Mrs. Jane, tailoress, 125 Baymiller
Monroe Morton, lab., Broadway Hotel
Monroe Randolph, twister, 86 W Front
Monroe Sarah, 409 W. 5th
Monsalt P., lab., wks. n.s. Front b. Lawrence and Pike
Monsen Chas., clothing, bds. 98 E. 3d
Monson Chas. C., salesman Thos. N. Dale & Co's., 90 W. 3d
Monsta M , molder, wks. Chamberlain & Co's.

Monsters Bernard, blksmith, 70 Abigail
Montag Charles, grocer, w.s. Vine b. Milk and Mulberry
Montag Jacob, dray. 420 W 2d
Montag Nicholaus tailor, 34 Hamer
Montag Peter, peddler, 62 Ham. Road
Montagni r Clementia, 100 John
Montagnier Frank G., salesman, 100 John
Montagnier Julius, 100 John
Montagnier Louise, teacher, 100 John
Montagnier Theodore, 100 John
Montague Mrs. C., bds. 183 Race
Montague Thos., bds. 125 W. 5th
Montague Wm., b.k., bds. 125 W. 5th
Montaldo Ignacio, French and Spanish teacher, 293 W. 4th
Monter Geo Henry, pressman, 26 Baum
Monter Henry, printer, 26 Baum
Montgomery Mrs. Almira, e.s Cutter b. Betts and Clinton
Montgomery Amanda, bds. 103 George
Montgomery Andrew, salesman, 30 W. 4th. h. 483 Elm
Montgomery Ann, e.s. Sycamore b. 7th and 8th
Montgomery Geo., ticket seller National Theater
Montgomery Geo., b.k., 34 W. 3d, h. Covington
Montgomery Henry J., auctioneer, 73 W. Pearl, h. 227 Baymiller
Montgomery J Curt, liquors &c., 284 Main, bds. 141 Longworth
Montgomery James, clk., 485 Elm
Montgomery James, saloon, 84 Sycamore
Montgomery James H., collar mkr., n.s. 5th b Race and Elm
Montgomery John, clk., bds. 174 Plum
Montgomery John, finisher, bds. 252 Walnut
Montgomery John, pipe fitter, wks. n.e. c. Walnut and Canal
Montgomery John, salesman, 174 W. 5th, bds. 174 Plum
Montgomery Margaret, 485 Elm
Montgomery Robert, brewer, bds. August a b. Smith and John
Montgomery Robert, clk., 73 W. Pearl, h. Covington
Montgomery Samuel J , mer., 13 Linn
Montgomery Wm., 141 Longworth
Montgomery Wm. clk., 485 Elm
Montgomery Wm., policeman, 99 Richmond
Montgomery Wm., salesman, n.e.c. 5th and Vine
Montgomery Wm. H., clk., 485 Elm
Montgomery Wm. clk., bds. 174 Plum
Mooar Daniel W., b.k., bds. w.s. Baymiller s. of Hopkins
Mooar Lavinia W., teacher, bds 49 Mansfield
Mooar Mark (Conkling, Young & Co.,) 49 Mausfield
Moodis Mary, 89 Martin
Moody Charles W., clk., 110 W. 3d, h. Newport, Ky
Moody Geo. A., clk., 110 W. 3d, h. Newport. Ky
Moody Rev. Granville, 28 Perry
Moody Jos. S., salesman, 51 W. Pearl, h. Selves' bldg
Moody Wm., clk., 85 Wade
Mook Jeannette, s.w.c. Central Av. and Everett
Mook Levi, tailor, 256 Walnut
Mook Peter, carver, 20 Cutter
Mook Sam'l, trader, 661 Central Av
Moonert Andrew, tinner, 152 Longworth
Moonert Augustus, tinner. 426 George
Mooney Andrew. lab., s.s. Friendship al. b. Pike and Butler
Mooney Andrew S., carp., 64 Mill
Mooney Christopher, saddler, 245 W 6th
Mooney James, saddler, 245 W. 6th
Mooney John, 445 W. 3d
Mooney John, lab., n.s. Fremont b. Harriet and Mill Creek
MOONEY JOHN B.,
Steam Engine Builder & Hoisting Apparatus Manufacturer, 116 W. 2d, h. 103 Baymiller
Mooney Mary, servt., 399 George

240 (MOO) CINCINNATI (MOO) DIRECTORY. (MOO)

Mooney Pat., lab., 189 E. Pearl
Mooney Thomas, lab , 37 Smith
Mooney Thomas. lab.. 58 Gano
Mooney Wm , cof. h , 136 W. 3d
Mooney Wm., tanner, 245 W. 6th
Moor Mrs. Ann, laundress, s.s. al. b Clay and Main and Canal and 12th
Moor August, 116 13th
Moor Frank, baker, bds. 320 W. 6th
Moor Hy., tanner, s.s. 6th b. Harriet and Horne
Moor Hugh, tinner, 409 John
Moor Jacob, mach , 233 Betts
Moor James, 204 Livingston
Moor John, carp., 169 Pleasant
Moor Levi, 95 St. Clair
Moor Peter, cooper, s w.c. Vine and Findlay
Moor Wm , finisher, 180 Elm
Moor Wm. S., salesman, n.w.c. 9th and Linn
Moorbrink Barney, tailor, near Catholic Church. Mt Adams
Moorbrink George, tailor, 35 Observatory
Moore Alabamus L., clk., bds. 1212 E. Front
Moore Albert, pressman, Times office. bds. Mt. Adams
Moore Albert, steward, 68 E. Front
Moore Albert C., show card writer, 65 W. 4th, h. 78 Gest
Moore & Albrecht (John C. M. & Frank C. A) carriage manuf., 64 E. Front, and 121 E. 2d, warerooms 106 E. 2d
Moore Alexander. distiller, 62 Butler
MOORE AMOS, Publisher, "Free Nation." 247 W. 5th, and Book Store, 436 W. 5th
Moore Amos, tannery, Providence b. Oliver and Findlay, h. 92 14th b. Elm and Plum
Moore Anna, servt , n.w.c. 3d and Kilgour
Moore Arthur G., supt., 124 W. 9th,
Moore Augustus, clk., n.s. Front b. Lawrence and Pike, h Avondale
Moore Cadwallader C., atty., 379 Main, h. 400 John
Moore Caroline, h. 54 E. 7th
Moore Caroline. 435 George
Moore Catharine. b 14. 122 Central Av
MOORE Chas. L. (Chas. L. M. & Co.), h. Covington, Ky
MOORE CHAS L. & CO (Chas. L. M. & Wm. A. Applegate) Wholesale Grocers and Commission Merchants. 28 and 30 Main
Moore Chas. W., b.k., bds. 504 Freeman
MOORE CORNELIUS, Editor of Masonic Review, 117 Walnut, h. 504 Freeman
Moore Danl., blksmith, 31 E. 7th
Moore David, lab., bds. n.e.c. 3d and Butler
Moore Edward, 38 Providence
Moore Edward D., salesman; Hunter, Edmeston & Co.'s, h. Fairmount
Moore Edward L. printer, 25 W. 4th, h. 331 Longworth
Moore Ellis, house mover, 104 E. Liberty
Moore Eliza, 331 Longworth
Moore Elizabeth, 104 Sycamore
Moore Emily, 157 Central Av [Av
Moore Frances, 491 W. 9th w. of Central
Moore Francis M., architect, 365 W. Front, h. n. s. Livingston b. Baymiller and Freeman
Moore Frederick R.,b,k . bds. 274 Longworth
Moore George, dray. 105 Vanhorn
Moore George, grocery, 341 W. 8th
Moore George, peddler, 327 W. 2d
Moore Geo A. (G. A. M. & Co.) h. 87 Pendleton
Moore G. A. & Co. (G. A. M. & H. Tumler) feed mill, 324 Broadway
Moore Geo. B, currier, 551 Central Av
Moore Hamilton, draughtsman, bds. 274 Longworth
Moore Miss Harriet, dress mkr, bds. 200 W. Front
Moore Hy., clk., n.e.c. Richmond and Cutter
Moore Hy., painter, wks. Crane, Breed & Co's

Moore Hy. B., b k., 117 Walnut
Moore Hugh, iron roofing, h. Mt. Adams
Moore Isaac, printer, 14 Charles
Moore Isaac, teamster, 172 W. Front
Moore Isaac V. D., carp., 134 Smith
Moore J. P., bds. Dennison House
Moore J. & P (John & Peter) blksmiths, 78 Race
Moore J. S., printer, 32 Smith
Moore Jackson M. (M & Ray) 36 Br'dway
Moore Jacob, turner, 233 Betts
Moore James, 327 W. 2d
Moore James, clk , 27 E. Front
Moore James, dray, 178 Broadway
Moore James, jeweler, bds. 327 W. 2d
Moore James, lab.. wks. Crane, Breed & Co's
Moore James, lab., 100 W. Court
Moore James, lab., s.w.c. Freeman and Richmond
Moore James, mach., bds. 327 W. 2d
Moore James salesman, s.s. 3d b. Canal and Kilgour
Moore James C., mate, n.s. E. Front e. of Vance
Moore James M., painter , 364 Central Av., h. 275 W. Court w. of Central Av
Moore James W., lab., s.s. 6th b. Broadway and Culver
Moore Mrs. Jane. 302 W. 8th
Moore Jefferson L., cigar mkr. 490 John
Moore Jared S., printer 132 Smith
Moore Jeremiah, carp. 312 Van Horn
Moore Joanna, 207 Everett
Moore John, blksmith, 103 W. Front
Moore John, blksmith, 125 W. Front
Moore John, blksmith, 139 Mound
Moore John, clk., 8 Pub. Landing, h. 173 Laurel
Moore John (J. & P. M.) 78 Race
Moore John, lab., wks Heatt & Wood's
Moore John, molder, wks. 222 E. Front
Moore John, asst. surgeon, U. S. A., bds. Burnet House
Moore John, teamster, wks. central saw mill. 17th ward
Moore John C. (M. & Albrecht) bds. John S Carouther's
Moore John D., tanner, 92 14th
Moore John, boots and shoes, 245 Central Av
Moore John H , clk., 173 Laurel
Moore John T., carp., 1198 E. Front
Moore Joseph, carriage painter. w.s. Broadway b. Franklin and Woodward
Moore Joseph, tailor, s.e.c. Logan and Liberty
Moore Julia Ann, 32 Providence
Moore Julia A., bds. 363 Race
Moore Kenney, carp., 20 W. Court w. of Central Av.
Moore Margaret, s.w.c. 3d and Central Av.
Moore Margaret, 290 W. 8th
Moore Margaret, servt , wks. 61 Cutter
Moore Martha, 270 Hopkins
Moore Martha, s e c. Plum and 2d
Moore Mary A., 210 W. 7th
Moore Matthew, blksmith, bds, 212 W. Court
Moore Michael, blksmith, 171 W. Front
Moore Michael, carriage mkr , 212 W. Court
Moore Nancy J., 1158 and 1160 E. Front
Moore Nathaniel, cook, 50 E. 2d
Moore Nettie, bds. 51 Stone st. b. 5th and 6th
Moore Nicholas, lab., h. 142 Spring
Moore Oliver, cigar mkr, bds 69 W. 6th
MOORE OSCAR F., Freight Agent, Indianapolis and Cincinnati Railroad. s.s. Front near Wood, h. 399 W. 4th
Moore Patrick, dray, 23 Lock n, of 8th
Moore Patrick, lab., 402 W. 7th
Moore Patrick, porter, h. 402 W. 7th
MOORE PERRY J., Plumber and Gas Fitter, 221 W. 5th, h. 333 Longworth
Moore Peter, cooper, n.s.c. Vine and Findlay
Moore Peter (J & P. M.), 58 W. Court w. of Central Av

Moore Peter, shoemkr, 62 Hopkins
Moore R. H., phys., 74 W. 8th
Moore Rachael, 18 Richmond b. Elm and Plum
Moore & Ray (Jackson M. M. & Samuel R) barbers, 36 Broadway
Moore Richard, blksmith, 78 Race, h. 25 Kossuth
Moore Richard, harness mkr., s.w.c. 5th and Broadway
Moore Richard. tailor, 57 Kossuth
MOORE RICHARD B., Measurer of Stone, Brick and Plastering Work, 263 Plum, h. 173 Laurel
MOORE & RICHARDSON (Robert M. & John G. R.), Locomotive and Marine Engine Builders, n.s. Front b. Lawrence and Pike
Moore Robert, 409 John
Moore Robert, atty., 22 W. Court, b. Green tp.
Moore Robert. bk. layer, s.s. Dayton b. Coleman and Western Av
Moore Robert, bk. molder, 179 W. Court w. of Central Av.
MOORE Robert, (M. & Richardson) 274 Longworth
Moore Robert, molder, wks. Niles works
MOORE Robert, (Robert M. & Co.) h. College Hill
Moore Robert. tailor, 90 W. 2d
MOORE ROBERT & CO.. (Robert M. & Matthew Allen) Produce and Commission Merchants and Dealers in Cotton, Pig and Bloom Iron, 49 Walnut
Moore Rosa, 57 Pendleton
Moore Sarah, 77 George
Moore Sarah, 397 George
Moore Sarah, 228 Laurel
Moore Sarah, 4 Providence
Moore Tarlton G., express driver, s.w.c. Vine and Front
Moore Thomas, h. 38 Providence
Moore Thos., heater, bds. s.e.c. Smith and Front
Moore Thos., peddler. 40 Mill
Moore Thos. E., finisher, 114 E. 3d e. of Whittaker
Moore Thos. H., salesman 67 W. Pearl, h 240 George
Moore Thos. S , salesman 109 W. Pearl. h. 98 Longworth
Moore Thos W., blksmith, 99 Providence
Moore Timothy, 209 W. 4th
Moore Wilhemina, bds. 398 W. 7th
Moore Wm., n.w.c. Linn and 9th
Moore Wm., 122 Laurel
Moore Wm., b.k., 409 John
Moore Wm., bk. mason, 944 E. Front
Moore Wm., clk., 534 Vine
Moore Wm., eng., 49 E. 2d, h. Mt. Adams
Moore Wm., pattern mkr., wks. Adams, Peckover & Co.'s
Moore Wm., photographer, 63 Lodge
Moore Wm. E., printer, 331 Longworth
Moore Wm. F. A., b.k. 140 W. Front, h. 61 Gest
Moore Wm. G , clk. 303 Central Av., bds. 47 Chestnut
Moore Wm. H., b.k. 28 Main, h. 265 W. 4th
Moore Wm. H., clk., 245 Central Av.
Moore Wm. H., grocery, 1212 E. Front
MOORE Wm. H., (Moore, Wilstach, Keys & Co.) h. Walnut Hills
Moore Wm. H., plasterer. 215 Wade
MOORE, WILSTACH, KEYS & CO., (Wm. H. M.. Chas. F. W., Saml. B. K. & Frank H. Baldwin) Publishers, Booksellers and Stationers, 25 W. 4th
Moorehead Edward, driver, 313 W. 9th w. of Central Av.
Moorehead Edward, molder, 313 w. 9th w of Central Av.
Moorehead John P., currier, 35 Baymiller Av
Moorehead Samuel, molder, 117 Van Horne
Moorehead Samuel, pattern mkr. 117 Van Horne
Moorehead Wm., currier, 117 Van Horne
Mooren Owen, porter, Clifton House

(MOR) CINCINNATI (MOR) DIRECTORY. (MOR) 241

MOORES & CO., (Wm. B. M., James C. Moores & Robert B. Moores) Saddles, Harness and Trunk Manufacturers. 89 Main
Moores Emanuel M., clk. 12 E. Pearl, h. 464 John
MOORES James C., (Moores & Co.) h. Avondale
Moores John A., saddler, 480 W. 9th w. of Central Av.
Moores John B. C., 265 Plum, res. Glendale
MOORES Robert B, (Moores & Co.) h. Glendale
MOORES WM. B., Lime. Cement, Plaster Paris, &c., 265 Plum, res. Glendale
Moorhern Hy., molder, 18 Woodward
Moorhead Josiah, molder, 230 W. Court w. of Central Av.
Moorhead Peter, finisher, wks. n.w.c. Plum and Wade
Mooring Herman, porter. 684 Main
Moorman Barney J., boots and shoes, 39 E. 7th
MOORMAN FRANK, Furniture Manufacturer and Dealer, 437 Main
Moorman Hy., chair factory, 214 Cutter
Moorman Joseph E., 269 Cutter
Moorman Benj., 14 Orchard
Moormann A. Gerhard, grocery, 97 Buckeye
Moormann Bernhard H., dry goods, 496 Main
Moormann Ferdinand H., grocery, 258 W. 5th
Moormann Fred., umbrella mender, 376 Broadway
Moormann H. & Co., (Hy. M. & Wm. Tangemann) cigar manufs., 617 Main
Moormann Hy., (H M. & Co.) 617 Main
Moormann J. Benj., jr., pressman, 14 Orchard
Moormann John J., boots and shoes. 351 W. 6th
Moormann Joseph, boots and shoes, 596 Main
Moormann Louis, (Kohus & M.) 84 Broadway
Moormann Barney, driver, h. 162 E. 5th
Moors Hy. T., carp., 237 John
Moorwood John, pipeman, 219 W. George
Moorwood Thos., lab., 219 George
Moose Solomon, clk., 321 W. 8th
Moralli John, confec., s.w.c. 9th and Elm
Moran Ann, 59 E. 8th e. of Lock
Moran Bernard, lab., 660 E. Front
Moran Bridget, chambermaid, Spencer House
Moran Cornelius, lab., e.s. Oregon b. 3d and 6th
Moran Ellen, cof. h., 212 E. 6th
Moran Ellen, chambermaid, Spencer House
Moran James, stone mason, 209 W. 7th
Moran John, carp., 174 Cutter
Moran John, driver, 519 W. 8th
Moran John, lab., w.s. Langdon al. b. 6th and 7th
Moran John, marble cutter, 48 W. Court w. of Central Av.
Moran John, millwright, 174 Cutter
Moran Kate, w.s. Langdon al. b. 6th and 7th
Moran Lawrence, lab., Burnet House
Moran Margaret, 20 Lock n. of 6th
Moran Michael, lab., w.s. Sycamore b. Hunt and Abigail
Moran Michael, lab., 429 W 2d
Moran Michael, lab., w.s. Langdon al. b. 6th and 7th
Moran Neil, dray, 225 Barr
Moran Patrick, lab., 658 E. Front
Moran Richard, horse trader, 99 Gest
Moran Thos., lab., n.s. Pearl b. Smith and Park
Moran Thos., policeman, 305 W. 2d
Moran Thos. B., meats, 187 W. 5th, h. 155 Central Av.
Moran Thos. J., janitor, 116 Webb
Moran Wm., lab., 90 W. 2d
Moran Wm., porter 93 W. Pearl, h. 90 W. 2d

Moran Wm., trader, 37 Rittenhouse
Moran Thos., trader, 19 W. Court w. of Central Av.
Morath Herman, lock mkr., wks. s.w.c. Elm and Front
Morath John J., clk., w.s. Walnut b. Allison and Mercer
More Richard, foreman, e.s. Harriet b. Budd and 8th
Morehead J. E., teller, 51 W. 3d, h. Clifton
Morehead Peter, molder, 14 Lock n. of 8th
Morehead Robt., peddler, 276 John
Morehouse John M., clk., 198 George
Morehouse Mary, variety store, n.e.c. 6th and Broadway
Morehouse Wm., mer., 198 George
Moreland Agustine, 345 W. 8th
Morgan David, n.s. Corporation al. b. Price and Young
Morgan David D., molder. 28 Elizabeth
Morgan Edward H., n s. Corporation al. b. Young and Price
Morgan Elizabeth, seamstress, e.s. Johnson al. b. Canal and 12th
Morgan Ephraim, printer, s.w.c. Bedinger and Miami Canal, h. Storrs Tp.
Morgan Evan, carp., 537 Freeman
Morgan Evan, molder, foot of Harrison
Morgan Fannie, 55 George
Morgan Francis H , foreman, 77 Walnut
Morgan Frank M., lab., s.s. Elizabeth b. Central Av. and John
Morgan Geo. E., 59 Gest
Morgan & Gunning, (Thos. M. & Danl. G.) boots and shoes, n.w.c. Main and 7th
Morgan Howell, boiler, bds. s.e.c. 2d and Smith
Morgan Hugh, lumber. s.w.c. Smith and W. W. Canal, h. 337 W. 3d
Morgan Isaac M., clk. Adams Express Co., bds. 397 Race
Morgan Jas., wks. J. Whittaker's, Deer Creek Valley
Morgan Jas., lab., 28 Accommodation
Morgan Jas., stone cutter, 543 Race
Morgan Jas. A., bk. binder, 43 Main
Morgan Jas. & Co., slaughter house, n. e.c. Harriet and Richmond
Morgan Jas. T., 264 W. Court w. of Central Av.
Morgan Jerry S., driver, 209 W. 3d
Morgan John, blksmith, 5 Central Av.
Morgan John, boiler, bds. s.e.c. 2d and Smith
Morgan John, molder, bds. 28 Elizabeth
Morgan John, shoe mkr., 621 Central Av.
Morgan John F , plasterer, 258 Clinton
Morgan John W., 77 Hopkins
Morgan Margaret, n.e.c. 5th and North
Morgan Margaret, servt., 141 Linn
Morgan Mary, servt., 108 Broadway
Morgan Mury E., bds. 382 Race
Morgan Patrick, blksmith, 37 Central Av.
Morgan Patrick, lab., 172 Cutter
Morgan Rice, cab. mkr , 38 Barr
Morgan Robert, (Johson, Stephens & M.) h. Newport
Morgan Samuel, printer, 60 E. 4th
Morgan Samuel W., steward, 109 E. 3d
Morgan Sarah, 27 Gano
Morgan Sarah, dry goods. 537 Freeman
Morgan Thos., boat mkr., n.s. 6th b. Broadway and Sycamore
MORGAN THOMAS, Lumber Yard, s.e.c. 12th and Plum, bds. 77 Hopkins
Morgan Thos., (M. & Gunning) 55 E. 8th
Morgan Thos. F., jr., plumber, wks. 230 Main
Morgan Watkin, 464 W. Front
Morgan Wilby, pipeman, s.s. E. Front e. of Vance
Morgan Wm., carp., 1208 E. Front
Morgan Wm., carp., e.s. Bank al. b. 3d and 4th, h. Covington
Morgan Wm., wagon mkr., bds. 49 Race
Morgan Wm. C., 244 Betts
Morgan Wm. C., clk., 256 W. 4th
Morgan Wm H., teacher, n.s. Poplar b. Freeman and Western Av

Morgan Willoughby C., carp., s.s. Front E. of Ferry
Morgenroth Falk,, peddler, 607 Race
Morgenstein Chas., blksmith, 102 Bremen
Morgenthaller Catharine, 463 Elm
Morgenthaller Jacob, waiter Madison House
MORGENTHAU H. & L., (Hy. and Louis) Importers and Dealers in Brandies, Wines and Cigars, 74 Main
MORGENTHAU Hy., (H. & L. M.) 119 W. Court
MORGENTHAU Louis, (H. & L. M) 119 W. Court
Morgenthau Saml., clk. 74 Main, h. 163 W. Court
Morgenthau Saml., clothing, 127 E 5th
Morgraf Louis, tailor, 193 Carr
Morgua Jacob. bds. Clifton House
Moriarty Mary, e.s. Crippen al. b, 7th and 8th
Moriarty Michael. clk., 86 Milton
Moriarty Wm. W., lab. 401 Central Av
Morin Ann, 591 W. 6th
Morin Matthew, scale mkr. 8 W. 2d, h. 187 Water
Morin Michael, porter, 124 W. 2d
Morlo Catharine, w.s. Long al. b. Woodward and Franklin
Moritz August, cattle dealer, 66 13th
Moritz, Bro. & Co., (Mayer M., Sol. M. & A. Nathan), clothiers, 26 W. Pearl
Moritz Emanuel, drover, 549 Vine
Moritz Godfrey, lab., 10 Commerce
Moritz Mayer, (M. Bro. & Co.) 14 Arch
Moritz Sol., (M. Bro. & Co.) h. Indianapolis
Mork David, clothier. 297, Elm
Mork Jacob, clothier, 297 Elm
Mork Moses S., b. k. 68 W. Pearl. bds. 21 and 23 E. Pearl
Morland Stephen, lab., Pennock al. b. Mound and Cutter
Morley Wm., dray, 99 Gest
Morman Benj., tailor, 612 W. 8th
Morman Fred., lab., 404 Longworth
Morman Geo., tailor, bds., 124 Carr
Morman Hy., teamster, wks. n. s. Miami Canal W. of Elm
Morman John, tailor, 612 W. 8th
Morman Hermann, 114 Butler
Morman Theodore, finisher, 417 W. 3d
Morn John, lab c. Park and Marsh
Morn Thos., lab., wks. 375 W. 3d
Mornan Herman, fireman, e.s. Park b. 2d and W. W. Canal
Morne John, lab., 130 Water
Morningstar Eugene. wks. Cin. Type Foundry
Morningstar Gottlieb, finisher, 50 Plum
Morningstar John, pipe fitter, wks. n.e. c. Walnut and Canal [8th
Moroney John, s.s. Accomodation e. of
Moroney Patrick, dray, s.s. Accomodation e. of 8th
Morr John, lab, n.w.c. 3d and Collard
Morran Hugh, grocery, s.w.c, 3d and Mill
Morrell August, brewer, 395 Sycamore
Morrell Nahum, b.k., bds. s.w.c. Franklin and Broadway
Morrenn August, brewer, n.s. Mulberry b. Main and Sycamore
Morritz Kate, sert., Henrie House
Morrill Hy.. A., teacher, bds. 310 Elm
Morrin Michael, lab., 187 Water
Morris Anson R., 306 W. 3d
Morris Benj., hatter, 149 Main
Morris Rev. Benj. F., 367 John
Morris C. N. & Co., (Chas. N. M. & Hy Brachmann), printers, 79 W. 3d
Morris & Chalfant, (W. G M & F. P. C.), tobacco mers., 46 W. Front
Morris Chas. N., (C. N. M. & Co.) 257 Longworth
Morris Cornelius, dray, 57 Woodward
Morris Dorothea, 8 W. Mulberry
MORRIS Edward C. (Holenshade, M. & Co.), 547 W. 8th
Morris Elizabeth, bds. 131 W. 5th
Morris Emeline, bds., 150 Baymiller
Morris Frances, tailoress, bds 148 Van Horne

23

242 (MOR) CINCINNATI (MOR) DIRECTORY. (MOS)

Morris Francis H., cof. h., 192 Sycamore
Morris Frank., boots and shoes, 14 W 5th h. 371 John
Morris Geo. A., librarian Y, M. M. L. A. h. 371 John
Morris Gottfried, blksmith, 532 Sycamore
Morris Hy., grainer, bds. Observatory st. Mt. Adams
MORRIS HENRY H.,
Justice of the Peace n.s Nassau b. Reed and Broad, 17th Ward
Morris Herman, lab, 404 Longworth
Morris Isaac H. carp., 163 Linn
Morris J., clk. 101 W. 4th, h. 264 Race
Morris J. B., jeweler. 175 Mound
Morris James, barber, w.s. Ramsey n. of Front
Morris James, driver, 21 Hannibal
Morris John, 228 W. 3d
Morris John, clk., bds. 264 Race
Morris John, lab., 550 W. 3d
Morris John B., jewelry &c., s.e.c. 2d and Sycamore, h. 173 Mound
Morris John C., bk. layer, 113 Mill
Morris John M., 277 Richmond
Morris John M., blksmith, bds. Pennsylvania Hotel
Morris John M., blksmith, s.e.c. Front and Pike
Morris Joseph, clk., 31 E. Pearl, h. 84 Barr
Morris Levi, carp., bds. 3 E. 3d e. of Parsons
Morris Maggie, 349 W. 5th
Morris Mary, servt., 13 Linn
Morris Mary, laundress, 148 Vanhorne
Morris Mary, C., bds. 115 Mill
Morris Mary J., dress mkr., 228 W. 3d
MORRIS NICHOLAS,
Confectionery, 264 Race
Morris Patrick, expressman, 48 Plum
Morris Peter, 77 George
Morris & Reith, (Thos. M. & Francis R) file manufs. 185 Central Av
Morris Rob. T., printer. 228 W 3d
Morris Saml., confec., 197 Central Av. h 306 W. 5th
Morris Saml., lab., 24 Commerce
Morris Thos., (M. & Reith), 177 Longworth
Morris Thos., painter, 44 Campbell al.
Morris Timothy, eng., 207 W. Front
Morris Wm., grainer, bds, Observatory st Mt. Adams
Morris Wm., lab., s.s. 6th b. Broadway and Culvert
Morris Wm., painter, 130 Sycamore
Morris Wm. C., (M. & Chalfant) h. Newport
Morris Wm. H., blksmith, wks. s.e.c. Water and Smith
Morris Wm. H., painter, Observatory st. Mt. Adams
Morrisey Bridget, servt., 155 John
Morrisey D., bds., Black Bear Hotel
Morrisey John. stone mason, Observatory st. Mt. Adams
Morrissey Ellen, chambermaid, Spencer House
Morrissey Patrick, lab, 187 W. Canal
Morrissey Wm., lab., wks. 830 Central Av.
Morrison Charles, 244 Broadway
Morrison Chas., e.s. Sycamore b 7th and 8th
MORRISON CORDUKES & CO. (James M., Thos. C. & John Morrison,) Pork Packers, 16 and 18 E. Canal
MORRISON & CROWTHER (Joseph M. and George H C.) Silverplaters and Engravers, 65 W. 4th
Morrison D. W, b.k. Cin. Gazette Co h. 30 Gest
Morrison Edwin L., clk. L. M. R. R., res Mt. Washington
Morrison Geo. E. B., conductor, bds. 484 W. 8th
MORRISON & HEWES, (Wm. M. & Orrin H.) Boots and Shoes, 212 W. 5th
MORRISON James, (M. Cordukes & Co) b. Clifton
Morrison James D., wagon mkr., 84 Betts

MORRISON James C., (Peter Neff & Sons.) 264 W. 9th
Morrison John, lab., bds. 11 Pub. Landing b Main and Walnut
MORRISON John, (Morrison, Cordukes & Co.) 350 Race
Morrison Joseph, shoe mkr. 483 Race
MORRISON Joseph. (M. & Crowther) 210 Findlay
Morrison Mary, E. 3d b. Parsons and Baum
Morrison Patrick, shoe mkr. 130 Mound
Morrison Rebecca, 483 Race
Morrison Robert, salesman, 30 Walnut h 212 Longworth
MORRISON Wm., (M. and Hewes,) h. 212 W. 5th
Morrison Wm., lab., 15 Water
Morrison Wm., paper carrier, 483 Race
Morrison Wm., porter, 146 W. Pearl
Morrison Wm., shoe mkr., 569 Sycamore
MORRISON Wm., (Wm. M. & Co.) 212 Longworth
MORRISON WM & CO., Wholesale Dealers in Foreign Fruits, Refined Sugar &c 30 Walnut
Morrison Wm. F., printer, 166 Central Av
Morrow Joseph H., auctioneer, 84 Barr
Morrow Robert, meats, 375 W. 6th
Morrow Louisa, h. 316 John
Morrow Saml., 207 Hopkins
Morrow Stephen C., 36 Main, h. 420 George
Morsch Hy., cof. h., 545 Elm
Morschell Geo., turner, 115 Clay
Morscher Geo., pro. Fireman's Hall, 65 W. 5th
Morse Agustus S., photographer, bds. 238 Race
Morse Edward (Lynn & M.) 34 Longworth
Morse Emanuel, (M. Bloom & Co.) 464 John
Morse Francis, w.s. Henderson al. b. 7th and 8th
Morse Nathan M., exchange office s.e.c. 3d and Race
Morse Royal, porter, 103 Park
MORSE STEPHEN, Prest. American Ins. Co., Office 12 Pub. Landing h. 377 W. 8th
Morse Theodore, saddler, 190 John
Morten Aaron G. G., clk., bds. 221 Mound
Morten Albert, saddler, h. 283 Longworth
Morten & Brother, (Hy. & Edward W.) underwriters, warehouse, 78 W. Front
Morten Edward W., (M. & Bro.) 134 Betts
Morten Hy., Prest. Central Ins. Co. 283 Longworth
Morten James L., produce mer., 78 W. Front, h. Walnut Hills
Morten Wm. C., clk., 221 Mound
Morthorst Bernard H., lab., 18 Mansfield
Mortimer John M., carp., 23 David
Mortimer Joseph, grocer, 318 E. Pearl
Mortimer Philip, cab. mkr., 114 Clinton
Mortimer Wm., blksmith, 53 Observatory Road
Mortlock Wm., baker Burnet House
Morton Aaron G. G., salesman, 3 W. Pearl, bds. 219 Mound
Morton Agnes, bds. 32 Harrison
Morton Charles S., salesman, 3 W. Pearl bds. 219 Mound
MORTON Daniel H., (Johnson M. & Co.) h. Walnut Hills
Morton Edward W., com. mer., 134 Betts
MORTON J. R. & CO., (John R. M., & Calvin W Thomas) Bankers, 29 W. 3d
Morton J. W., bds. Dennison House
Morton James, cook, 180 Clay
Morton James W., artificial leg mkr., 392 W. 3d
MORTON John R., (J. R. M. & Co.,) 264 Vine
Morten Joseph, clk., 56 Rittenhouse
Morton Joseph A. G., clk., bds. 1363 E. Front

Morton Joseph, lab., 1260 E. Front
Morton Joseph B., clk. 29 W. 3d, h. 264 Vine
Morton Miles, foreman, bds. 1383 E. Front
Morton Munroe, lab., 178 Water
Morton Nathan R., saw mill, 1379 E. Front, h. 1363 E. Front
Morton Sarah, rear 328 Linn
Morton Wellington L., policeman, 159 Linn
Morton Wm. C., salesman, 3 W. Pearl, bds. 219 Mound
Mosby Ann, 606 W. 9th
Mosby James, tobacconist, 22 L'Hommedieu al.
Mosby Mrs. Jane, 51 New
Mosby Wm., mcr., bds. 606 W. 9th
Moschel Jacob, baker, 159 Bremen
Moseby James, twister 22 L'Hommedieu
Mosenmeier B., phys., 465 Elm
Moser Anna M., 15 Mary
MOSER Charles, (Hoffmann & M.,) 329 Walnut
MOSER FREDERICK, Family Grocery, 56 Elder
Moser, Hy., watch mkr., bds. 43 W. Court
Moser John. clk., 494 Sycamore
Moser Martin, tailor, 192 Clark
Moser Robert, lab., 129 W. Liberty
Moser Vincent, bakery, 64 Duckeye
Mosert Michael, lab., 708 Vine
Moses Aaron, tailor, s. e. c. 5th and Home
Moses Aaron, renovator, 205 Plum, h. 502 W. 5th
Moses & Co. (Simeon M.) exchange office, n.e c. 3d and Sycamore
Moses Edward, 51 Gest
Moses Edward J., agency office, s. e. c. 3d and Walnut, b. 59 Richmond
Moses Hyman, n.w.c. Walnut and 7th
Moses Isaac, peddler, 25 Lodge
Moses Jacob, 17 Lodge
Moses John, plasterer. 58 Water
Moses Leo, clk., 126 Main, h. 36 W. 7th
Moses Levi. peddler, 23 Harrison
Moses Morris, clk., bds. 59 Richmond
Moses Nathan, salesman, 126 Main, h. 186 Sycamore
Moses Phineas, broker, bds. s. w. c. 3d and Broadway
Moses Simeon, (M. & Co.) 59 Richmond
Moses Solomon, bds. 56 W. 7th
Moses Solomon, 200 Richmond
Moses Sol, clk., 126 Main, h. 36 W. 7th
Mosey Nelson, 136 E. 6th
Mosig & Hesterberg, (Julius M., & Hy. H.,) machs, 543 Vine
Mosig Julius, (M. & Hesterberg,) 14 Mary
Moskewts Benjamin, 82 W. Court
Mosler Gustavus, b. k., 269 Walnut
Mosier Hy., artist, 269 Walnut
Mosier Julius, cigar mkr., 269 Walnut
Mosler Max, (Max M., & Kupferle,) 269 Walnut
Mosler Max, & Kupferle, (Max Mosler & Geo. K.,) cigars, &c., 269 Walnut
Moss Abel, 56 Richmond
Moss Bernhardt H., stable, n.w.c. Linn and Clark
Moss Francis, 507 W. 3d
Moss " Frank " W., printer, 179 Broadway
Moss Fredrick, 475 Broadway
Moss Frederick, lab., 32 Mulberry
Moss Hy., clothing, 291 Main
Moss Hy., cof. h, 365 W. 5th
Moss Joseph, carp., s.e.c. Baymiller and Richmond
Moss Joseph Hy., feed store, 941 Central Av.
Moss Louisa, grocery, 1069 Central Av.
Moss Michael J., (Solomon M. & Co.) 174 Main
Moss' Samuel, finisher, 7 Pierson
Moss Tony, lab., rear 65 Woodward
Moss W. O., clk. O. & M. R. R. Office, h. 608 W. 9th
Moss Wm., wagon mkr., 34 Stone
Mosse Gustavus, bds. Dumas Hotel

Mossel Wm., shoe mkr., 58 Elder
Mosser ———, at National Theatre
MOSSER John, (Roth & M.) 18 Longworth
Mosser Nicholas, bar k., n.w.c. Vine and Longworth
Mossman Mrs. E., w.s. Sycamore b. Reeder and Mount
Mosta Hy., cab. mkr., 86 Clinton
Motsch Hy., foreman, 43 Jackson
Mott Alfred, carriage painter, 128 Hopkins
Mott E., clk., 413 Elm
Mott Frank, pyrotechnist, 540 E. Front
Mott Hy., lab., s.s. 6th b. Harriet and Horne
Mott Peter, brass molder, 7 E. 3d e. of Parsons
Mott Samuel, cooper, n.s. al. b. Canal and 19th and Vine and Race
Motz Fred, blksmith, wks. C. T. Dumont's
Motzer Wm., bar k., 187 Vine
Mougey Desire, blksmith, 13 Orchard
Mougey Peter, porter, 13 Orchard
Moul George, blksmith, 66 Pleasant
MOULINIER CHARLES P., Wholesale Grocer and Commission Merchant, 13 W Front, h. 34 Clark
Moulton Charles, coal dealer, 518 W. 5th h. Storrs Tp.
Moulton J. F., American Ex. Co., bds. Broadway Hotel
Moulton Jos. H., 69 Hopkins
Moulton Porter, coal yard, 518 W. 5th h. 511 W. 5th
Mountel Frank, driver, 60 Findlay
Mount Hy. S., barber, 6 E. 2d, h. 25 Macalister
Mount Joseph, driver, 79 Augusta
Mt. Adams Observatory, n.s. Siderial w. of Mitchell
Mountain Patrick, baker, 325 W. 9th w. of Central Av.
Mouse Geo., 184 W. Court
Mouse Joseph, lab., wks. 222 E. Front
Moussbon Geo., bds. Dumas Hotel
Mower George, wagon mkr., bds. 69 W. 6th
Mowes Frederick, molder, 16 Madison
Mowinkel Hy. A., shoe mkr., 5 Mary
MOWRY A. L. & CO.,
(Albert L. M. & Co.)
Bankers, n.e.c. 3d and Walnut
MOWRY Albert L., (A. L. M. & Co.,) car wheel and chilled tire manufacturers, s.e.c. Front and Lewis, h. 214 W. 4th
Moyer Geo., clk., bds. 174 Plum
Moyer Joseph, Sr., 138 W. 9th
Moyer Mary, n.e.c. Wade and Dudley
Moyer Peter, teamster, 107 Betts
Moylan John, lab., 453 W 2d
Moylan John, lab., Anderson al. b. 2d and Front
Moylan James, lab., bds. Congress St. House [amore
Mucker Barney, shoe mkr., bds. 10 Sycamore
Muckerheide O., mach., wks. n.s. Front b. Lawrence and Pike
Mudd Dr. Jerome, school 298 Elm
MUDGE H. B.,
Bedstead Manufacturer, 95 W. 2d, h. 130 W. 7th
Mudge Wm. C., clk., 95 W. 2d, h. 130 W. 7th
Muduska Joseph, finisher, bds. s.e.c. 2d and Plum
Muecke Caroline, 648 Vine
Mueggenburg Hy., shoe mkr., 20 Webster
Muehlhauser Juliana, bds. 549 Vine
Mueller A. Frederick, tailor, 26 Allison
Mueller Adam, dray, 62 Ham. Road
Mueller Adam, lab., 137 Ham. Road
Mueller Andrew, painter, 612 Vine
Mueller Anthony, sewing machines, 148 W. Liberty
Mueller August, bar k., s.s. Allison b. Walnut and Vine
Mueller August, bakery, 427 Central Av
Mueller August, silver plater, h. 104 13th
Mueller Balthazar, painter, s.s. Ohio al. b. Plum and Elm and 15th and Adams

Mueller Bernhard, grocery, 74 15th, h. e.s. Race b. 12th and 13th
Mueller Caroline, 57 15th
Mueller Caspar, brewer, wks. J. Kauffman & Co's.
Mueller Catharine, 46 Pleasant
Mueller Chas., 493 Race
Mueller Chas., carp., 26 15th
Mueller Chas., shoe mkr., 21 Woodward
Mueller Christiana, 64 Ham. Road
Mueller Christopher, shoe mkr., 538 Elm
Mueller Clemens, lab., 612 Vine
Mueller Conrad, tailor, 1 Mulberry
Mueller Constantine, cof. h., 539 Vine
Mueller Daniel, tailor, 56 Ham. Road
Mueller David, shoe mkr., 65 Buckeye
Mueller Edward, brewer, 55 Harrison Pike
Mueller Ernst, stereotype molder, 19 Buckeye
Mueller Eve, 58 Buckeye
MUELLER Ferdinand, (M. & Gogreve,) 79 Pike
Mueller Ferdinand, painter, 662 Race
Mueller Fidel, shoe mkr., 554 Vine
Mueller Francis J., tailor, 157 Bremen]
Mueller Frank, finisher, wks. n. e. c. Walnut and Canal
Mueller Franz, carp., 11 Adams
Mueller Franz, lab., rear 166 Clay
Mueller Frederick, carp., 501 Walnut
Mueller Frederick, dray, 553 Vine
Mueller Fred, driver, 60 Findlay
Mueller Frederick, gilder, 598 Elm
Mueller Frederick, grocery, s.s. Findlay, b. Bremen and Franz
Mueller Frederick, tailor, 21 Franklin
Mueller Frederick C., cigar mkr., bds. 64 Ham. Road
Mueller Frederick W., b k., 503 Race
Mueller Gabriel, lab., 195 Pleasant
Mueller George, 110 Mohawk
Mueller George, cof. h., 245 W. 6th
Mueller George, lab., s.s. Charlotte, b. Linn and Baymiller
Mueller George, peddler, 60 Buckeye Vine
MUELLER & GOGREVE, (Fred. M. & Christian H. G.,) Congress Brewery, s.w.c. Pike and Pearl
Mueller Helena, 20 Mercer
Mueller Henrietta, washwoman, 599 Sycamore
Mueller Hy., 649 Elm
Mueller Hy., baker. 523 Sycamore
Mueller Hermann F., tailor, 464 Main
Mueller Johanna, seamstress, 20 Mercer
Mueller Jacob, cof. h , 538 Race
Mueller Jacob, lab., 69 Buckeye
Mueller Jacob, mach., 123 W. Liberty
Mueller Jacob, musician, 78 W. Liberty
Mueller Jacob G., sawyer, 86 Bremen
Mueller Jacob H., cof. h., 518 Vine
Mueller John, bk. binder, 29 Elder
Mueller John, brewer, wks. J. Kauffman & Co 's
Mueller John, carp., bds. 550 Main
Mueller John, carver, 108 Everett
Mueller John, cooper, 64 Ham Road
Mueller John, locksmith, bds. 502 Walnut
Mueller John, painter. 697 Race
Mueller John, phys., 345 Vine
Mueller John, soap mkr., 543 Race
Mueller John, tanner, 557 Race
Mueller John C., cigar mkr., bds. 64 Ham. Road
Mueller John G., shoe mkr., 13 15th
Mueller John H., cof. h., 602 Walnut
MUELLER JOHN M., Stone Yard, s.e.c. Plum and Madison, h. 33 Madison
Mueller Joseph, bakery, 116 Ham. Road
Mueller Joseph, tailor, 200 Mound
Mueller Joseph, wagon mkr., 150 Ham. Road, h. 571 Race
Mueller Josepha, n.e.c. Race and 15th
Mueller Rev. Lewis, e.s. Race, b. W. Liberty and 15th
Mueller Lorenz, shoemkr., 61 Bittenhouse
Mueller Ludwig, (Greiner & M.,) 128 Walnut
Mueller Magdalena, n.e.c. Race and 15th
Mueller Martin, cook, 66 Ham. Road

Mueller Martin, lab., 50 Pleasant
Mueller Mary, 522 Main
Mueller Mary, 565 Vine
Mueller Mathias, 557 Vine
Mueller Matilda, teacher, 420 Sycamore
Mueller Michael, cigar mkr., 66 Buckeye
Mueller Nicholas, cof. h., 647 Central Av
Mueller Nicholas, lab., 60 Buckeye
Mueller Peter mason, 63 Buckeye
Mueller Peter, saddles, &c., 453 Vine
Mueller Phillip, lab., 98 Clay
Mueller Rudolph, lab., 47 Pleasant
Mueller S., clk., 140 Main, b. 493 Race
Mueller & Schimpf, (Wm. M. & Louis S.,) painters, 26 Logan
Mueller Sebastian, lab., 540 Plum
Mueller Theodore, cigar mkr., 142 Pleasant
Mueller Wilhelmine, 112 Pleasant
Mueller Wm., blksmith, 39 Moore
Mueller Wm., lab., 700 Race
Mueller Wm., lab., 446 Linn
Mueller Wm., (M. & Schimpf,) 12 Moore
Mueller Wm., painter, 12 Moore
Mueller Wm., shoemkr, 608 Elm
Mueller Wm., shoemkr, 105 Woodward
Mueller Wm. G., finisher, 526 Main
Mueller Wm. J. L., carpet mkr., 38 Pleasant
Mueller Xavier, cooper, 613 Race
Muellerhaus Wm., lab., 52 15th
Muellmann John, lab., 12 Hamer
Muench G. & Co., (Geo. M. & Chas. Bode,) coppersmiths, 644 Vine
Muench Geo., (G. M. & Co.,) 644 Vine
Muench John H., blksmith, 524 Main
Muench Philip A., tailor, 78 W. Liberty
Muenchen Peter, tailor, 9 Buckeye
Muennich Gerhard J., painter, 93 Pendleton
Muenstermann Frederick, brush mkr., rear 26 Franklin
Muenter John, lab., bds. 9 Franklin
Mues Frederick, tanner, 8 Dunlap
Mues Margaret, seamstress, 224 John
Muettman Miss Margaret, teacher, 432 Vine
Mugal Peter, cof. h., 790 Central Av
Mugenberg Hy., butcher, junction Walnut Hills and Reading Road
Muggenberg Joseph, tanner, 923 Central Av
Muggenburg Joseph, carp., s.w.c. Abigail and Spring
Muggenburg Ferdinand, cooper, bds. 109 Browne
Muggenburg Hy., driver, rear 58 Abigail
Muggenburg Hy., lab., wks. 14 and 16 Water
Muggeridge Mark, b.k., 154 E. Front, h. Newport, Ky.
Mugiven John, finisher, 225 E. 6th
Muhall Michael, clk., 207 Smith
Muhlberg Wm., drug store, n.w.c. Wade and Central Av
Muhle Bernard H., dry goods, 369 George
Muhlenkamp Dena, rear 379 Broadway
Muhlhauser Mrs. Christiana, grocer, 275 Ham. Road
MUHLHAUSER G. & H., (Gottlieb & Henry,) Mineral Water Manufacturers, and Proprietors Elm Street Flour Mill, 724 and 726 Elm
Muhlhauser Gottlieb, 275 Ham. Road
MUILHAUSER Gottlieb, (G. & H. M.) 726 Elm
Muhlhauser Gottlieb, lab., 725 Ham. Road
MUHLHAUSER Hy., (G. & II. M.,) 275 Ham. Road
Muhlhauser J. U., cof. h., 709 Vine
Muhlhauser Michael, varnisher, e. s. Vine, near Auburn Av
Muhlig Wm., lab., s.s. 6th, nr. Harriet
Muhr Br. Boniface, director St. Francis School
Muhr John, billiards, n.w.c. Vine and Longworth, h. 228 Walnut
Muhrman C., clk., 140 Main, h. 199 Race
Muhrmann John P., cof. h., 207 and 209 Vine, h. 191 Race
Muhrmen Peter, watch mkr., 205 Main
Muigebler Jacob, paper carrier, 28 Allison
Muinchov John F., tailor, bds. 46 Elder

244   (MUL)   CINCINNATI   (MUL)   DIRECTORY.   (MUR)

Muir James, carp., 14 W. Mulberry
Muir James, molder, wks. n.e.c. Canal and Walnut
Muir John, carp., 134 Clark
Muir W. O., cutter, h. s. e. c. 3d and Broadway
Muirkead Thomas, lab., 290 Main
Mulahan Anna, hoop skirt mkr., 335 Cutter
Mulally Wm., lab., c. E. 8th and Accommodation
Mulane Andrew J., (Dennis & M.,) 99 Dudley
Mularky Thomas, lab., 170 E. Front
Mulberry Rebecca, servt., 137 E. 5th
Malcahy Ellen, millinery, 372 W. 5th
Mulcahy Margaret, n.e.c. 3d and Wood
Mulcahy Michael, lab., 238 Water
Mulcahy Patrick, lab., 1 Budd
Mulcahy Wm., lab., 135 W. 9th, w. of Central Av
Mulcare Dennis, teamster, 131 Sycamore
Mulcare Patrick, lab., 102 Sycamore
Mulchy James, lab., Maiden al. b. Anderson al. and Gas al
Mulchany John, lab., 42 Pierson
Muldoon Daniel, lab, 195 E. 6th
Muldoon Jeremiah, lab., 112 Butler
Muldoon Joseph, 33 Pierson
Muldoon Patrick, lab., 110 Butler
Muley Hy., tinner, 451 Main
Mulford Charles W., clk., 17 W. Pearl, h. 359 John
Mulford Julius Q., clk., Auditor's office L. M. R.R., h. 359 John
Mulford L., salesman, 14 W. 4th
Mulford Wm., b.k., 63 Milton
Mulhare Anna, 402 W. Front
Mulholland Hy., stone yard, n.e.c. 14th and Plum, h. 453 Plum
Mulholland John, lab., 79 Abigail
Mulholland Mary, 28 W. Court, w. of Central Av
Mulholland Thomas, clk., 11 E. Pearl, h. 25 Hathaway
Mulholm Barney, lab., rear 53 Woodward
Mull Sophia, 66 Dunlap
Mullah Darby, peddler, n. s. 6th, e. of Lock
Mullalley Cerilda, 175 Water
Mullaley Geo., bksmith, wks. 11 Freeman, h. 11 Sargent
Mullalley Nancy, 11 Sargent
Mullaly Johanna, 182 E. Pearl
Mullane Andrew J., (W. B. Dennis & Co.,) 99 Dudley
Mullane Wm., trimmings, 91 Mound
Mullanney Patrick, saloon, w.s. Central Av. b. 2d and W.W. Canal Basin
Mullarke Thos., plumber, bds. 169 W. Front
Mullen Albert W., (Geo. M., Hord & Co.) 201 Barr
Mullen Bernard, carp., 5 Longworth w. of Stone
Mullen Edward, lab., n.s. Cherry al. b. Plum and Central Av.
Mullen Edward, watchman, 47 Plum
Mullen Mrs. Ellen, 55 Dudley
Mullen Ellen, n.s. Cherry al. b. Plum & Central Av.
Mullen Gertrude, 731 Elm
Mullen Hugh, lab., s.w.c. E. Pearl and Canal
Mullen Hugh, produce, 483 Broadway
Mullen Jas., 110 Water
Mullen Jas , photographer, 100 W. 4th
Mullen John, 5 Longworth w. of Stone
Mullen John, bds. 431 W. 8th
Mullen John, 731 Elm
Mullen John, blk. smith, 55 Dudley
Mullen John, lab., e s. Hand al. b. Court and Clark
Mullen John, lab., n.s. Fremont b. Harriet and Mill Creek
Mullen John, mach., n.s. Cherry al. b. Plum and Central Av.
Mullen John, printer, bds. 5 W. 4th
Mullen Joseph, cab. mkr., bds. 431 W. 8th
Mullen Nancy, bds. 290 W. 4th
Mullen Nelson D., b.k., 70 and 72 Vine, h. 470 W. 3d
Mullen Saml., clk., 73 W. 4th, bds. 470 W. 3d
Mullen Saml. Sr., market master, 470 W. 3d

Mullen Theresa, tailoress, s.s. E. Front e. of Reed
Mullen Thos., saddler, bds. 125 W. 5th
Mullen Wm., mate, 1220 E Front
Mullen Wm. P., atty., 291 W. 7th
Mullen Wm., 182 Barr
Mullene Wm., variety store, n.e.c. Bank and Baymiller, h. 81 Mound
Mullenger Robt., carriage mkr., 50 W. Court w. of Central Av.
Muller August, butcher, 6 Mulberry
Muller Barney, bk. layer, 164 Clark
Muller Conrad, Sr., 136 W. Liberty
Muller Conrad, jr., meats, 130 W. Liberty
Muller Edwin, grocery, 373 Central Av.
Muller Florence, porter, 583 Main
Muller Frank, 139 Pleasant Av.
Muller Fred, boots and shoes, 713 Central
Muller Fred., cof. h., s e.c. Liberty and Central Av.
Muller Fred., dray, 554 Vine
Muller Hy., dray, 537 W. 8th
Muller Hy., tanner. bds. 701 Elm
Muller Hermon, bds. 335 Walnut
Muller Jacob, lab., bds. 13 Freeman
Muller John, lab., s.s. 6th near Mill Creek
Muller John B., teamster, rear 73 Abigail
Muller John H., boots and shoes, 84 Hunt
Muller John, eng., 59 Rittenhouse
Muller Lawrence, shoe mkr., 61 Rittenhouse
Muller Louis, cof. h., 106 Hunt
Muller Louis D., b.k., Duhme & Co.'s, h. 44 New
Muller & May, (Michael M. & Nathan M.,) leather, &c., 220 Main
Muller Mary, milliner, 335 Walnut
Muller Michael, (M. & May,) 158 Sycamore
Muller Michael, rope mkr., s.s. 3d opp. Stone
Muller Nicholas, upholsterer, 139 W. 4th
Muller Richard, tanner, 119 Dunlap
Muller Theodore, cigar mkr. 142 Pleasant
Muller Theodore, clk., 373 Central Av.
Mulleran Joseph, grocery, 2 Abigail
Mullet Augustine, clk., 73 W. 4th, bds. Wm. Tell
Mullett Fred , clk., 140 Main, h. 110 W. 6th
Mullettore Harmon, lab., 91 Spring
Mullevin Conrad, lab., 19 Mill
Mullich Louis, tailor, 97 E.Pearl
Mulligan Anna, e.s. Kilgour b. Pearl and 3d
Mulligan Patrick, bar k., 337 Elm
Mulligan Pat., lab., s.s. 6th b. Broadway and Culvert
Mulligan Thos., stereotyper, 162 W. 5th
MULLIKEN Edward W., (Gillmore, Dunlap & Co.,) bds. 414 W. 3d
Mullin Ann, cof. h., n.s. 6th e. of Lock
Mullin Christopher, lab., 15 Vine
Mullin Cornelius, lab., 30 Lock n. of 8th
Mullin M., lab., bds. Pennsylvania Hotel
Mullin Patrick, boatman, 72 Water
Mullin Pat., lab., n.s. W. W. Canal b. Smith and Park
Mullin Rachel, 579 Central Av.
Mullin Sampson, 579 Central Av.
Mullinger Robt., wks 340 W. 3d
Mullinger Robt., carriage mkr., wks. 136 W. Pearl
Mullinger Wm., blk. smith, wks. 136 W. Pearl
Mulloy John, driver, 333 W. 2d
Mullun Fanny, 431 W. 8th
Mulvaney John, 78 E. 7th
Mulmeier Marg, 191 Hopkins
Mulready Wm., shoe mkr., 345 W. 9th
Mulroy Wm., lab., s.s. Friendship al. b. Pike and Butler
Multner Rachael, servt., 395 W. 6th
Mulvahan Cornelius, lab., 19 Mill
Mulvanny Jas., dray, s.s. 5th b. Wood and Stone
Mulvany Matthew, shoe mkr., 108 Culvert

Mulvehill Dominick, stone mason, 55 E. 8th e. of Lock
Mulvehill Margaret, servt., 362 W. 7th
Mulvehill Michael, plasterer, 15 Accommodation
Mulvey Jas., cooper, 103 E. 2d
Mulvey John, clk., 86 Gest
Mulvey Pat., n.s. New b. Culvert and Broadway
Mulville John, lab., 614 W. 8th
Mulvy Ann, servt., 34 Elizabeth
Mulvy Ann, 36 Elisabeth
Mulvy Cornelius, watchman, 413 W. Front
Mulvy Jas., cooper, 103 E. 2d
Mulvy Peter, lab., 189 Cutter
Mumberg Gustave, shoe mkr., 62 Dunlap
Mumford & Co., (Lucian C. M. & M. C. Barnitz,) stationers, 38 W. 4th
Mumford Lucian C., (M. & Co.,) res. N. York
Mumke John H., tailor, 501 Main
Mumm Chas., cigar mkr., 538 Main
Mummberg Lewis, varnisher, bds. 72 W. Liberty
Mummert Jacob, 467 Vine
Mun Dominick, blk. smith, 397 Vine
Munce Jas., b.k., bds. 272 W. 7th
Munce John H., mach., bds. s.w.c. 3d and Sycamore
Munch Anthony, 154 York
Munch Jas. H., b.k.. n.e.c. Race and 5th
Munchenbach Danl., lab., 9 Pendleton
Munchhof Hy., bar k., n.e.c. Central Av and Court
Munchhof Joseph, cof. h., 277 Central Av.
Munchweiler Mauritz, 151 W. 6th
Mund Christian, baker, bds. 222 W. 6th
Mund Christian, cab mkr., 73 David
Mund Hy., musician, 537 Race
Mundel Geo., lab., 360 Broadway
Munder Frank, tanner, 14 Dunlap
Mundey Hy., cab mkr., 591 Walnut
Mundhenk Hy., tailor, 17 Abigail
Mundorf John, grocery, 171 W. Liberty
Mundowney Jeremiah, grocer, 198 Webb
Mundwil Joseph, box mkr., bds. s.e.c. 2d and Plum
MUNDY FREEMAN, Livery Stable, 389 W. 6th, h. 322 W. 9th b. John and Mound
Mundy Thos., cof. h., 317 W. 2d
Mundy Wm., drays, bds. 317 W. 2d
Mungavin Martin, lab., rear 406 Sycamore
Munich Peter, lab, 584 Plum
Munnett Geo., lab., wks. 25 Water
Munnich Fred., lab., 548 Plum
Munnich Gerhard, (M. & Ronnebaum,) 93 Pendleton
Munnich & Ronnebaum, (Gerhard M. & Ferdinand R.,) painters, 105 Woodward
Munninghoff Hy., lab., bds. 146 Clark
Munro Alex., clk., 130 Hopkins
Munroe Chas., real estate agt., 186 Longworth
Munroe Chas. F., clk., 186 Longworth
Munroe Horace, 186 Longworth
Munroe Michael, lab., 62 Butler
Munson John H., clk. U. S. Ex. Co.
Munson Saml. B., engraver, 58 W. 9th
Munson Wm. H., sawyer, 232 Clark
Munson Wm. S., clk., Sellew & Co's h. 58 W. 9h
Munster Geo., 205 W. Liberty
Muntal Herman, lab., 360 Broadway
Muntal Jared J., lab., 74 Abigail
Muntel Henry, molder, 13 Woodward
Munter Ellen, servt., Burnet House
Munter Wm., waiter, Burnet House
Munts Mary E , 33 E. 3d
Muntte John, finisher, wks. n.e.c. Walnut and Canal
Munty Abraham B., at Galt House
Munts Catharine, servt., 379 W. 6th
Munts Frances, servt., 395 W. 6th
Munz Gotthard, tailor, 40 Findlay
Munzemeier August, cof. h., 7 12th
Murch Bernard, shoe mkr., 48 Richmond
MURCH CHAUNCEY M., Pianos and Melodeons, 72 W. 4th, h. 216 Poplar

(MUR) CINCINNATI (MUR) DIRECTORY. (MUR) 245

Murdoch Jas. jr., stamp and brand cutter, 388 W. 9th
Murdock Anna, 457 Vine
Murdock Atty, 50 E. 2d
Murdock Chas. C., Judge Court Com. Pleas, 457 Vine
Murdock D. J., pilot, bds. 37 Longworth
Murdock Henry K., paper carrier, Observatory st., Mt. Adams
Murdock Henry K., clk., 46 E. 3d, h. Mt. Adams
Murdock James, paper carrier, 388 W. 9th w. of Central Av.
MURDOCK John G., (M. & Lacey,) 388 W. 9th
Murdock John, teamster, s. s. E. Front b. Willow and Leatherbury
MURDOCK & LACEY, (John G. M. & Nicholas L.) Plumbers, Pump and Hydrant Makers, 46 E. 3d
Murdock Margaret, 463 Plum
Murdock Sarah, 7 W. Court, w. of Central Av.
MURDOCK Thos., (Paul & Murdock,) h. nr. Cumminsville
Murley Chas., type mkr., 371 Longworth
Murnahan John, 79 E. 8th, e. of Lock
Murnahan Thomas, wagon mkr., 79 E. 8th e. of Lock
Murnin Hugh, dray, 559 Sycamore
Murnin Miss Rosanna, seamstress, 559 Sycamore
Murphy Anna, seamstress, wks. 53 W. 4th
Murphy Ann, servt, 430 W. 6th
Murphy Bridget, servt, 453 W. 6th
Murphy Bridget, servt, 390 W. 6th
Murphy Bridget, 209 W. Front
Murphy Catharine, 168 E. 5th
Murphy Catharine, 286 W. 6th
Murphy Catharine, 37 Central Av.
Murphy Chas., carp., bds. 16 Perry
Murphy Chas., lab., n.s. Taylor al. e. of Kilgour
Murphy Chas., lab., n.s. Taylor al. w. of Kilgour
Murphy Columbus, carp., n. s. R. Road e. of Hazen
Murphy Cornelius, b. k., 60 W. 2d, h. s.e.c. Sycamore and New
Murphy Cornelius, lab., s. s. 6th b. Broadway and Culvert
Murphy Cornelius, plasterer, 126 E. 8th
Murphy D. J., bar k., Dennison House
Murphy David, lab., bds. 60 Baum
Murphy Daniel, tailor, bds. 186 Race
Murphy Daniel, tailor, bds. 186 W. 5th
Murphy Daniel C., salesman, 57 E. 8th e. of Lock
Murphy David L., finisher, wks. n. e. c. Walnut and Canal
Murphy Dennis, Cramsey Alley, b. Mound and Cutter
Murphy Edward, rear 61 Barr
Murphy Edward, lab., 22 E. 5th
Murphy Elnora, s. s. 6th b. Broadway and Culvert
Murphy Ellen, bds. 32 Harrison
Murphy Ellen, servt, 342 W. 7th
Murphy Ellen, servt, 380 W. 5th
Murphy Frank, lab., 403 Sycamore
Murphy Hannah, servt, 496 W. 4th
Murphy James, cof. h., 273 Central Av.
Murphy James, dray, wks. s.w.c. Broadway and 5th
Murphy James, 150 Water
Murphy James, lab., bds. n.s. Augusta b. John and Smith
Murphy James, lab., 333 W. 5th
Murphy James, meat dealer, 10 Lock
Murphy James, painter, 546 W. 5th
Murphy James, plasterer, h. 17 Accommodation
Murphy James, shoe mkr., 115 Hopkins
Murphy Jane. 161 Longworth
Murphy Jeremiah, huckster, s.w.c. 6th and Broadway
Murphy Jeremiah, boots and shoes, 313 Central Av.
Murphy Johanna, servt, Galt House
Murphy John, clk., s.e.c. John and 6th
Murphy John, dray, 654 Sycamore
Murphy John, lab., w.s. Central Av. b. W.W. Canal and 2d
Murphy John, lab., 38 Lock n. of 8th

Murphy John, lab., 60 Gano
Murphy John, pipe fitter, wks. n. e. c. Walnut and Canal
Murphy John, shoe mkr., 398 Broadway
Murphy John, tinner, n s. 6th b. Harriet and Skaats
Murphy John, trunk mkr., wks. 31 Broadway
Murphy John, waiter, Burnet House
Murphy John A., phys., 209 W. 7th, bds. 282 W. 8th
Murphy Justin, clk., s. w. c. 3d and Smith
Murphy Kate, servt, 488 W. 7th
Murphy L. J., b. k., 48 W. 2d, h. n.e.c. Lawrence and Pearl
Murphy Margaret, servt., 116 E. 4th
Murphy Margaret, e.s. Oregon b. 3d and 6th
Murphy Margaret, n.s. W. W. Canal b. Smith and Park
Murphy Maria, E. 8th, e. of Lock
Murphy Martin, 68 Longworth
Murphy Mary, s.s. 6th b. Broadway and Culvert
Murphy Mary, 158 W. Front
Murphy Mary, 48 E. 7th
Murphy Mary, b. h., 158 W. Front
Murphy Mary, servt, 425 W. 6th
Murphy Mary, servt, 270 George
Murphy Mary, rervt, Henrie House
Murphy Mary, servt, 148 John
Murphy Merrick, rag dealer, 33 Water, h. w. s. Smith 2d door from 3d
Murphy Michael, 389 W. 2d
Murphy Michael, grocery, 162 W. 3d
Murphy Michael, lab., 64 Richmond
Murphy Michael, lab., s.s. 6th b. Broadway and Culvert
Murphy Michael, lab., 16 Kossuth
Murphy Michael, lab., 250 Water
Murphy Michael, paver. 165 Linn
Murphy Michael, plasterer, 20 Lock n. of 8th
Murphy Michael, saddler, bds. 74 Longworth
Murphy Michael, saloon, 193 Cutter
Murphy Nancy, n. s. R. Road e. of Hazen
Murphy Nancy, n. s. Augusta b. John and Smith
Murphy Owen, lab., 11 8th above Lock
Murphy Pat., 262 W. 8th
Murphy Patrick, 47-Lodge
Murphy Patrick, blksmith, 37 W. 9th
Murphy Patrick, horse shoer, wks. 152 W. Court
Murphy Patrick, lab., s.s. Phoebe al. b. Plum and Central Av.
Murphy Pat., lab., bds. 10 Pub. Landing, b. Main and Walnut
Murphy Patrick, lab., 269 W. Front
Murphy Pat., shoe mkr., bds. 281 Central Av.
Murphy Peter, 114 Water
Murphy Peter, lab., 540 W. Front
Murphy Phillip, boatman, bds 78 Water
Murphy Rufus, clk., s.w.c. 3d and Smith
MURPHY Samuel M., (Foote, Nash & Co.) bds. 282 W. 8th
Murphy Sarah, chambermaid, Broadway Hotel
Murphy Stephen, shoe mkr., 375 Broadway
Murphy Thos., 37 W. 9th w. of Central Avenue
Murphy Thos., tailor, w. s. Lock b. 8th and Court
Murphy Thos. A., coal agent, 168 E. 5th
Murphy Timothy, bds. 42 Lock n. of 8th
Murphy Timothy, carp., 225 W. Front
Murphy Timothy, huckster, w.s. Langdon b. 6th and 7th
Murphy Timothy, huckster, 191 E. Pearl
Murphy Wm. H., carp., wks. gas works
Murr Jacob, carp., 2 Louisa
Murran Kate, al. b. 4th and 5th and Central Av. and John
Murphy Mrs., 50 Rittenhouse
Murray Bridget, bds. 37 Smith*
Murray & Reiring, (Martin M. & John G. R.) ladies shoes, s.e.c. 6th and Central Av.
Murray Catharine, 119 W. 6th

Murray Chas., type founder, bds. s. s. Longworth below Stone
Murray Chas. R., clk., n. e. c. 8th and Central Av., bds. U. S. Hotel
Murray Daniel, tel. op., bds. 131 Longworth
Murray Ellen, s. s. 6th b. Broadway and Culvert
Murray F. W., printer, Press office, s.w. c. 3d and Sycamore
Murray Francis, lab., 59 Rittenhouse
Murray Geo., instrument mkr., 90 Longworth
Murray Hy., lab., wks. Chamberlain & Co.'s
Murray Hy., blksmith, wks. w.s. Sycamore b. Hunt and Abigail
Murray Hy., nailer, 405 Sycamore
Murray Hugh, lab., 19 Accommodation
Murray Hugo, tailor, 31 Rittenhouse
Murray James, bds. 62 Riddle
Murray James, dray, 124 E. 8th
Murray James, fruit dealer, 153 Central Avenue
MURRAY James H., (Riggs & M.) 24 Elizabeth
Murray John, 90 Longworth
Murray John, box mkr., 509 Plum
Murray John, cab. mkr., 206 W. Court w. of Central Av.
Murray John, dray, 11 Bedinger
Murray John, grocery, 19 York
Murray John, horse shoe nail manuf., n.w c. Sycamore and Canal
Murray John, lab., 34 Butler
Murray John, molder, 35 Elizabeth
Murray John, shoe mkr., 36 Kossuth
Murray John C., painter, 274 John
Murray John D., salesman, 9 W. 5th, h. 25 Race
Murray Maria, 48 Rittenhouse
Murray Martin, (M. & Reiring,) 380 George
Murray Mary, 111 George
Murray Mary A., dress mkr., 111 George
Murray Michael, lab., 36 Butler
Murray Oscar S., 381 Elm
Murray Patrick, h. 65 George
Murray Patrick, w.s. Miami Canal, b. 6th and 8th
Murray Patrick, blksmith, 232 W. Court
Murray Patrick, lab., E. 8th e. of Lock
Murray Patrick, lab., w.s. Lebanon Road b. Liberty and Corp Line
Murray Patrick, shoe mkr., 396 Broadway
Murray Patrick, stone mason, 25 Accommodation
Murray Theodore. artist, 103 Richmond
Murray Thos., plasterer, rear 291 Elm
Murray Thos. F., carrier, bds. n. w. c. Race ank Water
Murray Wm., 52 Riddle
Murray Wm., jr, w.s. Elm b. 5th and 6th
Murray Wm., 90 Longworth
Murray Wm., carp., 205 Elm
Murray Wm., molder, wks. n.e.c. Canal and Walnut
Murray Wm., lab., 60 Melancthon
Murray Wm. H., dray, 119 Everett
Murrell Samuel, twister, 86 W. Front, 189 W. 3d
Murroney Geo., tailor, n.s. 7th b. Broadway and Sycamore
Murry Barney, lab., 209 W. 2d
Murry C. J., painter, 203 Walnut
Murry Chas., lab., 97 E. Pearl
Murry Daniel, jr., tel. op., 131 Longworth
Murry Francis W., printer, 33 E. 3d
Murry Jas., lab., 132 Central Av.
Murry Jas., waiter, Madison House
Murry John, dray, 77 Walnut, h. Bedinger al.
Murry John, horse shoe nail mkr., 434 Sycamore
Murry John, lab., 170 W. Front
Murry John D., carp., 273 Cutter
Murry Joseph, lab., 129 W. Front
Murry Julia, servt., 233 W. 4th
Murry Margaret, 116 Barr
Murry Margaret. 186 E. 6th
Murry Martin, lab, 198 Water
Murry Mary, 127 Webb

246 (MYE) CINCINNATI (MYR) DIRECTORY. (NAS)

Murry Mary, cook, 133 W. Miami Canal
Murry Michael, molder, 186 E. 6th
Murry Michael lab., s s. Phoebe al. b. Plum and Central Av.
Murry Orlando S., salesman 61 W. Pearl, h. 381 Elm
Murry Patrick, lab., 116 Barr
Murry Patrick, lab., 46 Kossuth
Murry Patrick J., turner, 12 Park
Murry Peter, driver, 123 Van Horn
Murry Wm., lab., 369 W. 2d
Murry Wm., lab., wks. n.w.c. Plum and Wade
Murry Wm., molder, wks. n.w.c. Plum and Wade
Murtagh Thos., clk., bds. 41 George
Murteu Thos., clk. 112 W. 5th, h. s.w.c. George and Elm
Muschal Nicholas, stone mason, n.s. Front near Corporation Line
Muschler Peter, barber, 235 W. 5th
Muscroft Chas. E., phys., 447 Central Av.
Muse Hy., grocery, 351 W. 5th
Musgrave H. B., phys. and gas cooking stoves, 272 W. 6th
Musgrave Jas., lab., 111 York
Musgrove Chas. M., baker, 245 Cutter
Musgrove Hiram, tailor, 207 Hopkins
Musgrove Peter, blksmith, 245 Cutter
Mushak Gustav. C., shoe mkr., wks. 681 Vine
Mushalen Adolph, 584 Plum
Musselman Edwin M., salesman 180 Main, h. 326 Clark

MUSSEY R. D., Physician and Surgeon, 70 W. 7th

MUSSEY W. H., Physician and Surgeon, 70 W. 7th

Must Fred., bds. Cincinnati House
Mustard Alexander, carp., 60 George, h. 247 Laurel
Mustin E. C. L., trimmings, 96 W. 4th, h. 603 Freeman
Mustin S. C., b.k. 65 W. 3d. bds. 414 W. 4th
Muszmeyer John, lab., n.e.c. River and Ludlow

MUTH AUGUSTUS, Bakery and Confectionery 28 W. 5th

MUTH CHARLES F., Family Grocery and Provisions, 1070 Central Av.

Muthert George H., carp., 137 Baymiller
Mutsch Hy., foreman, 63 Jackson
Mutsch John, lab., wks. s.e.c. Canal and Vine
Mutter James, lab., 21 Mill
Mutual Benefit Life Ins. Co. of Newark, N. J., agency, 4 Pub. Landing
Mutual Life Insurance Co. of New York, agency, 80 W. 3d
Mutz Frederick, saddler, s.w.c. Pearl and Ludlow
Myer Andrew, tailor, 492 Elm
Myer Augusta, 399 Broadway
Myer Bernard, lab., rear 1184 E. Front
Myer Wm., whitewasher, w.s. Ridgway al. b. 14th and 15th
Myer Catharine, rear 70 Hunt
Myer Chas., baker, bds. 1184 E. Front
Myer Chas., tailor, 483 W. 3d
Myer Elizabeth, servt., 461 W. 6th
Myer Fred., 59 Abigail
Myer Geo., porter, h. n.e.c. Richmond and Baymiller
Myer H., tailor, bds. 343 Walnut
Myer Hy., b.k. s.e.c. Pearl and Walnut, bds. 2 Lucy
Myer Herman H., lab., rear 53 Woodward
Myer Jacob, tin shop, 63 Wade
Myer John, lab., n.s. Kemper's Lane b. Hill and E. Front
Myer Joseph, maltster, bds. s.e.c. Longworth and Hoadly
Myer Joseph, molder, 420 Sycamore
Myer Martes, carp., 293 Linn
Myer Martin, 268 Hopkins
Myer Mary, servt., 49 Barr
Myer Mary, servt., 374 W 6th
Myers Abraham, b.k., 243 W. 5th
Myers Anholt M , agent, 308 George
Myers Ann E., 27 Cutter

Myers Anton, cab. mkr., 320 Longworth
Myers Barney, sawyer, 363 W. 8th
Myers Benjamin H., carp., bds. 36 Dayton
Myers Braxton, clk. 310 Main, h. e.s. Carr s. of 6th
Myers Casper, cartman, 202 Cutter
Myers Catharine, servt., 279½ Longworth
Myers Chas. O., salesman, 137 Walnut
Myers Conrad, cof. h., 1032 Central Av.
Myers Cornelia, servt., 281 Central Av.
Myers Cornelius, porter, 52 Main

MYERS E. & CO., (John M. & Elkanah M.) Wholesale Confectioners and Candy Manufacturers,52 Main

Myers Edward, mach., 254 Clark
Myers Edward P., clk., 291 Main
Myers Edward Y., watchman, s.s. 3d b. Canal and Kilgour
MYERS Elkanah, (E. M. & Co.) 58 Mound
Myers Frank, lab., wks. 267 W. 5th
Myers Frederick, lab., wks. n.w.c. Pearl and M. Canal
Myers Geo, lab., 213 W. Court w. of Central Av.
Myers Geo , peddler, 129 Bremen
Myers Geo., spice mill, 327 Main
Myers H., blksmith, wks. n.s. Front b. Lawrence and Pike
Myers H. A., tobacconist, wks. 12 Main
Myers Hy., clk., 337 Main
Myers Hy., clothing, 337 Main
Myers Hy., lab., 140 Freeman
Myers Hy., lab., wks. n.e.c. Park and Marsh
Myers Hy., salesman 14 W. Pearl, h. E. Walnut Hills
Myers Hy , teamster, 49 Betts
Myers Hy. W., b.k. 52 Main, h. 94 Barr
Myers Herman, tailor, bds. 343 W. Court
Myers Jacob, boots and shoes, Carr near c. 6th
Myers Jacob R., eng., 110 E. 3d
Myers Jas., foreman, 95 Longworth
Myers Jas , teamster, 322 W. 8th
Myers Jane, servt., 33 McFarland
Myers Jeremiah, steward, 29 Gano
Myers John, bds. 1032 Central Av.
Myers John, cab. mkr., 399 Longworth
Myers John, grocer, 265 Freeman
Myers John. lab., 62 Abigail
MYERS John, (E. M. & Co.) h. E. Walnut Hills
MYERS John, (M. & Lamping) h. Walnut Hills
Myers John, molder, 67 Spring
Myers John F., tailor, 8 W. 3d, h. 508 Central Av.
Myers John N , b.k. 103 W. Pearl
Myers Joseph, carp., 101 Elder
Myers Kate, bds. 604 Race

MYERS & LAMPING, (John M. & Frederick L.) Plumbers, Pump and Hydrant Makers, 397 Vine

Myers Lewis, express driver, 566 E. Front
Myers Linia, 50 E. 2d
Myers Louisa, bds. 514 W. 7th
Myers Maurice W , librarian Cin. Law Library, h. s.s. 3d b. M. Canal and Kilgour
Myers Margaret, bds. 216 Longworth
Myers Martin, carp., 293 Linn
Myers Martin, molder, wks. Chamberlain & Co.'s
Myers Mary, servt., North Elm
Myers Rebecca, bds. 624 Race
Myers Thos., lab., 61 Mill
Myers Thos., tobacconist, 120 Richmond
Myers Valentine, clk., 352 Main
Myers Wm., dray, s.s. Van Horn b. Linn and Cutter
Myers Wolf, 468 Race
Myersseek Frederick, cigar packer, n.s. Budd b. Harriet and Mill Creek
Mygatt P. V., mess. American Express Co.
Mygatt Philip V., grocery, s.w.c. Mill and 4th
Myler Jas., lab., 928 E. Front
Myre Ferdinand, lab., wks. n.w.c. Plum and Wade
Myrick Jennie, 405 George

N

Naber Andrew, blksmith, 186 Barr
Naber Barney, blksmith, 525 W. 8th
Naber Benjamin, mach., wks. J. A. Fay & Co.'s
Naber Geo , blksmith, wks. C., H. & D. R.R. blksmith shop
Naber Hy., carriage mkr., s.w.c. Linn and Bank

NABER WM., Chair Factory, 567 Race, h. 662 Race

Nabor Geo., lab., wks. 1565 E. Front
Nacbengast Michael, lab., 69 Buckeye
Nachtigal John F., cab. mkr , 16 Grant
Nademann Casper, carp., 9 Pleasant
Naderman Albert, blksmith, 156 14th
Naderman Hy., lab., 19 Franklin
Naderman Albert, blksmith, 65 14th
Nadir Josephine, h. 431 W. 3d

NADLER FERDINAND, Turner, 487 Vine

Nae Hy., cab. mkr., s.e.c. Baymiller and Clinton
Naegel Elizabeth, rear 362 Ham. Road
Naegel Maria, 574 Elm
Naegule Joseph, cab. mkr., 34 Campbell al.
Naeher Frederick, lock mkr., 117 Betts
Naeher Simon, carver, 462 Elm
Nafew S. B., flour inspector, bds. National Hotel
Nagel Chas., cigar mkr., bds. 26 Mulberry
Nagel Christopher, bk. layer, rear 26 Mulberry
Nagel Frederick, carp., 166 Spring
Nagel Frederick, driver, 13 Mulberry
Nagel Geo., tailor, 126 Ham. Road
Nagel Hy., cigar mkr., 17 Chestnut
Nagel Hy., cigar mkr., 195 Broadway
Nagel Hy., grocery, 29 Ham. Road
Nagel Jacob, lab., 78 Buckeye
Nagel Joseph, huckster, 61 Hamer
Nagel Margaret, servt., wks. 434 Broadway
Nagel Martin, seed dealer, 86 Buckeye
Nagel & Spreen, (Wm. N., & Gottlieb S.,) liquors &c., 611 Central Av.
Nagel Wm., feed mill, s. w. c. Sycamore and Webster
Nagel Wm., foreman, 31 Webster
Nagel Wm. F., rope mkr., 505 Race
Nagele Vital, watch mkr., 564½ Front
Nagle John, cutter, 307 Findlay
Nagle Michael, blksmith, 31 W. Court w. of Central Av.
Nagle Nicholas, barber, 179 E. Front
Nagle Philip, tailor, w.s. Lebanon Road near Channing
Nagle Richard, lab., bds. s.s. Railroad e. of Kelly
Nagle Rudolphus H., bridge builder, 579 W. 5th
Nahen John, dray, 46 Barr
Nahring Hy., cigar box mkr., 93 Clay
Nahrung Wm., whitewasher, w. s. Ridgway al. b. 14th and 15th
Nallor John, mess., 51 E. 6th

NAISH Wm. J., (O'Donoghue & N.,) 154 W. 5th

Naler Andrew, lab., 51 Martin
Nanenger Charles, stone mason, 70 Martin
Nantrup Hy., produce, 320 Baymiller
Napier John, carriage smith, 69 W. 6th
Narey Matthew, cof. h. 343 Central Av. h. 125 Betts
Narwold Richard, cooper, 309 W. Liberty
Nase Noah, saddler, 325 W. 8th
Nash ———, saddler, bds. 579 W. 5th
Nash Betsey, 14 E. 8th e. of Lock
Nash Boanerges, cof. b., 128 Vine, bds. s.s. 6th b. Vine and Race
Nash David, police, 63 E. 8th
NASH Job M., (Foote N. & Co.,) bds. Burnet House
Nash John, car wheel manufac, 243 E. Pearl e. of Broadway, h. 36 E. 7th
Nash John, dental depot, 38 W. 4th, h. n.e.c. 7th and North
Nason Cyrus, teacher, 194 Richmond

Nast Gottlieb C., mailer, 49 Milton
NAST Dr. Wm., Editor of the Christian Apologist, Methodist Book Concern
Natebus Wm., clk., 597 Main
Nathan Abraham, (Moritz Bro. & Co.,) 189 Longworth
Nathan Jacob, clothing, 203 Main, h. 4 Harrison
Nathan & Levy, (Max N. & Jos. L.,) jewelry, 100 Walnut
NATHAN M. & CO., (Moritz N. & Max Nathan,) Wholesale Wines, Liquors and Cigars, 25 Vine
Nathan Marks, rag dealer, 529 Race, h. 464 Race
NATHAN Max, (M. Nathan & Co.,) 135 Central Av.
NATHAN Moritz, (M. N. & Co.,) 135 Central Av.
Nathmann Elizabeth. bds. 634 Race
NATIONAL CLAIM AGENCY, Harvey, Collins and Brace, (Fred L. Harvey, Washington City; John F. Collins, New York City; and Julius Brace, Cincinnati,) Branch Office, 66 W. 3d
National Hall, 200 and 202 Vine
National Hall, 402 Vine, Frank Klotter prop'r.
NATIONAL HOTEL, e.s. Sycamore b. 3d and 4th John Bates Proprietor
NATIONAL INSURANCE CO., John Burgoyne President, s.w.c. Main and Front
NATIONAL THEATER e.s. Sycamore b. 3d and 4th John Bates, Proprietor
Natman Wm., porter, 42 Jones
Nau Valentine, varnisher, 14 Mary
Nauber Gerhard, blksmith, n.e.c. Smith and Augusta
Naue Hy., lab., s s. Charlotte b. Linn and Baymiller
Nauer Adam, molder, 161 Pleasant
Nauer Francis, lab., 246 Pleasant
Naumann Chas., saddler, 29 Schiller
Naumann Frederick, trunk mkr., 29 Schiller
Naumann Gottlieb, saddler, 29 Schiller
Nauson Joseph, s.w.c. Pike and 3d
Navergold Frederick, furnaceman, 535 E. Front
Nayless Patrick, lab., 21 Central Av
Nayless James, fireman, 21 Central Av.
Naylor Ann E., tailoress, bds. 58 Martin
Naylor Charles W., 58 Martin
Naylor Elizabeth, 58 Martin
Naylor Geo., clk., 166 W 8th
Naylor Hy., grocery, 87 Martin
Naylor Margaret J., tailoress, bds. 58 Martin
Naylor Wm., watchman, s.s. Front e. of Willow
Neaber Wm., cooper, 15 Park
Nead James, blksmith, 331 W. 3d
Nead James, brewer, 331 W. 3d
Neagle Hy., lab, 10 York
Neagle James, lab., 20 Ann
Neagle Morris, lab., n. e. c. 3d and Butler
Neahous Joseph, carp., w. s. Harriet b. Sloo and Front
Neal Catharine, 144 Barr
Neal Celeste, 291 Livingston
Neal Emanuel, cab. mkr., 157 Linn
Nealaus John, lab , 29 E. 8th
Neale Máry, 10 Race [Av.
Nealon John, driver, wks. 165 Central
Nealon Patrick, driver, wks. 165 Central Av.
Nealy Kate, bds. 30 Patterson al.
Neaman August, clk., 16 E. Pearl, h. s.s. Liberty b. Main and Walnut
Neaman Bernard, cab. mkr., 135 Abigail
Neaman Hy., wagon mkr., 26 Logan
Neaman Wm., bar k., 71 Sycamore
Neamann John, lab., 20 Cutter
Neamann Joseph, clk., bds. 175 Broadway
Neameller Ferdinand, stone mason 16 Dudley
Neander Alexander, cab. mkr., 14 Milton

Neaport Wm., hostler, s. w. c. John and Front
Neaporte Anton, cooper, 63 Bremen
Neary Ed., walter, Burnet House
Neary Mary. 68 Avery
Nease Charles, dray, 417 W. 3d
Nease Hy., shoe mkr., 417 W. 3d
Nease Herman, bk. layer, 190 Walnut
Neather Augustus, salesman, 146 Baymiller
NEAVE Alexander C., (N. Ward & Co.) h. Clifton
NEAVE Halsted, (Neave Ward & Co.,) h. Clifton
Neave Martin, (T. Neave & Son,) 176 W, 4th
Neave T. & Son, (Thompson M. & Martin & Thompson Jr.,) iron, 65 and 67 Main
Neave Thompson, (T. Neave & Son,) 163 W. 4th
Neave Thompson, Jr., (T. N., & Son,) 445 W. 9th
NEAVE, WARD & CO., (Alex C. N., Robert B. W., & Halsted Neave,) Dealers in Saddlery Hardware and Carriage Trimmings, 37 and 39 Main
Nebe Andrew, 44 Hughes
Nebauer Joseph, lab., n.s. al. b. Poplar and Vine, and Ham. Road and Buckeye
Nebel Hy., clk., n.w.c. 5th and Central Av. bds. 315 W. 7th
Nebel Jacob, blksmith, 517 E. Front
Nebers Geo., policeman. 96 Ham. Road
Neblett James, steamboat agent, n. e. c. Pearl and Lawrence
Nebling Frantz. 54 W. 5th
Neblitt Chas., dray, 105 E. Pearl
Nebrage Benjamin, porter, 305 Cutter
Neckel Peter, shoe mkr., bds. 323 George
Neckert Wm., miller, n. w. c. Court and Broadway
Nedkraus Mary, 56 Martin
Neddermann Frank, cutter, 191 W. Canal
Neddermann Hy., shoe mkr., 191 W. Canal
Neddermann Hy., grocery, 191 W. Canal
Nedler John, lab., 242 Pleasant
Need Adam, lab , wks. 25 Water
Neehouse Hy., tailor, 428 Sycamore
Neekamp.Clemens. cutter, 150 E. 5th
Neelin Andrew. blksmith, wks. n. e. c. Canal and Walnut
Neely James, dray, 503 W. 4th
Neely James, lab, 444 W. 3d
Neely Wm., dray, 325 Clinton
Neemeier Wm., cooper, 42 W. 2d
Nees C., turner. wks. John Mitchell's
Nees Chas., cab. mkr., wks. s.w.c. Canal and Elm
Nees Geo., cooper, 335 Baymiller
Nees Hy., carver, 417 W 3d
Neesen John, porter, 190 Pleasant
Neff Aaron W., clk., 101 W. 4th, bds. 167 W, 9th
Neff Bros., & Co., office s.w.c. 2d & Main
Neff Edward W. S., at s. e. c. Canal and Vine, bds. 142 Broadway
Neff Edwin W., traveling agt., Diebold Bahmann & Co , safe manufac., h. 159 W. Front
Neff Geo. W., 140 Broadway
Neff Mary A., 13 Plum
Neff Moritz blksmith, 61 Findlay
NEFF Peter. (Peter N. & Son,) 296 Walnut
NEFF Peter Rudolph, (Peter Neff & Sons,) Storrs Tp.
NEFF PETER & SONS, (Peter, Wm. H., Peter R. Neff & James C. Morrison) Importers of Hardware, 93 W. Pearl
NEFF WM. CLIFFORD, Pork Packer and Commission Merchant, s.e.c. Canal and Vine, h. 142 Broadway
NEFF Wm. Howard (Peter Neff & Sons) 296 Walnut
NEFFLEN LOUIS G., Physician and Surgeon, 669 R ce
Negel Henriette 167 W. Liberty

Neher Frederick, locksmith, 117 Betts
Nehls Frederick J., shoemkr, 74 Bremen
Nebring Wm., porter, 83 W. Front
Nehrung Wm., porter, 83 W. Front
Neibel Hy., carriage mkr., wks. 55 E. 5th
Neiber G. Fred (N. & Tefft) 476 W. 4th
Neiber & Tefft (G Fred. N. & Albert T.) carps., 156 W. 3d
Nelbert Martin, lab., 1031 Central Av
Neider Aaron, shoemkr, 237 E. 5th
Neiderhauser F., store keeper, Burnet House
Neiderhelm Frederick, al, b. Linn and Baymiller and Liberty and Wade
Neidhard Valentine, cof. h., 662 Race
Neidlahner Leonhard, driver, 186 W. 9th
Neier Hy., boots and shoes, 52 Dudley
Neighbor Andrew, blksmith. 188 Barr
Neighbor Wm., cooper. 15 Park
Neighbours Thomas E., butcher, e.s. Bremen b. Elder and Findlay
Neihaus Barney, bk. mkr., s.s. Ringgold b. Price and Young
Neihaus George. teamster, w.s. Freeman opp. George, h. 193 W. 8th
Neihause Hy., tailor, 53 Bank
Neihause Jacob, lab., 185 W. Canal
Neiles Michael. lab., 21 Mill
Neillis James, lab., 21 Central Av
Neils Patrick, lab., 21 Central Av
Neill Samuel B., cof. h., 61 E. 3d
Neilly James, lab., 444 W, 3d
Neilson Wm. G., gauger, 18 W. Front, h Walnut Hills
Neiman Charles, lab., 33 Dunlap
Neiman Ida, 16 York
Neiman John, boots and shoes, 604 Central Av.
Neiman Margaret, 211 Clinton
Neimayer Joseph, porter, 82 W. Pearl
Nelmeier Hy., lab., 181 Baymiller
Neimelster John, lab., h. 810 W. Front
Neimer Frederick J., cof. h., 262 E.Front
Neimer Hy., lab., wks. 222 E. Front
Neimeyer Chas , hinge fitter, wks. n.e.c. Walnut and Canal
Neimeyer Hy., lab., n w.c. 4th and Lock
Neineman Conrad, lab., wks. n.w.c. Plum and Wade
Neisel Francis, cooper, n.e.c. Elm and Elder
Neisen Christina, 38 Green
Neisen Frank, printer, 57 13th
Neiters Hy , liquors, 42 Front
Neithart Albert, carp., rear 466 Walnut
Nelans Wm. H., paper hanger, wks. 161 Walnut
Nelke Edward, gilder, 71 Woodward
Nelson Mrs. ——, bds. s.w.c. Race and 3d
NELSON'S COMMERCIAL COLLEGE, s.e.c. 4th and Vine, Richard Nelson, Principal
Nelson Elizabeth, 103 W. Court w. of Central Av.
Nelson Fanny, 110 W. 5th
Nelson Hy., lab., 117 Betts
Nelson J. H., clk., bds. Clifton House
Nelson J W., clk., bds. National Hotel
Nelson Jacob, mate, 404 George
Nelson James. cof. h., 105 W. 3d
Nelson John. boatman, 57 E. 8th e. of Lock
Nelson John F., mach., 103 W. Court w. of Central Av
Nelson Louisa, servt., 88 E. 5th
Nelson Oliver, steward. 18 New
NELSON RICHARD, Principal, Nelson's Commercial College, s.e.c. 4th and Vine, 4th story, h. 174 Longworth
Nelson Robert T., liquors, 18 Broadway, h. Newport
Nelson Sarah, bds 139 W. Front
Nelson Wm., butcher, n.s. Deer Creek Road e. of Liberty
Nenecht Victor, molder, 616 Central Av
Nenninger John, tailor. 639 Vine
Nentrup Hy., cooper, 694 Race
Nepper Deitrich. tanner, 147 Ham. Road
Nepper Ernst. tanner, 124 Ham. Road
NEPPER GUSTAV. F., Tannery, 17 Dunlap, h. 134 Ham. Road
Nepper Richard, tanner, 147 Ham. Road
Nepplet Wm., bar k., 87 Providence

248 (NEW) CINCINNATI (NEY) DIRECTORY. (NID)

Nerney John, lab., 373½ W. 7th
Nerz Michael, cab. mkr., s.e.c. Front and John
NESMITH Thos. A. (Thompson & N.), 203 W. 3d
Nesler Mary, servt., 126 E. 4th
Nestler August, tinner, 123 York
Netermann Bernard, tailor, 67 Spring
Netherlan Chas., paper box mkr., 187 Main
NETIRON CHAS. C., Basket Maker, 66 Pleasant
Nettelton Nelson G., banker, 213 W. 4th
NETTER Jacob (Kuhn, N. & Co.) 99 W. 8th
Netterville Alvina, teacher, 59 Mansfield
Nettle Mary, laundress, 104 Spring
Nettler Lewis, cook, 72 W. Court w. of Central Av
Neubacher Francis, salesman, 36 W. Pearl
Neuber George, trimmer, 151 Buckeye
Neuborger Jacob, lab., 1 Wade b. Elm and Plum
Neuderfer Michael, lab., s.s. Johnson al. b. Canal and 12th
Neuell Rebecca, bds. 402 W. 7th
Neufarth Hy., distiller, rear 550 Walnut
Neufort Jacob, gardener, Garden of Eden
Neufurth ——, eng., wks. 221 and 223 Walnut
Neuhaus Frederick I., variety store. 493 Sycamore
Neukam Catharine, seamstress, 8 W. Mulberry
Neukam Johanna, huckster, 8 W. Mulberry
Neukamm Anthony, baker, 607 Vine
Neukum Saml., teamster, 112 Hunt
Neuman David, painter, wks. Crane, Breed & Co's
Neuman Fred., 594 Vine
Neuman George, shoemkr. 33 Jones
Neumann August, cab. mkr., 56 Laurel
Neumann David, painter, bds n,e c. Clay and Allison
Neumann Edward, tailor, 494 Elm
Neumann Emanuel, drover, e.s. Ridgway al. b. Liberty and 15th
Neumann Ferdinand, wagoner, 14 Hamer
Neumann Joseph A., tailor, 175 W. 5th
Neumann Wm., finisher, wks. s.w.c. Elm and Front
Neumeyer Anselm, phys., 523 Vine
Neumeyer Gottfried, baker, wks. 450 Main
Neumeyer Julius A., clk., 65 E. Pearl, bds, Cincinnati House
Neuporter Rudolph, driver, wks, 450 Walnut
Neustoeckel Mrs. ——, laundress, 510 Walnut
Nevers King G., collector, 200 Vine
Neville Bridget. dress mkr., 21 W. Court w. of Central Av
Neville Wm., lab., 21 W. Court w. of Central Av
Nevin Mary, s e.c. Lawrence and Pearl
Nevins ——, bds. s.w.c. 3d and Broadway
New Church Herald, Sabin Hough, publisher, College bldg., e.s. Walnut b. 4th and 5th
New Wm. H., clk., h. 204 Longworth
Newbauer Fred. L., carp., 115 Clinton
Newbauer Ludwig, cab. mkr., 115 Clinton
Newbaur Susannah, servt., 15 Chestnut
Newberg Mrs. Sarah, chair caner, 108 Longworth
Newberger Frederick, blksmith, wks. 55 and 57 E. 5th
Newberry Geo., lab., 504½ Main
Newberry Wm., teamster, 504½ Main
Newbrandt Jacob F., stone cutter, 593 W. 6th
NEWBURGER Moses, (Kornblith & Co.) 45 W. 7th
Newburgh L., bds. Gibson House
NEWBURGH Louis, (N. & Schott,) 256 Vine
NEWBURGH Nathaniel, (Aub, Fenkel & Co.) h. 118 E. 7th

NEWBURGH & SCHOTT, (Louis N. & Gustave S.) Importers and Dealers in Leaf Tobacco. 21 Walnut
Newcomb ——. butter mer., bds. 318 W. 5th
Newell Harvey, fireman, 112 W. 5th
Newell John, caulker, 1290 E. Front
Newell Robert, carp, bds. 221 Central Avenue
Newell Robert A., clk., bds. 112 John
Newell Samuel B., (N., Wilmot & Co.,) 49 Main
Newell Wm., 21 Providence
Newell Wm., eng., 112 John
Newell, Wilmot & Co. (Samuel B. N. & Wm. W. W. & Co.) Tobacconists, 49 Main
Newhall A. H., clk., 171 Vine, h. 293 George
Newhall Isabella, teacher, 293 George
Newhall Joshua, eng., 12 Harrison
Newhall Mary W., 293 George
Newhall Pliny, com. mer., 39 Water, h. n.s. Poplar 2 doors w. of Freeman
Newhall Wilhelmina, teacher, 293 George
Newhaus Christopher, lab., s.s. Court e. of Broadway
Newhaus Louis, finisher, w.s. Bank al. b. 3d and 4th
Newhause Theodore, silversmith, 24 W. 5th
Newhouse Gabriel, clothing, 149 W. Pearl
Newhouse Hy., cartman, 99 Barr
Newhouse Herman, porter. 36 Elm
Newhouse Isaac, clk., 37 Broadway
Newhouse John, cartman, 99 Barr
Newhouse Pauline, servt, 363 W. 9th
Newington Hy., conductor, 184 W. 4th
Newjent E., carriage painter, wks. Crane, Breed & Co.
Newkirk Wm. H., dray, 118 W. 9th w. of Central Av.
Newkirk Wm. H., shoe mkr., wks. 184 Linn
Newlen Tipton, lab.. 374 E. Front
Newman August, cab. mkr., 56 Laurel
Newman Chas., 70 E. 7th
Newman Chas., clk., bds. 174 Plum
Newman Elizabeth, servt, 403 W. 6th
Newman Elizabeth, laundress, 114 Avery
Newman Emma, servt, 103 Broadway
Newman Geo. W., clk., n.w.c. Vine and 5th, h 307 Richmond
Newman John, b. h., 205 W. 7th
Newman John H., (Weber & N.,) 76 Gano
Newman Margaret, 171 Central Av.
Newman Mary A., servt, 403 W. 6th
Newman Thos. J., plumber, 149 W. 5th b. 147 George
Newman Wm. clk., 108 W. 5th, bds. w.s. Walnut b. Court and 9th
Newman Wm., hats and caps, 78 E. Pearl
Newman Ferdinand, wagon mkr., 40 Commerce
Newmann John H., hardware, 74 Gano
Newmann Mary, 669 Central Av
New Orleans House, 10 Sycamore
Newstead Bainbridge, mach., bds. 355 Central Av
Newton Chas., carp., bds. 579 W. 5th
Newton John, clk., bds. 453 W. 6th
Newton John, mate, bds. 212 W. Front
Newton John M., clk., 75 W. 3d, h. 63 McFarland
NEWTON O. E., (N. & Scudder,) 102 W. 7th
NEWTON R. S., Physician, Office 98 W. 6th h. n.w.c. Vine and 6th
Newton S. Chipman, b k., 4 Hopkins
NEWTON & SCUDDER, (O. E. N. & Jno. M S.,) Physicians and Surgeons, Office 102 W. 7th
New York and Erie R.R. Office, 4 College Hall Building
New York Life Insurance Co. Agency, 65 W. 3d
NEY JACOB P., Family Grocery and Provisions, 643 Elm
Ney John A., teacher, 551 Vine

Ney Phoebe, servt., 466 Sycamore
Ney Theresa, bds. 551 Vine
Niagara Fire Insurance Co. Agency, 65 W. 3d
Niblett Charles, dray, bds. Ludlow House
Nichol Andres, watchman, e.s. Branch, b. Findlay and Ham. Road
Nichol James. blksmith, s.s Front, b. Lawrence and Pike. h. 38 Pike
Nicholas Alfred, lab., 99 E. 6th
Nicholas Geo., clk., 90 Clark
Nicholas Lerona, waiter, Dennison House
Nicholaus Louis, grocery, 55 Martin
Nichols Asa, miller, wks. 33 Lock
NICHOLS B. F., (W. B. Bisby & Co.) res. Pennsylvania
Nichols & Coburn, (George H. N. & Augustus S. C.) boots and shoes, 56 W. Pearl
Nichols David K., salesman, s.e.c. 4th and Vine, bds. 376 W. 4th
Nichols Elizabeth, servt., 327 Walnut
Nichols Frank, blksmith, bds. 177 Hopkins
Nichols Frederick, porter, Ludlow, 3 doors below 3d
NICHOLS FREEMAN, Coal Yards, n.e.c. Mill and 2d, and n e.c. Baymiller and Poplar, h. s.s. Madison, b. East Row and Saratoga, Newport
Nichols George H., (N. & Coburn,) bds. 168 W. 4th
Nichols J. R., phys. at 135 Elm
Nichols James, blksmith, 38 Pike
Nichols Joseph, miller. bds. 57 E. 3d
Nichols Nathan B., 824 E. Front
Nichols Peter, blksmith, 40 Gest
Nichols Vesper, com. mer., 361 Walnut, h. 281 W. Court
Nichols Wm., driver, e.s. Ludlow, b. Pearl and 3d
NICHOLS Wm. N., (C. B. Camp & Co.,) s.w.c. Race and 8th
Nicholson Alexander, carp., 93 Clark
Nicholson Ann, 133 W. Front
Nicholson Catharine, servt, 328 W. 6th
Nicholson Daniel, undertaker, 4 New
Nicholson John, tailor, h. 61 Mulberry
Nicholson John, teamster, n.s. Front, e. of Foster
Nicholson Julia, teacher, 228 W. Court
Nicholson Margaret, chambermaid, B'dway Hotel
Nicholson Matilda J., 228 W. Court, w. of Central Av
Nicholson Moses H., shoemkr, bds. 281 Central Av
Nicholson Richard. finisher, 232 E. 6th
Nicholson Samuel, carp., 93 Clark
Nicholson Thomas, stair builder, 93 Clark
Nick Martin, 368 Clark
NICKEL Adolph, (N. & Bieler,) h, 376 Elm
NICKEL & BIELER, (Adolph N. & Henry B.,) Leather and Findings, 228 Main
Nickel Conrad, cab. mkr., 20 Buckeye
Nickel Hy., carriage smith, 40 Gest
Nickel Peter, blksmith, 40 Gest
Nickels Annie, servt., wks. 420 Broadway
Nickels Frank, blksmith, 177 Hopkins
Nickert Jacob, liquors, &c., 350 Main
Nickler August, turner, 609 Main
Nickles Samuel, phys., 50 15th
Niccolaus Martin, brewer, 1039 Central Avenue
Nickoll Frank, lab., 696 W. Front
Nickuley Lorenz, butcher, 30 Green
Nicol Donald, stair builder, 227 Clinton, h. 77 Clinton
Nicolai Henry, butcher, 4 Hamer
Nicolassen F. Alphons, (F. Alphons, N. & Co.,) h. n.w.c. 3d and Ludlow
Nicolassen F. Alphons & Co., (F Alphons, N. & Frederick A. Nicolassen,) grocery, n.w.c. 3d and Ludlow
Nicolassen Frederick A., (F. Alphon Nicolassen & Co.,) res. Porto Ricos West Indies
Nida Martin, tailor, 514 Main

Nie Herman, box mkr., n.w.c. Linn and Findlay
Nieander Alex., cab. mkr., 81 Sycamore, h. 14 Milton
Nieb Jacob, shoemkr. s.s. Charlotte, b. Freeman and Baymiller
Niebaum John, porter, 22 Mulberry
Niebaum Wm., mach., 55 Hughes
Niebaum Wm., porter, 87 W. 2d
Nieble Jacob, blksmith, wks. 109 Hunt
Niebruegge Benj., porter, 365 Cutter
Niebuhr John H., saloon, 223 Central Avenue
Nied John, shoemkr., bds. 37 Ludlow
Nied Simeon, 69 Mohawk
Nieder Fred., grocery, 228 Elm
Nieder George, stone mason, 14 15th
Nieder Louis, blksmith, bds. s. e. c. 2d and Plum
Niederer John, boiler mkr., 175 E. Front Av
Niederhauser Susana, 93 Ham. Road
Niederhelm Ernst, shoemkr, bds. n.w.c. Wade and Baymiller
Niederhelman Wm., lab., s.e.c. Western Av. and Findlay
Niederker Louis, blksmith, s.w.c. Elm and 2d
Niederschmidt Charles, bds. n.e.c. Sycamore and Abigail
Niedfeld Hy. W., carp., 419 Sycamore
Niedford John, watch mkr., 25 Abigail
Niedenecker Hy., bar k., bds. n.e.c. Liberty and Vine
Niehauff Barney, lab., s.s. Budd, b. Harriet and Millcreek
NIEHAUS & BACH, (Joseph N. & Geo. D.,) Propr's. Park Brewery and Ale and Porter Manufacturer, s.e.c. Race and 13th
Niehaus Barney, saddle tree mkr., 145 Carr
Niehaus Bernhard, foreman, 13 Woodward
Niehaus Charles, porter, 76 Spring
Niehaus Charlotte, 91 Woodward
Niehaus Christian F., blksmith, 608 Elm
Niehaus Elizabeth, 31 Buckeye
Niehaus Ferdinand, cooper, w.s. Spring, b. Abigail and Woodward
Niehaus Ferdinand, cooper, rear 97 Woodward
Niehaus Frank, wagon mkr., 110 Clinton
Niehaus Frank, tailor, n.e c. Hunt and Broadway
Niehaus Geo., cab. mkr., 312 Water
Niehaus George, lab., 593 W. 8th
Niehaus Hall, 442 Sycamore
Niehaus Hy., 43 Pleasant
Niehaus Hy., clk. 669 Race
Niehaus Hy., cooper, 368 Broadway
Niehaus Hy., foreman, wks. 17 Home
Niehaus Hy., lab., 476 W. 3d
NIEHAUS CAPT. HENRY, Mineral Water, Ginger Pop, Cider, Ale, and Porter Manuf., 450 Sycamore
Niehaus Hy., stone cutter, 43 Pleasant
Niehaus Hermann, brewer, bds. 701 Elm
Niehaus J. Clements, teamster, 293 Water
Niehaus John, porter, s.e.c. Pearl and Broadway
Niehaus John B., blksmith shop, 677 Central Av., h. 229 W. Liberty
Niehaus John C., stone mason, 172 Baymiller
Niehaus John G., chair mkr., 312 Water
Niehaus John H., dray, 117 Laurel
Niehaus John H., boots and shoes, 205 W. Front
NIEHAUS Joseph, (De Camp & N.,) 220 George
NIEHAUS Joseph, (N. & Bach,) 13 Woodward
Niehaus Matthew, tailor, rear 95 Woodward
Niebause Hy., tailor, bds. 428 Sycamore
Niebelman Hy., tanner, s.s. Liberty, b. Linn and Baymiller
Niehelman Rudolph, tanner, s.w.c. Oliver and Linn
Niehof Mary, 360 Broadway
Niehoff Harmon J., lab., s.s. Liberty, b. Walnut and Vine
Niehoff John B., bds. 545 Walnut
Niehoff John G., dry goods, 373 W. 5th
Niehoff John H., foreman, n.e.c. 9th and Sycamore, h. 545 Walnut 24

Niehouse Herman, porter, 36 Elm
Niehouse Joseph, hardware, 220 George
Niehs Leonhard, tanner, 193 Pleasant
Nieland Andrew, lab., 484 Elm
Niels Frank, 19 Central Av
Nieman Barney, turner, 133 Abigail
Nieman George, lab., 29 Observatory
Nieman Hy., carriage mkr., wks. 136 W. Pearl
Nieman Herman, cab. mkr., 362 Broadway
Nieman Herman, chair mkr., 197 W. Front
Nieman Hermann, hostler, bds. n.e.c. Clark and Linn
Nieman John, lab., rear 67 Abigail
Niemann Amelia, seamstress, 22 Madison
Niemann Bernhard, cab. mkr., 135 Abigail
Niemann Charles, tanner, bds. 602 Elm
Niemann Clemens, lab., 13 Abigail
Niemann D. Henry, lab., 19 Pendleton
Niemann Mrs. Elizabeth, 22 Madison
Niemann Frederick, tinner, 118 Abigail
Niemann Frederick W., cooper, 516 Race
Niemann George, porter, n.e.c. Hunt and Pendleton
Niemann George F., 514 Race
Niemann Henry, plasterer, w.s Ridgway al. b. 14th and 15th
Niemann Herman W., cab. mkr., 297 W. Front
Niemann Hermann H., merchant tailor, 546 Main
Niemann Herman H., clk., 546 Main
Niemann John, janitor, 59 Woodward
Niemann John H., lab., rear 17 Clay!
Niemann Joseph, tailor, bds c. Front and Pike
Niemann Phillip, carp., 20 E. Liberty
Niemann Theodore, painter, 8 E. Canal
Niemann Theodore, tailor, 424 Walnut
Niemann Theodore C. lab., 97 Pendleton
Niemann Wm., lab., 102 Bremen
Niemann Wm., grocery, 25 Ham. Road
Niemar Frederick, tanner, wks. Wm. Hepworth's tannery
Niemar Henry tanner, 19 Pendleton
Niemeier Francis, clk., 168 Clay
Niemeier Franz, lab., n.s. Miami b. Locust and Sycamore
Niemeier Frederick, porter, 44 Pleasant
Niemeier Henry, lab., e.s. Spring b. Abigail and Woodward
Niemeier Henry, porter, 29 Commerce
Niemeler Henry F., lab., 66 Bremen
Niemeier Jane, 91 Spring
Niemeier Mary, laundress, rear 93 Woodward
NIEMER F. J., Proprietor Front Street Hotel, 262 E. Front
Niemeyer Elizabeth, 18 Woodward
Niemeyer Fred., shade hanger, 44 Pleasant
Niemeyer Henry, shoemkr., 5 Jane
Niemeyer Henry, carriage manuf., 536 Walnut, h. 533 Walnut
Niemeyer Hermann, butcher, 65 Green
Niemeyer Joseph, bds. Cincinnati House
Niemeyer Joseph, porter. 16 Woodward
Niemeyer Mary, servt. 125 E. 5th
Niems Henry, baker, 625 Vine
Nienaber Geo., lab., rear 93 Woodward
Nienaber Henry, driver, wks. 23 W. 5th
Nienaber Herman A., shoe mkr., 144 Clinton
NIENABER J. B. J., Merchant Tailor, 205 Walnut
Nienaber Jno. H, shoe mkr., 144 Clinton
Nienaber John H., lab., n.e.c. Ramsey and Park al.
Nienaber Jno. F., shoe mkr., 144 Clinton
Nienaber Theodore, biksmith., 141 Abigail
Nienhuesen John A., shoe mkr., 411 Sycamore
Nienhaus John B , 66 Green
Nieper John. cooper, 306 Sycamore
Nieporte Diederich, s.e.c. Front and John

NIEPORTE HENRY, Coffee and Boarding House, s.e.c. Front and John
Nieporte Rudolph, hostler, bds. rear 450 Walnut
Niepper Hermann H., lab., 290 W. Front
Niermann Conrad, tailor, 44 Hughes
Niermann Geo., cab. mkr., 360 Freeman
Niermann Helen, n.w.c. Rittenhouse and Court
Niermann Sophia, 10 Woodward
Niesel Chas., second hand store, 173 E. Front
Niesen Franz, printer, 57 13th
Niesen John, tailor, 199 Pleasant
Niefs Leopold, tanner, 66 Dunlap
Nieske Henry, carp., 118 Clay
Niessler Anthony, brewer, 38 Findlay
Nieters Geo., boots and shoes, 643 Central Av
NIETERT Henry, (Goosmann & N.,) 22 Grant
Nietgen Peter, painter, 15 Wade w. of Linn
Nightengale John, cab. mkr., 16 Grant
Nihring Mary, 36 Hughes
Nikol Andreas, tanner, 30 Branch
Niles Drusilla H., 209 W. 8th
Niles Elon G., 227 Findlay
Niles Sarah J., ladies shoe store, 224 W. 5th
Niles Stephen R., blksmith, 1563 E. Front
Niles Sandford D., clk., bds 263 Clark
NILES WORKS, Hank's Bell and Brass Foundry, 120 E. 2d, Thomas Firth, supt.
Niles Works, Henry A. Jones Pres., 222 E. Front
Nilling Joseph, (B. H. Alfers & J. N.) 454 Vine
Nimsgern Francis, tailor. 45 Hamer
Nimsgern Peter, prop. Lafayette Hotel, 73 E. Front
Ninde Rev. William X., 391 W. 9th w. of Central Av
Ninninger Ignatius, butcher, 295 Freeman
Ninth Street Station House, s.s. 9th, City Buildings
Niplin Wm , cab. mkr., wks. s.w.c. Canal and Elm
Nipper Anthony, grocery, n.e.c. Hunt and Spring
NIPPER B. H., Family Grocery and Provisions 169 W. 9th
Nipper Henry, molder, n.s. Front b. Smith and John
Nipper John, carp., bds. 169 W. 9th
Nipper John, lab., 11 Hanibal
Nipper Joseph, grocery, 61 W. Liberty
Nippgen Michael, lab., 117 Bremen
Nirmann Joseph, cooper, 112 Abigail
Nirnberger August, 483 Race
Nisbett Ellen, 532 W. 7th
Nister Edward, lab., 36 Butler
Niven Wm , confec., n.w.c. Elm and 8th
Nixol Henry, shoe mkr., bds. 372 Broadway
Nixon Mrs. A., bds. 67 Longworth
NIXON, CHATFIELD & WOODS, (Thomas N., Wm. H. C. & Wm. W.,) Manufacturers and Wholesale Paper Dealers, 77 and 79 Walnut
Nixon James S., gas fitter, 678 Main
Nixon Laura O., teacher, bds. 28 Laurel
Nixon Laura O., teacher, bds. 294 W. 8th
Nixon Margaret D., teacher, bds. 28 Laurel
Nixon Margaret, teacher, 294 W. 8th
Nixon Samuel, 28 Laurel
NIXON Thos., (N., Chatfield & Woods) h. Springfield, O.
NIXON W. K., (Smith & N.), Avondale, O.
Nixon Wm. P., atty, 75 W. 3d
Nondmin Henry, cab. mkr., 187 Clark
Noah Nathan, peddler, 213 Walnut
Nobbe Catharina, 24 Abigail
Nobbe Frederick, carp., s.w.c. Main and Liberty
NOBBE HARMON, Family Grocery, 53 W. Court
Nobbe John Henry, grocery, 627 Main

250 (NOL) CINCINNATI (NOR) DIRECTORY.

Nobel John, blksmith, 12 Mary
Noble Daniel, lab., 606 E. Front
Noble Elisabeth, cof. h., 101 W. 5th
Noble Frank, huckster, 82 E. Abigail
NOBLE J. M.,
   City Treasurer,
   Office City Hall, h. 411 W. 3d
Noble James, b.k., bds. 274 W. 8th
Noble James, mach., 202 Barr
Noble James F., b.k., 18 Barr
Noble John, blksmith, 12 Mary
Noble Jonathan H., plasterer, 33 Mill
Noble Joseph, musician, 100 W. Front
Noble Martin, 43 Lodge
Noble Mary, 95 Freeman
Noble Nathan M., clk. L. M. R. R., h. 18 Barr
Noble Oscar, police, 66 Mill
Noble Thomas, eng., 636 W. 6th
Noble Wm P., artist and designer, bds. 28 W. 7th
Nock August, 68 Mohawk
Nock Stephan, tailor, s.s. Buckeye nr. Locust
NOCK Wm. S., (Dannenhold & N.), h. Covington
Nockel John, meats, 146 Bremen
Nocttor Matthew, dray, 357 Broadway
Nodermann Henry, lab., 19 Franklin
Noe John, lab., 10 Eden
Noe Lucinda, 236 Linn
Noe Mathias, shoe mkr., 564 Race
Noe Samuel, tinner, wks. 21 E. Front
Noel C., bds. Dennison House
Noel Clarence photographer, bds. s.e c. 3d and Broadway
Noelcke Edward, frame manuf., 207 Central Av., h. 71 Woodward
NOELKER JOHN F.,
   Proprietor Western Hotel,
   502 W. Front
Noell Franz, printer, 450 Vine
Noewer Henry J, grocery, 658 Elm
Noewer John G., clk., bds. 658 Elm
Noffsinger Daniel, cigar mkr., 233 Main
Nobe Fred. finisher, wks. n.e.c. Walnut and Canal [Canal
Nohe Wm., lab., wks. n.e.c. Walnut and
Nohl John B., finisher, 213 Barr
Nohoa Frank, cook, Galt House
Nolan Catharine, servt., 75 Barr
Nolan Catharine, dress mkr , 102 E. 5th
Nolan Charles, lab., n.e.c. 3d and Butler
Nolan Edward, dray, 173 W. Front
Nolan Emilie, dress mkr., 26 Abigail
Nolan James, cooper, w.s. Lock b. 8th and Court
Nolan James, lab., s.s. Front E. of Hazen
Nolan John, lab . 302 W. 4th
Nolan John, mason, 205 Cutter
Nolan Kate teacher, 102 E. 5th
Nolan Kate, 35 Rittenhouse
Nolan Lucy Ann, laundress, 13 Thuber al. b. Adams and Wade
Nolan Margaret, dress mkr., 102 E. 5th
Nolan Martin, porter, 495 W. 9th
Nolan Mary, n.s. Front e. of Kelly
Nolan Michael, lab., 28 Ann
Nolan Patrick, cof. h., 508 W. 4th
Nolan Patrick, lab., n.s. E. Front E. of Leatherbury
Nolan Peter, police, s.s. E. Pearl b. Pike and Butler
Nolan Wm., porter, 402 W. 7th
Nolan Wm., boots and shoes, s.e.c. Broadway and Woodward
Nold Chas. D., mess. C. H. & D. R. R., 181 Barr
Nold Chas. D., messenger U. S. Express Company
Nold Jacob C., clk., 137 George
Nold Nicholas, dray, 47 Pub. Landing
Nolker Francis, lab., 38 Pleasant
Nolker John C., (John C. N. & Fred. Krumdleck,) 64 Richmond
Nolker John C. & Fred. Krumdleck, stable, n.s. 9th b. Plum and Central Av.
Nolkers Frank, sawyer, 38 Pleasant
Noll Chas., 130 Mohawk
Noll Franz, painter, 450 Vine
Noll Gottfried, brewer, 615 Vine
Noll Henry, cab. mkr., 179 Barr
Noll John H., tin shop, 502 Sycamore
Noll Kasper, boots and shoes, 321 W. 6th

Noll Peter, lab., 125 Mohawk
Noll Robt., cof. h., e.s. Vine junction of Buckeye
Nolt Christian, cof. h., 72 Ham. Road
Nolte Anton, lab., 302 Findlay
Nolte August, clk., bds. 440 Sycamore
Nolte August, lab., 154 Pleasant
Nolte Christopher, 108 Clinton
Nolte Francis, eng., 437 John
Nolte Franklin, eng., 437 John
Nolte Gustavus, clk., 377 John
Nolte Hammond, stone mason 199 Everett
Nolte Hy., cab. mkr., 90 Melancthon
Nolte John, 250 Mulberry
Nolte John H., lab., w.s. Bremen b. Elder and Findlay
Nolting Chas. P. F., cab. mkr., 235 W. 6th
Nonweiler Gustavus, cab. mkr., 71 Pleasant
Noon Adam, carp., s. w. c. 6th and Broadway
Noonan John, gas fitter, wks. 221 W, 5th, h. n.w.c. 8th and Lock
Noonan John, lab., 50 Pike
Noonan John, roller, bds. s.e.c. 2d and Smith
Noone Anna, bds. 103 Court
Noone Lucy, bks. 103 W. Court
Noppenberger Adam, n.w.c. Schiller and Hughes
Noppenberger John, meats, n.w.c. Schiller and Hughes
Noppenberger Andrew, stone mason, 731 Elm
Norcese Chas., cook, 160 E. 6th
Nordeck Philip, blk. smith, 536 Race
Nordheim Christiana, 510 Race
Nordheim John M., messenger C. F. Adae & Co.'s
Nordheim Nary, servt., 471 Vine
Nordheim Michael, painter, 260 Main
Nordloh & Coleman, (John B. N. & Arnold H. C.,) boots and shoes, 431 W 2d
Nordloh Hy., driver, 217 Betts
Mordloh Hermon, cigar mkr., wks. 422 Walnut
Nordloh Herman, lab., e.s. Anderson b. 2d and Pearl
Nordloh John B., (N. & Coleman,) w.s. Park b. 2d and W. W. Canal
Nordloh Mary, 148 Abigail
Nordlohne John, 81 Pleasant
Nordman Frank A., bar k., n.e.c. 2d and Broadway
Nordman Frederick, molder, 11 15th b. Elm and Plum
Nordman Louisa, 11 15th, b. Elm and Plum
Nordmann Chas., cigars, &c., 226 W. 5th, res. country
Nordmann Frederick, carp., 27 Ham. Road
Nordmann Henry, cigar mkr., h. s.w.c. 6th and Smith
Nordmeier Anna, 609 Race
Nordmeier Hy., carp., 26 Madison
Norman Antony, porter, 52 W. Pearl, h. 311 W. 8th
Norman Thos., lab., 309 W. 8th
Norman W. T., wood engraver and printer. 230 Walnut
Norris Benj. A., clk., 303 Central Av., bds. 26 Clark
Norris David, 18 New
Norris Edward, stone mason, 368 Broadway
Norris Ethelbert D., 108 York
Norris Ethelbert D. jr., engraver, 477 W. 7th
Norris Jas., saloon, 131 W. 5th
Norris John C., 202 Sycamore
Norris Joseph, carp., 21 Ann
NORRIS RICHARD D , Cloak, Shawl and Mantilla House, and Fancy Dress Goods, 174 W. 5th
Norris Walter, clk., 202 Sycamore
North America Fire Ins. Co., agency 65 W. 3d
North Ann, 7 Pierson
North Catharine, seamstress, al. b. 13th and Mercer and Vine and Walnut
North Chas., shoe mkr., 117 Betts
North John, 21 Jackson

(OAK) CINCINNATI (O'B) DIRECTORY. (O'B) 251

Nuesberger John, trimmer, 139 W. Pearl
Nuesse Hermann, carp., n.s. Cassatt al. b. Main and Sycamore
Nuezel Geo., bakery, 148 E. Front
Nugent Edward, maltster, n.s. 8th b. Broadway and Sycamore
Nugent Edward P., carriage painter. 454 W. 8th
Nugent Francis H., clk., bds. 454 W. 8th
Nugent Geo E., asst. city engineer, bds. 454 W. 8th
Nugent Jas., carp., 14 Oliver
Nugent John, porter, 98 E. 5th
Nugent Michael, dray, 71 Pendleton
Nugent Wm., cof. h., 239 Broadway
Nulvin John, carp., 114 and 116 Buckeye
Nullmeier Frederick, carman, 67 Hughes
NULSEN ANTHONY, Cigars and Tobacco, 12 Main, h. 137 E. Liberty
Nulsen Clements, clk., 12 Main, h. 137 E Liberty
Nulty Thomas, currier, bds. 138 W. 3d
Nummenson Hy., hatter, wks. 144 Main
Numan Jane, 212 E. 6th
Numan John, b.k., 212 E. 6th
Nunefeld Herman, cartman, n.s. Taylor al. w. of Kilgour
Nuneker Wm., (Wm. Wilke & Co.,) 156 W. Pearl
NUNNINGMOLLER JNO. H., Cigars, Tobacco, Snuff, &c., 455 W. 5th, h. 457 W. 5th
Nuoffer Martin, peddler, rear 20 15th
Nupert John, cooper, 366 Sycamore
Nurmile John, lab., s.s. 8th b. Broadway and Sycamore
Nurre Bernhard, salesman, 60 13th
Nurre Herman H., carpet weaver 60 13th
Nurre Joseph, clk., 457 Main
Nurre Joseph, carpet weaver, 60 13th
Nurtney Ann, servt., 279 Longworth
Nusbaum Benjamin, drover, bds. 494 Race
Nusbaum Bernhard, bds. 494 Race
Nusbaum Meyer, drover, 494 Race
Nusbaum Peter, lab., 515 E. Front
Nusky Theo., teamster, 12 Lock
Nuss Peter, bakery, bds. 244 W. 6th
Nussbaum Jacob, 403 Elm
Nussberger Anthony, lab., 22 Allison
Nussberger Geo., trimmer, h. 139 W. Pearl
Nusz Catharine, bds. 107 W. Liberty
Nusz Magdalena, bds. 107 W. Liberty
Nuszbaum Hy., 58 Allison
Nuttel Bridget, cof. h., State b. Deer Creek Road and Accommodation
Nuttel John, lab., e. end of 6th
Nuttel Thos., lab , e end of 6th
Nuttker Anthony, lab., 375 Broadway
Nuttle Ann, w.s. Miami Canal b. 6th and 8th
Nuttle Thos., lab., wks. J. Whittaker's, Deer Creek Valley
Nutz Michael, cab. mkr., s.e.c. Front and John
Nuxoll Herman, lab , rear 73 Abigail
Nuxoll John W., boots and shoes, 220 Central Av.
NYE & DEMAREST, (H R. N. & G. L. D.) Publishers Star in the West and Universalist Book Store, n.w. c. 6th and Walnut
Nye Elipha, pork mer., bds. 98 E. 3d
Nye Elipha N., clk., bds. 98 E. 3d
NYE H. R., (N. & Demarest) h. Yellow Springs, O.
Nye Hy., finisher, h. 211 Clinton
NYE HENRY, Pork and Beef Packer and Commission Merchant, 327, 329, 331 and 333 Broadway, h. 340 W. 4th
NYE JOHN C., Pork Packer and Ham Curer, 12 and 14 E. Canal, h. 440 Broadway

O

Oak John, lab., wks. Hy. Nye's
Oakley Isabella, teacher at First Intermediate School
Oakley John, lab., 42 E. 8th e. of Lock

Oakley Wm., bds. 107 Broadway
Oakley Wm. R., b.k. 53 Main
Oates James C., harness mkr., bds. Main St. House
Oates Wm., dray, n.s. Avery b. Mill and Stone
Oates Wm. H., paper hanger, bds. n.s. Avery b. Mill and Stone
O'Bar David, stone cutter, wks. s.w.c. Broadway and 5th
O'Beirna Sarah, 317 Broadway
Obel John, lab., 181 Baymiller
Ober David, marble cutter, s.e.c. 6th and Culvert
Ober Frank, molder, wks. s.w.c. Front and Central Av.
Ober Hy., barber, 9 W. 6th
Oberdahn John, bk. binder, 11 E. Liberty
Oberdeen Wm., molder, bds. 11 Pierson
Oberding Peter, molder, n.s. 5th b. Hannibal and Freeman
Oberding Rudolph, molder, 632 W. 6th
Oberding Wm., molder, 11 Pierson
Oberdink Geo., tailor, 13 Providence
Oberfeld Mathias, tailor, 674 Race
Oberfeld Christian, porter, 215 Walnut
Obergfell Christian, porter 215 Walnut
Oberguenter Mary, w.s. Coggswell al. b. Franklin and Woodward
Oberhelmann Ernst, tanner, 54 Dudley
OBERHEU E. & F., (Ernst & Fred.) Grocers and Commission Merchants 112 W. Court
OBERHEU Ernst, (E. & F. O.) 112 W. Court
OBERHEU Frederick, (E. & F. O.) 112 W. Court
OBERHEU L. O., (E. & F. O.) 112 W. Court
Oberhinan John, clk., 26 E. Pearl
Oberklaus Gerhard, lab., 164 Pleasant
Oberklein Francis, miller. 145 Clay
Oberklein Fred., molder, 145 Clay
Oberklein Geo. H., grocery, s.w.c. Freeman and Liberty
Oberklein Wm., gilder, 145 Clay
Oberklein Wm., molder, bds. 145 Clay
Oberlander John, collector, 163 Clinton
Oberle August, cof. h., 142 Clay
Oberle Chas., cooper, rear 166 Clay
Oberle Geo., shoe mkr., 585 Race
Oberle John, cooper, 192 Clinton
Oberley Louisa, servt., 68 Pike
Oberly Balser, carp , n.s. Front e. of Lumber
Obermayer Simon, 136 Longworth
Obermeier Bernhard, painter, 122 Abigail
Obermeier Hy., tinner, 122 Abigail
Obermeier Joseph, teamster, 165 Linn
Obermeyer Andrew, lab., 58 Hunt
Obermeyer Andrew, 152 Hunt
Obermeyer August, horse dealer, 167 Laurel
Obermeyer Fanny, 301 W. 9th w. of Central Av.
Obermeyer Hy., (B. Sander & H. O.) 440 Walnut
Obermeyer John H., stable, 178 Linn
Obermeyer Samuel, student, bds. 301 W. 9th w. of Central Av.
Obermeyer Simon, 76 Clinton
Oberndorfer Wm., b k. 78 W. Pearl, h. 133 W. 5th
Obernesser Jacob, finisher, e.s. Johnson al. b. Canal and 12th
Oberst John B., clk. s.e.c. 4th and Hammond
O'Beirne Thos., lime dealer, 109 Clinton
O'Bierne Theobold, clk. 24 W. 2d
Obirclone Geo., finisher, 164 Pleasant
Obker Fred., lab., 191 W. Canal
Oblinger F. J., printer, Press office, h. 199 W. 3d
Oborne Samuel W., clk. bds. 197 Vine
Obracke Christopher H., carp., 137 Baymiller
O'Brian Chas., confec., 168 W. 5th
O'Brian Dennis, stone cutter, 59 Rittenhouse
O'Brian Hy., dray, n.s. Railroad e. of French
O'Brian Marts, shoe mkr., 146 Spring
O'Brian Mary, 59 Rittenhouse
O'Brian Mary, laundress, Gibson House
O'Brian Michael, lab., s.s. 6th b. Harriet and Horne

O'Bride Anna, confec., 302 W. 6th
O'Brien Mrs., 15 W. Court w. of Central Av.
O'Brien Andrew, n.s. 6th e. of Lock
O'Brien Anne, servt., Burnet House
O'Brien Bartel, lab., bds. 182 E. 6th
O'BRIEN BERNARD, Family Grocery and Provisions, 251 Sycamore
O'Brien Catharine, s.s. Arch b. Ludlow and Lawrence
O'Brien Catharine, servt., 103 Broadway
O'Brien Chas., dray, 50 E. 7th
O'BRIEN Daniel, (Alexander Brennan & Co.) bds. Gibson House
O'Brien Dennis, lab., s.s. E. Pearl b. Pike and Butler
O'Brien Edward, clk., 202 Longworth
O'Brien Edward, drover, n.e.c. Court and John
O'Brien Ellen, s.s. Pearl b. Pike and Butler
O'Brien Frank, lab., 67 Observatory Road
O'Brien Hanora, 112 W. Pearl
O'Brien Hy., blksmith, wks. n.e.c. 6th and Culvert
O'Brien James, dray, bds. 399 Sycamore
O'Brien James, hatter, 277 W. 9th
O'Brien John, b.k. s.w.c. 4th and Walnut, h 236 W. 5th
O'Brien John, clothing, 236 W. 5th
O'Brien John, carp., 163 Cutter
O'Brien John, clk., h. 53 E. 8th e. of Lock
O'Brien John, finisher, 31 Baum
O'Brien John, finisher, 399 W. 3d
O'Brien John, lab., s.s. 6th e. of Lock
O'Brien John, mach., wks. n.s. Front b. Lawrence and Pike
O'Brien John, paper folder, 53 E. 8th
O'Brien John, servt., 390 W. 6th
O'Brien John D., molder, wks. n.e.c. Canal and Walnut
O'Brien John Y., whitewasher, n.s. Patterson al. b. Main and Walnut
O'Brien Kate, milliner, bds. s.s. Wade w. of Baymiller
O'Brien Lewis, driver, e.s. Baymiller b. Clinton and Betts
O'Brien Margaret, servt., Burnet House
O'Brien Martin, lab., n.e.c. 4th and Wood
O'Brien Martin, blksmith, s.s. 6th b. Broadway and Culvert
O'Brien Martin J., lab., 61 Mill
O'Brien Mary, 205 E. 5th
O'Brien Mary, 15 W. Court w. of Central Av.
O'Brien Mary, laundress, Spencer House
O'Brien Mary, servt., n.e.c 3d and Pike
O'Brien Mary, al. b. 4th and 5th and Central Av. and John
O'Brien Mary, s.s. Accommodation e. of 8th
O'Brien Maurice, cooper, 9 Accommodation
O'Brien Michael, 53 E. 8th e. of Lock
O'Brien Michael, carp., 102 Sycamore
O'Brien Michael, carp., 396 Broadway
O'Brien Michael, lab., 61 Mill
O'Brien Michael, lab., 168 Freeman
O'Brien Michael, lab., bds. Ludlow House
O'Brien Michael, lab., 69 E. 8th e. of Lock
O'Brien Morris, lab., City Water Works office
O'Brien Owen, printer, s.e.c. Elm and 3d
O'Brien Patrick, 106 E. Liberty
O'Brien Patrick, assessor, 90 W. 2d
O'Brien Patrick, blksmith, 399 W. 3d
O'Brien Patrick, dray, 240 Richmond
O'Brien Patrick, lab , 59 Rittenhouse
O'Brien Patrick, lab., 134 Clark
O'Brien Patrick, lab., 302 Plum
O'Brien Patrick, lab., 118 Water
O'Brien Patrick, tailor, 236 W. 5th
O'Brien Robt. A., 236 W. 5th
O'Brien Thos., bklayer, n.s. Channing b. Price and Young
O'Brien Thos., lab., wks. C., H. & D. R. R. Depot
O'Brien Thos., ments, 614 W. 6th
O'Brien Thos., salesman 129 Main
O'Brien Thos. F., carp., 30 Kossuth
O'Brien Wm., dray, 424 Freeman

O'Brien Wm., dray, e.s. Oregon b. 3d and 6th
O'Brien Winefrede, 113 George
O'Byrne Patrick, tailor, 32 W. 5th
Ochmann Hy., carp., 131 Clark
Ochs Conrad, tailor, bds. 84 W. Court
Ochs Hy., tailor, s.w.c. Peete and Poplar
Ochs John F., boots and shoes, 54 Ham. Road
Ochsner Hy., cigar mkr., w.s. Broadway b. Court and Hunt
Ochsner Nicholas, cof. h., n.s. Corp. Line near Auburn
Ockle Andrew, teamster, n.s. Front e. of Ferry
O'Connell Bridget, servt., 261 W. 6th
O'CONNELL Daniel, (M. E. Reeves & Co.) 428 W. 4th
O'Connell Daniel, bar k., 328 Central Av.
O'Connell Daniel, dry goods, 234 Water
O'Connell Daniel, lab., wks. Lane & Bodley's
O'Connell Daniel, lab., s.e.c. Freeman and W. W. Canal
O'Connell David, phys., 345 W. 8th
O'Connell Donald, lab., n.s. Front e. of Kelly
O'Connell Edward, printer, bds. 31 E. 8th
O'Connell Jas., lab., 55 Plum
O'Connell Jeremiah, printer, bds. 31 E. 8th
O'Connell John, lab., 53 E. 8th
O'Connell John, plumber, n.e.c. 6th and John
O'Connell John, tailor, 3 Crippen al.
O'Connell John, waiter Burnet House
O'Connell Kate, 445 W. 4th
O'Connell Mary, laundress, Spencer House
O'Connell Maurice, lab., 31 E. 8th e. of Lock
O'Connell Michael, cof. h., s.s. 6th b. Broadway and Culvert and blksmith shop n.e.c. 6th and Culvert
O'Connell Morris, finisher, n.e.c. 6th and John
O'Connell Timothy, bookseller &c., n.w. c. 8th and Central Av., h. 254 W. 8th
O'Conner Edward, lab., n.s. Hopkins b Freeman and Garrard
O'Conner Edward, varnisher wks. n.w.c Smith and Front
O'Conner Elizabeth, servt. 375 W. 8th
O'Conner Hugh, shoe mkr., n.e.c. 9th and Central Av
O'Conner John, lab., 196 W. 7th
O'Conner Michael, lab., 3 Smith Court
O'Conner Rich., lab., al. b. 4th and 5th and Central Av. and John
O'Conner Wm., cooper, 197 Richmond
O'Conner Thos., lab., n.s. Cherry al. b. Plum and Central Av
O'Connor Andrew, lab., wks. s.w.c. Broadway and 5th
O'Connor Arthur, steward, bds. 33 Mill
O'Connor Andrew, lab., s.s. E. Court b. 6th and Observatory Road
O'Connor Bridget, n.s. Patterson al. b. Main and Walnut
O'Connor Edward, lab., s.s. Pearl b Pike and Butler
O'Connor, Edward, varnisher, wks. n.w c. Elm and Pearl
O'Connor Eliza, h. 184 Race
O'Connor Elizabeth, laundress, 107 Woodward
O'Connor Ellen, servt., 25 Harrison
O'Connor Ellen servt., 266 W. 7th
O'Connor James, grocery, s.e.c. Lodge and Gano
O'Connor James, grocery, 124 E. 8th
O'Connor James, lab., 191 E. Pearl
O'Connor Jeffry, tailor, 275 Sycamore
O'Connor Johanna, h. 197 Richmond
O'Connor, John, boots and shoes, 231 Race
O'Connor John, carp., 100 Race
O'Connor John, cof. h., 130 Central Av.
O'Connor John, lab., 43 Mill
O'Connor John, lab., 236 E. 6th
O'Connor John X., bds. 312 Longworth

O'Connor Margaret, n.s. Patterson al. b. Main and Walnut
O'Connor Maggie, n.s. Patterson-al. b. Main and Walnut
O'Connor Michael, n.s. New b. Culvert and Broadway
O'Connor Michael, butcher, 50 E. 8th e. of Lock
O'Connor Patrick, expressman, 306 Clark
O'Connor Patrick, fireman, 447 W. 2d
O'Connor Patrick, tailor, 6 New
O'Connor T. A., atty., 130 Vine, h. 22 W. 7th
O'Connor Wm., lab., 197 Richmond
O'Connor Wm., lab. 14 E 8th e. of Lock
O'Cook Mary, 84 Abigail
O'Darnall Hugh, cooper, wks. s.s. Gest, b. Freeman and Carr
O'Day John, lab., s.s. Friendship al. b. Pike and Butler
O'Day Patrick, grocery 132 E. 6th
Odd Fellows Hall, n.w.c. 3d and Walnut
ODIORNE T. G. Commission Merchant and Dealer in Cotton Goods, 43 Walnut, h. 127 W. 8th
Odkamp Dieterich, cab. mkr., 13 Mary
Odlum Thomas, clk., 384 W. 3d
Odom John, carp., 607 Main
O'Dould Bridget, servt., Henrie House
O'Donald James, dray, 245 Laurel
O'Donald Mary, servt., 379 Longworth
O'Donall P., bds. Dennison House
O'Donnahue Mary, 21 E. 8th
O'Donnell Ann, 249 Hopkins
O'Donnell Bridget, 61 Hopkins
O'Donnell Bryan, lab., Is., 35 Ludlow
O'Donnell Daniel, lab., 176 E. 3d e. of Collard
O'Donnell Edward, lab., 18 Kossuth
O'Donnell Eliza, servt., 113 E. 3d
O'Donnell Hugh, 264 Hopkins
O'Donnell Jeremiah, molder, 313 John
O'Donnell John, M.. cof. h., 175 Richmond
O'Donnell John, lab., 97 Central Av
O'Donnell John, cooper, 12 Commerce
O'Donnell Lucretia, 133 Smith
O'Donnell Margaret, trimmer, 245 Laurel
O'Donnell Mary, servt., 136 E. 3d
O'Donnell Michael, cooper, 349 Central Av
O'Donnell Michael, drover, 31 W. Court w. of Central Av
O'Donnell Mich., lab., 15 W. Court
O'Donnell Michael, lab., 412 Sycamore
O'Donnell Michael, moulder 81 Hopkins
O'Donnell Milas, trader, 40 Everett
O'Donnell Patrick, cooper,16 Commerce b. Walnut and Vine
O'Donnell Patrick, hatter, n.s. Oliver b, Baymiller and Linn
O'Donnell Patrick, lab., 14 Plum
O'Donnell Patrick, lab., 78 Abigail
O'Donnell Patrick, molder, wks. Wm. Resor & Co's
O'Donnell Patrick, porter, 14 Plum
O'Donnell Sarah, 305 Water
O'Donnell Thos., clk., 52 E. 8th
O'Donnell Wm., lab., n.w.c. Freeman and Richmond
O'Donnell Wm., lab. s.s. Cassatt al. b. Sycamore and Main
O'DONOGHUE James (O'D. & Naish.) 164 W. 5th
O'Donoghue John, marble cutter, 62 W. Court
O'DONOGHUE & NAISH (James O'D & Wm. J. N.) Boots and Shoes, 164 W. 5th
O'Dowd B., dress mkr., 444 W. 5th
O'Dowd John, lab., 518 W. 3d
O'Dowd John, b k, 318 John
O'Dowd Thos., Recorder Probate Court, h. 72 Richmond
O'Down Sarah, servt., 428 W. 6th
O'Driscol Annie, servt., 342 W. 7th
O'DRISCOLL C. F., (Hills, O'D. & Co.) 144 Clark
O'Driscoll Cornelius F., stereotyper, 247 Clinton
O'Driscoll D. C., printer, 141 Main, bds. 127 W. 5th
O'Driscoll John, stereotyper, 141 Main, bds., 127 W. 5th

O'Driscoll Mary, 104 George
O'Driscoll Mary, e.s. Pancoast al. b. 7th and 8th
O'Dren Sarah, 314 W. 7th
Oechsle Fred., carp., w.s. Goose al. b. Liberty and Green
Oechsle John, pottery, 124 Findlay
Oechsle Philip, potter, 124 Findlay
Oede Wolfgang, baker, 510 Plum
Oeder Geo., bakery, n.e.c. Elm and Elder
Oeh Conrad, dry goods, 281 Ham. Road
Oeh Conrad, boots and shoes, 98 Pearl e. of Broadway
Oeh Fred., shoe mkr., s.s. Henry b. Elm and Dunlap
Oeh Geo., lab., 73 E. Front
Oeh John, n.e.c. Rice and Mulberry
Oeh John, lab., s.e.c. Pearl and Ludlow
Oehlemacher Philip, dray, 478 Linn
Oehler Benedict, porter, 112 Freeman
Oehler Benjamin, salesman, 112 Bremen
Oehler Fred., C.. shoe mkr., 275 Freeman
Oehler Jacob J., tailor, n.w.c. Freeman and Gest
Oehler John, gardener, w.s. Garrard b. Hopkins and Kenner
Oehler Lewis, wagon mkr., wks. I. & B Bruce's
Oehling Herman, cooper, bds. 87 Spring
OEHLMANN FREDERICK H., Recorder Ham. County, Office Court House, h. 35 Jackson
Oelert Chas., cigars &c., 344 Freeman
Oelgeklaus Wm. A. H., vinegar manuf., h. s.w.c. John and Clinton
Oelker C., carp., wks. 304 Broadway
Oelker Chas., grocery, 31 E. 7th
Oelschleger Hy., cooper, e.s. Orchard b. Main and Sycamore, h. 26 Orchard
Oelschleger John H., porter, e.s. Vine b Ham. Road and Buckeye
Oemisch Eberhard, phys , 29 Franklin
Oerlars John, varnisher n.e.c. Mound and Longworth
Oerthel Jacob, cooper, 24 Franklin
Oertle John, lab., 364 Race
Oesper Peter, dry goods, 36 Ham. Road
Oester John, cof. h., 415 Sycamore
Oester John H, baker, 55 Sycamore
Oesterle John Geo., blksmith., 195 Bremen
Oesterman Frank, lab., 29 Observatory
Oestler Edward cooper, bds. 172 Clay
Oeter John, tailor, 146 Ham. Road
Oeter John W., baker, 510 Plum
Oeter Wolfgang, tailor, 146 Ham Road
Oetjen Hy , tobacconist. 221 Main, h. 13 Buckeye
Oetting Hy., shoe mkr., 525 Sycamore
Oeyen Max, lithographer, s.w.c. 4th and Walnut
O'Fallon Michael stone mason, 46 Kossuth
O'Farrell Wm., clk. s.w.c. 6th and Freeman
Ofenheiser Fred., baker , 120 W. 5th
Offerman Philip, carp , 363 Cutter
OFFICE CHIEF OF POLICE, City Building, John W. Dudley, Chief
Offner Alex., salesman, bds. 321 W. 8th
Offner Gustav, salesman, bds. 321 W 8th
Offner Hy., tinner, 321 W. 8th
O'Flaraty Patrick, tailor, 111 W. 3d
O'Gara Patrick, grocery, 48 Plum
O'Gara Patrick, lab., w s. Lawrence b 4th and 5th
O'Garr Elizabeth, 17 Macalister
O'Garr Mary, servt., wks., 194 Barr
O'Garra John, cof. h , 571 W. 5th
O'Garry Patrick, marble polisher, 333 W 2d
O'Garry Thos , cof. h., 170 W. Front
OGDEN Isaac A., (Gilbert, Jones & O.) bds. Walnut St. House
Ogden A. H. & Co., (Albert H. O., & Chas. H. Hubbell,) com. mer., 593 W. 5th
Ogden Albert H., (O. A. H. & Co.) 376 W. 3d
Ogden Alex., type caster, wks. 163 Vine
Ogden Celia, 51 Rittenhouse

(OHL) CINCINNATI (O'M) DIRECTORY. (OPH) 253

Ogden Hy. T., printer, 16 Gest
Ogden James R., 376 W. 3d
OGDEN JONATHAN,
  Merchant Tailor, 32 W. 4th, h. 195 W. 4th
Ogden Joseph O., 324 Longworth
Ogden Marcus G., pattern mkr. bds. 560 Webb
Ogden Robert, type caster, 88 Wade
Ogden Samuel, 424 W. 4th
Ogle Custina, h. 213 Water
O'Gorman John, bk. layer, 197 E. 6th
O'Hair Thomas, shoe mkr., n.e.c. Court and Mound
O'Hallonan Daniel, molder, n.s. Front e. of Kelly
O'Hara Ellen, tailoress, n.s. 5th b. John and Smith
O'Hara John, 50 E. 2d
O'Hara John, blksmith, 66 Richmond
O'Hara John, lab, 106 E 6th
O'Hara John, lab., wks. 100 Sycamore
O'Hara John, lab., s.s. 5th b. Macalister and Lawrence
O'Hara Michael, carp. e. s. Miami Canal b. 8th and Court
O'Hara Michael, lab., 100 Sycamore
O'Hara Patrick, lab., n.s. Pearl b. Central Av. and Plum
O'Hara Peter, e. s. Pancoast al. b. 7th and 8th
O'HARA THOMAS B., Attorney at Law, and Notary Public, 119 Walnut, h. 314 W 6th
O'Hara Thomas, mach., bds. Columbia House
O'Hara Timothy J., salesman, 174 W. 5th, bds. 60 Richmond
O'Hara William, s. e. c. 7th and Broadway
O'Hara Wm. A., mer., 403 W. 7th
O'Haran Michael, 297 W. 7th
O'Hare Mary, 3 Smith Court
O'Haron Wm., 52 E. 8th e. of Lock
O'Harra James, lab., 178 Cutter
O'Harra Jane, 252 Longworth
O'Harra John, clk., 66 Richmond, b. Plum and Central Av.
O'Harra Patrick, lab., 209 W. 2d
O'Harra Thomas, lab., s.w.c Vine and Front
O'Harra Timothy, mach., 66 Richmond
Ohe Anna, laundress, 29 Abigail
Ohe John, finisher, s w. c. Pearl and Ludlow
Ohe Wm. N., clk., 449 Sycamore
O'Heren Michael, lab., n. e. c. 5th and Broadway
O'Heren Thomas, lab., s.s. 6th b. Broadway and Culvert
O'Herring Thomas, lab., s. s. 6th b. Broadway and Culvert
O'Heron Lawrence, lab., 343 Broadway
Ohey Geo., lab., wks. 222 E. Front
Ohio College of Dental Surgery, J. Taft, Dean, 29 College
OHIO LIFE INSURANCE CO.,
  Augustus Isham, President
  64 W. 3d
Ohio Medical College, s. s. 6th b. Vine and Race
OHIO & MISSISSIPPI RAILROAD DEPOT,
  s.s. Front near Wood
OHIO & MISSISSIPPI RAILROAD OFFICE,
  n.s. Front b. Mill and Wood
OHIO RIVER SALT CO.,
  27 W Front
  W. A. Healy, Agent
OHIO VALLEY FARMER,
  (Monthly) B. F. Sanford Proprietor
  n.e.c. 4th and Walnut
Ohl Chas., finisher, 375 W 5th
Ohlenroth Bernhard, J., nail mkr., 579 Race
Ohler Jacob, mason, 27 Moore
Ohlger Hy., cooper, s. e. c. Jones and Melancthon
Ohling Mrs. Elizabeth, dress mkr., h. 703 Main
Ohlmann Morris, (agent Isaac Kohn,) 111 Main
Ohlsen Hy. C., carriage mkr., 143 Baymiller

Ohlslager Hy., cooper. wks. n. w. c. Freeman and 9th
Ohmann Elizabeth, 561 Vine
Ohmann Wm., cigar mkr., 105 Pleasant
Ohmer Geo , refreshment stand, L. M.R. R. Depot, h. 54 Lawrence
Ohmer John P., confec., 782 E Front, h. n.s. E. 3d e. of Parsons
O'Holland Wm., tailor, e.s. Haven al. b. 8th and 9th
Ohschlegar Frederick, 35 Milton
O'Kane James, dray, 68 W. Mulberry
O'Kane Tullius O., teacher, 115 York
O'Keefe Daniel, lab.. 65 E. 8th
O'Keefe James, feed store, 265 Central Av.
O'Keefe Kyran, grocery, 414 George
O'Keefe Margaret 6 Clinton
O'Keefe Thos., bar k., 110 W. 4th
Oker August cooper, s. s. Charlotte b. Central Av. and Linn
Oker Joseph, cof. h., 817 Central Av.
Okes David, express, 25 Lodge
Oks Hy., peddler, e. s. Western Av, b. Poplar and Findlay
Okum Kate, servt., 420 Broadway
Olaphant John, carp., n. e. c. Front and Whittaker
O'Lary Johanna, 50 Lock
Oldagarring Hy., molder, 62 Abigail
Oldem George W., printer, bds. 244 W. Court w. of Central Av.
Oldemeier Francis, lab.. 63 Findlay
Olden Wm., wagon mkr., 293 Linn
Oldendek Hy., cab. mkr., bds. n. e. c. Smith and Augusta
Oldrieve Chas., E., music teacher, 103 Barr
Oldrieve Louisa M. C. 103 Barr
Oldrieve Sylvan R., bk. binder, 103 Barr
OLEAN HOTEL,
  C. F. Tonnies, Proprietor,
  s.e.c. Central Av. Front
O'Leary Mrs., 8 W.
O'Leary Cornelius, lab., n. s. 7th b. Broadway and Sycamore
O'Leary Michael, lab., 149 George
Olemacher Christian, lab., 681 Vine
Olhaber Clement salesman, Adam Peckover & Co's., 66 Laurel
Olier John, tailor, 662 Vine
Olier Joseph, tailor, 671 Race
Olinger John, tailor, e. s. Goose al. b. Liberty and Green
Olive Branch House, s.w.c. Ludlow and Front
Oliver Alexander L., 68 Water
Oliver Andrew, brakesman, n. s. Patterson al. b. Main and Walnut
Oliver B. W., (Conkling, Young & Co.) 130 Butler
Oliver David W., alchohol &c., 68 Water h. Covington
Oliver Edmund, dray, 49 David
Oliver Emeline, n. s. Patterson al. b. Main and Walnut
Oliver Hy., painter. 716 W. 6th
Oliver James, blksmith, 62 Butler
Oliver James H., phys., bds. 264 Elm
Oliver Jane, 105 Richmond
Oliver John, carp., 870 E. Front
Oliver Joseph N., 158 W. 9th
Oliver Mary Jane, nurse, Commercial Hospital
Oliver Melancthon W., judge, Court Com. Pleas, 495 W. 7th
Oliver Richard. butcher, Bank b. Baymiller and Freeman
Oliver Robt E., steward, 105 E. 2d
Oliver Thomas, shoe mkr., 104 Water
Oliver Warner S., 68 Water, bds. 320 W. 3d
Oliver Wm. H., foreman, 56 Pike, h. 507 W. 5th [Court
Ollarich Hy., dray, w.s. Plum b. 9th and
Ollirack Wm., teamster, 223 Betts
Olman Daniel, pawn broker, 30 E. 6th
Olmstead Hiram B., b. k., Culbertson, Kilgour & Co's., 503 Freeman
O'Loughlen Rev. Francis, St. Xavier College, w. s. Sycamore b. 6th and 7th
Olsen Louis, confec., bds. 426 Vine
O'Maha John, watchman, n. s. Fremont b. Carr and Harriet

O'Maha Wm., lab., n.s. Fremont b. Carr and Harriet
O'Maley Annie, 433 W. 4th
O'Malley John, drover, 243 Clinton
O'Malley Michael, saloon, 40 E. 3d
O'Mallon James R., clk., 185 Cutter
O'Mara James, steward, Clifton House
O'Mara Jeremiah, distiller, 165 Richmond
O'Mara Thomas, lab., 54 E. 2d
O'Meara John, dray, 507 Sycamore
O'Meary Catharine, servt, 33 McFarland
O'Melia Mary, tailoress, bds. 138 Longworth
O'Mera Wm., porter, 54 E. 2d
Omohundro Littleton J., 143 Smith
Omohundro Sidney, 143 Smith
O'Neal ——, painter, bds. 241 Central-Av
O'Neal Miss Anna, book folder, bds. 98 E. 5th
O'Neal Chas., carp.. 37 York
O'Neal David, lab., h 184 W. Court
O'Neal Michael, polisher, wks. n.e.c. W. Canal and Elm
O'Neal Michael, blksmith, bds. 39 W. Mulberry
O'Neal Michael, foreman, Aaron Shaw's 29 Chestnut
O'Neil Timothy, lab., 385 Vine
O'Neil Amelia, n.w.c. Broadway and 6th
O'Neil Ann, n.w.c. Broadway and 6th
O'Neil Arthur, lab., 613 Central Av.
O'Neil Bridget, 399 W. 3d
O'Neil Bridget, servt., 601 Freeman
O'Neil Catharine, 399 W. 3d
O'Neil Edward, lab., 102 Butler
O'Neil Elizabeth, servt., 406 W. 6th
O'Neil Ellen, cof. h., 149 W. Miami Canal
O'Neil Felix, foreman, 71 Abigail
O'Neil Felix, shoe mkr., 62 Gano
O'Neil Hannah, servt., 111 Broadway
O'Neil James, 71 Abigail
O'Neil James, 202 Butler
O'NEIL James, (John A. Griffith & Co.) 171 W. 9th
O'Neil James, molder, 48 W. Court w. of Central Av.
O'Neil James, lab., e. s. E. Court b. 6th and Observatory Road
O'Neil James, lab., 54 E. 8th e. of Lock
O'Neil John, 432 Clinton
O'Neil John, carp., bds. 49 Race
O'Neil John, lab., 339 Plum
O'Neil Mary, 171 W. 9th
O'Neil Margaret, 79 Abigail
O'Neil Margaret, h. 365 Broadway
O'Neil Mary, 102 Butler
O'Neil Mary, n.w.c. Broadway and 6th
O'Neil Michael, boots and shoes, 238 W. 5th
O'Neil Michael, dray, 166 Spring
O'Neil Michael, lab., 61 Barr
O'Neil Michael, marble cutter, 234 W. Court
O'Neil Patrick, grocery, 111 E. 8th
O'Neil Patrick, lab., 107 Carr
O'Neil Patrick, saddler, 174 Longworth
O'Neil Sarah A., 142 Everett
O'Neil Thomas, lab., 740 W. 6th
O'Neil Wm., lab., 740 W. 6th
O'Neil Wm. P., confec., n.e.c. 6th and John
O'Neill Cornelius, butcher, bds. 25 Woodward
O'Neill Hugh, lab., 25 Woodward
O'Neill James, driver. bds. 25 Woodward
O'Neill James W., lab., n.s. Hopkins, b. Freeman and Garrard
O'Neill John, painter, 200 Elm, h. 393 W 5th
O'NEILL PETER,
  Coffee House,
  22 E. 5th
O'Neill Thomas, 560 W. 5th
O'Neill Wm., lab., wks. C. H. & D. R. R. depot
Oneto Joseph, confec., 130 Vine
O'Nett Angelo, cof. h., 116 W. Front
Oney Martin, policeman, n.s. Fulton Av., e. of Washington
Ong Thomas, com. mer., 179 Richmond
Onsley J. B., phys., bds. Madison House
Ophald Susan, 59 W. Court

254 (ORR) CINCINNATI (OSM) DIRECTORY. (OTT)

Opitz Frederick, paper hanger, 84 Bremen
Opitz John, lab., 725 Race
Oppenheimer A., cigar mkr., bds. w. s. Sycamore, b. Front and 2d
Oppenheimer Getz, expressman, 85 Pleasant
Oppenheimer H., b.k., 55 W. Pearl, h. 36 Hathaway
Oppenheimer Hy., n.s. 9th, b. Central Av. and John
Oppenheimer Harry H., carriage painter, 305 Clark
Oppenheimer Isaac, b.k., 72 W. Pearl, bds 335 W. 8th
Oppenheimer J., clk., bds. s.w.c. Race and 3d
Oppenheimer Solomon, 205 Clinton
Opperbeck George, chair mkr., 419 Longworth
Opperbeck Hy., chair mkr., 419 Longworth [Front
Opperman Geo., chair mkr., 213 W.
Opple John, eng., bds. w.s. Baymiller b. Wade and Liberty
Oppleker Alexander, tailor, s.e.c. Sycamore and Webster
Orange Benjamin, upholsterer, w.s. Celestial, b. 3d and Observatory Road
Orange J. C., mattress manuf., 78 E. 5th
Orange John C., druggist, bds. 80 E. 5th
Orchard Catharine, dress mkr., 101 Mound
Orchard Elizabeth, bds. 414 Broadway
Ordelman Wm., carp., s.e.c. 5th and Elm
Ordelmundt & Howard, (John W. O. & Saml. F. Howard,) carps., 181 Elm
Ordelmundt John W., (O. & Howard,) 179 W. 5th
O'Reilley Mary, n.e.c. 6th and John
O'Reilly Brothers, (Wm. J. O'R., Stephen O'R., James O'R.,) dry goods, 112 W. 5th
O'Reilly James, (O'R. Brothers,) 127 Richmond
O'Reilly Joseph, clk., 112 W. 5th, b. 127 Richmond
O'Reilly Patrick, grocery, 182 Cutter
O'Reilly Richard, clk., 112 W. 5th, b. 127 Richmond
O'Reilly Stephen, (O'R. Brothers,) 127 Richmond
O'Reily Thomas, horse trader, w.s. Wood, b. 4th and 5th
O'Reilly Wm. A., eng., 112 E. Pearl
O'Reilly Wm. J., (O'R. Brothers,) 127 Richmond
Orenstein Helena, notions, 20 W. 5th, h. 278 Main
Orick Wm., lab., w.s. Broad b. Front and River
O'Rieley James, 251 W. Front
O'Rielly John W., printer, bds. 207 Longworth
Oriental Powder Co., (Den. F. Carleston, agent,) n.e.c. Walnut and 2d
Orleman Hy., butcher, bds. 151 Dayton
Orleman Peter, butcher, 151 Dayton
Orling Casper, saddler, bds. 609 Walnut
Orlopp M. A., salesman, 140 Main, h. 423 Bremen
Ormston Ellen, 520 E. Front
Ormston Hy., 520 E. Front
Ormston Walter, 520 E. Front
Ormston Wm., eng., 520 E. Front
Orncluse John H., lab., 361 Broadway
Orndorff David H., auditor Adams Express Co., h. 330 Cutter
Ornung Catharine, 164 Clay
O'Roark John, dairy, 64 Butler
O'Roarke Peter, lab., wks. n.w.c. Plum and Wade
O'Rourk Elizabeth, servt., 390 W. 6th
O'Rourk Thomas, painter, 32 Mulberry
O'Rourke John, clk., 64 Butler
O'Rourke Michael, tailor, bds. 40 W. 5th
Orpermann Richard, painter, 27 Cherry al
Orr Mrs. A. C., laundress, 28 W. 6th
Orr Andrew, carp., 14 E. 6th
Orr Arthur, cab. mkr., 134 Clinton
Orr Elias M., phys., 82 E. 3d, h. n. s. Goodloe, b. Niagara and Willow
Orr Eliza J., 310 W. 5th
ORR GEO. P., Agent for Moore & Perkin's Sewing Machines, 138 W. 4th

Orr James, carp., 425 Freeman
Orr James H., clk., bds. 438 W. 4th
Orr Jane, 465 W. 3d
Orr Joshua W., wagon mkr., 263 Freeman
ORR ROBERT, Agent, C. S. Malthy, 11 W. 5th, h. 297 W. 9th
Orr Thos., paver, bds. 112 Richmond
Orr William, molder, 218 Cutter
ORR WILLIAM, New and Second Hand Clothing, Stamping and Embroidery, 107 W. Court
Orr Wm. M., scale mkr., 8 W. 2d, h. 150 Clark
Orr Wm. Y., periodicals, 209 Clinton
Orrenstein Helena, 287 Main
Orrling Hy., lab., 137 Baymiller
Orschel Peter, shoemkr, 14 Mercer
Ort Louisa, 126 Vine
Ort Michael, musician, 14 Allison
Ort Frank, butcher, 153 Everett
Orth David S., bds. 121 E. 3d
Orth Frank, butcher, 153 Everett
Orth Geo., driver 143 Baymiller
Orth John, tailor, 68 Bremen
ORTH JOHN A., Family Grocery n.e.c. Sycamore and 4th
Orting Adam, lab., 75 Hughes
Ortlieb Jacob, stone mason, 146 Clay
Ortman Frank, cab. mkr 253 Laurel
Ortman Fred., cigar mkr., wks. 213 Walnut
Ortmann Chas., F., cigar mkr. 13 Moore
Ortmann Chas. W., 11 Moore
Ortmann Christopher, lab., 17 Park
Ortmann Hy., cigar mkr, 62 Hughes
Ortmann Joseph lab., 513 Sycamore
Ortmann Joseph, salesman, 145 Main h 440 Walnut
Ortmann Wm. finisher, 97 Pendleton
Ortner John, cab. mkr. 14 Mary
Orton Garrett V., mach. wks. J. A. Fay & Co's
Ortzet John G., baker, 685 Race
Orum Morris, broker, 12 W. 2d (up stairs,) h. 163 Plum
Osborn Archibald, 63 E. 7th
Osborn Archibald K., cab. mkr., 25 Cutter
Osborn Hy., clk., bds. 153 W. 4th
Osborn Saml. R., finisher, wks n.e.c. Walnut and Canal
Osborn Thos. H., salesman, 95 W. Pearl bds. 155 W. 4th
Osborne John, mach., 57 E. 3d e. of Whittaker
Osborn John S., produce mer., 31 Vine, h. Walnut Hills
Oschga Theodore, butcher, 151 Clark
Oschwald John, 64 Dunlap
Osendale H., molder, wks. Chamberlain & Co's
Oser Ernst, mason, 107 Pleasant
Oser Francis, bksmith, 163 Pleasant
Oser Mary 157 Pleasant
Osford Joseph, bksmith, 107 Clay
O'Shaughnessy James sen., 139 E. 5th
O'Shaughnessy James jr., clk., 139 E. 5th
O'Shaughnessy Jas. F., clk., #5 W. 2d h. s.w.c. Pike and 5th
O'Shaughnessy John, carp., 53 Plum
O'Shaughnessy Patrick, lab., 387 W. 3d
Oskamp August, jewelry &c., 108 Main res Country
OSKAMP CLEMENS, Importer of Watches and Clocks and Manuf. of Jewelry, 62 Main, h. 152 E. 5th
OSKAMP LEWIS, Watches, Clocks and Jewelry, 108 Main, h 16 Sycamore
Oskamp Margaret 164 E. 5th
Oakendorf Wm., painter, 5 Buckeye
Osler Albert W., clk. 7 Pub. Landing, h. 18½ Betts
Osler Ell, dray, 14 Betts
Osler Francis H., dray, 14 Betts
Osman Barney, lab., e.s. Sycamore b. Abigail and Woodward
Osmeier Chas., baker, wks. 565 Main
OSMOND EDMUND, Dentist 272 Vine
Osmond John, pattern mkr., 234 Linn
Osmus Catharine, 427 Broadway

Osorowoska Casimer, cab. mkr., bds. 522 Main
Osseford Joseph, bksmith, 107 Clay
Osseforter Joseph, bksmith, 107 Clay
Osseforth Harman, bksmith, 646 Race
Ossege Hy., family grocery, s.w.c Race and Findlay
Ossege Hy., cof. h., 710 Race
Ossenbeck Fred., 31 E. 7th
Osseobick John W., mach., cor. Pearl and Central Av
Ossendary Bernhard, bksmith, 105 Woodward
Ostendarp Bernhard J., cooper, 50 Bremen
Ostendarp Frank., carp., 123 Pleasant
Ostendarp Frank, rope mkr., 65 14th
Ostendarp Frederick, cooper, 50 Bremen
Ostendarp Joseph, tailor, 65 14th
Ostendarp Mathias, tailor, 654 Race
Ostendarp Hermann H., tailor, 654 Race
Ostendorf Bernard H., boots and shoes, 382 Baymiller
Ostendorf John H., molder, 73 Pendleton
Ostendorf Joseph, lab., 28 13th
Oster John, quarryman, 400 Broadway
Osterbrink Rudolph, carp., 170 Spring
Osterbrook Louis, chair mkr., 367 Linn
Osterbruck Wm., box mkr., 522 Main
Osterhage John H., cof. h., 26 Green
Osterhaus Julius, lab., 6 Miami
Osterhof Anthony, lab., 142 Pleasant
Osterhoff Barney, tailor, 62 Laurel
Osterholt Anthony, porter, 75 Bremen
Osterkamp Joseph, carp., 384 Sycamore
Osterman John, plate printer, 29 Observatory
Ostermann Geo., painter, 719 Race
Ostermeier Thomas, hostler, Clearwater b. Baymiller and Freeman
Osteroth Christian, miller, 135 Ham. Road
Osterroth August F., tailor, 455 Main
Ostholthoff Bernhard, lab., 109 Clay
Ostmer Joseph, riverman, bds. 10 Sycamore
Ostwalt John, cooper, 662 Main
Osveld Jacob, butcher. 64 Wade
OSWALD AUGUSTUS, Manufacturer of Tin, Copper and Sheet Iron Ware, and Dealer in all Kinds of Stoves, 368 Broadway
Oswald Caspar, painter, 462 Elm
Oswald Charles, painter, n.e.c. Elm and 14th
Oswald Charles, shoemkr., 466 Vine
Oswald Emanuel, shoemkr., 109 Ham. Road
Oswald Jacob, lab., bds. 64 Wade
Oswald John, tanner, bds. 442 Main
Oswald Xavier, tanner, 64 Dunlap
Osweiler Philipine, 62 Ham. Road
O'Teefe Bartholomew, cutter, 17 Chestnut
Otis James, bksmith, 89 E. 3d
Otis James L., mach., 130 John
Otting Christopher, bksmith, s.s. Charlotte b. Linn and Baymiller, h. 296 Findlay
O'Toole Henry, lab., 163 E. 3d
O'Toole John, collector, 335 Central Av
O'Toole Mary R., bds. 246 W. 3d
O'Toole Michael, lab., 152 Cutter
Ott Anthony, rope mkr., s.s. Budd b. Harriet and Mill Creek
Ott Clemmens, lab., e.s. Riddle b. Bank and Harrison Road
Ott Conrad, jeweller, 141 Main, h. 22 Ham. Road
Ott David, lab., rear 67 Bremen
Ott Francois, mach., 65 12th
Ott George, 108 W. Liberty
Ott Geo., cab. mkr., 194 Bremen
Ott George, cooper, 7 15th b. Elm and Plum
Ott George, rope mkr., 194 Bremen
Ott Henry, lab., 246 Pleasant
Ott Henry, shoe mkr., 604 Elm
Ott John, box mkr., 73 Buckeye
Ott Louisa, 176 E. 3d e. of Collard
Ott Margaret, h. 125 Pleasant
Ott Marietta, laundress, 692 Main
Ott Peter, bakery, 201 Baymiller
Ott Philp, shoe mkr., 201 Baymiller

CINCINNATI (PAC) DIRECTORY. (PAL) 255

rd	Overbeck Hermann, blksmith, 23 Woodward	Packer M. A., constable, bds. Buttemiler's Hotel
145	Overbeck John G., w.s. Central Av. b. 3d and W. W. Canal	Packham Louis, b. k., 47 W. 2d, h. Newport
	Overbeck Mary, 61 W. Liberty	Paddack Albert, dep. clk. Probate Court, h. 156 Clark
	Overbeck Wm., lab., 92 Woodward	
15th	Overbeck Wm., turner, 33 Locust	PADDACK ALEXANDER, Probate Judge, Office, Court House, h. 393 W. 9th
Main	Overbecke Henry, carp., 46 E. 8th, h. Walnut Hills	
	Overber Henry, cof. h , 275 Sycamore	PADDACK Benjamin F., (James L. Haven & Co.) 106 Plum
	Overberg Anthony, lab., 52 McFarland	
ading	Overdick Charles. (H. & C. O.,) 253 Carr	Paddack James R., b. k., 16 E. 2d, h. 92 Clark
	Overdick H. & C., (Henry O. & Charles O), mineral water manuf., 17 Home	
145	Overdick Henrietta, 371 Broadway	Paddack John, 502 W. 9th
	Overdick Henry, (H. & C. O.), 501 W. 5th	Paddack Truman B., b. k., 502 W. 9th
		Padden Dormie, hostler, s.w.c. 4th and Plum
W.	Overend Charles P., printer, 121 Hopkins	Paddock Chas. J., clk., s.e.c. 3d and Walnut, bds. 503 W. 7th
ne	Overesch Henry, porter, 399 Broadway	PADDOCK WM. R., Banker and Publisher Bank Mirror, s.e.c. 3d and Walnut, h. 503 W. 7th
	Overhaus Conrad, broom manuf., e.s Gamble al. b. Melancthon and Liberth, h. 126 Clay	
.ong-	Overkamp Hermann, lab., h. 151 Abigail	PADDOCK'S BANK MIRROR, s.e.c. 3d and Walnut, Wm. R. Paddock, Publisher
	Overklwaft Henry, plasterer, 86 W. 2d	
anuf.	Overmann Frederick, salesmann, 165 W. 5th	Padgett Albert, clk., 79 Vine, h. 441 Broadway
vorth	Overshine Julia, e.s. John b. Betts and Clinton	Padgett Ebenezer S., 441 Broadway
Main	Overwater Clemens, box mkr., 90 Melancthon	Paff Susanna, seamstress, n. s. al. b. Poplar and Vine and Ham. Road and Buckeye
3d		
Wa-	Overwerser Frederick, lab., 72 Abigail	Paffe Joseph, shoe mkr., 209 W. 6th
	O'Walsh Michael, lab., wks. s.w.c. Br'dway and 5th	Page David O., salesman, 76 Park
Syc-		Page H. D., lab., bds. 12 E. Front
[eye	Owen Bernard M., foreman, bds. Cincinnati House	Page Henry, lab., 133 W. Miami Canal
Buck-		Page James A., wks. Wm. Resor & Co.'s
rt w.	OWEN CHARLES, Wholesale and Retail Dealer in Watches and Jewelry, n.w.c. 4th and Main, res. Newport	
e. of		Page Margaret, foot of Harrison
		Page Mary, 30 Baum
		Page Richard G., clk., 101 W. 4th, h. 499 W. 5th
.in	Owen Geo. H., lab., 91 Pleasant	
y	Owen Isabella, 272 Cutter	Page Walter, cook, 110 W. Canal
res.	Owen Jesse, dentist, 154 W. 6th	Page Wm., checkman, 30 Baum
	Owen Wm., jeweler, 385 W. 4th	Pagenstecher J. C. Louis, teacher, 644 Elm
er	Owen Wm. jr., clk., 385 W. 4th	
	Owen William, nailor, rear 23 Hughes	Pagett Edward, cheese mer., 37 Jones
	Owens Alfred D., collector, 203 W. Court	Pahls Henry, lab., 103 Gest
on	Owens Francis, b. k., n.w.c. Broadway and Pearl	Pahls John, confec., 33 Broadway
fain		Pahner Fred. W., blksmith, 679 Elm
	Owens Geo., trunk mkr., 315 Baymiller	Paige David O., salesman, 76 Park
Ham.	Owens John, lab., 71 Richmond	Paige Joseph, cof. h., s.e.c. New and Broadway
	Owens John, Washington Hotel, n.w.c. Walnut and Water	
Race		Paine Hannah, s.s. Budd b. Harriet and Mill Creek
t	Owens John W., broker, 119 Richmond	
	Owens Joseph A., b.k., 46 Walnut, h. 7 Pine	Paine Luther, carriage manuf., 109 W 7th, h. 77 Barr
	Owens Lewis, lithographer, 315 Baymiller	Paine Rufus K., clk. P. O., h. 196 W. Front
sette,		
	Owens Martin, blksmith, 23 Hughes	Painter J., wagon manuf., 57 Race, h. 53 Race
t and	Owens Matthew, marble cutter, n.s. Augusta b John and Smith	Painter James, blksmith, wks. 57 Race
h. 59	Owens Owen, 33 Harrison	Painter Joseph, blksmith, wks. 57 Race
	OWENS OWEN, JR., Insurance Agent, 14 Public Landing, h. 351 Clark	Palfreyman James, tailor, Harriet b. W. 9th and Richmond
Av		Palm Wm., teacher, 286 W. Front
	Owens Miss P., 33 Harrison	Palmer A , jr., musician, 197 Vine
	Owens Patrick, dray, 23 8th, above Lock	PALMER Barker B., (Keck & Shaffer,) bds. Buttemiller's Hotel
n.e.c.		
	Owens Samuel M., 66 W. 3d	PALMER CHAS. R., Tin Ware Manufacturer, 506 Central Avenue
	Owens Thomas, s.s. Forbus Alley b. Elm and Canal	
hort's		
	Owens Thornton, molder, bds. 186 Race	Palmer Chauncey D., phys., 65 Laurel
5th	Owens Wm., blksmith, wks. n.w.c. Sycamore and Canal	Palmer Collin R., printer, Times Office, bds. Newport, Ky.
d and		
	Owens Wm., phys., 80 Mound	Palmer Geo., policeman, 518 Main
	Owings John B., oysters, fish, &c., 27 W. 5th	Palmer James, blksmith. bds. 919 Central Av.
l Av.	Oxner Mary, n.e c. Hunt and Broadway	Palmer James M., printer, Commercial Office, h. Newport, Ky.
bds.	Oyant Mary, servt, 126 E. 5th	
		Palmer James R., 56 Bank
		Palmer John, fireman, 734 W. 6th
nt b.	**P**	Palmer Laura, teacher, at 8th District School
W.	Pabe Carolina, midwife, w.s. Goose al. b. Liberty and 15th	Palmer Lydia, h. 38 Harrison
		Palmer Mary, 63 W. Front
lley	Pabe Chas., w.s. Goose al. b. Liberty and 15th	Palmer Mary J., 236 Richmond
pkins		Palmer Micah, carriage smith, 65 Laurel
	Pabe Conrad, lab., 678 Main	Palmer Moses D., (Smith & P.,) 275 Longworth
Vood-	Pabodie Wm H., teacher, 6 Dayton	
	Pabst Hy. J., salesman, 80 W. Pearl, h. 153 Richmond	Palmer Sarah, 63 W. Front
419		PALMER SOLON, Importer and Manufacturer of Perfumery, Fancy Goods, &c., 36 W. 4th, h. 330 George
	Pace Henry, 294 W. 4th	
W.W.	Pacey Robt., lab., wks. Hieatt & Wood's	
	Pachond Peter, lab., 68 Butler	
hoes,	Packer James, lab., s.s. Clark b. Garrard and Mill Creek	Palmer Susan B., 209 Longworth
		Palmer Wm. E., 69 Longworth

256 (PAR) CINCINNATI (PAR) DIRECTORY. (PAT)

Palmetry Susan, dress mkr., 269 W. 3d
Pamelet Francois, scissors grinder, Boots al. b. Mercer and 13th and Vine and Walnut
Pancoast Joseph, agt. gas fixtures, 284 Main
Pandorf Chas., grocery, 1123 Central Avenue
Pangburn Alpheus, express man, 2 Scott
Paner Adam, cof. h., 147 Buckeye
Paner Adam, grocer, 134 E. 6th
Paner Sabina, 147 Buckeye
Panschort Conrad, cigar mkr., 21 Commerce
Panton Michael, dray, bds. Pennsylvania Hotel
Panzera Anthony, butcher, 989 Central Avenue
Pape Bernard, confec., 603 Walnut
PAPE E. W. & BROTHER, (Edward W. P. & Theodore P.,) Frame and Gilt Moulding Manufacturers, 217 Walnut
PAPE Edward W., (E. W. & Brother,) 492 Main
Pape Eliza, serv't, 279 Longworth
Pape Henry, cutler, 259 W. 3d
Pape Isaac, lab., 12 Abigail
Pape Louis, tanner, bds. n.w.c. Liberty and Poplar
PAPE Theodore, (E. W. Pape & Bro.,) 492 Main
Pape Wm., lab., 424 Sycamore
Papenberg Geo., shoemkr., 456 E. Front
Papin Phillip, steward, 103 E. 6th
PAPPENHEIMER & DREYFOOS, (Leopold P. & Samuel D.,) Importers of Hardware, Cutlery, Guns, &c., 107 W. Pearl
PAPPENHEIMER Leopold, (P. & Dreyfoos,) h. n e.c. 9th and Vine
Papst Chas., lab., 202 Pleasant
Papst John, lab., 70 Martin
Parana Stephen, driver, 461 W. 5th
Parcels Price, carriage trimmer, 167 Baymiller
Pardee W. W., confec., 29 E. 4th
Pardick Bernhard, chair mkr., 1818 spring h. s.w.c. Woodward and Spring
Pardick Elizabeth, 482 Elm
Pardick Frank H., clk., 65 E. Pearl, h. 482 Elm
Pardick Mathias, cooper, 19 Abigail
Pare John, clk., 53 W. Pearl, bds. 120 John
Pareira Solomon, clothing, 290 W. 5th
Parham Hartwell, lab., 197 George
Parham Otwell, twister, 197 George
Parham Susan, 197 George
Parham Wm. H., teacher, 286 W. Front
Paris Daniel, 121 Mill
Paris Francois, tailor, 108 Buckeye
Paris Levi, eng., wks. 196 W. Pearl
Paris Mary, rear 245 Broadway
Parish Levi, eng., s.s. Cherry al. b. Elm and Plum
Park H. S., bds. Dennison House
PARK JOHN D., Patent Medicines, Wines, Perfumery, Toilet & Fancy Goods, n.e.c. 4th and Walnut, res. 3 miles back of Covington
Park Ostrander C., phys., bds. 47 W. 7th
PARK Richard, (Rowe, P. & Co.) 332 Baymiller
Park Robert C., phys., h. 101 E. 3d e. of Whittaker
PARK Wm. S. (Rowe, Park & Co.,) bds. Dennison House
Parker Alvah, notary, 405 W. 7th
Parker Ann, n.s. Front e. of Lumber
Parker Augustus G., prof. of music, 101 Longworth
Parker Benjamin, lab. wks. s.w.c. Broadway and 5th
Parker Christopher, lab., 231 E. 5th
Parker David S., conductor, bds. 22 Hathaway
Parker Edward, b. k. e. s. Central Av. b. Elizabeth and Canal
Parker Edward, teamster, 212 Front
Parker Edward D., driver, bds. 212 W. Front
Parker Edward W., b. k., 402 Central Avenue
Parker Elijah, lab., s.s. Weller b. Carr and Harriet

Parker Elizabeth, s. s. 6th b. Harriet and Horne
Parker Henry, teamster, bds. s.e.c. Front and John
PARKER Isaac W., (Geo. R. Dixon & Co.) 158 W. 9th
Parker James, tailor, 58 Clinton
Parker James W., printer, 15 Betts
Parker John, painter, 167 George, h. 135 Barr
Parker John, cook, 201 W. Front
Parker John W., plasterer, bds. 75 Park
PARKER Joseph W., (Hobbs & P.) h. Covington, Ky.
Parker Joseph W., grocer, 417 George
Parker Lucy, 22 Baum
Parker Maria, e.s. Freeman b. York and Findlay
Parker Mason D., teacher, 528 W. 9th
Parker Owen, driver, n.w.c. 9th and Race
Parker Peter, molder, s.w.c. Everett and Central Av
Parker Peter, lab., wks. n.w.c. Plum and Wade
Parker Richard, barber, 20 E. 5th
Parker Samuel, lab., 394 W. 8th
Parker Samuel, pilot, s.s. Front e. of Ferry
Parker Thomas, painter, 159 Cutter
Parker Thos., saddler, 170 E. Pearl
Parker Wm., shoemkr, wks. 319 Main
Parker Wm. A., carp., 10 Observatory
Parker Wm. G., 347 W. 8th
Parkes James, tanner, n.e.c. Main and Orchard
PARKHILL JAMES, Bakery, 143 Linn
Parkhurst Asel R., 107 Pike
Parkhurst Willard, fireman, 576 E. 5th
PARKINS BROS. & HODGSON, Steel and File Manufacturers, 240 W. 7th, Jonathan Hattersley, Agt.
Parkinson Jane, b.h., 206 W. 5th
Parkinson Richard, eng., 208 E. 6th
Parks Albert, river man, 111 E. 3d e. of Whittaker
Parks Geo. D., jewelry, 341 Central Av., h. 363 W. 9th
Parks J. M., homeopathic pharmacy, 3 W. 4th, h. Hamilton
Parks Joseph, turner, s.s. Corporation al. b. Young and Wilson
Parle Mary, 1182 E. Front
Parlington Hy., molder, 51 Plum
Parlon Patrick, gardener, 33 E. 8th e. of Lock [John
Parmelee Benj. F., chandler, bds. 524
Parmelee Hy., mach., h. 522 John
Parmelee Nancy, bds. 479 W. 8th
Parmer Geo. F., compositor, wks. Meth. Book Concern
Parmer Warren, baker, 172 Elm
Parmerton Alonzo B., billiard saloon, n. w.c. Longworth and Central Av., h. 105 Mound
Parnand Joseph, stone mason, 17 15th b. Central Av. and Plum
Parnell Chas. M., carp., 60 Everett
PARR GEORGE, Printer, 167 Walnut, res. 1st Race
Parr James, confec., 317 W. 6th
PARR J. C. & CO. (Jno. C. P. & Wm. H. Butler) Writing Fluid Manufacturers, 656 W. 5th
PARR JOHN C., Druggist and Apothecary, 554 W. 5th
Parr Michael, druggist, bds. 554 W. 5th
Parrol Peter L., clk., 224 Main, h. Mt. Auburn
Parrington James, tailor, 8 W. 3d
Purris Edward L., turner, wks. n.w.c. Smith and Front
Parrish Mrs. M. J., bds. 316 John
Parrott George, 55 Mansfield
Parry Augustus C., 150 Longworth
Parry Hester, 121 W. Front
Parry J. Maurice, b.k., 198 Main. h. 99 Clark
Parry Jemima, notions, 121 W. Front
Parry John, clk., 397 Central Av., h. Walnut Hills

Parry Joseph W., boiler, 291 Water
Parsell Benjamin F., feed store, s.e.c. Elm and M. Canal, h. 390 Race
Parsell Geo., tinner, 294 W. 5th, h. n.w. c. Smith and 6th
Parshall David, tailor, 27 Cutter
Parshall Edward, tailor, 27 Cutter
Parshall John B., phys., 115 W. 6th, h. 205 George
Parson Hy., cooper, w.s. Western Av. b. Bank and Harrison Road
Parson Wm., porter, w.s. Cassatt al. b. Sycamore and Main
Parsons Bryant, carp., 636 E. Front
Parsons George L., clk., 86 W. 5th w. of Central Av
Parsons Wm., 183 W. 4th
Partello Benj., bds. 199 W. 5th
Partello Wm. H., actor, 158 Sycamore
Parthey Gustav. F., mach., 588 Race
Partington Thomas, molder, bds. 192 W. 6th
Partl Frank F., barber, n.w.c. 8th and Freeman, bds. 65 Webster
Partl John, boots and shoes, 65 Webster
Partl Joseph, carver, 65 Webster
Partl Joseph, barber, bds. 65 Webster
Partl Wenzel, jeweler, Duhme & Co's., h. 65 Webster
Partmann Frederick, dray, e.s. Kilgour b. 3d and 4.
Partridge Charles A., e.s. Auburn, near Bigelow [low
Partridge Peck, e.s. Auburn near Bigelow
Parvin David H., trunk mkr., wks. 31 Broadway
Parvin Dorsey A., drugs, paints, oils, &c., junction 2d and Front, h. 122 E. 5th
Parvin & Johnson, (Wm. P. & John H. J.) trunk manufs, 31 Broadway
PARVIN S. H., Advertising and Collecting Agent, 63 W. 4th, h. Brooklyn Hights
Parvin Wm., (P. & Johnson) 398 Central Av
Paschen Frederick, lab., 53 Pendleton
Paschen William, cigar mkr., bds. 705 Main
Paschin Wm., shoemkr, 705 Main
Pasbau Fred., lab., wks. 222 E. Front
Paskerl Wm., tailor, 21 David
Pasquier Chas. (Ried & P.) 62 Stark
Passauer, Christian, cigar mkr, 6 Peete
Passauer John, lab., 19 Peete
Passaur Louis, lab., bds. 602 Elm
Passbeck Frank, baker, 69 Abigail
Passenger Railroad Comp. of Cin., receiver's office, 641 W. 5th
Patberg Wm. F., lab., 679 Race
Paton John, stationery, bds. n.w.c. Mill and Front
Paton Wm., hostler, 203 Race
PATRICK & GOULD (J. W. P. & R. G.) Forwarding and Commission Merchants, 9 W. Front
Patrick John H., tailor, 242 Clark
PATRICK J. W. (P. & Gould), 376 W. 7th
Pattan Angel, teacher, at St. Xavier College
Pattee Eliza, bds. 202 Betts
Patten Alexander J., 204 Cutter
Patton Elizabeth, 254 E. 6th
Patten Sallie, bds. s e.c. Walnut and 9th
Patterson ———, baggage master, I. & C. R.R., bds. 512 W. Front
Patterson A., driver, Adams' Exp. Co., bds. Commercial Saloon
Patterson Mrs. A. W., bds. 241 W. 7th
Patterson Ann, notions, 44 Lock
PATTERSON, BRO. & CO., (J. W. P. & W. M. P.) Produce and Commission Merchants, 42 Vine
Patterson Edward M., liquors, 150 John
Patterson Ellen, 58 Elm
Patterson Emanuel, boatman, 120 E. 8th
Patterson Geo., blksmith, 620 W. 6th
Patterson Hannah J., 103 Pendleton
Patterson Hy., porter, 6 North
Patterson India, bds. bds. 188 W. Court, w. of Central Av
PATTERSON J. W. (P., Bro. & Co.) bds. 162 Elm
Patterson James, upholsterer, 271 W. Court w. of Central Av

INNATI (PEC) DIRECTORY. (PEN) 257

Paver John M., clk., 404 George
Paver Mary A., bds. 404 George
Pawlowski John, grocery, 275 Clinton
PAXTON Thomas B., (Matson & P.,) bds. 92 Broadway
Payler George W., plasterer, 400 Longworth
Payler Wm., 884 W 6th
Payne A & Co., brewers, w.s. Miami Canal b. Liberty and Findlay street bridges
Payne Alta, bds. Dumas Hotel
Payne Benj., barber. 2 W. Court
Payne Harrison, teamster, n.s Pearl b. Lawrence and Pike
Payne Margaret, servt., Junction Ludlow and Lawrence
Payne Martha, d e c. Richmond and Cutter
Payne Theodore, clk., bds. 334 Richmond
Pea Maria. servt.. 443 W. 7th
Peabody Joseph H., roofer, n.w.c. 5th and Vine
Peach Wm., butcher. w.s. Lebanon Road b. Liberty and Corporation Line
Peachey Hy., asst. cashier Lafayette Banking Co., h. Walnut Hills
Peacock Adonijah plow manuf., 16 W. 7th, h. 562 Main
Peacock Simeon, plow manuf., h. 562 Main
Peake Patrick, upholsterer. 31 Webb
Peake Richard, huckster, 31 Webb
Peal John, carp , 209 W. Liberty
Peale Frank M., teacher, 168 W. Court
Peale Samuel, n.e c. Court and Rittenhouse
Peale Thos. J., phys., 35 Everett, bds. 168 W. Court w. of Central Av.
Peaper August, bar k., 13 E. Pearl
Pearce Mrs., s.e c. Elm and 3d
Pearce Christopher G., superintendent Louisville and Cincinnati mail line, 116 Broadway
Pearce D. J., n.w.c. 4th and Pike
PEARCE Henry, (Gould, Pearce & Co.) 33 Harrison
PEARCE James, (Gould, P. & Co.,) 146 E. 5th
Pearce Jas., lab., bds. n.w.c. Front and Central Av.
Pearce Martin, dray, 518 W. 3d
Peare Geo , lab at gas works
PEARE W , (W. P. & H Winter,) h West Covington
PEARE W. & H. WINTER, Plumbers, 206 W 6th
PEARL STREET HOUSE, John Frey Proprietor, s.w.c. Race and 3d
Pearl M rgaret, 245 W. Front
Pearl Street Station House, cor. Pearl and Central Av.
Pearle Anna, 341 Central Av.
Pearsey Wm., hostler. s.w c. Lodge and Gano
Pesrson Chas., paper hanger, w.s. Langdon al. b. 6th and 7th
Pearson Hy., tailor, n. s. Montgomery nr. M dison Road
Pearson Jas , maltster, s.e.c. Bank and Baymiller
Pearson Jas. R., photographer, 49 12th
Pearson John A., tailor, 326 W. 9th w. of Central Av.
Pease Catharine M., 128 Walnut
Peace Chas. O., conductor O. & M. R. R , h. 185½ Barr
Peat & Cornell, (Jas. P. & Wm. C.,) attys., 365 Main
Peat James, liquors, 295 Main, h. Hamilton Co., O.
Peat Jas., (P. & Cornell,) h. Pleasant Ridge
Pechiney Peter F , printer, bds. s.e.c. 9th and Walnut
Pechstedt Christian, tailor. 236 Pleasant
Pecht Mrs. Rosa, 84 Divison
Pechtler Christian, harness mkr., w.s. Vine b. 14th and 15th
Peck Alex. G., clk , 469 W. 7th
Peck Geo. E., clk., bds. 509 Freeman
Peck John M., 460 W. 7th

Peck Phillip, packer, wks. w.s. Lock b. 4th and 5th
Peck Wm. H., conductor, bds. 81 Wade
Pecker Anthony, mason, 168 Pleasant
Peckman Philip, baker, 59 E. 5th
PECKOVER Joseph, (Adams, P. & Co.,) 224 W. Court w. of Central Av.
Peckruhn John P., carver, bds. s.w.c. John and Pearl
Peckruhn Paul, carver bds. s.s. W. W. Canal b John and Smith
Pedel Joseph. mattress mkr., 16 Hamer
Pedretti F., (Ferrari & Co.,) 177 Vine
Pedretti F., fresco painter, room 20 Pike's Opera House, h. n.w.c. Baymiller and York
Peebles & Bro., (Daniel M P. & Alfred W. Stephenson.) candle manufs., s. s. Miami Canal b. Elm and Plum
Peebles Daniel M., (P. & Bro.,) 153 W. 8th

PEEBLES JOSEPH R., Staple and Fancy Groceries, n.e.c. 5th and Race, h. 398 W. 3d

Peebles S. S., salesman 70 Vine, h. Covington
Peel Eliza, (Peel & Son.) 274 Walnut
Peel Hy., (Peel & Son.) 274 Walnut
Peel Saml., h. 27 Clark
Peel & Son, (Mrs. Eliza P. & Henry P.) dye house, 274 Walnut
Peet John, molder, 638 W. 5th
Peet John F., molder, 638 W. 5th
Peet Thos., 18 Carr
Peet Wm., molder, 638 W. 5th
Peiffen Catharine, w.s. Poplar b. Buckeye and Ham. Road
Peiger Conrad, tailor, bds. 97 E. Pearl
Peiker John, lab., bds. s.w.c. Race and 2d
Pein John, carp.. 1268 E. Front
Peiner Martin, lab., 83 W. Front
Peiper Herman, tailor. 80 Abigail
Peiper John, lab , n.w.c. 5th and Hannibal
Peirano Anionio, confec., 403 Main
Peirce Alex. N., b.k., wks. n.w.c. Wade and Plum
Peirce II. W., bds Walnut Street House
Peirce Harvey, 447 W. 2d
Peirce Jas , hardware, 466 W. 9th w. of Central Av.
Peirce John D., 524 E. Front
Peirce Mary, servt., 11 Arch
Peirce Samuel N , b.k., 462 W. 7th
Peircey Wm. L , clk. Post Office, 61 Longworth
Peirson Joseph, lab., bds. 49 W. 12th
Peitzer Lewis, cab. mkr., 50 W Liberty
Pellan Mary J , 133 W. Pearl
Pellance Geo. W., clk., 404 Baymiller
Pellard Geo., lab., Oliver b. John and Linn
Pelle L., cutter, 84 W. Pearl, h. Newport
Pellegrini Pellegrino, n.w.c Main and Court
Pellens A. J., clk., n.w.c. 4th and Walnut
Pellens George W., clk. at G. & P. Bogen's, h 404 Baymiller
Pellenvessel Hy., 305 W. 3d

PELLING RICHARD C., Agent Johnson, Fry & Co.'s, 45 W. 4th, b. s.s. Findlay 3d door from Freeman

Pellott Geo , lab., wks. s.e.c. Canal and Vine
Pelogue Joseph, porter, wks. 34 Vine
Pelser Catharine, servt., 151 Elm
Pelser Fred , blk. smith, 86 Hunt
Pelser John, 361 Broadway
Pelster Hy., shoe mkr., bds. cor. 9th and Walnut
Pelster Mary, 580 W. 6th
Pelton Chas., teamster, bds. 479 W. 8th
Pelton Wm., confec , 479 W. 8th
Pelzer Alfred B., cof. h., 410 Sycamore
Penberger Eliza, 306 Race
Penco Emma Maria, bds. 170 W. 4th
Pendegest Margaret, bds. 205 Baymiller
Pendegrass Catharine, w s. Langdon al. b 6th and 7th
Pendegrast Frank, sawyer, 205 Baymiller

Pender Michael, hostler, s.w.c. Lodge and Gano [3d
Pendery Alexander, watchman, 195 W.
Pendery Alex. jr., clk., 6° E. Pearl
PENDERY & CO., (John D. P. & Thos. S. P.,) Tea Dealers, n.w c. 5th and Walnut, and t6 E. Pearl
PENDERY John B., (P. & Co.,) 135 Linn
PENDERY Thos. S., (P. & Co.) rooms 46 W. 7th
Pendery Wilson, phys., 188 W. Court
Pendleton Cynthia, 66 Avery
Pendleton Edwin II., 114 E. 4th
Pendleton Elliott, bds. 110 E 4th
PENDLETON AND FIFTH STREET R. R. Office, George McLaughlin Treasurer, 7e2 E. Front
Pendleton Geo., agt. N. Y. & E. R. R., 4 College Building, bds. Spencer House
PENDLETON GEO. H., Attorney at Law, 21 W. 3d h. 104 E. Liberty
Pendleton H., clk. L. M. R. R. freight office
Pengeman Bernhard, (John Hauck & Co ,) 58 Laurel
PENGEMANN JOHN T., Coffee House, 390 Sycamore
Penger John R., mill stone cutter, 61 Race
Penick Elizabeth, h. 15 Betts
Penkamen Burney, flour dealer, 58 Laurel
Penner Hy., lab., 91 Spring
PENNEY GROVE J., Produce, Commission Merchant and Grain Dealer, 27 Vine, h. 18 Clinton
Penning Geo., grocer, e.s. Vine junction of Mulberry [worth
Penning George, chair mkr., 418 Longl ennington Jas. grocer, 205 Elm
Pennsylvania Hotel, Bruns & Fisher propr's., s.w.c. Pike and Front
Penny Richard, cutter, 5d Barr
Penny Wm. F., cutter, bds. 42 E. Pearl
Penrod Daniel, eng , n s. Front w. of Hill
Penshaw Conrad, cigar mkr., bds. 23 Commerce
Pensinger Maria, 172 W. 6th
Pentecost Hy. C., salesman s.w.c. Walnut and Pearl, h. 102 W. 8th
Pentermann Hermann H , oil mat mkr., 12 Orchard
Penton Mary E., bds. n.w.c. Central Av. and George
Penton Thos., lab., 11 14th b. Central Av. and Plum
Peoplemann Hy , lab., 418 Walnut
Peoples John R. H., carp., bds. 59 Clinton
Peoples Margaret, 170 W. Court w. of Central Av.
Peoples Susan, dress mkr., bds. 491 Sycamore
Peper Geo., porter, 523 Sycamore
Peperkorn Fred., painter, 61 Hughes
Peppard Daniel, harness mkr., 150 Spring
Peppe Christ , shoe mkr., 50 McFarland
Peppe John, lab., 21 Hughes
Pepper Albert, lab., wks. Crane, Breed & Co.'s
Pepper Caroline, 19 E. Liberty
Pepper Gottlieb, carp., Richmond b. Freeman and Carr
Pepper Granville M., printer, bds. 132 Broadway
Pepper John R., printer, bds. 132 Barr
Pepper Sophia, 19 E. Liberty
Pepper W. T., com. mer., 11 Water
Pequitnot Peter, lab., 202 Water
Perchment Wm., carp., wks. n.e.c. Canal and Walnut
Percival Hy., die sinker, bds. s.w.c. 5th and Broadway
Perez Joseph, bar k., n.w.c. Central Av. and Longworth
Perham Wm., lab., n.e.c. 5th and Elm
PERIN, GOULD & CO., (Oliver P., John G., Thomas Gad & Jas. W. Gaff) Commission Merchants, 88 and 90 W. Front

Perin Lyman, 117 E. Pearl, res. Newport
PERIN Oliver, (P., Gould & Co.) 115 Broadway
Perkey David, carp., 406 W. 8th
Perkison Ann, n.s. Taylor b. Carr and Freeman
Perkins Barzilla, mach., 79 Augusta
Perkins Chas., eng., 534 W. 5th
Perkins Chas. D., 364 W. 7th
Perkins Chas. W., eng., 534 W. 8th
Perkins Constantine, lab., 65 Abigail
Perkins D. C., mess. P , C. & C. R.R., rooms Union Block
Perkins E. Payson, music teacher, bds. 36 Barr
Perkins Hy., n.s. Corp. al. b. Price and Young
Perkins Hy. A., salesman 22 Main, h. Covington
Perkins John E., mach., wks. s.e.c. Plum and Pearl
PERKINS John H., (Thorton & P.) res. Covington
Perkins John J., clk. 57 Main, h. 364 W. 7th
PERKINS John S., (M. E. Reeves & Co.) 364 W. 7th
Perkins Jos. H., steward, 101 W. Court w. of Central Av.
Perkins Thos. H., silver plater, 65 Abigail
Perkins Wm. T., b.k. Culbertson, Kilgour & Co.'s, bds. 285 W. 7th
Perkle Frederick, saddler, 427 Sycamore
Perle Victor, cigar mkr., bds. Cincinnati House
Permap Hy., cof. h., 15 Martin
Pernice John, confec., n.e.c. Race and 8th
Pero D. orter, 27 Walnut
Perrin J. n E., clk. L. M. R.R., Depot, h. Baum
Perrin Man M., steward, rear 11 Richmond
Perry — , b.k 49 Clark
Perry Mrs., 356 W. 5th
PERRY Aaron F., (Taft & P.) res. Mt. Auburn
Perry Amanda, bds. 353 Central Av.
Perry Cornelia A., bds. 99 Mound
Perry Edmund, fireman, 60 Stone al. b. 5th and 6th
PERRY Edward, (P. & Warren), 371 George
Perry Edward M., finisher, s.w.c. Longworth and Stone
Perry Elizabeth, 99 Clark
Perry Francis C., wagon mkr , 35 Hathaway
Perry Frank, wagon mkr., bds. 35 Hathaway
Perry Geo., 218 Findlay
Perry H. L., saddler, 215 W. 7th
Perry Horatio, sadler, 215 W. 7th
PERRY J. T. (Cincinnati Gazette Co.) n.e.c. Vine and 4th
Perry John, janitor. 36 E. 3d
Perry Mrs. L. P., bds. 170 Plum
Perry Louisa, 116 Findlay
Perry Major, shoe mkr., bds. 99 Mound
Perry Mary, 270 W. 3d
Perry Mary A., n.s. Front e. of Perry
Perry Mary E., millinery, 274 W. 5th, h. 133 Longworth
Perry Mary J., dress mkr., 11 W. 7th, h. Pendleton
Perry N. & Co., (Nehemiah P. & Thos. W. Sprague) clothing, n.w.c. Central Av. and Longworth
Perry Nancy A., 353 W. 6th
PERRY Nehemiah, (N. Perry & Co,) Newark, N. J.
Perry Richard, boiler mkr., w.s. Mulberry al. b. Pearl and 3d
Perry Samuel H., bds 24 Perry
PERRY & WARREN, (Edward P. & Alfred W.) Booksellers and Stationers, 235 Central Av.
Perry Wm., 24 Perry
Persinger James, lab., 668 W. Front
Persinger Jerry, eng., 716 E. Front
Peter Amand, saloon, 202 Linn
Peter Chas., lab., 196 Pleasant
Peter Chas. H., (Künkler & P.) h. Vine St. Hill

Peter Felix, tailor, 196 Pleasant
Peter Francis Ch., tailor, 196 Pleasant
Peter Geo. A., paper store, 505 W. 7th
Peter Gottfried, shoe mkr., s.s. Pearl b. Pike and Butler
Peter Hy , driver, 37 Hughes
Peter Hy., express man, 12 Hughes
Peter Hy., porter, s.s. Schiller b. Main and Hughes.
Peter Jacob, eng., 70 Bank
Peter Madison, paper hanger, 275 Richmond
Peter Meinrod, Peter's. Exchange, 199 E. Front
Peter Michael, huckster, 70 Bank
Peter Monroe, rodman, city engineer's office, bds. 505 W. 7th
Peter Philip, barber, bds. 22 W. 9th
Peter Sarah, n.s. 30 b. Lawrence and Pike
Peter Savour, carp., n.s. Front e. of Lewis
Peter Simon, brewer, 100 Sycamore
PETER THOMAS J., City Engineer, Office, City Building, h. 505 W. 7th
PETER THOMAS J., Wall Paper, 127 W. 5th, h. 505 W. 7th
Peter Wilbrand, wagon mkr., rear 583 Main
Peterman Geo., clk. P. O., 24 Grant
Petermann Herman, tailor, n.e.c. Hunt and Broadway
Petermann Lewis A., tailor, 47 12th
Petermann Martin, grocery, 35 Providence
PETERS A. C. & BRO., (Alf. C. P. & John L. P.) Music Store and Musical Instruments, 94 W. 4th
Peters Adam, brush mkr., wks. 41 E. 2d
PETERS Alfred C., (A. C. P. & Bro.) bds. Gibson House
Peters August, grocery, 506 Vine, h. 63 Allison
Peters Chas., tinner, s.s. Calhoun b. Madison and Vine
PETERS CHAS. F., Family Grocery and Provisions n.w.c. Elm and 6th
Peters Frederick, lab., 52 Dudley
Peters Fredericka, 567 Main
Peters Hy., bk. mkr., e.s. Western Av. b. Dayton and Bank
Peters Hy., blksmith, wks. 602 Main
Peters Hy , plow mkr., 587 Main
Peters Hy., lab., al. b. Charlotte and Findlay and Plum and Central Av.
Peters Hy., lab., 45 Rittenhouse
PETERS Isaac. (H. Campbell & Co.) h. Cin. Furnace
Peters James K., tinner, wks. 13 W. 5th
Peters Jeremy, 307 W. 4th
PETERS John, (H. Campbell & Co.) h. Ironton, Ohio
Peters John, cab. mkr., 293 W. Front
PETERS John L., (A. C. P. & Bro.) h. St Louis
Peters John H., cab. mkr., 293 W. Front
Peters John M., tinner, wks. 17 W. 5th
Peters Julius, pattern mkr., 107 E. 2d
Peters Mary, w s. Fountain b. Rice and Alexander
Peters Nicholas, jeweler, 119 Bremen
Peters Rudolph, blksmith, 87 Buckeye
Peters Stephen, lab , 768 E. Front
Peters Theodore H., lab., 109 Woodward
Peters Wm., express, 311 Findlay
Peters W. M., music, &c., 59 W. 4th, h. 113 Smith
Petersmann Joseph H., carman, 125 Bremen
Peterson Baltimore, cook, 18 Union
Peterson Chas., coach mkr., bds. 29 W. 7th [more
Peterson Chas., currier, bds. 390 Sycamore
Peterson Chas., painter, n.s. Elder b. Elm and Campbell al.
Peterson Geo., cigars, &c., 530 Central Av.
Peterson Geo. Christ., tailor, 37 Schiller
Peterson Hy. L., carriage mkr., 29 W. 7th
Peterson John, carp., n.s. Railroad e. of Hazen

Peterson John, currier, bds. 390 Sycamore
Peterson Mary Ann, seamstress, 366 Central av
Pethry Philipp, baker, h. 471 Vine
Petitt Julia, 89 E. 3.1
Petitt Theodore, printer, 87 12th
Petsch Chas., cap mkr., 540 Race
Petterson Chas., porter, 56 E. 7th
PETTIBONE Alex., (Ross, Pettibone & Co.) office 115 Vine, h. 293 Longworth
Pettibone Joseph E., 492 Vine
Pettinzer Peter, boots, &c., 3 Budd
Pettis Samuel L., carp., n.s. Goodloe b. Willow and Leatherbury
Pettit John H., printer, 80 Clark
Pettit John R., printer, h. n.w.c. Plum and 7th
Pettitt Julia, tailoress, 25 Martin
Pettitt Levey, printer, n.w.c. Plum and 2d
Pettit Samuel S., printer, Enquirer office, bds. Mt. Auburn
Petty Geo., porter, n w.c. 3d and Main
PETZSCH GUSTAVE C., Third Street Shades, 31 W. 3d
Peultier Philipp, carp., 394 Broadway
Peyton Brian, tailor, 32 North
Peyton John, cook, h. 870 E. Front
Peytona Barbara, washwoman, 501 E. Front
Pfaef Phillip, 40 Mohawk
PFAFFLIN WM., Manufacturer of Mustard and Dealer in all kinds of Liquor, n. s. Pearl, b. Lawrence and Pike
Pfaff Gottlieb, bar k., bds. n. e. c. Elm and 15th
PFAFF Jno., (P. Webb & McCabe,) 128 Richmond
Pfaff Maria F., 121 Cutter
PFAFF, WEBB & McCABE, (John P. Joseph T. W. & John W. McC.) Varnish Manufacturers, 54 W. 2d
Pfaffenberger Geo., lab., 116 Ham. Road
Pfaffinger Geo. N., clk., 78 W. Liberty
Pfalein John P., carp., s.s. High, e. of Washington
Pfalzgraf Philip, cab. mkr., 670 Vine
Pfander Victoria, 217 Barr
Pfanner Phillip, barber, 400 Sycamore, h. rear 61 Abigail
Pfannkuchen Christian, tailor, 693 Race
Pfannkuchen Fred., barber, n.w.c. Main and Court
Pfau Frank, harness mkr., bds. 1076 Central Av
PFAU J. & J. M., (Jacob & John M. P.,) Liquor Dealers, and Agents for Bogen's Catawba Wines, 258 Main
Pfau Jacob, stoves, &c., 1003 Central Avenue
PFAU Jacob, (J. & J. M. P.,) 83 W. 9th
Pfau John, harness mkr., bds. 1076 Central Av
Pfau John, safe mkr., 557 Main
PFAU John M., (J. & J. M. P.,) 83 W. 9th
Pfau Phillip, s. s. 8th b. Broadway and Sycamore
Pfau Phillip, cof. h., 62 Webster
Pfau Wm., clk., 232 Walnut, h. 278 W. 5th
Pfaul John, lab., wks. s.e.c. Canal and Vine
Pfeffer Chas. A., cigars, &c., 535 Vine
Pfeffer John, pattern mkr., wks. 109 W. 2d
Pfefferle Jacob, stoves, &c., 113 Ham. Road
Pfeifer Hannah, n e.c. Central Av. and Pearl
Pfeifer Jacob, cook, 172 W. 6th
Pfeiffer Adam, cutler, 23 15th
Pfeiffer Anthony, florist and nurseryman, 201 Walnut, h Avondale
PFEIFFER FREDERICK, Boarding House, s.e.c. Vine and 9th
Pfeiffer Jodocus, carp., 485 Walnut
Pfeiffer John, wks. w. s. Brighton, nr. Benckenstein's garden

Pfeiffer Peter, cooper, 628 Vine
Pfeil Hy., brewer, wks. J. Kauffman & Co.'s
Pfend Michael, lab., 3 Hamer
Pfennigworth E., carver, wks. John Mitchell's
Pfennigworth Otto, carver, 490 Race
Pferdmann Christian, shoemkr., 8 E. Canal
Pfiermann Conrad, tailor, 97 Ham. Road
Pfiester Jacob, b.k., 125 Main, h. 351 Main
Pfiester Michael, butcher, 26 Findlay
Pfif Hy., tailor, 524 Sycamore
Pfifer Hy., dry goods, 1000 Central Av
Pfifer Jacob, shoemkr, 282 Central Av
Pfiffer John, pattern mkr., bds. s.e.c. 2d and Plum
Pfiffer Jacob, lab., s. s. Montgomery Pike, nr. Lebanon Road
Pfil Valentine, shoemkr. 68 Rittenhouse
Pfirmann Frederick, bksmith, 67 Elder
PFIRRMANN ANDREW, Liquors, Wines, Cigars, &c., 359 Walnut, h. 119 W. Court
PFIRRMANN C. & CO., (Conrad P. & John B Hartwig,) Wines, Liquors, Cigars, &c., 19 W. Canal
PFIRRMANN Conrad, (C. P. & Co.,) 12 Abigail
Pfirrmann Rose, 18 Lock, n. of 8th
Pfister Frederick, boots and shoes, 351 Main
Pfister Hy., cab. mkr., 36 Pleasant
PFISTER Hy., (P. & Metzger,) 97 Pleasant
PFISTER & METZGER, (Henry P. & Gottlieb M.,) Locksmiths, 30 W 6th
Pfister Michael, waiter, 23 15th
Pfister Peter, boots and shoes, 146 Clay
Pfisterer Hy., shoemkr, 262 Ham. Road
Pfistorer John S., grainer, bds. 362 Ham. Road
Pfisterer Theresa, 4 Harrison Pike
Pfistwer Wm., painter, 85 Hamburg
Pfistner Ignatz, carp., 85 Hamburg
Pfitzer Charles, porter, 36½ W. 5th
Pfitzer Wm., porter, 15 Race
Pfitzer Wm., salesman, 228½ Bremen
Pflueger John M., books, &c., 26 Mercer
Pfluz August, cooper, w. s. Bernard b. Bank and Harrison Pike
Pfluz Wentelin, cap mkr., 570 Walnut
Pfnum Andrew, bar k., 40½ 12th
Pfnum Anna, 404 12th
Pfnum Gotfried, tailor s.s. 6th b. Harriet and Horne
Pfordt Michael, lab., 54 Mohawk
Phalen Catharine, washwoman, s. s. 6th b. Broadway and Culvert
Phares Abram, (Phares, Taylor & Co.,) 332 W. 7th
Phares Alexander, exchange office, 174 E. Pearl, e. of Broadway, h. 88 E. Pearl e. of Broadway
Phares James, carp., 186 E. Pearl
Phares John, (P. Taylor & Co) Mt. Horeb
Phares John P., agt., 169 Walnut, h. 552 W. 5th
Phares Taylor & Co., (John P., John C. T. & Abram Phares,) boots and shoes, 49 W. Pearl
Pheifer John, bds. s.s. 6th, b. Harriet and Horne
Phelan Dennis, grocery, s.e.c. Plum and Court
Phelan Thomas, bksmith, 12 Commerce
Phelen Edward, porter, s.e.c. Court and Plum
Phelps C. H., clk., 59 W. Pearl, bds. s.w.c. Race and George
Phelps Chas., real estate, 166 Vine
Phelps Mrs. Eliza, h. 166 Vine
Phelps Oscar F., card writer, bds. 27 Longworth
Phelps Wm. H., keeper Hammond St. station house, 151 Sycamore
Pheney Andrew, lab., bds. Michael Corcoran's
Phile David, instrument mkr., 346 Main
Phile Joseph, instrument mkr., s.e.c. 6th and Plum
Philips Daniel, general agt., 60 W. 4th, h. 233 Longworth

Philley Hy., broker, 221 Vine, h. 70 Longworth
Phillipa Sister, St. Clare Convent, n.w. c. 3d and Lytle
Phillips Wm., soap mkr., wks. 830 Central Av
Phillip Louis, tailor, h. 202 Broadway
Phillipp Bernhard, dry goods, 41 Freeman
Phillip Daniel, cutter, 233 Longworth
Phillippe Wm., lab., 1 York
Phillips —, cab, mkr., bds. n.s. Augusta b. John and Smith
Phillips Anna, n.w.c. George and Central Avenue
Phillips Ambrose, 33 Chestnut
Phillips B. M., porter, bds. 70 Sycamore
Phillips Benj., 39 Pleasant
Phillips Chas, clk., bds. 157 Elm
Phillips Elizabeth, n. s. Railroad, opp. French
Phillips Elizabeth R., teacher, 4 Wilson
Phillips Ellen, s.e.c. Elm and Water
Phillips Elmira, 120 W. 9th, w. of Central Av
Phillips F., carp., wks. 304 Broadway
Phillips Francis J., b.k., 79 W. Pearl, h. 410½ W. 9th
Phillips Geo, carriage painter, n.s. Court b. Mound and Cutter
PHILLIPS George, (P. & Son,) res. Covington
Phillips Geo., presser, 3 Pine
PHILLIPS GEO. W., Family Medicines and Physician, 50 W. 6th, h. 292 W. 7th
Phillips Geo. W. jr., provision broker, 5 College Bldg., h. 87 Harrison
Phillips Hy., stone cutter, wks. H. Rosenberg's, bds. 59 Findlay
Phillips Hy. C., bk. peddler, w.s. Wilson b. Milton and Liberty
Phillips Horace, b.k., 79 W. Pearl, bds. 410½ W 9th
Phillips J. Howard, b.k., 97 W. 3d, bds 251 W. Court, w. of Central Av
Phillips Jackson B., clk., 30 Pub. Landing, h. 46 Arch
Phillips Jacob, cook, n.w.c. Vine and Longworth
Phillips Jacob, driver. 47 14th
Phillips James, b.k., 410½ W. 9th, w. of Central Av
Phillips James A., eng., 303 W. 7th
Phillips Jane, 363 W. 7th
Phillips Jennie, tailoress, bds. 355 Central Av
Phillips John, conductor, 295 Findlay
Phillips John, porter, 246 W. 3d
Phillips John M., b.k. Methodist Book Concern, h. 131 Smith
Phillips Louis, bksmith, n.e.c. Pendleton and Abigail
Phillips Maggie, bds. rear 33 Dunlap
Phillips Margaret, rear 33 Dunlap
Phillips Mary, 44 Lock, n. of 8th
Phillips Phinens, 34 New
Phillips Peter, bds. rear 33 Dunlap
PHILLIPS ROBERT C., Civil Engineer and Surveyor, n.e.c. Walnut and 9th, h. 251 W. Court, w. of Central Avenue
Phillips Robert G., civil engineer, Metropolitan bldg., h. 270 Cutter
Phillips Sidney, furnishing goods, 269 Center st. bds. 286 W. 6th
Phillips Silas, boat stores, 30 Pub. Landing, h. 16 Arch
Phillips Solomon, painter, 122 W. Court, w. of Central Av
PHILLIPS & SON, (Thomas & George,) Licking Iron Works, 58 and 60 E. 2d
Phillips Susan, 37 Plum
PHILLIPS Thos., (P. & Son,) 114 W. 4th
Phillips Wm., 168 Race
PHILLIPS WM., Attorney at Law, n.e.c. Walnut and 9th, h. Mt. Hope
Phillips Wm. H., real estate broker, 83 W. 3d, h. 19 E. 3d, e. of Parsons
Philomina Sister, St. John's Hospital, n.w.c. 3d and Plum
Phinegan Louis, hinge fitter, wks. n.e.c. Walnut and Canal

260 (PIE) CINCINNATI (PIN) DIRECTORY. (PLA)

Phiney D N., salesman, 169 E. 3d
PHIPPS Gardner, (Gardner, P. & Co.) 118 E. 4th
PHIPPS GARDNER & CO., (Gardner P. & Chas. G. Enyart,) Pork Packers and Commission Merchants, n. w. c 9th and Broadway, and 301 Broadway
Phipps Margaret, 654 W. 8th
PHIPPS Wm. R., (M. E. Reeves & Co.,) h. Avondale
Phipps Wm. T., 285 Richmond
PHISTER Benjamin, (P. & How,) res. Maysville, Ky
Phister Charles, currier, 606 E. Front
PHISTER & HOW, (Benjamin P. & Fulton M H.,) Tobacco Warehouse. Pearl b. Plum and Central Avenue
Phister John, lab., 63 Providence
Phister Lena, cap mkr., 53 12th
Phobe Caroline, s.s. Phoebe al. b. Plum and Central Av.
Phœnix Hall, 200 Vine
PHOENIX INSURANCE CO., of Hartford, Conn., Branch Office 33 W. 3d, R H. & H. M. Magill, General Agents
Phoenix Insurance Co. of New York, agency. room 33 Pike's Opera House
PHYSIO MEDICAL COLLEGE, Literary and Scientific Institute, 135 Elm, A. Curtis. M D., Dean
Piatt Chas., student. bds. 137 Race
Piatt Wm , student. bds. 137 Race
Pichner Anthony, cigar mkr., wks. 646 Race
Pick Joseph, molder, 462 Race
Pick Sebastian. cooper, 723 Race
Pickard Geo. W., b k. 144 Main, h. 92 Richmond
Pickard John, sen., carp.. 19 Brighton
Pickard John, jr., clk, 117 Main, h. 19 Brighton
Pickel Frederick, lab., h. 9e Ham. Road
PICKEL MAX, Stoves, Hollow Ware, Tin Ware, &c., 243 W. 6th
Pickel Peter, 21 Mulberry
Pickens Ellen, b. h., 138 W. 8th
Pickens Ellen, 363 W. 3d
Picker Hy., shoe mkr., 155 Pleasant
Pickerd Lehman, clk., bds. 51 Longworth
Pickering Alfred, salesman 198 Main, bds. Walnut St. House
Pickering Chas. H., printer, bds. 38 Chestnut
Pickering Elizabeth, 38 Chestnut
Pickering Geo. M., clock mkr , 9 E. 7th
Pickering Geo. W., salesman 137 W. 9th
PICKERING JOSEPH M., Ladies' Dress Trimmings, 96 W. 4th, h. 414 W. 4th
Pickering Marcellus, 9 E. 7th
PICKERING Tilghman, (Joseph W. Wayne & Co.) bds. Walnut Street House
Pickering Wm. E., clk. 28 Pub. Landing, bds. 15 E. 6th
Pickers John A., printer, Cin. Gazette, h. Newport
Picket Lehman. b k. 22 W. Front, bds. 51 Longworth
Picket Sophia. 164 Spring
Pickett John, cof. h., 206 Broadway
Pickleman Geo., finisher, s.w.c. Pearl and Plum
Pickles Michael F., foreman, McCormick, Gibson & Co., h. Mt. Auburn
Picquet Harriet, shirt mkr., 295 Water
Picquet Louise, dress mkr.. 272 W. 3d
Pieber Gerhard, porter, 523 Sycamore
Piennig John H., cab. manuf., 23 Mercer, h. 507 Main
Piepenbring Christena. 346 Ham Road
PIEPENBRING FRANK, Proprietor Broadway Exchange n.e.c 2d and Broadway
Piepenmeier Frederick, 71 Milton
Pieper Elizabeth, 19 Franklin
Pieper Francis, lab., 219 Franklin
Pieper Frederick, varnisher. 19 Franklin
Pieper Geo., porter, wks. 17 W. 5th
Pieper Louis, cof. h., 598 Walnut
Piepho Chas., clk. 613 Vine

Pierce Alexander N., b.k., 308 Clark
Pierce Benj. F., clk., 184 George
Pierce Caleb. mach., n.s. Fremont b. Harriet and Mill Creek
Perce D. J., laundry, 218 Sycamore
Pierce Ed., servt., Burnet House
Pierce Hy. H., clk., bds. Walnut Street House
PIERCE JAMES, Commission Merchant, 31 Vine, h. Covington
Pierce James, salesman 65 Main, h. 466 W. 9th
Pierce Joseph, Inspector, 16 Pub. Landing, h 184 George
Pierce Samuel, bk. mkr., Richmond b. Harriet and Millcreek
Pierce Wm. H., inspector. 16 Pub. Landing, h. e.s. Lawrence b. 3d and 4th
Piermont Thos., bksmith, wks. n.e.c. Walnut and Canal
Pierpont Moses D., shoe mkr., 19 Observatory Road
Pierson Ann, 49 12th
Pierson Chas. E., clk., 274 W. 7th
Pierson Daniel, bds, 107 Broadway
PIERSON D. B. & CO., (Danl. B. P. & Robt. McCullough) Lumber Yard, 381 Plum
Pierson D. W., teller Evans & Co., 75 and 77 W 3d
PIERSON Daniel B., (D. B. P. & Co.) h. College Hill
Pierson Frederick, cooper, 49 12th
Pierson James, photographer. 49 12th
Pierson Joseph, painter, 49 12th
Pierson W. T., salesman, n.e.c. 5th and Vine
Piersey Wm., clk. post office, bds. 61 Longworth
Piersey Wm., fireman, 31 E. 7th
Piersey Wm., eng., w s. Crippen al. b. 7th and 8th
Pletsch Anthony. cab. mkr., 140 Everett
PIETZ BERNHARD, Coffee and Boarding House, 426 Vine
Pigg Joseph, 17 Providence
Piggott Chas. J., fancy goods, 164 W. 5th. h. Philadelphia
Pigram Lot, steward, n.s. Patterson al. b. Main and Walnut
PIKE Samuel N., (Samuel N. P. & Co) 355 W. 4th
PIKE SAMUEL N. & CO., Wholesale Liquor Dealers, 18 and 20 Sycamore
Pike Wm., lab., 654 W. 8th
Pike Wesley, carp., 72 E. 3d e. of Whittaker
PIKE'S OPERA HOUSE, s.s. 4th b. Vine and Walnut
PIKET A. & SON, (Anthony & Louis) Architects, 168 Vine
PIKET Anthony, (A. P. & Son) 274 Hopkins
Piket Ignatius painter, 36 Ellen
PIKET Louis, (A. Piket & Son) bds. 274 Hopkins
Pilger Christian. tailor, 224 Bremen
Pilger Daniel, tailor, bds. 224 Bremen
Pilger John P., tailor, bds. 420 W. 3d
Pilgram Hy., bksmith, wks. n w.c. Race and Burrows
PILKINGTON JOHN O. C., Family Grocery. s.w.c. 9th and Linn, h. 63 Linn
Pilmann Hy., driver, 11 Hannibal
Pillars L. W., cutter. 164 Elm
Pille Frederick, salesman, 408 Longworth
Pille Hy., clk., 478 Main
Pille J Hy., tinner, wks. 598 Main
Pilleng Hy., basket mkr., 14 Jackson
Pillsbury Andrew J., porter, 34 Walnut
Pilton Wm. F , dray. 99 Gest
Pincavea Frank, lab., 70 Abigail
Pinder Bernard, plow mkr., 67 Spring
Pinder Constan, gardener. w.s. Western Av. b. Dayton and Bank
Pine Leroy, chair mkr.. bds. 175 W, Court w. of Central Av.
Pine Leroy, painter, bds. 175 W. Court w. of Central Av.

Pine Noah. carp., 134 Clark
Pine Simon, cof. h., mkr., 200 Clark
Pinet Alphonso, cof. h., 561 Vine
Pinger Adam, butcher, w.s. Campbell al. b. Elder and Findlay
Pinger Christian, 716 Elm
Pinger Jacob, w.s. Campbell al. b. Elder and Findlay
Pinger Jacob, butcher, 716 Elm
Pinger Louis, bds w. s. Campbell al. b. Elder and Findlay
Pinger Philip, butcher, w.s. Campbell al. b. Elder and Findlay
Pinger Philip, butcher, 718 Elm
Pingsterhaus Hy., lab., 71 Green
Pinkfaus Lewis, porter, e.s. Kilgour b. 3d and 5th
Pinn Sanders, presser, 66 Everett
Pinn Sanders, whitewasher, 66 Avery
Pinner Samuel, tailor, s.w.c. Court and Walnut
Pinney Geo. E., coach painter, rooms 227 Central Av.
Pinney Maria, 196 W. 7th
Pinney Sidney A., clk. post office, h. Groesbeck, Ohio
Pinney Wm. A., harness mkr., 196 W. 7th
Pioneer Association, City Building, Wm. Moody, seargant-at-arms
Pipe Jas., liquor mer., bds. 273 Walnut
Pipemier Hy., cooper. 179 Baymiller
Pipenbring Chas., policeman. 84 Ham. Road
Pipenbring Phillip, 80 Mohawk
Piper Francis. dray, 548 W. 3d
Piper Frederick, varnisher, 16 Franklin
Piper Robt., lab.. 548 Race
Piper Susan, 460 W. 9th w. of Central Av.
Pipmeier John F., bksmith, 71 Milton
Pipp Philip, lab., 492 Elm
Pirrung Theobald, dray, 634 Elm
Pister Conrad, tailor, 524 Vine
Pister Joseph, cooper, 518 Main
Pister Peter. lab , n.s. al. b. Canal and 12th and Vine and Race
Pistler Wm., grocery. 74 Bremen
Pistner Christopher, cof. h., 18 Hamer
Pistner Godfrey, barber. 62 Findlay
Pistner John, boots and shoes. 653 Vine
Pistner Leo, carp., bds. 18 Hamer
Pistner Martin, bar k., bds. 18 Hamer
Pistner Stephan, lab., 639 Vine
Pistor Chas. confec , 80 W 6th
Pistor Jacob, bakery, 208 W. Liberty
PITMAN BEN., Phonographic Institute. Carlisle Building, h. Walnut Hills
Pittel Hy., turner, 150 Ham. Road
Pittinger Abraham, boots and shoes, 280½ W. 5th, h. 241 Laurel
Pittman Isaac A., (Grant & P.) 230 Main
Pittner Eliza, h. 244 Bremen
Pittner Florina, seamstress, 653 Vine
Pittner Peter. mason, 28 Green
Pitton Anthony, dye house. 96 13th
Pitton Chas.. cab. mkr. 96 13th
Pitton John P , dyer, 96 13th
Pitts Anthony, cab. mkr. , 140 Everett
Pitts John A., grocery, 234 Cutter, h. 244 Cutter
Pitzer Andreas, tailor, 677 Race
Placke Bernard, hatter, 414 Longworth
Placke Herman, candy mkr., 414 Longworth
Plager Barney, lab., 219 Betts
Plantholt Frank, phys., s.w.c. 8th and Carr
Planz Andreas, cof. h., 109 Bremen, h. 111 Bremen
Plappert Anna, 61 Avery
Plappert Geo., lab., 61 Avery
Plaspohl Hy., clk., 155 York
Plasphol Hy. E., grocery. h. 179 Barr
Plate Fred., lab., 64 Richmond
Plater Hannah, 199 Webb
Platt Alanson S., 8 Clinton Court
Platt Geo., mach., 234 Richmond
Platt Herman S. (L. B. Liatt & Co) bds. Spencer House
Platt L. B., (L. B. P. & Co.) res. Buffalo
Platt L. B. & Co., (L. Beach P. & Herman S. Platt) oysters, &c., s.e.c. 3d and Sycamore
Platta Anna, servt., 421 Freeman

Platscher John, carriage mkr., s.s. 6th near Mill Creek
Platz Albert, barber, 233 W. 5th
Plaut Michael, clothing, 604 Central Av
Pluuth Frederick, lab., 43 Race
Plea Joseph, mach., 406 Longworth
Pleasant David, tobacconist, 197 Webb
Plehs Hermann, tailor, 345 W. 5th
Pleimann Bernhard, clk., 594 Race
Pleisteiner John G., fancy store, 555 Vine
Pleoff Frederick, cooper, s. w. c. Cutter and Melancthon
Plettner Theodore, tailor, 484 Elm
Plimmer Wm., stone cutter, 407 Elm
Plimpton Albert, mess., 6 Dayton
PLIMPTON FLORUS B., Editor Daily Commercial, 205 W. 3d
Ploch Caroline, servt., 393 Vine
Plocher Hy., lab., s.w.c. Abigail and Spring
Plochy Anthony, dry goods, 513 Main
Plouman Barney, lab., 246 Clark
Plogmann Christopher, tailor, 103 Woodward
Plogsted Frederick, cab. mkr., 187 Clark
Plogsterth Hy., lab., 53 Hughes
Ploner John, brush mkr., 109 Ham. Road
Pluemer Wm., clk., 648 Main
Pluger Barney, lab., 219 Betts
Pluikebreum Frank, cigar mkr., 623 Elm
Plumb Charles, expressman, bds. 134 W. 3d
Plumb Frederick, stone cutter, 123 Clay
Plumb Geo. W., millinery, 204 W. 5th
Plumb Hy., lab, 118 Clay
Plumb Julia C, 204 W. 5th
Plumb Wolfgang, butcher. s. s. Montgomery Pike near Reading Road
Plumer Sarah, 402 W. 7th
Plumer Wm., lab., 407 Elm
Plummer Bernard, porter, 594 Race
Plump Frederick, stone cutter. s. s. Melancthon b Jones and Cutter
Plump (My. J., clk., 16 Mulberry
Plumridge Thomas R., bklayer, 60 15th
Plunket Hy., mach., 220 Betts
Plunkett Anna, bds. 61 David
Plunkett Michael, tailor, n. s. Pearl b. Central Av. and Plum
Ply Joseph, lab, 406 Longworth
POAGE Thos K., (Thos. K. P. & Co.,) 150 W. 3d
POAGE THOMAS K., & CO., Commission Merchants, Dealers in Flour and Grain, 148 and 150 W. 3d
Poath John, driver, bds. 463 W. 9th w. of Central Av.
Poath M., lab., 483 W. 9th w. of Central Av.
Pocock Lucy C., millinery, 287 Central Av.
Pochsner Mary, s. w. c. 9th and Central Av.
Podesta A, & Co., (A. P. & F. Podesta) confec., 130 Walnut
Podesta Anthony, (A. P. & Co.) n. s. 5th b. Vine and Race
Podesta Frank, (A Podesta & Co.) n. s. 5th b Vine and Race
Podesta James, confec., 301 Central Av.
Podesta John, confec., s.w.c. Main and Canal
Podesta Louis, confec., s. e. c. 4th and Central Av.
POE Adam, (P. & Hitchcock,) 52 Franklin
Poe Andrew, clk. Methodist Book Concern, b. 439 Broadway
POE & HITCHCOCK. (Adam P., & Luke H.,) Agents Methodist Book Concern, s.w.c. 8th and Main
Poehl Hy Wm., cigar mkr., 57 13th
Poel Frederick, lab.. s. s. Budd b. Donnersberger and Harriet
Poeling Herman, lab., n. e. c. Smith and Water
Poeppe Hy., lab., 123 Clay
Poeppelmann Hy., teacher, 579 Sycamore
Poeppelmeier Bernhard, cooper 55 Buckeye
Pogue Hy., (P. & Jones,) 208 George

Pogue Isabella, 208 George
Pogue James, dray, n. s. Freeman b. Richmond and Harriet
Pogue James, dray, Richmond b. Freeman and Carr
Pogue and Jones, (Hy. T. & Edward G. J.,) dry goods, 128 W. 5th
Pogue Samuel, dry goods, bds. 208 George
Pogue Thomas, clk., bds 208 George
Pogue William. clk., bds. 208 George
Pohard Lewis, saddler, 60 15th
Pohl Barney H., boots and shoes, 188 Linn
Pohl Hy., lab., rear 512 Walnut
Pohl Wm., shoe mkr., 188 Linn
Pohlman Frank. cutter, 45 New
POHLMAN GEO. W., Military Furnisher, 102 W. 4th h. 356 W. 9th
Pohlman Hy., carp., bds. n. e. c. Sycamore and Abigail
POHLMAN HENRY, Saddles Harness and Trunks, 349 Broadway
Pohlman Hy., W., mechanic, 47 Pendleton
POHLMAN JOHN, . Wines and Liquors, 35 and 37 W. Court
Pohlman Jno. W., carriage smith, 132 Clinton
Pohlman Philip, box mkr., wks. 509 Plum
Pohlmann Bern. r l, stove mounter, 188 Linn
Pohlmann Elizabeth, 132 Clinton
Pohlmann Frank, cutter, 45 New
Pohlmann H., blksmith, wks. Chamberlain & Co's
Pohlmann Hy., 669 Race
Pohlmann Hy., lab., 132 Clinton
Pohlmann Hy., tailor, 596 Main
Pohlmeier Herrmann J., lab., 592 Race
Pohlmeier J. Hy., quarryman, 93 Pendleton
Pohlmeier Chas. H., flour dealer, 11 W Canal. b. 445 Sycamore
Pohlmeyer John, teamster, 79 Gest
Pohrmann Mary, seamstress, s. s. Cassatt al. b. Sycamore and Main
Pohrmeier Hy., lab., 26 Green
Points Samuel, porter. 99 Park
Polack Mrs. Francis, 488 W. 9th
Poland Frederick, butcher, n.w.c. Front and Sycamore
Poland & Henry, (Patrick P. & John H.,) grocers, 60 and 62 W. 2d
Poland James drugs. rear 19 Milton
Poland Patrick (P. & Henry,) 188 Sycamore
Po'e nan Barney, lab., 186 Linn
POLICE COURT, City Building, s. s. 9th b. Central Av. and Plum, James Saffin Judge
Poles Hy., cigar mkr., 62 Laurel
POLK James E., (Ellis McA. & Co.,) bds. s.w.c. 3d and Broadway
Poll Geo., tailor, 91 Spring
Poll Hy , tailor, 374 Broadway
Poll Herman, tailor, 374 Broadway
POLL JOHN A., Merchant Tailor, 241 Central Av. h. 244 Main
Poll John B , cutter, 183 Walnut, bds. 244 Main
Poll Wm., tailor, 374 Broadway
Pollack Abraham, rag dealer, 612 Elm
Pollack John, janitor, 15 E. 8th
Pollard Eliza, 106 14th
Pollard James, confec., 227 Sycamore
Pollard John, fireman, 441 W. 2d
Pollard Nicholas, grocery, n.w.c. Whittaker and Front
Pollio Eugene, jewelery, bds. 174 Plum
Pollitz Jacob, b. k., 36 W. Pearl, h. 281 Vine
Pollman Adam, carriage smith, 17 Providence
Pollmann Hy., feed store, e. s. Vine b. Ham. Road and Buckeye, h. w. s. Race b. Findlay and Elder
Pollock Elizabeth, 18 Plum
Pollock Geo. W., (Pollock & Son,) 140 W. Front

POLLOCK & GILMOR, (Robert H. P., and Robert G.) Editors, Publishers and Proprietors. Presbyterian Witness, Office room No 6 Neave's Building, n. w. c. Race and 4th
Pollock James, janitor, 165 Vine
Pollock James S., (P. & Son,) 140 W. Front
Pollock John, clk., 141 Walnut, h. 182 W. Court w. of Central Av.
Pollock Joseph, fureman, 323 W. 4th
Pollock Joseph, salesman, 22 Main, h. 323 W. 4th
Pollock Joseph C., 323 W 4th
POLLOCK Rev. Robert H., (P. & Gilmor) 155 Dayton
Pollock Samuel, potter, s.e.c Whiteman and Dayton
Pollock & Son, (James S. P., & Geo. W. J .,) foundry 140 W. Front
Pollock Thomas, fireman, 212 Water
Pollock Thos., teamster, n. s Water b. Plum and Central Av
Pollock Wm., blksmith, 179 W. Front
Pollock Wm. saddler, 136 Baum
Pollord John, fireman, s.s. 2d b. Park and Mill
Polmise John, lab, wks. n. w. c. Plum and Wade
Polster August, jeweler, 417 Vine
Polster Robert C., baker, e. s. Goose al. b. Liberty and 15th
Polytechnic College, n. w. c. Vine and Longworth
POMEROY James P., (Robbins & Pomeroy.) h. n w.c. 3d and Baum
POMEROY James P., (R. M. Pomeroy & Co.) bds. Burnet House
POMEROY R. M., & CO., (Ralph M. P., James P. Pomeroy, Daniel Ahl Jr , & Aaron S. Betts,) Wholesale Dealers in Boots and Shoes, 59 W. Pearl
POMEROY Ralph M., (R. M. P., & Co.) n w.c. 3d and Baum
POMEROY S. WYLLYS, Pomeroy Coal Mines, Office, 54 E. 3d, h. E. Walnut Hills,
Pomeroy Anna E., bds. 73 W. 7th
Pompilly Judah, T., teacher, 149 Elm
Ponbacx Mary, n. e. c. Sycamore and Abigail
Ponreth Hy., shoe mkr., 129 Clark
Ponsett Mary, 36 E. 8th e. of Lock
Poutsack Frank, cab. mkr., s s. Betts b. Baymiller and Freeman
Pool Harriet, 232 E. 6th
Pool Mary E., teacher, 101 Baymiller
Pool Solomon, 60 E. 7th
Poor ——, clk., rooms 56 E 3d
Poor Chester M., 225 Walnut
Poor & Co., (Henry W. P., & Wm. C. P.,) grocers, 235 Walnut
Poor Hy. W , (P. & Co.,) h. Camp Washington
Poor John H., asst. librarian Ohio School Library, bds. s. e. c. 3d and Broadway
Poor Margaret, 61 Mound
Poor N. Peabody, librarian Public Library, Mechanics' Institute, bds s.e c. 3d and Broadway
Poor Standish H., Adams Express Co., bds. 77 E. 3d
Poor Wm., clk. Burnet House
Poor W'm , dray. 19 Webb
Poor William C., (P. & Co.,) h. 326 Baymiller
Poore R. B., mess. American Express Co., bds. Broadway Hotel
Popert David M., 103 Longworth
Popp Christian (Steiuer & P.,) bds. 451 Vine
Popp Geo., lab, 100 Buckeye
Popp Mary. servt., 31 W. 7th
Popp Michael, lab,, 1 Wade b. Elm and Plum
Poppe Frederick, sr. lab, 531 Walnut
Poppe Fred. jr , painter, 531 Walnut
Popping Joseph, prop. Indiana House, 536 W. Front
Poppino Daniel. phys. 466 W. 5th
Poppino Mary Jane, dress mkr., 466 W. 5th
Popst Michael, express driver, bks. 14 E Front

Porckenhagen Wm., wheel mkr., 537 Walnut
Pormeier Ferdinand, 147 Abigail
Pornobrun Benj. A., shoe mkr., e.s. Main b. Liberty and Mulberry
Porte H., lab., wks. 18 Sycamore
Porter Andrew, carp., 43 Gest
Porter Anna R., n.e.c Court and John
Porter Chas., J. 88 W 8th
Porter Fred. W., jeweler, 65 W. Court w of Central Av
Porter Geo S., messenger, M. & C. R. R., bds. Dennison House
Porter Hy., janitor, s.s. Court b. John and Mound
Porter Hy. E., bk. layer, 25 Hannibal
Porter J., finisher, wks C. T. Dumont's
Porter James, painter, 298 W. 5th, h. 25 Chestnut
Porter James H., tinner, 35 Chestnut
Porter John, lab., s.s. 6th b. Broadway and Culvert
PORTER John H., (Chas. Davis and Co.), 59 W. 9th
Porter John K., salesman, 103 W, Pearl bds. 102 Plum
Porter Joseph, finisher, 163 E 3d
Porter Joshua A., kpr. 9th street station house, 174 Richmond
Porter Lucy, cof. h., 144 E. 6th
Porter Mary, s e c. North and New
Porter Mary J., 88 W. 8th
Porter Miss N. C., bds. 59 W. 9th
Porter Osmon, plumber, s.s. Dayton b. Coleman and Western Av.
Porter Saml., boiler mkr., 592 E. Front
Porter Simon, carp , 592 E. Front
PORTER Thos. P. jr., (Hinde & P.) h. Covington
Porter W. T., scenic artist, Pike's Opera House
Porter Wm., foreman Commercial office h. 56 Hathaway
PORTER Wm. H., (Sechler & P.) h. Covington
Porter Wm. S., photographist, 106 W 4th b Latonia Springs
Porteus Geo W., upholsterer, bds. 580 E Front
Portier Chas., compositor, 122 Clark
PORTSMOUTH FIRE & MARINE Insurance Co., Joseph S. Ross President, S. W Reeder Sec'y, n.w c. Walnut and 3d
Portune John, barber. 30 Ham. Road
Portz Peter, butcher, bds. n.s. Browne nr. Ham. Road
Posener Bertha, n.e.c. 5th and Race
Posey Asbury, porter A L Mowry & Co's
Posey Edward, lab., wks 196 W, Pearl
POSEY Oliver, (Robbins & P.) 162 Elm
Poshner Hy., cook, n.s. Grandin al. b. Elm and Plum
Poske Dietrich J., shoe mkr., 9 Woodward
Poske Herman, dray 30 Walnut
Poske Rudolph, cooper, bds, 9 Woodward
Poss Catharine, servt. 458 Broadway
Post Aaron, auctioneer, 119 Mound
Post Anthony, cooper, 247 Clark
Post Francis, cooper, 188 Hopkins
Post Frank, (Peter Jacob & Co.), 188 Hopkins
Post Geo., tailor, 303 Clark
Post Hy. G., lab., 626 Vine
Post John, cof. h , n.s. Harrison Pike nr. Mill Creek
Post John, lab., 18 Commerce b. Walnut and Vine
Post John, porter, 18 Commerce
Post John A., cooper, 179 Baymiller
Post John B., cooper, 235 Clark, h. 179 Baymiller
Post Joseph G., cooper, 305 Linn
Post L. W., bds. 530 W. 5th
POST OFFICE. John C. Baum, Postmaster, s.w.c. 4th and Vine
Post Saml. P., clk , 70 Vine, h. 155 W. 4th
POST Simon S., (McCallum Bridge Co.), h. Jersey City, N. J.
Post Strange S., clk., 43 Pub. Landing
Postel Amelia, n.w.c Walnut and 9th
Postel Fred., shoe mkr., 194 Clark

Postel John, 677 Elm
Postman John, shoe mkr., bds. Cherry al. b. Plum and Central Av
Pot Wm., 69 Milton
Potne Peter, plasterer, 152 Van Horn
Potsmith Chas., shoe mkr., bds. 353 Central Av
Pott Herman H., grocery, 145 Linn
Potter Mrs. Ann. 149 Bank
Potter Barney, clk., 610 Central Av
Potter Daniel, atty., rooms 1 and 2 Masonic Temple h 425 W. 8th
Potter James, huckster, 17 New
Potter Jonathan, conductor, C. H. & D. R. R , h. 339 Longworth
POTTER JOSEPH F., Physician, Office 36 W. 4th, h. 302 Walnut
POTTER L. F. & WILSON, (Luther F. P. & James P W .) Commission Merchants, and Dealers in Machinery, 98 and 100 E. 2d
POTTER LUTHER F., Agent, Pomeroy Rolling Mill Co. 100 E. 2d, h, 109 Smith
POTTER M. D. & CO., (Martin D. P., Murat Halstead & Constantine D Miller), Proprietors Cincinnati Daily and Weekly Commercial, n.e. c. 4th and Race
POTTER Martin D., (M D, P. & Co.) 137 Central Av
Potter Mary. h. 17 New
POTTER Russell, (Thos. P. Saunders & Co), h. Hamilton O.
Potter Wm., 17 New
Potthaust Hy., cab. mkr., 14° Laurel
Potthoff Hy., bakery, 484 Walnut
Pottker Bernard, tailor, 147 Abigail
Pottker Hy., porter, 60 W. 13th
Pottmaer Anton, shoe mkr., 414 Longworth
Potts Rev. ——, bds. 297 W. 6th
Potts Hy. J., cab. mkr., 12 Mary
Potts John H., finisher, 12 Mary
Pottsdam Philip, 182 George
POUNSFORD Arthur H., (Applegate & Co.), 304 Richmond
Powdrell Wm., stone cutter, 28 Lock
Powe Saml. 69 Mohawk
Powell David A. foundry, 30 Butler, h. w.s. Kilgour b. 3d and Pearl
Powell E. W., bds. 158 W. 3d
Powell Edward W., clk. w.s. Kilgour b. 3d and Pearl
Powell Eliza, s.w c. 3d and Butler
Powell Hy., brass finisher, s.s. Central Av. b. Auburn Av. and Lebanon Road
Powell Hy., lab., n.s. Channing b Price and Young
Powell Hy., shoe mkr., bds. 283 W. 6th
POWELL Hy., (Wm. Powell & Co.), h. Mt. Auburn
Powell Rev. Howell, 43 New
Powell J. B., atty., 66 W. 3d, bds. D. A Powell's, Kilgour St
Powell J. N., n.w c. Kilgour and Pearl
POWELL James, (Wm. Powell & Co) 122 Mill
Powell John A., 145 E 3d
Powell John M., phys., bds. 47 W. 7th
Powell John R. clk. 204 W 6th
Powell Joseph, com. mer., 285 W. 7th
Powell Louisa, seamstress. 148 Clark
Powell Mary, servt., 386 W. 6th
Powell Michael lab, wks. Hy , Nye's
POWELL PALEMON Guns and Pistols, 160 Main, h. 51 Race
Powell Rich., grocers, s e c. Broadway and 7th
Powell Rich., lab., n.s. Van Horn b. Linn and Cutter
POWELL THOMAS Attorney at Law, 12 Masonic Temple, h Mt. Auburn
Powell Thos, bleacher, 90 Clark
Powell Thos R., carp., 200 Cutter
Powell Watkin, finisher, n.e.c. Daum and Observatory Road
Powell Watt E., (Vandevier & P.), 98 Sycamore
Powell Wm., 95 St. Clair

Powell Wm., 143 W. Court w. of Central Av
Powell Wm., collector, 138 Livingston
Powell Wm., foundryman, 368 W. 4th
Powell Wm. jr. com. mer., 109 Sycamore, h 401 W. 4th
POWELL WM. & CO., (James & Hy, P.) Brass Founders and Finishers 247 and 249 W. 5th
POWELL WM. F. & CO. Fruit Dealers, 337 Walnut
POWELL Wm. F., (Wm. F. P. & Co.)
Power Edward, tanner, wks. H. & G. R. Martin's
Power John M., student, bds. 47 W. 7th
Power Joseph F., painter, bds. 296 W. 5th
Power James lab., 210 E. 6th
Power Lewis B., student 204 W. 9th
Power Mary. e.s. Carl b. 3d and 4th and Mill and Stone
Power Rob., cof h., 028 E. Front
Power Wm. H., clk., 135 Main, bds. 416½ W. 9th
Powers Anna. waiter Dennison House
Powers Catharine, servt., 112 Broadway
Powers Catharine, 47 Betts
Powers Ellen, servt., Spencer House
Powers Franklin, carp., 1260 E Front
Powers Geo , N , clk., n.w.c. 5th and Central Av, bds. 316 Clark
Powers Hy. C., printer, bds. 182 Race
POWERS HIRAM, Asst. City Prosecuting Atty, Office City Bldg., h. Mt. Auburn
Powers James, pipe fitter, wks. n.e.c. Walnut and Canal
POWERS & JONES, Attorneys at Law, Room 8 Shorts Bldg., s.e.c. 4th and Walnut
Powers John, carp , bds. 445 Main
Powers Jno., lab., n.e.c. Richmond and Freeman
Powers John, lab., wks. C. H. & D. R. depot
Powers John, paper carrier, 15 Oliver
Powers Joseph J., carp., 316 Clark
Powers Margaret servt, 112 Broadway
Powers Mary, servt., 329 Longworth
Powers Mary, n.s. Margaret b Jane and Baymiller
Powers Michael, coachman, bds. 221 Central Av
Powers Michael, hackman, 341 W. 6th
Powers Nellie, bds. 476 W. 5th
Powers Rich., clk., Haughton & Reid's, h. 232 Broadway
Powers Thos., cooper, n.e. c. Lock and 6th
Powers Thos., salesman, bds. 177 Sycamore
Powers Wm., packer, 86 W. Front
Powers Wm., porter, n.e.c. Race and 5th
Pownell Thos., lab., 46 Baum
Prach Louis, printer. 63 Providence
Pracke John, pressman wks s.w c Vine and Longworth
Prndel Chas., clk , 492 Elm
Praeszler Jacob J., bar k., 283 Bremen
Praluse Hy., drays, s.e.c. Milton and Broadway
Prain Christopher, wagon mkr , 32 Dudley
Praschili Frank, huckster, e.s. Vine junction of Mulberry
Prater Jas., pilot. s.s. Pole b. Park and Rose
Prather Chas. B., mattress and bedding, 51 E 3d, h. 287 W. 8th
Pratl Chas , cap mkr., 492 Elm
Pratt Gertrude, bds. 51 Stone al
Pratt Hy. A., teacher, 575 W. 8th
Pratt John, lab., bds. n.e.c. Vine and Water
PRATT LEVERETT A , Proprietor Spencer House, n.w c. Front and Broadway
Preasker Andy, carp., 190 Linn
Prehn Christian, wagon mkr., 32 Dudley
Prein Chas., blk. smith, 300 Linn
Preis Margaret, seamstress, 142 Clay
Prell John 137 Linn
Prell Ludwig, brewer, n.s. Henry rear Elm
Prendegast Maurice, 134 Mound

Prendergast Richard W., clk., 134 Mound
Prenhagin Hy., painter, s.s. 6th b. Broadway and Culvert
PRESBYTER, THE Monfort & Wampler Editors and Proprietors, 25 W. 4th
Presbyterian Boards of Foreign and Domestic Missions, Education, Publication and Church Extention Agencies, 72 W. 4th
PRESBYTERIAN BOOK DEPOSITORY, J D. Thorpe, Depositary, 72 W. 4th
PRESBYTERIAN WITNESS, Pollock & Gitmor Publishers, n.w.c. 4th and Race
Presler Barbara, s s. Weller b. Carr and Harriet
Pressel Mary, 261 W. 3d
Preasenger Francis, tailor, s.e.c. 4th and Vine, bds. Henri House
Pressler Jacob, bar k., 283 Bremen
PRESS PRINTING CO., Samuel B. Keys & S. W. Swiggett Proprietors, 136 Vine
Preston Catharine, n.e.c. 5th and Park
Preston Chas. M., shoe mkr., bds. 236 Richmond
Preston Douglas, shoe mkr, bds, 281 Central Av.
Preston Edward J., carp., 122 Baymiller
Preston Frank, bk. layer, bds. 302 W. 5th
Preston Geo W., shoe mkr, 236 Richmond
Preston Wm., bds. 57 E. 3d
Presuhn Casper, tailor, bds. 412 Vine
Preuer Franz, cigar manuf., 53 13th
Preuer Fred., cigar mkr., 47 Jackson
Preum Theodore, box mkr., 616 W. 8th
Price Alex., barber, e.s. al. b 4th and 5th and Park and Mill
Price D. D., bds. Walnut Street House
Price David, blk. smith, foot of Harrison
Price Edward N., finisher, 108 Barr
Price John, lab., w.s. Linn b. Dayton and York
Price John, mer., 61 W. 9th w. of Central Av.
Price John, painter, 48 Elizabeth
Price John D., (T. & J. P.) 32 Observatory
PRICE John Z., (Dickinson, P. & Bishop,) h. Covington
Price Lewis, coach mkr., bds. 168 Longworth
Price Margaret, 55 E. 8th e. of Lock
Price Mary, servt , 390 Longworth
Price Sidney, 191 Smith
Price T. & J., (Timothy & John,) buckskin dressers and glove manuf., 312 Main
Price Thos., white washer, 197 W. 3d
Price Timothy, (T. & J. P.,) bds s.w.c. 8th and Broadway
Price Wm., cof. h., 235 Main
Prichard Edward H., teacher, h. 48 Mulberry
PRICHARD GEORGE A., Wholesale Dealer in Boots and Shoes, 105 W. Pearl, bds. Burnet House
Prichard John, molder, 48 W. Mulberry
Prichard Richard, carp., 48 W. Mulberry
Prichard Wm., molder, wks. n.e.c. Canal and Walnut
Priesber Wilhelmina, res. 582 Main
Prieshof Hy., cooper, 71 Buckeye
Prier Kraker, cof. h., 903 Central Av
Prigodius Valentine, tailor, 673 Race
Prigge Hy., lab., 127 Livingston
Prim Abraham, b.k., s.e.c. Front and Lawrence, h. Newport, Ky.
Prime Chas. E., n.s. 8th b. Broadway and Sycamore
Prime Wm , barber, 22 E. 7th
Prime Wm. H., barber, s.s. 7th b. Main and Sycamore
Primm Chas., blk. smith, 360 Linn
Prince David, b.k. 90 W. 3d., h. 137 Mound
Prince Jas. C., druggist, 153 W. 5th
Prince Jas. H., salesman n.w c. 4th and Vine, h. 52 E. 6th
Printz Valentine, lab., 2 Lucy
Prior Christopher W., carp., n.w.o. Everett and Baymiller, h. 40 Jones

Prior John, dray. 96 Cherry al. b. Plum and Central Av.
Prior John, lab., wks. s.w.c. John and and W. W. Canal
Pristner Mary, packer, wks. 726 Central Av
Pritchard John, molder, h. 73 Pike
Pritner Hughes, stone cutter, bds. 69 W. 6th
Pritz S. W., salesman 154 Main, h. 187 Broadway
Pritzner John, lab., n.s. Montgomery Pike nr. Reading Road
PROBASCO Henry, (Tyler, Davidson & Co.,) 221 W. 4th
PROBASCO W. B., Attorney at Law, 68 W. 3d h. Glendale
PROBATE COURT, Alex. Paddack, Judge, Office, Court House
Probst Ernst, shoe mkr., 101 W. Front
Probst Ignatz, cof. h 72 12th
Procter Alex., clk., 76 W. 6th, bds. Walnut Hills
Procter Edward, tailor, 333 W. 5th
PROCTER & GAMBLE, (Wm. P., Wm. A. Procter, Jas. G., & Saml. Lowry,) Soap and Candle Manufacturers, 830 Central Av., store 24 W. 2d
Procter Geo. H., clk. 24 W. 2d, bds 297 Race [4th
Procter Thos. W., plumber, wks. 45 E.
PROCTOR Wm., (P. & Gamble,) 297 Race
PROCTER Wm. A., (P. & Gamble,) h. 343 Race
Procior Alex., clk., 24 Pine
Proctor Ann, 24 Pine
Proctor Jas., butcher, 144 Baymiller
PRODUCE EXCHANGE, Wm. Kehlenbach, Proprietor, 419 Main
Proniaius Frank, cof. h., s.e.c. Liberty and Clay
Prophater Adam, (J. & A. P.,) 664 Race
Propheter Geo , driver, 764 Race
Propheter J. & A., (John & Adam,) pine coopers, 639 Race
Propheter John, cof h., 664 Race
Propheter John, (J. & A. P.,) 664 Race
Propheter Michael, bar k., 90 13th
Propheter Michael, 641 Race
Propheter Oliver, bk. binder, h. s.s. 6th b Harriet and Sloo
Propheter Thos., wks. junction 6th and Front
Prosa Jacob, lab., 62 Ham. Road
Proser Conrad, blk. smith, 61 Findlay
Pross Geo. W., bk. layer, 16 Hanibal
Pross Larrison. cab. mkr., 261 W. 9th
Prosser Phillip T., s.e.c. Richmond and John
Prout Anna J., 213 W. 7th
Providence Washington Ins. Co, agency 70 W. 3d
Prows Jas. A., grocery, 1558 E. Front
Prows Samuel, cooper, s.s. Goodloe b. Willow and Niagara
Prows Thos. L., 1188 E. Front
Prucell Thos , blk. smith, 824 W. Front
Pruden Andrew J., atty., 57 W. 3d, h. 76 Hopkins
Pruden Eliza, bds. 162 Elm
Prues Bernard H., grocery, 176 E. 5th
Prues John H., shoe mkr., 72 Abigail
Pruess John H., shoe mkr., 45 Wade
Prugel Adam, 140 Freeman
Prun Louis, box mkr., wks. Livingston near Linn
Pruss Chas., waiter, Galt House
Pryor Frank, (Sullivan & P.,) 33 E. 5th
Pryor Pat., peddler, w.s. Langdon al. b. 6th and 7th
Pryse Rev. Jas. M., 278 Broadway
Pucher E., stocking mkr., wks. 413 Main
PUCHTA LORENZ, Boarding House and Coffee House, n.w.c. Pike and Pearl
Puechner Theresa, w.s. Goose al. b. Green and Elder
Pues Wm., cooper, 55 Buckeye
Puff Chas., willow basket manuf., 382 Vine

PUGH ACHILLES, Book and Job Printing Office, 120 Main, h. Waynesville
Pugh Albert W., b.k., 101 W. Pearl, h. Covington
Pugh David W., salesman 113 W. Pearl, bds. 162 Elm
PUGH GEORGE E., Attorney at Law, 73 W. 3d, h. 118 E. 3d
Pugh Hy. A., clk. C. H. & D. R. R. Depot, h. 577 W. 5th
Pugh Hiram, surveyor Queen City Ins. Co., h. 577 W. 5th
Pugh Hugh, grocery, s.w.c. Laurel and Cutter
Pugh J. D , printer, bds. Bevis House
Pugh Jas., driver. 4d Central Av.
Pugh Jas B., salesman 55 W. Pearl, h. s.s. Clinton 2d door e. of Linn
Pugh John D., bk. layer. 47 Hopkins
Pugh John M., clk. County Clerk's Office
Pugh Wm., teamster, 48 Central Av.
Puhlaman Herman, varnisher, wks. n.w. c. Front and Smith
Puihl Barbara, 685 Race
Pulaski Joseph, gun mkr., bds. s.s. 5th b. Walnut and Vine
Pulston Jas., lab., 518 E. Front
Pullen & Banks, (Wm. P. & John D, B.,) atty's. n.w.c. Walnut and 3d
Pullen Wm., (P. & Banks,) 130 Dayton
PULLEN Wm., manager of Tappan, McKillop & Co., s.w.c. 3d and Walnut, h. 130 Dayton
Puls Mary, 181 Baymiller
Puls Wm., stone mason, 679 Sycamore
Pulsch Emmert, porter, 485 Walnut
Pulskamp H., plow mkr., wks. 10 W. 7th
Pulskamp Hy., chair mkr., bds. 13 Bremen
Pulson Jas., 518 E. Front
PULTE J. H., Physician and Surgeon, Office and Residence 293, Walnut
Pummill Jas., printer, 13 W. 4th
Pummill John, carriage mkr , 136 Betts
Pummill L. H., 136 Betts
Pummill Wm., carriage mkr., 93 Richmond
Pumphrey Jas. R., salesman 23 W. Pearl h. 479 W. 7th
Punch David, molder, 174 Webb
Punch Elizabeth, 17 Stone
Punch Mary, 17 Stone
Punch Samuel, lab., 110 Gest
Punch Wm. H., clk., 17 Stone
Pund Hy., mach., wks. n.s. Front b. Lawrence and Pike
Pung Geo., (Geo. P. & Bro.,) 23 13th
Pung Geo. & Bro., (Geo. & Henry P.,) boots and shoes. 23 13th
Pung Henry, (Geo. P. & Bro.,) 23 13th
Punghorst Henry, finisher, wks. n.e.c. Walnut and Canal
Puning Ferdinand, lab., 639 W. Front
Puning Gerhard, chair mkr., 418 Longworth
Punt Dietrich, lab., rear 71 Abigail
Pupp Joseph, tailor, 41 12th
PURCELL VERY REV. EDWARD, v. g , Editor Catholic Telegraph, s.w.c. Vine and Longworth, res. rear of Cathedral
Purcell Geo., cigar mkr., bds. 191 Smith
Purcell James, bds. 24 Bank
Purcell John, clk., 24 E. 5th, h. s.e.c. Macalister and 5th
PURCELL John, (Looker, Purcell & Co.,) 165 Central Av
Purcell John, salesman, e.s. Macalister b. 4th and 5th
PURCELL MOST REV. JOHN B., Archbishop of Cincinnati, s.e.c. 8th and Central Av
Purcell Kate, seamstress, 3 New
Purcell Patrick, grocer, n.e.c. Court and Baymiller
Purcell Pat., lab., w.s. Pole al. b. 2d and Pearl
Purcell Robert, policeman, 183 Water
Purchase Levi. shoemkr., 56 Hughes
Purchase Thomas, shoemkr. 56 Hughes
Purden Ann, dress mkr., 34 Mulberry

Purdon Mrs. Mary, laundress. rear 16 E. Mulberry
Purk John, porter, 45 Broadway
Purkey David. carp , 406 W 8th
Purlier Mrs Ann, 112 Betts
Purlier Napoleon, bk. layer. 112 Betts
Purnell Thomas F., salesman, s.w.c. Walnut and Pearl, h. Covington
Purnhagen Clements, shoemkr., 160 W. Court
Pursel J. H. bds. 89 E. 4th
Pursel Wm. M , b.k., 36 Vine, h. E. Walnut Hills
Pursell B & J. R., (Brison & Joseph R., upholsterers, 10 E. 4th
Pursell Brison, (B. & J. R. P.) h. California, O.
Pursell Joseph R., (B. & J. R. P.,) h. California, O. [W Court
Pursell Patrick, horse shoer, wks. 152
Purser John, blksmith, 91 E. Front, h. Newport
Purvis Eliza, 90 Carr
Puttast Henry. carp., 148 Laurel
Puthoff Barnard. tailor, 164 Dayton
Puthoff Dene, servt., 355 W. 7th
Puthoff Frank H., tailor, 260 Main
Puthoff Frederick, b.k., 110 Abigail
Puthoff Henry, 110 Abigail
Puthoff Henry, lab., 185 Linn
PUTHOFF HENRY, JR., Coffee House (Washington Saloon), 110 Abigail
Puthoff Henry, porter, 133 Baymiller
Puthoff Henry, tailor, 9 Ann
Puthoff John B., tailor, 99 W. 2d
Putter Barney. tailor, wks n w c. Main and Court
Puttmann Anthony, blksmith., s.e.c. Ramsey and Park al., h. 509 W. Front
Puttmann Frank J., blksmith, bds. 509 W. Front
Puttmann Ferdinand. blksmith., bds. 509 W. Front
Putz Adam, tailor, 29 Abigail
Putz Catharine, 50 McFarland
Pyatt George, potter, 164 Bank
Pye Eliza J., teacher. bds. s.w.c. 5th and Broadway
Pye Josiah R., hatter, 48 W. 5th
Pye Robert, stone cutter, 304 Linn
Pyle Alex., harness mkr., 93 George
Pyle Elenora. bds 123 Linn
Pyles Nelson, lab., s.s. 6th b. Broadway and Culvert
Pyne Wm. H., hats, caps, &c., e.s. Walnut b. 5th and 6th, bds. Dennison House
Pyper Wm., clk., s.e.c. 5th and Wood

Q

Quaill Ann, 146 George
Quaning Henry, brick yard, s.e.c. Dudley and Liberty
Qualls Judy, 7 Pancoast al.
Quante D. H., cab. mkr., 467 Walnut
Quante Henry, boots and shoes, 35 Broadway, h. 60 Plum
Quante W. C. H., clk., s.e.c. Main and Canal
Quarter Master's Office. U. S. A., John H Dickerson, assist. Quarter Master, 56 W. 3d
Quarter Master's Office. U. S. A., 103 E. 3d, Capt. Charles Schmidt
Quartuin Elizabeth. 97 Hopkins
Quebe Frederick, boots and shoes, 1514 E. Front. h 1515 E. Front
Queen City Distillery, w.s. Colerain Pike n. of Brighton House
Queen City Hall. G. W. Skaats, propr., n. w.c. 8th and Freeman
QUEEN CITY INS CO., Fire and Marine, James A. Devou, Sec'y, Wm. McCammon, Pres., Hiram Pugh, Surveyor, Office 34 W. 3d
Queen City Mantleized Iron Mantle Works, Hand, Whitehouse & Co., 205 and 2 7 W. 5th
QUEEN CITY VARNISH CO., F. F. Brooks, 43 Vine

Queen N. W., mess. M. & C. R. R., h. Covington
Queen Wm , blksmith, bds. Pennsylvania Hotel
Quellhorst Christiana, cof. h., 493 Walnut
Quellhorst Ludwig, carriage painter, n.e. c. Hughes and Schiller
Quelong Samuel, lock smith, s.s. Pearl b. Central Av. and Plum
Quentin Henrietta, teacher, 495 Race
Quentin Hermann, bakery, 387 Vine
Quepman Henry, driver, s.e.c. Hoadly and Longworth
Querner Catharine, 107 Bremen
Querry Mrs. Annetta, tail ress, s.s.Goodloe b. Willow and Niagara
QUICK Israel, (Hoag & Q.), h. Covington
Quick Thomas, shoe mkr., 58 Barr
Quient Mary, laundress, 404 Main
Quigley Charles, cooper, c Weller and Skaats
Quigley George, paper hanger, 458 W. 6th
Quigley James, waiter Burnet House
Quigley John, butcher, bds. 241 W. 4th
Quigley John, lab., s.s. Charlotte b. Linn and Baymiller
Quigley John H., plasterer, 157 Baymiller
Quigley Joseph, lab, wks. 110 W. 2d
Quigley Joseph, manufac. drugs, 357 W. 3d
Quigley M., lab, Burnet House
Quigley Mary, 39 Race
Quigley Mary J., teacher, bds. s.w.c. 5th and Broadway
Quigley Thomas, clk., 143 Sycamore
Quigley Wm., cooper, c. Skaats and Weller
Quin Hugh, hat bleacher, 202 Plum
Quinmann Catharine, 171 W. Front
Quinby Joseph B., daguereotypist, 224 Central Av
Quindelsaider Stephen, shoe mkr., 211 Clinton
Quinke Eberhard, tailor, 526 Main
Quinke Francis, tailor. 526 Main
Quinke John H , tailor, 93 Pendleton
Quinlan & Green, (Mark A. Q. & Robert B. G.) saloon. 12 Broadway
Quinlan John, huckster, 75 Mill
Quinlan John, shoe mkr., s.w.c. 9th and Central Av
Quinlan Margureth, 339 W. 8th
Quinlan Mark A., (Q. & Green), res. Covington
Quinlan Mary, laundress, Spencer House
Quinlan Mary, s.w.c. 9th and Central Av
Quinlan Mary Ann, servt., Burnet House
Quinlan Michael, huckster, 487 W. 5th
Quinlan Michael, waiter, Spencer House
Quinn Ann, servt., Spencer House
Quinn Arch J.. n.w.c. 5th and Elm
Quinn Bernard, 70 McFarland
Quinn Bridget, chambermaid, Spencer House
Quinn David, atty., s.w c. 9th and Main, h. 532 W. 7th
Quinn Elizabeth, millenery, n.w.c. 5th and Elm
Quinn Ellen, 29 Accomodation
Quinn Francis, land office. 74 Gest
Quinn Frank, lime and cement depot, 350 Central Av , h. n.s. Gest below Freeman
Quinn Frank R., b.k., 108 W. Pearl, h. 1-6 Elm
Quinn Hugh, dray, 86 Water
Quinn Hugh, stable, s.w.c. Lodge and Gano, h. 126 Elm
Quinn James, dray, 79 Abigail
Quinn James, bk. layer, wks. gas works
Quinn James, harness mkr., 68 Avery
Quinn James, lab., wks. n.w.c. Wood and 3d
Quinn James, selve mkr., 427 E. 4th
Quinn John, 639 W. 6th
Quinn John, fireman, bds 401 W. 2d
Quinn John, lab., 504 Race
Quinn John, lab., s.w.c. Central Av. and W. W. Canal
Quinn John, lab , 31 Lock n. of 8th
Quinn John, shoe mkr., 157 Cutter

Quinn John E., collar mkr., bds. 273 Walnut
Quinn John J., physician, 123 W. 7th
Quinn Margaret, 68 Avery
Quinn Martin, tailor, 8 New
Quinn Mary, asst. cook, Commercial Hospital
Quinn Matthew, asst clk. Police Court
Quinn Matthew J., b k., 108 W. Pearl, h. 126 Elm
Quinn Michael, blksmith., bds. 18 Landing b. Broadway and Ludlow
Quinn Michael, lab., 30 Water
Quinn Patrick, cof. h., 29 E. 5th
Quinn Patrick, grocery, 275 W. 6th
Quinn Patrick, harness mkr., wks. 30 E. 5th
Quinn Patrick, lab , 209 W. 2d
Quinn Peter, waiter. bds. 205 Plum
Quinn Robert A., conductor, bds. 427 W. 4th
Quinn Robert R , grocery, 427 W. 4th
Quinn Rodger, shoe mkr., 163 Richmond
Quinn Thomas, cof. h , s.w.c. Vine and Front
Quinn Thomas, lab., 191 Cutter
Quinn Thomas, lab., 141 E. Front
Quinn Thomas, lab., 149 W. Front
Quinn Thomas G., tin shop 308 Central Av
Quinn Wm., carp., 144 Baymiller
Quinn W., lab. wks. C. T. Dumont's
Quinnley Ann, 29 Accommodation
Quintin Henriette. teacher, 459 Race
Quinton E. J., teller, Culbertson, Kilgour & Co's. bds 256 Race
Quirk Michael, lab., n.w.c. 6th and Harriet
Quirk Richard, 313 W. 2d
Quiter Anthony, cof. h., s.e.c. Water and Walnut

R

Raabe Hy., bds. Cincinnati House
Raabe Peter, periodicals, 609 Main
Raabe Phillip. confec., 529 Main
Rabb Elisabeth, 160 Carr
Rabb Frans. tailor, 520 W. Front
Rabb Geo., bk. mkr , bds. 160 Carr
Rabb Hy., bk. molder. 89 Gest
Rabb John, cooper, 160 Carr
Rabo John, jr., bk. mkr., bds. 160 Carr
Rabb Mary. 675 Vine
Rabbe Emily S., teacher, 450 Vine
Rabbe Hy, G , bk. binder, 130 Main, h. 450 Vine
Rabbe John Hy., grocery, 450 Vine
Rabbe Mary, s.w.c. 2d and Ludlow
R-bbe Wm., cab. mkr., 133 Hopkins
Rabe Catharine, 77 Abigail
Rabe Francis I., chair mkr., 303 W. Front
Rabe George H., cof. h., s.e.c. 5th and Home
Rabe Hy. A., cigar box manuf., rear 93 Clay
Rabe John, cof h., 235 W. 6th
Rabe Joseph, plasterer, 392 Broadway
Rabe Mary, 17 Miller
Rabens Frederick, boots and shoes, 562 Main, h. 555 Main
Rabens Hy., grocery, 119 Bremen
Raber Rudolf, clk. 71 Spring
Racefield Mary. seamstress, wks. 53 W. 4th
Rach Wm., bakery, 324 Sycamore
Rachilu Barny, lab., 64 Baum
Racine Mrs. R. A., 95 W. 8th
Rademacher Frederick, driver. 140 Barr
Radcliff Hy., clk , bds. 291 Home
Radcliffe Thos. B., comedian, 155 Broadway
Raddamacker Richard, lab , wks. Wood & McCoy's
Raddy John, lab., 16 E. 5th e. of Lock
Raddy Richard, huckster, w.s. Langdon al. b. 6th and 7th
Radebaugh George. eng., 475 W 4th
Radebaugh Joel, sec'y. C . W. & Z R.R. s.w.c. Sycamore and 3d, h. 122 Hopkins
Rademacher Benedicta, 499 Race
Rademaker Dietrich. lab., 71 Spring
Rademaker Geo., porter, 222 Linn

(RAI) CINCINNATI (RAN) DIRECTORY. (RAS) 265

Rademaker Mrs M., millinery. 222 Linn
Radeloff Ferdinand, lab., 56 Rittenhouse
Radermann Frank, cab. mkr., 73 Clay
Radermann Kate, 590 Race
Radford Chas. W., clk., bds. 280 Richmond
Radina Casper, gardener, s.s. 5th b. Stone and Wood
Radina Michael A., cooper, 13 Pine
Radlay Louisa, 147 Livingston
Radle Frank, wks. Mitchell & Rammelsberg's
Radloff Anna. seamstress, 18 Hughes
Radlow A., clk., bds. Bevis House
Rady Patrick, lab., 40 Freeman
Rae Hermon, barber, s.e.c. Linn and York
Raepple John, turner. 662 Race
Raffe Chas., lab., 44 Peete
Raff Frederick. dray, 104 Ham. Road
Raff Frederick. dray, 241 Pleasant
Raffe Louis. tailor, bds. 701 Elm
Raffel Abraham, hoop skirt manuf., 321 Central Av., h. s.w.c. 6th and Broadway
Raffel Chris., bar k., bds. 205 Ham. Road
Rafferty Dani., carp., n.e.c. Richmond and Freeman
Rafferty Henry, lab., s.s. Hunt e. of Liberty
Rafferty John, lab., s.s. Hunt e. of Liberty
Rafferty John, lab., n.s. Front b. Foster and Kelly
Rafferty Martin. carp., 237 W. 5th
Rafferty Richard. dray, n w.c. Freeman and Richmond
Raft Frederick, tailor, 564 Elm
Rafter Catharine. 61 Mill
Rafter Joseph. stone cutter, s.w.c. John and Elizabeth
Rafter Mary, 321 John
Rafter Thomas, dray, 464 W. 5th
Ragan Barny, hostler, e.s. Elm b. 4th and 5th
Ragan Edmond, lab., 556 W. Front
Ragan James, driver. 212 W. 2d
Ragan James, lab., 180 E. Pearl
Ragan Jane, milliner, bds. 353 Central Av
Ragan John, lab., 212 W. 2d
Ragan Martin, drover, 157 Hopkins
Ragan Michael, lab., 202 W. Front
Ragan Michael, lab., rear 249 Broadway
Ragan Patrick, dray, 212 W. 2d
Ragan Wm. H., blksmith, bds. s.w.c. 8th and Broadway
Ragen Thomas, lab., 260 Water
Ragendurf Morris, cigars, &c.. 322 Main
Rager Hy., lab., wks. 1365 E. Front
Raggan Jeremiah. lab., 58 Kossuth
Rahbaun Frederick, n.w.c. Elm and Water
Rahe Barbara, servt., s.w.c. Franklin and Broadway
Rahe Frederick, blksmith, 21 New
Rahe Hy., jr. cooper, 61 Bremen
Rahe Hy., lab., 11 Peete
Rahe John. molder, wks. n.e.c. Walnut and Canal
Rahenkamp John, 41 Milton
Rahill James, n.s. 7th b. Sycamore and Broadway
Rahmeier Regina, seamstress, rear 62 W. Mulberry
Rahn Adam, grocery, 49 E. 3d e. of Whittaker
Rahn Christopher. driver, n.s. Dayton near Western Av
Rahn John, lab., 55 E. 3d e. of Whittaker
Rahn John W., mach., 55 E. 3d e. of Whittaker
Rahskopf Wm., lab., 155 Bremen
Raible Frederick, clk., 63 Richmond
Raible Paul, brewer. wks. s.w.c. Pearl and Pike
Raich Wm., printer, wks. Volksblatt office
Raichrath Frank, blksmith, s.e.c. Wade and Central Av
Raidt Hy., painter, 38 Peete
Railman August lab., wks. 190 W. Pearl
Railroad Building, n.w.c. Main and Court

Railroad House, Louis Dieckmann, 580 W. 6th
Raindon Owen, lab., 654 E. Front
Raine Wm., print' r, 72 W. Liberty
Rainear Wm G., huc(ster, 9 Pine
Rainay James, foreman, 39 Vine, h. 21 Commerce
Rainer Wm., mach., wks. 216 W, 2d
Rainey Kate. s.e c. New and Broadway
Rainey Wm. S., salesman. 83 W. Pearl, bds. Winnie House
Rainsberger Andrew, 767 Vine
Rainy Martin, lab., 197 Cutter
Raipe John J. (Slimer & R.) h. Newport
Rairdan Mary, 39 Plum
Rairden John. lab., s.s. 3d b. Ludlow and Lawrence
Raledon Wm., pattern mkr., c Front & Central Av
Rairsheld G. W., salesman, 23 W. Pearl, bds. 82 W 6th
Raisin Hanson, clk., bds. 98 Broadway
Raisz Matthew, brush mkr., 597 Sycamore
Rakers Geo.. bk. layer, rear 67 Abigail
Rakers Geo., lab., s.w.c Abigail and Spring
Rakers Gerrard, lab., 246 Clark
Rakers Hy., lab., 114 Hunt
Rakers Hy., shoemkr, 67 Spring
R iley F. H., bds. Dennison House
Rall Josiah V., carp., 268 W. Liberty
Rall Lewis, phys., 269 Baymiller
Rall Peter, 276 Richmond
Rallins Margaret, laundress, e.s. John b Betts and Clinton
Ralphy John, cook, 16 Stone
Ralsion John, foreman, 79 W. 3d
Ralston John, printer, 193 W. 3d
Ralston W., driver, wks 324 Broadway
Ralston Wm., feed store, 90 Milton
Rambo Francis, sen., dry goods, 328 W. 6th. h 307 W. 8th
Rambo Francis. jr. clk., 307 W. 8th
Rambold Christian, finisher, 70 E. 3d e. of Whittaker
Ramboldt Chris., mach., 76 E. 3d e. of Lock
Ramel Christian, bk. layer, 129 Pleasant
Ramier Wm., driver, 52 York
Ramizo Benj., lab., w.s. Langdon al. b. 6th and 7th
RAMLER Joseph (Warburg & R.), 243 Clark
Ramlock Joseph, cof. h . n.s. Calhoun b, McMillan and Clifton Av
Rammas Hy., cooper, s.w.c. Abigail and Sycamore
Rammelsberg Ernest, salesman, s e.c. 2d and John, bds 143 Elm
RAMMELSBERG Fred. (Mitchell & R.) L, 143 Elm
Rammler Ernst, varnisher, wks. Mitchell & Rammelsberg's
Rampf Saml., bk. layer, 195 Richmond
Rampelmann Franz, shoemkr, n.s. Pearl b. Butler and Canal
Rampendahl Hy., cof. h., 511 Sycamore
Rampermann Frank, shoemkr, 178 E. Pearl
Ramph Geo., cof h , 450 Race
Rams Hy., cooper, bds. 309 Sycamore
Ramsey Miss , house keeper, Gibson House
Ramsey John, hinge fitter, wks. n.e.c Walnut and Canal
Ramsey Wm. M., atty., 68 W. 3d, h. 297 Richmond
Rumpsperger M., tanner, 689 Elm
Rand Morris, tinner, 27 Commerce
Randall Alice, 14 14th b. Central Av. and Plum
Randall Amanda, lab., 152 Cutter
Randall David A., carp., 226 Barr
Randall Geo., plumber, 378 Cutter
Randall George W., plumber, s.e.c Betts and Cutter
Randall Harrison, saloon, 112 E. 3d
Randall Thos. B , prop., Randall's Pine Salve, bds. Indiana House
Randall Wm. H , 139 Smith
Randall Wm. H., clk. n.e.c. 8th and Walnut, bds. 460 W. 9th
Randall Wm. S, dray, 460 W. 9th w. of Central Av.
Randalls Flora, h. 118 E. 6th

RANDOLPH James F., (T. F. R. & Bro..) 27 ' George
Randolph Mary, hair dresser. 15 Home
Randolph Simon F., phys., 924 Central Av. near Mohawk Bridge, h. 996 Central Av.
R ANDOLPH T. F., & BRO.. (Theodore F , & James F. R..) Coal Oil Lamps, Coal Oil, Mathematical Instruments, &c., 67 W. 6th
RANDOLPH Theodore F., (T. F. R., & Bro..) 272 George
Rank Michael, lab., 23 Dunlap
Bank Wm., 59 E. 7th
R ANKIN AUGUSTUS, Tea Store, n. w. c. 6th and Central Av., h. 358 W. 7th
RANKIN Charles S., (Macy B. & Co..) 358 W. 7th
Rankin Geo. W., 358 W. 7th
Rankin Hy., lab., s.s. Avery b. Park and Mill
Rankin Johanna, 358 W. 7th
Rankin Joseph, baker, 154 Longworth
Rankin L. C., salesman, 11 W. Pearl, h. Covington
Rankin O., tinner, wks. n. w. c. Race and 2d
Rankin Oliver L., clk., bds. 358 W. 7th
Rankin William, photographer, 82 W. 5th, h. 357 W. 6th
Rankins Julia, 50 Lock, n. of 8th
Randle Wm., painter, 131 Laurel
Rannin Patrick, lab.. bds. 248 W. 3d
Ranns Andrew, express, 61 Mill
Rannsiek Hy., clk., 77 E. Pearl
Ranor Wm , lab., 333 W. 8th
Ranselman Hy., mach., wks. 365 W. Front
Ranshaw Hy., foreman, s. w. c Ramsey and W W. Canal
Ransley James, confec., 230 W. 8th
Ransman Antony, lab. 680 W, 6th
Ransom Chauncey M , agt., 77 Baymiller
Ransome Christopher, huckster, 73 Bank
Hanson Thos , carp., s.s. Avery al. w. of Wood
Rany Mary. servt., Burnet House
Ranz Michael, cook, bds. 81 E Pearl
Raper Joseph H., real estate broker, 75 W. 3d, h n.w.c. John and George
R APHAEL WILLIAM, Physician, Office and Residence, 59 E. 5th
Raplee Luke, 868 E. Front
Rapp —, huckster, 124 Pleasant
Rapp Francis John, physician, 483 Elm
Rapp Fred, nurse. Commercial Hospital
Rapp Frederick. n w.c. Linn & Poplar
Rapp Gabriel, peddler, 458 Main
Rapp George. blksmith, 68 W. Court
Rapp Jacob. stone cutter, rear 507 Elm
Rapp John, cooper, 106 Elder
Rapp Joseph, cooper, 78 Charlotte
Rapp Louis, pattern mkr., 47 Allison
Rapp Margaret, 16 Hamer
Rapp Mathias, cof. h., n.w.c. Plum and Ann
Rapp Peter, grocery, 28 Allison
Rapp Phillip, barber, s.s. Harrison Pike b. Division and Brighton
Rapp Valentine, carp., s. s. Taylor b. Carr and Harriet
Rappamus H., lab., wks. Chamberlain & Co's.
Rappermaker Mary, 275 Sycamore
Rappold Peter, rope mkr., n. s. 15th b. Elm and Plum
Raquet C., & J. Bandle, (Christian R. & Jacob B..) gun smiths, 424 Main
Raquet Christian, (C. R. & J. Bandle,) Main
Rarden Johanna, 291 Elm
Rardin Patrick, lab., 22 Lock n. of 8th
Raridan Jeremiah, driver, s s. Phoebe al. b. Plum and Central Av.
Rasch Louis T., eng., 55 Milton
Rische Edward, tanner, 58 Stark
Rasche Frederick A., floor store, 38 Elder
R ASCHE HENRY, Tannery, 26 Canal near Mohawk bridge, h. 682 Race
Rasche John, dray, 61 Lock

J. C. SHACKLEFORD &

SADDLE, HARN

—AND—

TRUNK MANUFACT

No. 208 Main Street, east side, above

CINCINNATI, OHIO.

P. J. MOORE,
PLUMBER, STEAM AND GA
221 Fifth Street, bet. Elm and Plum, Cincinnati

 Hydrants, Pumps, Water Rams, Baths, Water Closets, Basins, Slabs, &c., &c. S
Lead Pipes, Steam Fitting in all its branches. Wrought Iron Steam Gas and W
of all sizes, always on hand. Gas Fixtures of all kinds.—Chandeliers,
dants, Brackets, Portable Gas Stands, Drop Lights, Globes, Bells, &c
REPAIRING PROMPTLY ATTENDED TO.

WASH. KEMP

PLUMB
MANUFACTURER
LEAD PI

CHAIN, LIFT, FORCE, AND AL

No. 230 Main Street, between Fifth a

CINCINNATI, OHIO.

Rasche Marcus, tanner, 682 Race
Raschig Rev. Franz, e.s. Elm b. 2th and 14th
Raschig Herman H., teacher, e. s. Elm b. 12th and 14th
Rasebrough Joseph, jr., 100 14th
Rasin Hansel P., bds. 98 Broadway
Raskup Frederick W.M., 747 Vine
Rasler John, cooper, 64 David
Rasp Paul, gardener, 71 14th   [Front
Ratcliff Proctor, magh , 4b Lock
Ratcliffe Chas., biksmith. w. s. Butler b. Pearl and Front, h. 249 E 5th
Ratcliffe Delany, h, 124 Richmond
Ratcliffe Geo., at. bt. decorator, 89 E. Front
Rath Chas. b., harness mkr., 89 Main
Rath John, lab., bds. 576 Elm
Rath Michael, 59 E 7th
RATHBORNE Gorges L., (R. & Wallace,) Mt. Auburn
RATHBORNE & WALLACE, (Gorges L. R., & Wm. P. W ,) Wholesale Hats, Caps and Straw Goods, 134 Walnut
Rathgeber Christina, 538 Main
Rathgeber Frederick, baker, 538 Main
Rathgens John, plow mkr., 86 milton
Rathmann Ferdinand, cab, mkr., bds. 133 Baymiller
Rathmann Frederick, shoe mkr , 540 Race
Ratker Matthew, porter, 68 Walnut, h. 117 Clay
Ratkins John, plow mkr., wks. 10 W. 7th
Ratstake Dina, bds. 13 Abigail
Rattelsdufer Catharine, 42 W. Front
Ratterman A. D., salesman, 179 Main, h. 186 Linn
Ratterman Barney, shoe mkr., w.s. Jordon b. Gest and Clark
Ratterman Herman, blksmith, wks. 55 and 57 E. 5th
Ratterman Bernard, salesman, 186 Linn
Ratterman Bernhard, (R Gebbe & Co.) 125 W. Liberty
Ratterman Francis, 538 Sycamore
Rattermann, Gebbe & Co.. (Bernhard R., Henry G. & Geo. Helmig,) varnish manufac., 125 W Liberty
RATTERMANN HENRY A., Secretary German Mutual Insurance Company, 400 Vine, h. 183 Laurel
Ratterman J. H., b. k., 59 W. Front, h. s.w c. Race and Liberty
Ratterman Louisa, seamstress, 508 Sycamore
Ratwall Thomas, carp., 371½ W. 7th
Ratz P., clk., Burnet House
Rau Cornelius, lab., 419. Sycamore
Rau Frederick. carp., 607 Elm
Rau Louis, clk., s.w.c. 3d and Vine
Rau Michael, safe mkr., 160 Pleasant
Rau Rebecca, 107 Martin
Raubert Joseph, tobacconist, 133 Linn
Rauber Felix, weaver, 413 Sycamore
Rauber Wm., boots and shoes, 77 Dudley
Rauch Chas.. clk., 100 Walnut
Ruuch Ernst. clk P.O., 16 Jackson
RAUCH FRED W., Music Publisher and Manufacturer of Rauch's Cordial, 399 Race
Rauch Wm.. lab., 70 Lock
RAUH BROTHERS, (Lipman Siegmund R., and Solomon B. R.) Wholesale Clothiers and Dealers in Cloths, Cassimeres and Gents' Furnishing Goods, 58W. Pearl
Rauh John, foreman, 28 Mansfield
RAUH Lipman, (R. Brothers,) 187 John
Rauh Michael, lock mkr., 169 Pleasant
Rauiss Jacob, 611 Vine
Raulman Adolph, blksmith, 17 Webb
Raulmann Bernhard, s. s. Abigail b. Sycamore and Main
Raum Herman, druggist, 154 Clark
Rausch Adam, much., 22 Mercer
Rausch Anna M., 131 Everett
Ruscher Jacob, cof. h., 31 Bremen
Ruscher Jacob, eng., 162 E. 5th
Raushoff Nathan, 198 Bremen
Rauter Hy., tailor, 141 Everett
Rauth Chas., clk., 70 Main, h. n. s. 12th b. Walnut and Vine

Rauth Francis, grocery, 80 E. Pearl, h 44 12½th
Ravencramp Hy., blksmith, Spring b. Hunt and Abigail
Ravens Herman, cof. h., 558 W. 8th
Raver Nicholas. cooper, 31 Dunlap
Raver Wm., driver, 630 W 8th
Ravie Catharine, 347½ W. 7th
Rawdon Milan D , b. k. 52 Walnut, h. Covington
Rawe Joseph. boots and shoes, 578 E.
Rawl Josiah V., carp., n. w c. John and Liberty
Rawling Robert, finisher, wks. n. e. c. Walnut and Canal
Rawlings James D., horse dealer, 18 Harrison
Rawlins Priscilla, 237 Clinton
Rawlins William R., currier, bds. s e. c. 9th and Walnut
Rawls Mary, laundress, 127 Avery
RAWSON Alonzo R.., (R. Wilby & Co.,) res. Louisville, Ky.,
Rawson Joseph, pork packer, e.s Sycamore b. 9th and Court, h. 318 Race
Rawson Warren. clk., 318 Race
RAWSON, WILBY & CO., (Alonzo R., Joseph H. W., E. B Hinman & Charles S. Holmes,) Tobacco Factors, 8 W. Front
Ray Andrew J., plasterer, 1297 E. Front
Ray Bernard, carp., 82 Melancthon
Ray Charles J., painter, 71 George
Ray David, 422 Broadway
Ray James. 81 Bank
Ray Mary B., bds. 633 W. 7th
Ray Samuel, (Moore & R.,) 57 W. 7th
Ray Sarah, 51 W. 7th
Rayan Ann, 202 W. Court
Rayer Michael, lab., 21 Commerce
RAYMOND Daniel, (R. Hilsinger & Co.) 44 Mulberry
Raymond Daniel F., clk. Adams Ex. Co., room 21, w. end Union Block
RAYMOND, HILSINGER & CO., (Daniel R., Jacob H. & John Hilsinger) Plow Manufacturers, 614 Main
Raymond Otto, eng., 79 W. Front
Raymond Philip, saddler, 32 E. 5th
Rayner Wm., lab, 664 E. Front
Raynor Uriah, clk., 97 W. 9th w. of Central Av.
Rayster Wm., barber, 46 W. 6th, h. 181 George
Razline Geo., 114 Browne
Rea David, carriage mkr., 20 Carr
Rea Joseph, driver. 67 Clay
Rea Martin, teacher, 20 Carr
Rea Thos., 20 Carr
Reacher Frank, rope mkr., s.e.c. Rice and Fountain
Read Frank. silver smith, 76 Main
Read Hy., cab. mkr., w.c. Cutter and Betts
READ Joshua, (S. N. Marsh, Corliss & Co.) h. New York
Read Margaret, teacher of penmanship, 326 George
Read Mary, laundress, 5 North
Read Rebecca 108 Pleasant
Reader Alexander, cof. h., 54 Clay
Reading Hy., shoe mkr., 47 E. 3d e. of Whittaker
Reading Sarah, 758 W. Front
Readkar Wm., lab., 152 Baymiller
Readpath Margaret, 297 W. 5th
Ready Kate, 24 Commerce
Reagan Edward, lab , n.s Front b. Mill and Wood
Reagan Martin, lab., 33 Kossuth
Reagan Patrick, dray, wks. 7 Commercial Row
Reagin Reason, butcher, 19 Wade
Reahl Philip, lab., 70 Martin
Reakamp Barney, lab, 307 Race
Reake Frank, carp., 250 Clark
REAKIRT Charles, (J. & C. R.) h. Mt. Auburn
REAKIRT J. & C., (Joseph & Chas.) Wholesale Druggists and Importers of Chemicals, 52 W. 2d
Reakirt John C., clk. 52 W. 2d, bds. 364 W. 4th
REAKIRT Joseph, (J. & C. R.) h. Mt. Auburn

Realge A., tinner, wks. n.w.c. Race and 2d
Ream Erastus P., mess. P., C. & C. R. R., h. 70 Laurel
Reaman Ernst, tailor, 42 Rittenhouse
Reamin Joseph, lab., 149 Abigail
Reamond Margaret, w.s. Lebanon Road near Montgomery Pike
Reany Wm., n.e.c. Burt and Broad
Rearidan John, lab., wks. s.w.c. W. W. Canal and Smith
Reardon Cornelius, tailor, w.s. Langdon al. b. 6th and 7th
Rea don Michael, porter, 19 W. 2d
Reber Balthasar, huckster, 69 Buckeye
Rebber Hy., porter, 58 David
Rebenstein Conrad, baker, 369 Central Av.
Rebenstein Geo., baker, 369 Central Av.
Rebhotz Paul, baker, 540 Race
Rebimus Hy., lab., rear 376 Broadway
Rebmann Jacob, lab , 405 Vine
Rebold Geo., stove store, 659 Vine and 2d Ham. Road
Rebold Michael, cof. h., 668 Vine
Rekold John, tanner, 389 W. Liberty
Rebush Hy., driver, 207 W. Front
Reccord Hy., printer, 312 Plum
Rech Christian, shoe mkr., s s. Charlotte b. Linn and Baymiller
Rech Frederick painter, 58 E. 5th
Rech Hy., grocery, 636 Race
Rechel Adam, carp., 129 Hopkins
Rechel Catharine, 705 Vine
Rechel Conrad, tailor, 145 Buckeye
Rechel Daniel, tailor, 145 Buckeye
Rechkamp Elizabeth, 95 Hopkins
Rechtin Barney H., boots and shoes, 476 W. 3d
Rechtin Frank, bk. binder, 54 Baum
RECHTIN G. H., Wholesale Dealers in Groceries and Liquors, 76 E. Pearl, h. 80 Pike
Rechtin Herman Hy., lab., 140 Hopkins
Reck Louisa, teacher, 43 Clinton
Recker Hy., porter, w.s. Abigail b. Spring and Pendleton
Recker Julius, blksmith, 14 Allison
Reckers Hy., chair mkr., 20 Abigail
Reckers Hy., chair mkr., s.s. Cassatt al. b Sycamore and Main
Reckers Hy., tailor, 98 Buckeye
Reckers Hermann, lab., s.s. Cassatt al. b. Sycamore and Main
Reckers John C , bk. layer, s.s. Cassatt al. b. Sycamore and Main
Reckes John, tailor, 91 Pendleton
Reckitts Thos. R., watchman, 362 W.9th w. of Central Av
Reckter Barney, 156 Bank
Redcamp Hy., lab., wks. n.e.c. Walnut and Canal
Reddehase Chas., tailor, 71 Milton
Redden Edward. lab., bds. 71 Park
Redding James H., lab., bds. 346 Main
Redden Mary, servt., 96 E. 4th
Redden Patrick, trader, 71 Park
Reddencase Fred., porter, 59 Walnut
Redder Fred., renderer, h. Findlay b. John and Central Av.
Redding Harriet, teacher, 23 Commerce
Reddish John C., 581 W. 6th
Reddish Steven, 168 W. 9th
Reddy John, lab., wks. Hieatt & Wood's
Reddy Patrick, lab., 40 Freeman
Redeer Geo., candy mkr , 65 12th
Redeer Jacob, wood dealer, 65 12th
Redeker Ferd., clk. 98 W. Pearl, h. 30 Mercer
Redeker Hy., salesman, 43 Race
Redekin Frederick, clk., 30 Mercer
Redel Jacob, paper hanger, bds 27 Jackson
Redel John, umbrella mkr., 50 Allison
Redel John, umbrella mkr., 27 Jackson
Redelmann John, lab., 112 Hunt
Reden Amie, 101½ W, 4th
Reden Nicholas, cab. mkr., wks. n.w.c. Canal and Elm
Reder Hy., cooper, 508 Main
Redge Chas., lab., 90 Gest
Redhusen Lewis, varnisher, 63 Laurel
Redhead Moses, carp., 205 Cutter
Redhead N. D., cashier, 23 Sycamore
Redhead Nicholas D., (R. Beal & Co.) 412 Freeman

GEORGE McGREGOR,

No. 133 Fifth Street, between Vine and Race, CINCINNATI, O.

MANUFACTURES

Bank Locks, Jail Locks, Car and Switch Locks, Night Latches, Front Door Locks, Mortice Locks, Rim Locks, superior article of Pad Locks, Silver-plated Bell Pulls, Door Plates. Hangs Bells and puts up Speaking Trumpets in the most approved manner. Also, attends to Repairing and Fitting Keys.

N. B.   Has on hand an assortment of Builders' Hardware at the very lowest prices.

JOSEPH W. HART,
ENGRAVER ON WOOD.

Views of Buildings,　　Bill Heads,
　Machinery,　　　　　Druggists' Labels,
　　Landscapes,　　　　Society Seals,
　　　Portraits,　　　　Newspaper Heads,
　　　　Animals,　　　　&c., &c., &c.

Illustrations for Colored Printing.

Office, Enquirer Building, Vine Street,

CINCINNATI, OHIO.

T. WHITE & SON,
MARBLE WORKS,

255 and 257 West Fifth Street,

Between Plum and Central Avenue,

CINCINNATI, OHIO.

Monuments and Mantels,

ALWAYS ON HAND.

(REE) CINCINNATI (REH) DIRECTORY. (REI) 269

Redick Hy., 25 Woodward
Redix Mary, servt 423 Freeman
Redlon Daniel M., druggist, 251 W. 4th
Redlon Mary P., 251 W. 4th
REDMAN BENJAMIN T., Merchant Tailor, 126 Walnut, h. 40 Barr
Redman Benjamin T., jr., clk., 377 W. 7th
Redmon Matthew, clk., 686 E. Front
Redmond Bridget, s. s. Front e. of Foster
Redmond Mary, grocery, 157 W. 3d
Redmond Miles J., grainer, 278 W. 5th, h. 229 Barr
REDWAY Albert J., (R. & Burton) 18 Clinton
REDWAY & BURTON, (Albert J. R. & Stephen R B.) Wrought Iron Stove Manufacturers, 17 W. 5th
Redwood Mary J , laundress, 115 E. 5th
Reeb Chas., tailor, s w c Linn and York
Reeb Hy., cooper, 71 Elder
Reeb Hy., cooper. 71 Findlay
Reece Michael M., clk., 47 Hopkins
Reed —, printer, bds. 297 W. 6th
Reed Ann, 162 W. Pearl
Reed Catharine, s.s. Pleasant Court e. of Elm
Reed Chas., barber, 334 Central Av.
Reed Enos B., printer, 317 Clark
Reed Geo , turner, 233 Betts
Reed Geo. W., blksmith, 186 E. Pearl
REED GEO. W., Dealer in Wall Paper, Window Curtains, &c., 343 Central Av. h. 160 Hopkins
Reed Hannah, laundress, 173 Webb
REED HENRY, Editor, h. 379 Longworth
Reed Isaac W., blksmith, 331 Baymiller
Reed Isaiah, carp., 233 Broadway
Reed Israel D., porter, 161 W. Court w. of Central Av.
REED J R., General Freight Agent C., H. & D. R. R., Office at Depot, res. East Fairmount
Reed J. W., bds Walnut St. House
Reed Jas. H., salesman 9 W. 5 b. h. 55 Richmond
Reed John, dray, n s. Augu s . John and Smith
Reed John C., grist mill manu ., 351 W. Front
Reed John W., cab. mkr., 554 W. Front, h. 297 Clark
Reed Joseph, express man, 488 John
Reed Mary, n e.c. 3d and Sycamore
Reed Mary H., teacher. bds. n.e.c. Betts and John
Reed Mary M., teacher, 726 George
Reed Robert, auction, 223 Main, res. Fulton
REED SAMUEL R., Editor Cincinnati Gazette, h. 21 Hathaway
Reed Violet, tailoress, 23 Martin
Reed Wm., auctioneer 223 Main, res. Fulton
Reed Wm., (Hughes & R.) 204 W. Front
Reed Wm. A., lab , 249 W. Front
Reeder Atlas D., carp., 121 Mound
Reeder Chas. A., clk. L. M. R.R., 274 George
REEDER EDEN B., Contractor, 75 W. 3d, h. Mt. Auburn
Reeder John, exchange office, 127 Sycamore
Reeder John, tinner, 59 E. 3d
Reeder John, turner, #23 Central Av.
Reeder Joseph A., variety store, 1162 E. Front
Reeder S. W., sec. Portsmouth Fire and Marine Ins Co., h. Mill Creek Tp.
Reeder Wm., bds. Pennsylvania Hotel
Reeford John, butcher, 449 Linn
Reehel Christian, upholsterer, 129 Hopkins
Reehl Thos., butcher, 473 Elm
Reeker John, blksmith, 303 Broadway
Reekers Hy. G., boots and shoes, 423 Vine
Reeks Thos., lab., bds. s.e.c. Front and John
REEME Josiah B., (R., Wallingford & Co.) 95 Barr

REEME, WALLINGFORD & CO., (Josiah B. R.. Joel M W. & Co.,) Commission Merchants. 29 Vine
Reemelin Chas., atty. and assignee of C. Wolff & Co., 373 Main, h. 341 Vine
Reedy James, grocery, 331 W. 6th
Reedy Patrick, grocer, s. e. c. Sycamore and New
Reenan Lochman, blksmith. 25 E. 8th, e. of Lock
Reenan Mary, rear 406 Sycamore
Rees Edward, molder, 97 Mulberry
REES GRIFFITH, Drugs, Medicines, Chemicals, &c., n.w.c. 7th & Linn, h. 438 W. 7th
Rees John, expressman, n. e. c. 6th and Miller
Rees John, mate, w s. Mulberry al. b. Pearl and 3d
Rees John E., instrument maker, 436 W. 8th
Rees Lewis M., phys., 270 Everett
Rees Thomas. tailor, 38 E. 3d
REES WILLIAM Z., Manufacturer of Surgical and Dental Instruments. 71 W. 6th
Reese Charles, mate, foot of Harrison
Reese David, carp., 198 Broadway
Reese David, pilot, 317 W. 8th
Reese Frederick, lab., 31 Locust
Reese George, lab., wks. n.s. Front b. Lawrence and Pike
Reese Isadore, peddler, 402 John
Reese Richard, porter, 44 Pub. Landing
Reese Robt., 343 Central Av
Reese Solomon, sexton, s.s. 6th b. Race and Vine
Reeves A. S., b.k., 46 Walnut, h. Covington
REEVES Austin S., (Reeves & Co.,) h. Covington
REEVES & CO., (John R. & Austin S. Reeves,) Insurance Agents, 32 W. 3d
Reeves Harrison, dray, 93 Richmond
REEVES JOHN, (R. & Co.,) h. 186 Longworth
REEVES M. E & CO.. (Mark E. R., Wm. B. Phipps, John S. Perkins, & Daniel O'Connell,) Wholesale Boots and Shoes. 121 Walnut
REEVES Mark E., (M. E. R. & Co.) 212 W. 4th
Reeves Martha. teacher 5th dist. school
Reeves Rhoda, 413 John
Reeves Spencer C., musician, 3 E 3d, e. of Parsons
Reeves Thomas, lab., 440 W. Front
Regan Ann, 170 W. 5th. h. 108 Mound
Regan B , lab., s.s. Pleasant Court, e. of Elm
Regan John, driver, 260 Water
Regan John, grocery, 65 E. 8th
Regan Mary, servt , 287 Richmond
REGAN MICHAEL, Staple and Fancy Dry Goods, 90 W. 5th, h. 43 York
Regar Joseph, stone mason, 71 Woodward
Regelin John, lab., w. s. Oregon b. 3d and 6th
Regenfuss Joseph, lab., 119 Bremen
Reger Frank, rope mkr., w.s. Fountain, back of Jackson Hill
Reger Michael, lab., wks. n.e.c. Elm and Canal
Regg Andrew, cof. h., 700 Freeman
Regg Andrew, cooper, e. s. Freeman b. Bank and Dayton
Regh Peter, bar k., 57 W. 3d
Rehberger John, cooper, s.s. Henry b. Elm and Dunlap
Rehbock Hy., oil cloth mkr., 584 Walnut
Rehe Hy., cooper, rear 9 E. Liberty
Rehe Hy., sawyer, 166 Clay
Rehe John H., boots and shoes, 484 W. 5th
Rehe Joseph J., (R. & Luetkehaus,) 67 Clay
Rehe & Luetkehaus, (Joseph J. R. & Frank L.,) lard oil manufacturers, 13 W. Canal
Reher Theodore, hostler, 400 Sycamore
Rehfuss Catharine, bds. 51 Elizabeth

Rehg John, cooper, s. s. Pearl b. Pike and Butler
Rehkamp Dena. 95 Hopkins
Rehkamp Lizzie, 95 Hopkins
Rehl John, 417 W. 5th
Rehl Peter. cab mkr , 275 Freeman
Rehle Hermann, lab., 93 Woodward
Rehm John, cab. manuf., 1047 Central Avenue
Rehm John, shoemkr., 4 Walnut, h. 6 Walnut
Rehm Phillip. sawyer. bds. 400 W. 7th
Rehmann Kunegunde. 611 Race
Rehme Mathias, shoeinkr., wks. s. e. c. Vine and 6th
Rehment Wm , driver, 155 W. 2d
Rehn Frederick, butcher, 240 Pleasant
Rehrs Franz, carp , 301 Linn
Rehse Fred., (Ginandt & R.,) 464 W. 5th
Rehse Theodore. lab., 16 Commerce
Rehselage Frederick, lab., 67 Rittenhouse
Reibel Geo., lab., 83 Ham. Road
Reibel Hy., e. s. Bremen, b. Elder and Findlay
Reiber Andrew, switch tender, E. 3d b. Baum and Parsons
Reich Adam, shoemkr, 583 Main
Reich Emil, saddler, 14 Mary
Reich Francis. carp., 217 Barr
Reich S., clk, 106 W. Pearl, bds. 22 Longworth
Reichard Christian, tailor, 60 W. Mulberry
Reichard Martha. rear 102 Clay
Reichart Geo. A., bar k., 469 Vine
Reichart Rudolph, cab mkr.. 10 Mary
Reichden Herman, cooper, bds. e.s. Western Av., b Bank and Harrison Pike
Reiche Gottlieb, gardener, 217 Ham. Road
Reichel Martin, finisher, 72 Buckeye
Reicheldt Chas., tinner, 483 W. 3d
Reichelt John, sheet iron worker, 495 W. 3d
Reichenbach Damon, glass stainer, 227 Broadway
Reichenbacher John, dray, 161 Bremen
Reichert Christian, teamster, 141 Everett
Reichert Christian. cutter, 61 W. Pearl
Reichert Ernst, cof. h., 226 Walnut
Reichert Franciska, 654 Race
Reichert John, cof. h., s.w.c. Grant and Elm
Reichert John V., carp., rear 15 Adams
Reichert Joseph, dray, 608 Vine
Reichert Magnus, carp., 615 Race
Reichinger John, rag dealer, 13 Thuber al
Reichling Barbara, seamstress, 581 Sycamore
Reichling John, plumber, 581 Sycamore
Reichmann Frank, lab., 112 Buckeye
Re ckel Adolphus. 605 Elm
Reickert George, tailor, n e c. Pendleton and Abigail
Reickert Richard, tailor, n. e. c. Pendleton and Abigail
Reictter Hy., bk mkr., 230 Betts
Reid Catharine, cof. h., 246 W. 3d
Reid Geo. W., blksmith, 186 E. Pearl
Reid James, (Haughton & R ,) res. Ireland
REID James H., (R. & Pasquier.) 826 W. Front
Reid John, saddles, &c., 30 E. 5th, h. 315 Clark
Reid Mary, servt., 126 and 128 Central Avenue
REID & PASQUIER, (James H. R. & Chas. P.,) Carpenters and Builders, 539 W 9th
Reid Quartus, carp., 108 Pleasant
Reid Robert, printer, bds 297 W. 6th
Reid Wm., stair builder, 233 Betts
Reid Wm., letter carrier, 213 George
Reidelbuch John, shoemkr, 420 Vine
Reider Barbara, servt., 286 Longworth
Reider Christopher, cof. h., n.s. Front, e. of Foster
Reider Nicholas, cab. mkr., 606 Race
Reidhaar Francis. teacher, 592 Vine
Reidimaker Wm., lab., 33 Oest
Reidle Joseph, finisher, 205 W. Liberty
Reidy James. printer, 136 Vine, bds n. s. 5th b. Park and Mill

CINCINNATI ADVERTISEMENTS.

HOLSTEIN & HAMMER,

MANUFACTURERS OF

OVAL FRAMES,

SUITABLE FOR

CABINET MAKERS AND OTHERS,

Which we are making on our Improved OVAL MACHINE, for which Letters Patent were granted on the 11th day of March, 1862, to HOLSTEIN & HAMMER, the inventors thereof.

No. 31 Smith, corner of Augusta Street,

CINCINNATI, OHIO.

PREMIUM AWARDED AT OHIO MECHANICS' INSTITUTE FAIR, 1858.

CHAS. W. JORDAN,
PLAIN AND FANCY
PAPER BOX MANUFACTURER,
North-East Cor. Fifth and Walnut Streets.

☞ Constantly on hand a good assortment of Dry Goods and Druggists' Boxes, &c., &c.

R. BUCHANAN & SON,
COMMISSION AND FORWARDING MERCHANTS,
No. 26 COLUMBIA STREET, CINCINNATI, OHIO.

ALSO, AGENTS FOR THE

Covington Rail Mill Company, and the Cooper & Covington Cotton Factories.

D. S. CARRICK,
SADDLE, HARNESS, AND TRUNK MAKER,
NO. 112 MAIN STREET, BETWEEN THIRD AND FOURTH,

CINCINNATI, OHIO.

JOHN D. GIESTING.   GERHARD GIESTING.

J. D. & G. GIESTING,
WHOLESALE AND RETAIL MANUFACTURERS OF
LADIES, GENTS, & CHILDREN'S BOOTS & SHOES,
No. 52 WEST FIFTH STREET,

Between Walnut and Vine, opposite the Market House,   CINCINNATI, OHIO.

N. B. Particular attention paid to CUSTOM WORK.

Reif Adam, cutter, 443 Walnut
Reif Andrew, painter, 126 Ham. Road
Reif August, 19 Franklin
Reif Chas., cab. mkr., 19 Franklin
REIF FRANCIS, SR., Family Grocery and Wine Dealer, 126 Ham. Road
Reif Francis, grainer, 19 Franklin
Reif Francis, Jr., salesman, 126 Ham. Road
Reif Jacob, turner, 19 Franklin
Reif Jacob, tailor, e.s. Milk b. Calhoun and Vine
Reif Joseph, tailor, e. s. Milk b. Vine and Calhoun
Reif Nicholas, huckster, w.s. Bremen b. Elder and Findlay
Reif Peter, tailor, e. s. Milk b. Vine and Calhoun
Reif Petzr, tailor, rear 23d W. 7th
Reifel John F., lab., 601 Walnut
Reifert David, clk., bds. 1070 Central Avenue
Reiffle Conrad, stone mason, e.s. Logan b. Elder and Liberty
Reifle George Jacob, waxon mkr., e. s. Walnut b. Allison and Liberty
Reifschneider Conrad. lab , 10 Hamer
Reifschneider Elizabeth, cof h. e.s. Reading Road, nr. Montgomery Pike
Reigel John P., printer, 47 Clay
Reiger Christian cooper, 16 Brighton
Reiger Hermann, tailor, 151 Abigail
Reigert Charles, tanner, n.w.c. Hamburg and Mohawk
Reigger Casper, lab., 111 York
Reigger John, tailor, rear 111 York
Reigold Emil, glazier, 571 Main
Reika Fred., cigar mkr., 42 Gest
Reikert Rudolph, finisher, 12 Mary
Reil Adam, s.e.c Bank and Baymiller
Reil Philipp, lab., 615 Race
Reilng Fred., grocery, 438 Walnut
Reiley Edward, wks. 340 W. 3d
Reiley Hy., lab , 20 Commerce
Reiley John. conductor, 318 Longworth
Reiley Michael. lab., wks. Hieatt & Wood's
Reiley Patrick, lab., wks. s. w. c. Broadway and 5th
Reiley Robert T., clk., 35 Barr
Reiley Terrance E., plumber, 39 E. 6th
Reillnberger Anthony, cab. mkr., 165 Linn
Reilley John L , clk., bds. 138 Sycamore
Reilley Margaret, 53 E. rth
Reilly Edward, carriage mkr., bds. 28 W. 5th
Reilly Edward, lab., 57 Park
Reilly James, molder, 836 W. Front
Reilly Martin. mach., 181 Plum
Reilly Mary, 28 Ellen
Reilly Mary A. , n.s. Pearl b. Lawrence and Pike
Reilly Patrick J , lab., 826 E. Front
Reilly Thos., carp., 37 Smith
Reilly Wm. W., grainer, 248 E. 6th
Reily Edward, lab., 22 Park
Reily Hugh, lab., Cramsey al. b. Mound and Cutter
Reily John L., clk. 34 W. Pearl
Reily John T., conductor, 318 Longworth
Reily John W., tobacco inspector, 318 Longworth
Reily Michael, 836 W. Front
Reily Peter, lab., 225 E. 6th
Reily Philip, boiler, 65 E. 3d e. of Whittaker
Reily Robert, 341 W. 8th
Reimann David, 381 Vine
Reimers August, mason, 165 Buckeye
Reimert Chas., molder, 76 Bremen
Reimuth John, shoe mkr., 77 Peete
Rein Nicholaus, stone cutter, 55 Elder
Reinauer Leopold, cof. h., 202 Walnut
REINBOLD Rudolph, (John Kaufmann & Co.) 12 Hamer
Reineken Herman. tailor, 382 Baymiller
Reineke Frederick, cigar mkr., 99 Pendleton
Reineke Frederick U., tailor, 50 Dudley
Reineke Gustave, cigar mkr., 99 Pendleton
Reineman Clement, cooper, wks. 216 Clark

Reinemann Catharine, 109 Woodward
Reinemann Hermann, saddler, 109 Woodward
Reiner Geo., cof. h., 66 W. Liberty
Rei er Joseph, 275 W. Liberty
Reiner Joseph, pattern mkr., wks. n.e.c. Canal and Walnut
Reiner Leopold, lab., 656 Vine
Reiner Rudolph, tailor, 45 Hamer
Reinermann Clemens, grocery. 21 York
Reinermann Mrs. Elizabeth, 13 Peete
Reinermann Hermann, collar mkr., 109 Woodward
Reinganum Jacob, barber, 79 W. 5th, h. 191 W. 5th
Reinhagen Peter Wm., 328 Baymiller
Reinhard Dedrick, grocery, s.w c. Brighton and Harrison Pike
Reinhard Frank, grocery, h. 584 Elm
Reinhard Hy., student, bds. 137 Race
Reinhard Margaret, 395 Vine
Reinhardt Baltus, 80 Peete
Reinhardt Edward cigar mkr., e.s. Campbell al. b. Green and Elder
Reinhardt Hy., tailor, 67 Bremen
Reinhart ——, lab., 17 Mulberry
Reinhart Hy., driver, Findlay b. Central Av and John
Reinhart Jon. N. ; cof. h., 465 Walnut
Reinhart Nicholas, driller, wks s.w.c. Elm and Front
Reinhart Sarah, e.s. Western Av. b. Poplar and Findlay [erty
Reinhold Just. H., bklaver. 110 W. Liberty
Reinka Hy., lab., wks. Wood & McCoy's
Reinkamp August, grocery, s.e.c. Pearl and Butler
Reinke Chas., carp., w.s. Bremen b. Elder and Findlay
Reinke Hy., cab mkr., 40 Pleasant
Reinke Hy., lab., rear 4-6 Walnut
Reinle Joseph. tailor, e.s. Ham. Road b. Poplar and Vne
Reinlein Kate, bds. 364 W. 9th w. of Freeman
REINLEIN PAUL, Druggist and Apothecary, n.w c 8th and Freeman. h. 384 W 9th w. of Freeman
Reinold Edward, cap mkr., 608 Race
Reinold John, lab., 125 Ham. Road
Reinsburg Jacob, peddler, 34 Providence
Reinsmann Frank cutter, 253 Main
Reinstetler Brecher, (Peter R. & Antony h . s.w.c Race and 2d
Reis ———— (R. & Bescher) s.w.c. Race and
Reinelle Patrick, n.e.c 2d and Broadway
Reis Andrew Lewis O., shoe mkr., 52 Bremen
Reisuan Frank, cutter, 140 Cutter
Reinstein Michael, tailor, e. s. Vine junction of Calhoun
Beiring Benjamin, bds. 461 W. 7th
Beiring My H., grocery, 461 W. 7th
Reiring John G., (Murray & R.) 400 George
Reis Conrad, baker, 392 Race
Reis Elizabeth, servt , 23 15th
Reis Frederick, porter, 127 Bremen
Reis Fred., trunk mkr , 127 W. Court
Reis Geo., express man, h. 128 Ham. Road
REIS HENRY, Bakery. 86 W. 6th
Reis Jacob, cof. h., 166 Ham. Road
Reis Jacob, tailor, 28 Observatory
Reis John, blksmith. 128 Clay
Reis John, lab , 138 W. Liberty
Reis Mary A., 31 Hamer
Reis Michael, baker, 57 Ham. Road,
Reis Myer, trader, 42 Everett
Reis Nicholas, grocery, 459 Main
Reis Peter, bk binder, 67 Buckeye
Reis Peter, lab., s.s. 6th near Harriet
Reis Solomon, clk., bds. 22 Longworth
Reis Xavier, cab. mkr., 188 Everett
Reise George, huckster, 779 Vine
Reisenbary Barney, lab., 165 Curr
Reisenweber Nicholas, porter, w.s. Bank al. b. 3d and 4th
Reiser Abrahan, peddler, 9 14th b. Central Av. and Plum
Reisigen Joseph, lab., Pleasant b. Findlay and Henry

Reising Andress, cooper, 31 Dunlap
Reising Geo., lab., 31 Locust
Reising John, musician 116 Ham. Road
Reising Leonhard. lab., e.s. Goose al. b. Green and Elder
Reisinger Frederick, lab., w.s. Goose al. b. 14th and 15th
Reisinger Jacob, brush mkr., wks. 41 E. 2d
Reisinger John shovel mkr., wks. rear 180 Buckeye
Reisler John, butcher, 180 Buckeye
Reisman Adolphus, salesman 107 W. Pearl, h. 131 Hopkins
Reisor Hy., molder, 477 Broadway
Reiss John., molder, wks. n.e.c. Canal and Walnut
Reiss Philipp, sausage machine mkr., 473 Walnut
Reisz Alexander, brewer, wks. J. Kauffman & Co.'s
Reiszer Geo. M , gardener, 601 Walnut
Reiter Francis A., lab, 40 Buckeye
Reiter Frederick, tinner. 23 Buckeye
Reith Francis, (Morris & R.) 185 Central Av.
Reither Frederick, cooper, 193 Pleasant
Reitt Geo., lab., 61 Woodward
Reitlinghaus Hermann, rear 477 Broadway
Reitkamp Theodore, bakery, 513 Main
Reitler Jacob, second hand store, 116 Sycamore
Reitmann Christopher, lab., rear 477 Broadway
Reitmann David, brewer, e. end of Mohawk
Reity James, wks. Junction 6th and Front
Reitz John, cigar mkr., wks. n.e.c. 2d and Ludlow, h. Newport
Reitzel Chas., finisher, wks. 825 Central Av.
Reizer Frederick, dray, 11 Bremen
Rekel E., tailor, 643 Elm
Reker Marie, 122 Abigail
Rekers Hy., shoe mkr., 354 Central Av.
Rekop Wm., 641 Elm
Relage Fred., hats and caps. 449 Main
Releiner Lambert, tailor, 139 W. Pearl
Reler Joseph, carp., 84 Mohawk
Relkan Benjamin. tailor, s.s. Weller b. Carr and Harriet
Rembis Nicholas, tanner, 30 Branch
Rembold Hy., lab., h 7 E. 3d near Whittaker
REMKIER John D., (Meier & R.) 53 Hughes
Remer Hy., cartman, 111 Clark
Remer Herman, shoe mkr., 255 Richmond
Remler Andrew, pipe fitter, wks. n.e.c. Walnut and Canal
Remler Edward, pattern mkr., 579 Main
Remley Jacob, 534 Central Av.
Remlinger Margaret, bds. 465 Vine
Remke Frederick, varnisher, 115 Woodward
Remke Hy., baker, wks. 565 Main
Remke John, tailor, 113 Woodward
Remme Hy. W., boots and shoes, 624 Main
Remmert Hy., cab. mkr., 66 Bremen
Rehmig Michael, oil mkr., 630 Main
Remminger ——, w.s. Sycamore b. Schiller and Mulberry
Remmlein Francis, cof. h., 596 Elm
Rempe Wm., n.w.c. Mansfield and Liberty
Rempert Nicholas, e.s. Branch b. Findlay and Ham. Road
Rempler Elizabeth, n.s. Calhoun b. Clifton Av. and McMillan
Renau Caroline, (T. & C R.) 186 W. 5th
Renau T. & C., (Theresa & Caroline) milliners, 186 W. 5th
Renau Theresa, (T. & C R.) 186 W. 5th
Renau Wm., tobacconist, 117½ W. 3d
RENCK MICHAEL, Tannery. 23 Dunlap
Rendell Geo., chiropodist, 60 W. 4th
Rendler Frederick, stone mason, s.s. Henry b. Elm and Dunlap
Reneck Hy., express man, 10 Whiteman

CINCINNATI ADVERTISEMENTS.

H. TOBIAS,
FASHIONABLE
CAP MANUFACTURER,
No. 186 MAIN STREET,
Between Fourth and Fifth Sts., CINCINNATI.

Military and all kinds of Caps, of the latest styles, constantly on hand. Trade supplied at the shortest notice.

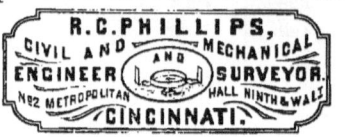

PHISTER & HOW,
PEARL STREET, BET. PLUM AND CENTRAL AVENUE,
CINCINNATI, OHIO,
TOBACCO WAREHOUSE,

Established under City Ordinance for Inspection and Sale of LEAF TOBACCO. Fees fixed by ordinance. Storage three months free. Auction Sales Tuesday, Thursday, and Saturday Mornings, at 9 o'clock. Especial attention to Private Sales every day.

HOFFMANN & MOSER,
MANUFACTURERS OF
PURE WHITE LEAD,
Paints, Putty and Artists' Colors,

Importers of Artists, Grainers, Gilders, and Painters' Materials. Also, Dealers in Oils, Varnishes, Brushes, Window Glass, &c., &c.

No. 222 East side Main St., bet. 5th & 6th, CINCINNATI.

J. F. & J. W. CLARK,
Wholesale & Retail Dealers in & Shippers of

FISH, GAME,
BERRIES, & FRUITS OF ALL KINDS,
No. 163 West Fifth Street, CINCINNATI.

J. H. EHLEN,
LEATHER AND FINDINGS,
216 and 218 MAIN ST., CINCINNATI, OHIO.

DRS. NEWTON & SCUDDER,
PHYSICIANS & SURGEONS,
OFFICE, No. 102 WEST SEVENTH STREET,
Cincinnati, O.

O. E. NEWTON, M. D.—Office Hours, from 7 to 8½ o'clock, A. M., from 1 to 2½ o'clock, P. M., from 6 to 8 o'clock, P. M. Residence, 102 W. Seventh Street.
J. M. SCUDDER, M. D.—Office Hours, from 9½ to 10½ o'clock, A. M., from 2½ to 3½ o'clock, P. M., from 6 to 8 o'clock, P. M. Residence, 92 Seventh Street.

H. WEBER,
TEACHER OF MUSIC,
N. E. Cor. 5th and Vine Sts., Cincinnati.
Cole & Hopkins' Building, Room No 8, up stairs.

JOSEPH MORRISON, Silver Plater. G H CROWTHER, Engraver.
MORRISON & CROWTHER,
HOUSE AND CARRIAGE PLATERS AND ENGRAVERS,
65 W. Fourth St., Cincinnati, O, Room No. 1, up stairs.

WM. WISWELL, Jr.
Importer, Manufacturer, and Dealer in LOOKING GLASSES, GILT MOULDINGS, German, French, and English ENGRAVINGS, LITHOGRAPHS, &c.
No. 70 West Fourth St., Cincinnati.

STEARNS & FOSTER,
MANUFACTURERS OF
WADDING & BATTING,
Cor. Clay and Liberty Streets,
CINCINNATI, O.

JOHN RIECKELMAN & CO.
MERCHANT TAILORS,
No. 143 Main Street,
West side, below Fourth, **CINCINNATI.**

Custom Ready-Made Clothing,
Constantly on hand.

F. & C. ANDRESS,
Manufacturers and Importers of
Paper Hangings,
No. 60 West Fourth St.,
CINCINNATI, OHIO.
Rooms Papered with neatness and dispatch. All work warranted.

M. FRINTZ,
Merchant Tailor,
—AND—
GENTS' FURNISHER,
No. 80 West Fourth St.,
Gazette Building,   CINCINNATI, O.

Reneger Ann, 103 Providence
Reneker Hy., grocery, n.w.c. Baymiller and Laurel
Rengenback Fred., cof. h., 532 Central Av.
Renhert Wm., driver, wks. 131 Race
Renker Barney, driver, wks. 333 W. 2d
Renk John J., teamster, s.w.c Gest and Harriet
Renka Frauk, lab., 185 Hopkins
Renke John, 150 Everett
Renker John, 557 Main
Renkert Ludwig, actor, 541 Elm
Renn Barnard, N 4 W. Liberty
Renn Isaac, lab., 21 Melancthon
Rennek Eliza, 187 Webb
Rennekamp August, grocery, s. e. c. Pearl and Butler
Rennekamp Bernhard, grocer, 23 Mill
Rentekamp Joseph, carp., 345 Clark
Rennekamp Lewis, grocery, n.w.c. Clark and Garrard, h. 358 Clark
Renneker Jacob, boots and shoes, n w.c. Main and 9th
Renneker Hy., 235 Betts
Renneker Hy., lab., wks. s.w.c. Park and W. W. Canal
Rennemeler Herman. lab., 69 Hughes
Renner —— clk, 23 W. 6th
Renner Adam, barber, 6 Walnut
Renner Andrew, butcher, n.w.c. Ravine al. and Browne
Renner Anthony, lab., 41 Moore
Renner August, lab., n.e.c. Young and Slack
Renner Elisabeth, 142 Bremen
Renner Chas., butcher, 470 Linn
Renner Christopher, lab., 2 Linnaeus
Renner Frederick, clk., 222 Main, bds. 15 K. 9th
Renner Fred., lab., bds. 114 Hunt
Renner J. W., b.k , Harrison Road b. Brighton and Barnard
Renner Jacob, butcher, 316 Baymiller
Renner Jacob, butcher, n.s. Karrison Pike b. Brighton and Western Av.
Renner Jacob, butcher, n.s. Montgomery Pike nr. Reading Road
Renner Jacob, carp., 16 15th
Renner Jacob, express man, sl. b. Vine and Walnut and 13th and Mercer
Renner Jacob, lab., 32 Buckeye
Renner Jacob, clk., n.s. Harrison Pike b. Brighton and Western Av.
Renner Joseph, finisher, wks. n.e.c. Walnut and Canal
Renner Joseph, lab., n e.c. Young and Slack
Renner Joseph, molder, 656 Vine
Renner Martin, 656 Vine
Renner Michael, tailor, n.w.c. Main and Court
Renner Oscar, finisher, wks. n.e.c. Walnut and Canal
Renner Otto, lab., 656 Vine
Renner Wm., n.s. Harrison Pike b. Brighton and Western Av
Rennick Geo. N., conductor, 462 W. 6th
Renniker Bernhard H., lab., e.s. Anderson b. 2d and Pearl
Renniker Hy., l.b., e.s. Anderson b. 2d and Pearl
Reno Emily, n.e.c. 7th and Sycamore
Rener Wm., cutter, 533 W. 8th
Renschen John H., boots and shoes, 401 Sycamore, h. 413 Sycamore
Renschen Hy. J., shoe mkr., e.s. Coggswell al b. Abigail and Woodward
Renschler Jacob, clk., 486 Walnut
Renschler Jacob, finisher, 486 Walnut
Rentigs Hy., cutter, 126 main, h. Vine Street Hill
Rentner Herman G., tailor, 537 Walnut
Rentschler Geo., meats, 680 Main
Rentschler Michael, tailor, 30 Buckeye
Rentz Augustus, atty., s.w.c. 8th and Main, h. n.s. Reeder b, Locust and Sycamore
Rentz Chas , printer, s.w.c. Vine and Longworth
Rents & Fryer, (Joseph R. & Lewis F.,) steamboat carps., River b. Ludlow and Lawrence
Rentz Joseph, cof. h., 294 Main
Rentz Joseph, (R. & Fryer,) h. Newport

Renworth Jas., cooper, n.s. Pearl b. Central Av. and Plum,
Renz Jacob, blk. smith, bds. 502 Walnut
Renz Jacob, lab., s.s. Mount nr. Sycamore
Renz Jacob, tinner, s.e.c. Allison and Walnut
Renz Nicholas, tannery, 183 Hamilton Road, h. 185 Ham. Road.
Renz Theo., druggist, s.s. Harrison Pike b. Riddle and Divison
Renzelmann Christopher, grocery, 22 Mansfield
Renzelmann Fred., lab., 18 E. Liberty
Renzenbrenk Wm., painter, 111 Clay
Renzenbrinck Fred., cigar mkr., bds. 9 E Liberty
Renzenbrinck Frederick, lab., 105 Woodward
Renzenbring Wm , painter, 111 Clay
Rentgehausen Ferdinand, cutter, n.w.c. 8th and Main, h. M. Auburn
Reoder Hermon, blk. smith, 71 Clay
Repholtz Geo , plasterer, 29½ Findlay
Repka Wm., lab., 61 Kossuth
Repold Peter, rope mkr., n.e.c. 15th and Plum
Reppe Darney, lab., 107 Gest
Reppet Joseph, fruits, 172 Broadway
Repphau Julius, saddler, 76 Bremen
Repple John, turner, w.s. Franz b. Elder and Findlay
Rercks Hy., shoe mkr., 12 Whiteman
Resch Geo. tailor, 73 Green
Resch Mathias, tailor, 636 Vine
Reschulder Christopher, lab., 179 Hopkins
Rese Benj., tanner, w s. Reading Road nr Montgomery Turnpike
Resener Hy., blk smith, e.s. Vine junction of Buckeye
Resing Fred., tailor, w.s, Sycamore b. Mount and Saunders
Resing Joseph chair mkr., 52 Commerce
Resolute Fire Insurance Co., agency 76 W. 3d
Resor I Burnet, clk. 13 and 15 Main, h. Clifton
RESOR Jacob, (Wm. Resor & Co.,) h. 172 W. 4th
RESOR William, (Wm. R. & Co.,) h. Clifton
Resor Wm. jr., b.k. 13 Main, h. 35 York
RESOR WM. & CO., (Wm. R. & Jacob R.,) Manufacturers of Stoves and Hollow Ware. 13 and 15 Main
Russ Valentine. carp., 192 Clinton
Ressebach Fred., dye house, 44 12th
Resta John, butcher, n.w.c. Smith and 3d
Restemeyer Fred., tailor, 162 Clark
Restemeyer Louisa, 162 Clark
Rester Joseph, butcher, 134 W. Miami Canal
Retg Christopher, lab. 29 Carr
Rotig Martin, brewer, 154 Ham. Road
Retkermann Herman, blk. smith, 530 Central Av.
Retman Geo. F., varnisher, cor. Liberty and Main
Rett Nicholas, blk. smith, 16 Commerce
Retterman Barney, shoe mkr., bds. w.s. Jordan b. Clark and Gest
Retterman Geo., carp., bds. w.s. Jordan b. Clark and Gest
Rettig John, cof. h. 599 Elm
Rettig Joseph, cab. mkr., 276 W. Front
Rettig Louis. finisher, wks. n.e.c. Walnut and Canal
Reuderman Barney, lab., 102 Spring
Reul Philip, bds. 60 Broadway
Reulmann Adolph, blk. smith, Webb al. b. Smith and Mound
Reum H. F., drugs s.e.c. Broadway and M.
Reum Herman, apothecary, 377 John
Reuply Jacob, dray, 464 Linn
Reuschel Catharine, teacher, 123 W. Liberty
Reuschel Lorenz, 123 W. Liberty
Reuscher Andreas, carp., w.s. Geese al. b. Green and Elder
Reusch John, cooper, 20 Brighton
Reusing Jacob, lab., 120 Ham. Road
Reusing John, lab., 30 Green

Reusse Diedrich, cooper, 634 Main
Reutemann Benj., tailor, 260 E. Front
Reutener Conrad, gilder, bds. 19 W. 5th
Reutepobler Christ., cooper, s.s. Gest b. Freeman and Carr, b. n.s. 14th b. Plum and Central Av.
REUTEPÖHLER Fred., (F. & G. R.,) 477 Race
REUTEPÖHLER F. & G., (Fred. & Geo.,) Fruit and Produce Store, 137 W. Court
REUTEPÖHLER George, (F. & G. R.,) 477 Race
Reuter Conrad. wks. Cin. type foundry
Reuter Fred., baker, 634 Elm
Reuter John, candle mkr., 13 Mulberry
Reuter John, lab., 32 Jones
Reuter Sophia, 685 Race
Reuter Wm., tinner, 149 Buckeye
Reuthe Chas., carriage trimmer, wks. Chas. Behlan & Co's.
Reuther Gottlelb, e.s. M. Canal b. 8th and Court
Reuther Hermann, huckster, 636 Vine
Revane Michael, lab., 210 Cutter
Reve Mary, 22 Grant
Reve Hy., lab., 22 Grant
Rever John C., carp., 59 14th
Levers Harman, molder, wks. Chamberlain & Co's.
Rewald Chas. tailor, bds. 147 Baymiller
Rewald Hy., blk. smith, 147 Baymiller
Rewalt Hy., eng., wks. n.e.c. Elm and Canal
Rewer Hy , lab., h. 34 Mercer
Rewer Christian, lab., w.s. Hanover b. Franklin and Woodward
Rewwer Hermann, molder, 73 Pendleton
Rexer John, lab., wks. 222 E. Front
Rexinger Gustave, clk., bds. 18 K. 6th
Rey Barbara, cook, n.e.c. 5th and Sycamore
Reymann Otto, eng., 79 W. Front
Reymond Philip, saddler, 30 E 5th
Reyner Jas., blk. smith, n.e.c. Central Av. and Court
Reynolds Abram S., teacher, Beech st. Walnut Hills
Reynolds, Alex., dray, 32 David
Reynolds C. A., R. R. agt , h. 204 Sycamore
Reynolds C. C., gov. agt., bds. Broadway Hotel
Reynolds Dashe, bds. 204 Plum
Reynolds Miss E.J., teacher, Mt. Auburn Institute
REYNOLDS Edward B., (Bonaparte & R.,) 182 Sycamore
Reynolds Eliza J., stamping, 760 Central Av
Reynolds F., harness mkr., bds. Henrie House
Reynolds George, 1060 Central Av
Reynolds Geo. D., photographer, s.w.c. 9th and Main, h Newport
Reynolds Isaac, 102 W. 9th
Reynolds Jabez, at Lane and Bodley's, 455 W. 6th
Reynolds James, butcher, 417 Baymiller
Reynolds James, paver. 198 Mound
Reynolds James, photographer, 120 W. 4th
Reynolds James, salesman, bds. 61 W. 6th
Reynolds James J., molder, 100 W. 5th
Reynolds John, dray, 19 North
Reynolds John, grocery, 249 W. Front
Reynolds John, M. D., 91 Sycamore
Reynolds John, shoe mkr., s.e.c. 7th and Broadway
Reynolds John W., eng., 151 E. 3d e. of Collard
Reynolds Lizzie, 186 W. Court w. of Central Av
Reynolds Martha, 413 Baymiller
Reynolds Mary, servt., Galt House
Reynolds Mary, 62 Clark
Reynolds Michael jr., carp., bds. 11 Gest
Reynolds Michael, lab., e.s. Crippen al. b. 7th and 8th
Reynolds Michael, lab. 11 Gest
Reynolds Michael P., carp., 11 Gest
Reynolds Pat., expressman, 12 George
Reynolds Patrick, lab., n.s. Cherry al. b. Plum and Central Av

274   (RIC)   CINCINNATI   (RIC)   DIRECTORY.   (RIC)

Reynolds Patrick, lab., 98 Race
Reynolds Patrick, mason, Burnet House
Reynolds Rachel, 398 W. 6th
Reynolds Richard, lab., 500 E. Front
Reynolds Robert R., ice house, 399 Baymiller
Reynolds Rosanna, dress mkr., 100 W. 5th
Reynolds Sackett, printer, 171 Clinton
Reynolds Stephen J., driver, bds. s.e.c. Pearl and Pike
Reynolds Mrs. W., 189 Cutler
Reynolds Wm., grocery, 333 W. 3d
REYNOLDS Wm., (Thomas Asbury & Co.,) 62 Clark
Reynolds Wm. T., molder, wks. W. W. Hane's
Rhaesa Chas., physician, 362 W. 6th
Rhegenness John, dray, 111 Carr
Rhegenness Sarah A., bds. 92 Gest
Rhegenness William, dray, 92 Gest
Rhegenness Wm. E., painter, 92 Gest
Rhein Frank, lock mkr., 673 Central Av
Rhein Jacob, cooper, wks. rear 463 Sycamore
Rhein Jacob, grocer, e.s. Vine Junction of Calhoun
RHEIN JOSEPH, Coffee and Boarding House, 480 Vine
Rhein Nicholaus, 612 Elm
Rheinberger John A., cigars &c., 465 Vine
RHEINBOLD Rudolph, (J. Kauffman & Co.)
Rheinhardt August, tailor, n.w.c. Grant and Elm
Rheman Wm., chair mkr., 214 Water
Rhinbold Henry, lab., 7 E 3d e. of Parsons
Rhineyearson Mary, tailoress, 146 Van Horne
Rhoder Mary, 41 W. 9th w. of Central Av
Rhoderulser Frank, cooper, wks. Oehler al. b. Freeman and Ganard
Rhodes C. W., clk., Adams Express Co., bds. Broadway House
Rhodes J., bds. Clermont Hotel
Rhodes Joseph H., treasurer Adams Express Co., h. 319 George
Bialy James, finisher, n.e.c. Walnut and Canal
Rianhard Adelaide, 126 Clinton
Rianhard Charles B., collector, 126 Clinton
Rianhard Jno. A., clk., 126 Clinton
Rianhard Lewis A., b.k., 57 Laurel
Rianhard Wm. E., b k., 564 W. 9th
Ribel Jacob, tailor, 9 Wade b. Elm and Plum
Ricard John F, clk., 252 Main
Rice Andrew S., gas fitting, bds. 140 Clark
Rice Charles, cashier 103 W. 4th, h. 473 Walnut
Rice Chas., printer, 44 E. 3d
Rice Comodore. lab., n.s. Ringgold b. Price and Young
Rice Cornelia, dress mkr., bds. 138 W. 8th
RICE FERMAN W., Coffee House, 48 Sycamore
Rice Fred., porter, 127 Bremen
Rice George, bds., 34 Milton
Rice George W., butcher, wks. 509 Sycamore
Rice Geo. W. sr., publisher, 324 W. 3d
Rice Geo. W. jr., clk., 324 W. 3d
Rice Herman, lab., 304 W. 2d
Rice J., molder, wks. Chamberlain & Co.'s
Rice Jacob, 61 E. 3d e. of Whittaker
Rice Jacob, 103 Longworth
Rice James. 269 W. 3d
RICE James, (John Rice & Co.,) 140 Clark
Rice James J., butcher, 140 Clark
Rice John, blksmith, 128 Clay
Rice John jr., butcher, bds. 140 Clark
RICE John, (John R. & Co.,) 140 Clark
Rice John, meats, 74 Mohawk
Rice John B., carp., n.s. Railroad e. of Vance

RICE JOHN & CO., (John R. and James Rice) Pork Packers, n.w.c. David and Cutter
Rice John G., b. h. 173 W. 3d
Rice Joseph, 68 W. Pearl, h. n.w.c. John and Longworth
Rice Josephene, 60 Clinton
Rice Lena, 138 Everett
Rice Louis, eng., bds. 10 Sycamore
Rice Lucretia. bds. 34 Stone
Rice Paul, lab., n.s. Railroad e. of Wallace al.
Rice Maria J., dress mkr., 188 W. 5th
Rice Sidney, contracting agt., Ind. & C. R. R Co., 66 W 3d, h. Newport
RICE SOLOMON G., Box Manufacturer and Pitch Pine Kindling Wood 872 Central Av, h. 31 Hathaway
Rice Uriah, teacher, 451 John
Rice Valentine, 74 Mohawk
Richard G. H. C., physician, 7 Pendleton
Richard George, lab., 154 Hopkins
Richard John Henry, shoe mkr.. 519 Sycamore
Richard Sarah. laundress, w.s. Mulberry al. b. Pearl and 3d
Richard Wm.. b.k., 25 State
Richards Albert C., agt., 543 W. 8th
Richards Ann, clk., 2x.8 Sycamore
Richards Anna, 299 W 3d
Richards Eliza, 401 W. 6th
Richards F. W., printer, 159 W. 3d
Richards Geo., cigars &c., 572 Central Av
Richards Geo. W., n.s. 7th b. Harriet and Mill Creek
Richards H. C. G., instrument mkr., wks. 71 W. 6th
Richards Hattie, 198 Plum
Richards Henry, lab., wks. 222 E. Front
Richards James. book store, 208 Sycamore, res. Newport
Richards John, agt. steam cooper manufac., 113 E. 9th, h. 215 Broadway
Richards John, coachman, 111 Br'dway
Richards Mary, servt., 328 W. 4th
Richards Samuel, clk., h. e.s. Auburn b. Coggswell Av. and Central Av
Richards Sarah, n.s. Oregon b. 3d and 5th
Richards Sarah, 116 E. 3d e. of Whittaker
Richards Stephen, carp., 48 Baum
Richards Stephen, lab., wks. n.s. Front b. Lawrence and Pike
Richards Thomas B., salesman, 13 W. 5th, h. 61 Milton
Richards Wm., finisher, 10 Observatory
Richards Wm. Joseph, cook, bds. 51 Jackson
Richardson Ann, 57 E. 4th
RICHARDSON B. F., Physician and Surgeon, 292 Race
Richardson Geo., (R., Wilson & Hale,) h. Covington
Richardson H. N. B., cof. h. 248 Vine
RICHARDSON J. C. & CO., (James C. R. & Wm. W. Thompson,) Manufacturers and Importers of Straw, Silk and Fancy Goods, 95 and 97 W Pearl, up stairs
RICHARDSON JAMES, Gents Furnishing Goods, 68 W. 4th, h. Sedamsville
Richardson James, lab., wks. 1565 E. Front
Richardson James, lab.. 1517 E. Front
Richardson James, molder, s.s. Front e. of Ferry
Richardson James, physician, 909 Central Av
RICHARDSON James C., (J. C. R. & Co.,) bds. 153 W. 4th
Richardson Jane, 237 Richmond
Richardson John, 490 W. 3d
Richardson John C., dry goods, 95 and 97 Ma'n, h. 27 Chestnut
RICHARDSON John G., (Moore & R.,) h. Newport
Richardson John W., (Ellis & R.,) 210 Vine
Richardson Joseph, clk. Cin. Gas Light and Coke Co.. 467 W. 5th
Richardson Joseph V., artist, s.w.c. Providence and Wade

Richardson Joseph, dentist, 121 W. 7th
Richardson Mrs. M. W., academy of design. 30 W. 4th, h. 467 W. 8th
Richardson Malachi H., salesman, 95 W. Pearl, bds. 153 W. 4th
Richardson Robert, roller, bds. 97 W. Front
Richardson Samuel, b k., 65 W. 3d, h. Mt. Auburn
Richardson Sarah F., h. 72 E. 3d e. of Whittaker
Richardson T., molder, wks. Chamberlain & Co.'s
Richardson W. M., sec'y City Ins. Co., bds. s e.c. 6th and Race
Richardson Wm., bds. 226 Race
Richardson Wm., cook, Gibson House
Richardson Wm. S., photographer, s.w.c. 9th and Main
Richardson Wm. W., clk., 251 W. 4th
Richardson, Wilson & Hale, (Geo. R., Wm. Wilson & Jno. R. H.,) com. mer., 22 Water
Richber Henry, sawyer, 224 W. 6th
Riche Julius, tailor, 29 Mansfield
Richenback Michael, teamster, 33 Madison
Richenberger Fanny, 20 Miller
Richert Geo., lab., 154 Hopkins
Richey David, carp., 198 Freeman
Richey Robert W., clk., 51 W. 3d, h. 304 Vine
Riching Mathias, tailor, w. s. Whiteman b. Bank and Dayton
Richmond Anna, b. h.. 183 Race
Richmond John, boots and shoes, 42 Richmond
Richmond Mary, 505 Race
Richter August, bonnet bleacher 89 13th
Richter August, tailor, 547 Walnut
Richter Benjamin, britannia ware mkr., rear 54 Abigail
Richter Dietrich, n.e.c. Hunt and Broadway
Richter Elizabeth, midwife, 122 Clay
RICHTER Francis, (W. Richter & Son.) 512 Vine
Richter Fritz, lab., 762 W. Front
Richter Hy., grocery, 396 W. 6th
Richter Hy., lab., rear 52 Abigail
Richter Hy., lab., 31 Buckeye
Richter Hy., lab., s. s. College al. b. Hunt and Abigail
Richter Herman chair mkr., 24 W. Mulberry
Richter Herman, lab., s. s. College al. b. Hunt and Abigail
RICHTER J. H., (R. & Verkamp,) 401 Longworth
Richter John, finisher. wks. 600 W. 5th
Richter John, lab., n. s. Sloo e. of Harriet
Richter Julius, blksmith, 14 Allison
Richter Joseph, cooper, 11 Pendleton
Richter Joseph, dray, 95 Hopkins
Richter Joshph, finisher, 52 Abigail
Richter Joseph, molder, rear 52 Abigail
Richter Mary, servt., 62 E. 4th
RICHTER Norbert, (N. R. & Son.) 512 Vine
RICHTER NORBERT & SON, (Norbert and Francis.) Jewelry and Watches, 512 Vine
RICHTER THEODORE, Stationery, Prints, Looking Glass Plates, Frames, Fancy Goods, 563 Vine
RICHTER & VERKAMP, (J. H. R. & G. H. V.,) Youths' and Boys' Clothing, 246 W. 5th
Richter Wm., lab., 538 Plum
Richter Wm., tailor, 681 Vine
Richthammer Anthony, blksmith, 2 Hamer
Richard B. S., printer, bds. Dennison House
Richard Edward C., baker, 71 E. Front
Richard J., bds. Dennison House
Richard James V., clk., 45 E. 4th, bds 268 W 5th
Ricke Bernhard, lab., 148 Pleasant
Ricke Frederick, cigar mkr., bds. 104 Gest
Ricke Frederick, stone mason, 147 Baymiller
Ricke John, teamster, 102 14th
Rickel Wilhelm, millinery, 425 Vine

(RIE) CINCINNATI (RIG) DIRECTORY. (RIL) 275

Rickenmann Michael, cof. h., 10 Dunlap
Ricker Gustavus, clk., 3 E. Front, h. Covington
Ricker Hy., porter, 31 W. Pearl, b. c. Hunt and Pendleton
Ricker John G., cigar mkr., bds. 390 Broadway
Ricker Leonora, 162½ W. 6th
Ricker Priscilla, 162½ W 6th
Ricker Theodore, blksmith, 390 Broadway
Rickers Annie, seamstress, 98 Locust
Rickers Michael, drays, 56 Mansfield
Rickert Chas. F., tinner, 71 Pleasant
Rickert Mary, w. s. Hanover b. Franklin and Woodward
Rickert Wm., carp., 219 Betts
Ricketts Sarah, 161 Longworth
Ricketts Wm., plumber, 45 E. 4th
Rickey Albert, clk., L. M. R. R., res. Covington
RICKEY & CARROLL, (John J. R. & Robert W C.,) Publishers, Booksellers and Stationers, 73 W. 4th
RICKEY John J., (R. & Carroll,) 217 Longworth
Rickey Wm. H., salesman, 73 W. 4th, bds. 98 W. 9th
Rickhoff Chas , carriage mkr., 33 Moore
Ricking Bernard, grocery, s.w.c. Laurel and Baymiller
Ricking John H., clothing, 6 Landing b. Broadway and Ludlow, h. 77 E. Pearl
Rickles Harriet, w.s. Langdon al. b. 6th and 7th
Rickoff Andrew J., academy, n. e. c. 9th and Elm, bds. Mt. Adams Observatory
Ridder Frederick, boots and shoes 102 13th
Ridder Rev. Hy., Trinity Church, s. s. 5th b. Smith and Park
RIDDLE ADAM N., Attorney at Law, 224 Main, h. n. w. c. Auburn and Saunders, Mt. Auburn
Riddle Alfred C., c. Colerein Pike and Corporation Line
Riddle Frederick, cab. mkr., n.w.c. Baymiller and George
Riddle George, conductor, 320 W. 3d
Riddle Lewis, shoe mkr., bds. 409 W. 8th
Riddle Mary, n. w. c. Baymiller and George
Riddleman Peter, stone mason, 74 Dunlap
Riddeldey John. 70 Mohawk
Ridenour Fannie J., bds. 133 Barr
Ridenour Monfort, clk., bds. 262 Race
Ridenour Samuel H., type caster, 121 Betts
Ridenour Wm., salesman, 52 W. Pearl bds. 266 Race
Rider Alex, second hand store, 340 W. 5th
Rider Charles E. I., auction stable, 17 E. 5th, h. Mt. Auburn
Rider Daniel, carp , 25 Commerce
Rider Hy. J., cof. h., 17 E. 5th, b. 19 Hannibal
Rider Mary, servt., 550 W. 5th
Rider W , tinner, wks. n.w.c. Race and 2d
Rider Wm., carp., 1170 E. Front
Ridgley Thomas, butcher, s. s. Harrison Pike b. Riddle and Division
Ridgway Alex H , gen'l index clk , County Recorder's Office
Ridgway John N , Co. commissioner, office, Court House, h. 521 Vine
Ridimann John, dry goods, 475 Vine
Riebel Catharine, 201 Baymiller
Riebel George, basket mkr , 76 W. Mulberry
Riebel Solomea, 76 W. Mulberry
Riebley Christian, brick mkr., 253 Carr
Riechler Barbara, servt., s.w.c. Pearl and Ludlow
Rieck Charles, tailor, 305 W. 6th
Riecke Hermann H., stone mason, 11 Madison
Rieckelman H. H. Jr., & Co., (Herman H. R. & John R.) tailors, s. w. c. 9th and Central Av.
Rieckelman Herman H., tailor, 13 Elisabeth

Rieckelman Herman H. Jr., (H. H. R. & Co.,) 13 Elizabeth
RIECKELMAN John, (John R. & Co.) 228 Water
RIECKELMAN JOHN & CO., (John R. & H. H. Rieckelman) Merchant Tailors, 143 Main
Rieckert Emil, blksmith, 13 Madison
Ried Mary, h. 313 Clark
Ried Sallie, 61 Vine
Riedel Chas., bk. binder, 302 W. 8th
Riedel Geo., cof. h , 510 Race
Riedel Joseph. lab., 246 Richmond
Riedenger Conrod, meats, Mill, junction 2d and Front
Rieder Felix, collector, 80 W. 3d, h. 76 W. 3d
Rieder Margaretha, 275 Bremen
Riedinger Peter, butcher, 240 Pleasant
Riedy Aloysius, clk., 1472 E. Front
Riedy Joseph, cigar mkr., n. s. Browne b. Ham. Road and Mohawk
Rief Frederick, painter, 19 Franklin
Riefenstahl Chas., tailor, 15 Hughes
Riefenstahl Christian, boots and Shoes, 682 Main
Riefenstohr Conrad, lab., 603 Main
Riefle Jacob, wagon mkr , 528 Walnut
Riegelmann Charles, clk., 45 Clinton
Rieger Chas., hat and cap store, 461 Main
Rieger Floriean, tailor, n. s. Garden b. Freeman and Western Av.
Rieger John, cof. h., 514 Walnut
Riegert Sophia, 25 Mulberry
Riegger Sebastian, baker, 31 W. 5th
Riehl Andreas, carp., 105 York
Riehl John, lab., wks. Cincinnati Chemical Laboratory
Riehl Wm., finisher, 148 Clinton
Riehle Ignatz, meats, 126 W. Front
Riehle Martin, grocer, 105 York
Riehlt Ferdinand, scourer, 234 W. 5th, h Covington
Rieka Hermann, cigar mkr., h. 42 Gest
Rieke Harmon, cigar mkr., bds. 104 Gest
Rieke Hy., cooper, 100 Gest
Rieke Sophia, h. 104 Gest
Rieker Jacob, malt kiln mkr., 507 Walnut
Rieley James N., carp., 293 W. 8th
Rieller Bernhard, lab., 54 Buckeye
Rielly James, lab., Von Seggern al. b. Abigail and Woodward
Rielly John W., printer, 202 Longworth
Rielly Wm., express, 190 Mound
Rieman Edward, cutter, 184 Main, h. 42 Rittenhouse
Rieman Wm., mach., 214 Water
Riemann Catharine, 25 Buckeye
Riemann Joseph, porter, 149 Abigail
RIEMEIER HERMANN H., Carpenter and Builder, 13 Ham. Road
Riemeyer John F., grocery, 82 Bremen, h. 16 14th
Rienlander Hy., grocery, 164 Everett
Riering Hy., grocery, 438 W. Front
Ries Charles, tanner, al. b. 13th and Mercer and Vine and Walnut
Ries Dorothea. 612 Race
Ries Frederick, mason, 31 Locust
Ries Hy., bds. Cincinnati House
Riesche Hy , blksmith, wks. Niles Works
Riesenbeck Bernhard, lab., 111 Woodward
Riesenberg Barney, porter, wks. 600 W. 5th
Riesenberg Hy., lab., 772 W. Front
Riesenberger Nicholas, shoe mkr., rear 176 Clay
Riesing Adam, butcher, bds. 64 Ham. Road
Riester John B., mason, 556 Vine
Riesterer Elizabeth, 126 Ham. Road
Riesz Wm., porter, 71 Walnut, h. 592 Elm
RIETH CHARLES, Coffee and Boarding House, 254 E. Front
Rieth Elizabeth, 491 Vine
Riffelmacher George, stocking mkr., 30 Ham. Road
Rigdon Isaac, (Wm. Huddart & Co.), 288 George

Rigg J. W., bds. Dennison House
Rigg John, b.k. 68 W. 4th
RIGGIN WM. G., Train Despatcher. O. & M. R. R. Office, 522 W. Front, h. 85 Mill
Riggins Peter, carp., 125 Avery
Riggles Wm. T., cutter, 176 Vine b. Covington
Riggney John, lab., 27 Mill
Riggs John H., policeman, 5 E. 3d e of Parsons
RIGGS Joseph, (R. & Murray), 19 Chesnut
Riggs M. B., b.k. 37 Walnut, h. Mt. Auburn
RIGGS & MURRAY, (Joseph R. & James H. M.,) Steamboat. House and Sign Painters, 29 E. Front
Rigke Hy., cooper, wks. s.s. Gest b. Freeman and Carr
Rigney Edward, lab., s.s. 9th. b. Harriet and Mill Creek
Rigney John, lab., rear s.e c. Pearl and Lawrence
Rigney John, lab., 27 Mill
Rigney Mary, 954 E. Front
Rigney Michael, lab., bds. 583 E. Front
Rigney Michael, lab., s.s. 9th b. Harriet and Mill Creek
Rigney Wm., porter, 60 W. 2d, bds. 49 Race
Rihrwie Jacob, tailor, 13 Madison
RIKHOFF JOHN G., Merchant Tailor, s.w.c. 9th and Main, h. 397 Elm
Riley Ann, s.w.c. 4th and Stone
Riley Ann, 674 Central Av
Riley Benj. F., coach mkr., 168 Longworth
Riley Bernard, rectifier, 17 Water
Riley Betsy, servt., 99 E. 3d
Riley Bridget, 212 W. 7th
Riley Charles, paver, 66 W. Court w. of Central Av
Riley D. & P., (Daniel & Parker), livery stable, 7 E. 6th
Riley Daniel, 26 E. 6th
Riley Daniel, (D. & P R.,) 180 Sycamore
Riley Dennis, teamster, 156 Freeman
Riley Edmund, butcher, 90 Abigail
Riley Edward, lab., 22 Park
Riley Ellen, n.s. Augusta b. John and Smith
Riley Ephraim, lab., 82 Baymiller
Riley Ephraim, policeman. 115 Mound
Riley James, atty , 20 W. 6th
Riley James, blksmith, wks. Chas. Graham & Bro's.
Riley James, mach., h. 24 Park
RILEY James W., (Benjamin & Co.) bds Dennison House
Riley John, b.k. 4 E. 4th, 228 Barr
RILEY John, (John Leist & Co.), 402 W. 7th
Riley John, lab., s.s. 6th b. Broadway and Culvert
Riley John, lab., n.s. Goodloe b. Willow and Niagara
Riley John, lab., 754 E. Front
Riley Letitia, teacher, bds. 14 George
Riley Luke, servt., Burnet House
Riley Maria, 132 Broadway
Riley Martin, lab., n.s. Fremont b. Harriet and Mill Creek
Riley Michael, carp., 136 Freeman
Riley Michael, conductor, 462 George
Riley Michael, wk. wks., 100 Sycamore
Riley Michael, lab., 20 E 8th e. of Lock
Riley Moses, lab., 101 E. 6th
Riley Parker, (D. & P. R.,) 20 E. 6th
Riley Patrick, lab. s.s. Budd b. Harriet and Mill Creek
Riley Patrick, lab., 44 Elm
Riley Pat., stone cutter, bds. 184 Race
Riley Patrick H., carp., 159 Barr
Riley Peter, miller, 148 Baymiller
Riley Philip, lab., wks. 196 W. Pearl
Riley Philip, mess. Adams Express Co., room 208, Burnet House
Riley Rich., tailor, 112 W Pearl
Riley Robert shoe mkr., 641 Race
Riley Rosa, laundress, w.s. Mulberry al b. Pearl and 3d
RILEY SHEPHERD G., Livery Stable, 82 Baymiller h. 84 Baymiller

276 (RIP) CINCINNATI (RIV) DIRECTORY. (ROB)

Riley Thos. C., 105 W. Pearl, h. 435 W. 8th
Riley Thos., contractor, s.s Peete b Vine and Poplar
Riley Thos., driver, 48 Butler
Riley Thos., lab., bds. 192 Sycamore
Riley Terrence, plumber, 39 E. 8th e. of Lock
Rill Hy., lab., 166 E. Front
Rinck Chas., watchman, 166 Pleasant
Rinck Michael, tailor, 166 Pleasant
Rickenberger Philip, bar k., 533 Walnut
Rinckhoff Adolphus A., clk., 87 Lock h 186 E 6th
Rinderle Geo J., tailor, 723 Race
Rindfleish Philip. cook., Burnet House
RINDSKOPF Adolph (Rindskopf Bros. & Co.) h. New York
R INDSKOPF BROS. & CO., (Morris R., Simon R., Adolph R., Raphael Buchman & Joseph Zeiller,) Importers and Wh. Dealers in Dry Goods, Clothing and Notions, 79 W. Pearl
RINDSKOPF Morris, (R. Bros. & Co.) 395 W. 6th
RINDSKOPF Simon, (R. Bros. & Co.) 395 W. 6th
Rindskopf Theodore, clk., h. 395 W. 6th
Rinear Thos. J, paper hanger, 141 Hopkins
Rinear Wm., L., paper hanger, 14 Stone
Rinehardt Christopher, fireman, 455 W. 2d
Rinehard John, huckster, 31 Barr
Rinehart M., molder, wks n.s. Front b. Lawrence and Pike
Rindhardt Michael, clk. 62 Allison
Rinehart Fred., lab., Oehler al. b Freeman and Garrard
Rinehart Theodore, plumber, Barr b. Mound and Cutter
Rinehart Wm., engraver, 465 Walnut
Ring Dennis, lab., 62 Hunt
Ring Jacob, bds. 48 E. Pearl
Ring John, clk., Burnet House Restaurant
Ring John, hostler, 487 W. 8th
Ring John, lab., wks. Chamerlain & Co's
Ring John. lab, e.s. Pendleton, b Woodward nad Liberty
Ringel Frank., salesman, 134 Walnut, b 380 W. 9th
Ringel Ludwig, lab., 679 Race
Ringen Frank G., hats and caps, 380 W 9th w. of Central Av
Ringen Lewis, box mkr., 137 Bremen
Ringer John, hinge fitter, wks. n e c. Walnut and Canal
Ringer Julia, seamstress, 102 Abigail
RINGGOLD Fred.. G., (E. G. Webster & Co.) 57 W. 7th
Ringgold Thos., salesman, 63 W. Pearl, h. 341 Clark
Ringgold Thos. H., clk., 344 Clark
Ringier Chas., tailor, e.s. Goose al. b. Liberty and 15th
R INGWALT & AVERY, (J. C. R & S. D. A.,) Importers and Dealers in Carpeting, 69 W. 4th
RINGWALT J. C., (R. & Avery.) h Clifton
Rinkelman Hermon, butcher, n.s. Montgomery pike nr. Madison Road
Rinn John, blksmith, 60 Kossuth
Rinshier Anton cooper, s.s. Dudd b. Harriet and Mill Creek
Rintz Mary, seamstress, s.e c. 4th and Vine
Rintz Sebastian, dry goods, 463 W. 5th
Rintz Caroline, 65 15th
Riordan Cornelius, porter, 103 W. Pearl
Riordan Fanny, 263 John
Riordan Jeremiah, boots and shoes 23 Central Av
Riordan Matthew, grocery, 15 E. 7th
Riordan Wm., carp., bds. n.w.c. Front and Central Av
Ripke Hermann, shoe mkr., h. s e c. Elm and Longworth
R IPLEY GEORGE, Feed Store, 162 John
Ripley Hy., feed store, 1071 Central Av.

Rippe Caroline, seamstress, s.e.c. Gest and Carr
Rippe Hy., carp., bds. 557 Elm
Ripsch John, shoe mkr., n.s. al. b Poplar and Vine and Ham. Road and Buckeye
Risen Allen, lab. s.s. E Front e. of Reed
Rising J., wks. A. G. Cheever & Co's
Risk Thos., boatman, 109 W. M. Canal
Riskamp Frank., lab. wks. s.w.c. W. W. Canal and Smith
Risser Daniel, b k. at Brighton House
Rist Leonard china &c., 624 Vine
Riston Mary, 343 W. 5th
Ristow John C. F., teamster, 571 Race
Ritchie C. & J. (Casper & Jaque,) dry goods, 65 and 67 E Pearl
Ritchie Casper, (C. & J. R.,) res. Ludlow Ky.,
Ritchie Casper sen., cashier, 63 E. Pearl h. 473 Walnut
Ritchie Christopher C., teamster, 154 Daymiller
Ritchie James, harness mkr., 127 Spring
Ritchie James T., clk,, P. O., bds. 102 W 8th
Ritchie Jaque, (C. & J. R.,) 91 E Liberty
Ritchie Margaret, 230 W. 6th
Ritchie Wm., finisher, 14 W Mulberry
Ritger John, cof. h., 596 Elm
Rithmann Chas., varnisher, n.w.c. Liberty and Mansfield
Ritschard Peter. teamster, 293 Water
Rittenhouse John, grocery, 448 W. 5th
Rittenhouse Jonathan C., prop. Cin. Harrison and Brookville Omnibus line, 109 Walnut, h. Harrison O
Ritter Anton, mineral water manuf., 468 Vine, h. 466 Vine
Ritter., Carl G., phys., e s. Lawrance b. 3d and 4th
Ritter Christian, cage mkr. 491 Vine
Ritter Conrad, barber. 744 W. 6th
Ritter Fred., lab, w.s. Goose al. b. Liberty and 15th
Ritter Fred., lab., Findlay b. Central Av and John
Ritter Geo. W., meats, 241 W. 4th
Ritter Hy. M., hinge mkr., wks. n.e c. Walnut and Canal
Ritter Jacob, baker, 63 Oliver
Ritter Jacob, baker, bds., 320 W. 6th
Ritter Jacob, tailor, 704 Dayton
Ritter James S., baker., 90 W. 2d
Ritter John, cigar. mkr., 140 Bremen
Ritterhoff John, foreman, Wood & McCoy's, h. 18 Spring
Ritter John, molder, 82 John
Ritter John, tailor, s.s. Ringgold b. Young and Price
Ritter Joseph, notions, &c., 67 Broadway, h. Newport
Ritter Lorens, lab, w.s. Ridgway al. b. Liberty and 15th
Ritter Lorens, lab., 180 Bremen
Ritter Lorens, mineral water mkr., 466 Vine
Ritter Louise, 18 W. 9th
Ritter Peter, lab., s.s. Dover al. b. Elm and Plum
Ritter Peter, lab., e.s. Plum b. Adams & Liberty
Ritter Peter, stone cutter, w.s. Thuber al. b. Wade and Liberty
Ritter Rupert, stone cutter, 673 Race
Ritler Sophia, teacher. 333 Vine
Ritterhoff Wm., bds. 79 Everett
Rittmann John, bar k.., h. 26 Elder
Ritur Ferdinand, lab., 100 Carr
Ritweger Phillip, bds. 57 E. Pearl
Rittweger Wm., barber, 3 E. 4th
Rittweger Wm. R., clk., bds. 292 Central Av
Ritz Leopold, driver, wks. 131 and 133 Race
Ritzel Adam, stone mason, n.s. Railroad e. of Wallace al
Ritzer Joseph, harness, &c., 1076 Central Av
Rivard John C., bakery, 46½ E. 3d
Rive Leon. teacher, 157 W. 8th
Rivers John H., recorder, co. clk's office, 503 Plum

Rivers Joseph, lab., wks. 335 Broadway
Rivers Wm. M., salesman, 137 Walnut, bds. 503 Plum
Rivoux Louis F., clk., s.e.c. Lawrence and Pearl
Rivy Antonio, confec., 346 W. 5th
Rixer Hy., lab., al. b. Vine and Walnut and 13th and Mercer
Rixmann Geo., grocery, 26 Franklin
Rixse Hy., express man, al. b. 13th and Mercer and Vine and Walnut
Roa Frederick W., grocery, 628 Vine
Roa Nicholaus, cab. mkr., bds. 628 Vine
Roach Annie, servt., 137 Plum
Roach Bridget. s.w.c. Laurel and Cutter
Roach David, carp., 14 E. 7th
Roach Frank, lab., e s. Ludlow b. 2d and Pearl
Roach John, salesman, 5P3 W. 8th
Roach Joseph, clk., 291 W. 3d
Roach Matthew, tailor, s.e.c. 7th and Broadway
Roach Michael, lab., 65 E. 8th
Roach Mollie, 259½ W. 5th
Roach Nancy, 538 W. 7th
Roach Patrick E. (Boyle & R.) 583 W. 8th
Roach Wm., lab., s.s. 5th b. Macalister and Lawrence
Roak Hy., harness mkr., bds. 173 W. 3d
Roark John, cof. h , 92 W. Front
Roark Margaret, seamstress, 353 W. 6th
R OBACK CHARLES W., Scandinavian Laboratory. 18 Hammond. office 6 E. 4th, h. 297 George
Robard John, salve mkr., 65 Oliver
Robb ——, driver, U. S. Express Co
Robb A. W., b.k., n e c 5th and Vine, b. Loveland
Robb Alexander, clk., 7 Canal
Robb Alexander, soliciting freight agt., M. and C. R. R., 3 Burnet House, res. Loveland
Robb Carrie W., n.e.c. Linn and Everett
Robb D. T., clk., 101 W. 4th, h. Loveland
Robb Joseph, pilot, 189 Broadway
Robb Septimus F., driver, 604 E. Front
Robben Dinah, grocery, 56 13th
Robben Hy., lab., 152 Hopkins
Robbin Barney, tailor, 257 Main
ROBBINS Adam B. (Robbins & Posey) 130 Broadway
Robbins Charles J., distillery, s.e.c. Freeman and Liberty
Robbins Charles R , stable, s.e.c. Freeman and Liberty
Robbins Charlotte, milliner, 518 Main
Robbins Frederick, boots and shoes, 553 Main
Robbins James, blk. layer, 88 Longworth
Robbins John I , com. mer., 25 W. Front, h. Covington
Robbins John V., (R. & Pomeroy) h. Madison, Wis.
Robbins Martin, mach., 247 W. 5th, h. 403 Clark
R OBBINS & POMEROY (John V. R., Ralph M. P., Samuel L. Robbins, Adam B. Robbins & James P. Pomeroy). Wholesale Dealers in Boots and Shoes, 57 W. Pearl
R OBBINS & POSEY (Samuel L. R., Oliver P. & Adam B. Robbins) Wholesale Boots and Shoes, 95 and 97 W. Pearl
ROBBINS Samuel L. (R. & Posey) bds. 130 Broadway
ROBBINS Wm. M. (Marshall & R.) Clermont Hotel
Roberg Augustus B., n.e.c. 9th and Baymiller
Roberg G. A., b.k., 172 Sycamore, h. 20 Barr
Roberg Gerhard, n.e.c., Daymiller and 6th
Robelman Richard, lab., wks 179 W.M. Canal
Robens Herman, cooper. 503 Race
Rober John, lab., 26 Mohawk
Robers Benjamin, cab. mkr., 435 W. 2d
Robert Bernard. lab., 67 Butler
Robert J. Warren, carriage painter, 448 W. 7th
Roberts ——, clk., bds. 57 Broadway

Roberts Angeline, 20 Lock n. of 8th
Roberts Catharine, 251 W. Front
Roberts Catharine D., 449 W. 5th
Roberts Catharine C., 351 W. 6th
Roberts David, lab., bds. 337 W. 3d
Roberts David, saddles, &c., 341 W. 5th
Roberts David J., harness mkr., 160 W. 3d
Roberts Dorothea A., laundress, 207 Clinton
Roberts E. & Co. (Edward R. & Louis P. Roberts) china, glass, &c., s.w.c. Sycamore and Pearl
Roberts Edw., boiler mkr., 129 Butler
Roberts Edward (E R. & Co.) res. Mt. Washington
Roberts Edward, finisher, 129 Butler
Roberts Edward, salesman, 337 W. 3d
Roberts Elizabeth, n.s. Front e. of Ferry
Roberts Elizabeth, 448 W. 7th
Roberts Elizabeth, 207 Clinton
Roberts Elizabeth, seamstress, 77 Pendleton
Roberts Hy , finisher, 133 Linn
Roberts Hy. J., harness mkr., 341 W. 5th
Roberts John, blksmith, 136 W. Pearl
Roberts John, carriage manuf., 136 W. Pearl h. 137 Barr
Roberts John, salesman, 144 Main, h. 250 Vine
Roberts John, stone cutter, 138 Spring
Roberts James C., plane mkr. 67 E. 8th e. of Lock
Roberts John E., trimmer, 449 W. 5th
Roberts John J., painter, 203 George
ROBERTS & JOHNSON, (Joseph R. & John T. J.) Tobacco Warehouse, 134 W. 2d
ROBERTS Joseph (R. & Johnson) h. 264 Everett
Roberts Kate, 133 Linn
Roberts Lizzie, 17 Macalister
Roberts Louis (E. Roberts & Co.) res. Amelia
Roberts Maria, 4 12th
Roberts Mary, seamstress, 522 Main
Roberts Mary, seamstress, 192 Sycamore
Roberts Mary, bds. 506 W. 5th
Roberts Robert, shoemkr., 303 W 8th
Roberts Samuel J., harness mkr., 341 W. 5th
Roberts Sanderson, renderer, s.s. Deer Creek Road n. of Court, office 17½ W. 3d. h. Mt. Auburn
Roberts Warren J. L., painter, bds. 448 W. 7th
Roberts Wm , finisher, bds. 133 Linn
Roberts Wm. M , mer., 11 David
Robertson Alexander, millwright, 413 W. Front. h. Mt. Auburn
Robertson Alexander, clk., n.s. Walker b. Ringgold and Boal
Robertson Geo. W., huckster, 31 W. Front
Robertson John, mach., wks. 222 E. Front
Robertson Mary, servt., 110 W. Canal
Robertson Robert, mach., c. Harriet and Canal
Robertson Sarah, cof. h., 179 Central Av
Robertson Wm., b.k., 303 W. 9th w. of Central Av
Robertson Wm. D., clk., 55 E. 5th, bds. Evans House
Robertson Wm. C., boots and shoes, 319 Central Av., h. 74 Clinton
Robertson Wm. M., b k. ,Gilmore, Dunlap & Co.'s, h. s. s. 9th b. Mound & Cutter
Robins Wm., bds. Dumas Hotel
Robinson Adam, lab., 178 W. Court w. of Central Av
Robinson Alex. M., transportation quartermaster, 18 Betts
Robinson Amanda, bds. 16 McFarland
Robinson Andrew M , saddler, 322 Main
Robinson Ansel L., molder, 127 Hopkins
Robinson Anson D., b.h., 57 Broadway
Robinson Anthony W., dray, 209 Freeman
Robinson Arthur, printer, 241 Longworth
Robinson Benjamin, 201 Longworth
Robinson Benjamin, lab., s.s.6th b. B'dway and Culvert

Robinson Buckner, painter, 230 Longworth, h. 203 Longworth
ROBINSON & BRUNS, (Nicholas R & Henry B.) Planing Mill, 572 Central Av
Robinson Chas. D., eng , 237 John
Robinson Chas. M., blksmith, 1 Scott
Robinson Daniel, butcher, n. s. Bank b. Linn and Baymiller
Robinson Daniel B., printer, bds. 57 Broadway
Robinson Edward R., ham curer, 179 Sycamore, h. Walnut Hills
Robinson Edwin, finisher, bds. 57 Br'dway
Robinson Rev. Edwin T., bds. 262 W. 8th
Robinson Eliza, 62 Accommodation
Robinson Elizabeth. s. s. Friendship al. b. Pike and Butler
Robinson Elizabeth, 335 W. 3d
Robinson Elizabeth A., 146 Hopkins
Robinson Frank, barber, 186 Walnut, h. 26 Pierson
Robinson Gabriel J., river man, w.s. Whittaker b. 3d and Front
Robinson Geo., with Davidson & Bro., n. e.c. Main and 5th
Robinson George T., carp., bds. 462 W. 7th
Robinson H. F., painter, 298 W. 5th, h. 203 Longworth
Robinson Hy. A., printer, wks. 168 Vine, h. Walnut Hills
Robinson H. H., 215 George
Robinson Hy. H., clk., 215 George
Robinson Hy. P., pilot, bds. n.e.c. Pearl and Pike
Robinson Horace. printer, 215 George
Robinson Isaac B., bklayer, 146 Hopkins
Robinson J S., conductor, 106 W. 6th
Robinson James, cof. h., 418 W. 2d
Robinson Jas., finisher, wks. n.e.c. Walnut and Canal
Robinson Jas. D., clk., 119 Dudley
Robinson Jas. M., wks. 340 W. 3d
Robinson Jas. W., 383 W. 3d
Robinson John, 89 W. 7th
Robinson John, blksmith, bds. 65 Broadway
Robinson John, bk. yard, foot of W. 9th
Robinson John, milkman, Pavillion b. Observatory and 3d
ROBINSON JOHN M., Drugs, Medicines and Chemicals, s.w.c. Everett and Central Av.
Robinson John M., wheelwright, wks. Royer, Simonton & Co's
Robinson John W., carp., bds. 462 W. 7th
Robinson Joshua, molder, 172 E. 3d e. of Whittaker
Robinson L., bell boy, Spencer House
Robinson Lawrence, butcher, 343 W. Liberty
Robinson Levi L., molder, bds. 57 Broadway
ROBINSON Lorenzo D., (Wilder, R. & Co.) 521 W. 5th
Robinson Louisa, n.w.c. Court and Main
Robinson Mrs. M., bds. s.e.c. Plum and 5th
Robinson Martha J., n.e c. Burt and Reed
Robinson Mary, 522 Main
Robinson Mary G., 93 Dudley
Robinson Nicholas,n.s. Charlotte b. Linn and Baymiller
Robinson Nicholas J., butcher, 343 W. Liberty, h. s.e.c. Liberty and Linn
ROBINSON Nicholas, (R. & Bruns) h. n.s. Charlotte b. Linn and Baymiller
Robinson Thos., lab., s.w.c. Goodloe and Willow
ROBINSON Thomas G., (Gilmore, Dunlap & Co.) res. Glendale
Robinson Wm., bds. 65 Broadway
ROBINSON WM., General Collector, Residence, 282 George
Robinson Wm., lab. s.w.c. Central Av. and 5th
Robinson Wm., plasterer, 510 W. 9th
Robinson Wm. H., molder, bds. 57 Broadway

Robison Anna, 367 Longworth
Robison Isabella, 121 Cutter
Robison John C., bk. mkr., 261 Richmond
Robson & Co., (Wm. R., Geo. W. Robso.& Wm. H. Robson) brass founders and wrought iron steam pipe manufs. and fitting shop, 154 E. Front
ROBSON Geo. W., (Wm. & Geo. W. R.) h. Mt. Vernon, Ky.
Robson Joseph, stone mason, bds. Indiana House
Robson Richard S., plumber, 174 E. Pearl e. of Broadway. bds. e.s. Broadway b. 2d and Pearl
ROBSON Wm., (Wm. & Geo. W. R.) h. Mt. Vernon, Ky.
ROBSON WM. & GEO. W., Coppersmiths, 156 and 158 E. Front
Robson Wm. H., molder, bds. 57 Broadway
Robson Wm. II . (R. & Co.) h. Newport
Roby Franklin H , cab. mkr., bds. Dennison House
Roby Jane, 334 George
Rocap Ed., stable, n.s. Patterson al. b. Main and Walnut, h. 23 Lodge
Rocap Eli D., (R. & Farrelly) h. Mill Creek Tp.
Rocap & Farrelly, (Eli D. R. & Owen B. F.) com. mers , 224 and 225 Sycamore
Rocap Jas., blksmith, n.s. Patterson al. b. Main and Walnut, h. 76 W, 6th
Roch Wm., carp., 186 Pearl
Roche Edward, contractor, 583 W. 8th
Roche Joseph, porter, 209 W. 3d
Roche Peter, blksmith, 127 Cutter
Roche Thos., blksmith, s.w.c. Laurel and Cutter
Rochel H., lab., wks. n.s. Front b. Lawrence and Pike
Roches Frederick, finisher, s.s. Peete b. Vine and Poplar
Rochr Peter, blksmith, 187 Cutter
Rock Mena. 352 Ham. Road
Rockel John, shoe mkr , 25 14th
Rockel L., lab., wks. Hughes and Foster's
Rockemann Hy., bklayer, 528 Walnut
Rockenfield Abraham. 27 Margaret
Rockenfield Margareth, 184 George
Rockerman Christ., stone cutter, 472 Freeman
Roskey Geo., bds. 53 Broadway
Rockey Geo. W., clk., n.w.c. Front and Ludlow
Rockey Hy., cashier, Suire, Eckstein & Co., h. 120 E. 4th
Rockey Margaret. 69 Martin
Rocklige Elizabeth, servt., 418 W. 6th
Rockwood Chas. A., mer., 135 W. 8th
Rockwood Frank, rear 62 Mohawk
Rockwood Norman, cigar mkr., 9 Charles
Rod L., finisher, wks. 217 W 5th
Rodde Edmond, porter, n.e.c. 13th and Vine
Roddermann Barney, lab., 22 Pierson
Roddy Bridget, tailoress, bds. n.e.c. 3d and Stone
Roddy Francis, shoe mkr., n.e.c. 3d and Stone
Roddy Jas., lab., 583 W. 5th
Roddy Michael, n.e c. 3d and Stone
Rode Bernard, cigar mkr., bds. 202 W. Front
Rode Frederick J., tailor, 97 Buckeye
Rode Hy., tailor, bds. n.w.c. Central Av. and Front
Rode Lewis. finisher, 477 W. 3d
Rodefer Elizabeth J., b.h., 14 Sycamore
Rodefer Joseph, measurer of carpenter's work., 263 Plum. b. 303 John
Rodefield Wm., stone mason, 301 Linn
Rodel John, clk., 56 Allison
Rodemeister Francis, clk., 70 Main, h. 146 Clay
Rodemer Andrew, cooper, 185 W. 2d
Roden Mary. bds. 160 Sycamore
Rodenberg Hy , cof. h. s.e c. Harrison Pike and Western Av.
Rodenberg Hy., lab., 61 Lock
Rodenberg Hy., lab., bds. s.w.c. Central Av. and Harrison Road

278 (ROE) CINCINNATI (ROH) DIRECTORY. (ROL)

Rodenberg Wm., cooper, bds. 139 Baymiller
Rodenstein John, collar mkr., bds. 180 Race
Rodepuller Christ., cooper, 9 14th b. Central Av. and Plum
Rodert John F., shoe mkr., 8 Buckeye
Robert Louisa, servt., 532 Main
Rodeter Barney, bk. mkr., s.s. Ringgold b. Price and Young
Rodgerman Hermann, lab., bds. Pennsylvania Hotel
Rodgers Andrew, driver, n.s. Pearl b. Central Av. and Plum
Rodgers Alexander H., clk., 395 George
Rodgers C. G., b.k. s.w.c. 3d and Walnut, h. Covington
Rodgers James C, paper carrier, 26 Pine
Rodgers John, paver, 245 W Front
Rodgers Patrick, lab., 24 Kossuth
Rodgers Thos., lab., n.w.c. Front and Whittaker
Rodin Mary, 172 Sycamore
Bodin Sarah, 172 Sycamore
Roe Catharine, servt., 391 W. 6th
Roe Ephraim, lab., 660 W. Front
Roe Miss R, bds. s e c. Plum and 5th
Roeadt John, lab., 207 Clinton
Roebling Hy. C. P., dry goods, 69 E. Pearl, bds. 55 Sycamore
Roedel Jacob, cab. mkr., 136 W. Liberty
Roedelsheimer Lewis, tailor, 290 Linn
Roeder Nicholas, carp., 606 Race
Roedersheimer Jacob, meats 544 W. 5th
Roed er Magdalene. rear 184 Clay
Roedter Hy., gardener, n.s. Corporation Line near Auburn
Roedter Theres; 235 Richmond
Roege Francis, butcher, 427 Sycamore
Roege Hy., lab., rear 164 Clay
Roege Hy.. meats, 427 Sycamore
Roeger Michael, lab., 593 Elm
Roehm Martin, tailor, 581 Sycamore
Roehrig Philip, huckster, 251 E. Pearl e. of Broa lway
Roehrs Louis C., bar k., 520 W. Front
Roeling John, brewer. s.s. Montgomery Pike near Reading Road
Roeling John, lab., wks. 728 Central Av.
Roelker Fred., phys., 122 W. 7th
Roelker Hy., porter, e.s. Kilgour b. 3d and 5th
Roelof Rev. Roman, St. Xavier College, w.s. Sycamore b. 6th and 7th
Roember F. H, teacher, 326 W. 9th w. of Central Av.
Roeng Anthony, cab. mkr., 129 Linn
Roenham Hy., (A. Louis & Co.) 525 W. 7th
Roenkamp John, lab., 41 Milton
Roenttgen Phillip, blksmith, 649 W. 8th, h. 537 W. 8th
Roenttgen Phillipp H., blksmith, 537 W. 8th
Roepenack Frederick, actor, 1 Mary
Roepking Hy., lab., s. Hanover b. Woodward and Franklin
Roeppiler Theodore, goldsmith, 487 Sycamore
Roerig August, agt., 579 Race
Roerig August, jr., druggist, 579 Race
Roerig Catharine, teacher, 579 Race
Roerig Elizabeth, milliner. 579 Race
Roerig Geo., watch mkr., 579 Race
Roerig Kate, teacher. 579 Race
Roermann Casper, wagon mkr., bds s.e. c. Brighton and Harrison Pike
Roesch John, bakery, 88 Woodward
Roesch John, bar k. Ludlow House
Roeschi Chas. F , carp., 679 Race
Roescher Leopold, b k. 35 W. Pearl, bds. s w.c 7th and Walnut
Roese John W., cab. mkr., h. 99 Ham. Road
Roese Wm., carp., 99 Ham. Road
Roesener Hermann, lab.; 13 Woodward
Roesher Leopold, b.k., bds. 281 W. 7th
Roesi Chas.. carp., 615 Race
Raesi Margaret, 615 Race
Roesi Martin, varnisher, 615 Race
Roesler John, cooper, 94 Everett
Roesler John N., lithographer, 26 Jackson
Roesner Hy., lab., 60 Findlay

Roesner Hy., molder, wks. n.e.c. Canal and Walnut
Roestel Julius C., tailor, 522 Main
Roetcker Mathias, porter, 117 Clay
Roettger Chas.., lab., n.s. Niles al. b. Main and Sycamore
Roettiech Louis, molder, 162 Oliver
Roettker Hy., gardener, n.s Montgomery Pike nr. Madison Road
Roever Frederika, shirt mkr., 81 W. 3d up stairs
Roewer Hy.., cab. mkr., 34 Pleasant
Roff Hy., dray, 151 Bremen
Rofferty Hannah, servt., 1466 E. Front
Rogan Pat., lab., 166 W. 8th
Roger Williams, Ins. Co., agency 76 W. 3d
Rogers ——, painter, bds. 27 Longworth
ROGERS Adolphus D., (R. W. Booth & Co..), h. 268 Race
Rogers Ann, servt., Burnet House
Rogers Bridget, servt., 459 W. 6th
ROGERS Caleb B., (J. A. Fay & Co.,) res. Norwich, Conn.
Rogers. Chas. S., supt telegraph L. 'M. & C & X. R. R., res. Linnwood
Rogers Cordelia D., 58 Betts
Rogers Emma, 46 Plum
Rogers Geo. B., 404 W. 9th w. of Central Av.
ROGERS Geo. P., (H. Campbell & Co.) h. Ironton, Ohio
Rogers Hy., wheelwright, s. w. c. Park and Brooks
ROGERS HIRAM D., Wholesale Grocer. Produce and Commission Merchant, 26 and 30 E. 2d. h. 58 Betts
Rogers Isaac, sheet iron worker, 792 E. Front
Rogers John, blk. smith, 155 Linn
Rogers John, clk., 33 E. 3d, bds. Henrie House
Rogers John, molder, wks. n.w.c. Plum and Wade
Rogers John, plasterer, bds. 33 W. Front
Rogers Joseph F., harness mkr., bds. Australia House
Rogers Kate, servt., 106 Broadway
ROGERS & KURDLEMEYER, (Wm. G. R. & Geo. K.,) Ladies Shoe Manufactory, n. w. c. Main and Pearl
Rogers Levi M., phys., s.s. Front b. Foster and Kelley
Rogers Mary, 219 Longworth
ROGERS DR. MELANCTHON, Dentist, Office and Residence, 170 Race
Rogers Michael, grocery, 156 Cutter
Rogers Michael, dray, e.s. Broadway b. Liberty and Milton
Rogers Pat., steam engine bldr., h. 100 E. Pearl e. of Broadway
ROGERS Robert C., (McGroarty, & R.,) 132 Barr
Rogers Robert F., 218 Longworth
Rogers Saml. J., blk. smith, 41 Jackson
Rogers Thos., 46 Plum
Rogers Thos. C., b k., 100 E. Pearl
Rogers Thos. J., printer, 13 W. 4th
Rogers Thornton F., clk., 111 W. Pearl
ROGERS Wm G., (R & Kurdlemeyer,) h. E. Walnut Hills
Rogers Wm. H., 218 Longworth
Rogerson James, printer, bds. 70 Longworth
Rogg Chas. carp., s.e.c. Bank and Western Av.
Rogg John B., saddler, 1302 E. Front
Roggendorf John, cigar mkr., 107 W. Liberty
Roggenkemper Hy., tailor, 112 Abigail
Rogin Ann, servt., 423 Freeman
Roh John, lab., 33 Locust
Rohan A. H., b.k. 167 Walnut, h. 53 Jackson
Rohan David, carp., 12 Jackson, h. 376 Elm
Rohde Casper F , shoe mkr., 174 W 9th
Rohden Hy., cigar mkr., s.w.c. Elm and 12th
Rohder Hy., tailor, bds. n.w.c. Front and Central Av.
Rohder John, tailor, bds. n.w.c. Front and Central Av.

Rohe Frank, 308 Main
Rohe H., musician, 348 Main
Rohe Hy., chair mkr., 369 W. 5th
Rohe Hy., cof. h, 348 Main
Rohe Hy., lab., 111 Clark
Rohkasse Fred., lab , 446 John
Rohl Hy., cof. h., n.s. 6th b. Harriet and Horne
Rohlfing Fred., cigar mkr., 103 Gest
Rohlfing Hy., cigar mkr., 102 Gest
Rohlfing Wm., porter, 149 Buckeye
Rohling Geo , lab., 158 E. 5th
Rohling Herman, carp , wks. 48 E. 8th, h. E. Walnut Hills
Rohling John H., carp., 172 Spring
Rohm Phillip, lab., 278 W. Liberty
Rohman Adam, tailor. w.s. Ridgway al. b. Liberty and 15th
Rohman Frank, tailor, 526 Sycamore
Rohman John, tailor, w.s. Ridgway al. b. Liberty and 15th
Rohman Michael, tailor, w.s. Ridgway al. b. Liberty and 15th
Rohmann Francis, tinner, bds. 606 Vine
Rohmann Matinas, baker, 40 Hamer
Rohmann Theodore, cab. mkr., bds. 155 W. Front
Rohmer R. C., Deputy U. S. Marshal, bds. 80 E. 5th
Rohmueller Andrew, lab., 100 Buckeye
Rohney Marla, servt., Burnet House
Rohol Joseph, cooper, 42 W. Front
Rohr John, dray, 24 Mercer
Rohrbach Wm., polisher, 550 Vine
Rohrstees Francis, lab., wks. n.e.c. Walnut and Canal
Rohs Sarah, brewery, s.w.c. Corporation Line and Clifton Av.
Rohwens Hermann, cooper, wks. 33 Bremen
Roiche John, boatman. 202 E. 6th
Rogoahn Hy., lab., 525 Sycamore
Roke Christian, lab., 98 Martin
Rokel Benj., express, n.e.c. Pendleton and Abigail
Rokmeiur Wm., stone cutter, wks. n.e.c Elm and Canal
Roland Geo., painter, bds.87 Longworth
Rolf Antone. s.w.c. 8th and Carr
Rolf Arnold H., lab., 2 W. Mulberry
Rolf Bernard H., shoe mkr., bds. 261 Central Av.
Rolf Dora. servt., 298 George
Rolf Fred., blk. smith, bds. 2 Mulberry
Rolf Fritz, grocery, L.e.c. Logan and Green
Rolf Wm., shoe mkr., s.e.c. 3d and Whittaker
Rolfer Hy., lab., rear 53 Woodward
Rolfes Christian, 343 W. 5th
Rolfes Edward, tailor, e.s. Western Av. b. Bank and Dayton
Rolfes Frank, cooper, 21 Hughes
Rolfes Fred , cigar mkr., 406 W. Front
Rolfes Fred. J., lab., 39 Abigail
Rolfes Hy., grocery, 61 Abigail
Rolfes Mary, cook, 70 Sycamore
Rolfes Theodore, rope mkr., 442 W. 2d
Rolles Theodore, cigars, &c., 466 W. Front
Rolfing Hy., carp., 218 Betts
Rolfus Deny, servt., 211 W. 7th
Rolfus Hy., molder, wks. n.e.c. Canal and Walnut
Rolher Hy., meats. 463 Linn
Roling Hy., sheet iron worker, 145 Abigail
Roling Herman, lab., 597 Race
Roling Jas, bds. Devis House
Rolink Hy., lab., 145 Abigail
Roll Chas., butcher. 699 Race
ROLL CHRISTOPHER, Coffee House, 175 E. Front
Roll Clements, baker, 638 Central Av.
Roll Edward, lock smith. n.w.c. Ham. Road and Findlay, b. 165 Hamilton Road
Roll Hy., V., trimmer, 58 Bank
Roll Irene, teacher. 1565 E. Front
Roll Louisa O. teacher, 1565 E Front
Roll Pat., lab., 139 W. Front
Rolle Ernst, s.w.c. Hughes and Schiller
Roller Augustus, butcher, 150 Everett
Rollins Adeline, h. 610 W. 6th
Rollins Edward E., 470 W. 7th

(ROO) CINCINNATI (ROS) DIRECTORY. (ROS) 279

Rollins Michael, bds. 158 W 3d
Rollins Phoebe, b. h., 185 W. 3d
Rollins Wm., currier, bds, s.e.c. Walnut and 9th
Rolliston Jas., paper carrier, 334 Mound
Rollmann Bernard, peddler, 39 Buckeye
ROLLO G. D. V. agt. Grover and Baker's Sewing Machines, 58 W. 4th, h. s.w.c. Race and 7th
Rolls Emma, rear 66 Peete
Rolls Jeremiah, 140 W. Pearl
Rolls Wm., blk. smith, e.s. Stone b. 4th and 5th
Rollwagen Fred, tailor, 668 Main
ROLLWAGEN LOUIS. Merchant Tailor and Clothier 562 Central Av.
Rolph F. A., clk., 49 Walnut, h. 388 Central Av.
Rolsan Bernard, express man, 64 Abigail
Roltgen Frank, lab., wks. n.e.c. Walnut and Canal
Roltgen Ferdinand, sen., finisher, 37 Pleasant
Roltgen Ferdinand, jr., butcher, 37 Pleasant
Rolvering John A., tailor, bds. 498 W. Front
Rolvers Elizabeth, servt., 306 Longworth
Rom John J., fancy goods, 60 13th
Romanovitz Lucas, cab. mkr., 278 Front
Rombach Burkhart, saddlery, 684 Central Av.
Rombach Chas. H., clk., 252 Main
Rombach Gertrude, 62 12th
Rome Geo., lab., wks. 335 Broadway
Romeiser Peter, porter, 530 Walnut
Romelsberg Marks, 691 Elm
Romer Alex., painter, 219 Broadway
Romer Chas., tailor, 19 Abigail
Romer Frank. cooper, bds e.s. Sycamore b. Abigail and Woodward
Romer John H., grocery, w.s. Kilgourb. 3d and 4th
Romer Joseph, shoe mkr., 10 Abigail
Romes Hy., clk., 424 Walnut
Romminger Jacob, tailor, bds. 32 E. Front
Ronecker Barney, tobacconist, 51 Martin
Roneldson John, agt., bds. s.s. Findlay, b. Freeman and Western Av
Roneldson Thomas, agt., h. s.s. Findlay, b. Freeman and Western Av
Roney John, lab. 71 Richmond
Roney Martin, lab., s. s. Friendship al. b. Pike and Butler
Roney Wm., tanner, 991 Laurel
Ronfort Mary, 210 Sycamore
Ronger Joseph, candle mkr., wks. 728 Central Av
Ronger Louisa, packer, wks. 728 Central Av
Ronger Martin, cof. and b. h., 23 Water
Ronnebaum Francis, lab., 16 Abigail
Ronnebaum Francis, painter, 5 Mary
Ronnebaum Ferdinand, (Munnich & R.) 5 Mary
Ronsheim Joseph, mer., 20 Gano
Roof Caroline, 50 Dudley
Roof Gusty, 50 Dudley
Ronnan Margaret, 53 Race
Rooney Charles, printer, bds. 199 W. 3d
Rooney John C., printer, Press office, bds. 199 W. 3d
Rooney L., student, 91 Sycamore
Rooney Margaret, servt., 283 Longworth
Roop Mary, 403 John
Roos Rev. Ernst. n. e. c. Bremen and 15th
Roos Geo., stone cutter, 18 Ann
Roos John. baker, 81 Bremen
Roos M., bds. Hart's Hotel
Roos Philip, teacher at St. Xavier College
Root Leonard. chemist, bds. 462 W. 7th
Root Oliver J., clk., bds. 462 W. 7th
ROOT OLIVER W., Attorney at Law. s.w.c. 3d and Sycamore, h. Newport
Roothwin John, brass finisher, 13 Home
Roots & Coe, (Guernsey Y. R., Erastus P. C. & John H. Aydelott,) commers. W.W. Canal Basin b. Central Av. and John

Roots George, barber, bds. 204 Broadway
Roots Guernsey Y., (R. & Coe,) res. College Hill
Roots Thomas E., barber, 144 Vine, bds. 204 Broadway
Roova Margaret, dress mkr., bds. 171 W 3d
ROPES N. & CO., Lard Oil and Candle Manufacturers, w.s. Lock, b. 4th and 5th
ROPES Nathaniel, (N. R. & Co.,) 300 W. 4th
Ropes Nathaniel, jr., clk., 300 W. 4th
Ropes Wm. A., b.k., 300 W. 4th
Ropp August. hostler, 44 E. 6th
Ropp Jno. H. R., carp., 397 Race
Rorar Nicholas, lab., rear 517 E. Front
Rorhy Julia. servt., 94 E. 4th
Rork Wesley, lab., 482 W. 9th, w. of Central Av
Rosa Hy., eng, 379 Broadway
Rosa Wm., baker, 215 Betts
Roschenkemper Bernhard, cigar mkr., s.w.c. 5th and John
Roschenkemper Hy., cigars, s.w.c. 5th and John
Rose Mrs. 169 E. 3d
ROSE ADEL C., Agent United States Express Company, 122 W. 4th, bds. 162 Elm
Rose Anna, millinery, 86 Hopkins
Rose Arthur, b.k., 58 Walnut, h. 308 Findlay
Rose Barbara, bds. 546 Race
Rose Charles W., cooper, 180 E. Pearl
Rose Daniel P., furniture, 126 Sycamore, h. 375 W. 4th
Rose Edward E , painter, bds. 72 Laurel
Rose Ezekiel. driver, bds. s.w.c. Franklin and Broadway
Rose Harrison, 120 W. Court, w. of Central Av
Rose Hy., wks. Cincinnati type foundry
Rose Hermann, grocery, n.s. 6th, b. Harriet and Horne
Rose Jacob, lab, 22 Commerce
Rose John, 93 George
Rose John, bksmith, 75 Pendleton
Rose John, eng., 24 Parsons
Rose John, lab., 75 Pendleton
Rose John, lab.. wks. n.s. Front, b. Lawrence and Pike
Rose Margaret, 76 W. 3d
Rose Saml D., printer, 72 Laurel
ROSE SAMUEL K., Notary Public and Patent Medicine Depot, 184 W. 6th, h. 173 W. 6th
Rose Solomon, n. s. Everett b. John and Cutter
Rose Thomas S. B., plumber, 86 Hopkins
Rose Wm., phys., 28 Mound
Rosebolt Charles, lab., 160 W. Liberty
Roseboom Wm. H., pipeman, 29 Chestnut
Rosebrough Joseph, cooper, 100 14th
Rosebrough Richard, clk., 100 14th
Rosecrans Ephraim D., 126 Clinton
Rosecrans Rt. Rev. Dr. Sylvester, s.e.c. 8th and Central Av
Rosekamp Joseph, cab. mkr., 235 Betts
Rosemeier Frederick, molder, 176 E. Pearl
Rosemeier Mrs. Margaret, washwoman, 40 Webb
Rosemier Jno., salesman, 144 Walnut, h. 40 Webb
Rosemer Charles, cigar mkr., wks. 361 Vine
Rosen John, carp., 421 Vine
Rosenacker August, wks. w.s. Brighton, nr. Benckenstein's Garden
Rosenbarker Adam, lab., 64 Barr
Rosenbaum A. lab., wks. 335 Broadway
Rosenbaum Adam, peddler, 15 Miller
Rosenbaum & Bro., (Levi & Meyer,) tinners, 20 W. 5th
Rosenbaum Charles, lab., s. s. e.c. Vine and Pearl, bds. 61 Cutter
Rosenbaum Frederick, 61 Cutter
Rosenbaum Isaac, second hand store, 247 Broadway
Rosenbaum Jacob, 191 W. 5th
Rosenbaum John H., wagon mkr., 532 Sycamore
Rosenbaum Levi, (R. & Bro.) 191 W. 5th

Rosenbaum M., clk., 140 Walnut, h. 61 Cutter
Rosenbaum Meiers, stoves, &c., 191 W. 5th
Rosenbaum Wm., clk., 502 Sycamore
Rosenberg Alex., clothing, 272 Central Avenue
Rosenberg Hy., stone yard, s.s. Wade, b. John and Cutter, h. 66 David
Rosenberg Hy., watchman, 61 Locke
Rosenberg Joseph, peddler, rear 20 15th
Rosenberger Casper, tailor, 65 W. Court
Rosenblander Chas., turner, 71 Hughes
Rosenbring Wm., chair mkr., 15 Mercer
Rosendale Alonzo, clk., s. w. c. Everett and Central Av., bds. 17 Hopkins
Rosendale Lemuel, trader. 17 Hopkins
Rosenfeld Albert, phys., 23 W. 8th
Rosenfeld Julius, tailor, 60 14th
Rosenfeld & Kaufman, (Leopold R. & Henry K.,) clothiers, 64 W. Pearl
Rosenfeld Leopold, (R. & Kaufman,) 277 W. 8th
ROSENFELD SOLOMON, Hoopskirt Manufacturer, 257 Central Avenue and 198 W. 5th. h. 365 Central Av
Rosenfeld Wm., paper box mkr., 512 Walnut
Rosenfelder August, tanner, 97 Pendleton
Rosenfelder Lewis F. J., cof. h., 90 13th
Rosenheim Isadore, salesman, 36 W. Pearl, bds. n.w.c. 7th and Walnut
Rosenheim Morris, (Rossmann & R.,) bds. 264 Vine
Rosenham Hy., (A. Louis & Co.,) h. 525 W. 7th
Rosenmear Hy., tailor, bds. n. s. Front nr. Stone
Rosenplath Louis, umbrella manufacturer, 481 Central Av
Rosenecker Frank, lab., wks. Queen City Distillery
Rosenstein Lewis S., dry goods, 108 W. 5th
Rosenstein S., cigar mer., bds. 250 Walnut
Rosenstock Morris, b.k., s.w.c. 4th and Walnut, h. 459 Plum
Rosenstock John, b.k , b. 459 Plum
Rosenstiel Michael, clk., s s. al. b. Clay and Main and Canal and 12th
Rosenstiel Lewis, dry goods mer., 341 Walnut
Rosenthal Chas., meats. 448 Main
Rosenthal Emanuel, 169 W. 5th
Rosenthal Hy., clk., 94 Providence
Rosenthal Joseph, student, bds. 172 Longworth
Rosenthal Joseph, tailor, 200 W. Court
Rosenthal Samson, drover, 34 Providence
Rosenthal Samuel, printer, 565 Vine
Roser Geo., liquors, &c., 135 W. Court, h. n.s. Court b. Race and Vine
Roser Joseph, blksmith, wks. n. w. c. Race and Burrows
Rosey —, student, bds. 335 Central Av
Rosig John, bds. Dennison House
Rosienkiewez Mrs. L., 43 George
Rosin John, lab., 6 Elm
ROSING ADOLPHUS C. A., Importer and Dealer in Wines, Liquors, Cigars, &c., 62 and 64 E. 2d, h. 206 Mound
Rosing Anton, (Krusemeir & R.,) rear 302 Ham. Road
Rosinna Christ, teamster, wks. 630 Central Av
Rositer John, stone cutter, bds. 182 Elm
Rositer Mary, 182 Elm
Rositer Thomas, much., bds. 182 Elm
Roskup Fred. W., 747 Vine
Rosler Jno., cooper, 54 David
Rosmann Christina, 623 Race
Rosmann Clemens J , carp., 168 Pleasant
Rosmann Gerhard B., 168 Pleasant
Rosmann Hy. J., carp., 168 Pleasant
Rosnagle Elizabeth, b.h., 55 Betts
Rosnagle Isaiah, blksmith, 150 Wade
Rosner H., lab., wks. Chamberlain & Co.'s
Rosner Hy., blksmith, 711 Vine, h. n. e. c. Buckeye and Vine
Ross A. L., jr., proprietor Cin. & Leb. omnibus line, 169 Walnut, b. Leb.O.

280 (ROS) CINCINNATI (ROT) DIRECTORY. (ROV)

Ross A. Q., pilot, 22 Barr
ROSS Abraham, (R. Pettibone & Co.,) h. 64 Hopkins
ROSS ALBERT, Drugs, Medicines, Chemicals, &c., s.w.c. 8th and Central Av., h. 404 W. 9th
Ross Alexander, fireman, n.e.c. 5th and c Broadway, h. 84 Pike
Ross Alexander, lab., 444 W. 5th
Ross Andrew, watchman, 119 Betts
Ross Angeline, washwoman, bds. 148 Van Horn
Ross Apollo M., surveyor Citisens Insurance Company, 54 Clark
Ross Arthur W., clk., 355 Central Av., h. 64 Hopkins
Ross Britton, painter, 139 W. Court, w. of Central Av
Ross Charles, 267 W. 9th
Ross Chas. C., bk. layer, h. 25 Cutter
Ross Chas. R., pipe fitter, wks. n. e. c. Walnut and Canal
ROSS & CO., Commission and Forwarding merchants and Steamboat Agents, 33 Sycamore
ROSS Chas W., (McDonald & R.,) h. Covington
Ross David A., jr., painter, bds. 353 Central Av
Ross David A., M. D., 203 W. 4th, h. 353 Central Av
Ross Emery C., Cin. machine works, n. e.c Front and Lawrence, h. 284 Longworth
Ross Ezekiel, ins. solicitor and inspector, h. 139 W. 8th
ROSS Frederick (Metcalf & R.), n.e.c, Main and 8th
Ross Geo., butcher, 129 Everett
Ross George, lab., 52 Abigail
ROSS Geo. W. (Ross, Pettibone & Co.), 10 Dayton
Ross Hy. cof. h., 50 W. Front
Ross Hugh B., carp., 179 George
Ross Hy. E., cab. mkr., bds. 353 Central Av
Ross J. H. M., mailer, Meth. Book Concern, n. Newport, Ky
Ross James J., cooper, 409 Plum
Ross James M., teacher, 53 Chestnut
Ross James W., carp., bds. 335 Clark
Ross Jessie, 53 Chestnut
Ross John, 81 Abigail
Ross John, bksmith, bds. 997 Central Av
Ross John, carp., 421 Vine
Ross John, driver, 434 Linn
Ross John, huckster, 130 Baymiller
Ross John, lab, bds. 70 Sycamore
Ross John, molder, 559 Sycamore
Ross John, porter, bds. Liberty Tree House
Ross John L., paper warehouse, 45 W. 2d, h. 120 E. 3d
Ross Joseph, carp., bds. 206 W. 5th
Ross Joseph, lab., 58 Clark
Ross Joseph S., pres't. Portsmouth Ins. Co., h. 20 Richmond
Ross Kate, servt., 237 Richmond
Ross Lilly, bds 191 W. 5th
ROSS M. B., (R. & Co.) 12 W 9th
Ross Nicholas, lab., s.s. Charlotte b. Linn and Baymiller
Ross Noble G., mach., 151 E. Front, h. c.s. John b. Court and Richmond
ROSS, PETTIBONE & CO. (Abraham R., Alex. P. & Geo. W. Ross) Coal Dealers, 115 Vine, n.e.c. W. W. Canal and 3d, n.w.c. 5th & Mound, and 358 Central Av
Ross Robert, eng., n. s. Goodloe b. Willow and Niagara
Ross Simon, mach., 65 Lodge
Ross Spaulding N., b k Lafayette Banking Co., h. w s Freeman n. of Findlay
Ross Stephen B., wire weaver, wks. 191 Walnut
Ross Theodore P., bds. 353 Central Av
Ross Valentine, w.s. Vine b. Milk and Mulberry
Ross Wellington, clk., 64 Hopkins
Ross Wm., lab., 530 W. 9th
Rossmann Adolph (R. & Rosenheim)264 Vine

Rossmann & Rosenheim (Adolph R. & Morris R.) notions, 36 W. Pearl
Rosster Rev. Wm. D., 310 W. 8th
Rosswinkel Barney A., b.k., 372 Main. bds. 84 Pike
Rosswinkel Herman, cof. h., 1 Landing, h. 84 Pike
Rost Conrad, lab., 86 Peete
Rost Jacob, tinner, 517 Elm
Rosteuscher Napoleon, lab., 41 Jones
Rostert Louis, lithographer, 64 W. 4th b. 2d and Pearl
Rotard Stephen, lab., e.s. Anderson al. b. 2d and Pearl
Rote August, waiter, 426 Walnut
Rote Peter, lab, n.s. Front e. of Ferry
Rotert Bernhard H., w.s. Goose al. b. Green and Elder
Rotert Frank, cab mkr., 226 Betts
Rotert Geo., lab., wks. Wood & M'Coy's
Rotert Hy., clk., bds. 91 Spring
Rotert Hy., cooper, 173 Clay
Rotert Hy., cof. h, 104 Abigail
Rotert Hy., shoemkr, 357 George
Rotert John G., lab., rear 176 Clay
Rotetwieser Frank, cooper, bds. 118 Gest
Rotger Francis, dray, 16 Harrison
Rotgerman John H., packer, 64 E. Pearl, h c. Pike and Front
Roth August, baker, n.e.c. Court and Elm
ROTH Balthazar (R. & Moser) 181 E. 3d
Roth Barney, tailor, e.s. Ramsey n. of Front
Roth Bernhard, 95 Buckeye
Roth Bernhard, brewer, 666 Race
Roth Carolina, servt., 181 E. 3d
Roth Conrad, baker, 149 Bremen
Roth Conrad, shoemkr., C6 W. Liberty
Roth Edward, cigar mkr., s.w.c. 12th and Elm
Roth Elizabeth, s.s. 6th b. Harriet and Horne
Roth Geo., carp., 290 W. Liberty
Roth Gottlieb, carp., n.s. Railroad e. of French
Roth Hy., lab., 1111 Central Av
Roth Jacob, shoemkr. 38 E. 2d
Roth John, boiler mkr., bds. Ludlow House
Roth John, brewer, 466 Elm
Roth John, butcher, 309 Freeman
Roth John, lab., 14 Hamer
Roth John, lab., 28 Mansfield
ROTH JOHN, Physician, Office 524 E. 5th, Residence Storrs Township
Roth John, pork packer, 309 Freeman
Roth Lawrence, bksmith, 542 E. Front
Roth Lewis, finisher, bds 606 Vine
Roth Joseph, candy store. 87 W. Liberty
ROTH Joseph, (McKee & R.,) 245 W. 7th
Roth Joseph, pork house, 236 Clark, h. n.w.c. Clark and Baymiller
Roth Joseph, tailor, 169 Bremen
ROTH & MOSER, (Balthazar R. & John M.) St. Nicholas Exchange, n.w.c. Vine and Longworth
Roth Nathan, tailor, 245 W, 7th
Roth Peter, sawyer, bds. 9 15th
Roth Philip, baker 196 Bremen
Roth Valentine mach., 69 W. Liberty
Rotthaus Louis, baker, 270 W. Liberty
Rothacker Margaret, 567 Sycamore
Rothacker Sophia, 119 Mound
Rothan Francis, 99 Darr
Rothan John, carp., 97 Barr
Rothe Joseph, 52 McFarland
Rothen John, carp., 266 Carr, h. 97 Barr
Rothenbush Mary A., 153 Everett
Rother Wm., lab., s. e. c. Clinton and Linn
Rothergi Ludwig, carp., s.w.c. 6th and Plum
ROTHERT August (J. H. Rothert & Sons,) 640 Central Av.
Rothert August, carp., 240 Mulberry
Rothert Francis H., (R. & Groene,) res. Clifton
Rothert Frederick, cab. mkr., 60 Melancthon
Rothert Gerhard, cooper, h. 147 Clay
Rothert & Groene, (Francis H. R. & Frederick H. G.) brewery, e. s. Denman b. Bank and Central Av.

ROTHERT Henry W., (J. H. Rothert & Sons,) 640 Central Av.
Rothert Hermann, tailor, wks. 488 Race
ROTHERT Herman R.,(J. H. Rothert & Sons.) res. Keokuk, Iowa
ROTHERT John H., (J. H. Rothert & Sons,) 640 Central Av.
ROTHERT J. H. & Sons, (John H. R., August R., Herman R. & Henry W. R.,) Stoves Hardware Iron, Tools &c., 640 and 642 Central Av.
Rothfus Albert, cigar mkr., 1015 Central Ax.
Rothfus Elizabeth, 540 Plum
Rothfus Frederick, meats, 114 W. Liberty
Rothfus Geo., cof. h., 714 Vine
Rothfus Paul, cigar mkr., 1015 Central Av
Rothfuss Henriette, 677 Vine
Rothfuss Lewis F., brewer, 677 Vine
Rothhan Fred, cof. h., 592 Elm
Rothje Mary, rear 545 Sycamore
Rothje Wm., porter, rear 395 Sycamore
Rothkamp Dieterick, cab. mkr., 13 Mary
Rothkopf Hy , carp., 115 Laurel
Rothkopp Jno. H., carp., 115 Laurel
Rothlauf Christopher, turner, 284 Bremen
Rothman Hy., lab., wks. s.e.c. 5th and Culvert
Rothrink William, lab., n. e. c. Sloo and Harriet
Rothschild Abraham, 339 Central Av.
Rothschild Louis, butcher. 129 Everett
Rothschild Mariana, 22 15th
Rothschild Maier, watches and jewelry, 238½ W. 5th
Rothschild Raphael, trader, 292 John
Rothwell Wm., turner, 656 Sycamore
Rott Chas, bksmith, 439 Vine
Rott Chas., bksmith, bds. 493 Vine
Rott Elizabeth, 71 Spring
Rott Hy., shoe mkr., bds. 254 W. 5th
Rott John H. W., boots and shoes, 254 W. 5th
Rottcher Louis, bakery, s.w.c. John and Clinton
Rottenhuss Frederick, lab., 227 E. 5th
Ruttgen Wm., wagon mkr., 615 Elm
Rottger Frank H., dry goods, 567 Main
Rottger George, clk., 121 Main, bds. 25 Franklin
Rotthass Elizabeth, bakery, 270 W. Liberty
Rotti Barney, porter, 30 Sycamore
Rottler Wm., saloon, n. w. c. 3d and Main, bds. Teutonia Hotel
Rottman Casper, stone mason, 28 Mansfield
Rottman Frank, lab., 68 Lock
Rottman Geo. S., grocery, 531 W. 8th
Rottman Hy. P., lab., 10 Peete
Rottner Wm., cigar mkr., 468 Race
Rouch John, teamster, e. s. Division b. Bernard and Harrison Pike
Rough Adam, bksmith, Mercer, b. Walnut and Vine
Rouhe George, n. s. Ham. Road head of Elm
Rouland H., mach., wks. n. s. Front b. Lawrence and Pike
Rouney Patrick, coppersmith, bds. s.w.c. 5th and Broadway
Rourke Charles, lab., s. s. Yeatman b. Broadway and Sycamore
Rourke John, porter, bds. 33 W. Front
Rourke Martin, lab. 64 Richmond
Rourke Thomas, clk., 118 Laurel
Rouscher John M., varnisher, 175 Carr
House Crawford, rear 820 Broadway
Rouse Ellis, barber, 39 Central Av.
Rouse George, turner, wks. 375 W. 3d
Rouse Simeon, watchman, 459 W. 3d
Rouse Thomas, plasterer. s. s. Charlotte b. Central Av. and Linn
Rouselot Victor, cook, Spencer House
Rouskoup Wm., carp., Oehler al. b. Freeman and Garrard
Router Hy., baker, bds. 222 W. 6th
Rover Barney H., clothing, 614 Central Av
Rover Chas., cab. mkr., wks. s.w.c. Canal and Elm
Rover Guard's Armory, 108½ Vine
Rover Rudolph, cab. mkr., 71 David

Rowald Henry, lab., bds 519 Main
Rowan Patrick. dray, 48 Butler
Rowds S. A., clk., bds Madison House
Rowe Daniel, policeman, 216 Water
Rowe Ernst. clk., 16 Jackson
Rowe Frank, 248 W. 7th
Rowe Geo., bds. 294 W. 5th
Rowe James, bds. Dennison House
ROWE James, (R. Park & Co.,) 150 Spring
Rowe James C., salesman, 124 Walnut. h. 269 W. 7th
ROWE JOHN, Saw Manufacturer, 238 W 7th, h. 296 W. 5th
ROWE John, (R. & Kendall,) h. n.s. 7th b. Central Av. and John
Rowe John T., sculptor, 409 John
Rowe Julia, bds. 248 W. 7th
ROWE & KENDALL, (John R. & Henry H. K.,) Hats and Caps, n w.c. 9th and Central Av
Rowe Lewis, b.k., bds. 64 Longworth
ROWE, PARK & CO., (James R., Richard P. & William S. Park,) Saddles, Harness and Trunk Manufacturers, 216 Main and 23 E. 5th
Rowe Stanhope S., teller, 23 W. 3d, h. 144 John
Rowe Thomas A., b.h., 177 Sycamore
Rowe Wm., wheelwright, 400 W 3d
Rowe Wm. B , shoe mkr., 179 Baymiller
Rowe Wm. H., b.k., 129 Main, h. Covington
Rowecraft Jonathan H., b.k., 71 W.Court w. of Central Av.
Rowekamp Barney, lab , 162 Freeman
Rowekamp Bernhard, lab., 604 Race
Roewekamp Bernhard tailor, 116 Clay
ROWEKAMP FREDERICK H., Justice of the Peace, n e.c. Hunt and Main, h. 101 Dayton
Rowekamp Henry, stone mason, 609 Race
Rowekamp Joseph, varnisher, rear 14 13th
Rowekamp Mary, teacher, 101 Dayton
Rowell & Alexander, (John R. & Henry A.,) bk. binders. 74 W. 3d
Rowell Samuel, salesman, 52 W. Pearl, bds. Madison House
Rowell Wm., printer, 48 Harrison
Rowen Edward J., lab., n s. Railroad e. of Wallace al.
Rower Frederick, tailor, 524 Sycamore
Rowland Charles W., grocer, 46 W. 2d, h n.e.c. 3d and Kilgour
Rowland Jennie, bds. 296 W. 5th
ROWLAND Thomas C., (Mitchell & R.,) h. e. s. Auburn b. Central Av. and Corporation Line
Rowley Ann, 477 W. 4th
Rownd Lewis, cooper, 332 John
Rox F. & Co., (Frank R. & Harris Stiff), furniture, 362 Central Av
Rox Frank, (F. R. & Co.,) 362 Central Av
Royal Fire and Life Ins. Co., agency 62 W. 3d
Royalty Samuel, bksmith, bds. 112 Laurel
Royan John, lab., e.s. Ludlow b. 2d and Pearl
ROYER, SIMONTON & CO., (Theodore R., Joseph S. & John Young), Wheel, Spoke, Hub and Felloe Manufacturers, 340, 373 and 375 W. 3d
ROYER Theodore, (R., Simonton & Co.) 286 W. Court w. of Central Av
Royse Noble K., teacher, 464 Sycamore
Royse Southwell, 464 Sycamore
Royse Thomas S., (E.'S. Butler & Co.,) 464 Sycamore
Royster Wm., barber, 181 George
Ruan John, lab , 196 Clark
Rubbe Hannah Barbara, 32 Mulberry
Ruben Moritz, 99 W. 2d
Rubenbau Nicholaus, lab., 263 Pleasant
Rubenow Ernst, tinner, 534 Main
Ruberg Bernard, clothing, 162 Bank
Ruberg Hermann, shoe mkr., bds. 667 W. 6th
Ruberg J. Henry, mason, 106 Abigail
Ruberg A. Maria, e.s. Spring b. Abigail and Woodward

Rubrecht Diedrich, cab. mkr., 18 Madison
Rubusch Arnold, varnisher, 25 Commerce
Rubusch Fred., sawyer, 25 Commerce
Rubury Henry, lab., 671 W. 6th
Rucfrigel John, s.s. Mohawk b. N. Elm and Hamburg
Ruckdeschel Andrew, 61 Hamer
Rucker Henriette, 125 Race
Ruckert Alex., grocery, 569 Main. bds. w.s. Main b. Allison and Liberty
Ruckhaber Charles, reporter, 29 Franklin
Ruckstuhl Christian, shoe mkr., 562 Elm
Ruckstuhl Peter, cigar mkr., 96 Ham. Road
Rudd Richard, grocery, 73 Park
Rudd Richard, fireman. 73 Park
Rudisyl Sylvester. saddler, bds. e.s. Main b 4th and 5th
Rudolf Jacob, stone cutter, rear 507 Elm
Rudolph Adam, grocer, s.s. 6th nr. Harriet
Rudolph Brockmeier, tailor, 138 Pleasant
Rudolph Christian, stone cutter, 507 Elm
Rudolph Jacob, shoe mkr., 184 Linn
Rudolph John, barber, 85 Bremen, h. 81 Bremen
Rudolph Margaret, bds. 65 Bremen
Rudolph Wm. blksmith, 140 Freeman
Rudu Wilhelmina, laundress, 111 Clay
Rudy Henry, dray, 125 W. 9th w. of Central Av.
Ruebel Ernst. tailor, 165 Ham. Road
Ruebush Henry, lab., 207 W. Front
Ruehl Chas., cab. mkr., 275 Freeman
Ruehl John, painter, 64 W. Liberty
Ruehl Lewis, boots and shoes, w.s. Vine b. Milk and Mulberry
Ruehrwein Frederick, shoe mkr., 68 14th
Ruehrwein Wm., mach., wks., 141 W. 2d
Ruel John, blksmith, 231 W. Court
Ruese Conrad, grocery, 513 Sycamore
Ruese Henry, molder, 523 Sycamore
Ruetter Hermann, lab., 97 Woodward
Ruettermann Bernhard. lab., 102 Abigail
Ruewe Clemens, policeman, 495 Elm
Ruf Alexander, grocery, 603 Elm
Ruf Chas. C., tailor, bds. 671 Race
Ruf & Eha, (John R. & Gottlieb E.), boots and shoes, 671 Race
Ruf Henry, cigar mkr , wks. 381 Vine
Ruf John, carp., 6 W. Mulberry
Ruf John, (J. R. & G. Eha,) 671 Race
Ruf Christ. pipeman, 24 Webster
Ruf Eliza, 17 Freeman
Ruf Louisa, 28 Allison
Ruf John D., b.k., 20 Broadway
Ruf Robert, expressman, 30 Peete
Ruffin Elinor, 381 Longworth
Ruffin J. L. & Co., (James L. R., Sam'l Baylis & Gus. Colcher,) detective police agency, n.w.c. 3d and Main
Ruffin James L., (J. L. R. & Co.,) 99 Longworth
Ruffin John B., clk. P. O., s.s. Front e. of Vance
Ruffin Samuel, printer, 381 Longworth
Ruffing Theobald, lab., e.s. M. Canal b. 8th and Court
Ruffle Mathias, lab., 88 Buckeye
Ruffmann Barney, lab., n.s. Front e. of Kelly
Ruffner David, 100 George
Ruffner Henry W., painter, 227 Broadway
Ruffregen Philippina, servt., 401 Vine
Rufle Josephine, wks. Hieatt & Woods' candle factory
Rufle Mary, wks Hieatt & Woods' candle factory
Rufli Michael, saloon. 7 Weller b. Carr and Harriet
Rugan Margaret, 55 Observatory Road
Ruggles Henry B., agt. L. M. R. R. Omnibus Co., 174 Race
Ruh Anthony, tailor, 74 Bremen
Ruh Benj., tailor, 14 Mary
Ruhe Joseph, tinner, bds. 113 Clay
Ruhl Charles, cab. mkr., 275 Freeman
Ruhl Henry, peddler, s.s. Liberty b. Linn and Baymiller
Ruhl Nicholas, cab. mkr., 208 Clark
Ruhl Paul, tailor, 22 Ham. Road

Ruhl Peter, carp., 275 Freeman
Ruhoff Bernhard, bar. k., bds. 496 W. Front
Ruhol Joseph, lab., 42 W. Front
Ruhrwien Wm., mach., 562 Elm
Ruhrwien Wm., tailor, 133 Pleasant
Ruickert Alexander, mer., bds. 577 Main
Ruiter Cornelius, type mkr., 199 Linn
Rukin John. lab., 363 George
RULE CHARLES, Steam Marble Works, s.w c. Broadway and 5th, h. 148 Broadway
Rule James, marble worker, s.w.c. Br'dway and 5th
Rulison Hiram M., phys. 235 Central Av., h. s.w.c. Dayton and Coleman
Rum George, carp., 11 Hughes
Rumbach Andreas, express driver, 100 13th
Rumenbecker John, tailor, 179 Linn
Rumke Christian, carp., bds. 568 Vine
Rump Anthony, tailor, 239 Hopkins
Rump Henry, shoe mkr., wks. 5 Casilly's Row
Rump Jacob, cab. mkr., 58 David
Rump Johanna, Moore al. b. W. 6th and 9th and Plum and Elm
Bumpert Gottfried, cooper, n.s. Charlotte b. Linn and Baymiller
Rumpf Mary, teacher, h 2 Milton
Rumpker Joseph, blksmith, bds. s.w.c. Abigail and Broadway
Rumpler Anton, cof. h., 50 York
Rumpler Wm., finisher. wks. Fritsch, Burkhardt & Co.'s
Runck Barbara, servt., 304 W. 5th
Runck Frederick, toves, &c., 509 Vine
Runck Peter, lab., 125 Clay
Rund Frederick, tailor, 194 Pleasant
Runegar Geo , lab., Junction Walnut Hills and Reading Road
Rung Geo., finisher, 273 Franz
Runge Victor Wm., carriage mkr., 591 Main
Runge Wm., blksmith, 591 Main
Runge Wm., porter, 53 14th
Runge Wm., porter, 18 Main, h. 21 E. Liberty
Runion Geo. W., printer, 19 Hathaway
Runk Charles, carver, 153 Pleasant
Runk Frederick, carp., 153 Pleasant
Runk Hy., painter, s.s. Findlay b. Freeman and Western Av.
Runk Louis, butcher, 153 Pleasant
Runk Peter, whitewasher, 153 Pleasant
Runkle Chester F., druggist, n.e.c. 8th and Walnut
Runkle Wm. H., apothecary, n.w.c. Court and Mound
Runnebaum Hy., lab., 16 Abigail
Runnebaum Mary, 12 13th
Runscer Joseph, lab., 475 W. 8th
Runte Adam, teacher, Catholic school, Mt. Adams
Runte Frederick W., turner, 475 Broadway
Runte Wm., cab mkr., 475 Broadway
Runtz Geo., cutter, 22 Arch
Runtz Marcus, tailor, 207 Clinton
Runyan Geo. W., carp., 183 Mound
Runyan Geo. W., printer, 10 Jane
Ruoff Caroline, teacher, 11 15th
Ruof Johanna, h. 11 15th
Rupking Catharine, 64 Abigail
Rupp Frederick, potter. 59 Buckeye
Rupp Ily., tailor, e.s. Vine b. Auburn Av. and Calhoun
Rupp Isaac, butcher, bds. 505 Linn
Rupp Jacob, cab. mkr., 58 David
Rupp John P., clk., 126 W. 5th
Rupp Joseph, baker, bds. 680 Vine
Rupp Valentine, 58 Stark
Ruppel John, dray, 164 Clay
RUPPELT HERMAN, Music, Book and Job Printer, 30 W. Court
Ruppersberg Jacob, stone mason, bds. 701 Elm
Ruppert Geo., 691 Elm
Ruppert Michael, cooper. 20 Brighton
Ruppert Nicholas, w.s. Milk b. Vine and Calhoun
Ruppett Joseph, confec., 242½ Vine, h. e s. Broadway b. 5th and 6th
Ruppiler Adolf, 491 Race
Ruppiler Fedor, jeweler, 467 Sycamore

282 (RUT)   CINCINNATI   (RYA)   DIRECTORY.   (SAA)

Rupprecht Lorenz, meats, 15 Ham. Road
Rupprecht Margaret, servt., 500 W, 7th
Rupprecht Margaret B , 15 Ham. Road
Rupprecht Mrs. Mary, teacher, e.s. Coggswell al. b. Franklin and Woodward
Ruroede John, tailor. 50 W. Mulberry
Rusche Mrs. Bella, tailoress 91 Clay
Rusche Benjamin, trunk mkr., 25 Abigail
Rusche Bernard, painter, 108 Baum
Rusche Frank H., grocery, 366 Broadway
Rusche Frederick. sawyer, 25 Abigail
RUSCIIE JOHN H., Staple and Fancy Dry Goods, Store 639 Vine
Rusche Joseph, tailor, 42 W. Front
Rusche Lewis, peddler, 77 W. Front
Rusche Vincent, carp., 77 W. Front
Ruschkupt Louisa, servt., 23 Ellen
Ruschorde Gerhard G., lab., 20 Abigail
Ruschutte Geo., porter, 81 W. 2d
Ruse Hy., lock mkr., wks. n e.c. Walnut and Canal
Ruse Hy., tailor, 63 W. 2d
Rush Jas , painter, 146 Linn
Rusk Jas., turner, 507 W. 3d
Rusk Wm. W., salesman 184 W. 5th, res Walnut Hills
Ruskaup Barney, mason, 160 Peete
Ruskaup Wm., carp., wks. 13 Rittenhouse
Ruskenbeck Frank, carp., e.s. Hand al. b. Court and Clark
Russ Gotthart, brewer, bds. 426 Vine
Russ Mungo, driver, 8 E. 8th e. of Lock
Russcamp Hy., stone cutter, bds. 622 Race
Russel Jas., blksmith, 53 Freeman
Russel Mary, bds. 170 W. 5th
Russel Miss P., 195 Vine
Russell Mrs., 218 John
Russell Alfred R., salesman, 163 Oliver
Russell Anna E., dress mkr., bds. 84 Hopkins
Russell Anthony O., 114 Mill
Russell Bridget, s.s. 6th e. of Lock
Russell Catharine, h. 431 George
Russell Catharine, 218 John
Russell Eliza, 47 Plum
Russell Hy., tailor, 218 John
Russell Isaac W., b.k. at S. A. Sargent's, bds. 46 Clinton
Russell James. carp., w.s. Central Av. b. 2d and W. W. Canal
Russell Jennie. bds. 128 Laurel
Russell Lutellus L., tinner, h. 187 W. Court w. of Central Av.
Russell Mary, rear 14 Richmond
Russell Mary, e.s. Carl b. 3d and 4th and Mill and Stone
Russell Michael, lab., 16 Hannibal
Russell Richard G., (H. Gibbs & Co.) 212 Plum
Russell Robert, foreman, 170 E. 3d e. of Collard
Russell Wm., blksmith, 598 Freeman
Russell Wm., horse shoeing shop, 695 Central Av
Rust A. M., b.k.. bds. 371 W. 9th
Rust D., mer., bds. 371 W. 9th w. of Central Av.
Rust Frederick. shoe mkr . 586 Race
Rust Herman, bakery, 145 Bremen, h. 35 Elder
Rust Rev. Herman, 10 15th b. Elm and Plum
Rust Justina, 467 Vine
Rust Lawrence, tinner, 467 Vine
Rust Lorenz, tin smith, 467 Vine
Rust Paul, chair mkr., wks. John Mitchell's
Rutburg Hiram. molder, wks. n.e.c. Canal and Walnut
Ruteniek Albert, drug store, &c., a.w.c. Bremen and Liberty
Ruter Geo., carp., rear 92 Dudley
Ruter Robert. tailor, 60 14th
Ruthemeyer Gerhard, grocery, 152 Linn
Ruthenburg Simon, tanner, 83 Spring
Ruthenburg Solomon, currier, 83 Spring
Rutherford Daniel E., salesman s.w.c. 3d and Vine, h. n.e.c. Scott and 8th, Covington
Rutherford Jas., lab., 84 W. 2d

Rutherford John, mach., 212 W. Front
Rutherman Wm., 735 Vine
Rutherman Wm., porter, wks. 190 W. 6th
Rutherman Mrs. M., H.. 757 Vine
Ruthman Gerhard, blksmith, 705 Race
Ruthmann Hy., blksmith, 462 Elm
Ruthmann Hy., carriage mkr., 462 Elm
Ruthmeier Herman, 163 Linn
Ruths Peter. blksmith, wks. n.e.c. Walnut and Canal
Ruths Philip, blksmith, 646 Vine
Ruthven John, brass foundry, 216 W. 2d, h. 13 Home
Rutlage Wm., lab., 60 Water
Rutlidge Jane, seamstress, 520 W. 7th
Ruttele Blaus. gardener, s.s. Bank b. Freeman and Coleman
Rutter Hy . locksmith, 17 Richmond
Rutter John H., printer, 28 W. 4th, bds. Walnut St House
Ruttinger Geo. C., prof. of music, 364 W. 5th
Ruttinger Valentine, cof. b., 711 Central Av.
Ruttinghouse Joseph, clk., 87 Spring
RUTZ JACOB. Band and Paper Box Manufacturer, n.w c. Main and Court
Rutz Susanna n.w.c. Court and Main
Ruve Frank, lab., n.e.c. Hunt and Broadway
Ruwe Casper, stone mason, 57 Hughes
Ruwe Hermann, driver. s.s. Abigail b. Main and Sycamore
Ruwe Joseph. boots and shoes, s.e.c. Elm and Longworth
Ruwe Joseph. cof. h., 292 Broadway
Ruyustaoul John, deck han l, 115 Carr
Ruzicka Joseph J.. clk 98 W. Pearl, h. s.w.c. 12th and Vine
Ryal W., bds. Dennison House
Ryall Thos , currier, wks. 215 Main
Ryan Ann, servt., Burnet House
Ryan Anna, bds. 134 W. Pearl
Ryan Anna, servt., n.e.c. 3d and Lawrence
Ryan Anna, bds. 138 Longworth
Ryan Bridget, 26 Kossuth
Ryan Bridget, servt., 403 W. 7th
Ryan Bridget, e.s. M. Canal b. 8th and Court
Ryan Catharine, 4 Elm
Ryan Catharine, 37 Chestnut
Ryan Catharine, 118 Butler
Ryan Catharine, 121 Lock
Ryan Conrad, dray, wks. 18 Water
Ryan Cornelius, dray, n.s. Augusta b. John and Smith
Ryan Dennis, lab., wks. 46 E. 3d
Ryan Dennis, lab., e.s. Ludlow b. Pearl and 3d
Ryan Dennis, lab., s.s. 6th b. Broadway and Culvert
Ryan Edward. wks. w.s. Brighton near Benckenstein's garden
Ryan Edward, lab., 33 Lock n. of 8th
Ryan Edward, lab., 213 E. 3d
Ryan Edward, packer, 202 W. Court w. of Central Av.
Ryan Elizabeth. pinking and stamping, 445 Central Av., bds. 75 Laurel
Ryan Elizabeth, 20 Stone
Ryan Ellen, al b. Central Av. and John and Augusta and Front
Ryan Ellen, servt., Spencer House
Ryan Hugh, porter, Burnet House, 224 E. 6th
Ryan Jas., s.s. 2d b. Rose and Mill
Ryan Jas., tailor, 53 E. 8th
Ryan Jefferson, lab., w.s. Kilgour b. 3d and 4th
Ryan Jeremiah, harness mkr., e.s. M. Canal b. 8th and Court
Ryan Johanna, al. b. 4th and 5th and Central Av. and John
Ryan John, bds. 207 Webb
Ryan John, blksmith, wks. n.e.c. Canal and Walnut
Ryan John, blksmith, wks. 222 E. Front
Ryan John, cof. h., 296 E. 6th
Ryan John, cof. h., 283 Central Av.
Ryan John, cooper, e.s. North b New and 7th
Ryan John, dray, 407 Race
Ryan John, driver, 213 E. 3d
Ryan John, fireman, Pike's Opera House

Ryan John, grocery and cof. h., s.e.c. Ludlow and 3d
Ryan John, lab., 614 W. 6th
Ryan John, lab., 168 Freeman
Ryan John, lab., s.e.c. 6th and Baum
Ryan John, lab., s.e.c. 5th and Butler
RYAN John B., (John B. R. & Co.) 221 Broadway
RYAN JOHN B. & CO. Proprietors and Manufacturers, of Dodge's Patent Grates and Stoves, 17 W. 5th Foundry 43 E. 7th
Ryan John J., clk., s.e.c. Ludlow and Arch
Ryan John W., lab., n.e.c. 3d and Stone
Ryan Joseph, bds. 20 Stone
Ryan Joseph, lab., Gas works
Ryan Julia. servt. Burnet House
Ryan Kate, dress mkr., bds 218 E. 6th
Ryan Mrs. Margaret, w.s M. Canal b. 6th and 8th
Ryan Margaret, 169 Sycamore
Ryan Margaret, h. 163 E. 3d
Ryan Martin, (R. & Wasteney.) 253 W. Court
Ryan Mary, servt., 378 W. 6th
Ryan Mary B., 459 Sycamore
Ryan Matthew, lab., 86 Hughes
Ryan Michael, carp , 48 Barr
Ryan Michael, clk., s.e.c. Ludlow and 3d
Ryan Michael, grocery, 585 W. 6th
Ryan Michael, lab., n.s E. Front e. of Leatherbury
Ryan Michael, lab., 591 W. 6th
Ryan Michael, lab., 716 E. Front
Ryan Michael, lab., n.w.c. Longworth and Smith
Ryan Michael, varnisher, wks. 165 Central Av
Ryan Michael, lab., w.s. Ludlow b. 3d and 4th
Ryan Nicholas, waiter, Spencer House
Ryan P. C., 28 E. 2d, h 127 W. 7th
Ryan Patrick, 121 Lock
Ryan Pat., dray, wks. 577 W. 6th
Ryan Patrick, lab., 261 John
Ryan Patrick, s.s. Avery al. w. of Wood
Ryan Patrick, lab , 46 E. 8th e. of Lock
Ryan Patrick. mer., 127 W. 7th
Ryan Patrick, steward. s.s. Pleasant Court e. of Elm
Ryan Peter, bk. layer, 172 Hopkins
Ryan Philip, lab, 12 Park
Ryan Rich., lab., Burnet House
Ryan Rich., porter, 248 W. 3d
Ryan Sarah, chambermaid Burnet House
Ryan Stephen, lab., 469 George
Ryan Thos., finisher, bds. 61 Butler
Ryan Thos., fireman, 247 W. Front
Ryan Thos., lab., n.s Augusta b. John and Smith
Ryan Thos., lab., 153 Cutter
Ryan Thos., lab., 60 E. 5th
Ryan Thos., lab., 61 Butler
Ryan Thos., policeman. 386 W. Liberty
Ryan Thos., saloon. 45 E 6th
Ryan Thos. H., n.s. Cherry al. Plum and Central Av
Ryan Timothy, baker, 708 Vine
Ryan & Wasteney, (Martin R. & John W.) horse shoeing, 253 W. Court
Ryan Wm., lab., n.s. 8th b. M. Canal and Lock
Ryan Wm., lab., 61 Mill
Ryan Wm F., upholsterer, 247 W. Front
Ryan Wm. J., rope mkr., bds., 20 Stone
Ryan Winne, servt., Burnet House
Ryans James, N. grocer, 45 Wood
Rybold Stephen, plasterer, 228 Findlay
Rybold Stephen J.. clk. 228 Findlay
Ryder Letitia, teacher, 15 George
Ryland Anne. h 324 W. 4th
Ryling John. upholsterer and awning mkr., 22 E. 8th
RYMAN GIDEON E. Proprietor Indiana House 159 W 5th
Rymert Chas., molder, 76 Bremen
Rynd Betsey, servt., 445 W. 7th

S

Saal Godfrey, baker, 28 W. 5th

(ST.X)　　CINCINNATI　(SAN)　DIRECTORY.　(SAN)　283

Saas Felix, cof. h., s.w.c. Liberty and Race
Sabath Hy., lab. 74 Rittenhouse
Sabbert John Hy.. eng., 72 Rittenhouse
Sabin Abbv, 431 Broadway
Sabrine Chas. bakery 173 W. Court
Sachs Augustus, peddlar. 213 Elm
Sachs Caspar, carp., 231 Bremen
Sachs Chas. D., saddler, bds. 674 W. 6th
Sachs Hy., finisher, e.s. Johnson al. b. Canal and 12th
Sachmuller Joseph, 117 Browne
Sack Hy , porter, E. Pearl b. Pike and Butler
Sack Jacob, varnisher, s.s. Woodward b. Sycamore and Broadway
Sackett Augustus N., salesman, 101 W. Pearl, h. 79 Laurel
Sackett Geo. painter, bds. 786 E. Front
Sackett Geo. H., (Gault & S.) 786 E. Front
Sackett Mary E., teacher, Wesleyan Female College
Sackett Wm. A., salesman, 98 W. Pearl. h. 79 Laurel
Sackhoff Hy., tailor, 20 Hughes
Sackhoff Hy. F., tailor, 674 Race
Sacksteder John, sewing machine manuf n.w.c. Laurel and Central Av. h 501 Plum
Sacs Casper, box mkr. 233 Bremen
SADD GEO. F, Banker, 30 W. 3d, Masonic Temple, Residence Covington
Saddelfelt John H., 106 Clay
Sadelfeld Fred., driver. 75 12th
Sieler Krezer, lab., 52 Mohawk [Av
Selmeyer Hy., shoe mkr., 604 Central
Saendker Joseph, blksmith, s.e.c. Green and Pleasant
Saenger Anthony, carp., 107 W Liberty
Saenger Barnh., 107 W. Liberty
Safdi Leon, confec., 91 Sycamore
Saffin James Judge, police court, office City Bldgs. h. 415 W. 8th
Saffin Wilson, clk. Co. Treas. office, bds. Burtemiller's Hotel
Sage Hy. W., v3 W. 4th. h. 44" W. 9th
Sage Marshal W., collector Cin. Gazette b. n. Fairmount
Sage Orrin N. jr., b.k. 47 W. Pearl, bds. 61 Longworth
Sazer Joseph. 99 Providence
Sizers Geo., lab., 162 Freeman
Sahlmaer Fred., varnisher, 179 Everett
Sahlmeaer Mary, servt., 295 Richmond
Saile Geo., lab., 650 Vine
Sain bury Wm., b.k. B. D. George & Co s h. 7E. 3d
St. Aloysius German Orphan Asylum, 264 W. 3d
ST. CHARLES EXCHANGE, Geo Selves, Proprietor 30 and 32 B 3d
ST. CLAIR H., (Jno. A. Clark & Co.), 420½ George
St. Clair Isaac, teamster, 298 W. Front
St. Clair Convent, sisters of the poor of St. Francis, n w.c. 3d and Lytle
St. Denny Charlotte, 3 al. b. 4th and 5th and Park and Mill
St. Francis school, e. s. Vine b. Liberty and Huber
St. Helen Edward, painter, w s. Goose al b. 14th and 15th
ST. JOHN'S HOSPITAL, n w.c. Plum and 3d. Sister Anthony, Matron
St. Mary's Hospital, n.s Betts b. Linn and Baymiller
ST. NICHOLAS RESTAURANT, Roth & Mosser, Propr's n.w.c. Vine and Longworth
St. Patrick School, n.s. 3d b. Park and Mill
St. Paulus school, e.s. Spring b. Abigail and Hunt
St Peter's Academy, Sister Gertrude superior. n.s. George b. John and Smith
ST. XAVIER COLLEGE AND Church, w.s. Sycamore b. 6th and 7th
St. Xavier Free School Rev. Francis Acmal director, w.s. Sycamore b. 7th and 8th

Sakreide Hy., F., tailor, rear 63 David
Salamons B., fruits &c., 195 Elm
Salender Wm. varnisher, wks. n w.c. Smith and Front
Salesbury Nathaniel, molder, n.s McDowell e. of Hill
Salfdi Leon, confec. 91 Sycamore
Salisbury Maria L., teacher, 409 W. 5th
Sallada Sebastian, collar mkr., bds. 141 Sycamore
Salloushin Davis, hats and caps. 182 George
Salpius August, druggist 440 Walnut
Salter August, rope mkr., 29 Grant
Salter, Elizabeth P , dry goods 263 Main
Salzer John, tailor. 100 Abigail
Salzmann Anthony, shoe mkr., 102 Bremen
Sam Theresa, seamstress. h 470 Race
Samburg, Geo., lab., 70 Lock
Samelson David b.k. 65 West Pearl, h. 391 Walnut
Sample James, eng., 55 Pierson
Sampson Emma J., teacher, 569 W. 9th
Sampson Frank., salesman, n.w.c. Pearl and Walnut, h. 276 Barr
Sampson Geo. b.k. bds. 236 Barr
Sampson Hy. W , baker, 419 W. 5th
Sampson John, teamster, 209 W. 4th
Sampson John P., porter, Adams Express Co
Sampson Julia M., 167 Poplar
Sampson Wm. S., 119 W. 8th
Sampson Wm. S., jr., b.k. 57 Main,h. 119 W. 8th
Samuels & Holzman, (Jacob J. S. & Joseph H,) clothiers, 18 W. Pearl
Samuels & Jacob, (Moses S. & Hy. H. J.) Lyon's Catawba brandy, 45 E 2d
Samuel Jacob J, (S. & Holzman), 16 E. 5th [W. 5th
Samuels Joel, (S. Samuels and Co), 559
Samuels Moses, (S. & Jacob). 55 Longworth
Samuels S. & Co. (Saml. S. & Joel Samuels) liquor store, 559 W. 5th
Samuels Saul.. (S. S. & Co.) 550 W. 5th
Saad Adolphus, (Burgert S. & Co.) bds. s.w.c. Dudley and Liberty
Sand Barney, dray, 53 Plum
Sand Barney, lab., wks. Hy. Nye's
Sand George, lab., 150 Baymiller
Sand Geo., lab., 187 Webb
Sand Hy., 135 Abigail
Sand Hermann J., lab , 11 Abigail
Sand John H., clk., 273 Main, bds. 13 Mansfield
Sand John, refreshments, C. H. & D. R. R. depot, h. 496 W. 4th
Sand Joseph, porter. 53 Mill
Sand Lewis D., farmer, 193 Vine
Sand Wm., carp., 13 Mansfield
Sandau Christ, blk. smith, 17 E. 7th, h. 14 Grant
Sandau Christian, cistern bldr., 470 Freeman
Santee Hy. H., molder, wks. n.e.c. Walnut and Canal
Sandell Edward, grocery, s,w.c. Elm and 12th
Sandel Jacob, clk, 10 W. 5th, res. Newport
Sander August, druggist, n.s. Front w. of Hill
Sander B & H. Obermeyer, (Benj. S. & Henry O ,) cigars, &c., 203 Elm
Sander Ben., (B. S. & H. Obermeyer), 36 Elm
Sander Casper, 604 Race
Sander Charlotte, servt., 522 Main
Sander Fred , lab., 611 Race
Sander Gottleib, blk. smith, 320 E Pearl
Sander Harmon, clk., s.e.c. Sycamore & Webster
Sander Hy., porter. 62 E. Pearl
Sander Hy., tailor, wks. 353 Main
Sander Herman, clk., s.w.c. Poplar and Freeman
Sander Joseph, carriage smith, bds. 68 Abigail
Sander Wm., lab., 522 Main
Sanderlin Holland steward, n.s Adams b. Plum and Elm
Sanderlin Kinrick, steward, 76 Pleasant
Sanderman J. Hy., molder, 95 Pendleton

Sanders Albert, conductor, s.w.c. 7th and Baymiller
Sanders Alex., tobacconist, 18 L'Hommedieu al.
Sanders Amelia, servt., 17 Arch
Sanders Andrew, shoe mkr., bds. 773 Vine
Sanders Anna, 76 W. 3d
Sanders Chas., peddler, w.s. Langdon al. b. 6th and 7th
Sanders David A., asst. commissary, 418 Broadway
Sanders Elizabeth, 227 George
Sanders Geo., 65 Kossuth
Sanders George, shoe mkr., bds. 773 Vine
Sanders Jas., printer, 93 Longworth
Sanders John, tailor, s.e.c. 8th and Walnut
Sanders John H., cooper, 361 Broadway
Sanders Joseph, blk. smith, bds. s.w.c. Abigail and Broadway
Sanders Joshua dray, 20 Stone
Sanders Lucy, dry goods, s.e.c. Liberty and Sycamore, h. 418 Broadway
Sanders Martha, bds. 14 Gest
Sanders Wm., driver, w.s Lebanon Road b. Liberty and Corp. Line
Sanders Wm. I., clk., 301 W. 5th, h. 227 George
Sanderson Geo., cof. h., 380 Central Av.
Sanderson Gen., printer, n e c. Central Av. and Court
Sanderson Jas., harness mkr., bds. 313 Walnut
Sanderson St. Clair, printer, 331 W. 6th
Sanderson Wm., harness mkr., 313 Walnut
Sandihus Louis, cof. h., 72 E. Front
Sandbeger Christopher, wines and liquors, 25 W. Court
Sandker Hy., shoe mkr. bds. 101 York
Sandle Benjamin, molder. wks. n.e.c. Walnut and Canal
Sandle Sml. H , molder, wks. n.e.c. Walnut and Canal
Sandmann Frederick. porter, 50 Walnut
SANDMAN J. Hy., (S. & Lackman,) h. 365 W 6th
SANDMAN & LACKMAN, (J. Henry S. & Herman L.,) Brewery, 443 and 445 W. 6th
Sandman Lonis, clk., n.w.c. Richmond and Mound
Sandmann Hy., brewer, 365 W. 6th
Sandmann Hy., cooper, 691 Race
Sandmann Joseph, cigar manufac., 218 W. Front
Sands Alex. C., U. S. Marshal Southern dist. of Ohio. Office Custom House, bds. 162 Broadway
SANDS GEO. F., Principal, 14th District School, Residence. 175 York
Sands John, lab., wks. 10 E. Canal
Sands John, lab. 90 Freeman
Sands Joseph, porter, 53 Mill
Sands Saml. B., carp., 175 York
SANDS THOMAS, National Saloon. National Theater Building, e. s. Sycamore b. 3d and 4th
Sandtmann Fred., tailor, 257 Main
Saner Christopher, wagon manufac., 763 Central Av.
SANFORD Benjamin F.. (S. & Bush,) res Latonia Springs Ky ,
SANFORD & BUSH, (Benj. F. S. & Wm. S B., Editors of the Ohio Valley Farmer, 22 W 4th
Sanford Wm. M., teller at Culbertson, Kilgour & Co's., h. 134 York
Sanfelt Harmon, lab., e.s. Campbell al. b. Elder and Liberty
Sanftleben Hy., lock smith, 513 Sycamore
Sanger Andy, carp., 107 W. Liberty
Sanger Florence, cab. mkr., 181 Hopkins
Sanger John. 146 Findlay
Sanger Joseph E. bleacher and presser, 175 W. 4th
Sanger Wm., cigar mkr., 194 Pleasant
Saning Albert, lab., bds. 9 Woodward

Sankey Thos., wood and willow ware, 4 W. 5th, res. 73 Mulberry
Sanning John H., carp. and builder, 505 Plum
Sanconbaugher Christian, 417 Freeman
Sansconbaugher Eve, 540 Elm
Santer Jacob, cof h., 19 Martin
Sauters Hy., waiter, n.w.c. Vine and Longworth
Santmyer Joseph P., b.k., 353 Clark
Sappington Matilda, bds. 120 John
Sarcanowski Harmon, n.s. 8th b. Broadway and Sycamore
Sard Albert, blk. smith, s s. Sloo e. of Harriet
Sardink Hermann, shoe mkr., 19 Green
Sargeant Dolly, bds. 19 Accommodation
Sargent Col. Chas. H., bds. Broadway Hotel
Sarcamp Fred., driver, 81 Findlay
Sargent Daniel B., bds. s s. 3d b. Canal and Kilgour
SARGENT Edward, (W. B. Smith & Co.,) 115 W 8th [berry
Sargent Edwin. shoe mkr., rear 12 Mulberry
Sargent Francis, engraver, Carlisle Building, h. Newport
Sargent Geo. C., stable, 11 Sargent
Sargent Josephine. servt , 1 4 W. 3d
SARGENT LEMUEL H., Grocer and Commission Merchant, Produce Dealer, and Agent for Mason City Salt Co., 31 Walnut, h. 285 W. Court w. of Central Av.
Sargent Margaret, s s. 3d b Ludlow and Lawrence
SARGENT SAMUEL A.. Real Estate Agent, 2 Apollo Building, n.w.c. 5th and Walnut, h. 46 Clinton
SARLE WM R., Foreman, 16 W. 4th, h. 285 Longworth
Sarles Jas. A., boots and shoes, s.w.c. Richmond and Mound
Sarline Richard, saddles. 447 Main
Sarran Felix, agt. 295 Main, h. S. W. 9th
Sarsfield Morris. tailor, 5½ E. 5th
Sarson Edward, dray, 331 John
Sarstedt Adolph carver, wks 13 Bremen res. W. Covington
Sarita! Mrs. Madalaine 99 York
Sarver John, bds. s.w.c. 5th and Broadway
Sarzedas David A., stage manager, h. 49 E. 3d
Sa-che J nnie, servt., 374 W 7th
Saslar John, turner, 46 Dunlap
Sass John, cab mkr., 49 15th
Sasse Frank, (Kinker & S.,) 55 Woodward
Satchell Wm. white washer, 92 Freeman
Satkamp Bernhardine, 604 Race
Satt Joseph, lab., 6 Pleasant
Sattler Ernst, millinery, 543 Main
Sattler Geo., phys., 495 Race
Sauder Jacob, boiler mkr., wks McIlvain Spiegel & Co's
Sauer Adam. meats, 593 Walnut
Sauer Conrad, boots and shoes, 598 Central Av.
Sauer Francis, shoe mkr., 273 Bremen
Sauer Frank, l.b., s.e.c Hopkins and Baymiller
Sauer Geo., shoe mkr., 158 Webb
Sauer Jacob, lab., 31 poplar
Sauer John, lithographer, n. w. c. Main and Court
Sauer John, shoe mkr., 169 Main
Sauer Martin, boots and shoes, 1017 Central Av.
Sauer Mary, 37 Green
Sauer W., cab. mkr., 325 W. 5th
Sauer Xavier, lab., 104 Ham. Road
Sauerbeck Geo., cof. h., 1166 E. Front
Sauerbrück Geo , grocery, 515 Plum
Sauerwein Conrad, tailor, 169 P easant
Sauers John, clk., n.e.c. 3d and Vine, h. Newport, Ky.,
Baumann Anthony. tailor, 163 Clay
Saun Frederick, cab. mkr.. 67 Mulberry
Saun Jacob, cab mkr., 67 Mulberry
Saunders Albert B., clk. 66 Walnut, h. 104 W 6th
Saunders & Baldwin, (Wm. A. S & Jas. H. B.,) painters, 217 W. 5th
Saunders David, harness mkr., 177 Sycamore

Saunders David, roller, 69 Park
Saunders David I., lab., 69 Park
Saunders Esco, finisher, 20 Pierson
Saunders John, costumer, Pike's Opera House
Saunders John H., cooper, 361 Broadway
SAUNDERS THOS. P. & CO., (Thos. P S. & Russell Potter.) Proprietors Burnet House, n.w.c. 3d and Vine
SAUNDERS Thos. P. (Thos. P. S & Co.,) Burnet House
Saunders Wm., barber, 146 E. 6th
Saunders Wm, whitewasher, 104 E. 6th
Saunders Wm. A., (Baldwin & S.,) 240 Clark
Saure Rev. Conrad, n.e.c. Franklin and Sycamore
Saurkamp Hy., driver, 83 Findlay
Saurs Saml., molder, bds. Bevis House
Sausser H. M., (A G. Wright & Co.,) h. Lebanon, Ohio
Sauter Jo eph, shoe mkr., 93 St. Clair
Savage Allen, 47 Pleasant
Savage F A., Secretary Great Western Coal and Oil Co. of Newark, Ohio, 13 W. 4th, h. Newark, Ohio
SAVAGE JOSEPH A., Machinist, 93 E. 8th, h. 352 George
Savage Nancy, 123 Mill
Savage Pamelia, teacher, 123 Mill
Savill Leonard, (Ham & S.,) 127 Hopkins
Saway Margaret. 291 Water
Saway Mary A., 291 Water
Saway Patrick. dray, 50 W. Front
Sawyer Almond, conductor, 91 Everett
Sawyer Augustus, b.k., bds. 141 Hopkins
Sawyer, J. A., b.k., 49 W. 2d, h. 334 Cutter
Sawyer Joseph A., currier. 119 Laurel
SAWYER & KIRK, (Milo S & Wilson J. K.,) Manufacturers and Dealers in Window Shades and Oil Cloths, &c.. 8 College bldg., e.s. Walnut b. 4th and 5th
Sawyer L. W , auctioneer, 154 Main, bds. Henrie House
Sawyer Margaret, 50 Hopkins
SAWYER Milo (S & Kirk,) 310 W. 8th
Sawyer Robert, salesman, s.e.c 4th and Vine [tillery
Sawyer S-, lab., wks Queen City Distillery
Saxe ——, saddler bds. 674 W. 6th
Saxes Otto, bds. Cincinnati House
Saxton John, huckster, s. w c. Longworth and Elm
Saxton Joseph C., broom manufacturer, 67 Longworth
Saxton Patrick, car inspector, bds. 99 Freeman
Saxton Sarah B., h. 97 Longworth
SAYLER MILTON, Superintendent Mt. Auburn Young Ladies' Institute. rooms n w c 4th and Race
SAYLER NELSON, Professor of Ancient Languages and Natural Sciience Mt. Auburn Young Ladies' Institute, rooms n. w. c. 4th and Rice
Saylor John, 47 York
Saylor Sebastian, mach., h. 47 York
Sayre Deborah, h. 314 9th. w. of Central Av
Sayre Hy. upholsterer, bds. 324 W. 9th w. of Central Av
Sayre John L., upholsterer, bds. 314 W. 9th. w. of Central Av
Sayre Joseph J., stamp cutter, bds 314 W. 9th, w. of Central Av
Sayre L. G , livery stable, 27 and 29 W. 9th, bds. Bevis House
SAYRE LEONARD, Auction and Commission Merchant, 231 Walnut, h. 349 Race
Sayre Samuel M., upholsterer, bds. 314 W. 9th w. of Central Av
Sayre W H., clk., s. w. c Front and Main, h. Walnut Hills
Sayre W. H., clk., s. w. c Front and Main, h. Walnut Hills
Scale Louis, cooper, 42 Jones
Scales Ellen, 43½ E. 3d
Scallan James, cutter, 53 W. 4th, bds. Dennison House

(SCH) CINCINNATI (SCH) DIRECTORY. (SCH) 285

SCHAEFFER JOHN ADAM, Brewery, 653 Main
Schaefer John G., peddler, 59 Buckeye
Schaefer John N., dray, 81 Melanchthon
Schaefer Louis, wagon mkr., bds. 104 Hunt
Schaefer M., servt, 442 Main
Schaefer Michael, lab., 56 Martin
Schaefer Michael, (S & Buschle,) 98 Liberty
Schaefer Philipp, expressman, 537 Vine
Schaefer Philipp, (G. F. & P. S.,) 503 Vine
Schaefer Thekla, bds. 512 Race
Schaefer Wm., cof. h., s. w. c. 6th and Plum
Schaefer Wm., lab., 25 Moore
Schaeffer Adam. 40 Dunlap
Schaeffer Andy, (S. & Co.,) h. 717 Freeman
Schaeffer & Co., (Andy S. & Wm. Ehlerding,) blksmiths, 1046 Central Av
Schaeffer Frank, w.s. Fountain, b. Rice and Alexander
Schaeffer Frederick, cooper, 149 Poplar
Schaeffer Hy., 41 Mulberry
Schaeffer Hy., s.w.c. Price and Clinton
Schaeffer Herman, lab., Pleasant b. Findlay and Henry
Schaeffer Jacob, provisions, &c., 682 Vine
Schaeffer Jacob, tanner, 691 Elm
Schaeffer John N., lab., wks. 728 Central Av
Schaeffer Peter. 961 Central Av
Schaeffer Gottlieb, 32 Dunlap
Schaer Joseph, barber, 136 Elm
Schaerf John, bk layer, 6 Findlay
Schaettle Joseph, baker, 695 Race
Schaeuffelen Lewis, tanner, s. s. Front e. of Ferry
Schaeven Joseph, cof. h., 46 Elder
Schafer Adam, tinner, 40 Dunlap
Schafer Albert, baker, bds. 144 Pleasant
Schafer Andrew, blksmith, 717 Freeman
Schafer Anthony, police, 67 Spring
Schafer Barbara, servt., 52 Sycamore
Schafer Bernard, mechanic, 57 Woodward
Schafer Edward, lab., 210 Mound
Schafer Jacques, tanner, 691 Elm
Schafer Ferdinand, (S & Wormann,) h. s.e.c. Liberty and Spring
Schafer George, cof. h., 30 Adams
Schafer Hy., lab, 164 Dayton
Schafer Hy. II., teamster, 52 Webster
Schafer Joseph, baker, bds. 144 Pleasant
Schafer Matthew, stone cutter, 267 Cutter
Schafer Michael, cnf b., 98 W. Liberty
Schafer Richard, barber, 4 E. 6th
Schafer Sophia, servt, 359 W. 7th
Schafer Theresa, 55 Rittenhouse
Schafer Wm., cab. mkr., 45 Kossuth
Schafer & Wormann, (Ferdinand S. & John B. W.,) livery stable, s. s. Gano b. Main and Walnut
Schaf Peter, lab, 26 Brighton
Schaffer Augustus, painter, 360 Central Avenue
Schaffer Benj., lab., wks. Henry Nye's
Schaffer Edward, lab., wks. 375 W. 3d
Schaffer Frederick, n.s. al. b. Pearl and 3d and Lawrence and Pike
Schaffer Hy., tailor, 413 Elm
Schaffer John, lab., h. 50 Observatory
Schaffer Louis cooper, 286 Linn
Schaffer Wm., lab., 45 Riddle
Schaffert Frederick, butcher, 148 Findlay
Schaffhauser Chas., cof. h., s. e c. Elm and Findlay
Schaffner Joseph, finisher, wks. s. w. c. Elm and Front
Schaffner Sophia, 273 Bremen
Schaffner Valentine, baker, bds. 273 Bremen
Schafstall Charles F., cigar mkr., 60 Mound
Schafstall Hy., lab., 79 Spring
Schag John, tinner, 217 Barr
Schaible Conrad, clk., 343 Vine
Schaible Philip shoemkr, 125 Bremen
Schaive John, clk., 145 Abigail
Schaler John, lab., wks. n.e.c. Walnut and Canal
Schaliter Joseph. blksmith, 65 Barr

Schaller Gustoff, 373 Cutter
SCHALLER H. SCHMIDT, Dentist, 333 Vine
SCHALLER JOSEPH, Eagle Brewery, s.e.c. Plum and Canal, h. Delhi Township
Schalley John. student, bds. 137 Race
Schallwitz Charles, bk. binder, 137 Baymiller
Schamerioh Hy., cof. h., n.s. Front e. of Kelly
Schampatist Bernhard, mason, 68 Green
Schana Antony, lab., 16 Commerce
Schandt ing John, rope mkr , 21 Providence
Schanor Mary, servt, 30 Findlay
Schanling Geo., barber, 674 Central Av
Schantz Michael cof. h., s.w.c. Coleman and Harrison Pike
Schanz George, wagon mkr., wks. 347 Broadway
Schaper Hy., shoemkr, w. s. Linn b. York and Dayton
Schapmann Hy., porter, 113 Avery
Schappi John,pleasure garden, 244 Ham. Road
Scharcer Leonhardt,cab.mkr. 19a Clinton
Scharden Geo., shoemkr, 21 Green
Schardt Fred, printer, 67 Bremen
Schardt Michael, locksmith, 443 Sycamore
Schrenhorst Hy , grocery, 543 Race
Scharer John, finisher, wks. n.e.c. Walnut and Canal
Scharges Chas. E., brewer, 632 Race
Scharinghaus Hy. cab. mkr, 47 Kossuth
Scharman Hy., cooper, 34 Webster
Scharman Mary. 31 Webster
Scharstein Hy., painter, n.s. Charlotte b. Linn and Baymiller
Scharstein John. painter, 170 Poplar
Scharta John, butcher, 788 Central Av
Schartwang Peter, tailor, 136 Pleasant
Schaser Michael, tailor, e.s. Oregon b. 3d and 6th
Schath Michael, cof. h., 510 Walnut
Schatz Martin, lab , 414 E. Front
Schatten George, shoemkr, 21 Green
Schatthouse Mary, s.s. al. b. Pike and Lawrence and Pearl and 3d
Schattinger Catharine, laundress, 146 Clay
Schattinger John, bk. layer. s.s. Bank b. Freeman and Coleman
Schatzman J., music plate engraver, 94 W. 4th
Schatsman Jacob, n.s. Front w. of Foster
Schatzmann Frederick, carp., 108 Martin
Schaub Conrad, carp , 233 Bremen
Schaub Hy., 35 Mulberry
Schaub John, carp , 249 Bremen, h. e.s. Goose al. b Green and Elder
Schauder Ulrich. shoemkr, 114 Clinton
Schaufert Hy., lab., 295 W. Liberty
Schaurer Elizabeth, 23 Buckeye
Schaurer Jacob, lab., 628 Vine
Schauter Michael. 121 Buckeye
Schaveny Louis, painter, 33 Dunlap
Schawb Hy., lab., 19 12th
Schawe Hy., grocery, 451 Plum
Schawe Herman, porter, 174 Abigail
Schawe John H., cigars, &c., 3 9 Main
Schawe Joseph, clk., 145 Abigail
Schawk Joseph, lab., e.s. Campbell al. b. Elder and Liberty
Schawtz David, 374 Elm
Schayrmann Frank, clk., 764 W Front
Scheur Thomas, tailor, bds, Cincinnati House
Scheurer Kate, servt , Galt House
Scheben Harney, n.s. Friendship al. b. Lawrence and Pike
Scheben Lorenz, b h., 57 E Pearl
Scheddinger Jacob, butcher, bds. e.s. Linn b. Wade and Liberty
SCHEER WM H., Hats and Caps, 143 Main, h. 173 W 4th
Scheffel Geo. C., grocery, 646 Vine
Scheffel Peter, basket mkr., 76 W. Mulberry
Scheim John J., grocery, 240 Pleasant
Schehr Elizabeth, seamstress, 119 Bremen
Schehr Jacob, lab., 119 Bremen

Schehr Peter, lab., 20 Hamer
Scheible Hy., clk., 142 W. 5th
Scheid Barbara, 179 W. Liberty
Scheid Chas.. carp., 17 Mary
Scheidler John, wagoner, 588 Elm
Scheidt Hy., shoemkr, 514 Walnut
Scheier Abraham, jewelry, n.e c. Race & 45th
Scheier Lorenz, huckster, 247 Ham. Road
Scheifele Wm., bakery, 1019 Central Av
Scheifele Wm., cook, 123 Ham. Road
Scheifers August, clk., 82 Sycamore
Scheifers Frank R., clk , 150 E. 5th
Scheiffer Wm., cook, Burnet House
Scheile Anthony, barber, 421 W. 6th
Schein Geo., cab. mkr., n.e.c. Smith and Water
Scheiner John, cooper, 56 W. Court
Scheinhof Hy., baker, rear 375 Broadway
Scheinhof John, organ bldr , w. s. Sycamore b. Schiller and Liberty, h 537 Sycamore
Schelaud Wm., driver, 109 Clark
Schelcher Edward, cook, 14 Bremen
Schele Behrt, printer, 601 Main
Scheleine Mathias, n.s. Rice head of Fountain
Scheleine Peter, tailor, n.s. Rice head of Fountain
Scheler Frederick, tailor, 279 Bremen
Scheiera Edwd., cook, Burnet House
Schelhorst Anthony, tailor, rear 400 B'dway
Schelzopf Christina, seamstress, 541 Main
Schell & Brinkman, (Jacob S. & Christ. B.) painters. w.s. Fillmore b. Richmond and Gest
Schell Hy, A., porter, n.s. Pearl b. Lawrence and Pike
Schell Jacob, (S. & Brinkman,) w.s. Fillmore b. Gest and Richmond
Schell Lewis J., city collector, 54 Hopkins
Schell Nicholas, brewer, bds 59 Harrison Pike
Schell Sebastian, cof. h., e.s. Logan b. Green and Elder
Schelle Anton, baker, 63 Clay
Schellenbaum John J., printer. 404 Elm nut
Schellenberger Joseph, bakery, 444 Walnut
Schelt David, hats and caps. 10 Home
Schelt Joseph, hats and caps. 10 Home
Schelter Frederick, hatter, 3 Mary
Schemann Theodore, (S. & Wirsing)res. Newport
Schemann & Wirsing (Theodore S & August W), lock smiths,53 Sycamore
Schembri Antonio, confec., 320 W. 5th, h. 102 York
Schemel Andrew, 262 Ham. Road
Schemer John, 41 Mansfield
Schemmell Leonhardt, cof. h., 264 Ham. Road
Scheu Brian, 14 Dunlap
Schenemann Mary, saleswoman, 172 Sycamore
Scheuleld Frank, eng., 381 Broadway
Schenk Adam, lab., 25 Hughes
Schenk Anthony, porter, 19 Abigail
Schenk Elizabeth, ., 6. Hopkins
Schenk Hertsen, carp., s s Logan b. Elder and Liberty
Schenk Wm., architect, bds. Teutonia Hotel
Schenke Bernard, shoemkr., s s. Hopkins b Cutter and Linn
Schenke Tony. porter. 19 Abigail
Schencel Paul, finisher, 114 Gest
Scheuring John, lab., wks. Hieatt & Wood's
Schep Hy., lab., 72 Hunt
Scheperslos Frederick, stone mason. 50 W. Mulberry
Scheppan John F., sawyer, 69 Bremen
Scheppmann Frederick,dray, 66 Findlay
Scherb Hy., terra cotta wkr., 156 W. Liberty
Scherberg Barney, pipe fitter, wks. n.e. c. Walnut and Canal
Scherberger Hy., walter. 29 W. 3d
Scherer Wm., tailor, e.s. Oregon b 3d and 6th

286 (SCH) CINCINNATI (SCH) DIRECTORY. (SCH)

Scheren Elizabeth, seamstress, 510 Plum
Scheren Maria, 510 Plum
Scherer Francis M., lab., 632 Race
Scherer Hy. W., upholsterer, 204 Pleasant
Scherer Jacob, grocery, 527 Race
Scherer John, cab. mkr., 115 Buckeye
Scherer John, lab., h 601 Vine
Scherer John A., grocery, 70 W. Liberty
Scherer Joseph, barber, 612 Elm
Scherer Joseph, lab, wks. Hieatt & Wood's
Scherer Joseph, painter, 66 Findlay
Scherer Joseph (Wentzel & S.) h. 65 W. 15th
Scherer Joseph, wagon mkr., w.s. Reading Road near Montgomery Pike
Scherer Josephine, wks. Hieatt & Wood's candle factory
Scherer Mary A., 661 Vine
Scherer Peter, grocery, 646 Central Av
Scherer Philip, barber, 10 E 3d
Schering Geo., lab., 94 Dudley
Scherle Anthony, lab., 102 E. 5th
Scherle Joseph, cab. mkr, 26 Madison
Scherlen Michael, cof. h., 70J Main
Scherley Anton, 6J Dunlap
Scherm Andrew, lab., 1 Wade b. Elm and Plum
Schermann George, cab mkr. n s. Liberty b Main and Sycamore
Schermann Hy., cooper, wks. 30 Webster
Scherinbeck Hy., lab., 517 Race
Scherp Hy., stone cutter, n e c. Liberty and Pleasant
Scherpf Peter, lab., 101 Bremen
Scherr Joseph, c b. mkr., 36 Madison
Scherr Peter, tailor, 594 Race
Scherrer Joseph, tailor, 98 W. Liberty
Scheryer Leonard, cab. mkr., 168 Clinton
Schetmer Jacob, tailor, 636 Main
Scheu Brian, 14 Dunlap
SCHEU George (Huber, S. & Liest), 90 Findlay
Scheuer Adam, cof. h., 845 Central Av
Scheuer Wm., dray, 64 13th
Scheutele John, bakery, 21 15th b. Elm and Plum
Scheufele Thomas, cab. mkr. 597 Walnut
Scheurmann Martin, driver, s.s. Friendship al. b. Pike and Butler
Scheve J. Hy., chair mkr., 320 George
Scheve John, (Heeke & S.,) n s. Ham. Road near Mohawk bridge
Scheve Joseph, grocery, 103 Clark
Schevene Philip, 463 Linn
Schevine Jacob, tanner, e. s. Branch b. Findlay and Ham Road
Scheven Ferdinand, cof. h., 22 E. Liberty
Schewene August, 69 Mohawk
Schewene John, 349 Ham Road
Schewene John J., painter, 593 Race
Scheuny Wm., bds. Cincinnati House
Schibley Nicholas, lab., s. s. Friendship al. b. Pike and Butler
Schicke Chas. G., music teacher, 536 Main
Schickling John, cab mkr. 663 Vine
Schidle Catharine, seamstress, 103 Abigail
Schidkamp Hy., lab., 312 Water
Schiefers August, clk. 70 E. Pearl, h. 82 Sycamore
Schlicht Franciska, huckster, 143 Clay
Schield Jacob, 126 W. 9th
Schielddecker Frederick, lab., n.w.c. Pearl and Kilgour
Schierg John, carp., s.w.c. 2d and Ludlow
Schierbarz Joseph, 25 Mill
Schierberg Joseph 1481 E. 5th
Schierholtz Adelhalt laundress, 473 Race
schierland Joachim J., tailor, 84 Bremen
Schierloh Hy., grocery, 552 W. 5th
Schierstein Chas., cigar mkr., 7 Jackson
Schiese Balzar, meat store, 920 Central Av.
Schiese Louis, butcher, bds. 920 Central Av.
Schiess Chas., grocery, 123 Ham. Road
Schiess Louis G., clk., P. O., 123 Ham. Road

Schieutz Fred pattern mkr. wks. n. e. c. Canal and Walnut
Schiewe Barney, carp., 213 Hopkins
Schifer Peter, driver, 212 Van Horn
Schiff Isaac, boots and shoes, 183 Vine
Schiff John, malt house, Colerain Pike n of Brighton House, h. Delhi Tp.
Schiffmacher Anthony, (F. Buschmann & Co.,) 648 Elm
Schildmeier John J., shoe mkr., 552 Walnut
Schilderink Hy., lab., 645 W. Front
Schiffmeier Jos., shoe mkr., rear 550 Walnut
Schilderink John, tailor, 26 Jackson
Schildknecht Jacob, boots and shoes 503 Elm
Schildmeyer Hy., fireman Front b. Vine and Walnut
Schildmayer Hurmon H., carp., 333 W. 6th
Schilter George, lab , 271 Freeman
Schiller Gustavus, cof. h., 679 Central Av.
Schiller Margaret, 58 Dudley
Schillerlag Hy., tailor, 20 Mercer
Schilli Wendelin, plasterer, 120 Ham. Road
Schilling Chas., printer, 3 Lucy
Schilling Dora, 326 Main
Schilling Frederick, shoe mkr., 12 Hughes
Schilling Joseph, b. k , n. w. c. Calhoun and Corporation Line
Schilling Ludwig, saddler, bds. 674 W. 6th
Schilling Mary, rear 94 Clay
Schillinger John, carp., 344 E. Front
Schillinger William, liquor inspector, 344 W. 6th
Schilmiller Frank, porter, s. s. Front b. Elm and Plum
Schilmiller Philander, porter, 169 W. Front
Schilowsky Paul, collar mkr., bds. Congress Exchange
Schimmel Clemens, cab. mkr., 661 Race
Schimmelpfenig John G., cooper, 598 Elm
Schimmer Francis, bksmith, 95 Ham. Road
Schimmoeler Hy., cooper, 052 Main
Schimpf Jacob. 62 Mohawk
SCHIMPF Louis, (Mueller & S.,) 12 Moore
Schimmer Francis, farrier, w. s. Ham. Road b. Findlay and Race
Schindeldecker Gottfried, lab. wks. Cincinnati Chemical Laboratory
Schindeldecker Hy. lab., Vine St. Hill
Schindler Hy., teamster, s.w.c. Freeman and Richmond
Schingle Philip, huckster, 104 Browne
Schingledecker Fred, baker, bds. 28 W. 5th
Schinick Michael, lab., 24 Lock n. of 8th
Schinner John, shoe store, 224 Linn
Schinner Michael, boots and shoes, 1460 E. Front
Schipper Herman, shoe mkr , 104 Pleasant
Schirmeister Wm., barber, 500 Vine
Schirmer Frederick, clk., bds. 61 W. Court
Schirufile Thomas, cab. mkr., 587 Walnut
Schiveggeman Barney, molder, wks. n. w.c Canal and Walnut
Schlamman Hy., bksmith. wks 109 Hunt
Schlafer Doretha, 49 Bremen
Schlafer Gotfried, cigar mkr., 49 Bremen
Schlafer John carp., 489 Walnut
Schlageter Jacob, carp., s.e.c. John and Front
Schlagerman August C., turner, 171 Webb
Schlebbe John T., tailor, 343 Main, h. 14 Jackson
Schleich Constantine, musician, n. s. al. b. Poplar and Vine and Ham. Road and Buckeye
Schlee Geo., tinner, wks. 30 W. 5th
Schlee Hy., cof. h., 137 Ham. Road
Schlelein Geo L, tailor 16 Ham. Road
Schlegelseker Jacob, cigar mkr., 32 Rittenhouse

Schlegel Edward, cooper, 29 Franklin
Schlel Michael, lab., 598 E. Front
Schleich Anthony, soap mkr., n e.c. Elm and Green
Schleich Gregory, lab., n. e. c. Linn and Findlay
Schleich Mary, grocery, n. s. Front b. Foster and Kelly
Schleicher Conrad, brewer, 60 Elder
Schleier Christian, carp., 180 W. Liberty
Schleiminger Joseph, mach., e. s. Ridgway al b Liberty and 15th
Schleiminger Lewis, lock smith, e. s. Ridgway al. b. Liberty and 15th
Schleiter Fred, lab. n.s. Channing b. Price and Young
Schleke Dietrich, sawyer, 5 Pleasant
Schleman Catharine w. s. Broadway b. Hunt and Abigail
Schlemm Christopher, turner, 171 W. 3d
Schlemmer Hy., tailor, 656 Vine
Schlemmer Hermann eng., 681 Vine
Schlenk Peter, lab 62 Dunlap
Schlenker Christina, servt., 493 Vine
Schlenker Jacob, baker, bds. 43 Pub. Landing
Schlenker John, barber, 99 Central Av.
Schlenker John, cof. h., 24 15th
Schlenker John, cooper, 19 14th
Schlenker John, cooper, 19 Bremen
Schlenker Thomas, turner, n.e.c. Linn and York
Schlenker Thomas, dray. 142 Clay
Schlenker Thomas, Jr., cigar mkr., 142 Clay
Schlermann Hy., bksmith, 114 Hunt
Schlermann Herman H., lab., 81 Spring
Schlesinger Annette, millinery, 161 Race
Schlesinger Bernhard, 161 Race
Schlesinger Leopold, peddler, 5 Mulberry
Schlesinger Samuel, tailor, 19 15th b. Elm and Plum
Schlett John, 23 Buckeye
Schlicht Joseph, driver, 100 W. Liberty
Schlicht Peter, teamster, 2 Hamer
Schlichter Christ, 73 E. Front
Schlick Francis, bk. binder, 61 Buckeye
Schlick Joseph, cigar mkr., 61 Buckeye
Schlick Margaret 61 Buckeye
Schlickman Hy., porter, 513 Sycamore
Schliffel John, grocery, 64 W. Mulberry
Schlitzberger, Hy , cutter, 337 W. 5th
Schlitzberger Hy., tailor, wks. 36 Elder
Schlochtermaer Birney, driver, s. e. c. Mound and Clark
Schloemer Hy., sawyer, bds. 24 Woodward
Schloemann Eugene, butcher, 504 John
Schloendorn Christian, fancy store, 492 Main
Schloendorn Wilhelmine, 117 Clay
Schlomer Bernhard J., shoe mkr., 671 W Front
Schloss Clements, shoe mkr., bds. 10 Sycamore
Schloss Jos. A., clk., bds. 16 Richmond
Schloss Joseph M., clothier, s. w. c. Pearl and Broadway, h. 201 Harrison
Schloss Lehman, clothing, 53 Longworth
Schlosser Francis. 108 13th
Schlosser Frederick, s. s. Stark b Canal and Dunlap
Schlosser Hy , painter, 9 Moore
Schlothman Gerhard, carp., n. s. Liberty near Baymiller
Schlotman Hy., venitian blinds, 55 Milton
Schlotterbeck John, stone cutter, 135 Ham. Road
Schlottman Wm., tailor, 30 Adams
Schlottmann Geo. H., carp., n.w.c. Liberty and Baymiller
Schlueter Chas., cab. mkr., 112 Bremen
Schlueter Francis H., lab , 594 Elm
Schlueters Eliza. bds. 11 Abigail
Schlumberger John, clk , 41 Moore
Schlund Radina, 113 Avery
Schluter Frederick, cab. mkr., W. B. Budd's & Co's.
Schluter Hy., team tar, n.s. Budd b. Harriet and Mill Creek
Schluter John brewer, s.s. W. W. Canal b. John and Smith
Schluter Peter, hostler, 51 W. 5th
Schluther Frederick, lab., 682 Main

(SCH) CINCINNATI (SCH) DIRECTORY. (SCH) 287

Schmaar Christina, servt., 378 George
Schmackers Anton, cab. mkr., 61 Laurel
Schmackers Hy., cab. mkr., 52 Laurel
Schmahl Herman, painter, wks. s. w. c. Elm and Front
Schmahle Joseph, blksmith, 588 Race
Schmalstig Charles, coppersmith, 56 13th
Schmidt Chas., carp., s.w.c. Laurel and Baymiller
Schmalzigang Frederick, butcher, 471 Vine
Schmalzigang Mathias, grocery 471 Vine
Schmand August, tailor, w.s. Harriet b. Bloo and Front
Schmare Andrew, lab., 18 Sargent
Schmars Hy., lab., 18 Commerce
Schmees Bernard, boots and shoes, n.s. Pearl b. Pike and Butler
Schmees Hermann, lab., bds. 19 Abigall
Schmees Hy., po ter, 18 Commerce
Schmeing Hy., lab., 161 Pleasant
Schmeiser Ernst, tailor, 533 Walnut
Schmoker Frederick, tailor, rear 12 Madison
Schmeltz Hy, butcher, e.s. Logan b. Greene and Elder
Schmeltzer John, cab. mkr., wks. n.s. Augusta b. Smith and Rose
Schmelz Franz, carp., 13 15th b. Elm and Plum
Schmelzer Chas., shoe mkr., wks. 624 Main
Schmelzpfennig Joseph, carp., 612 Race
Schmeiztel John, brewer, 299 Elm
Schmerling Reginia, candle mkr., wks. 728 Central Av.
Schmet John, chair mkr., 148 Laurel
Schmid Anna, h. 451 Sycamore
Schmid Conrad, lab., 170 Ham. Road
Schmid Christoph, bakery, 633 Elm
Schmid Geo, lab., s.s. Corporation al. b. Young and Wilson
Schmid Geo., tanner, 28 Canal
Schmid Gustav, millwright, wks. 825 Central Av
Schmid Hy., n.e.c. Liberty and Broadway
Schmid Hy., bakery, 57 Hopkins
Schmid Joseph, goldsmith, 60 13th
Schmidgall Frederick, clk., 642 Race
Schmidhorst Rudolph, bidayer, 503 Freeman
Schmidinghoff Joseph, finisher, 54 Jones
Schmidlin Ambrose malt kiln manuf., 29 Allison, h 28 Allison
Schmidt —, baker, 224 W. 6th
Schmidt Abraham, lab., n.s. Charlotte b. Linn and Baymiller
Schmidt Adam, 24 Charlotte
Schmidt Adam, lab., 67 Martin
Schmidt Adam, shoe mkr., s.e. Hubbard b. 5th and 6th
Schmidt Alice, tailoress, 24 Franklin
Schmidt Andreas, painter, 700 Race
Schmidt Anthony, baker, rear 554 Walnut
Schmidt Anthony, cutter, 471 Vine
Schmidt Anton, tailor, 164 Clark
Schmidt August barber, 21 Woodward
Schmidt August. finisher, 164 Pleasant
Schmidt August, harness mkr., 36 Elder
Schmidt Barbara, 69 Buckeye
Schmidt Barney, lab., 95 Woodward
Schmidt Benjamin, lab., 43 Race
Schmidt Bernard, clk. 95 Main, h. 543 Sycamore
Schmidt C. & W., (Chas. & Wm.) flour dealers, 361 Walnut
Schmidt Caroline, 68 Bank
Schmidt Catharine, 61 Hughes
Schmidt Catharine, seamstress, n.s. al. b. Poplar and Vine and Ham. Road and Buckeye
Schmidt Chas., (C & W. S.) 528 Main
Schmidt Chas., clk., bds. 137 Race
Schmidt Chas., cook, Galt House
Schmidt Chas., cooper, 19 Mercer
Schmidt Chas., druggist, 632 Main
Schmidt Chas., lab., bds. 14 E. Front
Schmidt Chas., pocket book mkr., 300 Findlay
Schmidt Chas., porter, 418 Walnut
Schmidt Chas, shoe mkr., 109 Ham. Road
Schmidt Capt. Charles D., asst. quartermaster U. S. A., office 101 E. 3d

Schmidt Chas. F., peddler. 63 Peete
Schmidt Chas. Hy., tinner, rear 31 Madison
Schmidt Chas. P., cof. h., 622 Vine
Schmidt Cornelius, finisher, rear, 556 Walnut
Schmidt Christian, cof. h., 1120 Central Av.
Schmidt Christian, grocer, 195 Freeman
Schmidt Christian, stone mason, 23 Hughes
Schmidt Christian, publisher, bds. Teutonia Hotel
Schmidt Christopher, mach., 658 Vine
Schmidt Eliza, servt., 371 W. 8th
Schmidt Elizabeth, 580 Main
Schmidt Ferdinand, cab. mkr., 13 Adams
Schmidt Ferdinand, confec., s.w.c. 6th and Race
Schmidt Ferdinand, phys., 439 Walnut
Schmidt Francis, fireman, 90 W. Court
Schmidt Francis, shoe mkr., 76 W. Court
Schmidt Frank 609 Main
Schmidt Frank, grocery, 207 Freeman
Schmidt Frederick, cooper, 470 Main
Schmidt Frederick, finisher, 62 Lock
Schmidt Fred., lab., 101 York
Schmidt F——ia.., Findlay b. Central Av. & John
Schmidt Frederick, sawyer, 42 Rittenhouse [lin
Schmidt Frederick; turner, rear 24 Frank-
Schmidt Fred. Wm., cutter, 113 Main
Schmidt Geo., blksmith, 65 W. Court
Schmidt Geo., brewer, 110 Ham. Road
Schmidt Geo., cab. mkr , 222 W. Front
Schmidt Geo. A. 112 Ham. Road
Schmidt Gottfried, baker, 420 Vine
Schmidt Gottlieb, 85 Ham. Road
Schmidt Gottlieb, pyrotechnist, 89 Ham. Road
Schmidt Gottlieb, tailor, s.s. Harrison Pike b. Riddle and Division
Schmidt Grace, laundress, 172 E. 5th
Schmidt Gustavus, finisher, 685 Race
Schmidt Hartmann, mach., 607 Race
Schmidt Rev. Heinrich, rear of church, e.s. Race b. 13th and 14th
Schmidt Hy., 138 Buckeye
Schmidt Hy., 43 Jones
Schmidt Hy., blksmith, bds. 628 Race
Schmidt Hy., boots and shoes, 29 Elder
Schmidt Hy., cab. mkr., 11 Adams
Schmidt Hy., clk., e.s. Walnut b. 12th and 13th
Schmidt Hy., finisher, wks. s.w.c. Elm and Front
Schmidt Hy., foreman, 418 Walnut
Schmidt Hy., furniture, 442 Walnut
Schmidt Hy , lab., n.s. Rice b. McGrew and Fountain
Schmidt Hy., lab., 8 E. Canal
Schmidt Hy., lab., 26 Mansfield
Schmidt Hy., pipe fitter, wks. n e.c. Walnut and Canal
Schmidt Hy., porter, 514 Race
Schmidt Hy , shoe mkr., 11 12th
Schmidt Hy., show case mkr., 577 Walnut
Schmidt Hy., wagon mkr., s.s. 6th b. Harriet and Horne
Schmidt Hy. F., tailor, 514 Race
Schmidt Herman, cooper, 692 Main
Schmidt Herman, tailor, 614 Central Av.
Schmidt Jacob, bds. Cincinnati House
Schmidt Jacob, clk., 84 Broadway
Schmidt Jacob, finisher, 652 E. Front
Schmidt Jacob, lab., 567 Sycamore
Schmidt Jacob, tinner, 145 Clay
Schmidt Jas., dray, bds. n.w.c. Pike and Pearl
Schmidt John, b. h., 86 W. Court
Schmidt John, blksmith, 639 Race
Schmidt John, brewer, s.s. Montgomery Pike near Reading Road
Schmidt John, finisher, 165 Buckeye
Schmidt John, tailor, 497 Walnut
Schmidt John B., blksmith, 52 Commerce
Schmidt John B., jr., porter, 543 Sycamore
Schmidt John C., lab., 658 Vine
Schmidt John G., shoe mkr., 108 Hunt
Schmidt John F., blksmith 619 Race
Schmidt John H.. carp., 89 Pendleton
Schmidt John H., shoe mkr., bds. n.w.c. Wade and Baymiller

Schmidt John Hy., stone breaker, rear 692 Main
Schmidt Joseph, s.s. Cross b. Hamburg and North Elm
Schmidt Joseph, meats, s.w.c. Linn and Clinton
Schmidt Joseph, shoe mkr., bds. 76 W. Court
Schmidt Joseph, wagon shop, 549 W. 8th, h. 523 W. 8th
Schmidt Lawrence, carp., 227 Betts
Schmidt Leonard, blksmith. 569 Main
Schmidt Lewis, cooper, 15 Mulberry
Schmidt Lina, teacher, 542 Sycamore
Schmidt Louis. bk. binder, 123 Liberty
Schmidt Louis, chair varnisher. 48 Jones
Schmidt Louis, cof. h., 767 Vine
Schmidt Ludwig, bk. binder, 123 W. Liberty
Schmidt Margaret, 652 E. Front
Schmidt Maria A., laundress 488 Walnut
Schmidt Martin. lab., 172 Baymiller
Schmidt Mary 1019 Central Av.
Schmidt Mary E., 8 E Canal
Schmidt Menna, 532 Main
Schmidt Michael, cooper, 67 Providence
Schmidt Michael, lab., s.e.c. Bank and Baymiller
Schmidt Nicholas, driver, bds. s.e.c. Pearl and Pike
Schmidt Peter, cigar mkr., 26 Allison
Schmidt Peter, hostler, wks. 578 Walnut
Schmidt Peter, tailor, 20 Mercer
Schmidt Philipp, lab., 365 Sycamore
Schmidt Philipp, printer, 75 Bremen
Schmidt Robert, baker, 613 Vine
Schmidt Sigmund, 507 Main
Schmidt Sophia, 53 Rittenhouse
Schmidt Wm., carriage painter, 778 Vine
Schmidt Wm., (C. & W. S.), 534 Main
Schmidt Wm., cooper, 67 Providence
Schmidt Wm., flour store, 532 Main
Schmidt Wm., foreman, 7 Pendleton
Schmidt Wm., grocery, s.e.c. Baymiller and Richmond
Schmidt Wm., lab., 368 Broadway
Schmidt Wm., meat store, 25 Bank
Schmpider Anthony, dray, 26 Jones
SCHMIDT-SCHALLER HENRY, Surgeon Dentist, 335 Vine
Schmied John G., lab., s.s. Dover al. b. Elm and Plum
Schmieder Adam, cab. mkr., 509 Vine
SCHMIEDT EDWARD, Cigars, Tobacco, Snuff, Pipes, &c., 34 E. Front
Schmiesing Frank, 164 Spring
Schmiesing Hendrick, carp , 213 Hopkins
Schmiesing Henry, stone cutter, bds. 628 Race
Schmiet Anthony, shoe mkr., 462 Elm
Schmieg John, shoe mkr., e.s. Bremen b. Elder and Findlay
Schmit Agatha, 14 Mary
Schmit Catharine, seamstress, 525 Sycamore
Schmit Christopher, baker, 202 Clark
Schmit Christopher, lab., 318 E Pearl
Schmit Fred , baker, 202 Clark
Schmit Henry, cigar mkr., 512 Main
Schmit Henry Jr., lab., 91 Pendleton
Schmit John, blksmith, 542 Main
Schmit John, lab., rear e.s. Plum b. Adams and Liberty
Schmit Tony, cigar mkr., 518 Main
Schmit Wm., lab., 23 Martin
Schmitterloew Adelaide, 572 Race
Schmitheimer Geo., baker, bds. 172 Sycamore
Schmitker Ernst, lab., 38 Hughes
Schmitt Abraham, box mkr., n.s. Charlotte b. Linn and Baymiller
Schmitt Adam, bk. binder, 35 Elder
Schmitt Anna, shirt mkr., 508 Walnut
Schmitt Anthony, bakery, 628 W. 6th
Schmitt Barbara, 564 Vine
SCHMITT & BRO (Wm. & Michael), Show Case Manufacturers, 66 Main
Schmitt Catharina, h. 126 W Liberty
Schmitt Catharine, 10 Buckeye
Schmitt Christian, wagon mkr., 56 Buckeye

288 (SCH) CINCINNATI (SCH) DIRECTORY. (SCH)

Schmitt Eliza, 197 Goose al. b. Liberty and Green
Schmitt Elizabeth, 761 Vine
Schmitt Frank, butcher, n.s. Browne w. of Ravine al.
Schmitt Frank, grocery, 141 Buckeye
Schmitt Frank policeman, 123 Pleasant
Schmitt Frederick, n.w.c Calhoun and Vine
Schmitt George, cof. h., 939 Central Av
Schmitt Geo., cooper, n s. Bank b. Central Av. and Clarkson, h. 937 Central Av
Schmitt Geo. M., barber, n.w.c. Main and Court
Schmitt Henry, barber, 625 Main
Schmitt Henry jr., cooper, 25 Brighton
Schmitt Henry J., cab. mkr., 18 Buckeye
Schmitt Jacob, boots and shoes, 64 13th
Schmitt Jacob, lab., e.s. Division b. Bank and Harrison Road
Schmitt Jacob H., barber, 621 Race
Schmitt John, cigar mkr , 508 Walnut
Schmitt John, cook, Clifton House
Schmitt John, cof h., 7 Mary
Schmitt John, teacher, 492 Main
Schmitt Joseph, cooper, rear 362 Ham. Road
Schmitt Julius, cook, Clifton House
Schmitt Margaret, 132 Bremen
Schmitt Mary. 73 E. Front
SCHMITT Michael, (S. & Bro.), res. New York
Schmitt Nicholaus, cof. h., 637 Race
Schmitt Nicholas. cof. h., 430 Vine
Schmitt Peter A., barber, 625 Main
Schmitt Philippina 197 Goose al. b. Liberty and Green
Schmitt Simon, mason, 42 Elder
Schmitt Valentine. 26 Allison
SCHMITT Wm., (S. & Bro.), e.s. Walnut b. 12th and 13th
Schmitter J. Henry, cooper, bds. 20 Buckeye
Schmitz Anthony, cigar mkr., 518 Main
Schmitz Bernhard, cigar mkr., 518 Main
Schmitz Charles, clk., 127 Main, h. 137 Race
Schmitz George, lab., 126 Main
Schmitz Henry. blksmith, 107 Clark
Schmitz Henry. varnisher, wks. Mitchell & Rammelsberg's
Schmitz Henry E., lab , 598 Elm
Schmitz Herman, finisher, 57 13th
Schmitz John H.. cigar mkr., 518 Main
Schmitz Margaret, 401 Sycamore
Schmitz Mary A , bds. 518 Main
Schmitzrider Chas., shoe mkr., 70 E. 3d E. of Whittaker
Schmock Rosa, 369½ W. 7th
Schmudde Wm. H., cooper, wks. 28 Sycamore
Schmutte Henry, cof. h., 117 E. 8th
Schnab Louis, peddler, 530 John
Schnaback Wm., lab., 16 Dudley
Schnabel Frederick, tailor, 109 Ham. Road
Schnabel Rudolph, painter, 143 Pleasant
Schnaham J. H., wks. n.e.c. Canal and Walnut
Schnautz Henry, pattern mkr., 78 Bremen
Schnapp Geo., safe mkr., 626 Race
Schnarb Peter, cooper, 692 Main
Schnarrenberger George, porter, 525 Sycamore
Schnear Anthony, finisher, 531 W. 8th
Schnebeck Henry, teamster, 23 Dudley
Schnebeck Wm., cab. mkr., 63 Dudley
Schnebecke Wm., stone sawyer, wks. John M. Mueller's
Schnebel Godfrey, shoe mkr., 267 Cutter
Schnecheim Henry J., finisher, 146 Bremen
Schneck Herman, cab. mkr., 61 15th
Schneckkburg Henry, cooper, bds s.e c. Brighton and Harrison Pike
Schneke Charles H., pattern mkr., Findlay b. Linn and John
Schnee Joseph, watch mkr., 683 Race
Schnee Norbert, lab , 99 Smith
Schneebeck Wm., 63 Dudley
Schneeberg D., tailor, n.s. al. b. Race and Ham. Road n. of Findlay
Schneeberger John, shoe mkr., 302 W. Liberty

Schneemann Wm., stone cutter, 63 Pleasant
Schneider Adam, porter, 473 Walnut
Schneider Andrew, chair mkr., 232 Linn
Schneider Andrew, stone mason, 49 Hughes
Schneider August, 53 Fountain
Schneider Baptist, 361 Ham. Road
Schneider Barbara, seamstress, 518 Plum
Schneider Blasius, 705 Race
Schneider Bonifacius, carp., 194 Bremen
Schneider Casper, cof. h., 673 W. 6th
Schneider Caspar. peddler, 618 Vine
Schneider Charles, bds. Olean Hotel
Schneider Chas., lab., 247 Ham Road
Schneider Chas.. lab., 1031 Central Av.
SCHNEIDER CHARLES A., Physician and Surgeon, Office and Residence 325 Vine
Schneider Christian J., shoe mkr., 300 W. 8th
Schneider Christopher, 267 Clinton
Schneider & Co., (Mrs. Eliza S. & Christopher Gobrecht,) grocers, s.s Harrison Pike b. Division and Brighton
Schneider Conrad, bk. m : , bds. 674 W. 6th
Schneider Daniel, 35 Ham. Road
Schneider David, butcher, rear 14 Allison
Schneider Dorsette, 97 Peete
Schneider Eliza, (S. & Co ,) s s. Harrison Pike b Division and Brighton
Schneider Elizabeth, 529 E. Front
Schneider Ferdinand, tailor, w.s. Bremen b. Elder and Findlay
Schneider Francis, 151 Everett
Schneider Francis A., lab., 18 Hamer
Schneider Frederick, 69 Mulberry
Schneider Frederick, ta. er, 311 Findlay
Schneider Fred., tailor, 39 Broadway
Schneider Frederick, stone yard, w.s. Sycamore b Woodward and Franklin, h. 441 Sycamore
Schneider Frederick, sawyer, 557 Elm
Schneider Fredericka, dry goods, 441 Sycamore
Schneider Gallus, brewer, wks. J. Kaufman & Co.'s
Schneider Geo., blksmith, n.e.c. Smith and Water
Schneider Geo., cof. h., 14 E. Front
Schneider Geo., confect. 434 Vine
Schneider Geo., harness mkr., 29 Hughes
Schneider Geo., lab., bds. s.w.c. Race and 2d
Schneider George, lab., 6 Miami
Schneider George, lab., 518 Plum
Schneider George A., clk., n.e.c. Smith and Water
Schneider Gustave, tailor, s.w.c. Gest and Harriet
Schneider Henry, 226 Linn
Schneider Henry, 28 Brighton
Schneider Henry, cof. h. 400 Sycamore
Schneider Henry, bakery, e.s. Vine b. Calhoun and Auburn
Schneider Henry, clk., 65 E. Pearl, bds. Cincinnati House
Schneider Henry, tailor, 29 Dunlap
Schneider Henry, tailor, 612 Sycamore
Schneider Henry, varnisher, 153 George
Schneider Henry H., chair mkr., bds. 51 Riddle
Schneider Herman, cof. h., 512 Elm
Schneider Hermann, porter, 116 Abigail
Schneider Ignatz, cof. h., n.s. Stark b. Mohawk Bridge and Dunlap
Schneider Mrs. J., 70 Peete
Schneider Jacob, n.s. Stark b. Dunlap and Mohawk Bridge
Schneider Jacob, blksmith., 987 Central Av
Schneider Jacob, broom mkr., 22 E. Liberty
Schneider Jacob, cigar mkr., 655 Vine
Schneider Jacob, cooper, 581 Walnut
Schneider Jacob, foreman Evans & Swift's, 12 Woodward
Schneider James, n.e.c Smith and Water
Schneider John, wks. w s. Brighton nr. Benckenstein's Garden
Schneider John, bakery, 452 Vine
Schneider John, carver, 60 Buckeye
Schneider John, cof. h., 1122 Central Av.

Schneider John, lab., e.s. Ridgway al. b. Liberty and 15th
Schneider John, plasterer, 2 Miami
Schneider John, (S. & Schaaf.) 11 Jones Road
Schneider John, shoe mkr., 164 Ham. Road
Schneider John B., jewelry, 43 Ham. Road
Schneider John M., tailor, 110 W. Liberty
Schneider John P., lab., e.s. Vine b. Milk and Mulberry
Schneider John Wm., grocery, 519 Sycamore
Schneider Jordan, lab., 50 Pleasant
Schneider Joseph, cutter, 494 Walnut
Schneider Julius, shoe mkr., 300 W. 8th
Schneider Lewis, baker, w.s. Ridgway al. b. 14th and 15th
Schneider Lewis, cof. h., 557 Walnut
Schneider Lorenz, cab. mkr., 47 Findlay
Schneider Louis, brewer, wks. s.e.c. Plum and Canal
Schneider Louis cab mkr., 47 Findlay
SCHNEIDER LOUIS, City Brewery, n.s. Augusta. b. John and Smith h. 177 Baymiller
Schneider Margaret. 108 Bremen
Schneider Martin, lab., 225 Cutter
Schneider Martin, mason, 477 W. 3d
Schneider Martin, mach., 225 Cutter
Schneider Mary, Ailanthus b. Bank and Clearwater
Schneider Mary, dairy, 2 Miami
Schneider Mary, 51 Riddle
Schneider Mary, seamstress. 2 Miami
Schneider Michael, clk., 667 Vine
Schneider Michael, molder, 278 W. Front
Schneider Michael, painter, 276 W. Front
Schneider Nicholas, mason, 112 Buckeye
Schneider Oswald, cab. mkr., 11 Jones
Schneider Peter, gardener, wks. n.w.c. Main and Liberty
Schneider Phillip, carp., s.e.c. Bank and Whiteman
Schneider Phillip, lab., 167 Sycamore
Schneider Phillip, lab., n.w.c. Abigail and Sycamore
Schneider & Schaaf, (John S. & Oswald S.,) chair factory, 11 Jones
Schneider Stephen, 584 Plum
Schneider Sophias, 12 Woodward
Schneider Sophronius, teacher, 592 Vine
Schneider Valentine, lab., 640 Elm
Schneider Wm., n.e.c Smith and Water
Schneider Wm., cooper, 700 Freeman
Schneiders Anton, tailor, bds. 365 W. 5th
Schneiker Mary, h. 304 Findlay
Schneiner Geo., 267 Ham. Road
Schnekke Charles, gardener, Garden of Eden
Schnell Frank, shoe mkr., s.s. 5th bet. Vine and Race
Schnell Joseph, painter, 66 Findlay
Schnelle Fred. H., shoe mkr., 72 Bremen
Schneller Andrew, 807 Vine
Schneller Lorenz, stone mason, e.s. Vine b. Mulberry and Milk
Schnetker Herman, lab., e.s. Anderson b. 2d and Pearl
Schnetker Wm., carp., 40 Rittenhouse
Schnetzer Fred , lab., 68 Hughes
Schneyder Joseph, cutter, 494 Walnut
Schnick Hy., shoe mkr., 61 15th
Schnick Geo., shoe mkr., 494 Elm
Schnicke Chas. A., porter, b. s.s. Findlay b. John and Linn
Schnier Chas , grocery, 14 Madison
Schnier Louis, grocery, &c., n.w.c. Richmond and Mound
Schnike Chas., piano teacher, 95 Findlay
Schnilliker Rudolph, s w.c. 4th and Walnut
SCHNITGER JOHN H., Family Grocery and Coffee House, s.e.c. 15th and Elm
Schnitker Wm., porter, 50 Webster
Schnitker Hy., carp., 238 Everett
Schnitker J. M., clk., 101 W. 4th, h. Covington
Schnorbus Adam, meat store, 329 W. 5th

(SCH) CINCINNATI (SCH) DIRECTORY. (SCH) 289

Schnoutz Hy., pattern mkr., wks. Crane, Breed & Co's
Schnucks Barney, ale bottler, 41 Race
Schnoabenland Valentine, shoe mkr., 62 W. Liberty
Schoats Wm., carp., 198 Hopkins
Scholarg Geo., lab., 161 Pleasant
Schobert Adam, bakery, 516 Vine
Schoch Louis, cab. mkr., wks. s.w.c. Canal and Elm
Schoch Ludwig, lab., 612 Elm
Schock Anton, wks. w.s. Brighton nr. Benckenstein's Garden
Schock Benedict, candle mkr., w.s. Thuber b. Wade and Liberty
Schock Daniel, n.w.c. Dunlap and Stark
SCHOCK FRED., Family Grocery and Provisions, n.s. Charlotte b. Linn and Baymiller
Schockliter Joseph, blk. smith, 65 Barr
Schockmin Geo., shoe mkr., 108 Avery
Schodel Hy., carp., s.s. Weller b. Harriet and Carr
Schodel Theo., turner. 247 Clark
Schoder Elizabeth, 104 Avery
Schodrowsky Fred., key mkr., h. 65 12th
Schoe Lena, 713 Central Av
Schoeder Hermann, stone sawyer, 45 Pleasant
Schoef Hy., porter, 194 Hopkins
Schoefenacker Geo., painter, 56 13th
Schoemacker Martin, wks. S W. 6th
Schoemer Nicholas, tailor, 576 Main
Schoen John, cab. mkr., 233 W. 6th
Schoen Susanna, milliner, 584 Walnut
Schoenbein Adolph, phys., 517 Elm
Schoenbein John, phys., 477 Elm
Schoenberg Alphonso, cof. h., s.e.c. Vine and Court
Schoenberger Joseph, porter, 553 Central Av. [5th
Schoenberger Margaretha, b. h., 160 W.
Schoenberger Michael, varnisher, w.s. Goose al. b. 14th and 15th
Schoenebaum John H., porter, 634 Main
Schoenefeld Lewis, lab., 28 Buckeye
Schoeneberger Lewis, paper carrier, h. 168 Pleasant
Schoenfeld Lotte, 427 Sycamore
Schoenheft Joseph, lab., 410 Broadway
Schoenlamb A., lab., wks. Chamberlain & Co's.
Schoenlaub Adam, lab., 62 Buckeye
Schoenling Valentine, lab., wks. Hieatt & Wood's
Schoenmacher Barney, shoe mkr., bds. n.w.c. Main and 9th
Schoepmann Fred., tinner, 55 15th
Schoepmann Wm., tinner, 55 15th
Schoeppner John, grocery, 594 Vine
Schoester John F., lab., 304 Water
Schoettner John H., express man, 568 Race
Schofield Edward, molder, 29 Observatory
Schofield Hugh, molder. n.e.c. Lawrence and Front, b. Newport
Schofield John, 333 John
Schuh John H., lab., 199 Pleasant
Schohl Wm., peddler, 629 Vine
Schoide Joseph, lab., 161 Pleasant
Scholes Wm. A., tinner, 239 Longworth
Scholhammer Lawrence, meats, 544 Central Av.
Scholl Cyprian, teacher, St. Francis School
Scholl Daniel, cooper, 277 Bremen
Scholl Mathias, cof. h., 109 Pleasant
Scholl Stephen, shoe mkr., 73 Green
Scholl Waldburger, bds. 29 Elder
Schollare Thos., lab., 69 Woodward
Scholle Hy., wks. s.s. 8th b. Broadway and Canal
Scholle Herman, cab. mkr., s.s. W. W. Canal b. Carr and Harriet
Scholuka Benedict, lab., 363 George
Schomaker Miss, teacher, 98 W. 14th
Schomaker Bernhard H., agt. 407 Main, h. 14 Abigail
Schomaker Geo. H., (G. H. S. & Co.,) 407 Main
Schomaker G. H. & Co., (Geo. H. S. & Mary Schomaker,) clothing, 407 Main
28

Schomaker Hy., carp., n.s. Railroad e. of Lewis
Schomakers Geo. W., tailor, 357 W. 5th
Schomackers Hy., shoe mkr., wks. 147 Sycamore
Schombart John, 700 Freeman
Schomberg Hy., lab., s.s. Montgomery Pike nr. Reading Road
Schomborg Fred., lithographer, 18 Gano
Schon Jacob, tailor, w.s. Goose al. b. Green and Elder
Schon Phillip, cof. h., 187 W. 6th
Schonebaum Bernard H. L., grocery, 413 John
Schoner Paul, boots and shoes, s.w.c. Bremen and Findlay
Schoufeldt Ludwick, lab., 28 Buckeye
Schonhoff Hy., baker, e.s. Broadway b. Abigail and Hunt
Schons Geo., wagon mkr., 102 Hunt
Schooey Louis, tanner, bds. s.e.c. 9th and Broadway
Schooley John, lab., bdd. 114 Hunt
Schooley John C., 375 W. 6th
Schooley Stephen, pork packer, 155 W. Court, h. 99 E. 4th
Schoolfield Stephen, chair mkr., 8 E. 4th
Schoonmaker Julia, 116 Findlay
Schoon naker Lloyd, 133 Barr
Schoonmaker Nicholas, clk, County Treasurer's Office, 98 14th
Schopmann Bernhard, lab., 19 Pendleton
Schoppelrei Chas , musician, 93 W. Liberty
Schoppenhorst Christina, laundress, 64 Wade
Schopper David, saddler, s.s. York b. Baymiller and Linn
Schopper Gottleib, saddler, 1109 Central Av.
Schork Matthew, lab., 73 Green
Schorr Adam, tailor, 60 W. Mulberry
Schorr David, cutter, 60 W. Mulberry
Schorr Geo., cof. h., n.w.c. Ham. Road and Main
Schorr John, cooper, 686 Main
Schorske Johanna, 34 Ham. Road
Short Valentine, dray, 76 Ham. Road
Schoster John B., shoe mkr., bds. 191 W. 6th
Schott Bonesne, e.s. Division b. Bernard and Bank
Schott Caroline, 194 Longworth
SCHOTT CHAS., Book Binder and Frame Manufacturer, 22 W. Court, h. 417 Main
Schott Christian, mach , 405 Elm
Schott Christopher, 51 Jackson
Schott Ferdinand, porter, 113 Ham. Road
Schott Frederick, cof. h., 66 W. Court
Schott Geo., clk. 354 Main, h. 113 Ham. Road
Schott Gustave, (Newburgh & S.) 256 Vine
Schott John, 108 Clinton
Schott John, bar tender, s.e.c. Harrison Pike and Patterson
Schott John, millwright, wks. n.w.c. Pearl and M. Canal
Schott John, tailor, 51 Fountain
Schott Lorenz, lab., 66 W. Liberty
Schott Louis, brewer, 664 Main
Schott Roman, plasterer, 470 Linn
Schotte Conrad, dray, s.s. Corporation b. Young and Wilson
Schotte Hy., lab. e.s. Vine b. Milk and Mulberry
Schottelkotte John L., grocery, 47 Pendleton
Schottmann Chas., tailor, 621 Sycamore
Schottmueller Johannah, 20 Webster
Schotwell Geo., clk., 160 George
Schotzman John, watchman, 158 Bank
Schoutmann Theresa, 14 Dunlap
Schovee Eliza, 183 W. 4th
Schowe Ernst, grocery, 108 13th
Schrader Bernard, cigar mkr., wks. 49 Main
Schrader Christopher, grocery, 465 W. 6th
Schrader Clemens, clk., 16 Baum
Schrader Fred., 594 Vine
Schrader Geo., 45 Jones

SCHRADER H. & CO., (Herman S. & Herman J. Gott) Importers of Fancy Goods and Toys, 70 Main
Schrader Hy., clk., 11 Orchard
Schrader Hy., collar mkr., 54 15th
Schrader Hy., cooper, wks. n.w.c. Freeman and 9th
Schrader Hy., mach., 41 Race
Schrader Hy. B., locksmith, 186 Hopkins
SCHRADER Herman, (H. S. & Co.) 340 Race
Schrader Louisa, servt., 433 Broadway
Schrader Wm., cap mkr , n.e.c. Everett and Gorman
Schrader Wm., cap mkr., 135 Bremen
Schratzki Ben , clothing. 190 W. Court
Schradzki Isador, (M. & I. S.) 170 W. 9th
Schradzki M. & I., (Michael & Isador) clothiers. 184 Main
Schradzki Michael, (M. & I. S.) 190 W. Court
Schraeder Hy., saddler, 54 15th
Schraer Bernard. lab., 181 E. 3d
Schraffenberger Michael, boots and shoes, 40 E. Front
Schrage Barney, dray, 583 W. 6th
Schrage Victor, finisher, 688 Main
SCHRAM A. D., (A. D. S. & Co.) h. Covington
SCHRAM A. D. & CO., (A. D. S. & Pat. Cleary) Steamboat Agents, 21 Pub. Landing
Schram Augusta, 530 Main
Schramm Frederick, lab., 571 Race
Schramm Louis, butcher, bds. n.w.c. Poplar and Baymiller
Schramm Peter, watchman, 17 Wade
Schrapp John, n.e.c. 6th and Lock
Schrand Barney, carp., 417 Longworth
Schrand Geo., stair builder, 233 Betts
Schrand Helena, 91 Clay
Schrand John, harness mkr., 104 Browne
Schrand Wm., plasterer, n.s. Wade b. Dudley and Daymiller
Schranker Barney, brewer, 72 Mohawk
Schrantz John, shoe mkr., 65 Buckeye
Schratz B., blksmith, wks. 103 Hunt
Schraudenbach Ferdinand, cooper, 71 Elder [Race
Schraudenbach Wm., bk. binder, 544
Schray Gottleib, bakery, 451 Sycamore
Schreader Albert, tailor, 141 Abigail
Schreck Andrew, lab., E. 3d b. Baum and Parsons
Schreckt John, tailor, bds. 51 W. 5th
Schreder Wm., cap manuf., 201 and 202 Everett
Schreiber Benjamin, cooper, w.s. Sycamore b. Franklin and Webster, h 513 Sycamore
Schreiber Catharine, w.s. Goose al. b. Liberty and 15th
SCHREIBER JOHN L., Fencing Apparatus, Lithographic Printing Presses, Iron Railing Manufacturer and Lock Smith, 550 Vine, h. 7 Mary
Schreiner Jacob, lab., 590 Race
Schremper Christ., lab , rear 71 Hughes
Schrenk John, turner, 612 Elm
Schrenke Barney, 72 Mohawk
Schrenke John, lab., 72 Mohawk
Schrenke John, cof. h., 1 Wade b. Elm and Plum
Schriber Joseph, cooper, 422 W. Liberty, h. 424 W. Liberty
Schriber Louis, seminarian, Catholic church, Mt. Adams
Schrichte J. Hy., clk , 307 Main
Schrichten Geo., 262 Main
Schrick A., sen., lab., wks. C. T. Dumont's
Schrick A., jr., molder, wks. C. T. Dumont's
Schrider Hermann, lab., 19 Dunlap
Schrieber Hy., grocery, 22 W. Mulberry
Schrieckell Frederick, meats, 64 Ham. Road
Schriefer Hy., grocery, 25 E. Liberty
Schrienker Barney, lab., wks. n.w.c. Plum and Wade
Schriever Edward H., currier, 291 W. 3d
Schrihter Hermann, tailor, n.s. Corporation al. b. Young and Price

Schrimer Conrad, n.s. Rice near Fountain
Schrimper Wm., porter, Gibson House
Schriner Geo., huckster, 641 Elm
Schriner John, teamster, n.s. Front e. of Lumber
Schriner Wenzel, butcher, 703 Vine
Schring John, 69 Mohawk
Schristen Gottleib, painter, n.e.c. Milton and Sycamore
Schriver Geo., butcher, bds. 137 W. 7th
Schriver Mary E., servt., w.s. Franz b. Elder and Findlay
Schroat Andrew, butcher, 69 Poplar
Schroder Barney, lab., w.s. Ramsey n. of Front
Schroder Chas., cigar mkr., n.e.c 15th and Pleasant
Schroder Chas., driver, 137 Everett
Schroder Chas., lab., 169 Oliver
Schroder Fred., driver, 191 W. Canal
Schroder Fred., (Ten Beig & S.) 19 12th
Schroder Hy., cab. mkr., wks. 129 W. 2d
Schroder Hy., lab., 185 W. Canal
Schroder Hy., rope mkr., 435 W. 2d
Schroder John B., lock smith, 188 Hopkins
SCHRODER JOHN D., Family Grocery and Provisions, 336 W. 7th
Schroder John H., cutter, 499 Main
SCHRODER John H., (John H. S. & Co.) h. 81 Laurel
SCHRODER JOHN H. & CO. (John H. S., Lawrence & Richard Schroder) Locksmiths and Bell Hangers, 53 W. 3d, Factory 2d near John
SCHRODER Lawrence. (John H. Schroder & Co.) h. St. Bernard
Schroder Matilda, 81 Laurel
SCHRODER Richard, (John H. Schroder & Co.) St. Bernard
Schrodrowsky Hy., key mkr., 65 12th
Schroeder Adam, express man, 681 Vine
Schroeder Adam H., lab., rear 525 Sycamore
Schroeder B., dry goods, 126 Main, h. 181 Broadway
Schroeder Caroline, tailoress, 472 Freeman
Schroeder Chas., grocery, 628 Race
Schroeder Chas., tailor, 567 Main
Schroeder Chas., teamster, 137 Everett
Schroeder Chas., varnisher, bds. 382 Broadway
Schroeder Chas A., cof. h., 78 W. Court
Schroeder Clemens, clk. 62 E. 2d
Schroeder Elizabeth, 380 Broadway
Schroeder Frederick, baker, 104 13th
Schroeder Frederick, baker, 511 Race
Schroeder Frederick, carp., 29 Jackson
Schroeder Frederick, carp., 15 Mary
Schroeder Frederick, tailor, 567 Main
Schroeder Frederick, tool mkr., s.s. Boal b. Broadway and Sycamore
Schroeder Fred. H., blksmith, s.s. Boal b. Sycamore and Broadway
Schroeder Fritz, shoe mkr., bds. 165 W. 5th
Schroeder H. F., clk. 4 Main, h. Covington
Schroeder Hy., cooper, 193 Pleasant
Schroeder Hy., lab., 669 W. Front
Schroeder Hy., lab., wks. n.w.c. Wood and 3d
Schroeder Hy., lab., rear 523 Sycamore
Schroeder Hy., meats, 172 E. 5th
Schroeder Hy., porter, 11 Orchard
Schroeder Hy., rope mkr., 442 W. 2d
Schroeder Hy., (S. & Klopp) bds. 12th b. Vine and Bremen
Schroeder Hy., shoe mkr, 493 Walnut
Schroeder Herman H., lab., 45 Pleasant
Schroeder John, hats and caps, 418 Vine
Schroeder & Klopp, (Hy. S. & Philipp K.) carriage manuf., 446 Race
Schroeder Louisa, 50 Rittenhouse
Schroeder Martin, bklayer, 70 12th
Schroeder Martin, mason, 235 Bremen
Schroeder S., sawyer, wks. John Mitchell's
Schroeder Samuel, mer., 23 Gano
Schroeder Sophia, servt., 399 Sycamore
Schroeder Wm., cigar mkr., 382 Broadway
Schroeder Wm., lab. 134 Bremen

Schroeder Wm. H., cooper, 147 Pleasant
Schroeer Stephen H., grocery, 12 Mary
Schroer Christiana, 511 Race
Schroer Barney, lab., w.s. Harriet b. 6th and Sloo
Schroer Darney, plasterer, 92 Woodward
Schroer Bernhard, cooper, 216 Clark, h. 162 Clark
Schroer Bernhard, jr., molder, 105 Woodward
Schroer Bernhard H., lab., 105 Woodward
Schroer Hy., brick mkr., 216 Laurel
Schroer Hy., dray, 126 Clay
Schroer Hy. C., carriage trimmer, 464 Elm
Schroer Herman, sash manuf., w. s. Spring b Liberty and Woodward, h. 420 Sycamore
Schroer Hermann, shoemkr, 488 Main
Schroer John H., carp., rear 420 Sycamore
Schroerlucke Hy., grocery, s. e. c. Baymiller and Everett
Schroeter Ferdinand, dray, bds. 674 W. 6th
Schrond Geo., carp., 233 Betts
Schror H. & H. Stock, (Henry S. & Henry S.) boots and shoes, 405 Main
Schror Henry, (H. S. & H. Stock), s.e.c. Main and Abigail
Schror John, 89 Bank
Schrot Geo., bakery, 123 Bremen
Schrot John, meats, s.s. Harrison Road, b. Coleman and Patterson
SCHROTH ANDREW, Family Grocery, 768 Central Avenue
Schroth Chas., musician, 134 Bremen
Schroth John, bakery, 50 Ham. Road
Schroth John, baker, wks 217 Everett
SCHROTH MATTHEW, Meat Store, 332½ W. 6th
Schrotke Christian H., b.k., 31 Ham. Road
Schrotke Hermann, clk., 31 Ham. Road
Schrots John, soap mkr., wks. w. s. St. Clair b. 7th and 8th
Schrover Theresa, 145 Livingston
Schub K., wks. A. G. Cheever & Co.'s
Schubert Francis, saddler, 522 Race
Schubert Gotthelf, shoemkr, s. s. Calhoun b. Madison and Vine
Schubert John, lab. jat G. & P. Bogen's, h. w.s. Baymiller, b. Bank and Dayton
Schubert Mary, seamstress, 538 Main
Schuch Geo., cab. mkr., 223 Findlay
Schuch Lewis, cab. mkr., 210 Livingston
Schuch Ulrich, e s. Carr b. 6th and Taylor
Schuchard Philip, cab. mkr., 458 W. 6th
Schuchardt Frederick, carp., 603 Vine
Schuchardt Harmon, barber, 9 W. 6th
Schuchter Anthony, blksmith, 34 Hamer
Schuchter Nicodemus, blksmith, 34 Hamer
Schuck Andrew, tanner, bds. s. w. c. Henry and Elm
Schuckman John, shoemkr, 108 Avery
Schuckmann Barney, grocery, 12 Dunlap
Schuderer George, atty., 22 W. Court
Schuefele Fred, meats, 450 Linn
Schuehler Fredericka, 107 Ham. Road
Schuele Jacob, cof. h., 4 W. Court
Schueler Frederick, shoemkr, 49 Hamer
Schueler Joseph, cab. ware, 67 Elder, h. 71 Elder
Schuelkins John H., chair mkr., 66 Lodge
Schuer Frank, bds. 90 E. 2d
Schuermann Chas., cooper, 28 Buckeye
Schuermann Francis, phys, 24 W. 8th
Schuermann Henry, cab. mkr., 33 15th
Schuessel Valentine, tailor, 95 Ham. Road
Schuester Albert, lab., 56 David
Schuester John, 13 Jones
Schuester John, blksmith, bds. rear 7 Bank
Schuester John, blksmith, n. e. c. Linn and Bank
Schuette Catharine, seamstress, 89 Clay

Schuette Christian, miller, bds. 31 Webster
Schueitenheimer Jacob, 19 Mercer
Schueterle Mathias, dry goods, 524 Race
Schuettmueller Chas., baker, 102 Ham. Road
Schuetze Katharine, bds. 38 Green
Schuetz Christian, tailor, 26 Hamer
Schuetz Hy., lab., 563 Walnut
Schugar Lewis, chair mkr., 490 W. 3d
Schugar Margaret, 490 W. 3d
Schuh Chas., lab., 62 Ham. Road
Schuh Christian, tinner, 609 Elm
Schuh Daniel, shoemkr, 614 Vine
Schuh John, cooper, 6 Buckeye
Schuhmacher Geo., shoemkr, h.33 Buckeye
Schuhmacher Hy., shoemkr, 725 Race
Schuhmacher Michael, 30 Green
Schuhmann Geo., tailor, 610 Race
Schuhmann August, cof. h., 614 Vine
Schuhmann Francis, brewer, 244 Pleasant
Schuhmann Frederick, lab., 517 Race
Schulask, saddler, bds. s. w. c. Ludlow and Pearl
Schuler A., shoemkr, 100 W. 6th, bds. n.s. 6th b. Elm and Plum
Schuler Barbara, s.w.c. 3d and Wood
Schuler Christian, bk layer, 10 Moore
Schuler Frank, b.k., 71 Walnut, bds. 564 Vine
Schuler Fred, cooper, wks. 28 Sycamore
Schuler John, cigar mkr., 564 Vine
Schuler John, clk., 56 Broadway
Schuler John, cooper, 84 Division
Schuler Theodore, cooper, 438 W. 8th
Schuler John, grocer, 84 Division
Schulhof Hy., clk., n. w. c. Vine and Longworth, h. 55 David
Schulinger John, finisher, wks. n. e. c. Walnut and Canal
Schuller David, tinner, wks. 144 and 146 W. 3d
Schulmeier Wm., cigar mkr., 40 Peete
Schulta Benj., lab., 91 Spring
Schulta Elizabeth, n.w.c. Baymiller and Gest
Schulta Hy., lab., wks. Wood & McCoy's
Schulta Richard, porter, 86 Hunt
Schulte August H., cigar mkr., al. b. 13th and Mercer and Vine and Walnut
Schulte B. H., 609 Race
Schulte Bernard L., cooper, 55 Kossuth
Schulte Bernhard H., (S. & Temmen,) 609 Race
Schulte Ernst W. H., grocery, 26 E. Pearl
Schulte Frances, 155 Pleasant
Schulte Garrett, lab., 402 Longworth
Schulte George, boots and shoemkr, 236 Water
Schulte Geo., cooper, 154 Hopkins
Schulte Geo., lab., w.s. Spring b. Abigail and Hunt
Schulte Geo., lab., e. s. Ramsey n. of Front
Schulte Gerhart, carp., 13 Adams
Schulte Hy., sawyer, 13 Adams
Schulte Hy., lab., bds. n.w.c. Linn and Clark
Schulte Hy., molder, 151 Abigail
Schulte Hy., teacher, e.s. Spring b. Hunt and Abigail
Schulte Herman, blksmith, 27 Spring
Schulte Herman, chair manuf., 144 Laurel
Schulte Hermann, lab., 386 Broadway
Schulte Herman, (Wenke & S.,) 91 W. Court
Schulte Hermon, teamster, wks. 381 Plum
Schulte Herman H., cooper, n. w. c. Schiller and Hughes
Schulte John, cigar store, s. w. c. Clark and Cutter
Schulte John, clk., 26 E. Pearl
Schulte John, grocery, 70 Buckeye
Schulte John, lab., 144 Laurel
Schulte Joseph, lab., 161 Pleasant
Schulte Karl, cof. h., s. w. c. 6th and Smith
Schulte M., lab., wks. Hieatt & Wood's
Schulte Mrs. Maria Bernardine, seamstress, n.w.c. Hughes and Schiller

Schulte Martin, lab., 28 13th
Schulte Mary, servt., 307 George
Schulte & Temmen, (Bernhard H. S. & John H. T.,) iron, &c., 240 Main
Schulte Wm., carp., 181 Hopkins
Schulte Wm., carp., 382 Baymiller
Schulte Wm., carpet weaver, bds. 24 Abigail
Schulte Wm., shoemkr., bds. 363 W. 5th
Schulten Barney, lab , w s. Campbell al. b. Elder and Findlay
Schulten Barney, shoemkr., wks. 147 Sycamore
Schulten Elizabeth, servt., 366 W. 7th
Schulten John H., boots and shoes, 46 Woodward
Schulter Bernard, e.s. Miami Canal, nr. Mohawk Bridge
Schulter George, lab., 26 Mohawk
Schulter Geo., lab., bds. 34 Abigail
Schulter Hy., lab., 418 Walnut
Schulter Hy., sawyer, wks. H. Rosenberg's. h. 13 Adams
Schulter Joseph, 150 Everett
Schulter Reuben, shoemkr, 170 Hopkins
Schultheis August, druggist, 19 Ann
Scultheis Hy., baker, bds. 420 Vine
Scultheis Jacob, bar k., 493 Vine
Schultheis John, 356 W. 5th
Schulthouse Mary, s.s. al. b. Pike and Lawrence and Pearl and 3d
Schultheis John S , lab., 62 Lock
Schultian Hy., tailor, n. w. c. Pleasant and Green
Schultice Casper, 116 Mohawk
Schultice John, 129 Mohawk
Schultice Michael, finisher. 114 Brown
Schultz Adam, cooper, 92 Woodward
Schultz Anton, porter, bds. 249 W. Court
SCHULTZ & BRO., (Wm. J. S. & Conrad S.,) Brewers, 485 E. Front
Schultz Catharine. cof. h., 16 Allison
Schultz Charles, clk., 411 W. 5th
Schultz Charles, steamboat man, 311 Freeman
Schultz Chas., tailor, 163 Pleasant
SCHULTZ Conrad. (S. & Bro.,) s.s. 3d, b. Lock and Kilgour
Schultz Daniel, cof. h., 531 Walnut
Schultz Daniel, millwright, 16 Allison
Schultz Frank, cof. h., 249 W. Court
Schultz Frank, lab., n.s. Garden b. Freeman and Western Av
Schultz Frederick, harness mkr., bds. Australia House
Schultz Frederick, millwright, 16 Allison
Schultz George, 72 Dunlap
Schultz George, tailor, 45 Elder
Schultz George, whitewasher, 99 Clay
Schultz George W., clk., bds. 488 E. Front
Schultz Hy., cooper, 20 Madison
Schultz Hy., phys., 488 E. Front
Schultz Hy., shoe mkr., bds. 70 Sycamore
Schultz Hy J., tailor, 67 Elder
Schultz Hy. M., brewer, bds. 488 E. Front
Schultz Herman, clk., 63 E. Pearl, h. Newport
Schultz Herman, lab., 210 Hopkins
Schultz Herman, teamster. wks. 381 Plum
Schultz Herman H., clk. P. O., h. 113 Everett
Schultz John, bds. s. e. c. Smith and Front
Schultz John, millwright, 16 Allison
Schultz Rev. J. John, St. Xavier College, w.s. Sycamore b. 6th and 7th
Schults John, teamster. 299 Linn
Schultz John W., musician, 518 Main
Schultz Julius R., s.e.c. 5th and Home
Schultz Louis R., clk. P. O., h. 388 Vine
Schultz Margaret, books &c., 77 Spring
Schultz Peter. miller, 491 Vine
Schultz Peter T. , printer, 70 Spring
Schultz R. J., 226 Longworth
Schultz Robert, mach., 148 W. Liberty
Schultz Wm., cab. mkr., 28 Broadway
Schultz Wm , shoe mkr., 92 Hunt
SCHULTZ Wm. J., (S. & Bro.) s. s. 3d b. Lock and Kilgour

SCHULTZE F. & CO,. (Frederick S. & Charles Ahrenfeldt,) French China and Foreign Glassware 127 Main
SCHULTZE Frederick, (F. S. & Co.,) h. Avondale
Schultze Hy. F., clk., 48 W. 2d, h. Covington
Schuly John, plasterer, rear 567 Sycamore
Schuly John Jr., plasterer, rear 567 Sycamore
Schulz Adam, cooper, 92 Woodward
Schulz Albert, tailor, 593 Vine
Schulz Mrs. Anna, tailoress, 117 Buckeye
Schulz August, clk., 549 Sycamore
Schulz Catharine, seamstress, bds. 679 Vine
Schulz Franz, shoe mkr., 19 14th
Schulz Joachim H., lab., 3 John
Schulz Joseph, bds. 649 Central Av.
Schulz Lorenz, mach., bds. 264 Central Av.
Schulz Louisa, w.s. Poplar b. Buckeye and Ham. Road
Schulze Diedrich, cooper, 20 Madison
Schulze Hy., cooper, 16 Madison
Schulse John G., clk., 173 Main, h. 415 John
Schulze Martin, painter, 90 Abigail
Schulze Wm., carpet weaver, bds. 24 Abigail
Schum Adam, tailor, bds. 45 Hamer
Schumacher August, dray, rear 579 Main
Schumacher Bernhard H., tailor, 14 Abigail
Schumacher John, cof. h., 72 12th
Schumacher John, cutter, n. s. 12th b. Bremen and Race
Schumacher John J., tailor, 403 Central Av.
Schumacher John H., mer. tailor, 367 W. 5th
Schuhmacher Paul, driver, wks. s. w. c. Plum and Canal
Schumaker Mary, servt., 15 Harrison
Schuman Catharine, servt., 35 McFarland
Schuman Ernst, porter, wks. 221 and 223 Walnut [nut
Schuman Geo., blksmith, bds. 502 Walnut
Schumann Caspar, 41 Jones
Schumann Chas., baker, 369 Central Av. h. 365 Central Av.
Schumard Dr. Geo., bds. s w. c. 3d and Broadway
Schumback Frederick, lab., n. s. Front e. of Kelly
Schunefeld Frederick, dray, 27 Kossuth
Schunk Andreas, tanner, 246 Pleasant
Schuntermuch Mrs. Elizabeth, n. s. Browne w. of Ravine al.
Schupp Mrs. Caroline, laundress, rear 14 15th
Schupper Gottlieb, 135 York
Schurb George, 172 Charlotte
Schurman Frank, clk., 674 W. Front
Schussler Charles H., clk., bds. 416 George
Schuster Geo., lab., 715 Race
Schuster Geo., teamster, 7 John
Schuster John, cof. h., 44 Sycamore
Schuster Mary, 714 Vine
Schutkamp Barney, lab., w. s. Ramsey al. n. of Front
Schutrath Christ, tanner, n. w. c. Stark and Dunlap
Schutt John, plasterer, 723 Race
Schutte Benjamin, shoe mkr., 638 W. 6th
Schutte Hy., stone mason, 19 Mulberry
Schutte John, shoe mkr., 22 Mill
SCHUTTE Joseph, (Taphorn & S.,) 493 W. Front
Schuttenhelm Jacob, brass finisher 466 E. Front
Schutz Frederick, tailor, 156 Pleasant
Schutz H., 150 Pleasant
Schuyler Alfred F., bk. layer, 274 Broadway
Schuyler Mrs. M. E., 281 George
Schwaab Nancy, servt., 422½ George
Schwab Catharine, servt., 186 Sycamore
Schwab Chas., peddler, 136 Bremen
Schwab Daniel, cooper, w. s. Lawrence b. 2d and Pearl

Schwab Frederick, stone mason, 14 15th
Schwab Frederick A., carp., 205 Clinton
Schwab Geo. J., bar k., 65 12th
Schwab George, clk., 555 Sycamore
Schwab Gottlieb, cab. mkr., 251 Laurel
Schwab Hy., cigar mkr., w. s Milk b. Calhoun and Vine
Schwab Hy., tanner. 691 Elm
Schwab Jacob, lab., wks. Cincinnati Chemical Laboratory
Schwab John, 691 Elm
Schwab Magdalene, 112 Clinton
Schwab Manuel, peddler, 65 Pleasant
Schwab Mary, 5 Whiteman
Schwab Mathias, organ builder, 555 Sycamore
Schwab Michael, porter, 14 W 2d
Schwab Paul, rope mkr., 511 Plum
Schwab Rosa servt., n.e.c. 2d and Broadway
Schwab Sebastian, finisher, bds 614 Vine
Schwab Thomas, lab., w. s. Goose al. b. Green and Elder
Schwabe George, carman, 28 Madison
Schwabenland Valentine, shoe mkr., 62 W. Liberty
Schwaegerle Adam, cof. h. 609 Main
Schwaemlein John, 141 Clay
Schwalb Hy., printer, 196 Pleasant
Schwald Martin, huckster, 124 Pleasant
Schwalmeier Margaret, 511 Race
Schwan Peter, cigars &c., 599 Vine
Schwaner Philip, tailor, 502 John
Schwaner Wernart. tailor, 502 John
Schwang Lucas. 675 Race
Schwangle E., lab., wks. Evans, Gaines & Co's.
Schwap Michael, lab., 14 Commerce b. Walnut and Vine
Schwap Susan, cof. h., 466 E. Front
Schwarb Fred. cigar mkr., 609 Vine
Schwarb Peter, lab., 609 Vine
Schwarm Charles, cof. h. 494 Walnut
Schwartz Anna, 615 Race
Schwartz Frederick, cab. mkr., 139 Everett
Schwartz Geo., 69 Mohawk
Schwartz Geo., shoe mkr., 17 David
Schwartz & Hafner (Henry S., & John A. H.,) dry goods, 434 Main
Schwartz Hy., (S. & Hafner,) 434 Main
Schwartz Hermon, bk. mkr., s.s. Ringgold b. Price and Young
Schwartz Isaac, dry goods, 505 Vine
Schwartz Jacob, shoe mkr., 510 Race
Schwartz Jacob, tailor, 708 Freeman
Schwartz Joseph, cof. h., n.s. Augusta b. John and Smith
Schwartz Joseph, shoe mkr., bds. 6 Walnut
Schwartz Lawrence, tinner, 713 Central Av.
Schwartz Lazarus E., b.k., 340 Vine
Schwartz Michael, b. k., 11 Main, h. 22 Webster
Schwartz Nicholas, butcher, bds. 65 Bank
Schwartz Nicholas, shoe mkr., 44 Hamer
Schwarz Balthazar, cigar mkr., 622 Race
Schwarz Catharine, 613 Race
Schwarz Celestin, grocery, 679 W. 6th Mercer and Vine and Walnut
Schwarz David, hats and caps, 159 Main, h 6 Harrison
Schwarz David, clk. 104 Main, h. 6 Harrison
Schwarz David, finisher, 381 Vine
Schwarz George, cof. h., 615 Main
Schwarz Hy., cigar mkr., 38 Green
Schwarz Hy., tailor, 663 Race
Schwarz Jacob, shoe mkr., 510 Race
Schwarz John, essence of coffee, 33 Ham. Road
Schwarz Katharina, servt., 669 Vine
Schwarz Martin, varnisher, 662 Central Av.
Schwarz Max, essence of coffee manuf., 603 Main
Schwarz Michael, tailor, 241 Pleasant
Schwarzenberg Nathan, clothing, 139 Main, h. 197 Broadway
Schwarzman Albert, clk Cincinnati Chemical Laboratory, h. 81 Martin
Schwebel John, lab., 66 Spring
Schwebel Louis, musician, 24 Orchard

292 (SCH) CINCINNATI (SCO) DIRECTORY. (SEA)

Schwecke Ferdinand, tanner, 612 Elm
Schwecke Frederick C., candy mkr., 503 Race
Schwecke Margaret, 503 Race
Schweer J. George, grocer, 188 Clark
Schweer Magdeline, 110 E. 2d
Schweers Frank J., porter, 15 Richmond
Schweers Joseph, porter, 59 W. Pearl, h. 15 Richmond
SCHWEGMAN BERNHARD, New York Coffee and Eating House, 30 Pub. Landing, h. 77 Pike
Schwegman Francis, confec., 361 Main
Schwezman Hy., lab., 63 Lock
Schwegmann Anna, 22 Woodward
Schwegmann Clara, seamstress 22 Woodward
Schwegmann Clemens, confec. 548 Walnut
Schwegmann Fred., lab., 60 Hughes
Schwegemann Hy., lab., 97 Woodward
Schwegmann Hy., shoe mkr., 12 Buckeye
Schwegmann Herman H., millstone cutter, 51 Plum
Schweickr. Geo., grocery, 63 Laurel
Schweickert John, cooper, 65 Lock
Schweiger Joseph, cooper, 23 Brighton
Schweigert Fred., shoe mkr., 620 Vine
Schweigert Louis, printer, 69 Buckeye
Schweigman Anton, carver, 457 Walnut
Schweikert Fred., flour store, 8 15th
Schweilher John H., cof. h., 4 Public Landing b. Broadway and Ludlow, h. 169 W. Front
Schwein Farques, tanner, 30 Branch
Schwein Geo. F., meats &c., n.e.c John and Chestnut
Schwein Hy., meats, n.w.c. Hunt and Broadway, h. 15 York
Schwein John, cof. h., 601 Vine
Schwein Martin, tailor, s.s. Front e. of Lewis
Schweinefus John H., grocery and cof. h., 716 E. Front
Schweinzer Louis, finisher, 110 W. Court
Schweiring Louis, grocery, s.e.c. Linn and Dayton
Schweithert Harmon, mach., 152 Hopkins
Schweitzer Caspar, mason, 696 Race
Schweitzer Fred., pipeman, bds. Commercial House
Schweitzer Fred., tinner, bds. n.e.c. 7th and Central Av
Schweitzer Geo. P., printer, e.s. Walnut n. of 12th
Schweitzer Jacob, janitor, n.w.c. Main and Court
Schweitzer Joseph, grocer, 1122 Central Av
Schweitzer Joseph, lab., 604 W. Front
Schweizer Christian, carp., 404 Walnut
Schweizer Geo., stocking mkr., 424 Walnut
Schweizer Hy., weaver, 32 Allison
Schweizer Josephine, servt., 643 Vine
Schweizer Wm., tanner, 130 Ham. Road
Schweizerhof Fred., carp., 402 Race
Schweller John, cigar mkr., h. 612 Race
Schwemann Bernhard, blksmith, 493 Race
Schwemberger Chas. sen., saddles &c., 609 Walnut
Schwemberger Chas. jr., saddler, 609 Walnut
Schwemberger Joseph, cof. h., 26 E. Canal, h. n.e.c. Vine and Liberty
Schwenck Christopher, lab., 448 Race
Schwenck Peter, lab., bds. 622 Vine
Schwendenmann Otmar, porter, 512 Vine
Schweng Wm., dray, wks. 830 Central Av
Schwener John, porter, 20 Commerce
Schwenker Fred., 178 Sycamore
SCHWENKER FREDERICK W., Oil Cloth and Window Shade Manufacturer, 570 Walnut
Schwenninger Gustav, lab., 550 Race
Schwenninger Julius, cigars &c., 89 Ham. Road
Schwent Christopher, cof. h., 445 W. 2d
Schwer Anton, cab. mkr., 401 Sycamore
Schwerdtfeyer Fred., gilder, 154 Bremen

Schwere Joseph, organ manuf., 766 Central Av
Schwers H., cooper, 33 Bremen
Schwert Fiedel, brewer, bds 606 Vine
Schwertfegers Hy., brewer, 745 Vine
Schwerzel Joseph, cutter, 180 Walnut
Schwick Diedrich, lab., 351 Sycamore
Schwienher Bernard, cof. h., s.w.c. Freeman and Central Av.
Schwierking Hy., cigar mkr., wks. 361 Vine [kins
Schwietert Bernard, pressman 152 Hopkins
Schwielert Hermann, eng., bds. 152 Hopkins
Schwil Alfred, bds. Cincinnati House
Schwill Ferdinand. com. mer., 64 Sycamore
Schwind Francis P., meats, 63 Hamer
Schwind Geo, A., carp., 157 Pleasant
Schwing Caroline, 122 Pleasant
Schwing John, lab., 155 Bremen
Schvingmeier Gottlieb, lab., 10 Buckeye
Schwink John, stone cutter, 7 Wade b Elm and Plum
Schwign Justus, cof. h., 160 Ham. Road
Schwisinger Adam, 99 Calhoun
Schwitzer Barbara, candle mkr., wks. 728 Central Av.
Schwitzer Fred., lab., 22 Commerce
Schwitzer Geo., stocking weaver, 424 Walnut
Schwoop Christian, lab., 52 Martin
Sciutti Michael, confec., 130 W. 4th, h. 142 W. 4th
Scivington Michael, lab., 649 W. Front
Scogin John L., clk., 171 Vine, h. Newport
Scola Peter, lab., 141 Clay
Scolen Catharine, laundress, 99 Mercer
Sconce George, carp., s.s. Broad b. Front and River
Sconce John, carp., w.s. Broad b. Front and River
Sconce John, carp., s. w. c. Front and Hazen
Sconce Samuel B., carp., s.w.c. Front & Hazen
Scope Antony, tailor, 304 Longworth
Scorp Conrad, shoemkr, 155 Water
Scott ——, s.w.c. 6th and Broadway
Scott Alexander, millwright, 66 Linn
Scott Alexander, paver. bds. U. States Hotel
Scott Alex. M., carp., bds. al. b. Vine & Race and 12th and Canal
Scott Alfred J., kpr. of city prison, s.s. Court e. of Broadway
Scott Alice, 63 E. 7th
Scott & Allgaier (John S. & Sebastian A. A.), cof. h., s.w.c. 6th and Central Av
Scott Ann T., bds. 22 Rittenhouse
Scott Benj. F., tinner. bds. 247 W. 6th
Scott Daniel, walter, Spencer House
Scott David B., b.k., 287 W. 6th
Scott David L., clk., 76 W. 5th, bds. Cincinnati House
Scott Edward S., compositor, 185 Mound
Scott Francis, books, &c , 229 Race
Scott Fred., shoe mkr., 462 Race
Scott Geo., pottery 690 W. Front
Scott Geo. P., tailor. 56 Barr
Scott Gustavus, mer., 256 Vine
Scott Hy. M., clk., 171 Vine
Scott Hugh, agt., 22 Carr
Scott James, lab., 225 George
Scott James, printer, 229 Race
Scott James, waiter, Walnut St. House
Scott James M., salesman, 81 W. Pearl, bds. 107 Pike
Scott John, cooper, 103 Lock
Scott John, druggist, n.w.c. 7th and Broadway
Scott John, printer, Am. Bank Note Co. h. 136 Mound
Scott Jno., jr., bank note printer, h. 136 Mound
Scott Jno. (S. & Allgaier) 136 Mound
Scott Capt. John, 147 W. Front
Scott John A., saloon, s.w.c. 3d and Central Av
Scott Louis, tobacconist, 94 Everett
Scott Margaret, bds. s.s. Railroad e. of French
Scott Margaret, bds. s. s. Railroad e. of French

Scott Marion, engraver, Carlisle bldg., h. Newport
Scott Mary, 456 John
Scott Nelson, cook, 56 E. 7th
Scott Peter, lab., 197 Cutter
Scott Robert, b k. Dantlin & Compton's. h 323 Broadway
SCOTT Robt. (H. Campbell & Co.), h. Mt. Vernon Furnace
Scott Samuel, tobacconist, 92 Everett
Scott Samuel S., cab. mkr., 168 Linn
Scott Virginia. trimmer, 95 W. 3d
Scott W. K., mess., I. & C. R. R., bds. Burnet House
Scott Wm., hostler, h. s.w.c. Freeman and Front
Scott Wm., Sabbath school book and bible depository, 28 W. 4th, h. 185 Mound
Scott Wm. B., japanner, 119 Main, h. Covington
Scott Wm. H., salesman, 27 Hopkins
Scott Wm. H., jr., ins. agent, No. 2 Burnet, bds. Burnet House
SCOTT Wm. R. (Buchanan & Co.) h. Covington
Scott Wilson, barber, s.e.c. Central Av. and Longworth
SCOTTI JOHN, Steam and Gas Fitter, 406 Vine
SCOVILL A. L. & CO., (Amon L. S. & Abel D. Breed,) Patent Medicines, 12 W. 6th
SCOVILL Amon L. (A. L. S. & Co.), 260 Longworth
Scrader Frederick, 767 Vine
Scrader Hy., bds. s.w.c. Henry and Race
Scranage John, barber, s.s. 6th b. Culvert and Broadway
Scrolke Harmon, lab., 79 Gest
Scruggs Catharine, 92 W. Front
Scudder Aletta, 400 Longworth
SCUDDER John M. (Newton & S.) 92 W: 7th
Scuffle Lawrence, peddler, 79 Martin
Scull Joseph, carriage mkr., bds. 65 W. 5th
Scull Joseph P., carriage mkr., bds. 61 W. 5th
Sculler Ann, servt., 143 Elm
Sculley Dennis, dray, 115 W. Court w. of Central Av
Sculley Wm., s.s. Calhoun b. McMillan and Clifton Av
Scully Bridget, s.s. 6th b. Broadway and Culvert
Scully Daniel, shoemkr. 546 W. 5th
Scully John, lab., n.s. 7th b. Broadway and Sycamore
Scully John, stone cutter, 255 Water
Scully Patrick, lab., wks. C., H. & D. R. R. depot
Scully Robert, plasterer, 20 Lock n. of 8th
Sculte Wm., porter, 86 Hunt
Scultetus Charles L., dray, 61 Allison
Scurrah Miss S. A., millinery, 26 E. 4th
Seager John. lab., 158 E. 5th
Seagel Geo., shoemkr., 278 W. Liberty
Seals Chas. A., lumber, 710 W. Front
Seals Gerhard, molder, rear 73 Abigail
Seaman Arthur, 34 North
Seaman August M., cutter, 358 W. 6th
Seaman Benj. M., carp., bds. 323 George
Seaman Chas., molder, wks n.e.c. Walnut and Canal
Seaman Frank, brakesman, 431 Central Av
Seaman Geo. W., stair bldr., 456 John
Seaman Henry, lab., n.e.c. Walnut and Canal
Seaman Hiram, carp., 323 George
Seaman J. H., carp., 220 John, h. 323 George
Seaman John, 80 12th
Seaman Jno. blksmith., 600 W. Front
Seaman Mrs. Joseph, cof. h., 13 W. 6th
Seaman Sophia, s.e.c. 7th and North
Seaman Wm., carp., 62 15th
Seamann Henry, molder, 43 Peete
Senmer August, tailor, 678 W. Front
Seamer Barney, lab., 230 Hopkins
Senmer Benjamin. molder, 401 Broadway
Senmer Conrad H , upholsterer, 374 Elm
Seamon George, lab., 464 E. Front

Seamon Geason, clk., bds. 225 W 4th
Scapet Elizabeth, servt., 158 Franklin
SEARLES A. M., pres. Merchants and Manufac. Ins. Co., h. 121 W 8th
Searles John H., clk., L. M. R. R., h. 70 Lodge
Sears C. P., cab. mkr., 91 St. Clair
Sears Mrs. Sarah, 171 W. 3d
SEASONGOOD Jacob, (Heidelbach, S. & Co.,) 58 W. 8th
SEASONGOOD Lewis, (Heidelbach, Seasongood & Co.,) s.e.c. 8th and Vine
Seasser Jacob, steward, 43 Race
Seaton Adam, lab., s.s. Phœbe al. b. Plum and Central Av
Seave Anthony, porter, 92 W. Court
Sebach John, wagon mkr., 1 Wade b. Elm and Plum
Sebastian Adolph, shoe mkr., 587 Race
Sebastian Benjamin, bk. layer, 157 Clinton
Sebastian John, pilot, 416 W. 9th w. of Central Av
Sebastiani Joseph, asst. sec'y German Mutual Ins. Co., h. 221 Linn
Sebille Celestine, saleswoman, 30 W. 4th, h. 210 Sycamore
Sebille Louis, candy mkr., bds. 210 Sycamore
Sebille Mrs. Mary, 210 Sycamore
Sebley Casper, sawyer, 164 Cutter
Sebolskie Lodwick, tailor, 293 Linn
SECHLER Daniel M., (S. & Porter), 304 George
SECHLER & PORTER, (Daniel M. S. & Wm. H. P.,) Wholesale Dealers in Pig, Bar, Boiler and Sheet Iron, &c., 54 W. 2d
Seck Henry, porter, n.s. Pearl b. Butler and Pike
Seckbart Adolph, lab., n.s Poplar b. Freeman and Western Av
Seckfort Henry, carp., 90 W. 2d
Seckmann Diederich, lab., 54 Baum
Seckunt Powell, shoe mkr., bds. 48 E. Pearl
Secor Robert F., policeman, 63 Pendleton
Secrist Hamilton, feed store, n.e.c. 12th and Central Av., h. 36 David
Secrist Henry C., com. mer., 153 Dayton
SECRIST JOHN M., Commission Merchant, Wholesale Dealer in Grain, 21 and 23 W. Front, h. 143 Dayton
Secrist John W., clk., n.e.c. 12th and Central Av
Secrist Joseph H., 73 Bank
Secrist Margaret, 21 Betts
Sedam Geo. W., b.h., 127 W. 5th
SEDAM J. Percival, (Athearn & S.,) 135 Longworth
Seddens John, pump mkr., River b. Vine and Race, bds. 204 W. Front
Seddens Thomas R., bk. layer, 31 W. Court w. of Central Av
Sedgebeer J., patent mills, s.w.c. Race and 3d
Sedger Henry, bds. s w.c. Race and Henry
Sedgwick Wm. S., clk., 20 E. Pearl, res. Newport
Sedkamp Richard, br. mkr ,242 Hopkins
Sedlecke Ferdinand, h. 66 Abigail
Sedorius Nicholas, lab , n.w.c. Ramsey and Park al,
See & Havens, (James S. & James H.), salesmen for cattle, &c., Brighton Stock Yards
See James, salesman. s s. Harrison Pike b. Division and Brighton
See Wm., cutter, 32 W. 4th
See Wm. Henry, 126 Laurel
Srebach Francis, millwright, 81 Bremen
Seebach Jacob, tailor, 502 W. 5th
Seebour Elizabeth, 101 Ham. Road
Seeds Chas., pilot, 287 Elm
Seeds Maria, n.s. Charlotte b. Linn and Baymiller
Seegar Florence J., teacher Wesleyan Female College
Seegar Henry, brass molder, wks. 247 W.
Seegar Jabez, phys. 291 W. 5th, res. Fairmount
Seegar John, clk., n.e.c. 2d and Walnut, h. 208 Livingston

Seeger Charlotte, teacher, 495 Race
Seeger Dorothea, teacher, 495 Race
Seeger Frank, locksmith, bds. 190 W. 6th
Seegers Daniel, lab. 179 Hopkins
Seegers George, boots and shoes, 48 W. Front
Beehuetter George J. G., 425 Sycamore
Seckamp Dietrich, porter. 232 Main
Seel George, bar. k., 74 W. 3d, h. 91 Clay
Seelen August, (H B. Ehlmann & S.,) s.s. Orchard b. Main and Sycamore
Seeley Edmond B., salesman 24 W. Pearl, h. 57 McFarland
Seeman Gerson, mer., bds. 17 Lodge
Seeman John, (Crowley & Co.,) bds. 328 W. 5th
Seep Barney, shoe mkr., 41 E. 7th
Seeren August, cooper, 9 Orchard
Seery Andrew, carp., 14 Kossuth
Seery Andrew, printer, bds. 80 Baymiller
Seery C. J., printer, bds. 80 Baymiller
Seery James, carp., s.s. Findlay b Freeman and Western Av
Seery Mary, 80 Baymiller
Seery Patrick, s.s. al. b. 9th and Richmond and Baymiller and Linn
Seessmann Augustus, gunsmith, 238 Main
Seevering Anthony, lab., bds. Pennsylvania Hotel
Sefrin John, 1 Wade b. Elm and Plum
Segale Francisco, peddler, 461 W. 5th
Segar Frank, cab. mkr , 439 W. 5th
Segar John, clk., 205 Livingston
Segbers Wm., cigar mkr., wks. 361 Vine
Segelken Henry, coachman, 13 15th
Seger Henry, grocery, s.e.c. Front and Vine
Seger Hermann, bar., 103 Clay
Seger Louis, lab., 168 W. Front
Seger Wessel, 103 Clay
Segkon Henry, driver; 13 15th b. Elm and Plum
Segmann Frederick, miller, 259 Ham. Road
Seguens Jno., tanner, 34 Ham. Road
Seguine Walter H., carriage mkr., n.e.c. Wade and Dudley
Sehl Wm., piano mkr., bds. 674 W. 6th
Sehr Jacob, cooper, bds. 29 Bernard
Seib Wm. C., mach., bds. 412 Freeman
Seibel Frederick, cof- h., s.w.c. Division and H irrison Pike
SEIBEL HENRY, Marble Works. 472 Race
Seibel Henry P., b.k., 139 Walnut, h. 19 Madison b, Elm and Plum
Seibel Jacob, meats 616 Vine
Seiberlich Adam. n.w.c. Elm and Liberty
Seibert Adam, 33 Locust
Seibert Barbara, notions, 230 W. 6th
Seibert Caroline, midwife, 460 Elm
Seibert Conrad, lab., e.s. Whittaker b. Front and 3d
Seibert George, millwright, 392 W. 3d
Seibert George, printer. 460 Elm
Seibert Gertrude, 193 Pleasant
Seibert Mary, wks. Hieatt & Woods' candle factory
Seibert Phillip, watch mkr., 460 Elm
Seiboldt Gottfried, butcher. 602 Main
Seickfort Ernst H., carp., 90 W. 2d
Seidel John, lab., 37 Buckeye
Seidel Joseph, cof. h., 570 Race
Seidenfaden George, tailor. 109 York
Seidenspinner Gottlieb, meats, 457 W 3d
Seidensticker Albin, watch mkr., 19 Main, h. 539 Race
Seidensticker Frederick, cof. h., 539 Race
Seidensticker Genther Wm., musician, 539 Race
Seiers David, lab., 32 E. Front
Selfel Henry, lab., 434 Linn
Seiferg Geo., eng., 34 Vine
Seifers James K., porter, P. O., 73 Pendleton
Seifers John, lab , 79 Abigail
Seifert Adam, lab., 119 Bremen
Seifert Catharina, 119 Bremen
Seifert Francis, 105 Dayton
Seifert Francis, bakery, 727 Race
Seifert Michael, carp., n.e.c. Linn and Bank

Seifert Michael, molder, 56 Martin
Seiffert Jacob, bk. binder, wks. 43 Main
Seiffert John, butcher, 705 Elm
Sniffert Stephen, 58 Stark
Seifried Adam, carp., 149 Bremen
Seifriet Joseph, blksmith, 919 Central Av
Seig Charles, millwright, wks., n.w.c. Pearl and M. Canal, h. Newport
Szigbert Henry, lab., 103 Carr
Seigel Lawrence, tailor, bds. 158 W, 3d
Seigen Wm., 335 Ham. Road
Seilacher Henry, tailor, 33 Moore
Seilar Lewis, carp., wks. 390 W. 8th
Seiler Anthony, eng., 34 Ham. Road
Seiler F., boots and shoes, Junction of Auburn and Vine
Sciler Henry, 167 Pleasant
Seiler Ignatius, mach., 673 Race
Seiler Jacob, lab., 93 Ham. Road
Seiler Leonhard, lab., 60 Elder
Seiler Martin, baker, bds. 47 12th
Seiler Rosina, 673 Race
Seiler Wendelin, tailor, 71 Peete
Seilmann John, blksmith, 244 Pleasant
Seimer George, dray. 137 Baymiller
Seimer Peter, 106 Hunt
SEINECKE Adolphus, (C. F. Adae & Co.). h. 646 Main
SEINSHEIMER BERNHARD, Paper Dealer, 297 Main, h. 14 W. 8th
Seinsheiber Solomon, tailor, 61 St. Clair
SEIP EMIL, Physician and Surgeon, Office and Residence 433 Vine
SEIP GEO., Coffee, Mustard and Spice Mills 133 Bremen
Seip Mary, 31 E. 7th
Seissiger Geo., cooper, s.s. Bank b. Freeman and Riddle
Seit Andrew, lab., 526 W. 8th
Seiter August, blk. smith, 675 Race
Seiter Charlotte, millinery, 55 Ham. Road
Seiter Geo., baker, n.e.c. Elm and 8th
Seiter Geo. T., conductor, bds. n.e.c. Elm and 8th
Seiter Harry, baker, 31 W. 5th
Seiter John, shoe mkr., bds. 65 W. 5th
SEITER JOSEPH, Family Grocery, 606 Freeman
Seiter Joseph, tailor, 58 Broadway
Seiter Joseph, upholsterer, 144 W. 8th
Seiter Wm , 197 Vine
Seiter Wm. A., clk., 40 W. Court, bds. n.e.c. Elm and 8th
Seitz August, cab. mkr., 53 Pine
Seitz Emily, cof. h., 20 Commerce
Seitz Hy., meats, 48 Buckeye
Seitz Leopold, St. Francis School
Seitz Louis, confec., 293 Main
SEITZER GEO., Proprietor Telegraph House, 338 Central Av.
Seiver John S., porter, 56 W. Liberty
Sievers August, trimmer, 94 Clay
Selvert Fred., tailor. 211 Clinton
Seixer Julius, 122 W. 5th
Séjbert Herman, bk. mkr., s.s. Findlay b. Freeman & Western Av.
Selbmeir Fred., varnisher, 139 Everett
Selby Thos. M., bds. 477 W. 4th
Seldon John R., clk. County Auditor's Office, rooms 26 Selves Building
Seleken Edward, brewer, wks. J. Kauffman & Co.'s
Selfe Wm., salesman, 11 Walnut, h. Covington
Selfstead Hy., harness mkr., 684 Central Av.
Selhaus Theodore, shoe mkr., 432 Sycamore
Selig Saml., 140 Everett
Seling John H., blk. smith, 13 Hunt
Selke Gottfried bk. binder, bds. 27 Franklin
Selke Wm., blk. layer, 71 Woodward
Sell Herman, baker, bds. 222 Clark
Sellars ———, clk., bds. 152 W. 4th
Seller Hy., lab., 91 Spring
Sellers Jane, bds. 137 Linn
Sellers Wm. G., salesman 144 Main, bds. 152 W. 4th

| 294 | (SEV) | CINCINNATI | (SHA) | DIRECTORY. | (SHA) |

SELLEW & CO., (Wm S., Enos Sellew & Osman Sellew,) Britannia Ware Manufactory, and Dealers in Metals, 214 Main h. 93 E. 8th
SELLEW Enos, (Sellew & Co.,) h. 58 W. 9th
SELLEW Osman, (Sellew & Co.,) res. Reading
SELLEW Wm., (S. & Co.,) 60 W. 9th
Sellins John, 254 Clinton
Selman Richard, (Smith & Co.,) 115 Sycamore
Selter Hy., lab., al. b. 13th and Mercer and Vine and Walnut
Seltzer Wm., lab., s.s. Front e. of Ferry
SELVES BUILDING, s.s. 3d, b. Main and Walnut
Selves Chas., h.k. St. Charles, 30 E. 3d
SELVES GEO., St. Charles Exchange, 30 and 32 E. 3d, h. 28 E. 3d
Selwest August, lab., 112 Gest
Semaly Huston, lab., 99 E. 6th
Semanson Mary, 54 Baum
Semar Joseph H. carp., 59 Woodward
Semmons Ily.. salesman, 82 W. Pearl
Semp Jacob, cooper, bds. 29 Bernard
Semple Jas., eng., 55 Pierson
Semple Jas. A., clk.. s.e.c. Front and Broadway, res. Newport
Semple Ro' ert S., clk., 44 Pub. Landing, h. Covington
Senadick Mrs. A., s.s. Woodward b. Sycamore and Broadway
Send Wm., lab., 50 Abigail
Sender Frank, cooper, bds. 141 Pendleton
Senf Ernst H., baker, 131 Bremen
Sengenberger Michael, expressman, 146 Clinton
Senger Eva C., 30 Mercer
Sengler John, carpet weaver, 29 Elder
Senior Abraham, (Levi S. & Co.,) 15 College
Senkler Lendler, 38 Mohawk
Senn John S., grocery, n.e.c. Elm and 14th
Sennett Albert W., molder, 291 W. Front
Sennett Johnson A., molder, 476 W. 4th
Sennett Olive. bds. 291 W. Front
Senour Wm., engraver, bds. 135 Central Av.
Sensel John, finisher, wks. s.w.c. Pearl and Plum
Sensner Hy. T., carp., 76 Barr
Sentelbeck John, lab., 72 Buckeye
Sentif Frank, 141 Abigail
Sentoff Geo., lab.. 417 W. 3d
Senzenberger John, carp., 42 Pike
Sercksteden Frank, cof. h., 361 Ham. Road
Seren Martin, cof. h., w.s. Butler b. Pearl and Front
Serer Philip, barber, bds. 48 E. Pearl
Sergeant Chas. E., b.k. Burnet House, h. 12 Hopkins
Sergeant Hy. C, bds. 12 Hopkins
Sergen Phillip, gardener, 259 Everett
Serodino Herman, jeweler, 487 Sycamore
Serrels George, tinner, cor. John and Livingston
Serrin Ruth, bds. 118 Vanhorne
Sertige Geo, clk., 210 Hopkins
Seseng Anthony, carp., 248 Clark
Seshuell J. T. steward U. S. Hotel
Settelmeyer Joseph, butcher, e.s. Clarkson b. Bank and Central Av.
Settle Wm. H., carp., 446 W. 9th w. of Central Av.
Settler Michael, wagon mkr., 110 Ham. Road
Seubert Joseph, w.s. Vine b. Milk and Mulberry
Seuer John, lab., 85 Hamburg
Seufert Constantine, cof. h., n.s. Front nr. Corp. Line
Scuffehalt Andrew, cooper, e. end of Mohawk, h. 264 Ham. Road
Seufferle Chas., cooper, 296 Findlay
Seufferle Christian, cooper, 140 Livingston, h. s.w.c. Findlay and Linn
Seve Hy., shoe mkr., bds. 220 Central Av.

Sevey Jacob, b.k., 204 Everett
Seville Louis, candy mkr., 210 Sycamore
Seward Geo. W., cutter, bds. 298 W. 5th
Seward Jas., drover, 16 W. Mulberry
Seward Wm. C., bk. layer, 152 Cutter
Seward Wm. H., undertaker, 540 W. 7th
Sewerin Franz, tailor, rear 611 Main
Sextbroe Mary, 214 Water
Sexton Chas., dentist, 114 W. 6th
Sexton Fenwick, painter, 372 George, h. 110 Barr
Sexton Rebecca, 110 Barr
Sexton Thos., lab., 186 Barr
Seymour Albert, shoe mkr., 94 W. Court
Seymour Benj., molder, wks. Chamberlain & Co.'s [5th
Seymour Chas. S., tinner, wks. 111 W.
Seymour Chas. W., painter, s.w.c. Barr and Daymiller
Seymour Eliza M., piano teacher, h. 102 Barr
Seymour Geo., carp., 148 Baymiller
Seymour Jacob, lab., 466 E. Front
Seymour John, lab., bds. 346 Main
Seymour John, salesman 65 Main, res. Newport
Seymour Sarah, 91 Mound
Seyppel Ferdinand, pipe store, 427 Vine
Shabe John, lithographer, 403 John
Shaber B., eng., wks. n.s. Front b. Lawrence and Pike
Shackelton John, wks. Cincinnati type foundry
SHACKLEFORD J. C. & CO., Saddles and Harness, 208 Main
Shackleford Jas., mer., 34 Dayton
Shackleford Jas. U., carp., h. 97 Freeman
SHACKLEFORD John C., (J. C. S. & Co.,) 133 W. 8th
Shackleford Wm., rooms s.w.c. 8th and Central Av.
Shackleford Wm. W., driver, bds. 97 Freeman
SHADDINGER GEORGE A., Coppersmith, 123 and 125 E. Pearl, h. 22 George
Shaddinger Jacob W., butcher, 300 Linn
SHADDINGER JOSEPH, Boiler Yard, s.e.c. Pearl and Ludlow, h. 24 George
Shaddinger Matilda, 158 W. 6th
Shaddinger Wm., coppersmith, bds. 158 W. 6th
Shade Wm. steward, Gibson House
Shadley Hy., n.e.c. Milk and Vine
Shaefer —, fireman. 463 W. 3d
Shaefer Emma, 236 Vine
Shaefer M., atty., 142 W. 4th
Shaeffer Geo., cooper, 63 Oliver
Shafer Clemens, stone cutter, 360 Central Av.
Shafer Geo., 412 Race
Shafer Henry, (Henry S. & Co.,) 412 Race
Shafer Henry & Co., (Henry S. & Michael Ziegler.) pork packers, n.s Canal h. Vine and Race
Shafer John, grocery, 360 Central Av.
Shafer Mendal. atty., room 5 Masonic Temple, h. 149 Elm
Shaffer Ann, 248 Clinton
Shaffer D., bds. Denuison House
Shaffer Frank, tinner, bds. 368 Clark
Shaffer Fred., cigar mkr., bds. 292 Pleasant
Shaffer Hy., shoe mkr., wks. 439 Main
Shaffer Hy., tailor, 139 W. Pleasant
SHAFFER Wm., (Keck & S.,) 251 W. 7th
Shafer Savilla, teacher, 248 Clinton
Shaffner Lewis, varnisher, 217 Barr
Shahan David, lab., e.s. Hand al. b. Clark and Court
Shahan Jas., stone mason, e.s. Hand al. b. Court and Clark
Shahan Margaret, 47 Betts
Shai Thomas, bar k., 502 W. Front
Shaible Michael, cooper, bds. s.w.c. Dudley and Liberty
Shamp I. D., bar k., 277 Walnut
Shanahan Michael, lab., e.s. Crippen al. b. 7th and 8th

Shane Chas. G., clk., L. M. R. R. Depot
Shane Geo., 362 Broadway
Shane Hy., 49 Clinton
Shane Hy., carp., 234 W. Front
Shane Johanna, servt., Broadway Hotel
Shanfeld Frank, 381 Broadway
Shanhof Joseph, lab., City Water Works Office
Shank Alfred J., trunk mkr., bds. Henrie House
Shank Mrs. Emily, 273 Cutter
Shank Jacob C., harness mkr., 195 Vine
Shanks Alex., dancing accademy, n.e.c. Central Av. and 5th
Shanley Kate. servt., 113 Pike
Shannehan Michael, packer, b. 217 W. 3d
Shannon Bernard, lab., 107 Mulberry
Shannon Charles, carp., 319 Clark
Shannon Chas. C., printer, e.s. Mound b. 7th and 8th
Shannon Chas. H., pattern mkr., wks. n.e.c. Walnut and Canal
SHANNON EDWARD L., Secretary Sun Insurance Company 75 W. 3d, h. 89 Laurel
Shannon Edward L. jr., b.k. Cin. Gazette Co., bds. 89 Laurel
Shannon Geo., driver, 36 Pike
Shannon Jamis, lab., 58 Gano
Shannon James, watchman, Burnet House
Shannon M., 104 John
Shannon John, lab., w.s. Central Av. b. W. W. Canal and 3d
Shannon John, shoe mkr., w.s. Central Av. b. W. W. Canal and 3d
Shannon John, lab., molder, bds. 114 Hunt
Shannon Kate, servt., Henrie House
Shannon Margaret, 107 Mulberry
Shannon Mary, bds. 30 Patterson al
Shannon Mary, 56 Water
Shannon Michael. porter, 217 W. 3d
Shannon Peter, baker, 253 Broadway
Shannon Peter, lab., 236 Elm
Shannon Peter, lab., 333 W. 5th
Shannon Robert, Junction Torrence and Mound
Shannon Robert H., shoe mkr., 82 Mound
Shannon Wm., lab., s.s. Sloo w. of Freeman
Sharf Conrad, 361 Ham. Road
Sharket Mrs., w s. Central Av. b. 2d and W. W. Canal
Sharkey Barnard, lab., 976 E Front
Sharkey Pat., expressman, s.w.c. Pearl and Canal
Sharp Alex., molder, wks. n.w.c. Plum and Wade
Sharp C., clk., bds. 91 Sycamore
Sharp Chas., 950 E. Front
Sharp Chas., (Woods & S.), 603 W. 6th
Sharp Elizabeth, 950 E. Front
Sharp Geo., tailor, 106 George
SHARP Isaac (Hughes & S.) res. Storrs tp
Sharp James, 106 George
Sharp James, book binder, h. n. s. Grandin al. b. Elm and Plum
Sharp John, agt., bds. 406 W 5th
SHARP Joseph, (Gow & S.,) 97 E. 3d e. of Whittaker
Sharp Peter, wks. w.s. Brighton nr. Denckenstein Garden
Sharp Saml. M., feed store. 31 Hannibal
SHARP Thomas, (Chas H. Wolf & Co) h. Springfield O.
Sharp Thos., n.s. Grandin al. b. Elm and Plum
SHARP Thomas T., (Jones & S.) 362 W. 6th
Sharpless Geo., student., 487 W. 4th
Sharpless Nicholas F., 487 W. 4th
Shart Bertha, dyer, 156 W. 4th
Sharwath Peter, clk., n.e.c. Hunt and Broadway
Shattinger Adam, harness mkr., 406 6th
Shattuck Benj., pass. agt. L. M. C. & X. & C. H. & D. R. R., h. 303 W. 6th
Shatu E. M., porter, 27 W. Front bds, Cincinnati House
Shatzman Christian, lab., 515 E. Front

Shatzman Christopher, finisher, 492 E. Front
Shaughnessey John, sawyer, 52 Plum
Shaute Wm., tailor, 186 Everett
Shaw A. B. bk. mason, 69 Longworth
Shaw Aaron, furniture, 12 E. 4th, bds. s.e.c. 3d and Broadway
Shaw Albert. clk., 335 Race
Shaw & Anderson, (Saml. S. & John R. A.,) grocery, 103 E. Pearl
Shaw Ann, servt., 92 E. 3d
SHAW BARBOUR & CO., (Chas. G. S., Lucius B. & Goodrich H. B.) Importers and Jobbers of Dry Goods, 81 W. Pearl
Shaw & Bonny, (Thos. S., & Andrew B.) feed store, n.w.c. Court and Cutter
Shaw Chas., carp., 19 Martin
SHAW Chas. G., (S. Barbour & Co.) 285 W. 8th
Shaw Daniel, painter, 63 Providence
Shaw Daniel B., harness mkr., bds. 316 W. 3d
Shaw Dora, actress, bds. 125 W. 5th
Shaw Emily, w.s Coggswell al. b Woodward and Abigail
SHAW HARRY E., New and Second hand Furniture, 16 E. 4th, h. 24½ E. 4th
Shaw Jas., dray, 57 Betts
Shaw James C., b.h. 127 W. 5th
Shaw John, cartman, 140 Laurel
Shaw John, fireman, 315 W. 2d
Shaw John A., (John A. S. & Co.) 282 Sycamore
Shaw John A. & Co., (John A. S. & Edward T. Latham), pork packers, 282 Sycamore
Shaw Joseph, finisher, 403 W. 6th
Shaw Julia, 107 Betts
Shaw Peter, lab., 30 Lock w. of 8th
Shaw Robt. n.w.c. Everett and Central Av
Shaw Saml., (S. & Anderson,) res. back of Newport
Shaw Saml. C., bk. layer, 17 Melancthon
Shaw Saml. J., 25 E. 8th
Shaw Sarah, n.w.c. Everett and Central Av
Shaw Thos., (S. & Bonny) 153 W. Court w. of Central Av
SHAW Thos. F., (Stedman, Carlisle & S.,) 335 Race
Shaw W. H., upholsterer, bds. 53 E. 3d
Shaw Wm., blocks and rigging, River b. Ludlow and Lawrence, h. 65 Butler b. Pearl and 3d
Shaw Wm. H., upholsterer, 34 E. 4th
Shaw Wm. M., sewing machine manuf. 31 Mulberry
Shawk Adam, lab., w.s. Riddle b. Bank and Harrison Road
Shawk Chas., lab., e.s. Division b. Harrison pike and Barnard
Shay Bernard, lab., 238 Broadway
Shay Catharine, e.s. Henderson al. b. 7th and 8th
Shay John, tailor, 227 Central Av
Shay Joseph, cook, bds. 13 Race
Shay Laura, saleswoman, 19d W. 5th, bds. 237 W. 5th
Shay Mary, n.s. 7th b. Broadway and Sycamore
Shay Rich., lab., 21 Mill
Shay Thos., bds. Cincinnati House
Shay Thos., stone cutter, e.s. Culvert b. 5th and 6th
Shay Tim., stone mason, 487 W. 5th
Shay Wm., 11 Race
Shay Wm., shoe mkr., 69 Avery
Shays Chas. C., produce, 467 Elm, res. Clifton
Shays John W., pork packer, 346 Walnut, h. Mt. Auburn
Shea Catharine, h. s.e.c. 6th and Culvert
Shea Dennis, grocery, s.e.c. Front and Ludlow
Shea Hy. P. O., tailor, n.e.c. Longworth and Plum
Shea James, lab., wks. C. H. & D R. R depot
Shea John, n.s. 6th b. Culvert and Broadway

Shea Luke, cof. h., n.e.c Front and Vine
Shea Matthew, tailor, 161 Cutter
Shea Patrick, bds. 502 W. 4th
Shea Philip, lab., s.s. 6th b. Broadway and Culvert
Shea Thos., stone cutter, w.s. Culvert b. 5th and 6th
Shean Matthew, tailor, 154 Cutter
Shearer Adeline, n.w.c. Hazen and Rail Road
Shearer Andrew, carp., 932 E. Front
Shearer Ann, 277 George
Shearer Delia, n.w.c. Hazen and Rail Road
Shearer E. C., clk., 101 W. 4th, bds. 27 Longworth
Shearer Hy., carp., 916 E. Front
Shearer Jacob, carp., 1192 E. Front
Shearer John, police, 946 E. Front
Shearer John, printer, 277 George
Shearer John P., carp., n.s Rail Road e. of Hazen
SHEARER LUDWICK, Residence 932 E. Front
Shearn John, lab., 65 Oliver
Shearon Dennis, buckster, 160 Mound
Shears Thos., roller, s.e.c. Race and Commerce
Sheehan Cornelius, clk., 200 W. 5th, h. n.e.c. 6th and Baum
Sheehan James, lab., 836 W. Front
Sheehan Jerry, cof. h., 293 Central Av.
Sheehan Johanna, tailoress, bds. 102 E. 6th
Sheehan Patrick, hostler, 81 Baymiller
SHEEHAN PIERCE, Tea Dealer, Grocer and Dealer in Flour, Grain, and all kinds of Feed, n.w.c. Court and Broadway, h. 315 Broadway
SHEEN FREDERICK, Flour, Meal and Groceries, 70 E. Pearl
Sheen Isaac, editor, n.e.c. Goodloe and Niagara
Sheen James, paper carrier, 231 Laurel
Sheen Pierre, grocer, 815 Central Av
Sheeren John, hostler, w. end of Longworth w. of Park
Sheets Geo., dray, 468 W. 7th
Sheffield Maria, n.e.c. 5th and Race
Sheffield Melia, 309 Richmond
Sheffler Fred, cooper, w.s. Western Av b. Bank and Harrison Road
Shehan Cornelius, clk., s.e.c. 6th and Baum
Shehan John, lab., 205 E. 6th
Shehan Wm., s.e.c. New and Broadway
Sheibert Emil, saddler, 518 W. 9th
Sheilds Chas., hostler, 256 W. 9th w. of Central Av
Skelby John, lab., e.s. Henderson al. b. 7th and 8th
Shelby Louisa, w.s. Jones b. Liberty and Everett
Sheldon Ben., expressman, w.s. Butler b. Pearl and Front
Sheldon Elisha, carp., 436 George
Sheldon James, clk., O. & M. R. R., h. 608 W. 9th
Sheldon Martin I., printer, bds. 390 Race
Sheldon Thaddeus S., agt. sewing machines, n.e.c. 4th and Race
Shelds C., hostler, s.w.c. Freeman and Front
Shell Louis, cooper, 42 Jones
Shelly Fred., molder, wks. n.w.c. Plum and Wade
Shelt Joseph, cap. manuf., 120 Main h. 10 Home
Shelt Wm., traveling agt., 120 Main, h. 10 Home
Shelton Rev. Wallace, 243 Longworth
Sheman W. H. E., coach trimmer, 118 Laurel
Shemick Gerhard, varnisher, 05 David
Shen Matthew, walter, Madison House
Shenfeld Dick, mach., 74 Spring
Shenk John, 69 Mulberry
Shepard Chas. J., teacher, 13 Hopkins
Shepard Elisha Y., bk. mkr., 538 W. 9th
Shepard Hy. A., car painter, bds. 13 Hopkins
Shepard Oscar F., clk., O. & M. R.R., h. 87 Barr

Shepardson Daniel, principal Woodward High School, h. 100 W. Court w. of Central Av.
Shepen Leonora, servt, 362 W. 7th
Sheper Hy., shoe mkr., 463 Linn
Shepfield Chas., lab., 403 W. 2d
Shepherd Geo. W. J., carriage painter, bds. 160 Sycamore
Shepherd J. W., cutter 109 W. Pearl, h. 136 John
Shepherd Mary J., 68 Butler
Shepherd Thos., lab. 175 Water
Shepherdson Jno, grocery, n.e.c. George and Linn
Shepman Fred., porter, 60 Freeman
Sheppard Chas, butcher, n.s. Montgomery Pike nr. Reading Road
Sheppard Ellen, 49 Rittenhouse
Sheppard Fred., shoe mkr., 124 W. 3d
SHEPPARD G. W. & CO., (Geo. W. S. & John Holland.) Manufacturers of Gold Pens, 6 W. 4th
SHEPPARD Geo W., (G. W. S. & Co.) res. Aurora, Ind.
Sheppard Jas., driver, bds. s.e.c. Pearl and Pike
Sheppard John W., cutter, 136 John
SHEPPARD JOHN W., Wholesale and Retail Dealer in Fancy Goods, 20 W. 4th
Sheppard Simon hackman, 16 New
SHEPPARD W. B., (Warden, Forrest & S.,) 125 W. 9th
Sheppell Wm., molder, 24 Ann
Shepperd Geo. painter, bds. s.e.c. Sycamore and 5th
Sher Benj., molder, wks. n. e. c. Canal and Walnut
Sherar Albert, cab, mkr., 35 Mill
Sheren Thos., salesman, 272 W. 9th
Sherer Anna, 93 E. 3d e. of Whittaker
Sherer Fred., carp., 504 E. Front
Sherer John, publisher, 126 Linn
Sheriff Amelia D , servt., 373 W. 8th
Sherrick Benj. J., stove mounter, s.e.c. Smith and 2d
Sherick John, bk. binder, wks. 137 Walnut
Sherick Mary A., 277 George
Sheridan Bridget. servt. Burnet House
Sheridan Cornelius, 503 Sycamore
Sheridan Edward, lab., s.s. Phoebe al. b. Plum and Central Av.
Sheridan Ellen, 245 W. Front
Sheridan Jas., lab., 48 Plum
Sheridan Jas., varnisher, 245 W. Front
Sheridan Jas., waiter Burnet House
Sheridan John, lab., 17 Freeman
Sheridan John B., drays, 105 W. Court w. of Central Av.
Sheridan M., waiter Burnet House
Sheridan Martin, fireman, 215 W. 2d
Sheridan Mary, servt., 135 Plum
Sheridan Michael, currier, 503 Sycamore
Sheridan Minnie, servt., Heurie House
Sheridan Pat., lab., 209 W. 3d
Sheridan Richard, driver, 209 W. 3d
Sheridan Wm., lab., wks. C. H. & D. R. R. Depot
SHERIFF'S OFFICE, Court House Building, John B. Armstrong, Sheriff
Sherlock Ann. h. 429 Walnut
Sherlock Edward, butcher. 26 State
Sherlock Jas., butcher, 26 State
Sherlock John, butcher. 28 State
Sherlock John, b k., 20 Broadway, h. 353 John
Sherlock Peter, renderer. cor. State and Deer Creek Road, h. 28 State
SHERLOCK THOMAS, Steamboat Agent, 20 Broadway and President City Insurance Company, h. Clifton
Sherman Fred., dray, 11 14th b. Central Av. and Plum
Sherman Geo., lab., wks. n. w. c. Wood and 3d
Sherman Hy., cof h., 393 Race
Sherman Nehemiah, eng., n.s. R. Road opp. French
Sherman Fred., porter. h. 63 W. Court
Shermann Geo., driver, 476 W. 3d
Shermann Mary, tailoress, bds. 476 W. 3d

Sherman O. S., bls. Dennison House
Sherrick Sam., printer, 43 Mill
Sherridan Wm., lab., n.s. Taylor b. Carr ank Freeman
Sherrike Chas , butcher, 141 Spring
Sherrike Edward, 141 Spring
Sherry Pat., butcher, n.s. Deer Creek Road b. Liberty and Tunnel
Sherwin W. G., atty., room 7 Masonic Temple
Sherwood Hy. R., dental instrument manuf., 269 Walnut
Sherwood Jas. E., 243 W. Court
Sherwood John. carp., h. w. s. Central Av. b. W. W Canal and 3d
Sherwood Wm., carp., wks. C. H. & D. R. R. depot paint shop, h. Delhi Tp.
SHERWOOD WM., Physician and Surgeon, Office and Residence, 243 W. Court
Shetland Casper, tinner, n.s. McDowell e. of Hill
Sheve Hy , plasterer, 19 Gorman
Shewan Geo., cab mkr., 492 W. 7th
Shey Thos., grocer, 116 Barr
Shey Timothy, rear of 37 New
Shick Conrad, 68 Mohawk
Shick Joseph, 69 Mohawk
Shidermandle John, 30 Canal
Shiel Nicholas, coach trimmer, 127 Clay
Shield Eben, fireman, 465 W. 3d
Shield Edward M., mach., 75 E. Front, h. 17 Clark
Shield Geo., Chief Eng. Water Works, h. 45 Ellen
Shield Geo. jr., mach , 75 E. Front, bds. 17 Clark
Shield Geo., B. M. eng., 45 Ellen
Shield Michael, cab mkr., bds 165 Barr
Shields ———, hack driver, bds. 81 E. Pearl
Shields Abraham, lab., 465 W. 3d
Shields Chas., lab., 506 W. 9th
Shields Cornelius, s.e.c. 6th and Central Av.
Shields Elizabeth 314 W. 7th
Shields Kate, dress mkr., 316 W. 5th
Soichls Martin, lab., 97 E. Pearl
Shields Mary, w.s. Langdon al. b. 6th & 7th
Shields Milton, b.k., 63 Walnut, bds. 243 W. 5th
Shields Patrick, 316 W. 5th
Shields Thomas D , bk layer,144 Mound
Sniffert Reuben, bliksmith, wks. s.w.c. Betts and Central Av
Shigling Michael. butcher, n.w.c. Bank and Dannm
Shilling Martin, lab., 37 Baum
Shillinger John. carp , 517 E. Front
Shillings Isaac, tailor, 60 Gano
SHILLITO Geo. (Geo. S. & Co.) 84 W. 9th [W. 9th
SHILLITO Geo., jr., (Geo. S. & Co.) 84
SHILLITO GEO. & CO. (George S., sen. & George S , jr.) Candle, Soap and Lard Oil Factory, cor. Findlay and John, Store 39 Sycamore
SHILLITO John. (John S & Co.) s.w. c 4th and Pike
SHILLITO JOHN & CO. Dry Goods. Carpeting, &c., 101, 103 and 105 W 4th
SHILLITO Wallace (John S. & Co.) s. w.c. 4th an l Pike
Shindle Mary A., 14 Harrison
Shindler Hy . teamster, wks.n.w.c. Freeman and 9th
Shine Daniel B., tobacconist, 17 Main
Shiner Geo. W., pipeman, 702 W. Front
Shiner Hy, G., 236 Longworth
Shinglelecker Isaac, carp., 434 W. 8th
Shinnick Richard, (T. & R. S.) 196 E. 6th
Shinnick T. & R (Thomas & Richard), carps., 168 W 8th
Shinnick Thos. (T. & R. S.) 124 E. 8th
Shipe David, cooper, 15 Park
Shipler Deborah, seamstress, 5 Pleasant
Shipler Stephenson H., chair mkr., 5 Pleasant
Shipley Caroline, 427 W. 6th
Shipley Charles, draughtsman, 129 W. 8th

Shipley Chas. J., artist, bds. 129 W. 8th
SHIPLEY Henry H. (S. & Smith), 118 W. 6th
Shipley Joseph, carp., s.s. Pearl b. Pike and Butler
SHIPLEY Murray (Murray S. & Co.), 329 W. 7th
SHIPLEY MURRAY & CO. (Murray S , Thomas C. Shipley & W. H. Hoover) Wholesale Fancy Dry Goods, 94 W. Pearl
SHIPLEY & SMITH (Henry H. S. & James E. S.) Visiting and Wedding Card Engravers, 22 W. 4th
SHIPLEY Thomas C. (Murray Shipley & Co) 129 W. 8th
Shipley Wm., b. k., 94 W. Pearl, bds. 129 W. 8th
Shipman Hy., lab., 113 Avery
Shipp Thomas, barber, 154 W. 8th
Shiras Wm. M. 289 W. Court w. of Central Av
Shire Hy., cooper, w. s. Central Av. b. Findlay and Charlotte
Shire Jacob, b.k., 31 Sycamore, h. 7 George
Shires Wm., manager, National Theater, h. 179 W. 3d
Shisheler Joseph. lab., 386 Broadway
Shivanan Hugh, lab., 67 Cherry al
Shlappner Elizabeth, 557 W. 8th
Shlemall Frank, painter, bds. 371 Br'd-way
Shlesinger Annetta, millinery, 106 W. 5th, h. 101 Race
Shlink M., bds. Cincinnati House
Shlitzberger Ferdinand, grocer, 114 Carr
SHLOFMAN Henry (Wm W. Carpenter & Co.) 55 Milton
Shmieg John, frame mkr., 111 Ludlow
Shneer Anthony, mach., 531 W. 8th
Shneider Jacob, lab., s.w.c. Riddle and Harrison Pike
Shnelle Louis. basket manuf., 109 W. Court, h. 132 W. Court
Shobbreck John H., harness mkr, 16 W. Court w. of Central Av
Shobe John, lithographer, 403 Race
Shober Chas. W. A., cab. mkr., 18 Harrison e. of Broadway
Shober Chas. W. A., sexton, 17 Hopkins
Shober Wm. H., b. k., h n.s. Harrison e. of Broadway
Shoberg George J., lab., 161 Pleasant
Shockley Dewitt C., clk., 214 Barr
Shockman B., lab., wks. 335 Broadway
Shoeldheis J., porter, 34 E. 5th
Shoemaker Adam G., carver, 311 Freeman
Shoemaker Adam, stone cutter, 36 Grant
Shoemaker Andy, carp., 533 W 8th
Shoemaker E. M., quartermaster, bds. Spencer House
Shoemaker Frederick, rope mkr., 442 W. 2d
Shoemaker Herman, tailor, 62 Laurel
Shoemaker Marion, lab., 15 Park
Shoemaker Martin, 83 W. Front
Shoemaker Paul, waiter, Gibson House
Shoemaker Theodore, carp., 198 Hopkins
Shoemate Alexander, bds. Dumas Hotel
SHOENBERGER G & J H. & CO. (Geo. K. S., John H. S. & Wm. H. S.,) Juniata Nail Works, 15 Pub. Landing
Shoenberger George. clk., 160 W. 5th
SHOENBERGER Geo. K., (G. & J. H. S. & Co) 111 Broadway
Shoenberger Hy., butcher, r°2 Bank
Shoenberger John, butcher, 405 Baymiller
SHOENBERGER John H., (G & J. H. S. & Co.) h. Pittsburgh Pa.
Shoenberger Joseph, n. e c. Logan and Liberty [Race
Shoenberger Michael, varnisher, 522
Shoenberger Philip, blksmith, bds. 919 Central Av.
SHOENBERGER Wm. H., (G. & J. H. S. & Co.,) b. Vine St. Hill
Shoenbrun Amelia, teacher of music 352 Race
Shoenbrun Isaac, 352 Race
Shoenbrun Leopold, 84 W. Pearl, h. 352 Race

SHOENLE W., reporter. Volksfreund, h. s.e.c. 12th and Elm
Shoepfel Jacob, clk., 22 W. 5th, res. Covington
Shohl Elias, clk., 62 W. Pearl, bds. 628 Vine
SHOHL Simon, (S. B. & Co.,) 205 W. Pearl
SHOHL SIMON & CO., (Simon S. & Bernhard Bettmann,) Importers and Dealers in Gents' Furnishing Goods, Notions &c., 62 W. Pearl
Sholl Elizabeth, h 417 W. Liberty
SHOLL GEORGE W., Manufacturer of Trunks, Valises and Carpet Bags, also of Terra Cotta Burial Cases, n.w.c. Walnut and 2d, h. 100 Everett
Sholl John, trunk mkr., wks. 509 plum
Shomblew Hy., lab., n.s. Front e. of Foster
Shomeyer Samuel, molder, wks. n.e.c. Walnut and Canal
Shonharst Harman H., chair mkr., 200 Cutter
SHONTER ANTHONY, Attorney at Law, 363 Main h. 397 Elm
Shore John G., blksmith, n. s. Front b. Pike and Butler, h. 88 Butler b. 5th and 3d
Short Charles, lab., w. s. Ramsey n. of Front
Short Charles A., 483 W. Front
Short Frederick, printer, rear 67 Bremen
SHORT FRED. H., Secretary, C. H. & D. R. R., Office in Depot, h. 51 Mound
Short Geo. M., (J J. Stagg & Co.) res. Mt. Washington
Short Thomas O., baggage master, C. H. & D. R. R., h. 598 W. 6th
Shorten James, agt., 34 E. 4th
Shorten James B., trunk mkr., n. w. c. Main and Patterson al.
Shorten John, s. s, New b. Culvert and Broadway
Shorten Mary, 437 John
Shorten Richard, trunk manufac., n.w.c. Main and Patterson al.
Shorten Richard, gold pen mkr., 120 E. Liberty
Shorten Richard Jr., trunk mkr., n.w.c. Main and Patterson al.
Shorten Wm., box mkr., wks. n. w. c. Main and Patterson al.
Shorter Chas., whitewasher, 114 Avery
Shorter Wm., whitewasher, 114 Avery
Shotfield George, real estate agent, 180 George [more
Shotley James, grocer. bds. 193 Syca-
Shott Adam, n.e.c. Ludlow and Pearl
Shotter Hy., molder, wks. n. e. c. Canal and Walnut
Shottsman Jacob, 30 Baum
Shotwell Cassius, clk., 61 W. 3d, bds. 180 George
Shotwell Mrs. E. A., Embroidery &c., 70 W. 5th, h. 138 W. 4th
SHOTWELL GEORGE H., Real Estate Broker, 75 W. 3d h. 180 George
SHOTWELL Theodore, (Chambers Stevens & Co.) 578 W. 9th
Shous Wm., clk., bds. n. w. c. Central Av. and Longworth
Shout Hy., pipeman, 3 Crippen al.
Show Geo., 111 W. Court w. of Central Av.
Showell Ely, carriage mkr., 740 Vine
Shreiner Conrad, packer, 11 E. 9th, h. Jackson Hill
Shreve Albert P., cashier, n. e. c. Vine and 5th, bds. 236 W. 3d
Shreve Hy., clk., Tappan McKillop & Co's., 236 W. 3d
Shreve Lizzie D., bds. 236 W. 3d
Shreve R. J., at Tappan McKillop & Co's., h. 236 W. 3d
Shreve Rebecca, bds. 233 W. 3d
Shreve Richard J., clk., bds. 236 W. 3d
Shriever Frank, 291 W. 3d
Shrimpton Harry, mach., 129 Richmond
Shriner Christian, n.w.c. Linn and Findlay

CINCINNATI (SIE) DIRECTORY. (SIM) 297

Sickles William, salesman, bds. 203 Longworth
Sickmann Richard, lab. 45 Wood
Sidal Xavier, cof. and b. h., 249 W. 6th
Siddall John B., real estate broker, 77 W. 3d, h. 290 W. 7th
Siddle Jonathan, mach., n.s Front e. of Kelly
Sidenberg Louisa, servt., 142 Broadway
Siebel Thomas. lab., 101 Martin
Siebel William, tanner, 713 Central Av
Siebenfercher Anthony, bar k., 280 Central Av
Sieber Andrew, carp., 679 Vine
Sieber Ernst, printer, 197 Smith
Sieber Wm., 421 Walnut
SIEBERN J. N. & BROS., (John N., Peter H. & Stephen W.,) Wholesale Dealers in Groceries, Produce and Liquors, 8 E. Pearl
SIEBERN John N., (J. N, S. & Bros.,) res. Pleasant Ridge
SIEBERN Peter H., (J. N. J. & Bros.,) 8 E. Pearl
SIEBERN Stephen W., (J. N. S. & Bros.,) 421 E. Pearl
Siebert Conrad, core mkr., w.s. Whittaker b. Front and 3d
Siebert Henry G., carp., 169 Pleasant
Siebrecht Christian, pattern mkr., 95 Clay
Siebrecht Wm., 26 Orchard
Sieckmeier, Christian C., cooper, 25 Franklin
Siodie August, clock mkr., 8 Hughes
Siefe Henry, tailor, 451 W. 6th
Siefermann Joseph, bds. 637 Race
Siefermann Anselm, cigar mkr., 652 Race
Siefers Mrs., 94 Clay
Siefert Chas., 59 12th
Siefert Eve, 105 Martin
Siefert Geo., lab., 43 Ham. Road
Siefert Joseph, mason, 59 12th
Siefert Lorenz, mason, 144 Bremen
Sieferts James K., porter P. O., 73 Pendleton
Siefke Hy., grocer, s e.c. Linn and 8th
Siegel Christiana, n. s. al. b. Poplar and Vine and Ham. Road and Buckeye
Siegel Gottfried J., carp., 107 W. Liberty
Siegel Gottlieb, cooper, n. s. al. b. Poplar and Vine and Ham. Road and Buckeye
Siegel Hy., brass founder, 540 Walnut
Siegel Jacob, finisher, 486 Walnut
Siegel Joseph, clk., 363 Main
Siegel L , bds. 158 W. 3d
Siegel Leopold, peddler, 22 15th
Siegel Louis, rag dealer, 27 15th b. Elm and Plum
Sieger John, tailor, 55 Elder
Siegers Francis, cab. mkr., 432 W. 5th
Siegler John, rope mkr., s.s. Budd b. Harriet and Mill Creek
Siegler Sebastian, finisher, 73 Hunt
Siegmann Augustus, shoemkr, 773 Vine
Siegmann Margaret, s.w.c. Abigail and Spring
Siegrist John, cook, St. Nicholas Restaurant
Siegwolf John, cof. h., 1102 Central Av.
Sickel Mandall, e.s. Branch b. Ham. Road and Findlay
Sielschelt Barney, confec., 200 Sycamore
Siemann Hy., 2 W. Mulberry
Siemann J. Frederick, cof. h., 26 Orchard
Siemer Ann, chair caner, 594 Main
Siemer John D., grocery, 594 Main
Siemon, August, tailor, 607 W. Front
Siering Barbara, 517 Buckeye
Siermann Andrew, lab., 56 Buckeye
Siermann Edward, tailor, 559 Vine
Sieter Albert agt., 57 Allison
Sieve Bernard, clk., s.e c. Bank and Baymiller
Sieve Clemons, peddler, 7 Buckeye
Sieve Herman, cigars, 555 Walnut
Sieve John, cigar mkr., bds. s.w.c. Liberty and Main
Siever John T., lab., 56 W. Liberty
Sieverding Hy., lab., 25 Franklin
Sieverding John D., porter, 18 Abigail
Sievering Hy., cab. mkr., 193 Pleasant

Sieverink Anthony, (Veeneman & Co.,) 566 Race
Sieverling Frederick, carp., 130 Pleasant
Sievert John G., tailor, 29 Moore
Sievin Frederick, driver, bds. 102 Gest
Siews Joseph, grocery, 215 Betts
SIEWERS CHARLES G., Saw and Cabinet Tool Manuf., 93 E. 8th, res. Newport
Siewig Hy., carp., bds. 25 Franklin
Sigel Hy., brass molder, wks. n.s. Front b. Lawrence and Pike
Sigel Jacob, mach., wks. n.s. E. Front b. Lawrence and Pike
Sigel Joseph, mach., wks. n.s. Front b. Lawrence and Pike
Sigerson Wallace, bds. 137 W. 9th
Siggers George. lab., 162 Freeman
Sigloch Jacob M , porter, 18 Webster
Sigloch John, porter, 18 Webster
Sigman Randolph, driver, 59 Abigail
Sigmund Alfred, bds. Cincinnati House
Sigmund Louis, bds. Cincinnati House
Signer Charles, varnisher, 338 Clark
Silas Catharine, s.w.c. Water and Plum
Silbermann Jacob, horse trader, 533 Walnut
Silbernagel Conrad, cof. h. 548 Vine
Silbernagel Michael, blk.smith, 70 W. Liberty
Silbernagel Simon J., meats, 97 W. 5th
Siller Geo., carp., n.e.c. Court and Elm
Sillinger Herman, Cin. type foundry
Sillit Thomas, baker, bds. 553 W. 5th
Sills Jacob, lab., wks. 25 Water
Sills John, lab., wks. 222 E. Front
Silmon John, lab. e.w. E. Front, e. of Reed
Silsbee Samuel, phys., 260 Walnut, h. 1457 E. Front [Hotel
Silsey Hy., cigar mkr., bds. Teutonia
Silver Jonathan J , wagon mkr., n.s. 6th b. Harriet and Horn
Silverman Hannah. 9 David
SILVERS James H., secy. Franklin Ins. Co. of Cin., 31½ W. 3d, h. 549 W. 7th
Silverstein Barnard, peddler, 132 Spring
Silverstone Jacob, 151 W. Pearl
SILVESTER HOUSE, Jno. Silvester, Proprietor, 4 and 6 W. 6th
SILVESTER JOHN, Proprietor Silvester House, 4 and 6 W. 6th
Silz Jacob, butcher, 25 15th b. Elm and Plum
Simann Catharine, 618 Vine
Simbe Wm., bds. Cincinnati House
Simcox Samuel, mach., wks. gas works
Simcox Wm., lab., wks. gas works
Simington Andrew, lab., 177 E. Front
Simmen Hy., box mkr., 11 Wade, b. Elm and Plum
Simmer Morris, lab., 30 Richmond, b. Elm and Plum
Simmerman Lawrence, baker, bds. w. s. Elm, b. 3d and McFarland
Simmon Jacob, 212 Laurel
Simmonds Adam, bk. layer, 180 Central Avenue
Simmonds George, agent, 267 George
Simmonds Maurice, 267 George
Simmonds Parmelia, 295 Cutter
Simmonds Mrs. Ann, 670 Central Av
Simmons Benjamin, whitewasher, 118 E. 6th
Simmons George, painter, 187 W. Court, w. of Central Av
Simmons Geo., (O. E Hotchkiss & Co.) 86 Broadway
Simmons H. D., bds. s.w.c. Race and 3d
Simmons Hy., clk., 16 Hathaway
Simmons Hugh, inspector, 18 W. Front, h. 424 George
Simmons Jacob, box mkr., wks. Livingston near Linn
Simmons James, waiter, Madison House
Simmons Lewis C., measurer, s.s. Findlay b. Freeman and Western Av
Simmons Martha, bds. 92 E. 5th
Simmons Ralph, 12 Race
Simmons Robert B., carp , bds. 424 George
Simmons Samuel, policeman, 110 W. 5th
Simmons Thomas, shoemkr. bds. n. s. Goodloe b. Willow and Niagara

Simms Mary, 162 W. Pearl
Simms Robert, eng., 182 Water
Simms Sarah C., servt., 408 W. 6th
SIMON B. & CO., (Benj. S., Ezekiel Simon, Max Thurnauer & Max Mack,) Wholesale Dry Goods, n. e. c. Pearl and Main
Simon Benjamin, clk., bds. 37 Broadway
Simon Benjamin, (B. S. & Co.,) 48 W. 8th
SIMON Benjamin, jr., (G. Simon & Son,) h. Riddle Av
Simon David, furniture, 189 W. 5th
SIMON Ezekiel, (B. Simon & Co.) 187 Broadway
SIMON G. & SON, (Gabriel & Benjamin, jr.,) Wholesale Clothiers, 37 W. Pearl, and Ladies and Gents Furnishing Goods, 12 W. 5th
SIMON Gabriel, (G. S. & Son,) 17 Longworth
Simon George, lab., 464 E. Front
Simon Isaac, atty., bds. 37 Broadway
Simon Jacob, foreman M. & C. R.R., 466 E. Front
Simon Jacob, mason, 13 Mulberry
Simon John, family grocery, 656 Vine
Simon John A., 470 Linn
Simon Joseph, 37 Broadway
Simon Joseph, gaiter cutter, bds. 206 W. 5th
Simon Lotte, 45 W. 8th
Simon Nicholas, cof. h., 346 Ham. Road
Simon Samuel, bakery, s. w. c. George and Central Av
Simon Samuel, tailor, s. w. c. Plum and Longworth
Simon Wm., furnisher, 121 Longworth
Simons Eunice R., 286 W. 9th, w. of Central Av
Simons Thomas, carp., h 21 Oliver
SIMONTON Joseph, (Royer & Co.) h. Front st. Covington
Simonton Richard L., clk., 340 W. 3d, h. Covington
Simpelson J. R., molder, bds. Bevis House
SIMPKINSON Alfred, (J. Simpkinson & Co.) h. Cheviot Pike
Simpkinson Chas., clk., 34 W. 5th
SIMPKINSON Henry, (J. Simpkinson & Co.) 149 John
SIMPKINSON J. & CO., (John, Alfred & Henry S.) Wholesale Dealers in Custom Made and Eastern Boots and Shoes, 99 W. Pearl
SIMPKINSON John, (J. S. & Co.,) 402 W. 4th
Simpson Alexander, plumber, wks. 200 Vine
SIMPSON CHARLES T., Physician and Surgeon, 483 E. Front, h. 52 W. 9th
Simpson Christina, 103 Longworth
Simpson George A., (Wm. T. Simpson & Son,) 46 Mound
Simpson Hy. F., auctioneer, bds. 321 Walnut
SIMPSON J. ALEX., Jr., Attorney and Counsellor at Law, n.w.c. 4th and Sycamore, h. Country
Simpson James, mach., wks. gas works
Simpson James E., salesman, 30 W. 4th, res. Covington
Simpson James J, 162 Longworth
Simpson June, 812 E. Front
Simpson John A., salesman, 30 W. 4th, res. Covington
Simpson Josephine, seamstress, 13 W. 6th
Simpson Margaret, 14 Lock
Simpson Mary, 460 W. 5th
Simpson Thomas, express driver, 460 W. 5th
Simpson Thomas, watchman, Junction High and Kempers Lane
Simpson Wm. T., (Wm. T. S. & Son,) 46 Mound
Simpson Wm. T. & Son, (Wm. T. & Geo. A.) meats, n. w. c. 6th and Mound
Simrall J. W. G., adjuster Ætna Ins. Co., 171 Vine, h. Covington
Sims Robert, 353 John
Sims Robert, eng., Enquirer bldg. n.e.c. Vine and Burnet

Sims Robert A., b.k., 110 Richmond
Sims Samuel A., carp., 75 Pleasant
Sims Wm., b. h., 269 Central Av
Sinzenbaher John, carp., 42 Pike
Sinclair Jno. H. H., clk., 136 Richmond
SINCLAIR Nimrod H., (Baker & Co.) h. Covington
Sinderman Hy., hinge molder, wks. n.e. Walnut and Canal
Singer Chas., barber, s.s. 6th nr. Broadway
Singer Jacob, shoemker, 282 W. 6th
Singer John, cooper, 135 Laurel
Singer John, finisher, wks. n. e. c. Walnut and Canal
Singer Lawrence, e.s. Vine, nr. Auburn Avenue
Singer Nettie, bds. s.e.c. 6th and Smith
Singer Peter, cooper, 257 Carr
Singer Peter, cooper, wks. Oehler al. b. Freeman and Garrard
Singer Phillip, tailor, wks. 305 W. 6th
Singerburger Ernst, lock mkr., wks. n.e. c. Walnut and Canal
SINGHOFF JOHN A., Drugs, Medicines, Paints, Oils, &c., 416 George
Singhose Christian, type dresser, 46 Central Av
Singleton John, clk. Billiard Room, Burnet House
Singleton John J 53 E. 3d
Singleton Thomas, driver, bds. s. e. c. Harrison Road and Brighton
Singleton Sarah, 53 E. 3d
Sining John, molder, wks. n.w.c. Plum and Wade
Sinkey P. S., bds. Walnut St. House
Sinks H. B., clk Walnut St. House
Sinnatt Patrick, lab., 407 Longworth
Sinner Berghard, carp., 118 Bremen
Sinner Hy., driver, wks s.e.c. Grant and Plum
Sinnett Ann, 26 George
Sinnett Patrick, driver, wks. n.w.c. Court and Rupe
Sinning John A., lab., 14 Madison
Sinseemann Hy., 16 Hughes
Sintal Hy., lab, 70 Abigail
Sinton David, (S. & Means,) 240 W. 4th
Sinton & Means, (David S. & Thos. W. M.,) pig iron, 25 W. 3d
Sippel Geo., tailor, 126 Walnut, h. 36 Pleasant
Sisters of Mercy, s. s. 4th b. Central Av. and John
Sisters of Notre Dame Academy, s. s. 6th b. Sycamore and Broadway, sister Louisa, superior
Sites Joseph, lab., 633 W. Front
Sitsman Barbara, servt., 456 W. 3d
Sittel Theodore, phys., 794 Pike
Sitterding Geo., salesman, 338 Main, h. 175 Clay
Sitterding Hy. J., shoemkr, 93 Pleasant
Sitterlie Robert, finisher, 24 Franklin
Siverman Hy., shoemkr. 66 W. Front
SKAATS & ANGEVINE, (Geo, S. & Chas. E. A.) Coal Dealers, n. w. c. 6th and Freeman and s.w.c. Mound and Court
Skaats Catharine, 269 W. 3d
SKAATS George, (S. & Angevine,) h. Delhi Tp.
Skaats James K., car. mkr., n.s. Taylor b. Freeman and Carr
Skaats Mary A., 641 W. 5th
Skahan Thomas, lab., 550 Race
Skally Peter, lab., 184 E. Pearl
SKARDON JAMES, Agent for Singer's Sewing Machines, n. e. c. 4th and Race, up stairs, h. 527 W. 5th
Skardon Wm., tailor, 46 Elizabeth
Skean John S., clk., 141 John
Skenn Lavinda, 141 John
Skelley John., lab., 10 E. 8th, e. of Lock
Skelton Josiah H., mer., 348 W. 7th
Skerrett David P., shoemkr. 96 Clinton
Skiff Frank D., clk., 16 W. Front, h. Covington
Skid Jno. A., com. mer., 16 W. Front, h. Covington
Skillman Annie bds. 333 Cutter
Skillman Edwin, teamster, 29 Pleasant
Skillman Ely M., steward, bds. 220 W. 9th, w. of Central Av

Skillman Mary, 220 W. 9th, w. of Central Av
Skinner Alfred, salesman, bds. Walnut St. House
SKINNER Frank, (Frank S. & Co.) 455 W. 8th
SKINNER FRANK & CO., Commission and Produce Merchants, 85 W. 2d
Skinner Lewis E., clk. L. M. R.R. Depot, h. 76 Baum
Skinner John A., cab. mkr., 459 W. 7th
Skinner Joseph F., clk., 65 W. 2d, bds. 455 W. 8th
Skinner Wm., clk., Adams Express Co. bds. 459 W. 7th
Skinner Wm. H., mess. O. & M. R.R., room 196 Burnet House
Skully Lawrence, lab., 564 Race
Slack Elijah, phys., n.s. Boal b. Young and Price
Slack Ily., 100 Milton
Slack James, carp., 136 Baymiller
Slack Saml., cooper, s.w.c. Hopkins and Central Av
Slack Wm., carp., 134 Baymiller
Slade Laura, bds. 294 W. 4th
Slagger Francis, cab. mkr., s.s. Weller b Carr and Harriet
Slake Hy., bksmith, 147 Clark
Slamer Hy., lab., 143 Abigail
Slane Dominick, lab., Maiden Lane b. Gas al. and Anderson al.
Slater Geo. lab., wks. w.s. Lock b. 4th and 5th
Slattery John, butcher, s.s. Hunt e. of Liberty
Slattery Patrick T., grocer, 108 E. 6th
Slattery Roda, lab., wks. Hieatt and Wood's
Slaughter Anna, w.s. Ramsey n. of Front
Slaughter Elizabeth, laundress, 3 al. b. 4th and 5th and Park and Mill
Slaughter James, printer, 98 Race
Slaughter Josephine, h. e.s. Race b. 3d and Pearl
Slea Casper, molder wks Chamberlain & Co's
Sleator Geo., lab., n.s. Friendship al. b. Lawrence and Pike
Sledge Geo. C., provision broker, (College Bldg., bds. Burnet House
Sledge Rich., porter, e.s Pancoast al. b. 7th and 8th
Slee Cosper, molder, 102 Hunt
Sleeper Hy., carp., 438 W. 5th
Sleer W. M. lab. wks. Wood & McCoy's
Sleeseman Elizabeth, 12 W. Mulberry
Sleet Louis O., clk., 24 E. 2d, bds. Buttemillers Hotel
Sleight John H., 306 Findlay
Sleihman-Joseph, lab., 103 W. Front
Slekters Mary, 29 Commerce
Slenderman Chas., cook, Clifton House
Slenger Enoch, lab. n.s. Rice nr. Fountain
Slenz Hy., tailor, s.s. Doal b. Broadway and Sycamore
Slep Hy., dray, Observatory street. Mt. Adams
Slicker John, lab., 13 Abigail
SLEVIN J. & J., (James and John), Importers and Wholesale Dealers in Fancy and Staple Dry Goods 146 Main
SLEVIN James, (J. & J. S.,) h. Philadelphia
Slevin Jas. L., clk., 424 W. 6th
SLEVIN John, (J. & J. S.,) 424 W. 6th
Slevin John A., clk., 424 W. 6th
Slevin Thos. E., student, 424 W. 6th
Slick Michael, carp., n.s. Sloe e. of Harriet
Slick Tony, saddletree mkr., s.w.c. Harriet and Budd
Slight John, lab., 306 Findlay
Sliker Christopher, (S. & Matthews), bds 26 Harrison
Sliker & Matthews, (Christopher S. & Hy. M.,) boots and shoes, 63 E, Pearl
Sliker Valentine, boots and shoes s.e.c. Pearl and Sycamore, res. Country
Slimer Geo. (S. & Raipe) 677 Elm
Slimer Hy., 28 Accomodation

Slimer & Ralpe, (Geo. S. & John J. R.) meats &c., 25 Pub. Landing
Slimmer Christian, rear 42 Mohawk
Slimmer Hermann. eng., 681 Vine
Slimmer John, wagoner, 52 Kossuth
Sling Robert, barber, n.e.c. Race and Water
Slints Rosina, 123 York
Sloan Chas., butter and eggs, 138 Dayton, h, 154 York
Sloan Ella, bds. n.s. Rail Road, e. of Kelly
Sloan Isabella, nurse, 587 Central Av
Sloan Rich., caner, 433 Central Av
Slone Sallie M., saleswoman, 286 Longworth
Sloan Saml., 45 David
Sloan Sarah M., bds., 286 Longworth
Slober John S., harness mkr., 202 Elm
SLOCOMB Rufus T., (Egan & S.) 139 W. 9th
Slocum Chas. H., 121 E. 3d
Slocum Elizabeth, 121 E. 3d
Slocum Theodore clk., 121 E. 3d
SLOCUM J. J., Commission and Produce Merchant, south end C. H. & D. R. R. Depot
Sloman Morris, clk., 89 W. Court
Slone Jane, n.s. Front e. of Lumber
Stone John, clk., 145 Longworth
Stone Wm., sawyer, n.s. Front opp. Ferry
Sloop Geo., carp., 99 W. M. Canal
Sloop Jacob, carp., 99 W. M. Canal
Sloop Jacob H., painter, bds. 380 Race
Sloop Washington, candy mkr., 99 W. M. Canal
SLOSSON M. H., Homopathic Physician, Office and Residence 102 W. 8th
Slotman Hy., lab., e.s. Anderson b. 2d and Pearl
Slough Jno. P., atty., 343 W. 4th
S,rggh M. A., b.k. 114 W. Court
Slough Martin, meats, n.e.c. Richmond and Mound, h. 435 W. 7th
Slusser Peter, driver, 46 Sycamore
Slyder Fred., teamster, 293 Water
Small Bridget, servt., 101 Pike
Small Geo., wagon mkr., n.s. Corporation line, nr. Auburn Av
Small Geo. W., walter, s.w.c. Smith and Longworth
Small I. K., (I. K. S. & Co.), 3 George
Small I. K. & Co., merchandise brokers, 37 Walnut
Small John, coach trimmer, 10 Bedinger
Small Joseph, helper, wks. n.e.c. Walnut and Canal
Small Patrick, lab., 228 E. 6th
Small Rich., shoe mkr., 10 Bedinger
Small Wm., deputy, U.S. Marshall h 172 Smith
Small Wm· H. H., clk. 172 Smith
Smallhouse Edwin, saddler, bds 125 W 5th
Smallhouse Wm., saddler, bds. 125 W. 5th
Smallwood Chas. C., carp., 220 W. Liberty
Smallwood Rich., blksmith, w.s John b. Laurel and Betts, h. 128 Everett
Smallwood Saml., 140 Everett
Smallwood Wm., blksmith., 286 W. Liberty
Smallwood Wm. T., blksmith, w.s. John b. Laurel and Betts, h. 88 Liberty
Smare Wm., Rider al Hamburg and Mohawk
SMART HENRY, Chimney Cleaning, 244 W. Court
Smeed Chas., huckster, 84 W. 2d
Smead Hy. D., printer, h. College Hill
Smears Christina, s.s Cross 2d door W of Hamburg
Smears Philip, mason, s.s. Cross 2d door w. of Hamburg
Smeing Hy., eng., wks. n.w c. Race and Burrows
Smeltz Hy., butcher, bds. w.s. Campbell al, b. Green and Elder
Smerk Hy., mason, 82 Mohawk
Smidberger —, lab., 196 Clark
Smidt Francis, fireman, 90 W. Court
Smdt Hy., stone cutter, 43 Jones

Smilan John. grocery, 62 E. Pearl, h. 94 W. 7th
Smiley Saml., 42 New
Smilk Abbg. Maiden Lane b. Gas. al and Anderson al
Smith ——, 183 Broadway
Smith ——, clk., L. M. depot, bds. 22 Daum
Smith ——, molder, bds. 158 W. Front
Smith ——, tinner, wks. 149 W. 5th
Smith A.D. clocks, 12 E 5th bds Dennison House
Smith Mrs., dress mkr., bds 297 W. 6th
Smith A. H. & Co., (Adolphus H. S & Hy. O. Gilbert), distillery, w.s. Colerain pike n. of Brighton House
Smith A. M., clk. s.e.c. 2d and Main
Smith Aaron, harness mkr., 19 Gest
Smith Adam, 337 Walnut
Smith Adam, molder, wks. 222 E. Front
SMITH Adolphus H., (S. & Gilbert) n. s. Dayton b. Central Av and John
Smith Albert, pilot, 1248 E. Front
Smith Alice, laundress, 176 Broadway
Smith Alice, e.s. Park b. Longworth and 6th
Smith Allen, artist, 234 Baymiller
Smith Amanda, 87 Wade
Smith Amanda M., 216 W. Front
Smith Amelia. 93 Freeman
SMITH AMOR, Star Candles, Lard Oil, and Crackling Manufacturer, 17, 19, & 21 Webster, h. 23 Webster
Smith Amor jr., clk., 23 Webster
Smith Andrew, mach., s.e.c. John and and Court
Smith Andrew M., clk., bds 228 Barr
Smith Ann. 16 York
Smith Anne, bds. 43 Lodge
Smith Ann E., 407½ Longworth
Smith Anna, 343 W. 5d
Smith Anne, servt., 91 Sycamore
Smith Anthony. mach., s.e.c. Court and John
Smith Asa C., 72 Hopkins
Smith August L., watchman, 138 Hopkins
Smith Austin, paver, 470 W. 8th
Smith Barbara, 32 Pike
Smith Barbara. teacher, 337 Walnut
Smith Barney. carp., 414 Longworth
Smith Bart., clk., 109 Mound
Smith Benedict P., baker, 85 George
Smith Ben., 12 Richmond b. Elm and Plum
Smith Benj., baker, 85 George
Smith Benj., policeman, bds. 12 Hopkins
Smith Benj., porter, 123 W. 2d
Smith Benj. C., coal agency, s.e.c. 6th and Central Av., h 351 Race
Smith Benj. F., grocery, 752 E. Front
Smith Bennett, blksmith, 52 Elm
Smith Benson. bds. 120 John
Smith Bernard. copper smith, 403 W 3d
SMITH & BOERNER, (Harry R. S. & Chas. G. B.,) Dealers in Jewelry Watches &c., 6 W. 4th
SMITH Brainard T., (Henry R. S. & Son), res. Mt. Adams
Smith Bridget, 185 W. 2d
Smith & Bro (Martin & Wright) crackling factory, n.w.c. John and Poplar
Smith Budd. finisher, bds. 158 W. Front
Smith Mrs. C.. 68 W. 7th
Smith Carrie E., teacher, 278 Court w. of Central Av
Smith Cassandra, 310 W. 7th
Smith Catharine, 228 Barr
Smith Catharine, 277 Broadway
Smith Catharine, servt., 365 W. 6th
Smith Chas., bds. s.w.c. 7th and Race
Smith Chas., 300 Findlay
Smith Charles, blksmith, 407½ Longworth
Smith Charles, cook, 63 Clay
Smith Charles. molder, w.s. Pancoast al. b. 7th and 8th
Smith Charles, shoe mkr., bds. 65 W. 5th
Smith Charles G. E. S., mach., 495 W. 5th
Smith Chas. H. clk.. 53 Walnut
Smith Charles H., type founder. s. e. c. 7th and Race
SMITH Charles J., (S. & Hawley,) h. 305 W. 8th

Smith Charles J. W., (S. & Winters,) 268 W. 8th
Smith Charles McD., bds. 228 Barr
Smith Charles R., clk., 437 W. 7th
SMITH Charles S., (T. H. Weasner & Co.,) s.e.c. 7th and Elm
Smith Charles W., sec'y. Niles Works 69 Observatory
Smith Charles R., steward, 60 W. Front
Smith Christian, wagon mkr., 56 Buckeye
Smith Christopher, printer, wks. 120 Main, h. 32 Pike
Smith Christopher, teamster, 1478 E. Front
Smith Clara, saleswoman, 30 W. 4th, h 105 Richmond
Smith & Co., produce dealers, 125 W. 5th
Smith Cornelius, lab., wks. 267 W. 5th
Smith Daniel, varnisher, 152 Baymiller
Smith Daniel H., baggage master, 12 New
Smith Daniel J., bakery, s. e. c. Court and John, h. 320 W. 6th
Smith David, 64 Mohawk
Smith David S., turner, 525 W. 8th
Smith David S., mach., 383 Longworth
Smith DeWitt Clinton, paper hanger, 96 Richmond
SMITH & DITSON, (Jas. R. S. & Oliver D.,) Proprietors Smith & Ditson's Hall 24 W. 4th
SMITH & DITSON'S HALL, Entrance 24 W. 4th
Smith Abby, 450 W. 4th
Smith Edward, w.s. Jordan b. Clark and Gest
Smith Edward, bk. layer, s. e. c. Everett and John
Smith Edward, cigars &c., 34 E. Front
Smith Edward, molder, 401 Central Av.
Smith Edward, shoe mkr., bds. 115 Baymiller
Smith Edward A., stable, 13 E. 5th h. 156 Sycamore
Smith Edward G., block and rigging mkr., River b. Ludlow and Lawrence h. Newport
Smith Elijah, tailor, 44 Cutter
Smith Ellen, 28 Rittenhouse
Smith Ellen, 44 Elm
Smith Ellen, talloress, 44 Elm
Smith Elizabeth, teacher, 65 Milton
Smith Elizabeth, s.s. 15th b. Plum and Elm
Smith Elizabeth, talloress, 1248 E. Front
Smith Emma, seamstress, rear 539 Main
SMITH Erastus M., (S. & McAlpin.) res. Ernst Station. C. H. & D. R. R.
Smith Esther, 63 Cutter
Smith Eugene, 468 W. 4th
SMITH Fayette, (Lincoln S. & Warnock) 396 W. 3d
Smith Francis A., b h., 57 E. 3d
Smith Franklin, fruit and produce, 198 W. 4th
Smith Fred. bar k., Gibson House
Smith Frederick, hostler, h. 487 W. 8th
Smith Frederick, lab., wks. John Mitchell's
Smith Frederick, mach., 62 Lock
Smith Fred, (S. & Selman,) 515 Sycamore
Smith Frederick W., paper hanger, bds. 337 Walnut
SMITH G. W., (Mitchell, Allemong & Co.,) bds. 36 Longworth
Smith Geo., 487 W. 5th
Smith Geo., blksmith, n.s. 7th b. Broad way and Sycamore
Smith Geo., candy manufac., 30 W. 6th
Smith Geo., cof. h., 54 W. Court
Smith Geo., harness mkr., 15 Gest
Smith Geo., lab., n.s. Livingston b. John and Linn
Smith Geo., mattress mkr., 407½ Longworth
Smith Geo., policeman, 55 Findlay
Smith, Geo., tailor, 486 Walnut
Smith Geo. A., lime burner, 416 W. 3d
SMITH Geo. D, (S. & Palmer,) h. 275 Longworth
Smith Geo. F., liquors, 4 Commercial Row, h. Covington

300 (SMI) CINCINNATI (SMI) DIRECTORY. (SMI)

Smith Geo. H., 37 W. Court w. of Central Av
Smith Geo. H., upholsterer, 25 E. 3d, h. 405 Longworth
Smith Geo. R. K., b. k., 53 W. Pearl, h. Covington
Smith Geo. W., pressman, Cin. Gazette, h. 115 Court
Smith Geo. W., clk., 3 W. 4th, h. 117 Hunt
Smith Geo. W., photographer, 100 W. 4th
Smith Geo. W.. teacher, bds. 296 W. 5th
SMITH & GILBERT, (A. H. S. & Henry O. G.) Bankers, 34 W. 3d
Smith Gottfried, bakery, 420 Vine
Smith Gottfield, pyrotechnist, 85 Ham. Road
Smith H., s.w.c. Corporation Line and North Elm
Smith H. Benson, clk., 166 W. 4th, bds. 120 John
SMITH H. Howard, (S. & Palmer,) bds. 275 Longworth
Smith Harriet, 17 Richmond
SMITH Harris R., (Hamlen & S.,) 3 W. 4th
Smith Harry, pilot, 30 E. 7th
Smith Harry D., clk., 8 E. 2d, h. 162½ Broadway
SMITH Harry R., (S. & Boerner,) res. Mt. Auburn
Smith and Hawkins, (Pleasant S. & Julius H.,) barbers, 161 W. 5th
SMITH & HAWLEY, (Charles J. S. & David H.,) Wholesale and Retail Furniture Ware Rooms, 136 and 138 W. 2d and 69 W. 5th, Factory n.w.c. Elm and Pearl
Smith Hy., w.s. Canal b. 6th and 8th
Smith Hy., blksmith, 678 E. Front
Smith Hy., cab. mkr., 11 Adams
Smith Hy., carp., 268 Cutter
Smith Hy., carriage smith, 167 Clark
Smith Hy., eng., 29 Hathaway
Smith Hy., safe mkr., 185 W. 2d
Smith Hy., shoe mkr., 082 Central Av.
Smith Hy., upholsterer, 55 Kossuth
SMITH HENRY A., Surgeon Dentist 118 W. 6th bds. Clifton House
Smith Hy. H., mach., 82 Baum
Smith Hy. J., millinery, 24 W. Pearl, rooms Carlisle Building
Smith Hy. J., professor of music, s.w.c. 4th and Walnut
Smith Hy. P., stair builder, 466 W. 6th, h. 33 Hathaway
Smith Hy. R., carp., 25 W. 7th
Smith Hy. R., (Henry R. S. & Son,) res. Mt. Adams
Smith Hy. R. & Son, (Henry R. S. & Brainerd T. S.,) teas, &c., s.e.c. Walnut and 5th
Smith Hy. T., clk., Aetna Ins. Co., 171 Vine
Smith Herman, blksmith, w.s. Jordan b. Clark and Gest
Smith Herman, cooper. 59 Woodward
Smith Hiram, phys., 189 W. Court, w. of Central Av.
Smith Holland, w. s. Auburn Av. near Central Av.
Smith Isaac, driver, 12 E. 8th, e. of Lock
Smith Isaac F., gents furnisher, 10 E. 5th, h. Avondale
Smith Isaac S., bds. 63 Cutter
Smith Isabel, servt., Dumas Hotel
Smith J. H. & Co., (Jesse H. S., Wm D. S., James S. S., and Alfred Lyons) brokers, 58 W. 3d
Smith J. J., mess. American Ex. Co. bds. Burnet House
Smith J. R., (J. R. S. & Co.,) h. Newport
Smith J. R. & Co., exchange office, 135 W. 6th
Smith J. W., mer., 81 W. 8th
Smith Jacob, blksmith, Clay b. Liberty and Allison
Smith Jacob H., barber, 10 E. 3d, h. 621 Race
Smith James, 36 Pleasant
Smith James. bds. Dennison House
Smith James, 173 W. Front

Smith James, carp., w. s. Culvert b. 4th and 5th
Smith James, clk., 143 John
Smith James, lab., 458 W. 5th
Smith James, lithographer, n. w. c. 3d and Main
Smith James, mach., 516 Main
Smith James, printer, bds. e. s. Park b. 6th and Longworth
Smith James, printer, h. 33 Wade
Smith James, sawyer, wks. 1565 E. Front
Smith James A., plate printer, 30 W. Court
SMITH JAMES B., Physician and Surgeon, Office and residence 284 W. 6th
Smith James D., sawyer, n.s. Railroad e. of Vance
Smith James D. (Jas. D. S. & Co.,) h. Newport
Smith James D. & Co., (Jas. D. S. & Samuel Bate,) millinery, 24 W. Pearl
SMITH James E., (Shipley & S.,) 366 W. 8th
Smith James F., phys., s. w. c. 4th and Broadway, h. n.w.c. 6th and Broadway
Smith James H., sexton, e.s. Vine b. 8th and 9th
Smith James P., blksmith, bds. Dennison House
Smith James R., physician, office and residence 133 W. 7th
SMITH James R., (S. & Nixon,) h. Clifton
Smith James S., (J. H. Smith & Co.,) h. 58 W. 3d
Smith Jane M., gents' furnisher, 60 W. Front
Smith Jason P., clk. City Water Works, h. 221½ Laurel
Smith Jennie, 23 Webster
Smith Jesse H., (J. H. S. & Co.,) 58 W. 3d
Smith Job, Jr., b. k., 9 Pub. Landing
Smith John, 351 Race
Smith John, bar k., s.w c. 6th and Plum
Smith John, blksmith, 12 Hannibal
Smith John, blksmith, 40 Hannibal
Smith John, boots and shoes, s.e.c. Main and Orchard
Smith John, carp., bds. 69 W. 6th
Smith John, expressman, rear 148 W. Court w. of Central Av.
Smith John Sr., finisher, wks n. e. c. Walnut and Canal
Smith John, Jr., finisher, wks. n. e. c. Walnut and Canal
Smith John, lab., w.s. Central Av. b. 3d and W. W. Canal
Smith John, lab., 608 E. Front
Smith John, lab., s s. Yeatman b. Broadway and Sycamore
Smith John, lab., n.s. Railroad e. of Wallace al.
Smith John, stable, h. 122 W. Front
Smith John, molder, n. s. Railroad e. of Wallace al.
Smith John, saloon, 48 & 50 E. 3d
Smith John, stone cutter, 117 Lock
Smith John, tailor, 262 W. 5th
Smith John, teacher, 492 Main
Smith John, upholsterer, 8 Phoebe
SMITH JOHN A., Staple and Fancy Dry Goods, 22 W. 5th, h. 49 Ellen
Smith John B., clk. Daily Times, bds. 114 Park
Smith John F., Japanner, 67 W. Court
Smith John G., salesman, 78 W. 4th, h. 268 Richmond
Smith John H., salesman, 30 W. 4th
Smith John J., bar k., 26 Vine, h. 44 Elm
Smith John K., bds. Cincinnati House
Smith John P., molder, 310 W. 5th
Smith John R., b. k., 269 Main, h. 202 Freeman
Smith John S., bk. layer, 29 Elizabeth
Smith John T., pilot, s. s. Front e. of Vance
SMITH John W. H., (Holliday & S.,) 343 George
Smith Joseph, s.s. Front e. of Torrence
Smith Joseph, 149 George
Smith Joseph Jr., coal agt, s.e.c. Front and Lawrence, h. 490 W. 7th

Smith Joseph A., wagon mkr., 64 Mohawk
Smith Joseph B., pipe fitter, wks. n.e.c. Walnut and Canal
Smith Joseph K., clk. L. M. R. R. depot, h. 35 Ellen
Smith Joseph K., sec'y Cin. Equitable Ins. Co., 30 W. 3d, h. Vine Street Hill
Smith Joseph L., policeman, 152 Barr
Smith Joseph M., bds. 174 E. Pearl
Smith Joseph M., driver, 154 Longworth
Smith Josiah B., blk. smith, n s. Oregon b. 3d and 5th
Smith Julia, 350 W. 6th
Smith Kate, teacher, 41 George
Smith Kilburn W., clk., 358 George
Smith Lamora, 161 Longworth
Smith Laur. C., bds. 217 Poplar
Smith Leander, salesman, 23 Webster
Smith Lena, bds. 522 Sycamore
Smith Lewis A., varnisher, 320 W. 9th w. of Central Av
Smith Lewis H., clk. 124 Main, h. Newport
Smith Lorenz, cab. mkr., 286 Water
SMITH Lorin W., (Austin & S.), 183 Br'dway b. Harrison and 6th
Smith Louis, waiter, Gibson House
Smith Louisa, bds. 30 Patterson al.
Smith Lucy H., s.w.c. Ohio Av. and Corporation Line
Smith Luman W., printer, 69 Observatory
Smith Lyman, carriage mkr., 1554 E. Front
Smith M., servt., Burnet House
SMITH & McALPIN, (Erastus M. S., & Wm. McA.), P oduce and Commission Merchants, 62 Walnut
Smith Maggie, cook, 198 Plum
Smith Margaret, 278 W 6th
Smith Margaret, servt., 381 George
Smith Maria, servt., 13 E. 6th
Smith Martha A., 90 Hopkins
Smith Martin, (S. & Bro.), s.s. Everett b. Cutter and Linn
Smish Martin J., grocery, 249 Broadway
Smith Martin L., cooper, 29 Broadway
Smith Mary, bds. 169 Sycamore
Smith Mary, al. b. Vine and Walnut and 13th and Mercer
Smith Mary, 53 E. 5th
Smith Mary, h. 65 Milton
Smith Mary, servt., 31 Harrison
Smith Mary, servt., s.w.c. Race and 3d
Smith Mary E., 10 Richmond
Smith Mathew, blacking mkr., n.w.c. Elm and Water
SMITH MATTHEW, Livery Stable, s.e.c. 3d and Vine, h. 124 W. Front
Smith Michael, clk., 65 Milton
Smith Michael, lab., 23 Ann
Smith Michael, stair builder, 60 David
Smith Mollie, bds. 87 E. Front
Smith Moses, driver, 218 E. 6th
Smith Mrs. N. B., b.h., 162 Elm
Smith Nancy F., 271 W. 6th
Smith Nelson, cook, Broadway Hotel
Smith Nicholas, cigar mkr., wks. 213 Walnut
SMITH & NIXON, (Jas. R. S. & W. K. N.,) Piano Dealers, 24 W. 4th
Smith Noah, blksmith., s s. Front e. of Foster
Smith Oliver, (S. Wayne & Co.) h. Covington
Smith Oliver W., carpenter, 383 Longworth
Smith Omay, grocery, s.e.c. Central Av. and Longworth
Smith Owen, lab., wks., 18 Sycamore
SMITH & PALMER, (Geo. D. S., H. Howard S. & Moses D. P.,) Leather Dealers, 51 Main
Smith Patrick, grocer, n.e.c. Richmond and Freeman
Smith Patrick, hackman, 59 George
Smith Patrick, lab., 16 6th e. of Lock
Smith Patrick, lock manufac., 45 Sycamore
Smith Patrick, saloon, 21 River Landing b. Ludlow and Broadway
Smith Perry, blksmith, wks 9 W. 7th

Smith Peter, 391 Broadway
SMITH PETER, Importer and Dealer in Ambrotype and Photograph Materials, 36 W. 5th. h. 192 W. 7th
Smith Peter, hackman, 54 George
Smith Peter, lab., 548 Race
Smith Phillip, wagon mkr., s.e.c. Elm and Water
Smith Pleasant, (S. & Hawkins,) 30 Barr
Smith R., molder, wks. Chamberlain & Co.'s
SMITH R. B. & CO., (Robt. B. S., and Graff, Rea & Co.,) Coal Yard, s.w. c. Elm and Water, 499 Central Av. 444 Race, and n.w.c. Hopkins and Central Av
Smith Rachael, 203 Plum
Smith Raymond, gents' furnisher, 34 W. 4th
SMITH RICHARD, Cincinnati Gazette Co., h. 189 George
Smith Richard, japanner, wks. n.w.c. Race and 2d
Smith Robert, bridge bldr., 90 Carr
Smith Robert, clk.. bds. 256 Longworth
Smith Robert, cooper, s.s. 6th e. of Lock
Smith Robert, lab. 19 Accommodation
Smith Robert, salesman, 100 W. 4th, h. e.s. Race b. 4th and 5th
Smith Robert, waiter, Burnet House
SMITH Robert B., (R. B. S. & Co) 289 George
Smith Robert H., porter, 2 New
Smith Robert H., roller, 25 W. 2d
Smith Robert L., salesman, 53 Main, h. 137 W. 7th
Smith Robert L., clk. 27 W. Pearl, bds. 256 Longworth
Smith Robert W., clk., bds. n.w.c. Mill and 3d
Smith Robert W., twister, 86 W. Front
Smith Rosa, 92 Baymiller
Smith Royal A., bds. 63 Cutter
Smith Rufus P., salesman, bds. 306 George
Smith Russell, bds. Clermont Hotel
Smith S. S., (S. S. & Co..) h. Clifton
Smith S.S.jr., (S. S. & Co) h. 105 Dayton
Smith S. S. & Co , (S. S. S. & S. Smith Jr.,) liquors, 56 W. 2d
Smith S. W., carp., 216 John
Smith Samuel W., (S. W. S. & Co.,) 406 W. 6th
Smith S. W. & Co., (S. W. S. & R. G. Hunting,) com. mers., 29 Water
Smith Sallie, 282 Richmond
Smith Samuel jr., slaughter house, s.w c. John and Findlay
Smith Samuel A., fireman, 259 Richmond
Smith Samuel A., mer., 168 George
Smith Samuel L., pass. agt. P. Ft. W. and C. R. R., s.e c. Front and Broadway, res. Newport
Smith Samuel P., bds. 68 W. 7th
Smith Samuel R., circular saw mill bldr., 141 Barr
Smith Sanford D., foreman 25 W. 4th, h. 458 W. 9th w. of Central Av.
Smith Sarah, 131 E. 5th
Smith Sarah H., 192 W. Front
Smith & Selman, (Fred. Smith and Richard S.,) cof. h., 115 Sycamore
Smith Sheldon, clk. 54 W. 2d, res. Covington
Smith Silas, carriage mkr., 36 W. 8th
Smith Silas, coach mkr., 308 W. 8th
Smith Soby C., salesman 69 Main, h. Loveland
Smith Spencer, 714 E. Front
Smith T. A , clk., 12 E. 5th, bds. Dennison House
Smith T. W., clk., 358 George
Smith Thaddeus A., clk., bds. n.e.c. Dayton and Whiteman
Smith Thomas, agt., 117 Hunt
Smith Thomas, lab., 35 E. 8th e. of Lock
Smith Thomas, lab., 12 Skaats
Smith Thomas, shoe mkr., 441 John
Smith Thomas A., distiller, bds. 27 Brighton
Smith Thomas B , land agt., 390 Race
SMITH Thomas B., (Meader & Co.,) 45 Barr

SMITH THOMAS G., Dealer in Pig Iron 53 W. 2d h. Walnut Hills
Smith Thomas J., clk., 22 E. 9th, h. 81 W. 8th
Smith Thomas J., printer, h. 392 W. 3d
Smith Col. Thomas Kelby, 294 W. Court w. of Central Av
SMITH THOMAS S., Iron and Steel Perforating Establishment, s. e. c. Plum and Pearl, h. 495 W. 5th
Smith Thomas T., carp., 1172 E. Front
Smith Theodric, (S. & Williamson,) n. w.c. 6th and John
Smith Valentine, huckster, 122 Gest
SMITH W. B. (W. B. Smith & Co.,) b. Clifton
SMITH W. B. & CO., (W. R. S. & Edward Sargent) Publishers and Book Sellers, 137 Walnut
Smith W. P., mech., 373 W. 7th
Smith W. W., supt. Ind. & Cin. R. R. Telegraph, h. 271 W. 7th
Smith W. W., telegraph operator, h. 242 Plum
Smith Walter, (Walter S. & Co.,) 391 W. 6th
Smith Walter & Co., (Walter S., Augustus S. Winslow & Wm. L. Lay,) Miami oil works, office 9 W. 2d
Smith Wayne & Co., (Oliver S., James S. W. & Wright Smith,) liquors, 10 W. Front
Smith Whitner, printer, Press office, bds. 293 W. 4th
Smith Willard H., bds. 129 Butler
Smith Wm., carp., 48 Pierson
Smith Wm , chair mkr., 335 W. 3d
Smith Wm , lab., 203 Plum
Smith Wm., molder, 403 George
Smith Wm., police, 49 Race
Smith Wm., (S. & Co..) bds. 280 W. 6th
Smith Wm., steward, 93 Pleasant
Smith Wm., stone cutter, bds. 338 Central Av
SMITH WM., Superintendent Merchant's Exchange, and Publisher Cin. Price Current, College Hall Bldg., Walnut b. 4th and 5th, h. 298 George
Smith & Williamson, (Theodric S. & Alex W. W.,) planing mill, s.w.c. 3d and John
Smith Wm. A., clk., 86 Richmond
Smith Wm. A., marble cutter, 386 Central Av
Smith Wm. B., (J. H. Smith & Co.,) h. Newport
SMITH WM. C., Wholesale Grocer and Commission Merchant, 22 and 24 E. 9th, h 300 Vine
Smith Wm. F., lab., s.s. McFarland e. of Hill
Smith Wm. G., clk., 221½ Laurel
Smith Wm. H., clk., h. North Elm
Smith Wm. H., clk., 221½ Laurel
Smith Wm. H., omnibus propr. C. H. & D. R. R., h. 284 W. 9th w. of Central Av
Smith Wm. H., paper hanger, 122 Mound
Smith Wm. H., saloon, 229 Central Av
Smith Wm. Henry, clk. P. O., b. Vine Street Hills
Smith Wm. M , R. R. agt., office 11 W. Front, h. Newport
Smith Wm. P., bk. binder, 211 Mound
Smith Wm. P., mach., 373 W. 7th
Smith Wm. W., atty., bds 47 W. 7th
Smith Wilson F., clk. City Water Works, h. 221½ Laurel
Smith & Winters, (Chas. J. W. S. & Wm. W.,) real estate agts. and auctioneers, 221 Vine
Smith Wright, (M. & W. S.,) 554 Freeman
Smith Wright jr., salesman, 55 W. Pearl, b. Covington
Smitherman Jesse, hostler, 53 E. 8th
Smithers Samuel H., bds. Spencer House
Smitt Frederick, bar. h. Gibson House
Smoll Frank, lab., bds. 50 W. Liberty
Smollnhawnk Peter, w.s. Pole b. 2d and Pearl
Smolt Charles, carp., s.w.c. Laurel and Baymiller

Smudde Wm., clk., bds. 477 Race
Smutta Wm., lab., 60 Plum
Smylie Henry H., salesman, bds. 121 E. 3d
Smyth Albert L., b.k. 12 Pub. Landing, h. 34 York
Sneath John, e.s. Ludlow b. Pearl and 3d
Snedecker Isaac, shoe mkr., 625 W. 6th
Sneider Adam, cab. mkr., 289 W, Liberty
Snelbaker David T., atty., 239 W. 9th, h. 162 Linn
Snell Abraham B., bk. binder, 53 Betts
Snell Alex., painter, 12 Richmond
Snell Arthur W., conductor, 380 Baymiller
Snell John, carp , 12 Richmond
Snell Jonas, cab. mkr., 152 Cutter
Snell Valentine, driver, 62 Laurel
Snell Wm., lab., 1520 E. Front
Snell Wm., teamster, 62 Laurel
Snider Francis, lab., 63 Lock
Snider Jacob, lab., 65 Martin
SNIDER LOUIS, Paper Warehouse, 232 Walnut, res. Hamilton, O.
Snider Matthias, clk., 196 W. 5th
Snippel Hy., (H. H. Macke & Co.,) n.s. Front, e. of Lewis
Snitker Geo., cooper, 466 Linn
Snitker Hermann, cooper, 95 York
Snodgrass Chas. W., b k., 256 Main, h. 317 Elm
Snodgrass Elizabeth, 271 W. Court, w. of Central Av.
Snodgrass Jno. A., salesman, 19 W. 4th, h. 11 George
Snodgrass Silas L., carp., 866 Central Av., h. 69 Dayton
SNODGRASS WM. W., Dealer in Leather, Hides, Oil and Furs, 256 Main, h. 317 Elm
Snook Nathan H., stable, s.w.c. 5th and Sycamore. res. Clarksville, O.
Snow Mrs. E. N., 142 W. 8th
SNOW HENRY, Atty. at Law, room 7 Masonic Temple, res. Mt. Auburn
Snow John, lab., n.s 8th, b. Broadway and Sycamore
Snow Norbert, lab. 99 Smith
Snow Robert, lab., 18 Woodward
Snow Walter M., b. k., bds. 142 W. 8th
SNOWDON & OTTE, (Theodore M. S. & Geo. F. O.,) Dealers in Carpets and Oil Cloths, 175 Main
Snowdon Susan B., teacher, 142 W. 8th
SNOWDON Theodore M., (S. & Otte,) 46 W. 9th
Snyder Christian, lab., 402 Longworth
Snyder Christopher, lab., 308 Longworth
Snyder D. H., clk., Adams' Express Office, bds. Burnet House
Snyder Mrs. E., dress maker, h. 156 W. 4th
SNYDER Mrs. Eliza, (S. & Gobrecht,) s.s. Harrison Pike, b. Division and Brighton
Snyder Frank, lab., wks. 33 Lock
SNYDER FREDERICK, Wholesale and Retail Grocery, 55 W. Court
Snyder Geo., bds. Dennison House
Snyder Geo., penny post, 160 Clark
Snyder Geo. H., coach trimmer, bds. 414 Broadway
SNYDER & GOBRECHT, (Mrs. Eliza S. & Christian G.,) Grocery, s.s. Harrison Pike, b. Division and Brighton
Snyder Hy., dray, 664 Sycamore
Snyder Hy., furniture car, 236 Hopkins
Snyder Jacob, blk.smith, wks. John Ewin's
Snyder Jennie, 51 Stone al., b. 5th and 6th
Snyder Jerry, lab., 430 E. Front
Snyder John, 63 Webster
Snyder John, 672 Central Av
Snyder John, bakery, 223 W. 6th
Snyder John, shoemkr. bds. s.s. Findlay b. Freeman and Western Av.
Snyder John, tailor, 217 Betts

302 (SOL) CINCINNATI (SPA) DIRECTORY. (SPE)

SNYDER JOHN M., Measurer of Carpenters' Work, w. s. St. Clair b. 8th and 9th, h. 414 Broadway
Snyder Joseph, baker, 602 Vine
Snyder Joseph, grocery, n.w.c. Laurel and Cutter
Snyder Joseph, lab., 417 Longworth
Snyder Joseph Y., shoemkr., n.e.c. 5th and Elm, h. 156 W. 4th
Snyder Louis, brewery, 177 Baymiller
Snyder M., atty., s.w.c. Main and Court, h. Mt Airy
Snyder Mary, 70 Jones
Snyder Peter, confec., 306 W, 5th
Snyder Rose, rear 194 W. 5th
Snyder Sallie, 155 W. 9th
Snyder Sanul, printer, 0 Home
Snyder Thos. D. Jr, clk. at S. A. Sargent's, h. Newport, Ky.
Snyder Valentine 255 Richmond
SNYDER WILLIAM, Drugs, Medicines, Chemicals, &c., n.w.c. 4th and Race, h. 92 Barr
Snyder Wm., porter, Madison House
SNYDER WM., Coal and Wood Dealer, 65 Water and foot of Lawrence, h. s.e.c. 4th and Butler.
Soards J. & Son. (John & Wm. H.,) undertakers, 175 W. 6th
Soards John, (J. S. & Son,) 88 W. 9th
Soards John A., clk., 222 Longworth
Soards L., student, bds. 88 W. 9th
Soards Wm. H., (J. S. & Son,) 540 W. 7th
Soden Chas. T. tobacconist, 12 Main
Soden Edward, molder, wks. s.w.c. Front and Central Av., res. Covington
Soden John M., molder, wks. s.e.c. Canal and Walnut
Soden Paul H., molder, s.w.c. Front and Central Av.
Soechting Chas., trimmings, 489 Vine
Soechting T., mach., wks. n. s. Front b. Lawrence and Pike
Soehnchen Catharina, dom. w.s. Goose al. b. 14th and 15th
Soeller Matthew, basket mkr., 670 E. Front
Soenichen Wm., lab., 512 Race
Soerweide B., tailor, bds. 701 Elm
Sogell Hy., driver, n.s. 5th b. Smith and Mound
Sogle Hy. D., fireman, 162 Smith
Soguel Chas. W., eng., 536 W. 7th
SOHN John G., (Geo. Klotter & Co.,) h. 48 Mohawk.
Sokup Albert, lab., 14 Hamer
Sokup Francis, cigar mkr., 45 Elder
Sokup Frans., Sr., lab., 14 Hamer
Sokup John, blk.smith, 14 Hamer
Solliday Solomon, saddler, bds. 141 Sycamore
Solair Frank, s. s. Henry b. Elm and Dunlap
Solari Augustus, confec., n.w.c. Smith and 3d
Solar Hermann, chair mkr., 365 Linn
Solar John J., eng., 232 Betts
Sotar Michael, 10 Ann
Soldiers' Friend and Army Record, Van Winkle & Dussert publishers, 8 W. 3d
Soldner Frederick, rope mkr., 442 W. 2d
Solern Andrew, confec., 185 Race, h. 139 W. 5th
Solimano Lorenzo, fruits, 192 Walnut
Solleis Margaret, 65 Oliver
Soller Barbara, gardener, n. s. Flint, b. Freeman and Mill Creek
Soller George, baker, 10 Commerce
Seller John J., eng., 336 Betts
Sullivan Geo., teamster, bds. 40 Rittenhouse
Solomon Dennis, lab., 67 E. 8th, e. of Lock
Solomon Eve, 614 W. 8th
Solomons George, (S. Moss & Co.,) 174 Main
Solomons Morris, (Solomons, Moss & Co.,) 236 W. 5th, w. of Central Av.
Solomons Moss & Co., (Geo. S., Michael J. M. & Morris Solomons,) cigars, &c., 174 Main
SOLOMON Wm., (Mohr S. & Mohr,) h. Newport

Somers Wm., blksmith, wks. n.e.c. Walnut and Canal
Somhorst Christian, tailor, 26 Jackson
Somhorst Eva, 5 Wade, b. Elm and Plum
Somhorst John, tailor, 5 Wade b. Elm and Plum
Sommer Alexander locksmith, 612 Vine
Sommer Andreas, lab., 640 Race
Sommer Chas., lab., 246 Bremen
Sommer Ferdinand, cigar mkr., 164 Spring
Sommer Frederick, lab., 114 Abigail
Sommer Geo., 540 Race
Sommer Hy., lab., 550 Main
Sommer Jacob, lab., 10 Abigail
SOMMER Joseph, (S. & Meyer,) 228 Water
SOMMER & MEYER, (Joseph S. & Fred. M.,) Wh. Grocers, Liquor and Commission Merchants, 36 E. Pearl
Sommer Simon, drover, 494 Race
Sommerkamp Caspar H., carp., n.w.c 15th and Goose al., h. 525 Race
Sommerkamp John, carp., 139 Everett
Sommers Ann, n.e.c. Peddleton and Liberty
Sommers Hy., locksmith, 310 Cutter
Sommers James, waiter, Burnet House
Sommers M., waiter, Burnet House
Sommers Martin, Sen., s. s. 6th, e. of Lock
Sommers Martin, Jr., lab., s. s. 6th, c. of Lock
Sommers Solomon, drover, 450 W. Liberty
Sommitt Wm., carp., 79 Gest
Sonar Alexander, painter, 168 Hopkins
Sonder Hermann, 674 Elm
Sonder Theresa, 159 Clay
Sonnemeyer Hy. J., blk.smith, bds. 502 W. Front
Sonner Louis, bar k., wks. n.w.c. Main and Liberty
Sonnet Louis, molder, 79 Augusta
Sontag Cassenno, blk.smith, 14 Grant
Sontag Chas, clk., 171 George
Sontag Michael, boots and shoes, 101 Ham. Road
Sontan John, porter, h. 42 Elm
Sorg David, blk.smith, 192 Clark
Sorg George, lab., n. s. Railroad, e. of Lewis
Sorg Hy., lab., 192 Clark
Sorg John, tailor, bds. 701 Elm
Sorg Paul, molder, 192 Clark
Sorg Rosina, 69 Buckeye
Sorge Chas., porter, 25 Franklin
Sorge Wm., porter, 25 Franklin
SORGEL GEORGE, Proprietor Congress Exchange, s.w.c. Pearl and Ludlow
Sorgel Miene, servt., 60 Broadway
Sorin John W., cab. mkr., s.e.c. Richmond and Carr
Souders George W., jeweler, 486 W. 9th, w. of Central Av.
Souders John, 85 Milton
Souer A., bakery, 425 W. 3d
Sourd Frederick, painter, wks. Crane, Breed & Co's
Sourenbroug Herman, tanner, s. s. Liberty b. Linn and Baymiller
Soutder Christina, 20 Webster
Soutder Margaret, 20 Webster
South Annie, actress, National Theatre
South James, 280 Broadway
Southall Nathaniel, rear 51 New
Southgate Hy. H., cashier L. M. R. R., res. Covington
Sovereign Daniel L., 71 E. 3d e. of Whittaker
Soward Alfred, b.k., 16 Main, bds. 115 W. 9th
Sowden Adam, grinder and polisher, wks. s.w.c. Pearl and Plum
Sowry Wm J., salesman, 140 Main
Spach Gustav, drugs, 491 Vine
Spacke Margaret, 92 Adams
Spade Fred., cigar mkr., 64 Ham. Road
Spader R. P., 83 W. 4th
Spaen Pat., grocery, 184 W. Court
Spaendler Peter, tailor, 1031 Central Av
Spaeth & Co., (Alois S. & Fred. Speckman,) Ice house, 323 Broadway
Spaeth Alois, (A Spaeth & Co.,) 323 Broadway

Spaeth David, cigar mkr., 90 Buckeye
Spaeth Frederika, 283 Bremen
Spaeth John C., cigar mkr., wks. 663 Vine
Spaeth Joseph, Ice mer., 323 Broadway
Spaeth Sam., bk. binder, 103 Martin
Spaeth Seth, lab., 323 Broadway
Spahe Francis A., brewer, 651 Vine
Spahn Frank, 594 Vine
Spakeman Hy., lab., wks. 222 E. Front
Spamer Hy., cooper, al. b. Charlotte and Findlay and Plum and Central Av.
SPAMER HENRY, Apothecary and Chemist, 408 Vine
Spamer Jacob, gardener, n.s. Corp. Line nr. Auburn
Spamer Mary, seamstress, s.s. Ringgold b. Young and Price
Spangler Fred., posementier, 223 Everett
Spangler Fred. C. T. fringe mkr., 80 W. 5th, b. 223 Everett
Spangler Joseph, paper carrier, e.s. Bremen b. Elder and Findlay
Spangler Philip. mach. 42 Jones
Spangler Saml. S., gilder, 151 Livingston
Spangman Fred., lab, 235 Betts
Spanger Magdalena, servt., 86 Pike
Spankuch I. Caspar, cof. h , 545 Main
Spankuch Otto, bar k., s.e.c. Cutter and Liberty
Spankuch Otto J., barber, 108 W. Liberty
Spannherst Mary, 16 Woodward
Sparka Jacob, trunk mkr., 22 Adams
Sparker Margaret, wks. Hieatt & Wood's candle factory
Sparkes Wm. B., clk., 18 Broadway, h. 426 W. 8th
Sparks Edward. lock mkr., wks. n.e.c. Walnut and Canal
Sparks Ephriam, clk., 11 Gorman
Sparks Jesse M., wagon mkr., 704 W. 6th
Sparks Mary L., bds. s.s. R. Road e. of Brooklyn
Sparks Rebecca, bds. s.s. R. Road e. of Brooklyn
Sparks Sarah, s.s. R. Road e. of Brooklyn
Sparks Sarah E., bds. s.s. R. Road e. of Brooklyn
Sparrow Pat., lab., junction High and Kemper's Lane
Spater Robert, 45 E. Front
Spath John saloon, s.e.c. 3d and John
Spatswood Peter, cook, 142 W. Pearl
Spatz C., blk. smith, Hamer b. Vine and Ham. Road
Spare Morris, lab., 464 E. Front
Speaker John, blk. smith, 52 Elm
Speaker John G., wagon mkr., 52 Commerce
SPEAR & CO., (Morgan S., Luke A. Bassett & John L. Hull,) Coal Oil, Lamps, Burning Fluid, &c., 165 Walnut
SPEAR Morgan, (S. & Co.,) 353 W. 7th
Spear John B., b.k., 402 W. 9th w. of Central Av.
Spear Wm , b.k., 364 Clark
Spears Wm., 17 E. 6th
Spears Christian, cab. mkr., 131 Pleasant
Specht Hy., blk. smith, 50 Bernard
Speck Ignatius, cab. mkr., 612 Vine
Speckback Fred., driver, 156 E. 5th
Specker J. B., clk., 27 Commerce
Specker Mary A., 27 Commerce
Speckman Chas. H., driver, n.e.c. Hunt and Sycamore
Speckman Fred., boiler mkr., 56 Pike, h. Newport
Speckman Fred., (Spaeth & Co.,) 323 Broadway
Speckman Geo. H., feed store, n.e.c. Hunt and Sycamore, h. 69 Clay
Speckmann Dorothea, seamstress, rear 31 Hughes
Speckmeyer Har k., 69 Clay
Specman Louis, clothing, 288 W. 5th
Speer Alfred, bk. mkr., 16 Freeman
Speer Chas. W., b.k., 158 Main, h. 508 Main
Speer Emily, seamstress, e.s. Spring b. Woodward and Abigail

h	Spencer W. (W. M. S. & Co.,) h. Covington
8 W.	Spencer Wm., grocer, bds. n.w.c. Central Av. and Longworth
7th	SPENCER Wm. F., (Haynes, Lewis & S.,) 102 Barr
	Spencer Wm. W., stamp cutter, 22 Gest
	Spener Hy., cooper, 641 Race
Jacob	Spengeman Fred, tanner, 235 Betts
	Spengeman Wm., chair mkr., 130 Betts
lack-	Spenney Eliza, 607 Vine
Court	Spenney Eliza H., 163 George
	Sperber Edward, barber, 353 Vine
., 211	Speth Mrs., cloth shoe mkr., 615 Main
	Speth Francis, brass finisher, 303 Race
Court	SPEYER BENNO, Commission Merchant, Notary Public, Passenger Agent for Foreign Steamers and Merchants Despatch, and R. Road Ticket Agent, 7 and 9 W. 3d, bds. St. Charles
in	
Co's,	
al. b.	Speyer Julius, 2 Clinton Court
w. of	Spher John, eng., bds. n.s. 6th b. Harriet and Horne
	Spicer Sarah, 83 Mulberry
	Spicker Augustus, salesman, 123 Main, bds. 167 Baymiller
. Lib-	Spicker Fred., (G. & F. Spicker,) 167 Baymiller
	Spicker G. & F. (Gottlieb S. & Fred. S.) hardware, 123 Main
lar b.	Spicker Gottlieb, (G. & F. Spicker,) 167 Baymiller
r, 115	SPIEGEL G. C., Tannery, w.s. Front e. of Jamestown Ferry, h. n.s. Front near McDowell
	Spiegel Stephen, bakery, 14 15th
i Syc-	SPIEGEL Wm., (McIlvain, S. & Co.,) h. Newport
atha-	Spiekerman John T., boots and shoes, 96 Baymiller
aker's	Spies Andrew, n.w.c. Linn and Poplar
tel, n.	Spies Christian, cab. mkr., 131 Pleasant
	Spies Elizabeth, 640 Vine
Syca-	Spies Geo. M., phys., s.e.c. W. 9th and Mound
	Spies Jacob, cooper, 124 Clay
64 W.	Spies Robert, Franklin Hotel, w.s. Lebanon Road b. Liberty and Corporation Line
, n.w.	Spiller & Bro., (Ferdinand & W. H. S.,) printers, 170 Sycamore
ain	Spiller Ferdinand, b.k, 144 Livingston
& S.,)	Spiller Ferdinand, (W. H. S. & Bro.) s.s. Maple W. of Freeman
	Spiller Frank, lab., wks. 137 W. 2d
vin al.	Spiller Hy., driver, 90 Butler
ail	Spillman James W., bds. n.s. Taylor, b. Carr and Freeman
.14th	SPILLS JOHN C., Professor of Dancing and Music, n. w. c. 6th and Walnut, h. 79 Everett
urt w.	
	Spilman Hy., clk., 36 Walnut, bds. 88 E. 4th
is. 80	Spindler David, lab., w. s. Western Av. b. Findlay and Dayton
	Spindler John, lab., 202 Pleasant
	SPINING & BROWN, (Chas. E. S. & Chas. B.) Wholesale Grocers and Produce and Commission Merchants, 49 W. 2d, and Soap and Candle Manuf., 80 Poplar
	SPINING Chas. E., (S. & Brown,) res. Glendale
.c. W.	Spining Pierson A., com. mer., 25 W. 2d, b. 153 W. 4th
s Ins.	Spinner Chas., finisher, 187 Ham. Road
	Spinner John, pipe fitter, wks. n. e. c. Walnut and Canal
	Spinney James A., shoemkr, 326 Elm
	Spinning Isaac P., clk., bds. U. S. Hotel
	Spinning Jacob T., bk. layer, 465 W. 8th
3d	Spinning Jonathan, salesman, 198 Main, h. Covington
ilgour	Spinninweber Jacob, varnisher, bds. cor. York and John
	Spintler Jacob, lab., s. w. c. Dudley and Liberty
th and	Spissman Geo. J., cof. h., Findlay b. Central Av. and John
	Spitz Frances, 571 Race
s	Spitzer Geo., lab., 42 Peete
	Spitzer Joseph, 260 W. 6th
& E.	Spitzmeeler Bernard, carp., n.s. Liberty b. Baymiller and Freeman, h. 450 Liberty
19 W.	

	Spitzmiller George, cof. h., e.s. Vine b. Calhoun and Auburn Av
	Spitzner Adrian, wagoner, 66 W. Liberty
	Splane John, lab., 122 Accomodation
	Splenter Hy., lab., s.w.c. Gest and Carr
	Splinters Mary, servt., 444 Sycamore
	Spofford Jacob F., com. mer., 265 Richmond
	Spohr Andrew, musician, 42 12th
	Spohr Wm., lab., 38 Green
	Spone Anna, 233 W. 6th
	Sponsel Christian, cook, 98 Ham. Road
	Sponsler Harriet, b.h., 16 Miller
	Spooner Catharine, servt., 289 Longworth
	Spooner Eliza, servt., 377 W. 6th
	SPOONER & LAWDER, (Wm. L. S. & John F. L.,) Attorneys at Law, Room 3, Railroad Buildings, n.w.c. Main and Court
	SPOONER William L. (S. & Lawder.) h. cor. Ohio Avenue and Corporation Line
	Sportman's Hall, Stephen R. Garrison, s.s. Front, e. of Corporation Line
	Sprague Andrew, foreman, 1202 E. Front
	Sprague E. T., salesman, s e.c. 4th and Vine, bds. 376 W. 4th
	SPRAGUE T. W. & CO., (Thomas W. S. & Nehemiah Perry,) Fashionable Tailors and Manufacturers of Ready Made Clothing, s. e. c. 4th and Vine
	SPRAGUE Thomas W., (T. W. S. & Co.,) 376 W. 4th
	Sprague Wm. B., salesman, s. e. c. 4th and Vine, bds. 376 W. 4th
	Sprain Louisa, servt., 293 Richmond
	Sprankel John, sawyer, 42 Hamer
	Spraten John, lab., wks. 335 Broadway
	Spratt James, huckster, 168 Sycamore
	Spreel Wm C. F., b.k., bds. 213 George
	Spreen August, lab., 19 Buckeye
	Spreen C. F. W., clk., bds. 213 George
	Spreen Chas., grocery, n.e.c. Court and Linn
	Spreen Chas., tailor, 90 Pleasant
	Spreen Christian, (F. W. Spreen & Bro.) 85 George
	Spreen F. & Bro., (Frederick W. & Christian,) bakery, 222 W. 6th
	Spreen Frederick W., (F. W. S. & Bro.) 222 W. 6th
	Spreen Louisa, 90 Pleasant
	Spreen Mena, servt., 14 McFarland
	Sprehe Francis H., cooper, 55 Buckeye
	Sprehn Lewis, cigar box mkr., 49 Pleasant
	Sprehn Ludwig, cigar box manufacturer, al. b. Vine and Walnut and 13th and Mercer, h. 49 Pleasant [gail
	Sprengelmeier John H., teacher, 70 Abigail
	Sprengelmeier Mary, 76 Abigail
	Sprenger Christian, turner, 101 Bremen
	SPRENGER & EMRICH, (Frederick S. & Philip E.,) Manufacturers of Shears and Cutlery, 340 Main
	SPRENGER Frederick, (S. & Emrich,) h. 340 Main
	Sprenger John, lithographer, 45 Kossuth
	Sprenger Sophia, laundress, rear 26 Franklin
	Sprenkel John, cab. mkr., 46 Hamer
	Sprey August, lab., wks. 304 Broadway
	Spreyer Peter, cooper, 507 Elm
	Sprigg Georgiana, washwoman, 29 L'Hommedieu al
	Spriggs Jane, 99 W. 9th, w. of Central Avenue
	Sprigman Julius A., b.k., 38 Walnut, h. 589 Freeman
	Spring Bridget, 16 E. 8th, e. of Lock
	SPRING GROVE CEMETERY, Office Melodeon Buildings, Room 3, n.w.c. Walnut and 4th
	Spring John, mattresses, &c., 29 Public Landing
	Spring Lucas, painter, wks. Crane, Breed & Co.'s
	Springer Albert, lab., 181 E. 3d
	Springer Ernst, wagon mkr., 99 W. Front
	Springer Frederick, mach., wks. 116 W. 2d
	Springer John, polisher, 40 Rittenhouse
	Springer Max, cigars, &c., 38 Broadway, bds. Broadway Hotel

304 (STA) CINCINNATI (STA) DIRECTORY. (STA)

Springer Reuben R., 180 W. 7th
Springer Samuel, cap mkr., 62 E. 5th
SPRINGER & WHITEMAN (Lewis W., Granville J. Williams, & Wm. I. Whiteman.) Wholesale Grocers and Commission Merchants, 16 and 18 W. 2d
Springett Abraham, tailor, 75 Mulberry
Springmann Ignatius, lab., w. s. Thuber al. b. Wade and Adams
Springmayer Wm., lab., 79 Gest
Springmeier Ferdinand J., (Hackmann & S.,) 23 Woodward
Springmeier Henrietta, 511 Sycamore
Springmeier Wm., tailor, 28 Mansfield
Springmeyer John, porter, 861 Gest
Sprinsly Philip, shoemkr, bds. 76 W. Court
Spritzke Christopher, tailor, 686 Main
Spritzke Hy., cof. h., 436 Vine
Spritzke Hy., cof. h., 442 Vine
Sproeder John N., butcher, 26 Pleasant
Sprong Sarah, bds. 122 Baymiller
Sproul Edward, b.k. binder, wks. s. w. c. 8th and Main
Sprow Wm., carp., 224 Findlay
Sprung Wm., lab., bds. 346 Main
Sprung Wm., lab., 33 Moore
SPRUTZKI HENRI, Saloon, 436 Vine
Spuele Francis, lab., 68 Green
Spumgord Chas., wagoner, Commercial Hospital
Spunaugle John, bk. mkr., Richmond b. Harriet and Millcreek
Spurling Martha, bds. 30 Patterson al
Spurlock Thomas W., 315 Ham. Road
Squires Henderson, sheet iron worker, 132 George
Sraszburger Nicholas, cof. h., 160 Bremen
Staab John, shoemkr, n. e. c. Elm and Elder
Stnat Geo., cooper, 20 Webster
Stucco Frank, sheet iron worker, wks. n.w.c. Pearl and M. Canal
Stacer Remmick, shoemkr, 35 Mulberry
STACEY GEORGE, Gasometer and Iron Bridge Builder, w. s. Ramsey n. of W. Front, h. Covington, Ky.
Stacey J. & J. W., (Joshua & John W.) fruits, &c., 53 E. 3d
Stacey John W., (J. & J. W. S.,) 22 E. 4th
Stacey Joshua, (J. & J. W. S.,) bds. Gibson House
STACY JOHN A., Plumber, Pump and Hydrant Maker, and Dealer in Lead Pipe and Sheet Lead, 253 Central Av., h. 444 W. 8th
Stachschulte Anna, servt., wks. 301 W. 8th
STACKHOUSE GEO., City Auditor's Office, City Hall, h. 232 Clinton
Stockman Hy., jeweler, 207 Longworth
Stactter Geo , tailor, 20 W. Court, w. of Central Avenue
Stacum Margaret, servt., 110 Broadway
STADLER, BROTHER & CO., (Max Martin, Wm. Kraus & Moses Stadler,) Wholesale Clothiers, and Importers of Dry Goods, 106 W. Pearl
Stadler Geo., lab., 52 15th
Stadler Jacob, shoemkr, 7 Buckeye
Stadler Martin, lab., wks. s. e. c. Canal and Vine
STADLER Martin, (Stadler, Brother & Co.) 117 W. 6th
STADLER Max, (Stadler, Bro. & Co.,) 262 W. Court, w. of Central Av
STADLER Moses, (Stadler, Brother & Co. , 64 Longworth
Stadlmair Helena, notions, 463 Main
Stadthagen Jacob, clothing, 100 W. Front
Stadtler Jacob, shoemkr, s.w.c. Buckeye and Main
Stadtler Leonard, lab., 804 W. Front]
Stadtmueller Anna M., 40 Buckeye
Staeb Donald, milkman, e. s. Millcreek, s. of Harrison Road
Staehelhart Barney, cooper, 181 York
Staehl Conrad, tailor, Allison b. Walnut and Vine

Staehle August, cab. mkr., 636 Main
Staffermann Herman, chair mkr., s.w.c. Clark and Cutter
Staffin Wm., wagon mkr., bds. rear 7 Bank
Stafiney Charles, n. s. Stark, b. Dunlap and Mohawk Bridge
Stafford Hy., lab., 50 Kossuth
Stafford James, tanner, n.s. Findlay b. Elm and Logan
Stafford John, clk., 27 Mound
Stafford Martha J., teacher, 193 3d
Stafford Thomas, mach., 27 Mound
Stafford Wm., lab., w. s. Whittaker b. 3d and Front
Stagaman Hy. jewelry, &c., 16 Sycamore, h. 207 Longworth
Stagenborg Barney, porter, 18 Commerce
Stager Chas., molder, "ks. n. e. c. Canal and Walnut
Stagg J. J. & Co., (John J. S., Geo. M. Short & David A. Winston,) grocers, 102 E. Pearl
Stagg John J., (J. J. S. & Co.,) res. Mt. Washington
Stagg Elizabeth, n.e.c. George and Linn
Stagge Frederick, 40 15th
Stagge George Hy., finisher, rear 523 Sycamore
Stagge Hy., 51 15th
Staggenwald Frank, tailor, 237 Bremen
Stegman Louis W., hardware, 20 E. Pearl, h. 13 Grant
Stahl Anthony, cooper. 715 Race
STAHL August, (S. & H , 203 Baymiller
Stahl Elizabeth, e. s. Johnson al. b. Canal and 12th
Stahl Elizabeth, 123 W. Liberty
Stahl Frank, la., h. 4 Mohawk
Stahl Frederick, eng., wks. s. w. c. Augusta and Smith
Stahl Frederick, cab. mkr., 298 Findlay
Stahl Hy., baker, 652 Vine
STAHL & HUST, (August S. & Jacob H.) Wines, Liquors, Cigars, &c., 32 Ham. Road
Stahl John A., lab., 115 Carr
Stahl Joseph, miller, 641 Race
Stahl Lena, vest mkr. 10 Orchard
Stahl Louisa, 532 Sycamore
Stahl Peter P., porter, 70 W. Pearl
Stahl Peter P., tailor, 383 Vine
Stahl Ulrich, 529 Race
Stahl Wm. F., carp., 298 Findlay
Stahlberg Herman H., lab., 403 Broadway
Stahlmann Fred.. saddler, bds. Teutonia Hotel
Staieb Sebastian, pattern mkr., 48 Lock
Stakum Bridget, servt., n.e.c. 4th and Pike
Stal Gerhard, shoemkr, bds. 64 E. 5th
Stalbox Sebastian, lab., wks. Hy. Nye's
Staley Valentine, lab., s.w.c. 8th and Sycamore
Stalkamp Hy., grocery, 10 Green
Stalkamp John H., hostler, 450 Walnut
Stalkamp John H., lab., 70 Abigail
STALL Bernard G., (S. & Meyer), h. Walnut Hills
Stall Frank, shoe fitter, 488 Sycamore
Stall Hy. A., grocery, 680 Central Av
Stall John F., grocery, s.w.c. Broadway and New
Stall Joseph, bar k., 30 Pub. Landing
Stall Martin, clk., 161 Linn
STALL & MEYER (Bernard G. S. & Henry A. M.) Wholesale Grocers and Dealers in Liquors, 64 and 66 W, 2d
Stall Robert A , sheet iron ware manuf., 40 W. 2d, bds. 197 Broadway
Stallnight Jno. A., undertaker, 120 Richmond
Stallo Ann, 94 Woodward
Stullo Geo., hinge fitter, wks. n.e.c. Walnut and Canal
STALLO John B. (S. & McCook,) 19 W. Court
STALLO John H. (S., Tafel & James), h. 456 Broadway
STALLO & McCOOK, (John B. S. & Robt. L. McC.) Attorneys at Law, 19 W. Court

STALLO, TAFEL & JAMES, (John H. S., Gustav. T. & T. M. James) Attorneys at Law, n.w.c. Main and Court
Stambuch Clements, foreman, 97 Bremen
Stamm Faltine, stone cutter, 1019 Central Av
Stammbusch Hy. B., carp., 62 14th
Stammel Antoinette, teacher, 221 Court
Stample Amanda, s.e.c. Elm and Union
Stamput Edward, driver, Pennock al. b. Cutter and Linn
Stanbach Ambrose, cooper, 40 John
Stanberry Hy., atty , 3 Masonic Temple, res. Campbell co., Ky
Standard Fire Ins. Co. Agency, 76 W. 2d
Stander Gottfried, painter, s s Charlotte b. Linn and Baymiller
Stander Phillip, cigars, &c., s.s. Bank b. Whiteman and Linn
Standish W. C., clk. 64 E. Pearl
STANFORD & BICKNELL (Richard S. & Edward M. B.) Fruit, Produce and Commission Merchants, 21 Broadway
Stanford John, painter, bds. n.w.c. Baymiller and Richmond
Stanford Julia, cof. h., 23 E. 3d
Stanford Otis W., carp., 391 Central Av.
STANFORD Richd. (S. & Bicknell), res. Country
Stang Reinhard, bk. binder, 539 Main
Stang Geo., tailor, 47 Findlay
Stangle Martha, n.w.c. Baltimore and Sycamore
Stanhope Chas. B., com. mer., bds. Henrie House
Stanhope Phillip W., 237 Barr
Stanley ——, 51 Freeman
Stanley B., bds. Dennison House
Stanley Chas., steam pipe fitter, wks. 250 E. Front
Stanley Daniel, (S. & Johnson), 100 Dudley
Stanley Elizabeth, 20 Pine
Stanley Hy., brass finisher, 15 Harrison
Stanley Hy., cook. 970 E. Front
Stanley John W., finisher, bds. 312 W. 6th
Stanley & Johnson (Daniel S. & George J.) mach's., 175 W, 2d
Stanley Michael, lab , 40 Elizabeth
Stanley Michael, watchman, Clifton House
Stanley Pat., waiter, Burnet House
Stanlin Geo., bksmith, wks. s.s. 8th b. Main and Sycamore
Stannus Aaron, mess. Adams' express, h. 452 W, 8th
Stannus James, not. pub., 273 W. 7th
Stannus Robt. B., salesman, 99 W. 4th, h. 273 W. 7th
Stannus Trevor, saddler, bds. 273 W. 7th
Stansberry James, lab., 97 E. Front
Stansberry John, 968 E. Front
Stansberry L., salesman. bds. 162 Plum
Stansberry Usual, 968 E. Front
Stansberry Wm., bds. 974 E. Front
Stanton Bridget, Maiden Lane b. Gas al. and Anderson al
Stanton Catharine, seamstress, Maiden Lane b. Gas al. and Anderson al
Stanton John, bksmith, 81 Hopkins
STANTON JOHN, Stamp & Brand Cutter, 139 W 5th, bds. 296 W. 5th
Stanton Johanna, grocery, 131 E. 6th
Stanton Martin, lab., 385 Vine
Stanton Mary, 122 W. Front
STANTON WM., Attorney at Law and Notary Public, s.e.c. 4th and Vine, bds. 61 Longworth
Staple Joseph, pewter wkr, bds. 171 Webb
Stapler Frederick, s.w.c. Linn and Charlotte
Stapleton Dennis, carriage trimmer, 205 Plum
Stapleton E., eng., Burnet House
Stapleton Edward, cooper, s.e.c. 6th and Culvert
Stapleton James, lab., 162 Livingston
Stapleton James, sawyer, 162 Livingston
Stapleton James, teamster, 103 E. 2d

(STE) CINCINNATI (STE) DIRECTORY. (STE) 305

Stapleton John, eng., 205 Plum
Stapleton John, lab., 544 Race
Stapleton John, mason, 357 W. 2d
Stapleton Kate, servt., 93 E.3d
Stapleton Patrick, carp., 162 Livingston
Stapleton Philip, upholsterer, 329 W. 2d [Av
Stapleton Richard D., porter, 220 Central
Stapleton Wm., 205 Plum
Stapleton Wm., jr., shoemkr, 205 Plum
Stapleton Wm., confec., 224 Walnut
Stapp Elizabeth, tailoress, bds s.s. Oliver b. John and Central Av
Stapp Wm., wks. Cin. type foundry
Star Emanuel, cigar manuf., 40 W. 7th
Star Hy. E., cigars, &c., 177 W. 5th
STAR IN THE WEST, Nye & Demarest, Publishers, n.w.c. 6th and Walnut
STARBUCK ALEXANDER, Amusement Editor, Daily Times, bds. 168 Smith
Starbuck Almira, teacher, 299 W. 8th
STARBUCK C. W., Proprietor, Cin. Daily Times, 62 W. 3d, h. 118 Mound
Starbuck Frank W., clk., Daily Times, bds. 118 Mound
Starbuck S., lnb., wks. 335 Broadway
Starck Frederick, tailor, 157 Pleasant
Starck John, lab., s.s. Buckeye b. Poplar and Vine
Starck Wendelin, tailor, 624 Vine
Starfarman Herman, chair mkr., s.w.c. Cutter and Clark
Stark Gustav., tailor, 448 Race
Stark Jacob, 767 Vine
Stark Joseph, turner, 69 14th
Stark M. D., agt Union railroad ticket office, n.w.c. 3d and Vine, h. 370 W. 7th
Stark Theodore, express, 757 Vine
Stark Wm. C., pewterer, 22 Woodward
Starling Jacob L., sutler, 420 W. 5th
Starr Mrs. ——, 62 Clinton
Starr Anthony J., gilder, 135½ Linn
Starr Rev. D. J., 661 Elm
STARR Edgar P. (Vent, S. & Co.), res Walnut Hills
Starr Edwin F., alcohol manuf., s.w.c. John and W. W. Canal, res. Walnut Hills
Starr Jacob, cooper, 181 Longworth
Starr James A., gilder, 135½ Linn
Starr James S., bk, layer, 37 Chestnut
Starr Joseph J., b k., 5d E. 2d, h. 443 Broadway
Starr Nathan B., w.s. Wilson b. Liberty and Milton
Startsman John W., b.k., Johnson, Morton & Co.)
STARTSMAN Samuel (Johnson, Morton & Co.) h. n.e.c. McDowell and Hill
Stattler Martin, lab., 596 Vine
Staubach Eberhard, tailor, s.e.c. Central Av. and Wade
Staubacher Baldwin, shoemkr, bds. 508 Vine
Staubitzer John B., finisher, h 185 W. 2d
Staubroch Ambrose, cooper, 40 Jones
Staud John, lab., 526 Main
Staudt Chas., reporter, bds. 137 Race
STAUDT John James, asst. editor Volksfreund, s.w.c. Vine and Longworth
Staufermann Elizabeth, 597 Race
Stauferman Frank, driver, 597 Race
Staughton J., conductor, bds. Clifton House
Staughton John McL., bds. 281 W. 8th
Staup Andrew, blksmith, 123 W. Front
Stautberg Hy., carriage painter, wks. 55 and 57 E. 5th
Stautberg Herman, cooper, wks. 586 Walnut
Stautigel Geo., tailor, 64 Elder
Stauverman Hy., lab., 187 Hopkins
Staverding Joseph, lab., wks. n. s. Front b Lawrence and Pike
Steadle Frederick, tanner, bds. 701 Elm
Steal Conrad, tailor, s. w. c. Walnut and Allison
Stealy George, porter, s. w. c. Sycamore and 8th
Stealy Valentine, porter. s.w.c. Sycamore and 8th 30

Stearn Mary F., teacher, 67 Milton
Stearns Benjamin B., 67 Milton
STEARNS & FOSTER, (Geo. S. S. & S C. F.), Wadding, Batting and Printing Ink Manufacturers. s.w.c. Clay and Liberty
Stearns G. E., atty., 14 Walnut, h. Madisonville
STEARNS George S. (S. & Foster) res. near Lockland
Stearns Louis, 200 Linn
Steavens Wm. H., contractor, 184 Sycamore
Stebler Joseph, bar k.. 26 13th
Stecher Albin, clay mkr., s.s. Allison b. Vine and Walnut
Stecher Anna, 85 Peete
Stecht Ferdinand, painter, wks. I. & B. Bruce's
Steckenreiter John, wagon mkr., 116 Ham. Road
Stecker Christina. 590 Elm
Stecker Hy., candle mkr., 139 Pleasant
Steekinger Balderson, cook Galt House
Steckmer Fred., cigar mkr., wks. 503 Main
Stedle John, 37 Dunlap
STEDMAN, CARLISLE & SHAW, (Geo. Carlisle, Geo. T. S., Wm. T. C. & Thos. F. S.,) Wholesale Dry Goods, 17 W. Pearl
STEDMAN George T., (S., Carlisle & Shaw,) 133 Plum
Steel Joseph, policeman, 62 Cutter
Steel Maria, 207 W. 9th w. of Central Av.
Steel Theo., lab., wks. s.w.c. 7th and Smith
Steele Anna, 259½ W. 5th
Steele Anton, cooper, 715 Race
Steele Daniel, salesman, bds 170 W. 4th
Steele John, 35 Pleasant
Steele Wm., 23 Chestnut
Steelman H——, clk., 100 Water
Steelman Horatio, bds. 159 W. Front
Steelman Hosea, sen., hoop pole and wood dealer, 97 and 99 Water
Steemer Chas., jeweler, 491 Walnut
Steemer Chas., enameller, 546 Walnut
Steemer George, gas fitter, wks. 14 W. Court
Steen Isaiah, agency, 1 Sycamore, h. 10 Sycamore
Steen Letitia, 365 Broadway
Steer Harriet, 61 Longworth
Steer Sarah R., teacher, 61 Longworth
Stefanni Joseph, huckster, e.s. Pleasant nr. Findlay
Steffel Joseph, paper box mkr., b. 545 Main
Steffen John Conrad, tailor, h. 19 Mulberry
Steffner Peter, tailor, rear 65 Woodward
Steffens Arnold, musician, 18 Allison
Steffens John, clk., bds. 10 Orchard
Steffens John, molder, 14 Hughes
Steffens John. sen., 18 Allison
Steffens Margaret, 10 Orchard
Stegeman Frank, boots and shoes, 498 Vine
Stegeman John H., grocery, 94 E. 2d, bds. cor. Ludlow and Pearl
Stegemann Anthony, lab., 108 Buckeye
Stegemann Francis, lab., bds. 24 Woodward
Stegemann Theo., cigar mkr., bds. n.w. c. Poplar and Buckeye
Stegemann Victor, cof. h., 197 W. 6th
Stegemeier Hy., carp., 141 Baymiller
Stegemneller Louisa, 19 Buckeye
Stegen Christopher, founder, 53 Pendleton
Steggermann Hy., lab., 91 Spring
Steglern Jacob, lab., 502 Vine
Stegman Fred., porter, 55 W. 4th
Stegmann Barney, whitewasher, 216 W. Liberty
Stegmann Conrad, lab., e.s. Vine b. Milk and Mulberry
Stegmann Ernst B., watch mkr., 17 Green
Stegmann Frederick, cigar mkr., 112 Abigail
Stegmann Fred., porter. 10 Peete
Stegner Adam, lab., 540 Plum
Stegner Geo., 560 Elm

Stegner Hy. J., b.k., 400 Sycamore, h. 560 Elm
Stegner Lewis, grocery. 560 Elm
Stegner Xavier, butcher, 11 Mulberry
Stehle Rev. Euglebert, 206 Linn
Stehle Jacob, carver, 541 Elm
Stehle Martin, policeman, 74 W. Mulberry
Stehmann Herman, carp., 623 Race
Stehmann Joseph, carp., 623 Race
Steib Sebastian, pattern mkr., h. 48 Lock
Steide Joseph, grainer, 471 Vine
STEIDEL Jacob, (Born & S.,) 564 Vine
Steidel Joseph, tailor, 161 Bremen
Steiding Christian, 30 Mohawk
Steidle John, tanner, 37 Dunlap
Steidle Joseph, gilder, 471 Vine
Steiernagel Valentine, lab., 594 Race
Steiernagle Michael, lab., wks. Hieatt & Wood's
Steigeneier Hy., driver, 54 Dudley
Steiger Casper, carp., 15 Bank
Steiger Chas., potter, 716 E. Front
Steiger John, lab., 40 Pike
Steiger Martin, 461 Walnut
Steigert Hy., finisher, s.w.c. Elm and Findlay
Steigert Leopold, finisher. 114 Elder
Steigerwald Adam, lab., 36 Elder
Steigerwald Geo., butcher, bds. 35 Elder
Steigerwald Sebastian, blk. smith 610 Race
Steigle John, finisher, 59 Findlay
Steigleman Jacob, sen., mach., wks. n. w.c Pearl and M. Canal
Steigleman Jacob. jr., mach., wks. n.w. c. Pearl and M. Canal
Steigman Jacob, finisher, 47 Observatory
Steigmuller Fred., baker, bds. 222 W. 6th
Steikel Hy., lab., wks. Hieatt & Wood's
Steilberg Herman F., 477 Broadway
Steimel Ferdinand, steward, 212 E. 6th
Stein Albert W., st. bt. captain, 190 W. 4th
Stein Chas., packer, 4 Lucy
Stein Charlotte, 4 Louisa
Stein Hy., trader, 252 Elm
Stein Joseph, carp., 716 E. Front
STEIN JOHN V., Photograph Gallery, 465 Vine
Stein Louis, driver, 58 Providence
Stein Magdelena, millinery, 62 Laurel
Stein Mrs. Mary, h. 512 Vine
Stein Mathilda, fancy goods, 156 W. 5th
Stein Michael, cof h., 136 Bremen
Stein Peter, mach., 209 Barr
Stein Philip, 256 Walnut
Stein Simeon, 156 W. 5th
Stein Theresa, s.w.c. Longworth and Elm
Stein Valentine, copper smith, n.e.c. 6th and Miller
Stein Wm., express man, 72 12th
Steinacher Hy., lab., 128 Mohawk
Steinau Joseph, 94 14th
Steinauer Anton, carp., 19 Mercer, h. 351 Vine
Steinauer Ursula, embroidery, 351 Vine
Steinbach Julius, copper smith, 21 Woodward
Steinbauer Wm., mach., 579 Main
Steinbeker Hy., teamster, 293 Water
Steinberg F., wig manuf., 132 Walnut, h. Mill Creek Township
Steinberg Geo. H., huckster, 505 Race
Steinberg Michael, peddler, 89 George
Steinborn Hy. J., boots and shoes, 73 W. Court
Steinbrecher Joseph, shoe mkr., 150 Clay
Steinbrecker Werner F., music teacher, 142 Sycamore
Steinburg Hy., molder, 27 Commerce
Steincamp Fred., grocery, s.e.c. Freeman and Liberty
Steindle Geo., lab., 311 Findlay
Steinemann Fred., chair mkr., n.e.c. Abigail and Broadway
Steinemann Geo., express man, 11 Moore
Steiner & Bier. (Michael S. & Emanuel B.,) clothiers, 22 W. Pearl

Steiner Fred., (S. & Popp,) 451 Vine
STEINER GEO.,
  Wine Dealer,
  35 E. 3d, h. 33 E. 3d
Steiner H., chair mkr., wks. John Mitchell's
Steiner Jacob, dray, 71 Green
Steiner Jacob, jr., lab., wks. Hieatt & Wood's
Steiner Jacob, sen., lab., wks. Hieatt & Wood's
Steiner Jacob. lab., 166 Freeman
Steiner John H., clk. C. H. & D. R. R. Depot, res. Glendale
Steiner Joseph, 115 Laurel
Steiner Michael, (S. & Bier,) 21 Richmond
Steiner Michael, brass molder, 525 Sycamore
Steiner & Popp, (Fred. S. & Christian P.,) tailors, 451 Vine
Steiner Wm., stone cutter, 407 Elm
Steinfelts Myer, peddler, 569 Central Av
Steingrebber Barney, shoe mkr., s.w.c. 13th and Main
Steinhelber Conrad, n.e.c. 2d and Broadway
Steinhelber Dora, chamber maid, n.e.c. 2d and Broadway
Steinhoff Fred., lab., 368 Broadway
Steinigweg Hy. Wm., blk. smith, 65 Pleasant
Steinkamp Benj., turner, bds. 400 W. 7th
Steinkamp Caroline. 160 Oliver
Steinkamp Christian, clk. n.e.c Webster and Mausfield
Steinkamp Elizabeth, seamstress, bds. 76 Bremen
Steinkamp F, lab., wks. Wood & McCoy's
Steinkamp Fred., clk., n.e.c. 9th and John
Steinkamp Fred., cooper, 586 Walnut
Steinkamp Geo., carman, 50 Rittenhouse
Steinkamp Geo., eng., e.s. Kilgour b. 3d and 5th
Steinkamp Geo., porter 66 Bremen
Steinkamp Geo. L., lab., 62 Bremen
Steinkamp Hy., upholsterer, bds. 400 W. 7th
Steinkamp John B., cab. mkr., 76 Bremen
Steinkamp Joseph, wheelwright, 401 W. 7th
Steinkamp Mary, seamstress, bds. 76 Bremen
Steinkamp Richard, wks. 65 Water
Steinkamp Theo, dry goods 488 Main
Steinke Geo., blk. smith, 15 Green
Steinke Gerhard, blk. smith, 201 Bremen
Steinker Rudolph, 55 David
Steinkonig August, grocery, 205 W. Liberty
Steinkop John, peddler, 99 Ham Road
Steinlage Albert, grocery, s.w.c. Abigail and Broadway
Steinlage D., lab., wks., 137 W. 2d
Steinle Andreas, porter, 427 Sycamore
Steinle Andrew, salesman, Benziger Brother's n.w.c. Vine and Longworth
Steinle Caroline, 634 Vine
Steinle Chas., cigar mkr., wks. 213 Walnut
Steinle Herman, brewer, bds. 59 Harrison Pike
Steinle Leo., cigar mkr., wks. 213 Walnut
Steinman Abraham, cab mkr., 12 15th
Steinman L. E. & Co., (Louis E. S., John D. Meyer & Daniel E. Kline,) furniture warerooms, 66 Sycamore, factory 470 W. 6th
Steinman Louis E., (L. E. S. & Co.), 34 Hathaway
Steinman Wm., shoe mkr., bds. 27 Pub. Landing
Steinmann Barney, lab., 87 Spring
Steinmetz Andrew, tailor, 83 Peete
Steinmetz John, tailor, n. s. Front w. of Hill
Steinmeyer Sophia, teacher 50 Mansfield
Steinnagel Francis, lab , 35 Elder
Steinnauer Ignatz, cab. mkr., 516 Main
Steinoen David, watchmkr., 428 John

Steinput Edward, driver, rear 204 Richmond
Steins A. Hy., tailor, 64 E. 5th
Steinsults Mary, 96 Buckeye
Steintker John,,porter, wks. 51 W. 2d
Steinwart Hy., grocery. 489 Walnut
Stele Benj., cooper, 181 York
Stell Mary, n.s. Montgomery pike nr. Madison Road
Stella Chas., carp., 10 Eaton
Stellwag Sebastian, lab., 510 Plum
Steltenkamp Frank., lab., 377 Broadway
Steltenkamp Theodore, fireman, e.s. Spring b. Woodward and Abigail
Steltenkamp Theodore, lab., 114 Clay
Steltunpohl Anton,lab., 8 Pleasant
Steltenpohl Hy. J., lab., wks. s.w.c. W. Canal and Smith
Steltenphol Joseph H., lab., 401 Longworth
Stem E; D., bds., 29 W. 3d
Steman, John, carp., 168 Pleasant
Steman Chas. J., b.k. 25 Main, bds. 94 14th
Stemberg Simon, cigar mkr., bds. n.s. 5th b Elm and Race
Stemke Fred., shoe mkr., 172 Everett
Stemler Danl., blksmith, wks. Niles Works
Stemler Louis, finisher, wks. C. T. Dumont's
Stemmens Chas., cof. h., 358 W. 5th
Stemmer Remidus, tailor, 86 Bremen
Stemmerding Bernhard, cigar mkr., 110 Pleasant
Stemmermann Emily, grocery, n.e.c. Linn and Everett
Stemmermann Hy., n.e.c. Linn and Everett
Stemmermann Wm., grocery, 225 W. Front [13th
Stemmler Charles., pattern mkr., 102
Stempler Hy., lab., wks. Wood and McCoy's
Stengel Francis, carp., 57 Hamer
Stengel Mary, 646 Vine
Stengel Philip, boots and shoes 132 W. Court
Stengel Theodore, shoe mkr., 586 Race
Stengen Elizabeth, 48 Elder
Stenger John, cooper, 66 Ham. Road
Stenglein Fred., tailor, 95 Buckeye
Stengler John, e.s. Branch b. Findlay and Ham Road
Stenglin Joseph, 69 Mohawk
Step Conrad, lab., rear 517 E. Front
Stepelcamp Geo , cof h., 83 W. Front
STEPHAN Antonio, (Conrad S. & Co.) 433 Walnut
Stephan Benedict, cab. mkr., 505 Vine
Stephan Chas., bakery, 505 Vine
STEPHAN Conrad, (Conrad S. & Co.), rear 8 12th
STEPHAN CONRAD & CO., (Conrad S., Sylester Stephan, & Antonio Stephan.) Pork Packers and Produce Dealers, 8 12th
Stephan Francis Ch., tailor, 673 Race
Stephan Geo., boots and shoes, 497 Vine
Stephan Hy., foreman, 35 Moore
STEPHAN Sylvester, (Conrad S. & Co) 435 Walnut
Stephens Elijah, tailor, 18 Gest
Stephens Hopkins, mach., wks. 222. E. Front
Stephens Jacob, (Speer & S.) res Ind.
Stephens James E., (Johnson, S. & Morgan) bds. 398 Central Av
Stephens James, H. K., foreman, A. S Butterfield, h. 196 Barr
Stephens Job., pork packer, 273 Sycamore, h Avondale
Stephens John, blksmith, s.w.c. Bank and Whiteman
Stephens John, molder, 734 W. 6th
Stephens John, bk. molder, 181 Clinton
Stephens John B., s.w.c Longworth and rge
Stephens John C., 62 Kossuth
Stephens Saml. D., com. mer., 39 Mill, h. 633 W. 7th
Stephens Sarah, 53 E. 3d e. of Whittaker
Stephenson Alfred W., (Peebles & Bro) 225 W. 4th

Steurer Geo., barber, 14 E. Front
Steurer Joseph, rope mkr., 273 Freeman
Steuwer Hy., lab., 70 Pleasant
Steve Caroline, seamstress, 703 Race
Steve John H., cigar mkr., wks. e.s Linn b. Clark and Hopkins, h. 223 Betts
Steve Mrs. Lizzie, 215 Betts
Stevenback Frederick, 416 Longworth
Stevener Frederick, tailor, 9 Wade b. Elm and Plum
Stevens Alex C. b.k,49 W 4th h 6 Jane
Stevens Amanda, 272 W. 7th
Stevens Americus A., 267 Longworth
STEVENS B. R, Carriage Manufacturer, 55 and 57 E. 5th, h. Glendale
Stevens Barney, blksmith, 407 Walnut
Stevens Chas. clk., Duhme & Co's, h. Walnut Hills
Stevens Chas.. shoe mkr. 86½ Broadway
Stevens Chas. H., 8 E. 2d. h 196 Zarr
Stevens Edward, b.k 88 W. Front h. 345 George
Stevens Edward B., physician, 130 Richmond
Stevens Dr. Edward T., Cin. Lock Hospital. 76 W. 3d, bds. Spencer House
Stevens Edwin. clk., bds 345 George
Stevens Geo. E., 52 W. 9th
Stevens Geo. E., h. k., 39 W. 4th, bds. e.s. Elm b. 9th and Court
Stevens Harmon A , turner. 81 Pike
Stevens Hiram, finisher, wks. n.e.c. Walnut and Canal
STEVENS I. Blackford. (Harlow M. Merrell & Co.,) bds. Clifton House
Stevens Isaac L., blksmith, 211 W. 3d, h. 267 Longworth
Stevens Jacob, finisher 345 George
Stevens Jacob A., 320 Main
Stevens John, dray, wks. Crane Breed & Co's.
Stevens John F., tel, op., 142 W. 7th
Stevens John T., blksmith, s. e. c. Denman and Central Av., h. s.w.c. Bank and Whiteman
Stevens Joseph, molder, 100 W. 5th
Stevens Julia, teacher, 398 Central Av.
Stevens L. B., bds. Clifton House
Stevens Lemuel, 286 W. 9th w. of Central Av.
Stevens Levi, plasterer, bds 294 Linn
STEVENS Levi E., (Chambers S. & Co.) 166 W. 9th
Stevens Lewis bk. mkr., 88 Carr
Stevens Maria, 63 E. 7th
Stevens Mary Jane, 97 W. 9th w. of Central Av
Stevens Michael, lab., 15 Water
Stevens Montgomery, policeman, 23 Harrison
Stevens P. S., shoe mkr., rooms 56 E. 3d
Stevens Ruth A., n.s. Railroad e. of Hazen
STEVENS Sala, (W. B. Bisby & Co.,) res. Penn.
STEVENS Sherman J., (D. Banning & Co.,) h. Covington
Stevens Susan, 206 Longworth
STEVENS W. F., (Chambers S. & Co.,) h. Aurora Ind
Stevens Wm. W., mach., 11 Linn
Stevenson B. D., ticket agt. C. H. & D. R. R., office in depot, h. 130 Everett
Stevenson Benjamin, bds. 441 W. 2d
Stevenson David A., carp., 297 Central Av.
Stevenson Hy. D., com. mer., 136 Barr
Stevenson Johanna C., teacher, 56 14th
Stevenson Joseph, lumber dealer, w. s. Freeman opp. Barr, h. 414 W. 7th
Stevenson Joseph M., carp., 31 Elizabeth
Stevenson Luke, carp., 32 George
Stevenson Margaret A. B., teacher, h. 325 W. 6th
Stevenson Maria C., bds. 31 Elizabeth
Stevenson Mary H., teacher, 325 W. 6th
Stevenson Peter G., (Forbus & S.,) 58 14th
Stevenson Robert, 325 W. 6th
Stevenson Robert H., (Conkling Young & Co.,) 113 Bremen
Stevenson Samuel, bds. 20 Macalister

Stevenson Samuel, clk. C. H. & D. R.R. h. 325 W. 6th
Stevenson Wm., carp., 347 Central Av.
Stevenson Wm., mason, 56 14th
Stevenson Wm., painter, 180 Elm
Stevenson Wm. L., clk., bds. 414 W. 7th
Stevenson York W., grainer, s. s. Front e. of Selas
Stevick George, printer, 66 Plum
Stevick Wm., japanner, wks. n.w.c. Race and 2d
Steward Geo. B., clk., n.e.c. Clinton and John
Steward James D., carp., 97 W. Front
Steward James M., furniture &c., 300 W. 5th
Steward John, bds. 136 John
Steward Mary E., n.e.c. Clinton and John
Steward Wm. E., clk., 48 W. 5th, h. Newport, Ky.
Stewart Alexander, cigar mkr., bds. 179 Broadway
Stewart Alexander, plumber, 128 Mound
Stewart Alex, tin shop, 1520 E. Front, h. 230 W. 6th
STEWART ARCH V., Meat Store, n.e.c. Park and 5th
Stewart Benjamin F., pipeman, 103 Martin
Stewart Calvin, carp., bds. 214 W. Front
Stewart Calvin N. A., molder, bds. 214 W. Front
STEWART CARMICHAEL & CO., (H. S. & Robert C.,) Forwarding and Commission Merchants, n.e.c. Front and Wood
Stewart Catharine, dry goods, 230 W. 6th
STEWART CHARLES, (Cassady & S.,) 437 Broadway
Stewart Chas., foreman, wks. 509 Plum
Stewart Charles, painter, s. e. c. Adams and Spring Grove Av.
Stewart Daniel, pilot, n.e.c Park and 5th
Stewart David R., agt., 88 E. 3d
Stewart David R., salesman, 53 W. Pearl h. 23 E. 3d
Stewart Edward, trunk mkr., 77 Providence
Stewart Eliza, b. h. 155 W. 4th
Stewart Mrs. Elizabeth, bds. 505 W. 7th
Stewart Elsy, 128. Walnut
Stewart Ephraim. 96 Central Av.
Stewart Helen, teacher, 437 Broadway
STEWART Hugh. (Stewart, Carmichael & Co.,) 152 W. 4th,
Stewart James, barber, 504 Elm, h. 645 Sycamore
Stewart James H.. (Tullis & S.,) 697 W. 6th
Stewart John, butcher, n. e. c. York and Baymiller ant John, lab., Marsh al. b. Park
Steward Smith
Stewat John. lab., 130 Water
Stewart John T. B., grainer, s. w. c, 6th and Broadway
Stewart John W , clk., 88 E. 3d
Stewart Joseph P., clk., bds. 21 Barr
Stewart Nancy h. 12 15th b. Central Av. and Plum
Stewart Prosper, 27 Barr
Stewart Richard C., blksmith, wks. s.w.c. Elm and Pearl
Stewart Samuel, currier, wks. 322 Main
Stewart Thos , policeman, 266 Cutter
Stewart Virginia, s. w. c. 6th and Broadway
Stewart Walter, roller, 327 W. 6th
Stewart Wesley A., druggist clk., n e.c. 7th and Linn, bds. 54 Richmond
Stewart Wm., draughtsman, s. e. c. 4th and Walnut, bds. Dennison House
Stewart Wm., fireman, 116 Avery
Stewart Wm., (Gibson Early & Co,) 129 Laurel
Stewart William, mach., 311 W. 8th
Stewart Wm. B., pattern mkr., 9 Linn
STEWART WILLIAM H., Architect and Carpenter Shop, w. s. Plum b. Canal and Court, h. 365 W. 8th
Stewart Wm. P. printer, n. e. c. Lewis and Front

Stewart Wm. P., butcher, w. s. Spring Grove Av., b. Adams and Corporation Line
Stewer Christopher, organ builder, 549 Sycamore
Stewer Hy., 543 Sycamore
Stezle Hy . butcher, at G. & P. Bogen's
Sthufstall Fritz, cigar mkr., 60 Mound
Sthulte George, carp., w. s. Ramsey b. Front and W. W. Canal
Stibing Conrad, lab., 549 Race
Stichhelm John E., barber, 583 W. 6th, h. 563 W 5th
Stichtenoth Lewis, b. k.. 4 Louisa
Sticker Barney, lab., rear 67 Abigail
Sticker Wm., bds. 81 E. Pearl
Stickforth Fred, lab., rear 62 W. Mulberry
Stickler Chas , butcher, 505 Race
Stickler Hy., carp., 87 12th
Stickler Joseph, butcher, 129 Everett
STICKNEY Daniel, (Fay & S.,) 181 Mound
Sticksel Hy., cab. mkr., 87 Wade
Sticksel Peter, lab., 87 Wade
Stiedel John, cigar mkr., wks. 433 Main
Stiefel John G., driver, 669 Vine
Stiefel Mary, 65 Rittenhouse
Stiefel Otmar H , engraver, 512 Vine
Stiegenauld Andrew, lab., wks. 728 Central Av. [Vine
Steigler Anthony, boots and shoes, 556
Stiegler Joseph, furniture, 41 Moore
Stiel Jacob, painter, n.s. Adams b. Plum and Elm
Stieler Christian, printer, 589 Walnut
Stieler Geo , musician, 587 Walnut
Stien Charles, varnisher, 601 Elm
Stienall James, lab., wks. s. e. c. Canal and Vine
Stiene Dietrich, dry goods, n. s. 13th b. Walnut and Clay
Stieneker Herman E., tobacco &c., 526 W. 8th
Stiens Francis Jr., tinner, 156 Pleasant
STIENS Francis, (Dieckman & S.,) 150 Pleasant
Stiens Frank X., clk., s.w.c. 3d and Vine bds. 420 W. 3d
Stiens G. IIy., tailor, 2 Abigail
STIENS JOHN, Merchant Tailor, 420 W. 3d
Stier Christian porter, 5 Lawrence
Stier Christopher, lab., 5 Lawrence
Stieringer Jacob, carp., n.s. Cassatt al. b. Sycamore and Main
STIERLE ADOLPH, Drugs, Medicines, Chemicals, Oils &c., 652 Race
Stierle Chas., inst. mkr , 48 Elder
Stierle Emma, teacher. 48 Elder
Stierle Herman, druggist, 48 Elder
Stierle Jacob, stocking manufac., 228 Walnut
Stierle Pauline, 48 Elder
Sterling ——, cab. mkr., 22 Mercer
Stierling Jacob, painter, bds. 65 W. 5th
Stietin Wm., cooper, 100 Gest
Stievens Bernhard, blksmith, 467 Walnut
STIFEL ADAM, Wines Liquors &c., 380 and 382 Main, h. n.e.c. Walnut and Allison
Stifel Geo., clk., 379 Vine
Stifel John, student, n.e.c. Walnut and Allison
Stiff Harris, (F. Rox, & Co.,) h. 362 Central Av.
Stigeler Rosa, 523 Vine
Stigeler Theresa, 523 Vine
Still Ily., lab., al. b. Vine and Walnut and 13th and Mercer
Stiles Francis, butcher, s.w.c. Linn and Bank
Stiles H. L. & Co., (Henry L. S. & Timothy M. S.,) com. mer., 53 Walnut
Stiles Ily. L., (H. L. S. & Co.,) 389 W. 9th w. of Central Av.
Stiles Timothy M., (II. L. Stiles & Co.,) bds. Walnut St. House
Stille Ernst, cab. mkr., 18 Madison
Stiller James, carp., 141 George
Stilley James, carp., n.s. L'Hommedieu al. b. Central Av. and John, h. 141 George

308 (STO) CINCINNATI (STO) DIRECTORY. (STO)

Stillinger, Chas., furniture, 658 Central Av.
Stillman Catharine, 114 W. Front
Stillman Geo. H., photographer, 106 W. 4th
STILLMAN GEORGE K., Wood Engraver, s.w.c. 4th and Walnut, h. 295 Baymiller
Stillman James, carp., 143 E. 2d
Stillman James, lab., 114 W. Front
Stillman Julius, 74 Stark
Stillwell Elias, molder, 196 W. Front
Stillwell John, carriage mkr., 333 John
Stillmiller Joseph, hostler. 34 Butler
Stimits John, lab., wks. 1505 E. Front
Stimper George, lab., 110 Culvert
Stimson Rachael, 472 Broadway
Stine Frederick A., b. k., s. e. c. Lawrence and 5th, res Newport
Stinelager Geo., lab., w. s. Pike b. Pearl and 3d
Sting Jacob, cof. h., n.e.c. Allison and Clay
Sting Rianhard, bk. binder, n.e.c. Franklin and Main
Stinger George, mach., bds. 144 Hopkins
Stinger Geo. A., silver smith, 2 W. 4th, h. 144 Hopkins
Stinkel Hermon, bds. 687 Central Av.
Stiritz Gottfried, lab., 1460 E. Front
Stirnkorb John, tailor, 20 Hamer
Stites Benj. carp., Walnut Hills
Stith Charlotte, matron, asylum for col'd orphans, n. s. 9th, b. Elm and Front
Stits Benjamin, carp., wks. 76 Betts
Stittleberg Caroline, 502 Main
Stitzle Gerhard, lab., 81 Bremen
Stitzle Geo. G., lab., 81 Bremen
Stivers L. B., clk., 101 W. 4th, bds. 119½ Clinton
Stiving Louis, upholsterer, 642 Elm
STIX Aaron (Stix, Krouse & Co.,) 282 Race
STIX Ily, (S. Krouse & Co.,) 156 W. 8th
STIX, KROUSE & CO., (Henry S., Jacob K. and Aaron Stix,) Wh. Clothiers, Importers of Cloths, Cassimeres, Vestings, &c, 61 W. Pearl
STIX Louis, (Louis S. & Co.,) h. 261 Race
STIX LOUIS & CO., (Louis S.. Joseph Swartz and Nathan Stix,) Importers and Wholesale Dealers in Staple and Fancy Dry Goods, 164 Main
STIX Nathan, (Louis Six & Co.,) b. 156 W. Court, w. of Central Av.
Stock Adam, (S. & Co.,) 674 Race
Stock Adam & Co , (Adam S. and Peter Hachn,) cof. h., 674 Race
Stock Conrad, n. w. c. Mohawk and Hamburg
Stock Hy., (H. Shror & H. S.,) 187 Linn
Stock Hy., lab., 54 Buckeye
Stock Jacob, saddler, e. s. Vine b. Ham. Road and Buckeye
Stock Margaret, seamstress, 367 W 5th
Stock Michael. saddler, e. s. Vine b Buckeye and Ham. Road
Stocker Michael, finisher, 103 Bremen
Stockett E., clk., Adams Express Co., h. Newport
Stockfish John H., 42 Elm
STOCKHOFF BERNHARD, Blacksmith and Wagon Maker, 65 W. Liberty
Stockhoff Charles, grocer, s.e.c. Milton and Broadway
Stockhove Dora, 24 Mansfield
Stockhove Fred., candy mkr., 24 Mansfield
Stockle Geo., mason, 59 Buckeye
Stockman Catharine, laundress, 110 Clay
Stockman John, porter, Madison House
Stockmeier Ernst, s.w.c. Price and Milton
Stocks Elizabeth, 25 Mill
Stocks Rachel, 180 W. 7th
Stocks Wm., wagon mkr., 186 W. 7th
Stockton James B., ticket agt , 242 Barr
Stockum Fred., butcher, 54 Providence
Stockum John, butcher, 56 Providence

Stockwell Emmons, phys., bds. 127 Laurel
Stoddard ——, actor, National Theater
Stoddard Marshall W., mach., 45 Cutter
Stoddart Alex., trav. agt. Ætna Ins. Co., 171 Vine
Stoddart Jane, bds. 206 W. Court, w. of Central Av.
STOECKLE, J. N., Com. Mer. and Real Estate Broker, 64 W. 3d, b. 3½ W 7th
Stoecker Charles, clk., 24 Allison
Stoeffer Frank, brewer, 42 Mohawk
Stoehr Leonard, catter, 666 Central Av.
Stoeher Philipp, carp., s.w.c. Vine and Mound
Stoeklin John I., shoemkr., 597 Race
Stoel Mary, 709 Central Av.
Stoeppelmann Joseph, plasterer, 9 Moore
Stoeppig Mrs. Elizabeth, h. 542 Race
Stoerle Chas., carp., 10 Eden
Stoever John C., tailor, 19 Mulberry
Stoffel Michael, shoemkr., 542 Main
Stoffel Peter, cooper, 201 Baymiller
Stoffer Constantine, confed., 574 Elm
Stoffregen Wm., hats and caps, 595 Central Av.
Stoke Sebastian, meat store, 987 Central Av.
Stoker Jane, 58 W. 6th
Stokes Benjamin, bk. layer, 101 Barr
Stokes Clara. dress mkr., bds. 315 W. 9th, w. of Central Av.
Stokes Edward, bk. layer, 101 Barr
Stokes John S., bds 34 Milton
Stokes John S., butcher, wks. 509 Sycamore
Stokes Robert, blk.smith, e. s. Vine, near Auburn Av.
Stokes Samuel, (Cooper & S.,) 57 Richmond
Stokes Theodore, mathematical instrument mkr., 7 W. 4th, b. 130 George
Stolberg Herman, cooper, College al. b. Woodward and Abigail
Stolkamp Hy., driver, wks. 450 Walnut
Stoll Christian, teamster, 10 Webb
Stoll Hy., boots and shoes, 269 John
Stoll Wm., bk. binder, bds. 709 Central Av.
Stoll Wm., tailor, 84 W. Court
Stollen Chas , lab., s. s. 6th b. Harriet and Horne
Stollman John, huckster, e. s. Western Av b. Poplar and Findlay
Stolss Benjamin, lab., 534 W. 2d
Stoltz Jacob, tailor, bds. 17 Poplar
Stoltz John, 510 Walnut
Stolz Jacob, tailor, 33 Peete
Stolz Simon, boots and shoes, 541 Race
Stolzer Andrew, cof. h., e. s. Milk b. Vine and Calhoun
Stoman Michael, lab., rear 400 Sycamore
STOMS Wm., (John F. Dair & Co.,) 77 Baum [more
Stone Abram, exchange office, 83 Sycamore
Stone B. T. & Co., (Benjamin T. S. & Benjamin W. Putnam,) com. mers., 18 E. 2d
Stone Benjamin T., (B. T. S. & Co.,) 1466 E. Front
STONE & CHAMPLIN, (Richard II. S. & L. D. C.,) Attorneys at Law, 13 W. Court
Stone Charles. tinner, bds. 267 W. Court, w. of Central Av.
Stone Edward, furniture, 275 Central Av., h. 151 Baymiller
Stone Emily A., bds. 118 Baymiller
STONE FRANCIS M., Wholesale Paper Warehouse, 141 Walnut, bds. Walnut St. House
Stone Guilford, clk., 275 Central Av.
Stone Jesse, hostler, 175 E. Front
Stone John, clk., 145 Longworth
Stone John, lab. bds. 48 Pearson
Stone John, porter, n.e.c. 2d and Broadway
Stone John, E., b. k., bds. 109 W. 7th
STONE, L. & M., (L. G. E. S. & M. W. Stone) Commission Merchants and Flour and Grain Dealers, 34 Vine

Stone Leonidas, grocery, n. s. [E. Front, opp. ferry
STONE Leverett G. E., (L. & M. S.,) 366 W 7th
Stone Louis P., druggist, s. w. c. Front and Waldon
STONE Medad W., (L. & M. Stone,) 497 W. 7th
STONE Richard R.. (S. & Champlin,' h. 111 Richmond
Stone Samuel A.. clk., bds. s.e.c 3d and Broadway
Stone Washington J., molder, 233 Central Av.
Stone Wm., confec., 455 W. 5th, h. 82 Mound
Stoneback, W., tel. op., h. 174 Plum
Stonebraker Augustine F., molder, bds. 53 Jackson
Stonebraker John, cooper, e. s. Plum b. Elder and Findlay, h. w. s. Logan b. Elder and Findlay
Stonebraker Sebastian E., carp., 53 Jackson
Stonebreaker Thomas, molder, wks. n.e.c. Canal and Walnut
Stonefeld Louis, peddler, rear 238 W. 7th
Stonefield Benjamin H., finisher, 51 Observatory
Stonegrebber Geo., chairmkr , wks. John Mitchell's
Stonemetz Ruth, 160 Webb
Stoner Edward, tinner, 19 15th b. Central Av. and Plum
Stookey Isaac, confec., 36 E. 3d
Stoomfuld Benj., mach , wks. 222 E. Front
Stoops Geo., carp., w. s. Whittaker b. 3d and Front
Stopelkamper Hy., tailor, 135 Abigail
Stopher Hy., shoe mkr., 471 W. 4th
Stopker Clemens, driver, wks. 450 Walnut
Storch Cornelius, brush mkr , rear 22 Hughes
STORCH Gustave F., (Hunt & S.,) 444 Broadway
Storck Frank, bar k., Galt House
Stordeur Hy., box manufacturer. Livingston near Linn, h. 115 Findlay
Stordeur Martin, box mkr.. wks. Livingston near Linn
Storer Belamy, judge Superior Court of Cincinnati, 16 W. 9th
Storey Frederick, cigar mkr., s. s. 4th, b. John and Smith
Storing Wm. D., cigars, &c., e. s. Linn b. Clark and Hopkins
Stork Hy., bk. mkr., rear 23 Bank
Storm Geo., blksmith, 600 Race
Storm George, printer, 6 W. 2d, rooms 51 Broadway
Storm Peter, painter, n. w. c. Hopkins and Baymiller
Stormann August, 72 Mohawk
Sturmont David, mer., 18 Linn
STOBRS REV. HENRY M., Pastor 1st Orthodox Congregational Church, h. 374 W. 6th
Stortz George, locksmith, 597 Race
Stertz John, shoemkr, 36 Elder
Story Adam, shoemkr., 519 Sycamore
Story James S., eng., 21 Gest
STORY Jeremiah H., (Cameron S. & Malone,) 21 Gest
Story John P., carp., 21 Gest
Story Joseph M., eng., 21 Gest
Storz Christian, cof. h., 641 Race
Storz Joseph, mason, 7 Buckeye
Stossmeister Chas., gunsmith, 281 Main
Stossmeister Wm., foreman Mitchell & Rammelsberg's, h. 145 John
Stouffer John, pipe fitter, wks. n. e. c. Walnut and Canal
Stouder John, steward Broadway Exchange, n.e.c. 2d and Broadway
Stous Richard, cooper. 145 Livingston
Stout Mrs., 13 Home
Stout Franklin, plasterer, n. s. Everett b. Linn and Jones
Stout Hy. H , (Brown, S. & Butler,) h. Mt. Auburn
Stout Ira L., blk. layer, 325 Findlay
Stout Jesse, plasterer, 47 Betts
Stout John, locksmith, 187 Laurel

Stout John, printer, e. s. Main b. Woodward and Franklin
Stout Mary A., 422 John
Stout Richard, cooper, 145 Livingston
Stout Saml. H. J., carp., wks. n.e.c. Canal and Walnut
Stout Wm., lock mkr., 187 Laurel
Stoverman D., brick mkr., 226 Hopkins
Stow Daniel C., tinner, 164 Barr
Stow Harry B., clk. American Express Co., 92 W. 4th
Stow Warren, b.k., 10 W. 2d
Stowder Catharine, 93 E. 3d, e. of Whittaker
Stowder John W., finisher, 10 Observatory
Stowe Warren, b.k., 149 Longworth
Stowell Elizabeth, 120 John
Stowpitcher John, cab. mkr., 158 W. 2d
Stoz Wilhelmina, 587 Walnut
Strabel Ignatz, cab. mkr., 53 Pine
Strack Louis, whitewasher, 553 Elm
Straden Joseph J., carp., wks. e. s. Bremen, b. Elder and Findlay
Strader August, tailor, bds. 192 Sycamore
Strader Benjamin F., 104 E. 4th
STRADER P. WILSON, General Ticket Agent L. M. & C. & X. R. R., & C. H. & D. R. R. Companies, Office, s.e.c. Front and Broadway, res. Spencer Tp.
Stradtman Hy. B. C., bIksmith, 493 Race
Stradtmann Hy. C., bIksmith, 493 Race
Straeffer Geo., carp., 57 12th
Straeffer Michael, carp., 12 Jackson, h. 27 12th
Strafer Geo., carp., 27 12th
Strafer L. M., teacher, 316 Elm
Straffer John, baker, 174 W. Liberty
Strable F., driver Adams Express Co., bds. 54 Ludlow
Strahle Joseph, 80 Mohawk
Strahleman Hy., lab., w. s. Oregon b. 3d ank 6th
Strait H., trunk box mkr., n.e.c. 3d and Sycamore
Strait Hiram, artist, n.e.c. 3d and Sycamore
STRAIT T. J., Attorney at Law, 230 Walnut, res. College Hill
STRAIGHT, DEMING & CO., (Seymore S., Wm. S. D., & James McFarlan,) Wholesale Grocers and Commission Merchants, n.e.c. Vine and 2d
STRAIGHT Seymore, (S. Deming & Co.) bds. 269 W. 7th
Strak Adam, barber, 668 Main
Strale Fred, lab., 2 Linnaeus
Straleh Fred, foreman, wks. 530 Central Avenue
Straley John, lab., 419 W. Liberty
Straling Geo., presser, wks. 728 Central Avenue
Straling John, presser, wks. 728 Central Avenue
Stralman Joseph, hostler, wks. e. s. St, Clair b. 8th and 9th
Strancamp Joseph, wagon mkr., 401 W. 7tb
Strang Louisa, seamstress, bds. 69 Allison
Strange Gabriel, shoemkr, 196 Elm, h. 56 New e. of Broadway
Strange Moses, porter, 258 E. 6th
Strange William, shoemkr, bds. 56 New
Strangmann Geo. W., tailor, 11 Wade b. Elm and Plum
Strankamp Francis, molder, 181 Webb
Strankamp Wm., molder, 227 W. 7th
Strankmeir Gerhard, tailor, 685 Race
Strasburg & Bro., (Hermann & Theophilus,) dry goods, 202 W. 5th
Strasburg Herman, (S. & Bro) 202 W. 5th
Strasburg Theophilus, (S. & Bro.,) 202 W. 5th
Strasel Peter, lab., 644 Race
Straser John, trader, 549 Vine
Strassburger George, cigar mkr., bds. 160 Bremen
Strassel Michael, tailor, 60 W. Mulberry
Strassell Mrs., 187 W. Court, w. of Central Avenue

Strasser Lewis, clk, 187 Walnut, bds. 225 W. 4th
Strassner August, stone mason, 155 Everett
Strassner Hy., tinner, 155 Everett
Straszburger Bernhard, bk. binder, bds. 150 Bremen
Stratch John, lab., wks. n. w. c. Plum and Wade
Stratemeier Hy., watchman, 13 Peete
Straten Bernhard, tailor, 120 Walnut
Stratiger Hy., cutter, 244 Main
STRATIGHER Hermann, (E. Gobs & Co.,) 478 Main
Stratman Mrs. Elizabeth, h. 5 John
Stratman Hy., lab., wks. Henry Nye's
Stratton Matthew, polisher, wks. n. e. c. Elm and Canal
Stratton Samuel S., clk., gas works, h. 326 George
Stratton Wm. P., surveyor City Insurance Co., h. 261 W. 8th
Straub Hy. F., foreman. 16 McFarland
STRAUB ISAAC, Manufacturer of Corn, Wheat and Saw Mills, and Engine Builder, n. w. c. John and Front, res. 8 miles in Kenton Co., Ky.
Straub Jacob, cigar mkr., 73 Buckeye
Straub Johanna, 198 Pleasant
Straub John, shoemkr, bds. 48 E. Pearl
Straub Mary, 73 Buckeye
Straub Michael, constable, 115 Ham. Road
Straub Nicholas, cab. mkr., 198 Pleasant
Straub Oliver B., 16 McFarland
Straub Walter F., attorney at law, room 3, Masonic Temple
Straughtker Hy., lab., 223 Cutter
Straughtker Lewis, lab., 6d Rittenhouse
Strauley Frederick, driver, 54 Ludlow
Straus Abraham, 51 Providence
Straus Alexander, b.k., 106 W. Pearl, bds. Silvester House
Straus Alexander, b.k., 43 W. 7th
Straus David, clothing, 316 Walnut
Straus H., shoemkr, 240 Main
Straus Hattie. 7 North
Straus Hy., furniture, 71 W. 5th, h 43 W. 7th [3d
Straus Isaac, b.k., 109 W 6th, h. 175 W.
Straus Jacob, gilder, 202 Elm
Straus Joseph, trunk mkr., wks. 509 Plum
Straus Moritz, salesman, 126 Main, bds. Silvester House
Straus Moses, agt., 436 Main
Straus Raphael, artist, 169 W. 6th
Straus Samuel, clk., 159 Main, bds. 197. Broadway
Straus Samuel, shoe store, 239 Main
Straus Samuel, watch mkr., 63 Providence
Straus Mrs. Sarah, 49 Longworth
Straus Sulzman, clothing, &c, 50 Sycamore
Straus Tobias, clothing, 226 W. 6th
Strausberger X., rope mkr., wks. s. s, Budd b. Harriet and Millcreek
Strause Mrs. C. H., 7 Clinton Court
Strauser Joseph, trunk mkr., 293 W. Liberty
Strauss Abraham, station house keeper, 53 Providence
Strauss Chas., b.k., bds. Silvester House
Strauss F. & Bro., (Ferdinand S. & Sol. S.,) liquors, &c., 54 Main
Strauss Ferdinand, (F. S. & Bro.,) 26 Perry
STRAUSS I. P. & BRO., (Isaac P. & Joseph,) Clothing, 211 Main
STRAUSS Isaac P., (I. P. S. & Bro.,) 211 Main
Strauss John N., grocery, s. e. c. 15th and Plum
STRAUSS Joseph, (I. P. S. & Bro.,) n.s Harrison. b. Broadway and Pike
Strauss Mary A., 33 Chesnut
Strauss Raphael, artist, 169 W. 5th
Strauss Rowena, s.w.c. New and North
Strauss Simon, furniture, 82 W. 7th
Strauss Sol., (F. S. & Bro.,) 263 Longworth
Strauss Solomon. fur dealer, 107 Longworth

Strauswell Peter, lab, 684 Race
Strausz John, carp., 67 Buckeye
Strawman Theodore, carp., n. s. 6th b. Harriet and Horne
Streaker Barney, clothing, 46 Sycamore
Streatelmeyer Sophia, grocer, 443 Linn
Strebbe Frank, blksmith, 186 Clark
Strebel James, lab., 154 Pleasant
Streeder Geo. W., foreman, 1220 E. Front
Street John, finisher, 99 Baum
Street Robert H., clk., 9 Main, h. 428 John
Streeter Chas. E., clk., 1226 E. Front
Streeter Eliza, grocery, 1226 E. Front
Streeter James F., carp., n. s. Railroad, opp. French
Streeter John L., carp., 1246 E. Front
Streetman Herman porter, 86 W. 2d
STREHLI VALENTINE W., Family Grocery and Provisions, 634 Elm
Strehly John dry goods, 631 Central Av
Streif Andrew, barber, 221 W. 6th
Streif Joseph, cig. mkr., 764 Central Av
Streigler August, tailor, w. s. Hamburg, b. Cross and Mohawk
Streiker Jacob, sawyer, wks. 205 Freeman
Streit Bernard, shoemkr., 61 W. 4th, h. 51 14th
Streit Chas., cab. mkr., 200 Pleasant
Streit Eve. 11 Moore
Streit Joseph, shoemkr, 200 Pleasant
Streitmann Joseph, driver, n.s. Friendship al b. Lawrence and Pike
Strenker John, stone mason, 70 Rittenhouse
Stretelmier Rudolph, tailor, 52 Dudley
Streube Ernst, dray, 87 W. 2d
Streuve Henry H., b.k , 66 13th
Stribick Michael, gardener, n.s. Liberty b. Freeman and Millcreek
Stricker Bernhard, shoe mkr., bds. s.w. c. 9th and Walnut
Stricker Charles, boots and shoes, 222 Clark
Stricker Frank, boots and shoes, 698 Vine
Stricker Jacob, steward, 55 Findlay
Stricker Mary Jane, 353 Race
Stricker, Ross. A. A., bar. k. 239 Clinton
Stricker Samuel, clothing, 161 W. Court
Stricker Wm., lab., 53 Woodward
Strickle Sebastian, 731 Elm
Strickler Geo. W., carp., 68 Clark
Striebel Francis J., peddler, n.w.c. Wade and Baymiller
Striebel Mary, servt., 403 Vine
Striecker Frank, (S. & Bro.), s.w.c. Abigall and Spring
Stried Joseph, cof. h., n.w.c. Liberty and Dudley
Striegel Sebastian, Elm b. Ham. Road and Findlay
Striehtmann Fred. (H. & F. S.), rear 156 Clay
Striehtmann H. & F., (Hermann S. and Frederick S.) coopers. rear 156 Clay
Striehtmann Hermann, (H & F. S.) rear 156 Clay
Striehtmann John H., cooper, 156 Clay
Striehtmann Marie, 156 Clay
Striehtmann Frank, clothing, 53 Broadway, h. c. Spring and Abigail
Striel Andrew, finisher, wks. n e.c. Walnut and Canal
Striel Henry, finisher, wks. n.e.c. Walnut and Canal
Strietelmeier Ernst, grocer, 625 Elm
Strietelmeier Henry, bds. 625 Elm
Strietelmeier John H., boots and shoes, 61 Findlay
Striethorst Frederick, dray, 42 Rittenhouse [3d
Striethorst Henry, clk., s.w.c. Race and
Striethorst Sophia, 59 Buckeye
Strietmann Gerhard, grocery, 577 Walnut
Strietmeier & Fisbigh, (Wm. S. & Wm. F.,) brick yard, w.s. Western Av. b. Bank and Harrison Road
Strietmeier Wm., (S. & Fisbigh,) w.s. Western Av. b. Bank and Harrison Road

310 (STR) CINCINNATI (STU) DIRECTORY. (SUE)

Striff Margaret, 54 Kossuth
Striff Margaret, servt., 99 E. 4th
Striker Jacob, carp., 350 Clark
String Wm., 42 Elizabeth
Stringer Joseph, saw mkr., 292 W. Front
Strithen Geo., driver, 35 Smith
STROBEL Charles, (Chas. S. & Bro.,) 415 Elm
STROBEL CHAS. & BRO., (Chas. & Louis.) Manufacturers of Pocket Books, Cases, &c., 150 Walnut
STROBEL JOHN, Hats, Caps, Furs, &c., 265 Central Av.
Strobel John M., music teacher, h. 24 Jackson
Strobel Leonhard, carp., 604 Walnut, h. 591 Walnut
STROBEL Louis, (Chas. S. & Bro..) h Chicago, Ill
Strobel Louis A., gilder, h. 265 Central Av
Strohle Wm., trunk mkr., 227 Liberty
STRODRIDGE Hines, (Middleton, S. & Co.) h. Linnwood, O,
Strodman Frank, cooper, bds. n.s. Abigail b Sycamore and Main
Stroebel August, gilder, n.w.c. George and Central Av
Stroebel Elizabeth, w.s. Bremen b. Elder and Findlay
Stroeher Michael, tailor, 228 Bremen
Stroehmann Frederick Wm., carp., 100 Buckeye
Stroehr Barney, cab. mkr., rear s.s. Abigail b. Broadway and Sycamore
Stroetz Geo., shoe mkr., 99 Bremen
Stroh Peter, wagon mkr., wks. S. G. Rice's
Strohle Geo., candle mkr., 51 Wade
Strohm John, caf. h., 248 E. Front
Struhman Joseph, 395 W. 3d
Strohmeier August, lab., bds. 592 Main
Strohmeier Michael, clk., bds. Spencer House
Stromberg Philip, agt. cigars, &c., 187 Walnut, h. 225 W. 4th
Strong Mrs., 272 W. 4th
Strong ——, lab., 52 Kossuth
Strong Adolf, turner, 233 Betts
Strong Chas. L. b.k. Wilson & Hayden's, h. 32 Perry
Strong Frederick, n.w.c. Broadway and Liberty
Strong Eben B., finisher, 52 Kossuth
Strong James, lab., wks. n.e.c. Park and Marsh
Strong Joseph, bds. 107 Broadway
Strong Joseph, clk., bds. 118 Broadway
Strong R. W., bds. Burnet House
Strong Robert, b.k. 19 W. 2d, bds. Burnet House
Strong Wm. E., clk., bds. Burnet House
Stroodman Geo. J. G , sawyer. s.e. Cassalt al. b Sycamore and Main
Stroop John J., printer Cin. Gazette, n e.c. Vine and 4th
Strontman Joseph, blksmith, 360 Broadway
Stroscell John, lab., 187 W. Court w. of Central Av
Strothmann Henry, carp., rear 290 Linn
Strothmann Henry, distiller, 18 Madison
Strothmann Heinrich, tailor, n.w.c. Mansfield and Liberty
Strotkamp Theodore, carp., 23 Green
Strotkamp Henry, driver, wks. Livingston nr. Linn
Strotman G. & H., (George & Henry,) dry goods, 95 W. Court
Strotman George, (G. & H.,) 95 W. Court
Strotman Henry, (G. & H.) s.e.c. Woodward and Broadway
Strotman John, blksmith, 360 Broadway
Strotmann Henry, lab., 609 Race
Strombel Charles, tailor, 76 Melancthon
Strough John, lab., wks Deer Creek Mills
Strouss Henry, bar k., Clermont Hotel
Strouts John, shoe mkr., 1029 Central Av
Strowmeyer Anna, 229 E 5th
Strubbe August, cooper, bds. 75 Buckeye
Strubbe August H., clk., 29 Abigail
Strubbe Ernst, dray, 511 Sycamore

Strubbe Fred., grocery, 126 Findlay
Strubbe Henry, carp., e.s. Dudley b. Poplar and Liberty
Strubbe Henry, dray, bds. 139 Baymiller
Strubbe Henry, tailor, 788 Central Av.
Strubbe Henry W., grocery, h. 243 Everett
Strubbe John H., carp., 94 Dudley
Strubbe John H., cooper, 222 Clark
Strubbe Rudolph, tailor, 45 Elder
Strubbe Wm. sr., 511 Sycamore
STRUBBE WM. F., Family Grocery, 29 Abigail
Struempler Wm., lab., 39 Moore
Strueve Charles H , clk. R. G. Dun & Co.'s, h. 340 Ham. Road
Strueve Henry F., watch mkr., 255 Main
Strueve Herman R., jewelry &c., 205 Main, res. 4 miles on Harrison Road
Strueve Wm., lab., 11 Abigail
Strueve Wm. F., brewer, 340 Ham. Road
Strueving Gerhard, peddler, 22 Peete
Strueving Henry, cigar mkr., rear 26 Franklin
Strueving Gerhard, peddler, 96 Buckeye
Skrule Henry, tailor, n.e.c. Linn and Betts
Strunk Mary A., grocery, 12 E. 8th
Strunk Simon, lime agt., 23 Abigail
Strunk Simon H., harness mkr., 23 Abigail
Strunk Wm., teacher, 93 Abigail
Struppert Rosa, 276 W. Liberty
Struve W., billards, 486 Main
Struwe Henry, cooper, bds. 71 Hughes
Stryker A. A., bar k., 239 Clinton
Stuart C. A. & Co., (Chas. A. S. & Horace T. Miller,) phys., 11 E. 3d
Stuart Chas. A., (C. A. S. & Co.) 154 Broadway
Stuart Elizabeth, b. h., 22 Home
Stuart James, printer, 554 W. Front
Stuart Wm., grocer, 120 Laurel
Stubbaman Frank, lab., 40 Freeman
Stubbe B rney, tailor, 26 Race. bds. s.s. Commerce b. Vine and Walnut
Stubbe Christopher, fireman, Gibson House
Stubbs Mary, s.s. 4th b. Vine and Race
Stube Charlotte, 466 Walnut
Stubenrauch Jacob, 20 Mercer
Stubenrauch Jacob F., meats, 607 Vine
Stubenrauch John, cigar mkr., n.w.c. Main and Court
Stubenrauch John E., cigar mkr., 161 Bremen
Stubenrauch Joseph, sawyer, 161 Bremen
Stuberman Frank, lab., 40 Freeman
Stubert John, clk., 54 W. Pearl, h. 463 W. 7th
Stubs Elizabeth, e.s. Coggswell al. b. Abigail & Woodward
Stuck Henry, shoe mkr., 187 Linn
Stuck Jacob, bar k., wks. s.e.c. Race and 13th
Stuck John, cof. h., 134 W. Court
Stackenberg Fred, blksmith, 20 Baum
Stuckenberg Herman H., dry goods, 593 Central Av
Stuckenberg Herman H., 593 Central Av
Stuckert Henry, shoemkr. 64 Stark
Stueckhof Fred , rear 375 Broadway
Stuckle Carolina, teacher of music, 297 Main
Stuckwich Gerhard H., eng., 97 Milton
Stuckwich John, 532 Sycamore
Studt Fred., porter, s.e.c. Milton and Sycamore
Studt John, porter, n.e.c. Milton and Sycamore
Studt Wm., lab., 15 Hughes
Stuebe Frederick, tinner, w.s. Long al. b. Woodward and Franklin
Stuebe Fred. Wm., 51 13th
Stuebe Wm., tinner, 538 Main
Stueve Henry, b. k., n.e.c. Elm and Elder
Stueve John H., rulle man, 703 Race
Stuewe Wilhelmina, 524 Main
Stuhlfaut Barbara, 549 Elm
Stuhlfauth Christopher, lab., 194 Bremen
Stuhlmueller Jos., hostler, American Ex. Co

Stuhtenoth Louis, jeweler, 4 Lucy
Stuimbel Bernard, lab., 6 Pleasant
Stuke Elizabeth, 25 Abigail
Stukenberg Frederick, tool dresser, 18 Baum
Stull John, barber, 217 Barr
Stultz Abraham, 115 John
Stultz Hermann, packer, 103 Bremen
Stum Christian, clks, 43u Walnut
Stump Frank, dray, 58 Providence
Stump Hy., lab., 734 Central Av
Stump Hy., stone mason, 19 Mulberry
Stump Hugh, carriage mkr., 410 Race
Stump John, lab., 724 Central Av
Stumn Wesley, coach mkr., bds. 263 Main
Stump Wm., carriage mkr., bds. 410 Race
Stump Wm., jr., carriage mkr., 410 Race
Stumpe Anton, painter. bds. s.s Bank b. Freeman and Coleman
Stumpe August, druggist, s.e.c. Race & 2d, bds. s.e.c. 5th and Vine
Stumpe August, clk, bds. 444 Sycamore
Stumpel Bernard, grocery. 636 W. 5th
Stumpf Anthony, blksmith, bds. 399 Sycamore
Stumpf Hy., shoemkr, bds. 24 Allison
Stumpf Margaret, seamstress, 724 Central Av
Stumpmeyer Conrad, nurse, Commercial Hospital
Stunderbach Frederick, shoemkr, 478 W. 5th
Stunt Hy., saddle tree mkr., 153 Carr
Stuntebeck Frank F., tailor, 98 Hunt
Stuntebeck Frank H., cigars, &c., w.s. Sycamore b. Baltimore and Dorsey
Stuntebeck Fred., shoemkr, 478 W. 5th
Stuetebeck Hy., tailor, 435 Broadway
Stuntebeck John H., tailor, 360 Broadway, h. 455 Broadway
Stuntz Chauncey R., teacher, 132 Hopkins
Sturla Mary, 217 Barr
Sturlia Bartholomew, confec., s.e.c. Court and Elm
Sturm Geo., lab., 600 Race
Sturm John, 961 Central Av
Sturm John B., shoemkr, bds. 560 W. 5th
Sturm Wm., phys., 40 W. 4th, res Storrs tp.
Sturenberg Benjamin, varnisher, 60 Abigail
Sturenberg Herman, blksmith, 60 Abigail
Sturnberg Bernard, varnisher, 60 Abigail
Sturow Ludwig, cooper, 261 Pleasant
Sturtz George, finisher, 497 Race
Sturtz William, boots and shoes, 533 W. 8th, h. 531 W. 8th
Sturwold Hy., shoemkr. 90 Gest
STURWOLD JOHN HY., Custom House Saloon, 520 W. Front
Stutz Daniel, grocery, 22 and 24 Ham. Road
Styles Benj. E., brass molder, 644 E. Front
Styvesant Mrs. E., 20 Longworth
Subelist F. W., bds Teutonia Hotel
Suchanek John, blk smith, 642 Main
Suckoff John, blksmith, 14 Hamer
Sudback Wm., carp., 61 David
Sudbeck Anthony, molder, 110 Culvert
Sudbeck H., molder, wks. n. s. Front b. Lawrence and Pike
Sudbeck F. Hy., clk., n. w. c. Pearl and Broadway, h. 100 Culvert
Suddendorf Hy., lab., rear 164 W. Liberty
Sudfeld Charles F., porter, n. s. Liberty b. Main and Walnut
Sudfeld Charles S., porter, 15 W. Liberty
Suding Herman H. porter, 91 Pendleton
Sudings Hy., lab , wks. 70 Water
Suedebeck Anna C., peddler, 95 Woodward
Suelfstede Hy., blksmith, s.w.c. Race & Findlay
Suetterle Robert, locksmith. 24 Franklin

Sullivan John, tanner, 50 Findlay
Sullivan John, waiter, Clifton House
Sullivan John B., clk., s.w.c. Race and 3d
Sullivan John D., grocery, 392 Broadway
Sullivan John W., printer, 122 W. Court w. of Central Av
Sullivan Joseph A., driver, 158 Freeman
Sullivan Julia, servt., 276 Longworth
Sullivan Lucy, 458 Elm
Sullivan Mrs. M. P., 51 E. 3d
Sullivan Margaret, servt., 98 Broadway
Sullivan Mary, 234 Water
Sullivan Mary, servt., 566 W. 9th
Sullivan Michael, tailor, c. 3d and Hill
Sullivan Morris, tailor, n. e. c. 9th and John
Sullivan Owen, lab., 62 Gano
Sullivan Patrick, stable, 165 Central Av
Sullivan Patrick, painter, 8 Bedinger
Sullivan Peter J., atty., 447 W. 4th
Sullivan Phillip, hostler, 183 W. 6th
Sullivan Philip, lab., 260 W. 6th
Sullivan Phillip, tailor, 349 Central Av
Sullivan & Pryor (John S. & Frank P.), cof. h., 33 E. 5th
Sullivan Samuel, 186 Cutter
Sullivan Sarah, dress mkr., 233 Race
Sullivan Septimus, salesman. 11 E. 4th
Sullivan Thomas, shoemkr, 228 Elm
Sullivan Thomas, lab., 45 Observatory Road
Sullivan Timothy, contractor, rear 66 Woodward
Sullivan Timothy, coppersmith, 23 E. 7th
Sullivan Timothy, finisher, bds. n.s. 7th b. Broadway and Sycamore
Sullivan Timothy, lab., s. e. c. Sycamore and 7th
Sullivan Timothy, lab., 14 E. 8th e. of Lock
Sullivan Wm., bds. 37 Longworth
Sullivan Wm., lab., w. s. Central Av. b. 2d and W. W. Canal Basin
Sullivan Wm., jr., clk., P. O., h. 587 W. 8th
Sulthouse Hy., lab., n. w. c. Wade and Baymiller
Sulz Jacob, tailor, 42 Hamer
'Sulzbacher Hy. (Guiterman & S.) h. Chillicothe
Sum George, barber, 198 Sycamore
Summe Barney, grocery, n.w.c. Hopkins and Baymiller
Summe Hy., lab., 58 Abigail
Summer Frank, cigar mkr, 164 Spring
Summer Hy., lab., s.w.c. 6th and Smith
Summer John, at Jewish Hospital, n.w. c. Cutter and Betts
Summer Mary, 164 Spring,
Summer Peter, lab. 138 Bank
Summerfield Elizabeth, 519 W. 8th
Summerfield Wolf, second hand store, 154 W. Front
Summers Anna, bds. 154 Baymiller
Summers Anna S., seamstress, bds. s.w. 5th and Broadway
Summers. David, brick yard, Clark, b. Baymiller and Linn, h. 145 Baymiller
Summers Ellen, servt., 369 Longworth
Summers Jas., lab., w.s. Langdon al. b. 6th and 7th
Summerton Fred., shoe mkr., 299 W. 6th
Summorah John, clk., bds. 80 E. 5th
Sumner Jas. H., hack, 14 New
Sumner Nancy, 47 Wade
Sumner Wm., hackman, 14 New
SUMNER Wm. (Wm. S. & Co.,) h. Pittsburgh, Penn.
SUMNER WM. & CO., (Wm. S. & J. R. Wright,) Agents for Wheeler & Wilson's Sewing Machines, 77 W. 4th
Sumwalde Conrad, carp., 143 Pleasant
Sumwall Edward T., salesman, 25 W. 4th, bds. 89 E. 4th
SUN MUTUAL INSURANCE CO., 75 W. 3d
E. L. Shannon, Sec'y.
Sund Bernard, shoe mkr, 101 York
Sund Bernhard H., tailor, 4 Mary
Sund Geo., tailor, 101 York
Sund J. Gerhard, tailor, 93 Pendleton

Sunday Moritz, baker, 347 Central Av.
Sunder Adolphus, clk., 501 Walnut
Sunderhuse Hermann, varnisher, 80 Melanethon
Sunderman Hy., lab., 509 W. 8th
Sunderman Wm., blind mkr., 509 W. 8th
Sundermann Elizabeth, 125 Bremen
Suneberg Hy., lab., 15 Commerce, b. Walnut and Vine
Suntine Sarras, 199 W. Court
Supe Richard, grocery, 239 Hopkins
Suppe Fred., carp., 717 Elm
Suppleman Hy., carp., s.w.c. Abigail & Spring
Supper Fred., shoe mkr., bds. 275 Freeman
Suptus Wm., trunk mkr., 20 Mercer
Surberg Geo., lab., 482 W 5th
Surguy Jas. O., printer, 225 Richmond
Surguy Thos., printer, 225 Richmond
Surguy Thomas N , printer, 233 Richmond
Surliene Bernhard, lab., bds. 113 Clay
Surmann Anton, tailor, 32 W. Court, h. 97 W. Court
Surmann Peter, grinder, 419 Sycamore
Surminn Clemens, tailor, 521 W. 8th
Surne Hy., lightning rod mkr., rear 58 Abigail
Surran John, pipe fitter, wks. n e.c. Walnut and Canal
Susman Louis, tailor, 199 Bremen
Susman Simon, grocer, 33 W. 7th
Sussmann Merger, lab., 20 E. Liberty
Suter Geo. T., painter, 108 George
Suter Jas. A., bds. 323 W. 3d
Suter Jas. Z., carp, 108 George
Suter Leonard, paper hanger, 108 George
Sutherland Catharine, servt., 177 Broadway
Suthof Hy., 486 Broadway
Suthoff Sarah, servt., 301 Richmond
Sutkamp Ferdinand, clk, bds. 97 W. Court
Sutter Adolphus, glass stainer, 190 Walnut, h. 49 Jackson
Sutter Alex., stone mason, 96 Bremen
Sutter Anthony, presser, wks. w.s. Lock b. 4th and 5th
Sutter Philip, boots and shoes, 325 W. 2d
Sutterer Frances, 46 Buckeye
Sutterer Geo., teacher, 151 York
Sutterer John, saddler, bds. 734 W. 6th
Suttle Joseph, cigar mkr., 99 York
Sutton Cornelius, grocery, 302 W. 5th
Sutton Jas , salesman, 34 Vine, h. Newport
Sutton Jas. N., sawyer, 516 W. 7th
Sutton John, finisher, n.s. Charlotte b. Linn and Baymiller
Sutton John, mach., 176 Charlotte
Sutton Peter, caulker, n.s. E. Front e. of Vance
Sutzman Joseph, 35 E. 6th
Suydam Geo. W., furniture, 21 E. 4th, res. Blanchester
Swab Paul, rope mkr., 442 W. 2d
Swabedise August, lab., 101 W. Front
Swager Jacob, eng., 68 Lock
Swaile Elizabeth, bds. s.s. Goodloe b. Willow and Niagara
SWAIN & CHENOWETH, (Wm. P. S. & Wm B. C.,) Carpenters and Builders, n.w.c. Barr and Linn
Swain Ralph A., bar k., s.s. Goodloe b. Willow and Niagra
Swain Thos. B., salesman, 90 W. 5th, bds. 61 E. 4th
SWAIN Wm. P., (S. & Chenoweth,) 600 W. 9th
Swan Eliza B., teacher Mt. Auburn Institute
Swan Frank, bds. 77 E. 3d
Swan Frank, purchasing agent L. M. R. R.
Swan Geo. C., 36 Longworth
Swan John, printer. Am. Bank Note Co.
Swan Nancy, 301 Elm
Swaney Andrew, hostler, h. 23 Commerce
Swaney Andy, lab., w.s. Denman bet. Kenner and Flint

312   (SWE)   CINCINNATI   (TAB)   DIRECTORY.   (TAN)

Swaney Ann, servt., n.e.c. 3d and Pike
Swaney Michael, lab., bds. 249 W. 6th
Swaney Wm., 2. Dayton
Swanston Wm., mach., n.s. R. Road e. of Kelly
Swap Louis, molder, wks. n.e.c. Canal and Walnut
Swarcarte Nicholas, cooper, wks. Deer Creek mills
SWARTS J. L., (Louis Stix & Co.,) 280 Race
Swartz Joseph, 26 Gano
Swartz Anna, teacher, 102 E Liberty
Swartz Benj. A., atty., 143 Walnut, h. Avondale, Ohio
Swartz Charlotte, s.s. 6th b. Broadway and Culvert
Swartz Fred., bakery, e.s. Western Av. b. Poplar and Findlay
Swartz Geo., lab., n.s. 6th b. Harriet & Horne
Swartz John, carp., rear 290 Linn
Swartz John C., 139 Everett
SWARTZ Leonard, County Commissioner, office Court House, res. Avondale
Swartz Martin, carp., 63 Laurel
Swartzott Conrad, stocking weaver, 68 Peete
Swasey Edwin A., wh grocer, 24 W. 9th
Swasey Edwin A.)r., bds 24 W. 9th
Swasey John. ir., clk., 169 W. 7th
SWASEY John, (John S. & Co.,) 169 W. 7th
SWASEY JOHN & CO., (John S, Allen Collier, Wake Hubbell & Joseph T. Swasey,) Wholesale Groceries, Liquors and Foreign Fruits, 23, 25 and 27 Sycamore
SWASEY Joseph T., (John Swasey & Co.,) 169 W. 7th
SWASEY MOSES, Wholesale Grocer and Produce Dealer, 45 Broadway, h. 51 W. 9th
Swayne Joseph A., clk., Walnut Street House
Swear Anthony, chair mkr., n.e.c. Sycamore and Abigail
Swear Edward, trimmer, 45 14th
Sweatnam Daniel, clk., bds. 197 Vine
Sweeney Andrew, lab., 22 Commerce
Sweeney Daniel, currier, 124 E. 8th
Sweeney Elizabeth, servt., Spencer House
Sweeney Geo., shoe mkr., Friendship al. b. Pike and Butler
Sweeney Hy., cof. h., 169 W. Front
Sweeney Jas., lab., s.s. Friendship al. b. Pike and Butler
Sweeney Jas., suloon, 329 W. 6th
Sweeney John, lab., 44 Pierson
Sweeney John, lab., 133 W. 9th w. of Central Av.
Sweeney Mary, s.s. 6th e. of Lock
Sweeney Mary, w.s. Central Av. b. 2d and W. W. Canal
Sweeney Pat., lab., 8 Pleasant
Sweeney Rodolph, wagon mkr., 58 W. Court e. of Central Av.
Swerney Thomas, lab., 59 E. 8th e. of Lock
Sweeny Catharine, cof. h., 43 Race
Sweeny Dennis, porter, 20 Broadway
Sweeny Ellen, servt., 333 W. 8th
Sweeny John, lab., 21 Commerce
Sweeny John, lab., 143 E. 2d
Sweeny John, sawyer, wks. 196 W. Pearl
Sweeny Julia, chambermaid, Burnet House [4th
Sweeny Mary, seamstress, wks. 53 W.
Sweeny Michael, lab., 33 Lock n. of 8th
Sweeny Morgan M., lab., s.s. Oliver b. John and Linn
Sweeny Thomas, e.s. Ludlow b. 2d and Pearl
Sweeny Thomas, lab., 6 Linnaeus
Sweeny Thomas, presser, wks. 830 Central Av.
Sweet Chas. b.k., 34 E. 5th, h. 28 Elizabeth
Sweet Margaret, w.s. Langdon al. b. 6th and 7th
Sweet Martha, w.s. Langdon al. b. 6th and 7th

Sweet R. R., clk. Methodist Book Concern, bds 354 W. 8th
Sweitzer Adam, 391 W. 2d
Sweny M. & Co., (Merrit Sweny & Co.,) grocers, 14 Main
Sweny Merrit, (M. S. & Co.,) bds. 179 Broadway
Sweny Michael, huckster, n.w.c. Lodge and Gano
Swere Edward, carriage trimmer, 45 14th
Swett John, painter, 627 W. 7th
Swidersky Francis, mason, 152 Bremen
SWIFT Abram, (S. Evans & Co.,) res. country
Swift Alex., (Alex. S. & Co.,) bds. Burnet House
Swift Alex & Co., (Alex. S. & Seth Evans,) sheet and boiler iron manuf, office 3 E. Front
SWIFT Briggs, (Evans & Co.,) h. 57 W. 8th
Swift C., bds. Black Bear Hotel
Swift Chas., mer., bds. s.s. 9th b. Harriet and Mill Creek
SWIFT E. E. C. & CO., (Eugene E. C. S. & Henry C. Swift,) Commission Merchants and Dealers in Ginseng Bags, Feathers and Beeswax, s.w.c. Water and Walnut
SWIFT Eugene E. C., (E. E. C. S. & Co.) bds. 104 Broadway
SWIFT, EVANS & CO., (Abram S., Benj. E. & Jas. McKeehan,) Pork Packers and Commission Merchants, n.w.c. 9th and Sycamore
SWIFT Henry C., (E. E. C. Swift & Co.,) bds. 104 Broadway
SWIFT Mrs. Lucy C., bds. 186 Plum
SWIFT Lot. P., (Stevens, Chambers & Co.,) 290 W. 6th
Swift Martin, lab., 176 E. Pearl
Swift Myron L., clk., 39 Water, bds. 104 Broadway
Swift Theodore, b.k., Swift, Evans & Co's, bds. Clifton House
Swiger Joseph, cooper, 27 Brighton
SWIGGETT SETH W., Press Printing Co., 136 Vine h. 426 W. 5th
Swine John, butcher, s.e.c. Hopkins and Baymiller, h. 251 Hopkins
Swinenger Louis, lab., Oehler al. b. Freeman and Garrard
Swing Hy., lab., 175 Hopkins
Swischart Jacob, lab., e. s. Western Av. b. Poplar and Findlay
Switzer Mollie, bds. 248 W. 7th
Switzer Fred, expressman, s. w. c. Pearl and Butler
Swivle Joseph, lab., wks. C. T. Dumont's
Syberg Francis, actor, 69 W. Liberty
Syfers Asa M., (S. & Jones,) 78 Baum
Syfers & Jones, (Asa M. S. & Charles P. J.,) grocery, n.e.c. Broadway and 5th
Sykes John, blksmith, 556 W. Front
Sylvester A., bds. Gibson House
Sylvester Abram, clk. 21 Walnut, h. 256 Vine
Sylvester Ann. 225 Barr
Sylvester Wm., lab., 253 Laurel
Symonds Abraham J., (Symonds Bro., & Co.,) bds. St. Charles
Symonds Benjamin W., (S. Bro. & Co.) 121 W. 9th
Symonds Brother & Co., (Benjamin W. S., Abraham J. S. & Philip Symonds.) clothing 143 Walnut
Symonds Philip, (Symonds Bro. & Co.) 121 W. 9th
Syng Mary, hoop skirt mkr., 367 Central Av., bds. 333 Cutter
Synnestvedts George C., clk., 118 Central Av.
Szotzski John. manufac, of bitters, s. s. Liberty b. Clay and Main

T

Tabb Vincent, with Charles Rodman, 59 and 61 W. Front
Tabben Anthon, porter, 319 Main
Tabe Barney, tailor, 105 W. 2d
Tabeling Hy., lab., 100 Buckeye

Taberle Frank, cigar mkr., 788 Central Av.
Tabke Anthony, lab., 410 Broadway
Tablin Patrick, lab., s. s. Court e. of Broadway
Tablor Bennet, mach., 248 W. 3d
Tabor Hy., tailor, 15 Park
Tach Isaac, clothing, 259 Main
Tachesser Thomas, lab., 69 Buckeye
Tacke Hy., carp., 53 15th
Tacke Margaret, 511 Race
Tackenberg Hy., molder, 179 W. 2d
TACKENBERG HERMAN, Family Grocery, 547 Walnut
Tae Peter, driver, 105 E. 2d
Tafel Albert, (T. & Bogeler,) n.e.c. Walnut and Allison
TAFEL Gustav, (Stallo T. & James,) n.e.c. Allison and Walnut
Tafel & Vogeler, (Albert T. & Frederick V.,) druggists, n.e.c. 6th and Main
TAFT Alphonso, (T. & Perry,) res. Mt. Auburn
Taft Francis, atty., e. s. Auburn near Bigelow
TAFT JONATHAN, Dentist, 56 W. 4th h. 431 Broadway
Taft Peter O., e.s. Auburn near Bigelow
TAFT & PERRY, (Alphonso T. & Aaron F. P.,) Attorneys at Law, Rooms 1 & 2 Masonic Temple
Taft Samuel H., office 512 Central Av. h. 22 Hopkins
TAGART GEORGE W., Job Printer, 19 W. 4th h. 71 Hopkins
Taggart James, porter, Adams Express Co., bds. 282 Main
Taglauer Martin, mach., s. s. Liberty b. Vine and Race
Taiker Frederick, cooper, 258 Pleasant
Tait Benj., F., clk., bds. 196 W. 6th
TAIT GEORGE, Wholesale and Retail Grocer, 196 W. 5th
Tait Geo B., clk., Co. Treas. Office, e. s. Baymiller b. Laurel and Hopkins
Talbert Ellen, cof. h., 135 W. 3d
Talbert Nancy, confec., 610 W. 5th
Talbott Charles A., b. k., bds. 400 W. 7th
Talbott Isaiah, carp., 254 Clark
Talbott John, b. k., 99 W. Pearl, h. 307 Elm
Talbott John L., b. k., bds. 400 W. 7th
Talbott John L., teacher, Friends Academy, s. s. 5th b. Central Av. and John. h. 400 W. 4th
Talbott J. T., salesman, 140 Main, h. n. w.c. 9th and Elm
Talbott John W., finisher, bds. 178 Barr
Talbott Joseph, builder, 400 W. 7th
Talbott Oliver, bk. layer, 178 Barr
Talbott Virginia, bds. 400 W. 7th
Talbott Wm.. H., salesman, s.w.c. Walnut and Pearl, h. n.w.c. 9th and Elm
Taley Thomas, finisher, wks. n.e.c. Walnut and Canal
TALIAFERRO & BUCKNER, (Wm. T. T. & James H. B.,) Physicians and Surgeons, n.w.c. 6th and Walnut
TALIAFERRO Wm. H., (T. & Buckner,) h. 52 W. 7th
Talliferro Mathilda, 157 W. 6th
TALLMADGE CHARLES S., Dealer in Coal Oil, Lamps &c., 241 Vine
Tallman Philip, bds. Gibson House
Tallon Thomas, carp., bds. 131 E. 5th
Talmadge H. P., act., bds. Clifton House
Talp Hy., cooper, 67 Green
Tambush Joseph, blksmith, s. s. Liberty b. Walnut and Vine
Tandrop Mary, 64 York [Race
Tandrop Ulrich C., fresco painter, 392
Tangeman Frederick, cof. h., 686 W. Front
Tangeman Joseph, clk. 224 W. 6th
Tangemann ——. boiler mkr., s.s. 6th b. Harriet and Horne
Tangemann Wm., (H. Moormann & Co.) 634 Main
Tanger Ferdinand, carp., s.w. c. Liberty and Baymiller

CINCINNATI (TAY) DIRECTORY. (TEB) 313

|dway | Tauch Martin, tanner, 32 Dunlap
| Tauchert Chas., bk. layer, 28 Allison
sta b. | Tauchert Chas bk. layer, 539 Main
| Taulkr Frederick, cooper, 58 David
| Taulkr Hermann, cooper, 50 Melancthon
| Taulman Chas., pressman Methodist Book Concern, h. Walnut Hills
| Taulman P. J., pressman Meth. Book Concern. h. Walnut Hills
| Taulwetter Charles,. compositor, wks. Meth. Book Concern
| Taup Jacob, 767 Vine
| Taus Andreas, cigar mkr.. 602 Elm
h and | Tauwald Hy., cigar mkr., 60 Findlay
| Tavaist Anthony, butcher, bds. 17 Wade
38 W. | Tavan Pat., s e.c. Park and Marsh
| Tavin Michael, lab., c. Park and Marsh
3road— | Tawlk John S., cigar mkr., wks. 122 Linn
utte,) | Taxis Otto, clk., 76 Broadway
| TAYLOR A M. & CO., (Abraham M.
(John | T. & David H. Taylor.) Hides, Oil
chant | and Leather, 20 and 22 W. 2d, Tannery s.w.c. Liberty and Linn
ziger | TAYLOR Abraham M., (A. M. T. & Co.)
Long— | 425 W. 6th
| Taylor Albert G., exchange office, 37 E. 3d, h. Covington
| TAYLOR & ANTHONY, (John S. T.,
99 W. | Geo. T. & John G. A.,) Insurance Agents, 76 Walnut
r., | TAYLOR & BROTHER, (R. M. W.
n In— | T. & S. Lester. T.,) Wholesale Grocers and Commission Merchants, 45 Walnut
| Taylor Chas., eng., 419 George
s. 322 | Taylor Chas. W., clk., bds. 139 W. 8th
| Taylor Chas. W., clk., 112 Main, h. 461 W. 6th
| Taylor Charlotte S., 153 Clinton
| TAYLOR David H., (A. M. Taylor & Co.,) res. country
a and | Taylor David M., polisher, 409½ Longworth
9th w. | Taylor E. B., wig mkr., 13 E. 4th
20 W. | Taylor Edward J., mer., 139 W. 8th
| Taylor Edward, whitewasher n.s. Gandin al. b. Elm and Plum
n. 86 | Taylor Rev. Edward G.. 66 Hopkins.
| Taylor Elizabeth, bds. 36 Richmond
| Taylor Enoch, forward. and com. mer., 3 E. Front, h. 144 W. 4th
h. 190 | Taylor F. P., exchange office. 15 Hammond, bds. 91 Sycamore
r, 15 | Taylor & Faulkner, (Joseph T. & Stephan F.,) planing mill, 487 Freeman
| Taylor Geo., clk., bds. 568 Freeman
| Taylor Geo., lab., 240 E. Front
e near | TAYLOR George, (T. & Anthony,) h. E. Walnut Hills
e and | Taylor Griffin. President Cincinnati Equitable Ins. Co., 30 W. 3d, h. Clifton
5 Elm | Taylor Hy. W. 154 Livingston
| Taylor Hiram, edge tool manuf., 53 E. 8th, h. 53 Jackson
| Taylor Howland, clk. L. M. R. R., res.
Mul— | Morrow
| Taylor Hugh, shoe mkr., 253 Hopkins
| TAYLOR & IRWIN, (Jas. T. & Jas.
Long— | T. Irwin,) Dentists, 171 Race
is. 322 | TAYLOR Isaac H., (Suire, Eckstein & Co.,) h. 422 W. 4th
| Taylor J. D., clk., 9 Water, h. Covington
entral | Taylor J. L., clk. 9 Water, h. Covington
| Taylor Jas., 427 W. 6th
y Ho— | Taylor Jas., 47 Plum
| TAYLOR James, (T. & Irwin,) h. Terrace Garden Nurseries, Ky.
e | Taylor Jas. D., 235 W. Court
Broad— | Taylor James A., huckster, 127 Race
| Taylor Mrs. Jane, 72 E. 7th
| Taylor John, bakery, 164 W. 3d
| Taylor John, b.k., 103 W. 4th, h. 29 Baum
| Taylor John, dray, 479 W. 3d
nt, h. | Taylor John, dray, 48 Elm
| Taylor John, iron worker, wks. s. w. c.
entral | Ramsey and W.W. Canal
| TAYLOR John, (Jno. T. & Co. & Geo.
P. Bo— | Coon & Co.,) h. 158 Dayton
| Taylor John, porter, 119 Sycamore
t w. of | Taylor John C., (Pharos, T. & Co.,) h. 192 George

TAYLOR, JOHN & CO., (John T. & Joseph T.) Wholesale and Retail Grocers, 1021 and 1025 Central Av
Taylor John F., cof. h., 35 W. 5th, res. Covington
Taylor John J., clk., 153 W. 6th, h. 43 Barr
Taylor John R., b.k., bds. 139 W. 8th
Taylor John R., dray, 136 Carr
TAYLOR John S., (T. & Anthony,) h. E. Walnut Hills
Taylor John S. jr., clk., s. e. c. Front and Broadway, bds. n. e. c. 6th and Race
Taylor John W., carpenter, 119 Mound
Taylor Jonah R.. real estate agt., 130 Vine, h. 114 Hopkins
Taylor Joseph. eng., rear 26 Mulberry
TAYLOR Joseph, (John Taylor & Co., & Geo. Coon & Co.,) 406 Baymiller
Taylor Joseph, (T. & Faulkner,) 568 Freeman
Taylor Joshua, lab., wks. 179 W. Canal
Taylor Leonard, lab., 183 George
Taylor Luke. porter, s.w.c. Race and 2d
TAYLOR MRS. M. A., Millinery Store, 106 W. 4th
Taylor M. M., clk. county clk's. office, h. 139 W. 8th
Taylor M. R., city gauger, office Minor & Andrews, h. E. Walnut Hills
TAYLOR Mark, (Thayer & T.,) res. Covington
Taylor Mary A., bds. 408 W. 7th
Taylor Mary A., h. 92 Broadway
Taylor Michael M., copyist, bds. 139 W. 8th
Taylor Mrs. N. B., 294 Plum
Taylor Noah, porter, 28 Pleasant
Taylor Phillip, porter, 139 W. Front
Taylor Pressley N., carp., 388 W. 8th, h. 20 Elizabeth
Taylor R. E., dentist, 229 College, h. 29 W. 7th [4th
TAYLOR R. M. W., (T. & Bro.,) 93 E.
Taylor Robert B., shoemkr, Cramsey al. b. Mound and Cutter
TAYLOR S. Lester, (T. & Bro.,) h. 577 W. 8th
Taylor Samuel, boatman, n. s. Accommodation e. of 8th
Taylor Samuel, mate, 10 Observatory
Taylor Sylvester, clk., 55 W. 4th, h. 171 Poplar
Taylor Thos. T., 233 W. Court
Taylor Wesley, b.k., 67 Walnut, h. 461 W. 6th
Taylor Wm., blksmith, s. s. Court b. Main and Sycamore, h. 25 State
Taylor Wm., butcher, 815 Vine
Taylor Wm., eng., 644 E. Front
Taylor Wm., grocer, s. w. c. Linn and Bank
Taylor Wm., lab., 64 Pleasant
Taylor Wm., porter, Cramsey al. b. Mound and Cutter
Taylor Wm. C., 106 W. 4th
Taylor W. F., clk., 9 Water, h. Covington
TAYLOR W. H., Gentlemen's Furnishing Goods, 160 W. 5th, h. 185 George
Taylor Wm. H., salesman, 49 W. Pearl, bds. 192 George
Taylor Wm. H., phys., 100 W. 8th
Taylor Wm. H. H., eng., s. s. Wade b. Baymiller and Dudley
Taylor Wm. P., 35 W. 5th
Taylor Zachariah, clk., bds. 262 E. Front
Teale Hy., mach., 508 W. 9th
Teulen David, carp., 1202 E. Front
Teamann George, carp., 332 George
Teangelbacker Christopher, butcher, 742 W. Front
Tearl Jacob, tailor, 451 Linn
Tearne Saml. S., printer, wks. Times office
Teasdale Hy. L., clk., n. w. c. Walnut and Gano, bds. 207 Walnut
Tensdale William, dye house, n. w. c. Walnut and Gano, h. Green Tp
Teaters Michael, teamster, 102 Freeman
Tebbe Hy., wagon mkr., 15 Park
Tebbe John P., chair mkr., wks. Bird, Burrows & Co.'s

314 (TEM) CINCINNATI (TEU) DIRECTORY. (THE)

Tebben Bernard H., carp., 59 14th
Tebber Barney, box mkr., 65 14th
Tebelman John, (Becker & T.,) 128 Clark
Tebermann Joseph, lab., 708 Freeman
Tebold Max., 69 Mohawk
Teceng Frank, soap mkr., n. s. Bank b. Riddle and Division
Teckel Joseph, shoemkr, 417 Longworth
Teders John B., lab, rear 115 Woodward
Tedeschi Laiona, fruit dealer, 47 E. 3d
Tedmann Wm. F., varnisher, bds. 125 W. 2d
Tedrow John, lab., wks. n. w. c. Plum and Wade
Tedrow John, molder, wks. C. T. Dumont's
Tedtmann Martin F. C., tailor, 50 15th
Teeats D. R., tailor, bds. s. w. c. 5th and Broadway
Teefe Mary A., 200 Clark
Teefe Wm., turner, 200 Clark
Teeman Hy., finisher, wks. n. e. c. Walnut and Canal
Teenafer Wm., grocer, 602 W. 8th
Teepe Wm., carp., Oehler al. b. Freeman and Garrard
Teermon Laura, 383 W. 7th
Tuetor Hy., butcher, 1607 Central Av
Teetzel Ezra, agt., bds. Gibson House
Teetzell Mahlon, clk., 76 W. 5th
Teevens John, dray, 86 Butler
Teey Catharine, servt., 372 W. 6th
Tefeluwe Mrs. Philamina, 404 Longworth
Teff Joseph, cigar mkr.. bds. 201 Clark
Teffinger Gottlieb, cigar mkr., 140 Ham. Rond
Tefft Albert, (Neiber & T.,) 205 Mound
Tegelkamp Frank, blksmith, 406 Longworth
Tehn Jenny, bds. 176 W. 6th
Tehn Mary, bds. 176 W. 6th
Tehn Timothy, lab., 343 Broadway
Tehne Anthon, tailor, 615 Race
Tehr Ludwig, whitewasher, 168 Hopkins
Teichmann Frederick, cab. mkr., 99 Buckeye
Teichmann Sophie, 113 Ham. Road
Teike Hy. E., shoemkr, 165 Linn
Teiman John, cab. mkr., 654 Sycamore
Teiman John, molder, 261 Carr
Teilmeier Elizabeth, 108 Clinton
Teilmeier Gus. cigar mkr., 105 Clinton
Teitmeier Herman, tailor, 108 Clinton
Tekoppel Gerhard W., tailor, 23 Green
Tekot John, 496 Broadway
Tekulre Geo., shoemkr, bds. 361 W. 5th

TELEGRAPH HOUSE,
Geo. Seitzer, Proprietor,
338 Central Avenue

Telfer John, b.k., 145 Main
Telfer Louisa, 1464 E. Front
Telgheder Hy., lab., 17 15th b. Elm and Plum
Telka Frederick, cigar mkr., 99 Pendleton
Telkamp Hy., blksmith, 63 Woodward
Telkink Hy., grocer, 234 Broadway
Tell Jas. W., lab., Weiler, nr. Harriet
Telthester Hy., cab. mkr., 49 15th
Teltrup Frank, molder, 50 Plum
Teman George, whitewasher, 30 Jones
Tembleiton John, bds. Dumas Hotel
Tembusch Anton lab., w.s. Goose al. b. Green and Elder
Temme Joseph, cab. mkr., 28 13th
Temmen John B., grocery, n.w.c. Clark and Baymiller
Temmen John H., (Schulte & T.) 604 Race
Temmeng Joseph, blksmith, 52 Commerce
Temmering Herman, varnisher, wks. n. w.c. Elm and Pearl
Temming Joseph, blksmith, wks. 55 E. [5th
Temper George, clk.. bds. 305 Race

TEMPEST & CO., (Michael T. & Frederick Dallas,) Ham. Road Pottery, 283, 285 and 287 Ham. Road

TEMPEST Michael, (T. & Co.,) 283 Ham. Road
Tempest Nimrod, potter, s s. Cross w. of Hamburg
Templars Magazine, monthly, 112 Hopkins

Temple George D., clk., Adams Express Co., bds. 305 Race
Temple Hy., mess. Ohio & Miss. R.R., h. 234 Barr
Temple Lottie, 383 W. 8th
Temple Luther, agt., 81 W. Pearl, bds. Henrie House
Templeton, actor, National Theatre
Templeton Aaron H., lab., 38 Lock
Templeton Nicholas J., cooper, w. s. Culvert b. 6th and 7th, h. 175 Broadway
Templeton Pompey, lab., 101 E. 6th
Templeton Wm., 38 Lock
Ten Beig John, (T. & Schroder,) 19 12th
Ten Beig & Schroder, (John Ten B. & Fred S.,) cof. h., 15 12th
Tenbusch John W., cigar mkr., 118 Ham. Road
Tenbusch Joseph, blksmith, 21 Green
Tenbusz Joseph, lab., 67 W. Liberty

TENCH GEO. G.,
House Furnishing Store,
329 Central Avenue

Tenderlein Lorenz, lab., 39 Moore
Tenear Samuel, finisher, wks. n. e. c. Walnut and Canal
Tenear Frank, finisher, wks. n.e.c. Walnut and Canal
Tenger Benjamin, shoemkr, 92 E. 5th
Tenger John, lab., 693 Race
Tenguman Geo., cigars, &c., 602 Central Avenue
Tenges Frederick R., tailor, 62 Findlay
Tenhundfeld Herman, lab., s.s. Taylor b. Harriet and Carr
Tenhundfeld Joseph, grocer, 554 W. Front
Tenkler Hy., cab. mkr., 12 Mary
Tenland Kate, servt., 137 John
Tennis Theodore, tailor, College al. b. Woodward and Abigail
Tennian Jerome, blksmith, wks. s. e, c. Race and Water
Tenningham Jerome, blksmith, 136 W. Front
Tennison Mark, ladies shoe manuf., 310 Main, h. s e c. Young and Corp. al.
Tennis Barbara, 628 Vine
Tennis Mary, 14 Mary
Tenseng Albert, expressman, 30 Observatory
Tensey Patrick, finisher, n. w. c. Plum and 2d
Theobald John, lab., 98 Ham. Road
Tepe Bernhard, grocery, 85 Abigail
Tepe Frank W., tailor, 468 Race
Tepe Henry, cab. mkr., 435 W. 2d
Tepe Jernard, engraver, Carlisle Bldg., h. 85 Abigail
Tepe Jno. H., porter, 108 Clinton
Tepe Rienhard, lab., Oehler al. b. Freeman and Garrard
Tepf Joseph, cigar mkr., 201 Clark
Tepke Geo., shoe mkr., 377 Broadway
Tepp John, 69 Buckeye
Teppe Henry, cab. mkr., 435 W. 2d
Terape Henry, 550 Central Av
Terhage Herman, grocery, e.s. Kilgour b. 3d and 5th [5th
Termarth Henry, wagon mkr., 478 W.
Terrell Charles A., awning mkr., 12 Sycamore, bds. 102 W. 6th
Terry Elizabeth, bds. 30 Patterson al.
Terry G. W., (G. W. Terry & Co.), 468 W. 4th
Terry G. W. & Co., map mounting and coloring, 52 E. 3d
Terry James, lab., 241 W Front
Terwort Wm., shoe mkr., bds. 677 W 6th
Teseck Caspar, tanner, bds. n.w.c Baymiller and Wade
Tesch Henry, butcher, 106 York
Tesing Herman, blksmith, 35 Milton
Tetus John, baker, 40 Pike
Tetter Francis, lab., 204 Clark
Tetzlelf August, h. 524 Main
Teuchter Wm., teacher Nelson's Commercial College
Teup John, printer, 139 Plum
Teuting Lizzie, seamstress, 11 Mausfield

TEUTONIA HOTEL,
J. B. Bollmann & Co.,
17 and 19 E. 9th

Tewes Henry, (T. & Herking.) n.s. Front e. of Kelly
Tewes & Herking, (Henry T. & Wm. H.,) grocers, n.s. Front e. of Kelly
Tezlawa August, saddler, 522 Main
Thacker John A., phys., 240 Race, h. 392 George
Thale Barney, express driver, 55 Pendleton
Thale Henry, runner, bds. 55 Pendleton
Thaler Mary, 37 Green
Thornbury Richard H., 203 Elm
Tharp, Edmund, grocery, 1244 E. Front
Tharp John, driver, s.s. Pearl b. Pike and Butler
Tharp John, s.s. Goodloe b. Willow and Niagara
Tharp Oliver P., supt. Cin. Street R. R. s.s. Goodloe b. Willow and Niagara
Thatcher David, 329 George

THAUWALD THEODORE, Coffee House, Billard Saloon and Restaurant, s.w c. 7th and Main

THAYER & ALDRICH, (Wm. H. T. & E. R. A.,) Wholesale Millinery, Silk and Straw Goods, &c., 92 W. Pearl

Thayer Geo. H., eng., 241 Laurel
Thayer Henry, 393 W. 3d
Thayer Mary, bds. 248 Hopkins

THAYER S. H., (T. & Taylor,) res. nr. Avondale

Thayer Simon, woolen machinery mkr., wks. foot of W. 9th

THAYER & TAYLOR, (S. H. T. & M. Taylor,) Wool Agents and General Commission Merchants, 9 Water

Thayer Thomas B., 97 W. 3d, bds. Clifton House
Thayer Theodore, mer., bds. Clifton House
Thayer Wm. H., mess. U. S. Express Co.

THAYER Wm. H., (T. & Aldrich,) h. Storrs Tp.

Theanes Peter, porter, h. 301 W. 6th
Theders John R., sawyer, 504 Central Av
Thedick Fred., turner, h. 24 13th
Thedieck Bernhard, blksmith, 9 Mary
Thedieck John F., salesman, 175 Main, res. Storrs Tp.
Thedy August, painter, 128 Ham. Road
Theldick Theodore, plumber, 24 13th
Thellengerdes Brunke, box mkr., w.s. Long al. b. Woodward and Franklin
Theilmann Philip, cab. mkr., 99 Ham. Road
Theis Edward, clk., 45 Jackson
Theis George, cigar mkr., n.e.c. Clifton Av. and Calhoun
Theis Henry, box mkr., wks. Livingston nr. Linn
Theis Jacob, cigar mkr., s.s. Calhoun b. McMillan and Clifton Av

THEIS JACOB,
Hat and Cap Manufacturer
185 Main, h. 45 Jackson

Theis Philipp J., 108 Bremen
Thelsing John, cab. mkr., wks. s.w.c. Canal and Elm
Theisinger Adam, shoe mkr., bds. 40 E. Front
Theisinger Jacob, cab. mkr., 541 Race
Theissen Harmon A., dry goods, 205 Linn
Thekemeyer Fred., blksmith, wks. n.e. c. Walnut and Canal
Thele Wm., miller, s.s. Dayton b. Coleman and Western Av
Thenes Peter, confec., 301 W. 6th
Theobald Carolina, bds. 502 Race
Theobald Caspar, porter, al. b. Vine and Walnut and 13th and Mercer
Theobald Conrad, butcher, 238 Pleasant
Theobald Christina, seamstress, 487 Walnut
Theobald Jacob, al. b. Vine and Walnut and 13th and Mercer
Theobald Jacob, baker, bds. 249 W. 6th
Theobald Jacob jr., cigar mkr., al. b. Vine and Walnut and 13th and Mercer
Theobald John, cigar mkr., 15 Mary
Theobald John, lab., 98 Ham. Road

(THO) CINCINNATI (THO) DIRECTORY. (THO) 315

Theobald John, tailor, 51 Clay
Theobald Kunigunde, 502 Race
THEOBALD Philip K., (T. & Theurkauf,) 456 Broadway
THEOBALD & THEURKAUF, (Philip K T. & Albert T.,) Foreign Books, Prints and Stationery, 9 Court House Building
Theodor Cornelius, broom mkr., 400 Broadway
Theodore Louise, actress, h. 541 Elm
THE OHIO VALLEY FARMER, Sanford and Bush, Editors, 42 W. 4th
THE RAILROAD RECORD, Wrightson & Co.. Proprietors, Office 167 Walnut
Theresa Sister, St. Clare Convent, n.w. c. 3d and Ludlow
Theringer David, meats, 342 Freeman
Thesing Wm., rope mkr., wks. 442 W. 2d
THEURKAUF Albert, (Theobald & T.,) h. 458 Sycamore
They Louis, tailor, s.s. Calhoun b. McMillan and Clifton Av
Thiebald ——, carp., bds. n.e.c. 7th and Central Av
Thiedemann Wm., tailor, rear 26 Franklin
Thieke Edward, cab. mkr., wks. s.w.c. Canal and Elm
Thieke John H., 50 Webster
Thiel Carolina, variety store, 473 Walnut
Thiel Oscar, lithographer, 473 Walnut
Thiel S. W., bds. Olean Hotel
Thiele Anna, 52 Bremen
Thiele Elizabeth, gilder, 109 Woodward
Thielebein Fred., cab. mkr., 520 Walnut
Thielen Caspar, grocery, 675 Race
Thielen Michael, tailor, 207 Pleasant
Thielman Henry, pattern mkr., bds. 199 E. Front
Thielmann Geo. O., atty., 9 W. Court, h. 39 Dayton
Thiemeyer Catharine, 21 Green
Thien Bernhard, lab., 100 Abigail
Thien Wm., lab., 312 Water
THIERY MICHAEL, Stoves, Hollow and Tin Ware, 61 Elder
Thies Jacob, tinner, bds. 145 E. 2d
Thiese John H., lab., n.s. Railroad e. of Wallace al.
Thiesing Fred. H., liquors, 374 Main, h. c. Webster and Mansfield
Thiesing Geo. H., hardware, 19 E. Pearl
Thiesing John, teamster, s.e.c. Front and John
Thight Catharine, 418 W. 2d
THILL Geo., (Geo. T. & Co.,) 626 Vine
THILL GEO. & CO, (Geo. T. & Nicholaus T.), Hat and Cap Manufacturers, 626 Vine
THILL Nicholaus, (Geo. Thill & Co.,) 626 Vine
Thiman Herman H., lab., 293 Water
Thime Charles, lock manufac., 644 Central Av
Thin Bernard, lab., 149 Abigail
Thinnis Peter, huckster, 56 Pleasant
Thierkield T. F. & Co., who. grocers, 27 Main
Thirkield Thornton F., (T. T. F. & Co.,) 6 Hopkins
Thistlethwaite Isaac, b.k. at 465 W. 2d, h. Newport
Thistlethwaite James, belt mkr., wks. s.w.c. Frost and Butler
Thobaben Ludwig, cab. mkr., 152 Hopkins
Thobe John J., cigar mkr., wks. 218 W. Front
Thoeny Elias, cof. h., 620 Vine
Thoia Joseph, eng., 83 W. Front
Thole Henry, boots and shoes, 3 Gilmore's Wharf, h. 23 E. Liberty
Thole Henry, lab., 4 Louisa
Thole Henry, watchman, 31 Webster
Thole Richard, lab., s.e.c. Clark and Baymiller
Tholen John D., tailor, 463 Vine
Thom David, blksmith, bds. n.w.c. Rose and Columbia
Thom James, n.e.c. Wade and Freeman
Thom Nathaniel G., eng., 107 Smith

Thoma Frederick, caner, bds. 218 Bremen
Thoma Henry, cooper, 94 Water
Thoma Martin, caner, 218 Bremen
Thomae Francis, cigar mkr., 653 Vine
Thomann Herman H., saloon, 187 Central Av
THOMAS Alex S., (Ball & T.,) h. 120 W. 4th
Thomas Alfred, porter, 132 Vanhorne
THOMAS Alfred C., (Fox, T. & Wardlow,) res. Hamilton
Thomas Albert L., c'k., 100 W. 5th, h. 235 Clark
Thomas Andrew, mason, 60 Buckeye
Thomas Mrs. C., 59 Clinton
THOMAS Calvin W., (J. R. Morton & Co.,) 418 W. 9th w. of Central Av
Thomas Chas., candy manuf., 320 Main, h. 122 W. 8th
Thomas Chas. W., clk., n.w.c. Race and 2d, h. 122 W. 9th
Thomas David H., carp., w.s. Pike b. Pearl and 3d
Thomas David S., 311 York
Thomas Mrs. E. S., 248 Longworth
Thomas Edward, carp., 59 York
THOMAS EDWARD B., Physician and Surgeon, 256 Race
Thomas Edwin D., baker, bds. 3 Mulberry
Thomas Ellen, 396 W. 8th
THOMAS Elbridge L., (N. W. T. & Co.,) h. 62 W. 8th
Thomas George L., bds. 142 E. Liberty
Thomas Geo. W., 237 W. Court
Thomas Henry, salesman, 30 W. 4th; res. Covington
Thomas Henry, tanner, 80 Abigail
Thomas Hugh J., collector, 25 W. 3d bds Henrie House
Thomas J. H., police, 14 Baum
Thomas Jacob, carriage trimmer 63 Bremen
THOMAS James K., (Fox T. & Wardlow,) res. Hamilton
Thomas John, bds., s.e.c. 2d and Smith
Thomas John, cooper, 620 W. 8th
Thomas John, lab., 55 Elder
Thomas John, plasterer. s.e.c. Court and Mound
Thomas Jno., trader, bds. 184 Race
Thomas John M., teamster, 274 Cutter
Thomas Joseph, teamster, 133 Barr
Thomas Joseph K., pork packer, 172 Richmond
Thomas Lizzie, servt., 120 E. 3d
Thomas Lizzie, 306 W. 4th
Thomas Margaret, bds. 144 John
Thomas Martha M., 248 Longworth
Thomas Mary J., 161 Court w. of Central Av
Thomas Melissa, n.s. Taylor b Carr and Freeman
Thomas Morris, boiler mkr., bds. 90 E. 2d
THOMAS N. W. & CO., (Nicholas W T. & Elbridge L. Thomas,) Curers of Extra Hams, and Pork Packers, s.w.c. Canal and Kenner
Thomas Nannie B. 306 W. 4th
Thomas Nathan W., candy store 579 Main
THOMAS Nicholas W., (N. W. T. & Co.) 62 W. 8th
Thomas Oliver H., teamster 212 W Front
Thomas Phoebe, s.s. Phoebe al. b. Plum and Central Av
Thomas R. J., roller, 18 L'Hommedieu
Thomas Robt., blksmith, bds. n.e.c. 7th and Central Av
Thomas Robt., bklayer, 205 Cutter
Thomas Robt., cooper, 458 W. 8th
Thomas Robt., mach. belt mkr., w.s. Freeman b. Findlay and Dayton
Thomas Saml. J., detective police, 73½ Betts
THOMAS SAMUEL P. Merchant Tailor, s.e.c. 4th and Walnut. h. c. 4th and Lawrence
Thomas Sophia, servt., 420 W. 6th
Thomas Susan, 248 Longworth
Thomas Washington, salesman, 102 Walnut, h. 131 W. 7th
Thomas Wm., bds, 158 W. 3d

Thomas Wm., carp, n.s. Rail Road e. of Kelly
Thomas Wm., eng., 62 Pierson
Thomas Wm., waggoner, 200 Cutter
Thomas Wm., wagon mkr., h. s.s. Montgomery pike nr Madison Road
Thomas Wm. C., clk. 102 Walnut, h. 131 W. 7th
Thomas Wm. H., clk. 320 Main, h. 122 W. 8th
Thomas Wm. P. clk. 12 W Pearl, rooms Neaves bldg
Thomas Wm. R., mach., 142 E. Liberty
Thomasmeyer H., cigar mkr., 65 Oliver
Thomason Adolph, lithographer, s.w.c. 4th and Walnut
Thons Frank, packer. wks. 131 Race
Thommann John. cof. h., 601 Walnut
Thompson ——, 584 E. Front
Thompson Mrs., bds. 272 W. 7th
Thompson Abel B., clk., 37 E. 3d, h. 33 E. 3d
Thompson Agnes W. 142 W. Court w. of Central Av
Thompson Alburtus, baker, bds. 55 Sycamore
Thompson Alex., lab. h. 48 Butler
Thompson Alfred V., tailor, 120 W. 6th, h. 256 E. 6th
Thompson Alva, carp., h. n.s. Nassau b. Broad and Waldon
Thompson Amanda, e.s. Pierson b. 5th and 6th
Thompson Andrew, molder, wks. n.e.c. Canal and Walnut
Thompson Belle, 13 E. 5th
Thompson Charles A., b.k. 95 W. Pearl bds. 36 Longworth
Thompson Chas. W., clk., n.e.c. 4th and Main, bds. 138½ Richmond
Thompson Dillworth, supt. St. R. R. 293 Baymiller
Thompson Edward chair mkr wks John Mitchell's
THOMPSON Egbert A., (T. & Nesmith) n.w.c. 4th and Broadway
Thompson Eliza, 346 W. 6th
Thompson Elizabeth, 26 E. 8th e. of Lock
Thompson Frances, b. h. 180 Race
Thompson Frank. R., produce broker, 305 W. 4th
Thompson Geo., roofer, 654 W. 8th
Thompson Geo., stocking weaver, 66 W. Mulberry
Thompson Geo. D., stone cutter, 232 W Court
Thompson H., salesman, 74 W. 4th
Thompson Harriet, 473 W. 4th
Thompson J. B., salesman, n.e.c. 5th and Vine
Thompson J. C., clk., 13 E. 5th, h. 36 E. 5th
Thompson J. L., deputy co. auditor h. Columbia
Thompson J. Y., b k. 81 W. Pearl, bds Henrie House
Thompson James, lab., 100 Elm
Thompson James lab., 30 George
THOMPSON JAMES T., Real Estate Dealer, Rail Road Bldg. s.w.c. 3d and Sycamore, bds Madison House
Thompson Jas. W., printer, 112 Water
Thompson Jane, 114 E. 3d e. of Whittaker
Thompson Jenny, 180 Central Av
Thompson John, hinge fitter, wks. n.e. c. Walnut and Canal
Thompson John, sheet iron worker, bds, Black Bear Hotel
THOMPSON JOHN B., Salesman n.e.c. Vine and 5th bds. n.e.c. Plum and McFarland
Thompson John C., tailor, s e.c. Sycamore and 5th
Thompson J. C., cutter, h. 202 W. 5th
Thompson John W., carriage trimmer 30 George
Thompson Julia, bds. 171 E. 3d
THOMPSON M. F. & CO., Manufacturers and Wholesale Dealers in Hats, Caps, Straw Goods and Ladies Furs, 96 W. Pearl
THOMPSON M. F. (M. F. T. & Co.) 364 W. 4th
Thompson Margaret, 211 Elm

Thompson Margaret Y., 161 Barr
THOMPSON MATTHEW, Umbrella and Parasol Manufacturer, 167 Main, h. 45 Chestnut
Thompson Rev. Matthew LaRue P., h. 121 Broadway c. 4th
Thompson Mary, bds. 171 E. 3d
Thompson Mary, 337 Elm
Thompson Mary, 13 E. 6th
Thompson Mary, 92 E. 5th
THOMPSON & NESMITH, (Egbert A T. & Thomas A. N.) Attorneys, at Law, Office 15 W. 3d
Thompson Rachel, 245 Broadway
Thompson Richard, b.k. John Mitchell's bds. Clifton House
Thompson Robert, plumber, wks, 46 E. 3d
Thompson Robert, shoemkr., 42 Cutter
Thompson Robert E., b.k. Cin. Gazette Co., h. 42 Dayton
Thompson Robt. H., clk., bds. 238 Race
Thompson Robt. J., clk., 42 Cutter
Thompson Rob P., foreman printing department Methodist Book Concern h. 167 W. Court w. of Central Av
THOMPSON Saml. J., (King & T.) h, Glendale
Thompson Saml, S., 28 E, 8th e of Lock
Thompson Thomas, finisher, 448 George
Thompson Thomas, lab., 34 Central Av
Thompson Theodore M. teacher 12 dist. school
Thompson W. H, & Co. (Wm. H. T. & Burwell S. Goode,) grocers 9 Pearl and 71 Main
Thompson Wendall, clk., 293 Baymiller
Thompson Wm., lab., 14 Race
Thompson Wm., lab., bds. 9 Pub. Landing b. Main and Walnut
Thompson Wm., foreman, wks. s.w-c, Broadway and 5th
Thompson Wm., mach., 24 Park
Thompson Wm., salesman, 167 Main, h. 25 Elizabeth
Thompson Wm, H., peddler, n.s. Front e. of Lumber
Thompson Wm. H., (Wm, H, T, & Co), res. Storrs tp
Thompson Wm. L. civil eng., 140 Richmond
Thompson Wm. L., fireman, s.e.c North and New
Thompson Wm. M., bds. Henrie House
THOMPSON Wm. W., (J. O Richardson & Co.) bds. 36 Longworth
Thompson Wm. X., 95 Dudley
Thoms Andrew, mach., 638 W 8th
Thoms Eliza, n.w.c. Brighton and Harrison pike
Thoms Joseph, n.w.c. Brighton and Harrison pike
Thoms Lewis, n.w.c. Brighton and Harrison pike
Thoms Marion, 638 W. 8th
Thoms Robert, n.w.c. Brighton and Harrison Av
Thomson Hy. W., receiver City Pass. R. R. 1117 Central Av, h 203 Baymiller
Thomson James, leather belt manufacturer, s.w.c. Front and Butler, bt Columbia tp
Thomson James A. blksmith, bds. 168 Vine
Thomson Joshua J., cook, 186 Cutter
THOMSON PETER, Wholesale Wines, Liquors & Cigars, 55 W. 3d, h 129 W 9th
Thomson S. I., b.k, bds. 23 W. 9th
Thomson Seth. L., b.k. 113 W Pearl bds 93 E. 4th
Thomson Saml. D. asst. supt. 3d and 4th st. R. R. h 292 Baymiller
THOMSON SANDY, Coffee House, 19 E. 3d
Thomson R, b.k., bds. Clifton House
Thomson Robt. B., belt mkr., w.s. Freeman b York and Dayton
Thomson Thomas, lab., 34 Central Av
Thomson Wm. N., b.k., s.w.c. Front and Butler, b, Newport Ky
Thorbeke Joseph, tailor, bds. 466 W. Front
Thorburn Robert T., steward, 312 W. 8th

Thorburn Wm., jewelry. 348 George
Thorn Nancy, 110 W, 5th
Thorn Stephen, brakesman, 196 Freeman
Thornburg Thos., molder, 203 Elm
THORNE Joseph, (Wm. F. T. & Co.) 436 W 4th
Thorne Frank, cigar mkr., 653 Vine h Waynesville O
THORNE Wm. F., (Wm. F. T. & Co.) 407 W. 6th
THORNE WM. F. & CO., (Wm. F. T. & Joseph Thorne), Wholesale Boots and Shoe Dealers, 142 Walnut
THORNER Saml., (Heidelbach, Seasongood & Co.), 11 Arch
Thornley Mira P., tailoress, 445 W. 4th
Thornton Albert M., teacher, bds. 419 W 7th
Thornton Jennie, bds. 116 Findlay
Thornton John, 221 Longworth
Thornton Joseph, 223 Longworth
Thornton Joseph L., principal Hughes high school, h. 419 W 7th
Thornton Mary A., h. h. 279 Main
THORNTON & PERKINS, (Wm. M. K. T. & John H, P.,) Slicking. Raising, Creasing, Dressing and Finishing Machines, s.e.c. Plum and Pearl
THORNTON RICHARD, Glove and Mitten Manufacturer, Tanner and Buckskin Dresser 314 Main h Reading Road
Thornton Wm. H., clk., n.w.c. Central Av and Longworth bds Clifton House
THORNTON Wm. M. K. (T. & Perkins) res. Covington
Thornton Wm. F. phys., h 310 W 6th
Thorp Andrew J., collector, 101 W. Pearl, h. Waynesville, O.
Thorp Chas. E., salesman, bds. 269 W. 7th
Thorp Chevie. 126 Mound
Thorp Francis H., bk. binder, 106 Liberty
Thorp Geo. A., bk. layer, 237 Cutter
Thorp James, driver, 3d and 4th str. R. R.
Thorp John, clk., 230 Cutter
Thorp Kate, 139 Clinton
Thorp Oliver, printer, 126 Mound
Thorp Paris B., clk., 7 Pub. Landing, h. e. s. John b. Laurel and Betts
Thorp Phoebe, s.w.c. Front and Broadway
Thorp Susan, bds. 139 Clinton
Thorp Theo., printer, bds. 297 W. 6th
Thorpe Mrs. A. F., ladies' cap store, 193 Plum
Thorpe Andrew J., distiller, 54 Lock
Thorpe & Brother, (Geo. & Fred.,) painters, 122 Vine
Thorpe Francis H., bk. binder, 106 E. Liberty
Thorpe Frederick, (T. & Brother,) h.Covington, Ky.
Thorpe Geo., (T. & Bro.,) h. Covington, Ky.
Thorpe Israel, lab., 363 W. 6th
Thorpe John, clk., 14 E. 4th, b. 239 Cutter
THORPE, JOHN D., Publisher, Bookseller & Stationer, 72 W. 4th, h. Mt. Auburn
Thorpe W. Coleman, atty., bds. 41 George
Thoss Bernard, spice packer, wks. 164 W. 3d
Thous Frank, packer. wks. 131 Race
Thraenert Hy. F., cof, h., 58 Ham. Road
Thrasher Hannah, s.w.c. Park and 5th
Threlkeld H. C., clk., 36 Main, bds. 159 Race
Threm Hy., hatter. 438 Walnut
Threm John, turner, 443 Walnut
Throy Mary, 399 W. 3d
Thsieng Herman, blk.smith, wks. 136 W. Pearl
Thuenemann Hy., cab. mkr., 137 Everett
Thuenemano John B., chair mkr., wks. H. Clastermann's
Thueringer & Busch, (David T. & Wm. B.,) meats, 526 Race

Thueringer David, (T. & Busch,) 546 Race
Thuire Hy., tailor, rear e. s. Plum b. Adams and Liberty
Thummel John F., venetian blind manuf., 45 E. 5th, b. 34 E. 7th
Thuma Hy., cooper, 18 Commerce, b. Walnut and Vine
Thumann John G., tailor, 64 Findlay
Thuning Hy., mach., 375 W. 5th
Thurmann Wm., tinner, 254 W. 6th
Thurmauer Chas., clothing, 320 Walnut
Thurmauer Mack, mer., 125 W. 8th
Thurston Mary J., bds 98 Broadway
TIBBATTS ISAAC, Solicitor, h. s.e.c. Stevens and 13th, Covington
Tibbetts Ephraim N., painter, 173½ Freeman, h. n. s. 9th b. Freeman and Carr
Tibbetts Richard, carp., 45 Gest
TIBBITTS Hy., (Henry T. & Son,) 393 George
TIBBITTS Hy. C., (Henry Tibbitts & Son., 393 George
TIBBITTS, HENRY & SON, (Henry & Henry C.,) Commission Merchants, s.e.c. Hathaway and Baymiller
Tibbitts John W., b. k., 393 George
Tibbitts Wm. T., salesman, 393 George
Tibbles Chas. F., printer, Commercial office
Tiber Ignatius, tinner, 65 Lock
Tice Charles W., b. k., 102 W. Pearl, h. 250 Longworth
Tice Elizabeth, s. s. Cross b. North Elm and Hamburg
Tice Ellen, teacher, 244 Clinton
Tice Geo, carriage mkr., 244 Clinton
Tice Isaac F., 297 Baymiller
Tice Jane, bds. 37 Chestnut
Tice John O., salesman, 139 Walnut, bds. 256 W. 3d
Tice Joseph M., pipe fitter, wks. n. e. c. Walnut and Canal
Tice John, ins. agt., 33 W: 3d, h. 244 Clinton
Tice Orceneth F., salesman, 119 Main, bds. 244 Clinton
Tice Solomon, foreman, 256 W. 3d
Tice Wm. II., salesman, 96 W, Pearl, bds. 256 W. 3d
Ticie Wm., carp., wks. n.e.c. Canal and Walnut
Tick Martin, butcher, w. s. Western Av. b Dayton and Bank
Tidball Valentine C., (Frankland & T.,) 1 Gorman
Tidings John, butcher, 61 E. 8th, e. of Lock
Tiebermann Richard, soap cutter, 212 W. Liberty
Tiecken Bernard, clk., wks. 77 W. Court
Tiefel Herman, carp., 9 Pendleton
Tiehl Leonard, 51 Wade
Tieka Lina, servt., 291 Richmond
Tieken Geo., sawyer, rear 14 13th
Tieken Hy., molder, rear 14 13th
Tielke Frederick, cig. mkr., 99 Pendleton
Tiellmann August, cab. mkr., 52 15th
Tieman Agnes, rear 375 Broadway
Tieman Chas, boots and shoes, 87 Sycamore, bds. 91 Sycamore
Tieman Hy., lab., 60 Abigail
Tieman Hy., shoe mkr., n.w.c. Plum and 2d
Tieman Hermann, lab, bds. 370 Broadway
TIEMAN PHIL., International Saloon and Billiard Rooms, 91 Sycamore
Tieman Philipp E., carver, 179 Spring
Tiemann Margaret, teacher, h, 1 Budd
Tiemann Dina, 122 Pleasant
Tiemann Frederick, varnisher, e. s. Hand al. b. Court and Clark
Tiemann Frederick H., salesman, 524 Main
Tiemann Harmon H., varnisher, 52 Eltenhouse
Tiemann Hy., lab., 370 Broadway
Tiemann John H., grocer, 630 W. 8th
Tiemann Joseph, salesman, w. s. Spring b. Woodward and Liberty

(TIM)　　CINCINNATI　　(TOA)　　DIRECTORY.　　(TOM)　　317

Tiemann Wm., varnisher, 52 Laurel
Tiemeyer Hy., tanner, 181 Baymiller
Tiemeyer John H., lab., 47 Kossuth
Tiemhaus Agnes, seamstress, 116 Abigail
Tiermann Wm., varnisher, 52 Laurel
Tiernan Michael, bds. 159 W. 3d
Tiernon Thomas G., city commissioner, h. 532 W 8th
Tierney Anna, bds. s.w.c. 6th and Broadway
Tierney Jane, 154 Broadway
Tierney John, watchman, Clifton House
Tierney Michael, porter, 55 W. Pearl
Tierney Pat., lab., s.w.c. Pearl and Canal
Tierney Rosa, servt., 427 W. 6th
Tierney Wm, peddler, bds. 177 E. Front
Tiers Rev. Montgomery C., 114 Dudley
Tiese Gottlieb. lab", 18 Mausfield
Tiesing Frederick, sexton, c. s. Race b. 13th and 14th
Tieter John, lab., wks. Adams, Peckover & Co's.
Tietig Hy., lab., h. 52 15th
Tiffenbach Joseph, w. s. John b Liberty and Oliver
Tift Cornelius Tacetus, (G. W. Coffin & Co.,) 18 Arch
Tigh Chas., porter, n. s. Clinton b. Central Av. and John
Tigh Eliza, servt., 103 Pike
Tigh Julia. 398 Broadway
Tighe Charles, porter, s. e. c 3d and Vine
Tighe Frank, dray, 191 E. Pearl
Tigurs Francis, 26 Jones
Tihatmer Bernard, lab., rear 60 Abigail
TILDEN, MYRON H.,
(Wm. B. Caldwell & M H. & W. T.) h Avondale
TILDEN Wm., (Wm. T. & Nephew,) h. New York
TILDEN Wm., (B. Caldwell & W. H. & W. T.,) bds. Gibson House
TILDEN, WM. & NEPHEW, (Wm. T. & W. T. Blodgett.) Manufacturers of Varnishes, 99 Walnut
Tiley John W., 315 Ham. Road
Tiley S. G., 47 Barr
Tilford Lewis whitewasher, e.s. North b. New and 7th
TILGHMAN THOMAS E.,
General Collector, n e.c 7th and Mound
Tilken Christina, servt., 283 Richmond
Tille John, fireman, 167 Clay
Tille Wm., druggist, 139 Abigail
Tillett Elizabeth, 189 Mound
Tilley George, copper smith, n. s. Kemper's Lane b Hill and E. Front
Tilley John, sheet iron wkr., bds. n. s. Kemper's Lane b Hill and Front
Tilling F. eng , bds 91 Sycamore
Tilling Hy., teamster, 91 Sycamore
Tilling Mary, servt., 91 Sycamore
Tillinghast D. J., printer, "Commercial" office, n. 108 Longworth
Tillinghast Kate, b.h., 243 W. 5th
Tillinghast W. T., printer, bds. 243 W. 5th
Tillmon Maria, bds. Dumas Hotel
Tillotson James, watchman, 25 E. 7th
Tillotson Mary A., teacher, 135 W. 9th
Tillotson Rebecca, 25 E. 7th
TILLY WM. Drugs, Medicines, Paints, s.w.c. Abigail and Spring, h. 129 Abigail
Tillyon Hy., lab , n.s , Charlotte b. Linn and Baymiller,
Tilney Joseph,b.k., 18 Sycamore, h. 371 W. 8th
Tilney Thomas, 371 W. 8th
Tilson Mary, bds. 135 Plum
Tilton Joseph M., printer, 34 E. 3d, h. 124 Hopkins
Timan Martin, undertaker, 53 Race
Timberlake Edward. printer, 75 W. 6th
Timberman Chas. C., bk. layer, 81 Betts
Timberman Christian, 278 Cutter
Timberman Ily., express man, 66 Spring
Timberman James, plasterer, bds. 475 W. 7th
Timberman John D., express man, 475 W. 7th

Timberman William, express man, 66 Spring
Timerman Harman, lab., 104 Gest
Timerman Margaret, 20 Hannibal
Times Building, n. s. W. 3d b. Walnut and Vine
Timm John, cab. mkr. 1 Mulberry
Timme Hy., tailor, n.s. Jail al. b. Sycamore and Main
Timmer Francis J., teacher, 205 Linn
Timmer Hy., driver, e. s. Kilgour b. 3d and 5th
Timmer John, whitewasher, bds. 19 Abigail
Timmer John G., (Wernke & T.). e. s. Kilgour b. 3d and 5th
Timmerding Hermann, varnisher, 90 Woodward
Timmerman Anna M., 90 Woodward
Timmerman John H., grocery, h. n.e.c. Carr and 6th
Timmermann Dietrich, carp., 519 Main
Timmermann Hermann G., tailor, 390 Sycamore
Timmermann Maria A., 90 Woodward
Timmers G. H., foreman, 93 Pendleton
Timmers Hy. G., foreman, 95 Pendleton
Timmers Wm., lab., 111 Woodward
Timmerwilke Bernhard, express man, w. s. Hanover b. Franklin and Woodward
Timon Martin, cooper, 54 Water
Timoney Geo., lab., n.s. Augusta b. John and Smith
Timperman John H., lab., 403 Longworth
Timpert John, cigar mkr., 471 George
Timroth August, shoemkr, 607 Main
Tinbrook Geo. H., cof. h., 527 Vine
Tindal Jackson, bk. binder, 129 York
Tingley Lucy B., teacher, 99 E. 5th
Tinlers Wm., hinge fitter, wks. n. e. c. Walnut and Canal
Tinkelacker Frederick, butcher, 770 W. Front
Tinker Frederick, lab.,wks. s.w.c. Broadway and 5th
Tinker Frederick. eng., bds. 120 E. 5th
Tinkler Joseph, clk. C. H. and D. R. R. depot, h. 199 Barr
Tinley Martha, teacher, 233 John
Tin ley Terry, lab., 390 Vine
Tinley Wm., lab , 130 W. Court
Tinnemeier Frederick, cigar mkr., 27 Ham. Road
Tinnemeier Wm., 33 Jones
Tinnemeyer & Bro. (Henry T. & Conrad T.) carps., rear 250 Mulberry
Tinnemeyer Conrad (T. & Bro.), 250 Mulberry
Tinnemeyer Hy. (T. & Bro.), 246 Mulberry
Tinner F., lab., wks. Chamberlain & Co's
Tipney Thos., printer, wks. Times office h. Newport, Ky
Tinsley Wm., architect, n. w. c. 6th and Walnut, h. Covington, Ky
Tipkemper Francis, tailor, 719 Race
Tippetts Sarah, 266 Central Av
Tisch Daniel, butcher, 280 W. Liberty
Tischler Gustave, tanner,bds, 105 Logan
Tischler Robert, tanner, 105 Logan
Tischler Sebastian, tanner 14 Dunlap
Tisdault Charles, finisher, w. s. Observatory b. Hill and Observato,y Road
Tisinger P., servt., n. w. c. Cutter and Betts
Tisinger Phillip, sawyer, 94 Betts
Tissct Hy , wagoner n.s. Cussatt al. b. Main and Sycamore
Titcomb Chas. S. W., clk., bds. 158 W. 5th
Titcomb Rufus, books, &c., 158 W. 5th
T ichkr Marga e, 63 Pecte
TITUS John (A. H. Wells & Co.) res. Glendale
Titus Joseph B., atty., 42 W. 4th, res. Green tp
Tivehus Joseph, cigar mkr., 11 Hannibal
Tivis Joseph, cigar mkr, 11 Hannibal
Tlowe F., tinner, wks. n.w.c. Race and 2d
Toackim Casper, lab., 576 E. Front
Toakan Jas., molder, wks. n. e. c. Canal and Walnut

Toaklyn Thomas, lab , 60 Pierson
Toal Patrick, dray, 182 E. 6th
Tobalt Jo hn, lab., 114 Gest
Tobe Charles, tailor, bds. 137 Race
Tobe Fred.. (T. & Hollman) 216 Vine
Tobe & Hollman (Fred. T. & Henry H.) tailors, 216 Vine
Tobey Cornelius, collector, 137 Longworth
Tobey Ellen, servt., 267 Richmond
Tobias Hy., cap manuf., 186 Main
Tobin John, lard oil manuf., 224 Broadway
Tobin John, tailor, bds. Fireman's Hall
Tobin John, walter, 178 W. 6th
Tobin John J., clk., 163 Richmond
Tobin Julia, 34 Lock n of 8th
Tohin Wm. J., lard oil factory,294 John, h. 379 W. 6th
Tubirn George, dray, 329 W. 9th w. of Central Av
Toborben Ludwig, cab. mkr., 152 Hopkins
Tocher John, books, &c., s.e.c. 4th and Main, h. Newport
Tocke Barney, 200 Linn
Tod Saml. B., coffee stand, 211 W. 6th
TODD Alex., (Haines, T. & Lytle), h. E. Walnut Hills
Todd Benjamin F., cab. mkr., bds. 47 W. 7th
Todd Frank, cab. mkr., bds. 47 W. 7th
Todd George W., mach., bds. 100 Broadway
Todd Harry, mach., 3 Providence
Todd Hy., mach., 200 Richmond
TODD JAMES,
Agent for Oyster Companies, 253 Walnut
TODD JAMES,
Foundry and Machine Shop, s.w.c. 7th and Smith, h. College Hill
Todd Joseph, lab., 700 W. Front
Todd Lewis, molder, h. Richmond near Harriet
Todd Samuel, teamster 49 Betts
Todd Thomas, carp., s. e. c. Front and Brooklyn
Tedenbler Andrew, peddler, 141 Pleasant
Todenbier George, cigar mkr., 634 Race
Todtle Hy., shoemkr., bds. 928 Central Av
Toebbe Rev. A., n. s. Pearl b. Pike and Butler
Toebler Wm., shoemkr, 62 Findlay
Toenges Ernst, porter, 11 Wade b. Elm and Plum
Toenges Frederick, lab., 197 Pleasant
Toenies Rudolph, cigar mkr., wks. 55 14th
Togel Rodney, n. s 6th b. Culvert and Broadway
Tohler Hy., lab., 92 Baum
Tohlking Bernard, lab., e.s. Anderson b. 2d and Pearl
Tokup Frank, cigar mkr., 45 Elder
Tolan Anthony lab., n.s. Front b. Canal and Kilgour
Toland James. lab., e. s. Whittaker b. Front and 3d
Toland Patrick, huckster, 336 Clark
Tolbert Martin, merch , 21 Ellen
Tolbert Michael, dry goods, 31 E. Pearl, h. e.s. Elm b. 3d and 4th
Tolbert Nathaniel, carp., 14 Gest
Tole Barney, lab., 59 Abigail
Tole Joseph, foreman, s e. c. Vine and Water
Tolcy Nicholas, lab., 30 Lock
Toll Barney, wks 242 E. Front
Toll Sarah H., Malden Lane b. Gas al. & Anderson al
Tolle Micajah. eng., 176 W. 3d
Tollena Mary, 97 Baum
Tulley John., lab., Maiden Lane b. Gas al. and Anderson al
Tolly Wm., lab., s. s. Avery al. w. of Wood
Tolliver Phillip, jr., mess., 216 E. 6th
Tomasini Charles, confec., n. w. c. Linn and George
Tombach Andrew, finisher, wks. n. e. c. Walnut and Canal
Tombach August, finisher, bds. 606 Race
Tombach Theodore, grinder, 600 Race

Tombregel Joseph, locksmith, 306 Linn
Tomholt John. bds. s. w. c, Abigail and Broadway
Tomlinson Miss Annie, milliner, bds. 214 W. Front
Tomlinson Horatio, carp . 221 Freeman
Tomlinson James (McLaughlin, T. & Co.), 223 Richmond
Tomlinson John, dray, 402 George
Tomlinson John S.. printer, 141 Longworth
Tomlinson Robt., 36 Pike
TOMLINSON SAM'L. B., Physician and Surgeon, Office and Residence 43 Everett
Tomlinson Will. compositor, Cin. Gazette, h. 143 Race
Tompkins Elizabeth, 314 W. 7th
TOMPKINS Garret (E. Leighton & Co.) 126 York
Tompkins Hy., shoemkr, 34 Rittenhouse
Tompkins James, furniture. 33 Ellen
Tompkins James, painter, 252 E. 6th
Tompkins Julia, bds. 57 Broadway
Tompson H., salesman, bds. s.w.c. Race and 9th
Tomsett Lydia, s.s. Front e. of Selas
Ton Peter, lab., w. s. Pole b. 2d and Pearl
Tone Thomas J., teacher, 115 Mill
Tonegas Ernst, porter, 17 Jefferson
Toner Julia, 17 Lock n. of 8th
Toney Wm. J., barber, 50 E. 5th, h. 74 E. 7th
Tonn Anthony, blksmith, 61 W. Liberty
Tonner James, printer, bds. 10 Sycamore
Tonnes Hy., lab., 62 Pierson
Tonnes Joseph, teamster, 7 John
TONNIES BERNHARD, Merchant Tailor, 335 W. 5th
TONNIES BERNHARD II., Family Groceries, 297 W. Front
TONNIES C. F., Proprietor Olean Hotel, s.e.c. Front and Central Av.
Toohey John, lab., s. s. Accommodation e. of 8th
Toohey Margaret, servt., 273 W. 4th
Toohey Matthew, lab., 63 E. 8th e. of Lock
Toohey Matthew, lab., 35 E. 8th e. of Lock
Toohey Michael, watchman, 331 W. 3d
Toohey Patrick, carp., wks. n. s Patterson al. b. Main and Walnut
Toolug Johanna, 63 W. Front
Tooker Amos, bk. layer, 230 Laurel
Toon Emma, 641 E. Front
Toomey Jeremiah, bar k., Spencer House
Toomey Thomas, lab., 16 E. 8th e. of Lock
Tooze John, cab. mkr., wks. Mitchell & Rammelsberg's
Top John, shoe mkr., s. s. 6th b. Plum and Central Av.
Topf Otto, s.s. Calhoun b Clifton Av. and McMillan
Tophy Anthony, lab., wks. n. s. Front b. Lawrence and Pike
Tophy Frederick, lub. wks. n. s. Front b. Lawrence and Pike
Tophy Joseph, blksmith, wks. n.s. Front b. Lawrence and Pike
Topy Wm., blksmith, n.s. Front b. Lawrence and Pike
Topic Gerhard F., expressman 28 Buckeye
Topie Frederick, lab., 26 Buckeye
Topie Hy., lab., 9 Peet
Topoel Ennis, porter, 448 Walnut
Toppelmiller Hy., lab., 158 Webb
Toppert Rev. Hy., Church of the Immaculate Conception, Mt Adams
Topphorn George, tailor, Pavilion near Observatory
Torbarg Harman, dray, 87 W. 2d
Torbeck Hy., lab., n. w c. Ramsey and Park al.
Torhmann Emeline, servt., 143 Elm
Tormeller Frederick, cooper, 30 Jones
Tornburg Thomas, molder, 203 Elm
Turner Hy., (Dorsch T. & Co.) s. s. Freeman b. Bank and Dayton

Torner Wm., bds. e.s. Freeman b. Bank and Dayton
Torrence Aaron, clk., 94 W. 9th
TORRENCE JAMES F., Forwarding and Commission Merchant. 67 and 69 W. Miami Canal, res. E. Walnut Hills
Torrence John F., 94 W. 9th
TORRENCE Joseph, (Chas. W. West & Co.) 94 W. 9th
Torrence Samuel, b. k., I. & E. Greenwald's, h. 94 W. 9th
Torrence W. I., clk., 94 W. 9th
Tosseny Brian lab., s. s. Culvert b. 5th and 6th
Tosso Julius, scale repairer, 7 Pub. Landing, h. 15 Oliver b. Central Av. and John
Tosspot George, (Lewis & T.,) 158 W. Pearl
Tosspott Jonathan, barber, 6 W. 3d, h. 16 Union
Totten Wm, J., clk., L. M. R. R., h. 272 Vine
Tout James, carp., s.s. Front e. of Reed
Tower Edward C., druggist, s. e. c. 5th and Mill
Tower Martin, cof. h., s.e.c. Plum and 2d
Towers Chas. C., clk., 56 W. 3d, h. Newport Ky.
Towers Ellen, 653 W. Front
TOWERS J. C. & CO., (John C. T. & James E. Bonneville,) Hatters and Furriers, 149 Main
TOWERS John C., (J. C. T. & Co.,) h. Newport. Ky.
Towers Robert, molder, wks. n.w.c. Plum and Wade
Towle Aaron B., real estate agt. 1 George
Towle Wm., b. k., 103 W. 4th, h. f George
Towner Samuel, finisher, 181 W. 2d
Townley Edward E., b. k., 67 W. Pearl h. Mt. Auburn
Townley Eugene G., asst. sec'y Com. Ins. Co. h. Mt. Auburn
Townley Geo. E., clk., bds. 21 W 8th
Townley Geo. W., lumber dealer, 21 W. 8th
Townley J. A., sec'y Commercial Ins. Co., h. Clifton Av.
Townley John, bk. layer. 86 Vanhorne
Townley Major J., lumber yard, 445 Vine h. 430 Broadway
Townley Richard, bk. layer, 110 Barr
Townley Robert, lab., s. s. Goodloe b. Willow and Niagara
Townley Wm. E., clk., bds. 21 W. 8th
Townsend E. B., 1st ass't. city auditor, h. 305 Race
Townsend George W., caulker, n. w. c. Front and Broad
Townsend Honora, 363 W. 6th
Townsend James, carp., 205 Poplar h. 201 Poplar
Townsend James W., clk. O. & M. R. R. Freight Office, h. 164 Longworth
Townsend Oliver, bds. 185 W. 3d
Townsend Sophia. 579 Central Av.
Townsend Wm. C., collector McMicken University, 141 Main, bds. 105 Race
Townsend Wm. H., saddler, bds. 180 Race
Townsley Alfred L., drug manufac., 171 Mound
Towolster Patrick, lab., s. s. Yeatman b. Broadway and Sycamore
Towsley Wm., teamster, s. w. c. 8th and Crippen al.
Towsley Wm., fireman, s. s. 8th b Broadway and Sycamore
Toy Alfred I., bds. 214 George
Tuy Isaiah, carp., 57½ Hopkins
Toy Napoleon, bk. layer, 214 George
Toys Mike, lab., bds. 67 Oliver
Tozier E. L., b. k., s.w.c. Richmond and Harriet
Tozier Edward, clk., bds. Richmond b. Harriet and Mill Creek
TRABER & AUBERY, (Jacob T. Jr. & Wm. A.,) Wholesale Grocers and Commission Merchants, and Dealers in Pig Iron, 7 Pub. Landing
TRABER Jacob, Jr., (T. & Aubury,) s.s. 3d e. of Kilgour
Tracey A. E., captain, bds. Clifton House

(TRO)   CINCINNATI   (TRU)   DIRECTORY.   (TUL)   819

Trendlecamp Barney, 17 Park
Trener W. K., painter, 100 W. 6th, h. Walnut Hills
Trenkamp Clemens, cigars &c., 462 Main, h. 404 Main
Trenkamp Geo., stone breaker, 96 Bremen
Trenkamp Hy., carp., rear 94 Clay
Trenkel Hy , tailor, 394 Vine
Trenkle Joseph, cof. h., 96 Ham. Road
Trenter James, finisher, wks. 247 W. 5th
Trentman Mille, servt., 337 Longworth
Trentmann Christopher, shoe mkr., bds. 165 Pleasant
Trentmann Francis, lab.. n.s. Cassatt al. b. Sycamore and Main
Trentmann Hy. G., boots and shoes, 165 Pleasant
Trephold Gerhard, cigar mkr., 141 Clark
Trer Lewis. dray, 492 E. Front
Treseler Wm , varnisher, 103 Woodward
Tresh Francis, tailor, bds. 232 Walnut
Tresler Benj., n.e.c. 3d and Wood
Tresler Hy., lab., 74 Abigail
Tressler John, watchman. 29 Webb
Tretsch Margaret, 166 Freeman
Trevor Caleb 399 George
Trevor John B., teacher, bds. 399 George
Trevor Kate, teacher, 399 George
TREVOR Samuel. Secretary O. & M. R. R. office, n s. Front b. Mill and Wood, h. 437 W. 6th
Trevor Susan. teacher, 399 George
Trevor Wm. M., clk. County Clerk's office, h. 437 W. 6th
Triberg John, lab., 62 Spring
Tricke Barney, box mkr., wks. Livingston's, nr. Linn
Trickler Barney, clk., 233 W. 6th
Trickler Hy., 15 Betts
Trier Geo., painter, 525 Freeman
Trier Phillip, lab., wks. Cin. Chemical Laboratory
Triggs Pat., lab., 46 E. 8th e. of Lock
Trimbell Mrs. Ann, laundress, Commercial Hospital
Trimble Geo., express, 14 New
Trimble Isabella, dress mkr., 9 Walnut
Trimble Jas., cof. h., 9 Walnut
Trimble Joseph, b.k., 17 E. M. Canal, b. Reading Road
Trimble Julia A., dress mkr., 9 Walnut
Trimble Pat., lab., 32 Kossuth
Trimble Theodore, tobacconist, 49 Main
Trimble Geo., grocery, 569 Vine
Trimpe Barney, grocery, 101 Hunt
Trimpe Elizabeth, servt., 13 Woodward
Trimpe Frank, pewter worker, 596 Race
Trimpe Hy., tailor, bds. 144 E. Front
Trimpe Hy. A., clk., s.s. Front b. Niagra and Willow
Trimpe Herman H., carp., 14 Hughes
Trimpe John, 796 E. Front
Trimpe John H., boots and shoes, 144 E. Front
Trimpe Martin A., grocery, 792 E. Front h. 796 E. Front
Trimpe Mary A., 596 Race
Trindle John, packer, 668 Sycamore
Trinker John G., bar k., 207 Vine
Triplett Alfred, steward, 29 Mercer
Tripp Albert E., teacher, 4 Dayton
Tritsch Andrew. porter, 166 Freeman
Tritsch Seraphin, butcher, 239 Bremen
Tritschler Chas., shoe mkr., 37 Ham. Road
Tritschler Leo., tailor, 14 Peete
Troddee John, finisher, wks. n.e.c. Walnut and Canal
Troeger Andrew, lab., 109 Buckeye
Troeger John, ck. 40 Main, h. s.w.c. Buckeye and Locust
Troendle Anthony, varnisher, s. w. c. Vine and 12th
Troendler Anton, varnisher, 41 12th
Troescher Catharina, 30 Peete
Troescher Christian F., turner, 475 Vine
Troescher Fred., boots and shoes, 342 Main
Trollman August, carp., e.s. Central Av. b. Liberty and Wade
Tronk John, tailor, 437 Linn
Troops Catharine, bds. 104 Plum
Tropf Jacob, cof. h., s.e.c. Freeman and 8th

Tropper Peter, tailor, e.s. Milk b. Vine and Calhoun
Trosky Fred., rear 420 Sycamore
Trosky Wm., rear 430 Sycamore
Trost Edward. cooper, bds. 624 Vine
Trost John, lab., 150 Charlotte
Trost Joseph, jewelry, 187 Sycamore
Trost Lena. dress mkr., bds. 181 Race
Trost Valentine, lab., w.s. Ridgway al. b. Liberty and 15th
Trost Wm., tailor, 17 Allison
Trost Wolf, mer., 347 Vine
Troste Hy.. sawyer, 8 Pleasant
Trotman Joseph, saddle tree manuf., 413 W. 6th
Trotter Jeremiah, watch mkr., 393 Central Av
Trotter Rudolph, painter, 807 Vine
Trotter Sallie, bds. 191 Longworth
Trotter Wm., barber, 36 Broadway
Trotter Wm., bds. e.s. Macalister b. 4th and 5th
TROUNSTINE A. & J. & CO., (Joseph T., Abram T.. Chas. Kiefer & Henry Hess,) Importers and Dealers in Cloths, Cassimeres and Clothing, s.e. c. Pearl and Vine
TROUNSTINE Abram, (A. & J. T. & Co.,) h. 347 W. 6th
TROUNSTINE Joseph, (A. & J. T. & Co.,) 271 W. 8th
Trout John, meats, 604 E. Front
Troutman John, harness mkr., bds. 160 W. 3d
Trowbridge Ann, h. 378 Race
TROWBRIDGE Geo. W. (Jas. Beatty & Co.,) 378 Race
Trowbridge Minerva, bds. Burt, b. Reed and Broad
Trowbridge Mollie, bds. s.e.c. Front and Reed
Trowbridge Sarah, Burt, b. Reed and Broad
Troy Bridget n.e.c. Elizabeth and John
Troy Chas., lab., 954 E. Front
Troy Edward, baker, wks. 118 W. 5th
Troy Ernst, b.k., 66 W. Pearl, h. 279 W. 8th
Troy I. M. & T. A., (Isaac M. & Theodore A.,) boots and shoes, 128½ W. 3d
Troy Isaac M., (I. M. & T. A. T.,) s.s. Commerce b. Elm and Plum
Troy Jas., shoe mkr., 90 E. 2d
Troy Saml., shoe mkr., 123 Race, h. s.s. Cherry al. b. Elm and Plum
Troy Simeon, blk. smith, bds. s.s. Front e. of Foster
Troy Theodore A., (I. M. & T. A. Troy) bds. s s. Commerce b. Elm and Plum
Truax Ed. A., b.k. 26 Main, h. 395 W. 7th
Trucker Mrs. A., 336 W. 5th
TRUE BENJAMIN C , Justice of the Peace, s.e c. 9th and Central Av., h. 248 Hopkins
Truesdale Chas., foreman Wm. Razor & Co's, h. 291 W. Front
Truesdale Dwight, molder, 42 Stone
Trum August, clk., bds. 113 W. Court
Trum Bernard, dry goods, 77 E. Court, h. 113 W. Court
Truman Wm. H., 240 Baymiller
Trumble John, ven. blind mkr., 34 E. 7th
TRUMBOWER & HICKMAN, (John P. T. & H. J. H.,) Cigars, Tobacco, &c., n.w c 2d and Broadway
TRUMBOWER John P., (T. & Hickman,) res. Campbell county, Ky.
Trumbull Charlotte, 7 Longworth w. of Stone
Trumter John C., whitewasher, 105 W. Liberty
Trunce Theo. P., barber, 108 W. 4th, h. Covington
Tranck Michael, cigar mkr., 437 Linn
Truscteh Casper, blk smith, s.e.c. Brighton and Harrison Pike
Trusell Martin, candle mkr , bds. n.w.c. Front and Central Av.
Truss Jonathan, police, 307 Longworth
Truss Thos., driver, 260 Clinton
Trussell Moses, grocery, s.w.c. Betts and Cutter, h. 75 Betts

Trussen John, lab., 131 W. Front
Trust Isaac, com. mer., 181 Race
Tachira Edward, painter, 59 E. 3d
Tachira Wm , painter, 27 Franklin
Tubbel Joseph, cooper, s. e. c. Bank and Freeman
Tubesing Hy., grocery, 593 Elm
Tuch Jacob, (M. & J. T.,) 274 Central Av.
Tuch Joseph, (M. & J. T.,) 371 Main
Tuch M. & J., (Morris T. & Jacob T.,) clothing, 231 Main
Tuch M. & J., (Morris & Joseph T.,) clothing, 371 Main
Tuch Morris, (M. & J. T.,) 274 Central Av.

TUCHSCHMID ULRICH, Coffee House, 232 E. Front
Tuchter Abraham, lab., rear 55 Woodward
Tucker Ann S., 309 W. 4th
Tucker Geo. H., harness mkr., wks. 33 W. 5th
Tucker Geo. W., harness manuf., 33 W. 5th, h 330 W Court w. of Central Av.
Tucker Geo. W., tailor, 319 W. 3d
Tucker Isaac, pattern mkr., 98 E. 3d e. of Whittaker
Tucker Jas. H., (Gurney & T.,) 17 Observatory Road
Tucker John C., baggage master Ind. & Cin. R. R., bds. 504 W. Front
Tucker Johnson, 102 Clinton
Tucker Rosanna, 36 Mitchell, Mt. Adams
Tucker Wm., 606 Freeman
Tucker Wm. H., civil eng., 395 Longworth
Tudleburg Chas., cigar mkr., 31 E. 3d, h. 21 Gano
Tudor Ann, servt., 430 W. 6th
Tudor Abraham, policeman, 301 W. Liberty
Tudor Eliza D., bds. 247 Plum
Tudor Hugh, boiler mkr., 94 E. 5th
Tudor John M., exchange broker, 113 Walnut, h. 461 W. 9th w. of Central Av.
Tudor John M., jr., clk. 4 Main, h. 461 W. 8th
TUDOR R. & CO., (Richard T. & Wm. Tudor,) Boiler Yard, s.s. 3d b. Butler and M. Canal
TUDOR Richard, (R. Tudor & Co.,) 325 W. 3d
TUDOR Wm., (R. T. & Co.,) 94 E. 5th
Tuemler Hy., miller, 360 Broadway
Tueting Fred., teamster, 11 Mansfield
Tuey John, 647 Sycamore
Tuechter Rudolph, lab., 49 15th

TUFFLI MRS. URSULA, Saloon, 319 W. 6th
Tungis John, water-cart man, rear 72 Hunt
Tugman Anna, dress mkr., bds. 144 W. 7th
Tuhey Matthew, lab., 63 E. 8th, e. of Lock
Tuhl Peter, dray, bds. n.w.c. Pike and Pearl
Tuite Edward, 167 Longworth
Tuite Edward J., jr., clk., 375 Central Av., h. 167 Longworth
Tuiting John G., dray, 13 E. Liberty
Tuke John, feed store, 605 W. 8th
Tuke John, jr., dray, 605 W. 8th
Tulken Jacob, cigar mkr., 11 Mulberry
Tulley John, lab., s.s. Phoebe al. b. Plum and Central Av.
Tulley Julia, s.s. Phoebe al. b. Plum and Central Av.
Tulley Michael, lab., wks. 82 Baymiller
Tulley Michael, lab. h 132 Linn

TULLIS ANDREW J., Attorney at Law and Notary Public, 243 W. 9th
Tullis David, (T. & Stewart,) s.s Taylor al. b. Freeman and Carr
Tullis Hannah, bds. n.e. R. Road e. of Hazen
Tullis & Stewart, (David T. & Jas. H. S) blk. smiths, 620 W. 6th
Tulloch Adam, carp., 522 Freeman

320 (TUR) CINCINNATI (TYL). DIRECTORY. (UMH)

Tully Andrew E., coke mkr., 351 W. 5th
TULLY ANDREW J., Book Keeper n.e.c. Main and 4th, bds. Walnut Street House
Tully Elizabeth, 255 Hopkins
Tully Mrs Mary, Cramsey al. b. Mound and Cutier
Tumber John, cigar mkr., 471 George
Tumer N. P., salesman, bds. 110 W. 6th
Tumey Jeremiah, lab., 419 W. 5th
Tumler Hy., (G. A. Moore & Co.,) 360 Broadway
TUMY Hiram L., (J. C. & H. L. T.,) h. 507 W. 7th
TUMY J. C. & H. L. (Jesse C. & Hiram L.,) Book Binders, 43 Main
TUMY Jesse C., (J. C. & H. L. T.,) h. Newport
Tunemann Bernhard, lab., h. e.s. Ramsey nr. Park al.
Tunemeyer Fred., cigar mkr., 25 Ham. Road
Tungelas A., tinner, wks. n.w.c. Race and 2d
Tunne Anthony, blksmith, 49 W. Liberty
Tunney Michael, lab., n.w.c. 7th and Plum
Tunney Wm., clk , 50 Rittenhouse
Tunnicliff John. stoves, &c., w.s. Celestial b. 3d and Observatory Road
Turajaki Peter, boots and shoes, 101 Elder
Tnrbit Nicholas, s.s. 6th e. of Lock
Turcka Herman H., lab., 416 Longworth
Turcke Chas., b.k. Monnig & Artman's, bds. 323 Walnut
Turcke Rev. Charles E., 323 Walnut
Turcke Sophia, teacher, h. Lutheran church, w.s. Walnut b. 8th and 9th
Turling Bernard, carp., s.s. Hopkins b. Linn and Baymiller
Turmath Henry, wks. 340 W. 3d
Turnace James, tinner, bds. 445 Main
Turner B. F., dry goods, 367 W. 6th
Turner Barr, barber, Dennison House, h. 20 McAlister
Turner David, cof. h., 138 W. Front
Turner E. B., 114 George
Turner Edward, cigar mkr., n.e.c. Milton and Sycamore
Turner Edwin. phys , 315 W. 8th
Turner Eliza, s.w.c. 3d and Whittaker
Turner Elizabeth. 24 Harrison
Turner Everard B., bk. binder, 190 W. 7th
Turner Frank, n.s. Harrison Pike b. Brighton and Western Av
Turner Frederick, lab., 90 Baum
Turner Henry, grocer, n.e.c. Pendleton and Abigail
Turner Henry, lab., n.s. Channing b. Price and Young
Turner Isaac, bds. Dumas Hotel
Turner J. D., bds. Gibson House
Turner Rev. J. D., church s.s. 6th b. Race and Elm
Turner James, shoe mkr., w.s. Stone al. b. 6th and Longworth
Turner James P., furniture, 163 W, 5th
Turner John, 66 E. 7th
Turner John, s.w.c. Front and Broad
Turner John, clk., bds. w.s. Pendleton b. Woodward and Abigail
Turner John, cooper, 700 Freeman
Turner John, waiter, Walnut St House
Turner Joseph, foreman Pierces' factory, 46 Baum
Turner Joseph, bk. layer, bds. n.e.c. Central Av. and Pearl
Turner Joseph S., cab mkr., 303 Water
Turner & Kearney, (Theodore T. & Edward K.,) boots and shoes, 135 W. 4th
Turner Maria, bds 272 W. 8th
Turner Mary, 41 New
Turner N. P., clk , bds. 110 W. 6th
Turner Robert, shoe mkr., n.e.c. Lewis and Front
Turner Samuel, books, s.w.c. Pearl and Broadway, h. Newport
Turner Samuel, ins. agt., 55 Cutter
Turner Samuel C , druggist, 409 Main, h. 52 W. 9th
Turner Mrs. Susan, 243 W. Court

Turner Theodore, (T. & Kearney,) 135 W. 4th
Turner Thos., lab., s.s. Friendship al. b. Pike and Butler
Turner Thomas, lab., s.s. 6th e. of Lock
Turner Thomas, (Chos. T. & Co.,) bds. Clermont Hotel
Turner Thomas, stone cutter, n.s. Corporation al. b. Young and Price
Turner Thomas & Co., boots, shoes, &c., 75 E. Pearl
Turnette Wm., lab., bds. n.e.c. 7th and Central Av
Turnpaugh James. mech., Richmond b. Harriet and Mill Creek
Turrah Annie, tailoress, bds. 397 Broadway
Turtle Richard, lab., s.s. 6th e. of Lock
Tussey Wm. H., butcher, 73 Bank
Tutor John, shoe mkr., wks 310 Main
Tuttle Charles, publisher, 111 Main, bds. 140 E. 5th
TUTTLE E. W. & CO., Exchange and Banking House, n.w.c. 3d and Sycamore
TUTTLE Elias W., (E. W. T. & Co.,) 54 Milton
Tuttle John F., bk. layer, 155 Baymiller
Tuttle John N.. blksmith., 352 Central Av., h. 68 Richmond b. Mound and John
Tutton Sarah, 357 George
Tuxworth Andrew J., moldei, bds. 70 Clinton
Twachtmann Christian, policeman, 520 Race
Twachtmann John, policeman, 457 W. 2d
Twachtmann Lewis, cab. mkr., 63 Pleasant
Twaddle John, lab., 120 Vanhorne
TWEED A. D. E., (T. (T. & Sibley,) 175 Elm
TWEED & ANDREWS, James A., John P. T., B. F. Brannen & Daniel A.,) Wholesale Grocers, 31 and 33 W. Pearl
Tweed Evans A. B., com. mer., 175 Elm
Tweed James, butcher, n.s. Garden b. Freeman and Western Av
TWEED.John P., (T. and Andrews,) 426 W. 6th
TWEED & SIBLEY, (A. D. E. T., J. W. S. & J, H. French,) Flour and Produce Dealers and Commission Merchants, 40 Walnut
Tweedy Ann, 19 E. 7th
Twehus Gertrude, servt., 592 Race
Twehus Margaret, servt., 592 Race
Twenhofel Benjamin, rope mkr., 442 W 2d
Twiford Catharine, bds. 295 Findlay
Twiford Henry, finisher, wks. n.e.c. Walnut and Canal
Twilling Henry, bk. mkr., s.e c. Dudley and Liberty
TWITCHELL Henry, (James Forster jr. & Co.,) 206 Everett
Twitchell John, 103 Broadway
Twitchell Thos. J., clk., bds. Dennison House
Twohig Hannah, b. h., 286 W. 6th
Twohig James, carp., s.s. 6th b. Broadway and Culvert
Twohig James, boot mkr., n.w.c. Br'dway and 6th
Twombly Mary A., teacher. Industrial School, n.e.c. Race and Commerce
Tydd Thomas R., printer Cin. Gazette, 138 Longworth
Tydings Eliza, 334 W. 6th
Tyfe Samuel, clk. 100 W. 5th, h. 132 Broadway
TYLER Edward M., (Applegate, T. & Co.,) bds. Gibson House
Tyler Henry, barber, 4 W. 4th, h. 235 Brodway
Tyler Wellington C., principal Cin. Female Seminary, s.w c. 7th and Mound, h. 354 W. 4th
TYLOR Albert O., (T. & Barrett), h. Avondale
TYLOR & BARRETT, (Albert O. T. & Silas M. B.,) Wholesale Wood and Willow Ware Dealers, n.e.c. Front and Walnut

TYLOR Erastus D., (Sam'l Cloon & Co.), h. Louisville, Ky.
TYLOR James E., (Sam'l Cloon & Co.,) h. Avondale
TYLOR Sam'l T., (Sam'l Cloon & Co.,) h. Louisville, Ky.
Tynan Mrs. Bernhard, 115 Everett
Tynan Jane, seamstress 205 Cutter
Tyrell John, shoe mkr., 52 Baum
Tyrell Thomas & Co., boots, shoes, &c., 74 Canal
Tyrell Wm. sen., shoe mkr., 52 Baum
Tyrell Wm. jr., shoe mkr., 52 Baum

U

Ude Augustus, box mkr., bds. al. b. 3d and Pearl and Lawrence and Pike
Uderstadt August, shoemkr, 639 Vine
Uderstadt Chas., shoemkr, 639 Vine
Uderstadt Hy. E., shoemkr, 639 Vine
Uetrecht Christian, porter, n. e. c. Race and 15th
Uetrecht Mrs. Dorothea, seamstress, 20 Madison
Uetrecht Wm., lab., 25 Madison
Uehlein Adam, basket mkr., 37 Green
Uffenheimer Bernhard, 475 Race
Uffman Hy., cab. mkr., 131 Clark
Uffman Henry, cigar mkr., 76 Rittenhouse
Uhl Anthony, cof. h., 67 Buckeye
Uhl David, teamster. 298 W. Front
Uhl John, miller, 104 Abigail
Uhland Herman H., mason. 1 Mulberry
Uhlenberg Mary A., 67 Rittenhouse
Uhlenhacke Wm., cooper, 20 Buckeye
Uhlfelder Loeb. sausage mkr. 184 W. 6th
Uhlhorn John Y., printer, 34 Pleasant
Uhlmann Frederick H., groceries, 41 Elder
Uhlrich Frederick, chair mkr., wks. John Mitchell's {men
Uihlein Philipp J., musician, 96 Bremen
Ulam Joseph, grocer, 244 Cutter
Ulbrenk Herman, lab., 20 Race
Ulchaver George, cab. mkr., 17 Madison
Ulerick Charles, cab. mkr., 641 Clay
Ulery Wm., clk., 101 W. 4th, room 25 Selve's bldg
Ulland Frederick, confec., 104 Gest
Ulland George, carp., wks. n. s. Canal, w. of Elm
Ullent George, carp., 18 E. Liberty
Ullman Daniel, broker, 60 W. 6th, h. 30 E. 6th
Ullman Jacob, 147 W. Pearl
Ullmer John, e. s. Western Av. b. Bank and Harrison Pike
Ullmer John P., tailor, 90 Bremen
Ullrick Valentine, molder, 59 Dudley
Ulm Emil, cigar mkr., 553 Elm
Ulm Mary, seamstress, 533 Elm
Ulmann Hy., fruit dealer, 26 Gano
Ulmer Andrew, tailor, 159 W. 8th
Ulmer Conrad, hats and caps. 280 Main
Ulmer Conrad, paper hanger, bds. 442 Main
ULMER FREDERICK, Hats and Caps, 113 Main h. 106 13th
Ulmer John, tailor, 54 Sycamore, h. Madison, Ind.
Ulmer John, waiter, Gibson House
Ulmer John M., tailor, s. e. c. 7th and Central Av
Ulmer Joseph, dray, 177 Clinton
Ulmer Julia E., 56 Rittenhouse
Ulpmann Hy., lab., 615 Race
Ulrich A. F., harness mkr., 89 Main
Ulrich Anthony, chandler, 284 W. Liberty
Ulrich Augustus, dining saloon, 60 Broadway
Ulrich Chas., cab. mkr., 644 Race
Ulrich Frederick, driver, 19 E. Liberty
Ulrich Heinrich, blksmith, wks. s.w.c. Elm and Front
Ulrich Valentine, molder, 57 Dudley
Ulrich Wm., cigars, &c., 133 Central Av
Ulrici Frederick, driver, 19 E. Liberty
Ultzhoefer George, cab. mkr , 17 Madison
Umbert May, 293 Water
Umevehr Frederick, varnisher, 115 Carr
Umhols John, col. h., 41 12th

CINCINNATI .(VAL) DIRECTORY. (VAN) 321

yer &	Urban Andrew, salesman, 441 Walnut	Vallandingham Geo., lab., wks. N. W. Thomas & Co's
'al Av	Urban Chas., lab., 105 W. Liberty	
s. Mc-	Urban Herman. foreman, 441 Walnut	Vallandingham Nelson W., bklayer, 60 Laurel
	Urban John, safe mkr., 53 Plum	
). Lo-	Urban John jr., wire mkr., bds 53 Plum	Vallandingham Rich., foreman 284 Sycamore, h. 46 Richmond
	Urban Joseph, brush mkr., 93 Bremen h 93 Bremen	
		VALLEAU Chas. M., (V. & Jacobs), h Clifton
ing b.	Urban Wilhelmine, 441 Walnut	
	Urd Jacob, butcher, 54 Dunlap	VALLEAU & JACOBS, (Chas. M. V.
York	Urlage Arnold, lab., 514 Woodward	& Enoch J.), Iron Jail Builders 86, 88, 90 & 92 Elm
	Urlage Bernard, cooper, n.w.c. Wade and Baymiller	
nt		Vallette Hy., 347 W 4th
	Urlage John A., lab., 514 Main	Vallis Rebecca, 22 Stone
n Av.	Uruer David, b.k. s.w.c Canal and Walnut, h. 60 Franklin	Vallo & Bagge, (Hy V. & Frank B.), meats, 98 E. Liberty
. 15th	Urner Edward C., clk. National Ins. Co. s.w.c. Main and Front, h. 94 E. 3d	Vallo Hy., (V. & B.) 118 Abigail
		Van John, salesman, 17 W. 5th, h. 130 George
s. 15th	Urner Hy. C., secy. National Ins Co. s.w c. Main and Front, h. 94 E. 3d	
		Van Louis N , sheet iron worker, 232 Water
r	Urner Nathan D., 94 E 3d	
arl	Uruer Wm., clk., 60 Franklin	Vanaghtovan Antony, cooper, w.s. Pole b. 2d and Pearl
Linn	Urwiler Geo. S., b.k., n.e.c Vine and 2d bds. 200 Richmond	
		Vanaghtovan Max., 18 Park
56 W.	Urwiler John, pattern mkr, 200 Richmond	Vanamor Barney. lab., wks. n e.c. Walnut and Canal
	Usher James, 132 Baymiller	Van Amringe Benj. F. b.k bds 162 Barr
entral	Usnet Frank. shoemkr, bds. 23 Water	Van Amringe Edwin A., b.k., 30 Walnut, h. 162 Barr
	Usbey Michael, butcher, s.s. Dayton b. Freeman and Coleman	
s. 728		Van Amringe Eliza, 162 Barr
	Utley A., clk., U. S. express, bds. 162 Elm	Van Amringe Ella L., teacher, 162 Barr
		Van Amringe John. b.k., bds. 102 Barr
	Utley Carlton, mach, 391 George	Van Antwerp Lewis, b.k. 137 Walnut, h. 443 W. 8th
2TER	Utley Hasting. boots and shoes, s.e.c. Front and Walnut, h. 391 George	
		Vanauker John D , clk. at City clerks office, h. 39 York
	Utt Frank . lab., wks., 25 Water	
4½ W.	Utt Louisa, w.s. Langdon al. b. 6th and 7th [Clay	Vanausdal Mary, bds. 61 E. 4th
		Vanausdol Garrett, 363 W. 6th
ANY,	Uttendoerfer Gustave, cab. mkr., 142	Vanausdol Lydia J., n.e.c. Wade and Freeman
'., E.	Uttendoerfer Otto, paper carrier, 142 Clay	
5 Pub-		Vanausloi Mary R., bds. 85 Mill
	Utter Elisa, servt., 180 Broadway	Vanbeuschoteu Benj., carp., rear 956 E. Front
! OF-	Utterman Christopher wagon mkr., 10 Buckeye	
s.e. c.		Vanburkalow Franklin. eng., 145 E 3d
	Utz Louis H., clk., s.w.c. Race and Longworth, h. 134 W. 9th	Van Brunhorst Anton, lab., 169 Linn
bigail		Van Camp, James H., salesman, 56 W. Pearl, b. 67 W· 8th
Court	Utz Andreas, flour store, 65 Elder	
, s. w.	Utz Chas. P., grocary, n.e.c. Richmond and Cutter	Vance Amos S., carp., 1292 E. Front
		Vance Catharine, 101 Hopkins
58 W.	Utz Conrad, tailor's, 46 Elder	Vance Chas., saw mill 1297 E. Front
	Utz John, blacksm'h, Canal h 124 W 9th w. of Central	Vance E., land ag't., 183 Walnut
lding,		Vance Elisha, 112 George
	Utzuber Peter, 2 amber, 70 Plum	Vance Ella J., teacher, E. Front b. Hill and Stone
OUSE,	Uzuber Peter, butcher, s.e.c. Plum and 2d	
, Cus-		Vance James, lab., 1212 E. Front
c. 4th		Vance James L. carraige mkr. 197 Poplar
		Vance Wm. D., carp., h. 1253 E Front
W. 4th	**V**	Van Cleeff Herman, dry goods, 58 Elder
1 CO.,		
	Vaal August, lab., 147 Pleasant	Vandenbergh John A. A, awning mkr. 28 Franklin
Race	Vabor John F., porter, bds. 227 E. 5th	
at and	Vagt T., cigars &c , 213 Walnut, h. n.w. c. Elm and Charles	Vande Beugel Emanuel, clothing, 239 W. 5th
rs Of-	Vahan Philip, lab., s.s. 8th b. Broadway and Sycamore	Vanderbilt Albert L., printer, bds. s.e.c. 9th and Walnut
pector		
le, In-	Vahn Michael, lab., n.s. Montgomery pike nr. Reading Road	VANDEBBILT W. C. (David Gibson & Co.) 261 Vine
House		
ine	Vahrenholz Charlotte, 563 Walnut	Vandergrift Benj. B., lumber yard, 121 Water
corner	Vahria Herman, mach., n.s 6th b. Carr and Harriet	
		Vanderberg James. saddler 35 Elizabeth
ustom	Vaiglinger Mars 504 Walnut	Vandervort Robert, billiards, 74 W. 3d bds. 316 W. 3d
Vine,	VAIL & DANBY, (Hiram S. V. & Chas. D.,) Lumber Dealers, 344 Broadway	
		Van Deursen Peter. auditor, O. & M. R. R. n.s. Front b Mill and Wood, h. 311 Longworth
ce, 101	VAIL Hiram S.. (V. & D..) 58 Franklin	
) Pub-	Vakeler Elizabeth, bds. 33 Gest	
	Vakner Conrad, painter 246 Clark	Vandever Peter, eng., bds. s.w.c. 5th & Smith
y, 62	Valentine Fred., cab. mkr., 72 12th	
	Valentine James, shoemkr, n.s. Rail Road e. of Wallace al	Van DeWater, bk. binder, wks. s.w.c. Main and 8th
dward		
	Valentine Lyda, h. s.s Front e of Vance	Vandivier & Powell Wm. V. & Watt E. P.) saloon, 98 Sycamore
Carr	Valentine Saml. G., 267½ George	
Eden	Valentine Wm. teamster, s e.c. Front and Ferry	Vandivier Wm., awning manuf., 49 E. 3d, h. 49 George
	Valentine's Express Co 3 E Front Enoch Taylor, agt	Van Dokkiem Lewis tailor, e.s. Goose al b Liberty and 15th
	Valerius Mark,. cab. mkr., 196 Clinton	
	Valkenhaus John H., stone cutter 162 Bank	VAN DOKKUM & FORMAN, (John J. Van D. & Wm. H. F.) Merchant Tailors, 125 Main
V. 7th,		
	Volkers Peter, frame manuf., 336 Main	VAN DOKKUM John J., (Van D & F.) h. 158 W Court w.of Central Av
more	Vallandingham A. W., foreman, N. W. Thomas & Co's	
113 W.		Vandolah Mrs. Mary, 130 Laurel
	Vallandingham Anderson W., bklayer, n.s. Poplar b. Freeman and Western Av	Vandousan James, clk., L. M. Depot bds. 22 Baum
nerce		
amore		Van Duck Cornelius, bar k. 14 Bremen
chell,	Vallandingham Anna E., teacher, 3d w. of Freeman	Van Duncan, Eliza, 207 9th w. of Central Av
32		

322 (VAN) CINCINNATI (VEL) DIRECTORY. (VIE)

Vanduzen Benj. C., sheet iron manufac., 9 E. Front, res. Newport
Vanduzen Ezra, W., (G. W. Coffin & Co.) res. Deerfield O.
Van Duzen James. clk. L. M. R. R., h. e.s. Baum n. of 3d
Van Dyke ———, peddler, bds. Indiana House [7th
Van Dyke Benj., watch mkr., bds. 53 W
Vanfelde Geo., huckster, 28 Dudley
Van Gorder Rosa. 119 W. 5th
VAN HAMM WASHINGTON, Attorney at Law, Office 65 W. 3d h. 292 W. 4th
Van Harlingen G. H., salesman, bds. 239 Race
Van Hart Emanuel, teamster, 405 John
Van Hart Jacob, teamster. 49 Laurel
Van Hart Mahlon, student, bds. 49 Laurel
Van Hart Thomas, teamster 52 Hopkins
Van Horn Cornelius, lab., bds. 566 Race
Van Horn Francis M., painter, bds. 93 Gest
Van Horn John, baggage master, n s. Fulton Av. e. of Washington
Van Horn Joseph, tailor, Pavillion near Observatory
Van Houten C. & J. B., (Chas. & J. B.) silverware manufac., n e.c. George and Central Av
Van Houten Chas. (C. & J. B. Van H.)
Van Houten Jos., (C. & J. B. Van H.)
Van Houten Margaret, 42 Kossuth
Van Hove Frank, 220 E 6th
Vanke Barney, carp., 498 W. Front
Vankirk Lucinda, bds 441 W. 7th
Van Kooten Herman, broom manuf., 102 Betts
Vanlahr John H, bds. 1080 Central Av
Van Leunen Gerrard, wig mkr, 79 W. 4rh
Van Leunen John sewing mach. shuttle mkr., 189 Linn
Van Lewis N., sheet iron worker, 232 Water
Van Liew Herman, foreman, 23 Grand
Van Liew Ira C., dray, 335 W 9th w. of Central Av
Van Loo Leon, photographer, 24 W 4th bds. n.e.c. 6th and Race
Van Lue Hurmon, painter, 23 Grant
Vanlunen Cornelius, blksmith, 129 Linn
Van Matre Hy., 130 W. 9th
Vann Walter, ointment mkr. 145 George
Vanname Thomas, R. R. conductor, 422½ George
Vannarp Lewis, bk. binder, 443 W. 8th
Vannewman Cornelius, finisher, w.s. Linn b. Clark and Court
Vanpelt James. car painter, 35 Hathway
VANPELT M. C., Commission Merchant, 361 Walnut, h. 373 W 8th
Van Pelt Wm. H., finisher, 246 Cutter
Vansant Elizabeth, Richmond b. Harriet and Mill Creek
Vansant Higbee, caulker, s.s. Front b. Broad and Waldon
Vansant James E., 152 W. Front
Vansant Saml., hatters goods 117 Main h. n.w.c. Elm and Front
Vansant Wm. A., clk. 28 E. 3d
Vanslick Mary, 1212 E. Front
Van Stratton Robt., peddler 147 George
Van Tielen Wm., porter, 459 Schiller
VanTicin Leonard, 112 Hunt
VonVulkenburgh Hy., b. k., 171 E. 3d
VanVliet Jane, b. h 10 Clinton
VanWest Abraham, peddler, 215 Elm
VanWinkle & Dussert, (Wm. Von W. & Thomas D.,) attys., 8 W. 3d
VanWinkle Wm., (Van W. & Dussert,) 413 W. 7th
VanWordragen Hy., cab. mkr., 107 W. M. Canal
VanWordragen John, cab. mkr., bds. 107 W. M. Canal
VAN WORMER ASA, Wholesale and Retail Grocer and Produce Merchant, 57 W. Court
VanWormer Erastus, dray, rear 461 Elm
Van Wormer John, cab. mkr., 165 Richmond

VanZant Chas. G., driver, 26 R. 6th
VanZile Almira P., dress mkr., n.w.c. Elm and 5th, up stairs
VanZile Mary, servt., 275 W. 9th
VanZyle Fanny, servt., 21 Chestnut
Varhan Frederick, barber, 336 W. 5th
Varllmer Frederick, shoe mkr., 404 Longworth
Varmin John, lab., wks. Deer Creek, foot of 8th
Varnau August, shoe mkr., 57 Ham. Road
Varney Wm. R., cooper, c. Weller and Skaats
Varnhomberg Joseph, foreman, 524 W. 3d
Varniker Barney, lab., 131 Everett
Varsel Nick, varnisher, 595 Race
Varwig Hy, bakery, 149 W. Court, w. of Central Av.
Varwig Louisa, 84 Bremen
Vaske Elizabeth, 46 Findlay
Vatchet Francis, grate setter, 232 Barr
Vatchet Wm. D, 232 Barr
Vatt Toelke, cigar mkr., 363 Elm
Vatter Hy., cooper, s. s. Charlotte b. Linn and Baymiller
VATTIER JOHN L., Physician and Surgeon, Office and Residence, 160 W. 9th
Vaughan Charles H., Jr., salesman, 70 W. Pearl, b. 318 Baymiller
Vaughan John, n. h. s. Railroad, e. of Hazen
Vaughan N. F., compositor Cin. Gazette, h. 110 W. 6th
Vaughan Patrick, wks. J. Whitaker's, Deer Creek Valley
Vaughan Wm., clk., 34 W. Pearl, bds. 318 Baymiller
Vaughen Antony, lab., 546 W. Front
Vaughn Eli, carp., n. s. Railroad, e. of Hazen
Vaunu John, teamster, n. s. Railroad, e. of Lewis
Vayhinger Frederick, peddler, 26 Franklin
Veatch Chas. W., carriage painter, 392 W. 3d
Veckel Hy., cab. mkr. 547 Walnut
Vedder Conrad, grocery, n.e.c. Woodward and Broadway
Vedder Hy., clk., 907 Linn
Vedder Rudolph, grocery, 207 Linn
Vedelmann Hermann, lab., 139 Pleasant
Veder Jacob, tailor, s. s. Ringgold b. Young and Price
VEERKAMP BERNHARD, Coach and Carriage Manufacturer, 469 Walnut, h. 55 Jackson
Veerkamp Geo., blk.smith, 1 Lucy
Veenema A & Co.,(Anthony V. & Anthony Sieverink,) grocery, 566 Race
Veeneman Anthony, (V. & Co.,) 566 Race
Veeneman H., shoemkr., 62 W. Front
Veeneman Hermann, shoemkr., 276 W. Front
Veeneman John H. D., shoemkr., 276 W. Front
Veenemann Bernhard, cof. h., 556 Walnut
Veenemann Hy., shoemkr., 556 Walnut
Veenemann John, shoemkr., 295 W. Front
Veñan Christian, bds. 100 Sycamore
Vehorn August, cof. h., 226 Linn
Vohring Barney, brk.mk., s.e.c. Dudley and Liberty
Vohrkampf Lewis, porter, 99 Walnut
Veil Alex., peddler, 487 Central Av
Veinhaye Hy., porter, Henrie House
Veissmann Jacob, tanner, bds. 701 Elm
Voit Philipp, porter, 1019 Central Av.
Veitermann Frank, bds. 703 Vine
Veith Sigismund, teacher, h. 201½ W. 4th
Veldich Frank, chairmkr., 595 Race
Veldman Johanna, n. s. Mercer b Vine and Walnut
Veldmann Mariues, painter, 296 Linn
Veldmann Mary, 60 Mound
Velingt Mrs. Mary, 367 Linn
Velka John H., shoemkr., bds. w. s Park b. 2d and W. W. Canal
Velatte Arthur E., clk., 90½ Barr

Vellatte Mary L., 95½ Barr
Vellengerhoff Fred., stone mason, 22 Mansfield
Velp George, 76 Abigail
Velp George, lab., n.w.c. Wade and Baymiller
Velp Hy., cooper, w. s. Green b. Campbell al. and Plum
Velpeau Eugene, (Jackson Herbert & Co.,) 167 Sycamore
Veluve John T., (V. & Kohrmann) 680 W.6th
Veluve & Kohrmann, (John T. V. & Henry K.,) painters, 680 W. 6th
Venbergan Frederick, hostler, n. w. c. Plum and 2d
Vencler John H., lab., n.w.c. Stone and 3d
Vender George, plasterer, 615 Central Av.
Venneman Antony, clk., 442 W. 2d, h. 463 W. 3d
Venneman Dina, servt., 499 W. 5th
Venneman Hy., painter, 23 Woodward
Veneman Johanna, bds. 494 Main
Venstrope Barney, lab., 191 W. Canal
VENT Chas. F., (V. Starr & Co.,)
VENT, STARR & CO., (Chas. F. V. & Edgar P. S.,) Western & Southern School Agency and Publishers, 6 W. 4th
Venter Margaret, 40 Mohawk
Venttering Theodore, chair mkr., 512 Walnut
Verchan Adolph, cig mkr., 52 Allison
Verdin John, lab., wks. n.w.c. Plum and Vine
Verdin Michael, town clock manuf., 396 Vine
VERDIN Nicholas, (M. Werk & Co.,) Marienheim, France
Verbase Hy., mineral water manuf., n.s. c. Lodge and Gano, h. 224 Race
Verkamp Geo. H., shoe fitter, 144 Laurel
VERKAMP Geo. H., (Richter & V.,) 420 Longworth
Verkoss Bernard, lab., 391 W. Liberty
Vermillion James, shoe mkr., 302 Plum
Verndren John, finisher, wks. s.e.c. Walnut and Canal
Vernezobre Edward, waiter, s.w.c. Race and 3d
Vernhomberg Joseph, miller, 524 W. 3d
Verschoor John, awnings &c, 28 Franklin
Vert David, bksmith, 48 Elm
Vessels Hy., h. n.w.c. Liberty and Baymiller
Vessenburgh Frederick, boiler mkr., 178 E. Pearl
Vesten Anton, tailor, s.s. Cross b. North Elm and Hamburg
Vestirfelt Elizabeth, seamstress, wks. 53 W. 4th
VETERINARY SURGEON, John Wilson, Brown's Livery Stable, 9 E. 6th
Vether John, watchman, 479 Race
Vetier John, mason, s. e. c. Jones and Melancthon
Vetman John, 75 Mohawk
Vett John, bk. mkr., 31 Jackson
Vette Gerhard Hy., blksmith, rear 176 Clay
Vette Hy., blksmith, wks. 602 Main
Vetter George, rope mkr., 75 Buckeye
Vetter George, shoe mkr., 330½ W. 6th
Vetter John, fireman, 479 Race
Vetter Josephine, 26 Mercer
Vetter Muthine, lab., s.w.c. Freeman and Dayton
Vetter Peter, sawyer, 533 Sycamore
Veve Jennie, bds. 96 E. 4th
Vibbard Timothy, produce, 269 W. 6th
Vick Frederick, porter, 69 Walnut
Vicka Julius, cab. mkr., 236 Clark
Vickman Joseph, soap manufac., s.s. Oliver b. John and Linn, h. s. e. c. Oliver and Linn
Victor Edward, huckster, 22 Hamer
Victor Jacob, (M. Hess & Co.,) 100 W. 9th
Vidder Hy., shoe mkr., 524 Sycamore
Viebe Hermann, shoe mkr., 60 13th
Vieman Ernst, cab. mkr., 116 Betts

'ront	Voellmecke Frederick, organ builder, 165 W. 5th	Volk John, cigar mkr., w. s. Franz b. Elder and Findlay
Front	Voellmelke Frederick, carver, bds. 165 Carr	Volk John V., lab , 104 Bremen
ıen b.	Voellmelke Joseph, cab. mkr., 165 Carr	Volk Rudolf, cooper, n. s. Bernard b. Division and Brighton, bds. s. w. c. Harrison Pike and Brighton
Biden-	Voet Clements, cof. h., 7 Landing b. Broadway and Ludlow, h. 68 E. Pearl	Volka Gerhard, lab., 364 Broadway
ny V.		Volkart Caspar, carp., 142 Buckeye
!., 25	Vogedes Bernhard, tailor, s. w. c. Race and Elder	Volker Philip, lab., rear 680 Main
	Vogeding August, bakery, 314 W. 5th	Volker Barney, dray, n.e.c. Vine and 2d
ıl Ve-	Vogeding Wm., tailor, 216 Laurel	Volkert Adam, cigar mkr., 680 Main
0 Syc-	Vogel Adam, brewer, wks. s.w.c. Plum and Canal	Volkert Philip, hatter, 680 Main
		Volkmann John, rag dealer, 612 Race
fouse	Vogel Albert, carriage mkr., n.s. 6th b. Carr and Harriet	Volkner Gerrard, lab., wks. 196 W. Pearl
lurnet	Vogel August, coach mkr., bds. 90 E. 2d	VOLKSBLATT, Stephen Molitor, Proprietor, Office Court House Building, s.e.c. Main and Court
ı, 183	Vogel Charles, cof. h., 461 Walnut	
	Vogel Charles, porter, George b. Linn and Baymiller	
. e. dT		VOLKSFRUEND, DAILY & WEEK-LY, Joseph A. Hemann Editor and Proprietor, Office s.w.c. Vine and Longworth
	Vogel Christian, turner, al. b. Vine and Walnut and 13th and Mercer	
nore	VOGEL FREDERICK, jr., Family Grocery, n.e.c. Clinton and John	
Hop-		Volkson Mary, servt., 290 George
		Volkweisz Jacob, tailor, 29 Buckeye
:. Syc-	Vogel Frederick, tailor, 205 Clinton	Voll Casper, 18 Abigail
	Vogel Frederick, turner, 292 W. Front	Voll Catharine, 46 15th
nt	Vogel George, carp., 89 Martin	Voll Ferdinand, planer, 104 Bremen
Cen-	Vogel Jacob, huckster, 983 Central Av.	Voll Frederick, molder, 46 15th
	Vogel John, boots and shoes, 62 W. Liberty	Voll George, lock smith, 554 Walnut
		Voll Hy., molder, 46 15th
	Vogel Mary, rear 80 Peete	Voll Joseph, varnisher, bds. 46 15th
y and	Vogel Wm. J., tailor, n.e.c. Clinton and John	Voll Michael, butcher, 569 Walnut
		Voll Michael, shoe mkr., e.s. Vine b. Calhoun and Auburn Av.
'. Lib-	Vogelbach Francis, X. cof. h., 613 Vine	
	Vogelbach Michael, lab., 673 W. 6th	Vollbert Wendelin, tailor, 55 Elder
ıh	Vogeler Benjamin, 336 Central Av.	Vollmecke Francis, paper carrier, n.s. Taylor b. Freeman and Carr
e and	Vogeler Edward, tailor, 13 Madison	
	Vogeler Frederick, (Tafel & V.,) n.w.c. Broadway and Franklin	Vollmeke Frank, teacher, n.s. Taylor al. b, Canal and 6th
	Vogeler Wm., b. k., 51 Bremen	Vollmer John, porter, rear 466 Walnut
E. 6th	Vogelsang Hy., lab., 145 Abigail	Vollweiler Wendelin, cab. mkr., 37 Moore
	Vogelsang John H., lab., 293 W. Front	
	Voghmann Herman, lab., 116 Clay	Volmer Caroline, 29 Clinton
th, h.	Voght Hy., blksmith, 101 Hunt	Volmer Frederick, cooper, 19 Mercer
	Voglebach Frank, blksmith, 613 Vine	Volmer Mrs. Mary, 588 Race
Hos-	Vogler Edward, tailor, 465 Elm	Volmer Sophia, bds. 29 Clinton
	Vogler Frederick, druggist 427 Broadway	Volmer Theodore, lab., 512 Walnut
ır and		Volpert Frank, carriage mkr., Hay al. b. 13th and Mercer and Vine and Walnut
	Vogler Wm., clk., 51 Bremen	
	Vogt Chas., porter, 41 Mansfield	
'ront	Vogt Charlotte, servt., 287 Longworth	Volpert Frank, saddler, bds. 252 Walnut
y	Vogt Christian, 529 Sycamore	
tin	Vogt Ciriak, lab., 65 Buckeye	Volpert Franz, blk. smith, e.s. Walnut b. 13th and Allison
ıy	Vogt Clements, chair mkr., wks. H. Clostermann's	
au b.		Volpert Joseph, lab., 46 Dunlap
r., &	Vogt George H., dry goods, 97 W. Court	Vois Chas., finisher, 28 Broadway
		Volter Christ, tailor, s.e.c. Young and Ringgold
	Vogt Hy., carp., 36 Lodge	
ı near	Vogt Hy., lab., wks. Wood and McCoy's	Voltering Hy., sawyer, wks. n.e.c. Elm and Canal
Wood-	Vogt Hy., lab., 99 W. Court	Voltermire Geo., lab., wks. s.w.c. W. W. Canal and Smith
	Vogt Hy., lab., 25 Buckeye	
	Vogt Hy., clk., bds. 97 W. Court	Volters Anthony, lab., 1 Lucy
ilding	Vogt Herman, shoe mkr., 53 Jones	Voltz Felicitas, 18 Hamer
	Vogt John, lab., n. s. Poplar b. Freeman and Western Av.	Voltz Joseph, trunk mkr., 149 Hopkins
h. 484	Vogt Jacob, A., carp., 197 Carr	Voltz Nicholas, 26 Brighton
	Vogt Jacob L., carp., 197 Carr	Volvert Rogers, w.s. Vine b. Milk and Mulberry
h and	Vogt John A., cigar mkr., 600 Race	
	Vogt John G., baker, 471 Vine	Volz Barbara, seamstress, bds. 473 Walnut
	Vogt Joseph, cook, 25 Hughes	
	Vogt Louis, turner, 41 Mansfield	Volz Constantine, grocery, 664 Main
	Vogt Mary, 12 Green	Volz Cosmos, 664 Main
	Vogt Victoria, 12 Green [ant	Volz Ernst, cap mkr., 55 Woodward
Rich-	Vogtmann Herman, porter, 38 Pleasmore	Volz Geo., tanner, wks. s s. 6th b. Harriett and Horne
c. Ca-	Voige George, brush mkr., 531 Sycamore	Volz Geo., peddler, 34 Hughes
nd	Voight Charles, varnisher, 395 Walnut	Volz Ignatz, cigar mkr., 18 Hamer
Hop-	Voight Lewis, paper hanger, 50 Richmond	VOLZ LEONHARD, Coffee House, 641 Vine
nut	Voigt Caspar, lab., 108 Ham. Road	
	Voigt Chas., varnisher, 593 Walnut	Volz Leonard. cof. h... e.s. Bremen b. Elder and Findlay
	Voigt Hy., compositor, 531 Sycamore	
Foun-	Voigt Jacob, finisher, 13 Mary	Volz Nicholas, cigar mkr., 33 Locust
	Voigt Nicholas, lab., 40 Peete	Vumbuemmel Hermann, b. h., 662 W. 6th
ark	Voigts Carsten, grocery, s. e. c. Elm and Union	
ine		Vompach John, cigar mkr., 273 Clinton
es, 80	Volareus John, box mkr , 198 Clinton	Vonax John, lab., wks. 72? Central Av.
	Volbenheim Frank, mason, 589 Race	Von Bargen Otto, (J. W. Meal & Co.,) 16 Bremen
ı Ham	Volders Elizabeth, 615 Race	
	Volfvender Joseph, mach., 60 Hunt	VON BEHREN HENRY W., Stoves, Tin and Hollow Ware, 557 Race
b. Bre-	Volk Andrew, cigar mkr , 680 Vine	
	Volk Charles, tailor, 572 Elm	
	Volk Hy., tanner, s. e. c. Henry and Dunlap	Von Berend Christian, tinner, 584 Walnut
ne		

324 (VOO) CINCINNATI (WAC) DIRECTORY. (WAG)

Von Berg Chas., lab., 36 Elder
Von Bokern Hy., lab.. 301 W Front
Von Bund Gerhard, (Metzeler & Von B.) 19 Hughes
Vondenfange Hy. R., 17 E Liberty
Vondenbeumen Anthony, lab., 14 Buckeye
Vonderahe Barney, shoe store, 118 W. Front
Vonderahe Geo. H., (D. Hoppe & Co.,) n e.c. Walnut and 13th, h. 452 Walnut
Vondergotten H. & Son, (Henry V. & Geo. Klein,) barbers, 61 Broadway
Vondergotten Hy., (H. V. & Son,) 99 E. 2d
Von Derha Clemens, 20 Webster
Vonderha Geo., grocery, 13th b. Walnut and Clay
Vonderha Gerhard, lab , 128 Clay
Vonderha Hy., lab., 122 Clay
Vonderheid John, saddler, bds. 508 Main
Vonderheid Leonard, lab., 179 Baymiller
Vonderheide Frank, rope manuf., 249 W. 3d, h. 261 W. 3d
Vonderheide Hy., confec., 104 13th
Vonderheide Joseph, confec., 127 Sycamore, h. 49 E. 3d
Vonderheide Joseph B., harness manuf., 929 Central Av., h. 923 Central Av.
Von Der Muillen, painter, 55 Hughes
Von Der Paul John, lab., w.s. Hanover b Franklin and Woodward
Von Derwellen John H., lab., 120 Abigail
Vonder Wesche Herman, chair mkr., 67 Rittenhouse
Von Di l Wm., clk., 551 Sycamore
Von Dung Jacob, lab., 105 Pleasant
Von Eye Fred., fam. grocery, n.e.c. Court and John
Von Eye Joseph, rear 521 Sycamore
Von Genechten Michael, cab. mkr., 568 Vine
Von Gries Conrad, watchman, 609 Main
Von Groeninger Herman, upholsterer, s.w.c. 5th and Smith
Von Hagel Fred., grocery, 141 Clark
Von Hagel Henry, shoe mkr., 8 E. Canal
Vonhagel Hy., shoe mkr., bds. 64 E. 5th
Von Handoff Mrs. Eliza, laundress. 102 Abigail
Von Heigel Barney, cooper, bds. c. Rittenhouse and Clark
Vonhol Joseph, tailor, 9 Woodward
Vonlahr John G., shoe mkr., 223 W. Front
Von Langberg Alex., bds. 637 Race
Vonler Christ J., tailor, s.e.c. Young and Ringgold
Von Mittendorf John, carp., 548 Walnut
Von Moos Francis, stone cutter, 44 Peete
Von Nederhauser Gottleib, lab., 546 Walnut
Vonnemann John, candle mkr., s.s. 6th b. Harriett and Horne
Von Niederhausen Fred., carpet shoe mkr., 60 Allison
VON PHUL Henry, (Baker & Von P.,) h Mt. Auburn
Von Rohr Joseph, stone cutter, 510 Plum
VON SEGGERN Christopher, (Mallon & Von S.,) 57 Webster
Von Seggern Frederick, policeman, 164 Spring
Von Seggern Herman, 493 Race
Von Seggern John R., clk. County Recorder's office, h. 493 Race
Von Stein Geo. Phillip, cutter, h. 28 Grand
Von Wald Barney, driver, 216 Betts
Vonwelder Hy., n.s. Bank b. Riddle and Division
Von Wetten Joseph, shoe mkr., bds. 478 W. 5th
Vonwick Arnaldi, apothecary, 923 Central Av.
Voorhies Lorenzo D., bk. mkr., 281 Richmond
Voorhis Benj. S., carp., bds. 353 Central Av.

Vordenberge Herman, porter, 22 Mansfield
Vorderlage Wm., painter, 94 Butler
Vorge Geo., clk., 531 Sycamore
Vorheer John, cof. h., 119 Findlay
Vorholt Wm., porter, 313 Main
Voris Wm , clk., 12 Dayton
Vormohr Anton, lab., s.s. 6th b. Harriet and Horne
Vormohr Casper, blk.smith. 2 Abigail
Vormohr Francis, lab., 2 Abigail
Vormohr Joseph, weaver, 2 Abigail
Vorndick John G., lock smith, 105 Buckeye
Vorndiecke John, grocery, 105 Buckeye
Vorney Hy., tailor, n.e.c. Young and Slack
Vornhagen John Hy., porter, 60 E. 2d
Vornholt Hy., lab., 435 W. 2d
VORNHOLT JOHN F., Staple and Fancy Dry Goods, 315 Main
Vornholt John H., b.k., bds. 315 Main
VORNHOLZ J. Henry, (Goodman & V.) 327 George
Vorspohl Bernard, weaver, 164 Clark
Vortran John, molder, 646 Race
Vorwald Catharine, bakery, 397 Broadway
Vorwald Fred , baker, 397 Broadway
Vorwohr C., blk. smith, wks. 103 Hunt
Vos August, clk. at S. A. Sargent's, bds. 258 Carr
Vos Hy., tailor, 260 Carr
Vos Joseph, grocery, n.w.c. Broadway and Woodward
Vosburg Sheldon S., carp., 154 Everett
Vosen Wm., cap mkr., n.e.c. 9th and Central Av.
Vosh Peter, box mkr., wks. Livingston nr. Linn
Voskotte Hermann, carp., s.s. Liberty b. Linn and Baymiller
Voskotter Hy., bk. layer, 253 Clark
Vosmeier August, molder, 205 Baymiller
Vosmer F. August, turner, s.s. Everett b. Linn and Cutter
Vosmer Wm., carp., 143 Everett
Voss August, carp, 129 Betts
Voss Bern rd, cooper, 42 Jones
Voss Frederick, lab., 19 Buckeye
Voss Fred., Wm., watch mkr., 54 W. 5th
Voss Henry, baker, 568 Race
Voss Hy., cigar mkr., 164 Clark
Voss Hy , soap factory, 66 Dudley
Voss Joseph S., jewelry, &c., 54 W. 5th, h. Covington
Voss Julius, jewelry, &c., 10 W. 5th, h. Sedamsville
Voss Leo., watch mkr., 109 Clark
Votel Geo., stone cutter, 374 Broadway
Votel John H., carp., 145 Abigail
Vottler Fred., finisher. 602 Race
Vough Jacob S., clk. L. M. R.R., bds. 104 E 4th
Vreman Wm. J., shoe mkr., 388 Broadway
Vrieck Jacob, bk. binder, 317 Broadway
Vrooman Jacob, molder, 214 W. Front
Vurthner J. F., saddler, 524 Sycamore

W

Waarbrock L., cof. h., 59 W. Court
Waas Christiana, teacher, 210 Findlay
Wabholding Fred , bds. Cincinnati House
Wachendorf Mary, e. s. Ridgway al. b. Liberty and 15th
Wachman Abraham D., jewelry, 389 Central Av
Wachs Julius, harness mkr., bds. s. w. c. Court and Main
Wachs Theodore, cof. h., s.w.c. Court & Main
Wachsmann August, carp., 74 12th
Wachsmuth August L., porter, 60 Ham. Road
Wachsmuth Christiana, teacher, 32 Pleasant
Wachtendorf Hy., bar k., 222 W. 6th
Wachtendorf Ann. 232 W. 6th
Wachtendorf Frederick, finisher, 115 Carr
Wachter Rev. Nicholas, 229 Bremen

Wachtler Hermann, tanner, s. s. 6th b. Harriet and Horne
Wachtman Wm., 312 Linn
Wacke Phillip, plow mkr., 587 Main
Wacker Charles L., blksmith, wks. 614 Main
Wacker John P., blksmith, wks. 614 Main
Wacker Louis, plow mkr , 150 Clay
Wackhorst Anna M., 65 Abigail
Waddel Orrin J., tel. op. M. & C. R. R., bds. Dennison House
Waddle George, lab., s. w. c. Vine and Front
Wade Andrew, lab., E. 3d b. Parsons & Baum
Wade David E., phys., 86 Everett
Wade John, lab., 82 Water
Wade Philip, st. bt. capt., 336 W. 8th
Wade Richard, carp., 178 W. Court w. of Central Av
Wade Robert, tailor, 5 E, 4th
Wade Mrs. Sarah, 218 Clark
Wade Stephen J., com. mer., 55 E. 4th
Wadlow Chas., lithographer, 64 W. 4th
Wadsworth Joshua, publisher Templars' Magazine, 112 Hopkins
Waecter John. tailor, rear 64 W. Mulberry
Waehrle J. T., show case mkr., 66 Main
Waeibel Hy., tailor, 153 Bremen
Waffenschmidt Geo., clk., s.e.c. Elm and 12th
Waffenschmidt Hy., druggist, s.e.c. Elm and 12th
Waffenschmidt Jacob, clk., wks. n. e. c. Elm and 12th
Wafieeschmidt John, clk., 440 Walnut
Waffenschmidt Wm., lithographer, s.e.c. 12th and Elm
Wagenheiser Geo., lab., 20 Hamer
Waggoner Alice, n.s. Grandin al. b. Elm and Plum
Waggoner Conrad, painter, 246 Clark
Waggoner George, tailor, s. s. 6th b. Harriet and Horne
Waggoner Hy. H., pattern mkr., 271 W. 7th
Waggoner John, finisher, wks. n. e. c. Walnut and Canal
WAGGONER JOHN, Real Estate and Money Broker, 56 W. 6th, h. Avondale
Waggoner John J., S w. 6th
Waggoner M , s. s. Oliver b. John and Linn
Waggoner Mary, h. s. e. c. Ludlow and Arch
Waggoner Samuel S., oyster depot, 203 Central Av., res. Avondale
Waggoner W. W., wood engraver, 58 W. 6th
Wagmann Simon, 184 Linn
Wagner Andrew, lithographer, 348 Main
Wagner Anton, brush mkr, s.s Bank b. Freeman and Coleman
Wagner August, cook, n.w.c. Court and Main
Wagner August, drugs, &c., 512 Main, h. 141 E. Liberty
Wagner Bernhard (Abrahams & W.) bds 117 Lodge
Wagner Conrad, cof. h., 40 Hughes
Wagner Dennis, painter, 19 Oliver
Wagner Elliott, driver. 461 W. 2d
Wagner Emil, furniture, 10:6 Central Av., h. 1069 Central Av
Wagner Ernst, baker, 6 4 Vine
Wagner Frank, b. k , 86 W Pearl, h. 19 Gest
Wagner Frederick, blksmith, 614 E. Front
Wagner Frederick, blksmith, 609 E. Front
Wagner Frederick, dray, 31 Buckeye
Wagner Geo. M., grocery, 514 Elm
Wagner Gertrude, seamstress, 624 Race
Wagner Hy., jr., cab. mkr., 447 Walnut
Wagner Hy., cof. h., 447 Walnut
Wagner Hy., cooper 574 Walnut
Wagner Hy., lab., 619 Race
Wagner Hy., tailor, 13 Mulberry
Wagner Hy., trunk mkr, 53 Ham. Road
Wagner John, 901 Central Av
Wagner John, cab. mkr., bds. 141 Longworth

(WAI) CINCINNATI (WAL) DIRECTORY. (WAL) 325

Wagner John, cigar mkr., 63 Poplar
Wagner John, finisher, Goose al. b. Elder and Green
Wagner John, lab., 619 Race
Wagner John, lithographer, 614 E. Front
Wagner John, shoemkr. 462 Race
Wagner John, tanner, 682 Vine
Wagner John B., molder, s.s. Avery al. w. of Wood
Wagner John F., molder, w. s. Goose al. b. Green and Elder
Wagner John J., cof. h., 318 E. Pearl
Wagner Lewis, tailor, 14 Mary
Wagner Louisa, servt., 53 12th
Wagner M, mer., bds. 17 Lodge
Wagner Mary, n.s. Angusta b. John & Smith
Wagner Michael, carriage trimmer, n. s. Corwin b. Walnut and Ham. Road
Wagner Nicholas, painter, s. s. Bank b. Freeman and Coleman
Wagner Philip, lab, n.s. Dayton b. Western Av and Coleman
Wagner Phillipp G., shoemkr, 13 Woodward
Wagner Rachael, 603 E Front
Wagner Stephen, b.k., 137 Main, h. 444 Sycamore (eye
Wagner Theodore, lab., rear 180 Buck-
Wagner Tobias, eng., 770 W. 6th
Wagner Valentine, paper carrier, 39 Mulberry
Wagner Wm., carver, 447 Walnut
Wagner Wm. F., tailor. 401 Vine
Wagner Wm. T., stamp clk., P. O., h. 34 Jackson
Wagner Wolf, 431 Elm
Wagstaff Joseph, blksmith. 175 Race
Wagoner Anna, 61 Vine
Wagoner Frank, tanner, 574 Central Av
Wagoner George, n.s. Ham. Road, head of Elm
Wagoner Hy., cab. mkr., wks. s.w.c. Canal and Elm
Wagoner Hy., tinner, 70 Lock
Wagoner John, cab. mkr., wks. s. w. c. Canal and Elm
Wagoner Joseph, dyer, e.s. Kilgour b. 3d and 5th
Wagoner Kelly, agt. 71 W. 3d
Wagoner Mary, s. s. Cathoun b. Vine & Madison
Wagoner Samuel, e. s. Division b. Bernard and Harrison Pike
Wagoner Wm., n.e.c. Logan and Green
Wagoner Wm., eng., e. s. Kilgour b. 3d and 5th
Wagonmaker Nicholas, n.w.c. Calhoun & Vine
Wahking Christian, porter, bds. 408 Main
Wahking Frederick, dray, 18 Dudley
Wahking Hy., porter, 464 Main
Wahl Anthony, carp., 137 Ham. Road
Wahl Catharine, 50 12th
Wahl Fred., wks. P W. 8th
Wahl John, carp., 666 Race
Wahlbrinck Hy F. C., mason, n.s. Cassatt al. b. Sycamore and Main
Wahle Joseph, cab. mkr, s. e. c. Mound and Clark
Wahler John, molder, 14 Bremen
Wahlers Conrad, dye house, 24 14th
Wahlike George, driver, n. s. Pearl b. Pike and Butler
Wahmes John B., clk., 52 W. 5th
Wahner John S., wagon mkr., bds. n.s. Front e of Lock
Waholl Birney, b.h., 428 Sycamore
Wahrenberger Ulrich, varnisher, 671 Sycamore

WAHRHEITSFREUND,
  Jos. A. Hemann, Editor and Proprietor, s.w.c. Vine & Longworth
Waibel Joseph, cook, 21 Woodward
Waichselfelter Ellen, servt., 39 Harrison
Waidner Farques, tanner, 701 Elm
Waigand Adam, porter, 215 W. Front
Waightman Thomas, 22 Park
Wailand Margaret, 136 Linn
Wainright Mrs. Elizabeth, 174 E. 3d e. of Collard
Wainright Jas. W., paper box mkr., 117 W. 5th
Wainright Wm., carp., 174 E. 3d e. of Collard

Wait Alice, 142 W. Court w. of Central Av
Wait Noah, grainer, 142 W. Court w. of Central Av
Wait Wm., painter, 142 W. Court w. of Central Av
Waites Joseph, cab. mkr., 568 E. Front
Waithman Charles, 308 W. 5th
Waitz Richard, photographist, 406 Vine
Wakelam Sarah, bds, 9 Gest
Wakeler Michael, carp., 184 W. Court
Waklyn John, baker, 376 Broadway
Walber Jacob. lab., 93 Bremen
Walberech Chas., box mkr., 11 15th b. Elm and Plum
Walburg Francis. tanner, 174 Everett
Walburg Hy., tanner, 232 Linn
Walch Thomas, flag man, n.s. Taylor b. Freeman and Carr
Walck Simon, lab., 13 Pendleton
Walcott David, pattern mkr., bds. 361 W. 3d
Wald Edward D., salesman, 353 W. 5th
Wald Jeannette, bds. 260 W. 7th

WALD LEWIS, Importer of Hosiery, Jackets, Baskets, &c., Wholesale Dealer in Notions and Fancy Goods, 80 W. Pearl, h. 391 W. 7th

Waldack Chas, photographer, 24 W. 4th
Waldapple Charles,rope mkr., s.s. Budd b. Harriet and Mill Creek
Waldau Gustave, show case manuf., 27 E. 3d
Walde Wm., lab., 62 Lock
Waldenmayer Hy., cooper,455 Sycamore
Waldenmeyer Adolph, b.k., C. F. Adae & Co.'s, h. Newport
Walder ——, actor, National Theater
Walder August, cigars, &c., 128 Walnut
Walder Catharine, 503 John
Walder Francis, lab., 261 Pleasant
Walder George, 32 Dunlap
Walder Hy., tailor, 225 Everett
Walder Peter, cab. mkr., 22 Pierson
Waldering Hy., lab., 106 Bremen
Waldernspiel Caroline, 76 Melancthon
Walsheim Sarah, grocery, n.e.c. 8th and Walnut
Walding Hy., lab., 99 Baum
Waldmann Jacob, tailor, 664 Race
Waldmann Julius, shoemkr, 134 Bremen
Waldmann Margaret M., 604 Race
Waldo Arabella, teacher, 17th district school, res. E. Walnut Hills

WALDO FRED AUG.,
  Nye Infirmary, s.w.c. 4th and Sycamore, h. 170 Race
Waldon Mary, n. s. Goodloe b. Willow and Niagara
Waldren Hy., lab., 189 Laurel
Waldren Thos., lab., 187 Linn
Waldron Corbe S., dry goods, n. w. c. Everett and Central Av
Waldron David, n.w.c. Everett and Central Av
Waldron David A., tailor, 46 W. 5th, h. 181 W. 4th
Waldron Dorcas, 197 W. 3d
Waldron Jane E., 146 Smith
Waldron John, lab., 173 Hopkins
Waldron Rev. John, 302 Baymiller
Waldron Pat., blksmith, rear 14 Richmond
Waldschmid Andrew, wood dealer, 534 Plum
Walerius Mathias, cooper, 196 Pleasant
Walkenhorst Casper H., 55 Milton
Walkenhorst Frank, s. w. c. Milton and Price
Walkenhorst Joseph H., blksmith, n. s. Front, w. of Hill
Walker Adaline A., 95 Betts
Walker Agnes. bds. 130 Hopkins
WALKER Andrew, (Walker & Co.,) 71 Webster
WALKER Archibald, (J. Walker & Co.) 566 Freeman
Walker C. S., cashier, 74 W. 4th, bds. Gibson House
Walker Catharine, E. Court above E. 6th
WALKER D. B., (J. P. & D. B. W.,) 96 W. 7th
Walker David, baker, 1184 E. Front
Walker Edward H., clk., 93 Main, bds. Madison House

Walker Elizabeth C., bds. 18 Harrison
Walker Ellen, servt, 345 W. 8th
Walker Eunice, 159 Dayton
Walker Ferdinand, driver, 50 Hathaway
Walker Frederick, collar mkr., bds. 253 Walnut
Walker Hy., dray, e. s. Pierson b. 5th and 6th
Walker Hy., fisherman, 132 W. Miami Canal

WALKER J. & CO.. (James W., Andrew Walker, William Walker, & Archibald Walker,) Brewery, 391 Sycamore
Walker J. H. & S , (James H. & Samuel.) dry goods, 20 W. 5th
WALKER J. P., (J. P. & D. B. W.,) 96 W. 7th

WALKER J. P. & D. B.,
  Physicians and Surgeons,
  219 Broadway

Walker Jacksel, omnibus driver, s. s. Front b Kelly and Foster
Walker James, 566 Freeman
WALKER James, (J. W. & Co.,) 566 Freeman
Walker James H., (J. H. & S. W.,) 20 W. 5th
Walker James M., clk., 95 Betts
Walker John, carp., n.w.c. Calhoun and Vine
Walker John, lab., 55 E. 8th e. of Lock
Walker John, shoemkr. bds. Australia House
Walker John B., clk., 101 Sycamore, h. Covington, Ky.
Walker John T., printer, 241 W. 3d
Walker Julian C., carp., 314 Water
Walker Lucy, 513 W. 5th
Walker Margaret, 50 Elm
Walker Marion M., 130 Hopkins
Walker Mary, servt., 358½ George
Walker Mathilda, 53 W. 6th
Walker Richard, n w.c 6th and Plum

WALKER ROBERT,
  Dyer and Renovator, 63 E. 3d,
  h. 300 Freeman

Walker Robert A., yard master M. & C. Depot. h. 50 Baum
Walker Rudolph, e. s. Vine b. Calhoun and Auburn Av
Walker Samuel, (J. H. & S. W.,) 304 Vine
Walker Wm., bds. Cincinnati House
Walker Wm., brewer. 316 W. 4th
Walker Wm., carp., 740 E. Front
Walker Wm., carp., 636 E. Front

WALKER WM., Sr., Coal Yards, e. s. Freeman b. 5th and 6th, and n. w. c. Court and Race, h. 500 W. 5th

Walker Wm., jr., clk., 500 W. 5th
Walker Wm., foreman, 100 Sycamore
Walker Wm., huckster. 522 Main
WALKER Wm., (J. Walker & Co.,) 440 Freeman
Walker Wm., trimmer, 21 W. 7th

WALKER WM. F.,
  Walker's Exchange,
  7 Sycamore

Walker Wm H., shoemkr, bds. 281 Central Avenue
Walkinburgh Hy., b.k., 57 W. Pearl, b. s.s. 3d b. Pike and Butler
Wall Jacob, cof. and b. h., 144 E. 2d
Wall James, stable, 114 Sycamore
Wall John, 313 Walnut
Wall John, jailor, w.s Sycamore b. Canal and Abignil
Wall John, lab., 663 Race
Wall John, lab. 26 15th
Wall Julia F., 571 Central Av
Wall Thomas, lab., 32 North
Wall Wm., lab., 42 Lock, n. of 8th
Wall Wm., porter, 12 W. 8th
Wallace Albert, lithographer, wks. n. w. c. 3d and Main. res. Walnut Hills
Wallace Anna, 108 W. 5th
Wallace David, rear 122 Mohawk
Wallace David S., notions. bds. 111 John
Wallace Edward. clk. bds. 409 Broadway
Wallace Henrietta, 152 Hopkins
Wallace J. C., phys., n e.c. 5th and Sycamore
Wallace J. Gibson, salesman, 92 W. Pearl, bds. 137 W. 7th

Wallace James, mail agt., bds. 120 John
Wallace John, carp., s.w.c. Laurel and Cutter
Wallace Joshua, 53 Webster
Wallace Maria, 40 Plum
Wallace Michael, lab., 21 E. 8th
Wallace Richard, saddler, 470 Broadway
Wallace Samuel, dray, 223 Clinton
Wallace Sebina, s.e.c. New and Broadway
Wallace Thomas, brass finisher, 441 W. 2d
Wallace Thomas, lab., 142 Spring
Wallace Thomas, lab., wks. 80 Poplar
Wallace Wm., saddler, 542 Race
WALLACE Wm. P., (Rathborne & W.) 117 W. 6th
Wallbracht Chas., cigar box manuf., 10 13th b. Central Av. and Plum
Wallending Hy., lab., wks. Lane & Bodley's
Wallenstein A , 47 Longworth
Waller John, 119 Mohawk
Waller John, lab., wks. n.w.c. Plum and Wade
Waller John, molder, 16 14th
Waller Mrs. Mary, w. end of Mohawk
Wallerauch John, mason, 14 Hamer
Wallers Mary, 654 Sycamore
Wallimann John, sr., lab., wks. Hieatt & Wood's
Wallmann John, jr., wks. Hieatt & Wood's
Wallin Wm., harness mkr., 89 Main
Walling Bell, 5 Home
Walling David C., mach., bds. 462 W. 7th
WALLINGFORD Joel M., (Reeme W. & Co.,) 196 W. 4th
Wallinghoff Hy., carp., 92 Broadway
Wallington J. M., com. mer., 196 W. 4th
Walimann Bernhardt J., boots and shoes, 345 W. 5th
Wallmann Frederick, shoemkr, 404 Longworth
Wallo Anthony, egg packer, 64 E. Pearl, bds. cor. Front and Pike
Walls E., 35 Harrison
Walmer Geo., blksmith, wks. s. w. c. Smith and Water
WALNUT STREET BANK, G. H. Bussing & Co., n.w.c. Walnut and 3d
WALNUT STREET HOUSE, H H. Davis, Proprietor, e.s. Walnut b. 6th and 7th
Walpert Frederick cof. h., 56 Mohawk
Walser Andrew, carriage mkr., 701 Elm
Walser H., painter, 89 13th
Walsh ——, conductor, n.w c. John and Linn
Walsh Edward., lab., wks. Foote, Nash & Co.'s
Walsh George, tailor, 228 Broadway
Walsh J. W., cutter, bds. Madison House
Walsh Jacob, driver, 53 Mill
Walsh James, foreman, Foote, Nash & Co.'s, h. Newport
Walsh James, grocery, 256 Central Av
Walsh James, saloon, 80 Sycamore
Walsh John, lab., n.s. W.W. Canal b. Smith and Park
Walsh John, lab, 61 Mill
Walsh John, tailor, bds. s. w. c. 5th and Broadway
Walsh John P., bookseller, publisher, and book and job printer, 170 Sycamore
Walsh John W., cutter, May & Cobn's, bds. Madison House
Walsh Julia, 242 Richmond
Walsh Maurice, police, 495 W. 4th
WALSH MICHAEL, Hides, Oil and Leather, 7 Commercial Row, h. 24 Harrison
Walsh Patrick, cof. h , 704 W. Front
Walsh Patrick, upholsterer, 152 Baymiller
Walsh Rebecca L., dress mkr., 32 Mound
Walsh Thos , clk , 254 W. 9th
Walsh Thomas, salesman, 96 W. 5th, h. s.w.c. 9th and Central Av
Walsh Timothy W., conductor, 3 Linn
Walsh Wm., cooper, wks. 44 E. 2d
Walsh William, lab., 638 W. Front
Walsh Wm. P., policeman, bds. 270 Everett

Walsmith George, carriage mkr., 361 Cutter
Walsterman Frederick, blksmith, Oehler al. h. Freeman and Garrard
Walt Hy , lab., n.s. Front, e. of Lewis
Waltehr Geo., carp., 16 Bremen
Waltemath Charles, tailor, 0 E. Liberty
Waltemath Wm., lab., 0 E. Liberty
Walter Aloisius, lab., 15 Mary
Walter Anna M., huckster, 454 Walter
Walter Barney, shoe mkr., bds. n.w.c. Plum and Water
Walter Charles, hatter, 107 Pleasant
Walter Edward, cof. h., 366 Sycamore
Walter Frederick, carp., 118 Gest
Walter Fred, wagon mkr., bds. 177 Hopkins
Walter George H., b.k. 33 Walnut
Walter Jacob, butcher, bds. 202 Hamilton Road
Walter Jacob F., tailor, 679 Vine
Walter John, 366 Sycamore
Walter John, hats and caps, 554 Vine
Walter John, porter, 335 Broadway
Walter John, shoe mkr., bds. 413 Sycamore
Walter Julius, brass finisher, 219 Freeman
Walter Lorenzo, cab mkr., 219 Freeman
Walter Louis, watchman, 212 Clinton
Walter Mason, cigar denler, 49 Elizabeth
Walter Nicolaus, feed store, 554 Elm
Walter Nicholaus, musician, 145 Bremen
Walter Peter, cab. mkr., 22 Pierson
Walter Phillip, photographer, 10 W. 5th, h. 6 E. 6th
Walter Rudolph, tailor, wks. 97 E. Pearl
Walter Samuel, clk., 514 W. 7th
Walter Valentine, grocery, 29 Moore
WALTER WM. Architect, s.e.c. 4th and Walnut, (up stairs,) h. 32 Clark
Walter Wm. F., 68 Alligan
Waltermann Barney, tailor, n.w.c. 3d and Stone
Walters Mrs., actress, National Theater
Walters Barbara, 69 Mulberry
Walters Catharine, seamstress, 447 Main
Walters Charles, actor, bds. 38 E. 4th
WALTERS CHAS J., Agent Virtue & Co., s e.c. 4th an l'Hammond
Walters Charles M., clk., 41 Broadway
Walters Elnora, rear 210 Cutter
Walters Francis, bds. 27 Elisabeth
Walters John, cigar mkr., 44 E. 8th e. of Lock
Walters John S , salesman, 113 W. Pearl, h. 215 W. 4th
Walters Joseph, clk., 103 Smith
Walters William, driver, 100 Clark
Walthauser Martin, lab , 19 Hughes
Walther Charles, carp., 1260 E. Front
Walther Chas., hatter, 107 Pleasant
Walther Conrad, varnisher, 10 Buckeye
Waltman Henry, shoe mkr , 73 W. Court
Walton Chas., b.k. L. M. R. R. Freight office, res. Branch HHH
Walton E. H., clk., 378 W. 9th w. of Central Av
Walton Geo. N., clk. L. M. R. R. depot, res. Branch HHH
Walton James, dray, 268 E. Pearl e. of Broadway
Walton Joshua A., foundry, 275 George
WALTON Joshua P., (Macy, Rankin & Co.,) h. 275 George
Walton Louis, watchman, 211 Clinton
Walton Wm., dray, wks. 109 E. Pearl
Walton Wm. W., carp., 143 E. 2d
Waltz Charles F., cof. h , 72 W. Liberty
Waltz George, waiter, Gibson House
Waltz Henry, bk. lxyer, bds. 72 W Liberty
Waltz Joseph, bar k., bds. 72 W. Liberty
Waltz Julius, butcher, s.s. Harrison Road nr. Brighton
Waltz Louis, bk. molder, bds. 72 W. Liberty
Walz Frank A., liquors, &c., 340 Walnut, h. 239 Linn
Walzer Henry, miller, wks. 164 W. 2d
Walzer Josephine. 40 Fin Hay
Wambagans Frederick, n.s. Harrison Pike nr. Mill Creek
Wamhoff Frederick, cooper, bds. 75 Buckeye

Warning Joseph, lab., 175 Hopkins
Wumpach Bernard, cigar mkr., 263 Clinton
Wampe Henry J. A., turner, bds. 662 Race
Wampler John M., (Monfort & W.,) 385 W. 8th
Wuppenstein Joseph, engraver, 453 Sycamore
Wamstead John, 396 Central Av
Wanford John. molder, wks. 267 W. 5th
Wangart Franciska, 128 W. Liberty
Wangelin Edward, clk. 28 ,W. Pearl, b. 95 Dayton
Wangelin Gustav, b. k., 520 Main
Wangemann Henry, music teacher, 31 Jackson
Wangemann Rudolph, instrument mkr., bds. 31 Jackson
Wanelin Edward, clk., bds 95 Dayton
Wanike Henry, lab., 14 Abigail
Wanke Gerhard J., turner, 566 Elm
Wankelmann Fred., cigars &c., 361 Vine and 56 15th
Wanken Frederick, tailor, 47 Pleasant
Wankey Frederick, dray, b. 91 and 93 Martin
Wankey John, dray, 101 Martin
Wankmueller Jacob, meats., 38 Hamilton Road
WANN C. & T., (Christopher & Thos.,) Lard Oil Manufacturers, 57 W. Miami Canal
WANN Christopher, (C. & T. W.,) bds. Deboit Exchange
WANN Thomas, (C. & T. W.,) bds. Deboit Exchange
WANNER Hermann, (Lang & W.,) 47 Dunlap
Wansbacher Henry, cigars, &c , 74 13th
Wansbrough Henry, locksmith, 182 Central Av., res Covington
Wanstarth John H., lab., 13 15th b. Elm and Plum
Wanstradt C., lab., wks. n.s. Front b Lawrence and Pike
Wanstrat George, lab., s.s. Woodward b. Sycamore and Broadway
Wanstroth Joseph, cof. b., 99 Woodward
Wanzer John, (Langstaff & W.), res. Wilmington, O.
Warber Hermann, s.w.c. Price and Milton
WARBURG John B., (W. & Ramler,) 206 Main
WARBURG & RAMLER, (John B. W. & Joseph Ramler,) Merchant Tailors, 260 Main
Ward Mrs., clock mkr., 392 W. 3d
WARD Andrew P., (W. & Ward,) 65 McFarland
Ward Arthur, eng. Meth. Book Concern, h. 204 Livingston
Ward Atha. eng , 204 Livingston
Ward Betty, servt., 32 Elizabeth
Ward Charles, s.s. Phoebe al. b. Plum and Central Av
Ward Charles, clk., 22 Plum
Ward Charles, carriage painter, 259 Hopkins
Ward Chas., porter, 10 Main
Ward Charlotte, 140 E. 5th
Ward Cylvestus, bds. Dumas Hotel
Ward Edward, deputy co. auditor, res. Reading Road
Ward Edward F., cab. mkr., 203 Wade
Ward Eliza A., 438 John
Ward Emily, rear 221 Water
Ward Hamilton, cab. mkr., s.s. 9th b. Harriet and Mill Creek
Ward Henry, 264 W. 8th
Ward James, bk. layer, 212 W. Court w. of Central Av.
Ward John, lab., 255 W. 3d
Ward Julia, s.s. 6th b. Broadway and Culvert
Ward L. M., painter, 259 Hopkins
Ward Levi, plasterer, 10 W. 9th
Ward Luke, carriage painter, 259 Hopkins
Ward Margaret 71 E. Front
Ward Owen, lab., 41 Ludlow
Ward Patrick, lab., s.s. 6th b. Broadway and Culvert
Ward Robert, meats, s.e.c. George and Central Av., h. 137 W. 7th

Warner Lizzy, bds 382 W. 9th
Warner Maria, 76 Barr
Warner Miles G., 68 Clark
Warner Warren, foreman, Miles Greenwood's, h. 68 Clark
Warner Wm. H., tinner, 200 Clark
Warning John, lab., 70 Water
Warnken Fred. J., tailor, 47 Pleasant
Warnken Geo., clk., 135 Clinton
Warnking Hy., b k., s.e.c. Augusta and Smith, h. 298 Water
WARNOCK James, (Lincoln, Smith & W.) 8 E. 2d
Warrander Maria, 380 W. Liberty
WARREN Alfred, (Perry & W.) 14 Pine
Warren Chas., prof. of music, 486 W.5th
Warren Geo., measurer of stone and brick work, 299 George
Warner Geo. K., eng., 268 Cutter
WARREN J. T. & CO. (John T. W. & Co.) Wholesale Dealers in Foreign Fruits, &c., 53 Main
Warren James, lab., 334 W. 5th
Warren John B., atty., n. w. c. 6th and Walnut, h. 465 Sycamore
Warren John T., conductor, bds. Spencer House
WARREN John T,, (J. T. W. & Co.) 101 Pike
Warren Mary, 520 W. 5th
Warren Samuel B., salesman, 53 Main, h. 101 Pike
Warren Susan J., 66 Peete
Warren Wm., block and rigging mkr., wks. 87 E. Front
WARREN WM., (Knight & W.) h. Walnut Hills
Warrick Arrison, lab., wks. s.e.c. Canal and Vine
Warrington Geo., carp., 127 Laurel
Warrington Oswald, picture depot, s. s. W. 4th, nr. Main, h. 127 Laurel
Warrington Robert, bar k., 56 Plum
Warstern Chas. 23 W. Liberty
Wartcki Moses, collector, 173 W. 9th
Warter Kate, seamstress, e.s. Walnut, nr. 13th
Warth Chas., printer, 647 Sycamore
Warth Marcus, 129 Spring
Warthman Eliza, fancy store, 308 W.5th
Wartman Jacob, 110 W. Liberty
WARTMAN Wm., (Wm.W. & Co.,) 657 Elm
Wartman Wm., clk., s. w. c. Elm and Findlay
WARTMAN WM. & CO., (Wm. W. & Jacob Haeusler.) Findlay Market Meat Store, No. 657, Elm, c. Findlay
Wartman Jacob, steward, 102 W. Liberty
Wartman John, wagon mkr., 110 Liberty
Wartz John, driver, 163 Bank
Warwick Pat., porter, Broadway Hotel
Warwick Sam., carriage trimmer, bds. 43 Plum
Warwick Truman B., carp., 132 Livingston
Warwood Benj., blk.smith, wks. J. A. Fay & Co's
Warwood Emanuel, blk.smith, 638 W.5th
Warwood Emanuel, music teacher, 538 W. 5th
Warwood Thos., blk.smith, 637 W. Front
Wasem Jacob, hatter, n. w. c. Main and Court
Washabaugh Geo. H., printer, Cin. Gazette, h. 193 Longworth
Washburn Andrew, driver, 3d and 4th st. R. R.
Washburn Elisha W., paper hanger, 198 W. Front
Washburn Ephraim, tailor, 184 Longworth
WASHINGTON BREWERY, Schultz & Bro., 485 E. Front
Washington Fire Ins. Co., Agency 76 W. 3d
Washington Hy., lab., 137 E. 6th
Washington Hotel, John Owens, n w.c. Walnut and Water
Washington House, 231 Walnut

WASHINGTON INSURANCE CO., Wm. Goodman, President, 41 Main
Washington Sam., porter, w.s. Henderson al. b. 7th and 8th
Wasmer Maxamilian, locksmith, 94 Findlay
Wasmus H. Theod., teacher, 32 Pleasant
Wasmusz Hy., sen., 32 Pleasant
Wasmusz Hy., jr., teacher, 32 Pleasant
Wassenich Jos., bakery, 65 Allison
Wassmer Chas. A., cooper, n.e.c. Liberty and Vine
Wasson Clinton, lab., Cramsey al., b. Mound and Cutter
Wasson Wm., eng., 44 Barr
Wastekamp Hy., butcher, 163 W. 5th
Wasteney John, (Ryan & W.) res. Walnut Hills
Wasteney John, horse shoer, 253 W. Court
Wasterbaka Clem., porter, 22 Commerce
Waterhause Hy., carp., n.e.c. Canal and Walnut
Waterman Barney, sawyer, 304 Longworth
Waterman Clemens, foreman, wks. Livingston, nr. Linn
Watermann Geo., driver, 435 W. 2d
WATERS ASA B., Gen.Freight Agt, Marietta & Cin. R. R., and Agent for Zaleski Coal Co., Office 3 Burnett House, h. 268 Everett
WATERS & BARRETT, (J. M. W. & S.M. B.) Washboard and Steam Bending Manufacturers & Planing Mill, n.w.c. Freeman and 9th
WATERS BYRON, Steam and Water Pipe, Gas Fixtures, Chandeliers, Lamps &c., Main, h. 169 Elm
WATERS Chas. H., (Chas. H. W. & Co.,) 277 W. Court, w. of Central Av.
WATERS CHAS. H., (Chas H. W. & Eben Dole,) Manufacturers and Wholesale Dealers in Wood and Willow Ware, Washboards, Brooms, Cordage, Twine &c., 3 Pub. Landing, and 4 Main
Waters Enoch, currier, wks. 232 Main
Waters Gardner, h. 263 Hopkins
WATERS Jabez M., (W. & Barrett,) 259 W. Court, w. of Central Av.
Waters James, clk. 371 Central Av.
Waters Pliny F. b. k., 55 W. 4th, h. 1 Clinton Court
Waters Wm. H., clk, Adams Express Co., h. Newport
WATKIN HARRY, Book and Job Printer, 140 W. 3d, h. Carthage
Watkins Margaret, 311 Elm
Watkins Mary, 104 Sycamore
Watkins Nelson, groceries, n. e. c 5th and Smith
Watkins Thos. D., car builder, 23 Kossuth
Watson Abijah, steward, Commercial Hospital
Watson Andrew, cab. mkr., bds. 27 Mound
Watson Augustus A., clk., Henrie House
Watson Frank F., supt., Henrie House
Watson James, (L. D. Watson & Bro.,) Henrie House
WATSON JAMES, Proprietor Henrie House, n.s. 3d b. Main and Sycamore
Watson James W., porter, 221 E. 6th
Watson John, capt., 40 Lock
Watson John, compositor, Cin. Gazette, h. 23 Webb
Watson John, lab., 23 Webb
Watson John A., policeman, 52 Lock
Watson Joseph, carp., 72 Richmond b. Plum and Central Av.
Watson Joseph, carp, s. s. Front E. of Vance
Watson Joseph, wire weaver, 63 Everett
Watson L. D. & Bro., (Lewis D. & James,) Kanawha Salt agency, 9 Main
Watson Lewis D., (L. D. W. & Bro.) bds. Henrie House

328 (WEA) CINCINNATI (WEB) DIRECTORY. (WEB)

Watson Robert B., cab. mkr., wks. n.w.c. Elm and Pearl
Watson Sarah, dress mkr., 332 W. 5th
Watson Thomas, printer, Cin. Gazette Office
Watson Thomas, tanner, 260 Linn
Watson William, carp., Pennock al. b. Linn and Baymiller
Watson Wm., tinner, 185 W. 3d
Watson Wm. E., b. k., s. w. c. 7th and Smith, h. College Hill
WATT Andrew, (Hart & W.,) 25 Broadway
Watt Ellen, w. s. Johnson al. b. Canal and 12th
Watt Maggie, bds. 20 Kossuth
Watt Richard, paper carrier, 507 Sycamore
Watt Wm. K., mach., 507 Sycamore
Watterberry John, baggage master, O. & M R.R., bds. 480 W. 4th
Watters James M., principal Bartlett's Com. College, h. 295 George
Watters Wm. E., teamster, 466 John
Watterson James, lab., 224 Freeman
Wattreah Jacob. shoe mkr., 130 Poplar
Watts Alfred, freight agt., O. & M. R. R. h. 486 W. Front
Watts David, 532 W. 5th
Watts Lewis, eng., 118 Vanhorne
Watts Mark, boiler, 425 W. 2d
Watts Nancy, dress mkr., 5 North
Watts Lovice, 20 Charles
Watts Wm., bar k., wks. n.e.c. 9th and Central Av.
Watts Wm., shoe mkr., w. s. Jones b. Everett and Liberty
Wavanbrunkherst Anthony, lab., 189 Linn
Waxler Benj., boots and shoes, 220 Cutter
Waxler Francis E., car trimmer, 220 Cutter
Waxler Geo. W., shoe mkr., 220 Cutter
Wayand Hy., bar k., 447 Main
Waybold D., lab., wks. n. s. Front b. Lawrence and Pike
Wayland Francis H., clk., 59 Broadway h. Newport
Wayman Kate, bds. Black Bear Hotel
Wayne Anthony, salesman, 124 Main, h. Country
Wayne Edward S., chemist. s. s. 3d, b. Canal and Kilgour
Wayne Mrs. Emma, 72 E. 7th
Wayne Francis. lab., e. s. Whittaker, b. Front and 3d
Wayne Hy., finisher, 24 Perry
WAYNE J. L. & SON, (Jacob L. & Jacob L. Jr.,) Hardware, Cutlery &c., 124 Main, and 20 Hammond
WAYNE Jacob L., (J. L. W. & Son,) 156 W. 4th
WAYNE Jacob, Jr., (J. L. Wayne & Son,) 25 W. 8th
Wayne James S., (Smith W. & Co.,) h. Covington
WAYNE Joseph W., (Joseph W. W. & Co.,) 301 W. 8th
WAYNE JOSEPH W. & CO., (Joseph W. W. & Tilghman Pickering,) Hardware. Tools, Cutlery &c., 196 and 198 Main
Weaberclink Barney, CO 13th
Weafer Ann, 31 E. 7th
Weafer Joseph, sawyer, s. s. Woodward b. Sycamore an 1 Broadway
Weakheart Francis, blksmith. wks. 10 W. 7th
Weakheart Hy. blksmith, wks. 10 W.7th
Weakheart Wm., blksmith, wks. 10 W. 7th
Weakly Thos., lab., 96 Hunt
Wealsh James. 236 Central Av.
WEASNER Thomas H., (T. H. W. & Co.,) s. e. c. 7th and Elm
WEASNER THOMAS H. & CO., (T. H. W. & Chas. S. Smith,) Lumber Yard, 371 Plum
Weatherby Caroline, 76 Providence
Weatherby Chas. S., dry goods, 110 W. 5th, h. 166 W. 8th
Weatherly Geo. P., photographer, 76 Providence
Weatherby Jas. A., bk. binder, 25 W. 4th h. 76 Providence

Weatherby James S., harness &c., 176 Main. h. 110 George
Weatherby James S., jr., salesman, 176 Main, h. 110 George
Weatherby Philip G., clk., 560 W. 9th
Weatherby Walcott R., finisher, 69 Abigail
Weatherby Wallace, paper hanger, 163 Main, h. 58 Hunt
Weatherby Wm., pipe fitter, wks. n.e.c. Walnut and Canal
Weatherherad Robt,, 40 W. 9th, w. of Central Av,
Weatherspoon James, molder, wks. 162 E. Front
Weathorn Catharine, servt., 286 George
Weaver ——, 123 Betts
Weaver Augusta, h. 26 Mohawk
Weaver Augustus, clk., 61 Martin
Weaver Augustus, carp., 61 Martin
Weaver Casper, tailor, 10 Commerce
Weaver Catharine, 143 Baymiller
Weaver Charles H., carp., 78 Mound
WEAVER CLARK G., Tin Ware Manufacturer, 417 W. 4th
Weaver Edward, conductor, 437 W. 5th
Weaver Eliza, 142 W. Pearl
Weaver Fanny, servt., 71 Webster
Weaver George, mach. wks. n.w.c. Pearl and M. Canal
Weaver Hy., carp., bds. 61 Martin
Weaver Hy., lab., 562 E. Front
Weaver Hy., riverman, 109 E 3d e. of Whittaker
Weaver Hy. A., actor, 136 John
Weaver J., molder, wks. Chamberlain & Co's.
Weaver Jacob, lab., 54 Baum
Weaver Jacob, wagon mkr., s. s. Reading Pike near Tunnel, h. 646 Race
Weaver Jacob, teamster, s. s. Friendship al. b. Pike and Butler
Weaver John, carp., ●●, 61 Martin
Weaver John, lab., 451 W. Front
Weaver John, lab., wks. n. s. Front b. Lawrence and Pike
Weaver John G., auctioneer, 471 W. 5th
Weaver John J. Jr., exchange office, 354 W. 5th, h. s.e.c. 4th and Mill
Weaver Joseph, lab., wks. John Mitchell's
Weaver Kate, dress mkr., 158 W. 6th, bds. Clifton House
Weaver Louis, lab., 493 E. Front
Weaver Margaret, 562 E. Front
Weaver Martin, driver, 47 Plum
Weaver Mary, servt., 562 W. 5th
Weaver Mary, 25 Martin
Weaver Michael, s.s. Front b. Broad and Waldon
Weaver Peter, shoe mkr., 98 Clinton
Weaver Philip, lab., wks. 1563 E. Front
Weaver Philip L., boiler mkr., 78 Mound
Weaver Thomas J., clk., Co. Auditor's Office, 437 W. 5th
Webb Albert A., cigar mkr., bds. 30 David
WEBB ALEX., 392 W. 4th
Webb Benjamin, lab., 239 Everett
Webb Ezra, sr., bds. Spencer House
Webb Ezra jr., bds. Spencer House
Webb Geo. molder, wks. W. W. Hanes
Webb Harriet E., 30 David
Webb Hy., b. k., bds. 261 W. 8th
Webb Hy., lab., wks. Gas Works
Webb John, bds 362 W. 4th
Webb John, lab., 92 W. Front
WEBB JOHN, Jr., Fancy Millinery and Variety Goods, 152 & 154 W. 5th
Webb John A., clk., 73 W. 4th, bds. 242 Plum
WEBB Joseph T., (Pfaff J., McCabe,) bds. 393 W. 6th
Webb Maria. 363 W 6th
Webb Rosa, 92 Baymiller
Webb Samuel, lab., wks. Gas Works
Webb Samuel, molder, 16 Carr
Webb Thomas, b. k., 133 Main h. 215 Plum
Webb Thomas, lab., 162 W. Pearl
Webb Thomas, porter, 171 Vine, h. 62 W. Pearl

Webb Thomas B , 245 Plum
Webb Wm., white washer, s e.c. Elm and Pearl
WEBB Wm A., (Bradley & W.,) 182 Richmond
Webber Bernard. tailor, 304 Findlay
Webber Charles T., artist, 14 E. 4th, h. Covington
Webber Fred Wm., grocery, 15 Providence
Webber Hy., cooper, 107 W. M.Canal
Webber Hy., lab., wks. n.w.c. Plum and Wade
Webber John 614 Sycamore
Webber John, lab., 3 Linneus
Webbin Bernard. tailor. w. s Observatory b. Hill and Observatory Road
Webbin Bernard H., clk., 79 W. Pearl, b. Mt. Adams
Webbwine John, eng., 548 W. 3d
Webenstetten Clemens, blk.smith, 388 Broadway
Weber Ada. bds. 204 Plum
Weber Adam, shoemkr., 586 Race
Weber Adam, porter, 145 W. Front
Weber Anastasius, lab., rear 175 W. Liberty
Weber Anton, dray, e. s. Ramsey, n. of Front
Weber Bartholomew, phys., 351 Vine
Weber Benjamin, varnisher, wks. H. Clostermann's
Weber Bernhard, lab., 55 15th
Weber Caroline. bds. 646 Race
Weber Caroline, 561 Vine
Weber Chas , harness mkr., bds. 453 Vine
Weber Christian, boots and shoes, 60 Elder
Weber Christian, lab., 25 15th
Weber Conrad, wks. n.w.c. Freeman and 9th
Weber Daniel, lab., e.s. Kilgour b. 3d and 5th
Weber Eleanora, 151 Everett
Weber Frank, butcher, Findlay b. Central Av, and John
Weber Franziska, 679 Vine
Weber Frederick, cigar mkr., 511 Race
Weber Frederick, shoemkr., 660 Main
Weber Fred., stone cutter, bds. 628 Race
Weber Fred., watch mkr, 16 Sycamore
Weber Fred Hy. L., grocery, 684 Main
Weber George. 514 Plum
Weber Geo., b k., Galt House
Weber Geo.. cof. h., 246 Sycamore
Webor Geo.. cof. h., 20 E. 8th
Weber Gottfried, (W. & Newman,) 360 Main
Weber Hy., butcher, bds. n.s Browne nr. Ham Road
Weber Hy. clk., 309 Main
Weber Hy., cooper. 521 Race
Weber Hy., lab, 67 Hughes
Weber Hy., lab., 227 E. 5th
Weber Hy., salesman, 78 W 4th, h. 309 Main
Weber Herman H., musician, 29 Buckeye
Weber Jacob, brewer, 60 Green
Weber Jacob, huckster, e.s Bremen b. Elder and Findlay
Weber Jacob, lab. 54 Baum
Weber John, 65 Rittenhouse
Weber John, bar k., 82 Walnut, bds. 57 W. Front
Weber John, cof. h., 729 Race
Weber John, lab., w.s Ramsey n. of W. Front
Weber John, tailor, 87 Ham. Road
Weber John A., cof. h., 567 Vine
Weber John D., presser. wks. 729 Central Av.
Weber John C., teacher, 26 Abigail
Weber John F., cigar mkr., 511 Race
Weber John F., porter, ugr. E. 5th
Weber John L., cof. h., 482 E. Front
Weber Joseph, n.w. c. Linn and Poplar
Weber Joseph, bds. 90 Freeman
Weber Joseph, lab., 64 Elder
Weber Joseph, varnisher, bds. 561 W. Front
Weber Julius, shoe mkr., 530 Walnut
Weber Louis, cooper, 512 Plum
Weber Margaret, wks. Hieatt & Wood's candle factory

Weber Martin, boots and shoes, 562 Elm
Weber Martin, clk., 15 Pub. Landing, h. 90 W. 2d
Weber Martin, tailor, 679 Vine
Weber Martin, tanner, 91 W. Findlay
Weber Mary, 646 Race
Weber Mary, 143 Abigail
Weber Mux.. cab. mkr., 27 Moore
Weber Michael, n s. Stark b. Dunlap and Mohawk bridge
Weber Michael, blk.smith, 22 Bank
Weber Michael, cof. h., 19 14th
Weber & Newman (Gottfried W. & John H. N.,) iron, &c., 360 Main
Weber Nicholas, cigar mkr., 602 Elm
Weber Nicholas, wks. Cin. type foundry, s.w.c. Vine and Longworth
Weber Peter, 359 Ham. Road
Weber Peter, lab., 20 York
Weber Peter, rope mkr , wks. 442 W. 2d
Weber Phillip, cigar mkr., 154 Smith
Weber Philip, lab , 466 E. Front
Weber Philip, painter, bds. s.s. Bank b. Freeman and Coleman
Weber Philip, shears, &c., 16 W 5th
Weber Rudolph, finisher, 24 Ham. Road
WEBER W., Music Teacher, n.e.c. 5th & Vine, h. 238 Hopkins
Weber Wm , cigar mkr., 115 Ham. Road
Weber Wm., music teacher, 109 Mulberry
Weber Zacharias, wagon mkr.. 646 Race
Weberler Harman, tailor, 225 Betts
Webers Charlotte, 45 Pleasant
Webert Michael, meats, 135 Ham. Road
Webling Hy., hinge molder, wks. n e c. Walnut and Canal
Websey Ephraim, cooper. 29 Pleasant
Webster Andrew, clk., bds. 154 Broadway
Webster David B., grocery, 593 W. 6th
WEBSTER E. G. & CO., (Edmund G. W. & Frederick G. Ringgold,) Wholesale Dealers in Boots and Shoes, 63 W. Pearl
WEBSTER Edmund G., (E. G. W. & Co.,) h. Ky.
Webster Ellen, 519 W. 8th
WEBSTER GEO. P., Attorney at Law, Office, 11 E. 3d, res. Newport
Webster John, watchman. s.s. Torrence nr. Railroad
Webster John T., pipeman, n.e.c. Torrence and Forest Av.
Webster Joseph, carp., junction E. Front and Torrence
Weburg Geo., lab., 626 W. 6th
Wechsel Moses. lab., 30 Adams
Wechsler Caroline, bds. 127 E. 5th
Wuchsler Emanuel, 17 Chestnut
Wechsler John A., butcher, 238 Pleasant
Wecht Adam, tailor, 516 Main
Weddendorf Catharine, n.w.c. Price and Ringgold
Weddendorf Hy., clk., n.w.c. Price and Ringgold
Weddendorf Hy., grocery, n.w.c. Price and Ringgold
Weddendorf Mary, 53 Dudley
Wedding Bernard, painter, 398 Baymiller [6th
Wedekind Julius, cigars. &c., 255 W.
Wedenkamp Hy., tailor, 38 Green
Wedgewood Hy., bk layer, 156 Mound
Weed Geo. L., publisher, 28 W. 4th, h. 32 McFarland
Weed Julia, 340 W. 5th
Weed Porter L., clk., 32 McFarland
Weeger Casper, carp., 110 E. 2d
Weekman Lucy, servt., n.s. Poplar b. Freeman and Western Av.
Weeks Chas., carp., 732 E. Front
Weeks Edward, druggist, 2 E. 5th
Weeks Eliza H.. dry goods, w.s. Broad b. Front and Burt
Weeks Hy., carp., 732 E. Front
Weeks John, cargo wheels and capstans, c. Burt and Broad, h. w.s. Broad b. Front and Burt
Weeks Matthew T., carp., 732 E. Front
Weeks Thomas J., policeman, 1290 E. Front
Weeks Sylvester H., carp., Burt e. of Broad

Weeler Eliza., servt., 143 Clinton
Weeligmann John, tailor, 601 Sycamore
Weeman Hy., lab., 226 Water
Wefensiedt Clement, blksmith, wks. n. w.c. Race and Durrows
Wefer Bernard W., carp., n.e.c. Logan and Green
Wefer Joseph, sawyer, 420 Sycamore
Wegefort Elizabeth, servt., wks. 456 Broadway
Wegemeier Peter, lab., bds. 401 Sycamore
Wegfort Jette, servt., 640 Race
Weghorn Geo., varnisher, 58 David
Weglehner David, brewer, rear 450 Vine
Weglein Julius, clk., bds. 320 Walnut
Wegmann Hy., butcher, 15 Adams
Wegner Adelbert, mach., 549 Elm
Wegner Chas., blksmith, 641 Elm
Wegner Chas., blksmith, e.s. Campbell al. b. Elder and Liberty
Wehage Herman, lab., 103 Clay
Wehage Tobins, 103 Clay
Wehagen Herman. finisher, wks Fritsch, Burkhardt & Co's
Wehart Fred.. blk.smith, 73 David
Wehebrink Bernhard H., lab., 49 Pendleton
Wehhaus Wm., lab., 169 Clay
Wehking Hy., lab , 464 Main
Wehking Wm., lab., 406 Main
Wehl Hy., stocking weaver, 164 W. Liberty
Wehling John, cab. mkr., 193 Pleasant
Wehlman Barney, lab., e.s. Young b. Boal and Ringgold
Wehlman Hy., lab., e.s. Young b. Boal and Ringgold
Wehlman Michael, bk mkr., n.e.c. Price and Liberty
Wehlmann Fred. H., clk., 50 Clay
Wehlmann Mary, 50 Clay
Wehmeg Hy., lab., 185 Linn
Wehmeier Andrew, cof. h., 11 Landing b. Broadway and Ludlow, res. Newport
Wehmer Catharine, 121 Clay
WEHMER CHAS.. Proprietor Western Republic Coffee House, 600 Main
Wehmer Chas. F., teacher, h. 121 Clay
Wehmer Hy. L., miller, 121 Clay
Wehmer Louisa, saleswoman, 121 Clay
Wehmer Wilhelmina, 121 Clay
Wehmloff John D., cof. h., n.w.c. Canal and Main
Wehmier Christian, cooper, e.s. Western Av. b. Bank and Harrison Pike
Wehming Hy. J., carp., n.e c. 12th and Race
Wehner Casper, n.e.c. Mulberry and Vine
Wehning Hy., bds. 36 Green
Wehns Fred., shoemkr., wks. 209 W. 6th
Wehouse Henrietta, servt., 310 George
Wehr Fred. Wm., cof. h., 199 W. 6th
Wehr Mathias, painter, 55 15th
Wehre Frank, lab., 28 13th
Wehrle Chas., stocking manufac , 616 Central Av.
Wehrle Jacob, restaurant, 7 W. 5th
Wehrle Joseph, carver, 10 Webb
Wehrman Wm., plate printer, 57 Milton
Wehrmann A. M., grocer, n.w.c. John and Wade
Wehrmann Hy. C., baker, wks. 217 Everett
Wehrmann Joseph, (Lindemann & W.,) 70 12th
Wehrmann Louis F., furniture, 23 W. 5th, h. 9 Gorman
Wehrmann Christian H. bakery, 217 Everett
Wehrmeir Wm., lab., 72 Abigail
Wehrmeister Oscar, varnisher, 154 Baymiller
Wehrmuth Wm., gilder, 528 Elm
Wehrung Jacob, wagon manuf., junction Montgomery pike and Reading Road
Wehry Hy., confec., 51 13th
Weiand Geo., lab. n.s. al. b. Sycamore and Main and Canal and Abigail

Weibel Frank, musty ale, 116 Main, h. 261 Clark
Weibell Stephen, dray, 49 Walnut, h. 196 Betts
Weiber, Fred., clk,, 363 Central Av
Weible Stephen, dray, 196 Betts
Weibolt & Klotter. (Hy. W. & Hy. K.) tailors, 477 Main
Weibolt Hy., wagon mkr., 70 Pleasant
Weich Geo., tailor, 9 Buckeye
Weich Joseph, cooper. 709 Race
Weichering Wm., cigar mkr. 63 Walnut h 5 Fillmore
Weichgrever Hy., shoemkr., 424 Freeman
Weickis Sophia, servt., 528 W. 9th
Weideman Frank, watch mkr., 62 Main, res. Vine St. Hill
Weidenmann Andrew, brush manf., 592 Central Av
Weidemann Fred., cab. mkr., 114 Canal
Weidener Chas. H., bds. Galt House
Weidens Geo., tailor, bds. 566 Race
Weiderman Joseph, lab., rear 529 E. Front
Weideweber Cecilia, 709 Race
Weidgenant Wm., grocery, 570 Walnut
Weidinger John S., grocery, n.e.c. 3d and John
Weidler Geo. B., b.k., 143 W. 4th
Weidler Hy., cigar mkr., wks. 422 Walnut
Weidman Geo., shoemkr., bds. 502 Walnut
Weidman Joseph, carriage mkr., n.s. 6th w. of Harriet
Weidman Joseph, tanner, n.s. 6th b. Harriet and Horn
Weidman Martha, teacher, n.s. W. 6th b. Skaats al and Harriet
Weidman Mary K., teacher, n.s. W. 6th b. Skaats al and Harriet
Weier Fred., cooper, 72 Hughes
Weifering Frank. H., cook., n.e.c. B'dway and 2d
WEIGHELL John, (John W. & Son) h Clifton
WEIGHELL JOHN & SON, (John W. & John T. W.) Excelsior Tobacco Works, 210 & 212 Elm
WEIGHELL John T. (John W. & Son) 210 Elm
Weighell M. V., clk., 210 Elm h. Clifton
Weightman Thomas, sprinkler, 22 Park
Weightman Thomas F. butcher, 73 Dayton
Weigle Geo., boots and shoes, w.s. Lebanon Road nr. Montgomery pike
Weigle Arnold, fancy goods, 400 W. 5th
Weigler Wilhemina, millinery 502 Main
Weiglow Hy., cook 20 Plum
Weigman Joseph, harness mkr., 612 Central Av
Weigman Joseph, lab., 35 Baum
Weihe Fred., cooper, 72 Hughes
Weihe Mary, seamstress. 72 Hughes
Weihe Moritz, meats, 152 E. Front
Weihert Fred., driver, 203 Hopkins
Weihreh Ferdinand, tailor, 1 Harrison pike
Weihs Bernhardt, chair mkr., 65 Pendleton
Weik Chas., cigar mkr., 26 Findlay
Weikamp John. lab., 297 Broadway
Weikel Adam, shoe mkr, 506 Vine
Weiking Christian, porter, bds. 468 Main
Weil Andrew, fam. grocery, 166 E. Front
Weil Annie, seamstress, 205 Elm
Weil Asher, peddler, 185 Bremen
Weil Caroline, 126 Bremen
Weil & Bro., (Isaac & Solomon), clothing 311 Main
Weil Duvid, (W. & Meyer), h 257 W. 8th
Weil David, carp., 146 Bremen
WEIL Edward, (Max, Weil & Co.), s.w c. Vine and 12th
Weil Frank, cof. h , 135 York
Weil Frank, salesman, 192 Main, h. 135 York
Weil Hy., plasterer, 111 Buckeye
Weil Isaac, baker, 202 Elm
Weil Isaac, mer., 116 W. 5th
Weil Isaac, (W. & Bro.), 311 Main
Weil Jacob, mer., 103 W. 4th
Weil Jacob, lab., 115 Clay

830 (WEI) CINCINNATI (WEI) DIRECTORY. (WEL)

Weil John, cof. h., 665 Central Av
Weil John, feed store, 667 Central Av, h. 665 Central Av
Weil John, huckster, 549 Elm
WEIL MAX, (Max W. & Co.) s.w.c Vine and 12th
WEIL MAX & CO., (Max & Edward), Books and Stationery, s. w c, Vine and 12th
Weil Meyer, indigo blue manuf., 500 Central Av
Weil & Meyer (David W. & Adolph M.) furniture, s e c. Plum and 5th
Well Michael, peddler, 126 Bremen
Weil Saml. peddler, 21 Providence
Weil Saml., peddler, 152 Bremen
Well Solomon, huckster, 63 15th
Well Solomon, (W. & Brother), 311 Main
Weilage John D., salesman, 101 W Pearl h. s.e.c. Vine and 9th
Weiland Andrew, lab., 21 E 3d e. of Parsons
Weilenberg Ily., tailor, 71 Spring
Weilend Wm., shoemkr, s.s. Calhoun b Clifton Av and McMillan
Weiler Benj., express driver, s.e c. Elm and Findlay
Weiler Geo., lab., wk. n.e.c Canal and Walnut
Weiler Geo. F. boots and shoes, 12 Green
Weiler John, carriage mkr., n.s. Court b Walnut and Vine
Weiler John, dray, s.s. Budd b Harriet and Mill Creek
Weiler Lipman, peddler, 404 Walnut
Weiler Max L., b.k. 28 Sycamore, bds. 404 Walnut
Weiler Michael, wh. clothier, 5 E. 4th, h 113 W. 7th
Weiler Simeon, 289 Vine
Weiler Wm., dry goods, 178 W. 5th, h 90 W. 7th
Weiler Willoughby H., 192 Betts
Weiler Wolf, mer. 90 W. 7th
Weilken Ily , finisher, bds. 14 13th
Weill Meir, peddler, 159 Pleasant
Weillemann John, 120 Mohawk
Weilman Jacob, clk., 45 E. 2d
Wely Rob., lab., at gas works
Weizel Godfried, 126 13th
Weiman Barney, cab. mkr., 455 E. 5th
Weiman Christopher, stone mason 112 Gest
Weimann Conrad, butcher, 720 Race
Weimann Conrad, teamster, 709 Race
Weimann Frank, cooper, 156 Clay
Weimann Fred., cof. h., 103 W. Court
Weimar Ernst- cof h, 73 Daymiller
Weimar George, wood sawyer, 534 Plum
Weimeng Joseph, lab. wks. n.w.c. Plum and Wade
Weimer Barbara, servt., 388 George
Weimer Fred., cooper, 267 Ham. Road
Weimer John, teamster, bds, 17 Wade
Weimer Nicholas, 306 Linn
Weinantz Geo., blksmith, 10 Moore
Weinberg Louis, lab., 46 Buckeye
Weinewuth Ily., bklayer, 114 Clay
Weingardner Frank J., brick mkr., 148 Carr
Weingartiner John J., clk., 40 Richmond
Weingartner Lawrence, grocery, n.w.c. Richmond and John
Weingartner Wm., cof. h., 553 W. 5th
Wejnheimer Anton, cutter, 22 W. Pearl
Weinheimer Valentine, baker, 490 Walnut
Weinien Frank, lab. 362 Freeman
Weinkam Peter, cof. h., n.e.c. Central Av and Pearl
Weinmann Geo. B., finisher, w.s. Race b Findlay and Ham. Road
Weinmann Jacob J., tailor, 581 Race
Weinmann Matthew, clk., bds. n.e.c. Court and Vine
Weinz Robt., stone mason, 13 Madison
Weir James, painter, 333 Central Av
Weir John, plumber, 27 Hannibal
Weir Joseph, carpet weaver, 143 W. 5th h 24 Park
Weir Martha, bds. 23 Hannibal
Weir Mary, bds. 23 Hannibal
Weir Peter, finisher, wks. n.e.c. Walnut and Canal

Weir Solomon, peddler, e.s. Little al. b. 14th and 15th
Weirich Anna, 551 Vine
Weirich Peter, peddler, 20 W. Mulberry
Weirich Wm., lab., 401 Race
Weirndorff Anthony, clk. 305 Central Av, h. 180 Hopkins
Weirs Barnard, chair mkr., 65 Pendleton
Weis Alfred, carp , 91 12th
Weis Anton, 170 W. Liberty
Weis Balthasar, tanner, 142 Pleasant
Weis Benj., clk., 121 Main, bds. 267 Longworth
Weis Bernard, clk. 38 W. Pearl, h. 233 Walnut
WEIS CHARLES, Coffee House 92 W Court
Weis Chas., baker, 5 Whiteman
Weis Charles, varnisher, 581 Sycamore
Weis David, cigars &c. 233 Walnut
Weis Fred., driver, n.s. 9th b, Central Av and Plum
Weis Fred. driver, s.s Richmond b Plum and Central Av
Weis Geo., lab., 430 Plum
Weis Geo., trader, 46 15th
Weis Gottlieb, driver, s.s. Richmond b. Plum and Central Av
Weis Gottlieb, drivwr. n.s. 9th. b. Plum and Central Av
Weis Jacob, carp , 262 Pleasant
Weis Jacob, shoemkr, 494 Main
Weis John, cof. h., 91 Ham. Road
Weis John, grocery, 109 Ham. Road
Weis Joseph, gilder, 27 Franklin
Weis Joseph, pipe mkr., rear 376 Broadway
Weis L & Co., cigars, &c., 273 Walnut
Weis Leopold, (L. W. & Co.,)
Weis Martin, cook. rear 478 Walnut
Weis Peter, cigar mkr., wks. 551 Vine
Weis Sophia, packer, wks. 728 Central Avenue
Weis Theresa, 144 Ham. Road
Weis Valentine, expressman, 28 E. Front
Weisbard L. II., cutter, 78 W. Pearl
Weisbecker Tobias, grinder, 657 Vine
Weisbrod Hy., tailor, 11 Mulberry
Weisbron Wm., tailor, 636 Main
Weise Adeline, s e.c. Mound and Clark
Weise Bernard, conductor, s. e. c. Baymiller and Dank
Weise Bernard, lab., 86 Mohawk
Wejse Chas., varnisher, bds. 581 Sycamore
Weise David, carp., n.e.c. Front and Parsons
Weise Frederick, hostler, wks. e. s. St, Clair b. 6th and 9th
Weise Frederick, lab , 134 Bremen
Weise Herman, wood finisher, 68 Hughes
Weise Mitchel. s.e.c. Baymiller and Bank
Weise Phillip J., lab., 32 Dunlap
Weisel Hy., cooper. 563 Walnut
Weiselman Peter, tailor, 15 Ann
Weisenborn H., teacher of music, 82 W. 5th
Weiser Christina, servt., 532 W. 7th
Weiser Herman W., varnisher, 68 Hughes
Weisgerber John, brush mkr., e. s. Vine, b. Milk and Mulberry
Weishardt Christian, lab., bds. n. w. c. Smith and Augusta
Weishaupt Anthony, stone cutter, 517 Sycamore
Weishaupt Frederick, bk. layer, 245 Pleasant
Weishorn Barbara, servt., 9 15th
Weisker Bernhard, (W. Brothers,) h. New York
Weisker Brothers, (Charles W., Bernhard W., Charles Brandis, & Julius Esselborn,) millinery, 321 Main
Weisker Charles, (W. Brothers,) h. New York
Weiskittel Chas., bakery, 347 W. 5th
Weiskoff Abram, 37 E. 6th
Weiskopf Chas., painter, 561 Vine
Weiskopf Hy., painter, 198 Pleasant
Weislinger Chas., painter, 628 Vine
Weislogel Jacob G., tailor, 101 Bremen
Weisman Joseph. lab., 76 Abigail
Weismann Ily., 762 W. Front
Weismueller Diedrich, cigar mkr., 634 Main

Weiss Bernard, lab., 86 Mohawk
Weiss Charles, n. w. c. Browne and Vernon alley
Weiss Chas. II., tailor, 156 Bremen
Weiss Christian, bakery, 68 Wade
Weiss David, tanner, 246 Henry
Weiss Elizabeth, 2 Hamer
Weiss Frederick, cab. mkr. and carver, 200 Cutter
Weiss Geo. W., carver, 25 Elder
Weiss Gottlieb, cab. mkr., 103 Bremen
Weiss Hy. G., cab. mkr., 103 Bremen
Weiss John, lab , s.s. Harrison Road b. Riddle and Brighton
Weiss Joseph, bk. binder, 25 W. 4th, h. 27 Franklin
Weiss Joseph, 142 Ham. Road
Weiss Lewis, cigar mkr., wks. 392 Race
Weiss Mary, bds. 103 Bremen
Weiss Samuel N., n w.c. Plum and 2d
Weiss Seraphimus D., cof. h., 73 W 3d, h. n.w.c 2d and Plum
Weisshach George, carp., w. s. Linn b Dayton and York
Weissfloch Tobias, bakery, 30 Hughes
Weissman August, carp., 16 York
WEISSMAN FRED., Wholesale and Retail Groceries, &c., n. w. c. Clinton and Central Avenue
Weissman Mary, 346 Sycamore
Weist August, cab mkr., wks. 126 W. 2d
Weist John, cof. h., 56 W. Court
Weist Daniel, lab., 246 Pleasant
Weisz John, cab mkr., h. 608 Vine
Weiss John A., tailor, 109 Ham. Road
Weiss Peter, driver, 63 Ham. Road
Weiss Wolfgang, baker, 142 Ham. Road
Weiszmann Lewis, cigar mkr., 395 Vine
Weitershagen John, 89 Bank
Weith Joseph, tailor, 156 E. 5th
Weithhaupt August, finisher, bds. n. s. Augusta b. John and Smith
Weitler Hy., fireman, 6 Crippen al.
Wehman Geo., bds. Cincinnati House
Weitman Louis, 527 Plum
Weitter Casper, carringe mkr., 67 Clay
Weitzel Adam, cof. h., n.w.c. John and Findlay
Weitzel Conrad, lab., 11 Mulberry
Weitzel Hy., dyer, 6 W. 9th, h. 75 Pendleton
Weitzel John, n. s. Browne b. Mohawk and Ham. Road
Weitzel John C., meats, n w.c. Hughes and Liberty
Weitzel Peter. mason, n. s. Browne b. Mohawk and Ham. Road
Weitzel Peter, tailor, 187 W. Court, w. of Central Av
Weitzenecker Geo., salesman, 136 Walnut, h. 238 Vine
Weitaer Frank C., shoemkr, 93 Pendleton
Weitzler Hy., tailor, 75 Pendleton
Welzel Conrad, barber, 67 Buckeye, h. 48 Buckeye
Weizenecker Alexander, dry goods, 388 Vine
Weizenecker Geo., clk., 388 Vine
Weizenekner Fred., confec., 357 Vine
Welage Bernhard, lab , 29 Woodward
Welage Mrs. Catharine, 29 Woodward
Welage Catharine, milliner, 29 Woodward
Welage Fredericka, milliner, 29 Woodward
Welage Joseph F., 73 Wade
Welbroch Christopher, shoemkr, bds. 149 Carr
Welbrock Ferdinand, cab. mkr., 149 Carr
Welch Cyrus, saw mill, s.e.c. Front and Vance, h. s s. Front e. of Vance
Welch Cyrus, jr., sawyer, s. e. c. Front and Vance
Welch David, painter, 134 Van Horne
Welch Edward, huckster, 254 W. 7th
Welch Elizabeth, b.h., 227 W. 5th
Welch Elizabeth, laundress, Gibson House
Welch James, lab., wks. 1565 E. Front
Welch John, currier, 53 Martin
Welch John, lab , 208 W. 7th
Welch Julia, 51 Wade
Welch Mary, 163 Cutter
Welch Mary, cook, 111 Broadway
Welch Michael, lab., wks. C. T. Dumont's

Welch Richard, w. s. Central Av. b. 2d and W.W. Canal
Welch Thomas, dray, 242 Richmond
Welch Thos. H., b.k. , 25 Carr
Welch Wm., cooper, bds. 90 E. 2d
Weldan Oliver, tailor, 19 Hannibal
Wellen Richard, bark., bds. 41 Public Landing
Welding John, painter, e. s. Findlay b. Freeman and Western Av
Welding Mary J., b.h , 198 Plum
Weldy H. C., salesman, 222 W. 5th
Welferts John, expressman, rear 64 Hunt
Welker Wendell, stone mason, n.s. Rail road e. of Stone
Well —, grocer. e. s. Auburn b. Coggswell Av. and Central Av
Well Frederick, lab , 215 W. Front
Well ince Gottfried, cooper. bds. 701 Elm
Welland Hy., cof. h., 56 W. 6th
Wellarding Charles. cab. mkr., 196 Clinton
Wellderley Clemens, e. s. Division b. Bernard and Harrison Pike
Wellenbach Frank, cigar mkr., n. e. c. Sycamore and Woodward
Weller Anthony, lab., 209 Wade
Weller Catharine, n. s. Margaret b. Jane and Baymiller
Weller Eliza, 21 Green
Weller Elizabeth, 37 Ham. Road
Weller Garluch, lab., 217 Barr
Weller H. B., b.k., Cobb, Williams & Co's b Covington
Weller Hy., cooper, bds. 113 Clay
Weller James M., real estate agent, 197 Plum, h. 321 W. 3d
Weller John, books, &c., h. 21 Green
Weller John, policeman, n. s. Margaret, b. Jane and Baymiller
Weller John H., shoemker, 600 Race
Weller Mary, bds. 21 Green
Weller Mary, servt, n.e.c. 2d and Broadway
Weller Wm., carp., 21 Green
Weller Wm., paper hanger, bds. 577 Main
Wellerding Anthony, mach., 50 E. 8th e. of Lock
Wells Alsop, b.k. , Sellew & Co.'s, h. 35 Harrison
Wellington A., mach., wks. n. s. Canal w. of Elm
Wellin-ton Frederick, turner, bds/ 166 York
Wellington James F., clk., 237 Clark
Wellkamp John, carp., 20 York
Wellman Anthony, (Geise & W.,) 89 Hunt
Wellman Barney, hinge fitter, wks. n.e.c. Walnut and Canal
Wellman Eliza, 99 York
Wellman Frederick, lab., wks. 82 Baymiller
Wellman Fred. H., jr., clk., J. H. Lohr's, h. 50 Clay
Wellman George, lab., 17 Gorman
Wellman Hy , carp., 614 W. 8th
Wellman Hy., dray, 32 Rittenhouse
Wellman Hy., lab. 149 Bank
Wellman Herman H., clk., 363 Central Av., h. 134 Hopkins
Wellman Louis B., w. s. Freeman b. Liberty and Poplar
Wellmann Bernard, 58 York
Wellmann Chas., e. s. Linn b. Poplar and Findlay
Wellmann Hy. B., dry goods, 132 W. 5th
Wellmann Lewis, dry goods, 424 Freeman
Wellner A. M., bar k., 81 W 4th
Wellner Charles, b.k., 460 Sycamore
Wellner Charles, tailor, 25 Ham. Road
Wells —, bds. National Hotel
WELLS A. H. & CO. (Augustus H. W., John Titus & John K. Sterrett). Wholesale Grocers, 33 and 35 Main
Wells Anthony, lab., s.s. Friendship al., b. Pike and Butler
Wells Anthony, umbrella mkr., 564 Race
WELLS Augustus H. (A. H. W. & Co.) h. Mt. Auburn

WELLS Chas., secretary and treasurer, Cin. type foundry, s w. c. Vine and Longworth, h. Avondale
Wells Chas. J., printer, s. w. c. 8th and Main, h. Newport
WELLS J. C. (W. & Miles), h. Rising Sun, Ind.
WELLS J. D. & CO., (Jacob D. W. & Wm. H. Adderley) Drugs, Medicines. Paints. Chemicals, &c., n.w.c. 4th and Central Av
WELLS Jacob D. (J. D. W. & Co.) n.w. c. 4th and Central Av
Wells Lemuel T. (G. W. Foster & Co.), h. Hamilton co.
Wells M., dentist. 97 W. 7th
WELLS & MILES (J. C. W. & H. S. M.) Auctioneers and Commission Merchants, 59 W. Pearl
Wells Noah B., clk., Cin. Gas Light and Coke Co., bds. Spencer House
Wells Robert, lab., s.s. 8th h. Accommodation and State
Wells Sarah, 29 E. 8th e. of Lock
WELLS W. W., (Gould & W.) h. Covington
Wells Wm. B., Cin. type foundry, h. 506 W. 5th
Well-hear Wm. A., b.k., 28 McFarland
Welmer Anne, seamstress, 602 Race
Welmer Antonia, seamstress, 602 Race
Welmer Casper, carp., e s. Vine b. Mulberry and Milk
Welmer Jerry, carp., 592 Race
Welmer Martin A., carp., 602 R...
Welpley John, stone mason, 23 W. Court w. of Central Av
Welscher Hy. G., shoemkr, 102 Clay
Weisenbach Adam, bksmith, 69 Peete
Welser Andrew, 701 Elm
Welsh Andrew, grocery, n.s. Front e. of Lumber
Welsh Anna, seamstress, wks. 53 W. 4th
Welsh Anthony, boiler mkr, wks. s.s. 3d b. Butler and M. Canal
Welsh Bridget, s. s. al. b Pike and Lawrence and 3d and Pearl
Welsh Bridget, servt., 1521 E. Front
Welsh Bridget, 176 E. Pearl
Welsh Catharine, 213 E. 3d
Welsh Catharine, 388 Race
Welsh Catharine, 520 Elm
Welsh Eliza, n. s. New b. Culvert and Broadway
Welsh Elizabeth, 172 Central Av.
Welsh Ellen, seamstress, wks. 53 W. 4th
Welsh Ellen, servt., 226 George
Welsh Hanorah, seamstress, wks. 53 W. 4th
Welsh James, bds. Dumas Hotel
Welsh James, boiler mkr, wks. s.s. 3d b. Butler and M. Canal
Welsh James, lab., 25 Hill
Welsh James, jab., 42 Pierson
Welsh James, lab., 64 Richmond
Welsh John, bksmith, 135 W. Front
Welsh John, dray, 68 Butler
Welsh John, lab., wks.830 Central Av
Welsh John, lab , n.s. Hopkins b. Freeman and Garrard
Welsh John, lab., 230 Water
Welsh John, lab., n. s. 6th e. of Lock
Welsh John, lab., E. 3d b. Parsons and Daum
Welsh John, lab., 36 Butler
Welsh John, dairy, e. s. Milk b. Vine & Calhoun
Welsh John, stone mason, 33 Race
Welsh John, tailor, bds. 228 Broadway
Welsh John, tailor, bds. s. w. c. 5th and Broadway
Welsh John, wagon mkr, 126 W. Front
Welsh Keron, lab., n. s. Goodloe b. Willow and Niagara
Welsh Lawrence, waiter, 172 E. 5th
Welsh Luke, cof. h., 133 W. Front
Welsh Margaret, n.s. Goodloe b. Willow and Niagara
Welsh Margaret, servt., 14 Barr
Welsh Martin. express man, 196 Water
Welsh Mary, 33 Broadway
Welsh Mary, servt. n.e.c. 4th and Pike
Welsh Mary, servt., 390 W. 6th
Welsh Mary, seamstress, wks. 53 W. 4th
Welsh Michael, lab., 22 E. 8th e. of Lock

Welsh Michael, lab., s.s. Marsh b. Smith and Park
Welsh Michael, polisher, 37 New
Welsh Nicholas, dray, rear 200 E. 6th
Welsh Nicholas, lab., n. s. Front e. of Kelly
Welsh P. R., tailor, wks. 126 Walnut
Welsh Patrick, huckster, s. w. c. Central Av. and W. W. Canal
Welsh Patrick, lab., w. s. Oregon b. 3d and 6th
Welsh Patrick, lab., n.s. Augusta b.John and Smith
Welsh Patrick lab., n e.c. 4th and Lock
Welsh Patrick, lab., 385 W. 2d
Welsh Patrick W., coppersmith, s. s. Front e. of Torrence
Welsh Philip, policeman, n. s. Railroad e. of Vance
Welsh Richard, lab., n. s. Railroad e. of Hazen
Welsh Richard, porter, s.w.c. 3d and Sycamore
Welsh Richard, twister, 86 W. Front
Welsh Robert, boot fitter, 559 Sycamore
Welsh Thomas, 17 8th above Lock
Welsh Thomas, lab., 103 W. Front
Welsh Thomas, flagman, C., H. & D. R. R. depot
Welsh Timothy, n. s. 6th b. Culvert and Broadway
Welsh Timothy, lab., 172 E. 5th
Welsh Wm., lab., n.s. E. Front e. of Leatherbury
Welt John, cooper, n. w. c. Linn and Findlay
Welte Fiedel, carp., 56 Elder
Welton John, hinge fitter, wks. n. e. c. Walnut and Canal
Welton John, lab., n.e.c. 3d and Butler
Welzer Wm., 80 Mohawk
Wempe Clemens A., stone cutter, 127 Clay
Wempe Joseph A., clk., bds. 577 Main
Wempel Frank, lab., al. b. 13th and Mercer and Vine and Walnut
Wemper Wm., bksmith, wks. n. e. c. Walnut and Canal
Wendel Adam, brush mkr., 36 Hamilton Road
Wendel Catharine, shoe binder, 49 Bremen
Wendel Marie Elizabeth, rear n. w. c. Hughes and Schiller
Wendel Frederick. bksmith, 36 Ham. Road
Wendelsteine Martz,lab., n.w.c. Freeman and Liberty
Wenderberger Frank, bksmith, n.s. Augusta b. John and Smith
Wenderth Julius, b.k., 243 W. Court w. of Central Av
Wendland Louis, liquors, 64 Kossuth
Wendlandt C. L., salesman, 306 Main, h. 64 Kossuth
Wendlandt George, bakery, 546 W. 5th
Wendt Charles, clk., 218 Main, h. Newport
Wendt Hy., bksmith, 108 E. 2d, res. Newport
Wenger Charles, lab., 28 E. Front
Wengle Albert, cigars, &c., 10 W. Court
Wenke Barney, driver, 81 Findlay
Wenken Frederick, lab., 29 Mercer
Wenker Hy., dray, 26 Mansfield
Wennemann Hy., shoemkr, bds. 686 W. Front
Wennemer Anthony, lab., 65 Pendleton
Wenner John, cooper, 21 Mulberry
Wenner John G., bar k., s.w.c. Pearl & Ludlow
Wenner Margaret, huckster, 553 Elm
Wenner Philip, tailor, 696 Race
Wenning Hy. N , 309 Race
Wenning Wm. (Wm. W. & Co.), 120 Laurel
Wenning Wm. & Co. (Wm. W. & August Fresenborg) soap and candle manufacs., 40 E. 8th
Wenpe Herman, currier, 272 Broadway
Wenpe Joseph, currier, 272 Broadway
Wensing Mrs. Ferdinand. College al. b. Woodward and Abigail
Wensing Herman, carriage trimmer, 7 Pleasant
Wensing Joseph, 72 10th

Wensing Joseph, 422 Race
Wensler John, tailor. s. w. c. Logan and Elder
Wenstel Joseph, 125 Pleasant
Wenstrop Bernard, shoemkr, 191 W. M. Canal
Wenstrup John II., cutter, 59 E. 8th e. of Lock
Wenta Herman, salesman, 138 Walnut, h. 594 Main
Wentker Barney, dray, w. s. Kilgour b. 3d and 4th
Wentling Jacob, molder, 36 Chestnut
Wentworth A. Sydney (W. & Hanly) 99 Pike
Wentworth Geo. W., salesman, 36 Main, h. 149 Barr
Wentworth & Hanly (A. Sydney W. & Joseph C. H.,) dry goods, 87 W. Pearl
Wentworth John G., foreman, n.s. Goodloe b. Willow and Niagara
Wentworth R. P., clk., 101 W. 4th, h. 446 W. 8th
Wentworth Saml. S., foreman, 159 E. Front, h. Newport
Wentworth Thos. S., printer, 263 W. Court w. of Central Av
Wentworth Wm., teamster, 29 Parsons
Wenz Adam, basket mkr., 612 E. Front
Wentz Peter, baker, 407 Elm
Wentzel Benjamin (W. & Scherer), 18 Jackson
Wentzel & Scherer, (Benj. W. & Joseph S.) flour dealers, 342 Walnut
Wentzler Chas., sawyer, 509 W. 8th
Wenzel Chas., lab., 124 Clark
Wenzel Emil, bar k., 13 Mercer
Wenzel Frederick, carver, wks. Mitchell & Rammelsberg's
Wenzel Hannah, 14 Hughes
Wenzel Hy., blksmith, s. s. Dayton b. Freeman and Coleman
Wenzel Ily., music teacher, bds, 138 Longworth
Wenzel Ily. L., music teacher, bds. 214 George
Wenzel John F., wood yard, 496 Central A., h. 449 Plum
Wenzler Geo. cof. h., 682 Vine
Wenzler John M., bar k., 689 Vine

WENZLER MATHIAS, Coffee House, 680 Vine

WENZLER MATHIAS, Coal Yard, s.e.c. Elder and Race, h. 636 Vine

Weortz Chas., tailor, wks. 604 Elm
Wepler Catharine, 109 York
Weppner Fred., barber, 606 E. Front
Werbers Herman, lab., 91 Dudley
Wergan Adolph, cig.mkr., 52 Allison
Werhardt Hy., tailor, 700 Freeman
Werhman Wm., printer, 57 Milton

WERK M. & CO., (Michael W., Thos. Kirby, John Kirby, Nicholas Verdin & Jeremiah S. Hewlett,) Manufacturers of Adamantine, Star and Tallow Candles, Soap and Lard Oil, Depot Werk's Catawba Wine, 11 Main. Factory, Poplar, nr Central Av

WERK Michael, (M. W. & Co.) res. Harrison Pike
Werle Frank, bar.k., 7 Sycamore
Werle Jacob, porter, 57 W. 3d
Werle John, cof.h., 51 W. 3d, h. 207 Longworth
Werle John, painter, 538 Plum
Werle Jos., carver, 10 Webb
Werling Herman G., sawyer, 497 Race
Worling John D., cig.mkr., 141 Pleasant
Werly Peter, 319 W. 6th
Werman Conrad, grocery. 189 Bremen
Wermaster Oscar, lab., 154 Baymiller
Wermeier Arnold, tailor, 52 Dudley
Wermel Andrew, 126 Mohawk
Wermer Edward, tailor, 612 Sycamore
Wernder Joseph, turner, 52 Milton
Werner A. V., salesman, 404 Main, h. 220 Linn
Werner Andreas, lab., 35 Elder
Werner August, blk.smith, n.e.c. Elder and Elm
Werner August, cab. mkr., n.e.c. Elm and Elder

Werner Chas., cigar mkr., 108 Buckeye
Werner Christopher, hardware, 503 Vine h. 114 Clinton
Werner Fred., butcher, s. s. Harrison Pike, b. Riddle and Division
Werner Frederick, lab., rear 123 York
Werner Frederick J., clk., Co. clk's office h. 49 Allison
Werner Jacob. varnisher, 268 W. Liberty
Werner John Charles, barber, 220 Linn
Werner Julius, gardener, 70 Hughes
Werner Nicholas, cab.mkr., 263 Clinton
Warner Sophia, servt., 61 Webster
Wernert Ambros. brewer, 95 Buckeye

WERNERT & GOETTHEIM, (J.B. W. & Francis G.) Vermicelli, Maccaroni and Chocolate manuf. and Produce Dealers, 597 & 599 Main

WERNERT John B , (W. & Goettheim,) 597 Main
Wernig John, 486 Broadway
Wernigck Phillip J., meats, 129 Bremen
Wernke Elizabeth, 388 Sycamore
Wernke Hy., (W. & Timmer,) 388 Sycamore
Wernke Hy., grocery, s.e.c Mound and Clark
Wernke & Timmer, (Henry W. & John G. T.) undertakers, 388 Sycamore
Wernsing Bernard H., carriage painter, 9 Pleasant
Wernsing Fred., blksmith, 20 Woodward
Wernsing Herman, trimmer, 101 Pleasant
Werns Mathaeus, cr... 42 Ham. Road
Werr Lawrence, atty., 509 Elm
Werr Leonhardt, w.s. Vine, b. Milk and Mulberry
Werring Barnard, lab., 293 Linn
Werry Geo., (Geo. & Hy. W.) 52 Butler
Werry Geo. & Hy , blk.smiths, River, b. Ludlow and Lawrence
Werry Hy., (Geo. & Hy. W.) 52 Butler
Werry Mary, 74 W. Liberty
Wersel Geo., carver, bds. 596 Race
Wersel Nicholas, paper hanger, 596 Race
Wershy Augustus, painter, b. 920 Central Av
Wershy Wm., carriage trimmer, bds. 920 Central Av
Wert George, auctioneer, bds. Henrie House
Wert Geo. J., clk., 154 Main
Wert Wm. W., auction, 154 Main, h 442 W. 7th
Werter Francis, foreman, 396 Vine
Werth Barbara. 164 Cutter

WERTHEIMER Arnold, (Heidelbach W. & Co) 308 W. 7th
Wertheimer Isaac II , (W. Marks & Co.) 355 W. 5th
Wertheimer Isaac J., clothing, 243 Main h. 333 Race
Wertheimer Jacob, tailor, 479 Vine
Wertheimer Leopold, b. k., 108 Main, h. 355 W. 5th
Wertheimer, Marks & Co. (Isaac H. W., David M. & Morritz Wertheimer,) clothiers, 128 Main
Wertheimer Moritz. (Wertheimer, Marks & Co.) res. Dayton
Wertheimer Saml, b.k., Benno Speyer's, bds, 15 Lodge
Werthwein Christian, butcher, 207 Ham. Road
Werthwein Gottlieb, driver, 402 Race
Werthwein John, driver, rear 550 Walnut
Werts Elizabeth, h. s. s. Adams, b. Plum and Elm
Werts Frits, cooper, s. w. c. Baymiller and Bank
Werts Peter, trunk mkr., n.s. Adams, b. Plum and Elm
Werts Valentine, grocery, n.e.c. Adams and Plum
Wertsch Friz, blk.smith, h. 65 W. 12th and Mercer and Vine and Walnut
Wertz Adeline, seamstress, al. b 13th and Mercer and Vine and Walnut
Wertz Eleanor, 119 York
Wertz Frederick, cooper, s.e.c. Bank and Baymiller
Wertz, Jacob M., tailor, 80 Providence

Wertz Peter. stone mason, n. s. Adams b. Plum and Elm
Wertz Peter, trunk mkr., 34 Adams
Wertz Regina, al. b. 13th and Mercer and Vine and Walnut
Wertzborger Joseph, cooper, 362 Broadway
Wesby Ephraim, cooper, 29 Pleasant
Weschmier Casper, porter, 85 W. 2d
Wescott Charles. carp., wks. J. Whitaker's, Deer Creek Valley
Wescott David, lab., 90 Plum
Wesdorp Eman., shoemkr., bds. 55 Sycamore
Wesdorp John, plumber, 52 Abigail
Wesdrup Imen, bds. Cincinnati House
Weseling Bernhard. lab., n.w.c. Race and Green

WESENER CHRISTOPHER, Commission Merchant, 1 Walnut, h. 328 W. 7th
Weshel John D., cooper, 390 Broadway
Wesing Anna. 104 13th
Wesing Fred. F., 104 13th
Weskamp Hy., s.s. Charlotte b. Linn and Baymiller
Weslemau Louis, finisher, 143 Cafr
Weslenq John, cooper, 435 W. 2d
Wesler Fred., wig manuf., 108 W. 4th, h. 323 George
Wesler Hy., 85 Hamburg
Wesler Joseph, lab., Pavillion b. Observatory and 3d
Wesles Hy., cab. mkr., bds. w. s. Clay b. 12th and 13th
Wesley Joseph, lab. wks. n. s. Front b. Lawrence and Pike
Wesley Wm., cab. mkr., wks. s.w.c. Canal and Elm
Wesleyan Cemetery Office, s.w.c. 8th and Main

WESLEYAN FEMALE COLLEGE, Rev. Robert Allyn, Pres't, w. s. Vine b. 6th and 7th
Wesling Barney, porter, 63 Kilgour
Wesling Dietrich, lab., rear 490 Walnut
Wesling H., lab., wks. Hieatt & Wood's
Wesling Hy., cof. h., n.w.c. Water and Central Av
Wesling Hy., grocer, s. w. c. New and North
Wesling J. Hy., grocer, n. e. c. New and Broadway
Wesling John H., lab., 94 Clay
Wesling Margaret, 19 Providence
Wesling Wm., lab., 94 Clay
Wesly Frank, hostler, wks. e.s. St. Clair b. 5th and 6th
Wessel Ann M., 97 Hopkins
Wessel August, clk., n.w.c. Central Av. and Longworth

WESSEL AUGUSTUS, (Agent Wm. Jessop & Sons.) Steel Manufs , 7 W. 2d, h. Walnut Hills
Wessel Benj., cooper, bds. 383 Main
Wessel Bernard, carp., 293 Linn

WESSEL BERNARD H, Coal Dealer, n.w.c. Wood & 3d, h. 271 George
Wessel Christian, lab., 11 Wade b. Elm and Plum
Wessel Frederick, brklayer, rear 176 Clay
Wessel Frederick, lab., 67 Hughes
Wessel Frederick, tailor, 50 Abigail
Wessel Frederick, teamster, rear 387 W. Liberty
Wessel Hy., cooper, s.s. Court, b. Main and Sycamore, h. 554 W. Front
Wessel Hy., molder, wks. n.w.c. Plum and Wade
Wessel Hy , tailor, 46 Woodward
Wessel Hy., wood dealer, 65 14th
Wessel Jacob, n. s. Ham. Road, head of Elm
Wessel John, clk. 271 George
Wessel John, cooper, 390 Broadway
Wessel John, tailor, 89 12th
Wessel John H., b. k., bds. 271 George
Wessel John Henry, lab., 178 Clay
Wessel Joseph, clk., 271 George
Wessel Joseph, shoemkr., 2 Abigail
Wessel Lewis, lab., e. s. Hanover b. Franklin and Woodward
Wesselman Anthony, cooper, rear 14 13th

(WES)　　CINCINNATI　　(WES)　　DIRECTORY.　　(WHA)　　333

selman F. H., painter, wks. John Mitchell's
selman Louis, blk.smith, Carr b. 7th and 8th
selmann Anna, servt., 351 W. 7th
selmann Hy., shoemkr., bds. 383 Main
selman Joseph, foreman, 369 Broadway
seln Lambert, shoe store, 28 Race
sels Barney H., lab, 435 W. 2d
sels Hy., porter, 21 Pub. Landing
sendarp Mathias, tailor, s.e.c. Findlay and Race
sendorf Mary, servt., wks. 122 Abigail
sing Frank H., (Cotter & W.,) 9 Landing b. Broadway and Ludlow
sling Mrs. Anna E., s. s. Milton b. Price and Young
sling Dietrich W., grocery, 99 Barr
sling George porter, 127 Walnut
sling Geo. H., (Geo. H. W. & Bro.,) 280 W. 6th
sling Geo. H. & Bro., (Geo. H. & Henry.) grocery, 280 W. 6th
sling Hy., b. k., n.w.c. Walnut and 2d
sling Hy., (Geo. H. Wesling & Bro.) 280 W. 6th
sling Mrs. Mary, h. 176 E. 5th
sling Samuel, wks Cin. Saw Mill, Junction 6th and Front
sner Jacob, tailor, 100 Clay
t Alfred, clk., bds. n. e. c. Elm and 8th
t Augustus, cab. mkr., w.s. Jordan b. Clark and Gest
EST C. W. & CO., (Charles W. W. & Joseph Torrence,) White Water Flour Mill, Junction W. 3d and Front
ST Chas. W., (C. W. W. & Co.,) bds. St. Charles Hotel
EST CYRUS, Ornamental Plasterer, 109½ W. 3d, bds. 199 W. 3d
t Euel, hatter, 19 Ann
t Frederick C., freight agent, I. & C. R. R., Office 66 W. 3d, h 202 Mound
EST HENRY F., Importer and Wholesale Dealer in China, Glass and Queensware, n.w.c. Pearl and Walnut, h. Avondale
t Isaac, boiler manufc., 56 Pike, h. n.w.c. 3d and Kilgour
t Isaac E., com. mer., 176 W. 7th
t James, artist, bds. 195 Broadway
t John, lab., 33 Baum
t John, porter, n.e.c Vine and 2d
t John B., grocery, 19 Abigail
t Lauelle, 155 W. 9th
t Mary, 125 W. 7th
t Orange S., painter, 431 Central Av
t Samuel, 16 W. Mulberry
t Wm., piano mkr., wks. 283 Main
t Wm. P., bds. 39 New
tberg Frank, lab., rear 92 Clay
tberg Mattheus K., lab., bds. 363 W. 5th
tberg Mathias, lab., 94 Clay
tbrock Mary, servt., 460 Main
tbrock Theodore, lab., rear 16 Madison
tcamp Henry, lab, wks. n.w.c. Plum and Wade
tcott Leonard W., teamster, 91 Carr
tcott Mary R., 91 Carr
tdorf John, lab., 52 Abigail
thusch Theresa, seamstress, 13 15th b. Elm and Plum [7th
temeyer Frederick, teamster, 551 W.
tenberger Moses, mer., 91 Richmond
tenberger Clemon, porter, 20 Commerce
tenbro Cornelius, tanner, wks. R. Culbertson's
tendick Francis, painter, 669 Race
tendorf Barney, salesman, 73 Spring
tendorf Henry, blksmith, s.s. Woodward b. Main and Sycamore
tendorf Henry E., cab. mkr., 73 Clay
tendorf Joseph, carriage painter, 67 14th

Westendorf Joseph, shoe mkr., bds. 70 Sycamore
Westendorf Joseph J., boots and shoes, 147 Sycamore
Westendorf Phillip, 147 Abigail
Westerbeck Henry, dray, e.s. Kilgour b. 3d and 5th
Westorhall Barney, hostler, bds. 24 Gano
Westerhaus Henry, lab., 523 Sycamore
Westerhaus Herman H., lab., 406 Longworth
Westerhoff Anthony, waiter, Galt House
Westerhoff Anthony, carp., wks. John H. Luhn's
Westerhoff Geo. F., chair mkr., wks. H. Clostermann's
Westerhouse Dena, servt., 40 Plum
Westerkamm Edward, boots and shoes, 1084 Central Av
Westerkamp Frank H., boots and shoes, 37½ Broadway
Westerkamp Henry, brewer, 264 Ham. Road
Westerkamp Wm., carp., 40 Pleasant
Westerman Christian, mach., 23 Commerce
Westerman Henry, chair caner, 399 Br'd'y way
Westerman Henry, lab., 67 Butler
Westermann Eliza, 21 Commerce
Westermann Fred., sawyer, 20 W. Mulberry
Westermann Frederick, teamster, 290 Linn
Westermann Henry, upholsterer, bds. 61 W. 5th
Westermann John G., varnisher, 12 Pleasant
Westermann John H., shoe mkr., 165 Carr
Westermann Lambert, propr. Frey's Exchange 61 W. 5th
Western Charlotte, 28 Barr
WESTERN CHRISTIAN ADVOCATE, Rev. Calvin Kingsley, Editor, s.w.c. 8th and Main
Western Coal Oil Co., s.s. 2d b. Rose and Mill
WESTERN HOTEL, John F. Noelker, Prop'r., 502 W. Front
WESTERN INS. CO., Fire and Marine, Thos. F. Eckert, Pres., J. A. Colling, Sec'y, R. Loheyde, Surveyor, Office 2 Pub. Landing
Western Massachusetts Insurance Agency, 65 W. 3d
Western Museum, e.s. Sycamore b. 3d and 4th
WESTERN UNION TELEGRAPH CO., Chas. Davenport, Division Supt., s.w.c. 3d and Walnut
Western Theophilus B., clk., 29 Barr
Westfall Henry, foreman, 97 Central Av
Westfield Charles, awning manuf., 100 Sycamore
Westheidemann Sophie, w.s. Goose al. b. Liberty and 15th
Westheimer Gustavus L., gen'l agt. Ehrgott, Forbriger & Co., h. 216 George
Westjohn Henry, jr., carp., 7 E. 7th
Westjohn Henry, sen., 7 E. 7th
Westjohn Hermann H., 69 E. Pearl
Westjohn Theresa, millinery, 310 W. 5th
Westjohn Wm., clk., 7 E. 7th
Westkamp Henry L., molder, wks. n.w. c. Plum and Wade
Westkamp Wm., lab., wks. n w c. Plum and Wade
Westlenk Henry, carp., w.s. Kilgour b. 3d and 4th
Westling Barney, porter, e.s. Kilgour b. 3d and 5th
Westling George, porter, e.s. Kilgour b. 3d and 5th
Westman Geo., teamster, 203 Water
Westmeier Casper, janitor, 68 W. 3d
Westmeier Henry, carp., s.e.c. Locust and Baltimore
Westmeier John Henry carp., s.s. Baltimore b. Locust and Sycamore
Westmeyer Casper, cab mkr., 68 W. 5th
Westmeyer Henry W., sawyer, h. 10 Webb
Westmeyer Hy., W., sawyer, 10 Webb
Westmeyer Wm., sawyer, 10 Webb

Weston Chas. F., clk., n.s. Wade b. Freeman and Dudley
Weston Edward R., watchman, 131 Betts
WESTON J. HENRY, Lightning Rod Works, 29 W. 6th, res. E. Walnut Hills
Westphalen Henry, cigar mkr., 595 Race
Westrup Walter, mess. Gilmore, Dunlap & Co.'s
Westwood Henry, steel yard mkr., 51 Observatory Road, h. 49 Observatory Road
Westwood John, supt. gas works, 436 W Front
Wetch Fred., blksmith, 65 12th
Wetenkamp John D., shoe mkr., 589 Race
Wetherby Coleman, bk.layer. 246 Clinton
Wethered Benjamin, blksmith., 183 Baymiller
Wetherherd Wm. Albert, student, 25 W. 3d, bds. 40 W, 9th w. of Central Av
Wetherill Augustus E., with Suire, Eckstein & Co., room 8 Railroad Bldg.
Wetmore M. W., real estate agt., bds. Spencer House
Wetmore Wm. P., plasterer, 101 Providence
Wettberg Henry, cooper, 12 Buckeye
Wettekan Anthony, meats, 101 Clark
Wettemeier George, lab., s.s. 6th nr. Mill Creek
Wettengel Christopher, trimmings, 165 W. Liberty
Wettengel Jacob, barber, 22 W. 9th
Wettengel Valentine, barber, 8 Court House Building, h. 92 W. 9th
Wetterer Bernhard, baker, 205 Vine
Wetterer Chas., finisher, 39 Pike
Wetterer John, vinegar manuf., 30 Plum
Wetterer Paul, shoe mkr., 21 E. 3d e. of Parsons
Wettering Constantine, musician, 41 Pleasant
Wettermann Michael, teamster, bds. s.w. c. Corporation Line and Clifton Av
Wettig Frederick H., cab. mkr., wks. n.s. Augusta b Smith and Rose
Wettig Geo., chair mkr., 42 Rittenhouse
Wettig Louis, cab. mkr., wks. Mitchell Rammelsberg's
Wettscharreck Peter, cof. h., 640 Elm
Watsdine Henry, tailor, 109 W. Court
Wetzel Henry, bk. molder, bds. 101 Gest
Wetzel Jacob, s.w.c. Railroad and French
Wetzel John, carp., n.s. Railroad e. of Vance
Wetzel John, stone cutter, 430 Plum
Wetzel Peter, tailor, 187 W. Court w. of Central Av
Wetzenbach Andrew, painter, 395 Walnut
Wetzler Joseph, agt., bds. 480 Vine
Weurt Catharine, tailoress, 102 Abigail
Weust A., turner, wks. 128 W. 2d
Weust Wm., propr. Commercial House, n.e c. Central Av. and 7th
Wewell John H., ice mer., 172 E. 5th
Weweler John H., lab., n.w.c. 3d and Stone
Wewer Henry, bar k., s e c. 5th and Home
Wexelberg August, salesman Sellew & Co.'s, h. Covington
Wexler Salomon, Jewish synagogue, e.s. Lodge b. 7th and Gano
Weyand Chas., cof. h., 1011 Central Av
WEYAND & JUNG, (Peter W. & Daniel Jung,) Western Brewery, 1039 Central Av
WEYAND Peter, (W. & Jung,) Allanthus b. Clearwater and Bank
Weyl Gustave, s e c. Clinton and John
Weyland L. H. millinery, 205 Elm
Weyler Leopold, 159 W. Court
Weyre Mary, 518 John
Weyres Br. Amedeus, teacher St. Francis school
Wexler Mary, 402 Vine
Wegel Mary, laundress, 24 13th
Whaling Bridget, 63 Avery
Whalling Margaret, 247 Pearl b. Canal and Kilgour
Whalan Anu, 109 Water
Whalan James, station house keeper, c. Pearl and Central Av
Whalan Michael, lab., 93 Water

334 (WHI) CINCINNATI (WHI) DIRECTORY. (WHI)

Whalen Thos., blksmith., s.e.c. Race and Water
Whalen Thomas, lab., n.s. Taylor b. Carr and Freeman
Whaland Bridget, 84 Water
Whaland Mary, 485 W. 3d
Whalen James, lab, n.s. Taylor b. Freeman and Carr
Whalen Patrick, lab., Anderson al. b. Front and 2d
Whaley John R., 4 Baker, h. 18 McFarland
Whalon Julia. 217 E. 6th
Whann Geo , clk., 114 Findlay
Wharty Daniel, lab., 445 W. 2d
Whateley H. & Co., (Henry W. & Erastus A. Baldwin,) saw mill, Junction 6th and Front
Whateley Henry, (H. W. & Co.,) h. Sterrs Tp.
Whaylan Martin, lab., n.w.c. Elm and Water
Whealand Thomas, cof. h., n.s. 6th b. Culvert and Miami Canal
Wheat James E., sawyer, 60 Everett
Wheatley Louisa. s.s. Phoebe al. b. Plum and Central Av
Wheatly Thomas, produce, bds. 298 W. 5th
Wheeland Michael, cook, 57 E. 7th
Wheeldon Thomas B., cutter, 201 Richmond
Wheelen John, paver, 254 E. 6th
Wheelen Wm., lab, 525 W. 8th
Wheeler Miss, actress National Theater
Wheeler Mrs., w.s. Campbell al b. Findlay and Elder
Wheeler Aquilla J., banker, 150 Richmond
WHEELER BENJ. D., Surgeon Dentist, 93 W. 7th
Wheeler Catharine, 505 Race
Wheeler David, lab., 92 E. 5th
Wheeler G. W., collecting agent, 365 W. 7th
Wheeler Geo. A., 309 George
Wheeler John W., clk., 301 Walnut, res. Covington
Wheeler Joseph, vet; surgeon, 180 Smith
Wheeler Milton G., baker, 46 Plum
Wheeler Stephen, 250 E. Pearl e. of Broadway
Wheeler Thomas, paper carrier, 6 W. 4th
Wheeler Wilber B., principal 11th district school. res. Walnut Hills
WHEELER & WILSON'S SEWING MACHINES. Wm. Sumner & Co., agents, 77 W. 4th
Wheelright Jas , mer., bds. Madison House
Whelan Barry S., lab. , n.s. Margaret b. Jane and Baymiller
Whelan Dennis, rubber, wks. n.e.c. Canal and Elm
Whelan John, candy mkr., s. w.c. 2d and Plum
Whelan John, lab., s. e. c. Front and Plum
Whelan John, shoe mkr., 9 New
Wheller John, 125 E. Pearl
Whellin Dennis D., lab., s.s. Court e. of Broadway
Whelpley A. W., printer, 319 Elm
Whetley Rachael A., 1 York
Whetstone F. D. S. & Co., manuf., Linseed oil, n. s. 8th b. Broadway and Miami Canal
Whetstone Frank D S. (F. D. S. W. & Co.,) h. Mt. Auburn
Whetstone Jacob V., druggist, 116 John
Whetstone John, 262 Vine
Whetstone Rev. Hy. H., lab., wks. 13 E. Front
Whetstone John L., clk., 262 Vine
Whichear Louis. trimmer, 195 W. Court
Whieran Adam, shoe mkr., 708 Freeman
Whinger Michael, molder, 704 W. 6th
Whipper Fred., can mkr., 28 Dudley
Whipple Eliza M., 284 Main
Whipple Emma, 7 Harrison
Whipple Geo., clk., bds. Indiana House
Whipple Geo. M., 210 Longworth
Whipple Geo. W., bds. Indiana House

Whipple Julia, 210 Longworth
Whipple W. B., teller, 51 W. 3d, h. Walnut Hills
Whiriskey Pat., shoe mkr., n.s. 7th b. Main and Sycamore
Whitaker Elizabeth, 144 Baymiller
Whitaker Fred., eng., wks. n. e c. Walnut and Canal
Whitaker Hy., saddler, wks 89 Main
Whitaker Jane, laundress, e.s. al. b. 4th and 5th and Park and Mill
Whitaker John S., lab., 177 W. Court w. of Central Av.
Whitaker Joseph, carp., junction of Torrence and Front
WHITAKER JOSEPH, Bristles, Hair, Lard, Tallow, Neat's Foot Oil, Grease and Sausage Casings Manufactory, Deer Creek Valley, h. Hathaway Lane E. Walnut Hills
Whitaker Thomas, mach., bds. 144 Baymiller
WHITCHER Wm. C.. (Wm. C. W. & Co.,), 370 W. 4th
WHITCHER WM. C. & CO , (Wm. C. W. & Co.,) Wholesale Dealers in, Hats and Caps, Hatter's Trimmings and Straw goods, 139 Walnut
Whitcomb Mrs. Geo. B., Richmond, b. Freeman and Carr
Whitcomb John, 58 Richmond b. Plum and Central Av.
White Albert, barber, wks. 186 Walnut
White Albert, clk., Canal, h. Foster's Crossing.
White Alfred, marble wks., 136 Clark
WHITE Alfred; (T. White & Son,) 136 Clark.
White Alice, 198 Webb
White Amelia, servt., 299 Longworth
White Andrew, saddler, 488 Race
White Ann, h. s. e. c. Lawrence and Pearl
White Anthony, blksmith, River b. Ludlow and Lawrence, h. 87 E. 3d b. Whittaker and Collard
WHITE & ANTRAM, (Julian W. & Micajah T. A.,) Importers and Wholesale Dealers in Fancy Dry Goods and Notions, 47 W. Pearl
White Archibald, lab., 27 Accommodation
White Avander D., clk., 290 John
White Benj., bk. binder, bds. 169 Longworth
White, Brother & Co., (Mordecai M. & Francis T. W.,) grocers, 83 and 85 Walnut
White Chas., gas fitter, 214 Sycamore
White Chester B , bar k., bds. 109 E. 2d
White Chas. R., foreman Enquirer printing establishment, h. 215 Walnut
White David, cof. h., 129 Sycamore
WHITE David A., (T. R. Biggs & Co.) bds. Spencer House
White Dominick, plasterer, 603 W. 8th
White Mrs. E., bds. 271 W. 6th
White Edward F., 197 W. Court
White Elizabeth, b. h., 351 Central Av.
White Elizabeth, n w.c. Mill and 4th
White F. T., bds. Dennison House
White Francis, janitor, 11 Bedinger
White Francis T., (W., Brother & Co.,) 420 W. 6th
White Frank, n.e.c. 9th and Elm
White Frank M., com. mer., 20 E. Canal h. Foster's Crossing [Lock
White Geo. W., mach., 87 E. 3d, e. of
White Hamilton, lab. 44 W. 7th
White Hy., boots and shoes, 3 Landing b. Broadway and Ludlow, h. 521 Sycamore
White Isaac H., b.k. 25 W. 4th and treas. Mt. Auburn Young Ladies' Institute. h. Mt Auburn
White J. F., bds. 231 Walnut
White Jas., blksmith, 87 E. 3d e. of Whittaker
White James, (Jas. W. & Co.,) h. Newport
White Jas. & Co., (Jas. W. & Charles Bilks,) blksmiths, River b. Ludlow and Lawrence

White Jas. M , blksmith, bds. 87 E. 3d b. Whittaker and Collard
White Rev Jas. M., 451 W. Liberty
WHITE JAMES S., Attorney at Law, 260 Walnut, h. 45 W. 9th
White Jane I., b.k., 44 W. 7th
White John, cook, bds. 10 Sycamore
White John, lab., n.s. Cherry al. b. Plum and Central Av.
White John, servt., Burnet House
WHITE JOHN F., Physician and Surgeon, Office n.w.c. Race and 4th, h. n.e.c. 4th and Plum
White John P., drug store, s.w.c. Race and Front
White John T , salesman, 19 W. Pearl. bds. Dennison House
White Joseph, lab., 18 Commerce
White Rev. Joseph J., 98 George
WHITE Julian, (W. & Antram,) 576 W. 9th
White Lemuel H., salesman 56 W. Pearl, bds Dennison House
White Leonard M , grocery, n.e.c. Hopkins and Freeman
White Lewis, clk., bds. 170 W. 3d
White Lewis H., cooper, bds. 2d Buckeye
White Malinda, 127 Longworth
White Mary, n.s. 6th e. of Lock
White Mary, bds. 41 W. Front
White Mary, servt., 162 Barr
White Mary A , w.s. Kilgour b. 3d and 5th
White Mary D , teacher, 20 Gest
White Mary E.. teacher, bds. s.w.c. Franklin and Broadway
White Matthew, tailor, 48 E. 3d
White Michael, lab., 47 Observatory Road
White Mill Distillery, w.s Western Av. b. Bank and Harrison Av.
White Mordecai M , (W.,Brother & Co.) 420 W. 6th
White Oliver D., atty., n.w.c. 3d and Main
White Pat., lab , 118 Betts
White Pat., lab , 191 Linn
White Pat., tailor, s. w. c. Pearl and Canal
White Pat., walter Walnut Street House
White Pat. H., s.s. Phoebe al. b. Plum and Central Av.
White Peter A., office, 50 Main, h. 133 Broadway
White Peter N., painter, bds. River b. Ludlow and Lawrence
White Robt., 265 W. 5th
White Robt., carp., 442 George
White Robert, pattern mkr., wks. n.e.c. Canal and Walnut
WHITE ROSWELL M., Lumber Yard, 418 Central Av., h. 443 W. 7th
White S. M., music teacher, 195 Vine
WHITE T. & SON.(Thos. & Alfred,) Marble Works. 255 and 257 W. 5th
White Thaddeus E , cab. mkr., bds. n.s. Augusta b. John and Smith
White Thayer D , cab. ware manuf., 5 Augusta, bds. n.s. Augusta b. John and Smith
White Thomas, cooper, 153 Cutter
White Thomas, dray, 96 Hunt
White Thomas, lab., wks. s.w.c. Front and Smith
WHITE Thos., (T. & Son.) s.s. Livingston b. Linn and Baymiller
WHITE W. O., Freight Agent Cincinnati and Chicago Air Line Railroad, Office 115 Vine
White Wm., blksmith, n.s. Front e. of Kelly
White Wm., blksmith, 51 Observatory Road, h. 54 Observatory Road
White Wm., carp., 96 Clinton
White Wm. clk., bds. Teutonia Hotel
White Wm., feed store, n.w.c. Pearl and Lawrence, h. 79 E. 3d e. of Whittaker
White Wm., finisher, s.s. Pearl b. Pike and Butler
White Wm., finisher, wks. C. T. Dumont's

(WHI) CINCINNATI (WIE) DIRECTORY. (WIL) 335

te Wm., mer., 187 Richmond
ite Wm., molder, wks. n.e.c. Canal and Walnut
ite Wm., (R. Brown & Co.,) 187 Richmond
te Wm., servt., Burnet House
ite Wm., wagon mkr., 96 Clinton
ite W. McLinn, 298 Vine
ite Wm. M., salesman, 46 W. 2d, bds. 7 Water
ite Wm. G., clk. Post Office, rooms No. 1 Ohio Medical College
iteley George, s.s. Avery al. w. of Wood
iteley Wm. G , carp., s.s. Avery al. w. of Wood
ITEMAN B. B., sec'y Merchants and Manufacturers' Ins. Co., h. Clifton
ITEMAN John P., sec'y Washington Ins. Co , h. 158 York
ITEMAN Wm. I., (Springer & W.,) h. E. Walnut Hills
ilehead Edward, blksmith, 14 Richmond
itehead Mrs. Geo., n. s. Front e. of Kelly
itehead James, finisher, 238 E. 6th
ITEHOUSE Joseph, (Hand, W. & Co.,) 430 John
teside James, porter, 7 Providence
iteside Wm., upholsterer, 7 Providence
tford Wm. M., agt., 197½ Plum, h. 277 John
thaufer Wm., marble cutter, wks. n. e.c. Elm and Canal
ITMAN Henry C., (Kebler, W. & Force,) bds. s.e.c 4th and Race
tmore John, shingler, bds. 444 W. Front
tmore Seth H., mach., 54 Lawrence
itmore T. & Co., (Thomas W. & Wm. Johnson,) hoop skirt manuf., s.w.c. 4th and Central Av.
tmore Thos., (T. W. & Co.,) w.s. Central Av. b. 3d and 4th
tney Amos, molder, 36 Plum
tney Decatur, carp., bds. 567 W. 9th
tney Hy., paper carrier, 213 W. Court, w. of Central Av.
tney James, molder, 36 Plum
tney James, printer, bds. 567 W. 9th
tney John, teacher, 239 W. 9th, w. of Central Av.
tney Margaret, 491 W. 9th, w. Central Av.
itney Michael, molder, 174 Water
tney Patrick, expressman, 171 Water
tney Thomas, molder, 489 W. 9th, w. of Central Av.
ITNEY Vincent, (W. F. & V. W.,) 232 Laurel
ITNEY Wm F., (W. F. & V. W.,) bds. 232 Laurel
HITNEY W. F. & V., (Wm. F. & Vincent,) Lumber Yard, 515 Central Av.
tridge Mrs. E. A., regalia manuf., 128 Walnut, h. 160 Race
tson Caleb C., 112 Barr
tson Clarkson S., printer, bds. 112 Barr
ttaker A., wks. junction 6th and Front
ttaker Martha, tailoress, 445 W. 4th
ttaker Samuel B., mach., Richmond b. Freeman and Carr
ttaker Wm , carp., 22 E. 5th
HITTEMORE JAMES B., Drugs, Medicines, &c., 51 Broadway, h. 22 Dayton
ttemore Thos., messenger, bds. 71 Longworth
tten Francis, 180 W. 6th
tten Hanora, 166 W. Court, w. of Central Av.
tten Wm., 149 Culvert
ttington Roland J., blksmith, 56 Avery
ttlesey Joseph, 8 Observatory Road
tton Chas. H., actor, bds. 168 W. 3d
tton John M. M., at W. U. Telegraph Co., bds n. w. c. Central Av. and Longworth

Wholaver Daniel, clk., bds, s. w. c Mill and 4th
Wholihan Michael, shoemkr., 398 Broadway
Whylaw Andrew, lab., wks 222 E. Front
Wibben Gerhard H., tailor, bds. 19 Abigail
Wibriede Catharine. servt., 33 Clark
Wibudeke J. H., 287 George
Wich Philip, 93 Ham. Road
Wichant Francis, cig. mkr., bds. 602 Elm
Wichard Franz, blk. smith, 11 Adams
Wichwar Louis, coach trimmer, bds. 195 W. Court, w. of Central Av.
Wichgar Rose, 195 W. Court, w. of Central Av.
Wichman Joseph, chair mkr., 104 Clay
Wickemeyer Wm., lab., e.s. Plum b Adams and Liberty
Wicker Wm. M., carp., n. s. Yeatman b. Broadway and Sycamore, h. Newport

WICKERSHAM OSWALD J., Dentist, 342 W. 5th

WICKERSHAM THOMAS, Artist, Portrait and Photograph Painter, Room No. 19 Pike's Opera House, res. 10 Pine

Wickham Aretas, porter, bds. 460 W. 8th
Wickham Andrew, dray, 460 W. 8th
Wickham Peter, lab., n.w.c. 3d and Ellen
Wickham Thomas, auction, 26 W. 5th
Widfau Louis, lab., 82 E. Pearl
Widdle August. horse shoer, 147 Hunt
Widdifield W. S., salesman, 83 W. Pearl bds Winnie House
Widdop Edward, lab., 667 Sycamore
Wideler George, clk., bds. 143 W. 4th
Widemer Enoch, lab., s.e.c. 5th and Culvert
Widick Hy., cooper, 27 Woodward
Widlinger John G., tailor, 73 Green,
Widmann Laurence, rope mkr., 527 Plum
Widmore Fred., stone mason, 35 Dunlap
Widner Wm. W., shoe mkr., n.e.c. Richmond and John
Wieber Hy., cooper, s w.c. Race and 15th
Wieber Michael, peddler, 145 Buckeye
Wiebold Hy., 477 Main
Wiebold Hy., grocery, 220 Walnut
Wiechelman John. C., h. 130 W. Court
Wiecher Harmon F., grocer, n.e.c. Barr and Freeman
Wiechers Diedrich, cab. mkr., rear 26 Mulberry
Wiechers William, tailor, 573 Main
Wiechert Charlotte, 24 Franklin
Wiechmann Joseph, chair mkr., 104 Clay
Wiedard Wm., blksmith, 50 Bremen
Wiedemann Geo., foreman, 37 Moore
Wiedemer Francis X., 442 Broadway
Wiedemer Ignatius, candle mkr., wks. 15 W. Front
Wiedemer M. L., soap, candles &c., 15 W. Front, h. 442 Broadway

WIEDERRECHT HENRY, Furniture Manufacturer, Warerooms 242 W. 2d, Factory n.s. Augusta b. Central Av. and John, h. 522 W. 3d

Wiederman Joseph, finisher, s.w.c. Elm and Grant
Wiederstein Adolph, upholsterer, 403 W. 8th
Wiederstein Ludwig, boots and shoes, 498 E. Front
Wiedmann August, tailor, 660 Vine
Wiedow Mary, seamstress, 18 Liberty
Wiegand Louis, clk Volksfreund Office, h. 75 Spring
Wiegand Milius, musician, 23 Franklin
Wiegand Valentine, music teacher, 504 Walnut
Wieger Adolph, carver, 102 13th
Wieger Wm., cab. mkr., 717 Race
Wiegers Theodore. 503 W. 8th
Wiegbels John N., cooper, 93 Woodward
Wiegbels Wm., tailor, bds. 70 Sycamore
Wieggrefe Hy. J., shoe mkr., 424 Freeman

Wiegmann Joseph, lab., Baum near 5th
Wiehe John H., edge tool mkr., 170 E. 5th
Wiekerin Wm., cigar mkr., w.s. Fillmore b. Gest and Richmond
Wiel Moses 573 Central Av.
Wielenberg John H., shoe mkr., n. w. c Main and 9th
Wielenga Hersel, lab., 19 Woodward
Wielert Charles, tinner, 61 W. Court
Wielert Lewis, tinner, bds. 61 W. Court
Wiaman Frederick, stone mason, 160 Gest
Wieman Hy., stone mason, 147 Livingston
Wiemann Hy. stone mason, 102 Gest
Wiemann Ernst, chair mkr., 116 Betts
Wiemann John, 58 Buckeye
Wiemann Rudolph, cooper, 19 Adams
Wiemeller Mary, 50 Richmond
Wiemon Christopher, stone mason, 112 Gest
Wienberg Lewis, blksmith, wks. 55 E. 5th
Wiener Elizabeth, seamstress, 24 13th
Wiening Christian, dray, 124 Clay
Wienziger Philip, cook, 404 Vine
Wiepking August. bakery, 3 Mulberry
Wiepking Frederick, musician, bds. 3 Mulberry
Wier John, dray, 13 Accommodation
Wierk Wm., porter, P. O., s. w. c. Race and 14th
Wierth Fred. cab. mkr., 88 Bremen

WIESER ISAAC, China Glass and Queens Ware, 488 Vine. h. 50 Allison

WIESMANN CLEMENS, Family Groceries, n.w.c. Pleasant and Green

Wiesner Christian, brewer, 415 Sycamore
Wiesner Ignatius, lab., 22 Locust
Wiesnewski Francis, chemist, e. s. Poplar near Ham. Road
Wiess Martin, cook, St. Charles Exchange
Wiest Hy., bk. layer, 100 W. Court
Wieste Hy., cigar mkr., bds. Cincinnati House
Wiethauper Wm., stone mason, 139 Pleasant
Wiethaupt Frederick, cigar mkr., 592 Race
Wiethe Mary G., servt., 24 Woodward
Wietholter Hy. A., stable, w.s. Lodge b. 5th and 6th, h. 13 College
Wiethop F. K., cigar mkr., 592 Race
Wiethorn Bernard G., grainer, 303 W Front
Wietkamp Hy., dray, 526 W. 8th
Wigand Frank, cigar mkr., 602 Elm
Wigand Philip, cof. h., 138 W. Liberty
Wigger Mina. 519 Sycamore
Wiggeringloh Bernard, carp , 104 Hunt
Wiggeringloh Theodore, grocery, n.w.c Vine and Front
Wiggers Hy., cab. mkr., bds. n. w. c. Cutter and Melancthon
Wiggers Hy. L., cab mkr., 286 Linn

WIGGINS SAMUEL, Office. 66 W 3d h. 337 W. 4th

Wiggins Orville B., clk., n.e.c. Court and Canal, h. Covington, Ky.

WIGHTMAN A. F., Exchange Office, 16 E. 3d, h. 19 Harrison

Wigman Gerhard H., lab., 111 Clay
Wihbrink Barney, salesman, n. w. c. Pendleton and Woodward
Willbank Margaret, 251 W. 4th

WILBER MRS. MARY C., Young Ladies' Seminary, 326 Race

Wilber L. E., salesman, 142 Walnut, h. s.w.c. Longworth and John
WILDY Joseph H., (Rawson W. & Co.) 340 W. 7th
Wilch Kate, h. 301 Linn
Wilcox Daniel, lab., rear s.e.c. Pearl and Lawrence
Wilcox George W. clk, bds. 942 E. Front
Wilcox Helen, house keeper, Burnet House
Wilcox Hy., driver, bds. 284 W. 9th w. of Central Av.

336 (WIL) CINCINNATI (WIL) DIRECTO:

Wilcox Hy., shoemkr, bds. 29 W. 7th
Wilcox Mary, 62 14th
Wilcox Richard, mach., wks. gas works
Wilcox Thos., (Leaman & W.,) Walnut Hills
Wilcox Wm., stone cutter, F5 Gest
Wilcox Wm., iron worker, wks. s. w. c. Ramsey and W.W. Canal
Wild George, 170 Ham. Road
Wild John M., lab., 5 Buckeye
Wild Nicholas, lab., 20 Ham. Road
Wild Peter, candle mkr., 35 Elder
WILDE Augustus, (J. Eggers & W.,) 95 E. Liberty
Wilde Robert, shoemkr, 641 Race
Wilde Wm., stoves, &c., s. e. c. Liberty and Mansfield
Wilder John R., 74 W. Court, w. of Central Av
WILDER Josiah, (W. Robinson & Co.) h. Covington, Ky.
WILDER, ROBINSON & CO.,) Josiah W., Lorenzo D. R. & Wm. H. Bellows, Manufacturers of Agricultural Implements and Machinery, 270 Walnut
Wilder Stephen L., 435 W. 4th
Wildey Augustus, lab., 194 Carr
WILDEY WM. D., Stoves. Grates and Hollow Ware, 378 Main, h. s.e.c. Mansfield and Liberty
Wildmann Wm., shoemkr, 53 Dudley
Wildt Thos. E., painter, w.s. Main b. 5th and 6th
Wiles Eliza, servt., Burnet House
Wiley Aaron, mach., 100 Broadway
Wiley Alonzo, shoemkr, 108 Dongworth
Wiley Decatur, brick yard, foot of Richmond
Wiley James, cof. h., 435 George
Wiley James, gas fitter, 226 Main
Wiley Mrs. Jane, b.h., 100 Broadway
Wilfert John A., stocking manuf., 466 Elm
Wilherm Charles F., cutter, 575 Walnut
Wilhelm C., trader, 141 Buckeye
Wilhelm Charles F., tailor, w.s. Vine b. Milk and Calhoun
Wilhelm Elizabeth, h. 9 Moore
Wilhelm Geo., lab., 9 Buckeye
Wilhelm H., chair mkr., wks. John Mitchell's
Wilhelm Ignatz, tailor, 179 Baymiller
Wilhermsdoerfer Julius, b.k., 61 W. Pearl. h. 216 George
Wilke Barney, driver, bds. 176 W. Front
Wilke Frederick H., lab., 26 Buckeye
Wilke George, driver, e. s. Western Av. b. Bank and Dayton
Wilke Gerhard H., shoemkr. 367 W. 5th
Wilke Hy., carp., 370 Broadway
Wilke Hy., dray, bds. 514 Main
Wilke Hy., shoemkr, e. s. Fountain b. Rice and Alexander
Wilke Hy., teamster, 11 Mansfield
Wilke J. Gerhard Henry, lab., 24 Madison
Wilke John, shoemkr, bds. 104 Hunt
Wilke Tony, shoemkr, 360 Broadway
Wilke Wm., (Wm. W. & Co.,) h. 156 W. Pearl
Wilke Wm. & Co., (Wm. W. & Wm. Nuneker,) mineral water manuf., 156 W. Pearl
Wilkemaer Hy., lab., e. s. Sycamore b. Abigail and Woodward
Wilkemake Rosina, 26 Abigail
Wilken Mrs. Dekler, n.w.c. Hopkins and Baymiller
Wilken Hy., carriage finisher, 14 13th
Wilkening Hy., huckster, 514 Race
Wilkens John D., grocery, 48 Ham. Road
Wilkens Hy., 528 Walnut
Wilkens Wm., lab., 53 Pendleton
Wilker Barney, dray, 122 Richmond
Wilker Hy., lab., 38 Elm
Wilker Hermann, painter, 537 Main
Wilkermaer Fritz, lab., rear 60 Abigail
Wilkerson Hy., w. s. Jones b. Everett and Liberty
Wilkerson John, clk., bds. Evans' Hotel
Wilkerson Lucinda, washwoman, 127 Avery
Wilkerson Saml., 19 David
Wilkes Daniel, painter, bds. 65 W. 5th

Wilking Hermann H., cab. mkr., 444 Sycamore
Wilkins Asa, foreman, W. M. Cameron & Co.'s, h. 32 Hathaway
Wilkins George, salesman, 11 Walnut, h 33 W. Front
Wilkins John D., grocery, 117 Betts
Wilkins John L., b.k., 146 John
Wilkinson Benjamin B., barber, e. s. Cherry al. b. Vine and Race
Wilkinson Hy., e. s. John b. Betts and Clinton
Wilkinson John, clk., bds. 65 Broadway
Wilkinson John, molder, wks. n. e. c. Canal and Walnut
Wilkinson Joseph C., at 140 Main
Wilkinson Meridith, carp., Commercial Hospital
Wilkinson Meredith M., carp., 130 Spring
Wilkinson Mat., expressman, 6 K. 7th
Wilkinson Rhoda, washwoman, 31 David
Wilkinson Robert, lab., 144 Baymiller
WILKINSON WM., Dining Saloon and Coffee House, 110 W. 4th
Wilks Hy., bk. mkr., s. s. Ringgold b. Price and Young
Wilkymackey Harmon H., 61 Laurel
Wilkymackey Hy., grocery, 61 Laurel
Will Barney, molder, 225 W. Front
Will Francis, shoemkr, 16 Moore
Will George, salesman, 95 W. Pearl, h. 91 High, c. of Whittaker
Will Jacob, bk. layer, 78 W. Liberty
Will Joseph, lab., poplar
Will Simon, cab. mkr., 92 Mound
Will Valentine, grocer, 1057 Central Avenue
Wille Charles, teacher, 48 Milton
Wille Gerhard, packer, 205 Walnut
Willeke Joseph, watch mkr., bds. 369 Main
Willeke Wm., bk layer, 04 Abigail
Willem Jacob, cof. h., 13 Hughes
Willem Michael, dray, 640 Elm
Willem Sophia, 13 Hughes
Willenborg Cremens, lab., 122 Abigail
Willenborg Herman, tailor, n.e.c. Baymiller and Richmond
Willenborg John B., grocery, s.e.c. John and David
Willenborg John H., cigar mkr., 18 Commerce
Willenborg Joseph, grocery, 360 Freeman
Willer Hy., tailor, 38 Pleasant
Willerding Charles, cab. mkr., 189 Clinton
Willet Jacob, cab. mkr., 428 Main
Willes Joseph, waiter Spencer House
Willey Chas. G. A., teacher, 46 Milton
Willey James, yawl builder, wks. 704 E. Front, h. 794 E. Front
Willey L., n.s. Catharine, 424 Sycamore
Williamsborg Catharine, 424 Sycamore
WM TELL EXCHANGE, Fred. Diserens, Proprietor, 29 W. 5th
Williams ——— clk., bds. n. w. c. Longworth and Central Av
WILLIAMS, A. P. & CO. Auctioneers & Commission Merchants, 22 and 24 E. 3d
Williams Abner, watchman, 143 W.
Williams Albert, mess. U.S. Express co. carver, wks. 416 W. 5th
WILLIAMS Albert P., (A. P. W. & Co.) h. 90 Clinton
Williams Alice, 70 George
Williams Amelia, teacher, Water, b. John and Smith
WILLIAMS AMERICUS V., Residence, 184 Barr
Williams Anna, 325 W. 8th
Williams August, bds. n.s. Wade, b. Freeman and Dudley
Williams Benj., hardware, bds. 27 Longworth
Williams Bennett, sawyer, n. w. c. Burt and Waldon

Williams Thomas D., carp., 167 W. Front
Williams Thos. J., (T. J. W. & Co.) 37 Harrison
Williams Thos. S., (Evens & W.) 239 Laurel
Williams Vachel, carp., 44 Freeman
Williams Victor, professor of music, 378 W 7th
Williams W. G., 131 Longworth
Williams Wm., 30 Pearson
Williams Wm., barber, 383½ W. 6th
Williams Wm., boiler mkr., 37 Parsons
Williams Wm., boiler mkr. rear 24 Park
Williams Wm., butcher, w.s. Reading Road nr. Montgomery pike
Williams Wm., clk., bds. 445 Main
Williams Wm., grocery, 23 Bank
Williams Wm., grocery. Mitchell, Mt. Adams
Williams Wm., mer., 104 Richmond
Williams Wm., plasterer, 163 Barr
Williams Wm., roller, 86 W Front
Williams Wm. C., salesman, 29 W Pearl h. 37 Harrison
Williams Wm. C., penny post, 227 Cutter
Williams Wm. E., baker, wks. 194 W. 6th
Williams Wm. G., atty., 148 Walnut
Williams Wm. H., b.k., 87 W. 2d, bds. 298 W. 8th
Williams Wm. O., painter, 676 E. Front
Williams Wm. R., miller, s.s. Goodloe b. Willow and Niagara
Williamson Aldert H., pilot, 332 Linn
Williamson Alex. W., (Smith & W.) 235 W. 4th
Williamson Chas. C., sawyer, s.s. Railroad e. of French
Williamson Daniel D., salesman, 102 W Pearl, h. 64 McFarland
Williamson Geo. H., n.s. 3d b, Elm and Plum
Williamson & Hatfield (Joseph T. W. & Clark S H.,) druggists, 41 Walnut
Williamson James, clk., L. M. R. R., h. 35 Ellen
Williamson James T., atty., bds. n.s. 3d b Elm and Plum
Williamson Jane, n.s. 3d b. Elm and Plum
Williamson Jennie, music teacher, bds. 475 W. 4th
Williamson John, wine grower's depot, 68 W. 3d
Williamson John G., policeman. 521 W. 3d
Williamson Joseph T., (W. & Hatfield.) 99 Clifton
Williamsor Lucy. 84 W. 2d
Williamson Martha S., teacher, 4th dist school, cor. Broad and Nassau
Williamson Mary, servt., 323 Longworth
Williamson May, n.s. 3d b Elm and Plum
Williamson Ovid C., capt., 30 Laurel
Williamson Robt. mate, 475 W. 4th
Williamson S., bds. Gibson House
Williamson Saml., tea dealer, 14 E. 2d h 166 Vine
Williamson Saml., (Goodhue & Co.) h. Deer Creek
Williamson Wm. blksmith, n.s. Betts b Linn and Baymiller
WILLIAMSON WM., Commission Merchant, 24 E, 2d res. Walnut Hills
Williamson Wm. F., n.s. 3d b Elm and Plum
Williamson Wm. R., 360 W. 7th
Willimbrink Ily., porter, 21 E. 2d
Willinger Bernard, cof. h., s.w.c. Riddle and Harrison pike
Willingter & Conrad, (Lewis W. & Geo. C.) Trunks &c., w.s. Walnut b. 4th and 5th
Willingter Lewis, (W. & Conrad), n.e.c. Liberty and Price
Willis Alex. F., notary public and real estate agt., 181 Walnut h. 23 Longworth
Willis Hy. W., bakery, 309 Central Av
Willis John, shoe mkr., s.w.c Court and Baymiller
Willis John A., millwright, bds Black Bear Hotel
Willis Martha J., shirt mkr., 522 Elm

Willis Wm., stable, 95 E. 2d, h. 171 Broadway
Willmann Fred., cooper, 293 W. Liberty
Willmann Harriet, 46 Pleasant
WILLMANN MATHIAS, Family Grocery, 422 Vine
Willmas Wm., clk., 126 W. 5th, h. 190 Linn
Willmers Wm., shoe mkr., 190 Linn
Willmig John, tailor, 106 Freeman
Willming Ily., box mkr , 493 Race
Willmott Geo., confec., s.e.c. 9th and Plum
Willobring Ily., porter 210 Mound
Willoe Chas., chair mkr., wks. John Mitchell's
Willotson Jane, bds. 79 George
Wills Garrett J., paper mkr , 19 Elizabeth
Willis Hy., bksmith, 229 E. 5th
Willis James M., nurse and waiter, 55 E. 8th
Willis John, lab., 92 W. Front
Wilmas Wm., grocery, 273 Freeman
Wilmeng John, cooper, 275 Sycamore
Wilmer Barney, dray, 71 Baymiller
Wilmer Geo., lab. rear 55 Woodward
Wilmerion John, cof. h., 99 W. 3d
Wilmer Lucas, lab., 224 E. 6th
Wilmes Jacob, tailor, 95 Woodward
Wilmes John H., quarryman, rear 115 Woodward
Wilming Gerhard, cooper, 692 Main
Wilming Hy., cooper, 64 Pitt
Wilming Herman H., cooper, bds. 20 Buckeye
Wilming John, cooper. 275 Sycamore
Wilmington Fanny, bds, 114 Mill
Wilmot Wm. W., (Newell, W. & Co.) h. 89 E. 4th
Wilmouth Bronson, phys. 188 W. Court
WILMS JOHN C., Watches and Jewelry, 1 College Bldg. e.s. Walnut b. 4th and 5th. h. 67 Laurel
Wilmsman Casper, lab., 102 13th
Wilp Hy., cooper, n.e.c. Pleasant and Green
Wilner Frank, lab., 96 Abigail
Wilshire Geo., 101 E. 4th
Wilson Mrs., w.s. Central Av b. 2d and W. W. Canal
Wilson Adam. cof. h., 32 E. Front
WILSON ADAM B., Fancy and Staple Groceries, 224 W. 6th, h. 87 George
Wilson Alex., carp., 451 W. 8th
Wilson Alex., molder, 22 Milton
Wilson Alfred, b.k. 18 W. Front, bds. 225 Baymiller
Wilson Amelia, 160 Broadway
Wilson Andrew, roofer, n.s. Pleasant Court e. of Elm
Wilson Andrew J., policeman, 166 E 6th
Wilson Ann, 208 Laurel
Wilson Ann, dress mkr., 160 Broadway
Wilson Ann, 204 W. 3d
Wilson Anna, teacher, n.e.c. Plum and 3d [way
Wilson Augusta, dress mkr., 160 Broadway
Wilson Benj. R., ins. agt. 279 W. 7th
Wilson Caroline, servt., 264 W. 9th w. of Central Av
Wilson & Carson, (Wm. H. W. & W. L. C.) liquors, 18 W. Front
Wilson Catharine, 64 Plum
Wilson Chas., clk., 186 W. 9th
Wilson Chas., finisher, wks. 154 E. Front
Wilson Chas., pattern mkr., n. s. 9th b. Plum and Central Av.
Wilson Charles A., 447 John
Wilson Christopher, clk., 81 W. Pearl, h. 87 George
Wilson Christopher, cab. mkr., n.e.c. Central Av. and Pearl
Wilson Christopher C., carp., 260 W. 5th
WILSON & CLARK, (Jos. T. W. Jno. E. W., & Augustus J C.) Shirt Manufacturers and Gent's Furnishers, s.e.c. 4th and Walnut
Wilson Clarinda, 100 George
Wilson David, (S. & D. W.) 277 Sycamore

Wilson David, phys., 115 W. 6th, bds 2115 George
Wilson David M. N., clk., 297 Central Avenue
Wilson Edward J., cook, 46 Lodge
WILSON Edward J., (Harrison & W.) h. Fairmount
WILSON, EGGLESTON & CO., (John M. W., James B. W. & Benjamin E.) Commission Merchants, 21 W. Canal
Wilson Eli, lab., 654 E. Front
Wilson Elizabeth, bds. 17 Kossuth
Wilson Elizabeth A., 28 W. Court w. of Central Av.
Wilson Emeline, 186 E. 6th
Wilson Ezekiel H., b. k., 30 E. 5th, h. 198 W. Court
Wilson Florence, 155 W. 9th
Wilson Frances, 131 Betts
Wilson Francis W., clk., bds. 69 W. 8th
Wilson Frank W., clk., 18 Sycamore, h. 69 W. 8th
Wilson George, 194 E 6th
Wilson George, clk., 504 W. 5th
Wilson Georgiana, e.s. Sycamore b. 7th and 8th
Wilson George W., clk., 78 W. 4th, bds. 269 W. 7th
WILSON Harvey T., (W., Hicks & Kinsey,) h. Covington
WILSON & HAYDEN, (Pollock W. & Peter H.) Saddlery and Coach Hardware and Carriage Trimmings, 22 and 24 Main
Wilson Hellen, bds. 424 W. 7th
Wilson Henry, 531 Sycamore
Wilson Henry, drays, 552 Sycamore
Wilson Henry, lab., wks. Hieatt & Wood's
Wilson Henry C., traveling ag't, 624 E. Front
WILSON, HICKS & KINSEY, (Harvey T. W., Levi T. H., & Thomas W. K.,) Produce and Commission Merchants, 39 Walnut
Wilson Hiram, clk., 306 Main, h. 485 W. 7th
Wilson Hosea, carp., 270 Hopkins
Wilson Hugh, clk., 128 W. 5th, bds. s.s. 9th nr. Freeman
Wilson Isaac B., carp., 590 W. 8th
WILSON ISRAEL, Physician,Drugs, Medicines. Chemicals, &c., 337 Main, h. 96 E. 4th
Wilson J. E., clk., bds. 162 Plum
Wilson J. H., packer, bds. 87 W. Front
Wilson James, carp., 424 W. 7th
Wilson James, jr., clk., bds. 69 W. 8th
Wilson James, currier, wks. 215 Main
Wilson James, finisher, 237 E. 5th
Wilson James, lab., bds. 442 W. Front
Wilson James, mathematical instrument mkr., 7 W. 4th
Wilson James, tailor, 145 W. 3d
WILSON James B. (W., Eggleston & Co.) 69 W. 8th
WILSON James F. (L. F. Potter & W.), 237 E. 5th e. of Lock
Wilson James S., clk., 10 W. 2d
Wilson James S., shoemkr, 111 Barr
Wilson James W., 455 W. 7th
Wilson Jane, 424 W. 7th
Wilson Jennie, bds. 18 Gest
Wilson John, bell boy, Spencer House
Wilson John, clk., bds. 69 W. 8th
Wilson John, clk., s. s. Ringgold b. Walker and Davis
Wilson John, eng., n.s. Goodloe b. Willow and Niagara
Wilson John, lab., 551 Central Av.
Wilson John, pipe man, h. s. e. c. Arch and Ludlow
WILSON JOHN, Veterinary Surgeon, at Brown & Bro's. Livery Stable, 9 E. 6th
Wilson John C., shoemkr, c. Weller and Harriet [Plum
WILSON Jno. E., (W. & Clark,) 162
Wilson John G., silk manuf., 238 Betts
Wilson John J., mach., 346 Clark
Wilson John L., architect, bds. 125 W. 5th
WILSON John M. (W. Eggleston & Co.) 69 W. 8th

Wilson Joseph, joiner's tool mkr., 224 E. 6th st. Hill
Wilson Joseph, s.s. Ringgold b. Walker and Davis
WILSON Jos. T. (W. & Clark,) 375 W. 9th w. of Freeman
Wilson Kate, 134 W. Pearl
Wilson Lauchlan, carp., 426 W. 7th
Wilson Lucy, 698 Central Av.
Wilson Margaret, bds. 61 E. 4th
Wilson Marin, 493 W. 5th.
Wilson Martha L., dry goods, 451 W. 8th
Wilson Mary, millinery, 148 W. 5th
Wilson Mary, 110 E. 5th
Wilson Mary, 110 John
Wilson Mildred, 429 W. 5th
Wilson Nancy A., 224 W. 6th
Wilson Obed J., correspondent W. B. Smith & Co., h. 1 George
Wilson Pri-cilla, 186 E. 6th
Wilson Peter, huckster, 68 E. 7th
WILSON Pollock (W. & Hayden), 384 W. 6th
Wilson Rheasylvia. 68 Milton
Wilson Richard, b.k., 61 Walnut, h. 148 W. 5th
Wilson Richard A., clk., 44 Walnut, h. Glendale
Wilson Robert, pattern mkr., wks: n.e c. Canal and Walnut
Wilson Robert, (S. & D. Wilson), 277 Sycamore
Wilson Rosa, bds. 298 John
Wilson S. & D. (Samuel & David), stable, 303 Sycamore
Wilson Samuel, carp., 96 W. Front
Wilson Samuel, huckster, 70 E. 7th
WILSON SAMUEL, Importer and Manufacturer of Mantillas and Cloaks, and Dealer in Shawls, Dress Trimmings,&c., 78 W.4th, bds. Burnet House
Wilson Samuel (S. & D. W.) 277 Sycamore
Wilson Sarah, milliner, 89 Pike
Wilson Sarah A., teacher, 299 W. 4th
Wilson Thos., hostler, Brighton House
Wilson Thomas, lab., 442 W. Front
Wilson Thomas, phys., 248 W. 5th
Wilson Wm., basket mkr, 260 W. 5th, h. n.s. Longworth b. Plum and Elm
Wilson Wm., blksmith, 13 Kossuth
Wilson Wm. (Richardson, W. & Hale). s.w.c. 9th and Sycamore
WILSON REV. WM., D.D., LL.D., Pastor, Church of the Covenanters, h 258 W. 9th
Wilson Wm. H (W. & Carson)h. Green Tp.
Wilson Wm. H., whitewasher, 29 E. 8th e. of Lock
Wilson Wm. M., printer, h. 170 Sycamore
Wilson Wm. P., 303 George
Wilson Wm. S., carp., 13 Kossuth
Wilson Wm. S. (French, W. & Co.) 219 Barr
WILSTACH Chas. F. (Moore, W., Keys & Co.) 287 W. Court w. of Central Av.
Wilt Andrew, printer, bds. s.s. Betts near Freeman
Wilt Fred., shoemkr, 1017 Central Av
Wilt Mary, 25 Hughes
Wilton Michael, lab., wks. s. e. c. Canal and Vine
Wiltberger Stephen, carp., s.s. 3d b. Canal and Kilgour
Wilton Ellen, 19 E. 8th
Wilts Alexander, carriage trimmer, bds. 48 Mansfield
Wilts John, carriage manuf., 244 Sycamore, h. 48 Mansfield
Wiltsee Catharine, dry goods, 356 W. 6th
Wiltsee Isaac C., clk., n.w.c. Plum and Longworth
Wiltsee J. W. (Kimball & W.) h. Walnut Hills
WILTSEE JOHN F., Undertaker, n.w.c. Plum and Longworth
Wiltsee Wm. F., clk., bds. 465 W. 8th
Wiltsee Wm. H., clk., Cin. Gas Light & Coke Co., h. 465 W. 8th
Wimbe Joseph, clk., bds. 577 Main

Wimeschlage Geo., carp., bds. 25 Franklin
Wimmer Christian J., cof. h., 9 15th
Wimsey Catharine, bds. 507 Freeman
Wimsey Della, servt., 100 E. 4th
Wimsey Patrick, lab., 4 Pleasant
Win John, lab., 162 E. 6th
Winsi Alex. W., b.k., Isaac Straub's, h. 137 Smith
Winall Geo. W., blksmith, s.w.c. Smith and Water, h. 32 Chestnut
Winall James W., clk., 14 Main, h. 39 Chestnut
Winall Samuel S. (Harper & W.), 398 Race
Winans Chauncey, carp., 573 Sycamore
WINCHELL Charles C. (Geo. D. Winchell & Bro.) bds. 52 W. 9th
WINCHELL Geo. D. (Geo. D. W. & Bro) h. Price's Hill
WINCHELL GEO. D. & BROTHER (Geo. D. W. & Charles C. W.), Pump and Machine Works, 141 and 143 W. 2d
WINCHELL GEO. D., MARSH & CO., (Geo. D. W., Augustus W. M. & Asahel A. Upson), Japanners, Tin, Sheet Iron, and Zinc Manufacturers, n.w.c. Race and 2d
Wincher Christopher, lab , s.s. Weller b. Carr and Harriet
Winckel Dietrich, shoemkr, 370 Broadway
Winckler Chas., lab., 63 Buckeye
Winckler Frederick, bk. binder, 81 Melancthon
Windel Hy., cab. mkr, 16 Hughes
Windeler Arnold, e.s. Race b, Liberty & 15th
Windeler Jacob, 160 Freeman
Winder Daniel, printer, 388 W. 9th w. of Central Av.
Winder John B., cook, s. w. c. 6th and Plum
Winder John W., photograph gallery, 373 Central Av., h. 32 Richmond
Winder Samuel, mach., 238 Baymiller
Winder Wm H., daguerreotypist, bds. 32 Richmond
WINDER WM. W., House and Sign Painter, 120 W. 3d, h. 108 Richmond
Windgaste Edward, finisher, 535 Main
Windhauz George, lab., 73 Wade
Windhor Anton cigar mkr, h. n.e.c. 3d and Sycamore
Windhorst Frederick, carp., bds. 141 Baymiller
Windhorst John F., seed store. 52 Everett
Windhorst Sophie,52 Everett
WINDISCH Conrad (Moerlein & W.) 722 Elm
Windisch John, lab., wks. G. & H. Muhlhauser's
Windisch John, miller, bds. 701 Elm
Windisch Simon, turner, 66 Findlay
Windler Benj., (Lowenthal & W.), 270 Longworth
Windler Geo. H., clk., 270 Longworth
Windmeier Gerhard. dray, 104 Clay
Windmueller Hy., lab., 12 Eden
Windoffer Bernard, bakery, 380 Baymiller
Windsor James M., n.s. Kemper's Lane b. Hill and E. Front
Windsor Phoebe, n.e.c. Washington and Front
Windsteg Jacob, 546 Race
Wineman Andrew (Henry W. & Son) h. 219 W. 6th
Wineman Henry (Henry W. & Son) 212 W. 6th
Wineman Henry & Son (Henry & Andrew), clothing, 219 W. 6th
Wines Chas., grocer, n. w. c. 7th and John
Wines Peter, baker, wks 224 W. 6th
Wing B. G., b.k., Walnut Hills
Wing Margaret, teacher, 145 Longworth
Winga Charles, 30 E. Front
Wingbermuhle Elizabeth, 169 Webb
Wingbermuhle Hy., bds. 169 Webb
Wingerberg George, driver, 165 Carr
Wingerberg Hy., cigar mkr, 602 Race

(WIN) CINCINNATI (WIR) DIRECTORY. (WIT) 839

Wingerd Jacob, cab. mkr., 301 Clark
Wingert Jacob, cab. mkr., 301 Clark
Wingerter Lewis, lab., 25 15th
Winkelhorst John, tailor, 61 Bank
Winkelmann Chas., gold beater,502 John
Winkelmann Fredrick, mason, 481 Walnut
Winkelmann Hy., bk. binder, 14 E.Mulberry
Winkelmann Hy., cab. mkr., s s. 6th b. Harriet and Horne
Winkelmann Hy., lab., s.s. 6th b. Harriet and Horne
Winkelmann Hy., tailor, 727 Elm
Winkelmann Hy. W., cooper, 53 Pendleton
Winkelmann Herman H., wagon mkr., 518 Freeman
Winkelmann Wm., cooper. 680 Main
Winkelmeyer Rudolph, shoemkr, 542 Main
Winken Frederick, sawyer, bds. 29 Ann
Winkler Anna, 108 Buckeye
Winkler Charles, tailor, 686 Main
Winkler Frederick, bk. binder, 81 Melancthon
Winkleman Hy., cooper, 53 Pendleton
Winkle John, cab. mkr., wks. s.w.c. Canal and Elm
Winkle John, carp., 409 W. 7th
Winkler Jacob, manuf. of hair and bristles, 982 Central Av
Winkler John, 108 Buckeye
Winkler Jehn, cooper, 72 Hughes
Winkler Xavier, brewer, 1031 Central Av
Winn Benjamin. lab., w. s. Central Av. and W. W. Canal
Winn Frank, lab., e s. Whittaker b. Front and 3d
Winn Mary, 35 E. 3d e. of Parsons
Winnemann Hy., lab., 56 Martin
Winner Charles N., clk., 27 W. 3d. bds. 29 W. 7th
Winner J. A., saloon, Broadway Hotel
Winner Wm. N. carriage painter, bds. 160 Sycamore
Winnermann Burnhard H., shoemkr., 822 E. Front
Winnes James J., bds. 178 Barr
Winnes Wm. W., bk. binder, 178 Barr
Winram John, 486 W. 4th
Winschel Anthony, turner, 577 Walnut,
Winschel John, cab mkr., 18 Hamer
WINSLOW AUGUSTUS S., Railroad Materials, (and Walter Smith & Co.) 9 W. 2d, h. 338 W. 7th
Winslow Harmon S., dentist, 102 Broadway
Winsrung Hy., lab. wks. 222 E. Front
Winstel Emil, bar k., 13 Mercer
Winstel Frank, tanner, 125 Pleasant
Winstel John, 66 Stark
Winston Alexander V., clk., 113 W. Pearl, h. Covington
Winston David A. (J. J. Stagg & Co.), res. Newport
Winston George, clk., 113 W. Pearl, h. Covington
Winston Herbert, dray, 302 Plum
WINSTON John P. (W. & Johnston), h. Covington
WINSTON & JOHNSTON, (John P. W. & Wm. B J.) Wholesale Dry Goods, 113 W. Pearl
Winston Mary, bds. 58 Hopkins
Wintel Hy., driver, 172 E. 5th
Winter ——, printer, bds. 27 Longworth
Winter Adolph, printer, 59 Jackson
Winter Alfred A., printer, 136 Vine,bds. 267 W. 8th
Winter Charles, peddler, 150 Everett
Winter Edwin E., b k., 238 W. Court w. of Central Av
Winter Elizabeth, dress mkr., 140 W.7th
Winter Francis, servt., 379 W. 6th
Winter Frederick, porter, 596 Main
Winter George, 15 Madison
Winter George, upholsterer, 577 Sycamore
WINTER Henry (Peare & Co.) 612 E. Front
Winter Hy. S., salesman, 31 Main
Winter John, clk., 15 W. 3d, h. 353 W. 3d

Winter John, gun mkr, 117 Richmond
Winter John, shoe mkr., w.s. Bank al. b. 3d and 4th
Winter John, tanner, wks. 183 Ham. Road
Winter Joseph, peddler, 116 Ham Road
Winter Laura S., teacher, 353 W. 3d
Winter Margaret, seamstress, 121 Providence
Winter Martin. peddler, 100 Buckeye
Winter Mary, 353 W. 3d
Winter Peter, carp., 71 Abigail
Winter Simon, paper box mkr., 347Walnut
Winter T., bleacher, 267 W. 8th
Winter Thomas, 118 Linn
Winter Thomas, clk., City Infirmary, bds. Walnut St. House
Winter & Bro., (Vincent and Xavier,) meat store. s.e.c. 5th and Smith
Winter Vincent, (V. W. & Bro.,) s.e.c. 5th and Smith
Winter Wm., 238 W. Court w. of Central Av
Winter Wm., saloon, 287 W. 5th
Winter Xavier, (V. W. & Bro.,), s.e.c. 5th and Smith
Winterberger Frank, blksmith, n.s. Augusta b. John and Smith
Winterburn Chr, carp., 310 W. 9th W. of Central Av
Winterburn John, carp., 92 Baymiller
Winterfield James, cigar mkr., 475 Race
Winterhalter Constant, barber, 3 E, 4th
WINTERHOLER ANDREAS, Coffee House, 47 12th
Winterholer Mathias, warehouse man, 17 E. M. Canal
Winterich Caroline, tailoress, al. b. Vine and Walnut and 13th and Mercer
Wintering Geo., chair mkr., 703 Race
Wintering Theodore, chair mkr., rear 512 Walnut
Wintermeyer Francis, porter, 45 Elder
Winters Augustus, cigar mkr., 163 W. Front
Winters David, lab., wks. Deer Creek Mills.
Winters Geo., cook, bds., c.w.c. 2d and Lawrence
Winters John, 703 Vine
Winters John A., cigar mkr., 163 W. Front
Winters William (Smith & W.,) 290 Longworth
Winters Wm , watchman, 2 Scott
Winton Mary, 207 Poplar
Winton Wm., M. E. B., 273 W. 4th
Wintzinger Joseph, candy peddler, s.e c. Walnut and 6th
Wintzke Gustav, shoe mkr., bds. 481 Vine
Wipert John, janitor, Melodeon, bds. Silvester House
Wipkenberg Joseph, tinner. 455 Sycamore
Wipling John H., Ailanthus b. Bank and Clearwater
Wipper Henry, cab, mkr., 28 Dudley
Wipper Henry J. D., cab. mkr., 28 Dudley
Wipperding Manns., carpet weaver, 60 13th
Wirkner Anthony, sawyer, 630 Race
Wirkner Ottilia, seamstress, 630 Race
Wirsching Gottlieb, bk. binder, 508 Vine
Wirsing August, (Schemann & W.,) res. Newport
Wirsing Frederick, gun mkr., bds. 132 Broadway
Wirth Charles, wagon mkr., 54 Ham. Road
Wirth George, cof. h., 613 Main
Wirth George, wagon mkr., 613 Main
Wirth Henry, clk., bds. 150 W. 6th
Wirth Henry H., clk., 150 W. 8th
Wirth Herman, grocery, 608 Vine
Wirth Jacob, porter, 127 Main. h. Newport
Wirth Lewis, peddler, 53 Dudley
Wirth Mary, w.s. Baymiller b. Bank and Dayton
Wirth Michael, lab., wks. 17 Webster
Wirth Paul, tailor, n.s. Mulberry b. Main and Sycamore

Wirthelm David, trader, 492 John
Wirthlin Nicholas, boots and shoes, 101 E. Pearl, h. c. Parson and High
Wirthlin Nicholas, shoe mkr., 121 Martin
Wirthlin Thaddeus, carriage trimmer, n. s. Front b. Ferry and Hill
Wirthwine Charles A., jr., butcher, 208 Ham. Road
Wirthwine Charles C., butcher, 206 Ham. Road
Wirtz George. lab., 538 Plum
Wirtzberger Anthony, shoe mkr., 21 Clinton
Wirz Andreas, grocery, 36 Elder
Wisbey Ann, n.s. Corporation Line nr. Mt. Auburn
Wisbey Lewis, asst. eng. Fire Depart., 92 George, h. 277 W. 5th
Wischmeyer Mary, 56 Rittenhouse
Wisdell Wm., 48 York
Wise Frederick, second hand store, 259 W. 6th
Wise Frederick, distiller, 134 Bremen
Wise Geo., bds. Dennison House
Wise Isaac, bds. 57 Broadway
WISE Isaac M., (Block & Co.,) h. College Hill
Wise John, conductor O. & M. R. R., 141 Clinton
Wise John, ladies shoes, n.w.c. Main and Court, h. 171 Richmond
Wise James S., 408 George
Wise John W., painter, 343 Central Av
Wise Joseph A., jewelry, 64½ W. 5th, bds. Dennison House
Wise Margaret, dress mkr., bds. 160 Broadway
Wise Mary, 770 W. 6th
Wise Michael, dray, 277 Broadway
Wise Richard, student, bds. 137 Race
Wise Wesley, mate, bds. 57 Broadway
Wise Wm. H., dray, 69 W. Front
Wisebart Frances, teacher, 93 Smith
Wisebarb Lewis H., cutter, 93 Smith
Wisemann Joe, blksmith., wks. 21 W. 7th
Wisser Henry, tailor, al. b. Vine and Walnut and 13th and Mercer
Wishart Marion. 426 Broadway
Wisher Barney, (Bruns & W.,) Pennsylvania Hotel
Wishmeier August, lab., 158 W. 2d
Wislinger Charles, painter, 628 Vine
Wisler George, tailor, s.s. Calhoun b. Madison and Vine
Wisling Henry, dry goods, nr. Junction 6th and Front
Wismann Joseph, lab., s.s. al. b. Abigail and Woodward and Sycamore and Broadway
Wiss Edward, bakery, 65 Bremen
Wissel Peter. carp., 533 Sycamore
Wissing Bernhard H., shoe mkr., 19 Green
Wissing Mary, 66 Hughes
Wiswell Chas. E., clk., bds. 322 W. 3d
WISWELL EBEN, Looking Glass and Cabinet Ware Manufacturer, s.w.c. Plum and Ann. h. 322 W. 3d
Wiswell Elizabeth, 322 W. 3d
Wiswell Geo., clk., bds. 277 Vine
WISWELL WM., JR., Manufacturer and Dealer in Looking Glasses and Engravings, 70 W. 4th, h. 277 Vine
Wiswell Wm. W., cigars, &c., 42 W. 4th, h. 407 W. 4th
Wisz Henry, lab., s s. Cassatt al. b. Sycamore and Main
Witfrau Miller, 22 Gano
Withar Bernhart, molder, 102 13th
Withare Hermann, lab., 113 Clay
Withauer Fred., clk., 70 Main, bds. 66 W. Court
Withenbury Thos. N., b.k. A. L. Mowry & Co.'s, bds. s.e.c. 6th and Race
Withered Benjamin, blksmith., 183 Baymiller
Witherill E. C., phys., 44 W. 7th
Withers Charles A., (C. A. W. & Wright) h. Covington
Withers C. A. & Wright, (Chas. A. W. & Thos. H. W.,) tobacco &c., 86 W. Front

340 (WOC) CINCINNATI (WOL) DIRECTORY. (WOL)

Withington Henry, baker, wks. 118 W 5th
Withmer Chas., turner, wks. Mitchell & Rammelsberg's
Withorn Jacob, tanner, 11 Dunlap
Witherup Joseph, carp., s.s. 9th b. Harriet and Mill Creek
Witmer John A., wood engraver, n.w.c. 4th and Race
Witmer Samuel H., railroad contractor, 420 W. 7th
Witner Margaret, n.e.c. Plum and River
Witrock Abraham, whitewasher, 403 Central Av
Witrock Bernard, tailor 405 Central Av
Witschger, Chas., clk., 89 W. Court
Witschger Louis. coach trimmer, bds. 195 W. Court w of Central Av
Witschger Rosa, 195 W. Court W. of Central Av
Witt Adolph, jewelry, &c., 19 Main, b. 22 Charles
Witt Bertha, 22 Charles
WITT Richard. (Dunn & W.,) bds. 295 Central Av
Witt Wm. B., shoe mkr., 107 Vanhorne
Witte Chas., carp., 162 Oliver
Witte Ferdinand, agt, 17 E. Front, h. 151 Dayton
Witte Frederick, tailor, 13 Mary
Witte Gasper, grocery, 353 Clark
Witte Harmon, butcher, 17 Wade w. of Linn
WITTE HERMANN, Agt., Pork Packer, n.s. Wade b. Linn and Baymiller
Witte John F. C., musician, 91 Bremen
Witte John II., 131 Pleasant
Witte John II., carp., 172 Everett
Witte L. H., clk. n.w.c. Walnut and 6th, bds n.w.c. 3d and Elm
Wittebrock Gerhard J., shoe mkr., 30 Green
Wittefeld John, varnisher, 70 Pleasant
Wittefeld Rudolph, varnisher, 70 Pleasant
Wittefett Heinrich, varnisher, Oehler al. b. Freemen and Garrard
Wittemiller Mary, 371 Broadway
Witten J. L., bds. Clermont Hotel
Witten Jerry, bds. Clegmont Hotel
Witten Matilda, seamstress, n.e.c. 9th and Central Av
Wittenburg Ernst, confec., n.w.c. Cutter and Hopkins
Wittenburg Herman, lab., 364 W 2d
Wittenbury Thos., bds. 236 Race
Wittengel Michael, packer, wks. 131 Race
Witterock Ernst, lab., 149 Pleasant
Witthake Benj., bar. k., 52 Abigail
Witthoff Henry, gauger 22 Madison
Witthoff Mauritz, cab. mkr., 104 Betts
Wittich Albert, meat store, 640 W. 6th
Wittikamp Anthony, lab., 144 Pleasant
Wittkamp Theodore, tailor, 9 Buckeye
Wittler Theodore, lab., w.s. Harriet b. 5th and Sloo
Wittman C. H. W., turner, bds. 426 Vine
Wittmann Francis, shoe mkr., 57 Hamer
Wittmann Gottlieb, cooper, 8 Henry
Wittmann Mathilda, servt., 409 Vine
Wittmann Nickolas A., confec., 485 Vine
Wittmann Peter, teamster, 725 Race
Wittmann Theresa, servt., 485 Vine
Wittof Maurice, cab. mkr., 104 Betts
Wittrock Ernst, lab., 149 Pleasant
Wittrock John II., grocery, s.w.c. Central Av. and Elizabeth
Witu Ily., confec., 315 Central Av.
Witvy Francis, 10 Carr
Witzelberger Martin, cooper, 160 Pleasant
Witzigmann John G., shoemkr., n.w.c. Race and Union
Witsigmann Nicholas, lab., 271 Bremen
Woark Thos., bds. Cincinnati House
Wohkenberg Ily., 339 Main
Wocher Adolph, porter Post Office, 52 Bank
Wocher John, stone cutter, 48 Ham. Road
Wocher Leopold, shoemkr., 09 Clay

WOCHER LOUIS, Truss, Brace, Bandage, Surgical and Dental Instrument Manufacturer, 318 Main
WOCHER MAX, Surgical and Dental Instrument mkr, Ohio Medical College, 6th, b. Vine and Race h. 11 College
Woebgenberg Joseph, tinner, 455 Sycamore
Woehle Harmon, turner, 232 Betts
Woehle Hermann, turner, 240 Betts
Woelf Joseph, 623 Vine
Woelfer August, tailor, 518 Main
Woelfer Gustavus, tinner, 660 Elm
Woellert Theodore, carp., 665 Vine
Woellner Chas., b.k. s.e.c. 2d and John, h. 460 Sycamore
Woellner John, tailor, 557 Race
Woells John, clk., 3 Mary
Woelts John A., bk layer, 3 Mary
Woenstein Chas. pipe fitter, wks. n.e.c. Walnut and Canal
Woerle Joseph, tailor, 160 Bremen
Woerner Jacob. baker, 632 Race
Woerner Joseph T., tailor, s.e.c. 7th and Central Av.
Woerner Lorenz, tailor, s.e.c. 7th and Central Av.
Woerz Ignatius, turner, 505 Race
Woeste John B., tailor, bds 165 W. 5th
Woestman Geo., driver, 893 Water
Woever Jacob, molder, 14 Humer
Wogkenant Isadore, lab, bds. Black Bear Hotel
Wogkenant Joseph, porter Black Bear Hotel
Wohrmeyer Wm., lab., 172 Abigail
Wowender W., cof. h., 60 Hunt
Woard Noah, paper carrier, 618 W. 6th
Wolcott David P., pattern mkr., 353 Central Av
Wolcott Fred J., clk. Magnolia Ins. Co., h. Covington
Woldering Ily., lab., 136 Pleasant
Wolderman John, saddle-tree mkr., 15 Park
Woldran Thos., lab., 188 W. Front
Wolereck Ily., lab., 439 Linn
Wolf A. J., student, 110 Main, b. 94 W. 8th
WOLF A. & I. & CO., (Abraham, Isaac. & Daniel Wolf,) Wholesale Clothiers and Dry Goods, 76 Main
WOLF Abraham, (A. & I. W. & Co.,) 94 W. 8th
Wolf Adam, butcher, 1011 Central Av.
Wolf Adeline, s. w.c. Longworth and Elm
Wolf Andrew, bakery, 524 Walnut
Wolf Andrew, lab., 12 Bremen
Wolf August, me its, 622 Central Av.
Wolf Charles, 139 Wade
Wolf Chas., clk., 1041 Central Av.
Wolf Chas., clk., 201 W. Court
Wolf Chas., lab., 69 York
Wolf Chas., (Wolf & Co.,) 209 W. Court
Wolf Christian, clk. mkr., 112 Clinton
Wolf Christian J., molder, 301 W. Front
Wolf & Co., (Joseph W. & Chas. Wolf,) liquors, &c., 369 Main
WOLF Daniel, (A. & I. W. & Co.,) 50 W. 8th
Wolf David 282 Linn
Wolf Emanuel, watchman, 65 Longworth
Wolf Francis, bds. 136 Linn
Wolf Frank, carp., 374 W. Liberty
Wolf Fred., lab , 153 Bremen
Wolf Fred., cof. h., 343 Walnut
Wolf Geo., cof. h, 449 Walnut
Wolf Geo., lab., 23 Green
Wolf Geo., mach., 68 Mulberry
Wolf Georgette, teacher, 52 Betts
Wolf Ily., butcher, 108 Buckeye
WOLF Isaac, (A. & I. W. & Co.,) 270 Race
Wolf J. F., clk. 101 W. 4th, h. c. John and Clinton
Wolf Jacob, atty., 19 W. 3d, bds. Walnut Street House
Wolf Jacob, grocer, 49 New
Wolf Jacob, peddler. 204 W. Liberty
Wolf John, cab. mkr., 107 Carr
Wolf John, cigars, &c., 95 Ham. Road
Wolf John, lab., 108 Buckeye

Wolf John, mach., 31 Ham. Road
Wolf John, tailor, e.s Vine b. Milk and Mulberry
Wolf John, teacher, 519 Elm
Wolf John, teacher, n.s. 13th b. Walnut and Vine
Wolf John, jr., trunk mkr., 519 Elm
Wolf John B., tailor, 15 Kossuth
Wolf John Ily., upholsterer, 57 Milton
Wolf John K., bklayer. 207 Cutter
Wolf Joseph, wks. 8 W. 6th
Wolf Joseph, billiard table mkr., n.e.c. Liberty and Vine
Wolf Joseph, cigar mkr., 170 Ham. Road
Wolf Joseph, (W. & Co.,) 203 W. 7th
Wolf Lawrence, bk. layer, 15 14th b. Central Av. and Plum
Wolf Lewis, clk., bds 249 W. 6th
Wolf Lewis W., b.k. 52 W. 2d, h. 89 E. 4th
Wolf Margaret, seamstress, 108 Buckeye
Wolf Mary, 52 Betts
Wolf Mary, 1041 Central Av.
Wolf Mary, seamstress, 68 W. Mulberry
Wolf Matthew, lab., 31 Ham. Road
Wolf Michael cigars, &c., 663 Vine
Wolf Moses, 524 John
Wolf Nicholas, bds. 525 Vine
Wolf Nicholas, clk., 1041 Central Av.
Wolf Nicholas, tailor, 74 Broadway, h. 72 Pike
Wolf Nicholas, cook, St. Charles Ex.
Wolf Nicholas, cooper, s.e.c. Melancthon and John, h. 532 John
Wolf Peter, finisher, 8 Moore
Wolf Simon A., com. mer., 392 W. 4th
Wolf Theresa, seamstress, h. rear 490 Walnut
Wolf Wilhelmine, variety store, 519 Elm
Wolfart Lawrence, rag dealer, 32 Adams
Wolfe C., chair mkr, wks. John Mitchell's
Wolfe John, clk., 30 E. 5th
Wolfe John H., upholsterer, 57 Milton
Wolfe Mary, 112 W. 9th w. of Central Av.
Wolfe Mary, bds. 14 E. 8th e. of Lock
Wolfe Napoleon B., phys., 86 E. 4th
Wolfel John, mach., wks. Nile's works
Wolfenden Elizabeth. laundress, s.s. 6th b. Broadway and Culvert
Wolfer Christena, 404 Vine
Wolfer Joseph, tailor, s.w.c. Logan and Elder
Wolff Adolph, molder, 18 Allison
Wolff Alfred, salesman, 145 Walnut, bds. 89 E. 4th
Wolff Barbara, 618 Vine
Wolff C. A., clk. at C. Wolff & Co's, bds. 99 E. Liberty
Wolff C. & Co., (Chas. W., Louis W. & Wm. W.,) iron, steel and hollow ware, 373 Main, Chas. Reemelin assignee
Wolff Chas. jr., clk. at C. Wolff & Co's. h. 201 Court
Wolff Chas. jr., b.k., 99 E. Liberty
Wolff Chas., (C. W. & Co.,) 99 E. Liberty
WOLFF CHARLES, Furniture Factory, 50 E. 6th
WOLFF Chas II., (Chas. H. W. & Co.) h. Mt. Washington
WOLFF CHARLES H. & CO., (Chas. H. W., Thomas Sharp & Geo. H. Wolff.) Importers and Wholesale Dealers in Dry Goods, 145 and 147 Walnut
Wolff Christian, lab. 544 E. Front
WOLFF DANIEL, Newport Iron Works, Warehouse 119 and 121 E. Pearl, h. Newport
Wolff Daniel, jr., clk. 119 E. Pearl, bds. 201 W. Court
Wolff Edward, clk., 115 E. Pearl
WOLFF George II., (Chas. H. Wolff & Co.,) 30 Clark
Wolff Ily., shoemkr., n.s. 12th b. Vine and Bremen
Wolff John C., hardware, 115 E. Pearl
Wolff John C., molder, 103 W. Front
Wolff Louis, (C. Wolff & Co.,) h. Green tp.

Wood Geo. B., foreman, 272 W. 5th
Wood Hiram J., painter, 12 Rittenhouse
Wood Horatio, bds. 202 W. 4th
Wood Ira, 399 W. 3d
Wood James, plasterer, s. s. Friendship al. b. Pike and Butler
Wood James, plumber, n.e.c. Richmond and Cutter
Wood James, shoemkr, n. w. c. 6th and Lock
Wood John, agt., 72 W. 3d
Wood John, lab., 26 Brighton
Wood John H., lumber dealer, 224 Barr
Wood Joseph C., weaver, 228 Walnut, res. Newport
Wood Laura, 89 W. 9th, w. of Central Avenue
Wood Mary M., variety store, 272 W. 5th
WOOD & McCOY, (Wm. W. & T. J. McC.,) Eagle White Lead and Color Works, 20 Spring
Wood Nancy, 90 W. 2d
Wood Reuben, blind mkr., 236 Vine
Wood Reuben, carp., 90 W. 2d
Wood Samuel, clk., 19 W. 5th, res. Newport
WOOD SEELY, Superintendent Am. Tract Society, 163 Walnut, h. Mt. Auburn
Wood Silva, 463 Plum
WOOD THOMAS, Physician and Surgeon, Office and Residence 112 W 6th
Wood Thompson, blksmith, 116 E. 3d, e. of Whittaker
WOOD WILLIAM, . Livery Stable, n w.c Longworth and Race, h. 46 Longworth
WOOD Wm., (W. & McCoy,) res. Mt. Washington
Wood Wm. C., clk., Wood & McCoy's, h. n.e.c. Ellen and 3d
Wood Wm., jr., b.k., n.e.c. 3d and Ellen
Wood Wm. H., clk., 224 Barr
Woodard Samuel S., op O. & M. R. R. tel. office 522 W. Front, bds. Columbia House, cor. 5th and Wood
WOODARD W. R. J., Operator O. & M. Railroad. Telegraph Office, 522 W. Front, bds. Columbia House. cor. 5th and Wood
WOODBURN Robert, (Juegling & W.,) 602 Central Av
Woodbury Lucy, 280 Richmond
Woodhouse Nancy, 351 W. 5th
Woodington Mollie, servt., n.e.c. 2d and Broadway
Woodlock Wm., bk. binder, bds 296 W. 5th
Woodmansel G. C., salesman, Cole & Hopkins, n.e.c. 5th and Vine
WOODNUTT Thomas, (Acton & W.,) 372 W. 7th
WOODROUGH Joseph, (W. & McParlin,) res. Hamilton, O.
WOODROUGH & McPARLIN, (Joseph W., Michael Mc. P. & Henry C. Dunn,) Manufacturers of Patent Ground Saws, 10 W. 2d
WOODROW David T., (H. Campbell & Co.,) h. 404 W. 6th
Woodrow Howard C., 404 W. 6th
Woodruff Aaron, shoemkr, 43½ E. Front
Woodruff Aaron T., shoemkr, 34 E. Front
Woodruff Adella, teacher, 392 W. 3d
Woodruff Archibald, 162 W. 8th
WOODRUFF Charles S., (Mills & W.,) 66 Baum
Woodruff Charles S. jr., b.k., 3 W. Pearl h. 66 Baum
Woodruff Charles, driver, bds. 97 Freeman
WOODRUFF EDWARD, Attorney at Law, 6 E. 5th, h. 162 W. 8th
Woodruff Emmet C., 13 Kossuth
Woodruff Geo W., clk., 380 Race
WOODRUFF J. B., Reporter Cincinnati Daily Times, bds. 402 George
Woodruff Joab, (Day & W.,) residence country
Woodruff Jonathan, builder, 392 W. 3d
Woodruff Joseph C., bds. 162 W. 8th

Woodruff Joseph H., constable, 161 Plum
Woodruff Leonard, editor, 403 Vine
Woodruff Nellie, bds. 188 W. 5th
Woodruff Samuel W., watchman, 138 Carr
Woodruff Walter, b.k., 392 W. 3d
Woodruff W., bds 149 Elm
WOODRUFF WM. H., Family Groceries, Provisions, &c., 380 Race
Woods ——, shoemkr, n. w. c. 12th and Vine
Woods Alice, s. s. 6th b. Broadway and Culvert
Woods Amanda, teacher, 366 W. 8th
Woods Eunice, 366 W. 8th
Woods Fanny, 7 Lock n of 8th
Woods Hy., shoemkr, n s. 12th b. Vine and Bremen
Woods James, bk. layer, 54 Richmond
Woods James, shoemkr, 7 Lock n. of 8th
Woods James, lab., s. s. Pearl b. Park and Smith
Woods James, steward, bds. 141 Sycamore
Woods John, lab., 26 Brighton
Woods John B., student, bds. 47 W. 7th
Woods Laura, bds. 271 W, 6th
Woods Lemuel, butcher, n. s. Accomodation e. of 8th
Woods Mrs. M., 56 W. 4th
Woods Mark, painter, 161 W. Court, w. of Central st
Woods Mary, 113 W. 3d
Woods Michael, fireman, bds. n.s. Front b. Mill and Wood
Woods Nancy, bds. Dumas Hotel
Woods Patrick, horse shoe nail mkr., 2 New
Woods Robt., freight agt., C. H. & D. R.R., bds. 275 W. 9th
Woods Robert R., (W. & Sharp.,) res. Covington
Woods & Sharp, (Robert R. W. & Chas. S.,) feed store, 603 W. 6th
Woods Silas, b.k., s. e. c. 4th and Vine, h. 275 W. 9th
Wood's Theater, George Wood manager, s.e.c. Vine and 6th
Woods Thomas, s. s. Forbus al. b. Elm and Canal
Woods Virginia, 231 W. 6th
WOODS Wm., (Nixon, Chatfield & W.) 408 W. 6th
Woods Wm., porter, 122 E. 6th
WOODS Wm H., (Hieatt & W.,) bds. 121 E. 3d
Woodside John, clk., bds. Dennison House
Woodside Samuel, salesman, 70 Walnut
Woodson Jesse, cab. mkr., 217½ W. 5th h. 117 Park
WOODWARD CHAS., Physician and Surgeon, Office and Residence. 116 W. 6th
Woodward Chas., rout agt., 329 Elm
Woodward Chas. jr , salesman, 7 Public Landing, h. 116 W. 6th
WOODWARD E. W., Superintendent L. M. R. R., Office at Depot. res. Morrow
Woodward Edward, e. s. Campbell al. b. Elder and Liberty
Woodward Geo. W., bds. Burnet House
Woodward High School, Franklin b Sycamore and Broadway
Woodward J. M., clk., 97 W. 8th
Woodward Job, clk., 97 W. 8th
Woodward John H., atty., room 7, Short's building. h. 116 W. 6th
Woodward Joseph, sr., driver, at 271 Cutter
Woodward Samuel, fuel agt., L. M. R. R. bds. National Hotel
Woodward W. W., dentist, 116 W. 6th
Woodward Warren R., phys., 116 W. 6th
Woodwarm James M., carp., 275 Clinton
Woodworth Douglass, pewter worker, wks. H. Homan's
Woodworth Richard, lab., wks. C. H. & D. R R. depot
Woodworth T. H., bds. Gibson House
Woodyer Wm., lab. 27 E. 8th e. of Lock
Wool Alexander, drover, 53 Providence

Wooley Newton, bk. binder, h. 297 Central Av
Woolford Fritz, lab., 59 Wood
Woolley Chas. W., atty., 111 Pike
Woolley David, bds. 333 Cutter
WOOLLEY & GERRY, (Richard W. & Arad G.,) Leather and Findings, 166 Main
Woolley Reuben H., grate mkr., 177 Smith
WOOLLEY Richard, (W. & Gerry,) 423 W. 5th
Woolley Wm. H., carp., 61 David
Woolman Wm. R., teacher, 2d district school
Wooster Andrew, 128 Walnut
Wootley James W., children's dress and linen store, 131 W. 4th
Wooze Hy., cab. mkr., wks. s. w. c. Canal and Elm
Worden Oscar, driver, 325 W. 5th
Wordmann John W., teacher, 106 Abigail
Work Henry, 32 Dunlap
Work Mary, 125 Water
Work Rosa. wks. Hieatt & Wood's Candle Factory
Workmaster Joseph, cigar mkr., bds. 86 W. Court
Work Alphonso, cook, United States Hotel
Works Anna, dress mkr., 174 W. 6th
Works Charlotte, w. s. Plum b. Water and River
Works Rachael, seamstress, 11 Ann
Workum Jacob L., 84 E. 3d
WORKUM Levi J., (Freiberg & W.,) 84 E 3d
World Anna, servt., 476 W. 5th
World Jacob, agt., 187 Walnut, h. 340 Main
Worlds John, steward, 135 Everett
Worley Cassandra, 492 W. 4th
Worley David, molder, 492 W. 4th
Worley Herman, lab., 64 Hunt
Worley Jacob, 340 Main
Worley Jesse, police, s. e. c. 4th and Wood
Worley Maria, n. s. Railroad e. of Hazen
Worley Wm., feed store, s. e. c. Front and Niagara
Worley Wm., prop. Drovers' Inn, 862 E. Front
Worman Wm., boots and shoes, 138 Richmond
Worman Hy., lab , 67 Rittenhouse
Wormann John B., (Schafer & W.,) s.w. c. Main and Gano
Wormberger Adam, lab. s.s. Mount near Sycamore
Wormley Samuel, steward, 204 Broadway
Worms August, cooper, 641 Race
Worms Herman, (Mack & W.) 161 Broadway
Worms Isidore, cof. h., s.s. 6th near Mill Creek
Wornfeldt Anna, rear 70 Hunt
Worpenburge Conrad, core mkr., wks. 137 W. 2d
Worrall Hy., teacher of music, 32 Laurel
Worrall Jr., prof. of drawing, Wesleyan Female College
Worrell C. B., (Hubbard & W.) h. Mt. Harrison
Worst Augustus, watchman, 358 Clark
Worteramnn Hy., cigars &c., 687 Central Av.
Worth David A., clk., 91 George
Worth John, hustler, bds. Bevis House
Worth Sylvester, boots and shoes, 116 Clinton
Worthing John, lab., 968 E. Front
Worthington Alfred A., teamster, 200 W. Front
WORTHINGTON & CO., (Lewis W. & Joseph Kinsey,) Manufacturers Bar, Boiler, Sheet, and Sash Iron and Wire, 42 and 44 W. 2d, (Globe Iron and Wire Works, 413 W. Front
Worthington Edward, clk., 23 W. 3d, h. 113 Pike

Worthington Hy., free stone dealer, and pres. Great Wes. Coal Oil Co. of Newark Ohio, 13 W. 4th, h. Covington
WORTHINGTON James T.. (W. & Matthews.) 147 W. 7th
WORTHINGTON Lewis, (W. & Co.,) 239 W. 4th
Worthington Lewis S.. Not. Pub., 116 Main, h. 239 W. 4th
WORTHINGTON & MATTHEWS, (Vachel W. & James T. Worthington,) Attorneys at Law, 23 W. 3d
WORTHINGTON Vachel, (W. & Matthews,) 113 Pike
Worthlin Stephen, dray, n. s. Front, w. of Hill
Wortman August, boot mkr., bds. 373 Broadway
Wortman Wm., teacher, n. e. c. Spring and Abigail
Wortmann Lewis, cooper, 24 Buckeye
Worton James, japanner. 121 Main
Wortz Charles, tailor, 49 Hughes
Worwick Jos., (P. Lukens & Co.,) h. Springborough
Wossmeier John H., feed store, 471 W. 3d, h. 560 W. 3th
Wosten Hy. J., bksmith, 48 Pleasant
Woyke Gottlieb, mach., 29 Hughes
Woyki John, finisher, wks. n. e. c. Walnut and Canal
Wrampelmeier Fred, painter, w. s. Main b 5th and 6th, h. 9 Mary
Wratten James, lab., s. e. c. Poplar and Freeman
Wray Hy. G., jeweler manufac., 141 Main, h. College Hill
Wrede Edward, teamster, 469 W. 8th
Wrede Frederick, turner, 11 15th, b. Elm and Plum
Wrede Frederick, w. s. Franz b. Elder and Findlay
Wrede Hy., cigar mkr., 538 Plum
Wren Ellen servt., 337 W. 8th
Wrench Wm., bksmith, n.s. Sun b. Mill and Park, h. 23 Mill
Wrenn Lawrence, porter, 103 W. Pearl, b. Walnut Hills
Wrenshaw Joseph, chair mkr., 119 Elm
Wride August, policeman, 56 W. Liberty / (anon O.
Wright A. G., (A. G. W. & Co.,) h. Lebanon O.
Wright A. G. & Co., (A. G. W., H. M. Sausser, L. T. Barr and E. B. W.,) com. mers. n.s. 6th near Main
Wright Amelia S., teacher, 160 Longworth
Wright Amzi J., 217 Plum
Wright Ann, 43 E. Liberty
Wright Anna, s.e.c. Race and Court
Wright Anna, s.e.c. Front and Hazen
Wright Andrew, e. s. Baymiller, near Bank
Wright Andrew, 402 Baymiller
Wright Arthur W., dry goods, n. w. c. Pearl and Broadway, res. E. Walnut Hills
Wright B., bds. 294 Vine
Wright Benjamin T., b. k., 404 W. 7th
Wright Benjamin F., bk binder, n. e. c. 3d and Elm
Wright Benjamin F., 229 W. 4th
Wright C. W., clk., Cin. Gas Light and Coke Co , h. Avondale
Wright Charles, carp., 223 Laurel
WRIGHT COL. CRAFTS J., 229 W. 4th
Wright D. J., phys., 8 George
Wright D. Thew, atty., 60 W. 3d, h. Storrs Tp.
Wright E. B., (A. G. Wright & Co.,) h. Lebanon O.
Wright Edwin, b. k., 50 Everett
Wright Eliza, young ladies school, s. s. 6th b. Race and Elm, h. 22 E. 6th
Wright Frederick, pattern mkr., 39 Mulberry
Wright Geo., carriage finisher, 79 Woodward
WRIGHT GREG. G., Lightning Rod Manufacturer, 23 W. 6th, bds. 246 Plum

Wright George J., clk., n. e. c. 2d and Walnut
Wright H. P., carp., s. w. c. Richmond and Central Av.
Wright Hannah, 324 W. 9th, w. of Central Av.
Wright Hiram W., artist, 134 Broadway
WRIGHT J. R., (Wm. Sumner, & Co.,) h. Glendale
Wright Jacob H., dining saloon, 8 E. 4th h. 48 Elizabeth
Wright James F., phys., 307 Elm
Wright John, b. h., 579 W. 5th
Wright John, clk., Times Office, h. 320 W. 5th
Wright John, mach., 441 W. 2d
Wright John, mach., 263 W. 3d
Wright John C., clk., bds. 3 George
Wright John E., b. k., 51 W. 3d, h. Lockland
Wright John J., 43 E. Liberty
Wright John V., cutter, 53 W. 4th, h. 18 Elizabeth
Wright Joseph, carp., 59 Pierson
Wright Joseph, clk. L. M. R. R., b. s. s. E. 3d second door w. of Kilgour
Wright Joseph, teamster, 139 E. 3d
Wright Joseph P., asst. surg , U. S. A. 101 E. 3d, bds. Burnet House
Wright Leman, 116 E. Liberty
WRIGHT M. BURR, Physician and Surgeon, Office and Residence 294 Vine
Wright Martin, clk., L. M. R. R., h. s.s. 3d b. Lock and Kilgour
Wright Matilda, h. 63 E. 7th
Wright Nathaniel, 140 Elm
WRIGHT Nat, jr., (Foulds & W.,) 140 Elm
Wright Robt., dry goods, 397 Central Av.
Wright Robt., mach., s. s. Lock b. 3d and 4th
Wright Robt. H., carp., 223 Laurel
Wright Samuel, n. s. Calhoun b. McMillan and Clifton Av.
Wright Samuel, dray, 146 Linn
Wright Sarah, servt. 374 W. 7th
WRIGHT SMITHSON E., Treasurer L. M. R. R., Office s.e. c. Pearl and Kilgour, h. s. s. 3d b. Lock and Kilgour
Wright Sylvanus, com. mer. 26 W. Front, b. Walnut Hills
WRIGHT T. J., Physician and Surgeon, Office and Residence 8 George
Wright Thomas, bksmith, bds. 1234 E. Front
Wright Thomas C., bksmith, 23 Abigail
Wright Thomas H., (C. A. Withers & W.,) 430 W. 6th
Wright Thos. J., copper smith, 113 Clinton
Wright Thomas W., bellows mkr., wks. 54 E. 2d
WRIGHT TILGHMAN, Pattern Maker., 156 W. 3d, h. 440 W. 9th
Wright W. Martin, clk., h. s.s. 3d b. Canal and Kilgour
Wright Wm., bds. 294 Vine
Wright Wm., packer, wks. 131 Race
Wright Wm. C., painter, bds. 324 W. 9th w of Central Av.
Wright Wm. H., 97 Main, h. Walnut Hills
Wright Wm. G. S., dray, 249 E. Pearl, e. of Broadway
Wright Wm. L., clk., 43 Main, h. Newport
Wright Wm. S., com. mer., 68 W. 3d, h. 134 Elm
WRIGHTSON & CO., Book and Job Printers, 157 Walnut
WRIGHTSON Thos. (Wrightson & Co.) h. Cherry Hill Farm Campbell Co. Ky.
WRIGHTSON Wm., 157 Walnut
Wrightley Jacob, loan office, 113 Sycamore
Wrigley Wright, currier, 472 W. 5th
Wromping Mrs., 194 Hopkins
Wubolding Ferdinand, clk., 65 E. Pearl
Wuck Wm., cab. mkr., 73 New
Wuebbel Frederick, 14 Green

CINCINNATI (YON) DIRECTORY (YOU) 843

Wyler Louis, salesman, 66 W. Pearl, h. 279 W. 8th
Wylie Decatur, bkmaker, 682 W. 6th
Wyman Chas. J., shoemkr., s. w. c. 8th and Central Av.
Wyman Jacob, teacher, 212 Water
Wymond Francis. (Chambers, Stevens & Co.,) h. Aurora, Ind.
Wyner Humphrey, actor, bds. National Hotel
Wynja Louis, awning mkr., 69 Sycamore, h. n.w.c. 3d and Sycamore
Wynne Catharine, 9 Home
Wynne David R., clk., 101 W. Pearl, h. 160 Longworth
WYNNE Gomer, (J. E. Wynne & Co.,) 235 Longworth
WYNNE, HAINES & CO., (John W., Seth S. H. & Co.,) Wholesale Dealers in Foreign and Domestic Dry Goods, 101 W. Pearl
WYNNE J. E. & Co., (Jabez E., W., George H. Christian, Gomer, Wynne and Noah H. Chapman.) Wholesale Dealers in Dry Goods and Notions, 91 W. Pearl
WYNNE Jabez E.. (J. E. Wynne & Co.,) 294 W. 7th
WYNNE John, (W. Haines & Co.,) h Mt. Auburn
Wynne Jonathan A., salesman, 96 W. Pearl, bds. 294 W. 7th
Wynne Thomas F., clk., 9 Home
Wynne Wm., jr., clk., 101 W. Pearl, h. Covington

X

Xavier Christian, trader, 542 Race
Xavier Defile, stone cutter, 540 Plum
Xavier Frank, lab., 120 Gest

Y

Yackle Rachael, 606 E. Front
Yackley Valentine, wks. 8 W. 6th
Yaeger Henry, bk. layer, 14 Mercer
Yager Fred., lab., n.s. 6th b. Harriet and Horne
Yager John H., lab., s. s. Front e. of Hill
Yancey John, trunk mkr., 110 Betts
Yancey Leroy, trunk mkr., n.e.c. Wade and Central Av.
Yanson Hy., gardener, 745 Freeman
Yarnell David, sawyer, 742 W. 6th
Yarnell John, teamster, 41 Freeman
Yarrington Wm., saloon, Henrie House, h. 145 Sycamore
Yeager Charles, carp., 322 Baymiller
Yeager Henry, 180 W. Liberty
Yeager John, carp., n.s. Elder b. Campbell al. and Elm
Yeakle Jacob J., clk., 250 Hopkins
Yeakle John J., boots and shoes, 250 Hopkins
Yeatman Francis M., 205 Longworth
Yeatman Griffin, rooms 56 E. 3d
Yeatman Stephen B., broker, 205 Longworth
Yeatman T. Henry, wine dealer, 120 Main
Yeatman Walker M., salesman, 17 W. Pearl, res. Glendale
Yecks Chas., tanner, bds. 519 Main
Yehnsing B H., teamster, s. s. Abigail e. of Pendleton
Yelarius John, box mkr., 198 Clinton
Yelarius Mathias, carp., 196 Clinton
Yentz Samuel, lab., 13 Pendleton
Yeomans Richard, printer, Cin. Gazette, h. Covington
Yerker Enoch, boots and shoes, 542 E. Front
Yochman David, carp., 293 Linn
Yockmann David, carp., bds. 293 Linn
Yocum Jesse E., grocer, n.w.c. 6th and Smith, h. 486 W. 9th w. of Central Avenue
Yonke John, brewer, 59 Abigail
Yongling H., lab, wks. Wood & McCoy's
Yonk Sebastian, brewer, 55 Harrison Pike

Yope Jacob, n. s. Browne b. Mohawk and Ham. Road
York Francis, lab., n. s. Railroad e. of Vance
York Louisa, 103 E. 2d
Yorke Joshua, 49 E. 4th
Yorston Amelia, bds. 21 Chestnut
Yorston Matthew M., clk.. s.w.c. Chestnut and Central Av., bds. 21 Chestnut
Yose Fred., 316 Linn
Yost Benjamin, driver, 3d and 4th street R. R.
Yost Geo., clk., 103 E. Pearl, h. 13 15th
Yost Hy., carp., 208 W. Liberty
Yost Jacob, blksmith, 530 John
Yost John, lab., 716 W. 6th
Yost Margaret, 13 15th
Yost Peter, lab., 649 W. Front
Yost W m., tailor, 85 W. 3d. h. 145 W. 3d
Youmans Peter, printer, bds. 50 Monroe
Young Abel, sheet iron wkr., bds. Pennsylvania Hotel
Young Adam, cooper, 23 Abigail
Young Albert K., sheet iron wkr., h. s.s. 3d b. Canal and Kilgour
Young Andrew, carriage mkr., wks. 11 Freeman
Young Anna, Harriet b. W. 9th and Richmond
Young B. F., printer, s.e.c. 9th and Walnut
Young Bridget, cook, National Hotel
Young Charles, 57 Hopkins
Young Chas., lab., 1031 Central Av.
Young Chas., wagon mkr., 1041 Central Avenue
Young Chas. B., student, bds. 375 W. 3d
Young Chas. E., cook, 1216 E. Front
Young Chas. J., b.k., 162 Main, bds. 110 W. 6th
Young Clara M., seamstress, n. e. c. Longworth and Plum
Young Chas. W., finisher, 48 Kossuth
Young Courtland H., music printer, bds. 47 W. 7th
Young Daniel, n.s. 6th b. Culvert and Broadway
YOUNG Elias, (Heller & Y.) 467 W. 3d
Young Eliza, 208 Broadway
Young Eliza, 576 E. Front
You g Elizabeth, bds. s.w. c. 3d and Broadway
Young Emma L., dress mkr., 19 Longworth
Young Geo. H., bk. binder, 260 Clinton
Young Harvey, 54 New
Young Henry C., cashier, s.w.c. Walnut and Pearl, b. 106 Smith
Young Isaac, bel boy, Spencer House
Young Jacob, cooper, 23 Abigail
Young Jacob, lab., 492 E. Front
Young Jacob, meats, s.e.c. Clinton and Cutter
Young Jacob, trunk mkr., 64 Findlay
Young James, carp., s.s. Railroad e. of French
Young James S., clk., 204 W. Cout w. of Central Av.
Young James W., dray, 204 W Court w. of Central Av.
Young Jesse. eng. 1526 E. Front
Young Jesse J. policeman 5 Providence
Young John, (Conkling, Y. & Co.) 177 Spring [tp.
YOUNG John (Fallis, Y. & Co) h Storrs
Young John, gas metre mkr., 280 Main
Young John, gas metre mkr., 464 Walnut
Young John lab., wks. n.s. Front b. Lawrence and Pike
Young John, lab., 80 Poplar
Young John, pipeman, 389 Vine
YOUNG John (Royer, Simonton & Co) h. Storrs tp.
YOUNG John, (R. W. Booth & Co.) h Storrs tp
Young John P., printer, bds. 61 Ham. Road
Young Kate, 23 E. 3d e. of Parsons
YOUNG LADIES MT. AUBURN INSTITUTE, w.s. Auburn Av. Mt Auburn
Young Margaret, 107 Barr
Young Martha. O., teacher, 260 Richmond

344   (ZAP)   CINCINNATI   (ZIE)   DIRECTO

Young Martin, 32 Dunlap
Young Mary A., 107 Barr
Young Mens Bible Society depository 28 W 4th
YOUNG MEN'S GYMNASTIC ASSOCIATION,
n e.c 4th and Race
YOUNG MEN'S MERCANTILE Library Association, College Bldg. e.s. Walnut b. 4th and 5th, Geo. A Morris Librarian
Young Milton H., molder, 534 Main
Young Nancy, 427 W. 9th w. of Central Av
Young Pat., walter, Burnet House
Young Patrick H., waiter 100 Race
Young Philip, clk., s.w.c. 7th and Walnut
Young Philip, blksmith, n.s Ham. Road b Dunlap, and Hamburg
Young Philip J. B. caulker 796 E Front
Young Sabina, rear 73 Abigail
Young Thomas, tailor, 127 Barr
Young Thomas, tinner, 210 Mound
Young Violetta, bds 73 W 7th
Young W., artist, 25 W. 4th b. Mt. St. Mary's
Young Mrs. W. R., bds. 53 E. 3d
Young Wm.. dray, 26 Richmond, b. Elm and Plum
Youngblood Geo., carp., 14 W. Mulberry
Youngblood Mary, 151 Cutter
Youngblood Nicholas, cof. h., n.s. Front e. of Foster,
Younger Geo. gardener Garden of Eden
Younger Wendlin, gardener, Garden of Eden
Younglass August, tinner, bds. 225 W. 6th
Youngs Clark D., bridge bldr., h. n.s. 6th b. Harriet and Horne
Yourtee Rev, Saml. L., 575 W 8th
YOUSE JAMES F.,
b.k. Commercial Office,
h. 320 Clark
Yoxon Saml., carriage painter, 493 John
Yoxon Wm., lab., 493 John
Yungblut Joseph S., clk., n.e.c. 4th and Main, bds 189 Sycamore
Yunger Chas., lab., 71 Hughes
Yuukurg Nicholas, waiter Gibson House

Z

Zachary Hy., b.k. 9 W 2d, h. 34 Longworth
Zacklikowski Chas., tailor. 2 Mary
Zachritz Ewalte Hy., barber, n.e c. Walnut and Gano
Zachritz Jacob H., barber, 52 Sycamore
Zachritz John L., barber, 1120 Central Av, h. w.s, Denman, b. Central Av. and Bank
Zachritz Philip J., baber, 1076 Central Av
Zaehnder Francis, barber, 124 Bremen
Zahn Francis, lock mkr., 163 Pleasant
Zahn Frank, tool mkr , wks. 8 Main
Zahn Geo., cigar mkr., bds. w.s. Freeman b. Dayton and York
Zahn Herman H., tailor, s.s. Melancthon b Cutter and Jones
Zahn Jacob, finisher, 35 Observatory
Zahn Joseph, expressman. 13 Clinton
Zahneis John, lab., 63 Buckeye
Zahrringer Frank. C., barber, 91 Spring
Zamart Arnold, upholsterer 290 W Front
Zamhamer John, brewer, 262 Ham. Road
Zammart Ferdinand, lab., 70 Van Horn
Zammert Albert, tailor, 107 Pleasant
Zammert Ferdinand, clk , 99 Walnut
Zanis Geo., lab , City Water Works Office
ZANONE John B., (G. Gatti & Z.) 80 Broadway
Zanone Joseph, confec n.w.c. 7th and Central Av
Zanoni Antonio, cof. h., 60 W 5th
Zapf Jacob, cigar mkr., 1015 Central Av
Zapf John, s.s. Mercer b. Vine and Walnut
Zapf Michael, lab. 24 14th
Zapf Veit, tailor, 64 Ham. Road

Zapp Nicholas, tailor, 587 Main
Zaverinck A., lab., wks. 196 W. Pearl
Zaverinck Joseph, cab. mkr., wks. 196 W. Pearl
Zear Geo., huckster, n.w.c Freeman and Liberty
Zebold Robt. blind mkr., 52 W 6th
Zech Frank, cof. h., 41 E. Front
Zeeb Jacob, carp., 118 Bremen
Zeeb John M., gardener, 520 Freeman
Zeh Michael, shoe mkr., 24 Allison
Zehfus Gustave, teacher, 537 Walnut
Zehler Charles. baker, s.s. Ohio al. b. Elm and Plum and 15th and Adams
Zehler George, bakery, 54 W. Liberty
Zehn Adam, carp., s.w.c. Freeman and Dayton
Zehn Joseph, cigar mkr., bds. s.w.c. Freeman and Dayton
Zehnder Christian, cab mkr., 125 Bremen
Zehner Michael, eng., 367 W. 5th
Zehner Michael, lithographer, 144 Bremen
Zeid'er Richard D., clk. 50 Walnut, h Delhi tp.
Zeigle Archy, lab., 49 Providence
Zeigler George, butcher, 729 Elm
Zeigler John, 123 Mohawk
Zeigler John, butcher, 57 Providence
Zeigler Ludwig, cof. h., s s North Elm b. Cross and Warner, h. 490 Vine
Zeigler Michael, butcher, 609 Elm
Zell Joseph, spinner, n.s. Mercer b. Vine and Walnut
Zeiller & Friedman, (Isaac Z. & Morris F.,) clothiers, &c., 72 W. Pearl
Zeiller Isaac, (Z. & Friedman,) 175 W. 3d
ZEILLER Joseph, (Bindskopf Bros. & Co.,) 168 Elm
Zeis John, upholsterer, 82 Mound
Zeisken Ernst, lab., 135 Ham. Road
Zeisz Philipp, lab., n.e.c. Smith and Water
Zeitz Chas., baker, 65 Buckeye
Zeiger Francis, 49 Findlay [7th
Zeiger Ferdinand, e.s. Canal b. 6th and
Zeller Catharine, 178 W. 6th
ZELTNER JOHN E.,
Coffe House,
402 Vine
Zeltner John, jr., bar k., 402 Vine
Zeltner Michael, bar. k., 402 Vine
Zemar Michael, lab., e.s. Western Av, b, Poplar and Findlay
Zender Martin, n. e. c. Sycamore and Milton
Zenger Geo., dray, 149 Pleasant
Zenger Jacob G., turner, 36 Mercer
Zentner Henrietta, cof. h., 276 W. Liberty
Zeoller Leopold, cof.h., n. w. c. Augusta and Smith
Zeppenfeld Francis, cof. h., 14 Mary
Zeppenfeld Herman, meats, 65 Abigail
Zerfas John, tailor, 501 Walnut
Zerhusen Theodore, blksmith, s.s. 2d b. Race and Vine
Zettle & Stallo (Wm. Z. & J H. Stallo) patentees, new fruit jar, 9 R. R. Bldg., n.w.c. Court and Main
Zettle Wm. (Z. & Stallo), bds. Teutonia Hotel
Zettler Martin, carp., h. s. w. c. 2d and Ludlow
Zeuner Chas., pattern mkr, 54 Allison
Zibold John G., lab., 91 Bremen
Zidler Louis, ma h., wks. Lane & Bodley's
Ziefle Joseph, paper hanger, 13 Mary
Ziegler Conrad, express driver, n. c. c. Ham. Road and Vine
Ziegler Hy., cof. h., n. e. c. Front and Pike
Ziegler John, shoemkr, 127 Ham. Road
Ziegler Soseph, bk. binder, 639 Vine
Ziegler Louisa, h. 19 Peete
ZIEGLER LUDWIG,
Coffee House and Brewery,
490 Vine
Ziegler Margaret, 64 Ham. Road
Ziegler Martin, lab., 729 Race
Ziegler Michael, (Hy. Shafer & Co.)
Ziegler Michael, butcher, n. w. c. Henry and Pleasant, h. 699 Elm

(ZUB) CINCINNATI (ZUM) DIRECTORY. (ZYP) 345

'cher Chas., b.k., W. 9th, b. Harriet and Millcreek
t Anton, tailor, 74 Dunlap
ercher Christian, cab. mkr., 25 Monroe
'INER Paul W,, (Harris & Z.) 297 W. 8th
lair M., 62 Mohawk
lhans Fred , lab., 116 Buckeye
ll Burkhard, mason, e.s. Goose al., b. Green and Elder
llais Frederick, lab., 118 Buckeye
ller Andrew, cof.h., 245 W. 6th
ller Fritz, salesman, 174 W 5th, bds. 340 Vine
ller John, blksmith, 708 Vine
ller Wm. E., bkbinder, 25 W. 4th, b. 67 W. 6th
mbahlen Clemens, cutter, 540 Plum
mmer Wm., blksmith, al b. Linn and Baymiller an 1 Wade and Liberty
pf Adam, tailor, 186 Everett
pf Nicholaus, baker, 64 W. Liberty
pfy Caroline, rear 26 Franklin
rb Conrad, shoe mkr., 153 Water
rge Joost J., porter, 25 W. 4th
rge Wm., porter, 23 Walnut, bds. 25 Franklin
rger Rejier, porter, 25 Franklin
rnes Andrew J., mate, 63 Butler
st John, cof.h., 195 Bremen
uber John A., porter, 536 Vine
.ber John A., porter, 536 Vine

Zudora Charles, lab., 43 Race
Zuercher Ulrich, baker, bds. 550 Main
Zuest Jacob, grocer, 32 Dunlap
Zufall Bernhard, barber, e.s. Johnson al. b. Canal and 12th
Zufang Euchar, shoe mkr., bds. 22 Hughes
Zufang Stephen. lab., 11 E. Liberty
Zugler Saml . finisher. wks. n e.c. Walnut and Canal
Zuleger Joseph, mason, w. s. Goose al. b. Green and Elder
Zuleger Joseph, tailor, w.s. Vine, b. Milk and Mulberry
Zullur Herman, c b.mkr., 303 Linn
Zumar Elizabeth, 149 Elm
Zumbahlen Hy., painter 540 Plum
Zumbahlen Elizabeth, 538 Plum
Zumbiel Geo., salesman, 85 Main
Zumbusch Ferdinand M., jewelry, 673 Vine
Zumdresch Elizabeth, 7 Mary
Zumear Elizabeth, b h., 149 Elm
Zumstein Chas., bar k., 185 Vine
Zumstein Frank., brush mkr., wks. 578 Main

ZUMSTEIN FRANK M.,
Coffee House,
185 Vine

Zumstein Geo., cigars, &c., 183 Vine. h. 185 Vipe
Zumstein Hy., cof h., 189 Vine

ZUMSTEIN JOHN,
Coffee House,
s.w.c. 5th and Walnut

Zumstein Peter, bar.k., 189 Vine
Zumwalde Hy., lab , 587 Race
Zurburn Casper, watch mkr., 62 Main. h. 27 Harrison
Zurcher Conrad, painter, 43 14th
Zurhusen Herman H., tailor, 105 W. 2d
Zurin John, saddler, 463 Walnut
Zurkamp Hy., chair mkr., bds. 662 Race
Zurkamp John, varnisher, bds 662 Race
Zurlein Frank, cab.mkr., 14 13th
Zurliene Fred., sawyer, 6 Ramsey
Zurliene Hy., boots and shoes, 390 Broadway
Zurline Catharine, bds. 15 Franklin
Zurline Dietrich, saddler, 15 Franklin
Zurline Frederick, bds. e.s. Ramsey, nr. Park al
Zurmuhlens John, grocery, 78 Wade
Zusi Victor, macht., 532 Central Av
Zwekbronner Wm , baker, h. 706 Central
Zwick Geo. A., clk., 76 Broadway
Zwick J. M., druggist. bds. Henrie House
Zwick Madame Joanne, hair jewelry and ladies' wig manuf , 40 W. 4th
Zwlering Juseph, lab., bds. 9 Woodward
Zwitzler John, expressman, 26 Findlay
Zyburth John, shoe mkr., 13 Pendleton

DODGE'S PATENT

IMPROVEMENT IN

GRATES AND STOVES.

IT PRODUCES DOUBLE THE HEAT WITH HALF THE FUEL.

It is simple, efficient, and practicable; saving fuel, radiating the heat into the room instead 'allowing it to pass up the chimney; suppressing the cold draught of air through the room, to ie fire, and is as good for Wood as for Coal.

**Over 50,000 Persons are now using this Patent, with entire satisfaction.
All who value Economy, Comfort, or health, should adopt it at once.**

Counting coal at 15 cents per bushel, this improvement will save its cost in one season, and afford ich comfort as can not be produced by any other arrangement.

We have Circulars, giving the unqualified recommendations of many well known citizens, in early all the principal cities of the United States.

Address, **JOHN B. RYAN & CO.,**

Proprietors of Dodge's Patent,

eave Orders at Eagle Stove Store, No. 17 West Fifth Street, **CINCINNATI, OHIO.**

CINCINNATI
Business Mirror;

A Directory of Business Persons, Firms and Institutions,

ARRANGED ACCORDING TO THEIR VARIOUS BUSINESS PURSUITS.

Agents.
(Advertising.)
PARVIN SYLVESTER H., 63 W. 4th.

Agents.
(Claim.)
Hartshorn Chas., 101 E. 3d
NATIONAL CLAIM Agency 66 W. 3d
Scott Wm. H. jr. 2 Burnet
Van Winkel & Bussert, 8 W. 3d

Agricultural Implements
DAIR JOHN F. & CO., 40 and 42 E. Pearl
FLETCHER R., 61 Sycamore
McCULLOUGH J. M. & SON, 200 Main & 3 E. 5th
WARWOOD JOSEPH, 510 W. Front
WILDER, ROBINSON & Co., 230 Walnut

Alcohol, Pure Spirits, &c.
BARTLETT R. & CO., s.w.c. Front and Walnut
BOYLE & CO., 51 to 53 E. 2d
FLETCHER L. HOBART & Co., s.w.c. Front & Vine
Littner & Austing, Pearl b. Kilgour and Lock
Oliver David W. 68 and 70 Water
PIKE S. N. & CO., 18 and 20 Sycamore
Starr E. P., s.w.c. Pearl and John

Ale and Porter Manufac.
(See also Breweries.)
Billerbeck Clements A, 189 E. Pearl
Holls Charles, 126 Cutter
Lepare Val, 144 Buckeye
NIEHAUS CAPT. HENRY, 450 Sycamore
NIEHAUS JOSEPH, 13 Woodward

Ambrotypes.
(See Photographic Artists.)

Apothecaries.
(See Druggists & Apoth's.)

Apple-Butter and Mince Meat.
Hunt John, n.e.c. Central Avenue and Ann

Architects.
ANDERSON & HANNA-FORD, n.e.c. 3d and Race
Bochman C. V., 544 Elm
KELLY & BRITT, 77 W. 3d
McLAUGHLIN JAS. W., 125 Central Av.
Moore Francis W. 305 W. Front
PIKE A. & SON, 168 Vine
Tinsley Wm. n.w.c. 6th and Walnut
WALTER WILLIAM, s.e.c. 4th and Walnut

Artificial Flowers.
Jamelson Mrs. Mary, 121 W. 5th
Ottenheimer A., 113 W. 5th

Artificial Limbs.
Bly Douglas, s.w.c. 6th and Vine
Daniels Dr. D. N., n.w.c. 4th and Main
MARSH, CORLISS & CO., 5 W. 4th.

Artists.
Aubery John, 14 E. 4th
Beard James H. 6 Carlisle Building
Eaton J. O. room 20 Pike's Opera House
Lindsay Thomas C. 28 W. 4th
Norton E. L. 23 W. 4th
Pedretti P., room 20 Pike's Opera House
Richardson Miss M. W.
Webber Chas. T. 14 E. 4th
WICKERSHAM THOS. room 19 Pike's Opera House
Young Wm. 23 W. 4th

Artist's Materials.
HOFFMAN & MOSER, 222 Main
EGGERS & CO., 165 Main

Attorneys at Law.
ABRAHAM J., room 10 Masonic Temple
Adams Wm. A. 8 Short's bldg.
APPLEGATE JOHN W., 51 W. 4th
Ast John A., s.e.c. Main and Court
Avery Wm. L., 21 W. 3d
Baker John S., 148 Walnut
Baldauf Phillip, 478 Vine
BALDWIN & BALDWIN, 51 W. 3d
BALL & JORDAN, 6 E. 3d
BATEMAN WARNER M., 21 W. 3d
BATES & SCARBOROUGH, 58 W. 3d
BELL PETER, 10 Court House
Bevan John jr. Masonic Temple
Biddle Francis J., 22 W. Court
Biddle Wm. P, 31 Bank bldg.
BIRD NICHOLAS, s.w.c. 3d and Sycamore
Black Samuel F., 33 E. 3d
BOCKING A. H., 51 W. 4th
Bofinger Ben. 211 W. 9th
Boyle James, n.w.c. Main and Court
Bradstreet Edw'd P., 23 W. 3d
BROWER ABM., 4 Masonic Temple
BROWN CHAS. BRADY, 19 W. 3d
Brown J., s.w.c. Court and Main
Brown Louis G. 14 E. 2d
Brown O. & E. T. s.w.c. Main and Court
BRUNER MARTIN, 20 W. Court
Burgoyne John, Jr., s.e.c. Main and Court
BURROWES WM. S., 6 W. 4th

Cady David K, jr. 57 W. 3d
CALDWELL & CALDWELL, 379 Main
CALDWELL WM. B. & M. H. & W. TILDEN, 9 Masonic Temple
CARPENTER SAML. S., 23 W. 3d
Carter A. G. W., 8 Masonic Temple
Carter S. B., s.w.c. Main and Court
Clark Stephen, 22 W. Court
Clason Marshal B. 21 W. 3d
CLEMMER J. H., n.e.c. 7th and Main
Coles Stephen, 120 Main
COLLINS & HERRON, 148 Walnut
Colton F. 17 E. 3d
Conklin T., 9th E. of Cent. Av
Constable A. G. A. 11 Short's bldg
Coppock Wm. J. 9 Masonic Temple
COREY W. M., n.e.c. 9th and Walnut
CORWINE R. M., 7 Short's bldg
Cox Joseph, n.w.c. Fifth and Walnut
Craig James G. 7 Masonic Temple
CRANCH & CHALLEN, s.e.c. 4th and Vine
CRAPSEY JACOB T., n.w.c. 6th and Walnut
CRAWFORD SAML. T., 30 W. 4th
Creutz Jacob, s.e.c. Main and Court
CURWEN M. E. 66 W. 3d
Day Henry, 58 W. 3d
Denzler F. N. 22 W. Court
DICKSON W. M., 6 E. 3d
Disney Wm., 208 W. 7th
Dobmeyer Joseph G. n.w.c. Main and Court
DODD & HUSTON, 14 E. 2d up stairs
DOUGLASS JOHN G., 42 W. 4th un stairs
DUTTON AARON R., 6 E. 3d
Eaton John B., n.w.c. 6th and Walnut
Edwards Edwin, 148 Walnut
EGLEY JOSEPH E.
n.e.c. Main and Court
FERGUSON & McGINNIS 65 W. Third
Flinn Jacob, 11 Richmond
Folsom Richard, s.w.c. 4th and Walnut
FOX, HARRIS & FOX, 156 Main
FRENCH & CUNNINGHAM, 57 W. 3d
Freon J., n.w.c. 3d and Main
Fulton & Karr, 148 Walnut
GAINES THEOPHIL'S, Pros. Atty Court House
GALLAGHER T. J. 148 Walnut
Garrard Jeptha, s.e.c. 4th and Vine
Gasser John J., n.w.c. Main & Court
GETZENDANNER J. H. 15 W. 3d
GIBBONS JOS. G., 35 W. 3d

Glazier Wm. B., s.s. 9th b. Plum and Central Av.
GROESBECK WM. S., 21 W. 3d
Grosvenor Mason, n.w.c. 6th and Walnut
HAGANS & BROADWELL 148 Walnut
HAINES, TODD & LYTLE, 15 W. 3d
Hale Joseph, 17 W. 3d
Hamilton R. S. 180 Walnut
HANOVER M. D. 57 W. 3d
Henderson T. J., 15 E. 3d
Houdricks G. 211 W. 5th
Hill A. P., s.w.c. 3d Main
HILTON GEO. H. 13 W. 3d
HILTS CHARLES, 22 W. Court
Hopple Matthew, 11 E. 3d
HOLLISTER G. B., 230 Walnut
Hunter John E. 75 W. 3d
HUTCHESON E. E., 65 W. 3d
Jackson & Johnson, 13 Mas. Tem
JAMES CHARLES P. 15 Masonic Temple
James Thomas M., 3 Masonic Temple
JOACHIM WENDELL, 22 W. Court
JOHNSON JAMES W., 17 Bank bldg
JOHNSTON & COLLIER, 13 Masonic Temple
JOHNSTON ROBERT, 4 Masonic Temple
Jolliffe John, 80 W. 4th
JONES & BURNET, 5 Masonic Temple
Jones Jeremiah H. 148 Walnut
JONES & SHARP, 8 Masonic Temple
KEBLER, WHITMAN & FORCE, 11 Masonic Tem.
KERR WM. H., Asst. Pro. Atty., Court House
KING & THOMPSON, Worthington's bldg.
KIRBY CLINTON, n.w.c. 6th and Walnut
Kittredge E. W. 8 Carlisle bldg
Langdon E. Bassett, n.e.c. 9th and Walnut
Lathrop Wm. H. 9 Masonic Temple
LEE & FISHER, 33 W. 3d
Lewis J. H., n.w.c. Main and Court
LINCOLN F. D., 56 Main
LINCOLN, SMITH & WARNOCK, 8 E. 2d
LOGAN THOMAS A., 73 W. 3d
LONG & HOEFFER, 21 W. 3d
LUDLOW AUGUSTUS, s.e.c. 4th and Vine
LYNCH JOHN A. 7 Short's bldg
Lynd Staughton, 7 Masonic Temple
McClymons J. B., n.w.c. 3d and Main
McDougal Joseph, 57 W. 3d
McGROARTY & ROGERS, 2 Short's bldg
McGUFFEY ALEX. H., 120 Main

CINCINNATI

McLEAN N. C., Custom House bldg
MALLON P. & C. VON SEGGERN, Dubolt bldg
Mansfield Chas. D., 6 E. 5th
MATSON & PAXTON, 21 W. 3d
Matthews Sam'l R., 23 W. 3d
Matthews Stanley, 23 W. 3d
MILLER FRANCIS W., 65 W. 3d
MILLER I. J., 34 Bank bldg
MILLS & GOSHORN, 17 W. 3d
MINER JNO. L., 57 W. 3d
MITCHELL T. G. 116 Main
Moore O, C., 379 Main
Moore Robert, 22 W. Court
Mullane And. J., 114 Plum
Nixon Wm. P., 75 W. 3d
O'Connor T. A. 130 Vine
O'HARA T. B. 119 Walnut
Paul H. D., 25 W. 3d
Peat & Cornell. 363 Main
PENDLETON GEO. H., Worthington's bldg.
PHILLIPS WM., n.e.c. Walnut and 9th
Potter Daniel F., 1 and 2 Masonic Temple
POWELL JOSEPH B., 66 W. 3d
POWELL THOMAS, 12 Masonic Temple
PROBASCO WM. B., 68 W. 3d
Pruden A. J., 57 W. 3d
PUGH GEO. E., 73 W. 3d
Pullen & Banks, n.w.c. 3d and Walnut
Ramsay Wm. M. 68 W. 3d
Reemelin Charles, 373 Main
RIDDLE ADAM N., 284 Main
Riley James, 20 W. 6th
ROOT O. W. s.w.c. 3d and Sycamore
Schuderer Geo. 22 W. Court
Shafer Mendal, 5 Masonic Tem.
Sherwin W. G., Masonic Temple
SHONTER ANTHONY, 363 Main
SIMPSON J. ALEX. n.w.c. 4th and Sycamore
Snelbaker David T., 239 W. 9th
SNOW HENRY, 7 Masonic Temple [Court
Sayder M. s.w.c. Main and
SPOONER & LAWDER, n.w.c. Main and Court
STALLO & McCOOK, 19 W. Court
STALLO & TAFEL, n.w.c. Main and Court
Stanbery H., 3 Masonic Temple
Stanton Wm., 83 W 4th
Stearnes Geo. E., 148 Walnut
STEPHENSON & NOYES, 148 Walnut
STONE & CHAMPLIN, 13 W. Court
STRAIT T. J. 230 Walnut
STRAUB & JAMES, 3 Masonic Temple
Swartz Benj. A., 118 Walnut
TAFT & PERRY, 1 and 2 Masonic Temple
Thielmann Geo. O. 9 W. Court
THOMPSON & NESMITH, 25 W. 3d
Titus Jos. B. 42 W. 4th
Tullis A. J. 243 W. 9th
VAN HAMM WASH. 65 W. 3d
Van Winkle & Dussert, 8 W. 3d
WARD & WARD, s.e.c. 3d and Walnut
Warden, Forrest & Sheppard, 20 W. Court
WARE THOMAS, City Solicitor, City bldg
Warren Jno. D., n.w.c. 6th & Walnut.
WEBSTER GEO. F., 17 E. 3d
WHITE J. S., 230 Walnut
White O. D., 49 Bank bldg.
Williams E. M. 284 Main
WILLIAMS PETER T., n.e.c. Walnut and 5th
Williams Wm. G., 148 Walnut
Wolf Jacob, 19 W. 3d
WOODRUFF EDWARD, over 6 E. 5th

WORTHINGTON & MATTHEWS, 23 W. 3d
Wright D. Thew., 66 W. 3d
Zinn Peter, n.w.c. Main and Court

(Patent.)
Clough Wm., 122 Main

Astrologer.
RAPHAEL WM. 59 E. 5th

Auctioneers.
(Book trade Sales.)
HUBBARD'S, G., 21 W. 5th

(Dry Goods.)
Johnston Thos., 98 Main
Kahn Julius, 9 W. 5th
Montgomery Henry J. 73 W. Pearl
Wells & Miles, 25 W. Pearl

(Furniture.)
Chew Jas. P. 21 E. 4th
WILLIAMS A. P. & CO. 22 and 24 E. 3d
Furniture at Private Houses, Real Estate and Variety.
Cooper & Stokes, 14 E. 4th
GRAFF, JACOB & KUHL, 20 East Fourth
WAGGONER JOHN, 56 W. 6th

(Groceries.)
BRASHEARS G. & LAWS, 57 and 59 Main
Kissick James, 217 Main
SAYRE L., 234 Walnut

(Horse.)
Carney Daniel, 19 E. 5th.
Day & Woodruff, 26 E. 5th
Miller James M, 21 E. 5th
Rider Chas. E., 17 E. 5th

(Real Estate.)
Hickman J. L. & Co. 60 W. 3d
HANOVER J. C. 57 W. 3d
Smith & Winters, 221 Vine

(Miscellaneous.)
Dell N. C. 219 Main
HUBBARD & HEATON, 21 W. 5th
Pauson H. n.w.c. Elder and Vine
Roed Robert, 223 Main
West Wm. W. 154 Main
Wickham Thos. B. 26 W. 5th

Awnings, Tents, &c.
Alcorn W. E., 85 Sycamore
Gordon George. 150 Sycamore
Hogbin Thomas, 210 Central Av
Lee Robert R. n.w.c. Central Av. and 5th
Lee Wm. H., 222 Central Av
Ryling John, 22 E. 8th
Terrell Charles A. 12 Sycam'r
Vandivier Wm., 49 E. 3d
Verschoor John, 23 Franklin
Westfield Chas., 100 Sycamore
Wynja Louis, 68 Sycamore

Bakeries.
Amreihn B., 547 Race
Arnhold A., 351 Central Av
BAILIE JOHN & CO. s.e.c. 2d and Ludlow
Balley Martin, 347 W. 5th
Barnberger John, 144 Ham. Rd
Beck John A. 527 Freeman
Beckenhaupt J., 18 Freeman
Bedel T., 342 Ham. Road
Bender John, 461 Elm
Bengel Geo., 69 Wade
Bengel Philip, 623 Vine
Bennet C. H., 89 W. Court
Bertrams Benj., 522 Race
Birtsch John, 637 Central Av.
Bogershausen J., 3 7 Cen'l Av
Braun John, 681 Race
Breiling Arnold, 167 Pleasant
Brendel Geo. 535 Walnut
Brisbo F., 23 Findlay
Bruce Alex., s.e.c. 6th and Culvert
Brucknor W. 263 Main
Bruggemann August, 456 Vine
Bruno Fred. 134 W. Front
Bryce F. F. 506 Sycamore
BURBECK & HAIGHT, 58 and 60 Commerce
Burkhart Frank, 564 Central Av.

Burnett Thomas N. 217 Freeman
CAVAGNA B., 31 W. 5th
Christie E. 146 W. 6th
CLOON SAMUEL & CO. 21 Public Landing
Cole James 194 W. 4th
Cooper Jas. C., n.e.c. Walnut and Water
Cooper R. A., 28 & 30 E. Pearl
DUNHOLTER H., 244 W. 6th
Dunstorf Wm., 176 W. Front
Eckert D., n.w.c. 6th and Culvert
Engelke F., 635 Central Av
Feleng Wm. 420 W. 4th
Feuss Wm., 207 Cutter
Field R. B. 118 W. 5th
Fischer Chris. 272 Main
Froehlich John. 134 Linn
Fritz John, 609 Vine
Gasner John, 74 Ham. Road
Gates George, s.w.c. Pike and Butler
Gegner J., 211 W. 6th
Gellenbeck & Duttman, 93 Abigail
Golden Mrs. Isaac, 172 and 174 Elm
Gollinger F., s.e.c. Central Av. and Baymiller
Goodwin A. 43 Public Land'g
Gruter C. 718 Front
Griffig M., 106 Buckeye
Hablitz F., 720 Vine
Hahneman C., 549 Vine
Hauckman B., 237 Pine
Hart August, s.w.c. Linn and 8th
Heinrichdorf Otto, 19 W. 5th
Hjensman George, n.s. 6th b. Harriet & Horne
Honhouser B., 63 E. 8th
Honhouser John, 90 Hunt
Hunt J., 620 Central Av.
Hurster D., 456 W. 3d
Hurt John, 265 Vine
Jahr B., 582 Main
Kerner J., 8 Walnut
KESSLING HENRY J. s.e.c. Linn and Clinton
Kirchhof L., 642 Main
Knaul & Co., 137 York
Lauther Adam t2 13th
Link Martin, w.s. Elm b. McFarland and 3d
Littleford J. S. S., 14 E. Pearl
Lohmann Ed. 33 Mulberry
Ludeke C., 505 Main
LUERS MRS. JOHN B., 172 Sycamore
McCartney John, 444 W. 5th
Macauley R. E. 278 W. 5th
McGowern P. H., s.w.c. Plum and Front
Maier John, 118 Pleasant
Merkel John, 72 E. Pearl
Metzger Geo., 91 Bremen
Moser Vincent, 64 Buck
Mueller A. 427 Central Av.
Mueller J., 116 Ham. Road
Muth A., 26 W. 5th
Nuber J., 95 York
Nusel Geo., 148 E. Front
Oeder Geo., n. e. c. Elm and Elder
Ott Peter, 201 Baymiller
PARKHILL J., 143 Linn
Pistor Jacob, 208 W. Liberty
Potthoff H., 484 Walnut
Quentin Herman, 387 Vine
Rach Wm. 524 Sycamore
Reis Henry, 186 W. 5th
Roesch John, 88 Woodward
Rivard J. C., 42½ E. 3d
Roettcher Louis, s.w.c. John and Clinton
Rotthaas E. 270 W. Liberty
Rust Herman, 35 Elder
Rust Herman, 145 Bremen
Sabine Chas., 173 W. Court
Scheifele Wm. 1019 Central Av.
Schellenberger Joseph, 444 Walnut
Schonfele John, 21 18th
Schmidt C. F., 633 Elm
Schmidt Chris., 202 Clark
Schmidt Henry, 57 Hopkins
Schmitt Anthony, 628 W. 6th
Schneider Henry, e.s. Vine b. Calhoun and Auburn Av.
Schneider John, 652 Vine
Schroth John, 50 Ham. Road
Schobert Adam, 316 Vine
Schray Gottleib, 451 Sycamore
Schrut George, 123 Bremen
Seifert Francis, 727 Race
Seiter G., n.e.c. 8th and Elm

itkamp Theodore, 515 Main
mner A., 6 Walnut
ter C. 744 W. 6th
binson F., 186 Walnut
ots T. E., 114 Vine
use Ellis, 32 Central Av.
yster Wm., 46 W. 8th
dolph John, 83 Bremen
unders Wm. 146 E. 6th
hlenker John, 99 Central Av
hnell C., 103 Ham. Road
hnling Geo., 674 Central Av
huhardt Harmon, 9 W. 6th
hmitt Henry, 625 Main
ipp Thos., cor. 6th & Walnut
ing Robert, c. Race and
Water
ith Jacob H., 10 E. 3d
ith & Hawkins, 161 W. 5th
erber E., 383 Vine
urer Geo. 14 E. Front
wart James, 504 Elm
ichelm J. E., 583 W. 28th
rack Adam, 688 Main
ney Wm. J., 50 E. 5th
aspot J., 6. W. 3d
rner Burr. Dennison House
rhein F., 356 W. 5th
ndergotten H., & Son, 61
Broadway
sael Conrad, 67 Buckeye
rner John C. 220 Linn
tengel V., 8 Court House
Building
lliams Wm. 233½ W. 5th
chritz E. Henry, Walnut
Street House
chritz John L, 1120 Central
Av.
chritz Phillip, 1078 Cen'l Av
chritz J. H. 52 Sycamore
nder Frank, 124 Bremen
apelmann P., 497 Cen'l Av

isket Manuf. & Deal's
*(e also Wood and Willow
Ware.)*
ss Thomas, 206 W. 5th
ONER JOHN
36 W. 5th
ADY D. K.,
n.e.c. Fifth and Walnut
pins & Discher, 560 Main

Bath Tubs.
LATCHFORD & CO.
168 Vine
)HNSTON J. & J. M.,
219 and 221 W. 3d

Bath Houses.
RRICO ANTONIO,
108 W. 4th
scho & Gordon, 95 W. 5th
URNET HOUSE BATH
ROOMS
hof John, 137 Sycamore
ltengel V., Court House
bldg

Baths, (Chemical)
ibee Samuel, 280 Walnut

dstead Manufacturers
e also Cab. Ware Manuf.)
LBRO HENRY,
196 W. Pearl
ENSHAW G. & SONS,
26 Sycamore
EADER & CO.
41 W. 2d
ITCHELL & RAMMELS-
BURG, 99 W. 4th
UDGE H. B.,
95 W. 2d
ITH & HAWLEY,
69 W. 5th

Bedstead Fastener.
ion Peter, 257 W, 7th

Bell Hangers.
Locksmiths & B. Hangers)

ll and Brass Founders.
ARK WM. H.,
122 Main
hn G. W. & Co., 102 E. 2d
MMINGS S. & SON,
162 E. Front
ger Jacob, 48 Public Land
BSON J. D. & T.,
200 Vine
AVEN J. L. & CO,
173 W. 2d
UME JAMES,
65 Lodge
RKUP WM. & SON,
250 E. Front

Kuchner Chas. F. 9 Allison
Leuchtweis Ant., 46 12h
NILES WORKS CO.,
123 and 125 E. 2d
POWELL WM. & CO.,
217 and 219 W. 5th
Robson, & Co., 154 E. Front
Ruthven John, 216 W. 2d

Bellows Manufctrs.
ENGLISH C. L.,
41 E. 2d
HYNDMAN W. G.
54 E. 2d

Belting and Hose.
(See Hose and Belting Manuf.)

Billiard Saloons.
(See also Coffee Houses.)
Apollo Saloon, Apollo Build'g.
n.w.c. 5th and Walnut
Bakhaus Chas. n.w.c. Main
and 7th
BOLLMANN J. B. & CO.
15 E. 9th
Botherton Louis, 430 Main
Buckeye, 76½ W. 4th
DAUM MICHAEL,
30 Broadway
Harrison & Collins, n.w.c. 5th
and Central Av.
Hesse Ernst H. n.e.c. Pearl
and Race
INTERNATIONAL,
91 Sycamore
Jennys Wm. C. 286 Main
Johnson Edward P. Apollo
bldg
Loring & Hartshorn, 76½ W.
4th
Metcalfe & Ross, n.e.c. Main
and 8th
Parmorton A.B. n.w.c. Long-
worth and Central Av
ST. CHARLES,
30 E. 3d
ST. NICHOLAS,
n.w.c. Vine & Longworth
Scott & Allgair, s.w.q. 5th
and Central Av.
Struwe W., 488 Main
TIEMAN PHIL.
w.s. Sycamore b. 3d & 4th
Vandervort Robert, 74 W. 3d
Wach Theodore, s.w.c. Main
and Court

Billiard Table Manufs.
Balke Julius, n.e.c. 8th and
Main
BRUNSWICK J. M. & BRO.
8 W. 6th

Bird Fancier.
Miller George, 28 W. Court
Espich Chas., s.s. 6th b. Main
and Walnut

Bill Posters.
Chapman J. Q. A. Enquirer
Office
Head S. H., Commercial Office

Blacking Manufs.
Butler Thos. S., Agt. 39 Vine
Sneers Noah W., 61 Walnut
King H. L., 230 Walnut

Blacksmiths.
Appel Joseph, s.s. 6th nr. Horne
Baum John, 7 Bank
Beard G. H., 213 W. 2d
Bell Thomas, 152 W. Court
Belliew Patrick, s.s. 8th b.
Main and Sycamore
Bleckman Henry C. w.s. John
b. Laurel and Betts
Boges Samuel, 124 E. 2d
Bolser Mahlon, s.w.c. 5th and
Lock
Brauning Carl, s.s. Reading
Pike nr. Tunnel
Breier Fred, 214 Clark
Bristol Wm. H. n.e.c. Marsh
and Park
Burdorff H., 103 Hunt
Bussi Fred. 218 Clark
Clark John N., 36 E. 6th
Daganer H., 907 Central Av
Dilany P., 206 W. 7th
Doyle Ed., Freeman, nr C. H.
and Dayton R.R.
Dexheimer John, 559 Walnut
Dorn Conrad, 600 Walnut
Dorrmann Fred, 509 Elm
Duffy Ed., 416 W. 2d
Felix Geo. M., 987 Cen'l Av
Fischer Lewis, 796 Cen'l Av

Fischer John F., n.e.c. Liberty
and Freeman
Francis A. W., 93 E. 8th
Fritz Henry, 139 Ham. Road
Galvin Thomas, n.w.c. Canal
and Sycamore
Geiger Geo, 313 Ham. Road
Gosling Thomas, 69 Hunt
GRAHAM CHAS. & BRO.,
277 W. Front
Hanlein J. A., 135 Wade
Hegger John, 449 W. 2d
Haller Justus, 41 W. 9th w. of
Central Av.
Housman Fredk. e.s. Sycamore
b. Abigail and Woodward
Hutton J. & E., Commerce b.
Elm and Plum
Jones Jos., 66 E. Front
Kamp Peter, 152 W. Court w.
of Cen'l Av
Kaus & Bachmann, s.e.c.
Harrison Road & Division
Kenely Pat, n.s. Pearl b. Cen.
Av and John
Klug P., 1032 Central Av
Kipp Fred. 617 Elm
Kreimborg John, 19 Ham. Rd
Linebaugh Samuel, 143 Water
McCormick Patrick, n.s, Pat-
terson al. b. Main and Wal-
nut
McKone L. w.s. Butler b.
Front and Pearl
Maloney Martin, e.s. Front e.
of Weeks
Maus Nick. 337 Broadway
Meier Frank, 173 Hopkins
Menke John B. 65 12th
Meyer & Dwyer, 27 Lodge
Moore John and Peter, 78 Race
Nichol James, s.s. Front b.
Lawrence and Pike
Niehaus Jno. B. 677 Central Av
Niles S, B., 1563 E. Front
O'Connell M., n.e.c. 6th and
Culvert
Otting C., s.s. Charlotte b.
Linn and Baymiller
Palmer F.W., 679 Elm
Purser John, 91 E. Front
Puttman A. N. s.e.c. Ram-
sey and Pearl av.
Ratcliff Charles, w.s. Butler
b. Pearl and Front
Roberts John, 136 and 138 W.
Pearl
Recap James, n.s. Patterson
al. b. Main and Walnut
Roentigen P. H., 549 W. 8th
Rosner Henry, 711 Vine
Russel James, 23 Freeman
Ruthman G. 705 Race
Sandau C., 17 E. 7th
Sauder C., 320 E. Pearl
Schaeffer & Co. 1046 Central Av
Schatz Fred, s.s. 6th nr. Horne
Shore John G. n.s. Front b.
Pike and Butler
Silbernagel Mich, 70 W. Lib'ty
Silver Jonathan J. n.s. 6th b.
Harriet and Horne
Smallwood Rich. w.s. John b.
Laurel and Betts
Smith Noah, s.s. Front e. of
Foster
Stevens J. L., 211 W. 2d
Stevens John T. s.e.c. Denman
and Central Av.
STOCKHOFF BERNARD,
65 W. Liberty
Street R. Co., 521 W. 8th
Taylor Wm., s.s. Court b.
Main and Sycamore
Tullis & Stewart, 620 W. 6th
Tuttle J. N., 352 Central Av
Utz John, 9 Conal
Walkenhorst Jo., n.s, Front b.
Louisand Vance
WARWOOD JOSEPH,
663 W. Front
Worry Henry & G., Landing
b. Ludlow and Lawrence
Wendt Henry, 108 E. 2d
Whalen Thomas, s.e.c. Race
and Water
White Anthony, River b. Lud-
low and Lawrence
White James & Co., River b.
Ludlow and Lawrence
White Wm. 51 Observatory
Whitehead Ed. 14 Richmond
Winall George W., s.e.c. Smith
and Pearl
Wolfington S. & R, 133 W. 2d
Young Phillp, n.s. Ham. Rd,
b. Dunlap and Hamburg

Blocks and Riggings.
Harcourt & Mook, 87 E. Front
Shaw William, Land, b. Lud-
low & Lawrence

CINCINNATI

Boarding-Houses.
(See also *Hotels and Taverns*.)

Alberger Ellen, 104 Plum
Ammann Joseph, 346 Main
Arnetz Peter, 92 W. Court
Baer Jacob, 37 Ham. Road
Bauer Ulrich, 347 Walnut
Bagley Jane, 61 E. 4th
Bauman John, 74 E. Pearl
Bean Dabney J., 297 W. 6th
Beckmann John H., 109 E. 2d
Becksmith Henry, s.w.c. 6th and Broadway
Bindhammer Powell, 340 Vine
Bishop Mrs. L. L. 137 W. 7th
Bissell Mrs. E. F. 111 W. 6th
Bockholt Fred. 51 W. 5th
Bode Christian H, 592 Main
Boschert Bernhard, 620 Main
Botts John, 212 W. Front
Brickley Margaret, 158 W. 3d
Brockerhoff Ant., 519 Main
Brokamp Henry, n.w.c. Hunt and Pendleton
Brown Pat. II, 20 River Land.
Bunnell Susan, 209 Central Av
BURHOFF BARNEY, s.w.c. 5th and Smith
Busch John, 68 E. Front
Caden John, n.w.c. Ludlow and River
Carlisle Mary Ann, 37 Longworth
Carty E. B., 29 W. 7th [worth]
Clark Peter H. 25 Macalister
Classick Michael, 134 Main
Coffin Levi, s.w.c. Franklin and Broadway
Coleman Kate, s.w.c. Broadway and 5th
Collins Mary V. 206 W. 5th
Connelly Thomas, n.e.c. Vine and Water
Connor Wm., n.e.c. Ludlow and Front
Daily Christopher, 84 E. 5th
Daniels Mrs. L. D. 77 E. 3d
Darling Mary, s.w.c. 7th and Race
Dauman Henry, 125 Ham. Rd
DAWSON JAMES, 208 W. 5th
Deininger Henry, 34½ E. Front
Devitt Cash., 180 Race
DENNISON HOUSE, s.s. 5th b. Main and Sycamore
Doyle Patrick, 100 Freeman
Druffel John H. 90 E. 2d
Dryer Salome, s.e.c. Plum and Water
Dubois Wm. S., 109 W. 5th
Dumas Hotel, e.s. Macalister b. 4th and 5th
Duncan Samuel W. 316 W. 3d
Dunn Mary, 47 W. 7th
Earl Ben. W., 162 Broadway
Eisenheimer J., Geo. 412 Vine
Engelhart Jacob, 217 W. 5th
Evans Mrs. W. P., 239 Race
Ferguson Eliza, 162 Plum
Fiche Catharine, 113 Clay
Flaherty Patrick, 177 E. Front
Fox Catharine, 214 W. Front
Fox Ellen J. 159 W. Front
Frantz M. s.e.c. 2d and Plum
French Maynard, c.s. Auburn b. Northern and Central Av
Friederick Chris. 502 Walnut
Furst Charles, 48 E. Pearl
Gardner Robert, c.s. Walnut and 8th
Gelifus Louis, 701 Elm
Gluss Roberta, 204 W. 4th
Graf Joseph, 209 W. 6th
Green Elizabeth, 305 Race
Greenland Paulina, 230 Walnut
Griffith Samuel, 31 W. Front
Haley Patrick, 35 Ludlow
Hall Wm. 123½ E. Front
Haskell Joseph, 130 W. 5th
Hushart John, 334 Ham. Road
Hennibal Wm. 60 Wade
Herrmann Ernst, n.w.c. Lawrence and 2d
Hildreth Lewis A. s.w.c. 3d and Broadway
Hughes John, 174 E. Pearl
John Catharine, 27 Jackson
Jenni Henry, 550 Main
King Kate, n.w.c. Longworth and Central Av.
King Mrs. Lewis, 38 E. 4th
Kohule Anton, 674 W. 6th
Koo Wm., 80 Freeman
KRUCH LOUIS, 232 Walnut
Lafon Felix, 80 E. 5th
Langenheim Charles, 36 and 38 E. 5th
Larue Chas. 180 Broadway
Lathrop Mrs. G. 174 Plum

Legg Elizabeth, 208 W. 5th
Lomas Wm. 33 W. Front
Long John, 221 W. 5th
Lorence Basilius, 40 Pike
McCurdy Samuel, 89 E. 4th
McKee Eliza, 170 W. 5th
Maloy Mary, 162 W. 5th
Martens Henry, 137 Race
Meyer Francis A. 14 18th
Molley Betsey, 318 W. 5th
Morris Frances H. 192 Sycam'r
Moses Jacob, 15 and 17 Lodge
Mueller Geo. 225 W. 6th
Murphy Mary, 158 W. Front
Newman John, 205 W. 7th
NIEPORTE HENRY, s.e.c. Front and John
O'Connor Eliza, 184 Race
Parkinson Jane, 206 W. 5th
Peter Meinrad, 199 E. Front
PFEIFFER FREDERICK, s.e.c. 9th and Vine
Pickens Ellen, 139 W. 8th
PIETZ BERNHARD, 446 Vine
PUCHTA LORENZ, n.w.c. Pike and Pearl
Refnauer Leopold, 202 Walnut
Rice John G. 173 W. 3d
Richmond Anna, 183 Race
RIETH CHARLES, 254 E. Front
Robinson Anson D., 57 Broadway
Rodefer Elizabeth J. 145 Sycamore
Rollins Phoebe, 185 W. 3d
Ronger Martin, 23 Water
Rosmagle Elizabeth, 55 Betts
Ross David A., 353 Central Av
Rowe Thos. A., 177 Sycamore
Schafer Wm. s.w.c. 6th and Plum
Schehen Lorenz, 57 E. Pearl
Scherlen Michael, 703 Main
Schmidt John, 86 W. Court
Schneider George, 14 E. Front
Schoenberger Margrethea, 109 W. 8th
Schwartz Joseph, n.s. Augusta b. John and Smith
Sedam Geo., W. 127 W. 5th
Shaw James C., 127 W. 5th
Sidal Xavier, 249 W. 6th
Sims William, 269 Central Av.
Smith Francis A. 57 E. 3d
Smith Mrs. Nancy B., 162 Elm
Smith Patrick, 21 River Land
Spence Rebecca, 281 Cent'l Av
Stewart Eliza, 155 W. 4th
Stuart Elizabeth, 22 Home
Thompson Frances, 180 Race
Tillinghast Kate, 243 W. 5th
TREIDER FREDERICK, 362 Ham. Road
Turner Mary H. 52 W. 9th
Twohig Hannah, 286 W. 6th
Tydd Thos. E., 138 Longworth
Van Vliet Janc, 10 Clinton
Vonbuemmel Herman, 882 W. 6th
Waholl Barney, 428 Sycamore
Wall Jacob, 144 E. 2d
Wehr Frederick W. 199 W. 6th
Welch Elizabeth, 227 W. 5th
Westermann Lambert, 61 W. 5th
White Elizabeth, 355 Central Av
Wicchelman John C. 130 W. Court
Williams Elizabeth, 120 E. 5th
Wilson Adam, 32 E. Front
Wiley Jane, 100 Broadway
Wolf Frederick, 343 Walnut
Wrigh John, 579 W. 5th
Zeoller Leopold, n.w.c. Augusta and Smith
Ziegler Henry, n.e.c. Front and Pike
Zimmerman Chas. 161 E. Front
Zumear Elizabeth, 119 Elm

Boat Stores.
BARKER, HART & COOK, 44 Public Landing
Giddings James, 38 Public Landing
Hazlett John, 13 & 15 E. Front
Isham Fischer & Co. 47 Public Landing
Phillips Silas, 30 Public Land

Boiler Manufrs.
FAY J. A. & CO, s.w.c. Front and John
Hirshauer Ph., 147 E. Front
Holabird & Dumont, 355 W. Front
JONES JAMES & JAMES, s.s. Pearl e. of Ludlow
McLean & Shaddinger, s.e.c. Ludlow and Pearl

McILVAIN, SPIEGEL & Co w.s. Lawrence b. 2d and Pearl
SHADDINGER JOSEPH, s.e.c. Pearl and Ludlow
TUDOR R. & CO. s.s. 3d b. Butler and Miami Canal
West Isaac, 56 Pike

Bonnet Bleachers and Pressers.
Millson James, 139 W. 6th
Quinn Hugh, 302 Plum
Richter August, 89 13th
Sanger Joseph, 175 W. 4th

Bonnets.
(See *Millinery*.)

Book Binders.
Bardes Louis C., College hall
Bartscher A., 25 14th
BRADLEY & WEBB, 135 Main
Breisch J. F., Court House bldg
Brickley R. H. & Co. 160 Vine
Byrne J. & Co. 111 Main
Cropper C., 111 Main
Daniels Hector L. 58 W. 3d
DeForrest D., 62 W. 3d
ECKERT LORENZ, n.w.c. Walnut and 13th
Evers A. P., 120 Main
Hinkle A. H. & Co, 137 Walnut
Johnson, Stevens & Morgan, 141 Main
METHODIST BOOK CONCERN, s.w.c. Main & 8th
MOORE, WILSTACH, KEYS & Co., 25 W. 4th
Rabbe Henry G. 120 Main
Rowell & Alexander, 74 W. 3d
Schott Charles, 22 W. Court
TUMY J, C. & H. L., 43 Main
WRIGHTSON & CO., 167 Walnut

Bookbinders' Stock and Tools.
EGGERS J. C., 168 Main
HOOLE JOHN R., 27 E. Third

Booksellers and Publishers.
AM. S. S. UNION, (George Crosby agt.,) 41 W. 4th
AM. TRACT SOCIETY, 163 Walnut, S. Wood agt.
APPLEGATE & CO., 43 Main
BENZIGER & BROS. Catholic Institute Bettinger Peter, 3 Budd
BIRD M. H. 297 Central Av
Blanchard Geo. S. 39 W. 4th
Bloch & Co., 32 W. 6th
Buchman Bar. 26 W. 3d
CLARKE ROB. & CO., 65 W. Fourth
CROSBY GEORGE, 41 W. 4th
Dennis Lewis, 375 W. 5th
Dietz Fred. W. 611 W. 8th
ECKERT LORENZ, n.w.c. Walnut and 13th
EGGERS J. & WILDE, 317 Main
FLYNT MRS, M. D., n.w.c. Court & Cent. Av
GALVAGNI JOHN, 513 Vine
Gillard Wm., 182 W. Court
Hageney Anton W. 19 Linn
Harpel Oscar H. 344 W. 5th
Hartwell W. D., 192 W. 5th
HAWLEY J. R. 164 Vine
JAMES U. P., 167 Walnut
JOHNSON, FRY & CO. 13 W. 4th
Kelly A. A., 28 W. 4th
KENNEDY WARREN, 160 Vine
LEWIS GEORGE N. 28 W. 4th
LeBlond Robert. 120 W. 6th
McArthur & Son, 162 Vine
Mayle Ebenezer, s.w.c. 5th and Walnut & 334 Central Av
MACDONALD ALEX., 9 W. 4th
Magoling Charles, 668 Main
MEIS HENRY, 501 Main
MENDENHALL E., 157 Main
METHODIST BOOK CONCERN, s.w.c. Main & 8th

Moore Ames, 436 W. 5th
MOORE CORNELIUS, 117 Walnut
MOORE WILSTACH, KEYS & Co., 25 W. 4th
NYE & DEMAREST, n.w.c. 6th and Walnut
O'Connell T.. n.w.c. 8th and Central Av
Perry Edward, s.e.c. Main and 3d
PERRY & WARREN, 235 Central Av
Pettinger Peter, 3 Budd
Plueger J. M., 26 Mercer
Richards James, 248 Sycamore
RICKEY & CARROLL, 75 W. 4th
Schultz Marg., 77 Spring
Scott Francis, 229 Race
SMITH W. B. & CO, 137 Walnut
THEOBALD & THEURKAUF, 9 Court House bldg
THORPE JOHN D., 74 W. Fourth
Titcomb R., 153 W. 5th
Tucher J., s.e.c. 4th and Main
Turner Samuel, s.w.c. Pearl and Broadway
Tuttle Charles, 111 Main
Vierschilling & Bidenhorn, 25 Green
VIRTUE & CO. s.e.c. 8th and Hammond
WALSH JOHN P., 170 Sycamore
WEIL MAX & CO. s.w.c. 12th and Vine
Weller John, 23 Green
WOOD SHEL'Y, 163 Walnut

Boots and Shoes.
(*Wholesale*.)
AMBERG & LINDAUER, 97 W. 3d
AMBURG BROTHERS, 68 W. Pearl
Andrews & Biggs, 11 W. Pearl
Burnet Jacob, jr., 92 W. Pearl
Burton Gideon, 32 W. Pearl
Cahill John, 52 W. Pearl
Cluflin Aaron & Co., 7 W. 3d
COMSTOCK WM. H. & CO., 14 and 16 W. Pearl
DETERS J. H., 53 W. Fourth
Dittman Isadore, 140 Walnut
EAGAN & SLOCOMB, 73 W. Pearl
GATES JOHN & CO. 54 W. Pearl
GEORGE G. W. 102 Walnut
HART WM. & CO., 95 Walnut
HEWES & M'CANN, 31 W. 5th
JOHNSON C. E. & CO. 51 W. Pearl
KING WM. H., 27 E. Pearl
Kohlman Charles, 97 W. 3d
LYON JOHN, 281 W. 6th
MANSS L. & SONS, 39 and 41 E. Pearl
Nichols & Coburn, 56 W. Pearl
POMEROY R M. & CO. 59 W. Pearl
PRICHARD GEO. A. 105 W. Pearl
REEVES M. E. & CO., 121 Walnut
ROBBINS & POMEROY, 57 W. Pearl
ROBBINS & POSEY, 95 and 97 W. Pearl
SIMPKINSON J. & CO. 98 W. Pearl
Slikter & Matthews, 83 E. Pearl
THORNE W. F. & CO., 112 Walnut
WEBSTER E. G. & CO., 63 W. Pearl

Boots & Shoes.
(*Retail*.)
Abeling Henry, 19 Landing b. Main and Walnut
Ahlborn Wm. sr., 499 John
Ahlers John H., 406 Sycamore
Albers Anthony J. 31 Green
Alf John D., 322 E. Front
ALLAN & KLISTER, 147 Main
Ashman James, 549 Central Av
Assum Andrew, 50 Martin
Assum Henry P., 508 Vine

BUSINESS MIRROR. 351

Ausdenmoere Henry, 89 Central Av
BARBOUR ABIN E., 140 W. 5th
Becker Simon, 42 Pike
Beckman John H. n.w.c. Wade and Baymiller
Beckmann Theo., 615 Race
Behler Frank L., 172 W. Front
Behmer August, 40 E. 3th
Belle James B. s.w.c. Barr and Arnold
Bell J. B., 209 Cont. Av
Benzer Charles, 457 Walnut
Berger Herman K. 64 E. 5th
Berger John T., 438 W. 5th
Berling Henry, 682 Central Av
Berling Herman H. 917 Cen'l Av
Bernard Christian, 612 Vine
Berning Anthony William, 7 Pleasant
Berning Casper, 361 W. 5th
Bertelt Frank, 179 Linn
Bloch Abraham, 206 W. 6th
Blumberg Wm. 417 Central Av
Boeres John, 660 Elm
Bohl John, 10 Sycamore
Bollman Theodore, 35 Baum
Borger Fred., 459 Main
Brandewiede R., 671 W. Front
Brenner John C., 139 York
BRODFUEHRER & BRO., 52 W. 6th
Buecker August, 382 Race
Bubriage Fred'k, n.c.c. 15th and Plum
Buhrmann Geo. L... 579 Cen'l Av
Bunyan Maurice, 207 Broad'y
Burger Frank J. 328 W. 5th
Burger Philip R., 324 Main
Burterner Frank, 5 Casilly's Row
Busse Fred., 60 Plum
Cahill John, 315 Central Av
Clark Alex. P., 3385½ W. 5th
Cleary John, 128 Lock
Collins Henry, 151 Central Av
Conrad Peter, 553 Walnut
Crooks John, 268 Main
Cummins J. & Son, 56 Everett
Cunningham Felix, 37 Central Av
Curley Luke, s.s. Pearl b. Pike and Butler
Deckelman Henry, 1265 E. Frnt
Degenhard Ph., s.s. 6th nr. Horne
Derome John. 1029 Central Av
DETERS JNO. H., 83 W. Fourth
Dietz John, 923 Central Av
Dinkelman Geo, H. 32 Rittenhouse
Denbush Frederick, 185 W. 2d
Droppelmann John H. 345 Central Av
Duffel Casper, 37 Ludlow
Eck Peter, 623 Central Av
Eckelmann Henry B., 6 E. 5th
Edmondson Robert, w.s. Broadway b. Pearl and 3d
Elseley Francis, n.w.c. 6th and Freeman
Ellis Jonathan, 195 Smith
Englert Fred, 146 Ham. Road
Everlage Otto H., 174 W. 5th
Ewald Joseph J., 383 Main
Falk Chas. W., 526 Sycamore
Fangman Joseph, 66 W. Front
Farming John, 174 Broadway
Felden Fred., 311 Freeman
Feldmann Herm. C, 620 Race
Feltmann Geo. H., 231 W. 6th
Fink John P., 94 W. Court
Finke Barney, 30 E. Pearl
Finke Henry, 717 Race
Flaig Andrew, 613 R ice
Foppe & Lenglaud, 402 W. 5th
Forst Fred. 161 Richmond
Frohle Joseph, 33 W. 7th
Franke F. H. 502 Main
FURSTE FREDERICK, 440 W. 5th
Gainer John, s.w.c. Vine and Court
Gamel John P., 687 Race
Gerks Richard, 426 Freeman
Gesling Frank A. 388 Baymiller
Gilbert Geo., 270 W. 6th
Gioss Ferdinand, 63 E. Pearl
Giose Joseph, 55 E. Pearl
GIESTING J. D. & G., 52 W. 5th
Gossten holt Geo., 61 12th
Gradel John, 587 Walnut
Groen Geo. & John, 201 Plum
Green John, 142 Vine
Gross Jacob, 77 W. 5th
Grosardt George, 410 Freeman
Grosskopf Barbara, w.s. Baymiller b. George and Barr

HALDY F. P., 61 W. 4th
Halmer Charles, 414 Vine
Hambacher Jacob, 537 Vine
Hamberg Herman, 200 Linn
Hawmann Anton, 75 12th
HART WM. & CO. 18 W. 5th
Hefner George, 151 W. Court
Hoffmann John B., 497 Race
Holthaus Benjamin, 104 Hunt
Hoffman Fk. G., act, 486 Main
Helmich Henry, 154 Bremen
Hoksning John, 704 Elm
Henke John H.. 209 Elm
HEWES & McCANN, 51 and 364 W. 5th
Hinsen Emanuel, 1413 Cen'l Av
Henderaman Henry, 116 W. Liberty
Hocker Frank, 467 W. 9th W. of Central Av
HOCKER GEORGE, s.e.c. Richmond & Central Av
Hocker Herman B., 36 Elm
Hocker Martin, 92 Central Av
Hoffman M., 106 E. 6th
Hoffmann Henry, 385½ E. Front
Hoffmann Jacob, 494 Walnut
Holdridge A., n.s. 6th nr. Main, 4th floor
Holthaus Bernard H. 62 E. Front
Hopper Morris S. 25 E. Pearl
Hormann C., 76 W. Court
Herstscheider J., 165 W. 5th
Houck G. W., 356 W. 6th
Houvet Herman, 336 Central Av
Inwalle Barnard, 87 Butler
Inwalle Henry, 60 W. 5th
Jaeger Gottlieb, 666 Elm
Joering Frederick, 5½ Landing b. Broadway and Ludlow
Joering Henry, 249 Hopkins
Joyce Edwin, 123 Lock
Kallmayer Geo. H., 357 Main
Kallmeier Harmon, 235 Richmond
Kamp Gerhard H., 121 W. 3d
KATHMAN & Bro., 483 Main & 247 Central Av
Kavert Gavert, 222 W. Front
Kean Michael, 232 Broadway
Kelley Michael, 192 E. 6th
Kelly Francis, 130 W. Front
Kemna Henry, 412 W. 3d
KENT WILLIAM & CO. 126 W. 5th
Kettich Magnus. 278 W. Lib'y
KING WILLIAM H. 27 E. Pearl
Kleinbohahorst Frank, 8½ Landing b. Broadway and Ludlow
Kleistank John, 686 W. Front
Klusmann H. Gottlieb, 544 Main
Klute John H., 634 Main
Knestman Chas., 27 Pub. Landg
Koehle Pankraz, n.s. 12th b. Vine and Bremen
KOEHLER CHRISTIAN 169 Main
Korts Frans Hy., 17 Mulberry
Kostars Frank, n.e.c. Barr & Linn
Kraemer Chas., 663 Vine
Kramer John G. 133 Butler
Krug Martin, 138 Everett
Krueger Fred., 633 Cont. Av
Kuhlmann Henry D. s.e.c. Vine and 6th
Kunstman Sebastian, 51 Mohawk
Kurtz John, 100 W. Court
Lamb George W. 269 Cun'l Av
Lamb John W. 281 Central Av
Lampe John B., 6 E. Canal
Lampling John H., 191 W. 6th
Lange Anton J. 400 W. 5th
Lange Charles, 81 12th
Langmead John, 205 Central Av
Lasz Joseph, 740 Vine
LAWSON J. W. 96 W. 5th
Leach John, 98 Clinton
Lee William, 130 Vine
LEININGER JOHN D., 315 Vine
LEWIS W. & CO., 82 W. 4th
Liester W., 665 W. Front
Loindemann & Wehrman, 70 12th
Lockhoss George, 62 & 61 Hunt
Lohrer Martin, 128 Clinton
Lotz John, 616 Central Av
Luchmann H. W., n.c.c. Race and 15th
McCullough Hugh, 29 Broad'y
McDonald Wm, 256 W. 6th

McGrath John, 82 E. 3d
McKenzie Duncan, 10 W. 6th
Macke Wm. 599 Main
Maufrleln Daniel, 638 Vine
Marks David, 436 Main
Manver Henry, s.s. Harrison Pike b. Division and Riddle
MANSS L, & SONS, 39, 41 and 79 E. Pearl
Melzer Fred., s.s. Henry b. Elm and Dunlap
Menke Arnold, 72 Sycamore
Meyer Fred., 50 Sycamore
Moyer Wm., 191 E. 6th
Moyers John, 95 Dayton
Mesch John H. 111 W. Court
Mothvon Alex., 535 Central Av
Miller Joseph, w.s. Smith b. Augusta and 2d
Mills Wm. A. s.e.c. Poplar and Dudley
Moore John D., 215 Central Av
Moore Peter, 62 Hopkins
Moormann Barney J, 39 E. 7th
Moormaan John J, 351 W.6th
Moormann Jos., 596 Main
Morgan & Gunning, n.w.e. Main and 7th
Morris Frank, 14 W. 5th
MORRISON & HEWES, 212 W. 5th
Mueggenburg Michael, 20 Webster
Mueller Fred, 713 Central Av
Muller John H., 81 Hunt
Murphy Jeremiah, 313 Cen'l Av
Myers Jacob, Carr u. 6th
Neier Henry, 32 Dudley
Nieman John, 664 Central Av
Niehaus John H. 233 W. Front
Nienuher John H. 144 Clinton
Nietera Geo., 643 Central Av.
Nilos Sarah J., 224 W. 5th
Nolan Wm. s.e.c. Broadway and Woodward
Noll Kusner, 381 W. 6th
Nordloh & Coleman, 431 W. 2d
Naxoll John W., 220 Cen'l Av
Ochs J. F., 54 Ham. Road
O'Connor John, 231 Race
O'DONOGHUE & NAISH, 164 W. 5th
Oeh Conrad, 98 E. Pearl E. of Broadway
Oehler Fred. C. 275 Freeman
O'Neil Mich., 238 W. 5th
Ostendorf Bernard H. 382 Baymiller
Ottke Peter, 475 Main
Overbeck Hy. W. 210 Broadway
Papenberz George, 466 E. Frnt
Partl John, 65 Webster
Paul August, 174 Charlotte
Pauli Peter, w.s. Observatory b. Hill and Observatory Ed
Pfeister Fredk., 381 Main
Pfister Peter, 116 Clay
Pistner John, 683 Vine
Pittinger A., 238½ W. 5th
Pohl Barney H., 183 Linn
Prues John H. 72 Abigail
Puag Geo. & Bro. 83 13th
Quante Henry, 55 Broadway
Quehn Fred, 1514 E. Front
Rabena Fred., 502 Main
Rauber W. s. 77 Dudley
Rawe Joseph, 578 E. Front
Rechtin Burney H., 476 W. 3d
Reckers Henry G. 423 Vine
Rehe John H, 464 W. 5th
Rohn John, 4 Walnut
Remme Henry W., 624 Main
Renneker Jacob, n.w.c. Main and 9th
Renschen John H, 401 Sycamore
Richmond John. 42 Richmond
Ridder Fred, 102 13th
Riefenstahl Christian, 682 Main
Rierdan Jeremiah, 23 Central Av
Robertson Wm. C., 319 Cen'l Av
Rott John H. W., 254 W. 5th
Ruchi Lewis, w.s. Vine b. Mulberry and Milk
Ruf & Elm, 671 Race
Ruwe Joseph, s.e.c. Elm and Longworth
Sarles James A. s.w.c. Richmond and Mound
Sauer Conrad, 598 Central Av
Sauer Martin, 1017 Cen'l Av
Schadle Joseph, 431 Linn
Schiebel Godfrey, 207 Cutter
Schiff Isaac, 183 Vine
Schildknecht Jacob, 503 Elm
Schinner John, 224 Linn
Schinuor Mich., 149 W. 5th
Schmees Ber, n.s. Pearl b. Pike and Butler
Schmidt Henry, 23 Elder

Schmidtt Jacob, b. 61 11th
Schoner Paul, s.w.c. Bremen and F'ndlay
Schraffenberger Michael, 40 E. Front
Schror H. & H. Stock, 403 Main
Schulto Geo. 220 Water
Schulten John H. 46 Woodward
Schulte Hen., 408 W. 6th
Schulte John, 22 Mill
Seegers George, 38 W. Front
Seiler F., junction of Auburn Av, and Vine
Shannon Robert H. 83 Mound
Shulta Reuben, s.s. Hopkins b. Cutter and Linn
Shurmann John J., 178 W. 5th
Sibley Geo, 128 Walnut
Siegmann Aug., 773 Vine
Sliker & Matthews, 83 E. Pearl
Sliker Valentine, s.e.c. Pearl and Sycamore
Smith John, s.e.c. Main and Orchard
Sontag M., 101 Ham. Road
Spellmayer Geo, n.w.c. Plum & Water
Spiekerman John T., 96 Baymiller
Stegoman Frank, 498 Vine
Steinhorn Henry J., 73 W. Court
Stengel Philip, 132 W. Court
Stephan George, 497 Vine
Stern Edward, 521 Main
Stiegler Anthony, 579 Vine
Stoll Henry, 260 John
Stolz Simon, 541 Race
Strange Gabriel, 196 Elm
Straus Samuel, 230 Main
Stricker Frank, b. 698 Vine
Stricker Charles, 222 Clark
Strietelmeier John H., 61 Findlay
Sturts Wm., 533 W. 8th
STURWOLD HENRY, 90 Geat
Sutter Philip, 323 W. 2d
Tapking Hy. W., 299 W. 6th
Thole Henry, 3 Gilmore Wharf
Tieman Chas., 87 Sycamore
Trentmann Hy. G. 165 Pleas't
Tilmpe John H. 144 E. Front
Tritschler Charles, 37 Ham. Rd
Troescher Fred., 312 Main
Troy J. M. & T. A. 123¾ W 3d
Troy Samuel, 123 Race
Turner & Kearney, 135 W. 4th
Turner Thos. & Co. 75 E. Pearl
Utley Hastin, s.e.c. Walnut & Front
Veenenam H., 62 W. Front
Veeneman J. H. D., 276 W. Front
Vigeon Robert, 183 Longworth
Voegeli John W, 80 W. Liberty
Vozel John, 62 W. Liberty
Vonderabe Barney, 118 W. Frnt
Vonlahr Jno. G., 223 W, Front
Wallman Bern. J, 315 W. 5th
Waxler Denj., 220 Cutter
Weber Christian 60 Elder
Webor Martin, 562 Elm
Weigle Geo, w.s. Lebanon Rd. nr. Montgomery Pike
Weller George F. 13 Green
Wessels Lambert, 23 Race
Westendorf Joseph J. 147 Sycamore
Westerkamm Edward, 1084 Central Av
Westerkamp Frank H., 373 Broadway
Westerman John H. 165 Carr
White Henry, 3 Casilly's Row
Wiederstein L., 498 E. Front
Willis John, s.w.c. W. Court and Baymiller
Wirthlin Nicholas, 101 E. Pearl
Worth Sylvester, 138 Clinton
Wuest Albert, 600 Elm
Wutsmann Henry, n.c.c. Baymiller and Hopkins
Wander Robert, s.e.c. 15th and Central Av
Wurth Antony, n.e.c. Clinton and Baymiller
Yerker Enoch, 512 E. Front
Zorb Conrad, 17 Elm
Zurliene Henry, 330 Broadway

(Ladies.)
Carter James, 230 W. 5th
Collauer Stephen P. 234 Central Av
GIESTING J. D. & G. 52 W. 5th
HURRELL WM. F. 104 W. 4th
JAMES ROBERT, 172 W. 5th
LEWIS W. & CO. 82 W. 4th

CINCINNATI

Murray & Reiring, s.e.c. 6th and Central Av
ROGERS & KURDLE-MEYER, n.w.c. Main and Pearl
Tennison Mark, 310 Main
Wise John, n.w.c. Main and Court

Bottler.
(Ale and Porter.)
NIEHAUS JOS., 13 Woodward

Box Manufrs.
(Band and Paper.)
JORDAN CHAS. W., n.e.c. Walnut and 5th
JORDAN D. B., s.e.c. Main and 5th
Lentz John, 76 W. 3d
Lonshach H., 117 W. 5th
RUTZ JACOB, n.w.c. Court and Main
STORDEUR HENRY, Livingston nr. Linn
Melcher & Ahrens, rear 350 Main

(Cigar.)
Rabe H. A., 93 Clay
Sprehn Ludwig, alley b. Vine and Walnut and 13th and Mercer
Wallbracht Charles, 10 15th b. Central Av. and Plum

(Packing.)
Anderson J. Bauk Alley b. 3d and 4th
Bultman D. L., 141 Water
Cook M. H. & Co., w.s. W.W. Canal nr. C.H. & D.R.R. Depot
JOHNSTON J. & J. M., 219 and 231 W. 3d
Larman B. 6 Commerce
Luhn Jno. H., s.s. W.W. Canal b. Carr and Harriet
Meyer F. J., 137 Race
RICE SOL. G., 672 Central Av

Box Wood Dresser.
Curry Ed. P., 120 Main

Brand & Stamp Cutters.
(See Stamp Cutters.)

Drewers.
BECK & BAUER, 59 Harrison Road
BILLIOD FREDK., 161 Ham. Road
Boss & Co., s.e.c. Sycamore and Abigail
Burkholz John, Lebanon Rd
CONGRESS BREWERY, Mueller & Gogreve s.w.c. Pike and Pearl
Drum Thomas, n.w.c. Smith and 2d
Fortman Francis, c. Clay and 12th
Glossner & Bro., 456 Vine
HARRIES DAVID, 100 Sycamore
Heints Charles, foot of Walnut Hills
HERANCOURT G. M., n.s. Harrison Rd. nr. Mill Creek Bridge
Hochenluitner Joseph, s.w.c. Harrison Pike and Division
Huser Gus A., Ham. Road nr. Boundary
KAUFFMAN JOHN & CO. 604 Vine
KLEINER & BRO., 284 Hamilton Road
KLOTTER GEO. & CO., (Hamilton Brewery) 330 Ham. Road
KOEHLER GOTTFRIED, co., 63 Buckeye
MOERLEIN & WINDISCH, (Elm St. Br'y) 721 Elm
MUELLER & GOGREVE, (Congress Brewery) s.w.c. Pike and Pearl
NIEHAU'S & DACH, n.e.c. Race and Main
Payne A. & Co., s.s. M. Canal b. Liberty and Findlay
Rohs Sarah, s.w.c. Corp. line and Clifton Av
Rothert & Groene, e.s. Denman b. Bank and Central Av
SANDMAN & LACKMAN, 6th b. Stone and Baymiller
SCHAEFER JOHN A., 652 Main

SCHALLER JOSEPH, s.e.c. Plum and Canal
SCHNEIDER L., Augusta b. John and Smith
SCHULTZ & BRO., (Washton Br'y.) 485 E. Front
WALKER'S BREWERY, 391 Sycamore
WALKER WM., n.w.c. Smith and 2d
WEYAND & JUNG, (Western Brewery,) 1039 Central Av
ZEIGLER LUDWIG, 490 Vine

Brick Layers.
(Builders.)
Allen David P., 310 George
Bowers Wm. T., 140 Baymiller
Craven Wm., 271 Richmond
DeCamp Hiram, 233 W. 7th
Dosh Daniel, 154 York
Hoke Dav. T., 142 Carr
Shaw A. B., 69 Longworth
Spinning Jacob, T. 456 W. 5th

Brick Layers.
(Jobbers.)
DeCamp Lamb., 78 Laurel
Jones Paul, 138 Betts
Leonard Hy. R., 63 Hopkins
NUCKOLS W. W., 322 W. 9th

Brick Yards.
Cook Henry, s.w.c. Ringgold and Price
Honroth William, w.s. Western Av. b. Bank and Harrison Rd.
Robinson John, foot of W. 9th
Strietmeier & Fisbigh, w.s. Western Av. b. Bank and Harrison Road
Summers David, Clark, b. Baymiller and Linn

Bridge Builders.
MCCALLUM BRIDGE CO. 75 W. 3d

Bridle Manufrs.
(See also Saddles, Harness and Trunks.)
Clark H. S., 196 Walnut

Bristles.
BULLOCK A. D. & CO. 12 and 14 W. 2d
WHITAKER JOSEPH, Deer Creek Valley
Winkler Jacob, 982 Cent. Av

Britannia Ware Manufs.
HOMAN HENRY, 11 E. 7th
SELLEW & CO., 214 Main

Brokers, Exch. & Mon.
(See Banks and Bankers.)

Brokers.
(Note and Bill.)
BASCOM SILAS, 15 W. 3d
Grant James B., 39 Walnut
GREGG & HARVEY, 19 W. 3d
Hickman J. L. & Co. 60 W. 3d
HEWSON W. M. F., 21 W. 3d
Loraldo Ed., 47 Walnut
Marsh Wm., N. 59 W. 3d
Philley H., 221 Vine
Phillips Wm. H. 83 W. 3d
Smith J. H. & Co. 58 W. 3d

(Produce.)
JOHNSON, BROOKS & CO Enquirer Bldgs, Room 2.
King Geo. C. & Co. 273 Sycamore
McFarland Wm. Y. 5 College bldg
Orum Morris, 12 W. 2d
Phillips Geo. W., Jr., 5 College Hall bldg
Sledge Geo. C., 4 College bldg
Small I. K. & Co. 37 Walnut

Brokers, Real Estate.
(See also Real Estate Dealers.)
GREGG & HARVEY, 19 W. 3d
HALE & CO., 120 Walnut
Hickman J. L. & Co. 60 W. 3d

HORTON HENRY V., n.w.c. 5th and Walnut
Knight Geo. C. n.w.c. 5th and Walnut
KNIGHT N. S. n.w.c. 5th and Walnut
Lyan & Morse, 227 Vine
Lamphear Edward P. 82 W. 3d
Magill G. W., n.w.c. 3d and Walnut
Philley Henry, 221 Vine
Phillips Wm. H. 83 W. 3d
SARGENT SAMUEL A., n.w.c. 5th and Walnut
SHOTWELL GEORGE, 75 W. 3d
Smith & Winters, 221 Vine
STOECKLE J. N., 64 W. 3d
Taylor J. R., 130 Vine
Willis A. F., 161 Walnut
Williams C.H. 80 W. 3d

Brokers.
(Stock.)
GREGG & HARVEY, 19 W. Third
HEWSON W. M. F., 23 W. 3d
Hickman J. L. & Co. 60 W. 3d
Hall D. P., 168 Walnut
Luralde Ed., 47 Walnut
KIRK & CHEEVER, 57 W. 3d
Rieder Felix, 73 W. 3d
SARGENT SAM. A., c.w. Fifth and Walnut
STOECKLE J. N., 64 W. 3d

Brooms, Manufacs., and Dealers.
BROWN JAS. R. & CO. 27 Walnut
MOORE ROBERT, 49 Walnut
Overbuss C. s.s. Gamble b. Melancthon and Liberty
TYLOR & BARRETT, 79 e.c. Walnut and Front
Vankooten Harmann, 102 Betts
WATERS CHAS. H. & CO. 4 Main and 3 Pub. Land.

Brush Manufs.
BROMWELL WM. & CO. 161 Walnut
CLAASEN O. & W., 578 Main
CRAIG ROBT. S. 219 Central Av.
Dallman H., 456 Main
ENGLISH C. L., 41 E.
Garringer Phillip, 637 Elm
Hilsinger Hy., 105 W. Court
Koepf Geo. F. 41 Ham. Road
Mayer Charles H. 399 Vine
Metzeler & Von Bund, 23 Hughes
Urban Joseph, 95 Bremen
WATERS CHAS. H. & CO. 4 Main and 3 Pub. Land.
Weidenmann Andrew, 262 Central Av

Bucket Manufs.
MILLER & JESSUP, s.s. Court c.c. of Broadw'y

Buckskin Dressers and Glove Manuers.
KESSLER HENRY & SON, 215 Main
Price T. & J., 312 Main
THORNTON RICHARD, 314 Main

Builders' Material.
CRAWFORD GEO. & CO. 288 Walnut
HINKLE, GUILD & CO., 305 W. Front

Bung and Plug Factory.
Kirby Josiah, Watson Alley

Burial Cases.
(Metallic.)
CRANE, BREED & CO., s.s. 8th b. Harriet and Millcreek
EPPLY JOHN P., n.w.c. 5th and Plum
FAY LUCIAN, e.c. Plum and Canal
(Terra Cotta.)
SHOLL G. W., 57 Walnut

Burning Fluid.
BARTLETT R. & CO., s.w.c. Walnut and Front
Kendall Omar H. 98 Betts
SPEAR & CO., 195 Walnut
Starr Edwin F., s.w.c. John and W. W. Canal

Butchers.
(See Meat Stores.)

Butter, Eggs, &c.,
BANNING D. & CO., 42 Walnut
Banning J. W., 32 Walnut
Barnes Geo. D. 323 W. 5th
Barth Herman H., 295 W. 6th
Benjamin & Co., 19 and 197 Walnut
CLARK & ROGERS, 28 & 30 E. 2d
FOOTE JOS. W., 199 Central Av
HOLT AMOS, 32 W. 5th
HOLT WILLIAM, 88 E. Pearl
Maescher John V. 52 E. Pearl
MOORE ROBERT, 49 Walnut
NOURSE J. G. 166 W. 4th and 34 Walnut
Sloan Charles, 138 Dayton

Button Manufs.
Lammert Joseph, 521 Main

Cabinet Ware Manufs. and Dealers.
Adams W., n.s. Laurel near John
Alms G. H., 115 W. Liberty
Applehans Henry, 14 Dudley
AVERY CHARLES, 277 Main
Bailey & D. Camp, 133 E. Frnt
Bailer Kasper, 197 Elm
Becker Wm. n.s. L'Hommedieu st. b. Central Av. and John
BICHARD P. 547 Vine
Bihl John, 502 Elm
Bird, Burrows & Co. 20 E. 3d
Blinn O. & Co. 201 W. 5th
Block Louis, 193 Broadway
Brasel & Taenschi, n.w.c. Laurel and Central Av
Bonan Theodore, w.s. Cutter b. Clinton and Betts
Bultman D., 141 W. 5th
CABINET MAKERS' UNION, Jacob Diehl agt., n.s. Augusta b. Smith & Rose
Callahan George, 328 W. 6th
Carter John W, 133 Sycamore
Carter Wm., 34 E. 5th
CLOSTERMAN HENRY, s.e.c. Augusta & Smith
Coolidge J. K., 185 & 187 W. Fifth
Cook Anthony, 531 Central Av
Cook Ben. 253 Hopkins
COATES JOHN F., 150 W. 5th
Collins James, 350½ W. 5th
Crane L. M. 81 Sycamore
Damen Wm., 517 Main
Dubell E. B., 106 E. Pearl
Douson John, 500 Sycamore
Duchscher P. 209 W. 5th
Ekelmann Bernard, Gramercy al. b. Mound and Cutter
Fernburg Louis, 632 Central Av
GEYER JOHN, 8 E. 4th
Ginandt & Rehse, 148 W. 6th
Hackman G. E. 79 W. Court
Hatke & Larbez, 610 Race
Haupt Moritz, 318 W. 5th
Hempel Fredk., 36 W. Court
HENSHAW G. & SONS, 26 Sycamore
Herwegen Henry, 241 W. 5th
Hoffman John J. 677 Vine
Kelsall Thomas, n.w.c. 7th & Baymiller
Klecmann Peter, 961 Cent'l Av
Knoblangh F. H. 126 Sycam'r
Knost Fred. 128 W. 2d
KRAMER ANTHONY, 830 Main
KRAMER MRS. CATH., 835 Main
Lammers Henry, al. b. Vine and Walnut and 13th and Mercer
Luhmann C. H. 12 Mercer
MEADER & CO., 41 & 43 W. 2d
Meiss L., 205 W. 5th
Meier John H. 809 Race
Mestemaker Jos. 15 Bremen

BUSINESS MIRROR. 353

ine Mrs, Margaret, 108 E.5th
rtschoke Henrietta, 599 Sycamore
hner Louis, 34 E. Pearl
th Jos, 87 W. Liberty
ville Louis, 44 E. 6th
onc Wm, 82 Mound
omas N. W. 579 Main
oinns Charles, 320 Main
mone Jos., n.w.c. 7th and Central Av

Cap Manufs.
(See also Hats and Caps.)
rton J. N. 22 E. 4th
ORCHHEIMER M. S. 102 and 104 Pearl
acs S., 104 Main
iller Saml, n.s. Brown b. Mohawk and Ham. Rd
EYBERG & HELLMAN, 124 Walnut
hwarz D. 159 Main
elt Jos. 120 Main
orpe A. F. 147 Plum
bliss H., 186 Main

arpenters & Builders.
iderson John, e.s. Bank al. b. 3d and 4th
plegate B. W. 191 Mound
ALDWIN JOS., 302 Elm
ARR & AYERS, 120 Central Av
rr Henry H. n.s. Front b. Torrence and Kelly
arly Geo. s.s. Clinton b. Linn and Baymiller
cket George, s.s. 8th b. Main and Sycamore
hrens & Abernethy, s.s.
Baker b. Walnut and Vine
scher Philip, 436 Linn
ndley James, w.s. Lawrence b. 2d and Pearl
chard Peter, e.s. Ridgway al. b. Liberty and 15th
ancy Wm., 112 Park
LEY A. & BRO.,
n.e.c. Baymiller & Liberty
odley P. F., 454 W. 9th W. Central Av
own Warren H, 466 W. 6th
arhaus D. J., w.s. Lawson al. b. 4th and 5th
yrn John, n.w.c. 5th and Stone al.
ALDWELL A., 910 E. Front
ALDWELL SYLV. G., 190 Race
AMERON W. M. & CO., s.e.c. 6th and Hoadly
arson R. & W., 414 W. 9th
nter I. S. & H. H, 56 George
ilds M., 40 E. 2d
oke Richard, 45 E. 3d
OTTERAL & GOLDSWORTHY, 328 Elm
IRONE BENJAMIN, w.s. Cutter b. Betts and Clinton
unningham J. P., 410 George
aun Joseph, 543 W. 3d
avis James H. & Co. 38 W.9th w. of Central Av
avis Samuel, n.w.c. 5th and John
oCamp J. & D., 130 W. Court w. of Central Av
etchen Henry, 295 Elm
iehl Jacob, 42 Buckeye
reyer Hermann B.,s.s. Charlotte, b. Linn & Baymiller
rumbar Enos, e.s. Sycamore b. Hunt and E. Canal
eldkamp B. J., w.s. Coggswell al. b. Woodward and Franklin
illmore E. H., s.w.c. Front and Lawrence
inch B. P. s.s. George b. Baymiller and Freeman
ischer David, 6 Moore
lanagan Pat. n.s. Patterson al. b. Main and Walnut
oley John, 138 Race
EIST CASPER, 500 Sycamore
erlach John, 139 W. Court
irt Ernst, rear 482 Walnut
lasgow H., 134 Race
lemser F. rear 480 Walnut
oble Wm. 191 Mound
orman E. J., s.s. David bet. John and Cutter
oss Fred, rear 480 Walnut
ottschalk Conrad, 543 W. 3d
aehl Jacob, Freeman b. Bank and Central Av
ambleton James H. 1263 E. Front

Handy & Bro., 74 Pendleton
Harrison Henry, s.e.c. Mound and George
Harter Mathias, e.s. Goose al b. Liberty and Greene
Harwood & Elliot, s.s. Avery b. Park and Mill
Henning J., 7 Home
Hixdon & Farrell, 117 Linn
HINKLE, GUILD & CO., 365 W. Front
Hoffman J. S., 131 & 133 Central Av
Hoffmann Jacob, e.s. Bremen b. Elder and Findlay
Holtzinger & Edwards,167 Geo.
Hughes & Sharp, 5 Augusta
JENKINS J. & T. & CO., 390 W. Eighth
Johnson John, s.s. 2d b. Smith and Rose
Johnston Wm. 63 E. 3d
KELLY & BRITT, n.e.c. Linn & Richmond
Kennedy Geo. W. 231 John
King T. 133 Longworth
Krenning Wm. 15 Jones
Landwehr H. H., 15 Rittenhouse
Leutsch & Eich, s.s. 12th b. Vine and Race
Luken Barney, 215 Baymiller
McBride Lyman, 173 Pleasant Conrt
McCONNELL THOMAS S. 476 W. 8th
McCord J. S. & D. A., c. Gest and Pinn
McDonnell M. Patterson al
Magill C. W. & W. W., 51 Richmond
Masson M. B. s.s. Liberty b. Broadway and Man field
Menkhaus J. F., 202 Pleasant
Mierenfeld John, 876 E. Front
Miller & D. Camp. 458 George
MILLS & STELMIRE, 40 Everett
Morgan Wm., Bank al
Mustard Alex., 60 George
Neiber & Toft, 156 W. 3d
Neill Samuel B, 61 E. 3d
Nicol Donald, 227 Clinton
O'Brien M., 193 Sycamore
Ordemann & Howard, 181Elm
Overbeck H., 48 E. 8th
Prior Christ, W. n.w.c. Everett and Baymiller
Rafferty Martin, 217 W. 5th
Rents & Fryer, River b. Ludlow and Lawrence
REID & PASQUIER, 539 W. 9th w. of Cen'l Av
RIEMRIER H. H. 13 Ham. Road
Roese Wm. 99 Ham. Road
Ruhan David, 12 Jackson
Rothan John, 216 Carr
Sanning John H. 505 Plum
Schauh John, 219 Bremen
Seaman J. H., 220 John
Sewar J. H. 59 Woodward
Shinnick T. & R., 168 W. 8th
Shubert Wm. 140 Race
Snodgrass L. L., 356 Cen'l Av
Sommerkamp Caspar H. n.w.c. 15th and Goose al.
Spitzmeiler B. n.s. Liberty b. Baymiller and Freeman
Steinauer Anton, 19 Mercer
STEWART W. H. w.s. Plum b. Canal and Court
Stilley James, n.s. L'Hommedieu b. Central Av. & John
Straeffer Michael, 12 Jackson
Strobel Leonard, e.s. Walnut b. Liberty and Ham. Road
SWAIN & CHENOWETH, n.w.c. Burr and Linn
Taylor & Faulkner, 487 Freeman
Taylor F. N., 383 W. 8th
Tiunemeyer & Bro. rear 230 Mulberry
Townsend James, 205 Poplar
Vogt Henry, 30 Lodge
Wicker Wm. N. n.s. Yeatman b. Broadway and Sycam'c
Woodson Jesse, 217½ W. 5th

Carpets, Oil Cloths, &c.
Greeble Mrs. & Bro. 331 Central Av
HAMMETT & CHESELDINE, s.e.c. Main and Pearl
HURD EDWARD, 11 E. 4th
Marshall & Brothers, 56 W.5th

McDOWELL ALEX. 100 W. 4th
RINGWALT & AVERY, 69 W. 4th
SAWYER & KIRK, College Hall
SHILLITO JOHN & CO., 101, 103 and 105 W. 4th
SNOWDON & OTTE, 175 Main

Carpet Slippers.
Brown Michael, n.s. 7th b. Broadway and Sycamore

Carpet Weavers.
Baschang Geo, 273 W. 6th
Deckebach Geo., 173 W. Court
Fricke Burney, 422 Race
Hilmer Joseph, 173 W. 5th
Horstman N., 14 Abigail
Weir Jos., 143 W. 5th

Carriage Bolts.
Calloway Joseph, 71 12th
GREEN J. B. & BRO. 4 Public Landing
HOLLENSHADE, MORRIS & Co., s.w.c. Central Av and Betts

Carriage Manufacs.
BARKER EDWARD, 11 E. 6th
Behlen Charles & Co. 513 Vine
Brickell Wm., 11 Freeman
BRUCE J. & B. s.e.c. Vine and 3d
Butters Edmund, 509 Cen'l Av
Conradi Frederick, n.w.c. 12th and Bremen
Ernst Wm., 886 Central Av
Ewin John, 981 Central Av
GOSLING J. W., s.w.c. 6th and Sycamore
Gryden Hans, 888 Central Av
Hussing & Co., 58 and 60 12th
Howell Richard S, 56 Bank
Jacobs Geo. 86 and 88 Ham. Rd
Kintzer & Sasse, 16 E. 8th
LOOKER, PURCELL & CO. w.s. Central Av. b. 4th and 5th
MILLER GEO. C. & SONS, 19 and 21 W. 7th
Moore & Albrecht, 106 E. 2d
Niemeier Henry, 536 Walnut
Paine Luther, 199 W. 7th
Roberts John, 136 W. Pearl
Smith Lyman, 1534 E. Front
STEVENS B. R., 55 E. 5th
Schroeder & Klopp, 446 Race
VEERKAMP D. 463 Walnut
Wilts John, 283 Sycamore

Carriages.
(Childrens.)
CADY DAVID K. n.e.c. 5th and Walnut
Marqua P. J. & Co. w.s. John b. 2d & Front
TENCH GEO. G. 320 Central Av.

Carriage Shaft Fastener.
Chapman Wm. S. s.e.c. 3d and Vine

Carriage Trimmings.
CLARK S. & S. S., 189 Main
NEAVE, WARD & CO., 37 and 39 Main
HUNTER, EDMESTON & Co., 168 Main
WILSON & HAYDEN, 22 Main

Car Wheel Manfs.
Mowry Albert L., s.e.c. Front and Lewis
Nash John, 213 & 215 E. Pearl E. of Broadway

Carvers.
ANDERSON A. W., 132 W. 3d
Fitzgerald Fred. 413 W. 5th
FRY H. L., 321 Central Av
Mierenfeld John A. 272 Linn
Weiss Fred. 200 Cutter

Cemetery Offices.
SPRING GROVE CEM'RY Cyrus Davenport, Sec'y, office Melodeon bldg
WESLEYAN CEMETERY, Cumminsville, office s.w. c. Main & 8th

Chair Manufacs.

Bird, Burrows & Co., n.e.c. 3d and Hammond
CLOSTERMAN HY., n.e.c. Smith and Augusta
Cook Anthony, 331 Central Av
Cook H., s.s. Melancthon nr. Jones
Delliott John. 470 W. 9th W. of Central Av
FRYE HENRY, 367 Broadway
Grosenbrink Wm., 15 Mercer
Hocke & Shove, n.s. Ham. Rd nr. Mohawk bridge
HENSHAW G. & SONS, 26 Sycamore
Kampmayer & Bro. 175 Clintn
Kaveman Fredk. & Bro., 116 Hopkins
KRAMER ANTHONY, 530 Main
Krumme Frank. 230 Hopkins
MEADER & Co., 41 and 43 W. 2d
MITCHELL JOHN, 239 W. 2d
Munkadick Theo. s.e.c. Hunt and Pendleton
Moormann Henry, 211 Cutter
NABER WM., 367 Race
Pardick Bernhard, 181 Spring
Schneider And. 2½ Linn
SMITH & HAWLEY, n.w.c. Elm and Pearl
Stillinger Chas. 658 Central Av
Wulfsek Victor, 505 Sycamore

Chair Rims and Seats.

Waters & Barrett, e. Freeman and 9th

Cheese Dealers.

BANNING D. & CO. 42 Walnut
Banning J. W. 32 Walnut
CLARK & ROGERS, 28 and 30 E. 2d
Freeman Joseph, 56 Buckeye
KEHLENBACH WM. 418 Main
NOURSE J. G. 34 Walnut
Stiles H. L. & Co. 53 Walnut
STRAIGHT, DEMING & CO., n.e.c. 2d and Vine

Chemical Laboratories.

BAUM J. C., e.s. Canal b. Findlay and Ham. Road
FRIES ALEXANDER, O. pst 101 Main
GORDON W. J. M. & BRO. office n.w.c. 8th & Central Avenue
GRASSELLI EUGENE, 440 E. Front
MARSH & HARWOOD, n.w.c. M. Canal & Dunlap
WELLS J. D. & CO., n.w.c. 4th & Central Av

Chemists, Analytical.

GARRISON H. D, 235 Central Av
GORDON W. J. M. & BRO. n.w.c. Central Av & 8th
GRASSELLI EUGENE, 440 E. Front
Locke Joseph M., 31½ W. 3d

Chimney Caps.

Fairclough T., 191 Richmond
LOTZE ADOLPHUS, 219 Walnut
Mapers Henry, c. Vine and Mulberry

China, Glass and Queens Ware.

Atkinson John V., 21 E. 4th
Beste Henry A., 538 Main
BROOKMAN C. E. 244 Main
Burnett P. C. 302 Central Av
Dormond John J., 330 Central Avenue
Fiehe Herman, 60 E. Pearl
FUNK JOHN H. c. Vine & Court
HACKMAN JOHN G., 1164 W. 5th
HUNNEWELL, HILL & Co., 87 Main
HUNTINGTON & BROOKS Room 7, s.w.c. 4th and Walnut
HUNTINGTON, BROS. & Co., 119 Main
Ihle Michael, 479 Vine
Kelly James W. B. 123 W. 5th

KISTNER EDW., 311 Main
Kolbe Werner, 522 Main
Meis F., n.e.c. Court & Vine
MOHLENHOFF JOHN A. 44 W. 5th
Rintz Sebastian, 463 W. 5th
Rist L., 624 Vine
Roberts & Bro. s.w.c. Pearl and Sycamore
SCHULTZE F. & CO., 127 Main
TENCH G. G., 321 Cent. Av
Ware F. J. H. n.w.c. Vine and Court
WEST HENRY F. n.w.c. Pearl and Walnut
WIESER ISAAC, e.s. Vine b. Mercer and Allison

Chiropodist.

Barnett James, 187 Sycamore
Rendall George, 60 W. 4th

Chocolate Manufs.

Heschong Michael, 571 Walnut
WERNERT & GOETHEIM, 597 and 599 Main

Churn Manufacturer.

Baum George, 1601 Central Av

Cigars and Tobacco.

Abrahams & Wagner, 131 W 5th
Alig John, 119 Btemen
Amann & Bro., 56 Broadway
Arndt D., 531 Vine
Bancroft G. H. n.s.c. 8th and Walnut
Barbaro Dominick S, 10 B'way
Becker & Totelmann, 188 Walnut
BECKMAN S. E. 17 E. 3d
Bell Joseph, 108 Hunt
Beinhardt, M. 167 W. Liberty
Benge Fred. n.w.g. Liberty and John
Berger M. 109 Buckeye
BERGER JOHN, 228 Vine
BESUDEN H., 93 Walnut
BILTZ AUGUST, 235 Main
Boduman Fred. 273 Main
Bowman Jno., 279 Walnut
BRACHMAN R., 86 W. 3d
Brockland H., 579 Main
Brand Andrew, 618 Vine
BREED R. E. 118 and 120 W. 2d
Brichler Thomas, 98 Ham. Rd.
Burns Geo. W. 31 E. 3d
CAHN L. & BRO. Spencer House
Chruler Chriss. 210 W. Liberty
Colet John, 1111 Central Av
Cooper & Co., 10 E. Front
Cramer Charles F. 67 Wade
Crouse Geo. W. s.w.c. Court and Central Av
Cuslaer & Baschelder, 237 Main
DAVIS N. H. & G. H., 89 Walnut
Deickmann J., F. H. & Co, 40 Elder
Dreher Martin, 33 Green
DUNKER JOHN, 8 13th
Duwelius Christian, 530 Main
Ebke John F., 443 Central Av
Eggert W., 279 Central Av
EGGERT & BRENTANO, 42 Main
EICHHOLZ M. & BRO. 318½ Main
Euphrat Charles, 479 Walnut
Euphrat Louis, 160½ Walnut
Fafler Charles, 215 W. 6th
FAEHR & MEYER, 439 Main
Feiertag Geo. 59 15th
Fischer Wm. s.e.c. 6th and Walnut
Fischer F. 495 Elm
Fischer Valentine, 405 Central Av
Fry Wm. R. 133 Vine
FUHRMAN V. 7 Main
Faldner Philin, 196 Clinton
Funck Chas. E., 148 W. 5th
Garland Herman, 153 W. 5d
Gans Justus, 119 Clinton
Gollanburg George, 503 Main
Gerland W., 14 E. 5th
Gunther N., 98 W. Court
Gusdorf Morris, 110 Vine
Hanstein Emil, 452 Vine

Haskamp Kasper, 105 W. 2d
Hasemeier Hy., 59 W. Liberty
Hobel Wm., 61 Liberty
Heber Lewis, 635 Vine
Herkelrath C. & H., 105 Sycamore
Heidelman J. 464 Linu
Heyne H. W., 490 Walnut
Higgins Mrs. E. 28½ Broa'wy
Hilgeman Fred, 588 Elm
Hilgemann F. 55 12th
HILL EDWARD D., 5 Main
Hiunau G., 441 Vine
HOFER CHAS., 268 Vine
Hoffheimer Bros., 32 E. 2d
Hoffman Philip, 1013 Cen'l Av
Hopf Peter, 62 Ham. Road
Huck & Leudre, n.e.c. 2d and Ludlow
Huermann Henry, 416 Vine
Hunemann Henry, 422 Walnut
Husman & Co., 13 Broadway
Hutsteiner Edward, 405 Vine
Jackson John W. jr., 429 Central Av
Jirauth E., 597 Vine
Jones Wm. 14 Pub. Landing
Kaiser Chas., 262 W. Front
KASTING & KRUSE, 23 W. Front
KENNETT JOHN, 14 Public Landing
KING & DALY, s.w.c. 2d and Sycamore
Kircher John, jr 88 W. Court
Kissinger Wm. 676 Main
Kline Daniel, 38 E. 3d
Kluge Fred. 107 W. Liberty
Klueber V. J. 646 Race
Klugman Jno. N. 452 Main
Knaebel G. L., 634 Central Av
LABROT A., 6 W. Front
Lang Thomas, 18 Ham. Rd
Laugerman Chris, 243 Elm
Laagermann Ch., 623 Cen'l Av
Leary Robert L. 106 Vine
Leuchtenburg John F. 626 Central Av
LEVIS & BROS. 228 Main, 221 & 223 Wal't
Lewis M. H. & Co, 16 Broad'y
Lindsay Alex. A. 375 Central Av
Loewen Peter, 381 Vine
Lohman Benj. 554 W. Front
Louchelm Sam. 115 Main
Lowenthal & Windler, 6 W. Pearl
Louis A. & Co., 56 & 58 Main
Macke D., 68 Hunt
MARIENTHAL LEHMAN 246 Walnut and 36 W. 6th
Martheus A. W. 63 Walnut
Meier Clemens, 382 Race
Meuzel Jacob, 10 Walnut
Metz B. M. E., 2d & Sycamore
Metz G., 645 Central Av
Meyer C. F. & Bro. 72 w. Court
Meyer Henry, 347 Vine
Meyer John G. 549 Main
MILLER PETER, e.s. Vine nr. Auburn Av
MILLER WM. 385 Main
Moormann H. & Co., 617 Main
Mosler & Kupferle, 269 Walnut
Mueller Nicholas, 617 Central Av
NATHAN M. & CO., 25 Vine
Nicolausin Alphonso & Co., n.w.c. 3d and Ludlow
Nordmann Chas., 724 W. 5th
NUELSEN FRANCIS, 233 Main
NULSEN ANTHONY, 12 Main
NUNNINGMOLLER J. H. 433 W. 5th
Oetert Charles, 311 Freeman
Otten Henry, 185 Main
Patterson Jos. A., 162 W. 4th
Peterson Geo., 530 Central Av
PFAU J. & J. M., 218 Main
Pfeffer Chas. A. 535 Vine
Preuer Franz, 54 13th
Ragendorff M., 322 Main
RAWSON, WILBY & CO., 24 W. Front
Rheinberger J. A., 465 Vine
Richards George, 572 Cen'l Av
Rolfes T. 406 W. Court
Rosenkemper H., s.w.c. 5th and John
ROSING A. C. A., 63 and 64 E. 2d

Sander B. & H. Obermyer, 203 Elm
Sandmann Jos. 218 W. Front
Schawe John H., 333 Main
SCHMIEDT EDWARD, 34 E. Front
Schwan Peter, 599 Vine
Schweninger J., 89 Ham. Road
Shulte John, s.w.c. Clark and Cutter
Sieve H., 555 Walnut
Spels Herman, 66 Abigail
Springer Max, 36 Broadway
Stander P. s.s. Bank b. Linn and Whiteman
Starr H. E., 177 W. 5th [8th
Stieneker Harmon E., 526 W.
Stering Wm. & Co. s.s. Linn b. Clark and Hoskins
STRASSER LEW., 189 Walnut
Stromberg Philip, 187 Walnut
Stuntebeck Frank H. w.c. Sycamore b. Dorsey and Baltimore
Taphorn Gerhard H., 277 Br'dwy
Tesguman Geo. 662 Central Av
Tronkamp C., 462 Main
TRUMBOWER & HICKMAN, n.w.c. 2d and B'way
Ulrich W., 333 Central Av
Vage T., 213 Walnut
Vonderheide Frank, 249 W. 3d
Walder August, 128 Walnut
Wankelman Fred., 361 Vine
Wankelmann Fred., 56 13th
Wansbacher Henry, 74 13th
WATERS CHAS. H. & CO. 4 Main & 3 P'sh. Landing
Wedekind Julius, 235 W. 6th
WEIGHEL J. & SON, 210 Elm
Weis L. & Co. 233 Walnut
Wengle Albert, 10 W. Court
Wiswell Wm. W., 42 W. 4th
Wolf John, 95 Ham. Rd
Wolf Michael, 663 Vine
Wortermann Henry, 687 Cent'l Av
Zins Jacob, 573 Main
ZUMSTEIN GEORGE, 183 Vine

"City Criers.

Hewson John, 131 Longworth
Rider H. J., 19 E. 5th

Cloaks and Mantillas.

DELAND & GOSSAGE, 74 and 76 w. 4th
Ivens & Co. 28 W. 4th
Lewis Geo., 92 w. 4th
NORRIS R. D., 174 w. 5th
Phillips C., n.w.c. Fourth & Walnut
SHILLITO JNO. & CO. 104 W. 4th
WILSON SAMUEL, 78 W. 4th

Clocks.

(Town.)
Verdin M., 396 Vine

Clock Dealers.

(See also Jewelry, Watches &c.)
Blakeslee E., 229 Main
Bornschein Ed. 531 Central Av
KENT LUKE, s.w.c. 6th & Main
Muhle B. H. 368 George
PARKS O., 425 Central Av
Pickering G. M., 9 E. 7th
Smith A. D., 12 E. 5th

Clothiers.

(Wholesale.)
ACKERLAND A., 66 W. Pearl
AMBURGH & BROS., 65 W. Pearl
AUD, FRENKEL & CO., 30 W. Pearl
Baker George, 63 Broadway
Banberger F. & Co. 363 Main
BARWISE & KING, 171 Main
BISCHOF & MARCH, 33 W. Pearl
COHEN A. 194 Main
COHEN, GUITERMAN & Co., 82 W. Pearl
COHEN & WOLF, 191 Main
Drahmann J. H. & Co. 56 Sycamore
Elsas Jacob, 109 W. Pearl
Enneking & Hurwe, 7 Br'way

BUSINESS MIRROR. 355

FECHHEIMER MARCUS, 84 W. Pearl
FRIEDL & BRO., 60 Main
Freidman & Stern, 122 Walnut
GLASER & CO., 98 and 100 w. Pearl
Goodman & Vornholz, 307 Main
Guiterman & Sulzbacher, 60 W. Pearl
HEIDELBACH, SEASON-GOOD & CO., s.w.c. Third and Vine
HEIDELBACH, WERT-HEIMER & CO., 86 W. Pearl
Heinsheimer J. H. & Co., 123 Walnut
Jacobs F. & Son, 483 Vine
KLEINE, HEGGER & CO. 127 Walnut
KORNBLITH J. & CO, 70 W. Pearl
Kraft, Hoffman & Co., 88 Main
KRAMER & KROGER, 62 Broadway
KUHN, NETTER & CO., n.e.c. 3d and Vine
Leon, Marks & Co, 5 W. Pearl
Leopold & Goodheart, 74 W. Pearl
Levinson J. & M. 170 B'way
Liebenstein Isaac, 9 E. Penn.
Loewenstine J. H. & Bros., 50 W. Pearl
MACK & BROS., 78 W. Pearl
Mack & Worms, 190 Main
MENDERSON & FROHMAN 111 W. Pearl
Moritz, Bro. & Co, 26 W. Pearl
RAUH & BROTHERS, 58 W. Pearl
RINDSKOPF BROS. & CO., 79 W. Pearl
Rosenfeld & Kaufman, 64 W. Pearl
Samuels & Holzman, 18 W. Prl
Schradski M. & I., 344 Main
SIMON G. & SON, 87 W. Pearl
SPRAGUE T. W. & CO. s.e.c. 4th and Vine
STADLER, BROS. & CO., 106 W. Pearl & 117 W. 3d
STEINER & DIER, 22 W. Pearl
STIX, KROUSE & CO., 61 W. Pearl
STRAUSS I. P. & BROS. 211 Main
Symonds Bro. & Co., 143 Walnt
TROUNSTINE A. & J. & Co., 75 W. Pearl
Weiler M. & E. 4th
WERTHEIMER, MARKS & CO., 128 Main
WOLF A. & I. & CO., 76 Main
Zeiller & Freidman, 72 W. Pearl

Clothing Stores.

(See also Tailors.)

AHLERING J. F., 39 Broadway
Amberg Joshua, 257 W. 6th
AMBURG & BROS., 40 Public Landing
Bamberger P. & Co, n.w.c. 8th and Main
BARWISE & KING, 171 Main
Becker Ferd. 3 Sycamore
Berliner Abram, 189 Broad'w'y
Bermann David, 54 Pub. Land
Bing M. & Brothers, 391 Main
BROOKE J. H., 66 W. 5th
Cohen A. & Co. 41 E. 4th
COHEN A., 194 Main
Cohen Isaac, 96 W. Front
COHEN WOLF, 191 Main
Drahmann J. H. & Co., 56 Sycamore
Enneking P., 355 Main
Fechheimer Wolf, 627 Vine
Gleick Leopold, 668 Central Av
Goodman & Vornholz, 307 Main
Gottlieb & Bro. 1107 Central Av
Greiwe E. 353 Main
Harris A., s.e.c. 5th and Main
Hart Isaac, 615 Vine
Heerdt Adam, 558 Central Av
Heidkamp Jos., 411 Main
Hess M. & Co., 317 Main
Himmelreich S., 511 Vine
Hirschberg Jacob, 287 Main
Joseph & Bro., 253 & 311 Main

Kessing & Greifenkemp, 4 River Landing
Koke Joseph, 10 Landing b. Broadway and Ludlow
Kottenbrock Hy., 2 Cassily's
KRAMER & KROGER, 252 Main
Landauer Aaron, 473 Vine
Lazarus David, 398 W. 8th
Leiser Marx 359 Main
Liebman A. s.e.c. Elm and Eider
Lobenstein A., 37 Broadway
Lowenstein & Guiterman, n.e.c. Pub. Landing and Syc.
MARTIN EDWARD, 134 Walnut
Mode Solomon, 227 Main
Maue Fred. 70 Broadway
Moss H., 231 Main
Nathan Jacob, 203 Main
Pureira Solomon, 290 W. 5th
Perry N. & Co., n.w.c. Central Av. and Longworth
Plant Michael, 604 Central Av
Ricking J. H., 6 Landing b. Broadway and Ludlow
ROLLWAGEN LOUIS, 562 Central Av
Rosenberg Alex, 273 Cen'l Av
Rover B. H. 614 Central Av
Ruberg Bernard, 162 Bank
Schloss Jos. M., s.w.c. Pearl and Broadway
Schomaker G. H. & Co. 407 Main
Schradski M & I. 397 Main
Schroeder B. 126 Main
Schwarzenberg N. 139 Main
SPRAGUE T. W. & CO., s.e.c. Vine and 4th
Straus & Sulzman, 50 Sycamore
STRAUSS I. P. & BRO., 211 Main
Streaker B. 46 Sycamore
Stricker Frank, 53 Broadway
Tach Isaac, 269 Main
Trame Wm. 40 Pub. Landing
Trame Henry, 51 Pub. Land.
Tuch M. & J., 371 Main
Ulmer John, 54 Sycamore
Waldron D. A., 46 W. 5th
Weil & Bro. 311 Main
Wertheimer Isaac J., 213 Main
Wineman Henry & Son, 212 W. 6th
Wise Leopold, 55 Broadway
Wolfson Israel, n.e.c. Main and Front

Clothing.

(Ladies.)

Perry Mrs. Mary J., 33 W. 7th

Clothing.

(Youth's.)

BECK WM., 266 W. 5th
BROOKE J. H., 66 W. 5th
Frankel B. & W., 68 Findlay
May & Cohn, n.w.c. 5th and Main
O'Brien John, 236 W. 5th
RICHTER & VEIKAMP, 245 W. 5th
Waldron D. A. 46 W. 5th

Cloths Cassimeres and Vestings.

(See also Dry Goods, Wh.)

ACKERLAND A., 66 W. Pearl
ACTON & WOODNUTT, 108 W. Pearl
AMBURG & BROS., 65 W. Pearl
AUB, FRENKEL & CO., 30 W. Pearl
CHAMBERS, STEVENS & CO., 23 W. Pearl
COHEN, GUITERMAN & CO., 82 W. Pearl
Elsas Jacob, 69 W. Pearl
FECHHEIMER MARCUS, 84 W. Pearl
Friedman & Stern, 122 Walnut

Goodman & Vornholz, 307 Main
Guiterman & Sulzbacher, 60 W. Pearl
HEIDELBACH, SEASON-GOOD & CO., s.w.c. 3d and Vine
HEIDELBACH. WERT-HEIMER & CO., 86 W. Prl
Heinsheimer J. H. & Co., 123 Walnut
KLEINE, HEGGER & CO., 127 Walnut
KORNBLITH J. 70 W. Pearl
Kraft, Hoffman & Co., 88 Main
KUIN, NETTER & CO., n.e.c. 3d and Vine
Leopold & Goodheart, 74 W. Pearl
Lowenstein J. H. & Bros. 50 W. Pearl
MACK & BROS., 78 W. Pearl
MARKS HENRY & CO., 12 W. Pearl
MENDERSON & FROHMAN, 23 W. Pearl
Moritz, Bro. & Co. 26 W. Pearl
RAUH & BROTHERS, 58 W. Pearl
RINDSKOPF BROS. & CO. 79 W. Pearl
Rosenfeld & Kaufman, 64 W. Pearl
Samuels & Holzman, 18 W. Pearl
SIMONS B. & CO. n.e.c. Main and Pearl
STADLER, BRO. & CO., 106 W. Pearl
STEDMAN, CARLISLE & SHAW, 17 W. Pearl
STIX LOUIS & CO, 164 Main
STIX, KROUSE & CO., 61 W. Pearl
TROUNSTINE A. & J. & CO., 75 W. Pearl
WERTHEIMER, MARKS & CO., 231 Main
WOLF A. & I. & CO. 76 Main
WOLFF CHAS. H. & CO. 145 Walnut
WYNNE, HAINES & CO., 101 W. Pearl
Zeiller & Freidman, 72 W. Pearl

Coal

(Wholesale.)

McGrew James, s.e.c. Front and Lawrence
POMEROY S. WYLLYS, 5 E. 3d
Smith Joseph, s.e.c. Front and Lawrence

Coal Yards.

Abel F. & Co., w.s. Park b. W. W. Canal and 2d
Ashcraft Jesse, Front b. Pike and Lawrence
BERTRAM & CO. 197 E. Front
Blackman J. L. 68 Smith
BROWN LEONARD W., s.w.c. Plum and Court, and n.w.c. Vine and 7th
BUCHANAN ALFRED, 333 W. Front
Buchanan & Adams, 333 W. Front
BUSHNELL J., e.s. Cen'l Av b. 2d & Pearl
CINCINNATI FUEL CO., s.w.c. 3d and Ludlow
Cochnower J., 28 W. 3d
CRITTENDEN L. B. & CO., 46 Mill
CHURCH CHARLES, n.w.c. 3d and John
Davis I. B. 25 W. Front
DODSWORTH T. & M., s.e.c. Lawrence & Front and n.e.c. Court & Wal't
Gardner Jacob, 521 E. Front
GORDON ROBT, n.w.c. M. Canal and 6th and s.w.c. Front and M. Canal
Graff Alex. C. s.e.c. Central Av and 3d
GREAT WESTERN COAL AND OIL CO., 13 W. 4th
Green W. 1513 E. Front
HUTCHINSON E., s.w.c. Front and Butler
Hendricks J. G., n.e.c. Hunt and Main

Jones E. P. & Sons, s.e.c. Lawrence and 5th
Johannigmann M. 611 Elm
Meyer Casper, s.w.c. Cutter and Hopkins
McGrew James, s.e.c. Front and Lawrence
Moulton Porter, s.w.c. Linn and W. Court
NICHOLS FREEMAN, s.e.c. Carmiller & Poplar
ROSS, PETTIBONE & CO., n.w.c. 5th and Mound; 115 Vine; 358 Central Av.; and n.e.c. W. W. Canal and 3d
SKAATS & ANGEVINE, n.w.c. 6th and Freeman and s.w.c. Mound and George
SMITH R. B. & CO. s.w.c. Elm and Water; 489 Central Av.; and 444 Race
Smith Joseph, agent, s.e.c. Front and Lawrence
SNYDER WM., 85 Water
WALKER WM., sr., n.w.c. Race and Court
WARDEN WM. G. e.s. Central Av. b. 2d and Front
WATERS ASA D. 3 Burnet House
WENZLER MATHIAS, s.e.c. Elder and Race
WESSEL BERNARD H. n.w.c. Wood and 3d

Coal Oil.

(See Oils.)

Coffee.

(Burners.)

Doll Samuel, 466 Walnut

(Essence of)

DREIDEL THEO., 10 N. Providence
Schwars Max, 603 Main
Schwarz John, 33 Ham. Road
Weil Meyer, 510 Central Av

Coffee Houses.

Adams Solomon, e.s. Broadway b. 3d and Pearl
Adleta Martin, 580 Central Av
Ahlers Charles, 40 W. Court
Ahlers Fred. H., 771 Vine
Albert Louis, 13 Ham. Road
Allen James, 371 W. 2d
ALMS HENRY, 27 and 29 W. Third
Ammaun Joseph, 346 Main
Amtaur Henry, 121 Linn
Anton John, 708 Central av.
Aptel Jacob, 464 Walnut
Araldo Vincent, 84 W. Front
Arbeiter Halle, e.s. Walnut b. 13th and Allison
Arendt Daniel, n.e.c. 6th and Lock
Arneta Peter, 92 W. Court
Armeader John, n.e.c. Court and Elm
Arnold Henry F. 470 Vine
Art Catherine, 510 Plum
Auel Conrad, 277 Freeman
Ayres Isaac W. 401 Central av.
Badrack Samuel, 172 Broadway
Baer Jacob, 87 Ham. Road
Bahn Wm. H., s.w.c. 6th and Elm
Bake Wm. A., n.s. Ham. Road ar. Mohawk Bridge
Baker Leopold, 807 Vine
Ball Gabriella, 321 Central Av.
Bamberger George, 516 Walnut
Bange Barney, 392 W. 5th
Banziger Chas. 404 Vine
Bardo John, 280 Ham. Road
Barkan Henry, n.w.c. Browne and Vernon al.
Barmann Henry, 188 W. Canal
Barnhorn Clemens, 50 W. Court
Barrett Geo. W., 376 W. 6th
Barter John, 672 Central av.
Bartils Augustus, 11 Sycamore
Basler John, 661 Vine
Bassey Wm., n.e.c. Bank and Linn
Batsche Frank, n.e.c. Smith and Water
Bauer Conrad, 133 Ham. Road
Bauer Jacob, s.e.c. Pearl and Pike
Bauer John, 29 W. Front
Bauer John, 187 Ham. Road
Bauerfeld Charles, n.e.c. Harrison Pike and Spring Grv. av

BATHIANY RUDOLPH, 475 and 477 Walnut
Baukuochl Frank, 68 13th
Bauman John, 74 E. Pearl
Bawer Ulrich, 317 Walnut
Bayersdoerfer John, 640 Vine
Beaugrand Louis, 58 E. 5th
Beck John C. 72 Broadway
Becker Jacob, 634 Race
Becker John, 506 Vine
Becker Joseph, 7 Buckeye
Beckman Henry, s.w.c. Broadway and Hunt
Becksmith Frank, 169 W. 5th
Becksmith Henry, s.w.c. 8th and Broadway
Beers Charles H., 68 E. Pearl
Bender Peter, 17 E. 8th
Benjamin Bernhard, 25 Providence
Benedict Ben., 222 Vine
Bentel Wm., 67 Elder
Berberich John, n.w.c. Pearl and Kilgour
Bertken Richard, 71 Sycamore
Bigger Henry, 21 E. 5th
Binder Jacob, s.c.c. 6th and Freeman
Binder Oswald, 24 E. Front
Blach Charles, 541 Elm
Blackburn Henry, 440 W. Front
Blatter John, 458 Walnut
Blaw Fred. M, 277 W. 5th
Blendinger John, 510 Cen'l Av
Blum Frederick, 526 E. Front
Bockholt Fred. 51 W. 5th
Bockholt Henry B. 216 Walnut
Bode Christian H. 5 2 Main
Bode Margaret, 557 Elm
Botkin Samuel, 14 Vine
Boehinger Louis, 331 Vine
Bolger John, 34 Butler
Boehmerle John, 408 Main
Bola Henry, 86 W. 2nd
Bollinger Peter, 120 Clinton
Bollmann Fred. G. 38 Green
BOLLMAN J. B. & CO. 15 and 17 E. 9th
Bonger Martin, 23 Water
Bookwood Charles, 238 Vine
Borgerding J. Henry, 8 E. Front
Borns Christian, 517 E. Front
Boschert Bernhardt, 620 Main
Bothner Louis, 430 Main
Botter Gerhard H. 18 13th
Brabender Hubert, 18 Mercer
Bracken Wm. 8 Landing b. Broadway and Ludlow
Brady James, 267 John
Brahm John H. 3 Casilly'sRow
Bratzler Chas. 218 E. Front
Brenner John, 80 W. Court
Brichler George, n.c.c. Elm and Green
Briggs John Y. 2 Commercial Row
BRIGHTON HOUSE, Harrison Pike, head of Central av.
Brinkmann Wm. 341 Main
Brock Louis, 181 Walnut
Brockmann Herman H., 373 Broadway
Brockmann Theodore, 73 W. 6th
Brockerhoff Anthony, 519 Main
Brokamn Hy, n.w.c. Hunt and Pendleton
Brossarts Frank, 97 W. Miami Canal
Drossmer Francis S., Hill b.
Brown Mary, s.s. 6th b. Broadway and Culvert
Brown P. H., 20 Riv. Landing
Brown Susan A., 180 Central av.
Brown William, 1008 Cen'l Av
Brittain John, 204 W. 6th
Brittan John D., 4 W. 3d
Brubacker Jacob, n.w.c. Melancthon and Central av.
Bruck Valentine, 438 E. Front
Brueggemann Bern., 602 Elm
BRUNS JOHN R., 480 W. Front
Bucher Frederick, 16 E. Front
Buchheit Mathias, 41 14th
Buckman Joseph, cor. Lawrence and Newport Ferry Landing
Buehler Andrew, 187 Vine
Bugganoor Peter, 502 W. 3rd
Bulger James, n.w.c. Front and Washington
Burckhard Geo. 100 W. Liberty
Burg Ludwig, 51 Ham. Road
Burhoff Barney, s.w.c. 5th & Smith
Burke Thomas, 512 W. Front
Burke Thomas, 401 W. 2nd

Burkrle Martin, 78 Mohawk
Busam Michael, 652 Central Av
Busch Francis K. 654 Race
Busch John, 68 E. Front
Bussmann B., 155 W. Front
Butscha Fred. R, 463 Vine
Butz Margaret, 365 Sycamore
Caden John, c. Ludlow and River
Cahill Patrick. 53 Commerce
Campbell J. L., 352 W. 5th
Carroll Elizabeth, 42 Lock n. of 8th
Carroll John, n.w.c. Carr and W. W. Canal
Carroll Patrick, 218 Water
Carroll William, 215 W, 3rd
Carvin John, 587 W. 5th
Chambers Nich, 132 W. Front
Choate Evan P. 271 Main
Clark Patrick, 253 W, 6th
Class Charles, 108 Vine
Cline Henry, n.s, Front e. of Kelly
Cloyd Julian, 195 W. 6th
Coakly Thomas, 127 Water
Cohn Matthew A. 68 W. 6th
Collins Wm. n.s. 6th c. of Lock
Connelley Thomas, 48 Pike
Connelly Fisty, 70 E. Front
Connelly Patrick, 51 Commerce
Connelly Thomas, n.e.c. Vine and Water
Connor Wm., n.é.c. Ludlow and Front
Conrad Christian, 797 Central av.
Constamz Charles, 400 Vine
Conway Michael, s.e.c. 8th and Sycamore
Cook Barney, 606 Central av.
Coony Pat. 972 E. Front
COOPER THOMAS, 76 W. 3d
Coors Fred., 1512 E. Front
Corcoran Edward. 232 Elm
Corcoran Michael, 18 Landing b. Broadway and Ludlow
Corcoran Thomas, s.w.c. Vine and Water
Correvont Francis, 1112 Central av.
Cosgrove Thomas, h. n.s. 8th b. Broadway and Sycam'e
Cotter & Wessing, 9 Landing, b. Broadway and Ludlow
Coulcy Martin, 48 W. Front
Crage William, 202 W. 6th
Cramp Michael, 440 Elm
Cregar Samuel P, n.e.c. Elm and 15th
Creiger August, 718 Central av.
Creppel Fred., s.s. Front w. of Hill
Creppel Henry, 325 W. 5th
Dads Henry, 89 Allison
Darlis Andrew, s.s. Reading road nr. Montgomery pike
Dasch Charles, 617 Vine
DAUM MICHAEL, 30 Broadway
Daumann Henry, 125 Ham. Rd
Daaman John, 67 W. Liberty
DEBOLT EXCHANGE, s.e.c. Main and Court
Deck Abraham, s.w.c. Central Av and Clarkson
Dee Michael, 34 Elm
Deierling Jacob, 546 Race
Deininger Henry, 31½ E. Front
Deinweig John Phillip, 530 Walnut
Deller John, 140 Buckeye
Denach Michael, 704 Central av.
Deperetz Daniel, 156 Ham. Rd.
DeRaay Peter, n.w.c. 7th and Plum
Dermity Joseph, 35 Accommodation
DENAX P. 2., 80 and 82 Walnut
Deters Frank, 50 Race
Dewoin Wm. 384 W. 2nd
Deyer John, 27 Mercer
Dieckmann Louis, 919 W. 6th
Diehl John, 28 Elder
Dieterle Andrew, 919 Central av.
DISERENS FRED., 23 W. 5th
Distel Conrad, 52 Elder
Doll George J, 58 Liberty
Doll Jacob, 76 Ham. Road
Doll Robert, 554 Walnut
Dollar Adam, 321 Broadway
Donnelly Michael, 189 W. 6th
Donohue John, s.e.c. 3d and Walnut
Dooley John, 23 Accommodation

Doppler Andrew, 764 Cen'l Av
Dorn F., 271 Freeman
Dorna Christian, 529 E. Front
Dornhoefer Moritz, 94 Buckeye
Dotzauer Fred. 353 W. 5th
Dougherty David, 616 Cent. av.
Doyle Patrick, 100 Freeman
Draude August, 961 Central av.
Draude Henry F., 691 Elm
Drech Louis, 847 Sycamore
DRESCHER CHARLES, 251 W. 6th
Druck Frank, 33 E. 3d e. of Parsons
Druffel J. H., 90 E. 2d
Dubeck Chris. n.e.c. Central av. and Court
Duan Cornelius, 120 E. 8th
Duran Charles, 330 Central av
Ebding Christian, 4 Moore
EBERLE CLEMENTS C. s.c.c. Abigail and Broadway
Ebert Fred. h. 533 Main
Eckhardt Charles, 84 W. 3rd
Eckers Henry, 630 Central av.
Edelmann Michael, 17 Ham. Road
Effinger Jno., 6 Sycamore
Egland Fred. 194 Broadway
Ehmer Joseph, 166 Bremen
Ehrinzer Ehrhart, 842 E. Frnt
Eich Peter, 282 W. Liberty
Elchenlaub Fred. 280 W. Liberty
Eichenlaub G. F. 543 Central av.
Eichhorn George, 601 Main
Elsen Anton, s.w.c. Freeman and Dayton
Eisfelden Louis, 22 Bank
Eisle Joseph, 37 Dunlap
EITH BRENHARD, n.s. Ham. Rd., b. Race & Elm
Elble Chris, 106 Walnut
Ellis & Richardson, 199 Vine
Ellman Joseph, 5 Landing b. Broadway and Ludlow
Eisenheimer J., Geo. 412 Vine
Engberson William, n.s. Front e. of Foster
Engel Frederick, 675 Vine
Englehardt Jacob, 575 W. 5th
Engelhart Jacob, 217 W. 6th
English John, 220 Broadway
Enpens & Bro. 9 E. Liberty
Eschenbach John, 157 Pleasant and Walnut
Esmann Joseph, n.w.c. Court and Walnut
Estinger John 440 Main
Eversfield John, 14 E. 7th
Evermann Peter, 814 W. 5th
Freelage Ben. 9 12th
Fabry Bonyparc, 641 Elm
Farrow James, 134 Culvert
Faulkner John, 49 W. 5th
Felix Matthew, w.s. Brown nr Hum. Road
FENGER ANTON, 500 W. Front
Fencer John, 5 Lawrence
FENNESSY ED. s.c.c. Race and Commerce
Ferari Giovani, 101 Race
Ferdinand Charles, 78 Sycam'e
Ferera Andrew, 102 W. Front
Fernin Miles, n.s. Montgomery pike nr. Reading road
Ferrari & Co. 177 Vine
Ferrell Anna M. 176 Central av.
Ferry & Co., 20 E. 5th
Ferry Hannah, n.e.c. North and New
Ferry James, 212 W. 7th
Feuerstein Henry, s.s. Harrison pike b. Riddle and Brighton
Fev Henry, 215 Bremen
FEY SEBASTIAN, 621 Vine
Fiedler Edward, 206 Vine
Finnegan Richard, n.s. Augusta b. John and Smith
Fischer Frederick, 214 Vine
Fischer Jacob, 611 Main
Fitzgerald Oliver, s.w.c. Race and Pearl
Flach Frances, w.s. Western av. b. Bank & Harrison av.
Flaherty Patrick, 177 E. Frnt
Flaig Jacob M., 82 E. Front
Flanagan John, n.e.c. Ludlow and Pearl
Flannery Martin, 12 Landing b. Main and Walnut
Flanagan Edward, n.s. R. Front e. of Leatherbury
Flatlich Jacob F. 469 Vine
Fletcher James, 585 E. Front
Flick Joseph, w.s. Lebanon Road nr. Channing

Foerster Andrew, 237 Ham. road
Fool Frank H., 71 Baymiller
Foughney Martin, 15 Water
Foy Michael, 9 Landing b. Main and Walnut
Frank Anton, 98 Gest
Frank E. I. 74 W. Court
Franzreb Jacob, 412 Freeman
Frey August, 18 W. Court
Frey Charles, 583 Main
Freyermuth Peter, 607 Elm
Fricke Fred. L. 235 Sycamore
Friederick Christopher, 502 Walnut
Friedlein George, 62 Buckeye
Friedlein John, 53 Sycamore
Froehlich Chas 527 Central av
Fruhweld Matthias, 64 Lock
Fuchs Julius, s.w.c. Melancthon and Central av.
Fuchs Lorenz, 35 Elder
Fuchs Peter, 424 Vine
Fuldner John, 192 Clinton
Furst Charles, 48 E. Pearl
Fussner John, 561 Walnut
Fury Bernard, 94 Freeman
Gabel Gabriel, n.e.c. 6th and Walnut
Gabennesch Chr. u.s. Harrison pike b. Brighton and Riddle
Gallmann Louis, 1 E. 8th
Gans Casper, 519 Walnut
Gandolph Frank, 59 Vine
Gardner Adam, 673 Race
Gardner Jacob, 70 E. 3rd e. of Whittaker
Gass Henry, 172 Clay
Gass, John, 650 Vine
Gaussen Wm. E., 71 W. 3d
Gavin Michael, 16 Landing b. Broadway and Ludlow
GEISER JOSEPH, 23 W. Court
Geldreich Joseph, 179 W. Liberty
Gentsch Wm. 393 Vine
Gerhold Louis, 210 E. Front
Gerth Valentine, 110 W. Liberty
Gibbons John, 15 Landing
Gibbons Mary A. River b. Ludlow and Lawrence
Gill Charles, 49 Water
Gillon James, 2 E. Pearl
GINANDY GEO., 349 Walnut
Glaser Jacob, 417 Main
Glabier Andrew J. 178 Central av.
Goddard Richard, 192 W. 6th
Goebel Henry, 584 W. 6th
Goetz John G. 577 Elm
Goetz Philip, 337 Ham. Road
Good Matthew, 462 Race
Gorian Patrick, n.w.c. Race and Water
Gorman John, 179 W. Court
Gorman Thomas, s.w.c. Court and John
Gorrer John, 17 Poplar
Gorrien Henry, 78 Water
Gottbohcede Bernard H. 113 & 115 Woodward
Gotts John, 35 W. 3d
Gottschalk Fred, 982 Cent. av.
Goydst John H. 687 Central av.
Grabbage Nicholas, 43 Vine
Graf Joseph, 209 W. 6th
Grannin James, n.e.c. 9th and Central av.
Greasa George, 227 E. 5th
Green James, 151 Culvert
Gregson John, 132 W. 6th
Greichelmer Jacob, 359 Ham. Road
Greslin Carl, 318 Main
Griffith Samuel, 31 W. Front
Grigois Christopher, 180 Buckeye
Grimme Harmon, 7 Landing
Gronette Harney, s.w.c. Union and Race
Grothues Joseph H. 494 Main
Gruesser Benedict, 635 Vine
Grunkemeyer H. & J. n.w.c. Central av. and W. Water Canal
Guhmann Jacob, 401 Vine
Gukolberger Geo. 462 Walnut
Gulick Geo. H. 346 W. 6th
Guth Jacob, s.w.c. 2nd and Vine
Guthardt Conrad, s.e.c. Melancthon and John
Guttenberg Fred. 394 Vine
Haake Anthony, 107 E. 2d
Haas Charles J, 483 Vine
Hacket Robert, 134 Water
Haders John, 763 Vine
Hafner Stephen, 707 Elm
Hagan James, 258 Walnut

BUSINESS MIRROR.

Halo Nicholas, 564 E. Front
Haley Thom. 10 River Landing
Hallron John, 229 W. 6th
Hall Bish, 201 Vine
Hall Wm 1214 E. Front
Hamburger S, 22 W. 6th
Hamann Abel, 1 Mary
Hardle Henry, 762 Central av
Hardling John, s.w.c. John and Wade
Harnold Jacob, 638 Vine
Harriett Margaret, 323 W. 6th
Harrigan Thomas H. 62 E. 5th
Harrington Bridget, 11 River Landing
Harsch John, 52 Water
Hart Henry, 421 Vine
Hätke Berhard, 13 Landing b. Broadway and Ludlow
Hattersley Saml., 514 W. Front
Hauck Jacob, s.e.c. Race & Findlay
Hauck William, s.w.c. Wade and John
Hauenschild H. C., 577 Main
Hauser Jacob, 442 Main
Healy Thomas, 163 Central av.
Hearn Patrick, 86 E. 5th
Hecker Jacob, 481 Vine
Heger Simon, 95 W. M. Canal
Heidacher Joseph, s.e.c. Ham. road and Elm
Heimrod Adolph, 504 W. Front
Helde Jacob, 104 Freeman
HELFFERICH FRANCIS,
    367 Main
Hellstern Joachim, 552 Vine
Helmsdorfer Fred, 1121 Central Avenue
Hengfling John, 48 Ham. road
Hemmer Jacob, 243 Ham. road
Henneker Henry, 537 Main
Hennessy Thomas, 40 Accommodation
Henzie Michael, 544 W. Front
Herancourt P., 1066 Cent. av.
Herrmann Ernest, n.w.c. Lawrence and 2d
Herty Daniel, 205 E. 6th
Hesse Ernest H, n.e.c. Pearl and Race
Hestor T., s.w.c. 6th & John
Hey Jacob, 535 Walnut
Hey William, 323 Main
Heymann Charles, n.s. Front e. of Lewis
Hickey Ann, 33 Lock n. of 8th
Hickey John S., s.w.c. 6th & Pierson
Hiedgerken John, 404 W. 5th
Rieck Mike, 464 E. Front
Hill James, 41 Public Landing
Hills J., n. w. c. Butler & Front
Hinchy Thomas, 546 W. Front
Hinkelmann Louis, 300 Findly
HOBBS WM. H.
    183 W. 6th
Hoeft Henry, 600 Main
Hoer Catharine, w.s. Fountain b. Rice and Alexander
Hoess Anton, 56 Ham. Road
HOFACKER CHRIST.
    35 E. 3rd
Hoffmann Fred, 132 Bremen
Hoffmann John, 10 Landing b. Broadway and Ludlow
Hoffmann Julius, n.s. 13th b. Walnut and Vine
Hoffmann Math, 1462 E. Front
Hogan Johanna, s.s. 6th b. Broadway and Culvert
Hogan John, 182 Central av.
Hogan Patrick, 241 W. 6th
Hohneck Valentine, 614 Vine
HOLTER B.,
    c. Main & River
Holthenrichs Wm. 13 E. Pearl
Holthous Bernard, n.s. R. R. e. of Stone al
Honing Frank, 470 Main
Honkomp Fred, 145 W. 5th
Horn George, 272 Main
Horner J., s.s. Reading Pike, nr. Franklin Brewery
Hotel George, s.s. Budd b. Harriett and Millcreek
Howell Ellis, 154 Baymiller
HUBER J. EDWARD,
    56 W. 3rd
Hudson Wm. S., 280 Cen'l Av
Hugel John, 6 Buckeye
Hukill Richard, 156 Main
Hurley Daniel, 36 Lock n. of 8th
Husman Andrew, s.e.c. Ann and Central av
Huser Fred, 137 Everett
Icefelder Louis, 22 Bank
Ilg Anthony, 106 Ham. road
Ilg George, 478 Vine
Imhof John, 343 Broadway
INTERNATIONAL,
    91 Sycamore

Inwalle John H. jr. 451 W. 6th
Jacobs Jane, foot of 5th, nr. Freeman
Jacobs Joseph, w.s. Vine b. Milk and Mulberry
Jackson Albert G. 305 Elm
Jaequet Joseph, 68 12th
Jaokel George, 60 W. Mulberry
Jeffers James, 58 Water
Jenni Henry, 320 Main
Jenny's Wm. C. 386 Main
Jenz Geo, s.w.c. 15th & Plum
Johnson Caleb, 186 Central Av
Johnton Overton J, e.s. M'Allister b. 4th and 5th
Jones Priscilla, 138 Culvert
Joy Thomas, 48 Lock
Junck Clayton, s.s. Court bet. Main and Sycamore
Jutzler Heinrich, 448 Vine
Kuin John, 34 E. 8th e. of Lock
Kaiser William, 15 W. Court
Kaiser Philip, n.s. Harrison Pike b. Brighton & Riddle
Kaiser Xavier, 890 Vine
Karmau Andrew, s.e.c. Cutter and Liberty
Karman A., s.w.c. Wade and Central av.
Keegan James, 48 Freeman
Keegan Matthew, 61 Water
Keller Valentine, e.s. Vine b. Culhoun and Auburn Av.
Keenan Nich. n.e.c. Richmond and John
KEHLENBACH WM.,
    418 Main
Keiser Anthony, 65 Wade
Kelbert Herrmann, s.w.c. Gest and Liberty
Kelley Wm, 30 Water
Kenkel Daniel, 105 E. 2nd
Kenler Michael, 482, Linn
Kennedy Margaret, 117 Sycamore
Kennedy Michael, 111 W. 3rd
Kennett Charles, 619 Elm
Kenny Edward, 740 W. 6th
Keown & Manly, n.w.c. Front and Broadway
Kestner Wm, 140 Carr
Ketterer Andrew, 712 Vine
Kettler Wm, 412 Sycamore
Kialy Thomas, 122 Freeman
Kiefer John, 1028 Central Av
Kihn Valentine, 55 Elder
Kindel Gabriel, n.s. Charlotte b. Elm and Baymiller
Kindervater Theo., 202 Vine
King Julis, 8 Commerce
Kirkland Joseph M. 54 B'way
Kukpatrick Wm, s.e.c. 6th and Culvert
Klein Peter, 147 Carr
Klensoh Fred. 78 W. Liberty
Klingler Joseph C. 144 Bremen
Klotter Frank, 402 Vine
Knauber Geo, 19 Providence
Knuepfer Henry J, 657 Vine
Koble Michael, Findlay b. Central Av. and John
Kobmann Frederick C, 81 Bremen
Koch John, s.s. Harrison Road b. Coleman and Patterson
KOCH LOUIS,
    57 W. 3rd
Koebel Joseph, 43 Riddle
Koeble Pankraz, n.w.c. Vine and 12th
Koehler Albert F. 319 Walnut
Koehler Fred. 11 E. Liberty
Koelling Fred. 159 Vine
Kohlka Julius, b. 27 15th
Koo William, 90 Freeman
Kopp Felix, 488 Walnut
Koppel John A. 279 Everett
Korte John F., 42 E. 5th
Kracht Theodore, 679 W. Front
Kraft Francis, 467 Vine
Kramer George, 6. Front
Kramer Franz, 578 Walnut
Kraus Charles, 87 Ham. Road
Krees Henry, 1080 Central Av
Kringel Gustave, 218 Vine
Krippner Adam, n.e.c. Clark and Baymiller
Kroger Jame, 1 Budd
Kronlage Bernhard, 538 Walnt
Krog Julius, w.s. Ham. Road nr. Brighton House
Kruch Louis, 232 Walnut
Krusius John G., 766 E. Front
Kuchler August, 39 Ludlow
Kuchler Casper, s.e.c. Harrison pike and Brighton
Kuegler Chas, w.s. Central Av b. Findlay and Poplar
Kung Peter, s.e.c. s.e.c. Riddle and Harrison Pike
Kunning Henry, s.s. W. W. Canal b. John and Smith

Kuntz Peter, 634 Vine
Lachtrop Henry, 18 Webster
Ladonkotter &c., 106 Abigail
Laenkering Henry J, 520 Main
Lehring H. & J. 496 W. Front
Lamping J. D., 193 W. 6th
Lander Max, 597 W. 5th
Lang Charles, 544 Race
Lang John, 649 Vine
Lang Thomas, 18 Ham. Road
Laugion John, 119 W. 5th
Langenhein Charles 38 E. 5th
Lasch Charles, 52 W. Liberty
Lauck Michael, n.s. Ham. R1. b. Poplar and Vine
Laufer Michael, 24 W. 6th
Laux Joseph, 606 Vine
Lawler Elisabeth, 371 Sycam'r
Lechler Christ. s.w.c. Liberty and Plum
Leddy Daniel, 137 E. 6th
Ledger Hannah, 175 W. Court
Lee George, 414 W. Front
Lennamore Wm. 177 Walnut
Leuse Charles, 35 Moore
Leweroby C. 68 W. Front
Leyman John, 502 W. 5th
Lidia John, 163 Sycamore
Linke Louis, n.w.c. 9.h and Walnut
Littlemann F. Herman, w.s. Vine b. Milk and Mulberry
Lochner Frederick, 753 Vine
LOEWE JOSEPH O.
    437 Vine
Lohrer Jacob, 576 Elm
Lomas Wm. 33 W. Front
Loree Samuel, s.o.c. 6th and Lodge
Lorence Basilius, 40 Pike
Lotz Peter, 40 Findlay
Loughuan Michael, 460 W. Front
Loventhal Benj. S. s.e.c. Race and Third
Ludders Doderich E. s.e.c. Bank and Whiteman
Luning Frank, 467 Walnut
Luning Frederick, 497 Main
Lutz Lorenz, 154 Ham. Rd.
Lynch Elizabeth, 18 Lock n. of 8th
Lynch Thomas, 237 W. 6th
McAvoy Mary, n.e.c. Ludlow and 3d
McCarty John, n.s. Front w. of 8th
McCarty Randall, 16 Lock n. of 8th
McClellan James, 1072 Central Av.
McConville John, 754 E. Front
McCormack Thos. 23 E. 5th
McCormick Phillip, 53 Accommodation
McCulloch Charles, 320 Brdwy
Mc Dermott Mrs. B. 8 River Landing b. Main & Walnut
McDonald Mary, 113 W. 3d
McDonald Wm. 64 Broadway
McGovern Michael, 140 Culvert
McGuire Austin, 9 E. 4th
McHugh Patrick, 320 Plum
McHugh Wm. 17 Landing b. Broadway and Ludlow
McLane Wm., 42 E. Front
McLaughlin John, 74 E. 5th
McLaughlin Wm., 157 W. 5th
McManus John, 218 W. 3d
McNally Peter, 32 Water
MAAG FRED & SON,
    443 Main
Maag Henry, s.e.c. 6th and Vine
Macke Frank, n.e.c. Sycamore and Abigail
Macke R. & Co., n.s. Front e. of Lewis
Mackey —, 107 W. 3d
Mackey Christopher, s.s. 6th e. of Lock
Mackey John sr., Melodeon Buildings, n.w.c. 4th and Walnut
MACKENTEPE B.
    n.w.c. Vine and 2d
Maerts Bernard, 201 W. 6th
MAGERHAUS AUGUST F.
    n.e.c. 12th and Walnut
Maguire Thomas, s.e.c. Central Av. and Pearl
Mahoney Eliza, 209 E. 6th
Maier Simon, n.e.c. Vine and Ham. Road
Malascher Sebastian, s.s. Front b. Lawrence and Pike
Mandler Paul, s.e.c. Walnut and 12th
Manuel John, basement 182 Walnut

Marek David, 14 Landing b. Ludlow and Broadway
MARHOFFER PHILLIP,
    509 W. 6th
Martin John, n.e.c. Vine and Milk
Martin Wm. J. n.w.c. Front and Ludlow
MARTIN WILSON,
    240 W. 6th
Master Casper, 23 13th
Mathews Peter, 177 W. Liberty
Maul Robert, 511 Plum
Mayer George, 327 Main
Mayloben A Butterfass, 2 Wlnt
Mayloben Ph., 16 Walnut
MEINER CHARLES,
    n.e.c. Mercer and Vine
Mofer Aug, s.e.c. 5th and Elm
Meininger Carl, 184 Walnut
Menge Robert C. 134 Bremen
Mentor Almon, 81 W. 4th
Menzel Jacob, 40 Walnut
Mert Benedict, e.s. Vine b. Mulberry and Milk
METCALFE & ROSS,
    n.e.c. Main and 8th
Moyenschein Juo. 154 Pleasant
Meyer Barney H. 42 Elm
Meyer Charles H. 52 15th
Meyer Christian, 165 Clay
Meyer Christian. n. w.c. Front and Wood
Meyer Francis A. 11 13th
Meyer Fred, A. n.w.c. Freeman and Richmond
MEYER GEORGE,
    117 Bremen
Meyer George, w.s. Western Av. b. Dayton and Back
Meyer Louis, w.s. Ham. Road nr. Brighton House
Meyer Martin, 76 W. Liberty
Meyer Philip, 1031 Central Av
Meyer William, n.e.c. Elm and Pearl
Meyers John D. 20 Central Av
Miller John, 263 Clinton
Millar Nicholus, n.s. R. R. c. of Wallace al.
Miller Phillip, s.s. Calhoun b. McMillan and Madison
Miller Wm. 100 Elm
Miller Patrick, 82 Water
Moeller Henry, 580 Main
Moerk Ernst F. 669 Vine
Moessner James, 16 12th and Main
Molique John, 13 Freeman
Monday Joseph, s.w.c. Dudley and Liberty
Montgomery Jas., 81 Sycamore
Mooney William, 176 W, 3d
Moran Ellen, 212 E. 6th
Morris Francis H. 182 Sycamore
Morach Henry, 545 Elm
Moss Henry, 365 W. 5th
Mueller Bernhard, 74 12th
Mueller Constantine, 510 & 511 Vine
Mueller George, 223 W. 6th
Mueller Jacob, 588 Race
Mueller John II. 602 Walnut
Mueller Nicholas, 617 Cent. Av
Mueller Jacob II., 518 Vine
Mugal Peter, 790 Central Av.
Muhlhauser J. P., 701 Vine
MUHRMANN JOHN F.
    207 and 219 Vine
Mullanny Pat. w.s. Central Av b. 21 and W. W. Canal
Muller Fred. s.e.c. Liberty and Central Av.
Muller Louis, 105 Hunt
Mullen Ann, n.s. 6th c. of Lock
Mundy Thomas, 317 W. 21
Munscher Joseph, 277 Cent. Av
Munzemeier August, 7 12th
Murphy Michael, 193 Cutter
Murphy Jas., 273 Cent. Av.
Myers Conrad, 1012 Central Av.
Nagel Henry, 20 Ham. Road
Narey Matthew, 313 Central Av
Nash Bonnergas, 123 Vine
Nauber Gerhard, n.e.c. Smith and Augusta
Neidhard Valentine, 662 Race
NIEMER J.
    262 E. Front
Nelson James, 105 W. 3d
Niebuhr John H. 221 Cent. Av.
Niemann Wm. 21 Ham. Road
Noble Elizabeth, 101 W. 5th
Nolan Patrick, 508 W. 4th
Null Robert, e.s. Vine junction of Buckeye
Nolt Christian, 72 Ham. Road
Norris James, 131 W. 5th
Nuber John, s.w.c. Linn and York

Nugent William, 230 Broadway
Nuttel Bridget, State b. Deer Creek Road and Accommodation
Oberle August, 142 Clay
O'Connell Michael, s.s. 6th b. Broadway and Culvert
O'Connor John, 130 Cen'l Av
Ochsner Nicholas, n.s. Corporation line nr. Auburn
Oester John, 413 Sycamore
O'Garra John, 571 W. 5th
O'Garry Thomas, 170 W. Front
Oker Joseph, 817 Central Av.
O'Malley Michael, 40 E. 3d
O'Neil Ellen, 149 W. M. Canal
O'Neill Peter, 22 E. 5th
O'Nett Angelo, 116 W. Front
Ossege Henry, 719 Race
Osterhage John H. 20 Green
Otto Lawrence, 909 Cen'l Av.
Outred Richard, 395 Central Av
Overbur Henry, 275 Sycamore
Paige Joseph, s.e.c. Broadway and New
Paner Adam, 147 Buckeye
Panckner Adam, 462 Vine
Pelzer Alfred B. 410 Sycamore
Pengemann John T. 350 Sycamore
Perman Henry, 17 Martin
PETZSCH GUSTAVE C. 31 W. 3d
Pickett John, 206 Broadway
PIEPENDRING FRANK, n.e.c. 21 and Broadway
Pieper Louis, 528 Walnut
Pietz Bernard, 420 Vine
Pinot Alphonse, 561 Vine
Pistner Chris., 19 Hamer
Plana Andreas, 209 Bremen
Porter Lucy, 141 E. 6th
Post John, n.s. Harrison Pike nr. Millcreek
Power Robert, 628 E. Front
Price Wm. 225 Main
Prier Kraktor, 905 Central Av.
Probst Ignatz, 74 12th
Profeter John, 964 Race
Pronizius Fr., s.e.c. Clay and Liberty
Puchta Lorenz, n. w. c. Pike and Pearl
PUTHOFF HENRY jr. 110 Abigail
Quellhorst Chris., 409 Walnut
Quinlan & Green, 12 Broadway
Quinn Patrick, 21 E. 5th
Quinn Thomas, s.w.c. Vine and Front
Quetel Anthony, s.e.c. Water and Walnut
Rabe George H. s.e.c. 5th and Home
Rabe J., 245 W. 6th
Rambendahl Henry, 511 Sycamore
Rambock Joseph, n.s. Calhoun b. McMillan and Clifton Av
Ramph George, 440 Race
Rapp Mathias, n.w.c. Plum and Ann
Rauscher Jacob, 31 Bremen
Ravens Hermann, 538 W. 8th
Reader Alex. 54 Clay
Rebold Michael, 668 Vine
Regan John, 16 E. 8th
Reeg Andrew, 710 Freeman
Reichert Ernst, 225 Walnut
Reichert John, s.w.c. Grant and Elm
Reider Christopher, n.s. Front o. of Foster
Reischneider Elizabeth, e.s. Reading Road nr. Montgomery pike
Reinauer Leopold, 202 Walnut
Reiner George, 66 W. Liberty
Reinhardt John B., 465 Walnut
Reinkamp August, s.e.c. Pearl and Barlet
Reinstetler A. Bescher, s.w.c. Race and 21
Reis Jacob, 175 Ham. Road
Remmlein Francis, 596 Elm
Rengenbach Fred. 532 Central Av.
Rettig John, 559 Elm
Rentz Joseph, 2d Main
RHEIN JOSEPH, 480 Vine
RICE FERMAN W. 46 Sycamore
Richardson H. N. B. 218 Vine
Richenmann Mich'l, 10 Dunlap
Rider Henry J. 17 E. 5th
Ried Catherine, 216 W. 3d
Riedel George, 329 Race
Rieger John, 511 Walnut
RIETH CHARLES, 251 E. Front
Ritger John, 598 Elm

Roark John, 92 W. Front
Robertson Sarah, 172 Cent. Av.
Robinson James, 419 W. 2d
Rodenberg Henry, s.e.c. Harrison Pike and Western Av.
R he Henry, 348 Main
Rohl Henry, n.s. 6th b. Harriet and Horne
ROLL CHRIS. 175 E. Front
Rosenfelder Lewis F. J. 90 13th
Ross Henry, 50 W. Front
Rosswinkle Herman, 1 Cassilly's Row
ROTH & MOSSER, n.w.c. Vine & Longworth
Roltier Wm. n.w.c. 3d & Main
Rotert Henry, 104 Abigail
Rothfus George, 714 Vine
Rothhan Fred. 592 Elm
Rumpler Anton, 50 York
Ruttinger Valentine, 711 Central Av.
Ruwe Joseph, 292 Broadway
Ryan John, 298 E. 6th
Ryan John, 326 Central Av.
Ryan John, s.e.c. Ludlow and Third
Ryan Michael, 585 W. 6th
Ryan Thomas, w.s. 6th, 6th
Saas Felix, n.w.c. Liberty and Race
ST. CHARLES, 30 and 32 E. 3d
ST. NICHOLAS EXCH'GE n.w.c. Vine and Longworth
Sanderson George, 380 C'tri Av
Sandhas Louis, 72 E. Front
Santer Jacob, 19 Martin
Sauerbeck Geo. 1186 E. Front
Schafer Wm. s.w.c. 6th and Plum
Schaefer Geo. 30 Adams
Schaeven Joseph, 46 Elder
Schäfer Michael, 98 W. Lib'ty
Schaffhauser Chas. s.e.c. Elm and Findlay
Schanta Mich'l, s.w.c. Coleman and Central Av
Schappi John, 214 Ham. Rd.
Schath Michael, 510 Walnut
Schell Sebastian, e.s. Logan b. Elder and Green
Schemmel Leonhardt, 264 Ham Road
Scherien Mich. 709 Main
Schett Frederick, 66 W. Court
Scheuer Addm, 815 Central Av.
Schewen Ferdinand, 32 E. Liberty
Schiller Gustav, 678 Central Av
Schlee Henry, 137 Ham. Road
Schlinker John, 21 15th
Schmid Christian, 1120 Central Av
Schmidt Charles P. 623 Vine
Schmidt Louis, 21 Poete
Schmidt Louis, 707 Vine
Schmidt Geo. 239 Central Av
Schmitt John, 7 Mary
Schmitt Louis, 430 Vine
Schmitt Nicholas, 637 Race
Schmitte, Hy., 117 E. 8th
Schnears George, 913 Main
Schneider Casper, 673 W. 6th
Schneider Geo. 14 E. Front
Schneider Henry, 400 Sycam'e
Schneider Herman, 592 Elm
Schneider Ignatz, n.s. Stark b. Dunlap and Mohawk bridge
Schneider John, 1122 Cen'l Av
Schneider Louis, 567 Walnut
SCHNITTGER JOHN H. s.e.c. 15th nr. Elm
Schoenberg Alph-two, s.e.c. Vine and Cear
Scholl Mathias, e.' Pleasant
Schon Phillip, P. W. 6th
Schorr George, n.w.c. Elm Rd. and Main
Schottelkotte John L. 47 Pendleton
Schrenker John, 1 Wade b. Elm and Plum
Schroeder Charles A., 78 W. Court
Schudle Jacob, 21 W. Court
Schumann August, 514 Vine
Schulte Karl, s.w.c. 6th and Smith
Schultz Catharine, 16 Allison
Schultz Daniel, 531 Walnut
Schultz Frank, 249 W. Court
Schumacher John, 74 12th
Schumann Fre'l. 531 Race
Schuster John, 41 Sycamore
Schwagerle Adam, 409 Main
Schwap Susan, 868 E. Front
Schwarm Charles, 494 Walnut
Schwartz Joseph, n.s. Augusta b. John and Smith

SCHWEGMAN BERNH'D, 30 Pub. Landing
Schwieher John H. 4 Casilly's Row
Schwein John, 650 Vine
Schweinefus John H. 716 E. Front
Schwemberger Chas, sr., 607 Walnut
Schwemberger Joseph, n.e.c. Vine and Liberty
Schwemberger Joseph, 20 E. Canal
Schwenck Christop., 448 Race
Schwent Christopher, 445 W. 2d
Schwienher Bernard, s.w.c. Central Av. and Freeman
Schwinn Justus, 160 Ham. Rd.
Scott & Allgaier, s.w.c. 8th and Central Av.
Scott John A. s.w.c. 3d and Central Av
Seaman Mrs. Joseph, 13 W. 6th
Seibel Frederick, s.w.c. Division and Harrison Pike
Seidel Joseph, 570 Race
Seidensticker Fred. 539 Race
Seits Emil, 20 Commerce
Serekstoder Frank, 361 Ham Rd
Seren Martin, w.s. Butler b. Pearl and Front
Seufert Constantine, n.s. Front nr. Corp. Line
Shea Luke, n.e.c. Front and Vine
Sheehan Jerry, 293 Central Av
Sherman Henry, b 303 Race
Sidal Xavier, 219 W. 6th
Siegwolf John 1108 Cen'l Av
Siemann J. Fred. 26 Orchard
Silbernagel Conrad, 548 Vine
Simon Nicholas, 346 Ham. Rd
Smith Geo. 54 W. Court
Smith John, 50 E. 3d
Smith Patrick, 21 River Land.
Smith & Selman, 115 Sycamore
Smith Wm. H., 220 Central Av
Spankuch I. Casper, 515 Main
Spath John, s.e.c. 3d and John
Speekmaas Geo. E. n.e.c. Hunt and Sycamore
Spissmann Geo. J. Findlay b. Court Av. and John
Spitzmiller Geo., e.s. Vine b. Calhoon and Auburn Av
Spritzke Henry, 499 Vine
Stanford Mrs. Julia, 24 E. 3d
Stegemann Victor, 197 W. 6th
Stein Mich, 136 Bremen
Steincamp Fred. s.e.c. Liberty and Freeman
Stommens Charles, 358 W. 5th
Stouder Jacob, n.e.c. Central Av. and Canal
Sting Jacob, n.e.c. Allison & Clay
Stock Adam & Co. 674 Race
Stock Yard Exchange, s.e.c. Harrison Pike and Patt'son
Stolzer Andrew, e.s. Milk b. Vine and Calhoun
Storr Christian, 561 Race
Strasburger Nicholas, 160 Bremen
Strieff Joseph, n.w.c. Liberty and Dudley
Strunk Mary A. 12 E. 8th
Stuck John, 134 W. Court
STURWOLD JOHN HY., 520 W. Front
Stutz Daniel, 22 Ham. Road
Sullivan & Pryor, 28 E. 5th
Sweeney James, 329 W. 6th
Sweeny Catharine, 43 Race
Talbert Ellen, 133 W. 3d
Tangeman Fred. 636 W. Front
Tapharn Gerird B. 277 B'way
Taylor John F. 35 W. 5th
Ten Belz & Schroder, 15 12th
Thoeny Elias, 620 Vine
Thoman Herman H. 187 Cent'l Av
Thousman John, 601 Walnut
THOMPSON SANDY, 12 E. 3d
Thranert Henry F. 58 Ham. Road
Tiubrack Geo. H. 527 Vine
Tower Martin, s.e.c. Plum and 2d
Tracy Thomas, 19 Landing b. Broadway and Ludlow
Trame B. H. & Co., n.w.c. Main and River Landing
Trenklo Joseph, 96 Ham. Road
Trimble James, 9 Walnut
Tropf Jacob, s.e.c. Freeman and Main
TUCHSCHMID ULRICH, 232 E. Front
TUFFLI URSULA, 319 W. 6th

Turner David, 138 W. Front
Uhl Anthony, 67 Buckeye
Umhols John, 41 13th
Vandervert Robert, 74 W. 3d
Vandevier & Powell, 98 Sycamore
Veeneman Bernard, 556 Walnut
Vehorn August, 228 Linn
Vincent Geo. S., 283 W. 5th
Vitrick Arnold, n.e.c. 14th and Central Av
Vocke Henry, 125 W. 2d
Voelker Adam, 69 Allison
Voet Clements, 7 Landing b. Broadway and Ludlow
Vogel Charles, 491 Walnut
Vogelbach Francis X, 613 Vine
Vols Leonard, 641 Vine
Vombusmmel Hermann, 862 W. 6th
Vorheer John, 119 Findlay
Waarbrock D. 59 W. Court
Wacha Theodore, s.w.c. Main and Court
Wagner Conrad, 40 Hughes
Wagner Henry, 447 Walnut
Wagner John J. 318 E. Pearl
WALKER WM. F., 7 Sycamore
Wall Jacob, 144 E. 2d
Walpert Fred. 56 Mohawk
Walsh James, 80 Sycamore
Walsh Patrick, 701 W. Front
Walter Edward, 366 Sycamore
Waltz Charles F., 72 Liberty
Waustroth Joseph, 99 Woodward
Weber George, 20 E. 8th
Weber John, 712 Race
Weber John A. 507 Vine
Wehr John L., 282 E. Front
Weber Michael, 19 14th
Wehmeier Andrew, 11 Landing b. Broadway and Ludlow
Wehmbol John D. n.w.c. M. Canal and Main
Wehr Frederick W. 199 W. 6th
Weibel Frank, 110 Main
Weil Frank, 135 York
Weil John, 665 Central Av
Weimar Ernst, 73 Baymiller
Weimann Fred. 195 W. Court
Weingartner Wm. 553 W. 5th
Weinkam Peter, n.e.c. Cent'l Av. and Pearl
Weis John, 91 Ham. Road
Weis Seraphinus D. 73 W. 3d
Weist John, 56 W. Court
Weltzel Adam, n.w.c. John and Findlay
Welland Henry, 56 W. 6th
Welsh Luke, 133 W. Front
Wenzler Charles, 682 Vine
WENZLER MATHIAS, 680 Vine
Werle John, 51 W. 3d
Werns Mathaeus, 142 Ham Rd
Wesling Henry, n.w.c. Front and Central Av
Westermann Lambert, 61 W. 5th
Wettschureck Peter, 640 Elm
Weynand Charles, 1031 Central Av
Wheatand Thomas, n.s. 6th b. Culvert and Miami Canal
White David, 123 Sycamore
Wiebold Henry, 220 Walnut
Wigand Philip, 138 W. Lib'ty
WILKINSON WM. 110 W. 4th
Wiley James, 433 George
Williams James, 338 W. 2d
Williams Maria, 43 Sycamore
Williams Samuel, 11 E. 6th
Wilem Jacob, 13 Hughes
Willinger Bernard, s.w.c. Harrison Av and Riddle
Wilmerton John, 99 W. 3d
Wilson Adam, 32 E. Front
Winner J. A., Broadway Hotel
Winter Wm., 2-7 W. 5th
WINTERKOLER ANDREAS, 47 12th
Wirth George, 613 Main
Wimmer Christian J. 9 15th
Wohlwender Wauliorld, 60 Hunt
Wolf Frederick, 813 Walnut
Wolf George, 469 Walnut
Worms Isidor, s.s. 6th nr. Millcreek
Wuebben John H., 511 Main
Yarrington Wm., Henrio House
Youngblut Nicholas, n.s. Front e. of Foster
Zech Frank, 41 E. Front
ZEIGLER LUDING. N. Elm b. Cross and Warner
Zeltner John, 402 Vine
Zontner Henrietta, 276 W. Liberty

BUSINESS MIRROR. 359

Zeppenfeld Francis, 14 Mary
ZUMSTEIN FRANK,
 185 Vine
Zumstein Henry, 180 Vine
ZUMSTEIN JOHN,
 s.w.c. 5th and Walnut
Ziegler Henry, u.e.c. Front and Pike
Zimmerer Henry, s.e.c. Wade and Central Av
Zimmerman Charley, 164 E. Front
Zoller A., 254 W. 6th
Zost John, 195 Bremen

Coffee and Spice Mills.
BATHGATE CHAS.
 242 W. 6th
DIXON G. R, & CO.,
 213, 215 and 217 Sycamore
HARRISON & WILSON,
 131 and 133 Race

Collectors and Agents.
Douglas Peter, 62 E. 4th
HYATT JNO. T.,
 20 W. 3d
PARVIN S. H.
 63 W. 4th
Rieder Felix, 80 W. 3d
ROBINSON WM.,
 286 George
TILGHMAN THOS. E.,
 n.e.c. 7th and Mound

Colleges.
(*Commercial.*)
BACON'S COLLEGE, c. 6th and Walnut, J. H. Doty, Principal
BARTLETT R. M.,
 s.w.c., Walnut and 3d
GUNDEY JOHN,
 n.w.c. Walnut and 5th
Herold M., n.w.c. 4th & Race
NELSON'S COMMERCIAL COLLEGE, s.e.c. 4th and Vine, R'd Nelson, Principal

Comb Manuf.
CALVERT WM. H. & CO.
 67 W. Pearl
SHEPPARD J. W.,
 20 W. 4th

Commissioners of Deeds for Different States.
ABRAHAM J.,
 Bank bldg
APPLEGATE JOHN W.,
 s.w.c. 4th and Walnut
Burke Jos., 15 W. 3d
Bocking A. H., s.w.c. 4th and Walnut
CARPENTER S. S.,
 23 W. 3d
CHALLEN JAMES R.,
 s.e.c. 4th and Vine
DOUGLASS JOHN G.,
 n.e.c. 4th and Walnut
Jackson J. P. Masonic Temple
JOACHIM WM.
 22 w. Court
JONES TALBOT,
 Masonic Temple
LYNCH JNO. A.,
 17 W. 3d
M°DOUGAL JOS.,
 57 W. 3d
M°GUFFEY A. H.,
 120 Main
MILLER ISAAC J.,
 34 Bank bldg
Paul H. D. 25 W. 3d
SHEPPARD WM. B.,
 20 W. Court
STEARNS GEO. E.,
 148 Walnut
THIELMAN GEO. O.,
 9 W. Court
THOMPSON E. A.,
 23 W. 3d

Commissioners.
(*United States.*)
Bocking A. H., s.w.c. 4th and Walnut
DUTTON A. R.,
 Chase's bldg
FORCE MANNING F.
 Masonic Temple
Halliday Frankland, Custom House
HAGANS MARCEL. B.,
 148 Walnut
LEE GEO. M.,
 53 W. 3d
Paul H. D. 25 W. 3d

Commission, Produce & Forwarding Merchants.
ANDREW P. & CO.
 n.w.c. Kilgour & Front

Andrew Robt., 58 W. Front
ARNOLD & CRAWFORD,
 22 E. Canal
ATHEARN & SEDAM,
 5 E. Front
BABBITT, GOOD & CO.,
 18 & 19 Public Landing
Bailey M. & Co. s.w.c. Wal't
BAKER D. P. & CO., [& 2d
 s.e.c. Walnut and 2d
BAKER & CO.,
 29 Main
BANNING D. & CO.
 42 Walnut
Banning J. W. 32 Walnut
BARTLETT R. & CO.
 s.w.c. Walnut and Front
BEATTIE JOHN,
 51 and 53 W. Front
BENJAMIN & CO.,
 199 Walnut
BEATTY JAMES & CO.,
 s.w.c. Race and M. Canal
Bernard N. L., 29 W. M. Canal
BIGGS T. T. & CO.,
 s.w.c. Main and 2d
Bishop J. G. & J. W. 16 Main
BISHOP R. M. & CO.,
 36 Main
Bornstein L. 35 W. Front
Bowen Aaron S. 5 E. Front
BRASHEARS G. & LAWS,
 57 and 59 Main
BROWN H. W. & CO.,
 25 E. Front
BROWN JOSEPH R. & CO.
 27 Walnut
BROWN M. J.
 s.e.c. Main and 7th
BROWN E.
 s.e.c. Sycamore & Court
Brown, Stout & Butler, 44 Walnut
BUCHANAN R. & SON,
 26 E. 2d
BUCKINGHAM CHAS. J. & CO., 117 E. Pearl
BUCKINGHAM & MATHERS, 114 W. Court
BULLOCK D. & CO.,
 12 & 14 W. 2d
BURBECK & HAIGHT,
 107 E. Pearl
Butler S. & Co. 7 E. Front
BURCKHARDT & CO.,
 107 Sycamore
Byrne & Co., 63 W. Canal
CALKINS J. P. & CO.,
 21 Walnut
CANFIELD J. W. & CO.
 70 Walnut
Carpenter Daniel R. s.s. W.W. Canal b. Central Av. & John
Carpenter & Ford, 14 w. Front
Cecil & Clark, 19 E. Mi. Canal
CHAPIN, JONES & CO.
 33 Water and 17 Gilmore's Wharf
Cinnamon John, 40 Walnut
CHIPMAN W. DOUGLAS,
 s.s. W.W. Canal Basin
Christopher A. H. 20 W. Front
CLARK & CARR,
 29 Walnut
CLARK JOHN A. & CO.
 38 Vine
CLARK & ROGERS,
 28 and 30 E. 2d
CLARKE C. R.
 11 Walnut
Cleanay Joseph S. & Son, 42 Vine
Clenesy Wm. & Son, 51 Walnut
COBB, WILLIAMS & CO.
 35 Water and 18 Pub. Land
CODY P.,
 17 and 19 Water
Coffin D. H. B., 20 E. Pearl
Conklin W. H. & Co., 56 W. Front
Cooper R., 28 & 30 E. Pearl
Cooper S. S., 59 Walnut
Cooper & Stokes, 11 E. 4th
COPEN A. P.,
 90 Water
Coyle & Co. 25 Broadway
Crane James C. 3'6 Walnut
CRAWFORD GEO. & CO.,
 209 Walnut
CULLEN JAMES,
 46 Pub. Landing
CUNNINGHAM & BENNETT, 21 Public Landing
CUNNINGHAM JAMES F. & Co., 20 Public Landing
CUNNINGHAM & SON,
 231 Sycamore
DAVIS WM. W.
 40 W. Front
Daniel Hiram, 41 Vine
DAVIS GEO. F. & CO.,
 11 Sycamore

DEAN & HALE,
 19 and 21 Sycamore
Dell N. C. 218 Main
DICKINSON D. L.,
 51 W. Front
DILLS W. R.
 91 and 93 W. Miami Canal
DOMINICK GEO. & BRO.,
 25 and 27 Water
Dubois & Augur, 87 W. 2d
DUGAN HUGH,
 37 Walnut
DUGAN JOHN A. & CO.
 21 and 23 W. 2d
EGAN & SLOCOMB,
 73 W. Pearl
Eagleson D., 33 W. Canal
Ellis H. & J., 21 Water
Emerson N.W. & Co, 47 Walnut
FAGIN LEWIS,
 33 Look
FENTON S. & CO.
 38 Walnut
FEIGLRY & DAVIS,
 247. Walnut
FERRIS, DUNLEVY & FOWLER, 51 W. 2d
Fosdick C. R. 46 Walnut
FOULDS & WRIGHT,
 596 and 598 W. 5th
FOX THOMAS & WARDLOW, 2 E. Miami Canal
FRAZER JAS. A. & CO.
 66 and 68 Walnut
French, Wilson & Co., 27 E. Frnt
Gale John A. 80 W. Front
Gardiner & Magee, 20 Water
GATTI & ZANONE,
 80 Broadway
GEORGE D. B. & CO.,
 n.e.c. Pearl and Broadway
Gerard & Co., 44 E. Pearl
GERARD JOHN H. & CO.,
 207 Broadway
GIBSON D. & CO.,
 48 W. 2d
Gibson, Early & Co., 50 W. 2d
GILBERT, JONES & OGBORN, 595, 597 & 599 W. 5th
GILPIN W. T.
 17 E. Canal
GLENN WM. & SONS,
 70 and 72 Vine
GOEPPER M.,
 3 Court House
GOODHART J. H. & CO.,
 7 W. Front
GOULD GEO. W.,
 11 and 13 E. 9th
GRAFF J. & KOHL,
 25 E. 4th
Graham Wm. M. & Co., w.s. Main b Water and Front
Grawe & Hullman, 421 Race
GRAY WM. C.
 17 W. Front
Griese D., 3 Commercial Row
Griggs Louis, 80 Plum
Hafer & Daddy, 65 Walnut
Hale G. S., 21 W. Front
Hatley D. & Bros., 5 Water
Hammar & Dave, 52 Walnut
Hauks Richard, 32 Vine
HARPER D. & SON,
 38 Walnut
Harper & Wimall, 12 E. 2d
HARRISON & HOOPER,
 50 W. 2d
Harvey & Kemper, 18 Water
HATCH & HALL,
 36 Vine
Haughton & Reid, s.w.c. Canal and Sycamore
Hayes C. & Bro. 15 Walnut
Hazard W. S., 65 W. Canal
Hazlett John, 13 E. Front
Henness Bros., s.w.c. Canal and Vine
HINDE & PORTER,
 4 W. 2d
HIATT & WOODS,
 Deercreek n. of Court
HOBBS & PARKER,
 10 Main
HOLDEN R. A. & CO.,
 67 Vine
Hoppe D. & Co. 25 Walnut
HOLT WM.,
 88 E. Pearl
Hord Geo. M. & Co., 69 W. Front
Horner & Gall, 38 Main
HOSEA ROBT. & CO.,
 s.w.c. Front and Main
HUBBARD & HEATON,
 21 W. 5th
Hubbard & Worrell, 33 Walnut
Hughes & Reed, 37 Water
Hull Julius, 7 W. Canal
HURIN JAMES K.,
 577 and 579 W. 6th
HUSER E.,
 372 Main

Ireland Wm., 507 Central Av
JACOB C., Jr. & CO.
 50 Walnut
JENNINGS & BUTTERFIELD, n.w.c. Main and 6th
John Jas. C. 199 W. 5th
JOHNSON, BROOKS & CO.
 134 Vine
JOHNSON C. E. & CO.
 57 W. Pearl
Johnston Thomas, 93 Main
Jones John E., 105 W. 5th
Kauffman Julius, 22 W. Front
KECK & SHAFFER,
 9 and 11 E. Canal
Kemper Hugh F., 18 Water
Kennedy Hy. B. 31 Vine
KENNETT JOHN,
 14 Public Landing
King Geo. C. & Co., 273 Syca's
Kissick James, 217 Main
LABROT A.,
 6 W. Front
LANE GEO.,
 23 and 25 Canal
LANGLEY & KINKEAD,
 31 Water
LAWRENCE CHARLES,
 50 Main
LEHMER JAMES D.
 81 and 83 W. 2d
LOUDON JAS. A. & CO.
 30 Vine
Lukens P. & Co., s.w.c. Walnut and 2d
Lykins & Son, c. Main & Wtr
M°BIRNEY HUGH & CO.
 69 Vine
M°KEEHAN & EVANS,
 n.e.c. Sycamore and 9th
McLauchlin, Tomlinson & Co.,
 46 Walnut
MAGILL JAMES,
 152 W. Court
Manning S. & Co. 64 Walnut
MARMET C. & F.,
 305 Main
Marsh Richard, 23 W. Front
Marthen Albert W. 63 Walnut
Meal J. W. & Co., 12 & 14 Wal
MILLER BRUNING &
 DECKMAN, 33 Sycamore
Mills & King, 18 Main
MINOR & ANDREWS,
 s.e.c. Main and 2d
MITCHELL, ALLEMONG & CO., 13 Water
MITCHELL JOHN,
 30 Water
MITCHELL & LADD,
 357 and 359 Plum
Montgomery Henry J., 73 W. Pearl
MOORE CHAS. L. & CO.
 28 and 30 Main
MOORE ROBERT & CO.
 49 Walnut
MORRISON, CORDUKES & CO., 13 E. Canal
Morton James L. 70, 80 and 82 W. Front
NEFF WM. CLIFFORD,
 s.e.c. Vine and Canal
Newhall P. 39 Water
Nichols Vesper, 36 Walnut
NOURSE J. G.,
 31 Walnut
NYE HENRY,
 323 Broadway
OBERHUE E. & F.,
 112 W. Court
O'BORNE THOMAS G.,
 43 Walnut
Ogden A. H. & Co., 583 W. 5th
Owings John B., 27 W. 5th
PATRICK & GOULD,
 9 W. Front
PATTERSON, BRO. & CO.
 42 Vine
PAUL & MURDOCK,
 14 Water
PENNY C.,
 27 Vine
Pepper W. T., 11 Water
PERIN GOULD & CO.,
 88 W. Front
Phillips Geo. W. jr. 4 College Hall
PHIPPS, GARDNER & CO.
 n.w.c. 9th and Broadway
PIERCE JAMES,
 118 and 120 W. 3d
POAGE T. K. & CO.,
 Poland & Henry, 60 w. 2d
Poor & Co., 225 Walnut
POTTER F. & WILSON,
 98 E. 2d
Powell Wm. jr. 102 Sycamore
RAWSON, WILBY & CO.,
 3 W. Front

CINCINNATI

REEME, WALLINGFORD & Co., 23 Vine
Richardson, Wilson & Hale, 22 Water
Robbins John I., 25 W. Front
Rocap & Farrelly, 221 Sycam're
Roots & Coo, n.s. W, W.Canal Basin b. Cent. Av, & John
ROSS & CO., 33 Sycamore
ROWLAND CHAS. W. 46 W. 2d
Sackett W. A., 170 Water
SARGENT L. H., 31 Walnut
SAYRE LEONARD, 231 Walnut
Schwill Ferd'inand,64 Sycamore
SECRIST J. M., 21 and 23 w. Front
Shays John W., 346 Walnut
Shunard John II, 10 E. 2d
SIEBERN J. N. & BROS., 8 E. Pearl
SKIFF J. A., 16 W. Front
SKINNER FRANK & CO., 85 W. 2d
SMITH & McALPIN, 62 Walnut
Smith S. W. & Co., 29 Water
SMITH WM. C., 22 E. 8th
SOMMER & MEYER, 36 E. Pearl
SPEYER B., 7 and 9 W. 3d
Spencer W. M. & Co. 19 W. Front
SPINING & DROWN, 49 W. 2d
Spining P. A. 25 W. 2d
SPRINGER & WHITEMAN, 16 and 18 W. 2d
STANFORD & BICKNELL 21 Broadway
Stephens S. D. 39 Mill
STEWART, CARMICHAEL & Co., n.e.c. Front and Wood,
Stiles H. L. & Co., 53 Walnut
STONE B. T. & CO., 18 E. 2d
STONE L. & M., 31 Vine
STRAIGHT, DEMING & Co., n.e.c. Vine and 2d
SWASEY JOHN & CO., 23, 25 and 27 Sycamore
SWASEY M., s.w.c. 2d and Broadway
Sweny M. & Co. 14 Main
Swift R. E. C. & Co., s.w.c. Walnut and Water
SWIFT, EVANS & CO., n.w.c. 9th and Sycamore
TAYLOR & BRO., 45 Walnut
Taylor Enoch, 3 E. Front
THAYER & TAYLOR, 9 Water
THOMAS N. W. & CO., s.w.c. Canal & Walnut
TIBBITTS HY. & SON, n.e.c. 6th and Baymiller
TORRENCE JAMES F., 67 and 69 W. Canal
TRABER & AUBERY, 7 Public Landing
TRENCHARD E. P. s.w.c. Walnut and 2d
TWEED & SIBLEY, 40 Walnut
VAN PELT, M. C., 361 Walnut
Watson L. D. & Bro. 9 Main
Warner C. K., 287 w. 4th
WESENER C., 1 Walnut
WELLS & MILES, 21 w. Pearl
WERNER & GOETTHEIM 587 and 590 Main
Wert Wm. W. 151 Main
White Fran M. 20 E. Canal
WILLIAMSON WM., 21 E. 2d
WILSON, HICKS & KINSEY, 39 Walnut
WILSON, EGGLESTON & CO., 21 W. Canal
WOOD ADOLPH & CO., 31 W. Canal
WRIGHT A. G. & CO., n.s. 6th nr. Main
Wright Sylvanus, 20 W. Front

Confectioners.

Arath Rosa, 57 Broadway
Arseno Joseph, 60 W. 5th
AUSTIN & SMITH, 8 E. Second

Bacciocco Jos. C. 4th & Elm
Bacciocco S., 176 W. 5th
Balle Geo. 637 Vine
Barnet James, 60 Mound
Becker August, 412 W. 5th
Behar J., 368 Central Av
Boehm Wm., 417 Vine
Bogelt H., 46 E. 6th
Bolley Alexander, n.s. 6th b. Jane and Baymiller
Boomer John, 461 W. 5th
Boro'r & Bro., n.e.c. 3d and Elm
Bosch John, 302 W. 8th
Brizzolara Chas., n.e.c. Race and Front
Brizzolara Jno., 28 E. 4th
Brueck Charles, 522 Main
Carbin Wm., s.e.c. 8th and Walnut
Carroll Mrs. J., 97 Central Av
Cassady & Glass, 26 Vine
Chiappe Andrew, 5 E. Front
Chicsa John, n.w.c. Race and 9th
Clayton Mrs. M., 325 W. 9th w. of Central Av
Colona John, 154 Sycamore
Conie Jos., 19 Broadway
CORBETT MICHAEL, 210 Sycamore
Cornelius Mrs. R. A. 234 Elm
Davis Mrs. E. s.e.c. Findlay and Baymiller
Day & Bro., 209 Walnut
DEMAND MATTHIAS, 207 Main
Devoto A. & Co., 6 W. 5th
Dondoros G. 93 W. 5th
Dryer Jas., 172 W. 5th
Elsenheimer John J. 409 Vine
Englehard J., 265 Main
Finley William, 89 Sycamore
Fischer Wm., s.e.c. 6th and Walnut
Fricke Fred. 235 Sycamore
Gandolfo Peter, n.w.c. 5th and Broadway
Ginochio D. & Co., 23 Broad'y
GATII & ZANONE, 80 Broadway
Gatti John B. & Bro, 122 W. 3d
Gazole Peter, 26 Pub. Landing
Gazole James, 45 Pub. Landing
Gazole Anthony, 56½ Broad'y
Ghio A. J. 136 Vine
Ghiardelli Jerome, s.w.c. Pike and 3d
Ginochio Ang. 210 Vine
Ginochio D., 28 E. 5th
Ginochio Lewis, n.w.c. Broad way and 6th
Grillo Joseph J. 232 W. 5th
Grundhoefer Charles, 630 Vine
Hebern Catharine, 221 Central Av
Helmig Henry, 1260 E. Front
Henry Jacob, 479 Main
Herberding Frank, s.w.c. 9th and Walnut
Hogbin Thomas, 210 Central Av
Hughes Eliza M, 225 Cen'l Av
Jonas Henry W., 50 E. 4th
Kaufman & Fernich, 26 W.6th
Kennealy Patrick, 122 Central Av
Keppler Geo., 273 W. 4th
Kifel Charles, 52 Sycamore
King Lewis, s.e.c. 4th and Sycamore
Kochman Jos, L. 79 Sycamore
Kocks Henry, 322 Central Av
Landt Mrs. Bell, 207 Walnut
Latiner G. A., 282 Walnut
Lewis John I., 24 Broadway
Littlefield Henry, 383½ W. 5th
Livellari J. B., 70 W. 3d
Longinotte J. B. & Bro., 216 W. 6th
Longshore John, 73 12th
Lorch Alex., 111 W. 6th
Louderback M. C., s.e.c. 8th and Baymiller
Luthy Samuel, 508 Walnut
Mcffale Martin, e.s. Walnut b. 5th and 6th
MANGOLD SIMON, 577 Central Av
Massa Nicholas, 216 W. 6th
Mayleben & Butterfass, 2 Walnut
Morrall John, s.w.c. 9th and Elm
MORRIS NICHOLAS, 264 Race
Morris Samuel, 197 Cent'l Av
MYERS C. & CO., 85 Main
Niven Wm. n.w.c. Elm and Clarkson
O'Bride Anna, 302 W. 6th
O'Brien Charles, 168 W. 5th
Ohmer Geo. L. M. R. R. Depot

Ohmer John P. 782 E. Front
O'Nell W.P.n.e.c. 6th & John
Oneto Joseph, 130 Vine
Ott William, 372 Vine
Pabla John, 33 Broadway
Pape Bernard, 603 Walnut
Pardee W., W. 29 E. 4th
Parr James, 317 W. 6th
Peirano Antonio, 403 Main
Pernice John. n.e.c. Race and 8th
Pistor Charles, 80 W. 6th
Podesta A. & Co. 130 Walnut
Podesta James, 301 Central Av
Podesta John, s.w.c. Main and Canal
Podesta L., c. Cen'l Av & 4th
Pollard James, 227 Sycamore
Raabe Philip, 529 Main
Ransley James, 259 W. 8th
Rittweger Phillip, 282 Cent'l Av
Rivy Antonio, 316 W. 5th
Ruppert Joseph, 242½ Vine
Safd L., 91 Sycamore
Schemerl Antonio, 320 w. 5th
Schmidt Ferd., c. 6th and Race
Schneider George, 434 Vine
Schwegman F., 361 Main
Sciutti M., 130 W. 4th
Seits Louis, 293 Main
Sielscheit Barney, 200 Sycam're
Simon Samuel, s.w.c. George and Central Av
Smith Daniel J, 320 W. 6th
Snyder Peter, 306 W. 5th
Solari Andrew, 185 Race
Solari Augustus, n.w.c. Smith and 3d
Stapleton Wm. 221 Walnut
Stone Wm., 455 W. 5th
Stookey Dr. Isaac, 36 E. 3d
Sturllu B., s.e.c. Court & Elm
Talbort Nancy, 610 W. 6th
Thenaus Peter, 301 W. 6th
Tomasaini Charles, c. George & Linn
VONDERHEIDE HERM'N 12 Sycamore
Ward Levi, 10 W. 8th
Webry Henry, 51 13th
Weil I., 202 Elm
Weizenaker Fred. 357 Vine
Willmott George, s.e.c. 9th and Plum
Witz Henry, 315 Central Av
Wittenburg R. n.w.c. Hopkins and Cutter
Wittman Nich. A, 485 Vine
Zanone Jos. c. 7th and Central Avenue

Coopers.

Baird Wm., 39 Bremen
Beck Adolph, w.s. Pleasant b. 12th and 14th
Behner Henry, 692 Main
Bunder George, Oehler al. b. Freeman and Garrard
Benus C., Schilier nr. Main
Best Adam., 277 Ham. Road
Buehl John & Anthony, n.s. Liberty b. Main and Sycamore
Boerger Francis, 635 Race
Bowes John, 105 W. Canal
Bricks G. 2·8 Pleasant
Brockmann Il., 531 Pleasant
Bross Paul, rear 413 Sycamore
BUCKTON ABRAHAM, 93 Vine
Butler Thomas, 44 E. 2d
Butts James, 218 W. Liberty
Clansheide Henry, 75 Buckeye
Cole Wm. A. 15 E. 2d
Conkling, Young & Co. 20 Spring
COPEN ALFRED P. 90 Water
Coughlin D., 41 Lock n. of 8th
Dagen J., s. s. Poplar w. of Freeman
Debus L., 167 W. 2nd
Dieringer Celestin, Pleasant b. Findlay and Henry
Dorsch, Turner & Co. s.s. Dayton b. Freeman and West'n Av
Fey William, n.s. Bank b. Central Av. and Clarkson
Fox & Baker, 474 Elm
Fox Charles, 109 Browne
Fries Michael, c.s. Brighton b. Harrison Pike and Bernard
Fritch A., 511 Sycamore
Guild George, n.s. Mi. Canal b. Main and Walnut
Guinthal Henry, 634 Main
Hemmelkalk H., 380 Sycamore
Hoberg H., e. Wade & Cutter
Hoffmann & Krode, 30 Webster
Hormann Wm. 179 Baymiller

Houck George, rear 29 Bernard
Jacobs Peter, c. Clark & Kossuth
Jacob P. & Co. s.w.c. Cutter and Clinton
Jonte & Bro., 158 Poplar
JONTE PETER N., 484 Race
Jungling Wm. n.s. Brighton b. Harrison Pike and Bernhard
Kemp r H. D., 563 Walnut
Knost Frederick, n.s. al. b. Race and Ham. Road
Koch Frederick, 2 Peete
Kollmeier F., 695 Main
Koors B. H. 543 W. 3d
Laumann John, 20 Peete
Lotters Lawrence, rear 29 Hughes
Meyers Wm., 134 Wade
Oelschleger Henry, s.s. Orchard U. Main and Sycamore
Oker August, s.s. Charlotte b. Central Av. and Linn
Post J. B. 235 Clark
Propheter J. & A., 639 Race
Pues Wm. 55 Buckeye
Rahe Henry, jr., 61 Bremen
Renworth James, n.s. Pearl b. Central Av. and Plum
Rentepohler Chr's., Gest, b. Freeman and Carr
Richards John, 113 E. 8th
Schmidt Mich., 67 Providence
Schmitt George, n.s. Bank b. Central Av. and Clarkson
Schneider Jacob, 581 Walnut
Schreiber Ben. w.s. Sycamore b. Franklin and Webster
Schriber Joseph, 422 W. Lib'ty
Schroer B, 216 Clark
Schwab Daniel, w.s. Lawrence b. 2d and Pearl
Schwers Henry, 33 Bremen
Seeren August, 9 Orchard
Seufferle Christian, Livingston b. Linn and Baymiller
Seuffenlah Andrew, c. end of Mohawk
Shire Henry, w.s. Cin. Av. b. Findlay and Charlotte
Steinkamp Fred. 586 Walnut
Stonebraker John, e.s. Plum b. Elder and Findlay
Strichtmann H. & F. 156 Clay Templeton N. J., w.s. Culvert b. 6th and 7th
Thomas Henry, 94 Water
Uhlenbacke Wm. 20 Buckeye
Vatter Hy, Charlotte, b. Linn and Baymiller
Volk Rudolph, n.s. Bernhard b. Division and Brighton
Wehmier Christian, e.s. Western Av. b. Bauk and Harrison Pike
Wessel Hy, s.s. Court, b. Main and Sycamore
Wiemann Rudolph, 19 Adams
White Thomas. 153 Cutter

Coppersmiths.

Berg August, 134 W. Court
Britt Peter, 42 Pub. Landing
DECKEBACH F. C. & CO., 171 W. Court
Horrocks J. R. & Son, 6 Com Row
Kiersted & Hoffman, 89 E. Frnt
Lape W. H. & Co., 1 E. Frnt
Musnch Geo. & Co., 644 Vine
Robson W. & G. W., 156 and 158 E. Front
SHADDINGER GEO. A., 123 & 125 E. Pearl
Vanduzen C. D., 9 E. Front

Cordage.

(See Ropes and Cordage.)

Corks and Corkwood

FISCHER & FEINTHEL, 34 W. Court

Corn Mills.

(See Mills.)

Costumer's Fancy.

BECK WILLIAM, 208 W. 5th
Vanhorn A. R., 216 W. 5th

Cotton.

(Dealers In.)

CUMMINGS & JONES, 81 and 83 W. 2d
MOORE ROBT., 49 Walnut

BUSINESS MIRROR.   361

ite Geo. F., 55 W. 7th
sz Phillip, 143 Ham. Road
AMLEN & SMITH,
  2 W. 4th
ARDY J. C.,
  87 W. 7th
rt Wm. M. 97 W. 7th
adrick L. A. jr., 56 W. 5th
UNTER W. M.,
  296 Vine
kson Gamaliel, 131 W.4th
nes C. H., 97 W. 7th
NOWLTON P.
  136 W. 4th
ufer M., 24 W. 6th
reus A., 151 W. 6th
redish P., 132 W. 6th
SMOND EDMUND,
  272 Vine
en Jesse, 154 W. 6th
chardson Joseph, 121 W. 7th
OGERS M.
  170 Race
tton Charles, 114 W. 6th
HMIDT SCHALLER H.,
  335 Vine
MITH HENRY A.
  118 W. 6th
AFT JONATHAN,
  56 W. 4th
AYLOR & IRVIN,
  171 Race
for E. E. 22 College
ARDLE SAMUEL,
  97 W. 7th
ills M, 97 W. 7th
HEELER BENJ. D.,
  93 W. 7th
ICKERSHAM O. J.
  342 W. 5th
INSLOW H. S.,
  102 Broadway
odward W. W, 114 W. 6th

esigning and Perspective Drawing.
ard James C., Carlisle bldg.
gart John H. 25 W. 4th
nes T., s.e.c. 4th & Walnut
ble W. P., c. 4th & Walnut
ggoner Wm. W., 56 W. 6th

etective Police Agency.
iffin J. L. & Co. 4 Bank bld

Dining Saloons.
ee *Restaurants and Eating Houses*).

Distillers.
OYLE & CO.,
  53 E. 2d
OON GEO. & CO.
  n.e.c. Riddle and Bank
wis T. D., w.s. Western Av
  b. Bank and Harrison Rd
xter E. & Sons, 49 Sycamore
LETCHER L. HOBART &
  CO., s.e.c. Front & Vine
EYKER F. & M.
  n.e.c. Clinton and Cutter
OOTE, NASH & CO.,
  c. Pearl & Kilgour
IBSON D. & CO.,
  48 W. 2d
EVI S. & BROS.,
  221 and 223 Walnut
itmer & Austing, Pearl, b.
  Kilgour and Canal
OIR, SOLOMON &
  MORN, 159 W. 3d
oner V. J., 119 E. 5th
oore & Pfeffer, Harrison Rd
ueen City Distillery, Ham.
  Road nr. Brighton House
IKE S. N. & CO.,
  18 Sycamore
MITH A. H. & Co.
  w.s. Colerain Pk. n. of
  Brighton House

Dress Makers.
See also *Millinery and Dress Making, &c.*)
ain Adelia, 171 W. 3d
rent Elizabeth, 179 Smith
ade Pruline, 214 Longworth
alvert Hannah J., 22 McFarland
arman Julia, 31 W. 8th
hild Mrs. S. D., 347 W. 7th
row Emily P., 83½ George
aily Margaret, 222 W. 5th
urham Elizabeth, 274 Elm
uvorney Antoinette, 203 Elm
olger Mary A., 238 Cutter
alvorsen Mary, 102 W. 5th
ardy Mrs. B. B., 350 W. 8th
rving Mrs. J. T., 164 W. 6th
ones Amandia M., 548 Sycamore

Kenneally Mrs. M. E. 112 W. 4th
Kinnan Mrs. William, 171 Sycamore
Kysor Mary, 51 W. 7th
Lyon Sarah J., 325 W. 4th
McDermott J. R., 167 Race
McKinsey Mary A., 180 Smith
Minier Melicent, n.e.c. 5th and Park
O'Dowd Miss B., 444 W. 5th
Perry Mary J., 31 W. 7th
Poppino Mary Jane, 406 W.5th
Rice Maria J., 188 W. 5th
Shields Kate, 316 W. 5th
Snyder Mrs. E., 156 W. 4th
Trimble Julia A., 9 Walnut
Vauzile Almira P., n.w.c. Elm and 5th, up stairs
Watson Sarah, 332 W. 5th
Watts Nancy, 5 North
Weaver Kate, 158 W. 6th
Young Emma L., 19 Longworth
Zimmermann Catharine, 259 Ham. Road

Druggists.
(*Wholesale.*)
ALLEN & CO.,
  s.w.c. Main and 5th
BURDSALL & BROTHER
  n.w.c. Main and Front
DAVIDSON WM. F.
  n.e.c. 5th and Main
Greene C. B., 24 E. Pearl
GORDON W. J. M. & BRO,
  b. e.c. Central Av & 8th
HARRISON WM. H. & CO
  23 W. 4th
Keeshan John, n.w.c. 6th and Walnut
MACREADY ROBERT,
  58 and 60 Walnut
MERRELL WM. S. & CO.,
  110 W. 3d
REAKIRT J. & C.,
  52 W. 2d
SCANLAN E. & CO.,
  n.e.c. 4th and Main
SUIRE, ECKSTEIN & CO.,
  n.w.c. 4th and Vine
Williamson & Hatfield, 41 Walnut

Druggists and Apothecaries.
ADDERLY W. H.,
  n.e.c. 6th and Mound
Alexander S., 1015 Cen'l Av
Armstrong J. L., s.w.c. 7th and Broadway
Bakhaus Chas, c. 7th and Main
Beal R. & Co. u.e.c. Freeman and Everett
Bennett D. M., 435 Cen'l Av
BODE C. H.,
  n.w.c. Linn & Hopkins
Boettcher W., s.w.c. Vine and Findlay
Brand F. W., 525 Race
Brown John M., n.w.c. Walnut and 4th
Burdsal Sam., 400 Main
Castle E. I., n.e.c. Linn and Clinton
Coolidge Wm. H. n.e.c. Pearl and Sycamore
COOPER J. M.,
  s.w.c. Cutter and Court
CROWTHER E. W.,
  334 w. 7th, and s.w.c. 6th and Central Av
CROWTHER F. A. & BRO.,
  n.w.c. Baymiller & Richmond
DAVIDSON WM. F.
  n.e.c. 5th and Main
Debolt Joseph H., 1216 E. Front
EBERLE CHAS.,
  s.e.c. 5th and Central Av
Eckel Herman, 128 Ham. Road
EMERSON E. S.,
  s.e.c. Pearl and Broadway
Emrick D. L., n.w.c. John and Clinton
ENSLIN A.
  590 Main
FAHRENHOLTZ WM.
  n.e.c. Baymiller and York
Fennel Adolph, 444 Sycamore
FRITSCU HENRY,
  n.w.c. Freeman and Cent
Gerhard J. C., n.w.c. Clinton and Cutter
Glenny Wm., 383 Central Av
GORDON W.J.M. & BRO.,
  s.e.c. 8th & Central Av
Greene Caleb D., 24 E. Pearl
GREVE T. L. A.,
  s.e.c. 6th and John
Griffith S. A., 51 Broadway

GRONEWEG LOUIS,
  s.w.c. Court and Walnut
Haulin Wm., n.w.c. Front and Elm
Hayden S. L. 6th and Freeman
Heermance H., 983 E. Front
HEUN EDWARD,
  s.w.c. 5th and Vine
HEINEMANN O.,
  c. Linn and Laurel
HELMAN CHAS. M.,
  n.w.c. Findlay and Baymiller
HILL A. C.
  s.w.c. 3d and Smith
HILL H. H. & CO.
  s.e.c. 5th and Race
HILLERG A.,
  76 Broadway
HOEVELER JOS.,
  n.e.c. 6th and Central Av
Huebner A., 497 Elm
JOHNSTON & FOERTMEYER, n.e.c. Elm & 6th
Karrmann Wm., 5th & Smith
Keeshan John, 6th & Walnut
Kinsbach P., 515 Vine
Koerlitz Emil, c. Green & Vine
LANGENBECK A.,
  490 Main
LIPPERT O.
  915 Central Av
MERRELL H. M. & CO.,
  u.w.c. Court and Plum
Muhlberg W., c. Wade and Central Av
PARR J. C.,
  554 W. 5th
Parvin D. A., c. Front and 2d
PAULSEN AUGUSTUS,
  n.e.c. 8th and Vine
REES GRIFFITH,
  n.w.c. 7th and Linn
Renz T., s.s. Harrison Pike b. Riddle and Division
Reum Herman, 377 John
Reum H. F. s.e.c. 5th and Broadway
REINLEIN PAUL,
  171 Freeman
ROBINSON J. M.
  s.w.c. Everett and Cent'l Av
Roerig August, jr., 579 Race
ROSS ALBERT,
  s.w.c. Cent'l. Av. and 8th
Runkle C. F., 453 W. 5th, and n.e.c. 8th and Walnut
Runkle Wm. H., n.w.c. W. Court and Mound
Rutenick Albert, c. Bremen and Liberty
Salpius August, 440 Walnut
Sander August, n.s. Front w, of Hill
SCANLAN E. & CO.,
  152 Main
Schaefer F. 504 Walnut
Schmidt Chas., 632 Main
Scott John, n.w.c. 7th and Broadway
SHUESLER & CHAPMAN,
  s.w.c. 6th and Vine
SINGHOFF JOHN A.
  c. George & Baymiller
SNYDER WILLIAM,
  n.w.c. 4th and Race
Spach Gustav, 491 Vine
SPAMER HENRY,
  408 Vine
STIEFLE ADOLPH,
  652 Race
SUIRE, ECKSTEIN & CO.,
  n.w.c. 4th and Vine
Stone Louis P., s.v.c. Front and Waldon
Tafel & Vogeler, n.s.c. 6th and Main
Tilly William, s.w.c. Abigail and Spring
Tower E. C., c. 5th and Mill
VILTER CHAS.,
  s.e.c. Race and 2d
Vonwyck Amaldi, 923 Central Avenue
Waffenschmidt Henry, s.e.c. Elm and 12th
WAGNER A.,
  512 Main
WELLS J. D. & CO.
  n.w.c. 4th and Cent'l Av
White John P., c. Race & Frnt
WHITTEMORE J. R.,
  51 Broadway
WILSON ISRAEL,
  337 Main

Druggists Label Gilders
Overdick H. & C., 17 Home
Scott W. D. 119 Main

362　CINCINNATI

Drug Mills.

MERRELL WM. S. & CO., 110 W. 3d
Overdick H. & C., 17 Home
SHROYER JAS. C., 164 w. 2d

Drum Manufacturer.

Gleieh Bolser, 61 Clay

Dry Dock.

MARINE RAILWAY & DRY DOCK CO., s.s. Front b. Rice and Walnut, 17th Ward
Freeman Samuel Canal above Ham. Road

Dry Goods.
(*Wholesale.*)

ACKERLAND ABRAH'M 66 W. Pearl
ACTON & WOODNUTT. 103 W. Pearl
ALEXANDER, BRENNAN & Co., 129 Main
AMBURGH & BROS. 65 W. Pearl
ANTRAM M. T. & CO. 47 W. Pearl
BOHM, MACK & CO., 30 W. Pearl
Chambers C. C. & W., 53 E. Pearl
CHAMBERS STEVENS & Co., 23 W. Pearl
COHEN, GUITERMAN & Co 82 W. Pearl
CRAWFORD JOHN, 76 W. 5th
DELAND & GOSSAGE, 74 and 76 W. 4th
DEVOU & CO. 83 and 85 W. Pearl
ELLIS, McALPIN & CO., 108 W. Pearl
FECHHEIMER MARCUS, 84 W. Pearl
Guiterman & Sulsbasher, 60 W. Pearl
HAMMETT & CHESELDINE, s.e.c. Pearl & Main
HAYNES, LEWIS & SPENCER, 130 Walnut
HEIDELBACH, SEASONGOOD & CO., s.w.c. 3d & Vine
HEIDELBACH, WERTHEIMER & CO., 86 W. Pearl
HEINSHEIMER J. H. & CO., 123 Walnut
JONES BROS. & CO., 19 W. Pearl
KORNBLITH J. & CO. 70W. Pearl
KUHN; NETTER & CO., n.e.c. 3d and Vine
Leopold & Goodheart, 74 W. Pearl
Lockard & Ireland, 88 and 90 W. Pearl
Loewensteine J. H. & Bros. 50 W. Pearl
MACK & BROS., 78 W. Pearl
MARKS HENRY & CO.; 12 W. Pearl
MILLS & WOODRUFF, 1 and 3 W. Pearl
MORITZ BROS. & CO. 26 W. Pearl
RAUH BROS. 58 W. Pearl
Richardson J. C., 95 & 97 Main
Ritchie C. & J., 67 E. Pearl
RINDSKOPF, BROS. & CO., 79 W. Pearl
Schroeder B., 126 Main
SHAW, BALBOUR & CO. 81 W. Pearl
SHILLITO JOHN & CO., 101, 103 and 105 W. 4th
SHIPLEY MURRAY & CO., 94 W. Pearl
SIMON B. & CO., n.e.c. Main and Pearl
SLEVIN J. & J., 116 Main
STADLER, BRO. & CO., 106 W. Pearl and 117 W. 3d
STEDMAN, CARLISLE & SHAW, 17 W. Pearl
STIX, KROUSE & CO. 61 W. Pearl
TROUNSTINE A. & J. s.e.c. Vine and Pearl
Wentworth & Hanley, 87 W. Pearl
WHITE & ANTRAM, 47 W. Pearl

WINSTON & JOHNSON, 113 W. Pearl
WOLF A. & I. & CO., 76 Main
WOLFF CHAS. H. & CO., 145 and 147 Walnut
WRIGHT, DALTON & CO., 95 and 97 Main
WYNNE, HAYNES & CO., 101 W. Pearl
WYNNE J. E. & CO., 91 W. Pearl
Zeller & Friedman, 72 W. Prl

Dry Goods.
(*Retail.*)

ALMS H. A., 571 Vine
Assur A., 120 W. 5th
Aszmann H. F., 363 Cen'l Av
Betty Wm., 100 W. 5th
Bollmer John H., 517 Race
Borcherding Wm., 143 Everett
Brechtner Casper, 1064 Central Av
Brockhof John A. 121 Hopkins
Buddemeyer & Ummethan, 307 Central Avenue
Burtanger A., 48 Elder
Busch M., 400 Broadway
Busken J. H. & Bro., 236 W. 6th
Chambers C. C. & W., 53 E. Pearl
Cobb Mrs Nancy, 515 W. 5th
Cohrs H. F., 501 Vine
COHEN SIMON M. 130 W. 5th
CRAWFORD JOHN, 76 W. 5th
DALTON JAMES, 146 W. 5th
DELAND & GOSSAGE, 74 W. 4th
Donzelman H., 31 Ham. Rd
Dopke Fred., 92 Martin
Downard Mary A., 154 W. 4th
DRAKE SAMUEL C., 449 w. 5th
DUHME H. H., 74 W. 5th
Duwelius H. H., 375 Elm
Eaton Jane, 136 Dayton
Eggers George, 158 Baymiller
EVESLAGE JOSEPH, 472 Main
Feldman John W., 644 Race
Feltman H., 29 Green
Feldman Wm., 585 Race
Fihe John, 610 Central Av
Fletcher Simon, 196 w. 5th
Fischer Julius, 77 E. Pearl
Fisher F. C., 131 Carr
Focks John A., 571 Main
Freking B., 450 W. 2d
Frieling B., 248 W. 6th
Gibson G. & J., 3 w. 5th
GOHS E. & CO., 478 and 480 Main
Greeble Mrs. & Bro., 391 Central Av
Guilford Mrs. J., 303 W. 5th
HAMBURGER JACOB, n.w.c. Race and Elder
HAMMETT & CHESELDINE, s.e.c. Main & Pearl
Hatke Geo., 104 13th
Hoers F. H., 480 Walnut
Hoffman Wm., 213 W. Front
HOPKINS L. C. & CO., n.e.c. Vine and 5th
Jannings Mary, 139 Laurel
Kammann H. W., 499 Vine
Kirkland John A., 58 W. 5th
KNABE ALBERT, n.e.c. Race and Liberty
Kroger John H., 548 Cen'l Av
Krumberg Theodore, 399 Main
KRUSE J. F. & H. s.w.c. Race and Elder
Kunst Beni., 213 Linn
LEBOUTTILLIER & BROS. 30 W. 4th
Liebmann Anthony, s.e.c. Elm and Elder
Lindemann Hy. 531 Main
Lullmann Mrs. R., 22 13th
McComas, M. P., 575 Cen'l Av
McDonald William, 236 w. 6th
McGregor Elizabeth, 116 Loek
Mann John H. 2W W. 5th
Mantel Henry, 701 W. 6th
Marks Liepman, 189 Main
MARSHALL & BROS., 56 w. 5th
Menke & Schnite, 91 W. Court
Mentel H., 313 Freeman
Metz M. & L., 50 w. 5th
Miller J. N., 300 W. 5th
MILLS JOHN & CO., 303 Central Av
Moller Joseph, 101 Woodward
Monnig Fred., 81 Spring

Moorman B. H., 496 Main
Morgan Mrs. Sarah, 537 Freeman
Muhle B. H., 369 George
Niehoff J. P., 373 W. 5th
NORRIS RICHARD D., 174 W. 5th
O'Connell Daul., 234 Water
Oeh C., 281 Ham. Rd
Oesper Peter, 36 Ham. Road
O'Reilly Brothers, 112 W. 5th
Pfefer Henry, 1009 Central Av
Phillip B., 41 Freeman
Ploehg Anton, 513 Main
Pogue & Jones, 128 W. 5th
REGAN M., 90 W. 5th
Ridimann John, 475 Vine
Rintz Sebastian, 463 W. 5th
Ritchie C. & J. 65 & 67 E. Pearl
Roebling H. C. P., 69 and 71 E. Pearl
Rottger F. H., 567 Main
Rosenstiel Lewis S., 108 W. 5th
RUSCHE J. H., 639 Vine
Salter E. P., 263 Main
Sanders Lucy, s.e.c. Sycamore and Liberty
Schneider Mrs. Frederieka, 441 Sycamore
Schwartz & Hafner, 434 Main
Schwartz Isaac, 505 Vine
SHILLITO JOHN & CO., 101, 103 and 105 W. 4th
Schuetterle M., 524 Race
Sicking Henry, 26 Green and 80 Bank
SMITH JOHN A., 22 W. 5th
Steinkamp Theodore, 488 Main
Stewart Mrs. Cath., 230 W. 6th
Stiene Dederick, n.s. 13th 1 Walnut and Clay
Strasburger & Bro., 202 w. 5th
Strehly Jno., 611 Central Av
Strotman G. & H., 95 W. Court
Stuckenberg H. H., 599 Central Avenue
Theissen H. Aug., 205 Linn
Tolbert M., 31 E. Pearl
Trum Bernard, 77 W. Court
Vancliff Henry, 58 Elder
Vieman Henry, 143 Henry
Vogt George H., 97 w. Court
VORNHOLT J. F., 315 Main
Waldron C. S., n.w.c. Everett and 'entral Av
Walker J. H. & S., 20 W. 5th
Weatherby C. S., 110 W. 5th
Weeks Eliza H., w.s. Broadway Burt and Pearl
Wellman H. B., 132 W. 5th
Wellman Lewis, 424 Freeman
Weiler Wm., 178 w. 5th
Weizgnecker A., 338 Vine
Westjohn Mrs. T., 310 W. 5th
Williams J. D., 33 E. Pearl
Williams Mrs. S., 44 Freeman
Wilson Martha, 451 w. 8th
Wiltsee Mrs. C., 336 W. 6th
Wisseling H. Junction & Front Pearl and Broadway
Wright Arthur W., n.w. Pearl and Broadway
Wright R., 397 Central Av

Dyers.

Cortis Thomas, 214 Elm
Doeller A., 18 11th w. of Carr
Gibbs H., & Co, 212 Plum
Harris Mrs. E., 374 W. 5th
HARMEIER JOHN, 218 Walnut
Harmeyer John F., 10 Woodward
Hesselbach Fred., 44 12th
Jobe Mrs. H., 134 W. 6th
Kampe F., 109 W. 3d
Kinkel Dan. 103 E. 3d
Kuhlmann Geo., 44 E. 6th and 142 W. 6th
Peel & Son, 274 Walnut
Piton Anthony, 96 13th
Short Mrs. B., 156 W. 4th
Teasdale Wm., 235 Walnut
Trefzger A., 489 Main
Wahlers C., 28 14th
WALKER ROBERT, 65 E. 3d
Weitzel Henry, 6 W. 9th

Eating Houses.

BESUDEN HERMAN, 50 E. Pearl
Bracken Wm., 8 Landing b Broadway and Ludlow
BUCKEYE DINING S LOON, 170 Vine
Carothers John S., 23 E. Pearl
Conner J. Q. A., 197 Vine

BUSINESS MIRROR. 363

tson J. C. & Co., 28 E. 3d
one Abram, 69 Sycamore
ylor A. G., 37 E. 3d
ylor F. P., 15 Hammond
dor John M., 113 Walnut
OTTLE E. W. & CO.,
 n.w.c. 3d and Sycamore
aver J. J., jr., 354 W. 5th
WIGHTMAN A. F.,
 16 E. 3d

Exchange Dealers.
(Foreign.)
DAE C. F. & CO.,
 s.w.c. 3d and Main
rry Wm. B. & Co.; 76 W.
 3d,
PEYER BENNO,
 7 and 9 W. 3d
IGGERS & CO.,
 170 Main
ALLIS, YOUNG & CO.,
 s.w.c. 3d and Main
ILMORE, DUNLAP & CO.
 Masonic Temple
OMANS & CO.,
 13 W. 3d
ELINE J. F.;
 Shorts's bldg

Eye Infirmaries.
arens A., 151 W. 6th
OTTER J. F.,
 36 W. 4th
VALDO FRED. A., M. D.,
 s.w.c. 4th and Sycamore
VILLIAMS E.,
 163 Race

Express Companies.
DAMS EXPRESS CO.,
 67 W. 4th
MERICAN EX. CO.,
 92 W. 4th
UROPEAN & AMERICAN
 Ex. Co., 5 W. 3d
erchants' Despatch Co. 7 W 3d
NITED STATES EX. CO.,
 122 W. 4th
S. DESPATCH CO.,
 122 W. 4th
alentine & Co., 3 E. Front

Fancy Goods.
(Importers and Wholesale Dealers.)
llen C. & W. H., 117 Main
NTRAM M. T. & CO.
 47 W. Pearl
ohl Valentine, 73 E. Pearl
OHM, MACK & CO.,
 80 W. Pearl
rown R., & Co., s.e.c. Pearl
 and Walnut
ALVERT WM. H. & CO.
 67 W. Pearl
OHERTY CHARLES C. &
 Co., 34 W. Pearl
UHME & CO.,
 s.w.c. 4th and Walnut
AYNES, LEWIS &
 SPENCER, 136 Walnut
nle John, 104 Walnut
UNTINGTON, BROS. &
 CO., 119 Main
oth M., 121 Main
ICHARDSON J. C. & CO.
 93 and 97 W. Pearl
CHRADER H. & CO.,
 70 Main
CHULTZE F. & CO.,
 127 Main
HAW, BARBOUR & CO.
 81 W. Pearl
HIPLEY MURRAY & CO.
 W. Pearl b, Vine and Race
HOHL S. & CO.,
 62 W. Pearl
TIX LOUIS & CO.,
 164 Main [Pearl
entworth & Hanly, 87 W.
VALD LEWIS,
 80 W. Pearl
YNNE J. E. & CO.,
 91 W. Pearl

Fancy Goods, Notions, &c.
ddis Wm., 200 Walnut
llan Mrs. J., 186 W. 4th
tkins Geo., 102 W. 5th
ART & HICKOX,
 49 W. 4th
edgood Mrs. Martha, 19 East
ottmann M., 80 W. 5th
ONER JOHN,
 36 W. 5th
ADY D. K.,
 n.e.c. 5th and Walnut
rompton Mrs. M., 214 W. 5th
oward Mrs. M. A. 154 W. 7th
reifus Mrs. C., 64 w. 5th

Franklin L. M., 94 Main
GALVAGNI JOHN,
 513 Vine
Harder Mary, n.s. 5th b. Main
 and Walnut
Kohn I., 111 Main
Levi Joseph, 168 W. 5th
Menken S. & Sons, 62 W. 5th
Mullane Wm., 81 Mound
PARK JOHN D.,
 n.e.c. 4th and Walnut
PICKERING J. M. & CO.
 96 W. 4th
Pleisteiner John G. 555 Vine
Piggott Chas. J. 104 W. 5th
RICHTER THEODORE,
 563 Vine
Rom John J. 50 13th
Schloendorn Christian, 492
 Main
SCHRADER H. & CO.,
 70 Main
SCHULTZE F. & CO.,
 127 Main
SHEPPARD J. W.,
 20 W. 4th
Stein Miss M., 156 W. 5th
Taylor Ezra B., 13 E. 4th
Titcomb R., 158 W. 5th
Waithman Mrs. Eliza, 308 W.
 Fifth
WEBB JOHN, Jr.,
 152 W. 5th
Wentworth & Hanly, 87 W.
 Pearl

Faucet Manufact.
Fuller Albert & Co. 118 E. 2d

Feathers.
HOLDEN R. A. & CO.,
 67 Vine
SWIFT E. C. & CO.
 s.w.c. Water and Walnut

Feed Stores.
Alfers B. H. & J. Nilling, 454
 Vine
AMBS JOSEPH,
 219 Ham. Road
Baumer Theo., s.w.c. Findlay and Central Av
Box Wm., 263 Broadway
BUNNING JOHN H.
 81 Baymiller
Cregar S. P. n.e.c, Elm & 15th
Fenley Patrick, 170 Water
Fisher J.W. & Co., 539 Central
 Av
Focke Joseph, s.s. Harrison Rd
 b. Western Av. & Milc'k
French, Wilson & Co., 27 E.
 Front
Geise & Wellman, 86 Hunt
Grawe & Hullman, 424 Race
Grothe & Baruing, 207 Freemn
Hagedorn J., 500 Walnut
Haley B. & Bros., c. Central
 Av. and Liberty
Hoefler N., jr., n.w.c. Baymiller and 8th
Hughes & Reed, 37 Water
Kehsen Henry, 1114 Cen'l Av
Kerbert Hernson, s.w.c. Geest
 and Harriet
King John, 984 E. Front
Koch Henry, 570 Main
Koch John, 728 Elm
Krode Barney, 192 Hopkins
Krusemier & Rosing, 362 Ham.
 Road
Kuhling Clement, 230 Clark
Laurens J., s. s. Harrison
 Road c. Division
Lower Peter, 171 E. Front
Luke John, 605 W. 8th
McLean & Bro., 132 Ham. Rd
Moore Geo. A., 324 Broadway
Moss Jos. Henry, 941 Cent. Av
Parsell Benj. F., s.e.c. Elm
 and Canal
Pollmann Henry, Vine b. Ham
 Road and Buckeye
RIPLEY GEO.
 160 John
RIPLEY HENRY,
 1071 Central Av
Secrist Hamilton, n.e.c. 12th
 and Central Av
Shaw & Busby, s.w.c. Court
 and Outter
SHEEHAN P.,
 319 Broadway
Speckman Geo. H., n.e.c.
 Hunt and Sycamore
Spellman Samuel D., 404 W.
 6th
Steiter L. 601 Elm
Taubald Geo., 1064 Central Av
Vossmeier Hy. & Co., 471 W.
 Third
Walder N., s. e. c. Elm and
 Liberty

Walter Nicholas, 554 Elm
Weil John, 667 Central Av
White William, n.w.c. Pearl
 and Lawrence
Wills Andrew N., Walnut Hill
Woods & Sharp, 603 W. 6th
 and 7 W. W. Canal Basin
Worley Wm., s.e.c. Front and
 Niagara
Wassmier John H., 471 W. 3d

File Manufa.
Hopf & Gebhardt, 28 Ham. Rd
Morris & Roith, 185 Cent. Av
PARKIN, BROS. & HODGSON, 240 W. 7th

Fire Brick and Clay.
BUCHANAN A.,
 333 W. Front
Cochnower J., 28 W. 3d
GRAFFA, C.,
 s.e.c. 2d and Central Av
HUTCHISON R.,
 n.e.c. Butler and Front
McCracken R. B. & Co., 76 E.
 Front
TEMPEST & CO.,
 c. Ham. Road and Dunlap

Fire Works.
Diehl H. P., Laboratory, Mt.
 Adams nr. Observatory
MYERS E. & CO.,
 52 Main
STEVENS CHARLES,
 320 Main

Fishing Tackle.
BONER JOHN,
 36 w. 5th
CADY D. K. & CO.,
 n.e.c. Walnut and 5th
Spicker G. & F., 121 Main

Flag Manufact.
Gracnaind H. M., 1 Court Ho.
 bldg
Longley & Bros., 164 Vine

Flatboat Dealers.
Gibner & Hall, n.e.c. Race
 and Landing

Flooring Mills.
CAMERON, STORY
 MALONE, Storrs Towns
CAMERON W. M. & G.
 s.e.c. 6th and Hoadley
CHOATE, BARDER &
 EVANS, 567 Race
Cline John, 159 and 161 E. Front
Cook M. H. & CO., w.s. W. W.
 Canal b. 5th & 6th
FAY & STICKNEY,
 304 Broadway
Gilpin Thomas, n.s. Canal nr.
 Elm
HINKLE, GUILD & CO.,
 365 W. Front
Horsley & Ehler, 248 W. Front
HUGHS & FOSTER,
 92 John
LAPE J. S.,
 512 Central Av
ROBINSON & BRUNS,
 872 Central Av
Smith & Williamson, s.w.c. 3d
 and John
Taylor & Faulkner, 487 Freeman
WATERS & BARRETT,
 n.w.c. Freeman and 9th

Flour and Grist Mills.
Anshutz Jacob, n.w.c. 8th &
 Broadway
Barr & Gudgeon, n.s. Front b.
 Terrence and Kelly
BRADBURY WM. E.,
 266 Broadway
BRINCKMAN HENRY
 11 Hunt
CAMERON LYCURGUS,
 s.w.c. Central Av & Clark
Crout Henry, junction of Leatherbury and N. Front
Elstner Jos., agent, 294 Broadway
Elstner & Fisher, w.s. Lock b.
 4th and 5th
ERKENBRECHER AND.,
 Lock, 5th and 6th
FAGIN LEWIS,
 33 Lock
French, Wilson & Co, 165 E.
 Front
Hamer William W. 120 W. 3d
HURIN J. K.,
 577 W. 6th

CINCINNATI

Meal J. W., 206 Broadway
MUHLHAUSER G. & H.,
726 Elm
Nagel Wm., s.w.c. Sycamore and Webster
SHEEHAN PIERCE,
127 Spring
Smith A. H. & Co., Ham. Rd.
Utz A. 65 Elder
WEST C. W. & CO.,
junction 3d and Front

Flour Dealers.
Armstrong J. M. & A. E, s.c. e. Walnut and Canal
BEATTIE JOHN,
51 W. Front
BERNARD N. L.,
59 W. Miami Canal
BURBECK & HAIGHT,
107 and 109 E. Pearl e. of Broadway
BUCKINGHAM CHARLES J. & CO, 117 E. Pearl
BROWN JOS. R. & CO.
27 Walnut
Byrne & Co., 63 M. Canal
CHIPMAN W. D,
s.s. W. W. Canal Basin
CLOON SAML. & CO.,
21 Pub. Landing
Cutter E., 249 Walnut
DEAN & HALE,
19 and 21 Sycamore
DICKINSON D. L.,
11 W. Front
DICKENHORST & ARENS
e. s. c. W. Main and Canal
Ellis H. & J., 21 Water
Fosdick C. R. & Co., 46 Walnut
Frommeyer J. F. & Son, 432 Main
GELLENBECK B. & SON,
426 & 428 Main
Harvey & Kemper, 16 Water
Hanelt John & Co, 372 Wlnt
Hord Geo. M. & Co, 69 W. Frnt
Kraemer Jacob, 568 Vine
Kramig F. & Co, 605 Walnut
Meal J. W. & Co., 14 Walnut
Monnig & Bongfeld, 83 Spring
MOORE ROBERT,
49 Walnut
Pohlmeyer Chas., 11 W. Canal
Rasche F. & A., 38 Elder
MUILHAUSER G. & H.
726 Elm
Roots & Coe, W. W. Canal Bas
Schmidt C. & W., 361 Walnut
Schweikert Fred., 8 15th
SUEREY FREDK.,
70 E. Pearl
SHEEHAN PIERCE,
n.w.c. Court and Broad'y
STONE L. & M,
34 Vine
TWEED & SIBLEY,
40 Walnut
Utz A. 65 Elder
Wentzel & Scherer, 342 Walnut

Forges.
(Portable)
ENGLISH C. L.,
41 E. 2d
HYNDMAN W. G.,
54 E. 2d

Frame Manuf.
BOETIG T. G.
s.w.c. John and 2d
BONTE A. P. C.,
118 W. 4th
Bosse Henry, 59 W. 5th
BOWN THOS.,
30 E. 4th
EGGERS & CO.,
168 Main
Henochsberg M. 283 Main
Hornblow W., 8 E. 6th
Hogan A. 16 E. 4th
KOHL WM. M.
3 College bldg
Noelcke E. 207 Cent'l Av
PAPE E. W. & BRO.,
217 Walnut
WISWELL WM. Jr.
70 W. 4th
Schott Charles, 22 W. Court

Fringes, Cords, &c.
Atkins Geo., 102 W. 5th
HAMBO Mrs. M,
142 W. 5th
Hfürbich F. 29 15th b. Elm and Plum
Hoffmeister F., 98 W. 5th
Lammert Joseph, 505 Main
Mustin E. O. L., 96 W. 4th
PICKERING J. M. & CO.
96 W. 4th
POHLMAN GEORGE W.,
102 W. 4th
Spangler F., 80 W. 5th

Fruits, Foreign.
(Wholesale)
BATES JOHN,
e. s. Sycamore, b. 3d & 4th
BOWN & DEMING,
40 Main
Devoto A. & Co. 6 W. 5th
GATTI G. & ZANONE,
80 Broadway
MORRISON WM. & CO.
30 Walnut
REUTEPOHLER F. & G,
137 W. Court
SWASEY JNO. & CO.,
23, 25 and 27 Sycamore
WARREN J. T. & CO.,
53 Main

Fruit Stores.
(See also Confectioners.)
Ader A., 337 Walnut
Bacciocco John, 124 W. 5th
Bacciocco Joseph, n.e.c. 4th and Elm
Bacciocco S., 176 W. 5th
Bennet Mrs. J, 423 Sycamore
Bickley H. T, 111 E. Pearl
Bonfanti Samuel, n.w.c. 4th and Main
Coyle & Co., 25 Broadway
Coyle Phillip, e. Walnut & 5th
Dixon George R, 163 W. 5th
FISCHER & FEINTHAL,
34 W. Court
Ginassi John. 107 Ham. Road
Gozzolo Samuel, n.e.c. 4th and Walnut
Hathaway J.A., 6 College bldg.
Keown Hugh, n.w.c. 5th and Walnut
McVean Peter, 222 Walnut
MORRISON WM. & CO.
30 Walnut
Platt L. B. & Co, s.e.c. 3d and Sycamore
Smith Franklin, 198 W. 6th
Solimano Lorenzo, 192 Walnut
Stacey J. & J W., 53 E. 3d
STANFORD & BICKNELL,
21 Broadway

Fur Dealers.
Buerkle John C. 137 Main
KESSLER HENRY & SON,
215 Main
MEIER & ISPHORDING,
8 Main
SNODGRASS WM. W.
236 Main

Furnaces.
(Hot Air.)
HELLER & YOUNG,
292 Main
LOTZE ADOLPHUS,
219 Walnut
McCracken R. B. & Co. 76 E. Front
Marlow George, 378 Main

Furnishing Goods.
(Gents.)
ACKERLAND A.,
66 W. Pearl
Barrett Samuel, 115 Walnut
BARWISE & KING,
156 Main
Bicknell E. M. 54 W. 4th
BISCHOF & MARCH,
95 W. Pearl
BOHM, MACK & CO.,
(wh.) 80 W. Pearl
Brown R. & Co., cr. Pearl and Walnut
COHEN S. M.
130 Main
Efray A., 174 Vine
Gultermau & Sulzbacher, 60 W. Pearl
HEIDELBACH, SEASONGOOD & CO., s.w.c. 3d and Vine
Heller Bro. & Co. 228 W. 5th
Johnson Mrs. E. e.s. Walnut b. 5th and 6th
KEPPNER L. A.
107 W. 5th
KLEINE, HEGGER & CO.
127 Walnut
Kohn Isaac, 111 Main
KUHN, NETTER & CO.,
n.e.c. 3d and Vine
LEAVITT & BEVIS,
s.w.c. 5th c. Vine
Lockwood C. L., 143½ W. 4th
Loth M. 131 Main
LOWMAN J. & BRO,
(wh.) 38 W. Pearl
McCRACKEN K. C.,
19 W. 4th

Marks Henry & Co., 12 W. Pearl
Montgomery H. J., 78 W. 5th
Phillips S., 267 Central Av
RAUH BROS.,
56 W. Pearl
RICHARDSON JAMES,
68 W. 4th
SHOHL SIMON & CO.,
62 W. Pearl
Smith Isaac N., 10 E. 5th
Smith Mrs. J. M., 60 W. Front
Smith Raymond, 34 W. 4th
SPRAGUE T. W. & CO.
s.c.c. 4th and Vine
SIMON G. & SON,
12 W. 5th
Steiner & Dier. 22 W. Pearl
STRAUSS I. P. & BRO.,
211 Main
TAYLOR WM. H.,
160 W. 5th
VAN DOKKUM & FORMAN, 125 Main
WALD LEWIS,
80 W. Pearl
Wentworth & Haaly, 87W. Pearl
WILSON & CLARK.
s.c.c. 4th and Walnut
WOLF A. & I. & CO.,
76 Main

Furnishing Goods.
(House.)
Carter Wm., 34 E. 5th
Desmond J. J., 332 Cent. Av
GOOCH CHARLES,
355 Central Av
Hackman G. E., 79 W. Court
HUNTINGTON BROS. &
co., 119 Main
Mackelfresh Chas., 204 W. 5th
STEPHENSON HY. W.
30 W. 5th
TENCH GEO. G.,
323 Central Avenue

Furnishing Goods.
(Ladies)
COHEN SIMON M.
130 Main
Johnson Mrs. E., e.s. Walnut b. 5th and 6th
LEAVITT & BEVIS,
n.w.c. 5th and Vine
MONTGOMERY H. J.
78 W. 5th
Phillips Sidney, 267 Cent'l Av
RICHARDSON JAMES,
68 W. 4th
SIMON G. & SON,
12 W. 5th

Furniture Dealers.
See also Cabinet Ware.
BICHARD PETER,
547 Vine
Carter Wm, 34 E. 5th
Crane L. M, 81 Sycamore
Dobell Edward R., W. 6th b.
Harriet and Horne
Duchescher Pierre, 134 Sycam'e
Duescher Peter, 231 Clinton
Eilers John, 47 W. 5th
Goelkel A., 45½ E. 3d
Haug J., 541 Race
HENSHAW G. & SONS,
26 Sycamore
Hofmann Jacob, 204 Elm
Kirshner A., 59 Broadway
Laske Barbett, 101 Sycamore
McDonald C. M. n.e.c. John and 5th
MITCHELL & RAMMELSBERG, 99 W. 4th and 23 and 25 E. 2d
Schmidt C. & W. 361 Walnut
SMITH & HAWLEY,
136 W. 3d and 69 W. 5th
Straus Hy., 71 W. 5th
Suydam Geo. W., 45 W. 5th
Wiederrecht. H., n.s. Augusta, b. Central Av and John
Wolf Charles, 50 E. 8th
Wulfek Victor, 503 Sycamore

Garden Rake Manuf.
WARWOOD JOSEPH,
563 W. Front

Gas.
CINCINNATI GAS LIGHT & COKE CO., 269 Vine

Gas Apparatus.
McHENRY & CARSON,
162 Main

Gas Burners.
DANNENHOLD & NOCK,
99 W. 5th
McHENRY & CARSON,
162 Main

Gas Stoves.
WATERS BYRON,
226 Main
MUSGRAVE H. B.,
272 W. 6th

Gas Fixtures & Fitters
BAKER & VON PHUL,
62 W. 4th
DANNENHOLD & NOCK
99 W. 5th
FRANZ CONRAD,
60 W. Court
GIBSON J. B. & T.
200 and 202 Vine
McHENRY & CARSON,
162 Main
McIntire Geo. G., 296 W. 5th
MOORE P. J.,
221 W. 5th
Pancoast J., Agent, 284 Main
Scott John, 406 Vine
WATERS B.,
226 Main

Gasometers.
Green R. B., 79 E. Front
STACEY GEO.,
Ramsey b Front and W.W Canal

Gas, Spirit.
(See Burning Fluids.)

Gent'n Collar Manuf.
DRAKE LOUIS P.,
58 W. 4th

Gilders.
BOETIG T. G.
s.e.c. 2d and John
BONTE A. P. C.,
118 W. 4th
BOWN THOMAS,
30 E. 4th
KOHL W. M.
College Building
PAPE E. W. & BRO.
217 Walnut
WISWELL WM., Jr.,
70 W. 4th

Gilt Moulding.
EGGERS & CO.,
168 Main

Ginseng.
SWIFT R. C. & CO.
s.w.c. Water and Walnut
HOLDEN R. A. & CO.,
67 Vine

Glass Blowers.
(Fancy.)
Greiner & Mueller, 24 E. 4th

Glass Signs.
CUMMINGS & BERNE,
n.e.c. 3d and Race
HOPKINS H. P.
s.s. Baker nr. Vine
Scott W. B, 123 Main

Glass Stainers.
BURGUND HENRY,
47 E. 3d
Sutter Adolphus, 190 Walnut
Tschira Edward, 61 E. 3d

Glassware.
(See also China, Glass and Queensware.)
Coulter Wm., 102 and 104 E. 2d
GRAY, HEMINGRAY &
BRO., 20 E. 2d

Glove Manuf.
(Buckskin.)
Buerkle Jno. C. 137 Main
KESSLER H. & SON,
215 Main
Price T. J., 312 Main
THORNTON RICHARD,
314 Main

Glue Manuf.
BULLOCK A. D. & CO.
12 W. 2d
Goss John H, 11 Dunlap
James D. A, Cummingsville, Address Cin. P. O.

Gold Frames.
BONTE A. P. C.,
118 W. 4th
BOETIG T. G.,
s.e.c. 2d and John
BOWN THOMAS,
30 E. 4th
KOHL W. M.
College Building
PAPE E. W. & BRO.
217 Walnut

BUSINESS MIRROR. 365

WISWELL WM.; Jr., 70 W. 4th
Gold Beater.
LESLIE JAMES, n.w.c, 4th and Race (up stairs)
Lockwood & Maguire, 181 Wlnt
Gold Pen Makers.
SHEPPARD G. W. & CO, 6 W. 4th
Grainers.
Griffin P. C., 221 Elm
McCarthy Daniel, 100 W. 6th
Grain Dealers..
n.e.c. 6th and Vine
(See *Flour Mills and Dealers, and Com. and Produce Merchants.*)
Grates.
EVANS C. B. & CO., 142 W. 3d
HAND, WHITEHOUSE & Co., 205 w, 5th
MACY, RANKIN & CO. 8 Burnet House
Grocers.
(Family.)
Abel Henry, 467 W. 5th
Abel Henry, s.w.c. Mill & 5th
Adam Jesse M. 815 Vine
Ader Frank, 129 Clay
Ahaus Joseph, s.e.c. Dudley and Liberty
AHLERS CONRAD, 628 Main
Ahlers Fred. H., 771 Vine
Ahlers John, 165 Ham. Rd
Ahlers Wm. H, 24 Buckeye
Ahrens Herman, s.e.c. Mound and Richmond
Ahrens Peter, s.e.c. Sycamore and 7th
Akins Samuel, 812 E. Front
Alf Mary, 9 Woodward
Ambrose Patrick, 45 E. 8th E. of Lock
Ammann Benedict, 47 Dunlap
Arendt D., n.e.c. 6th & Lock
Arnold Margaret, 64 Elder
Aselarge Henry, 518 Walnut
Atkinson Elizabeth, 62 Butler
Aufderheide D. H. 469 W. 8th
Arendt J., s.w.c. Bank and Whiteman
AUSTIN JAMES S., n.e.c. 5th and Elm
Austing John B. 60 Abigail
Avermaat John, 165 Bremen
Awverwater Casper, n.e.c. York and Linn
Baer Conrad, 703 Vine
Bahns Andrew, 24 W. Court w. of Central Av
Bailey John A. 425 Sycamore
Ballmeier Henry, 11 Mulberry
Bamer Bernard H. 67 Abigail
Banan Owen, 144 Culvert
BARKER, HART & COOK, 61 Pub. Landing
Barr J., n.c. George & Elm
Bascher Philip, 436 Linn
BATES JOHN, s.s. Sycamore b. 3d and 4th
BATHGATE CHARLES, 242 W. 6th
BATHGATE JAMES, 67 W. Court
Bathgate Richard, 204 W. 6th
Batter John Theodore 204 Linn
Bauer Gottfried, 73 Peete
BECK NICHOLAS, 72 W. 5th
BECKMANN GEO. H. 458 W. 3d
Beckman Henry, 106 Clay
Beegan John W., s.e.c. Plum and Longworth
Behrens Frederick, 33 E. 6th E. of Lock
Behrens John, 102 Elder
Beirlein Francis, 96 Bremen
Belleden Francis J. 95 E. 5th
Bente H., s.w.c. Wood and 5th
Berens Theodore J, s.w.c. Water and Plum
Bergfeld Henry, 93 Spring
Bernens Joseph, 309 w. 5th
Bertling Matthew, 706 Cent. av
Beyerle Cuthar., n.w.c. Park and Longworth
Bien Anthony, 772 W. 6th
Bigler & Co., 155 w. 5th
Binheim Herman, 57 Hughes
Bischoff Samuel, 19 Mercer
Blatnau Peter, 618 Vine
Blumberg Henry, 12 15th b.
BOCKLAGE JOHN H. s.w.c. Smith and 2d
Bode Henry, 59 Findlay

Boedker Hermann, s.e.c. Cutter and Court
Bohlke George H., 303 Freem'n
Boohan Dennis, 29 Accomodation
Bostle John, n.w.c. Front and Lewis
Botter Gerhard H., 18 13th
Branan Patrick, n.s. Cherry al b. Plum and Central Av
Braun Ferdinand, 99 Ham. Rd
Braun Gottlieb, 434 Walnut
Brendel Jacob, 20 Hamer
Breslin Michael, 69 Woodward
Bresnan Daniel C., 61 E. 8th
Brethorst Henry, 10 W.Mulb'y
BRICKETT & CO., n.e.c. 6th and Vine
BRINKEMEIER FRED. W, 490 w. 3d
Broadwell & Edwards, 1454 E. Front
Brockhaus Margaret A., 270 Longworth
Brockman Henry, s.e.c. Elm and Water
Brockmann Herman H., 375 Broadway
Broring Arnold, 312 Baymiller
Bruder George, 560 Vine
Bruggemann Adolph, n.w.c. Liberty and Walnut
Bruning Fred, 52 Baum
Bruns Antony, 183 Hopkins
Bruns Joseph, 98 Clay
Brown Mary, s.w.c. 4th and Stone
Bryson Charles, 634 w. 5th
Buckler Henry, 63 Woodward
Buckmann Fredericka, 57 12th
Buening Anthony, 590 Elm
Bulger James, n.w.c. Washington and E. Front
Buning Frank, s.w.c. Freeman and Dayton
BUNING JOHN H., 81 and 83 Baymiller
Burke John, 130 W. 6th
Burke Mary, 121 Lock
Burwinkel Anton, 24 Woodward
Bushkamp Joseph, 323 Plum
Byrna Margaret, s.e.c. 9th and Elm
Callan James, n.w.c. 7th and Cutter
Callinan Peter W., 57 W. 7th
Campbell John, s.w.c. John and Betts
Cappelman Henry, 349 John
Carey Dennis, 142 E. 6th
CARBERY JOSEPH P. 163 Smith
Carnes Adolphus, 238 w. 6th
Carney Ann, 126 E. 6th
Carney Michael, n.s. 6th b. Culvert and Broadway
Carrigan Phillip, n.e.c. 3d and Joseph
Cashen Wm, 203 W. 7th
CAVAGNA, B., 31 W. 5th
Christian John, 654 E. Front
Cisale Josep. s. w. c. Chestnut and John.
Clark Frazee. 1521 E. Front
Clark Wm. 85 E, 3d, east of Whittaker
Cline Alex, 36 Butler
Coesmeier Barney, 18 Donnersberger
Coffin Levi, n.w.c. Hunt and Broadway
COFFIN Z. B., 32 w. 5th
Cohrs Henry C, 71 Elder
Coleman Patrick, 40 Kossuth
Colter Aaron A, 319 Main
Combrinck Bernhard, 140 Hopkins
Conclin Wm, 25 W. 5th
Conroy Cha, n.e.c. 3d & Cent. Av
Corcoran Edw'd, n.w.c. Smith and Longworth
Cordes Dietrich, n.w.c. Baymiller and York
Crain Martin, 47 Plum
Cramer John B, 329 W. 9th, w. of Central Av
Creed Daniel, n. e. c. Jackson and 12th
Crone Geo. P., 147 Clinton
Crother John H. 582 Cent. Av
Crowley & Co. 328 W. 5th
Cruces Mary, 230 Broadway
CUSCADEN ALEX. s.w.c. Elm and 3d
Daepke Phillip, 16 Mulberry
Daganer Louis, 309 Findlay
Dankel Fred'k, 9 Franklin

Dass Martin 834 E. Front
Deckebach Phillip, 286 W, Liberty
Docker Geo., s.s. Harrison Av, Brighton
Decker Jacob, s.s. Harrison Av b. Divison and Brighton
De Graw A., 246 w. 6th
Dohner Daniel, s. s, 6th, b. Harriet & Horne
Delaney Cornelius, s.e.c. New and North
Delaney Jas. 184 W. Front
Deloksen Henry, 23 Green
Doller John, 140 Buckeye
Dempsay Michael, n. w.c. North and New
Dempsey John S., s.e.c. 6th and Plum
Deters Frank, 50 Race
Daveney Jas., n.w.c. Cutter and Barr
DEWALD MICHAEL, s.w.c. Linneus & Cen. av
Dewin John W., 537 E. Front
DICKMAN MARTIN, n.w.c. Plum and 3d
Dieckmaun Aug. F. s.e.c. Sycamore and Webster
Dieckmann Bernhard, 176 Linn
Dieckmann Herman, s.w.c. Poplar and Freeman
Dirks Aug., n.w.c. Grant&Elm
Dobell Wm T, 286 W. 8th
Docker John A, 91 Hopkins
Donohuu John, 62 W. Court, w. of Central Av
Dorgau Stephen 581 W. 2nd
Dougherty Edw, 514 E. Front
Drake & Fillmore 521 W. 4th
Dresbach J., s.e.c. Linn & 5th
Dreyer Henry, 913 Central Av
Driesman J. F., 135 Laurel
Drum Mrs. C., s.w.c. 7th&Laurel
Duffner F., s.w.c. Poplar and Linn
Duffey James, 78 E. 7th
Duncan Anthony 223 Clark
Duncan Sam. W., 467 w. 5th
Dunphy M., s.e.c. 5th & Butler
EBERLE CLEMENTS C. s.e.c. Abigal and Broadw
Ebker John H., 103 Gest
Ebeier Barney, 474 Linn
Eiler John, 50 Jones
Eiker H., s. s. Logan b. Elder and Findlay
Ehinger Erhart, 512 E. Front
Ehll C., c. Harriet &W. Front
Eichelberger J., 108 W.Liberty
Eishenlaub Frederick, 280 W. Liberty
Einhoun Frank H, 444 Linn
Eisenacher John, 310 Cutter
Elfels Joseph. 509 W. 7th
Eagherson William, n.s. Front e. of Foster
Eayart J. L., 1000 Central Av
Eppons & Bro 9 E. Liberty
Ernst George, 578 Elm
Erpiensstein Joseph, s.s. Budd, b. Donnersberger & Harriet
Eschenbrenner Chas, 723 Race
Espel Henry, 52 Elm
Espel M., n.e.c. 6th a Sycamore
Evans Ebenezer, 178 Broadway
Evers John, 87 Wade
Eversmann H. H., n.w.c. Cutter and Richmond
Eversmann Peter, 644 w. 5th
Exler Joseph, s.e.c. 6th & Carr
FACKLER GEORGE, 581 Sycamore
Fannasy P., s.e.c. Mill and 3d
Faske Herman b. 185 Hopkins
Feken Aaron,H.,s.w.c.4th&Lock
Feldkamp B., 391 W. Liberty
Feldmann H. J., 235 Linn
Feldwisch John H., 36 & 38 cor. Hughes
Feldhouse, n.e.c. Liberty and Broadway
Fenker John, e.s. Ramsey, nr. Park al
FENNESY EDWARD, s.e.c. Race and Commerce
FERGUSON JOHN, s.e.c. 9th and Vine
Fermann B. H., 18 Abigail
Foye George, n.e.c. Sycamore and Woodward
Fibbe H., s.w.c. 12th & Race
Fiedler Fred. n.w.c. Elm and Court
Finke Frederick, 312 Linn
Finuarn Michael, n.w.c. Wade and Cutter
Fisher Bernhard, 31 Abigail
Fisher W m., 446 w. 3d
Fitzgerrald J. C., 39 Everett
FITZGERALD JAS. W. s.w.c. 5th aud Broadway

Fitzpatrick Michael, 136 W. Front
Fleming Jno & Jas II, 339 Central av
Flinn Timothy, 53 E. 8th
Fogarty James, 613 Central Ay
Foster Thomas, 100 Pearl c. of Broadway
Foy Bridget, 40 Pierson
Francis Peter, 591 W. 6th
FRANK AUGUSTUS W., 120 W. 5th
Frank G. A., n.w.c. Elizabeth and Central Av
FRANK S. H., 379 Vine
Frantzreb Hy., 135 Liberty
Frazee Clark. 1524 E. Front
Frocke Frederick, 57 13th
Fries John, 218 Findlay
Fries Wm. s.e.c. David &Cutter
Fritz Frederick, 43 Moore
Gassar B., 643 W. Front
Gathaus Henry, 70 Hunt
Gauspohl J. B., s.e.c. Plum & Front
Geiger John, 70 Pleasant
Geilfus Louis, 701 Elm
GEORGE D. B. & CO., n.e.c. Pearl and Broadway
GERDSEN H. H., 519 Vine
Germann Mary, n.w.c. 13th and Main
Gerry Wm, 368 Central Av
Gettman Frank, 213 Cutter
Giese C. L., agt. 56 Rittenhaus
Ginther John 152 Clark
Glass Lorenz, s.e.c. 4d & Smith
Glenaou Thomas G., 537 W. 6th
Goetzel Cha., 572 Race
Goff Mary M., n.s. Front, e. of Kelly
Gold George, 70 Martin
GOLD PETER, s.w.c. 2d and Ludlow
Golden Isaac, 172 Elm
Gosiger Fred. J., s.e.c. George and Cutter
Gottbehode Bernard H., 115 Woodward
Graham James, 151 Hopkins
Grassardt Mario, 168 Clay
Graway Joseph, 156 Bank
Greive George, 665 Vine
GREIVING GEORGE E., s.w.c. Elm & Longworth
Greiwe John II. 70 Abigail
Grene John II., 61 Mill
Grimmelsmann Francis, n.w.c. Hanszibal and 5th
Groenes J. H. F. 43 Race
Groger Theodore W., 411 W. 8th
Gronweeg Frederick, 501 Walnut
Gronotte Barney., s.w.c. Race and Union
Grote Clemens, s. w. c. cor. Hopkins and Linn
Grothoff John, 309 Sycamore
Grothues Ludwig A., 42 Elder
Gugenbergur Chas., 717 Elm
Haag Michael, head of Cu'l Av
Haagen John, 60 Ham. Road
Haas Jacob, 61 Peete
Haas Nicolas, 621 Sycamore
HACKMAN H. JOSEPH s.e.c. Longworth and Hoadley
Hagenbuch Henry, 28 Mercer
Hagerdorn Conrad, s.s.Calhoun b. Vine and Madison
Hagermann A., 114 Bank
Halenkamp G. H., 20 Cutter
Hall Wm., n.s. 9th b. Harriet and Millcreek
Hallenkamp Geo. H., s. w. c. George and Smith
Haller Frod., 230 Linn
Hamberg John H., n.e.c. Pearl and Pike
Hanser Margaret, 188 Clinton
Hansler, John, 706 Central Av
Harconrt Lemuel C., 27 W. 5th
Hardt Phillipp, 623 Vine
Hare P. O., n.e.c. 4th & Smith
Harmyer Henry, s'e.c. Logan and Liberty
Hartlaub Peter, 60 Observatory
Hartling George, 262 Baymiller
Hartzel Thos. 168 W. 3d
Hanhold Fred., 141 Everett
Haverkamp Clemens,160 Freeman
Hayes Wm., 133 E. 6th
Healey Martin, s.e.c. Court & Mound
Healy John, 278 Central Av
Herrmann F. W., 927 Cen'l Av
HEET BERNARD G., 654 Sycamore

CINCINNATI

866

Heidaeeker Fred'iok, 678 Main
Heimrath C. H., 20 Milton
Helgenhold H., 1236 E. Front
Helie Richard, 599 Race
Helling J. A. n.w.c. 3d & Stone
Helmig George, 149 Bank
Helmig, Joseph, 708 Freeman
Hempelman B., n.w.c. Findlay and Linn
Herles Henry, 108 Baum
Heskamp John G., 65 Hunt
Heskamp, Margaret, 33 Baum
Hespeng Herman, cor. Baymiller and W. Liberty
Hesselberger Theodore H., s.e.c. W. 8th and Mound
Hessler Frederick, 174 W. 6th
Hildreth David, s.w.c. Cutter and
Hill Mary A. T. n. e. c. Baum and Observatory Rd
Hill Sarah, 19 E. 8th
Hillebrand Frederick, 30 Dudley
Hillert & Fahlbusch, 449 Sycamore
Hipp Jacob, s.w.c. John & 9th
Hinghouse Wm., 46 Rittenhse
Hinken J. & G., n.e.c. Race and Water
Holmes J. & Co., s.w.c. 5th and Plum
Hirshburg Meyer, agt., 573 Central Av
Hoban Joseph, 302 W. 3d
Hoffmann Christian, 46 Hamer
Hofinghoff Chas. 110 W. Court
Hogan Mrs. Bridget, 321 John
Hogan Thomas, 45 E. Third e. of Whitaker
Hohnstedt Henry, s.e.c. 14th and Race
Holt Wm., 22 W. 5th
HOLT WM., 84 & 86 E. Pearl
Hoppe Dominick, 546 Cen'l Av
Hornung Peter, 19 Hughes
Hubbell & Coney, 626 Main
HUBING JOHN W., 452 W. 2d
Huneke Henry, 507 Sycamore
Hunzicker Jacob, 118 Bremen
Hulbert Lambur n.w.c. Linn and Court
Husmann Barny, 49 Woodwrd
Huss Charles, 1116 Central Av
Imm Charles, n.w.c. Poplar & Linn
Immenhort Henry, 511 Race
Inott Wm., 589 Central Av
Jackson Murray M., s.s. Front, e. of Brooklyn
Jacobs Christopher, 118 Gest
Janson Martin, 15 Mulberry
Jaquillard Christian, 930 Central Avenue
Johnson D., n.e.c. Barr and Baymiller
Johnson Francis, 46 E. Front
Jokem Mathias, 355 Ham. Road
JONES RYAN W., 513 W. 5th
Joyce Michael, 982 E. Front
Karsper John G., 141 Pleasant
Kasting G. H., 66 Ham. Road.
Kasser Christian n.w.c. Everett and Plum
KATTENHORN ARND, 381 Main
Kating, Andrew, w.s. Lebanon Road b. Liberty and Corporation Line
Kattenhorn John H., n.e.c. 3d and Lock.
Katterer Joseph, 725 W. 6th
Kauser Henry, n.w.c. Linn & Oliver
KAVANAUGH MICHAEL A., n.e.c. Hunt & Brdway
Keegan Jas. 48 Freeman
Keenan Lawrence, 213 W. Front
KESHAN EDWARD n.e.c. 9th and Elm
Keidel Wm. H., 658 Race
Keraker J. G., s.e.c. Green and Pleasant
Kelly John G., n.w.c. John & Court
Kelley Martin, n.e.c. Linn and Poplar
Kelley Matthew, 307 W. 3d
Kempus Frank, 270 Clark
Kennedy James, 54 E. 8th, e. of Lock
Kennedy Patrick, 217 E. 6th,
Kern Frank, 694 Central Av
Kerney John H., n.e.c. 3d and Stone
Kessing Frank, 49 Plum
KESTNER A. H., 432 Main
Kidner Daniel, 140 Water

KESTNER GEORGE F., s.e.c. Canal and Main
Kilduff, Margaret, s.w.c. John and Elizabeth
King D., s.s. 8th b. Broadway and Sycamore
King Thomas, 71 W. Court, w. of Central Av
Kirby Mary. 67 Observatory Road
Kirker, John & Co., 32 E. 5th
Klefot Frederick, 96 Hunt
Kleiman Wm., e. s. Fountain, b. Rice and Alexander
Klein, Anthony, n.w.c. Court & Baymiller
Klein George Peter, 660 Vine
Klein Jacob, 63 Hamilton Rd
Klemper Henry, 492 W, Front
Kline Chrlotte, n.s. Goodloe b. Willow and Niagara
Klotter Geo., 119 Browne
Kluber J., 162 Baymiller
Klumper Joseph, n.w.c. George and Cutter
Knecht Wm., 502 John
Knollman R., n.e.c. Cutter & Betts
Koch Chas. L., 267 Ham, Road
Koch Michael, 665 Race
Koch Wm. 211 Clinton
Koehl John, e.s. Reading Rd. n r. Montgomery Pike
Konig H. H., 27 Buckeye
Koenig Raymond, 98 Ham. Rd.
Konerman Henry, 207 W. Frnt
Korte Albert, n.w.c. 7th and Sycamore
Kottman Harman, 9 John
Kovermann Ed'rd, 30 Buckeye
Kramer Clement, 159 Laurel
Kramer Frederick, 83 W. Frnt
Kramer John, s.s. Front, nr. Jamestown Ferry
Kreyenbrock John C., n.w.c. George and Central Av
Kroger Anton, 1 Pine
Kronlage Henry, 384 Sycamore
Kruse C. H., n.w.c. 15th and Pleasant
Kruse H., 49 Woodward
Kruse H., 602 Race
Kruse H. F. W., 484 Elm
KRUTHAUP J. J. FRED. n.e.c. Pearl and Butler
Kuhlman Joseph, 704 W. 5th
Kunckel Deborah, 1476 E. Frnt
KUSGOERD H. & A., s.w.c. 3d and Park
Kyte Joseph, n.w.c. 8th & Lock
Labold R., n.w.c. John and Everett
Laddenkotter Jos., 106 Abigail
Lahmann H. A., 170 W. Court w. of Cent. Av
Lambers John H., n.e.c. Budd and Donnersberger
Lambur A., s.e.c. Smith & 2d
Lamping B. H., 491 Race
Lamping H. A., 19 Franklin
Landwer Anthon, s.e.c. Liberty and Hunt
Lange John G., 363 George
Lang Robt., Sr., n.e.c. 7th & Linn
Lauther John, 930 E. Front
Lavin Peter, 423 w. 2d
Lesch Andrew, n.w.c. Baum and Observatory Road
Lehmann Hart, 201 Elm
Lebunkpohler E. H., 173 Clay
Leonard Patrick, 31 Race
Letsche Matthew, 613 Elm
Levi Amelia, s.s. Front b. Broad and Waldon
Leydon M. B., s.w.c. Central Av and Pearl
Lillie F., n.e.c. Budd & Dudley
Limke Francis A., 48 Green
Litmer Henry, 526 Main
Lobkar Herman, 291 Clark
Lodder Henry, 39 Pike
Lodders J. F., 519 Race
Lohn Fred. F., n.w.c. Freeman and Poplar
Louze Jared, 52 Abigail
LOVE ALEX, H. n.w.c. 5th & Sycamore
Loventhal H. S., s.e.c. Race and Third
Lubbe R. & G., 480 W. 5th
Lubbelman Geo., 430 Walnut
Luken Joseph 36 Elm
LUTHY & FOX. n.e.c. Main and 7th
Lynch Michael D., 216 Central Avenue
Lyons M. R., s.s. 5th, b. Macalister and Lawrence
McAllister Michael, n.w.c. Frnt and Race
McCaffray Nich. 71 Richmond

McCarthy Wm., 97 Sycamore
McCarty Martin, 289 Gen'l Av
McCloy Henry, 19 Freeman
McClure David, 33 Cutter
McConvill John, 754 E. Front
McCormack John, s.e.c. 5th & John
McCormic Mathew, 219 E. 6th
McCullan Jas., 158 E. 6th
McDermott Michael, 495 w. 4th
McGOLDRICK EDWARD, s.e.c. 6th and Mound
McGuire Thos., s.e.c. 6th and Baum
McLaughlin Mary, 117 Lock
McMann Mrs. Mary, 54 E. 7th
McNair & Co. 105 E. Pearl E. of Broadway
McNamar J. C., 165 E. Front
McQuaid W. S., 258 w. 6th
Macke Francis, 278 W. Front
Macke M., F., s. w. c. Freeman and Richmond
MACKENTEPE BERNARD, 57 Vine
Maescher John V., 82 E. Pearl
Mahan John, n.s. 6th, b. Culvert and Broadway
Maher Antony, 420 w. 2d
Mahony Mary E., s.e.c. 4th & Wood
MANGOLD ADAM, 107 W. 5th
Manning John, 128 W. Front
Manne Charles, 8 13th
Marty Francis J., s.w.c. 8th and John
Masker Casper, 28 13th
Matthews William R., n.w.c. Burr and Baymiller
Meyer J., 13 Junes
Meagher John, 52 Plum
Meidel Anton, w.s. Vine, b. Milk and Mulberry
Meier Henry, n.e.c. Mansfield and Webster
Melcher F., 209 Wade
Menke G. M., n.e.c. Cutter & Clinton
Mesher Fred., s.w.c. Longworth and Smith
Metzler Jacob, 147 Bremen
Mewhinney Sylvanus, s.e.c. Poplar and Freeman
Meyer A. N., s.e.c. Wilson & Milton
MEYER FREDERICK W., n.w.c. 4th and Park
Meyer Harmer H., s w.c. Cutter and Melancthon
Meyer John B., 189 W. Front
Meyer J. M., 218 John
Meyers H., n.w.c. Cutter and Everett
MEYERS JOHN D., Jr., n.e.c. Water & Cen'l Av
Moyers Wm., 676 Central Av
Muedcking H., n.e.c. 9th and John
Miller A., 78 Buckeye
Miller Gustave, s.e.c. 6th and Central Av
Miller Jacob, n.w.c. Mound and 8th
Miller Rudolph, s.w.c. Mansfield and Liberty
Miller S. B., s.e.c. Sycamore and Webster
Moder Anthony, 553 Vine
Mohrhaus Bernhard, 540 Plum
Mondoway Jer., 313 W. 7th
Mone Nicholas, 624 W. 6th
Munchen Wm., n.s. Pearl, b. Smith and Park
Montag Charles. w. s. Vine b. Milk and Mulberry
Moore George, 281 W. 8th
Moor Wm. M., 1242 E. Front
Moormann G. A., 97 Buckeye
MOHRMANN FERD. H., 258 W. 5th
Morran Hugh, s. w.c. 3d & Mill
Moser Frederick, 50 Elder
Moss L., 1069 Central Av
Muller Bernad, 74 12th
Mueller F., s.s. Findley, b. Bremen and Franz
Muhlhauser C., 275 Ham. Rd
Muller E., 273 Central Av
Mulleran Jos., 2 Abigail
Munderf J., 171 W. Liberty
Murphy M., 102 W. 3d
Murray John, 19 York
Muse Henry, 331 W. 5th
MUTH CHARLES F., 1070 Central Av
Myers John, 265 Freeman
Mygazz Philip V., s.w.c. Mill and 4th
Nagel Henry, 29 Ham. Road
Naylor Henry, 87 Martin
Nedderman Hy., 191 W. Canal

NEY JACOB P., 648 Elm
Nicholaus Louis, 55 Martin
Nicolaus P., Alphons & Co., n.w.c. 3d and Ludlow
Nieder Frederick, 290 Elm
Niemann Wm., 25 Ham. Road
Nipper Anthon, n.e.c. Munt and Spring
NIPPER B. H., 169 W. 9th
Nipper Joseph, 61 W. Liberty
NOBBE HERMANN, 53 W. Court
Nobbe John H., 637 Main
Nower Henry J., 657 Elm
OBERHUE E. F., 112 W. Court
Oberkline G. H., s.w.c. Freeman and Liberty
O'BRIEN BERNARD, 251 Sycamore
O'Conner James, 124 E.8th
Oday Patrick, 132 E. 6th
Oelker Chas., 31 E. 7th
O'Gara Patrick, 48 Plum
O'Keefe Kyran, 414 George
O'Neil, Patrick, 111 E. 8th
O'Reilly Patrick, 182 Cutter
OLTH J. A., n.e.c. 4th and Sycamore
Ossege Henry, s.w.c. Race and Findlay
Ottenschultz J. B., 177 Water
Otting Henry, 139 Baymiller
Otting Wm., 76 Spring
Pandorf Charles H., 1123 Central Av
Pauer Adam, 154 E. 6th
Pawlowski John, 275 Clinton
PEEBLES JOSEPH F., n.e.c. 5th and Race
Penning George, e.s. Vine Junction of Mulberry
Pennington Jas., 296 Elm
Peterman Martin, 35 Providence
Peters Aug., 506 Vine
Peters Chas. F., n.w.c. 6th & Elm
Phelon Dennis, s.e.c. Plum & Court
PILKINGTON JOHN O. C., s.w.c. Linn and 9th
Pistler Wm., 74 Bremen
Pitts John J., 234 Cutter
Plasphol Henry E., 179 Barr
Pollard Nicholas, n.w.c. Whitaker and Front
Poor & Co., 225 Walnut
Pott H. H., 145 Linn
Powell Richard, s.w.c. 7th & Broadway
Prues B. H., 176 E. 5th
Prows James A., 1558 E. Front
Pugh Hugh, s.w.c. Cutter and Laurel
Purcell Patrick, n.e.c. Court and Baymiller
Quinn Patrick, 275 W. 6th
Rabbe John Henry, 656 Vine
Rabens Henry, 129 Bremen
Rahn Adam, 49 E. 3d, e. of Whitaker
Rapp Peter, 28 Allison
Rech Henry, 636 Race
Reedy Jas., 331 W. 6th
Reedy Patrick, e. s. Sycamore and New
Regan John, 65 E. 8th
REIF FRANCIS, SEN'R., 128 Ham. Road
Reilag Fred., 438 Walnut
Reinerman Clemmens, 21 York
Reinhard D., s.w.c. Harrison Av and Brighton
Reinhard Frank, 534 Elm
Reinkamp A., s.e.c. Pearl and Butler
Reiring Henry H., 461 w. 7th
Raring Henry, 433 W. Front
Reis Nicholas, 430 Main
Rencker Henry, n.w.c. Baymiller and Laurel
Rennekamp Derah't, 23 Mill
Rennekamp L., n.w.c. Clark and Garrard
Rennekamp Louis, 353 Clark
Renzelmann Christopher, 22 Nansfield
Reynolds John, 249 W. Front
Reynolds Wm., 333 W. 5th
Rhein Jacob, e.s. Vine, Junction of Calhoun
Richter Henry, 396 w. 5th
Ricking Barnard, s.w.c. Laurel and Baymiller
Riehle Martin, 195 York
Riemeyer John F., 82 Bremen
Rienlander Hy., 144 Everett
Riordon Matthew, 15 E. 7th
Rittenhouse John, 448 W. 5th
Rixmann Geo., 26 Franklin

Roa Frederick, 628 Vine
Robben Dinah, 56 13th
Rogers Michael, 156 Cutter
Rolf Frits, n.e.c. Logan and Green
Rolfes Henry, 61 Abigail
Romer John H., w.s. Kilgour, b. 3d and 4th
Rose Hermann, n.s. 6th, b. Harriet and Horne
Rotert Henry, 104 Abigail
Rolhfust Geo., 714 Vine
Rotjmann Geo. S., 531 w. 8th
Rueckert Alexander, 569 Main
Rudd Richard, 72 Park
Rudolph Adam, 6th b. Harriet and Horne
Rueso Conrad, 513 Sycamore
Ruf Alexander, 603 Elm
Rusche Prof. H., 366 Br'dway
Ruthemeyer Gerh't. 152 Linn
Ryan John, s.e.c. 3d & Ludlw
Ryan Michael, 583 W. 6th
Ryans Jas. N., 45 Wood
Sandell Edward,s.w.c. Elm & 12th
Suuerbeck Geo., 515 Plum
Schaefer Geo., 32 Adams
Schaefer Jacob, 137 Carr
Scharenhorst H., 543 Race
Schawe H., 451 Plum
Scheffel G. C. 646 Vine
Schehl John J., 246 Pleasant
Scherer Jacob, 527 Race
Scherer John A., 70 W. Librty
Scherer Peter, 646 Central Av
Scheve Joseph, 103 Clark
Schierloh Hy, 552 W. 5th
Schkiess Chas., 123 Ham. Road
Schleick Mary, n.s. Front b. Foster and Kelly
Schliffel John, 54 W. Mulberry
Schmatsigang M., 471 Vine
Schmidt Christian, 195 Freeman
Schmidt Frank, 207 Freeman
Schmidt William, s.e.c. Baymiller and Richmond
Schmitt Frank 141 Buckeye
Schweider & Co., s.s. Harrison Pike, b. Division & Brighton
Schneider J. W., 519 Sycamore
Schnier Charles, 14 Madison
Schnier Louis, n.w.c. Richmond and Mound
SCHNITGER JOHN H., s.e.c. 15th & Elm
SCHOCK FREDERICK, n.s. Charlotte, b. Linn & Baymiller
Schoeppner John, 594 Vine
Schonebaum B. H. L., 413 John
Schottelkotte John L., 47 Pendicton
Schewe Ernst, 108 12th
Schrader Chris., 405 W. 6th
Schrieber H 22 W. Mulberry
Schriefer Henry, 25 E. Liberty
Schroeder Charles, 628 Race
Schroeer Stephan H., 12 Mary
Schroerlucke Hy, s.e.c. Baymiller and Everett
SCHROEDER J. D., 336 W. 7th
SCHROTH ANEREW, 786 Central Av
Schuckmann Bernard, 12 Dunlap
Schuler John 81 Division
Schulte R. H. W., 26 E. Pearl
Schulte John, 70 Buckeye
Schwars Celestin, 679 W. 6th
Schwer John Geo., 188 Clark
Schweikert Geo., 63 Laurel
Schweinafus John H., 716 E. Front
Schweiring Louis, s.e.c. Linn and Dayton
Schweitzen Joseph. 1122 Central Av
Seger Henry, s.e.c. Front & Vine
SEITER J., 606 Freeman
Senn J. S., n.e.c. Elm & 14th
Shafer John, 360 Central Av
Shaw & Anderson, 103E. Pearl
Shey Dennis, s.e.c. Front and Ludlow
SHEEHAN PIERCE, n.w.c. Court and Broadway
SHEEN FREDERICK 70 E. Pearl
Shepherdson John, n.e.c. George and Linn
Shey Thomas, 116 Barr
Shiltzberger John, 14 Carr
Shwere Theodore, 45 Freeman
Sickols Robert, n.w.c. 6th and John
Siefke Henry, s.e.c. Linn and 6th
Siemann J. Fred., 26 Orchard

Siemer John D., 594 Main
Simon Joseph, 215 Betts
Simon John, 656 Vine
Slattery Patrick T., 108 E. 6th
SMITH B. F., 752 E. Front
Smith Martin J., 219 Broadway
Smith Omay, s. e. c. longworth and Central Avenue
Smith Patrick, n.e.c. Richmond and Freeman
SNYDER FREDERICK, 55 W. Court
SNYDER & GOBRECHT, s.s. Harrison Pike, b. Division and Brighton
Snyder Joseph, n. w. c. Cutter and Laurel
Spaen Patrick, 184 W. Court
Spreen Charles, n.e.c. of W. Court and Linn
Stagg J. J. & Co., 102 E.Pearl
Stalkamp Henry, 10 Green
Stall Henry A., 680 Cent. Av
Stall John F., s.w.c. Brodwy and New
Stanton Johanna, 131 E. 6th
Stogeman J. H., 94 E. 2d
Stegne. Lewis, 560 Elm
Steinkamp Frederick, s.e.c. Freeman and Liberty
Steinkonig A., 235 W. Liberty
Steinlaga Albert, s.w.c. Abigail and Broadway
Steinwart, Henry, 469 Walnut
Stemmermann Emily, n.e.c. Linn and Everett
Stemmermann W., 225 W. Front
STERRITT DAVID B., 541 Main
Stockhoff Charles, s.e.c.Broadway and Milton
Stone L., n.s. Front, below Jamestown Ferry
Straus J., s.e.c. Plum & 15th
Streatolmeyer Sophia,445 Linn
Streeter Mrs. Eliza J., 1226 E. Front
STREHLI V. W., 634 Elm
Strietmann George, 577 Walnut
Strictolmeier Ernest, 625 Elm
Strubbe Henry W., 213 Everett
Strubbe Fred., 126 Findlay
STRUBBE WM. F., 29 Abigail
Strunk Mary Ann, 12 E. 8th
Stumpel Barney, 636 W. 5th
Stutz Daniel, 24 Ham. Road
Suhr Xavier, n.w.c. Baymiller and George
Sullivan, Ellen,Junct'n Reading Rd. & Montgomery Pike
Sullivan J.D., 398 Broadway
Summe Barney, n. w. c. Hopkins and Baymiller
Supe Richard, 299 Hopkins
Susman Simon, 33 W. 7th
Sutton C., 302 W. 5th
Syfers & Jones, n.e.c. Broadway and Fifth
TACKENBURG HERMAN, 547 Walnut
Taylor Wm., s.w.c. Linn and Bank
Telkink Henry, 274 Broadway
Tenafee Wm., 603 W. 8th
Temman J. B., n.w.c. Clark and Baymiller
Tenhundfeld J., 394 W. Front
Tepe Bernard, 85 Abigail
Terhage Herman, e.s. Kilgour b. 3d and 5th
Tewes & Herking, n.s. Front, e. of Kelly
Tewes Wm., n.s. Front b. Foster and Kelly
Thielen Casper, 675 Race
Tharp Edmund, 1214 E. Front
Tiemann John H., 630 W. 8th
Timmerman John H., n.e.c. Carr and 6th
TONNIES BERNHARD, 237 W. Front
Tracy Patrick, 126 and 128 Central Avenue
Trader Moses W., n.e.c. 4th & Mill
Trembaur George, 569 Vine
Trimpe John B., 101 Hunt
Trimpe Martin A., 702 E. Frnt
Troessner John, 30 Poeta
Trussell Moses, s.w.c. Cutter and Betts
Tubesing Henry, 593 Elm
Turner Henry, n.s.c. Abigail and Pendleton
Uhlmann Frederick, 41 Elder
Utz C. P., n. e. c. Cutter and Richmond
Van, Wormer A., 57 W. Court
Vedder Conrad, n.e.c. Woodward and Broadway

Vedder R., 207 Linn
Veenoman A. & Co., 566 Race
Vodde Joseph, 205 Richmond
Voegoli G. M., 58 Stark
VOGEL FREDERICK, Jr., n.e.c. Clinton and John
Voigts Carstan, s.e.c. Union & Elm
Volz Constantine, 664 Main
Von Eye Fred., n.e.c. Court and John
Von Nagel Fred., 141 Clark
Vorndlecke John., 105 Buckeye
Vos Joseph, n.w.c. Broadway and Woodward
Wagner G. M., 514 Elm
Walsh James, 256 Central Av
Walter Valentine, 29 Moore
Wanstroth Jos., 99 Woodward
Warner George, 89 E. 3d, e. of Whittaker
Watkins Nelson, n.e.c. 5th & Smith
Webber Fred. Wm., 15 Providence
Weber Fred. Henry L., 084 Main
Webster David B., 595 W. 6th
Weddendorf Henry, n. w. c. Price and Ringgold
Wehrmann A. M., n. w. c. Wade and John
Weidgenant Wm., 570 Walnut
Weidlager John S., n.e.c. 3d and John
Weil Anthony, 166 E. Front
Weingartner Lawrence,n.w.c. Richmond and John
Weis John, 109 Ham. Road
WEISSMANN F., w. c. Clinton and Central Avenue
Welch Andrew, n.s. Front e. of Lumber
Werman Conrad, 189 Bremen
Wernke Henry, s.e.c. Mound and Clark
Werts Valentine, n.e.c. Adams and Plum
Wessling Henry, s.w. c. New and North
Wessling J. Henry, n.e.c. Broadway and New
Wessling Deidrich, 99 Barr
Wessling G. H., 260 W. 6th
West John B., 19 Abigail
White Leonard M., n.e.c. Hopkins and Freeman
Wiebold Henry, 220 Walnut
Wischer H. F., n.e.c. Barr & Freeman
Wiesmann Clements. n.w.c. Green and Pleasant
Wiggeringloh Theodore, n.w.c. Vine and Front
Wilkins John D., 117 Betts
Wilkens John D., 48 Ham. Rd.
Wilkymacky H., 61 Laurel
Will Valentine, 1057 Cen'l Av
Willenborg Joseph, 362 Freeman
Willenborg J. B., s.e.c. John and Davis
Williams Wm., Mitchell, Mt. Adams
Williams Wm., 23 Bank
WILLMANN MATHIAS, 422 Vine
Wilson A. B., 324 W. 8th
Wilmas Wm., 273 Freeman
Winne Charles, n.w.c. 7th, & John
Wirth Herman, 608 Vine
Wirz Andreas, 36 Elder
Witte Gasper, 233 Clark
Wittrock John H., s.w.c. Central Av. and Elizabeth
Wolking John C., s.w.c. 6th and Broadway
WOODRUFF WM. H., 380 Race
Wuennemann John B., n.e.c. 4th and Lock
Yocum Jesse E., n.w.c. 6th & Smith
Zuest Jacob, 32 Dunlap
Zurmuhlen John, 57 Wade

Grocers.
(Wholesale.)

BABBITT, GOOD & CO., 18 and 19 Pub. Landing
BAKER B. P. & CO., s.e.c. 2d and Walnut
BAKER & CO., 29 Main
BIGGS T. R. & CO., s.w.c. Main and 2d
Bishop J. G. & J.W., 16 Main
BISHOP R. M., & CO., 36 Main

BROWN M. J., s.e.c. Main and 7th
Brown, Stout & Butler, 44 Walnut
CANFIELD J. W. & CO. 70 Walnut
CLARK & CARR, 29 Walnut
CLARK J. A. & CO., 38 Vine
CLARK & ROGERS. 28 & 30 E. 2d
CODY F., 17 and 19 Water
Coffin D. H. D., 20 E. Pearl
COFFIN Z. Z., 32 W. 5th
Colter Aaron A., 319 Main
Coonor Robert A., 24 & 30 E.Prl
CUNNINGHAM JAS. F. & CO., 20 Pub. Landing
DUGAN J. A. & CO., 21 & 23 w. 2d
Emerson R. W., & Co., 47 Walnut
FERGUSON JOHN, s.e.c. 8th and Vine
FERRIS, DUNLEVY & FOWLER, 51 w. 2d
FICKEN JOHN, 16 E. Pearl
Foster Thos., 100 Pearl, e. of Broadway
FRAZER JAMES A. & CO. 66 and 68 Walnut
GEORGE D. B. & CO., n.e.c. Pearl & Broadway
Gerard & Co., n.w.c. Pearl & Sycamore
Gibson, Early & Co., 50 W. 2d
GLENN WM. & SONS, 70 & 72 Vine
Griese B., 3 Commercial Row
Graham W. M. & Co., 4 and 5 Commercial Row
Hanks Richard, 32 Vine
HANLY WM. W., 23 Main
Harper & Winall, 12 E. 2d
HARRISON & HOOPER, 50 W. 2d
HATCH & HALL, 36 Vine
HOBBS & PARKER, 10 Main
HOLT WM., 84 & 86 E. Pearl
HOSEA ROBERT & CO., s.w.c. Main and Front
Isham, Fisher & Co., 47 Pub. Landing
JENNINGS, & BUTTERFIELD n.w.c. Main & 6th
KATTENHORN A., 381 Main
KESTNER GEO. F., s.e.c. Main and Canal
KESTNER A. H., 432 Main
KING & DALY, s.w.c. 2d and Sycamore
KISSICK JAMES, 235 Main
Lewis Charles, 64 E. Pearl
LOUDON J. A. & CO., 30 Vine
LUTHY & FOX, 16 7th And Main
McGECHIN THOMAS s.e.c. Main and 6th
Manning S. & Co., 64 Walnut
Meader & Ludington, 32 c. Pearl
Mohuor Louis, 34 E. Pearl
Meyers John D. jr., n. e. c. Water and Central Av
MILLER, BRUNING & DIECKMAN, 33 Sycamore
Mills & Kline, 18 Main
MINOR & ANDREWS, s.e.c. 2d and Main
MOORE CHAS. L. & CO., 28 & 30 Main
MOULINIER C. P., 13 W. Front
OBEIHEU E. & F., 112 W. Court
Poland & Henry, 60 W. 2d
Poor & Co., 225 Walnut
Rauth Francis, 85 E. Pearl
RECHTIN G. H., 75 E. Pearl
Rowland Chas. W., 40 W. 2d
SAYRE L., 214 Walnut
SAYRE & WHITE, 15 Public Landing
Schultes E.W. II., 20 E. Pearl
Shaw & Anderson, 103 E. Pearl
Shea Dennis, s.e.c. Front and Ludlow
SIEBERN J. N. & BROS., 8 E. Pearl

CINCINNATI

Smilan John, 62 E. Pearl
SMITH WM. C.,
  22 and 24 E. 9th
SOMMER & MEYER,
  36 E. Pearl
SPINING & BROWN,
  49 W. 2d
SPRINGER & WHITEMAN,
  16 and 18 W. 2d
Stagg J. J. & Co., 102 Pearl,
  e. of Broadway
STALL & MEYER,
  64 and 66 W. 2d
STONE B. T. & CO.,
  18 E. 2d
STONE L. & M.,
  47 Vine
STRAIGHT, DEMING & CO., n.e.c. Vine and 2d
SWASEY JOHN & CO.,
  23 and 25 Sycamore
SWASEY M.,
  s.w.c. Broadway and 2d
Sweny M. & Co., 14 Main
TAIT GEORGE,
  196 W. 6th
TAYLOR L. & BRO.,
  45 Walnut
TAYLOR J. & CO.,
  1025 Central Av
Thirkield, T. F. & Co. 27 Main
THOMPSON WM. H. & Co,
  71 Main
TRABER & AUBERY,
  7 Pub. Landing
TRENCHARD E. P. & Co.
  s.w.c. Walnut and 2d
TWEED & ANDREWS,
  31 and 33 W. Pearl
WELLS A. H. & CO.,
  33 Main
White, Bro. & Co., 83 Walnut

Gun Powder.
AUSTIN & SMITH,
  8 E. 2d
Carleton B. F., n.e.c. Walnut and Second
DONOHUE J. W. & CO.
  n.e.c. 2d and Walnut
LAWRENCE CHAS.,
  50 Main

Guns, Pistols, &c.
BOOTH R. W. & CO.,
  s.w.c. Pearl and Walnut
BROWN IRA,
  218 Main
Cox A., 251 W. 5th
Eberle A., 345 Vine
Eckel Chas., 480 Walnut
GANO, HOWELL & CO.,
  138 Walnut
GRIFFITH JOHN,
  165 Main
Kettler Edward, 611 Cent. Av
KITTREDGE B. & CO.,
  134 Main
PAPPENHEIMER, DREYFOOS & CO., 107 W. Pearl
POWELL P.,
  160 Main
Rapner C, & J. Bandle, 429 Main
Schemann & Wirsing, 53 Sycamore
Spicker G. & F., 121 Main

Gutta Percha Roofing.
GAY JAMES P.,
  1 Apollo bldg

Gymnasiums.
Catholic Institute Gymnaseum
  n.w.c. Vine & Longworth
GERMAN GYMNASTIC SOCIETY, Walnut, near Liberty
YOUNG MENS GYMNASTIC ASSOCIATION, n.e.c. Race and 4th

Hair Braiding
Soechting C., 417 Main
Taylor E. B., 13 E. 4th
Zwick Mad., 40 W. 4th

Hair Dye Manufacturer.
ARRICCO ANTONIO,
  108 W. 4th

Ham Curers.
(See Pork and Beef Packers,
  Ham Curers, &c.)

Hardware.
AUPERLE ALEX.,
  26 Ham. Road
BOECKLEY MRS. KATE
  537 Vine

BOOTH R. W. & CO.,
  s.w.c. Walnut and Pearl
BORCHERDING E. & H.,
  503 Freeman
BULTMANN C. F.,
  s.c.c. Main and 9th
DAVIDSON TYLER & CO.,
  140 and 142 Main
DE CAMP & NIEHAUS,
  270 Central Av
Eyrman Chas., 403 Main
Fischer G., 156 Baymiller
FROELKING & MARMET,
  1023 Central Av
GANO HOWELL & CO.,
  138 Walnut
GASTEN, DICKSON & Co., 53 W. Pearl
GOOCH CHARLES,
  335 Central Av
GLAESCHER G. W.,
  534 Main
GREENWOOD M. & CO.,
  396 Walnut
HAMMETT HENRY,
  90 Main
HAVEN JAS. L. & CO.,
  173 and 175 W. 2d
Herder Gustave, 338 Main
HOLENSHADE, MORRIS & CO., 553, 555 & 557 Central Av
HOLLIDAY & SMITH,
  n.e.c. 5th and Central Av
King John W., 224 George
KRUSE & BAHLMAN,
  389 Main
LANGHORST H. A.,
  810 Main
Lender F., 1065 Central Av
LEONARDE G. & CO.,
  55 W. Pearl
LOHRJ H.,
  n.e.c. Main and 9th
MERNA JOSEPH,
  192 Main
Neave T. & Sons, 67 Main
Neff, Bro. & Co., s.w.e. Main and 2d
NEFF PETER & SONS,
  93 W. Pearl
PAPPENHEIMER, DREYFOOS & CO., 107 W. Pearl
RESOR WM. & CO.,
  13 and 15 Main
ROTHERT J. H. & SONS,
  n.e.c. Central Av & Wade
Schrichten & Luther, 262 Main
Schulte & Temmen, 240 Main
Siebrecht Wm., 464 Main
Spicker G. & F., 121 Main
Stuzman L., W., 20 E. Pearl
THIESSING GEO. T.,
  19 E. Pearl
WAYNE J. L. & SON,
  124 Main
WAYNE JOS. W. & CO.,
  196 Main
Weber & Newman, 306 Main
Werner Christ., 503 Vine
Wolff John O., 115 E. Pearl

Hardware.
(Saddlery.)
BANTLIN & COMPTON,
  n.e.c. Court and Main
CLARK S. & S. S.,
  180 Main
GREENWOOD M. & CO.,
  396 Walnut
HUNTER, EDMESTON & CO., 168 Main
NEAVE, WARD & CO.,
  33 Main
ROTHERT J. H. & SONS,
  640 and 642 Cent. Av
THORNTON & PERKINS,
  s.e.c. Pearl and Plum
WILSON & HAYDEN,
  22 & 24 Main

Hats and Caps.
(Wholesale.)
ADKINS DUDLEY M.,
  114 Walnut
CAMP C. B. & CO.,
  95 W. 3d
DODD WM. & CO.,
  144 Main
DICKINSON, PRICE & BISHOP, 112 & 114 W. Pearl
FORCHEIMER MEYERS,
  64 W. Pearl
MASON GEO.,
  73 W. Pearl
Meybeig & Hollman, 121 Walnut
RATHBORNE & WALLACK, 134 Walnut
REEVES M. E. & CO.,
  121 Walnut

SIMPKINSON J. & CO.
  e. Race and Pearl
THOMPSON M. F. & CO.,
  56 W. Pearl
WHITCHER W. C. & CO.,
  139 Walnut
Williams T. J. & Co., 29 W. Pearl
Zeiller & Friedmann, 72 W. Pearl

Hats, Caps and Furs.
ADKINS DUDLEY M.,
  114 Walnut
Alley D. R., 41 Broadway
Benjamin Joseph, 327 Central Avenue
Biedenbender J., 212 Main
BORN & STEIDEL,
  564 Vine
CAMP C. B. & CO.
  95 W. 3d
Debo Wm., 190 Linn
DODD WM. & CO.,
  144 Main
Evers Chas., 35 E. Pearl
Fisler Louis, 502 Vine
Friederich C., 569 Central Av
Hendley G. W., 262 W. 5th
HIBBERT BROS.,
  51 E. Pearl & 210 W. 5th
ISAACS SAMUEL, AGT.,
  104 Main
Jones Abraham, 40 E. Pearl
Kerr Geo., 92 W. 5th
Keller Sam'l, n.s. Browne, b. Mohawk & Ham. Road
Kling Mrs. Catharine, 495 Vine
Kohlbrand Aug., 452 Walnut
MANSS L. & SONS,
  79 E. Pearl
Mason Edwin, 42 W. 5th
McCarthy John, 172 E. 5th
Newman Wm., 78 E. Pearl
Otte H. F., 304 Main
Pye J. R., 48 W. 5th
Pyne Wm. H., e.s. Walnut b. 5th and 6th
Relage Fred., 449 Main
Rieger Chas., 461 Main
ROWE & KENDALL, n.w.c. 9th and Cent. Av
Samuels & Benjamin, 51 E. Pearl
Schaefer & Busche, 138 W. 2d
SCHEER W. H.,
  145 Main
Schroeder J., 418 Vine
Schwarz D., 159 Main
Shelt Joseph, 120 Main
Shroder Wm., 61 E. Pearl
Stoffregen Wm., 595 Cent. Av
STROHEL JOHN,
  245 Central Avenue
THEIS JACOB,
  185 Main
THRILL GEO. & CO.,
  626 Vine
Tobias Henry, 186 Main
TOWERS J. C. & CO.,
  149 Main
Ulmer C., 280 Main
ULMER F.,
  113 Main
Van Sant Samuel, 117 Main
Walter John, 534 Main
Wasem J., e. Main and Court

Hat Blocks.
Carver Wm. H., 63 E. 3d

Hatters' Goods.
(See Wholesale Hats & Caps.)

Hides.
(See Leather, Hides and Oil.)

Homœopathic Pharmacy
Parks Jno M., 3 W. 4th

Hoop Poles.
COPEN ALFRED P.,
  90 Water
Hoban Pat., 51 Water
Steelman Hosea sr., 99 Water

Horse Auctions.
Biggs, J. S., 21 E. 5th
Caruey D., 119 E. 5th
Rider C. E, I., 17 E. 5th

Horse Shoers.
Bell Thomas, 152 W. Court
Burdick Frederick, n.s.12th b. Bremen and Vine
Fluke Henry, 702 Vine
Kordes, J. F., 874 Vine
Rocap James, al. b. 5th and 6th and Main and Walnut
Russell Wm., 695 Cent. Av
Ryan & Westoney, 253 Court
Widdel Aug., 109 Hunt

Hoop Skirt Manufact'rs.
Alley Chas. C., 220 W. 5th
Lazarus David, 371 Cen. Av
Plumb Mrs. G. W. 204 W 5th.
Raffel Abraham, 381 Cent. Av
ROSENFELD SOL.
  275 Cent. Av & 198 W. 5th
Whitmore T. & Co., s.w.c. 4th and Cent. Av

Hops. (Dealer in.)
GOEPPER MICHAEL,
  3 Court House

Horse Collar Manufact.
CARRICK D. S.
  112 Main
Dumler & Bro., 35 Barmen
McGovern J. R., Jr., 208 Central Av
MOORES & CO.,
  89 Main

Horse Shoe Nail Manufs.
Kendall U., 693 Cent. Av
McGrath Pat., n.s. Sycamore b. Hunt and Abigail
Murray Jno., n.w.c. Sycamore and Canal
Woods Patrick, 2 New

Hose and Belt Manuf.
Kennell Geo., 19 W. Front
GOW & SHARP,
  65 Walnut
Thomson Jas., 185 E. Front

Hosiery.
(See also Furnishing Goods.)
Bottmann M., 80 W. 5th
Brown R. & Co., Pearl and Walnut
CALVERT WM. H. & CO.,
  67 W. Pearl
Huie John, 104 Walnut
LEAVITT & BEVIS,
  n.w.c. 5th and Vine
LOWMAN J. & BRO.,
  36 W. Pearl
Phillips S., 250 Cent. Av
RICHARDSON JAS.,
  68 W. 4th
SHILLITO JOHN & CO.
  101 W. 4th
SHOLL, SIMON & CO.,
  52 W. Pearl
Stierle J., 228 Walnut
TAYLOR W. H.,
  160 W. 5th
WALD L.,
  n.s. Pearl b. Vine and Race
WEBB J., JR.,
  154 W. 5th
WYNNE J. R. & CO.,
  91 West Pearl

Hotels and Taverns.
Allegheny House, foot of Walnut
AMERICAN HOTEL,
  e. 5th and Sycamore
American Hotel, n.s. Front e. of Lewis
Australia House, 273 Walnut
Benkenstein Chris., Har'sn Rd
BEVIS HOUSE,
  s.e.c. Walnut and Court
Black Bear Tavern, s.w.c. 9th and Sycamore
BOHL PETER,
  10 Sycamore
Brighton House, junction Harrison & Coleman Pikes
BROADWAY HOTEL,
  s.e.c. Broadway and 2d
Brookville House, n.w.c. Frnt and Central Avenue
BURNET HOUSE,
  n.w.c. Vine and 3d
BUTTMILLERS HOTEL
  40 W. Court
CINCINNATI HOUSE,
  55 Sycamore
CLERMONT HOTEL,
  e.s. Broadway b. 3d & Fri
CLIFTON HOUSE,
  s.e.c. 6th and Elm
Commercial House, n.e.c. 7th and Central Avenue
CONGRESS EXCHANGE
  s.w.c. Pearl and Ludlow
DENNISON HOUSE, s.s. 5th b. Main and Sycamore
Detzel Frank, 36 E. Front
Drovers Inn, 882 E. Front
Dunnas Hotel, McAlister st.
Ebert Conrad, River, b. Ludlow and Lawrence
Evans Hotel, 65 Broadway
Ewan House, 326 Central Av
Farmer's Hotel, 1512 E. Front
FARMERS HOTEL,
  n.e.c. Race and Vine
Fireman's Hall, 65 W. 5th
FREY'S HOTEL,
  421 and 423 Main

BUSINESS MIRROR. 369

Front Street House, 55 W. Frnt
GALT HOUSE,
e. s. Main and 6th
GIBSON HOUSE,
w. s. Walnut b. 4th & 5th
Hartleb Carl, s. w. c. Ludlow &
E, Front
Hart's Hotel, 21 W. 6th
HENRIE HOUSE, n. s. 3d
b. Sycamore and Main
Hollerback John, 43 E. Front
INDIANA HOUSE,
159 W. 5th
INDIANA HOUSE,
536 W. Front
INTERNATIONAL HOTEL
e. s. Sycamore b. 3d and 4th
Jefferson House, c. Ludlow &
Landing
LIBERTY TREE HOUSE,
70 Sycamore
Lower Market Exchange, 57
Sycamore
Ludlow House, n. w. c. Ludlow
and 2d
MAAG FRED. & SON,
443 Main
MADISON HOUSE,
w. s. Main b. Front and 2d
Main Street House, 234 Main
McKernan John, n. e. c. Ludlow and River
Macke H. H. & Co., n. s. c.
Front, E. of Lewis
MECHANICS HALL,
s. e. c. Smith and Front
Mill Street House, n. w. c. Mill
and Front
MONONGAHELA HOUSE,
12 E. Front
NAPOLEON HOUSE,
442 Main
NATIONAL HOTEL,
e. s. Sycamore b. 3d & 4th
NEW ORLEANS HOUSE,
10 Sycamore
Nimzerrn Peter, 71 E. Front
OCEAN HOTEL,
s. e. c. Cen'l Av and Front
PEARL STREET HOUSE,
s. w. c. 3d and Race
Pennsylvania Hotel, s. w. c.
Pike and Front
Phoenix Hotel, n. s. Front nr.
Tollgate, 17th Ward
Rail Road House, 578 W. 6th
SILVESTER HOUSE,
6 and 6 W. 6th
SIXTH ST. HOUSE,
s. w. c. 6th and Plum
Sollman John, n. s. 6th. b.
Horne and Mill Creek
SPENCER HOUSE,
n. w. c Front & Broadway
Spies Robert, w. s. Lebanon
Road, b. Liberty & Corporation Line
Sportsman's Hall, E. Front n.
Corpo. Line
TELEGRAPH HOUSE,
338 Cent. Av
TEUTONIA HOUSE,
15 E. 9th
TREMONT HOUSE,
s. e. c. Vine and 5th
United States Hotel, c. 6th and
Walnut
Union Exchange, 512 W. Front
WALNUT ST. HOUSE,
264 and 266 Walnut
Washington Hotel, 231 Walnut
Washington House, n. w. c. Water and Walnut
WESTERN HOTEL,
502 W. Front

Ice Chests.
(See Refrigerators.)

Ice Dealers.
ASBURY THOMAS & CO.,
s. e. c. Grant and Plum
BLAIR SAMUEL & CO.,
s. e. c. Plum and 12th
CULLEN JAMES,
46 Pub. Landing
Deller Peter, 110 Buckeye
Gandolfo P., 375 Elm
Marks Isaac, Canal b. 15th and
Wade and 31 College
Knorr A. H., s. e. c. Findlay
and Plum
Marks Isaac, 531 Plum and 21
College
Reynolds Robt. R., 389 Daymiller
Spaeth & Co., 323 Broadway
Witte F., 17 E. Front

**India Rubber & Gutta
Percha Goods.**
BART & HICKOX,
49 W. 4th

DAVIDSON TYLER & Co.,
140 and 142 Main
FENWICK & CO.,
56 W. 4th

Indigo Blue manufact.
APPENZELLER J. C.
n. w. c. Oliver and Plum
Well Meyer; 500 Central Av

Ink.
(Printing.)
FRANKLIN TYPE FOUNDRY, 168½ Vine
HARRIS J. N. & CO.,
7 College Hall bldg
JAMES U. P.,
167 Walnut
NIXON, CHATFIELD &
Woods, 77 and 79 Walnut
Smith Walter & Co., 11 w 2d
SNIDER LOUIS,
232 Walnut
STEARNS & FOSTER,
c. Clay and Liberty
STONE F. M.,
141 Walnut
(Writing.)
BUTLER J. J., AGT.,
39 Vine
BERNIRGHOUSE RICH'D,
11 Carr
Deveren John, 149 George
GUNDRY JOHN,
n. w. c. 5th and Walnut
PARR J. C. & CO.,
536 W. 5th
Spies Noah W., 61 Walnut

Instruments.
(Mathematical and Philosophical.)
FOSTER JAS., JR. & CO.,
s. w. c. 5th and Race
RANDOLPH T. F. & BRO.,
67 W. 6th
WARE HENRY,
7 W. 4th
WOCHER MAX,
w. s. 6th, b. Race & Vine
WOCHER LOUIS,
318 Main
(Optical.)
FOSTER JAS., JR., & CO.
s. w. c. 5th and Race
Hall F., 11 E. 3d
WARE HENRY,
7 W. 4th
WOCHER MAX.,
105 W. 6th
(Surgical and Dental.)
REES WM. Z.,
71 W. 6th
Sherwood H. R., 200 Walnut
WOCHER LOUIS,
318 Main

Insurance.
(City Companies.)
AMERICAN,
12 Public Landing
BUCKEYE STATE,
16 Public Landing
CENTRAL,
7 Public Landing
CINCINNATI,
4 Public Landing
CINCINNATI EQUITABLE
30 w. 3d
CITIZENS',
18 Main
City, 8 Public Landing
COMMERCIAL,
n. w. c. Main and Front
EAGLE,
73 W. 3d
FIREMAN'S,
n. e. c. Main and Front
FRANKLIN,
31½ W. 3d
GERMAN MUTUAL,
400 Vine
MAGNOLIA,
15 Public Landing
MERCHANT'S AND MANUFACTURER'S, 11 Public
Landing
NATIONAL,
s. w. c. Main and Front
OHIO LIFE,
68 W. 3d
PORTSMOUTH,
n. w. c. Walnut & 3d
QUEEN CITY,
s. w. c. Walnut and 3d
SUN MUTUAL,
73 W. 3d
UNION,
5 Public Landing
WASHINGTON,
41 Main
WESTERN,
2 Public Landing

(Agencies.)
ÆTNA, of Hartford, Ct.,
Agency for Western States,
J. B. Bennett Gen'l Agent,
office 171 Vine. (See advertisement.)
American Exchange, 76 W. 3d
Atlantic, 76 W. 3d
BENNETT J. B.,
171 Vine. (See advertisement.)
Berne J. J., 33 W. 3d
BONSALL CHARLES,
4 Public Landing
CARTER & BEATTIE,
171 Vine
City Ins. Co., of Hartford,
Conn., 80 W. 3d
Commonwealth of N. Y., 62 W. 3d
Connecticut, 80 W. 3d
DAVIES GEO. C.,
67 W. 4th
EVANS & LINDSEY,
68 w. 3d
Gaddum Wm. L., 455 Vine
Germania, 76 W. 3d
Goodhue, 76 W. 3d
HARTWELL J. W.,
4 Pub. Landing
Hartford, 80 W. 3d
HEDRICK H.,
80 W. 3d
HOLLINGSHEAD M.,
71 W. 3d.
Home Ins. Co. N. Y., 65 W. 3d
HOME INS. CO., N. H.,
Agent 76 w. 3d
HORTON H. V.
n. w. c. 5th and Walnut
Hope, 76 W. 3d
Indemnity, 76 W. 3d
KNIGHT & WARREN,
s. w. c. 3d and Main
Lamar, 76 W. 3d
Law John S., 62 W. 3d
LAW JOHN H.,
62 W. 3d
Lorillard, 76 W. 3d
MAGILL R. H. & H. M.,
33 W. 3d.
Manhattan Life Ins, 76 W. 3d
Market, 76 W. 3d
Mercantile of N. Y., 62 W. 3d
Mutual Life, 80 W. 3d
Mutual Benefit Life, of Newark, N. J., 4 Pub. Land'g
OWENS OWEN, Jr.,
14 Public Landing
PHŒNIX INS. CO.
33 W. 3d
Providence Washington Ins.
Co., 76 W. 3d
REEVES & CO.,
62 W. 3d
Resolute, 76 W. 3d
Roger Williams Ins., 76 W. 3d
Royal Fire and Life Ins. Co. of
Liverpool, 62 W. 3d
Security Fire Ins. Co., 65 W. 3d
Standard, 76 W. 3d
TAYLOR & ANTHONY,
76 W. 3d
Tice John, 33 W. 3d
Unity Ins. Co. of London 62 W. 3d
URNER HENRY C.,
s. w. c. Main and Front
Western Mass. Ins. Co., 65 w. 3d
Washington Ins. Co., 70 W. 3d

Intelligence Offices.
Allen Richard, 23 E. 4th
HALE O.,
128 Walnut
Jones Wm. P., 25 E. 4th

Iron Bridges.
STACEY GEORGE,
s. w. c. Ramsey and W. W.
Canal
GREENWOOD MILES,
n. e. c. Canal & Walnut
McCALLUM BRIDGE CO.,
75 W. 3d

Iron Founders.
ADAMS, PECKOVER & Co.
181 and 183 W. 5th
ASHCRAFT SAMUEL S.,
n. w. c. Plum and Wade
BAKER T. F.,
275 W. 5th
BURROWS J. H. & CO.,
180 W. 2d
CHAMBERLAIN & CO.,
(Hunt. c. of Broadway
Cincinnati Machine Works, n.
e. c. Front and Lawrence
CRANE, BREED & CO.,
s. s. 8th b. Harriet & Millcreek
DAVIS F. P. & CO.,
n. w. c. Main and 2d

Dumont C. T., Front b. Ludlow and Lawrence
EAGLE IRON WORKS,
(M. Greenwood,) n. e. c.
Walnut and Canal
ELMER & FORKNER,
662 W. 5th
Fritsch, Burkhardt & Co., 536
Vine
Goodhue & Co., n. w. c. Plum
and Commerce
GREENWALD J. & E.,
n. w. c. Pearl & M. Canal
HAND, WHITEHOUSE &
Co., 263, 267 & 269 W. 5th
HANES WM. W.,
259 & 261 West Front,
HAVEN JAMES L. & CO.,
173, 175 & 177 W. 2d
Holabird A. B. & Co., s. s.
Front b. Smith & Rose
Howden & Co., 714 W. 6th
LANE & BODLEY,
s. e. c. John and Water
MACY, RANKIN & CO.,
s. w. c. Elm and Pearl
MOORE & RICHARDSON,
Front b. Lawrence & Pike
Niles Works, 222 E. Front
PATTERSON N. & CO.,
26 Main
Pollock & Son, 140 W. Front
Powell D. A., 30 Butler
RESOR WM. & CO.,
13 and 15 Main
RYAN J. B.,
n. s. 7th b. Broadway and
Sycamore
Swift Alex. & Co., Office 3 E.
Front
TODD JAMES,
c. 7th and Smith
Wolff C. & Co., 375 Main
WORTHINGTON & CO.,
413 W. Front

Iron Jail Builders.
BAKER T. F.,
275 W. 5th
MACY, RANKIN & CO.,
s. w. c. Elm and Pearl
VALLEAU & JACOBS,
86, 83, 90 and 92 Elm

Iron Mantels and Grates.
EVANS C. D. & CO.,
112 W. 3d
HAND, WHITEHOUSE &
Co., 263, 265, 267 and 269
W. 5th
MACY, RANKIN & CO.,
8 Burnet House and s. w. c.
Pearl and Elm

**Iron Monuments and
Vaults.**
Dieckmann Ferdinand, Harrison Rd. nr. Benckensteins

Iron, Nails, &c.
CAMPBELL H. & CO.,
19 E. 2d
CHAMBERLAIN & CO.,
51 and 53 Vine
GAYLORD, SON & CO.,
90 and 92 Broadway
HOLENSHADE, MORRIS
& CO., 533, 535 & 537 Central Av
JESSOP WM. & SONS,
11 W. 3d,
MERNA JOSEPH,
102 Main
Neave T. & Sons, 67 Main
NEFF PETER & SONS,
93 W. Pearl
PATTERSON N. & CO.,
36 Main
PHILLIPS & SON,
58 and 60 E. 2d
POTTER LUTHER F.,
100 E. 2d
ROTHERT J. H. & SONS,
610 and 612 Central Av
Schulte & Temmen, 230 Main
SECHLER & PORTER,
51 W. 2d
SHOENBERGER G. & J. H.,
15 Pub. Landing
Weber & Newman, 360 Main
Wolff C. & C. & CO., 375 Main
WOLFF DAN'L.,
119 & 121 E. Pearl

Iron.
(Pig and Bloom.)
Brown, Stout & Butler, 44
Walnut
BUCHANAN R. & SON,
26 E. 2d

CINCINNATI

CAMPBELL, ELLISON & Co., 19 and 21 E. 2d
MOORE ROBT. & CO., 49 Walnut
SECHLER & PORTER, 54 W. 2d
Sinton & Means, 25 W. 3d
SMITH T. G., 53 W. 3d
TRABER & AUBERY, 7 Public Landing

Iron Railings.
BAKER T. F., 275 W. 5th
Espach J. & Bro., 941 Central Avenue
GAYLORD T. G. & CO., 92 Broadway
Heeman Lamburt, 467 Walnut
MACY, RANKIN & CO., s.w.c. Pearl and Elm
Monning & Artman, n.w.c. Race and Burrows
SCHREIBER JOHN L., 550 Vine
VALLEAU & JACOBS, 86, 88, 90 & 92 Elm

Iron Safes.
DIEBOLD, BAHMANN & Co., s.w.c. Elm & Front
DODDS WM. B. & Co., s.s. Pearl b' Elm & Plum
HALL JOSEPH L., & CO., s.w.c. Pearl and Plum
(Dealers in.)
NEFF PETER & SONS. 73 W. Pearl

Iron & Steel Perforating Works.
SMITH THOS. S., s.e.c. Plum and Pearl

Iron Ware.
(Enamelled.)
BAKER T. F. & CO., 275 W. 5th
EVANS C. B. & CO. 112 W. Third
HAND, WHITEHOUSE & CO., 255 W. 5th
MACY, RANKIN & CO., s.w.c. Pearl and Elm
Massman Lewis, c.s. Spring b.
Woodward and Abigail
Wolf C. & Co., 375 Main

Japanned Ware.
Crumpton E., n.e.c. George and Central Av
Scott Wm. B., 121 Main
Smith John F., 67 W. Court
WINCHELL GEO. D., Mausll & Co., n.w.c. Race and 2d

Jewelry Manufacturers
Carley S. T., s.w.c. 4th and Main. (Up Stairs.)
CLAPP WM. B., 81 W. 4th
DUHME & CO., s.w.c. 4th and Walnut
FROESE RUDOLPH, 210 Vine
Hendy Frank T., 5 W. 4th
Keck H., 2 W. 4th
Klausing Clemens, 485 Main
Lange J. & Bro., 52 W. 4th
Lohde Adolp., s.w.c. 4th, & Main
Meyer Leopold, 180 Walnut
Wray H. G., 111 Main

Jewelry, Silver Ware, Watches &c.
See also Watches, Jewelry &c.
Allen C. & W. H., 117 Main
Ausshenmoore H., 663 Cent. Av
Barth Fred., 367 Vine
Berding Ernst, 426 Walnut
Bexell & Hill, 103 Main
Bude Ferdinand, 411 Sycamore
Bornhein E. W., 584 Cen'l Av
CLAPP W. B., 81 W. 4th
Cook Chas., 370 W. 5th
Daller John, 731 Vine
DORLAND GARRET T. n.w.c. Main and Pearl
DUHME & CO., s.w.c. 4th & Walnut
Escalos M., 110 Walnut
Evans Wm. M., 280 Main
ENSTER ANDW. A., 271 Central Av
GREBNER WM., 517 Vine
Honer J. B., 203 Walnut
Konkel C. Henry, 516 Main
Kenkel J. George, 550 Cent Av

KENT LUKE, s.w.c. 6th and Main
KINSEY DAVID, 21 W. 5th
Koch Marcus, 585 Central Av
Korf Henry 365 Main
LOVELL THOS., n.w.c. 5th & Race
MCGROW WM. WILSON n.w.c. 4th and Main
Marmet Fredk., 61 Broadway
Meyer L., 180 Walnut
Mitthoefer H. W., 440 Main
OSKAMP CLEMENS, 62 Main
OSKAMP AUGUST, 108 Main
OWEN CHARLES, n.w.c. Main and 4th
Parks G. D., 341 Central Av
RICHTER, NORBERT & SON, 512 Vine
Scheler A., 528 Race
Schmidt Jos., 60 13th
Schneider J. B., 43 Ham. Road
Struve H. F., 255 Main
Trotter John, 393 C'nut. Av
Voss Julius, 10 W. 5th
Voss J. S., 54 W. 5th
Wachman A. D., 389 Con'l Av
WILMS J. G., College bldg
Wise Jos. A., 64½ W. 5th
Zumbusch Ferdinand M., 673 Vine
(Hair.)
Zwick Madame Joanna, 40 W. Fourth

Justices of the Peace.
ALDRICH WM. L., 78 W. 3d
CHIDSEY WM., 20 W. 5th
Clark H. N., 10 Court House bldg
FISHER DAVID, n.s. 9th b. Plum & Cen'l Av
HANSELMAN CHRIS. F., 82 E. 2d
McLEAN THOS., 478 Vine
Marchant Nathan, 42 E. 2d
Martin P. K., 118. 3d
MORRIS HENRY, H. n.s. Nassau b. Reed & Broad
ROWEKAMP FREDK. H., n.s.c. Main and Hunt
TRUE BENJ. C., s.o.c. 9th & Cent. Av

Lamps and Chandeliers.
Aldrich Otis, 74½ W. 3d
BAKER & VON PUHL, 62 W. 4th
Brown John D. 4 e. 4th
DANNENHOLD & NOCK, 89 W. 5th
GRAY, HEMINGRAY & BRO., 20 E. 2d
Greene Chas. A., 981 W. 5th
HUNNEWELL, HILL & CO., 87 Main
McHENRY & CARSON, 162 Main
RANDOLPH T. F. & BRO. 67 W. 6th
SPEARS & CO., 165 Walnut
TALLMADGE CHAS. S., 215 Vine
Union Coal Oil and Lamp Co., 74½ W. 3d
WATERS BYRON, 236 Main
Lamps.—(Coach,)
McGowan Alex., 72 W. 6th
Lard Oil.—(See Oils.)

Laundries.
Bartley J., 5th above Baum
Caring F., 77 W. Front
Kessler Frederick, 235 Elm
Pierce D. J., 218 Sycamore
Siddall Jno. B., s.w.c. Race & Longworth

Lead Pipe.
GIBSON J. B. & T., 220 Vine
KEMPER WASIL., 230 Main
McCORMICK, GIBSON & Co., 17 E. 9th
STACEY JOHN A., 231 Cent. Av

Leather and Findings.
BANTLIN & COMPTON, n.e.c. Court and Main
Deitman Chas. 288 Main

DIEKMANN GERHARD, 349 Main
EASTON S., 232 Main
ECKERT M., 179 Main
Eblen J. H., 216 & 218 Main
FIEDELDY J. H., 5 12th
Fleishhauer & Eiseman, 25 & 27 W. Canal
Flickner J. O., 235 Main
Forbus & Stevenson, 254 Main
HELMERS C., 8 Main
Hnewe J. H., 359 Vine
KESSLER, HENRY & SON, 215 Main
Krais W., 557 Main
LEIST JOHN & CO., 313 Main
Luhring & Michael, 334 Main
MEIER & ISPHORDING, 8 Main
Mulle- & May, 220 Main
NICKEL & BIELER, 238 Main
PAUL J., 181 Main
SMITH & PALMER, 51 Main
SNODGRASS WM. W., 236 Main
WOOLLEY & GERRY, 166 Main
Warmser B., 317 Central Av

Leather, Hides & Buckskin.
KESSLER H. & SON, 215 Main

Leather, Hides and Oil,
BANTLIN & COMPTON n.e.c. Court and Main
Cahill John, 52 W. Pearl
DIEKMANN G., 349 Main
EASTON S., 212 Main
ECKERT MICHAEL, 179 Main
Forbus & Stevenson, 254 Main
HUNTER, EDMESTON & Co., 168 Main
Kramer Chas., 150 Bremen
McCabe A., 352 Main
MEIER & ISPHORDING, 8 Main
PAUL JOSIAH, 181 Main
SMITH & PALMER, 51 Main
SNODGRASS W. W., 236 Main
TAYLOR A. M. & CO., 20 and 22 W. 2d
Walsh Michael, 7 Commercial Row
WILSON & HAYDEN, 21 and 21 Main
WOOLEY & GERRY, 166 Main

Leather.
(Patent.)
CLARK S. & S. S., 190 Main
(Belt.)
GOW & SHARP, 63 Walnut
Thomson James, 181 E. Front

Lightning Rods.
MAYO ENOCH M., 245 Sycamore
RANDOLPH F. & BRO., 67 W. 6th
WESTON J. H., 23 W. 6th
WRIGHT G. G., 23 W. 6th

Lime and Cement.
Bargy John, 600 Central Av
Fairclough Thos., 193 Richmond
McGlincy Hugh, 332 Cent. Av
Marsh & Co., 4th and Sycamore
MOORES W. B. 265 Plum
Quinn Frank, 350 Central Av

Linseed Oils.
(See Oils.)
(See Wines and Liquors.)

Lithographers.
EHRGOTT, FORBRIGER & Co., s.w.c. 4th & Walnut
Fleetwood C. W., 32 E. 3d
GIBSON & CO., n.w.c. 3d and Main
Macbrair A., over 11 E. 4th

MENZEL G. A. & CO., 257 & 259 Walnut
MIDDLETON, STROBRIDGE & CO., 64 W. 4th
Sauer John, n.w.c. Main and Court

Livery and Sale Stables
Arstingstall J. S., 20, 22 and 24 Hammond
Bard S. W., Betts, nr. John
BOHRER GEO. A., 551 Elm
BROWN & BRO., 9 E. 6th
Bucholz Fred., 348 W. 6th
BUCHHOTZ GEO., 216 W. 7th
Butler Wm., 183 W. 6th
BUTTEMILLER JOHN, e. St. Clair st. and Court
Carney Daniel 19 E. 5th
Cutter A., 78 W. 6th
Dickman & Steins, 627 Race
Dunham & Higdon, 177 W. 6th
Ehlmann H. D., 353 Main
EPPLY JOHN F., n.w.c. 9th and Plum
HACKMAN & DUESTERBERG, n.s. 13th b. Clay and Walnut
Hale A. C., 22 Lodge
HAPGOOD L. E., alley b. 5th and 6th Main and Sycamore
Henermann John, 15 W. 6th
Hust H., n.w.c. Ham. Road & Locust
Jenifer Benjamin c. Walnut & 12th
Johnson Isaac D., St. Clair b. 8th and 9th
Lingers G. H., 341 W. 6th
McDonough J., s.s. 5th, b. Broadway and Lawrence
MILLER J. & CO., 234 Walnut
Moss B. H., n.w.c. Linn and Clark
MUNDY F., 389 W. 6th
Nolker John C. & Fred. Krumdieck, n.s. 9th b. Plum and Central Avenue
Quinn H., 53 Lodge
Riley D. & J., 7 E. 6th
RILEY S. P., 82 Baymiller
Rocap E., Patterson alley
Sayre L., 27 and 29 W. 9th
Schafer & Wormann, 17 Gano
SMITH MATTHEW, s.e. Vine & 3d
Sullivan Patrick, 165 & 167 Central Av
Wall Amos, 114 Sycamore
Uphoff Geo. H., 20 W. 7th
Wietholter H. A.; 11 and 13 Lodge
Willis Wm., 95 E. 2d
Wilson S. & D. 303 Sycamore
WILTSEE, JOHN F., Longworth b' Plum and Central Av
WOOD GEO., 203 Race
WOOD WM., n.w.c. Longworth and Race

Locksmiths and Bell Hangers.
AUPERLE ALEX., 26 Ham. Road
DECAMP & NIEHAUS, 270 Central Av
Delarue O., 518 Walnut
Garbeck C., 426 Sycamore
Gott Fredk., 92 Clinton
Laware N., 236 Elm
Luhman M., 532 Vine
Naybach John F., 33 12th
McGREGOR GEORGE, 133 W. 5th
PFISTER & METZGER, 30 W. 6th
SCHREIBER JOHN L., 530 Vine
SCHRODER J. H. & CO., 53 W. 3d
Smith Pat., 45 Sycamore
Thiue Chas., 644 Cent. Av
Voeglin Geo. H., 104 Ham. Rd
Wansbrough Henry, 182 Cent. Avenue

Locomotive Builders.
MOORE & RICHARDSON, Front b. Lawrence and Pike
Niles Works, 222 E. Front

BUSINESS MIRROR.

Looking Glasses.
(*See Frame Makers.*)

Lumber Dealers.
Bailey E, 518 Front
BISHY W. B. & CO., 133 Freeman
Carson & Dexter, 449 Freeman
Cline John, 159 & 161 E. Front
Corwin H. R., 214 E. Pearl
Dunlap J. & Co., 534 Vine and 435 Freeman
FARRIN THOS. W. & CO., n.e.c. 6th and Baymiller
FRAZER & CO.,
GLENN M. & L., 1565 E. Front
Greiwe J. H., Hunt nr. Br'dway
Hanna J. J. & Co., n.w.c. Clinton and Linn
Hartman F. W., 287 Linn
Higbee W. W. & Co., n.e.c. Elm and Water
HINKLE, GUILD & CO., 1451 e. Front & 365 w. Front
Horsley & Ehler, 248 W. Front
JOHNSON, MORTON & CO s.e. Front b. Kelley and Foster
JOHNSTON J. & J. M., c. 3d and W. W. Canal
Kirby J. J. & Daniel, 93 E. Front
MEIER & REMEIER, head of Race
MILLER P., 567 Elm
MITCHELL & ROWLAND, 522 Vine
Morgan Hugh, s.w.c. W. W. Canal and Smith
MORGAN T., c. 12th and Plum
PIERSON D. B. & CO., 381 Plum
Smith & Williamson, s.w.c. 3d and Vine
Stephens S. D., 39 Mill
Stevenson J., w.s. Freeman b. 6th and 7th
Townley M. J., 445 Vine
VAIL & DANBY, 314 Broadway
VANPELT M. C., 361 Walnut
Ward W. W., c. Harrison Rd and Western Av
WEASNER THOMAS H. & Co., 371 Plum
Whatel y H. & Co., june. 6th and Front
White R. M., 418 Central Av
WHITNEY W. F. & V., 515 Central Avenue

Lumber Inspector.
McGREW ROBT., 53 Laurel

Machinery.
(*Wood Working.*)
FAY J. A. & CO., s.w.c. Johnand Front
LANE & BODLEY, s.e.c. John and Water
STEPTOE & McFARLAN, 216 W. 2d
Wilson Jas. F., 98 E. 2d

Machinists.
ADAMS, PECKOVER & Co., s.w.c. Front & Cent. Av
BURROWS J. O. & CO., 180 W. 2d
CUMMINGS S. & SON, 162 E. Front
Cincinnati Machine Works, n. e.c. Front and Lawrence
Darling J., 80 W. Court, w. of Cent. Av
Dietz Louis, 718 Vine
Donaldson Alex., s.w.c. John and Augusta
Dumont Chas. T., 65, 67 and 69 E. Front
EVENS P., JR., 64 W. 4th
FRIDGE JACOB, rear 48 ' nb. Ldng
Fritsch, Burkhardt & Co., 546 Vine
GREENWALD I & E., n.w.c. Pearl & M. Canal
GREENWOOD MILES, n.e.c. Canal and Walnut
Griffey David, s.s. Pearl b. Ludlow and Lawrence
Gury Jno, P. J., 80 W. Cours
HANES WM. W., 259, 261 & 263 W. Front

Hey A. M., 216 W. 2d
Holabird A. B. & Co., 355 W. Front
Hordesman H J. & D. Dierker, 137 & 139 W. 2d
KRIEGER JOHN, 625 Cent. Av
KETTERLINUS CHAS. W., 408 Walnut
LANE & BODLEY, s.e.c. Water and John
Latta A. B. & E., 179 Race
Lawarre Nicholas, 230 Elm
Maddock S. J., 190 Walnut
Meinecke Wm., 105 Ham. Rd
MOONEY J. B., 116 w. 2d
MOORE & RICHARDSON, n.s. rout b. Lawrence and Pike
Mosig & Hesterberg, 543 Vine
Niles Works, 222 E. Front
POTTER L. F. & WILSON, 98 E. 2d
Powell D. A., 30 Butler
Robbins Martin, 247 W. 5th
Ross N. G., 154 E. Front
Ross S., 65 Lodge
SAVAGE J. A., 93 E. 8th
Shield E. M., 75 E. Front
Stanley & Johnson, 175 w. 2d
STRAUB ISAAC, s. w. c. John and Front
THORNTON & PERKINS, s.e.c. Plum and Pearl
TODD JAMES, c. 7th and Smith

Malt Houses.
BEATTY JOHN & CO., Front b. of Water Works
BRANDT A. R., 113 John
Drum Thos., n.w.c. Smith and Second
HERANCOURT GEO. M., e.s. Harrison Pike ur. Mill Creek
KOEHLER GOTTFRIED & Co., 124 Ham. Road
Schiff John, Colerain Pike, n. of Brighton House

Map Colorers and Mounters.
Graenland M., 1 Court House bldg
Terry Geo. W. 52 E. 3d

Map Publishers.
Barnitz Mack B., 38 & 40 W. 4th
Larrance Isaac. 235 E. 6th
MENDENHALL E., 157 Main

Marble Work.
Albert Wm. & John, 88 13th
Bolles David, 243. Vine
BROOKFIELD WILLIAM, s.e.c. Plum and 6th
FOSTER JOSEPH, n.e.c. Elm and Canal
Fettweis Chas. L., w.s. Ham. Rd b. Findlay & Race
GOODALL WM., 244 W. Court
Gresse Joseph, n.s. Betts, b. Linn and Baymiller
Hoerating Henry, 201 Linn,
Johnson J. B., e.s. Cent. Av. b. 12th and Ann
KELLEY CHARLES J., s.e.c. Linn & Hopkins
MAHON THOMAS, 339 Broadway
RULE CHARLES s.e.c. 5th and Broadway
SEIBEL HENRY 474 Race
WHITE J. & SON, 237 W. 5th
BALDWIN & CO., c. Flint and Freeman
WATERS CHAS. H. & CO. 4 Main
Burgert, Sand & Co., 60 Dudley

Mathematical Instruments.
(*See Instruments.*)

Mattress and Bedding Manufacturers.
Alcorn W. E., 87 Sycamore
ELLIS ROBERT, 136 Sycamore
GEIS ADAM, 67 W. 5th
Grabstein Charles, 224 Central Avenue

HARRIS G. W., 130 Sycamore
Orange J. C., 78 E. 5th
Prather C. B., 51 E. 3d
Pursell D. & J R., 19 E. 4th
Ryling John, 22 E. 8th
SNOWDON & OTTE, 175 Main
Spring John, 29 Pub, Landing
Suydam G, W., 45 W. 5th
Wehrman L. F., 2 W. 5th

Measurers.
(*Carpenter Work.*)
Rodefer J., 203 Plum
SNYDER J. M., St. Clair b. 8th and 9th
(*Stone and Brick Work.*)
MOORE R. B., 203 Plum
Ridgway John N., 521 Vine

Meat Stores.
Bardes Hy., 667 Vine
Bardes Jacob, 596 Vine
Burth Fred., 104 W. Liberty
Baumgoerner Jacob, 628 Race
Becker F., 87 Bremen
Beck Henry, 160 Curr
Billigheimer Louis, 180 W. 6th
Bogart Sam'l, 385 Central Av
Bohn John, s.w.c. Liberty & Baymiller
Bohlander John, 59 W. Court, w. of Central Av
Bolander Nathaniel, w.s. Pike b. Pearl and 3d
Bordick Christian, 168 Linn
Breur Juo. B., 521 Main
Brodhag Wm., 54 Lock
Buck Wm., s.s. Harr. Road b. Brighton and Division
Busk Ferdinand, 293 Freeman
Chaplin Henry, n.w.c. Park and 4th
Clancey James, 616 W. 6th
Clasor Chas. 636 Elm
Cramer Joseph, 239 Broadway
Cramp Michael, 460 Elm
Crepo Wm., 169 Richmond
Donnewald C., 54 Dudley
Dinkelbacker C. & F., 139 W. 5th
D rn Philip, 93 Ham. Road
Drussler Martin, n.c.e. Linn and Betts
Eckele P., 67 12th
Eckerle M., 72 13th
Engelke Wm., 39 Abigail
Ellis G. S., s.e.c. Longworth and Mound
Felt Henry, 14 15th, b. Cent. Av and Plum
FENTON & BECK, n.w.c. 6th and Plum
Fries M., 671 Vine
Fries Phillip, 642 Vine
Frey Lewis, 16 Mary
Freund Ernst, 1106 Cent. Av
Froomor J., 57 15th
Fuernadder John, 580 Main
Fuchs John, 17 Allison
Ganss Michael, 53 12th
Geeks A., 59 E. Front
Gebert F., 107 Clark
Gegner John, 727 Race
Gerhlein Frank, 268 E. Pearl, e. of Broadway
Gelser Wm., 496 Walnut
Gescher Casper, 799 Cent Av
Gettis Frank, n.s. Ham. Road head of Elm
Glanb Adam, 112 Buckeye
Glesser Fred, 570 Vine
Goldsmith N., 236 W. Liberty
Gottsenalk Robert, 323 W. 8th
Greise Christian, 84 Buckeye
Gurney & Tucker 292 E. 5th
Hall Ed. H., 571 Cent. Av
Hamann Lewis, e.s. Race, b. Liberty and 15th
Hannan & L'urney, c. 6th and Sycamore
Harizet Thos., 168 W. 3d
Harmann B., s.s. Abigail, b. Broadway and Spring
Hause Chas., 286 Linn
Herold John, 94 W. Front
Hugger August, c.Sycamore & Milton
Hunt X., 118 Bank,
Hunter G. V., s.e.c. Linn and Walnut
Keetirs Valentine, 731 Elm
Kerdolf J. A., cor. George & Linn
Klumh Henry, 26 Central Av
Knight J., c. 6th & Harriet

Kuntzmann Jno., s.w.c. Liberty and Broadway
Loewenstein Herman, n.w.c, John and 9th
Longwish Henry, s.e.c. Baymiller and Court
McNurny Thos., n.e.c. 7th & Broadway
Meier Conrad, 662 Main
Mergle Jos., n.w.c. 3d & Park
Metsker Philip, 431 W. 7th
Meyer Chas., 536 Central Av
Meyerle C., 236 W. 6th
Miller Joseph, 40 Race
Miller Richard, 47 Wade
Miller Samuel B., s.c.c. Sycamore and Webster
Miller Thos., 696 Central Av
Moran T. B., 187 W. 5th
Mueller Conrad, s.e.c. Liberty and Pleasant
Nockel Jno., 46 Bremen
Nopenberger John, 43 Hughes
O'Brien Thomas, 614 W. 6th
Pollaway P., 991 Central Av
Renner Jacob, 198 Linn
Reutschler Geo., 620 Main
Rice John, 74 Mohawk
Riehle Ignatz, 126 W. Front
Rittenger Conrad, cor. Mill and 2d
Ritter Geo. W., 241 W. 4th
Roehler Henry, 463 Linn
Roedersheimer J., 544 W. 5th
Roege Henry, 427 Sycamore
Rosenthal Chas., 448 Main
Rothfuss Fred., 114 W. Liberty
Ruprecht Lorentz, 15 Ham. Road
Schaefer Henry, 466 Main
Sauer Adam, 593 Walnut
Schmidt J., s.w.c. Linn and Clinton
Schmidt Wm., 25 Bank
Schnorbus A., 329 W. 5th
Scholhammer, L., 544 Cent.av
Schinc B', 920 Central Avenue
Schrecker Fritz, 64 Ham. Road
Schroder Henry 172 E. 5th
SCHROTH MATTHEW, 332 W. 6th
Schrot Jno., s.s. Harrison Rd b. Coleman and Patterson
Schuefesle Fred., 450 Linn
Schwein G. F., c. John & Chesnut
Schwein Henry, n.w.c. Hunt and Broadway
Schwind F. P., 83 Hamer
Seidenspinner G. 457 W. 3d
Siebel Jacob, 616 Vine
Sietz Henry, n.e.c. Buckeye and Locust
Silbernagle S. jr., 97 W. 5th
Simpson W. T, & Son, e. 6th & Mound
Slimer & Raipe, 28 Pub. Ldng
Slough Martin, cor. Richmond and Mound
STEWART A. V., s.e.c. Park and 5th
Stickler Chas., 505 Race
Stoke S., 987 Central Av
Stubenrauch Jacob F., 607 Vine
Swine John, s.e.c. Hopkins & Baymiller
Theringer David, 322 Freeman
Thuringer B., Bauch, 526 Race
Troiler John, 449 Vine
Trout John, 104 E. Front
Vallo & Bagge, 78 E. Liberty
Wankmueller, J., 604 Ham. Rd
Ward Robt., 238 Cent. Av
Warner G. W., 89 W. 3d, e. of Findlay
WARTMAN WM. & CO., 15 Ham. and Findlay
Webert M., 135 Ham. Road
Weihe M., 152 E. Front
Wernigok P., 121 Bremen
Wettchan A., 101 Clark
Witte F., Apt.. 17 E. Front
Winter V. & Bro., s.e.c. 3 W. 5th and Smith
Wittich Albert, 610 W. 6th
Wolf August, 122 Central Av
Wunder Edward, 509 Sycamore
Young Jacob, s.e.c. Clinton & Cutter
Zeppenfeld H., 65 Abigail
Ziegler M., n.w.c. Henry and Pleasant
Zimmerman C., 314 Findlay

Medicines.
(*Patent and Family.*)
BANFORD C. F., 103 Barr
Forsha A. W., 415 W. 5th
HARRIS J. N. & CO., 7 College Building.

Hunshall J. G. (Agent B. Keith & Co., 1106 W. 6th
PARK JOHN D., n.e.c. 4th and Walnut
PHILLIPS GEO. W., 50 W. 6th
ROBACK DR. C. W., 6 E. 4th
ROSE SAM'L K., 184 W. 6th
SCOVILL L. & CO., 12 W. 8th
SHEPPARD J. W., 20 W. 4th
Townsley A. L., 171 Mound

Mercantile Agencies.
BRADSTREET J. M. & SON, 27 W. 3d
DUN R. G. & CO., 51 and 53 Walnut
TAPPAN, McKILLOP & CO., s.w.c. 3d and Walnut

Metals.
DAVIDSON TYLER & CO. 140 Main
HOMAN HENRY, 11 E. 7th
LAWSON F. H. & CO., 178 Main
MERNA JOSEPH, 132 Main
RESOR WM. & CO., 13 and 15 Main
SELLEW & CO., 214 Main
STEPHENSON H. W., 30 W. 4th
WAYNE JOS. W. & CO., 106 Main
WINCHELL GEO. D., MARSH & CO., n.w.c. Race and 2d

Military Goods.
BONER JOHN, 36 W. 5th
HAMLIN HANNIBAL G., JR., 67 W. 4th
Hoffmeister F., 114 W. 5th
POHLMAN GEO. W., 102 W. 4th

Millinery Goods.
(See Wholesale Silk and Straw Goods.)

Millinery and Dress Making.
(See also Dress Makers.)
Algoe M. F., 222 W. 5th
Alms H. August, s.w.c. Vine and Liberty
Alma Wm., 642 Race
Barton Mrs. J. N., 22 E. 4th
Baston Robert, 144 W. 5th
Baumgartner J. & Co., 592 Vine
Becker Mrs., 128 W. 5th
Bell Mary, 252 W. 5th
Bice Mrs. E., 479 W. 7th
Bigeon Madam Mary, 211 W. 5th
Blonz Miss S. H., 106 W. 4th
Buhl Mrs. V., 73 E. Pearl
BORN & STEIDEL, 552 Vine
Brondamonte S., 107 Cent. Av
Brinkhoff E., 374 Broadway
BRITTING M. & P., 227 W. 7th
Brockington J. C., 130 W. 5th
Bryan L., 210 W. 5th
Costello, 128 W. 5th
COUDEN E. B., 7 E. 4th
Dominict Julia A., 162 W. 5th
Dopke Fred. 91 and 93 Martin
DOUGHERTY CHAS. C. & CO., 34 W. Pearl
Droitus C., 64 W. 5th
Ennis M., 194 W. 5th
EPPLY ADAM, 20 W. Pearl
Feakins Mrs. Marg., 24 E. 4th
Feldman Wm., 584 Race
Fisher Julius, 77 E. Pearl
Flur O., 452 Vine
Focks John A., 571 Main
Garre M. & E., 591 Main
Gaesling C., 818 Main
Goldenberger Jno., 423 Vine
Hanover Harriet A., 190 W. 5th
Hatke Geo., 104 14th
HENDERSON J. A., 18 W. 5th
HENLEY I. & H., 21 W. 4th
Hett M., 92½ Central Av
Hineral Annie, 236 W. 5th
Irving J. S., 164 W. 6th
Jamison M., 121 W. 5th
Knox Edward C., 120 W. 4th
Laird Eliza, 210 W. 5th

Lennon A., 218 W. 5th
Lindemann H., 331 Main
McCLURE EMILY, 17 W. 4th
McDermott M., 207 Wade
Marklan Anna, 166 W. 5th
Marks Ann, 70 W. 5th
Menkeos S. & Son, 62 W. 5th
Millson James, 130 W. 6th
Mulcahy Ellen, 372 W. 5th
Muller Mary, 335 Walnut
Orchard C., 101 Mound
Perry Mary E., 274 W. 5th
Ploohg Anthony, 513 Main
Plumb Geo. W., 204 W. 5th
Pocock Lucy C., 287 Central Av
Quinn Elizabeth, n.w.c. 5th & Elm
Ronau T. & C., 186 W. 5th
Riekel Wilhelm, 425 Vine
Rodemaker Mrs. M., 223 Linn
Rose Anna, 86 Hopkins
Rottger Frank H., 567 Main
Sattler Erust, 542 Main
Scurrah S. A., 26 E. 4th
Selter Charlotte, 85 Ham. Rd
Shlesinger B., 106 W. 5th
Sullivan Sarah, 233 Race
TAYLOR M. A., 106 W. 4th
Thorne A. F., 197 Plum
WEBB JOHN, JR., 14 W. 5th
Weigler Wilhelmina, 502 Main
Weigler Arnold, 400 W. 5th
Weisker Brothers, 121 Main
Westjohn Theresa, 310 W. 5th
Weyland N. H., 205 Elm
Wilson Mary, 148 W. 5th
Wilson Sarah, 80 Pike
WILSON SAMUEL, 78 W. 4th

Mills.
(Portable.)
BRADFORD JAMES & CO., 65 Walnut
BRADFORD T. & CO 59 Walnut
BURROWS J. H. & Co., s.s. 180 W. 2d
Cochran Robt., 44 W. Front
GREENWALD I. & E., n.w.c. Pearl and M. Canal
Hamer M. W., 120 W. 3d
Holabird A. D. & Co., 345 W. Front
Niles Works, 222 E. Front
STRAUB ISAAC, n.w.c. John and Front
TODD JAMES, s.w.c. 7th and Smith

Mill Stones.
(Burr.)
BRADFORD JAS. & CO., 65 Walnut
BRADFORD T & CO., 59 Walnut
BURROWS J. H. & CO., n.s. 2d b. Elm and Plum
Cochran Robert, 44 W. Front

Mineral Water.
Alwois H. & J., 127 W. 2d
Born & Grolwe, 530 Walnut
MUILLAUSER G. & H., 724 Elm
NIEHAUS CAPT. HENRY, 450 Sycamore
Overdick H. & C., 17 Home
Ritter A., 468 Vine
Vorhage Henry, 66 Gano
Wilku & Co., 150 W. Pearl

Mineral Water.
(Medicinal.)
BERGER ALEX. M., 128 W. 4th

Mouldings.
(Gilt.)
EGGERS & CO., 168 Main
BONTE A. P. C., 217 Walnut
EGGERS & WILDE, 317 Main
PAPE E. W. & BRO., 217 Walnut
THEOBALD & THEURKAUF, Court House bldg
WISWELL WM., JR., 70 W. 4th

Moulding Manufs.
Bechman F. W., 354 Ham. Rd
BONTE A. P. C.
HOLSTEIN & HAMMER, n.e.c. Augusta and Smith
MITCHELL & RAMMELSBERG, 99 W. 4th
PAPE E. W. & BRO., 217 Walnut

Mourning Goods.
DELAND & GOSSAGE, 74 W. 4th
SHILLITO J. & CO., 101 W. 4th

Museum.
Western Museum, 78 Sycamore

Music.
(Bands.)
Geyer's Cornet Band, 30 W. Crt
Heidel's Cornet Band, 197 Vine
Menter's Amer. Cornet Band, 81 W. 4th
SPILLS J. C., n.w.c. 6th and Walnut

Music.
(Professors.)
(See also Teachers.)
Aiken Chas., 152 E. Liberty
Boldwin E. H., 36½ Carr
Brooks, Theodosia, n.w.c. Longworth and Central Av
DeRicoles J., 118 John
Fasig Mary C., 264 George
Geyer John, 30 W. Court
Greenleaf M. H. L., s.w.c. 3d and Broadway
Hahn H., 157 Smith
Klausmeyer Wm., 413 Elm
Knapp F. W., 60 Elder
Langake Ed. A., 21 E. 4th
Locke E., 144 George
Mason L. W., 86 Barr
Menter A., 81 W. 4th
Rattinger Geo. C., 364 W. 5th
Shoenbran Amelia, 352 Race
Steinbrecher W. F., Sycamore b. 4th and 5th
Stuckle C., 297 Main
Warren John 193 W. 5th
WEBER W., n.e.c. 5th and Vine
Wisenborn H., 82 W. 4th
Williams Victor, 378 W. 7th
Worrall Henry, 52 Laurel

Music.
(Sheet.)
CHURCH J. Jr., 66 W. 4th
Fonda C. Y., 72 W. 4th
PETERS A. C. & BRO., 94 W. 4th
Peters W. M., 50 W. 4th
RAUCH F. W., 349 Race

Musical Instruments.
Allen G. W. H., 117 Main
BRITTING & BROS., 227 W. 5th
CHURCH J. Jr., 66 W. 4th
Colburn Wm. F., 94 W. 4th
Fonda C. Y., 72 W. 4th
Gleich R., 61 Clay
Gleich J. F., Metropolitan bldg
Kaiser & Koffler, 471 Walnut
KRELL ALBERT, 180 Vine
MITCHELL & RAMMELSBERG, 99 W. 4th
MURCH C. M., 72 W. 4th
PETERS A. C. & BRO., 94 W. 4th
Peters W. M., 50 W. 4th
RAUCH F. W., 349 Race
SCHROEDER H. & CO., 70 Main
SMITH & NIXON, 40 W. 4th
WURLITZER RUDOLPH, 123 Main

Mustard Manuf.
APPENZELLER J. C., n.w.c. Oliver and Plum
DIXON G. R. & CO., 213, 215 and 217 Sycamore
HARRISON & WILSON, 131 and 133 Race
PFAEFLIN W., n.s. Pearl b. Lawrence & Pike
SEIP GEORGE, 133 Bremen

Morocco Dresser.
Forbus Jno. F., e.s. Plum n. of Findlay

Nail Manufacturers.
Graff Norbert, 1104 Cent. Av
SHOENBERGER O. & J. H. & CO., 15 Public Landing

Naval Stores.
BARTLETT R. & Co., s.w.c.w. and Front

MOORE ROBERT, 49 Walnut

News Depot.
(See Periodical Depots.)

Newspaper Agency.
PARVIN SYLVESTER H., 63 W. 4th

Newspapers and Periodicals.
(Daily, English.)
CIN. ENQUIRER, n.e.c. Vine and Burnet
CIN. TIMES, 62 W. 3d
CIN. COMMERCIAL, n.e.c. 4th and Race
CIN. GAZETTE, n.e.c. 4th and Vine
CIN. PRESS, Vine opp. Custom House
LAW BULLETIN, 19 W. 4th

(Daily, German.)
Union, s.w.c. Court & Main
VOLKSBLATT, Court House bldg
VOLKSFREUND, c. Vine and Longworth

WEEKLY (English.)
CATHOLIC TEL. & ADVOCATE, s.w.c. Vine and Longworth
CHRISTIAN HERALD, 21 W. 4th
CHRISTIAN PRESS, 28 W. 4th
CIN. PRICE CURRENT, Walnut b. 4th and 5th
DOLLAR COMMERCIAL, n.e.c. Race and 4th
DOLLAR TIMES, 62 W. 3d
ENQUIRER, n.e.c. Vine and Burnet
ISRAELITE, 32 W. 6th
LETTER SHEET P. CURRENT, Col. Hall
LID. HALL & GAZETTE, n.e.c. 4th and Vine
NEW CHURCH HERALD, College Building
PRESBYTER, 21 W. 4th
RAILROAD RECORD, 167 Walnut
STAR IN THE WEST, n.w.c. 6th and Walnut
WEST. CHRIST. ADVOC., s.w.c. Main and 8th

WEEKLY (German.)
CHRISTIAN APOLOGIST, s.w.c. Main and 8th
CIN. VOLKSFREUND, c. Longworth and Vine
DEBORAH, 32 W. 6th
KIRCHENBOTE & VOLKSBOTE, 428 Main
VOLKSBLATT, Court House bldg
WAHRHEITS FREUND, c. Vine and Longworth
ZEITBLATTER, 432 Walnut

SEMI-MONTHLY (English.)
CHRISTIAN ERA, 162 Vine
LORD'S COUNFT. DETR., 6 W. 3d
PADDOCK'S BANK MIRROR, s.n.c. 3d & Walnut
PRESBYTN. WITNESS, n.w.c. 4th & Race
SUN. S. ADVOCATE, s.w.c. Main and 8th
SUN. S. BELL, s.w.c. Main and 8th

MONTHLY.
AM. CHRIST. REVIEW, 41 W. 8th
LADIES REPOSITORY, s.w.c. Main and 8th
Laucet & Observer, 120 Richmond
MASONIC REVIEW, 117 Walnut
MISSIONARY ADVOC., s.w.c. Main and 8th
OHIO VAL. FARMER, 42 W. 4th
PADDOCK'S BANK MIRROR, s.n.c. 3d and Walnut
PHONOGRAPHIC MAGAZINE, 51 W. 4th

BUSINESS MIRROR. 373

Soldiers' Friend & Army Record, 8 W. 3d
Tem'p'r'nce Mag'zine, 112 Hpkns
UNION COUNTERFEIT DETECTOR, 8 W. 3d

QUARTERLY.

DENTAL REGISTER, 38 W. 4th

YEARLY.

WILLIAMS' CIN. DIRECTORY, 194 Walnut

Night Carts.

Byl Leondert, 36 Stone

Notaries Public.

ABRAHAM JOS., Masonic Temple
ALDRICH WM. L., 78 W. 3d
APPLEGATE JOHN W., 51 W. 4th
Ast John A., s.e.c. Court and Main
Avery Wm. L., 21 W. 3d
Baldauf F., 478 Vine
BALL FLAMEN, JR., 6 E. 3d
BATEMAN W. M., 23 W. 3d
BATES J. H., 56 W. 3d
BELL PETER, 10 Court House bldg
BEATRIE JNO. H., 171 Vine
Bevan J. Jr., Masonic Temple
Biddle F. J., 22 W. Court
BIRD NICHOLAS, 4 Railroad bldg
Blakely J. L., 53 W. 3d
Booking A. H., Carlisle bldng
Bofinger Benj., 221 W. 6th
BRADSTREET EDW. P., 25 W. 3d
BROWER A., 4 Masonic Temple
BROWN C. BRADY, 19 W. 3d
Brows E. T., s.w.c. Court & Main
BRUNER MARTIN, 20 W. Court
BROOKE CHAS. F., 27 W. 3d
Burgoyne Jno. Jr., s.e.c. Main and Court
BURNET JACOB, 5 Masonic Temple
Cady D. K., Jr., 57 W. 3d
CALDWELL J. W., 379 Main
Caldwell Sam., 379 Main
CARPENTER SAML. S., 23 W. 3d
Carter S. D., Court and Main
CHALLEN JAMES R., s.e.c. 4th and Vine
CHAMPLIN L. D., 13 W. Court
Clark Ste., 22 W. Court
CLEMMER J. A., s.e.c. 7th and Main
Coles Stephen, 120 Main
Collier Chas. D., Masonic Temp
Conklin T., 9th nr. Cent. Av
Coppock W. J., Mason, Temp.
Cox Edwin, 23 W. 3d
Cox Jos., n.w.c. 5th and Wlnt
CRANCH & CHALLEN, s.e.c. 4th and Vine
CRAWFORD S. T., 30 W. 4th
Creutz Jacob, s.e.c. Main and Court
Day H. M., 58 W. 3d
Dengler F. X., 22 W. Court
Disney Wm., City Bldngs
DOBMEYER JOS. J., n.w.c. Main and Court
DOUGLASS JOHN G., 42 W. 4th
DUTTON AARON R., Chase's bldg
Edwards Edwin, 148 Walnut
EGLY JOS. E., s.e.c. Court and Main
Elmes Webster, 6 E. 3d
FERGUSON & McGINNIS, 65 W. 3d
FISHER SAML. S., 53 W. 3d
Forrest Wm. T., 20 W. Court
FOX CHAS. H., 116 Main
Freon Jozef, n.w.c 3d & Main
Garrard Jeptha, s.e.c. 4th and Vine
GIBBONS J. G., 35 W. 3d

GOODMAN T. S., 17½ W. 3d
GOSHORN ALFRED T., 17 W. 3d
Grosvenor Mason, n.w.c.6th & Walnut
HAGANS MARCEL. B., 148 Walnut
Hamilton Robert S., 180 Wlnt
HANOVER JNO. C., 57 W. 3d
Hanselman W. F., 52 E. 2d
HARVEY JOSHUA, 19 W. 3d
Heinsheimer D., 19 W. Court
Hendricks G. W., 241 W. 9th
HERRON JOHN W., 148 Walnut
Hill A. P., Bank bldg.
Hill Rich., n.w.c. 3d & Sycamore
HILTS CHAS., 22 W. Court
HOLLINGSHEAD MARK, 77 W. 3d
Hooker John J., n.s. Front nr. Hill
Hunter Jno. R., 75 W. 3d
HUSTON A. B., 14 E. 2d
HUTCHINSON E. E., 65 W. 3d
James Thos. M., 3 Mas. Temple
Jeuney H., Masonic Temple
JOACHIM WENDELL, 22 W. Court
JOHNSON JAMES W., n.w.c. 3d and Main
JOHNSTON ROBT. A., Masonic Temple
JONES & SHARP, Masonic Temple
KERR WM. H. Court House
Kemper Theophilus, 8 E. 2d
KIRBY CLINTON, n.w.c. 6th and Walnut
Kittredge E. W., 51 W. 4th
Langdon E. Bassett, Metropolitan Building
LATHROP WM. H., Masonic Temple
Lawder John F., n.w.c. Court and Main
LINCOLN T. D., 8 E. 2d
LOGAN THOS. A., 73 W. 3d
LONG ALEX., 25 W. 3d
LUDLOW AUGUSTUS, s.e.c. 4th and Vine
LYNCH JOHN A., 7 Short's Building
Lynd Staughton, 7 Masonic Temple
McClymon J.B., n.w.c 3d and Main
McDougal Jos., 57 W. 3d
McGUFFEY ALEX. H., 120 Main
McManama A. B., 57 W. 3d
Mansfield Chas. D., 6 E. 5th
MATSON L. B., 21 W. 3d
Matthews S. R., 23 W. 3d
MILLER F. W., 65 W. 3d
Miller Geo. W., n.w.c. 3d and Walnut
MILLER ISAAC J., 34 Bank Bldg
MINER J. L., 57 W. 3d
Morse Edward, 227 Vine
Mulane A. J., 146 Plum
Munroe Chas., 186 Longworth
NESMITH T. A., 23 W. 3d
Nixon Wm. Penn, 75 W. 3d
NOYES EDW'D R., 23 W. 3d
Outcalt P., s.w.c. 3d & Main
O'HARA THOMAS B., 119 Walnut
Paul Har. D., 23 W. 3d
PAXTON T. B., 21 W. 3d
Potter Daniel, 1 and 2 Masonic Temple
POWERS HIRAM, 8 Short's Building
Powell J. B., 66 W. 3d
POWELL THOMAS, Masonic Temple
REEDER STEPHEN W., 73 W. 3d
Richards Channing, Jr., s.e.c. 4th & Vine
ROGERS R. C., 1 Short's bldg

ROSE SAMUEL K., 194 W. 6th
Searles A. M., 11 Pob. Ldng
SHEPPARD WM. D., 20 W. Court
Sherwin W. G., Masonic Tem.
SHONTER A., 363 Main
SNOW HENRY, 7 Masonic Temple
SPRYER BENNO, 7 & 9 W. 3d
SPOONER W. L., n.w.c. Court and Main
STALLO JOHN B., 15 W. Court
Stearns Geo. E., 148 Walnut
STRAIT EDWIN F., 230 Walnut
STRAUB W. F., 3 Masonic Temple
Swartz Benj. A., 148 Walnut
TAFEL G. n.w.c. Main and Court
Thielmann Geo. O., s.s. Court nr. Main
Taylor J. R., 130 Vine
THOMPSON E. A., 25 W. 3d
TODD ALEX., 15 W. 3d
Titus Joseph. B., 12 W. 4th
TRUE BENJ. C., s.e.c. 9th and Cent. Av
TULLIS A. J., 243 W. 9th
VON SEGGERN C., s.e.c. Court and Main
WHITE J. S., 200 Walnut
White O. D., 49 Bank Bldg
Williams E. M., 284 Main
Willis A. F., 181 Walnut

Notions.

(See Fancy Goods, also Variety Stores.)

ANTRAM M. T. & CO., 47 W. Pearl
Arnold Lester, 11 W. 6th
BOHM, MACK & CO., 80 W. Pearl
COHEN SIMON M., 130 Main
DYER CHAS. S., 37 Everett
EPPLY ADAM, 20 W. Pearl
Harder Maria, n.s. 5th b. Main and Walnut
HANNES, LEWIS & SPENCER, 136 Walnut
Herder Mary, 85 E. Pearl
Huie John, 104 Walnut
HUNT & STORCH, 28 W. Pearl
Jones John G., s.e.c. Linn & 7th
Kauts Mary, 650 Central Av
Lewis Jno., 24 Broadway
Lewis Annette, 126 W. 9th
McFadden G. & H., 98 W. 5th
Masmeister Laura, 83 E. Pearl
Ovenstolu Helena, 90 W. 5th
Parry Jemina, 121 W. Front
Patterson Anna, 44 Lock
Ritter Joseph, 67 Broadway
Rossman & Rosenheim, 30 W. Pearl
SHEPPARD J. W., 20 W. 4th
SHIPLEY, MURRAY &CO. 94 W. Pearl
Stadlmair Helena, 463 Main
Stern Simon, 118 Clinton
WALD LEWIS, 80 W. Pearl

Nurseries, Seedsmen, &c.

(See Seed Stores.)

Oculists.

Long John C., 278 W. 6th
Marcus A., 151 W. 6th
POTTER J. F., 30 W. 4th
WALDO F. A., s.w.c. 4th and Sycamore
WILLIAMS E., 163 Race

Oil Cloth Manufacturers.

SAWYER & KIRK, 8 College Building
SCHWENKER F. W., 579 Walnut
SNOWDON & OTTE, 175 Main

Oil Manufacturers.

(Castor.)

WOOD & McCOY, 20 Spring

(Coal.)

Aldrich Otis, 74½ W. 3d
BARTLETT R. & CO., s.w.c. Walnut & Front
Brown J. D., 4 E. 4th
Crumpton E., n.e.c. Cent. Av & George
DONOHUE J. W. & CO. s.e.c. Walnut & 2d
GREAT WESTERN COAL & OIL CO., 13 W. 4th
Kendall O. H., 98 Betts
McHENRY & CARSON, 162 Main
RANDOLPH T. F. & BRO. 67 W. 6th
Smith Walter & Co., office 9 W. 2d
SPEAR & CO., 105 Walnut
TALLMADGE C. S., 241 Vine
Union Coal Oil and Lamp Co. 74½ W. 3d

(Lard.)

BARTLETT R. & CO., s.w.c. Walnut & Front
BOGEN G. & P., Ham. Road n Brighton H.
BURCKHARDT & CO., 107 Sycamore
Cheever A. G. & Co., 11 W. Front
Conkling J. L., 109 E. 5th
Cronin T. & Co., 28 Water
EMERY THOS. & SON, s.e.c. Water and Vine
Ford Wm., s.s. Front b. Reed and Broad
HIATT & WOODS, s.s. Deer Creek Road, n. of Court
JONES & CONAHAN, 728 Central Av
Litmer Casper, 63 Hunt
Miami Oil Works, 9 W. 2d
Peebles & Bro., s.s. Canal b. Elm and Plum
PROCTER & GAMBLE, 14 W. 2d
Rehs & Lutkehaus, 13 W. Canal
ROPES N. & CO., Lock b. 4th and 5th
SHILLITO GEO. & CO., 30 Sycamore
SMITH AMOR, 17, 19 and 21 Webster
Smith, Walter & Co., 9 W. 2d
TAYLOR A. M. & CO., 20 & 22 W. 2d
Tubin W. J., 214 John
WANN C. & T., 57 W. Miami Canal
WERK M. & CO., 11 Main
Wiedemer M. L., 15 W. Front

(Linseed.)

CASSADY & STEWART, s.e.c. 9th & Sycamore
Gordon James, c. 4th & Lock
Whetstone F. D. S. & Co., n. s. 8th b. Broadway & Canal

(Neats Foot.)

WHITAKER JOS., Deer Creek Road

(Tanner's.)

(See Leather, Hides and Oil.)

(Vitriol.)

MARSH & HARWOOD, 313 Ham. Road

Oils and Turpentine.

(See also Druggists.)

BARTLETT R. & CO., s.w.c. Walnut & Front
COFFIN & SON, 3 Water
HARRISON W. H. & CO., 25 W. 4th
Miami Oil Works, 9 W. 2d
MOORE ROBERT, 49 Walnut

Omnibus Manuf.

BRUCE I. & B., s.e.c. Vine and 3d

Omnibus Lines.

Batavia & Williamsburg Omnibus office, 139 W. 6th
Cincinnati, Covedrain, Venice & New London, 109 Walnut
Cincinnati & St. Louis L. R. n.e.c. Park and Mound
C. Bainnati, Harrison & Brookville, 169 Walnut
Cincinnati & Lebanon, 169 Walnut

Opticians.

Davis W. M., 217 W. 5th
Kelly Charles, 196 W. Front

374 CINCINNATI

FOSTER JAS., Jn., & CO.,
137 W. 5th & Race
Hall F., 11 E. 3d
WARE HENRY,
7 W. 4th

Organ Builders.
Close John, 407 Central Av
KOEHNKEN & CO.,
553 Sycamore
Schwer D., 706 Cent Av
Voellmcoke Fred., 165 W. 5th

Ornamentor & Decorator
BOETIG T. J.,
s.e.c. John & 2d

Oyster Depots.
Barber John, 77 W. 5th
CLARK JAS. L.,
55 W. 5th
GESNER ISAAC O.,
223 Walnut
Kaufman Julius, 22 W. Front
Keith Robt., 81 W. 5th
MALTBY C. S.,
11 W. 5th
ORR ROBT.,
11 W. 5th
Owings John D., 27 W. 5th
Platt L. B. & Co., s.e.c. 3d &
Sycamore
TODD JAS.,
233 Walnut
Waggoner S. S., 203 Cent Av

Oysters, Fish and Game
Clark J. F. & J. W. 46 E. 3d
CLARK J. L.,
55 W. 5th
Keith Robert, 81 W. 5th
Owings J. D., 27 W. 5th
TODD JAS.,
233 Walnut

Painters.
(House and Sign)
Allan & Kettell, 201 Plum
Barbenchon & Jones, n.e.c.
6th and Walnut
Bates H. M., 11 W. 9th
Becker Jno. C., 111 Ham. Rd.
Bennett Morris, 222 Elm
Bogart & Son, Van Horn, b.
Baymiller and Freeman
Bogart J., jr., 76 Butts
Bogart John H., 23 W. 4th
Bray C. W., 224 Elm
Brossamle Fred., 660 Elm
BURUND HENRY,
47 E. 3d
Buschmann F. & Co., 500 Sycamore
Coates & Lecount, 110 Laurel
Clark Chester M., 72 W. 3d
Conway M. A., e.s. Cent. Av,
b. 7th and 8th
Cox Wm. E., 455 W. 3d
CUMMINGS & BEIRNE,
n.e.c. 3d and Race
Dierlein Fred., 27 Bremen
Dickson Samuel, 191 W. 4th
Duvel Henry, 22 Abigail
Emerson Sam'l W., 41 E. 3d
Fick Fred., 133 Clinton
Forristall C. T., 122 Vine
Frank Simon, 30 W. Court
Freeman W. D., 420 W. 8th
Gault & Sackett, s.s. Front e.
of Leatherbury
Gorman J. J., 45½ E. 3d
Hackmann & Springmeier, 26
Woodward
Haynes & Bro., 132 Race
Hollman T., 371½ Broadway
Hoizbach Wm., 776 Central Av
HOPKINS H. P.,
s.s. Baker, b. Vine and
Walnut
HUSTON J. M.,
67 W. 3d
Klingelhoefer F., 57 W. 3d
Knaggs Thomas, n.e.c. 3d and
Park
Leaman & Wilcox, n.e.c. John
and Everett
Lovell J. D. & Co., 43 E. 2d
Lyford L., 154 W. 5th
McCord J. H., 103 W. 6th
McCoy J., 61 George
McKitrick John, 489 W. 5th
Moore Jas. M., 364 Central Av
Mueller John, 697 Race
Mueller & Schimpf, 26 Logan
Musick & Ronnebaum, 105
Woodward
Murry C. A., 374 Walnut
O'Neill John, 300 Elm
Parker John, 107 George
Rech Fred., 38 E. 5th
RIGGS & MURRAY,
28 E. Front
Robinson B., 200 Longworth

Robinson H. F., 298 W. 5th
Saunders & Baldwin, 217 W.
5th
Schell & Brinkman, w.s. Fillmore b. Richmond & Gest
Sexton F., 372 George
Thorpe & Bro., 122 Vine
Tibbetts E. N. 173½ Freeman
Troner Worth K., 100 W. 6th
Tschira Ed., 59 E. 3d
Velure & Kohlmann, e.s. Carr,
nr. 6th
Walze. H., 80 13th
Ward J., s.w.c. 4th & Sycamre
WINDER W. W.,
120 W. 3d
Wrampelmeier F., 205 Main

Paints, Oils and Glass.
(See also Druggists.)
Glenny Wm., 383 Cen'. Av
HARRISON WM. H. & CO.,
23 W. 4th
HOFFMAN & MOSER,
222 Main
Williamson & Hatfield, 41
Walnut

Paint Manufacturer.
(Air and Water-Proof.)
BAUM J. C.,
Canal nr. Mohawk Bridge
WOOD & McCOY,
20 Spring

Paper Dealers.
Ahr Conrad, 646 Central Av
Bachelor, De Camp & Co., 61
Walnut
BIEDINGER PETER,
548 Elm
BRADLEY & WEBB,
135 Main
Craven Moses, 12 E. Pearl
GIBSON & CO.,
n.w.c. 3d and Main
Hahn Emanuel, 543 Elm
HOF GUSTAVUS,
282 Main
Koehnke Xavier, 605 Race
Karlsruher & Adler 344
Walnut
Metzker G., 455 Main
NIXON, CHATFIELD, &
WOODS, 77 and 79 Walnut
Ross John L., 45 W. 2d
SEINSHEIMER B.,
237 Main
SNIDER LOUIS,
232 Walnut
Speer & Stephens, 158 Main
STONE FRANCIS M.,
141 Walnut

Paper Box Makers.
(See also Boxes, Paper.)
JORDAN CHAS. W.,
191 Walnut
JORDAN D. B.,
187 Main
Leo John, 76 W. 3d
Lohmshuck Mrs. H., 117 W.5th
McKim Chas., 102 Gest
RUTZ JACOB,
n.w.c. Court & Main

Paper Hangings.
Andress C. O., agt., 103 Main
Andreas F. & C., 60 W. 4th
Bannister J., 505 W. 8th
BRENEMAN H. H.,
57 W. 4th
Constantine W. L., 100 W. 6th
Fleischer Emil, 321 Central Av
Frazer & Meyer, 161 Walnut
Hain & Savill, 211 Central Av
HOLMES S. & SON,
65 W. 4th
Metzger Gottlieb, 455 Main
PETER T. J.,
127 W. 5th
REED GEO. W.,
343 Central Avenue
Schlencken C., 492 Main
WILLIAMS C. CURRY,
85 Main

Patent Agents.
Clough Wm., 122 Main
Grant, Pittman & Co., 8 W. 3d
KNIGHT BROS.,
n.e.c. 4th and Vine

Pattern Makers.
ADAMS, PECKOVER&CO.,
161 and 163 W. 5th cor.5th
Berger Peter, 109 W. 2d
Cavon Wm., 51 Vine
Cooke G. T. & Wm. E., s.w.c.
John and Augusta
FRY H. L.,
224 Central Avenue

HARRIS, & ZOINER,
n.s. 8th b. Horn and Harriet
WRIGHT T.,
156 W. 3d

Penmanship.
(See Commercial Colleges.)
Herold M., 124 W. 4th

Pension Agents.
Barry W. B. & Co., 76 W. 3d
BORDEN H. C.,
75 W. 3d
KIRK & CHEEVER,
37 W. 3d

Perfumery.
BERNINGHAUS RICHR'D
13 Carr
David Henry, 278 Main
PALMER SOLON,
36 W. 4th
PARK J. D.,
n.e.c. 4th and Walnut

Periodical Depots.
BLOCH & CO.,
32 W. 6th
Brigham Chas. F., 279½ Walnut
Church H. B., s.e.c. 4th &Vine
Downing Robert, 288 W. 6th
FLYNT M. D.,
n.w.c. Court and Cent Av
Hartwell W. D., 192 W. 5th
Keller W. H., 504 W. Front
LEWIS GEO. N.,
29 W. 6th
Mayle E., 384 Central Av
Orr Wm. Y., 209 Clinton
Rabbe H. G., 120 Main
Trainer Jos. H., 8 Broadway
Turner Samuel, s.w.c. Pearl
and Broadway
WEIL MAX & CO.,
s.w.c. 15th and Vine

Photographic Artists.
Albright S. & Co., 20 W. 5 h
APPLEGATE, TYLER &
CO. 26 W. 5th
Ball J. P., 30 W. 4th
BALL & THOMAS,
120 W. 4th
Bloom A. S., 22 W. 5th
Bishop Justin B., 58 W. 4th
Burgert P., s.w.c. Dudley and
Liberty
Carpenter M., 22 W. 5th
Currevont Leonard, s.s. Pearl
b. Pike and Butler
Cowan Henry, 92 W. 5th
Donave M. J. & Co., 23 W. 4th
Dewey J. M., 112 W. 5th
Hellebrog Chas. G., e. Ham.
Road and Vine
HOAG & QUICK,
100 W. 4th
Howland Chas., n.w.c. 5th &
Main
JOHNSON C. A.,
s.w.c. 5th and Main
Layman Jno. W., s.w.c. 6th &
Cent. Av
Lusby Jno. R., 58 Broadway
Luedeke Christ., 505 Main
Merritt Jno. T., 188 W. 5th
Porter Wm. S., 106 W. 4th
Rankin Wm., 82 W. 5th
Schaefer G. F., 303 Vine
Stein John 465 Vine
Van Loo Leon, 24 W. 4th
Waitt H., 405 Vine
Walter Phillip, 10 W. 5th
Waldack Chas., 21 W. 4th
Winder J. W., 373 Central Av

Physicians.
Alexander John, s.s. 6th 2nd
door w. of Broadway
ALMY S. O.,
161 W. 4th
Allen A. H., 365 Central Av
Allen Nirum, 95 W. 7th
Alwin Lewis, 13 E. 6th,
Ames Fisher W., 18 Hathaway
AVERY CHAS. L.,
89 W. 7th
BAKER A. H.,
316 W. 6th
Barthel F., 389 Vine
BASFORD CHAS. F.
103 Barr
BAUER ADOLPHUS,
344 Race
Bauriedel Wm. Henry, 42 12th
Bayer Jacob, 58 14th
Bettman A., 245 Elm
Beyrer Jno. N., 96 Ham. Rd.
Betscher Caspar, 658 Vine
BIGLER G. W.,
59 W. 7th

Blackburn Geo. S. 59 W. 7th
BLACKMAN G. C.,
113 W. 8th
BONAPARTE & REYNOLDS, 182 Sycamore
BONNER STEPHEN,
189 W. 7th
Bonner S. F., 189 W. 7th
Boynton Samuel W., 316 W. 5th
Brown Sam'l, 46 E. 4th
BROWN W. T.,
174 Freeman
Brown W. C., 46 E. 4th
Bruhl Gustavus, 146 Laurel
Buckner Kenyon, Henderson al
Buelow Henry, 515 Sycamore
Buckner C. F., 10 Paneoast al
Campbell J. B., 195 John
Carroll T., 358 W. 5th
Carter R. C., 112 George
Carson Wm., n.e.c. 3d and
Broadway
Cleaveland C. H., 203 W. 4th
CLENDENNIN WM.,
s.e.c. 7th and Vine
Comegys Cornelius G., n.e.c.
7th and Elm
COOK A. L.,
s.w.c. 4th & Broadway
Connar W. J., 316 W. 6th
Cook Wm. H., 132 W. 6th
COOPER L. & J. R.,
s.w.c. Cutter and Court
Cox Wm. H., 113 W. 6th
Cropper A. H., 133 Laurel
CURTIS A.,
135 Elm
Culver J. D.,
216 Walnut
DANDRIDGE A. S.,
n.e.c. 3d and Broadway
Daniels D. W., n.w.c. 4th and
Main
DAVIS JOHN,
323 Elm
Davis Wm. B., 315 Elm
Dimmick Miss Ada, 171 W. 4th
DODGE ISRAEL S.,
313 Race
DOHERTY GEO. A.,
224 Broadway
EBERLE C. C.,
91 Spring
EHRMANN BENJAMIN,
46 W. 7th
Ehrman Frederic, 84 W. 7th
Emmert Fred. L., 65 13th
Esmann Louis, 73 Clay
Fishburn Cyrus D., s.e.c. Vine
and Ham. Rd
Fischer C. W. F., 648 Main
Fischer Val., 137 Laurel
Foss S., 53 W. 6th
Foote Henry E., 263 W. 4th
Ford A. J., 131 Race
Fore Pryor, n.e.c. 7th & Vine
Forsha S. W., 415 W. 5th
Foster Nathaniel, n.e.c. 3d and
Broadway
Fowler H. W., 135 Elm
Frank Isaac, 216 Elm
Freeman E., 271 W. 6th
FREEMAN Z.,
276 W. 6th
FRIES GEO.,
n.w.c. Vine and 8th
Fuller F. M., 185 Richmond
Gans D. S., 348 Race
GARRETSON JESSE,
274 W. 4th
GARRISON H. D.,
245 Central Av
Gerwe F. A. J., 306 Longworth
Goode B. P., 304 Baymiller
Goodson Edw. W., St. John's
Hospital
Graham James, 119 W. 7th
Greenwald S., 998 Central Av
Grover J. H., 48 Sycamore
Hall Ivers S. P., 56 W. 4th
HARPER THOS. L.,
215 Plum
Harringous Alfred, 490 John
Hassett J. H., 233 W. 7th
Henshall J. G., 106 W. 6th
Henshall James A., 106 W. 6th
Hill N., s.s. 6th b. Broadway
and Culvert
Homburg F. W., 415 Walnut
Hovey D. W., 55 E. 3d
Howe A. Jackson, 2 W. 4th
HUNT JAMES G.,
278 Walnut
Hussey W. C., 56 W. 4th
Hussey Z., 135 Elm
Jackson, Herbert & Co., 167
Sycamore
Johnson E. H., 139 W. 6th
Jones A. E., 866 E. Front
Jones Geo. E., 481 W. 7th
Judge J. F., 116 Dudley
Judkins David, 301 Race

BUSINESS MIRROR. 375

ith Hiram, 189 W. Court,
 W. of Cent. Av
MITH J. B.,
 284 W. 6th
ith Jas. F., s.w.c. 4th and
 Broadway
MITH J. R.,
 133 W.7th
vens Edw. B., 130 Richm'd
vens Edward T., 76 W. 3d
irm Wm., 40 W. 4th
iart C. A. & Co., 11 E. 3d
ALIAFERRO & BUCKNER
 n.w.c. 6th and Walnut
ylor Wm. H., 100 W. 8th
acker John A., 240 Race
THOMAS E. B.,
 258 Race
ornton W. P., 310 W. 6th
OMLINSON S. B.,
 43 Everett
NZICKER JOS.,
 423 Walnut
ATTIER J. L.,
 160 Vine
ALDO F. A.,
 s.w.c. 4th and Sycamore
ALKER J. P. & D. B.
 219 Broadway
allace J. C., n.e.c. 5th and
 Sycamore
eber B., 351 Vine
WHITE JOHN F.,
 1 Neave's bldg. Race c.
 4th
hite Jno. P., s.w.c. Race &
 Front
ilson David, 115 W. 6th
ilson Thos., 248 W. 5th
WILSON ISRAEL,
 337 Main
itherell Edwin O., 44 W. 7th
WOOD THOS.,
 112 W. 6th
WOODWARD CHARLES,
 116 W. 6th
oodward W. R., 116 W. 6th
WRIGHT M. B.,
 294 Vine
right D. J., 8 George
WRIGHT T. J.,
 8 George
right Jas. F., 307 Elm

Physicians' Saddlebags.
ark H. S., 196 Walnut

Piano Forte Dealers.
 (see also Musical Instruments.)
RITTING & BRO.,
 227 W. 5th
itting John, 236 Vine
CHURCH JOHN, Jn.,
 64 W. 4th
ilburn W. F., 94 W. 4th
anreuther A., 407 Cen'l Av
MITCHELL & RAMMELS-
 BERG, 99 W. 4th
MURCH C. M.,
 72 W. 4th
PETERS A. C. & BRO.,
 94 W. 4th
eters W. M., 50 W. 4th
SMITH & NIXON,
 24 W. 4th

Piano Manufacturers.
lackburn Thos. R., 283 Main
BRITTING & BRO.,
 227 W. 5th
ritting John, 236 Vine

Pipe Stores.
om Jno. J., 60 13th
eis Joseph, 376 Broadway

Plane Manufacturers
 (See also Edge Tools.)

Planing Mills.
 (See also Flooring Mills.)
CHOATE, BARBER &
 EVANS, 567 Race
line John, 159 & 161 E. Front
look M. H. & Co., w.s. W.
 W. Canal opp. C. H. & D.
 R. R. Depot
GAY & STICKNEY,
 304 Broadway
Iilpin Thos., n.s. M. Canal b.
 Elm and Plum
HINKLE, GUILD & CO.,
 365 W. Front
Horsley & Ebler, 248 W. Frnt
HUGHES & FOSTER,
 s.w.c. Augusta and John
ROBINSON & DRUNS,
 672 Central Av
Smith & Williamson, s.w.c. 3 1
 and John
Taylor & Faulkner, 487 Free-
 man
WATERS & BARRETT,
 n.w.c. 9th and Freeman

Platers.
Clark John, 10 E. 6th
Davison W. C., 72 W. 6th
MILLER H.,
 217 Elm
MORRISON & CROW-
 THER, 65 W. 4th
POWELL WM. & CO.,
 247 W. 5th
Vanhouten C. and J., n.e.c.
 George and Central Av

Plaster Statuary.
Fazzi James, 47 E. 4th

Plasterers.
Allen D. P., 310 George
DeCamp Joh, 78½ Laurel
Fairclough T., 193 Richmond
Fisher Daniel M., 241 Findlay
Harrison E., 246 Hopkins
NUCKOLS W. W.,
 332 W. 9th
Rybolt Stephen, 228 Findlay

Plastering, Ornamental.
 (Stucco Work.)
Fazzi Jas., 47 E. 4th
Kinsey Pearson, 165 Pearl
WEST CYRUS,
 109 1-2 W. 3d

Pleasure Gardens
Ackva Wm., n.w.c. Main and
 Liberty
Benckenstein Chris., n.w.c.
 Harrison Pike and Spring
 Grove Av
Getz Matthew, 781 Vine
LOEWE JOSEPH O.,
 437 Vine
Schappi Jno., 214 Ham. Rd

Plow Manufacturers.
Garrett & Cottman, 9 W. 7th
MILLER GEO. C. & CO.,
 11 W. 7th
Peacock A., 10 W. 7th
RAYMOND, HILSINGER
 & CO., 614 Main

Plow Handles.
COLEMAN J. & Co.,
 91 a.s. 8th b. Broadway
 and Culvert
WATERS & BARRETT,
 n.w.c. 9th and Freeman

Plug and Bung Factory.
Kirby Josiah, Watson al. b.
 Main & Sycamore

Plumbers, Pump and Hydrant Makers.
Attlesey Jas., 321 Vine
Gardner C. D., 387 W. 6th
GIBSON J. B. & T.,
 200 Vine
GIBSON JNO. & CO.,
 290 Main
Johnson Henry C., 440½ W. 5th
JUEGLING & WOODBURN
 602 Central Av
KEMPER WASH.,
 230 Main
KIRK DAVID,
 215 Walnut
McCOLLUM HUGH,
 101 W. 6th
McNEIL JOHN,
 n.e.c. 7th & Walnut
MOORE P. J.,
 221 W. 5th
MURDOCK & LACEY,
 46 E. 3d
MEYERS & LAMPING,
 307 Vine
Newman T. J., 119 W. 5th
PEARE & WINTER,
 206 W. 6th
Ricketts Wm., 45 E. 4th
STACY JOHN A.,
 233 Central Av

Pocket Book Manufac.
HOOLE J. H. & CO.,
 21 E. 3d
STROBEL CHAS. & BRO.,
 150 Walnut

**Pork and Beef Packers,
 Ham Curers, &c.**
BEATTY JAS. & CO.,
 s.w.c. Race and Canal
BOGEN G. & F.,
 Ham. Rd. nr. Brighton
BONTE PETER C.
 619 Cent. Av
BROWN ROBERT,
 s.e.c. Sycamore and Court
BUCKINGHAM & MATH-
 ERS, 111 W. Court
Cassard G. H., 61 Hunt

COBB, ARMEL & FLET-
 CHER, 335 Broadway
Coleman J. W., 13 W. Court
CUNNINGHAM & SON,
 281 Sycamore
DAVIS CHAS. & CO.,
 272 Sycamore and n.w.c.
 8th and Sycamore
DAVIS GEO. F. & CO.,
 11 Sycamore
DAVIS, Jn., & CO.,
 303 to 313 Broadway
DAVIS WM. W.,
 40 W. Front
DOMINICK GEO. & BRO.,
 23 and 27 Water
Evans, Gaines & Co., c. Court
 and Broadway
EVANS & SWIFT,
 21 E. 9th
FIEDELDEY JOHN C.,
 56 E. Pearl
FLORER N. M.,
 9 Sycamore
Frietsch Sigmund, n.w.c. N.
 Elm & Ohio Av
GERARD JNO. H. & CO.,
 207 Broadway
Gilmore & Cordukes, c.a. Sy-
 camore b. Court and Canal
Griggs Lewis, 80 Plum
Haughton & Reed, s.w.c.
 Canal and Sycamore
Henry Jacob, 249 Cutter
HEATT & WOODS,
 Deer Creek Valley
Jacob & Brill, 214 Walnut
JACOB CHAS. Jn. & CO.,
 50 Walnut
JACOB CHAS. & LOUIS,
 n.e.c. 2d and Sycamore
Jacob Louis, Sr., 16 E. 2d
KECK & SHAFFER,
 9 and 11 E. Canal
Kingan & Co., n.e.c. Court &
 Sycamore
Kistner J. R., 8 & 10 E. Canal
LANG GEO.,
 23 and 25 E. Canal
Langstaff & Wanzer, e.s Miami
 Canal nr. Mohawk Bridge
LEIGHTON E. & CO.,
 270 Sycamore
Leonard H. & Co., 487 Elm
McKEEHAN & EVANS,
 n.e.c. and s.e.c. Syca-
 more and 8th
MAGILL JAMES,
 154 W. Court
Michener I., 126 W. Canal
MITCHELL & LADD,
 357 Plum
MORRISON, CORDUKES
 & CO., 16 and 18 E. Canal
NEFF WM. CLIFFORD,
 s.e.c. Vine and Canal
NYE HENRY,
 327 Broadway
NYE J. C.,
 12 and 14 E. Canal
PHIPPS G. & CO.,
 n.w.c. 9th and Broadway
Rawson J., e.s. Sycamore b. 9th
 & Court
RICE JOHN, & CO.,
 337 Cutter
Robinson Ed. H., 179 Sycamore
Roth Joseph, 246 Clark
Roth Jno., Oehler al., b. Free-
 man and Garrard
Recap & Farrelly, 221 Sycamre
Schooley Stephen, 155 W. Court
Shafer H. & Co., n.s. Canal b.
 Race and Vine
Shaw J. A. & Co., 282 Sycamore
Shays J. W., 346 Walnut
SMITH AMOR,
 17, 19 & 21 Webster
Spencer Andrew, cor. 14th and
 Plum
Steele John & Co., 52 and 54
 Hunt
STEPHAN CONRAD & CO.
 8 12th
Stevens Joh, 273 Sycamore
SWIFT, EVANS & CO.,
 c. 9th and Sycamore
THOMAS S. W. & CO.,
 s.w.c. Walnut and Canal.
WANN C. & T.,
 34 Sycamore
WITTE HERMAN,
 n. s. Wade b. Linn and
 Baymiller

Portrait and Landscape Painters.
Aubery John, cr. 11 E. 4th
Baldwin A., s.c.c. 4th & Walnt

CINCINNATI

Board Jas. H., Carlisle bldg
Cridland C. E., 60 E. 3d
Duncannon R. S., 51 Pierson
Eaton J. O., Pike's Opera House
Frankenstein Jno., 14 E. 4th
Kenner H. W., 21 W. 4th
WICKERSHAM THOS.,
Pike's Opera House

Potteries.

BUHN ANDREW,
219 Ham. Road
Bromley Wm., 1077 Cent. Av
Lessel Peter, 94 Hunt
MAPPES H.,
s.e.c. Vine and Mulberry
Occhsle John, 124 Findlay
Scott Geo., 690 W. Front
TEMPEST & CO.,
281, 285 and 287 Ham. Road

Preserved Fruits, Pickles, etc.

Bickley H. T., 111 E. Pearl c. of Broadway

Printers.
(Book and Job.)

BLOCH & CO.,
32 W. 4th
Boyd Jos. B., 25 W. 4th
BRADLEY & WEBB,
135 Main
BROWNE P. C.,
s.e.c. 3d and Sycamore
CIN. DAILY TIMES,
62 W. 3d
CIN. ENQUIRER,
n.e.c. Vine & Burnet
CIN. GAZETTE CO.,
n.e.c. 4th and Vine
Conway & Co., 8 w. 3d
Doyle Wm., 74 W. 3d
EGGERS J. & WILDE,
317 Main
FARAN & McLEAN,
e.s. Vine b. 3d and 4th
Frankland & Tidball, 28 W. 4th
FREDEWEST & DON-
NERSBERGER, 428 Main
GIBSON & CO.,
c. 3d and Main
Grant & Pittman, 8 W. 3d
Harpel Jeremiah c. 3d & Vine
HART & WATT,
25 Broadway
Johnson, Stephens & Morgan,
141 Main
Kalbfell Wm., & Co., 21 E. 3d
Lang Fred., & Co., 9 W. Court
Luthor C. T. Elw., 452 Walnut
Marshall A. Hefley, 6 W. 2d
METH. BOOK CONCERN,
c. 8th and Main
MOORE, WILSTACH,
KEYS & Co., 25 W. 4th
Monfurt & Wampler, 247 W. 5 h
Morgan Ephraim, s.w.c. Miami
Canal and Bedinger
Morris C. N. & Co., 79 W. 3d
Moore Amos, 27 W. 5th
Norman W. T., 230 Walnut
POTTER M. D. & CO.,
n.e.c. 4th and Race
PRESS PRINTING CO.,
136 Vine
PUGH ACHILLES,
120 Main
RUPPELT H.,
30 W. Court
Ryan Elizabeth, 443 Cent. Av
Spiller & Bro., 170 Sycamore
STARBUCK C. W. & CO.,
62 W. 3d
TAGART G. W.,
19 W. 4th
Tifton Joseph M., 34 E. 3d
VOLKSBLATT,
Court House bldg
VOLKSFREUND OFFICE,
s.w.c. Vine and Longw'th
WALSH JOHN P.,
170 Sycamore
WATKIN HENRY,
110 W. 3d
WRIGHTSON & CO.,
167 Walnut
Young Courtland H., 187 Wint

(Copperplate.)

AMERICAN BANK NOTE
CO., 118 Main
ELLICOTT, FORBRIGGER
& CO., s.w.c. 4th & Walnut
GIBSON & CO.,
c. Main and 3d
MIDDLETON, STROBRIDGE & CO., 64 W. 4th
SHIPLEY & SMITH,
22 W. 4th

(Lithographic.)
(See Lithographers.)

Printers' Materials.

CIN. TYPE FOUNDRY,
c. Longworth & Vine
Day W. T. & S. D. & Co., 173, 175 and 177 W. 2d
FRANKLIN TYPE FOUNDRY, 168 1-2 Vine
Hill Reuben, 168 W. 2d

Printing Press Manufacs

CIN. TYPE FOUNDRY,
c. Longworth and Vine
Day W. T. & S. D. & Co., 173, 175 and 177 W. 2d
FRANKLIN TYPE FOUNDRY, 168½ Vine
Lawyer Geo. H., c. Walnut & Canal

Produce and Commission Merchants.
(See also Com., Forwarding and Produce Merchants.)

Andrews Robt., 58 W. Front
ARNOLD & CRAWFORD,
22 E. Canal
Bailey M. & Co., s.w.c. Walnut and 2d
Bernard Nich. L., 59 W. Miami Canal
BROWN J. R. & CO.,
27 Walnut
DILLS W. R.,
91 W. Miami Canal
Gale John A., 80 W. Front
Hoppe E. & Co., 25 Walnut
Hubbard & Worrell, 33 Wint
JACOBS C., JR. & CO.,
50 Walnut
KOHLENBACH WM.,
418 Main
Lewis Chas., 64 & 66 E. Pearl
Lukens P. & Co., s.w.c. 2d & Walnut
Lykins & Son, c. Main & Water
MARMET C. & F.,
395 Main
MITCHELL, ALLEMONG
& CO., c. 13 Water
MOORE, ROBERT & CO.,
49 Walnut
Morten James L., 78 W. Front
Nantrup H., 320 Baymiller
Osborne Jno. S., 31 Vine
PENNEY GROVE J.,
27 Vine
REUTERPOHLER F. & G.,
137 W. Court
SECRIST JOHN M.,
21 W. Front
Shays Chas. C., 467 Elm
Smith & Co., 125 W. 8th
STANFORD & BICKNELL,
31 Broadway
STEPHAN CONRAD & CO.
8 12th
SWASEY M.,
s.w.c. 3d & Broadway
WERNERT & GOETTHEIM
507 & 599 Main

Publishers.
(See Booksellers.)

Pump Makers.

GIBSON J. B. & T.,
200 Vine
JUEGLING & WOODBURN,
602 Central Av
Harcourt & Mock, 87 E. Front
McCOLLUM H.,
101 W. 6th
Newman Thos. J., 149 W. 5th
Seddens John, River b. Race & Vine
Seddens Marshall, 87 E. Front
Shaw Wm., 153 E. Front

Pumps.
(Force.)

WINCHELL G. D. & BRO.,
141 and 143 W. 2d

Pumping Engines.

WINCHELL G. D. & BRO.,
141 and 143 W. 2d

Rag Dealers.
(See also Paper Dealers.)

Bachelor DeCamp & Co. 61 Wal
BIEDENGER PETER,
518 Elm
Karlsruher & Adler, 344 Walnut
Karlo Xavier, 605 Race
Murphy M., 33 Water
Nathan Marks, 820 Race
NIXON, CHATFIELD & WOODS, 77 & 79 Walnut
SNIDER LOUIS,
242 Walnut
Zimmermann Anthony, 23 Locust

Railroad Agents.

Brecount Geo. S., 5 College Building
BROWN H. W. & CO.,
25 E. Front
Brown G. B., 77 W. 3d
BUCHANAN R. & SON,
26 E. 2d
Burch Jno. W., 35 W. 3d
BRUCE W. E.,
77 W. 3d
DEVENNY LAFAYETTE,
77 W. 3d
Gettler T. J., 4 College Bldg
HECKERT H. F.,
3 E. Front
Henderson Dewitt C., 5 College Building
KIMBALL THOS. L.,
46 W. 5th
Pendleton Geo., 4 College bldg
Rice Sidney, 66 W. 3d
Smith W. M., 11 W. Front
SPEYER BENNO,
3 E. Front
WATERS A. B., 3 Burnet House
WHITE W. O.,
115 Vine

Railroad Depots

CIN. & CHICAGO AIR
LINE, at C. H. & D. R. R.
CIN., HAM. & DAYTON,
c. 6th and W. W. Canal
INDIANAPOLIS & CIN.,
Front nr. Wood
KENTUCKY CENTRAL,
Covington
LITTLE MIAMI,
Front, c. of M. Canal
MARIETTA & CIN.,
s.s. Front c. of Water Wks
OHIO & MISSISSIPPI,
Front nr. Wood

Railroad Materials.

GREEN J. B. & BRO.,
6 Public Landing
MOWRY A. L.,
River b. Custer & Front
17th Ward
WINSLOW A. S.,
9 W. 2d

Railroad Offices.

Air Line, 115 Vine
CIN & CHICAGO,
73 W. 3d
CIN., COL. & CLEVEL'D,
4 College Hall
CIN., HAM. & DAYTON,
c. 6th and W. W. Canal
Cin. Passenger, n.w.c. 4th & Main
Cincinnati Street, 162 Vine
CIN., WILMINGTON AND
ZANESVILLE, s.w.c. 3d & Sycamore
Cleveland, Columbus & Cin.,
4 College Hall bldg
DAYTON & CINCINNATI,
(Short Line,) 13 W. 4th
Hannibal & St. Joseph, 35 W. 3d
INDIANAPOLIS & CIN.,
66 W. 3d
LITTLE MIAMI,
c. Pearl and Kilgour
MARIETTA & CIN., (Works
s.s. Front c. of Water
OHIO & MISSISSIPPI,
Front nr. Mill
PENDLETON & 5TH ST.
MARKET, n.s. Front c. of Washington

Railroad Ticket Offices.

CIN., HAM. & DAYTON &
EATON & HAM., c. Front & Broadway and n.w.c. 3d and Vine
INDIANAPOLIS & CIN.,
1 Burnet House
KENTUCKY CENTRAL,
2 Burnet House
LITTLE MIAMI,
1 E. Front c. Broadway
MARIETTA & CIN.,
3 Burnet House
OHIO & MISSISSIPPI,
Burnet House
UNION OFFICE,
1 E. Front & Burnet House

Ranges.
(Cooking.)

Blunt R. D., 221 Main
HELLER & YOUNG,
292 Main
LOTZE A. & CO.,
219 Walnut

REDWAY & BURTON,
17 W. 5th

Real Estate Agents.
(See also Brokers Real Estate.)

Cooper Abner M., 35 W. 3d
Cooper Andrew J., 75 W. 3d
Dennis W. B. & Co, 146 Plum
Dora Wm. N., 57 W. 3d
GREGG & HARVEY,
19 W. 3d
HALE & CO.,
128 Walnut b. 3d and 4th
Herron Andrew C., 65 W. 4th
James W. P., 9 Water
King Henry W., s.w.c. Poplar and Dudley
Lynn & Morse, 227 Vine
McNamara A. B., 57 W. 3d
Munroe Chas., 186 Longworth
SARGENT S. A.,
2 Apollo bldgs
SHOTWELL GEO. H.,
75 W. 3d
Smith & Winters, 221 Vine
STOECKLE J. N.,
64 W. 3d
TILGHMAN THOS. E.,
n.e.c. 7th and Mound
WAGGONER JNO.,
54 W. 6th
Weller Jas. M., 197 Plum
Weller J. M., 197 Plum
Wood John H., 78 W. 3d

Real Estate Brokers.
(See also Brokers.)

Real Estate Dealers.

Cochran Geo. W., n.e.c. 3d & Race
Phelps Chas., 166 Vine
WAGGONER JOHN,
56 W. 6th
Willis A. F., 181 Walnut

Rectifiers.
(See also Wines and Liquors.)

Block E. & L., 28 Sycamore
BOYLE & CO.,
53 to 59 E. 2d
Conkling W. H. & Co., 56 W. 3d
Dexter E. & Sons, 51 Sycamore
FLETCHER L. C. HOBART
& Co., s.e.c. Front & Vine
FOOTE, NASH & CO.,
17 & 19 W. 2d
Hoffheimer Bros., 31 E. 2d
GIBSON D. & CO.,
46 W. 2d
HUDEPOHL LOUIS,
372 Main
King James J., s.w.c. 6th and Freeman
LANHAM R. J., 9 Water
LEVI S. & BRO.,
221 & 223 Walnut
Loder W. & B., 270 Main
MARIENTHAL LEHMAN
& CO., 235 Walnut
MOHR, SOLOMON & MOHR
159 and 161 W. 3d
PFIERMANN C. & CO.,
19 W. Canal
POHLMAN JOHN,
35 and 37 W. Court
PIKE S. N. & CO.,
18 and 20 Sycamore
SIEBERN J. N. & BROS.,
8 E. Pearl
Smith S. W. & Co., 29 Water
Smith, Wayne & Co., 10 & 12 W. Front
SOMMER & MEYER,
36 E. Pearl

Refrigerators.

BLATCHFORD & CO., 166 Vine & 205 Freeman
JOHNSTON J. & J M.,
221 and 223 W. 3d

Regalia.

Addis Wm., 260 Walnut
Manning Chas. G., 126 Walnut
Whitridge Mrs. E. A. 128 W. Walnut

Renderers.

Butchers' Melting Ass., n.w.c. Central Av & Findlay
Bowman E. Co., s.s. Deer Crk Rd, n. of Court
Roberts Sanderson, Deer Creek Road

BUSINESS MIRROR. 377

anecker J. P. J., 118 Findlay
OULD, PEARCE & CO., 48 Walnut
OLD PETER, 111 E. 2d
AKMAN H., 442 W. 2d
ACOBS CHAS. C., 24 W. Front and Budd w. of Harriett
ng C. C., 498 John
cLACHLAN JOHN, n. w. c. Main and Water
OORE ROBERT, 49 Walnut
YLOR & BARRETT, n. e. c. Walnut and Front and 51 W. 2d
ONDERHEIDE F. 249 W. 3d
ATERS CHAS. H. & CO., 4 Main

Saddlery and Coach Trimmings.
LARK S. & S. S., 180 Main
REENWOOD M. & CO., 396 Walnut
UNTER, EDMESTON & Co., 168 Main
EAVE, WARD & CO., 37 and 39 Main
ILSON & HAYDEN, 22 and 24 Main

Saddles and Harness.
nder Frank X., 651 Vine
OEGER JOHN, 30 W. Court
ockman B., 112 E. Pearl
UTTERFIELD A. S., 242 Main
ARRICK D. S., 112 Main
niels Jacob, 205 W. 6th
genhart A., 6th b. Harriet and Carr
chl & Co., 679 Vine
ldson Geo., 103 W. 3d
EGNER L. & CO., 30 W. Court
endorf Geo., 384 Vine
nder Gustav, 59 Ham. Road
llmeyer Fred., 508 Main
olp Louis, 621 Cent. Av
tsch Bernard, 620 W. Front
tch V., 620 W. Front
tz J., 612 Central Av
artin Xavier, w. s. Ludlow b Front and 2d
OORES & CO., 69 Main
nller Peter, 453 Vine
OHLMAN HENRY, 349 Broadway
eid John, 30 E. 5th
itzher Jos., 1076 Central Av
oberts D., 341 W. 5th
ogg John, 1302 E. Front
ombach B., 684 Cent. Av
OWE, PARK & Co., 29 E. 5th and 206 Main
arline Richard, 447 Main
hopper G., 1109. Central Av
ihwemberger Chas., sen., 609 Walnut
HACKLEFORD J. C. & CO. 208 Main
ucker Geo. W., 33 W. 5th
onderheide Jos. B., 929 Cent. Av
eatherby Jas. S., 176 Main

Saddle Trees.
athrew & Gosker, 131 Carr
rotman Jos., 413 W. 6th

Salt Agencies.
angley & Kinkead, 31 Water
HIO RIVER SALT CO. 27 W. Front
OMEROY S. WYLLYS, 51 E. 3d
ARGENT LEMUEL H., 31 Walnut
atson L. D. & Bro., 9 Main

Sash, Doors and Blinds.
ARR HENRY, n. s. Front b. Torrence and Kelley
ook M. H. & Co., W. W. Canal opp. C. H. & D. R. R. Depot
vans & Williamson, 519 Central Av
HINKLE, GUILD & CO., 365 W. Front
lorsley & Ehler, 248 W. Front
UGHES & FOSTER, s. w. c. John and Augusta
lughes & Sharp, 5 Augusta
ones Wm., 167 E. Front

Jones Wm., 167 E. Front
KOLKER & McCAMMON, n. w. c. John & Laurel
LAPE J. S., 512 Central Av
ROBINSON & BRUNS, 872 Central Av
Schroer Herman, w. s. Spring b. Liberty & Woodward
Smith Henry P., 466 W. 6th
Smith & Williamson, s. w. c. John & 3d
Sommerkamp H., 26 15th

Saw Manufacturers.
Kimball & Wiltsee, 41 W. Crt
LEE & LEAVITT, 130 W. 2d
ROW J., 238 W. 7th
SIEWERS C. G., 93 E. 8th
WOODROUGH & McPARLIN, 10 W. 2d

Saw Mills.
ALBRO HENRY, 196 W. Pearl
Baily Ezra, 518 W. Front
CAMERON, STORY & MALONE, Storrs Township
GLENN M. & L., 1565 E. Front
JOHNSON, MORTON & CO., n. s. Front b. Kelly and Foster
Morton M. R., 1379 E. Front
Welch Cyrus, s. e. c. Front and Vance
Whateley H. & Co., Junction 6th and Front

Saw Mill Manufs.
FAY J. A. & Co., cor. John and Front
Franke & Jones, 124 W. 2d
LANE & BODLEY, s. e. c. John and Water
LEE & LEAVITT, 130 W. 2d

Scales.
Huddart M. & Co., 8 W. 2d
KISTNER JOHN, 394 Vine
Tosso Julius, 7 Public Landng

Sculptors.
Frankenstein Jno., 14 E. 4th
Jones Thos. D., 47 E. 4th

School Furniture.
Kelsall Thos. George nr. C. H. & D. R. R. Depot
VENT, STARR & CO., 6 W. 4th

Seal Presses.
EVENS PLATT, JR., 64 W. 4th
Hall Mrs. C. F., 14 W. 4th

Seal Engravers.
(See Engravers.)

Second Hand Stores.
Batty Wm., 620 W. 6th
Berliner A., 189 Broadway
Berliner Sol., s. e. c. Main & 8th
Block L., 193 Broadway
Blumenthal P., 481 Central Av
Callaghan Michael, 237 Brdwy
Cohen A. & Co., 41 E. 4th
Cohn Levi, 367 Central Av
Cohn Isaac, w. s. Elm b. Front and Commerce
Onlian M., 175 W. Front
DRURY THOMAS, 146 W. Front
Fitzsimmons M., 155 W. 3d
Gabriel R., 31 E. 5th
Garrison D. R., 323 Cent. Av
Goldsmith Benj., 639 Cent. Av
Hassenbush B., 148 Sycamore
Hazlebush L., 103 W. 5th
Husselberger Saml., 334 W. 5th
Kleine Mrs. A., 867 Cen'l Av
Kirstner A., 53 Broadway
Lasker D., 149 Sycamore
Lavendorff S., 180 W. Front
Levy S., 115 W. 5th
McDonald Chas. H., n. e. c. John and 5th
McDonough P., 218 Plum
Manogue Thos., 46 E. Front
Mase Chas., 351 Central Av
Menogue Nicohlas, 142 Race
Myers Levi, 330 W. 5th
Niesel Chas., 173 E. Front
ORR WM., 107 W. Court
Reiter Jacob, 116 Sycamore
Rider Alexander, 340 W. 5th
SHAW HARRY E., 18 E. 4th
Rosenbaum I., 247 Broadway

Simon & Reeder, 189 W. 5th
Spillman Louis, 288 W. 5th
Stadthagen Jacob, 100 W. Frnt
Straus Tobias, 226 W. 6th
Sugarman Louis, 276 W. 5th
Sugenheim J., 36 Race
Summerfiel W., 154 W. Front
Treaman M., 483 Central Av
Vander B. E., 23 W. 5th
Weil & Meyer, 305 Cent. Av
Wise Bernhard, 253 W. 6th

Seed Stores.
DAIR JNO. F. & CO., 40 and 42 E. Pearl
McCULLOUGH J. M. & Son, 200 Main & 3 E. 5th
McNair & Co., 105 E. Pearl
MOORE ROBERT, 49 Walnut
REUTEPOHLER F. & G., 187 W. Court
SMITH WM. C., 22 E. 9th
WILDER, ROBINSON & Co., 230 Walnut
Windhorst J. F., 52 Everett

Seminaries and Select Schools.
See also Colleges in City Guide.
Armstead Miss L., n. w. c. Hopkins and Cutter
Cincinnati Female Seminary, s. w. c. 7th and Mound
Clive Geo., 264 W. 7th
Collins Lethy, 299 Clark
Friends' Academy, s. s. 5th b. Cent. Av. and John
HERRON'S SEMINARY, 64 W. 7th
Horton Caroline, 119 E. 3d
Howells Mary, 162 Oliver
Iliff Martha, s. s. Clinton b. Cutter and Linn
Mudd Dr. Jerome, 298 Elm
Notre Dame Academy, s. s. 6th b. Sycamore and Broadway
Nourse Clara, 48 W. 9th
Oldrieve Louisa C., 103 Barr
Rickoff A. J., s. e. c. 9th & Elm
St. Joseph's School, s. e. c. Linn and Laurel
ST. XAVIER'S COLLEGE, Sycamore b. 6th and 7th
WESLEYAN FEMALE COLLEGE, 249 Vine
WILBER MARY C., 326 Race
Wright Eliza, s. s. 6th b. Race & Elm
YOUNG LADIES' MOUNT Auburn Inst., Mt. Auburn

Sewing Machines.
Caffrey Jas., s. w. c. John and Augusta
Colburn Wm. F., 94 W. 4th
Davis Wm. M., 247 W. 5th
Empire Sewing Machine, 100 W. 5th
EVENS PLATT JR., 64 W. 4th
Gantenberg B., 264 Central Av
GROVER & BAKER, 58 W. 4th
Gury G. F. G., 90 W. Court
Krans John, 482 Walnut
PARKER SEWING MACHINE Co., Western Agency, 46 W. 5th
Ladd, Webster & Co., 94 W. 4th
MASTERS GEO. L. & Co., s. w. c. John and Front
ORR GEO. P., AGT., 138 W. 4th
Raquet C. & J. Bandle, 428 Main
Sheldon T. S., n. e. c. 4th and Race
Sachsteder John, 511 Plum
SKARDON JAMES, n. e. c. 4th & Race
SUMNER WM. & CO., 77 W. Fourth
Williams & Orvis, Agency, n. e. c. 4th and Race

Sewing Silk.
Jouvet John H., 72 W. 4th

Ship Chandlers.
BARKER, HART & COOK, 41 Pub. Landing
Hagarty & Co., 48 Pub. Landg
Isham, Fisher & Co., 47 Pub. Landing

Shirt Manufacturers.
Barrett Samuel, 115 Walnut
Bicknell E. M., 54 W. 4th

378 CINCINNATI

DRAKE LOUIS P.,
58 W. 4th
Effray Alex. 174 Vine
KEPPNER L. A.,
107 W. 6th
LOWMAN J. & BRO.,
36 W. Pearl
McCRACKEN RALPH C.,
19 W. 4th
RICHARDSON JAMES,
68 W. 4th
Rolver Fredericka, 31 W. 3d
Walthman Eliza, 308 W. 5th
WILSON & CLARK,
s. e. c. 4th and Walnut

Shoe Maker's Tools.
EASTON S.,
232 Main
MEIER & ISPHORDING,
6 Main

Show Cards.
Doubleday Henry J., 120 Main
Moore A. C., 65 W. 4th
Scott Wm. B., 119 Main

Show Case Manufs.
Dolphe Moses, s. e. c. 4th and Walnut
SCHMITT & BRO.,
66 Main
Waldau Gustav, 25 & 27 E. 3d

Silk and Straw Goods.
BRITTING M. & P.,
227 W. 5th
DEVOU & CO.,
83 and 85 W. Pearl
DICKINSON, PRICE & BISHOP, 102 & 104 W. Pearl
DOHERTY CHAS. C. & CO.
31 W. Pearl
FORCHHEIMER MEYERS
64 W. Pearl
EPPLY ADAM,
20 W. Pearl
HAYNES, LEWIS & SPENCER, 136 Walnut
HENLY I, & H.,
3 E. 4th
Knox Edward C., 68 W. 4th
MASON GEORGE,
73 W. Pearl
Menken S. & Sons, 103 W. 5th
Meyberg & Hellman, 124 Wlnt
PICKERING J.
96 W. 4th
RATHBONE & WALLACE
131 Walnut
RICHARDSON J. C. & CO.,
95 and 97 W. Pearl
SMITH J. D. & CO.,
21 W. Pearl
THAYER, & ALDRICH
92 W. Pearl
THOMPSON M. F. & CO.,
96 W. Pearl
Williams T. J. & Co., 29 W. Pearl
Winter Thos., 207 W. 8th
ZILLER & WISE,
72 W. Pearl

Silver Ware.
(See also Jewelers.)
DUHME & CO.,
s. w. c. 4th & Walnut
KINSEY DAVID,
21 W. 5th
McGREW WM. WILSON,
s. w. c. 4th and Main
OSKAMP CLEMENS,
62 Main
OWEN CHAS.,
n. w. c. Main and 4th
SMITH & BOERNER,
6 W. 4th
Vanhouten C. & J. B., n. s. c. Cent. Av. and George

Slate Roofers.
DUNN & WITT,
146 W. 3d
FAY LUCIAN,
349 Plum

Slaughter Houses.
Beresford F., s. s. Court b. M. Canal and Lock
BOGEN C. & P.,
Harrison Pike nr. Brightn
Bowman & Co., s. s. Deer Crk Rd. n. of Court
DAVIS & CO.,
s. s. Deer Creek Rd. n. of Court

DOMINICK GEO. & BRO.,
n. s. Deer Creek Rd. n. of Court
Fieber John, 950 Central Av
Flach Chas. s. s. Montgomery Pike dr. Reading Road
Gall W. B. & J. A., Clarkson nr. Bank
HIEATT & WOODS,
Deer Creek Valley
Hoffman M., 421 Baymiller
Kahn Chas., n. e. c. John and Poplar
Lawrence John, n. s. Deer Crk. Road b. Liberty & Tunnel
Leggett Charles, s. s. Wade, w. of Baymiller
Otte Martin, w. s. Reading Rd nr. Montgomery Pike
Slimmers Geo., Deer Creek Val
Smith Sam'l., Jr., s. w. c. John and Findlay
Thompson George, Mill Creek Bottom nr. Harrison Rd
WHITTAKER J.,
Deer Creek Valley

Soap.
(Fancy.)
David Henry, 22 W. 7th
HILL GEO. H. & CO.,
31 Main

Soap and Candle Manufs
Cheever A. G. & Co., 11 W. Front
Hesselbrock Henry, n. s. Deer Creek Road n. of Court
HILL GEO. H. & CO.,
31 Main
JONES & CONAHAN,
726 Cen'l Av
KIRBY THOS.,
477 Vine
Logermann B., n. s. Bank b. Riddle and Division
Meyer Michael, Browne n. of Ham. Road
PROCTER & GAMBLE,
21 W. 2d
SHILLITO GEO. & CO.,
30 Sycamore
SPINING & BROWN,
80 Poplar
Teceng Frank, n. s. Bank b. Riddle and Division
Vickman Joseph, s. s. Oliver b. Linn and John
Wechman & Co., Oliver bet. Linn & York
Wenning Wm. & Co., 46 E. 8th
WERK M. & CO.,
11 Main
Wiedemer M. L., 15 W. Front

Soap Curbs, Cisterns, Stills, etc.
Dobus Louis, 167 W. 2d

Spoke, Felloe and Hub Manufs.
ROYER, SIMONTON & CO.,
375 W. 3d

Stair Builders.
Goble Wm., 191 Mound
Hunter Geo. W., s. e. c. 6th and Hoadley
KOLKER & McCAMMON,
n. w. c. Laurel & John
Nicol Donald, 227 Clinton
Nicholson Thos., 93 Clark

Stamp Cutters.
AUTENRIETH L.,
s. w. c. 4th and Walnut
Breidenbuecher Geo., 492 Vine
STANTON JOHN,
139 W. 5th

Starch Manufs
ERKENBRECKER A.,
s. s. Lock b. 5th and 6th
Fox Thos. & Geo., 71 Walnut
PROCTER & GAMBLE,
24 W. 2d

Stationers.
(See also Booksellers.)
APPLEGATE & CO.,
43 Main
BENZIGER BROS.,
n. w. c. Vine & Longwrth
BIRD M. H.,
207 Central Avenue
Blanchard Geo. S., 30 W. 4th
BRADLEY & WEBB,
135 Main
Buchman B., 26 W. 3d
CROSBY GEO.,
41 W. 4th
EGGERS & CO.,
168 Main

EGGERS J. & WILDE,
317 Main
Ernst. J. & Co., 107 Main
HAWLEY J. R.,
164 Vine
KENNEDY WARREN,
160 Vine
McArthur & Son, 162 Vine
MACDONALD ALEX,
9 W. 4th
McMullen J. & Co., 167 Wal
MOORE, WILSTACH KEYS & CO., 25 W. 4th
Mumford & Co., 54 W. 4th
RICKEY & CARROLL,
77 W. 4th
SMITH W. B. & CO.,
137 Walnut
THEOBALD & THEU RAUF, Court House
THORPE JNO. D.,
72 W. 4th
WEIL MAX & CO.,
s. w. c. 12th and Vine

Steamboat Agents.
ATHEARN & SEDAM,
5 E. Front
BROWN H. W. & CO.,
25 E. Front
CUNNINGHAM & BENNI
20 Pub. Landing
Butler E. S. & Co., 7 E. Fro
Graham Wm. & Co., 4 Cor Row
MEMPHIS & OHIO RIVE PACKET OFFICE, 16 Pu lic Landing
PAUL & MURDOCK,
13 Water
ROSS & CO.,
33 Sycamore
SCHRAM A. D. & Co.,
21 Pub. Landing
SHERLOCK THOS.,
20 Broadway
SPEYER DENNO,
7 & 9 W. 3d

Steamboat Builders.
Hambleton S. T. & Co., s Front. e. of Hasen
Horsley & Ehler, 248 W. Fro
JOHNSON, MORTON & 565 Front
Litherbury John, s. s. Front Leatherbury & Reed

Steamboat Cabin Build
Horsley & Ehler, 248 W. F

Steamboat Inspector
Guthrie J. V., Custom Ho
Haldeman T. J., Custom Ho
Pierce Jos. 16 Pub. Landi
Pierce Wm. H., 16 Pub. L

Steam Pipe.
BAKER & VON PHUL,
62 W. 4th
DANNENHOLD & NOCI
90 W. 5th
GAYLORD T. G. & CO.
90 & 92 Broadway
GREENWOOD M.
c. Walnut and Canal
Griffey Day., Congress b. L low and Lawrence [Fr
Robson & Westover, 158
WATERS B.,
226 Main

Steel Manufs.
PARKINS BROS & HOD SON, 240 W. 7th
WESSEL A., Agt. Wm. J sop & Sons, 7 W. 2d

Stencillers.
Ernst Thomas J., 187 Wal
LANPHEAR W. K. & C
102 W. 4th
MACKENZIE J. D.,
180 Walnut

Stereotypers.
CIN. TYPE FOUNDRY,
c. Vine and Longworth
FRANKLIN TYPE FOU DRY, 168 Vine
HILLS, O'DRISCOLL &
141 Main

Stock Dealers & Brok
(See Brokers.)

Stock & Die Manuf
BRINKMAN RUDOLPH
216 W. Court
MAYO E. M.,
245 Sycamore

BUSINESS MIRROR. 379

LOTZE ADOLPHUS, 219 Walnut
Mackelfresh C. W., 294 W. 5th
Martin Peter, 149 W. 5th
Merrill J. F., 219 W. 5th
Michel D., 145 E. 2d
OSWALD T. A., 368 Broadway
PATTERSON N. & CO., 26 Main
Pfau Jacob, 1003 Central Av
Pfefferle Jacob, 113 Ham. Rd
PICKEL MAX, 243 W. 6th
Rebold Geo., 659 Vine and 20 Ham. Rd
REDWAY & BURTON, 17 W. 5th
RESOR WM. & CO., 13 and 15 Main
Rosenbaum M., 191 W. 5th
ROTHERT J. H. & SONS, 642 Central Av
Runck F., 509 Vine
RYAN J. S. & CO., 17 W. 5th
Thiery Michael 61 Elder
VON BEHREN HENRY W. 557 Race
Wildey Wm. D., 378 Main
Wolf C. d., 375 Main

Surveyors.
(See Engineers, Civil.)

Tailors, Merchant.
(See Also Clothiers.)
Abel George, 939 Central Av
AHLERING, JOHN F., 39 Broadway
Amenskamp G., 257 Main
Baker George, 63 Broadway
BARNES R. G., 155 Main
Bartels Charles, 767 Vine
BARVISE & KING, 171 Main
Bauer A., 121 Ham. Road
Buchmann J., 1020 Central Av
BEESLEY J. W., 105 Main
BELL MAX, 161 Main
Berger P. A., 512 Walnut
Bieber & Bro., 230 Main
BILLAU ADAM, 97 E. Pearl
Billian M., 13 Mary
Bitter Peter, 210 W. 6th
BOEBINGER A. & J., 490 Walnut
BOYD ALEXANDER, 33 E. 3d
Boyd Sam'l 27 E. 4th
BROKAMP & LAKE, 464 Main
BROOKE J. H., 66 W. 5th
Brummer J. B, & Co., 244 Main
Buff & Blosafeld, 313 W. 6th
BUFF JACOB, 126 Vine
Burford R. G., 227 Central Av
Cain Alex., 201 Broadway
CLARK GEO., 146 Walnut
Callahan Patrick, 26 Broadway
Davis Adolph, 76 E. 5th
Dettmer B., 183 Walnut
Drahmann J. H. & Co., 56 Sycamore
Dreyling Wm., 485 Walnut
Ebbers Henry, 418 Walnut
Enneking & Huwe, 7 Br'dway
Englehardt P., 535 E. Front
EVERETH WM. H., 18 W. 4th
Finney John, 120 W. 6th
Fisher George, 257 Walnut
Flamm B., 442 W. 5th
Fresenberg Hy. 202 Broadway
Friel & McGuire, 256 Walnut
FRINTZ MICHAEL, 80 W. 4th
Goodman Samuel, 156 W. Frnt
Gruber F., 642 Elm
Groutman Henry, 176 W. Frnt
Guhe Henry, n.e.c. Cent. Av, and Front
Guthardt Elias, 565 Vine
Haddix N., 228 Walnut
Hallagan Pat., 505½ E. 5th
Hamburg Hy., 183 Linn
Harper M. A., 200 Walnut
Hartye John H., 51 Plum
Hawlekhorst Hy., 560 W. 5th
Heck Bernhard, 632 Vine
Heil Philip, 657 Vine
Helleman Bernard, 26 Race
Henke Wm. L., 493 Race
Hirsh Nathan, 212 Vine
Holch Matthew, 476 Vine
Irving John T., 164 W. 6th

JENNINGS M. C., 11 W. 4th
Joring B., 403 Broadway
Kampe Fred., 109 W. 3d
Kathmann C., 25 Mill
Kauther P. J., 107 Martin
Kein John, 37 Moore
Keller Henry, 61 15th
Kenning A., 96 W., Cou.t
Kleswetter G., 219 Elm
Klonne Adam H., 218 Linn
Knapman J. H., Court H. bldg
Knodel F., 81 W. 5th
KOCH H. & J., 178 Walnut
Kohus & Moorman, 260 E. Front and 84 Broadway
Kolhoff Jos., 165 W. 5th
KRAMER & KROGER, 62 Broadway & 252 Main
Kraper W. F., 507 Race
Lammers & Jeckel, 268 Central Av
Lassance Aug., 120 W. Front
LEININGER JOHN G., 317 Vine
Linck F., 27 Ham. Road
Loeb & Bros., 2 Burnet House
Lohmann A., 521 Main
Lohmeyer C., 622 Main
LUHN J. H., 8 E. 5th
LUKEN JNO. B., 285 Main
Luning J. & H., 150 Hopkins
McARDLE E. & J., 176 Vine
Marks Elias, 64 W. Front
Macke Bernard, 42 W. Front
McCord Wm., 292 W. 6th
M'KEE & ROTH, 48 w. 4th & 159 Walnut
MEIFIELD JOHN G., 147 W. 5th
Mette Wm., 76 E. Front
Meyer Jno. B., 23 Broadway
Meyer Werner, 24 13th
Miller Peter, 157 W. 6th
Myers Jno. F., 8 W. 3d
Newmann Joseph A., 175 W. 5th
NIEMANN HERMAN H., 546 Main
NIENABER J. B. J., 205 Walnut
Oberfeld Matthias, 674 Race
OGDEN & JONATHAN, 30 W. 4th
Osterroth A. Fred., 455 Main
Pistor C., 525 Vine
POLL JOHN A., 211 Central Av
Puthoff Frank H., 260 Main
Quinn Mart'n. 8 New
REDMAN B. T., 128 Walnut
Ries Thos., 38 E. 3d
RICHTER & VERKAMP, 215 W. 5th
Rieckelman H. H. & Co., s.w.c. 9th and Cent. Av
Rieck Charles, 305 W. 18th
RIECKELMAN JOHN & Co. 143 Main
RIKHOFF JOHN G., s.w.c. 9th & Main
Rover B. H., 614 Central Av
Rower Frederick, 524 Sycamore
Schlebbe J. T., 343 Main
Schlelein G. L., 16 Ham. Rd
Schloss J. M., s.w.c. Pearl & Broadway
Schoemer N., 576 Main
Schumaker J. H., 367 W. 5th
Schumacher J. H., 403 Central Av
SEITER JOS., 58 Broadway
Sharp Geo., 106 George
Siermann Edward, 359 Vine
Slomon Aug., 687 W. Front
Sippel Geo., 120 Walnut
SPRAGUE T. W. & CO., s.e.c. 4th and Vine
Steiner & Popp, 451 Vine
Sterger John, 68 W. Court
Stiens John, 420 W. 5d
Stoll Wm., 84 W. Court
Strubbe Rudolph 45 Elder
Stuntebeck Frank F. 98 Hunt
Stuntebeck Jno. H., 360 Brdwy
Sullivan Philip, 349 Con'l Av
Surman Anton, 32 W. Court
TAPHORN & SCHUTTE, 498 W. Front
Tepe Frank Wm., 488 Race
THOMAS S. P., 43 W. 4th & Walnut
Thompson Alfred V., 120 W. 6th
TONE & NOLAN, 216 Vine

TONNIES BERNARD, 335 W. 5th
Trame, Meyer & Co., 21 Broadway & 51 E. Front
Ulmer John, 54 Sycamore
VAN DOKKUM & FORMAN, 125 Main
Waldron D. A., 46 W. 5th
WALKER S., 59 E. 3d
WARBURG & RAMLER, 266 Main
Wiebold & Klotter 477 Main
W lenborg Herman, n.e.c, Baymiller and Richmond
WILLIAMS JNO. A., 169 Sycamore
Woerner L., s.e.c. Central Av and 7th.
Wolf Nich., 74 Broadway
Wurdemann John, 51 15th
Yost Wm., 65 W. 3d

Tailors' Shears.
SPRENGER & EMRICK, 340 Main
Weber Philip, 16 E. 5th

Tailors' Trimmings.
DALE THOS. N. & CO., 90 W. 3d
GRIFFITH J. A. & CO., 51 W. 4th

Tanners.
BALLANCE J. H., 108 W. Canal
Bodmann F. J., s.e. 6th, b. Harriet and Horne
Culbertson Robert, Elm nr. Findlay
Dorst Isaac, rear 23 Dunlap
EASTON S., 232 Main
ECKERT MICHAEL, 964 Cen'l Av
Fell J. F., Culvert nr. 5th
Fuhrmann L., Deer Creek b. 8th & Court
Grossman J., n.s. Front b. Stone and Hill, 17th Ward
Hepworth Wm., Deer Creek Valley
HUBER, SCHEU & LEIST 669 Elm
KESSLER HENRY & SON, e.s. Plum n. of Findlay
Kirchner Francis M., 930 Central Av
LANG & WANNER, 39, 41 & 43 Dunlap
M'Cabe Alex., Deer Creek, foot of 8th
MARTIN H. & G. R., 694 Elm
Moore Amos, Providence, b. Oliver and Findlay
NEPPER G. F., 17 Dunlap
RASCH HENRY, 26 Canal, n. Moh'k bridge
RENCK MICHAEL, 21 Dunlap
Rens N., 173 Ham. Road
SPIEGEL G. C., s.s. Front, above Jamestown Ferry
TAYLOR A. M. & CO., s.w.c. Linn and Liberty
THORNTON R., w.s. Lebanon Rd, near Montgomery Pike

Tanners' and Curriers' Tools.
EASTON S., 232 Main
PAUL JOSIAH, 181 Main

Tea Dealers.
COFFIN J. D., 32 W. 5th
GRIFFITHS G. n.w.c. 5th & Central Av
MADDUX BROS., 27 W. Pearl
PENDERY & CO. n.w.c. 5th and Walnut & 88 E. Pearl
RANKIN A. n.w.c. Central Av & 5th
SHEEHAN PIERCE, n.w.c. Court & Br'dway
Smith Henry K. & Son, s.e.c. 5th and Walnut
Williamson Samuel, 14 E. 2d

Telegraph Office.
W'N UNION TELEGRAPH CO., s.w.c. 3d and Walnut

Terra Cotta Works.
Hennler & Molk, Plum b. Everott and Wade

Teachers.
(French and Spanish.)
Grienmard Ch., 97 Mound
Montaldo Ignatius, 293 W. 4th
(Music.)
(See also Music Professors of.)
Geyer John, 30 W. Court
Groenlesf Mrs. H. L., s.w.c. 3d and Broadway
Hahn H., 157 Smith
Klausmeyer Wm., 413 Elm
Mason Luther W., 36 Barr
Ruttinger Geo. C., 364 W. 5th
Shoenbrun Amelia, 352 Race
Stuckle Caroline, 237 Main
Weisborn H., 82 W. 5th
Williams Victor, 378 W. 7th
WEBER W., n.e.c. 5th and Vine

Theaters.
NATIONAL THEATER, e.s. Sycamore b. 3d and 4th
PIKE'S OPERA HOUSE, s.s. 4th b. Vine & Walnut
Woods' Theater. c. Vine & 6th

Tin, Copper and Sheet Iron Workers.
Beckmann Aug., 571 Race
Beckman Charles, 525 W. 8th
Behren H. W., 557 Race
Bickel Edward A., 256 W. 5th
Britt Peter, 42 Pub. Landing
BROPHY JOHN L., 114 W. 9th
BUSSE JOSEPH, 495 Main
Caldwell John, 569 Central Av
COOK C., n.w.c. Richmond and Central Av
Crompton Ebenezer, n. e. c. George & Cent. Av
DAWSON BENJ. 251 W. 6th
Dieckmann Joseph, 75 W. Crt
Dobbins Thos., 68 W. Court, w. of Cent. Av
Doerler John, 222 Broadway
FAKES & MILLER, 5. W. 5th
Gaertner S., 566 Vine
Greeninger C., 44 Linn
GROSSIUS JOHN, 33 W. Court
Hanaway E., 202 W. 6th
Herpst Herman, 223 Linn
Hoeltge Wm., 307 Linn
Hitchcl John, 433 Central Av
HOFFNER JACOB, 38 E. Pearl
HOPKINS JOHN B., s.w.c. Sycamore & 7th
Horrocks J. R. & Son, 6 Com. Row
Johnson W. & J. S., 429 Central Av
KEELER, I. M., 13 & 15 W. 5th
Kiechler C., 110 Baymiller
King John W., 224 George
Konsheim August, 208 Ham. Rd
Kunkler & Peters, 311 Vine
Lallay Michael, 20 Race
Lape W. H., & Co., 21 E Front
Lilge Wm., s.s. 6th ar. Horne
LILLER M. & J., 533 Vine cor. 15th
Lohn John, 533 W. 5th
LOTZE ADOLPHUS, 219 Walnut
Mackelfresh C. W., 294 W. 5th
Maish Andw., 213 W. 6th
Martin P., 149 W. 5th
Mayer Chas., 478 Walnut
Muloy Henry, 451 Main
Myer Jacob, 63 Wade
Noll John H., 552 Sycamore
OSWALD AUG., 368 Broadway
PALMER CHAS. R., 506 Cent. Av
PATTERSON N. & CO., 26 Main
Pfefferle Jacob, 113 Ham. Rd
PICKEL MAX, 243 W. 6th
Quinn Thos. G., 898 Cent. Av
Rebolt Geo., 20 Ham. Road
REDWAY & BURTON, 17 W. 5th
Rosenbaum & Bro., 20 W. 5th
Rosenbaum Miers, 191 W.5th
Schult C., 609 Elm
Stall Robt. A., 40 W. 2d
Stein Valentine, n.e.c., 6th and Miller

CINCINNATI

STEPHENSON H. W., 30 W. 5th
Stewart Alex., 1520 E. Front
Strassner Hy., 155 Everett
VON BEHREN HENRY W., 257 Race
Vanduzen B. C., 9 & 11 E. Frnt
Weaver Clark G., 417 W. 4th
Wielert Chas., 61 W. Court
WINCHELL GEORGE D., Marsh & Co., n.w.c. Race & 2d
Wolff & Co., 373 Main
Wolfer Gustave, 660 Elm

Tinman's Tools.
HULL J. E., 95 E. 8th
LAWSON F. H. & CO., 178 Main
WINCHELL GEO. D., Marsh & Co., n.w.c. Race & 2d

Tobacco Agents & Dealers.
Bodman Chas., 59 W. Front
BESUDEN HENRY, 93 Walnut
Bornstein L., 35 W. Front
BREED R. E., 120 W. 2d
Carpenter & Ford, 14 W. Front
Dressing & Otting, 57 Sycamore
Hafer & Duddy, 65 Walnut
KASTING & KRUSE, 24 W. Front
KENNETT JOHN, 14 Public Landing
McLaughlin, Tomlinson & Co., 46 Walnut
MADDUX BROS., 22 W. Pearl
Morris & Chalfant, 46 W. Frnt
NEWBURG & SCHOTT, 21 Walnut
Otten Fred., 504 Vine
PHISTER & HOW, Pearl b. Central Av. and Plum
RAWSON, WILBY & CO., 8 W. Front
Withers C. A. & Wright, 86 W. Front

Tobacconists.
(See also Cigars and Tobacco.)
BESUDEN HENRY, 93 Walnut
FAEHR & MEYER, 438 Main
McLaughlin, Tomlinson & Co., 46 Walnut
Morsmann Henry, 17 Main
Newell, Wilmot & Co., 40 Main
Runau Wm., 171½ W. 3d
Ronker Barney, 51 Martin
ROBERTS & JOHNSON, 133 W. 2d
Withers C. A. & Wright, 86 W. Front

Toys and Fancy Goods.
(See also Fancy Goods.)
BONER J., 30 W. 5th
Bochheit Peter, 62 Martin
CADY D. K., n.e.c. 5th and Walnut
Franklin L. M., 94 Main
SCHRADER H. & CO., 70 Main
SCHULTZE F. & CO., 127 Main
Schwegmann F., 361 Main
SHEPPARD J. W., 20 W. 4th

Trimming Stores.
Atkins Geo., 102 W. 5th
AUB, FRENKEL & CO., 30 W. Pearl
Burstinger J., 352 Main
Costello Thos., 138 W. 5th
GRIFFITH JNO. A. & CO., s.w.c. 4th and Walnut
HA MARY, 5th
Hoffmeister F., 114 W. 5th
James Chas. E., 206 W. 5th
Levinson Leah, 268 W. 5th
MARKS H. & CO., 12 W. Pearl
Mulane Wm., 81 Mound
Mustin R. C. L., 96 W. 4th
PICKERING J. M., 96 W. 4th
POHLMAN GEORGE W., 102 W. 4th
Suechting Chas., 489 Vine
Wettengel O., 165 W. Liberty

Trunk Makers' Stock.
MERNA JOSEPH, 192 Main

WAYNE J. L. & ON, Main
WAYNE JOS. W. & CO., 196 Main

Trunks.
BUTTERFIELD A. S., 242 Main
CERRICK D. S., 112 Main
FLYNT MARTIN D., 182 Walnut
Grumbine J., 204 Vine
Kruger Henry, 479 Cen'l Av.
LEONARD & COOK, n.e.c. Main & 2d and 54 Elm
M'Nutt & Armstrong, 69 W. 3d
MOORES & CO., 89 Main
Parvin & Johnson, 31 Br'dway
Reid John, 30 E. 5th
ROWE, PARK & Co., 206 Main, and 23 E. 5th
SHACKELFORD J. C. & CO., 208 Main
SHOLL O. W., n.w.c. Walnut and 2d and 509 Plum
Shorten Richard, n.w.c. Main and Patterson Alley
Tucker G. W., 33 W. 5th
Weatherby J. S., 176 Main
Willington & Conrad, Gibson House

Trusses.
Daniels D. N., 2 W. 4th
FORSBERG A. O., 5 E. 4th
KATES DR. J., 153 Sycamore
MARSH. S. N., CORLISS & CO., 5 W. 4th
REES WM. Z., 71 W. 8th
WOCHER LEWIS, 318 Main
WOCHER MAX, 105 W. 6th

Turners.
Adams Wm., John and Laurel
Bechmann Fred., 261 Ham. Rd
Blannerhassett A. T., n.e.c., Stone and Avery
Bolz Adam, n.w.c. Laurel and Central Av
Clark Benj., 146 W. 6th
Cunning Jas., Lawson al.
Drehm Frank, 498 Walnut
Geier Fred, Locke b. 5th & 6th
Gleich B., 61 Clay
Gleich J. F., (Ivory) n.e.c. Walnut & 9th
Lech & Jno. II., 386 Vine
Mahone Lom & Co., 518 Cent'l Avenue
Moyer Jos., 138 W. 9th
NADLEIG F., 487 Vine
Schaeffer & Buschle, 128 W. 2d
Threm John, 445 Walnut
Wrede Frederick, 11 15th b. Elm and Plum

Type Foundries.
CIN. TYPE FOUNDRY, c. Longworth and Vine
Foster G. W. & Co., (copper-cage) 139 W. 5th
FRANKLIN TYPE & STEREOTYPE FOUNDRY, 168 1-2 Vine

Type Manfs.
(Wood.)
Day W. T. & S. D. & Co., 173, 175 & 177 W. 2d

Umbrella Manufs. and Dealers.
COLE JAS. C., 98 W. 4th
Fox Jacob, 227 Central Av
LINDSKOFF, BROS. & CO., 79 W. Pearl
Rosenplatt Louis, 481 Cent. Av
THOMPSON M., 167 Main

Undertakers.
BOHRER GEO. A., 554 Elm
CORD SAM'L, 143 Sycamore
Ehlmann H. B. & Seelen, 593 Elm
EPPLY JOHN P., n.w.c. 9th and Plum
HACKMAN & DUSTERBERG, 450 Walnut
Hust Henry, n.w.c. Ham. Rd and Locust

Jenkins John & C. W., 138 Sycamore
McCarthy T. J., 221 Sycamore
Meyer Lewis, 69 12th
Moss B. H., n.w.c. Linn and Clark
Nicholson Daniel, 4 New
Soards J. & Son, 175 W. 6th
Sullivan Patrick, 165 Cen'l Av
Wernke & Timmen, 388 Sycamore
WILTSEE JOHN F., n.w.c. Plum & Longwrth

Underwriter's Warehouse
Morton & Bro., 78 W. Front

Upholsterers.
COATES JOHN F., 150 W. 8th
Cramsey W. Mound and Longworth
ELLIS ROBT., 136 Sycamore
GEIS ADAM, 67 W. 5th
Grebenstein C., 224 Cen'l Av
Hall John C., 27 E. 3d
HARRIS G. W., 130 Sycamore
Hoffmann Jacob, 204 Elm
MOREHOUSE & CO., 134 Sycamore
Prather C. B. & Co., 51 E. 3d
Pursell B. & J. R., 19 E. 4th
Ryling John, 22 E. 8th
SNOWDON & OTTE, 179 Main

Variety Stores & Notions
(See also Fancy Goods.)
Atkins George, 102 W. 5th
Averbeck Ferdinand, 360 Broadway
Binghams Mrs. Ann, 1310 E. Front
Fishwick James, 415 Cen'l Av
Fletcher Rebecca, 188 W. 5th
Frech Fredericka, 636 Main
Hall Samuel, 242 W. 5th
Hand Caleb, C., 147 Linn
Isaacs Simeon, 239 Main
Kimber H., 327 Findlay
Lutz Caroline, 458 Vine
McCleary Sam'l 170 Cent. Av
Midgley Ernstein, 419 Cent. Av
Morehouse Mary, n.e.c. 6th & Broadway
Mullane Wm., n.e.c. Baymiller & Bank
Newhouse F. I., 403 Sycamore
Pocock L. C., 287 Central Av
Reeder Jos. A., 1162 E. Front
Schwagman F., 361 Main
Seymour Geo., 148 Baymillor
Third C., 473 Walnut
Wolf W., 519 Elm
Wood Mary, 272 W. 5th

Varnish Manufs.
BARTLETT R. & CO., s.w.c. Walnut and Front
BERNINGHAUS R., 13 Carr
HARRISON W. H. & CO., 23 W. 4th
HOFFMANN & MOSER, 222 Main
PFAFF, WEBB & M'CABE, 54 W. 2d
QUEEN CITY VARNISH CO., 43 Vine
Ratterman, Gebbe & Co., 125 W. Liberty
ROGERS M., Office 170 Race
Tilden Wm., & Neph, 99 Walnut

Veneers.
ALDRO HENRY, n.s. Pearl b. Plum & Elm
M'ALPIN, HINMAN & CO., 103 Walnut

Venetian Blinds.
CARPENTER W. W. & CO., 82 W. 6th
COOMBS S. B., 236 Vine
HESSELER W. H., 147 Sycamore
HOLLANDER C. P. & A., 397 Walnut
Thumsel John F., 45 E. 5th
VICTH A., 140 Sycamore

Vermicelli, Maccaroni & Chocolate Manufac.
Guillon Antoine, 374 Walnut
Heschong M., 571 Walnut
WERNERT & GOETHEIM, 597 & 599 Main

Veterinary Surgeons.
BOWLER G. W., n.w.c. 6th and Walnut
Carrick A. L., 226 Broadway
Estell John, 168 W. Front
Collins Chas. W., 24 Dayton
Kuhlman G., 44 E. 5th
Wheeler J., 180 Smith
WILSON JOHN, 9 E. 6th

Vinegar Manufac.
Bender Wm., 582 Central Av
Bickley H. T., 111 E. Pearl
Conkling W. H. & Co., 56 W. Front
Droste & Kuhn, n.s. Yeatman b. Broadway & Sycamore
Elbrey H., 395 Broadway
Frederick Conrad 660 Cent Av
HERBSTREIT M., 461 Vine
Hummell J., 160 Hopkins
Ill D., 449 Plum
Johnson A. W., 47 E. 2d
Loehmann Wm. & Co., 106 E. Pearl
MILLER, BRUNING & DICKMAN, 33 Sycamore
Pfirrman A., 359 Walnut
PFIRRMANN C. & CO., 19 W. Canal
Senn John S., n.e.c. Elm and 14th
STAHL & HUST, 16 Locust
Thiesing Fred. H., 374 Main
Wetterer John, 430 Plum

Wedding Manufacs.
STEARNS & FOSTER, 183 Clay

Wagon Makers.
Alf Wm., 223 W. Liberty
Boake John H., 64 W. Canal
Bonte John H., s.e.c. 9th and John
Dreier F., 214 Clark
Conradi Fred., n.w.c. Bremen and 12th
Creger Sam'l P., n.e.c. Elm & 15th
Crowder James, 1275 E. Front
Dodt Barney H., 103 Hunt
Dolt Clem, 347 Broadway
Eberhardt & Wust, n.s. Ham. Rd, nr. Mohawk Bridge
Fisher Lewis, 706 Central Av
Freyer F., 828 E. Front
Gastner Nicholas, 313 Ham. Rd
Grietz D., n.s. Ham. Road b. Dunlap and Hamburg
Growe Joseph, 173 Hopkins
Henge Paul, 792 Cent. Av
Hill Thos., 524 Central Av
HUTTON J. & H., 164 W. Front
Kralaus F., 681 Central Av
Lampe Henry, 19 Ham. Road
Laudenbach H. H., 109 Hunt
Malone Frank, s.s. Front, b. Lawrence and Pike
Meick Henry, 509 Walnut
Mueller Joseph, 180 Ham. Rd
Painter J., 57 Race
Rottger Wm., 65 Elm
Sauer Christ, 763 Central Av
Schmidt Hy. s.s. Sixth b. Harriet and Horne
Schmidt Joseph, 549 W. 8th
Schroeder & Klopp, 446 Race
Schoer Geo., n.w.c. Ham. Rd and Main
Silver J. J., W. 6th b. Harriet and Horne
Sparks J. M., 620 W. 6th
Weaver Jacob, s.s. Reading Pike, nr. Tunnel
Wehring Jacob, Junction Montgomery Pike & Reading Road
Winkelman H. H., 518 Freeman
Young Chas., 1041 Central Av

Wagon Yards.
BUTTEMILLER JOHN, s.s. Court b. Walnut and Main
Weust Wm., n.e.c. Cent. Av, and 7th

Washboards.
COLEMAN J. & Co., s.s. 8th b. Culvert and Broadway
WATERS & BARRETT, n.w.c. 9th and Freeman
WATERS CHAS. H. & CO., 4 Main and 3 W. Front
WAYNE JOS. W. & CO., 196 Main

BUSINESS MIRROR. 381

Washing Machines.
WAYNE JOS. W. & CO., 196 Main

Watch Cases, Materials & Tools.
Allen C. & W. H., 117 Main [Walnut
Doll Francis, s.w.c. 4th and
DORLAND GARRETT T., n.w.c. Main & Pearl
DUHME & CO., 4th and Walnut
Morris John B., s.s.c. 2d and Sycamore
Struve H. R., 205 Main

Watch Makers.
(See also Jewelry, Watches, &c.)
Allen C. & W. H., 117 Main
Beatus H., 78 Main
Closs Fred, 57 Ham. Road
DORLAND GARRETT., n.w.c. Main and Pearl
Dees A., 309 Main
DUHME & CO., s.w.c. 4th & Walnut
Dornseifer H., 353 Central Av
Draper Jos., 16 W. 4th
Elias E. H., n.w.c. Public Landing and Broadway
Escales M., 140 Walnut
EYSTER ANDREW A., 271 Central Av
Honer John B., 203 Walnut
Keller Stephan, 43 W. Court
Kenkel J. Ger., 550 Central Av
KOCH MARCUS, 585 Cent. Av
Korf Hy., 309 Main
LOVELL THOS. n.w.c. 5th and Race
Marmet F. W., 65 Broadway
Mayer A., 72 Main
McGREW WM. WILSON, n.w.c Main and Fourth
Meyer L., 180 Walnut
Morris John B., s.e.c. 2d and Sycamore
Nathan & Levy, 100 Walnut
OSKAMP CLEMENT, 52 Main
Oskamp Aug., 108 Main
OWEN CHAS., n.w.c. Main and 4th
Parks Geo. D., 341 Cent. Av
Rothschild Maier, 238½ W. 5th
SMITH & BOERNER, 6 W. 4th
Struve H. R., 205 Main
WILMS J. C., 1 College Hall bldg, Walnut b. 4th & 5th

Water Coolers & Filters.
HUNTINGTON BROS. & CO., 119 Main [Vine
WINCHELL GEORGE D., Maish & CO., n.w.c. 2d and Race

Weighers City.
ASHLEY E. W., 1 Water
Broadwell Wm. H., 13 Water

Wheel, Hub and Spoke Manufacs.
ROYER, SIMONTON & CO., 375 W. 3d

Whips, Thongs, &c.
AMER. WHIP CO., 17 E. 3d

White Lead and Putty Manufacs.
BAUM J. C., Canal nr. Mohawk Bridge
CONKLING B. & CO., Main nr. 8th
HARRISON W. H. & CO., 23 W. 4th
HOFFMAN & MOSER, s.w.c. M. Canal & 6th
WOOD & McCOY, 20 Spring

Wig Makers.
Steinberg F. 152 Walnut
Taylor E. B., 13 E. 4th
Van Luenen G., 79 W. 4th
Wesler Fred., 108 W. 4th
Zwick Joanna, 40 W. 4th

Window Shades.
BENEMAN H. H., 57 W. 4th

CARPENTER W. W. & CO., 82 W. 6th
ELLIS ROBERT, 136 Sycamore
Pursell B. & J. R., 19 E. 4th
SAWYER & KIRK, 8 College Hall
SCHWENKER F. W., 579 Walnut
SNOWDON & OTTE, 175 Main

Wines, Liquors, &c.
Andrews Robert, 58 W. Front
BABBITT, GOOD & CO., 18 and 19 Pub. Landing
BATES JOHN, 94 Sycamore
Bealer C., Agt., 18 Broadway
Bender W. 582 Central Av
Bergmann J. F., 660 Cen'l Av
Block E. & Bros. 22 E. 2d
Block E. & L., 28 Sycamore
Born Philip, 665 Race
BOYLE & CO., 53 to 59 E. 2d
Boyle & Roach, 208 Main
BRACHMANN H., 81 W. 34
Byron & Co., s.w.c. Central Av and 5th
BUCHANAN & CO., 12 Public Landing
Clark C. E., 11 Walnut
CODY P., 17 and 19 Water
Conkling W.H.&Co.,56 W. Frnt
CONROY CHARLES, n.c.c. 3d & Central Av
CONSTANT H., 88 E. 2d
DAVIS N. H. & G. H., 69 Walnut
DEAN & HALE, 19 and 21 Sycamore
Dexter E. & Sons, 49 Sycamore
FAEHE, BOTTLER & CO., 438 Main
FICKEN JOHN, 16 E. Pearl
Fitzgerald & Jackson, 113 E. Pearl
FOOTE, NASH & CO., 17 and 19 W. 3d
Frank C. & Co., 38 W. Court
FREIBERG & WORKUM, 13 Sycamore
Friend J. H., 123 W. 3d
GATTI G. & ZANONE, 80 Broadway
GOOSMAN & XIETERT, 133 W. Court
Griese Benj. H., 3 Com, Row
Graham Wm. M. & Co., 4 and 5 Com. Row
Groene J, H. F., 43 Race
Gnkelberger Geo., 462 Walnut
Hauser Matthew 70 13th
HERBSTREIT MATH., 461 Vine
HERCKELRATH C. & H., 105 Sycamore
HEYKER F. & M., 308 Cutter
Hilb Max, 376 Main
Hirsch A., 108 W. 6th
HOFER CHAS., 208 Vine
Hoffheimer Bros., 34 E. 2d
Holmes & Co., 19 E. Front
Hotchkiss O. E. & Co., 86 Broadway
HUDEPOHL LEWIS, 372 Main
Isetzki Jno., s.s. Liberty b. Main and Clay
JACOB ISAAC, 45 E. 2d
Kaufman S. & Bro., 31 Sycamore
KATTENHORN A., 381 Main
KING & DALY, s.w.c. 2d and Sycamore
Koebling G. 422 E. 2d
LABROT AUG. A., 6 W. Front
LACK CHAS., 342 Walnut
Lauham R. J., 9 Water
Levi Sen'r & Co., 103 Sycamre
LEVIS & BROS., 221 & 223 Walnut
Levy Jas. & Bro., 7 W. Front

Lewis M. H. & Co., 16 Brdwy
Loder W. & B., 270 Main
Loehmann W. & Co., 106 E. Pearl
Louis A. & Co., 56 Main
McDONALD & ROSS, 22 Water
McIlvain Hugh L., 5 E. Front
MACKENTEPE B., 2d and Vine
Mackenzie Robt. H., 306 Main
MARIENTHAL, LEHMAN & CO., 236 Walnut & 36 W.
Mehner Louis, 34 E. Pearl [6th
Meyer Samuel, 141 W. Pearl
MILLER, BRUNING & DIECKMAN, 33 Sycamore
Mills & Kline, 18 and 20 Main
Monheimer Isaac, 62 Walnut
MOHR, SOLOMON & MOSS, 139 W. 3d
gomery J. C., 281 Main
MORGANTHAU H. & L., 74 Main
Nagel & Spreen, 611 Cent. Av
NATHAN M. & CO., 25 Vine
Nickert Jacob, 350 Main
Pattison Edw., 11 E. Pearl
Peat James, 205 Main
PFAEFFLIN WM., 88 Pearl E. of Lawrence
PFAU J. & J. M., 238 Main
PFIRRMANN ANDW., 359 Walnut
PFIRRMANN C. & CO., 18 W. Canal
PIKESAM'L N. & CO., 18 and 20 Sycamore
POHLMANN JOHN, 35 and 37 W. Court
Rabe John, 237 W. 6th
Rauth Francis, 80 E. Pearl
REIF FRANCIS, 126 Ham. Road
Roser Geo., 135 W. Court
ROSING A. C. A., 62 & 64 E. 2d
Samuels S. & Co., 550 W. 5th
Samuels & Jacob, 45 E. 2d
Sandheger C., 25 & 27 W. Court
SIEBERT J. N. & BRO., 8 E. Pearl
Smith S. S. & Co., 56 & 58 w. 2d
Smith, Wayne & Co., 10 & 12 West Front
SOMMER & MEYER, 36 E. Pearl
Smith S. W. & Co., 29 Water
Smith Geo. F., 4 Com. Row
STAHL & HUST, 82 Ham. Road
STALL & MEYER, 64 and 66 W. 2d
STEINER GEO, 35 E. 3d
STIFEL ADAM, 383 Main
STETTER & MANGOLD, 233 W. 6th
Straus F. & Bro., 54 Main
SWASEY JOHN & CO., 23 Sycamore
Thiesing Fred. H., 374 Main
THOMSON PETER, 55 W. 3d
Wals Frank A., 340 Walnut
Williamson John, 68 W. 3d
Wilson & Carson, 18 W. Front
Wolf & Co., 362 Main

Wine Manufacturers & Dealers.
(Native.)
BOGEN G. & P., Ham. Road n. Brighton H.
BUCHANAN ROBT. & SON, 24 E. 2d
FAEHR, BOTTLER & CO., 438 Main
LONGWORTH N., s.s. 6th E. of Broadway
PARK JOHN D., n.e.c. 4th and Walnut
WERK M. & CO., 11 Main
Williamson John, 68 W. 3d
ZIMMERMANN & CO., 586 W. 6th

Wire Manufac.
WORTHINGTON & CO., 42 and 44 W. 2d

Wire Workers.
BROMWELL WM. & CO., 161 Walnut
Gundersdorf Casper, 65 Wade

Wood Dealers.
Blackmun J. L., 68 Smith
Blangy Wm F., 109 Water
Bohlander Geo., Ham. R'd nr. Mohawk Bridge
Carlin Joseph; s.e.c. Smith & W. Canal
Cassedy L., n.w.c. Smith & W. Canal
Coleman G. W., s.w.c. 5th and Front
Darling J., 87 W. Court W. of Central Av
Estell D. & Son, n.e.c. Elm & River
Hornberger F. s.e.c. Elder and Race
Hornberger J., s.e.c. Plum & Liberty
JOHNSTON G.W.C., 145 Water
Lancaster Isaac, s.s. 8th b. Broadway and Lock
LIPPELMAN H. H., 424 Central Avenue
MAINS JOHN, SEN., n.w.c. River and Vine
Parsell Ben. S., s.e.c., Elm and Canal
SNYDER WM., 83 Water
Steelman Hosea, sen., 99 Water
Ware Geo. W., 314 W. 7th
Waldschmidt A., 334 Plum
Warrington Robt, Central Av b. Front & 2d
Wenzel J. F., 496 Central Av
Wonsmeier John H., 471 W. 3d

Wood Working Mach'ry.
(See Machinery Wood Working)

Wood and Willow Ware.
Baker H., 349 Vine
BONER JOHN, 36 W. 5th
CADY D. K., s.s. 8th & Walnut
Clegg Thos., n.s. Mulberry, b. River and Vine
Degner E. L., 176 Broadway
Detch Geo., 211 W. 5th
Hartman Frank, 76 Mulberry
Puff Chas., 382 Vine
Sankey Thomas, 4 W. 5th
Schnelle L., 109 W. Court
TENCH GEO. G., 329 Central Av
TYLOR & BARRETT, n.e.c. Front and Walnut
WATERS CHAS. H. & CO., 4 Main
Woodson Jesse, 217½ W. 5th

Wood Dealers.
BALLANCE JNO. H., 108 W. Miami Canal
BULLOCK A. D. & CO., 12 and 14 W. 2d
THAYER & TAYLOR, 9 Water

Woolen Machinery manufacturers.
Brown A. C., 9th w. of Harriot

Yawl Builder.
Gominger J. & Co., 704 E. Frnt

Miscellaneous.
Baynes J. H., Agt., Bone Dust man., 214 Clark
BRANSON MISS SUSAN, AGT. for Knitting Machine 104 W., 4th
BAUM JOHN C., Prussiato of Potash man., s.s. Canal, b. Findlay & Ham. Rd
BURSTINGER JOSEPH, Tassel & Fringe Manufac. 352 Main
Cohen Simon, Lead Pencil Man., 222 Walnut
CULLEN JAMES, dealer in Vegetables, Fruits &c., 46 Pub. Landing
Feener Louis, Phonographic Reporter, 19 W. 4th
Hagarty & Co., chain manuf., 48 Pub. Landing
Hirschauer P., chain manuS., 147 & 151 E. Front
TREIBER FREDERICK, BULL HEAD TAVERN, 362 Ham. Road
ROTHEET J. H. & SONS, dealers in Tools, 640 & 642 Cent. Av
Vann Walter, Manufacturer of Ointment, 113 George
Wootley Jas. W., children's dress & linen store, 131 W. 4th
Zetlle & Stallo, dealers in patent fruit jars, n.w.c. Court and Main

Post Office Information.

JOHN C. BAUM..................POSTMASTER.
WM. H. CONKLIN..................ASSISTANT POSTMASTER.
WM. T. WAGNER,..................CASHIER.

OFFICE :—United States Custom House and Post Office Building, s.w.c. Fourth and Vine.

RATES OF POSTAGE, ETC.

Letters in the United States, per ½ ounce (fractions same), not over 3000 miles, 3 cents, prepaid ; over 3000 miles, 10. Letters dropped for delivery only, 1 cent. Advertised Letters, 1 cent extra. To or from the Provinces, not over 3000 miles from the line, 10 cents per half ounce, over 3000, 15 cents, prepaid or not.

Transient Newspapers, Periodicals, unsealed Circulars, or other articles of printed matter, not exceding three ounces in weight, to any part of the United States, prepaid, 1 cent. Each additional ounce, or fraction of an ounce, prepaid, 1 cent.

Regular Newspapers or Periodicals, paid yearly or quarterly in advance, when circulated in the State where published, not weighing over 1½ ounces, ¼ cent ; over 1½ ounce and not over 3 ounces, ½ cent ; every additional ounce or fraction, ½ cent. When circulated OUT OF THE STATE, all weighing 3 ounces or less, ½ cent, and each additional once or fraction, ½ cent.

Books bound or unbound, not weighing over 4 pounds, under 3000 miles, 1 cent per ounce, prepaid ; over 3000 miles, 2 cents, prepaid.

Publishers of Newspapers and Periodicals, are allowed a free exchange of one copy, and may also send to each actual subscriber, enclosed in their publications, bills and receipts for the same, free.

All printed matter must be sent without cover, or in a cover open at the ends or sides. There must be no word or communication printed on the same after its publication, or upon the cover, except the name and address of the person to whom it is to be sent. There must be no paper, or other thing enclosed in or with such printed paper.

LETTERS TO OR FROM GREAT BRITAIN OR IRELAND.—Each ½ ounce, 20 cents ; 5 cents extra for California or Oregon. Prepayment optional.

NEWSPAPERS.—Two cents each, payable in the United States.

PERIODICALS AND PAMPHLETS. Not over two ounces, 2 cents each, and 4 cents, an ounce or fraction of an ounce, if they exceed two ounces. No pamphlet over 8 ounces, or Periodical over 16 ounces, can be sent unless for letter postage. Payable in the United States.

A CLOSED MAIL, consisting of Letters and Newspapers, for States and cities of the German-Austrian Postal Union, and Denmark, Norway, Sweden, Poland, Russia, Greece, Ionian Islands, etc.; is sent from the N. Y. office semi-weekly. By this conveyance, called the "PRUSSIAN CLOSED MAILS," the postage on Letters varies from 30 to 45 cents per half ounce. Newspapers, 6 cents each paid in full.

France and Algeria, by either United States, British or French packet, direct or through England, 15 cents the single letter of ¼ ounce or under—prepayment optional. Newspapers 2 cents each, Periodicals, pamphlets, etc., 1 cent an ounce or fraction of an ounce—prepayment required, being United States postage only.

Postage between the United States and Hamburg, 10 cents the single letter of ½ an ounce or under—prepayment optional. Newspapers three cents each, prepayment required.

Single rate letter postage to or from Bremen, by the Bremen line, 10 cents—prepayment optional. Newspapers each 3 cents, United States postage, prepayment required, Letters and Newspapers to other parts of the Continent may also go by this line, subject to various rates.

N. B.—All letters to and from foreign countries (the British North American Provinces excepted) are to be charged with single rates of postage, if not exceeding the weight of half an ounce ; double rates if exceeding half an ounce, but not exceeding an ounce ; quadruple rates if exceeding an ounce, but not exceeding two ounces ; and so on, charging two rates for every ounce or fractional part of an ounce over the first ounce. As this rule differs from that followed in respect to domestic letters, great care is requisite to prevent mistakes. By the French mails the single rate is reckoned on the ¼ ounce, each additional quarter ounce being an additional rate.

Mails for Mexico will be dispatched tri-monthly, by the New Orleans and Vera Cruz United States Steamship Line. United States letter postage 10 cents under 2,500, 20 cents over 2,500 miles from the mailing office—to be prepaid when sent from, and collected when received in the United States. Newspapers 2 cents each, to be collected in the United States as above.

Single rate letter postage to Havanna and the British West Indies, 10 cents under 2,500, and 20 cents over 2,500 miles ; newspapers 2 cents ; and to West Indies (not British,) Carthagena, Honduras, and St. Juan, (Nicaragua,) 34 cents under 2,500, and 44 cents over 2,500 miles. Newspapers, 6 cents each ; pre-payment required.

GENERAL OBSERVATIONS.

All letter postage within the United States must be prepaid by stamps.

All transient printed matter must be prepaid by stamps.

The upper right hand corner of a letter is the most suitable place to put the stamp.

Parties should be particular in having legible directions, with as little flourishing as possible. The County and State should always be designated, as well as the Post Office.

Any writing whatever on printed matter, or the enclosure of a circular, handbill, or any other thing, whatever, subjects the same to letter postage.

A card printed on an envelope or wrapper of printed matter, subjects it to letter postage.

Stamps cut out of Post Office envelopes are not reckoned as postage when used on letters, etc.

Stamps cut in pieces are not received as postage.

The U. S. P. O. Dispatch stamps do not pay postage, but are for paying the conveyance of letters to the office, or the delivery of letters by carriers, within the city limits.

Letters for the carriers are delivered to them at 7½ A. M., and 12 M., at which time they take all for delivery in their respective districts.

Letters dropped in the carriers' boxes for city delivery, should have on two U. S. P. O. Dispatch stamps.

Those to be mailed should have on one to pay the carrier for delivery at the Post Office—besides the regular postage.

Persons wishing their letters delivered to them by the carriers, should hand into the Post Office a written direction to that effect ; the charge for delivery is two cents.

Persons changing their residence should notify, (in writing) the carriers of the change.

Persons wishing their letters forwarded to another office, should hand in written directions to that effect ; all verbal orders should be avoided.

Letters addressed to Postmasters on Post Office business, should be marked as such.

Letters uncalled for are advertised but once—on the Monday subsequent to their arrival at the office ; German letters three times a week.

Persons applying for advertised letters should state that they are such, giving DATE and number of list.

All letters remaining in the office over three months are returned to the dead letter office at Washington, where they are examined ; if containing any thing of value are returned to the writer at the office at which they were originally mailed.

Letters to be registered must be brought to the office by 5 P. M.

Letters for Great Britain, Germany, etc., may be registered on the payment of 5 cents in addition to the postage.

In applying tt the office for letters, care should be taken to apply at the proper windows, thus avoiding unnecessary trouble and often misunderstanding.

The Box delivery is in the Main Hall of the Post Office Building. For the accommodation of those having Lock Boxes the Main Hall is open until 10 o'clock, P. M., and on Sundays till 12 M. The Box Delivery is closed from 9 to 10 A. M., for the distribution of the Eastern mail, and the General Delivery on Saturdays from 3 to 4 o'clock, P. M., to prepare the Letter List.

The Letter list is published every Sunday morning in the "Daily Enquirer."

The General delivery is in the west side of the building.

Ladies Boxes and delivery between the Main Hall and General delivery.

Gentlemen applying for ladies' letters should ask at the first window in the General Delivery, no one but females are waited on at the ladies' window.

All complaints, of whatever nature, should be made to the Postmaster or his Assistant. No controversy should be held with the clerks.

PENALTIES FOR VIOLATION OF P. O. LAW.

For obstructing or retarding the passage of the mail, or of any driver or carrier, or of any horse or carriage carrying the same, a fine of $100.

To rob a mail-carrier, imprisonment. Second conviction, death.

To obstruct the correspondence of another, or to pry into his business or secrets, or to secrete, embezzle, or destroy any letter or packet belonging to another, a fine not exceeding $500, and imprisonment not exceeding 12 months.

To counterfeit the handwriting of a Frank, $500.

Opening newspapers by a person not addressed or authorised, $20. Stealing newspapers, imprisonment.

Enclosing letter or memorandum, or other thing in any newspaper or other printed matter, or writing thereon, $5 for each offense.

To counterfeit postage stamps of the United States, or any other Government, imprisonment.

Any person carrying the mail to carry letters out of the mail, $50.

Owner of Stage, Railroad Car, Steamboat, or other vehicle, carrying letters or packets out of the mail, $100.

Sending letters or packets, (mailable matter,) by Express or other unlawful means, unless the same be enclosed in stamped envelopes, $50. N. B. A letter with a postage stamp merely can not be so sent.

Enclosing two or more letters directed to different persons in the same envelope, $10.

To use or attempt to use any postage stamps or stamped envelopes which have been used before, or to attempt to take the stamp of one envelope upon any other, $50.

Selling a postage stamp or stamped envelope by a postmaster, or other person, for any larger sums than that indicated on its face, $10 to $300.

LIST OF POST OFFICES

IN THE

UNITED STATES AND TERRITORIES.

ALABAMA.

Autauga co.
Antaugaville
Chestnut Creek
Crystal Springs
Hartwood
Huntington
Independence
Kingston (c h)
Milton
Mulberry
Prattville
Ranch

Baldwin co.
Blakely (c h)
Dannelley's Mills
Honey Cut
Stockton
Tensaw

Barbour co.
Adkison's
Buck Branch
Buford
Bushville
Choctawhatchie
Clayton (c h)
Cowikes
Eufaula
Fort Browder
Fort Williams
Glennville
Jernigan
Kings
Louisville
Midway
Mount Andrew
New Topia
Renoldsville
Texasville
White Oak Springs

Bibb co.
Affonee
Caudle's Shop
Centreville (c h)
Maplesville
Mars
Randolph
Scottsville
Six Mile

Blount co.
Blount Spring
Blountsville (c h)
Brooksville
Campbell's Store
Chapultepec
Hanna's
Little Warrior
Mount Alvis
Murphree's Valley
Ogee
Sapp's ⋈ Roads
Summit
Village Springs
Violy
Walnut Grove

Butler co.
Armadillo
Butler's Spring
Davidville
Dawson
Dead Fall
Didaske
East Georgia
Friendship
Georgiana
Greenville (c h)
Honoroville
Jackson's Mills
Kirkville
Long Creek
Manningham
Millville
Monterey
Oaky Streak

Pigeon Creek
Rainersville
Sal Soda
South Butler
Starlington
Three Runs
Toluca

Calhoun co.
Abernethy
Alexandria
Cainland
Corn Grove
Cave Creek
Cross Plains
Fair Play
Jacksonville (c h)
Kemp's Creek
Ladiga
Lead Mines
Loydville
Middleton
Morrisville
Mount Polk
Narrow Valley
New Bethel
Oak Level
Oxford
Palestine
Peak's Hill
Rabbittown
Reavesville
Ripley
Rosewood
Shoal Creek
Sulphur Springs
Ten Islands
Watt's Creek
Wehoga
White Plains

Chambers co.
Bethlehem
Beulah
Chambers (c h)
Cusseta
Fredonia
Hickory Flat
Kendall's ⋈ Roads
Milltown
Mount Hickory
Mount Jefferson
New Harmony
Oak Bowery
Osanippa
Waverly

Cherokee co.
Ball Play
Blue Pond
Cedar Bluff (c h)
Cedar Springs
Centre
Cobb's Mills
Coloma
Davis ⋈ Roads
Gadsden
Gaylesville
Gnatsville
Goshen
Hannegan
Hoke's Bluffs
Howell's ⋈ Road
King's Hill
Kirk's Grove
Leesburgh
Little River
Oceola
Pleasant Gap
Ringgold
Rio Grande
Sand Rock
Sterling
Spring Garden
Tranquility
Turkeytown
Water Cure

Choctaw co.
Barryton

Creek
Bladen Springs
Bogueloosa
Butler (c h)
Desotoville
Emery Creek
Hurricane Creek
Isney
Mount Sterling
Nicholson's Store
Oakuppa (b)
Old Washington (c
Pelham
Puscus
Pushmataha
Red Creek
Tompkinsville
Williams' ⋈ Roads
Yancey

Clark co.
Air Mount
Bashi
Choctaw Corner
Coffeeville
Dead Level
Gainestown
Grove Hill
Jackson
Morvin
Saint Paul
Suggsville

Coffee co.
Busbeeville
Cane Brake
Coffee Corner
Elba
Geneva
Indigo Head
Old Town
Perdue
Wellborn (c h)

Conecuh co.
Belleville
Brooklyn
Commerce
Evergreen
Fort Crawford
Jamestown
Lewis' Station
Nathansville
Orison
Rural Hill
Sepulga
Sparta (c h)

Coosa co.
Adams' Store
Bradford
Buyoksville
Central Institute
Coosa Valley
Equality
Good Water
Hanover
Marble Valley
Mount Olive
Nixburgh
Rockford (c h)
Socoopatoy
Traveler's Rest
Weogufka
Wetumpka

Covington co.
Andalusia (c h)
Conecuh River
Leon
Losago
Road Level
Rose Hill
Westover
Williams' Mill

Dale co.
Barnes' ⋈ Roads
Beaver Creek

Big Creek
Clopton
Daleville
Dothan
Echo
Goline
Haw Ridge
High Bluff
High Fall
Newton (c h)
Ozark
Pondtown
Rocky Head
Skipperville
Summer Hill
Sylvan Grove
Westville

Dallas co.
Bellevue
Burnsville
Cahaba (c h)
Cambridge
Carlowville
Elm Bluff
Forts
Liberty Hill
Moseley's Grove
Orrville
Pleasant Hill
Portland
Richmond
Selma
Summerfield
Woodlawn

De Kalb co.
Annawalka
Atwood
Coxville
Duck Spring
Greenwood
Head Spring
Hendricksville
Laurel Creek
Lebanon (c h)
McCammac
North Bend
Pierceville
Porterville
Rawlingsville
Reese's Mills
Reubensville
Sand Mountain
Valley Head
Van Buren
Worth

Fayette co.
Asbury
Beaverdale
Big Pond
Brown
Cave Spring
Cordova
Davis' Creek
Dublin
Fayette (c h)
Folis
Handy
Hester's
Hill
Military Springs
Milfnort
Mud Creek
New River
Newtonville
Olinda
Pilgrim's Rest
Sheffield
Yellow Creek

Franklin co.
Allsboro'
Barton
Blue Lick
Burleson
Cherokee
Chickasaw

Dickson
Frankfort
La Grange
Mountain Spring
Nauvoo
Newburgh
Pleasant Site
Rock Creek
Russellville (c h)
South Florence
Spruce Pine
Tuscumbia (c h)
Waco

Greene co.
Boligee
Clinton
Eutaw (c h)
Forkland
Greensboro'
Harrison
Havana
Hollow Square
Hopewell
Knoxville
Mount Hebron
Newbern
New Prospect
Pleasant Ridge
Springfield
Union
Welton

Hancock co.
Clear Creek Falls
Houston
Littlesville

Henry co.
Abbeville
Columbia
Cureton's Bridge
Egypt
Flag Pond
Franklin
Hilliardsville
Lawrenceville
Mercy Bay
Open Pond
Otho
Shorterville

Jackson co.
Bellefonte (c h)
Big Coon
Bolivar
Bridgeport
Dodsonville
Estill's Fork
Langston
Larkin's Fork
Larkinsville
Long Island
Lyonville
Parks' Store
Princeton
Redman
Rocky Spring
Rustic Bower
Sauta
Scott's Mills
Stevenson
Straight Fork
Trenton
Woodville (c h)

Jefferson co.
Cedar Grove
Chester
Elyton (c h)
Jonesboro'
Mexico
Mount Pinson
Nebo
Oregon
Rockville
Taylor's
Truss
Vinesville
Waldrop's Mills

Lauderdale co.
Bailey's Springs
Centre Star
Florence (c h)
Gravelly Spring
Green Hill
Lexington
Little Cypress
Masonville
Oakland
Rogersville
Waterloo
Westmorelandville

Lawrence co.
Avoca
Brickville
Camp Spring
Concord
Courtland
Dry Creek
Kinlock
Landersville
Leighton
Marietta
Moulton (c h)
Mountain Home
Mount Hope
Oakville
Town Creek

Limestone co.
Athens (c h)
Centre Hill
Gilbertsboro'
Good Spring
Lucky Hit
Mooresville
Mount Roszell
Pettusville
Shoal Ford

Lowndes co.
Benton
Bragg's
Farmersville
Fort Deposit
Hayneville
Helicon
Letohatchee
Lowndesboro'
Manack
Mount Willing
Panola
Sandy Ridge
Steep Creek

Macon co.
Aberfoil
Auburn
Chunonuggee
Cotton Valley
Cross Keys
Cubehachohie
Dick's Creek
Enon
Fort Decatur
Guerryton
Hardaway
Hernando
La Place
Loachapoka
Lockland
Magnolia
New Potosi
Notasulga
Person's
Ridge Grove
Society Hill
Suspension
Tuskegee (c h)
Union Springs
Uphaupee
Warrior Stand

Madison co.
Berkley
Haden's
Hayes' Store

384 Arkansas.

Huntsville (c h)
Madison ⋈ Roads
Madison Station
Maysville
Meridianville
New Hope
New Market
Owen's ⋈ Roads
Triana
Whitesburgh

Marengo co.
Clay Hill
Dayton
Demopolis
Dixon's Mills
Hampden
Jefferson
Linden (c h)
McKinley
Macon
Nanafalia
Pineville
Shiloh
Spring Hill
Sweet Water

Marion co.
Aheda
Allen's Factory
Aston's Store
Barnesville
Beaverton
Bexar
Bigalow
Chalk Bluff
County Line
Detroit
Hackleburgh
Haley's
Moscow
Palo
Pikeville (c h)
Toll Gate

Marshall co.
Aurora
Big Spring
Claysville
Cottonville
Guntersville
Henrysville
Hillian's Store
Kennamer
McCloskey's
Meltonsville
Mount High
Oleander
Red Hill
Sydney
Warrenton (c h)
Zachary

Mobile co.
Citronelle
Miller Creek
Mobile (c h)
Mount Vernon
Seal's Precinct
Whistler

Monroe co.
Bell's Landing
Buena Vista
Burnt Corn
Claiborne (c h)
Clauselville
Cokerville
Monroeville
Mount Pleasant
Newtown Academy
Old Texas
River Ridge

Montgomery co.
Arcadia
Argus
Cotoma
Hickory Grove
Line Creek
Montgomery (c h)
Mount Meigs
Oak Grove
Oakley
Pine Level
Pintlala
Ramer
Sharpesville
Snowdoun
Strata

Morgan co.
Apple Grove
Basham's Gap
Blue Spring
Cedar Plains
Danville
Decatur
Flint River
Gandy's Cove
Ivy Bluff
Lacey's Spring
Somerville (c h)
Valhermoso Spring

Perry co.
Brush Creek
Bucksnort
Chestnut Hill
Five Mile
Ford's Mill
Hamburgh
Jericho
Marion (c h)
Morgan Spring
Oakmulga
Perryville
Pinctucky

Plantersville
Radfordsville
Uniontown

Pickens co.
Antioch
Bridgeville
Carrollton (c h)
Cochran's Mills
Fairfield
Gordo
Hinton's Grove
Mantua
Memphis
Olney
Palmetto
Pickensville
Pleasant Grove
Providence
Raleigh
Reform
Vienna
Yorkville

Pike co.
Arborvitae
Bibb
Bruceville
Brundige
Buck Horn
China Grove
Farriersville
Gainer's Store
Hallsville
Indian Creek
Little Oak
Milo
Monticello (c h)
Mount Hilliard
New Providence
Oluste Creek
Orion
Pea River
Perote
Pine Grove
Troy (c h)
Wesley Chapel
White Water

Randolph co.
Almond
Arbacoochee
Buchanan
County Line
Delta
Dowdell
Eastville
Fish Head
Gold Ridge
Haywood
Hebron
Ingram
Lumar
Louina
Mellow Valley
Milner

Molino
Oakfusky
Roanoke
Rockdale
Rock Mills
Warren
Weedowee
Wehadkee
Wesobulga
Winston

Russell co.
Colbert
Crawford (c h)
Dover
Girard
Hatchechubbee
Lamington
Mechanicsville
Opelika
Oswichee
Salem
Sand Fort
Seale's Station
Uchee
Vilula
Waccoochee
Watoola
Yongesborough

Saint Clair co.
Ashville (c h)
Beaver Valley
Beobe Springs
Bennettsville
Blairsville
Branchville
Broken Arrow
Coosa Valley
Cropwell
Greensport
Kelly's Creek
Mount Niles
Round Pond
Springville
Trout Creek
Wolf Creek

Shelby co.
Bridgeton
Columbiana (c h)
Harpersville
Highland
Hillsboro'
Montevallo
Mullins
Nelson
Shelby Spring
Sterrett
Wilsonville
Woodsboro'

Sumter co.
Anvil
Belmont
Bluffport

Brewersville
Gainesville
Gaston
Intercourse
Jones' Bluff
Livingston (c h)
Payneville
Rosserville
Sumterville
Sydenham
Warsaw

Talladega co.
Alpine
Bluff Spring
Bowdon
Brownsville
Chandler's Spring
Childersburg
Chinnibee
Coleta
Conehardee
Court Hill
Curry
Dido
Easta Boga
Fayetteville
Fife
Flat Rock
Hatcher's
Hillabee
Iron Works
Kelly's Springs
Kimulga
Lincoln
Mardisville
Middle Ridge
Mountain
Pinckneyville
Pine Flat
Silver Run
Sylacauga
Talladega (c h)
Weewokaville
Winterboro'

Tallapoosa co.
Beckettsville
Bulger's Mills
Camp Hill
Chanahachee
Chapman's Ford
Dadeville (c h)
Daviston
De Soto
Dudleyville
Emuckfaw
Fish Pond
Goldville
Horse Shoe Bend
Island Home
Jackson's Camp
Kowaliga
New Site
Realtown
Souchahatchee

Stow's Ferry
Tallassee
Tehopeka
Wind Creek
Youngsville

Tuskaloosa co.
Addison
Blockers
Carthage
Cushing
Fernvale
Foster's
McConnell's
McMath's
Moore's Bridge
New Lexington
Northport
North River
Oregonia
Plum
Romulus
Sipsey Turnpike
Trion
Tuskaloosa (c h)
Woodstock

Walker co.
Arkadelphia
Bartonville
Blackwater
Democrat
Eldridge
Fairview
Gap
Hanby's Mill
Holly Grove
Jasper
Kansas
Thornhill
York

Washington co.
Escatawpa
McIntosh Bluff
New Wakefield
Pleasant Valley
Saint Stephens

Wilcox co.
Allenton
Bethel
Camden
Clifton
Creagh's Mill
Fatama
Lilly's Store
Lower Peach Tree
Pine Apple
Pine Hill
Prairie Bluff
Rehoboth
Sebastopol
Snow Hill
Wilcox Springs

ARKANSAS.

Arkansas co.
Arkansas Post
Clear Point
Crain River
Crockett's Bluff
Cummins
Dewitt (c h)
Fair Dale
Long Point
Molina del Rey
Mount Adams
Pearson's Mill
Saint Charles
Sharon
South Bend
Swan Lake

Ashley co.
Berlin
Chester
Elon
Fountain Hill
Hamburgh (c h)
Lake Enterprise
Litona
Long View
Marie Salome
Orion
Portland
Shiloh

Benton co.
Apple Orchard
Bentonville
Bloomington
Double Springs
Equality
Hico

Hickory
Jenning's Ferry
Maysville
Osage Mills
Pea Ridge
Roller's Ridge
Spavinaw
Twin Springs
Two Mills
Trott's Mill

Bradley co.
Adamsville
Eagle Creek
Gravel Ridge
Hermitage
Lagle
Lamark
Mount Elba
Sumpter
Warren (c h)

Calhoun co.
Hampton
Locust Bayou
Thomas' Store

Carroll co.
Berryville
Carrollton
Crooked Creek
Elm Wood
King's River
Mountain Spring
Mount Pleasant
Osage

Cherokee Nation co.
Baptist Mission
Flint
Fort Gibson
Grand Saline
Marble Salt Works
Tahlequah
Webber's Falls

Chickasaw Nat. co.
Fort Washita
Pontotoc
Tishemingo

Chicot co.
Columbia
Eudora
Gaster's Landing
Grand Lake
Hawkins's Landing
Lake Village
Masona

Choctaw Nation co.
Armstrong Academy
Bogy Depot
Choctaw Agency
Donksville
Eagletown
Fort Arbuckle
Hochubboe
Lukfiahtah
Tohoxby
Wheelock

Clark co.
Alpine
Amity
Auvil
Arkadelphia (c h)
Beech Creek
Clear Spring
De Gray
Genoa
Hickory Grove
Highway
McNeely's Ridge
Okalona
Point Cedar
Rome
Springvale
Terre Noir

Columbia co.
Calhoun
Dorcheat
Falcon
Hicksville
Hobson's Store
Liddesdale
Magnolia
Palestine
Sulphur Spring

Conway co.
Cadron
Cane Creek
East Fork
Greenbrier
Green Grove
Lewisburgh
Old Hickory

Olive Creek
State Rock
Springfield

Crawford co.
Belmont
Lee's Creek
Natural Dam
The Narrows
Van Buren (c h)

Creek Nation co.
Creek Agency
Micco

Crittenden co.
Bledsoe's Landing
Cat Island
Council Bend
Edmondson
Grayson
Hopefield
Marion (c h)
Oldham

Dallas co.
Beech Bluff
Cachemasso
Chambersville
Chappell
Como
Fairview
Holly Springs
Princeton (c h)
Stover
Tulip

Desha co.
Antwerp
Butler
Campbell
Cypress Creek
Florence
Laconia
Napoleon
Red Fork
Selma
White River

Drew co.
Barkada
Branchville
Cut Off
Cornersville
Dearmond's Mills
Green Mount
Ion
Lacey
Mars Hill
Monticello (c h)
Montonea
Rolf's Bluff
Wolf Creek

Franklin co.
Cass
Charleston
Constitution
De Rosey
Ozark (c h)
Pleasant Hill
Roseville
Short Mountain
Sub Rosa

California. 385

Fulton co.
Bennett's Bayou
Bennett's River
Cross Plains
Eagle
Franklin
Pilot Hill (c h)
Rapp's Barrens
Union

Greene co.
Campobella
Chalk Bluff
Crowley
Gainesville (c h)
Greensboro'
Lorado
Oak Bluffs
Oak Ridge
Petra
Shakespear
Wolcott

Hempstead co.
Albany
Clark's Mills
Columbus
Fulton
Graves
Hickory Creek
Justus' Mills
Moscow
Nashville
Ozan
Spring Hill
Washington (c h)

Hot Springs co.
Antioch
Dividing Ridge
De Roche
Fair Play
Fitzhugh's Mills
Henderson
Hot Springs
Magnet Cove
Midway
Rockport
Sheriff's Ridge

Independence co.
Alder Brook
Batesville (c h)
Big Bottom
Black Oak
Buck Horn
Conveniences
Curia
Galloway
Graham
Hickory Valley
Merrittaville
Oil Trough
Pleasant Plains
Poke Bayou
Rock Point
Rust's
Sullivan Springs
Sulphur Rock
Wallace Creek
Walnut Grove
Wolf Bayou

Izard co.
Benbrook's Mills
Big Spring
Blue Mountain
Greenbush
Mill Creek
Mount Olive
North Fork
Rich Woods

Rocky Bayou
Sylamore
Table Rock
Violet Hill
Wild Haws

Jackson co.
Augusta
Brown's Creek
Colerain
Elgin
Grand Glaze
Jachin
Jacksonport
Kenyon
Mount Pinson

Jefferson co.
Brooks
Byrd's Spring
Camp Creek
Darysaw
Egypt
Flat Bayou
Lehi
Locust Cottage
Monday
New Gascony
Pastoria
Peach Grove
Pine Bluff
Plum Bayou
Richland
Waterssky
White Sulphur Springs
White Bluff
White Oak

Johnson co.
Clarksville
Cobbsville
Eubank's Mills
Horse Head
Patterson's Bluff
Pekin
Piney
Pittsburgh
Point Meers
Shoal Creek

La Fayette co.
Covington
Forest Grove
Lewisville (c h)
Line Ferry
Oak Hill
Rondo
Spring Bank
Walnut Hill

Lawrence co.
Ash Flat
Calamine
Camanche
Canton
Clover Bend
Cuba
Evening Shade
Hazel Grove
Houghton
Jackson
Linwood
Martin's Creek
Mount Sylvan
Osborn's Creek
Paw Paw
Reed's Creek
Sidney
Smithville
Stranger's Home
Strawberry
Sugar Grove

Madison co.
Clifty
Huntsville (c h)
Jupiter
Kingston
Little Spring
Marble
Saint Paul
War Eagle
Wesley.

Marion co.
Big Pond
Buffalo City
Clear Creek
Dubuque
Lead Hill
Rolling Prairie
Whiteville
Yellville

Mississippi co.
Barfield
Rickman's Bend
Holly Grove
Osceola (c h)
Pecan Point
Shawnee Village

Monroe co.
Aberdeen
Clarendon
Cypress
Lawrenceville
Moro
Pine Grove
Pleasant Lake
Surrounded Hills
Valley Grove

Montgomery co.
Big Fork
Caddo Cove
Centreville
Crystal Hill
Harold
Mazarne
Mount Ida

Newton co.
Borland
Cave Creek
Jasper (c h)
Mount Judea
Mount Parthenon
Walnut Fork
Watkinsville
Whiteley's

Perry co.
Casa
Cypress Mills
Onyx
Perryville (c h)
Tyler's Bluff

Philips co.
Askew
Beech Grove
Edwardsburg
Gillens Landing
Helena (c h)
Jeffersonville
La Grange
Marianna
North Creek
Oldtown
Planters
Sterling
Trenton
Walnut Bend
Wayne

Pike co.
Antoine
Brocktown

County Line
Huddleston
Murfreesboro'
Royston
Wilton

Poinsett co.
Caseyville
Cold Water
Goldsboro'
Harrisburgh
Johnson
Lockbee
Santa Fe

Polk co.
Big Bend
Cove
Dallas
Edge Hill
Gap Springs
Mountain Fork
Quito
Reardon

Pope co.
Dayton
Dover
Gally Creek
Gally Rock
Geeseville
Glass Village
Gum Log
Hebron
Moreland
Norristown (c h)
Rock Hill
Russellville

Prairie co.
Brownsville
Centre
Cherryville
Clear Lake
Des Arc
Duvall's Bluff
Gumwood
Hamilton
Hickory Plain
La Grue
Lake Bluff
Larissa
Oakland Grove
Walnut Plains
Watensaw

Pulaski co.
Bayou Metoe
Good Hope
Little Rock (c h)
Mary
Maumelle
North Point
Palarm
Pennington's Mills
Liberty
Waverly

Randolph co.
Baptist Fork
Black's Ferry
Cherokee Bay
Crosson's Store
Fourche Dumas
Hix's Ferry
Lima
Pocahontas (c h)
Spring Creek

St. Francis co.
Calvert
Cotton Plant
Eureka
Gage's Point

Jones' Hill
Lauguelle
Linden
Madison
Mill Ridge
Oakland
Taylor's Creek
Willsburgh

Saline co.
Akin's Store
Belfast
Benton (c h)
Bland's
Brazil
Cherry Grove
Collegeville
Hickory Flat
Hungary
Lost Creek
Owensville
Prattsville
Whittington

Scott co.
Black Jack
Boonville (c h)
Chismville
Cedar Creek
Olio
Parks
Reviles
Texas
Trouble Hill
Tumlinsonville
Waldron

Searcy co.
Big Flat
Burrowsville
Calf Creek
Lebanon (c h)
Locust Grove
Marshall Prairie
Point Peter
Providence
Rock Fish
Tomahawk
Wett's Springs
White Oak Shoals
Wiley's Cove

Sebastian co.
Back Bone
Bloomer
Breckinridge
Bruner
Chocoville
Fort Smith
Greenwood (c h)
Hodge's Prairie
James' Fork
Jenny Lind
Long Prairie
Sugar Loaf
Vache Grass
Valley

Sevier co.
Adrian
Brownstown
Centre Point
Farmington
Millwood
Mineral Hill
Nelta Bec
Norwoodsville
Paraclifta
Richmond
Rocky Comfort
Ultama Thule
White Oak Shoals

Union co.
Atlanta
Champagnolle

Eldorado
Hillsboro'
Lisbon
Meeks
Mount Holly
New London
Pigeon Hill
Scotland
Three Creeks
Tremont
Union Springs
Wilmington

Van Buren co.
Clinton
Cumfort
Kinderhook
Liberty Springs
Middletown
Quitman

Washington co.
Ada
Billingsly
Boonsboro'
Boone's Grove
Buchanan
Cincinnati
Elm Springs
Evansville
Fayetteville (c h)
Greenville
Hermannsburgh
Hilochee
Lynch's Prairie
Maguire's Store
Spring Mill
Taney
West Fork

Washita co.
Buchanan
Buena Vista
Buffalo
Camden (c h)
Caney
Carouse
Freco
Hermannsburgh
Lamartine
Liberty
Lone Grove
Luda
Mount Moria
Ouachita
Petersburgh
Seminary
Woodlawn

White co.
Centre Hill
Cold Well
Judson
Kentucky Valley
Muddy Bayou
Rose Bud
Royal Colony
Searcy (c h)
Stony Point
Velvet Ridge
West Point

Yell co.
Bluffton
Chikalah
Danville (c h)
Dardanelle
Dutche's Creek
Gravelly Hill
Parkersburgh
Petite Jean
Pleasant Valley
Rock Creek
Rover
Walnut Tree

CALIFORNIA.

Alameda co.
Alameda
Alvarado
Brooklyn
Centreville
Oakland
San Leandro
San Lorenzo

Amador co.
Drytown
Ione City
Jackson
Sarahville
Sutter Creek
Volcano

Butte co.
Bangor
Bidwell's Bar
Brush Creek
Butte Mills
Cherokee
Chico
Forbestown
Hamilton
Hansonville
Lassens
Oroville
Pea Vine
Rio Seco
Thompson's Flat
Yankee Hill
ndot Wyate

Calaveras co.
Angel's Camp
Camp Seco
Chili
Double Springs
Fourth Crossing
Jenny Lind
Mill Valley
Mokelumne Hill
Mountain Ranch
Murphy's
Musquito
North Branch
O'Byrne's Ferry
Poverty Bar
Reynold's Ferry

Rich Gulch
San Andreas
Vallicita
West Point

Colusi co.
Colusi (c h)
Grand Island
Jacinto
Monroeville
Moon's Ranch
Princeton
Tehama

Contra Costa co.
Alamo

Antioch
Lafayette
Martinez (c h)
San Pablo
San Ramon

Del Norte co.
Ferry Point
Happy Camp

El Dorado co.
Bottle Hill
Cedarville
Clarksville
Cold Spring
Coloma (c h)

Diamond Springs
Durno
Eldorado
Fiddletown
Garden Valley
Georgetown
Greenwood
Grizzly Flats
Indian Diggings
Kelsey
Newton
Pilot Hill
Placerville
Salmon Falls
Spanish Flat
Ycomet

Connecticut.

Fresno co.
Scottsburg

Humboldt co.
Bucksport
Eel River
Eureka
Uniontown

Klamath co.
Cottage Grove
Crescent City (c h)
Elk Camp
Forks of Salmon
Orleans
Sawyer's Bar
Trinidad
Weitchpec

Los Angeles co.
Fort Tejon
Los Angeles
Monte
San Gabriel
San Pedro
Tejon

Marin co.
Novato
Olema
San Rafael (c h)
San Quentin
Tomales

Mariposa co.
Agua Fria
Bear Valley
Bondville
Colorado
Gwin
Hornitas
Indian Gulch
Mariposa (c h)
Maxwell's Creek
Mt. Ophir
New Potosi
Ophir
Quartzburgh
Wyatt's Store

Mendocino co.
Anderson
Clairville

Mendocino
Punta Arenas
Ukiah

Merced co.
Merced Falls
Snelling's Ranch

Monterey co.
Monterey (c h)
Natividad
Salinas
San Antonio
San Juan

Napa co.
Big Valley
Lower Lake
Napa City (c h)
Sebastopol
Uncle Sam
Upper Clear Lake

Nevada co.
Alpha
Grass Valley
Indian Springs
Little York
Moores Flat
Mountain Well
Nevada City (c h)
North Bloomfield
North San Juan
Omega
Patterson
Red Dog
Rough and Ready
Sweetland

Placer co.
Auburn
Bath
Coon Creek
Damascus
Dutch Flat
Grizzly Bear House
Illinoistown
Iowa City
Lisbon
Michigan Bluff

Mountain Springs
Neilsburgh
Ophirville
Oro City
Rattlesnake Bar
Secret Ravine
Todd's Valley
Virginia
Yankee Jims

Plumas co.
Meadow Valley
Nelson's Creek
Onion Valley
Quincy

Sacramento co.
Cosumne
Elk Grove
Folsom City
Michigan Bar
Mormon Island
Onisbo (c h)
Sacramento City
Salsbury
Sutter
Walnut Grove

San Bernardino co.
San Bernardino (c h)

San Diego co.
San Diego (c h)

San Francisco co.
San Francisco (c h)
Woodside

San Joaquin co.
Foreman's Ranch
Fourteen Mile House
French Camp
Fugitt
Half Way House
Knight's Ferry
Marietta
Orr's Ranch
Poland

Staples' Ranch
Stockton (c h)
Wood's Ferry

San Luis Obispo co.
San Luis Obispo (c h)

San Mateo co.
Belmont
Redwood City
Searsville

Santa Barbara co.
Santa Barbara (c h)

Santa Clara co.
Gilroy
McCartysville
Mayfield
Mission San Jose
Mountain View
Milpitas
Santa Clara
San Jose (c h)

Santa Cruz co.
Santa Cruz (c h)
Soquel
Watsonville

Shasta co.
American Ranch
Cottonwood
French Gulch
Horsetown
Red Bluff
Shasta
Whiskey Creek

Sierra co.
Alleghany
Downieville
Eureka North
Forest City
Gibsonville
Goodyear's Bar
La Porte
Plum Valley
Saint Louis
Table Rock

Siskiyou co.
Callahan's Ranch
Fort Goff
Healey
Ottitiewa
Scott River (c h)
Seiad Valley
Yreka

Solano co.
Benecia (c h)
Denverton
Fairfield
Putah
Rio Vista
Rockville
Suisun
Vacaville
Vallejo

Sonoma co.
Bloomfield
Bodega
Clover Dale
Healdsburgh
Lakeville
Pacific Home
Petaluma
Santa Rosa (c h)
Smith's Ranch
Sonoma
Stony Point
Windsor

Stanislaus co.
La Grange

Sutter co.
Johnson's Ranch
Nicolaus
Yuba City

Tehama co.
Grove City
Rock Creek

Trinity co.
Big Bar
Burnt Ranch
Lewiston
Minersville

Trinity
Trinity Centre
Weaverville (c h)

Tulare co.
Keesaysburgh
Keysville
King's River
Petersburg
Visalia

Tuolumne co.
Big Oak Flat
Chinese Camp
Columbia
Don Pedro's Bar
Garrote
Green Springs
Horr's Ranch
Jacksonville
Jamestown
Montezuma
Shaw's Flat
Sonora
Springfield

Yolo co.
Antelope
Buck Eye
Cache Creek
Charleston
Fremont
Grafton
Prairie
Willow Point
Yolo

Yuba co.
Camptonville
Cascade City
Empire Ranch
Foster's Bar
Greenville
Honcuts
Long Bar
Marysville (c h)
Oregon House
Owsley's Bar
Park's Bar
Round Tent
Strawberry Valley
Timbuctoo

CONNECTICUT.

Fairfield co.
Ball's Pond
Banksville
Bethel
Black Rock
Bridgeport
Brookfield
Cold Spring
Danbury (c h)
Darien
Darien Depot
Easton
Fairfield (c h)
Georgetown
Glenville
Greenfield Hill
Greenwich
Hawleyville
High Ridge
Huntington
Limestone
Long Ridge
Minnus
Mill Plain
Monroe
New Cannan
New Fairfield
Newton
North Greenwich
North Stamford
North Wilton
Norwalk
Redding
Redding Bridge
Ridgebury
Ridgefield
Round Hill
Saugatuck
Sherman
Smith's Ridge
South Norwalk
Southport
Stanford
Stanwich
Stepney
Stepney Depot
Stratford
Trumbull
Trumbull Long Hill
Weston
Westport

West Norwalk
West Redding
Wilton
Winnipauk

Hartford co.
Avon
Berlin
Bloomfield
Bristol
Broad Brook
Buckland
Burlington
Canton
Canton Centre
Collinsville
East Berlin
East Granby
East Hartford
East Windsor
East Windsor Hill
Enfield
Farmer's Village
Farmington
Forestville
Glastenbury
Granby
Hartford (c h)
Hartlandt
Hazardville
Hockanum
Kensington
Manchester
Manchester Station
Marion
Marlboro'
New Britain
Newington
North Canton
North Granby
Plainville
Plantsville
Poquonock
Rainbow
Rocky Hill
Scitico
Simsbury
South Glastenbury
Southington
South Manchester
South Windsor

Suffield
Tariffville
Thompsonville
Unionville
Warehouse Point
West Avon
West Granby
West Hartford
West Hartland
West Suffield
Wethersfield
Windsor
Windsor Locks
Windsorville

Litchfield co.
Bakersville
Bantam Falls
Barkhamsted
Bethlehem
Bridgewater
Burrville
Campville
Canaan
Chapinville
Colebrook
Colebrook River
Cornwall
Cornwall Bridge
Cornwall Hollow
East Canaan
Ellsworth
Falls Village
Goshen
Harwinton
Hitchcockville
Hotchkissville
Huntsville
Joyceville
Kent
Lakeville
Lanesville
Limo Rock
Litchfield (c h)
Marble Dale
Merwinsville
Mill Brook
Milton
New Hartford
New Hartford Centre
New Milford

New Preston
Norfolk
North Cornwall
North Colebrook
Northfield
North Goshen
North Norfolk
Northville
Ore Hill
Pequabuck
Pine Meadow
Pleasant Valley
Plymouth
Plymouth Hollow
Roxbury
Salisbury
Sharon
South Canaan
South Farms
South Kent
South Norfolk
Southville
Terrysville
Torringford
Torrington
Warren
Washington
Watertown
West Cornwall
West Goshen
West Norfolk
West Winsted
Winchester
Winchester Centre
Wolcottville
Woodbury
Woodville

Middlesex co.
Centre Brook
Chester
Clinton
Cobalt
Cromwell
Deep River
Durham
Durham Centre
East Haddam
East Hampton
Essex
Haddam (c h)
Haddam Neck

Hadlyme
Higganum
Killingworth
Leesville
Middlefield
Middle Haddam
Middletown (c h)
Millington
Moodus
North Killingworth
Portland
Saybrook
Saybrook Ferry
West Brook
Winthrop

New Haven co.
Ausonia
Beacon Falls
Bethany
Branford
Brook's Vale
Cheshire
Derby
East Haven
Fair Haven
Guilford
Hamden
Madison
Meriden
Middlebury
Milford
Mount Carmel
Naugatuck
New Haven (c h)
North Branford
Northford
North Guildford
North Haven
North Madison
Oakville
Orange
Oxford
Prospect
Rockland
Seymour
South Britain
Southbury
Southford
Stoney Creek
Wallingford

Waterbury
Waterville
West Cheshire
West Haven
West Meriden
Westville
Whitneyville
Wolcott
Zoar Bridge

New London co.
Bozrah
Bozrahville
Centre Groton
Chesterfield
Colchester
Franklin
Gates' Ferry
Gardner's Lake
Greenville
Griswold
Groton
Hamburgh
Jewett City
Lebanon
Ledyard
Liberty Hill
Lisbon
Lord's Bridge
Lyme
Montville
Mystic
Mystic Bridge
Mystic River
New London (c h)
Niantic
Noank
North Lyme
North Stonington
Norwich (c h)
Norwich Town
Pendleton Hill
Poquonoc Bridge
Poquetanuck
Preston
Salem
South Lyme
Stonington
Uncasville
Waterford
West Cheshire
Yantic

Delaware, Florida, Georgia.

Tolland co.
Andover
Bolton
Columbia
Coventry
Coventry Depot
Eagleville
Ellington
Gilead
Hebron
Mansfield
Mansfield Centre
Mansfield Depot

Mashapang
Merrow Station
Moose Meadow
Mount Hope
North Somers
Quarryville
Rockville
Somers
Somersville
South Coventry
Square Pond
Stafford
Stafford Springs

Staffordville
Tolland (c h)
Union
Vernon
Vernon Depot
West Stafford
West Willington
Willington

Windham co.
Abington
Ashford
Brooklyn (c h)

Campbell's Mills
Canterbury
Central Village
Chaplin
Collamer
Eastford
East Killingly
East Woodstock
Fishersville
Hampton
Killingly
Moosop
New Boston

North Ashford
North Windham
North Woodstock
Oneco
Phœnixville
Plainfield
Pomfret
Pomfret Landing
Putnam
Scotland
South Killingly
South Windham
Sterling

Sterling Hill
Thompson
Voluntown
West Ashford
Westford
West Killingly
Westminster
West Thompson
West Woodstock
Willimantic
Windham
Woodstock
Woodstock Valley

DELAWARE.

Kent co.
Arthursville
Camden
Canterbury
Dover (c h)
Farmington
Felton Station
Frederica
Harrington
Haslettville
Hollyville
Kenton
Leipsic

Leipsic Station
Little Creek Landing
Magnolia
Marshy Hope Bridge
Masten's Corner
Milford

Smyrna
Vernon
Whiteleysburgh
Williamsville
Willow Grove

New Castle co.
Black Bird
Centreville
Chippewa
Christiana
Claymont
Cooch's Bridge
Delaware City
Fieldsboro'
Glasgow [tory
Henry Clay Factory
Loveville
McClellandsville

McDonough
Mermaid
Middletown
Newark
Newcastle (c h)
New Port
Odessa
Pleasant Hill
Port Penn
Red Lion
Saint George's
Stanton
Summit Bridge
Talleyville

Townsend Station
Wilmington (c h)
Sussex co.
Angola
Black Water
Bridgeville
Bull's Mills
Cannon's Ferry
Cedar Creek
Concord
Cove Dale
Dagsboro'
Draw Bridge
Frankford

Georgetown (c h)
Gumborough
Hall's Store
Hollyvie
Horsey's ⋈ Roads
Laurel
Lowes
Middleford
Millsboro'
Milton
St. Johnstown
Seaford
Selbyville
Tunnell's Store

FLORIDA.

Addison co.
Sandy Ford
Alachua co.
Gainesville
Micanopy
Morrison's Mills
Newnansville (c h)
Sikesville
Sugar Grove
Waldo
Benton co.
Augusta
Homasassa
Brevard co.
Indian River
Calhoun co.
Long Cane
Ochesee
Columbia co.
Barber's
Cherry Hill
Columbus
Durham
Ellisville
Huntsville
Ichetucknee
Lake City
Little River
New Boston
Newburgh
New River
Olustee
Palestine
Providence

St. Helena
Saint Louis
Spring Grove
Stark
Suwannee Shoals
Trail Ridge
Tustenugee
Dade co.
Miami
Duval co.
Baldwin
Chesuwiskia
Hibernia
Jacksonville (c h)
Magnolia Mills
Mandarin
Mayport Mills
Middleburg
Yellow Bluff
Escambia co.
Pensacola (c h)
Warrington
Franklin co.
Apalachicola
Gadsden co.
Aspalaga
Chattahoochee
China Hill
Concord
Mount Pleasant
Quincy (c h)
Rickoe's Bluff
Ridleysville

Hamilton co.
Bellville
Jasper
Jennings
White Springs
Hernando co.
Bay Port
Cadar Tree
Crystal River
Fort Dade
Fort Tyler
Monroe's Ferry
Pierceville
Hillsborough co.
Alafia
Ichepuckesassa
Tampa
Holmes co.
Cerro Gordo
Home Spring
Ponce De Leon
Jackson co.
Campbelton
Crowell
Greenwood
Marianna (c h)
Millwood
Jefferson co.
Boseley
Monticello (c h)
Walker's Mills
Waukeenah
La Fayette co.
Fayetteville

McQueen
Old Town
Leon co.
Bailey's Mill
Centreville
Chaires'
Hodgeson's Distillery
Jackson's Bluff
Miccosukee
Tallahassee (c h)
Levy co.
Atsena Otis
Black Dirt
Clay Landing
Long Pond
Wekeiva
Liberty co.
Blue Creek
Ridleysville
Madison co.
Cherry Lake
Clifton
Finkholloway
Fort Hamilton
Hamburg
Madison (c h)
Mosely Hall
Sandy Ford
Manatee co.
Manatee
Marion co.
Camp Izard
Cottage

Flemington
Iola
Long Swamp
Ocala
Orange Lake
Orange Springs
Silver Spring
Waeahootie
Monroe co.
Key West (c h)
Nassau co.
Callahan
Fernandino
King's Ferry
Lewisville
Orange co.
Hawkinsville
Jernigan
Mellonville (c h)
New Smyrna
Orlando
Putnam co.
Fort Gates
George's Lake
Lake George
Pilatka
Welaka
Santa Rosa co.
Austinville
Coon Hill
McLellanville
Milton

St. John's co.
Orange Mills
Picolata
St. Augustine (c h)
Sumter co.
Adamsville
Lake Griffin
Lake Harris
Mossy Grove
Palmyra
Pine Level
Sumpterville
Volusia co.
Enterprise
Volusia
Wakulla co.
Benhaden
Newport
Oil Works
Saint Marks
Shell Point
Sopehoppy
Walton co.
Alaqua
Almirante
Douglassville
East River
Knox Hill
Uchee Anna
Washington co.
Econfina
Orange Hill
St. Andrews Bay
Vernon

GEORGIA.

Appling co.
Cook's Store
Hall
Holmesville (c h)
Middleton's Store
Rushville
Baker co.
Albany
Bond's Mills
McSweensville
Milford
Newton (c h)
Pryor
Baldwin co.
Black Spring
Milledgeville (c h)
almage
Berrien co.
Milltown
Nashville

Bibb co.
Eleanor
Macon (c h)
Brooks co.
Naakin
Bryan co.
Way's Station
Bullock co.
Bengal
Mill Ray
Statesboro (c h)
Burke co.
Alexander
Fryer's Ponds
Girard
Green Cut
Herndon
Holcombe
Hopeful
Joy's Mills

Lester's District
Midville
Millin
Sardis
Waynesboro (c h)
Butts co.
Cork
Indian Springs
Jackson (c h)
Seven Islands
Stark
Wothville
Calhoun co.
Beckcom's ⋈ Roads
Morgan
Pachitta
Camden co.
Centre Village
Jeffersonton (c h)
Langshury
Saint Marys

Campbell co.
Campbellton (c h)
Cedar Branch
Chapel Hill
County Line
Dark Corner
Empire Mills
Fairburn
Gartrell
New Manchester
Palmetto
Riverlown
Salt Springs
Sandtown
Carroll co.
Rowden
Bowenville
Buffalo
Burnt Stand
Carrollton (c h)
Central Point
Chanceville

Hickory Level
Laurel Hill
Mistletoe Bower
Rotherwood
Sand Hill
Tallapoosa
Villa Rica
Wimberly
Cass co.
Adairsville
Allatoona
Cartersville
Cassville (c h)
Kiowah
Euharley
Kingston
Little Prairie
Mountain House
Pine Log
Stilesborough
Catoosa co.
Catoosa Springs
Graysville

Ringgold
Wood's Station
Charlton co.
Trader's Hill
Chatham co.
Savannah (c h)
Chattahoochee co.
Cottage Mill
Cusseta
Halloca
King
Chattooga co.
Alpine
Chattoogaville
Dirt Town
Farmersville
Melville
Subliqua
Summerville (c h)
Telogn Springs
Trion Factory
Valley Store

Georgia.

Cherokee co.
Ball Ground
Canton (c h)
Fort Buffington
Foster's Mills
Freemansville
Hammett
Hickory Flat
Little River
Macedonia
Ophir
Orange
Sharp Top
Sutallee
Troy
Wafesca
Woodstock

Clark co.
Athens (c h)
Farmington
Salem
Watkinsville

Clay co.
Fall Creek
Pomaria

Clinch co.
Carter's Ridge
Cow Creek
Homersville
Magnolia (c h)
Troublesome

Cobb co.
Acworth
Boltonville
Brown's
Fulton
Lost Mountain
Marietta (c h)
Mill Grove
Moon's
Nelson
Newtown
Noonday
Powder Springs
Roswell

Coffee co.
Byrd's Mills
Douglas
Feronia
Ocmulgeeville
Red Bluff

Colquitt co.
Greenfield
Moultrie

Columbia co.
Appling
Berzelia
Columbia Mine
Eubanks
Kiokee
Lombardy
Nebraska
Raysville
Saw Dust
Thompson
White Oak
Winfield
Wrightsboro (c h)

Coweta co.
Grantville
Haralson
Kidron
Location
Lodi
Newnan (c h)
Paris
Rio
Salada
Turin
Willow Dell
Willow Grove

Crawford co.
Hickory Grove
Hopewell
Knoxville (c h)
Pine Level

Dade co.
Hobbie
Lookout Station
Rising Fawn
Salula Farm
Trenton (c h)

Dawson co.
Dawsonville

Decatur co.
Attapulgus
Bainbridge (c h)

Blowing Cave
Cairo
Faceville
Pine Hill
Sofkey
Steam Mill
Tired Creek

De Kalb co.
Cross Keys
Decatur (c h)
Lythonia
Stone Mountain
Utoy

Dooly co.
Byromville
Drayton (c h)
Gum Creek
Millwood
Vienna

Dougherty co.
Gillon's

Early co.
Blakely (c h)
Cedar Springs
Damascus
Fort Gaines
Hulmes
Saffold
Spring Creek
Stamperville

Effingham co.
Eden
Egypt
Guyton
Sister's Ferry
Springfield (c h)

Elbert co.
Amandaville
Anthony Shoals
Broad River
Cold Water
Cook's Law Office
Craftsville
Eagle Grove
Elberton (c h)
Fishdam
Grove
Harmony
Ruckersville
Summervale
Webster Place

Emanuel co.
Battle Ground
Canoochee
Ohoopee
Swainsboro' (c h)

Fannin co.
Hot House
Mineral Bluff
Morganton (c h)
Ida
Rollin
Skoinah
Vanzandt's Store

Fayette co.
Fayetteville (c h)
Glenn Grove
Jonesborough
Red Oak
Rough and Ready
White Water

Floyd co.
Armuchee
Barker's Store
Cave Spring
Coosa
Dyke's Store
Everett's Spring
Floyd Springs
McGuire's Store
Missionary Station
Rome (c h)
Thomas' Mills
Vann's Valley
Yarborough

Forsyth co.
Ami
Bethlehem
Big Creek
Coal Mountain
Cumming (c h)
Davis Creek
Hartford
High Tower
Sawney's Mountain
Sheltonville
Vickery's Creek
Warsaw

Franklin co.
Aquilla
Auburn Hill
Bald Spring
Belton
Bowersville
Bushville
Carnesville (c h)
Erastus
Fairview
Flintsville
Ford's Store
Franklin Springs
Georgian
Goodwill
Grove Level
Middle River
Mosely's Store
Nail's Creek
Parker's Store
Phi Delta
Walnut Hill
Webb's Creek

Fulton co.
Atlanta (c h)
Irbyville
Oak Grove

Gilmer co.
Alma
Blue Ridge
Cartīcay
Cherry Log
Chesnut Gap
Edom
Ellejay (c h)
Mountain Town
Pierceville
Prince Edward
Rock Hill
Santa Lucah
Tail's Creek
White Path

Glasscock co.
Gibson

Glynn co.
Bethel
Brunswick (c h)
Frederica
Mount Pleasant

Gordon co.
Calhoun (c h)
Fair Mount
Free Bridge
Red Bud
Resaca
Sonora
Sugar Valley

Greene co.
Curtright
Greensboro' (c h)
Ida
Penfield
Public Square
Scull Shoals
Union Point
White Plains
Woodville

Gwinnett co.
Auburn
Berkshire
Cain's
Chinkapin Grove
Lawrenceville (ch)
Pinckneyville
Rock Bridge
Suwance
Sweet Water
Yellow River

Habersham co.
Allandale
Batesville
Blue Creek
Clarksville (c h)
Crosby
Duane Street
Hollingsworth
Leo
Loudsville
Mount Yonah
Nacoochee
Leakesville
Tallulah
Walton's Ford

Hall co.
Argo
Chesnut Mountain
Gainesville (c h)
Gillsville
Hog Mountain

Oakland
Polksville
Poplar Springs
Reacher
Shoal Creek
Skitt's Mountain
Sugar Hill
War Hill
Wolleysford

Hancock co.
Bulah
Culverton
Island Creek
Long's Bridge
Mount Zion
Powellton
Shoals of Ogeehee
Sparta (c h)

Haralson co.
Buchanan
Newsville
Repose

Hart co.
Air Line
Bio
Hartwell
Henley's Store(ch)
Montevideo
Oak Bower

Harris co.
Cataula
Ellerslie
Goodman's Cross
Roads
Hamilton (c h)
Mountain Hill
Mulberry Grove
Piedmont
Waverly Hall
Whitesville
Wisdom's Store

Heard co.
Corinth
Enon Grove
Franklin (c h)
Houston
Saint Cloud
State Line
Union Mills

Henry co.
Bear Creek
Bershefa
Flat Rock
Gleantsville
Locust Grove
McDonough (c h)
Mount Carmel
Sandy Ridge
Spring
Stockbridge
White House

Houston co.
Busbayville
Fort Valley
Hayneville
Henderson
Houston Factory
Perry (c h)
Powersville
Wellboru's Mill

Irwin co.
Edenfield
House Creek
Irvinsville (c h)
Orel
Pennsborough
Vineyard

Jackson co.
Bascobel
Delay
Harmony Grove
Jefferson (c h)
Marcus
Maysville
Mulberry
Pond Fork

Jasper co.
Gladesville
Hillsboro'
Monticello (c h)
Palo Alto
Shady Dale

Jefferson co.
Fenn's Bridge
Louisville (c h)
Pope Hill

Reedy Creek
Speir's Turnout
Woodburn

Jones co.
Blountsville
Cardsville
Clinton (c h)
Cornucopia
Griswoldville
Poverty Hill
Wallace

Laurens co.
Buck Eye
Dublin (c h)
Laurens Hill
Lime Sink

Lee co.
Chickasawhatchie
Flat Pond
Renwick
Sneed
Starkville (c h)
Sumterville

Liberty co.
Beard's Creek
Hinesville (c h)
McIntosh
Ricebore
Taylor's Creek
Walthourville

Lincoln co.
Clay Hill
Double Branches
Goshen
Leathersville
Lincolnton (c h)
Lisbon

Lowndes co.
Anderson
Ava
Clyattsville
Flat Creek
Grand Bay
Griffin's Mills
Hahira
Morven
Okapilco
Piscola
Radford's Mills
Tallokas
Tronpville (c h)

Lumpkin co.
Amicalola
Auraria
Barrottsville
Catoosa
Crossville
Dahlonega (c h)
Juno
New Bridge
Pleasant Retreat
Round Hill
Smithville
Yellow Creek

McIntosh co.
Darien (c h)
Juhuston's Station
South Newport

Macon co.
Creek Stand
Etna
Grangersville
Hamburg
Lanier (c h)
Marshallsville
Montezuma
Oglethorpe
Winchester

Madison co.
Brookline
Danielsville (c h)
Fort Lamar
Madison Springs
Paoli
Planter's Stand

Marion co.
Buena Vista
Church Hill
Fragoletta
Glonalta
Pine Knot Mills
Pineville
Poindexter
Tazewell (c h)

Meriwether co.
Erin
Farmer's
Flat Shoals
Greenville (c h)
Holly
Jones' Mills
Magdalena
Oak Ridge
Rocky Mount
Warm Springs
Warnerville
White Sulphur
  Springs
Woodberry

Miller co.
Colquit

Milton co.
Alpharetta

Mitchell co.
Camilla
Gum Pond
Viola

Monroe co.
Colaparchee
Culloden
Forsyth (c h)
Johnstonville
New Market
Proctor's Store
Russellville
Unionville

Montgomery co.
Boxville
Hot House
Little York
Mount Vernon (ch
Seward
Sterling

Morgan co.
Buck Head
Ebenezer
Fair Play
High Shoals
Madison (c h)
Rutledge

Murray co.
Chaseville
Cohuttah Springs
Cooswattee
Fancy Hill
Hassler's Mills
Holly Creek
Spring Place (c h)
Woodlawn

Muscogee co.
Columbus (c h)
Jamestown
Steam Factory
Upatoie
Water Oak

Newton co.
Brick Store
Conyers
Covington (c h)
Middle Ridge
Newborn
Newton Factory
Oak Hill
Oxford
Rocky Plains
Sheffield
Snapping Shoals
Starrsville

Oglethorpe co.
Bairdstown
Crawford
Lexington (c h)
Maxey
Millstone
Philomath
Point Peter
Stephens

Paulding co.
Dallas (c h)
De Soto
Drake Town
Etna
Huntsville
Pumpkin Vine

Pickens co.
Jasper (c h)
Jerusalem
Marble Works
Rich Mountain
Saunder's Town
Talking Rock

Illinois.

Pierce co.
Blackshear
Zero

Pike co.
Barnesville
Griffin
Liberty Hill
Milner
Zebulon (c h)

Polk co.
Cedartown
Esom Hill
Pumpkin Pile
Van Wert
Yellow Stone

Pulaski co.
Cross Creek
Hawkinsville (c h)
Lawson
Long Street

Putnam co.
Avlona
Clopton's Mills
Dennis
Eatonton (c h)
Glades ⋈ Roads
Hearnville
Rockville
Stanfordville

Rabun co.
Clayton (c h)
Head of Tennessee
Pine Mountain
Tiger
War Woman

Randolph co.
Benevolence
Brooksville
Buford
Cotton Hill
Cuthbert (c h)
Georgetown
Hamlet
Linwood
Nochway

Ochohdkee
Verona

Richmond co.
Allen's
Augusta (c h)
Belair
McBean Depot
Richmond Factory

Scriven co.
Black Creek
Buck Creek
Halcyon Dale
Middle Ground
Mill Haven
Mobley Pond
Ogechee
Scarborough
Sylvania (c h)

Spaulding co.
York

Stewart co.
Bladen Creek
Compton
Florence
Friendship
Hannahatchee
Lumpkin (c h)
Millard
Richland
Scienceville

Sumter co.
Americus (c h)
Andersonville
Bottsford
Danville
Lake Harris
Plains of Dura
Pondtown
Providence
Quebec

Talbot co.
Belleview
Bluff Spring
Box Spring
Centre

Geneva
Pleasant Hill
Prattsburgh
Quito
Red Bone
Talbotton (c h)

Taliaferro co.
Crawfordsville (c h)
Raytown
Sharon

Tatnall co.
Bull Creek
Long Branch
Matlock
Perry's Mills (c h)
Reidsville
Watermelon

Taylor co.
Butler
Daviston
Howard
New Agency
Reynolds

Telfair co.
Cobbville (c h)
Copeland
Jacksonville (c h)
Lumber City
McRae's Store
Sugar Creek
Temperance

Terrell co.
Chenuba
Dawson
Dover
Osceola

Thomas co.
Arabia
Boston
Dry Lake
Duncanville
Eastwood
Glasgow
Grooverville

Station
Tatesville
Thomasville (c h)
Youngsville

Towns co.
Hinwassee (c h)
Mountain Scene
Mount Eolis

Troup co.
Antioch
Asbury
Hoganville
La Grange (c h)
Long Cane
Mountville
O'Neal's Mills
Troup Factory
Vernon
West Point

Twiggs co.
Jeffersonville
Marion (c h)
Tarversville
Twiggsville

Union co.
Blairsville (c h)
Brasstown
Choestoe
Gaddistown
Ivy Log
Mill Creek
Rose Hill
Shady Grove
Stock Hill
Track Rock
Young Cane

Upson co.
Double Bridges
Flint RiverFactory
Thomaston (c h)
The Rock
ThunderingSprings
Waynmanville

Walker co.
Cane Creek
Cassandra
Cotoosa Springs
Cedar Grove
Chesnut Flat
Duck Creek
Frick's Gap
Greenbush
High Point
Lafayette (c h)
Naomi
Pond Spring
Rock Spring
Rossville
Snow Hill
Villanow

Walton co.
Cut Off
Good Hope
Loganville
Monroe (c h)
Social Circle
Walnut Grove
Windsor

Ware co.
Burrell
Isabel
Kettle Creek
Strickland's
Waresboro' (c h)

Warren co.
Double Wells
Jubilee
Mayfield
Republican
Tannville
Warrenton (c h)

Washington co.
Curry's Mills
Davisboro'
Hebron
Irwin's ⋈ Roads
Oconee
Sandersville (c h)
Tennille
Warthen's Store

Wayne co.
Bennettsville
Doctor Town
Satilla
Waynesville (c h)

Webster co.
Preston
Weston

Whitfield co.
Anderson
Dalton
Fillmore
Gordon Springs
Green Woods
Red Clay
Rural Vale
Tilton
Tunnell Hill
Upper King's
Bridge
Varnell's Station

Wilcox co.
Adams

Wilkes co.
Centreville
Danburgh
Delhi
Mallorysville
Rahobeth
Washington (c h)

Wilkinson co.
Cool Spring
Gordon
Irwinton (c h)
McIntire
Milton
Stephensville
Toombsborough

Worth co.
Bloomfield
Brooks
Deer Land
Isabella (c h)
Minton
Warwick

ILLINOIS.

Adams co.
Adams
Beverly
Big Neck
Burton
Camp Point
Clayton
Coatsburgh
Columbus
Elm Grove
Fair Weather
Fowler's Station
Houston
Keene
Liberty
Lima
Marcelline
Mendon
New Paloma
Payson
Pitman
Quincy (c h)
Richfield
Stone's Prairie
Ulm
Ursa
Woodville

Alexander co.
Alexandria
Cairo
Clear Creek Landing
Dogtooth
Santa Fee
Thebes
Unity

Bond co.
Beaver Creek
Cottonwood Grove
Elm Point
Greenville (c h)
Mulberry Grove
Old Ripley
Pocahontas

Boone co.
Beaverton
Belvidere
Bonus
Boone

Burton's Corners
Caledonia Station
Garden Prairie
Kossuth
Leesville
Park's Corners
Poplar Grove

Brown co.
Buck Horn
Cooperstown
Mount Sterling
Ripley
Versailles
Walker's Neck

Bureau co.
Arlington
Buda
Bureau Junction
Dover
Enon
Hollowayville
Lamoille
Limerick
Macon
Malden
Milo
Mineral
Neponset
New Bedford
Ohio
Pettit
Princeton
Providence
Selby Station
Sheffield
Tiskilwa
Truxton
Walnut
Wyanet
Yorktown

Calhoun co.
Belleview
Deer Plain
Farrowtown
Gilead
Hamburgh
Hardin (c h)

Monterey
News
Vedder

Carroll co.
Argo
Bluffville
Cherry Grove
Elk Horn Grove
Fair Haven
Milledgeville
Mount Carroll (c h)
Polsgrove
Rock Creek
Savanna
Spring Valley

Cass co.
Arenzville
Ashland
Beardston
Berryton
Chandlersville
Hagley
Jersey Prairie
Lancaster
Virginia

Champaign co.
East Bend
Homer
Mahomet
Newcomb
Pera Station
Pesotum
Point Pleasant
Rantoul Station
Saint Josephs
Sidney
Sodorus
Tolona
Urbana (c h)
West Urbana

Christian co.
Assumption
Blueville
Buckhart
Kippersville
Mount Auburn
Owaneco
Pana

Rosemond
Stonington
Taylorsville (c h)

Clark co.
Anderson
Casey
Clark Centre
Darien
Darwin
Dolson
Johnson's Mills
Livingston
Margaretta
Marshall (c h)
Martinsville
Melrose
Parker
Sacton
Westfield

Clay co.
Bible Grove
Clay City (c h)
Flora
Hard
Ingraham Prairie
Larkinsburgh
Louisville
Sutton's Point
Xenia

Clinton co.
Aviston
Carlyle (c h)
Collins Station
Germantown
Jamestown
Keysport
Looking Glass
Shoal Creek Station
Trenton
Wittemberg

Coles co.
Arcola
Ashby
Ashmore
Bourbon
Brushy Fork
Camargo

Campbell
Charleston
Fuller's Point
Hermitage
Matoon
Milton Station
Oakland
Paradise
Rural Retreat
Springville
Tuscola

Cook co.
Ainsworth Station
Barrington Station
Bloom
Brickton
Chicago (c h)
Comoru
Elk Grove
Evanston
Glencoe
Grosse Point
Hope
Jefferson
Lemonte
Leyden
Leyden Centre
Lyons
Lyonsville
Maine
Mainville
Matteson
New Bremer
Niles
Northfield
Noycesville
Orland
Palos
Plum
Proviso
Ringgold
Shaumburgh
South Northfield
Strasburg
Thornton
Thornton Station
West Northfield
West Wheeling
Wheeling
Winnetka
Worth

Crawford co.
Annapolis
Bell Air
Eaton
Elkton
Flat Rock
Hardinsville
Hutsonville
New Hebron
Oblong
Palestine (c h)
Robinson (c h)
Stiflesville
Vernon
York

Cumberland co.
Cornton
Greenup
Hazle Dell
Johnstown
Majority Point
Neoga
Woodbury

De Kalb co.
Blood's Point
Courtland Station
Doerfield Prairie
De Kalb Centre
Dorset
Freeland
Genoa
Hick's Mills
Kingston
Lacey
La Clair
Malta
New Lebanon
Ney
North Kingston
Ohio Grove
Pierceville
Ross' Grove
Sandwich
Shabbona's Grove
Somonauk
South Grove
Squaw Grove
Sycamore (c h)
Van Buren

Illinois.

De Witt co.
Clinton (c h)
De Witt
Santa Anna
Tunbridge
Wapella
Waynesville

Du Page co.
Addison
Babcock's Grove
Big Woods
Bloomingdale
Bonaparte
Cass
Cottage Hill
Danby
Downer's Grove
Fullersville
Lisle
Naperville
Sagone
Turner
Warrensville
Wayne
Wayne Centre
Wheaton
Winfield
York Centre

Edgar co.
Baldwinville
Bloomfield
Bonwell
Dudley
Elbridge
Grand View
Kansas
Logan
Paris (c h)
Vermillion

Edwards co.
Albion (c h)
Mills Prairie
Maple Grove
West Salem

Effingham co.
Edgewood
Effingham
Elliottstown
Ewington
Freemanton
Mason
Salt Creek
Teutopolis

Fayette co.
Bowling Green
Cumberland
Farina
Hickory Creek
Howard's Point
La Clede
London City
Prairie Mound
Ramsey
Shobonier
Vandalia (c h)

Franklin co.
Benton (c h)
Big Muddy
Cave
Crittenden
Ewing
Fitts Hill
Frankfort (c h)
Hall
Little Muddy
Marey
Osaga
Parrish
Pleasant Shade
Town Mount
Webb's Prairie

Fulton co.
Astoria
Avon
Bernadotte
Canton
Copperas Creek
Cuba
Duncan's Mills
Ellisville
Fairview
Farmington
Fiatt
Fulton Centre
Ipava
Lewistown
Liverpool
Maple's Mills
Marietta

Middle Fork
Middle Grove
Midway
Otto
Saint Augustine
Summum
Table Grove
Troy Mills
Vermont
Virgil

Gallatin co.
Buffalo
Cuttonwood
Christmasville
Crawford
Equality (c h)
New Haven
New Market
Overton
Robinett
Saline Mills
Shawneetown
South Hampton

Greene co.
Athensville
Bluff Dale
Breese
Carrollton (c h)
Fayette
Greenburg
Greenfield
Jalapa
Kane
Negro Lick
Pisgah
Rockbridge
White Hall

Grundy co.
Gardner
Mazon
Minooka
Morris (c h)
Sandy Ridge
Vietta

Hamilton co.
Belle Prairie
Buck
Griswold
Lane's X Roads
Logansport
Lovilla
McLeansboro' (c h)
Night's Prairie
Palo Alto
Rectoville

Hancock co.
Appanese
Augusta
Basco
Carthage (c h)
Chili
Chili Centre
Dallas City
Durham
Elvaston
Fountain Green
Golden's Point
Hamilton
La Harpe
McGary
Middle Creek
Nauvoo
Pilot Grove
Plymouth
Pontoosae
Pulaski
Rough and Ready
Saint Albans
Saint Marys
Sylvan Dale
Walker
Warsaw
Webster
West Point
Wythe

Hardin co.
Cave in Rock
Elizabetown (c h)
Martha Furnace
Rosiclare

Henderson co.
Biggsville Station
Hopper's Mills
Olena
Oquawka
Oquawka Junction
Raritan
Rozetta
Shokokon
Terre Haute

Henry co.
Andover
Annawan

Atkinson
Bishop Hill
Burns
Cambridge
Colona Station
East Cambridge
Galva
Geneseo
Green River
Kewannee
Minersville
Morristown (c h)
Mount Vista
Munson
Orion
Oxford
Pink Prairie
Saxon
Sharon
Weller
Wethersfield
Woodhull

Iroquois co.
Ash Grove
Ashkum
Beaverville
Belwood
Bulkley
Chebanse
Clifton
Courtright's Mills
Del Rey
Democrat
Donovan
Farmer's Farm
Gilman
Iroquois
Lavine
L'Erable
Middleport (c h)
Milford
Oakulla
Onargo
Plato
Rinosa

Jackson co.
Ava
Bradley
Carbondale
De Soto
Grand Tower
Markanda
Murphysborough
Worthington

Jasper co.
Cartersville
Hidalgo
Island Creek
Newton (c h)
Pickwick
Rose Hill
Saint Marie
Shorb
Wetweather
Willow Hill
Yale

Jefferson co.
Blue Ridge
Fair Play
Ham's Grove
Linchburgh
Moore's Prairie
Mount Vernon (c h)
Rome
Spring Garden

Jersey co.
Delhi
Fidelity
Fielding
Grafton
Jersey Landing
Jerseyville
Newbern
Otter Creek

Jo Daviess co.
Apple River
Avery
Council Hill
Council Hill Station
Derinda
Dunleith
Elizabeth
Galena (c h)
Greenvale
Guilford
Hanover
Ira
Millville
Mount Sumner
Nora
Pleasant Valley
Plum River
Rush

Scales Mound
Small Pox
Stockton
Thompson Mills
Ward's Grove
Warren
Willow

Johnson co.
Cedar Bluff
Cross Roads
Cypress Creek
Gray's Mill
Vienna (c h)

Kane co.
Aurora
Batavia
Big Rock
Blackberry
Blackberry Station
Burlington
Campton
Clintonville
Dundee
Elgin
Geneva
Grouse
Hampshire
Jericho
Kaneville
King's Mills
Lodi Station
Montgomery
New Plato
New Virgil
North Plato
Pingree Grove
Rutland
Saint Charles
Sugar Grove
Udina
Winthrop

Kankakee co.
Aroma
Bloomville
Bulbonnas Grove
Essex
Grand Prairie
Kankakee Depot
Limestone
Manteno
Momence
Rockville
Saint Anne
Sherburneville
Simoda
Yellowhead Grove

Kendall co.
Bristol
Bristol Station
Kendall
Lisbon
Little Rock
Mansfield
Naausay
Newark
Ohio Farm
Oswego
Pavilion
Plano
Plattville
Seward
Specie Grove

Knox co.
Abingdon
Centre Point
Douglass
Eugene
Farmer's Hall
Galesburgh
Gilson
Henderson
Hermon
Hulsford
Knoxville
Maquon
Milroy
North Prairie
Oneida
Ontario
Saluda
Truro
Uniontown
Victoria
Walnut Grove
Wataga
Yates City

Lake co.
Angola
Antioch
Deerfield
Diamond Lake
Ela
Emmet

Forksville
Fort Hill
Fox Lake
Fremont Centre
Gage's Lakes
Gilmer
Hainesville
Half Day
Hickory
Lake Zurich
Libertyville
Long Grove
Millburn
Newport
Oak Hill
Otsego
Port Clinton
Warrenton
Wauconda
Waukegan (c h)
Wellington
Wentworth

La Salle co.
Alum Rock
Arrow
Asbury
Cornville
Crotty
Dayton
Deer Park
Eagle
Earlville
Farm Ridge
Freedom
Galloway
High Prairie
Lasalle
Leland
Lowell
Manlius
Marseilles
Mendota
Miner's
Mission Point
New Rutland
Northville
Norway
Ophir
Ottawa (c h)
Peru
Scott
Serena
Tonica
Triumph
Troy Grove
Utica
Vermillionville

Lawrence co.
Bridgeport
Hadley Station
Hershey's Mill
Lawrenceville (c h)
Old Farm
Olive
Petty's
Russellville
Saint Francisville
Sumner

Lee co.
Amboy
Dixon
East Paw Paw
Four Mile Grove
Franklin Grove
Gap Grove
Lee Centre
Malugin Grove
Nachusa
Nelson
Ogle Station
Paw Paw Grove
Shelburn
Sublette
Willow Creek

Livingston co.
Amity
Ancona
Cayuga
Chatsworth
Dwight
Fairburgh
Hickory Point
Indian Grove
Long Point
New Michigan
Odell
Pontiac
Reading
Rook's Creek
Sunbury

Logan co.
Atlanta
Boynton

Broadwell
Elkhart City
Eminence
Laenna
Lawndale
Lincoln (c h)
Middletown
Mount Pulaski
Prairie Creek

McDonough co.
Argyle
Bardolph
Blandinsville
Bruce
Burnsville
Bushnell
Colchester
Colmar
Friendship
Good Hope
Hill's Grove
Industry
Johnson
Macomb
Prairie City
Tennessee
Young

McHenry co.
Alden
Algonquin
Barreville
Belden
Bliven's Mills
Cary Station
Chemung
Coral
Crystal Lake
Dearborn
Deep Cut
English Prairie
Erin
Greenwood
Harmony
Hartland
Harvard
Hebron
Huntley Grove
Lawrence
McHenry
Marengo
Ostend
Richmond
Ridgefield
Riley
Ringwood
Romeo
Solon Mills
Union
West Hebron
Woodstock (c h)

McLean co.
Bloomington
Cheney's Grove
Chenoa
Delta
Dry Grove
Gridley
Heyworth
Hudson
Le Roy
Lexington (o h)
Lytlesville
McLean
Padua
Randolph's Grove
Selma
Senox
Shirley
Stout's Grove
Towanda
Wilkesborough

Macon co.
Decatur (c h)
Harristown
Hopewell
Maros
Niantic
Oakley
Sangamon
South Macon
Wilson

Macoupin co.
Barr's Store
Brighton
Bunker Hill
Carlinville (c h)
Chesterfield
Gillespie
Girard
Hoover's Point
Hornsby
Miles' Station
Milwood
Palmyra
Piasa

Illinois. 391

Plain View
Rhoades Point
Rising Sun
Scottville
Shaw's Point
Shipman
Staunton
Stirrup Grove
Vancil's Point
Virden
Woodburn

Madison co.
Alhambra
Alton (c h)
Bethalto
Collinsville
Dorsey
Edwardsville (c h)
Fosterburg
Godfrey
Highland
Lamb's Point
Madison
Marine
Moultonville
Moro
Omph Ghent
Paddocks' Grove
Ridgeley
Saint Jacob
Toluca
Troy
Upper Alton
Venice
Wanda

Marion co.
Alma
Central City
Centralia
Foster's
Green Dale
Hickory Hill
Kinmundy
New Middleton
Oden
Omega
Patoka
Racoon
Salem (c h)
Sandoval
Walnut Hill

Marshall co.
Belle Plain
Crow Meadows
Henry
Lacon (c h)
La Prairie Centre
Lawn Ridge
Sparland
Steuben
Washburn
Wenona Station
Whitefield

Mason co.
Bath (c h)
Crane Creek
Egypt
Havana
Mason City
Matanzas
Moscow
Prairie
Quiver
San Jose
Walker's Grove

Massac co.
George's Creek
Hickory Grove
Metropolis City
Pellonia

Menard co.
Athens
Greenview
Petersburgh
Robinson's Mills
Smoot's Point
Sweet Water
Talula

Mercer co.
Aledo
Carbon
Centre Ridge
Eliza
Ferdinand
Hamlet
High Point
Keithsburgh
Millersburgh (c h)
New Boston

Perryton
Pope Creek
Preemption
Richland Grove
Sunbeam
Viola

Monroe co.
Burksville
Columbia
Eagle Cliffs
Hardscrabble
Harrisonville (c h)
Hecker
Mitchie
Monroe City
Renault
Rush Island Bend
Waterloo

Montgomery co.
Audubon
Bear Creek
Butler
Fillmore
Herndon
Hillsboro' (c h)
Hurricane
Irving
Litchfield
Nokomis
Shop Creek
Walshville
White Oak
Zanesville

Morgan co.
Alexander
Arcadia
Bethel
Concord
Emerald Point
Epler
Evans' Mill
Franklin
Jacksonville (c h)
Lynnville
Maradosia
Orleans
Sinclair
Waverly
Zion

Moultrie co.
Lovington
Marrow Bone
Sullivan

Ogle co.
Adeline
Baileyville
Barclay
Brookville
Byron
Daysville
Dement Station
Eagle Point
Fitz Henry
Foreston
Grand Detour
Haldane
Hale
Killbuck
Kyte River
Lane Depot
Lindenwood
Luda
Monroe Centre
Mount Morris
Ogle
Oregon
Paine's Point
Pine Creek
Polo
Taylor
Wales
White-Rock
Woosung

Peoria co.
Akron
Brimfield
Brunswick
Chillicothe
Edwards' Station
Elmore
Elm Wood
Helena (c h)
Kickapoo
Kingston Mines
Mossville
Mount Hawley
North Hampton
Orange Prairie
Pooria (c h)
Princeville
Robins' Nest
Rome Farms

Rosefield
Smithville
Southampton
Southport
Summerville
Timber
Trivoli

Perry co.
Carnent Prairie
Duquoin
Galum
Grand Cote Prairie
Pinckneyville (c h)
St. Johan
Tamaro

Piatt co.
Bement
Centerville
Cerro Gordo
Monticello (c h)
Piatt

Pike co.
Atlas
Barry
Bedford
Chambersburg
Detroit
El Dara
Fish Hook
Florence
Gilgal
Griggsville
Kinderhook
Martinsburgh
Milton
Montezuma
Monument
Nebo
New Hartford
New Maysville
New Salem
Pearl
Perry
Pittsfield (c h)
Pleasant Hill
Pleasant Vale
Rockport
Summer Hill
Time

Pope co.
Allen's Springs
Breckinridge
Broad Oak
County Line
Golconda (c h)
New Liberty
Rock
Rock Quarry
Walnut Shade
Wool
Zion Hill

Pulaski co.
Ash Ridge
Burkeville
Caledonia
Mound City (c h)
Ullin
Valley Forge
Wallbridge
Wetaug

Putnam co.
Florid
Granville
Hennepin (e h)
Magnolia
Mount Palatine
Oxbow
Snackwine

Randolph co.
Bremen
Chester
Cobb
Coultersville
Dog Wood
Ellis Grove
Evansville
Jones' Creek
Jordan's Grove
Kaskaskia (c h)
Laurel Hill
Prairie du Rocher
Preston
Red Bud
Ruma
Shiloh Hill
Sparta
Steeles Mills

Richland co.
Bon Pas
Boot
Calhoun
Clermont
Dundas
Fransonia
Noble
Olney (c h)
Parkersburgh
Stringtown
Wakefield
Wilsonburgh

Rock Island co.
Buffalo Prairie
Camden Mills
Carbon Cliff
Coal Valley
Copper Creek
Cordova
Drury
Edgington
Hampton
Haslett
Illinois City
Izoria
Murcia
Mill Creek
Moline
Pennsylvania
Pleasant Ridge
Port Byron
Prairiefield
Rapids City
Rock Island (c h)
Rural
Watertown

Saint Clair co.
Bellville (c h)
Casseyville
Fayetteville
Freeburg
French Village
Illinoistown
Lebanon
Lenaburg
Lively
Marissa
Mascoutah
Millstadt
Mud Creek
O'Fallon Depot
Prairie De Long
Risdon
Shiloh
Smithton
Summerfield

Saline co.
Eldorado
Gallatia
Harrisburg
Hartford
Mitchellsville
Raleigh (c h)
Somerset
South America
Stone Fort

Sangamon co.
Auburn
Bates
Berlin
Carter
Chatham
Dawson
Illeopolis Station
John's Creek
Loami
Mechaniesburg
Pawnee
Pleasant Plains
Reed
Richland
Rochester
Salisbury
Springfield (c h)
Watson
Williamsville
Woodside

Schuyler co.
Birmingham
Brooklyn
Browning
Camden
Doddsville
Erwin
Fredericksville
Huntsville
Jasper
Littleton
Mount Meacham
Pleasant View
Rushville
Sheldon's Grove

Steam Mill
Sylva
Wayland
Woodland

Scott co.
Exeter
Glasgow
Manchester
Naples
Winchester (c h)

Shelby co.
Big Spring
Cold Spring
Mode
Moweaqua
Oconee Station
Prairie Bird
Shelbyville (c h)
Westminster
Windsor

Stark co.
Bradford
Camp Grove
Dorrance
Elmira
La Fayette
Osceola
Pleasant Green
Slack Water
Toulon (c h)
Valley
West Jersey
Wyoming

Stephenson co.
Buena Vista
Cedarville
Dakota
Damascus
Davis
Freeport (c h)
Howardsville
Jackson
Kent
Lena
Loran
Louisa
McConnell's Grove
Nevada
New Eria
Oneco
Orangeville
Ridotts
Rock Grove
Rock Run
Silver Creek
Waddam's Grove
Winneshiek
Winslow
Yellow Creek

Tazewell co.
Armington
Bellfame
Boynton
Circleville
Deer Creek
Delavan
Dillon
Groveland
Hopedale
Little Detroit
Mackinaw
Norton
Pekin
Spring Lake
Tremont (c h)
Washington
Wesley City

Union co.
Anna
Dongola
Jonesboro' (c h)
Mount Pleasant
South Pass
Toledo
Union Point
Western Saratoga

Vermillion co.
Blue Grass
Catlin
Conkey's Store
Danville (c h)
Essex
Fairmount
Georgetown
Higginsville
Indianola
Jordan
Kentucky
Marysville

Myersville
North Fork
Pilot
Prospect City
Richardson
Ridge Farm
Ten Mile Grove

Wabash co.
Armstrong
Friend Grove
Friendsville
Gard's Point
Mier
Mount Carmel
New Hope
Rochester Mills
Siloam

Warren co.
Berwick
Cameron
Cane Run
Denny
Duck Creek
Ellison
Greenbush
Ionia
Little York
Monmouth
New Lancaster
Roseville
Spring Grove
Swan Creek
Utah
Young America

Washington co.
Ashley
Dubois
Elk Horn
Hoyleton
Nashville (c h)
Okaw
Osborn
Plum Hill
Richview

Wayne co.
Black Oak
Blue Point
Brush Creek
Enterprise
Fairfield
Hopkins' Grove
Jeffersonville
Johnsonville
Keeuville
Long Prairie
Maulding's Mills
Morlan's Grove
Mount Erie
New Franklin
New Baltimore
New Massillon
Pin Oak
Pleasant Grove
Wabash
Zif

White co.
Burnt Prairie
Carmi (c h)
Duncanton
Emma
Enfield
Grayville
Mill Shoals
Phillipstown
Rattlesnake
Roland

Whitesides co.
Albany
Clyde
Como
Empire
Erie
Fulton
Garden Plain
Genessee Grove
Hemlo
Jefferson's Corners
Kingsbury
Lyndon
Morrison
Mount Prospect
New Clyde
New Genesee
New Jordan
Portland
Prophetstown
Round Grove
Spring Hill
Sterling
Summit Hill

392 Indiana.

Will co.
Arnon
Channahon
Chelsea
Crete
Dupage
East Wheatland
Elwood
Endor
Gooding's Grove
Green Garden
Hadley
Joliet (c h)

Lillecash
Lockport
Long John
Mokena
Monee
Peotone
Pierce
Plainfield
Spencer
Tamarack
Tracy
Wallingford
Wheatland
Wilmington

Williamson co
Attilla
Bainbridge
Blairsville
Bolton
Crab Orchard
Fredonia
Lake Creek
Locust Grove
Marion (c h)
Prairie Hill
Saline
Sarahsville

Sugar Creek
Sulphur Springs

Winnebago co.
Burritt
Cherry Valley
Clairville
Durand Station
Elida
Harlem
Harrison
Kishwaukee
Laona

New Milford
Pecatonica
Rockford (c h)
Rockton
Roscoe
Shirland
South Bend
Tyler
Winnebago Depot

Woodford co.
Cruger

El Paso
Eureka
Farmsville
Kappa
Low Point
Metamora
Minonk
Panola Station
Roanoke
Secor
Spring Bay
West Britain
Woodford

INDIANA.

Adams co.
Canoper
Decatur (c h)
Kirkland
Limber Lost
Linn Grove
Monmouth
Pleasant Mills

Allen co.
Aboite
Arcola
Chamberlain
Fort Wayne (c h)
Hall's Corners
Harlan
Holler's Corners
Lee
Little River
Maples
Massillon
Monroeville
New Haven
Nine Mile
Perry
Po
Randall
Ridge Road
Root
Surinam
Taw Taw

Bartholomew co.
Azalia
Burnsville
Clifford
Columbus (c h)
Elizabethtown
Goldsborough
Hartsville
Hope
Jonesville
Kansas
Moore's Vincyard
Mount Healthy
Newbern
Rock Creek
Taylorsburgh
Taylorsville
Wallesboro'
Waynesville

Benton co.
Ontalpa Grove
Mount Gilboa
Oxford (c h)
Parish Grove

Blackford co.
Dundee
Hartford City (c h)
Montpelier
Priam

Boone co.
Elizaville
Jamestown
Lebanon (c h)
New Brunswick
Northern Depot
Northfield
Reese's Mill
Royalton
Thorntown
White Lick
Whitestown
Zionsville

Brown co.
Bean Blossom
Christiansburg
Cleona
Gold Creek
Milo
Mount Liberty
Mount Moriah
Nashville (c h)
New Belleville
Spearsville

Carroll co.
Burlington
Camden
Carroll
Cornucopia
Deer Creek
Delphi (c h)
Fetherhuff's Mills
Lockport
Mount Jefferson
Pittsburgh
Prince William
Rockfield
Wild Cat

Cass co.
Amsterdam
Anoka
Crittenden
Fitch
Galveston
Lewisburg
Lincoln
Logansport (c h)
Metea
Montez
New Waverly
Onward
Royal Centre
Spring Creek
Twelve Mile
Walton

Clark co.
Bennettsville
Bethlehem
Blue Lick
Bowyer's Landing
Charlestown (c h)
Hubbard
Jeffersonville
Memphis
Muddy Fork
New Providence
New Washington
Oregon
Polk Run
Sellersburg
State Cut
Sylvan Grove
Utica

Clay co.
Anguilla
Ashboro
Belle Air
Bowling Green (c h)
Brazil
Centre Point
Christy's Prairie
Cloverland
Cuffee
Farm
Harmony
Howesville
Marta
Poland
Staunton
Van Buren

Clinton co.
Barnesville
Bertin
Colfax
Frankfort (c h)
Geetingsville
Jefferson
Kirk's ½ Roads
Michigantown
Middle Fork
Rossville
Russinville
Winship's Mill

Crawford co.
English
Fredonia (c h)
Graunsburg
Leavenworth

Magnolia
Marengo
Mifflin
Milltown
Mount Prospect
Nebraska
Pilot Knob
Wickliffe

Daviess co.
Alfordsville
Black Oak Ridge
Clark's Prairie
Epsom
High Rock
Hudsonville
Mayeville
Montgomery's Station
Owl Prairie
Plainville
Raglesville
Washington (o h)

Dearborn co.
Aurora
Braysville
Bright
Cochran
Coopersville
Dillsborough
Farmer's Retreat
Guilford
Guionsville
Holman
Jones's Station
Kelso
Lawrenceburgh (c h)
Lawrenceville
Logan
Manchester
Moore's Hill
New Alsace
Saint Leon
Sparta
Van Wedding's Station
Wilmington
Wright's Corners
Yorkville

Decatur co.
Adams
Cave Spring
Clarksburgh
Clifty
Forest Hill
Greensburgh (o h)
Jackson
Kingston
McCoy's Station
Millhousen
Rossburgh
Saint Omer
Saint Paul
Sardinia
Smyrna
Spring Hill
Waynesburgh
Westport
Williamtown
Wintersville

De Kalb co.
Artic
Anburn (c h)
Butler
Coles' Corners
Corunna
De Kalb
Fairfield Centre
Iba
Mount Hope
Newville
Norristown
Spencerville
Taylor's Corners
Victor
Woolsey

Delaware co.
Albany
Anthony
Daleville
Eaton
Granville
Harrison
Muncie (c h)
New Burlington
New Corner
Richwoods
Selma
Sharon
Wheeling
Yorktown

Dubois co.
Birdseye
Celestine
Ditney Hill
Ferdinand
Haysville
Holland
Huntingburgh
Ireland
Jasper (c h)
Ludlow
Porterville
Worth

Elkhart co.
Benton
Bristol
Cook's Station
Elkhart
Fish Lake
Goshen (c h)
Locke
Middlebury
Mount Olive
New Paris
Pine Creek
South West
Vistula

Fayette co.
Alquina
Bentonville
Columbia
Connersville (o h)
Everton
Falmouth
Harrisburgh
Longwood
Null's Mills
Orange
Waterloo

Floyd co.
Edwardsville
Floyd Knobs
Galena
Georgetown
Greenville
New Albany (c h)
Scottsville

Fountain co.
Attica
Cole Grove
Covington (c h)
Fountain City
Harveysburg
Headley's Mills
Hillsboro
Newtown
Portland
Rob Roy
Steam Corner
Wallace

Franklin co.
Andersonville
Blooming Grove
Blue Creek
Brookville (o h)
Cedar Grove
Drewersburgh
Fairfield

Jennings
Laurel
Metamora
Mixersville
Mount Carmel
New Trenton
Oak Forest
Oldenburgh
Peppertown
Saint Peters
South Gate
Springfield
Stip's Hill
Whitcomb
Wynn

Fulton co.
Akron
Aubbeenaubbee
Bloomingsburgh
Blue Grass
Bruce's Lake
Fulton
Green Oak
Indian Field
Kewanna
Mill Ark
Rochester (o h)

Gibson co.
Bovine
Buckskin
Dangola
Fort Branch
Francisco
Haubstadt
Hazleton
Marsh Creek
Owensville
Patoka
Port Gibson
Princeton (c h)
Somerville
West Buena Vista

Grant co.
Arcana
Grant
Greenbush
Jadden
Jalapa
Jonesboro'
Marion
Mier
Oak Woods
Point Isabel
Rigdon
Slash
Trask
Walnut Creek

Greene co.
Blanton
Bloomfield (o h)
Buck Creek
Hobbleville
Jasonville
Linton
Lone Tree
Marco
Newberry
Owensburgh
Pleasant Ridge
Point Commerce
Scotland
Solsberry
Worthington
Wright

Hamilton co.
Avoada
Boxley
Carmel
Cicero
Clarksville
Deming
Eagletown
Edgewood
New Britton
Noblesville

Sheeillyville
Strawtown
Westfield

Hancock co.
Charlottesville
Cleveland
Eden
Greenfield (c h)
Harvey
Kinder
McCordsville
Mount Comfort
Philadelphia
Sugar Creek
Walpole
Warrington
Westland
Willow Branch
Woodbury

Harrison co.
Barren
Bradford
Byrneville
Corrydon (c h)
Crisp's ¼ Roads
Elizabeth
Hancock
Knob Creek
Laconia
Lauesville
Mauckport
New Amsterdam
New Salisbury
Palmyra
Rosewood
Sharp's Mills
Spring Dale
White Cottage

Hendricks co.
Amo
Belleville
Brownsburgh
Cartersburgh
Cincinnatus
Clayton
Coatesville
Danville (c h)
New Elizabeth
New Winchester
North Salem
Pecksburg
Pittsboro'
Plainfield
Springtown
Stilesville

Henry o.
Ashland
Blountville
Cadis
Dan Webster
Devon
Greensboro'
Knightstown
Lewisville
Luray
Mechanicsburgh
Middletown
Millville
New Castle (o h)
New Lisbon
Ogden
Raysville
Rogersville
Spiceland
Sulphur Springs
Wenona

Howard co.
Alto
Cassville
Centre
Greentown
Jerome
Kokomo (c h)
New London
Oakford

Indiana. 393

Poplar Grove
Shanghai
Vermont
West Liberty

Huntington co.
Antioch
Australia
Bayou Mills
Branch Creek
Huntington (c h)
Mahon
Majenica
Markle
Mount Etna
Price
Roanoke
Warren

Jackson co.
Baker's Mills
Brownstown (c h)
Cortland
Craine's Mills
Crothersville
Dudleytown
Ewing
Freetown
Houston
Mecora
New Farmington
Newry
Reddington
Rockford
Seymour
Sparksville
Tampico
Valley Farm
Valonia
Woodville

Jasper co.
Brook
Carpenter's Creek
Davison
Morocco
Pilot Grove
Pleasant Grove
Rensselaer
Walkersville
White's Grove

Jay co.
Bear Creek
Bluff Point
Boundary
Dunkirk
Gillum
Half Way
Huctor
Jay (c h)
Monroe
New Corydon
New Mount Pleasant
Pennville
Salamonia
Westchester

Jefferson co.
Barbersville
Bryantsburgh
Camargo
Canaan
Dupont
Graham
Home
Kent
Lancaster
Madison (c h)
Manville
Mud Lick
North Madison
Saluda
South Hanover
Stony Point
Swanville
Volga
Wirt

Jennings co.
Benville
Brewersville
Butlerville
Cana
Hopewell
Montgomery
Oakdale
Otter Creek
Paris
Queensville
San Jacinto
Scipio
Six Mile

Tripton
Vernon (c h)
Weston
Zonas

Johnson co.
Amity
Bluff Creek
Edinburg
Franklin (c h)
Greenwood
Musselman
Ninevoh
Trafalgar
Worthsville

Knox co.
Bruceville
Busseron
Decker's Station
Edwardsport
Lecompton
Lovely Dale
Maria Creek
Oak Station
Paw Paw Band
Pond Creek Mills
Spaldingville
Vincennes (c h)
Wheatland.

Kosciusko co.
Beaverdam
Boydston's Mills
Claypool
Clear Spring
Deed's Creek
Etna Green
Farmers
Leesburgh
Milford
North Galveston
Oneida
Oswego
Palestine
Pierceton
Rose Hill
Sevastopol
Silver Lake
Syracuse
Warsaw (c h)
Wooster
Yellow Creek

La Grange co.
Brighton
Brushy Prairie
Fly Creek
Greenfields Mills
Haw Patch
La Grange (c h)
Lima
Marcy
Mongoquinong
Ontario
Ringgold
South Milford
Utah
Wolcott's Mills

Lake co.
Cedar Lake
Crown Point (c h)
Deep River
Dyer
Eagle Creek
Gibson's Station
Hanover
Hobart
Lake Station
Merrillville
Orchard Grove
Outlet
Ross
Saint John
West Creek
Winfield

Laporte co.
Bigelow's Mills
Big Springs
Callao
Crossing
Door Village
Haskell
Hudson
Kankakee
Kingsbury
Laporte (c h)
Michigan City
New Durham
Puddletown
Rolling Prairie
Roselli
Sauk Village
Union Mills
Westville

Lawrence co.
Avoca
Bedford (c h)
Bono
Bryantsville
Fayetteville
Fort Rituer
Georgia
Guthrie
Heltonville
Huron
Juliet
Lawrenceport
Leatherwood
Leesville
Mitchell
Pinhook
Silverville
Spring Mill
Springville

Madison co.
Alexandria
Alfont
Anderson (c h)
Bock's Mills
Chesterfield
Curtis
Duck Creek
Fishersburg
Forestville
Frankton
Huntsville
Mendon
Oceola
Ovid
Pendleton
Perkinsville
Prosperity
Santa Claus
Summitville
Zinsburg

Marion co.
Acton
Adair
Augusta Station
Bridgeport
Broad Ripple
Castleton
Clermont
Cumberland
Fall Crock
Gallaudet
Germantown
Glenn's Valley
Indianapolis (c h)
Lawrence
Millersville
Southport
West Newton

Marshall co.
Alden
Argos
Bourbon
Bremen
Fairmount
Lyceurgus
Maxinkuckee
Plymouth (c h)
Sidney
Sligo
Tippecanoetown
Tyner City
Wolf Creek
Yellow River

Martin co.
Dover Hill
Dys
Halbert's Bluff
Keck's Church
Loogootee
McCameron
McCormickstown
Mountain Spring
Mount Pleasant
Natches
Trinity Springs
Willow Valley

Miami co.
Cary
Chili
Five Corners
Gilead
Leonda
Mexico
Miami
Nicoza
Palos
Paw Paw
Perrysburgh
Peru (c h)
Reserve
Santa Fe

Stockdale
Wawpecong
Wheatville
Xenia

Monroe co.
Bloomington (c h)
Bryant's Creek
Ellistsville
Harrodsburgh
Mount Tabor
Smithville
Stanford
Unionville

Montgomery co.
Alamo
Ashby's Mills
Rock's Corners
Brown's Valley
Crawfordsville (c h)
Darlington
Ludoga
Linden
Mace
New Richmond
New Ross
Parkersburgh
Pleasant Hill
Prairie Edge
Shannondale
Sugar River
Waveland
Waynetown
Whitesville
Youatsville

Morgan co.
Brooklyn
Centerton
Centre Valley
Eminence
Hall
Mahalasville
Martinsville (c h)
Monrovia
Mooresville
Morgantown
Mount Washington
Sheasville
Waverly
White River

Noble co.
Albion (c h)
Avilla
Bourie
Cold Springs
Cromwell
Huela
Kendallsville
Ligonier
Lisbon
Merriam
Noble (c h)
Northport
Simon's Corners
Springfield Mills
Swan
Wawaka
Wilmot
Wolf Lake

Ohio co.
Aberdeen
Bear Branch
Hartford
Rising Sun (c h)

Orange co.
Campbell
Chambersburgh
French Lick
Leipsic
McDonalds
Newton Stewart
Orangeville
Orleans
Paoli (c h)
Stamper's Creek
Valeone

Owen co.
Alligator
Araey
Atkinsonville
Cataract
Cuba
Deem
Freedom
Gosport
Hauzertown
Jordan Village
Patricksburg
Quincy
Spencer (c h)
Stockton
Vandalia
White Hall

Parke co.
Annapolis
Armiesburgh
Banner Mills
Bellmore
Bethany
Bridgeton
Bruin's X Roads
Clinton Lock
Delta
Gallatin
Hollandsburgh
Howard
Ionia
Lick Branch
Lodiville
Mansfield
Medelline
Montesuma
Numa
Parkville
Piattsville
Rockville (c h)
Roseville
Russell's Mills
Sylvania
Wright's Mills

Perry co.
Cannelton
Derby
Don Juan
Foster's Ridge
Leopold
Lilly Dale
Lusher's
Rome
Rono
Tell City
Troy (c h)

Pike co.
Delectable Hill
Hawthorn's Mills
High Banks
Kinderhook
Petersburgh
Union
White Oak Grove
Winslow

Porter co.
Boon Grove
Coffee Creek
Hebron
Porter's X Roads
Tassinnong Grove
Valparaiso
Wheeler

Posey co.
Blairsville
Cynthiana
Farmersville
McFadden
Mount Vernon (c h)
New Harmony
Parker's Settlement
Poseyville
Saint Wendels
Stewartsville
Wadesville
West Franklin

Pulaski co.
Francesville
Medarysville
Monterey
Muoresburg
Oak
Pulaski
Two Mile Prairie
Winnamae (c h)

Putnam co.
Alma
Bainbridge
Brunerstown
Carpentersville
Cloverdale
Greencastle (c h)
Groveland
Manhattan
Mount Meridian
New Mayaville
Nicholsonville
Norton
Portland Mills
Putnamville
Roelsville
Russellville

Randolph co.
Arba
Balaka
Bartonia

Bloomingsport
Cerro Gordo
Deerfield
Emmettsville
Fairview
Farmland
Harrisville
Jordan
Losantville
Lynn
Mar's Hill
Neff
New Pittsburgh
Parker
Ridgeville
Snow Hill
Spartansburgh
Trenton
Union City
Winchester (c h)
Windsor

Ripley co.
Ballstown
Batesville
Cross Plains
Delaware
Elrod
Hart's Mills
Hermann
Holton
Milan
Morris
Napoleon
New Marion
North Hogan
Olean
Osgood
Pierceville
Poston
Spade's Depot
Stringtown
Summan
Versailles (c h)
Way

Rush co.
Beech Grove
Bloom
Carthage
Groves
Hannegan
Homer
Manilla
Melrose
Milroy
Moscow
New Salem
Raleigh
Richland
Rushville (c h)
Smelser's Mills
Star
Steele's
Swain's Mills

St. Joseph co.
Cottage Hill
Lakeville
Mishawaka
New Carlisle
North Liberty
Notre Dame
Oscola
Richardson
South Bend (c h)
Sumption Prairie
Terre Coupee
West York
Woodland

Scott co.
Afton
Alpha
Austin
Lexington (c h)
Mayfield
New Frankfort
Pigeon Roost
Vienna

Shelby co.
Blue Bell
Blue Ridge
Conn's Creek
Davisville
Fairland
Flat Rock
Freeport
London
Manwarings
Marietta
Martin's Corners
Moral
Morristown
Mount Auburn
Noah

Iowa.

Pleasant View
Shelbyville (c h)
Smithland
Sulphur Hill
Winterrowd

Spencer co.
Dale
Enterprise
French Island
Fulda
Gentryville
Grand View
Midway
New Boston
Oakland
Rockport (c h)
Santa Claus

Stark co.
Bogus Run
Clear Lake
Grovertown
Knox
Lake City
North Bend
San Piere
Toto

Steuben co.
Alvarado
Angola (c h)
Crooked Creek
Fish Creek
Flint
Fremont
Hamilton
Mets
North East
Orland
Pleasant Lake
Salem Centre
Sandy Ridge
Turkey Creek
York Centre

Sullivan co.
Ascension
Batham
Black Creek
Brick Mill
Carlisle
Currysville
Greysville
Hymera
Merom
New Lebanon
Sullivan (c h)
Turman's Creek

Switzerland co.
Allensville
Bennington
Craig
Florence
Grant's Creek
Jacksonville
Moorefield
Mount Sterling
Patriot
Pleasant
Quercus Grove
Rutherford
Sugar Branch
Vevay (c h)

Tippecanoe co.
Americus
Baker's Corners
Battle Ground
Buchanan
Clark's Hill
Concord
Dayton
Lafayette (c h)
Pettit
Romney
Shawnee Mound
Sugar Grove
Transitville
West Point
Wyandotte

Tipton co.
Curtisville
Nevada
New Lancaster
Normanda
Pine Creek
Prailie
Shtrpsville
Tesersburg
Tipton (c h)
West Kinderhook
Windfall

Union co.
Beechy Mire
Billingsville
Brownsville
Clifton
Cottage Grove
Dunlapsville
Liberty (c h)

Vanderburgh co.
Armstrong
Evansville (c h)
McCutehonville
Nash Depot
Oakdam
Saundersville

Vermillion co.
Clinton (c h)
Eugene
Highland
Indiana Furnace
Newport (c h)
Perrysville
Toronto

Vigo co.
Cookerly
Fruit Hill

Lewis
Manrius
New Goshen
Pimento
Prairie Creek
Prairieton
Riley
Saint Mary's
Sandford
Terre Haute (c h)

Wabash co.
America
Belden
Dora
La Fontaine
La Gro
Laketon
Liberty Mills
Lodi
New Holland
North Manchester
Somerset
Urbana
Wabash

Warren co.
Baltimore
Independence
Marshfield
Pine Village
Poolsville
Rainsville
State Line
West Lebanon
Williamsport (c h)

Warrick co.
Boonville (c h)
Canal
Crowville
Hartsboro
Lea
Lynnville
Newburgh

Polk Patch
Yankeetown

Washington co.
Beck's Mills
Campbellsburg
Canton
Chestnut Hill
Claysville
Flower Gap
Forester's Station
Fredericksburgh
Hardinsburgh
Harristown
Hitchcock
Kossuth
Little York
Livonia
Martinsburgh
New Philadelphia
New Retreat
Organ Spring
Pekin
Prowsville
Salem (c h)
Saltilloville
South Boston
Texas
Walnut Ridge

Wayne co.
Abington
Bethel
Boston
Cambridge
Centreville (c h)
Chester
Cox's Mills
Dalton
Dublin
East Germantown
Economy
Green's Fork
Hagerstown
Jacksonburgh

Milton
Neil's Station
New Garden
Olive Hill
Richmond
Webster
White Water
Williamsburgh

Wells co.
Barber's Mills
Bluffton (c h)
Fox
Lake Creek
Liberty Centre
Murray
Nottingham
Ossian
Roifisburg
Vera Cruz
Zanesville

White co.
Brookston
Buffalo
Burnett's Creek
Catheart
Flowerville
Monon
Monticello (c h)
Mudge Station
Reynolds

Whitley co.
Churubusco
Coesse
Collamer
Columbia City
Fuller's Corners
Laud
Saturn
South Cleaveland
South Whitley
Summit
Washington Centre

IOWA.

Adair co.
Adair
Arbor Hill
Fontanelle
Greenfield
Hebron
Holaday's

Adams co.
Canaan City
Carl
Corning
Mount Etna
Nevinville
Queen City
Quincy

Allamakee co.
Allamakee
Capoli
Clear Creek
Cleaveland
Dorchester
Elon
French Creek
Hardin
Ion
Lansing
Lybrand
Lycurgus
Makee
New Galena
Neseka
Ossian
Postville
Rossville
Union Prairie
Village Creek
Volney
Waterville
Wawkou
Wexford
Willson's Ford

Appanoose co.
Bectrace
Caldwell
Centreville
Cincinnati
Hibbsville
Iconium
Jerome
Johnstown
Livingston
Memphis
Milledgeville

Moravia
Numa
Parsonville
Sharon
Unionville
Welland
Wells' Mills

Audubon co.
Exira
Hamlin Grove
Oakfield

Benton co.
Benton City
Burk
Gomersal
Gwinville
Linwood
Pickaway
Shellsburgh
Taylor's Grove
Unity
Urbanna
Vinton (c h)
Williams
Woods

Black Hawk co.
Barclay
Blakeville
Cedar Falls (c h)
Cedar Valley
East Waterloo
Enterprise
Gilbertsville
Hudson
Laporte City
Lester
Mullarky's Grove
Waterloo

Boone co.
Boonesboro'
Carson's Point
Mineral Ridge
Prairie Hill
Rapids
River Side
Swede Point

Bremer co.
Breckinridge
Bremer
Frederica
Grove Hill

Horton
Jaynesville
Leroy
Nautrill
Polk Precinct
Spring Lake
Sumner
Waverley

Buchanan co.
Atlanta
Brandon
Buffalo Grove
Cana
Chatham
Erie
Erin
Fairbank
Hazelton
Independence (c h)
Perry Valley
Pine
Quasquoton

Butler co.
Algonquin
Boylin's Grove
Butler Centre
Elm Springs
Island Grove
Leoni
New Hartford
Parkersburg
Sholl Rock
Swanton
Willoughby

Carroll co.
Carrollton

Cass co.
Edna
Hedge's Grove
Lewis
Lura
Turkey Grove

Cedar co.
Apollo
Cedar
Downey
Durant
Gower's Ferry
Harwell
Inland

Lowden
Massillon
Mechanicsville
Onion Grove
Pedee
Pleasant Hill
Red Oak
Rochester
Rosette
Spring Dale
Tipton (c h)
West Branch
Woodbridge

Cerro Gordo co.
Clear Lake City
Mason City
Owen's Grove
Shell Rock Falls

Cherokee co.
Cherokee

Chickasaw co.
Beaver City
Bradford
Chickasaw
Deerfield
Fredericksburg
Jacksonville
Maplesville
Nashua
New Hampton
North Washington
Stapleton
Williamstown

Clark co.
Bartlettville
Glenn's
Hopeville
Jackson
Lacello
La Porte
Liberty
Milford
Osceola
Ottawa
Prairie Grove
Riley
Shelby

Clay co.
Peterson

Clayton co.
Cass
Clayton
Communia
Cox Creek
Elkader
Elkport
Farmersburgh
Garnavillo
Gem
Giard
Grand Meadow
Gottenburg
High Grove
Highland
Honey Creek
Little Port
Locust Hill
McGregor
Millville
Monona
National
New Stand
Panther Creek
Peck's Ferry
Read
Spencer
Strawberry Point
Volga City
Yankee Settlement

Clinton co.
Boon Spring
Brookfield
Buena Vista
Burgess
Calmus
Camanche
Charlotte
Clinton
De Witt
Elk River
Elvira
Low Moore
Lyons
Orange
Spring Rock
Toronto
Welton
Wheatland

Crawford co.
Boyer River
Denison

Dallas co.
Adel
Alton
Boone
Chattanooga
Chicago
Greenvale
Pierce Point
Snyder
Wicotta

Davis co.
Albany
Bloomfield (c h)
Chequest
Drakesville
Floris
Fox
Harbor
Monterey
Mount Calvary
Nottingham
Oak Spring
Pulaski
Salt Creek
Savannah
Stiles
Stringtown
Taylor
Troy
West Grove

Decatur co.
Decatur
Franklin
Garden Grove
High Point
Leon
New Buda
Nine Eagles
Prairieville
Spring Valley

Delaware co.
Almoral
Barryville
Campton
Coffin's Grove
Cold Water
Colony
Delhi (c h)
Earlville
Forestville
Grove Creek
Hazle Green
Hartwick
Hopkinton
Mauchester
Mount Hope

Iowa.

Plum Spring
Poulton
Rockville
Sand Spring
Tower Hill
Uniontown
Viola
York

Des Moines co.
Albright's
Augusta
Burlington (c h)
Danville
Dodgeville
Franklin Mills
Hawk Eye
Kingston
Kossuth
La Vega
Limestone
Linton
Middletown
Northfield
Parrish
Pleasant Grove
South Flint
Vandyke
Yellow Spring

Dickenson co.
Emmet
Okoboji
Spirit Lake

Dubuque co.
Bally Clough
Buncombe
Cascade
Cottage Hill
Derrinana
Dubuque
Durango
Dyersville
Epworth
Farley
Fillmore
Glassnevin
Jefferson
Millroy
Moreau
New Vienna
Oakland
Ogden
Peosta
Pin Oak
Rockdale
Sherrill's Mount
Tara
Tivoli
Weld's Landing

Fayette co.
Bethel
Bremer
Brush Creek
Clermont
Corn Hill
Douglas
Eden
El Dorado
Elgin
Illyria
Luo
Lima
Mill
Oran
Otsego
Richfield
Taylorsville
Waucoma
Westfield
West Union
Windsor

Floyd co.
Beelar's Grove
Flood Creek
Floyd
Howardsville
Riverton
Rockford
Rock Grove City
St. Charles City
Ulster
Watertown

Franklin co.
Geneva
Hampton
Maysville
Otisville
Union Ridge

Fremont co.
Austin
Buchanan
Cory

Gaston
McKissack's Grove
Manti
Plum Hollow
Sidney
Tabor

Green co.
New Jefferson
Rippey

Grundy co.
Bois D'Arc
Grundy Centre
Taylor Hill

Guthrie co.
Bear Grove
Dalmanutha
Dodge
Guthrie Centre
Morrisburg
Orange Grove
Penora
West Milton

Hamilton co.
Eagletown
Homer
Lakin's Grove
Rose Dale
Webster City

Hancock co.
Elk Grove
Upper Grove

Hardin co.
Alden
Dolanti
Eldora
Fontaine
Hardin City
Iowa Falls
La Yerba
Lithopolis
New Providence
Point Pleasant
Quebec

Harrison co.
Calhoun
Howsier
Jeddo City
Little Sioux
Magnolia
Melrose
Modail
Olmstead
Woodbine
Yazoo

Henry co.
Cotton Grove
East Grove
Hillsborough
Lowell
Marshall
Mount Pleasant
New London
Rome
Salem
Trenton
Vega
Wayne
Winfield

Howard co.
Chester
Foreston
Howard
Howard Centre
Jamestown
Lime Spring
New Oregon
Osborne
Saratoga
Sturgis
Vernon Springs

Ida co.
Ida

Iowa co.
Amish
Cono
Downard
Genoa Bluff
Homestead
Jone
Keszta
Marengo
Millersburgh
North English

Jackson
Andrew (c h)
Bellevue
Bridgeport
Canton
Cobb
Cottonville
Emeline
Farmer's Cree
Fulton
Garry Owen
Hickory Grove
Higginsport
Iron Hills
La Motte
Maquoketa
Monmouth
Mount Algor
Ozark
Rolley
Sabula
Saint Donatus
Spring Brook
Spruce Mills
Sterling
Sullivan
Summer Hill
Van Buren
Wagonersburgh
Waterford
Wickliffe
Zwingle

Jasper co.
Bush
Clyde
Galesburgh
Greencastle
Lynnville
Monroe
Newton
Pleasant View
Prairie City
Vandalia

Jefferson co.
Abingdon
Abscom
Botavia
Brookville
Fairfield (c h)
Germanville
Glasgow
Harmony
Libertyville
Lockridge
Parsonville
Pleasant Plain
Salina
Walnu
Wooster

Johnson co.
Belle Air
Bon Accord
Carthage
Copi
Danforth
Frank Pierce
Iowa City (c h)
Malvern
Newport
Newport Centre
North Liberty
Oxford
Palestine
Seventy Eight
Seventy Seven
Shueyville
Solon
Windham

Jones co.
Anamosa (c h)
Bowen's Prairie
Castle Grove
Duane
Edinburgh
Fairview
Fuller's Mills
Highland Grove
Isabell
Johnson
Longworthy
Madison
Monticello
Scotch Grove
Temple Hill
Walnut Fork
Wyoming

Keokuk co.
Aurora
Butler
Chandaller
Ioka
Lancaster (c h)
Martinsburg

Richland
Sigourney (c h)
South English
Springfield
Tullyrand
Webster
White Pigeon
Wimer's Mills

Kossuth co.
Algona
Cresco
Irvington
Kossuth Centre
Lott's Creek

Lee co.
Belfast
Big Mound
Charleston
Clay's Grove
Cono
Croton
Denmark
Dover
Fort Madison
Franklin Centre
Jeffersonville
Jollyville
Keokuk
Montrose
Pilot Grove
Primrose
Summitville
Vincennes
Warren
West Point

Linn co.
Banner Valley
Boulder
Cedar Rapids
Central City
Centre Point
Dry Creek
Forfax
Kingston City
La Fayette
Lisbon
Marion (c h)
Mondieu
Mount Vernon
Nugent's Grove
Necot
Palo
Prospect Hill
Saint Marys
Sisley's Grove
Spring Grove
Springville
Valley Farm
Wapsa
Waubeck
Western College

Louisa co.
Burris
Cairo
Columbus City
Forest Hill
Grand View
Morning Sun
Ouonwa
Palo Alto
Port Allen
Port Louisa
Spring Run
Toolsborough
Virginia Grove
Wapello (c h)

Lucas co.
Argo
Belinda
Cedar Grove
Chariton (c h)
Freedom
Freeland
Greenville
La Grange
Macceville
Tallahome
Time

Madison co.
Brooklyn
Charlottsville
Clanton
Heaton
Middle River
North Branch
Peru
Queen's Point
Saint Charles
Winterset

Mahaska co.
Agricola
Auburn
Belle Fountain
Cherry
Flint
Fremont
Granville
Hopewell
Indianapolis
Laredo
New Sharon
Oskaloosa (c h)
Peoria
Rose Hill
Scott

Marion co.
Attica
Bennington
Caloma
Columbia
Dallas
Ely
English Settlement
Gosport
Hamilton
Jola
Knoxville
Mennon
Newbern
Newark
Newtown
Pella
Pleasantville
Red Rock
Wheeling

Marshall co.
Albion
Bangor
Green Mountain
Illinois Grove
Le Grand
Marietta
Marshalltown
Minerva
Reedsville
Timber Creek
Vienna

Mills co.
Alps
Cerro Gordo
Fayette
Glenwood
Indian Creek
Ingraham
Mapleton
Pacific City
Wahughbonsy
White Cloud

Mitchell co
Cardiff
Doran
Leoti
Mitchell
Nelson
Newburgh
North Bend
Osage
Otranto
Saint Ansgar
Staceyville
Wentworth

Monona co.
Bellevidere
Mapleton
Onawa City

Monroe co.
Albia (c h)
Avery
Bluff Creek
Cuba
Georgetown
Gray's Creek
Half Way Prairie
Henn
Lovilia
Osprey
Weller

Montgomery co.
Coe's Grove
Frankfort
Red Oak Junction
Ross Grove
Sciola

Muscatine co.
Atalissa
Bower Landing
Durant

Fairport
Melpine
Minerva
Moscow
Muscatine (c h)
Pleasant Prairie
Prairie Mills
Strawberry Hill
Summit
Sweetland Centre
West Liberty
Wilton Junction

Page co.
Centre
Clarinda
College Spring
Harder's Corner
Hawleysville
Nodaway Forks
Tarkio

Palo Alto co.
Emmetsburg
Paoli

Polk co.
Adelphia
Apple Grove
Avon
Bloomington
Des Moines (c h)
East Des Moines
Frcel
Kirkwood
Peoria City
Polk City
Ridgedale
Rising Sun
Summerset
Taylorsville

Pottawattamie co
Big Grove
Council Bluffs
Crescent City
Macounis
Newtown

Poweshiek co.
Bear Creek
Deep River
Forest Home
Grinnell
Malcom
Mill Grove
Montezuma (c h)
Sugar Grove
Victor

Ringgold co.
Caledonia
Cross
Eugene
Mount Ayr
Prairie View
Providence
Redding
Silver Street

Sac co.
Sac City

Scott co.
Allen's Grove
Amity
Big Rock
Blue Grass
Buffalo
Davenport
Dixon
Gilbert
Le Claire
Linn Grove
Mount Joy
New Liberty
Pleasant Valley
Princeton
Round Grove
Walnut Grove
Wolcott

Shelby co.
Manteno
Shelbyville
Simoda

Story co.
Cambridge
Camden
Iowa Center
Nevada
New Philadelphia
Sheffield
Story City

Tama co.
Butterville
Buckingham
Collins' Grove
Crystal
Eureka
Heath

Kentucky.

Helena
Kinisaw
Ola
Redman
Spring Creek
Tamaville
Toledo
West Irving
Wolf Creek

Taylor co.

Bedford
Brushy
Gravity
Litchfield
Lone Office
Memory
Plattville

Union co.

Afton
Kings
Lexington
Myers
Ohio
Philo

Platt
Union City

Van Buren co.

Benton's Port
Birmingham
Bonaparte
Business Corner
Farmington (c h)
Gainesborough
Hickory
Home
Iowaville
Keosauqua (c h)
Kilbourn
Lebanon
Milton
Mount Sterling
NewMarket
Oak Point
Pittsburg
Portland
Upton
Utica
Vernon
Winchester

Wapello co.

Agency City

Amador
Ashland
Chillicothe
Christinsburgh
Competine
Dahlonega
Eddyville
Greene
Kirkville
Ottumwa (c h)
Point Isabelle
Port Richmond

Warren co.

Carlisle
Dorrville
Fort Plain
Hammondsburgh
Handsome View
Hartford
Indianola (c h)
Lacona
Lawrenceburg
Lynn
Montpelier
New Virginia
Palmyra
Pyra

Sandysville
Somerset

Washington co.

Amboy
Brighton
Clay
Crawfordville
Davis' Creek
Dutch Creek
Merceilus
New Haven
Pottsville
Richmond
Valley
Washington (c h)
Wassonville
Yatton

Wayne do.

Bethlehem
Cambria
Clio
Corydon
Genoa
Grand River
Lewisburg
New York
Promise City

South Fork
Warsaw
Wayne ⋈ Roads
Xnifin

Webster co.

Belleville
Border Plains
Fort Dodge
Hesperian
Homer
McLaughlins Grove
Otho
West Dayton

Winnebago co.

Forest City

Winneshiek co.

Aquilla Grove
Bluffton
Burr Oak
Burr Oak Springs
Calmar
Canoe
Castalia
Decorah
Fort Atkinson
Frankville

Freeport
Hesper
Locust Lane
Moneek
Morgan
Old Mission
Plymouth Rock
Twin Spring
Winneshiek

Woodbury co.

Morris
Sergeant's Bluff
Sioux City
Smithland

Worth co.

Bristoe
Lena
Northern
Oakvale

Wright co.

Bach Grove
Belmond
Fryeburgh
Gold Field
Luni
Rosodale

KENTUCKY.

Adair co.

Breeding's
Cane Valley
Casey Creek
Columbia (c h)
East Fork
Glen's Fork
Gradyville
Millersville
Milltown
Neatsville

Allen co.

Butlersville
Cedar Spring
Gainesville
Mount Aerial
New Roe
Scottsville (c h)

Anderson co.

Camdenville
Chesher's Store
Johnsonville
Lawrenceburgh
Rough and Ready
Van Buren

Ballard co.

Adamsville
Belle Ombre
Blandville (c h)
Chestnut Hill
Elm
Hazlewood
Lovelaceville
Melvin
Milburn
Sebastopol

Barren co.

Bear Wallow
Black Walnut
Blue Spring Grove
Centre
Caval Hill
Cross Plains
Dry Fork
Edmonton
Glasgow (c h)
Horsewell
Merry Oaks
Nobob
Pace's
Pageville
Park
Peter's Creek
Prewitt's Knob
Randolph
Rockland Mills
Rocky Hill
Roseville
Sugar Plant
Temple Hill
Three Forks
Woodland

Bath co.

Bethel
Eastville
Gill's Mills

Laurel Fork
Marshall
Olympian Springs
Owingsville (c h)
Peeled Oak
Rockhouse
Sharpsburgh
Wyoming

Boone co.

Beaver Lick
Boone
Bullittsville
Burlington (c h)
Constance
Elijah's Creek
Florence
Hamilton
Hebron
Northcutt's Store
Petersburgh
Union
Verona
Walton

Bourbon co.

Centreville
Clintonville
Flat Rock
Houston (c h)
Hutchisons
Jacksonville
Millersburgh
Moreland
North Middletown
Paris (c h)
Ruddle's Mills
Shawhan
Stony Point

Boyle co.

Danville
Mitchellsburgh
Parksville
Perryville

Bracken co.

Augusta
Berlin
Bridgeville
Brookville (c h)
Browningsville
Foster
Locust Mills
Milford
Mount Olivet
Powersville
Santa Fe

Breathitt co.

Frozen Creek
Jackson (c h)
Jett's Creek
Lost Creek

Breckinridge co.

Dewleyville
Big Spring
Cedar Grove
Clifton Mills
Cloverport

Hardinsburgh (c h)
Hudsonville
Lost Run
Planter's Hall
Rock Lick
Stephensport
Union Star
Webster

Bullitt co.

Belmont
Bitter Water
Brook's Station
Cane Spring
Mount Washington
Pitts Point
Shepherdsville(c h)
Shortsville

Butler co.

Berry's Lick
Hurreldville
Honaker's Ferry
Logansport
Morgantown (c h)
Quality Valley
Rochester

Sugar Grove
Welch's Creek
Woodberry

Caldwell co.

Burnsville
Farmersville
Fredonia
Long Pond
Pollard's Tan Yard
Princeton
Walnut Grove

Callaway co.

Callawaytown
Clark's River
Cold Water
Hico
Locust Grove
Murray
New Concord
Oakley
Pine Bluff
Radford
Shiloh
Snow Hill
Wadesboro' (c h)

Campbell co.

Alexandria (c h)
California
Carthage
Cold Spring
Dale
Flagg Spring
Grant's Licks
Indian Spring
Newport (c h)
Tibbatt's ⋈ Roads

Carroll co.

Carrollton
Ghent
Sandefer's Store
Worthville

Carter co.

Bell's Trace
Bruin
Caves
Grass Land
Grayson (c h)
Knaps
Mount Pleasant
Mount Savage
Olive Hill
Star Furnace
Upper Tygart

Casey co.

Freedom
Liberty
Middleburgh
Mintonville
Poplar Hill

Christian co.

Atkinson
Bainbridge
Belleview
Beverly
Cottonwood
Fruit Hill
Garretsburgh
Grissam's Chapel
Hopkinsville (c h)
La Fayette
Long View
Mills
Newstead
Oak Grove
Pembroke
Williams
Woodridge's Store

Clark co.

Dunaway's
Fryville
Goode's Precinct
Jones' Nursery
Kiddville
Pine Grove
Ruckerville
Stoner
Walnut Valley
Winchester (c h)

Clay co.

Flat Creek
Jacksonville
New Harrison
Robison's
Sampson
Snooksville
Manchester (c h)
Sexton's Creek

Clinton co.

Albany (c h)
Alpha
Green Grove
Seventy Six

Crittenden co.

Bell's Mines
Camp Creek
Crittenden Springs
Dycusburgh
Ford's Ferry
Marion
Shady Grove
Walker's
Westonburgh

Cumberland co.

Amandaville
Burkesville (c h)
Marrow Bone

Davies co.

Crow's Pond
Curdsville
Knottsville
Long Falls Creek
McLean's Retreat
Masonville
Mount Dallas
Oakford
Owensboro' (c h)
Pleasant Point
Sand Spring
Whitesville
Yelvington

Edmonson co.

Bee Spring
Big Ready
Brownsville
Dripping Spring
Mammoth Cave
Sun Fish

Estill co.

Cottage Furnace
Estill Furnace
Irvine (c h)
Old Landing
Red River Iron Works

Fayette co.

Athens
Cleaveland
Lexington (c h)
Walnut Hill

Fleming co.

Elisaville
Flemingsburgh(ch)
Hillsboro
Mount Carmel
Oak Woods
Pleasant Grove Mills
Plummer's Mill
Poplar Plains
Sherburne Mills
Tilton
Triplett
White Oak Hill

Floyd co.

Burning Spring
Coal Grove
Hueysville
Langsville
Prestonburgh (c h)

Franklin co.

Bald Knob
Benson
Bridgeport
Farmdale
Forks of Elkhorn
Frankfort (c h)

Military Institute
Puck'n Mills
Springbank

Fulton co.

Compromise
Hickman
Lodge
Middle Grand
State Line

Gallatin co.

Glencoe
Napoleon
Sugar Creek
Warsaw

Garrard co.

Back Creek
Bryantsville
Buck Eye
Lancaster (c h)
Lowell
Paint Lick

Grant co.

Cordova
Crittenden
Downingsville
Dry Ridge
Gouge's
Macedonia
Stateley's Run
Williamstown (c h)

Graves co.

Cuba
Depot
Dublin
Fancy Farm
Farmington
Feliciana
Hickory Grove
Kansas
Leander
Mayfield
Oak Ridge
Symsonia
Viola Station
Wilson's Creek

Grayson co.

Big Clifty
Caneyville
Falls of Rough
Gausaway's
Grayson Springs
Litchfield (c h)
Millerstown
Short Creek

Greene co.

Allendale
Barrick
Catalpa Grove
Clover Hill
Felixville
Greensburgh (c h)
Haskinsville
Summersville
Union Hall

Kentucky.

Greenup co.
Amanda
Ashland
Callahan
Cannonsburg
Catlettsburg
Greenup (c h)
Hood's Run
Lynn
Oldtown
Three Prong
Truittsville
Tygert's Creek

Hancock co.
Bennettsville
Blackford
Hawesville
Lewisport

Hardin co.
Buck Snort
Claiborne
Elisabethtown (ch)
Franklin ⋈ Roads
Glendale
Howell's Springs
Howe's Valley
Otter Creek
Phillinsburg
Red Hill
Robertsville
Stephensburgh
Vine Grove
West Point

Harlan co.
Big Rock
Calloway
Clover Fork
Friendship
Harlan (c h)
La Fontaine
Poor Fork
Smithville

Harrison co.
Berry's Station
Boyd's Station
Broadwell
Buena Vista
Claysville
Colemansville
Connersville
Curry's Run
Cynthiana (c h)
Havilandaville
Kentontown
Leesburgh
Oddville
Raven Creek
Robertson's Station
Rutland

Hart co.
Bacon Creek
Clear Point
Glen Brook
Green River
Hammonville
Monroe
Munfordsville
Rio
Three Springs
Woodsonville

Henderson co.
Cairo
Corydon
Hebbardsville
Henderson (c h)
Poole's Mill
Smith's Mills
Spotsville
Steamport
Wise's Mill
Zion

Henry co.
Bethlehem
Campbellsburgh
Drennon
Eminence
Franklinton
Jericho
Lockport
Midview
New Castle (c h)
Pleasureville
Port Royal
Sligo
Smithfield
Springport

Hickman co.
Baltimore
Clinton
Columbus (c h)
Moscow
New Texas
Wesley

Hopkins co.
Ashbysburgh
Burnett
Carlow
Chalk Level
Charleston
Clyde
Day's Store
Hall
Little Prairie
Madisonville (c h)
Nebo
Providence
Slaughtersville
Underwood
Vandenburgh

Jefferson co.
Cedar Creek
Donosit
Falls of Harrod
Fern Creek
Fisherville
Grassy Pond
Hay's Spring
Jeffersontown
Lacona
Long Run
Louisville (c h)
Middletown
O'Bannon
Portland
Saint Matthews
Salina

Jessamine co
Cogar's Landing
Hanly
Jessamine
Keene
Mount Freedom
Nicholasville (c h)
Pekin
Potts' Mills
Sulphur Well

Johnson co.
Hood's Fork
Paintsville (c h)

Kenton co.
Covington
Dry Creek
Fowler's Creek
Independence (c h)
Kenton
Latonia Springs
Morning View
Visalia

Knox co.
Barboursville (c h)
Clear Creek
Cumberland Ford
Flat Lick
Lynn Camp
Yellow Creek

La Rue co.
Buffalo
Hodgensville
Magnolia
Salt Lick
Uptonville

Laurel co.
Bush's Store
Laurel Bridge
Londou
Mershon's ⋈ Roads
Middle Fork
Rose Hill
White Lilly
Whippoorwill

Lawrence co.
Blains
Bolton
Bolt's Fork
Cherokee
Falls of Blaine
Louis (c h)
New Store
Peach Orchard
Prosperity
Warfield

Letcher co.
Cornett's Mill
Indian Bottom
Whitesburgh (c h)

Lewis co.
Cabin Creek
Clarksburgh (c h)
Concord
Kinnieoniek
Marine
Martin's Fork
Poplar Flat
Quincy
Rock Creek
Tolesboro
Vanceburgh

Lincoln co.
Crab Orchard
Hall's Gap
Hustonville
Milledgeville
Stanford (c h)
Walnut Flat
Waynesburgh

Livingston co.
Berry's Ferry
Carrsville
Ross' Ferry
Salom (c h)
Smithland

Logan co.
Adairville
Baugh's Station
Escipion
Cordonville
Hague
Henrysville
Hesper
Keysburgh
Logan Mills
Rabbitsville
Richlieu
Russellville (c h)
South Union
Volney

Lyon co.
Eddyville (c h)
Saratoga

McCracken co.
Exchange
Massack
Paducah (c h)
Woodville

McLean co.
Bremen
Calhoun (c h)
Livermore
Rumsey
Social Hill
Worthington

Madison co.
Berea
Big Hill
Boonesboro'
Doylesville
Elliston
Goochland!
Joe's Lick
Kingston
Kirksville
Menelos
Mill Grove
Pruty's Mill
Richmond (c h)
Speedwell
Union Meeting House
White Hall

Marion co.
Bradfordsville
Chicago
Haysville
Lebanon (c h)
Loretto
Manton
New Market
Raywick
Saint Mary's

Marshall co.
Aurora
Barksdale
Benton (c h)
Birmingham
Briensburgh
Fair Dealing
Olive
Palma
Watson's

Mason co.
Dover
Fern Leaf
Germantown

397

Helena
May's Lick
Maysville
Millwood
Minerva
Mount Gilead
Murphoysville
North Fork
Orangeburg
Sardis
Slack
Washington (c h)

Mead co.
Brandenburgh (ch)
Flint Island
Garrett
Garnettsville
Meadville
Rock Haven
Stapleton

Mercer co.
Bohan
Cornishville
Duncan
Harrodsburgh (c h)
McAfee
Nevada
Pleasant Hill
Salvisa

Monroe co.
Centre Point
Fleppin
Fountain Run
Hilton
Mud Lick
Rock Bridge
Sulphur Lick
Tompkinsville (ch)

Montgomery co.
Aaron's Run
Camargo
Cash's Knob
Howard's Mill
Levee
Mount Ida
Mount Stirling(ch)
Side View

Morgan co.
Black Water
Bloomington
Caney
Cassity's Mill
Christy's Fork
Grassy Creek
Hampton's Mills
Hazle Green
Johnson's Fork
Licking Station
Little Saudy
Swiftville
West Liberty (c h)
Woodlawn

Muhlenburg co.
Airdrie
Earles
Ellwood
Greenville (c h)
Laurel Bluff
Lead Hill
Luro
Model Mills
Pond River Mills
South Carrolton
Sulphur Springs
Wickland

Nelson co.
Bardstown (c h)
Bloomfield
Boston
Chaplin
Cox's Creek
Deatsville
Fairfield
High Grove
Nelson Furnace
New Haven
New Hope
Poplar Neck
Rolling Fork
Wickliffe

Nicholas co.
Blue Lick Springs
Buzzard Roost
Carlisle (c h)
Forest Retreat
Head Quarters
Irvinesville
Moorefield
Pleasant Valley Mills
Weston

Ohio co.
Beaver Dam
Briggs' Mills
Buck Horn
Buford
Ceralvo
Cool Spring
Cromwell
Fordsville
Hartford (c h)
Hines' Mills
Pleasant Grove
Point Pleasant
Tippecanoe

Oldham co.
Ballardsville
Beard's Station
Brownsborough
Centrofield
Floydsburgh
Goshen
La Grange
Oldhamburgh
Pewee Valley
Westport (c h)

Owen co.
Dallasburg
Eagle Hill
Gratz
Harmony
Lusby's Mill
Monterey
New Columbus
New Liberty
Owenton (c h)
Poplar Grove
Rock Dale
Savern
Sparta

Owsley co.
Bear Creek
Beatyville
Booneville (c h)
Devils' Creek
Gray Hawk
Green Hall
Maulden
Proctor
South Fork
Spruce Grove
Traveller's Rest

Pendleton co.
Aspen Grove
Callensville
Catawba
Clayton
De Mossville
Falmouth (c h)
Flower Creek
Gardnersville
Meridian
Morgan
Motier
Wright's Station

Perry co.
Brashersville
Hazard (c h)

Pike co.
Breckinridge
Democracy
Elliottville
Hamilton's Store
Lonville
Piketon
Robinson Creek

Powell co.
Stanton

Pulaski co.
Adams' Mills
Cato
Dabney
Dallas
Dobbsville
Grundy
Line Creek
Somerset (c h)
Telico
Thompsonville
Waterloo
Waitsboro'
Wightsville
Woodstock

Rockcastle co.
Mount Vernon (ch)
Round Stone
Scaffold Cane

Rowan co.
Farmers
Morehead

Russell co.
Creelsburg
Horse Shoe Bottom
Jamestown
Mount Airy
Rowena
Royalton
Russell Spring

Scott co.
Georgetown (c h)
Great Crossings
Griffee's Mill
Jones's
Little Eagle
Newtown
Oxford
Payne's Depot
Ray's Fork
Stamping Ground
Turkey Foot
White Sulphur

Shelby co.
Chestnut Grove
Christiansburgh
Clay Village
Consolation
Cropper's Depot
Finchville
Graefenberg
Harrisonville
Jesse's Store
Shelbyville (c h)
Simpsonville
Six Mile
Southville

Simpson co.
Franklin (c h)
Galway
Hickory Flat
Temperance Mount

Spencer co.
Elk Creek
Smileytown
Taylorsville (c h)
Van Dyke's Mills
Waterford
Wilsonville

Taylor co.
Campbellsville
Manusville
Saloma

Todd co.
Allensville
Clifty
Daysville
Elkton (c h)
Fairview
Graysville
Hadensville
McLean's Mill
Pilot Knob
Roscoe
Trenton

Trigg co.
Cadiz (c h)
Canton
Donaldson
Empire Iron Works
Golden Pond
Laura Hill
Lindsay's Mills
Roaring Spring
Rock Castle
Wallonia

Trimble co.
Abbottsford
Bedford (c h)
Garriott's Landing
Milton
Winona

Union co.
Bordley
Caseyville
Clay
Curlew
Cypress
Gum Grove
Huntsville
Morganfield (c h)
Raleigh
Uniontown

Lousiana.

Warren co.
Alma
Bowling Green (ch)
Claypool
Doughty's Creek
Green Castle
Ingleside
Pleasantville

Polkville
Smith's Grove
Temperance Hill
Woodburn

Washington co.
Beech Fork
Beechland

Fredericktown
Mackville
Sharpsville
Springfield (c h)
Texas
Willisburgh

Wayne co.
Clio

Mill Springs
Monticello (c h)
Newberry
North Hill
Robertsport

Whitley co.
Burk Camp Mills
Clear Fork

Craig's Ferry
Lot
Marsh Creek
Meadow Creek
Pine Tree
Rockhold's
Whitley (c h)
Wild Cat
Woodbine

Woodford co.
Dorcey
Midway
Mortonsville
Munday's Landing
Spring Station
Troy
Versailles (c h)

LOUISIANA.

Ascension Parish
Dominique's Store
Donaldsonville (ch)
Live Oak
New River
Tureaud

Assumption par.
Albemarle
Assumption (c h)
Church
Crane's Forge
Paincourtville
Star

Avoyelles par.
Big Bend
Evergreen
Holmesville
Mansura
Marksville (c h)
Moreauville
Simms' Post

Bienville par.
Arcadia
Brush Valley
Duckhorn
Iverson
Loggy Bayou
Mount Lebanon
Mud Branch
Ringgold
Saline
Salt Spring
Sparta
Walnut Creek

Bossier par.
Belleview (c h)
Bistoneau
Bossier Point
Collinsburg
Cotton Valley
Fillmore
Knox Point
Orchard Grove
Plainville
Rouky Mount
Sentell's Store
Tono's Bayou

Caddo par.
Adams
Albany
Bayou La Chute
Cook's Store
Greenwood
Mooring's Port
Shreveport (c h)
Spring Ridge
Summer Grove
Sunny Side

Calcasieu par.
Hamburgh
Hickory Flat
Lake Arthur
Lake Charles

Caldwell par.
Alpha
Augusta

Castor
Columbia (c h)
Copenhagen
Long Lake
Mount Pleasant

Carroll par.
Ashton
Caledonia
Deerfield
Floyd
Joe's Bayou [(c h)
Lake Providence
Monticello
Oak Bluffs
Oak Grove
Pecan Grove
Vista Ridge

Catahoula par.
Aimwell
Casto Springs
Enterprise
Finlay's
Ford's Creek
Funny Louis
Green's Creek
Harrisonburgh (ch)
Sicily Island
Trinity
White Sulphur Springs

Claiborne par.
Allen's Settlement
Argus
Athen's (c h)
Cane Ridge
Dorcheat
Flat Lick
Forest Grove
Gordon
Haynesville
Homer (c h)
Lanier
Lisbon
Minden
Quay
Rose Hill
Scottsville
Shungaloo
Sugar Creek
Wiseville

Concordia par.
Black Hawk Point
Fairview
Flowery Mound
South Bend
Tooley's
Vidalia

De Soto par.
Black Jack
Grand Cane
Keatchie
Kingston
Logansport
Long Street
Mansfield (c h)
Pleasant Grove
Pleasant Hill
Red Bluff

E. Baton Rouge, par.
Baton Rouge (c h)
Greenwell Springs
Magnolia Springs
Manchac
Plain's Store
Stony Point

E. Feliciana par.
Clinton
Jackson (c h)
Oakland
Port Hudson
Woodland

Franklin par.
Boeuff Prairie
Hurricane
Oakly
Pullaway
Red Mouth
Warsaw
Winnsborough (c h)
Yellow Bluff

Iberville par.
Bayou Goula
Gross Tete
Plaquemine
Rosedale
St. Gabriel (c h)

Jackson par.
Brookline
Douglass
Plankville
Timberville
Vernon (c h)
Vienna
Woodville
Wyatt's ⋈ Roads
Vernon (c h)
Vienna
Woodville
Wyatt's ⋈ Roads

Jefferson par.
Carrollton (c h)
Jefferson
Kenner's
La Fayette City

La Fayette par.
Cote Gelee [(c h)
Vermillionville

La Fourche par.
Raceland
Thibodeaux (c h)

Livingston par.
Bayou Barbary
Benton's Ferry
Cecik
Independence
French Settlement
Hollywood
Ponchatoula
Springfield
Walker

Madison par.
Chickamaw Bend

Dallas
De Soto
Milliken's Bend
New Carthage
Quebec
Richmond (c h)

Morehouse par.
Bastrop (c h)
Ion
Line
Lind Grove
Plantersville
Point Jefferson
Prairie Mer Rouge
Tipton

Natchitoches par.
Adaies
Campti
Cloutierville
Coushattee Chute
Kisatchee
Marthaville
Natchitoches (c h)

Orleans par.
Algiers
Fort Pike
New Orleans (c h)

Plaquemines par.
Dalize
Buras Settlement
Graud Prairie
Jesuit's Bend
Point a la Hache
Point Michael
Southwest Pass

Point Coupee par.
Alabama Bayou
Centre Port
Cypress Point
False River
Hermitage
Livonia
Morgana
Point Coupee (c h)
Red River Landing
The Village
Waterloo
Williamsport

Rapides par.
Alexandria (c h)
Barnwell
Bear Creek
Big Creek
Chenayville
Cotile
Hineston
Huddleston
Lecompte
Liberty Creek
Lucky Hit
Spring Creek

Sabine par.
Anacoca
Burr's Ferry
Columbus
Dillonsburg

Fort Jessup
Manny (c h)
Mill Creek
Nashboro'
Negreet
Toro

St. Bernard par.
Bienvenu

St. Charles par.
M'Cutchin's Landing
St. Charles (c h)
Taylor

St. Helena par.
Amite City
Darlington
Dennis' Mills
Greensburg (c h)
Hog Branch
Kemp's Mills
Prospect Hill
Roberts' Mills
Tangapaha

St. James par.
Cantrelle
Convent
Grande Pointe
Vacherie Road

St. John Baptist par
Bonnet Carre
Edgard

St. Landry par.
Arnaudville
Atchafalaya
Ballew's Ferry
Bayou Boeuf
Bayou Chicot (c h)
Big Cane
Dunbarton
Grand Coteau
Leonvile
Mormenton
Opelousas
Plaquemine Brulee
Pouppeville
Ville Platte
Washington

St. Martin's par.
Bayou Chene
Breaux's Bridge
Chicot Pass
Fausse Point
La Place
Myrtle Grove
New Iberia [(c h)
Saint Martinsville

St. Mary's par.
Alligator
Berwick
Brashear
Centreville
Charenton
Franklin (c h)
Jeanerett's
Pattersonville

St. Tammany par.
Covington (c h)
Lima
Madisonville
Mandeville
O'Rourke's
Parkerville
Sun

Tensas par.
Ashwood
Kirk's Ferry
Mound Bayou
St. Josephs (c h)
Water Proof

Terre Bonne par.
Houma (c h)
Laurence
Tigerville

Union par.
Cherry Ridge
D'Arbone
Downsville
Farmersville (c h)
Lindville
Marion
Ouachita City
Pipesville
Shiloh
Spear's Store
Union ⋈ Roads

Vermillion par.
Abbville
Grand Chenier
Perry's Bridge

Wachita par.
Indian Village
Monroe (c h)
Prevost
Spring Place
Trenton

Washington par.
Bailey's Mills
Davidson
Franklinton
Palestine
Roberts
Shady Grove
Stubb's Mill

W. Baton Rouge par.
Bruly Landing
Lobdell's Store

W. Feliciana par.
Bayou Tunica
Laurel Hill
St. Francisville (c h)

Winn par.
Bertrand Prairie
Good Water
Kyishe
Louisville
Montgomery
Pine Ridge
Saint Maurice
Saline Mills
Wheeling
Winfield (c h)

MAINE.

Androscoggin co.
Auburn
Danville
Durham
East Livermore
East Poland
East Turner
East Wales
Greene
Greene Corner
Leeds
Leeds Junction
Lewistown

Lisbon
Little River Village
Livermore
Livermore Centre
Livermore Falls
Mechanics Falls
Minot
North Auburn
North Leeds
North Livermore
North Turner
North Turner Bridge

Poland
Sabatus
South Durham
South Leeds
South Livermore
Turner
Wales
Webster
West Auburn
West Danville
West Durham
West Minot
West Poland

Aroostook co.
Amity
Aroostook
Bancroft
Bancroft Mills
Bridgewater
Castle Hill
Conway
Easton
Fort Fairfield
Fort Kent
Fremont
Haynesville

Hodgdon
Houlton (c h)
Limestone
Linneus
Littleton
Lyndon
Madawaska
Maple Grove
Mar's Hill
Masardis
Monticello
Moro
New Limerick
North Linneus

Number Three
Orient
Presque Isle
Rawson
Rockabema
Salmon Brook
Smyrna
Smyrna Mills
South Moluneus
Van Buren
Weston
West Van Buren

Maine.

Cumberland co.
Bolster's Mills
Bonny Eagle
Bridgeton
Brunswick
Cape Elizabeth Depot
Casco
Cumberland
Cumberland Centre
East Auburn
East Baldwin
East North Yarmouth
East Otisfield
East Raymond
East Standish
East Windham
Edes' Falls
Falmouth
Freeport
Gorham
Gray
Harrison
Naples
New Casco
New Gloucester
North Baldwin
North Bridgeton
North Gray
North Pownal
North Raymond
North Windham
North Yarmouth
Oak Hill
Oak Hill Station
Otisfield
Portland (c h)
Pownal
Raymond
Saccarappa
Sandy Beach
Scarboro'
Sebago
South Bridgeton
South Casco
South Freeport
South Windham
Standish
Steep Falls
Stevens' Plains
Upper Gloucester
Webb's Mills
West Baldwin
West Bridgeton
West Cumberland
West Falmouth
West Gloucester
West Gorham
West Pownal
Windham
Yarmouth

Franklin co.
Avon
Carthage
Chesterville
East New Sharon
East New Vineyard
East Strong
East Wilton
Farmington
Farmington Falls
Freeman
Industry
Jay
Kingfield
Madrid
New Sharon
New Vineyard
North Chesterville
North Jay
North Wilton
Phillips (c h)
Rangeley
Salem
South Chesterville
Strong
Temple Mills
Weld
West Freeman
West's Mills
Wilton

Hancock co.
Amherst
Aurora
Blue Hill
Blue Hill Falls
Brooklin
Brooksville
Buck's Mills
Bucksport
Bucksport Centre
Castine (c h)
Cranberry Isles
Dedham
Deer Isle
East Buckport
East Eden
East Sullivan
East Trenton
Eden
Ellsworth
Ellsworth Falls
Franklin
Gouldsboro'
Great Pond
Green's Landing
Hancock
Mount Desert
North Blue Hill
North Bucksport
North Castine
North Ellsworth
North Hancock
North Haven
North Mariaville
North Penobscott
North Sedgwick
Oceanville
Orland
Otis
Penobscot
Prospect Harbor
Salisbury Cove
Seal Cove
Seaport
Sedgwick
South Brooksville
South Deer Isle
South Penobscot
South West Harbor
Sullivan
Surry
Swan's Island
Tilden
Tremont
Trenton Point
Waltham
West Brookville
West Eden
West Ellsworth
West Gouldsboro'
West Sedgwick
West Trenton
Winter Harbor

Kennebeck co.
Albion
Augusta (c h)
Belgrade
Belgrade Mills
Benton
Brown's Corners
Centre Sidney
China
Clinton
Curtis' Corner
East Benton
East Monmouth
East Pittston
East Readfield
East Vassalboro'
East Winthrop
Fayette
Gardiner
Hallowell
Kent's Hill
Litchfield
Litchfield Corners
Monmouth
Mount Vernon
North Belgrade
North Fayette
North Monmouth
North Pittston
North Sidney
North Vassalboro'
North Vienna
North Wayne
Pishon's Ferry
Pittston
Readfield
Readfield Depot
Rome
Seward's Mills
Sidney
South Albion
South China
South Litchfield
South Monmouth
South Vassalboro'
South Windsor
Strickland's Ferry
Togus Springs
Vassalboro'
Vienna
Waterville
Wayne
Weck's Mills
West Gardiner
West Sidney
West Waterville

Windsor
Winslow
Winthrop

Lincoln co.
Alma
Booth Bay
Bristol
Cooper's Mills
Cushing
Damariscotta Mills
Dresden
Dresden Mills
Edgecomb
Friendship
Hodgdon's Mills
Jefferson
Matinicus
Monhegan Island
New Castle
Nobleesboro'
North Boothbay
North Edgecomb
North Newcastle
North Union
North Waldoboro'
North Washington
North Whitefield
Owl's Head
Pemaquid
Rockland
Round Pond
Saint George
Sheepscott Bridge
Somerville
South Dresden
South Jefferson
Southport
South St. George
South Thomaston
Tenant's Harbor
Thomaston
Union
Waldoboro'
Warren
Washington
West Jefferson
Westport
West Washington
Whitfield
Wiscasset (c h)

Oxford co.
Albany
Andover
Bethel
Brownfield
Bryant's Pond
Buckfield
Byron
Canton
Canton Mills
Centre Lovell
Denmark
Dixfield
East Dixfield
East Fryeburgh
East Hebron
East Rumford
East Stoneham
East Sumner
Fryeburgh
Fryeburgh Center
Gilead
Grafton
Greenwood
Hanover
Hartford
Hebron
Hiram
Letter B
Locke's Mills
Lovell
Mexico
Milton Plantation
Newry
North Albany
North Buckfield
North Fryeburgh
North Lovell
North Newry
North Paris
North Waterford
North Woodstock
Norway
Oxford
Paris (c h)
Peru
Porter
Roxbury
Rumford
Rumford Centre
Rumford Point
Snow Falls
South Andover
South Hartford
South Newry

South Paris
South Waterford
Stow
Sumner
Sweden
Waterford
Welchville
West Bethel
West Paris
West Peru
West Sumner
Wilson's Mills
Woodstock

Penobscot co.
Alton
Alton Village
Argyle
Bangor (c h)
Bradford
Brewer
Brewer Village
Burlington
Carmel
Carroll
Charleston
Chester
Corinna
Corinna Centre
Corinth
Deerfield
Dexter
Dixmont
Dixmont Centre
East Bradford
East Corinth
East Dixmont
East Eddington
East Exeter
East Hampden
East Holden
East Lowell
East Newport
East Orrington
East Stetson
Eddington
Edinburgh
Enfield
Etna
Etna Centre
Exeter
Exeter Mills
Garland
Glenburn
Great Works
Greenbush
Hampden
Hampden Corner
Hermon
Hermon Pond
Holden
Howland
Hudson
Kenduskeag
La Grange
Lee
Levant
Lincoln
Lincoln Centre
Lowell
Mattawamkeag
Maxfield
Milford
Newburg
Newburg Centre
Newport
Nickatou
North Bradford
North Carmel
North Dixmont
North East Dixmont
North Hermon
North Howland
North Newport
North Woodward
Olamon
Oldtown
Orono
Orrington
Passadumkeag
Patton
Plymouth
Six Mile Falls
South Charleston
South Corinth
South Dexter
South Exeter
South Levant
South Lincoln
South Newburg
South Orrington
South Winn
Springfield
Stetson
Upper Stillwater
Veasie
West Bangor
West Charleston

West Corinna
West Enfield
West Garland
West Glenburn
West Great Works
West Hampden
West Levant
Woodville

Piscataquis co.
Abbot
Atkinson
Blanchard
Bowerbank
Brownsville
Centre Guilford
Dover (c h)
Dover South Mills
East Dover
East Sangerville
Elliottsville
Foxcroft
Greenville
Guilford
Katahdin Iron Works
Kilmarnock
Kingsbery
Milo
Monson
Mount Kineo
North Brownville
Orneville
Parkman
Parkman Centre
Saugerville
Sebec
Shirley
Shirley Mills
South Atkinson
South Dover
South Parkman
South Sangerville
South Sebec
Wellington
West Dover
Williamsburgh

Sagadahoc co.
Bath
Bowdoin
Bowdoin Centre
Bowdoinham
East Bowdoinham
Georgetown
Parker's Head
Phipsburg
Richmond
Richmond Corner
Small Point
Topsham (c h)
West Bowdoin
Winnegance
Woolwich

Somerset co.
Anson
Athens
Bingham
Bloomfield
Brighton
Cambridge
Canaan
Canada Line
Carritunk
Concorv
Cornville
Dead River
Detroit
East Madison
East New Portland
East Pittsfield
Embden
Embden Centre
Fairfield
Fairfield Corners
Flag Staff
Harmony
Hartland
Highland
Kendall's Mills
Larone
Lexington
Madison
Madison Centre
Mercer
Moose River
New Portland
Norridgewock (c h)
North Anson
North Fairfield
North New Portland
Palmyra [land
Parlin Pond
Pittsfield
Ripley
Saint Albans

Skowhegan
Smithfield
Solon
Somerset Mills
South Norridgewock
South Solon
Stark
The Forks
West Anson
West Embden
West Moscow
West Ripley

Waldo co.
Belfast (c h)
Belmont
Brooks
Burnham Village
Camden
Carver's Harbor
Centre Lincolnv'l
Centre Montville
East Knox
East Montville
East Northport
East Palermo
East Thorndike
Ellingwood's Cor.
Frankfort
Frankfort Mills
Freedom
Hope
Islesboro'
Jackson
Knox
Liberty
Lincolnville
McLain's Mills
Monroe
Monroe Centre
Montville
Morrill
North Appleton
North Frankfort
North Islesboro'
North Monroe
North Palermo
Northport
North Prospect
North Searsmont
North Searsport
Palermo
Palermo Centre
Prospect Ferry
Rockport
Rockville
Sandy Point
Searsmont
Searsport
South Brooks
South Freedom
South Hope
South Liberty
South Montville
Stockton
Swanville
Thorndike
Troy
Troy Centre
Unity
Waldo
West Camden

Washington co.
Addison Point
Alexander
Baileyville
Baring
Beddington
Calais
Charlotte
Columbia
Cooper
Crawford
Cutler
Dablois
Dennysville
East Machias
Eastport
Harrington
Indian River
Jackson Brook
Jonesboro'
Jonesport
Lane's Brook
Lubec
Lubec Mills
Machias (c h)
Machias Port
Marion
Medybemps
Milbridge
Milltown
Narraguagus
North Cutler
Northfield
Pembroke
Perry

400 Maryland.

Plantation No 14	York co.	East Parsonfield	Kittery Depot	North Limington	South Parsonfield
Princeton	Acton	Elliot	Kittery Point	North Newfield	South Sanford
Red Beach	Alfred	Elliot Depot	Lebanon	North Parsonfield	Springvale
Robbinston	Bar Mills	Emory's Mills	Limerick	North Shapleigh	Waterboro'
South Beddington	Biddeford	Goodwin's Mills	Limington	Ogunquit	Waterboro' Centre
South Princeton	Bonny Eagle	Hollis	Lyman Centre	Parsonfield	Wells
Steuben	Buxton	Hollis Centre	Newfield	Ross' Corners	Wells' Depot
Topsfield	Buxton Centre	Kennebank	North Acton	Saco	West Buxton
Waite	Cape Neddick	Kennebank Depot	North Berwick	Sanford	West Lebanon
Wesley	Centre Lebanon	Kennebank Port	North Hollis (Port	Shapleigh	West Newfield
West Laben	Cornish	Kezar Falls	North Kennebunk	South Acton	West Parsonfield
Whiting	East Limington	Kittery	North Lebanon	South Berwick	York (c h)
Whitneyville					

MARYLAND.

Alleghany co.	Rossville	*Cecil co.*	Foxville	Savage	Great Mills
Accident	Saint Dennis	Battle Swamp	Frederick (c h)	Simpsonville	Leonardtown (c h)
Barrallville	Shawan	Bay View	Graceham	Woodstock	Milestown
Barton	Stablersville	Blue Ball	Greenfield Mills		Mount Olive
Bloomington	Stocksdale	Bohemia Mills	Ijamsville	*Kent co.*	Oakville
Brady's Mill	Sweet Air	Brick Meeting-	Jefferson	Chestertown (c h)	Ridge
Cumberland (c h)	Towsontown	House	Johnsville	Chesterville	St. Clement's Bay
Flint Stone	Union Meeting	Cecilton	Kemptown	Galena	St. Inigos
Frostburgh	House	Charlestown	Ladiesburgh	Hanesville	
Glade Mills	Upperco	Cherry Hill	Lewistown	Harmony	*Somerset co.*
Grantaville	Upper Falls	Chesapeake City	Liberty Town	Head of Sassafras	Barren Creek
Johnstown	Warren	Elkton (c h)	Linganore	Massey's ⋈ Roads	Springs
Lonaconing	Weisesburgh	Fair Hill	Mechanicstown	Millington	Crow's Mills
Mount Savage	Westerman's Mills	Farmington	Middletown	Rees' Corner	Dame's Quarter
Oakland	Wetheredville	Northeast	Monrovia	Rock Hall	Deal's Island
Oldtown	White Hall	Perryville	Mount Pleasant	Rogers' Store	Fork Town
Orleans	Woodberry	Port Deposit	Myersville	Still Pond	Kingston
Rawling's Station	Woodensburgh	Port Herman	New London	Urieville	Princess Ann (c h)
Shelbysport	Zoucksville	Principio	New Market		Quantico
Shade Mill		Principio Furnace	Oak Orchard	*Montgomery co.*	Roachville
Summitville	*Calvert co.*	Rising Sun	Petersville	Barnesville	Salisbury
Swanton	Dunkirk	Rock Springs	Point of Rocks	Brookville	Sharp Town
Western Port	Huntingtown	Rowlandsville	Sabillisville	Burnt Mills	Shelltown
Winston	Lower Marlboro'	Saint Augustine	Unionville	Clarksburg	Tyaskin
	Port Republic	South Milford	Urbana	Colesville	Upper Trappe
Ann Arundel co.	Prince Frederick-	Warwick	Utica Mills	Concord	Whitehaven
Annapolis (c h)	town (c h)	Westnotsingham	Walkersville	Cottage	
Annapolis Junc-	Saint Leonards	Zion	Weverton	Damascus	*Talbot co.*
tion	Sunderlandville		Wolfsville	Darnestown	Bay Hundred
Bristol		*Charles co.*	Woodsborough	Drayton	Chapel
Crownsville	*Caroline co.*	Allen's Fresh		Forest Oak	Easton (c h)
Davidsonville	Bethlehem	Beantown	*Harford co.*	Goshen	Oxford
Forest Home	Boonsville	Benedict	Abingdon	Great Falls	Royal Oak
Friendship	Bridgetown	Bryantown	Bel-Air (c h)	Hyattstown	Saint Michaels
Governor's Bridge	Burraville	Doncaster	Churchville	Laytonsville	Skipton
Johnson's Store	Denton (c h)	Duffield	Cottage Home	Middlebrook	Trappe
Millersville	Fowling Creek	Gallant Green	Clayton	Monocacy	
Patuxent	Greensboro'	Glymont	Clermont Mills	Olney	*Washington co.*
Saint Margaret's	Hillsboro'	Nanjemoy	Darlington	Poolesville	Bakersville
South River	Melville	Newport	Dublin	Rockville (c h)	Beaver Creek
Tracy's Landing	New Hope	Patuxent City	Emmorton	Sandy Spring	Benevola
West River	Potter's Landing	Pisgah	Fallstone	Trindolphia	Boonsboro'
	Preston	Pomonkey	Federal Hill	Unity	Brownsville
Baltimore co.	Smithville	Port Tabacco (c h)	Forest Hill		Cavetown
Baltimore (c h)		Tompkinsville	Glenville	*Prince George's co.*	Chewsville
Black Rock	*Carroll co.*		Greyrock		Clear Spring
Buchanan	Bachman's Mills	*Dorchester co.*	Hall's ⋈ Roads	Aquasco	College of St.
Brooklandville	Bark Hill	Airey's	Havre De Grace	Beltsville	James
Butler	Bird Hill	Big Mills	Harford Furnace	Bladensburgh	Dowsville
Salverton Mills	Bruceville	Bucktown	Hickory Tavern	Brandywine	Fair Play
Carrollton	Cambridge (c h)	Hopewell ⋈ Roads	Buena Vista	Fairview
Catonsville	Double Pipe Cr'k	Cedar Creek	Jarrettsville	Collington	Four Locks
Chase's	Finksburgh	Church Creek	Jerusalem Mills	Croom	Funkstown
Cockeysville	Franklinville	Cornersville	Lapidum	Horse Head	Green Spring Fur-
Ellengowan	Freedom	Crotcher's Ferry	Magnolia	Hyattsville	nace
Fork Meeting H'se	Hampstead	Drawbridge	Michaelsville	Laurel Factory	Hagerstown (c h)
Freeland	Harney	East New Market	Mill Green	Long Old Fields	Hancock
Gorsuch's Mills	Houd's Mills	Federalsburgh	Perrymansville	Nottingham	Indian Springs
Govanstown	Houck's Store	Fishing Creek	Pleasantville	Piscataway	Keedysville
Grave Run Mills	McKinstry's Mills	Galestown	Pylesville	Queen Ann	Lappon's ⋈ Roads
Greenwood	Kroh's Mills	Golden Hill	Sandy Hook	Surratt's	Leitersburgh
Harewood	Manchester	Harrison	Shawsville	Upper Marlboro'	Millstone Point
Hereford	Middleburgh	Hicksburgh	Taylor		Ringgold
Hookstown	Mount Airy	Hill's Point	Thomas' Run	*Queen Ann co.*	Rohrersville
Lauraville	New Windsor	Lakesville	Upper ⋈ Roads	Broad Creek	Sharpsburgh
Little Gunpowder	Piney Creek	Taylor's Island		Centreville (c h)	Smithsburgh
Long Green Acad-	Poolsburgh	Tobacco Stick	*Howard co.*	Church Hill	Williamsport
emy	Porters	Vienna	Alberton	Crumpton	
Lutherville	Nam's Creek	Williamsburgh	Clarksville	Long Marsh	*Worcester co.*
Maryland Line	Silver Run		Cooksville	Queenstown	Berlin
Monkton Mills	Sykesville	*Frederick co.*	Elk Ridge Land-	Roesville	Bishopsville
Mount Washington	Taneytown	Adamstown	ing	Sudlersville	Derickson's Cross
North Branch	Union Bridge	Barry	Millcott's Mills	Templeville	Roads
Owing's Mills	Union Mills	Bolivar	Glenelg	Wye Mills	Newark
Paper Mills	Uniontown	Bridgeport	Ilchester Mills		Newtown
Parkton	Wakefield	Buckey's Town	Lisbon	*St. Mary's co.*	Powellville
Philopolis	Warfieldburgh	Burkittsville	Marriottsville		Salut Martins
Pike's Hill	Westminster	Cotocton Furnace	Matthews' Store	Chapt	Sandy Hill
Randallstown	Winfield	Creagerstown	Piercaland	Charlott Hall	Snow Hill (c h)
Reisterstown	Woodbine	Emmitsburgh	Poplar Springs		Whaleysville

Massachusetts.

MASSACHUSETTS.

Barnstable co.
Barnstable (c h)
Brewster
Centreville
Chatham
Cotuit Port
Dennis
East Brewster
East Dennis
East Falmouth
Eastham
East Harwich
East Orleans
East Sandwich
Falmouth
Harwich
Harwichport
Hatchville
Hyannis
Marston's Mills
Monument
North Chatham
North Eastham
North Falmouth
North Sandwich
North Truro
Orleans
Osterville
Pocasset
Provincetown
Sandwich
South Dennis
South Harwich
South Orleans
South Sandwich
South Wellfleet
South Yarmouth
Spring Hill
Truro
Waquoit
Wellfleet
West Barnstable
West Brewster
West Chatham
West Dennis
West Falmouth
West Harwich
West Sandwich
West Yarmouth
Wood's Hole
Yarmouth
Yarmouth Port

Berkshire co.
Adams
Alford
Ashley Falls
Bancroft
Beckot
Berkshire
Blackinton
Boston Corner
Cheshire
Cold Spring
Curtisville
Dalton
East Lee
East Sheffield
East Windsor
Egremont Plain
Florida
Glen Dale
Great Barrington
Hancock
Hartsville
Hinsdale
Hinsdale Depot
Hoosatonic
Housatonic
Lanesborough
Lee
Lenox (c h)
Lenox Furnace
Mill River
Monterey
Montville
New Ashford
New Boston
New Lenox
New Marlboro'
North Adams
North Becket
North Egremont
Otis
Peru
Pittsfield
Richmond
Sandisfield
Savoy
Sheffield
South Egremont
Southfield
South Lee

South Williamstown,
State Line
Stockbridge
Tyringham
Van Deusenville
Washington
West Becket
West Otis
West Pittsfield
West Stockbridge
West Stockbridge Centre
Williamstown
Windsor

Bristol co.
Attleboro'
Berkley
Dartmouth
Dighton
East Freetown
East Taunton
Easton
Fairhaven
Fall River
Freetown
Long Plain
Mansfield
Miriokville
New Bedford (c h)
North Attleboro'
North Dartmouth
North Dighton
North Easton
North Fairhaven
North Rehoboth
North Swansea
North Westport
Norton
Rehoboth
Seekonk
Somerset
South Attleboro'
South Dartmouth
South Easton
South Seekonk
South Westport
Swansea
Taunton (c h)
West Mansfield
Westport
Westport Point

Dukes co.
Chilmark
Edgartown (c h)
Holmes' Hole
West Tisbury

Essex co.
Amesbury
Andover
Annisquam
Ballard Vale
Beverly
Beverly Farms
Boxford
Bradford
Byfield
Clifton Dale
Danvers
Danvers Centre
Danversport
East Haverhill
East Salisbury
Essex
Georgetown
Gloucester
Groveland
Hamilton
Haverhill
Ipswich (c h)
Lanesville
Lawrence
Lynn
Lynnfield
Lynnfield Centre
Manchester
Marblehead
Methuen
Middleton
Nahant
Newburyport (c h)
North Andover
North Andover Depot
North Beverly
Pigeon Cove
Rockport
Rowley
Salem (c h)
Salisbury
Saugus

Saugus Centre
South Amesbury
South Danvers
South Groveland
Swampscott
Topsfield
Wenham
West Amesbury
West Boxford
West Gloucester
West Newbury

Franklin co.
Adamsville
Ashfield
Bernardston
Buckland
Charlemont
Colerain
Conway
Deerfield
East Charlemont
East Shelburne
East Whately
Erving
Gill
Greenfield (c h)
Grout's Corners
Hawley
Heath
Leverett
Leyden
Lock's Village
Monroe
Montague
New Salem
Northfield
Northfield Farms
North Leverett
North New Salem
North Orange
Orange
Rowe
Shelburne
Shelburne Falls
Shutesbury
South Deerfield
South Hawley
Sunderland
Warwick
Wendell
Wendell Depot
West Hawley
West Northfield
Whately
Zoar

Hampden co.
Agawam
Ashleyville
Blanford
Bond's Village
Brimfield
Chester
Chester Factories
Chicopee
Chicopee Falls
Collins' Depot
East Brimfield
East Granville
East Long Meadow
Feeding Hills
Holland
Holyoke
Indian Orchard
Ireland
Long Meadow
Ludlow
Mittineague
Monson
Montgomery
North Blanford
North Chester
Palmer
Russell
Southwick
South Wilbraham
Springfield (c h)
Thorndike
Three Rivers
Tolland
Wales
Westfield
West Granville
West Springfield
Wilbraham
Willimansett

Hampshire co.
Amherst
Belchertown
Chesterfield
Cummington

Cummington West Village
East Hampton
Enfield
Florence
Goshen
Granby
Greenwich
Greenwich Village
Hadley
Hatfield
Haydenville
Huntington
Middlefield
North Amherst
Northampton (c h)
North Hadley
North Prescott
Norwich
Pelham
Plainfield
Prescott
Ringville
South Amherst
Southampton
South Hadley
South Hadley Falls
Ware
West Hampton
West Worthington
Williamsburgh
Worthington

Middlesex co.
Acton
Ashby
Ashland
Assabet
Auburn Dale
Bedford
Belmont
Billerica
Boxboro'
Braggville
Brighton
Burlington
Cambridge (c h)
Cambridgeport
Carlisle
Charlestown
Chelmsford
Cochituate
Concord (c h)
Dracut
Dunstable
East Cambridge
East Holliston
East Lexington
East Pepperell
East Woburn
Feltonville
Forge Village
Framingham
Groton
Graniteville
Greenwood
Hayden Row
Holliston
Hopkinton
Lexington
Lincoln
Littleton
Lowell
Middlesex Village
Malden
Mapleweed
Marlboro'
Medford
Melrose
Mount Auburn
Natick
Newton
Newton Centre
Newton Lower Falls
Newton Upper Falls
Newtonville
North Billerica
North Cambridge
North Chelmsford
North Reading
North Sudbury
North Towksbury
North Wilmington
North Woburn
Pepperell
Reading
Rock Bottom
Saxonville
Sherborn
Shirley
Shirley Village
Somerville
South Acton

South Framingham
South Groton
South Malden
South Natick
South Reading
Stoneham
Stow
Sudbury
Tewksbury
Townsend
Townsend Harbor
Tyngsboro'
Waltham
Watertown
Wayland
West Acton
West Cambridge
West Chelmsford
Westford
West Groton
West Medford
West Newton
Weston
West Townsend
Wilmington
Winchester
Woburn
Woodville

Nantucket co.
Nantucket (c h)

Norfolk co.
Bald Hill
Bellingham
Braintree
Brookline
Canton [lage
Charles River Village
Cohasset
Dedham (c h)
Dorchester
Dover
East Foxboro'
East Medway
East Randolph
East Sharon
East Stoughton
East Walpole
East Weymouth
Fairmount
Foxborough
Franklin
Franklin City
Grantville
Harrison Square
Jamaica Plain
Mattapan
Medfield
Medway
Milton
Needham
Neponset Village
North Bellingham
North Cohasset
North Weymouth
North Wrentham
Plainsville
Quincy Point
Quincy
Randolph
Rockville
Roxbury
Sharon
Sheldonville
South Braintree
South Dedham
South Franklin
South Randolph
South Walpole
South Weymouth
South Wrentham
Stoughton
Walpole
West Dedham
West Foxboro'
West Medway
West Roxbury
West Wrentham
Weymouth
Wrentham

Plymouth co.
Abington
Bridgewater
Campello
Carver
Chiltonville
Cochesett
Duxbury
East Abington
East Bridgewater

East Marshfield
East Middleboro'
East Wareham
Halifax
Hanover
Hanson
Hingham
Hull
Kingston
Marshfield
Mattapoisett
Middleboro'
North Abington
North Bridgewater
North Carver
North Marshfield
North Middleboro'
North Pembroke
North Plympton
North Rochester
North Scituate
N'th West Bridgewater
Pembroke
Plymouth (c h)
Plympton
Rochester
Rock
Scituate
Scotland
Sippican
South Abington
South Carver
South Hanson
South Hingham
South Middleboro'
South Plymouth
South Scituate
Wareham
West Bridgewater
West Duxbury
West Scituate
West Wareham

Suffolk co.
Boston (c h)
Chelsea
East Boston
North Chelsea
Winthrop

Worcester co.
Ashburnham
Ashburnham Depot
Athol
Athol Depot
Auburn
Baldwinsville
Barre
Barre Plains
Berlin
Blackstone
Bolton
Boylston
Boylston Centre
Brookfield
Burrageville
Charlton
Charlton Depot
Cherry Valley
Clappville
Clinton
Cold Brook
Cordaville
Dana
Douglass
Dudley
East Brookfield
East Douglass
East Princeton
Farnumsville
Fiskedale
Fitchburgh
Gardner
Globe Village
Grafton
Hardwick
Harvard
Holden
Hubbardston
Lancaster
Leicester
Leominster
Lunenburgh
Mendon
Milford
Millbury
Millville
New Braintree
New England Village
North Blackstone
Northboro'
Northbridge

402   Michigan.

Northbridge C'ntr	Otter River	Saundersville	Spencer	Wachusett Village	Westminster
North Brookfield	Oxford	Shrewsbury	Sterling	Warren	West Rutland
North Dana	Paxton	Southboro'	Still River	Webster	West Sterling
North Leominster	Petersham	Southbridge	Sturbridge	Westboro'	West Sutton
North Oxford	Phillipston	South Gardner	Sutton	West Boylston	Whitinsville
North Spencer	Princeton	South Lancaster	Templeton	West Brookfield	Wilkinsonville
North Uxbridge	Royalston	South Milford	Upton	West Fitchburgh	Winchendon
Oakdale	Rutland	South Royalston	Uxbridge	West Millbury	Worcester (c h)
Oakham					

MICHIGAN.

Alcona co.
Harrisville

Allegan co.
Allegan (c h)
Bradley
Cheshire
Ganges
Gun Marsh
Hopkins
Lake
Leighton
Manlius
Martin
Monterey
New Casco
Otsego
Overisel
Pine Plain
Plainwell
Proctor
Saugatuck
Silver Creek
Wayland

Alpena co.
Alpena

Antrim co.
Elk Rapids

Arenac co.
Arenac

Barry co.
Assyria
Baltimore
Barryville
Bristolville
Carlton
Cedar Creek
Glass Creek
Gun Lake
Hastings (c h)
Hickory Corners
Irving
Johnstown
Maple Grove
Merritt
Middleville
Milo
North Irvin
Orangeville Mills
Prairieville
South Assyria
Woodland
Yankee Spring

Berrien co.
Bainbridge
Berrien Centre
Berrien Spring (c h)
Bertrand
Buchanan
Coloma
Dayton
Galien
Milburgh
New Buffalo
Niles
Pipestone
Saint Joseph
Three Oaks
Watervliet
Weesaw

Branch co.
Algansee
Batavia
Bethel
Branch (c h)
Bronson's Prairie
Butler
California
Cold Water (c h)
East Gilead
Gilead
Girard
Kinderhook
Mattison
Noble Centre

Quincy
Round Lake
Sherwood
Union City

Calhoun co.
Absoota
Albion
Athens
Battle Creek
Bedford
Burlington
Cedar Lake
Ceresco
Clarence
Clarendon
Clarendon Centre
Convis
Convis Centre
East Leroy
Emmett
Homer
Lyon Lake
Marengo
Marshall (c h)
Newton
Partello
Penfield
Pine Creek
Scotlia
Tekonsha
West Leroy

Cass co.
Adamsville
Brownsville
Cassapolis (c h)
Dowagiac
Edwardsburgh
La Grange
Liberty Church
Little Prairie
Roude
Marcellus
Newburg
Picket's Corner
Pokagon
Shave Head
Summerville
Union
Vandalia
Williamsville

Chebovgan co.
Duncan

Chippewa co.
Sault de St. Marie
Sugar Island

Clinton co.
Bath
Bengal
Dallas
De Witt
Duplain
Eagle
Elsie
Essex
Geary
Goss
Greenbush
Keystone
Maple Rapids
North Eagle
Olive
Ovid
Ovid Centre
Riley
Saint Johns
South Riley
Victor
Waconsta
Westphalia

Delta co.
Cedar Fork
Escanawba

Eaton co.
Bellevue
Brookfield

Camp Creek
Carlisle
Centre
Charlotte
Chester
Delta
Eaton Rapids
Elmira
Grand Ledge
Kalamo
Mud Creek
Olivet
Oneida
Roxana
South Sunfield
Sunfield
Vermontville
West Benton
West Windsor
Windsor

Emmett co.
Bear River
Charlevoix
Saint James

Genesee co.
Argentine
Atlas
Crockersville
Davison Centre
East Thetford
Elgin
Elk
Fentonville
Flint
Flushing
Forest
Gaines
Gaines' Station
Genesee Village
Goodrich
Grand Blane
Kearsley
Linden
Montrose
Mount Morris
Mundy
Pine Run
Richfield
Stony Run
Swartz Creek
Thetford
Valeria

Grand Traverse co.
Grand Traverse
Mapleton
Omena
Traverse City
Whitewater

Gratiot co.
Alma
Elm Hall
Forest Hill
Ithaca
Lafayette
Monticello
Newark
North Star
North Shade
Pompei
Saint Louis
Stella
Spring Brook

Hillsdale co.
Amboy
Cambria Mills
Camden
Cass
Edinburgh
Florida
Hillsdale (c h)
Jefferson
Jonesville
Litchfield
Morganville
Moscow
Mosherville
North Adams
Ransom

Reading
Somerset
South Wright
Sparta
Sylvanus
Wheatland Centre
Wood's Corners

Houghton co.
Algonquin
Clifton
Eagle Harbor
Eagle River
Fort Wilkins
Houghton
Keweenaw Bay
North West Mines

Huron co.
Barnettsville
Port Austin
White Rock
Willow Creek

Ingham co.
Alverson
Aurelius
Bunker Hill
Dansville
Delhi Centre
Eden
Felt's
Fitchburg
Lansing
Le Roy
Leslie
Mason
North Aurelius
Norton
Onondaga
Phelpstown
Rod Bridge
Sanford
Stockbridge
West Delhi
White Oak
Williamstown

Ionia co
Avon
Boston
Campbell
Danby
Ionia (c h)
Kiddville
Kossuth
Lake City
Lyons
Maple
Matherton
Muir
North Plains
Orange
Otisco
Palo
Patterson's Mills
Pewamo
Plains
Portland
Rix
Ronald Centre
Saranac
Schewa
Smyrna
South Boston
South Cass
Wheatland

Isabella co.
Albany
Salt River
Wiota

Jackson co.
Arland
Baldwin's Mills
Barry
Brooklyn
Cayuga
Columbia
Concord
Franciscoville

Gidley's Station
Grass Lake
Hanover
Henrietta
Jackson (c h)
Leoni
Liberty
Michigan Centre
Napoleon
Norvell
Otter Creek
Portage Lake
Pulaski
South Henrietta
South Jackson
Spring Arbor
Springport
Tompkins
Waterloo
West Rives

Josco co.
Ausable
Tawas City

Kalamazoo co.
Alamo
Brady
Charleston
Climax Prairie
Comstock
Cooper
Galesburgh
Kalamazoo (c h)
Oshtemo
Pavilion
Portage
Prairie Ronde
Richland
Schoolcraft
Wakshma
West Climax
Yorkville

Kent co.
Ada
Algoma
Alto
Alton
Ashley
Austerlitz
Bowne
Bracevile
Buck Creek
Caledonia
Cannonsburgh
Cascade
Cedar Springs
Cortlandt
Cortlandt Center
Cuba
Englishville
Erin
Fallsburgh
Flat River
Gainesville
Grahamville
Grand Rapids (c h)
Grandville
Grattan
Indian Creek
Kelloggsville
Laphamville
Loominsville
Lowell
Nelson
North Brownsville
Oakfield
Pleasant
Sparta Centre
Spencer's Mill
Vergennes
White Swan
Whitneyville

Lapeer co.
Allison
Almont
Arcadia
Columbiaville
Dryden
Farmer's Creek

Goodland
Hadley
Hunter's Creek
Imlay
Lapeer (c h)
Marathon
Metamora
North Branch
Pool
Thornville
Whigville

Leelanaw co.
Glen Arbor
Herring Creek
Leland
Northport
North Unity

Lenawee co.
Addison
Adrian
Attica
Blissfield
Cambridge
Canandaigua
Clayton
Clinton
Deerfield
Dover
East Ogden
Fairfield
Geneva
Hudson
Lake Ridge
Macon
Medina
Morenci
North Adrian
Oakford
Palmyra
Ridgeway
Riga
Rollin
Rome
Seneca
Springville
Tecumseh (c h)
Tipton
Wellsville
West Ogden
Woodstock
Wolf Creek

Livingston co.
Brighton
Cohoctah
Conway
Deer Creek
Fleming
Fowlerville
Genoa
Green Oak
Hamburgh
Hamburgh Village
Hartland
Hollister
Howell (c h)
Iosco
Madison
Marion
Middletown
North Brighton
Oak Grove
Osceola Centre
Parshallville
Pinckney
Plainfield
Tyrone
Unadilla

Macomb co.
Armada
Disco
East Union
Lenox
Macomb
Memphis
More
Milton
Mount Clemens (c h)

Minnesota. 403

Mount Vernon
New Baltimore
New Haven
Plumb Brook
Ray
Ray Centre
Red Run
Richmond
Romeo
Roseville
Scottsville
Utica
Vienna
Warren
Washington

Manistee co.
Manistee
Portage Creek

Marquette co.
Marquette
Negaunee

Mason co.
Freeman's Mills
Little Sauble
Pere Marquette

Mecosta co.
Grove
Leonard
Pierson

Michilimackinac co
Mackinac (c h)

Midland co.
Midland

Monroe co.
Brest
Clark City
Dundee
East Raisinville
Erie
Exeter
Grafton
Ida
Lambertville
La Salle
London
Milan
Monroe (c h)
Newport
North Raisinville
Oakville
Ottawa Lake
Summerfield

Montcalm co.
Bloomer Centre
Bushnell Centre
Cato
Clear Lake
Crystal
Fair Plains
Greenville
Montcalm
W at Bloomer

Newago co.
Ashland
Big Prairie
Bridgeton
Croton
Newago (c h)
Weaversville

Oakland co.
Auburn
Austin
Ball Mountain
Big Beaver
Birmingham
Brandon
Clarkston
Commerce
Davisburgh
Drayton Plains
Farmington
Four Towns
Franklin
Gilbert
Groveland
Highland
Holly Mills
Jersey
Kensington
Lakeville
Mahopac
Milford
Mount Pleasant
New Hudson
North Farmington
North Oxford
Novi
Oakland
Oakwood
Orion
Ortonville
Oxford
Pontiac (c h)
Rochester
Rose
Royal Oak
Southfield
South Lyon
Springfield
Springs Mills

Strait's Lake
Summit
Troy
Walled Lake
Waterford
West Bloomfield
West Novi
White Lake

Oceana co.
Clay Banks
Benona
Greenwood
Marr
Pent Water
White River

Ontonagon co.
Adventure
Greenland
Minnesota Mine
Ontonagon
Pewabic
Rockland

Ottawa co.
Allendale
Berlin
Big Spring
Casenovia
Coopersville
Crimea
Dalton's Mills
Day
Eastmansville
East Muskegon
Forest City
Georgetown
Grand Haven (c h)
Holland
Jamestown
Lamont
Mill Point
Muskegon
Ottawa Centre
Pintler's Corners
Ravenna
Robinson
Sebastopol
Six Corners
Tallmadge
Wright
Zealand

Saginaw co.
Bay City
Birch Run
Blumfield
Bridgeport
Bridgeport Centre
Ohessaning

East Saginaw
Frankenlust
Frankenmuth
Jay
Mickleville
Portsmouth
Saginaw (c h)
Saint Charles
Taymouth
Tittabawasee
Zilwaukee

Saint Clair co.
Algonac
Belle River
Brockway
Campbellton
Casco
Casco
China
Clyde Mills
Columbus
Cottrellville
Kenockee
Lake Port
Lynn
Marysville
Merrillsville
Port Huron
Pottersburgh
Ruby
Saint Clair (c h)
Swan Creek
Tara's Hall
Thornton
Wales
West Berlin

Saint Joseph's co.
Burr Oak
Centreville (c h)
Colon
Constantine
Fawn River
Florence
Flowerfield
Howardsville
Leonidas
Mill Creek
Mottville
Nottawa
Oporto
Park
Parkville
Sturgis
Three Rivers
White Pigeon

Sanilac co.,
Buel
Davisville

Farmers
Forest Bay
Forestville
Forrester
Lexington
Puck
Port Sanilac
Sanilac Mills
Stevens' Landing

Shiawassee co.
Antrim
Bennington
Burns
Byron
Corunna (c h)
Enterprise
Fremont
Hartwellville
Hazleton
Maple Valley
Middleburgh
Nebraska
North Vernon
Owasso
Perry
Pittsburgh
Shiawasseetown
Vernon
West Haven
Wheelerville
Woodhull

Tuscola co.
Akron
East Dayton
Fair Grove
Millington
Pine Grove
Sibbiwaing
Vasser
Wahjamega
Watrousville
Worth

Van Buren co.
Arlington
Bloomingdale
Breedsville
Brewerville
Decatur
Hamilton
Hartford
Hunter
Keelersville
Lake Mill
Lawrence
Lawton
Matawan
Paw Paw (c h)

Porter
Prospect Lake
Saint Paul
South Haven
Waverly

Washtenaw co.
Ann Arbor (c h)
Base Lake
Benton
Bridgewater
Chelsea
Dexter
Fredonia
Gravel Run
Iron Creek
Lima
Lodi
Manchester
Paint Creek
Salem
Saline
Scio
Superior
Sylvan
Union District
Webster
Whitmore Lake
York
Ypsilanti

Wayne co.
Belleville
Borodino
Brownstown
Conner's Creek
Dearbornville
Detroit (c h)
East Nankin
Ecorce
Elm
Gibraltar
Greenfield
Grosse Isle
Huron
Livonia Centre
Mead's Mills
Moulin Ridge
Nankin
Northville
Oak
Plank Road
Plymouth
Rawsonville
Redford
Romulus
Smithville
South Plymouth
Trenton
Wayne
Wyandotte

MINNESOTA.

Anoka co.
Anoka
Cedar Valley
Saint Francis
Wenstown

Benton co.
Big Lake
Clear Lake
Itasca
Langola
Princeton
Sauk Rapids
Watab

Big Sioux co.
Sioux Falls City

Blue Earth co.
Butternut Valley
Cereseo
Garden City
Judson
Liberty
Mankato
Mapleton
Shelbyville
South Bend
Tivoli
Vernon
Watanwon
Waverly
Winnebago Agency

Brown co.
Cottonwood
Leavenworth
New Ulm

Pajutasee
Sioux Agency
Wacapa

Carver co.
Camden
Carver
Chaska
Chanhassen
Elm Grove
Scandia
Watertown
Young America

Cass co.
Leaf City
Pakagamon Falls
Wadena

Chisago co.
Amador
Centre City
Chisago City
Middle Branch
Muskootink
Rusheeby
Sunrise City
Taylor's Falls
Wyoming

Crow Wing co.
Crow Wing

Dakotah co.
Castle Rock
Christiania
Empire City
Farmington
Fort Snelling

Hampton
Hastings
Lakeville
Lewiston
Mendota
Nininger
Pine Bend
Rich Valley
Rosemount
Waterford
West Saint Paul

Dodge co.
Ashland
Avon
Berne
Claremont
Concord
Ellington
Hallowell
Hector
Mantorville
Rice Lake
Sacramento
Union Springs
Wasioga

Douglas co.
Alexandria

Faribault co.
Bass Lake
Blue Earth City
Grapeland
Lura
Minnesota Lake
Verona
Winnebago City

Fillmore co.
Alba
Bellville
Bergen
Big Spring
Canfield
Carimona
Chatfield
Cherry Grove
Deer Creek
Elkhorn
Elliotta
Etna
Ettaville
Fairview
Farmer's Grove
Fillmore
Forestville
Free Soil
Granger
Highland
Lenora
Looking Grass
Newburg
Odessa
Peterson
Pilot Mound
Preston
Riceford
Richland
Rushford
Spring Valley
Vailville
Washington
Waukokee

Freeborn co.
Albert Lea
Bancroft
Bear Lake

Buckeye
Clark's Grove
Freeborn
Freeborn Springs
Geneva
Guildford
Hartland
Moscow
Nunda
Oakland
Oakvale
Riceland
St. Nicholas
Shell Rock
Sumner
Trenton

Goodhue co.
Cannon River Falls
Central Point
Crystal Springs
Fair Point
Feather Stone
Florence
Goodhue Centre
Hader
Kenyon
Miami
Norway
Pine Island
Poplar Grove
Red Wing
Roscoe
Spencer
Stanton
Sunapec
Waconta
Wanamingo
Wastedo

Westervelt
Zumbrota

Hennepin co.
Bloomington
Champlin
Crystal Lake
Dayton
Eden Prairie
Excelsior
Fremont
Greenwood
Harmony
Harrisburgh
Island City
Leighton
Maple Plain
Medicine Lake
Minneapolis
Minnetonka
Osseo
Perkinsville
St. Anthony Falls
Tamarack
Wyzata

Houston co.
Brownsville
Caledonia
Dodham
Freeburgh
Hackett's Grove
Hokah
Houston
La Crescent
La Villa
Lorettee
Looneyville
Money Creek

Mississippi.

Portland
Riceford
San Jacinto
Sheldon
Spring Grove
Union
Winnebago Valley
Yucatan

Isanti co.
Cambridge
Spencer Brook

Jackson co.
Jackson

Lake co.
Burlington

Le Sueur co.
Anawauk
Cleveland
Cordova
Elysian
German Lake
Gorman
Hillsdale
Kasota
Kilkenny
Lanesburgh
Le Sueur
Le Sueur City
Lexington
Marysburg
Maylardsville
Oral
Ottawa
Waterville
West Troy

Manomin co
Manomin

Martin co.
Chain Lake Centre
Fairmount
Lake Puzah

McLeod co.
Cedar
Glencoe
Glendale
Hutcherson
Plato
Winsted

Meeker co.
Acton
Forest City

Green Lake
Harrison
Kingston
Mananah

Midway co
Medary

Monongalia co
Irving

Morrison co.
Belle Prairie
Granite City
Langola
Little Falls
Swan River

Mower co.
Austin
Frankford
Grand Meadow
Lansing
Le Roy
Madison
Mineral Springs
Mower City
Nevada
Pleasant Valley

Nicolet co.
Hebron
Hilo
La Fayette
Nicolett
Oshaway
Red Stone
Saint Peter
Swan City
Travers des Sioux

Olmsted co.
Bear Grove
Dover
Fairfield
Greenfield
High Forest
Kalmar
Marion
New Haven
Oronoco
Pleasant Grove
Quincy
Rochester
Rock Dell
Salem
Stewartville
Waterloo
Zumbro

Pembina co.
Leech Lake
Pembina
Saint Josephs

Pierce co.
Fort Ridgely

Pine co.
Chengwatana

Ramsey co.
Centerville
Columbus
Howard's Lake
Little Canada
Mound's View
Oak Grove
Otter Lake
Roseville
St. Paul (c h)
White Bear Lake

Rice co.
Cannon City
Chester
Dundas
East Prairie
Faribault
Fowlersville
Hazelwood
Millersburg
Morristown
Northfield
Shieldsville
Union Lakes
Walcott
Warsaw
Wheatland

Scott co.
Bellefontaine
Belle Plaine
Cedar Lake
Helena
Louisville
New Dublin
St. Lawrence
Sand Creek
Shakopee

Sherburne co.
Brantford
Clear Lake
East Monticello

Elk River
Orlando
Santiago

Sibley co.
Arlington
Dryden
Eagle City
Faxon
Henderson
Jessen Land
Johnatown
Kelso
New Auburn

Stearns co.
Clinton
Cold Spring City
Kennebec
Marysville
Neenah
Paynesville
Rockville
St. Augusta
Sauk Centre
Saint Cloud
Torah
Woodstock
Yarmouth

Steele co.
Aurora Centre
Berlin
Clinton Falls
Cooleysville
Deerfield
Dodge City
Elwood
Juno
Lemond
Medford
Meriden
Oak Glen
Owatatauna (c h)
St. Marys
Somerset
Swavesey

St. Louis co.
Buchanan
Duluth
Fon du Lac
Oneota

Superior co.
Beaver Bay
Grand Portage

Todd co.
Long Prairie

Toombs co.
Breckinridge
Otter Tail City
Waseata

Wabashaw co.
Bear Valley
Cook's Valley
Elgin
Forest Mound
Greenville
Hyde Park
Independence
Jacksonville
Lake City
Mazeppa
Minniski
Mt. Pleasant
Plain View
Pleasant Prairie
Reed's Landing
Smithfield
South Troy
Toepeeotah
Wabashaw
Wantopa
West Albany

Wahnahta co.
Fort Ripley

Waseca co.
Iosco
Janesville
Maxson Grove
Okaman
Otisco
Silver Lake
Vivian
Wilton

Washington co.
Afton
Cottage Grove
Dolphin
Gray Cloud
Lake Land
Marine Mills
Milton Mills
Newport
Oakdale
Point Douglass

MISSISSIPPI.

Adams co.
Jackson Point
Kingston
Natchez
Washington (c h)

Amite co.
Armstead
Centreville
Jacksonwood
Liberty (c h)
Rose Hill
Smithdale
Toler's
Wall's Store
Zion Hill

Attala co.
Attalaville
Bluff Springs
Burkittsville
Centre
Cuba
Edgefield
Kosciusko (c h)
Muttona Springs
Newtonville
Rocky Point
Wells

Bolivar co.
Boulah
Bolivar (c h)
Carson's Landing
Concordia
Glencoe
Miles' Landing
Prentiss
Rosedale
Victoria

Calhoun co.
Benela
Big Creek
Cherry Hill
Concord
Erin
Hopewell
Pittsborough
Sabougiy
Sarepta
Short Branch
Slate Spring

Carroll co.
Black Hawk
Carrollton (c h)
Ceralvo
Duck Hill
Gorenton
Greenwood
Hays Creek
Jefferson
Last Chance
Leflora
Middleton
Providence
Shongalo
Sidon
Smith's Mills
Valley Hill

Chickasaw co.
Buena Vista
Dalton
Dix Creek
Hohenlinden
Houlka
Houston (c h)
Montpelier
Okolona
Palo Alto
Pikeville
Prairie Mount
Sparta

Choctaw co.
Bankston
Bellefontaine
Bywyah
Cadereta
Dido
Fame
French Camps
Grahamsville
Greensborough (c h)
Green's × Roads
Huntsville
Kilmichael
Little Black
Lodi
Monte Vista
Oakley
Pigeon Roost
Poplar Creek
Saowville
Stateland
Steam Mill
White Hill
Wilcox

Claiborne co.
Grand Gulf
Grindstone Ford
Oakland College
Port Gibson (c h)
Rocky Spring

Clark co.
Beaverdam
De Soto
Enerzy
Enterprise
Mackaville
Quitman
Shoobota

Coahoma co.
Delta

Friar's Point
Hopson's
Mound Place
Robsou's Landing
Shufordsville
Sunflower Landing
Swan Lake

Copiah co.
Dahala
Burtonton
Caseyville
Crystal Springs
Gallatin
Georgetown
Hazle Hurst
Linden
Mount Hope
Pearl River
Pine Bluff
Pine Ridge
Rockport
Saudifer's Mills

Covington co.
Dry Creek
Jaynesville
Mount Carmel
Mt. Olive
Oakohay
Santee
Wilkesburg
Williamsburgh (c h)
Zion Seminary

De Soto co.
Areabutla
Centre Hill
Cockrum
Crockett
Elm Grove
Flewellin's × Roads
Greenleaf

Harkleroad
Hernando (c h)
Horn Lake
Looxahoma
Olive Branch
Pleasant Hill
Senatahoba

Franklin co.
Friendship
Hamburg
Homochitto
Knoxville
Little Spring
McCall's Creek
McRosville
Meadville (c h)
Veto

Greene co.
Adamsville
Buck Creek
Leakesville
McLeod's
Vernal

Hancock co.
Beppo
Gainesville
Habolochitto
Pearlington
Pinetucky
Riceville
Shieldsboro' (c h)

Harrison co.
Biloxi
Flint Creek
Handsboro
Mississippi City
Pass Christian
Rescue
Rosales

Missouri.   405

La Fayette co.
Abbeville
Banner
Caswell
College Hill
Dallas
Delay
La Fayette Springs
Liberty Hill
Maple Springs
Oxford (c h)
Paris
Spring Dale
Taylor's Depot
Wyatt

Lauderdale co.
Alamutcha
Battlefield
Chunkeyville
Daleville
Hurricane Creek
Lauderdale Springs
Marion (c h)
Marion Station
Markwell
Meridian
Oakatibbe
Rawsonville
Sookalena
Spring's Depot
Why Not
Zero

Lawrence co.
Brookhaven
Fair River
Monticello (c h)
Oakvale
Rayville
White Sand

Leake co.
Carthage (c h)
Edinburgh
Good Hope
High Hill
Pensacola
Standing Pine
Thomastown
Walnut Grove
Yorka

Lowndes co.
Caledonia
Columbus (c h)
Crawfordsville
Mayhew's Station
Tibby Station
Toland's Depot
Vinton
Waverly
West Point

Madison co.
Battle Springs
Beatie's Bluff
Calhoun
Camden
Canton (c h)
Kirkwood
Livingston
Madisonville
Sharon
Sulphur Springs
Vernon
Way's Bluff

Marion co.
Columbia (c h)
Fordsville
Rocky Hill
Sandy Ridge
Spring Cottage

Marshall co.
Bethlehem
Byhalia
Chulahoma
Cold Water
Cornersville
Early Grove
Holly Springs
Hudsonville
Lamar
Moody
North Mt. Pleasant
Oak Grove
Pink Hill
Seales
Snow Creek
Tacaluche
Tallaloosa (c h)
Tiro
Wall Hill
Waterford
Watson's

Monroe co.
Aberdeen
Ashland
Athens
Buttahatchie
Camargo
Cotton Gin Port
Hamilton (c h)
Mormon Springs
Quincy
Smithville
Splung
Temperance Hill

Neshoba co.
Coffadeliah
Dixon
Herbert
Hill's Bluff
Laurel Hill
Neshoba Springs
Pearl Valley
Philadelphia

Newton co.
Conehatta
County Line
Decatur (c h)
Evergreen
New Ireland
Union

Noxubee co.
Armitage
Barry
Bigbee Valley
Brooksville
Cooksville
Gholson
Macon
Mashulaville
Parkeville
Prairie Point
Shuqualak

Oktibbehah co.
Ash Creek
Cedar Bluff
Choctaw Agency
Double Springs

Hickory Grove
Line Creek
Long Branch
Siloam
Starkville (c h)
Steelsville
Tampico
Whitefield

Panola co.
Batesville
Byaum's Creek
Central Academy
Como Depot
Eureka
Keel Boat
Longtown
Panola (c h)
Peach Creek
Pleasant Mount
Robinia
Sardis
Springport

Perry co.
Augusta (c h)
Carlile's Mills
Enon
Monroe
Try Again

Pike co.
Bogue Chitto
China Grove
Conerly's
Holmesville (c h)
Magnolia
Osyka
Summit

Pontotoc co.
Bartersville
Birmingham
Buncomb
Cherry Creek
Chesterville
Coonewar
Corona
Ellistown
Fredonia
Harrisburgh
New Albany
Oak Hill
Oldtown Creek
Palmetto
Pontocola
Pontotoc
Poplar Spring
Raudolph
Red Land
Rocky Ford
Tallbencia
Tardyville
Toccopola
Turkland
Wallersville

Rankin co.
Brandon (c h)
Cato
Goshen Springs
Monterey
Orion
Pulahatches
Pilahatchee
Steen's Creek

Scott co.
Damaseus
Hillsboro' (c h)

Homewood
Ludlow
Morton
Sebastopol
Sherman Hill

Simpson co.
Harrisville
Mount Zion
New Dublin
Old Hickory
Saunders' Creek
Westville (c h)

Smith co.
Bunker Hill
Flower's Place
Pineville
Raleigh
Taylorsville
Trenton

Sunflower co.
McNutt
Shell Mound
Spring Bluff

Tallahatchee c.
Big Mound
Charleston
Eolia
Mitchell's X Roads
Tuscahoma

Tippah co.
Canaan
Claysville
Cotton Plant
Dumas
Hickory Flat
Irene
Jonesborough
Lebanon
McLean's Store
Molino
Orizaba
Pleasant Ridge
Ripley
Ruckersville
Salem
Shelby Creek
Spring Hill
Silver Springs
Union Mills

Tishemingo co.
Barne's Store
Bay Springs
Big Spring
Black Land
Bone Yard
Burnsville
Burton's
Cairo
Cane Creek
Carolina
Carrollsville
Cartersville
Corinth
Cripple Deer
Cross Ridge
Danville
Dry Run
Eastport
Farmington
Hazle Green
Hickory Plains
Highland
Iuka

Jacinto (c h)
Kossuth
Rienzi
Tripoli

Tunica co.
Anderson
Austin (c h)

Warren co.
Bethesda
Bovina
Cardiff
Hurricane
Ingraham
Villdalo
Vicksburgh (c h)
Warrenton

Washington co.
Egg's Point
Greenville (c h)
Point Worthington
Princeton (c h)

Wayne co.
Brotherton
Bucatta
Miltonville
State Line Station
Waynesborough
Winchester (c h)

Wilkinson co.
Buffalo
Cold Spring
Fort Adams
Holly Retreat
Hopewell Church
Newtonia
Perey's Creek
Woodville (c h)

Winston co.
Ashfordsville
Buckhorn
Fearn's Springs
Louisville (c h)
New Prospect
Noxapater
Plattsburgh
Randall's Bluffs
Rome
Singleton
Webster

Yalobusha co.
Coffeeville (c h)
Cole's Creek
Cuddyhunk
Gatewood
Graysport
Gronada
Jones' Mills
Mount Nubo
Oakachickama
Oakland
Pine Valley
Post Oak
Preston
Troy
Water Valley

Yazoo co.
Benton
Cypress
Deasonville
Dover
Satartia
Yazoo City

MISSOURI.

Atchison co.
Allena
Center Grove
El Paso
Irish Grove
Linden
North Star
Rich
Rockport

Audrian co.
Hickory Creek
John's Branch
Littleby
Loutre
Mexico (c h)
Salt River
Young's Creek

Barry co.
Cassville
Clay Hill
Flat Creek

Gadfly
Hazle Bottom
McDowell
Roaring River
Washbourn Prairie

Barton co.
Bakers Grove
Lamar
Horse Creek

Bates co.
Butler
Cove Creek
Crescent Hill
Elk Fork
Fancy Hill
Johnstown
Little Osage
Marvel
Papinsville
Pleasant Gap
Prairie City
Spruce
West Point

Benton co.
Bishop's Store
Boyler's Mill
Cole Camp
Colerain
Duroc
Haw Creek
Leasley
Mount View
Prairie Lea
Warsaw (c h)

Bollinger co.
Beseville
Buchanan
Castor
Greeno
Paton
Perkins Creek
White Water

Boone co.
Ashland
Centralia

Claysville
Columbia (c h)
Eureka
Germantown
Grand View
Hallsville
Providence
Rocheport
Rome
Sturgeon

Buchanan co.
Birming
De Kalb
Easton
Platte River
Rockhouse Pairie
Rushville
Saint Joseph
Sparta (c h)
Walnut Hill

Butler co.
Braunmsburgh
Cane Creek
Poplar Bluff (c h)

Caldwell co.
Grand River
Hamilton
Kingston (c h)
Mirabile

Callaway co.
Boydville
Concord
Cote Sans Dessein
Fulton (c h)
Hibernia
Jones' Tan Yard
Millersburg
New Bloomfield
Pierce
Portland
Readsville
Reform
Saint Aubert
Shamrock
Springfield's Store
Williamsburgh

Missouri.

Camden co.
Cave Pump
Cherry
Green Dale
Linn Creek
Little Niangua
Max Creek
Might Point
Toronto
Tuckerville
Wet Glaze
Whitesburgh

Cape Girardeau co.
Appleton
Cape Girardeau
Gravel Road
Hickory Ridge
Jackson (c h)
Oak Ridge
People's
Pocahontas
Sheffield

Carroll co.
Carrollton (c h)
De Witt
Mills' Landing
Mandeville
Manlius
Miles Point
Newport
Pleasant Park
San Francisco
Tagart's Mill

Cass co.
Austin
Cause Prairie
Dayton
Everett
Harrisonville (c h)
Jonesville
Morristown
Ovid
Pleasant Hill
Plum Grove
Rockford
Rural Home
Wadesburg

Cedar co.
Bear Creek
Brown
Cane Hill
Clintonville
Coplinger's Mills
Eaton
Hall's Point
Mule Creek
Rector's Store
Silver Creek
Stockton
White Hare

Chariton co.
Brunswick
Bynumville
Elk Spring
Keytesville (c h)
Westland

Clarks co.
Acasta
Alexandria
Ashton
Athens
Bonita
Cahoka
Chambersburg
Eldorado
Fairmount
Fenkeville
Saint Francisville
St. Patrick
Sugar Creek
Waterloo (c h)
Winchester
Wrightville

Clay co.
Barry
Kendall
Liberty (c h)
Missouri City
Paradise
Smithville

Clinton co.
Beehive
Cameron
Carpenter's Store
Castile
Hainesville
Plattsburg (c h)
Plum Creek

Cole co.
Brazito
Elston Station
Hickory Hill
Jefferson City
Look Out
Marion (c h)
Osage City
Osage Bluff
Russelville
St. Thomas
Stringtown
Taos

Cooper co.
Bell Air
Bullingsville
Boonville (c h)
Clark's Fork
Coal Bank
Cold Neck
Connor's Mills
Fair Point
Gooch's Mill
La Mine
Midway
Otterville
Pilot Grove
Pisgah
Pleasant Green
Round Hill
Syracuse
Vermont

Crawford co.
Amanda
Argo
Avery
Bourbon
Elm Grove
Harrison's Mills
High Grove
Knob View
Little Prairie
Maramec
Osage
Steelsville (c h)

Dade co.
Dadeville
Greenfield (c h)
King's Point
Rock Prairie
Sons Creek
Turnback

Dallas co.
Buffalo
Cross Plains
Long Lane
Louisburg
Paseo
Shady Grove
Spring Grove
Urbana

Daviess co.
Cravensville
Crittenden
Gallatin (c h)
Jamesport
Pattonsburg
Victoria

De Kalb co.
Roxford
Grindstone Point
Locust
Maysville (c h)
Osborn
Stewartsville
Third Fork

Dent co.
Dent (c h)
Lake Spring
Sarvis Spring
Short Bend
Sylvan
Winston

Dodge co.
St. John

Dunklin co.
Beech
Chillitecaux
Four Mile
West Prairie

Franklin co.
Berger
Beaufort
Boone
Beouff Creek
Burbois
Calvy
Campbellton (c h)
Cedar Fork
Dry Branch
Dundee

Gray's Summit
Grubville
Iron Hill
Jeffriesburgh
Labaddie
Mount Helicon
New Haven
Oakfield
Pacific
Port Hudson
Rucker's Prairie
Shotwell
South Point
Stanton Copper Mines
St. Clair
Union
Virginia
Young's Mills

Gasconade co.
Bem
Canaan
Delphi
Gall's Prairie
Gasconade Ferry
Hermann
Jake's Prairie
Leander
Mount Sterling
Oak Hill
Owensville
Woollam

Gentry co.
Alanthus Grove
Albany
Allendale
Douglas
Gentryville
Grant's Hill
Hugginsville
Liland City
Lot's Grove
New Castle
Philander
Rose Hill
Sampson Creek
Smithton
Yolo

Greene co.
Ash Grove
Bowark
Crab Tree
Fair Grove
Henderson's
Hickory Barren
Kenton
Little York
Ozark
Pallas
Richland
Springfield (c h)
Walnut Forest
Walnut Grove
White Oak Grove
Willard
Wilson Creek

Grundy co.
Alpha
Buttsville
Edinburg
Hickory Port
Howard Corner
Lyndley
Perkins' Grove
Trenton

Harrison co.
Atlanta
Bethany (c h)
Blue Ridge
Eagle
Jay
Pleasant Ridge
Snell's Mill
Trail Creek
Woodbine

Henry co.
Bolton
Browning's Ferry
Cainsville
Calhoun
Clinton
Deep Water
Huntingdale
Leesville
Lucas
Norris Fork
Roscoe
Shawnee Mound
Toledo
Windsor
Zion

Hickory co.
Black Oak Point
Bledsoe
Cornersville
Cross Timbers
Elkton
Hermitage (c h)
Pittsburgh
Quiney

Holt co.
Forest City
Jones 'Point
Lowell
North Point
Olive Branch
Oregon (c h)
Rushbottom

Howard co.
Boon's Lick
Fayette (c h)
Franklin (c h)
Glasgow
Land Mark
Myers

Howell co.
Fulton Valley
Lost Camp
West Plains

Iron co.
Ironton (c h)
Marble Creek
Middlebrook
Pilot Knob
Pine Grove

Jackson co.
Big Cedar
Blue Springs
Cogswell's Landing
Independence (c h)
Kansas
Lone Jack
New Santa Fee
Oak Grove
Pink Hill
Sibley's
Stony Point
Westport

Jasper co.
Blytheville
Breckenridge
Carthage (c h)
Coon Creek
Diamond Grove
Dogwood Grove
Dry Fork
Fidelity
French Point
Jasper
Joka
Mudoc
Minersville
Port Royal
Sarcoxie
Sherwood
Valley Forge

Jefferson co.
Avoca
Dolew's Creek
De Soto
Hematite
High Ridge
Hillsborough Station
Hillsborough (c h)
Isle au Bois
Jefferson Mills
Kimmswick
Morse's Mill
Pevely
Platin
Sandy Mines
Sulphur Springs Landing
Tyro

Johnson co.
Basin Knob
Big Creek
Chilhower
Columbus
Cornelia
Fayetteville
Hayden
Globe
Holden
Kingsville
Knobnoster
Milford
Post Oak
Prairie Home
Sissonville
Warrensburgh (c h)
Wall's Store

Knox co.
Bee Ridge
Colony
Edina
Goodland
Greensburgh
Locust Hill
Millport
Muddy Fork
Newark
Novelty

Laclede co.
Brush Creek
Competition
Dry Glaze
Forkner's Hill
Hazle Green
Jericho
Lebanon
May Apple
Oakland
Osage Fork
Sharon

La Fayette co.
Afrek
Berlin
Chapel Hill
Cooke's Store
Dover
Elk Grove
Freedom
Greenton
Hempland
Lexington (c h)
Moss
Napoleon City
Renick's Mills
Snibar
Tabo
Wagon Knob
Waverly
Wellington

Lawrence co.
Bower's Mills
Centre Creek
Chesapeake
Dunkle's Store
Hall
Kain
Long Hollow
Mount Vernon
Phelps
Spring River
Verona

Lewis co.
Bunker Hill
Canton
Deer Ridge
Durgan's Creek
La Belle
La Grange
Monticello (c h)
Oyster
Primrose
Williamstown

Lincoln co.
Auburn
Cap au Gris
Chantilly
Cuivre
Hawk Point
Lost Branch
Lost Creek
Louisville
Millwood
New Hope
Old Alexandria
Troy (c h)
Truxton

Linn co.
Laceledo
Linnæus (c h)
North Cutt
North Salem
Saint Catherine
Salem
Wyandott

Livingston co.
Austinsville
Bedford
Chillicothe (c h)
Culliersville
Dawn
Dido
Grassy Creek
Livingston
Spring Hill
Utica

McDonald co.
Beaver Spring
Bethpage
Elk Mills
Enterprise
Erie
Honey Creek
Pineville
Loomiesville
Rutledge (c h)
Shell's Mills
White Rock Prairi

Macon co.
Berier
Bloomington (c h)
Callao
Carbon
College Mound
Coulter's Store
East Fork
Economy
La Plata
Macon City
New Boston
Newburgh
Pankas
Rice's Ferry
Stockton
Ten Mile
Tullvania
Woodville

Madison co.
Brunot
Fredricktown (c h)
Mine La Motte

Marion co.
Dear Creek
Brookville
Emerson
Hannibal
Hanson
Hester
Marion City
Nelsonville
Palmyra
Philadelphia
Sharpsburg
Warren
West Ely

Maries co.
Bloom Garden
Clifty Dale
Flat Woods
Lacoa
Painswick
Pay Down
Vienna

Mercer co.
Goshen
Mercer
Middlebury
Modesta
Princeton (c h)
Ravanna
Rosemont
Saline

Miller co.
Iberia
Pleasant Farm
Pleasant Mount
Rocky Mount
Tuscumbia (c h)
Ulman's Ridge

Mississippi co.
Birdsville
Charleston
Hopewell
Rush Ridge
Wolf Island

Moniteau co.
California
Clarksburgh
Cold Springs
Felix
High Point
Jamestown
Oak Point
Tipton

Monroe co.
Crooked Creek
Florida
Granville
Indian Creek
Long Branch
Madison
Middle Grove
Paris (c h)

New Hampshire.

Santa Fe
Somerset
Woodlawn

Montgomery co.
Big Spring
Danville (c h)
Elk Horn
Flint Point
Green Hill
High Hill
Lead Creek
Middletown
Montgomery City
New Florence
Prairie Fork
Price's Branch
Rhineland
Stockland
Tiviot
Wellsville

Morgan co.
Dogwood Grove
Florence
Lone Grove
Minerva
Mining
Stone House
Syracuse
Versailles (c h)
Wheatland

New Madrid co.
New Madrid (c h)
Ogden
Point Pleasant

Newton co.
Almeda
Capp's Creek
Cedar Creek
Gates
Grandby
Grand Falls
Jones Creek
Juliru
Kent
Neosho (c h)
Newtonia

Noddaway co.
Graham
Guilford
Hallsa's Ferry
Littsville
Maryville
Narrows
Reindeer
Sweet Home
White Cloud
Xenia

Oregon co.
Birch Tree
Huddleston
Jobe
Low Wassie
Mammoth Spring
Thomasville (c h)
Warm Fork
Webster
Woodside

Osage co.
Bailey's Creek
Bonnots
Castle Rock
Chamois
Fredericksburg
Lane's Prairie
Linn (c h)
Lisle
Loose Creek

Medora
Prior's Mill
Rich Fountain
Wallace's Landing
Westphalia

Ozark co.
Gowskin
Forest Store
Helen
Isabella
Mulissa
Red Bud
Rockbridge (c h)
Saint Leger
Selden

Pemiscot co.
Caruthersville
Cottonwood Point
Gayoso (c h)
Solitude

Perry co.
Altenburg
Perryville

Pettis co.
Arator
Crane Creek
Dunksburg
Fairview
Georgetown (c h)
Green Ridge
Lamonte
Longwood
Priceville
Rowletta
Spring Fork
Spring Garden

Pike co.
Ashley
Ashburn
Bowling Green
Charlemont
Clarkesville
Frankford
Louisiana
New Harmony
Paynesville
Prairie Mound
Prairieville
Spencerburgh
Vannoy's Mill

Platte co.
Camden Point
Farley
Hampton (c h)
Jatan
New Market
Parkville
Platte City (c h)
Ridgley
Union Mills
Weston

Polk co.
Bolivar (c h)
Brighton
Fair Play
Half Way
Humansville
Orleans
Rondo
Sentinel Prairie

Pulaski co.
De Bruin
Humbolt
Little Piney
Nebo
Relfe

Spring Creek
Waynesville (c h)

Putnam co.
Ayersville
Chariton Mills
Hartford
Locustville
Martinstown
Mendota
Newtown
Pleasant Home
Scotland Ridge
Shoneytown
Springville
St. John
Unionville
West Liberty

Quapaw co.
Crawford Seminary

Ralls co.
Cincinnati
Hydesburgh
Lick Creek
Madisonville
New London (c h)
Pigeon Creek
Saverton
Sidney

Randolph co.
Allen
Darksville
Fort Henry
Huntsville
Jacksonville
Milton
Randolph
Roanoke

Ray co.
Camden
Crab Orchard
Hardin
Knoxville
McClain's Mills
Millville
Otsego
Prospect Hill
Richmond (c h)
Tinney's Grove

Reynolds co.
Alamode
Centreville
Egg Hill
Lesterville
Logan's Creek
Munger's Mill

Ripley co.
Doniphan (c h)
Dry Spring
Gutewood
Little Black
Martinsburg
Mill Creek
Neelyville
Pike Creek
Van Buren

St. Charles co.
Augusta
Cottleville
Femme Osage
Flint Hill
Hamburg
Hickory Grove
Missourian
Naylor's Store
New Melle
Oakwood
O'Fallon
Portage des Sioux

Saint Charles (c h)
St. Peter
Snow Hill
Wellsbargh
Wentyville

St. Clair co.
Chalk Level
Howard's Mills
Hoyle's Creek
Jenkin's Bridge
Monagan
Oseola
Pleasant Sight
Weaubleau

St. Francois co.
Big River Mills
Black Wells Station
Blairsville
Cross Roads
Farmington (c h)
French Village
Hasie Run Mills
Iron Mountain
Locust Ridge
Silver Spring
Stono

St. Genevieve co.
Avon
New Bremen
Plank Road
Punjaub
St. Genevieve (c h)
Saint Marys'

St. Louis co.
Allenton
Barrett's Station
Bellemoute
Bonhomme
Bridgeton
Carondelet
Central
Cheltenham
Creve Cœur
Des Peres
Ellisville
Fee Fee
Fenton
Florisant
Fox Creek
Glencoe
Jefferson Barracks
Kirkwood
Manchester
Matese
Melrose
Normandy
Rock Hill
Saint Louis (c h)
Sappington
Waltonham

Saline co.
Arrow Rock
Brownsville
Bryan
Cambridge
Cow Creek
Elm Wood
Finney's Creek
Hazle Grove
Jonesboro'
Marshall (c h)
Miami
Petra
Ridge Prairie
South Grove

Schuyler co.
Cherry Grove
Green Top
Inkerman

Lancaster (c h)
Pedee

Scotland co.
Arbela
Bible Grove
Billupsville
Etna
Laura
Memphi
Middle Fable
Pleasant Retreat
Prospect Grove
Sand Hill
Unity
Wyaconda

Scott co.
Benton (c h)
Commerce
Cypress
Kelso
Pleasant Plains
Price's Landing

Seneca co.
Looniesville

Shannon co.
Eminence (c h)
Hanpeck
Pine Hill
Richmond Hill
Willow Spring

Shelby co.
Bethel
Clarence
Cherry Box
Hagor's Grove
Hawkins' Store
Lakeland
Lakeman
Oakdale (c h)
Shelbyville
Shelbina
Tiger Fork
Walkersville
West Springfield

Stoddard co.
Augusta
Bloomfield
Indian Ford
Lakeville
Piketon

Stone co
Curran
Galena (c h)
Robertson's Mill

Sullivan co.
Bairdstown
Green Castle
Jackson Corners
Kiddville
Milan
Owasco
Pennville
Scottsville
Vulparaiso
West Locust
Wintersville

Taney co.
Arno
Bald Knob
Banff
Big Beaver
Bull Mills
Forsyth (c h)
Swan Creek
Taney City

Texas co.
Blooming Rose
Casto Valley
Cedar Bluff
Ellsworth
Hickory Springs
Houston (c h)
Jack's Fork
Licking
Montauk
Plato
Plum Valley
Roubidoux
Stanford

Vernon co.
Deerfield
Dry Wood
Hardwood
Montevallo
Nevada

Warren co.
Brandt's Rock
Spring
Camp Branch
Holstein
Loutre Island
Marthasville
Pinckney
Pin Oak
Pitts
Warrenton (c h)
Wright City

Washington co.
Boyer
Cadet
Caledonia
Fourche a Renault
Harmony
Hopewell Furnace
Irondale
Mineral Point
Old Mines
Potosi (c h)
Richwoods
Rock Spring

Wayne co.
Brunot
Cold Water
Greenville (c h)
Greenwood Valley
Lowndes
Otter Creek
Patterson

Webster co.
Bristol
Dallas
Finley
Marshfield
Mornington
Norma
Orr
Panther Valley
St. Luke
St. Mark
St. Paul
Waldo

Wright co.
Alma
Astoria
Cave Spring
Hartsville (c h)
Hazelwood
Mint Spring
Pleasant Valley
Sacramento
Whetstone
Wolf Creek
Woodbury
Wood's Fork

NEW HAMPSHIRE.

Belknap co.
Alton
Barnstead
Centre Barnstead
Centre Harbor
East Sanbornton
Gilford Village
Gilmanton
Gilmanton Iron Works

Laconia (c h)
Lake Village
Lower Gilmanton
Meredith Centre
Meredith Village
New Hampton
North Barnstead
North Sanbornton
Sanbornton
Sanbornton Bridge
Upper Gilmanton

Weir's Bridge
West Alton

Carroll co.
Bartlett
Brookfield
Centre Conway
Centre Ossipee
Centre Sandwich
Conway
East Madison

East Moultonboro'
East Wakefield
Easton Centre
Effingham
Effingham Falls
Freedom
Horn's Mills
Leighton's Corners
Lower Bartlett
Mackerel Corner
Madison

Melvin Village
Moultonboro'
North Conway
North Sandwich
North Wakefield
North Wolfboro'
Ossipee (c h)
Sandwich
South Tamworth
South Wolfboro'
Tamworth

Tamworth Iron Works
Tuftonboro'
Union
Wakefield
Water Village
West Ossipee
Wolfboro'
Wolfboro' Centre

Cheshire co.
Alstead

New Jersey.

Ashuelot
Chesterfield
Chesterfield Factory
Drewsville
Dublin
East Jaffrey
East Sullivan
East Westmoreland
Fitzwilliam
Gilsum
Harrisville
Hinsdale
Jaffrey
Keene (c h)
Marlboro'
Marlboro' Depot
Marlow
Munsonville
Nelson
New Alstead
North Richmond
Paper Mill Village
Pottersville
Richmond
Rindge
South Stoddard
Stoddard
Sullivan
Surry
Swanzey
Troy
Walpole
Westmoreland
Westmoreland Depot
Westport
West Swanzey
Winchester
Coos co.
Berlin
Berlin Falls
Carroll
Clarksville
Colebrook
Columbia
Coos
Crawford's House
Dalton
Errol
Gorham
Groveton
Jackson
Jefferson
Lancaster (c h)
Milan

Northumberland
Pittsburgh
Randolph
Shelburn
Stark
Stewartstown
Stratford
Wentworth's Location
West Stewartson
Whitefield
West Milan
White Mountain House
Grafton co.
Alexandria
Bath
Benton
Bethlehem
Bridgewater
Bristol
Campton
Campton Village
Canaan
Danbury
Dorchester
East Canaan
East Haverhill
East Landaff
East Lebanon
Ellsworth
Enfield
Enfield Centre
Flume
Franconia
Grafton
Grafton Centre
Groton
Hanover
Hanover Centre
Haverhill (c h)
Haverhill Centre
Hebron
Hill
Holderness
Landaff
Lebanon
Lincoln
Lisbon
Littleton
Lyman
Lyme
Monroe
North Dorchester
North Groton
North Haverhill

North Lisbon
North Littleton
North Monroe
Orford
Orfordville
Piermont
Plymouth (c h)
Profile House
Rumney
South Danbury
Sugar Hill
Thornton
Warren
Wentworth
West Campton
West Canaan
West Enfield
West Lebanon
West Littleton
West Plymouth
West Rumney
West Thornton
Woodstock
Hillsboro' co.
Amherst (c h)
Amoskeag
Antrim
Bedford
Bennington
Brookline
Deering
East Weare
Francistown
Goffstown
Goffstown Centre
Greenfield
Hancock
Hillsboro'
Hillsboro' Bridge
Hillsboro' Centre
Hollis
Hudson
Lyndeboro'
Manchester
Mason
Mason Village
Milford
Mount Vernon
Nashua
New Boston
New Ipswich
North Branch
North Lyndeboro
North Weare
Oil Mill Village

Pelham
Peterboro'
Reed's Ferry
South Lyndeboro'
South Merrimack
South Weare
Temple
Thornton's Ferry
Weare
West Wilton
Wilton
Merrimack co.
Allenstown
Andover
Boscawen
Bow
Bradford
Canterbury
Chichester
Concord (c h)
Contoocook Village
Dunbarton
East Andover
East Concord
Epsom
Fisherville
Franklin
Henniker
Hooksett
Hopkinton
Loudon
Loudon Centre
Loudon Ridge
Mast Yard
Newbury
New London
North Chichester
North Dunbarton
Northfield Depot
North Sutton
Pembroke
Pittsfield
Rowe's Corner
Salisbury
Shaker Village
South Bradford
South Newbury
Suncook
Sutton
Warner
West Andover
West Boscawen
West Concord
West Henniker

West Hopkinton
West Salisbury
Wilmot
Wilmot Flat
Rockingham co.
Atkinson
Atkinson Depot
Auburn
Brentwood
Candia
Candia Village
Chester
Danville
Deerfield
Deerfield Centre
Derry
East Chester
East Kingston
East Northwood
Epping
Exeter (c h)
Fessenden Mills
Fremont
Greenland
Greenland Depot
Hampstead
Hampton
Hampton Falls
Kensington
Kingston
Londonderry
Newington
New Market
Newton
North Hampton
North Hampton Depot
North Londonderry
North Salem
Nottingham
Nottingham Turnpike
Plaistow
Portsmouth (c h)
Raymond
Rye
Salem
Sandown
Seabrook
South Deerfield
South Hampton
South Kingston
South New Market
Stratham
West Northwood

West Windham
Windham
Strafford co.
Barrington
Centre Strafford
Dover (c h)
Downing's Mills
Durham
Farmington
Gonic
Great Falls
Lee
Madbury
Middleton
Milton
Milton Mills
North Barrington
North Strafford
Rochester
Salmon Falls
Strafford
Strafford Blue Hill
Strafford Corner
Wadley's Falls
West Milton
Sullivan co.
Acworth
Charlestown
Claremont
Cornish Flat
Croydon
Croydon Flat
East Lempster
East Plainfield
East Unity
East Washington
George's Mills
Goshen
Grantham
Langdon
Lempster
Meriden
Mill Village
Newport (c h)
North Charlestown
North Grantham
Plainfield
South Acworth
South Charlestown
Springfield
Sunapee
Unity
Washington
West Claremont
West Springfield

NEW JERSEY.

Atlantic co.
Absecon
Atlantic City
Bargaintown
Decosta
Egg Harbor City
Leed's Point
May's Landing (c h)
Port Republic
Smith's Landing
Somer's Point
Weymouth

Bergen co.
Carlstadt
English Neighborhood
Fort Lee
Godwinville
Hackensack (c h)
Hohokus
Lodi
Pasknck
Ramsey's
Saddle River
Schraalenburgh
Spring Valley

Burlington co.
Arneytown
Batsto
Beverly
Bordentown
Bridgeboro'
Brown's Mills
Burlington
Cinnaminson
Columbus
Cookstown
Crosswicks
Crowleyville
Delanco
Fellowship

Florence
Georgetown
Harrisville
Jacksonville
Jacobstown
Jobstown
Julinstown
Lower Bank
Lumberton
Marlton
Medford
Moorestown
Mount Holly (c h)
Mount Laurel
New Gretna
New Lisbon
Palmyra
Pemberton
Pointville
Progress
Rancocas
Recklesstown
Sykesville
Tuckerton
Vincentown
Wading River
Wrightstown

Camden co.
Blackwoodtown
Camden (c h)
Chew's Landing
Cross Keys
Ellisburgh
Glen Dale
Gloucester City
Haddonfield
Hurfville
Long-a-Coming
Mount Ephraim
Waterford Works
Williamstown
Winslow
White Horse

Cape May co.
Beesley's Point
Cape Island
Cape May (c h)
Cold Spring
Dennisville
Dias Creek
East Creek
Fishing Creek
Goshen
Green Creek
Petersburgh
Rio Grande
Seaville
Townsend Inlet
Tuckahoo

Cumberland co.
Bridgeton (c h)
Cedarville
Deerfield Street
Dividing Creek
Ewing's Neck
Fairton
Greenwich
Leesburg
Mauricetown
Millville
Newport
Port Elizabeth
Roadstown
Shiloh

Essex County.
Belleville
Bloomfield
Caldwell
Craneville
Elizabeth Port
Elizabeth
Feltville
Franklin
Irvington
Livingston

Millburn
Newark (c h)
New Providence
Orange
Plainfield
Scotch Plains
South Orange
Springfield
Vernon
West Bloomfield
Westfield

Gloucester co.
Barnaborough
Bridgeport
Carpenter's Landing
Clarksboro'
Fislerville
Franklinville
Glassboro'
Hardingville
Harrisonville
Malaga
Mullica Hill
Paulsborough
Swedesboro'
Westville
Woodbury (c h)

Hudson co.
Bergen Point
Harrison
Hoboken
Hudson
Jersey City
New Durham
Salterville
West Hoboken

Hunterdon co.
Baptistown
Bethlehem
Bloomsbury

Centreville
Cherryville
Clarksville
Clinton
Clinton Station
Clover Hill
Copper Hill
Cokesburgh
Croton
Everittstown
Fair Mount
Flemington (c h)
Frenchtown
High Bridge
Holland
Kingwood
Klinesville
Lambertville
Lebanon
Little York
Locktown
Milford
Mountainville
Mount Pleasant
New Germantown
New Hampton
Oak Dale
Oak Grove
Patenburg
Perryville
Pittstown
Pleasant Run
Pottersville
Quakertown
Raven Rock
Readington
Rosville
Ringoes
Rowland Mills
Sand Brook
Sergeantsville
Sidney
Stanton
Stockton
Tumble

Wertsville
White Hall
White House
Mercer co.
Baker's Basin
Dutch Neck
Edinburgh
Ewingville
Greensburgh
Groveville
Hamilton Square
Hightstown
Hopewell
Lawrenceville
Mount Rose
Pennington
Port Mercer
Princeton
Robbinsville
Titusville
Trenton (c h)
Van Hiseville
Windsor
Woodville
Yardville

Middlesex co.
Cranberry
Jamesburgh
Kingston
Metuchen
New Brunswick (c h)
New Market
Old Bridge
Perth Amboy
Plainsborough
Rahway
South Amboy
South Brunswick
South River
Spotswood
Woodbridge

New York.   409

Monmouth co.
Allentown
Chanceville
Chapel Hill
Clarksburgh
Black's Mills
Colt's Neck
Eatontown
Englishtown
Farmingdale
Fillmore
Freehold (c h)
Holmdel
Imlaystown
Key Port
Leedsville
Long Branch
Lower Squankum
Manalapan
Marlborough
Middletown
Middletown Point
New Bedford
New Sharon
Ocean Port
Perrineville
Red Bank
Riceville
Runsom Landing
Shrewsbury
Tinton Falls
Turkey
Walnford

Morris co.
Berkshire Valley
Boonton
Budd's Lake
Chatham
Chester
Danville
Dover
Drakesville
Drakestown
Flanders
German Valley
Hanover
Hanover Neck
Long Hill
Madison
Mendham
Millington
Milton
Morristown (c h)
Neighborville
Newfoundland
New Vernon
Parsippany
Passaic Valley
Pine Brook
Pompton Plains
Rockaway
Schooley's Mont'n
Stephensburgh
Sucksunny
Walnut Grove
Waterville
Woodport

Ocean co.
Barnegat
Bergen Iron Works
Cassville
Cedar Creek
Davisville
Forked River
Hornerstown
Jackson's Mills
Manahawkin
Metedecook
New Egypt
Point Pleasant
Potter's Creek
Red Oak Grove
Shark River
Shelltown
Squan Village
Tom's River
West Creek
Wiretown

Passaic co.
Bloomingdale
Little Falls
Mead's Basin
Passaic
Paterson (c h)
Pompton
West Milford

Salem co.
Allowaystown
Canton
Centreton
Daretown
Eldridge's Hill
Elmer
Hancock's Bridge
Pedricktown
Penn's Grove
Pitt's Grove
Salem (c h)
Scullville
Sharptown
Woodstown

Somerset co.
Baskenridge
Blawenburgh
Boundbrook
Flaggtown
Griggstown
Harlingen
Lesser Cross Roads
Liberty Corner
Martinsville
Middlebush
Millstone
Neshanie
North Branch
Peapack
Pluckemin
Raritan
Rocky Hill
Six Mile Run
Somerville (c h)
Warrenville
Weston

Sussex co.
Andover
Augusta
Beemerville
Bevans
Branchville
Culesville
Deckertown
Flatbrookville
Franklin Furnace
Freedon
Gratitude
Hainesville
Hamburgh
La Fayette
Libertyville
Middleville
Monroe
Montague
Mount Salem
Newton (c h)
Papokating
Pleasant Valley
Sparta
Stauhope
Stillwater
Stockholm
Swartswood
Tranquility
Tuttle's Corner
Vernon
Wallpack Centre
Waterloo
Wawayanda
Wykertown

Warren co.
Allamuchy
Anderson
Asbury
Beatyestown
Belvidere (c h)
Blairstown
Brainard's
Bridgeville
Broadway
Brotzmanville
Calno
Carpentersville
Columbia
Danville
Delaware Station
Hackettstown
Hainesburgh
Hardwick
Harmony
Hope
Howard
Johnsonburgh
Karrsville
Knowlton
Markslorough
Millbrook
Mount Bethel
Musconetcong
New Village
Oxford Furnace
Paulina
Phillipsburgh
Polkville
Rooksburgh
Serepta
Stewartsville
Still Valley
Townsbury
Vienna
Springtown
Walnut Valley
Washington

NEW YORK.

Albany co.
Albany (c h)
Berne
Bethlehem Centre
Boght
Callanan's Corners
Cedar Hill
Clarksville
Coeymans
Coeymans Hollow
Cohoes
Cooksburgh
Dormansville
Dunnsville
East Berne
Green Island
Guilderland [tre
Guilderland Cen-
Indian Fields
Ireland Corners
Keefer's Corners
Knowersville
Knox
Lisha's Kill
Medusa
New Salem
New Scotland
Newtonville
Norman's Kill
Potter's Hollow
Preston Hollow
Reidsville
Rensselaerville
South Berne
South Westerlo
Union Church
Watervliet Centre
Westerlo
West Township
West Troy

Allegany co.
Alfred
Alfred Centre
Allen
Allen Centre
Alma
Almond
Andover
Angelica (c h)
Belfast
Belvidere
Belmont
Birdsall
Birdsall Centre
Black Creek
Bolivar
Burns
Caneadea
Canaseraga
Centre Almond
Centreville
Ceres
Chautauque Val-
  ley

Cuba
East Rushford
Elm Valley
Fillmore
Friendship
Granger
Grove
Hallsport
Houghton Creek
Hume
Independence
Knight's Creek
Little Genesee
Mills' Mills
Nile
North Almond
Oramel
Phillips' Creek
Richburgh
Rockville
Rushford
Scio
Seymour
Shougo
Short Tract
South Bolivar
Spring Mills
Swainsville
Transit Bridge
Ward
Wellsville
West Almond
West Clarksville
Whitesville
Whitney's Cross-
  ing
Wirt
Wiscoy

Broome co.
Barker
Binghamton (c h)
Castle Creek
Centre Lisle
Centre Village
Chenango
Chenango Forks
Colesville
Conklin Centre
Crandallville
Doraville
East Maine
Glen Aubrey
Glen Castle
Gulf Summit
Harpersville
Hawleyton
Hooper
Killawog
Kirkwood
Lisle
Maine
Milburn
Nanticoke Springs
New Ohio
Nineveh

North Sanford
Osborne Hollow
Ouaquaga
Port Crane
Randolph Centre
Sanford
Tracy Creek
Triangle
Union
Union Centre
Unitaria
Upper Lisle
Vallonia Springs
Vestal
Vestal Centre
West Colesville
West Windsor
Witney's Point
Windsor

Cattaraugus co.
Allegany
Ashford
Ash Park
Buck Tooth
Cadiz
Cattaraugus
Conewanga
Cottage
Dayton
East Ashford
East Leon
East Otto
East Randolph
Eddyville
Elgin
Ellicottsville (c h)
Elton
Fairview
Farmersville
Five Mile Run
Franklinville
Freedom
Friend's Ferry
Gowanda
Great Valley
Haskell Flatts
Hinsdale
Humphrey
Ischua
Kill Buck
Leon
Limestone
Little Valley
Machias
Napoli
New Albion
Olean
Onoville
Otto
Perrysburgh
Plato
Portville
Randolph

Rawson
Sandusky
Sugartown
Tuna
Versailles
West Yorkshire
Yorkshire
Yorkshire Centre

Cayuga co.
Auburn (c h)
Aurelius
Aurora
Cato
Cayuga
Conquest
Dresserville
East Genoa
East Venice
Fair Haven
Five Corners
Fleming
Fosterville
Genoa
Ira
Kelloggsville
King's Ferry
Ledyard
Levanna
Locke
Martville
Meridian
Montezuma
Moravia
Niles
North Sterling
Owasco
Owasco Lake
Puntico
Poplar Ridge
Port Byron
Scipio
Scipioville
Sempronius
Seneca River
Sennet
Sherwood's
Sterling
Summer Hill
The Square
Throopsville
Union Springs
Venice
Venice Centre
Victory
Weedsport
Westbury

Chautauque co.
Arkwright Sum-
  mit
Barcelona
Blockville
Brigham

Brockton
Busti
Cassadaga
Centre Sherman
Charlotte Centre
Cherry Creek
Clear Creek
Clymer
De Wittville
Dunkirk
Ellery
Ellery Centre
Ellington
Falconer
Fentonville
Findley's Lake
Fluvanna
Forestville
Fredonia
French Creek
Frewsburgh
Friends
Gerry
Hamlet
Harmony
Hartfield
Irving
Jamestown
Kiantone
Laona
Levant
Magnolia
Marvin
Mayville (c h)
Mina
Nashville
Oregon
Panama
Poland Centre
Portland
Ripley
Sheridan
Sherman
Silver Creek
Smith's Mills
South Stockton
Stedman
Stockton
Vermont
Villanova
Volusia
Westfield

Chemung co.
Baldwin
Beaver Dams
Big Flats
Breesport
Catlin Centre
Chemung
Chemung Centre
Elmira
Erin
Horseheads
Mill Port

North Chemung
Pine Valley
Post Creek
Seely Creek
South Erin
Southport
State Road
Sullivanville
Van Ettenville
Veteran
Webb's Mills
Wellsburgh

Chenango co.
Afton
Ayeshire
Bainbridge
Bennettville
Cheshireville
Church Hollow
Columbus
Coventry
Coventryville
East German
East Greene
East Guildford
East McDonogh
East Pharsalia
Genegantslet
German
Greene
Guilford
Guilford Centre
King's Settlement
Linklaen
McDonogh
Mount Upton
New Berlin
New Berlin Centre
North Linklaen
North Norwich
North Pharsalia
North Pitcher
Norwich (c h)
Otselic
Oxford
Pharsalia
Pitcher
Pitcher Springs
Plymouth
Preston
Rockdale
Sherburne
Smithville Flats
Smyrna
South New Berlin
South Otselic
South Oxford
South Plymouth
West Bainbridge
White's Store

Clinton co.
Altona
Beekmantown

New York.

Black Brook
Cadyville
Chainplain
Chazy
Churubusco
Clintonville
Dannemora
East Beekmantown
Ellenburgh
Ellenburgh Centre
Frontier
Garlick Falls
Ingraham
Mooer's
Moore's Forks
Morrisonville
Perry's Mills
Peru
Plattsburgh (c h)
Redford
Rouse's Point
Saranac
Schuyler's Falls
Sciota
South Plattsburgh
Union Falls
Valcour
West Chazy
West Plattsburgh

Columbia co.

Ancram
Ancram Lead Mines
Austerlits
Canaan
Canaan Centre
Canaan Four Corners
Chatham
Chatham Centre
Chatham Four Corners
Churchtown
Claverack
Clermont
Copake
Copake Iron Works
East Chatham
Elizaville
Flat Brook
Gallatinville
Germantown
Ghent
Glenco Mills
Green River
Harlemville
Hillsdale
Hudson (c h)
Humphreysville
Kinderhook
Linlithgo
Livingston
Malden Bridge
Martindale Depot
Mellenville
Moffett's Store
New Lebanon
New Lebanon Centre
New Lebanon Springs
Niverville
North Chatham
North Copake
Philmont
Smoky Hollow
Spencertown
Stockport
Stuyvesant
Stuyvesant's Falls
Taghkanick
Valatie
West Taghkanick

Cortlandt co.

Blodgett Mills
Cincinnatus
Cortland Village
Cuyler   [(c h)
East Homer
East Scott
East Virgil
Freetown Corners
Glen Haven
Harford
Homer
Hunt's Corners
Keeney's Settlement
Lapeer   [ment
Little York
McGrawville
Marathon
Messengerville
Preble
Solon
Scott

South Cortlandt
Taylor
Texas Valley
Truxton
Union Valley
Virgil
Willet

Delaware co.

Andes
Barbourville
Bloomville
Bovina
Brushland
Cabin Hill
Cadosia Valley
Cannonsville
Clark's Factory
Clovesville
Colchester
Croton
Davenport
Davenport Centre
Delhi (c h)
Deposit
Downsville
East Branch
East Roxbury
Fergusonville
Franklin
Griffin's Corners
Halcottsville
Hale's Eddy
Hamden
Hancock
Harpersfield
Harvard
Hobart
Kortright
Lordsville
Lumberville
Margarettville
Masoville
Meredith
Moresville
New Kingston
New Road
North Franklin
North Hamden
North Harpersfield
North Kortright
Oulcout
Pepacton
Roxbury
Shavertown
Sidney
Sidney Centre
Sidney Plains
South Kortright
Stamford
Stockport Station
Stratton's Fall
Tremper's Kill
Trout Creek
Walton
West Brook
West Davenport
West Kortright
West Meredith

Dutchess co.

Adriance
Amenia
Amenia Union
Arthursburgh
Attlebury
Baugall
Barrytown
Beekman
Bull's Head
Carthage Landing
Chesnut Ridge
City
Clinton Corners
Clinton Hollow
Clinton Point
Clove
Crouse's Store
Crum Elbow
Dover
East Fishkill
Federal Store
Fishkill
Fishkill Landing
Fishkill Plains
Freedom Plains
Glenham
Green Haven
Hart's Village
Hibernia
Hughsonville
Hull's Mill
Hyde Park
Jackson Corners
Johnsville
La Fayetteville
La Grangeville
Leedsville
Lithgow
Little Rest

Locust Glen
Mabbettsville
Manchester Bridge
Mansfield
Matteawan
Milan
New Hackensack
New Hamburgh
North East
North East Centre
North East Station
Oblong
Oswego Village
Pawling
Pine Plains
Pleasant Plains
Pleasant Ridge
Pleasant Valley
Poughkeepsie (c h)
Poughquag
Pulver's Corners
Quaker Hill
Red Hook
Rhinebeck
Rhinebeck Station
Rock City
Salt Point
Schultsville
Sharon Station
South Amenia
South Dover
Sprout Creek
Staatsburgh
Stanfordville
Stormville
Tivoli
Upper Red Hook
Verbank
Wappinger's Falls
Washington
Washington Hollow
Wassaic
Wing's Station

Erie co.

Akron
Alden
Alden Centre
Angola
Big Tree Corners
Black Rock
Boston
Bowmansville
Brant
Buffalo (c h)
Buffalo Plains
Cheectowaga
Clarence
Clarence Centre
Clarksburgh
Colden
Collins
Collins Centre
Crittenden
East Amherst
East Aurora
East Eden
East Evans
East Hamburgh
Eden
Eden Valley
Eggertsville
Elma
Ellicott
Evans
Farnham
Getzville
Glenwood
Grand Island
Griffin's Mills
Hamburgh
Hamburgh on the Lake
Harris Hill
Holland
Lancaster
Langford
Looneyville
Marilla
Marshfield
Nill Grove
Morton's Corners
New Oregon
North Boston
North Buffalo
North Clarence
North Evans
Patchin
Pontiac
Protection
Reserve
Sardinia
Shirley
South Wales
Spring Brook
Springville
Tonawanda
Town Line

Wales
Wales Centre
Water Valley
West Falls
West Seneca
West Seneca Centre
Westwood
White's Corners
Williamsville
Willink
Winspear
Woodward's Hollow

Essex co.

Au Sable Forks
Bloomingdale
Crown Point
Elizabethtown (c h)
Essex
Jay
Keene
Keeseville
Lewis
Minerva
Moriah
New Russia
North Elba
North Hudson
Olmstedville
Port Henry
Port Kent
Schroon Lake
Schroon River
Ticonderoga
Upper Jay
Wadham's Mills
Westport
Whallonsburgh
Willsborough
Wilmington

Franklin co.

Alder Brook
Audrusville
Bangor
Bombay
Brush's Mills
Burke
Chateaugay
Chateaugay Lake
Cook's Corner
Dickinson
Dickinson Centre
Duane
East Constable
East Dickinson
Fort Covington
Fort Covington Centre
Franklin Falls
Hogansburgh
Hunter's Home
Malone (c h)
Moira
North Bangor
North Burke
Saranac Lake
South Bombay
Titusville
Trout River
West Bangor
West Constable

Fulton co.

Bleeker
Broadalbin
Cranberry Creek
Crum Creek
Ephratah
Garoga
Gloversville
Jackson Summit
Johnstown (c h)
Keck's Centre
Kingsborough
Lassellsville
Lotville
Mayfield
Mill's Corners
Newkirk's Mills
Northampton
North Broadalbin
Northville
Oppenheim
Osborn's Bridge
Perth
Rockwood
Sammonsville
Stratford
Union Mills
Vail's Mills
Westbush
West Galway
West Perth
Whitesburgh

New York.

Danmark
Diana
Diana Centre
Glensdale
Greig
Harrisburgh
Harrisville
High Market
Houseville
Indian River
Leyden
Lowville
Lyonsdale
Lyons' Falls
Martinsburgh (c h)
Montague
Naumburgh
New Boston
New Bremen
Osceola
Pinkney
Port Leyden
South Harrisburgh
Sterling Bush
Turin
Watson
West Leyden
West Lowville
West Martinsburgh
Wrightsvale

Livingston co.
Avon
Brooks' Grove
Byersville
Caludonia
Conesus
Conesus Centre
Cuylerville
Dansville
East Avon
East Groveland
East Hill
East Springwater
Geneseo (c h)
Gibsonville
Greigsville
Groveland
Groveland Centre
Hemlock Lake
Hunt's Hollow
Inverness
Kysonville
Lakeville
Lima
Livonia
Livonia Station
Moscow
Mount Morris
North Sparta
Nunda
Nunda Station
Oakland
Ossian
Piffard
Ridge
Scottsburgh
South Avon
South Lima

South Livonia
Sparta
Spring Water
Tuscarora
Union Corners
West View
York

Madison co.
Bennet's Corners
Bouckville
Bridgeport
Brookfield
Canastota
Cazenovia
Chittenango
Chittenango Falls
Clockville
Cowaselon
De Lancey
De Ruyter
Earlville
East Hamilton
Eaton
Erieville
Fenner
Georgetown
Hamilton
Hubbardsville
Lakeport
Lebanon
Lenox
Leonardsville
Madison
Morrisville (c h)
Munsville
Nelson
New Woodstock
North Brookfield
Oneida
Oneida Lake

Oneida Valley
Perryville
Peterboro'
Pine Woods
Pooleville
Pratt's Hollow
Shed's Corners
Siloam
Solsville
South Brookfield
South Hamilton
Stockbridge
Sullivan
Wampsville
West Eaton

Monroe co.
Adams' Basin
Brighton
Brockport
Bushnel's Basin
Charlotte
Chili
Churchville
Clarkson
Clarkson Centre
Clifton
East Clarkson
Egypt
Fairport
Gates
Greece
Handford's Landing
Henrietta
Honeoye Falls
Irondequoit
Mendon
Mendon Centre
Mumford
North Chili
North Clarkson
North Greece
North Parma
North Rush
Ogden
Parma
Parma Centre
Penfield
Pittsford
Redman's Corners
Riga
Rochester (c h)
Rush
Scottsville
South Greece
Spencerport
Sweden
Webster
West Brighton
West Greece
West Henrietta
West Rush
West Webster

Montgomery co.
Amos
Amsterdam
Auriesville
Buel
Burtonsville
Canajoharie
Charleston
Charleston Four Corners
Cranesville
Flat Creek
Fonda (c h)
Fort Hunter
Fort Plain
Frey's Bush
Fultonville
Glen
Hagaman's Mills
Hallsville
Minaville
Minden
Mindenville
Palatine
Palatine Bridge
Port Jackson
Root
Saint Johnsville
Scotch Bush
Spraker's Basin
Sprout Brook
Stone Arabia
Tribes Hill

New York co.
Haerlem
King's Bridge
Manhattanville
New York
Washington Heights
Yorkville

Niagara co.
Beech Ridge
Bergholtz

Cambria
Coomer
County Line
Dickersonville
East Porter
East Royalton
East Wilson
Gasport
Hartland
Hess Road
Hickory Corners
Johnson's Creek
Lake Road
La Salle
Lewiston
Lockport (c h)
Locust Tree
Mapleton
Martinsville
Middleport
Newfane
Niagara Falls
North Hartland
North Ridge
North Wilson
Olcott
Orange Port
Pekin
Pendleton
Pendleton Centre
Ransomville
Rapids
Roynale's Basin
Royalton
Shawnee
Somerset
South Pekin
South Royalton
South Wilson
Suspension Bridge
Walmore
West Somerset
Wilson's
Wright's Corners
Youngstown

Oneida co.
Alder Creek
Augusta
Ava
Babcock Hill
Big Brook
Blossvale
Booneville
Bridgewater
Camden
Cassville
Clark's Mills
Clayville
Clinton
Dinasville
Deerfield
Delta
Durhamville
East Florence
Florence
Floyd
Forest Port
Glenmore
Hawkinsville
Hecla Works
Higginsville
Hillsboro'
Hill Side
Holland Patent
Hurlbutville
Kirkland
Knox Corners
Lairdsville
Lee
Lee Centre
Lowell
McConnellsville
Marcy
Marshall
New Hartford
New London
New White Lake
New York Mills
North Bay
North Bridgewater
North Gage
North Western
Oneida Castle
Oriskany
Oriskany Falls
Paris
Prospect
Remsen
Rome (c h)
Sangerfield
Sauquoit
Seconndoa
South Trenton
Stanwix
State Bridge
Steuben
Stittville
Stokes
Taberg

Trenton
Trenton Falls
Utica
Vernon
Vernon Centre
Verona
Vienna
Walesville
Washington Mills
Waterville
West Branch
West Camden
Westernville
Westmoreland
West Vienna
Whitestown (e h)

Onondago co.
Amber
Apulia !
Baldwinsville
Belle Isle
Borodino
Brewerton
Camillus
Canal
Cardiff
Cicero
Clay
Collamer
Delphi
De Witt
Elbridge
Euclid
Fabius
Fair Mount
Fayettsville
Geddes
Hart Lot
Howlet Hill
Jack's Reef
Jamesville
Jordon
Kirkvale
La Fayette
Lamson's
Linn
Liverpool
Lysander
Maufana
Manlius
Manlius Centre
Manlius Station
Marcellus
Marcellus Falls
Marietta
Messina Springs
Mestville
Navarino
North Manlius
Onondaga
Onondaga Castle
Onondaga Valley
Oran
Otisco
Plainville
Plank Road
Polkville
Pompey
Pompey Centre
Salina
Skaneatles
South Onondaga
Spafford
Spafford Hollow
Syracuse (c h)
Thorn Hill
Three River Point
Tully
Tully Valley
Van Buren
Van Buren Centre
Vesper
Watervale
West Onondaga

Ontario co.
Academy
Allen's Hill
Bristol
Bristol Centre
Canadice
Canandaigua (c h)
Chapinville
Cheshire
Clifton Springs
East Bloomfield
East Farmington
Farmington
Fishers
Flint Creek
Geneva
Gorham
Gypsum
Hall's Corners
Honeoye
Hopewell
Hopewell Centre
Manchester
Manchester Centre

Naples
North Bloomfield
Norton's Mills
Oaks' Corners
Orleans
Phelps
Port Gibson
Reed's Corners
Richmond Mills
Seneca Castle
Shortsville
South Bristol
Stanley Corners
Taylorville
Victor
West Bloomfield
West Farmingto

Orange co.
Amity
Belvale
Blooming Grove
Bullville
Buttermilk Falls
Centre Point
Chester
Circleville
Coldenham
Collaburgh
Cornwall
Craigsville
Cuddebackville
Edenville
Florida
Fort Montgomery
Goshen (c h)
Greenwood Works
Highland Mills
Howell's Depot
Huguenot
Little Britain
Middle Hope
Middletown
Minisink
Monroe
Monroe Works
Montgomery
Moodna
Mortonville
Mount Hope
Newburgh (c h)
New Hampton
New Milford
Otisville
Otterville
Oxford Depot
Pine Bush
Port Jervis
Ridgebury
Saint Andrews
Salisbury Mills
Savill
Scotchtown
Searsville
Slate Hill
Sparrow Bush
Sugar Loaf
Turner's
Unionville
Walden
Warwick
Waterloo Mills
Wells' Corner
West Point
West Town

Orleans co.
Albion (c h)
Barre Centre
Carlton
Clarendon
Eagle Harbor
East Carlton
East Gaines
East Shelby
Gaines
Hindsb
Holley
Hulberton
Jeddo
Kendall
Kendall Mills
Knowlesville
Lyndonville
Medina
Millville
Murray
North Ridgeway
Oak Orchard
Ridgeway
Shelby
Shelby Basin
South Barre
Waterport
West Barre
West Carlton
West Gaines
West Kendall
West Shelby
Yates

Oswego co.
Amboy Centre
Barnhard's Bay
Bowen's Corners
Boylston
Butterfly
Cartersville
Caughdenoy
Central Square
Cleaveland
Colosse
Constantia
Constantia Centre
Dagway
Fair Dale
Fulton
Gilbert's Mills
Granby Centre
Greensboro'
Hannibal
Hannibal Centre
Hastings
Hastings Centre
Hinmansville
Kasoag
Kinney's Four Corners
Mexico
Minetto
Molino
New Centroville
New Haven
North Scriba
North Volney
Orwell
Oswego (c h)
Oswego Falls
Palermo
Parish
Pennellville
Phoenix
Port Ontario
Pulaski
Redfield
Salmon River
Sand Bank
Sandy Creek
Scriba
Seneca Hill
South Albion
South Granby
South Hannibal
South Richland
South West Oswego
Texas
Union Settlement
Union Square
Vermillion
Volney
West Amboy
West Monroe
Williamstown

Otsego co.
Burlington
Burlington Flats
Butternuts
Centre Brook
Chaseville
Cherry Valley
Colliersville
Cooperstown (c h)
Decatur
East Springfield
East Worcester
Edmeston
Exeter
Fly Creek
Garrattsville
Hartwick
Hartwick Seminary
Laurens
Maple Grove
Maryland
May Flower
Middlefield
Middlefield Centre
Milford
Morris
Mount Vision
New Lisbon
Oaksville
Oneonta
Oneonta Plains
Otego
Otsego Lake
Otsdawa
Pittsfield
Pleasant Brook
Portlandville
Richfield
Richfield Springs
Rosboom
Salt Springville
Schenevus
Schnyler's Lake
South Edmeston
South Hartwick

South Valley
South Worcester
Spooner's Corners
Springfield
Springfield Centre
Toddsville
Unadilla
Unadilla Centre
Unadilla Forks
West Burlington
West Edmeston
West Exeter
Westford
West Laurens
West Oneonta
Westville
Worcester

Putnam co.
Brewster's Station
Carmel (c h)
Cold Spring
Dykeman's
Farmer's Mills
Garrison's
Haviland Hollow
Kent
Ludingtonville
Mahopac
Milltown
Patterson
Red Mills
Towner's

Queens co.
Astoria
Cedar Swamp
College Point
East Norwich
Farmingdale
Flushing
Freeport
Glen Cove
Hempstead
Hicksville
Jamaica
Jericho
Jerusalem South
Jerusalem Station
Locust Valley
Little Neck
Manhasset
Maspeth
Merrick
Mineola
Newtown
North Hempstead (c h)
Oyster Bay
Queens
Ravenswood
Rockaway
Rockaway Beach
Rockville Centre
Roslyn
South Oyster Bay
Syosssett
Whitestone
Woodbury

Rensselaer co.
Alps
Berlin
Brainard
Castleton
Centre Berlin
Centre Brunswick
Cropseyville
Defreestville
Eagle Bridge
Eagle Mills
East Grafton
East Greenbush
East Nassau
East Poestenkill
East Schodack
Grafton
Greenbush
Haynerville
Hoag's Corner
Hoosick
Hoosick Falls
Johnsonville
Junction
Lansingburgh
Nassau
North Hoosick
North Nassau
North Stephentown
Petersburgh
Petersburgh Four Corners
Pittstown
Poestenkill
Potter Hill
Quacken Kill
Raymertown
Sand Lake
Schaghticoke

Schodack Centre
Schodack Depot
Schodack Landing
South Berlin
South Sand Lake
South Schodack
South Stephentown
Stephentown
Tomhannock
Troy (c h)
Valley Falls
West Berlin
West Hoosick
West Sandlake
West Stephentown
Wynantskill

Richmond co.
Bay View
Bentley
Kreischerville
Lemon Creek
Long Neck
Marshland
New Brighton
New Springville
North Shore
Port Richmond
Richmond (c h)
Richmond Valley
Rossville
South Side
Stapleton
Tompkinsville

Rockland co.
Blauveltville
Clarkstown (c h)
Haverstraw
Monsey
Nanuet
North Haverstraw
Nyack
Nyack Turnpike
Palisades
Piermont
Ramapo Works
Rockland Lake
Sloatsburgh
Spring Valley
Suffern
Tappantown

St. Lawrence.
Black Lake
Brasher Falls
Brasher IronWorks
Brier Hill
Buck's Bridge
Canton (c h)
Chase's Mills
Colton
Crary's Mills
De Kalb
De Peyster
East De Kalb
East Pierpont
East Pitcairn
Edenton
Edwards
Edwardsville
Fine
Flackville
Fowler
Fullersville Iron Works
Gouverneur
Grass River
Hailesburough
Hammond
Helena
Hermon
Heuvelton
Hopkinton
Lawrenceville
Lisbon
Lisbon Centre
Louisville
Louisville Landing
Macomb
Madrid
Massena
Massena Centre
Morley
Morristown
Nicholville
Norfolk
North Lawrence
North Potsdam
North Russell
North Stockholm
Oak Point
Ogdensburg
Parishville
Pierpont
Pitcairn
Pope's Mills
Potsdam
Racket River

Raymondville
Rensselaer Falls
Richville
Rossie
Russell
Shingle Creek
Somerville
South Edwards
Southville
Stockholm
Stockholm Depot
Waddington
Wegatchie
West Potsdam
West Stockholm

Saratoga co.
Bacon Hill
Ballston (c h)
Ballston Centre
Barkersville
Datchellerville
Bemus' Heights
Burnt Hills
Charlton
Clifton Park
Corinth
Coveville
Crescent
Day
Dunn's Corners
Dry Dock
East Galway
East Line
Edinburgh
Fortaville
Galway
Gansevoort
Grangerville
Greenfield Centre
Groom's Corners
Hadley
Half Moon
Jonesville
Ketcham's Corners
Malta
Maltaville
Mechanicsville
Middle Grove
Moreau Station
Mosherville
Mount Pleasant
North Galway
North Greenfield
Northumberland
Porter's Corners
Providence
Quaker Springs
Rexford Flats
Rock City Mills
Saratoga Springs
Schuylersville
South Ballston
South Corinth
South Galway
South Glenn's Falls
Stillwater
Victory Mills
Vischer's Ferry
Waterford
West Charlton
West
West Greenfield
West Hadley
West Milton
West Providence
Whiteside's Corners
Wilton

Schenectady co.
Braman's Corners
Duanesburgh
East Glenville
Glennville
Hoffman's Ferry
Marionville
Quaker Street
Schenectady (c h)
Scotia

Schoharie co.
Argosville
Barnerville
Barton Hill
Breakabeen
Broome Centre
Carlisle
Central Bridge
Charlotteville
Cobleskill
Cobleskill Centre
Conesville
East Cobleskill
Eminence
Engellville
Esperance
Franklinton
Fultonham

Gallupville
Gardenville
Gilboa
Grovenor's Corners
Hunter's Land
Hyndsville
Jefferson
Lawyersville
Leesville
Livingstonville
Lutheranville
Manor Kill
Middleburgh
Morseville
North Blenheim
Richmondville
Schoharie (c h)
Seward
Sharon
Sharon Centre
Sharon Springs
Shutter's Corners
Sloansville
South Gilboa
Summit
Waldensville
Warnerville
West Conesville
West Fulton
West Gilboa
West Richmondville

Schuyler co.
Alpine
Altay
Burdett
Catharine
Cayuta
Cayutaville
Croton Corners
Havanna (c h)
Hector
Logan
Mecklenburgh
Moreland
North Hector
Odessa
Orange
Perry City
Pine Grove
Reading
Reading Centre
Reynoldsville
Searsburgh
Sugar Hill
Townsend
Tyrone
Watkins
West Cayuta
Weston

Seneca co.
Canoga
Covert
Cruso
East Varick
Farmer
Fayette
Junius
Kidder's Ferry
Lodi
Lodi Centre
Ovid
Romulus
Romulus Centre
Rose Hill
Seneca Falls
Sheldrake
Townsendville
Trumansburgh
Tyro [Landing
Varick
Waterloo (c h)
West Fayette
West Junius

Steuben co.
Addison
Addison Hill
Avoca
Bath (c h)
Bennett's Creek
Big Creek
Bonny Hill
Bradford
Buena Vista
Cameron
Cameron Mills
Campbelltown
Canisteo
Caton
Centre Canisteo
Cohocton
Cooper's Plains
Corning
Crosbyville
Doty's Corner

East Painted Post
East Troupsburg
Gibson
Goff's Mills
Greenwood
Haskinville
Hornby
Hornellsville
Howard
Jasper
Kanona
Lindleytown
Loon Lake
Mead's Corners
Mitchellville
Mount Washington
North Cameron
North Cohocton
North Reading
North Urbana
Painted Post
Perkinsville
Prattsburgh
Pultney
Purdy Creek
Rathboneville
Rexville
Risingville
Riker's Hollow
Savona
Sonora
South Addison
South Bradford
South Dansville
South Hill
South Howard
South Pultney
South Thurston
South Troupsburgh
Stephens' Mills
Thurston
Towlesville
Troupsburgh
Urbana
Wallace
Wayland Depot
Wayne
Wayne Four Corners
West Addison
West Cameron
West Greenwood
West Jasper
West Troupsburgh
West Union
Wheeler
Wileysville
Woodhull
Young Hickory

Suffolk co.
Amagansett
Amityville
Atlanticville
Babylon
Baiting Hollow
Bell Port
Blue Point
Bridgehampton
Centre Moriches
Centreport
Cold Spring Harbor
Commack
Coram
Cutchogue
Deer Park
Dix Hills
East Hampton
East Marion
East Moriches
Fire Island
Fireplace
Flanders
Fresh Pond
Good Ground
Greenport
Hauppauge
Huntington
Islip
Jamesport
Lakeland
Manorville
Mattituck
Middle Island
Miller's Place
Moriches
Mount Sinai
New Village
Northport
Orient
Patchogue
Peconic
Penntaquit
Port Jefferson
Quogue
River Head
Sag Harbor
Saint James
Sayville

Selden
Setauket
Shelter Island
Smithtown
Smithtown Branch
Southampton
South Haven
Southold
Speonk
Springs
Stony Brook
Success
Suffolk Station
Thompson's Station
Upper Aquebogue
Wading River
West Hills
Yaphank

Sullivan co.
Barryville
Beaver Brook
Beaver Kill
Beech Wood
Bethel
Bloomingburgh
Bridgeville
Burlington
Bushville
Callicoon
Callicoon Depot
Claryville
Cochecton
Cochecton Centre
Delaware Bridge
Fallsburgh
Forestburgh
Fosterdale
Fremont
Fremont Centre
Galen
Glen Wild
Grahamsville
Hasbrock
Homowack
Jeffersonville
Liberty
Liberty Falls
Loch Sheldrake
Long Eddy
Lumberland
Mamakating
Mongaup
Mongaup Valley
Monticello (c h)
Moraston
Narrowsburgh
Neversink
North Branch
Parksville
Phillipsport
Pike Pond
Pond Eddy
Purvis
Robertsonville
Rockland
Sandburgh
Shin Creek
Stevensville
Thompsonville
West Brookville
White Lake
Woodbourne
Wurtsboro
Youngsville

Tioga co.
Apalachin
Barton
Berkshire
Campville
Candor
Canfield's Corner
Catatonk
East Berkshire
East Candor
Factoryville
Flemingsville
Halsey Valley
Hooper's Valley
Jenksville
Ketchumville
Newark Valley
Nichols
North Barton
Owego (c h)
Richford
Smithsboro
South Owego
Spencer
Strait's Corners
Tioga Centre
Waverly
Weltonville
West Candor
West Newark
West Richford
Willseyville
Wilson Creek

North Carolina. 413

Tompkins co.
Bennettsburgh
Caroline
Caroline Centre
Danby
Dryden
East Lansing
Enfield
Enfield Centre
Etna
Forest City
Groton
Groton City
Ithaca (c h)
Jacksonville
Lake Ridge
Lansingville
Ludlowville
McLean
Mott's Corners
Newfield
North Lansing
Peruville
Pony Hollow
Pugsley's Depot
Rawson Hollow
Slaterville
South Danby
South Lansing
Speedsville
Trumansburgh
Trumbull Corners
Varna
West Danby
West Dryden
West Groton

Ulster co.
Accord
Amesville
Bearsville
Brunswick
Clintondale
Denning
Dwaarskill
Ellenville
Esopus
Evensville
Fly Mountain
Galeville Mills
Glasco
Greenfield
High Falls
Hurley
Jamesburgh
Kerhonkson
Kingston (c h)

Krippelbush
Kyserike
Lackawack
Lake Hill
Libertyville
Loyd
Malden
Marbletown
Marlboro'
Milton
Modena
Napanock
New Hurley
New Paltz
New Paltz Landing
Ohioville
Olive
Olive Bridge
Perrine's Bridge
Phoenicia
Pine Hill
Plattekill
Port Ewen
Quarryville
River Side
Rondout
Rosendale
Samsonville
Saugerties
Shandaken
Shawangunk
Shokan
Stone Ridge
The Corner
Tuthill
Ulsterville
Wawarsing
West Camp
West Hurley
West Shandaken
Wilbur
Woodland
Woodstock

Warren co.
Athol
Bolton
Caldwell (c h)
Chestertown
Creek Centre
French Mountain
Glenn's Falls
Hague
Horicon
Johnsburgh
Luzerne
Mill Brook
North Creek

Pottersville
Queensbury
Stony Creek
The Glen
Thurman
Wardboro'
Warrensburgh

Washington co.
Adamsville
Argyle
Bald Mountain
Battenville
Belcher
Buskirk's Bridge
Cambridge
Centre Cambridge
Centre White Creek
Coila [ing
Comstock's Land-
East Greenwich
Easton
East Salem
Fort Ann
Fort Edward [tre
Fort Edward Cen-
Fort Miller
Galesville
Granville
Greenwich
Griswold's Mills
Hampton
Hartford
Hebron
Jackson
Kingsbury
Lake
Low Hampton
Middle Granville
North Argyle
North Cambridge
North Easton
North Granville
North Greenwich
North Hebron
North White Creek
Patten's Mills
Putnam
Salem (c h)
Sandy Hill (c h)
Shushan
Slateville
Smith's Basin
South Argyle
South Easton
South Granville
South Hartford

West Fort Ann
West Hebron
White Creek
Whitehall

Wayne co.
Alloway
Alton
Arcadia
Clyde
East Palmyra
Fairville
Huron
Joy
Lock Berlin
Lyons (c h)
Macedon
Macedon Centre
Marengo
Marion
Newark
North Huron
Ontario
Palmyra
Paltneyville
Red Creek
Rose
Savannah
Sodus
Sodus Centre
Sodus Point
South Butler
South Sodus
Walworth
West Butler
West Walworth
Williamson
Wolcott

Westchester co.
Armonk
Bedford (c h)
Bedford Station
Boscobel
Boutonville
Bronxville
Chappaqua
Cross River
Croton Falls
Croton Landing
Dobbs' Ferry
East Chester
Fordham
Golden's Bridge
Harrison
Hastings upon
Hudson
Irvington

Jefferson Valley
Katonah
Kensico
Lewisboro'
Lamaroneck
Moringville
Morrisania
Mott Haven
Mount Kisko
Mount Vernon
Neperan
New Castle
New Rochelle
North Castle
North Salem
Peekskill
Pelham
Pine's Bridge
Pleasantville
Port Chester
Poundridge
Purdy's Station
Rye
Salem Centre
Scarsdale
Shrub Oak
Sing Sing
Somers
South Salem
South Yonkers
Spuyten Duyvil
Tarrytown
Throg's Neck
Tuckahoe
Verplank
Vista
West Chester
West Farms
West Somers
White Plains (c h)
Williams' Bridge
Yonkers
Yorktown

Wyoming co.
Attica
Attica Centre
Bennington
Castile
China
Covington
Cowlesville
Dale
Eagle
Engle Village
Voak
East China
East Gainesville

East Java
East Koy
East Orangeville
Fast Pike
East Warsaw
Folsomdale
Gainesville
Hermitage
Java
Java Centre
Java Village
Johnsonsburgh
La Grange
North Java
North Sheldon
North Wethersfield
Orangeville
Pearl Creek
Peoria
Perry
Perry Centre
Pike
Portageville
Saint Helena
Sheldon
South Warsaw
Strykersville
Varysburgh
Warsaw (c h)
Wethersfield
Wethersfield
Wyoming [Springs

Yates co.
Barrington
Benton
Benton Centre
Big Stream Point
Bluff Point
Branch Port
Dundee
Eddytown
Ferguson's Corners
Italy Hill
Italy Hollow
Middlesex
Milo
Milo Centre
Penn Yan (c h)
Potter
Rock Stream
Rushville
Sherman's Hollow
Starkey
Voak
West Dresden
Yatesville

NORTH CAROLINA.

Alamance co.
Company's Shops
Curtis' Mills
Graham
Hartshorn
Haw River
Holt's Store
Lindley's Store
McCray's Store
McDaniel
Mebanesville
Melville
Morton's Store
Patterson's Store
Pleasant Grove
Rock Creek
Saxapahaw
Shallow Ford
Smith's Store
Snow Camp
South Side
Watsonville

Alexander co.
Elk Shoal
Little River
Mountain Female
Seminary
Mount Pisgah
Stony Point
Taylorsville (c h)
Wittenberg

Anson co.
Ansouville
Cedar Hill
Deep Creek
Frank'nburgh
Jones' Creek
Lanesboro'
Lilesville
Morven
Peedee
Wadesboro' (c h)
White's Store

Ashe co.
Beaver Creek
Cherry Lane
Chestnut Hill
Elk n Roads
Elk Creek
Gap Civil
Gap Creek
Glade Creek
Helton
Horse Creek
Jefferson (c h)
Laurel Springs
Nathan's Creek
Nettle Knob
North Fork
Potato Creek
Scottville
South Fork
Walnut Hill
Weaver's Ford

Beaufort co.
Bath
Belleview
Blount's Creek
Campbell's Creek
Durham's Creek
Fork Swamp
Goose Creek Island
Hunter's Bridge
Leechville
North Creek
Pantego
Punzo Creek
South Creek
Washington (c h)

Bertie co.
Colerain
Hotel
Merry Hill
Mill Landing

Roxobel
Windsor (c h)

Bladen co.
Baker's Creek
Bryant's Swamp
Beatty's Bridge
Cypress Creek
Deserett
Downingville
Elizabethtown (c h)
Ellizville
French Creek
Gravelly Hill
Melvinsville
Pleasant Exchange
Prospect Hall
West Brook
Western Prong
White Oak
White's Creek

Brunswick co.
Black Rock
Huckleberry
Lockwood's Folly
Maxwell
Robeson
Smithville (c h)
Supply

Buncombe co.
Ashville (c h)
Avery's Creek
Democrat
Dick's Creek
Fairview
Flat Creek
French Broad
Rommen's Creek
Reem's Creek
Sandy Mush
Shufordville

Stocksville
Sulphur Springs
Swannano
Turkey Creek
Turnpike
Walnut Creek
Warm Springs

Burke co.
Bridgewater
Brindletown
Drowning Creek
Happy Home
Linville River
Morgantown (c h)
Perkinsville

Cabarras co.
Rost's Mills
Coddle Creek
Concord (c h)
Garmon's Mills
Harris Depot
Kirkland
Klutt's Tan Yard
Mill Hill
Mount Pleasant
Oak Lawn
Parks' Store
Pioneer Mills

Caldwell co.
Catawba View
Colletts ville
Copenhagen
Deal's Mill
Fort Defiance
Globe
Hazel Dell
King's Creek
Lenoir (c h)
Lovelady
Patterson

Camden co.
Camden (c h)
Shiloah
South Mills'

Carteret co.
Beaufort (c h)
Caroline City
Hadnots
Morehead City
Portsmouth
Smyrna
Straits

Caswell co.
Anderson's Store
Blackwell
Graves
Hudson
Independence
Leasburgh
Locust Hill
Milton
Moore's Store
Newtonville
Prospect Hill
Purley
Yanceyville

Catawba co.
Bunker's Hill
Fishers
Flint Rock
Jacob's Fork
Long Island
Mountain Creek
Mull Grove
Newton (c h)

Chatham co.
Beaumont
Bellevoir
Branch
Cane Creek

Carbonton
Fall Creek
Glenaloon
Goldston
Grove
Hackney's x Roads
Hadley's Mills
Haywood
Jenny Lind
Kimbolton
Little Lick
Martha's Vineyard
Moringville
Mud Lick
Oakland
Pedlar's Hill
Pittsboro (c h)
Rialto
Riggsbee's Store
Saint Lawrence
Sandy Grove
Snipe's Store
The Gulph
William's Mills

Cherokee co.
England's Point
Fort Hembree
Fort Montgomery
Laurel Valley
Marble Spring
Murphey (c h)
Nottla
Peach Tree
Persimmon Creek
Stikoih
Turtle Town
Turquiles
Valley Town
Wolf Creek

Chowan co.
Ballard's Bridge
Edenton (c h)

North Carolina.

Cleveland co.
Birchettsville
Broad River
Buffalo Paper Mills
Camp Call
Camp's Creek
Clingman
Double Shoal
Duncan's Creek
Erwinsville
Garners Ford
Knob Creek
Mooresboro'
Muddy Fork
Nicholsonville
Piercevville
Polkville
Shelby (c h)
Stice's Shoal
Swangstown
White Plains

Columbus co.
Beach's Mills
Big Swamp
Cerro Gordo
Fair Bluff
Green Swamp
Peacock's Store
Pleasant Plain
Whitesville (c h)

Craven co.
Bay River
Newbern (c h)
Swift Creek Bridge

Cumberland co.
Argyle
Barclaysville
Blockers
Chalk Level
Fayetteville
Gibb's ⋈ Roads
Grays Creek
Harrison Creek
Inverness
Johnsonville
Kingsbury
Kinnie's Creek
Kyle's Landing
Little Rock Fish
Mauchosar
Mary's Garden
Montrose
Northington
Terebinthe

Currituck co.
Coinjock
Cowell's Bridge
Currituck (c h)
Dey's Mill
Indiantown
Knott's Island
Moyock
Poplar Branch
Powell's Point

Davidson co.
Abbott's Creek
Cedar Bush
Clemmonsville
Cotton Grove
Fair Grove
Hamby's Creek
Hamersville
Healing Springs
Holtsburgh
Jackson Hill
Lexington (c h)
Midway
It ch Fork
Shady Grove
Silver Hill
Spencer
Thomasville
Waller's Mill
Yadkin Institute

Davie co.
Calahaln
Clarksville
County Line
Farmington
Fulton
Jerusalem
Mocksville
Smith Grove

Duplin co.
Albertson's
Battle Hill
Bear Swamp
Branch's Store
Buena Vista
Chinkapin
Faison's Depot

Hallsville
Island Creek
Kenansville (c h)
Magnolia
Outlaw's Bridge
Prescott
Rosson
Rock Fish
Teachey's
Warsaw

Edgecombe co.
Battleboro'
Joyner's Depot
Rocky Mount
Sparta
Stantonsburg
Tarboro' (c h)
Wilson

Forsyth co.
Bethania
Kernersville
Mount Tabor
Muddy Creek
Old Richmond
Rural Hall
Salem
Sedges Garden
Vienna
Walkertown
Waughtown
Weavel's Mills
White Road
Winston (c h)

Franklin co.
Bakers' ⋈ Roads
Cedar Rock
Franklinton
Laurel
Louisburg (c h)
Pacific
Pugh's Hill

Gaston co.
Castania Grove
Catawba Creek
Crowder's Creek
Crowder's Mountain
Dallas (c h)
Erasmus
King's Mountain
Mountain Island
Nail Factory
Old Furnace
Pleasant Ridge
South Point
Stanley's Creek
Stowesville
Woodlawn

Gates co.
Buckland
Gatesville
Mintonsville
Reynoldson
Sunbury

Granville co.
Asylum
Berea
Blue Wing
Brookville
Brownsville
Buchanan
Butchville
Fairport
Henderson
Kittrell
Knap of Reeds
Millbank
Oak Hill
Oxford (c h)
Sassafras Fork
Tabb's Creek
Tally Ho
Townesville
Tranquility
Waller's
Waterloo
Williamsboro'
Wilton
Woodworths
Young's ⋈ Roads

Greene co.
Ball Head
Hookerstown
Maysville
Snow Hill (c h)
Speight's Bridge

Guilford co.
Alamance
Battle Ground
Bloomington
Brick Church
Centre
Deep River

Fentriss
Friendship
Gibsonville
Gilmer's Store
Greensboro'
High Point
Hillsdale
Jamestown
McLeansville
Monticello
New Garden
Oak Ridge
Shaw's Mills
Summerfield
Summer's Mills
Westminster

Halifax co.
Brinkleyville
Enfield
Halifax (c h)
Heathsville
Littleton
Palmyra
Ringwood
Scotland Neck
Sycamore Alley
Weldon
Westland

Harnett co.
Averysboro'
Buey's Creek
Burns' Level
Harrington
Norval
Summerville
Winslow

Haywood co.
Big Spring
Crab Tree
Fine's Creek
Forks of Pigeon
Jonathan's Creek
Ivy Hill
Ocona Lufty
Peru
Pigeon River
Qualiatown
Waynesville

Henderson co.
Bear Wallow
Blue Ridge
Boilston
Boman's Bluff
Calhoun
Cathey's Creek
Cedar Mountain
Cherryfield
Claytonville
Davidson River
Dana's Rock
Edneyville
Flat Rock
Green River
Hendersonville (c h)
Mill River
Mud Creek

Hertford co.
Bartonsville
Harrellsville
Murfreesboro'
Pitch Landing
Saint John
Winton

Hyde co.
Enterprise
Fairfield
Hatteras
Lake Comfort
Lake Landing
Middletown
Ocracoke
Sladesville
Swan Quarter (c h)
Wysoking

Iredell co.
Amity Hill
Bolt's Bridge
Bethany Church
Boyden
Chesnut Grove
Cool Spring
Deep Well
Eagle Mills
Enola
Fallstown
Fancy Hill
Granite Hill
Houstonville
Liberty Hill
Mount Mourne
New Hope
New Stirling

Olin
Oak Forest
Snow Creek
Statesville (c h)
Sweet Home
Tulin
Turnersburgh
Union Grove
Williamsburg

Jackson co.
Cashiers Valley
East Laport
Georgeown
Heady Mountain
High Top
Hogback Valley
Horse Cove
Webster

Johnson co.
Bentonsville
Beulah
Boonhill
Clayton
Creachville
Earpsborough
Elevation
Lowell
Pine Level
Saint Charles
Sandy Level
Smithfield (c h)

Jones co.
Comfort
Pollocksville
Trenton

Lenoir co.
Kinston (c h)
Lenoir Institute
Moseley Hall
Pink Hill
Sandy Foundation
Strabane

Lincoln co.
Beattie's Ford
Catawba Springs
Chronicle
Cottage Home
Dry Ponds
Early Grove
Killian's Mills
Lantz Grove
Lincolnton (c h)
Lowrance's Mills
Sherrill's Ford
Siegel's Store
Spring Hill Forge
Vesuvius Furnace

Macon co.
Cowee
Forks of Tennessee
Franklin
Governor's Island
Nantahala
Niyohih
Skeench
Tennessee River

Madison co.
Big Laurel
Clay
Cross Rock
Gabriel's Creek
Ivy Bend
Ivy Gap
Jewel Hill
Lapland
Marshall
Raysville
Spring Creek
Walnut Mountain
White Rock

Martin co.
Hamilton
Jamesville
Williamston

McDowell co.
Black Mountain
Cain's Branch
Dysortville
Marion (c h)
Minersville
North Cove
Old Fort
Stone Mountain
Sugar Hill
Turkey Cove

Mecklenburg co.
Alexandriana
Bloomingdale

Charlotte (c h)
Clear Creek
Cowan's Ford
Creaghead
Davidson College
Fullwood's Store
Hopewell
Hornet's Nest
Martindale
Morrison's Tan Yard
Orrville
Pineville
Providence
Ranaleburgh
Roservale
Sharon
Steele Creek
Tackassa
White Hall

Montgomery co.
Auman's Hill
Clark's Creek
Edinboro'
Harrisville
Hunsucker's Store
Macedonia
Milledgeville
Mount Gilead
Pekin
Pine Grove
Rush's Mills
Sanders Hill
Swift Island
Troy
Wind Hill

Moore co.
Buffalo
Caledonia
Calton
Carthage
Centreville
Crain's Creek
Curriersville
Gold Region
Jackson Springs
Lawhon's Hill
Long Street
Mooshannee
New Gilead
Pharr's Mill's
Pocket
Prosperity
Reedy Branch
Rollin's Store
Solema Grove
Watson's Bridge

Nash co.
Botanic Hill
Castalia
Hilliardstown
Nashville (c h)
Peach Tree Grove
Ransom's Bridge
Springhope
Stanhope
Stony Hill
Sunny South

New Hanover co.
Angola
Bannerman
Black River Chapel
Burgaw Depot
Caintuck
Colvin's Creek
Dogwood Grove
Harrell's Store
Long Creek
Moore's Creek
Scott's Hill
Sill's Creek
Spring Garden
Topsail Sound
Wilmington (c h)

Northampton co.
Garysburgh
Gaston
Green Plains
Jackson (c h)
Margaretsville
Pleasant Hill
Potecasi
Rich Square
Seaboard
Summit
Wheelersville
Woodland

Onslow co.
Aman's Store
Catharine Lake
Golden Grove
Haw Branch
Onslow (c h)

Palo Alto
Piny Green
Richlands
Snead's Ferry
Stone's Bay
Swansboro'
Wolf Pit

Orange co.
Big Falls
Caldwell
Cedar Grove
Chapel Hill
Clover Garden
Clover Orchard
Durham's
Enoe Mills
Flat River
Hawfields
Hillsboro' (c h)
Meadow Creek
Mount Willing
Oaks
Orange Factory
Red Mountain
Rock Spring
Round Hill
South Lowell
Stagville
University Station
Walnut Grove
West Orange
West Point
White Cross

Pasquotank co.
Elizabeth City (c h)
Hintansville
Newbegon Creek

Perquimans co.
Durant's Neck
Hertford (c h)
Newby's Bridge
Woodville

Person co.
Allensville
Bushy Fork
Centre Grove
Cunningham's Store
Daniel's Mills
Five Forks
Gordonton
Hester's Store
Mount Tirzah
Olive Hill
Roxboro' (c h)
Van Hook's Store
Woodsdale

Pitt co.
Bethel
Boyd's Ferry
Coxville
Falkland
Greenville (c h)
Johnson's Mills
Marlboro'
Pactolus
Pleasant Mount
Ridge Spring

Polk co.
Columbus
Tyron

Randolph co.
Ashboro' (c h)
Brower's Mills
Brush Creek
Buffalo Ford
Caraway
Cedar Falls
Cheek's Mills
Cox's Mills
Eden
Foust's Mill
Franklinville
Gladesborough
Hill's Store
Hoover Hill
Jones' Mine
La Grange
Lassiter's Mills
Long's Mills
Marley's Mills
Moffitt's Mills
New Market
New Salem
Reed Creek
Salem Church
Sandy Creek
Sawyersville
Science Hill
Soap Stone Mount

Ohio.

Stone Lick
Trinity College
Troy's Store
White House

Richmond co.
Bear Branch
Bostick's Mills
Covington
Dockery's Store
Dumas' Store
Dunning Creek
Gibson's Store
Laurinburgh
Lothe
Linton
Little's Mills
McDonald's Mills
Mangum
Montpelier
Powellton
Rockingham
Springfield

Robeson co.
Alfordsville
Anna Perenna
Brooklin
Clay Valley
Cowper Hill
Dundarrack
Fair Play
Floriesville
Gaddeyville
Gilopolis
Howellsville
Leesville
Lumber Bridge
Lamberton (c h)
Melrose
Philadelphus
Queensdale
Rendalsville
Red Sorings
East Swamp
Saint Pauls
Smith Bridge

Rockingham co.
Clarksburgh
Dan River
Eagle Falls
Elm Grove

Groganville
Hogan's Creek
Lawsonville
Leaksville
Lenox Castle
Madison
Mayfield
Mayo
Monroeton
Oregon
Pleasantville
Rawlinsburgh
Reidsville
Staceyville
Thompsonville
Troublesome
Wentworth (c h)

Rowan co.
Bringle's Ferry
Calaabria
Euharla
Gold Hill
Laurel Branch
Miranda
Mount Ulla
Mount Vernon
Rockville
Roseman's Store
Rowan Mills
Salisbury (c h)
Wood Leaf

Rutherford co.
Brittain
Butler
Cedar Creek
Chimney Rock
Cooper's Gap
Caba
First Broad
Golden Valley
Grassy Knob
Green Hill
Hicksville
High Shoals
Island Ford
Logan's Store
Oak Spring
Other Creek
Patton's Home
Rutherfordton (c h)
Sandy Plains
Suck Creek
Webb's Ford

Sampson co.
Areysville
Bonnett's X Roads
Blackman's Mills
Clinton (c h)
Dobbinsville
Draughon's Store
Hawley's Store
Horringsville
Monk's Store
Newton Grove
Owensville
Piney Grove
Six Runs
Taylor's Bridge
Wardsville

Stanly co.
Albemarle (c h)
Alpine
Efird's Mills
Kendall's Store
Leo
Norwood

Stokes co.
Ayersville
Blakely
Colesville
Crooked Creek
Danbury (c h)
Francisco
Germanton
Little Yadkin
Martin's Lime Kiln's
Neatman
Old Town
Peters Creek
Pilot Mountain
Pine Hall
Red Shoals
Smith's Valley
Walnut Cove
Westfield
Wilson's Store

Surry co.
Dobson
Elkin
Flat Shoal
Fisher's Gap
Hay Stack

Judesville
Mount Airy
Rockford (c h)
Rusk
Roaring Gap
Siloam
State Road
Stony Ridge
Tom's Creek

Tyrrel co.
Columbia (c h)
Fort Landing
Gum Neck

Union co.
Beaverdam
Coburn's Store
Jenkin's Store
Lano's Creek
Love's Level
Monroe (c h)
Morgan's Mills
Oak Grove
Oakville
Olive Branch
Raywood
Richardson Creek
Stevens' Mills
Walkersville
White Hill
Winchester
Wolf Pond
Wolfsville

Wake co.
Auburn
Brassfield
Cary
Eagle Rock
Fishdam
Forestville
Green Level
Holly Spring
Middle Creek
Milbernie
Morrisville
New Hill
New Light
Raleigh (c h)
Rogers' Store
Rolesville
Wakefield

Warren co.
Cheathamville
Exchange
Grove Hill
Macon Depot
Merry Mount
Nutbush
Ridgeway
Shocco Springs
Warren Plains
Warrenton (c h)

Washington co.
Long Ridge
Mackey's Ferry
Plymouth (c h)
Souppernong
Union

Wautauga co.
Blowing Rock
Boone (c h)
Cranberry Forge
Moreti Mill
Rotherwood
Stoney Fork
Sugar Grove
Sweet Water
Valle Crusis
Watauga Falls

Wayne co.
Everittsville
Falling Creek
Goldsborough
Jericho
Mount Olive
Nahunta
Pikeville
Sleepy Creek

Wilkes co.
Ausburnville
Brier Creek
Bugaboo
Elk Spur
Elkville
Hay Meadow
Hunting Creek
Job's Cabin
Lewis' Fork
Lovelace

Mulberry
New Castle
Purlour's Creek
Reddie's River
Swan Pond
Trap Hill
Warrior Creek
Wilkesboro' (c h)
Wilbar
Zimmerman

Wilson co.
Black Creek
Saratoga

Yadkin co.
Bald Knob
Boonville
Chestnut Ridge
East Bend
Five Mile Fork
Forbush
Hamptonville
Huntsville
Jonesville
Locust Shade
Mount Nebo
Oak Level
Panther Creek
Red Plains
Republic
Richmond Hill
Walnut Lane
Yadkinville
Zion

Yancey co.
Bakersville
Bald Creek
Burnsville (c h)
Childsville
Day Book
Egypt
Falls
Fork Mountain
Grassy Creek
Ivy
Ledger
Paint Gap
Ramseytown
Red Hill
Rose's Creek
Yellow Mountain

OHIO

Adams co.
Bensley's Fork
Buton ville
Blue Creek
Bradysville
Cherry Fork
Dunbarton
Dunkinville
Eckmansville
Emerald
Gustin
Hill's Fork
Locust Grove
Lovett's
Manchester
Marble Furnace
May Hill
Mount Leigh
Osmons
Rockvill
Scott
Stouts
Tranquility
Vineyard Hill
Waggoner's Ripple
West Union (c h)
Wheat Ridge
Youngsville

Allen co.
Acadia
Allentown
Beaver Dam
Blue Lick
Bluffton
Crameryille
Cranberry
Donnel's
Elida
Gomer
Herring
Hog Creek
Lima (c h)
Middle Spring
South Warsaw
West Cairo
Westminster

Ashland co.
Albion
Ashland (c h)
Hayesvill
Jeromesville
Lake Fork
Loudonville
McKay
Mifflin
Mohican
Nankin
Nova
Perote
Perryville
Polk
Row's
Ruggles
Savannah
Sullivan

Ashtabula co.
Amboy
Andover
Ashtabula
Austinburgh
Cherry Valley
Clark's Corner
Conneaut
Cork
Denmark
Dorset
Eaglevillo
East Plymouth
East Trumbull
Geneva
Harpersfield
Hart's Grove
Jefferson (c h)
Kelloggsville
Kingsville
Lenox
Leon
Lindenville
Monroe Centre
Morgan
New Lyme
North Sheffield
Orwell
Osbornville

Phelps
Pierpont
Richmond Centre
Rome
Saybrook
South Ridge
Steamburgh
Trumbull
West Andover
West Williamsfield
Williamsfield
Windsor

Athens co.
Amesville
Athens (c h)
Big Run
Calvary
Canaan ville
Chauncey
Coolville
Federalton
Garden
Guysville
Hartleyville
Hebbardsville
Hockingport
Horton
Hulls
Lee
Lottridge
Lowry
Marshfield
Medill
Millfield
Mineral
Nelsonville
New England
Pleasanton
Rock Oak
Torch
Trimble
Woodyard's

Auglaize co.
Cridersville

Deep Cut
Frysburgh
Kossuth
Minster
Moulton
New Bremen
New Hampshire
New Knoxville
Rinehart
Saint John's
Saint Marys
Uniopolis (c h)
Wapakoneta
Waynesfield

Belmont co.
Armstrong's Mills
Atlas
Bailey's Mills
Barnesville
Bell Air
Belmont
Bethesda
Bridgeport
Captina
Coleruin
Dumos
Dille's Bottom
East Richland
Flushing
Glencoe
Hundrysburgh
Hunter
Jacobsburgh
Kennon
Lamira
Loydsville
Martin's Ferry
Morristown
Pilcher
Plank Road
Powhatan Point
Pugh
Ring's Mills
St. Clairsville (c h)
Sewelsville
Shepherdstown
Somerton

Temperanceville
Uniontown
Warnock
Wegee

Brown co.
Aberdeen
Arnheim
Ash Ridge
Bloom Rose
Clover Valley
Decatur
De La Palma
Fayetteville
Feesburgh
Fincastle
Five Mile
Georgetown (c h)
Hamersville
Higginsport
Lewis
Locust Ridge
Maple
Mount Orab
New Harmony
New Hope
Ripley
Russelville
Sardinia
Todd's Run
White Oak Valley

Butler co.
Alert
Bethany
Blue Ball
Bunker Hill
College Corner
Collinsville
Contreras
Darrtown
Hamilton (c h)
Jacksonboro'
Jones' Station
Le Sourdsville
McKonigloe's Stat'n
Middletown
Millville
Monroe

Okeana
Overpeck's Station
Oxford
Paddy's Run
Philanthropy
Piszah
Poast Town
Port Union
Princeton
Reiley
Ross
Saint Charles
Seven Mile
Somerville
Trenton
Union Corner
West Chester

Carroll co.
Algonquin
Augusta
Cabello
Carrollton (c h)
Harlem Springs
Hibbutt's
Kilgore
Lamertine
Leavitt
Leesville
Malvern
Mechanicstown
New Harristown
Oneida Mills
Palerma
Pekin
Ross
Scroggsfield
Sherodsville
Wattsville

Champaign co.
Bakers
Brinton
Careysville
Chalfant

Ohio.

Christiansburg
Mechanicsburg
Millerstown
Mutual
North Lewisburg
St. Paris
Springhill
Terre Haute
Urbana (c h)
Westville
Woodstock

Clark co.

Bowlesville
Catawba
Donnellsville
Enon
Harmony
Medway
New Carlisle
Northampton
Selma
South Charleston
Springfield (c h)
Tremont
Vienna ⋈ Roads

Clermont co.

Amelia
Angola
Bantam
Batavia (c h)
Belfast
Bethel
Branch Hill
California
Cedron
Chilo
Clover
Edenton
Felicity
Goshen
Henning Mills
Laurel
Locust Corner
Loveland
Marathon
Miamisville
Milford
Monterey
Moscow
Mount Carmel
Mount Olive
Mount Pisgah
Mulberry
Neville
New Palestine
New Richmond
Newtonville
Nicholsville
Olive Branch
Owensville
Perin's Mill
Point Isabel
Point Pleasant
Rural
S one Lesh
West Woodville
Williamsburgh
Withamsville

Clinton co.

Blanchester
Bloomington
Clarksville
Clinton Station
Clinton Valley
Cuba
Farmer's Station
Lee's Creek
Lumberton
Martinsville
Morrisville
New Antioch
New Burlington
New Vienna
Oakland
Port William
Reesville
Sabina
Sligo
Snow Hill
Westboro'
Wilmington (c h)

Columbiana co.

Achor
Bayard
Bucks
Calcutta
Cannon's Mill
Clarkson
Columbiana
Damascoville

Dunganon's
East Fairfield
East Liverpool
East Palestine
East Rochester
Elkton
Franklin Square
Gavers
Glasgow
Greenhill
Hanoverton
Inverness
Little Beaver
  Bridge
Millport
Moultrie
New Alexander
New Chambersburg
New Garden
New Lisbon (c h)
New Waterford
North Georgetown
St. Clair
Salem
Salineville
Sandy
Summitville
Unity
Washingtonville
Wellsville
West Beaver
West Point

Coshocton co.

Bacon
Bakersville
Boyd's Mill
Canal Lewisville
Chili
Clark's
Coshocton (c h)
Evansburg
Franklin Station
Jone's Corners
Keene
Linton Mills
Mohawk Village
Munnsville
New Bedford
New Castle
New Guilford
New Moscow
Plainfield
Roscoe
Spring Mountain
Tiverton
Tyrone
Wakatomia
Walhonding
Warsaw
West Bedford
West Carlisle
West Lafayette
White Eye Plains
Will's Creek
Yankee Ridge

Crawford co.

Broken Sword
Bucyrus (c h)
Camp Run
Chatfield
Crestline
De Kalb
Galion
Leesville ⋈ Roads
Liberty Corners
Likens
New Washington
North Robinson
Oceola
Poplar
Sulphur Spring
Tim
Wellersville

Cuyahoga co.

Barry
Bedford
Berea
Brecksville
Brooklyn
Chagrin Falls
Cleveland (c h)
Coe Ridge
Collamer
Dover
East Cleveland
East Rockport
Euclid
Gate's Mills
Independence
Mayfield
Middleburgh
Newburgh
North Dover

North Royalton
North Solon
Olmsted
Parma
Rock Port
Solon
Strongsville
Warrensville
West View

Darke co.

Ansonia
Arcanum
Bismaville
Brock
Castine
Concordia
Darke
Dawn
Do Lisle
Fort Jefferson
German
Gettysburgh
Gordon
Greenville (c h)
Hill Grove
Horatio
Ithaca
Jaysville
Mitchett
Mississinawa
Mount Heron
New Madison
North Star
Painter Creek
Pittsburgh
Poplar Ridge
Republican
Rose Hill
Seven Mile Prairie
Stelvideo
Tampico
Versailles
Webster
Woodland
Woodington
Yankeetown

Defiance co.

Arrowsmith
Ayersville
Brunersburgh
Cicero
Defiance (c h)
Evansport
Farmer
Hickville
McCauley's
Milldale
Milo
Ney
Panama

Delaware co.

Alum Creek
Ashley
Boile Point
Berkshire
Centre Village
Condit
Constantia
Delaware (c h)
East Orange
Galena
Genoa ⋈ Roads
Harlem
Killbourne
Kingston Centre
Leonardsburgh
Lewis Centre
Maxwell
Norton
Orange Station
Ostrander
Patterson
Porter
Powell
Radnor
Sunbury
Tanktown
Unison
Van's Valley
White Sulphur

Erie co.

Berlin Heights
Berlin Station
Berlinville
Birmingham
Bloomingville
Castalia
Florence
Huron
Kelly's Island
Milan
Sandusky (c h)

Seven Mile House
Venice
Vermillion

Fairfield co.

Amanda
Baltimore
Basil
Bremen
Carroll
Cedar Hill
Clear Creek
Clear Port
Dumontville
Green Castle
Hamburg
Lancaster (c h)
Lithopolis
Lockville
Macey
Millersport
New Salem
North Berne
Pickerington
Pleasantville
Royalton
Rushville⁴
Stoutsville
Sugar Grove
Walnut
West Rushville

Fayette co.

Bloomingburgh
Convenience
Good Hope
Jasper Mills
Jeffersonville
Moons
New Martinsburgh
Pancoastburgh
South Plymouth
Staunton
Washington (c h)
West Lancaster
White Oak

Franklin co.

Alton
Black Lick
Blendon
Bronson's Station
Canal Winchester
Center College
Clintonville
Columbus (c h)
Darby
Dublin
Gahanna
Georgesville
Grove City
Grove Port
Harrisburgh
Hilliards
Hope
Lockbourne
Midianville
North Columbus
Ovid
Park's Mills
Pleasant Corners
Reynoldsburgh
Shadesville
Westerville
Worthington

Fulton co.

Ai
Archbold
Beta
Blanc
Chesterfield
Delta
Elmira
Emery
Gorham
Haudy
Lavona
Lena
Lyons
Metamora
Mill Creek
Ottokee (c h)
Pettisville
Swanton
Todrow
Wasscon
West Barre
Winnamac

Gallia co.

Addison
Anselm
Bay's Bottom
Cheshire
Ewington
Gallia Furnace
Gallipolis (c h)

Harris
Kyger
Little Bullskin
McDaniels
Mercerville
Northrop
Patriot
Pine Grove
Racoon Island
Rio Grande
Rodney
South Newcastle
Swan Creek
Thivener
Thurman's
Vinton
Wales
Waterloo

Geauga co.

Auburn
Bissell's
Bridge Creek
Bundysburgh
Burton
Chardon (c h)
Chester ⋈ Roads
Claridon
East Claridon
Fo
Fowler's Mills
Hampden
Huntsburgh
Middlefield
Montville
Mulberry Corners
Newbury
North Newbury
Parkman
Pond
Russell
South Thompson
Thompson
Welshfield

Greene co.

Alpha
Bellbrook
Bowersville
Byron
Cedarville
Clifton
Clio
Fairfield
Grape Grove
Jamestown
Kneisly
New Jasper
Osborn
Paintersville
Spring Valley
Xenia (c h)
Yellow Springs
Zimmerman

Guernsey co.

Antrim
Bird's Run
Buffalo
Cambridge (c h)
Claysville
Creighton
Cumberland
Dyson's
Fairview
Galigher
Gibson's Station
Gomber
Indian Camp
Kimbolton
Leatherwood
Londonderry
Middlebourne
Milnersville
North Salem
Salesville
Senecaville
Spencer's Station
Washington
Winchester

Hamilton co.

Bevis' Tavern
Carthage
Cherry Grove
Cheviot
Cincinnati (c h)
Cloves
College Hill
Columbia
Delhi
Dent
Dry Ridge
Dunlap
East Sycamore
Elizabethtown
Fulton
Glendale

Groesbeck
Harrison
Indian Hill
Linwood
Lick Run
Lockland Station
Ludlow
Madisonville
Miami
Montgomery
Mount Airy
Mount Healthy
Mount Washington
Newtown
Plainville
Pleasant Ridge
Pleasant Run
Preston
Reading
Sharonville
Sixteen Mile Stand
Spring Dale
Storrs
Sweet Wine
Taylor's Creek
Tompkins
Transit
Walnut Hills

Hancock co.

Alba
Arcadia
Arlington
Benton Ridge
Big Lick
Blanchard's Bridge
Cannonsburgh
Cass
Clement
Eagle
Elm Grove
Finley (c h)
Hassan
McComb
Mount Blanchard
North Ridge
Oak Ridge
Portage Centre
Van Biron
Vanlue
West Independence

Hardin co.

Ada
Dudley
Dunkirk
Forest
Hale
Hudsonville
Huntersville
Kenton (c h)
McDonald
Mount Victory
North Washington
Round Head
Sylvia

Harrison co.

Archer
Bowerstown
Cadiz (c h)
Cassville
Cold Spring
Conotton
Deersville
Fife
Freeport
Germano
Harrisville
Hopedale
Jewett
Laceyville
Means
Moorefield
New Athens
New Rumley
Nottingham
Scio
Short Creek
Smyrna
Station 15
Tappan
Tippecanoe

Henry co.

Colton
Damascus
Durand
Florida
Liberty Centre
Napoleon (c h)
New Bavaria
Odessa
Ridgeland
Ridgeville Corners
Shunk
Texas

Ohio.

Highland co.
Allensburgh
Bell
Berryville
Buford
Carmel
Centrefield
Dallas
Dodsonville
East Monroe
Economy
Elmville
Fairfax
Greenfield
Highland
Hillsborough (c h)
Hollowtown
Home
Leesburgh
Lynchburgh
Marshall
Mowrystown
Neven
New Corwin
New Market
New Petersburgh
North Uniontown
Paint
Pricetown
Rainsborough
Russell's Station
Samantha
Sicily
Sinking Spring
Sonner's Mill
Sugar Tree Ridge
Willettville

Hocking co.
Ash Cave
Black Jack
Ewing
Gibsonville
Gore
Islesboro'
Logan (c h)
Middle Fork
Rock House
South Bloomingv'le
South Perry
Starr

Holmes co.
Benton
Berlin
Black Creek
DeWitt Ridge
Holmesville
Humphrey's Villa
Killbuck
Millersburgh (c h)
Mount Hope
Nashville
Plimpton
Salt Creek
Saltillo
Walnut Creek
Winesburgh

Huron co.
Bellevue
Bronson
Carson
Centreton
Clarksfield
East Clarksfield
East Townsend
Fitchville
Four Corners
Greenwich Station
Hartland
Havana
Monroeville
New Haven
New London
North Fairfield
Norwalk (c h)
Olena
Peru
Plymouth
Pontiac
Ripleyville
Sherman
Steuben
Wakeman

Jackson co.
Agatha
Berlin X Roads
Buckeye Furnace
Camba
Clay
Cove
Dawkin's Mills
Hays
Iron Valley
Jackson (c h)

Jackson Furnace
Keystone
Levi
Mabee's
Meadow Branch
Munroe Furnace
Oak Hill
Rays
Rocky Hill
Sampsonville

Jefferson co.
Adena
Amsterdam
Annapolis
Bloomingdale
Cope's Mills
Cross Creek
Croxton
East Springfield
Elliottsville
Fair Play
Hammondsville
Holmes' Mill
Island Creek
Jeddo
Knoxville
Linton
Mitchell's Salt Works
Moore's Salt Works
Mount Pleasant
Nebo
New Alexandria
New Somerset
Philipsburgh
Port Homer
Richmond
Rush Run
Sloane Station
Smithfield
Steubenville (c h)
Unionport
Updegraffs
Warrenton
Wintersville

Knox co.
Bladensburgh
Brandon
Centreburgh
Chanticleer
Danville
Democracy
Fredericktown
Gambier
Greersville
Jelloway
Knox
Levering's
Lock
Lucerne
Martinsburgh
Milfordton
Millwood
Monroe Mills
Mount Liberty
Mount Vernon (c h)
Nonpareil
North Liberty
Shaler's Mills
Wolf

Lake co.
Concord
Hillhouse
Kirtland
Madison
Mentor
Painesville (c h)
Perry
South Kirtland
Unionville
Wickliffe
Willoughby

Lawrence co.
Aid
Arabia
Athalia
Bartramville
Burlington
Coal Grove
Greasy Ridge
Hanging Rock
Ironton (c h)
Kelley's Mills
Kennedy's X Roads
Miller's
Quaker Bottom
Rock Camp
Russell's Place
Scott's Town
South Point
Symmes' Run
Walnut Ridge

Licking co.
Alexandria
Appleton
Beach
Brownsville

Chatham
Clay Lick
Columbia Centre
Croton
Etna
Fallsburgh
Fredonia
Granville
Gratiot
Green
Hanover
Hawk Eye
Hebron
Homer
Jacksontown
Jersey
Johnstown
Kirkersville
Linnville
Long Run
Newark (c h)
New-way
Outville
Pataskala
Perryton
Rocky Forks
Saint Louisville
Toboso
Utica
Vanatta
Wilkin's Run

Logan co.
Bell Centre
Bellefontaine (c h)
Bloom Centre
De Graff
East Liberty
Harper
Huntsville
Lewistown
Loganville
Mark
Machinippe
New Richland
Pickereltown
Quincy
Rushylvania
West Liberty
West Middleburgh
Zanesfield

Lorain co.
Amherst
Avon
Avon Lake
Black River
Brighton
Brownhelm
Camden Station
Columbia Station
Copopa
Crandall
Elyria (c h)
Grafton
Henrietta
Huntington
La Grange
La Porte
North Camden
North Eaton
North Ridgeville
Oberlin
Penfield
Pittsfield
Plato
Rawsonville
Rochester Depot
Sheffield
Sheffield Lake
Wellington

Lucas co.
East Toledo
Hardy
Hickory
Java
Maumee City
Monclova
Providence
Riga
Sylvania
Toledo (c h)
Waterville
White House

Madison co.
Big Plains
Cross Roads

Darby Creek
La Fayette
London (c h)
Mount Sterling
Rosedale
South Solon
Summerford
Tradersville
Wahoo
West Canaan
West Jefferson

Mahoning co.
Berlin Centre
Boardman
Boswell
Briar Hill
Canfield (c h)
Coitsville
Cornersburgh
East Lewistown
Ellsworth
Frederick
Greenford
Hanna's Mills
Lowellville
Milton
New Albany
New Middletown
New Springfield
North Benton
North Jackson
North Lima
Orange
Patmos
Petersburgh
Poland
Smithfield Station
Youngstown

Marion co.
Big Island
Caledonia
Cochranton
Green Camp
Larue
Lestimberville
Marion (c h)
New Bloomington
Prospect
Three Locusts
Underwoods
Waldo

Medina co.
Abbeyville
Brunswick
Chatham Centre
Granger
Guilford
Hinckley
Homersville
Leroy
Litchfield
Liverpool
Lodi
Mallett Creek
Medina (c h)
Poe
Remson's Corners
River Styx
Sharon Centre
Spencer
Wadsworth
Weymouth
Whittlesey

Meigs co.
Alfred
Apple Grove
Rashan
Beach Grove
Burlingham
Chester
Dexter
Downington
Great Bend
Harrisonville
Hemlock Grove
Langsville
Leturi Falls
Long Bottom
Middleport
Minersville
Mount Blanco
Olive Centre
Pomeroy (c h)
Portland
Racine
Rutland
Salem Centre
Silver Run
Syracuse
Tupper's Plains
Valley Ford

Mercer co.
Noctis
Carthagena
Cilina (c h)

Chickasaw
Cold Water
Cranberry Prairie
Fort Recovery
Macedon
Maria Stein
Mendon
Mercer
Montezuma
Neptune
Reservoir
Saint Henry's
Shane's Crossings
Skeel's X Roads

Miami co.
Allen's
Brandt
Casstown
Conover
Covington
Fidelity
Fletcher
Greenford
Hyattsville
Laura
North Clayton
Piqua
Pleasant Hill
Potsdam
Troy (c h)
West Charleston
West Milton

Monroe co.
Antioch
Beallsville
Calais
Cameron
Centre View
Clarington
Graysville
Hannibal
Hope Ridge
Jolly
Laing's
Lecompton
Lewisville
Malaga
Masterton
Miltonsburgh
Mount Carrick
Ozark
Round Bottom
Sardis
Stafford
Wittens
Woodsfield (c h)
Young's Mills

Montgomery co.
Alexandersville
Brookville
Centre
Cantreville
Chambersburgh
Clayton
Dayton (c h)
Dodson
Farmersville
Fishburg
Germantown
Harshmansville
Hay's Store
Henby
Johnsville
Liberty
Little York
Miamisburgh
Miami City
New Lebanon
Pyrmont
South Arlington
Taylorsville
Union
Vandalia
West Baltimore

Morgan co.
Bishopville
Bristol
Chester Hill
Deavertown
Elliott's X Roads
Hall's Valley
Log Cabin
McConnellsville (o h)
Malta
Meigs' Creek
Meigsville
Mill Grove
Moscow Mills
Neelysville
Penisville
Pleasant Valley
Ringgold
Rokeby

Rosseau
Roxberry
Stockport
Todd's
Triadelphia
Wood Grove

Morrow co.
Andrews
Bennington
Bloomfield
Cardington
Chesterville
Corsica
Gray's Corners
Iberia
Indigo
McEwen's X Roads
Macon
Marengo
Marit's
Mount Gilead (c h)
Pulaskiville
Shauck's
Sparta
Vail's X Roads
Westfield
Whetstone
Woodview

Muskingum co.
Adams' Mills
Adamsville
Blue Rock
Bridgeville
Chandlersville
Coal Dale
Cottage Hill
Dresden
Duncan's Falls
Frazeysburgh
Freeland
Fultonham
High Hill
Hopewell
Licking Valley
Meadow Farm
Nashport
New Concord
Norwich
Otsego
Philo
Putnam
Rich Hill
Rix's Mills
Roseville
Rural Dale
Sago
Saintfield
Shannon
Sonora
Stovertown
Symmes' Creek
West Zanesville
White Cottage
Young Hickory
Zanesville (c h)
Zene

Noble co.
Ava
Batesville
Berne
Caldwell (c h)
Crooked Tree
Claytonia
Enoch
Gardner
Harriettsville
Hiramsburgh
Hoskinsville
Keith's
Kennonsburgh
McCleary
Middle Creek
Mount Ephraim
Noblesville
Olive Green
Olive
Renrock
Rochester
Sarahsville
Sharon
South Olive
Summerfield
Wharton's
Whigsville

Ottawa co.
Elmora
Genoa
Graytown
Locust Point
Marblehead
Marin
Ottawa
Port Clinton (c h)

Ohio.

Paulding co.
Antwerp
Charloe
Cranesville
Emmet
Hamer
Junction
McGill
Murat
Paulding (c h)
Payne
Reid's

Perry co.
Asbury
Buchanan
Buckeye Cottage
Chapel Hill
Dow Creek
East R'ish Creek
McClinsy
Maxville
Mount Perry
New Lexington (ch)
Oakfield
Pike
Porterville
Rehoboth
St. Joseph's College
Sego
Somerset
Straitsville
Thornville
Whipstown
Worth

Pickaway co.
Ashville
Backert's Store
Camp Charlotte
Circleville (c h)
Darbyville
Deer Creek
East Ringold
Five Points
Hedges' Store
New Holland
Kinderhook
Palestine
Prospect lle
South Bloomfield
St. Paul's
Tarlton
Tearird'n
Williamsport

Pike co.
Beaver
Byington
Cynthiana
Flat
Gibson
Jasper
Latham
Meggin's Fork
Omera
Piketon
Waverly (c h)

Portage co.
Atwater
Aurora
Blair
Brimfield
Charlestown
Deerfield
Edinburgh
Franklin Mills
Freedom
Garrettsville
Hiram
Mantua Centre
Mantua Station
Nelson
New Milford
Palmyra
Parisville
Randolph

Rapids
Ravenna (c h)
Rootstown
Shalersville
Streetsboro'
Suffield
Windham
Windham Station

Preble co.
Brinley's Station
Camden
Campbelltown
Eaton (c h)
El Dorado
Enterprise
Fair Haven
Gratis
Greenbush
Lewisburgh
Morning Sun
New Paris
New Westville
Sugar Valley
Upshur
West Alexandria
West Elkton
West Florence
West Manchester
West Sonora

Putnam co.
Belmore
Back Eye
Dog Creek
Fort Jennings
Franconia
Gilboa
Kalida (c h)
Leipsic
Pendleton
Pleasant
Sugar Ridge
Vaughnsville

Richland co.
Adario
Barnes
Belleville
Butler
Ganges
Hastings
Lexington
Lucas
Mansfield (c h)
Newville
Olivesburgh
Ontario
Plymouth
Riblet's
Richland
Rives
Shelby
Shenandoah
West Windsor

Ross co.
Adelphi
Austin
Bainbridge
Burnville
Chillicothe (ch)
Clarksburgh
Frankfort
Gillespieville
Greenland
Halleville
Hoop Pole
Kingston
Lattas
Lyndon Station
Richmond Dale
Roxabell
Schooley's Station
South Salem
Vigo
Walter
Yellow Bud

Sandusky co.
Black Swamp
Clyde
Exeter

Fremont (c h)
Greensburgh Cross Roads
Rollersville
Townsend
West Fremont
Wester's Station
Woodville

Scioto co.
Brushy Fork
Franklin Furnace
Friendship
Hale's Creek
Haverhill
Iron Furnace
Lilly
Lucasville
Nairs
Ottway
Pond Creek
Pond Run
Portsmouth (c h)
Powellsville
Rarden
Scioto
Sciotoville
Wheelersbargh

Seneca co.
Adams
Adrian
Attica
Bascom
Berwick
Battaville
Bloomville
Butternut Ridge
Flat Rock
Port Seneca
Fostoria
Green Spring
Kanas
Melmore
Palo Alto
Reedtown
Republic
Tiffin (c h)
Watson's Station
West Lodi

Shelby co.
Anna
Dinsmore
Hardin
Houston
Jackson Centre
Lockington
Loramie's
Montra
Pemberton
Plattsville
Pratt
Russia
Sidney (c h)
Tawawa
Wynaut

Stark co.
Alliance
Barryville
Cairo
Canal Fulton
Canton (c h)
East Greenville
Freese's Store
Greentown
Hartville
Lake
Limaville
Louisville
McDonaldsville
Magnolia
Mapleton
Marlborough
Massillon
Maximo
Middle Branch
Minerva
Mount Union
Navarre
New Baltimore
New Berlin
New Franklin
North Industry
North Lawrence
Osnaburgh
Pallow
Paris
Pierce
Waynesburgh
West Brookfield

Summit co.
Akron (c h)
Bath
Clinton
Copley
Cuyahoga Falls
Ghent
Hudson
Inland
Johnson's Corners
Macedonia Depot
Middlebury
Mogadore
Montrose
New Portage
Nimisilla
Northfield
North Springfield
Norton Centre
Peninsula
Richfield
Stow
Summit
Tallmadge
Twinsburgh
Western Star

Trumbull co.
Bazetta
Braceville
Bristolville
Brookfield
Burgh Hill
Church Hill
Duck Creek
Farmington
Fowler
Girard
Greensburgh
Gustavus
Hartford
Howland
Hubbard
Johnsonville
Kinsman's
Lordstown
Mecca
Mesopotamia
Newton Falls
Niles
North Bloomfield
Ohl's Town
Oil Diggins
Orangeville
Southington
State Line
Vernon
Vienna
Warren (c h)
Willow Dale

Tuscarawas co.
Albany
Bolivar
Brady
Buena Vista
Cadwallader
Canal Dover
Deardorff's Mills
Dundee
Gilmore
Guadenhutten
Milligan
Mineral Point
New Comerstown
New Cumberland
New Philadelphia (c h)
Pioli
Port Washington
Rocksford
Rogersville
Rush
Sandyville
Shanesville
Stillwater
Stone Creek
Strasburgh
Tabor
Tuscarawas
Uhricksville
Winfield
Zoar
Zoar Station

Union co.
Allen Centre
Bake's Creek
Byhalia
Coberly's
Darby Plains
Irwin

Jerome
Marysvil's (c h)
Milford Centre
New California
New Dover
Pharisburgh
Raymond's
Richwood
Rush Creek
Taylor Centre
Unionville Centre
Watkins
Wilkins
York

Van Wert co.
Auglaize
Delphos
Dixon
Leslie
Middle Point
Tally
Van Wert (c h)
Willshire

Vinton co.
Allensville
Big Sand Furnace
Dundas
Eagle Mills
Elk
McArthur (c h)
Mingo
New Plymouth
Prattsville
Road's Mills
Swan
Vinton Station
Wilkesville
Zaleski

Warren co.
Butlerville
Carlisle Station
Dallasburgh
Deerfield Village
Danlevy
Edwardsville
Fort Ancient
Foster's Crossings
Franklin
Harveysburgh
Hopkinsville
Lebanon (c h)
Level
Mainville
Mason
Morrow
Mount Holly
Oregon
Pleasant Plain
Red Lion
Ridgeville
Springboro'
Twenty Mile Stand
Waynesville

Washington co.
Barlow
Bartlett
Belpre
Beverly
Boaz
Brown's Mills
Centre Belpre
Coal Run
Constitution
Decaturville
Dunbar
Dunham
Fearing
Fillmore
Flints Mills
Grand View
Harmar
Lawrence
Layman
Liberty Hill
Little Hockhocking
Lowell
Lower Lawrence
Lower Newport
Lower Salem
Marietta (c h)
Moss Run
New Matamoras
Newport
Olds
Ostend
Requier's Mills
Saltpeter
Tunnell
Veto

Vincent
Waterford
Watertown
Wesley

Wayne co.
Amwell
Apple Creek
Baughman
Big Prairie
Blacklysville
Burbank
Canaan
Cedar Valley
Chippewa
Congress
Dalton
Easton
East Union
Fredericksburgh
Golden Corners
Kosh's
Madisonburgh
Marshallville
Mill Brook
Moorland
Mount Eaton
New Pittsburgh
New Prospect
Old Hickory
Orrville
Plain
Reedsburgh
Shreve
Smithville
West Lebanon
West Salem
Wooster (c h)

Williams co.
Bridgewater
Bryan (c h)
Deer Lick
Domestic
Dirbin's Corners
Edgerton
Lockport
Lake's Corners
Montpelier
Nettle Lake
North West
Pioneer
Primrose
Pulaski
Saint Joseph
Spring Lake
Stryker
West Bridge Water
West Buffalo
West Unity
Williams Centre

Wood co.
Bloom
Bowling Green
Brown's Corner
Gilead
Haskins
Holt
Lovett's Grove
Millbury
Milton Mills (Roads)
Montgomery K
New Rochester
New Westfield
Perrysburgh (c h)
Portage
Prairie Depot
Scotch Ridge
Stony Ridge
Tontogany
West Mill Grove
Woodbury

Wyandott co.
Belle Vernon
Bowshersville
Carey
Kirby
Little Sandusky
McCutchenville
Marseilles
Mexico
Nevada
Seal
Sycamore
Tymochtes
Upper Sandusky (ch)
Whartonsburgh
Wyandott

Oregon, Pennsylvania.

OREGON.

Benton co.
Corvallis (c h)
King's Valley
Liberty
Starr's Point
Tampico

Clackamas co.
Hood River
Milwaukie
Needy
Oregon City (c h)
Oswego
Sandy

Clatsop co.
Astoria

Columbia co.
Rainier
St. Helen (c h)

Coos co.
Empire City

Curry co
Port Orford

Douglas co.
Alder Brook
Galesville
Myrtle Creek
North Canyonville
Oakland
Roseburgh (c h)
Round Prairie
Winchester

Jackson co.
Applegate
Ashland Mills
Gold River
Jacksonville (c h)
Phœnix

Josephine co.
Kerby
Leland
State Creek
Vannoy
Waldo

Lane co.
Cottage Grove
Eugene City (c h)
Frauklin
Freedom
Grand Prairie
Long Tom
McKenzie
Othello
Pleasant Hill
Suislaw
Smithfield
Willamette Forks

Linn co.
Albany (c h)
Calaponya
Central
Diamond Hill
Harrisburgh
Peoria
Pino
Santiam City
Union Point
Washington Butte

Marion co.
Ashland Mills
Aurora Mills
Butteville
Champoeg
Fairfield
Parkersville
Salem (c h)
Silverton
Sublimity

Multnomah co.
Portland (c h)

Polk co.
Bloomington
Bridgeport
Dallas (c h)
Eola
Etna
Independence
Lawn Arbor
Luckiamute
Monmouth
Plum Valley
Salt Creek
Valfontis

Umpqua co.
Elkton (c h)
Kellogg's
Locust Grove

Scottsburg
Umpqua City
Yoncolla

Wascopum co
Wascopum (c h)

Washington co
Forest Grove
Hillsborough (c h)
Souvies Island
Wapato

Yam Hill co
Amity
Dayton
Lafayette (c h)
McMinville
Mount Hood
Muddy
North Yam Hill
Washington
Willamina

PENNSYLVANIA.

Adams co.
Abbottstown
Arendtsville
Bendersville
Bigler
Cashtown
East Berlin
Fairfield
Fountain Dale
Gettysburgh (c h)
Grateushurgh
Granite Hill
Green Mount
Hampton
Heidlersburgh
Hunterstown
Littlestown
McSherrystown
Mendlon
Mummusburgh
New Chester
New Oxford
Round Hill
Square Corner
Table Rock
Two Taverns
York Sulphur Springs

Alleghany co.
Alleghany
Arsenal
Bakerstown
Braddock Fields
Brodhead
Buchanan
Buena Vista
Carrick
Clinton
Coal Valley
Courtneyville
Culmerville
Dorseyville
Duquesne
Eakin
Elizabeth
Ewing's Mill
Fayette
Gumble's
Gill Hall
Glen Shaw
Green Tree
Harmarville
Herriottsville
Hope Church
Houston
Hulton
Library
McKeesport
Monroeville
Moon
Mount Lebanon
New Texas
Noblestown
Parnassus
Perrysville
Pittsburgh (c h)
Port Perry
Remington
Rich Valley
Rural Ridge
Sewickilyville
Sharpsburgh

Shirland
Shoustown
Spring Dale
Street's Run
Surgeon's Hall
Tally Covey
Tarentum
Temperanceville
Turtle Creek
Upper Saint Clair
Walker's Mills
West Elizabeth
West Manchester
Wexford
White Ash
Wilkins
Wilkinsburgh
Woodville

Armstrong co.
Adams
Apollo
Belknap
Blanket Hill
Brady's Bend
Cochran's Mills
Cowansville
Davis
Dayton
Echo
Eddyville
Elderton
Freeport
Kiskiminitas
Kittaning (c h)
Lawrenceburgh
Leechburgh
Long Run
Miller's Eddy
Oakland
Olivet
Orrsville
Phoenix
Pine Township
Putneyville
Red Bank Furnace
Rosston
Rural Valley
Scrub Grass
Slate Lick
South Bend
Spring Church
Worthington

Beaver co.
Baden
Baker Bank
Beaver (c h)
Black Hawk
Brush Creek
Cornetsburgh
Darlington
Economy
Elder's Mill
Fallston
Frankfort Springs
Freedom
Georgetown
Harshaville
Hookstown
Industry
Kendall
McClary
New Brighton
New Galilee

New Scottville
New Sheffield
North Sewickly
Ohio
Parkison
Poe
Rochester
Service
Seventy Six
Smith's Ferry
Water Cure

Bedford co.
Alum Bank
Bedford (c h)
Bloody Run
Charlesville
Clearville
Cumberland Val'y
Dry Ridge
Dublin Mills
El biasville
Hopewell
Mann's Choice
Pattonville
Rainsburgh
Ray's Hill
Robinsonville
Saint Clairsville
Schellsburgh
Six Mile Run
Stonerstown
West End
Woodbary
Yellow Creek

Berks co.
Albany
Baumstown
Bechtelsville
Beckersville
Bernville
Bethel
Birdsboro'
Boyerstown
Brower
Brumfieldville
Clayton
Colebrookdale
Coxtown
Cross Kill Mills
Cuuru
Dale
Douglassville
Dryville
Earlville
Fetheroffsville
Fredericksville
Furnace
Geiger's Mills
Gougersville
Greshville
Grimville
Hamburgh
Hereford
Host
Joanna Furnace
Klinesville
Kuaner's
Kutztown
Kutzville
Landis' Store

Leesport
Lenartsville
Lesher's
Leinbach's
Lobachsville
Long Swamp
Lower Bern
Maiden Creek
Manatawny
Maxatawny
Mertztown
Mohn's Store
Mohrsville
Molltown
Monterey
Morguntown
Moselem
Mount Aetna
New Jerusalem
Nora
Oley
Pike Township
Pricetown
Reading (c h)
Rehrersburgh
Robeson
Seisholtzville
Shanesville
Shartleysville
Sinking Spring
South Evansville
Spangsville
Stonersville
Stouchburgh
Strausstown
Temple
Tuckertown
Tulpehocean
Umstead's
Virginsville
Wernersville
Windsor Castle
Wintersville
Womelsdorf

Blair co.
Altoona
Antestown
Arch Spring
Canoe Creek
Clover
Duncansville
East Freedom
Fostoria
Frankstown
Hollidaysburgh (c h)
Martinsburgh
Newry
Olivia
Sabbath Rest
Sarah
Sinking Valley
Spang's Mills
Springfield Furnace
Tipton
Tyrone
Williamsburgh
Yellow Spring

Bradford co.
Alba
Asylum
Athens (c h)
Bently Creek

Browntown
Burlington
Camptown
Canton
Columbia Cross Roads
Durell
East Smithfield
East Springhill
East Troy
Edsallville
Elwell
Franklindale
French's Mills
Frenchtown
Granville
Granville Summit
Havensville
Herrick
Herrickville
Highland
Hornbrook
Laddsburch
Leonard Hollow
Le Raysville
Le Roy
Liberty Corners
Lime Hill
Litchfield
Macedonia
Merryall
Milan
Monroeton
Myersburgh
Narkonks
New Albany
New Era
North Orwell
North Rome
North Smithfield
North Towanda
Old Hickory
Orcutt Creek
Orwell
Overton
Pike
Potterville
Ridgebury
Rome
Rummerfield Cr'k
Sheshequin
South Creek
South Hill
South Warren
Springfield
Spring Hill
Standing Stone
Stevensville
Sugar Run
Sylvania
Tioga Valley
Towanda (c h)
Troy
Ulster
Warren Centre
Warrenham
West Burlington
West Franklin
West Warren
West Windham
Windham
Wyalusing
Wysox

Bucks co.
Andalusia
Applebachsville
Attleboro'
Badminter
Bridge Valley
Bridgewater
Bristol
Browsburgh
Buckingham
Bucksville
Bunker Hill
Barsonville
Carversville
Centre Bridge
Danboro'
Davisville
Dulington
Doylestown (c h)
Dublin
Durham
Edidngton
Edgewood
Emilie
Erwinna
Fallsington
Feasterville
Gardonville
Gery's
Hagersville
Hartsville
Hilltown
Hulmesville
Kiutnersville
Labaska
Lumberville
Mechanicsville
Milford Square
Morrisville
New Britain
New Hope
Newportville
Newtown
Oakford
Ottsville
Oxford Valley
Pineville
Pipersville
Pleasant Valley
Plumsteadville
Point Pleasant
Quakertown
Richboro'
Richlandtown
Riegelsville
Seller's Tavern
Spinnerstown
Springtown
Steinsburgh
Taylersville
Trumbaursville
Tullytown
Upper Black Eddy
Warminster
Warrington
Whitehallville
Wrightstown
Yardleyville

Butler co.
Anandale
Anderson's Mills

Pennsylvania.

Baldwin
Barnhart's Mill
Bovard's Store
Breakneck
Brownington
Bruin
Butler (c h)
Coultersville
Coyleville
Double Sale
Glade Mills
Harmony
Harrisville
Jacksville
McCandless
Maple Furnace
Middle Lancaster
Murrinsville
North Hope
North Oakland
Ogle
Petersburgh
Portersville
Prospect
Riddle's Cross Roads
Sarversville
Saxenburgh
Slippery Rock
Utena
Whitestown
Zelienople

Cambria co.
Bemis Creek
Bethel Station
Carrolltown
Chess Springs
Cresson
Ebensburgh (c h)
Fallen Timber
Gallitzin
Glen Connell
Hemlock
Johnstown
Loretto
Mineral Point
Munster
Pershing
Platteville
Roseland
Saint Augustines
Scalp Level
Sonman
Summer Hill
Summit
Wilmore

Carbon co.
Albrightsville
Beaver Meadows
Carbon
East Penn
Hickory Run
Lehigh Gap
Lehighton
Little Gap
Mauch Chunk (c h)
Nesquehoning
New Mahoning
Parryville
Penn Haven
Rockport
Stombersville
Summit Hill
Tresckow
Weatherly
Weissport

Centre co.
Aaronsburgh
Bellefonte (c h)
Benner
Bouldsburgh
Buffalo Run
Centre Hall
Centre Hill
Centre Line
Farm School
Fillmore
Fleming
Half Moon
Hannah
Howard
Hublersburgh
Julian Furnace
Madisonburgh
Marshcreek
Milesburgh
Millheim
Mountain Eagle
Nittany
Phillipsburgh
Pin Grove Mills
Pine Swamp
Pleasant Gap
Port Matilda
Potter's Mills
Rebersburgh
Rock Spring
Snow Shoe

Spring Mills
Stover's Place
Walker
Wolf's Store
Woodward
Zion

Chester co.
Avondale
Black Horse
Blue Rock
Brandywine Manor
Caln
Chaulterville
Chatham
Chester Springs
Chester Valley
Chesterville
Coatsville
Cochransville
Collamer
Dilworthtown
Doe Run
Downingtown
East Nantmeal
Elk Dale
Embreeville
Ercildoun
Fairville
Forestville
Frazer
Glen Roy
Gothenville
Gum Tree
Guthriesville
Hamorton
Hayesville
Hickory Hill
Honey Brook
Hopewell Cotton Works
Jennersville
Kemblesville
Kennett's Square
Kimberton
Lewisville
Lionville
Loag
London Grove
McWilliamstown
Marlborough
Marsh
Marshallton
Milltown
Mortonville
Mount Vernon
New Centreville
New Garden
New London
Nottingham
Oxford
Paoli
Parkersville
Parkesburgh
Penningtonville
Phœnixville
Pickering
Pughtown
Rockville
Russellville
Sadsburyville
Saint Mary's
Saint Peters
Schuylkill
Setzler's Store
Spread Eagle
Steelville
Street Road
Strickersville
Sugartown
Talbotville
Thornbury
Thorndale Iron Works
Unionville
Uwchland
Valley Forge
Vincent
Wagontown
Wallace
Warren Tavern
Waterloo Mills
Westchester (c h)
West Grove
West Vincent
West Whiteland
Willistown Inn

Clarion co.
Black Fox
Brinkerton
Callensburgh
Callph Furnace
Clarion (c h)
Curllsville
Frampton
Fryburgh
Helen Furnace
Jefferson
Kerr's Store
Kingsville

Knox
Kossuth
Lamartine
Leatherwood
Limestone
Lineville
Lucinda Furnace
Matildaville
New Bethlehem
North Pine Grove
Piny
Reidsburgh
Rimersburgh
River
Scotch Hill
Shannondale
Shippensville
Stant's Store
Strattonville
Tylersburgh
Watterson's Ferry
West Freedom

Clearfield co.
Ansonville
Bald Hill
Bloomville
Bower
Breckinridge
Burnside
Chest
Clearfield (c h)
Clearfield Bridge
Curwinsville
Cush
Frenchville
Glen Hope
Grahampton
Grampian Hills
Jefferson Line
Jeffries
Karthous
Kylertown
Lecoute's Mills
Lumber City
Luthersburgh
Marvon
Morrisdale
New Washington
Ostend
Penfield
Rockton
Salt Lick
Shawsville
Smith's Mills
Troutville
Tyler
Woodland

Clinton co.
Beech Creek
Birch Island
Cameron
Carroll
Cedar Springs
Chatham Run
Cook's Run
Defranceville
Dunnsburgh
Drury's Run
Farraudsville
First Fork
Flemington
Hiner's Run
Keating
Lamar
Leidig
Lockhaven (c h)
Logan Mills
McElhattan
Mill Hall
Salona
Rauch's Gap
Sinnamahoning
Sugar Valley
Tylersville
Westport
Young Womenst'n

Columbia co.
Beaver Valley
Benton
Berwick
Bloomsburgh (c h)
Briar Creek
Buckhorn
Catawissa
Central
Cole's Creek
Espy
Evansville
Fishing Creek
Forks
Foundryville
Fowlersville
Greenwood
Jerseytown
Light Street
Lime Ridge
Mainsville

Mifflinville
Millville
Monsicolo
Mordansville
Orangeville
Polkville
Rhoadestown
Rohrsburgh
Rupert
Sereno
Stillwater
Van Camp
Welliversville

Crawford co.
Adamsville
Beaver Centre
Bloomfield
Blooming Valley
Burns
Centreville
Chapinville
Cochranton
Connsautville
Crossingville
Cussawago
Custard's
Espyville
Evansburgh
Grinnels
Guy's Mills
Harmonsburgh
Hartstown
Hayfield
Kerr's Hill
Kingsville
Line Mills
Little Cooley
McDowell's
Marshall's Corners
Mead Corners
Meadville (c h)
New Richmond
North Shenango
Oil Creek
Penn Line
Randolph
Riceville
Rockdale
Royalton
Rundells
Saegerstown
Sandy Creek
Silverlings
South Shenango
Spartansburgh
Spring
Steamburgh
Steuben
Sugar Lake
Sutton's Corners
Tamarac
Teepleville
Titusville
Troy Centre
Turnersville
Unity
Venango
West Greenwood
Woodcock

Cumberland co.
Allen
Big Spring
Bloserville
Boiling Springs
Carlisle (c h)
Carlisle Springs
Dickinson
Eberly's Mill
Good Hope
Hogestown
Kerrsville
Lee's X Roads
Lisburn
Mechanicsburgh
Mt. Holly Springs
Mount Rock
Newburgh
New Cumberland
New Kingstown
Newville
Oakville
Plainfield
Shepherdstown
Shippensburgh
Shiremantown
Stonghstown
Walnut Bottom
West Fairview
West Hill
White House

Dauphin co.
Benvonan
Berrysburgh
Dauphin
Derry Church
Elizabethville
Enders

Enterline
Fisherville
Gratz
Halifax
Harrisburgh (c h)
Hockersville
Hummelstown
Linglestown
Lykens
Mamada Hill
Middletown
Millersburgh
Pillow
Powl's Valley
Short Mountain
Susquehannah
Union Deposit
West Hanover
Wiconisto

Delaware co.
Booth Corner
Chadd's Ford
Chelsea
Chester (c h)
Cheyney
Concordville
Darby
Edgemont
Glen Mills
Glen Riddle
Haverford
Howellville
Ivy Mills
Kellysville
Leipersville
Lenni Mills
Lima
Marple
Media
Newtown Square
Oakdale
Radnor
Ridleyville
Rose Tree
Spread Eagle
Tharlow
Upper Darby
Village Green
West Haverford

Elk co.
Arroyo
Benezett
Bentinger
Caledonia
Hellen
Hick's Run
Kerseys
New Highland
Pine Street
Ridgeway (c h)
Second Fork
Williamsville

Erie co.
Albion
Belle Valley
Carter Hill
Cherry Hill
Cook
East Greene
Edenville
Edinboro'
Elk Creek
Erie (c h)
Fairview
Franklin Corners
Girard
Greenfield
Harbour Creek
Lehoeuf
Lundy's Lane
McKean
Moorheadville
North East
Northville
Oak Grove
Platea
Springfield X Rd's
Sterrettania
Stewart
Swan Station
Union Mills
Waterford
Wattsburgh
Wayne
Wells' Corners
Wesleyville
West Springfield

Fayette co.
Belle Vernon
Brownsville
Connellsville
Cookstown
Davison's Ferry
Dawson

East Liberty
Elm
Farmington
Fayette Springs
Flatwoods
Heisterburgh
High House
McClellandtown
Masontown
Merritstown
Morris X Roads
New Geneva
New Salem
Peansville
Perryopolis
Red Stone
Reppert's Cross Roads
Searight's
Smithfield
Spring Hill Furnace
Tippecanoe
Tyrone Mills
Uniontown (c h)
Upper Middletown
Woodvale

Forest co.
Clarington
Foxburgh
Marionville

Franklin co.
Amberson's Valley
Chambersburgh (c h)
Concord
Doylesburgh
Dry Run
Fannettsburgh
Fayetteville
Green Castle
Green Village
Jackson Hall
Keefer's Store
Loudon
Marion
Mercersburgh
Mont Alto
New Guilford
Orrstown
Pleasant Hall
Quincy
Roxbury
Saint Thomas
Scotland
Spring Run
State Line
Sylvan
Upper Strasburgh
Upton
Waynesboro'
Welsh Run

Fulton co.
Burnt Cabins
Fort Littleton
Harrisonville
McConnellsburgh
New Granada
Spearsville
Waterfordburgh
Webster's Mills
West Dublin

Greene co.
Carmichael's
Clarksville
Crow's Mills
Davistown
Dunkard
Day's Store
Greensboro'
Harvey's
Hunter's Cave
Jefferson
Jollytown
Kirby
Mapletown
More Docks
Mount Morris
New Freeport
Oak Forest
Rice's Landing
Rogersville
Ruff Creek
Ryerson's Station
Sprang's
Waynesburgh (c h)
White Cottage
Whitely
Willow Tree
Windridge

Huntingdon co.
Airy Dale
Alexandria

Pennsylvania. 421

Anghwick Mills
Barre Forge
Birmingham
Bread Top
Calvin
Cassville
Coulmont
Coffee Run
Colerain Forge
Cottage
Crowmover's Mills
Cummingsville
Donation
Eagle Foundry
East Barre
Ennisville
Graysville
Greenwood Furnace
Huntingdon (c h)
James' Creek
McAlevy's Fort
M'Connellstown
Maddensville
Mauor Hill
Mapleton Depot
Meadow Gap
Mill Creek
Monroe Furnace
Mount Union
Orbisonia
Paradise Furnace
Shade Gap
Shaver's Creek
Shirelysburgh
Spruce Creek
Three Springs
Todd
Vineyard Mills
Warrior's Mark
Water Street
West Barre

Indiana co.
Armagh
Ayers
Black Lick
Black Lick Station
Blairsville
Brady
Brush Valley
Chambersville
Clarksburgh
Coal Port
Cookport
Decker's Point
Delhi
Ebenezer
Elder's Ridge
Hillsdale
Horton's
Indiana (c h)
Kent
Mahoning
Marchaud
Mitchell's Mills
Newman's Mills
Penn Run
Philip's Mill
Plumville
Saltsburgh
Shelocta
Smicksburgh
Smitten
Strongstown
Tannery
Tunnel
Utah
West Lebanon
Willet

Jefferson co.
Alvan
Big Run
Brockwayville
Brookville (c h)
Drown's Mills
Cool Spring
Corsica
Frostburgh
Hamilton
Packer
Porter
Punxatawney
Reynoldsville
Richardsville
Ringgold
Schoffner's Corners
Sprankle's Mills
Summersville
Warsaw

Juniata co.
Academia
East Salem
East Waterford
Evendale
Honey Grove

McAllisterville
McCoysville
McCulloch's Mills
Mexico
Mifflintown (c h)
Mohontongo
Oakland Mills
Patterson
Peru Mills
Pleasant View
Port Royal
Richfield
Spruce Hill
Thompsontown
Walnut
Waterloo

Lancaster co.
Adamstown
Bainbridge
Bareville
Bart
Bartville
Beartown
Bellemonte
Bethesda
Binkley's Bridge
Blue Ball
Bowmansville
Brickerville
Brinkley's Bridge
Buck
Cain's
Camargo
Cambridge
Chesnut Level
Chickies
Christiana
Churchtown
Clonmell
Cocalico
Colemanville
Colerain
Columbia
Conestoga
Durlach
East Hempfield
Elisabethtown
Enterprise
Ephratah
Falmouth
Farmersville
Fertility
Fulton House
Gap
Goodville
Gordonsville
Greene
Greenland
Groff's Store
Hempfield
Highville
Hinkleton
Intercourse
Kinzers
Kirk's Mills
Kirkwood
Lampeter
Lancaster (c h)
Landis Valley
Landisville
Leacock
Liberty Square
Litiz
Lyles
Manheim
Manor
Marietta
Martickville
Martinsville
Mastersonville
May
Maytown
Mechanic's Grove
Millersville
Mount Hope
Mount Joy
Mount Nebo
Mountville
Muddy Creek
Neffsville
New Danville
New Holland
New Milltown
New Providence
Nine Points
Oak Hill
Oak Shade
Oetoraro
Old Line
Oregon
Paradise
Penn
Peter's Creek
Piquea
Pleasant Grove
Pusayville
Quarryville
Rawlinsville
Reamstown

Reinholdsville
Rothsville
Safe Harbor
Salisbury
Schoeneck
Silver Spring
Slack Water
Smithville
Smyrna
Soudersburgh
South Hermitage
Sporting Hill
Strasburgh
Swarr's Mills
Swartzville
Terre Hill
Vogansville
Wakefield
West Earl
Wheatland Mills
Willow Street
Weaver's Mill
White Oak

Laurens co.
Chenango
Cross Cut
East Brook
Edinburgh
Enon Valley
Harlensburgh
Hillsville
Irish Ripple
Marr
Marvin
Mount Jackson
Neshannock Falls
New Bedford
Newcastle (c h)
New Wilmington
Plain Grove
Princeton
Pulaski
Rose Point
Volant
Wurtemberg

Lebanon co,
Achey's Corner
Annville
Bellview
Campbelltown
Colebrook
Cornwall
East Hanover
Fredericksburgh
Heilman's Dale
Jonestown
Lebanon (c h)
Meyerstown
Millbach
Minsemer Mills
Mount Zion
Ono
Palmyra
Richland Station
Shaefferstown
Union Forge

Lehigh co,
Allentown (c h)
Breinigsville
Catasauqua
Centre Valley
Clausville
Cooperburgh
Dillingerville
Emaus
Fogelsville
Friedensville
Germansville
Hensingerville
Hosensack
Jacksonville
Laury's Station
Lehigh Valley
Lowhill
Lynnville
Lyon Valley
Macungie
New Tripoli
North Whitehall
Orefield
Ritterville
Rucksville
Ruppsville
Saucon Valley
Schneckesville
Seiberlingsville
Shimerville
Shoenersville
Slatington
South Whitehall
Stinesville
Troxlertown
Weisenburgh
Wescosville
Whitehall Station

Luzerne co.
Albert's
Archbald
Bailey Hollow
Bald Mount
Beach Haven
Bear Creek
Blakeley
Black Creek
Cambra
Campbell
Carbondale
Carverton
Clark's Green
Clifton
Conyngham
Daleville
Dallas
Dorrance
Drum's
Dunmore
Dunnings
Eckley
Exeter
Fair Mount Spr'gs
Fleetville
Forty Fort
Gouldsboro'
Green Grove
Harveyville
Hazleton
Hendricksburgh
Hobbie
Humphreysville
Hunluck Creek
Huntsville
Hyde Park
Jeansville
Kingston
Kunckle
Lackawanna
Lake
Lehman
Milwaukee
Moosic
Morrison
Moscow
Muhlenburgh
Nauticoke
Nescopeck
New Columbus
Old Forge
Orange
Peneader
Pittston
Plainsville
Plymouth
Port Blanchard
Providence
Ransom
Red Rock
Scranton
Shickshinny
Sloyersville
Stoddardsville
Stockton
Sweet Valley
Sybertsville
Town Hill
Town Line
Truckaville
Wallsville
Wapwallopen
Waverly
West Nanticoke
White Haven
Wilkesbarre (c h)
Wyoming

Lycoming co.
Alvira
Barbour's Mills
Bastross
Bodine
Cedar Run
Chesnut Grove
Clinton Mills
Cogan House
Corson's
Elimsport
Delaware Water-Gap
Effort
Experiment
Fennersville
Henrysville
Kellersville
Kresgeville
Larry's Creek
Linden
Loyalsock
Lycoming Creek
Montoresville
Moreland
Muncy
Newburry
Nipponose
Oval
Phelps' Mills
Ralston

Road Hall
Salladyburgh
Texas
Tomb's Run
Trout Run
Unityville
Warrensville
Waterville
White Deer
White Pine
Williamsport (ch)
Wolf Run

McKean co.
Alleghany Bridge
Annin Creek
Bradford
Burtville
Clermontville
Eden
Farmer's Valley
Glenn
Kendall Creek
La Fayette
Norwich
Port Allaghany
Prentiss Vale
Sartwell
Shippen
Smithport (c h)

Mercer co,
Balm
Centretown
Clark
Delaware Grove
French Creek
Harthegig
Henderson
Hermitage
Hill
Indian Run
Irishtown
Jamestown
Leesburgh
London
Maysville
Mercer (c h)
Milledgeville
New Hamburgh
New Lebanon
New Vernon
North Liberty
North's Mill
Perrine
Salem
Sandy Lake
Satterfield
Sharon
Sheakleyville
West Greenville
West Middlesex
West Salem
Worth
Willow Brook
Wolf Creek

Mifflin co,
Allensville
Atkinsou's Mills
Belleville
Decatur
Kishacoquillas
Lewiston (c h)
Locke's Mills
McVeytown
Menno
Milroy
Newton Hamilton
Reedsville
Strode's Mills

Monroe co.
Analomink
Bartonville
Bossardsville
Brodheadville
Coolbaugh's
Coveaville
Delaware Water-Gap
Effort
Experiment
Fennersville
Henrysville
Kellersville
Kresgeville
Kunkletown
Long Valley
Marshall's Creek
Merwinsburgh
Nagleaville
New Mount Pleasant
Paradise Valley
Pocopoming
Priceburgh
Rossland
Shawnee

Shoemaker's
Snydersville
Spruce Grove
Stormville
Stroudsburgh (c h)
Tannersville
Treibleville
White's Tannery

Montgomery co.
Abington
Barren Hill
Blue Bell
Bridgeport
Broad Axe
Cabinet
Centre Square
Cheltenham
Conshohocken
Crooked Hill
Douglass
Eagleville
Fagleysville
Fairview Village
Fitzwatertown
Franconia
Frederick
General Wayne
Gilbertsville
Gulf Mills
Gwynedd
Harleysville
Hatboro'
Hickorytown
Hillegass
Hoppenville
Horsham
Huntingdon Valley
Jeffersonville
Jenkintown
King of Prussia
Kulpsville
Lederachsville
Limerick
Limerick Bridge
Line Lexington
Lower Merion
Montgomeryville
New Hanover
Norristown (c h)
Norritonville
Pennsburgh
Penn's Square
Perkiomen Bridge
Perkiomenville
Pleasant Run
Plymouth Meeting
Port Kennedy
Port Providence
Pottstown
Prospectville
Red Hill
Royer's Ford
Safordville
Schwenck's Store
Shaunonville
Shoemakertown
Skippack
Sorrell Horse
Spring House
Sumneytown
Three Tons
Trappe
Tyler's Port
Union Square
Upper Dublin
White Marsh
Willow Grove
Worcester
Zieglersville

Montour co.
Danville (c h)
Exchange
Limestoneville
Mooresburgh
Roaring Creek
Washingtonville
White Hall

Northampton co.
Bath
Belfast
Berlinsville
Bethlehem
Blue Mountain
Boston
Bush Kiln Centre
Butztown
Cherryville
Danielsville
Dill's Ferry
Easton (c h)
Flicksville
Freemansburgh
Hanoverville
Hecktown
Hellertown
Iron Hill

Pennsylvania.

Kessler's
Kluckuersville
Kreider'sville
Laubach
Leithsville
Lower Saucon
Martin's Creek
Middaugh's
Monoc'stown
Mount Bethel
Nazareth
Newhart's
Petersville
Richmond
Seidersville
Sinteford
South Easton
Stockertown
Stone Church
Uhlerstown
Weaversville
Wind Gap

Northumberland co.
Augusta
Bear Gap
Chillisquaque
Chulasky
Dalmatia
Dewart
Elysburgh
Fisher's Ferry
Greenbrier
Herndon
Hickory Corners
Kline's Grove
Line Mountain
McEwensville
Mahanoy
Milton
Mount Carmel
Northumberland
Paxinos
Pott's Grove
Rebucks
Rushtown
Shamokin
Snydertown
Sunbury (c h)
Troverton
Turbotville
Union Corner
Watsontown

Perry co.
Andersonburgh
Andesville
Blain
Donally Mills
Duncannon
Elliottsburgh
Ickesburgh
Juniata
Landisburgh
Liverpool
Marklesville
Millerstown
Montgomery's Ferry
Morleytown
New Bloomfield
New Buffalo
New Germantown
Newport
Roseburgh
Sandy Hill
Sherman's Dale
Sterrett's Gap
Warm Springs

Philadelphia co.
Andora
Bleckley
Bridesburgh
Bustleton
Byberry
Chesnut Hill
Falls of Schuylkill
Feltonville
Fox Chase
Frankford
Germantown
Holmesburgh
Kensington
Kingsessing
Leverington
Manayunk
Milestown
Mount Airy
Oxford Church
Philadelphia (c h)
Port Richmond
Rising Sun
Somerton
Tacony

Pike co.
Blue Eddy
Bushkill

Delaware
Dingman's Ferry
Egypt Mills
Fulmerville
Lackawaxen
Lord's Valley
Masthope
Matamoras
Milford (c h)
Narrows
Nyces
Paupac
Shehola
Tafton
Westfall

Potter co.
Ayer's Hill
Bingham
Brookland
Hartville
Carter Camp
Clara
Colesburgh
Cowdersport (c h)
Cross Forks
Dounally
East Homer
East Sharon
Eleven Mile
Ellisburgh
Eulalia
Genesee Fork
Germania
Harrison Valley
Hebron
Hector
Homer
Kettle Creek
Lymansville
Mill Port
Nelsonport
North Wharton
Oswayo
Pike Mills
Pike Valley
Raymond's
Roulette
Sharon Centre
Shinglehouses
Sweden
Turner Creek
Ulysses
Ulysses Centre
West Pike
Wharton
White's Corners
Williston

Schuylkill co.
Ashland
Auburn
Barry
Bearmout
Branch Dale
Broad Mountain
Cressona
Donaldson
Elwood
Focht's Forge
Freidensburgh
Gordon
Hecksherville
Hegins
Hendler
Hepler
Hughes
Klingerstown
Landingville
Llewellyn
Lower Mahantango
McKeansburgh
Middleport
Minersville
North Penn
Orwigsburgh (o h)
Pine Grove
Pitman
Port Carbon
Port Clinton
Pottsville
Ringtown
Rough and Ready
Sacramento
Saint Clair
Schuylkill Haven
Silver Creek
Summit Station
Swatara
Tamaqua
Tremont
Tuscarora
Upper Mahantango
West Penn
Woodside

Snyder co.
Beaver Springs
Beavertown

Chapman
Cosgrave Hall
Freeburgh
Kantz
Kratzerville
Kreamer
McKee's Half F'ls
Middleburgh
Mount Pleasant Mills
Penn's Creek
Port Treverton
Selin's Grove
Shamokin Dam
Troxelville

Somerset co.
Addison
Bakersville
Benford's Store
Berkley's
Berlin
Buckstown
Davidsville
Drakestown
Elk Lick
Forwardstown
Gebhart's
Harnedsville
Jenner's X Roads
Lavansville
Meyer's Mills
New Lexington
Pocahontas
Shade Furnace
Sipesville
Somerfield
Somerset (c h)
Southampton
Stanton's Mills
Stony Creek
Stoyestown
Summit Mills
Turkey Foot
Wellersburgh
Wittenberg

Sullivan co.
Campbellville
Cullny
Davidson
Dushore
Eagle's Mere
Eldredville
Forkville
Hill's Grove
Laporte
Millview
Muncy Bottom
Robinson's Lake
Shunk
Sonestown

Susquehannah co.
Ararat
Auburn Centre
Auburn Four Corners.
Birchardville
Brackney
Brookdale
Brooklyn
Choconut
Clifford
Dimock
Dundaff
Fairdale
Forest Lake
Friendsville
Gibson
Glenwood
Great Bend
Harford
Hop Bottom
Jackson
Jackson Valley
Lathrop
Lathrop's Lake
Lanesboro'
Lawsville Centre
Lenox
Lenoxville
Little Meadows
Lynn
Montrose (c h)
Montrose Depot
New Milford
Niven
North Jackson
Oakley
Rush
Rushville
Saint Joseph
Silver Lake
Smiley
South Auburn
South Gibson
Springville
Summers
Susquehannah Depot

Taylor
Thompson
Union Dale
Upsonville
West Auburn

Tioga co.
Bailey Creek
Blossburgh
Brookfield
Charleston
Chatham Valley
Cherry Flats
Covington
Crooked Creek
Daggett's Mills
East Charleston
Elkland
Elk Run
Farmington Centre
Gaines
Gray's Valley
Hammond's Creek
Knoxville
Lawrenceville
Liberty
Little Marsh
Mainesburgh
Mansfield
Maple Ridge
Middlebury Centre
Mitchells Creek
Mixtown
Morris
Nauvoo
Nelson
Osceola
Ogdensburgh
Pine Creek
Rutland
Sabinsville
Stony Fork
Sullivan
Tioga
Wellsboro'
Westfield

Union co.
Buffalo X Roads
Forest Hill
Hartleton
Laurelton
Lewisburgh
Locust Hill
Middle Creek
Millinburgh
New Berlin (c h)
New Columbia
Port Treverton
White Deer Mills
Winfield

Venango co.
Agnew's Mills
Big Bend
Canal
Cass
Cherry Tree
Clintonville
Cooperstown
Cornplanter
Cranberry
Dempseytown
East Sandy
Emlenton
Fertigs
Franklin (c h)
Holland
Howe
Maple Grove
McCalmont
Nebraska
Perry
Plum
Plumer
Polk
Porterfield
President Furnace
Rockland
Seneca
Stewart's Run
Sunville
Ten Mile Bottom
Tionesta
Tyrrel
Utica
Wallaceville
Wesley
Wilson's Mills

Warren co.
Columbus
Corydon
Eagle
East Pine Grove
Freehold
Garland
Germany
Jackson Run
Irvine

Kinzua
Lottsville
Pattonia
Pine Valley
Pittsfield
Russelsburgh
Sheffield
South West
Spring Creek
Star
Steam Mill
Sugar Grove
Tidionte
Warren (c h)
West Sheffield
West Spring Creek
Youngsville

Washington co.
Amity
Bavington
Beallsville
Bentleyville
Bower Hill
Brush Run
Buffalo
Burgettstown
Candor
Cannonsburgh
Cherry Valley
Claysville
Clokey
Coal's Bluff
Commettsburgh
Coon Island
Cross Creek Vil'ge
Dunningsville
East Bethlehem
East Finley
Eldersville
Finleyville
Florence
Fredericktown
Ginger Hill
Good Intent
Hickory
Hillsboro'
Independence
Kerr's Station
Lindly's Mills
Locust Hill
Millsboro'
Monongahela City
Munntown
Murdocksville
North Star
Paris
Patterson's Mills
Pike Run
Prosperity
Simpson's Store
Sparta
Strabano
Taylorstown
Ten Mile
Thompsonville
Van Buren
Venice
Washington (c h)
West Alexander
West Brownsville
West Finley
West Middletown
Woodrow
Zollersville

Wayne co.
Aldenville
Ariel
Beach Pond
Berlin Centre
Bethany (c h)
Canaan
Cascade
Cherry Ridge
Cold Spring
Damascus
Dyberry
East Sterling
Eldred
Equinunk
Galilee
Hamlinton
Hawley
High Lake
Hollisterville
Honesdale
Indian Orchard
Jericho
Ledge Dale
Middle Valley
New Foundland
Pleasant Mount
Preston
Priceville
Prompton
Purdyville
Rileyville

Rock Lake
South Sterling
Starrucca
Sterling
Stevenson's Mills
Tallmansville
Tannar's Falls
Waymart
White Mills

Westmoreland co.
Adamsburgh
Bolivar
Duquette
Bradenville
Branch Junction
Barrell
Cavettsville
Conemaugh Furnace
Crab Tree
Donegal
Fitz Henry
Fulton
Greensburgh (c h)
Harrison City
Harvey's Five Points
Hillside
Hill's View
Irwin's Station
Jones' Mills
Larimer's Station
Latrobe
Laughlintown
Laurelville
Ligonier
Livermore
Lockport Station
Lucesco
Madison
Manor Dale
Manor Station
McKean's Old Stand
McLaughlins Store
Mendon
Milligan's Mills
Millwood
Mount Pleasant
Murrysville
New Alexandria
New Derry
New Florence
New Stanton
North Washington
Oakland X Roads
Parnassus
Perryton
Pleasant Unity
Rostraver
Salem X Roads
Sardis
Shearer's X Roads
Stahlstown
Stewartsville
Sutersville
Tinker Run
Verona
Walts' Mills
Weaver's Old St'd
Webster
West Fairfield
West Newton
Youngstown
Yeloghany

Wyoming co.
Bella Sylva
Bowman's Creek
Braintrem
Centre Moreland
Clinton Corners
Eaton
Evan's Falls
Factoryville
Falls
Forkston
Furnan Hill
Golden Hill
Jenningsville
Keelersburgh
Keiserville
Laceyville
LaGrange
Lemon
Lovelton
Mehoopany
Messhoppin
Nicholson
North Flat
Pierceville
Russell Hill
Scottsville
Skinner's Eddy
South Eaton
Tunkhannock (c h)
Vernon

Rhode Island, South Carolina. 423

York co.
Apple Grove
Bald Eagle
Bryansville
Castle Fin
Chanceford
Clear Spring
Codorus
Cross Roads
Dallastown
Davidsburg
Dillsburgh
Dover
Emigsville
Etter's
Farmer's
Fawn Grove
Franklintown
Glen Rock
Grahamville
Hall
Hanover
Hanover Junction
Hellam
Hetricks
Hopewell Centre
Jefferson Station
Lewisberry
Loganville
Lower Chanceford
McCall's Ferry
Manchester [nace
Margaretta Fur-
Mount Campbell
Muddy Creek Frks
Newberrytown
New Bridgeville
New Freedom
Peach Bottom
Pine Hill
Porter's Seidling
Rail Road
Rossville
Seven Valleys
Shrewsbury
Sidonsburgh
Slate Hill
Slate Ridge
Smith's Station
Spring Forge
Stewartown
Strawbridge
Stringstown
Union
Wellsville
Windsor
Wrightsville
Yocumtown
York (c h)
York Furnace
Xenia

RHODE ISLAND.

Bristol co.
Barrington
Bristol (c h)
Nayatt Point
Warren

Kent co.
Centreville
Coventry
East Greenwich (c h)
Escohoag
Natick
Nooseneck Hill
Pawtuxet
Phenix
Quidnick

Rice City
Summit
Warwick
Warwick Neck
West Greenwich Centre

Newport co.
Adamsville
Bliss Four Corners
Jamestown
Little Compton
Newport (c h)
New Shoreham
Portsmouth
South Portsmouth
Tiverton

Tiverton Four Corners

Providence co.
Albion
Burrillville
Centredale
Chepachet
Cumberland Hill
Diamond Hill
Fiskeville
Foster
Foster Centre
Georgiaville
Greenville
Harmony
Knightsville

Lime Rock
Lonsdale
Manton
Manville
Mapleville
Mohegan
Mount Vernon
North Scituate
Olneyville
Pascoag
Pawtucket
Providence (c h)
Rockland
Slaterville
South Foster
South Scituate

Valley Falls
West Gloucester
Woonsocket Falls

Washington co.
Allenton
Arcadia
Ashaway
Carolina Mills
Charlestown
Davisville
Dorrville
Exeter
Hopkinton
Kingston (c h)
La Fayette

Narragansett
Peace Dale
Perryville
Pine Hill
Potter Hill
Quonochontaug
Rockville
Shamrock Mills
Slocumville
Tower Hill
Usquepaugh
Wakefield
Westerly
Wickford
Woodville
Wyoming

SOUTH CAROLINA.

Abbeville District.
Abbeville (c h)
Bordeaux
Calhoun's Mill
Cambridge
Cherokee Heights
Cokesbury
Diamond Hill
Donnaldsville
Dorn's Gold Mines
Due West Corner
Fraziersville
Gentzville
Gilbertville
Greenwood
Harper's Ferry
Harrisburgh
Hodges
Indian Hill
Level Laud
Long Caue
Lowndesville
Mapleton
Mill Way
Monterey
Mountain View
New Market
Ninety Six
Park's Creek
Sandover
Smithville
Swancy's Ferry
Temple of Health
Warrenton
White Hall
Wideman's
Willington
Wilson's Creek

Anderson's District
Anderson (c h)
Andersonville
Belton
Brushy Creek
Buchanan
Butlersville
Calhoun
Churubusco
Craytonville
Double Branches
Douthet
Equality
Evergreen
Five Forks
Golden Springs
Holland's Store
Honey Path
Locust Hill
Melville
Moffetsville
Moutain Creek
Newell
Orrville
Pendleton
Pierce Town

Queensboro'
Rock Mills
Rocky Ridge
Saddler's Creek
Seneca
Shallow Ford
Silver Glade
Slab Town
Steele's
Storeville
Townville
Twenty-Six
Varonnes
Williamston

Barnwell District.
Aiken
Allendale
Barker's Mills
Bamberg
Barnwell (c h)
Blackville
Buford's Bridge
Cowpen Branch
Davis' Mills
Duck Branch
Dunbarton
Erwinton
Four Mile Branch
Graham's Turnout
Greenland
Hammond
King Creek
Lower Three Runs
Merritt's Bridge
Midway
Millersville
Mims
Silverton
Smyrna
Speedwell
Tinker's Creek
White Pond
Williston
Windsor
Woodward

Beaufort District.
Beach Branch
Beaufort (c h)
Bluffton
Brighton
Danielton
Gillisonville
Grahamville
Greenland
Hardeesville
Hickory Hill
Hilton Head
Horse Gall
Lawtonville
Long Branch
Pocotaligo
Robertsville
Sand Hill

Silver Hill
Steep Bottom
Whippy Swamp

Charleston District.
Black Oak
Charleston (c h)
Danner's ⋈ Roads
Echaw
Haddrell's
Holly Hill
Monk's Corner
Mount Holly
North Santee
Pineville
Roadville
Summerville

Chester District.
Black Stocks
Baton Rouge
Beckansville
Carmel Hill
Cedar Shoal
Chester (c h)
Cornwell Turnout
Crosbyville
Halsellville
Hazlewood
Landsford
Lewisville
Lowrysville
Rich Hill ⋈ Roads
Rossville
Saudersville
Tomsville
Torbit's Store
Wallace
Well Ridge

Chesterfield District
Catarrh
Cheraw
Chesterfield (c h)
Hornsborough
Jefferson
Mount Croghan
Old Stone
Pine Tree
White Plains

Clarendon District.
Friendship
Fulton
Manning
New Zion
Wright's Bluff

Colleton District.
Adam's Run
Ashapoo Ferry
Blue House
Broxton's Bridge
Buckhead Causey
Edisto Island
Elmville
Jacksonborough Depot

Jedsburgh
Reevesville
Ridgeville
Rumph's Bridge
Saint Georges
Saltketcher Bridge
Walker's
Walterboro'

Darlington District
Cartersville
Darlington (c h)
Florence
Gully
Hartsville
Leavensworth
Lisbon
Lydia
Merchant's Bluff
Philadelphia
Society Hill
Sparrow Swamp
Swift Creek
Tan's Bay
Thomas' ⋈ Roads
Timmonsville
Wood Shop

Edgefield District.
Bath
Beech Island
Big Creek
Cairo
Cold Spring
Coleman's ⋈ Roads
Colliers
Dorn's Mill
Duntonsville
Dyson's Mills
Edgefield (c h)
Edisto Mills
Elton
Fruit Hill
Germanville
Graniteville
Grove Hill
Hamburgh
Higgin's Ferry
Ivy Island
Kirksey's ⋈ Roads
Longmire's Store
Lotts
Meeting Street
Mine Creek
Mount Willing
Oakland
Parks'
Perry's ⋈ Roads
Phenix
Pleasant Lane
Poverty Hill
Rehoboth
Richardsonville
Ridge
Shatterfield
Sister Springs
Tucker's Pond

West Creek
Woodlawn

Fairfield District.
Alston
Bell's Store
Brown's
Buck Head
Doko
Feasterville
Gladden's Grove
Jackson's Creek
Lilesford
Long Run
Monticello (c h)
Ridgeway
Rocky Mount
Shelton
Strother
Winnsboro'
Youngesville

Georgetown District
Georgetown (c h)
North Santee
Rhyme
Yanhanna

Greenville District.
Buena Vista
Cedar Falls
Chick's Springs
Clear Spring
Cottage Hill
Cripple Creek
Dublin
Dunklin
Fairview
Fountain Inn
Gilder
Golden Grove
Gowensville
Grove Station
Greenville (c h)
Highland Grove
Highway
Huntersville
Lavinda
Lickville
Lima
Line Creek
Marietta
Merrittsville
Milburg
Milford
Mush Creek
Plain
Pleasant Grove
Pliny
Sandy Flat
Sterling Grove
Traveler's Rest
White Horse
White Sand

Horry District.
Blanton's ⋈ Road
Bucksville
Bug Swamp
Conwaysborough (c h)
Dogwood Neck
Little River

Kershaw District.
Auniedell
Bee Tree
Camden (c h)
Flat Rock
Hanging Rock
Liberty Hill
Lynchwood
Red Hill
Russell Place
Tiller's Ferry

Lancaster District
Belair
Butler
Craigsville
Cureton's Store
Dry Creek
Dudley
Flint Ridge
Hickory Head
Jacksonham
Lancaster (c h)
Longstreet
Pleasant Hill
Pleasant Valley
Wild Cat

Laurens District.
Bluff Rabun
Brewerton
Centreville
Clinton
Cold Water
Cross Hill
Eden
Highland Home
Huntington
Laurens (c h)
Marenzo
Martin's Depot
Milton
Montroe
Mount Gallagher
Mount Pleasant
Mountville
North Creek
Pleasant Mound
Power's Shop
Reynos
Scuffletown
Simpson's Mills
Spring Grove
Tumbling Shoals
Tylersville
Waterloo
Young's Store

Tennessee.

Lexington District.
Beaver Pond
Calk's Ferry
Clark's Mills
Countsville
Dean Swamp
Draft's Mill
Edisto
Hollow Creek
Hope Station
Leesville
Lexington (c h)
Long Hollow
Oakville
Pleasant Spring
Rish's Store
Rockville
Rocky Well
Sandy Run
Sawyer's Mills
Steedman's
Williamson's Mills

Marion District.
Allen's Bridge
Britton's Neck
Campbell's Bridge
Catfish
Centenary
Effingham Station
Ella's Grove
Flintville
Floydville
Forestville
Friendfield
Gilchrist's Bridge
Gum Swamp
Jeffrey's Creek
Little Rock
Lynche's Creek
Marion (c h)
Mar's Bluff
Molunais Bridge
McGuces
Mullin's Depot
Oak Grove
Oakton
Peedee
Red Bluff
Reedy Creek
Selkirk
Sugar Hill

Temperance Hill
Willow Creek

Marlborough Dist.
Adamsville
Bennettsville
Brightsville
Brownsville
Olio
Parnassus
Powell's Store

Newberry District.
Beth Eden
Belmont
Chappell's Bridge
Cotswood
Glymphville
Indian Creek
Jalappa
Jolly Street
Kinnard's Turnout
Liberty Hall
Little Mountain
Long Pond
Maybinton
Mount Bethel
Newberry (c h)
Pomaria
Prosperity
Saluda Mills
Shop Spring
Walton
Whitemires

Orangeburgh Dist.
Branchville
Bull Swamp
Fort Motte
Halfway Swamp
Jamison
Jordan's Mills
Kitching's Mills
McCantsville
Orangeburgh (o h)
Poplar
Rowe's Pump
Saint Matthews
Vance's Ferry
White Cane
Willow Swamp

Pickens District.
Anderson's Mills
Arnold's Mills
Bachelor's Retreat
Bounty Land
Branch Island
Cain Creek
Camp Ground
Cheohee
Claremont
Clayton's Mills
Colonel's Fork
Dacusville
Eastaloe
Eighteen Mile
Fair Play
Five Mile
Flat Shoal
Fowler's Creek
George's Creek
Glassey Mountain
Holly Spring
Horse Shoe
Long Creek
Martin's Creek
Maxwell's Mills
Nine Times
Oakway
Oconee Station
Pickens (c h)
Pickensville
Salubrity
Snow Creek
Symm's Mills
Table Mountain
Toxaway
Tunnel Hill
Twelve Mile
Walhalla
Warsaw
Whetstone
White Hill
Wolf Creek

Richland District.
Cedar Creek
Columbia (c h)
Gadsden
Hopkins Turnout
Wateree

Spartanburgh District.
Algood
Arrowood
Barleywood
Batesville
Bivingsville
Boiling Springs
Briantsville
Buck Creek
Burnt Factory
Campobella
Cannon's Store
Cashville
Cedar Springs Asylum
Clarksville
Cowpens
Cowpen Furnace
Crawfordsville
Cross Anchor
Crowsville
Damascus
Earlesville
Enoree
Fingerville
Fort Prince
Glen Springs
Grassy Pond
Hebron
Hobbysville
Hurricane
Jackson Hill
Limestone Springs
Millville
Moultrie
Mount Lebanon
Mountain Shoals
New Prospect
Poolsville
Reidsville
Rogers' Bridge
Smith's Store
Sparta
Spartanburgh (c h)
Templeman's Mills
Valley Falls
Vernonsville
Wallace's Factory
Walnut Grove
Woodruff's

Sumter District.
Bethlehem
Bishopville
Black River
Bradford Springs
Bradleyville
Brewington
Plowerton
Harmony College
Lynchburgh
Manchester
Mayesville
Mechanicsville
Mill Grove
Packsville
Plowden's Mills
Privateer
Providence
Salem
Shiloh
Stateburgh (c h)
Sumter
Taylor's

Union District.
Cedar Bluff
Cold Well
Coopersville
Cross Keys
Draytonsville
Fair Forest
Fishdam
Goshen Hill
Gowdeysville
Jonesville
Kelton
McDuffie
Meansville
Mount Joy
Mount Tabor
Pacolett Mills
Simsville
Skull Shoals
Timber Ridge
Unionville (c h)
West's Spring
Wilkinsville

Williamsburgh District.
Black Mingo

Camp Ridge
Cedar Grove
Deer
Gourdines
Grape
Indiantown
Johnsonville
Kingstree (c h)
Lanude's Ferry
Lynche's Lake
Murray's Ferry
Myersville
Natural Grove
Plantersville
Potato Ferry
Singletarysville
Tisdale
Vine

York District.
Allison Creek
Antioch
Bethany
Bethel
Blairsville
Boydton
Bullock Creek
Cherokee Iron Works
Clark's Fork
Clay Hill
Coate's Tavern
Ebeneserville
Fort Mill
Jamestown
Grand Hill
Guthriesville
Harmony
Hickory Grove
Hopewell
McConnellsville
Meek's Hill
New Centre
New House
Rock Hill
Sharon Valley
Smith's Ford
Smith's Turnout
Taylor's Creek
Tirza
Yorkville (c h)
Zeno

TENNESSEE.

Anderson co.
Clinton (c h)
East Fork
Live Well
Loy's X Roads
Monroe's Rest
Oliver's
Robertsville
Ross
Wallace's X Roads
Wilson's

Bedford co.
Bell Buckle
Fairfield
Flat Creek
McGowansville
Normandy
Palmetto
Richmond
Rover
Rowesville
Shelbyville (c h)
Unionville
Wartrace Depot

Benton co.
Camden
Chaseville
Coxburg
Morgan's Creek
Onward
Point Mason
Rockport
Will's Point

Bledsoe co.
Bee Creek
Fillmore
Foster's X Roads
Grassy Cove
Mount Airy
Nine Mile
Orme's Store
Pikeville (c h)
Pitt's X Roads
Roberson's X Road
Spencer Hill
Stephen's Chapel

Blount co.
Brick Mill
Cade's Cove
Chilhowee
Clover Hill
Cloyd's Creek
Ellejoy
Friendsville
Gamble's Store
Louisville
Marysville
Montvale Springs
Morgantown
Rockford
Tuckaleechee Cove
Unitia

Bradley co.
Charleston
Cleaveland (c h)
Maple Grove
Meesville
Muskrat Springs
Potter's Branch
Stony Point
Wausville

Campbell co.
Archer'sville
Buffalo Creek
Coal Creek
Fincastle
Gibson's Store
Grantsboro'
Jacksboro'
Straight Fork

Cannon co.
Auburn
Bradyville
Mechanicsville
Woodbury (c h)

Carroll co.
Atwood
Buena Vista
Christmasville
Clarksburgh

Hecla
Hico
Huntingdon (c h)
Lavinia
McLemoresville
Macedonia
Marlborough
Sandy Bridge
South Carroll
Terry

Carter co.
Butler
Carter's Depot
Cave Spring
Doe River Cove
Dugger's Ferry
Elizabethtown (o h)
Elm Grove
Happy Valley
Limestone Cove
Peoplesville
Roan Mountain

Cheatham co.
Chesnut Grove
Henrietta
Sewanee
Shaw's Store
Sycamore Mills

Claiborne co.
Big Barren
Clearfield
Cumberland Gap
Head of Barren
Howard's Quarter
Oldtown
Pleasant
Powell's River
Rob Camp
Speedwell
Sycamore
Tazewell (c h)
Woodson's X Roads
Yellow Springs

Cocke co.
Bridgeport
Cato
Hackletooth
Newport (c h)
Parrottsville
Taylorsburgh
Wilsonville
Wilton's Springs
Wolf Creek

Coffee co.
Beech Grove
Forest Mills
Hickory Creek
Hillsboro
Manchester
Oak Hill Seminary
Pocahontas
Summitville
Tullahoma

Cumberland co.
Crossville
Grassy Cove
Maple Spring
Pleasant Hill
Pomona
Sandy Mills
Yellow Creek

Davidson co.
Capital View
Donelson
Elm Hill
Franklin College
Goodlettsville
Hamilton's Creek
Madison
Marrowbone
Nashville (c h)
Ridge Post
Stewart's Ferry
Tank
White Bend

Decatur co.
Brodie's Landing

Decaturville
Douglass Springs
Etna
Hermitage
Howesville
Perrysville

De Kalb co.
Alexandria
Laurel Hill
Liberty
Pine Creek
Smithville (c h)
Temperance Hall

Dickson co.
Barton's Creek
Bellsburgh
Charlotte (c h)
Danielsville
Independence
Laurel Furnace
Turnbull
White Bluff
Williamsville

Dyer co.
Booth's Point
Chestnut Bluffs
Dyersburgh
Forrest Hill
Friendship
Grove Mount
Miller's Chapel
Newbern

Fayette co.
Championville
Egypt
Elba
Fayette Corner
Galway
Hickory Withe
Lagrange
Macon
Moscow
Mount Comfort
Oakland
Pierce

Rossville
Somerville (c h)
Willis' Station
Wolf River

Fentress co.
Boatland
Coopersville
Hale's Mills
Jamestown (c h)
Pall Mall
Pine Springs
Rocky Branch
Travisville

Franklin co.
Anderson
Cowan
Dechard
Elk River
Estill Springs
Hawkersville
Hurricane
Pettysville
Salem (c h)
Winchester (c h)

Gibson co.
Antioch
Bluff Springs
Chester
Eaton
Enterprise
Gibson's Wells
Holly Leaf
Hope Hill
Humboldt
Pond Hill
Poplar Grove
Quincy
Shady Grove
Shiloh
South Gibson
Trenton
Tuckerville
Waterford
Yorkville

Tennessee.

Giles co.
Bethel
Bodenham
Bradshaw
Brick Church
Bunker's Hill
Campbellsville
Cornersville
Elkmont Spring
Elkton
Gibsonville
Holyoke
Lamartine
Lynnville
Midbridge
Oak Flat
Poplar Hill
Prospect
Pulaski (c h)
Vale Mills

Granger co.
Bean's Station
Blain's ✕ Roads
Cedar Cliff
Cedar Ford
Clear Spring
Haynes
Horner's Store
Marshall's Ferry
Noe's Ferry
Powder Spring Gap
Red Hill
Rocky Springs
Rutledge (c h)
Spring House
Tampico
Thorn Hill

Greene co.
Camp Creek
Caney Branch
Cedar Creek
Clear Creek
Fullens
Graysburg
Greenville (c h)
Gourley's Bridge
Gustavus
Henderson's Mill
Horse Creek
Laurel Gap
Limestone Springs
Little Chucky
Newmansville
Ones
Rheatown
Romeo
Timber Ridge
Warrensburgh

Grundy co.
Altamont (c h)
Beruboa Springs
Pelham
Tracy City

Hamilton co.
Birchwood
Chattanooga
Chickamoga
Double Branch
Harrison (c h)
Leonard Springs
Limestone
Loddy
Long Savannah
Sall Creek
Snow Hill
Zion Hill

Hancock co.
Alanthus Hill
Mulberry Gap
Sneedsville
War Creek

Hardeman co.
Amity Hill
Black Oak Grove
Bolivar (c h)
Crainsville
Grand Junction
Hickory Valley
Jenkins' Depot
Matamora
Middleburgh
New Castle
Salisbury
Toone Station
Van Buren
Whiteville

Hardin co.
Bon Ean
Chalk Bluff
Gillis' Mills
Hamburg

Herbertsville
Ingleside
Lowryville
Monticello
Saltillo
Savannah (c h)
Smith's Forks
Swallow Bluff

Hawkins co.
Bull's Gap
Lee Valley
Lyons' Store
Marble Hall
Mill Rend
New Canton
Quarrysville
Red Bridge
Rogersville (c h)
Saint Clair
Van Hill
War Gap
Yellow Store

Haywood co.
Bell's Depot
Brownsville
Cageville
Carolina
Daneyville
Forked Deer
Lanefield
Wellwood
Wesley
Woodville

Henderson co.
Centre Point
Farmville
Jack's Creek
Juno
Lexington
Middle Fork
Mifflin
Oak Forest
Pleasant Exchange
Poplar Spring
Red Mound
Scott's Hill
Shady Hill
Spain's
Tobasco

Henry co.
Albany
Barren Hill
Buchanan
Caledonia
Chanceford
Cheap Valley
Como
Conyersville
Cottage Grove
Ell Grove
Hagleaville
Manlyville
Mansfield
Mount Holyoke
Mount Vista
Mouth of Sandy
New Boston
North Fork
Paris (c h)
Sandy Hill

Hickman co.
Bluff Point
Bon Aqua
Centreville
Duck River
Dunnington
Lick Creek
Pine Wood
Pleasantville
Totty's Bend
Vernon (c h)
Whitfield

Humphreys co.
Big Bottom
Buffalo
Fowler's Landing
Hall's Creek
Honey Point
Silesia
Sugar Wood
Turkey Point
Waverly (c h)
Weaw
White Oaks

Jackson co.
Bennett's Ferry
Buck Point
Butler's Landing
Celina

Clementsville
Double Springs
Equality
Flynn's Lick
Fort Blount
Frank's Branch
Gainsboro' (c h)
Granville
Hamilton Landing
Highland
Lodi
Mayfield
Meigsville
New Columbus
North Springs
Pekin
Rocky Mount
White Plains
Whitleyville

Jefferson co.
Chestnut Hill
Chucky Bend
Cynthiana
Dandridge (c h)
Flat Gap
Green Vale
Kansas
Leadvale
Mill Spring
Morristown
Mossy Creek
Nebraska
New Market
Oak Grove
Panther Springs
Russellville
Snoddyville
Springvale
Strawberry Plains
Talbot Mills
Trion
Whitesburgh
Wittsville

Johnson co.
Baker's Gap
Cable's Valley
Cobb's Creek
Little Doe
Pandora
Shady
Shown's ✕ Roads
Taylorsville (c h)
Trade

Knox co.
Ball Camp
Beaver Ridge
Church Grove
Concord
Flint Gap
Gallaher's
Gap Creek
Kidd's Hill
Knoxville (c h)
McMillan
Mecklenburgh
North Hope
Raccoon Valley
Roseberry
Thorn Grove
Vandergriffs

Lauderdale co.
Cane Bottom
Cottage Hill
Double Bridges
Dry Hill
Durhamville
Fulton
Goldin's Ridge
Leesville
Ripley (c h)
Walnut Post

Lawrence co.
Appleton
Blanche
Cass
Glen Rock
Henryville
Lawrenceburg (c h)
Palo Alto
Wayland's Springs
West Point

Lewis co.
Newburgh (c h)
Palestine

Lincoln co.
Boon's Hill
Camargo
Cane Creek
Charity
Chestnut Ridge

Cordova
County Line
Craighead
Cyruston
Fayetteville (c h)
Gas Factory
George's Store
Gill's Store
Goshen
Kinderhook
Lynchburgh
Marble Hill
Millville
Molino
Mulberry
Norris Creek
Oregon
Petersburgh
Pleasant Plains
Robinson's Store
Viney Grove

McMinn co.
Athens
Calhoun
Cantrell's ✕ Roads
Cog Hill
Facility
Fountain Hill
Hamilton ✕ Roads
Jalapa
Middle Brook
Middle Creek
Mount Harmony
Oxford
Pine Ridge
Riceville
Rodger's Creek

McNairy co.
Adamsville
Anderson's Store
Chawalla
Gravel Hill
Hatchie
Monterey
Montezuma
Morse Creek
Mud Creek
Purdy (c h)
Rose Creek
Stantonville

Macon co.
Alton Hill
Brooks' Tan Yard
Echo
Eclipse
Eulia
La Fayette
Meadorville
Pugehcon Camp
Red Boiling Springs

Madison co.
Andrew Chapel
Centre
Cotton Grove
Denmark
Gadsden
Jackson (c h)
Medon
Mount Pinson
Poplar Corner
Spring Creek

Marion co.
Cheeksville
Crown Point
Dunlap
Jasper (c h)
Looney's Creek
Niojuck
Running Water
Wallden's Ridge
Walnut Valley

Marshall co.
Belfast
Berlin
Caney Spring
Chapel Hill
Farmington
Globe Creek
Holt's Corner
Lewisburg (c h)
Medium
Mooresville
New Hope
Spring Place
Tyrone

Maury co.
Ashwood
Beard's Store
Bigbyville

Cartersville
Columbia (c h)
Cross Bridge
Hampshire
Hardison's Mill
Hopewell
Hurt's ✕ Roads
Isom's Store
Mount Pleasant
Pleasant Grove
Rally Hill
Santa Fe
Silver Creek
Spring Grove
Spring Hill
Union
Williamsport

Meigs co.
Decatur
Goodfield
Kelly's Ferry
Kincannon's Ferry
Moore's ✕ Roads
Mouth of Hiwassee
Pine Land
Sewee
Ten Mile Stand

Monroe co.
Ball Play
Belltown
Chota
Citico
Coker Creek
Coytee
Four Mile Branch
Hiwassee College
Johnston's Mill
Madisonville
Mount Vernon
Philadelphia
Riverside
Rockville
Sweet Water
Tellico Plains
Towee Falls

Montgomery co.
Clarksville (c h)
Daley's
Fairmount
Fredonia
McAllister's Cross Roads
New Providence
New York
Oakwood
Onecho
Palmyra
Peacher's Mills
Pea Ridge
Pleasant Mound
Poplar Spring Iron Works
Port Royal
Richardson's
Ringgold
Sailor's Rest
Woodford
Woodlawn
Yellow Creek Furnace

Morgan co.
Crooked Fork
Glades
Morgan (c h)
Owl Hill
Pine Top
Sagefield

Obion co.
Clover Lick
Fremont
Jacksonville
Mason Hall
Mount Prospect
Silver Top
Troy (c h)
Union City

Overton co.
Fox Spring
Hilham
Livingston (c h)
Locust Shade
Monroe
Mount Pisgah
Mouth of Wolf
Netherland
Nettle Carrier
Oakley
Oak Hill
Olympus
Walnut Grove
West Fork

Perry co.
Beardstown
Britt's Landing
Cedar Grove Furnace
Linden
Lobelville
Wood's

Polk co.
Bell's Mill
Benton
Brush Creek
Canasauga
Copper Mines
Ducktown
Higdon's Store
Kimsey's Store
Lousville
Ocoa
Parksville
Springtown
Wetmore

Putnam co.
Bear Creek
Byrne
Cookville
Falling Water

Rhea co.
Big Elm
Lake
Prestonville
Smith's ✕ Roads
Sulphur Spring
Washington (c h)

Roane co.
Barnardsville
Bellville
Cross Keys
Emory Iron Works
Erie
Gray's Hill
Hackberry
Hope's Creek
Kingston (c h)
Lenoir's
London
Paw Paw Ford
Post Oak Springs
Tabor
Welckers' Mill
Wood's Hill
Wrightsville

Robertson co.
Barren Plain
Black Jack
Cherry Mount
Cooperstown
Cross Plains
Millersville
Mitchellville
Red River
Rose Hill
Sadlersville
Slaydensville
Springfield (c h)
Thomasville
Turnersville

Rutherford co.
Carlockville
Fosterville
Hall's Hill
Independent Hill
Jefferson
Jordan's Valley
Las Casas
La Vergne
Middletown
Milton
Murfreesboro (c h)
Readyville
Smyrna
Versailles

Scott co.
Clarsboro
Fort Brandon
Good Water
Horse Shoe Bend
Huntsville (c h)
Pouch Creek
Winfield

Sequatchie co.
Newberry

Sevier co.
Boyd's Creek
Cannon's Store
Fair Garden
Gatlinburch
Henderson's Spring

Texas.

Henry's ⋈ Roads
Pigeon Forge
Sevierville (c h)
Trundle's ⋈ Road
Waldon's Creek
Wear's Cove

Shelby co.
Arizonia
Big Creek
Colliersville
Cuba
Delta
Fisherville
Germantown
Green Bottom
Hagan's Landing
Hazel Flat
High Hill
Jessamine
Memphis
Morning Sun
Nashville
Raleigh (c h)
Sulphur Well

Smith co.
Bagdad
Bairdsville
Carthage (c h)
Chestnut Mound
Convenient
Dixon's Springs
Gibb's ⋈ Roads
Goose Creek
Gordonsville
Jennings Forks
Lancaster
Montross
New Middleton
Peyton's Creek

Pleasant Shade
Rome

Stewart co.
Big Rock
Bowling Green
Cable's Valley
Cumberland Iron Works
Dover (c h)
Great Western
Hope
Indian Mound
Iron Mountain
Lineport
Magnolia
Mint Spring
Standing Rock
Tobacco Port

Sullivan co.
Arcadia
Beaver Creek
Blountville (c h)
Campbell's Rest
Clover Bottom
Eden's Bridge
Edgeworth
Fordtown
Gott's ⋈ Roads
Hilton's
Holston Valley
Kingsport
Millpoint
Morrell's Mill
Paperville
Piney Flats
Poor Hill
River Bend Forge
Rockhold's
Union Depot

Sumner co.
Beech
Castalian Springs
Enon College
Fountain Head
Gallatin (c h)
Gretna Green
Hanna's
Hurtsville
Hendersonville
Rockhouse
Saundersville
Trammel
Tyree Springs

Tipton co.
Bloomington
Covington
Mountain
Mount Zion
Portersville
Randolph
Sharon

Union co.
Big Barren Forge
Cedar Ford
Lost Creek
Maynardville (c h)
Woodbourne

Van Buren co.
Mill's Branch
South Rock Island
Spencer (c h)

Warren co.
Caney Fork
Clearmont
Increase
Irving College
McMinnville

Morrison
Mountain Creek
Pine Bluff
Rocky River
Rough and Ready
Trousdale
Viola

Washington co.
Blue Plum
Boon's Creek
Broylesville
Buffalo Ridge
Cherry Grove
Clear Branch
Cox's Store
Falls Branch
Flag Pond
Freedom
Indian Creek
Johnson's Depot
Jonesboro' (c h)
Knob Creek
Leesburgh
Locust Mount
Longmire
Swingleville
Washington College
West's Store

Wayne co.
Ashland
Carrollville
Clifton
Craven's Mills
Factor's Fork
Houston
Middle Cypress
Patriot
Sorby

Victory
Waynes
Whitak

Wea
Alma
Black O
Boydsvi
Cedar H
Dedham
Dresden
Dukedo
Elm Tr
Fleming
Irvine's
Locust
Mount
Old Ric
Pillowv
Poland
Winstor

W
Bon Air
Bon Air
Calf Kil
Cassvill
Cave
Clarksv
Claysvi
Cumber
tute
Dry Va
Frank's
Green T
Newark
River P
Rock Is
Solen
Sparta

TEXAS.

Anderson co.
Barton
Beaver
Bethel
Hendersonville
Ioni
Kickapoo
Magnolia
Marietta
Mitto
Palestine (c h)
Parkersville
Plenitude
Prewitt's Tan Yard
Roudville
Tennessee Colony

Angelina co.
Chusland
Elysium
Fort Turan
Herrington
Homer
Marion (c h)

Atascosa co.
Pleasanton
Tordilla Mound

Austin co.
Bellville
Cat Spring
Hartville
Industry
Hempstead
Millheim
New Ulm
San Felipe (c h)
Sempronius
Shelby
Travis
Waller's Store

Bandera co.
Bandera

Bastrop co.
Alum Creek
Bastrop (o h)
Cedar Creek
Cunningham's
Young's Settlement

Bell co.
Belton
Howard
Salado
South Nolan

Bexar co.
Fort Clark
Fort Davis
Fort Lancaster
Fort McKavitt
Leal
Leon Springs
Lodi
Post Oak
San Antonio (c h)
San Lucas Springs
Selma
Sutherland Springs
Tenaha

Blanco co.
Blanco
Twin Sisters

Bosque co.
Cyrus
Mag Pond
Meridian
Neill's Creek

Bowie co.
Boston (c h)
De Kalb
Moore's
Myrtle Springs

Brazoria co.
Brazoria
Columbia
Gulf Prairie
Liverpool
Sandy Point
Velasco

Brazos co.
Boonville (c h)
Millican

Brown co.
Brownwood

Burleson co.
Blue Branch
Brazos Bottom
Caldwell (c h)
Chance Prairie
Lexington
Prospect
Sand Fly

Burnet co.
Burnet (c h)
Burns' Ford
Double Horn

Mahomet
Mormon Mills
Oatmeal
O'Havis Hill
Stricklinas

Caldwell co.
Albade
Lockhart (c h)
Plumb Creek
Prairie Lea
Sour Springs

Calhoun co.
Indianola
Port Lavaca (c h)
Saluria

Cameron co.
Brazos Santiago
Brownsville (c h)
Point Isabel
Santa Rosa

Cass co.
Alley's Mills
Courtlandt
Cusseta
Douglassville
Forest Home
Havana
Hickory Hill
Jefferson (c h)
Linden
Point Monterey
Smithland
Unionville

Cherokee co.
Alto
Box Creek
Griffin
Jacksonville
Knoxville
Larissa
Linwood
Mount Comfort
Pine Town
Rusk (c h)
Shooks Bluff
Sulphur Springs

Collin co.
Farmersville
Highland
Lone Tree
McKinney (c h)
Mantas
Millwood

Plano
Rock Hill
Roseland
Rowlett's Creek
Weston

Colorado co.
Columbus (c h)
Eagle Lake
Freisburgh
Ridge
San Bernard

Cooke co.
Fish Creek
Gainesville (c h)

Comal co.
Boerne
Crain's Mills
Hodge's Mills
New Braunfels (c h)
Sattler's
Sisterdale
Smithson's Valley
Spring Branch

Comanche co.
Cora
Resly's Creek

Coryell co.
Gatesville
Henson's Creek
Rainey's Creek
Station Creek

Dallas co.
Breckinridge
Buck & Breck
Cedar Hill
Dallas (c h)
Duck Creek
Eagle Ford
Farmer's Branch
New Lorem
Palace Hill
Pleasant Run
Reunion
Scyene
Trinity Mills

Denton co.
Alton (c h)
Clear Creek

Denton
Lewisvi
Little E
Pilot Po
Spear's
Stewart
Vallette

De
Clinton
Concret
Live Oa
Meyers
Pierpon
Price's
Yerktov

El
Brocksv
Chambe
Cumming
Milford
Red Oal
Tellico
Waxaha

El 1
El Paso
Fort Qu
Isleta
San Eliz

Er
Erath
Palaxy
Stephen

Fa
Alta Sp
Carolina
Elm Cre
Jena
Marlin (

Fan
Bois D'
Bonham
Caney C
Garnette
Honey G
Ladonia
Licke
Oakhill
Orangev
Warren

Fay
Cistern
Fayette

Texas. 427

Grayson co.
Basin Springs
Clayton
Ferguson
Kentuckytown
Macomb
Pilot Grove
Sherman (c h)
Springville
Woodboro'

Grimes co.
Anderson (c h)
Grimesville
Navasota
Piedmont Springs
Plantersville
Prairie Plains
Retreat

Guadaloupe co.
Bonite
Nockenut
Seguin (c h)
Valley

Harris co.
Baytown
Cypress Top
Harrisburgh
Hockley
Houston (c h)
Lynchburgh
Prairie Anna
Rose Hill
San Jacinto

Harrison co.
Ash Spring
Elysian Fields
Freedom
Friendship
Galatea
Glade Spring
Jonesville
Marshall (c h)
Port Caddo
Powellton

Hays co.
Cannonville
Dripping Springs
Manchac
Round Mountain
San Marcos

Henderson co.
Aberdeen
Athens
Brownsborough
Buffalo (c h)
Finoastle
Mulakoff
Science Hill
Scottsville

Hidalgo co.
Edinburgh
Rudyville

Hill co.
Covington
Crimea
Fairview
Fort Graham
Greenwade's Mills
Hillsborough (c h)
Peoria
White Rock

Hopkins co.
Black Jack Grove
Black Oak
Bright Star
Charleston
Pleasant Hill
Retina
Sulphur Bluff
Tarrant (v h)
White Oak
Woodland

Houston co.
Augusta
Coltharp's
Crockett (c h)
Hancock
Naches
Pennington
Prairie
Randolph

San Pedro
Shady Grove
Telegraph Mills

Hunt co.
Greenville (c h)
Hooker
Shiloh
South Sulphur
Tidwell Creek
Timber Creek

Jack co.
Antelope
Jacksborough

Jackson co.
Morales De Lavaca
Texana (c h)

Jasper co.
Bevilport
Cairo
Erin
Jasper (c h)
Magnolia Spring
Meritt's
Walnut Run
Wiess' Bluff

Jefferson co.
Beaumont (c h)
Concord
Pine Island
Sabine City
Village Creek

Johnson co.
Alvarado
Buchanan
Camanche Peak
Grand View
Noland's River
Rock Creek

Karnes co.
Ecleto
Helena
Home Place
Pana Maria

Kaufman co.
Cedar Grove
College Mound
Eureka
Kaufman (c h)
Kemp
Prairieville
Rockwall
Trinidad
Turner's Point

Kerr co.
Camp Verde
Comfort
Kerrsville

Kinney co.
Camp Hudson
Fort Clarke (c h)

Lamar co.
Ben Franklin
Blossom Prairie
Paris (c h)
Prairie Mount
Price's Store
Shockey's Prairie

Lampases co.
Lampasas
McAnelly's Bend

Lavacca co.
Antioch
Bearden
Halletsville
Hope
Moulton
Oaklund
Petersburgh (c h)
Sweet Home
Woodpoort

Leon co.
Bowling
Cane Branch
Centreville
Clapp's Creek
Frankville
Kidd's Mills
Leona (c h)
Look Out
Moody's ⋈ Roads

Navarro
Ringgold

Liberty co.
Cedar Bayou
Chambursia
Grand Cane
Johns
Liberty (c h)
Swartwout
Tarkington's Prairie
Wallisville
West Liberty

Limestone co.
Beargrass
Eutaw
Mount Calm
Personville
Springfield (c h)
Stoele's Creek
Tewookony Springs

Live Oak co.
Echo
Gussettville
Oakville

Llano co.
Cherokee
Llano

McLennan co.
Amonda
Bold Springs
Gilbert
Jackson
Middle Bosque
Perry
Sardis
Stark Grove
Waco Village

Madison co.
Bedi
Madisonville
Midway

Mason co.
Hedwig's Hill
Mason

Matagorda co.
Caney
Deming's Ridge
Kenner
Matagorda (c h)

Maverick co.
Eagle Pass (c h)

Medina co.
Castroville (c h)
D'Hanis
New Fontaine

Milan co.
Bryant's Station
Cameron
Nashville (c h)
Port Sullivan
San Anders
San Gabriel
Willow Springs

Montgomery co.
Danville
Montgomery (c h)

Nacogdoches co.
Cherino
Douglass
Green wood
Linn Flat
Lucknow
Melrose
Nacogdoches (c h)

Navarro co.
Corsicana (c h)
Dresden
Muskete
Richland Crossings
Rural Shade
Spring Hill
Taos

Newton co.
Biloxi
Burkoville
Cotland
Newton
Salem

Nueces co.
Corpus Christi (c h)
Ingleside

Orange co.
Bunn's Bluff
Duncan's Woods
Orange

Palo Pinto co.
Golconda
Pleasant Valley
Russell's Store (ch)

Panola co.
Anacostia
Beckville
Bethany
Carthage (c h)
Fair Play
Grand Bluff
Lineville
Long Branch
McMillan's
Pulaski
Reed's Settlement
Sugar Hill
Sweeton
Walnut Hill
Wood's

Parker co.
Balch
Copper Hill
Gamma
Nowburg
Veal's Station
Weatherford
Weatherstield

Polk co.
Cold Spring
Colita
Dayton
Livingston
Morganville
Moscow

Red River co.
Clarksville (c h)
Flinthan's Tan Yard
Kiomatia
Mill Creek
Pine Bluff
Robbinsville
Savannah
Spencer

Refugio co.
Aransas
Copano
Crescent Village
Lamar
Refugio (c h)
St. Marys

Robertson co.
Owensville
Wheelock (c h)
Willow Creek

Runnels co.
Fort Chadbourne

Rusk co.
Alma
Anadorca
Belleview
Caledonia
Cotton Plant
Fredonia
Harmony Hill
Henderson (c h)
Iron Mountain
London
Millville
Minder
Mount Enterprise
Murval
New Danville
New Salem
Reagon

San Cosme
Walling's Ferry
Wherrys

Sabine co.
Bear Creek
Fairmount
Milam (c h)
Sabinetown

San Agustine co.
San Augustine (c h)

San Patricio co.
Alguna
San Patricio (c h)

San Saba co.
San Saba

Shelby co.
Buena Vista
Clay's Mound
Graham's Mills
Hamilton
Hilliard
Shelbyville (c h)
Truit's Store
White Cottage

Smith co.
Flora
Garden Valley
Jamestown
Mount Carmel
Mount Sylvan
Ogburn
Seven Leagues
Starville
Tyler (c h)
Troup

Starr co.
Rio Grande City (c h)
Roma

Tarrant co.
Ashland
Atchison's Point
Birdsville
Estill's Station
Fort Worth
Gilleland
Grapevine
Hawkinsville
Johnson's Station
Merrilltown
Robinson's Mills
Webberville

Titus co.
Daingerfield
Ella
Goldsborough
Gray Rock
Green Hill
Hagansport
Lone Star
Monticello
Mount Pleasant (c h)
Snow Hill
Union Bridge

Travis co.
Austin (c h)
Bluff Springs
Case's Mills
Gilleland Creek
Hornsby
Merrilltown
Perdinales
Webberville

Trinity co.
Beasly's Store
Lake
Sumpter

Tyler co.
Billum's Creek
Caney Head
Pamplin's Creek

Paulineville
Peach Tree Village
Providence Hill
Town Bluff
Woodville (c h)

Upshur co.
Calloway
Carrollton
Coffecville
Earpville
Gilmer (c h)
Lafayette
Omega
Pine Tree
Pittsburgh
Point Pleasant
Red Rock
Simpsonville
West Mountain

Uvalde co.
Sibinai
Uvalde

Vanzandt co.
Barren Ridge
Big Rock
Canton
Edom
Four Mile Prairie
Hamburgh
Jordan's Saline (c h)

Victoria co.
Anaqua
Mission Valley
Victoria (c h)

Walker co.
Goshen
Huntsville (c h)
McKenzie
Newport
Tuscaloosa
Waverly

Washington co.
Brenham (c h)
Chapel Hill
Day
Duddville
Evergreen
Gay Hill
Independence
Long Point
Union
Vine Grove
Washington
Ye Gus

Webb co.
Carrizo
Laredo (c h)

Wharton co.
Egypt
Waterville
Whartou (c h)

Williamson co.
Bagdad
Circleville
Corn Hill
Cross Roads
Florence
Gabriel Mills
Georgetown (c h)
Liberty Hill
Pond Spring
Post Oak Island
Round Rock

Wise co.
Cactus Hill
Catlett's Creek
Decatur
Odessa
Prairie Point

Wood co.
Holly Spring
Lake Fork
Quitman (c h)
Sand Spring
Webster
Winnesborough

Young co.
Brazos Agency
Fort Belknap

VERMONT.

Addison co.
Addison
Bridport
Bristol
Brooksville
Chimney Point
Chipman's Point
Cornwall
East Middlebury
Ferrisburgh
Granville
Hancock
Larrabee's Point
Leicester
Lincoln
Middlebury (c h)
Monkton
New Haven
New Haven Mills
North Ferrisburgh
Orwell
Panton
Ripton
Salisbury
Sandusky
Shoreham
South Starksboro'
Starksboro'
Vergennes
West Addison
West Cornwall
West Salisbury
Weybridge Lower Falls
Whiting

Bennington co.
Arlington
Bennington
Bennington Centre
Boudville
Dorset
East Dorset
East Rupert
Factory Point
Heartwellville
Landgrove
Manchester (c h)
North Bennington
North Dorset
North Pownal
Peru
Pownal
Pownal Centre
Readsborough
Rupert
Sandgate
Searsburgh
Shaftsbury
South Dorset
South Shaftsbury
Stamford
Sunderland
West Arlington
West Rupert
Winhall
Woodford

Caledonia co.
Barnet
Burke
Danville (c h)
East Burke
East Hardwick

Groton
Hardwick
Lower Waterford
Lyndon
Lyndon Centre
McIndoe's Falls
Newark
North Danville
Passumsic
Peacham
Ryegate
Saint Johnsbury
St. Johnsbury Centre
St. Johnsbury East
Sheffield
South Hardwick
South Ryegate
South Walden
Sutton
Walden
Waterford
West Barnet
West Burke
West Danville
West Waterford
Wheelock

Chittenden co.
Bolton
Burlington (c h)
Charlotte
Colchester
Essex
Hinesburgh
Huntington
Jericho
Jericho Centre
Jonesville
Milton
Painesville
Pleasant Valley
Richmond
Saint George
Shelburn
Underhill
Underhill Centre
West Bolton
Westford
West Milton
Williston
Winooski Falls

Essex co.
Bloomfield
Brunswick
Canaan
Concord
East Haven
Granby
Guildhall (c h)
Island Pond
Lemington
Lunenburgh
Victory
West Concord

Franklin co.
Bakersfield
Berkshire
Buck Hollow
East Berkshire
East Fairfield
East Franklin
East Georgia

East Highgate
East Richford
East Sheldon
Enosburgh
Enosburgh Falls
Fairfax
Fairfield
Fletcher
Franklin
Georgia
Georgia Plain
Highgate
Highgate Spring
Montgomery (tre
Montgomery Cen-
North Fairfax
North Sheldon
Richford
Saint Albans (c h)
Saint Alban's Bay
Saxe's Mills
Sheldon
Swanton
Swanton Centre
West Berkshire
West Enosburgh
West Georgia

Grand Isle co.
Alburgh
Alburgh Springs
Grand Isle
Isle La Motte
North Hero (c h)
South Hero
West Alburgh
Windmill Point

Lamoille co.
Belvidere
Cady's Falls
Cambridge
Eden
Elmore
Hyde Park (c h)
Jeffersonville
Johnson
Morristown
Morrisville
North Cambridge
North Hyde Park
North Wolcott
Stow
Waterville
Wolcott

Orange co.
Bradford
Bradford Centre
Braintree
Brookfield
Chelsea (c h)
Copperas Hill
Corinth
East Brookfield
East Corinth
East Orange
East Randolph
East Thetford
Fairlee
Newbury
North Randolph

North Thetford
North Tunbridge
Orange
Post Mill Village
Randolph
South Newbury
South Strafford
Strafford
Thetford
Thetford Centre
Topsham
Tunbridge
Union Village
Vershire
Wait's River
Washington
Wells River
West Braintree
West Fairlee
West Randolph
West Topsham
Williamstown

Orleans co.
Albany
Barton
Barton Landing
Brownington
Coventry
Craftsbury
Derby
Derby Line
East Charleston
East Craftsbury
East Greensboro'h
Glover
Greensboro
Holland
Irasburgh (c h)
Jay
Lowell
Morgan
Newport
North Craftsbury
North Greensboro'
North Troy
Troy
West Albany
West Charleston
West Derby
Westfield
West Newport
Willoughby Lake

Rutland co.
Benson
Benson Landing
Brandon
Castleton
Centre Rutland
Chittenden
Clarendon
Clarendon Springs
Cuttingsville
Danby
Danby Four Corners
East Clarendon
East Hubbardton
East Poultney
East Wallingford
Fairhaven
Forest Dale
Healdville

Hortenville
Hubbardton
Hydeville
Ira
Mechanicsville
Mendon
Middletown
Mount Holly
North Clarendon
Pawlet
Pittsfield
Pittsford
Poultney
Rutland (c h)
Sherburne
Shrewsbury
South Wallingford
Sudbury
Sutherland Falls
Tinmouth
Wallingford
Wells
West Haven
West Pawlet
West Rutland

Washington co.
Barre
Berlin
Cabot
Calais
East Calais
East Montpelier
East Roxbury
East Warren
Marshfield
Middlesex
Montpelier (c h)
Moretown
North Duxbury
Northfield
North Montpelier
Plainfield
Roxbury
South Barre
Waitsfield
Warren
Waterbury
Waterbury Centre
Woodbury
Worcester

Windham co.
Athens
Bartonsville
Bellows Falls
Brattleboro'
Brookline
Cambridgeport
Dover
Dummerston
East Putney
Fayetteville (c h)
Grafton
Green River
Guilford
Guilford Centre
Halifax
Houghtonville
Jacksonville
Jamaica
Londonderry
Marlboro'
Putney
Rockingham

Saxton's River
South Halifax
South Londonderry
South Wardsboro'
South Windham
Stratton
Townsend
Vernon
Wardsboro'
West Brattleboro'
West Dover
West Dummerston
West Halifax
West Marlboro'
Westminster
Westminster West
West Townshend
West Wardsboro'
Whitingham
Williamsville
Wilmington
Windham
Windsor co.
Andover
Ascutneyville
Barnard
Bethel
Bridgewater
Brownsville
Cavendish
Chester
East Barnard
East Bethel
Felchville
Gassett's Station
Gaysville
Hartford
Hartland
Hartland Four Corners
Ludlow
North Chester
North Hartland
North Springfield
Norwich
Perkinsville
Plymouth
Pomfret
Pompanoosuc
Proctorsville
Quechy
Reading
Rochester
Royalton
Sharon
Simonsville
Snow's Store
South Pomfret
South Reading
South Royalton
South Woodstock
Springfield
Stockbridge
Tatisville
Tyson Furnace
Upper Falls
Weathersfield
Weathersfield Centre
West Hartford
Weston
West Rochester
White River Junction
Windsor
Woodstock

VIRGINIA.

Accomack co.
Accomack (c h)
Belle Haven
Chincoteague
Guildford
Horntown
Jenkins' Bridge
Locust Mount
Locustville
Messongo
Metompkin
Modestown
New Church
Onancock
Pungoteague
Savageville
Temperanceville
Wagram
Wisoville

Albemarle co.
Batesville
Bentivoglio
Boyd's Tavern
Brown's Cove
Carter's Bridge
Charlottesville (c h)
Cobham
Covesville
Earlysville
Free Union
Garland's
Greenwood Depot
Howardsville
Hydraulic Mills
Ivy Depot
Kesnick Depot
Mechum's River

Millington
Moreman's River
North Garden
Nortonsville
Scottsville
Shadwell
Stony Point
University of Virginia
Warren
Yancey's Mills

Alexandria co.
Alexandria (c h)
Globe Cottage

Alleghany co.
Callaghan's
Clifton Forge

Covington (c h)
Cowpasture Bridge
Cypress Island
Morris Hill
Mountain House
Red Sweet Springs
Rich Patch
Selma

Amelia co.
Amelia (c h)
Chula Depot
Deatonsville
Dennisville
Elk Hill
Finney Mills
Jetersville
Lodore
Maunboro'

Mataox
Morven
Painesville
Pride's Church
Rich Woods
Winterham

Amherst co.
Allen's Creek
Amherst (c h)
Buffalo Springs
Burford's Summit
Cool Well
Galt's Mills
Hockett's Bottom
New Glasgow
Oronoco
Pedlar's Mills
Pryor's Vale

Rose Mills
Salt Creek
Sandidge's
Stony Fork
Temperance

Appomattox co.
Appomattox
Bent Creek
Evergreen
Nebraska
Oakville
Reedy Spring
Spanish Oaks
Spout Spring
Spring Mills
Stone Wall Mills
Tower Hill
Walker's Church

Virginia.

Augusta co.
Arbor Hill
Barter Brook
Burke's Mills
Churchville
Craigsville
Deerfield
Fishersville
Greenville
Hermitage
Jenning's Gap
Lebanon White
 Sulpher Springs
Long Glade
Middlebrook
Mint Spring
Moffatt's Creek
Mossy Creek
Mount Meridian
Mount Sidney
Mount Solon
New Hope
Parnassus
Pond Gap
Rockland Mills
Saggersville
Sherando
Staunton (c h)
Steele's Tavern
Stribling Springs
Stuart's Draft
Summerleon
Swoope's Depot
Waynesboro'
West View

Barbour co.
Belington
Burnersville
Calhoun
Hackersville
Meadowville
Melon
Nestorville
Overfield
Peel Tree
Phillippa (c h)

Bath co.
Bath (c h)
Bath Alum
Cady's Tunnel
Cleek's Mills
Green Valley
Healing Spring
Hot Springs
Letcher
Millboro' Springs
Mountain Grove
Sun Rise
Williamsville

Bedford co.
Big Island
Body Camp
Buford's
Bunker Hill
Chamblisburg
Charlemont
Chesnut Fork
Cross Roads
Davis' Mills
Davis' Store
Emaus
Fancy Grove
Forest Depot
Goodview
Hendrick's Store
Holcomb's Rock
Horeb
Ivy Creek Mills
Kasey's
Liberty (c h)
Lisbon
Lone Pine
Loving Creek
Lowry
Otter Bridge
Peaks of Otter
Peaksville
Piercville
Wade's
White Rock

Berkeley co.
Arden
Darkesville
Falling Waters
Gerrardstown
Glengary
Hainesville
Hedgesville
Jones' Spring
Little Georgetown
Martinsburgh (c h)
Mill Creek
North Mountain

Shanghai
Tomahawk Spring
Van Clevesville

Boone co.
Bald Knob
Ballardsville
Coon's Mills
Hewittville
Mud River
Peytona
Slash Branch
Turtle Cleck

Botetourt co.
Amsterdam
Blue Ridge
Catawba
Cloverdale
Dagger's Springs
Fincastle (c h)
Finkes
Junction Store
Old Hickory
Pattonsburg
Rio Mills
Roaring Run
Rocky Point Mills
Saltpetre Cave
Tinker Knob
Waskey's Mills

Braxton co.
Beech Bottom
Birchtown
Braxton (c h)
Buffalo Fork
Bulltown
Brown's Mountain
Flat Woods
Hacker's Valley
Holly River
Middleport
Perkin's Mills
Rock Camp
Salt Lick Bridge
Sideling Hill
Two Lick Run

Brooke co.
Bethany
Cherry Hill
Fowler's
Short Creek
Wellsburgh (c h)

Brunswick co.
Benton
Burntville
Crichton's Store
Diamond Grove
Edmunds'
Gholsonville
Harper's Home
Jonesboro'
Kennedy's
Lawrenceville (c h)
Lewisville
Pleasant Oaks
Powellton
Smoky Ordinary
Stony Mount
Sturgeonville
White Plains

Buchanan co.
Grundy

Buckingham co.
Austin
Buckingham (c h)
Buckingham Mine
Centenary
Curdsville
Diana Mills
Glenmore
Gold Hill
Gravel Hill
Mount Vinco
New Canton
New Store
Staunton's Precinct
Virginia Mills
Well Water

Cabell co.
Bloomingdale
Cabell (c h)
Falls Mill
Green Bottom
Griffithsville
Guyandotte
Hamlin
Mud Bridge
Paw Paw Bottom
Ten Mile
Thorndike

Calhoun co.
Brooksville
Minnora

Campbell co.
Arnoldton
Brook Neal
Campbell (c h)
Castle Craig
Concord D
Green Hill
Hat Creek
Leesville
Lynchburgh
Marysville
Morris Church
Mount Athos
Mount Zion
Pigeon Run
Yellow Branch

Caroline co.
Apple Wood
Bowling Green (c h)
Central Point
Chilesburgh
Flippo's
Golansville
Guiney's
Milford
Penola
Port Royal
Ruther Glen
Sparta
Turner's Store
White Chimneys

Carroll co.
Cranberry Plains
Dug Spur
Gladesborough
Grayson Sulphur
 Springs
Hillsville
Laurel Fork
Lovel's Creek
Stone Mountain
Wolf Glade

Charles City co.
Apperson's
Charles City (c h)
Edna Mills
Wilcox's Wharf

Charlotte co.
Aspen Wall
Charlotte (c h)
County Line Cross
 Roads
Cub Creek
Drake's Branch
Dupree's Old Store
Harvey's Store
Keysville
Mossing Ford
Red House
Red Oak Grove
Roanoke Bridge
Rolling Hill
Rough Creek
Talcott
Wylliesburgh

Chesterfield co.
Blackheth
Chester
Hallsboro'
Manchester
Midlothian
Proctor's Creek
Skinquarter
Winterpock

Clarke co.
Berryville
Berry's Ferry
Castleman's Ferry
Millwood
Wadesville
White Post

Clay co.
Clay (c h)

Craig co.
Craig's Creek
Francisco's Mills
Level Green
Midway
Middle Mountain
New Castle (c h)
Simmonsville
Sinking Creek

Culpeper co.
Boston
Brandy Station
Castleton
Culpeper (c h)
Eldorado
Griffinsburgh
Homeland
Jeffersonton
Kellysville
Mitchell's Station
Oak Shade
Raccoon Ford
Rapid Ann Station
Richardsville
Shepard's Grove
Stevensburgh
Waylandsburgh

Cumberland co.
Ca Ira
Cartersville
Cumberland (c h)
Oak Forest
Royal Oaks
Stony Point Mills
Sunny Side
Woodson

Dinwiddie co.
Bothwick
Crimea
Dinwiddie (c h)
Ford's Depot
Goodwynsville
Malonesville
Mulberry Inn
Petersburgh
San Marino
Sutherland
Wilson's Depot

Doddridge co.
Central Station
Cold Water
Greenbrier Run
Greenwood
Long Run Station
McElroy
New Milton
Sayre's Mill
Smithton
West Union (c h)

Elizabeth City co.
Hampton (c h)
Old Point Comfort

Essex co.
Bestland
Centre Cross
Dunnsville
Lloyds
Loretto
Miller's Tavern
Montague
Mount Landing
Occupacia
Tappahanock (c h)

Fairfax co.
Accotink
Anandale
Anna
Ayr Hill
Burke's Station
Centreville
Chantilly
Dranesville
Dye's Mill
Fairfax (c h)
Fairfax Station
Falls Church
Friendship
Herndon
Langley
Mount Pierce
Peach Grove
Pleasant Valley
Prospect Hill
Republican Mills
Sangster's Station
Spring Vale
Theological Seminary

Fauquier co.
Auburn
Bealeton
Bristersburg
Broad Run Station
Catlett
Clift Mills
Elk Run
Foxville

Markham Station
Millview
Morrisville
New Baltimore
New Brighton
Orlean
Paris
Piedmont Station
Pine View
Rectortown Station
Saint Stephen
Salem Fauquier
Somerville
The Plains
Upperville
Warrenton (c h)
Warrenton Springs
Waterloo
Weaversville
Wheatley

Fayette co.
Clifty
Cotton Hill
Fayetteville (c h)
Gauley Bridge
Hawk's Nest
Locust Lane
Mountain Cove
Oak Hill
Pack's Branch
Rocky Hill

Floyd co.
Copper Hill
Copper Valley
Floyd (c h)
Greasy Creek
Huffville
Indian Valley
Little River
Simpson's
West Fork Furnace
Willis Ridge

Fluvanna co.
Bremo Bluff
Central Plains
Chapel Hill
Columbia
Fork Union
La Fayette Hill
Palmyra (c h)
Seven Islands
Union Mills
Wilmington

Franklin co.
Bonbrook
Boone's Mill
Carron Furnace
Cooper's
Dickinson's
Gill's Creek
Glade Hill
Gogginsville
Hale's Ford
Long Branch
Lynanville Mills
Paffs'
Penhook
Pig River
Prillaman's
 Retreat
Rocky Mount (c h)
Shady Grove
Snow Creek
Sontag
Starry Creek
Sydnorsville
Taylor's Store
Union Hall
Villa
Young's Store

Frederick co.
Acorn Hill
Back Creek Valley
Brucetown
Cedar Creek
Collinsville
Gainsboro'
Gravel Spring
High View
Middletown
Mountain Falls
Mount Vernon Tannery
Newton Stephensburg
Stephenson's Depot
White Hall
Winchester (c h)

Giles co.
Bell Point
Egglestons Springs
Kimberlin

Mechanicsburgh
Newport
North View
Pearisburg
Pembroke
Staffordsville
White Gate

Gilmer co.
Arnoldsburgh
Big Bend
Cox's Mills
De Kalb
Glenville (c h)
Letter Gap
Normantown
Pine Creek
Steer Creek
Stout's Mills
Townsend Mills
Troy

Gloucester co.
Glenn's
Gloucester (c h)
Hayes' Store
Hickory Fork
New Upton
Wood's ⋈ Roads

Goochland co.
Caledonia
Coal Hill
Dover Mills
Fife's
Goochland (c h)
Hadensville
Issequena
Johnson's Springs
Loch Lomond
Pemberton
Perkinsville
Shannon Hill

Grayson co.
Big Meadow
Bridle Creek
Carsonville
Elk Creek
Grayson (c h)
Independence (c h)
Meadow Creek
Mouth of Wilson
Peach Bottom
Point Hope
Spring Valley
White Top

Greenbrier co.
Alvon
Big Clear Creek
Blue Sulpher
 Springs
Bunger's Mill
Clintonville
Falling Spring
Frankford
Grassy Meadows
Green Sulphur
 Springs
Letcher
Lewisburgh (c h)
Lowry's Mills
Marshalleville
Maysville
Meadow Bluff
Meadow Grove
Millbrook
Palestine
Renick's Valley
Second Creek
White Sulpher
 Springs

Greene co.
Dawsonville
McMullen's Mill
Ruckersville
Standardsville (c h)
Swift Run

Greenville co.
Hicksford (c h)
Poplar Mount
Ryland's Depot

Halifax co.
Barksdale
Black Walnut
Bloomsburgh
Brookly'n
Clover Depot
Halifax (c h)
Harmony
Henry's Mills
Hyco
Hyco Falls
Mayo

430 Virginia.

Meadville
Mount Carmel
Mount Laurel
Newn Ferry
Omega
Providence
Red Bank
Republican Grove
Scottsburgh
South Boston Depot
Vernon Hill
Whitesville
Whitlock

Hampshire co.
Bloomery
Burlington
Capon Bridge
Capon Springs
Cold Stream
Dillon's Run
Forks of Potomac
Frankfort
Frouchburg
Green Spring Run
Hanging Rock
Hartmonsville
Higginsville
Hook's Mills
New Creek Station
North River Meet-
 inghouse
North River Mills
Okonoko
Patterson's Depot
Piedmont
Pleasant Dale
Purgitsville
Ridgeville
Romney (c h)
Sheetz Mill
Slanesville
Smith's Gap
Springfield
Wardville
Yellow Spring

Hancock co.
Fairview
Freeman's Land-
 ing
Holliday's Cove
New Cumberland

Hanover co.
Ashland
Auburn Mills
Beaver Dam Depot
Chickahomeny
Ellen
French Hay
Hanover (c h)
Junction
Montpelier
Morris
Negro Foot
Old Church
Rockville
Spring Level
Taylorsville
Verdon

Hardy co.
Baker's Run
Fabius
Greenland
Howard's Lick
Inkermann
Kettsman's
Lauretton
Lost River
Luney's Creek
Moorefield (c h)
Mount Hebron
Mount Storm
Peru
Raymoursville
Wardensville
Williamsport

Harrison co.
Adamsville
Bridgeport
Brown's Creek
Clarksburgh (c h)
Hepsville
Kincheloe
Lost Creek
Lumberport
New Salem
Prospect Valley
Quiet Dell
Romine's Mills
Shinnston
Wallace
W. Milford
Wilsonburgh
Wolf Summit

Henrico co.
Erin Shades
Richmond (c h)
West Ham Locks

Henry co.
Brockinridge
County Line Mills
Dyer's Store
Granville
Horse Pasture
Irisburgh
Leatherwood'
 Store
Martinsville (c h)
North Mayo
Oak Level
Prunty's
Ridgeway
Rough and Ready
 Mills
Traylorsville

Highland co.
Clover Creek
Doe Hill
Head Waters
Hightown
McDowell
Meadow Dale
Mill Gap
Monterey
New Hampden
Palo Alto
Spruce Hill
Strait Creek
Wilsonville

Isle of Wight co.
Barber's ⋈ Roads
Burwell's Day
Carraville
Franklin Depot
Smithfield (c h)
Windsor Station
Zun Station

Jackson co.
Angerona
Boggsville
Elk Fork
Fisher's Point
Frozen Camp
Grass Lick Fork
Hemlock
Jackson (c h)
Le Roy
Moore's Mills
Murrayville
Muse's Bottom
New Geneva
Pleasant View
Ravenswood
Reedy
Sandy
Wise

James City co.
Burnt Ordinary
Williamsburgh (c h)

Jefferson co.
Charlestown (c h)
Duffields
Halltown
Harper's Ferry
Kabletown
Kearneysville
Leetown
Middleway
Rippon
Shepherdstown
Summit Point

Kanawha co.
Blue Creek
Cannelton
Carbonvale
Chestnut Hill
Coalsmouth
Coondenin
Jarrott's Ford
Kanawha (c h)
Kanawha Saline
Newton
Osborne's Mill
Paint Creek
Pocotaligo
Shrewsbury
Sissonville
Tyler Mountain
Upper Falls of Coal

King & Queen co.
Bruington
Carlton's Store
Fleetwood Aca-
 demy
King and Queen
 (c h)
Little Plymouth

New Prospect
Newtown
Plain View
Saint Stephen's
 Church
Shakleford's
Stevensville
Walkerton

King George co.
Clifton
Comorn
Edge Hill
Hampstead
King George (c h)
Port Conway
Shiloh

King William co.
Acquinton
Aylett's
Enfield
King William (c h)
Lanasville
Mangohick
Rumford Academy
West Point

Lancaster co.
Kilmarnock
Lancaster (c h)
Litwalton
Lively Oak
Merry Point
White Stone

Lee co.
Beech Spring
Cany Hollow
Jonesville (c h)
Rocky Station
Ross Hill
Sticklysville
Turkey Cove
Walnut Hill
Whitesburg
White Oak Springs
Yocum Station
Zion's Mills

Lewis co.
Alkire's Mills
Bennett's Mills
Big Skin Creek
Bush's Mills
Fink's Creek
Hacker's Creek
Ireland
Jacksonville
Janelew
Leading Creek
Little Skin Creek
Weston (c h)
Wild Cat Run

Logan co.
Chapmanville
Green Shoal
Logan (c h)
Mouth of Pigeon
Pigeon Trace
Rich Creek
White's Mills

Loudon co.
Aldie
Arcola
Belmont
Bloomfield
Bolington
Broad Run
Circleville
Goresville
Hamilton
Hillsboro'
Hoylesville
Hughesville
Leesburgh (c h)
Lovettsville
Middleburgh
Morrisonville
Mount Gilead
Mountville
Necraville
Oatland's
Philomont
Potomac Furnace
Purcellville
Round Hill
Snickersville
Union
Waterford
Whaley's Store
Wheatland

Louisa co.
Alto
Ambler's Mills
Bulls ⋈ Roads

Cuckooville
Ellisville
Frederickshall
Gilboa
Gum Spring
Harris
Jackson
Locust Creek
Locust Level
Long Creek
Louisa (c h)
Mansfield
Mechanicsville
Poindexter's Store
Second Turn Out
South Anna
Thompson's ⋈
 Roads
Tolersville
Trevillian's Depot

Lunenburg co.
Brickland
Columbian Grove
Double Bridge
Halseysburgh
Laurel Hill
Lochleven
Lunenburgh (c h)
McFarland's
New Plymouth
Non Intervention
Plantersville
Pleasant Grove
Rehoboth
Tussekiah
Wattaboro'
Yatesville

McDowell co.
Dick's Creek
Gilead Spring
Peerysville

Madison co.
Criglersville
Dulinsville
Graves' Mill
Lesa
Locust Dale
Madison (c h)
Madison Mills
Oak Park
Peola Mills
Rochelle
Seville
Wolftown

Marion co.
Barracksville
Basnettsville
Beaty's Mills
Benton's Ferry
Bingamon
Boothsville
Fairmont (c h)
Farmington
Forksburgh
Glover's Gap
Gray's Flat
Hoodsville
Manningtown
Meredith's Tavern
Mill Falls
Nuzums
Palatine
Rivesville
Valley Falls
Worthington

Marshall co.
Adaline
Beeler's Station
Bolton
Benwood
Cameron
Dallas
Fair Hill
Fork Ridge
Glen Easton
Kossuth
Lynn Camp
Moundsville (c h)
Rock Lick
Rock Valley
Rosby's Rock
Sherrard
Slippery Ford
Wheeling Valley
Woodlands

Mason co.
Arbuckle
Clover Valley
Cologne
Deer Lick
Hartford City
Hereford's

Letart
Mason
Point Pleasant (c h)
Upland
Upper Flats
West Columbia

Matthews co.
Cobb's Creek
Matthews (c h)
North End

Mecklenburgh co.
Boydton (c h)
Cabbage Farm
Christiansville
Clarksville
Drapersville
Forksville
Joyceville
Lombardy Grove
Marengo
Oakley
Palmer's Springs
Randolph Macon
 College
Saint Tammany's
Shelton's Springs
South Hill
Stony Cross
Tanner's Store
Union Level
White House
Whittle's Mills

Mercer co.
Bethel
Camp Creek
Deep Lick
East River
Flat Top
Frenchville
Jumping Branch
Mercer Salt Works
Pipe Stem
Princeton (c h)
Spanishburg
The Rock

Middlesex co.
Church View
Freeshade
Harmony Village
Jamaica
Locust Hill
Harmony Village
Saluda (c h)
Sandy Bottom
Urbanna

Monongalia co.
Arnettsville
Blacksville
Casaville
Center
Clinton Furnace
Fort Martin
Granville
Ice's Ferry
Jake's Run
Jobe
Laurel Point
Maidsville
Miracle Run
Morgantown (c h)
Pentress
Pridevale
Stewartstown
Uffington
Wadestown
White Day

Monroe co.
Egypt
Gap Mills
Indian Creek
Johnson's ⋈ Roads
Lindside
Mount Vernon
Mouth of Indian
 Creek
Pack's Ferry
Peterstown
Red Sulpher
 Springs
Salt Sulpher
 Springs
Sink's Grove
Sweet Springs
Union (c h)
Wolf Creek

Montgomery co.
Alleghany Spring
Blacksburgh
Childress' Store
Christiansburg
 (c h)

Dry Valley
La Fayette
Laurel Creek
Lovely Mount
Matamoras
McDonald's Mill
Montgomery
 Springs
Shawsville
Shellville

Morgan co.
Alpine Depot
Berkeley Springs
 (c h)
Cacapon Depot
Cherry Run Depot
Oakland
Paw Paw
Sir John's Run
Sleepy Creek
 Bridge
Unger's Store
Valley Mills

Nansemond co.
Australia
Chuckatuck
Hargrove's Tavern
Holy Neck
Kingsville
Somerton
South Quay
Suffolk (c h)

Nelson co.
Afton
Avon
Faber's Mills
Green Field
Gulf Ford
Hardwicksville
Lovingston (c h)
Martin's Mills
Massie's Mills
Mount Horeb
Murrill's Shop
Robert's Mills
Rock Fish
Roseland
Tye River Ware-
 house
Variety Mills
Willow Bank

New Kent co.
Barhamsville
New Kent (c h)
Slatersville

Nicholas co.
Beaver Mills
Birch River
Fork Lick
Fowler's Knob
Keller's ⋈ Lane
Hookersville
Nicholas (c h)
Sandrun
Snow Hill
Rich Woods
Winston

Norfolk co.
Churchland
Deep Creek
Great Bridge
Hickory Ground
Lake Drummond
Norfolk (c h)
North West River
 Bridge
Portsmouth

Northampton co.
Bay View
Capeville
Eastville
Hadiock
Johnsontown
Sea View

Northumberland co
Burgess' Store
Heathsville (c h)
Lottsburgh
Union Village
Wicomico Church

Nottoway co.
Blacks and Whites
Burksville
Forkland
Jeffress' Store
Jennings' Ordinary

Virginia. 431

Nottoway (c h)
Wellville

Ohio co.
Clinton
Coleman's
Elm Grove
Triadelphia
Valley Grove
West Liberty
Wheeling (c h)

Orange co.
Barboursville
Germanna
Gordonsville
Jackson's Shop
Locust Grove
Madison Run Station
Mallory's Ford
Orange (c h)
Orange Springs
Somerset
Thornhill
Unionville
Verdierville

Page co.
Alma
Cedar Point
East Liberty
Grove Hill
Hope Mills
Leaksville
Luray (c h)
Marksville
Massanuton
Shenandoah Iron Works
Stoney Man
Valleyburgh

Patrick co.
Ararat
Ayo
Clark's Creek
Elamsville
Mayo Forge
Meadows of Dan
Nettle Ridge
Patrick (c h)
Penn's Store
Rock Castle
Rock Spring
Round Meadows
Sandy Plains
Spabrook Station
Tuggles' Gap
Union Furnace

Pendleton co.
Dry Run
Franklin (c h)
Harper's Mills
Mount Freedom
Mouth of Seneca
Oak Flat
Sugar Grove
Sweedlin Hill
Upper Tract

Pittsylvania co.
Aspen Grove
Axton
Bachelor's Hall
Berger's Store
Callaud's
Cartersburgh
Cascade
Chalk Level
Grafton
Danville
Glady Fork
Hill Grove
Laurel Grove
Mount Airy
Museville
Peytonsburg
Pittsylvania (c h)
Pleasant Gap
Riceville
Ringgold
Sandy Level
Sandy River
Spring Garden
Swansonville
Whitmell

Pleasants co.
Grape Island
Hebron
Saint Marys (c h)
Willow Island

Pocahontas co.
Academy
Big Spring
Dunmore

Gray
Frost
Green Bank
Hintersville (c h)
Marlin Bottom
Mill Point
Mount Murphy
Oldfield Fork of Elk
Sanset
Thorny Creek
Traveller's Repose

Powhatan co.
Balleville
Fine Creek Mills
Genito
Hullsboro'
Jefferson
Macon
Powhatan (c h)
Smithsville
Sublett's Tavern

Preston co.
Allbright
Amblersburgh
Brandonville
Bruceton Mills
Orancsville
Evansville
Fellowsville
German Settlement
Glade Farms
Gladesville
Greensburgh
Gasseman's Store
Horse Shoe Run
Kingwood (c h)
Masontown
Muddy Creek
Newburgh
Pariston
Recon
Reidsville
Rowlesburgh
Saddick Falls
Springdale
Tannery
Tunnelton
Valley Point

Prince Edward co.
Darlington Heights
Farmville
Green Bay
Hampden Sidney College
Moore's Ordinary
Pamplin's Depot
Prince Edward (c h)
Prospect
Rice Depot

Prince George co.
Brandon Church
City Point
Disputanto
Garysville
Prince George (ch)
Templeton

Princess Ann co.
Blossom Hill
Ives' Store
Kempsville
Land of Promise
London Bridge
Pleasant Ridge
Princess Anne (ch)

Prince William co.
Brentsville (c h)
Bristoe Station
Buckland
Dumfries
Evansport
Gainesville
Groveton
Haymarket
Independent Hill
Landsdown
Maple Valley
Neabsco Mills
Occoquan
Thoroughfare
Tudor Hall

Pulaski co.
Draper's Valley
Dublin
Newbern (c h)
Poplar Hill
Snowville

Putnam co.
Buffalo
Frazier Bottom
Hensonville
Hurricane Bridge
Mount Salem
Mouth of Poca
Red House Shoals
Sycamore Grove
Tease's Valley
Walnut Grove
Winfield

Raleigh co.
Coal River Marshes
Jarrold's Valley
Raleigh (c h)
Richman Falls
Round Glade
Shady Spring
Table Rock

Randolph co.
Beverly (c h)
Dry Fork
Fillmore
Huttonsville
Leadsville
Middle Fork
Mingo Flat
New Interest
Queen's Mills
Red Creek
Roaring Creek
Salina
Upper Cheat
Valley Head

Rappahanock co.
Amissville
Flint Hill
Gaines' X Roads
Laurel Mills
Rock Mills
Sandy Hook
Slate Mills
Sperryville
Washington (c h)
Woodville

Richmond co.
Durrettsville
Farnham
Stony Hill
Warsaw (c h)

Ritchie co.
Bone Creek
Cairo
Cornwallis
Ellenborough
Goose Creek
Highland
Mulehill
Oxford
Pennsboro'
Petroleum
Ritchie (c h)
Rusk
Webb's Mills
White Oak

Roane co.
Henrie's Fork
Reedyville
Roxalana
Spencer
Walton

Roanoke co.
Bent Mountain
Big Lick
Bonsack's
Botetourt Springs
Cave Spring
Gishe's Mills
Salem (c h)

Rockbridge co.
Alone
Alum Springs
Balcony Falls
Brownsburgh
Buena Vista Furnace
Caniselle
Cedar Grove Mills
Collierstown
Fairfield
Fancy Hill
Gilmore Mills
Glenwood
Goshen Bridge
Jordan's Springs
Kerr's Creek

Lexington (c h)
Longwood
Monmouth
Natural Bridge
Oakdale
Rapp's Mills
Rockbridge Bath
Sandors' Store
Summers
Thompson's Landing
Timber Ridge

Rockingham co.
Bowman's Mills
Bridgewater
Broadway Depot
Cherry Grove
Conrad's Store
Coote's Store
Cross Keys
Dayton
Dovesville
Edom
Green Mount
Harrisonburgh (ch)
Keezletown
Lacey Spring
McGaheysville
Melrose
Meyerhoeffer's Store
Mount Clinton
Mount Crawford
Port Republic
Tenth Legion
Timberville
Waverlie

Russell co.
Belfast Mills
Bickley's Mills
Dickensonville
Gibsonville
Guest's Station
Hansonville
Hendrick's Mills
Lebanon (c h)
New Garden
Pine Spring
Point Truth
Pound
Rock Farm
Rosedale
Willow Spring

Scott co.
Duncan's Mills
Estillville (c h)
Fort Blackimore
Holston Bridge
Holston Springs
Nickelville
Osborn's Ford
Pattousville
Quillinsville
Rocky Point
Rye Cove
Stock Creek
Wayland

Shenandoah co.
Columbia Furnace
Edinburg
Forestville
Fort Furnace
Hamburgh
Jacob's Church
Lantz Mills
Lebanon Church
Liberty Furnace
Lorenzoville Foundry
Moore's Store
Mount Clifton
Mount Jackson
Mount Olive
New Market
Orkney Springs
Paddy Mills
Saumisville
Seven Fountains
Strasburgh
Tom's Brook
VanBuren Furnace
Woodstack (c h)

Smyth co.
Blue Spring
Broadford
Chatham Hill
Marion (c h)
Olympia
Rye Valley
Seven Mile Ford
Sinclair's Bottom
Two Mile Branch

Southampton co.
Assinoosick
Berlin
Blunt's Depot
Bowers
Boykin's Depot
Branchville
Drewrysville
Falsonaville
Farmer's Grove
Green Level
Grueu Plain
Ivor
Jerusalem
Newsom's Depot
Nottaway Chapel
Pond's Shop
Vickaville

Spotsylvania co.
Andrews
Chancellorsville
Clover Green
Danielsville
Fredericksburgh
Lewis' Store
Matipony
Mount Pleasant
Partlows
Spotsylvania (c h)
Thorsburgh
Todd's
Twyman's Store
Wilderness

Stafford co.
Accokeek
Belifair Mills
Falmouth
Garrisonville
Hartwood
Stafford (c h)
Tackett's Mill

Surry co.
Bacon's Castle
Baileysburgh
Cabin Point
Spring Grove
Surry (c h)

Sussex co.
Blackwater
Coman's Well
Henry
Jarratts
Littleton
Newville
Parham's Store
Stony Creek Warehouse
Sussex (c h)
Wakefield Station
Waverly Station

Taylor co.
Fetterman
Flemington
Grafton
Harmony Grove
Pleasant Creek
Pruntytown (c h)
Simpson's Creek
Three Forks
Webster

Tazewell co.
Abb's Valley
Baptist Valley
Big Rock
Blue Stone
Burke's Garden
Cedar Bluff
Clear Fork
Cove Creek
Fine Oaks
Hicksville
Ironville
Knob
Maiden Spring
Richland
Rocky Gap
Springville
Tazewell (c h)
Thompson's Valley
Tug River
Tumbling Creek
Valley

Tucker co.
Black Fork
Bonifield's Mills
Hannahsville
Holly Meadows
Lead Mine
Pleasant Run
Saint George
Texas

Tyler co.
Kidwell
Lone Tree
Middlebourne (c h)
Moort's
North Bend Mills
Roppy's
Russell's Mills
Shirley
Sistersville
Wick

Upshur co.
Buckhannon (c h)
French Creek
Frenchton
Lorents' Store
Marple's Store
Overhill
Rude's Mill
Sago

Warren co.
Bentonville
Buckton
Chester's Gap
Confluence
Front Royal (c h)
Hambaugh's
Happy Creek Station
Linden [tion
Milldale
Ninevch
Overall's
Water Lick

Warwick co.
Warwick (c h)

Washington co.
Abingdon (c h)
Buffalo Pond
Clear Branch
Craig's Mills
Emory
Forks
Glade Spring Depot
Goodson
Holston
Kinderhook
Laurel
Liberty Hall
Ledi
Love's Mills
Magnolia
Mendecah
Mock's Mills
North Fork
Raven's Nest
Saltville
Smith's Creek
Sneadsville
Three Springs

Wayne co.
Adkinsville
Amacetta
Corado
Falls of 12 Pole
Falls of Tug
Forks of 12 Pole
Fort Gay
Palmetto
Round Bottom
Savage Grant
Twelve Pole
Wayne (c h)
White Creek

Westmoreland co.
Hague
Kinsale
Montross (c h)
Nominy Grove
Oak Grove
Oldham's X Roads
Rice's Store

Wetzel co.
Broad Tree Tunnel
Burton
Davenport
Knob Fork
Milo [(ch)
New Martinsville
Pine Grove
Portor's Falls
Proctor
Vau Camp

Wirt co.
Burning Spring
Freeport
Lees' Mills
Newark
Reedy Ripple
Spring Creek
Wirt (c h)
Zackville

Wisconsin.

Wise co.	Davisville	Parkersburgh (c h)	Jo's Branch	Cedar Springs	Sharon
Berge's Gap	Deer Walk	Pond Creek	Morgan Valley	Crab Orchard	Speedwell
Big Stone Gap	Fountain Spring	Stillwell	Oceana	Graham's Forge	Wytheville (c h)
Wise (c h)	Lee Creek	Walker	Sun Hill	Jackson's Ferry	*York co.*
Wood co.	Limestone Hill	Williamstown		Mack's Meadows	Bigler's Mills
Belleville	Lubeck		*Wythe co.*	Reed Island	Half Way House
Briscoe Run	New England	*Wyoming co.*	Austinville	Rural Retreat	Yorktown (c h)
Bull Creek		Craney	Browne Hill		

WISCONSIN.

Adams co.	*Chippewa co.*	Macfarland	Calumet Village	Sylvester	*La Crosse co.*
Big Spring	Bloomer Prairie	Madison	Dotyville	Walnut Springs	Bangor
Davis' Corners	Chippewa City	Mazo Manie	Eden	Willet	Burns
Dell Prairie	Chippewa Falls	Middleton	El Dorado		Burr Oak
Edna	Eau Claire	Mount Vernon	Empire	*Iowa co.*	Half Way Creek
Fountain	Lafayette	Oregon	Fair Water	Adamsville	La Crosse
Friendship	*Clark co.*	Paoli	Fond du Lac	Aruna	Mindoro
Germantown	Frankville	Peatville	Foster	Avoca	Mormon Cooley
Grand Marsh	Neillsville	Perry	Illensberg	Clyde	Neshonoc
Killdare	Pineville	Peirceville	Junius	Dodgeville	New Amsterdam
Lindenwold	Pleasant Ridge	Pine Bluff	Ladoga	Dover	Onalaska
Little Lake	Weston Rapids	Pleasant Branch	Lamartine	Helena	
Mill Haven	*Columbia co.*	Primrose	Marytown	Highland	*La Fayette co.*
Necedah	Arlington	Rockside	Metomen	Jennicton	Argyle
New Chester	Beaver Creek	Roxbury	Moria	Linden	Belmont
New Rome	Bellefountain	Rutland	Murone	Mifflin	Benton
Pilot Knob	Cambria	Spring Dale	Nanaupa	Mineral Point	Bethel Grove
Plainville	Columbus	Stoner's Prairie	New fane	Moscow	Blanchardville
Point Bluff	Dekorra	Stoughton	North Lamartine	Ridgeway	Calamine
Quincy	East Randolph	Sun Prairie	Oakfield	West Blue Mound	Cottage Inn
Roche-a-Cri	Empire Junction	Sweet Home	Oakfield Centre	Wyoming	Darlington
Strong's Prairie	Fall River	Utica	Oceola		Elk Grove
Twin Valley	Fort Winnebago	Verona	Ripon	*Jackson co.*	Etna
White Creek	Hampden	West Middleton	Rosendale	Black River Falls	Fayette
Wonewoc	Kilbourn City	Westport	Rush Lake	Cataraut	Georgetown
	Leeds	Windsor	Taycheeda	Garden Valley	Gratiot
Bad Ax co.	Leed's Centre	York	Wanpun	Melrose	Meeker's Grove
Bad Ax	Lodi		West Rosendale	Navary	New Diggings
Bergen	Lowville	*Dodge co.*		North Bend	North Elk Grove
Bloomingdale	Marcellon	Alderly	*Grant co.*	Pine Hill	Shullsburgh
Brockinridge	New Haven	Atwater	Banfield	Pole Grove	Snafford
Carvoaso	North Leeds	Beaver Dam	Beetown	Roaring Creek	White Oak Spring
Coon Prairie	Okeo	Burnett	Boscobel	Siscoott	Wiota
Debello	Oshaukuta	Chester Station	Bunker's Hill		Yellow Stone
De Soto	Otsego	Clyman	Cassville	*Jefferson co.*	
Goole	Pacific	Danville	Castle Rock	Ashippun	*La Pointe co.*
Harmony	Pardeeville	Emmett	Charlotte	Aztalan	Bayfield
Hillsborough	Pigeon Grove	Farmersville	Dickeyville	Bark River	Houghton
Hockley	Portage City	Fox Lake	Ellenboro	Cold Spring	La Pointe
Kickapoo	Port Hope	Hermann	Fair Play	Concord	Montreal Falls
Mount Tabor	Poynett	Horicon	Fennimore	Farmington	Odanah
New Brookville	Rio	Hastisford	Glen Haven	Fort Atkinson	Whittlesey
New Salem	Rocky Run	Iron Ridge	Hazel Green	Golden Lake	
Newville	Showcaw	Juneau	Homer	Helenville	*Manitowoc co.*
Ontario	Welch Prairie	Kekoskee	Hurricane Grove	Hubbleton	Branch
Readstown	West Point	Le Roy	Jamestown	Ixonia	Clark's Mills
Retreat	Wyocena	Louisa	Lancaster (c h)	Jefferson (c h)	Cooperstown
River Side		Lowell	Little Grant	Johnson's Creek	Eaton
Romance	*Crawford co.*	Mayville	Martinville	Koskonong	Hika
Sierra	Batavia	Napasha	Millville	Lake Mills	Larrabee
Springville	Belle Center	Neosho	Montford	Milford	Manitowoc
Star	Crow's Mills	Oak Grove	Mount Hope	Oak Hill	Manitowoc Rapids
Victory	Eastman	Portland	Mount Ida	Oakland	Maple Grove
Viroqua	Lower Lynxville	Reeseville	Muscoda	Palmyra	Meeme
Warner's Landing	Marietta	Rolling Prairie	New California	Richwood	Mishicot
Weister	Mount Sterling	Rubicon	Oliver's Mills	Rome	Neshoto
	Ocena	Theresa	Ora Oak	Sullivan	Newtonburgh
Brown co.	Prairie Du Chien	Woodland	Patch Grove	Transit	Niles
Denmark	Rising Sun		Platteville	Waiteville	Oslo
De Peru (c h)	Rolling Ground	*Door co.*	Potosi	Waterloo	Paquette
Fort Howard	Seneca	Chickatock	Rockville	Watertown	Two Rivers
Green Bay	Sladesburg	Fishcreek	Saint Rose		
Mukwa	Somerville	Gibraltar	Sinsinawa Mound	*Juneau co.*	*Marathon co.*
New Franken	Teller's Corners	Marcus	Smeltzer's Grove	America	Gesmeken
Oneida	Towerville	Nasuwakee	Tafton	Fowler's Prairie	Jenny
Suamico	Wauzeka	Sturgeon Bay	Washburn	Lemouweir	Wausau (c h)
Wequiock	Wright's Ferry	Washington Harbor	Wyalusing	Mauston	Weston
Wrightstown	Yankeetown	*Douglass co.*		Union Center	
		Superior	*Green co.*	Werner	*Marquette co.*
Buffalo co.	*Dane co.*	*Dunn co.*	Albany		Briggsville
Alma	Albion	Dunnville	Attica	*Kenosha co.*	Dartford
Buffalo	Ancient	Durand	Bem	Brighton	Grand Prairie
Fountain City	Ashton	Ean Galle	Broadhead	Bristol	Green Lake
Gilmantown	Belleville	Fall City	Brooklyn	Cypress	Greenwood
Glencoe	Berry	Frankfort	Cadis	Kenosha	Harrisville
Maxville	Black Earth	Pepin	Dayton	Liberty	Jeddo
Moudovi	Blue Mound	Rock Falls	Decatur	Marion	Kingston
Waumandee	Berke	Rockville	Exeter	Paris	La Cote St. Marie
	Cambridge	Wauska	Farmer's Grove	Salem	Lake Maria
Calumet co.	Christiana	Wauheok	Hamsick	Wheatland	Long Lake
Brant	Cottage Grove		Jordan	Wilmot	Mackford
Brillion	Cross Plains	*Eau Claire co.*	Juda		Manchester
Charlestown	Dane	Augusta	Monroe (c h)	*Kewaunee co.*	Markesan
Chilton	Deerfield	Half Moon	Monticello	Ahnapee	Marquette
Dundas	Door Creek	Otter Creek	Morefield	Casco	Midland
High Cliff	Dunkirk		New Glarus	Coryville	Montello
New Holstein	Eolis	*Fond du Lac co.*	Oakley	Dykesville	Moundville
Poquet	Fitchburgh	Alcove	Pedee	Kewaunee	Neshkoro
Rantout	Hanshettville	Ashford	Shuey's Mills	Sandy Bay	Ordine
Sherwood	Lake View	Auburn	Skinner	Walhaim	Oxford
Stockbridge	Leicester	Bothelle	Spring Grove		
		Brandon			
		Byron			

District of Columbia,—Kansas Territory.

Pakwaukee
Princeton
Roslin
Stone Hill
Westfield
West Green Lake

Milwaukee co.
Butler
Davis
Franklin
Good Hope
Granville
Greenfield
Hale's Corners
Lamberton
Milwaukee
New Berlin
New Keoln
Oak Creek
Root Creek
Ten Mile House
Wauwatosa
West Granville

Monroe co.
Angelo
Big Valley
Clifton
Dorset
Farmer's Valley
Fife
Glendale
Jacksonville
Leon
Meridian
Moore's Creek
Mountain
Mount Pisgah
Oakdale
Puckwana
Ridgeville
Solon
Sparta
Sultan
Tomah
Tunnel City
Wellington
Wilton

Oconto co.
Little Suamico
Marrinette
Menekaune
Oconto
Pensaukie
Peshtigo
Stiles

Outagamie co.
Appleton
Freedom
Greenville
Hortonville
Kaukauna
Keshena
Lansing
Little Chute
Medina
Shaw-wu-no
Shiocton
Stephensville
Sugar Bush
Wakefield

Ozaukee co.
Belgium
Cedarburg

Fredonia
Grafton
Horris Corners
Mequon River
Ozaukee
Saukville
Ulao

Pepin co.
Cippewa
Durand

Luna
Pepin
Stockholm

Pierce co.
Bay City
Beldenville
Big River
Clifton Mills
Diamond Bluff
El Paso
Maiden Rock
Martell
Perrytown
Pleasant View
Prescott (c h)
River Falls
Rush River
Trenton
Trim Belle

Polk co.
Cedar Valley
Falls of St. Croix
Osceola Mills
Stirling

Portage co.
Almond
Amherst
Badger
Buena Vista
Centralia
Eau Pleine
Emily
Linwood
Lone Pine
Madely
Mohawk
Plover (c h)
Randall
Saratoga
Stevens Point
Stockton

Racine co.
Burlington
Caldwell Prairie
Caledonia
Caledonia Centre
Ives' Grove
Kansasville
Mount Pleasant
North Cape
Norway
Pan Yan
Prairie
Racine
Raymond
Rochester
South Bristol
Sylvania
Trowbridge
Union Church
Union Grove
Waterford
Whitesville
Yorkville

Richland co.
Aken
Ashland
Boaz
Buckeye
Casenovia
Cincinnati
East Henrietta
Excelsior
Fancy Creek
Forest
Henrietta
Hoosier
Ithaca
Lone Rock
Lost Mountain
Loyd
Milan
Mill Creek
Neptune
Orion
Port Andrew
Richland Centre
Richland City
Ripley
Rockbridge
Sextonville
Sylvan
Viola
West Branch
Woodstock
Yuba

Rock co.
Afton
Alvaretta
Avon
Beloit
Center
Cooksville
Edgerton
Emerald Grove
Evansville
Fairfield
Footville
Fulton
Hanover
Janesville
Johnstown
Johnstown Centre
Leyden
Lima Centre
Magnolia
Milton
Ogden
Orfordville
Osborn
Rock Prairie
Shopiere
Spring Valley
Tiffany
Union

St. Croix co.
Bonches
Brookville
Glenmont
Hammond
Hudson
Huntingdon
Kinnick Kinnick
New Centreville
New Richmond
Prescott
Rushville
Somerset

Sauk co.
Adams
Baraboo (c h)
Bear Valley

Bluff
Buchanan
Cassell Prairie
Dellona
Delton
Garrison
Giddings
Humboldt
Ironton
Lavalle
Lime Ridge
Loganville
Merrimack
Newport
Oaks
Prairie Du Sac
Reedsburg
Russell's Corners
Sauk City
Sandusky
Spring Green
Wilson's Creek

Shawana co.
Embarras
Kesheno
Lamote

Sheboygan co.
Adell
Beech Wood
Cascade
Cedar Grove
Edwards
Elkhart
Gibbville
Greenbush
Hingham
Howard's Grove
Onion River
Our Town
Plymouth
Rathbun
Russell
Scott
Sheboygan (c h)
Sheboygan Falls
Wheat Valley
Winooski

Trempeleau co.
Arcadia
Galesville
South Bend
Sumner
Trempeleau

Walworth co.
Adams
Allen's Grove
Big Foot Prairie
Bloomfield
Darien
Delavan
Densmore's Mills
East Troy
Elk Horn (c h)
Geneva
Geneva Bay
Grove
Huart Prairie
Honey Creek
La Grange
Little Prairie
Lyons
Millard
Richmond
Sharon
South Grove

Springfield
Spring Prairie
State Line
Sugar Creek
Tirade
Troy
Troy Centre
Troy Lakes
Vienna
Walworth
Westville
White Water

Washington co.
Addison
Aurora
Barton
Boltonville
Cedar Creek
Fillmore
Freistadt
Hartford
Kewaskum
Mecker
Myra
Nenno
Newburgh
Richfield
Schleisingerville
Staatsville
Station
Toland's Prairie
West Bend
Young Hickory

Waukesha co.
Big Bend
Brookfield Centre
Colebrook
Delafield
Dodge's Corners
Dousman
Duplainville
Eagle
Elm Grove
Genesee
Hartland
Lake Five
Lannon Springs
Lisbon
Mapleton
Marcy
Menominee Falls
Merton
Monches
Monterey
Mukwonago
Muskego Centre
North Prairie Station
Oconomowoek
Ottawa
Pewaukee
Pine Lake
Prospect Hill
South Genesee
Stone Bank
Summit
Sussex
Vernon
Waterville
Waukesha

Waupaca co.
Bear Creek
Clintonville
Crystal Lake
Evanswood

Fremont
Gill's Landing
Iola
Lind
Little Wolf
Mukwa
New London
Northport
Northera
North Royalton
Ogdensburgh
Readfield
Rural
Scandinavia
Waupaca

Waushara co.
Adario
Blurton
Cedar Lake
Cole Brook
Coloma
Corfu
Dakota
Dodge's Corners
East Coloma
East Oasis
Elma
Hancock
Howe's Corners
Lincoln
Mount Morris
Oasis
Pine River
Poy Sippi
Plainfield
Ravine
Sacramento
Saxeville
Silver Lake
Spring Lake
Spring Water
Wautoma
Willow Creek

Winnebago co.
Algoma
Black Wolf
Butte des Morts
Campbell
Clairville
Delhi
Eureka
Fisk's Corners
Groveland
Kore
Menasha
Neenah
Napueskun
Nekama
Omro
Oshkosh
Poygan
Rat River
Vinland
Waukau
Weelaunce
Weyauweya
Winchester
Winneconne

Wood co.
Centralia
Dexterville
Frenchtown
Grand River
Hemlock
Horn River
Nasonville

DISTRICT OF COLUMBIA.

| *Washington co.* | Georgetown | Oak Grove | Tennallytown | Washington (c h) |

KANSAS TERRITORY.

Allen co.
Carlyle
Cofachiqui
Geneva
Humboldt

Anderson co.
Canton
Cresco
Elisabethtowa
Hyatt
Redes
Shannon
Springfield
Walker

Arrapahoe co.
Auraria
Montana

Atchison co.
Atchison
Eden
Huron
Lancaster
Mt. Pleasant
Monrovia
Pardee
Port William
Sumner

Bourbon co.
Barnesville
Cato
Dayton
Fort Scott
Hathaways
Mapleton
Marmaton
Osage
Turkey Creek
Xenia

Breckinridge co.
Agnes City
Allen
Emporia

Forest Hill
Orleans
Plymouth
Toledo
Waterloo
Waushara

Brown co.
Carson
Claytonville
Hamlin
Hiawatha
Kennekuk
New Eureka
Nohart
Padonia

Powhattan
Pony Creek
Robinson

Butler co.
Byard
Chelsea

Calhoun co.
Holton
Indianola

Coffee co.
Burlington
Camp Creek
Le Roy

Nashville
Neosha City
Ottuawa

Davis co.
Ashland
Kenton
Riley City
Zeandale

Doniphan co.
Charlestown
Doniphan
Elwood
Geary
Green Top

434 Nebraska, New Mexico, Utah, Washington.

Highland	Centropolis	Shawnee	Miami Village	Capioma	Ridgeway
Iowa Point	Hickory Creek	Spring Hill	Midway	Central City	Tecumseh
Lafayette	Minneola	Squiresville	New Lancaster	Clear Creek	Topeka
Palermo	Ohio City		Osawatomie	Pleasant Spring	Walton
Rogersville	Peoria	*Leavenworth co.*	Paola	Richmond	Williamsport
Troy	Shermanville		Stanton	Sabetha	Wilmington
Walnut Grove		Delaware City		Seneca	
Wathena	*Greenwood co.*	Easton	*McGhee co.*		*Weller co.*
Wenona	Eureka	Kickapoo City		*Pottawatamie co.*	Superior
White Cloud	Pleasant Grove	Leavenworth City	Brushville	Elden	
		Quindaro	Salisbury	Unadilla	*Wise co.*
Douglas co.	*Jefferson co.*	Wyandott	Spring City	Westmoreland	Cottonwood Falls
Big Springs	Crooked Creek		*Madison co.*	*Richardson co.*	Council Grove
Black Jack	Grasshopper Falls	*Linn co.*	Hartford	Walaunsee	*Woodson co.*
Clinton	Kaw City		Italia		Belmont
Davis	Middletown	Blooming Grove	Madison	*Riley co.*	Neosho Falls
Eudora	Mt. Florence	Brooklyn		Henryville	
Franklin	Oakaloosa	Centreville	*Marshall co.*	Junction City	*Counties Unknown.*
Kanwaka	Osawkie	Hawkswing		Kansas Falls	Beach Valley
Lawrence	Rising Sun	H Ilsborough	Barrett	Manhattan	Catholic Mission
Lecompton	Shields	Jackson	Bennett's Station	Ogden	Coraville
Mar on	Winchester	Monoka	Marysville	Randolph	Fort Leavenworth
McKinney		Mound City	New Dayton		Fort Riley
Prairie City	*Johnson co.*	Oakwood	Nottingham	*Shawnee co.*	Ottawa Creek
Palmyra	Gardner	Paris	Vermillion City	Auburn	Rock Creek
Twin Mound	Haysville	Rovella		Burlingame	Sac & Fox Agency
Wakarusa	Hilbard	Twin Springs	*Nemaha co.*	Mairestown	St. Mary's Mission
	Lexington		Albany	Richardson	Secondine
Franklin co.	Monticello	*Lykins co.*	America	Richland	Whitehead
Appanoose	Olathe	Lyons	Ash Point		

NEBRASKA TERRITORY.

Burt co.	*Cuming co.*	Lewisburg	Tecumseh	Syracuse	Salem
Decatur	De Witt	Wallace	Turkey Creek	Wyoming	Yankton
Tekamah	West Point		Vesta		
		Douglass co.		*Pawnee co.*	*Sarpy co.*
Cass co.	*Dakota co.*	Bellevue	*Jones co.*	Pawnee City	Fairview
Avoca	Covington	Chicago	Daniel's Rancho	Pleasant Valley	Forest City
Cleveland	Dakota	Elkhorn City		Table Rock	Larimer
Glendale	Logan	Florence	*L'Eau Qui Court co.*		Plattford
Kanoshe	Omadi	Omaha City	Bonhomme City	*Platte co.*	
Mt. Pleasant	Poncah			Buchanan	*Washington co.*
Plattes Mouth	Saint John	*Forney co.*	*Monroe co.*	Columbus	Cuming City
Rock Bluffs		Brownsville	Genoa	El Dorado	Desoto
Three Grove	*Dixon co.*		Monroe		Fort Calhoun
Weeping Water	Dixon	*Gaye co.*		*Richardson co.*	
Cedar co.		Beatrice	*Nemaha co.*	Archer	*Counties Unknown.*
Saint Helena	*Dodge co.*	Stewarts	Mount Vernon	Chasta	Aurora
St. James	Belle Creek		Nehama City	Falls City	Fort Laramie
Wacaponna	Fontanelle	*Hall co.*		Midcleburg	Fort Pierre
Chukamas co.	Franklin	Grand Island City	*Niobrara co.*	Monterey	Lancaster
Fort Kearny	Fremont	*Johnston co.*	Breckinridge	Nemaha Falls	Niolrara
Clay co.	Jalapa	Helena	*Otoe co.*	Rulo	O'Fallon's Bluff
Austin		Kingston	Nebraska City	Saint Stephens	Saint Vrain

NEW MEXICO TERRITORY.

Bernadillo co.	Fort Fillmore	*Rio Arriba co.*	San Miguel	*Socorro co.*	*Counties Unknown.*
Albuquerque	Fort Stanton	Los Luceros	Tecolota	Socorro	Bringhurst's
Fort Defiance	Gila City		Santa Ana co.		Fort Buchanan
	Las Cruzces	*San Miguel co.*	Algodones	*Taos co.*	Fort Craig
Dona Ana co.	Mesilla	Las Vegas	*Santa Fe co.*	Fernandez de Taoz	Tucson
Arizona	Tulac		Santa Fe	Fort Union	

UTAH TERRITORY.

Beaver co.	*Davis co.*	Parowan	Taylorsville	Cedar Valley	Heberville
Beaver	Centerville	Pine Valley	Union	Lehi City	Santa Clara
	Farmington			Payson	Tokersville
Box Elder co.	Kaysville	*Millard co.*	*San Pete co.*	Pleasant Grove	Washington
Brigham City	Stoker	Fillmore City	Ephraim	Provo City	
Carson co.			Manti	Santaquin	*Weber co.*
Carey's Mills	*Green River co.*	*Salt Lake co.*		Spanish Fork	Ogden City
Carson City	Fort Bridger	Draper	*Tooele co.*	Springville	Willard
Carson Valley		Gardner's Mills	Tooele		
Mott's Ranch	*Iron co.*	Mill Creek	*Utah co.*	*Washington co.*	*Counties Unknown.*
Cedar co.	Cedar City	Mormon	Alpine City	Harmony	Salt Creek
Camp Floyd	Fort Johnson	Salt Lake City	American Fork		Susanville

WASHINGTON TERRITORY.

Chehalis co.	*Cowlitz co.*	Seabeck	Oysterville	*Thurston co.*	*Walla Walla co.*
Bruceport	Monticello (c h)	Tuekalet	*Pierce co.*		Colville Valley
			Spanaway	Bakers	Fort Colville
Chilum co.	*Island co.*	*Lewis co.*	Steilacoom City	Grand Mound	Waileptu
New Dungerness	Coveland	Boist Fort	(c h)	Ilkumeen	
		Castle Rock		Oak Point	*Waukiakum co.*
Clark co.	*Jefferson co.*	Cla.quato	*Snamish co.*	Olympia (c h)	Cathlamet
Fisher's Landing	Port Townsend (ch)	Cowlitz	Arkada	Saunders Prairie	
Lake River		Highland	Oakland	Scatter Creek	*Whatcom co.*
Fort Ludlow	*King co.*	Neivauoum	Skokomish	Skookumchuck	Camp Simeahmee
Vancouver	Seattle (c h)			Yelm	Simeahmee
Washougal	*Kitsap co.*	*Parkis co.*	*Skamania co.*		Whatcom
	Port Madison	Chenkou	Cascades		

Newspapers.

Dailies.

Cincinnati Daily Commercial.
Published every morning except Sunday, at the north-east corner of Fourt and Race, by M D. Potter & Co. Terms $6.00 per annum. Cincinnati Dollar Commercial, published at same office, at $1,00 per annum.

Cincinnati Daily Enquirer.
Published every morning. Mondays excepted, by Faran & McLean, at north-east corner Vine and Burnet Terms $6.00 per annum. Cincinnati Weekly Enquirer, published at Enquirer Office, at $1,00 per annum.

Cincinnati Daily Gazette.
Published every morning except Sunday, at the north-east corner of Vine and Fourth, by the Cincinnati Gazette Company. Terms $8.00 per annum. Cincinnati Weekly Gazette, published at same office, at $1,00 per annum.

Cincinnati Daily Press.
Published every evening except Sunday, by the Press Printing Co., Vine street, opposite the Custom House. Terms, $1.00 per annum. Cincinnati Weekly Press, published at Daily Press office, at $1.00 per annum.

Cincinnati Daily Times.
Published every evening, Sunday excepted, at 62 West Third street, by C. W. Starbuck. Terms $6,00 per annum. Dollar Times, published at same office at $1,00 per annum.

Cincinnati Daily Volksblatt.
Published every morning, except Monday, in the north-west wing of Court House, by Stephen Mollitor, editor and proprietor. Terms $6.00 per annum. Cincinnati Weekly Volksblatt published every Thursday, at same office. Terms $1,00 per annum.

Cincinnati Daily Volksfreund.
Published every morning except Monday, at south-east corner of Vine and Longworth, by Joseph A. Hemann, editor and proprietor. Terms, $6,00 per annum. Cincinnati Weekly Volksfreund, published at same office.

Cincinnati Union.
Published every morning, except Sunday, at No. 9 West Court by Fred Lang, editor and proprietor. Terms $5,00 per annum.

Law Bulletin.
Office No. 10 West Fourth. W. W. Warden, proprietor. Published daily. Terms 15 cents per week.

Weeklies.

Catholic Telegraph and Advocate.
Office, south-west corner Vine and Longworth. Published every Saturday, by Joseph A. Hemann, at $3,00 a year.

Christian Apologist.
Published every Thursday, by Poe & Hitchcock, s. w. c. 8th and Main. Terms, $1.25 per annum.

Christian Herald, (*N. S. Presbyterian.*)
Office No. 26 West Fourth street L C. Ford, Publisher. Every Thursday morning, at $2,00 a year.

Christian Luminary.
Office No. 247 W. Fifth street. John Boggs, editor and proprietor. Every Thursday, at $1,50 a year.

Cincinnati Wahrheitsfreund.
Published every Thursday, at south-west corner of Vine and Longworth, by J. A. Hemann Terms $2,00 per annum.

Free Nation.
Office. 247 west Fifth street. Amos Moore, publisher. Terms, $2,00 per annum.

Journal and Messenger.
Published every Friday, by the Central Baptist Press Co. 59 West Fourth street. $1.50 a year.

New Church Herald.
Rev. Sabin Hough, editor and publisher. Office. College Hall Building. Published every Saturday, at $2,00 a year.

Presbyter, (*O. S. Presbyterian.*)
No. 25 West Fourth street. Monfort & Wampler, editors and proprietors. Published every Thursday morning, at $2,00 a year.

Presbyterian Witness.
No. 6 Neave's Building, (corner Fourth and Race,) Rev. R. H. Pollock and R. Gilmor, editors and proprietors. Every Wednesday $2,00 per year.

Protestantische Zeitblatter.
Corner of Walnut and 13th streets Christian Association, publishers. Every Thursday morning, at $1,00 per year.

The American Christian Review.
247 West Fifth street. Rev. Benjamin Franklin, editor and publisher. Every Tuesday, at $1.50 per year.

The Deborah.
Published every Friday, by Bloch & Co., at 32 West 6th street. Terms, $1,50 per year.

The Israelite.
Published every Friday, at 32 West 6th street, by Bloch & Co. Terms, $2,00 per annum.

The Railroad Record.
Published every Thursday, by Wrightson & Co. Office 167 Walnut street. Terms, $3.00 per annum.

The Star in the West.
Published Weekly, at north-west corner 6th and Walnut, by H. R. Nye and G. L. Demarest, editors and proprietors. Terms, $2.00 per annum.

The Western Christian Advocate.
Published every Wednesday, by Poe and Hitchcock, at the south west corner of 8th and Main. Terms $1,50 per annum.

CAMARGO MANUFACTURING COMPANY,
MANUFACTURERS OF
PAPER HANGINGS & WINDOW SHADES,
No. 57 WEST FOURTH STREET,

H. H. BRENEMAN,   CINCINNATI.

Railroads and Transportation Companies.

UNION TICKET OFFICES.

At which are sold Tickets for all routes leading out of the city, (except for Marietta and Cincinnati R.R.)

N. W. Corner of Third and Vine Streets, under Burnet House, — M. D. Stark, Jno. Glazier, Ticket Agents.

S. E. Corner Front and Broadway, opposite Spencer House, — R. M. Lea, A. Hamilton, Ticket Agents.

MARIETTA & CINCINNATI R. R. Ticket Office, No. 3 Burnet House, — B. F. Coan, Ticket Ag't.

Cincinnati, Hamilton & Dayton R. R.

DEPOT, Fifth and Sixth Sts. bet. Hoadly and W. W. Canal, FREIGHT OFFICE, at the Depot.

President,.... S. S. L'Hommedieu, Sedamsville,
Superintend't.Daniel McLaren. City,
Secretary,......F. H. Short, "
Gen'l Fr't Ag't, J. R. Reed, Country,
Gen. Tk't Ag't..P. W. Strader, "

STATIONS.

Cincinnati,..........	0	Hamilton	25
Mill Creek...........	1	Overpeck's..........	29
Brighton.............	2	Busenbarck's........	31
Ludlow...............	5	Trenton.............	33
Spring Grove.........	7	Middletown..........	37
Carthage.............	10	Poast Town.........	40
Lockland.............	12	Carlisle............	44
Glendale.............	15	Miamisburg..........	49
Princeton Pike.......	17	Carrollton..........	52
Jones'...............	19	**Dayton**..........	60
Schenck's............	22		

Cincinnati & Chicago Air Line R.R.

DEPOT, Cincinnati, Hamilton & Dayton Depot, FREIGHT OFFICE, 115 Vine Street, under Burnet House, W. O. White, Agent.

President,....... W. D. Judson, New York,
Superintendent, Jno. Brandt, jr., Richmond, Ind,
Treasurer,......Henry Morgan, "
Gen. Fr't Ag't..S. W. Chapman, Chicago,
Gen. Tk't Ag't..Chas. E. Follet, "

Connects with C. H. & D. R. R. at Hamilton.

STATIONS.

Cincinnati........	0	Tampico..........	79
Hamilton..........	25	Kokomo...........	84
(Ayton & Ham. R.R.)		Galveston........	90
Richmond......	70	Lincoln..........	93
Culbertson........	4	Anoka............	102
Centreville Pike..	7	Logansport.......	106
Washington........	10	Gebhard..........	111
Hagerstown........	17	Royal Centre.....	117
Millville.........	22	Rosedale.........	123
Ashland...........	25	Scarboro.........	126
New Castle........	28	Winnemac.........	131
Sulphur Springs...	34	Shakapee.........	141
Middletown........	41	Brandtwood.......	145
Anderson..........	49	English Lake.....	150
Clarks............	54	La Crosse........	156
Frankton..........	59	Montebello.......	160
Quincy............	63	Tenney...........	163
Windfall..........	71	Valparaiso.......	167
Nevada............	75	**Chicago**......	210

Cincinnati, Wilmington & Zanesville R. R.

DEPOT, at Little Miami Depot.

Receiver and Sup't..Wm.K. Bond, City,
Gen'l Fr't Agt......B. D. Abbott, Zanesville,
Gen. Tk't Ag't......C. G. Gove, City.

Connects with L. M. R. R. at Morrow.

STATIONS.

Cincinnati....	0	Williamsport.....	92
(Little Miami R. R.)		Yellow Bird......	97
Morrow........	36	Circleville......	103
Hicks.............	41	Stout's..........	110
Clarksville.......	46	Amanda...........	115
Sligo.............	51	Lancaster........	125
Wilmington........	55	Berne............	131
Wilson's..........	59	Bremen...........	135
Reesville.........	64	Wolf's...........	142
Sabina............	66	New Lexington....	147
Jasper............	72	McLuney..........	152
Washington........	77	Roseville........	158
New Holland.......	87	Putnam...........	167
Four Corners......	90	**Zanesville**...	168

Cincinnati and Indianapolis Junction R. R.

DEPOT, at Cin., Ham. and Day. Depot.

President,......J. M. Ridenour, College Corner, O.
Secretary and }
Gen. Tk't Ag't } J. Leach, Hamilton, O.
Gen. Ag't......Wm. M. Smith, Hamilton, O.

Connects with C. H. & D. R. R. at Hamilton.

STATIONS.

Hamilton..........	Oxford...........	
Hanover...........	McDonald's.......	
McGonigle's.......	College Corner...	
Rogersville.......	Swain's Station..	
Ogleton...........	**Liberty**...... 29

Central Ohio R. R.

DEPOT, Little Miami or Cin., Ham. & Day. Depot.
FREIGHT OFFICE, 77 West Third Street. L. Divinney, and G. W. Brown, Agents.

Pres't and Receiver,.. H. J. Jewett, Zanesville, O.
Gen. Fr't Ag't....... D. S. Gray, Columbus, O.
Gen. Ticket Ag't..... John W. Brown, "

Connects with Little Miami R. R. at Columbus.

STATIONS.

Columbus......	0	Norwich..........	73
Taylor's..........	8	Concord..........	78
Black Lick........	10	Cassel's.........	81
Columbia..........	16	Cambridge........	85
Pataskala.........	17	Campbell's.......	93
Kirkersville......	22	Gibson's.........	96
Union.............	27	Salesville.......	100
Newark........	33	Milwood..........	102
Clay Lick.........	39	Spencer's........	103
Black Hand,.......	44	Barnesville......	110
Claypool's........	47	Burr's Mill......	117
Pleasant Valley...	50	Belmont..........	119
Dillon's Falls....	53	Lewis' Mill......	122
Zanesville........	59	Glencoe..........	126
Coal Dale.........	63	Neff's Siding....	132
Sonora............	66	**Bellaire**.....	137

Cleveland, Columbus and Cincinnati R. R.

DEPOT. Little Miami, or Cin., Ham. and Day. Depot.
FREIGHT OFFICE, No. 4 Merchant's Exchange, Thos. J. Gettier, Agent.

President......L. M. Hubby, Cleveland, O.
Superintend't...E. S. Flint, "
Gen. Fr't Ag't...Addison Hills, "
Gen. Tk't Ag't...H. C. Marshall, "

Connects with L. M. and C. & X. R. R. at Columbus.

STATIONS.

Cincinnati....	0	Crestline........	59
(L. M. & C. & X. R.R.)		Shelby...........	67
Columbus......	120	Salem............	74
Worthington.......	8	Greenwich........	81
Orange............	13	New London.......	86
Berlin............	19	Rochester........	93
Delaware..........	20	Wellington.......	99
Eden..............	26	La Grange........	106
Ashley............	30	Grafton..........	110
Cardington........	35	Columbia.........	116
Gilead............	42	Berea............	122
Iberia............	49	**Cleveland**....	135
Galion............	54		

RAILROADS & TRANSPORTATION COMPANIES.

Dayton and Michigan R. R.

DEPOT, Cin., Ham. and Day. Depot.
FREIGHT OFFICE, No. 5 Merchant's Exchange, D. C. Henderson and G. L. Brecount, Agents.

President......C. Dietrich,
Superintendent..R. M. Shoemaker,
Gen Freight &
Ticket Ag't......M. Shoemaker, Toledo,
Connects with Cin., Ham. and Day. R. R. at Dayton.

STATIONS.

Cincinnati	0	Lima	71
Dayton	60	Cairo	77
Johnson's	7	Columbus Grove	84
Tippecanoe	14	Ottawa	91
Troy	20	Leipsic	98
Piqua	28	N. Ridge	103
Sidney	40	Milton	112
Careysville	46	Westfield	116
Botkins	52	Waterville	126
Wapakoneta	59	Perrysburg	133
Criderville	65	**Toledo**	142

Eaton and Hamilton R. R.

DEPOT, Cin., Ham. & Day. Depot.
President......David Barnett, Barnett's Station,
Superintendent.. David M Morrow, Eaton, O.
Secretary......E. W. McGuire, "
Connects with C. H. & D. R. R. at Hamilton.

STATIONS.

Cincinnati	0	Camden	45
(C. H. & D. R. R.)		Barnett's	47
Hamilton	25	Eaton	53
Seven Mile	32	Florence	60
Collinsville	36	**Richmond**	70
Somerville	39		

Greenville & Miami R. R.

DEPOT, Cin., Ham. and Day. Depot.
Pres't and Sup't..H. C. Stimpson, Dayton, O.
Sec. and Gen. Tk't.
Agent......Jno. L. Miller, "
Connects with C. H. & D. R. R. at Dayton.

STATIONS.

Cincinnati	0	Arcanum	26
Dayton	60	Delisle	28
Dodson's	15	Greenville	35
Baltimore	20	Union City	47

Indianapolis and Cincinnati R. R.

FREIGHT DEPOT, W. Front St., foot of Third,
PASSENGER DEPOT, at Ohio and Mississippi Depot.
OFFICES, 66 W. 3rd St., F. C. West and Sidney Rice, Agts.

Pres't and Sup't..H. C. Lord, City,
Gen. Fr't Ag't.....G. L. Barringer, City.
Gen. Tk't Ag't....W. H. L. Noble, Indianapolis,
Branches from O. & M. Track at Lawrenceburg.

STATIONS.

Cincinnati	0	McCoy's	60
(O. & M. R.)		Greensburg	64
O. & M. Junc		Adams	70
Lawrenceburg	20	St. Paul	75
Newtown	21	Waldron	77
Guilford	28	Prescott	80
Harmans	34	Shelbyville	84
Van Weddens	39	Fairland	91
Sunman	41	London	95
Spades	43	Brookfield	96
Morris	46	Acton	98
Batesville	49	Gallaudet	102
New Point	55	Poplar Grove	105
Smith's Crossing	57	**Indianapolis**	110

Kentucky Central R. R.

DEPOT AND GENERAL OFFICE, Covington,
Tickets sold at Union Ticket Office.
President......R. B. Bowler, Clifton,
Superintendent.G. W. Fulton, Covington,

STATIONS.

Covington	0	Robertson's	55
Ryland	13	Cynthiana	66
Benton	18	Kiser's	75
Demossville	25	Paris	80
Butler	28	Lexington	99
Irving	33	Providence	
Falmouth	39	Nicholasville	
Morgan	47	(Stages)	
Boyd's	50	**Danville**	

Little Miami and Columbus & Xenia R.R.

DEPOT, E. Front Street, E. of Miami Canal,
OFFICES at the Depot,
Pres't L. M. R. R.....W. H. Clement, Morrow.
" C. & X. R.R...Jos. R. Swan, Columbus,
Superintendent......E. W. Woodward, City.
Gen. Fr't Ag't......J. N. Kennedy, City.
Gen. Tk't Ag't......P. W. Strader, Country,

STATIONS.

Cincinnati	0	Xenia	65
Engine House	3	Xenia	65
Plainville	9	Yellow Springs	75
Milford	14	Springfield	84
Miamiville	17		
Branch Hill		Cedarville	73
Loveland	21	Selma	79
Foster's	27	South Charleston	84
S. Lebanon	32	Florence	90
Morrow	36	London	95
Fort Ancient	41	Glade Run	101
Freeport	45	West Jefferson	106
Corwin	51	Alton	114
Claysville	54	**Columbus**	120
Spring Valley	58		

Marietta and Cincinnati R. R.

PASSENGER DEPOT, at Little Miami Depot.
FREIGHT DEPOT. Front St. east of Little Miami.
FREIGHT & TICKET OFFICE, No. 3 Burnet House,
President......N. L. Wilson, Chillicothe,
Superintendent..John Durand, City,
Gen. Fr't Ag't...A. B. Walters, "
Gen. Tk't Ag't...Jno. H. Brummett, Chillicothe,
Auditor and Sec. Wm. S. Nye, "

STATIONS.

Cincinnati	0	Schooley's	103
(Little Miami R.R.)		Londonderry	108
Loveland	23	Raysvile	115
Gosh. & Wil. Pike	32	Cincin. Furnace	120
Blanchester	39	Hamden	126
		McArthur	170
Blanchester		Vinton Furnace	133
Westboro		Zaleski	137
Lynchburgh		Big Sand Furnace	142
Russells		Marshville	120
Hillsboro	76	Athens	147
Martinsville	48	Warren's	163
Vienna	55	New England	167
Lexington	60	Big Run	171
Leesburg	62	Cutler	176
Munroe	66	Vincent's	183
Greenfield	72	Tunnel	190
Lyndon	76	Scott's Landing	193
Frankfort	83	Marietta	156
Chillicothe	96	**Parkersburg**	202

Ohio & Mississippi R. R.

DEPOT, West Front Street, corner of Mill,
GENERAL OFFICES, Opposite the Depot,
FREIGHT OFFICE, 77 West Third Street, W. E. Bruce. Agt.

President......Geo. B. McClellan, U. S. A.
V. Pres. & Supt...Wm. J. McAlpin, City,
Assistant Sup't..A. H. Lewis "
Gen. Fr't Ag't...G R. Blanchard, St Louis,
Gen. Tk't Ag't... E. F. Fuller.

STATIONS.

Cincinnati	0	Seymour	87
Storrs	2	Brownstown	98
Cullums	5	Velonia	101
Delhi	10	Medora	106
North Bend	14	Fort Ritner	114
Gravel Pit	18	Scottville	121
I. & C. R. R. Junc	21	Mitchell	127
Lawrenceburg	21	Georgia	132
Aurora	25	Willow Valley	142
Cochran	27	Shoals	150
Dillsborough	33	Loogootee	158
Moore's Hill	40	Washington	173
Milan	42	Junc. E. & C. R. R.	191
Pierceville	45	Vincennes	193
Delaware	47	Lawrenceville	201
Osgood	52	Bridgeport	206
Poston	56	Sumner	211
Holton	58	Hadley	213
Nebraska	62	Claremont	217
Butlerville	66	Olney	222
North Vernon	73	Noble	231
Hardenbergh	79	Clay City	238

RAILROADS & TRANSPORTATION COMPANIES.

Flora	245	Breese	301
Xenia	213	Trenton	310
Middleton	250	Summerfield	3 3
Salem	260	Lebanon	316
Odin	275	O'Fallon	322
Sandoval	279	Caseyville	331
Carlyle	293	**East St. Louis**	310

Pittsburgh, Columbus & Cincinnati R. R.

Depot, Little Miami or Cin. Ham. & Day. Depot.
Freight Office, 77 W. Third St., L. Divinney, Gen. Ag't.
 President & Sup't.. Thos. L. Jewett, Steubenville,
 Audit r ....S. F. Scull,   "
 Gen. Fr't Ag't......D S. Gray, Columbus,
 Gen. Tk't Ag't.....Jno. W. Brown, "
 Gen. Pass. Ag't....Ira Hutchinson, "
Connects with L. M. and C. & X R. R. at Columbus.

STATIONS.

Cincinnati	0	Uhrichsville	100
(*L M C. & X. R. R.*)		P. [inde]lphia Road	105
Columbus	120	Bowerston	110
(*Cen. Ohio R R*)		Mastersville	1.2
Newark	33	New Market	116
Montgomery's	36	Fairview	121
Hanover	41	Cadiz Junction	125
Nashport Road	44	Miller's	127
Frazeesburg	40	Unionport	130
Dresden	55	Bloomfield	132
Adam's Mills	59	Skelley's	133
Conesville	62	Reed's Mill	136
Coshoct	64	Smithfield Station	134
Coshocton	69	Alexandria Road	142
W st Lafayette	75	Gould's	144
Oxford	76	Steubenville Junc	147
New Comerstown	83	Steubenville	150
Port Washington	89	(*Clev. & Pitts. R R.*)	
Lock No. 17	93	**Pittsburgh**	209
Trenton	97		

Sandusky, Dayton & Cincinnati R. R.

Depot. at Cin., Ham. & Day. Depot.
Freight Office, No 5 Merchants Exchange.
 President ....Oran Follett, Sandusky,
 Superintendent..Harvey Rice,
 G 'n Fr't Ag't...Jno. Osborn, Dayton,
 Gen. Tk't Ag't...M. O Clapp, Sandusky.
Connects with C. H. & D. R. R. at Dayton.

STATIONS.

Cincinnati	0	Belle Center	69
(*U H. & D. R. R*)		Yelverton	73
Dayton	60	Hudsonville	75
Drawbridge	1	Kenton	81
Harshman's	4	Patterson	91
Knessley's	7	Forest	94
Oak ru	10	Whartonsburgh	98
Kn	16	Carey	105
S	18	Adrian	110
Springfield	24	Berwick	112
Tremont	30	Tiffin	121
Lawrence	33	Watson's	127
Urbana	30	Green Springs	132
West Liberty	49	Clyde	137
Bellef'tnine	57	Castalia	144
Huntsville	63	**Sandusky**	154
Richland	67		

Erie R. R.
 Geo. Pendleton, General S. W. Agent,
 No. 4 Merchant's Exchange.

Baltimore and Ohio R. R.
 Henry Heckert, Agent, No. 3 E. Front Street.

Pennsylvania R. R.
 H. W. Brown & Co., Agents, N. 25 E. Front Street.

Hannibal & St. Joseph R. R.
 John W. Burch, Agent, No. 35 W. Third Street.

Pittsburg, Fort Wayne & Chicago, R. R.
 H. W. Brown & Co., Contracting Agents, No. 25 E. Front Street

Grand Trunk R. R.
 Taylor & Bro, Agents, No. 43 Walnut Street.

Logansport, Peoria & Burlington R. R.
 W. O White Contracting Agent, 115 Vine Street.

MAIL BOATS & PACKET LINES.

Cincinnati & Louisville Mail Boat.
 Capt. C. G. Pearce, Sup't., Wharfboat, foot of Broadway.

Madison Packet Line,
 Joseph Hallgath, Agent, foot of Main.

Big Sandy & Cincinnati Packet Line.
 Phillip J. Colbert, Agent, foot of Ludlow.

Cincinnati and Memphis Packet Co.
 16 Public Landing. James Bugher, Super't.

Maysville Packet Line,
 Andrew J. Harrangan, Agent, foot of Walnut.

Portsmouth Packet Line,
 James Neblett, Agent, foot of Ludlow.

EXPRESS COMPANIES.

American Express Company,
 No. 92 W. Fourth Street, Frank Clark, Agent.

Adams Express Company,
 No. 67 W. Fourth Street, Alfred Gaither, Agent.

United States Express,
 Office, No. 192 W. Fourth Street, A. C. Rose, Agent

Great Western Dispatch,
 Office, Cincinnati Ham. & Dayton Depot. J. McCune, Ag't

Merchants Dispatch,
 Office, 7 and 9 W Third Street, Beno Speyer, Agent

Foreign Passenger and Exchange Agency,
 Benno Speyer Nos. 7 and 9 W. Third Street,
 W. D Barry & Co., 76 W. Third Street.

STREET RAILROADS.

  (See Page 30.)

OMNIBUS & STAGE LINES.

Brookville Omnibus Line,
 Office, 169 Walnut, J. C. Rittenhouse, Proprietor.

Lebanon Omnibus Line,
 Office, 169 Walnut, Abner L. Ross, Jr., Prop'r.

New London Omnibus Line,
 Office, 169 Walnut, J. Bevis & Co., Prop'r.

Bethel & Georgetown, Omnibus Line,
 Office, S. C. Pearl and Broadway.

College Hill Omnibus Line,
 Starts from Walnut Street House.

Walnut Hills Omnibus Line,
 Stand, corner Fourth and Main.

Covington Omnibus Line,
 Stand s.w.c. Fifth and Walnut, Clayton & Young, Prop'rs.

Amelia Omnibus Line.
 Office N. E. C. Pearl and Broadway.

CINCINNATI ADVERTISEMENTS. 445

:EPH WHITAKER,
MANUFACTURER OF
ES, HAIR, CURLED HAIR,

V, NEATS' FOOT OIL, GREASE AND SAUSAGE CASINGS,

ESTABLISHMENT ON DEER CREEK.

ICE ADDRESS, Box 229, CINCINNATI, O.

Price paid for Bristles, Hair, or Grease of any description, in the rough.

J. COOK.

/ YORK TRUNK STORE.

ONARD & COOK.

Corner Main and Second Streets,

CINCINNATI, OHIO.

Manufacturers and Wholesale Dealers in

Packing Trunks, Valises, Carpet Bags, &c.

ring done at shortest notice. Trunks made to order.

MICHAEL BEBERGER.

HN GIBSON & CO.
PLUMBERS,
AND MANUFACTURERS OF

on & Co's Patent Improved Hydrant,

MAIN STREET, below Seventh, CINCINNATI, O.

AND LEAD PIPE, Wholesale and Retail.

T WESTERN AND NORTH-WESTERN LINE!

AND CINCINNATI RAILROAD!

0 miles. No change of Cars to Indianapolis, at which place it unites with all points in the West and North-west.

rains leave Cincinnati daily, from the foot of Mill and Front streets. s, Terre Haute, Lafayette and Chicago, in advance of all other routes. time shorter than any other route. Baggage checked through.

ood until used, can be obtained at the Ticket Offices, south-east corner of No. 1 Burnet House Corner, and at the Depot Office, foot of Mill and Front sary information may be had.

H. C. LORD, President.
W. H. L. NOBLE, Gen'l Ticket Agent.

CINCINNATI DAILY ENQUIRER,

Published every morning, Monday excepted, by

FARAN & McLEAN,

At North East Corner Vine and Burnet Streets.   Terms $600 per annum.

CINCINNATI WEEKLY ENQUIRER published at Enquirer Office, at $1,00 per annum.

We have the largest JOB OFFICE in the West and are prepared to do all kinds of

COLORED POSTERS, FOR CIRCUSSES, CONCERTS, &C,

MERCHANTS' PRINTING EXECUTED WITH NEATNESS AND DISPATCH.

FARAN & McLEAN.

THE Cincinnati Daily and Weekly Press,

OFFICE ON VINE STREET, BELOW FOURTH.

The only Ten Cents a Week Paper in Cincinnati.

ADVERTISEMENTS
Inserted at very low rates,

THE PRESS PUBLISHES THE LETTER LIST.

WEEKLY PRESS $1.00 PER YEAR.

Daily, Tri-Weekly & Dollar Weekly Times,
CINCINNATI, OHIO.

TERMS OF DAILY TIMES, (invariably in advance.)

One year, by Mail,..................................$5 00 | Three months, by Mail,..............................$1 50
Six months, " .... 2 50 | One month, " 50

TERMS OF TRI-WEEKLY TIMES, (invariably in advance.)

Per Year,..$3 00 | Four months,...................................... 1 00

THE TRI-WEEKLY TIMES will be (to the exclusion of advertisements) entirely devoted to reading matter, presenting with each issue the Latest Mail News, the Telegraphic Repor's in full. Editorial Comments on Passing Events, the Produce and Money Markets, and whatever else may be of interest to the general reader.

TERMS OF DOLLAR WEEKLY TIMES.

Single Copies,....$1.00 | Clubs of six,....$5.00 | Clubs of twelve,...$10 | Larger Clubs at same rates.

TIMES STEAM JOB OFFICE,

Pamphlets, Lawyer's Briefs, all kinds of Mercantile Printing, illustrated Store Bills, Insurance and Railroad Work, Posters, Programmes, Military Printing, etc., etc. at War Prices.

Daily and Weekly Volksfreund,

OFFICE, Corner Vine and Longworth Streets,
CINCINNATI, OHIO.

JOS. A. HEMANN, - - - PUBLISHER.

THE
CATHOLIC TELEGRAPH & WAHRHEITSFREUND

Are published in the same building.

Job Work done in all its Branches.

"To a young man just starting in life, a good education and no money is better capital than two thousand dollars joined to ignorance."—FRANKLIN.

"SCIENCE WAITS UPON LABOR."

1862. 1862.

"Acquire a good Commercial Education, and you will as surely succeed in life as that cause produces effect."
ABBOTT LAWRENCE.

"Let us then be up and doing, With a heart for every fate; Still achieving, still pursuing, Learn to labor and to wait."
LONGFELLOW.

North-West Cor. Sixth and Walnut Streets, CINCINNATI, OHIO.

J. H. DOTY, - - - Principal.

The College apartments are large and commodious, well ventilated, and elegantly furnished, making them the most desirable school rooms for Mercantile Instruction in this city or the West.

☞ The Principal has published an important "Practical Method of Computing Interest," with almost electric rapidity, alike at any per cent, being universally conceded the simplest and briefest ever devised. All should have a copy. The "Method" is given to students gratis.

Many other Business Calculations are alike shorn of very much of the usual circumlocution and tedious unmeaning prolixity. These, with other valuable improvements and additions, recently made to the Regular Course of

DOUBLE ENTRY BOOK KEEPING, &C.

Together with Daily Lectures on the Science of Accounts, Mercantile Calculations, Customs of Merchants, Principles of Book Keeping and Penmanship, Commercial Law, Political Economy, Art of Detecting Counterfeit Money, &c., make the Course of Study more practical and complete than ever, all being so arranged as to enable the student to get the largest amount of information in the shortest possible time. The mode of teaching is peculiar to this Institution, and confessedly merits, what it fully receives, the suitable signet of superiority. Proficiency is our motto.

BOYS' COURSE OF STUDY.

A course of Mercantile Instruction, especially adapted to Masters and Lads, with a view of fitting them for Clerkships and Counting House Assistants, is now in readiness as introductory to the more extended course. Those quite young, thus matriculating for instruction, can avail themselves, gratis, of the Penmanship and Lectures given to Full Course Students. Rates for this Course, liberal.

For Terms, &c., call at the College, or address the Principal for Catalogue. By arranging for a Course of Study in the above College, you will never regret it. Competent Assistants in constant attendance with the Principal.

☞ In confirmation of the true merit of the "Practical Method of computing Interest," above mentioned, read the following letters. Many others received from reliable sources, and of like import, are not here given, for want of space.

INDIANA ASBURY UNIVERSITY, Greencastle, Ind., March 6, 1861.

J. H. DOTY, Esq., Cincinnati, O.—DEAR SIR :—I have received and examined a copy of your "Practical Method of Computing Interest." It is, as you claim, accurate, comprehensive, brief, and simple, and certainly superior to the Rules and Tables generally in use. Yours respectfully, JOHN W. LOCKE, A. M., Prof. of Mathematics.

MIAMI UNIVERSITY, Oxford, O., March 18, 1861.

J. H. DOTY, Principal of Bacon's Mercantile College, Cincinnati, O.—DEAR SIR :—As to the excellence of the Method detailed in your Pamphlet, I give unhesitating assent. Very truly yours, R. H. McFARLAND, Prof. of Mathematics.

GEORGETOWN COLLEGE, KY., March 26, 1861.

J. H. DOTY, Principal of Bacon's Mercantile College, Cincinnati, O.—DEAR SIR :—I have, of recent years, examined many Methods of Computing Interest, but, I confess, yours to be the simplest and most succinct of them all.
Yours truly, REV. D. R. CAMPBELL, L. L. D., President.

☞ Students enter at any time. No Vacations. Review at pleasure.

NELSON'S
COMMERCIAL COLLEGE,

Opposite the Post Office,

CINCINNATI, - - - - OHIO.

Important Changes in the Art of Teaching Accounts.

THE COLLEGE CONVERTED INTO A TRAINING ESTABLISHMENT.

Business transacted between Teachers and Students as between Merchants.

Students prepared for Clerking as well as for Keeping Books.

All kinds of Business Paper, Business Forms, etc., in constant use.

NO COPYING FROM DAY BOOKS AFTER THE OLD ITALIAN METHOD.

RULES FOR JOURNALIZING IGNORED.

STUDY INTENSELY INTERESTING.

BOYS RECEIVED BY THE YEAR.   YOUNG MEN BY THE COURSE, AS USUAL.

TUITION. (*Payable in advance.*)

Full Course,	$40	For Clubs of two, Full Course,	$70
Partial Course,	25	" " three "	90

For Particulars see Circulars.

RICHARD NELSON, PRINCIPAL AND PROPRIETOR.

Nelson's Mercantile Arithmetic.

An entirely original method of teaching the science of Arithmetic, saving two thirds of the student's time.

The Science of Arithmetic revolutionized. Rules superseded by Principles.

New and simple methods of Computation adopted.

Interest rendered more simple than Long Division and introduced before that rule.

Antiquated calculations under compound numbers discarded and

Numerous forms of Bills, Invoices, Account Sales, Accounts Current, etc., substituted.

Average applied to Accounts, Account Sales and Storage.

Calculations for Modern French Goods, prepared by a Dry Goods Merchant.

Abbreviated methods for making extensions mentally.

Rules of Measurement of the Cincinnati Builders, with Trade's Price Lists and Calculations for Carpenters and Bricklayers.

A section for Farmers and an article for Ladies. An article on laying and repairing Roads.

A method of giving the answers which prevents their being copied.

Mailed free for Fifty Cents in Stamps, Address,

RICHARD NELSON, Principal of Nelson's Commercial College.

Or Applegate & Co., or Robert Clarke & Co., Cincinnati, Ohio.

INDEX TO CITY GUIDE.

American Protestant Association	18
Benevolent Institutions	20
Cemeteries	21
Church Directory	16
Cisterns	29
City Government	26
City Officers	26
City Water Works	22
Colleges	20
County Officers	31
Druids	18
Fire Department	28
Fire Plugs	30
Foreign Consuls	25
Good Fellows	19
Insurance Companies	21
Justices of the Peace	28
Libraries	23
Masonic	18
Odd Fellows	18
Order of Bene Berith	18
Public Buildings	17
Red Men	19
School Department	23
Secret Associations	18
Societies and Associations	19
Street Railroads	30
Street Directory	9
Temperance	19
Ward Boundaries	22

INDEX TO ADVERTISEMENTS.

ACID MANUFACTURERS.
Marsh & Harwoood 40

ALCOHOL MANUFACTURERS.
Levi S. & Co 32

ARTIST.
Wickersham T 78

ARTISTS' MATERIALS.
Hoffmann & Moser 272

ATTORNEYS AT LAW.
Crawford S T 92
Douglass John G 66

BAKING POWDER.
Bishoprick H. & Co 448

BANK NOTE ENGRAVERS.
American Bank Note Co 82

BELL HANGER.
McGregor Geo 268

BILLIARD TABLE MANUFAC.
Balke Julius 447
Brunswick J. M. & Bro 202

BLACKSMITHS.
Brinkman R 40
Graham C. & Bro 78

BLANK BOOK MANUFS.
Tumy J. C. & H. L 32

BOLOGNA SAUSAGE MANUFS.
Bogen G. & P 48

BOOK BINDERS.
Tumy J. C. & H. L 32

BOOKSELLERS.
Applegate & Co 72
Bird M. H 92
Clarke Robert & Co 68
Mendenhall E 86

BOOTS AND SHOES.
Brodfuehrer & Bro 56
Deters J. H 42
Giesting J. D. & G 270

BOX MANUFS, (Packing.)
Johnston J. & J. M 64

BOX MANUFS., (Paper.)
Jordan, Chas. W 270
Jordan D B 212

BRASS FOUNDERS.
Fridger Jacob 52
Kirkup Wm & Son 86
Powell Wm. & Co 4

BRISTLES.
Bullock A D. & Co 76
Whitaker Joseph 443

BRITANNIA WARE MANUF.
Homan H 76

BURIAL CASES, (Metallic.)
Crane, Breed & Co 214
Epply John P 90
Fay L ....
Sholl G. W., (Terra Cotta.) ... 42

CABINET HARDWARE.
McAlpin, Hinman & Co 70

CABINET TOOL MANUF.
Siewers C. G 88

CABINET MAKERS.
Cabinet Maker's Union 70
Coates J. F 70
Geyer John 40
Kramer Anthony 70
Shaw H E 212
Wolff Chas 70

CANDLE MANUFS.
Shillito Geo. & Co 448

CANDLE MOULDS.
Homan H 76

CAP MANUFACT.
Tobias H 272

CARPETS.
Ringwalt & Avery 70

CARRIAGE MANUF.
Gosling J. W 56
Stevens B. R 82

CARVERS.
Anderson A. W 447

CEMENT ROOFERS
Beckley J. & Co 38

CHAIR MAKERS.
Cabinet Maker's Union 70
Coates J. F 70
Geyer John 40
Kramer Anthony 70
Naber Wm 40
Wolff Chas 70

CHEMICAL LABORATORIES.
Grasselli E 84
Marsh & Harwood 40

INDEX TO ADVERTISEMENTS.

CHIMNEY TOPS.
Mappes Henry 4

CIGARS AND TOBACCO.
Levi S. & Bro 32
Nuelsen Francis 447

CINCINNATI LEAD WORKS.
McCormick, Gibson & Co 42

CIRCULAR SAW MILLS.
Hanes W. W 31
Lane & Bodley 46
Todd James 86

CIVIL ENGINEERS & SURVEYORS.
Huntington T. S 40
Phillips R. C 272

CLOTHIERS.
Brooke J. H 86
Cohen A 64
Rieckelman John & Co 272
Waldron D. A 447

COAL DEALERS.
Bertram & Co 52
Dodsworth T. & M 82
Gordon Robert 40
Hutchison E 52
Ross, Pettibone & Co 88

COFFEE AND SPICE MILLS.
Dixon Geo. R. & Co 88

COMMISSION MERCHANTS.
Bartlett R. & Co 44
Beatty James & Co 68
Bishop R. M. & Co 94
Bogen G. & P 48
Brown H. W. & Co 44
Buchanan R. & Son 270
Cody P 92
Davis Geo. F. & Co 48
Davis S. jr. & Co 48
Frazer James A. & Co 44
Gilbert, Jones & Ogborn 44
Glenn Wm. & Sons 68
Jacob Chas. jr. & Co 48
Magill James 68
Moore Robert & Co 68
Swift E. E. C. & Co 212
Thomas N. W. & Co 68
Traber & Aubery 44

COMMISSIONER OF DEEDS.
Douglass John G 66

COMPOSITION ROOFERS.
Beckley J. & Co 38

COPPERSMITHS.
Deckebach F. C. & Co 212

COTTON FACTORIES.
Buchanan R. & Son, Agts 270

CURLED HAIR AND BRISTLES.
Bullock A. D. & Co 76
Whitaker Joseph 445

DENTISTS.
Belknap Dr 50
Hamlen & Smith 202
Taft J 212
Taylor & Irwin 448
Wardle S 40
Wheeler D. D 38
Wickersham O. J 50

DIRECTORY.
Cincinnati Directory 3

DYER AND SCOURER.
Walker R 78

DYE HOUSES.
Harmeler John 94

EAR INFIRMARIES.
Waldo Fred. Aug 448
Williams E 94

ELECTRICIAN.
Belknap Dr 50

ELECTROTYPE FOUNDRIES.
Cincinnati Type Foundry 60
Franklin Type Foundry 36
Hills O'Driscoll & Co 62

EMBROIDERIES, &c.
Epply Adam 64

ENGRAVERS, (Bank Note.)
American Bank Note Co 82

ENGRAVERS, (General.)
Evens Platt, Jr 210
Morrison & Crowther 272

ENGRAVERS, (Wood.)
Hart Joseph W 269
Jones Theodore 346

ESSENCE OF COFFEE MANUF.
Dreidel Theodore 54

EYE INFIRMARIES.
Hunt Jas. G 212
Waldo Fred Aug 448
Williams E 94

FANCY BASKETS, &c.
Waters Chas. H. & Co 88

FANCY GOODS.
Cady D. K 66
Wurlitzer Rudolph 50

FEMALE SEMINARIES.
Mt. Auburn Young Ladies Institute .... *Frontispiece.*

FIRE BRICK AND CLAY.
Bertram & Co 52
Dodsworth T & M 82
Hutchison E 52

FIRE AND BURGLAR PROOF SAFES.
Diebold, Bahmann & Co 82

FLOUR MANUFACTURERS.
Cameron L 40
Erkenbrecher Andrew 447
Fagin Lewis 216

FORWARDING MERCHANTS.
Brown H. W. & Co 44
Buchanan R. & Son 270
Gilbert Jones & Ogborn 44

FRENCH BURR MILL STONE MANUFACTURERS.
Bradford T. & Co 64

GASOMETERS.
Stacey Geo 52

GILDERS.
Wiswell Wm., Jr 272

GLASS SIGNS.
Hopkins H. P 435

GLASS STAINER.
Burgund H 212

GLUE MANUFACTURER.
Bullock A. D. & Co 76

GOLD PEN MANUFACTURERS.
Sheppard G. W. & Co 78

GROCERS, WHOLESALE.
Bishop R. M. & Co 94
Cody P 92
Frazer James A. & Co 44
Glenn Wm. & Sons 68
Traber & Aubery 44

HAIR DRESSER
Arrico Antonio 447

HAIR DYE MANUFACTURER.
Arrico Antonio 447

HAM CURERS.
Beatty James & Co 68
Bogen G. & P 48
Davis Geo. F. & Co 48

INDEX TO ADVERTISEMENTS. 453

NAVAL STORES.
Bartlett R. & Co......... 44

NEWSPAPERS.
Daily Enquirer............ 446
Daily Press.............. 446
Daily Times.............. 446
Daily Volksfreund........ 446

NOTARIES PUBLIC.
Crawford S. T........... 92
Douglass Jno. G......... 66

OCULISTS.
Waldo Fred Aug......... 416
Williams E.............. 94

OILS, TURPENTINE, &C.
Bartlett R. & Co......... 44

OPTICIAN.
Foster James, jr. & Co... 92

OYSTER DEPOTS.
Clark J. F. & J. W....... 272
Clark J. L.............. 200
Gesner I. O............. 78

OYSTERS, FISH AND GAME.
Clark J. F. & J. W....... 272
Clark J. L.............. 200

PACKING BOX MANUFS.
Johnston J. & J. M....... 54

PAINTERS HOUSE AND SIGN.
Cummings H. & Berne..... 56
Hopkins H. P............ 455
Winder W. W............ 38

PAINTS, OILS, &c.
Hoffmann & Moser........ 272

PAPER BOX MANUF.
Jordan Chas. W.......... 270
Jordan D. B............. 212

PAPER DEALERS.
Snider Louis............ 76

PAPER HANGINGS.
Andress F. & C.......... 272
Camargo Manufacturing Co. 4 & 435
Williams C. Curry....... 64

PATENT AGENTS.
Knight & Bros........... 5

PATENT GRATES AND STOVES.
Dodges Patent (J. B. Ryan & Co.)........................ 345

PHOTOGRAPH GALLERIES.
Bishop J. R............. 40
Bonsall I. H............ 204

PHYSICIANS.
Hunt James G........ 212 & 447
Newton & Scudder....... 272
Pulte J. H.............. 92

PIG IRON DEALERS.
Traber & Aubery......... 44

PLATERS, SILVER AND GOLD.
Powell Wm. & Co......... 4

PLOW MANUFACTURERS.
Raymond, Helsingor & Co.. 31

PLUMBERS.
Gibson John & Co........ 445
Kemper Wash............ 266
Kirk David.............. 94
Moore P. J.............. 266
Peare Wm. & H. Winter... 64

PORK PACKERS.
Beatty James & Co....... 68
Bogen G. & P............ 46
Davis Geo. F. & Co...... 48
Davis S. Jr. & Co....... 48
Jacob Chas. Jr. & Co.... 48
Magill James............ 68
Thomas N. W. & Co....... 68

PORTRAIT AND PHOTOGRAPH PAINTER.
Wickersham T............ 78

POTTERIES.
Mappes Henry............ 4
Tempest & Co............ 52

PRINTERS.
Browne P. C............. 92
Faren & McLain.......... 416
Hemann Joseph A......... 446
Press Printing Co....... 446
Starbuck C. W........... 446
Wrightson & Co.......... 80

PRINTING MATERIALS.
Cincinnati Type Foundry. 60
Franklin Type Foundry... 36
Hills, O'Driscoll & Co.. 62

PRINT PUBLISHER.
Bird M. H............... 92

PRODUCE MERCHANTS.
Bishop R. M. & Co....... 94
Gilbert Jones & Ozborn.. 44
Jacob Chas. Jr. & Co.... 48
Moore Robert & Co....... 68
Swift E. E. Co. & Co.... 212

RAILROADS.
Central Ohio R. R....... 443
Cin. & Chicago Air Line. 440
Indianapolis & Cincinnati R. R. 445
Kentucky Central R. R... 442
L. M. & C. H. & D. R. R. 439
Marietta & Cincinnati R. R. 444
Ohio & Mississippi...... 441

RAILROAD AGENTS.
Brown H. W. & Co........ 44

RANGES.
Redway & Burton......... 456

REAL ESTATE AGENT.
Sargent Samuel A........ 92

REFRIGERATORS.
Johnston J. & J. M...... 54

RENOVATORS.
Harmeier John........... 94
Walker R................ 78

ROLLING MILLS.
Sechler & Porter, Agts.. 86

ROOFERS IRON.
Stacey Geo.............. 52

ROOFING MACHINES.
Fay L................... 40

ROOFERS METALLIC.
Fay L................... 40

SADDLERY HARDWARE.
Bantlin & Compton....... 92

SADDLES, HARNESS, &c.
Carrick D. S............ 270
Shackleford J. C. & Co.. 266

SALT AGENCIES.
Ohio River Salt Co., W. A. Healy, Agt.................. 54

SASH, DOOR AND BLINDS.
Kolker & McCammon....... 92
Whitney W. F. & V....... 64

SAW MANUFACTURERS.
Rowe John............... 84
Siewers C. G............ 88

SCALES.
Traber & Aubery, Agts. Fairbanks.................. 44

SEAL ENGRAVER.
Evens Platt, jr......... 210

SEAL PRESSES.
Evens Platt, Jr......... 210

SECOND HAND STORE
 Shaw H. E...................... 212
SEMINARIES.
 Mt. Auburn Young Ladies Institute......................
SEWING MACHINES.
 Evens Platt, Jr................ 210
 Grover & Baker Sewing Machine Co...... Inside back Cover.
 Skardon James................ 74
 Wheeler & Wilson's..........
    outside front Cover.
SILVER PLATERS.
 Morrison & Crowther.......... 272
SPOKE, HUB & FELLOE MANUFS.
 Royer, Simonton & Co......... 82
STAIR BUILDERS.
 Kolker & McCammon........... 92
STAMP AND BRAND CUTTER.
 Stanton John................... 92
STARCH MANUF.
 Erkenbrecher Andrew......... 447
STATIONERS.
 Applegate & Co................ 72
STEAMBOAT AGENTS.
 Brown H. W. & Co............ 44
STEAM ENGINE BUILDERS.
 Greenwood Miles.............. 204
 Hanes W. W.................. 31
 Lane & Bodley................ 46
 Potter L. F. & Wilson......... 208
 Todd James................... 86
STEAM AND GAS FITTER,
 Moore P. J................... 266
STEAM PIPE FITTINGS,
 Greenwood Miles.............. 204
 Kirkup Wm. & Son............ 80
STENCIL CUTTERS.
 Lanphear W. K. & Co......... 40
 Mackenzie J. D............... 212
 Stanton John.................. 92

STEREOTYPERS,
 Cincinnati Type Foundry...... 60
 Franklin Type Foundry........ 36
 Hills, O'Driscoll & Co......... 62
STOCK AND DIE CUTTER,
 Brinkmann R.................. 40
STOVES, HOLLOW WARE, &C.
 Busse John................... 92
 Chamberlain & Co............. 208
 Lotze Adolphus............... 94
 Redway & Burton............. 456
TANNERS,
 Lang & Wanner............... 78
 Martin H. & G. R............. 64
TEA DEALERS.
 Smith H. R. & Son............ 447
TEACHERS MUSIC,
 Weber H..................... 272
TELEGRAPH COMPANIES,
 Western Union................ 86
TIN AND SHEET IRON WORKER'S TOOLS
 Hull J. E..................... 40
TIN WARE,
 Busse Joseph................. 92
 Lotze Adolphus............... 94
TOBACCO WAREHOUSE,
 Phister & How................ 272
TOYS, &C.
 Cady D K.................... 66
TRANSPORTATION AGENTS,
 Brown H. W. & Co............ 44
TRUNK MAKERS' STOCK,
 Merna Joseph................. 42
TRUNK MANUFACTURERS,
 Carrick D. S................. 270
 Flynt M. D................... 208
 Leonard & Cook.............. 446
 Shackleford J. C. & Co........ 266
 Sholl G. W................... 42
TYPE FOUNDRIES,
 Cincinnati Type Foundry...... 60
 Franklin Type Foundry....... 36
UNDERTAKER,
 Epply John P................. 90

UPHOLSTERERS,
 Coates J. F................... 70
 Geis Adam.................... 40
UPHOLSTERERS' AND UNDERTAKERS' MATERIALS,
 McAlpin, Hinman & Co........ 70
VENETIAN BLIND MANUFAC.,
 Vieth A...................... 66
VETERINARY SURGEONS,
 Bowler G. W................. 447
 Wilson Jno................... 447
WADDING AND BATTING MANUF.,
 Stearns & Foster............. 272
WAGON MAKERS
 Hutton J. & R................ 38
WARM AIR FURNACES,
 Lotze Adolphus............... 94
WATCHES, CLOCKS, JEWELRY, &C.
 Eyster Andrew A............. 64
 Wilms J. C................... 212
WINE, (Catawba,)
 Bogen G. & P................. 48
WINE DEALERS,
 Faehr, Bottler & Co........... 52
WOOD DEALERS,
 Johnston G. W. C............. 64
WOOD ENGRAVERS,
 Hart Joseph W............... 266
 Jones Theodore............... 345
WOOD AND WILLOW WARE,
 Waters Charles H. & Co....... 88
WOOD WORKING MACHINERY,
 Hanes W. W.................. 31
 Lane & Bodley................ 46
YELLOW AND ROCKINGHAM WARE,
 Tempest & Co................. 52
YOUNG LADIES INSTITUTE,
 Mt. Auburn Young Ladies Institute............ *Frontispiece.*
YOUTHS' AND BOYS' CLOTHING,
 Brooke J. H.................. 86

www.ingramcontent.com/pod-product-compliance
Lightning Source LLC
Chambersburg PA
CBHW051721300426
44115CB00007B/411